P9-AOO-689

The Canadian World Almanac

& Book of Facts

1989

1989

JANUARY
S	M	T	W	T	F	S
(1)	2	3	4	5	6	7
8	9	10	11	12	13	14
15	16	17	18	19	20	21
22	23	24	25	26	27	28
29	30	31				

FEBRUARY
S	M	T	W	T	F	S
			1	2	3	4
5	6	7	8	9	10	11
12	13	14	15	16	17	18
19	20	21	22	23	24	25
26	27	28				

MARCH
S	M	T	W	T	F	S
			1	2	3	4
5	6	7	8	9	10	11
12	13	14	15	16	17	18
19	20	21	22	23	24	25
(26)	27	28	29	30	31	

APRIL
S	M	T	W	T	F	S
						1
2	3	4	5	6	7	8
9	10	11	12	13	14	15
16	17	18	19	20	21	22
23/30	24	25	26	27	28	29

MAY
S	M	T	W	T	F	S
	1	2	3	4	5	6
7	8	9	10	11	12	13
14	15	16	17	18	19	20
21	22	23	24	25	26	27
28	29	30	31			

JUNE
S	M	T	W	T	F	S
				1	2	3
4	5	6	7	8	9	10
11	12	13	14	15	16	17
18	19	20	21	22	23	24
25	26	27	28	29	30	

JULY
S	M	T	W	T	F	S
						(1)
2	3	4	5	6	7	8
9	10	11	12	13	14	15
16	17	18	19	20	21	22
23/30	24/31	25	26	27	28	29

AUGUST
S	M	T	W	T	F	S
		1	2	3	4	5
6	7	8	9	10	11	12
13	14	15	16	17	18	19
20	21	22	23	24	25	26
27	28	29	30	31		

SEPTEMBER
S	M	T	W	T	F	S
					1	2
3	(4)	5	6	7	8	9
10	11	12	13	14	15	16
17	18	19	20	21	22	23
24	25	26	27	28	29	30

OCTOBER
S	M	T	W	T	F	S
1	2	3	4	5	6	7
8	(9)	10	11	12	13	14
15	16	17	18	19	20	21
22	23	24	25	26	27	28
29	30	31				

NOVEMBER
S	M	T	W	T	F	S
			1	2	3	4
5	6	7	8	9	10	11
12	13	14	15	16	17	18
19	20	21	22	23	24	25
26	27	28	29	30		

DECEMBER
S	M	T	W	T	F	S
					1	2
3	4	5	6	7	8	9
10	11	12	13	14	15	16
17	18	19	20	21	22	23
24/31	(25)	26	27	28	29	30

Jan. 1 — New Year's Day; March 26 — Easter; July 1 — Canada Day; Sept. 4 — Labour Day; October 9 — Thanksgiving; December 25 — Christmas.

Metric Conversion Chart—Approximations

Symbol	When you know	Multiply by	To find	Symbol
Length				
mm	millimetres	0.04	inches	in
cm	centimetres	0.4	inches	in
m	metres	3.3	feet	ft
m	metres	1.1	yards	yd
km	kilometres	0.6	miles	mi
Area				
cm²	square centimetres	0.16	square inches	in²
m²	square metres	1.2	square yards	yd²
km²	square kilometres	0.4	square miles	mi²
ha	hectares (10 000m²)	2.5	acres	
Mass (weight)				
g	grams	0.035	ounce	oz
kg	kilograms	2.2	pounds	lb
t	tonnes (1000kg)	1.1	short tons	
Volume				
mL	millilitres	0.03	fluid ounces	fl oz
L	litres	2.1	pints	pt
L	litres	1.06	quarts	qt
L	litres	0.26	gallons (U.S.)	gal (U.S.)
L	litres	0.22	gallons (Imp.)	gal (Imp.)
m³	cubic metres	35	cubic feet	ft³
m³	cubic metres	1.3	cubic yards	yd³
Temperature (exact)				
°C	Celsius temp.	9/5 (+32)	Fahrenheit temp.	°F

Symbol	When you know	Multiply by	To find	Symbol
Length				
in	inches	*2.5	centimetres	cm
ft	feet	30	centimetres	cm
yd	yards	0.9	metres	m
mi	miles	1.6	kilometres	km
*1 in = 2.54 cm (exactly)				
Area				
in²	square inches	6.5	sq. centimetres	cm²
ft²	square feet	0.09	square metres	m²
yd²	square yards	0.8	square metres	m²
mi²	square miles	2.6	sq. kilometres	km²
	acres	0.4	hectares	ha
Mass (weight)				
oz	ounces	28	grams	g
lb	pounds	0.45	kilograms	kg
	short tons (2000 lb)	0.9	tonnes	t
Volume				
tsp	teaspoons	5	millilitres	mL
tbsp	tablespoons	15	millilitres	mL
fl oz	fluid ounces	30	millilitres	mL
c	cups	0.24	litres	L
pt	pints	0.47	litres	L
qt	quarts	0.95	litres	L
gal	gallons (U.S.)	3.8	litres	L
gal	gallons (Imp.)	4.5	litres	L
ft³	cubic feet	0.03	cubic metres	m³
yd³	cubic yards	0.76	cubic metres	m³

Temperature (exact)

°F	Fahrenheit temp.	(−32) 5/9	Celsius temp.	°C

The Canadian World Almanac

& Book of Facts

1989

GLOBAL PRESS

A Division of Canada Publishing Corporation
Toronto   Ontario   Canada

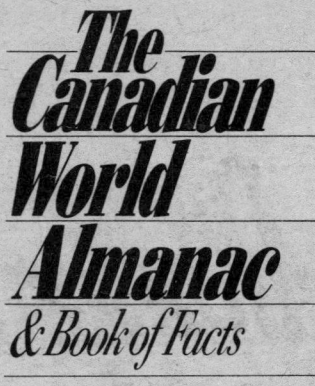

Publishing Director
Susan Yates

Editor
John Filion

Senior Editor and Co-ordinator
Nancy Nishikawa

Contributors to this Edition
Craig Hoskins
Mike Tuchscherer

Index
Barbara Czarnecki

Cover Design
Brant Cowie/Artplus Limited

Contributors to The Canadian World Almanac
Tap Aavasalmi
Paul Bilodeau
Peter Carey
Graham Draper
Ian Hundey
Kathleen Kenna
Mark Kennedy
Heather Milne Kerrigan
Paul Klodniski
Dave Laws
Paul Marshman
Mary Ann Mavrinac
Christopher Nicholls
Constantine Passaris

Technical Assistance
Eileen Brett
Ruby Miranda

In this third edition of The Canadian World Almanac users will find completely updated information, a revised layout and over 700 pages of essential facts for everyday reference.

The Canadian World Almanac is published annually in November.

The editors acknowledge with thanks the many letters of helpful comment and criticism from users of The Canadian World Almanac, and invite further suggestions and observations. Because of the volume of mail directed to the editorial offices, it is not possible to reply to each letter. However, all comments and suggestions receive careful attention. Letters should be sent to: Global Press, 164 Commander Blvd., Agincourt, Ont. M1S 3C7.

Copyright © 1988 Global Press
A Division of Canada Publishing Corporation
Toronto Ontario Canada

Copyright © 1988 Pharos Books
A Scripps Howard Company
New York, N.Y. 10166

All rights reserved. Reproduction in whole or part
is prohibited unless written permission is obtained
from the publisher. While every effort has been made
to ensure accuracy and completeness the publisher
cannot be held liable for errors or omissions.

ISBN: 0-7715-3997-5 (pb)
          0-7715-3998-3 (36-copy floor stand)
ISSN: 0833-532X

Contents

New Features

Canadian Overview ● Farm Population ● Number of Farms ● Type of Farms ● Farmland Use ● Farm Cash Receipts ● Value of Agricultural Products ● Number of Livestock ● Fruit Production ● Sales of Dairy Products ● Vegetable Production ● Egg Production ● Principal Crops ● Production and Use of Wheat ● Canada's Share of the World Wheat Market ● World Wheat, Rice and Corn Production

The Sun ● The Planets and the Solar System ● Planetary Missions ● Celestial Events Highlights 1989 ● The Earth ● The Moon ● Eclipses ● Auroras ● Constellations ● The Zodiac ● Largest Telescopes ● Eras ● Julian and Gregorian Calendars ● Days Between Two Dates ● Perpetual Calendar ● Holidays in Canada ● World Time Differences ● North American Time Differences ● Latitude, Longitude, Elevation of Canadian Cities

Governor General's Literary Awards ● Izaak Walton Killam Memorial Prize ● The Booker Prize ● Nobel Prize Winners

Canada's Largest Corporations ● Industry Leaders ● Largest Employers ● Largest Exporters ● Corporate Profits and Losses ● Business Turnarounds ● Largest Foreign-Owned Companies ● Largest Subsidiaries ● Largest Financial Institutions ● Top Acquisitions ● Crown Corporations ● Investment Terms ● How to Buy Stocks ● Most Active Stocks ● Stock Exchange Trading ● TSE Index ● Labor Unions Directory ● Union Membership

Widely-Known Canadians of the Present ● Widely-Known Canadians of the Past

Events of 1988 ● Historical Anniversaries–20 Years Ago ● 50 Years Ago ● 100 Years Ago ● 200 Years Ago ● 400 Years Ago ● 500 Years Ago

Contents

Contents

Chronology of the Year's Events

(Oct. 15, 1987 to Oct. 14, 1988)

October

International

Stock Prices Plunge Worldwide—Stock prices around the world plummetted **Oct. 19**, known as Black Monday, in a wave of panic selling reminiscent of the stock market collapse that triggered the Great Depression 58 years earlier. The Dow Jones industrial average plunged 508.32 points or 22.6 percent—easily surpassing its previous record 12.82 percent drop in 1929. The Toronto Stock Exchange's TSE 300 index fell 407.2 points or 11.32 percent. The Hong Kong market was closed for a week after values fell 11 percent on Oct. 19. The London market declined 21 percent on Oct. 19 and 20 while markets in Frankfurt, Mexico City, Paris, Sydney and Tokyo also fell sharply. The selling wave appeared to be caused in part by anxiety over U.S. international trade and federal budget deficits. A more immediate cause may have been criticism of West Germany's economic policies by U.S. Treasury Secretary James Baker, who had also hinted at a willingness to let the U.S. dollar decline further against other currencies. Most analysts also blamed program trading, a new fad on Wall Street, in which computers automatically ordered the buying or selling of a large volume of shares when certain circumstances for which the computers were programmed occurred.

Canada

Commonwealth Leaders Endorse Further Sanctions Against South Africa—Commonwealth heads of government meeting in Vancouver said **Oct. 17** that they were committed to further economic sanctions against South Africa. The leaders said such measures would help force an end to apartheid, even if they were not supported by Great Britain. British Prime Minister Margaret Thatcher, holding her own press conference, repeated her opinion that sanctions "harden attitudes rather than promote progress."

November

International

Deng Steps Down in China—On **Nov. 1**, at the conclusion of the 13th Chinese Communist Party Congress in Beijing, Deng Xiaoping stepped down as China's top leader. Although expected to continue to influence party policy, Deng, 83, gave up most of his positions. Premier Zhao Ziyang, Deng's protege, was elected general secretary of the party **Nov. 2**. Deng also resigned from the ruling Politburo and the Central Committee. The newly elected Central Committee contained many new and younger members who supported the economic reforms advocated by Deng and Zhao. Zhao supported private enterprise, including allowing the marketplace to set the price for most products. He also favored more foreign investment in China.

Gorbachev Rebukes Stalin—Soviet leader Mikhail Gorbachev, addressing 6 000 party officials and visitors in the Kremlin **Nov. 2** accused the late Soviet leader Joseph Stalin of "wholesale repressive measures and acts of lawlessness". He added that a commission would investigate the possibility of rehabilitating the reputations of innocent victims of Stalin's regime. In a speech marking the 70th anniversary of the Bolshevik revolution, Gorbachev also praised Stalin for his policy of farm collectivization and for his leadership during World War II.

Van Gogh Sets Another Record—*Irises* (1889) by Vincent van Gogh, set a record **Nov. 11** for a painting sold at auction—$53.9 million, including commission. The buyer was not identified. The previous record, $39.9 million, had been set in March 1987 by Van Gogh's *Sunflowers*. *Irises* had been painted after the artist entered a mental asylum. Philanthropist Joan Whitney Payson had bought the painting for less than $85 000 in 1947. It was put up for auction by her son, John Whitney Payson.

Poles Reject Government Reforms—In what was believed to be an unprecedented repudiation of a Communist government, Polish voters **Nov. 29** witheld endorsement of economic and political reforms supported by the regime. Two referenda were presented. One asked voters to accept hardships as part of a "radical healing" of the economy. The second supported democratization of political life, including more civil rights. An absolute majority of all eligible voters was required for approval. But only 68 percent of the voters turned out, and neither referendum carried, although both got a majority of votes actually cast. Solidarity, the dissident labor union, urged Poles not to vote.

Canada

Mulroney Promotes Free Trade—Prime Minister Brian Mulroney defended the recently-negotiated free trade pact **Nov. 14**, saying it would allow Canada's poorer regions to enjoy the same economic prosperity as Ontario. "We can't have 2 Canada's, one rich and one poor," he said. "We've got to have one Canada."

Johnson Resigns as PQ Leader—Parti Québécois leader Pierre Marc Johnson resigned **Nov. 10** following internal dissent caused by hardliners who refused to accept a party vote in June to take a moderate approach twoards Quebec independence. "I do not wish to preside over the weakening, the splintering of nationalist forces in Quebec," Johnson said in a speech to the national assembly.

Senates Passes Drug Patent Bill—A constitutional crisis was averted **Nov. 19** when the Liberal-dominated Senate bowed to pressure to pass the Conservative government's new drug patent legislation. After rejecting the bill several times after it had been passed by the House of Commons, most Liberal senators abstained after Liberal Leader John Turner urged the Senate to allow passage of the legislation. The new bill gave makers of newly-patented drugs a 10-year monopoly on the drug. Previously, companies could make low-cost generic copies of brand name prescription drugs. Opposition parties argued that the law would lead to higher costs for prescription drugs. The Conservatives said the new law would encourage drug companies to spend more on research and development.

Bell Named MVP—Toronto Blue Jay George Bell became the first player of a Canadian-based team to win baseball's Most Valuable Player Award. Bell led the American league in runs batted in (134), was second in home runs (47) and posted a .308 average.

December

International

Reagan, Gorbachev Sign INF Treaty—U.S. Pres. Ronald Reagan and Soviet leader Mikhail Gorbachev met in Washington, D.C. and signed an unprecedented agreement that would eliminate the superpowers' medium-range intermediate nuclear forces. The IMF treaty had been worked out in intense negotiations preceding the summit meeting. In an interview **Dec. 3** Reagan defended the treaty against criticism by some conservatives, who he said did not understand what the treaty contained.

He suggested that some of them seemed to think "that war is inevitable." Gorbachev arrived in Washington **Dec. 7** after meeting with British Prime Minister Margaret Thatcher in Oxfordshire, England. The INF treaty was signed by both leaders **Dec. 8**. It provided for the dismantling of all 1 752 U.S. and 859 Soviet missiles having a range between 500 and 5 500 km. As part of the inspection agreement, it was reported **Dec. 8** that Soviet inspectors would be stationed near a plant in Magna, Utah that made missile components. U.S. on-site inspection teams would be allowed to visit some 75 East-bloc localities, mostly in the Soviet Union. Soviet inspectors could visit 9 U.S. sites and others in Europe.

Palestinian Youths Fight Israelis—Violent protests by Palestinians broke out in territories occupied by Israel. More than 20 of the demonstrators were killed. The trouble began in the crowded Gaza Strip, from which 60 000 workers commuted to Israel daily. On **Dec. 8**, 4 Arabs were killed and 17 injured in the collision of an Israeli army truck and several vans. Widespread protests occurred **Dec. 9**, and on **Dec. 11** many workers stayed home in protest. A general strike began **Dec. 12** on the West Bank, another occupied territory. The Israeli authorities sought to force Arab merchants to open for business. Palestinians, mostly young men, threw stones and Molotov cocktails at Israeli soldiers, who fired back, using live ammunition, officials said, only after rubber bullets and tear gas failed to work. Aside from the Palestinians killed, many others were wounded or beaten badly. Israeli Prime Minister Yitzhak Shamir **Dec. 13** blamed the demonstrations on "the terrorism of a few." The Arab League **Dec. 15** denounced Israeli "massacres." On **Dec. 18**, soldiers stormed a Gaza hospital, arrested wounded suspects and beat doctors and nurses. Crowds of Arab teenagers demonstrated in Jerusalem **Dec. 19**, and on **Dec. 21**, more than 100 000 Arab residents of Israel joined in a general strike to protest the army's behaviour. The U.N. Security Council, with the United States abstaining, unanimously adopted a resolution **Dec. 22** denouncing Israeli actions.

1 600 Drown—A Philippine inter-island ferry and a Philippine tanker collided in the Tablas Strait, 175 km south of Manila **Dec. 20**. More than 1 600 persons drowned; only 26 were rescued. The ferry's manifest listed 1 583 passengers and 60 crew members, but there was speculation that more than 3 000 persons were aboard. The tanker had a crew of 13, 2 of whom survived. The ferry carried travelers bound for Manila for Christmas. Seas were calm but visibility was poor at the time of the collision, after which the tanker's cargo ignited and fire engulfed both vessels. The toll in the disaster was the highest in 20th century peacetime maritime history. About 1 500 had died in the sinking of the Titanic in 1912.

Canada

Stevens Guilty of Conflict of Interest—Former Mulroney Cabinet Minister Sinclair Stevens violated conflict of interest guidelines 14 times, according to a report tabled in the House of Commons **Dec. 3**. Mr. Justice William Parker, who conducted the inquiry into allegations of wrongdoing by Stevens, concluded that he had "used his public office for private advantage." Six of the violations involved Stevens' continued involvement with Magna International Inc. after he learned that his wife obtained a $2.6 million loan with a former executive of the auto parts firm.

Free Trade Details Unveiled—Details of the Canada-U.S. free trade agreement, approved in principle in Oct., were detailed in 5 kg of documents tabled in the House of Commons **Dec. 11**. Both the Liberals and New Democrats renewed calls for an election on the free trade agreement and said they would scrap the deal if elected. The treaty would take effect in 1989 if approved by Parliament and the U.S. Congress.

Shellfish Causing Illness—Federal officials announced **Dec. 15** that 5 species of Atlantic shellfish—mussels, oysters, clams, quahogs and cockles—had been taken off the market and destroyed because of health hazards from toxins. The announcement came after 2 men—one from Montreal and the other from Scarborough—had died after eating mussels. Another 104 cases of people becoming ill after eating mussels were reported in P.E.I.

Air Canada Strike Ends—A 3-week shutdown of Air Canada ended **Dec. 16** when a settlement was reached with 8 500 members of the International Association of Machinists and Aerospace Workers. The employees had been locked out Nov. 27 following a series of rotating strikes. The major item of dispute was a union demand for indexed pensions, which Air Canada eventually agreed to.

January

International

Palestinian-Israeli Clashes Continue—Unrest in Israel's occupied territories continued throughout January. Israel also struck by sea and air at Palestinian targets in Lebanon **Jan. 2**, killing 21 and wounding 14, according to Lebanese police. The fatal shooting of an Arab woman in the West Bank by an Israeli soldier **Jan. 3** triggered a new round of demonstrations. On observing the wretched conditions at a refugee camp in Gaza **Jan. 4**, David Mellor, minister of state in the British Foreign Office, said "Israel cannot duck its responsibilities" for what he called "an affront to civilized values." The U.N. Security Council, in response to Israel's announced plans to deport 9 Palestinians, voted unanimously **Jan. 5** to ask Israel "to refrain from deporting any Palestinian civilians from the occupied territories." Citing the 1949 Geneva Convention, which prohibited deportation from occupied territories, the United States cast its first vote against Israel in the Council in 6 years. An Israeli army spokesman described the 9 as "chief instigators" of the unrest. Four of the 9 were in fact expelled **Jan. 13**. They were flown into Lebanese territory—despite Lebanon's objections—and turned loose. The Palestinian protests began to build anew, and on **Jan. 15** Israeli police entered 2 of Islam's holiest shrines in Jerusalem and beat male and female worshipers. To discourage media coverage, Israeli officers declared many areas off-limits to reporters. With 38 Palestinians having been shot to death, Israel shifted strategy to one of "force, might, beatings" in the words of Israeli Defence Minister Yitzhak Rabin. The Israelis used clubs to break the hands of suspected demonstrators so that they could not throw rocks. Entire families were often beaten, and the hospitals filled with the injured.

Haitians Elect President—The voters of Haiti chose Leslie Manigat, a university professor who had spent 23 years in exile, as president in January. An attempt to have an election in November failed when soldiers and thugs disrupted it and caused the deaths of 34 people. The 4 leading candidates in the November voting, refused to run in January, charging that the government was controlling the electoral process. Accusations of fraud in the **Jan. 17** voting were widespread. The electoral council announced **Jan. 24** that Manigat had won 50 percent of the votes and that no other candidate had gotten more than 20 percent.

Canada

Reagan Promotes Free Trade—Canadians need not fear losing their national identity as part of a free trade agreement with the United States, U.S. President Ronald Reagan said in a radio broadcast **Jan. 9**. Speaking one week after he and Prime Minister Brian Mulroney had signed the agreement, Reagan said Canada has "a national character that will not only survive but flourish in an environment of free trade and expanding opportunities." Meanwhile, the Wall Street Journal, in an editorial published **Jan. 5**, urged the U.S. Congress to end its "protectionist binge" and support the free trade deal.

Report Urges Halt On Nuclear Reactors—A moratorium on nuclear reactor construction should be imposed until there are better methods of waste disposal, according to a House of Commons committee report released **Jan. 19**. The report, resulting from hearings held in 1987, said that Canada had already generated 12 400 tonnes of spent reactor fuel. By 2024, it was estimated that the total amount of radioactive waste would reach 100 000 tonnes.

Supreme Court Rules Abortion Law Unconstitutional—In a landmark decision handed down **Jan. 28**, the Supreme Court of Canada ruled that the nation's abortion law violated provisions in the *Charter of Rights and Freedoms* which guarantee life, liberty and security of the person. The ruling struck down a section of the Criminal Code, which allowed abortions to be performed only in accredited hospitals after a committee of doctors determined that a woman's continued pregnancy would be a threat to her life or health. The Court's ruling was the result of an appeal brought by Dr. Henry Morgentaler, who had been found guilty of performing illegal abortions by an Ontario Court of Appeal decision. Morgentaler based his appeal on the grounds that Canada's abortion law, passed by Parliament in 1969, violated the 1982 Charter.

February

International

Kennedy Approved for U.S. Supreme Court—U.S. Appeals Court Judge Anthony Kennedy was approved by the Senate **Feb. 3** to fill a vacancy on the U.S. Supreme Court. Kennedy was President Ronald Reagan's third nominee for the position. The first, Judge Robert Bork, was rejected by the Senate in October because of his right wing views. Reagan's second nominee, Judge Douglas Ginsburg, withdrew in November after acknowledging he had smoked marijuana "a few times" during the 1970s.

Panamanian Leader Indicted by U.S.—U.S. grand juries indicted Panamanian strongman Gen. Manuel Noriega **Feb. 4** on charges of international drug dealing. The indictments charged that Noriega had assisted international drug traffickers and that he had allowed the laundering of drug profits through Panamanian banks. Noriega, chief of the Panama Defence Forces since 1983, denied the allegations. Panama's President Eric Arturo Delvalle tried to fire Noriega Feb. 25, but the general refused to quit and, on Feb. 26, the National Assembly ousted him instead. Delvalle denounced the assembly's action, called for a general strike, and went into hiding. A strike began Feb. 29 and was widely supported in the nation's capital.

Report Says Waldheim Knew of Crimes—A panel of international historians issued a report **Feb. 9** which found that Austrian Pres. Kurt Waldheim had known of war crimes committed by his units during World War II, but that he had not committed any crimes himself. The report found that Waldheim had concealed and misrepresented his service during the war. The historians noted that while serving in Greece and Yugoslavia from 1942 to 1944, Waldheim, who was responsible for compiling data on his unit's activities, must have been well-informed. Waldheim said he was happy the report found that he was not guilty of crimes and declared that "knowledge is not a crime." On **Feb. 15** he vowed not to resign his office.

Swaggart Admits Sin to Congregation—Jimmy Swaggart became the latest television evangelist to fall from grace **Feb. 21** when he publicly confessed to an unspecified sin and asked for forgiveness. In 1987, Swaggart had denounced another TV evangelist, Jim Bakker, as a "cancer on the body of Christ" after Bakker had been linked to sexual misbehavior. Swaggart had also accused Marvin Gorman—who, like Bakker and Swaggart, was an Assemblies of God minister—of adultery. Gorman later obtained photographs of Swaggart taken by a private detective that placed Swaggart at a motel frequently used by prostitutes. Gorman handed the evidence over to the Assemblies of God. While it was not made public, the evidence was sufficient for Swaggart to admit an indiscretion, and for the local leaders of the church to bar him **Feb. 22** from the pulpit for 3 months and impose a 2-year period of rehabilitation. Swaggart conducted the country's most popular religious broadcast, which brought in donations of $150 million a year.

Canada

Calgary Hosts Olympics—The XV Winter Olympics officially began **Feb. 13** in Calgary with more than 1 800 athletes from 57 participating countries. Although Canada failed to win gold during the 15-day competition, silver medals were awarded to figure skaters Elizabeth Manley and Brian Orser. Skier Karen Percy won 2 bronze medals, and another bronze was captured by the ice-dance duo of Tracy Wilson and Rob McCall.

Côté Fired From Cabinet—Supply and Services Minister Michel Côté was fired from Cabinet **Feb. 2** for violating conflict-of-interest guidelines. Côté failed to disclose a $250 000 personal loan from a businessman who reportedly received government contracts from Côté's ministry.

March

International

AIDS Threat to Heterosexuals Cited—The debate concerning acquired immune deficiency syndrome (AIDS) continued when 2 leading sex therapists warned that the threat to heterosexuals was greater than others had suggested. Dr. William Masters and Virginia Johnson held a press conference in New York City **Mar. 7** to announce findings in their book *Crisis: Heterosexual Behavior in the Age of AIDS*, written in collaboration with Dr. Robert Kolodny. The authors reported that the AIDS virus was prevalent among heterosexuals who had had at least 6 sex partners a year for the past 5 years. Among 400 men and women, ages 21 to 40, who had been studied, 7 percent of the women and 5 percent of the men were said to be infected. In a control group of 400 persons in longterm monogamous relationships, only 1 individual was infected. The authors recommended that pregnant women, convicted prostitutes, marriage-licence applicants and hospital inpatients 15 to 60 be tested for the virus. They estimated that 3 million North Americans were infected, and argued that under rare circumstances the virus could be spread by mosquitoes, kissing, dining in restaurants, or using toilet seats. Authorities on AIDS questioned the methodology and conclusions of Masters and Johnson.

U.S. Pressure Disrupts Panama—U.S. attempts to oust Gen. Manuel Antonio Noriega as the ruler of Panama plunged the country into political and economic turmoil. Panama's new president, Manuel Solis Palma, who had been chosen by Noriega, named a new cabinet that was sworn in **Mar. 1**. The ousted president, Eric Arturo Delvalle, who claimed from hiding that he was still head of the government, issued a proclamation Mar. 1 freezing all Panamanian assets outside Panama. The U.S. State Department advised U.S. banks **Mar. 2** not to disburse funds to Noriega, and on **Mar. 3** federal district courts restrained 4 banks from transferring funds to the Panamanian government. Panama, which used the U.S. dollar as its currency, became hard-pressed for cash. Popular opposition to the government took the form of a general strike that spread in early March to banks, companies, and commercial enterprises, especially in the capital. On **Mar. 4**, Panama ordered the nation's banks to close "until the supply of dollar bills can be regularized." Although the strike had ended, the bank closing devastated the economy again. The United States **Mar. 7** flew cash to Panama to pay Panama Canal workers. Spain agreed to offer Noriega asylum if the United States would drop its drug trafficking indictments against him.

New Irish-British Violence—Three violent incidents in March kept animosity between the Irish Republican Army and British authorities at a high point. British security forces in Gibraltar shot and killed 3 suspected Irish terrorists **Mar. 6**. British and Spanish authorities said that the 3, who were unarmed when killed, had been planning a car-bomb attack. Foreign Minister Sir Geoffrey Howe said **Mar. 7** that, when challenged, the men had "made movements" that prompted the military personnel who confronted them to conclude that their lives were in danger. On **Mar. 8**, Spanish authorities found a car to which one of those slain had keys; it contained explosives and ammunition. At the funeral **Mar. 16** in Belfast for those who had been killed, a man, later captured and identified as a Protestant, attacked the crowd of 10 000 mourners with grenades and an automatic pistol. Three mourners were killed and dozens injured. One of those killed **Mar. 16** was buried in West Belfast **Mar. 19**. Two British soldiers, armed but not in uniform, apparently drove into the funeral procession by mistake. When they attempted to drive away, their car was stopped, and the soldiers were overpowered, beaten and shot to death.

Ozone Layer Declines in North—Concern over the loss of ozone in the atmosphere grew when the U.S. National Aeronautics and Space Administration announced that the ozone layer was declining in the northern hemisphere. The NASA study, released **Mar. 15**, found that the decline had been significant over a period of 2 decades. It was already known that a seasonal hole in the layer occurred in Antarctica. Ozone in the atmosphere blocks ultraviolet radiation from the sun that contributes to skin cancer and other health problems. E.I. Du Pont de Nemours & Co. announced **Mar. 24** that it would phase out production of chlorofluorocarbons because of growing evidence that chlorine in these CFCs was reacting with the ozone and depleting it. Du Pont said it would try to come up with a substitute for CFCs—used as refrigerants and in producing plastic foam—within 5 years.

Canada

AIDS Hospice Opens—Canada's first AIDS hospice opened in Toronto in March, providing a place for victims of the disease to die with dignity. Casey House will be financed by private donations and funding from the provincial health ministry. There was immediately an 18-person waiting list for the home's 12 beds.

Fathers Can Receive Maternity Benefits—Fathers can collect maternity benefits if the mother of their baby dies or becomes disabled, under federal legislation approved **Mar. 29**. The new law was prompted by the case of a Kitchener, Ont. man who wanted to care for his baby daughter. The child's mother was declared brain dead when 8 months pregnant and was kept on life support systems until the baby was born.

April

International

PLO Military Leader Killed—The military leader of the Palestine Liberation Organization was assassinated **Apr. 16** in Tunis. Nine masked attackers—after killing 2 bodyguards and a driver—broke into the home of Khalil al-Wazir, the PLO military chief, and killed him. Subsequent reports said that 30 to 40 raiders had been put ashore in Tunis from an Israeli missile boat, and that the operation had been carried out by Israeli intelligence agents and naval and army units. Al-Wazir, known by the nom de guerre Abu Jihad, had been coordinating the Palestinian uprising in the territories occupied by Israel, which regarded him as responsible for terrorist raids against Israel. On hearing of the assassination, Palestinians in the territories rioted, and 14 were shot to death by Israeli soldiers in the bloodiest day since the unrest began. The U.S. State Department, without naming Israel, denounced the assassination **Apr. 18**. The *Washington Post* reported **Apr. 20** that the 10-member inner cabinet of Israel had discussed the assassination in advance.

Kuwait Airliner Hijacked—A Kuwait Airways jet with 112 persons aboard was seized in the air by Arab-speaking gunmen **Apr. 5**. It was forced to land at Mashhad, Iran, where one half of the hostages were released on **Apr. 6** and **7**. Kuwait rejected the hijackers' demands that 17 convicted Shiite terrorists be freed. The plane took off and, after being refused the right to land in Beirut, flew on to Larnaca, Cyprus and landed there. Two hostages were killed **Apr. 9** and **11**; 12 were released on **Apr. 12**. On **Apr. 13**, the refueled plane flew to Algiers with more than 30 hostages still aboard. Algerian officials negotiated the release of the remaining hostages **Apr. 20** and allowed the hijackers to leave the country.

"Ivan the Terrible" Convicted—John Demjanjuk, who had been extradited from the United States to Israel in 1986, was found guilty of war crimes by an Israeli court in Jerusalem **Apr. 18**. Survivors of the Treblinka, Poland death camp said he was the notorious sadist nicknamed "Ivan the Terrible" who had participated in the execution of Jews. Some 850 000 Jews had died there during World War II. Demjanjuk said he had never been to Treblinka and that he was the victim of mistaken identity. On **Apr. 25**, the 3-judge panel sentenced him to death.

Canada

Air Canada Up For Sale—Air Canada, one of the nation's largest Crown corporations, with assets of more than $3 billion,

will be put up for sale, Deputy Prime Minister Don Mazankowski announced **Apr. 12**. Mazankowski said the government would be introducing legislation to sell 45 percent of the airline's shares. The remaining 55 percent would be kept by the government but eventually they too would be sold.

Tories Elected in Manitoba—Manitoba voters elected a Progressive Conservative minority government **Apr. 26**. The Tories, led by Gary Filmon, won 25 of the 57 seats in the provincial legislature, compared to 20 for the Liberals and 12 for the New Democratic Party which had previously formed the government.

EXPO 86 Site Sold—British Columbia Premier Bill Vander Zalm announced **Apr. 27** that the EXPO 86 site would be sold to Hong Kong billionaire Li Ka-Shing. The 84 hectares of choice downtown Vancouver property had been owned by the B.C. Enterprise Corp., a Crown agency.

May

International

Labor Unrest Sweeps Poland—Workers demanding more pay and more political power went on strike throughout Poland in May. After workers who struck at Bydgoszcz **Apr. 25** got a big pay hike, a strike by about 15 000 workers began at the Lenin steel mill near Krakow **Apr. 26**. About 7 000 workers demanding more pay and recognition of Solidarity, the independent labor federation, struck the Lenin shipyard in Gdansk **May 2**. Nobel Peace Prize winner Lech Walesa, pleading ill health, played only a secondary role in the protest. Antigovernment demonstrators clashed with police in several cities, including Warsaw **May 3**. Police raided the Lenin steel mill **May 5** and put an end to the strike. More than 30 workers were injured and 38 arrested. Talks at Gdansk between workers and the shipyard management broke down **May 8** over legalization of Solidarity, and most of the workers returned to their jobs by **May 10**. The Polish parliament **May 11** approved emergency measures that strengthened the government's hand in economic matters. The legislation would allow strikes, but only by members of government-supervised unions.

Hungarian Leader Ousted—Janos Kadar, who had been the leader of Hungary since the time of the nation's ill-fated revolution against Soviet domination in 1956, was removed from power **May 22**. Kadar, the general secretary of the Socialist Workers (Communist) Party, lost that position during the party's first national conference in 3 decades. Kadar and 7 allies lost their seats on the Politburo, and delegates also replaced about 40 percent of the Central Committee. Kadar was succeeded by Karoly Grosz, who had served as premier since 1987. Trained as a printer, Grosz had risen through the party bureaucracy to serve on the Central Committee in 1980 and the Politburo in 1985.

Funding on Artificial Heart Ends—Dr. Claude Lenfant, director of the National Heart, Lung and Blood Institute of the U.S. National Institutes of Health, announced **May 12** that the government would cease to finance research on artificial hearts. He said that the human body "just couldn't seem to tolerate" an artificial heart. All 5 recipients of permanent implants, which were made between 1982 and 1985, died. William Schroeder, who died in 1986, survived the longest with an artificial heart, 620 days. The HLBI planned to focus its resources on implantable devices that worked with part of the real heart.

Cigarettes Found to Be Addictive—In a report issued **May 16**, U.S. Surgeon Gen. C. Everett Koop declared that cigarettes and other tobacco products were addictive. The report, the work of 50 scientists who studied 2 000 research articles, found that the "processes that determine tobacco addiction are similar to those that determine addiction to. . .heroin and cocaine." Koop recommended that vending machine sales be banned to protect young people and that tobacco products be labelled as addictive. The Tobacco Institute criticized the report's conclusion on addiction, noting that many smokers have been able to quit smoking.

Canada

Quebec Encourages Larger Families—The Quebec government announced **May 12** that it would pay families $500 cash for each of their first 2 babies and $3,000 for each subsequent child. The measure was designed to address Quebecers' concerns that their culture might be eroded by a low birthrate of 1.38 children per woman of childbearing age. Other steps taken to increase the rate to 1.8 in 5 years included 60 000 new day care spaces and interest-free loans on a new home.

Sopinka Named to Supreme Court—Defence lawyer John Sopinka was appointed to the Supreme Court of Canada, filling the vacancy created by the resignation of J.W. Estey. Sopinka, whose appointment was announced by Prime Minister Brian Mulroney **May 24**, was best known for his defence of nurse Susan Nelles and former cabinet minister Sinclair Stevens who was found guilty of violating federal conflict-of-interest guidelines.

Oilers Win Stanley Cup—Edmonton Oilers won the Stanley Cup **May 26**, defeating the Boston Bruins in a 4-game sweep. Wayne Gretzky, who led the Oilers to their fourth Cup victory in 5 years, was awarded the Conn Smythe Trophy as the most valuable player in the playoffs.

June

International

Two Million South African Blacks Strike—Resentment over a proposed new labor law and the banning of union political activity in February led **June 6-8** to a strike by about 2 million black South Africans. The law, being considered by Parliament, would curb wildcat strikes, outlaw sympathy strikes, and possibly open striking unions to suits. The Congress of South African Trade Unions, supported by the National Council of Trade Unions, led the strike. Most successful in its first day, the strike was believed to be the largest ever in South Africa.

Korean Student Marchers Thwarted—South Korean authorities prevented South Korean students from talking with their North Korean counterparts about reunification. In response to student pressure, Premier Lee Hyun Jai wrote North Korean officials **June 3**, suggesting that the 2 Koreas resume talks on various issues. The South Korean students, in the latest phase of their protest movement, said **June 3** that they would march to Panmunjom, in the demilitarized zone between the 2 Koreas, to talk with North Korean students about reunification. Violent clashes with police occurred **June 8** and **9**, and on **June 10** riot police blocked some 25 000 students from reaching Panmunjom.

Haitian General Ousts President—Lt. Gen. Henri Namphy ousted Pres. Leslie Manigat of Haiti and reclaimed power himself. Namphy had headed a military government in Haiti until Manigat was elected president in January 1988. On **June 14**, Namphy had ordered the transfer or retirement of 10 top military officials. Pres. Manigat rescinded the order **June 15**, objecting that he had not been consulted. Manigat dismissed Namphy **June 17** and placed him under house arrest. Soldiers loyal to Namphy freed him **June 19**. During the night of **June 19-20**, Namphy seized control and Manigat went into exile in the Dominican Republic. Namphy declared himself president **June 20**.

U.S. Sues to Oust Teamsters Leaders—Charging that the 1.7 million-member Teamsters Union had refused to clean up organized-crime influence and asserting that "we will," the U.S. Justice Department asked a federal court **June 28** to remove the leaders of the union and appoint a trustee to run it. In filing the suit in New York City, U.S. Attorney Rudolph Giuliani said that his goal was "to take back the Teamsters from the Mafia." The civil suit was brought under the Racketeer Influenced and Corrupt Organizations law, the first time the statute had been applied to an entire union. Giuliani noted that 4 of the last 5 Teamsters presidents had been indicted while in office and 3 of them had been imprisoned. He said organized crime had deprived union members of their rights through 20 murders as well as through shootings, bombings, beatings, extortion and theft. The trustee would run the union until new officers were elected. Weldon Mathis, the Teamsters' general secretary-treasurer, denied that the union had been controlled by organized crime and called the suit a "vicious anti-labor tactic."

Pres. Duarte Gravely Ill—Pres. José Napoleón Duarte of El Salvador underwent surgery **June 7** and was found to be terminally ill with cancer. Duarte's state of the union speech was read for him, **June 1**, by Vice Pres. (and acting president) Rodolfo Castillo. In it, Duarte said that his nation was fighting "economic and institutional collapse."

Russian Church Celebrates Millennium—The Russian Orthodox Church celebrated the 1 000th anniversary of the introduction of Christianity into Russia. The church dated its origin from the conversion to Christianity in 988 of a pagan prince Vladimir I of present-day Kiev. The current Kremlin leadership, including Mikhail Gorbachev, gave its own blessing to the celebration and, in fact, had signalled a new tolerance of religion. Christian leaders from around the world attended the formal opening of the celebration **June 5**, a mass in the Epiphany Cathedral in Moscow. The church conducted a general council, or meeting of bishops, at a monestary at Zagorsk **June 6-10**, only the 3d such conference permitted by the government since World War II. An open-air mass **June 12** at the 13th-century Danilov Monestary in Moscow concluded the celebration.

Tobacco Company Liable in Smoker's Death—A jury in New Jersey found **June 13** that a tobacco company was partly responsible for the death of a woman who had smoked the company's cigarettes. More than 300 such liability suits had been tried since 1954, and this one, in Newark, N.J. was the first in which damages were assessed against a cigarette manufacturer. Mrs. Rose Cipollone had smoked cigarettes for 40 years before her death of lung cancer at age 58 in 1984. During this time, she smoked brands of 3 companies, but she had smoked only the products of the Liggett Group Inc. before 1966, when a federal label law required that all cigarettes be labelled as dangerous to health. It was this labelling, the jury found, that spared the other companies from liability. But it found that Liggett had breached an express warranty of safety by promoting its cigarettes with such slogans as "Just what the doctor ordered." The jury found that because Mrs. Cipollone had learned of the dangers of smoking from other sources and had not quit smoking, she was 80 percent responsible for her death. The jury awarded $400 000 in compensation to Mr. Cipollone. The jury found that Liggett and the other defendants had not conspired to mislead the public about the dangers of smoking before 1966 and had not fraudulently misrepresented facts.

Earth Heating Up, Scientist Warns—The "greenhouse effect," long anticipated by scientists, had finally arrived, according to U.S. Congressional testimony. James Hansen of the National Aeronautics and Space Administration told a Senate committee **June 23** that the Earth had been warmer during the first 5 months of 1988 than at any time since records had been kept. He said that global temperatures had risen by a half-degree Fahrenheit in the hundred years before 1880, by another degree from then to 1950, and by more than half a degree since then. He asserted, "It is time to stop waffling so much and say that the evidence is pretty strong that the greenhouse effect is here." The effect is caused by atmospheric gases that prevent heat from the sun from radiating back into space. The burning of fossil fuels and the destruction of forests are chiefly responsible. Hansen warned that an "increasing tendency" to droughts could be expected in the future. Another consequence of the warming trend would be the melting of polar and glacial ice and the subsequent rise in sea levels and flooding of coastal areas.

Canada

Parliament Approves Meech Lake—The House of Commons gave final approval to the Meech Lake Accord **June 22**, with only 7 MPs voting against the pact. The Commons originally ratified the accord in Oct. 1987 but needed to vote on it a second time because the Senate had proposed amendments. In addition to Parliament, all 10 provinces must approve the agreement before it becomes law.

Summit Held in Toronto—Leaders of the world's 7 major industrial nations met in Toronto in June. In a communique at the end of the summit, leaders of the United States, Britain, France, West Germany, Japan, Italy and Canada spoke optimistically about global economic prospects. The leaders also announced plans to relieve the debts of some poor African nations and stated that they "strongly welcome" the Canada-U.S. free trade agreement.

July

International

U.S. Navy Missile Downs Iranian Airliner—A missile fired from a U.S. Navy warship in the Persian Gulf struck and destroyed a commercial Iranian airliner over the Persian Gulf **July 3**, killing all 290 persons on the plane. The U.S. government reported that Navy personnel had mistaken the airliner for an Iranian F-14 jet fighter. The incident occurred at a moment when tensions in the vicinity were high. At 10:10 a.m. **July 3**, Iranian gunboats fired on a reconnaissance helicopter from the cruiser *USS Vincennes*, one of the ships in the U.S. fleet that was seeking to keep sea lanes open in the Gulf during the Iran-Iraq war. The helicopter was not hit. The *Vincennes* and the U.S. frigate *Elmer Montgomery* attacked the boats beginning at 10:42 and sank or damaged 3 of them. At 10:47, the airliner took off from a joint civilian-military airport in Bandar Abbas, Iran, and flew southwest toward its destination, Dubai in the United Arab Emirates. This was flight 655, on a scheduled run across the Strait of Hormuz. At 10:49, the *Vincennes* began to radio warnings, reportedly 3 on civilian frequencies, 4 on military frequencies. These were not acknowledged. The plane was declared hostile at 10:51 and at 10:54, when it was 15 km distant, Capt. Will Rogers ordered his crew to fire 2 surface-to-air heat-seeking missiles. At least one struck the plane at a distance of about 10 km. The Navy reported that an Iranian fighter plane has been downed. The stunning announcement to the contrary came at a news conference conducted several hours later by Adm. William Crowe, chairman of the Joint Chiefs of Staff. Crowe told reporters that the plane was outside its designated commercial air corridor and was headed directly for the *Vincennes* and was descending. He said there were "electronic indications" that the plane was an F-14. The Navy began an investigation and the original account by Crowe did not hold up. By **July 5**, Pentagon officials were telling members of Congress that the plane had been well within the commercial air corridor. It was also subsequently determined that the plane was ascending, not dscending. Reagan said **July 11**, that the United States would pay compensation to families of the victims, who came from 6 countries in addition to Iran.

Communist Conference Backs Restructuring—The 19th All-Union Conference of the Soviet Communist Party concluded **July 1** with the declaration of support for *perestroika* (restructuring), the centrepiece of the reform movement supported by Soviet Leader Mikhail Gorbachev. The dramatic debate of the 3 previous days continued **July 1** when Boris Yeltsin, the ousted Communist Party chief in Moscow, endorsed Gorbachev's reforms but criticized conference procedures as undemocratic. Yegor Ligachev, regarded as the No. 2 man in the ruling Politburo and as cautious on reform, in turn called Yeltsin "a destructive force" and asserted that "perestroika has become the cause of my life." In his closing address, Gorbachev noted that "Nothing of this kind has occurred in this country for nearly 6 decades." The delegates, aside from endorsing economic, social, and political restructuring, also approved competitive elections and 10-year limits on the tenure of elected government and party officials. They also supported the principle of *glasnost* (openness) in the conduct of public affairs.

Democrats Nominate Dukakis—Gov. Michael Dukakis of Massachusetts received the presidential nomination of the Democratic Party **July 20**. Dukakis, who had obtained enough delegates by June to assure his nomination, defeated Rev. Jesse Jackson 2 876 votes to 1 218. On the recommendation of Dukakis, the party selected Texas Senator Lloyd Bentsen, 67, as his vice-presidential running mate. Bentsen had a more conservative record than Dukakis on national defence, supporting weapons such as the B-1 bomber and the MX missile that Dukakis opposed. Bentsen, unlike Dukakis, also supported aid to the Nicaraguan contras. In his acceptance speech **July 21**, Dukakis said his campaign was about competence rather than ideology. His themes included the importance of the family and traditional values, and of honesty in government.

Jordan Drops Claims to West Bank—King Hussein of Jordan said **July 31** in a televised address that he was renouncing all claims to the Israeli-occupied West Bank. This land, lying west of the Jordan River and the home of 850 000 Palestinians, had been ruled by Jordan from 1948 until 1967, when it fell to Israel as a result of its war with Jordan. After 1967, Jordan had

continued to provide services to the West Bank, regulating business, subsidizing hospitals and schools, and administering laws. Jordan also paid salaries to 21 000 public employees. The King said, "We respect the wish of the PLO, the sole legitimate representative of the Palestinian people, to secede from us in an independent Palestinian state."

Armenian Demands Rejected—The Presidium of the Supreme Soviet voted **July 18** to reject demands by the Nagorno-Karabakh Autonomous Region to split from the republic of Azerbaijan and join the Armenian republic. Armenians constituted an ethnic majority in the region. In conformity with the new policy of openness, the Soviet people were allowed to watch the Presidium's debate on television. Soviet Leader Mikhail Gorbachev opposed the territorial realignment and rebuked officials in the 2 republics for putting local needs ahead of national considerations.

Report Warns Against Fat in Diet—A U.S. government report released **July 27** warned that fat in the diet was a major cause of death from heart disease, cancer, strokes, diabetes, and atherosclerosis. The 712-page "Surgeon General's Report on Fitness and Health" had been 4 years in preparation. It found that dietary shortcomings were related to 2 of every 3 deaths in the United States in 1987. The report called for increased consumption of fibre and complex carbohydates from whole-grain foods, cereals, fruits, and vegetables. Limited consumption of salt and alcohol was recommended, and children and women of child-bearing age were advised to eat more foods rich in iron—lean meat, fish, beans, and cereals.

Canada

New Bilingual Legislation Approved—The House of Commons approved new legislation promoting bilingualism **July 7**. The bill, which updated the 19-year-old *Official Languages Act*, guaranteed the right to a trial in either French or English and provided greater opportunity for civil servants to work in the official language of their choice. The legislation was opposed by 9 dissident Tory MPs, some of whom argued that the bill would limit job opportunities for persons who spoke only one official language.

Senate To Force Election On Free Trade—The Liberals will use their majority in the Senate to block the Conservative government's free trade legislation and force an election on the issue, Liberal Leader John Turner announced **July 20**. "Call an election and let the people decide," Turner told Prime Minister Brian Mulroney in the House of Commons. Mulroney criticized Turner for using the Senate to block the will of the democratically-elected House of Commons.

Canada and Iran to Resume Relations—Canada and Iran will resume normal diplomatic relations for the first time in more than 8 years, External Affairs Minister Joe Clark announced **July 18**. The Canadian embassy in Tehran closed in 1980, shortly after Canadian diplomats helped smuggle 6 U.S. hostages out of Iran.

August

International

Iran, Iraq Implement Cease-Fire—A cease-fire in the Iran-Iraq war went into effect in August. U.N. Secretary Gen. Javier Pérez de Cuéllar said **Aug. 5** that he planned to send 250 military observers to monitor the truce in the Persion Gulf. He announced **Aug. 8** that the cease-fire would begin **Aug. 20**, and that both parties would begin to discuss a final settlement. On **Aug. 20**, as the truce took effect, members of the peacekeeping force took positions along the Iran-Iraq frontier. On **Aug. 25**, foreign ministers of the 2 countries began their talks in Geneva.

Pakistani President Dies in Crash—Pres. Zia ul-Haq of Pakistan died **Aug. 17** when the plane in which he was travelling exploded in the air over eastern Pakistan and crashed. All 30 aboard were killed, including the U.S. Ambassador to Pakistan and several high-ranking Pakistani military officers. The cause of the disaster was not known, but speculation was widespread that the C-130 Hercules transport had been shot down or sabotaged. Gulam Ishaq Khan, chairman of the Pakistani Senate, became acting president. He declared a state of emergency, but announced that general elections scheduled for Nov. 16 would take place.

Republicans Nominate Bush and Quayle—Vice President George Bush was his party's unanimous nominee for president at the Republican National Convention which opened **Aug. 15**. But much of the convention news coverage centred around his surprise choice as running mate, Senator Dan Quayle of Indiana. Quayle, 41, a conservative, was repeatedly questioned about his service in the National Guard during the Vietnam War. It was established that Quayle had sought help to get into the Guard, which was widely viewed during the 1960s as a means of avoiding combat in Vietnam. Quayle said he was proud of his Guard service. In his acceptance speech, Bush said his administration would produce 30 million new jobs and pledged not to raise taxes.

Crash at Air Show Kills 50—A spectacular performance by a precision flying team at an air show in West Germany ended in tragedy **Aug. 28**. Three jet planes being flown by members of an Italian team crashed in midair over a crowd of 300 000 people. The planes were sweeping low over the crowd at the time of the accident. One of the 3 jets plunged into a field filled with spectators attending the performance at Ramstein Air Base, a U.S. base 100 km southwest of Frankfurt. All 3 pilots involved in the crash were among those killed. The death toll was over 50. Some 500 persons were injured, with many suffering severe burns.

New Burmese Leader Resigns—Western diplomats estimated that as many as 1500 persons may have been killed in several days of clashes between Burmese demonstrators and Army troops. Another casualty was U Sein Lwin, who had come to power in July and then resigned **Aug. 12**. On **Aug. 19**, Burma's ruling party chose Attorney Gen. Maung Maung to lead the country. He was named chairman of the Burma Socialist Program Party and elected president by the People's Assembly. Students and others objecting to one-party rule continued to demonstrate against the regime.

Thousands Slain in Burundi—The government of Burundi said **Aug. 22** that at least 5000 persons had been killed in the central African country as the result of ethnic clashes between the ruling Tutsi tribe and the Hutu tribe. Although the Tutsi constituted only 15 percent of the population, they ran the government and army with a firm hand. Details of the violence were uncertain, but it may have begun with a small exchange in which a few persons were killed. A slaughter of the virtually defenseless Hutu by army troops appearently followed.

U.S. Soviet Scientists Conduct A-Test—On **Aug. 17**, in the Nevada desert, U.S. and Soviet scientists conducted a joint nuclear test for the first time. Forty-three Soviet scientists were among the observers as the United States detonated a nuclear device 2000 feet underground. The purpose was to refine techniques for verifying underground nuclear explosions.

Jury Finds That Hunt Brothers Conspired—A federal jury concluded, **Aug. 20**, in New York City that 3 of the Hunt brothers of Dallas, Tex., had engaged in a conspiracy with others to corner the silver market in 1979 and 1980. Nelson Bunker Hunt, William Herbert Hunt, and Lamar Hunt were found to have committed fraud and to have violated commodity and antitrust laws. The Hunts and the other defendants were ordered to pay more than $130 million in damages to a government-owned commodities company in Peru. The company, Minpeco S.A., said it had lost $151 million while the Hunts were manipulating the market.

Disasters—Some 400 people may have died **Aug. 6** when a ferry capsized in the Ganges River in India . . . An earthquake in India and Nepal **Aug. 21** killed more than 800 people.

Canada

Immigration Rule Eased—It will be easier for adult children to sponsor the immigration of their parents under new rules announced by Immigration Minister Barbara McDougall in

August. The new rule will allow anyone 18 years of age or older, and who has been a resident of Canada for at least 3 years, to sponsor parents of any age under the family class. Previously, this could be applied only to parents who were older than 60, infirm or widowed.

Canadian Troops Monitor Ceasefire—The first of 385 Canadian peacekeeping troops left for the Middle East in August as part of the United Nations' monitoring of the Iran-Iraq ceasefire. Fifteen members of the Canadian force were to be officers acting as observers; most of the remainder would be communicators and support staff in charge of the U.N. signalling operation.

Toxic Cloud Forces Evacuation—Three thousand people were forced from their homes by a toxic chemical cloud in St.-Basile-le-Grand, Que. **Aug. 24**. The cloud of thick smoke was caused by burning PCB-laced oil during a warehouse fire in the suburb east of Montreal.

Swimmer Conquers All 5 Great Lakes—Marathon swimmer Vicki Keith completed the crossing of Lake Ontario **Aug. 30**, successfully ending her quest to be the first person to swim all 5 Great Lakes. Keith was raising funds for charity.

September

International

Worst Hurricane of Century Hits Caribbean—At least 300 people were killed and a million left homeless as Hurricane Gilbert swept a path of destruction through the Caribbean and Mexico **Sept. 11-17**. The worst hurricane of this century brought torrential rains and winds of up to 320 km/h. In Jamaica alone, where Gilbert hit **Sept. 12**, damage was estimated at $10 billion.

Bangladesh Flood Leaves Millions Homeless—Raging floods covering 3-quarters of Bangladesh left 25 million people homeless in early September. The official death toll was given as 900, but unofficial reports listed it at 1 600. Various nations and international agencies quickly pledged $250 million in aid. Canada promised $5 million in assistance.

Fire Rages Through Yellowstone—Wyoming's Yellowstone National Park was closed to visitors for the first time in its 116-year history as forest fire conditions worsened there in September. The fires, which began in June, had already charred a third of the one million hectare park.

Canada

Tories Re-Elected in Nova Scotia—The Conservative government of Premier John Buchanan was returned for a fourth term by Nova Scotia voters **Sept. 6**. The Tories were re-elected with a reduced majority, winning 28 of the 42 seats in the provincial legislature. The Liberals won 21 seats, the New Democrats 2, and one independent was elected.

Native Land Settlement Reached—A tentative land claim settlement between the federal government and the 13 000 Dene and Métis of the Northwest Territories was signed **Sept. 5**. The agreement, reached after 13 years of negotiations, grants native ownership to 180 000 sq. km of land. The Dene and Métis would have full ownership of natural resources on 8 200 sq. km of this land and shared mineral and exploration revenue on the remainder. The boundaries of the land settlement were to be further negotiated. In addition, the Dene and Métis are to receive $500 million over the next 20 years.

Japanese-Canadians Receive Restitution—A formal apology to Japanese-Canadians interned during World War II was given by Prime Minister Brian Mulroney in the House of Commons **Sept. 23**. Mulroney also announced a $291 million compensation package. This included $21 000 tax-free for each survivor of the internment, $12 million to the Japanese-Canadian community for educational, social and cultural activities, and $24 million for a new Canadian Race Relations Foundation. The compensation, which was opposed by the Royal Canadian Legion and some Tory MPs, sparked renewed demands for restitution from other ethnic groups, such as the Ukrainian-Canadians who were interned during World War I.

sample had tested positive for Stanozolol, a banned drug used by some athletes to increase strength. Canadian Sports Minister Jean Charest immediately announced a lifetime ban on Johnson competing for Canada. In a press conference **Oct. 4**, Johnson said he never "knowingly" took drugs. But fellow sprinter Angela Issajenko said **Oct. 8** that both she and Johnson had been taking steroids for years. And sprinter Angela Bailey said **Oct. 9** that many Canadian runners had been taking drugs. The federal government announced that it would conduct an inquiry.

October

International

Ben Johnson Stripped of Gold Medal—Canadians were alternately thrilled and then dismayed as Ben Johnson won an Olympic gold medal in record-breaking time but 2 days later was stripped of both the medal and the record for taking anabolic steroids. Johnson, competing in the 100 m sprint against arch rival Carl Lewis of the U.S., **Sept. 24**, won the gold in 9.79 seconds. But on **Sept. 26** it was announced that Johnson's urine

Canada

Federal Election Called For November—Prime Minister Brian Mulroney ended months of speculation **Oct. 1** when he announced Nov. 21 as the date of the federal election. The election was expected to centre on the free trade issue.

Canadian Buys PTL—A businessman from North York, Ont. confirmed **Oct. 4** that he had purchased Jim and Tammy Faye Baker's PTL Christian empire. Stephen Mernick, who paid $115 million for PTL's assets, which include an 890-hectare property and the Heritage U.S.A. theme park, said he saw the purchase as "an excellent real estate opportunity."

Off-Beat News Stories of 1988

Gone But Not Forgotten—An Illinois man continued to live in his home for 9 years after his death, while his wife, a registered nurse, continued to tend to his corpse as if it were alive. "Although it was obvious he'd been dead 8 years, the family sincerely thought he was fine, the way he was being treated," said Knox County Sheriff Mark Shearer. "They changed his clothes and bedding just like he was sick. There's also evidence they moved him around the house to different rooms and chairs." Carole Stevens told friends and co-workers of her husband, Carl, that he was not receiving visitors, and managed to persuade her teenage children that their father was alive despite his grisly appearance, court was told. Though Steven's disappearance was investigated, his brother threatened a harassment lawsuit and "people stopped inquiring," a detective said.

One Down, Eight to Go—Reports of Smokey the cat's death were greatly exaggerated—as his startled owner discovered when he turned up alive and purring at her windowsill 2 months after she had ordered him put to sleep. Mickey Beswick, 70, of Toronto, decided her cat would be better off dead when it became distraught over the death of her husband and pet poodle. "He (Smokey) just cried day and night," she said. After paying a $40 bill and receiving a sympathy card from the veterinarian, Beswick considered the deed done. But the cat was spared when a visitor to the veterinary clinic offered the feline a new lease on life. Smokey, not one to hold a grudge, escaped from his benefactor and made the one-km trek home for a joyful reunion with Beswick.

Did She Receive Her Training in the Civil Service?—A Toronto-Dominion Bank teller foiled a robbery attempt by advising the would-be robber that he'd filled out the wrong form. Leonard Goodin presented the TD teller with a holdup note written on a Royal Bank of Canada withdrawal slip. "You have the wrong bank. This is the Toronto-Dominion, not the Royal," said the teller, handing back the note. Goodin pushed the note back to her, along with a paper bag into which the money was to be stuffed. When the teller again informed the would-be bandit that he was in the wrong bank, court was told, "the accused stared at the victim, shook his head and left the bank." An hour later he successfully robbed another bank—even though it wasn't a Royal branch either. Afterwards, authorities were aided in their search to find Goodin when he phoned the Toronto police to complain that some of the money he had stolen from the bank had, in turn, been stolen from him. When police officers responding to the call asked Goodin to state his occupation, he replied "bank robber".

Man's Best Friend Turns Him In—A Calgary man was charged with marijuana posession in May after authorities received an anonymous tip from his pet pooch. The dog knocked his master's phone off the hook and punched zero. A telephone operator, hearing rustling but no voice at the end of the line, became alarmed and had the call traced. An emergency medical crew arrived, followed by police who discovered a crop of 60 marijuana plants.

No, It Was Pvt. Doberman Who Was Played By The Dalai Lama—A Tibetan soldier who tried to tear off a British woman's Sgt. Bilko T-shirt became the first known case of someone mistaking Phil Silvers for the Dalai Lama. Kris Tait was on vacation in the town of Gyangste when the soldier noticed the shirt with the likeness of the character Silvers played in the 1950s television series. As he tried to remove the shirt, a crowd of Tibetans gathered, pointed at the portrait and chanted "Dalai Lama!" After finding a change of clothes, the tourist, an avid Sgt. Bilko fan, observed: "Looking back on it, I suppose he does look a bit like the Dalai Lama."

Divorce Lawyer Fights For Custody of Dog—Well-known U.S. lawyer Melvin Belli announced in July that he would take legal action to gain custody of his Italian greyhound, Rumproast. Belli's estranged wife, Lia, allowed him to take 3 of the couple's 4 dogs but refused to give up "Rumpy." "All I want is that the dog be with the other dogs; the dogs hate her (Lia)," Belli said. "I slept with those dogs for the past 5 or 6 years when I kicked her out of my bed."

Life In The Fast Lane—Robert Henshew was fined $58 for driving his van in the car pool lane. In Santa Ana, Calif., only vehicles with at least 2 people inside can use these lanes. Hanshew, who transports cadavers for a mortuary transportation service, claimed that the 4 frozen corpses in his van qualified as passengers. But a judge ruled that passengers must be alive to qualify for the fast lane.

What Happens If They Become Overstaffed?—When the Stockholm zoo discovered it didn't have enough space for a popular bear cub, officials decided to solve the problem by eating it. The 2-year-old cub, Molly, was served to staff at the Skansen Park Zoo. But the zoo's, caretaker, for one, refused to partake of the meal, saying "Molly was so nice I didn't take a bite."

You Can't Get There From Here—The Soviet Union's chief map maker announced that authorities had decided to begin releasing accurate maps of the country. Victor Yashchenko said that, for 50 years, almost all public maps had been deliberately falsified. "Roads and rivers were moved, city districts were tilted, streets and houses were incorrectly indicated," and on the tourist map of Moscow only the contours of the capital were accurate, he said. Tourist maps of other cities often did not even contain major streets. The falsification of maps began in the 1930s when the map-making administration was put under the control of the security police, which thought the incorrect maps would help protect the nation from aerial bombing and foreign intelligence. American diplomats and correspondents based in Moscow had found that the most reliable map of the city was produced in the United States by the Central Intelligence Agency.

Money Rains—A different kind of whiteout stopped motorists on Toronto's Gardiner Expressway last March when the back doors of an armoured vehicle blew open and $50 and $20, bills spilled out. As a police sergeant at the scene described "People were chasing money all over the place. From east and west (-bound) lanes, climbing over the guard rails. Everything." Though most motorists grabbed only loose bills, 2 made off with bags of money containing $75 000 apiece. Police demanded that the money be returned, but at least one bag and numerous loose bills were not recovered.

Sleepwalker Acquitted of Murder—A Pickering, Ont. man who beat and stabbed his mother-in-law to death was acquitted of the crime when it was found that he was sleepwalking at the time. The man, who was said to be under a great deal of stress when the crime occurred because of his addiction to gambling and theft of $32 000 from his employer, drove 23 km from his own home to the house of his in-laws where he attacked his mother-in-law and father-in-law. The case was the first of its kind in Canada and among only 30 to 35 similar cases documented worldwide.

Young Drivers of America Takes On New Meaning—In Port Chester, NY, 5-year-old Rocco Morabito and his 2-year-old sister borrowed their mother's car to take a ride. Four km from home they were stopped by a police officer who noticed that a station wagon—which was obeying all traffic rules—appeared to be driverless. "I observed that the car was being driven pretty well," remarked the officer, "but all I could see was a small girl standing in the back seat. It looked like the invisible man was driving the car." When pulled over, both children began to cry. Later, when the police told the kids that their mother would have to come and pick them up, Rocco explained, "My mommy can't come here because I have the only car. I can drive. I'll go get her."

Yankee Killer—The Toronto Blue Jays baseball club announced that it will pay a falconer $100 000 a year to scare away gulls from their new SkyDome stadium which will feature a retractable roof. The scavenging gulls from nearby Lake Ontario are expected to pose the same problems they have at Exhibition Stadium. The falcon will be called Winfield, in honor of the N.Y. Yankee outfielder who was arrested for killing a gull with a thrown ball in 1983.

They're Sure Glad Elephants Don't Fly—The Stoneham, Mass. police were forced to conduct daily Canada geese round-ups because of a multiplying gaggle that was stopping traffic, munching parched lawns, and making people careful of where they step. "The droppings are awesome," said town administrator Bill Reid. The birds stopped at the town in the course of their migration, were fed by the people, and stayed instead of moving on. Since Canada geese are a protected species, it is illegal to kill them. Residents shoo them off their lawns with brooms and honk their horns to get them out of the streets.

Poor Tippers Beware!—The mayor of Paris ridicules the idea, the police are skeptical, while some medical authorities certify that it will not kill cardiac patients. Parisian taxi drivers, in search of protection against thieves and muggers, are installing the "blazing seat," an electric cushion slipped under the passenger seat and attached to a powerful battery. At the touch of a button, the device delivers 52,000 volts of low-tension electric current to the back of the spine. It is more powerful than the police weapon known as the "stun gun," which delivers about 45 000 volts. Defenders of the "seat" argue that there are some 40 assaults on taxi drivers reported each month. "We are not sheep waiting to be slaughtered" a spokesman said.

Is That All There Is?—The average person's lifetime includes 6 years eating, 4 years cleaning and 2 years trying to return telephone calls to people who never seem to be in, according to a time-management study conducted by the consulting firm Priority Management Pittsburgh Inc. The year-long study also found that a person spends 6 months at stoplights, one year searching for misplaced objects, and eight months opening junk mail. In this telephone survey of over 1 000 married people, it was estimated that the average married couple spends 4 minutes a day in meaningful conversation and that working couples spend 30 seconds a day talking with their children.

Historical Anniversaries
1969—20 Years Ago

Richard M. Nixon was inaugurated as the 37th President of the U.S.

Apollo 11, launched from Cape Kennedy, landed the lunar module on the moon's surface on July 20; Neil Armstrong stepped out on the moon on July 21.

Two Mariner space probes sent back pictures of the surface of Mars.

The first U.S. troops were withdrawn from Vietnam.

Sirhan Sirhan was tried and convicted of the murder of Senator Robert F. Kennedy.

James Earl Ray was sentenced to 99 years in prison for the assassination of Rev. Martin Luther King, Jr.

The New Czech federal government was inaugurated.

Al Fatah leader Yasir Arafat was elected Chairman of the Executive Committee of the Palestine Liberation Organization, and shifted his main guerilla forces to Jordan.

Mrs. Golda Meir became Israel's fourth Prime Minister.

The British army sent 600 troops into Belfast, Northern Ireland, to quell the fighting between Protestants and Roman Catholics.

Canada's abortion law was liberalized.

U.S. Senator Edward M. Kennedy, driving a car at Chappaquiddick Island, Mass., plunged into a pond, and the body of a passenger, Mary Jo Kopechne, was found in the car.

The Woodstock Music and Art Fair, near Bethel, New York, attracted more than 300 000.

"Sesame Street" began on Public Service television stations.

The Ford Maverick was introduced to compete with Volkswagen and other foreign compact cars.

Doonesbury, the comic strip by Garry Trudeau, age 20, began syndication.

Penthouse magazine began publication; *The Saturday Evening Post* ceased, after 148 years.

Trousers became acceptable as everyday wear by women. Pantyhose production soared.

Saturday postal deliveries ended in Canada.

The breathalyzer came into use in Canada as a way of testing whether drivers were impaired by alcohol.

Books: *Portnoy's Complaint*, by Philip Roth; *The Godfather*, by Mario Puzo; *An Unfinished Woman*, by Lillian Hellman; *Slaughterhouse-Five*, by Kurt Vonnegut, Jr.; *Armies of the Night*, by Norman Mailer.

Art: "The Finn," by Andrew Wyeth; "Orange Yellow Orange," by Mark Rothko.

Theatre: "To Be Young, Gifted and Black," by Lorraine Hansberry; "No Place to Be Somebody," by Charles Gordone; "Last of the Red Hot Lovers," by Neil Simon; "Oh! Calcutta!"

Movies: "Midnight Cowboy"; "Easy Rider"; "Bullitt"; "Butch Cassidy and the Sundance Kid"; "M*A*S*H."

Music: "Get Back" (Beatles); "Honky Tonk Women" (Rolling Stones); "Everyday People" (Sly & The Family Stone); Aquarius/Let The Sunshine In" (5th Dimension).

Sports: Montreal Expos began their first season as baseball's 2 major leagues split into eastern and western divisions. The New York Mets won their first World Series by defeating the Baltimore Orioles 4 games to one. Montreal Canadiens won the Stanley Cup for the 4th time in 5 years. Phil Esposito of the Boston Bruins won the NHL scoring championship and Hart trophy as most valuable player. Ottawa Rough Riders won their 2nd consecutive Grey Cup. Rod Laver won the Grand Slam of tennis for the 2d time. For the 4th year in a row, and the 8th out of the previous 10, Wilt "the Stilt" Chamberlain was rebound leader in the NBA; he also held most of the other NBA records.

1939—50 Years Ago

World War II began one week after the Aug. 23 signing of a mutual nonaggression pact between Nazi Germany and Soviet Russia. Hitler occupied Bohemia and Moravia and annexed Memel. German troops and aircraft attacked Poland on Sept. 1. Britain and France declared war on Germany on Sept. 3, as a German U-boat sank the British ship Athenia off the Irish coast. Canada declared war on Germany one week later. Soviet troops invaded Poland from the east on Sept. 17; Warsaw surrendered to the Germans on Sept. 28, and Poland was partitioned on Sept. 28 between Germany and the USSR. Italy invaded Albania. Conscription was adopted in Britain; women and children were evacuated from London.

The Spanish Civil War ended on Mar. 28 with the fall of Madrid to Francisco Franco.

After the 1938 recession, the U.S. economy began to recover and by fall was booming, due to European countries' orders for arms and war equipment.

The possibility of self-sustaining nuclear fission was proved on Mar. 3 at Columbia Univ. in New York by Enrico Fermi, Hungarian-American physicist Leo Szilard and their colleagues. These and other findings were discussed by Niels Bohr with Albert Einstein at Princeton, N.J., after which Einstein wrote to Pres. Franklin D. Roosevelt: "This new phenomenon would lead also to the construction of bombs."

Radar stations were used in Britain to give early warnings of approaching enemy aircraft.

The first commercial transatlantic passenger air service began on June 28, as 22 passengers and 12 crew members took off from Port Washington, N.Y., for Marseilles via the Azores and Lisbon, aboard the Pan American Airways "Yankee Clipper."

The first turbojet aircraft was tested Aug. 28 at Rostock-Marienehe and was demonstrated in Oct. for high officials of the German Luftwaffe.

Igor Sikorsky, a Russian-American inventor, constructed the first helicopter. Paul Muller synthesized DDT. Polyethylene was invented. Nylon stockings first appeared. Cup-sizing for brassieres was introduced by Warner Brothers Company of Bridge-

port, Conn. Pall Mall cigarettes in a new 85-mm length became the first U.S. "king-sized" cigarettes. The first precooked frozen foods were introduced under the Birds Eye label by General Foods Corporation, which marketed a chicken fricasee and a criss-cross steak.

"Batman" was launched by U.S. cartoonist Bob Kane. *Glamour* magazine began publication. Pocket Books Americanized the paperback revolution in publishing begun by Britain's Penguin Books in 1936; the new paperback house put out 25-cent reprints of literary classics.

Books: *Finnegans Wake*, by James Joyce; *The Grapes of Wrath*, by John Steinbeck; *The Big Sleep*, by Raymond Chandler, which introduced private eye Philip Marlowe. Children's: *Madeline*, by Ludwig Bemelmans; *Mike Mulligan and His Steam Shovel*, by Virginia Lee Burton.

Art: 79-year-old Anna Mary Robertson—"Grandma Moses"—was discovered; "Reclining Figure" sculpture, by Henry Moore; "Poison and Objective Stimulation," by Rene Magritte; "Seated Man," by Willem de Kooning; "Handball," by Ben Shahn; "Retrato de Pita Amor," by Diego Rivera.

Theatre: "Life With Father," by Lindsay and Crouse; "The Man Who Came to Dinner," by Kaufman and Hart; "The Time of Your Life," by William Saroyan; "The Little Foxes," by Lillian Hellman; "The Philadelphia Story," by Philip Barry; "Du Barry Was a Lady."

Movies: "Gone With the Wind"; "The Wizard of Oz"; "Ninotchka," with Greta Garbo; "Stagecoach," by John Ford; "Good-Bye, Mr. Chips"; "Dark Victory"; "Gunga Din"; "The Hound of the Baskervilles"; "Intermezzo"; "Wuthering Heights"; "The Hunchback of Notre Dame"; "Of Mice and Men"; "Destry Rides Again"; "Mr. Smith Goes to Washington"; "Young Mr. Lincoln."

Music: New Jersey roadhouse singer Frank Sinatra, age 23, joined Harry James and his new band. Songs: "Moonlight Serenade," "In the Mood," "All or Nothing at All," "Three Little Fishes," "Beer Barrel Polka," "God Bless America."

Sports: Ted Williams was brought up by the Boston Red Sox. Yankee "Iron Horse" Lou Gehrig was stricken with amyotropic lateral sclerosis, and said a tearful goodbye to fans on July 4. Mel Allen began broadcasting Yankee baseball games for New York's CBS radio station. The first baseball game was broadcast on TV. The Baseball Hall of Fame was established at Cooperstown, N.Y. Football helmets were made mandatory in U.S. college football competition.

1889—100 Years Ago

A worldwide influenza pandemic began which would affect forty percent of the human race in the next two years.

Japan got its first constitution.

The first Pan-American Conference opened in Washington, D.C., to cement relations among Western Hemisphere nations.

The French Panama Canal Company went bankrupt after having spent hundreds of millions of dollars in an effort to build the canal, and after losing the lives of some 20 000 French, Chinese, Irish, and West Indian laborers to epidemics of malaria and yellow fever.

The first 1000 of the 7000 Canadian troops left for South Africa to assist Britain in the Boer War.

Alexandre Gustave Eiffel designed the 322 m Eiffel Tower for the Paris World Exhibition, celebrating the 100th aniversary of the French Revolution. The masterpiece of wrought-iron technology was built from a detailed set of plans: the 12 000 metal parts were all pre-fabricated and numbered for assembly, and most of the 2.5 million rivets were put into place before the structure was erected at the site.

Europe's Orient Express began to travel between Paris and Constantinople without change of train. The first run took 67 hours, 35 minutes.

The Johnstown flood of May 31 killed 2000 to 5000 Pennsylvanians in a city of 30 000. It was one of the country's worst peacetime calamities.

London's Savoy Hotel opened, the first British hotel to have private baths. Under the management of Swiss-born Cesar Ritz, it became the most successful luxury hotel in the world. Later Ritz would open hotels in major cities of the world, and the word "ritzy" would come to denote the ultimate in fashion and social status.

Science & Inventions

G.V. Schiaparelli discovered the synchronous rotations of the planets Mercury and Venus.

Von Mehring and Minkowski proved that the pancreas secretes insulin, preventing diabetes.

Europe's first electric trolley car went into service at Northfleet, Kent, England.

The world's first electric elevators were installed by the Otis Company in New York's Demarest Building on Fifth Avenue at 33rd Street.

Electric lights were installed at the White House. Since neither President Harrison nor his wife would touch the switch, an employee turned the lights on and off.

I.M. Singer introduced the first electric sewing machine and sold a million of them the first year.

The first electric train lighting system was patented by U.S. inventor Henry Ward Leonard, age 28, who had worked with Thomas Edison to introduce the central station electrical system for cities.

A coin-operated telephone patented by a Hartford, Conn. inventor, William Gray, was installed in the Hartford Bank.

New York's first real skyscraper, designed by Bradford Lee Gilbert, opened at 50 Broadway; it was 13 stories high.

Aunt Jemima pancake flour, invented at St. Joseph, Mo., became the first self-rising flour for pancakes and the first readymix food ever to be introduced commercially.

Arts & Entertainment

Mark Twain published *A Connecticut Yankee in King Arthur's Court*. *The Wall Street Journal* began publication. Vincent Van Gogh painted "Landscape with Cypress Trees," "The Starry Night," and "Self-Portrait with Bandaged Ear"; Paul Gauguin painted "Still Life with Japanese Print"; Winslow Homer painted "The Gulf Stream." John Philip Sousa wrote the "Washington Post March."

Sports

John L. Sullivan, age 30, defeated Jake Kilrain at Richburg, Miss., in July, in a 75-round fight that lasted for 2 hours and 16 minutes in 41°C heat. This was the last major bareknuckle fight.

Milestones

Born in 1889: Adolf Hitler, Charlie Chaplin, German philosopher Martin Heidegger, French author Jean Cocteau, and American playwright George S. Kaufman. English poet Robert Browning died.

1789—200 Years Ago

The first U.S. Congress met in New York City. George Washington was inaugurated as U.S. President; John Adams, Vice President; Thomas Jefferson, Secretary of State; and Alexander Hamilton, Secretary of the Treasury.

The French Revolution took place, with the Paris mob storming the Bastille, the French feudal system abolished and the Rights of Man declared.

The first steam-driven cotton factory opened in Manchester, England.

England's textile technology was transplanted to the U.S. by Derbyshire technician Samuel Slater, 21, the father of the American factory system.

Songs of Innocence, by William Blake, was published.

Elements of Chemistry, by Antoine Lavoisier, became the first modern chemical textbook.

Chrysanthemums were introduced from the Orient to Britain.

Hookworm got its name in a report by a German zoologist.

The Mutineers of the HMS Bounty settled on Pitcairn Island in the E. Pacific.

The first known American advertisement for tobacco appeared, with a picture of an Indian smoking a long clay pipe while leaning against a hogshead marked "Best Virginia."

The first bourbon whiskey was distilled by a Baptist minister, Elijah Craig, in the bluegrass country established the previous year as Kentucky County.

1589—400 Years Ago

Galileo Galilei became a professor of mathematics at the University of Pisa.

The Reverend William Lee of Cambridge invented the stocking frame, the first knitting machine.

The Bourbon dynasty that would rule France until 1792 was founded by Henri of Navarre, beginning a 21-year reign as Henri IV.

Forks were used for the first time at the French court.

1489—500 Years Ago

The first major European epidemic of typhus broke out in Aragon, where the disease was introduced by Spanish soldiers returning from Cyprus.

The symbols + (plus) and − (minus) came into use.

The Constitution of Canada

The Constitution is the supreme law of Canada. It is composed of written documents and unwritten conventions that define the powers and structure of Canadian government and the rights and freedoms of the Canadian people. Any federal or provincial law found by the courts to be inconsistent with the Constitution is invalid.

Canada's written constitution includes the following documents: (1) The *Constitution Acts, 1867 to 1982* (which includes the Canadian Charter of Rights and Freedoms); (2) The orders in council and statutes which admitted or created new provinces or altered boundaries; (3) The *Statute of Westminster, 1931;* (4) The *Canada Act 1982;* (5) Any amendments to the above documents.

The Constitution Act, 1867

The *Constitution Act, 1867* is now the official name for the *British North America (BNA) Act, 1867.* The BNA Act was passed by the United Kingdom Parliament in 1867 to confederate 3 of Britain's North American colonies: New Brunswick, Nova Scotia and Canada (now Ontario and Quebec).

Unlike the U.S. Constitution, which dealt in detail with a host of matters vital to the formation of a new, totally independent republic, the BNA Act was chiefly designed to provide a framework for a federal system of government in the new Dominion of Canada, and to define the spheres of authority for the federal Parliament and the provincial legislatures. Beyond these basic provisions, Canada would simply follow unwritten British constitutional conventions. It was still a British colony, and all of Canada's laws—whether federal or provincial—remained subject to imperial statutes by virtue of Britain's *Colonial Laws Validity Act, 1865.*

The Statute of Westminster

As Canada matured as a nation, its relationship with Britain began to change. In 1931, the U.K. Parliament enacted the *Statute of Westminster* to recognize the evolving independence of British Dominions. This act abolished the rule making colonial laws subject to imperial statutes and empowered the Canadian Parliament and provincial legislatures to amend any imperial statute affecting Canada—except the BNA Act which, at Canada's request, was to remain alterable only by the U.K. Parliament.

Furthermore, at the Imperial Conference of 1930, the U.K. adopted a convention that no laws extending to Canada would be passed except at Canada's request. Thus, although the power to amend the BNA Act remained in Britain, Britain would only exercise that power when specifically requested to do so by Canada.

The Canada Act

The impetus for modern constitutional change came in 1980 with the Quebec referendum on "sovereignty-association," a form of separation from Canada. During the campaigning that preceded the May 20 vote, federalist supporters assured the people of Quebec that defeat of the referendum would lead to constitutional changes that would accommodate fairly the special needs of Quebec within the Canadian confederation. The majority of Quebecers voted against sovereignty-association and the process of constitutional reform began shortly afterward with a series of federal-provincial conferences.

At first, no agreement on constitutional change could be reached; so a determined Prime Minister Pierre Trudeau proposed to have the federal government act without provincial consent to "patriate" the Constitution—that is, to eliminate the authority of the U.K. Parliament in Canadian constitutional matters.

The first version of the *Canada Act* was prepared. Following lengthy debates and numerous amendments, the text was passed as a "resolution" by the House of Commons and the Senate in April 1981.

But many provinces were dissatisfied. Manitoba, Quebec and Newfoundland all initiated court challenges to the federal action. They argued that the constitutional changes contained in the *Canada Act* would affect provincial legislative powers and that the federal Parliament, therefore, had no authority to make such changes without provincial consent.

On September 28, 1981 the Supreme Court of Canada ruled that although no provincial consent was required by law, "substantial" provincial consent was necessary by convention. The Court did not define "substantial" but did state that the consent of only 2 provinces was not enough. Since only Ontario and New Brunswick supported the federal package, it was clear that the federal government would be violating constitutional convention if it continued to act without a greater provincial mandate.

More federal-provincial discussions followed the Supreme Court's decision. In November, 1981, a new version of the constitutional bill was agreed to by every province except Quebec.

It was this new bill that was passed as a resolution by the House of Commons on December 2, 1981, and by the Senate on December 8, 1981.

The resolution consisted of a request formally asking the Parliament of the United Kingdom to pass a bill entitled the *Canada Act 1982.*

The Constitution Act, 1982

The *Canada Act 1982* was passed by the U.K. Parliament on March 29, 1982, but the constitutional reforms in the *Constitution Act, 1982* were not to become law until "proclaimed into force."

On April 17, 1982, Queen Elizabeth came to Ottawa and signed the proclamation that brought Canada's new constitution into effect.

The most important changes brought about by the *Constitution Act, 1982* were the introduction of the *Canadian Charter of Rights and Freedoms* and the procedures for amending the constitution in the future, without having to appeal to the British Parliament.

Canadian Charter of Rights and Freedoms

Part I of the *Constitution Act, 1982* consists of 34 sections comprising the *Canadian Charter of Rights and Freedoms.* The Charter does not create these rights. Rather, it formally recognizes them, provides constitutional protection to them, and introduces a remedy by which they can be enforced. It is the constitutional entrenchment of rights that makes the Charter different from the *Canadian Bill of Rights* which was passed by the federal government in 1960.

The Bill of Rights was an ordinary statute, not a constitutional document. It applied only to federal laws and could be repealed at any time by Parliament. The Charter, however, can only be amended or repealed by a special constitutional amendment procedure, and it applies to both federal and provincial levels of government.

Constitutional Amendment Procedures

The *Constitution Act, 1982* provides 2 procedures by which the Canadian constitution may be amended. The choice of procedure depends on the nature of the proposed amendment.

For example, amendments relating to such things as the office of the Queen, the Governor General or a provincial lieutenant-governor can only be made if they are authorized by the Senate, the House of Commons and the legislative assembly of every province. Some other matters, such as the powers of the Senate, may be dealt with in resolutions authorized by the Senate, the House of Commons and the legislative assemblies of at least two-thirds of the provinces, having at least 50 percent of the country's population. In other words, if the number of provinces and their relative populations remain as they are today, at least 7 provinces would have to authorize a constitutional amendment; one of the 7 would have to be either Ontario or Quebec because their combined population is more than 50 percent of Canada's total.

Meech Lake

In an effort to obtain Quebec's agreement on constitutional change, which it had rejected in 1982, Prime Minister Brian Mulroney and the 10 provincial premiers met privately at the federal government lodge at Meech Lake, Que, April 30, 1987. Here, and at a subsequent meeting June 2-3 in Ottawa, unanimous agreement was reached on a series of proposals which would shift some powers from the federal government to the provinces and would recognize Quebec as a "distinct society" within Canada. The major proposed changes are:
• all 10 provinces would have the power of veto over any changes in the structure or powers of the Senate, House of Commons or the Supreme Court
• persons to fill vacancies to the Senate and Supreme Court would be chosen by the federal government from among candidates submitted by the provinces
• the practice that 3 of the 9 Supreme Court justices be from Quebec would be enshrined in the Constitution
• a 10-year-old federal-provincial agreement giving Quebec power over selection of immigrants to the province would become part of the Constitution
• the creation of any new provinces would require the consent of all 10 existing provinces
• any province would have the right to opt out of national shared-cost programs in areas of provincial jurisdiction (such as day care or job training); the provinces could then take their share of the federal funds to set up their own programs
• a clause in the Constitution would recognize Quebec as a "distinct society" within Canada. Some opponents of the accord argued that this would allow the province to enact legislation which might over-ride the *Charter of Rights and Freedoms* which guarantees the equality of all Canadians.

As of Sept. 1988, the federal Parliament and 8 of the provinces had approved the accord. But New Brunswick Premier Frank McKenna said he wanted changes to the agreement and it was unclear whether the Manitoba legislature would support it. To become law, the Meech Lake accord must be approved, without change, by Parliament and all provincial legislatures, by June 1990.

Text of The Canadian Charter of Rights and Freedoms

Whereas Canada is founded upon principles that recognize the supremacy of God and the rule of law:

Guarantee of Rights and Freedoms

1. The *Canadian Charter of Rights and Freedoms* guarantees the rights and freedoms set out in it subject only to such reasonable limits prescribed by law as can be demonstrably justified in a free and democratic society.

Fundamental Freedoms

2. Everyone has the following fundamental freedoms: (a) freedom of conscience and religion; (b) freedom of thought, belief, opinion and expression, including freedom of the press and other media of communication; (c) freedom of peaceful assembly; and (d) freedom of association.

Democratic Rights

3. Every citizen of Canada has the right to vote in an election of members of the House of Commons or of a legislative assembly and to be qualified for membership therein.

4. (1) No House of Commons and no legislative assembly shall continue for longer than five years from the date fixed for the return of the writs at a general election of its members.

(2) In time of real or apprehended war, invasion or insurrection, a House of Commons may be continued by Parliament and a legislative assembly may be continued by the legislature beyond five years if such continuation is not opposed by the votes of more than one-third of the members of the House of Commons or the legislative assembly, as the case may be.

5. There shall be a sitting of Parliament and of each legislature at least once every twelve months.

Mobility Rights

6. (1) Every citizen of Canada has the right to enter, remain in and leave Canada.

(2) Every citizen of Canada and every person who has the status of a permanent resident of Canada has the right (a) to move to and take up residence in any province; and (b) to pursue the gaining of a livelihood in any province.

(3) The rights specified in subsection (2) are subject to (a) any laws or practices of general application in force in a province other than those that discriminate among persons primarily on the basis of province of present or previous residence; and (b) any laws providing for reasonable residency requirements as a qualification for the receipt of publicly provided social services.

(4) Subsections (2) and (3) do not preclude any law, program or activity that has as its object the amelioration in a province of conditions of individuals in that province who are socially or economically disadvantaged if the rate of employment in that province is below the rate of employment in Canada.

Legal Rights

7. Everyone has the right to life, liberty and security of the person and the right not to be deprived thereof except in accordance with the principles of fundamental justice.

8. Everyone has the right to be secure against unreasonable search or seizure.

9. Everyone has the right not to be arbitrarily detained or imprisoned.

10. Everyone has the right on arrest or detention (a) to be informed promptly of the reasons therefor; (b) to retain and instruct counsel without delay and to be informed of that right; and (c) to have the validity of the detention determined by way of *habeas corpus* and to be released if the detention is not lawful.

11. Any person charged with an offence has the right (a) to be informed without unreasonable delay of the specific offence; (b) to be tried within a reasonable time; (c) not to be compelled to be a witness in proceedings against that person in respect of the offence; (d) to be presumed innocent until proven guilty according to law in a fair and public hearing by an independent and impartial tribunal; (e) not to be denied reasonable bail without just cause; (f) except in the case of an offence under military law tried before a military tribunal, to the benefit of trial by jury where the maximum punishment for the offence is imprisonment for five years or a more severe punishment; (g) not to be found guilty on account of any act or omission unless, at the time of the act or omission, it constituted an offence under Canadian or international law or was criminal according to the general principles of law recognized by the community of nations; (h) if finally acquitted of the offence, not to be tried for it again and, if finally found guilty and punished for the offence, not to be tried or punished for it again; and (i) if found guilty of the offence and if the punishment for the offence has been varied between the time of commission and the time of sentencing, to the benefit of the lesser punishment.

12. Everyone has the right not to be subjected to any cruel and unusual treatment or punishment.

13. A witness who testifies in any proceedings has the right not to have any incriminating evidence so given used to incriminate that witness in any other proceedings, except in a prosecution for perjury or for the giving of contradictory evidence.

14. A party or witness in any proceedings who does not understand or speak the language in which the proceedings are conducted or who is deaf has the right to the assistance of an interpreter.

Equality Rights

15. (1) Every individual is equal before and under the law and has the right to the equal protection and equal benefit of the law without discrimination and, in particular, without discrimination based on race, national or ethnic origin, colour, religion, sex, age or mental or physical disability.

(2) Subsection (1) does not preclude any law, program or activity that has as its object the amelioration of conditions of disadvantaged individuals or groups including those that are disadvantaged because of race, national or ethnic origin, colour, religion, sex, age or mental or physical disability.

Official Languages of Canada

16. (1) English and French are the official languages of Canada and have equality of status and equal rights and privileges as to their use in all institutions of the Parliament and government of Canada.

(2) English and French are the official languages of New Brunswick and have equality of status and equal rights and privileges as to their use in all institutions of the legislature and government of New Brunswick.

(3) Nothing in this Charter limits the authority of Parliament or a legislature to advance the equality of status or use of English and French.

17. (1) Everyone has the right to use English or French in any debates and other proceedings of Parliament.

(2) Everyone has the right to use English or French in any debates and other proceedings of the legislature of New Brunswick.

18. (1) The statutes, records and journals of Parliament shall be printed and published in English and French and both language versions are equally authoritative.

(2) The statutes, records and journals of the legislature of New Brunswick shall be printed and published in English and French and both language versions are equally authoritative.

19. (1) Either English or French may be used by any person in, or in any pleading in or process issuing from, any court established by Parliament.

(2) Either English or French may be used by any person in, or in any pleading in or process issuing from, any court of New Brunswick.

20. (1) Any member of the public in Canada has the right to communicate with, and to receive available services from, any head or central office of an institution of the Parliament or government of Canada in English or French, and has the same right with respect to any other office of any such institution where (a) there is a significant demand for communications with and services from that office in such language; or (b) due to the nature of the office, it is reasonable that communications with and services from that office be available in both English and French.

(2) Any member of the public in New Brunswick has the right to communicate with, and to receive available services from, any office of an institution of the legislature or government of New Brunswick in English or French.

21. Nothing in sections 16 to 20 abrogates or derogates from any right, privilege or obligation with respect to the English and French languages, or either of them, that exists or is continued by virtue of any other provision of the Constitution of Canada.

22. Nothing in sections 16 to 20 abrogates or derogates from any legal or customary right or privilege acquired or enjoyed either before or after the coming into force of this Charter with respect to any language that is not English or French.

Minority Language Educational Rights

23. (1) Citizens of Canada (a) whose first language learned and still understood is that of the English or French linguistic minority population of the province in which they reside, or (b) who have received their primary school instruction in Canada in English or French and reside in a province where the language in which they received that instruction is the language of the English or French linguistic minority population of the province, have the right to have their children receive primary and secondary school instruction in that language in that province.

(2) Citizens of Canada of whom any child has received or is receiving primary or secondary school instruction in English or French in Canada, have the right to have all their children receive primary and secondary school instruction in the same language.

(3) The right of citizens of Canada under subsections (1) and (2) to have their children receive primary and secondary school instruction in the language of the English or French linguistic minority population of a province (a) applies wherever in the province the number of children of citizens who have such a right is sufficient to warrant the provision to them out of public funds of minority language instruction; and (b) includes, where the number of those children so warrants, the right to have them receive that instruction in minority language educational facilities provided out of public funds.

Enforcement

24. (1) Anyone whose rights or freedoms, as guaranteed by this Charter, have been infringed or denied may apply to a court of competent jurisdiction to obtain such remedy as the court considers appropriate and just in the circumstances.

(2) Where, in proceedings under subsection (1), a court concludes that evidence was obtained in a manner that infringed or denied any rights or freedoms guaranteed by this Charter, the evidence shall be excluded if it is established that, having regard to all the circumstances, the admission of it in the proceedings would bring the administration of justice into disrepute.

General

25. The guarantee in this Charter of certain rights and freedoms shall not be construed so as to abrogate or derogate from any aboriginal, treaty or other rights or freedoms that pertain to the aboriginal peoples of Canada including (a) any rights or freedoms that have been recognized by the Royal Proclamation of October 7, 1763; and (b) any rights or freedoms that may be acquired by the aboriginal peoples of Canada by way of land claims settlement.

26. The guarantee in this Charter of certain rights and freedoms shall not be construed as denying the existence of any other rights or freedoms that exist in Canada.

27. This Charter shall be interpreted in a manner consistent with the preservation and enhancement of the multicultural heritage of Canadians.

28. Notwithstanding anything in this Charter, the rights and freedoms referred to in it are guaranteed equally to male and female persons.

29. Nothing in this Charter abrogates or derogates from any rights or privileges guaranteed by or under the Constitution of Canada in respect of denominational, separate or dissentient schools.

30. A reference in this Charter to a province or to the legislative assembly or legislature or a province shall be deemed to include a reference to the Yukon Territory and the Northwest Territories, or to the appropriate legislative authority thereof, as the case may be.

31. Nothing in this Charter extends the legislative powers of any body or authority.

Application of Charter

32. (1) This Charter applies (a) to the Parliament and government of Canada in respect of all matters within the authority of Parliament including all matters relating to the Yukon Territory and Northwest Territories; and (b) to the legislature and government of each province in respect of all matters within the authority of the legislature of each province.

(2) Notwithstanding subsection (1), section 15 shall not have effect until three years after this section comes into force.

33. (1) Parliament or the legislature of a province may expressly declare in an Act of Parliament or of the legislature, as the case may be, that the Act or a provision thereof shall operate notwithstanding a provision included in section 2 or sections 7 to 15 of this Charter.

(2) An Act or a provision of an Act in respect of which a declaration made under this section is in effect shall have such operation as it would have but for the provision of this Charter referred to in the declaration.

(3) A declaration made under subsection (1) shall cease to have effect five years after it comes into force or on such earlier date as may be specified in the declaration.

(4) Parliament or a legislature of a province may re-enact a declaration made under subsection (1).

(5) Subsection (3) applies in respect of a re-enactment made under subsection (4).

Citation

34. This Part may be cited as the *Canadian Charter of Rights and Freedoms*.

Text of the Meech Lake Accord

The Constitution Act, 1987

Whereas first ministers, assembled in Ottawa, have arrived at a unanimous accord on constitutional amendments that would bring about the full and active participation of Québec in Canada's constitutional evolution, would recognize the principle of equality of all the provinces, would provide new arrangements to foster greater harmony and co-operation between the Government of Canada and the governments of the provinces and would require that annual first ministers' conferences on the state of the Canadian economy and such other matters as may be appropriate be convened and that annual constitutional conferences composed of first ministers be convened commencing not later than Dec. 31, 1988;

And whereas first ministers have also reached unanimous agreement on certain additional commitments in relation to some of those amendments;

Now therefore the Prime Minister of Canada and the first ministers of the provinces commit themselves and the governments they represent to the following:

1. The Prime Minister of Canada will lay or cause to be laid before the Senate and House of Commons, and the first ministers of the provinces will lay or cause to be laid before their legislative assemblies, as soon as possible, a resolution, in the form appended hereto, to authorize a proclamation to be issued by the Governor-General under the Great Seal of Canada to amend the Constitution of Canada.

2. The Government of Canada will, as soon as possible, conclude an agreement with the Government of Quebec that would:

(a) Incorporate the principles of the Cullen-Couture agreement on the selection abroad and in Canada of independent immigrants, visitors for medical treatment, students and temporary workers, and on the selection of refugees abroad and economic criteria for family reunification and assisted relatives;

(b) Guarantee that Quebec will receive a number of immigrants, including refugees, within the annual total established by the federal Government for all of Canada proportionate to its share of the population of Canada, with the right to exceed that figure by 5 per cent for demographic reasons, and;

(c) Provide an undertaking by Canada to withdraw services (except citizenship services) for the reception and integration (including linguistic and cultural) of all foreign nationals wishing to settle in Quebec where services are to be provided by Quebec, with such withdrawal to be accompanied by reasonable compensation, and the Government of Canada and the Government of Quebec will take the necessary steps to give the agreement the force of law under the proposed amendment relating to such agreements;

3. Nothing in this accord should be construed as preventing the negotiation of similar agreements with other provinces relating to immigration and the temporary admission of aliens;

4. Until the proposed amendment relating to appointments to the Senate comes into force, any person summoned to fill a vacancy in the Senate shall be chosen from among persons whose names have been submitted by the government of the province to which the vacancy relates and must be acceptable to the Queen's Privy Council for Canada.

Amending The Constitution Act, 1982

Motion for a resolution to authorize an amendment to the Constitution of Canada:

Whereas the *Constitution Act, 1982*, came into force on April 17, 1982, following an agreement between Canada and all the provinces except Quebec;

And whereas the Government of Quebec has established a set of five proposals for constitutional change and has stated that amendments to give effect to those proposals would enable Quebec to resume a full role in the constitutional councils of Canada;

And whereas the amendment proposed in the schedule hereto sets out the basis on which Quebec's five constitutional proposals may be met;

And whereas the amendment proposed in the schedule hereto also recognizes the principle of the equality of all the provinces, provides new arrangements to foster greater harmony and co-operation between the Government of Canada and the governments of the provinces and requires that conferences be convened to consider important constitutional, economic and other issues;

And whereas certain portions of the amendment proposed in the schedule hereto relate to matters referred to in Section 41 of the *Constitution Act, 1982*;

And whereas Section 41 of the *Constitution Act, 1982*, provides that an amendment to the Constitution of Canada may be made by proclamation issued by the Governor-General under the Great Seal of Canada where so authorized by resolutions of the Senate and the House of Commons and of the legislative assembly of each province;

Now therefore the (Senate) (House of Commons) (Legislative assembly) resolves that an amendment to the Constitution of Canada be authorized to be made by proclamation issued by Her Excellency the Governor-General under the Great Seal of Canada in accordance with the schedule hereto.

Schedule

Constitution Amendment, 1987
Constitution Act, 1867

1. The *Constitution Act, 1867*, is amended by adding thereto, immediately after Section 1 thereof, the following section:

2. (1) The Constitution of Canada shall be interpreted in a manner consistent with;

(a) The recognition that the existence of French-speaking Canadians, centred in Quebec but also present elsewhere in Canada, and English-speaking Canadians, concentrated outside Quebec but also present in Quebec, constitutes a fundamental characteristic of Canada; and;

(b) The recognition that Quebec constitutes within Canada a distinct society;

(2) The role of the Parliament of Canada and the provincial legislatures to preserve the fundamental characteristic of Canada referred to in paragraph (1)(a) is affirmed;

(3) The role of the Legislature and Government of Quebec to preserve and promote the distinct identity of Quebec referred to in paragraph (1)(b) is affirmed;

(4) Nothing in this section derogates from the powers, rights or privileges of Parliament or the Government of Canada, or of the legislatures or governments of the provinces, including any powers, rights or privileges relating to language.

2. The said Act is further amended by adding thereto, immediately after Section 24 thereof, the following section:

25. (1) Where a vacancy occurs in the Senate, the government of the province to which the vacancy relates may, in relation to that vacancy, submit to the Queen's Privy Council for Canada the names of persons who may be summoned to the Senate;

(2) Until an amendment to the Constitution of Canada is made in relation to the Senate pursuant to Section 41 of the *Constitution Act, 1982*, the person summoned to fill a vacancy in the Senate shall be chosen from among persons whose names have been submitted under Subsection (1) by the government of the province to which the vacancy relates and must be acceptable to the Queen's Privy Council for Canada.

3. The said Act is further amended by adding thereto, immediately after Section 95 thereof, the following heading and sections:

Agreements on immigration and aliens

95a. The Government of Canada shall, at the request of the government of any province, negotiate with the government of that province for the purpose of concluding an agreement relating to immigration or the temporary admission of aliens

into that province that is appropriate to the needs and circumstances of that province.

95b. (1) Any agreement concluded between Canada and a province in relation to immigration or the temporary admission of aliens into that province has the force of law from the time it is declared to do so in accordance with Subsection 95c(1) and shall from that time have effect notwithstanding Class 25 of Section 91 or Section 95.

(2) An agreement that has the force of law under Subsection (1) shall have effect only so long and so far as it is not repugnant to any provision of an Act of the Parliament of Canada that sets national standards and objectives relating to immigration or aliens, including any provision that establishes general classes of immigrants or relates to levels of immigration for Canada or that prescribes classes of individuals who are inadmissible into Canada.

(3) The *Canadian Charter of Rights and Freedoms* applies in respect of any agreement that has the force of law under Subsection (1) and in respect of anything done by the Parliament or Government of Canada, or the legislature or government of a province, pursuant to any such agreement.

95c. (1) A declaration that an agreement referred to in Subsection 95b(1) has the force of law may be made by proclamation issued by the Governor-General under the Great Seal of Canada only where so authorized by resolutions of the Senate and House of Commons and of the legislative assembly of the province that is a party to the agreement.

(2) An amendment to an agreement referred to in Subsection 95b(1) may be made by proclamation issued by the Governor-General under the Great Seal of Canada only where so authorized:

(a) by resolutions of the Senate and House of Commons and of the legislative assembly of the province that is a party to the agreement; or;

(b) in such other manner as is set out in the agreement.

95d. Sections 46 and 48 of the *Constitution Act, 1982*, apply, with such modifications as the circumstances require, in respect of any declaration made pursuant to Subsection 95c(1), any amendment to an agreement made pursuant to Subsection 95c(2) or any amendment made pursuant to Section 95e.

95e. An amendment to Sections 95a to 95d or this section may be made in accordance with the procedure set out in Subsection 38(1) of the *Constitution Act, 1982*, but only if the amendment is authorized by resolutions of the legislative assemblies of all the provinces that are, at the time of the amendment, parties to an agreement that has the force of law under Subsection 95b(1).

4. The said Act is further amended by adding thereto, immediately preceding Section 96 thereof, the following heading: "General".

5. The said Act is further amended by adding thereto, immediately preceding Section 101 thereof, the following heading: "Courts Established by the Parliament of Canada"

6. The said Act is further amended by adding thereto, immediately after Section 101 thereof, the following heading and sections:

Supreme Court of Canada

101a. (1) The court existing under the name of the Supreme Court of Canada is hereby continued as the general court of appeal for Canada, and as an additional court for the better administration of the laws of Canada, and shall continue to be a superior court of record.

(2) The Supreme Court of Canada shall consist of a chief justice to be called the Chief Justice of Canada and eight other judges, who shall be appointed by the Governor-General in Council by letters patent under the Great Seal.

101b. (1) Any person may be appointed a judge of the Supreme Court of Canada who, after having been admitted to the bar of any province or territory, has, for a total of at least 10 years, been a judge of any court in Canada or a member of the bar of any province or territory.

(2) At least three judges of the Supreme Court of Canada shall be appointed from among persons who, after having been admitted to the bar of Quebec, have, for a total of at least 10 years, been judges of any court of Quebec or of any court established by the Parliament of Canada, or members of the bar of Quebec.

101c. (1) Where a vacancy occurs in the Supreme Court of Canada, the government of each province may, in relation to that vacancy, submit to the Minister of Justice of Canada the names of any of the persons who have been admitted to the bar of that province and are qualified under Section 101b for appointment to that court.

(2) Where an appointment is made to the Supreme Court of Canada, the Governor-General in Council shall, except where the Chief Justice is appointed from among members of the Court, appoint a person whose name has been submitted under Subsection (1) and who is acceptable to the Queen's Privy Council for Canada.

(3) Where an appointment is made in accordance with Subsection (2) of any of the three judges necessary to meet the requirement set out in Subsection 101b(2), the Governor-General in Council shall appoint a person whose name has been submitted by the Government of Quebec.

(4) Where an appointment is made in accordance with Subsection (2) otherwise than as required under Subsection (3) the Governor-General in Council shall appoint a person whose name has been submitted by the government of a province other than Quebec.

101d. Sections 99 and 100 apply in respect of the judges of the Supreme Court of Canada.

101e. (1) Sections 101a to 101d shall not be construed as abrogating or derogating from the powers of the Parliament of Canada to make laws under Section 101 except to the extent that such laws are inconsistent with those sections.

(2) For greater certainty, Section 101a shall not be construed as abrogating or derogating from the powers of the Parliament of Canada to make laws relating to the reference of questions of law or fact, or any other matters, to the Supreme Court of Canada.

7. The said Act is further amended by adding thereto, immediately after Section 106 thereof, the following section:

106a. (1) The Government of Canada shall provide reasonable compensation to the government of a province that chooses not to participate in a national shared-cost program that is established by the Government of Canada after the coming into force of this section in an area of exclusive provincial jurisdiction, if the province carries on a program or initiative that is compatible with the national objectives.

(2) Nothing in this section extends the legislative powers of the Parliament of Canada or of the legislatures of the provinces.

8. The said Act is further amended by adding thereto the following heading and sections:

XII—Conferences on the Economy and Other Matters

148. A conference composed of the Prime Minister of Canada and the first ministers of the provinces shall be convened by the Prime Minister of Canada at least once each year to discuss the state of the Canadian economy and such other matters as may be appropriate.

XIII—References

149. A reference to this Act shall be deemed to include a reference to any amendments thereto.

The Constitution Act, 1982

9. Sections 40 to 42 of the Constitution Act, 1982 are repealed and the following substituted therefor:

40. Where an amendment is made under Subsection 38(1) that transfers legislative powers from provincial legislatures to Parliament, Canada shall provide reasonable compensation to any province to which the amendment does not apply.

41. An amendment to the Constitution of Canada in relation to the following matters may be made by proclamation issued by the Governor-General under the Great Seal of Canada only where authorized by resolutions of the Senate and House of Commons and of the legislative assembly of each province:

(a) The office of the Queen, the Governor-General and the Lieutenant-Governor of a province;

(b) The powers of the Senate and the method of selecting senators;

(c) The number of members by which a province is entitled to be represented in the Senate and the residence qualifications of senators;

(d) The right of a province to a number of members in the House of Commons not less than the number of senators by which the province was entitled to be represented on April 17, 1982;

(e) The principle of proportionate representation of the provinces in the House of Commons prescribed by the Constitution of Canada;

(f) Subject to Section 43, the use of the English or the French language;

(g) The Supreme Court of Canada;

(h) The extension of existing provinces into the territories;

(i) Notwithstanding any other law or practice, the establishment of new provinces; and;

(j) an amendment to this part.

10. Section 44 of the said Act is repealed and the following substituted therefor:

44. Subject to Section 41, Parliament may exclusively make laws amending the Constitution of Canada in relation to the executive government of Canada or the Senate and House of Commons.

11. Subsection 46(1) of the said Act is repealed and the following substituted therefor:

46. (1) The procedures for amendment under Sections 38, 41 and 43 may be initiated either by the Senate or the House of Commons or by the legislative assembly of a province.

12. Subsection 47(1) of the said Act is repealed and the following substituted therefor:

47. (1) An amendment to the Constitution of Canada made by proclamation under Section 38, 41 or 43 may be made without a resolution of the Senate authorizing the issue of the proclamation if, within 180 days after the adoption by the House of Commons of a resolution authorizing its issue, the Senate has not adopted such a resolution and if, at any time after the expiration of that period, the House of Commons again adopts the resolution.

13. Part VI of the said Act is repealed and the following substituted therefor:

Part VI Constitutional Conferences

50. (1) A constitutional conference composed of the Prime Minister of Canada and the first ministers of the provinces shall be convened by the Prime Minister of Canada at least once each year, commencing in 1988.

(2) The conferences convened under Subsection (1) shall have included on their agenda the following matters:

(a) Senate reform, including the role and functions of the Senate, its powers, the method of selecting senators and representation in the Senate;

(b) Roles and responsibilities in relation to fisheries; and

(c) Such other matters as are agreed upon.

14. Subsection 52(2) of the said Act is amended by striking out the word "and" at the end of paragraph (b) thereof, by adding the word "and" at the end of paragraph (c) thereof and by adding thereto the following paragraph:

"(d) any other amendment to the Constitution of Canada."

15. Section 61 of the said Act is repealed and the following substituted therefor:

61. A reference to the Constitution Act, 1982, or a reference to the Constitution Acts, 1867 to 1982, shall be deemed to include a reference to any amendments thereto.

General

16. Nothing in Section 2 of the Constitution Act, 1867, affects Section 25 or 27 of the Canadian Charter of Rights and Freedoms, Section 35 of the Constitution Act, 1982, or Class 24 of Section 91 of the Constitution Act, 1867.

Citation

17. This amendment may be cited as the Constitution Amendment, 1987.

Canada's System of Government

Canada is an independent, self-governing democracy whose form of government is a constitutional monarchy.

The Constitution

Canada's constitution consists of written documents and unwritten conventions. The written constitution is embodied in the *Constitution Acts 1867-1982.* The 1867 legislation (originally titled the *British North America Act*) established a federal state with a Parliament modelled on the British system. This federation is now composed of 10 provinces and 2 territories. The central government, based in Ottawa, is empowered by the constitution to legislate in areas, such as foreign policy, which affect the entire nation. The provinces have legislative power in other areas such as the administration of justice. The constitution prohibits either level of government from encroaching on the authority of the other.

Just as important as Canada's written constitution are the constitutional conventions, or principles, that have evolved in Britain and Canada. These include the role of the prime minister, an office not mentioned in the written constitution, and the requirement that the Sovereign exercise powers according to the principle of responsible government—meaning that power can be exercised only by government leaders who have the support of the nation's elected representatives. Although legislation passed by Parliament requires royal assent by the Queen's representative, the Governor General, this consent has never been denied.

The Parliament

Canada's Parliament consists of the Queen, an upper house known as the Senate, and the House of Commons. Senators are appointed by the Governor General on the advice of the prime minister; the 104 seats in the Senate are distributed on a regional basis. The House of Commons is an elected assembly in which each member represents one of 295 electoral districts distributed according to population.

Formation of Government

General elections to choose House of Commons members occur at least every 5 years. But they may take place more often if the prime minister decides to call an election or if the governing party loses the support of the majority of members of the House.

Following an election, the Governor General calls upon the leader of the party with the greatest House of Commons support to become prime minister. This is almost always the leader of the party with the most seats in the House but, under unusual circumstances, it could be the leader of another party which is able to gain majority support in Parliament with the help of a 3d party.

The prime minister selects the cabinet, usually from members of his party in the House of Commons. Formally, the prime minister and cabinet act as advisors to the Governor General. In practice, however, they wield executive power and the Governor General's role is mainly ceremonial.

Passage of Legislation

To become law, proposed legislation (known as bills) must be passed by a majority of members in both the House of Commons and the Senate and must then be given royal assent by the Governor General. Most bills are introduced by members of the government in the House of Commons. Typically, a bill is given 3 "readings" in the House. The first reading is simply to introduce the bill. The 2d reading is accompanied by debate on the principle of the bill. The bill is then voted on and, if approved, is sent to a House committee to be considered clause-by-clause. The committee prepares a report and submits it to the House of Commons along with any proposed amendments. These amendments, plus any others moved by any member of Parliament, are debated and usually voted on. A motion is then brought for the bill to be given 3d reading. If the vote is favorable, the bill is then introduced in the Senate where it undergoes a similar process. After a bill has been approved by both Houses, the Governor General gives it royal assent in a ceremony that takes place in the Senate chamber.

Defeat of a Government

Between elections, a government can be forced to resign if it is defeated in a vote on a major government bill. When this happens the government is considered to have lost the support of the majority of Parliament's elected representatives. This typically occurs only when the party in power has formed a minority government—that is, if it holds more seats than any other single party but fewer seats than the combined Opposition parties. This last happened federally in 1979 when a minority Conservative government, elected earlier that year, introduced a budget which was defeated by the combined votes of the Liberal and New Democratic Party members in the House. An election was called and the Liberals regained power.

The Monarchy

The British monarch (since June 2, 1953 Queen Elizabeth II) is Canada's official head of state through which the entire authority of the government is set in motion and in whose name laws are enacted. The Queen's role is set out in the *Constitution Act, 1867,* and that same act gives the monarch command-in-chief over Canada's armed forces.

In practice, however, the Queen has little or no part to play in Canadian government. She appoints the Governor General, but does so only on the prime minister's recommendation. Once appointed, it is the Governor General who performs the monarch's duties, and these duties have been mainly ceremonial for many years. Only during royal visits does the Queen carry out those functions normally performed in her name by the Governor General, such as the opening of Parliament.

The Governor General

The Governor General is selected by the prime minister and formally appointed by the Queen to act as her representative in Canada. The appointment is usually for 5 years but has sometimes been extended to 7.

Bills passed in the House of Commons and Senate do not become law until the Governor General has given them royal assent. The Governor General executes all orders-in-council and other state documents, appoints all superior court judges (on the advice of Cabinet) and summons, prorogues and dissolves Parliament (on the advice of the prime minister). Also, the Governor General invites the leader of the political party with the most support in the House of Commons to form a government. Thus, that leader becomes prime minister.

The Imperial Conferences of 1926 and 1930 established that the Governor General was not the representative or agent of the British government and should act only on the advice of the Canadian prime minister and Cabinet. Therefore, the Governor General is obliged to respect the principle of responsible government and to follow the wishes of Canada's elected representatives. Because of this, the role of the Governor General has become largely symbolic, with duties that are chiefly ceremonial.

Two members of the Royal Family have held the post: the Duke of Connaught (1911-16) and the Earl of Athlone (1940-46). The first Canadian Governor General was Vincent Massey (1952-59).

The House of Commons

The House of Commons is Canada's 295-member elected federal assembly. Its members are chosen in general elections held at least once every 5 years. By-elections are held if a member dies or resigns between general elections.

All bills governing matters within federal jurisdiction must be passed by a majority of members of Parliament to become law.

Members of Parliament usually belong to a political party and will normally vote with that party on any proposed legislation. Occasionally, members will break with their party on a vote and will sometimes leave the party with whom they were elected to sit as independents or to join another political party within the House. Members of Parliament can also be elected as independent candidates who do not belong to a political party, but this happens infrequently.

The prime minister is the leader of the political party able to command the support of a majority of the members of the House of Commons. If no party holds a clear majority of seats, a "minority government" is formed, usually led by the party with the most seats in Parliament—provided it has enough support from one of the other parties so that it can pass legislation.

When the House of Commons is in session it convenes at 2 o'clock daily and 11 o'clock on Fridays when the Speaker of the House takes the chair. After the mace is laid on the table in front of the Speaker and the daily prayer is read, business commences. Members of the government sit to the Speaker's right and the Opposition sits on the left. The leaders of other opposition parties sit on the left farther away from the Speaker's chair.

An important feature of Parliament is the daily question period at which time members question Cabinet ministers about their policies and actions. But most of Parliament's time is spent discussing proposed legislation introduced as "bills". Any member may introduce a bill, although this is usually done by a member of Cabinet. After readings in the House and detailed examination in committee, the bill will go for "third reading" in the House and if passed, will be forwarded to the Senate.

When a major piece of legislation introduced by the government is defeated in the House of Commons, the government is obliged to resign. The Governor General may then call on the leader of the Opposition to form a government but, in most cases, will call a general election so that the electorate can decide which party has the most public support for its policies.

The Senate

The Senate is the Upper House of the Canadian Parliament through which all legislation must pass before it becomes law. Its 104 members, appointed by the Governor General on the recommendation of the prime minister, hold office until age 75. (If appointed before June 1965 they hold office for life).

Seats in the Senate are apportioned on a regional basis: 24 from the Maritime provinces (Nova Scotia, 10; New Brunswick, 10; Prince Edward Island 4); 24 from Quebec; 24 from Ontario; 24 from the Western provinces (Manitoba, 6; Saskatchewan, 6; Alberta, 6; British Columbia, 6); 6 from Newfoundland; 1 each from the Northwest Territories and Yukon.

To be eligible for Senate appointment, a person must be a Canadian citizen, at least 30 years old, a resident of the province for which he or she is appointed, possess land in that province with an unencumbered value of $4 000 and have a net estate of $4 000. A Senator for Quebec must either be resident in the division for which he or she is appointed, or have property qualification there.

Technically, the Senate's legislative powers are equal to those of the House of Commons with 2 restrictions: first, on certain constitutional amendments, the Senate may delay resolutions of the House of Commons for up to 180 days, but cannot defeat them; second, the Senate cannot initiate money bills.

In practice, however, the Senate's chief role now is to provide technical reviews of legislation proposed in the House of Commons rather than to initiate political action. These reviews are done by Senate committees, which inspect each bill clause-by-clause and hear evidence from groups or individuals who may be affected by the proposed legislation.

In the past, the Senate rarely exercised its powers to impede legislation originating in the Commons. However, recent use of this power by the Liberal-controlled Senate to delay bills of Brian Mulroney's Progressive Conservative government has prompted a proposal to limit the Senate's role. Under this proposal, the Senate veto would be abolished, and the Upper House would be permitted to delay money bills by only 30 days, and other bills by only 45. Such a proposed change to the Senate involves constitutional amendment and would, therefore, require approval of 7 provinces with at least 50% of Canada's population.

The Cabinet

The Cabinet is a group of government ministers who, chosen and led by the prime minister, determine executive policies and are responsible for them to the House of Commons. Cabinet members are usually given responsibility for heading specific areas of the government—such as finance or foreign policy—and will introduce legislation pertaining to them in the House of Commons. They will also explain or defend government actions when questioned in the House.

Cabinet ministers are generally chosen from members of the government's party in the House of Commons, although Senators are sometimes appointed to provide Cabinet representation from all parts of the country. When Senators join the Cabinet they do not usually head a government department because a Senator is constitutionally forbidden to introduce tax or "money bill" legislation.

There are 5 categories of cabinet ministers:
1. Department Ministers who assume responsibility for running one or more government departments.
2. Ministers with special parliamentary responsibilities.
3. Ministers without portfolios who do not have responsibility for running a department and are often appointed to balance regional representation in the Cabinet.
4. Ministers of state for designated purposes who formulate and develop new policies outside normal departmental responsibilities.
5. Other ministers of state who may assist departmental ministers, though the departmental minister remains legally responsible for the duties and functions performed by the minister of state.

The Provincial Governments

Canada's provinces have a system of government which parallels that of the federal government in several ways. A premier, like the prime minister, leads the government by virtue of being leader of the party with the most support in the provincial legislature and forms a Cabinet from the elected members of the governing party. Members of a provincial legislature, like members of the federal Parliament, represent constituencies and approve legislation within their constitutional jurisdiction. A lieutenant-governor, like the Governor General, gives royal assent to the laws passed by the legislature.

The major difference between the provincial and federal systems is that the provinces have no equivalent body to Canada's Senate.

Government in the Yukon and Northwest Territories

Both the Yukon and Northwest Territories are administered by a commissioner, appointed by the federal government. In practice, however, the commissioners' role has become much like that of the provincial lieutenant-governors' in that they follow the wishes of the territories' elected representatives when exercising their authority.

In the Northwest Territories, real executive power is in the hands of a 24-person elected assembly whose members run for office as independents rather than as members of political parties. This assembly then chooses a government leader and elects 7 other members to serve on an 8-member executive council.

Yukon has a 16-member legislative assembly which operates on a political party system. Executive power is in the hands of an executive council, which functions like a provincial Cabinet. Its members are appointed by Yukon's commissioner on the advice of the government leader in the assembly. The government leader, like a provincial premier, is the leader of the political party supported by a majority of the assembly's elected representatives.

In both territories, the elected bodies have jurisdiction over such areas as education, housing, social services and renewable resources. The federal government retains control over non-renewable resources.

The National Flag

The National Flag was adopted by Parliament Oct. 22, 1964 and proclaimed by Queen Elizabeth II Feb. 15, 1965.

It is a red flag of the proportions two by length and one by width, containing in its centre a white square, the width of the flag, bearing a single, red, stylized maple leaf. The maple leaf has been looked upon as an emblem of Canada since the early 1700s. Red and white were declared Canada's official colors by King George V Nov. 21, 1921.

The National Flag is to be flown daily from sunrise to sunset at all federal government buildings, airports and military bases and establishments within and outside Canada. When flown with other flags, it should be given a place of honor.

The National Anthem: O Canada

The music of *O Canada* was composed by Calixa Lavallée and the lyrics were written in French by Adolphe-Basile Routhier in Quebec City. Originally called *Chant National* it was first performed at a banquet in Quebec City on June 24, 1880. The anthem grew in popularity in Quebec but was not heard in English until the early 1900s. There have been several English translations of the work, the most popular of which was written in 1908 by Robert Stanley Weir. In 1967 a Special Joint Committee of the Senate and the House of Commons was formed to recommend official versions of Canada's National and Royal Anthems. With a few minor changes, the official English version of *O Canada* is based on Weir's lyrics. On June 27, 1980 the House of Commons passed Bill C-36 designating both the music and lyrics of *O Canada* as Canada's national anthem. It was proclaimed in force July 1, 1980.

O CANADA

O Canada!
    Our home and native land!
True patriot love
    in all thy sons command.
With glowing hearts
    we see thee rise,
The True North
    strong and free!
From far and wide,
    O Canada,
We stand on guard
    for thee.
God keep our land
    glorious and free!
O Canada,
    we stand on guard for thee.
O Canada,
    we stand on guard for thee!

Ô CANADA

Ô Canada!
    Terre de nos aïeux,
Ton front est ceint
    de fleurons glorieux!
Car ton bras
    sait porter l'épée,
Il sait porter
    la croix!
Ton histoire
    est une épopée
Des plus
    brillants exploits,
Et ta valeur,
    de foi trempée,
Protégera nos foyers
    et nos droits,
Protégera nos foyers
    et nos droits.

Canadian History

Notable Dates in Canadian History

Circa 1000
Leif Ericsson and other **Vikings** visit Labrador and Newfoundland.

1497
John Cabot (Giovanni Caboto) claims Cape Breton Island (or possibly Newfoundland or Labrador) for Henry VII of England (June 24).

1498
Cabot makes his second voyage to North America.

1534
Jacques Cartier visits the Strait of Belle Isle (Newfoundland), and charts the Gulf of St. Lawrence (landing in Gaspé, July 14).

1535
Cartier sails up the St. Lawrence River to **Quebec** and **Montreal.**

1541
Cartier and the Sieur de Roberval found Charlesbourg-Royal, the **first French settlement** in America.

1577
Martin Frobisher of England makes the first of his 3 attempts to find a Northwest Passage, sailing as far as Hudson Strait.

1600
King Henry IV of France grants a **fur-trading monopoly** in the Gulf of St. Lawrence to a group of French merchants.

1605
Samuel de Champlain and the Sieur de Monts found Port Royal (Annapolis, N.S.).

1608
Champlain founds Quebec.

1609
Champlain supports the Algonquins against the Iroquois at Lake Champlain.

1610
Étienne Brûlé goes to live among the Huron and eventually becomes the first European to see Lakes Ontario, Huron and Superior. **Henry Hudson** explores Hudson Bay.

1617
Louis Hébert, the **first habitant (farmer),** arrives in Quebec.

1625
Jesuits arrive in Quebec to begin missionary work among the Indians.

1627
The **Company of One Hundred Associates** is founded (Apr. 29) to establish a French empire in North America.

1629
David Kirke captures Quebec for Britain (July 19).

1632
The **Treaty of Saint-Germain-en-Laye** returns Quebec to France.

1634-1640
The **Huron nation** is reduced by half from European diseases (smallpox epidemic, 1639).

1637
Kirke is named first governor of Newfoundland.

1642
Montreal is founded (May 18) by the Sieur **de Maisonneuve.**

1649
The Jesuit Father Jean **de Brébeuf** is martyred by the **Iroquois** at St-Ignace (Mar. 16). The Iroquois disperse the Huron nation (1648-1649).

1659
François **de Laval,** later to become Canada's first bishop, arrives in Quebec (June).

1660
Adam **Dollard des Ormeaux** makes his last stand against the Iroquois at Long Sault (May). The small party of French fights so well that the Iroquois decide not to attack Montreal.

1663
Quebec becomes a **royal province.**

1665
The Carignan-Salières regiment is sent from France to Quebec to deal with the Iroquois. Jean **Talon** becomes Quebec's intendant.

1667
Canada's **first census** counts 3 215 non-native inhabitants in 668 families.

1670
The **Hudson's Bay Company** is formed and granted trade rights over all territory draining into Hudson Bay (May 2).

1672
Comte **de Frontenac** becomes Governor of Quebec.

1673
Marquette and **Jolliet** explore the Mississippi to its junction with the Arkansas.

1674
Laval becomes first Bishop of Quebec.

1678-1679
Dulhut explores the headwaters of the Mississippi.

1682
La Salle explores the Mississippi to its mouth.

1686
De Troyes and **D'Iberville** capture the English posts of Moose Fort (June 20), Rupert House (July 3) and Fort Albany (July 26) on James Bay.

1689
The Iroquois kill many French settlers at Lachine.

1690
Sir William Phips captures Port Royal (May 11). Frontenac repels Phips's attack on Quebec (Oct.).

1697

The **Treaty of Ryswick** restores the *status quo* in the struggle between England and France. All captured territory is returned.

1701

The **War of the Spanish Succession** begins in Europe; the conflict spreads to North America (**Queen Anne's War**) the following year.

1710

Francis Nicholson captures Port Royal for England.

1713

The **Treaty of Utrecht** confirms British possession of Hudson Bay, Newfoundland and Acadia (except Cape Breton Island). France starts building Fort **Louisbourg.**

1739

La **Vérendrye** expedition explores Lake Winnipeg.

1740

The **War of the Austrian Succession** pits Britain against France; the European conflict spreads to North America (**King George's War**) in **1744.**

1745

Massachusetts Governor William Shirley takes the French fortress of **Louisbourg.**

1748

Louisbourg is returned to France by the **Treaty of Aix-la-Chapelle.**

1749

Britain founds **Halifax** to counter the French presence at Louisbourg.

1752

Canada's **first newspaper,** the Halifax *Gazette,* appears (Mar. 25).

1753

George **Washington**'s military expedition to the Monogahela is defeated by the French.

1754

Beginning of **French and Indian War** in America. Although war is not officially declared for another 2 years, this marks the final phase in the struggle between France and Britain in North America.

1755

Britain expels the **Acadians** from Nova Scotia, scattering them throughout her other North American colonies.

1756

Beginning of the **Seven Years' War** in Europe pits Britain against France. The Marquis **de Montcalm** assumes command of French troops in North America.

1758

The British under Generals Amherst and Wolfe take Louisbourg.

1759

Wolfe takes Quebec, defeating Montcalm on the Plains of Abraham (Sept. 13). Both generals are killed.

1760

General **James Murray** is appointed military governor of Quebec; he becomes civil governor in **1764.**

1763

France cedes its North American possessions to Britain by the **Treaty of Paris.** A Royal Proclamation imposes British institutions on Quebec (Oct.).

1768

Guy Carleton succeeds Murray as governor of Quebec.

1774

The **Quebec Act** provides for British criminal law but restores French civil law and guarantees religious freedom for Roman Catholic colonists.

1775

Americans under Montgomery capture Montreal (Nov.) and attack Quebec (Dec. 31).

1776

Under Carleton, Quebec withstands American siege until the appearance of a British fleet (May 6).

1778

Captain **James Cook** anchors in Nootka Sound, Vancouver Island (Mar. 29-Apr. 26).

1783

The American Revolutionary War ends; the border between Canada and the U.S. is accepted between the Atlantic Ocean and Lake of the Woods.

1784

United Empire Loyalists arrive in Canada. The province of **New Brunswick** is created. The **North West Company** is formed.

1789

Alexander Mackenzie journeys to the Beaufort Sea, following what would later be named the Mackenzie River.

1791

Constitutional Act divides Quebec into Upper and Lower Canada.

1792

George Vancouver begins his explorations of the Pacific coast.

1793

Alexander **Mackenzie reaches** the **Pacific.**

1794

Jay's Treaty (Nov. 19) between the U.S. and Britain promises British evacuation of the Ohio Valley forts. The treaty's appointment of officials to settle boundary disputes marks the beginning of international arbitration through its provisions for boundary settlements.

1797

David Thompson joins the North West Company as a surveyor and mapmaker.

1806

Le Canadien, Quebec nationalist newspaper, is founded.

1812

The U.S. declares war on Britain (June 18), beginning the **War of 1812.** Americans under General William Hull invade Canada from Detroit (July 11). The Red River settlement is begun in Canada's northwest (Aug.-Oct.). Battle of Queenston Heights (Oct. 13): Canadian victory.

1813

Americans burn York (Apr. 27). Battle of Stoney Creek (June 5): Canadian victory. Battle of Beaver Dams (June 23): Canadian victory; **Laura Secord** passes American sentries driving a cow and walks 32 km (20 miles) through dense bush to warn of American attack. Battle of Put-in-Bay, Lake Erie (Sept. 10): American victory. Battle of Moraviantown (Oct. 5): American victory; the Indian Chief **Tecumseh** is killed. Battle of Chateauguay (Oct. 25): Canadian victory. Battle of Crysler's Farm (Nov. 11): Canadian victory.

1814

Battle of Chippawa (July 5): American victory. Battle of Lundy's Lane (July 25): Canadian victory. A British naval force takes Washington (Aug. 24). Battle of Lake Champlain (Sept. 6-11): American victory. The **Treaty of Ghent** ends the War of 1812 (Dec. 24).

1816

Agents of the North West Company kill Robert Semple, governor of the Hudson's Bay Company's Red River colony, and 20 others at White Oaks (June 19).

1817

The **Rush-Bagot** agreement limits the number of battleships on the Great Lakes.

1818

The **49th Parallel** is accepted as **Canada's border** with the U.S. from Lake of the Woods to the Rocky Mountains.

1821

The Hudson's Bay Company and the North West Company are amalgamated as the HBC.

1829

The **Lachine** and **Welland Canals** are completed.

1835

William Lyon Mackenzie becomes the first mayor of Toronto.

1836

Opening of Canada's **first railway line,** from St. Johns, Que., to La Prairie, Que.

1837

Unsuccessful **Rebellions** in Upper and Lower Canada are led by Mackenzie and Louis-Joseph Papineau.

1839

Lord Durham's Report recommends union of Upper and Lower Canada and the establishment of responsible government.

1841

The **Act of Union** unites Upper and Lower Canada.

1842

The Ashburton-Webster Treaty settles the Maine-New Brunswick border dispute.

1843

Fort Victoria is built to bolster Britain's claim to Vancouver Island.

1848

Responsible government is achieved in the Canadas and in the Maritimes, thanks to the work of **Robert Baldwin** and **Joseph Howe.**

1849

The boundary of the 49th Parallel is extended to the Pacific Ocean.

1851

Britain transfers control of the colonial postal system to Canada.

1854

The **Reciprocity Treaty** between Canada and the U.S. is signed (June 6).

1857

Ottawa is named **Canada's capital** by Queen Victoria.

1860

Cornerstone of the **Parliament buildings** is laid (Sept. 1).

1861

The **Grand Trunk Railway** is completed.

1864

The **Charlottetown Conference** (Sept. 1-9) takes the first steps toward **Confederation.** The **Quebec Conference** (Oct. 10-27) sets out the basis for union.

1866

The **London Conference** (Dec. 4) passes resolutions which are redrafted to become the **British North America Act.** First raid into Canada by the **Fenians,** a radical Irish-American, anti-British group, takes place (June 2).

1867

Confederation. Britain's North American colonies are united by means of the **BNA Act** to become the **Dominion of Canada** (July 1). **Sir John A. Macdonald** is Canada's first prime minister.

1868

Confederationist **Thomas D'Arcy McGee** is **assassinated** by a Fenian in Canada's first political assassination.

1869

Canada purchases Rupert's Land from the HBC for £300 000.

1870

Louis Riel leads the Métis in resisting Canadian authority in Canada's northwest. The Manitoba Act creates the province of **Manitoba.**

1871

British Columbia joins Confederation.

1872

Macdonald's Conservatives win federal re-election.

1873

Prince Edward Island joins Confederation. A period of economic depression begins. The North-West Mounted Police are formed. **Alexander MacKenzie** becomes Canada's second prime minister after **Macdonald resigns** over the **Pacific Scandal.**

1874

Liberals win federal election.

1875

The **Supreme Court of Canada** is established.

1876

The **Intercolonial Railway** linking central Canada and the Maritimes is completed (July 1).

1878

Conservatives under Macdonald win federal election.

1879

Macdonald introduces **protective tariffs** as part of his **National Policy.**

1881

The **Canadian Pacific Railway** is incorporated.

1884

Riel returns to Canada.

1885

Métis and the NWMP clash at Duck Lake (Mar. 26). The Métis are defeated at Batoche (May 9-12). The **last spike of the transcontinental railway** is driven at Craigellachie in Eagle Pass, B.C., by Donald Smith (Nov. 7). Louis **Riel** is **hanged** in Regina (Nov. 16).

1887

Conservatives win federal election. Liberals choose **Wilfrid Laurier** as leader. The **first provincial premiers' conference** takes place, in Quebec City.

1890

Manitoba Liberals under Thomas Greenway halt public funding of Catholic schools in Manitoba (Mar.).

1891

Sir John A. **Macdonald dies.** Conservatives win federal election.

1896

The economic depression ends. Liberals under Laurier win federal election on **Manitoba Schools Question.** Gold is discovered in the Klondike (Aug. 16).

1897

Gold Rush begins in the Klondike.

1898

Yukon becomes a separate entity from the Northwest Territories.

1899

The first **Canadian troops** ever sent overseas are dispatched to the **Boer War** (Oct. 30).

1901

Marconi receives the **first transatlantic radio message**, at St. John's, Newfoundland.

1903

Canada loses the **Alaska Boundary dispute** when British tribunal representative Lord Alverstone sides with the U.S. (Oct. 20). In northern Ontario, Fred LaRose throws hammer at what he thinks are fox's eyes and hits world's richest silver vein.

1904

Liberals win federal election.

1905

The provinces of **Alberta** and **Saskatchewan** are formed.

1908

Liberals win federal election.

1909

The Department of External Affairs is formed. John McCurdy's Silver Dart is first heavier-than-air machine to achieve powered flight in Canada, at Baddeck, N.S. University of Toronto wins first Grey Cup football match.

1910

Laurier creates a Canadian navy via the Naval Service Bill.

1911

Robert Borden and the Conservatives win federal election, defeating Laurier on the Reciprocity issue.

1914

CP ship **Empress of Ireland** sinks in the St. Lawrence in 14 minutes after being rammed in fog, with the loss of 1 014 lives (May 29). **Canada is automatically at war** with Germany when Britain declares war (Aug. 4). The first Canadian troops leave for England (Oct. 3). Parliament passes the **War Measures Act,** allowing suspension of civil rights during periods of emergency.

1915

Canadians face German gas attack at **Ypres** (Belgium) (Apr. 22). John McCrae writes 'In Flanders Fields.'

1916

The Parliament buildings are destroyed by fire (Feb. 3). The unreliable, Canadian-made Ross rifle is withdrawn from war service (Aug.).

1917

Income tax is **introduced** as a "temporary wartime measure." Prime Minister Sir Robert Borden sits as a member of the Imperial War Cabinet (Feb. 23), giving Canada a voice in war policy. The Military Service Bill is introduced (June 11), leading to the **Conscription Crisis** between Quebec and English Canada. Unionist government under Borden wins federal election, in which **women vote** for the first time. Canadians capture Vimy Ridge (France) (Apr. 9-12). Canadians take Passchendaele (Belgium) (Nov. 6), in one of the war's worst battles. Explosion of a munitions ship in Halifax harbor wipes out 2 square miles (5.2 sq km) of Halifax, killing almost 2 000 and injuring 9 000 (Dec. 6).

1918

Canadians break through German trenches at Amiens (Aug. 8), 'the black day of the German army.' The period from this date until the end of the war becomes known as 'Canada's Hundred Days.' Armistice ends war (Nov. 11).

1919

Alcock and Brown take off from St. John's, Nfld. (June 14), on the first successful flight across the Atlantic, to Cliften, Ireland. A **general strike paralyzes Winnipeg** (May-June), where an armed charge by the RCMP kills one person and injures 30 (June 21).

1920

Canada joins the **League of Nations** at its inception (Jan. 10).

1921

Liberals under **Mackenzie King** defeat Conservatives under Arthur Meighen in federal election; the Progressive Party comes in second. **Agnes Macphail** becomes the first woman elected to Parliament. The world's fastest fishing schooner, the **Bluenose,** is launched at Lunenburg, N.S. (Mar. 26).

1922

The Canadian Northern and Canadian Transcontinental are merged to form the **Canadian National Railways.** Canada declines to rally to Britain's side during the Chanak Crisis. Sir Frederick Banting, Dr. Charles **Best,** Dr. J.J.R. MacLeod and J.B. Collip share Nobel Prize for the **discovery of insulin.** Foster Hewitt makes the world's first hockey radio broadcast.

1923

Canada signs the Halibut Treaty with the U.S. without a corroborating British signature. Mackenzie King leads opposition to a common imperial policy ('one voice for the empire') at an Imperial Conference in London.

1925

Although Conservatives win more seats in federal election, Mackenzie King's Liberals remain in power with the support of the Progressives.

1926

King's Liberals win federal election. An Imperial Conference defines British dominions as autonomous (Balfour Report).

1927

Britain's Privy Council awards Labrador to Newfoundland instead of to Quebec (Mar. 1). The Diamond Jubilee of Confederation (July 1) is marked by Canada's first coast-to-coast radio network broadcast.

1928

The Supreme Court of Canada rules that, according to the British North America Act, women are not "persons" who could hold public office. This decision is reversed by British Privy Council in 1929.

1929

The **Great Depression** begins.

1930

Conservatives under **R.B. Bennett** win federal election.

1931

The **Statute of Westminster** (Dec. 11) grants Canada full legislative authority domestically and in external affairs. The Governor General becomes a representative of the crown.

1932

Ottawa Agreements provide for preferential trade between Canada and other Commonwealth nations. The **Co-operative Commonwealth Federation (CCF)** is founded at Calgary.

1934

The Bank of Canada is formed. The **Dionne quintuplets** are born in Callander, Ont.

1935

Liberals under Mackenzie King win federal election.

1937

The **Rowell-Sirois Commission** is appointed to investigate the financial relationship between the federal government and the provinces. First regular flight of **Trans Canada Air Lines** (Sept. 1).

1938

Franklin D. Roosevelt becomes first U.S. President in office to visit Canada, meeting Mackenzie King at Kingston.

1939

Canada declares war on Germany (Sept. 10) after remaining neutral for a week following the British declaration. Quebec Premier Maurice Duplessis, who opposed Quebec participation in the war, is defeated by the Liberals on that issue (Oct. 26).

1940

Unemployment insurance is **introduced**. Liberals win federal election (Mar. 26). The Permanent Joint Defense Board is formed between Canada and the U.S.

1941

Canadians are captured when Hong Kong falls to Japanese (Dec. 25); about 300 of the POWs subsequently die in Japanese camps.

1942

In Canada's first European war action, many Canadians are captured or killed in the disastrous **Dieppe** raid (Aug. 19). Canadians of Japanese descent are moved inland from the coast of British Columbia as 'security risks'; their property is confiscated. A national plebiscite releases Mackenzie King from his pledge of no conscription but reveals deep divisions between Quebec and the rest of Canada.

1943

Canadians participate in the invasion of Sicily (July 10). Canadians win the Battle of Ortona (Dec. 20-28).

1944

Canadian troops push further inland than any other Allied unit on D-Day (June 6). Canadian forces fight as a separate army (July 23). Saskatchewan elects Tommy Douglas's CCF, the first socialist government in North America.

1945

War in Europe ends (May 5). Liberals win federal election (June 11). First **family allowance payments** are **made** (June 20). Canada joins the **United Nations** (June 26). Igor Gouzenko defects from the Soviet Embassy in Ottawa (Sept. 5) and reveals the existence in Canada of a Soviet spy network. Canada's first nuclear reactor begins operations at Chalk River, Ontario.

1947

Imperial Oil discovers the **Leduc oil field** (Feb. 13).

1948

Louis St. Laurent succeeds Mackenzie King as prime minister (Nov. 15).

1949

Under Premier **Joey Smallwood**, **Newfoundland** becomes Canada's 10th province (Mar. 31). Canada joins NATO. Canadian appeals to Britain's Judicial Committee of the Privy Council are abolished: Canada's Supreme Court becomes final court of appeal. Liberals under St. Laurent defeat Conservatives under George Drew in federal election (June 3).

1950

The Korean War begins (June 25); Canadian troops participate in the conflict as part of a United Nations force.

1951

The mid-century census reports Canada's population as 14 009 429. The Massey Royal Commission reports that Canadian cultural life is dominated by American influences.

1952

Vincent Massey becomes the first native-born Governor General of Canada. Canada's **first television** stations begin broadcasting, in Montreal (Sept. 6) and Toronto (Sept. 8).

1953

Canada's National Library is established in Ottawa (Jan. 1). The Stratford Festival opens (July 13). The Korean War ends (July 27); total Canadian casualties are 314 killed and 1 211 wounded. Liberals under St. Laurent defeat Conservatives under Drew in federal election (Aug. 10).

1954

An economic slump interrupts the post-war boom. Canada's **first subway** opens in Toronto (Mar. 30). Roger Bannister and John Landy run the 'miracle mile' at the British Empire Games in Vancouver (Aug.), the first time 2 men crack the 4-minute barrier in the same race. Sixteen-year-old Marilyn Bell becomes the first person to swim Lake Ontario (Sept. 9). **Hurricane Hazel** hits Toronto, killing 83 people (Oct. 15).

1955

The Canadian Labour Congress is formed. The suspension of Montreal Canadiens' hockey star Maurice 'Rocket' Richard leads to rioting in Montreal (Mar. 17).

1956

The Liberals use closure to limit the **Pipeline Debate** (May 8-June 6), a manoeuvre that contributes to their electoral defeat the following year.

1957

Conservatives under **John Diefenbaker** win federal election (June 10) and form minority government. Ellen Fairclough becomes the first woman federal cabinet minister. The Canada Council is created to help foster Canadian cultural life. **Lester B. Pearson wins Nobel Prize** (Oct. 12) for his role in resolving the Suez Crisis.

1958

Conservatives under Diefenbaker win 208 seats in federal election (Mar. 31). Coal mine disaster at Springhill, N.S., results in death of 74 miners.

1959

The **Avro Arrow** project is terminated, with a loss of almost 14 000 jobs (Feb. 20). The **St. Lawrence Seaway** is **opened** (June 26).

1960

Liberals under **Jean Lesage** win provincial election in Quebec (June 22), inaugurating the **Quiet Revolution.** A **Canadian Bill of Rights** is approved by Parliament. Indians and Inuit get the right to vote in federal elections.

1961

The **New Democratic Party** replaces the CCF.

1962

Conservatives are reduced to minority status in federal election (June 18). The Saskatchewan NDP introduces the first Canadian **Medicare** plan (July 1), and is opposed by a doctors' strike. **Trans-Canada Highway** officially opens (Sept. 3). Canadian-made satellite Alouette is launched (Sept. 29), making Canada the third nation in space. Canada's last execution, a double hanging, takes place (Dec. 11), at the Don Jail in Toronto.

1963

Liberals under Pearson win federal election (Apr. 8), and form a minority government. The Quebec separatist group **Front de Libération du Québec (FLQ)** sets off a series of bombs in Montreal (Apr.-May). A TCA flight crashes in Quebec, killing all 118 people aboard (Nov. 29).

1964

Canadians get Social Insurance cards (Apr.). Northern Dancer becomes the first Canadian horse to win the Kentucky Derby (May 2).

1965

Canada gets a new flag (Feb. 15). The **Autopact** between Canada and the U.S. is signed. Canadian Roman Catholic Churches begin to celebrate mass in English (Mar. 7). Liberals win federal election (Nov. 8), to continue as a minority government. Failure of an Ontario Hydro relay device at Queenston plunges eastern North America into a power blackout (Nov. 9).

1966

The Munsinger Affair becomes Canada's first major parliamentary sex scandal (Mar. 4). The **Canada Pension Plan** is established. The CBC begins color television broadcasting (Oct. 1).

1967

The Canadian army, navy and air forces are **unified** to become the Canadian **Armed Forces** (Apr. 25). Montreal hosts a World's Fair, **Expo '67** (opened Apr. 27). Canada celebrates its **Centennial** (July 1).French President Charles **de Gaulle** delivers his 'Vive Québec Libre' speech in Montreal (July 24).

1968

Pierre Elliott Trudeau succeeds Pearson as Prime Minister (Apr. 6), and leads Liberals to majority in federal election (June 25). A Royal Commission on the Status of Women is appointed. Canadian divorce law is reformed.

1969

Saturday postal deliveries end (Feb. 1). Abortion law is liberalized (May). English and French become **official languages** of federal administration (July 9). The breathalizer comes into use as a test for alcohol-impaired drivers (Dec. 1).

1970

The FLQ kidnaps British trade commissioner James Cross (Oct. 5), precipitating the **October Crisis.** Quebec labour and immigration minister Pierre Laporte is kidnapped (Oct. 10), and found murdered (Oct. 17). The federal government invokes the **War Measures Act** (Oct. 16), leading to the arrest of 465 people.

1971

A policy of **multiculturalism** is adopted by the federal government. Pierre Trudeau becomes the first prime minister to wed while in office when he marries 22-year-old Margaret Sinclair (Mar. 4). Canadian Gerhard Herzberg wins the Nobel Prize in chemistry for his studies of chemical reactions that help produce smog.

1972

Canada defeats the USSR in the first hockey series between the Soviets and Canadian professionals (Aug.-Sept.). Liberals win federal election with 109 seats to the Conservatives 107, with the NDP holding the balance of power at 31 (Oct. 30).

1973

The House of Commons passes a resolution (Jan. 5) criticizing U.S. bombing of North Vietnam. Dr. Henry Morgentaler is acquitted by a Montreal jury of having performed an illegal abortion (Nov. 13). The separatist Parti Québécois becomes the official Opposition in Quebec.

1974

Soviet ballet star Mikhail Baryshnikov defects in Montreal (June 29). Liberals under Trudeau win federal election and form majority government (July 8).

1975

The **CN Tower,** the world's tallest free-standing structure at 553.339 metres, is completed in Toronto (Apr. 2). Federal government announces (July 18) its intention to screen foreign investment in Canada, via the Foreign Investment Review Agency (FIRA). Television cameras are allowed inside the House of Commons for the first time. Federal government imposes **wage and price controls** in an effort to fight inflation (Oct. 14).

1976

Canada announces 200-nautical-mile coastal fishing zone (June 4). **Death penalty** is **abolished** (July 14). Montreal hosts **Olympic Games** (July 17-31). Team Canada wins the first **Canada Cup** (hockey) series (Sept. 15). The **Parti Québécois** under René Lévesque wins provincial election in Quebec (Nov. 15). T. Eaton Company discontinues catalogue sales after 92 years.

1977

Prime Minister Trudeau and his wife Margaret separate (May 27). Quebec government passes Bill 101, restricting English-language schooling to children whose mother or father had attended English elementary school in Quebec (Aug. 26). Highway signs in most of Canada become metric (Sept. 6).

1978

Soviet nuclear-powered satellite crashes in Canadian north (Jan. 24). The federal government orders birth control pills sold in Canada to include a warning that women over 30 who smoke, and all women over 40, should not use them. Sun Life Assurance Co. announces a head office move from Montreal to Toronto because of language laws and political instability in Quebec.

1979

Conservatives under **Joe Clark** win federal election (May 22). Canada's first gold bullion coin, the Maple Leaf, goes on sale (Sept. 5). 220 000 people are evacuated from Mississauga, Ont., because of derailed tanker cars containing chlorine and other chemicals (Nov. 10). Supreme Court of Canada declares Manitoba and Quebec legislation creating unilingual courts and legislatures unconstitutional (Dec. 13). Federal Conservatives lose non-confidence vote on budget (Dec. 13), forcing the government's resignation.

1980

Canada's ambassador to Iran, Ken Taylor, arranges the successful **escape of 6 American Embassy staff** from Tehran while their colleagues are held hostage (Jan. 28). Liberals win federal election (Feb. 18). Canada decides to boycott the Olympic Games in Moscow because of the Soviet invasion of Afghanistan. **Quebec votes "no"** to 'sovereignty-association' (separatism) **in a referendum** (May 22). **O Canada** becomes Canada's national anthem (June 27). The Supreme Court awards Rosa Becker half the assets accumulated during a 19-year common law relationship.

1981

Terry Fox dies of cancer at age 22 (June 29); his 'Marathon of Hope,' in which he tried to run across Canada on one leg after having lost the other to cancer, raised $25 million for cancer research. Quebec bans public signs in English (Sept. 23). The federal government and every province except Quebec reach agreement on a method for patriating Canada's constitution (Nov. 5).

1982

The Ocean Ranger, an offshore oil platform, sinks with the loss of 84 lives (Feb. 15). Bertha Wilson becomes Canada's first woman to be appointed a Justice of the Supreme Court (Mar. 4). The Quebec Court of Appeal rejects the Quebec government's claim of veto power over constitutional change (Apr. 7). Canada gains a new **Constitution** and **Charter of Rights and Freedoms** (Apr. 17). Canada's GNP falls 4.8% in the worst recession since the Great Depression of the 1930s.

1983

Canadian pay-TV channels begin operation (Feb. 1). **Jeanne Sauve** is Canada's first woman to be appointed Governor General (Dec. 23). Canada approves a U.S. plan to test unarmed **cruise missiles** in western Canada, beginning in 1984.

1984

Trudeau is succeeded as prime minister by **John Turner** (June 30). Conservatives under **Brian Mulroney** win federal election with 211 seats, the largest majority in Canada's history (Sept. 4). The **Pope visits Canada** (Sept. 9-20). **Marc Garneau** becomes the first Canadian in space, aboard U.S. space shuttle Challenger (Oct. 5).

1985

The voyage through the Northwest Passage of U.S. icebreaker 'Polar Sea' challenges Canada's **Arctic sovereignty.** Long-time premiers Bill Davis (Ont.), Rene Levesque (Que.) and Peter Lougheed (Alta.) retire. Prime Minister Mulroney and U.S. President Reagan declare mutual support for **Star Wars research** and **free trade** between the 2 nations at "Shamrock Summit" (Mar. 18) in Quebec City. The Liberals under Robert Bourassa defeat the Parti Quebecois (Dec. 2). Ontario Liberals under David Peterson end 4 decades of Conservative rule.

1986

The Canadian dollar hits an all-time low of 70.20 cents U.S. (Jan. 31). The **Expo 86** world's fair is held in Vancouver from May 2 to Oct. 13. The U.S. imposes stiff tariffs (May 22) on imported Canadian shakes and shingles. Canada joins other Commonwealth nations (Aug. 5) in adopting **economic sanctions against South Africa** because of its apartheid policy. One hundred and fifteen **Tamil refugees** from Sri Lanka are found drifting in lifeboats off the coast of Newfoundland (Aug. 11). Canada receives a United Nations award (Oct. 6) for providing a haven for world refugees. Canadian John Polanyi shares the Nobel Prize for chemistry.

1987

The Bank of Canada rate dropped to a 13-year low of 7.49% (Jan. 28); 6-month residential mortgages were as low as 7.5%. The **Meech Lake Accord,** proposing major constitutional amendments, was agreed to by Prime Minister Brian Mulroney and the 10 provincial premiers (Apr. 30). A tornado killed 26 and injured 250 others in Edmonton (July 20). Toronto sprinter Ben Johnson set a new world record (Aug. 30) for the 100-metre dash. Team Canada won the Canada Cup in a 6-5 victory over the Soviet Union (Sept. 15). A **free trade** agreement between Canada and the United States was reached (Oct. 3); the deal would still require ratification by both houses of Parliament and the U.S. Congress. **Stock prices tumbled** (Oct. 19) in Canada and throughout the world.

(For **1988,** see Chronology of the Year's Events, page 1)

The History of Canada

Exploration and First Settlements

The first people who came to North America arrived during the last Ice Age which began about 80 000 years ago and ended about 12 000 years ago. These Native People were hunters who crossed from Asia via a land bridge now submerged beneath the Bering Sea. Although there is continuing debate among archeologists as to how early humans might have settled in what is now Canada, the earliest accepted occupation site is at the Bluefish Caves in the Yukon. Here artifacts at least 12 000 to 17 000 years old have been found. As the glaciers of the Ice Age retreated, human settlements spread across Canada. Gradually, these first Canadians developed lifestyles based on the environments in which they lived. They obtained their food by hunting, fishing, gathering, and in the case of Eastern Woodland tribes, by farming. By the time explorers from Europe reached Canada, the Native People had well-developed trading patterns, arts and crafts, languages, writing, religious beliefs, laws and government.

There has been much conjecture as to who were the first Europeans to come to Canada. The suggestion that an Irish monk, St. Brendan, arrived about the year 550 has not been substantiated. But the theory that Vikings had settled in Newfoundland was confirmed by archeological excavations at L'Anse aux Meadows during the 1960s and 1970s. In 1978, this site in northern Newfoundland was declared a World Heritage Site by the United Nations.

A burst of European exploration took place during the Age of Discovery of the 15th and 16th centuries. In search of a route to the Far East, explorers found what they called a New World. In 1497, Giovanni Caboto (Cabot), an Italian sailing for England, landed on the Canadian coast, likely in Cape Breton or Newfoundland, and claimed the land for Henry VII. Cabot probably died on a 2d expedition in 1498, but his voyages helped open up the rich fishing grounds of the Grand Banks.

European navigators and fishermen continued to visit the shores of Canada, but the first real exploration was undertaken by Jacques Cartier. Cartier, searching for a passage to Asia, discovered the Gulf of St. Lawrence in 1534. The next year he travelled up the St. Lawrence River as far as Stadacona (Quebec) and Hochelaga (Montreal). On this voyage, Cartier picked up the Iroquoian word for village, Kanata (thought to be the origin of "Canada"), and used it to apply to the whole region he had discovered. Cartier's discoveries gave France a claim to Canada and led to the first French settlements.

In 1541-42, Cartier and the Sieur de Roberval established a short-lived settlement at Charlesbourg-Royal just above Quebec. In 1605, the Sieur de Monts and Samuel de Champlain established the colony of Port Royal in what is now Nova Scotia. Champlain went on to establish a settlement at Quebec in 1608, to explore the interior and to draw maps of New France. Champlain also started a fur-trading network with the Algonkians and the Hurons who inhabited the St. Lawrence and Great Lakes regions. This trade relationship became a military alliance as Champlain supported these groups against the Iroquois. This enmity between the French and the Iroquois prevailed throughout most of the history of New France.

The Growth of New France (1627-1660)

The economic foundation of New France was the fur trade. In fact, the French kings were content to let fur-trading companies run the colony. Although these companies expanded the fur-trading boundaries, they failed to encourage settlement. One of King Louis XIII's most able advisers, Cardinal Richelieu, tried to remedy this problem. In 1627, he granted a fur-trading monopoly to the Company of One Hundred Associates, on condition that it bring out several hundred settlers each year. However, war between England and France broke out and Quebec was captured in 1629. Even after peace was restored in 1633, the Company of One Hundred Associates failed to honor its commitment to bring out settlers.

Despite the lack of settlers, the colony was expanding in other ways. As governor, Champlain encouraged the expansion of the fur trade. The Jesuits had arrived in 1625 and were vigorously pursuing their missionary work among the Hurons. Montreal was founded in 1642 and soon became a centre of the fur trade.

However, problems soon arose. First, Champlain died in 1635, just 2 years after the colony was restored to France. No leader possessing his vision or drive emerged to replace him. Next, despite their conviction, the French missionaries made few converts among the Native People. Even Ste. Marie Among the Hurons, their central mission-post was abandoned in 1649 in the face of invasion by the Iroquois, who dispersed the Hurons, disrupting the French fur-trading network. Finally, the security of Montreal and the rest of the colony was threatened by the wars against the Iroquois. When they were renewed in 1659-1660, after a short period of peace, there were still only about 3 000 French settlers in the colony. Clearly, the French King would have to act to secure France's foothold in North America.

Royal Government in New France (1663-1700)

In 1663 King Louis XIV made New France a crown colony. Regular troops were sent out and undertook a successful campaign against the Iroquois, which resulted in the signing of a peace treaty in 1667. Several hundred of these regulars stayed on as settlers, thereby adding to the security of the colony. A system of government headed by a governor, an intendant, and a bishop was instituted. The governor, who was the king's representative, was charged with defence. The intendant was responsible for industry, trade, and administrative affairs. The bishop looked after religious matters, which included education. In theory, this system provided for a clear separation of powers; but, in practice, there were frequent disputes among the 3 officials. Still, this system survived intact for the remainder of the colony's history, and it provided New France with some remarkably dynamic officials. Two of these arrived in the first years of Royal Government.

The first intendant of New France, Jean Talon (1665 to 1672), introduced innovative measures, including awards for early marriage, to boost the population. As well, he attempted to build a diversified economy on the St. Lawrence by promoting crafts, farming, and local industry. Yet few other officials in New France shared Talon's concern for settlement or economic diversity. Most were more interested in profits from the fur-trade. This interest was visible in the career of Count Frontenac, governor for all but 7 years between 1672 and 1698. Frontenac's enthusiastic support for the fur trade not only raised profits but also encouraged exploration. Under his rule, French adventurers explored the Mississippi River from its upper reaches to the Gulf of Mexico, thereby greatly expanding the fur-trading boundaries of New France. Frontenac gained more fame when he withstood the attack of an English army which besieged Quebec in 1690.

But Frontenac had not only exceeded his powers in promoting territorial expansion, he had also undermined the security of the colony. With its limited population, New France now found itself competing for the fur-trade with the more populous English colonies. In the north, there was rivalry with the Hudson's Bay Company, founded in 1670. To the south, there was border warfare between French fur traders and their Indian allies, and the English with their Iroquois allies. New France fared well in the limited warfare of the 1680s and 1690s; but in the 18th century there was a series of major wars which resulted in disaster for the colony.

The Collapse of New France (1701-1763)

In the early years of the 18th century, New France stretched from Hudson Bay to the Gulf of Mexico, and from Newfoundland to the Great Lakes. Its population was thinly scattered in the north, south and west but its fur-trading posts in these regions gave legitimacy to its territorial claims. In the Atlantic region, there were several hundred colonists in Newfoundland and another 1 500 in Acadia. The heartland of New France was the settlement of about 20 000 colonists in Montreal, Quebec and in the small communities along the St. Lawrence. The prosperity of the French settlements was to be hurt by long periods of war.

The first of these was the War of the Spanish Succession, 1701-1713. Although the British failed to capture their main objective, the fortress city of Quebec, they succeeded at the bargaining table. By the Treaty of Utrecht, France gave up the Hudson Bay territory, all of Acadia except for Cape Breton, and Newfoundland.

During a 30-year period of peace, New France enjoyed limited prosperity. The population grew, farm yields increased, some industry was established, and furs were still exported. But military expenditure was turning the colony into a financial burden for France. Much of that expenditure went into the huge fortress of Louisbourg, built on Cape Breton Island to protect the offshore fisheries and guard the Gulf of St. Lawrence.

When the War of the Austrian Succession broke out in 1744, Louisbourg was a natural target. The fortress fell to the British, although it was returned to France at the war's end in 1748. This development led to the establishment, in 1749, of the British military and naval base at Halifax.

The fragile peace was broken in 1754, when fighting broke out between the English and French colonists in the Ohio Valley. Within 2 years, Britain and France were officially at war again. Despite some early victories, the French suffered the loss of Louisbourg in 1758. In the following year, General Wolfe defeated General Montcalm on the Plains of Abraham on the heights above the St. Lawrence at Quebec. Although Montreal did not fall until the next year, the loss of Quebec was an irreversible setback. The British army occupied New France, and in 1763 the treaty ending the Seven Years' War confirmed British sovereignty.

New France had fallen because of decisive military defeats at Louisbourg and Quebec, but more significant was the inability of France to supply its colony in the face of British naval supremacy. The British were now masters in North America.

The First Years of British Rule (1763-1812)

In 1763 a Royal Proclamation was imposed by the British government on the newly-acquired territories of New France. The intent of this proclamation was clear. By encouraging the establishment of Protestant schools, by promoting the Church of England, and by stipulating that an assembly be elected, the proclamation aimed at Anglicization. This intent was most visible in the matter of the assembly. Although the French inhabitants were in the majority, under British law no Roman Catholic could hold office. If an assembly were elected, a few hundred British settlers would control about 65 000 Canadiens (French Canadians).

Fortunately for the French in Canada, James Murray, the governor of Quebec from 1760 to 1768, felt that the loyalty of the French colonists could be gained by fair treatment. Murray refused to call elections for the assembly, and allowed French legal practices to continue. Murray's sympathies provoked a storm of protest by the British colonists in Quebec and he was recalled. But his successor, Guy Carleton, also realized that the Royal Proclamation of 1763 would only alienate the recently-defeated colonists. Carleton saw that even if Anglicization were carried out, few colonists from the Thirteen Colonies in America or immigrants from Britain would be lured to the rugged colony of Quebec. Consequently, Carleton advised the Government in London to replace the proclamation with more liberal legislation.

The result was the Quebec Act of 1774 which dropped the assembly in favor of an appointed council on which Catholics might serve. As well, the French system of civil law and the seigneurial system of land tenure were both guaranteed. Finally, the Quebec Act expanded the borders of the colony to include the rich lands of the Ohio Valley. The British had acted to win the support of the Canadiens. In doing so, however, the British government angered the citizens of the Thirteen Colonies, who resented the special treatment given to

their former enemies. These English colonists were especially upset over the loss of the Ohio Valley, a region into which they expected to expand.

The Quebec Act was not the only cause for complaint in the Thirteen Colonies. Protests over British taxation policies and trade restriction led to talk of revolution. That talk led to action, and in 1775 an invading American army took Montreal. Quebec held out against the American siege until relieved by British forces. Although there was some sympathy for the American cause in both Quebec and Nova Scotia, it was not a strong enough sentiment to cause these 2 colonies to join the revolution.

During and immediately after the American Revolution, some American colonists who wished to retain their British ties fled from the newly-created United States into the Maritimes and Quebec. The arrival of about 30 000 of these Loyalists in Nova Scotia resulted in the creation of a new colony, New Brunswick, in 1784. Similarly, the influx of 10 000 Loyalists into Quebec led to the division of the colony, and in 1791, the western part of the colony became Upper Canada. The remainder of the old colony was known as Lower Canada.

During these changes fur-trading remained an important economic activity in the interior of British North America. In fact, there was keen rivalry for furs between the Hudson's Bay Company and the newly-formed (1784) North West Company based in Montreal. This fur-trade rivalry led to a flurry of western exploration. Alexander Mackenzie, a partner in the North West Company, explored a river (now known as the Mackenzie) to its mouth on the Beaufort Sea in 1789, and found a route to the Pacific via the Fraser and Bella Coola Rivers in 1793. Two other North West Company employees, Simon Fraser and David Thompson, also carried out voyages of discovery. Fraser followed the river named after him to the Pacific in 1808, and Thompson travelled down the Columbia River to the coast in 1811. These voyages along with the earlier coastal explorations of James Cook in 1778 and George Vancouver in 1792-1795 helped establish Britain's claim to the northwest part of the continent.

The War of 1812

Although the British and Americans signed a peace treaty in 1783 to end the American War of Independence, there was still friction between them. One source of conflict was the British fur-trading posts in the Ohio Valley which now belonged to the United States. Although Britain surrendered these posts in 1796 as stipulated by Jay's treaty (1794), there were still American complaints that the British were arming the Indians of the interior. At the same time there was growing American resentment over British interference with shipping. The British, who were at war with France, claimed the right to search American ships for cargoes bound for the enemy. In the process, the British often forced American sailors on these ships to join the British navy. Resentment grew among Americans until June 1812, when the United States declared war on Britain.

In the first year of the war, the Americans under General William Hull crossed the Detroit River to invade Upper Canada. Hull expected Canadian sympathizers to flock to his cause but he was disappointed. Without fighting a major battle, he retreated to Detroit. British General Isaac Brock and Shawnees under Chief Tecumseh moved against Detroit and Hull surrendered. This British and Canadian victory was followed by a victory at Queenston Heights on the Niagara River. Brock was killed in this battle which nevertheless gave confidence to the defenders of the British colonies.

In 1813, the Americans carried out a successful raid on York (now Toronto), and also gained a foothold in the Niagara district. But by the summer of that year the Americans had been pushed back across the Niagara River by British victories at Stoney Creek and Beaver Dam. Meanwhile, the Americans were building up a large fleet on the Great Lakes, and in Sept. 1813 the Americans won control of Lake Erie at the Battle of Put-in-Bay. This victory prompted the British under General Proctor to abandon Fort Malden on the Detroit River. However, the American General Harrison caught the retreating forces at Moraviantown on the Thames River and defeated Proctor. The staunch British ally, Tecumseh, was killed in this battle. In the east, a two-pronged attack on Montreal was repulsed. The American invaders were defeated on the Chateauguay River and at Crysler's Farm near Cornwall in the fall of 1813.

In 1814, the Americans again invaded the Niagara district but were halted at the Battle of Lundy's Lane. From Halifax, British forces attacked targets in Maine, and occupied most of that state. Another attack from Halifax was launched on the American capital, Washington. The British raiders burned the government buildings there in retaliation for the destruction of York the previous year. Despite these successes, a major British offensive against Plattsburg on Lake Champlain failed. By now the war was in stalemate and both sides were tired. British and American negotiators signed the Treaty of Ghent in Dec. 1814, to end the war.

In the aftermath of the war, the 2 sides made an effort to settle outstanding differences. The Rush-Bagot Agreement of 1817 provided for naval disarmament on the Great Lakes. In the following year Britain and the United States agreed to accept the 49th parallel as the international boundary from the Lake of the Woods to the Rocky Mountains. In addition, they agreed to the joint occupation of the Oregon Territory for 10 years.

Rebellion and Reform (1814-1839)

In the years after the War of 1812, there was considerable growth in British North America. The population increased as immigrants from both the United States and Britain arrived to take up land that was free or inexpensive. The economy became more diversified as lumbering, farming, and shipbuilding developed in the Canadas and in the Maritimes. Finally, a sense of nationalism began to grow in parts of British North America. This feeling arose partly out of postwar patriotism and partly out of the shared experiences of a demanding colonial life.

As the colonies became more populous, political interest increased. In both the Canadas and the Maritimes friction between ruling elites and the ordinary colonists developed and was partially fueled by the form of government in each colony. British governors or lieutenant-governors picked their own officials, including the members of legislative and executive councils. There were elected assemblies in each colony, but their powers were limited. Legislation might pass the assembly but be turned down by the legislative council. The assemblies, the voices of the people, found themselves frustrated by the power of appointed officials.

By the mid-1830s, economic distress increased the discontent that had been building during the 1820s. In Lower Canada, where cultural prejudice against the Canadiens added to the tension, Louis Joseph Papineau emerged as leader of the radical Patriote Party. When the colonial authorities would not grant the reforms called for by Papineau and his followers, rebellion broke out in Nov. 1837. But loyalist forces quickly defeated the badly-organized and poorly-led rebels. Papineau and other leaders fled to the United States.

In Upper Canada, the reform movement was able to gain a majority in the assembly in several elections. Still, the reformers could not turn their program into legislation because of Tory control of the Legislative Council. When an anti-reform lieutenant-governor, Sir Francis Bond Head, took over in 1836 some reformers became more radical. The leader of this radical faction was William Lyon Mackenzie, a newspaper editor and member of the assembly. The Tories won the election of 1836, when Head directly intervened in the campaign. Mackenzie and his followers, spurred on by events in Lower Canada, took up arms in early Dec. of 1837. Mackenzie's disorganization, and a lack of widespread support among the colonists, doomed the rebellion. After a skirmish north of Toronto the main body of rebels fled. An uprising in the western districts of Upper Canada was equally unsuccessful. Throughout the following year some rebels and American sympathizers mounted raids on Upper Canada from the United States, but these received no popular support.

In the aftermath of the rebellions came political change. The British government sent out Governor General Lord Durham to investigate the rebellion. The Durham Report of 1839 contained 2 main recommendations: the first called for

the union of Upper and Lower Canada as a first step in the eventual assimilation of the French Canadians; the second recommended the granting of responsible government (in which the executive is responsible to the assembly). Since the reformers had long been demanding responsible government, the Durham Report may be seen as evidence of the success of the Rebellions of 1837.

The Road to Confederation (1840-1867)

The middle years of the 19th century were both satisfying and disturbing for British North Americans. Immigrants streamed into the colonies, more land was cleared, and towns grew. Local industries were started, while lumbering and shipbuilding activities increased. Montreal and Toronto became commercial centres and the ports of the Maritimes engaged in widespread shipping ventures. Transportation improved as roads, canals and, by the 1850s, railways were built. Some British North Americans had the vision to look beyond their borders to predict that the Hudson's Bay Company's Red River Settlement and the settlements in British Columbia might one day be part of a federation of British colonies.

Yet there were problems in British North America. Until the mid-1840s, the colonies had enjoyed a preferential trading relationship whereby Britain reduced tariffs on colonial products. This advantage was lost, however, in 1846 when Britain adopted free trade. At first, the colonies found some advantage in entering into a limited free trade arrangement with the United States. But this Reciprocity Treaty of 1854 was allowed to lapse by the Americans in 1866. British North Americans would have to look to themselves as trading partners.

There was also concern in British North America about the United States. That country seemed intent on fulfilling its 'Manifest Destiny' to take over North America. The threat was especially clear during and after the American Civil War. During the war, the Northern States were angered by British support for the South, and after the war, there was a fear that the large Northern army might march into British Territory.

As well, there was a serious political problem in the colony of Canada. The union of Upper and Lower Canada in 1841 had resulted in the creation of a single legislature for the new colony, Canada. By the 1860s, however, this legislature was barely functioning. No single party could gain enough support from both Francophones and Anglophones to gain a majority. There had been 12 different governments in 15 years, and Canadian politicians were desperate for a solution.

Three powerful figures in Canada's legislature, John A. Macdonald, George Brown and George-Étienne Cartier formed a coalition and proposed a larger union of British North America as a way to end the political deadlock. In addition, this proposal would solve the problem of trade, and provide security against the American threat. Meanwhile, on the east coast there was interest in a union too, a union of the Maritimes. A conference had been called for Charlottetown in Sept. 1864 to discuss that topic. When the leaders of the new Canadian coalition heard of this meeting, they asked to attend. At Charlottetown the British North American delegates decided on a federation of all the colonies. A 2d conference at Quebec in Oct., 1864 resulted in a plan for federal union. A federal government would control defence, trade and other matters of national interest. Provincial governments would have power over local matters such as roads and education. The final details were hammered out at another conference in London, England, in 1866.

The British government which supported this colonial initiative, passed the British North America Act in Mar. of 1867. On July 1, 1867 the provinces of Nova Scotia, New Brunswick, Ontario (formerly Canada West) and Quebec (formerly Canada East), became the Dominion of Canada.

The Nation Expands (1867-1885)

Soon after the Confederation of Ontario, Quebec, New Brunswick, and Nova Scotia in 1867, the new nation of Canada began to expand. Guided by the national vision of Prime Minister John A. Macdonald, the federal government in 1869 bought from the Hudson's Bay Company Rupert's Land, a huge territory which included most of modern Manitoba, as well as parts of Saskatchewan, Alberta and the North-west Territories. The few Ontario immigrants in the Red River Settlement welcomed this move; but the far more numerous Métis (descendants of French fur traders and Indians) were suspicious, especially because they had not been consulted beforehand. When Lieutenant-Governor William McDougall tried to enter the settlement before the territory had officially been transferred to Canada, the Métis turned back his party. In the absence of a legitimate government, the Métis under their leader, Louis Riel, seized Fort Garry on the Red River and proclaimed a provisional government. The Métis demanded the right to vote, land laws, the official use of both French and English, and the provision of both Roman Catholic and Protestant schools. The Métis list of rights became the terms for negotiating Manitoba's entry into Confederation in 1870.

In the same year, representatives from the colony of British Columbia arrived in Ottawa to discuss union. With the promise from Ottawa to build a transcontinental railway, British Columbia entered Confederation in 1871. Canada now stretched from sea to sea, but the work of nation building was still not complete.

In the Maritimes, Macdonald had faced a challenge to the union in 1868 when Nova Scotia elected an anti-Confederation provincial government and sent a delegation under veteran politician Joseph Howe to London to seek a repeal of the union. But Britain was unsympathetic, and in 1869 Macdonald seized the opportunity to offer Nova Scotia better terms and Howe a cabinet position. With the Nova Scotia situation resolved, Macdonald could turn to Prince Edward Island. The Islanders found union more attractive after an expensive railway project nearly bankrupted the colony. Macdonald agreed to assume the colony's debts, offered a cash subsidy, and promised a steamer service to the mainland. In 1873, Prince Edward Island agreed to the terms and became Canada's 7th province.

In the 1870s and 1880s railways were built to link the provinces of the new nation. The Intercolonial Railway joining central Canada to the Maritimes was completed in 1876, but construction of a rail link to British Columbia ran into several delays. First, Macdonald's government was defeated in 1873 over corruption associated with the railway project. Then, the new prime minister, Alexander Mackenzie, refused to fund extensive railway projects in the midst of a depression which hit Canada. However, after Macdonald's re-election in 1878, railway building began in earnest. In Feb. 1881 the Canadian Pacific Railway Company (CPR) was incorporated, and in Nov. 1885 the last spike was driven at Craigellachie in British Columbia to complete the link to the Pacific.

Even before it was fully completed, the CPR was used to carry troops to quell a rebellion in the spring of 1885. Trouble had started several years earlier when settlers in the North-West Territory (modern Alberta and Saskatchewan) complained to the government about land title, shipping rates, and the lack of an elected government. Among those who complained were the Métis, some of whom had moved farther west after the Red River troubles of 1870. When the federal government was slow to respond, the Métis, again under Louis Riel, rose up in Mar. 1885 against the territorial council appointed by Ottawa. By late Apr., 5 000 Canadian soldiers, who had travelled by the new railway, were on the march against Riel and his Métis and Indian followers. At the Battle of Batoche in May, the forces of General Middleton defeated the rebels. Riel was found guilty of treason and executed.

The Laurier Era (1896-1911)

Conservative Prime Minister John A. Macdonald died in 1891, soon after winning a federal election. The Conservatives could not find a suitable successor and ran through 4 prime ministers by 1896. In these years, the Conservatives had to deal with a crisis over school legislation introduced in Manitoba. The Manitoba legislature had replaced the dual school system (both Protestant and Catholic schools) which had been guaranteed in the terms of union, with a single Protestant system. Francophone Catholics across Canada already were bitter about Louis Riel's execution, following a trial before an English-speaking jury. Now the schools' legislation convinced them that English Protestant Canadians wanted to stamp out

French Catholic rights. Extremists on both sides inflamed the issue, and the Conservatives' inability to settle the matter hurt them in the election of 1896. The Liberals, under Wilfrid Laurier, formed a government.

Laurier settled the Manitoba schools question by adopting a compromise approach. Religious instruction would be allowed within the single system, and instruction in French could take place where numbers warranted. The issue died down but Laurier had to remain sensitive to the tensions between Anglophone Protestants and Francophone Catholics. Many English Canadians were swept up in a great wave of pro-imperial sentiment associated with the Diamond Jubilee of Queen Victoria. In Britain the event was seen as an opportunity to strengthen ties within the British Empire. Laurier acknowledged Canada's support for the Empire but resisted proposals for a closer relationship with Britain and the other colonies. The prime minister did not wish to yield Canadian autonomy, nor did he wish to lose support in French Canada. The issue of Canada's role in the Empire came to a head in 1899 during the Boer War. Once again steering a middle course, Laurier agreed to equip and transport Canadian volunteers to South Africa, but sent no official troops. Although this compromise did not satisfy all Canadians, it avoided a bitter dispute. For a time, imperial issues were forgotten, as Canadians enjoyed boom times after the turn of the century.

Laurier summed up the nation's mood when he declared that the "twentieth century is Canada's century." Impressive growth in both industrial and agricultural production provided support for his words. Canada's prospects appealed to immigrants who flocked to the industrial cities and to the farmland of the Prairies. Many of them were attracted by an extensive government advertising campaign and by the lure of free land in the west. As a result of this influx, 2 new provinces, Alberta and Saskatchewan, were created in 1905. The immigrant tide boosted Canada's population from 5 371 315 in 1901 to 7 206 643 in 1911. The mood of the country was so confident that 2 new transcontinental railway building projects got under way in the early years of the century.

The international scene, however, was not so bright. In 1903, the British sided with the Americans in a dispute over the international boundary near the Klondike gold fields. Canadians were dismayed; but Britain was less concerned about the Canadian claim than for the need to maintain good relations with the United States. Tension in Europe was increasing and Britain found itself outside of the alliance system which had developed there. This same concern led both the British government and Canadian pro-imperialists to pressure Laurier into providing money to build British warships. Again, Laurier staked out a middle position by introducing a Naval Service Act which created a Canadian navy that could help Britain where the need arose.

Laurier's naval policy satisfied neither side. Some French Canadians supported the views of Quebec nationalist Henri Bourassa who claimed Laurier had betrayed his people. Anglophone pro-imperialists complained that Laurier had not done enough. Canada's naval policy became an issue in the 1911 election. Another issue was the Liberal plan for free trade with the United States. The Conservative leader, Robert Borden, was able to use the two issues to characterize Laurier as disloyal to Britain and favoring annexation to the United States. The Conservatives won the election and Borden became prime minister. Laurier stayed on as leader of the Opposition, continuing to advocate conciliatory policies when the interests of French and English Canadians clashed.

Canada and the First World War (1914-1918)

In Aug. 1914, Britain declared war on Germany and Austro-Hungary. The declaration automatically applied to Canada, as part of the British Empire. At first, there was an enthusiastic response, especially among recent British immigrants. When the minister of militia, Sam Hughes, called for 25 000 volunteers, about 33 000 appeared. In 1915, when the government asked the Canadian public to buy $50 million in war bonds, they bought $100 million. But enthusiasm for war began to fade as the casualties mounted and the realities of trench warfare became known.

Canadian troops sailed for Europe in Oct. 1914 and, after training in Britain, went into action at Ypres, Belgium, in Apr.

1915. There they gained a reputation for courage, holding their positions in the face of a new weapon, poison gas. Canadians took part in the costly battles at St. Eloi and Mont Sorrel in 1916. By the Battle of the Somme, in late summer of 1916, Canada had 4 army divisions in France; in the spring of 1917, all 4 were deployed in the attack on Vimy Ridge, which resulted in the first real Canadian victory of the war. But by now it was clear that every battle would result in terrible losses. At Passchendaele in Oct. 1917, the Canadians sustained more than 15 000 casualties.

Voluntary recruitment could not keep pace with the high casualty rates. Prime Minister Borden was forced to consider conscription to draft soldiers into the army and took the issue to the electorate in 1917, unleashing one of the most bitterly-fought campaigns in Canadian history. In Quebec, Henri Bourassa rallied anti-conscription supporters and argued that Canada had done enough. In Ontario, Borden's supporters condemned French-Canadian anti-conscriptionists as traitors. For his part Borden introduced the Wartime Elections Act to help secure victory. This act removed the right to vote from enemy aliens, even though some were Canadian citizens. It also gave the right to vote to women relatives of soldiers. In the election Borden won in every province except Quebec where he was soundly rejected. Conscription had created a deep division between Quebec and the rest of Canada. The irony is that conscription had little impact on the course of the war. When the first 400 000 conscripts were called up, 90% of them appealed for exemption, and by the war's end only about 24 000 conscripts had reached the front.

While the conscription crisis raged at home, Canadian soldiers played a major role in the events leading to an Allied victory. They took part in the successful battle at Amiens in Aug. 1918 and helped to roll the Germans back to Mons by Nov. The Canadians were still fighting at Mons when the armistice was signed Nov. 11, 1918.

Canadians also served with distinction in other theatres of war. By 1918, Canadians made up almost 25% of the pilots in Britain's Royal Flying Corps. Other Canadians served in the Royal Navy or on coastal patrol in Canada's own small navy. Some served in forestry corps overseas and others operated the railways behind the British lines. Some, including women, served as ambulance drivers at the front. Many Canadian women also played key roles as nurses overseas, and in the munitions factories in Canada.

Canada's war effort won the country a place in the Imperial War Cabinet during the war, and a seat in the League of Nations afterwards. There were other benefits, too. Women's contributions to the war effort helped them win the right to vote in federal elections and in provincial elections in 7 of the provinces by 1919. Yet these advances came at a terrible cost. Overseas, 68 300 Canadians had died. At home bitterness over the conscription issue had created a division between French and English Canadians that would be remembered for decades.

Canada in the 1920s

As the soldiers returned home, many expected to find a Canada ready to reward them for their sacrifices. What they found was a nation in the midst of painful postwar readjustment. Industry had to convert to peacetime production, but interest rates were high so investment capital was scarce. Jobs were hard to find and wages were low, and tariffs on imported goods kept prices high. By 1921, 300 000 men and women—more than 15% of the work force—were unemployed. Farmers, especially on the Prairies, suffered too. During the war, the west had become the world's breadbasket, wheat prices had soared and many farmers had borrowed heavily to expand their production. But with the war's end, world markets collapsed; wheat prices fell by almost half within 2 years.

These conditions, along with resentment over wartime profiteering by big business, created unrest. Radical unionism flared briefly with the One Big Union movement centered in western Canada. This attempt to create a single union to represent all workers was partly responsible for the Winnipeg General Strike of 1919. Although the Winnipeg workers were striking over such issues as the right to collective bargaining, better wages and improved working conditions, the opponents of the general strike characterized it as a communist conspiracy. The federal government sided with the anti-strike forces. Immigration laws were amended to deport 'alien' labor radicals, the

strike leaders were arrested and the Royal North West Mounted Police fired into a rioting crowd on 'Bloody Sunday', June 21, 1919. The 6-week strike was over and so was a period of growth in the power of labor unions. In 1919 alone there were more than 400 strikes, but after the Winnipeg General Strike, most governments at the provincial and federal levels opposed union activities. Throughout the 1920s there was a decline in union membership.

Unrest and discontent had regional overtones in the 1920s. The government takeover of 5 financially-troubled railways had led to the creation of the Canadian National Railways in 1919. As a result of the takeover, railway rates in the Maritimes were raised 40% to bring them up to central Canadian levels. Angry over the rail rates and feeling that Ottawa was making decisions on the basis of central Canada's interests, many Maritimers protested. The Maritimes Rights movement aimed at winning transportation concessions and federal subsidies; at the same time it promoted regional rights and pride.

There were signs of discontent in other parts of the country too. Farmers, resentful over low prices for farm products, high rail rates and high prices for manufactured goods, formed the United Farmers movement. In 1919 in Ontario, in 1921 in Alberta, and in 1922 in Manitoba, United Farmers' parties won provincial elections. At the federal level, the Progressive Party embraced some of the program of the United Farmers' movement. The Progressives called for free trade, nationalization (especially in the case of railways) and more direct democracy (such as calling a referendum to decide a controversial issue). Although they were a new party, the Progressives were to play an important role in politics in the 1920s.

The election of 1921 marked new directions in Canadian politics. First of all, both major parties had new leaders: Arthur Meighen had replaced Borden as prime minister; William Lyon Mackenzie King had taken over as Liberal leader after Laurier's death. Of even greater significance was the choice offered to voters in this election of 1921. For the first time in a federal election Canadians could vote for a third party, the Progressives. In fact, although the Liberals won the election, the Progressives finished 2d. Their position in the House of Commons was even more important, however, after the 1925 election in which Meighen won the most seats but King remained in power by claiming the support of the Progressives. After 1925 the Progressives declined, and many of their supporters voted Liberal in King's 1926 election victory. But the influence of the Progressive movement was still felt as King's government, anxious to keep Progressive support, passed Canada's first Old Age Pension Act in 1927. For the first time, a third party movement had made an impact on Canadian politics.

In foreign affairs, King made sure that Canada played a cautious role in the League of Nations, because he feared that Canada would be drawn into international disputes. In imperial matters, his insistence on autonomy contributed to a redefinition of the empire at the Imperial Conference of 1926. There it was acknowledged that Canada and the other British dominions were autonomous even in their external affairs. As a result, by 1929, Canada had diplomatic posts in Washington, Paris and Tokyo and Britain had a high commissioner in Ottawa. The Governor General would now be a symbolic representative of the Crown rather than a representative of the British government.

At home, there were many signs that good times had finally come to Canada. World markets for Canadian manufactured goods had revived, and wheat prices were soaring to new levels. New mining and lumbering areas were developed. From the newly-developed primary industries of the Canadian Shield, more than a billion dollars worth of products were being extracted by 1928. Immigrants poured into Canada by the hundreds of thousands to provide labor in the growing industrial cities. Cars, radios, telephones, electrical appliances and other consumer goods were being bought, especially by middle-class Canadians, often using credit plans. Credit was also used to buy shares on the stock market, as the country became increasingly optimistic about its future. This confidence, along with the faster pace of life and the glamor of big city living, was reflected in the radio programs, the movies, the magazines, the fads and the fashions that were popular in Canada. On both sides of the Canadian-American border, the Roaring Twenties were in full swing and there seemed no end in sight to the good times.

The Great Depression (1929-1939)

In 1929, Canadians looked with confidence toward the next decade. That confidence made the effects of the Great Depression of the 1930s even more bitter. This Depression was world wide, but the effects were especially felt in Canada because about a third of the nation's gross national product was based on exports. The first signs of Canadian economic collapse appeared in Oct. 1929 when wheat prices began to fall. In the same month the stock market collapsed, ruining thousands of shareholders, some of whom, on paper at least, had been millionaires. By 1930, the number of unemployed had doubled, and by 1933, one in 5 Canadians was unemployed.

Western Canada was hardest hit because of its reliance on a single crop, wheat. The Prairie provinces also suffered from crop failure and drought during these hard times. The combined results were devastating. In Saskatchewan, for example, provincial income fell by 90% and two thirds of the province's population had to go on welfare. In the 1930s, welfare, or "relief" as it was then known, became a burden for municipal and provincial governments across the country. By 1935, 10% of Canadians were on relief.

But Bennett's government did not intervene to rebuild the economy. In the 1930s, politicians, economists and business leaders assumed that the Depression, like other downswings in the business cycle, would soon be followed by a recovery. Their own experience, and most economic theory at the time, did not encourage them to consider major government spending as a way to stimulate the depressed economy.

One of the few federally-financed programs involved sending single unemployed men to camps where they did manual work in return for their keep and a small allowance. Working in isolated conditions, often at meaningless tasks, many of the young men were discontent; those in the British Columbia camps took action. In 1935 about 1 500 camp inmates decided to present their complaints directly to Bennett in Ottawa. They began the On to Ottawa Trek by taking over freight trains heading east. By the time they reached Regina, there were about 2 000 protesters. The railway refused to provide further transportation. Representatives of the Trekkers met with Prime Minister Bennett in Ottawa, but the talks were inconclusive. When the delegation returned to Regina, Bennett decided to arrest the protest leaders. On July 1, there was a bloody riot in Regina involving the Trekkers, local police and the RCMP. The Trek was over and the protesters returned home over the next few days; but Bennett's handling of the affair hurt his image. In the election of 1935, the people turned to King, in the hopes that this time he could deal with the Depression.

After 1935, economic conditions began to improve slowly, yet federal politicians did little to speed this recovery. The failure of the Liberals and the Conservatives to deal with the Depression led to the rise of reform parties. A socialist party, the Co-operative Commonwealth Federation (CCF) won 7 seats in the 1935 election and elected members to several provincial legislatures. Other new parties appeared at the provincial level. In Alberta, the Social Credit Party promised $25 prosperity certificates to each resident; the plan fell flat because the province did not have the power to issue currency. In Quebec, Maurice Duplessis established the Union Nationale and promised economic reform. But the Union Nationale, like the other parties, could not end the Depression, the effects of which faded only with the outbreak of World War II, in 1939.

Canada in World War II (1939-1945)

While most Canadians focused attention on the effects of the Depression at home, events in Europe during the 1930s were moving the world closer to another global conflict. After taking over Austria and Czechoslovakia, Germany invaded Poland in 1939; Britain and France responded by declaring war. Following Britain's action, King quickly summoned Parliament. On Sept. 10, one week after Britain had entered the conflict, the Canadian Parliament declared war on Germany and its allies.

Parliamentary support for the war declaration was based in part on King's known preference for a limited Canadian role and his assurance that there would be no conscription. Initially, only one Canadian division was sent to Britain. But by 1940, France had fallen and Britain faced invasion. Now King abandoned the concept of limited participation and decided to dispatch more troops. By late 1942, Canada had 5 divisions overseas. Canadian soldiers first saw action in Dec. 1941 during the unsuccessful defence of Hong Kong. In Aug. 1942, 5 000 Canadians took part in the disastrous raid on the French port of Dieppe, suffering casualties of 2 200 killed or captured. Despite these setbacks, the Canadian army did play a major role in defeating enemy forces in Italy and took part in the Allied landings at Normandy in June of 1944. After taking key targets in France, Canadian soldiers moved northward to liberate Holland in 1945.

Canadians contributed to the war effort in other important ways. The Royal Canadian Navy grew from 6 destroyers and less than 2 000 personnel in 1939 to 471 warships, 99 688 men and 6 500 women by the war's end in 1945. The navy helped win the Battle of the Atlantic against German submarines by providing protection to the convoys carrying essential supplies from North America to Britain. Canadians also fought in the air as members of Britain's Royal Air Force, and, in increasing numbers throughout the war, in the Royal Canadian Air Force (RCAF). By 1945, there were 48 RCAF squadrons overseas. Other members of the RCAF were involved in the Commonwealth Air Training Plan. Operating from Canadian airfields, this plan trained 131 000 aircrew from around the British Commonwealth.

The air training scheme was just one example of the war effort on the Home Front. Canada produced a wide variety of munitions, and provided important food supplies to the Allied war effort. Much of Canada's war production went directly to Britain, so did more than $3 billion in financial assistance.

Despite the contributions of Canadian men and women to the war effort, the conflict caused some disturbing issues at home. In reversing his earlier stand against conscription, Prime Minister King called for a national plebiscite on the issue in 1942. In all provinces except Quebec the electorate voted for conscription; relations between Quebec and the rest of Canada were strained, although not as severely as in World War I. Another issue involved the internment of Japanese Canadians and the confiscation of their property in the name of national security. Although there was little outcry over these actions during the war, the issue has gained attention more recently.

By the war's end, more than a million Canadians had served in the armed forces and more than 42 000 had died. Canada's war effort enhanced its international image. At the same time, Canada had developed closer ties with the United States. The most dramatic indication of this new relationship was the establishment, in 1940, of the Permanent Joint Board on Defence.

Canada: 1945-1968

In the years following World War II, Canadians enjoyed a standard of living that was in stark contrast to the pre-war Depression years. The economy had boomed during the war and the gross national product had doubled. The war had prompted development in new industries, such as the chemical industry, which continued to expand in peacetime. Consumer spending had increased dramatically during the war, and continued to rise with the postwar baby boom. This boom, along with large numbers of European immigrants, resulted in a 40% population increase between the war's end and 1958. In Canada's quickly growing cities and suburbs, home ownership was made easier by the National Housing Act which made mortgages more readily available. This example of government involvement in the economy was characteristic of the times. By 1945, unemployment insurance and family allowance legislation had been passed and other social welfare measures were being discussed.

Prime Minister King retired in 1948, and was followed as Liberal leader by Louis St. Laurent. One of St. Laurent's first achievements was the entry of Newfoundland into Confederation in 1949. In 1951, his government increased old age pensions and, in 1957, introduced a hospital insurance plan. St. Laurent negotiated with the United States to build the St. Lawrence Seaway, an impressive feat of engineering completed in 1959. In 1956, however, St. Laurent's government had lost popularity over its use of closure to limit parliamentary debate about building a trans-Canada pipeline for oil and gas. In the election the following year, the Conservatives under John Diefenbaker won a minority victory. In 1958, to consolidate his position, Diefenbaker called another election. This time, the Conservatives swept the country, winning 208 of 265 seats.

Diefenbaker, popularly known as "Dief", had great appeal to the average Canadian. He spoke with vision about the opening of the Canadian north and he boosted western agriculture by arranging wheat sales to China. His government showed its concern for the rights of Canadians by introducing the Bill of Rights and granting Native Indians the right to vote in federal elections, both in 1960.

Diefenbaker's pride in Canada still left room for his strong support of the British Commonwealth, a popular cause in the 1950s. He looked to Canada's security at a time of international tension by signing the North American Air Defence Agreement (NORAD) with the United States. But Diefenbaker's government could not deal with an economic recession that led to a devalued dollar and high unemployment. Also, Diefenbaker took the controversial steps of cancelling production of the Canadian-made Avro Arrow fighter jet and refusing to allow nuclear warheads on the American missiles based in Canada. In the election of 1962, his government lost to the Liberals.

The earlier career of the new prime minister, Lester B. Pearson, provides a record of Canadian external relations in the late 1940s and the 1950s. In 1945 Pearson had attended the founding conference of the United Nations, and he had strongly supported Canada's membership in the North Atlantic Treaty Organization in 1949. As minister of external affairs, and then as president of the United Nations General Assembly, Pearson had favored Canadian involvement in the UN army during the Korean War, 1950-1953. In 1957, he had won the Nobel Peace Prize for his peaceful solution to the Suez Crisis of 1956. Pearson's role in that crisis reflected the reputation that Canada enjoyed as a middle power capable of mediating in dangerous international disputes.

As prime minister, Pearson concentrated on domestic matters. His government broadened social welfare by introducing Medicare, the Canada Pension Plan and the Canada Assistance Plan. Canadian nationalism was heightened with the adoption of the maple leaf flag, and the opening of the world's fair, Expo, in Canada's centennial year, 1967. At the same time, Pearson was sensitive to growing nationalism in Quebec. There, the Quiet Revolution, a transformation from traditional to modern attitudes towards education, social reform and industrialization, was taking place. The Quebec government was implementing the ideas of the Quiet Revolution and championed provincial rights with its slogan *maîtres chez nous* (masters in our own house). Pearson wanted to demonstrate that Quebec's interests could be served by the federal government. He established a Royal Commission on Bilingualism and Biculturalism, and encouraged some of those closely associated with the Quiet Revolution to run for federal office. One of these, Pierre Trudeau, was elected to the House of Commons in 1965 and, in 1967, was named minister of justice. In 1968, following Pearson's retirement, Trudeau became Liberal leader.

The Trudeau Years (1968-1984)

In the election campaign of 1968, the relatively young and charismatic Trudeau captured the attention of the media, and drew enthusiastic crowds. "Trudeaumania" carried the Liberals to a majority victory. Although associated with the Quiet Revolution, Trudeau was an avowed federalist, determined to show that Ottawa could promote the rights of French Canada. The *Official Languages Act* of 1969 recognized both English and French as official languages, and required federal institutions to provide services in both languages. Although the legislation was supported by all parties, there was some resentment in Anglophone parts of the country, especially in Ontario and the west.

Trudeau received more widespread support for his firm handling of the October Crisis of 1970. Separatist extremists belonging to the FLQ (Front de Libération du Québec) had kidnapped British Trade Commissioner James Cross, and had

killed Quebec cabinet minister, Pierre Laporte. Trudeau used the *War Measures Act* to apply emergency measures of arrest, detention and martial law. This move was generally popular but was criticized by advocates of civil rights, especially since the FLQ had little real support.

In his early years in power, Trudeau's attempt to concentrate decision-making in Ottawa, and particularly in the newly-created Prime Minister's Office led to complaints in western Canada that its interests were being ignored by an eastern-dominated federal government. At the same time the Opposition parties charged that Trudeau was undermining both the power of the cabinet and of Parliament. The Liberals were almost defeated in the election of 1972 but retained power through a minority government.

By 1974, the Liberals had regained a majority but were faced with a soaring inflation rate. Trudeau tried a variety of measures, including a 3-year imposition of wage and price controls under the Anti-Inflation Act of 1975. Although the controls may have had some effect, world conditions, especially the oil crisis, kept inflation high. While trying to deal with this economic problem, Trudeau had to face another crisis. In 1976, the separatist Parti Québécois under René Lévesque won the provincial election in Quebec. Public uncertainty over the future of Quebec, continuing inflation, and western alienation all undermined Liberal support. In the 1979 election, the Liberals lost, and Conservative leader Joe Clark became prime minister.

Trudeau had resigned as Liberal leader, but Clark's defeat on a non-confidence vote, and the calling of an election, drew the former prime minister out of retirement. The Liberals won the election of 1980, and Trudeau embarked on an eventful term of office. His own intervention, and that of his cabinet colleagues, helped to defeat the 1980 Quebec referendum on Sovereignty Association, which could have led to an attempt by Quebec to leave Confederation. Then, after a long and difficult campaign waged in Parliament, at federal-provincial meetings and in the media, Trudeau managed to get agreement on patriating the Canadian constitution (see pages 10-15). Patriation officially took place when Queen Elizabeth II proclaimed the new Constitution Act in Ottawa on Apr. 17, 1982. Finally, in his last term Trudeau enhanced his world image. He promoted a North-South dialogue between wealthy nations and underdeveloped countries, and in his last year of office undertook a personal peace initiative by travelling to world capitals to promote nuclear disarmament.

Despite his achievements, Trudeau had many critics in Canada. He had lost some of his popular appeal and was accused of being aloof and arrogant. Business leaders complained that the Foreign Investment Review Agency, set up in 1973 to protect the Canadian economy against foreign domination, discouraged investment. The National Energy Program, created in 1980, aimed at oil self-sufficiency and greater Canadian ownership in an industry dominated by American-owned companies. But westerners were angered by the program's tax and price-fixing features. Finally, Trudeau's emphasis on the constitution and global issues did not sit well with many Canadians suffering from the effects of the severe recession of the early 1980s. In 1984, Trudeau retired and John Turner became Liberal leader and prime minister.

Mulroney in Power

In the 1984 general election, Prime Minister Turner faced Brian Mulroney who had been elected Conservative leader in 1983. The Conservatives won a decisive victory, taking 211 of 282 seats in the House of Commons, including 58 seats in Quebec, a former Liberal stronghold.

Mulroney's major initiatives from 1984 to 1988 were the negotiation of a free trade agreement with the United States and an agreement (the Meech Lake accord) on constitutional amendments designed to end Quebec's boycott of the 1982 constitutional changes. But, as of the summer of 1988, the free trade agreement was blocked by the Liberal-dominated Senate, which refused to endorse it prior to a federal election on the issue, and the Meech Lake accord was in jeopardy because the legislatures of New Brunswick and Manitoba had not yet approved it.

In its first few years in office, Mulroney's Conservative government sought to strengthen ties with the United States and took steps to attract more foreign investment to Canada.

Biographies of Canada's Prime Ministers

Sir John A. Macdonald

Canada's first prime minister, Sir John A. Macdonald, was born at Glasgow, Scotland, Jan. 11, 1815, the son of Hugh Macdonald and Helen Shaw. At age 5 he came to Canada with his parents who settled at Kingston, Upper Canada. He attended Midland District Grammar School, and Rev. John Cruickshank's School in Kingston.

Called to the bar in 1836, Macdonald practised law in Kingston, and then in Toronto. He established a reputation as a corporation lawyer, company director, and businessman.

He was elected to the Legislative Assembly of the Province of Canada in 1844, and was re-elected in 1848, 1851, 1854, 1857, 1861 and 1863. In 1864, he joined a coalition with George Brown, leader of the Upper Canadian reformers, dedicated to bringing about Confederation. That same year, Macdonald was a delegate to the Charlottetown and Quebec Conferences, and became the principal author of the Confederation resolutions agreed upon in Quebec. He was chairman of the London Conference (1866-67), and his role was pivotal in bringing about Confederation.

Macdonald became Canada's first prime minister when the Conservative party, which he led, held a majority of seats in Parliament following the first post-Confederation general election in 1867. Though he was re-elected in 1872, Macdonald's second administration was marred by the so-called "Pacific Scandal" in 1873, when the Liberal opposition charged that his government had awarded the C.P.R. contract to Sir Hugh Allan in return for contributions Allan had made to party coffers. An investigation into these charges was held, and the government resigned on Nov. 5, 1873.

The general election of Sept. 17, 1878 saw Macdonald's Liberal-Conservatives returned to power, and Macdonald remained prime minister until his death in Ottawa on June 6, 1891.

During his first administration, Macdonald had seen the Dominion of Canada expand to include the provinces of British Columbia, Prince Edward Island, and the newly-created Manitoba.

The building of the transcontinental railway is the most memorable feature of his second administration, but other notable accomplishments include the establishment of the "National Policy"—a system of tariff protection to aid the development of Canadian industries (1879)—and the increased settlement of the Western provinces that followed the construction of the railway.

Alexander Mackenzie

Alexander Mackenzie was born on Jan. 28, 1822 near Dunkeld, Perthshire, Scotland. His father was also named Alexander Mackenzie, and his mother was Mary Fleming. He attended public schools at Moulin, Dunkeld, and Perth, Scotland, but left school and became a stonemason at the age of 14.

He emigrated to Canada in 1842 and became a contractor at Lambton, Ontario and then editor of the *Lambton Shield*. From 1866-1874, he was a major in the 27th Lambton Battalion Volunteer Infantry.

In 1861, Mackenzie was elected to the Legislative Assembly of the Province of Canada, where he gave his support to the Confederation plan. When George Brown was defeated in elections to choose the first Parliament after Confederation, Mackenzie became *de facto* leader of the Opposition, though it was not until after the 1872 elections that he formally accepted this title.

It was Mackenzie who led the attack on the Macdonald administration over the "Pacific Scandal"; when Macdonald resigned on Nov. 5, 1873, Mackenzie became prime minister.

During his 5-year term of office, Mackenzie introduced changes to election laws that included the secret ballot and universal male suffrage. The Supreme Court of Canada was established under Mackenzie's rule, and Wilfrid Laurier was brought into Mackenzie's cabinet.

Severe economic depression plagued Canada during the Mackenzie years, and in 1878, his Liberal party was routed at the polls.

Mackenzie retained his own seat, however, and was still a member of Parliament when he died Apr. 17, 1892, in Toronto.

Sir John Abbott

Sir John Joseph Caldwell Abbott, the son of Joseph Abbott and Harriet Bradford, was born Mar. 12, 1821 at St. Andrews, Lower Canada, making him the first prime minister to be born on Canadian soil.

After taking his law degree from University of McGill College, he was admitted to the bar in 1847 and practised law in Montreal. From 1855-1880 he was dean of the Faculty of Law, McGill University.

Abbott was elected to the Legislative Assembly of the Province of Canada in 1857, re-elected in 1861 and 1863, and sat until Confederation. He was then elected to the House of Commons in 1867, 1872, and 1874. He was last elected in 1882, and appointed to the Senate on May 12, 1887.

When Sir John A. Macdonald died in 1891, Abbott—though a senator—inherited the Conservative leadership. The three other leading Conservatives—Langevin, Tupper and Thompson—were unwilling or unable to assume the post. Abbott held the office of prime minister from June 16, 1891 until his resignation on Nov. 24, 1892. He died in Montreal on Oct. 30, 1893.

Sir John Thompson

Sir John Sparrow David Thompson was born in Halifax, N.S., on Nov. 10, 1845. His father was John Sparrow Thompson, his mother, Charlotte Pottinger.

Thompson attended Halifax Common School and Free Church Academy. He was called to the Nova Scotia bar in 1865, and was instrumental in founding Dalhousie Law School in 1883, where he eventually became a lecturer.

In May 1882, Thompson became premier of Nova Scotia, but when his government was defeated 2 months later, he retired from politics and became a judge of the Supreme Court of Nova Scotia.

Prime Minister Macdonald coaxed Thompson back into politics, making him Minister of Justice in 1885. When Macdonald died in 1891, Thompson was one of the leading Conservatives who might have succeeded him. But he declined, fearing that his conversion to Roman Catholicism in 1870 would hinder his party's fortunes. However, by the following year, Thompson changed his mind, and on Dec. 5, 1892, he became prime minister.

Though prime minister for just over 2 years, Thompson was largely responsible for the establishment of the Criminal Code and penetentiary reforms. He very nearly succeeded in bringing Newfoundland into Confederation in 1894, and successfully negotiated fisheries clauses in the Treaty of Washington.

He died while still in office on Dec. 12, 1894.

Sir Mackenzie Bowell

Mackenzie Bowell was born at Rickinghall, Suffolk, England on Dec. 27, 1823, and came to Canada in 1832. In 1834, he became an apprentice printer at Belleville, Upper Canada, and he was later editor and proprietor of the Belleville *Intelligencer*. He served in the Militia of the United Province of Canada during the American Civil War and the Fenian raids of 1866.

Bowell was elected to the House of Commons in 1867 for Hastings North, Ont., and was re-elected in 1872, 1874, 1878, 1887 and 1891.

As spokesman for the Orange Association of British America, Bowell was instrumental in having Louis Riel expelled from the Commons in 1874.

On Dec. 5, 1892, Bowell was called to the Senate and, after Thompson's death in 1894, was invited by the Governor General to form a government.

Perhaps the thorniest problem facing Prime Minister Bowell was the Manitoba Schools question. In 1890, Manitoba legislation had withdrawn school privileges from the Roman Catholic and primarily French minority in that province. By the time Bowell assumed office, attempts were being made to restore those lost school privileges by federal remedial legislation. Bowell was not equal to the political challenges facing him; he lost control of his cabinet ministers, several of whom eventually called for his resignation. Bowell denounced this cabinet rebellion as a "nest of traitors", but eventually he resigned on Apr. 27, 1896. He died in Belleville, Ont., on Dec. 10, 1917 at 93.

Sir Charles Tupper

Charles Tupper was born at Amherst, N.S., July 2, 1821, the son of Rev. Charles Tupper and Miriam Lockhart Low. He attended Horton Academy and took a degree in medicine at Edinburgh University. At the age of 22, he began practising medicine in Amherst, and became the first president of the Canadian Medical Association (1867-70).

The 1855 election that brought him to the Legislative Assembly of Nova Scotia was declared void on Feb. 24, 1857. But he was subsequently re-elected in a by-election that same year and was elected again in 1859 and 1863.

Tupper took a leading part in the Confederation movement, and was a delegate to the Charlottetown, Quebec and London Conferences. He was elected to the House of Commons in 1867, and re-elected 1870, 1872, 1874, 1878 and 1882. He resigned in 1884, and was High Commissioner for Canada in the United Kingdom from May 28 of that year to Jan. 26, 1887. In 1887, he was re-elected to the House of Commons, but resigned the following year and again served as High Commissioner from May 23, 1888 to Jan. 14, 1896.

In 1896, following the rebellion of Bowell's cabinet, Tupper became *de facto* leader of the administration until Bowell formally resigned on Apr. 27, 1896. At that time, the Governor General invited Tupper to form the government. Parliament was dissolved shortly thereafter and in the election that followed on June 23, Tupper's Conservatives were defeated. Tupper stayed on as leader of the Opposition until Feb. 5, 1901, then retired from public life. He died Oct. 30, 1915 at Bexley Heath, Kent, England.

Sir Wilfrid Laurier

Wilfrid Laurier, son of Carolus Laurier and Marie-Marcelle Martineau, was born at St-Lin, Canada East, Nov. 20, 1841. He first attended Collège de l'Assomption, and then took his degree from McGill University.

He was called to the bar of Lower Canada in 1865. He practised law at Montreal and at Arthabaskaville, Que. He

was also, for a short time, editor of *Le Defricheur* of Arthabaskaville.

First elected to the Legislative Assembly of Quebec in 1871, Laurier resigned in Jan. 1874 and later that year was elected to the House of Commons. He became leader of the Opposition in June 1887. Then, following the 1896 election that gave his party a 23-seat majority, Laurier became Canada's first French-speaking prime minister on July 11, 1896. The Liberals retained power in 1900, and won a landslide election victory in 1904.

Laurier's accomplishments included western settlement and a significant extension of Canadian autonomy. Immigration increased as Clifford Sifton, Laurier's minister of the interior from 1896-1905, mounted a powerful campaign to attract immigrants from Britain, the United States and Europe. In 1905, Laurier created the provinces of Alberta and Saskatchewan and vastly increased the size of Manitoba. During Laurier's years in power the Canadian West became a major world wheat producer. In 1909, Laurier established the External Affairs Department.

His government's controversial support for the creation of a Canadian navy, and his unpopular attempt to enter into a reciprocal trade agreement with the United States (an agreement that would have reduced or eliminated duties on many imported goods) spelled trouble for Laurier in 1911. His party was defeated in the Sept. 21 election. He remained an Opposition M.P. until his death on Feb. 17, 1919 in Ottawa.

Sir Robert Borden

Born at Grand Pré, N.S., June 26, 1854, Robert Laird Borden was the son of Andrew Borden and Eunice Laird. He attended Acacia Villia Seminary in Horton, N.S., but at age 14 he gave up formal schooling to become an assistant master in classical studies. He taught classics and mathematics at Glenwood Institute in Matawan, New Jersey in 1873, before returning to Nova Scotia to study law. He was admitted to the Nova Scotia bar in 1878, and practised first in Halifax, then in Kentville, N.S.

Borden was elected to the House of Commons in 1896 and 1900 and became leader of the Conservative party on Feb. 6, 1901. He served as leader of the Opposition until 1911, when he led his party to victory in the Sept. 21 election.

Borden was prime minister throughout World War I and during the war years his staunch support of the Ross Rifle— a weapon known to jam in battle—resulted in the debacle known as the Ross Rifle Scandal. He also suffered from the controversy surrounding the Shell Committee—established by Defence Minister Sir Sam Hughes to secure British munitions contracts. It was Borden's government that introduced the first federal income tax, nationalized Canadian Northern and Grand Trunk-Grand Trunk Pacific Railway systems, and introduced conscription in 1917.

In the election of Dec. 17, 1917, Borden led to victory a re-organized Union Government, comprising Conservatives and pro-conscription Liberals. Borden headed the Canadian delegation at the Paris Peace Conference in 1919, where the autonomy of Canada and other dominions within the British Commonwealth was successfully established. He resigned on July 10, 1920, and died in Ottawa June 10, 1937.

Arthur Meighen

Arthur Meighen was born at Anderson, Ont., June 16, 1874, the son of Joseph Meighen and Mary Jane Bell. He attended St. Mary's Collegiate Institute and the University of Toronto. Following his graduation from university in 1896, Meighen taught high school for a year, then moved to Winnipeg in 1898 to study law. He was called to the Manitoba bar in 1902, and practised at Portage La Prairie.

He was first elected to the House of Commons in 1908, re-elected in 1911, 1913 and 1917, defeated in 1921, and re-elected in 1922 and 1925.

Meighen first achieved national prominence in 1913 when he was instrumental in devising a closure rule which permitted the government to end debate on a bill which was to effect a $35-million contribution to the British navy. Prior to closure, the bill had been obstructed by a fierce and protracted Opposition party blockade.

Prime Minister Borden appointed Meighen his solicitor general on Oct. 2, 1915, and Meighen held this post for 2 years. A strong supporter of conscription, Meighen essentially drafted Canada's 1917 Conscription bill, and put it into operation. He was also the chief draughtsman of the *Wartime Elections Act*.

When Borden resigned on July 10, 1920, Meighen succeeded him as prime minister. His first administration was short-lived. In the general election of Dec. 6, 1921, Meighen's party was defeated. Though his Conservatives won a plurality of seats on Oct. 29, 1925, the Liberals were able to stay in power with the support of Progressive and Labour members.

Following the "King-Byng" controversy, which led to the resignation of William Lyon Mackenzie King's government on June 28, 1926, the Governor General invited Meighen to form a new ministry. This government was less than 3 months old, however, when it was defeated in the House of Commons (by only one vote) and Canadians again went to the polls.

Following a Liberal victory in the election of Sept. 14, 1926, Meighen resigned as Conservative leader in the House of Commons. He was called to the Senate on Feb. 3, 1932 during Richard Bennett's ministry. This made Meighen government leader in the Senate. Then, following King's victory in 1935, he became Senate Opposition leader. Meighen was thus the only person to have headed both Government and Opposition forces in both Houses of Parliament.

On Nov. 12, 1941, he once again became leader of the Conservative party, but failed in his bid to win a seat in the Commons in a federal by-election on Feb. 2, 1942. Following this defeat, he retired from politics and resumed his law practice in Toronto where he died Aug. 5, 1960.

Mackenzie King

William Lyon Mackenzie King was born in Kitchener (then called Berlin) on Dec. 17, 1874, the son of John King and Isabel Grace Mackenzie.

He took his B.A. and law degrees from the University of Toronto, and also studied at the University of Chicago and Harvard University.

He was deputy minister of labour and edited the *Labour Gazette* from 1900-1908.

He was first elected to the House of Commons in 1908, and succeeded Laurier as leader of the Liberal party in 1919. In the general election of Dec. 6, 1921, the Liberals were victorious and King became prime minister.

Though Meighen's Conservatives won a plurality of seats in the general election of Oct. 29, 1925, King stayed in office with the help of Progressive and Labour members whose support he gained by offering tariff reductions and old-age pension legislation. King had lost his own York North seat in the 1925 election but returned to the House of Commons as the member for Prince Albert, Sask., following a by-election on Feb. 15, 1926.

King's government was shaken in 1926 by the revelation that the Customs department was tainted with corruption and incompetence. In the furor that followed, King lost the support of many members of Parliament and, although never technically defeated in the House of Commons, decided that he could no longer hold his minority government. He appealed to the Governor General, Lord Byng, to dissolve Parliament, even though the government had not been defeated. Byng refused. King subsequently resigned on June 28, 1926, and the Governor General invited Arthur Meighen to become prime minister.

In the general election of Sept. 14, 1926, King's Liberals regained power and held it until 1930. But the disastrous fall in the price of wheat and other Canadian exports in 1929 soured Canadians on their government, and King was defeated by Bennett's Conservatives in the election of July 28, 1930.

Five years later, King was back in the prime minister's office, following the Liberal victory in the general election

of Oct. 14, 1935. In the coming years, King, an ardent supporter of Canada's autonomy within the British Commonwealth in the past, was now faced with the issue of Canada's participation in an impending European war. To soothe French-Canadian concerns over Canadian support of Great Britain, King promised there would be no conscription; Canada declared war in Sept. 1939. Later, however, heavy casualties in France and Italy in 1944 prompted King to break his promise and send conscripts overseas.

King's government began introducing post-war recovery legislation even before peace was declared. These measures included reconstruction plans and social security schemes such as mother's allowances.

King resigned as prime minister on Nov. 15, 1948, supporting St. Laurent as his successor.

In poor health in his final years, King died July 22, 1950 at Kingsmere, his estate in Wright County, Que.

Richard Bennett

Richard Bedford Bennett was born at Hopewell, N.B., July 3, 1870, the son of Henry John Bennett and Henrietta Stiles. After attending Hopewell Cape Public School and Provincial Normal School in Fredericton, Bennett went on to Dalhousie University to study law. He read and practised law in Chatham, N.B., from 1893-1897, before moving to Calgary where he entered a legal partnership with Senator James A. Lougheed (grandfather of former Alberta Premier Peter Lougheed).

Bennett was first elected to the House of Commons in 1911. He served as minister of justice in Arthur Meighen's 1921 cabinet, and minister of finance and minister of mines in Meighen's 1926 government.

Bennett was chosen to replace Meighen as Conservative leader at the party convention in Winnipeg in 1927. Three years later, he became prime minister following the Conservative victory in the general election of July 28, 1930.

Bennett had the unhappy task of governing Canada during the worst years of the Depression. Virtually every measure his government attempted ended in failure. High unemployment levels continued despite Bennett's efforts to reduce them. An attempt to negotiate a reciprocity treaty with the United States did not succeed. A plan of preferential tariffs agreed to in 1930 at the Imperial Conference did little to ease Canada's economic woes.

Then, in 1935, near the end of his term, Bennett took an unexpected step to the political left. He proclaimed that "the old order is gone" and that it was time for a new economic system. That new system was to include a state-planned economy, and new unemployment and health insurance legislation and old-age pension laws.

In the election of Oct. 14, 1935, Bennett's Conservatives suffered a devastating defeat, winning just 39 seats. Bennett remained in Opposition until 1937, when he retired to England. There he was given the title Viscount Bennett of Mickelham, Hopewell and Calgary.

Though most often remembered as the years of the Great Depression, Bennett's term also saw the creation of the Canadian Radio Broadcasting Corporation (the predecessor to the C.B.C.) and the Bank of Canada. As well, it was during Bennett's tenure that Canada received autonomy with the Statute of Westminster in 1931.

Bennett died June 27, 1947.

Louis St. Laurent

Louis Stephen St. Laurent was born at Compton, Que., Feb. 1, 1882, the son of Jean-Baptist Moise St. Laurent and Mary Broderick. He attended Collège St. Charles, Sherbrooke and Université Laval. Called to the Quebec bar in 1905, he practised law in Quebec City, and became Professor of Law at Université Laval. He was elected president of the Canadian Bar Association in 1930.

St. Laurent became justice minister in Mackenzie King's cabinet on Dec. 10, 1941. On Feb. 9, 1942, he was elected to the House of Commons in a by-election for Quebec East.

Originally planning to hold his cabinet post only during the war, St. Laurent was persuaded to stay on afterwards.

On Dec. 10, 1946, he became secretary of state for external affairs. A firm believer in collective security, St. Laurent was one of the architects of the North Atlantic Treaty Organization. On Aug. 7, 1948, he accepted his party's nomination to be King's successor, and on Nov. 15 became prime minister.

While in power St. Laurent persuaded India, Pakistan and Ceylon to remain in the Commonwealth (1948-49). He ended the former practice of appealing court cases to the Judicial Committee of the Privy Council in England, and made the Supreme Court of Canada the final Canadian court of appeal. He won the acceptance of a new apportionment of taxes in 1956 and, in negotiation with President Truman, laid the foundation for a U.S.-Canada agreement to develop the St. Lawrence Seaway.

In 1958, he retired and returned to Quebec City to practise law. He died July 25, 1973.

John Diefenbaker

John George Diefenbaker was born at Neustadt, Ont., Sept. 18, 1895, the son of William Thomas Diefenbaker and Mary Florence Bannerman. He attended public schools in Ontario before moving to western Canada with his parents in 1903. He attended Saskatoon Collegiate Institute, received his B.A. from the University of Saskatchewan in 1915, and his M.A. one year later.

After the outbreak of World War I, he joined the Canadian Officers' Training Corps, and served overseas as a lieutenant with the 105th Saskatoon Fusiliers' Regiment from 1916 to 1917.

Returning to Saskatchewan, he took his law degree from the University of Saskatchewan in 1919 and established a law practice at Wakaw. He later moved to Prince Albert.

After several unsuccessful attempts to gain a seat, first in the federal, then in Saskatchewan's provincial parliament, Diefenbaker was finally elected to the House of Commons in 1940. He was a candidate for leadership of the Progressive Conservative Party at the 1942 and 1948 conventions, but did not win the nomination until Dec. 14, 1956.

The P.C.s won the election of June 10, 1957, and on June 21, John Diefenbaker officially became prime minister. A year later, he called an election, hoping to turn his Conservative plurality into a clear majority. He was overwhelmingly successful, winning 208 of the 265 seats in the Mar. 31, 1958 election. He fared less well in the 1962 election, when only 116 P.C.s were elected, and in the general election of 1963, when a Liberal victory relegated Diefenbaker to the role of Opposition leader. Diefenbaker remained Conservative leader until Sept. 1967, when he was defeated by Robert Stanfield at the Progressive Conservative leadership convention.

The Diefenbaker years (1957-63) saw the passage of the Canadian Bill of Rights, a "roads-to-resources" program to encourage the development of northern resources, legislation providing support for agriculture, encouragement of technical training and improved health and welfare programs. Regional development was emphasized by significant public works such as construction of the South Saskatchewan Dam, and simultaneous translation was introduced in the House of Commons.

Diefenbaker died Aug. 16, 1979 at his home in Rockliffe Park, Ottawa.

Lester Pearson

Lester Bowles Pearson was born at Newtonbrook, Ont., on Apr. 23, 1897, the son of Edwin Arthur Pearson and Annie Sarah Bowles. He attended collegiate institutes at Toronto, Peterborough and Hamilton, and took his B.A. at the University of Toronto, and his M.A. at Oxford University.

After serving overseas in World War I, he became a history professor at the University of Toronto, where he taught from 1924-1928. He joined Canada's foreign service in 1928, became Canada's ambassador to the U.N. in 1945,

was appointed under-secretary of state for external affairs in 1946, and accepted the invitations of King and St. Laurent to become minister of external affairs in Sept. 1948.

Pearson handled the negotiations that eventually led to the formation of NATO in 1949.

In 1956, following the Anglo-French-Israeli invasion of Egypt, Pearson's work at the United Nations helped establish a U.N. Emergency Force which kept peace on the Israeli/Egyptian border for the next decade. His settlement of the Suez crisis brought him the Nobel Peace Prize in 1957—the only time a Canadian has been so honored.

Pearson was chosen leader of the Liberal Party Jan. 15, 1958. In the general election of Apr. 8, 1963, the Liberals won 129 seats in the House of Commons, and Pearson became the leader of a minority government.

In the 1965 election, the Liberals made slight gains, but were still short of a clear majority. Pearson announced his resignation in Dec. 1967 and, in Apr. 1968, was succeeded by Pierre Trudeau.

Under Pearson, the old age pension had been extended and a national health plan created. He secured—after much debate—the adoption of a national flag and established the Royal Commission on Bilingualism and Biculturalism.

Though he retired in 1968, his international reputation prompted the World Bank to commission him to prepare a report on international aid programs.

He died in Ottawa, Dec. 27, 1972.

Pierre Trudeau

Born in Montreal Oct. 18, 1919, Pierre Elliott Trudeau was the son of Charles-Émile Trudeau and Grace Elliott. He attended Collège Jean-de-Brébeuf, the University of Montreal, Harvard University, Université de Paris and the London School of Economics. He was called to the Quebec bar in 1943. From 1949-1951, he was a member of the Privy Council staff in Ottawa. In 1950, he co-founded the magazine Cité Libre. From 1952-1962, he practised law and was a journalist and broadcaster in Montreal. From 1962-1965 he was a law professor at the University of Montreal.

First elected to the House of Commons in 1965, Trudeau was named justice minister in Lester Pearson's cabinet in 1967. The following year, he won the Liberal leadership and became prime minister Apr. 19, 1968. In the general election of the same year, the Liberals won a solid majority.

During his first 4 years in power, Trudeau faced several politically volatile situations. The most dramatic of these occurred in Oct. 1970, when he invoked the War Measures Act, a statute giving the state broad powers of arrest and detention in times of emergency. The emergency in this case was the "F.L.Q. Crisis"—the kidnapping of British diplomat James Cross and Quebec cabinet minister Pierre Laporte by the radical separatist organization Front de Libération du Québec. Laporte was later murdered.

In the general election of 1972, Trudeau returned to power but with only a minority government. Two years later, he regained a majority, largely on his denunciation of the Progressive Conservative proposal to introduce wage and price controls in Canada. But one year later, in the face of escalating inflation, his own government introduced wage and price controls.

In the general election of 1979, the Progressive Conservatives under Joe Clark won a narrow victory, and were able to form a minority government. Trudeau announced his intention to retire; but when the Clark government fell later that year, Trudeau was convinced to remain as leader. In Feb. 1980, Trudeau's Liberals won another majority.

Trudeau's final term in office is best known for the constitutional reform which, for the first time, allowed Canada's Parliament to amend the constitution without appeal to the U.K. government. A constitutionally-entrenched Charter of Rights and Freedoms was also introduced.

Trudeau's introduction of a National Energy Program led to bitter disputes between the federal government and the energy-producing provinces, particularly Alberta. The NEP was aimed at increasing Canadian control of the oil industry, promoting energy self-sufficiency and generating more federal revenues in the energy sector.

During his final year as prime minister Trudeau launched a world peace initiative, visiting more than 40 world leaders to appeal for peace and an end to the nuclear arms race.

On Feb. 29, 1984, Trudeau announced his intention to resign. He was succeeded in June by John Turner and left politics, eventually joining a Montreal law firm.

Joe Clark

Charles Joseph "Joe" Clark was born at High River, Alta., on June 5, 1939, the son of Charles A. Clark and Grace Welch. He was educated at the University of Alberta where he received his B.A. and M.A. degrees.

Clark was first elected to the House of Commons in 1972. In 1976 he became leader of the Progressive Conservative Party and, in the general election of 1979, won enough seats to form a minority government. At 39, Clark was Canada's youngest prime minister. But his minority government fell in Dec. of that year on a vote of non-confidence in its proposed budget. In the Feb. 1980 election that followed, Trudeau's Liberals returned to power.

At a national general meeting of the Conservative party in Jan. 1983, Clark received the support of only two-thirds of the delegates and subsequently called for a national convention at which he would run again for the party leadership. At the convention in June 1983, Clark lost the leadership to Brian Mulroney in the 4th ballot. He remained an M.P. and, when Mulroney became prime minister in 1984, Clark joined the cabinet as secretary of state for external affairs.

John Turner

John Napier Turner was born at Richmond, Surrey, England on June 7, 1929, the son of Leonard Turner and Phyllis Gregory. He attended Ashbury College and St. Patrick's College in Ottawa, the University of British Columbia, Oxford University and Université de Paris. He was called to the bar in England in 1953 and the bar in Quebec in 1954. He lectured for a time in the Faculty of Commerce at Sir George Williams University.

First elected to the House of Commons in 1962, Turner entered Lester Pearson's cabinet in 1965. He became minister of consumer and corporate affairs in 1967. In 1968 he was a candidate for the Liberal leadership, finishing 3d on the final ballot.

In 1968, Turner was appointed minister of justice in Pierre Trudeau's cabinet. In 1972, he became minister of finance, a post he held until Sept. 1975, when he resigned from the cabinet. In Feb. 1976 he left politics and joined a Toronto law firm.

Turner remained in private practice until Trudeau's retirement in 1984, when he successfully ran for leader of the Liberal Party and became prime minister on June 30, though he did not have a seat in the House of Commons. He dissolved Parliament July 9, and in the ensuing general election suffered a crushing defeat at the hands of the Progressive Conservatives led by Brian Mulroney.

Turner won his own seat, however, and remained in Parliament as leader of the Opposition.

Brian Mulroney

Martin Brian Mulroney was born at Baie Comeau, Que., Mar. 20, 1939, the son of Benedict Mulroney and Irene O'Shea. He attended St. Francis Xavier University and Université Laval. Called to the bar of Quebec in 1965, Mulroney practised law in Montreal. In 1976, he joined the Iron Ore Company of Canada as executive vice-president, and was elected company president the following year.

Mulroney made an unsuccessful bid for the Progressive Conservative party leadership in 1976, finishing 3d. In 1983 he ran again, defeating the incumbent leader, Joe Clark, on the 4th ballot.

A by-election for the riding of Central Nova brought Mulroney into Parliament as leader of the Opposition. In the general election of 1984, he led the Conservatives to victory, winning the largest number of seats (211) in Canadian history.

In its first few years in power, Mulroney's government took steps to attract more foreign investment and sought to strengthen ties with the United States. Mulroney's major initiatives between 1984 and 1988 were the Meech Lake Accord—a package of constitutional changes designed to end Quebec's boycott of the 1982 constitutional reform—and the negotiation of a free trade agreement with the United States.

Faced with blockage of his free trade legislation by the Liberal-dominated Senate, Mulroney called a Nov. 1988 election with free trade as the major issue.

Fathers of Confederation

Union of the British North American colonies into the Dominion of Canada was discussed and its terms negotiated at 3 confederation conferences held at Charlottetown (C), Sept. 1, 1864; Quebec (Q), Oct. 10, 1864; and London (L), Dec. 4, 1866. The names of delegates are followed by the provinces they represented; Canada refers to what are now the provinces of Ontario and Quebec.

Adams G. Archibald, N.S. . . . . (C,Q,L)	Hector L. Langevin, Canada . . . . (C,Q,L)
George Brown, Canada . . . . (C,Q)	Jonathan McCully, N.S. . . . . (C,Q,L)
Alexander Campbell, Canada . . . . (C,Q)	A.A. Macdonald, P.E.I. (C,Q)
Frederick B.T. Carter, Nfld. . . . . (Q)	John A. Macdonald, Canada . . . . (C,Q,L)
George-Étienne Cartier, Canada . . . . (C,Q,L)	William McDougall, Canada . . . . (C,Q,L)
Edward B. Chandler, N.B. . . . . (C,Q)	Thomas D'Arcy McGee, Canada . . . . (C,Q)
Jean-Charles Chapais, Canada . . . . (Q)	Peter Mitchell, N.B. . . . . (Q,L)
James Cockburn, Canada . . . . (Q)	Oliver Mowat, Canada . . . . (Q)
George H. Coles, P.E.I. (C,Q)	Edward Palmer, P.E.I. (C,Q)
Robert B. Dickey, N.S. (C,Q)	William H. Pope, P.E.I. (C,Q)
Charles Fisher, N.B. . . . . (Q,L)	John W. Ritchie, N.S. . . . . (L)
Alexander T. Galt, Canada . . . . (C,Q,L)	J. Ambrose Shea, Nfld. . . . . (Q)
John Hamilton Gray, N.B. . . . . (C,Q)	William H. Steeves, N.B. . . . . (C,Q)
John Hamilton Gray, P.E.I. . . . . (C,Q)	Sir Étienne-Paschal Taché, Canada . . . . (Q)
Thomas Heath Haviland, P.E.I. . . . . (Q)	Samuel Leonard Tilley, N.B. . . . . (C,Q,L)
William A. Henry, N.S. . . . . (C,Q,L)	Charles Tupper, N.S. (C,Q,L)
William P. Howland, Canada . . . . (L)	Edward Whelan, P.E.I. . . . . (Q)
John M. Johnson, N.B. . . . . (C,Q,L)	R.D. Wilmot, N.B. . . . . (L)

Canadian Politics and Elections

Prime Ministers of Canada

Prime Minister	Party	Term(s)	Born	P.M. at age	Died	Age
Sir John A. Macdonald ...	Conservative	July 1, 1867 – Nov. 5, 1873 Oct. 17, 1878 – June 6, 1891	Jan. 11, 1815	52	June 6, 1891	76
Alexander Mackenzie	Liberal	Nov. 7, 1873 – Oct. 16, 1878	Jan. 28, 1822	51	Apr. 17, 1892	70
Sir John Abbott	Conservative	June 16, 1891 – Nov. 24, 1892	Mar. 12, 1821	70	Oct. 30, 1893	72
Sir John Thompson	Conservative	Dec. 5, 1892 – Dec. 12, 1894	Nov. 10, 1845	47	Dec. 12, 1894	49
Sir Mackenzie Bowell	Conservative	Dec. 21, 1894 – Apr. 27, 1896	Dec. 27, 1823	70	Dec. 10, 1917	93
Sir Charles Tupper	Conservative	May 1, 1896 – July 8, 1896	July 2, 1821	74	Oct. 30, 1915	94
Sir Wilfrid Laurier	Liberal	July 11, 1896 – Oct. 6, 1911	Nov. 20, 1841	54	Feb. 17, 1919	77
Sir Robert Borden	Conservative/ Unionist	Oct. 10, 1911 – Oct. 12, 1917 Oct. 12, 1917 – July 10, 1920	June 26, 1854	57	June 10, 1937	82
Arthur Meighen	Unionist/ Conservative	July 10, 1920 – Dec. 29, 1921 June 29, 1926 – Sept. 25, 1926	June 16, 1874	46	Aug. 5, 1960	86
Mackenzie King	Liberal	Dec. 29, 1921 – June 28, 1926 Sept. 25, 1926 – Aug. 6, 1930 Oct. 23, 1935 – Nov. 15, 1948	Dec. 17, 1874	47	July 22, 1950	75
Richard B. Bennett	Conservative	Aug. 7, 1930 – Oct. 23, 1935	July 3, 1870	60	June 27, 1947	76
Louis St. Laurent	Liberal	Nov. 15, 1948 – June 21, 1957	Feb. 1, 1882	66	July 25, 1973	91
John Diefenbaker	Prog. Cons.	June 21, 1957 – Apr. 22, 1963	Sept. 18, 1895	61	Aug. 16, 1979	83
Lester Pearson	Liberal	Apr. 22, 1963 – Apr. 20, 1968	Apr. 23, 1897	65	Dec. 27, 1972	75
Pierre Trudeau	Liberal	Apr. 20, 1968 – June 4, 1979 Mar. 3, 1980 – June 30, 1984	Oct. 18, 1919	48		
Joe Clark	Prog. Cons.	June 4, 1979 – Mar. 3, 1980	June 5, 1939	39		
John Turner	Liberal	June 30, 1984 – Sept. 17, 1984	June 7, 1929	55		
Brian Mulroney	Prog. Cons.	Sept. 17, 1984 –	Mar. 20, 1939	45		

The Canadian Cabinet[1]

(as of September, 1988)

(Titles: Minister unless otherwise stated or *Minister of State)

Brian Mulroney .... Prime Minister
Joe Clark .... External Affairs
Flora MacDonald .... Communications
John Crosbie .... International Trade
Don Mazankowski .... Deputy Prime Minister, Pres. of Privy Council, Privatization and Deregulation, Agriculture
Elmer Mackay .... National Revenue
Jake Epp .... Health and Welfare
Ramon Hnatyshyn .... Justice and Attorney-General
Robert R. de Cotret .... Regional Industrial Expansion, *Science and Technology
Perrin Beatty .... Defence
Michael Wilson .... Finance
Harvie Andre .... Consumer and Corporate Affairs
Otto Jelinek .... Supply and Services
Tom Siddon .... Fisheries and Oceans
Charles Mayer .... *Grains and Oilseeds
William McKnight ..... Indian Affairs and Northern Development, Western Economic Diversification
Tom McMillan .... Environment
Patricia Carney .... Treasury Board
Benoît Bouchard .... Transport
James Kelleher .... Solicitor General

Marcel Masse .... Energy, Mines and Resources
Barbara McDougall .... Employment and Immigration
Gerald Merrithew .... Veterans Affairs
Monique Vézina ... *Employment and Immigration, *Senior Citizens
Stewart McInnes .... Public Works
Frank Oberle .... *Science and Technology
Lowell Murray .... Leader of the Govt. in the Senate, *Federal-Provincial Relations
Paul Dick .... Associate Minister of Defence
Pierre Cadieux .... Labor
Jean Charest .... *Youth, *Fitness and Amateur Sport
Thomas Hockin .... *Finance
Monique Landry .... External Relations
Bernard Valcourt ..... *Small Business and Tourism, *Indian Affairs and Northern Development
Gerry Weiner ...... *Multiculturalism and Citizenship
Douglas Lewis .... *Treasury Board
Pierre Blais .... *Agriculture
Gerry St. Germain .... *Forestry
Lucien Bouchard .... Secretary of State
John McDermid ..... *International Trade, *Housing
Shirley Martin .... *Transport

Governors General of Canada, 1867-1988

Name	Date Appointed	Assumed Office	Term
Viscount Monck of Ballytrammon	June 1, 1867	July 1, 1867	1867-69
Baron Lisgar of Lisgar and Bailieborough	Dec. 29, 1868	Feb. 2, 1869	1869-72
The Earl of Dufferin	May 22, 1872	June 25, 1872	1872-78
The Marquis of Lorne	Oct. 5, 1878	Nov. 25, 1878	1878-83
The Marquis of Landsdowne	Aug. 18, 1883	Oct. 23, 1883	1883-88
Baron Stanley of Preston	May 1, 1888	June 11, 1888	1888-93
The Earl of Aberdeen	May 22, 1893	Sept. 18, 1893	1893-98
The Earl of Minto	July 30, 1898	Nov. 12, 1898	1898-1904
Earl Grey	Sept. 26, 1904	Dec. 10, 1904	1904-11
The Duke of Connaught	Mar. 21, 1911	Oct. 13, 1911	1911-16
The Duke of Devonshire	Aug. 19, 1916	Nov. 11, 1916	1916-21
Baron Byng of Vimy	Aug. 2, 1921	Aug. 11, 1921	1921-26
Viscount Willingdon of Ratton	Aug. 5, 1926	Oct. 2, 1926	1926-31
The Earl of Bessborough	Feb. 9, 1931	Apr. 4, 1931	1931-35
Baron Tweedsmuir of Elsfield	Aug. 10, 1935	Nov. 2, 1935	1935-40
The Earl of Athlone	Apr. 3, 1940	June 21, 1940	1940-46
Viscount Alexander of Tunis	Aug. 1, 1945	Apr. 12, 1946	1946-52
Vincent Massey	Jan. 24, 1952	Feb. 28, 1952	1952-59
Georges Vanier	Aug. 1, 1959	Sept. 15, 1959	1959-67
Roland Michener	Mar. 25, 1967	Apr. 17, 1967	1967-73
Jules Léger	Oct. 5, 1973	Jan. 14, 1974	1973-79
Edward Schreyer	Dec. 7, 1978	Jan. 22, 1979	1979-83
Jeanne Sauvé	Dec. 23, 1983	May 14, 1984	1984-

Members of Canada's Senate

(As of Sept. 1988; 96 Senators, 8 vacancies)

Senator	Birthdate	Date Appointed	Appointed by	Province
Willie Adams	June 22, 1934	Apr. 5, 1977	Trudeau	N.W.T.
Margaret Anderson	Aug. 7, 1915	Mar. 23, 1978	Trudeau	N.B.
Hazen Argue	Jan. 6, 1921	Feb. 24, 1966	Pearson	Sask.
Martial Asselin	Feb. 3, 1924	Sept. 1, 1972	Trudeau	Que.
Norm Atkins	June 27, 1934	July 2, 1986	Mulroney	Ont.
Jack Austin	Mar. 2, 1932	Aug. 19, 1975	Trudeau	B.C.
James Balfour	May 22, 1928	Sept. 13, 1979	Clark	Sask.
Estafious W. Barootes	Nov. 15, 1918	Dec. 21, 1984	Mulroney	Sask.
Jean Bazin	Jan. 31, 1940	Dec. 29, 1986	Mulroney	B.C.
Rhéal Bélisle	July 3, 1919	Feb. 4, 1963	Diefenbaker	Ont.
Ann Elizabeth Bell	May 26, 1924	Oct. 7, 1970	Trudeau	B.C.
Martha P. Bielish	Oct. 20, 1915	Sept. 27, 1979	Clark	Alta.
Mark Lorne Bonnell	Jan. 4, 1923	Nov. 15, 1971	Trudeau	P.E.I.
Peter Bosa	May 2, 1927	Apr. 5, 1977	Trudeau	Ont.
Sidney L. Buckwold	Nov. 3, 1916	Nov. 4, 1971	Trudeau	Sask.
Guy Charbonneau	June 21, 1922	Sept. 27, 1979	Clark	Que.
Ethel Cochrane	Sept. 23, 1937	Nov. 17, 1986	Mulroney	Nfld.
Michel Cogger	Mar. 21, 1939	May 2, 1986	Mulroney	Que.
Anne Cools	Aug. 12, 1943	Jan. 13, 1984	Trudeau	Ont.
Eymard Corbin	Aug. 2, 1934	July 9, 1984	Turner	N.B.
Ernest G. Cottreau	Jan. 28, 1914	May 8, 1974	Trudeau	N.S.
David A. Croll	Mar. 12, 1900	July 28, 1955	St. Laurent	Ont.
Keith Davey	Apr. 21, 1926	Feb. 24, 1966	Pearson	Ont.
Paul David	Dec. 25, 1919	Apr. 16, 1985	Mulroney	Que.
Pierre De Bané	Aug. 2, 1938	June 29, 1984	Trudeau	Que.
Azellus Denis	Mar. 26, 1907	Feb. 3, 1964	Pearson	Que.
C. William Doody	Feb. 26, 1931	Oct. 3, 1979	Clark	Nfld.
Richard J. Doyle	Mar. 10, 1923	Mar. 19, 1985	Mulroney	Ont.
Douglas Donald Everett	Aug. 12, 1927	Nov. 8, 1966	Pearson	Man.
Joyce Fairbairn	Nov. 6, 1939	June 29, 1984	Trudeau	Alta.
Jacques Flynn	Aug. 22, 1915	Nov. 9, 1962	Diefenbaker	Que.
Royce H. Frith	Nov. 12, 1923	Apr. 5, 1977	Trudeau	Ont.
Phillipe Deane Gigantès	Aug. 16, 1923	Jan. 13, 1984	Trudeau	Que.
Jerahmiel (Jerry) Grafstein	Jan. 2, 1935	Jan. 13, 1984	Trudeau	Ont.
B. Alasdair Graham	May 21, 1929	Apr. 27, 1972	Trudeau	N.S.
Joseph-Philippe Guay	Oct. 4, 1915	Mar. 23, 1978	Trudeau	Man.
Stanley Haidasz	Mar. 4, 1923	Mar. 23, 1978	Trudeau	Ont.
Earl A. Hastings	Jan. 7, 1924	Feb. 24, 1966	Pearson	Alta.
Daniel Hays	Apr. 24, 1939	June 29, 1984	Trudeau	Alta.
Jacques Hébert	June 21, 1923	Apr. 20, 1983	Trudeau	Que.
Henry D. Hicks	Mar. 15, 1915	Apr. 27, 1972	Trudeau	N.S.
William McDonough Kelly	July 21, 1925	Dec. 23, 1982	Trudeau	Ont.
Colin Kenny	Dec. 10, 1943	June 29, 1984	Trudeau	Ont.
Michael Kirby	Aug. 5, 1941	Jan. 13, 1984	Trudeau	N.S.
Leo Kolber	Jan. 18, 1929	Dec. 23, 1983	Trudeau	Que.
Daniel Lang	June 13, 1919	Feb. 14, 1964	Pearson	Ont.
Léopold Langlois	Oct. 2, 1913	July 8, 1966	Pearson	Que.

Senator	Birthdate	Date Appointed	Appointed by	Province
Edward M. Lawson	Sept. 24, 1929	Oct. 7, 1970	Trudeau	B.C.
Fernand E. Leblanc	July 1, 1917	Mar. 27, 1979	Trudeau	Que.
Roméo LeBlanc	Dec. 18, 1927	June 29, 1984	Trudeau	N.B.
Tom Lefebvre	Apr. 23, 1927	July 9, 1984	Turner	Que.
P. Derek Lewis	Nov. 28, 1924	Mar. 23, 1978	Trudeau	Nfld.
Paul Lucier	July 29, 1930	Oct. 23, 1975	Trudeau	Yukon
Finlay MacDonald	Jan. 4, 1923	Dec. 21, 1984	Mulroney	N.S.
John M. Macdonald	May 3, 1906	June 24, 1960	Diefenbaker	N.S.
Allan J. MacEachen	July 6, 1921	June 29, 1984	Trudeau	N.S.
Heath Macquarrie	Sept. 18, 1919	Oct. 3, 1979	Clark	P.E.I.
Len Marchand	Nov. 16, 1933	June 29, 1984	Trudeau	B.C.
Lorna Marsden	Mar. 6, 1942	Jan. 24, 1984	Trudeau	Ont.
Jack Marshall	Nov. 26, 1919	Mar. 23, 1978	Trudeau	Nfld.
Charles McElman	June 18, 1920	Feb. 24, 1966	Pearson	N.B.
Gildas L. Molgat	Jan. 25, 1927	Oct. 7, 1970	Trudeau	Man.
Hartland de M. Molson	May 29, 1907	July 28, 1955	St. Laurent	Que.
Robert Muir	Nov. 10, 1919	Mar. 26, 1971	Trudeau	N.S.
Lowell Murray	Sept. 26, 1936	Sept. 13, 1979	Clark	Ont.
Joan Neiman	Sept. 9, 1920	Sept. 1, 1972	Trudeau	Ont.
Nathan Nurgitz	June 22, 1934	Oct. 3, 1979	Clark	Man.
H.A. (Bud) Olson	Oct. 6, 1925	Apr. 5, 1977	Trudeau	Alta.
Gerry Ottenheimer	June 4, 1934	Dec. 30, 1987	Mulroney	Nfld.
Raymond J. Perrault	Feb. 6, 1926	Oct. 5, 1973	Trudeau	B.C.
William John Petten	Jan. 28, 1923	Apr. 8, 1968	Pearson	Nfld.
Orville H. Phillips	Apr. 5, 1924	Feb. 5, 1963	Diefenbaker	P.E.I.
Michael Pitfield	June 18, 1937	Dec. 22, 1982	Trudeau	Ont.
Maurice Riel	Apr. 3, 1922	Oct. 5, 1973	Trudeau	Que.
Pietro Rizzuto	Mar. 18, 1929	Dec. 23, 1976	Trudeau	Que.
Brenda Mary Robertson	May 23, 1929	Dec. 21, 1984	Mulroney	N.B.
Louis-J. Robichaud	Oct. 21, 1925	Dec. 21, 1973	Trudeau	N.B.
Duff Roblin	June 17, 1917	Mar. 23, 1978	Trudeau	Man.
Eileen Rossiter	July 7, 1929	Nov. 17, 1986	Mulroney	P.E.I.
Cyril B. Sherwood	July 1, 1915	Oct. 3, 1979	Clark	N.B.
Jean-Maurice Simard	June 21, 1931	June 26, 1985	Mulroney	Que.
Ian Sinclair	Dec. 27, 1913	Dec. 23, 1983	Trudeau	Ont.
Herbert Orville Sparrow	Jan. 4, 1939	Feb. 9, 1968	Pearson	Sask.
Mira Spivak	July 12, 1934	Nov. 17, 1986	Mulroney	Man.
Richard J. Stanbury	Oct. 14, 1944	Feb. 13, 1968	Pearson	Ont.
David G. Steuart	Jan. 26, 1916	Dec. 9, 1976	Trudeau	Sask.
John Stewart	Nov. 19, 1924	Jan. 13, 1984	Trudeau	N.S.
Peter Alan Stollery	Nov. 29, 1935	July 2, 1981	Trudeau	Ont.
L. Norbert Thériault	Feb. 16, 1921	Mar. 26, 1979	Trudeau	N.B.
Andrew E. Thompson	Dec. 14, 1924	Apr. 6, 1967	Pearson	Ont.
Arthur Tremblay	June 18, 1917	Sept. 27, 1979	Clark	Que.
Charles Turner	Mar. 24, 1916	July 9, 1984	Turner	Ont.
George C. van Roggen	July 22, 1921	Nov. 4, 1971	Trudeau	B.C.
David James Walker	May 10, 1905	Feb. 4, 1963	Diefenbaker	Ont.
Charlie Watt	June 29, 1944	Jan. 16, 1984	Trudeau	Que.
Dalia Wood	Aug. 21, 1924	Mar. 26, 1979	Trudeau	Que.

Members of Parliament

(As of Oct. 1988, prior to calling of a federal election)

Member	Riding	Party	Birthdate	First Elected[1]	Previous Occupation
Newfoundland					
George Baker	Gander-Twillingate	Lib.	1942	1974	Radio and TV announcer/producer
John C. Crosbie	St. John's West	P.C.	Jan. 30, 1931	1976*	Lawyer
Jack Harris	St. John's East	N.D.P.	Oct. 27, 1948	1987*	Lawyer/Journalist
Morrissey Johnson	Bonavista-Trinity-Conception	P.C.	Oct. 21, 1932	1984	Master mariner/Businessman
Joe Price	Burin-St. George's	P.C.	May 5, 1942	1984	Teacher
Bill Rompkey	Grand Falls-White Bay-Labrador	Lib.	May 13, 1936	1972	Educator
Brian Tobin	Humber-Port au Port-St. Barbe	Lib.	Oct. 21, 1954	1980	Radio/TV reporter/Announcer
Prince Edward Island					
Pat Binns	Cardigan	P.C.	Oct. 8, 1948	1984	Businessman
Mel Gass	Malpeque	P.C.	Dec. 21, 1938	1979	Businessman
vacant	Egmont				
Tom McMillan	Hillsborough	P.C.	Oct. 15, 1945	1979	Political scientist

Member	Riding	Party	Birthdate	First Elected[1]	Previous Occupation
		Nova Scotia			
Robert C. Coates	Cumberland-Colchester	P.C.	Mar. 10, 1928	1957	Lawyer
Gerald Comeau	South West Nova	P.C.	Feb. 1, 1946	1984	Professor
Howard E. Crosby	Halifax West	P.C.	Nov. 26, 1933	1978*	Lawyer
Lloyd R. Crouse	South Shore	P.C.	Nov. 19, 1918	1957	Business executive
Dave Dingwall	Cape Breton-East Richmond	Lib.	June 29, 1952	1980	Lawyer
Mike Forrestall	Dartmouth-Halifax East	P.C.	Sept. 23, 1932	1965	Businessman/Journalist
Elmer M. MacKay	Central Nova	P.C.	Aug. 5, 1936	1971*	Lawyer
Russell MacLellan	Cape Breton-The Sydneys	Lib.	Jan. 16, 1940	1979	Lawyer
Stewart McInnes	Halifax	P.C.	July 24, 1937	1984	Lawyer
Pat Nowlan	Annapolis Valley-Hants	P.C.	Nov. 10, 1931	1965	Lawyer
Lawrence I. O'Neil	Cape Breton Highlands-Canso	P.C.	Nov. 14, 1954	1984	Lawyer
		New Brunswick			
Roger Clinch	Gloucester	P.C.	Jan. 8, 1947	1984	School administrator
Dennis H. Cochrane	Moncton	P.C.	Oct. 26, 1950	1984	School principal
Robert A. Corbett	Fundy-Royal	P.C.	Dec. 14, 1938	1978*	Businessman
Al Girard	Restigouche	P.C.	Aug. 18, 1949	1984	Businessman
J. Robert Howie	York-Sunbury	P.C.	Oct. 2, 1929	1972	Lawyer
W.R. Bud Jardine	Northumberland-Miramichi	P.C.	May 31, 1935	1984	Retired naval officer
Fred McCain	Carleton-Charlotte	P.C.	Nov. 11, 1917	1972	Farmer
Gerry Merrithew	Saint John	P.C.	Sept. 23, 1931	1984	School principal
Fernand Robichaud	Westmorland-Kent	Lib.	Dec. 2, 1939	1984	Businessman
Bernard Valcourt	Madawaska-Victoria	P.C.	Feb. 18, 1952	1984	Lawyer
		Quebec			
Warren Allmand	Notre-Dame-de-Grace-Lachine East	Lib.	Sept. 19, 1932	1965	Lawyer
David Berger	Laurier	Lib.	Mar. 30, 1950	1979	Businessman
Gilles Bernier	Beauce	P.C.	July 15, 1934	1984	Radio announcer
Gabrielle Bertrand	Brome-Missisquoi	P.C.	May 15, 1923	1984	n.a.
André Bissonnette	Saint-Jean	P.C.	June 25, 1945	1984	Businessman/Food wholesaler
Jean-Pierre Blackburn	Jonquière	P.C.	July 6, 1948	1984	Marketing manager
Pierre Blais	Bellechasse	P.C.	Dec. 30, 1948	1984	Lawyer
Suzanne Blais-Grenier	Rosemount	P.C.	n.a.	1984	Sociologist/Economist
Anne Blouin	Montmorency-Orléans	P.C.	Sept. 14, 1946	1984	Executive assistant
Benoît Bouchard	Roberval	P.C.	Apr. 16, 1940,	1984	Professor
Lucien Bouchard	Lac-Saint-Jean	P.C.	Dec. 22, 1938	1988*	Lawyer
Lise Bourgault	Argenteuil-Papineau	P.C.	June 5, 1950	1984	Administrator
Pierre H. Cadieux	Vaudreuil	P.C.	Apr. 6, 1948	1984	Lawyer
Andrée P. Champagne	Saint-Hyacinthe-Bagot	P.C.	July 17, 1939	1984	Administrator
Michel Champagne	Champlain	P.C.	May 4, 1956	1984	n.a.
Jean. J. Charest	Sherbrooke	P.C.	June 24, 1958	1984	Lawyer
Gilbert Chartrand	Verdun-Saint-Paul	P.C.	Nov. 3, 1954	1984	Vice-president/Alderman
Michel Côté	Langelier	P.C.	Sept. 13, 1942	1984	Accountant
Marcel Danis	Verchères	P.C.	Oct. 22, 1943	1984	Lawyer
Robert de Cotret	Berthier-Maskinongé-Lanaudière	P.C.	Feb. 20, 1944	1978*	Economist
Vincent Della Noce	Duvernay	P.C.	Nov. 18, 1943	1984	Businessman
Gabriel Desjardins	Témiscamingue	P.C.	Feb. 14, 1949	1984	Teacher and Businessman
Edouard Desrosiers	Hochelaga-Maisonneuve	P.C.	Aug. 26, 1934	1984	Newspaper president
Suzanne Duplessis	Louis-Hébert	P.C.	June 30, 1940	1984	Professor
Marc Ferland	Portneuf	P.C.	Apr. 15, 1942	1984	Project co-ordinator
Sheila Finestone	Mount Royal	Lib.	Jan. 28, 1927	1984	Political analyst
Gabriel Fontaine	Lévis	P.C.	Sept. 17, 1940	1984	Administrative councillor
Alfonso Gagliano	Saint-Léonard-Anjou	Lib.	Jan. 25, 1942	1984	Chartered accountant
Raymond Garneau	Laval-des-Rapides	Lib.	Jan. 3, 1935	1984	Banker
François Gérin	Mégantic-Compton-Stanstead	P.C.	Aug. 3, 1944	1984	Lawyer
Michel Gravel	Gamelin	P.C.	Aug. 4, 1939	1984	Company president
Darryl L. Gray	Bonaventure-Îles-de-la-Madeleine	P.C.	Dec. 26, 1946	1984	Professor/Farmer
Richard Grisé	Chambly	P.C.	Jan. 15, 1944	1984	Insurance salesman
Gilles Grondin	Saint-Maurice	Lib.	Feb. 3, 1943	1986*	Director-student services
Jacques Guilbault	Saint-Jacques	Lib.	Oct. 29, 1936	1968	Engineer
Jean-Guy Guilbeault	Drummond	P.C.	Mar. 14, 1931	1984	Businessman
Charles Hamelin	Charlevoix	P.C.	Apr. 20, 1947	1984	Journalist
André Harvey	Chicotimi	P.C.	Sept. 16, 1941	1984	Teacher
Jean-Guy Hudon	Beauharnois-Salaberry	P.C.	Apr. 24, 1941	1984	Administrator
Gaston Isabelle	Hull-Alymer	Lib.	Nov. 14, 1920	1965	Physician
Carole Jacques	Montréal-Mercier	P.C.	June 12, 1960	1984	Lawyer
Donald J. Johnston	Saint-Henri-Westmount	Lib.	June 26, 1936	1978*	Lawyer
Jean-luc Joncas	Matapédia-Matane	P.C.	Dec. 16, 1936	1984	Businessman/Mayor
Fernand Jourdenais	LaPrairie	P.C.	Mar. 25, 1933	1984	Businessman
Thérèse Killens	Saint-Michel-Ahuntsic	Lib.	June 29, 1927	1979	Administrator

Member	Riding	Party	Birthdate	First Elected[1]	Previous Occupation

Quebec

Member	Riding	Party	Birthdate	First Elected[1]	Previous Occupation
Fernand Ladouçeur	Labelle	P.C.	Aug. 2, 1925	1984	Insurance broker
Monique Landry	Blainville-Deux-Montagnes	P.C.	Dec. 25, 1937	1984	Administrator
Claude Lanthier	LaSalle	P.C.	Jan. 24, 1937	1984	Engineer
Jean Lapierre	Shefford	Lib.	May 7, 1956	1979	Lawyer
Roch La Salle	Joliette	P.C.	Aug. 6, 1929	1968	Sales manager
Bob Layton	Lachine	P.C.	Dec. 25, 1925	1984	Engineer
Nic Leblanc	Longueuil	P.C.	Nov. 15, 1941	1984	Businessman
Ricardo Lopez	Châteauguay	P.C.	Feb. 13, 1937	1984	Businessman
Claudy Mailly	Gatineau	P.C.	Nov. 30, 1938	1984	Corporate advisor
Jean-Claude Malépart	Montréal-Sainte-Marie	Lib.	Dec. 3, 1938	1979	Administrator/Promotor
Charles-Eugène Marin	Gaspé	P.C.	Oct. 24, 1925	1984	Psychiatrist
Marcel Masse	Frontenac	P.C.	Mar. 27, 1936	1984	Marketing vice-president
Barry Moore	Pontiac-Gatineau-Labelle	P.C.	Aug. 21, 1944	1984	Certified general accountant
Brian Mulroney	Manicouagan	P.C.	Mar. 20, 1939	1983*	Lawyer/Corporate executive
André Ouellet	Papineau	Lib.	Apr. 6, 1939	1967*	Lawyer
Lucie Pépin	Outremont	Lib.	Sept. 7, 1936	1984	Nurse
Louis Plamondon	Richelieu	P.C.	July 31, 1943	1984	Professor/Businessman
André Plourde	Kamouraska-Rivière-du-Loup	P.C.	Jan. 12, 1937	1984	Businessman
Marcel Prud'homme	Saint-Denis	Lib.	n.a.	1964*	n.a.
Guy Ricard	Laval	P.C.	Aug. 2, 1942	1984	Engineer
Carlo Rossi	Bourassa	Lib.	Aug. 8, 1925	1979	Police detective (Lieut.)
Guy St-Julien	Abitibi	P.C.	Feb. 19, 1940	1984	Controller
Alain Tardif	Richmond-Wolfe	Lib.	Aug. 23, 1946	1979	Lawyer
Monique B. Tardif	Charlesbourg	P.C.	Jan. 8, 1936	1984	Administrator
Robert Toupin	Terrebonne	N.D.P.	Jan. 20, 1949	1984	Notary
Marcel R. Tremblay	Québec-Est	P.C.	Mar. 30, 1943	1984	Marketing consultant
Maurice Tremblay	Lotbinière	P.C.	Apr. 23, 1944	1984	Lawyer
Monique Vézina	Rimouski-Temiscouata	P.C.	July 13, 1935	1984	Administrator
Pierre H. Vincent	Trois-Rivières	P.C.	Apr. 2, 1955	1984	Lawyer
Gerry Weiner	Dollard	P.C.	June 26, 1933	1984	Pharmacist

Ontario

Member	Riding	Party	Birthdate	First Elected[1]	Previous Occupation
Iain Angus	Thunder Bay-Atikokan	N.D.P.	June 1, 1947	1984	Parks and recreation planner
Bill Attewell	Don Valley East	P.C.	Jan. 20, 1932	1984	Vice-pres., Corporate Planning
Perrin Beatty	Wellington-Dufferin-Simcoe	P.C.	June 1, 1950	1972	Public servant
Derek Blackburn	Brant	N.D.P.	June 16, 1934	1971*	Teacher
Don Blenkarn	Mississauga South	P.C.	June 17, 1930	1972	Lawyer
John Bosley	Don Valley West	P.C.	May 4, 1947	1979	Businessman
Don Boudria	Glengarry-Prescott-Russell	Lib.	Aug. 30, 1949	1984	Purchasing agent
Patrick Boyer	Etobicoke-Lakeshore	P.C.	Mar. 4, 1945	1984	Lawyer/Writer
Bud Bradley	Haldimand-Norfolk	P.C.	Apr. 30, 1938	1979	Dentist
A.H. Harry Brightwell	Perth	P.C.	Aug. 4. 1932	1984	Veterinarian
Ed Broadbent	Oshawa	N.D.P.	Mar. 21, 1936	1968	Professor
Pauline Browes	Scarborough Centre	P.C.	May 7, 1938	1984	Educator
Charles Caccia	Davenport	Lib.	Apr. 28, 1930	1968	Alderman
Jim Caldwell	Essex-Kent	P.C.	July 20, 1941	1984	Broadcaster
Murray Cardiff	Huron-Bruce	P.C.	June 10, 1934	1980	Farmer
Mike Cassidy	Ottawa Centre	N.D.P.	May 10, 1937	1984	Journalist
Terry Clifford	London-Middlesex	P.C.	Nov. 12, 1938	1984	Principal
Sheila Copps	Hamilton East	Lib.	Nov. 27, 1952	1984	Journalist
Jennifer Cossitt	Leeds-Grenville	P.C.	June 22, 1948	1982*	Businesswoman
vacant	Rosedale				
Stan Darling	Parry Sound-Muskoka	P.C.	July 16, 1911	1972	Realtor/Insurance Agent
David Daubney	Ottawa West	P.C.	July 23, 1947	1984	Lawyer
Roland De Corneille	Eglinton-Lawrence	Lib.	Mar. 19, 1927	1979	Clergyman
Marion Dewar	Hamilton Mountain	N.D.P.	Feb. 17, 1928	1987*	Mayor
Paul Dick	Lanark-Renfrew-Carleton	P.C.	Oct. 27, 1940	1972	Lawyer
Bill Domm	Peterborough	P.C.	July 24, 1930	1979	Businessman
Jack Ellis	Prince Edward-Hastings	P.C.	Oct. 21, 1929	1972	Businessman
Ernie Epp	Thunder Bay-Nipigon	N.D.P.	Sept. 28, 1941	1984	History professor
Scott Fennell	Ontario	P.C.	Jan. 9, 1928	1979	Insur. exec./Investor/ Developer
Maurice Foster	Algoma	Lib.	Sept. 8, 1933	1968	Veterinarian
Sid Fraleigh	Lambton-Middlesex	P.C.	Feb. 5, 1931	1979	Farmer
Girve Fretz	Erie	P.C.	Mar. 4, 1927	1979	Retailer
Doug Frith	Sudbury	Lib.	Mar. 5, 1945	1980	Pharmacist
Jean-Robert Gauthier	Ottawa-Vanier	Lib.	Oct. 22, 1929	1972	Chiropractor
Aurèle Gervais	Timmins-Chapleau	P.C.	Feb. 1, 1933	1984	businessman
Herb Gray	Windsor West	Lib.	May 25, 1931	1962	Laywer
Gary M. Gurbin	Bruce-Grey	P.C.	Dec. 13, 1941	1979	General practitioner
Bruce Halliday	Oxford	P.C.	June 18, 1926	1974	Physician
Elliott Hardey	Kent	P.C.	Jan. 3, 1932	1984	Farmer
Dan Heap	Spadina	N.D.P.	Sept. 24, 1925	1981*	Priest/Printer

Member	Riding	Party	Birthdate	First Elected[1]	Previous Occupation
		Ontario			
George Hees	Northumberland	P.C.	June 17, 1910	1950*	Businessman
Bob Hicks	Scarborough East	P.C.	June 4, 1933	1984	Principal
Tom Hockin	London West	P.C.	Mar. 5, 1938	1984	Businessman
Len Hopkins	Renfrew-Nipissing-Pembroke	Lib.	June 12, 1930	1965	Teacher
Bob Horner	Mississauga-North	P.C.	July 3, 1932	1984	Veterinarian
Ken James	Sarnia-Lambton	P.C.	Aug. 5, 1934	1984	Marketing Manager/Farmer
Otto Jelinek	Halton	P.C.	May 20, 1940	1972	Businessman
Jim Jepson	London East	P.C.	Apr. 4, 1942	1984	Businessman
Bob Kaplan	York Centre	Lib.	Dec. 27, 1936	1968	Lawyer
Jim Kelleher	Sault Ste. Marie	P.C.	Oct. 2, 1930	1984	Lawyer
Bill Kempling	Burlington	P.C.	Feb. 5, 1921	1972	Businessman
Allan Lawrence	Durham-Northumberland	P.C.	Nov. 8, 1925	1972	Lawyer
Steven W. Langdon	Essex-Windsor	N.D.P.	July 15, 1946	1984	Economist
Doug Lewis	Simcoe North	P.C.	Apr. 17, 1938	1979	Lawyer/Chartered Accountant
Flora MacDonald	Kingston and the Islands	P.C.	June 3, 1926	1972	Univ. Tutor/Administrator
John A. MacDougall	Timiskaming	P.C.	Apr. 20, 1947	1982*	Sales representative
Moe Mantha	Nipissing	P.C.	Dec. 13, 1933	1984	Proprietor
Sergio Marchi	York West	Lib.	May 12, 1956	1984	Alderman/Businessman
Shirley Martin	Lincoln	P.C.	Nov. 20, 1932	1984	Businesswoman
W. Paul McCrossan	York-Scarborough	P.C.	May 20, 1942	1978	Actuary
Howard McCurdy	Windsor-Walkerville	N.D.P.	Dec. 10, 1932	1984	Professor
John McDermid	Brampton-Georgetown	P.C.	Mar. 17, 1940	1979	Public relations/Marketing manager
Lynn McDonald	Broadview-Greenwood	N.D.P.	July 15, 1940	1982*	Sociologist
Barbara McDougall	St. Paul's	P.C.	Nov. 12, 1937	1984	Financial analyst
Walter McLean	Waterloo	P.C.	Apr. 26, 1936	1979	Minister
Gus Mitges	Grey-Simcoe	P.C.	n.a.	1972	Veterinarian
Aideen Nicholson	Trinity	Lib.	Apr. 29, 1927	1974	Social worker
Rob Nicholson	Niagara Falls	P.C.	Apr. 29, 1952	1984	Lawyer
John V. Nunziata	York South-Weston	Lib.	Jan. 4, 1955	1984	Lawyer
John Oostrom	Willowdale	P.C.	Sept. 2, 1930	1984	Senior executive
John Parry	Kenora-Rainy River	N.D.P.	Feb. 6, 1946	1984	Mayor
Keith Penner	Cochrane-Superior	Lib.	May 1, 1933	1968	Teacher
Bob Pennock	Etobicoke North	P.C.	Dec. 14, 1936	1984	Contractor
Peter Peterson	Hamilton West	P.C.	Feb. 22, 1953	1984	Stockbroker
Allan Pietz	Welland	P.C.	June 18, 1925	1984	Dairyman
Alan Redway	York East	P.C.	Mar. 11, 1935	1984	Lawyer
Joe Reid	St. Catharines	P.C.	Sept. 24, 1917	1979	Lawyer
John Reimer	Kitchener	P.C.	July 16, 1936	1979	Educator
John Rodriguez	Nickel Belt	N.D.P.	Feb. 12, 1937	1984	Teacher
Tony Roman	York North	Ind.	Jan. 17, 1936	1984	Regional council chairman
Bill Scott	Victoria-Haliburton	P.C.	Oct. 6, 1921	1965	Merchant
Geoff Scott	Hamilton-Wentworth	P.C.	Mar. 2, 1938	1978*	Broadcast journalist
Chris Speyer	Cambridge	P.C.	Mar. 24, 1941	1979	Lawyer
Reg Stackhouse	Scarborough West	P.C.	Apr. 30, 1925	1984	College principal
Ronald A. Stewart	Simcoe South	P.C.	Apr. 13, 1927	1979	Wholesale distributor
Sinclair Stevens	York-Peel	P.C.	Feb. 11, 1927	1972	Lawyer
Bill Tupper	Nepean-Carleton	P.C.	Oct. 7, 1933	1984	Professor/Businessman
Barry Turner	Ottawa-Carleton	P.C.	Apr. 11, 1946	1984	Marketing manager
Bill Vankoughnet	Hastings-Frontenac-Lennox and Addington	P.C.	Jan. 7, 1943	1979	Administrator
Norm Warner	Stormont-Dundas	P.C.	Dec. 23, 1943	1984	Insurance broker
Michael Wilson	Etobicoke Centre	P.C.	Nov. 4, 1937	1979	Sr. Exec./Investment dealer
William C. Winegard	Guelph	P.C.	Sept. 17, 1924	1984	Metallurgical engineer
John Wise	Elgin	P.C.	Dec. 12, 1935	1972	Farmer
Andrew Witer	Parkdale-High Park	P.C.	Nov. 23, 1946	1984	Management consultant
Neil Young	Beaches	N.D.P.	Aug. 28, 1936	1980	Tool and die maker
		Manitoba			
Lloyd Axworthy	Winnipeg-Fort Garry	Lib.	Dec. 21, 1939	1979	Professor
Bill Blaikie	Winnipeg-Birds Hill	N.D.P.	June 19, 1951	1979	Clergyman
Lee Clark	Brandon-Souris	P.C.	Dec. 16, 1936	1983*	Teacher
Léo Duguay	St. Boniface	P.C.	Mar. 13, 1944	1984	School administrator
Jake Epp	Provencher	P.C.	Sept. 1, 1939	1972	Teacher
Felix Holtmann	Selkirk-Interlake	P.C.	Dec. 5, 1944	1984	Hog farmer
Cyril Keeper	Winnipeg North Centre	N.D.P.	July 17, 1943	1980	Administrator
Charles Mayer	Portage-Marquette	P.C.	Apr. 21, 1936	1979	Farmer
Dan McKenzie	Winnipeg-Assiniboine	P.C.	Mar. 25, 1924	1972	Communications
George Minaker	Winnipeg-St. James	P.C.	Sept. 17, 1937	1984	Professional engineer
Rod Murphy	Churchill	N.D.P.	Oct. 16, 1946	1979	Teacher
Jack Murta	Lisgar	P.C.	May 13, 1943	1970*	Farmer
David Orlikow	Winnipeg North	N.D.P.	Apr. 20, 1918	1962	School trustee/administrator
Brian White	Dauphin-Swan River	P.C.	Jan. 17, 1951	1984	Pharmacist

Member	Riding	Party	Birthdate	First Elected[1]	Previous Occupation
Saskatchewan					
Vic Althouse	Humbolt-Lake Centre	N.D.P.	Apr. 15, 1937	1980	Farmer
Les Benjamin	Regina West	N.D.P.	Apr. 29, 1925	1968	Railway station agent and telegrapher
John Gormley	The Battlefords-Meadow Lake	P.C.	Aug. 2, 1957	1984	Journalist
William Andrew Gottselig	Moose Jaw	P.C.	Dec. 1, 1934	1984	Farmer
Len Gustafson	Assiniboia	P.C.	Nov. 10, 1933	1979	Farmer
Alvin Hamilton	Qu'Appelle-Moose Mountain	P.C.	Mar. 30, 1912	1957	Teacher
Ray Hnatyshyn	Saskatoon West	P.C.	Mar. 16, 1934	1974	Lawyer
Stan Hovdebo	Prince Albert	N.D.P.	Aug. 20, 1925	1979*	Educator
Simon de Jong	Regina East	N.D.P.	Apr. 9, 1942	1979	Small businessman
Bill McKnight	Kindersley-Lloydminster	P.C.	July 12, 1940	1979	Farmer
Lorne Nystrom	Yorkton-Melville	N.D.P.	Apr. 26, 1946	1968	Teacher
Don Ravis	Saskatoon East	P.C.	Feb. 28, 1940	1984	Small businessman
Jack Scowen	Mackenzie	P.C.	Dec. 12, 1925	1984	Farmer
Geoff Wilson	Swift Current-Maple Creek	P.C.	Sept. 24, 1941	1984	Lawyer
Alberta					
Harvie Andre	Calgary Centre	P.C.	July 27, 1940	1972	Professional engineer
Joe Clark	Yellowhead	P.C.	June 5, 1939	1972	University lecturer
Albert Cooper	Peace River	P.C.	June 19, 1952	1980	Businessman
Murray Dorin	Edmonton West	P.C.	May 21, 1954	1984	Chartered accountant
Jim Edwards	Edmonton South	P.C.	Aug. 31, 1936	1984	Broadcaster
Paul Gagnon	Calgary North	P.C.	Sept. 17, 1937	1984	Professional engineer
Jim Hawkes	Calgary West	P.C.	June 21, 1934	1979	Businessman
David Kilgour	Edmonton-Strathcona	P.C.	Feb. 18, 1941	1979	Lawyer
Alex Kindy	Calgary East	P.C.	Jan. 8, 1930	1984	Physician
Bill Lesick	Edmonton East	P.C.	June 10, 1923	1984	Pharmacist
Arnold Malone	Crowfoot	P.C.	Dec. 9, 1937	1974	Farmer
Don Mazankowski	Vegreville	P.C.	July 27, 1935	1968	Businessman
Steve Paproski	Edmonton North	P.C.	Sept. 23, 1928	1968	Business manager
Bob Porter	Medicine Hat	P.C.	Aug. 14, 1933	1984	Rancher/Businessman
Stan Schellenberger	Wetaskiwin	P.C.	Jan. 7, 1948	1972	Agrologist
Jack Shields	Athabasca	P.C.	Dec. 25, 1929	1980	Businessman
Barbara Sparrow	Calgary South	P.C.	July 11, 1935	1984	Businesswoman
Gordon E. Taylor	Bow River	P.C.	July 20, 1910	1979	Teacher/Businessman
Blaine Thacker	Lethbridge-Foothills	P.C.	Jan. 11, 1941	1979	Lawyer
Gordon Towers	Red Deer	P.C.	July 5, 1919	1972	Farmer
Walter Van De Walle	Pembina	P.C.	July 20, 1922	1986*	Farmer/Businessman
British Columbia					
Ross Belsher	Fraser Valley East	P.C.	Jan. 19, 1933	1984	Retail store manager
Bob Brisco	Kootenay West	P.C.	Dec. 29, 1928	1974	Chiropractor
Pat Carney	Vancouver Centre	P.C.	May 26, 1935	1980	Economist
Mary Collins	Capilano	P.C.	Sept. 26, 1940	1984	Businesswoman
Chuck Cook	North Vancouver-Burnaby	P.C.	July 28, 1926	1979	Lawyer
Patrick Crofton	Esquimalt-Saanich	P.C.	May 29, 1935	1984	Farmer/Businessman
Vincent M. Dantzer	Okanagan North	P.C.	Oct. 2, 1923	1980	Lawyer
John A. Fraser	Vancouver South	P.C.	Dec. 15, 1931	1972	Lawyer
Benno Friesen	Surrey-White Rock-N. Delta	P.C.	June 27, 1929	1974	Dean of students
Jim Fulton	Skeena	N.D.P.	Jan. 22, 1950	1979	Probation officer
Stan Graham	Kootenay East-Revelstoke	P.C.	Jan. 29, 1926	1979	Businessman
Lorne Greenaway	Cariboo-Chilcotin	P.C.	May 8, 1933	1979	Veterinarian
Pauline Jewett	New Westminster-Coquitlam	N.D.P.	Dec. 11, 1922	1963	Univ. prof./administrator
Fred King	Okanagan-Similkameen	P.C.	June 11, 1923	1979	Fruit grower
Jim Manly	Cowichan-Malahat-The Islands	N.D.P.	Oct. 29, 1932	1980	Clergyman
Lorne McCuish	Prince George-Bulkley Valley	P.C.	May 25, 1923	1979	Insurance claims manager
Allan McKinnon	Victoria	P.C.	Jan. 11, 1917	1972	Educator
Margaret Mitchell	Vancouver East	N.D.P.	July 17, 1925	1979	Social worker
Frank Oberle	Prince George-Peace River	P.C.	May 24, 1932	1972	Businessman
Nelson A. Riis	Kamloops-Shuswap	N.D.P.	Jan. 10, 1942	1980	Geographer/Administrator/Teacher
Svend J. Robinson	Burnaby	N.D.P.	Mar. 4, 1952	1979	Lawyer
Ted Schellenberg	Nanaimo-Alberni	P.C.	Aug. 11, 1952	1984	Broadcaster
Tom Siddon	Richmond-South Delta	P.C.	Nov. 9, 1941	1978*	Professional engineer
Ray Skelly	Comox-Powell River	N.D.P.	July 1, 1941	1979	Teacher
Gerry St. Germain	Mission-Port Moody	P.C.	Nov. 6, 1937	1983*	Contractor
John N. Turner	Vancouver Quadra	Lib.	June 7, 1929	1962	Lawyer
Ian Waddell	Vancouver Kingsway	N.D.P.	Nov. 21, 1942	1979	Lawyer
Robert Lloyd Wenman	Fraser Valley West	P.C.	June 19, 1940	1974	Businessman/Educator
Yukon Territory					
Audrey McLaughlin	Yukon	N.D.P.	Nov. 7, 1936	1987*	Consultant

Member	Riding	Party	Birthdate	First Elected[1]	Previous Occupation
Northwest Territories					
Dave Nickerson	Western Arctic	P.C.	Apr. 30, 1944	1979	Mining engineer
Thomas Suluk	Nunatsiaq	P.C.	Mar. 14, 1950	1984	Executive director

(1) General election unless * indicating by-election. n.a. - not available. P.C. - Progressive Conservative; Lib. - Liberal; N.D.P. - New Democratic Party; Ind. - Independent.

Salaries of Federal Political Figures

(as of Jan. 1, 1988)

Members of Parliament—$58 300, with $19 400 of this tax-free for expenses[1], and 64 travel destinations per year.

The following figures receive as *extra* salary on top of their M.P. salaries:

Prime Minister—$66 600
Cabinet Ministers—$44 500
Speaker of the House—$44 500 plus $1 000 motor vehicle allowance[2].
Official Opposition Leader—$44 500 plus $2 000 motor vehicle allowance[2].
Other Party Leaders—$26 800
Opposition House Leader—$21 700
Other House Leaders—$9 300
Government and Opposition Whips—$12 100
Other Party Whips—$6 900
Parliamentary Secretaries—$9 700

Senators— $58 300 with $9 300 of this tax-free for expenses, and 64 travel destinations per year.

The following figures receive as *extra* salary on top of their Senate salaries:

Leader of the Government—$44 500 plus $2 000 car allowance.
Leader of the Opposition—$21 700
Speaker of the Senate—$28 100 plus $3 000 residence allowance and $1 000 car allowance.
Deputy Leader of the Government—$13 600
Deputy Leader of the Opposition—$8 600
Government Whip—$6 900
Opposition Whip—$4 500

The **Governor General** receives $70 000[3] per year.

(1) 23 MPs representing remote or distant ridings are allowed $23 800 tax-free; 2 MPs representing N.W.T. ridings are allowed $25 600 tax-free. (2) Allowances have remained unchanged since 1931. (3) As of Apr. 1, 1985. In 1867, the Governor General's salary was set at £10 000 (British pounds) and remained unchanged until 1970 when it was converted to $48 666.63 (Canadian). This salary remained unchanged until 1985 when it was raised to $70 000.

Canadian Political Party Leaders

Progressive Conservative[1] Party

Leader	Term	Leader	Term
Sir John A. Macdonald	1854–July 6, 1891	R.B. Hanson[2]	May 13, 1940–Nov. 12, 1941
Sir J.J.C. Abbott	June 16, 1891–Dec. 5, 1892	Arthur Meighen	Nov. 12, 1941–Dec. 11, 1942
Sir John Thompson	Dec. 5, 1892–Dec. 12, 1894	John Bracken	Dec. 11, 1942–Oct. 2, 1948
Sir Mackenzie Bowell	Dec. 21, 1894–Apr. 27, 1896	George A. Drew	Oct. 2, 1948–Dec. 14, 1956
Sir Charles Tupper	May 1, 1896–Feb. 5, 1901	John G. Diefenbaker	Dec. 14, 1956–Sept. 9, 1967
Sir Robert Borden	Feb. 6, 1901–July 10, 1920	Robert L. Stanfield	Sept. 9, 1967–Feb. 22, 1976
Arthur Meighen	July 10, 1920–Oct. 11, 1926	Joe Clark	Feb. 22, 1976–Feb. 8, 1983
Hugh Guthrie[2]	Oct. 11, 1926–Oct. 12, 1927	Erik Nielsen[2]	Feb. 9, 1983–June 11, 1983
R.B. Bennett	Oct. 12, 1927–July 7, 1938	Brian Mulroney	June 11, 1983–
R.J. Manion	July 7, 1938–May 13, 1940		

Liberal Party

Leader	Term	Leader	Term
Alexander Mackenzie	Mar. 6, 1873–Apr. 27, 1880	Louis St. Laurent	Aug. 7, 1948–Jan. 16, 1958
Edward Blake	May 4, 1880–June 2, 1887	Lester B. Pearson	Jan. 16, 1958–Apr. 2, 1968
Sir Wilfrid Laurier	June 1887–Feb. 17, 1919	Pierre E. Trudeau	Apr. 6, 1968–June 16, 1984
Daniel D. McKenzie[2]	Feb. 1919–Aug. 1919	John N. Turner	June 16, 1984–
W.L. Mackenzie King	Aug. 7, 1919–Aug. 7, 1948		

New Democratic Party[3]

Leader	Term	Leader	Term
James. S. Woodsworth	Aug. 1932–July 1942	Tommy Douglas	Aug. 1961–Apr. 1971
M.J. Coldwell	July 1942–Aug. 1960	David Lewis	Apr. 24, 1971–July 7, 1975
Hazen Argue	Aug. 1960–Aug. 1961	Ed Broadbent	July 7, 1975–

(1) Name changed from Conservative to Progressive Conservative Dec. 1942. (2) Interim leader appointed to fill a vacancy until a party leadership convention could be held. (3) Prior to Aug. 1961 was called the Co-operative Commonwealth Federation.

Canadian Political Party Leadership Conventions

Liberal Party

1919

Candidates	First ballot	Second ballot	Third ballot
W.L. Mackenzie King	344	411	476
W.S. Fielding	297	344	438
George P. Graham	153	124	–
D.D. McKenzie	153	60	–

1948

Candidates	First ballot
Louis St. Laurent	848
James Garfield Gardiner	323
Charles G. "Chubby" Power	56

1958

Candidates	First ballot
Lester B. Pearson	1 074
Paul Martin	305

1968

Candidates	First ballot	Second ballot	Third ballot	Fourth ballot
Pierre Elliott Trudeau	752	964	1 051	1 203
Robert Winters	293	473	621	954
John Turner	277	347	279	195
Paul Hellyer	330	465	377	–
J.J. Greene	169	104	29	–
Allan MacEachen	165	11	–	–
Paul Martin	277	–	–	–
Eric Kierans	103	–	–	–

1984

Candidates	First ballot	Second ballot
John Turner	1 593	1 862
Jean Chrétien	1 067	1 368
Donald Johnston	278	192
John Roberts	185	–
Mark MacGuigan	135	–
John Munro	93	–
Eugene Whelan	84	–

New Democratic Party

1961

Candidates	First ballot
Tommy Douglas	1 391
Hazen Argue	380

1971

Candidates	First ballot	Second ballot	Third ballot	Fourth ballot
David Lewis	661	715	742	1 046
James Laxer	378	407	508	612
John Harney	299	347	431	–
Ed Broadbent	236	223	–	–
Frank Howard	124	–	–	–

1975

Candidates	First ballot	Second ballot	Third ballot	Fourth ballot
Ed Broadbent	536	586	694	984
Rosemary Brown	413	397	494	658
Lorne Nystrom	345	342	413	–
John Harney	313	299	–	–
Douglas Campbell	11	–	–	–

Progressive Conservative Party

1942

Candidates	First ballot	Second ballot
John Bracken	420	538
Maj. M.A. MacPherson	220	255
John G. Diefenbaker	120	79
Howard Green	88	–
Henry Herbert Stevens	20	–

1948

Candidates	First ballot
George A. Drew	827
John G. Diefenbaker	311
Donald M. Fleming	104

1956

Candidates	First ballot
John G. Diefenbaker	744
Donald M. Fleming	393
E. Davie Fulton	117

1967

Candidates	First ballot	Second ballot	Third ballot	Fourth ballot	Fifth ballot
Robert Stanfield	519	613	717	865	1 150
Duff Roblin	349	430	541	771	969
E. Davie Fulton	343	346	361	357	–
Alvin Hamilton	136	127	106	167	–
George Hees	395	299	277	–	–
John G. Diefenbaker	271	172	114	–	–
Donald M. Fleming	126	115	76	–	–
Wallace McCutcheon	137	76	–	–	–
Michael Starr	45	34	–	–	–
John P. McLean	10	–	–	–	–
Mary Walker Sawka	2	–	–	–	–

1976

Candidates	First ballot	Second ballot	Third ballot	Fourth ballot
Joe Clark	277	532	969	1 187
Claude Wagner	531	667	1 003	1 112
Brian Mulroney	357	419	369	–
Jack Horner	235	286	–	–
Flora MacDonald	214	239	–	–
Paul Hellyer	231	118	–	–
Patrick Nowlan	86	42	–	–
John Fraser	127	34	–	–
Sinclair Stevens	182	–	–	–
James Gillies	87	–	–	–
Heward Grafftey	33	–	–	–

1983

Candidates	First ballot	Second ballot	Third ballot	Fourth ballot
Brian Mulroney	874	1 021	1 036	1 584
Joe Clark	1 091	1 085	1 058	1 325
John Crosbie	639	781	858	–
David Crombie	116	67	–	–
Michael Wilson	144	–	–	–
Peter Pocklington	102	–	–	–
John Gamble	17	–	–	–
Neil Fraser	5	–	–	–

Election Results by Province and Party, September 4, 1984

Province	Total valid votes	Conservative	%	Liberal	%	New Democrat	%	Other	%
Newfoundland	241 159	138 867	57.6	87 778	36.4	13 993	5.8	521	0.2
Prince Edward Island	73 091	38 160	52.2	30 075	41.1	4 737	6.5	119	0.2
Nova Scotia	460 418	233 713	50.8	154 954	33.7	70 190	15.2	1 561	0.3
New Brunswick	377 350	202 144	53.6	120 326	31.9	53 332	14.1	1 548	0.4
Quebec	3 439 267	1 728 196	50.2	1 219 124	35.4	301 928	8.8	190 019	5.5
Ontario	4 399 974	2 113 187	48.0	1 323 835	30.1	921 504	20.9	41 448	0.9
Manitoba	513 834	221 947	43.2	112 123	21.8	139 999	27.2	39 765	7.7
Saskatchewan	522 800	218 000	41.7	95 143	18.2	200 918	38.4	8 739	1.7
Alberta	1 017 394	701 344	68.9	129 945	12.8	143 588	14.1	42 517	4.2
British Columbia	1 432 795	668 432	46.7	235 394	16.4	502 331	35.1	26 638	1.9
Yukon	11 704	6 648	56.8	2 535	21.7	1 884	16.1	637	5.4
N.W. Territories	19 510	8 059	41.3	5 254	26.9	5 511	28.2	686	3.5
Total votes	12 509 296	6 278 697	50.2	3 516 486	28.1	2 359 915	18.9	354 198	2.8
Seats	282	211	74.8	40	14.2	30	10.6	1	0.4

Voter Turnout for the 1984 Federal Election

Source: Elections Canada

	Eligible voters	Actual votes cast[1]	Voter turnout[2]		Eligible voters	Actual votes cast[1]	Voter turnout[2]
Canada	16 775 011	12 638 424	75%	Manitoba	704 585	516 053	73
Newfoundland	370 219	242 491	65	Saskatchewan	673 289	524 566	78
Prince Edward Island	87 215	73 801	85	Alberta	1 479 675	1 022 274	69
Nova Scotia	613 964	462 885	75	British Columbia	1 853 110	1 437 904	78
New Brunswick	491 169	379 850	77	Yukon	15 056	11 731	78
Quebec	4 575 493	3 485 815	76	Northwest Territories	28 916	19 638	68
Ontario	5 882 320	4 461 416	76				

(1) Valid and non-valid votes. (2) Percentage of actual votes to eligible voters.

Federal Election Results, 1867-1904

	1867	1872	1874	1878	1882	1887	1891	1896	1900	1904
Canada										
Conservative	101	103	73	137	139	123	123	89	80	75
Liberal	80	97	133	69	71	92	92	117	133	139
Other	–	–	–	–	–	–	–	7	–	–
Prince Edward Island[1]										
Conservative	–	–	–	5	4	–	2	3	2	3
Liberal	–	–	6	1	2	6	4	2	3	1
Nova Scotia										
Conservative	3	11	4	14	15	14	16	10	5	–
Liberal	16	10	17	7	6	7	5	10	15	18
New Brunswick										
Conservative	7	7	5	5	10	10	13	9	5	6
Liberal	8	9	11	11	6	6	3	5	9	7
Quebec										
Conservative	45	38	32	45	48	33	30	16	7	11
Liberal	20	27	33	20	17	32	35	49	58	54
Ontario										
Conservative	46	38	24	59	54	52	48	44	55	48
Liberal	36	50	64	29	37	40	44	43	37	38
Other	–	–	–	–	–	–	–	5	–	–
Manitoba[2]										
Conservative	–	3	2	3	2	4	4	4	4	3
Liberal	–	1	2	1	3	1	1	2	3	7
Other	–	–	–	–	–	–	–	1	–	–
British Columbia[3]										
Conservative	–	6	6	6	6	6	6	2	2	–
Liberal	–	–	–	–	–	–	–	4	4	7
Yukon[4]										
Conservative	–	–	–	–	–	–	–	–	–	1
Northwest Territories[2]										
Conservative	–	–	–	–	–	4	4	1	–	3
Liberal	–	–	–	–	–	–	–	2	4	7
Other	–	–	–	–	–	–	–	1	–	–

(1) Entered Confederation July 1, 1873. (2) Entered Confederation July 15, 1870. (3) Entered Confederation July 20, 1871. (4) Entered Confederation June 13, 1894.

Federal Election Results, 1908-1953

	1908	1911	1917[1]	1921	1925	1926	1930	1935	1940	1945	1949	1953
Canada												
Conservative	85	133	153	50	116	91	137	39	39	67	41	51
Liberal	133	86	82	117	101	116	88	171	178	125	190	170
Progressive	–	–	–	64	25	–	2	–	–	–	–	–
CCF	–	–	–	–	–	–	–	7	8	28	13	23
Social Credit	–	–	–	–	–	–	–	17	10	13	10	15
Other	3	2	–	4	3	38	18	11	10	12	8	6
Newfoundland[2]												
Conservative	–	–	–	–	–	–	–	–	–	–	2	–
Liberal	–	–	–	–	–	–	–	–	–	–	5	7
Prince Edward Island												
Conservative	1	2	2	–	2	1	3	–	–	1	1	1
Liberal	3	2	2	4	2	3	1	4	4	3	3	3
Nova Scotia												
Conservative	6	9	12	–	11	12	10	–	1	3	2	1
Liberal	12	9	4	16	3	2	4	12	10	8	10	10
CCF	–	–	–	–	–	–	–	–	1	1	1	1
New Brunswick												
Conservative	2	5	7	5	10	7	10	1	5	3	2	3
Liberal	11	8	4	5	1	4	1	9	5	7	7	7
Progressive	–	–	–	1	–	–	–	–	–	–	–	–
Other	–	–	–	–	–	–	–	–	–	–	1	–
Quebec												
Conservative	11	27	3	–	4	4	24	5	–	1	2	4
Liberal	53	37	62	65	60	60	40	55	61	54	66	66
Other	1	1	–	–	1	1	1	5	4	10	5	5
Ontario												
Conservative	48	72	74	37	68	53	59	25	25	48	25	33
Liberal	36	13	8	21	12	23	22	56	55	34	56	50
CCF	–	–	–	–	–	–	–	–	–	–	1	1
Progressive	–	–	–	24	2	4	–	–	–	–	–	–
Other	2	1	–	–	–	2	1	1	2	–	1	1
Manitoba												
Conservative	8	8	14	–	7	–	11	1	1	2	1	3
Liberal	2	2	1	2	1	4	1	12	14	10	12	8
CCF	–	–	–	–	–	–	–	2	1	5	3	3
Progressive	–	–	–	12	7	4	–	–	–	–	–	–
Other	–	–	–	1	2	9	5	2	1	–	–	–
Saskatchewan[3]												
Conservative	1	1	16	–	–	–	8	1	2	1	1	1
Liberal	9	9	–	1	15	16	11	16	12	2	14	5
CCF	–	–	–	–	–	–	–	2	5	18	5	11
Progressive	–	–	–	15	6	5	2	–	–	–	–	–
Social Credit	–	–	–	–	–	–	–	–	2	–	–	–
Other	–	–	–	–	–	–	–	–	2	–	–	–
Alberta[3]												
Conservative	3	1	11	–	3	1	4	1	–	2	2	2
Liberal	4	6	1	–	4	3	3	1	7	2	5	4
Progressive	–	–	–	10	9	–	–	–	–	–	–	–
Social Credit	–	–	–	–	–	–	–	15	10	13	10	11
United Farmers of Alta.	–	–	–	–	–	11	9	–	–	–	–	–
Other	–	–	–	2	–	1	–	–	–	–	–	–
British Columbia												
Conservative	5	7	13	7	10	12	7	5	4	5	3	3
Liberal	2	–	–	3	3	1	5	6	10	5	11	8
CCF	–	–	–	–	–	–	–	3	1	4	3	7
Progressive	–	–	–	2	1	–	–	–	–	–	–	–
Social Credit	–	–	–	–	–	–	–	–	–	–	–	4
Other	–	–	–	1	–	1	2	2	1	2	1	–
Yukon and Northwest Territories												
Conservative	–	1	–	1	1	1	1	–	1	1	–	–
Liberal	1	–	–	–	–	–	–	–	–	–	1	2
Other	–	–	–	–	–	–	–	1	–	–	–	–

(1) For the 1917 election, Conservative refers to "Unionists", a coalition of Conservatives plus pro-consciption Liberals; Liberals, for the 1917 election, are sometimes called "Laurier Liberals" because of their support for Laurier's anti-consciption stand. (2) Entered Confederation Mar. 31, 1949. (3) Entered Confederation Sept. 1, 1905.

Federal Election Results, 1957-1984

	1957	1958	1962	1963	1965	1968	1972	1974	1979	1980	1984
Canada											
Conservative	112	208	116	95	97	72	107	95	136	103	211
Liberal	105	48	99	129	131	155	109	141	114	147	40
NDP (CCF)[1]	25	8	19	17	21	22	31	16	26	32	30
Social Credit	19	–	30	24	5	–	15	11	6	–	–
Other	4	1	1	–	11	15	2	1	–	–	1
Newfoundland											
Conservative	2	2	1	–	–	6	4	3	2	2	4
Liberal	5	5	6	7	7	1	3	4	4	5	3
NDP (CCF)	–	–	–	–	–	–	–	–	1	–	–
Prince Edward Island											
Conservative	4	4	4	2	4	4	3	3	4	2	3
Liberal	–	–	–	2	–	–	1	1	–	2	1
Nova Scotia											
Conservative	10	12	9	7	10	10	10	8	8	6	9
Liberal	2	–	2	5	2	1	1	2	2	5	2
NDP (CCF)	–	–	1	–	–	–	–	1	1	–	–
New Brunswick											
Conservative	5	7	4	4	4	5	5	3	4	3	9
Liberal	5	3	6	6	6	5	5	6	6	7	1
Other	–	–	–	–	–	–	–	1	–	–	–
Quebec											
Conservative	9	50	14	8	8	4	2	3	2	1	58
Liberal	63	25	35	47	56	56	56	60	67	74	17
NDP (CCF)	–	–	–	–	–	–	–	–	–	–	–
Social Credit	–	–	26	20	–	–	15	11	6	–	–
Other	3	–	–	–	11	14	1	–	–	–	–
Ontario											
Conservative	61	67	35	27	25	17	40	25	57	38	67
Liberal	20	14	43	52	51	64	36	55	32	52	14
NDP (CCF)	3	3	6	6	9	6	11	8	6	5	13
Other	1	1	1	–	–	1	1	–	–	–	1
Manitoba											
Conservative	8	14	11	10	10	5	8	9	7	5	9
Liberal	1	–	1	2	1	5	2	2	2	2	1
NDP (CCF)	5	–	2	2	3	3	3	2	5	7	4
Saskatchewan											
Conservative	3	16	16	17	17	5	7	8	10	7	9
Liberal	4	–	1	–	–	2	1	3	–	–	–
NDP (CCF)	10	1	–	–	–	6	5	2	4	7	5
Alberta											
Conservative	3	17	15	14	15	15	19	19	21	21	21
Liberal	1	–	–	1	–	4	–	–	–	–	–
Social Credit	13	–	2	2	2	–	–	–	–	–	–
Bristish Columbia											
Conservative	7	18	6	4	3	–	8	13	19	1 6	19
Liberal	2	–	4	7	7	16	4	8	1	–	1
NDP (CCF)	7	4	10	9	9	7	11	2	8	12	8
Social Credit	6	–	2	2	3	–	–	–	–	–	–
Yukon											
Conservative	–	1	1	1	1	1	1	1	1	1	1
Liberal	1	–	–	–	–	–	–	–	–	–	–
Northwest Territories											
Conservative	–	–	–	1	–	–	–	–	1	1	2
Liberal	1	1	1	–	1	1	–	–	–	–	–
NDP (CCF)	–	–	–	–	–	–	1	1	1	1	–

(1) The New Democratic Party (NDP) replaced the Co-operative Commonwealth Federation (CCF) in Aug. 1961.

Voter Turnout at Canada's General Elections, 1867-1984

Source: Elections Canada

Year	Voter turnout[1]	Year	Voter turnout[1]	Year	Voter turnout[1]	Year	Voter turnout[1]
1867	73%	1904	84%	1940	71%	1968	76%
1872	70	1908	79	1945	76	1972	77
1874	75	1911	72	1949	75	1974	71
1878	71	1917	90	1953	68	1979	76
1882	72	1921	71	1957	75	1980	69
1887	70	1925	69	1958	81	1984	75
1891	65	1926	70	1962	80		
1896	61	1930	76	1963	80		
1900	79	1935	75	1965	76		

(1) Percentage of actual votes to eligible voters. In many early general elections, several electoral districts were won by acclamation; hence, no eligible voters nor actual votes were recorded. Furthermore, in some of the more remote districts, votes were cast but no voters' lists had been prepared.

Registered Federal Political Parties

Source: Elections Canada

(as of July 1988)

Communist Party of Canada—24 Cecil St., Toronto, Ont. M5T 1N2, (416) 979-2109; leader: George Hewison.

Confederation of Regions Western Party—6155-99th St., Edmonton, Alta. T6E 3P1, (403) 435-4185; leader: Elmer Knutson.

Green Party of Canada—3012 Yellow Point Rd., R.R. 3, Ladysmith, B.C. V0R 2E0, (604) 254-8165, 722-3349; leader: Dr. Seymour Trieger.

Liberal Party of Canada— ste. 200, 200 Laurier Ave. W., Ottawa, Ont. K1P 6M8, (613) 237-0740; leader: The Right Honourable John Turner.

Libertarian Party of Canada—ste. 1004, 11 Yorkville Ave., Toronto, Ont. M4W 1L3, (416) 323-0020; leader: Dennis Corrigan.

New Democratic Party—600-280 Albert St., Ottawa, Ont. K1P 5G8, (613) 236-3613; leader: The Honourable J. Edward Broadbent.

Parti Nationaliste du Québec—8469 rue Drolet, Montreal, Que. H2P 2H8, (514) 389-1033; leader: Bertrand Desrosiers.

Parti Rhinocéros—4534 de Bordeaux, Montreal, Que. H2H 2A1, (514) 524-5172; interim leader: Dominique Langevin.

Party for the Commonwealth of Canada—8377, rue St-Denis, Montreal, Que. H2R 2G9; leader: Gilles Gervais.

Progressive Conservative Party of Canada—ste. 200, 2d fl., 161 Laurier Ave. W., Ottawa, Ont. K1P 5J2, (613) 238-6111; leader: The Right Honourable M. Brian Mulroney.

Social Credit Party of Canada—Box 7000, Cambridge, Ont. N1R 6C7, (519) 291-2611; leader: Harvey G. Lainson.

Ministers of External Affairs

From 1867 to 1912, the secretary of state of Canada presided over the department of external affairs. The office of secretary of state for external affairs was created on Apr. 1, 1912. The prime minister was to hold the office *ex officio*, but this situation changed in 1946 with the appointment of a minister.

Minister	Appointed by	Term(s)
Secretaries of State of Canada:		
Hector L. Langevin	Macdonald	July 1, 1867–Dec. 7, 1869
James Cox Aikins[2]	Macdonald	Dec. 8, 1869–Nov. 5, 1873
David Christie[2]	Mackenzie	Nov. 7, 1873–Jan. 8, 1874
Richard William Scott[2]	Mackenzie	Jan. 9, 1874–Oct. 8, 1878
James Cox Aikins[2]	Macdonald	Oct. 19, 1878–Nov. 7, 1880
John O'Connor	Macdonald	Nov. 8, 1880–May 19, 1881
Joseph-Alfred Mousseau	Macdonald	May 20, 1881–July 28, 1882
Joseph Adolphe Chapleau	Macdonald	July 29, 1882–June 6, 1891
	Abbott	June 16, 1891–Jan. 24, 1892
James Colebrooke Patterson	Abbott	Jan. 25, 1892–Nov. 24, 1892
John Costigan	Thompson	Dec. 5, 1892–Dec. 12, 1894
Arthur Rupert Dickey	Bowell	Dec. 21, 1894–Mar. 25, 1895
Walter Humphries Montague	Bowell	Mar. 26, 1895–Dec. 20, 1895
Joseph Aldéric Ouimet[1]	Bowell	Dec. 27, 1895–Jan. 5, 1896
Thomas Mayne Daly[1]	Bowell	Jan. 6, 1896–Jan. 14, 1896
Sir Charles Tupper	Bowell	Jan. 15, 1896–Apr. 27, 1896
	himself	May 1, 1896–July 8, 1896
Richard William Scott[2]	Laurier	July 13, 1896–Oct. 8, 1908
Charles Murphy	Laurier	Oct. 9, 1908–Oct. 6, 1911

Minister	Appointed by	Term(s)
Secretaries of State for External Affairs:		
Robert Borden	ex officio	Apr. 1, 1912–Oct. 12, 1917
		Oct. 12, 1917–July 10, 1920
Arthur Meighen	ex officio	July 10, 1920–Dec. 29, 1921
Mackenzie King	ex officio	Dec. 29, 1921–June 28, 1926
Arthur Meighen	ex officio	June 29, 1921–Sept. 25, 1926
Mackenzie King	ex officio	Sept. 25, 1926–Aug. 7, 1930
Richard B. Bennett	ex officio	Aug. 7, 1930–Oct. 23, 1935
Mackenzie King	ex officio	Oct. 23, 1935–Sept. 3, 1946
	(to May 28, 1946)	
Louis St. Laurent	King	Sept. 4, 1946–Sept. 9, 1948
Lester B. Pearson	King;	Sept. 10, 1948–Nov. 15, 1948
	St. Laurent	Nov. 15, 1948–June 21, 1957
John Diefenbaker	himself	June 21, 1957–Sept. 12, 1957
Sidney Smith	Diefenbaker	Sept. 13, 1957–Mar. 17, 1959
John Diefenbaker[1]	himself	Mar. 19, 1959–June 3, 1959
Howard Green	Diefenbaker	June. 4, 1959–Apr. 22, 1963
Paul Martin	Pearson	Apr. 22, 1963–Apr. 20, 1968
Mitchell Sharp	Trudeau	Apr. 20, 1968–Aug. 7, 1974
Allan MacEachen	Trudeau	Aug. 8, 1974–Sept. 13, 1976
Donald Jamieson	Trudeau	Sept. 14, 1976–June 3, 1979
Flora MacDonald	Clark	June 4, 1979–Mar. 2, 1980
Mark MacGuigan	Trudeau	Mar. 3, 1980–Sept. 9, 1982
Allan MacEachen	Trudeau	Sept. 10, 1982–June 29, 1984
Jean Chrétien	Turner	June 30, 1984–Sept. 16, 1984
Joe Clark	Mulroney	Sept. 17, 1984–

(1) Acting. (2) Senator.

Ministers of Justice and Attorneys General

Minister	Appointed by	Term(s)
Sir John A. Macdonald	himself	July 1, 1867–Nov. 5, 1873
Antoine-Aimé Dorion	Mackenzie	Nov. 7, 1873–May 31, 1874
Sir Albert James Smith[1]	Mackenzie	June 1, 1874–July 7, 1874
Télesphore Fournier	Mackenzie	July 8, 1874–May 18, 1875
Edward Blake	Mackenzie	May 19, 1875–June 7, 1877
Toussaint Antoine R. Laflamme	Mackenzie	June 8, 1877–Oct. 8, 1878
James McDonald	Macdonald	Oct. 17, 1878–May 19, 1881
Sir Alexander Campbell[2]	Macdonald	May 20, 1881–Sept. 24, 1885
Sir John Thompson	Macdonald;	Sept. 26, 1885–June 6, 1891
	Abbott;	June 16, 1891–Nov. 24, 1892
	himself	Dec. 5, 1892–Dec. 12, 1894
Sir Charles Tupper	Bowell	Dec. 21, 1894–Jan. 5, 1896
Thomas Mayne Daly[1]	Bowell	Jan. 6, 1896–Jan. 14, 1896
Arthur Rupert Dickey	Bowell;	Jan. 15, 1896–Apr. 27, 1896
	Tupper	May 1, 1896–July 8, 1896
Sir Oliver Mowat[2]	Laurier	July 13, 1896–Nov. 17, 1897
David Mills[2]	Laurier	Nov. 18, 1897–Feb. 7, 1902
Charles Fitzpatrick	Laurier	Feb. 11, 1902–June 3, 1906
Sir Allen Bristol Aylesworth	Laurier	June 4, 1906–Oct. 6, 1911
Charles Joseph Doherty	Borden;	Oct. 10, 1911–July 10, 1920
	Meighen	July 10, 1920–Sept. 20, 1921
Richard B. Bennett	Meighen	Oct. 4, 1921–Dec. 29, 1921
Sir Lomer Gouin	King	Dec. 29, 1921–Jan. 3, 1924
Ernest Lapointe[1]	King	Jan. 4, 1924–Jan. 29, 1924
Ernest Lapointe	King	Jan. 30, 1924–June 28, 1926
Hugh Guthrie[1]	Meighen	June 29, 1926–July 12, 1926
Esioff-Léon Patenaude	Meighen	July 13, 1926–Sept. 25, 1926
Ernest Lapointe	King	Sept. 25, 1926–Aug. 7, 1930
Hugh Guthrie	Bennett	Aug. 7, 1930–Aug. 11, 1935
George Reginald Geary	Bennett	Aug. 14, 1935–Oct. 23, 1935
Ernest Lapointe	King	Oct. 23, 1935–Nov. 26, 1941
Joseph-Enoil Mishaud[1]	King	Nov. 27, 1941–Dec. 9, 1941
Louis St. Laurent	King	Dec. 10, 1941–Dec. 9, 1946
James Lorimer Ilsley	King	Dec. 10, 1946–June 30, 1948
Louis St. Laurent[1]	King	July 1, 1948–Sept. 9, 1948
Louis St. Laurent	King	Sept. 10, 1948–Nov. 15, 1948
Stuart Sinclair Garson	St. Laurent	Nov. 15, 1948–June 21, 1957
E. Davie Fulton	Diefenbaker	June 21, 1957–Apr. 8, 1962
Donald Fleming	Diefenbaker	Apr. 9, 1962–Apr. 22, 1963
Lionel Chevrier	Pearson	Apr. 22, 1963–Feb. 2, 1964
Guy Favreau	Pearson	Feb. 3, 1964–June 29, 1965

Minister	Appointed by	Term(s)
James McIlraith[1]	Pearson	June 30, 1965–July 6, 1965
Lucien Cardin	Pearson	July 7, 1965–Apr. 3, 1967
Pierre Trudeau	Pearson;	Apr. 4, 1967–Apr. 20, 1968
	himself	Apr. 20, 1968–July 5, 1968
John Turner	Trudeau	July 6, 1968–Jan. 27, 1972
Otto Lang	Trudeau	Jan. 28, 1972–Sept. 25, 1975
Ron Basford	Trudeau	Sept. 26, 1975–Aug. 2, 1978
Otto Lang[1]	Trudeau	Aug. 3, 1978–Aug. 8, 1978
Otto Lang	Trudeau	Aug. 9, 1978–Nov. 23, 1978
Marc Lalonde	Trudeau	Nov. 24, 1978–June 3, 1979
Jacques Flynn[2]	Clark	June 4, 1979–Mar. 2, 1980
Jean Chrétien	Trudeau	Mar. 3, 1980–Sept. 9, 1982
Mark MacGuigan	Trudeau	Sept. 10, 1982–June 29, 1984
Donald Johnston	Turner	June 30, 1984–Sept. 16, 1984
John Crosbie	Mulroney	Sept. 17, 1984–June 30, 1986
Ray Hnatyshyn	Mulroney	June 30, 1986–

(1) Acting. (2) Senator

Ministers of Finance

Minister	Appointed by	Term(s)
Alexander T. Galt	Macdonald	July 1, 1867–Nov. 7, 1867
John Rose	Macdonald	Nov. 8, 1867–Sept. 30, 1869
Sir Francis Hincks	Macdonald	Oct. 9, 1869–Feb. 21, 1873
Samuel Leonard Tilley	Macdonald	Feb. 22, 1873–Nov. 5, 1873
Richard John Cartwright	Mackenzie	Nov. 7, 1873–Oct. 8, 1878
Sir Samuel Leonard Tilley	Macdonald	Oct. 17, 1878–May 19, 1879
		May 20, 1879–Nov. 10, 1885
Archibald Woodbury McLelan	Macdonald	Dec. 10, 1885–Jan. 26, 1887
Sir Charles Tupper	Macdonald	Jan. 27, 1887–May 22, 1888
George Eulas Foster	Macdonald;	May 29, 1888–June 6, 1891
	Abbott;	June 16, 1891–Nov. 24, 1892
	Thompson;	Dec. 5, 1892–Dec. 12, 1894
	Bowell	Dec. 21, 1894–Jan. 5, 1896
Sir Mackenzie Bowell[1][2]	himself	Jan. 6, 1896–Jan. 14, 1896
George Eulas Foster	Bowell;	Jan. 15, 1896–Apr. 27, 1896
	Tupper	May 1, 1896–July 8, 1896
William Stevens Fielding	Laurier	July 20, 1896–Oct. 6, 1911
Sir William Thomas White	Borden	Oct. 10, 1911–Oct. 12, 1917
		Oct. 12, 1917–Aug. 1, 1919
Sir Henry Lumley Drayton	Borden;	Aug. 2, 1919–July 10, 1920
	Meighen	July 10, 1920–Dec. 29, 1921
William Stevens Fielding	King	Dec. 29, 1921–Sept. 4, 1925
James Alexander Robb	King	Sept. 5, 1925–June 28, 1926
Sir Henry Lumley Drayton[1]	Meighen	June 29, 1926–July 12, 1926
Richard B. Bennett	Meighen	July 13, 1926–Sept. 25, 1926
James Alexander Robb	King	Sept. 25, 1926–Nov. 11, 1929
Charles Avery Dunning	King	Nov. 26, 1929–Aug. 7, 1930
Richard B. Bennett	himself	Aug. 7, 1930–Feb. 2, 1932
Edgar Nelson Rhodes[2]	Bennett	Feb. 3, 1932–Oct. 23, 1935
Charles Avery Dunning	King	Oct. 23, 1935–Sept. 5, 1939
James Layton Ralston	King	Sept. 6, 1939–July 4, 1940
James Lorimer Ilsley	King	July 8, 1940–Dec. 9, 1946
Douglas Abbott	King;	Dec. 10, 1946–Nov. 15, 1948
	St. Laurent	Nov. 15, 1948–June 30, 1954
Walter Harris	St. Laurent	July 1, 1954–June 21, 1957
Donald Fleming	Diefenbaker	June 21, 1957–Aug. 8, 1962
George Nowlan	Diefenbaker	Aug. 9, 1962–Apr. 22, 1963
Walter Gordon	Pearson	Apr. 22, 1963–Nov. 10, 1965
Mitchell Sharp[1]	Pearson	Nov. 11, 1965–Dec. 17, 1965
Mitchell Sharp	Pearson	Dec. 18, 1965–Apr. 20, 1968
Edgar Benson	Trudeau	Apr. 20, 1968–Jan. 27, 1972
John Turner	Trudeau	Jan. 28, 1972–Sept. 9, 1975
Bud Drury	Trudeau	Sept.10, 1975–Sept.25, 1975
Donald Macdonald	Trudeau	Sept. 26, 1975–Sept. 15, 1977
Jean Chrétien	Trudeau	Sept. 16, 1977–June 3, 1979
John Crosbie	Clark	June 4, 1979–Mar. 2, 1980
Allan MacEachen	Trudeau	Mar. 3, 1980–Sept. 9, 1982
Marc Lalonde	Trudeau;	Sept. 10, 1982–June 29, 1984
	Turner	June 30, 1984–Sept. 16, 1984
Michael Wilson	Mulroney	Sept. 17, 1984–

(1) Acting. (2) Senator.

Ministers of Employment and Immigration

(The office of minister of employment and immigration was created Aug. 15, 1977. It superseded the office of minister of manpower and immigration which had been created Oct. 1, 1966 and abolished the office of minister of citizenship and immigration. This office had in turn superseded the office of minister of immigration and colonization which had been created by Order in Council effective Oct. 12, 1917.)

Minister	Appointed by	Term(s)
Ministers of Immigration and Colonization:		
James Alexander Calder	Borden;	Oct. 12, 1917–July 10, 1920
	Meighen	July 10, 1920–Sept. 20, 1921
John Wesley Edwards	Meighen	Sept. 21, 1921–Dec. 29, 1921
Hewitt Bostock[1] [2]	King	Jan. 3, 1922–Feb. 2, 1922
Charles Stewart[1]	King	Feb. 20, 1922–Aug. 16, 1923
James A. Robb	King	Aug. 17, 1923–Sept. 4, 1925
George Newcombe Gordon	King	Sept. 7, 1925–Nov. 12, 1925
Charles Stewart[1]	King	Nov. 13, 1925–June 28, 1926
Robert James Manion[1]	Meighen	June 29, 1926–July 12, 1926
Sir Henry Drayton[1]	Meighen	July 13, 1926–Sept. 25, 1926
Robert Forke	King	Sept. 25, 1926–Dec. 29, 1929
Charles Stewart[1]	King	Dec. 30, 1929–June 26, 1930
Ian Mackenzie	King	June 27, 1930–Aug. 7, 1930
Wesley Ashton Gordon	Bennett	Aug. 7, 1930–Feb. 2, 1932
Wesley Ashton Gordon[1]	Bennett	Feb. 3, 1932–Oct. 23, 1935
Thomas A. Crerar	King	Oct. 23, 1935–Nov. 30, 1936
Ministers of Citizenship and Immigration:		
Walter Edward Harris	St. Laurent	Jan. 18, 1950–June 30, 1954
John (Jack) Pickersgill	St. Laurent	July 1, 1954–June 21, 1957
E. Davie Fulton[1]	Diefenbaker	June 21, 1957–May 11, 1958
Ellen Fairclough	Diefenbaker	May 12, 1958–Aug. 8, 1962
Richard Albert Bell	Diefenbaker	Aug. 9, 1962–Apr. 22, 1963
Guy Favreau	Pearson	Apr. 22, 1963–Feb. 2, 1964
René Tremblay	Pearson	Feb. 3, 1964–Feb. 14, 1965
John Robert Nicholson	Pearson	Feb. 15, 1965–Dec. 17, 1965
Jean Marchand	Pearson	Dec. 18, 1965–Sept. 30, 1966
Ministers of Manpower and Immigration:		
Jean Marchand	Pearson;	Oct. 1, 1966–Apr. 20, 1968
	Trudeau	Apr. 20, 1968–July 5, 1968
Allan MacEachen	Trudeau	July 6, 1968–Sept. 23, 1970
Otto Lang	Trudeau	Sept. 24, 1970–Jan. 27, 1972
Bryce Mackasey	Trudeau	Jan. 28, 1972–Nov. 26, 1972
Robert Andras	Trudeau	Nov. 27, 1972–Sept. 13, 1976
Bud Cullen	Trudeau	Sept. 14, 1976–Aug. 14, 1977
Ministers of Employment and Immigration:		
Bud Cullen	Trudeau	Aug. 15, 1977–June 3, 1979
Ron Atkey	Clark	June 4, 1979–Mar. 2, 1980
Lloyd Axworthy	Trudeau	Mar. 3, 1980–Aug. 11, 1983
John Roberts	Trudeau;	Aug. 12, 1983–June 29, 1984
	Turner	June 30, 1984–Sept. 16, 1984
Flora MacDonald	Mulroney	Sept. 17, 1984–June 30, 1986
Benoit Bouchard	Mulroney	June 30, 1986–Mar. 31, 1988
Barbara McDougall	Mulroney	Mar. 31, 1988–

(1) Acting. (2) Senator.

Ministers of Agriculture

Minister	Appointed by	Term(s)
Jean-Charles Chapais[2]	Macdonald	July 1, 1867–Nov. 15, 1869
Christopher Dunkin	Macdonald	Nov. 16, 1869–Oct. 24, 1871
John Henry Pope	Macdonald	Oct. 25, 1871–Nov. 5, 1873
Luc Letellier de St-Just[2]	Mackenzie	Nov. 7, 1873–Dec. 14, 1876
Isaac Burpee[1]	Mackenzie	Dec. 15, 1876–Jan. 25, 1877
Charles Alphonse P. Pelletier[2]	Mackenzie	Jan. 26, 1877–Oct. 8, 1878
John Henry Pope	Macdonald	Oct. 17, 1878–Sept. 24, 1885
John Carling	Macdonald	Sept. 25, 1885–June 6, 1891
	Abbott	June 16, 1891–Nov. 24, 1892
Auguste Réal Angers[2]	Thompson	Dec. 7, 1892–Dec. 12, 1894
	Bowell	Dec. 21, 1894–July 12, 1895

Minister	Appointed by	Term(s)
Joseph Aldéric Ouimet[1]	Bowell	July 13, 1895–Dec. 20, 1895
Walter Humphries Montague	Bowell	Dec. 21, 1895–Jan. 5, 1896
Donald Ferguson[1] [2]	Bowell	Jan. 6, 1896–Jan. 14, 1896
Walter Humphries Montague	Bowell	Jan. 15, 1896–Apr. 27, 1896
	Tupper	May 1, 1896–July 8, 1896
Sydney Arthur Fisher	Laurier	July 13, 1896–Oct. 6, 1911
Martin Burrell	Borden	Oct. 16, 1911–Oct. 12, 1917
Thomas A. Crerar	Borden	Oct. 12, 1917–June 11, 1919
James Alexander Calder[1]	Borden	June 18, 1919–Aug. 11, 1919
Simon Fraser Tolmie	Borden	Aug. 12, 1919–July 10, 1920
	Meighen	July 10, 1920–Dec. 29, 1921
William Richard Motherwell	King	Dec. 29, 1921–June 28, 1926
Henry Herbert Stevens[1]	Meighen	June 29, 1926–July 12, 1926
Simon Fraser Tolmie	Meighen	July 13, 1926–Sept. 25, 1926
William Richard Motherwell	King	Sept. 25, 1926–Aug. 7, 1930
Robert Weir	Bennett	Aug. 8, 1930–Oct. 23, 1935
Thomas A. Crerar[1]	King	Oct. 25, 1935–Nov. 3, 1935
James Garfield Gardiner	King	Nov. 4, 1935–Nov. 15, 1948
	St. Laurent	Nov. 15, 1948–June 21, 1957
Douglas Harkness[1]	Diefenbaker	June 21, 1957–Aug. 6, 1957
Douglas Harkness	Diefenbaker	Aug. 7, 1957–Oct. 10, 1960
Alvin Hamilton	Diefenbaker	Oct. 11, 1960–Apr. 22, 1963
Harry William Hays	Pearson	Apr. 22, 1963–Dec. 17, 1965
John James Greene	Pearson	Dec. 18, 1965–Apr. 20, 1968
	Trudeau	Apr. 20, 1968–July 5, 1968
Bud Olson	Trudeau	July 6, 1968–Nov. 26, 1972
Eugene Whelan	Trudeau	Nov. 27, 1972–June 3, 1979
John Wise	Clark	June 4, 1979–Mar. 2, 1980
Eugene Whelan	Trudeau	Mar. 3, 1980–June 29, 1984
Ralph Ferguson	Turner	June 30, 1984–Sept. 16, 1984
John Wise	Mulroney	Sept. 17, 1984–

(1) Acting. (2) Senator.

Ministers of National Health and Welfare

    The office of minister of national health and welfare was created on July 24, 1944; that same year, the office of minister of pensions and national health was abolished. Prior to the creation of the office of minister of pensions and national health in 1928, the department of health—created in 1919—was presided over by the minister of another department. Until Sept. 21, 1921 the President of the Privy Council was designated to be *ex officio* the minister to preside over the department of health. On that date, the minister of immigration and colonization was designated to administer the department. During 1921-26 each successive minister of soldiers' civil re-establishment presided over the health department.

Minister	Appointed by	Term(s)
Ministers of Pensions and National Health:		
James Horace King[2]	King	June 11, 1928–June 18, 1930
James Layton Ralston	King	June 19, 1930–Aug. 7, 1930
Murray MacLaren	Bennett	Aug. 7, 1930–Nov. 16, 1934
Donald Sutherland	Bennett	Nov. 17, 1934–Oct. 23, 1935
Charles Gavan Power	King	Oct. 23, 1935–Sept. 18, 1939
Ian Mackenzie	King	Sept. 19, 1939–Oct. 17, 1944
Ministers of National Health and Welfare:		
Brooke Claxton	King	Oct. 18, 1944–Dec. 11, 1946
Paul Martin	King;	Dec. 12, 1946–Nov. 15, 1948
	St. Laurent	Nov. 15, 1948–June 21, 1957
Alfred Johnson Brooks	Diefenbaker	June 21, 1957–Aug. 21, 1957
Jay Waldo Monteith	Diefenbaker	Aug. 22, 1957–Apr. 22, 1963
Judy LaMarsh	Pearson	Apr. 22, 1963–Dec. 17, 1965
Allan MacEachen	Pearson;	Dec. 18, 1965–Apr. 20, 1968
	Trudeau	Apr. 20, 1968–July 5, 1968
John Munro	Trudeau	July 6, 1968–Nov. 26, 1972
Marc Lalonde	Trudeau	Nov. 27, 1972–Sept. 15, 1977
Monique Bégin	Trudeau	Sept. 16, 1977–June 3, 1979
David Crombie	Clark	June 4, 1979–Mar. 2, 1980
Monique Bégin	Trudeau;	Mar. 3, 1980–June 29, 1984
	Turner	June 30, 1984–Sept. 16, 1984
Jake Epp	Mulroney	Sept. 17, 1984–

(1) Acting. (2) Senator.

Ministers of National Defence

The statute which created the office of minister of national defence on Jan. 1, 1923 abolished the previous office of minister of militia and defence. During WW II, the offices of associate minister of national defence, minister of national defence for air, and minister of national defence for naval services were created. These offices were originally to exist only in periods of emergency, but a later statute provided for the appointment of an associate minister of national defence at any time.

Minister	Appointed by	Term(s)
Ministers of Militia and Defence:		
Sir George-Etienne Cartier	Macdonald	July 1, 1867–May 20, 1873
Hector L. Langevin[1]	Macdonald	May 21, 1873–June 30, 1873
Hugh McDonald	Macdonald	July 1, 1873–Nov. 4, 1873
William Ross	Mackenzie	Nov. 7, 1873–Sept. 29, 1874
William Berrian Vail	Mackenzie	Sept. 30, 1874–Jan. 20, 1878
Alfred Gilpin Jones	Mackenzie	Jan. 21, 1878–Oct. 8, 1878
Louis F. R. Masson	Macdonald	Oct. 19, 1878–Jan. 12, 1880
Sir Alexander Campbell[2]	Macdonald	Jan. 16, 1880–Nov. 7, 1880
Sir Joseph P.R.A. Caron	Macdonald;	Nov. 8, 1880–June 6, 1891
	Abbott	June 16, 1891–Jan. 24, 1892
Mackenzie Bowell	Abbott	Jan. 25, 1892–Nov. 24, 1892
James Colebrooke Patterson	Thompson;	Dec. 5, 1892–Dec. 12, 1894
	Bowell	Dec. 21, 1894–Mar. 25, 1895
Arthur Rupert Dickey	Bowell	Mar. 26, 1895–Jan. 5, 1896
Sir Mackenzie Bowell[1] [2]	himself	Jan. 6, 1896–Jan. 14, 1896
Alphonse Desjardins[2]	Bowell	Jan. 15, 1896–Apr. 27, 1896
David Tisdale	Tupper	May 1, 1896–July 8, 1896
Sir Frederick William Borden	Laurier	July 13, 1896–Oct. 6, 1911
Sir Samuel Hughes	Borden	Oct. 10, 1911–Oct. 12, 1916
Sir Albert Edward Kemp	Borden	Nov. 23, 1916–Oct. 12, 1917
Sydney Chilton Mewburn	Borden	Oct. 12, 1917–Jan. 15, 1920
James Alexander Calder[1]	Borden	Jan. 16, 1920–Jan. 23, 1920
Hugh Guthrie	Meighen	July 10, 1920–Dec. 29, 1921
George Perry Graham	King	Dec. 29, 1921–Dec. 31, 1922
Ministers of National Defence:		
George Perry Graham	King	Jan. 1, 1923–Apr. 27, 1923
Edward Mortimer Macdonald[1]	King	Apr. 28, 1923–Aug. 16, 1923
Edward Mortimer Macdonald	King	Aug. 17, 1923–June 28, 1926
Hugh Guthrie[1]	Meighen	June 29, 1926–July 12, 1926
Hugh Guthrie	Meighen	July 13, 1926–Sept. 25, 1926
James Alexander Robb[1]	King	Oct. 1, 1926–Oct. 7, 1926
James Layton Ralston	King	Oct. 8, 1926–Aug. 7, 1930
Donald Sutherland	Bennett	Aug. 7, 1930–Nov. 16, 1934
Grote Stirling	Bennett	Nov. 17, 1934–Oct. 23, 1935
Ian Mackenzie	King	Oct. 23, 1935–Sept. 18, 1939
Norman Rogers	King	Sept. 19, 1939–June 10, 1940
Charles Gavan Power[1]	King	June 11, 1940–July 4, 1940
James Layton Ralston	King	July 5, 1940–Nov. 1, 1944
Andrew McNaughton	King	Nov. 2, 1944–Aug. 20, 1945
Douglas Charles Abbott	King	Aug. 21, 1945–Dec. 11, 1946
Brooke Claxton	King;	Dec. 12, 1946–Nov. 15, 1948
	St. Laurent	Nov. 15, 1948–June 30, 1954
Ralph Osborne Campney	St. Laurent	July 1, 1954–June 21, 1957
George Randolph Pearkes	Diefenbaker	June 21, 1957–Oct. 10, 1960
Douglas Harkness	Diefenbaker	Oct. 11, 1960–Feb. 3, 1963
Gordon Churchill	Diefenbaker	Feb. 12, 1963–Apr. 22, 1963
Paul Hellyer	Pearson	Apr. 22, 1963–Sept. 18, 1967
Leo Cadieux	Pearson;	Sept. 19, 1967–Apr. 20, 1968
	Trudeau	Apr. 20, 1968–Sept. 16, 1970
Bud Drury	Trudeau	Sept. 17, 1970–Sept. 23, 1970
Donald Macdonald	Trudeau	Sept. 24, 1970–Jan. 27, 1972
Edgar Benson	Trudeau	Jan. 28, 1972–Aug. 31, 1972
Jean-Eudes Dube[1]	Trudeau	Sept. 1, 1972–Sept. 6, 1972
Bud Drury[1]	Trudeau	Sept. 7, 1972–Nov. 26, 1972
James Richardson	Trudeau	Nov. 27, 1972–Oct. 12, 1976
Barney Danson[1]	Trudeau	Oct. 13, 1976–Nov. 2, 1976
Barney Danson	Trudeau	Nov. 3, 1976–June 3, 1979
Allan McKinnon	Clark	June 4, 1979–Mar. 2, 1980
Gilles Lamontagne	Trudeau	Mar. 3, 1980–Aug. 11, 1983
Jean-Jacques Blais	Trudeau;	Aug. 12, 1983–June 29, 1984
	Turner	June. 30, 1984–Sept. 16, 1984
Robert Coates	Mulroney	Sept. 17, 1984–Feb. 11, 1985
Erik Nielsen	Mulroney	Feb. 27, 1985–June 30, 1986
Perrin Beatty	Mulroney	June 30, 1986–

(1) Acting. (2) Senator.

Federal and Provincial Legislative Authority

Because Canada is a federal state, legislative powers are divided between 2 levels of government: federal and provincial. (Municipal governments only exercise powers delegated to them by the provincial government).

Each level of government has a distinct sphere of authority. With a few exceptions, neither level is permitted to encroach on the legislative authority of the other.

The *Constitution Act, 1867* (formerly called the *British North America Act, 1867*) lists the classes of subject over which the federal and provincial governments have exclusive authority. The federal government, in addition to a general power to make laws for the "peace, order and good government of Canada," has exclusive power in a number of areas including criminal law, unemployment insurance, postal service, regulation of trade and commerce and defence. Matters exclusively within provincial legislative authority include property and civil rights, administration of justice, municipal institutions and matters of a merely local or private nature.

Many of the subject classes set out in the *Constitution Act, 1867* are broadly worded, and considerable debate has arisen over which level of government has authority to pass certain laws. Confusion has also arisen over the proper distribution of powers to regulate matters that could not have been foreseen by the Fathers of Confederation, such as air travel, radio and television broadcasting, etc. These difficulties have led to long political debates and frequently to court challenges which arise when a person adversely affected by a particular law claims that the law is invalid because it is *ultra vires* – beyond the powers of the level of government that enacted it. Prior to the passing of the *Constitution Act, 1982*, only statutes found to be *ultra vires* could be declared inoperative by the Constitution. Now, there is an additional restraint on the federal parliament and the provincial legislatures to comply with constitutional provisions, including the *Canadian Charter of Rights and Freedoms*.

Lieutenant-Governors of the Provinces[1]

Each of Canada's 10 provinces has a lieutenant-governor appointed by the Governor General on advice of the prime minister. The lieutenant-governor is the monarch's representative in the province and performs the same duties at the provincial level that the governor general performs at the federal level; the lieutenant-governor opens, prorogues and dissolves the provincial legislative assembly and gives royal assent to provincial legislation and provincial orders in council.

Lieutenant-governors are paid by the federal government and are usually appointed for a term of 5 years.

Province	Lieutenant-Governor	Birthdate	Date Appointed
Newfoundland	Hon. Jim McGrath	Jan. 11, 1932	July 18, 1986
Prince Edward Island	Hon. Lloyd G. MacPhail	Mar. 22, 1920	Aug. 1, 1985
Nova Scotia	Hon. Alan R. Abraham	Feb. 1, 1931	Dec. 23, 1983
New Brunswick	Hon. Gilbert Finn	Sept. 3, 1920	Aug. 20, 1987[2]
Quebec	Hon. Gilles Lamontagne	Apr. 17, 1919	Mar. 28, 1984
Ontario	Hon. Lincoln Alexander	Jan. 21, 1922	Sept. 20, 1985
Manitoba	Hon. George Johnson	Nov. 18, 1920	Dec. 12, 1986[2]
Saskatchewan	Hon. Sylvia O. Fedoruk	May 5, 1927	Sept. 7, 1988[2]
Alberta	Hon. Helen Hunley	Sept. 6, 1920	Jan. 22, 1985[2]
British Columbia	Hon. David C. Lam	July 25, 1923	Sept. 9, 1988[2]

(1) As of Sept. 1988. (2) Date installed in office.

Provincial Premiers: An Historical Listing

(as of Oct. 1988)

Source: Historical Statistics of Canada; Provincial Archives

Newfoundland

Premier	Term	Party	Elected or sworn in
Joseph R. Smallwood	1949-1972	Liberal	Apr. 1, 1949
Frank D. Moores	1972-1979	Conservative	Jan. 18, 1972
A. Brian Peckford	1979-	Conservative	Mar. 27, 1979

Prince Edward Island

Premier	Term	Party	Elected or sworn in
J. C. Pope	1873	Conservative	Apr., 1873
L. C. Owen	1873-1876	Conservative	Sept., 1873
L. H. Davies	1876-1879	Liberal (Coalition)	Aug.,1876
W. W. Sullivan	1879-1889	Conservative	Apr. 25, 1879
N. Mcleod	1889-1891	Conservative	Nov., 1889
F. Peters	1891-1897	Liberal	Apr. 27, 1891
A. B. Warburton	1897-1898	Liberal	Oct., 1897
D. Farquharson	1898-1901	Liberal	Aug., 1898
A. Peters	1901-1908	Liberal	Dec. 29, 1901
F. L. Haszard	1908-1911	Liberal	Feb. 1, 1908
H. James Palmer	1911	Liberal	May 16, 1911
John A. Mathieson	1911-1917	Conservative	Dec. 2, 1911
Aubin Arsenault	1917-1919	Conservative	June, 21, 1917

Prince Edward Island

Premier	Term	Party	Elected or sworn in
J. H. Bell	1919-1923	Liberal	Sept. 9, 1919
James D. Stewart	1923-1927	Conservative	Sept. 5, 1923
Albert C. Saunders	1927-1930	Liberal	Aug. 12, 1927
Walter M. Lea	1930-1931	Liberal	May 20, 1930
James D. Stewart	1931-1933	Conservative	Aug. 29, 1931
William J. P. MacMillan	1933-1935	Conservative	Oct. 14, 1933
Walter M. Lea	1935-1936	Liberal	Aug. 15, 1935
Thane A. Campbell	1936-1943	Liberal	Jan. 14, 1936
J. Walter Jones	1943-1953	Liberal	May 11, 1943
Alexander W. Matheson	1953-1959	Liberal	May 25, 1953
Walter Shaw	1959-1966	Conservative	Sept. 1, 1959
Alexander B. Campbell	1966-1978	Liberal	July 28, 1966
William Bennett Campbell	1978-1979	Liberal	Sept. 18, 1978
J. Angus MacLean	1979-1981	Conservative	May 3, 1979
James M. Lee	1981-1986	Conservative	Nov. 17, 1981
Joseph A. Ghiz	1986-	Liberal	May 2, 1986

Nova Scotia

Premier	Term	Party	Elected or sworn in
H. Blanchard	1867	Conservative	July 4, 1867
William Annand	1867-1875	Liberal	Nov. 7, 1867
P. C. Hill	1875-1878	Liberal	May 11, 1875
S. H. Holmes	1878-1882	Conservative	Oct. 22, 1878
John S. D. Thompson	1882	Conservative	May 25, 1882
W. T. Pipes	1882-1884	Liberal	Aug. 3, 1882
W. S. Fielding	1884-1896	Liberal	July 28, 1884
George H. Murray	1896-1923	Liberal	July 20, 1896
E. H. Armstrong	1923-1925	Liberal	Jan. 24, 1923
E. N. Rhodes	1925-1930	Conservative	July 16, 1925
Col. Gordon S. Harrington	1930-1933	Conservative	Aug. 11, 1930
Angus L. Macdonald	1933-1940	Liberal	Sept. 5, 1933
A. S. MacMillan	1940-1945	Liberal	July 10, 1940
Angus L. Macdonald	1945-1954	Liberal	Sept. 8, 1945
Harold Connolly	1954	Liberal	Apr. 13, 1954
Henry D. Hicks	1954-1956	Liberal	Sept. 30, 1954
Robert L. Stanfield	1956-1967	Conservative	Nov. 20, 1956
George Smith	1967-1970	Conservative	Sept. 13, 1967
Gerald A. Regan	1970-1978	Liberal	Oct. 28, 1970
John Buchanan	1978-	Conservative	Oct. 5, 1978

New Brunswick

Premier	Term	Party	Elected or sworn in
Andrew Wetmore	1867-1870	Conservative	1867
George King	1870-1871	Conservative	1870
George Hatheway	1871-1872	Conservative	1871
George King	1872-1878	Conservative	1872
James Fraser	1878-1882	Conservative	1878
D. L. Hannington	1882-1883	Conservative	1882
Andrew Blair	1883-1896	Liberal	1883
James Mitchell	1896-1897	Conservative	July, 1896
Henry Emmerson	1897-1900	Liberal	Oct. 29, 1897
L. J. Tweedie	1900-1907	Conservative	Aug. 31, 1900
William Pugsley	1907	Liberal	Mar. 6, 1907
Clifford Robinson	1907-1908	Liberal	May 31, 1907
John Douglas Hazen	1908-1911	Conservative	Mar. 24, 1908
James K. Flemming	1911-1914	Conservative	Oct. 16, 1911
George G. Clarke	1914-1917	Conservative	Dec. 17, 1914
James Murray	1917	Conservative	Feb. 1, 1917
Walter E. Foster	1917-1923	Liberal	Apr. 4, 1917
Peter Veniot	1923-1925	Liberal	Feb. 28, 1923
John B. M. Baxter	1925-1931	Conservative	Sept. 14, 1925
Charles D. Richards	1931-1933	Conservative	May 19, 1931
Leonard Tilley	1933-1935	Conservative	June 1, 1933
Allison Dysart	1935-1940	Liberal	July 16, 1935
John McNair	1940-1952	Liberal	Mar. 13, 1940
Hugh J. Flemming	1952-1960	Conservative	Oct. 8, 1952
Louis J. Robichaud	1960-1970	Liberal	July 12, 1960
Richard Hatfield	1970-1987	Conservative	Nov. 12, 1970
Frank McKenna	1987-	Liberal	Oct. 13, 1987

Quebec

Premier	Term	Party	Elected or sworn in
Pierre-Joseph-Olivier Chauveau ..	1867-1873	Conservative	July 15, 1867
Gédéon Ouimet	1873-1874	Conservative	Feb. 27, 1873
Charles E. Boucher deBoucherville	1874-1878	Conservative	Sept. 22, 1874
Henri Joly	1878-1879	Liberal	Mar. 8, 1878
J. Adolphe Chapleau	1879-1882	Conservative	Oct. 31, 1879
J. Alfred Mousseau	1882-1884	Conservative	July 31, 1882
John J. Ross	1884-1887	Conservative	Jan. 23, 1884
L. Olivier Taillon	1887	Conservative	Jan. 25, 1887
Honoré Mercier	1887-1891	Liberal	Jan. 29, 1887
Charles E. Boucher deBoucherville	1891-1892	Conservative	Dec. 21, 1891
L. Olivier Taillon	1892-1896	Conservative	Dec. 16, 1892
Edmund J. Flynn	1896-1897	Conservative	May 11, 1896
F. Gabriel Marchand	1897-1900	Liberal	May 24, 1897
S. Napoléon Parent	1900-1905	Liberal	Oct. 3, 1900
Lomer Gouin	1905-1920	Liberal	Mar. 23, 1905
L. Alexandre Taschereau	1920-1936	Liberal	July 9, 1920
Adélard Godbout	1936	Liberal	June 11, 1936
Maurice Duplessis	1936-1939	Union Nationale	Aug. 26, 1936
Adélard Godbout	1939-1944	Liberal	Nov. 8, 1939
Maurice Duplessis	1944-1959	Union Nationale	Aug. 30, 1944
Paul Sauvé	1959-1960	Union Nationale	Sept. 11, 1959
Antonio Barrette	1960	Union Nationale	Jan. 8, 1960
Jean Lesage	1960-1966	Liberal	July 5, 1960
Daniel Johnson	1966-1968	Union Nationale	June 16, 1966
Jean-Jacques Bertrand	1968-1970	Union Nationale	Oct. 2, 1968
Robert Bourassa	1970-1976	Liberal	May 12, 1970
René Lévesque	1976-1985	Parti Québécois	Nov. 25, 1976
Pierre-Marc Johnson	1985	Parti Québécois	Oct. 3, 1985
Robert Bourassa	1985-	Liberal	Dec. 12, 1985

Ontario

Premier	Term	Party	Elected or sworn in
J.S. Macdonald	1867-1871	Conservative	July 16, 1867
Edward Blake	1871-1872	Liberal	Dec. 20, 1871
Oliver Mowat	1872-1896	Liberal	Oct. 25, 1872
A. S. Hardy	1896-1899	Liberal	July 25, 1896
G. W. Ross	1899-1905	Liberal	Oct. 21, 1899
Sir J. P. Whitney	1905-1914	Conservative	Feb. 8, 1905
Sir William Hearst	1914-1919	Conservative	Oct. 2, 1914
E. G. Drury	1919-1923	United Farmers of Ontario	Nov. 14, 1919
G. H. Ferguson	1923-1930	Conservative	July 16, 1923
G. S. Henry	1930-1934	Conservative	Dec. 15, 1930
Mitchell F. Hepburn	1934-1942	Liberal	July 10, 1934
G. D. Conant	1942-1943	Liberal	Oct. 21, 1942
Harry S. Nixon	1943	Liberal	May 18, 1943
George Drew	1943-1948	Conservative	Aug. 17, 1943
T. L. Kennedy	1948	Conservative	Oct. 19, 1948
Leslie M. Frost	1949-1961	Conservative	May 4, 1949
John P. Robarts	1961-1971	Conservative	Nov. 8, 1961
William G. Davis	1971-1985	Conservative	Mar. 1, 1971
Frank Miller	1985	Conservative	Feb. 8, 1985
David Peterson	1985-	Liberal	June 26, 1985

Manitoba

Premier	Term	Party	Elected or sworn in
A. Boyd	1870-1871	n.a.	Sept. 16, 1870
M. A. Girard	1871-1872	Conservative	Dec. 14, 1871
J. H. Clarke	1872-1874	n.a.	Mar. 14, 1872
M. A. Girard	1874	Conservative	July 8, 1874
R. A. Davis	1874-1878	n.a.	Dec. 3, 1874
John Norquay	1878-1887	Conservative	Oct. 16, 1878
D. H. Harrison	1887-1888	Conservative	Dec. 26, 1887
T. Greenway	1888-1900	Liberal	Jan. 19, 1888
H. J. Macdonald	1900	Conservative	Jan. 8, 1900
Sir R. P. Roblin	1900-1915	Conservative	Oct. 29, 1900
T. C. Norris	1915-1922	Liberal	May 12, 1915
John Bracken	1922-1943	Coalition[1]	Aug. 8, 1922
S. S. Garson	1943-1948	Coalition	Jan. 8, 1943
D. L. Campbell	1948-1958	Liberal	Nov. 7, 1948

Manitoba

Premier	Term	Party	Elected or sworn in
Duff Roblin	1958-1967	Conservative	June 16, 1958
Walter Weir	1967-1969	Conservative	Nov. 25, 1967
Edward Schreyer	1969-1977	New Democratic	July 15, 1969
Sterling Lyon	1977-1981	Conservative	Oct. 24, 1977
Howard Pawley	1981-1988	New Democratic	Nov. 17, 1981
Gary Filmon	1988-	Conservative	Apr. 26, 1988

Saskatchewan

Premier	Term	Party	Elected or sworn in
Walter Scott	1905-1916	Liberal	Sept. 12, 1905
W. M. Martin	1916-1922	Liberal	Oct. 20, 1916
C. A. Dunning	1922-1926	Liberal	Apr. 5, 1922
J. G. Gardiner	1926-1929	Liberal	Feb. 26, 1926
J. T. M. Anderson	1929-1934	Conservative	Sept. 9, 1929
J. G. Gardiner	1934-1935	Liberal	July 19, 1934
W. J. Patterson	1935-1944	Liberal	Nov. 1, 1935
Tommy Douglas	1944-1961	C.C.F.[2]	July 10, 1944
W. S. Lloyd	1961-1964	C.C.F.-N.D.P.	Nov. 7, 1961
W. Ross Thatcher	1964-1971	Liberal	May 22, 1964
Allan E. Blakeney	1971-1982	New Democratic	June 30, 1971
Grant Devine	1982-	Conservative	May 8, 1982

Alberta

Premier	Term	Party	Elected or sworn in
Alex Rutherford	1905-1910	Liberal	Sept. 2, 1905
A. L. Sifton	1910-1917	Liberal	May 26, 1910
Charles Stewart	1917-1921	Liberal	Oct. 30, 1917
Herbert Greenfield	1921-1925	United Farmers of Alberta	Aug. 13, 1921
John E. Brownlee	1925-1934	United Farmers of Alberta	Nov. 23, 1925
Richard G. Reid	1934-1935	United Farmers of Alberta	July 10, 1934
William Aberhart	1935-1943	Social Credit	Sept. 3, 1935
E. C. Manning	1943-1968	Social Credit	May 31, 1943
Harry Strom	1968-1971	Social Credit	Dec. 12, 1968
Peter Lougheed	1971-1985	Conservative	Sept. 10, 1971
Don Getty	1985-	Conservative	Nov. 1, 1985

British Columbia

Premier	Term	Party	Elected or sworn in
J. F. McCreight	1871-1872	n.a.	Nov. 13, 1871
Amor De Cosmos	1872-1874	n.a.	Dec. 23, 1872
G. A. Walkem	1874-1876	n.a.	Feb. 11, 1874
A. C. Elliott	1876-1878	n.a.	Feb. 1, 1876
G. A. Walkem	1878-1882	n.a.	June 25, 1878
Robert Beaven	1882-1883	n.a.	June 13, 1882
William Smithe	1883-1887	n.a.	Jan. 29, 1883
A. E. B. Davie	1887-1889	n.a.	May 15, 1887
John Robson	1889-1892	n.a.	Aug. 2, 1889
Theodore Davie	1892-1895	n.a.	July 2, 1892
J. H. Turner	1895-1898	n.a.	Mar. 4, 1895
C. A. Semlin	1898-1900	n.a.	Aug. 15, 1898
Joseph Martin	1900	n.a.	Feb. 28, 1900
James Dunsmuir	1900-1902	n.a.	June 15, 1900
E. G. Prior	1902-1903	n.a.	Nov. 21, 1902
Richard McBride	1903-1905	Conservative	June 1, 1903
William J. Bowser	1915-1916	Conservative	Dec. 15, 1915
Harlan C. Brewster	1916-1918	Liberal	Nov. 23, 1916
John Oliver	1918-1927	Liberal	Mar. 6, 1918
John D. Maclean	1927-1928	Liberal	Aug. 20, 1927
Simon F. Tolmie	1928-1933	Conservative	Aug. 21, 1928
T. D. Pattullo	1933-1941	Liberal	Nov. 15, 1933
John Hart	1941-1947	Liberal[3]	Dec. 9, 1941
Byron Johnson	1947-1952	Liberal[3]	Jan. 18, 1947
W. A. C. Bennett	1952-1972	Social Credit	Aug. 1, 1952
David Barrett	1972-1975	New Democratic Party	Aug. 30, 1972
William R. Bennett	1975-1986	Social Credit	Dec. 11, 1975
Bill Vander Zalm	1986-	Social Credit	Aug. 14, 1986

(1) United Farmer/Progressive, 1922-27; Coalition, 1927-37; Liberal-Progressive, 1937-43. (2) Co-operative Commonwealth Federation. (3) Coalition; n.a. not available.

Provincial Election Results

Newfoundland

	1956	1959	1962	1966	1971	1972	1975	1979	1982	1985
Liberal	32	31	34	38	20	9	16	19	8	15
Progressive Conservative	4	3	7	4	21	33	30	33	44	36
New Democratic	–	–	–	–	–	–	–	–	–	1
Other	–	2	1	–	1	–	5	–	–	–
Size of legislature	36	36	42	42	42	42	51	52	52	52

Prince Edward Island

	1955	1959	1962	1966	1970	1974	1978	1979	1982	1985
Liberal	27	8	11	17	27	26	17	11	14	21
Progressive Conservative	3	22	19	15	5	6	15	21	18	11
Size of legislature	30	30	30	32	32	32	32	32	32	32

Nova Scotia

	1956	1960	1963	1967	1970	1974	1978	1981	1984	1988
Liberal	18	15	4	6	23	31	17	13	6	21
New Democratic[1]	1	1	–	–	2	3	4	1	3	2
Progressive Conservative[2]	24	27	39	40	21	12	31	37	42	28
Other	–	–	–	–	–	–	–	1	1	1
Size of legislature	43	43	43	46	46	46	52	52	52	52

New Brunswick

	1952	1956	1960	1963	1967	1970	1974	1978	1982	1987
Liberal	16	15	31	32	32	26	25	28	18	58
Progressive Conservative[3]	36	37	21	20	26	32	33	30	39	–
New Democratic	–	–	–	–	–	–	–	–	1	–
Size of legislature	52	52	52	52	58	58	58	58	58	58

Quebec

	1952	1956	1960	1962	1966	1970	1973	1976	1981	1985
Crédit Social	–	–	–	–	–	12	2	1	–	–
Liberal	23	20	51	63	50	72	102	26	42	99
Parti Québécois[4]	–	–	–	–	–	7	6	71	80	23
Union Nationale	68	72	43	31	56	17	–	11	–	–
Other	1	1	1	1	2	–	–	1	–	–
Size of legislature	92	93	95	95	108	108	110	110	122	122

Ontario

	1955	1959	1963	1967	1971	1975	1977	1981	1985	1987
Liberal	11	22	24	28	20	36	34	34	48	95
New Democratic[5]	3	5	7	20	19	38	33	21	25	19
Progressive Conservative[3]	84	71	77	69	78	51	58	70	52	16
Size of legislature	98	98	108	117	117	125	125	125	125	130

Manitoba

	1958	1959	1962	1966	1969	1973	1977	1981	1986	1988
Liberal	–	–	13	14	4	5	1	–	1	20
Liberal and Liberal Progressive	19	11	–	–	–	–	–	–	–	–
New Democratic[5]	11	10	7	11	28	31	23	34	30	12
Progressive Conservative[6]	26	35	36	31	22	21	33	23	26	25
Other	1	1	1	1	3	–	–	–	–	–
Size of legislature	57	57	57	57	57	57	57	57	57	57

Saskatchewan

	1952	1956	1960	1964	1967	1971	1975	1978	1982	1986
Liberal	11	14	17	33	35	15	15	–	–	1
New Democratic[7]	42	36	38	25	24	45	39	44	8	25
Progressive Conservative[8]	–	–	–	1	–	–	7	17	56	38
Other	–	3	–	–	–	–	–	–	–	–
Size of legislature	53	53	55	59	59	60	61	61	64	64

Alberta

	1952	1955	1959	1963	1967	1971	1975	1979	1982	1986
Liberal	4	15	1	2	3	–	–	–	–	4
New Democratic[1]	2	2	–	–	–	1	1	1	2	16
Progressive Conservative[6]	2	3	1	–	6	49	69	74	75	61
Social Credit	52	.37	62	60	55	24	4	4	–	–
Other	1	4	1	1	1	1	1	–	2	2
Size of legislature	61	61	65	63	65	75	75	79	79	83

British Columbia

	1956	1960	1963	1966	1969	1972	1975	1979	1983	1986[9]
Labour	1	–	–	–	–	–	–	–	–	–
Liberal	2	4	5	6	5	5	1	–	–	–
New Democratic[5]	10	16	14	16	12	38	18	26	21	20
Progressive Conservative[3]	–	–	–	–	–	2	1	–	–	–
Social Credit	39	32	33	33	38	10	35	31	35	49
Other	–	–	–	–	–	–	–	–	1	–
Size of legislature	52	52	52	55	55	55	55	57	57	69

(1) Known as the Co-operative Commonwealth Federation until 1962. (2) Known as the Conservative Party until 1946. (3) Known as the Conservative Party until 1943. (4) Formed in 1968. (5) Known as the Co-operative Commonwealth Federation until 1961. (6) Known as the Conservative Party until 1944. (7) Known as the Co-operative Commonwealth Federation until 1967. (8) Known as the Conservative Party until 1945. (9) Prior to recounting.
– = zero.

Leaders[1] of Major Provincial Political Parties

Newfoundland

Progressive Conservative Party

Noel Murphy	1962-66
G. R. Ottenheimer	1966-69
Leadership vacant	1969-70
Frank D. Moores	1970-79
A. Brian Peckford	1979-

Liberal Party

Donald Jamieson	1979-82
Len Sterling	1982-84
Stephen Neary	1984-85
Leo Barry	1985-87
Clyde Wells	1987-

New Democratic Party

Peter Fenwick	1981-

Prince Edward Island

Progressive Conservative Party

Melvin McQuaid	1973-76
Angus MacLean	1976-81
James M. Lee	1981-87
Leone Bagnall	1987-88
Melbourne Gass	1988-

Liberal Party

J. Walter Jones	1943-53
Alexander W. Matheson	1953-65
Alex Campbell	1965-78
Bennett Campbell	1978-81
Joseph Ghiz	1981-

New Democratic Party

Aquinas Ryan	1974-77
Vacant	1978-79
Douglas Murray	1979-81
David Burke	1982-83
Jim Mayne	1983-

Nova Scotia

Progressive Conservative Party[2]

Gordon S. Harrington	1930-40
Leonard Wm. Fraser	1940-46
Leadership vacant	1946-48
Robert Stanfield	1948-67
George I. Smith	1967-71
John M. Buchanan	1971-

Liberal Party

Gerald A. Regan	1965-80
A. M. (Sandy) Cameron	1980-85
Vincent J. MacLean	1985-
J. William Gillis	1985-86
Vincent J. MacLean	1986-

New Democratic Party[3]

Russell Cunningham	1945-52
Michael J. McDonald	1952-63
No member elected	1963-66
James Aitchison	1966-68
Jeremy Akerman	1968-80
Alexa McDonough	1980-

New Brunswick

Progressive Conservative Party[4]

Hugh John Flemming	1951-60
C. B. Sherwood	1960-66
Charles Van Horne	1966-69
Richard B. Hatfield	1969-87
Malcolm MacLeod	1987-

Liberal Party

Louis Robichaud	1958-71
Robert Higgins	1971-78
Joe Daigle	1978-81
Doug Young	1982-83
Frank McKenna	1985-

New Democratic Party

George Little	1980-88
Elizabeth Weir	1988-

Quebec

Parti Québecois

René Lévesque	1968-85
Pierre-Marc Johnson	1985-88
Jacques Parizeau	1988-

Parti Libéral

Georges-Emile Lapalme	1950-58
Jean Lesage	1958-70
Robert Bourassa	1970-77
Claude Ryan	1978-82
Robert Bourassa	1983-

Union Nationale

Joseph Sauvé	1959-60
J. Antonio Barrette	1960-
Daniel Johnson	1961-68
Jean-Jacques Bertrand	1968-73
R. Biron	1976-80

Ontario

Progressive Conservative Party		Liberal Party		New Democratic Party[5]	
Leslie Frost	1949-61	Farquhar Robert Oliver	1963-64	Edward B. Joliffe	1942-53
John Robarts	1961-71	Andrew E. J. Thompson	1964-66	Donald C. MacDonald	1953-70
William G. Davis	1971-85	Robert Nixon	1967-76	Stephen H. Lewis	1970-78
Frank Miller	1985-	Stuart Smith	1977-81	Michael Cassidy	1978-82
Larry Grossman	1985-87	David Peterson	1982-	Bob Rae	1982-

Manitoba

Progressive Conservative Party[6]		Liberal Party		New Democratic Party[5]	
Duff Roblin	1954-67	Robert Bend	1969-70	Lloyd Stinson	1952-60
Walter C. Weir	1967-70	Israel (Izzy) Asper	1970-75	A. Russell Paulley	1960-69
Sidney Spivak	1971-75	Charles Huband	1975-78	Edward R. Schreyer	1969-79
Sterling Lyon	1975-83	Doug Lauchlan	1980-82	Howard R. Pawley	1979-88
Gary Filmon	1983-	Sharon Carstairs	1984-	Gary Doer	1988-

Saskatchewan

Progressive Conservative Party[7]		Liberal Party		New Democratic Party[8]	
Alvin Hamilton	1949-57	A. (Hammy) McDonald	1955-60	John H. Brockelbank	1941-44
Martin Pederson	1958-68	Ross Thatcher	1961-71	Tommy Douglas	1944-61
Ed Nasserden	1969-73	Dave Steuart	1971-76	Woodrow Lloyd	1961-70
Dick Collver	1973-79	E.C. Ted Malone	1976-81	Allan Blakeney	1970-87
Grant Devine	1979-	Ralph E. Goodale	1981-88	Roy Romanow	1987

Alberta

Progressive Conservative Party[6]		Liberal Party		Social Credit		New Democratic Party[3]	
W. J. C. Cam Kirby	1958-60	J. Harper Prowse	1947-59	E. C. Manning	1943-68	Chester A. Ronning	1939-42
Ernest Watkins	1960-62	J. Walter Grant McEwan	1959-62	H. Strom	1968-73	Elmer Roper	1942-55
Milt Harradance	1962-64	David Hunter	1962-65	W. Schmidt	1973-75	Neil Reimer	1955-67
Peter Lougheed	1965-85	Mike Maccagno	1967-68	R. C. Clark	1975-80	W. Grant Notley	1968-82
Donald R. Getty	1985-	Nick Taylor	1974-	Rod Sykes	1980-82	Ray Martin	1982-

British Columbia

Social Credit		New Democratic Party	
W. A. C. Bennett	1952-72	Robert M. Strachan	1956-69
Bill Bennett	1972-86	Thomas Berger	1969-
Bill Vander Zalm	1986-	Dave Barrett	1969-84
		Bob Skelly	1984-87
		Mike Harcourt	1987-

(1) Includes up to 5 most recent leaders of the major parties. (2) Known as the Conservative Party until 1946. (3) Known as the Co-operative Commonwealth Federation until 1962. (4) Known as the Conservative Party until 1943. (5) Known as the Co-operative Commonwealth Federation until 1961. (6) Known as the Conservative Party until 1944. (7) Known as the Conservative Party until 1945. (8) Known as the Co-operative Commonwealth Federation until 1967.

Mayors of Incorporated Towns and Cities

Source: Canadian World Almanac Survey

(Population 75 000 and over as of 1986 census)[1]

City/Town	Mayor	First Elected	Re-elected	Term Expires
Brampton, Ont.	Kenneth (Ken) Whillans	Nov. 1982	1985[2]	Nov. 1988
Brantford, Ont.	Karen E. George	Sept. 1987[3]	–	Nov. 1988
Burlington, Ont.	Roland L. Bird	Nov. 1979	1980; 1982; 1985	Nov. 1988
Calgary, Alta.	Ralph Klein	Oct. 1980	1983; 1986	Oct. 1989
Cambridge, Ont.	Claudette Millar	Dec. 1969	1972; 1973; 1978; 1980; 1982; 1985	Nov. 1988
Charlottetown, P.E.I.	John E. Ready	Jan. 1987	–	Dec. 1989
Edmonton, Alta.	Laurence Decore	Oct. 1983	1986	Oct. 1989
Etobicoke, Ont.	Bruce Sinclair	Sept. 1984[3]	1985	Nov. 1988
Fredericton, N.B.	Brad Woodside	May 1986	–	May 1989
Gatineau, Que.	Robert (Bob) Labine	June 1988	–	Nov. 1991
Gloucester, Ont.	Harry Allen	Nov. 1985	–	Nov. 1988
Guelph, Ont.	John C.G. Counsell	Nov. 1985	–	Nov. 1988
Halifax, N.S.	Ron Wallace	Oct. 1980	1982; 1985	Oct. 1988

City/Town	Mayor	First Elected	Re-elected	Term Expires
Hamilton, Ont.	Robert Morrow	Nov. 1982	1985	Nov. 1988
Kitchener, Ont.	Dominic Cardillo	Nov. 1982	1985	Nov. 1988
LaSalle, Que.	Michel Leduc	Nov. 1983	1987	Nov. 1991
Laval, Que.	Claude LeFebvre	Nov. 1981	1985	Nov. 1989
London, Ont.	Thomas C. Gosnell	Nov. 1985	–	Nov. 1988
Longueuil, Que.	Roger Ferland	May 1987	–	Nov. 1990
Markham, Ont.	Carole Bell	Feb. 1984[3]	1985	Nov. 1988
Mississauga, Ont.	Hazel McCallion	Nov. 1978	1980; 1982; 1985	Nov. 1988
Montreal, Que.	Jean Doré	Nov. 1986	–	Nov. 1990
Montreal-Nord, Que.	Yves Ryan	Nov. 1963	1966; 1970; 1974; 1978; 1982; 1986	Nov. 1990
Nepean, Ont.	Benson A.J. Franklin	Nov. 1978	1980; 1982; 1985	Nov. 1988
North York, Ont.	Mel Lastman	Dec. 1972	1974; 1976; 1978; 1980; 1982; 1985	Nov. 1988
Oakville, Ont.	P. William Perras, Jr.	Nov. 1985	–	Nov. 1988
Oshawa, Ont.	Allan C. Pilkey	Nov. 1980	1982; 1985	Nov. 1988
Ottawa, Ont.	Jim Durrell	Nov. 1985	–	Nov. 1988
Quebec, Que.	Jean Pelletier	Nov. 1977	1981; 1985	Nov. 1989
Regina, Sask.	Larry P. Schneider	Oct. 1979	1982; 1985	Oct. 1988
Saint John, N.B.	Elsie E. Wayne	May 1983	1986	May 1989
Saint-Leonard, Que.	Raymond Renaud	Sept. 1984	1986	Nov. 1990
Saskatoon, Sask.	Cliff Wright	Oct. 1976	1979; 1982; 1985	Oct. 1988
Sault Ste. Marie, Ont. . . .	Joseph M. Fratesi	Nov. 1985	–	Nov. 1988
Scarborough, Ont.	Gus Harris	Nov 1978	1980; 1982; 1985	Nov. 1988
St. Catharines, Ont.	Joseph L. McCaffery	Nov. 1985	–	Nov. 1988
St. John's, Nfld.	John J. Murphy	Nov. 1981	1985[2]	Nov. 1989
Sudbury, Ont.	Peter Wong	Nov. 1982	1985	Nov. 1988
Thunder Bay, Ont.	Jack Masters	Nov. 1985	–	Nov. 1988
Toronto, Ont.	Art Eggleton	Nov. 1980	1982; 1985	Nov. 1988
Vancouver, B.C.	Gordon Campbell	Dec. 1986	–	Dec. 1988
Victoria, B.C.	Gretchen Brewin	Nov. 1985	1987	Nov. 1990
Whitehorse, Yukon	Donald W. Branigan	Feb 1979	1980; 1983; 1985	Nov. 1988
Windsor, Ont.	David Burr	Nov. 1985	–	Nov. 1988
Winnipeg, Man.	William A. Norrie	June 1979	1980; 1983; 1986	Nov. 1989
Yellowknife, N.W.T.	Pat A. McMahon	Jan. 1988	–	Nov. 1988
York, Ont.	Alan Tonks	Nov. 1982	1985	Nov. 1988

(1) Includes capital cities with less than 75 000. (2) By acclamation. (3) Appointed by Council to complete unexpired term of previous mayor.

Forms of Address-Titles to be Used in Canada

Source: Precedence of Canadian Dignitaries and Officials, Department of Secretary of State

All titles listed are for life, except those followed by an asterisk *, which indicates that the title is used only while in office.

Position	Title/Address	Salutation
Government		
Governor General of Canada	His/Her Excellency The Governor General* (address)/The Right Honourable (title)	Dear Governor General
husband/wife	His/Her Excellency*	Dear Sir/Madam
Lieutenant-Governor of a Province	His/Her Honour*, The Hon. _____, Lieutenant-Governor of the Province of _____	Dear Sir/Madam
husband/wife	His/Her Honour*	Dear Mr./Mrs.
Prime Minister of Canada	The Right Honourable _____, P.C., M.P., Prime Minister of Canada	Dear Mr./Madam Prime Minister, or Dear Prime Minister
Chief Justice of Canada	The Right Hon. The Chief Justice of Canada or The Rt. Hon. _____, P.C., Chief Justice of Canada	Dear Mr./Madam Chief Justice, or Dear Sir/Madam
Premier of a Province	The Honourable* _____, M.L.A., (use M.N.A. for Quebec, M.P.P. for Ontario) Premier (or for Quebec and Ontario – Prime Minister) of the Province of _____	Dear Sir/Madam
Privy Councillor, Member of the . . . . Federal Cabinet[1], Member of the Executive Council of a Province*	The Honourable _____, P.C. The Honourable _____, Minister of _____	Dear Mr./Mrs./Miss
Speaker of the House of Commons[2]	The Honourable* _____, Speaker of the House of Commons	Dear Sir/Madam
Senators	The Honourable _____ or if also a member of the Privy Council: Senator the Honourable	Dear Senator _____ or Dear Sir/Madam

Speaker of the Legislative Assembly of a Province	The Honourable* _____	Dear Mr./Mrs./Miss
Member of the House of Commons/	_____, Esq., M.P.	all may be addressed as
Member of a Provincial Government	_____, Esq. M.L.A.	Dear Sir/Madam, or as
	(use M.N.A. for Quebec, M.P.P. for Ontario)	Dear Mr./Mrs./Miss
Deputy Minister	Deputy Minister of _____	
	name of department	
Mayor of a Town or City	His/Her Worship Mayor _____*	Dear Sir/Madam, or
	or His/Her Worship the Mayor of _____*	Dear Mr./Madam Mayor

Diplomatic

Ambassador of a foreign country	His/Her Excellency, Ambassador of _____	Excellency, or Dear Sir/Madam, or Dear Mr./Mrs./Miss
High Commissioner of a British Commonwealth Country in Canada	His/Her Excellency, High Commissioner for _____	Your Excellency, or Dear Sir/Madam, or Dear Mr./Mrs./Miss
Canadian Ambassador (from a Canadian citizen)	_____, Esq., Canadian Ambassador to _____	Dear Sir/Madam, or Dear Ambassador, or Dear Mr./Mrs./Miss
Canadian High Commissioner (abroad)	_____, Esq., High Commissioner for Canada in _____	Dear High Commissioner, or Dear Sir/Madam, or Dear Mr./Mrs./Miss

Judiciary

The Chief Justice of Canada	The Rt. Hon. The Chief Justice of Canada or The Rt. Hon. _____, P.C., Chief Justice of Canada	Dear Sir/Madam, or Dear Mr./Madam Chief Justice
Chief Justice of a Province	The Hon. _____, Chief Justice of _____	Dear Mr./Madam Chief Justice, or Dear Sir/Madam
Judges of: The Supreme Court of Canada, Federal Court of Canada, Courts of Appeal, Courts of the Queen's Bench, Superior Court of the Province of Quebec, Supreme Courts of the Provinces, Supreme Courts of the Territories[3]	The Honourable Mr./Madam Justice _____	Dear Sir/Madam Justice _____
Judges of County and District Courts	The Honourable _____	Dear Judge _____, or Sir/Madam

Religion

Protestant

Archbishop	The Most Reverend _____, degrees, Archbishop of _____	Dear Archbishop or Most Reverend Sir/Madam
Bishop	The Most Reverend _____, degrees, Bishop of _____	Dear Bishop _____ or Rt. Reverend Sir/Madam
Minister	The Reverend _____	Reverend Sir/Madam, or Dear Mr./Mrs./Miss
Archdeacon	The Venerable The Archdeacon of _____ or The Venerable Archdeacon _____	Dear Mr./Mrs./Miss Archdeacon, or Very Reverend Sir/Madam
Dean	The Very Reverend _____, Dean of _____,	Dear Mr./Mrs./Miss/Dean, or Venerable Sir/Madam
Canon	The Reverend Canon _____	Dear Canon _____ or Reverend Sir/Madam
Moderator	The Rt. Reverend _____, degrees, Moderator of the Church	Right Reverend Sir/Madam, or Dear Dr. _____

Roman Catholic

Cardinal	His Eminence (first name), Cardinal (surname), Archbishop of _____	Your Eminence, or Dear Cardinal _____
Archbishop	The Most Reverend _____, Archbishop of _____	Most Reverend Sir, or Dear Archbishop
Bishop	The Most Reverend _____, Bishop of _____ The Rt. Reverend _____, Bishop of _____	Rt. Reverend Sir, or Dear Bishop
Monsignor	The Right Reverend _____	Rt. Reverend Monsignor, or Dear Monsignor _____
Canon	The Very Reverend _____	Very Reverend Canon, or Dear Canon _____
Priest	The Reverend _____	Reverend Sir, or Dear Father _____
Mother Superior	The Reverend Mother Superior, The Congregation of _____	Reverend Mother Superior, or Dear Mother Superior, or Dear Madam

Jewish

Chief Rabbi	The Very Reverend _____, Chief Rabbi	Dear Chief Rabbi, or Dear Sir
Rabbi	The Reverend Rabbi _____	Dear Rabbi, or Dear Sir

(1) Usually, although not always, federal Cabinet Ministers are also members of the Privy Council and thus retain the title "Honourable" for life. (2) Speakers of the House of Commons are often granted permission by the Governor General to retain the title "Honourable" after they have ceased to hold office. (3) These judges are eligible to be granted permission by the Governor General to retain the title of "Honourable" on retirement from the bench.

Provinces of Canada

Newfoundland

Capital: St. John's, metro pop. (1986) 161 901. **Date entered Confederation:** Mar. 31, 1949.
Population (Jan. 1988): 567 000; **Pop. density:** 1.5 per sq. km. **Pop. urban** (1986): 58.9%. **Language** (mother tongue, 1986): 99% English. **Religious distrib.** (1981): 63% Protestant; 36% Catholic.
Vital statistics: Rates (per 1 000 pop., 1985): **Birth:** 14.6; **Death:** male 7.1, female 5.2. **Life expectancy at birth** (1981): male 72; female 79.
Marital status (1986): 48% single; 45% married; 1% divorced and separated; 4% widowed. **Rates** (per 100 000 pop., 1985): **Marriage:** 550; **Divorce:** 97.
Geography: Total area 405 720 sq. km; **Land area** 371 690 sq. km; **Forested land** 142 000 sq. km; **Length of coastline** 19 720 km. **Climate:** ranges from subarctic in Labrador and northern tip of island to humid continental with cool summers and heavy precipitation. **Topography:** Island of Newfoundland: highlands of the Long Range Mtns. (elev. 900 m) along w. coast; barren and rocky central plateau descends to lowlands towards the n. east; coast is deeply indented with bays and fjords. Labrador: mountainous in the n.; rugged coast and interior plateau.
Economy: Gross Domestic Product (1985): $6.2 billion. **Per capita income** (1985): $10 767. **Employment distrib.** (1986): services 31%; trade 18%; manu. 12%; primary ind. 10%; govt. 11%; transp., comm. and util. 9%; construc. 6%;

finance 3%. **Unemployment rate** (1987): 18.6%. **Principal industries:** mining, manufacturing, fishing, pulp and paper, electricity production. **Value of industries** (1983 GDP in $ millions): manufacturing, 431; fishing, 116; forestry, 40; construction, 373; **Mineral production** (1986): $764 million: iron 92%; sand and gravel 2%; asbestos 2%; cement 1%; zinc 1%. **Electricity production** (1986, mwh): 40 407 174; hydro 97%. **Govt. finance: Revenue** (1984): $1 948 million. **Expenditure** (1984): **Total:** $2 233 million; education $591 million; health $461 million; social services $232 million. **Debt** (1986): $2.6 billion.
Agriculture: Farm cash receipts (1986): $44 million: poultry 27%; dairy 25%; eggs 20%; pigs 10%; nurseries 5%. **No. of farms** (1986): 415.
Education (1987-88): **No. of schools:** 583 elem. and sec.; 11 post-sec. **Enrolment:** 136 140 elem. and sec.; 14 610 post-sec.
International airports: Gander.
Provincial data: Motto: *Quaerite Prime Regnum Dei:* "Seek Ye First the Kingdom of God." **Flower:** Pitcher plant. **Bird:** none.
Politics: Premier: Brian Peckford (Prog. Cons.). **Leaders, opposition parties:** Peter Fenwick (N.D.P.), Clyde Wells (Lib.). **Date of last general election:** Apr. 2, 1985. **Lt. Governor:** Jim McGrath.

Prince Edward Island

Capital: Charlottetown, metro pop. (1986) 15 776. **Date entered Confederation:** July 1, 1873.
Population (Jan. 1988): 128 000; **Pop. density:** 22.6 per sq. km. **Pop. urban** (1986): 38.1%. **Language** (mother tongue, 1986): 94% English; 4% French. **Religious distrib.** (1981): 50% Protestant; 47% Catholic.
Vital statistics: Rates (per 1 000 pop., 1985): **Birth:** 15.8; **Death:** male 10.1, female 7.4. **Life expectancy at birth** (1981): male 73; female 80.
Marital status (1986): 46% single; 45% married; 3% divorced and separated; 6% widowed. **Rates** (per 100 000 pop., 1985): **Marriage:** 750; **Divorce:** 1 676.
Geography: Total area 5 660 sq. km; **Land area** 5 660 sq. km; **Forested land** 3 000 sq. km; **Length of coastline** 1 107 km. **Climate:** humid continental with temperatures moderated by maritime location. **Topography:** flat through gently rolling hills; sharply indented coastline; many streams but only small rivers and lakes.
Economy: Gross Domestic Product (1985): $1.3 billion. **Per capita income** (1985): $10 321. **Employment distrib.** (1986): services 37%; trade 17%; agr. 12%; govt. 10%; manu. 8%. **Unemployment rate** (1987): 13.3%. **Principal**

industries: agriculture, tourism, fisheries, light manufacturing. **Value of industries** (1983 GDP in $ millions): manufacturing, 79; fishing, 30; forestry, 0.2; construction, 56; **Mineral production** (1986): $1.7 million: sand and gravel 100%. **Electricity production** (1986, mwh): 11 868: steam 84%. **Govt. finance: Revenue** (1984): $442 million. **Expenditure** (1984): **Total:** $435 million; education $104 million; health $96 million; social services $50 million. **Debt** (1986): $169 million.
Agriculture: Farm cash receipts (1986): $193 million: potatoes 33%; dairy 16%; cattle 17%; pigs 13%; tobacco 5%. **No. of farms** (1986): 2 458.
Education (1987-88): **No. of schools:** 74 elem. and sec.; 3 post-sec. **Enrolment:** 24 660 elem. and sec.; 2 950 post-sec.
International airports: none.
Provincial data: Motto: *Parva Sub Ingenti:* "The small under the protection of the great." **Flower:** Lady's slipper. **Bird:** Blue Jay.
Politics: Premier: Joseph Ghiz (Lib.). **Leaders, opposition parties:** Melbourne Gass (Prog. Cons.) Jim Mayne (NDP). **Date of last general election:** Apr. 21, 1986. **Lt. Governor:** Lloyd G. MacPhail.

Nova Scotia

Capital: Halifax, metro pop. (1986) 295 990. **Date entered Confederation:** July 1, 1867.
Population (Jan. 1988): 881 000; **Pop. density:** 16.7 per sq. km. **Pop. urban** (1986): 54.0%. **Language** (mother tongue, 1986): 93% English; 4% French. **Religious distrib.** (1981): 58% Protestant; 37% Catholic.

Vital statistics: Rates (per 1 000 pop., 1985): **Birth:** 14.1; **Death:** male 9.3, female 7.4. **Life expectancy at birth** (1981): male 71; female 78.
Marital status (1986): 44% single; 47% married; 4% divorced and separated; 6% widowed. **Rates** (per 100 000 pop., 1985): **Marriage:** 770; **Divorce:** 265.

Geography: Total area 55 490 sq. km; **Land area** 52 840 sq. km; **Forested land** 41 000 sq. km; **Length of coastline** 5 934 km. **Climate:** humid continental with some moderating effects due to maritime location. **Topography:** Atlantic Uplands are segmented by river valleys; Cape Breton Is. rises from lowland in the s. to a high plateau; many rivers, lakes and jagged coastline.

Economy: Gross Domestic Product (1985): $11.6 billion. **Per capita income** (1985): $13 181. **Employment distrib.** (1986): services 32%; trade 20%; manu. 13%; govt. 9%; transp., comm. and util. 8%; construc. 6%; finance 5%; primary ind. 5%; agr. 2%. **Unemployment rate** (1987): 12.5%. **Principal industries:** manufacturing, fishing, mining, tourism, agriculture, forestry. **Value of industries** (1983 GDP in $ millions): manufacturing, 1 099; fishing, 192; forestry, 27; construction, 518; **Mineral production** (1986): $356.7 million: coal 49%; gypsum 14%; cement 6%; stone 6%; sand and gravel 7%. **Electricity production** (1986,

mwh): 7 411 398: steam 86%; hydro 14%. **Govt. finance: Revenue** (1984): $2.6 billion. **Expenditure** (1984): **Total:** $2.9 billion; education $697 million; health $734 million; social services $301 million. **Debt** (1986): $3.0 billion.

Agriculture: Farm cash receipts (1986): $267.3 million: dairy 30%; pigs 13%; poultry 11%; cattle 10%; eggs 7%. **No. of farms** (1986): 3 170.

Education (1987-88): **No. of schools:** 580 elem. and sec.; 25 post-sec. **Enrolment:** 172 400 elem. and sec.; 26 230 post-sec.

International airports: Halifax

Provincial data: Motto: *Munit Haec et Altera Vincit:* "One defends and the other conquers." **Flower:** Mayflower. **Bird:** none.

Politics: Premier: John M. Buchanan (Prog. Cons.). **Leaders, opposition parties:** Vincent J. MacLean (Lib.), Alexa McDonough (NDP). **Date of last general election:** Sept. 6, 1988. **Lt. Governor:** Alan R. Abraham.

New Brunswick

Capital: Fredericton, metro pop. (1986) 44 352. **Date entered Confederation:** July 1, 1867.

Population (Jan. 1988): 712 000; **Pop. density:** 9.9 per sq. km. **Pop. urban** (1986): 49.4%. **Language** (mother tongue, 1986): 96% English; 32% French. **Religious distrib.** (1981): 54% Catholic; 43% Protestant.

Vital statistics: Rates (per 1 000 pop., 1985): **Birth:** 14.1; **Death:** male 8.4, female 6.2. **Life expectancy at birth** (1981): male 71; female 79.

Marital status (1986): 44% single; 47% married; 4% divorced and separated; 5% widowed. **Rates** (per 100 000 pop., 1985): **Marriage:** 740; **Divorce:** 189.1.

Geography: Total area 73 440 sq. km; **Land area** 72 090 sq. km; **Forested land** 65 000 sq. km; **Length of coastline** 1 524 km. **Climate:** humid continental climate except along the shores where there is a marked maritime effect. **Topography:** northern upland; rolling central plateau; southern lowland plain with many rivers.

Economy: Gross Domestic Product (1985): $8.8 billion. **Per capita income** (1985): $12 244. **Employment distrib.** (1986): services 33%; trade 19%; manu. 13%; transp., comm. and util. 9%; govt. 9%; construc. 6%; primary 4%; finance 4%; agr. 2%. **Unemployment rate** (1987): 13.2%.

Principal industries: manufacturing, fishing, mining, forestry, pulp and paper. **Value of industries** (1983 GDP in $ millions): manufacturing, 953; fishing, 55; forestry, 138; construction, 337; **Mineral production** (1986): $526 million: zinc 39%; silver 10%; lead 10%; coal 5%; cement 2%; copper 3%; stone 2%. **Electricity production** (1986, mwh): 12 191 723: nuclear 43%; steam 31%; hydro 26%. **Govt. finance: Revenue** (1984): $2.3 billion. **Expenditure** (1984): **Total:** $2.5 billion; education $590 million; health $577 million; social services $331 million. **Debt** (1986): $2.2 billion.

Agriculture: Farm cash receipts (1986): $221.4 million: dairy 24%; potatoes 19%; poultry 11%; pigs 10%; cattle 10%. **No. of farms** (1986): 2 776.

Education (1987-88): **No. of schools:** 468 elem. and sec.; 12 post-sec. **Enrolment:** 139 400 elem. and sec.; 17 360 post-sec.

International airports: none.

Provincial data: Motto: *Spem Reduxit:* "Hope was restored." **Flower:** Purple Violet. **Bird:** Chickadee.

Politics: Premier: Frank McKenna (Lib.). **Leaders, opposition parties:** Malcolm MacLeod (Prog. Cons.), Elizabeth Weir (NDP). **Date of last general election:** Oct. 13, 1987. **Lt. Governor:** Gilbert Finn.

Quebec

Capital: Quebec, metro pop. (1986) 603 267. **Date entered Confederation:** July 1, 1867.

Population (Jan. 1988): 6 619 000; **Pop. density:** 4.9 per sq. km. **Pop. urban** (1986): 77.9%. **Language** (mother tongue, 1986): 81% French; 9% English; 2% Italian. **Religious distrib.** (1981): 88% Catholic; 6% Protestant; 2% Jewish; 1% Eastern Orthodox; 1% Eastern non-Christian.

Vital statistics: Rates (per 1 000 pop., 1985): **Birth:** 13.1; **Death:** male 8.0, female 5.9. **Life expectancy at birth** (1981): male 71; female 79.

Marital status (1986): 43% single; 47% married; 5% divorced and separated; 5% widowed. **Rates** (per 100 000 pop., 1985): **Marriage:** 560; **Divorce:** 240.

Geography: Total area 1 540 680 sq. km; **Land area** 1 356 790 sq. km; **Forested land** 940 000 sq. km; **Length of coastline** 10 839 km. **Climate:** varies from subarctic to continental. **Topography:** lowlands along the St. Lawrence R. valley separate the Laurentian Mtns. to the n. and the Appalachian Mtns. to the s.; Canadian Shield landscape dominates north.

Economy: Gross Domestic Product (1985): $108 625 million. **Per capita income** (1985): $16 441. **Employment distrib.** (1986): services 33%; manu. 20%; trade 18%; transp., comm. and util. 8%; govt. 7%; finance 5%; construc. 5%; agr. 3%; primary ind. 2%. **Unemployment rate** (1987):

10.3%. **Principal industries:** manufacturing, agriculture, electricity production, mining, meat processing, petroleum refining. **Value of industries** (1983 GDP in $ millions): manufacturing, 17 588; fishing, 40; forestry, 340; construction, 3 264; **Mineral production** (1986): $2.3 billion: gold 21%; asbestos 10%; cement 9%; stone 7%; copper 6%; zinc 2%. **Electricity production** (1986, mwh): 148 260 909: hydro 97%; nuclear 3%. **Govt. finance: Revenue** (1984): $26.3 billion. **Expenditure** (1984): **Total:** $27 billion; education $6.5 billion; health $5.5 billion; social services $6 billion. **Debt** (1986): $10.0 billion.

Agriculture: Farm cash receipts (1986): $3.2 billion: dairy 31%; pigs 21%; poultry 8%; cattle 7%; corn 4%. **No. of farms** (1986): 37 160.

Education (1987-88): **No. of schools:** 2 852 elem. and sec.; 87 post-sec. **Enrolment:** 1 154 720 elem. and sec.; 278 800 post-sec.

International airports: Dorval; Mirabel.

Provincial data: Motto: *Je me souviens:* "I remember." **Flower:** Fleur de Lis (Madonna Lily). **Bird:** Alouette (lark).

Politics: Premier: Robert Bourassa (Lib.). **Leaders, opposition parties:** Jacques Parizeau (Parti Quebecois). **Date of last general election:** Dec. 2, 1985. **Lt. Governor:** Gilles Lamontagne.

Ontario

Capital: Toronto, metro pop. (1986) 3 427 168. **Date entered Confederation:** July 1, 1867.
Population (Jan. 1988): 9 373 000; **Pop. density:** 10.5 per sq. km. **Pop. urban** (1986): 82.1%. **Language** (mother tongue, 1986): 76% English; 5% French; 3% Italian. **Religious distrib.** (1981): 52% Protestant; 36% Catholic; 2% Eastern Orthodox; 2% Jewish.
Vital statistics: Rates (per 1 000 pop., 1985): **Birth:** 14.6; **Death:** male 8.0, female 6.7. **Life expectancy at birth** (1981): male 72; female 79.
Marital status (1986): 42% single; 48% married; 5% divorced and separated; 5% widowed. **Rates** (per 100 000 pop., 1985): **Marriage:** 800; **Divorce:** 230.
Geography: Total area 1 068 580 sq. km; **Land area** 891 190 sq. km; **Forested land** 807 000 sq. km; **Length of coastline** 1 210 km. **Climate:** ranges from humid continental in south to subarctic in far north; westerly winds bring winter storms; the Great Lakes moderate winter temperatures. **Topography:** Rugged, rocky Canadian Shield plateau is broken by lowlands around Great Lakes, St. Lawrence R. and Hudson Bay.
Economy: Gross Domestic Product (1985): $184.3 billion. **Per capita income** (1985): $20 183. **Employment distrib.** (1986): services 31%; manu. 22%; trade 17%; transp., comm. and util. 7%; govt. 6%; finance 6%; construc. 5%; agr. 3%; primary ind. 1%. **Unemployment rate** (1987): 6.1%. **Principal industries:** manufacturing, finance, con-

struction, tourism, agriculture, forestry. **Value of industries** (1983 GDP in $ millions): manufacturing, 35 132; fishing, 19; forestry, 383; construction, 4 904; **Mineral production** (1986): $4.8 billion: nickel 17%; gold 15%; copper 12%; uranium 10%; zinc 8%; cement 6%; sand and gravel 4%; stone 4%; salt 3%. **Electricity production** (1986, mwh): 125 224 281: nuclear 46%; hydro 33%; steam 20%. **Govt. finance: Revenue** (1984): $23.7 billion. **Expenditure** (1984): **Total:** $26.1 billion; education $5.2 billion; health $7.8 billion; social services $4 billion. **Debt** (1986): $21.2 billion.
Agriculture: Farm cash receipts (1986): $5.5 billion: cattle 19%; dairy 17%; pigs 12%; corn 6%; poultry 6%. **No. of farms** (1986): 63 253.
Education (1987-88): **No. of schools:** 5 391 elem. and sec.; 52 post-sec. **Enrolment:** 1 876 560 elem. and sec.; 276 600 post-sec.
International airports: Pearson (Toronto); Ottawa.
Provincial data: Motto: *Ut Incepit Fidelis Sic Permanet:* "Loyal she began, loyal she remains." **Flower:** White trillium. **Bird:** Common Loon.
Politics: Premier: David Peterson (Lib.). **Leaders, opposition parties:** Andy Brandt (Prog. Cons.-interim leader); Bob Rae (NDP). **Date of last general election:** Sept. 10, 1987. **Lt. Governor:** Lincoln Alexander.

Manitoba

Capital: Winnipeg, metro pop. (1986) 625 304. **Date entered Confederation:** July 15, 1870.
Population (Jan. 1988): 1 082 000; **Pop. density:** 2.0 per sq. km. **Pop. urban** (1986): 72.1%. **Language** (mother tongue, 1986): 71% English; 6% German; 4% French; 4% Ukrainian. **Religious distrib.** (1981): 57% Protestant; 31% Catholic; 2% Eastern Orthodox; 2% Jewish.
Vital statistics: Rates (per 1 000 pop., 1985): **Birth:** 16.0; **Death:** male 9.2, female 7.2. **Life expectancy at birth** (1981): male 72; female 79.
Marital status (1986): 44% single; 47% married; 4% divorced and separated; 6% widowed. **Rates** (per 100 000 pop., 1985): **Marriage:** 780; **Divorce:** 216.
Geography: Total area 649 950 sq. km; **Land area** 548 360 sq. km; **Forested land** 349 000 sq. km; **Length of coastline** 917 km. **Climate:** continental with seasonal extremes. **Topography:** the land rises gradually south and west from Hudson Bay; flat plateau through south central region; countless lakes, streams and bogs.
Economy: Gross Domestic Product (1985): $17 993 million. **Per capita income** (1985): $16 764. **Employment distrib.** (1986): services 32%; trade 18%; manu. 12%; transp., comm. and util. 10%; agr. 9%; govt. 8%; finance 5%; construc. 5%; primary ind. 2%. **Unemployment rate** (1987):

7.4%. **Principal industries:** manufacturing, agriculture, slaughtering and meat processing, mining. **Value of industries** (1983 GDP in $ millions): manufacturing, 1 635; fishing, 10; forestry, 15; construction, 496; **Mineral production** (1986): $7.6 billion: nickel 34%; copper 19%; oil 12%; zinc 9%; cement 6%; gold 5%. **Electricity production** (1986, mwh): 24 051 907: hydro 99%. **Govt. finance: Revenue** (1984): $3.5 billion. **Expenditure** (1984): **Total:** $4 billion; education $835 million; health $1 billion; social services $510 million. **Debt** (1986): $3.3 billion.
Agriculture: Farm cash receipts (1986): $2.1 billion: wheat 23%; cattle 14%; pigs 11%; canola-rapeseed 6%; barley 6%. **No. of farms** (1986): 25 262.
Education (1987-88): **No. of schools:** 838 elem. and sec.; 16 post-sec. **Enrolment:** 219 500 elem. and sec.; 23 430 post-sec.
International airports: Winnipeg.
Provincial data: Motto: none. **Flower:** Prairie Crocus. **Bird:** none.
Politics: Premier: Gary Filmon (Prog. Cons.). **Leaders, opposition parties:** Sharon Carstairs (Lib.), Gary Doer (NDP). **Date of last general election:** April 26, 1988. **Lt. Governor:** George Johnson.

Saskatchewan

Capital: Regina, metro pop. (1986) 186 521. **Date entered Confederation:** Sept. 4, 1905.
Population (Jan. 1988): 1 011 000; **Pop. density:** 1.8 per sq. km. **Pop. urban** (1986): 61.4%. **Language** (mother tongue, 1986): 81% English; 4% German; 2% French. **Religious distrib.** (1981): 57% Protestant; 31% Catholic; 2% Eastern Orthodox; 2% Jewish.
Vital statistics: Rates (per 1 000 pop., 1985): **Birth:** 17.8; **Death:** male 9.0, female 6.7. **Life expectancy at birth** (1981): male 72; female 80.
Marital status (1986): 44% single; 47% married; 4% divorced and separated; 5% widowed. **Rates** (per 100 000 pop., 1985): **Marriage:** 700; **Divorce:** 189.
Geography: Total area 652 330 sq. km; **Land area** 570 700 sq. km; **Forested land** 178 000 sq. km; **Climate:** continental, with cold winters and hot summers. **Topography:** gently roll-

ing plains through south; higher, hilly plateaus in the s.w.; north is rugged Canadian Shield.

Economy: Gross Domestic Product (1985): $17 297 million. **Per capita income** (1985): $16 961. **Employment distrib.** (1986): services 30%; trade 18%; govt. 7%; transp., comm. and util. 7%; manu. 5%; construc. 5%; finance 5%; primary ind. 3%. **Unemployment rate** (1987): 7.3%. **Principal industries:** agriculture, mining, meat processing, electricity production, petroleum refining. **Value of industries** (1983 GDP in $ millions): manufacturing, 703; fishing, 2; forestry, 37; construction, 848; **Mineral production** (1986): $2.6 billion: oil 49%; uranium 17%; natural gas 5%; coal 4%. **Electricity production** (1986, mwh): 11 913 362: steam 68%; hydro 32%. **Govt. finance: Revenue** (1984): $3.6 billion. **Expenditure** (1984): **Total:** $3.9 billion; education $593 million; health $957 million; social services $512 million. **Debt** (1986): $631 million.

Agriculture: Farm cash receipts (1986): $4 billion: wheat 35%; cattle 10%; canola-rapeseed 7%; barley 6%; pigs 3%. **No. of farms** (1986): 60 809.

Education (1987-88): **No. of schools:** 1 034 elem. and sec.; 7 post-sec. **Enrolment:** 215 470 elem. and sec.; 25 170 post-sec.

International airports: none.

Provincial data: Motto: none. **Flower:** Western Red Lily. **Bird:** Prairie sharp-tailed grouse.

Politics: Premier: Grant Devine (Prog. Cons.). **Leaders, opposition parties:** Roy Romanow (NDP), vacant (Lib.). **Date of last general election:** Oct. 20, 1986. **Lt. Governor:** Sylvia O. Fedoruk.

Alberta

Capital: Edmonton, metro pop. (1986) 785 465. **Date entered Confederation:** Sept. 1, 1905.

Population (Jan. 1988): 2 385 000; **Pop. density:** 3.7 per sq. km. **Pop. urban** (1986): 79.4%. **Language** (mother tongue, 1986): 81% English; 3% German; 2% French. **Religious distrib.** (1981): 56% Protestant; 28% Catholic; 2% Eastern Orthodox; 2% Eastern non-Christian.

Vital statistics: Rates (per 1 000 pop., 1985): **Birth:** 18.6; **Death:** male 6.4, female 4.8. **Life expectancy at birth:** male 72; female 79.

Marital status (1986): 44% single; 47% married; 5% divorced and separated; 4% widowed. **Rates** (per 100 000 pop., 1985). **Marriage:** 840; **Divorce:** 345.

Geography: Total area 661 190 sq. km; **Land area** 644 390 sq. km; **Forested land** 349 000 sq. km. **Climate:** great variance in temperatures between regions and seasons; summer highs between 16°C and 32°C; winters as low as −45°C. **Topography:** Rocky Mtns. in s.w. to rolling prairie throughout southern region; far north is a forested plateau.

Economy: Gross Domestic Product (1985): $62 billion. **Per capita income** (1985): $26 084. **Employment distrib.** (1986): services 33%; trade 19%; transp., comm. and util. 8%; manu. 8%; agr. 8%; govt. 7%; primary ind. 6%; construc. 6%; finance 5%. **Unemployment rate** (1987): 9.6%.

Principal industries: oil production, mining, agriculture, beef ranching, manufacturing, construction. **Value of industries** (1983 GDP in $ millions): manufacturing, 3 265; fishing, 0.6; forestry, 37; construction, 3 218; **Mineral production** (1986): $8 billion: oil 46%; natural gas 35%; sulphur 5%; coal 3%. **Electricity production** (1986, mwh): 34 716 353: steam 90%; hydro 5%; gas turbine 5%. **Govt. finance: Revenue** (1984): $13.5 billion. **Expenditure** (1984): **Total:** $12 363 million; education $2.1 billion; health $2.9 billion; social services $1.2 billion. **Debt** (1986): $ + 18.7 billion (surplus).

Agriculture: Farm cash receipts (1986): $3.6 billion: cattle 31%; wheat 12%; canola-rapeseed 8%; pigs 7%; dairy products 6%. **No. of farms** (1986): 51 743.

Education (1987-88): **No. of schools:** 1 715 elem. and sec.; 25 post-sec. **Enrolment:** 475 300 elem. and sec.; 70 830 post-sec.

International airports: Edmonton; Calgary.

Provincial data: Motto: *Fortis et Liber:* "Strong and free." **Flower:** Wild Rose. **Bird:** Great horned owl.

Politics: Premier: Donald Getty (Prog. Cons.). **Leaders, opposition parties:** Ray Martin (NDP), Nick Taylor (Lib.). **Date of last general election:** May 8, 1986. **Lt. Governor:** Helen Hunley.

British Columbia

Capital: Victoria, metro pop. (1986) 255 547. **Date entered Confederation:** July 20, 1871.

Population (Jan. 1988): 2 961 000; **Pop. density:** 3.2 per sq. km. **Pop. urban** (1986): 79.2%. **Language** (mother tongue, 1986): 81% English; 3% Chinese; 3% German; 1% French. **Religious distrib.** (1981): 55% Protestant; 20% Catholic; 3% Eastern non-Christian; 1% Eastern Orthodox.

Vital statistics: Rates (per 1 000 pop., 1985): **Birth:** 14.9; **Death:** male 8.2, female 6.5. **Life expectancy at birth:** male 73; female 80.

Marital status (1986): 41% single; 48% married; 6% divorced and separated; 5% widowed. **Rates** (per 100 000 pop., 1985): **Marriage:** 770; **Divorce:** 288.

Geography: Total area 947 800 sq. km; **Land area** 929 730 sq. km; **Forested land** 600 000 sq. km; **Length of coastline** 17 856 km. **Climate:** maritime with mild temperatures and abundant rainfall in the coastal areas; continental climate with temperature extremes in the interior and northeast. **Topography:** mostly mountainous; deep river valleys and gorges, except for the n.e. area which is an extension of the Great Plains; indented coast with numerous bays and islands.

Economy: Gross Domestic Product (1985): $54 billion. **Per capita income** (1985): $18 665. **Employment distrib.** (1986): services 35%; trade 19%; manu. 12%; transp., comm. and util. 9%; govt. 7%; finance 7%; construc. 5%;

primary ind. 4%; agr. 2%. **Unemployment rate** (1987): 12.0%. **Principal industries:** forestry, mining, tourism, agriculture, fishing, manufacturing. **Value of industries** (1983 GDP in $ millions): manufacturing, 5 870; fishing, 146; forestry, 1 305; construction, 2 296; **Mineral production** (1986): $3.4 billion: coal 29%; copper 20%; natural gas 13%; oil 8%; zinc 5%; gold 4%. **Electricity production** (1986, mwh): 50 772 515: hydro 96%; steam 3%. **Govt. finance: Revenue** (1984): $9.6 billion. **Expenditure** (1984): **Total:** $10.6 billion; education $2.1 billion; health $3 billion; social services $1.7 billion. **Debt** (1986): $1.7 billion.

Agriculture: Farm cash receipts (1986): $1 billion: dairy products 23%; cattle 13%; poultry 10%; fruits 10%; vegetables 8%. **No. of farms** (1986): 13 699.

Education (1987-88): **No. of schools:** 1 889 elem. and sec.; 26 post-sec. **Enrolment:** 525 700 elem. and sec.; 59 090 post-sec.

International airports: Vancouver; Victoria.

Provincial data: Motto: *Splendor Sine Occasu:* "Splendor without Diminishment." **Flower:** Dogwood. **Bird:** none.

Politics: Premier: Bill Vander Zalm (Soc. Cred.). **Leaders, opposition parties:** Michael Harcourt (NDP). **Date of last general election:** Oct. 22, 1986. **Lt. Governor:** David C. Lam.

Yukon

Capital: Whitehorse, metro pop. (1986) 15 199. **Date entered Confederation:** June 13, 1898.

Population (Jan. 1988): 25 000; **Pop. density:** .05 per sq. km. **Pop. urban** (1986): 64.6%. **Language** (mother tongue, 1986): 88% English; 2% French.

Vital statistics: Rates (per 1 000 pop., 1985): **Birth:** 20.4; **Death:** male 7.2, female 3.5.

Marital status (1986): 48% single; 44% married; 6% divorced and separated; 2% widowed. **Rates** (per 100 000 pop., 1985): **Marriage:** 810; **Divorce:** 421.

Geography: Total area 483 450 sq. km; **Land area** 478 970 sq. km; **Forested land** 242 000 sq. km; **Length of coastline** 343 km. **Climate:** great variance in temperatures; warm summers, very cold winters; low precipitation. **Topography:**

main feature is the Yukon plateau with 21 peaks exceeding 3 300 m; open tundra in the far north.
Economy: Gross Domestic Product[1] (1985): $2 billion. **Per capita income** (1985)[1]: $27 284. **Principal industries:** mining, tourism. **Value of industries**[1] (1983 GDP in $ millions): manufacturing, 13.6; fishing, 0.8; construction, 343.5; **Mineral production** (1986): $183.5 million: gold 36%; zinc 37%; lead 13%. **Electricity production** (1986, mwh): 337 537: hydro 93%; internal combustion 7%. **Govt. finance: Revenue**[1] (1984): $761 million. **Expenditure**[1] (1984): **Total:** $694 million; education $121 million; health

$78 million; social services $43 million. **Debt** (1986): $ + 87 million (surplus).
Education (1987-88): **No. of schools:** 25 elem. and sec.; 1 post-sec. **Enrolment:** 4 900 elem. and sec.; 50 post-sec.
International airports: none.
Flower: Fireweed. **Bird:** Common Raven.
Politics: Commissioner: Ken McKinnon; **Govt. Leader:** Tony Penikett (NDP). **Leaders, opposition parties:** Jim McLachlan (Lib.—interim leader), Willard Phelps (Prog. Cons.) **Date of last general election:** May 13, 1985.

Northwest Territories

Capital: Yellowknife, metro pop. (1986) 11 753. **Date entered Confederation:** July 15, 1870.
Population (Jan. 1988): 52 000; **Pop. density:** .02 per sq. km. **Pop. urban** (1986): 46.3%. **Language** (mother tongue, 1986): 54% English; 28% Inuktitut; 2% French.
Vital statistics: Rates (per 1 000 pop., 1985): **Birth:** 28.2; **Death:** male 5.5, female 2.8.
Marital status (1986): 57% single; 38% married; 3% divorced and separated; 2% widowed. **Rates** (per 100 000 pop., 1985): **Marriage:** 450; **Divorce:** 141.
Geography: Total area 3 426 320 sq. km; **Land area** 3 293 020 sq. km; **Forested land** 615 000 sq. km; **Length of coastline** 111 249 km. **Climate:** extreme temperatures and low precipitation; arctic and sub-arctic. **Topography:** mostly tundra plains formed on the rocks of the Canadian Shield; the Mackenzie Lowland is a continuation of the Great Plains; the Mackenzie River Valley is forested.

(1) Includes Northwest Territories and Yukon.

Economy: Gross Domestic Product[1] (1985): $2 019 million. **Per capita income** (1985)[1]: $27 284. **Principal industries:** mining, mineral and oil and gas exploration; oil refining. **Value of industries**[1] (1983 GDP in $ millions): manufacturing, 13.6; fishing, 0.8; construction, 343.5; **Mineral production** (1986): $789.8 million: zinc 44%; gold 28%; oil 14%. **Electricity production** (1986, mwh): 534 899: hydro 65%; internal combustion 35%. **Govt. finance: Revenue** (1984)[1]: $761 million. **Expenditure**[1] (1984): **Total:** $694 million; education $121 million; health $78 million; social services $43 million. **Debt** (1986): $ + 149 million (surplus).
Education (1987-88): **No. of schools:** 75 elem. and sec.; 1 post-sec. **Enrolment:** 13 100 elem. and sec.; 250 post-sec.
International airports: none.
Flower: Mountain Avens. **Bird:** none.
Politics: Commissioner: John Parker; **Govt. Leader:** Dennis Patterson. **Date of last general election:** Oct. 5, 1987.

Lifetime Migration of Canadian-Born Population[1]

Source: Statistics Canada

(thousands)

This table shows the movement, from province to province, of persons born in Canada. For example, of 662 500 Canadians born in Newfoundland, 530 400 still live there while 69 600 have moved to Ontario.

Province of Residence

Province of birth	Nfld	PEI	NS	NB	Que	Ont	Man	Sask	Alta	BC	YT	NWT	Total (prov. of birth)
Newfoundland	530.4	1.0	19.0	5.5	8.3	69.6	3.0	1.4	13.9	9.4	0.3	0.8	662.5
Prince Edward Island	0.7	98.4	8.2	5.5	2.8	18.8	0.8	0.8	5.5	3.6	0.1	0.1	145.4
Nova Scotia	5.7	5.4	684.1	28.4	14.3	118.7	5.8	3.3	28.3	28.4	0.4	0.8	923.7
New Brunswick	2.2	3.3	24.4	570.6	49.9	80.0	3.8	2.0	19.4	16.8	0.3	0.5	773.2
Quebec	2.8	1.7	13.4	21.0	5 603.9	314.2	9.2	6.1	47.9	52.6	0.7	1.3	6 074.9
Ontario	10.0	5.2	35.6	23.8	134.1	5 643.7	46.2	29.3	170.8	173.3	2.7	3.5	6 278.3
Manitoba	0.6	0.3	3.3	2.0	9.8	92.3	727.0	41.6	87.0	129.7	1.1	2.8	1 097.7
Saskatchewan	0.3	0.3	2.6	1.3	6.3	75.5	48.9	746.0	195.3	201.8	1.6	2.1	1 281.8
Alberta	0.6	0.6	3.5	1.8	6.6	47.5	13.0	28.6	1 195.7	205.3	2.6	3.4	1 509.1
British Columbia . . .	0.6	0.4	3.7	1.6	6.1	46.1	5.4	12.4	79.6	1 254.9	3.3	1.4	1 419.5
Yukon	. . .	. . .	0.2	0.1	0.2	1.0	0.2	0.3	1.9	4.1	7.0	0.2	15.1
Northwest Territories.	0.1	. . .	0.1	. . .	0.8	1.1	0.4	0.9	3.6	2.0	0.2	25.8	35.1
Total (prov. of residence)	554.0	116.7	798.1	661.8	5 843.1	6 508.5	867.7	872.8	1 848.8	2 082.0	20.2	42.8	20 216.3

(1) As of June 1981.
. . . = too small to be included.

Population

Population of Provinces and Territories

Source: Censuses of Canada

(thousands of persons)

	Canada	Nfld	PEI	NS	NB	Que	Ont	Man	Sask	Alta	BC	YT	NWT
1867	3 463	n.a.	88	364	271	1 123	1 525	15	*	*	32	*	45
1871	3 689	n.a.	94	388	286	1 191	1 621	25	*	*	36	*	48
1881	4 325	n.a.	109	441	321	1 360	1 927	62	*	*	49	*	56
1891	4 833	n.a.	109	450	321	1 489	2 114	153	*	*	98	*	99
1901	5 371	n.a.	103	460	331	1 649	2 183	255	91	73	179	27	20
1911	7 207	n.a.	94	492	352	2 006	2 527	461	492	374	393	9	7
1921	8 788	n.a.	89	524	388	2 361	2 934	610	756	589	525	4	8
1931	10 377	n.a.	88	513	408	2 875	3 432	700	922	732	694	4	9
1941	11 507	n.a.	95	578	457	3 332	3 788	730	896	796	818	5	12
1951	14 009	361	98	643	516	4 056	4 598	777	832	940	1 165	9	16
1961	18 238	458	105	737	598	5 259	6 236	922	925	1 332	1 629	15	23
1971	21 568	522	112	789	635	6 028	7 703	988	926	1 628	2 185	18	35
1981	24 343	568	123	847	696	6 438	8 625	1 026	968	2 238	2 744	23	46
1986	25 354[1]	568	127	873[1]	710[1]	6 540[1]	9 114[1]	1 071[1]	1 010[1]	2 375[1]	2 889[1]	24	52
1988[2]	25 796	567	128	881	712	6 619	9 373	1 082	1 011	2 385	2 961	25	52

(1) Includes estimates, rather than actual counts, for the population of some Indian reserves and settlements which were not completely enumerated.
(2) Estimate as of Jan. 1
n.a. not available. * Included with the Northwest Territories.

Canadian Population Growth Components

Source: Statistics Canada

(thousands)

Census period	Population growth	Births	Deaths	Natural increase[1]	Immigration	Emigration	Net migration[2]	Total population[3]
1851-1861	793	1 281	670	611	352	170	182	3 230
1861-1871	460	1 370	760	610	260	410	−150	3 689
1871-1881	636	1 480	790	690	350	404	− 54	4 325
1881-1891	508	1 524	870	654	680	826	−146	4 833
1891-1901	538	1 548	880	668	250	380	−130	5 371
1901-1911	1 835	1 925	900	1 025	1 550	740	810	7 207
1911-1921	1 581	2 340	1 070	1 270	1 400	1 089	311	8 788
1921-1931	1 589	2 420	1 060	1 360	1 200	970	230	10 377
1931-1941	1 130	2 294	1 072	1 222	149	241	− 92	11 507
1941-1951	2 503	3 212	1 220	1 992	548	382	166	14 009
1951-1956	2 071	2 106	633	1 473	783	185	598	16 081
1956-1961	2 157	2 362	687	1 675	760	378	482	18 238
1961-1966	1 777	2 249	731	1 518	539	280	259	20 015
1966-1971	1 553	1 856	766	1 090	890	427	463	21 568
1971-1976	1 424	1 758	823	934	841	352	489	22 993
1976-1981	1 349	1 820	842	978	588	217	371	24 343
1981-1986[4]	1 247	1 874	886	988	500	241	259	25 588

(1) Births minus deaths. (2) Immigration minus emigration. (3) At the end of the census period. (4) Preliminary estimates.

Net Interprovincial Migration[1]

Source: Statistics Canada

	Nfld	PEI	NS	NB	Que	Ont	Man	Sask	Alta	BC	Yukon	NWT
1961-1966 .	− 15 213	−2 969	−27 124	−25 680	− 19 859	85 369	−23 471	−42 094	−1 983	77 747	−1 706	−3 017
1966-1971 .	− 19 344	−2 763	−16 396	−19 599	−122 736	150 712	−40 690	−81 399	32 005	114 964	1 781	3 465
1971-1976 .	− 1 857	3 754	11 307	16 801	− 77 610	−38 560	−26 827	−40 752	58 571	92 285	988	1 900
1976-1981 .	− 18 983	− 829	−7 140	−10 351	−156 496	−57 826	−42 218	−9 716	186 364	122 625	− 933	−4 497
1981-1982 ..	− 5 693	− 856	−1 936	−2 842	− 25 790	−5 665	−2 625	− 323	36 562	8 705	81	382
1982-1983 ..	1 829	636	3 791	3 554	− 24 678	23 585	2 544	3 580	− 11 650	−1 489	−1 653	−49
1983-1984 ..	− 2 026	797	3 804	1 792	− 17 417	36 400	339	2 133	− 31 986	6 636	− 435	−37
1984-1985 ..	− 3 445	250	2 557	− 678	− 8 020	33 885	− 595	− 1 425	− 20 771	−1 969	− 223	434
1985-1986 ..	− 5 716	− 76	−1 321	−1 891	− 5 349	33 562	−2 297	−6 939	− 3 831	−4 501	− 545	−1 096
1981-1986 .	− 15 051	751	6 895	−65	− 81 254	121 767	−2 634	−2 974	− 31 676	7 382	−2 775	−366
1986-1987[3] ..	− 4 950	− 232	− 288	−2 536	− 3 686	45 278	−3 097	−7 142	− 29 731	7 609	548	−1 773

(1) Represents the number of persons moving into a province minus the number of persons moving out of that province. (2) Preliminary estimate.

Population of Metro[1] Areas in Canada

Source: Censuses of Canada

	Population (000s)					Average annual % population change			
	1951	1961	1971	1981	1986	1951-61	1961-71	1971-81	1981-86
Calgary, Alta.	142.3	279.1	403.3	592.6	671.3[2]	9.6	4.5	4.7	2.7
Chicoutimi-Jonquière, Que.	91.2	127.6	133.7	135.2	158.5	4.0	0.5	0.1	3.4
Edmonton, Alta.	193.6	359.8	495.7	656.9	785.5[2]	8.6	3.8	3.3	3.9
Halifax, N.S.	138.4	193.4	222.6	277.7	296.0	4.0	1.5	2.5	1.3
Hamilton, Ont.	281.9	401.1	498.5	542.1	557.0	4.2	2.4	0.9	0.5
Kitchener, Ont.	107.5	154.9	226.8	287.8	311.2	4.4	4.6	2.7	1.6
London, Ont.	167.7	226.7	286.0	283.7	342.3	3.5	2.6	-0.1	4.1
Montreal, Que.	1 539.3	2 215.6	2 743.2	2 828.3	2 921.4[2]	4.4	2.4	0.3	0.7
Oshawa, Ont.	n.a.	n.a.	120.3	154.2	203.5	n.a.	n.a.	2.8	6.4
Ottawa-Hull, Ont.-Que.	311.6	457.0	602.5	718.0	819.3	4.7	3.2	1.9	2.8
Quebec, Que.	289.3	379.1	480.5	576.0	603.3	3.1	2.7	2.0	0.9
Regina, Sask.	72.7	113.7	140.7	164.3	186.5	5.6	2.4	1.7	2.7
St. Catharines-Niagara, Ont.	189.0	257.8	303.4	304.4	343.3	3.6	1.8	. . .	2.6
St. John's, Nfld.	80.9	106.7	131.8	154.8	161.9	3.2	2.4	1.7	0.9
Saint John, N.B.	80.7	98.1	106.7	114.0	121.3	2.2	0.9	0.7	1.3
Saskatoon, Sask.	55.7	95.6	126.4	154.2	200.7	7.2	3.2	2.2	6.0
Sudbury, Ont.	80.5	127.4	155.4	149.9	148.9	5.8	2.2	-0.4	-0.1
Thunder Bay, Ont.	73.7	102.1	112.1	121.4	122.2	3.9	1.0	0.8	0.1
Toronto, Ont.	1 261.9	1 919.4	2 628.0	2 998.7	3 427.2	5.2	3.7	1.4	2.9
Trois-Rivières, Que.	46.1	53.5	55.9	111.4	128.9	1.6	0.4	9.9	3.1
Vancouver, B.C.	586.2	826.8	1 082.4	1 268.1	1 380.8	4.1	3.1	1.7	1.8
Victoria, B.C.	114.9	155.8	195.8	233.5	255.6[2]	3.6	2.6	1.9	1.9
Windsor, Ont.	182.6	217.2	258.6	246.1	254.0	1.9	1.9	-0.5	0.6
Winnipeg, Man.	357.2	476.5	540.3	584.8	625.3	3.3	1.3	0.8	1.4

(1) For census metropolitan areas, which include neighboring municipalities from which the major urban centre draws its work force.
(2) Includes estimates of Indian reserves and settlements.
. . . = too small to be included; n.a. not available.

Population of Canadian Cities

(with 50 000+ population in 1986)

Source: Censuses of Canada

	Year incorporated[1]	Population (000s)					Average annual % population change		
		1966	1971	1976	1981	1986	1966-76	1976-81	1981-6
Beauport, Que.	1976	11.7	14.7	55.3	60.4	62.9	37.3	1.8	0.8
Brampton, Ont.	1974	36.3	41.2	103.5	149.0	188.5	18.5	8.8	5.3
Brantford, Ont.	1877	59.9	64.4	67.0	74.3	76.1	1.2	2.2	0.5
Brossard, Que.	1958	11.9	23.5	37.6	52.2	57.4	21.6	7.8	2.0
Burlington, Ont.	1974	65.9	87.0	104.3	114.9	116.7	5.8	2.0	0.3
Calgary, Alta.	1893	330.6	403.3	469.9	592.7	636.1	4.2	5.2	1.5
Cambridge, Ont.	1973	n.a.	64.8	72.4	77.2	79.9	n.a.	1.3	0.7
Charlesbourg, Que.	1976	24.9	33.4	63.1	68.3	69.0	15.3	1.6	0.2
Chicoutimi, Que.	1976	32.5	33.9	57.7	60.1	61.0	7.8	0.8	0.3
Coquitlam, B.C.[2]	1891	40.9	53.1	55.5	61.1	69.3	3.6	2.0	2.7
Dartmouth, N.S.	1961	58.7	64.8	65.3	62.3	65.2	1.1	-0.9	0.9
Delta, B.C.[2]	1879	20.7	45.9	64.5	74.7	79.6	21.2	3.2	1.3
East York, Ont.[3]	1967	74.2	104.8	107.0	102.0	101.1	4.4	-0.9	-0.2
Edmonton, Alta.	1904	376.9	438.2	461.4	532.2	574.0	2.2	3.1	1.6
Etobicoke, Ont.	1983	219.5	282.7	297.1	298.7	303.0	3.5	0.1	0.3
Gatineau, Que.	1975	17.7	22.3	73.5	75.0	81.2	31.5	0.4	1.7
Gloucester, Ont.	1981	23.2	37.1	56.5	72.9	89.8	14.4	5.8	4.6
Guelph, Ont.	1879	51.4	60.1	67.5	71.2	78.2	3.1	1.1	2.0
Halifax, N.S.	1841	86.8	122.0	117.9	114.6	113.6	3.6	-0.6	-0.2
Hamilton, Ont.	1846	298.1	309.2	312.0	306.4	306.7	0.5	-0.4	. . .
Hull, Que.	1875	60.2	63.6	61.0	56.2	58.7	0.1	-1.6	0.9
Jonquière, Que.	1976	29.7	28.4	60.7	60.4	58.5	10.4	-0.1	-0.6
Kamloops, B.C.	1973	10.8	26.2	58.3	64.0	61.8	44.0	2.0	-0.7
Kelowna, B.C.	1973	17.0	19.4	52.0	59.2	61.2	20.6	2.8	0.7
Kingston, Ont.	1846	59.0	59.0	56.0	52.6	55.0	-0.5	-1.2	0.9
Kitchener, Ont.	1912	93.3	111.8	131.9	139.7	150.6	4.1	1.2	1.6
Langley, B.C.[2]	1873	15.8	21.9	36.7	44.6	53.4	13.2	4.3	3.9
LaSalle, Que.	1958	48.3	72.9	76.7	76.3	75.6	5.9	-0.1	-0.2
Laval, Que.	1965	196.1	228.0	246.2	268.3	284.1	2.6	1.8	1.2

Town or City	Year incorporated[1]	Population (000s) 1966	1971	1976	1981	1986	Average annual % population change 1966-76	1976-81	1981-6
Lethbridge, Alta.	1906	37.2	41.2	46.8	54.1	58.8	2.6	3.1	1.7
London, Ont.	1855	194.4	223.2	240.4	254.3	269.1	2.4	1.2	1.2
Longueil, Que.	1920	25.6	97.6	122.4	124.3	125.4	37.8	0.3	0.2
Markham, Ont.[4]	1971	7.8	36.7	56.2	77.0	114.6	62.1	7.4	9.8
Matsqui, B.C.[2]	1892	16.2	23.6	31.2	42.0	51.4	9.2	6.9	4.5
Mississauga, Ont.	1974	93.5	156.1	250.0	315.1	374.0	16.7	5.2	3.7
Moncton, N.B.	1973	45.8	47.9	55.9	54.7	55.5	2.2	-0.4	0.3
Montreal, Que.	1832	1 222.3	1 214.4	1 080.5	980.4	1 015.4	-1.2	-1.9	0.7
Montreal-Nord, Que.	1959	67.8	89.1	97.3	94.9	90.3	4.4	-0.5	-1.0
Nepean, Ont.	1978	43.9	64.6	76.9	84.4	95.5	7.5	2.0	2.6
Niagara Falls, Ont.	1903	56.9	67.2	69.4	71.0	72.1	2.2	0.5	0.3
North Bay, Ont.	1925	23.6	49.2	51.6	51.3	50.6	11.9	-0.1	-0.3
North Vancouver, B.C.[2]	1891	48.1	57.9	63.5	65.4	68.2	3.2	0.6	0.9
North York, Ont.[4]	1979	399.5	504.2	558.4	559.5	556.3	4.0	...	-0.1
Oakville, Ont.[4]	1857	52.8	61.5	69.0	75.8	87.1	3.1	2.0	3.0
Oshawa, Ont.	1924	78.1	91.6	107.0	117.5	123.7	3.7	2.0	1.1
Ottawa, Ont.	1854	290.7	302.3	304.5	295.2	300.8	0.5	-0.6	0.4
Peterborough, Ont.	1905	56.2	58.1	59.7	60.6	61.0	0.6	0.3	0.1
Prince George, B.C.	1915	24.5	33.1	59.9	67.6	67.6	14.4	2.6	...
Quebec, Que.	1832	167.0	186.1	177.1	166.5	164.6	0.6	-1.2	-0.2
Red Deer, Alta.	1913	26.2	27.7	32.2	46.4	54.4	2.3	8.8	3.4
Regina, Sask.	1903	131.1	139.5	149.6	162.6	175.0	1.4	1.7	1.5
Richmond, B.C.[2]	1879	50.5	62.1	80.0	96.1	108.5	5.8	4.0	2.6
Saanich, B.C.[2]	1906	58.8	65.0	73.4	78.7	82.9	2.5	1.4	1.1
Saint-Hubert, Que.	1958	17.2	21.7	49.7	60.6	66.2	18.9	4.4	1.8
Saint John, N.B.	1785	51.6	89.0	86.0	80.5	76.4	6.7	-1.3	-1.0
Saint-Laurent, Que.	1955	59.5	63.0	64.4	65.9	67.0	0.8	0.5	0.3
Saint-Leonard, Que.	1963	25.3	52.0	78.5	79.4	75.9	21.0	0.2	-0.9
Sainte-Foy, Que.	1955	48.3	68.4	71.2	68.9	69.6	4.7	-0.6	0.2
St. Catharines, Ont.	1876	97.1	109.7	123.4	124.0	123.5	2.7	0.1	-0.1
St. John's, Nfld.	1888	79.9	88.1	86.6	83.8	96.2	0.1	-0.6	3.0
Sarnia, Ont.	1914	54.6	57.6	55.6	50.9	49.0	0.2	-1.7	-0.7
Saskatoon, Sask.	1906	115.9	126.4	133.8	154.2	177.6	1.5	3.0	3.0
Sault Ste. Marie, Ont.	1912	74.6	80.3	81.0	82.7	80.9	0.9	0.4	-0.4
Scarborough, Ont.	1983	278.4	334.3	387.1	443.4	484.7	3.9	2.9	1.9
Sherbrooke, Que.	1875	75.7	80.7	76.8	74.1	74.3	0.1	-0.7	0.1
Sudbury, Ont.	1930	84.9	90.5	97.6	91.8	88.7	1.5	-1.2	-0.7
Surrey, B.C.[2]	1879	81.8	98.6	116.5	147.1	181.4	4.2	5.3	4.7
Thunder Bay, Ont.	1970	104.5	108.4	111.5	112.5	112.3	0.7	0.2	...
Toronto, Ont.	1834	664.6	712.8	633.3	599.2	612.3	-0.5	-1.1	0.4
Trois-Rivières, Que.	1857	57.5	55.9	52.5	50.5	50.1	-0.9	-0.8	-0.2
Vancouver, B.C.	1886	410.4	426.3	410.2	414.3	431.1	...	0.2	0.8
Vaughan, Ont.[4]	1971	n.a.	15.9	17.8	29.7	65.1	n.a.	13.4	23.8
Verdun, Que.	1912	76.8	74.7	68.0	61.3	60.2	-1.1	-2.0	-0.4
Victoria, B.C.	1862	57.5	61.8	62.6	64.4	66.3	0.9	0.6	0.6
Waterloo, Ont.	1948	29.9	36.7	46.6	49.4	58.7	5.6	1.2	3.8
Windsor, Ont.	1892	192.5	203.3	196.5	192.1	193.1	0.2	-0.4	0.1
Winnipeg, Man.[5]	1873	257.0	246.2	560.9	564.5	594.6	11.8	0.1	1.1
York, Ont.	1983	134.7	147.3	141.4	134.6	135.4	0.5	-1.0	0.1

(1) As a city, unless otherwise indicated by footnote. (2) District Municipality. (3) Borough. (4) Town. (5) Includes St. James-Assiniboia, Man.
. . . = too small to be included; n.a. not available.

Population of Canadian Towns and Cities

(5 000 and over)

Source: Censuses of Canada

Town or city classification is made according to the official designations adopted by provincial or federal authority. Population by mother tongue is rounded to the nearest 5. *Indicates a city; all others are towns.

Town or City	Population 1981	1986	Area[1] (sq. km)	Mother Tongue[2] English	French	Other
			Newfoundland			
Carbonear	5 335	5 337	11.81	5 315	5	15
Channel-Port aux Basques	5 988	5 901	37.43	5 960	5	20
Conception Bay South	10 856	15 531	59.70	10 815	15	25
Corner Brook*	24 339	22 719	147.37	24 080	50	210
Gander	10 404	10 207	101.16	10 225	100	85
Grand Falls	8 765	9 121	29.72	8 655	15	80

Town or City	Population 1981	Population 1986	Area[1] (sq. km)	Mother Tongue[2] English	Mother Tongue[2] French	Other
Happy Valley-Goose Bay	7 103	7 248	306.42	6 990	110	90
Labrador City	11 538	8 664	6.47	10 785	535	215
Marystown	6 299	6 660	62.99	6 270	15	15
Mount Pearl	11 543	20 293	25.29	11 440	15	85
St. John's*	83 770	96 216	101.59	82 085	335	1 335
Stephenville	8 876	7 994	34.81	8 660	145	70
Windsor	5 747	5 545	26.94	5 735	5	10

Prince Edward Island

Town or City	1981	1986	Area	English	French	Other
Charlottetown*	15 282	15 776	6.99	14 675	315	290
Summerside	7 828	8 020	4.31	7 115	680	30

Nova Scotia

Town or City	1981	1986	Area	English	French	Other
Amherst	9 864	9 671	15.29	9 245	305	130
Antigonish	5 205	5 291	5.01	4 920	115	175
Bedford	6 777	8 010	39.79	6 370	160	245
Bridgewater*	6 669	6 617	13.35	6 455	90	125
Dartmouth*	62 277	65 243	58.58	58 850	1 830	1 595
Glace Bay	21 466	20 467	23.15	21 135	90	125
Halifax*	114 594	113 577	79.76	106 280	3 525	4 790
Kentville	4 974	5 208	17.12	n.a.	n.a.	n.a.
New Glasgow	10 464	10 022	10.36	10 125	130	210
New Waterford	8 808	8 326	5.26	8 415	290	110
North Sydney	7 820	7 472	5.38	7 700	50	50
Stellarton	5 435	5 259	8.55	5 310	55	70
Sydney*	29 444	27 754	23.49	28 050	440	955
Sydney Mines	8 501	8 063	10.91	8 435	30	40
Truro	12 552	12 124	38.09	12 205	95	255
Yarmouth	7 475	7 617	11.14	6 625	780	70

New Brunswick

Town or City	1981	1986	Area	English	French	Other
Bathurst*	15 705	14 683	90.94	8 115	7 445	145
Campbellton*	9 818	9 073	17.30	4 820	4 870	130
Chatham	6 779	6 219	10.36	6 115	590	70
Dalhousie	4 958	5 363	13.25	n.a.	n.a.	n.a.
Dieppe	8 511	9 084	52.90	2 425	6 055	35
Edmunston*	12 044	11 497	34.58	1 180	10 805	55
Fredericton*	43 723	44 352	129.58	39 805	2 605	1 315
Grand Falls (Grand-Sault)	6 203	6 209	17.73	1 110	5 060	40
Moncton*	55 743	55 468	141.09	35 950	17 945	850
Newcastle	6 284	5 804	14.09	5 755	480	50
Oromocto	9 064	9 656	22.26	8 250	650	160
Quispamsis	6 022	7 185	38.91	5 615	320	90
Riverview	14 907	15 638	34.26	13 765	985	155
Sackville	5 654	5 470	74.42	5 305	290	60
Saint John*	80 521	76 381	322.88	74 165	4 970	1 390
St. Stephen	5 120	5 032	12.35	4 920	155	45

Quebec

Town or City	1981	1986	Area	English	French	Other
Alma*	26 322	25 923	109.27	335	25 915	70
Amos*	9 421	9 261	108.05	155	9 195	75
Ancienne-Lorette*	12 935	13 747	7.87	215	12 630	90
Anjou*	37 346	36 916	13.65	3 130	30 600	3 615
Arthabaska*	6 827	7 244	8.94	60	6 735	35
Asbestos*	7 967	6 961	13.47	235	7 695	40
Aylmer*	26 695	28 976	91.21	9 845	15 835	1 010
Baie-Comeau*	12 866	26 244	352.27	505	12 280	85
Beaconsfield*	19 613	19 301	10.64	13 815	3 780	2 020
Beauharnois*	7 025	6 519	40.44	225	6 780	20
Beauport*	60 477	62 869	71.33	765	59 365	320
Bécancour*	10 247	10 472	434.29	100	10 070	75
Belœil*	17 540	17 958	24.01	1 140	16 150	245
Black Lake*	5 148	4 824	41.39	60	5 065	25
Blainville*	14 682	16 175	55.20	615	13 475	590
Boisbriand*	13 471	14 360	27.32	635	12 025	815
Boucherville*	29 704	31 116	69.33	1 230	27 850	625
Brossard*	52 232	57 441	44.98	9 845	35 780	6 610
Buckingham*	7 992	8 820	14.46	1 490	6 435	70
Candiac*	8 502	9 096	16.47	1 580	6 560	360
Cap-de-la-Madeleine*	32 626	32 800	17.30	610	31 875	140
Cap-Rouge*	8 492	12 101	6.39	285	8 095	115
Chambly*	12 190	12 869	25.06	1 575	10 310	300
Charlemagne*	4 827	5 331	1.76	n.a.	n.a.	n.a.

Town or City	Population 1981	Population 1986	Area[1] (sq. km)	Mother Tongue[2] English	Mother Tongue[2] French	Mother Tongue[2] Other
Charlesbourg*	68 326	68 996	67.36	1 155	66 610	560
Charny*	8 240	9 123	8.76	200	8 005	35
Châteauguay*	36 928	37 865	35.40	11 710	23 225	1 990
Chibougamau*	10 732	9 922	754.08	405	10 155	175
Chicoutimi*	60 064	61 083	156.66	655	59 085	320
Coaticook*	6 271	6 440	12.50	360	5 870	40
Côte-Saint-Luc*	27 531	28 592	7.21	17 720	2 555	7 255
Cowansville*	12 240	11 643	50.58	2 130	9 945	155
Deux-Montagnes*	9 944	10 531	6.05	3 670	5 950	325
Dolbeau*	8 766	8 554	46.36	85	8 640	40
Dollard-des-Ormeaux*	39 940	43 089	15.05	23 140	10 065	6 735
Donnacona*	5 731	5 435	20.12	105	5 610	15
Dorion*	5 749	5 469	3.70	785	4 855	110
Dorval*	17 722	17 354	20.64	10 130	6 080	1 510
Drummondville*	27 347	36 020	31.01	580	26 570	200
Farnham*	6 498	6 102	24.70	515	5 940	45
Gaspé*	17 261	17 350	1 105.11	2 970	14 265	25
Gatineau*	74 988	81 244	272.11	6 750	67 040	1 200
Granby*	38 069	38 508	72.60	1 885	35 755	430
Grand-mère*	15 442	14 582	71.13	355	15 000	85
Greenfield Park*	18 527	18 290	4.58	8 200	8 420	1 900
Hampstead*	7 598	7 451	1.77	5 480	850	1 270
Hull*	56 225	58 722	37.07	3 910	49 760	2 555
Iberville*	8 587	8 547	4.90	225	8 300	60
Ile-Perrot*	5 945	6 586	4.87	775	5 030	140
Joliette*	16 987	16 845	22.14	245	16 570	170
Jonquière*	60 354	58 467	209.63	1 255	58 845	255
Kirkland*	10 476	13 376	10.34	5 940	3 050	1 480
L'Assomption*	3 457	5 280	2.07	n.a.	n.a.	n.a.
La Baie*	20 935	20 753	261.69	760	20 120	60
La Prairie*	10 627	11 072	43.54	440	9 750	440
La Sarre*	8 861	8 622	148.30	75	8 750	30
La Tuque*	11 556	10 723	22.25	355	11 100	100
Lac-Mégantic*	6 119	5 732	20.21	110	6 000	15
Lachenaie*	8 631	10 177	42.79	230	8 315	80
Lachine*	37 521	34 906	17.38	11 455	22 875	3 195
Lachute*	11 729	11 586	96.24	2 005	9 580	135
LaSalle*	76 299	75 621	16.42	25 320	39 340	11 640
Lauzon*	13 362	13 620	16.40	165	13 165	30
Laval*	268 335	284 164	245.40	28 450	216 820	23 060
Le Gardeur*	8 312	9 230	44.00	160	8 090	55
LeMoyne*	6 137	5 634	.96	455	5 575	105
Lévis*	17 895	18 310	16.70	200	17 635	60
Longueuil*	124 320	125 441	42.68	6 845	112 150	5 320
Loretteville*	15 060	14 335	6.94	465	14 490	100
Lorraine*	6 881	7 334	5.46	1 040	5 645	200
Magog*	13 604	13 530	15.26	1 200	12 325	80
Maniwaki*	5 424	5 168	6.64	480	4 905	35
Mascouche*	20 345	21 285	107.95	1 270	18 795	280
Matane*	13 612	13 243	24.35	110	13 455	45
Mercier*	6 352	7 264	45.89	380	5 825	150
Mirabel*	14 080	13 875	492.26	420	13 550	110
Mistassini*	6 682	6 734	248.38	30	6 640	15
Mont-Joli*	6 359	6 670	9.11	70	6 285	—
Mont-Laurier*	8 405	7 937	82.05	90	8 275	40
Mont-Royal*	19 247	18 350	7.43	8 755	7 205	3 290
Mont-Saint-Hilaire*	10 066	10 588	48.17	1 140	8 695	225
Montmagny*	12 405	11 958	125.77	85	12 290	35
Montréal*	980 354	1 015 420	176.90	146 980	643 580	189 795
Montréal-Nord*	94 914	90 303	11.03	6 080	74 445	14 385
Montréal-Ouest*	5 514	5 382	1.63	4 215	460	835
Noranda*	8 767	8 870	32.48	1 010	7 385	370
Outremont*	24 338	23 080	3.68	3 360	15 920	5 055
Pierrefonds*	38 390	39 605	24.40	17 205	17 000	4 185
Pincourt*	8 750	9 121	8.27	3 355	5 055	340
Plessisville*	7 249	7 042	4.34	50	7 145	55
Pointe-Claire*	24 571	26 026	19.19	17 015	5 355	2 200
Port-Cartier*	8 191	6 858	74.47	290	7 805	95
Québec*	166 474	164 580	88.86	4 450	159 910	2 115
Repentigny*	34 419	40 778	24.42	800	33 230	385
Rimouski*	29 120	29 672	75.68	265	28 725	125
Rivière-du-Loup*	13 459	13 321	16.94	125	13 260	75
Roberval*	11 429	11 448	147.05	60	11 330	35
Rock Forest*	12 283	12 210	51.41	475	11 720	90
Rosemère*	7 778	8 673	10.20	2 540	4 820	420
Rouyn*	17 224	17 319	30.79	585	16 455	185
Roxboro*	6 292	6 138	2.23	2 880	2 620	795
Saint-Antoine*	7 012	7 691	9.84	130	6 835	45

Town or City	Population 1981	Population 1986	Area[1] (sq. km)	Mother Tongue[2] English	French	Other
Saint-Basile-le-Grand*	7 658	8 852	34.83	525	6 970	165
Saint-Bruno-de-Montarville*	22 880	23 103	41.79	4 910	17 080	890
Saint-Constant*	9 938	12 508	57.02	600	9 120	225
Saint-David-de-L'Auberivière*	5 380	5 769	10.90	45	5 315	20
Saint-Eustache*	29 716	32 226	70.03	2 150	27 150	415
Saint-Félicien*	9 058	9 324	167.90	75	8 965	20
Saint-Georges*	10 342	11 723	19.01	150	10 140	55
Saint-Georges-Ouest*	6 378	6 352	5.93	70	6 295	5
Saint-Hubert*	60 573	66 218	63.22	8 785	48 970	2 820
Saint-Hyacinthe*	38 246	38 603	36.63	415	37 525	310
Saint-Jean-Chrysostome*	6 930	8 797	82.90	90	6 815	20
Saint-Jean-sur-Richelieu*	35 640	34 745	47.40	1 810	33 015	815
Saint-Jérôme*	25 123	23 316	15.79	460	24 390	275
Saint-Lambert*	20 557	20 030	6.42	6 925	12 460	1 170
Saint-Laurent*	65 900	67 002	46.28	21 550	28 695	15 660
Saint-Léonard*	79 249	75 947	12.93	7 020	42 475	29 935
Saint-Luc*	8 815	10 951	51.22	355	8 355	110
Saint-Nicolas*	5 074	6 123	36.93	95	4 930	50
Saint-Pierre*	5 305	4 944	2.15	875	4 255	165
Saint-Rédempteur*	4 463	5 033	3.46	n.a.	n.a.	n.a.
Saint-Rémi*	5 146	5 288	79.67	70	5 015	65
Saint-Romuald*	9 849	9 953	18.34	180	9 615	50
Sainte-Agathe-des-Monts*	5 641	5 254	15.57	260	5 250	125
Sainte-Anne-des-Monts*	6 062	6 008	106.27	40	6 010	10
Sainte-Catherine*	6 372	7 020	9.06	270	6 045	60
Sainte-Foy*	68 883	69 615	83.86	3 150	64 350	1 385
Sainte-Julie*	14 243	15 502	47.91	410	13 625	210
Sainte-Marie*	8 937	9 536	105.49	55	8 860	30
Sainte-Marthe-sur-le-Lac*	5 586	6 143	9.01	320	5 175	90
Sainte-Thérèse*	18 750	19 336	10.09	850	17 050	855
Salaberry-de-Valleyfield*	29 574	27 942	35.74	1 310	27 970	295
Sept-Iles*	29 262	25 637	298.93	1 565	27 000	695
Shawinigan*	23 011	21 470	26.27	350	22 580	85
Shawinigan-Sud*	11 325	11 412	51.39	245	11 015	65
Sherbrooke*	74 075	74 438	55.42	4 465	68 285	1 325
Sillery*	12 825	12 784	6.73	1 120	11 400	305
Sorel*	20 347	19 522	9.65	375	19 850	120
Terrebonne*	11 769	31 310	73.17	295	11 260	210
Thetford Mines*	19 965	18 561	23.15	530	19 335	100
Tracy*	12 843	12 546	19.11	350	12 345	145
Trois-Rivières*	50 466	50 122	77.86	1 395	48 615	455
Trois-Rivières-Ouest*	13 107	15 538	28.70	280	12 705	120
Val-Belair*	12 695	13 105	68.54	335	12 275	85
Val d'Or*	21 371	22 252	1 217.16	1 255	19 485	635
Vanier*	10 725	10 208	4.66	135	10 550	45
Varennes*	8 764	10 489	93.96	205	8 495	65
Vaudreuil*	7 608	8 253	69.49	1 375	5 995	235
Verdun*	61 287	60 246	8.50	18 185	40 690	2 415
Victoriaville*	21 838	21 587	16.13	185	21 560	95
Westmount*	20 480	20 011	3.96	14 475	3 600	2 410
Windsor*	5 233	4 850	10.95	310	4 915	10
Ontario						
Ajax	25 474	36 550	67.70	22 880	415	2 180
Amherstburg	5 685	8 413	3.29	4 775	300	610
Ancaster	14 428	17 264	174.57	12 655	80	1 695
Arnprior	5 828	6 022	8.52	5 345	230	255
Aurora	16 267	20 905	49.16	14 875	170	1 225
Aylmer	5 254	5 248	4.78	4 340	55	860
Barrie*	38 423	48 287	73.40	35 395	675	2 350
Belleville*	34 881	36 041	29.13	32 765	440	1 670
Bracebridge	9 063	9 811	632.09	8 620	80	365
Bradford	7 370	8 825	7.43	5 075	85	2 215
Brampton*	149 030	188 498	265.04	121 015	2 405	25 605
Brantford*	74 315	76 146	70.81	64 315	975	9 025
Brockville*	19 896	20 880	20.24	18 395	430	1 065
Burlington*	114 853	116 675	177.41	99 935	2 240	12 680
Caledon	26 645	29 666	686.84	22 840	255	3 550
Cambridge*	77 183	79 920	115.06	62 610	1 185	13 380
Carleton Place	5 626	6 520	5.64	5 335	125	150
Chatham*	40 952	42 211	27.52	35 305	1 455	4 190
Cobourg	11 385	13 197	15.89	10 655	130	590
Collingwood	12 064	12 172	21.30	11 425	115	520
Cornwall*	46 144	46 425	63.49	28 630	15 960	1 545
Deep River	5 095	4 602	50.88	4 540	200	350
Dryden	6 640	6 462	16.86	5 705	190	745
Dundas	19 586	20 118	24.42	17 485	145	1 955

Town or City	Population 1981	Population 1986	Area[1] (sq. km)	Mother Tongue[2] English	French	Other
Dunnville	11 353	11 589	302.92	10 175	100	1 080
East Gwillimbury	12 565	14 644	245.14	11 270	140	1 155
Elliot Lake	16 723	17 984	756.79	11 150	4 560	1 010
Espanola	5 836	5 491	17.66	4 290	1 295	255
Essex	6 295	6 134	6.48	5 790	205	305
Etobicoke*	298 713	302 973	123.93	211 430	3 890	83 390
Fergus	6 064	6 272	6.87	5 790	45	230
Flamborough	24 470	26 142	489.90	21 325	225	2 925
Fort Erie	24 096	23 253	168.30	21 575	375	2 145
Fort Frances	8 906	8 870	26.05	7 745	225	935
Gloucester*	72 859	89 810	293.86	46 365	20 885	5 615
Goderich	7 322	7 352	6.74	6 940	90	295
Gravenhurst	8 532	8 926	524.01	7 975	95	460
Grimsby	15 797	16 956	68.12	13 060	160	2 575
Guelph*	71 207	78 235	68.69	60 830	910	9 470
Haldimand	16 866	17 701	638.15	15 550	145	1 170
Halton Hills	35 190	35 570	275.86	31 345	725	3 115
Hamilton*	306 434	306 728	122.69	231 190	5 755	69 490
Hanover	6 316	6 414	6.49	5 790	25	500
Hawkesbury	9 877	9 710	8.16	1 355	8 350	170
Hearst	5 533	5 559	28.85	730	4 625	180
Huntsville	11 467	12 131	700.90	10 835	90	540
Ingersoll	8 494	8 451	10.20	7 990	70	430
Iroquois Falls	6 339	6 191	689.94	3 180	2 970	190
Kanata*	19 728	27 519	132.19	17 190	1 085	1 450
Kapuskasing	12 014	11 378	83.92	4 250	7 125	635
Kenora	9 817	9 621	15.33	8 220	260	1 335
Kincardine	5 778	5 852	7.65	5 420	135	220
Kingston*	52 616	55 050	29.57	46 525	1 010	5 080
Kingsville	5 134	5 382	4.27	4 295	75	765
Kirkland Lake	12 219	11 604	270.01	8 635	2 335	1 250
Kitchener*	139 734	150 604	135.13	110 310	2 410	27 015
Leamington	12 528	12 828	8.75	7 830	260	4 435
Lincoln	14 196	14 391	163.43	11 000	165	3 030
Lindsay	13 596	14 455	15.19	12 960	90	545
Listowel	5 026	5 107	6.19	4 615	20	395
London*	254 280	269 140	162.21	220 140	3 120	31 020
Markham	77 037	114 597	211.53	63 855	990	12 195
Midland	12 132	12 092	16.01	10 690	625	815
Milton	28 067	32 037	367.20	24 810	345	2 905
Mississauga*	315 056	374 005	273.86	237 720	5 630	71 710
Nanticoke*	19 816	20 202	674.72	17 510	210	2 095
Nepean*	84 361	95 490	217.02	69 350	5 305	9 705
New Liskeard	5 551	5 286	6.42	3 890	1 515	145
Newcastle	32 229	34 073	607.79	29 010	350	2 865
Newmarket	29 753	34 923	35.91	27 290	340	2 120
Niagara Falls*	70 960	72 107	212.02	56 485	2 015	12 460
Niagara-on-the-Lake	12 186	12 494	131.11	8 560	135	3 495
Nickel Centre	12 318	11 469	378.36	8 170	3 315	835
North Bay*	51 268	50 623	312.88	39 870	8 550	2 855
North York*	559 521	556 297	176.87	364 885	8 240	186 395
Oakville	75 773	87 107	138.18	61 715	1 420	12 635
Onaping Falls	6 198	5 619	228.98	4 425	1 305	465
Orangeville	13 740	14 440	13.39	12 905	125	715
Orillia*	23 955	24 077	22.90	22 305	280	1 365
Oshawa*	117 519	123 651	143.41	100 190	2 800	14 530
Ottawa*	295 163	300 763	110.15	202 380	57 005	35 780
Owen Sound*	19 883	19 804	20.29	19 145	100	640
Paris	7 485	7 898	10.67	7 155	65	270
Parry Sound	6 124	5 977	14.98	5 840	95	190
Pelham	11 104	12 137	124.52	9 590	170	1 345
Pembroke*	14 026	14 131	14.83	12 060	1 185	780
Penetanguishene	5 315	5 576	9.40	3 750	1 445	115
Perth	5 655	5 673	8.92	5 455	80	120
Peterborough*	60 620	61 049	53.41	57 630	520	2 475
Pickering	37 754	48 959	226.52	33 540	610	3 605
Port Colborne*	19 225	18 281	122.82	14 665	1 260	3 295
Port Elgin	6 131	6 208	5.92	5 555	195	380
Port Hope	9 992	10 281	10.00	9 505	95	390
Rayside-Balfour	15 017	14 231	328.21	5 430	9 045	535
Renfrew	8 283	8 314	12.25	7 770	210	305
Richmond Hill	37 778	46 766	99.42	30 125	460	7 190
Sarnia*	50 892	49 033	32.76	43 710	2 020	5 165
Sault Ste. Marie*	82 697	80 905	221.52	65 745	3 770	13 185
Scarborough*	443 353	484 676	187.70	347 065	6 425	89 860
Simcoe	14 326	14 290	40.51	12 705	200	1 420
Smiths Falls	8 831	9 163	8.26	8 375	190	275

Town or City	Population 1981	Population 1986	Area[1] (sq. km)	Mother Tongue[2] English	French	Other
St. Catharines*	124 018	123 455	94.43	98 865	3 795	21 355
St. Marys	4 883	5 069	12.14	n.a.	n.a.	n.a.
St. Thomas*	28 165	28 851	18.10	25 560	370	2 240
Stoney Creek*	36 762	43 554	98.65	27 860	625	8 275
Stratford*	26 262	26 451	20.33	24 195	185	1 885
Strathroy	8 748	9 045	13.89	6 520	75	2 155
Sturgeon Falls	6 045	5 895	5.79	1 585	4 400	60
Sudbury*	91 829	88 717	262.73	55 095	22 050	14 685
Tecumseh	6 364	7 731	6.19	4 965	955	440
Thorold*	15 412	16 131	84.54	12 075	435	2 895
Thunder Bay*	112 486	112 272	322.86	85 550	2 935	24 005
Tillsonburg	10 487	10 745	20.58	8 865	200	1 425
Timmins*	46 114	46 657	3 004.39	23 905	17 625	4 590
Toronto*	599 217	612 289	97.15	372 185	10 395	216 640
Trenton*	15 085	15 311	11.69	13 945	420	720
Valley East	20 433	19 233	518.03	9 535	10 260	640
Vanier*	18 792	18 426	2.93	5 500	11 945	1 345
Vaughan	29 674	65 058	275.34	18 045	250	11 380
Walden	10 139	9 442	718.62	8 080	740	1 320
Wallaceburg	11 506	11 367	10.71	9 975	380	1 150
Wasaga Beach	4 705	5 124	52.10	n.a.	n.a.	n.a.
Waterloo*	49 428	58 718	64.45	40 870	635	7 930
Welland*	45 448	45 054	81.23	30 180	7 070	8 205
Whitby	36 698	45 819	142.99	32 515	525	3 655
Whitchurch-Stouffville	13 557	15 135	206.85	12 235	130	1 190
Windsor*	192 083	193 111	119.87	142 425	10 670	38 990
Woodstock*	26 603	26 386	24.53	23 395	345	2 860
York*	134 617	135 401	23.18	77 825	1 705	55 085

Manitoba

Town or City	Population 1981	Population 1986	Area[1] (sq. km)	English	French	Other
Brandon*	36 242	38 708	74.50	31 910	570	3 760
Dauphin	8 971	8 875	11.94	5 835	145	2 990
Flin Flon* (part in Man.; balance in Sask.)	7 894	7 243	11.55	6 780	190	925
Morden	4 579	5 004	10.53	n.a.	n.a.	n.a.
Portage La Prairie*	13 086	13 198	24.03	11 415	340	1 330
Selkirk	10 037	10 013	24.71	8 300	120	1 610
Steinbach	6 676	7 473	25.24	3 035	80	3 565
The Pas	6 390	6 283	28.46	5 300	250	840
Thompson*	14 288	14 701	16.85	11 940	440	1 910
Winkler	5 046	5 926	16.17	1 765	5	3 275
Winnipeg*	564 473	594 551	571.60	414 735	27 940	121 795

Saskatchewan

Town or City	Population 1981	Population 1986	Area[1] (sq. km)	English	French	Other
Estevan*	9 174	10 161	17.67	7 990	195	990
Humboldt	4 705	5 089	11.65	n.a.	n.a.	n.a.
Lloydminster[3]*	15 031	17 356	39.38	13 480	285	1 260
Melfort*	6 010	6 078	14.66	5 205	75	735
Melville*	5 092	5 123	15.41	3 390	50	1 650
Moose Jaw*	33 941	35 073	45.30	30 125	725	3 095
North Battleford*	14 030	14 876	37.06	11 185	575	2 270
Prince Albert*	31 380	33 686	64.97	25 645	1 670	4 070
Regina*	162 613	175 064	110.06	137 165	2 470	22 980
Saskatoon*	154 210	177 641	132.23	126 665	3 230	24 310
Swift Current*	14 747	15 666	20.50	12 015	245	2 490
Weyburn*	9 523	10 153	13.70	8 335	120	1 070
Yorkton*	15 339	15 574	23.16	10 940	100	4 305

Alberta

Town or City	Population 1981	Population 1986	Area[1] (sq. km)	English	French	Other
Airdrie*	8 414	10 390	13.37	7 770	140	500
Bonnyville*	4 454	5 470	14.39	n.a.	n.a.	n.a.
Brooks	9 421	9 464	15.81	8 235	145	1 040
Calgary*	592 743	636 104	534.82	492 175	13 075	87 490
Camrose*	12 570	12 968	24.43	10 510	135	1 920
Crowsnest Pass	7 306	6 912	171.79	5 860	110	1 335
Drayton Valley	5 042	5 290	7.95	4 455	140	450
Drumheller*	6 508	6 366	28.48	5 775	95	640
Edmonton*	532 246	573 982	669.95	402 560	17 205	112 475
Edson	5 835	7 323	25.89	5 070	170	590
Fort McMurray*	31 000	34 949	56.61	27 125	1 420	2 450
Fort Saskatchewan*	12 169	11 983	32.94	10 775	275	1 125

Town or City	Population		Area[1]	Mother Tongue[2]		
	1981	1986	(sq. km)	English	French	Other
Grande Prairie*	24 263	26 471	41.83	20 895	870	2 500
High River	4 792	5 096	10.42	n.a.	n.a.	n.a.
Hinton	8 342	8 629	22.52	7 170	480	690
Innisfail	5 247	5 535	9.82	4 865	115	265
Lacombe	5 591	6 080	11.40	4 970	45	575
Leduc*	12 471	13 126	22.42	10 905	235	1 335
Lethbridge*	54 072	58 841	119.90	44 590	560	8 952
Lloydminster[3]*	15 031	17 356	39.38	13 480	285	1 260
Medicine Hat*	40 380	41 804	96.17	33 100	490	6 785
Morinville	4 657	5 364	12.32	n.a.	n.a.	n.a.
Okotoks	3 847	5 214	11.67	n.a.	n.a.	n.a.
Peace River	5 907	6 288	21.20	4 935	380	590
Ponoka	5 221	5 473	9.81	4 485	50	680
Red Deer*	46 393	54 425	51.74	41 860	790	3 740
Rocky Mountain House	4 698	5 182	10.82	n.a.	n.a.	n.a.
Slave Lake	4 506	5 429	7.43	n.a.	n.a.	n.a.
Spruce Grove	10 326	11 918	19.56	9 195	210	925
St. Albert*	31 996	36 710	33.63	27 165	1 520	3 310
St. Paul	4 884	5 030	6.80	n.a.	n.a.	n.a.
Stettler	5 136	5 147	9.36	4 575	50	510
Stony Plain	4 839	5 802	26.51	n.a.	n.a.	n.a.
Taber	5 988	6 382	15.62	4 870	50	1 070
Vegreville	5 251	5 276	13.99	3 085	85	2 080
Wetaskiwin*	9 597	10 071	13.27	8 020	130	1 450
Whitecourt	5 585	5 737	25.40	4 920	300	265
British Columbia						
Castlegar*	6 902	6 385	16.16	5 350	60	1 490
Colwood	10 540	11 546	17.91	n.a.	n.a.	n.a.
Comox	6 607	6 873	7.88	6 135	135	335
Courtenay*	8 992	9 631	11.00	8 140	190	660
Cranbrook*	15 915	15 893	16.29	14 200	230	1 480
Dawson Creek*	11 373	10 544	20.30	10 040	245	1 090
Fernie*	5 444	5 188	13.64	4 705	100	640
Fort St. John*	13 891	13 355	19.53	12 540	245	1 100
Kamloops*	64 048	61 773	296.06	55 830	960	7 250
Kelowna*	59 196	61 213	212.56	47 305	1 140	10 750
Kimberley*	7 375	6 732	58.19	6 665	120	590
Langley*	15 124	16 557	10.18	13 280	240	1 605
Merritt*	6 110	6 180	8.34	4 845	185	1 075
Nanaimo*	47 069	49 029	88.20	41 885	680	4 505
Nelson*	9 143	8 113	6.51	7 685	105	3 355
New Westminster*	38 550	39 972	15.38	32 245	825	5 480
North Vancouver*	33 952	35 698	10.77	28 540	600	4 815
Parksville	5 216	5 828	10.66	4 750	75	390
Penticton*	23 181	23 588	40.79	19 455	435	3 295
Port Alberni*	19 892	18 241	17.51	16 035	555	3 300
Port Coquitlam*	27 535	29 115	26.91	23 800	435	3 300
Port Moody*	14 917	15 754	13.72	13 145	230	1 540
Prince George*	67 559	67 621	315.72	57 960	1 545	8 055
Prince Rupert*	16 197	15 755	53.56	13 050	255	2 890
Quesnel*	8 240	8 358	20.56	6 465	135	1 635
Revelstoke*	5 544	8 279	29.99	4 725	80	735
Sidney	7 946	8 982	5.02	7 345	80	525
Trail*	9 599	7 948	13.79	7 720	115	1 765
Vancouver*	414 281	431 147	112.94	274 305	7 215	132 760
Vernon*	19 987	20 241	22.67	16 315	260	3 405
Victoria*	64 379	66 303	18.78	55 820	1 075	7 485
White Rock*	13 550	14 387	5.05	11 835	205	1 505
Williams Lake	8 362	10 280	23.26	6 895	140	1 325
Yukon						
Whitehorse*	14 814	15 199	413.48	13 315	400	1 095
Northwest Territories						
Yellowknife*	9 483	11 753	102.38	7 910	385	1 190

(1) 1986 Census figures. (2) 1981 Census figures. (3) Includes both the Sask. and Alta. portions of Lloydminster.
n.a. not available.

Canadian Population by Country of Birth, 1981

Source: Census of Canada

	Total	%		Total	%
Total Population	24 343 181	100.0	Kampuchea	5 595	...
Total Foreign Born[1]	3 867 160	15.9	Kenya	9 225	...
Argentina	7 235	...	Laos	8 855	...
Australia	14 800	0.1	Lebanon	22 595	0.1
Austria	34 325	0.1	Malta	10 585	...
Barbados	14 310	0.1	Mexico	11 310	...
Belgium	25 250	0.1	Morocco	11 840	...
Brazil	4 340	...	Netherlands	138 760	0.6
Chile	15 330	0.1	Norway	11 555	...
China	52 395	0.2	Pakistan	15 140	0.1
Czechoslovakia	41 660	0.2	Poland	148 940	0.6
Denmark	26 345	0.1	Portugal	139 765	0.6
East Germany	34 285	0.1	Romania	24 350	0.1
Ecuador	5 835	...	South Africa	15 860	0.1
Egypt	21 870	0.1	South Korea	10 165	...
Fiji	10 120	...	Spain	12 855	0.1
Finland	21 660	0.1	Sri Lanka	4 195	...
France	56 175	0.2	Sweden	10 665	...
Greece	90 070	0.4	Switzerland	16 955	0.1
Guyana	38 060	0.2	Taiwan	54 320	0.2
Haiti	26 865	0.1	Tanzania	11 480	...
Hong Kong	58 980	0.2	Trinidad and Tobago	38 655	0.2
Hungary	64 735	0.3	Turkey	8 805	...
India	109 660	0.5	USSR	128 680	0.5
Ireland	16 755	0.1	United Kingdom	884 915	3.6
Israel	11 205	...	United States	312 015	1.3
Italy	386 505	1.6	Vietnam	50 710	0.2
Jamaica	78 165	0.3	West Germany	163 930	0.7
Japan	11 910	...	Yugoslavia	91 870	0.4

(1) Totals for individual countries have been rounded to the nearest 5.
. . . = too small to be included.

Canadian Population by Mother Tongue[1]

Source: Censuses of Canada

(thousands of persons and percent of total population)

	1941	%	1951	%	1961	%	1971	%	1981	%	1986	%
English	6 448	56.0	8 281	59.1	10 661	58.5	12 974	60.2	14 918	61.3	15 334	63.1
French	3 355	29.2	4 069	29.0	5 123	28.1	5 794	26.9	6 249	25.7	6 160	24.3
Italian	80	0.7	92	0.7	340	1.9	538	2.5	529	2.2	456	1.8
German	322	2.8	329	2.3	564	3.1	561	2.6	523	2.2	439	1.7
Chinese	34	0.3	28	0.2	49	0.3	95	0.4	224	0.9	267	1.0
Ukrainian	313	2.7	352	2.5	361	2.0	310	1.4	292	1.2	208	0.8
Portuguese	n.a.	n.a.	n.a.	n.a.	18	0.1	87	0.4	166	0.7	154	0.6
Dutch	53	0.5	88	0.6	170	0.9	145	0.7	157	0.6	124	0.5
Polish	129	1.1	129	0.9	162	0.9	135	0.6	128	0.5	123	0.5
Greek	9	0.1	8	0.1	40	0.2	104	0.5	123	0.5	110	0.4
Spanish	1	...	2	...	7	...	24	0.1	70	0.3	83	0.3
Indo-Pakistani	...	...	2	...	5	...	33	0.2	117	0.5	n.a.	n.a.
Yugoslav[2]	15	0.1	11	0.1	29	0.2	74	0.3	88	0.4	n.a.	n.a.
Native Indian	131[5]	1.1	166[5]	1.2	167[5]	0.9	165	0.8	127	0.5	74[6]	0.3
Hungarian	46	0.4	42	0.3	86	0.5	87	0.4	84	0.3	69	0.3
Vietnamese	n.a.	n.a.	n.a.	n.a.	n.a.	n.a.	n.a.	n.a.	30	0.1	42	0.2
Arabic	8	0.1	5	...	13	0.1	29	0.1	50	0.2	41	0.1
Finnish	37	0.3	32	0.2	45	0.2	37	0.2	33	0.1	25	0.1
Russian	52	0.5	39	0.3	43	0.2	32	0.1	31	0.1	25	0.1
Yiddish[3]	130	1.1	104	0.7	82	0.5	50	0.2	33	0.1	23	0.1
Czech[3]	38	0.3	46	0.3	51	0.3	45	0.2	43	0.2	23	0.1
Danish	19	0.2	16	0.1	35	0.2	27	0.1	26	0.1	21	0.1
Inuktituk[4]	131[5]	1.1	166[5]	1.2	167[5]	0.9	15	0.1	19	0.1	21	0.1
Japanese	22	0.2	18	0.1	18	0.1	17	0.1	20	0.1	18	0.1
Armenian	n.a.	n.a.	n.a.	n.a.	n.a.	n.a.	n.a.	n.a.	17	0.1	18	0.1
Norwegian	60	0.5	44	0.3	40	0.2	27	0.1	19	0.1	13	0.1
Swedish	50	0.4	36	0.3	33	0.2	22	0.1	17	0.1	12	...

(1) The language first spoken in childhood and still understood. (2) Includes Croatian, Serbian and Slovenian. (3) Includes Slovak. (4) The language of the Inuit. (5) Includes Native Indian and Inuktituk. (6) Includes Cree and Ojibway.
n.a. not available; . . . = too small to be included.

Canadian Population by Age Group

Source: Censuses of Canada

(thousands of persons)

		Total population	under 5 years	5-9 years	10-14 years	15-19 years	20-24 years	25-34 years	35-44 years	45-54 years	55-64 years	65 years and over
1851	male	1 250	233	173	152	136	112	168	116	78	46	35
	female	1 186	218	173	146	141	111	161	103	67	38	30
1861	male	1 660	277	218	203	187	154	232	156	107	70	54
	female	1 570	266	211	196	187	150	224	141	92	59	44
1871	male	1 869	276	264	243	202	172	249	175	132	86	74
	female	1 820	265	255	233	206	179	256	171	120	73	61
1881	male	2 189	304	284	262	240	215	302	217	161	111	94
	female	2 136	295	278	251	243	221	301	212	153	100	84
1891	male	2 460	309	300	282	262	242	366	263	191	131	115
	female	2 373	302	292	272	259	240	354	246	180	122	105
1901	male	2 752	326	313	297	283	260	412	331	234	157	139
	female	2 620	320	306	285	275	255	386	299	214	148	133
1911	male	3 822	450	396	356	355	390	684	475	334	209	171
	female	3 385	440	389	346	331	322	535	388	286	184	165
1921	male	4 530	534	529	462	405	352	693	630	434	276	215
	female	4 258	525	521	452	400	361	650	532	366	246	206
1931	male	5 375	543	573	543	526	464	778	707	590	356	295
	female	5 002	531	560	531	514	448	717	627	485	306	281
1941	male	5 901	534	529	556	565	518	920	745	649	494	391
	female	5 606	518	517	545	555	514	891	691	579	421	377
1951	male	7 089	879	714	575	532	538	1 066	950	728	557	551
	female	6 921	843	684	556	526	551	1 108	919	679	520	535
1956	male	8 152	1 012	920	732	587	567	1 209	1 079	838	588	623
	female	7 929	972	887	703	576	562	1 206	1 062	774	566	622
1961	male	9 219	1 154	1 064	948	729	587	1 258	1 191	959	655	674
	female	9 019	1 102	1 016	908	704	597	1 222	1 199	920	635	717
1966	male	10 054	1 129	1 173	1 071	929	727	1 249	1 275	1 041	743	717
	female	9 961	1 069	1 128	1 022	909	734	1 233	1 268	1 037	736	823
1971	male	10 795	930	1 152	1 181	1 074	942	1 462	1 286	1 132	854	782
	female	10 773	887	1 102	1 129	1 040	948	1 428	1 241	1 160	877	963
1976	male	11 450	889	967	1 165	1 196	1 066	1 823	1 315	1 226	928	876
	female	11 543	843	921	1 112	1 149	1 068	1 798	1 282	1 246	997	1 127
1981	male	12 068	914	912	985	1 182	1 174	2 105	1 497	1 257	1 030	1 011
	female	12 275	869	865	936	1 133	1 170	2 110	1 471	1 243	1 129	1 350
1986[1]	male	12 486	928	920	917	985	1 131	2 249	1 822	1 276	1 124	1 133
	female	12 824	882	875	870	940	1 122	2 278	1 819	1 269	1 204	1 564

(1) Excludes incompletely enumerated Indian reserves and settlements.

Demographic Comparison of Canada and Other Countries

Source: World Development Report 1988, World Bank

	Population 1986 (millions)	% Population growth[1]	Population density[2] 1986		Population 1986 (millions)	% Population growth[1]	Population density[2] 1986
Canada	25.6	1.1	2.6	Mexico	80.2	2.2	40.6
Australia	16.0	1.4	2.1	Nicaragua	3.4	3.4	26.2
Brazil	138.4	2.2	16.3	Pakistan	99.2	3.1	123.4
China	1 054.0	1.2	110.2	Peru	19.8	2.3	15.4
Egypt	49.7	2.7	49.7	Poland	37.5	0.9	119.8
France	55.4	0.5	101.3	South Africa	32.3	2.2	26.5
Greece	10.0	0.5	75.8	South Korea	41.5	1.4	423.5
Hong Kong	5.4	1.2	5 400.0	Sweden	8.4	0.1	18.7
Hungary	10.6	−0.1	114.0	Uganda	15.2	3.1	64.4
India	781.4	2.2	237.7	United Kingdom	56.7	0.1	231.4
Israel	4.3	1.7	204.8	United States	241.6	1.0	25.8
Italy	57.2	0.3	190.0	USSR	281.1	1.0	12.5
Jamaica	2.4	1.5	218.2	Vietnam	63.3	2.6	191.8
Japan	121.5	0.7	326.6	West Germany	60.9	−0.2	244.6
Libya	3.9	3.9	2.2	Yugoslavia	23.3	0.7	91.0

(1) Percent average annual growth 1980-86. (2) Persons per sq. km; area used in calculating population density includes both land and water areas.

Canada's Native People

Native Population of Canada, 1986

Source: Census of Canada

	Total native population[1]		Native Indian[2]	Métis[2]	Inuit[2]
	number	%			
Canada[3]	**711 725**	**100.0**	**548 945**	**151 605**	**36 460**
Newfoundland	9 555	1.3	4 695	1 435	4 120
Prince Edward Island	1 290	0.2	1 115	160	30
Nova Scotia[3]	14 220	2.0	13 060	1 110	315
New Brunswick[3]	9 375	1.3	8 700	750	185
Quebec[3].....................	80 940	11.4	63 585	11 435	7 360
Ontario[3]	167 375	23.5	150 715	18 265	2 955
Manitoba[3]	85 235	12.0	55 960	33 285	700
Saskatchewan[3]	77 650	10.9	55 215	25 695	190
Alberta[3]....................	103 930	14.6	68 965	40 125	1 125
British Columbia[3]	126 625	17.8	112 790	15 295	1 035
Yukon	4 995	0.7	4 775	220	65
Northwest Territories	30 530	4.3	9 380	3 825	18 360

(1) Figures represent individuals who identified their ethnic origin(s) as North American Indian, Métis and/or Inuit. (2) Figures do not add to total native population due to the double counting of individuals who identified more than one native ethnic origin. For example, a person who is a Métis and Inuit is counted twice, as both a Métis and an Inuit. (3) Excludes approximately 45 000 individuals in Canada living on incompletely enumerated Indian reserves and settlements.

Canada's Native People

Origin

Canada's natives are believed to have descended from peoples who migrated from Asia across a land bridge over what is now the Bering Strait separating Alaska and Siberia between 10 000 and 25 000 years ago. Some anthropologists also postulate a theory of development of indigenous peoples on the American continents, with people migrating northward from a heartland in central America.

Language

Dialects of 10 distinct linguistic groups involving over 50 languages are spoken by Canada's Indians, while the Inuit (singular: Inuk; formerly known as Eskimos, an Indian word meaning "flesh eater") people of the northern reaches speak variations of a common tongue, Inuktitut. About half the Indian population and 75 percent of the Inuit speak their native tongue today. The vast majority also speak English, while less than 2 percent speak French.

Lifestyle

Before European settlement of the American continent in the 16th century, the livelihood of the Indians varied widely. Agriculture was practised by many tribes occupying what is now southern Ontario, and the dwellers of the rocky sub-Arctic forests and coastal areas hunted and fished. The large plains bison, or buffalo, was the major staple of the nomadic tribes who inhabited the central Prairies.

The lifestyle of Indian people began to change with the first French settlements in what is now New Brunswick. Trapping fur-bearing animals such as beaver and lynx, and trading their pelts for manufactured goods, improved the standard of living of the native people.

With the interaction of races, a new people of mixed race began to develop. Neither Indian nor European, the early Metis (an old French word meaning "mixed blood") became guides and packers, known as coureurs de bois, who escorted French and later English traders by canoe and longboat across the expanse of rivers and lakes.

As European colonization expanded in the 17th and 18th centuries, the Indians began to be outnumbered, and their leaders made treaties with the newcomers. Inter-tribal warfare and disease introduced by the Europeans wiped out many Indians, and others moved westward.

Legislation and Treaties

The Royal Proclamation of 1763, on the heels of the Seven Years' War by which England took control of New France, is the cornerstone of British Indian policy and still forms the basis of native relations with the Canadian government. This proclamation by King George III preserved lands solely for Indian use and forbade anyone except governments from making treaties with Indians.

Over the next 200 years, Indians signed treaties by which they gave up claim to the land in return for reserve lands, per capita money grants, other benefits such as special fishing and hunting rights and farming equipment. Eleven major treaties signed between 1871 and 1921 extended the Canadian government's control from Ontario westward and northward. However, the many varied tribes of British Columbia (with the exception of Treaty 8 in northern B.C.), northern Quebec, the Northwest Territories and Newfoundland remained isolated in remote villages until more recent times and did not enter into treaty.

The *Indian Act* of 1876 consolidated regulations governing Indian reserve lands and created a legal definition of Indian, conferring special status on those who had made treaties with the government, and their descendants. Its aim was to protect Indians from exploitation while guiding them into gradual assimilation with Canadians. Status Indians were settled on reserves, not allowed to vote in Canadian elections, and were exempted from taxation.

Native people in remote areas who were left off official band lists drawn up by Indian affairs department officials came to be known as "non-status Indians". They are Native people who identify themselves as Indians but are not registered for the purpose of the *Indian Act*. They are not covered by the Act, not entitled to live on reserves, and do not receive special benefits. Non-status Indians and Metis have no special rights, with minor exceptions in Ontario, Alberta and New Brunswick, where they enjoy some special fishing and hunting concessions. In 1936, the Alberta government designated 12 areas in northern Alberta especially for Metis settlement. Eight Metis settlements still exist.

Revisions to the *Indian Act*, notably in 1951, narrowed its scope and reduced the number of people covered by excluding Indian women who married non-Indians. This provision of the Act was removed in 1985 following protests that it was discriminatory. The right to vote in federal elections was extended to Indians and Inuit in 1960.

In 1988, one of the first Indian-led changes to the *Indian Act*, Bill C-115 known as the "Kamloops Amendment", resulted in band councils having jurisdiction over all reserve land, including the power to levy taxes.

As of June 30, 1988, there were 592 Indian bands in the country, occupying 2 276 reserves or other categories of Indian lands. New bands and reserves are being created with the settlement of Indian claims for land and as some bands split their reserves in two.

It is estimated that only 8 percent of native people still make their living in the traditional occupations of hunting, trapping, fishing and craftsmanship. Unemployment among native people is 3 times the national average, income and education levels are lower, and housing conditions poorer. Total government payments to native programs was estimated at approximately $2.8 billion in 1986. In recent years, increased native participation in business, largely through investment of funds from land claim settlements, is seen to be slowly improving living standards.

The federal Department of Indian Affairs and Northern Development (DIAND) set up a special agency in 1974 to handle land claims. Under a 1985 reorganization, "comprehensive" land claims—those based on aboriginal rights and involving the traditional and continued use of the land by large tribal groupings—are negotiated under the department's self-government program. As of Mar., 1988, agreement had been reached on 3 of 28 "comprehensive" claims.

The James Bay and Northern Quebec Agreement of November, 1975, followed by the northeastern Quebec or Naskapi Agreement of 1978, made way for a large hydroelectric development, giving the 6 700 Cree Indians and 4 400 Inuit up to $500 million in land and benefits, title to 169 902 sq. km of land, and some self-government. In June 1984, the federal government signed a land claim settlement with 2 500 Inuit in the arctic region of the western Northwest Territories. This agreement gave the Inuvialuit people $85 million over 20 years and title to 90 650 sq. km of land.

In September 1988, after 13 years of negotiations with native leaders, the federal government signed an agreement in principal to turn over 186 000 sq. km of land to the 13 000 Dene and Métis of the Northwest Territories. The agreement guarantees the surface and subsurface title to about 10 000 sq. km and surface title, with mineral royalties, to another 176 000 sq. km. The actual boundaries of the land were to be the subject of further negotiations, with a final treaty possible by 1990. In addition, the Dene and Métis will receive $500 million over the next 20 years.

Other major comprehensive claims are still under negotiation, including that of the Inuit of the Tungavik Federation of Nunavit to land in the central and eastern Arctic.

A land claim by the Council of Yukon Indians, representing 6 000 Indians and Metis in the Yukon Territory, is also under negotiation. The Nishga Tribal Council of northwestern B.C., the Conseil Attikamek Montagnais in Quebec and the Labrador Inuit Association are also negotiating comprehensive land claims. Nineteen other claims await negotiations, including 17 in British Columbia, one in Newfoundland and one in the Northwest Territories.

Specific claims for compensation concerning land covered by treaties or under the jurisdiction of the *Indian Act* are negotiated under the lands, revenues and trusts program of DIAND.

Specific claims are grievances Indian people have relating to treaties or to other formal agreements, or to the administration of lands and other assets under the *Indian Act*.

As of July 31, 1988, 517 specific claims had been filed. Settlements had been reached in 38 claims, five were near completion, 42 had been rejected, 17 were in negotiation and another 77 were awaiting the development of mandates. Sixteen claims had been the subject of litigation. Seventy-four were suspended pending re-assessment by claimants and 23 files had been closed. Sixty-nine had been referred for administrative remedy and 156 claims were under active research.

Constitutional Discussions

Native people were accorded special status in the *Constitution Act of 1982* which enshrined existing aboriginal and treaty rights. "Aboriginal Peoples of Canada" were defined to include Inuit, Indian and Métis. Several major constitutionally-required conferences of Canada's prime minister, provincial premiers and native leaders, have been held to further define these rights but, as of mid 1988, these issues remain unresolved.

Native people are represented at these talks by leaders of the major native political organizations. The Assembly of First Nations represents status Indian interests, the Inuit Tapirisat of Canada represents the Inuit; Metis and non-status Indian interests are represented by the Native Council of Canada and the Metis National Council.

Native Indian Population[1], 1988

Source: Dept. of Indian and Northern Affairs

	Total Indian population	On reserve	Off reserve	On Crown land	Number of bands	Number of reserves	Area of reserves (hectares)
Canada	415 898	242 837	147 424	25 637	592	2 231	2 666 139
Atlantic Provinces	16 792	11 476	5 275	41	31	68	30 282
Quebec	41 227	26 532	9 411	5 284	39	29	72 272
Ontario	94 275	54 368	37 687	2 220	126	191	710 114
Manitoba	60 918	40 187	18 244	2 487	60	105	215 431
Saskatchewan	64 118	35 565	27 386	1 167	68	145	627 587
Alberta	52 053	33 533	16 079	2 441	41	90	656 221
British Columbia	71 866	40 662	30 256	948	196	1 576	337 473
Yukon	5 037	328	2 064	2 645	14	25	3 197
Northwest Territories	9 612	186	1 022	8 404	17	2	13 562

(1) Represents status Indians only.

Vital Statistics

Births and Deaths in Canada, 1925–1986

Source: Statistics Canada

	Live births	Birth rate[1]	Deaths	Death Rates[1] Both sexes	Males	Females
1925	249 365	26.1	102 528	10.7	10.3	9.5[2]
1930	250 335	23.9	113 283	10.8	11.2	10.2[3]
1935	228 396	20.5	109 724	9.9	10.2	9.2[3]
1940	252 577	21.6	114 717	9.8	10.5	9.0[3]
1945	300 587	24.3	117 325	9.5	10.3	8.5[3]
1950	372 009	27.1	124 220	9.1	10.1	7.9
1955	442 937	28.2	128 476	8.2	9.4	6.9
1960	478 551	26.8	139 693	7.8	9.0	6.6
1965	418 595	21.3	148 939	7.6	8.8	6.3
1970	371 988	17.5	155 961	7.3	8.5	6.1
1975	359 323	15.8	167 404	7.3	8.5	6.2
1980	370 709	15.5	171 743	7.2	8.2	6.1
1981	371 346	15.3	171 029	7.0	8.0	6.0
1982	373 082	15.1	174 413	7.1	8.0	6.1
1983	373 689	15.0	174 484	7.0	7.9	6.1
1984	377 031	15.0	175 727	7.0	7.9	6.1
1985	375 727	14.8	181 323	7.2	8.0	6.3
1986	372 913	14.7	184 224	7.3	8.1	6.5

(1) Per 1 000 population. (2) Excludes Que., Nfld., Yukon and NWT. (3) Excludes Nfld., Yukon and NWT.

Canadian Births[1] by Age of Mother, 1986

Source: Statistics Canada

Age of mother	Total births	1st	2d	3d	4th	5th	6th	7th	8th	9th	10+	Not stated
Under 15 yrs.	210	207	3	–	–	–	–	–	–	–	–	–
15 yrs.	761	739	22	–	–	–	–	–	–	–	–	–
16 yrs.	2 154	2 038	110	5	–	–	–	–	–	–	–	1
17 yrs.	4 024	3 603	400	20	1	–	–	–	–	–	–	–
18 yrs.	6 064	5 104	870	82	7	1	–	–	–	–	–	–
19 yrs.	8 449	6 442	1 710	276	19	1	–	–	–	–	–	1
20 yrs.	11 339	7 968	2 785	515	57	12	2	–	–	–	–	–
21 yrs.	14 631	9 336	4 245	879	154	13	3	1	–	–	–	–
22 yrs.	18 652	11 088	5 906	1 385	227	41	5	–	–	–	–	–
23 yrs.	22 438	12 491	7 373	2 054	401	89	23	2	3	–	–	2
24 yrs.	25 855	13 364	9 069	2 670	599	119	27	6	–	1	–	–
25 yrs.	28 806	13 951	10 556	3 338	760	139	51	8	3	–	–	–
26 yrs.	29 976	13 253	11 618	3 921	892	219	51	14	6	1	–	1
27 yrs.	29 789	11 981	11 933	4 430	1 061	269	89	20	4	2	–	–
28 yrs.	28 714	10 566	11 723	4 738	1 261	273	95	40	10	7	1	–
29 yrs.	26 278	8 833	10 866	4 719	1 350	338	115	36	10	8	3	–
30 yrs.	22 812	7 089	9 395	4 545	1 275	325	104	46	21	11	1	–
31 yrs.	19 387	5 440	7 860	4 217	1 326	309	151	44	25	11	4	–
32 yrs.	16 466	4 196	6 694	3 784	1 235	348	125	49	19	8	8	–
33 yrs.	12 643	2 962	4 928	3 080	1 100	325	139	64	25	11	9	–
34 yrs.	10 123	2 381	3 755	2 502	946	313	123	56	23	14	10	–
35 yrs.	7 739	1 793	2 758	1 924	782	279	105	42	20	15	21	–
36 yrs.	5 778	1 254	1 930	1 494	660	215	110	50	22	22	21	–
37 yrs.	3 998	810	1 327	997	492	185	82	40	31	17	17	–
38 yrs.	2 911	611	937	718	337	145	63	44	28	11	17	–
39 yrs.	1 993	419	582	473	265	123	58	26	18	14	15	–
40 yrs.	1 101	240	279	249	164	79	35	21	13	6	15	–
41 yrs.	684	120	152	162	102	64	29	18	14	9	14	–
42 yrs.	400	76	108	79	51	27	24	13	8	2	12	–
43 yrs.	246	42	56	48	35	15	13	12	8	4	13	–
44 yrs.	107	14	27	22	14	10	6	1	4	1	8	–
45 yrs.	61	10	12	10	6	4	5	2	4	3	5	–
46 yrs.	19	4	1	4	3	2	2	1	1	–	1	–
47 yrs.	5	1	–	–	2	–	–	–	1	–	1	–
48 yrs.	–	–	–	–	–	–	–	–	–	–	–	–
49 yrs.	1	–	1	–	–	–	–	–	–	–	–	–
50 years and over	–	–	–	–	–	–	–	–	–	–	–	–
Not stated	199	65	45	24	5	4	–	–	–	–	–	56
Total births	364 813	158 491	130 036	53 364	15 589	4 286	1 635	656	321	178	196	61

(1) Excludes Newfoundland.
– = zero.

85

Births and Deaths by Province, 1986

Source: Statistics Canada

	Live Births	Birth rate[1]	Deaths	Death Rates[1] Both sexes	Males	Females
Canada	372 913	14.7	184 224	7.3	8.1	6.5
Newfoundland	8 100	14.2	3 540	6.2	7.4	5.4
Prince Edward Island	1 928	15.2	1 121	8.9	10.0	7.7
Nova Scotia	12 358	14.2	7 255	8.3	9.3	7.3
New Brunswick	9 788	13.8	5 458	7.7	8.7	6.7
Quebec	84 634	13.0	46 892	7.2	8.2	6.2
Ontario	133 882	14.7	67 865	7.5	8.1	6.9
Manitoba	17 009	16.0	8 911	8.4	9.3	7.5
Saskatchewan	17 513	17.4	8 061	8.0	9.2	6.8
Alberta	43 744	18.5	13 360	5.7	6.5	5.0
British Columbia	41 967	14.6	21 213	7.4	8.2	6.6
Yukon	483	20.6	113	4.8	6.0	3.5
Northwest Territories	1 507	28.9	235	4.5	5.4	3.5

(1) Rate per 1 000 population.

Canadian Life Expectancy, 1921-1981

Source: Statistics Canada

	At birth male	female	At age 20 male	female	At age 40 male	female	At age 60 male	female	At age 80 male	female
1921[1]	n.a.	n.a.	49.1	49.2	32.2	33.0	16.6	17.1	6.0	6.1
1931	60.0	62.1	49.1	49.8	32.0	33.0	16.3	17.2	5.6	5.9
1941	63.0	66.3	49.6	51.8	31.9	34.0	16.1	17.6	5.5	6.0
1951	66.3	70.8	50.8	54.4	32.5	35.6	16.5	18.6	5.8	6.4
1956	67.6	72.9	51.2	55.8	32.7	36.7	16.5	19.3	5.9	6.8
1961	68.4	74.2	51.5	56.7	33.0	37.5	16.7	19.9	6.1	6.9
1966	68.8	75.2	51.5	57.4	33.0	38.2	16.8	20.6	6.4	7.3
1971	69.3	76.4	51.7	58.2	33.2	39.0	17.0	21.4	6.4	7.9
1976	70.2	77.5	52.1	59.0	33.6	39.7	17.2	22.0	6.4	8.2
1981	71.9	79.0	53.4	60.1	34.7	40.7	18.0	22.9	6.9	8.8

(1) Excludes Quebec.
n.a. not available.

Life Expectancy[1] of Canadians, by Age

Source: Statistics Canada

Age	Male % living to next age[2]	% dying[3]	Life expectancy	Age	Female % living to next age[2]	% dying[3]	Life expectancy
0	98.91	1.09	71.88	0	99.16	.84	78.98
1	99.92	.08	71.67	1	99.93	.07	78.65
2	99.94	.06	70.73	2	99.95	.05	77.70
3	99.95	.05	69.77	3	99.96	.05	76.74
4	99.95	.05	68.80	4	99.97	.03	75.77
5	99.96	.04	67.84	5	99.97	.03	74.79
6	99.97	.03	66.86	6	99.98	.02	73.81
7	99.98	.02	65.88	7	99.98	.02	72.83
8	99.98	.02	64.90	8	99.98	.02	71.84
9	99.98	.02	63.91	9	99.98	.02	70.86
10	99.98	.02	62.92	10	99.98	.02	69.87
11	99.97	.03	61.94	11	99.98	.02	68.88
12	99.96	.04	60.95	12	99.98	.02	67.90
13	99.95	.05	59.97	13	99.98	.02	66.91
14	99.93	.07	59.00	14	99.97	.03	65.93
15	99.91	.09	58.04	15	99.96	.04	64.95
16	99.89	.11	57.10	16	99.96	.04	63.97
17	99.87	.13	56.16	17	99.96	.04	63.00
18	99.86	.14	55.23	18	99.95	.05	62.02
19	99.85	.15	54.31	19	99.95	.05	61.05
20	99.85	.15	53.39	20	99.95	.05	60.08
21	99.84	.16	52.47	21	99.95	.05	59.11
22	99.84	.16	51.55	22	99.95	.05	58.14
23	99.84	.16	50.63	23	99.95	.05	57.16
24	99.85	.15	49.71	24	99.95	.05	56.19
25	99.85	.15	48.78	25	99.95	.05	55.22
26	99.86	.14	47.86	26	99.95	.05	54.25

Age	Male % living to next age[2]	% dying[3]	Life expectancy	Age	Female % living to next age[2]	% dying[3]	Life expectancy
27	99.86	.14	46.92	27	99.95	.05	53.27
28	99.86	.14	45.99	28	99.95	.05	52.30
29	99.87	.13	45.05	29	99.94	.06	51.33
30	99.87	.13	44.11	30	99.94	.06	50.36
31	99.87	.13	43.17	31	99.94	.06	49.39
32	99.87	.13	42.22	32	99.94	.06	48.42
33	99.86	.14	41.28	33	99.93	.07	47.45
34	99.86	.14	40.34	34	99.93	.07	46.48
35	99.85	.15	39.39	35	99.92	.08	45.51
36	99.84	.16	38.45	36	99.91	.09	44.55
37	99.83	.17	37.52	37	99.90	.10	43.59
38	99.81	.19	36.58	38	99.89	.11	42.63
39	99.80	.20	35.65	39	99.88	.12	41.68
40	99.78	.22	34.72	40	99.87	.13	40.73
41	99.76	.24	33.80	41	99.86	.14	39.78
42	99.73	.27	32.88	42	99.84	.16	38.84
43	99.70	.30	31.97	43	99.82	.18	37.90
44	99.67	.33	31.06	44	99.81	.19	36.97
45	99.63	.37	30.16	45	99.79	.21	36.04
46	99.59	.41	29.27	46	99.77	.23	35.11
47	99.54	.46	28.39	47	99.75	.25	34.19
48	99.49	.51	27.52	48	99.72	.28	33.28
49	99.43	.57	26.66	49	99.69	.31	32.37
50	99.37	.63	25.81	50	99.66	.34	31.47
51	99.31	.69	24.97	51	99.63	.37	30.57
52	99.23	.77	24.14	52	99.59	.41	29.68
53	99.15	.85	23.33	53	99.56	.44	28.80
54	99.07	.93	22.52	54	99.52	.48	27.93
55	98.97	1.03	21.73	55	99.47	.53	27.06
56	98.87	1.13	20.95	56	99.43	.57	26.20
57	98.76	1.24	20.18	57	99.37	.63	25.35
58	98.64	1.36	19.43	58	99.32	.68	24.51
59	98.51	1.49	18.69	59	99.26	.74	23.68
60	98.37	1.63	17.96	60	99.20	.80	22.85
61	98.22	1.78	17.25	61	99.13	.87	22.03
62	98.05	1.95	16.56	62	99.04	.96	21.22
63	97.86	2.14	15.88	63	98.95	1.05	20.42
64	97.66	2.34	15.21	64	98.85	1.15	19.63
65	97.44	2.56	14.57	65	98.74	1.26	18.85
66	97.21	2.79	13.93	66	98.62	1.38	18.09
67	96.95	3.05	13.32	67	98.49	1.51	17.33
68	96.68	3.32	12.72	68	98.34	1.66	16.59
69	96.40	3.60	12.14	69	98.19	1.81	15.86
70	96.09	3.91	11.58	70	98.02	1.98	15.14
71	95.76	4.24	11.03	71	97.82	2.18	14.44
72	95.38	4.62	10.49	72	97.60	2.40	13.75
73	94.98	5.02	9.98	73	97.35	2.65	13.08
74	94.54	5.46	9.48	74	97.09	2.91	12.42
75	94.07	5.93	9.00	75	96.79	3.21	11.78
76	93.56	6.44	8.53	76	96.46	3.54	11.15
77	93.00	7.00	8.09	77	96.06	3.94	10.54
78	92.39	7.61	7.66	78	95.62	4.38	9.95
79	91.75	8.25	7.25	79	95.13	4.87	9.39
80	91.06	8.94	6.85	80	94.60	5.40	8.84
81	90.32	9.68	6.48	81	94.01	5.99	8.32
82	89.52	10.48	6.12	82	93.34	6.66	7.82
83	88.66	11.34	5.78	83	92.62	7.38	7.34
84	87.76	12.24	5.45	84	91.84	8.16	6.88
85	86.80	13.20	5.14	85	91.00	9.00	6.45
86	85.77	14.23	4.85	86	90.01	9.91	6.04
87	84.68	15.32	4.57	87	89.09	10.91	5.65
88	83.53	16.47	4.30	88	88.02	11.98	5.28
89	82.31	17.69	4.05	89	86.87	13.13	4.93
90	81.03	18.97	3.82	90	85.65	14.35	4.60
91	79.67	20.33	3.59	91	84.34	15.66	4.29
92	78.23	21.77	3.38	92	82.93	17.07	3.99
93	77.68	22.32	3.19	93	82.45	17.55	3.71
94	78.00	22.00	2.96	94	82.90	17.10	3.39
95	77.77	22.23	2.65	95	82.75	17.25	2.99
96	75.56	24.44	2.27	96	80.47	19.53	2.51
97	69.91	30.09	1.84	97	74.52	25.48	1.99
98	58.76	41.24	1.41	98	62.66	37.34	1.50
99	43.03	56.97	1.05	99	45.90	54.10	1.10
100	25.89	74.11	.79	100	27.62	72.38	.81

(1) As of 1981. (2) Represents the percentage of the population that will live to the next age. (3) Represents the percentage of the population that will die before reaching the next age.

Suicides in Canada

Source: Statistics Canada

Age groups	1975				1985			
	Number		Rate[1]		Number		Rate[1]	
	male	female	male	female	male	female	male	female
5- 9 yrs.	1	2	0.1	0.2	1	—	0.1	—
10-14 yrs.	19	3	1.6	0.3	12	5	1.3	0.6
15-19 yrs.	186	48	15.9	4.2	186	35	18.4	3.6
20-24 yrs.	316	83	29.7	7.9	374	50	30.8	4.2
25-29 yrs.	244	82	25.2	8.5	321	72	27.5	6.1
30-34 yrs.	150	58	18.8	7.4	284	76	26.5	7.0
35-39 yrs.	154	74	23.3	11.6	237	77	23.9	7.8
40-44 yrs.	161	81	25.0	13.0	201	64	25.6	8.3
45-49 yrs.	152	84	24.3	13.5	162	67	25.0	10.4
50-54 yrs.	171	81	29.2	13.2	174	47	28.0	7.6
55-59 yrs.	136	60	28.4	11.9	165	54	27.9	8.8
60-64 yrs.	120	37	27.9	8.1	131	43	24.9	7.3
65-69 yrs.	93	44	28.5	12.1	104	38	25.9	8.0
70-74 yrs.	59	17	25.0	6.0	102	31	31.7	7.6
75-79 yrs.	28	14	19.1	6.8	53	21	25.6	7.1
80-84 yrs.	26	9	31.0	6.8	40	5	34.8	2.6
85 yrs. and over	7	1	13.2	1.0	18	8	26.4	5.1
Total Suicides	**2 030[2]**	**778**	**17.5**	**6.8**	**2 566[3]**	**693**	**20.5**	**5.4**

(1) Suicides per 100 000 population. (2) Includes 7 suicides for which the age was not stated. (3) Includes 1 suicide for which the age was not stated.
— = zero.

Abortions[1] in Canada

Source: Statistics Canada

Under a 1969 amendment to the Canadian Criminal Code, abortions are legal in Canada if performed by a doctor in an approved hospital after a therapeutic abortion committee has certified that continuation of a woman's pregnancy "would or would be likely to endanger her life or health."

	1970	1975	1980	1982	1983	1984	1985
Canada	11 152	49 311	65 751	66 254	61 750	62 247	60 928
Newfoundland	25	176	539	457	483	382	415
Prince Edward Island	17	77	23	26	14	12	11
Nova Scotia	261	1 017	1 662	1 691	1 678	1 703	1 698
New Brunswick	72	379	467	243	277	278	310
Quebec	534	5 579	8 940	9 671	9 406	9 720	9 527
Ontario	5 568	24 921	30 900	31 290	28 404	28 276	27 335
Manitoba	238	1 298	1 587	1 728	1 689	2 226	2 285
Saskatchewan	215	1 282	1 572	1 622	1 398	1 214	1 173
Alberta	1 154	4 333	7 131	6 617	6 484	6 668	6 547
British Columbia	2 901	10 076	12 673	12 566	11 597	11 449	11 264
Yukon	6	77	125	124	113	87	95
Northwest Territories	n.a.	95	126	218	205	226	254
Not stated	161	1	6	1	2	6	14

(1) Represents abortions performed in Canadian hospitals with approval of hospital abortion committees; data shows province of residence of persons having abortions.
n.a. not available.

Abortions in Canada,[1] by Age Groups

Source: Statistics Canada

Age groups	1975		1980		1983		1984		1985	
	Number	Rate[2]	Number	Rate[2]	Number	Rate[2]	Number	Rate[2]	Number	Rate[2]
Under 15 yrs.	597	1.3	559	1.4	499	1.3	451	1.2	489	1.3
15-17 yrs.	7 437	10.9	8 660	12.7	6 236	10.6	6 063	10.7	5 687	10.2
18-19 yrs.	7 413	16.7	10 277	21.8	8 647	18.8	8 173	18.8	7 761	19.3
20-24 yrs.	14 354	13.8	20 926	18.2	20 575	17.3	20 867	17.5	20 415	17.3
25-29 yrs.	9 584	10.0	12 866	12.1	12 846	11.2	13 292	11.5	13 123	11.2
30-34 yrs.	5 262	6.8	7 631	7.9	7 764	7.5	7 894	7.5	7 939	7.3
35-39 yrs.	3 165	4.9	3 492	4.5	3 978	4.4	4 278	4.5	4 250	4.3
40 yrs. and over	1 499	2.4	1 340	2.1	1 205	1.7	1 229	1.6	1 264	1.6
Total Abortions	**49 311**	**8.8**	**65 751**	**10.7**	**61 750**	**9.6**	**62 247**	**9.6**	**60 928**	**9.3**

(1) Represents abortions performed in Canadian hospitals with approval of hospital abortion committees; this data is for Canadian residents only. (2) Number of abortions per 1 000 females.

Causes of Accidental Death in Canada, 1986

Source: Statistics Canada

Age Groups	All accidents	Motor vehicle[1]	Falls	Fire	Poison	Drowning	Choking	Electro-cution	Guns	Light-ning
Total accidental deaths	9 096	4 048	2 012	475	380	371	349	52	50	5
less than 1 yr.	64	14	2	10	1	3	17	—	—	—
1- 4 yrs.	240	80	17	36	1	60	10	2	1	—
5- 9 yrs.	190	103	6	19	—	24	4	1	6	—
10-14 yrs.	182	111	3	23	3	10	3	—	4	2
15-19 yrs.	789	607	15	28	12	36	3	3	10	—
20-24 yrs.	980	713	25	28	43	39	6	4	5	1
25-29 yrs.	712	451	28	31	38	34	7	7	6	—
30-34 yrs.	578	325	26	46	35	27	16	9	3	—
35-39 yrs.	482	260	23	30	41	15	13	11	3	—
40-44 yrs.	436	214	34	28	37	17	10	3	3	—
45-49 yrs.	342	158	22	21	35	17	14	2	2	1
50-54 yrs.	364	152	35	26	28	10	12	6	—	—
55-59 yrs.	446	187	62	26	32	21	25	2	4	1
60-64 yrs.	398	146	75	23	20	14	28	—	1	—
65-69 yrs.	386	142	99	17	9	13	28	2	2	—
70-74 yrs.	443	147	147	20	16	13	31	—	—	—
75-79 yrs.	469	125	205	20	14	6	30	—	—	—
80-84 yrs.	545	69	333	23	10	6	42	—	—	—
85 yrs. and over	1 050	44	855	20	5	6	50	—	—	—

(1) Includes both traffic and non-traffic accidents involving motor vehicles.
— = zero.

Vital Statistics Comparision: Canada and Other Countries, 1986

Source: *World Development Report 1988*, World Bank

	Rate per 1 000 population			Life expectancy at birth		Fertility rate[2]	% use of contracep-tion[3]
	Birth rate	Death rate	Infant[1] mortality rate	male	female		
Canada	15	7	8	73	80	1.7	73
Australia	15	7	10	75	80	1.9	n.a.
Brazil	29	8	65	62	68	3.5	65
China	18	7	35	68	70	2.3	69
Egypt	34	10	88	59	63	4.6	32
France	14	10	8	74	80	1.8	n.a.
Greece	11	9	12	74	79	1.8	n.a.
Hong Kong	16	6	8	73	79	1.9	72
Hungary	12	14	19	67	75	1.8	73
India	32	12	86	57	56	4.4	35
Israel	22	7	12	73	77	2.9	n.a.
Italy	10	10	10	74	79	1.5	n.a.
Jamaica	26	6	19	71	76	3.0	52
Japan	12	7	6	75	81	1.8	64
Libya	44	19	85	61	63	6.9	n.a.
Mexico	29	6	48	65	72	3.7	48
Nicaragua	42	9	65	60	63	5.6	27
Pakistan	47	15	111	52	51	6.8	11
Peru	32	10	90	59	62	4.1	46
Poland	17	10	18	68	76	2.3	n.a.
South Africa	34	10	74	59	63	4.5	n.a.
South Korea	20	6	25	66	73	2.2	70
Sweden	12	11	6	74	80	1.7	78
Uganda	50	18	105	46	49	6.9	1
United Kingdom	13	12	9	72	78	1.8	83
United States	16	9	10	71	79	1.9	68
USSR	19	10	29	65	74	2.4	n.a.
Vietnam	34	7	47	63	68	4.5	20
West Germany	10	12	9	72	78	1.3	78
Yugoslavia	15	9	27	68	74	2.0	n.a.

(1) Less than one year old. (2) Represents the number of children that would be born to a woman if she were to live to the end of her childbearing years and bear children at each age in accordance with prevailing age-specific fertility rates. (3) Percent of women of child-bearing age (married or in long-term sexual relationships) who use contraception; data is for 1985.
n.a. not available.

Drinking and Driving

About 43% of driver fatalities tested for alcohol in 1986 were over the legal limit. This represents a slight increase over 1985 (40%). This increase occurred during the first full year in which new, tougher laws on impaired driving were in effect in Canada. A person is considered legally impaired with a blood alcohol concentration (BAC) over 80 mg%. BAC refers to the amount of alcohol in a person's blood and is usually expressed as the number of milligrams of alcohol in 100 millilitres of blood.

In Canada, it is a crime to drive, operate or be in control of a motor vehicle, vessel or aircraft while impaired by alcohol or a drug. It is also a crime to fail or refuse, without reasonable excuse, to give a breath or blood sample upon demand by a peace officer.

The **minimum penalties** for impaired-driving offences are:

First conviction—a fine of not less than $300 and a driving prohibition for 3 months or longer

Second conviction—not less than 14 days in jail and a driving prohibition of 6 months or longer

Subsequent convictions—not less than 90 days in jail and a driving prohibition of one year or longer

The **maximum penalties** are:

First conviction—maximum 5 years in prison and a driving prohibition of up to 3 years

Impaired driving causing bodily harm—maximum 10 years in prison and a driving prohibition of up to 10 years

Impaired driving causing death—maximum 14 years in prison and a driving prohibition of up to 10 years

Manslaughter and criminal negligence causing death—maximum life imprisonment and lifetime driving prohibition

How to Determine Your BAC Level

- find the body weight closest to yours in the left hand column
- move across the row and locate your estimated total BAC under the column corresponding to the number of drinks you have had or plan to have
- determine the number of hours it takes you to consume this many drinks; for every hour subtract 15 mg% from the total BAC estimated

For example: if you are a female weighing 57 kilograms and have had 3 drinks in the last 2 hours, the number (120) at the intersection of the 2 columns represents your blood alcohol level. Then subtract 15 for each of the 2 hours that has passed since you began drinking: 120 − 30 equals 90 mg%.

Females

Body weight kg	lb	No. of drinks[1] 1	2	3	4	5	6	7	8	9	10
45	100	50	101	152	203	253	304	355	406	456	507
57	125	40	80	120	162	202	244	282	324	364	404
68	150	34	68	101	135	169	203	237	271	304	338
79	175	29	58	87	117	146	175	204	233	262	292
91	200	26	50	76	101	126	152	177	203	227	253
102	225	22	45	68	91	113	136	159	182	204	227
114	250	20	41	61	82	101	122	142	162	182	202

Males

Body weight kg	lb	No. of drinks[1] 1	2	3	4	5	6	7	8	9	10
45	100	43	87	130	174	217	261	304	348	391	435
57	125	34	69	103	139	173	209	242	278	312	346
68	150	29	58	87	116	145	174	203	232	261	290
79	175	25	50	75	100	125	150	175	200	225	250
91	200	22	43	65	87	108	130	152	174	195	217
102	225	19	39	58	78	97	117	136	156	175	195
114	250	17	35	52	70	87	105	122	139	156	173

(1) One drink represents 341 mL of normal strength beer, 142 mL of table wine, 85 mL of strong wine, 43 mL of hard liquor.

Alcohol Use in Fatal Motor Vehicle Accidents[1]

Source: Traffic Injury Research Foundation of Canada

	Number of driver deaths[2]	% of deaths tested for alcohol[3]	Of fatalities tested: % with alcohol involvement by BAC level[4] no alcohol	under legal limit 1-49	50-80	over legal limit 81-150	over 150
1973	1 776	76.4	41.9	4.1	5.4	17.2	31.4
1974	1 962	76.7	43.8	6.0	5.2	15.6	29.3
1975	1 862	79.5	41.5	7.3	5.5	14.3	31.5
1976	1 640	77.2	40.8	5.8	6.2	14.4	32.9
1977	1 695	74.5	41.6	7.1	5.2	15.0	31.2
1978	1 601	75.5	42.4	6.5	4.1	13.4	33.6
1979	1 846	72.3	42.4	6.7	4.0	14.3	32.5
1980	1 832	67.3	40.6	6.9	4.5	14.1	33.8
1981	1 879	74.5	38.4	6.6	3.4	15.8	35.9
1982	1 571	75.2	40.1	6.3	4.6	14.5	34.6
1983	1 559	79.3	42.3	5.8	4.3	11.7	35.9
1984	1 483	80.0	45.0	6.1	3.9	13.6	31.5
1985	1 582	81.6	49.8	6.3	3.9	10.1	29.9
1986	1 597	84.9	50.2	4.2	3.1	11.6	31.0
male	1 296	85.6	45.0	4.4	3.2	13.0	34.3
female	301	81.7	73.2	3.3	2.4	5.3	15.9

(1) Excludes Nfld., N.S. and Que. (2) Excludes drivers of bicycles, snowmobiles, farm tractors and buses. (3) Not every fatality is tested for blood alcohol. About 15% of fatally injured persons die more than 6 hours from the time of the accident; this group of fatalities is tested infrequently because test results will not represent BACs at the time of the accident. In other cases, the condition of the body precludes meaningful tests (e.g., incineration or exsanguination). (4) Blood alcohol concentration (BAC) level refers to the amount of alcohol in a person's blood. It is usually expressed as the no. of milligrams of alcohol in 100 millilitres of blood. The legal limit in Canada is 80 mg of alcohol in 100 millilitres of blood.

Immigration

Canadian Immigration Totals, 1852-1987

Source: Dept. of Employment and Immigration

Year	Total	Year	Total	Year	Total	Year	Total
1852	29 307	1886	69 152	1920	138 824	1954	154 227
1853	29 464	1887	84 526	1921	91 728	1955	109 946
1854	37 263	1888	88 766	1922	64 224	1956	164 857
1855	25 296	1889	91 600	1923	133 729	1957	282 164
1856	22 544	1890	75 067	1924	124 164	1958	124 851
1857	33 854	1891	82 165	1925	84 907	1959	106 928
1858	12 339	1892	30 996	1926	135 982	1960	104 111
1859	6 300	1893	29 633	1927	158 886	1961	71 689
1860	6 276	1894	20 829	1928	166 783	1962	74 586
1861	13 589	1895	18 790	1929	164 993	1963	93 151
1862	18 294	1896	16 835	1930	104 806	1964	112 606
1863	21 000	1897	21 716	1931	27 530	1965	146 758
1864	24 779	1898	31 900	1932	20 591	1966	194 743
1865	18 958	1899	44 543	1933	14 382	1967	222 876
1866	11 427	1900	41 681	1934	12 476	1968	183 974
1867	10 666	1901	55 747	1935	11 277	1969	161 531
1868	12 765	1902	89 102	1936	11 643	1970	147 713
1869	18 630	1903	138 660	1937	15 101	1971	121 900
1870	24 706	1904	131 252	1938	17 244	1972	122 006
1871	27 773	1905	141 465	1939	16 994	1973	184 200
1872	36 578	1906	211 653	1940	11 324	1974	218 465
1873	50 050	1907	272 409	1941	9 329	1975	187 881
1874	39 373	1908	143 326	1942	7 576	1976	149 429
1875	27 382	1909	173 694	1943	8 504	1977	114 914
1876	25 633	1910	286 839	1944	12 801	1978	86 313
1877	27 082	1911	331 288	1945	22 722	1979	112 096
1878	29 807	1912	375 756	1946	71 719	1980	143 117
1879	40 492	1913	400 870	1947	64 127	1981	128 618
1880	38 505	1914	150 484	1948	125 414	1982	121 147
1881	47 991	1915	36 665	1949	95 217	1983	89 157
1882	112 458	1916	55 914	1950	73 912	1984	88 239
1883	133 624	1917	72 910	1951	194 391	1985	84 302
1884	103 824	1918	41 845	1952	164 498	1986	99 219
1885	79 169	1919	107 698	1953	168 868	1987	152 098

Canadian Immigration Patterns

The Post-Confederation Years

In 1867, Canada's population was less than 3.5 million—too small for the realization of Prime Minister John A. Macdonald's plans for economic and geographic expansion. Immigration then, as in later years, was seen as a solution to Canada's population and labor needs. Canadian policy during the early post-Confederation period generally encouraged the free entry of immigrants, although an 1885 "head tax" restriction on Chinese entrants was the first in a series of measures designed to restrict non-white immigration. During Canada's first quarter century, some 1.4 million immigrants arrived. Most were farmers from the British Isles, western Europe and the United States, lured by the offer of free land.

1900-1914

By the turn of the century, western European and American immigration had slowed to a trickle. Clifford Sifton, minister of the interior in the government of Sir Wilfrid Laurier, launched a plan to recruit farmers from central and eastern Europe to develop the Canadian West. Said Sifton: "I think that a stalwart peasant in a sheepskin coat, born on the soil, whose forefathers have been farmers for 10 generations, with a stout wife and a half-dozen children, is good quality." Sifton's efforts led to the first major immigration of Poles, Slovaks and Russians and triggered a period of population growth and industrial expansion. By 1912, Canada had become the world's third largest exporter of wheat. Between 1891 and the start of World War I in 1914, more than 3 million immigrants arrived, more than a million of them between 1911 and 1913 alone.

1915-1945

The 2 World Wars and the Great Depression of the 1930s greatly reduced immigration, although there was a steady flow of new arrivals during the 1920s when 73 000 Germans, 52 000 Poles and 59 000 Ukrainians added to the usual influx of immigrants from the British Isles. Although most were farmers, many also found jobs in the emerging cities. By 1941, the proportion of the population whose ancestry was British had declined to 49.7%, those of French heritage made up 30.3% and other ethnocultural groups had grown to 20% of Canada's population.

1946-1981

With the end of World War II, Canada experienced its second major surge of immigration in this century. Early post-war immigration included war brides, some European Jews and a large number of "displaced persons" from the communist satellite countries of eastern Europe. Average annual immigration exceeded 100 000 during the 1950s and reached a 1957 peak of 282 164, including refugees from the Suez and Hungarian crises.

The nation's post-war industrial expansion increased the demand for skilled manpower and laborers who were not sufficiently available in Canada. During the 1950s, more than 30 percent of Canada's immigrants came from Germany, Austria and Italy.

By the early 1960s, the government had developed a "point system" designed primarily to select immigrants who could best meet the country's labor needs. This policy resulted in increased multicultural immigration. The 1981 census showed substantial percentage increases for new Canadians born in Asia, the Caribbean and Latin America. The proportion of Canadian residents of neither British nor French ancestry had increased to about one-third of the population.

Recent Policy

The most recent changes to immigration policy were contained in the *Immigration Act* of 1976 (proclaimed in 1978) which specified the objectives of Canada's immigration program. These included demographic goals, cultural and social enrichment, family re-unification, the fulfillment of Canada's international obligations to refugees and the use of immigration to assist economic development. The Act also provides for increased consultation between the federal and provincial governments to determine regional demographic and labor needs.

One of the contemporary concerns of Canada's immigration program is the destination of immigrant arrivals. Since the Second World War, about 66% of new immigrants have chosen Montreal, Toronto or Vancouver for their permanent residence.

In the 1980s, Canadian immigration policy has responded to the prevailing high unemployment rates by strengthening the link between economic factors and immigration. Since 1982, all independent immigrants have been required to have firm employment offers before being admitted; immigrants in the business entrepreneurial category have been aggressively courted.

In 1988, the government announced a change in immigration rules to make it easier for families to be reunited.

Immigration[1] to Canada, 1956-1981

Source: Employment and Immigration Canada

	Total immigrants	United States	Total Asia	China	Hong Kong	India	Israel	Lebanon	Pakistan
1956	164 857	9 777	3 537	1 516	615	254	309	454	50
1957	282 164	11 008	3 244	856	866	186	482	401	83
1958	124 851	10 846	4 223	894	1 752	325	531	312	62
1959	106 928	11 338	5 368	519	2 018	585	1 490	377	62
1960	104 111	11 247	4 002	183	1 146	505	1 532	283	83
1961	71 689	11 516	2 706	118	710	568	652	293	72
1962	74 586	11 643	2 593	244	426	529	558	303	55
1963	93 151	11 736	3 553	179	1 008	737	688	456	121
1964	112 606	12 565	6 121	184	2 490	1 154	871	347	282
1965	146 758	15 143	11 215	197	4 155	2 241	822	602	423
1966	194 743	17 514	13 835	4 094[2]	4 094[2]	2 233	1 488	889	566
1967	222 876	19 038	20 740	6 409[2]	6 409[2]	3 966	2 345	1 096	648
1968	183 974	20 422	21 686	8 382[2]	8 382[2]	3 229	1 497	1 682	627
1969	161 531	22 785	23 319	8 272[2]	8 272[2]	5 395	863	1 196	1 005
1970	147 713	24 424	21 170	5 377[2]	5 377[2]	5 670	818	1 206	1 010
1971	121 900	24 366	22 171	47	5 009	5 313	600	928	968
1972	122 006	22 618	23 325	25	6 297	5 049	620	996	1 190
1973	184 200	25 242	43 193	60	14 662	9 203	984	1 325	2 285
1974	218 465	26 541	50 566	379	12 704	12 868	1 090	1 762	2 315
1975	187 881	20 155	47 382	903	11 132	10 144	1 527	1 506	2 165
1976	149 429	17 315	44 328	833	10 725	6 733	1 201	7 161	2 173
1977	114 914	12 888	31 368	798	6 371	5 555	957	3 847	1 575
1978	86 313	9 945	24 007	644	4 740	5 110	735	1 454	1 159
1979	112 096	9 617	50 540	2 058	5 966	4 517	831	1 747	1 117
1980	143 117	9 926	71 602	4 936	6 309	8 483	1 498	1 406	881
1981	128 618	10 559	48 831	6 550	6 451	8 256	1 785	1 122	731

	Philippines	Total Europe	United Kingdom	France	West Germany	Greece	Italy	Netherlands	Portugal
1956	n.a.	145 554	50 390	3 809	26 061	4 986	27 739	7 792	1 697
1957	n.a.	257 540	108 989	5 869	28 430	5 460	27 740	11 934	4 423
1958	n.a.	102 279	24 777	2 727	13 888	5 190	27 043	7 420	1 938
1959	n.a.	84 517	18 222	2 153	10 423	4 867	25 655	5 243	4 080
1960	n.a.	82 922	19 585	2 944	10 774	4 856	20 681	5 429	5 023
1961	n.a.	52 132	11 870	2 330	6 231	3 766	14 161	1 787	2 762
1962	n.a.	53 790	15 603	2 674	5 548	3 741	13 641	1 555	2 928
1963	n.a.	69 069	24 603	3 569	6 744	4 759	14 427	1 728	4 000
1964	n.a.	82 798	29 279	4 542	5 992	4 391	19 297	2 029	5 309
1965	1 502	108 285	39 857	5 225	8 927	5 642	26 398	2 619	5 734
1966	2 639	148 410	63 291	7 872	9 263	7 174	31 625	3 749	7 930
1967	2 994	159 979	62 420	10 122	11 779	10 650	30 055	4 401	9 500
1968	2 678	120 702	37 889	8 184	8 966	7 739	19 774	3 264	7 738
1969	3 001	88 363	31 977	5 549	5 880	6 937	10 383	2 494	7 182
1970	3 240	75 609	26 497	4 410	4 193	6 327	8 533	1 916	7 902
1971	4 180	52 031	15 451	2 966	2 275	4 769	5 790	1 301	9 157
1972	3 946	51 293	18 197	2 742	2 025	4 016	4 608	1 471	8 737
1973	6 757	71 883	26 973	3 586	2 564	5 833	5 468	1 898	13 483
1974	9 564	88 694	38 456	4 232	3 619	5 632	5 226	2 103	16 333
1975	7 364	72 898	34 978	3 891	3 469	4 062	5 078	1 448	8 547
1976	5 939	49 903	21 548	3 251	2 672	2 487	4 530	1 359	5 344
1977	6 232	40 748	17 997	2 757	2 254	1 960	3 411	1 247	3 579
1978	4 370	30 075	11 801	1 754	1 471	1 474	2 976	1 237	3 086
1979	3 873	32 858	12 853	1 900	1 323	1 247	1 996	1 479	3 723
1980	6 051	41 168	18 245	1 900	1 643	1 093	1 740	1 866	2 014
1981	5 859	46 299	21 154	2 089	2 188	958	2 043	1 797	1 886

	Switzer-land	Yugo-slavia	Carib-bean	South America	Total Africa	Egypt	South Africa	Austra-lasia	Central American[3]
1956	1 514	453	1 245	1 551	1 079	194	342	1 924	106
1957	1 800	1 048	1 414	2 376	2 970	421	464	3 345	172
1958	1 024	984	1 360	2 168	1 355	116	367	2 344	159
1959	855	958	1 369	1 750	843	120	287	1 512	160
1960	1 048	881	1 340	1 823	833	58	503	1 657	202
1961	805	852	1 307	1 301	1 088	31	531	1 432	147
1962	802	862	1 659	1 103	2 171	1 322	340	1 384	183
1963	999	781	2 443	1 779	2 431	1 476	296	1 692	168
1964	1 446	1 187	2 281	2 257	3 874	1 855	417	2 303	186
1965	2 169	1 230	3 215	2 471	3 196	1 378	545	2 711	205
1966	2 982	1 502	4 133	2 604	3 661	1 854	892	4 057	224
1967	3 738	2 089	8 582	3 090	4 608	1 728	1 366	6 168	422
1968	3 529	4 660	7 755	2 693	5 204	1 915	924	4 815	374
1969	2 307	4 053	13 315	4 767	3 297	1 429	599	4 411	593
1970	2 098	5 672	12 660	4 943	2 863	913	646	4 385	711
1971	1 024	2 997	11 017	5 058	2 841	730	729	2 902	636
1972	778	2 047	8 353	4 309	8 308	606	440	2 143	865
1973	953	2 873	19 563	11 057	8 307	905	766	2 671	1 141
1974	1 336	3 200	23 885	12 528	10 450	928	1 154	2 594	1 391
1975	1 272	2 932	17 973	13 270	9 867	892	1 567	2 174	1 510
1976	1 192	1 741	14 842	10 628	7 752	728	1 611	1 886	1 356
1977	944	1 408	11 911	7 840	6 372	598	2 458	1 545	1 276
1978	801	927	8 328	6 782	4 261	471	1 653	1 233	912
1979	1 073	887	6 366	5 898	3 958	511	1 339	1 395	694
1980	857	661	7 361	5 433	4 330	616	1 370	2 497	780
1981	863	743	8 634	6 163	4 889	683	1 428	2 253	991

(1) By country of last permanent residence. (2) Includes China and Hong Kong. (3) Includes Greenland and St. Pierre & Miquelon for 1956-1976.
n.a. not available.

Immigration[1] to Canada, 1982-1987

Source: Employment and Immigration Canada

	1982	1983	1984	1985	1986	1987	1980-1987 total	%
Total Immigrants	121 147	89 157	88 239	84 302	99 219	152 098	905 897	100.0
United States	9 360	7 381	6 922	6 669	7 275	7 967	66 059	7.3
Asia	41 686	36 906	41 920	38 597	41 600	67 337	388 479	42.9
Afghanistan	79	73	125	370	590	975	2 264	0.2
Bangladesh	58	78	84	94	449	473	1 385	0.2
China	3 571	2 217	2 214	1 883	1 902	2 625	25 898	2.9
Hong Kong	6 542	6 710	7 696	7 380	5 893	16 170	63 151	7.0
India	7 776	7 041	5 502	4 028	6 940	9 692	57 718	6.4
Iran	1 201	1 268	1 870	1 728	1 952	3 083	13 179	1.5
Iraq	201	325	495	359	242	296	2 380	0.3
Israel	1 392	584	429	676	1 206	1 461	9 031	1.0
Japan	630	333	250	205	273	446	3 644	0.4
Kampuchea	1 378	1 542	1 727	1 803	1 745	1 612	14 409	1.6
South Korea	1 506	1 017	801	934	1 143	2 276	10 063	1.1
Laos	375	434	870	379	636	456	10 282	1.1
Lebanon	1 190	813	1 245	1 657	2 348	3 414	13 195	1.5
Malaysia	688	399	356	332	418	717	4 320	0.5
Pakistan	868	836	611	479	643	991	6 040	0.7
Philippines	5 062	4 454	3 748	3 076	4 102	7 343	39 695	4.4
Sri Lanka	182	166	1 048	815	1 753	4 226	8 557	0.9
Taiwan	560	570	421	536	695	1 467	5 910	0.7
Vietnam	5 935	6 451	10 950	10 404	6 622	5 668	79 822	8.8
Europe	46 156	24 312	20 901	18 859	22 709	37 563	257 967	28.5
Czechoslovakia	853	1 259	924	903	835	922	7 900	0.9
England	13 332	4 730	4 116	3 639	4 193	7 028	68 482	7.6
France	2 393	1 651	1 380	1 401	1 610	2 290	14 714	1.6
West Germany	4 425	2 518	1 727	1 578	1 403	1 906	17 388	1.9
Greece	885	601	555	551	551	771	5 965	0.7
Hungary	405	484	374	614	697	717	4 173	0.5
Ireland	630	299	291	265	434	990	4 398	0.5
Northern Ireland	535	177	161	146	186	357	2 744	0.3
Italy	1 506	826	839	650	715	1 031	9 350	1.0
Netherlands	1 827	672	545	466	524	575	8 272	0.9
Poland	8 278	5 094	4 499	3 617	5 231	7 036	38 790	4.3
Portugal	1 388	820	855	910	1 970	5 977	15 820	1.7
Romania	988	946	840	852	858	1 550	7 413	0.8
Scotland	1 985	655	686	597	567	948	10 695	1.2

	1982	1983	1984	1985	1986	1987	1980-1987 total	%
Spain	440	323	266	103	119	216	2 224	0.2
Switzerland	796	423	389	376	361	633	4 698	0.5
USSR	377	212	140	110	107	225	4 118	0.5
Yugoslavia	773	527	465	478	481	1 059	3 783	0.4
Central America[2]	**10 317**	**10 864**	**9 706**	**11 143**	**14 947**	**18 100**	**92 843**	**10.2**
Barbados	303	250	258	284	259	325	2 386	0.3
Cuba	93	106	110	148	133	140	1 076	0.1
El Salvador	857	2 551	2 579	2 881	3 167	3 536	15 983	1.8
Guatemala	128	364	648	1 063	1 311	1 089	4 746	0.5
Haiti	3 468	2 827	1 397	1 297	1 727	2 121	18 137	2.0
Jamaica	2 593	2 423	2 479	2 922	4 652	5 422	26 205	2.9
Mexico	513	512	522	369	591	815	4 186	0.5
Nicaragua	31	50	114	468	716	1 073	2 488	0.3
St. Vincent	202	161	158	192	207	223	1 492	0.2
Trinidad and Tobago	992	787	595	670	940	1 721	7 611	0.8
South America	**6 871**	**4 816**	**4 085**	**4 356**	**6 686**	**10 801**	**49 184**	**5.4**
Argentina	675	280	243	218	243	567	3 142	0.3
Brazil	272	158	180	162	241	265	1 913	0.2
Chile	1 011	757	664	534	639	1 422	7 232	0.8
Colombia	356	234	243	213	256	374	2 244	0.2
Ecuador	187	163	183	210	249	363	1 821	0.2
Guyana	3 486	2 605	1 896	2 301	3 905	6 073	25 380	2.8
Peru	415	243	305	327	624	861	3 557	0.4
Venezuela	196	137	160	188	228	272	1 522	0.2
Africa	**4 513**	**3 659**	**3 552**	**3 545**	**4 770**	**8 501**	**37 759**	**4.2**
Egypt	844	498	449	394	507	1 066	5 057	0.6
Ethiopia	167	482	734	742	960	1 019	4 286	0.5
Ghana	85	134	122	194	234	956	2 088	0.2
Kenya	277	266	278	271	356	773	2 929	0.3
Morocco	481	390	251	338	395	516	3 173	0.4
South Africa	993	454	321	365	938	1 845	7 714	0.9
Tanzania	514	418	420	424	342	468	3 700	0.4
Australasia	**2 119**	**1 213**	**1 151**	**1 128**	**1 227**	**1 827**	**13 415**	**1.5**
Australia	564	334	377	355	338	530	4 162	0.5
Fiji	818	552	388	444	359	512	4 409	0.5
Mauritius	304	154	196	157	312	521	2 106	0.2
New Zealand	357	139	154	147	163	205	2 327	0.3

(1) By country of last permanent residence. (2) Includes the Caribbean.

Immigration by Province of Intended Destination

Source: Employment and Immigration Canada

	Total immigrants[1]	Nfld	PEI	NS	NB	Que	Ont	Man	Sask	Alta	BC	YT and NWT
1960	104 111	306	83	1 210	634	23 774	54 491	4 337	2 087	6 949	10 120	120
1961	71 689	365	69	901	770	16 920	36 518	2 527	1 333	4 823	7 326	137
1962	74 586	378	77	989	944	19 132	37 210	2 410	1 163	4 475	7 441	97
1963	93 151	349	78	1 198	769	23 264	49 216	2 792	1 438	4 731	9 254	62
1964	112 606	445	79	1 189	696	25 973	61 468	3 006	1 795	5 521	12 324	110
1965	146 758	604	137	1 612	1 074	30 346	79 702	3 948	2 649	8 049	18 502	135
1966	194 743	805	141	2 084	1 283	39 198	107 621	5 132	3 440	10 078	24 746	215
1967	222 876	984	147	2 406	1 322	45 717	116 850	9 313	3 754	15 004	27 215	164
1968	183 974	1 006	176	1 957	1 025	35 481	96 115	8 723	3 557	13 203	22 496	195
1969	161 531	832	182	2 167	1 239	28 230	86 588	6 380	2 492	11 274	21 953	194
1970	147 713	630	185	2 007	1 070	23 261	80 732	5 826	1 709	10 405	21 683	205
1971	121 900	819	172	1 812	1 038	19 222	64 357	5 301	1 426	8 653	18 917	183
1972	122 006	686	175	1 872	1 301	18 592	63 805	5 262	1 511	8 390	20 107	305
1973	184 200	984	273	2 548	1 729	26 871	103 187	6 621	1 866	11 904	27 949	268
1974	218 465	1 036	311	2 601	2 207	33 458	120 115	7 423	2 244	14 289	34 481	300
1975	187 881	1 106	235	2 124	2 093	28 042	98 471	7 134	2 837	16 277	29 272	290
1976	149 429	725	235	1 942	1 752	29 282	72 031	5 509	2 323	14 896	20 484	250
1977	114 914	583	192	1 587	1 158	19 248	56 594	5 058	2 231	12 694	15 395	174
1978	86 313	374	145	980	661	14 290	42 397	3 574	1 564	9 826	12 331	171
1979	112 096	553	289	1 336	1 145	19 522	51 947	4 903	2 760	12 778	16 586	208
1980	143 117	541	190	1 616	1 207	22 538	62 257	7 683	3 603	18 839	24 437	189
1981	128 618	483	128	1 405	990	21 182	55 032	5 370	2 402	19 330	22 095	201
1982	121 147	406	165	1 256	751	21 336	53 049	4 931	2 125	17 949	18 999	180
1983	89 157	275	105	833	554	16 374	40 036	3 978	1 735	10 688	14 447	132
1984	88 239	299	109	1 034	600	14 641	41 527	3 903	2 150	10 670	13 190	116
1985	84 302	325	113	974	609	14 884	40 730	3 415	1 905	9 001	12 239	107
1986	99 219	274	168	1 097	641	19 459	49 630	3 749	1 860	9 673	12 552	116
1987	152 098	458	159	1 227	642	26 822	84 807	4 799	2 119	11 975	18 913	152

(1) Includes immigrants whose province of intended destination was not stated.

Canadian Emigration by Province

Source: Statistics Canada

(number of persons moving from Canada)

	Canada	Nfld	PEI	NS	NB	Que	Ont	Man	Sask	Alta	BC	Yukon	NWT
1961-1966 ..	432 100	10 971	2 436	17 172	13 972	124 877	147 896	21 595	21 378	31 972	38 934	346	551
1966-1971 ..	472 400	13 901	2 390	17 549	20 517	144 078	179 523	15 330	15 907	23 974	38 127	333	771
1971-1976 ..	357 200	3 501	393	4 857	3 358	82 085	163 312	12 501	9 073	26 254	51 866	n.a.	n.a.
1976-1981 ..	278 641	3 551	921	8 967	7 027	43 439	127 740	11 311	6 548	34 012	33 969	379	777
1981-1982	45 338	261	48	432	874	6 963	21 184	1 570	780	6 769	6 374	61	22
1982-1983	50 249	372	78	373	708	8 402	23 448	1 487	842	7 315	7 125	70	29
1983-1984	48 826	253	87	398	665	8 146	22 319	1 745	954	7 200	6 981	45	33
1984-1985	46 252	332	71	350	612	7 203	21 916	1 255	837	6 214	7 389	44	29
1985-1986	44 816	245	66	371	710	6 141	22 385	1 299	936	5 677	6 893	42	51
1981-1986 ..	235 481	1 463	350	1 924	3 569	36 855	111 252	7 356	4 349	33 175	34 762	262	164
1986-1987[1]	41 090	303	57	329	563	5 612	20 487	1 475	612	5 126	6 451	42	33

(1) Preliminary estimate.
n.a. not available.

How to Become a Canadian Citizen

Source: Department of Secretary of State

Citizenship Requirements: You must have been lawfully admitted to Canada, i.e. as a landed immigrant. You must know either English or French well enough to make yourself understood in your community.

Age: You must be 18 years of age or older; if under 18, citizenship may be granted provided one parent is a Canadian citizen.

Residence: You must reside in Canada for a total of 3 years within the 4 years immediately prior to applying.

Restrictions: You cannot take the Oath of Citizenship if you: are considered a security risk, are on probation or parole; are in prison; have been convicted of an indictable offence within the past 3 years.

How to Apply: Obtain an application at the offices of a Secretary of State Citizenship Court, or through a citizenship officer who travels to your area.

Submit your application with: a birth certificate, passport, or other satisfactory evidence of your birth; 2 additional pieces of identification to establish identity; evidence of the date of your lawful admittance to Canada[1]; 2 black and white or color photographs, taken within the last year, each measuring 35 mm × 43 mm, with a 10 mm space at the bottom for your signature; a fee of $40 for adults, $25 for children.

Sign the photographs and swear or affirm that the statements made on the application are true, either at the citizenship court, or before a Notary Public, Commission for Oaths, or Justice of the Peace.

The Interview: If your application is found free of prohibitions, you will be interviewed before a Citizenship Judge, who reviews the application, speaks with you to determine your knowledge of English and/or French, questions you on your knowledge of Canada and the responsibilities of citizenship, and then decides whether to approve the application.

The Ceremony: Successful applicants are usually notified within 2 months following the interview of the date and place of the citizenship ceremony.

Applicants 14 years of age or over must swear or affirm the Oath of Citizenship in order to become a Canadian citizen:

"I swear/affirm that I will bear true allegiance to Her Majesty Queen Elizabeth the Second, Queen of Canada, Her Heirs and Successors, according to law and that I will faithfully observe the laws of Canada and fulfil my duties as a Canadian citizen."

After taking the Oath of Citizenship you receive various documents, including the certificate of citizenship.

Where to apply: Registrar of Canadian Citizenship: Department of Secretary of State, Sydney, N.S. B1P 646; or:

Citizenship Courts:

St. John's, Nfld.: Box 75, 8th Floor, Atlantic Place, 215 Water St., A1C 6C9; (709) 772-5566.

Halifax, N.S.: 5281 Duke St., B3J 3M1; (902) 426-2148.

Moncton, N.B.: Ste. 503, 860 Main St., E1C 1G2; (506) 857-7050.

Quebec, Que.: Complexe St. Amable, Ste. 155, 333 St. Amable St., G1R 5G2; (418) 648-3831

Montreal, Que.: Complexe Guy Favreau, 10th Floor, West Tower, 200 Dorchester Blvd. W., H2Z 1X4; (514) 283-1419; 5167 Jean Talon St. E., H1S 1K8; (514) 283-6817; 6420 St. Denis St., H2S 2R7; (514) 283-3943.

Ottawa, Ont.: 9th Floor, 150 Kent St., K1A 0M5; (613) 992-4485.

Kingston, Ont.: Ste. 210 Federal Bldg., 106 Clarence St., K7L 1X3; (613) 545-8014.

Oshawa, Ont.: 2nd Floor, 310 Simcoe St. S., L1H 4M7; (416) 723-1216

Toronto, Ont.: 1541 Bloor St. W., M6P 1A5; (416) 973-5656; Ste. 814, 55 St. Clair Ave. E., M4T 1M2; (416) 973-6424.

Mississauga, Ont.: Ste. 101, Confederation Place, 90 Dundas St. W., L5B 2T5; (416) 848-1900.

Scarborough, Ont.: Ste. 217, 200 Town Centre Court, M1P 4X8; (416) 973-4510

Hamilton, Ont.: Ste. 412, 150 Main St. W., L8P 1H8; (416) 572-2361.

Waterloo, Ont.: 70 King St. N., N2J 2X1; (519) 886-3120.

London, Ont.: Main Floor, Government of Canada Building, 451 Talbot St., N6A 5C9; (519) 679-4334.

Windsor, Ont.: 2nd Floor, 467 University Ave. W., N9A 5R2; (519) 252-7852.

Sudbury, Ont.: Rm. 326, Federal Building, 19 Lisgar St. S., P3E 3L4; (705) 675-0621.

Thunder Bay, Ont.: Rm. 234, Federal Building, 33 South Court Street, P7B 2W6; (807) 345-2316.

Winnipeg, Man.: Rm. 200, Grain Commission Bldg., 303 Main St., R3C 3G7; (204) 983-3792.

Regina, Sask.: Rm. 200 Financial Bldg., 2101 Scarth St., S4P 2H9; (306) 780-5535.

Saskatoon, Sask.: Ste. 505, Financial Bldg., 230-22nd St. E., S7K 0E9; (306) 975-4117.

Calgary, Alta.: Rm. 254, 220 4th Ave. S.E., P.O. Box 2498, Postal Station M, T2P 3C1; (403) 292-5539.

Edmonton, Alta.: Main Floor, Harley Court, 10045-111th St., T5K 1K4; (403) 420-3355.

Kelowna, B.C.: Rm. 102, 1433 St. Paul St., V1Y 2E4; (604) 763-5322.

Surrey, B.C.: 10447-137th St., V3T 4B1; (604) 585-5730.

Vancouver, B.C.: Ste. 200, Sinclair Centre, 757 West Hastings St., V6C 1A1; (604) 666-3971.

Victoria, B.C.: Rm. 105, Customs House, 816 Government St., V8W 1W9; (604) 388-3464.

Prince George, B.C.: Ste. 400A, Royal Bank Building, 550 Victoria St., V2L 2K1; (604) 561-5303.

(1) Other documents may be required depending upon individual circumstances.

Persons Granted Canadian Citizenship, 1920-1987[1]

Source: The Secretary of State

1920	3 004	1943	12 533	1966	60 852
1921	10 507	1944	12 827	1967	59 968
1922	10 360	1945	13 562	1968	60 055
1923	7 589	1946	9 047	1969	59 900
1924	7 659	1947	15 335	1970	57 556
1925	13 288	1948	11 410	1971	63 669
1926	15 403	1949	11 991[2]	1972	80 866
1927	16 917	1950	10 441	1973	104 697
1928	13 466	1951	10 301	1974	130 278
1929	13 099	1952	10 888	1975	137 507
1930	21 221	1953	13 562	1976	117 276
1931	21 392	1954	19 545	1977	123 655
1932	32 517	1955	58 711	1978	223 214
1933	23 613	1956	55 404	1979	156 699
1934	21 908	1957	95 462	1980	118 590
1935	20 903	1958	84 183	1981	94 457
1936	30 679	1959	71 280	1982	87 468
1937	31 744	1960	62 378	1983	90 328
1938	27 455	1961	56 476	1984	109 504
1939	21 418	1962	72 082	1985	126 466
1940	18 207	1963	69 468	1986	103 800
1941	15 594	1964	64 334	1987	72 791[3]
1942	14 213	1965	63 844		

(1) For fiscal year ending Mar. 31 for 1920 to 1951; calendar years 1952 onwards.(2) Does not include approx. 359 000 Newfoundlanders wh became Canadian citizens when Newfoundland became Canada's 10th province in 1949. (3) Preliminary figure.

Refugees to Canada

Source: Employment and Immigration Canada

Canada has a tradition of refugee and humanitarian assistance. Since the Second World War, about half a million refugees have found new homes in Canada and special humanitarian measures have helped thousands of others. Canada is also a leading contributor to international humanitarian agencies. Cash contributions to the Red Cross and UN High Commissioner for Refugees exceed $50 million per year, and more than $16 million in food aid is contributed annually to refugee relief efforts.

Canada's refugee policy has 2 main components: resettlement from abroad and protection in Canada.

Resettlement from Abroad

There are 10-15 million refugees in the world today. According to the United Nations, the preferred solution for most of these refugees is voluntary repatriation or local integration. For a small minority, however, resettlement in a third country is the best solution.

Applications for refugee resettlement can be made at any Canadian embassy or consulate outside the applicant's home country (except refugees designated as Political Prisoners or Oppressed Persons, who may apply inside their home country). Applications are assessed by a Canadian foreign service officer who interviews the candidate to determine his or her eligibility and admissibility. If accepted, the refugee is given a visa and becomes a permanent resident of Canada upon arrival.

Eligibility

There are 3 categories of people who are eligible for selection from abroad on humanitarian grounds:

Convention Refugees—persons who, by reason of a well-founded fear of persecution, for reasons of race, religion, nationality, political opinion or membership in a particular social group, are unable or unwilling to return to their home country.

Members of Designated Classes—persons in "refugee-like" situations who are in need of resettlement although they may not meet the strict definition of a Convention Refugee. There are 3 such designated classes: Indochinese (Kampuchea, Laos and Vietnam), Political Prisoners and Oppressed Persons

(Chile, El Salvador, Guatemala, Poland and Uruguay), and Self-Exiled Persons (Eastern Europe and U.S.S.R., except Yugoslavia).

Special Humanitarian Measures—resettlement of persons in need of humanitarian relief who do not meet other eligibility requirements, but for whom Canada has a special interest. These include persons, with close relatives in Canada, whose countries may be experiencing an emergency situation such as an earthquake, a flood, a revolution, or a war. Special measures are in effect for citizens of Guatemala, Iran, El Salvador, Lebanon, and Sri Lanka.

Admissibility

Refugees are not subject to the "point system" used to evaluate the skills and adaptability of independent immigrants. Nevertheless, the refugee's ability to successfully adapt to Canadian life is taken into account. The applicant's age, level of education, job skills, and knowledge of English or French are used as guides in determining whether he/she will be able to cope. Also, the amount of financial and other settlement assistance available to the applicant may determine admissibility. In some cases, a refugee may not be admitted because of security or health reasons.

The need for resettlement, however, is the over-riding consideration. If there are compelling humanitarian reasons, persons who do not meet statutory requirements, or who require urgent admission, may be issued Minister's Permits in order to waive admissibility requirements. There are also special initiatives to assist disabled refugees, women at risk, and unaccompanied minors.

Settlement Assistance

Although a person may be a genuine refugee, he or she may be judged unable to adapt successfully in Canada without short-term assistance. In such cases, private sponsorship can help by providing settlement assistance to refugees for up to one year. This assistance includes housing, food, clothing, incidental expenses, community orientation, help in finding a job and moral support. There are also a number of federal and provincial government services available to help refugees resettle in Canada (including interest-free loans to cover travel expenses to Canada, temporary health care, and language training). Refugees are also eligible for all benefits and social assistance programs available to permanent residents of Canada.

Protection in Canada

Under the 1951 Geneva Convention and Protocol, Canada is obliged to protect refugees on its territory against involuntary return to a country in which they fear persecution. In recent years, increasing numbers of economic migrants have been circumventing overseas selection by coming to Canada and falsely claiming refugee status. In 1986, 1 600 claims to refugee status were made within Canada. By 1988, the number had risen to over 27 000.

In May 1987, the federal government introduced legislation to speed up the processing of refugee claims, as well as to curb abuse of the refugee system by persons trying to bypass normal immigration procedures. In August 1987, new measures expanding the government's power to detain refugee claimants without identification and to deport those considered a security risk were introduced in the House of Commons. Many groups, including the United Nations High Commissioner for Refugees,

expressed concerns about the legislation, fearing it might endanger genuine refugee claims. After extensive study and amendment, the new legislation received Royal Assent in August 1988, and was scheduled to be implemented in early 1989.

The new process for refugee claimants includes the following:
• Every person arriving in Canada claiming to be a refugee will first be seen by a panel of 2 people: one, a member of the new Immigration and Refugee Board and the other, an immigration adjudicator.
• People with refugee status elsewhere and people arriving from safe third countries who had a reasonable opportunity to claim protection will be returned to those countries. People with no arguable basis for their claims will be returned to their country of origin. A unanimous decision is required to remove these people, and they retain the right of appeal by leave to the Federal Court, even though they are outside Canada.
• Those people with an arguable claim will be referred to the Refugee Board for an oral hearing.
• The oral hearing will be before 2 members of the Refugee Board: claimants accepted by the Board can apply for landing. A unanimous decision is required to reject the claim. Decisions of the Board may be appealed by leave to the Federal Court of Canada.

Recent Refugees to Canada by Country[1]

Source: Employment and Immigration Canada

	1980	1981	1982	1983	1984	1985	1986	1987
Total Refugees	40 348	14 981	16 929	13 970	15 345	16 760	19 147	21 565
Eastern Europe	4 062	5 013	7 965	4 147	3 499	3 897	5 388	6 843
Bulgaria	51	32	26	36	27	30	34	38
Czechoslovakia	1 015	948	683	1 117	765	764	697	762
Hungary	296	330	250	356	260	516	545	562
Poland	477	2 555	6 345	2 034	2 064	2 209	3 620	4 545
Romania	307	434	478	490	338	334	442	832
USSR	1 914	714	174	98	26	39	40	100
Indochina	34 637	8 684	5 506	4 957	5 761	6 163	6 065	5 874
Kampuchea	3 261	1 302	1 347	1 513	1 492	1 593	1 665	1 546
Laos	6 264	855	359	423	863	360	617	438
Vietnam	25 112	6 527	3 800	3 021	3 406	4 210	3 783	3 890
Middle East	37	35	329	799	1 054	1 150	1 139	1 208
Iran	16	17	292	541	608	819	874	994
Iraq	5	5	5	226	408	294	183	130
Lebanon	10	7	4	8	14	16	26	30
Africa	191	239	394	892	1 107	1 061	1 249	1 436
Ethiopia	72	61	139	457	685	709	905	869
Ghana	–	4	–	2	24	51	38	29
Nigeria	2	–	17	41	62	1	5	13
South Africa	16	16	13	37	36	17	53	34
Sudan	9	4	32	70	31	20	19	77
Uganda	3	5	20	83	117	113	54	73
Central America[2]	308	68	360	2 087	2 753	3 617	3 931	3 964
Cuba	293	13	52	33	23	55	41	20
El Salvador	1	38	266	1 758	2 030	2 491	2 459	2 368
Guatemala	2	4	10	169	490	546	710	549
Haiti	8	10	21	23	44	14	6	10
Honduras	–	–	1	2	13	50	39	25
Nicaragua	3	1	5	43	93	451	670	955
South America	396	423	407	324	305	289	407	492
Argentina	21	57	57	56	58	27	9	3
Chile	355	309	322	213	143	133	182	320
Guyana	1	–	–	8	41	83	154	104
Uruguay	14	25	12	27	32	26	22	8
Other	717	519	1 968	764	866	583	968	1 748
Afghanistan	7	32	68	66	100	346	539	801
Sri Lanka	1	–	6	1	32	123	265	599

(1) By country of last permanent residence. Represents total number of refugees admitted to Canada from abroad as Convention Refugees or members of Designated Classes. Excludes Special Humanitarian Movements. (2) Includes the Caribbean.
– = zero.

Refugees to Canada, 1959-1988

Source: Employment and Immigration Canada

1959	3 047	1967	1 499	1975	748	1983	13 643
1960	2 329	1968	820	1976	1 014	1984	15 400
1961	1 813	1969	799	1977	1 061	1985	16 550
1962	1 733	1970	1 387	1978	775	1986	18 625
1963	2 024	1971	626	1979	27 740	1987	20 673
1964	2 279	1972	365	1980	40 361	1988[2]	12 692
1965	2 131	1973	405	1981	14 996		
1966	2 058	1974	537	1982	16 908		

(1) Represents total number of refugees admitted to Canada from abroad as Convention Refugees or members of Designated Classes and those admitted on the strength of Minister's Permits (who have been selected from abroad on an emergency basis and are not granted permanent residence on arrival but are allowed to remain in Canada for up to one year and may apply for permanent residence after arrival). Excludes Special Humanitarian Movements. (2) Up to June.

Special Refugee and Humanitarian Movements, 1947-1988

Source: Employment and Immigration Canada

1947-52	Post-War European Movement	186 150
1956-57	Hungarian Movement	37 149
1968-69	Czechoslovakian Movement	11 943
1970	Tibetans	228
1972-73	Ugandan Asians	7 069
1973-79	Special South American Program	7 016
1975	Cypriots	700
1975-78	Special Vietnamese/Cambodian Program	9 060
1976	Kurds from Iraq	98
1976-79	Lebanese Movement	11 321
1978-84	Argentine Political Detainee Program	9
1982-85	Polish Special Movement	9 365
1982-present	Iranian Special Movement	3 369[1]
1982-present	El Salvadoran Special Movement	3 474[1]
1983-present	Lebanon Special Movement	4 958[1]
1983-present	Sri Lankan Special Movement	2 052[1]
1984-present	Guatemala Special Movement	1 111[1]

(1) Figure represents preliminary total up to end of June 1988.

Resettled Refugees[1] by Country, 1975-1986

Source: *World Refugee Survey, 1987*, U.S. Committee for Refugees

Resettlement country	Resettled refugees[1] 1975-1985	1986	Indigenous population (millions)	Ratio of refugees to population
Namibia	40 000	n.a.	1.3	1: 33
Australia	127 767	11 840	16.2	1: 116
Canada	178 781	22 920	25.9	1: 128
Sweden	36 789	13 419	8.4	1: 167
Denmark	14 512	9 299	5.1	1: 214
United States	1 030 529	70 831	243.8	1: 221
Switzerland	18 336	820	6.6	1: 345
France	145 959	10 645	55.6	1: 355
New Zealand	7 771	689	3.3	1: 390
Austria	14 171	1 432	7.6	1: 487
Norway	7 263[2]	835	4.2	1: 519
West Germany	54 224	8 893	61.0	1: 834
Netherlands	10 707	2 027	14.6	1:1 147
Spain	25 706	683	39.0	1:1 478
Belgium	3 842[2]	n.a.	9.9	1:2 577

(1) Resettled refugees are those who have been accepted for permanent settlement. The primary source for numbers of resettled refugees was the U.S. State Department. This ranking represents the top 15 countries among those for which refugee resettlement figures were available. (2) Statistics unavailable for 1975-1981, represents statistics for 1982-1985. n.a. not available.

Foreign Relations

Major International Organizations

Association of Southeast Asian Nations (ASEAN), was formed in 1967 to promote political and economic cooperation among the non-communist states of the region. Members in 1988 were Brunei, Indonesia, Malaysia, the Philippines, Singapore and Thailand. Annual ministerial meetings set policy; a central Secretariat in Jakarta, Indonesia and 9 permanent committees work in trade, transportation, communications, agriculture, science, finance, and culture.

Caribbean Community (CARICOM) was formed in 1973 providing economic co-operation through the Caribbean Common Market, co-ordination of foreign policy and co-operation in such areas as health, education, culture, sports, science and tax administration for its member states. Members include Antigua and Barbuda, Bahamas, Barbados, Belize, Dominica, Guyana, Jamaica, Montserrat, St. Kitts-Nevis, St. Lucia, St. Vincent and the Grenadines and Trinidad and Tobago.

Colombo Plan was founded in 1950 to promote the development of newly independent Asian countries. Since then, it has evolved into an association of nations with aims to promote interest and support for economic and social development and to accelerate this development through co-operative effort. Member countries include: Afghanistan, Australia, Bangladesh, Bhutan, Burma, Kampuchea, Canada, Fiji, India, Indonesia, Iran, Japan, South Korea, Laos, Malaysia, Maldives, Nepal, New Zealand, Pakistan, Papua New Guinea, the Philippines, Singapore, Sri Lanka, Thailand, the United Kingdom and the United States.

Commonwealth of Nations: see pages 100–101.

Council for Mutual Economic Assistance (COMECON) was founded by the USSR, Bulgaria, Czechoslovakia, Hungary, Poland and Romania. Later admissions were Albania (ceased participation in 1961), East Germany, Mongolia, Cuba, Vietnam and Yugoslavia (minor status). Afghanistan, Angola, Ethiopia, Laos, Mexico, Mozambique, Nicaragua and South Yemen attend COMECON sessions as observers. The aims of the Council are to promote socialist economic integration, planned development of national economies, economic and technical advancement and increased industrialization for Third World countries.

European Communities (EC, the Common Market) is the collective designation of three organizations with common membership: the European Economic Community (Common Market), the European Coal and Steel Community, and the European Atomic Energy Community. The 12 full members are: Belgium, Denmark, France, West Germany, Greece, Ireland, Italy, Luxembourg, the Netherlands, Portugal, Spain, United Kingdom. Some 60 nations in Africa, the Caribbean, and the Pacific are affiliated under the Lomé Convention.

A merger of the 3 communities executives went into effect July 1, 1967, though the component organizations date back to 1951 and 1958. A Council of Ministers, a Commission, a European Parliament, and a Court of Justice comprise the permanent structure. The communities aim to integrate their economies, coordinate social developments, and bring about political union of the democratic states of Europe.

European Free Trade Association (EFTA), consisting of Austria, Iceland, Norway, Portugal, Sweden, Switzerland and associated member Finland, was created Jan. 4, 1960, to gradually reduce customs duties and quantitative restrictions between members on industrial products. By Dec. 31, 1966, virtually all tariffs and quotas had been eliminated. The association entered into free trade agreements with the EC, Jan. 1, 1973. Trade barriers were removed July 1, 1976.

Latin American Free Trade Association (LAFTA) was formed on Feb. 18, 1961 to promote freer trade by eliminating customs duties and export quotas. Members include: Argentina, Bolivia, Brazil, Chile, Colombia, Ecuador, Mexico, Paraguay, Peru, Uruguay and Venezuela.

League of Arab States (The Arab League) was created Mar. 22, 1945, by Egypt, Iraq, Jordan, Lebanon, Saudi Arabia, Syria, and Yemen. Joining later were Algeria, Bahrain, Djibouti, Kuwait, Libya, Mauritania, Morocco, Oman, Qatar, Somalia, Sudan, Tunisia, United Arab Emirates, North Yemen and South Yemen. The Palestine Liberation Organization has also been admitted as a full member. The League fosters cultural, economic, and communication ties and mediates disputes among the Arab states; it represents Arab states in certain international negotiations. As a result of Egypt signing a peace treaty with Israel, the League, Mar. 1979, suspended Egypt's membership and transferred the League's headquarters from Cairo to Tunis.

North Atlantic Treaty Org. (NATO) was created by treaty (signed Apr. 4, 1949; in effect Aug. 24, 1949) among Belgium, Canada, Denmark, France, Iceland, Italy, Luxembourg, the Netherlands, Norway, Portugal, United Kingdom, and the United States. Greece, Turkey, West Germany, and Spain have joined since. The members agreed to settle disputes by peaceful means; to develop their individual and collective capacity to resist armed attack; to regard an attack on one as an attack on all, and to take necessary action to repel an attack under Article 51 of the United Nations Charter.

The NATO structure consists of a Council and a Military Committee of 3 commands (Allied Command Europe, Allied Command Atlantic, Allied Command Channel) and the Canada-U.S. Regional Planning Group.

Following announcement in 1966 of nearly total French withdrawal from the military affairs of NATO, organization headquarters moved from Paris to Brussels in 1967. In August, 1974, Greece announced a total withdrawal of armed forces from NATO, in response to Turkish intervention in Cyprus. Greece rejoined NATO's military wing, Oct. 20, 1980.

Organization of African Unity (OAU), formed May 25, 1963, by 32 African countries (50 in 1988) to coordinate cultural, political, scientific and economic policies; to end colonialism in Africa; and to promote a common defense of members' independence. It holds annual conferences of heads of state. Hq. is in Addis Ababa, Ethiopia.

Organization of American States (OAS) was formed in Bogota, Colombia, in 1948. Hq. is in Washington, D.C. The purpose of the OAS is to achieve peace and justice, to promote American solidarity and to recognize each member's sovereignty, territorial integrity and independence. There are 32 members, each with one vote in the Council of Organization: Antigua and Barbuda, Argentina, Bahamas, Barbados, Bolivia, Brazil, Chile, Colombia, Costa Rica, Cuba, Dominica, Dominican Republic, Ecuador, El Salvador, Grenada, Guatemala, Haiti, Honduras, Jamaica, Mexico, Nicaragua, Panama, Paraguay, Peru, St. Kitts-Nevis, St. Lucia, St. Vincent and the Grenadines, Suriname, Trinidad & Tobago, U.S., Uruguay and Venezuela. In 1962, the OAS excluded Cuba from OAS activities but not from membership.

Organization for Economic Cooperation and Development (OECD) was established Sept. 30, 1961 to promote economic and social welfare in member countries, and to stimulate and harmonize efforts on behalf of developing nations. Nearly all the industrialized "free market" countries belong, with Yugoslavia as an associate member. OECD collects and disseminates economic and environmental information. Members in 1988 were: Australia, Austria, Belgium, Canada, Denmark, Finland, France, West Germany, Greece, Iceland, Ireland, Italy, Japan, Luxembourg, the Netherlands, New Zealand, Norway, Portugal, Spain, Sweden, Switzerland, Turkey, United Kingdom, United States and Yugoslavia (special member). Headquarters is in Paris.

Organization of Petroleum Exporting Countries (OPEC) was created Nov. 14, 1960 at Venezuela's initiative. The group has often been successful in determining world oil prices, and in advancing members' interests in trade and development dealings with industrialized oil-consuming nations. Members in 1988 were Algeria, Ecuador, Gabon, Indonesia, Iran, Iraq, Kuwait, Libya, Nigeria, Qatar, Saudi Arabia, United Arab Emirates and Venezuela.

United Nations: see pages 101–103.

Warsaw Pact was created May 14, 1955, as a mutual defence alliance. Members in 1988 were Bulgaria, Czechoslovakia, East Germany, Hungary, Poland, Romania, and the USSR. Hq. is in Moscow. It provides for a unified military command; if one member is attacked, the others will aid it with all necessary steps including armed force.

Canadian Representatives to International Organizations

(as of Sept. 1988)

European Communities Commission, Brussels	Daniel Molgat, Amb., H.M.
FAO (Food and Agriculture Organization), Rome	G.H. Musgrove, P.R.
GATT (General Agreement on Tariffs and Trade), Geneva	John M. Weekes, Amb., P.R.
Habitat (U.N. Centre for Human Settlements), Nairobi	A. Raynell Andreychuk, P.R.
International Civil Aviation Organization, Montreal	D.M. Fiorita, P.R.
Mutual and Balanced Force Reductions Talks, Vienna	Michael Shenstone, H.D., Amb.
North Atlantic Council, Brussels	Gordon S. Smith, P.R., Amb.
Office of the U.N.; Conference on Disarmament, Geneva	de Montigny Marchand, P.R., Amb.
Office of the U.N.; U.N. Industrial Development Organization, International Atomic Energy Agency, Vienna	Michael Shenstone, P.R., Amb.
Organization of American States, Washington	vacant
Organization for Economic Co-Operation and Development, Paris	L. Michael Berry, P.R., Amb.
UNEP (U.N. Environment Program), Nairobi	A. Raynell Andreychuk, P.R.
UNESCO (U.N. Educational, Scientific and Cultural Organization), Paris	Jean Drapeau, Amb.
United Nations, New York	Yves Fortier, P.R., Amb.

H.D. = Head of Delegation; H.M. = Head of Mission; Amb. = Ambassador; P.R. = Permanent Representative; P.O. = Permanent Observer; P.D. = Permanent Delegate.

The Commonwealth

Source: Department of External Affairs

The Commonwealth is a loosely-structured, voluntary association of 48 independent states which were once part of the British Empire. Its roots can be traced to the early 1900s and the concept of autonomous nations within the Empire co-operating in such matters as foreign policy, out of a common allegiance to the Crown. The Commonwealth was more formally established in 1931 when the *Statute of Westminster* legally granted self-government to the Dominions within the Empire. Founding members were Britain, Canada, Newfoundland (which ceased to be an independent member upon entering Confederation in 1949), Australia, New Zealand and South Africa (which left in 1961 due to Commonwealth opposition to its racial policies).

The number of members grew quickly from the late 1940s into the 1960s as many Asian and African countries gained independence. In more recent years, many small Caribbean, Indian Ocean and Pacific Island countries have become member states. Current membership represents about a quarter of the world's population and about a third of the countries in the United Nations.

The Commonwealth has no written charter or constitution. It is a forum for pooling experience and expressing viewpoints. The highest level of Commonwealth consultation is the Heads of Government Meetings, held every 2 years. In 1971, the Commonwealth adopted 5 principles: the pursuit of international peace and order through the United Nations; the promotion of representative institutions and guarantees for personal freedom under the law; the recognition of racial equality and the need to combat racial discrimination; opposition to all forms of colonial domination and racial oppression; and dedication to lessening the disparities in wealth between different sections of mankind.

Aid is distributed to developing countries, and many economic, social and educational programs are sponsored through the Commonwealth Secretariat, which is funded by members under a system of assessed contributions.

Commonwealth Members[1]

Country	Year Joined	Country	Year Joined
Antigua and Barbuda	1981	Malta	1964
Australia	1931	Mauritius	1968
Bahamas	1973	Nauru[2]	1968
Bangladesh	1972	New Zealand	1931
Barbados	1966	Nigeria	1960
Belize	1981	Papua New Guinea	1975
Britain	1931	St. Christopher and Nevis	1983
Botswana	1966	St. Lucia	1979
Brunei Darussalam	1984	St. Vincent and The Grenadines	1979
Canada	1931	Seychelles	1976
Cyprus	1961	Sierra Leone	1961
Dominica	1978	Singapore	1965
The Gambia	1965	Solomon Islands	1978
Ghana	1957	Sri Lanka	1948
Grenada	1974	Swaziland	1968
Guyana	1966	Tanzania	1961
India	1947	Tonga	1970
Jamaica	1962	Trinidad and Tobago	1962
Kenya	1963	Tuvalu[2]	1978
Kiribati	1979	Uganda	1962
Lesotho	1966	Vanuatu	1980
Malawi	1964	Western Samoa	1970
Malaysia	1957	Zambia	1964
Maldives	1982	Zimbabwe	1980

(1) As of June 1988. (2) Special Member of the Commonwealth. Has right to participate in all meetings and activities except meetings of Commonwealth Heads of State.

United Nations

The 42d regular session of the United Nations General Assembly was scheduled to open in September, 1988.

UN headquarters are in New York, N.Y., between First Ave. and Roosevelt Drive and E. 42d St. and E. 48th St. The General Assembly Bldg., Secretariat, Conference and Library bldgs. are interconnected. A new UN office building-hotel was opened in New York in 1976.

A European office at Geneva includes Secretariat and agency staff members. Other offices of UN bodies and related organizations are scattered throughout the world.

The UN has a post office originating its own stamps.

Proposals to establish an organization of nations for maintenance of world peace led to the United Nations Conference on International Organization at San Francisco, Apr. 25-June 26, 1945, where the charter of the United Nations was drawn up. It was signed June 26 by 50 nations, and by Poland, one of the original 51, on Oct. 15, 1945. The charter came into effect Oct. 24, 1945, upon ratification by the permanent members of the Security Council and a majority of other signatories.

United Nations Secretaries General

Year	Secretary, Nation	Year	Secretary, Nation	Year	Secretary, Nation
1946	Trygve Lie, Norway	1961	U Thant, Burma	1982	Javier Perez de Cuellar, Peru
1953	Dag Hammarskjold, Sweden	1972	Kurt Waldheim, Austria		

Organization

The text of the UN Charter, and further information, may be obtained from the Office of Public Information, United Nations, New York, NY, U.S.A. 10017.

General Assembly. The General Assembly is composed of representatives of all the member nations. Each nation is entitled to one vote.

The General Assembly meets in regular annual sessions and in special session when necessary. Special sessions are convoked by the Secretary General at the request of the Security Council or of a majority of the members of the UN.

On important questions a two-thirds majority of members present and voting is required; on other questions a simple majority is sufficient.

The General Assembly must approve the budget and apportion expenses among members. A member in arrears will have no vote if the amount of arrears equals or exceeds the amount of the contributions due for the preceeding two full years.

Security Council. The Security Council consists of 15 members, 5 with permanent seats. The remaining 10 are elected for 2-year terms by the General Assembly; they are not eligible for immediate reelection.

Permanent members of the Council: China, France, USSR, United Kingdom, United States.

Non-permanent members are Argentina, W. Germany, Italy, Japan and Zambia (until Dec. 31, 1988); Algeria, Brazil, Nepal, Senegal and Yugoslavia (until Dec. 31, 1989).

The Security Council has the primary responsiblity within the UN for maintaining international peace and security. The Council may investigate any dispute that threatens international peace and security.

Any member of the UN at UN headquarters may participate in its discussions and a nation not a member of UN may appear if it is a party to a dispute.

Decisions on procedural questions are made by an affirmative vote of 9 members. On all other matters the affirmative vote of 9 members must include the concurring votes of all permanent members; it is this clause which gives rise to the so-called "veto." A party to a dispute must refrain from voting.

The Security Council directs the various truce supervisory forces deployed throughout the world.

Economic and Social Council. The Economic and Social Council consists of 54 members elected by the General Assembly for 3-year terms of office. The council is responsible under the General Assembly for carrying out the functions of the United Nations with regard to international economic, social, cultural, educational, health and related matters. The council meets usually twice a year.

Trusteeship Council. The administration of trust territories is under UN supervision. The only remaining trust territory is the Pacific Islands, administered by the U.S.

Secretariat. The Secretary General is the chief administrative officer of the UN. He may bring to the attention of the Security Council any matter that threatens international peace. He reports to the General Assembly.

Budget: The General Assembly approved a total budget for 1988 and 1989 of $1.77 billion.

International Court of Justice. The International Court of Justice is the principal judicial organ of the United Nations. All members are *ipso facto* parties to the statute of the Court, as are three nonmembers — Liechtenstein, San Marino, and Switzerland. Other states may become parties to the Court's statute.

The jurisdiction of the Court comprises cases which the parties submit to it and matters especially provided for in the charter or in treaties. The Court gives advisory opinions and renders judgments. Its decisions are only binding between the parties concerned and in respect to a particular dispute. If any party to a case fails to heed a judgment, the other party may have recourse to the Security Council.

The 15 judges are elected for 9-year terms by the General Assembly and the Security Council. Retiring judges are eligible for re-election. The Court remains permanently in session, except during vacations. All questions are decided by majority. The Court sits in The Hague, Netherlands.

Judges: 9-year term in office ending 1994: Ni Vhengyo, China; Jens Evensen, Norway; Manfred Lachs, Poland; Taslim Olawala Elias, Nigeria. **9-year term in office ending 1991:** Nagendra Singh, India; Jose Maria Ruda, Argentina; Robert Y. Jennings, United Kingdom; Guy Ladreit de Lacharriere, France; Keba Mbaye, Senegal. **9-year term in office ending 1988:** Robert Ago, Italy; Stephen M. Schwebel, U.S; Mohammed Bedjaoui, Algeria; Platon D. Morozov, USSR; Jose Sette Camara, Brazil.

Specialized and Related Agencies

These agencies are autonomous, with their own memberships and organs which have a functional relationship or working agreement with the UN (headquarters.)

International Labor Org. (ILO) aims to promote employment; improve labor conditions and living standards. (4 route de Morillons, CH-1211, Geneva 22, Switzerland.)

Food & Agriculture Org. (FAO) aims to increase production from farms, forests, and fisheries; improve distribution, marketing, and nutrition; better conditions for rural people. (Viale delle Terme di Caracalla, 00100 Rome, Italy.)

United Nations Educational, Scientific, & Cultural Org. (UNESCO) aims to promote collaboration among nations through education, science, and culture. (9 Place de Fontenoy, 75700 Paris, France.)

World Health Org. (WHO) aims to aid the attainment of the highest possible level of health. (20 Ave. Appia, 1211 Geneva, Switzerland.)

International Monetary Fund (IMF) aims to promote international monetary co-operation and currency stabilization; expansion of international trade. (700 19th St., NW, Washington, DC, 20431.)

International Maritime Org. (IMO) aims to promote co-operation on technical matters affecting international shipping. (4 Albert Embankment, London, SE1 7SR, England.)

World Intellectual Property Organization (WIPO) seeks to protect, through international cooperation, literary, industrial, scientific, and artistic works. (34, Chemin des Colom Bettes, 1211 Geneva, Switzerland.)

International Atomic Energy Agency (IAEA) aims to promote the safe, peaceful uses of atomic energy. (Vienna International Centre, PO Box 100, A-1400, Vienna, Austria.)

General Agreement on Tariffs and Trade (GATT) is the only treaty setting rules for world trade. Provides a forum for settling trade disputes and negotiating trade liberalization. (Centre William Rappard, 154 rue de Lausanne, 1211 Geneva 21, Switzerland.)

International Civil Aviation Org. (ICAO) promotes international civil aviation standards and regulations. (1000 Sherbrooke St. W., Montreal, Quebec H3A 2R2.)

Universal Postal Union (UPU) aims to perfect postal services and promote international collaboration. (Weltpoststrasse 4, 3000 Berne, 15 Switzerland.)

International Telecommunication Union (ITU) sets up international regulations of radio, telegraph, telephone and space radio-communications. Allocates radio frequencies. (Place des Nations, 1211 Geneva 20, Switzerland.)

World Meteorological Org. (WMO) aims to co-ordinate and improve world meteorological work. (Case Postale 5, CH-1211, Geneva, Switzerland.)

International Fund for Agricultural Development (IFAD) aims to mobilize funds for agricultural and rural projects in developing countries. (107 Via del Serafico, 00142 Rome, Italy.)

International Bank for Reconstruction and Development (IBRD) (World Bank) provides loans and technical assistance for economic development projects in developing member countries; encourages cofinancing for projects from other public and private sources. **International Development Association (IDA),** an affiliate of the Bank, provides funds for development projects on concessionary terms to the poorer developing member countries. (both 1818 H St., NW, Washington, DC, U.S.A. 20433.) **International Finance Corporation (IFC)** an affiliate of the Bank, promotes the growth of the private sector in developing member countries; encourages the development of local capital markets; stimulates the international flow of private capital. (1818 H St., NW, Washington, DC, U.S.A. 20433.)

United Nations Children's Fund (UNICEF) provides aid and development assistance to children and mothers in developing countries. (1 UN Plaza, New York, NY, U.S.A. 10017.)

Roster of the United Nations

(As of mid–1988)

The 159 members of the United Nations, with the years in which they became members.

Member	Year	Member	Year	Member	Year	Member	Year
Afghanistan	1946	Denmark	1945	Lesotho	1966	Sao Tome e Principe	1975
Albania	1955	Djibouti	1977	Liberia	1945	Saudi Arabia	1945
Algeria	1962	Dominica	1978	Libya	1955	Senegal	1960
Angola	1976	Dominican Rep.	1945	Luxembourg	1945	Seychelles	1976
Antigua and Barbuda	1981	Ecuador	1945	Madagascar (Malagasy)	1960	Sierra Leone	1961
Argentina	1945	Egypt[2]	1945	Malawi	1964	Singapore[1]	1965
Australia	1945	El Salvador	1945	Malaysia[1]	1957	Solomon Islands	1978
Austria	1955	Equatorial Guinea	1968	Maldives	1965	Somalia	1960
Bahamas	1973	Ethiopia	1945	Mali	1960	South Africa[5]	1945
Bahrain	1971	Fiji	1970	Malta	1964	Spain	1955
Bangladesh	1974	Finland	1955	Mauritania	1961	Sri Lanka	1955
Barbados	1966	France	1945	Mauritius	1968	Sudan	1956
Belgium	1945	Gabon	1960	Mexico	1945	Suriname	1975
Belize	1981	Gambia	1965	Mongolia	1961	Swaziland	1968
Benin	1960	Germany, East	1973	Morocco	1956	Sweden	1946
Bhutan	1971	Germany, West	1973	Mozambique	1975	Syria[2]	1945
Bolivia	1945	Ghana	1957	Nepal	1955	Tanzania[3]	1961
Botswana	1966	Greece	1945	Netherlands	1945	Thailand	1946
Brazil	1945	Grenada	1974	New Zealand	1945	Togo	1960
Brunei	1984	Guatemala	1945	Nicaragua	1945	Trinidad & Tobago	1962
Bulgaria	1955	Guinea	1958	Niger	1960	Tunisia	1956
Burkina Faso	1960	Guinea-Bissau	1974	Nigeria	1960	Turkey	1945
Burma	1948	Guyana	1966	Norway	1945	Uganda	1962
Burundi	1962	Haiti	1945	Oman	1971	Ukraine	1945
Byelorussia	1945	Honduras	1945	Pakistan	1947	USSR	1945
Cambodia (Kampuchea)	1955	Hungary	1955	Panama	1945	United Arab Emirates	1971
Cameroon	1960	Iceland	1946	Papua New Guinea	1975	United Kingdom	1945
Canada	1945	India	1945	Paraguay	1945	United States	1945
Cape Verde	1975	Indonesia[6]	1950	Peru	1945	Uruguay	1945
Central Afr. Rep.	1960	Iran	1945	Philippines	1945	Vanuatu	1981
Chad	1960	Iraq	1945	Poland	1945	Venezuela	1945
Chile	1945	Ireland	1955	Portugal	1955	Vietnam	1977
China[4]	1945	Israel	1949	Qatar	1971	Yemen	1947
Colombia	1945	Italy	1955	Romania	1955	Yemen, South	1967
Comoros	1975	Jamaica	1962	Rwanda	1962	Yugoslavia	1945
Congo	1960	Japan	1956	Saint Christopher		Zaire	1960
Costa Rica	1945	Jordan	1955	& Nevis	1983	Zambia	1964
Côte d'Ivoire	1960	Kenya	1963	Saint Lucia	1979	Zimbabwe	1980
Cuba	1945	Kuwait	1963	Saint Vincent and the			
Cyprus	1960	Laos	1955	Grenadines	1980		
Czechoslovakia	1945	Lebanon	1945	Samoa (Western)	1976		

(1) Malaya joined the UN in 1957. In 1963, its name was changed to Malaysia following the accession of Singapore, Sabah, and Sarawak. Singapore became an independent UN member in 1965. (2) Egypt and Syria were original members of the UN. In 1958, the United Arab Republic was established by a union of Egypt and Syria and continued as a single member of the UN. In 1961, Syria resumed its separate membership. (3) Tanganyika was a member of the United Nations from 1961 and Zanzibar was a member from 1963. Following the ratification in 1964 of Articles of Union between Tanganyika and Zanzibar, the United Republic of Tanganyika and Zanzibar continued as a single member of the United Nations, later changing its name to United Republic of Tanzania. (4) The General Assembly voted in 1971 to expel the Chinese government on Taiwan and admit the Beijing government in its place. (5) The General Assembly rejected the credentials of the South African delegates in 1974, and suspended the country from the Assembly. (6) Indonesia withdrew from the UN in 1965 and rejoined in 1966.

Canadian Ambassadors to the United Nations

Source: Dept. of External Affairs

Ambassador	Date appointed	Ambassador	Date appointed
Andrew McNaughton	Jan. 1948	Yvon Beaulne	Feb. 1969
John Holmes	Jan. 1950	Saul Forbes Rae	1972
Gerald Riddell	June 1950	William Barton	Aug. 1976
David Johnson	Oct. 1951	Michel Dupuy	May 1980
Robert MacKay	June 1955	Gérard Pelletier	Aug. 1981
Charles Ritchie	Nov. 1957	Stephen H. Lewis	Dec. 1984
Paul Tremblay	May 1962	Yves Fortier	Aug. 1988
George Ignatieff	July 1966		

Canadian Foreign Aid Policy

Canadian foreign aid totalled $2.5 billion in the 1986-87 fiscal year. About 75 percent of this is distributed through the Canadian International Development Agency (CIDA), whose primary goal is to help developing countries become self-sufficient in such areas as agriculture, energy and education. To accomplish this, CIDA mainly provides practical training, equipment and food rather than donations of money. The portion of the foreign aid budget not administered by CIDA goes to international organizations such as the United Nations and the World Bank, with a small amount to private agencies.

Canada's foreign aid projects started with contributions to the United Nations during the 1940s. In 1950, Canada supported the Colombo Plan, assistance aimed at the newly-independent Asian nations of India, Pakistan and Ceylon (now Sri Lanka).

During the next 2 decades, Canadian aid expanded to include the Caribbean (1958), Commonwealth Africa (1959), Francophone Africa (1961) and Latin America (1964).

By the time CIDA was created in 1968, Canadian foreign aid had begun focussing on self-sufficiency rather than its earlier goal of encouraging rapid industrial development. During the 1970s, Canadian aid was aimed at improving social conditions in very poor countries by assisting in such areas as rural planning and public health.

In 1980, the Canadian government announced its intention to increase foreign aid to 0.7 percent of the gross national product (GNP) by the end of this decade. Assistance is currently 0.50 percent of GNP (1987), about the same level it was in the late 1970s.

Canadian Expenditure on Foreign Aid, 1950-1987

Source: Canadian International Development Agency

(millions of dollars)

	Foreign aid[1]	% of GNP		Foreign aid[1]	% of GNP		Foreign aid[1]	% of GNP
1950	13	.08	1963	58	.13	1976	910	.53
1951	13	.07	1964	65	.14	1977	972	.49
1952	27	.12	1965	101	.20	1978	1 050	.49
1953	8	.03	1966	123	.22	1979	1 166	.49
1954	14	.05	1967	214	.34	1980	1 291	.47
1955	16	.06	1968	193	.29	1981	1 307	.43
1956	29	.10	1969	212	.28	1982	1 489	.43
1957	30	.09	1970	279	.34	1983	1 670	.46
1958	62	.18	1971	346	.40	1984	1 812	.45
1959	72	.20	1972	398	.41	1985	2 097	.49
1960	70	.19	1973	525	.47	1986	2 174	.46
1961	76	.20	1974	591	.46	1987	2 521	.50
1962	61	.15	1975	750	.49			

(1) For fiscal year ending Mar. 31.

Canadian Foreign Aid,[1] by Country

Source: Canadian International Development Agency

(millions of dollars; for fiscal year ending Mar. 31)

	1970	1975	1980	1985	1986	1987
Africa	37.39	208.01	285.67	548.28	449.61	557.14
Algeria	3.91	9.21	0.88	5.84	6.00	0.01
Angola	–	–	–	1.85	1.40	5.40
Benin	–	4.50	5.03	1.81	0.59	1.00
Botswana	–	7.20	3.56	7.56	4.65	15.18
Burkina Faso	–	4.02	18.09	11.21	16.82	16.60
Burundi	–	0.14	0.03	1.69	1.50	2.12
Cameroon	2.29	4.58	15.29	33.36	16.27	20.58
Chad	–	3.42	0.20	2.57	1.45	2.01
Congo	–	4.03	1.62	1.17	1.05	0.72
Côte d'Ivoire	1.11	4.24	16.99	17.88	14.35	13.78
Egypt	–	–	27.78	10.73	10.51	8.56
Ethiopia	0.03	6.47	2.09	47.00	56.70	25.82
Gabon	n.a.	0.77	–	0.87	3.11	5.02
Gambia	n.a.	–	0.03	0.95	0.87	1.67
Ghana	4.44	13.17	17.97	45.97	17.17	30.02

	1970	1975	1980	1985	1986	1987
Guinea	–	0.51	0.05	18.06	8.15	5.51
Guinea-Bissau	n.a.	n.a.	0.03	0.49	0.52	1.08
Kenya	1.99	5.20	12.78	38.71	31.90	36.90
Lesotho	–	0.62	7.02	4.67	4.16	5.44
Malawi	–	9.11	15.96	4.31	2.78	8.07
Mali	–	6.57	12.79	14.43	19.07	28.35
Mauritania	–	3.13	0.72	4.94	5.62	0.60
Morocco	0.50	4.86	2.58	8.58	3.16	9.09
Mozambique	–	–	0.06	13.14	3.26	9.18
Niger	1.11	16.84	4.08	21.87	26.74	28.69
Nigeria	4.63	10.20	0.56	1.70	1.20	1.09
Rwanda	0.86	3.68	5.84	15.03	12.19	8.13
Senegal	1.98	5.69	8.76	20.35	22.90	34.73
Sierra Leone	–	0.29	0.37	1.31	0.66	1.92
Somalia	–	0.99	0.02	0.96	1.08	1.15
South Africa	n.a.	–	–	0.98	2.19	3.28
Sudan	–	–	2.40	22.19	29.62	19.51
Swaziland	–	0.65	1.69	3.78	3.29	3.96
Tanzania	2.24	38.34	27.64	44.93	26.81	54.56
Togo	–	1.44	9.17	3.62	10.88	6.99
Tunisia	7.24	11.72	10.87	6.53	–	6.73
Uganda	1.17	0.36	0.27	3.83	1.86	4.17
Zaire	0.96	6.33	8.18	24.33	17.22	26.91
Zambia	–	4.39	15.98	22.89	18.56	19.78
Zimbabwe	–	0.01	0.04	18.07	17.29	14.10
Asia	**140.93**	**244.25**	**234.62**	**410.85**	**409.14**	**461.29**
Bangladesh	–	69.13	65.18	105.76	103.53	128.27
Burma	–	1.39	6.33	3.22	3.03	1.66
China	–	–	–	13.51	21.80	36.35
India	88.61	96.40	42.60	90.08	52.45	71.02
Indonesia	2.33	19.52	11.75	37.05	77.49	46.44
Jordan	n.a.	–	–	0.66	0.65	1.10
Lebanon	–	–	n.a.	1.11	1.48	3.39
Malaysia	1.57	1.61	1.75	3.17	3.19	5.08
Nepal	–	0.07	6.74	10.08	8.87	12.00
Pakistan	32.76	32.23	67.17	66.30	73.19	57.61
Philippines	–	0.02	0.37	8.34	8.06	16.65
Singapore	–	0.34	–	1.10	1.10	0.75
Sri Lanka	6.40	10.84	15.94	37.97	27.99	32.93
Syria	n.a.	–	–	–	0.20	1.06
Thailand	2.26	0.41	6.79	22.02	15.55	31.69
Central America	**n.a.**	**n.a.**	**42.16**	**145.06**	**n.a.**	**n.a.**
Antigua	n.a.	0.15	1.90	1.41	0.39	0.77
Barbados	0.40	0.77	2.16	9.10	3.95	1.86
Belize	0.46	1.39	3.77	4.22	4.74	7.98
Costa Rica	n.a.	0.15	0.17	8.07	8.70	15.36
Dominica	n.a.	0.56	1.95	9.57	7.62	2.69
Dominican Republic	n.a.	3.71	0.34	5.00	2.22	3.14
El Salvador	n.a.	1.42	1.37	1.51	1.80	9.23
Grenada	n.a.	0.24	0.07	3.89	6.85	5.85
Guatemala	n.a.	0.02	2.94	2.39	1.99	3.11
Haiti	n.a.	1.34	7.59	8.77	7.67	17.74
Honduras	n.a.	2.19	4.62	20.45	4.35	4.97
Jamaica	2.72	3.11	7.76	29.11	34.07	31.53
Mexico	n.a.	–	–	1.78	4.52	4.77
Nicaragua	n.a.	1.02	0.20	8.52	8.24	8.51
Panama	n.a.	–	–	0.77	0.64	1.53
St. Kitts/Nevis	n.a.	0.21	1.50	1.35	0.85	0.97
St. Lucia	n.a.	2.93	0.24	2.44	1.00	3.09
St. Vincent & the Grenadines	n.a.	0.76	–	0.62	2.82	6.61
Leeward & Windward Islands	5.81	3.31	3.01	4.15	5.63	6.14
South America	**n.a.**	**n.a.**	**24.02**	**52.87**	**n.a.**	**n.a.**
Argentina	n.a.	–	–	1.80	2.06	3.66
Bolivia	n.a.	0.99	1.01	3.28	2.93	11.07
Brazil	n.a.	1.44	2.39	8.38	6.35	7.07
Chile	n.a.	0.30	–	4.67	4.33	6.71
Colombia	n.a.	1.74	7.11	7.97	8.07	13.34
Ecuador	n.a.	3.33	0.30	1.58	1.56	2.81
Guyana	2.15	4.05	5.95	2.15	0.89	4.18
Peru	n.a.	1.61	4.02	16.90	18.84	30.46
Australasia	**n.a.**	**n.a.**	**0.42**	**3.05**	**2.31**	**6.23**
Papua New Guinea	n.a.	n.a.	n.a.	0.79	0.56	3.15
Vanuata	n.a.	n.a.	n.a.	0.26	0.29	1.09

(1) Includes only country-to-country aid—i.e., Canadian aid to specified countries. It does not include Canadian aid to international organizations such as the United Nations relief programs, international financial institutions dealing with foreign aid and the World Food Program. Country-to-country aid represents about ⅔ of all Canadian foreign aid.
– = zero; n.a. not available.

World Assistance to Developing Countries

Source: *World Development Report 1988*, World Bank

(millions of U.S. dollars)

	1965		1970		1975		1980		1985		1986	
Donor Country	Foreign aid	% of GNP[1]	Foreign aid	% of GNP[1]	Foreign aid	% of GNP[1]	Foreign aid	% of GNP[1]	Foreign aid	% of GNP[1]	Foreign aid	% of GNP[1]
Algeria	n.a.	n.a.	n.a.	n.a.	41	0.28	81	0.22	52	0.09	50	0.09
Australia	119	0.50	216	0.56	578	0.60	704	0.47	789	0.41	817	0.43
Austria	10	0.11	21	0.14	41	0.11	180	0.24	258	0.37	202	0.27
Belgium	102	0.63	122	0.47	394	0.68	583	0.49	426	0.52	516	0.57
Canada	96	0.19	362	0.44	950	0.58	1 042	0.41	1 634	0.46	1 606	0.44
Denmark	13	0.13	72	0.47	267	0.76	555	0.82	526	0.91	842	1.30
France	752	0.76	937	0.62	2 100	0.66	4 082	0.64	3 807	0.71	4 876	0.82
Italy	60	0.08	151	0.13	202	0.09	683	0.16	1 126	0.26	2 424	0.50
Japan	244	0.28	463	0.23	1 205	0.24	3 529	0.31	3 939	0.29	5 761	0.37
Kuwait	n.a.	n.a.	n.a.	n.a.	946	7.18	1 140	4.03	771	3.03	715	2.90
Libya	n.a.	n.a.	n.a.	n.a.	259	2.29	376	1.27	149	0.55	31	n.a.
Netherlands	70	0.36	206	0.62	686	0.84	1 688	0.99	1 150	0.85	1 747	1.20
New Zealand	. . .	. . .	4	0.06	73	0.51	75	0.35	57	0.23	73	0.30
Nigeria	n.a.	n.a.	n.a.	n.a.	14	0.04	35	0.05	45	0.06	52	0.08
Norway	11	0.16	50	0.47	236	0.89	593	1.12	671	1.12	921	1.43
Qatar	n.a.	n.a.	n.a.	n.a.	338	15.58	277	5.02	9	0.18	3	0.07
Saudi Arabia	n.a.	n.a.	n.a.	n.a.	2 756	7.76	5 682	5.77	2 630	2.64	3 575	4.29
Sweden	38	0.18	144	0.43	662	0.98	1 090	0.92	861	0.87	1 167	1.06
Switzerland	12	0.09	34	0.15	118	0.23	263	0.24	310	0.29	424	0.37
United Arab Emirates	n.a.	n.a.	n.a.	n.a.	1 046	11.68	1 118	4.10	71	0.26	72	0.35
United Kingdom	472	0.48	491	0.40	916	0.42	1 745	0.39	1 456	0.31	1 667	0.33
United States	4 023	0.57	3 125	0.31	4 139	0.26	7 179	0.26	9 294	0.23	9 395	0.22
Venezuela	n.a.	n.a.	n.a.	n.a.	31	0.11	135	0.26	32	0.06	85	0.16
West Germany	456	0.40	603	0.35	1 706	0.41	3 543	0.43	2 827	0.42	3 651	0.50

(1) Gross National Product. (2) Preliminary estimates.
. . . = too small to be included; n.a. not available.

Peacekeeping

Canada is recognized internationally as a peacekeeping nation, having sent more than 77 000 Canadian servicemen and women to restore or keep the peace in countries of conflict around the world during the past 4 decades.

Such operations have taken Canadian units to the Middle East, Indochina, Africa, India, Korea, West New Guinea and Cyprus.

One of the first peacekeeping operations began in Kashmir in the late 1940s when Canadian forces were involved in supervising a truce between India and Pakistan.

Then, in 1954, Canada was invited by the Geneva Conference on the Far East to join India and Poland in an International Commission for Supervision and Control in Indochina, where Canadians stayed for almost 20 years. They later joined Hungary, Poland and Indonesia in supervising an armistice there with the renamed International Commission for Control and Supervision, for 5 months in 1973. These commissions, established by the Geneva Conference, usually included representatives from a western state, a neutral country and a communist state, who helped monitor new boundaries, supervise elections and relocate populations as part of the provisions of the Geneva agreements.

But it was through the United Nations that Canada's worldwide reputation as a peacekeeper was firmly established.

Canada played a central role in diffusing the Suez Crisis, which was sparked in late 1956 when Britain, France and Israel invaded Egypt after that country took over the Suez Canal. Alarmed at the threat this posed to international relations and peace, the United Nations Security Council held emergency debates on the issue and voted for a ceasefire and immediate withdrawal. Lester B. Pearson, then Canada's secretary of state for external affairs and later its prime minister, proposed that the United Nations establish an emergency international force to secure and supervise an end to the hostilities. Canadian supply and service troops joined soldiers from other countries in setting up peacekeeping operations on both sides of the Gulf of Aqaba until 1967, and returned again in 1973.

Pearson won the Nobel Peace Prize in 1957 for his diplomatic efforts in the Suez Crisis, and during his years as prime minister, the government's defence policies made peacekeeping a top priority.

Not all peacekeeping operations were peaceful for the Canadian servicemen and women who participated. Some lost their lives during a tumultuous peacekeeping operation in the Congo (now Zaire) from 1960 to 1964, where Canada had sent a 300-member signals unit to provide communications for the UN force. Since 1953, 78 Canadians have died while serving on peacekeeping forces.

Canada joined the United Nations peacekeeping force in Cyprus in 1964, after that country's leaders appealed for help in putting an end to fighting between the Turks and Greeks. Today, the island is still a posting for 575 Canadian service people with the United Nations Peacekeeping Force in Cyprus.

Canadians served with the United Nations Emergency Force in the Middle East from 1973 until 1979 and continue to serve there. 224 Canadian officers provide communications, technical support and logistics aid for the United Nations Disengagement

Observer Force (UNDOF) in the Golan Heights and another 20 Canadian observers are with the United Nations Truce Supervisory Organization (UNTSO) in Israel.

Another Canadian foreign policy venture in the Middle East is with the Multinational Force and Observers (MFO), an operation outside the auspices of the United Nations which is monitoring the 1979 peace treaty between Egypt and Israel. 140 Canadian service people and 9 helicopters are stationed with the MFO in the Sinai Peninsula.

Pearson's influence has continued to be reflected in Canadian diplomatic efforts. For several months before Pierre Trudeau stepped down as prime minister in 1984, he toured the world, appealing to more than 40 world leaders, including the president

of the United States and leader of the Soviet Union to commit their countries to peace and an end to the nuclear arms race. He failed in winning support for a summit meeting of the world's 5 nuclear nations, but focussed world attention on reopening talks between the east and west superpowers. Trudeau's peace initiative won him the 1984 Albert Einstein Peace Award.

In 1988, Canada participated in 2 new UN peacekeeping operations. Five Canadians were sent as part of the 50-person unit monitoring the Soviet withdrawal from Afghanistan and the other Geneva Accords. With the signing of the ceasefire agreement in the Iran-Iraq war, Canada sent 15 persons as part of the UN Iran Iraq Military Observer Group (UNIIMOG). As well, Canada sent a 485-person communications and support team to monitor the ceasefire.

Visits by British Monarchs[1]

Sources: The Monarchist League of Canada and Department of the Secretary of State of Canada

1786 (June) Prince William, Captain of the *H.M.S. Pegasus* (later King William IV), lands on the coast of Newfoundland. This was the first time that a member of the Royal Family set foot on what is now Canada. The Prince arrived in Halifax Oct. 10 and left for the West Indies in Nov.

1787 (Oct. 26) Prince William returns to Halifax, staying there until Nov. 11.

1788 (Aug. 17) Prince William, now in command of the *H.M.S. Andromeda*, returns to Halifax, leaving Halifax to return to England in Apr. 1789.

1860 (July 26-Sept. 20) Albert Edward, the Prince of Wales (later King Edward VII), arrives at St. John's, Nfld., and tours the provinces of British North America.

1883 Prince George of Wales (who became King George V) visits his aunt, Princess Louise, whose husband the Marquess of Lorne is Governor General of Canada. The Prince travels to Toronto, Niagara, Ottawa, Montreal and Quebec.

1890 (Aug.) Prince George of Wales visits Halifax and attends a grand ball in Quebec City (he was commander of the Royal Navy in North American waters at the time).

1901 (Sept. 16-Oct. 21) The Duke and Duchess of Cornwall and York, the future King George V and Queen Mary, make a coast-to-coast tour.

1908 (July 22-29) The Prince of Wales (George V) attends Quebec's 300th anniversary celebrations.

1915 (May 15) Prince Albert (George VI), while serving as a cadet, arrives at Halifax and visits Montreal, Quebec, Toronto, Niagara Falls, the Thousand Islands, Gaspe and St. John's.

1919 (Aug. 12-Nov. 24) The Prince of Wales (Edward VIII) makes a nation-wide tour of Canada.

1923 (Sept. 13-Oct. 13) The Prince of Wales visits Quebec, Ottawa, Winnipeg, the E.P. Ranch[2] and Banff.

1924 (Sept. 22-Oct. 22) The Prince of Wales arrives at Ottawa, visits E.P. Ranch and Montreal.

1927 (July 30-Sept. 7) The Prince of Wales and his brother Prince George visit Quebec, open Princes' Gates in Toronto and visit E.P. Ranch.

1939 (May 17-June 15) King George VI, the first British monarch to visit Canada as sovereign, arrives at Wolfe's Cove, Que., and tours Canada with Queen Elizabeth.

1951 (Oct. 8-Nov. 12) Princess Elizabeth and Prince Philip travel coast to coast, mostly by train.

1957 (Oct. 14) In Ottawa, Queen Elizabeth II becomes the first sovereign to open Parliament.

1959 (June) Queen Elizabeth II and Prince Philip tour Canada; it is the Queen's first tour of the country as Canada's sovereign.

1964 (Oct. 5-13) The Queen and Prince Philip are in Prince Edward Island for the centenary of the Charlottetown Conference; the Queen addresses the Quebec Legislature in Quebec City, and hosts a state dinner with the provincial premiers in Ottawa.

1967 (June 29-July 5) The Queen presides at Canada's centennial in Ottawa, and travels to Montreal to attend Expo '67.

1970 (July 5-15) The Queen, Prince Philip, Prince Charles and Princess Anne tour the Northwest Territories and Manitoba.

1971 (May 3-May 12) The Queen, Prince Philip and Princess Anne tour British Columbia.

1973 (June 25-July 6) The Queen visits Ontario, Prince Edward Island, Saskatchewan and Alberta.

1973 (July 31-Aug. 4) The Queen visits Ottawa to open the first Commonwealth Conference held outside of the United Kingdom.

1974 (Jan. 27) The Queen makes a stopover at Ottawa, and holds an investiture at C.F.B. Uplands, en route to Australia and New Zealand.

1975 (Apr. 20-Apr. 30) The Prince of Wales[3] tours the Arctic, Ottawa and Hull on his first solo tour of Canada.

1976 (July 13-July 26) The Queen tours Nova Scotia and New Brunswick, then opens the Olympic Games in Montreal, accompanied by Prince Philip, the Prince of Wales, Princess Anne, Prince Edward, Prince Andrew and Captain Phillips. It is the first time all members of the immediate Royal Family are together on Canadian soil.

1977 (Oct. 14-Oct. 19) The Queen and Prince Philip visit Ottawa to celebrate the Silver Jubilee and travel to Wakefield, Que., by train.

1978 (July 26-Aug. 6) The Queen and Prince Philip tour Newfoundland, Saskatchewan and Alberta where she opens the Commonwealth Games in Edmonton, accompanied by Prince Andrew and Prince Edward.

1982 (Apr. 15-18) The Queen and Prince Philip visit Ottawa, where she proclaims Canada's revised Constitution.

1983 (Mar. 8-Mar. 11) The Queen and Prince Philip tour cities in British Columbia.

1983 (June 14-July 1) The Prince and Princess of Wales tour Nova Scotia, New Brunswick, Ottawa, Newfoundland, Prince Edward Island and Alberta.

1984 (Sept. 24-Oct. 7) The Queen and Prince Philip visit New Brunswick and Ontario (for its bicentenary), then the Queen continues on to Manitoba.

1986 (Apr. 30-May 7) The Prince and Princess of Wales arrive in Victoria on a tour of cities in British Columbia. On May 2 they open Expo '86 in Vancouver.

1987 (Oct. 9-24) The Queen and Prince Philip participate in the opening sessions of the Commonwealth Conference in Vancouver, visit Saskatchewan, then Quebec.

(1) On May 29, 1953, Queen Elizabeth was proclaimed Queen of Canada, a separate and distinct title that emphasizes both Canada's sovereignty and her own role as monarch of Canada. (2) E.P. Ranch, located near High River, Alta., had been purchased by the Prince of Wales for his personal use. The initials stand for Edward *Princeps*, *Princeps* being one of the names the first heir in line to the throne is entitled to use. The ranch was sold in the early 1960s. (3) Visits made by Charles, Prince of Wales, have been included because he is first in line to the throne.

Foreign Embassies and High Commissions in Canada

Source: Dept. of External Affairs

Algeria: Embassy of the People's Democratic Republic of Algeria, 435 Daly Ave., Ottawa, Ont. K1N 6H3. Tel: (613) 232-9453, -4.
Antigua and Barbuda: High Commission For Antigua and Barbuda, 112 Kent St., Ste. 205, Ottawa, Ont. K1P 5P2. Tel: (613) 234-9143, -4.
Argentina: Embassy of the Argentine Republic, Royal Bank Centre, 90 Sparks St., Ste. 620, Ottawa, Ont. K1P 5B4. Tel: (613) 236-2351, -4.
Australia: High Commission for the Commonwealth of Australia, 50 O'Connor St., Ste. 710, Ottawa, Ont. K1P 6L2. Tel: (613) 236-0841.
Austria: Embassy of the Republic of Austria, 445 Wilbrod St., Ottawa, Ont. K1N 6M7. Tel: (613) 563-1444, -5, -6, -7.
The Bahamas: High Commission for the Commonwealth of the Bahamas, 360 Albert St., Ste. 625, Ottawa, Ont. K1R 7X7. Tel: (613) 232-1724.
Bangladesh: High Commission for the People's Republic of Bangladesh, 85 Range Rd., Ste. 402, Ottawa, Ont. K1N 8J6. Tel: (613) 236-0138, -9.
Barbados: High Commission for Barbados, 151 Slater St., Ste. 210, Ottawa, Ont. K1P 5H3. Tel: (613) 236-9517, -8, 236-0014.
Belgium: Embassy of the Kingdom of Belgium, 85 Range Rd., Suites 601-604, Ottawa, Ont. K1N 8J6. Tel: (613) 236-7267, -8, -9.
Bénin: Embassy of the People's Republic of Bénin, 58 Glebe Ave., Ottawa, Ont. K1S 2C3. Tel: (613) 233-4429, -4866.
Bolivia: Embassy of the Republic of Bolivia, 77 Metcalfe St., Ste. 608, Ottawa, Ont. K1P 5L6. Tel: (613) 236-8237.
Brazil: Embassy of the Federative Republic of Brazil, 255 Albert St., Ste. 900, Ottawa, Ont. K1P 6A9. Tel: (613) 237-1090.
Britain: British High Commission, 80 Elgin St., Ottawa, Ont. K1P 5K7. Tel: (613) 237-1530.
Bulgaria: Embassy of the People's Republic of Bulgaria, 325 Stewart St., Ottawa, Ont. K1N 6K5. Tel: (613) 232-3215, -3453.
Burkina Faso: Embassy of the Burkina Faso, 48 Range Rd., Ottawa, Ont. K1N 8J4 Tel: (613) 238-4796, -7.
Burma: Embassy of the Socialist Republic of the Union of Burma, The Sandringham Apartments, 85 Range Rd., Ste. 902, Ottawa, Ont. K1N 8J6. Tel: (613) 232-6434, -5.
Burundi: Embassy of the Republic of Burundi, 151 Slater St., Ste. 800, Ottawa, Ont. K1P 5H3. Tel: (613) 236-8483, -9.
Cameroon: Embassy of the Republic of Cameroon, 170 Clemow Ave., Ottawa, Ont. K1S 2B4. Tel: (613) 236-1522.
Chile: Embassy of the Republic of Chile, 56 Sparks St., Ste. 801, Ottawa, Ont. K1P 5A9. Tel: (613) 235-4402, 235-9940.
People's Republic of China: Embassy of the People's Republic of China, 511-515 St. Patrick St., Ottawa, Ont. K1N 5H3. Tel: (613) 234-2706.
Colombia: Embassy of the Republic of Colombia, 150 Kent St., Ste. 404, Ottawa, Ont. K1P 5P4. Tel: (613) 230-3760, -1.
Costa Rica: Embassy of the Republic of Costa Rica, 150 Argyle St., Ste. 115, Ottawa, Ont. K2P 1B7. Tel: (613) 234-5762.
Côte d'Ivoire: Embassy of the Republic of Côte d'Ivoire, 9 Marlborough Ave., Ottawa, Ont. K1N 8E6. Tel: (613) 236-9919.
Cuba: Embassy of the Republic of Cuba, 388 Main St., Ottawa, Ont. K1S 1E3. Tel: (613) 563-0141.
Czechoslovakia: Embassy of the Czechoslovak Socialist Republic, 50 Rideau Terrace, Ottawa, Ont. K1M 2A1. Tel: (613) 749-4442.
Denmark: Embassy of the Kingdom of Denmark, 85 Range Rd., Ste. 702, Ottawa, Ont. K1N 8J6. Tel: (613) 234-0704, -0116.
Djibouti: c/o Consulate of Djibouti, 1420 Sherbrooke St. W., Ste. 900, Montreal, Que. H3G 1K5. Tel: (514) 282-0651.
Arab Republic of Egypt: Embassy of the Arab Republic of Egypt, 454 Laurier Ave. E., Ottawa, Ont. K1N 6R3. Tel: (613) 234-4931.
El Salvador: Embassy of El Salvador, 294 Albert St., Ste. 302, Ottawa, Ont. K1P 6E6. Tel: (613) 238-2939.
Finland: Embassy of Finland, 55 Metcalfe St., Ste. 850, Ottawa, Ont. K1P 6L5. Tel: (613) 236-2380, -9.
France: Embassy of France, 42 Sussex Dr., Ottawa, Ont. K1M 2C9. Tel: (613) 232-1795.
Gabon: Embassy of the Gabonese Republic, 4 Range Rd., Ottawa, Ont. K1N 8J5. Tel: (613) 232-5301, -2.
German Democratic Republic: Embassy of the German Democratic Republic, 150 Kent St., Ste. 710, Ottawa, Ont. K1P 5P4. Tel: (613) 234-4359
Federal Republic of Germany: Embassy of the Federal Republic of Germany, 1 Waverley St., Ottawa, Ont. K2P 0T8. Tel: (613) 232-1101, -2, -3, -4, -5.
Ghana: High Commission for the Republic of Ghana, 85 Range Rd., Ste. 810, Ottawa, Ont. K1N 8J6. Tel: (613) 236-0871.
Greece: Embassy of Greece, 76-80 MacLaren St., Ottawa, Ont. K2P 0K6. Tel: (613) 238-6271, -2, -3.
Guatemala: Embassy of the Republic of Guatemala, 294 Albert St., Ste. 500, Ottawa, Ont. K1P 6E6. Tel: (613) 237-3941, -2.
Guinea: Embassy of the Republic of Guinea, 112 Kent St., Ste. 208, Place de Ville, Tower B, Ottawa, Ont. K1P 5P2. Tel: (613) 231-1133.
Guyana: High Commission for the Co-operative Republic of Guyana, Burnside Bldg., 151 Slater St., Ste. 309, Ottawa, Ont. K1P 5H3. Tel: (613) 235-7240, -9.

Haiti: Embassy of the Republic of Haiti, 112 Kent St., Ste. 1308, Place de Ville, Tower B, Ottawa, Ont. K1P 5P2. Tel: (613) 238-1628, -9.
Holy See: Apostolic Nunciature, 724 Manor Ave., Rockcliffe Park, Ont. K1M 0E3. Tel: (613) 746-4914.
Honduras: Embassy of the Republic of Honduras, 151 Slater St., Ste. 300-A, Ottawa, Ont. K1P 5H3. Tel: (613) 233-8900.
Hungary: Embassy of the Hungarian People's Republic, 7 Delaware Ave., Ottawa, Ont. K2P 0Z2. Tel: (613) 232-1711, -1549.
India: High Commission for India, 10 Springfield Rd., Ottawa, Ont. K1M 1C9. Tel: (613) 744-3751, -2, -3.
Indonesia: Embassy of the Republic of Indonesia, 287 MacLaren St., Ottawa, Ont. K2P 0L9. Tel: (613) 236-7403.
Iran: Embassy of the Islamic Republic of Iran, 411 Roosevelt Ave., 4th Floor, Ottawa, Ont. K2A 3X9. Tel: (613) 729-0902.
Iraq: Embassy of the Republic of Iraq, 215 McLeod St., Ottawa, Ont. K2P 0Z8. Tel: (613) 236-9177, -8.
Ireland: Embassy of Ireland, 170 Metcalfe St., Ottawa, Ont. K2P 1P3. Tel: (613) 233-6281.
Israel: Embassy of the State of Israel, 410 Laurier Ave. West, Ste. 601, Ottawa, Ont. K1R 7T3. Tel: (613) 237-6450.
Italy: Embassy of the Republic of Italy, 275 Slater St., 11th Floor, Ottawa, Ont. K1P 5H9. Tel: (613) 232-2401, -2, -3.
Jamaica: High Commission for Jamaica, Standard Life Bldg., 275 Slater St., Ste. 402, Ottawa, Ont. K1P 5H9. Tel: (613) 233-9311, -4.
Japan: Embassy of Japan, 255 Sussex Dr., Ottawa, Ont. K1N 9E6. Tel: (613) 236-8541.
Jordan: Embassy of the Hashemite Kingdom of Jordan, 100 Bronson Ave., Ste. 701, Ottawa, Ont. K1R 6G8. Tel: (613) 238-8090.
Kenya: High Commission for the Republic of Kenya, 415 Laurier Ave. E., Ste. 600, Ottawa, Ont. K1N 6R4. Tel: (613) 563-1773, -4, -5, -6.
Korea: Embassy of the Republic of Korea, 151 Slater St., 5th Floor, Ottawa, Ont. K1P 5H3. Tel: (613) 232-1715, -6, -7.
Lebanon: Embassy of the Republic of Lebanon, 640 Lyon St., Ottawa, Ont. K1S 3Z5. Tel: (613) 236-5825, -55.
Lesotho: High Commission for the Kingdom of Lesotho, 202 Clemow Ave., Ottawa, Ont. K1S 2B4. Tel: (613) 236-9449, -0960.
Liberia: Embassy of the Republic of Liberia, Royal Trust Bldg., 116 Albert St., Ste. 805, Ottawa, Ont. K1P 5G3. Tel: (613) 594-5410.
Malawi: High Commission for Malawi, 7 Clemow Ave., Ottawa, Ont. K1S 2A9. Tel: (613) 236-8931.
Malaysia: High Commission for Malaysia, 60 Boteler St., Ottawa, Ont. K1N 8Y7. Tel: (613) 237-5182, -3, -4.
Mali: Embassy of the Republic of Mali, 50 Goulburn Ave., Ottawa, Ont. K1N 8C8. Tel: (613) 232-1501.
Mexico: Embassy of the United Mexican States, 130 Albert St., Ste. 206, Ottawa, Ont. K1P 5G4. Tel: (613) 233-8988, -9272, -9917.
Monaco: c/o Consulate of Monaco, 1 Place Ville Marie, Ste. 1200, Montreal, Que. H3B 4A8. Tel: (514) 866-9190.
Morocco: Embassy of the Kingdom of Morocco, 38 Range Rd., Ottawa, Ont. K1N 8J4. Tel: (613) 236-7391, -2, -3.
The Netherlands: Royal Netherlands Embassy, 275 Slater St., 3rd Floor, Ottawa, Ont. K1P 5H9. Tel: (613) 237-5030.
New Zealand: New Zealand High Commission, Metropolitan House, 99 Bank St., Ste. 727, Ottawa, Ont. K1P 6G3. Tel: (613) 238-5991.
Nicaragua: Embassy of the Republic of Nicaragua, 170 Laurier Ave. W., Ste. 908, Ottawa, Ont. K1P 5V5. Tel: (613) 234-9361.
The Niger: Embassy of the Republic of the Niger, 38 Blackburn Ave., Ottawa, Ont. K1N 8A2. Tel: (613) 232-4291, -2, -3.
Nigeria: High Commission for the Federal Republic of Nigeria, 295 Metcalfe St., Ottawa, Ont. K2P 1R9. Tel: (613) 236-0521.
Norway: Royal Norwegian Embassy, Royal Bank Centre, 90 Sparks St., Ste. 532, Ottawa, Ont. K1P 5B4. Tel: (613) 238-6571.
Pakistan: Embassy of the Islamic Republic of Pakistan, Burnside Bldg., 151 Slater St., Ste. 608, Ottawa, Ont. K1P 5H3. Tel: (613) 238-7881.
Peru: Embassy of the Republic of Peru, 170 Laurier Ave. W., Ste. 1007, Ottawa, Ont. K1P 5V5. Tel: (613) 238-1777, -9.
The Philippines: Embassy of the Republic of the Philippines, 130 Albert St., Ste. 606-609, Ottawa, Ont. K1P 5G4. Tel: (613) 233-1121, -2, -3.
Poland: Embassy of the Polish People's Republic, 443 Daly Ave., Ottawa, Ont. K1N 6H3. Tel: (613) 236-0468.
Portugal: Embassy of the Republic of Portugal, 645 Island Park Dr., Ottawa, Ont. K1Y 0B8. Tel: (613) 729-0883, -2922.
Romania: Embassy of the Socialist Republic of Romania, 655 Rideau St., Ottawa, Ont. K1N 6A3. Tel: (613) 232-5345, -3001.
Rwanda: Embassy of the Rwandese Republic, 121 Sherwood Dr., Ottawa, Ont. K1Y 3V1. Tel: (613) 722-5835, -7921.
San Marino: c/o Consulate of San Marino, 27 McNider Ave., Montreal, Que. H2V 3X4. Tel: (514) 871-3838.
Saudi Arabia: Embassy of the Kingdom of Saudi Arabia, 99 Bank St., Ste. 901, Ottawa, Ont. K1P 6B9. Tel: (613) 237-4100, -1, -2, -3.
Senegal: Embassy of the Republic of Senegal, 57 Marlborough Ave., Ottawa, Ont. K1N 8E8. Tel: (613) 238-6392.
Somalia: Embassy of the Somali Democratic Republic, 130 Slater St., Ste. 1000, Ottawa, Ont. K1P 6E2. Tel: (613) 563-4541.
South Africa: Embassy of the Republic of South Africa, 15 Sussex Dr., Ottawa, Ont. K1M 1M8. Tel: (613) 744-0330.
Spain: Embassy of the Kingdom of Spain, 350 Sparks St., Ste. 802, Ottawa, Ont. K1R 7S8. Tel: (613) 237-2193, -4.
Sri Lanka: High Commission for the Democratic Socialist Republic of Sri Lanka, 85 Range Rd., Suites 102-4, 201, Ottawa, Ont. K1N 8J6. Tel: (613) 233-8440, -9.
The Sudan: Embassy of the Democratic Republic of The Sudan, 457 Laurier Ave. E., Ottawa, Ont. K1N 6R4. Tel: (613) 235-4000, -4999.
Sweden: Embassy of the Kingdom of Sweden, 441 MacLaren St., 4th Floor, Ottawa, Ont. K2P 2H3. Tel: (613) 236-8553.
Switzerland: Embassy of Switzerland, 5 Marlborough Ave., Ottawa, Ont. K1N 8E6. Tel: (613) 235-1837, -8.
Tanzania: High Commission for the United Republic of Tanzania, 50 Range Rd., Ottawa, Ont. K1N 8J4. Tel: (613) 232-1509.
Thailand: Embassy of the Kingdom of Thailand, 180 Island Park Dr., Ottawa, Ont. K1Y 0A2. Tel: (613) 237-1517, -0476.
Togo: Embassy of the Republic of Togo, 12 Range Rd., Ottawa, Ont. K1N 8J3. Tel: (613) 238-5916, -7.
Trinidad and Tobago: High Commission for the Republic of Trinidad and Tobago, 75 Albert St., Ste. 508, Ottawa, Ont. K1P 5E7. Tel: (613) 232-2418, -9.
Tunisia: Embassy of the Republic of Tunisia, 515 O'Connor St., Ottawa, Ont. K1S 3P8. Tel: (613) 237-0330, -2.
Turkey: Embassy of the Republic of Turkey, 197 Wurtemburg St., Ottawa, Ont. K1N 8L9. Tel: (613) 232-1577, -8.
Uganda: High Commission for the Republic of Uganda, 231 Cobourg St., Ottawa, Ont. K1N 8J2. Tel: (613) 233-7797, -8.
Union of Soviet Socialist Republics: Embassy of the Union of Soviet Socialist Republics, 285 Charlotte St., Ottawa, Ont. K1N 8L5. Tel: (613) 235-4341, 236-1413.
United States of America: Embassy of the United States of America, 100 Wellington St., Ottawa, Ont. K1P 5T1. Tel: (613) 238-5335.
Uruguay: Embassy of the Eastern Republic of Uruguay, 130 Albert St., Ste. 1905, Ottawa, Ont. K1P 5G4. Tel: (613) 234-2727.
Venezuela: Embassy of the Republic of Venezuela, 294 Albert St., Ste. 602, Ottawa, Ont. K1P 6E6. Tel: (613) 235-5151, -4
Yugoslavia: Embassy of the Socialist Federal Republic of Yugoslavia, 17 Blackburn Ave., Ottawa, Ont. K1N 8A2. Tel: (613) 233-6289.
Zaire: Embassy of the Republic of Zaire, 18 Range Rd., Ottawa, Ont. K1N 8J3. Tel: (613) 236-7103.
Zambia: High Commission for the Republic of Zambia, 130 Albert St., Ste. 1610, Ottawa, Ont. K1P 5G4. Tel: (613) 563-0712.
Zimbabwe: High Commission for the Republic of Zimbabwe, 112 Kent St., Ste. 1315, Place de Ville, Tower B, Ottawa, Ont. K1P 5P7. Tel: (613) 237-4388, -9.

Geography

Canada is the largest country in the Western Hemisphere and the 2d largest in the world, with a total area of 9 970 610 sq. km. It stretches north to south from Cape Columbia on Ellesmere Island to Middle Island in Lake Erie, a distance of 4 634 km. The greatest east-west distance is 5 514 km from Cape Spear, Nfld. to the Yukon-Alaska border. Within this vast expanse, Canada contains an extremely wide variety of geographical features: the towering peaks of the Rockies, the flat Prairies, the rugged north and the gently rolling landscape of the east. But within this seemingly wide range of features, areas with similar characteristics are found. These areas are called landforms, and within the diversity of the Canadian landscape only 4 landforms are found. These landforms are: the Canadian Shield, the Appalachian Region, the Interior Plains and the Western Cordillera.

The Canadian Shield

Also known as the Precambrian Shield, this area is located in the central part of the continent and makes up more than half of Canada. The Shield is composed of ancient rock that was once lifted and broken by forces in the Earth to form mountains. Over thousands of years, ice, wind and water eroded the mountains into a rough and rocky surface. Swamps and lakes are characteristic of the Canadian Shield landscape.

The Appalachian Region

To the east of the Shield, this region was also once the site of massive mountain peaks. The rock which formed these peaks was not as old as the rock of the Shield and was also made through different processes which allowed it to be more easily eroded. Now, throughout the Appalachian Region, which runs in a northeasterly direction from the southern United States to Newfoundland, the landscape is one of rounded mountains and hills.

The Interior Plains

West of the Shield, rock which formed at the bottom of ancient seas gives the Prairies their distinctive flatness. This is the area of the Interior Plains. An extension of the Interior Plains forms the lowlands around the Great Lakes and the St. Lawrence River.

The Western Cordillera

The most geologically active area in Canada, the Western Cordillera is one of the most recent landforms to develop. Erosion has not yet worn away its sharply-etched mountains and valleys; thus the highest mountains are found in this landform area—which includes the mountain ranges of Canada's west.

Superlative Canadian Statistics

Source: Energy, Mines and Resources Canada; Statistics Canada

Largest province	Quebec	1 540 681 sq. km
Smallest province	Prince Edward Island	5 660 sq. km
Largest city[1]	Gagnon, Que	5 971.02 sq. km
Smallest city[1]	Ile Dorval, Que	0.18 sq. km
Largest island	Baffin, N.W.T.	507 451 sq. km
Northernmost point	Cape Columbia, Ellesmere Island, N.W.T.	83° 07'N.
Southernmost point	Middle Island, Lake Erie, Ont.	41° 41'N.
Easternmost point	Cape Spear, Nfld.	52° 37'W.
Westernmost point	Yukon-Alaska boundary	141° 00'W.
Northernmost community	Alert, Ellesmere Island, N.W.T.	82° 30'N.
Southernmost town	Pelee Island South, Ont.	41° 45'N.
Easternmost town	Blackhead, St. John's South District, Nfld.	52° 39'W.
Westernmost town	Beaver Creek, Yukon	140° 53'W.
Highest city	Rossland, B.C.	1 056 m at Railroad Stn.
Highest town	Lake Louise, Alta.	1 540 m
Longest river	Mackenzie, N.W.T.	4 241 km
Largest lake partly in Canada	Superior, Ont.	Total area within Canada: 29 888 sq. km (54 355 sq. km U.S.)
Largest lake entirely in Canada	Great Bear, N.W.T.	31 328 sq. km
Deepest lake	Great Slave, N.W.T.	614 m
Highest mountain	Mount Logan, Yukon	5 951 m
Highest waterfall	Takakkaw Falls, B.C.	503 m (more than one leap)
Greatest waterfall by volume	Horseshoe Falls, Niagara River, Ont.	5 365 cubic metres/second
Longest bridge	Pierre Laporte Suspension Bridge, Que.	668 m
Longest covered bridge	at Hartland, N.B.	391 m
Longest tunnel	Connaught Railway Tunnel, Rogers Pass, B.C.	8.08 km

(1) As of 1986 Census.

Climate

Within Canada, climate is primarily based on the presence of landforms, proximity to large bodies of water and the degree of latitude.

Landforms

Wind or any air mass is forced to rise over mountains which lie in its path. As this happens, the air cools and its ability to retain moisture is reduced. Condensation then occurs and precipitation falls in the form of snow or rain. For instance, Prince Rupert on the western side of the Coastal Mountains receives over 2 500 mm of precipitation annually.

On the leeward side of the mountains, the air mass descends, warms and is able to once again retain moisture. Thus precipitation is reduced and a rain-shadow effect is created. In a rain-shadow area, such as near Kamloops, B.C., desert-like conditions exist.

Water

Parts of Canada near large bodies of water have more moderate climates due to the differing abilities of land and water to gain or lose heat. Whereas water can act like a heat bank, releasing accumulated heat through the fall and early winter and warming the land nearby, the reverse is also true. In the spring and early summer, the water is cooler than the land and can keep the land temperature lower.

Wind direction also determines the degree to which this influence is felt. On the Pacific coast the prevailing westerlies blow off the water onto the land and the influence of the Pacific Ocean is keenly felt. On the Atlantic coast, the westerlies blow off the land onto the water so the effect of the Atlantic Ocean is not as pronounced. Victoria has a monthly low of 4.1°C and a range of only 11.5°C while Halifax has a monthly low of −3.6°C and a range of 22.4°C.

Latitude

Latitude is the distance north or south of the equator which is measured in degrees. Its effects are twofold: first, the curva- ture of the earth results in the sunlight spreading over a greater surface area which decreases the solar radiation per unit area of ground so that less warmth from the sun is felt; secondly, the earth's atmosphere is thicker at northern latitudes which again reduces the amount of solar radiation reaching the earth.

Other Factors

Because the prevailing wind direction is from west to east, the air masses move eastward across the continent picking up moisture from lakes and rivers and releasing it further along. Therefore, generally, precipitation increases with greater distance eastward from the central continent: the average precipitation in Winnipeg is 526 mm, Toronto 762 mm, Montreal 946 mm and Halifax 1 282 mm.

Also, the Labrador Current affects climate on the Atlantic coast. This cold current within the Atlantic Ocean flows south along the coast of Newfoundland and Labrador and reduces the moderating effect of the ocean on the land. It also causes the thick Newfoundland fog.

Canadian Climate Extremes

Source: Energy, Mines and Resources Canada

Highest temp.	45°C at Midale and Yellow Grass, Sask.	July 5, 1937
Lowest temp.	−63°C at Snag, Yukon	Feb. 3, 1947
Lowest mean monthly temp.	−47.9°C at Eureka, Ellesmere Island, N.W.T.	Feb. 1979
Warmest city	Victoria, B.C.	Mean annual temperature: 10.4°C
Coldest city	Yellowknife, N.W.T.	Mean annual temperature: −5.4°C
Sunniest city	Saskatoon, Sask.	with an average of 2 450 hours of sunshine per year
Rainiest place	Ocean Falls, B.C.	438.68 cm per year
Foggiest place	Argentia, Nfld.	with fog an average of 206 days a year
Highest monthly precipitation	223.54 cm at Swanson, B.C.	Nov. 1917
Greatest annual precipitation	812.24 cm at Henderson Lake, B.C.	1931
Heaviest snowfall in one day	118.1 cm at Lakelse Lake, B.C.	Jan. 17, 1974
Highest monthly snowfall	535.9 cm at Haines Alaska Petroleum Pipeline System No 2, B.C.	Dec. 1959
Heaviest seasonal snowfall	2 446.5 cm at Revelstoke/Mt. Copeland, B.C.	during the winter of 1971-2
Most sunshine in one month	621 hours at Eureka, Ellesmere Island, N.W.T.	May 1973
Strongest wind	(one hour duration) 203 km/h at Cap Hopes Advance Peninsula d'Ungava, Que.	Nov. 18, 1931

Vegetation

Coniferous forests dominated by spruce, fir and pine cover much of the Canadian landscape, sweeping across the continent in a broad band. Through the rest of the country there is a range of forest conditions. To the north, cold temperatures limit growth and the trees become small and fewer in number. At the tree line, trees grow only in sheltered river valleys. The tree line marks the northern extent of forests and the beginning of tundra conditions.

The massive spruce, fir and pine of the forests along the coast of British Columbia are encouraged by a friendly climate. The moisture-laden winds from the Pacific Ocean keep the land well-supplied with rain. Under these conditions tree growth is rapid: the soils are constantly being replenished with minerals by the rains, and plant decay is rapid in the damp conditions, thereby releasing more minerals for tree growth. With average monthly temperatures seldom going below freezing, the growing season is long. Coniferous trees thrive under such conditions.

The Interior Plains is one region of Canada that is not naturally covered by forests because there is not enough precipitation, or available moisture, to sustain tree growth. In Alberta, Saskatchewan and Manitoba forests gradually give way from north to south through a transitional area called the park belt, which contains both trees and grassland, before yielding to grasslands. Within these provinces, there are areas where moisture levels are insufficient to support grasslands and even hardy grasses have difficulty growing. In these provinces, during the 1930s, the lack of rainfall led to "dust bowl" conditions because vegetation could not grow enough to anchor the soil.

The forests of eastern Canada are mixed, containing both coniferous and deciduous trees. Adequate rainfall and warm temperatures allow the less hardy species such as oak, maple, hickory and walnut to flourish in southern Ontario and Quebec and the Maritime provinces.

The Arctic tundra is the other region of Canada that is not covered by forests. The Arctic is both very dry and so cold that the growing season is very limited. The vegetation of the tundra consists of mosses, lichen, dwarf bushes and heather. These plants are able to grow because they have adapted to the difficult conditions through characteristics such as small size and slow growth. Some shrubs and lichen grow so slowly that their development must be measured in centimetres per century.

Area[1] of Canadian Provinces and Territories

Source: Energy, Mines and Resources Canada

(sq. km)

	Land	Fresh Water	Total	% of total area	Forested land	Area north of treeline
Newfoundland	371 690	34 030	405 720	4.1	142 000	30 040
Island of Newfoundland	105 700	5 690	111 390	1.1	n.a.	—
Prince Edward Island	5 660	...	5 660	0.1	3 000	—
Nova Scotia	52 840	2 650	55 490	0.6	41 000	—
New Brunswick	72 090	1 350	73 440	0.7	65 000	—
Quebec	1 356 790	183 890	1 540 680	15.5	940 000	268 320
Ontario	891 190	177 390	1 068 580	10.7	807 000	17 610
Manitoba	548 360	101 590	649 950	6.5	349 000	19 680
Saskatchewan	570 700	81 630	652 330	6.5	178 000	—
Alberta	644 390	16 800	661 190	6.6	349 000	—
British Columbia	929 730	18 070	947 800	9.5	633 000	—
Yukon	478 970	4 480	483 450	4.8	242 000	34 190
Northwest Territories	3 293 020	133 300	3 426 320	34.4	615 000	2 358 960
Districts of: Franklin	1 423 560	19 430	1 442 990	14.5	n.a.	1 463 860
Keewatin	575 470	25 120	600 590	6.0	n.a.	454 800
Mackenzie	1 293 990	88 750	1 382 740	13.9	n.a.	440 300
Canada	**9 215 430**	**755 180**	**9 970 610**	**100.0**	**4 364 000**	**2 728 800**

(1) Areas have been rounded to the nearest 10 sq. km; forested area has been rounded to nearest 1 000 sq. km.
— = zero; . . . = too small to be included; n.a. not available.

Highest Point in each Province and Territory

Source: Energy, Mines and Resources Canada

Province / Territory	Highest Point	Elev. (m)
Newfoundland	Mt. Caubvick[1]	1 622
Prince Edward Island	46° 20' − 63° 25'	142
Nova Scotia	46° 42' − 60° 36' (Cape Breton Highlands)	532
New Brunswick	Mt. Carleton	820
Quebec	Mt. d'Iberville[2]	1 622
Ontario	Ishpatina Ridge	693
Manitoba	Baldy Mt.	832
Saskatchewan	Cypress Hills	1 468
Alberta	Mt. Columbia	3 747
British Columbia	Fairweather Mt.	4 663
Yukon	Mt. Logan	5 951
Northwest Territories	61° 52' − 127° 42'	2 773

(1) On the Nfld. / Que. border; also known as Mt. d'Iberville; next highest point in Nfld. is Cirque Mt. at 1 568 m.   (2) On the Nfld. / Que. border; also known as Mt. Caubvick; next highest point in Que. is Mt. Jacques-Cartier at 1 268 m.

Largest Lakes in Canada

Source: Energy, Mines and Resources

Lake	Area[1] (sq. km)	Lake	Area[1] (sq. km)
Superior, Ont.[2]	84 243	Winnipegosis, Man.	5 374
Huron, Ont.[3]	63 096	Nipigon, Ont.	4 848
Great Bear, NWT	31 328	Manitoba, Man.	4 624
Great Slave, NWT	28 568	Dubawnt, NWT	3 833
Erie, Ont.[4]	25 812	Lake of the Woods, Ont./Man.[6]	3 150
Winnipeg, Man.	24 387	Amadjuak, NWT	3 115
Ontario, Ont.[5]	19 001	Melville, Nfld.	3 069
Athabasca, Sask.	7 935	Wollaston, Sask.	2 681
Reindeer, Sask./Man.	6 650	Mistassini, Que.	2 335
Smallwood Reservoir, Nfld.	6 527	Nueltin, NWT/Man.	2 279
Nettilling, NWT	5 542	Southern Indian, Man.	2 247

(1) Total area, including islands. (2) Includes 54 355 sq. km in U.S. (3) Includes 23 623 sq. km in U.S. (4) Includes 12 932 sq. km in U.S. (5) Includes 8 613 sq. km in U.S. (6) Includes 1 322 sq. km in U.S.

Longest Rivers in Canada

Source: Energy, Mines and Resources Canada

River	Length (km)	Flows Into	River	Length (km)	Flows Into
Mackenzie	4 241	Arctic Ocean	Koksoak	874	Hudson Bay
Yukon	3 185	Bering Sea	Churchill (Que.)	856	Atlantic Ocean
St. Lawrence	3 058	Gulf of St. Lawrence	Coppermine	845	Arctic Ocean
Nelson	2 575	Hudson Bay	Dubawnt	842	Hudson Bay
Columbia	2 000	Pacific Ocean	Winnipeg	813	Hudson Bay
Saskatchewan	1 939	Lake Winnipeg	Kootenay	780	Columbia River
Peace	1 923	Slave River	Nottaway	776	Hudson Bay
Churchill (Man.)	1 609	Hudson Bay	Rupert	763	Hudson Bay
South Saskatchewan	1 392	Hudson Bay	Eastmain	756	Hudson Bay
Fraser	1 370	Str. of Georgia	Attawapiskat	748	Hudson Bay
North Saskatchewan	1 287	Hudson Bay	Kazan	732	Hudson Bay
Ottawa	1 271	St Lawrence River	Grande rivière de la Baleine	724	Hudson Bay
Athabaska	1 231	Arctic Ocean	Red Deer	724	Hudson Bay
Liard	1 115	Arctic Ocean	Porcupine	721	Pacific Ocean
Assiniboine	1 070	Hudson Bay	Hay	702	Arctic Ocean
Severn	982	Hudson Bay	Saguenay	698	St. Lawrence River
Albany	982	James Bay	Anderson	692	Arctic Ocean
Back	974	Arctic Ocean	Peel	684	Arctic Ocean
Thelon	904	Hudson Bay	Fairford	684	Hudson Bay
La Grande	893	Hudson Bay	Saint John	673	Bay of Fundy
Red	877	Lake Winnipeg			

Canada's Largest Waterfalls

Source: Energy, Mines and Resources Canada

Name	Vertical drop (metres)	Location	Latitude		Longitude	
Takakkaw Falls[1]	503	From the Daly Glacier, B.C.	51°	30'	116°	28'
Della Falls[1]	440	Della Lake, B.C.	49°	27'	125°	32'
Hunlen Falls	253	Atnarko River, B.C.	52°	17'	125°	46'
Panther Falls	183	Nigel Creek, Alta.	52°	11'	117°	03'
Helmcken Falls	137	Murtle River, B.C.	51°	57'	120°	11'
Bridal Veil Falls	122	Bridal Creek, B.C.	49°	11'	121°	44'
Virginia Falls	90	South Nahanni River, N.W.T.	61°	38'	125°	42'
Montmorency, Chute	84	Montmorency River, Que.	46°	53'	71°	09'
Ouiatchouane, Chute	79	Ouiatchouaniche River, Que.	48°	26'	72°	10'
Churchill Falls	75	Churchill River, Nfld.	53°	36'	64°	19'
Brandywine Falls	61	Brandywine Creek, B.C.	50°	02'	123°	07'
Marengo Falls	61	Marengo Creek, N.W.T.	61°	35'	125°	50'
Niagara Falls American Falls	59	Niagara River, U.S.A.	43°	05'	79°	04'
Horseshoe Falls	57	Niagara River, Ont.	43°	05'	79°	04'

(1) Falls with more than one leap.

Largest Islands in Canada

Source: Energy, Mines and Resources Canada

Island	Area (sq. km)	Island	Area (sq. km)
Baffin, NWT	507 451	Prince Patrick, NWT	15 848
Victoria, NWT	217 291	King William, NWT	13 111
Ellesmere, NWT	196 236	Ellef Ringnes, NWT	11 295
Newfoundland (main island)	108 860	Bylot, NWT	11 067
Banks, NWT	70 028	Cape Breton, N.S.	10 311
Devon, NWT	55 247	Prince Charles, NWT	9 521
Axel Heiberg, NWT	43 178	Anticosti, Que.	7 941
Melville, NWT	42 149	Cornwallis, NWT	6 995
Southampton, NWT	41 214	Graham, B.C.	6 361
Prince of Wales, NWT	33 339	Prince Edward Island (main island)	5 620
Vancouver, B.C.	31 285	Coats, NWT	5 498
Somerset, NWT	24 786	Amund Ringnes, NWT	5 255
Bathurst, NWT	16 042	Mackenzie King, NWT	5 048

Highest Peaks in Canada

Source: Energy, Mines and Resources Canada

Mountain	Range	Province/Territory	Elev. (m)
Mt. Logan	St. Elias Mts.	Yukon	5 951
Mt. St. Elias	St. Elias Mts.	Yukon/Alaska	5 489
Mt. Lucania	St. Elias Mts.	Yukon	5 226
King Peak	St. Elias Mts.	Yukon	5 173
Mt. Steele	St. Elias Mts.	Yukon	5 067
Mt. Wood	St. Elias Mts.	Yukon	4 838
Mt. Vancouver	St. Elias Mts.	Yukon/Alaska	4 785
Mt. Macaulay	St. Elias Mts.	Yukon	4 663
Mt. Slaggard	St. Elias Mts.	Yukon	4 663
Fairweather Mt.	St. Elias Mts.	B.C./Alaska	4 663
Mt. Hubbard	St. Elias Mts.	Yukon/Alaska	4 577
Mt. Walsh	St. Elias Mts.	Yukon	4 505
Mt. Alverstone	St. Elias Mts.	Yukon/Alaska	4 439
McArthur Peak	St. Elias Mts.	Yukon	4 344
Mt. Augusta	St. Elias Mts.	Yukon/Alaska	4 289
Mt. Kennedy	St. Elias Mts.	Yukon	4 238
Avalanche Peak	St. Elias Mts.	Yukon	4 212
Mt. Strickland	St. Elias Mts.	Yukon	4 212
Mt. Newton	St. Elias Mts.	Yukon	4 210
Mt. Cook	St. Elias Mts.	Yukon/Alaska	4 194
Mt. Craig	St. Elias Mts.	Yukon	4 039
Mt. Quincy Adams	St. Elias Mts.	B.C./Alaska	4 133
Mt. Waddington	Coast Mts.	B.C.	4 012
Mt. Robson	Rocky Mts.	B.C.	3 954
Mt. Root	St. Elias Mts.	B.C./Alaska	3 901
Mt. Malaspina	St. Elias Mts.	Yukon	3 886
Mt. Queen Mary	St. Elias Mts.	Yukon	3 886
Mt. Badham	St. Elias Mts.	Yukon	3 848
Mt. Tiedemann	Coast Mts.	B.C.	3 848
Combatant Mt.	Coast Mts.	B.C.	3 756
Mt. Columbia	Rocky Mts.	Alta./B.C.	3 747
North Twin	Rocky Mts.	Alta.	3 733
Asperity Mt.	Coast Mts.	B.C.	3 716

Geology of the Earth

Prior to the 1960s, geologists could not find a comprehensive theory that tied together all their isolated notions about the way the Earth worked. Their theories—about the formation of rocks and minerals, about the structure of the Earth, and about the forces that built mountains—lacked one concept that would unite all the individual research efforts. Then, in the late 1960s, geologists and geophysicists began to piece together information gained from examining the magnetism of rocks on the ocean floor and improved surveys of the topology of the ocean floor. They formed a new model of the structure of the Earth—the idea of continental drift.

Continental drift theory, or plate tectonics as it is often called, is based on the notion that the thin outer surface, or crust, of the Earth is divided into a number of rigid plates. These plates are not static but float on the asthenosphere, which is the outer layer of the Earth's mantle, 50 to 250 km below the surface. Under pressure from the rocks above, and heated from below by the hot interior of the Earth, the temperature of the rocks of the asthenosphere approaches the melting point and becomes capable of flowing very slowly in currents, like currents within an ocean. As this layer of molten rock moves, it carries the plates of the Earth with it.

When these plates are pulled apart, the magma from within the Earth can rise to reach the surface, and volcanoes erupt. Such splitting has occurred in the Atlantic Ocean midway between Africa and South America and between North America and Europe, where volcanoes have created an underwater chain of mountains known as the Mid-Atlantic Ridge. Iceland marks the northern location of this ridge. Sea-floor spreading is also occurring in the Indian and Pacific Oceans.

Such spreading would indicate that the Earth is expanding, but evidence has shown that the Earth's diameter is not increasing. There are places where parts of the crust are contracting—where the floating plates are being pulled towards each other. As when automobiles smash into each other, the leading edges of the vehicles, or plates, are crumpled. So, the collision of one plate into another produces mountains, such as those forming the western edge of North and South America, which were built by the folding and buckling of layers of rock.

When a plate that carries an ocean meets a plate under a continent, the oceanic plate is forced beneath the continental plate. As this happens the oceanic plate bends and produces deep trenches in the ocean floor parallel to the margins of the plates. The Mindanao Trench east of the Philippines is such a case.

Even with this theory of continental drift geologists have little understanding of the movements of the land masses prior to about 200 million years ago. They believe a single large continent existed at that time made up of all the land masses of the world. This supercontinent has been called Pangaea. By about 135 million years ago large rifts had appeared dividing the land mass into two portions, Laurasia and Gondwanaland. Laurasia included the present-day northern continents and Gondwanaland the rest. Movement of these land masses continued with large pieces breaking away and moving in different directions and speeds. South America, at one time completely separated from North America, moved west and northward to meet the northern continent. The Indian sub-continent, once broken free of Africa, smashed into the underbelly of Asia, in the process pushing up the massive Himalaya Mountains.

Since the movement of the Earth's plates is continuous, geologists have successfully measured the rate of movement of various parts of the crust. The North Atlantic Ocean is widening at a speed of about 2 cm/year, so that Iceland, astride the Mid-Atlantic Ridge, is being torn apart at that rate. North America is travelling westward at 2-3 cm/year. The Pacific plate, with a small portion of Mexico and California attached, is moving past the North American plate at speeds of up to 6 cm/year. Africa has continued to move northward. These motions are on-going, and landforms will continue to be created and shaped by pressures deep within the Earth's crust.

Geological Time Periods

Source: *Gage Canadian Dictionary* by Walter S. Avis, *et al.* Copyright © 1983 Gage Publishing Limited. Reproduced by permission.

Era	Period	Epoch	Years Ago	Changes and Characteristics
Precambrian Time .			4.5 bil.?	Cooling and melting of the earth's crust. Evidence of bacteria, the first known living things, about 3.5 billion years ago.
Paleozoic	Cambrian		575 mil.	Seas spread across North America. First fishes appear. Greatest development of invertebrates.
	Ordovician		480 mil.	Floods sometimes cover two-thirds of North America. Jawless fish appear. Algae become plentiful.
	Silurian		435 mil.	Coral reefs are formed. First amphibians and forests of fernlike trees appear.
	Devonian		405 mil.	Gas and oil are formed. Many kinds of fish in seas and fresh water. First insects appear.
	Carboniferous —Mississippian		350 mil.	Warm, moist climate produces great forests that later become coal beds. Fish and amphibians plentiful.
	—Pennsylvanian		310 mil.	Appalachian Mountains are formed. Large amounts of coal are formed. First reptiles appear.
	Permian		270 mil.	Ural Mountains are formed. Glaciers in southern hemisphere melt. Gas, oil and salt are formed. Reptiles developing.
Mezozoic	Triassic		225 mil.	Reptiles dominate the earth. First mammals appear.
	Jurassic		180 mil.	Shallow seas invade continents. Dinosaurs reach their largest size. First birds appear.
	Cretaceous		130 mil.	Seas spread over the land. Flowering plants appear. Dinosaurs die out. Most chalk deposits are made.
Cenozoic	Tertiary	Paleocene	65 mil.	Mountains become higher. Climates less uniform. Mammals, flowering plants become common.
		Eocene	50 mil.	Climate mild. Seas flood shores of continents. Primitive apes, early horses and elephants appear.
		Oligocene	38 mil.	Climate mild. Alps and Himalayas begin to rise. Many volcanoes. Oil and natural gas are formed.
		Miocene	27 mil.	Climate mild. Rocky Mountains and Sierra Nevadas forming. Flowering plants and trees resemble modern kinds.
		Pliocene	10 mil.	Climate cooling. Mountains rising in western Canada. Many volcanoes. Birds and mammals spread around the world. Humans appear near end of epoch.
	Quaternary	Pleistocene	1.5 mil.	Great ice sheets cover northern hemisphere. Climate cool. Mountains continue to rise in North America. Early humans reach Europe and North America.
		Recent, or Holocene	10 000	Glaciers melt and Great Lakes are formed. Climate warm. Humans live in most parts of the earth, develop agriculture, use metals, domesticate animals.

Geology of Canada

In a country as large as Canada it is necessary to speak of the physical environment in general terms—using categories to simplify the vast array of geologic conditions. Five landforms or physiographic regions are commonly used to describe the geology of Canada. These geological areas also form the basis of Canada's geographical landforms.

The Precambrian Shield

No other geologic area is so widely associated with Canada as the Precambrian Shield. Viewed from the air it is a vast inhospitable land of rocks, lakes and trees. It makes up roughly half of Canada's surface area sweeping around Hudson Bay like a giant horseshoe, but also underlies the rest of the continent like a basement or foundation. Some of the oldest rocks in the world are found in the Shield.

The Precambrian Shield has not always looked as it does today. Early in the Earth's history this area was the site of towering mountains, deep valleys and mighty rivers. The mountains were thrust up by volcanic activity as long as 3.8 billion years ago, during the Precambrian era. Over time, the forces of erosion—wind, water, freezing temperatures, ice— wore down the rocks that formed the mountain peaks and carried the materials away. Now all that remains are the roots of the once-mighty mountains.

The processes of volcanism present at the time of mountain-building caused minerals to form in the cooling rock of the Precambrian mountains. Deep inside the mountains minerals such as gold, silver, copper, and nickel came together into veins of ore. These ore bodies make the Precambrian Shield a rich storehouse of mineral wealth.

The Appalachian Region

As the youthful mountains of the present-day Precambrian Shield were being worn away, the debris was carried by rivers to the edge of the continent and deposited in the surrounding seas. Over time, thick layers accumulated. About 600 million years ago, for reasons not understood but assumed to be related to continental drift, the continent began to move east. The sediments on the edge of the Precambrian mountain range were jammed against the adjacent land mass, causing layers of rock to buckle and crack. This motion continued off and on until the Permian period, some 240 million years ago. Then, the continent began to move in a westerly direction, which has continued to this day.

The mountains that were formed on the eastern edge of the Precambrian mountains are known today as the Appalachian Region. This is an area of old deposits changed through the pressures of folding and buckling and the intrusion of magma. The mineral deposits found in the region reflect the complexity of the geology, and include gypsum, barite, salt, copper, zinc, lead, gold and silver. Since the end of the mountain-building period, erosion has worn off the tops of the mountains and filled the valleys with sediments, which gives the area its present-day less rugged appearance.

The Interior Plains

To the west of the Precambrian mountains, the eroded debris, or sediment, carried by the rivers and deposited into the sea eventually formed wide, flat, relatively undisturbed plains. The surface layers of the sedimentary rock which forms the plains have been dated to the Paleozoic era which ended about 250 million years ago. The remains of old coral reefs point to the marine conditions during the development of the plains.

The Interior Plains occupy the central portion of the continent. Minerals found in the Interior Plains include potash, a substance produced when lakes and shallow seas are evaporated leaving behind deposits. Potash deposits in Saskatchewan are among the largest in the world. Coal, oil and natural gas were formed from organic materials trapped by the sedimentary layers during Paleozoic times. An extension of the Interior Plains thrusts up between the Precambrian Shield and the Appalachian Region, forming the Great Lakes–St. Lawrence Lowlands landform area. Soils throughout the Interior Plains are fertile, since the sedimentary materials they are formed of break down easily.

Other lowlands areas were formed during the Paleozoic era as a result of the deposit of sediment which created the Interior Plains. The Hudson Bay Lowlands on the southwestern edge of Hudson Bay are relatively thin layers of sedimentary rock on top of the Precambrian Shield. The Arctic Lowlands, between the Shield and the Innuition Mountains of the high Arctic, are similar in age and characteristics to the material of the Interior Plains.

The Western Cordillera

As the Precambrian mountains eroded, the sedimentary layers were deposited over a great distance and formed the Appalachian Region to the east. These deposits also provided the material from which future landforms would be built to the west. These landforms are now known as the Western Cordillera.

When the continent started its westward movement about 200 million years ago, its leading edge was forced against the adjacent oceanic plate and the land moved overtop the ocean. Geologists speculate that the tremendous pressure exerted in the land during this process caused the sedimentary layers of the plate's edge to buckle into a massive dome. Magma from within the Earth flowed into the dome and formed a core which eventually collapsed between 65 and 160 million years ago, breaking the rock layers. This core, stretching along the edge of the continental plate, now acts like a bumper on an automobile by absorbing the pressure of the 2 plates as they press upon each other.

The Western Cordillera is an area of great complexity; rocks composed of different materials and through different processes are thoroughly mixed. The Coast Ranges which form the leading western edge of the continent are a perfect example of this complexity since they are composed of both igneous and metamorphic rocks. The interior of the Cordillera is a chaotic jumble of plateaus, folded and broken rock layers and recent volcanoes. Intrusive rocks, which underlay only about 20% of this area, are almost totally absent from the Rocky Mountains, the eastern edge of the Cordillera. The sedimentary rocks of the Rockies were folded and broken during a period of mountain-building in Eocene times, some 40-65 million years ago.

The Cordillera contains minerals associated with all the processes involved in its creation. The igneous rocks of the western part of the Cordillera have provided a major source of minerals including lead, zinc, silver, copper and gold. The sedimentary deposits of the eastern Cordillera are responsible for the coal and petroleum found there.

Innuitian Region

Mountain-building shaped the landforms of the high Arctic beginning about 405 million years ago (the Devonian period). The most recent activities appear to have occurred about 30 million years ago which was long after the mountain-building period that thrust up the Rocky Mountains in the Cordillera.

Little detail is known about this region because research is so difficult in the inhospitable climate, but some geologists have suggested mountain-building is the result of the North American plate advancing on the Eurasian plate.

The topography of this region is characterized by low plateau mountains, with ridges as high as 3 000 m. The area is composed mainly of sedimentary rocks but includes some metamorphic and volcanic rocks.

Glaciation

Virtually all of Canada was subjected to glaciation over the past one million years. The periodic advances of the glaciers stripped away the soil and helped to wear away the rocks at the surface. As the ice melted and the glaciers retreated the soils and rocks which had been suspended in the ice were deposited onto the surface below. These deposits, some of which are known as moraines, drumlins and outwash plains, contribute to the present-day topography of Canada.

Drainage patterns were severely disrupted by glaciation, and the countless lakes and swamps of the Canadian Shield are a product of the poorly-developed drainage system resulting from the last glacial period about 10 000 years ago.

Earthquakes

Most of the world's geological activity takes place at the edges of the earth's continental and oceanic plates. This activity is caused by plates moving away from each other, towards each other, or running past each other sideways. Virtually all major earthquakes are located at plate boundaries. Most of Canada is situated in the middle of the North American plate on a very stable foundation of ancient Precambrian rock. This is one of the most geologically stable areas of the world. Nevertheless, parts of the North American plate are still subject to earthquakes. For example, the fault zone that marks the division between the Precambrian Shield and the Appalachian Region is an area of weakness. Called Logan's Line it runs up the Hudson River in New York State to Quebec

City and then down the St. Lawrence River. Another fault zone in the Ottawa River valley is still active. Even the stable Precambrian Shield has sporadic earthquake activity and periods when the Earth's crust moves. Geologists believe this activity is simply a rebound effect as the crust recovers from its recent, in geological time, load of glacial ice.

The vast majority of earthquakes in Canada occur along the west coast where the North American and Pacific plates meet. The long and active Queen Charlotte Island fault runs parallel to the coast about 150 km offshore. The Coastal Range of mountains, which forms the western border of the continent, is part of the Circum-Pacific belt of intense earthquake and volcanic activity.

Nations of the World

The nations of the world are listed in alphabetical order. Initials in the following articles include UN (United Nations), OAS (Org. of American States), NATO (North Atlantic Treaty Org.), EC (European Communities or Common Market), OAU (Org. of African Unity), ILO (Intl. Labor Org.), FAO (Food & Agricultural Org.), WHO (World Health Org.), IMF (Intl. Monetary Fund), GATT (General Agreement on Tarriffs & Trade). **Sources:** U.S. Dept. of State; U.S. Census Bureau; The World Factbook; International Monetary Fund; UN Statistical Yearbook; UN Demographic Yearbook; International Iron and Steel Institute; The Statesman's Year-Book; Encyclopaedia Britannica. Literacy rates are usually based on the ability to read and write on a lower elementary school level. The concept of literacy is changing in the industrialized countries, where literacy is defined as the ability to read instructions necessary for a job or a license. By these standards, illiteracy may be more common than present rates suggest. All dollar amounts are $U.S.

Afghanistan

Democratic Republic of Afghanistan

De Afghanistan Democrateek Jamhuriat

People: Population (1989 est.): 16 592 000. **Pop. density:** 25 per sq. km. **Ethnic groups:** Pushtun 50%; Tajiks 25%; Uzbek 9%; Hazara 9%. **Languages:** Pushtu, Dari Persian (spoken by Tajiks, Hazaras), Uzbek (Turkic). **Religions:** Sunni Moslem (74%), Shi'a Moslem (25%).

Geography: Area: 654 610 sq. km. **Location:** Between Soviet Central Asia and the Indian subcontinent. **Neighbors:** Pakistan on E, S, Iran on W, USSR on N; the NE tip touches China. **Topography:** The country is landlocked and mountainous, much of it over 1 220 m above sea level. The Hindu Kush Mts. tower 4 800 m above Kabul and reach a height of 7 500 m to the E. Trade with Pakistan flows through the 56 km long Khyber Pass. The climate is dry, with extreme temperatures, and large desert regions, though mountain rivers produce intermittent fertile valleys. **Capital:** Kabul. **Cities** (1985 est.): Kabul 2 mln.

Government: Type: People's republic. **Head of state, and President of the Revolutionary Council:** Pres. Mohammad Najibullah; in office: Nov. 30, 1987. **Head of Government:** Prime Min. Sultan Ali Keshtmand; in office: 1981. **Head of Communist Party:** Sec. Gen. Mohammad Najibullah; in office: May 4, 1986. **Local divisions:** 29 provinces, each under a governor. **Defence:** 3.0% of GNP (1984).

Economy: Industries: Textiles, carpets, cement. **Chief crops:** Nuts, wheat, fruits. **Minerals:** Copper, coal, zinc, iron. **Other resources:** Wool, hides, karacul pelts. **Arable land:** 13%. **Livestock** (1985): cattle: 3.7 mln.; sheep 20 mln. **Electricity prod.** (1986): 1.3 bln. kwh. **Labor force:** cannot be estimated due to war.

Finance: Currency: Afghani (Mar. 1988: 50.60 = $1 US). **Gross national product** (1985): $3.3 bln. **Imports** (1985): $1.1 bln.; partners: USSR 48%, Jap. 10%. **Exports** (1985): $556 mln.; partners: USSR 65%, UK 10%. **International reserves less gold** (Feb. 1988): $288 mln. **Gold:** 965 000 oz t.

Transport: Motor vehicles: in use (1982): 30 000 passenger cars, 35 000 comm. vehicles. **Civil aviation** (1986): 140 mln. passenger-km; 7.4 mln. net ton-km.

Communications: Television sets: 20 000 in use (1986); **Radios:** 150 000 in use (1986). **Telephones in use** (1985): 31 000. **Daily newspaper circ.** (1986): 6 per 1 000 pop.

Health: Life expectancy at birth (1986): 42.5 male; 40.8 female. **Births** (per 1 000 pop. 1985): 48.9. **Deaths** (per 1 000 pop. 1985): 27.3. **Natural increase** (1985): 2.1%. **Hospital beds:** 6 875. **Physicians:** 1 215 (1982). **Infant Mortality** (per 1000 live births 1985): 189.

Education (1987): **Literacy:** 12%. Over 88% of adults have no formal schooling.

Major International Organizations: UN (World Bank, IMF).

Afghanistan, occupying a favored invasion route since antiquity, has been variously known as Ariana or Bactria (in ancient times) and Khorasan (in the Middle Ages). Foreign empires alternated rule with local emirs and kings until the 18th century, when a unified kingdom was established. In 1973, a military coup ushered in a republic.

Pro-Soviet leftists took power in a bloody 1978 coup, and concluded an economic and military treaty with the USSR.

Late in Dec. 1979, the USSR began a massive military airlift into Kabul. The three-month old regime of Hafizullah Amin ended with a Soviet backed coup, Dec. 27th. He was replaced by Babrak Karmal, a more pro-Soviet leader. Soviet troops, estimated at between 60 000-100 000, fanned out over Afghanistan, fighting rebels. Fighting continued for 8 years as the Soviets found themselves engaged in a long, protracted guerrilla war.

A UN-mediated agreement was signed Apr. 14, 1988 providing for the withdrawal of Soviet troops from Afghanistan, creation of a neutral Afghan state, and repatriation of millions of Afghan refugees. The U.S. and USSR pledged to serve as guarantors of the agreement. Afghan rebels rejected the pact and vowed to continue fighting while the "Soviets and their puppets" remained in Afghanistan.

The Soviets announced in May that during the war 13 310 soldiers were killed, 35 478 wounded, and 311 were missing.

Albania

Peoples Socialist Republic of Albania

Republika Popullore Socialiste e Shqipërisë

People: Population (1989 est.): 3 201 000. **Pop. density:** 111 per sq. km. **Urban** (1984): 33%. **Ethnic groups:** Albanian (Gegs in N, Tosks in S) 96%, Greek 2.5%. **Languages:** Albanian (Tosk is official dialect), Greek. **Religions:** officially atheist; (historically) mostly Moslems. All public worship and religious institutions were outlawed in 1967.

Geography: Area: 28 860 sq. km. **Location:** On SE coast of Adriatic Sea. **Neighbors:** Greece on S, Yugoslavia on N, E. **Topography:** Apart from a narrow coastal plain, Albania consists of hills and mountains covered with scrub forest, cut by small E-W rivers. **Capital:** Tirana. **Cities** (1986 est.): Tirana 272 000; Durres 127 000; Vlore 90 000.

Government: Type: Communist. **Head of state:** Pres. Ramiz Alia, in office: Nov. 22, 1982. **Head of government:** Premier Adil Carcani; in office: Jan. 18, 1982. **Head of Communist Party:** Ramiz Alia; b. Oct. 18, 1925; in office: Apr. 13, 1985. **Local divisions:** 26 districts. **Defence:** 10.9% of budget (1986).

Economy: Industries: Chem. fertilizers, textiles. **Chief crops:** Corn, wheat, cotton, potatoes, tobacco, fruits. **Minerals:** Chromium, coal, oil. **Other resources:** Forests. **Arable land:** 21%. **Livestock** (1985): cattle: 600 000; sheep: 1.2 mln. **Electricity prod.** (1986): 4.9 bln. kwh. **Labor force:** 50% agric; 50% ind. and commerce.

Finance: Currency: Lek (Nov. 1987: 6.19 = $1 US). **Gross national product** (1986) $2.8 bln. **Per capita income** (1985): $900. **Imports** (1985): $335 mln.; partners: Czech., Yugoslavia, Romania. **Exports** (1985): $345 mln.; partners: Czech., Yugoslavia, N. Korea, Italy.

Transport: Motor vehicles: in use (1971): 3 500 passenger cars, 11 200 comm. vehicles. **Chief ports:** Durres, Vlone.

Communications: Television sets: 187 000 in use (1985). **Radios:** 210 000 in use (1986). **Daily newspaper circ.** (1982): 52 per 1 000 pop.

Health: Life expectancy at birth (1985): 70.4 yrs. **Births** (per 1 000 pop. 1985): 27.0. **Deaths** (per 1 000 pop. 1985): 6.0. **Natural increase** 2.0%. **Hospital beds** (per 1 000 pop. 1982): 70. **Physicians** (1982): 4 476 doctors & dentists. **Infant mortality** (per 1 000 live births 1982): 44.0.
  Major International Organizations: UN (FAO, WHO).
  Education (1986): **Literacy:** 75%.
  Canadian Embassy: c/o Kneza Milosa 75, 11000 Belgrade, Yugoslavia.

  Ancient Illyria was conquered by Romans, Slavs, and Turks (15th century); the latter Islamized the population. Independent Albania was proclaimed in 1912, republic was formed in 1920. Self-styled King Zog I ruled 1925-39, until Italy invaded.
  Communist partisans took over in 1944, allied Albania with USSR, then broke with USSR in 1960 over de-Stalinization. Strong political alliance with China followed, leading to several billion dollars in aid, which was curtailed after 1974. China cut off aid in 1978 when Albania attacked its policies after the death of Chinese ruler Mao Zedong.
  Industrialization, pressed in 1960s, slowed in 1970s. Large-scale purges of officials occurred 1973-76. Enver Hoxha, the nation's ruler for 4 decades, died Apr. 11, 1985.

Algeria

Democratic and Popular Republic of Algeria

al-Jumhuriya al-Jazāiriya ad-Dimuqratiya ash-Shabiya

  People: Population (1989 est.); 25 063 000. **Age distrib.** (%): 0–14: 46.0; 15–59: 48.3; 60+: 5.7. **Pop. density:** 10.5 per sq. km. **Urban** (1987): 49%. **Ethnic groups:** Arabs 75%, Berbers 25%. **Languages:** Arabic (official), Berber (indigenous language), French. **Religions:** Sunni Moslem (state religion).
  Geography: Area: 2 388 092 sq. km. **Location:** In NW Africa, from Mediterranean Sea into Sahara Desert. **Neighbors:** Morocco on W, Mauritania, Mali, Niger on S, Libya, Tunisia on E. **Topography:** The Tell, located on the coast, comprises fertile plains 80-160 km wide, with a moderate climate and adequate rain. Two major chains of the Atlas Mts., running roughly E-W, and reaching 2 100 m, enclose a dry plateau region. Below lies the Sahara, mostly desert with major mineral resources. **Capital:** Algiers (El Djazair). **Cities** (1987 est.): El Djazair 1 483 000; Wahran 590 000; Qacentina 483 000.
  Government: Type: Republic. **Head of state:** Pres. Chadli Bendjedid; b. Apr. 14, 1929; in office: Feb. 9, 1979. **Head of government:** Premier Abdel Hamid Brahimi; in office: Jan. 22, 1984. **Local divisions:** 31 wilayaat (states). **Defence:** 2.0% of GDP (1984).
  Economy: Industries: Oil, light industry, autos, textiles, fertilizer. **Chief crops:** Grains, wine-grapes, potatoes, dates, tomatoes, oranges. **Minerals:** Mercury, iron, zinc, lead, mercury. **Crude oil reserves** (1987): 4.8 bln. bbls. **Other resources:** Cork trees. **Arable land:** 17%. **Livestock** (1985): cattle: 1.7 mln.; sheep: 13 mln. **Electricity prod.** (1986): 12 bln. kwh. **Crude steel prod.** (1985): 1.2 mln metric tons. **Labor force:** 30% agric.; 40% ind. and commerce; 17% government; 10% services.
  Finance: Currency: Dinar (Mar. 1988: 5.29 = $1 US). **Gross national product** (1985): $57.0 bln. **Per capita income** (1984): $2,085. **Imports** (1986): $10.1 bln.; partners: France 18%, W. Ger. 18%, lt. 11%, Japan 9%. **Exports** (1986): $7.8 bln.; partners: U.S. 51%, W. Ger. 14%, France 11%, lt. 7%. **National budget** (1985): $23.2 bln. **International reserves less gold** (Mar. 1988): $1.4 bln. **Gold:** 5.58 mln. oz t. **Consumer prices** (change in 1987): 7.5%
  Transport: Motor vehicles: in use (1986): 712 000 passenger cars, 471 000 comm. vehicles. **Chief ports:** El Djazair.
  Communications: Television sets: 1.5 mln. in use (1986). **Radios:** 3.2 mln. in use (1986). **Telephones in use** (1985): 769 000. **Daily newspaper circ.** (1986): 23 per 1 000 pop.
  Health: Life expectancy at birth (1984): 56.7 male; 58.9 female. **Births** (per 1 000 pop. 1985): 42.0. **Deaths** (per 1 000 pop. 1985): 10.0. **Natural increase** (1985): 3.2%. **Hospital beds** (1985): 49 000. **Physicians** (1986): 15 361. **Infant mortality** (per 1 000 live births 1985): 182

Education (1987) **Literacy:** 52%. **School:** Free and compulsory to age 13; Attendance: 86% primary, 31% secondary.
  Major International Organizations: UN (FAO, IMF, WHO), OAU, Arab League, OPEC.
  Canadian Embassy: 27 Bis rue d'Anjou, Hydra; P.O. Box 225, Gare Alger, Algiers; Tel: 260-66-11.

  Earliest known inhabitants were ancestors of Berbers, followed by Phoenicians, Romans, Vandals, and, finally, Arabs. Turkey ruled 1518 to 1830, when France took control.
  Large-scale European immigration and French cultural inroads did not prevent an Arab nationalist movement from launching guerilla war. Peace, and French withdrawal, was negotiated with French Pres. Charles de Gaulle. One million Europeans left.
  Ahmed Ben Bella was the victor of infighting, and ruled 1962-65, when an army coup installed Col. Houari Boumedienne as leader.
  In 1967, Algeria declared war with Israel, broke with U.S., and moved toward eventual military and political ties with the USSR. French oil interests were partly seized in 1971, but relations with the West have since improved.

Andorra

Principality of Andorra

Principat d'Andorra

  People: Population (1989 est.): 56 000. **Age distrib. (%):** 0–14: 19.0; 14–59: 68.5; 60+: 12.5. **Pop. density:** 116.9 per sq. km. **Ethnic groups:** Catalan 61%, Spanish 30%, Andorran 6%, French 3%. **Languages:** Catalan (official), Spanish, French. **Religion:** Roman Catholic.
  Geography: Area: 479 sq. km. **Location:** In Pyrenees Mtns. **Neighbors:** Spain on S, France on N. **Topography:** High mountains and narrow valleys over the country. **Capital:** Andorra la Vella.
  Government: Type: Co-principality. **Head of state:** Co-princes are the president of France and the Roman Catholic bishop of Urgel in Spain. **Local divisions:** 7 parishes.
  Economy: Industries: Tourism, tobacco products. **Labor force:** 20% agric.; 80% ind. and commerce; services; government.
  Finance: Currency: French franc, Spanish peseta.
  Communications: Television sets: 4 000 in use (1986). **Radios:** 8 000 in use (1986). **Telephones in use** (1982): 17 719.
  Health: Births (per 1 000 pop. 1986): 11.6. **Deaths** (per 1 000 pop. 1986): 3.8. **Natural increase** (1986): 0.7%.
  Education (1987): **Literacy:** 99%. School compulsory to age 16.

  The present political status, with joint sovereignty by France and the bishop of Urgel, dates from 1278.
  Tourism, especially skiing, is the economic mainstay. A free port, allowing for an active trading centre, draws some 10 million tourists annually. The ensuing economic prosperity accompanied by Andorra's virtual law-free status, has given rise to calls for reform.

Angola

People's Republic of Angola

República Popular de Angola

  People: Population (1989 est.): 8 971 000. **Pop. density:** 7.2 per sq. km. **Ethnic groups:** Ovimbundu 38%, Kimbundu 25%; Bakongo 15%, Lunda-Chokwe 8%; Nganguela 6%. **Languages:** Portuguese (official), various Bantu languages. **Religions:** Roman Catholic 68%, Protestant 20%, animist 2%.
  Geography: Area: 1 251 518 sq. km. **Location:** In SW Africa on Atlantic coast. **Neighbors:** Namibia (SW Africa) on S, Zambia on E, Zaire on N; Cabinda, an enclave separated from rest of country by short Atlantic coast of Zaire, borders Congo Republic. **Topography:** Most of Angola consists of a plateau elevated 900 to 1 500 m above sea level, rising from a narrow coastal strip. There is also a temperate highland area in the west-central region, a desert in the S, and a tropical rain forest covering Cabinda. **Capital:** Luanda (1987 est.): 1.1 mln.

Government: Type: Marxist People's republic, one-party rule. **Head of state:** Pres. Jose Eduardo dos Santos b. Aug. 28, 1942; in office: Sept. 20, 1979. **Local divisions:** 18 provinces. **Defence:** 14.3% of GNP (1984).

Economy: Industries: Food processing, textiles, mining, tires, petroleum. **Chief crops:** Coffee, bananas. **Minerals:** Iron, diamonds (over 2 mln. carats a year), copper, phosphates, oil. **Crude oil reserves** (1987): 1.9 bln. bbls. **Arable land:** 3%. **Fish catch** (1984): 112 000 metric tons. **Electricity prod.** (1986): 851 mln.kwh. **Labor force:** 75% agric., 15% industry.

Finance: Currency: Kwanza (Nov. 1987: 30.53 = $1 US). **Gross domestic product** (1985): $4.5 bln. **Imports** (1986): $1.1 bln.; partners: Portugal 15%, Fra. 12%; USSR 8%. **Exports** (1986): $1.4 bln.; partners: Bahamas 15%, U.S. 49%.

Transport: Motor vehicles: in use (1984): 56 000 passenger cars, 29 000 comm. vehicles. **Chief ports:** Cabinda, Lobito, Luanda.

Communications: Radios: 400 000 in use (1986). **Telephones in use** (1982): 40 000. **Daily newspaper circ.** (1984): 13 per 1 000 pop.

Health: Life expectancy at birth (1984): 42.0 male; 44.0 female. **Births** (per 1 000 pop. 1985): 47.0. **Deaths** (per 1 000 pop. 1985): 20.0. **Natural increase** (1985): 2.7%. **Hospital beds** (per 1 000 pop. 1985): 20 000. **Physicians** (1980): 436. **Infant mortality** (per 1 000 live births 1986): 200.

Education (1987): **Literacy:** 30%.

Major International Organizations: UN (ILO, WHO), OAU.

Canadian Embassy: The Canadian Embassy to Angola, c/o The Canadian High Commission, P.O. Box 1430, Harare, Zimbabwe.

From the early centuries AD to 1500, Bantu tribes penetrated most of the region. Portuguese came in 1583, allied with the Bakongo kingdom in the north, and developed the slave trade. Large-scale colonization did not begin until the 20th century, when 400 000 Portuguese immigrated.

A guerrilla war begun in 1961 lasted until 1974, when Portugal offered independence. Violence between the National Front, based in Zaire, the Soviet-backed Popular Movement, and the National Union, aided by the U.S. and S. Africa, killed thousands of blacks, drove most whites to emigrate, and completed economic ruin. Cuban troops and Soviet aid helped the Popular Movement win most of the country after independence Nov. 11, 1975.

S. African troops crossed the southern Angolan border June 7, 1981, killing more than 300 civilians and occupying several towns. The S. Africans withdrew in Sept.

Russian influence, backed by 25 000 Cubans, East Germans, and Portuguese communists, is strong in the Marxist regime. The U.S. is now providing military aid to a rebel group, The National Union for Total Independence of Angola (UNITA) which is fighting to overthrow the government.

Antigua and Barbuda

People: Population (1989 est.) 86 000. **Pop. density:** 193.3 per sq. km. **Urban:** 34%. **Ethnic groups:** Mostly African. **Language:** English (official). **Religion:** Predominantly Church of England.

Geography: Area: 445 sq. km. **Location:** Eastern Caribbean. **Neighbors:** approx. 48 km north of Guadeloupe. **Capital:** St. John's, (1983 est.) 27 000.

Government: Type: Constitutional monarchy with British-style parliament. **Head of State:** Queen Elizabeth II; represented by Sir Wilfred E. Jacobs. **Head of Government:** Prime Min. Vere Cornwall Bird; b. Dec. 7, 1910; in office Nov. 1, 1981.

Economy: Industries: manufacturing, tourists (195 000 in 1984). **Arable Land:** 18%.

Finance: Currency: East Caribbean dollar (Jan. 1987): 2.70 = $1 U.S. **Gross national product** (1984): $150 mln.

Health: infant mortality (per 1 000 live births 1985): 31.5.

Education (1987): **Literacy:** 90%.

Major International Organizations: UN, Commonwealth of Nations.

Canadian High Commission: The Canadian High Commission to Antigua and Barbuda, c/o The Canadian High Commission, P.O. Box 404, Bridgetown, Barbados.

Antigua was discovered by Columbus in 1493. The British colonized it in 1632.

The British associated state of Antigua achieved independence as Antigua and Barbuda on Nov. 1, 1981. The government maintains close relations with the U.S., United Kingdom, and Venezuela.

Argentina
Argentine Republic
República Argentina

People: Population (1989 est.): 32 617 000. **Age distrib.** (%): 0–14: 31.1; 15–59: 56.6; 60+: 12.3. **Pop. density:** 11.8 per sq. km. **Urban** (1986): 80%. **Ethnic groups:** Europeans 98% (Spanish, Italian), Indians, Mestizos, Arabs. **Languages:** Spanish (official), English, Italian, German, French. **Religion:** Roman Catholic 90%.

Geography: Area: 2 769 260 sq. km, second largest in S. America. **Location:** Occupies most of southern S. America. **Neighbors:** Chile on W, Bolivia, Paraguay on N, Brazil, Uruguay on NE. **Topography:** The mountains in W: the Andean, Central, Misiones, and Southern. Aconcagua is the highest peak in the Western hemisphere, alt. 6 960 m. E of the Andes are heavily wooded plains, called the Gran Chaco in the N, and the fertile, treeless Pampas in the central region. Patagonia, in the S, is bleak and arid. Rio de la Plata, 274 by 225 km, is mostly fresh water, from 4 000 km Parana and 1 600 km Uruguay rivers. **Capital:** Buenos Aires (the senate has approved the moving of the capital to the Patagonia region). **Cities** (1982 est.): Buenos Aires 2 908 000; Cordoba 969 000; Rosario 750 455; Mendoza 597 000; San Miguel de Tucuman 497 000.

Government: Type: Republic. **Head of state:** Pres. Raul Alfonsin; b. Mar. 3, 1926; in office: Dec. 10, 1983. **Local divisions:** 22 provinces, 1 natl. terr. and 1 federal dist., under military governors. **Defence:** 3.7% of GNP (1984).

Economy: Industries: Meat processing, flour milling, chemicals, textiles, machinery, autos. **Chief crops:** Grains, corn, grapes, linseed, sugar, tobacco, rice, soybeans, citrus fruits. **Minerals:** Oil, lead, zinc, iron, copper, coal. **Crude oil reserves** (1987): 2.1 bln. bbls. **Arable land:** 9%. **Livestock** (1986): cattle: 54 mln.; sheep: 29 mln.; pigs: 4 mln. **Fish catch** (1986): 406 000 metric tons. **Electricity prod.** (1986): 42.7 bln. kwh. **Crude steel prod.** (1986): 3.2 mln. metric tons. **Labor force:** 16% agric.; 37% ind. and comm.; 20% services.

Finance: Currency: Austral (June 1988: 9.20 = $1 US). **Gross domestic product** (1985): $65.4 bln. **Per capita income** (1978 est.): $2 331. **Imports** (1986): $4.7 bln.; partners: U.S. 18%, W. Ger. 9%, Braz. 14%, Jap. 10%. **Exports** (1986): $6.8 bln.; partners: USSR 13%, Neth. 9%, U.S. 9%. **Tourists** (1984): receipts: $602 mln. **National budget** (1986): $31.3 bln. expenditures. **International reserves less gold** (Jan. 1988): $1.4 bln. **Gold:** 4.37 mln. oz t. **Consumer prices** (change in 1987): 131.3%.

Transport: Railway traffic (1986): 10.7 bln. passenger-km; 9.5 bln. net ton-km. **Motor vehicles:** in use (1985): 3.7 mln. passenger cars, 1.3 mln. comm. vehicles. **Civil aviation:** (1986) 6.6 mln. passenger-km; 538 mln. net ton-km. **Chief ports:** Buenos Aires, Bahia Blanca, La Plata.

Communications: Television sets: 5.9 mln. in use (1985). **Radios:** 19 mln. in use (1985). **Telephones in use** (1985): 3.4 mln. **Daily newspaper circ.** (1982): 85 per 1 000 pop.

Health: Life expectancy at birth (1983): 66.8 male; 73.2 female. **Births** (per 1 000 pop. 1985): 24.0. **Deaths** (per 1 000 pop. 1985): 9.0 **Natural increase** (1985): 1.5%. **Hospital beds** (1980): 150 010. **Physicians** (1980): 79 000. **Infant mortality** (per 1 000 live births 1986): 34.1.

Education (1986): **Literacy:** 94%. School attendance 21.5% through secondary school.

Major International Organizations: UN (WHO, IMF, FAO), OAS.

Canadian Embassy: Suipacha 1111, 25th fl., Brunetta Bldg., Suipacah and Sante Fe; postal: Casilla de Correo 1598, Buenos Aires; Tel: 312-9081/8.

Nomadic Indians roamed the Pampas when Spaniards arrived, 1515-1516, led by Juan Diaz de Solis. Nearly all the Indians were killed by the late 19th century. The colonists won independence, 1810-1819, and a long period of disorders ended in a strong centralized government.

Large-scale Italian, German, and Spanish immigration in the decades after 1880 spurred modernization, making Argentina the most prosperous, educated, and industrialized of the major Latin American nations. Social reforms were enacted in the 1920s, but military coups prevailed 1930-46, until the election of Gen. Juan Peron as president.

Peron, with his wife Eva Duarte, effected labor reforms, but also suppressed speech and press freedoms, closed religious schools, and ran the country into debt. A 1955 coup exiled Peron, who was followed by a series of military and civilian regimes. Peron returned in 1973, and was once more elected president. He died 10 months later, succeeded by his wife, Isabel, who had been elected vice president, and who became the first woman head of state in the Western hemisphere.

A military junta ousted Mrs. Peron in 1976 amid charges of corruption. Under a continuing state of siege, the army battled guerrillas and leftists, killed 5 000 people, and jailed and tortured others. On Dec. 9, 1985, after a trial of 5 months and nearly 1 000 witnesses, 5 former junta members, including ex-presidents Jorge Videla and Gen. Roberto Eduardo Viola, were found guilty of murder and human rights abuses.

A severe worsening in economic conditions placed extreme pressure on the military government.

Argentine troops seized control of the British-held Falkland Islands on Apr. 2, 1982. Both countries had claimed sovereignty over the islands, located 402 km off the Argentine coast, since 1833. The British dispatched a task force and declared a total air and sea blockade around the Falklands. Fighting began May 1; several hundred lost their lives as the result of the destruction of a British destroyer and the sinking of an Argentine cruiser.

British troops landed in force on East Falkland Island May 21. By June 2, the British had surrounded Stanley, the capital city and Argentine stronghold. The Argentine troops surrendered, June 14; Argentine President Leopoldo Galtieri resigned June 17.

Democratic rule returned to Argentina in 1983 as Raul Alfonsin's Radical Civic Union gained an absolute majority in the presidential electoral college and Congress. The nation was plagued by severe financial problems as inflation remained high (more than 131% in 1987). In 1987, Argentina reached agreement with foreign banks on a repayment schedule and interest rate adjustments on its foreign debt.

Australia
Commonwealth of Australia

People: Population (1989 est.): 16 090 000. **Age distrib.** (%): 0–14: 22.7; 15–59: 62.3; 60+: 15.0. **Pop. density:** 2.1 per sq. km. **Urban** (1984): 85%. **Ethnic groups:** European 96%, Asian 2%, aborigines (including mixed) 1.5%. **Languages:** English, aboriginal languages. **Religions:** Anglican 26%, other Protestant 25%, Roman Catholic 25%.

Geography: Area: 7 712 120 sq. km. **Location:** SE of Asia, Indian O. is W and S, Pacific O. (Coral, Tasman seas) is E; they meet N of Australia in Timor and Arafura seas: Tasmania lies 240 km S of Victoria state, across Bass Strait. **Neighbors:** Nearest are Indonesia, Papua New Guinea on N, Solomons, Fiji, and New Zealand on E. **Topography:** An island continent. The Great Dividing Range along the E coast has Mt. Kosciusko, 2 228 m. The W plateau rises to 607 m, with arid areas in the Great Sandy and Great Victoria deserts. The NW part of Western Australia and Northern Terr. are arid and hot. The NE has heavy rainfall and Cape York Peninsula has jungles. The Murray R. rises in the South Wales and flows 2 575 km to the Indian O. **Capital:** Canberra. **Cities** (1986 est.): Sydney 3 430 000; Melbourne 2 942 000; Brisbane 1 171 000; Adelaide 993 000; Perth 1 000 000.

Government: Type: Democratic, federal state system. **Head of state:** Queen Elizabeth II, represented by Gov.-Gen. Ninian Martin Stephen; in office: July 29, 1982. **Head of government:** Prime Min. Robert James Lee Hawke; b. Dec. 9, 1929; in office: Mar. 11, 1983. **Local divisions:** 6 states, 2 territories. **Defence:** 2.8% of GNP (1986).

Economy: Industries: Iron, steel, textiles, electrical equip., chemicals, autos, aircraft, ships, machinery. **Chief crops:** Wheat (a leading export), barley, oats, corn, hay, sugar, wine, fruit, vegetables. **Minerals:** Bauxite, coal, copper, iron, lead, nickel, silver, tin, tungsten, uranium, zinc. **Crude oil reserves** (1987): 1.6 bln. bbls. **Other resources:** Wool (30% of world output). **Arable land:** 6%. **Livestock** (1985): cattle: 23 mln.; sheep: 155.2 mln.; pigs: 2.5 mln. **Fish catch** (1985): 168 000 metric tons. **Electricity prod.** (1986): 125 bln. kwh. **Crude steel prod.** (1986): 6.6 mln. metric tons. **Labor force:** 6% agric.; 51% service; 22% government; 21% mining and manufacturing.

Finance: Currency: Dollar (Mar. 1988: 1.23 = $1 US). **Gross national product** (1985): $153 bln. **Per capita income** (1984): $10 282. **Imports** (1987): $29.3 bln; partners: U.S. 21%, Jap. 22%, UK 7%. **Exports** (1987): $26.5 bln.; partners: Jap. 27%, U.S. 11%, NZ 5%. **Tourists** (1985): $1.0 bln. **National budget** (1986): $49 bln. expenditures. **International reserves less gold** (Mar. 1988): $9.3 bln. **Gold:** 7.93 mln. oz t. **Consumer prices** (change in 1987): 8.5%.

Transport: Railway traffic (1984): 39.2 bln. net ton-km. **Motor vehicles:** in use (1986): 8.7 mln. passenger cars, 1.2 mln. comm. vehicles; **Civil aviation** (1985): 24.3 mln. passenger-km.; 1.8 bln. freight ton-km. **Chief ports:** Sydney, Melbourne, Newcastle, Port Kembla, Fremantle, Geelong.

Communications: Television sets: 6.5 mln. (1985). **Radios:** 20 mln. (1985). **Telephones in use** (1985): 8.7 mln. **Daily newspaper circ.** (1982): 426 per 1 000 pop.

Health: Life expectancy at birth (1986): 72.3 male; 78.8 female. **Births** (per 1 000 pop. 1987): 15.2. **Deaths** (per 1 000 pop. 1987): 7.5. **Natural increase** (1987): .7%. **Hospital beds** (1985): 91 654. **Physicians** (1982): 27 500. **Infant mortality** (per 1 000 live births 1986): 9.6.

Education (1987): **Literacy:** 99%. **School:** compulsory to age 15; attendance 94%.

Major International Organizations: UN and all its specialized agencies, OECD, Commonwealth of Nations.

High Canadian Commission: Commonwealth Ave., Canberra A.C.T. 2600; Tel: (062)73-3844.

Capt. James Cook explored the E coast in 1770, when the continent was inhabited by a variety of different tribes. Within decades, Britain had claimed the entire continent, which became a penal colony until immigration increased in the 1850s. The commonwealth was proclaimed Jan. 1, 1901. Northern Terr. was granted limited self-rule July 1, 1978. Their capitals and 1987 population estimates:

	Area (sq. km)	Population
New South Wales, Sydney	804 700	5 581 300
Victoria, Melbourne	228 540	4 188 300
Queensland, Brisbane	1 734 174	2 616 300
South Aust., Adelaide	987 740	1 378 900
Western Aust., Perth	2 535 260	1 458 700
Tasmania, Hobart	68 120	448 600
Aust. Capital Terr., Canberra	2 340	267 600
Northern Terr., Darwin	1 351 480	150 300

Australia's racially discriminatory immigration policies were abandoned in 1973, after 3 million Europeans (half British) had entered since 1945. The 50 000 aborigines and 150 000 part-aborigines are mostly detribalized, but there are several preserves in the Northern Territory. They remain economically disadvantaged. On Jan. 26, 1988, some 15 000 aborigines demonstrated in Sydney to protest discrimination while the rest of the nation celebrated the 200th anniversary of the landing of the first European settlers.

Australia's agricultural success makes it among the top exporters of beef, lamb, wool, and wheat. Major mineral deposits have been developed as well, largely for exports. Industrialization has been completed.

Australia harbors many plant and animal species not found elsewhere, including the kangaroo, koala bear, platypus, dingo (wild dog), Tasmanian devil (racoon-like marsupial), wombat (bear-like marsupial), and barking and frilled lizards.

Australian External Territories

Norfolk Is., area 35 sq. km, pop. (1985) 1 800, was taken over, 1914. The soil is very fertile, suitable for citrus fruits, bananas, and coffee. Many of the inhabitants are descendants of the Bounty mutineers, moved to Norfolk 1856 from Pitcairn Is. Australia offered the island limited home rule, 1978.

Coral Sea Is. Territory, 2.6 sq. km, is administered from Norfolk Is.

Territory of Ashmore and Cartier Is., area 5.2 sq. km, in the Indian O. came under Australian authority 1934 and are administered as part of Northern Territory. **Heard** and **McDonald Is.** are administered by the Dept. of Science.

Cocos (Keeling) Is., 27 small coral islands in the Indian O. 2 800 km NW of Australia. pop. (1981) 569, area: 14 sq. km. The residents voted to become part of Australia, Apr. 1984.

Christmas Is., 135 sq. km, pop. (1983) 3 000, 368 km S of Java, was transferred by Britain in 1958. It has phosphate deposits.

Australian Antarctic Territory was claimed by Australia in 1933, including 6 427 200 sq. km of territory S of 60th parallel S Lat. and between 160th-45th meridians E Long.

Austria

Republic of Austria
Republik Österreich

People: Population (1989 est.): 7 555 000. **Age distrib.** (%): 0–14: 18.2; 15–59: 61.8; 60+: 20.0. **Pop. density:** 89.8 per sq. km. **Urban** (1986): 55.0%. **Ethnic groups:** German 98%, Slovene, Croatian. **Languages:** German 98%. **Religion:** Roman Catholic 85%.

Geography: Area: 84 172 sq. km. **Location:** In S Central Europe. **Neighbors:** Switzerland, Liechtenstein on W, W. Germany, Czechoslovakia on N, Hungary on E, Yugoslavia, Italy on S. **Topography:** Austria is primarily mountainous, with the Alps and foothills covering the western and southern provinces. The eastern provinces and Vienna are located in the Danube River Basin. **Capital:** Vienna. **Cities** (1987 cen.): Vienna 1 500 000.

Government: Type: Parliamentary democracy. **Head of state:** Pres. Kurt Waldheim; b. Dec. 21, 1918; in office: June 8, 1986. **Head of government:** Chancellor Franz Vranitzky; b. Oct. 4, 1937; in office: June 16, 1986. **Local divisions:** 9 lander (states), each with a legislature. **Defence:** 1.3% of GNP (1986).

Economy: Industries: Steel, machinery, autos, electrical and optical equip., glassware, sport goods, paper, textiles, chemicals, cement. **Chief crops:** Grains, potatoes, beets. **Minerals:** Iron ore, oil, magnesite. **Crude oil reserves** (1985): 116 mln. bbls. **Other resources:** Forests, hydro power. **Arable land:** 18.3%. **Meat prod.** (1985): cattle: 2.6 mln.; pigs: 3.9 mln. **Electricity prod.** (1986): 46.4 bln. kwh. **Crude steel prod.** (1986): 4.2 mln. metric tons. **Labor force:** 8% agric.; 35% ind. & comm.; 56% service.

Finance: Currency: Schilling (June 1988: 12.16 = $1 US). **Gross national product** (1986): $94.7 bln. **Per capita income** (1986): $12 521. **Imports** (1987): $32.7 bln.; partners: W. Ger. 41%, It. 9%, Switz. 5%. **Exports** (1987): $27.1 bln.; partners: W. Ger. 29%, It. 9%, Switz. 7%. **Tourists** (1985): receipts: $6.0 bln. **National budget** (1984): $20.3 bln. expenditures. **International reserves less gold** (Mar. 1988): $8.1 bln. **Gold:** 21.15 mln. oz t. **Consumer prices** (change in 1987): 11.4%.

Transport: Railway traffic (1985): 7.0 bln. passenger-km; 11.9 bln. net ton-km. **Motor vehicles:** in use (1985): 2.5 mln. passenger cars, 232 000 comm. **Civil aviation** (1986): 1.3 bln. passenger-km; 23.4 mln. freight ton-km.

Communications: Television sets: 2.4 mln. (1984). **Radios:** 2.6 mln. (1984). **Telephones in use** (1984): 2.6 mln. **Daily newspaper circ.** (1985): 312 per 1 000 pop.

Health: Life expectancy at birth (1981): 69.3 male; 76.4 female. **Births** (per 1 000 pop. 1985): 12.0 **Deaths** (per 1 000 pop. 1985): 13.0. **Natural increase** (1985): −.1%. **Hospital beds** (1985): 84 125. **Physicians** (1985): 21 513. **Infant mortality** (per 1 000 live births 1987): 10.6.

Education (1987): Literacy: 98%. School years compulsory 9; attendance 95%.

Major International Organizations: UN and all of its specialized agencies, EFTA, OECD.

Canadian Embassy: Dr. Karl Luegar Ring 10, A-1010, Vienna; Tel: 533-3961, -95; 533-6626, -28.

Rome conquered Austrian lands from Celtic tribes around 15 BC. In 788 the territory was incorporated into Charlemagne's empire. By 1300, the House of Hapsburg had gained control; they added vast territories in all parts of Europe to their realm in the next few hundred years.

Austrian dominance of Germany was undermined in the 18th century and ended by Prussia by 1866. But the Congress of Vienna, 1815, confirmed Austrian control of a large empire in

southeast Europe consisting of Germans, Hungarians, Slavs, Italians, and others.

The dual Austro-Hungarian monarchy was established in 1867, giving autonomy to Hungary and almost 50 years of peace.

World War I, started after the June 28, 1914 assassination of Archduke Franz Ferdinand, the Hapsburg heir, by a Serbian nationalist, destroyed the empire. By 1918 Austria was reduced to a small republic, with the borders it has today.

Nazi Germany invaded Austria Mar. 13, 1938. The republic was re-established in 1945, under Allied occupation. Full independence and neutrality were restored in 1955.

Austria produces most of its food, as well as an array of industrial products. A large part of Austria's economy is controlled by state enterprises. Socialists have shared or alternated power with the conservative People's Party.

Economic agreements with the Common Market give Austria access to a free-trade area encompassing most of West Europe.

An international panel of historians issued a report in 1988 concluding that Pres. Kurt Waldheim knew of war crimes in Greece and Yugoslavia while serving in the German army during World War II, did nothing to stop them, and later covered up his war record. The panel found no evidence that Waldheim committed war crimes.

The Bahamas

The Commonwealth of the Bahamas

People: Population (1989 est.): 247 000. **Age distrib.** (%): 0–14: 38.0; 15–59: 56.3; 60+: 5.7. **Pop. density:** 17.7 per sq. km. **Urban** (1987): 75%. **Racial groups:** black 85%, white 15%. **Language:** English. **Religions:** Baptist 29%, Anglican 23%, Roman Catholic 22%.

Geography: Area: 13 988 sq. km. **Location:** In Atlantic O., E of Florida. **Neighbors:** Nearest are U.S. on W, Cuba on S. **Topography:** Nearly 700 islands (30 inhabited) and over 2 000 islets in the western Atlantic extend 1 216 km NW to SE. **Capital:** Nassau. **Cities:** (1985 est.) New Providence 135 437; Freeport 16 000.

Government: Type: Independent commonwealth. **Head of state:** Queen Elizabeth II, represented by Gov.-Gen. Gerald C. Cash; b. May 28, 1917, in office: Sept. 29, 1979. **Head of government:** Prime Min. Lynden Oscar Pindling; b. Mar. 22, 1930; in office: Jan. 16, 1967. **Local divisions:** 18 districts.

Economy: Industries: Tourism (70% of GNP), rum, banking, pharmaceuticals. **Chief crops:** Fruits, vegetables. **Minerals:** Salt. **Other resources:** Lobsters. **Arable land:** 2%. **Electricity prod.** (1986): 885 mln. kwh. **Labor force:** 5% agric.; 25% tourism, 30% government.

Finance: Currency: Dollar (June 1988: 1 = $1 US). **Gross national product** (1985): $2.1 bln. **Per capita income** (1986): $7 598. **Imports** (1986): $1.6 bln.; partners: U.S. 74%, EC 30%. **Exports** (1986): $825 mln. (not incl. oil); partners: U.S. 41%, U.K. 7%. **Tourists** (1986): receipts: $1.1 bln. **National budget** (1986): $414 mln. expenditures. **International reserves less gold** (Mar. 1988): $211 mln. **Consumer prices** (change in 1986): 5.4%.

Transport: Motor vehicles: in use (1984): 88 000 passenger cars, 5 600 comm. vehicles. **Chief ports:** Nassau, Freeport.

Communications: Radios: 120 000 in use (1986). **Television sets** (1986): 40 000. **Telephones in use** (1985): 97 000. **Daily newspaper circ.** (1985): 136 per 1 000 pop.

Health: Life expectancy at birth (1987): 64.0 male; 70 female. **Births** (per 1 000 pop. 1985): 24.0. **Deaths** (per 1 000 pop. 1985): 6.0. **Natural increase** (1985): 1.8%. **Infant mortality** (per 1 000 live births 1985): 20.2.

Education (1988): Literacy: 93%; School compulsory through age 14.

Major International Organizations: UN (World Bank, IMF, WHO), OAS.

Canadian High Commission: c/o P.O. Box 1500, Kingston 10, Jamaica; Nassau: Out Island Traders Building, Ernest St., P.O. Box SS6371, Nassau; (809) 323-2124.

Christopher Columbus first set foot in the New World on San Salvador (Watling I.) in 1492, when Arawak Indians inhabited the islands. British settlement began in 1647; the islands became a

British colony in 1783. Internal self-government was granted in 1964; full independence within the Commonwealth was attained July 10, 1973.

International banking and investment management has become a major industry alongside tourism, despite controversy over financial irregularities.

Bahrain

State of Bahrain

Dawlat al-Bahrayn

People: Population (1989 est.): 483 000. **Age distrib. (%):** 0–14: 32.0; 15–59: 64.4; 60+: 3.6. **Pop. density:** 720.9 per sq. km. **Urban** (1984): 79%. **Ethnic groups:** Bahraini 63%, Asian 13%, other Arab 10%, Iranian 6%. **Languages:** Arabic (official), Persian. **Religions:** Sunni Moslem 30%, Shi'a Moslem 70%.

Geography: Area: 670 sq. km. **Location:** In Persian Gulf. **Neighbors:** Nearest are Saudi Arabia on W. Qatar on E. **Topography:** Bahrain Island, and several adjacent, smaller islands, are flat, hot and humid, with little rain. **Capital:** Manama. **Cities** (1985 est.): Manama 122 000.

Government: Type: Traditional monarchy. **Head of state:** Amir Isa ibn Sulman al-Khalifa; b. July 3, 1933; in office: Nov. 2, 1961. **Head of government:** Prime Min. Kahlifa ibn Sulman al-Khalifa; b. 1935; in office: Jan. 19, 1970. **Local divisions:** 6 towns and cities. **Defense:** 3.6% of GNP (1984).

Economy: Industries: Oil products, aluminum smelting. **Chief crops:** Fruits, vegetables. **Minerals:** Oil, gas. **Crude oil reserves** (1985): 173 mln. bbls. **Arable land:** 5%. **Electricity prod.** (1986): 6.8 bln. kwh. **Labor force:** 4% agric.; 84% ind. and commerce; 5% services; 19% gov.

Finance: Currency: Dinar (Mar. 1988: 0.38 = $1 US). **Gross national product** (1987): $4.6 bln. **Per capita income** (1982 est.): $11 900. **Imports** (1986): $2.4 bln.; partners: Sau. Ar. 60%, UK 6%, U.S. 9%. **Exports** (1936): $2.3 bln.; partners: UAE 18%, Jap. 12%, Sing. 10%, U.S. 6%. **National Budget** (1987): $2.6 bln. expenditures. **International reserves less gold** (Mar. 1988): $1.1 bln. **Gold:** 150 000 oz t. **Consumer prices** (change in 1986): −2.3%.

Transport: Motor vehicles: in use (1984): 72 000 passenger cars, 23 000 comm. vehicles. **Chief ports:** Sitra.

Communications: Television sets: 114 000 in use (1986). **Radios:** 200 000 in use (1986). **Telephones in use** (1985): 114 000.

Health: Births (per 1 000 pop. 1985): 30.0 **Deaths** (per 1 000 pop. 1985): 7.0. **Natural Increase** (1985): 3.5. **Medical Services:** free; there are 49 government hospitals and health centres.

Education (1987): **Literacy:** 74%.

Major International Organizations: UN (GATT, IMF, WHO), Arab League.

Canadian Embassy: c/o P.O. Box 25281, 13113 (Safat), Kuwait City, Kuwait.

Long ruled by the Khalifa family, Bahrain was a British protectorate from 1861 to 1971, when it regained independence.

Pearls, shrimp, fruits, and vegetables were the mainstays of the economy until oil was discovered in 1932. By the 1970s, oil reserves were depleted; international banking thrived.

Bahrain took part in the 1973-74 Arab oil embargo against the U.S. and other nations. The government bought controlling interest in the oil industry in 1975.

Saudi Arabia has built a 24 km causeway linking Bahrain with the Arab mainland.

Bangladesh

People's Republic of Bangladesh

Gana Prajätantrï Bangladesh

People: Population (1989 est.): 112 757 000. **Age distrib. (%):** 0-14: 44.3; 15-59: 50.4; 60+: 5.3. **Pop. density:** 780 per sq. km. **Urban** (1985): 20%. **Ethnic groups:** Bengali 98%, Bihari, tribesmen. **Languages:** Bengali (official), English. **Religions:** Moslem 83%, Hindu 16%.

Geography: Area: 144 555 sq. km. **Location:** In S Asia, on N bend of Bay of Bengal. **Neighbors:** India nearly surrounds country on W, N, E; Burma on SE. **Topography:** The country is mostly a low plain cut by the Ganges and Brahmaputra rivers and their delta. The land is alluvial and marshy along the coast, with hills only in the extreme SE and NE. A tropical monsoon climate prevails, among the rainiest in the world. **Capital:** Dhaka. **Cities** (1987 est.): Dhaka (met.) 3.4 mln.; Chittagong (met.) 1.4 mln.; Khulna (met.) 646 000.

Government: Type: Islamic republic. **Head of state:** Pres. Hossain Mohammad Ershad, b. Feb. 1, 1930, in office: Dec. 11, 1983. **Head of government:** Prime Minister Moudud Ahmed; in office: Mar. 27, 1988. **Local divisions:** 64 districts. **Defence:** 1.4% of GNP (1984).

Economy: Industries: Cement, jute, textiles, fertilizers, petroleum products. **Chief crops:** Jute (most of world output), rice. **Minerals:** Natural gas, offshore oil, coal. **Fish catch** (1986): 763 000 metric tons. **Electricity prod.** (1985): 4.8 bln. kwh. **Labor force:** 74% agric; 11% ind.; 15% services.

Finance: Currency: Taka (Mar. 1988: 31.50 = $1 US). **Gross national product** (1985): $15.0 bln. **Per capita income** (1986) $113. **Imports** (1986): $2.5 bln.; partners: Jap. 13%, U.S. 8%. **Exports** (1986): $953 mln.; partners: U.S. 10%, Sing. 11%; Pak 5%. **International reserves less gold** (Mar. 1988): $827 mln. **Gold:** 54 000 oz t. **Consumer prices** (change in 1986): 11.0%.

Transport: Railway traffic (1984): 6.2 bln. passenger-km; 724 mln. net ton-km. **Motor vehicles:** in use (1984): 38 000 passenger cars, 23 000 comm. vehicles. **Chief ports:** Chittagong, Mongla.

Communications: Radios: 775 000 (1985). **Television sets:** 300 000 (1985). **Telephones in use** (1984): 143 000. **Daily newspaper circ.** (1984) 6 per 1 000 pop.

Health: Life expectancy at birth (1986): 50.2 males; 49.2 females. **Births** (per 1 000 pop. 1986): 42.7. **Deaths** (per 1 000 pop. 1986): 16.3. **Natural increase** (1987): 2.6%. **Hospital beds** (1984): 21 370. **Physicians** (1984): 12 306. **Infant mortality** (per 1 000 live births 1985): 140.

Education (1985): **Literacy:** 33%. **Attendance:** 24% primary school; 4% secondary school.

Major International Organizations: UN (GATT, IMF, WHO).

Canadian High Commission: House CWN 16/A, Road 48, Gulshan; postal: G.P.O. Box 569, Dhaka; Tel: 607071, -7.

Moslem invaders conquered the formerly Hindu area in the 12th century. British rule lasted from the 18th century to 1947, when East Bengal became part of Pakistan.

Charging West Pakistani domination, the Awami League, based in the East, won National Assembly control in 1971. Assembly sessions were postponed; riots broke out. Pakistani troops attacked Mar. 25; Bangladesh independence was proclaimed the next day. In the ensuing civil war, one million died and 10 million fled to India.

War between India and Pakistan broke out Dec. 3, 1971. Pakistan surrendered in the East Dec. 15. Sheik Mujibur Rahman became prime minister. The country moved into the Indian and Soviet orbits, in response to U.S. support of Pakistan, and much of the economy was nationalized.

In 1974, the government took emergency powers to curb widespread violence; Mujibur was assassinated and a series of coups followed.

Chronic destitution among the densely crowded population has been worsened by the decline of jute as a major world commodity.

On May 30, 1981, Pres. Ziaur Rahman was shot and killed in an unsuccessful coup attempt by army rivals. Vice President Abdus Sattar assumed the presidency but was ousted in a coup led by army chief of staff Gen. H.M. Ershad, Mar. 1982. Ershad declared Bangladesh an Islamic republic in 1988. Bangladesh remains one of the world's poorest countries.

In 1987, floods brought devastation to much of Bangladesh; over 1,000 died, 20 million were made homeless, and damages were nearly $1 billion.

Barbados

People: Population (1989 est.): 256 000 **Age distrib. (%):** 0–14: 27.3; 15–59: 59.8; 60+: 12.9. **Pop. density:** 594 per sq. km. **Urban** (1985): 42%. **Ethnic groups:** African 80%, mixed

16%, Caucasian 4%. **Language:** English. **Religions:** Anglican 70%, Methodist 9%, Roman Catholic 4%.

Geography: Area: 431 sq. km. **Location:** In Atlantic, farthest E of W. Indies. **Neighbors:** Nearest are Trinidad, Grenada on SW. **Topography:** The island lies alone in the Atlantic almost completely surrounded by coral reefs. Highest point is Mt. Hillaby, 334 m. **Capital:** Bridgetown. **Cities** (1982 est.): Bridgetown 7 600.

Government: Type: Independent sovereign state within the Commonwealth. **Head of state:** Queen Elizabeth II, represented by Gov.-Gen. Hugh Springer. **Head of government:** Prime Min. Erskine Sandiford; b. Mar. 24, 1937; in office: June 1, 1987. **Local divisions:** 11 parishes and Bridgetown.

Economy: Industries: Rum, molasses, tourism. **Chief crops:** Sugar, corn. **Minerals:** Lime. **Other resources:** Fish. **Arable land:** 76%. **Electricity prod.** (1986): 389.0 mln. kwh. **Labor force:** 6.9% agric.; 12.7% ind. and comm.; 80.9% services and government.

Finance: Currency: Dollar (June 1988: 2.01 = $1 US). **Gross national product** (1985): $1.1 bln. **Per capita income** (1982): $3 040. **Imports** (1985): $552 mln.; partners: U.S. 47%, CARACOM 12%. **Exports** (1985): $352 mln.; partners: U.S. 42%, CARACOM 22%. **Tourists** (1986): $326 mln. receipts. **National budget** (1985): $330 mln. **International reserves less gold** (Mar. 1988): $154 mln. **Consumer prices** (change in 1987): 3.3%.

Transport: Motor vehicles: in use (1985): 32 000 passenger cars; 5 363 comm. vehicles. **Chief ports:** Bridgetown.

Communications: Television sets: 60 000 in use (1986). **Radios:** 335 000 in use (1986). **Telephones in use** (1986): 90 000. **Daily newspaper circ.** (1986): 156 per 1 000 pop.

Health: Life expectancy at birth (1984): 70.8. **Births** (per 1 000 pop. 1986): 16.1. **Deaths** (per 1 000 pop. 1986): 8.2. **Natural increase** (1986): .7%. **Hospital beds** (1983): 2 110. **Physicians** (1983): 213. **Infant mortality** (per 1 000 live births 1985): 14.

Education (1987): **Literacy:** 99%. **Years compulsory:** 9.

Major International Organizations: UN (FAO, GATT, ILO, IMF, WHO), OAS.

Canadian High Commission: Bishops Court Hill, St. Michael; P.O. Box 404, Bridgetown; Tel: 429-3550.

Barbados was probably named by Portuguese sailors in reference to bearded fig trees. An English ship visited in 1605, and British settlers arrived on the uninhabited island in 1627. Slaves worked the sugar plantations, but were freed in 1834.

Self-rule came gradually, with full independence proclaimed Nov. 30, 1966. British traditions have remained.

Belgium

Kingdom of Belgium

Koninkrijk België (Dutch)
Royaume de Belgique (French)

People: Population (1989 est.): 9 897 000. **Age distrib.** (%): 0–14: 20.0; 15–59: 61.4; 60+: 18.6 **Pop. density:** 323.2 per sq. km. **Urban** (1980): 73%. **Ethnic groups:** Fleming 55%, Walloon 33%. **Languages:** Flemish (Dutch) 57%, French 33%, legally bilingual 10%, German 1%. **Religion:** Roman Catholic 75%.

Geography: Area: 30 625 sq. km. **Location:** In NW Europe, on N. Sea. **Neighbors:** France on W, S, Luxembourg on SE, W. Germany on E, Netherlands on N. **Topography:** Mostly flat, the country is trisected by the Scheldt and Meuse, major commercial rivers. The land becomes hilly and forested in the SE (Ardennes) region. **Capital:** Brussels. **Cities** (1985 est.): Brussels (met.) 980 196; Antwerp (met.) 486 000; Ghent 234 000; Charleroi 211 000; Liege 202 000.

Government: Type: Parliamentary democracy under a constitutional monarch. **Head of state:** King Baudouin; b. Sept. 7, 1930; in office: July 17, 1951. **Head of government:** Premier Wilfried Martens; b. Apr. 19, 1936; in office: Dec. 17, 1981. **Local divisions:** 9 provinces; 3 regions; 3 cultural communities. **Defence:** 3.3% of GNP (1984).

Economy: Industries: Steel, glassware, diamond cutting, textiles, chemicals. **Chief crops:** Grains, fruits, potatoes, sugar beets. **Minerals:** Coal, coke. **Other resources:** Forests. **Arable land** (incl. Lux.): 26.5%. **Meat prod.** (1985): cattle: 3.1 mln.; pigs: 5.5 mln. **Fish catch** (1985): 44 000 metric tons. **Electricity prod.** (1986): 57.4 bln. kwh. **Crude steel prod.** (1986): 9.7 mln. metric tons. **Labor force:** 2% agric.; 26% ind. & comm.; 37% services & transportation; 23% public service.

Finance: Currency: Franc (June 1988: 36.15 = $1 US). **Gross national product** (1986): $111 bln. **Per capita income** (1986): $10 475. *Note:* the following trade and tourist data includes Luxembourg. **Imports** (1987): $83.2 bln.; partners: W. Ger. 18%, Neth. 15%, France 9%, UK 7%, U.S. 3%. **Exports** (1987): $84.0 bln.; partners: W. Ger. 19%, France 18%, Neth. 9%, UK 6%. **Tourists** (1985): receipts: $1.6 bln. **National budget** (1987): $43.5 bln. expenditures. **International reserves less gold** (Mar. 1988): $9.1 bln. **Gold:** 33.67 mln. oz t. **Consumer prices** (change in 1986): 1.6%.

Transport: Railway traffic (1985): 6.5 bln. passenger-km; 7.4 bln. net ton-km. **Motor vehicles:** in use (1985): 3.3 mln. passenger cars, 318 000 comm. vehicles. **Civil aviation** (1986): 5.5 bln. passenger-km; 594 mln. freight ton-km. **Chief ports:** Antwerp, Zeebrugge, Ghent.

Communications: Television sets: 3 mln. licensed (1985). **Radios:** 4.6 mln. licensed (1985); **Telephones in use** (1986): 4.3 mln. **Daily newspaper circ.** (1985): 272 per 1 000 pop.

Health: Life expectancy at birth (1985): 70.1 male; 76.7 female. **Births** (per 1 000 pop. 1985): 12.0. **Deaths** (per 1 000 pop. 1985): 12.0. **Natural increase** (1985) 0%. **Hospital beds** (1984): 91 638. **Physicians:** 28 828. **Infant mortality** (per 1 000 live births 1985): 10.

Education (1985): **Literacy:** 98%. School compulsory to age 16.

Major International Organizations: UN and all of its specialized agencies, NATO, EC, OECD.

Canadian Embassy: 2, Avenue de Tervuren, 1040 Brussels; Tel: 02/735 60 40.

Belgium derives its name from the Belgae, the first recorded inhabitants, probably Celts. The land was conquered by Julius Caesar, and was ruled for 1800 years by conquerors, including Rome, the Franks, Burgundy, Spain, Austria, and France. After 1815, Belgium was made a part of the Netherlands, but it became an independent constitutional monarchy in 1830.

Belgian neutrality was violated by Germany in both world wars. King Leopold III surrendered to Germany, May 28, 1940. After the war, he was forced by political pressure to abdicate in favor of his son, King Baudouin.

The Flemings of northern Belgium speak Dutch while French is the language of the Walloons in the south. The language difference has been a perennial source of controversy. Antagonism between the 2 groups has continued.

Belgium lives by its foreign trade; about 50% of its entire production is sold abroad.

Belize

People: Population (1989 est.): 179 400. **Age distrib.** (%): 0–14: 44.9; 15–59: 47.8; 60+: 7.3. **Pop. density:** 7.8 per sq. km. **Ethnic groups:** African, Mestizo, Amerindian, Creole. **Languages:** English (official), Spanish, native Creole dialects. **Religions:** Roman Catholic 50%, Protestant 50%.

Geography: Area: 23 054 sq. km. **Location:** eastern coast of Central America. **Neighbors:** Mexico on N., Guatemala on W. and S. **Capital:** Belmopan. **Cities** (1987 est.): Belize City 40 000.

Government: Type: Parliamentary. **Head of State:** Gov. Gen. Minita Gordon. **Head of government:** Prime Min. Manual Esquivel; b. 1940; in office: Dec. 17, 1984. **Local divisions:** 6 districts.

Economy: Sugar is the main export.

Finance: Currency: Belize dollar (Mar. 1988) 2 = $1 U.S. **Gross domestic product** (1984): $1 000. **Per capita income** (1984): $1 000. **Imports** (1985) $128 mln.; partners: U.S. 55%, UK 17%. **Exports:** (1985): 90.1 mln.; partners: U.S. 36%, UK 22%. **National Budget** (1986): $106 mln. expenditures.

Health: life expectancy (1981) 60 yrs. **Births** (per 1 000 pop. 1985): 38.0. **Deaths** (per 1 000 pop. 1985): 7.0. **Hospital beds** (1984): 584; **Physicians** (1984): 78. (1983). **Infant mortality** (per 1 000 live births, 1985): 54.

Education: (1985) **Literacy:** 80%.; **Years compulsory:** 9; attendance 55%.

Major International Organizations: UN (IMF, World Bank), Commonwealth of Nations.

Canadian High Commision: c/o P.O. Box 1500, Kingston 10, Jamaica.

Belize (formerly called British Honduras), Great Britain's last colony on the American mainland, achieved independence on Sept. 21, 1981. Guatemala claims territorial sovereignty over the country and has refused to recognize Belize's independence. British troops in Belize guarantee security.

Benin

People's Republic of Benin

République Populaire du Benin

People: Population (1989 est.): 4 551 000. **Age distrib. (%):** 0–14: 46.5; 15–59: 49.0; 60+: 4.5. **Pop. density:** 40.3 per sq. km. **Urban** (1985): 20%. **Ethnic groups:** Fon, Adja, Bariba, Yoruba. **Languages:** French (official), local dialects. **Religions:** Mainly animist with Christian, Moslem minorities.

Geography: Area: 113 056 sq. km. **Location:** In W Africa on Gulf of Guinea. **Neighbors:** Togo on W, Burkina Faso, Niger on N, Nigeria on E. **Topography:** most of Benin is flat and covered with dense vegetation. The coast is hot, humid, and rainy. **Capital:** Porto-Novo. **Cities** (1984 est.): Cotonou 330 000.

Government: Type: Marxist-Leninist. **Head of state:** Pres. Mathieu Kerekou; b. Sept. 2, 1933; in office: Oct. 27, 1972. **Local divisions:** 6 provinces, 84 districts. **Defense:** 2.6% of GNP (1983).

Economy: Chief crops: Palm products, peanuts, cotton, coffee, tobacco. **Minerals:** Oil. **Arable land:** 16%. **Fish catch** (1983): 21 000 metric tons. **Electricity prod.** (1986): 124 mln. kwh. **Labor force:** 60% agric; 30% serv. & comm.

Finance: Currency: CFA franc (Mar. 1988: 281 = $1 US). **Gross national product** (1984): $1.1 bln. **Per capita income** (1983): $290. **Imports** (1984): $225 mln.; partners: Fr. 27%, UK 13%, W. Ger. 6%, Neth. 6%. **Exports** (1984): $172 mln.; partners: Neth. 28%, Jap. 27%, Fr. 24%. **International reserves less gold** (Feb. 1988): $4.7 mln.

Transport: Railway traffic (1985): 137 mln. passenger-km; 176 mln. net ton-km. **Chief ports:** Cotonou.

Communications: Television sets: 17 000 (1984). **Radios:** 290 000 in use (1984). **Daily newspaper circ.** (1985): 3 per 1 000 pop.

Health: Life expectancy at birth (1984): 47.0 male; 51.0 female. **Births** (per 1 000 pop. 1985): 47. **Deaths** (per 1 000 pop. 1985): 16. **Natural increase** (1985): 3.1%. **Hospital beds** (1982): 4 902. **Physicians** (1982): 204. **Infant mortality** (per 1 000 live births 1985): 143.

Education (1987): **Literacy:** 28%. Years compulsory 6; attendance 43%.

Major International Organizations: UN (GATT, IMF, WHO), OAU.

Canadian Embassy: c/o The Canadian High Commission, P.O. Box 1639, Accra, Ghana.

The Kingdom of Abomey, rising to power in wars with neighboring kingdoms in the 17th century, came under French domination in the late 19th century, and was incorporated into French West Africa by 1904.

Under the name Dahomey, the country became independent Aug. 1, 1960. The name was changed to Benin in 1975. In the fifth coup since independence Col. Ahmed Kerekou took power in 1972; two years later he declared a socialist state with a "Marxist-Leninist" philosophy. The economy relies on the development of agriculturally-based industries.

Bhutan

Kingdom of Bhutan

Druk-Yul

People: Population (1986 est.): 1 538 000. **Age distrib. (%):** 0–14: 40.0; 15–59: 54.5; over 60: 5.5 **Pop. density:** 32.6 per sq. km. **Ethnic groups:** Ngalops and Sharchops 75%. Nepalese 25%, Lepcha (indigenous), Indians. **Languages:** Dzong-

kha (official), Nepali, English. **Religions:** Buddhist state religion 75%, Hindu 25%.

Geography: Area: 47 182 sq. km. **Location:** In eastern Himalayan Mts. **Neighbors:** India on W (Sikkim) and S, China on N. **Topography:** Bhutan is comprised of very high mountains in the N, fertile valleys in the center, and thick forests in the Duar Plain in the S. **Capital:** Thimphu. **City** (1987 est.): Thimphu 20 000.

Government: Type: Monarchy. **Head of state:** King Jigme Singye Wangchuk; b. Nov. 11, 1955; in office: July 21, 1972. **Local divisions:** 18 districts.

Economy: Industries: Handicrafts. **Chief crops:** Rice, corn, wheat. **Other resources:** Timber. **Arable land:** 2%. **Labor force:** 95% agric.

Finance: Currency: Ngultrum (Nov. 1987: 12 = 1 US) (Indian Rupee also used). **Gross national product** (1984): $135 mln. **Per capita income** (1985): $120. **Tourism** (1986): 2.2 mln. **Imports** (1986): $72.6 mln.; partners India 99%. **Exports** (1986): $22.2 mln.; partners India 99%.

Communications: Radios: 12 500 licensed (1986). **Telephones in use** (1982): 14 000.

Health: Life expectancy at birth (1986): 47.7 male; 46.3 female. **Births** (per 1 000 pop. 1986): 37.8. **Deaths** (per 1 000 pop. 1986): 17.3. **Natural increase** (1986) 0%. **Hospital beds** (1983): 831. **Physicians** (1983): 65. **Infant Mortality** (per 1 000 live births 1985): 122.

Education (1987): **Literacy:** 12%. School attendance: 21%.

Major International Organizations: UN (IMF, World Bank).

The region came under Tibetan rule in the 16th century. British influence grew in the 19th century. A monarchy, set up in 1907, became a British protectorate by a 1910 treaty. The country became independent in 1949, with India guiding foreign relations and supplying aid.

Links to India have been strengthened by airline service and a road network. Most of the population engages in subsistence agriculture.

Bolivia

Republic of Bolivia

República de Bolivia

People: Population (1989 est.): 6 876 000. **Age distrib. (%):** 0–14: 43; 15–59: 51.8; 60+: 5.2. **Pop. density:** 6.2 per sq. km. **Urban** (1987): 49%. **Ethnic groups:** Quechua 30%, Aymara 25%, mixed 30%, European 14%. **Languages:** Spanish, Quechua, Aymara (All official). **Religion:** Roman Catholic 95%.

Geography: Area: 1 102 829 sq. km. **Location:** In central Andes Mtns. **Neighbors:** Peru, Chile on W, Argentina, Paraguay on S, Brazil on E and N. **Topography:** The great central plateau, at an altitude of 360 m, over 800 km long, lies between two great cordilleras having 3 of the highest peaks in S. America. Lake Titicaca, on Peruvian border, is highest lake in world on which steamboats ply (3 752 m). The E central region has semitropical forests; the llanos, or Amazon-Chaco lowlands are in E. **Capitals:** Sucre, (legal), La Paz (de facto). **Cities** (1986 est.): La Paz 955 000; Santa Cruz 419 000; Cochabamba 304 000.

Government: Type: Republic. **Head of state:** Pres. Victor Paz Estenssoro, b. Oct. 2, 1907; in office: Aug. 6, 1985. **Local divisions:** 9 departments, 94 provinces.

Economy: Industry: Textiles, food processing, mining, clothing. **Chief crops:** Potatoes, sugar, coffee, barley, cocoa, rice, corn, bananas, citrus. **Minerals:** Antimony, tin, tungsten, silver, zinc, oil, gas, iron. **Crude oil reserves** (1985): 157 mln. bbls. **Other resources:** rubber, cinchona bark. **Arable land:** 3%. **Electricity prod.** (1986): 2.0 bln. kwh. **Labor force:** 47% agric., 19% ind. & comm, 34% serv. & govt.

Finance: Currency: Peso (Mar. 1988: 2 230 = $1 US). **Gross national product** (1986): $3.7 bln. **Per capita income** (1985): $536. **Imports** (1985): $552 mln.; partners: U.S. 16%, Jap. 13%, Arg. 14%, Braz. 22%. **Exports** (1985): $663 mln.; partners: Arg. 44%, U.S. 24%. **National budget** (1986): $669 mln. revenues; $4.7 bln. expenditures. **International reserves less gold** (Mar. 1987): $234 mln. **Gold:** 894 000 oz t. **Consumer prices** (change in 1987): +15%.

Transport: Railway traffic (1986): 736 mln. passenger-km; 590 mln. net ton-miles. **Motor vehicles:** in use (1983): 40 000 passenger cars, 36 000 comm. vehicles. **Civil aviation** (1986): 884 mln. passenger-km.; 27.7 mln. freight ton-km.

Communications: Television sets: 386 000 (1984). **Radios:** 480 000 in use (1984). **Telephones in use** (1983): 204 000. **Daily newspaper circ.** (1984): 40 per 1 000 pop.

Health: Life expectancy at birth (1985): 48.6 male; 53.0 female. **Births** (per 1 000 pop. 1985): 42.0. **Deaths** (per 1 000 pop. 1985): 15.0. **Natural increase** (1985): 2.9%. **Hospital beds** (per 100 000 pop. 1977): 228. **Physicians** (per 100 000 pop. 1977): 38. **Infant mortality** (per 1 000 live births 1986): 123.

Education (1986): **Literacy:** 75%. **Years compulsory:** ages 7-14; attendance 82%.

Major International Organizations: UN (IMF, FAO, WHO), OAS.

Canadian Embassy: c/o Casilla 1212, Lima, Peru; La Paz: Consulado del Canada, 2342 Avenida Arce, La Paz; Tel: 37-5224.

The Incas conquered the region from earlier Indian inhabitants in the 13th century. Spanish rule began in the 1530s, and lasted until Aug. 6, 1825. The country is named after Simon Bolivar, independence fighter.

In a series of wars, Bolivia lost its Pacific coast to Chile, the oilbearing Chaco to Paraguay, and rubber-growing areas to Brazil, 1879-1935.

Economic unrest, especially among the militant mine workers, has contributed to continuing political instability. A reformist government under Victor Paz Estenssoro, 1951-64, nationalized tin mines and attempted to improve conditions for the Indian majority, but was overthrown by a military junta. A series of coups and countercoups continued through 1981, until the military junta elected Gen. Villa as president.

In July 1982, the military junta assumed power amid a growing economic crisis and foreign debt difficulties. The junta resigned in October and allowed the Congress, elected democratically in 1980, to take power.

Botswana
Republic of Botswana

People: Population (1989 est.): 1 220 000. **Age distrib.** (%): 0–14: 48.1; 15–59: 46.1; 60+: 7.4. **Pop. density:** 2.0 per sq. km. **Urban** (1986): 21%. **Ethnic groups:** Batswana, 95%. **Languages:** English (official), Setswana (national). **Religions:** indigenous beliefs (majority), Christian 15%.

Geography: Area: 602 690 sq. km. **Location:** In southern Africa. **Neighbors:** Namibia (S.W. Africa) on N and W, S. Africa on S, Zimbabwe on NE; Botswana claims border with Zambia on N. **Topography:** The Kalahari Desert, supporting nomadic Bushmen and wildlife, spreads over SW; there are swamplands and farming areas in E, and rolling plains in E where livestock are grazed. **Capital:** Gaborone. **Cities** (1986): Gaborone 96 000.

Government: Type: Republic, parliamentary democracy. **Head of state:** Pres. Quett Masire; b. 1925; in office: July 13, 1980. **Local divisions:** 10 district councils and 4 town councils. **Defence:** 1.8% of national budget (1985).

Economy: Industries: Livestock, processing, mining. **Chief crops:** Corn, sorghum, peanuts. **Minerals:** Copper, coal, nickel, diamonds. **Other resources:** Big game. **Arable land:** 2%. **Electricity prod.** (1986): 533 mln. kwh. **Labor force:** 70% agric.

Finance: Currency: Pula (Mar. 1988: 0.40 = $1 US). **Gross national product** (1985): $900 mln. **Imports** (1985): $535 mln.; partners: S. Africa 88%. **Exports** (1984): $469 mln.; partners: Europe 67%, U.S. 17%, S. Africa 7%. **National budget** (1985): $241 mln. **International reserves less gold** (Mar. 1988): $2.0 bln. **Consumer prices** (change in 1987): 9.8%

Transport: Railway traffic (1984): 1.0 bln. net ton km. **Motor vehicles:** in use (1985): 14 000 passenger cars, 23 000 comm. vehicles.

Communications: Radios: 77 000 in use (1985). **Daily newspaper circ.** (1985): 22 per 1 000 pop.

Health: Life expectancy at birth (1985): 63.5. **Births** (annual per 1 000 pop. 1986): 45.6. **Deaths** (per 1 000 pop. 1986): 11. **Natural increase** (1986): 3.4%. **Hospital beds** (1985): 2 367. **Physicians** (1985): 155. **Infant mortality** (per 1 000 live births 1985): 63.

Education (1987): **Literacy:** 35% (in English).

Major International Organizations: UN (GATT, IMF, WHO), OAU, Commonwealth of Nations.

Canadian High Commission: c/o The Canadian High Commission, P.O. Box 1430, Harare, Zimbabwe.

First inhabited by bushmen, then by Bantus, the region became the British protectorate of Bechuanaland in 1886, halting encroachment by Boers and Germans from the south and southwest. The country became fully independent Sept. 30, 1966, changing its name to Botswana.

Cattle-raising and mining (diamonds, copper, nickel) have contributed to the country's economic growth. The economy is closely tied to S. Africa.

Brazil
Federative Republic of Brazil
República Federativa do Brasil

People: Population (1989 est.): 153 992 000. **Age distrib.** (%): 0–14: 36.4; 15–59: 57.0; 60+: 6.6. **Pop. density:** 18.0 per sq. km. **Urban** (1987): 74%. **Ethnic groups:** Portuguese, Africans, and mulattoes make up the vast majority; Italians, Germans, Japanese, Indians, Jews, Arabs. **Languages:** Portuguese (official), English. **Religion:** Roman Catholic 89%.

Geography: Area: 8 544 822 sq. km. **Location:** Occupies eastern half of S. America. **Neighbors:** French Guiana, Suriname, Guyana, Venezuela on N, Colombia, Peru, Bolivia, Paraguay, Argentina on W, Uruguay on S. **Topography:** Brazil's Atlantic coastline stretches 7 365 km. In N is the heavily-wooded Amazon basin covering half the country, its network of rivers navigable for 25 302 km. The Amazon itself flows 3 349 km in Brazil, all navigable. The NE region is semiarid scrubland, heavily settled and poor. The S central region, favored by climate and resources, has almost half of the population, produces 75% of farm goods and 80% of industrial output. The narrow coastal belt includes most of the major cities. Almost the entire country has a tropical or semitropical climate. **Capital:** Brasilia. **Cities** (1985 est.): Sao Paulo 10.1 mln.; Rio de Janeiro 5.6 mln.; Belo Horizonte 2.1 mln.; Fortaleza 1.9 mln.; Salvador 1.8 mln.; Porto Alegre 2.6 mln.

Government: Type: Federative republic. **Head of state:** Pres. Jose Sarney; b. Apr. 30, 1930; in office: Apr. 22, 1985. **Local divisions:** 23 states, with individual constitutions and elected governments; 3 territories, federal district. **Defence:** 0.8% of GNP (1985).

Economy: Industries: Steel, autos, textiles, ships, appliances, petrochemicals, machinery. **Chief crops:** Coffee (largest grower), cotton, soybeans, sugar, cocoa, rice, corn, fruits. **Minerals:** Chromium, iron, manganese, columbium, titanium, diamonds, gold, nickel, gem stones, coal, tin, tungsten, bauxite, oil. **Crude oil reserves** (1988): 2.3 bln. bbls. **Arable land:** 7%. **Meat prod.** (1985): cattle: 133 mln.; pigs: 30.5 mln.; heep: 19 mln. **Fish catch** (1984): 946 000 metric tons. **Electricity prod.** (1986): 175.7 bln. kwh. **Crude steel prod.** (1986): 21.2 mln. metric tons. **Labor force:** 40% services, 35% agric.; 25% ind.

Finance: Currency: Cruzeiro (June 1988: 163 = $1 US). **Gross national product** (1986): $250 bln. **Per capita income** (1978): $1,523. **Imports** (1986): $14.0 bln.; partners: U.S. 12%, Jap. 6%. **Exports** (1986): $22.4 bln.; partners: U.S. 25%, EC 27%. **Tourists** (1985): receipts: $1.7 bln. **National budget** (1979): $18.91 bln. revenues; $18.83 bln. expenditures. **International reserves less gold** (Jan. 1988): $6.2 bln. **Gold:** 2.4 mln. oz t. **Consumer prices** (change in 1987): 229%.

Transport: Railway traffic (1984): 15.4 bln. passenger-km; 92 bln. net ton-km. **Motor vehicles:** in use (1984): 10 mln. passenger cars, 1.1 mln. **Civil aviation** (1985): 18.2 bln. passenger-km: 907 mln. freight ton-km: **Chief ports:** Santos, Rio de Janeiro, Vitoria, Salvador, Rio Grande, Recife.

Communications: Television sets: 36 mln. in use (1986). **Radios:** 50 mln. in use (1986). **Telephones in use** (1985): 11 mln. **Daily newspaper circ.** (1986): 62 per 1 000 pop.

Health: Life expectancy at birth (1985): 60.9 male; 66.0 female. **Births** (per 1 000 pop. 1985): 30.6. **Deaths** (per 1 000 pop. 1985): 8.4. **Natural increase** (1985): 2.2%. **Hospital beds** (1982): 530 000. **Physicians** (per 100 000 pop. 1980): 68.1. **Infant mortality** (per 1 000 live births 1986): 70.

Education (1987): **Literacy:** 76%.

Major International Organizations: UN and most of its specialized agencies, OAS.

Canadian Embassy: Ave. des Nacoes, Number 16, Setor das Embaixadus Sul.; postal: Caixa Postal 07-0961, 70.410 Brasilia D.F.; Tel: (61) 223-7515.

Pedro Alvares Cabral, a Portuguese navigator, is generally credited as the first European to reach Brazil, in 1500. The country was thinly settled by various Indian tribes. Only a few have survived to the present, mostly in the Amazon basin.

In the next centuries, Portuguese colonists gradually pushed inland, bringing along large numbers of African slaves. Slavery was not abolished until 1888.

The King of Portugal, fleeing before Napoleon's army, moved the seat of government to Brazil in 1808. Brazil thereupon became a kingdom under Dom Joao VI. After his return to Portugal, his son Pedro proclaimed the independence of Brazil, Sept. 7, 1822, and was acclaimed emperor. The second emperor, Dom Pedro II, was deposed in 1889, and a republic proclaimed, called the United States of Brazil. In 1967 the country was renamed the Federative Republic of Brazil.

A military junta took control in 1930; dictatorial power was assumed by Getulio Vargas, who alternated with military coups until finally forced out by the military in 1954. A democratic regime prevailed 1956-64, during which time the capital was moved from Rio de Janeiro to Brasilia in the interior.

The next 5 presidents were all military leaders. Censorship was imposed, and much of the opposition was suppressed amid charges of torture. In 1974 elections, the official opposition party made gains in the chamber of deputies; some relaxation of censorship occurred.

Since 1930, successive governments have pursued industrial and agricultural growth and the development of interior areas. Exploiting vast mineral resources, fertile soil in several regions, and a huge labor force, Brazil became the leading industrial power of Latin America by the 1970s, while agricultural output soared. Democratic elections were held in 1985 as the nation returned to civilian rule.

However, income maldistribution, inflation and government land policies have all led to severe economic recession. Foreign debt is among the largest in the world. Brazil announced, Feb. 1987, that it was unilaterally suspending payment of interest on $68 billion of debt to foreign commercial banks.

Brunei Darussalam
State of Brunei Darussalam
Negara Brunei Darussalam

People: Population (1989 est.): 267 000. **Pop. density:** 46.1 per sq. km. **Ethnic groups:** Malay 65%, Chinese 20%. **Languages:** Malay (official), English, Chinese. **Religions:** Moslem 64%, Buddhist 14%, Christian 10%.

Geography: Area: 5 788 sq. km. **Location:** on the north coast of the island of Borneo; it is surrounded on its landward side by the Malaysian state of Sarawak. **Capital:** Bandar Seri Begawan. **Cities** (1982 est.): Bandar Seri Begawan 51 000.

Government: Type: Independent sultanate. **Head of Government:** Sultan Sir Muda Hassanal Bolkiah Mu'izzadin Waddaulah; in office: Jan. 1, 1984.

Economy: Industries: petroleum (about 90% of revenue is derived from oil exports). **Chief crops:** rice, bananas, cassava.

Finance: Currency: Brunei dollar (Dec. 1987: 2.10 = $1). **Gross domestic product** (1985): $3.4 bln. **Per capita income** (1987): $20 000.

Communications: Television sets: 48 000 (1986). **Radios:** 74 000 (1986). **Telephones:** 32 000 (1985).

Health: Infant Mortality (per 1 000 live births 1985): 12.1

Education (1987): **Literacy:** 95% among young.

Major international organizations: UN and some of its specialized agencies.

Health: Life expectancy at birth: (1987): 74 yrs. **Infant mortality:** (per 1000 live births 1985): 12.1.

Canadian Embassy: c/o The Canadian Embassy, P.O. Box 10990, 50732 Kuala Lampur, Malaysia.

The Sultanate of Brunei was a powerful state in the early 16th century with authority over all of the island of Borneo as well as parts of the Sulu Islands and the Philippines. In 1888, a treaty

was signed which placed the state under the protection of Great Britain.

Brunei became a fully sovereign and independent state on Jan. 1, 1984.

Bulgaria
People's Republic of Bulgaria
Narodna Republika Bulgaria

People: Population (1989 est.): 9 037 000. **Age distrib. (%):** 0–14: 22.2; 15–59: 60.2; 60+: 17.6. **Pop. density:** 78.7 per sq. km. **Urban** (1986): 65%. **Ethnic groups:** Bulgarian 85%, Turk 8.5%. **Languages:** Bulgarian, Turkish, Greek. **Religions:** Government promotes atheism; background of people is 85% Orthodox.

Geography: Area: 114 896 sq. km. **Location:** In eastern Balkan Peninsula on Black Sea. **Neighbors:** Romania on N, Yugoslavia on W, Greece, Turkey on S. **Topography:** The Stara Planina (Balkan) Mts. stretch E-W across the center of the country, with the Danubian plain on N, the Rhodope Mts. on SW, and Thracian Plain on SE. **Capital:** Sofia. **Cities** (1986 est.): Sofia 1 114 759; Plovdiv 377 637; Varna 297 090.

Government: Type: Communist. **Head of state:** Pres. Todor Zhivkov; b. Sept. 7, 1911; in office: July 7, 1971. **Head of government:** Premier Georgy Atanasov; in office: Mar 21, 1986. **Head of Communist Party:** First Sec. Todor Zhivkov; b. 1911; in office: Jan. 1954. **Local divisions:** 9 administrative counties. **Defence:** 3.9% of GNP (1984).

Economy: Industries: Chemicals, machinery, metals, textiles, fur, leather goods, vehicles, wine, processed food. **Chief crops:** Grains, fruit, corn, potatoes, tobacco. **Minerals:** Lead, bauxite, coal, oil, zinc. **Arable land:** 38%. **Meat prod.** (1985): cattle: 1.7 mln.; pigs: 3.9 mln.; sheep: 9.7 mln. **Fish catch** (1982): 121 000 metric tons. **Electricity prod.** (1986): 45 bln. kwh. **Crude steel prod.** (1986): 2.9 mln. metric tons. **Labor force:** 22% agric.; 43% ind. & comm.

Finance: Currency: Lev (Dec. 1987: 1.00 = $.85 US). **Gross National Product** (1985): $25 bln. **Per capita income** (1985): $2 806. **Imports** (1985): $14.0 bln.; partners: USSR 54%, E. Ger. 6%, W. Ger. 5%. **Exports** (1985): $13.7 bln.; partners: USSR 48%, E. Ger. 6%. **Tourists** (1984): revenues $288 mln. **National budget** (1983): $16.7 bln. expenditures.

Transport: Railway traffic (1986): 8.9 bln. passenger-km; 18 bln. net ton-km. **Motor vehicles:** in use (1985) 1 mln. passenger cars, 587 000 commercial. **Chief ports:** Burgas, Varna.

Communications: Television sets: 1.6 mln. licensed (1986). **Radios:** 2.1 mln. licensed (1986). **Telephones in use** (1986): 1.9 mln. **Daily newspaper circ.** (1985): 254 per 1 000 pop.

Health: Life expectancy at birth (1984): 68 male; 74 female. **Births** (per 1 000 pop. 1985): 13.0. **Deaths** (per 1 000 pop. 1985): 12.0. **Hospital beds** (1986): 84 300. **Physicians:** 25 000. **Infant mortality** (per 1 000 live births 1986): 16.1

Education (1987): **Literacy:** 95%. **Years compulsory:** Ages 7-16.

Major International Organizations: UN, Warsaw Pact.

Canadian Embassy: c/o Kneza Milosa 75, 11000 Belgrade, Yugoslavia.

Bulgaria was settled by Slavs in the 6th century. Turkic Bulgars arrived in the 7th century, merged with the Slavs, became Christians by the 9th century, and set up powerful empires in the 10th and 12th centuries. The Ottomans prevailed in 1396 and remained for 500 years.

A revolt in 1876 led to an independent kingdom in 1908. Bulgaria expanded after the first Balkan War but lost its Aegean coastline in World War I, when it sided with Germany. Bulgaria joined the Axis in World War II, but withdrew in 1944. Communists took power with Soviet aid; the monarchy was abolished Sept. 8, 1946.

Burkina Faso

People: Population (1989 est.): 7 704 000. **Pop. density:** 28.0 per sq. km. **Ethnic groups:** Voltaic groups (Mossi, Bobo), Mande. **Languages:** French (official), Sudanic tribal languages. **Religions:** animist 65%, Moslem 25%, Christian 10%.

Geography: Area: 275 259 sq. km. **Location:** In W. Africa, S of the Sahara. **Neighbors:** Mali on NW, Niger on NE, Benin, Togo, Ghana, Côte d'Ivoire on S. **Topography:** Landlocked Burkina Faso is in the savannah region of W. Africa. The N is arid, hot, and thinly populated. **Capital:** Ouagadougou. **Cities** (1986): Ouagadougou 366 000; Bobo-Dioulasso 202 000.

Government: Type: military. **Head of state:** Pres. Blaise Compaore; in office: Oct. 15, 1987. **Local divisions:** 30 provinces. **Defence:** 2.7% of GNP (1984).

Economy: Chief crops: Millet, sorghum, rice, peanuts, grain. **Minerals:** Manganese, gold, limestone. **Arable land:** 10%. **Electricity prod.** (1986): 159 mln. kwh. **Labor force:** 83% agric.; 12% industry.

Finance: Currency: CFA franc (Mar. 1988: 281 = $1 US). **Gross national product** (1985): $1.0 bln. **Per capita income** (1983): $150. **Imports** (1983): $279 mln.; partners: EC, Côte d'Ivoire. **Exports** (1983): $55 mln.; partners: Ivory Coast, EC, China. **International reserves less gold** (Jan. 1988): $324 mln. **Gold:** 11 000 oz t. **Consumer prices** (change in 1987): −2.7%

Transport: Motor vehicles: in use (1983): 21 000 passenger cars, 6 600 comm. vehicles.

Communications: Television sets: 41 000 in use (1986). **Radios:** 311 000 in use (1986). **Telephones in use** (1984): 14 000. **Daily newspaper circ.** (1984): 2 per 1 000 pop.

Health: Life expectancy at birth (1984): 42 yrs. **Births** (per 1 000 pop. 1985): 48. **Deaths** (per 1 000 pop. 1985): 22. **Natural increase** (1985): 2.6%. **Hospital beds** (1980): 4 587. **Physicians** (1984): 118. **Infant mortality** (per 1 000 live births 1985): 176.

Education (1984): **Literacy:** 8%. Only 8% attend school.

Major International Organizations: UN and many of its specialized agencies, OAU.

Canadian Embassy: c/o 01 P.O. Box 4101, Abidjan 01, Côte d'Ivoire.

The Mossi tribe entered the area in the 11th to 13th centuries. Their kingdoms ruled until defeated by the Mali and Songhai empires.

French control came by 1896, but Upper Volta (name changed to Burkina Faso on Aug. 4, 1984), was not finally established as a separate territory until 1947. Full independence came Aug. 5, 1960, and a pro-French government was elected. A 1982 coup established the current regime.

Several hundred thousand farm workers migrate each year to Côte d'Ivoire and Ghana. Burkina Faso is heavily dependent on foreign aid.

Burma

Socialist Republic of the Union of Burma

Pyidaungsu Socialist Thammada Myanma Naingngandaw

People: Population (1989 est.): 39 893 000. **Age distrib.** (%): 0–14: 41.2; 15–59: 52.8; 60+: 6.0. **Pop. density:** 58.6 per sq. km. **Ethnic groups:** Burmans (related to Tibetans) 68%; Karen 4%, Shan 7%, Rakhine 3%. **Language:** Burmese (official). **Religions:** Buddhist 85%; animist, Christian.

Geography: Area: 680 651 sq. km. **Location:** Between S. and S.E. Asia, on Bay of Bengal. **Neighbors:** Bangladesh, India on W, China, Laos, Thailand on E. **Topography:** Mountains surround Burma on W, N, and E, and dense forests cover much of the nation. N-S rivers provide habitable valleys and communications, especially the Irrawaddy, navigable for 1 440 km. The country has a tropical monsoon climate. **Capital:** Rangoon. **Cities** (1983 est.): Rangoon 2 458 712; Mandalay 458 000; Karbe (1973 cen.): 253 600; Moulmein 188 000.

Government: Type: Socialist republic. **Head of state:** Pres. U San Yu in office: Nov. 9, 1981. **Head of government:** Prime Min. U. Maung Maung Kha; b. Nov. 2, 1917; in office: Mar. 29, 1977. **Local divisions:** 7 states and 7 divisions. **Defence:** 4.2% of GNP (1985).

Economy: Chief crops: Rice, sugarcane, peanuts, beans. **Minerals:** Oil, lead, silver, tin, tungsten, precious stones. **Crude oil reserves** (1985): 733 mln. bbls. **Other resources:** Rubber, teakwood. **Arable land:** 15%. **Meat prod.** (1985): cattle: 9.9 mln.; pigs: 3.1 mln. **Fish catch** (1985): 643 000 metric tons.

Electricity prod. (1986): 1.7 bln. kwh. **Labor force:** 66% agric; 12% ind.

Finance: Currency: Kyat (Mar. 1988: 6.22 = $1 US). **Gross national product** (1985): $6.5 bln. **Per capita income** (1985): $179. **Imports** (1985): $648 mln.; partners: Jap. 34%, U.S. 12%, UK 9%, W. Ger. 9%. **Exports** (1985): $399 mln.; partners: Switz. 12%, Sing. 10%. **National budget** (1986): $4.3 bln. **International reserves less gold** (Mar. 1988): $29.9 mln. **Gold:** 251 000 oz t. **Consumer prices** (change in 1987): 23%.

Transport: Railway traffic (1986): 3.7 bln. passenger-km; 576 mln. net ton-km. **Motor vehicles:** in use (1980): 43 000 passenger cars, 44 000 comm. vehicles. **Civil aviation** (1985): 229 mln. passenger-km.; 23 mln. net ton-km. **Chief ports:** Rangoon, Sittwe, Bassein, Moulmein, Tavoy.

Communications: Television sets: 64 000 (1986). **Radios:** 800 000 in use (1986). **Telephones in use** (1986): 53 000. **Daily newspaper circ.** (1986): 14 per 1 000 pop.

Health: Life expectancy at birth (1986): 51.6 male; 54.6 female. **Births** (per 1 000 pop. 1985): 37.9. **Deaths** (per 1 000 pop. 1985): 12.7. **Natural increase** (1985): 2.5%. **Hospital beds** (1984): 25 919. **Physicians** (1984): 8 931. **Infant mortality** (per 1 000 live births 1986): 96.

Education (1986): **Literacy:** 66%. **Years compulsory:** 4; **Attendance:** 84%.

Major International Organizations: UN (World Bank, IMF, GATT).

Canadian Embassy: c/o The Canadian High Commission, G.P.O. Box 569, Dhaka, Bangladesh.

The Burmese arrived from Tibet before the 9th century, displacing earlier cultures, and a Buddhist monarchy was established by the 11th. Burma was conquered by the Mongol dynasty of China in 1272, then ruled by Shans as a Chinese tributary, until the 16th century.

Britain subjugated Burma in 3 wars, 1824-84, and ruled the country as part of India until 1937, when it became self-governing. Independence outside the Commonwealth was achieved Jan. 4, 1948.

Gen. Ne Win dominated politics from the 1960s to 1986 when he abdicated power. He led a Revolutionary Council set up in 1962, which drove Indians from the civil service and Chinese from commerce. Socialization of the economy was advanced, isolation from foreign countries enforced.

In 1987 Burma, once the richest nation in SE Asia, was granted least developed status by the UN. There were serious student riots in Sept.

Burundi

Republic of Burundi

Republika y'Uburundi

People: Population (1989 est.): 5 233 000. **Age distrib.** (%): 0–14: 44.3; 15–59: 49.6; 60+: 6.1. **Pop. density:** 187 per sq. km. **Urban** (1985): 8%. **Ethnic groups:** Hutu 85%, Tutsi 14%, Twa (pygmy) 1%. **Languages:** French, Rundi (both official). **Religions:** Christian 67%, traditional African 32%.

Geography: Area: 27 973 sq. km. **Location:** In central Africa. **Neighbors:** Rwanda on N, Zaire on W, Tanzania on E. **Topography:** Much of the country is grassy highland, with mountains reaching 2 713 m. The southernmost source of the White Nile is located in Burundi. Lake Tanganyika is the second deepest lake in the world. **Capital:** Bujumbura. **Cities** (1986 est.): Bujumbura 272 000.

Government: Type: Republic. **Head of state and head of government:** Major Pierre Buyoya; in office: Sept. 9, 1987. **Local divisions:** 15 provinces. **Defence** (1984): 3.5% of GNP.

Economy: Chief crops: Coffee (90% of exports), cotton, tea. **Minerals:** Nickel. **Arable land:** 50%. **Fish catch** (1985): 14 000 metric tons. **Electricity prod.** (1986): 44 mln. kwh. **Labor force:** 93% agric.

Finance: Currency: Franc (Apr. 1988: 131 = $1 US). **Gross national product** (1985): $1.1 bln. **Per capita income** (1984): $273. **Imports** (1984): $183 mln.; partners: Iran 14%, Belg.-Lux. 16%, Jap. 8%. **Exports** (1984): $99 mln; partners: U.S. 32%, Belg. 10%. **National budget** (1984): $160 mln. expenditures. **International reserves less gold** (Mar. 1988): $50.3 mln. **Gold:** 17 000 oz t. **Consumer prices** (change in 1987): 7.3%.

Transport: Motor vehicles: in use (1984): 7 500 passenger cars, 6 000 comm. vehicles.

Communications: Radios: 230 000 in use (1986). **Telephones in use** (1984): 6 000.

Health: Life expectancy at birth (1985): 42.4 male; 45.6 female. **Births** (per 1 000 pop. 1985): 47.6. **Deaths** (per 1 000 pop. 1985): 20.9. **Natural increase** (1985): 2.6%. **Hospital beds** (1983): 2 893. **Physicians** (1983): 216. **Infant mortality** (per 1 000 live births 1985): 137.

Education (1985): **Literacy:** 30%.

Major International Organizations: UN (GATT, IMF, WHO), OAU.

Canadian Embassy: c/o P.O. Box 8341, Kinshasa, Zaire.

The pygmy Twa were the first inhabitants, followed by Bantu Hutus, who were conquered in the 16th century by the tall Tutsi (Watusi), probably from Ethiopia. Under German control in 1899, the area fell to Belgium in 1916, which exercised successively a League of Nations mandate and UN trusteeship over Ruanda-Urundi (now 2 countries).

Independence came in 1962, and the monarchy was overthrown in 1966. An unsuccessful Hutu rebellion in 1972-73 left 10 000 Tutsi and 150 000 Hutu dead. Over 100 000 Hutu fled to Tanzania and Zaire. A bloodless coup on Sept. 4, 1987 ousted the 11-year old government of Col. Bagaza. The new leader, Major Buyoya, was given full support by the armed forces and promised fewer restraints on society, but Burundi remains one of the poorest and most densely populated countries in Africa.

Cambodia (Kampuchea)
Cambodian People's Republic

People: Population (1989 est.): 6 895 000. **Pop. density:** 40.0 per sq. km. **Ethnic groups:** Khmers 90%, Vietnamese 4%, Chinese 5%. **Languages:** Khmer (official), French. **Religions:** Theravada Buddhism 95%.

Geography: Area: 181 735 sq. km. **Location:** In Indochina Peninsula. **Neighbors:** Thailand on W, N, Laos on NE, Vietnam on E. **Topography:** The central area, formed by the Mekong R. basin and Tonle Sap lake, is level. Hills and mountains are in SE, a long escarpment separates the country from Thailand on NW. 75% of the area is forested. **Capital:** Phnom Penh. **Cities** (1987 est.): Phnom Penh 300 000.

Government: Type: No single authority controls the whole country. Vietnamese-installed government controls Phnom Penh. **Head of State:** Pres., People's Revolutionary Party Heng Samrin; in office: Jan. 7, 1979. **Head of government:** Premier Hun Sen; in office: Jan. 14, 1985. **Local divisions:** 20 provinces.

Economy: Industries: Rice milling, wood, rubber. **Chief crops:** Rice, sugar. **Minerals:** Iron, copper, manganese. **Other resources:** Forests, rubber, kapok. **Arable land:** 16%. **Meat prod.** (1980): beef: 17 000 metric tons; pork: 26 000 metric tons. **Fish catch** (1985): 68 000 metric tons. **Electricity prod.** (1986): 142.00 mln. kwh.

Finance: Currency: Riel (Jan. 1987: 4 = $1 US). **Per capita income** (1984): $100. **Imports** (1981): $103 mln. **Exports** (1981): $43 mln.

Transport: Railway traffic (1981): 54 mln. passenger-miles; 6.8 mln. net ton-miles. **Motor vehicles:** in use (1981): 700 passenger cars, (1981) 700 trucks. **Chief ports:** Kompong Som.

Communications: Television sets: 52 000 in use (1985). **Radios:** 200 000 in use (1985). **Telephones in use** (1981): 7 000.

Health: Life expectancy at birth (1986): 45.3 male; 48.2 female. **Births** (per 1 000 pop. 1985): 39. **Deaths** (per 1 000 pop. 1985): 18. **Natural increase:** (1985): 2.1%. **Infant mortality** (per 1 000 births 1985): 145.

Education (1987): **Literacy:** 48%.

Major International Organizations: UN.

Early kingdoms dating from that of Funan in the 1st century AD culminated in the great Khmer empire which flourished from the 9th century to the 13th, encompassing present-day Thailand, Cambodia, Laos, and southern Vietnam. The peripheral areas were lost to invading Siamese and Vietnamese, and France established a protectorate in 1863. Independence came in 1953.

Prince Norodom Sihanouk, king 1941-1955 and head of state from 1960, tried to maintain neutrality. Relations with the U.S.

were broken in 1965, after South Vietnam planes attacked Vietcong forces within Cambodia. Relations were restored in 1969, after Sihanouk charged Viet communists with arming Cambodian insurgents.

In 1970, pro-U.S. premier Lon Nol seized power, demanding removal of 40 000 North Viet troops; the monarchy was abolished. Sihanouk formed a government-in-exile in Beijing, and open war began between the government and Khmer Rouge. The U.S. provided heavy military and economic aid.

Khmer Rouge forces captured Phnom Penh April 17, 1975. Over 100 000 people had died in 5 years of fighting. The new government evacuated all cities and towns, and shuffled the rural population, sending virtually the entire population to clear jungle, forest, and scrub, which covered half the country. Over one million people were killed in executions and enforced hardships.

Severe border fighting broke out with Vietnam in 1978; developed into a full-fledged Vietnamese invasion. The Vietnamese-backed Kampuchean National United Front for National Salvation, a Cambodian rebel movement, announced, Jan. 8, 1979, the formation of a government one day after the Vietnamese capture of Phnom Pehn. Thousands of refugees flowed into Thailand. Widespread starvation was reported; by Sept., when the UN confirmed diplomatic recognition to the ousted Pol Pot government, international food assistance was allowed to aid the famine-stricken country.

On Jan. 10, 1983, Vietnam launched an offensive against rebel forces in the west. They overran a refugee camp, Jan. 31, driving 30 000 residents into Thailand. In March, Vietnam launched a major offensive against camps on the Cambodian-Thailand border, engaged Khmer Rouge guerrillas, and crossed the border instigating clashes with Thai troops. By Feb. 1985, Vietnamese forces had overrun all major Khmer Rouge bases.

Cameroon
Republic of Cameroon

People: Population (1989 est.): 10 874 000. **Age distrib. (%):** 0–14: 44.6; 15–59: 49.8; 60+: 5.6. **Pop. density:** 22.5 per sq. km. **Urban** (1985): 31%. **Ethnic groups:** Some 200 tribes; largest are Bamileke 30%, Fulani 7%. **Languages:** English, French (both official), 24 African groups. **Religions:** Animist 51%, Moslem 16%, Christian 33%.

Geography: Area: 482 477 sq. km. **Location:** Between W and central Africa. **Neighbors:** Nigeria on NW, Chad, Central African Republic on E, Congo, Gabon, Equatorial Guinea on S. **Topography:** A low coastal plain with rain forests is in S; plateaus in center lead to forested mountains in W, including Mt. Cameroon, 3 962 m; grasslands in N lead to marshes around Lake Chad. **Capital:** Yaounde. **Cities** (1985 est.): Douala 852 000; Yaounde 583 000.

Government: Type: Unitary republic. **Head of state:** Pres. Paul Biya; b. Feb. 13, 1933; in office: Nov. 6, 1982. **Local divisions:** 10 provinces. **Defence:** 6.5% of budget (1987).

Economy: Industries: Aluminum processing, oil products, palm products. **Chief crops:** Cocoa, coffee, peanuts, bananas, cotton. **Crude oil reserves** (1985): 531 mln. bbls. **Other resources:** Timber. **Arable land:** 14%. **Fish catch** (1985): 50 000 metric tons. **Electricity prod.** (1986): 4.2 bln. kwh. **Labor force:** 74% agric., 13% ind. and commerce.

Finance: Currency: CFA franc (Mar. 1988: 281 = $1 US). **Gross national product** (1985): $8.3 bln. **Per capita income** (1984): $802. **Imports** (1986): 1.7 bln.; partners: Fr. 47%, U.S. 8%. **Exports** (1986): $782 000; partners: Fr. 27%, U.S. 26%, It. 5%. **National budget** (1986): $1.6 bln. **International reserves less gold** (Jan. 1988): $62 mln. **Gold:** 30 000 oz t. **Consumer prices** (change in 1986): 3.2%.

Transport: Railway traffic (1986): 432 mln. passenger-km; 756 mln. net ton-km. **Motor vehicles:** in use (1985): 72 000 passenger cars, 41 000 comm. vehicles. **Chief ports:** Douala.

Communications: Radios: 800 000 in use (1986). **Telephones in use** (1984): 49 000. **Daily newspaper circ.** (1986): 6 per 1 000 pop.

Health: Life expectancy at birth (1983): 43.2 male; 45.6 female. **Births** (per 1 000 pop. 1985): 44. **Deaths** (per 1 000 pop. 1985): 17. **Natural increase** (1985): 2.8%. **Hospital beds** (1981): 24 541. **Physicians** (1982): 604. **Infant mortality** (per 1 000 live births 1985): 113.

Education (1987): Literacy: 65%. About 70% attend school.
Major International Organizations: UN, OAU, EC (Associate).
Canadian Embassy: Immeuble Stamatiades, Place de l'Hôtel de Ville, P.O. Box 572, Yaoundé, Cameroon; Tel: 23-02-03, 22-29-22.

Portuguese sailors were the first Europeans to reach Cameroon, in the 15th century. The European and American slave trade was very active in the area. German control lasted from 1884 to 1916, when France and Britain divided the territory, later receiving League of Nations mandates and UN trusteeships. French Cameroon became independent Jan. 1, 1960; one part of British Cameroon joined Nigeria in 1961, the other part joined Cameroon. Stability has allowed for development of roads, railways, agriculture, and petroleum production. In 1986, some 3 000 died as the result of clouds of toxic gas of volcanic origin emanating from Lake Nyos.

Cape Verde
Republic of Cape Verde
Republica de Cabo Verde

People: Population (1989 est.): 337 000. **Age distrib. (%):** 0–14: 45.6; 15–59: 47.7; 60+: 6.7. **Pop. density:** 83.6 per sq. km. **Urban** (1980): 26.2%. **Ethnic groups:** Creole 71%, African 28%, European 1%. **Languages:** Portuguese (official), Crioulo. **Religion:** Roman Catholic 80%.
Geography: Area: 4 032 sq. km. **Location:** In Atlantic O., off western tip of Africa. **Neighbors:** Nearest are Mauritania, Senegal. **Topography:** Cape Verde Islands are 15 in number, volcanic in origin (active crater on Fogo). The landscape is eroded and stark, with vegetation mostly in interior valleys. **Capital:** Praia. **Cities** (1986 est.): Mindelo 40 000; Praia 50 000.
Government: Type: Republic. **Head of state:** Pres. Aristide Pereira; b. Nov. 17, 1923; in office: July 5, 1975. **Head of government:** Prime Min. Pedro Pires, b. Apr. 29, 1934; in office: July 5, 1975. **Local divisions:** 14 administrative districts.
Economy: Chief crops: Bananas, coffee, sugarcane, corn, beans. **Minerals:** Salt. **Other resources:** Fish. **Arable land:** 10%. **Electricity prod.** (1985): 12 mln. kwh.
Finance: Currency: Escudo (Dec. 1987: 89.27 = $1 US). **Gross national product** (1985): $140 mln. **Per capita income** (1984): $350. **Imports** (1981): $104 mln.; partners: Port. 58%, Neth. 5%. **Exports** (1981): $6 mln.; partners: Port. 63%, Ang. 14%, UK 5%, Zaire 5%.
Transport: Motor vehicles: in use (1981): 4 000 passenger cars, 1 343 comm. vehicles. **Chief ports:** Mindelo, Praia.
Communications: Radios: 47 000 licensed (1985). **Telephones in use** (1984): 2 300.
Health: Life expectancy at birth (1985): 60.3 male, 64.0 female. **Births** (per 1 000 pop. 1985): 36. **Deaths** (per 1 000 pop. 1985): 10. **Natural increase** (1985): 2.5%. **Hospital beds** (1980): 632. **Physicians** (1980): 51. **Infant mortality** (per 1 000 live births 1985): 89.
Education (1986): **Literacy:** 37%.
Major International Organizations: UN (GATT, IMF, WHO), OAU.
Canadian Embassy: c/o P.O. Box 3373, Dakar, Senegal.

The uninhabited Cape Verdes were discovered by the Portuguese in 1456 or 1460. The first Portuguese colonists landed in 1462; African slaves were brought soon after, and most Cape Verdeans descend from both groups. Cape Verde independence came July 5, 1975. The islands have suffered from repeated extreme droughts and famines. Emphasis is placed on the development of agriculture and on fishing.

Central African Republic
Republique Centrafricaine

People: Population (1989 est.): 2 999 000. **Pop. density:** 4.8 per sq. km. **Ethnic groups:** Banda 27%, Baya 34%, Mandja 21%, Sara 10%. **Languages:** French (official), local dialects. **Religions:** Protestant 25%, Roman Catholic 25%, traditional 24%.

Geography: Area: 625 388 sq. km. **Location:** In central Africa. **Neighbors:** Chad on N, Cameroon on W, Congo, Zaire on S, Sudan on E. **Topography:** Mostly rolling plateau, average altitude 610 m, with rivers draining S to the Congo and N to Lake Chad. Open, well-watered savanna covers most of the area, with an arid area in NE, and tropical rainforest in SW. **Capital:** Bangui. **Cities** (1985 est.): Bangui (met.) 473 000.
Government: Type: Republic (under military rule). **Head of state:** Gen. Andre Kolingba; in office: Sept. 1, 1981. **Local divisions:** 14 prefectures. **Defence:** 4% of GNP (1984).
Economy: Industries: Textiles, light manuf., mining. **Chief crops:** Cotton, coffee, peanuts, corn, sorghum. **Minerals:** Diamonds (chief export), uranium, iron. **Other resources:** Timber. **Arable land:** 13%. **Electricity prod.** (1986): 61 mln. kwh. **Labor force:** 86% agric.
Finance: Currency: CFA franc (Mar. 1988: 281 = $1 US). **Gross national product** (1985): $700 mln. **Per capita income** (1982): $310. **Imports** (1984): $139 mln.; partners: Fr. 58%. **Exports** (1984): $145 mln.; partners: Fr. 52%, Bel.-Lux. 14%. **International reserves less gold** (Jan. 1988): $96.7 mln. **Gold:** 11 000 oz t.
Transport: Motor vehicles: in use (1984): 43 000 passenger cars, 3 861 comm. vehicles.
Communications: Radios: 135 000 in use (1986).
Health: Life expectancy at birth (1983): 44 years. **Births** (per 1 000 pop. 1985): 47. **Deaths** (per 1 000 pop. 1985): 19%. **Natural increase** (1985): 2.8%. **Hospital beds** (1984): 3 774. **Physicians** (1984): 112. **Infant mortality** (per 1 000 live births 1986): 134.
Education (1983): **Literacy:** 20%. **Attendance:** primary school 64%; secondary school 11%.
Major International Organizations: UN (GATT, IMF, WHO), OAU.
Canadian Embassy: c/o P.O. Box 572, Yaoundé, Cameroon.

Various Bantu tribes migrated through the region for centuries before French control was asserted in the late 19th century, when the region was named Ubangi-Shari. Complete independence was attained Aug. 13, 1960.

All political parties were dissolved in 1960, and the country became a center for Chinese political influence in Africa. Relations with China were severed after 1965. Elizabeth Domitien, premier 1975-76, was the first woman to hold that post in an African country. Pres. Jean-Bedel Bokassa, who seized power in a 1965 military coup, proclaimed himself constitutional emperor of the renamed Central African Empire Dec. 1976.

Emp. Bokassa's rule was characterized by virtually unchecked ruthless and cruel authority, and human rights violations. Bokassa was ousted in a bloodless coup aided by the French government, Sept. 20, 1979, and replaced by his cousin David Dacko, former president from 1960 to 1965. In 1981, the political situation deteriorated amid strikes and economic crisis. Gen. Kolingba replaced Dacko as head of state in a bloodless coup.

Chad
Republic of Chad
République du Tchad

People: Population (1989 est.): 5 714 000. **Age distrib. (%):** 0–14: 42.5; 15–59: 51.7; 60+: 5.8. **Pop. density:** 4.4 per sq. km. **Urban** (1986): 23%. **Ethnic groups:** 200 distinct groups. **Languages:** French, Arabic, (Both official), some 100 other languages. **Religions:** Moslem 44%, animist 23%, Christian 33%.
Geography: Area: 1 288 963 sq. km. **Location:** In central N. Africa. **Neighbors:** Libya on N, Niger, Nigeria, Cameroon on W, Central African Republic on S, Sudan on E. **Topography:** Southern wooded savanna, steppe, and desert, part of the Sahara, in the N. Southern rivers flow N to Lake Chad, surrounded by marshland. **Capital:** N'Djamena. **Cities** (1986 est.): N'Djamena 511 000.
Government: Type: Republic. **Head of state:** Pres. Hissen Habre; b. 1942; in office: June 19, 1982. **Local divisions:** 14 prefectures. **Defence:** 1.6% of GNP (1984).
Economy: Chief crops: Cotton. **Minerals:** Uranium. **Arable land:** 2%. **Fish catch** (1985): 115 000 metric tons. **Electricity prod.** (1986): 65 mln. kwh. **Labor force:** 81% agric.

Finance: Currency: CFA franc (Mar. 1988: 281 = $1 US). **Gross national product** (1985): $405 mln. **Per capita income** (1984): $88. **Imports** (1984): $114 mln.; partners: Fr. 47%. **Exports** (1984): $113 mln.; partners Fra, EDEAC countries. **International reserves less gold** (Jan. 1988): $62.1 mln. **Gold:** 11 000 oz t.

Transport: Motor vehicles: in use (1982): 7 000 passenger cars, 5 000 comm. vehicles.

Communications: Radios: 100 000 in use (1986). **Telephones in use** (1981): 1 000.

Health: Life expectancy at birth (1984): 43.0 male; 45.0 female. **Births** (per 1 000 pop. 1985): 51. **Deaths** (per 1 000 pop. 1985): 28. **Natural increase** (1985): 2.3%. **Hospital beds** (1980): 3 500. **Physicians** (1980): 94. **Infant mortality** (per 1 000 live births 1985): 140.

Education (1980): **Literacy:** 17%.

Major International Organizations: UN, (GATT, IMF, WHO), OAU, EEC.

Canadian Embassy: c/o P.O. Box 572, Yaoundé, Cameroon.

Chad was the site of paleolithic and neolithic cultures before the Sahara Desert formed. A succession of kingdoms and Arab slave traders dominated Chad until France took control around 1900. Independence came Aug. 11, 1960.

Northern Moslem rebels have fought animist and Christian southern government and French troops from 1966, despite numerous cease-fires and peace pacts.

Libyan troops entered the country at the request of the Chad government, Dec. 1980. On Jan. 6, 1981 Libya and Chad announced their intention to unite. France together with several African nations condemned the agreement as a menace to African security. The Libyan troops were withdrawn from Chad in Nov. 1981.

Rebel forces, led by Hissen Habre, captured the capital and forced Pres. Oueddei to flee the country in June 1982.

In 1983, France sent some 3 000 troops to Chad to assist Habre in opposing Libyan-backed rebels. France and Libya agreed to a simultaneous withdrawal of troops from Chad in Sept. 1984 but Libyan forces remained in the north until Mar. 1987 when Chad forces drove them from their last major stronghold. Libyan troops abandoned almost $1 billion of military equipment during their retreat.

Chile
Republic of Chile
República de Chile

People: Population (1989 est.): 12 866 000. **Age distrib.** (%): 0–14: 31.1; 15–59: 60.6; 60+: 8.3. **Pop. density:** 16.9 per sq. km. **Urban** (1986): 83%. **Ethnic groups:** Mestizo 66%, Spanish 25%, Indian 5%. **Language:** Spanish. **Religions:** Roman Catholic 89%, Protestant 11%.

Geography: Area: 759 868 sq. km. **Location:** Occupies western coast of southern S. America. **Neighbors:** Peru on N, Bolivia on NE, Argentina on E. **Topography:** Andes Mtns. are on E border including some of the world's highest peaks; on W is 4 240 km Pacific Coast. Width varies between 160 and 400 km.. In N is Atacama Desert, in centre are agricultural regions, in S are forests and grazing lands. **Capital:** Santiago. **Cities** (1986 metro est.) Santiago 4 804 000.

Government: Type: Military. **Head of state:** Pres. Augusto Pinochet Ugarte; b. Nov. 25, 1915; in office: Sept. 11, 1973. **Local divisions:** 12 regions and Santiago region. **Defence:** 4.2% of GNP (1984).

Economy: Industries: Steel, textiles, wood products. **Chief crops:** Grain, onions, beans, potatoes, peas, fruits, grapes. **Minerals:** Copper (27% world resources and 40% of export revenues), molybdenum, nitrates, iodine (half world output), iron, coal, oil, gas, gold, cobalt, zinc, manganese, borate, mica, mercury, salt, sulphur, marble, onyx. **Crude oil reserves** (1985): 224 mln. bbls. **Other resources:** Water, forests. **Arable land:** 7%. **Meat prod.** (1985): cattle: 3.5 mln.; pigs: 1.1 mln. **Fish catch** (1985): 4.9 mln. metric tons. **Electricity prod.** (1986): 13.9 bln. kwh. **Crude steel prod.** (1984): 684 000 metric tons. **Labor force:** 9% agric.; 32% ind & comm., 38% serv.

Finance: Currency: Peso (June 1988: 246 = $1 US). **Gross national product** (1985): $16.1 bln. **Per capita income** (1979): $1 950. **Imports** (1982): $2.6 bln.; partners: U.S. 29%, Braz.

7%. **Exports** (1986): $4.2 bln.; partners: W. Ger. 6%, Jap. 11%, U.S. 26%. **Tourists** (1985): $115 mln. receipts. **National budget** (1985): $5.1 bln. expenditures. **International reserves less gold** (Mar. 1988): $2.5 bln. **Gold:** 1.53 mln. oz. t. **Consumer prices** (change in 1987): 19.9%

Transport: Railway traffic (1986): 1.2 bln. passenger-km; 2.4 bln. net ton-km. **Motor vehicles:** in use (1985): 624 000 passenger cars, 257 000 comm. vehicles. **Civil aviation** (1986): 1.9 bln. passenger-km; 137 mln. net ton-km. **Chief ports:** Valparaiso, Arica, Antofagasta.

Communications: Television sets: 2.6 mln. in use (1984). **Radios:** 17 mln. in use (1986). **Telephones in use** (1985): 761 000.

Health: Life expectancy at birth (1983): 63.8 male; 70.4 female. **Births** (per 1 000 pop. 1985): 24. **Deaths** (per 1 000 pop. 1985): 6. **Natural increase** (1985): 1.8%. **Hospital beds** (1986): 33 000. **Physicians** (1985): 12 344. **Infant mortality** (per 1 000 live births 1985): 22.

Education (1983): **Literacy:** 90%. Compulsory ages 6-14.

Major International Organizations: UN and all of its specialized agencies, OAS.

Canadian Embassy: Ahumada 11, 10th fl., Santiago; Tel: 6962256, 7.

Northern Chile was under Inca rule before the Spanish conquest, 1536-40. The southern Araucanian Indians resisted until the late 19th century. Independence was gained 1810-18, under Jose de San Martin and Bernardo O'Higgins; the latter, as supreme director 1817-23, sought social and economic reforms until deposed. Chile defeated Peru and Bolivia in 1836-39 and 1879-84, gaining mineral-rich northern land.

Eduardo Frei Montalva came into office in 1964, instituting social programs and gradual nationalization of foreign-owned mining companies. In 1970, Salvador Allende Gossens, a Marxist, became president with a third of the national vote.

The Allende government furthered nationalizations, and improved conditions for the poor. But illegal and violent actions by extremist supporters of the government, the regime's failure to attain majority support, and poorly planned socialist economic programs led to political and financial chaos.

A military junta seized power Sept. 11, 1973, and said Allende killed himself. The junta named a mostly military cabinet, and announced plans to "exterminate Marxism."

Repression has continued during the 1980s with no sign of any political liberalization.

Tierra del Fuego is the largest (48 688 sq. km) island in the archipelago of the same name at the southern tip of South America, an area of majestic mountains, tortuous channels, and high winds. It was discovered 1520 by Magellan and named the Land of Fire because of its many Indian bonfires. Part of the island is in Chile, part in Argentina. Punta Arenas, on a mainland peninsula, is a centre of sheep-raising and the world's southernmost city (pop. 67 600); Puerto Williams, pop. 949, is the southernmost settlement.

China
People's Republic of China
Zhonghua Renmin Gonghe Guo

People: Population (1989 est.): 1 069 628 000. **Pop. density:** 111 per sq. km. **Urban:** (1985): 37%. **Ethnic groups:** Han Chinese 94%, Mongol, Korean, Manchu, others. **Languages:** Mandarin Chinese (official), Yue, Wu, Minbei, Minnan, Xiang, Gan. **Religions:** officially atheist; Confucianism, Buddhism, Taoism, are traditional.

Geography: Area: 9 634 014 sq. km. **Location:** Occupies most of the habitable mainland of E. Asia. **Neighbors:** Mongolia on N, USSR on NE and NW, Afghanistan, Pakistan on W, India, Nepal, Bhutan, Burma, Laos, Vietnam on S, N. Korea on NE. **Topography:** Two-thirds of the vast territory is mountainous or desert, and only one-tenth is cultivated. Rolling topography rises to high elevations in the N in the Daxinganlingshanmai separating Manchuria and Mongolia; the Tienshan in Xinjiang; the Himalayan and Kunlunshanmai in the SW and in Tibet. Length is 2 976 km from N to S, width E to W is more than 3 200 km. The eastern half of China is one of the best-watered lands in the world. Three great river systems, the Changjiang, the Huanghe, and the Xijiang provide water for vast farmlands. **Capital:** Beijing. **Cities** (1987 est.): Shanghai 7 mln.; Beijing 5.9 mln.; Tianjin 5.4 mln.; Canton 3.3 mln.; Shenyang 4.2 mln; Wuhan 3.4 mln.; Chengdu 2.6 mln.

Government: Type: Communist Party led state. **Head of state:** Pres. Li Xiannian; in office: June 18, 1983. **Effective head of government:** Premier Li Peng; in office: Nov. 24, 1987. **Gen. Secy. of Communist Party:** Zhao Ziyang; b. 1919; in office Nov. 2, 1987. **Local divisions:** 22 provinces, 5 autonomous regions, and 3 cities. **Defense:** 8.5% of GNP (1984).

Economy: Industries: Iron and steel, textiles, agriculture implements, trucks. **Chief crops:** Grain, rice, cotton, tea. **Minerals:** Tungsten, antimony, coal, iron, lead, manganese, mercury, molybdenum, phosphates, potash, tin. **Crude oil reserves** (1987): 18.5 bln. bbls. **Other resources:** Silk. **Arable land:** 11%. **Meat prod.** (1985): cattle: 66.9 mln.; pigs: 328 mln.; sheep: 94.2 mln. **Fish catch** (1984): 6.1 mln. metric tons. **Electricity prod.** (1986): 430 bln. kwh. **Crude steel prod.** (1986): 51.9 mln. metric tons. **Labor force:** 68% agric.; 18% ind. & comm.

Finance: Currency: Yuan (Mar. 1988): 3.72 = $1 US). **Gross national product** (1984?: $270 bln. **Per capita income** (1986): $258. **Imports** (1986): $42.9 bln.; partners: Jap. 31%, U.S. 14%, Hong Kong 11%. **Exports** (1986): $30.9 bln.; partners: Hong Kong 26%, Jap. 20%, U.S. 9%. **Tourism** (1985): $1.5 bln. receipts. **National budget** (1987): $66.1 bln. expenditures. **International reserves less gold** (Feb. 1988): 16.7 bln. **Gold:** 12.7 mln. oz t. **Consumer prices** (change in 1987): 7.3%.

Transport: Railway traffic (1986): 874 bln. net ton-km. **Motor vehicles:** in use (1985): 794 000 passenger cars, 2.2 mln. comm. vehicles. **Civil aviation** (1985): 11.7 bln. passenger km, 420 mln. net ton-km. **Chief ports:** Shanghai, Tianjin, Luda.

Communications: Television sets: 69 mln. in use (1986). **Radios:** 223 mln. in use (1986). **Telephones** (1986): 2.7 mln.; **Daily newspaper circ.** (1984): 22 per 1 000 pop.

Health: Life expectancy at birth (1985): 65.5 male; 69.4 female. **Births** (per 1 000 pop. 1985): 16. **Deaths** (per 1 000 pop. 1985): 8. **Natural increase** (1985): 0.8%. **Hospital beds** (1985): 2.4 mln. **Physicians** (1985): 1.4 mln. **Infant Mortality** (per 1 000 live births 1985): 50.

Education (1987): **Literacy:** 70%. Years compulsory 9; first grade enrollment 93%.

Major International Organizations: UN (IMF, FAO, WHO).

Canadian Embassy: 10 San Li Tun Rd., Chao Yang District, Beijing; Tel: 52-3536.

History. Remains of various man-like creatures who lived as early as several hundred thousand years ago have been found in many parts of China. Neolithic agricultural settlements dotted the Huanghe basin from about 5000 BC. Their language, religion, and art were the sources of later Chinese civilization.

Bronze metallurgy reached a peak and Chinese pictographic writing, similar to today's, was in use in the more developed culture of the Shang Dynasty (c. 1500 BC–c. 1000 BC) which ruled much of North China.

A succession of dynasties and interdynastic warring kingdoms ruled China for the next 3 000 years. They expanded Chinese political and cultural domination to the south and west, and developed a brilliant technologically and culturally advanced society. Rule by foreigners (Mongols in the Yuan Dynasty, 1271-1368, and Manchus in the Ch'ing Dynasty, 1644-1911) did not alter the underlying culture.

A period of relative stagnation left China vulnerable to internal and external pressures in the 19th century. Rebellions left tens of millions dead, and Russia, Japan, Britain, and other powers exercised political and economic control in large parts of the country. China became a republic Jan. 1, 1912, following the Wuchang Uprising inspired by Dr. Sun Yat-sen.

For a period of 50 years, 1894-1945, China was involved in conflicts with Japan. In 1895, China ceded Korea, Taiwan, and other areas. On Sept. 18, 1931, Japan seized the Northeastern Provinces (Manchuria) and set up a puppet state called Manchukuo. The border province of Jehol was cut off as a buffer state in 1933. Japan invaded China proper July 7, 1937. After its defeat in World War II, Japan gave up all seized land.

Following World War II, internal disturbances arose involving the Kuomintang, communists, and other factions. China came under domination of communist armies, 1949-1950. The Kuomintang government moved to Taiwan, 145 km off the mainland, Dec. 8, 1949.

The People's Republic of China was proclaimed in Beijing

Sept. 21, 1949, by the Chinese People's Political Consultative Conference under Mao Zedong.

China and the USSR signed a 30-year treaty of "friendship, alliance and mutual assistance," Feb. 15, 1950.

The U.S. refused recognition of the new regime. On Nov. 26, 1950, the People's Republic sent armies into Korea against U.S. troops and forced a stalemate.

By the 1960s, relations with the USSR deteriorated, with disagreements on borders, ideology and leadership of world communism. The USSR cancelled aid accords, and China, with Albania, launched anti-Soviet propaganda drives. High level talks were held with the USSR to seek improved trade and cultural contracts; little progress was reported.

On Oct. 25, 1971, the UN General Assembly ousted the Taiwan government from the UN and seated the People's Republic in its place. The U.S. had supported the mainland's admission but opposed Taiwan's expulsion.

U.S. Pres. Nixon visited China Feb. 21-28, 1972, on invitation from Premier Zhou Enlai, ending years of antipathy between the 2 nations. China and the U.S. opened liaison offices in each other's capitals, May-June 1973. The U.S., Dec. 15, 1978, formally recognized the People's Republic of China as the sole legal government of China; diplomatic relations between the 2 nations were established, Jan. 1, 1979.

In a continuing "reassessment" of the policies of Mao Zedong, Mao's widow, Jiang Qing, and other Gang of Four members were convicted of "committing crimes during the 'Cultural Revolution,' " Jan. 25, 1981.

Internal developments. After an initial period of consolidation, 1949-52, industry, agriculture, and social and economic institutions were forcibly molded according to Maoist ideals. However, frequent drastic changes in policy and violent factionalism interfered with economic development.

In 1957, Mao Zedong admitted an estimated 800 000 people had been executed 1949-54; opponents claimed much higher figures.

The Great Leap Forward, 1958-60, tried to force the pace of economic development through intensive labor on huge new rural communes, and through emphasis on ideological purity and enthusiasm. The program caused resistance and was largely abandoned. Serious food shortages developed, and the government was forced to buy grain from the West.

The Great Proletarian Cultural Revolution, 1965, was an attempt to oppose pragmatism and bureaucratic power and instruct a new generation in revolutionary principles. Massive purges took place. A program of forcibly relocating millions of urban teenagers into the countryside was launched.

By 1968 the movement had run its course; many purged officials returned to office in subsequent years, and reforms in education and industry that had placed ideology above expertise were gradually weakened.

In the mid-1970s, factional and ideological fighting increased, and emerged into the open after the 1976 deaths of Mao and Premier Zhou Enlai. Mao's widow and 3 other leading leftists were purged and placed under arrest, after reportedly trying to seize power. Their opponents said the "Gang of Four" had used severe repression and mass torture, which had sparked local fighting and had disrupted production. The new ruling group modified Maoist policies in education, culture, and industry, and sought better ties with non-communist countries.

Relations with Vietnam deteriorated in 1978 as China charged persecution of ethnic Chinese. In retaliation for Vietnam's invasion of Cambodia, China attacked 4 Vietnamese border provinces Feb. 17, 1979; heavy border fighting ensued.

Sweeping reforms of the central bureaucracy were announced March 1982. By the mid 1980's, China had enacted far-reaching economic reforms highlighted by the departure from rigid central planning and the stressing of market-oriented socialism.

Manchuria. Home of the Manchus, rulers of China 1644-1911, Manchuria has accommodated millions of Chinese settlers in the 20th century. Under Japanese rule 1931-45, the area became industrialized. China no longer uses the name Manchuria for the region, which is divided into the 3 NE provinces of Heilongjiang, Jilin, and Liaoning.

Guandong is the southernmost part of Manchuria. Russia in 1898 forced China to lease it Guandong, and built Port Arthur (Lushun) and the port of Dairen (Luda). Japan seized Port Arthur in 1905. It was turned over to the USSR by the 1945 Yalta agreement, but finally returned to China in 1950.

Inner Mongolia was organized by the People's Republic in 1947. Its boundaries have undergone frequent changes, reaching its greatest extent (and restored in 1979) in 1956, with an area of 1 175 800 sq. km, allegedly in order to dilute the minority Mongol population. Chinese settlers outnumber the Mongols more than 10 to 1. Pop. (1986 est.): 20 mln. Capital: Hohhot.

Xinjiang Uygur Autonomous Region, in Central Asia, is 1 647 885 sq. km, pop. (1986 est.): 13.6 mln. (75% Uygurs, a Turkic Moslem group, with a heavy Chinese increase in recent years). Capital: Urumqi. It is China's richest region in strategic minerals. Some Uygurs have fled to the USSR, claiming national oppression.

Tibet, 1 222 000 sq. km, is a thinly populated region of high plateaus and massive mountains, the Himalayas on the S, the Kunluns on the N. High passes connect with India and Nepal; roads lead into China proper. Capital: Lhasa. Average altitude is 4 500 m. Jiachan, 4 761 m, is believed to be the highest inhabited town on earth. Agriculture is primitive. Pop. (1986 est.): 1.9 mln. (of whom 500 000 are Chinese). Another 4 million Tibetans form the majority of the population of vast adjacent areas that have long been incorporated into China.

China ruled all of Tibet from the 18th century, but independence came in 1911. China reasserted control in 1951, and a communist government was installed in 1953, revising the theocratic Lamaist Buddhist rule. Serfdom was abolished, but all land remained collectivized.

A Tibetan uprising within China in 1956 spread to Tibet in 1959. The rebellion was crushed with Chinese troops, and Buddhism was almost totally suppressed. The Dalai Lama and 100 000 Tibetans fled to India.

Colombia

Republic of Colombia

República de Colombia

People: Population (1989 est.): 31 821 000. **Age distrib.** (%): 0–14: 35.5; 15–59: 47.1; 60+: 7.4. **Pop. density:** 27.9 per sq. km. **Urban** (1983): 65.4%. **Ethnic groups:** Mestizo 58%, Caucasian 20%, mixed 14%. **Language:** Spanish. **Religion:** Roman Catholic 95%.

Geography: Area: 1 138 826 sq. km. **Location:** At the NW corner of S. America. **Neighbors:** Panama on NW, Ecuador, Peru on S, Brazil, Venezuela on E. **Topography:** Three ranges of Andes, the Western, Central, and Eastern Cordilleras, run through the country from N to S. The eastern range consists mostly of high table lands, densely populated. The Magdalena R. rises in Andes, flows N to Carribean, through a rich alluvial plain. Sparsely-settled plains in E are drained by Orinoco and Amazon systems. **Capital:** Bogota. **Cities** (1985 cen.): Bogota 3 967 000; Medellin 1 664 000; Cali 1 450 000; Barranquilla 924 000.

Government: Type: Republic. **Head of state:** Virgilio Barco Vargas; b. Sept. 17, 1921; in office: Aug. 7, 1986. **Local divisions:** 23 departments, 8 national territories, and special district of Bogota. **Defence:** 2.1% of GNP (1985).

Economy: Industries: Textiles, processed goods, hides, steel, cement, chemicals. **Chief crops:** Coffee (50% of exports), rice, corn, cotton, sugar, bananas. **Minerals:** Oil, gas, emeralds (90% world output), gold, copper, lead, coal, iron, nickel, salt. **Crude oil reserves** (1987): 1.6 bln. bbls. **Other resources:** Rubber, balsam, dye-woods, copaiba, hydro power. **Arable land:** 5%. **Meat prod.** (1985): cattle: 20.5 mln.; pigs: 2.4 mln.; sheep: 2.7 mln. **Fish catch** (1985): 78 000 metric tons. **Electricity prod.** (1986): 29.5 bln. kwh. **Crude steel prod.** (1984): 498 000 metric tons. **Labor force:** 26% agric.; 21% ind.; 53% services.

Finance: Currency: Peso (June 1988: 290 = $1 US). **Gross national product** (1986): $31.0 bln. **Per capita income** (1981): $1,112. **Imports** (1986): $3.8 bln.; partners: U.S. 34%, EEC 14%, Jap. 11%. **Exports** (1986): $5.1 bln.; partners: U.S. 40%, EEC 38%. **Tourists** (1984): $205 mln. receipts. **National budget** (1987): $5.6 bln. **International reserves less gold** (Mar. 1988): $2.9 bln. **Gold** 819 000 oz t. **Consumer prices** (change in 1987): 23.3.

Transport: Railway traffic (1985): 228 mln. passenger-km; 780 mln. net ton-km. **Motor vehicles:** in use (1984): 509 000 passenger cars, 520 000 comm. vehicles. **Civil aviation** (1986):

1.9 bln. passenger-km; 252 mln. net ton-km. **Chief ports:** Buena Ventura, Santa Marta, Barranquilla, Cartagena.

Communications: Television sets: 3.8 mln. in use (1986). **Radios:** 7.9 mln. in use (1986). **Telephones in use** (1985): 2.0 mln. **Daily newspaper circ.** (1984): 44 per 1 000 pop.

Health: Life expectancy at birth (1985): 61.4 male; 66 female. **Births** (per 1 000 pop. 1985): 31. **Deaths** (per 1 000 pop. 1985): 7.7. **Natural increase** (1985): 2.3%. **Hospital beds** (1982): 28 880. **Physicians** (1983): 21 778. **Infant mortality** (per 1 000 live births 1985): 62.

Education (1986): **Literacy:** 80%. Only 28% finish primary school.

Major International Organizations: UN (World Bank, GATT), OAS.

Canadian Embassy: Calle 76, No. 11-52; postale: Apartado Aereo 53531, Bogata 2; Tel: 217-5555.

Spain subdued the local Indian kingdoms (Funza, Tunja) by the 1530s, and ruled Colombia and neighboring areas as New Granada for 300 years. Independence was won by 1819. Venezuela and Ecuador broke away in 1829-30, and Panama withdrew in 1903.

One of the Latin American democracies, Colombia is plagued by rural and urban violence, though scaled down from "La Violencia" of 1948-58, which claimed 200 000 lives. Attempts at land and social reform, and progress in industrialization have not yet succeeded in reducing massive social problems aggravated by a very high birth rate.

Comoros

Federal Islamic Republic of the Comoros

Jumhurīyat al-Qumur al-Itthādīyah al-Islāmīyah

People: Population (1989 est.): 459 000. **Pop. density:** 210.6 per sq. km. **Ethnic groups:** Arabs, Africans, East Indians. **Languages:** Shaafi Islam, (a Swahili dialect), French (official), Malagasy. **Religions:** Islam (official), Roman Catholic.

Geography: Area: 2 179 sq. km. **Location:** 3 islands (Grande Comore, Anjouan, and Moheli) in the Mozambique Channel between NW Madagascar and SE Africa. **Neighbors:** Nearest are Mozambique on W, Madagascar on E. **Topography:** The islands are of volcanic origin, with an active volcano on Grand Comoro. **Capital:** Moroni. **Cities** (1985 est.): Moroni (met.) 26 000.

Government: Type: Republic. **Head of state:** Pres. Ahmed Abdallah Abderemane; b. 1919; in office: May 23, 1978. **Head of govt.:** Prime Min. Ali Mroudjae; in office: Feb. 8, 1982. **Local divisions:** each of the 3 main islands is a prefecture.

Economy: Industries: Perfume. **Chief crops:** Vanilla, copra, perfume plants, fruits. **Arable land:** 35%. **Electricity prod.** (1986): 5 mln. kwh. **Labor force:** 87% agric.

Finance: Currency: CFA franc (Mar. 1988: 281 = $1 US). **Gross national product** (1985): $114 mln. **Per capita income** (1982): $339. **Imports** (1985): $25 mln.; partners: Fr. 51%, Madag. 6%, Pak. 13%, Ken. 5%. **Exports** (1985): $15 mln.; partners: Fr. 43%, U.S. 6%.

Transport: Chief ports: Dzaoudzi.

Communications: Radios: 41 000 in use (1986). **Telephones in use** (1981): 3 000.

Health: Life expectancy at birth (1984): 46.4 male; 49.7 female. **Births** (per 1 000 pop. 1985): 44. **Deaths** (per 1 000 pop. 1985): 15. **Natural increase** (1985): 2.9%. **Infant mortality** (per 1 000 live births 1985): 92.3.

Education (1987): **Literacy:** 15%; less than 20% attend secondary school.

Major International Organizations: UN (IMF, World Bank); OAU.

Canadian Embassy: c/o The Canadian High Commission, P.O. Box 30481, Nairobi, Kenya.

The islands were controlled by Moslem sultans until the French acquired them 1841-1909. A 1974 referendum favored independence, with only the Christian island of Mayotte preferring association with France. The French National Assembly decided to allow each of the islands to decide its own fate. The Comoro Chamber of Deputies declared independence July 6, 1975. In a referendum in 1976, Mayotte voted to remain French. A leftist regime that seized power in 1975 was deposed in a pro-French 1978 coup.

Congo

People's Republic of the Congo
République Populaire du Congo

People: Population (1989 est.): 2 031 000. **Pop. density:** 5.9 per sq. km. **Ethnic groups:** Bakongo 45%, Bateke 20%, others. **Languages:** French (official), Bantu dialects. **Religions:** Christian 50% (two-thirds Roman Catholic), animist 47%, Moslem 2%.

Geography: Area: 343 320 sq. km. **Location:** In western central Africa. **Neighbors:** Gabon, Cameroon on W, Central African Republic on N, Zaire on E, Angola (Cabinda) on SW. **Topography:** Much of the Congo is covered by thick forests. A coastal plain leads to the fertile Niari Valley. The centre is a plateau; the Congo R. basin consists of flood plains in the lower and savanna in the upper portion. **Capital:** Brazzaville. **Cities** (1984 est.): Brazzaville (met.) 595 000; Pointe-Noire 297 000; Loubomo 35 000.

Government: Type: People's republic. **Head of state:** Pres. Denis Sassou-Nguesso; b. 1943; in office: Feb. 8, 1979. **Head of government:** Prime Min. Ange Edouard Poungui; in office: Aug. 12, 1984. **Local divisions:** 9 regions and capital district. **Defence:** 2.5% of GNP (1985).

Economy: Chief crops: Palm oil and kernels, cocoa, coffee, tobacco. **Minerals:** Oil, potash, natural gas, lead, copper, zinc. **Crude oil reserves** (1985): 798 mln. bbls. **Arable land:** 2%. **Fish catch** (1985): 33 000 metric tons. **Electricity prod.** (1986): 262 mln. kwh. **Labor force:** 90% agric.

Finance: Currency: CFA franc (Mar. 1988: 281 = $1 US). **Gross national product** (1985): $1.9 bln. **Per capita income** (1978): $500. **Imports** (1984): $618 mln.; partners: Fr. 63%. **Exports** (1984): $1.3 bln.; partners: U.S. 50%, Ital. 21%. **Tourist receipts** (1985): $13 mln. **International reserves less gold** (Jan. 1988): $3.4 mln. **Gold:** 11 000 oz t. **Consumer prices** (change in 1986): 4.0%.

Transport: Railway traffic (1985): 432 mln. passenger-km; 516 mln. net ton-km. **Motor vehicles:** in use (1982): 41 000 passenger cars, 79 000 comm. vehicles. **Chief ports:** Pointe-Noire, Brazzaville.

Communications: Television sets: 5 500 in use (1986). **Radios:** 99 000 in use (1985). **Telephones in use** (1984): 18 000.

Health: Life expectancy at birth (1986): 44.9 male; 48.1 female. **Births** (per 1 000 pop. 1985): 44.5. **Deaths** (per 1 000 pop. 1985): 17.1. **Natural increase** (1985): 2.7%. **Hospital beds** (1978): 6 876. **Physicians** (1980): 278. **Infant mortality** (per 1 000 live births 1985): 110.

Education (1980): **Literacy:** 80%. Years compulsory 10; attendance 80%.

Major International Organizations: UN (GATT, IMF, WHO), OAU.

Canadian Embassy: c/o P.O. Box 8341, Kinshasa, Zaire.

The Loango Kingdom flourished in the 15th century, as did the Anzico Kingdom. of the Batekes; by the late 17th century they had become weakened. France established control by 1885. Independence came Aug. 15, 1960.

After a 1963 coup sparked by trade unions, the country adopted a Marxist-Leninist stance, with the USSR and China vying for influence. Tribal divisions remain strong. France remains a dominant trade partner and source of technical assistance, and French-owned private enterprise retains a major economic role. The government of Pres. Sassou-Nguesso, favoring a strengthening of relations with the USSR, adopted a socialist constitution in 1979.

Costa Rica

Republic of Costa Rica
República de Costa Rica

People: Population (1989 est.): 2 922 000. **Age distrib.** (%): 0–14: 35.0; 15–49: 51.8; 50+: 13.2. **Pop. density:** 57.4 per sq. km. **Urban** (1986): 50%. **Ethnic groups:** Spanish (with Mestizo minority). **Language:** Spanish (official). **Religion:** Roman Catholic 95%.

Geography: Area: 50 895 sq. km. **Location:** In central America. **Neighbors:** Nicaragua on N, Panama on S. **Topography:** Lowlands by the Caribbean are tropical. The interior plateau, with an altitude of about 1 200 m, is temperate. **Capital:** San Jose. **Cities** (1984 est.): San Jose 241 000, Limon 52 000.

Government: Type: Democratic republic. **Head of state:** Pres. Oscar Arias Sanchez; b. Sept. 13, 1941; in office May 8, 1986. **Local divisions:** 7 provinces and 80 cantons.

Economy: Industries: Fiberglass, aluminum, textiles, fertilizers, roofing, cement. **Chief crops:** Coffee (chief export), bananas, sugar, cocoa, cotton, hemp. **Minerals:** Gold, salt, sulphur, iron. **Other resources:** Fish, forests. **Arable land:** 12%. **Fish catch** (1985): 11 000 metric tons. **Electricity prod.** (1986): 2.7 bln. kwh. **Labor force:** 27% agric.; 34% ind. & comm.; 28% service and government.

Finance: Currency: Colone (Mar. 1988: 74 = $1 US). **Gross national product** (1985): $3.7 bln. **Per capita income** (1985): $1 352. **Imports** (1985): $1.0 bln.; partners: U.S. 40%, CACM 10%, Jap. 10%. **Exports** (1985): $928 mln.; partners: U.S. 47%, CACM 18%. **Tourists** (1985): **receipts: $118 mln. National budget** (1985): $603 mln. expenditures. **International reserves less gold** (Mar. 1987): $506 mln. **Gold:** 65 000 oz t. **Consumer prices** (change in 1987): 16.8%.

Transport: Motor vehicles: in use (1984): 106 000 passenger cars, 72 000 comm. vehicles. **Civil aviation** (1986): 558 mln. passenger-km; 29 mln. net ton-km. **Chief ports:** Limon, Puntarenas, Golfito.

Communications: Television sets: 470 000 in use (1986). **Radios:** 200 000 in use (1986). **Telephones in use** (1985): 314 000. **Daily newspaper circ.** (1985): 71 per 1 000 pop.

Health: Life expectancy at birth (1986): 67.5 male; 71.9 female. **Births** (per 1 000 pop. 1985): 31. **Deaths** (per 1 000 pop. 1985): 4. **Natural increase** (1985): 2.7%. **Hospital beds** (1982): 7 706. **Physicians** (1982): 1 929. **Infant mortality** (per 1 000 live births 1986): 15.2.

Education (1986): **Literacy:** 90%. Years compulsory 6; attendance 99%.

Major International Organizations: UN (FAO, ILO, IMF, WHO), OAS.

Canadian Embassy: 6th fl., Cronos Bldg., Calle 3y Ave. Central; postal: Apartado postal 10303, San José; Tel: 23-04-46.

Guaymi Indians inhabited the area when Spaniards arrived, 1502. Independence came in 1821. Costa Rica seceded from the Central American Federation in 1838. Since the civil war of 1948-49, there has been little violent social conflict, and free political institutions have been preserved.

Costa Rica, though still a largely agricultural country, has achieved a relatively high standard of living and social services, and land ownership is widespread.

Côte d'Ivoire

République de la Côte d'Ivoire

People: Population (1989 est.): 11 798 000. **Age distrib.** (%): 0–14: 45.1; 15–59: 50.2; 60+: 4.7. **Pop. density:** 36.4 per sq. km. **Urban** (1985): 42%. **Ethnic groups:** Baule 23%, Bete 18%, Senufo 15%, Malinke 11%, over 60 tribes. **Languages:** French (official), tribal languages. **Religions:** Moslem 25%, Christian 12%, indigenous 63%.

Geography: Area: 323 708 sq. km. **Location:** On S. coast of W. Africa. **Neighbors:** Liberia, Guinea on W, Mali, Burkina Faso on N, Ghana on E. **Topography:** Forests cover the W half of the country, and range from a coastal strip to halfway to the N on the E. A sparse inland plain leads to low mountains in NW. **Capital:** Yamoussoukro. **Cities** (1985 est.): Abidjan 1 850 000 (met.)

Government: Type: Republic. **Head of state:** Pres. Felix Houphouet-Boigny; b. Oct. 18, 1905; in office: Aug. 7, 1960. **Local divisions:** 34 departments.

Economy: Chief crops: Coffee, cocoa. **Minerals:** Diamonds, manganese. **Other resources:** Timber, rubber, petroleum. **Arable land:** 19%. **Livestock:** goats: 1.4 mln.; sheep: 1.4 mln. cattle: 760 000. **Fish catch** (1985): 93 000 metric tons. **Electricity prod.** (1986): 2.1 bln. kwh. **Labor force:** 85% agric.; forestry.

Finance: Currency: CFA franc (Mar. 1988: 281 = $1 US). **Gross national product** (1986): $9.3 bln. **Per capita income** (1986): $921. **Imports** (1985): $1.7 bln.; partners: Fr. 31%,

Venez. 8%, Jap. 5%, U.S. 5%. **Exports** (1985): $2.9 bln.; partners: Fr. 19%, Neth. 13%, U.S. 11%, It. 8%. **Tourists** (1984): $72 mln. receipts; **International reserves less gold** (Jan. 1988): $11.2 mln. **Gold:** 45 000 oz t. **Consumer prices** (changed in 1986): 6.7%.

Transport: Railway traffic (1986): 857 mln. passenger-km; 530 mln. net ton-km. **Motor vehicles:** in use (1984): 182 000 passenger cars, 52 000 comm. vehicles. **Chief ports:** Abidjan, Sassandra.

Communications: Television sets: 550 000 in use (1986). **Radios:** 1.2 mln. in use (1986). **Telephones in use** (1981): 88 000. **Daily newspaper circ.** (1984): 8 per 1 000 pop.

Health: Life expectancy at birth (1983): 46.9 male; 50.2 female. **Births** (per 1 000 pop. 1985): 48.0. **Deaths** (per 1 000 pop. 1985): 12.0. **Natural increase** (1985): 3.6%. **Hospital beds** (1982): 10 062. **Physicians** (1982): 502. **Infant mortality** (per 1 000 live births 1987): 121.

Education (1988): **Literacy:** 35%. **Years compulsory:** none; attendance 75%.

Major International Organizations: UN and all of its specialized agencies, OAU.

Canadian Embassy: Immeuble Trade Centre, 23 av. Nogues, Le Plateau; postal: 01 C.P. 4104, Abidjan 01; Tel: 32-20-09.

A French protectorate from 1842, Côte d'Ivoire became independent in 1960. It is the most prosperous of tropical African nations, due to diversification of agriculture for export, close ties to France, and encouragement of foreign investment. About 20% of the population are workers from neighboring countries. Côte d'Ivoire, which officially changed its name from Ivory Coast in Oct. 1985, is a leader of the pro-Western bloc in Africa.

Cuba

Republic of Cuba

República de Cuba

People: Population (1989 est.): 10 587 000. **Age distrib.** (%): 0–under 15: 25.9; 15–59: 62.8; 60+: 11.3. **Pop. density:** 92.5 per sq. km. **Urban** (1986): 70%. **Ethnic groups:** Spanish, African. **Language:** Spanish. **Religions:** Roman Catholic 42%, none 49%.

Geography: Area: 114 516 sq. km. **Location:** Westernmost of West Indies. **Neighbors:** Bahamas, U.S., on N, Mexico on W, Jamaica on S, Haiti on E. **Topography:** The coastline is about 4 000 km. The N coast is steep and rocky, the S coast low and marshy. Low hills and fertile valleys cover more than half the country. Sierra Maestra, in the E is the highest of 3 mountain ranges. **Capital:** Havana. **Cities** (1986 est.): Havana 2 013 000; Santiago de Cuba 358 000; Camaguey 260 000.

Government: Type: Communist state. **Head of state:** Pres. Fidel Castro Ruz; b. Aug. 13, 1926; in office: Dec. 3, 1976 (formerly Prime Min. since Feb. 16, 1959). **Local divisions:** 14 provinces, 169 municipal assemblies. **Defence:** 5.9% of GNP (1984).

Economy: Industries: Texiles, wood products, cement, chemicals, cigars. **Chief crops:** Sugar (75% of exports), tobacco, coffee, pineapples, bananas, citrus fruit, coconuts. **Minerals:** Cobalt, nickel, iron, copper, manganese, salt. **Other resources:** Forests. **Arable land:** 29%. **Meat prod.** (1985); cattle: 6.5 mln.; pigs: 2.4 mln.; sheep: 382 000. **Fish catch** (1985): 221 000 metric tons. **Electricity prod.** (1986): 14.0 bln. kwh. **Crude steel prod.** (1985): 412 000 metric tons. **Labor force:** 25% agric.; 47% ind. & comm.; 28% services & govt.

Finance: Currency: Peso (Dec. 1987: 1.28 = $1 US). **Gross national income** (1984): $26.9 bln. **Per capita income** (1983): $1 590. **Imports** (1985): $8.6 bln.; partners: USSR 67%. **Exports** (1985): $6.5 bln.; partners: USSR 72%. **Tourist** (1985): revenues: 130 mln.

Transport: Railway traffic (1986): 2.2 bln. passenger-km; 2.4 bln. net ton-km. **Motor vehicles:** in use (1985): 200 000 passenger cars, 164 000 comm. vehicles. **Civil aviation** (1986): 2.6 bln. passenger-km.; 33 mln. net ton-km. **Chief ports:** Havana, Matanzas, Cienfuegos, Santiago de Cuba.

Communications: Television sets: 1.5 mln. in use (1986). **Radios:** 3.2 mln. in use (1986). **Telephones in use** (1985): 515 000. **Daily newspaper circ.** (1985): 140 per 1 000 pop.

Health: Life expectancy at birth: (1980): 71.0 male; 74.0

female. **Births** (per 1 000 pop. 1986): 16.3. **Deaths** (per 1 000 pop. 1986): 6.1. **Natural increase** (1986): 0%. **Hospital beds** (1986): 56 000. **Physicians** (1986): 25 418. **Infant mortality** (per 1 000 live births 1986): 13.6.

Education (1985): **Literacy:** 96%. 92% of those between ages 6–14 attend school.

Major International Organizations: UN (GATT, WHO).

Canadian Embassy: Calle 30 No. 518 Esquina a7a, Miramar, Havana; Tel: 26421, -22, -23.

About 50 000 Indians lived in Cuba when it was discovered by Columbus in 1492. Its name derives from the Indian Cubanacan. Except for British occupation of Havana, 1762-63, Cuba remained Spanish until 1898. A slave-based sugar plantation economy developed from the 18th century, aided by early mechanization of milling. Sugar remains the chief product and chief export despite government attempts to diversify.

A 10-year uprising ended in 1878 with guarantees of rights by Spain, which Spain failed to carry out. A full-scale movement under Jose Marti began Feb. 24, 1895.

The U.S. declared war on Spain in April, 1898, after the sinking of the U.S.S. Maine in Havana harbor, and defeated it in the short Spanish-American War. Spain gave up all claims to Cuba. U.S. troops withdrew in 1902, but under 1903 and 1934 agreements, the U.S. leases a site at Guantanamo Bay in the SE as a naval base. U.S. and other foreign investments acquired a dominant role in the economy. In 1952, former president Fulgencio Batista seized control and established a dictatorship, which grew increasingly harsh and corrupt. Former student leader Fidel Castro assembled a rebel band in 1956; guerrilla fighting intensified in 1958. Batista fled Jan. 1, 1959, and Castro took power, becoming premier Feb. 16.

Some 700 000 Cubans emigrated in the years after the Castro takeover, mostly to the U.S.

Cattle and tobacco lands were nationalized, while a system of cooperatives was instituted. By the end of 1960 all banks and industrial companies had been nationalized, including over $1 billion worth of U.S.-owned properties, mostly without compensation.

Poor sugar crops resulted in collectivization of farms, stringent labor controls, and rationing, despite continued aid from the USSR and other Communist countries.

The U.S. imposed an export embargo in 1962, severely damaging the economy. On Apr. 17, 1961, some 1 400 Cubans, trained and backed by the U.S. Central Intelligence Agency, landed at the Bay of Pigs in an unsuccessful attempt to overthrow the regime.

In the fall of 1962, the U.S. learned that the USSR had brought nuclear missiles to Cuba. After an Oct. 22 warning from Pres. Kennedy, the missiles were removed.

In 1975-78, Cuba sent troops to aid one faction in the Angola Civil War. Cuban troops or advisers are stationed in several African countries. In 1983, 24 Cubans died and over 700 were captured, later repatriated, as a result of the U.S. led invasion of Grenada.

Cyprus

Republic of Cyprus

Kypriaki Dimokratia (Greek)
Kibris Cumhuriyeti (Turkish)

People: Population (1989 est.): 696 000. **Age distrib.** (%): 0–14: 25.0; 15–59: 61.0; 60+: 14.0. **Pop. density:** 75.2 per sq. km. **Urban** (1982): 53%. **Ethnic groups:** Greek 78%, Turk 18.7%, Armenians, Maronites. **Languages:** Greek, Turkish (both official), English. **Religions:** Orthodox 77%, Moslem 18%.

Geography: Area: 9 251 sq. km. **Location:** In eastern Mediterranean Sea, off Turkish coast. **Neighbors:** Nearest are Turkey on N, Syria, Lebanon on E. **Topography:** Two mountain ranges run E-W, separated by a wide, fertile plain. **Capital:** Nicosia. **Cities** (1984 est.): Nicosia 124 300.

Government: Type: Republic. **Head of state:** Pres. George Vassiliou; in office: Feb. 22, 1988. **Local divisions:** 6 districts. **Defence:** over 11% (1984) of govt. budget.

Economy: Industries: Wine, clothing, construction, chemicals. **Chief crops:** Grains, grapes, carobs, citrus fruits, potatoes,

olives. **Minerals:** Copper, pyrites, asbetos, gypsum, umber. **Arable land:** 47%. **Electricity prod.** (1986): 1.5 mln. kwh. **Labor force:** 21% agric.; 20% ind., 18% comm., 19% serv.
Finance: Currency: Pound (Mar. 1988: 1.00 = $2.17 US). **GNP** (1984): $2.3 bln. **Per capita income** (1983): $3 986. **Imports** (1985): $1.4 bln.; partners: UK 13%, Itl. 12%. **Exports** (1983): $561 mln.; partners: UK 17%, Sau. Ar. 7%. **Tourists** (1985): receipts: $298 mln. **National budget** (1985): $540 mln. revenues; $737 mln. expenditures. **International reserves less gold** (Mar. 1988): $873 mln. **Gold:** 459 000 oz. t. **Consumer prices** (change in 1986): 1.2%.
Transport: Motor vehicles: in use (1986): 126 000 passenger cars, 54 000 comm. vehicles. **Civil aviation** (1984): 1.1 bln. passenger-km; 26 mln. net ton-km. **Chief ports:** Famagusta, Limassol.
Communications: Television sets: 158 000 (1985). **Radios:** 300 000 (1985). **Telephones in use** (1983): 164 000. **Daily newspaper circ.** (1986): 144 per 1 000 pop.
Health: Life expectancy at birth (1984): 72.3 male; 76.0 female. **Births** (per 1 000 pop. 1985): 21. **Deaths** (per 1 000 pop. 1985): 8. **Natural increase** (1985): 1.3%. **Hospital beds** (1984): 3 588. **Physicians** (1984): 797. **Infant mortality** (per 1 000 live births 1985): 12.
Education (1984): **Literacy:** 99%. **Years compulsory:** 9; attendance 99%.
Major International Organizations: UN (GATT, IMF, WHO), Commonwealth of Nations, EC (Assoc.).
Canadian Embassy: c/o P.O. Box 6410, Tel Aviv 61063, Israel.

Agitation for enosis (union) with Greece increased after World War II, with the Turkish minority opposed, and broke into violence in 1955-56. In 1959, Britain, Greece, Turkey, and Cypriot leaders approved a plan for an independent republic, with constitutional guarantees for the Turkish minority and permanent division of offices on an ethnic basis. Greek and Turkish Communal Chambers dealt with religion, education, and other matters.

Archbishop Makarios, formerly the leader of the enosis movement, was elected president, and full independence became final Aug. 16, 1960. Makarios was re-elected in 1968 and 1973.

Further communal strife led the United Nations to send a peace-keeping force in 1964; its mandate has been repeatedly renewed.

The Cypriot National Guard, led by officers from the army of Greece, seized the government July 15, 1974, and named Nikos Sampson, an advocate of union with Greece, president. Makarios fled the country. On July 20, Turkey invaded the island; Greece mobilized its forces but did not intervene. A cease-fire was arranged July 22. On the 23d, Sampson turned over the presidency to Glafkos Clerides (on the same day, Greece's military junta resigned). A peace conference collapsed Aug. 14; fighting resumed. By Aug. 16 Turkish forces had occupied the NE 40% of the island, despite the presence of UN peace forces. Makarios resumed the presidency in Dec., until his death, 1977.

Turkish Cypriots voted overwhelmingly, June 8, 1975, to form a separate Turkish Cypriot federated state. A president and assembly were elected in 1976. Some 200 000 Greeks have been expelled from the Turkish-controlled area, replaced by thousands of Turks, some from the mainland.

A unilateral declaration of independence was announced by Turkish-Cypriot leader Rauf Denktash, Nov. 15, 1983. The new state, which was not recognized by other nations, was named the Turkish Rep. of Northern Cyprus.

Czechoslovakia

Czechoslovak Socialist Republic

Československá Socialistická Republika

People: Population (1989 est.): 15 661 000. **Age distrib.** (%): 0–14: 24.4; 15–59: 59.2; 60+: 16.4. **Pop. density:** 122.5 per sq. km. **Urban** (1985): 73%. **Ethnic groups:** Czech 64%, Slovak 31%, Hungarian, German, Polish, Ukrainian. **Languages:** Czech, Slovak (both official). **Religion:** Roman Catholic 65%.
Geography: Area: 127 845 sq. km. **Location:** In E central Europe. **Neighbors:** Poland, E. Germany on N, W. Germany on W. Austria, Hungary on S, USSR on E. **Topography:** Bohemia, in W, is a plateau surrounded by mountains; Moravia is hilly, Slovakia, in E, has mountains (Carpathians) in N, fertile Danube

plain in S. Vltava (Moldau) and Labe (Elbe) rivers flow N from Bohemia to G. **Capital:** Prague. **Cities** (1987 est.): Prague 1.2 mln.; Brno 385 000; Bratislava 413 000; Ostrava 327 000.
Government: Type: Communist. **Head of state:** Pres. Gustav Husak; b. Jan 10, 1913; in office: May 29, 1975; **Head of government:** Prime Min. Lubomir Strougal; b. Oct. 19, 1924; in office: Jan. 28, 1970. **Head of Communist Party:** Gen. Sec. Milos Jakes; in office: Dec. 17, 1987. **Local divisions:** Czech and Slovak republics each have an assembly. **Defence:** 7.5% of Gov't budget (1986).
Economy: Industries: Machinery, oil products, iron and steel, glass, chemicals, motor vehicles, cement. **Chief crops:** Wheat, sugar beets, potatoes, rye, corn, barley. **Minerals:** Coke, coal, iron. **Arable land:** 40%. **Livestock** (1985): cattle: 5 mln.; pigs: 6.6 mln.; sheep: 1 mln. **Electricity prod.** (1986): 83.0 bln. kwh. **Crude steel prod.** (1986): 15.1 mln. metric tons. **Labor force:** 14% agric.; 64% ind., comm.; 22% service, govt.
Finance: Currency: Koruna (Jan. 1988: 5.48 = $1 US). **Gross national product** (1985): $135.6 bln. **Per capita income** (1984): $8 300. **Imports** (1985): $18.1 bln.; partners: USSR 46%, E. Ger. 10%, Pol. 6%, W. Ger. 5%. **Exports** (1985): $18.0 bln.; partners: USSR 41%, E. Ger. 9%, Pol. 7%, Hung. 5%.
Transport: Railway traffic (1985): 19.8 bln. passenger-km; 66 bln. net ton-km. **Motor vehicles:** in use (1985): 2.6 mln. passenger cars, 425 000 comm. **Civil aviation** (1985): 1.1 bln. passenger-km; 60 mln. net ton-km.
Communications: Television sets: 4.3 mln. (1985). **Radios:** 4.2 mln. (1985). **Telephones in use** (1986): 3.5 mln. **Daily newspaper circ.** (1984): 284 per 1 000 pop.
Health: Life expectancy at birth (1985): 67.2 male; 74.4 female. **Births** (per 1 000 pop. 1985): 15. **Deaths** (per 1 000 pop. 1985): 12. **Natural increase** (1985): .3%. **Hospital beds** (1986): 123 000; **Physicians** (1986): 47 569. **Infant mortality** (per 1 000 live births 1985): 15.6.
Education (1987): **Literacy:** 99%.
Major International Organizations: UN (GATT, WHO), Warsaw Pact.
Canadian Embassy: Mickiewiczova 6, Prague 6; Tel: 32-6941.

Bohemia, Moravia and Slovakia were part of the Great Moravian Empire in the 9th century. Later, Slovakia was overrun by Magyars, while Bohemia and Moravia became part of the Holy Roman Empire. Under the kings of Bohemia, Prague in the 14th century was the cultural center of Central Europe. Bohemia and Hungary became part of Austria-Hungary.

In 1914-1918 Thomas G. Masaryk and Eduard Benes formed a provisional government with the support of Slovak leaders including Milan Stefanik. They proclaimed the Republic of Czechoslovakia Oct. 28, 1918.

By 1938 Nazi Germany had worked up disaffection among German-speaking citizens in Sudetenland and demanded its cession. Prime Min. Neville Chamberlain of Britain, with the acquiescence of France, signed with Hitler at Munich, Sept. 30, 1938, an agreement to the cession, with a guarantee of peace by Hitler and Mussolini. Germany occupied Sudetenland Oct. 1-2.

Hitler on Mar. 15, 1939, dissolved Czechoslovakia, made protectorates of Bohemia and Moravia, and supported the autonomy of Slovakia, which was proclaimed independent Mar. 14, 1939.

Soviet troops with some Czechoslovak contingents entered eastern Czechoslovakia in 1944 and reached Prague in May 1945; Benes returned as president. In May 1946 elections, the Communist Party won 38% of the votes, and Benes accepted Klement Gottwald, a communist, as prime minister.

In February, 1948, the communists seized power in advance of scheduled elections. In May 1948 a new constitution was approved. Benes refused to sign it. On May 30 the voters were offered a one-slate ballot and the communists won full control. Benes resigned June 7 and Gottwald became president. A harsh Stalinist period followed, with complete and violent suppression of all opposition.

In Jan. 1968 a liberalization movement spread explosively through Czechoslovakia. Antonin Novotny, long the Stalinist boss of the nation, was deposed as party leader and succeeded by Alexander Dubcek, a Slovak, who declared he intended to make communism democratic. On Mar. 22 Novotny resigned as president and was succeeded by Gen. Ludvik Svoboda. On Apr. 6, Premier Joseph Lenart resigned and was succeeded by Oldrich Cernik, whose new cabinet was pledged to carry out de-mocratization and economic reforms.

In July 1968 the USSR and 4 Warsaw Pact nations demanded an end to liberalization. On Aug. 20, the Russian, Polish, East German, Hungarian, and Bulgarian armies invaded Czechoslovakia.

Despite demonstrations and riots by students and workers, press censorship was imposed, liberal leaders were ousted from office and promises of loyalty to Soviet policies were made by some old-line Communist Party leaders.

On Apr. 17, 1969, Dubcek resigned as leader of the Communist Party and was succeeded by Gustav Husak. In Jan. 1970, Premier Cernik was ousted. Censorship was tightened and the Communist Party expelled a third of its members. In 1973, amnesty was offered to some of the 40 000 who fled the country after the 1968 invasion, but repressive policies continue to remain in force.

More than 700 leading Czechoslovak intellectuals and former party leaders signed a human rights manifesto in 1977, called Charter 77, prompting a renewed crackdown by the regime.

Czechoslovakia has long been an industrial and technological leader of the eastern European countries, though its relative standing has declined in recent years because of the government's rejection of economic reforms. The adoption of Soviet-style political and economic reforms was announced in 1988.

Denmark

Kingdom of Denmark

Kongeriget Danmark

People: Population (1989 est.): 5 074 000. **Age distrib.** (%): 0–14: 17.9; 15–59: 61.7; 60+: 20.4. **Pop. density:** 117.8 per sq. km. **Urban** (1985): 84%. **Ethnic groups:** Almost all Scandinavian. **Language:** Danish. **Religion:** Evangelical Lutheran 97%.

Geography: Area: 43 076 sq. km. **Location:** In northern Europe, separating the North and Baltic seas. **Neighbors:** W. Germany on S., Norway on NW, Sweden on NE. **Topography:** Denmark consists of the Jutland Peninsula and about 500 islands, 100 inhabited. The land is flat or gently rolling, and is almost all in productive use. **Capital:** Copenhagen. **Cities** (1985): Copenhagen 633 412; Arhus 252 071.

Government: Type: Constitutional monarchy. **Head of state:** Queen Margrethe II; b. Apr. 16, 1940; in office: Jan. 14, 1972. **Head of government:** Prime Min. Poul Schluter; b. 1929; in office: Sept. 10, 1982. **Local divisions:** 14 counties and one city (Copenhagen). **Defence:** 2.1% of GNP (1985).

Economy: Industries: Machinery, textiles, furniture, electronics. **Chief crops:** Dairy products. **Crude oil reserves** (1985): 533 mln. bbls. **Arable land:** 62%. **Livestock** (1985): cattle: 25 mln.; pigs: 9.4 mln. **Fish catch** (1985): 1.6 mln. metric tons. **Electricity prod.** (1984): 22.1 bln. kwh. **Crude steel prod.** (1985): 560 000 metric tons. **Labor force:** 8.2% agric.; 46% ind. & comm.; 13% serv.

Finance: Currency: Krone (June 1988: 6.57 = $1 US). **Gross national product** (1985): $57.9 bln. **Per capita income** (1985): $11 312. **Imports** (1986): $22.8 bln.; partners: W. Ger. 20%, Swed. 12%, UK 9%, Neth. 5%. **Exports** (1986): $21.2 bln.; partners: W. Ger. 15%, EC 42%, U.S. 8%. **Tourists** (1984): $1.3 bln. receipts. **National budget** (1980): $23 bln. expenditures. **International reserves less gold** (Mar. 1988): $10.7 bln. **Gold:** 2.0 mln. oz t. **Consumer prices** (change in 1987): 4.0%.

Transport: Railway traffic (1985): 4.7 bln. passenger-km; 1.7 bln. net ton-km. **Motor vehicles:** in use (1985): 1.5 mln. passenger cars, 346 000 comm. vehicles. **Civil aviation** (1986): 3.2 bln. passenger-km; 129 mln. net ton-km. **Chief ports:** Copenhagen, Alborg, Arhus, Odense.

Communications: Television sets: 1.9 mln. licensed (1986). **Radios:** 2 mln. licensed (1986). **Telephones in use** (1986): 4.0 mln. **Daily newspaper circ.** (1986): 363 per 1 000 pop.

Health: Life expectancy at birth (1986): 71.5 male; 77.5 female. **Births** (per 1 000 pop. 1986): 10.8. **Deaths** (per 1 000 pop. 1986): 11.4. **Hospital beds** (1985): 36 000. **Physicians** (1986): 12 975. **Infant mortality** (per 1 000 live births 1985): 8.

Education (1986): **Literacy:** 99%. Years compulsory 9; attendance 100%.

Major International Organizations: UN and all of its specialized agencies, OECD, EC.

Canadian Embassy: Kr. Bernikowsgade 1, 1105 Copenhagen K; Tel: (01) 12-22-99.

The origin of Copenhagen dates back to ancient times, when the fishing and trading place named Havn (port) grew up on a cluster of islets, but Bishop Absalon (1128-1201) is regarded as the actual founder of the city.

Danes formed a large component of the Viking raiders in the early Middle Ages. The Danish kingdom was a major north European power until the 17th century, when it lost its land in southern Sweden. Norway was separated in 1815, and Schleswig-Holstein in 1864. Northern Schleswig was returned in 1920.

The **Faeroe Islands** in the N. Atlantic, about 483 km NE of the Shetlands, and 1 368 km from Denmark proper, 18 inhabited, have an area of 1 404 sq. km and pop. (1985) of 45 000. They are self-governing in most matters.

Greenland

(Kalaallit Nunaat)

Greenland, a huge island between the N. Atlantic and the Polar Sea, is separated from the North American continent by Davis Strait and Baffin Bay. Its total area is 2 184 000 sq. km, 84% of which is ice-capped. Most of the island is a lofty plateau 2 700 to 3 000 m in altitude. The average thickness of the cap is 300 m. The population (1987 est.) is 54 000. Under the 1953 Danish constitution the colony became an integral part of the realm with representatives in the Folketing. The Danish parliament, 1978, approved home rule for Greenland, effective May 1, 1979. Accepting home rule the islanders elected a socialist-dominated legislature, Apr. 4th. With home rule, Greenlandic place names came into official use. The technically-correct name for Greenland is now Kalaallit Nunaat; its capital is Nuuk, rather than Gothab. Fish is the principal export.

Djibouti

Republic of Djibouti

Jumhouriyya Djibouti

People: Population (1989 est.): 327 000. **Pop. density:** 14.9 per sq. km. **Ethnic groups:** Issa (Somali) 60%; Afar 35%; European 5%. **Languages:** French, Arabic (both official); Somali, Saho-Afar, Arabic. **Religion:** Sunni Moslem 94%.

Geography: Area: 21 998 sq. km. **Location:** On E coast of Africa, separated from Arabian Peninsula by the strategically vital strait of Bab el-Mandeb. **Neighbors:** Ethiopia on N (Eritrea) and W, Somalia on S. **Topography:** The territory, divided into a low coastal plain, mountains behind, and an interior plateau, is arid, sandy, and desolate. The climate is generally hot and dry. **Capital:** Djibouti. **Cities** (1982): Djibouti (met.) 200 000.

Government: Type: Republic. **Head of state:** Pres. Hassan Gouled Aptidon b. 1916; in office: June 24, 1977; **Head of government:** Prem. Barkat Gourad Hamadou; in office: Sept. 30, 1978. **Local divisions:** 5 cercles (districts).

Economy: Minerals: Salt. **Electricity prod.** (1986): 140 mln. kwh.

Finance: Currency Franc (Jan. 1988: 176=$1 US). **Gross national product** (1986): $344 mln. **Per capita income** (1986): $400. **Imports** (1986): $197 mln.; partners: Fr. 47%, Jap. 8%, UK 8%. **Exports** (1986): $96 mln.; partners: Fr. 87%.

Transport: Motor vehicles: in use (1985): 12 000 passenger cars, 950 commercial vehicles. **Chief ports:** Djibouti.

Communications: Television sets: 4 000 in use (1986). **Radios:** 32 000 in use (1986). **Telephones in use** (1984): 6 400.

Health: Life expectancy at birth (1985): 50 years. **Births** (per 1 000 pop. 1985): 49.2. **Deaths** (per 1 000 pop. 1985): 18.3. **Natural increase** (1985): 3.0%. **Infant Mortality** (per 1 000 live births 1985): 132.

Education (1985): **Literacy:** 17%.

Major International Organizations: UN, OAU, Arab League.

Canadian Embassy: P.O. Box 1130, Addis Ababa, Ethiopia.

France gained control of the territory in stages between 1862 and 1900.

Ethiopia and Somalia have renounced their claims to the area, but each has accused the other of trying to gain control. There were clashes between Afars (ethnically related to Ethiopians) and Issas (related to Somalis) in 1976. Immigrants from both countries continued to enter the country up to independence, which came June 27, 1977.

Unemployment is very high. There are few natural resources; trade is the main contributor to domestic product. French aid is the mainstay of the economy and some 5 000 French troops are present.

Dominica
Commonwealth of Dominica

People: Population (1989 est.): 76 000. **Pop. density:** 101.0 per sq. km. **Ethnic groups:** nearly all African or mulatto, Caribs. **Languages:** English (official), French patois. **Religion:** mainly Roman Catholic.

Geography: Area: 751 sq. km. **Location:** In Eastern Caribbean, most northerly Windward Is. **Neighbors:** Guadeloupe to N, Martinique to S. **Topography:** Mountainous, a central ridge running from N to S, terminating in cliffs; volcanic in origin, with numerous thermal springs; rich deep topsoil on leeward side, red tropical clay on windward coast. **Capital** (1983 est.) Roseau 18 000.

Government: Type: Parlimentary democracy; republic within Commonwealth. **Head of state:** Pres. Clarence Augustus Seignoret; in office: 1984. **Head of government:** Prime Min. Mary Eugenia Charles; b. 1919; in office: July 21, 1980. **Local divisions:** 10 parishes.

Economy: Industries: Agriculture, tourism. **Chief crops:** Bananas, citrus fruits, coconuts. **Minerals:** Pumice. **Other resources:** Forests. **Arable land:** 23%. **Electricity prod.** (1984): 20 mln. kwh. **Labor Force** 40% agric.; 32% ind. & comm.; 28% services.

Finance: Currency: East Caribbean dollar (May 1988: 2.70 = $1 US). **Gross domestic product** (1986): $102 mln. **Imports** (1986): $63 mln.; partners: UK 12%, U.S. 27%, Can. 7%. **Exports** (1986): $35 mln.; partners: UK 47%. **Tourists** (1984): 23 826. **Consumer prices** (change in 1986): 3.0%.

Transport: Chief ports: Roseau.

Communications: Telephones in use (1985): 6 000.

Health: Life expectancy at birth (1987): 57 male; 59 female. **Births** (per 1 000 pop. 1985): 19. **Deaths** (per 1 000 pop. 1985): 6. **Natural increase** (1985): 1.3%. **Hospital beds** (1985): 292. **Physicians** (1985): 25. **Infant mortality** (per 1 000 live births 1985): 20.

Education: Literacy: 80%.

Major International Organizations: UN, OAS.

Canadian High Commission: c/o The Canadian High Commission, P.O. Box 404, Bridgetown, Barbados.

A British colony since 1805, Dominica was granted self government in 1967. Independence was achieved Nov. 3, 1978.

Hurricane David struck, Aug. 30, 1979, devastating the island and destroying the banana plantations, Dominica's economic mainstay. Coups were attempted in 1980 and 1981.

Dominica took a leading role in the instigation of the 1983 invasion of Grenada.

Dominican Republic
República Dominicana

People: Population (1989 est.): 7 307 000. **Age distrib.** (%): 0–14: 40.7; 15–59: 54.6; 60+: 4.7. **Pop. density:** 149.9 per sq. km. **Urban** (1985): 55%. **Ethnic groups:** Caucasian 16%, mixed 73%, black 11%. **Language:** Spanish. **Religion:** Roman Catholic 95%.

Geography: Area: 48 730 sq. km. **Location:** In West Indies, sharing I. of Hispaniola with Haiti. **Neighbors:** Haiti to W. **Topography:** The Cordillera Central range crosses the center of the country, rising to over 3 000 m, highest in the Caribbean. The Cibao valley to the N is major agricultural area. **Capital:** Santo Domingo. **Cities** (1987 est.): Santo Domingo 1 700 000; Santiago de Los Caballeros 422 000.

Government: Type: Representative democracy. **Head of state:** Pres. Joaquin Belaguer; in office: Aug. 16, 1986. **Local divisions:** 29 provinces and Santo Domingo. **Defence:** 1.5% of GDP. (1986).

Economy: Industries: Sugar refining, cement, pharmaceuticals. **Chief crops:** sugar, cocoa, coffee, tobacco, rice. **Minerals:** Nickel, gold, silver. **Other resources:** Timber. **Arable land:** 30%. **Livestock.** (1984): cattle: 1.9 mln. **Electricity prod.** (1984): 4.0 bln. kwh. **Labor force:** 45% agric.; 21% ind. & comm.; 34% serv. & govt.

Finance: Currency: Peso (Mar. 1988: 5.25 = $1 US). **Gross national product** (1986): $5.5 bln. **Per capita income** (1980): $1 221. **Imports** (1986): $1.2 bln.; partners: U.S. 35%, Venez. 21%, Mex. 11%. **Exports** (1986): $720 mln.; partners: U.S. 64%, Swit. 5%, Neth. 4%. **Tourists** (1984): $277 mln. receipts. **National budget** (1986): $781 mln. expenditures. **International reserves less gold** (Mar. 1988): $169 mln. **Gold:** 18 000 oz t. **Consumer prices** (change in 1986): 9.7%

Transport: Motor vehicles: in use (1983): 94 000 passenger cars, 55 000 comm. vehicles. **Chief ports:** Santo Domingo, San Pedro de Macoris, Puerto Plata.

Communications: Television sets: 500 000 in use (1986). **Radios:** 800 000 in use (1986). **Telephones in use** (1983): 175 054. **Daily newspaper circ.** (1985): 33 per 1 000 pop.

Health: Life expectancy at birth (1985): 60.7 male; 64.6 female. **Births** (per 1 000 pop. 1985): 34. **Deaths** (per 1 000 pop. 1985): 9. **Natural increase** (1985): 2.5%. **Hospital beds** (1980): 8 953. **Physicians** (1980): 2 142. **Infant mortality** (per 1 000 live births 1985): 74.

Education (1987): **Literacy:** 68%. Years compulsory 6; attendance 60%.

Major International Organizations: UN (World Bank, IMF, GATT), OAS.

Canadian Embassy: c/o Apartado 62302, Caracas 1060A, Venezuela. Santo Domingo: Consulate of Canada, Mahatma Gandhi 200, Corner Juan Sanchez Ramirez, Santo Domingo 1; P.O. Box 2054; Tel: (809) 689-0002.

Carib and Arawak Indians inhabited the island of Hispaniola when Columbus landed in 1492. The city of Santo Domingo, founded 1496, is the oldest settlement by Europeans in the hemisphere and has the supposed ashes of Columbus in an elaborate tomb in its ancient cathedral.

The western third of the island was ceded to France in 1697. Santo Domingo itself was ceded to France in 1795. Haitian leader Toussaint L'Ouverture seized it, 1801. Spain returned intermittently 1803-21, as several native republics came and went. Haiti ruled again, 1822-44, and Spanish occupation occurred 1861-63.

The country was occupied by U.S. Marines from 1916 to 1924, when a constitutionally elected government was installed.

In 1930, Gen. Rafael Leonidas Trujillo Molina was elected president. Trujillo ruled brutally until his assassination in 1961. Pres. Joaquin Balaguer, appointed by Trujillo in 1960, resigned under pressure in 1962. Juan Bosch, elected president in the first free elections in 38 years, was overthrown in 1963.

On April 24, 1965, a revolt was launched by followers of Bosch and others, including a few communists. Four days later U.S. Marines intervened against the pro-Bosch forces. Token units were later sent by 5 So. American countries as a peacekeeping force.

A provisional government supervised a June 1966 election, in which Balaguer defeated Bosch by a 3-2 margin; there were some charges of election fraud. The Inter-American Peace Force completed its departure Sept. 20, 1966.

Continued depressed world prices have affected the main export commodity, sugar.

Ecuador
Republic of Ecuador
República del Ecuador

People: Population (1989 est.): 10 490 000. **Age distrib.** (%): 0–14: 41.5; 15–64: 54.8; 65+: 3.7. **Pop. density:** 36.9 per sq. km. **Urban** (1986): 52% **Ethnic groups:** Indian 25%, Mestizo 55%, Spanish 10%, African 10%. **Languages:** Spanish (official), Quechuan, Jivaroan. **Religion:** Roman Catholic 95%.

Geography: Area: 284 656 sq. km. Location: In NW S. America, on Pacific coast, astride Equator. Neighbors: Colombia to N, Peru to E and S. Topography: Two ranges of Andes run N and S, splitting the country into 3 zones: hot, humid lowlands on the coast; temperate highlands between the ranges, and rainy, tropical lowlands to the E. Capital: Quito. Cities (1987 est.): Guayaquil 1 500 000; Quito 1 200 000.

Government: Type: Republic. Head of state: Pres. Leon Febres-Cordero Rivadeneira; b. Mar. 9, 1931; in office: Aug. 10, 1984. Local divisions: 20 provinces. Defense: 1.6% of GNP (1984).

Economy: Industries: Food processing, wood prods., textiles. Chief crops: Bananas (largest exporter), coffee, rice, sugar, corn. Minerals: Oil, copper, iron, lead, silver, sulphur. Crude oil reserves (1987): 1.2 bln. bbls. Other resources: Rubber, bark. Arable land: 9%. Livestock (1984): cattle: 3.3 mln.; pigs: 4.2 mln.; sheep: 2.3mln. Fish catch (1984): 159 000 metric tons. Electricity prod. (1984): 4.8 bln. kwh. Labor force: 34% agric., 12% ind., 35% services.

Finance: Currency: Sucre (June 1988: 475 = $1 US). Gross national product (1985): $12.1 bln. Per capita income (1985): $1 299. Imports (1987): $2.0 bln.; partners: U.S. 32%, EC 16%, Jap. 13%. Exports (1987): $2.0 bln.; partners: U.S. 64%. National budget (1986): $1.2 bln. International reserves less gold (Mar. 1988): $506 mln. Gold: 414 000 oz t. Consumer prices (change in 1987): 29.5%.

Transport: Railway traffic (1986) 43 mln. passenger-km; 11 mln. net ton-km. Motor vehicles: in use (1984): 248 000 passenger cars, 32 000 comm. vehicles. Civil aviation (1982): 862 mln. passenger-km; 39.4 mln. net ton-km. Chief ports: Guayaquil, Manta, Esmeraldas, Puerto Bolivar.

Communications: Television sets: 600 000 in use (1985). Radios: 1.9 mln. in use (1985). Telephones in use (1984): 295 000. Daily newspaper circ. (1985): 87 per 1 000 pop.

Health: Life expectancy at birth (1981): 59.8 male, 63.6 female. Births (per 1 000 pop. 1985): 36.0. Deaths (per 1 000 pop. 1985): 8.0. Natural increase (1985): 2.9%. Hospital beds (1984): 15 455. Physicians (1984): 11 000. Infant mortality (per 1 000 live births 1985): 63.

Education (1986): Literacy: 90%. Attendance through 6th grade—76% urban, 33% rural.

Major International Organizations: UN (IMF, WHO), OAS, OPEC.

Canadian Embassy: c/o The Canadian Embassy, Apartado Aero 53531, Bogota 2, Columbia; Tel: 458-016; 458-156, 458-578. Guayaquil: Consulate of Canada, Edificio Torres de la Merced, Oficina 11-Piso 4, General Cordova 800 y Victor Manuel Rendon, Guayaquil; Tel: (04) 303-580.

Spain conquered the region, which was the northern Inca empire, in 1633. Liberation forces defeated the Spanish May 24, 1822, near Quito. Ecuador became part of the Great Colombia Republic but seceded, May 13, 1830.

Ecuador had been ruled by civilian and military dictatorships since 1968. A peaceful transfer of power from the military junta to the democratic civilian government took place, 1979.

Since 1972, the economy has revolved around its petroleum exports, which have declined since 1982, causing severe economic problems. In 1987, following a Mar. 5-6 earthquake which left 20 000 homeless and destroyed a stretch of the country's main oil pipeline, Ecuador suspended interest payments, for 1987, on its estimated $8.2 billion foreign debt.

Ecuador and Peru have long disputed their Amazon Valley boundary.

The Galapagos Islands, 960 km to the W, are the home of huge tortoises and other unusual animals.

Egypt
Arab Republic of Egypt
Jumhūrīyah Misr al-Arabiya

People: Population (1989 est.): 54 779 000. Pop. density: 54.7 per sq. km. Urban (1985): 48.8%. Ethnic groups: Eastern Hamitic stock 90%, Bedouin, Nubian. Languages: Arabic (official), English. Religion: Sunni Moslem 90%.

Geography: Area: 1 001 346 sq. km. Location: NE corner of Africa. Neighbors: Libya on W, Sudan on S, Israel on E. Topography: Almost entirely desolate and barren, with hills and mountains in E and along Nile. The Nile Valley, where most of the people live, stretches 880 km. Capital: Cairo. Cities (1986 est.): Cairo 6 305 000; Alexandria 2 800 000; al-Jizah 1 600 000.

Government: Type: Republic. Head of state: Pres. Hosni Mubarak; b. 1929; in office: Oct. 14, 1981. Head of Government: Atef Sedki; in office: Nov. 10, 1986. Local divisions: 26 governorates. Defence: 8.2% of GNP (1987).

Economy: Industries: Textiles, chemicals, petrochemicals, food processing, cement. Chief crops: Cotton (one of largest producers), rice, beans, fruits, grains, vegetables, sugar, corn. Minerals: Oil, phosphates, gypsum, iron, manganese, limestone. Crude oil reserves (1987): 4 bln. bbls. Arable land: 4%. Livestock (1984): cattle: 1.8 mln.; sheep: 1.4 mln. Fish catch (1985): 138 000 metric tons. Electricity prod. (1986): 40.6 bln. kwh. Labor force: 41% agric.; 22% services; industry 14%.

Finance: Currency: Pound (June 1988: 2.28 = $1 US). Gross national product (1986): $30.0 bln. Per capita income (1983): $686. Imports (1986): $11.5 bln.; partners: U.S. 19%, W. Ger. 10%, It. 8%, France 8%. Exports (1986): $2.9 bln.; partners: It. 22%, Isr. 14%. Tourists (1985): $990 mln. receipts. National budget (1987): $12.2 bln. expenditures. International reserves less gold (Jan. 1988): $1.3 bln. Gold: 2.43 mln. oz t. Consumer prices (change in 1987): 19.7%.

Transport: Railway traffic (1984): 24.1 bln. passenger-km; 2.5 bln. net ton-km. Motor vehicles: in use (1985): 719 000 passenger cars, 292 000 comm. vehicles. Civil aviation (1986): 4.0 bln. passenger-km, 111 mln. freight ton-km. Chief ports: Alexandria, Port Said, Suez.

Communications: Television sets: 2 mln. in use (1986). Radios: 15 mln. in use (1986). Telephones in use (1985): 1.1 mln. Daily newspaper circ. (1985): 99 per 1 000 pop.

Health: Life expectancy at birth (1985): 55.9 male; 58.4 female. Births (per 1 000 pop. 1985): 40. Deaths (per 1 000 pop. 1985): 11. Natural increase (1985): 2.9%. Hospital beds (1984): 85 350. Physicians (1984): 73 300. Infant mortality (per 1 000 live births 1986): 102.

Education (1988): Literacy: 44%. Compulsory ages 6-12.

Major International Organizations: UN (IMF, World Bank, GATT), OAU.

Canadian Embassy: 6 Sharia Mohamed Fahmi el Sayed, Garden City, Cairo; postal: P.O. Box 2646, Cairo; Tel: 354-3110.

Archeological records of ancient Egyptian civilization date back to 4000 BC. A unified kingdom arose around 3200 BC, and extended its way south into Nubia and north as far as Syria. A high culture of rulers and priests was built on an economic base of serfdom, fertile soil, and annual flooding of the Nile banks.

Imperial decline facilitated conquest by Asian invaders (Hyksos, Assyrians). The last native dynasty fell in 341 BC to the Persians, who were in turn replaced by Greeks (Alexander and the Ptolemies), Romans, Byzantines, and Arabs, who introduced Islam and the Arabic language. The ancient Egyptian language is preserved only in the liturgy of the Coptic Christians.

Egypt was ruled as part of larger Islamic empires for several centuries. The Mamluks, a military caste of Caucasian origin, ruled Egypt from 1250 until defeat by the Ottoman Turks in 1517. Under Turkish sultans the khedive was hereditary viceroy had wide authority. Britain intervened in 1882 and took control of administration, though nominal allegiance to the Ottoman Empire continued until 1914.

The country was a British protectorate from 1914 to 1922. A 1936 treaty strengthened Egyptian autonomy, but Britain retained bases in Egypt and a condominium over the Sudan. Britain fought German and Italian armies from Egypt, 1940-42, but Egypt did not declare war against Germany until 1945. In 1951 Egypt abrogated the 1936 treaty. The Sudan became independent in 1956.

The uprising of July 23, 1952, led by the Society of Free Officers, named Maj. Gen. Mohammed Naguib commander-in-chief and forced King Farouk to abdicate. When the republic was proclaimed June 18, 1953, Naguib became its first president and premier. Lt. Col. Gamal Abdel Nasser removed Naguib and became premier in 1954. In 1956, he was voted president. Nasser died in 1970 and was replaced by Vice Pres. Anwar Sadat.

A series of decrees in July, 1961, nationalized about 90% of industry. Economic liberalization was begun, 1974, with more emphasis on private domestic and foreign investment.

The Aswan High Dam, completed 1971, provides irrigation for more than 400 000 ha of land. Artesian wells, drilled in the Western Desert, reclaimed 17 400 ha, 1960-66.

When the state of Israel was proclaimed in 1948, Egypt joined other Arab nations invading Israel and was defeated.

After terrorist raids across its border, Israel invaded Egypt's Sinai Peninsula, Oct. 29, 1956. Egypt rejected a cease-fire demand by Britain and France; on Oct. 31 the 2 nations dropped bombs and on Nov. 5-6 landed forces. Egypt and Israel accepted a UN cease-fire; fighting ended Nov. 7.

A UN Emergency Force guarded the 188 km long border between Egypt and Israel until May 19, 1967, when it was withdrawn at Nasser's demand. Egyptian troops entered the Gaza Strip and the heights of Sharm el Sheikh and 3 days later closed the Strait of Tiran to all Israeli shipping. Full-scale war broke out June 5 and before it ended under a UN cease-fire June 10, Israel had captured Gaza and the Sinai Peninsula, controlled the east bank of the Suez Canal and reopened the gulf.

Sporadic fighting with Israel broke out late in 1968 and continued almost daily, 1969-70. Military and economic aid was received from the USSR. Israel and Egypt agreed, Aug. 7, 1970, to a cease-fire and peace negotiations proposed by the U.S. Negotiations failed to achieve results, but the cease-fire continued.

In a surprise attack Oct. 6, 1973, Egyptian forces crossed the Suez Canal into the Sinai. (At the same time, Syrian forces attacked Israelis on the Golan Heights.) Egypt was supplied by a USSR military airlift; the U.S. responded with an airlift to Israel. Israel counter-attacked, crossed the canal, surrounded Suez City. A UN cease-fire took effect Oct. 24.

A disengagement agreement was signed Jan. 18, 1974. Under it, Israeli forces withdrew from the canal's W bank; limited numbers of Egyptian forces occupied a strip along the E bank. A second accord was signed in 1975, with Israel yielding Sinai oil fields. Pres. Sadat's surprise visit to Jerusalem, Nov. 1977, opened the prospect of peace with Israel, but worsened relations with Libya (border clashes, July 1977). On Mar. 26, 1979, Egypt and Israel signed a formal peace treaty, ending 30 years of war, and establishing diplomatic relations. Israel returned control of the Sinai to Egypt in April 1982.

Tension between Moslem fundamentalists and Christians in 1981 caused street riots and culminated in a nationwide security crackdown in Sept. Pres Sadat was assassinated on Oct. 6.

The **Suez Canal**, 166 km long, links the Mediterranean and Red seas. It was built by a French corporation 1859-69, but Britain obtained controlling interest in 1875. The last British troops were removed June 13, 1956. On July 26, Egypt nationalized the canal.

Egypt had barred Israeli ships and cargoes destined for Israel since 1948, and closed the canal to all shipping after the 1967 Arab-Israeli War. The canal was reopened in 1975.

El Salvador
Republic of El Salvador
República de El Salvador

People: Population (1989 est.): 5 548 000. **Age distrib.** (%): 0–14: 45.3; 15–59: 51; 60+: 4.7. **Pop. density:** 259.4 per sq. km. **Urban** (1986): 42%. **Ethnic groups:** Mestizo 89%, Indian 10%. **Languages:** Spanish, Nahuatl (among some Indians). **Religion:** Roman Catholicism prevails.

Geography: Area: 21 392 sq. km. **Location:** In Central America. **Neighbors:** Guatemala on W, Honduras on N. **Topography:** A hot Pacific coastal plain in the south rises to a cooler plateau and valley region, densely populated. The N is mountainous, including many volcanoes. **Capital:** San Salvador. **Cities** (1987 est.): San Salvador 1.4 mln.

Government: Type: Republic. **Head of state:** Pres., Rodolfo Castillo Claramount, act.; in office: May 30, 1988. **Local divisions:** 14 departments. **Defence:** 6.1% of GNP (1984).

Economy: Industries: Food and beverages, textiles, petroleum products. **Chief crops:** Coffee (21% of GNP), cotton, corn, sugar. **Other resources:** Rubber, forests. **Arable land:** 35%. **Meat prod.** (1984): cattle: 937 000; pigs: 379 000. **Electricity prod.** (1986): 1.7 bln. kwh. **Labor force:** 50% agric.; 22% ind.; 27% services.

Finance: Currency: Colon (Mar. 1988: 5.00 = $1 US). **Gross national product** (1986): $4.0 bln. **Per capita income** (1986):

$700. **Imports** (1986): $902 mln.; partners: U.S. 39%, CACM 22%. **Exports** (1986): $757 mln.; partners: U.S. 33%, CACM 23%. **National budget** (1986): $740 mln. expenditures. **International reserves less gold** (Mar. 1988): $195 mln. **Gold:** 469 000 oz t. **Consumer prices** (change in 1986): 31.9%.

Transport: Railway traffic (1984): 4.6 mln. passenger-km; 25 mln. net ton-km. **Motor vehicles:** in use (1984): 128 000 passenger cars, 19 000 comm. vehicles. **Chief ports:** La Union, Acajutla.

Communications: Television sets: 400 000 in use (1986). **Radios:** 1.2 mln. in use (1986). **Telephones in use** (1985): 123 000. **Daily newspaper circ.** (1982): 71 per 1 000 pop.

Health: Life expectancy at birth (1985): 62.6 male; 66.3 female. **Births** (per 1 000 pop. 1985): 34. **Deaths** (per 1 000 pop. 1985): 10. **Natural increase** (1985): 2.4%. **Hospital beds** (1985): 6 525. **Physicians** (1985): 1 592. **Infant mortality** (per 1 000 live births 1985): 71.

Education (1987): **Literacy:** 62% (urban areas); 40% (rural areas). Years compulsory 6; attendance 82%.

Major International Organizations: UN (IMF, WHO, ILO), OAS, CACM.

Canadian Embassy: c/o Apartado Postal 10303, San José, Costa Rica.

El Salvador became independent of Spain in 1821, and of the Central American Federation in 1839.

A fight with Honduras in 1969 over the presence of 300 000 Salvadorean workers left 2 000 dead. Clashes were renewed 1970 and 1974.

A military coup overthrew the Romero government, 1979, but the ruling military-civilian junta failed to quell the civil war which has resulted in some 50 000 deaths. Some 10 000 leftists insurgents, armed by Cuba and Nicaragua, control about 25% of the country, mostly in the east. Extreme right-wing death squads organized to eliminate suspected leftists were blamed for over 1 000 deaths in 1983. The U.S. has staunchly supported the government with military aid.

Voters turned out in large numbers in the May 1984 presidential election. Christian Democrat Jose Napoleon Duarte, a moderate, was victorious with 54% of the vote. Duarte was diagnosed as having terminal cancer iin 1988.

Leftist guerrillas have continued their offensive in 1988 as the civil war entered its 8th year.

Equatorial Guinea
Republic of Equatorial Guinea
República de Guinea Ecuatorial

People: Population (1989 est.): 389 000. **Age distrib.** (%): 0–14: 38.1; 15–59: 55.2; 60+: 6.7. **Pop. density:** 13.9 per sq. km. **Ethnic groups:** Fangs 80%, Bubi 15%. **Languages:** Spanish (official), Fang, English. **Religions:** mostly Roman Catholic

Geography: Area: 28 053 sq. km. **Location:** Bioko Is. off W. Africa coast in Gulf of Guinea, and Rio Muni, mainland enclave. **Neighbors:** Gabon on S, Cameroon on E, N. **Topography:** Bioko Is. consists of 2 volcanic mountains and a connecting valley. Rio Muni, with over 90% of the area, has a coastal plain and low hills beyond. **Capital:** Malabo. **Cities** (1986 est.): Malabo 34 980.

Government: Type: Republic. **Head of state:** Pres., Supreme Military Council Teodoro Obiang Nguema Mbasogo; b. June 5, 1942; in office: Oct. 10, 1979. **Local divisions:** 6 provinces.

Economy: Chief crops: Cocoa, coffee, bananas, sweet potatoes. **Other resources:** Timber. **Arable land:** 8%. **Electricity prod.** (1985): 15 mln. kwh. **Labor force:** 50% agric.; 40% public sector.

Finance: Currency: Bipkwela (Mar. 1988: 281 = $1 US). **Gross national product** (1985): $95 mln. **Per capita income** (1985): $250. **Imports** (1985): $41 mln.; partners: Spain 54%, China 17%. **Exports** (1985): $24 mln.; partners: Sp. 40%, Neth. 28%, W. Ger. 23%.

Transport: Chief ports: Malabo, Bata.

Communications: Radios: 90 000 in use (1984).

Health: Life expectancy at birth (1984): 44.4 male; 47.6 female. **Births** (per 1 000 pop. 1985): 42.2. **Deaths** (per 1 000

pop. 1985): 17.6. **Natural increase** (1985): 2.4% **Hospital beds** (1982): 3 200. **Infant mortality** (per 1 000 live births 1986): 142.

Education (1986): **Literacy:** 55%. About 65% attend primary school.

Major International Organizations: UN (IMF, World Bank), OAU.

Canadian Embassy: c/o The Canadian Embassy, P.O. Box 4037, Libreville, Gabon.

Fernando Po (now Bioko) Island was discovered by Portugal in the late 15th century and ceded to Spain in 1778. Independence came Oct. 12, 1968. Riots occurred in 1969 over disputes between the island and the more backward Rio Muni province on the mainland. Masie Nguema Biyogo, himself from the mainland, became president for life in 1972.

Masie's 11-year reign was one of the most brutal in Africa, resulting in a bankrupted nation. Most of the nation's 7 000 Europeans emigrated. In 1976, 45 000 Nigerian workers were evacuated amid charges of a reign of terror. Masie was ousted in a military coup, Aug., 1979.

The nation is heavily dependent on external aid.

Ethiopia

People's Democratic Republic of Ethiopia

Ye Etiyop'iya Hezbawi Dimokrasiyawi Republek

People: Population (1989 est.): 47 709 000. **Age distrib. (%):** 0–14: 46.5; 15–59: 47.3; 60+: 6.6. **Pop. density:** 39.0 per sq. km. **Urban** (1987): 11%. **Ethnic groups:** Oromo 40%, Amhara 25%, Tigre 12%, Sidama 9%. **Languages:** Amharic (official), Tigre (Semitic languages); Galla (Hamitic), Arabic, others. **Religions:** Orthodox Christian 40%, Moslem 40%.

Geography: Area: 1 221 805 sq. km. **Location:** In E. Africa. **Neighbors:** Sudan on W, Kenya on S. Somalia, Djibouti on E. **Topography:** A high central plateau, between 1 800 and 3 000 m high, rises to higher mountains near the Great Rift Valley, cutting in from the SW. The Blue Nile and other rivers cross the plateau, which descends to plains on both W and SE. **Capital:** Addis Ababa. **Cities** (1984 est.): Addis Ababa 1 412 000.

Government: Type: Unitary single-party people's republic. **Head of state:** Mengistu Haile Mariam; b. 1937; in office: Feb. 11, 1977. **Head of gov't:** Prime Min. Fikre Selassie Wogderess. **Local divisions:** 14 provinces. **Defence:** 9.8% of gov't budget (1986).

Economy: Industries: Food processing, cement, textiles. **Chief crops:** Coffee (61% export earnings), grains. **Minerals:** Platinum, gold, copper, potash. **Arable land:** 13%. **Livestock** (1985): cattle: 26.3 mln; sheep: 23.5 mln. **Electricity prod.** (1986): 722 mln. kwh. **Labor force:** 86% agric.

Finance: Currency: Birr (Mar. 1988: 2.07 = $1 US). **Gross national product** (1985): $4.6 bln. **Per capita income** (1984): $141. **Imports** (1985): $993 mln.; partners: USSR 22%, U.S. 15%, Italy 10%, Jap. 6%, W.Ger. 10%. **Exports** (1985): $333 mln.; partners: U.S. 20%, W. Ger. 18%, Italy 7%. **National budget** (1984): $1.7 bln. revenues; $1.8 bln. expenditures. **International reserves less gold** (Mar. 1988): $128 mln. **Gold:** 209 000 oz t. **Consumer prices** (change in 1987): −2.4%.

Transport: Railway traffic: 350 mln. passenger-km; 125 mln. net ton-km. **Motor vehicles:** in use (1985): 41 300 passenger cars, 19 000 comm. vehicles. **Civil aviation** (1983): 762 mln. passenger-km; 27.1 mln. net ton-km. **Chief ports:** Masewa, Aseb.

Communications: Television sets: 40 000 in use (1986). **Radios:** 2 mln. in use (1986). **Telephones in use** (1985): 122 000. **Daily newspaper circ.** (1986): 1 per 1 000 pop.

Health: Life expectancy at birth (1985): 41.3 male; 44.5 female. **Births** (per 1 000 pop. 1985): 49.2. **Deaths** (per 1 000 pop. 1985): 21.5. **Natural increase** (1985): 4.7%. **Hospital beds** (1984): 11 307. **Physicians** (1984): 539. **Infant mortality** (per 1 000 live births 1985): 168.

Education (1985): **Literacy:** 18%.

Major International Organizations: UN (IMF, WHO), OAU.

Canadian Embassy: African Solidarity Insurance Bldg., 6th fl., Churchill Ave., postal: P.O. Box 1130, Addis Ababa; Tel: 15 11 00, 15 12 28, 15 13 19, 15 92 00.

Ethiopian culture was influenced by Egypt and Greece. The ancient monarchy was invaded by Italy in 1880, but maintained its independence until another Italian invasion in 1936. British forces freed the country in 1941.

The last emperor, Haile Selassie I, established a parliament and judiciary system in 1931, but barred all political parties.

A series of droughts since 1972 have killed hundreds of thousands. An army mutiny, strikes, and student demonstrations led to the dethronement of Selassie in 1974. The ruling junta pledged to form a one-party socialist state, and instituted a successful land reform; opposition was violently suppressed. The influence of the Coptic Church, embraced in 330 AD, was curbed, and the monarchy was abolished in 1975.

The regime, torn by bloody coups, faced uprisings by tribal and political groups in part aided by Sudan and Somalia. Ties with the U.S., once a major arms and aid source, deteriorated, while cooperation accords were signed with the USSR in 1977. In 1978, Soviet advisors and Cuban troops helped defeat Somalia forces. Ethiopia and Somalia signed a peace agreement in 1988.

A world-wide relief effort began in 1984, as an extended drought caused millions to face starvation and death. Victories by Eriterean guerrillas forced the government to curtail the work of foreign aid workers in drought-stricken regions. Foreign relief officials expressed the fear that suspension of their work would lead to the death of hundreds of thousands.

Fiji

Dominion of Fiji

People: Population (1989 est.): 758 000. **Age distrib. (%):** 0–14: 38.2; 15–59: 56.9; 60+: 4.9. **Pop. density:** 41.5 sq. km. **Urban** (1986): 39%. **Ethnic groups:** Indian 50%, Fijian (Melanesian-Polynesian) 45%, Europeans 2%. **Languages:** English (official), Fijian, Hindustani. **Religions:** Christian 49%, Hindu 40%.

Geography: Area: 18 274 sq. km. **Location:** In western S. Pacific O. **Neighbors:** Nearest are Solomons on NW, Tonga on E. **Topography:** 322 islands (106 inhabited), many mountainous, with tropical forests and large fertile areas. Viti Levu, the largest island, has over half the total land area. **Capital:** Suva. **Cities** (1986 est.): Suva 69 000.

Government: Type: Republic. **Head of state:** Queen Elizabeth II, represented by Pres. Penaia Ganilau; in office: Dec. 5, 1987. **Head of government:** Prime Min. Kamisese Mara; b. May 13, 1920; in office: Oct. 10, 1970. **Local divisions:** 4 divisions.

Economy: Industries: Sugar refining, light industry, tourism. **Chief crops:** Sugar, bananas, ginger. **Minerals:** Gold. **Other resources:** Timber. **Arable land:** 12%. **Electricity prod.** (1986): 402 mln. kwh. **Labor force:** 44% agric.

Finance: Currency: Dollar (Mar. 1988: 1.00 = $.69 US). **Gross national product** (1986): $1.0 bln. **Per capita income** (1984): $1 086. **Imports** (1985): $447 mln.; partners: Austral. 34%, Jap. 16%, N.Z. 16%. **Exports** (1985): $240 mln.; partners: UK 42%, Aust. 18%. **Tourists** (1986): 235 000; receipts $163 mln. **National budget** (1986): $402 mln. expenditures. **International reserves less gold** (Mar. 1988): $167 mln. **Gold:** 11 000 oz t. **Consumer prices** (change in 1986): 2.0%.

Transport: Motor vehicles: in use (1986): 32 000 passenger cars, 22 000 comm. vehicles. **Civil aviation** (1986): 509 mln. passenger-km; 6.4 mln. net ton-km. **Chief ports:** Suva, Lautoka.

Communications: Radios: 400 000 in use (1985). **Telephones in use** (1983): 46 252. **Daily newspaper circ.** (1985): 76 per 1 000 pop.

Health: Life expectancy at birth (1986): 67.8 male; 72.1 female. **Births** (per 1 000 pop. 1985): 31. **Deaths** (per 1 000 pop. 1985): 7. **Natural increase** (1985): 2.4%. **Hospital beds** (1986): 1 736. **Physicians** (1986): 385. **Infant mortality** (per 1 000 live births 1985): 29.

Education (1985): **Literacy:** 80%. 95% attend school.

Major International Organizations: UN (IMF, WHO), Commonwealth of Nations.

Canadian High Commission: c/o P.O. Box 12-049, Wellington North, New Zealand.

A British colony since 1874, Fiji became an independent parliamentary democracy Oct. 10, 1970.

Cultural differences between the majority Indian community, descendants of contract laborers brought to the islands in the 19th century, and the less modernized native Fijians, who by law own 83% of the land in communal villages, have led to political polarization.

The discovery of copper on Viti Levu along with increased sugar production bodes well for the economy.

In 1987, a military coup ousted the government; order was restored May 21 when a compromise was reached. However, in Oct., Lt. Col. Sitiveni Rabuka, the coup's leader, once again took power, proclaimed a Republic and denounced Queen Elizabeth II as head of state.

declared its independence and in 1919 became a republic. On Nov. 30, 1939, the Soviet Union invaded, and the Finns were forced to cede 42 050 sq. km, including the Karelian Isthmus, Viipuri, and an area on Lake Ladoga. After World War II, in which Finland tried to recover its lost territory, further cessions were exacted. In 1948, Finland signed a treaty of mutual assistance with the USSR. In 1956 Russia returned Porkkala, which had been ceded as a military base.

Finland is an integral member of the Nordic group of five countries and maintains good relations with the Soviet Union.

Aland, constituting an autonomous department, is a group of small islands, 1 487 sq. km, in the Gulf of Bothnia, 40 km from Sweden, 24 km from Finland. Mariehamn is the principal port.

Finland
Republic of Finland
Suomen Tasavalta

People: Population (1989 est.): 4 990 000. **Age distrib. (%):** 0–14: 19.5; 15–59: 63.2; 60+: 17.3. **Pop. density:** 14.8 per sq. km. **Urban** (1986): 61%. **Ethnic groups:** Finns 94%, Swedes, Lapps. **Languages:** Finnish 94%, Swedish 6% (both official). **Religion:** Lutheran 90%.

Geography: Area: 336 982 sq. km. **Location:** In northern Europe. **Neighbors:** Norway on N, Sweden on W, USSR on E. **Topography:** South and central Finland are mostly flat areas with low hills and many lakes. The N has mountainous areas, 900-1 200 m. **Capital:** Helsinki. **Cities** (1987 est.). Helsinki 487 000; Tampere 170 000; Turku 160 000.

Government: Type: Constitutional republic. **Head of state:** Pres. Mauno Koivisto; b. Nov. 25, 1923; in office: Jan. 27, 1982. **Head of government:** Prime Min. Harri Holkeri; b. Jan. 6, 1937; in office: Apr. 30, 1987. **Local divisions:** 12 laanit (provinces). **Defence:** 1.5% of GNP (1985).

Economy: Industries: Machinery, metal, shipbuilding, textiles, clothing. **Chief crops:** Grains, potatoes, dairy prods. **Minerals:** Copper, iron, zinc. **Other resources:** Forests (40% of exports). **Arable land:** 8%. **Livestock** (1980): cattle: 1.5 mln.; pigs: 1.3 mln. **Fish catch** (1985): 160 000 metric tons. **Electricity prod.** (1986): 45.5 bln. kwh. **Crude steel prod.** (1986): 2.5 min. metric tons. **Labor force:** 11% agric.; 46% ind. & comm.; 28% services.

Finance: Currency: Markka (June 1988: 4.08 = $1 US). **Gross national product** (1985): $54.0 bln. **Per capita income** (1985): $11 007. **Imports** (1987): $19.8 bln.; partners: USSR 21%, Swed. 12%, W. Ger. 14%, UK 7%. **Exports** (1986): $16.3 bln.; partners: USSR 21%, Swed. 13%, UK 11%, W. Ger. 9%. **Tourists** (1985): $501 mln. receipts. **National budget** (1985): $18.6 bln. expenditures. **International reserves less gold** (Mar. 1988): $6.6 bln. **Gold** 1.9 mln. oz t. **Consumer prices** (change in 1987): 3.7%.

Transport: Railway traffic (1986): 2.6 bln. passenger-km; 6.9 bln. net ton-km. **Motor vehicles:** in use (1985): 1.5 mln. passenger cars, 188 000 comm. vehicles; **Civil aviation** (1986): 2.9 bln. passenger-km; 92 mln. freight ton-km. **Chief ports:** Helsinki, Turku.

Communications: Television sets: 1.7 mln. licensed (1986). **Radios:** 2.5 mln. in use (1986). **Telephones** in use (1986): 3.0 mln. **Daily newspaper circ.** (1986): 543 per 1 000 pop.

Health: Life expectancy at birth (1986): 70.4 male; 78.8 female. **Births** (per 1 000 pop. 1985): 12.7. **Deaths** (per 1 000 pop. 1985): 9.5. **Natural increase** (1985): 0.3%. **Hospital beds** (1985): 61 082. **Physicians** (1986): 10 193. **Infant mortality** (per 1 000 live births 1985): 6.0.

Education (1986): **Literacy:** 99%. Years compulsory 9; attendance 99%.

Major International Organizations: UN (IMF, GATT), EFTA, OECD.

Canadian Embassy: P. Esplanadi 25B, 00100 Helsinki 10; P.O. Box 779, 00101 Helsinki 10; Tel: 17-11-41.

The early Finns probably migrated from the Ural area at about the beginning of the Christian era. Swedish settlers brought the country into Sweden, 1154 to 1809, when Finland became an autonomous grand duchy of the Russian Empire. Russian exactions created a strong national spirit; on Dec. 6, 1917, Finland

France
French Republic
République Francaise

People: Population (1989 est.): 55 813 000. **Age distrib. (%):** 0–14: 21.1; 15–60: 60.6; 60+: 18.3. **Pop. density:** 97.7 per sq km. **Urban** (1985): 77.2%. **Ethnic groups:** A mixture of various European and Mediterranean groups. **Languages:** French; minorities speak Breton, Alsatian German, Flemish, Italian, Basque, Catalan. **Religion:** Mostly Roman Catholic.

Geography: Area: 571 486 sq. km. **Location:** In western Europe, between Atlantic O. and Mediterranean Sea. **Neighbors:** Spain on S, Italy, Switzerland, W. Germany on E, Luxembourg, Belgium on N. **Topography:** A wide plain covers more than half of the country, in N and W, drained to W by Seine, Loire, Garonne rivers. The Massif Central is a mountainous plateau in centre. In E are Alps (Mt. Blanc is tallest in W. Europe, 4 807 m), the lower Jura range, and the forested Vosges. The Rhone flows from Lake Geneva to Mediterranean. Pyrenees are in SW, on border with Spain. **Capital:** Paris. **Cities** (1982 cen.): Paris 2 188 918; Marseille 878 689; Lyon 418 476; Toulouse 354 289; Nice 338 486; Nantes 247 227; Strasbourg 252 264; Bordeaux 211 197.

Government: Type: Republic. **Head of state:** Pres. François Mitterrand; b. Oct. 26, 1916; in office: May 21, 1981. **Head of government:** Prime Min. Michel Rocard; b. Aug. 23, 1930; in office: Mar. 10, 1988. **Local divisions:** 22 administrative regions containing 95 departments. **Defence:** 19% of govt. budget. (1987).

Economy: Industries: Steel, chemicals, autos, textiles, wine, perfume, aircraft, electronic equipment. **Chief crops:** Grains, corn, rice, fruits, vegetables. France is largest food producer, exporter, in W. Eur. Wheat. **Minerals:** Bauxite, iron, coal. **Crude oil reserves** (1985): 221 mln. bbls. **Other resources:** Forests. **Arable land:** 34%. **Livestock:** (1985): cattle: 22.8 mln.; pigs: 10.9 mln.; sheep: 10.7 mln. **Fish catch** (1985): 738 000 metric tons. **Electricity prod.** (1985): 326 bln. kwh. **Crude steel prod.** (1986): 17.9 mln. metric tons. **Labor force:** 9% agric.; 45% ind. & comm.; 46% services.

Finance: Currency: Franc (June 1988: 5.82 = $1 US). **Gross national product** (1986): $724 bln. **Per capita income** (1986): $13 046. **Imports** (1987): $158 bln.; partners: EC 51%. **Exports** (1987): $148 bln.; partners: EC 50%, U.S. 9%. **Tourists** (1985) receipts: $7.9 bln. **National budget** (1987): $164 bln. expenditures. **International reserves less gold** (Feb. 1988): $31.1 bln. **Gold:** 81.85 mln. oz t. **Consumer prices** (change in 1987): 3.3%.

Transport: Railway traffic (1985): 60.7 bln. passenger-km; 58.4 bln. net ton-km. **Motor vehicles:** in use (1985): 20.8 mln. passenger cars, 3.3 mln. comm. vehicles; manuf. (1982): 3 mln. passenger cars; 466 000 comm. vehicles. **Civil aviation** (1984): 38.4 bln. passenger-km; 2.8 bln. net ton-km. **Chief ports:** Marseille, LeHavre, Nantes, Bordeaux, Rouen.

Communications: Television sets: 17.9 mln. in use (1986). **Radios:** 20 mln. in use (1983). **Telephones** in use (1985): 34 mln. **Daily newspaper circ.** (1985): 244 per 1 000 pop.

Health: Life expectancy at birth (1984): 70.9 male; 79.0 female. **Births** (per 1 000 pop. 1986): 14.1.-5bf Deaths (per 1 000 pop. 1986): 9.9. **Natural increase** (1986): 0.4%. **Hospital beds** (1983): 496 896. **Physicians** (1983): 114 000. **Infant mortality** (per 1 000 live births 1986): 8.2.

Education (1987): Literacy: 99%. Years compulsory 10; 17.7% of natl. budget.

Major International Organizations: UN and most of its specialized agencies, OECD, EC, NATO.

Canadian Embassy: 35 av. Montaigne, 75008 Paris VIIIᵉ; Tel: 4723-01-01.

Celtic Gaul was conquered by Julius Caesar 58-51 BC; Romans ruled for 500 years. Under Charlemagne, Frankish rule extended over much of Europe. After his death France emerged as one of the successor kingdoms.

The monarchy was overthrown by the French Revolution (1789-93) and succeeded by the First Republic; followed by the First Empire under Napoleon (1804-15), a monarchy (1814-48), the Second Republic (1848-52), the Second Empire (1852-70), the Third Republic (1871-1946), the Fourth Republic (1946-58), and the Fifth Republic (1958 to present).

France suffered severe losses in human resources and wealth in the first World War, 1914-18, when it was invaded by Germany. By the Treaty of Versailles, France exacted return of Alsace and Lorraine, French provinces seized by Germany in 1871. Germany invaded France again in May, 1940, and signed an armistice with a government based in Vichy. After France was liberated by the Allies Sept. 1944, Gen. Charles de Gaulle became head of the provisional government, serving until 1946.

De Gaulle again became premier in 1958, during a crisis over Algeria, and obtained voter approval for a new constitution, ushering in the Fifth Republic. Using strong executive powers, he promoted French economic and technological advances in the context of the European Economic Community, and guarded French foreign policy independence.

France had withdrawn from Indochina in 1954, and from Morocco and Tunisia in 1956. Most of its remaining African territories were freed 1958-62, but France retained strong economic and political ties.

In 1966, France withdrew all its troops from the integrated military command of NATO, though 60 000 remained stationed in Germany. France continued to attend political meetings of NATO.

In May 1968 rebellious students in Paris and other centres rioted, battled police, and were joined by workers who launched nationwide strikes. The government awarded pay increases to the strikers May 26. In elections to the Assembly in June, de Gaulle's backers won a landslide victory. Nevertheless, he resigned from office in Apr., 1969, after losing a nationwide referendum on constitutional reform. De Gaulle's policies were largely continued after his death in 1970.

On May 10, 1981, France elected François Mitterrand, a Socialist candidate, president in a stunning victory over Valéry Giscard d'Estaing. In September, the government nationalized 5 major industries and most private banks. In 1986, France began a privatization program in which some 80 state-owned companies would be sold. Mitterrand was elected to a 2d 7-year term in 1988.

France supported Chad in its war with Libya. On Oct. 23, 58 members of the French peacekeeping force in Lebanon were killed in a suicide terrorist attack.

Agents of France's external security service were responsible for the July 10, 1985 sinking of the *Rainbow Warrior*, flagship of the Greenpeace environmental movement, in the port of Auckland, New Zealand.

The island of **Corsica,** in the Mediterranean W of Italy and N of Sardinia, is an official region of France comprising 2 departments. Area: 8 759 sq. km; pop. (1975 cen.): 289 842. The capital is Ajaccio, birthplace of Napoleon.

Overseas Departments

French Guiana is on the NE coast of South America with Suriname on the W and Brazil on the E and S. Its area is 83 355 sq. km; pop. (1987): 92 038. Guiana sends one senator and one deputy to the French Parliament. Guiana is administered by a prefect and has a Council General of 16 elected members; capital is Cayenne.

The famous penal colony, Devil's Island, was phased out between 1938 and 1951.

Immense forests of rich timber cover 90% of the land. Placer gold mining is the most important industry. Exports are shrimp, timber, and machinery.

Guadeloupe, in the West Indies' Leeward Islands, consists of 2 large islands, Basse-Terre and Grande-Terre, separated by

the Salt River, plus Marie Galante and the Saintes group to the S and, to the N, Desirade, St. Barthelemy, and over half of St. Martin (the Netherlands portion is St. Maarten). A French possession since 1635, the department is represented in the French Parliament by 2 senators and 3 deputies; administration consists of a prefect (governor) and an elected General Council.

Area of the islands is 1 786 sq. km; pop. (1987 est.) 335 000, mainly descendants of slaves; capital is Basse-Terre on Basse-Terre Is. The land is fertile; sugar, rum, and bananas are exported; tourism is an important industry.

Martinique, one of the Windward Islands, in the West Indies, has been a possession since 1635, and a department since March, 1946. It is represented in the French Parliament by 2 senators and 3 deputies. The island was the birthplace of Napoleon's Empress Josephine.

It has an area of 1 105 sq. km; pop. (1987 est.) 329 000, mostly descendants of slaves. The capital is Fort-de-France. It is a popular tourist stop. The chief exports are rum, bananas, and petroleum products.

Mayotte, formerly part of Comoros, voted in 1976 to become an overseas department of France. An island NW of Madagascar, area is 374.4 sq. km, pop. (1987 est.) 73 000.

Reunion is a volcanic island in the Indian O. about 675 km E of Madagascar, and has belonged to France since 1665. Area, 2 519 sq. km; pop. (1987 est.) 565 000, 30% of French extraction. Capital: Saint-Denis. The chief export is sugar. It elects 3 deputies, 2 senators to the French Parliament.

St. Pierre and Miquelon, formerly an Overseas Territory, made the transition to department status in 1976. It consists of 2 groups of rocky islands near the SW coast of Newfoundland, inhabited by fishermen. The exports are chiefly fish products. The St. Pierre group has an area of 26 sq. km; Miquelon, 216 sq. km. Total pop. (1982 cen.), 6 041. The capital is St. Pierre. A deputy and a senator are elected to the French Parliament.

Overseas Territories

French Polynesia Overseas Territory, comprises 130 islands widely scattered among 5 archipelagos in the South Pacific; administered by a governor. Territorial Assembly and a Council with headquarters at Papeete, Tahiti, one of the Society Islands (which include the **Windward** and **Leeward** islands). A deputy and a senator are elected to the French Parliament.

Other groups are the **Marquesas Islands,** the **Tuamotu Archipelago,** including the **Gambier Islands,** and the **Austral Islands.**

Total area of the islands administered from Tahiti is 4 014 sq. km; pop. (1987 est.), 185 000, more than half on Tahiti. Tahiti is picturesque and mountainous with a productive coastline bearing coconut, banana and orange trees, sugar cane and vanilla.

Tahiti was visited by Capt. James Cook in 1769 and by Capt. Bligh in the Bounty, 1788-89. Its beauty impressed Herman Melville, Paul Gauguin, and Charles Darwin.

French Southern and Antarctic Lands Overseas Territory, comprises **Adelie Land,** on Antarctica, and 4 island groups in the Indian O. Adelie, discovered 1840, has a research station, a coastline of 296 km and tapers 1 984 km inland to the South Pole. There are 2 huge glaciers, Ninnis, 35 km wide, 158 km long, and Mentz, 18 km wide, 225 km long. The Indian O. groups are:

Kerguelen Archipelago, discovered 1772, one large and 300 small islands. The chief is 139 km long, 118 km wide, and has Mt. Ross, 1 960 m tall. Principal research station is Port-aux-Français. Seals often weigh about 2 tonnes; there are blue whales, coal, peat, semi-precious stones. **Crozet Archipelago,** discovered 1772, covers 507 sq. km. Eastern Island rises to 2 000 m. **Saint Paul,** in southern Indian O., has warm springs with earth at places heating to 50° to 200° C. **Amsterdam** is nearby; both produce cod and rock lobster.

New Caledonia and its dependencies, an Overseas Territory, are a group of islands in the Pacific O. about 1 784 km E of Australia and approx. the same distance NW of New Zealand. Dependencies are the **Loyalty Islands,** the **Isle of Pines, Huon Islands** and the **Chesterfield Islands.**

New Caledonia, the largest, has 16 978 sq. km. Total area of the territory is 22 225 sq. km; population (1987 est.) 152 000. The group was acquired by France in 1853.

The territory is administered by a governor and government council. There is a popularly elected Territorial Assembly. A deputy and a senator are elected to the French Parliament. Capital: Noumea.

Mining is the chief industry. New Caledonia is one of the world's largest nickel producers. Other minerals found are chrome, iron, cobalt, manganese, silver, gold, lead, and copper. Agricultural products include coffee, copra, cotton, manioc (cassava), corn, tobacco, bananas and pineapples.

In 1987, New Caledonian voters chose by a referendum to remain within the French republic. There were clashes between French and Melanesians (Kanaks) in 1988.

Wallis and Futuna Islands, 2 archipelagos raised to status of Overseas Territory July 29, 1961, are in the SW Pacific S of the Equator between Fiji and Samoa. The islands have a total area of 276 sq. km and population (1982 cen.) of 11 943. **Alofi,** attached to Futuna, is uninhabited. Capital: Mata-Utu. Chief products are copra, yams, taro roots, bananas. A senator and a deputy are elected to the French Parliament.

Gabon
Gabonese Republic
République Gabonaise

People: Population (1989 est.): 1 110 000. **Pop. density:** 4.1 per sq. km. **Urban** (1985): 40%. **Ethnic groups:** Fangs 25%, Bapounon 10%, others. **Languages:** French (official), Bantu dialects. **Religions:** Tribal beliefs, Christian minority.

Geography: Area: 267 645 sq. km. **Location:** On Atlantic coast of central Africa. **Neighbors:** Equatorial Guinea, Cameroon on N, Congo on E, S. **Topography:** Heavily forested, the country consists of coastal lowlands plateaus in N, E, and S, mountains in N, SE, and centre. The Ogooue R. system covers most of Gabon. **Capital:** Libreville. **Cities** (1985 est.): Libreville 235 000.

Government: Type: Republic. **Head of state:** Pres. Omar Bongo; b. Dec. 30, 1935; in office: Dec. 2, 1967. **Head of government:** Prime Min. Leon Mebiame, b. Sept. 1, 1934; in office: Apr. 16, 1975. **Local divisions:** 9 provinces, 37 prefectures. **Defence:** 2.1% of GNP (1984).

Economy: Industries: Oil products. **Chief crops:** Cocoa, coffee, rice, peanuts, palm products, cassava, bananas. **Minerals:** Manganese, uranium, oil, iron, gas. **Crude oil reserves** (1985): 623 mln. bbls. **Other resources:** Timber. **Arable land:** 2%. **Electricity prod.** (1986): 981 mln. kwh. **Labor force:** 65% agric.; 30% ind. & comm.

Finance: Currency: CFA franc (Mar. 1988: 281 = $1 US). **Gross national product** (1985) $3.3 bln. **Per capita income** (1983): $2 613. **Imports** (1986): $951 mln.; partners: Fr. 51%, U.S. 14%. **Exports** (1986): $1.9 bln.; partners: Fr. 26%, U.S. 25%. **Tourists receipts** (1984): $4 mln. **National budget** (1984): $1.3 bln. **International reserves less gold** (Jan. 1988): $120 mln. **Gold:** 13 000 oz t. **Consumer prices** (change in 1986): 6.3%.

Transport: Motor vehicles: in use (1983): 16 000 passenger cars, 10 000 comm. vehicles. **Civil aviation** (1983): 430 mln. passenger-km. **Chief ports** Port-Gentil, Owendo, Mayumba.

Communications: Television sets: 21 000 licensed (1985). **Radios:** 100 000 licensed (1985). **Telephones in use** (1984): 11 600.

Health: Life expectancy at birth (1985): 48.0 male; 51.4 female. **Births** (per 1 000 pop. 1985): 33.7. **Deaths** (per 1 000 pop. 1985): 19.9. **Natural increase** (1985): 1.3%. **Hospital beds** (1985): 4 617. **Physicians** (1985): 265. **Infant mortality** (per 1 000 live births 1985): 162.

Education (1985): **Literacy:** 65%. Compulsory to age 16; attendance: 84% primary, 14% secondary.

Major International Organizations: UN (World Bank), OAU, OPEC.

Canadian Embassy: P.O. Box 4037 Libreville; Tel: 72.41.54, .56, .69.

France established control over the region in the second half of the 19th century. Gabon became independent Aug. 17, 1960. It is one of the most prosperous black African countries, thanks to abundant natural resources, foreign private investment, and government development programs.

The Gambia
Republic of The Gambia

People: Population (1989 est.): 840 000. **Age distrib. (%):** 0–14: 45.9; 15–59: 54.4; 60+: 3.8. **Pop. density:** 74.4 per sq. km. **Urban** (1985): 21%. **Ethnic groups:** Mandinka 42%, Fula 16%, Wolof 16%, others. **Languages:** English (official), Mandinka, Wolof. **Religion:** Moslem 90%.

Geography: Area: 11 294 sq. km. **Location:** On Atlantic coast near western tip of Africa. **Neighbors:** Surrounded on 3 sides by Senegal. **Topography:** A narrow strip of land on each side of the lower Gambia. **Capital:** Banjul. **Cities** (1986 est.): Banjul 40 000.

Government: Type: Republic. **Head of state:** Pres. Dawda Kairaba Jawara; b. May 16, 1924; in office: Apr. 24, 1970 (prime min. from June 12, 1962). **Local divisions:** 5 divisions and Banjul.

Economy: Industries: Tourism. **Chief crops:** Peanuts (main export), rice. **Arable land:** 28%. **Fish catch** (1985): 11 000 metric tons. **Electricity prod.** (1986): 63 mln. kwh. **Labor force:** 75% agric.; 18% ind. & comm.

Finance: Currency: Dalasi (Mar. 1988: 1.00 = $1.50 US). **Gross national product** (1985): $179 mln. **Per capita income** (1985): $255. **Imports** (1985): $104 mln.; partners: UK 21%, China 11%. **Exports** (1985): $32 mln.; partners: EEC 40%. **Tourists** (1985): 65 000. **National budget** (1985): $57 mln. expenditures. **International reserves less gold** (Mar. 1988): $15.5 mln. **Consumer prices** (change in 1986): 56.6%.

Transport: Motor vehicles: in use (1986): 5 200 passenger cars, 720 comm. vehicles. **Chief ports:** Banjul.

Communications: Radios: 110 000 in use (1986). **Telephones in use** (1980): 3 500.

Health: Life expectancy at birth (1985): 40.9 male; 44.1 female. **Births** (per 1 000 pop. 1985): 47.5. **Deaths** (per 1 000 pop. 1985): 21.7. **Natural increase** (1985): 2.5%. **Hospital beds** (1980): 635. **Physicians** (1980): 65. **Infant mortality** (per 100 000 live births 1986): 217.

Education (1986): **Literacy:** 12%.

Major International Organizations: UN (GATT, IMF, WHO), OAU.

Canadian High Commission: c/o Box 3373, Dakar, Senegal.

The tribes of Gambia were at one time associated with the West African empires of Ghana, Mali, and Songhay. The area became Britain's first African possession in 1588.

Independence came Feb. 18, 1965; republic status within the Commonwealth was achieved in 1970. Gambia is one of the only functioning democracies in Africa. The country suffered from severe famine in 1977-78.

Gambia signed an agreement with Senegal Dec. 17, 1981 for confederation of the 2 countries under the name of Senegambia. The confederation began Feb. 1, 1982. The 2 nations retained their individual sovereignty but adopted joint defense and monetary policies.

Germany

Now comprises 2 nations: Federal Republic of Germany (West Germany), German Democratic Republic (East Germany).

Germany, prior to World War II, was a central European nation composed of numerous states which had a common language and traditions and which had been united in one country since 1871; since World War II it has been split in 2 parts.

History and government. Germanic tribes were defeated by Julius Caesar, 55 and 53 BC, but Roman expansion N of the Rhine was stopped in 9 AD. Charlemagne, ruler of the Franks, consolidated Saxon, Bavarian, Rhenish, Frankish, and other lands; after him the eastern part became the German Empire. The Thirty Years' War, 1618-1648, split Germany into small principalities and kingdoms. After Napoleon, Austria contended with Prussia for dominance, but lost the Seven Weeks' War to Prussia, 1866. Otto von Bismarck, Prussian chancellor, formed the North German Confederation, 1867.

In 1870 Bismarck maneuvered Napoleon III into declaring war. After the quick defeat of France, Bismarck formed the **German**

Empire and on Jan. 18, 1871, in Versailles, proclaimed King Wilhelm I of Prussia German emperor (Deutscher kaiser).

The German Empire reached its peak before World War I in 1914, with 540 700 sq. km, plus a colonial empire. After that war Germany ceded Alsace-Lorraine to France; West Prussia and Posen (Poznan) province to Poland; part of Schleswig to Denmark; lost all of its colonies and the ports of Memel and Danzig.

Republic of Germany, 1919-1933, adopted the Weimar constitution; met reparation payments and elected Friedrich Ebert and Gen. Paul von Hindenburg presidents.

Third Reich, 1933-1945, Adolf Hitler led the National Socialist German Workers' (Nazi) party after World War I. In 1923 he attempted to unseat the Bavarian government and was imprisoned. Pres. von Hindenburg named Hitler chancellor Jan. 30, 1933; on Aug. 3, 1934, the day after Hindenburg's death, the cabinet joined the offices of president and chancellor and made Hitler fuehrer (leader). Hitler abolished freedom of speech and assembly, and began a long series of persecutions climaxed by the murder of millions of Jews and opponents.

Hitler repudiated the Versailles treaty and reparations agreements. He remilitarized the Rhineland 1936 and annexed Austria (Anschluss, 1938). At Munich he made an agreement with Neville Chamberlain, British prime minister, which permitted Hitler to annex part of Czechoslovakia. He signed a non-aggression treaty with the USSR, 1939. He declared war on Poland Sept. 1, 1939, precipitating World War II.

With total defeat near, Hitler committed suicide in Berlin Apr. 1945. The victorious Allies voided all acts and annexations of Hitler's Reich.

Postwar changes. The zones of occupation administered by the Allied Powers and later relinquished gave the USSR Saxony, Saxony-Anhalt, Thuringia, and Mecklenburg, and the former Prussian provinces of Saxony and Brandenburg.

The territory E of the Oder-Neisse line within 1937 boundaries comprising the provinces of Silesia, Pomerania, and the southern part of East Prussia, totaling about 106 750 sq. km, was taken by Poland. Northern East Prussia was taken by the USSR.

The Western Allies ended the state of war with Germany in 1951. The USSR did so in 1955.

There was also created the area of Greater Berlin, within but not part of the Soviet zone, administered by the 4 occupying powers under the Allied Command. In 1948 the USSR withdrew, established its single command in East Berlin, and cut off supplies. The Allies utilized a gigantic airlift to bring food to West Berlin, 1948-1949. In Aug. 1961 the East Germans built a wall dividing Berlin, after over 3 million E. Germans had emigrated.

East Germany
German Democratic Republic
Deutsche Demokratische Republik

People: Population (1989 est.): 16 736 000. **Age distrib. (%):** 0–14: 19.2; 15–59: 61.5; 60+: 19.3. **Pop. density:** 154.7 per sq. km. **Urban** (1986): 76.6%. **Ethnic groups:** German 99%. **Language:** German. **Religion:** Protestant 47%, Roman Catholic 7%, none 45%.

Geography: Area: 108 171 sq. km. **Location:** In E. Central Europe. **Neighbors:** W. Germany on W, Czechoslovakia on S, Poland on E. **Topography:** E. Germany lies mostly on the North German plains, with lakes in N, Harz Mtns., Elbe Valley, and sandy soil of Bradenburg in centre, and highlands in S. **Capital:** East Berlin. **Cities** (1986 est.): East Berlin 1 200 000; Leipzig 553 000; Dresden 520 000.

Government: Type: Communist. **Head of state:** Chmn. Erich Honecker; b. Aug. 25, 1912; in office: Oct. 29, 1976. **Head of government:** Prime Min. Willi Stoph; b. July 9, 1914; in office: Oct. 29, 1976. **Head of Communist Party:** Sec.-Gen. Erich Honecker; in office: May 3, 1971. **Local divisions:** 14 districts. **Defence:** 7.7% of GNP (1984).

Economy: Industries: Steel, chemicals, electrical prods., textiles, machinery. **Chief crops:** Grains, potatoes, sugarbeets. **Minerals:** Potash, lignite, uranium, coal. **Arable land:** 47%. **Livestock** (1985): cattle: 5.8 mln.; pigs: 12.9 mln.; sheep: 2.5 mln. **Fish catch** (1985): 265 000 metric tons. **Electricity prod.** (1986): 118 bln. kwh. **Crude steel prod.** (1986): 7.9 mln metric tons. **Labor force:** 10% agric.; 42.5% ind. & construction.

Finance: Currency: Mark (Jan. 1988: 1.80 = $1 US). **Gross national product** (1984): $93 bln. (excl. service sector). **Per capita income** (1984): $10 000. **Imports:** (1985): $22.2 bln.; partners: USSR, E. Europe. **Exports** (1985): $23.9 bln.; partners: USSR, E. Europe. **Tourists** (1983): 933 000. **National budget** (1984): $78 bln.

Transport: Railway traffic (1985): 22.4 bln. passenger-km; 58 bln. net ton-km. **Motor vehicles:** in use (1985): 3.3 mln. passenger cars, 360 000 comm. vehicles. **Civil aviation** (1985): 2.5 bln. passenger-km; 71 mln. freight ton-km. **Chief ports:** Rostack, Wismar, Stralsund.

Communications: Television sets: 6.0 mln. licensed (1986). **Radios:** 6.6 mln. licensed (1986). **Telephones in use** (1986): 3.6 mln. **Daily newspaper circ.** (1986): 559 per 1 000 pop.

Health: Life expectancy at birth (1987): 68.8 male; 74.7 female. **Births** (per 1 000 pop. 1985): 14.0. **Deaths** (per 1 000 pop. 1985): 13.0. **Natural increase** (1985): 0.1%. **Hospital beds** (1986): 169 000. **Physicians** (1986): 37 000. **Infant mortality** (per 1 000 live births 1985): 13.1.

Education (1987): **Literacy:** 99%. **Years compulsory:** 10.

Major International Organizations: UN (IMF, GATT), Warsaw Pact.

Canadian Embassy: c/o Ulica Matejki 1/5, Warsaw 00-481, Poland.

The German Democratic Republic was proclaimed in the Soviet sector of Berlin Oct. 7, 1949. It was proclaimed fully sovereign in 1954, but Soviet troops remain on grounds of security and the 4-power Potsdam agreement.

Coincident with the entrance of W. Germany into the European Defence community in 1952, the East German government decreed a prohibited zone 4.8 km deep along its 966 km border with W. Germany and cut Berlin's telephone system in two. Berlin was further divided by erection of a fortified wall in 1961, but the exodus of refugees to the West continued, though on a smaller scale.

E. Germany suffered severe economic problems until the mid-1960s. A "new economic system" was introduced, easing the former central planning controls and allowing factories to make profits provided they were reinvested in operations or redistributed to workers as bonuses. By the early 1970s, the economy was highly industrialized. In May 1972 the few remaining private firms were ordered sold to the government. The nation was credited with the highest standard of living among Warsaw Pact countries. But growth slowed in the late 1970s, due to shortages of natural resources and labor, and a huge debt to lenders in the West.

West Germany
Federal Republic of Germany
Bundesrepublik Deutschland

People: Population (1989 est.): 60 162 000. **Age distrib. (%):** 0–14: 15.0; 15–59: 64.6; 60+: 20.3. **Pop. density:** 242.0 per sq. km. **Urban** (1985): 86%. **Ethnic groups:** German 93%. **Language:** German. **Religions:** Protestant 44%, Roman Catholic 45%.

Geography: Area: 248 556 sq. km. **Location:** In central Europe. **Neighbors:** Denmark on N, Netherlands, Belgium, Luxembourg, France on W, Switzerland, Austria on S, Czechoslovakia, E. Germany on E. **Topography:** West Germany is flat in N, hilly in centre and W, and mountainous in Bavaria. Chief rivers are Elbe, Weser, Ems, Rhine, and Main, all flowing toward North Sea, and Danube, flowing toward Black Sea. **Capital:** Bonn. **Cities** (1987 est.): Berlin 1.8 mln.; Hamburg 1.6 mln.; Munich 1.3 mln.; Cologne 919 000; Essen 622 000; Frankfurt 598 000; Dortmund 575 000; Dusseldorf 593 000; Stuttgart 561 000.

Government: Type: Federal republic. **Head of state:** Pres. Richard von Weizsacker; b. Apr. 15, 1920; in office: May 23, 1984. **Head of government:** Chan. Helmut Kohl; b. Apr. 3, 1930; in office: Oct. 1, 1982. **Local divisions:** West Berlin and 10 laender (states) with substantial powers. **Defence:** 5% of GNP (1985).

Economy: Industries: Steel, ships, autos, machinery, coal, chemicals. **Chief crops:** Grains, potatoes, sugar beets. **Minerals:** Coal, potash, lignite, iron. **Crude oil reserves** (1985): 289 mln. bbls. **Arable land:** 30%. **Livestock** (1985): cattle: 15.6 mln.; pigs: 24.3 mln.; sheep: 1.2 mln. **Fish catch** (1984):

305 000 metric tons. **Electricity prod.** (1984): 394 bln. kwh. **Crude steel prod.** (1986): 37.1 mln. metric tons. **Labor force:** 6% agric.; 42% ind. & comm.; 42% service.

Finance: Currency: Mark (June 1988: 1.72 = $1 US). **Gross national product** (1986): $898 bln. **Per capita income** (1986): $10 680. **Imports** (1987): $228 bln.; partners: Neth. 12%, Fr. 11%, It. 8%, Belg. 7%. **Exports** (1987): $294 bln.; partners: Fr. 14%, Neth. 8%, Belg. 7%, It. 8%. **Tourists** (1985): receipts $5.8 bln. **National budget** (1986): $151 bln. **International reserves less gold** (Mar. 1988): $73 bln. **Gold:** 95.18 mln. oz t. **Consumer prices** (change in 1987): 0.3%.

Transport: Railway traffic (1986): 41 bln. passenger-km; 60 bln. net ton-km. **Motor vehicles:** in use (1986): 26 mln. passenger cars, 1.3 mln. comm. vehicles; manuf. (1982): 3.7 mln. passenger cars; 286 000 comm. vehicles. **Civil aviation** (1986): 26.6 bln. passenger-km; 2.9 bln. freight ton-km. **Chief ports:** Hamburg, Bremen, Lubeck.

Communications: Television sets: 23.0 mln. in use (1986). **Radios:** 25 mln. in use (1986). **Telephones in use** (1986): 39.1 mln. **Daily newspaper circ.** (1986): 417 per 1 000 pop.

Health: Life expectancy at birth (1985): 67.2 male; 73.4 female. **Births** (per 1 000 pop. 1985): 10.2 **Deaths** (per 1 000 pop. 1986): 11.5. **Natural increase** (1986): −0.1%. **Hospital beds** (1984): 682 747. **Physicians** (1985): 153 000. **Infant mortality** (per 1 000 live births 1985): 9.

Education (1987): **Literacy:** 99%. **Years compulsory:** 10; attendance 100%.

Major International Organizations: UN and all of its specialized agencies, EC, OECD, NATO.

Canadian Embassy: Friedrich Wilhelm Str. 18, 5300 Bonn 1; Tel: (0228) 23 10 61.

The Federal Republic of Germany was proclaimed May 23, 1949, in Bonn, after a constitution had been drawn up by a consultative assembly formed by representatives of the 11 laender (states) in the French, British, and American zones. Later reorganized into 9 units, the laender numbered 10 with the addition of the Saar, 1957. Berlin also was granted land (state) status, but the 1945 occupation agreements placed restrictions on it.

The occupying powers, the U.S., Britain, and France, restored the civil status, Sept. 21, 1949. The U.S. resumed diplomatic relations July 2, 1951. The powers lifted controls and the republic became fully independent May 5, 1955.

Dr. Konrad Adenauer, Christian Democrat, was made chancellor Sept. 15, 1949, re-elected 1953, 1957, 1961. Willy Brandt, heading a coalition of Social Democrats and Free Democrats, became chancellor Oct. 21, 1969.

In 1970 Brandt signed friendship treaties with the USSR and Poland. In 1971, the U.S., Britain, France, and the USSR signed an agreement on Western access to West Berlin. In 1972 the Bundestag approved the USSR and Polish treaties and East and West Germany signed their first formal treaty, implementing the agreement easing access to West Berlin. In 1973 a West Germany-Czechoslovakia pact normalized relations and nullified the 1938 "Munich Agreement."

In May 1974 Brandt resigned, saying he took full responsibility for "negligence" for allowing an East German spy to become a member of his staff. Helmut Schmidt, Brandt's finance minister, succeeded him.

West Germany has experienced tremendous economic growth since the 1950s. The country leads Europe in provisions for worker participation in the management of industry.

The NATO decision to deploy medium-range nuclear missiles in Western Europe sparked a demonstration by some 400 000 protesters in 1983. Chancellor Kohl supports the U.S. "Star Wars" antimissile program.

Helgoland, an island of 52.6 ha in the North Sea, was taken from Denmark by a British Naval Force in 1807 and later ceded to Germany to become a part of Schleswig-Holstein province in return for rights in East Africa. The heavily fortified island was surrendered to UK, May 23, 1945, demilitarized in 1947, and returned to W. Germany, Mar 1, 1952. It is a free port.

Ghana

Republic of Ghana

People: Population (1986 est.): 14 786 000. **Age distrib.** (%): 0–14: 46.6; 15–59: 48.9; 60+: 4.5. **Pop. density:** 62.0 per

sq. km. **Urban** (1984): 31%. **Ethnic groups:** Akan 44%, Moshi-Dagomba 16%, Ewe 13%, Ga 8%, others. **Languages:** English (official), 50 tribal languages. **Religions:** Christian 24%, traditional beliefs 38%, Moslem 24%.

Geography: Area: 238 515 sq. km. **Location:** On southern coast of W. Africa. **Neighbors:** Côte d'Ivoire on W, Burkina Faso on N, Togo on E. **Topography:** Most of Ghana consists of low fertile plains and scrubland, cut by rivers and by the artificial Lake Volta. **Capital:** Accra. **Cities** (1984 est.): Accra 859 000.

Government: Type: Military. **Head of government:** Pres. Jerry Rawlings; b. 1947; in office: Dec. 31, 1981. **Local divisions:** 10 regions.

Economy: Industries: Aluminum, light industry. **Chief crops:** Cocoa (70% of exports), coffee. **Minerals:** Gold, manganese, industrial diamonds, bauxite. **Crude oil reserves** (1980): 7 mln. bbls. **Other resources:** Timber, rubber. **Arable land:** 12%. **Fish catch** (1985): 254 000 metric tons. **Electricity prod.** (1986): 3.6 bln. kwh. **Labor force:** 60% agric.; 10% ind.

Finance: Currency: Cedi (Mar. 1988: 1.00 = $.05 US). **Gross national product** (1985): $4.9 bln. **Per capita income** (1980): $420. **Imports** (1986): $783 mln.; partners: UK 18%, W. Ger. 12%, Nigeria 12%. **Exports** (1986): $863 mln.; partners: UK 16%, U.S. 16%, Neth. 9%, W. Ger. 9%. **International reserves less gold** (Mar. 1987): 631 mln. **Gold:** 314 000 oz t. **Consumer prices** (change in 1987): 15.0%.

Transport: Railway traffic (1985): 201 mln. passenger-km; 73 mln. net ton-km. **Motor vehicles:** in use (1983): 52 000 passenger cars, 24 000 comm. vehicles. **Civil aviation** (1986): 298 mln. passenger-km; 6.9 mln. freight ton-km. **Chief ports:** Tema, Takoradi.

Communications: Television sets: 140 000 in use (1986). **Radios:** 3.0 mln. in use (1986). **Telephones in use** (1985): 72 000.

Health: Life expectancy at birth (1985): 50.3 male; 53.7 female. **Births** (per 1 000 pop. 1985): 47.0. **Deaths** (per 1 000 pop. 1985): 14.6. **Natural increase** (1985): 3.2%. **Physicians** (1982): 1 435. **Infant mortality** (per 1 000 live births 1985): 98.

Education (1983): **Literacy:** 30%.

Major International Organizations: UN and all of its specialized agencies, OAU.

Canadian High Commission: 42 Independence Ave.; P.O. Box 1639, Accra; Tel: 228555, 228502.

Named for an African empire along the Niger River, 400-1240 AD, Ghana was ruled by Britain for 113 years as the Gold Coast. The UN in 1956 approved merger with the British Togoland trust territory. Independence came March 6, 1957. Republic status within the Commonwealth was attained in 1960.

Pres. Kwame Nkrumah built hospitals and schools, promoted development projects like the Volta R. hydroelectric and aluminum plants, but ran the country into debt, jailed opponents, and was accused of corruption. A 1964 referendum gave Nkrumah dictatorial powers and set up a one-party socialist state.

Nkrumah was overthrown in 1966 by a police-army coup, which expelled Chinese and East German teachers and technicians. Elections were held in 1969, but 4 further coups occurred in 1972, 1978, 1979, and 1981. The 1979 and 1981 coups were led by Flight Lieut. Jerry Rawlings.

Greece

Hellenic Republic

Elliniki Dimokratia

People: Population (1989 est.): 10 048 000. **Age distrib.** (%): 0–14: 20.9; 15–59: 61.0; 60+: 18.1. **Pop. density:** 75.9 per sq. km. **Urban** (1981): 58.1%. **Ethnic groups:** Greek 98.5%. **Languages:** Greek, others. **Religion:** Greek Orthodox 97%.

Geography: Area: 132 458 sq. km. **Location:** Occupies southern end of Balkan Peninsula in SE Europe. **Neighbors:** Albania, Yugoslavia, Bulgaria on N, Turkey on E. **Topography:** About 75% of Greece is non-arable, with mountains in all areas. Pindus Mts. run through the country N to S. The heavily indented coastline is 15 016 km long. Of over 2 000 islands, only 169 are inhabited, among them Crete, Rhodes, Milos, Kerkira (Corfu), Chios, Lesbos, Samos, Euboea, Delos, Mykonos. **Capital:** Athens. **Cities** (1981 est.): Athens (met.) 3 016 457; Thessaloniki (met.) 800 000; Patras 120 000.

Government: Type: Presidential parliamentary republic. **Head of state:** Pres. Christos Sartzetakis; in office: Mar. 30, 1985. **Head of government:** Prime Min. Andreas Papandreou; b. Feb. 5, 1919, in office: Oct. 21, 1981. **Local divisions:** 51 prefectures. **Defence:** 5% of GDP (1985).

Economy: Industries: Textiles, chemicals, metals, wine, food processng, cement. **Chief crops:** Grains, corn, rice, cotton, tobacco, olives, citrus fruits, raisins, figs. **Minerals:** Bauxite, lignite, oil, manganese. **Crude oil reserves** (1985): 35 mln. bbls. **Arable land:** 30%. **Livestock** (1983): sheep: 7.9 mln.; goats: 1.1 mln. **Fish catch** (1984): 100 000 metric tons. **Electricity prod.** (1986): 29.5 bln. kwh. **Crude steel prod.** (1986): 1.0 mln. metric tons. **Labor force:** 28% agric.; 29% ind., 42% service.

Finance: Currency: Drachma (June 1988: 137.00 = $1 US). **Gross national product** (1985): $32.8 bln. **Per capita income** (1984): $3 260. **Imports** (1986): $11.3 bln.; partners: W. Ger. 18%, It. 9%, Fr. 7%. **Exports** (1986): $5.6 bln.; partners: W. Ger. 19%, It. 8%, U.S. 8%. **Tourists** (1985): $1.4 bln. receipts. **National budget** (1986): $12.4 bln. expenditures. **International reserves less gold** (Mar. 1988): $2.2 bln. **Gold:** 3.3 mln. oz t. **Consumer prices** (change in 1986): 23.0%.

Transport: Railway traffic (1986): 1.6 bln. passenger-km; 708 mln. net ton-km. **Motor vehicles:** in use (1985): 1.1 mln. passenger cars, 589 000 comm. vehicles. **Civil aviation** (1984): 6.1 bln. passenger-km; 78.1 mln. freight ton-km. **Chief ports:** Piraeus, Thessaloniki, Patrai.

Communications: Television sets: 1.7 mln. in use (1986). **Radios:** 4 mln. in use (1986). **Telephones in use** (1985): 3.5 mln. **Daily newspaper circ.** (1982): 88 per 1 000 pop.

Health: Life expectancy at birth (1985): 72 male; 75 female. **Births** (per 1 000 pop. 1986): 11.3. **Deaths** (per 1 000 pop. 1986): 9.2. **Natural increase** (1986): 0.2%. **Hospital beds** (1984): 57 081. **Physicians** (1984): 27 607. **Infant mortality** (per 1 000 live births 1985): 13.8.

Education (1985): **Literacy:** men 96%, women 89%. **Years compulsory:** 9.

Major International Organizations: UN (GATT, IMF, WHO, ILO), EC, NATO, OECD.

Canadian Embassy: 4 Ioannou Gennadiou St., Athens 115 21; Tel: 7239-511 to 519.

The achievements of ancient Greece in art, architecture, science, mathematics, philosophy, drama, literature, and democracy became legacies for succeeding ages. Greece reached the height of its glory and power, particularly in the Athenian city-state, in the 5th century BC.

Greece fell under Roman rule in the 2d and 1st centuries BC. In the 4th century AD it became part of the Byzantine Empire and, after the fall of Constantinople to the Turks in 1453, part of the Ottoman Empire.

Greece won its war of independence from Turkey 1821-1829, and became a kingdom. A republic was established 1924; the monarchy was restored, 1935, and George II, King of the Hellenes, resumed the throne. In Oct., 1940, Greece rejected an ultimatum from Italy. Nazi support resulted in its defeat and occupation by Germans, Italians, and Bulgarians. By the end of 1944 the invaders withdrew. Communist resistance forces were defeated by Royalist and British troops. A plebiscite recalled King George II. He died Apr. 1, 1947, and was succeeded by his brother, Paul I.

Communists waged guerrilla war 1947-49 against the government but were defeated.

A period of reconstruction and rapid development followed, mainly with conservative governments under Premier Constantine Karamanlis. The Centre Union led by George Papandreou won elections in 1963 and 1964. King Constantine, who acceded in 1964, forced Papandreou to resign. A period of political manoeuvers ended in the military takeover of April 21, 1967, by Col. George Papadopoulos. King Constantine tried to reverse the consolidation of the harsh dictatorship Dec. 13, 1967, but failed and fled to Italy. Papadopoulos was ousted Nov. 25, 1973.

Greek army officers serving in the National Guard of Cyprus staged a coup on the island July 15, 1974. Turkey invaded Cyprus a week later, precipitating the collapse of the Greek junta, which was implicated in the Cyprus coup.

The military turned the government over to Karamanlis, who named a civilian cabinet, freed political prisoners, and sought to solve the Cyprus crisis. In Nov. 1974 elections his party won a large parliamentary majority, reduced by socialist gains in 1977. A Dec. 1974 referendum resulted in the proclamation of a republic.

Greece was reintegrated into the military wing of NATO in October 1980, and it became the 10th full member of the European Community on Jan. 1, 1981.

The 1981 victory of the Panhellenic Socialist Movement (Pasok) of Andreas Papandreou has brought about substantial changes in the internal and external policies that Greece has pursued for the past 5 decades. Since 1985, Greece has been victimized by several incidents of international terrorism.

Grenada
State of Grenada

People: Population (1989 est.): 87 000. **Pop. density:** 252.6 per sq. km. **Ethnic groups:** Mostly African descent. **Languages:** English (official), French-African patois. **Religions:** Roman Catholic 64%, Anglican 22%.

Geography: Area: 344 sq. km. **Location:** 145 km N. of Venezuela. **Topography:** Main island is mountainous; country includes Carriacon and Petit Martinique islands. **Capital:** St. George's. **Cities** (1980 est.): St. George's 7 500.

Government: Type: Independent state. **Head of state:** Queen Elizabeth II, represented by Gov.-Gen. Paul Scoon, b. July 4, 1935; in office: Sept. 30, 1978. **Head of government:** Prime Minister: Herbert Blaize; b. Feb. 26, 1918; in office: Dec. 4, 1984. **Local divisions:** 6 parishes and one dependency.

Economy: Industries: Rum. **Chief crops:** Nutmeg, bananas, cocoa, mace. **Arable land:** 41%. **Electricity prod.** (1986): 24 mln. kwh. **Labor force:** 33% agric.; 31% services.

Finance: Currency: East Caribbean dollar (Apr. 1988: 2.70 = $1 US). **Gross national product** (1986): $103 mln. **Per capita income** (1977): $500. **Imports** (1986): $68 mln.; partners: UK 19%, Trin./Tob. 25%. U.S. 17%. **Exports** (1986): $27 mln.; partners: UK 35%, CARICOM countries 38%. **Tourists** (1986): $26 mln. receipts. **National budget** (1987): $83.8 mln. expenditures. **International reserves less gold** (Jan. 1988): $23 mln.

Transport: Motor vehicles: in use (1981): 4 700 passenger cars, 1 000 comm. vehicles. **Chief ports:** Saint George's.

Communications: Radios: 50 000 in use (1986). **Telephones in use** (1985): 5 000.

Health: Life expectancy at birth (1985): 68.5 male; 72.5 female. **Births** (per 1 000 pop. 1985): 27. **Deaths** (per 1 000 pop. 1985): 7. **Natural increase** (1985): 2.0%. **Infant mortality** (per 1 000 live births 1987): 16.7.

Education (1987): **Literacy:** 95%; **Years compulsory:** 6.

Major International Organizations: UN (IMF, WHO), OAS.

Canadian High Commission: c/o The Canadian High Commission, P.O. Box 404, Bridgetown, Barbados.

Columbus sighted the island 1498. First European settlers were French, 1650. The island was held alternately by France and England until final British occupation, 1784. Grenada became fully independent Feb. 7, 1974 during a general strike. It is the smallest independent nation in the Western Hemisphere.

On Oct. 14, 1983, a military coup ousted Prime Minister Maurice Bishop, who was put under house arrest, later freed by supporters, rearrested, and, finally, on Oct. 19, executed. U.S. forces, with a token force from 6 area nations, invaded Grenada, Oct. 25. Resistance from the Grenadian army and Cuban advisors was quickly overcome as most of the population welcomed the invading forces as liberators. U.S. troops left Grenada in June 1985.

Guatemala
Republic of Guatemala
República de Guatemala

People: Population (1989 est.): 9 412 000. **Age distrib.** (%): 0–14: 45.9; 15–59: 49.4; 60+: 4.7. **Pop. density:** 86.4 per sq. km. **Urban** (1986): 33%. **Ethnic groups:** Maya 55%, Mestizos 44%. **Languages:** Spanish, Indian dialects. **Religions:** mostly Roman Catholic

Geography: Area: 108 880 sq. km. **Location:** In Central America. **Neighbors:** Mexico N, W; El Salvador on S, Honduras, Belize on E. **Topography:** The central highland and mountain areas are bordered by the narrow Pacific coast and the lowlands and fertile river valleys on the Caribbean. There are numerous volcanoes in S, more than half a dozen over 3 300 m. **Capital:** Guatemala City. **Cities** (1986 est.): Guatemala City 1 800 000.

Government: Type: Republic. **Head of state:** Pres. Marco Vinicio Cerezo Arevalo; b. Dec. 26, 1942; in office: Jan. 14, 1986. **Local divisions:** Guatemala City and 22 departments. **Defence:** 2.2% of GNP (1986).

Economy: Industries: Prepared foods, tires, textiles. **Chief crops:** Coffee (one third of exports), sugar, bananas, cotton, corn. **Minerals:** Oil, nickel. **Crude oil reserves** (1985): 500 mln. bbls. **Other resources:** Rare woods, fish, chicle. **Arable land:** 16%. **Electricity prod.** (1986): 2.2 bln. kwh. **Labor force:** 50% agric.; 27% ind. & comm., 12% services.

Finance: Currency: Quetzal (Apr. 1988: 2.50 = $1 US). **Gross national product** (1985): $8.9 bln. **Per capita income** (1985): $1 000. **Imports** (1983): $619 mln.; partners: U.S. 34%, CACM 8%. **Exports** (1986): $655 mln.; partners: U.S. 34%, CACM 20%. **National budget** (1986): $1.7 bln. expenditures. **International reserves less gold** (Mar. 1988): $206 mln. **Gold:** 523 000 oz t. **Consumer prices** (change in 1987): 12.3%.

Transport: Railway traffic. Motor vehicles: in use (1983): 188 000 passenger cars, 58 000 comm. vehicles. **Civil aviation** (1985) 143 mln. passenger-km; 21 mln. freight ton-km. **Chief ports:** Puerto Barrios, San Jose.

Communications: Television sets: 300 000 in use (1986). **Radios:** 500 000 in use (1986). **Telephones in use** (1983): 128 000. **Daily newspaper circ.** (1983): 30 per 1 000 pop.

Health: Life expectancy at birth (1986): 55 yrs. **Births** (per 1 000 pop. 1985): 42. **Deaths** (per 1 000 pop. 1985): 10. **Natural increase** (1985): 3.2% **Health:** There are about 1 250 doctors, 60 hospitals, and 100 dispensaries. **Infant mortality** (per 1 000 live births 1985): 67.

Education (1987): **Literacy:** 48%. **Years compulsory:** 6; **Attendance:** 35%.

Major International Organizations: UN (IMF, World Bank), OAS.

Canadian Embassy: Galerias Espana, 6th fl., 7 Avenida 11-59, Zona 9; postal: P.O. Box 400, Guatemala, C.A.; Tel: 321411, -13, -17, -18, -19.

The old Mayan Indian empire flourished in what is today Guatemala for over 1 000 years before the Spanish.

Guatemala was a Spanish colony 1524-1821; briefly a part of Mexico and then of the Fed. of Central America, the republic was established in 1839.

Since 1945 when a liberal government was elected to replace the long-term dictatorship of Jorge Ubico, the country has seen a swing toward socialism, an armed revolt, renewed attempts at social reform, a military coup, and, in 1986, civilian rule. The Guerrilla Army of the Poor, an insurgent group founded 1975, led a military offensive by attacking army posts and succeeded in incorporating segments of the large Indian population in its struggle against the government.

Dissident army officers seized power, Mar. 23, 1982, denouncing the Mar. 7 Presidential election as fraudulent and pledging to restore "authentic democracy" to the nation. Political violence has caused some 200 000 Guatemalans to seek refuge in Mexico. A second military coup occurred Oct. 8, 1983. The nation returned to civilian rule in 1986.

Guinea
Republic of Guinea
République de Guinée

People: Population (1989 est.): 6 147 000. **Pop. density:** 25.0 per sq. km. **Urban** (1986): 26%. **Ethnic groups:** Foulah 40%, Malinké 25%, Soussous 10%, 15 other tribes. **Languages:** French (official), tribal languages. **Religions:** Moslem 85%, Christian 10%.

Geography: Area: 245 938 sq. km. **Location:** On Atlantic coast of W. Africa. **Neighbors:** Guinea-Bissau, Senegal, Mali on N, Côte d'Ivoire on E, Liberia on S. **Topography:** A narrow coastal belt leads to the mountainous middle region, the source of the Gambia, Senegal, and Niger rivers. Upper Guinea, farther inland, is a cooler upland. The SE is forested. **Capital:** Conakry. **Cities** (1983 est.): Conakry 656 000; Labe 273 000; N'Zerekore 250 000; Kankan 278 000.

Government: Type: Republic under Military Committee For National Recovery. **Head of state:** Pres. Brig. Gen. Lansana Conte; b. 1944; in office: Apr. 5, 1984. **Local divisions:** 33 districts. **Defence:** 3.3% of GNP (1983).

Economy: Chief crops: Bananas, pineapples, rice, corn, palm nuts, coffee, honey. **Minerals:** Bauxite, iron, diamonds. **Arable land:** 6%. **Electricity prod.** (1986) 236 mln. kwh. **Labor force:** 82% agric.; 11% ind. & comm.

Finance: Currency: Franc (Jan. 1988: 339 = $1 US). **Gross national product** (1985): $1.9 bln. **Per capita income** (1984): $305. **Imports** (1984): $403 mln.; partners: Fr. 36% USSR 11%, U.S. 6% It. 6%. **Exports** (1984): $537 mln.; partners: U.S. 18%, Fr. 13%, W. Ger. 12%, USSR 12%. **National budget** (1982): 140 mln.

Transport: Motor vehicles: in use (1982): 10 000 passenger cars, 10 000 comm. vehicles. **Chief ports:** Conakry.

Communications: Radios: 200 000 in use (1986).

Health: Life expectancy at birth (1985): 38.7 male; 41.8 female. **Births** (per 1 000 pop. 1985): 46.8. **Deaths** (per 1 000 pop. 1985): 23.5. **Natural increase** (1985): 2.3%. **Physicians** (1980): 301. **Infant mortality** (per 1 000 live births 1985): 159.

Education (1983): **Literacy:** 48%. **Years compulsory:** 8; attendance: 34% primary, 15% secondary.

Major International Organizations: UN and most specialized agencies, OAU.

Canadian Embassy: P.O. Box 99, Conakry; Tel: 46-37-32, -33.

Part of the ancient West African empires, Guinea fell under French control 1849-98. Under Sekou Toure, it opted for full independence in 1958, and France withdrew all aid.

Toure turned to communist nations for support, and set up a militant one-party state. Western firms, as well as the Soviet government, have invested in Guinea's vast bauxite mines.

Thousands of opponents were jailed in the 1970s, in the aftermath of an unsuccessful Portuguese invasion. Many were tortured and killed.

The military took control of the government in a bloodless coup after the March 1984 death of Toure.

Guinea-Bissau
Republic of Guinea-Bissau
Republica da Guiné-Bissau

People: Population (1989 est.): 929 000. **Pop. density:** 25.7 per sq. km. **Ethnic groups:** Balanta 30%, Fula 20%, Manjaca 14%, Mandinga 13%. **Languages:** Portuguese (official), Criolo, tribal languages. **Religions:** Traditional 65%, Moslem 30%, Christian 4%.

Geography: Area: 36 123 sq. km. **Location:** On Atlantic coast of W. Africa. **Neighbors:** Senegal on N, Guinea on E, S. **Topography:** A swampy coastal plain covers most of the country; to the east is a low savanna region. **Capital:** Bissau. **Cities** (1979): Bissau 109 500.

Government: Type: Republic. **Head of government:** Gen. Joao Bernardo Vieira; b. 1939; in office: Nov. 14,1980. **Local divisions:** 9 regions. **Defence:** 8.4% of GNP (1984).

Economy: Chief crops: Peanuts, cotton, rice. **Minerals:** Bauxite. **Arable land:** 10%. **Electricity prod.** (1986): 28 mln. kwh. **Labor force:** 90% agric.

Finance: Currency: Peso (Jan. 1988: 649 = $1 US). **Gross national product** (1985): $150 mln. **Per capita income** (1983): $165. **Imports** (1982): $61 mln.; partners: Port. 32%, It. 11%, Fr. 7%. **Exports** (1982): $13 mln.; partners: Port. 65%.

Communications: Radios: 26 000 receivers (1986). **Daily newspaper circ.** (1984): 7 per 1 000 pop.

Health: Life expectancy at birth (1985): 42 years. **Births** (per 1 000 pop. 1985): 39. **Deaths** (per 1 000 pop. 1985): 20. **Natural increase** (1985): 1.9%. **Infant mortality** (per 1 000 live births 1985): 137.

Education (1985): **Literacy** 15%. **Years compulsory:** 4.

Major International Organizations: UN, OAU.

Canadian Embassy: c/o P.O. Box 3373, Dakar, Senegal.

Portuguese mariners explored the area in the mid-15th century; the slave trade flourished in the 17th and 18th centuries, and colonization began in the 19th.

Beginning in the 1960s, an independence movement waged a guerrilla war and formed a government in the interior that achieved international support. Full independence came Sept. 10, 1974, after the Portuguese regime was overthrown.

The November 1980 coup gave Joao Bernardo Vieira absolute power.

Guyana
Co-operative Republic of Guyana

People: Population (1989 est.): 779 000. **Age distrib. (%):** 0–14: 37.5; 5–59: 56.5; 60+: 6.0. **Pop. density:** 3.6 per sq. km. **Urban** (1983): 32%. **Ethnic groups:** East Indian 51%, African and mixed 43%. **Languages:** English (official), Amerindian dialects. **Religions:** Christian 57%, Hindu 34%.

Geography: Area: 214 953 sq. km. **Location:** On N coast of S. America. **Neighbors:** Venezuela on W, Brazil on S, Suriname on E. **Topography:** Dense tropical forests cover much of the land, although a flat coastal area up to 64 km wide, where 90% of the population lives, provides rich alluvial soil for agriculture. A grassy savanna divides the 2 zones. **Capital:** Georgetown. **Cities** (1985 est.): Georgetown 170 000.

Government: Type: Republic within the Commonwealth of Nations. **Head of state:** President Hugh Desmond Hoyte; b. Mar. 9, 1929; in office: Aug. 6, 1985. **Head of Government:** Prime Min. Hamilton Green; in office: Aug. 6, 1985. **Local divisions:** 10 regions. **Defence:** 9% of GDP (1985).

Economy: Industries: Cigarettes, rum, clothing, furniture, drugs. **Chief crops:** Sugar, rice, citrus and other fruits. **Minerals:** Bauxite, diamonds. **Other resources:** Timber, shrimp. **Arable land:** 2%. **Electricity prod.** (1986): 500 bln. kwh. **Labor force:** 33% agric.; 45% ind. & comm.; 22% services.

Finance: Currency: Dollar (Mar. 1988: 10.00 = $1 US). **Gross national product** (1985): $460 mln. **Per capita income** (1983): $457. **Imports** (1985): $209 mln.; partners: U.S. 21%, CARICOM 33%. **Exports** (1985): $214 mln.; partners: UK 28%, U.S. 18%, CARICOM 17%. **National budget** (1985): $1.5 bln. **International reserves less gold** (Feb. 1988): $6.8 mln. **Consumer prices** (change in 1986): 7.9%.

Transport: Motor vehicles: in use (1985): 25 000 passenger cars, 7 000 comm. vehicles. **Chief ports:** Georgetown.

Communications: Radios: 350 000 in use (1986). **Telephones in use** (1985): 33 000. **Daily newspaper circ.** (1985): 99 per 1 000 pop.

Health: Life expectancy at birth (1985): 70 years. **Births** (per 1 000 pop. 1985): 28.0. **Deaths** (per 1 000 pop. 1985): 7.0. **Natural increase** (1985): 2.1% **Health** (1982): 270 doctors, 29 hospitals, 149 health centers. **Infant mortality** (per 1 000 live births 1985): 32.

Education (1985): **Literacy:** 86%. **Years compulsory:** ages 5–14.

Major International Organizations: UN (GATT, ILO, IMF, World Bank), CARICOM, Commonwealth of Nations. **Canadian High Commission:** High and Young Streets; postal: P.O. Box 10880, Georgetown; Tel: 72081-5; 58337.

Guyana became a Dutch possession in the 17th century, but sovereignty passed to Britain in 1815. Indentured servants from India soon outnumbered African slaves. Ethnic tension has affected political life.

Guyana became independent May 26, 1966. A Venezuelan claim to the western half of Guyana was suspended in 1970 but renewed in 1982. The Suriname border is also disputed. The government has nationalized most of the economy which has remained severely depressed.

The Port Kaituma ambush of U.S. Rep. Leo J. Ryan and others investigating mistreatment of American followers of the Rev. Jim Jones' People's Temple cult, triggered a mass suicide-execution of 911 cultists in the Guyana jungle, Nov. 18, 1978.

Haiti
Republic of Haiti
Républiqe d'Haiti

People: Population (1989 est.): 6 216 000. **Age distrib. (%):** 4–14: 39.2; 15–59: 52.5; 60+: 8.3. **Pop. density:** 224.0 per sq. km. **Urban** (1986): 29%. **Ethnic groups:** African descent 95%. **Languages:** French, Creole (both official). **Religions:** Roman Catholic 80%, Protestant 10%; Voodoo widely practiced.

Geography: Area: 27 747 sq. km. **Location:** In West Indies, occupies western third of I. of Hispaniola. **Neighbors:** Dominican Republic on E, Cuba on W. **Topography:** About two-thirds of Haiti is mountainous. Much of the rest is semiarid. Coastal areas are warm and moist. **Capital:** Port-au-Prince. **Cities** (1986 est.): Port-au-Prince 557 000.

Government: Type: Military. **Head of state:** Gen. Henri Namphy; b. Nov. 2, 1932; in office: June 20, 1988. **Local divisions:** 26 provinces, 1 federal dist. **Defence:** 1.6% of GNP (1984).

Economy: Industries: Sugar refining, textiles. **Chief crops:** Coffee, sugar, bananas, cocoa, tobacco, rice. **Minerals:** Bauxite. **Other resources:** Timber. **Arable land:** 32%. **Livestock** (1986): cattle: 1.3 mln.; goats: 1.1 mln. **Electricity prod.** (1986): 332 mln. kwh. **Labor force:** 75% agric.; 18% ind. & comm.; 7% services.

Finance: Currency: Gourde (Apr. 1988: 5.00 = $1 US). **Gross national product** (1986): $1.8 bln. **Per capita income** (1983): $300. **Imports** (1986): $340 mln.; partners: U.S. 45%. **Exports** (1986): $200 mln.; partners: U.S. 59%. **Tourists** (1984): receipts $9 mln. **National budget** (1987): $258 mln. expenditures. **International reserves less gold** (Mar. 1988): $17 mln. **Gold:** 18 000 oz t. **Consumer prices** (change in 1987): −11.5%.

Transport: Motor vehicles: in use (1985): 34 000 passenger cars, 11 000 comm. vehicles. **Chief ports:** Port-au-Prince, Les Cayes.

Communications: Television sets: 25 000 in use (1986). **Radios:** 200 000 in use (1986). **Telephones in use** (1983): 38 000 **Daily newspaper circ.** (1985): 4 per 1 000 pop.

Health: Life expectancy at birth (1985): 51.2 male; 54.4 female. **Births** (per 1 000 pop. 1985): 35.6. **Deaths** (per 1 000 pop. 1985): 13.0. **Natural increase** (1985): 2.2%. **Hospital beds** (1980): 3 964. **Physicians** (1985): 803. **Infant mortality rate** (per 1 000 live births, 1985): 107.

Education (1987): **Literacy:** 23%. **Years compulsory:** 6; attendance 20%.

Major International Organizations: UN and some of its specialized agencies, OAS.

Canadian Embassy: Edifice Banque Nova Scotia, Route de Delmas; postal: C.P. 826, Port-au-Prince; Tel: 2-2358, 2-4231.

Haiti, visited by Columbus, 1492, and a French colony from 1677, attained its independence, 1804, following the rebellion led by former slave Toussaint L'Ouverture. Following a period of political violence, the U.S. occupied the country 1915-34.

Dr. Francois Duvalier was voted president in 1957; in 1964 he was named president for life. Upon his death in 1971, he was succeeded by his son, Jean-Claude. Drought in 1975-77 brought famine, and Hurricane Allen in 1980 destroyed most of the rice, bean, and coffee crops.

Haiti is the poorest nation in the Western hemisphere; unemployment was estimated at 50% in 1987.

Following increasing unrest, President Jean-Claude Duvalier fled Haiti aboard a U.S. Air Force jet Feb. 7, 1986, ending the 28-year dictatorship by the Duvalier family. A military-civilian council, headed by Gen. Henri Namphy, assumed control. In 1987, voters approved a new constitution.

The Jan. 17, 1988 elections led to Leslie Manigat being named president; opposition leaders charged widespread fraud. Gen. Namphy seized control June 20, and named himself president of a military government.

Honduras
Republic of Honduras
Republica de Honduras

People: Population (1989 est.): 5 106 000. **Age distrib. (%):** 0–14: 46.9; 15–59: 48.6; 60+: 4.5. **Pop. density:** 45.6 per sq. km. **Urban** (1986): 40.0%. **Ethnic groups:** Mestizo 90%, Indian 7%. **Languages:** Spanish, Indian dialects. **Religions:** Roman Catholic, small Protestant minority.

Geography: Area: 112 079 sq. km. **Location:** In Central America. **Neighbors:** Guatemala on W, El Salvador, Nicaragua on S. **Topography:** The Caribbean coast is 800 km long. Pacific coast, on Gulf of Fonseca, is 64 km long. Honduras is mountainous, with wide fertile valleys and rich forests. **Capital:** Tegucigalpa. **Cities** (1985 est.) Tegucigalpa 571 000; San Pedro Sula 372 000.

Government: Type: Democratic constitutional republic. **Head of State:** Pres. Jose Azcona Hoyo; b. 1927; in office: Jan. 27, 1986. **Local divisions:** 18 departments. **Defence:** 7% of govt. budget (1987).

Economy: Industries: Clothing, textiles, cement, wood prods, cigars. **Chief crops:** Bananas (chief export), coffee, corn, beans. **Minerals:** Gold, silver, copper, lead, zinc, iron, antimony, coal. **Other resources:** Timber. **Arable land:** 16%. **Livestock:** (1985): cattle: 2.3 mln. **Electricity prod.** (1986): 1.4 bln. kwh. **Labor force:** 62% agric.; 20% services; 9% manuf.

Finance: Currency: Lempira (Apr. 1988): 2.00 = $1 US). **Gross national product** (1986): $2.6 bln. **Per capita income** (1985): $815. **Imports** (1985): $1.5 bln.; partners: U.S. 39%, Jap. 5%. **Exports** (1985): $958 mln.; partners: U.S. 52%, W. Ger. 8%, Jap. 5%. **Tourists** (1983): $23 mln. receipts. **National budget** (1984): $805 mln. revenues; $1.3 bln. expenditures. **International reserves less gold** (Mar. 1988): $87.5 mln. **Gold:** 16 000 oz t. **Consumer prices** (change in 1987): 2.5%.

Transport: Motor vehicles: in use (1985) 66 000 passenger cars, 18 000 comm. vehicles. **Civil aviation** (1983): 348 mln. passenger-km; 2.3 mln. freight ton-km. **Chief ports:** Puerto Cortes, La Ceiba.

Communications: Television sets: 90 000 in use (1986). **Radios:** 300 000 in use (1986). **Telephones in use** (1985): 45 000. **Daily newspaper circ.** (1984): 58 per 1 000 pop.

Health: Life expectancy at birth (1984): 58.7 yrs. **Births** (per 1 000 pop. 1985): 41. **Deaths** (per 1 000 pop. 1985): 8. **Natural increase** (1985): 3.3%. **Hospital beds** (1985): 5 220. **Physicians** (1985): 1 900. **Infant mortality** (per 1 000 live births 1985): 73.

Education (1987): **Literacy:** 56%. **Years compulsory:** 6; attendance 70%.

Major International Organizations: UN, (IMF, WHO, ILO), OAS.

Canadian Embassy: c/o Apartado Postal 10303, San José, Costa Rica.

Mayan civilization flourished in Honduras in the 1st millenium AD. Columbus arrived in 1502. Honduras became independent after freeing itself from Spain, 1821 and from the Fed. of Central America, 1838.

Gen. Oswaldo Lopez Arellano, president for most of the period 1963-75 by virtue of one election and 2 coups, was ousted by the army in 1975 over charges of pervasive bribery under United Brands Co. of the U.S.

The government has resumed land distribution, raised minimum wages, and started a literacy campaign. An elected civilian government took power in 1982, the country's first in 10 years.

The U.S. has provided military aid and advisors to help the covert war against Nicaragua and help block arms shipments from Nicaragua to anti-government forces in El Salvador. Some 3 200 U.S. troops were sent to Honduras after the Honduran border was violated by Nicaraguan forces, Mar. 1988.

Hungary
Hungarian People's Republic
Magyar Népköztáraság

People: Population (1989 est.): 10 571 000. **Age distrib.** (%): 0–14: 21.4; 15–59: 60.4; 60+: 18.2. **Pop. density:** 113.6 per sq. km. **Urban** (1986): 56%. **Ethnic groups:** Magyar 92%, German 2.5%. **Language:** Hungarian (Magyar). **Religions:** Roman Catholic 67%, Protestant 25%.

Geography: Area: 93 023 sq. km. **Location:** In East Central Europe. **Neighbors:** Czechoslovakia on N, Austria on W, Yugoslavia on S, Romania, USSR on E. **Topography:** The Danube R. forms the Czech border in the NW, then swings S to bisect the country. The eastern half of Hungary is mainly a great fertile plain, the Alfold; the W and N are hilly. **Capital:** Budapest. **Cities** (1986 est.): Budapest 2 080 000; Miskolc 211 000; Debrecen 212 000.

Government: Type: Communist. **Head of state:** Pres. Karoly

Nemeth; in office: June 25, 1987. **Head of government:** Prem. Karoly Grosz; b. 1930; in office: June 25, 1987. **Head of Hungary Socialist Workers Party:** Karoly Grosz; in office: May 22, 1988. **Local divisions:** 19 counties, 5 cities with county status. **Defence:** 4.1% of GNP (1984).

Economy: Industries: Iron and steel, machinery, pharmaceuticals, vehicles, communications equip., milling, distilling. **Chief crops:** Grains, vegetables, fruits, grapes. **Minerals:** Bauxite, natural gas. **Arable land:** 57%. **Livestock:** (1985): cattle: 1.7 mln.; pigs: 8.2 mln.; sheep: 2.4 mln. **Electricity prod.** (1986): 27.2 bln. kwh. **Crude steel prod.** (1986): 3.7 mln. metric tons. **Labor force:** 20% agric.; 31% ind.; 40% services.

Finance: Currency: Forint (Mar. 1988: 47 = $1 US). **Gross national product** (1985): $80.1 bln. **Per capita income** (1982): $4 180. **Imports** (1987): $10.8 bln.; partners: USSR 29%, W. Ger. 11%, E. Ger. 7%, Czech. 5%. **Exports** (1987): $10.5 bln.; partners: USSR 34%, E. Ger. 6%, W. Ger. 7%, Czech. 6%. **National budget** (1983): $13.4 bln. **Tourists** (1985): $506 mln. receipts. **Consumer prices** (change in 1987): 8.7%.

Transport: Railway traffic (1985): 11.2 bln. passenger-km; 22.3 bln. net ton-km. **Motor vehicles:** in use (1986): 1.4 mln. passenger cars, 157 000 comm. vehicles. **Civil aviation** (1986): 1.1 bln. Passenger-km; 23.6 mln. net freight-km.

Communications: Television sets: 2.9 mln. licensed (1985). **Radios:** 5.5 mln. licensed (1985). **Telephones in use** (1985): 1.4 mln. **Daily newspaper circ.** (1986): 236 per 1 000 pop.

Health: Life expectancy at birth (1985): 65.6 male; 73.6 female. **Births** (per 1 000 pop. 1986): 12.1. **Deaths** (per 1 000 pop. 1986): 13.8. **Natural increase** (1986): 0.1%. **Hospital beds** (1986): 102 000. **Physicians** (1986): 30 000. **Infant mortality** (per 1 000 live births 1985): 20.2

Education (1985): **Literacy:** 98%. **Years compulsory:** to age 16; attendance 99%.

Major International Organizations: UN (IMF, World Bank, GATT), Warsaw Pact.

Canadian Embassy: Budakeszi ut. 32, 1021 Budapest; Tel: 767-686, 676-312, 767-512.

Earliest settlers, chiefly Slav and Germanic, were overrun by Magyars from the east. Stephen I (997-1038) was made king by Pope Sylvester II in 1000 AD. The country suffered repeated Turkish invasions in the 15th-17th centuries. After the defeats of the Turks, 1686-1697, Austria dominated, but Hungary obtained concessions until it regained internal independence in 1867, with the emperor of Austria as king of Hungary in a dual monarchy with a single diplomatic service. Defeated with the Central Powers in 1918, Hungary lost Transylvania to Romania, Croatia and Bacska to Yugoslavia, Slovakia and Carpatho-Ruthenia to Czechoslovakia, all of which had large Hungarian minorities. A republic under Michael Karolyi and a bolshevist revolt under Bela Kun were followed by a vote for a monarchy in 1920 with Admiral Nicholas Horthy as regent.

Hungary joined Germany in World War II, and was allowed to annex most of its lost territories. Russian troops captured the country, 1944-1945. By terms of an armistice with the Allied powers Hungary agreed to give up territory acquired by the 1938 dismemberment of Czechoslovakia and to return to its borders of 1937.

A republic was declared Feb. 1, 1946; Zoltan Tildy was elected president. In 1947 the communists forced Tildy out. Premier Imre Nagy, in office since mid-1953, was ousted for his moderate policy of favoring agriculture and consumer production, April 18, 1955.

In 1956, popular demands for the ousting of Erno Gero, Communist Party secretary, and for formation of a government by Nagy, resulted in the latter's appointment Oct. 23; demonstrations against communist rule developed into open revolt. Gero called in Soviet forces. On Nov. 4 Soviet forces launched a massive attack against Budapest with 200 000 troops, 2 500 tanks and armored cars.

About 200 000 persons fled the country. In the spring of 1963 the regime freed many anti-communists and captives from the revolution in a sweeping amnesty. Nagy was executed by the Russians.

Soviet troops are stationed in Hungary. Hungarian troops participated in the 1968 Warsaw Pact invasion of Czechoslovakia.

Major economic reforms were launched early in 1968, switching from a central planning system to one in which market forces and profit control much of production. Productivity and living standards have improved.

Iceland

Republic of Iceland

Lýoveldio Island

People: Population (1989 est.): 251 000. **Age distrib. (%):** 0–14: 25.5; 15–59: 60.1; 60+: 14.4. **Pop. density:** 2.4 per sq. km. **Urban** (1986): 85% **Ethnic groups:** Homogeneous, descendants of Norwegians, Celts. **Language:** Icelandic. **Religion:** Evangelical Lutheran 95%.

Geography: Area: 102 994 sq. km. **Location:** In Northern Atlantic O. east of Greenland. **Neighbors:** Nearest is Greenland. **Topography:** Iceland is of recent volcanic origin. Three-quarters of the surface is wasteland: glaciers, lakes, a lava desert. There are geysers and hot springs, and the climate is moderated by the Gulf Stream. **Capital:** Reykjavik. **Cities** (1986 est.): Reykjavik 89 000.

Government: Type: Constitutional republic. **Head of state:** Pres. Vigdis Finnbogadottir; b. Apr. 15, 1930; in office: Aug. 1, 1980. **Head of government:** Prime Min. Thorsteinn Palsson; in office: July 8, 1987. **Local divisions:** 23 counties.

Economy: Industries: Fish products (some 80% of exports), aluminum. **Chief crops:** Potatoes, turnips, hay. **Arable land:** 0.5%. **Livestock** (1985): lamb: 14 000 metric tons. **Fish catch** (1986): 1 600 000 metric tons. **Electricity prod.** (1986): 4.4 bln. kwh. **Labor force:** 7% agric.; 49% ind. & comm.; 30% services & govt; 14% fisheries.

Finance: Currency: Kronur (Mar. 1988: 38.9 = $1 US). **Gross national product** (1985): $2.5 bln. **Per capita income** (1984): $10 216. **Imports** (1984): $842 mln.; partners: USSR 8%, W. Ger. 12%, UK 9%, Den. 10%. **Exports** (1984): $744 mln.; partners: U.S. 28%, UK 19%. **Tourists** (1984): receipts: $76 mln. **National budget** (1985): $704 mln. expenditures. **International reserves less gold** (Mar. 1988): $287.9 mln. **Gold:** 49 000 oz t. **Consumer prices** (change in 1987): 18.2%.

Transport: Motor vehicles: in use (1986): 100 000 passenger cars, 12 000 comm. vehicles. **Civil aviation** (1985): 2.3 bln. passenger-km ; 22.4 mln. freight ton-km . **Chief ports:** Reykjavik.

Communications: Television sets: 70 000 in use (1985). **Radios:** 70 000 licensed (1985). **Telephones in use** (1985): 97 245. **Daily newspaper circ.** (1985): 415 per 1 000 pop.

Health: Life expectancy at birth (1985): 73.5 male; 79.5 female. **Births** (per 1 000 pop. 1985): 18. **Deaths** (per 1 000 pop. 1985): 7. **Natural increase** (1985): 1.1%. **Hospital beds** (1985): 2 678. **Physicians** (1985): 574. **Infant mortality** per (1 000 live births 1985): 6.2.

Education (1986): **Literacy:** 99%. **Years compulsory:** 8; attendance 99%.

Major International Organizations: UN (GATT), NATO, OECD.

Canadian Embassy: c/o Oscar's Gate 20, 0352 Oslo 3, Norway.

Iceland was an independent republic from 930 to 1262, when it joined Norway. Its language has maintained its purity for 1 000 years. Danish rule lasted from 1380-1918; the last ties with the Danish crown were severed in 1941. The Althing, or assembly, is the world's oldest surviving parliament.

India

Republic of India

Bharat

People: Population (1989 est.): 833 422 000. **Age distrib. (%):** 0–14: 36.8; 15–59: 56.4; 60+: 5.8. **Pop. density:** 254.1 per sq. km. **Urban** (1985): 26%. **Ethnic groups:** Indo-Aryan groups 72%, Dravidian 25%, Mongoloid 3%. **Languages:** 16 languages, including Hindi (official) and English (associate official). **Religions:** Hindu 83%, Moslem 11%, Christian 3%, Sikh 2%.

Geography: Area: 3 280 228 sq. km. **Location:** Occupies most of the Indian subcontinent in S. Asia. **Neighbors:** Pakistan on W, China, Nepal, Bhutan on N, Burma, Bangladesh on E. **Topography:** The Himalaya Mts., highest in world, stretch across India's northern borders. Below, the Ganges Plain is wide, fertile, and among the most densely populated regions of the world. The area below includes the Deccan Peninsula. Close to one quarter the area is forested. The climate varies from tropical heat in S to near-Arctic cold in N. Rajasthan Desert is in NW; NE Assam Hills get 1 016 cm of rain a year. **Capital:** New Delhi. **Cities** (1981 cen.): Calcutta 9.1 mln.; Bombay (met.) 8.2 mln.; Delhi 5.2 mln.; Madras 4.3 mln.; Bangalore 2.9 mln.; Hyderabad 1.5 mln.; Ahmedabad 2.5 mln.; Kanpur 1.7 mln.; Pune 1.7 mln.; Nagpur 1.3 mln.

Government: Type: Federal Republic. **Head of state:** Pres. Ramaswamy Vepkataraman; b. Dec. 4, 1910; in office: July 25, 1987. **Head of government:** Prime Min. Rajiv Gandhi, b. Aug. 20, 1944; in office: Oct. 31, 1984. **Local divisions:** 25 states, 7 union territories. **Defence:** 3.9% of GNP (1984).

Economy: Industries: Textiles, steel, processed foods, cement, machinery, chemicals, fertilizers, consumer appliances, autos. **Chief crops:** Rice, grains, coffee, sugar cane, spices, tea, cashews, cotton, copra, coir, juta, linseed. **Minerals:** Chromium, coal, iron, manganese, mica salt, bauxite, gypsum, oil. **Crude oil reserves** (1987): 4.3 bln. bbls. **Other resources:** Rubber, timber. **Arable land:** 57%. **Livestock** (1985): cattle: 185 mln.; pigs: 9 mln.; sheep: 54.4 mln. **Fish catch** (1985): 2.8 mln. metric tons. **Electricity prod.** (1986): 170 bln. kwh. **Crude steel prod.** (1986): 1.8 mln. metric tons. **Labor force:** 70% agric.; 13% ind. & comm.

Finance: Currency: Rupee (June 1988: 13.51 = $1 US). **Gross national product** (1985): $194 bln. **Per capita income** (1977): $150. **Imports** (1986): $15.4 bln.; partners: U.S. 12%, USSR 8%, W. Ger. 6%, Iran 11%. **Exports** (1986): $9.4 bln.; partners: U.S. 11%, USSR 18%, UK 6%, Jap. 9%. **Tourists** (1985): receipts: $1.0 bln. **National budget** (1988): $56 bln. expenditures. **International reserves less gold** (Jan. 1988): $6.3 bln. **Gold:** 10.4 mln. oz. t. **Consumer prices** (change in 1987): 8.8%.

Transport: Railway traffic (1986): 250 bln. passenger-km; 213 bln. net ton-km. **Motor vehicles:** in use (1985): 1.5 bln. passenger cars, 952 000 comm. vehicles. **Civil aviation:** (1986): 15.4 bln. passenger-km; 566 mln. freight ton-km. **Chief ports:** Calcutta, Bombay, Madras, Cochin, Vishakhapatnam.

Communications: Television: 5.0 mln. licensed (1986). **Radios:** 25 mln. (1985).**Telephones in use** (1984): 3.2 mln. **Daily newspaper circ.** (1985): 16 per. 1 000 pop.

Health: Life expectancy at birth (1981): 52 male; 50 female. **Births** (per 1 000 pop. 1986): 29.6. **Deaths** (per 1 000 pop. 1986): 11.5. **Natural increase** (1986): 1.8%. **Hospital beds** (1984): 599 000. **Physicians** (1984): 284 000. **Infant mortality** (per 1 000 live births 1985): 101.

Education (1981): **Literacy:** 36%.

Major International Organizations: UN (IMF, World Bank).

Canadian High Commission: 7/8 Shantipath, Chanakyapuri, New Delhi 110021; postal: P.O. Box 5207, New Delhi; Tel: 60-8169.

India has one of the oldest civilizations in the world. Excavations trace the Indus Valley civilization back for at least 5 000 years. Paintings in the mountain caves of Ajanta, richly carved temples, the Taj Mahal in Agra, and the Kutab Minar in Delhi are among relics of the past.

Aryan tribes, speaking Sanskrit, invaded from the NW around 1500 BC, and merged with the earlier inhabitants to create classical Indian civilization.

Asoka ruled most of the Indian subcontinent in the 3d century BC, and established Buddhism. But Hinduism revived and eventually predominated. During the Gupta kingdom, 4th-6th century AD, science, literature, and the arts enjoyed a "golden age."

Arab invaders established a Moslem foothold in the W in the 8th century, and Turkish Moslems gained control of North India by 1200. The Mogul emperors ruled 1526-1857.

Vasco de Gama established Portuguese trading posts 1498-1503. The Dutch followed. The British East India Co. sent Capt. William Hawkins, 1609, to get concessions from the Mogul emperor for spices and textiles. Operating as the East India Co. the British gained control of most of India. The British parliament assumed political direction; under Lord Bentinck, 1828-35, rule by rajahs was curbed. After the Sepoy troops mutinied, 1857-58, the British supported the native rulers.

Nationalism grew rapidly after World War I. The Indian National Congress and the Moslem League demanded constitutional reform. A leader emerged in Mohandas K. Gandhi (called Mahatma, or Great Soul), born Oct. 2, 1869, assassinated Jan.

30, 1948. He advocated self-rule, non-violence, removal of untouchability. In 1930 he launched "civil disobedience," including boycott of British goods and rejection of taxes without representation.

In 1935 Britain gave India a constitution providing a bicameral federal congress. Mohammed Ali Jinnah, head of the Moslem League, sought creation of a Moslem nation, Pakistan.

The British government partitioned British India into the dominions of India and Pakistan. Aug. 15, 1947, was designated Indian Independence Day. India became a self-governing member of the Commonwealth and a member of the UN. It became a democratic republic, Jan. 26, 1950.

More than 12 million Hindu & Moslem refugees crossed the India-Pakistan borders in a mass transferral of some of the 2 peoples during 1947; about 200 000 were killed in communal fighting.

After Pakistan troops began attacks on Bengali separatists in East Pakistan, Mar. 25, 1971, some 10 million refugees fled into India. India and Pakistan went to war Dec. 3, 1971, on both the East and West fronts. Pakistan troops in the east surrendered Dec. 16; Pakistan agreed to a cease-fire in the west Dec. 17.

India and Pakistan agreed to withdraw troops from their borders and seek peaceful solutions. In Aug. 1973 India released 93 000 Pakistanis held prisoner since 1971. The 2 countries resumed full relations in 1976.

In 2 days of carnage, the Bengali population of the village of Mandai, Tripura State, 700 people, were massacred in a raid by indigenous tribal residents of the area, June 8-9, 1980. A similar year-long campaign against Bengali immigrants had been going on in Assam State.

Prime Min. Mrs. Indira Gandhi, named Jan. 19, 1966, was the 2d successor to Jawaharlal Nehru, India's prime minister from 1947 to his death, May 27, 1964.

Long the dominant power in India's politics, the Congress Party lost some of its near monopoly by 1967. The party split into New and Old Congress parties in 1969. Mrs. Gandhi's New Congress party won control of the House.

Threatened with adverse court rulings in a voting law case, an opposition protest campaign and strikes, Gandhi invoked emergency provisions of the constitution June, 1975. Thousands of opponents were arrested and press censorship imposed. Measures to control prices, protect small farmers, and improve productivity were adopted.

The emergency, especially enforcement of coercive birth control measures in some areas, and the prominent extra-constitutional role of Indira Gandhi's son Sanjay, was widely resented. Opposition parties, united in the Janata coalition, scored massive victories in federal and state parliamentary elections in 1977, turning the New Congress Party from power.

With 350 candidates of her party winning seats to Parliament, Indira Gandhi became prime minister for the second time, Jan. 14, 1980. Gandhi was assassinated by Sikh extremists Oct. 31, 1984. Widespread rioting followed causing over 1 000 deaths. Rajiv, her son, replaced her as prime minister.

On Dec. 3, 1984, methyl isocyanate, a deadly gas, escaped from a tank owned by the Union Carbide Corp. at Bhopal and killed over 2 500, in history's worst industrial accident.

Extremist Sikhs ignited several violent clashes during the 1980s. The government's May 1987 decision to bring the state of Punjab under the rule of the central government led to increased violence. Forty-six died during a government siege of the Golden Temple at Amritsar, the holiest Sikh shrine, May 1988.

As India's population passed 800 million, government officials expressed alarm that the failure to control the birthrate would lead to disaster.

Sikkim, bordered by Tibet, Bhutan and Nepal, formerly British protected, became a protectorate of India in 1950. Area, 7 124 sq. km; pop. 1981 cen. 315 000; capital, Gangtok. In Sept. 1974 India's parliament voted to make Sikkim an associate Indian state, absorbing it into India.

Kashmir, a predominantly Moslem region in the northwest, has been in dispute between India and Pakistan since 1947. A cease-fire was negotiated by the UN Jan. 1, 1949; it gave Pakistan control of one-third of the area, in the west and northwest, and India the remaining two-thirds, the Indian state of Jammu and Kashmir, which enjoys internal autonomy. Repeated clashes broke out along the line.

There were also clashes in April 1965 along the Assam-East Pakistan border and in the **Rann** (swamp) **of Kutch** area along the West Pakistan-Gujarat border near the Arabian Sea. An international arbitration commission on Feb. 19, 1968, awarded 90% of the Rann to India, 10% to Pakistan.

France, 1952-54, peacefully yielded to India its 5 colonies, former French India, comprising Pondicherry, Karikal, Mahe, Yanaon (which became Pondicherry Union Territory, area 481 sq. km, pop. 1981, 604 136) and Chandernagor (which was incorporated into the state of West Bengal).

Goa, 3 715 sq. km, pop., 1981, 1 mln., which had been ruled by Portugal since 1505 AD, was taken by India by military action Dec. 18, 1961, together with 2 other Portuguese enclaves, **Daman** and **Diu,** located near Bombay. They became states of India in 1987.

Indonesia
Republic of Indonesia
Republik Indonesia

People: Population (1989 est.): 187 726 000. **Age distrib.** (%): 0–14: 39.2; 15–59: 56.5; 60+: 5.2. **Pop. density:** 98.6 per sq. km. **Urban** (1985): 25%. **Ethnic groups:** Malay, Chinese, Irianese. **Languages:** Bahasa Indonesian (Malay) (official), Javanese, other Austronesian languages. **Religion:** Moslem 88%.

Geography: Area: 1 904 197 sq. km. **Location:** Archipelago SE of Asia along the Equator. **Neighbors:** Malaysia on N, Papua New Guinea on E. **Topography:** Indonesia comprises 13 500 islands, including Java (one of the most densely populated areas in the world with 3 900 persons to the sq. km), Sumatra, Kalimantan (most of Borneo), Sulawesi (Celebes), and West Irian (Irian Jaya, the W. half of New Guinea). Also: Bangka, Billiton, Madura, Bali, Timor. The mountains and plateaus on the major islands have a cooler climate than the tropical lowlands. **Capital:** Jakarta. **Cities** (1985 est.): Jakarta 7 800 000; Surabaja 2 345 000; Bandung 1 633 000; Medan 1 110 000.

Government: Type: Independent Republic. **Head of state:** Pres. Suharto; b. June 8, 1921; in office: Mar. 6, 1967. **Local divisions:** 28 provinces, 282 regencies. **Defence:** 2.6% of GNP (1984).

Economy: Industries: Food processing, textiles, light industry. **Chief crops:** Rice, coffee, sugar. **Minerals:** Nickel, tin, oil, bauxite, copper, natural gas. **Crude oil reserves** (1987): 8.4 bln. bbls. **Other resources:** Rubber. **Arable land:** 11%. **Livestock:** (1985): cattle: 6.9 mln.; pigs: 4.3 mln.; sheep: 5.1 mln. **Fish catch** (1985): 2.2 mln. metric tons. **Electricity prod.** (1985): 27.7 bln. kwh. **Labor force:** 66% agric.; 23% ind. & comm.; 10% services.

Finance: Currency: Rupiah (June 1988: 1 673 = $1 US). **Gross national product** (1986): $85 bln. **Per capita income** (1982): $560. **Imports** (1986): $10.7 bln.; partners: Jap. 23%, U.S. 2%, Sing. 9%. **Exports** (1986): $14.8 bln.; partners: Jap. 47%, U.S. 20%, Sing. 10%. **Tourists** (1985): $519 mln. receipts. **National budget** (1986): $13.8 bln. **International reserves less gold** (Feb. 1988): $5.0 bln. **Gold:** 3.10 mln. oz t. **Consumer prices** (change in 1987): 9.3%.

Transport: Railway traffic (1986): 6.3 bln. passenger-km; 1.1 bln. ton-km. **Motor vehicles:** in use (1985): 958 000 passenger cars, 1 mln. comm. vehicles. **Civil aviation** (1985): 8.8 bln. passenger-km; 157 mln. freight ton-km. **Chief ports:** Jakarta, Surabaja, Medan, Palembang, Semarang.

Communications: Television sets: 4.9 mln. in use (1985). **Radios:** 32 mln. in use (1985). **Telephones in use** (1984): 795 000.

Health: Life expectancy at birth (1986): male: 53.9; female 56.7 years. **Births** (per 1 000 pop. 1986): 29.8. **Deaths** (per 1 000 pop. 1986): 11.7. **Natural increase** (1986) 1.8%. **Hospital beds** (1985): 106 000. **Physicians** (1985): 18 447. **Infant mortality** (per 1 000 live births 1985): 90.3.

Education (1984): **Literacy:** 72%. 86% attend primary school; 15% secondary school.

Major International Organizations: UN and all of its specialized agencies, ASEAN, OPEC.

Canadian Embassy: 5th fl. WISMA Metropolitan, Jalan Jendral Sudirman; postal: P.O. Box 52/JKT, Jakarta; Tel: 510-709.

Hindu and Buddhist civilization from India reached the peoples of Indonesia nearly 2 000 years ago, taking root especially in Java. Islam spread along the maritime trade routes in the 15th century, and became predominant by the 16th century. The Dutch replaced the Portuguese as the most important European trade power in the area in the 17th century. They secured territorial control over Java by 1750. The outer islands were not finally subdued until the early 20th century, when the full area of present-day Indonesia was united under one rule for the first time.

Following Japanese occupation, 1942-45, nationalists led by Sukarno and Hatta proclaimed a republic. The Netherlands ceded sovereignty Dec. 27, 1949, after 4 years of fighting. West Irian, on New Guinea, remained under Dutch control.

After the Dutch in 1957 rejected proposals for new negotiations over West Irian, Indonesia stepped up the seizure of Dutch property. A U.S. mediator's plan was adopted in 1962. In 1963 the UN turned the area over to Indonesia, which promised a plebiscite. In 1969, voting by tribal chiefs favored staying with Indonesia, despite an uprising and widespread opposition.

Sukarno suspended Parliament in 1960, and was named president for life in 1963. Russian-armed Indonesian troops staged raids in 1964 and 1965 into Malaysia, whose formation Sukarno had opposed.

Indonesia's popular, pro-Peking Communist Party tried to seize control in 1965; the army smashed the coup, later intimated that Sukarno had played a role in it. In parts of Java, communists seized several districts before being defeated; over 300 000 communists were executed.

Gen. Suharto, head of the army, was named president in 1968, reelected 1973, 1978 and 1988. A coalition of his supporters won a strong majority in House elections in 1971. Moslem opposition parties made gains in 1977 elections but lost ground in the 1982 elections. The military retains a predominant political role.

In 1966 Indonesia and Malaysia signed an agreement ending hostility. After ties with Peking were cut in 1967, there were riots against the economically important ethnic Chinese minority. Riots against Chinese and Japanese also occurred in 1974. Indonesia and China agreed to begin bilateral trade talks in 1985.

Oil export earnings, and political stability have made Indonesia's economy stable.

Iran

Islamic Republic of Iran

Jomhori-e-Islami-e-Irân

People: Population (1989 est.): 51 005 000. **Age distrib. (%):** 0–14: 44.4; 15–59: 50.3; 60+: 5.2. **Pop. density:** 31.0 per sq. km. **Urban** (1980): 50%. **Ethnic groups:** Persian 63%, Turkoman & Baluchi 19%, Kurd 3%, Arab 4%. **Languages:** Farsi, Turk, Kurdish, Arabic, English, French. **Religion:** Shi'a Moslem 93%.

Geography: Area: 1 647 872 sq. km. **Location:** Between the Middle East and S. Asia. **Neighbors:** Turkey, Iraq on W, USSR of N (Armenia, Azerbaijan, Turkmenistan), Afghanistan, Pakistan on E. **Topography:** Interior highlands and plains are surrounded by high mountains, up to 5 400 m. Large salt deserts cover much of the area, but there are many oases and forest areas. Most of the population inhabits the N and NW. **Capital:** Teheran. **Cities** (1985 est.): Teheran 5 751 000; Isfahan 1 121 000; Mashhad 1 103 000; Shiraz 834 000.

Government: Type: Islamic republic. **Religious head (Faghi):** Ayatollah Ruhollah Khomeini, b. 1901. **Head of state:** Pres. Sayyed Ali Khamenei. **Head of government:** Prime Minister Mir Hussein Moussavi; b. 1937; in office: Oct. 29, 1981. **Local divisions:** 24 provinces. **Defence:** 7.2% of GNP (1984).

Economy: Industries: Petrochemicals, cement, sugar refining, carpets. **Chief crops:** Grains, rice, fruits, sugar beets, cotton, grapes. **Minerals:** Chromium, oil, gas. **Crude oil reserves** (1987): 36.5 bln. bbls. **Other resources:** Gums, wool, silk, caviar. **Arable land:** 9%. **Livestock:** (1985): cattle: 8.3 mln.; sheep: 34.5 mln. **Electricity prod.** (1984): 37.1 bln. kwh. **Crude steel prod.** (1986) 1.2 mln. metric tons. **Labor force:** 40% agric.; 33% ind. & comm; 27% services.

Finance: Currency: Rial (Mar. 1988: 66.83 = $1 US). **Gross national product** (1986): $75 bln. **Per capita income** (1986): $1 667. **Imports** (1986): $10.5 bln.; partners: W. Ger. 16%, Jap. 13%, UK 6%. **Exports** (1986): $13.3 bln.; partners: Jap. 16%, It. 10%. **National budget** (1983): $33.3 bln. expenditures. **Consumer prices** (change in 1985) 4.4%.

Transport: Motor vehicles: in use (1983): 2.1 mln. passenger cars, 313 000 comm. vehicles. **Chief ports:** Bandar Abbas.

Communications: Television sets: 2.1 mln. in use (1985). **Radios:** 10 mln. in use (1985). **Telephones in use** (1986): 1.8 mln. **Daily newspaper circ.** (1986): 13 per 1 000 pop.

Health: Life expectancy at birth (1985): 58.0 male; 58.3 female. **Births** (per 1 000 pop. 1985): 43. **Deaths** (per 1 000 pop. 1985): 12. **Natural increase** (1985): 3.1%. **Hospital beds** (1983): 67 734. **Physicians** (1983): 15 945. **Infant mortality** (per 1 000 live births 1986): 110.

Education (1986): **Literacy:** 48%.

Major International Organizations: UN (IMF, WHO), OPEC.

Canadian Embassy: 57 Javad-Sarafraz St., Ostad-Motahhari Ave, P.O. Box 11365-4647, Tehran; Tel: 623177, -548, -549, -192.

Iran was once called Persia. The Iranians, who supplanted an earlier agricultural civilization, came from the E during the 2d millenium BC; they were an Indo-European group related to the Aryans of India.

In 549 BC Cyrus the Great united the Medes and Persians in the Persian Empire, conquered Babylonia in 538 BC, restored Jerusalem to the Jews. Alexander the Great conquered Persia in 333 BC, but Persians regained their independence in the next century under the Parthians, themselves succeeded by Sassanian Persians in 226 AD. Arabs brought Islam to Persia in the 7th century, replacing the indigenous Zoroastrian faith. After Persian political and cultural autonomy was reasserted in the 9th century, the arts and sciences flourished for several centuries.

Turks and Mongols ruled Persia in turn from the 11th century to 1502, when a native dynasty reasserted full independence. The British and Russian empires vied for influence in the 19th century, and Afghanistan was severed from Iran by Britain in 1857.

The previous dynasty was founded by Reza Khan, a military leader, in 1925. He abdicated as shah in 1941, and was succeeded by his son, Mohammad Reza Pahlavi.

Parliament, under Premier Mohammed Mossadegh, nationalized the oil industry in 1951, leading to a British blockade. Mossadegh was overthrown in 1953; the shah assumed control. Under his rule, Iran underwent economic and social change but political opposition was not tolerated.

Conservative Moslem protests led to 1978 violence. Martial law in 12 cities was declared Sept. 8. A military government was appointed Nov. 6 to deal with striking oil workers. Prime Min. Shahpur Bakhtiar was designated by the shah to head a regency council in his absence. The shah left Iran Jan. 16, 1979.

Exiled religious leader Ayatollah Ruhollah Khomeini named a provisional government council in preparation for his return to Iran, Jan. 31. Clashes between Khomeini's supporters and government troops culminated in a rout of Iran's elite Imperial Guard Feb. 11, leading to the fall of Bakhtiar's government.

The Iranian revolution was marked by revolts among the ethnic minorities and by a continuing struggle between the clerical forces and westernized intellectuals and liberals. The Islamic Constitution established final authority to be vested in a Faghi, the Ayatollah Khomeini.

Iranian militants seized the U.S. embassy, Nov. 4, 1979, and took hostages including 62 Americans. The militants vowed to stay in the embassy until the deposed shah was returned to Iran. Despite international condemnations and U.S. efforts, including an abortive Apr., 1980, rescue attempt, the crisis continued. The U.S. broke diplomatic relations with Iran, Apr. 7th. The shah died in Egypt, July 27th. The hostage drama finally ended Jan. 21, 1981 when an accord, involving the release of frozen Iranian assets, was reached.

The ruling Islamic Party, increasingly dissatisfied with President Abolhassan Bani-Sadr, declared him unfit for office. In the weeks following Bani-Sadr's dismissal, June 22, 1981, a new wave of executions began. The political upheavals have brought Iran to almost total isolation from other countries.

A dispute over the Shatt al-Arab waterway that divides the two countries brought Iran and Iraq, Sept. 22, 1980, into open warfare. Iraqi planes attacked Iranian air fields including Teheran airport. Iranian planes bombed Iraqi bases. Iraqi troops occupied Iranian territory including the port city of Khorramshahr in October. Iranian troops recaptured the city and drove Iraqi troops back across the border, May 1982. Iraq, and later Iran, attacked several oil tankers in the Persian Gulf during 1984. Saudi Arabian war planes shot down 2 Iranian jets, June 5, which they felt were threatening Saudi shipping. A U.S. Navy warship shot down an Iranian commercial airliner, July 3, 1988, after mistaking it for an F-14 fighter jet; all 290 aboard the plane died.

Iran and Iraq continued to fight during 1988; in August, both sides agreed to a ceasefire and Canada provided troops as part of a United Nations force monitoring the truce.

Iraq
Republic of Iraq
al Jumhouriya al 'Iraqia

People: Population (1989 est.): 17 610 000. **Age distrib. (%):** 0–14: 46.9; 15–59: 48.8; 60+: 4.3. **Pop. density:** 40.5 per sq. km. **Urban** (1985): 70.0%. **Ethnic groups:** Arab, 75% Kurd, 15% Turk. **Languages:** Arabic (official), Kurdish, others. **Religions:** Moslem 95% (Shiite 60%, Sunni 35%), Christian 5%.

Geography: Area: 434 890 sq. km. **Location:** In the Middle East, occupying most of historic Mesopotamia. **Neighbors:** Jordan, Syria on W, Turkey on N, Iran on E, Kuwait, Saudi Arabia on S. **Topography:** Mostly an alluvial plain, including the Tigris and Euphrates rivers, descending from mountains in N to desert in SW. Persian Gulf region is marshland. **Capital:** Baghdad. **Cities** (1985 est.): Baghdad (met.) 3 400 000.

Government: Type: Ruling council. **Head of state:** Pres. Saddam Hussein At-Takriti, b. 1935 in office: July 16, 1979. **Local divisions:** 18 provinces. **Defence:** 42% of GNP (1984).

Economy: Industries: Textiles, petrochemicals, oil refining, cement. **Chief crops:** Grains, rice, dates, cotton. **Minerals:** Oil, gas. **Crude oil reserves** (1987): 40 bln. bbls. **Other resources:** Wool, hides. **Arable land:** 13%. **Livestock:** (1985): cattle: 1.5 mln.; sheep: 8.5 mln; goats: 2.3 mln. **Electricity prod.** (1986): 22.5 bln. kwh. **Labor force:** 50% agric.

Finance: Currency: Dinar (Mar. 1988: 1.00 = $3.21 US). **Gross national product** (1985): $35 bln. **Per capita income** (1984): $1 740. **Imports** (1985): $10.5 bln.; partners: W. Ger. 16%, Jap. 14%, Fr. 7%. **Exports** (1986): $7.5 bln.; partners: It. 13%, Tur. 11%, Braz. 22%, Jap. 6%.

Transport: Railway traffic (1984): 1.2 bln. passenger-km; 1.2 bln. net ton-km. **Motor vehicles:** in use (1984): 393 000 passenger cars, 118 700 comm. vehicles. **Civil aviation** (1982): 1.7 bln. passenger-km; 54.7 mln. freight ton-km. **Chief ports:** Basra.

Communications: Television sets: 605 000 in use (1986). **Radios:** 2.8 mln. in use (1986). **Telephones in use** (1985): 886 000. **Daily newspaper circ.** (1986): 21 per 1 000 pop.

Health: Life expectancy at birth (1985): 55.9 male; 59.1 female. **Births** (per 1 000 pop. 1985): 45.1. **Deaths** (per 1 000 pop. 1985): 11.5. **Natural increase** (1985): 3.3%. **Hospital beds** (1984): 26 657. **Physicians** (1984): 4 428. **Infant mortality** (per 1 000 live births 1985): 80.

Major International Organizations: UN (IMF, WHO, ILO), Arab League, OPEC.

Education (1987): **Literacy:** 70%. Compulsory age 6 to grade 6.

Canadian Embassy: Street: Hay Al-Mansour, Mahalla, Street 1, House 33; Postal: P.O. Box 323 Central Post Office, Baghdad; Tel: 542-1459. -1932, -1933.

The Tigris-Euphrates valley, formerly called Mesopotamia, was the site of one of the earliest civilizations in the world. The Sumerian city-states of 3000 BC originated the culture later developed by the Semitic Akkadians, Babylonians, and Assyrians.

Mesopotamia ceased to be a separate entity after the conquests of the Persians, Greeks, and Arabs. The latter founded Baghdad, from where the caliph ruled a vast empire in the 8th and 9th centuries. Mongol and Turkish conquests led to a decline in population, the economy, cultural life, and the irrigation system.

Britain secured a League of Nations mandate over Iraq after World War I. Independence under a king came in 1932. A leftist, pan-Arab revolution established a republic in 1958, which oriented foreign policy toward the USSR. Most industry has been nationalized, and large land holdings broken up.

A local faction of the international Baath Arab Socialist party has ruled by decree since 1968. Russia and Iraq signed an aid pact in 1972, and arms were sent along with several thousand advisers. The 1978 execution of 21 communists and a shift of trade to the West signalled a more neutral policy, straining relations with the USSR. In the 1973 Arab-Israeli war Iraq sent

forces to aid Syria. Within a month of assuming power, Saddam Hussein instituted a bloody purge in the wake of a reported coup attempt against the new regime.

Years of battling with the Kurdish minority resulted in total defeat for the Kurds in 1975, when Iran withdrew support. Kurdish rebels continued their war, 1979; fighting led to Iraqi bombing of Kurdish villages in Iran, causing relations with Iran to deteriorate.

After skirmishing intermittently for 10 months over the sovereignty of the disputed Shatt al-Arab waterway that divides the two countries, Iraq and Iran, Sept. 22, 1980, entered into open warfare when Iraqi fighter-bombers attacked 10 Iranian airfields, including Teheran airport, and Iranian planes retaliated with strikes on 2 Iraqi bases. In the following days, there was heavy ground fighting around Abadan and the adjacent port of Khorramshahr as Iraq pressed its attack on Iran's oil-rich province of Khuzistan. In May 1982, Iraqi troops were driven back across the border. A fierce border war continued through 1985 with both sides suffering heavy casualties.

Israeli airplanes destroyed a nuclear reactor near Baghdad on June 7, 1981, claiming that it could be used to produce nuclear weapons.

Iraq and Iran expanded their war to the Persian Gulf in Apr. 1984. Several attacks on oil tankers were reported.

The bloody war with Iran continued until August 1988, when a ceasefire was announced. Canada provided troops as part of a United Nations force monitoring the truce.

Ireland

People: Population (1989 est.): 3 734 000. **Age distrib. (%):** 0–14: 30.5; 15–59: 54.5; 60+: 15.0. **Pop. density:** 53.1 per sq. km. **Urban** (1985): 57%. **Ethnic groups:** Celtic, English minority. **Languages:** English predominates, Irish (Gaelic) spoken by minority. **Religions:** Roman Catholic 94%, Anglican 4%.

Geography: Area: 70 279 sq. km. **Location:** In the Atlantic O. just W of Great Britain. **Neighbors:** United Kingdom (Northern Ireland). **Topography:** Ireland consists of a central plateau surrounded by isolated groups of hills and mountains. The coastline is heavily indented by the Atlantic O. **Capital:** Dublin. **Cities** (1986 est.): Dublin 502 000; Cork (met.) 133 000.

Government: Type: Parliamentary republic. **Head of State:** Pres. Patrick J. Hillery; b. May 2, 1923; in office: Dec. 3, 1976. **Head of government:** Prime Min. Charles Haughey; in office: Mar. 10, 1987. **Local divisions:** 26 counties. **Defence:** 1.8% of GNP (1985).

Economy: Industries: Food processing, auto assembly, metals, textiles, chemicals, brewing, electrical and non-electrical machinery, tourism. **Chief crops:** Potatoes, grain, sugar beets, fruits, vegetables. **Minerals:** Zinc, lead, silver, gas. **Arable land:** 14%. **Livestock.** (1985): cattle: 5.7 mln.; pigs: 994 000; sheep: 2.7 mln. **Fish catch** (1985): 179 000 metric tons. **Electricity prod.** (1986): 12.6 bln. kwh. **Crude steel prod.** (1985): 203 000 metric tons. **Labor force:** 16% agric.; 27% manuf. & construction; 20% services.

Finance: Currency: Pound (June 1988: 0.64 = $1 US). **Gross national product** (1986): $21.34bln. **Per capita income** (1986): $6 000. **Imports** (1987): $12.6 bln.; partners: UK 43%, U.S. 17%, W. Ger. 8%, Fr. 5%. **Exports** (1987): $15.9 bln.; partners: UK 33%, Fr. 9%, W. Ger. 9%. **Tourists** (1985): receipts: $549 mln. **National budget** (1986): $8.6 bln. expenditures. **International reserves less gold** (Mar. 1988): $5.0 bln. **Gold:** 359 000 oz. t. **Consumer prices** (change in 1987): 3.1%.

Transport: Railway traffic (1985): 948 mln. passenger-km; 552 mln. net ton-km. **Motor vehicles:** in use (1985): 709 000 passenger cars, 98 000 comm. vehicles. **Civil aviation:** (1985): 2.4 bln. passenger-km; 85 mln. freight ton-km. **Chief ports:** Dublin, Cork.

Communications: Television sets: 918 000 receivers (1986). **Radios:** 2 mln. receivers (1986). **Telephones in use** (1985): 942 000. **Daily newspaper circ.** (1986): 200 per 1 000 pop.

Health: Life expectancy at birth (1986): 70.1 male; 75.6 female. **Births** (per 1 000 pop. 1985): 19. **Deaths** (per 1 000 pop. 1985): 9. **Natural increase** (1985): 1.0%. **Hospital beds** (1984): 32 000. **Physicians** (1984): 4 250 **Infant mortality** (per 1 000 live births 1986): 10.5

Education (1986): **Literacy:** 99%. **Years compulsory:** 9; attendance 91%.

Major International Organizations: UN (GATT, IMF, World Bank), EC.

Canadian Embassy: 65 St. Stephen's Green, Dublin 2; Tel: 781-988.

Celtic tribes invaded the islands about the 4th century BC; their Gaelic culture and literature flourished and spread to Scotland and elsewhere in the 5th century AD, the same century in which St. Patrick converted the Irish to Christianity. Invasions by Norsemen began in the 8th century, ended with defeat of the Danes by the Irish King Brian Boru in 1014. English invasions started in the 12th century; for over 700 years the Anglo-Irish struggle continued with bitter rebellions and savage repressions.

The Easter Monday Rebellion (1916) failed but was followed by guerrilla warfare and harsh reprisals by British troops, the "Black and Tans." The Dail Eireann, or Irish parliament, reaffirmed independence in Jan. 1919. The British offered dominion status to Ulster (6 counties) and southern Ireland (26 counties) Dec. 1921. The constitution of the Irish Free State, a British dominion, was adopted Dec. 11, 1922. Northern Ireland remained part of the United Kingdom.

A new constitution adopted by plebiscite came into operation Dec. 29, 1937. It declared the name of the state Eire in the Irish language (Ireland in the English) and declared it a sovereign democratic state.

On Dec. 21, 1948, an Irish law declared the country a republic rather than a dominion and withdrew it from the Commonwealth. The British Parliament recognized both actions, 1949, but reasserted its claim to incorporate the 6 northeastern counties in the United Kingdom. This claim has not been recognized by Ireland. *(See United Kingdom — Northern Ireland.)*

Irish governments have favored peaceful unification of all Ireland. Ireland cooperated with England against terrorist groups.

Ireland has suffered economic hardship during the 1980s; unemployment reached 18% in 1987.

Israel

State of Israel

Medinat Israel

People: Population (1989 est.): 4 477 000. **Age distrib.** (%): 0–14: 32.6; 15–59: 55.0; 60+: 12.4. **Pop. density:** 220.3 per sq. km. **Urban** (1985): 89%. **Ethnic groups:** Jewish 83%, Arab 16% **Languages:** Hebrew and Arabic (official), Yiddish, various European and West Asian languages. **Religions:** Jewish 83%, Moslem 13%

Geography: Area: 20 322 sq. km. **Location:** On eastern end of Mediterranean Sea. **Neighbors:** Lebanon on N, Syria, Jordan on E, Egypt on W. **Topography:** The Mediterranean coastal plain is fertile and well-watered. In the centre is the Judean Plateau. A triangular-shaped semi-desert region, the Negev, extends from south of Beersheba to an apex at the head of the Gulf of Aqaba. The eastern border drops sharply into the Jordan Rift Valley, including Lake Tiberias (Sea of Galilee) and the Dead Sea, which is 389 m below sea level, lowest point on the earth's surface. **Capital:** Jerusalem. Most countries maintain their embassy in Tel Aviv. **Cities** (1983 est.): Jerusalem 431 000; Tel Aviv-Yafo 330 000; Haifa 227 000.

Government: Type: Parliamentary democracy. **Head of state:** Pres. Chaim Herzog; b. Sept. 17, 1918; in office: May 5, 1983. **Head of government:** Prime Min. Yitzhak Shamir; b. 1915; in office: Oct. 20, 1986. **Local divisions:** 6 administrative districts. **Defence:** 24.4% of GNP (1984).

Economy: Industries: Diamond cutting, textiles, electronics, machinery, food processing. **Chief crops:** Citrus fruit, vegetables. **Minerals:** Potash, copper, phosphates, manganese, salt, sulphur. **Crude oil reserves** (1987): 700 000 mln. bbls. **Arable land:** 21%. **Livestock** (1985): cattle: 310 000; sheep: 230 000. **Fish catch** (1984): 22 000 metric tons. **Electricity prod.** (1986): 16.3 bln. kwh. **Crude steel prod.** (1981): 114 000 metric tons. **Labor force:** 6% agric.; 23% ind., 30% public services.

Finance: Currency: Shekel (May 1988: 1.58 = $1 US). **GNP** (1986): $25.9 bln. **Per capita income** (1986): $5 995. **Imports** (1986): $10.7 bln.; partners: U.S. 21%, W. Ger. 11%, UK 9%. **Exports** (1986): $7.1 bln.; partners: U.S. 34%, W. Ger. 5%, UK 7%. **Tourists** (1985): receipts $1.1 bln. **National budget** (1985): $23 bln. expenditures. **International reserves less gold** (Jan. 1988): $5.7 bln. **Gold:** 1.01 mln. oz t. **Consumer prices** (change in 1987): 19.8%.

Transport: Railway traffic (1986): 205 mln. passenger-km; 942 mln. net ton-km. **Motor vehicles:** in use (1984): 599 000 passenger cars, 125 000 comm. vehicles. **Civil aviation** (1985): 542 mln. passenger-km; 49 mln. freight ton-km. **Chief ports:** Haifa, Ashdod, Eilat.

Communications: Television sets: 620 000 in use (1986). **Radios:** 700 000 (1986). **Telephones in use** (1986): 1.7 mln. **Daily newspaper circ.** (1986): 263 per 1 000 pop.

Health: Life expectancy at birth (1984) Jewish pop. only 72.1 male; 75.7 female. **Births** (per 1 000 pop. 1985): 23.2. **Deaths** (per 1 000 pop. 1985): 7. **Natural increase** (1985): 1.6%. **Hospital beds** (1983): 26 402. **Physicians** (1983): 9 000. **Infant mortality** (per 1 000 live births 1985): 13.

Education (1987): **Literacy:** 88% (Jewish), 70% (Arab).

Major International Organizations: UN (GATT).

Canadian Embassy: 220, Hayardon St., Tel Aviv 63405; P.O. Box 6410, Tel Aviv 61063; Tel: (03) 228122, -6.

Occupying the SW corner of the ancient Fertile Crescent, Israel contains some of the oldest known evidence of agriculture and of primitive town life. A more advanced civilization emerged in the 3d millenium BC. The Hebrews probably arrived early in the 2d millenium BC. Under King David and his successors (c.1000 BC-597 BC), Judaism was developed and secured. After conquest by Babylonians, Persians, and Greeks, an independent Jewish kingdom was revived, 168 BC, but Rome took effective control in the next century, suppressed Jewish revolts in 70 AD and 135 AD, and renamed Judea Palestine, after the earlier coastal inhabitants, the Philistines.

Arab invaders conquered Palestine in 636. The Arabic language and Islam prevailed within a few centuries, but a Jewish minority remained. The land was ruled from the 11th century as a part of non-Arab empires by Seljuks, Mamluks, and Ottomans (with a crusader interval, 1098-1291).

After 4 centuries of Ottoman rule, during which the population declined to a low of 350 000 (1785), the land was taken in 1917 by Britain, which in the Balfour Declaration that year pledged to support a Jewish national homeland there, as foreseen by the Zionists. In 1920 a British Palestine Mandate was recognized; in 1922 the land east of the Jordan was abandoned.

Jewish immigration, begun in the late 19th century, swelled in the 1930s with refugees from the Nazis; heavy Arab immigration from Syria and Lebanon also occurred. Arab opposition to Jewish immigration turned violent in 1920, 1921, 1929, and 1936. The UN General Assembly voted in 1947 to partition Palestine into an Arab and a Jewish state. Britain withdrew in May 1948.

Israel was declared an independent state May 14, 1948; the Arabs rejected partition. Egypt, Jordan, Syria, Lebanon, Iraq, and Saudi Arabia invaded, but failed to destroy the Jewish state, which gained territory. Separate armistices with the Arab nations were signed in 1949; Jordan occupied the West Bank, Egypt occupied Gaza, but neither granted Palestinian autonomy. No peace settlement was obtained, and the Arab nations continued policies of economic boycott, blockade in the Suez Canal, and support of guerrillas. Several hundred thousand Arabs left the area of Jewish control; an equal number of Jews left the Arab countries for Israel 1949-53.

After persistent terrorist raids, Israel invaded Egypt's Sinai, Oct. 29, 1956, aided by British and French forces. A UN cease-fire was arranged Nov. 6.

An uneasy truce between Israel and the Arab countries, supervised by a UN Emergency Force, prevailed until May 19, 1967, when the UN force withdrew at the demand of Egypt's Pres. Nasser. Egyptian forces reoccupied the Gaza Strip and closed the Gulf of Aqaba to Israeli shipping. In a 6-day war that started June 5, the Israelis took the Gaza Strip, occupied the Sinai Peninsula to the Suez Canal, and captured Old Jerusalem, Syria's Golan Heights, and Jordan's West Bank. The fighting was halted June 10 by UN-arranged cease-fire agreements.

Egypt and Syria attacked Israel, Oct. 6, 1973 (Yom Kippur, most solemn day on the Jewish calendar). Egypt and Syria were supplied by massive USSR military airlifts; the U.S. responded with an airlift to Israel. Israel counter-attacked, driving the Syrians back, and crossed the Suez Canal.

A cease fire took effect Oct. 24; a UN peace-keeping force went to the area. A disengagement agreement was signed Jan. 18, 1974. Israel withdrew from the canal's W bank. A second withdrawal was completed in 1976; Israel returned the Sinai to Egypt in 1982.

Israel and Syria agreed to disengage June 1; Israel completed withdrawing from its salient (and a small part of the land taken in the 1967 war) June 25.

In the wake of the war, Golda Meir, long Israel's premier, resigned; severe inflation gripped the nation. Palestinian guerrillas staged massacres, killing scores of civilians 1974-75. Israel aided Christian forces in the 1975-76 Lebanese civil war.

Israeli forces raided Entebbe, Uganda, July 3, 1976, and rescued 103 hostages seized by Arab and German terrorists.

In 1977, the conservative opposition, led by Menachem Begin, was voted into office for the first time. Egypt's Pres. Sadat visited Jerusalem Nov. 1977 and on Mar. 26, 1979. Egypt and Israel signed a formal peace treaty, ending 30 years of war, and establishing diplomatic relations.

Israel invaded S. Lebanon, March 1978, following a Lebanon-based terrorist attack in Israel. Israel withdrew in favor of a 6 000 strong UN force, but continued to aid Christian militiamen.

A 5-day occupation of Israeli forces in southern Lebanon took place April 1980, in retaliation to the Palestinian raid on a kibbutz earlier that month. Violence on the Israeli-occupied West Bank rose in 1982 when Israel announced plans to build new Jewish settlements.

Israel affirmed the entire city of Jerusalem as its capital, July, 1980, encompassing the annexed Arab East Jerusalem.

Israel shot down, Apr. 28, 1981, two Syrian helicopters Israel claimed were attacking Lebanese Christian militia forces in the Beirut-Zahle area of Lebanon. Syria responded by installing Soviet-built surface-to-air missiles in Lebanon. Both the U.S. and Israel were unable to persuade Syria to withdraw the missiles, and Israel threatened to destroy them.

On June 7, 1981, Israeli jets destroyed an Iraqi atomic reactor near Baghdad that, Israel claimed, would have enabled Iraq to manufacture nuclear weapons.

In a close election, June 30, 1981, Prime Min. Menachem Begin was able to assemble a narrow coalition, he survived a no confidence motion in the Knesset by one vote, May 1982. He retired Oct. 1983.

Israeli jets bombed Palestine Liberation Organization (PLO) strongholds in Lebanon April, May 1982. In reaction to the wounding of the Israeli ambassador to Great Britain, Israeli forces in a coordinated land, sea, and air attack invaded Lebanon, June 6, to destroy PLO strongholds in that country. Israel and Syrian forces engaged in the Bekka Valley, June 9, but quickly agreed to a truce. Israeli forces encircled Beirut June 14. Following massive Israeli bombing of West Beirut, the PLO agreed to evacuate the city.

Israeli troops entered West Beirut after newly-elected Lebanese president Bashir Gemayel was assassinated on Sept. 14. Israel received widespread condemnation when Lebanese Christian forces, Sept. 16, entered 2 West Beirut refugee camps and slaughtered hundreds of Palestinian refugees. Israeli Defense Minister Ariel Sharon resigned Feb. 11, 1983, after Israel's State Board of Inquiry cited him for neglect of duty during the massacre. Israeli troops withdrew from Lebanon in June 1985.

In 1988, there were firebombings and arson by Palestinians protesting the Israeli military occupation of the West Bank and Gaza Strip; protesters and Israeli troops clashed frequently.

Italy

Italian Republic

Repubblica Italiana

People: Population (1989 est.): 57 439 000. **Age distrib.** (%): 0–14: 19.9; 15–59: 61.3; 60+: 18.8. **Pop. density:** 190.7 per sq. km. **Urban** (1985): 71%. **Ethnic groups:** Italian, small minorities of Germans, Slovenes, Albanians. **Languages:** Italian. **Religion:** Predominantly Roman Catholic.

Geography: Area: 301 202 sq. km. **Location:** In S Europe, jutting into Mediterranean S. **Neighbors:** France on W, Switzerland, Austria on N, Yugoslavia on E. **Topography:** Occupies a long boot-shaped peninsula, extending SE from the Alps into the Mediterranean, with the islands of Sicily and Sardinia offshore. The alluvial Po Valley drains most of N. The rest of the country is rugged and mountainous, except for intermittent coastal plains, like the Campajna, S of Rome. Apennine Mts. run through centre of peninsula. **Capital:** Rome. **Cities** (1985 est.): Rome 2.8 mln.; Milan 1.5 mln.; Naples 1.2 mln.; Turin 1.0 mln.

Government: Type: Republic. **Head of state:** Pres. Francesco Cossiga; b. July 26, 1929; in office: July 9, 1985; **Head of government:** Prime Min. Giovanni Goria; b. July 30, 1943; in office: July 29, 1987. **Local divisions:** 20 regions with some autonomy, 94 provinces. **Defence:** 2.5% of GNP (1986).

Economy: Industries: Steel, machinery, autos, textiles, shoes, machine tools, chemicals. **Chief crops:** Grapes, olives, citrus fruits, vegetables, wheat, rice. **Minerals:** Mercury, potash, gas, marble, sulphur, coal. **Crude oil reserves** (1987): 951 mln. bbls. **Arable land:** 41%. **Livestock** (1985): cattle: 8.9 mln.; pigs: 9.1 mln.; sheep: 9.6 mln. **Fish catch** (1985): 428 000 metric tons. **Electricity prod.** (1985): 182 bln. kwh. **Crude steel prod.** (1986): 22.8 mln. metric tons. **Labor force:** 10% agric.; 30% ind. and comm.; 49% services and govt.

Finance: Currency: Lira (June 1988: 1 283 = $1 US). **Gross national product** (1986): $368 bln. **Per capita income** (1986): $6 447. **Imports** (1987): $125 bln.; partners: W. Ger. 16%, Fr. 12%, U.S. 7%. **Exports** (1987): $111 bln.; partners: W. Ger. 16%, Fr. 15%, U.S. 7%, UK 6%. **Tourists** (1985): receipts $8.7 bln. **National budget** (1983): $173 bln. expenditures. **International reserves less gold** (Apr. 1988): $29 bln. **Gold:** 66.67 mln. oz t. **Consumer prices** (change in 1987): 4.7%.

Transport: Railway traffic (1986): 40 bln. passenger-km; 17.5 bln. net ton-km. **Motor vehicles:** in use (1985): 22.3 mln. passenger cars, 1.9 mln. comm. **Civil aviation** (1986): 13.9 bln. passenger-km; 859 mln. freight ton-km. **Chief ports:** Genoa, Venice, Trieste, Taranto, Naples, La Spezia.

Communications: Television sets: 15.0 mln. in use (1986). **Radios:** 14 mln. in use (1986). **Telephones in use** (1985): 25.6 mln. **Daily newspaper circ.** (1985): 109 per 1 000 pop.

Health: Life expectancy at birth (1983): 73.0 male; 79.1 female. **Births** (per 1 000 pop. 1985): 10.2. **Deaths** (per 1 000 pop. 1985): 10. **Natural increase** (1985): 0%. **Hospital beds** (1983): 500 828. **Physicians** (1981): 97 003. **Infant mortality** (per 1 000 live births 1985): 12.

Education (1985): Literacy: 97%. **Years compulsory:** 8.

Major International Organizations: UN and all of its specialized agencies, NATO, OECD, EC.

Canadian Embassy: Via G.B. de Rossi 27, 00161 Rome; Tel: 855-341, -342, -343.

Rome emerged as the major power in Italy after 500 BC, dominating the more civilized Etruscans to the N and Greeks to the S. Under the Empire, which lasted until the 5th century AD, Rome ruled most of Western Europe, the Balkans, the Near East, and North Africa. In 1988, archeologists unearthed evidence showing Rome as a dynamic society in the 6th and 7th centuries B.C.

After the Germanic invasions, lasting several centuries, a high civilization arose in the city-states of the N, culminating in the Renaissance. But German, French, Spanish, and Austrian intervention prevented the unification of the country. In 1859 Lombardy came under the crown of King Victor Emmanuel II of Sardinia. By plebiscite in 1860, Parma, Modena, Romagna, and Tuscany joined, followed by Sicily and Naples, and by the Marches and Umbria. The first Italian parliament declared Victor Emmanuel king of Italy Mar. 17, 1861. Mantua and Venetia were added in 1866 as an outcome of the Austro-Prussian war. The Papal States were taken by Italian troops Sept. 20, 1870, on the withdrawal of the French garrison. The states were annexed to the kingdom by plebiscite. Italy recognized the State of Vatican City as independent Feb. 11, 1929.

Fascism appeared in Italy Mar. 23, 1919, led by Benito Mussolini, who took over the government at the invitation of the king Oct. 28, 1922. Mussolini acquired dictatorial powers. He made war on Ethiopia and proclaimed Victor Emmanuel III emperor, defied the sanctions of the League of Nations, joined the Berlin-Tokyo axis, sent troops to fight for Franco against the Republic of Spain and joined Germany in World War II.

After Fascism was overthrown in 1943, Italy declared war on Germany and Japan and contributed to the Allied victory. It surrendered conquered lands and lost its colonies. Mussolini was killed by partisans Apr. 28, 1945.

Victor Emmanuel III abdicated May 9, 1946; his son Humbert II was king until June 10, when Italy became a republic after a referendum, June 2-3.

Reorganization of the Fascist party is forbidden. The cabinet normally represents a coalition of the Christian Democrats, largest of Italy's many parties, and one or 2 other parties.

The Vatican agreed in 1976 to revise its 1929 concordat with the state, depriving Roman Catholicism of its status as state religion. In 1974 Italians voted by a 3-to-2 margin to retain a 3-year-old law permitting divorce, which was opposed by the church.

Italy has enjoyed an extraordinary growth in industry and living standards since World War II, in part due to membership in the Common Market. Italy joined the European Monetary System, 1980. A wave of left-wing political violence began in the late 1970s with kidnappings and assassinations and continued through the 1980s. Christian Dem. leader and former Prime Min. Moro was murdered May 1978 by Red Brigade terrorists.

The Cabinet of Prime Min. Arnaldo Forlani resigned, May 26, 1981, in the wake of revelations that numerous high-ranking officials were members of an illegally secret Masonic lodge. The June 1983 elections saw Bettino Craxi chosen the nation's first Socialist premier. Craxi's government faced a severe crisis as the result of a chain of events sparked by the Oct. 17, 1985 hijacking of the Italian cruise ship *Achille Lauro* and the subsequent U.S. downing on Italian soil of an Egyptian aircraft carrying the 4 hijackers and Abul Abbas, a PLO leader suspected of planning the hijacking. Craxi's release of Abbas and refusal to turn the 4 hijackers over to the U.S. caused an internal crisis that almost saw his government fall. Craxi ended the longest tenure of an Italian leader since World War II by resigning Mar. 1987.

Sicily, 25 808 sq. km, pop. (1986) 5 084 000, is an island 290 by 193 km, seat of a region that embraces the island of **Pantelleria,** 83 sq. km, and the **Lipari** group, 114 sq. km, including 2 active volcanoes: **Vulcano,** 491 m and **Stromboli,** 911 m. From prehistoric times Sicily has been settled by various peoples; a Greek state had its capital at Syracuse. Rome took Sicily from Carthage 215 BC. **Mt. Etna,** 3 369 m active volcano, is tallest peak.

Sardinia, 24 183 sq. km, pop. (1986) 1 638 000, lies in the Mediterranean, 185 km W of Italy and 12 km S of Corsica. It is 257 km long, 109 km wide, and mountainous, with mining of coal, zinc, lead, copper. In 1720 Sardinia was added to the possessions of the Dukes of Savoy in Piedmont and Savoy to form the Kingdom of Sardinia. Giuseppe Garibaldi is buried on the nearby isle of Caprera. **Elba,** 224 sq. km, lies 9.6 km W of Tuscany. Napoleon I lived in exile on Elba 1814-1815.

Trieste. An agreement, signed Oct. 5, 1954, by Italy and Yugoslavia, confirmed, Nov. 10, 1975, gave Italy provisional administration over the northern section and the seaport of Trieste, and Yugoslavia the part of Istrian peninsula it has occupied.

Jamaica

People: Population (1989 est.): 2 362 000. **Age distrib.** (%): 0–14: 36.7; 15–59: 52.8; 60+: 8.5. **Pop. density:** 215.5 per sq. km. **Urban** (1986): 49%. **Ethnic groups:** African 76%, mixed 15%, Chinese, Caucasian, East Indian. **Languages:** English, Jamaican Creole. **Religion:** Protestant 70%.

Geography: Area: 10 960 sq. km. **Location:** In West Indies. **Neighbors:** Nearest are Cuba on N, Haiti on E. **Topography:** The country is four-fifths covered by mountains. **Capital:** Kingston. **Cities** (1984 est.): St. Andrews 393 000, Kingston 100 000.

Government: Type: Independent state. **Head of state:** Queen Elizabeth II, represented by Gov.-Gen. Florizel A. Glasspole; b. Sept. 25, 1909; in office: Mar. 2, 1973. **Head of government:** Prime Min. Edward Seaga; b. May 28, 1930; in office: Oct., 1980. **Local divisions:** 14 parishes; Kingston and St. Andrew corporate area. **Defence:** 1.1% of GDP (1986).

Economy: Industries: Rum, molasses, cement, paper, tourism. **Chief crops:** Sugar cane, coffee, bananas, coconuts, citrus fruits. **Minerals:** Bauxite, limestone, gypsum. **Arable land:** 24%. **Livestock** (1985): cattle: 318 000; goats: 420 000. **Electricity prod.** (1986): 1.5 bln. kwh. **Labor force:** 35% agric.; 19% services; 13% manuf.

Finance: Currency: Dollar (Apr. 1988: 5.48 = $1 US). **Gross national product** (1986): $2.0 bln. **Per capita income** (1981): $1 340. **Imports** (1987): $1.2 bln.; partners: U.S. 44%, Venez. 11%, Neth. Ant. 10%, UK 17%. **Exports** (1987): $649 mln.; partners: U.S. 33%, UK 17%, Can. 16%. **Tourists** (1986): receipts: $482 mln. **National budget** (1986): $584 mln. **International reserves less gold** (Feb. 1988): $172 mln. **Consumer prices** (change in 1987): 6.7%.

Transport: Railway traffic (1985): 40 mln. passenger-km; 129 mln. net ton-km. **Motor vehicles:** in use (1985): 42 000

passenger cars, 23 000 comm. vehicles. **Civil aviation** (1986): 1.7 bln. passenger-km; 19.0 mln. freight ton-km. **Chief ports:** Kingston, Montego Bay.

Communications: Television sets: 350 000 in use (1986). **Radios:** 910 000 in use (1986). **Telephones in use** (1985): 143 000. **Daily newspaper circ.** (1986): 36 per 1 000 pop.

Health: Life expectancy at birth (1984): 65 years. **Births** (per 1 000 pop. 1985): 26. **Deaths** (per 1 000 pop. 1985): 6. **Natural increase** (1985): 2.0%. **Hospital beds** (1984): 6 066. **Physicians** (1985): 319. **Infant mortality** (per 1 000 live births 1986): 28.0.

Education (1987): **Literacy:** 73%. Compulsory to age 14.

Major International Organizations: UN (World Bank, GATT), OAS.

Canadian High Commission: Royal Bank Bldg., 30-36 Knutsford Blvd., Kingston 5; postal: P.O. Box 1500, Kingston 10; Tel: 926-1500, -1, -2, -3, -4.

Jamaica was visited by Columbus, 1494, and ruled by Spain (under whom Arawak Indians died out) until seized by Britain, 1655. Jamaica won independence Aug. 6, 1962.

In 1974 Jamaica sought an increase in taxes paid by U.S. and Canadian companies which mine bauxite on the island. The socialist government acquired 50% ownership of the companies' Jamaican interests in 1976, and was reelected that year. Rudimentary welfare state measures were passed, but unemployment increased. Jamaica has broken diplomatic relations with Cuba.

Japan

Nippon

People: Population (1989 est.): 123 231 000. **Age distrib.** (%): 0–14: 20.4; 15–59: 63.9; 60+: 15.7. **Pop. density:** 326.2 per sq. km. **Urban** (1980): 76.2%. **Language:** Japanese. **Ethnic groups:** Japanese 99.4%, Korean 0.5%. **Religions:** Buddhism, Shintoism shared by large majority.

Geography: Area: 377 738 sq. km. **Location:** Archipelago off E. coast of Asia. **Neighbors:** USSR on N, S. Korea on W. **Topography:** Japan consists of 4 main islands: Honshu ("mainland"), 228 293 sq. km; Hokkaido, 78 374 sq. km; Kyushu, 36 696 sq. km; and Shikoku, 18 327 sq. km. The coast, deeply indented, measures 26 646 km. The northern islands are a continuation of the Sakhalin Mts. The Kunlun range of China continues into southern islands, the ranges meeting in the Japanese Alps. A group of volcanoes, mostly extinct or inactive, including 3 776 m Fuji-San (Fujiyama) near Tokyo rises in a vast transverse fissure crossing Honshu E-W. **Capital:** Tokyo. **Cities** (1987 est.): Tokyo 8.3 mln.; Osaka 2.6 mln.; Yokohama 3.0 mln.; Nagoya 2.1 mln.; Kyoto 1.4 mln.; Kobe 1.4 mln.; Sapporo 1.5 mln.; Kitakyushu 1 mln.; Kawasaki 1.1 mln; Fukuoka 1.1 mln.

Government: Type: Parliamentary democracy. **Head of state:** Emp. Hirohito; b. Apr. 29, 1901; in office: Dec. 25, 1926. **Head of government:** Prime Min. Noboru Takeshita; in office: Nov. 6, 1987. **Local divisions:** 47 prefectures. **Defence:** Less than 1% of GNP (1984).

Economy: Industries: Electrical & electronic equip., autos, machinery, chemicals. **Chief crops:** Rice, grains, vegetables, fruits. **Minerals:** negligible. **Crude oil reserves** (1985): 26 mln. bbls. **Arable land:** 13%. **Livestock** (1986): cattle: 4.6 mln.; pigs: 10.3 mln. **Fish catch** (1986): 12.6 mln. metric tons. **Electricity prod.** (1986): 601 bln. kwh. **Crude steel prod.** (1986): 98.2 mln. metric tons. **Labor force:** 9% agric.; 34% manuf; 53% services & trades.

Finance: Currency: Yen (May 1988: 125 = $1 US). **Gross national product** (1986): $1.9 trl. **Per capita income** (1984): $11 266. **Imports** (1987): $150 bln.; partners: U.S. 20%, Middle East 26%, SE Asia 22%, EC 6%. **Exports** (1987): $231 bln.; partners: U.S. 37%, EC 12%, SE Asia 23%. **Tourists** (1985): $1.1 bln. receipts. **National budget** (1988): $450 bln. expenditures. **International reserves less gold** (Mar. 1988): $84 bln. **Gold:** 24.23 mln. oz. t. **Consumer prices** (change in 1987): 0.0%.

Transport: Railway traffic (1985): 330 bln. passenger-km; 22.1 bln. net ton-km. **Motor vehicles:** in use (1986): 27.8 mln. passenger cars, 17.3 mln. comm. vehicles. **Civil aviation** (1985): 65.5 bln. passenger-km; 3.0 bln. freight ton-km. **Chief**

ports: Yokohama, Tokyo, Kobe, Osaka, Nagoya, Chiba, Kawasaki, Hakodate.

Communications: Television sets: 31.3 mln. in use (1986). **Radios:** 94 mln. in use (1986). **Telephones in use** (1985): 66.6 mln. **Daily newspaper circ.** (1986): 569 per 1 000 pop.

Health: Life expectancy at birth (1986): 75.1 male; 80.8 female. **Births** (per 1 000 pop. 1986): 11.4. **Deaths** (per 1 000 pop. 1986): 6.2. **Natural increase** (1986): 0.5%. **Hospital beds** (1986): 1.4 mln. **Physicians** (1986): 179 000. **Infant mortality** (per 1 000 live births 1985): 6.0.

Education (1987): **Literacy:** 99%. Most attend school for 12 years.

Major International Organizations: UN (IMF, GATT, ILO), OECD.

Canadian Embassy: 3-38 Akasaka 7-chome, Minato-ku, Tokyo 107; Tel: 408-2101, -8.

According to Japanese legend, the empire was founded by Emperor Jimmu, 660 BC, but earliest records of a unified Japan date from 1 000 years later. Chinese influence was strong in the formation of Japanese civilization. Buddhism was introduced before the 6th century.

A feudal system, with locally powerful noble families and their samurai warrior retainers, dominated from 1192. Central power was held by successive families of shoguns (military dictators), 1192-1867, until recovered by the Emperor Meiji, 1868. The Portuguese and Dutch had minor trade with Japan in the 16th and 17th centuries; U.S. Commodore Matthew C. Perry opened it to U.S. trade in a treaty ratified 1854. Japan fought China, 1894-95, gaining Taiwan. After war with Russia, 1904-05, Russia ceded S half of Sakhalin and gave concessions in China. Japan annexed Korea 1910. In World War I Japan ousted Germany from Shantung, took over German Pacific islands. Japan took Manchuria 1931, started war with China 1932. Japan launched war against the U.S. by attack on Pearl Harbor Dec. 7, 1941. Japan surrendered Aug. 14, 1945.

In a new constitution adopted May 3, 1947, Japan renounced the right to wage war; the emperor gave up claims to divinity; the Diet became the sole law-making authority.

The U.S. and 48 other non-communist nations signed a peace treaty and the U.S. a bilateral defense agreement with Japan, in San Francisco Sept. 8, 1951, restoring Japan's sovereignty as of April 28, 1952. Japan signed separate treaties with China, 1952; India, 1952; a declaration with USSR ending a technical state of war, 1956. In Dec. 1965 Japan and South Korea agreed to resume diplomatic relations.

On June 26, 1968, the U.S. returned to Japanese control the Bonin Is., the Volcano Is. (including Iwo Jima) and Marcus Is. On May 15, 1972, Okinawa, the other Ryukyu Is. and the Daito Is. were returned to Japan by the U.S.; it was agreed the U.S. would continue to maintain military bases on Okinawa. Japan and the USSR have failed to resolve disputed claims of sovereignty over 4 of the Kurile Is. and over offshore fishing rights.

In 1972, Japan and China resumed diplomatic relations.

Industrialization was begun in the late 19th century. After World War II, Japan emerged as one of the most powerful economies in the world, and as a leader in technology.

The U.S. and EC member nations have criticized Japan for its restrictive policy on imports which has given Japan a substantial trade surplus.

Jordan
Hashemite Kingdom of Jordan
al Mamlaka al Urduniya al Hashemiyah

Population (1989 est.): 3 031 000. **Age distrib.** (%): 0–14: 48.1; 15–59: 46.9; 60+: 4.0. **Pop. density:** 31.0 per sq. km. **Urban** (1986): 70%. **Ethnic groups:** Arab 98%, Circassians, Armenians, Kurds. **Languages:** Arabic (official), English. **Religions:** Sunni Moslem 93.6%, Christian 5%.

Geography: Area: 97 731 sq. km. **Location:** In W Asia. **Neighbors:** Israel on W, Saudi Arabia on S, Iraq on E, Syria on N. **Topography:** About 88% of Jordan is arid. Fertile areas are in W. Only port is on short Aqaba Gulf coast. Country shares Dead Sea (389 m below sea level) with Israel. **Capital:** Amman. **Cities** (1986 est.): Amman 833 000; az-Zarqa 285 000; Irbid 150 000.

Government: Type: Constitutional monarchy. **Head of state:** King Hussein I; b. Nov. 14, 1935; in office: Aug. 11, 1952. **Head of government:** Prime Min. Zaid Rifai; b. 1937; in office: Apr. 4, 1985. **Local divisions:** 8 governorates. **Defence:** 12% of GNP (1985).

Economy: Industries: Textiles, cement, food processing. **Chief crops:** Grains, olives, vegetables, fruits. **Minerals:** Phosphate, potash. **Arable land:** 5%. **Electricity prod.** (1986): 2.8 bln. kwh. **Labor force:** 20% agric. 20% manuf. & mining.

Finance: Currency: Dinar (Mar. 1988: 0.33 = $1 US). **Gross national product** (1985): $4.0 bln. **Imports** (1986): $2.4 bln.; partners: Saudi Ar. 19%, U.S. 11%, Jap. 8%. **Exports** (1986): $733 mln.; partners: Saudi Ar. 12%, Ind. 13%, Iraq. 26%. **Tourists** (1985): receipts: $555 mln. **National budget** (1985): $2.2 bln. revenues; $2.68 bln. expenditures. **International reserves less gold** (Mar. 1988): $146 mln. **Gold:** 1.0 mln. oz t. **Consumer prices** (change in 1987): −0.3%.

Transport: Motor vehicles: in use (1982): 118 900 passenger cars, 43 600 comm. vehicles. **Civil aviation** (1984): 3.6 bln. passenger-km; 139 mln. freight ton-km. **Chief ports:** Aqaba.

Communications: Television sets: 181 000 in use (1985). **Radios:** 550 000 in use (1985). **Telephones in use** (1983): 86 000. **Daily newspaper circ.** (1985): 68 per 1 000 pop.

Health: Life expectancy at birth (1985): 60.3 male; 64.2 female. **Births** (per 1 000 pop. 1985): 45.3. **Deaths** (per 1 000 pop. 1985): 9.1. **Natural increase** (1985): 3.6%. **Hospital beds** (1984): 3 578. **Physicians** (1984): 2 310. **Infant mortality** (per 1 000 live births 1985): 51.

Education (1980): **Literacy:** 31%.

Major International Organizations: UN (WHO, IMF), Arab League.

Canadian Embassy: Pearl of Shmeisana Bldg. SH Shmeisani, Amman; Postal: P.O. Box 815403, Amman; Tel: 666-124, -5, -6.

From ancient times to 1922 the lands to the E of the Jordan were culturally and politically united with the lands to the W. Arabs conquered the area in the 7th century; the Ottomans took control in the 16th. Britain's 1920 Palestine Mandate covered both sides of the Jordan. In 1921, Abdullah, son of the ruler of Hejaz in Arabia, was installed by Britain as emir of an autonomous Transjordan, covering two-thirds of Palestine. An independent kingdom was proclaimed, 1946.

During the 1948 Arab-Israeli war the West Bank and old city of Jerusalem were added to the kingdom, which changed its name to Jordan. All these territories were lost to Israel in the 1967 war, which swelled the number of Arab refugees on the East Bank. A 1974 Arab summit conference designated the Palestine Liberation Organization as the sole representative of Arabs on the West Bank. Jordan accepted the move, and was granted an annual subsidy by Arab oil states.

King Hussein actively promoted rejection of the Egyptian-Israeli peace treaty.

Kenya
Republic of Kenya
Jamhuri ya Kenya

People: Population (1989 est.): 23 727 000. **Age distrib.** (%): 0–14: 52.3; 15–59: 43.2; 60+: 4.5. **Pop. density:** 40.7 per sq. km. **Urban** (1985): 16%. **Ethnic groups:** Kikuyu 21%, Luo 13%, Luhya 14%, Kelenjin 11%, Kamba 11%, others, including Asians, Arabs, Europeans. **Languages:** Swahili (official), English. **Religions:** Protestant 38%, Roman Catholic 26%, Moslem 6%, others.

Geography: Area: 582 601 sq. km. **Location:** On Indian O. coast of E. Africa. **Neighbors:** Uganda on W, Tanzania on S, Somalia on E, Ethopia, Sudan on N. **Topography:** The northern three-fifths of Kenya is arid. To the S, a low coastal area and a plateau varying from 900 to 3 000 m. The Great Rift Valley enters the country N-S, flanked by high mountains. **Capital:** Nairobi. **Cities** (1987): Nairobi 959 000; Mombasa 401 000.

Government: Type: Republic. **Head of state:** Pres. Daniel arap Moi, b. Sept., 1924; in office: Aug. 22, 1978. **Local divisions:** Nairobi and 7 provinces. **Defence:** 4.8% of GDP (1985).

Economy: Industries: Tourism, light industry, petroleum prods. **Chief crops:** Coffee, corn, tea, cereals, cotton, sisal.

Minerals: Gold, limestone, diatomite, salt, barytes, magnesite, felspar, sapphires, fluospar, garnets. **Other resources:** Timber, hides. **Arable land:** 4%. **Livestock** (1985): cattle: 12.5 mln. **Fish catch** (1985): 91 000 metric tons. **Electricity prod.** (1986): 1.9 bln. kwh. **Labor force:** 17% agric.; 18% ind. and commerce; 13% services; 50% public sector.

Finance: Currency: Shilling (Mar. 1988: 17.02 = $1 US). **Gross national product** (1986): $6.7 bln. **Per capita income** (1986): $322. **Imports** (1986): $1.6 bln.; partners: UK 14%, W. Ger. 8%, Jap. 8, Saudi Ar. 17%. **Exports** (1986): $1.2 bln.; partners: W. Ger. 11%, UK 18%, Ugan. 9%. **Tourists** (1985): receipts: $128 mln. **National budget** (1985): $2 bln. **International reserves less gold** (Mar. 1988): $265 mln. **Gold:** 80 000 oz t. **Consumer prices** (change in 1987): 5.2%.

Transport: Motor vehicles: in use (1984): 122 000 passenger cars, 96 000 comm. vehicles. **Civil aviation** (1985): 1.1 bln. passenger-km; 136 mln. freight ton-km. **Chief ports:** Mombasa.

Communications: Television sets: 192 000 in use (1986). **Radios:** 2.1 bln. in use (1986). **Telephones in use** (1983): 216 000. **Daily newspaper circ.** (1986): 16 per 1 000 pop.

Health: Life expectancy at birth (1983): 56.3 male; 60.0 female. **Births** (per 1 000 pop. 1985): 55.1. **Deaths** (per 1 000 pop. 1985): 14.0. **Natural increase** (1984): 4.1%. **Hospital beds** (1985): 30 886. **Physicians** (1985): 2 752. **Infant mortality** (per 1 000 live births 1985): 83.

Education (1985): **Literacy:** 50%. 83% attend primary school.

Major International Organizations: UN and all of its specialized agencies, OAU, Commonwealth of Nations.

Canadian High Commission: Comcraft House, Hailé Sélassie Ave.; P.O. Box 30481, Nairobi; Tel: 334-033, -4, -5, -6.

Arab colonies exported spices and slaves from the Kenya coast as early as the 8th century. Britain obtained control in the 19th century. Kenya won independence Dec. 12, 1963, 4 years after the end of the violent Mau Mau uprising.

Kenya has shown steady growth in industry and agriculture under a modified private enterprise system, and has had a relatively stable political life. This stability was shaken in 1974-5, with opposition charges of corruption and oppression.

In 1968 ties with Somalia were restored after 4 years of skirmishes. Tanzania closed its Kenya border in 1977 in a dispute over the collapse of the East African Community.

Kenya has close ties to the West.

Kiribati
Republic of Kiribati

People: Population (1989 est.): 65 000. **Pop. density:** 94.4 per sq. km. **Ethnic groups:** nearly all Micronesian, some Polynesians. **Languages:** Gilbertese and English (official). **Religions:** evenly divided between Protestant and Roman Catholic.

Geography: Area: 689 sq. km. **Location:** 33 Micronesian islands (the Gilbert, Line, and Phoenix groups) in the mid-Pacific scattered in a 5.2 mln sq. km chain around the point where the International Date Line cuts the Equator. **Neighbors:** Nearest are Nauru to SW, Tuvalu and Tokelau Is. to S. **Topography:** except Banaba (Ocean) I., all are low-lying, with soil of coral sand and rock fragments, subject to erratic rainfall. **Capital** (1985): Tarawa 21 000.

Government: Type: Republic. **Head of state and of government:** Pres. Ieremia Tabai, b. Dec. 16, 1950; in office: July 12, 1979.

Economy: Industries: Copra. **Chief crops:** Coconuts, breadfruit, pandanus, bananas, paw paw. **Other resources:** Fish. **Electricity prod.** (1986): 8 mln. kwh.

Finance: Currency: Australian dollar. **Gross national product** (1985): $25 mln.

Transport: Chief port: Tarawa.

Communications: Radios: 10 000 in use (1986). **Telephones in use** (1984): 1 400.

Health: Hospital beds (1983): 263; **Physicians:** 19.

Education: Literacy (1985): 90%.

Canadian High Commission: c/o The Canadian High Commission, P.O. Box 12-049, Wellington North, New Zealand.

A British protectorate since 1892, the Gilbert and Ellice Islands colony was completed with the inclusion of the Phoenix Islands,

1937. Self-rule was granted 1971; the Ellice Islands separated from the colony 1975 and became independent Tuvalu, 1978. Kiribati (pronounced *Kiribass*) independence was attained July 12, 1979.

Tarawa Atoll was the scene of some of the bloodiest fighting in the Pacific during WW II.

North Korea
Democratic People's Republic of Korea
Chosun Minchu-chui Inmin Konghwa-guk

People: Population (1989 est.): 21 964 000. **Pop. density:** 182.2 per sq. km. **Urban** (1985): 62%. **Ethnic groups:** Korean. **Language:** Korean. **Religions:** activities almost nonexistent; traditionally Buddhism, Confucianism, Chondokyo.

Geography: Area: 120 529 sq. km. **Location:** In northern E. Asia. **Neighbors:** China, USSR on N, S. Korea on S. **Topography:** Mountains and hills cover nearly all the country, with narrow valleys and small plains in between. The N and the E coast are the most rugged areas. **Capital:** Pyongyang. **Cities** (1981 est.): Pyongyang 1 283 000.

Government: Type: Communist state. **Head of state:** Pres. Kim Il-Sung; b. Apr. 15, 1912; in office: Dec. 28, 1972. **Head of government:** Premier Li Gunmo; in office: Dec. 29, 1986. **Head of Communist Party:** Gen. Sec. Kim Il-Sung; in office: 1945. **Local divisions:** 9 provinces, 4 municipalities. **Defence** (1984): 23.3% of GNP.

Economy: Industries: Textiles, petrochemicals, food processing. **Chief crops:** Corn, potatoes, fruits, vegetables, rice. **Minerals:** Coal, lead tungsten, graphite, magnesite, iron, copper, gold, phosphate, salt, fluorspar. **Arable land:** 19%. **Livestock** (1985): cattle: 1.1 mln.; pigs: 2.8 mln. **Fish catch** (1985): 1.7 mln. metric tons. **Crude steel prod.** (1986) 9.0 mln. metric tons. **Electricity prod.** (1986): 41 bln. kwh. **Labor force:** 48% agric.

Finance: Currency: Won (Jan. 1988): 0.94 = $1 US). **Gross national product** (1985): $24 bln. **Imports** (1985): $1.7 bln.; partners: China 17%, USSR 22%, Jap. 18%. **Exports** (1985): $1.3 bln.; partners: USSR 26% China 17%, Saudi Ar. 9%, Jap. 9%.

Communications: Television sets: 1 mln. in use (1984). **Radios:** 4.1 mln. in use (1984).

Transport: Chief ports: Chonglin, Hamhung, Nampo.

Health: Life expectancy at birth (1984): 65 male; 72 female. **Births** (per 1 000 pop. 1985): 30. **Deaths** (per 1 000 pop. 1985): 7. **Natural increase** (1985): 2.3%. **Hospital beds** (1982): 244 000. **Physicians** (1982): 45 000. **Infant mortality** (per 1 000 live births, 1985): 30.

Education (1986): **Literacy:** 99%. **Years compulsory:** 11.

The Democratic People's Republic of Korea was founded May 1, 1948, in the zone occupied by Russian troops after World War II. Its armies tried to conquer the south, 1950. After 3 years of fighting with Chinese and U.S. intervention, a cease-fire was proclaimed.

Industry, begun by the Japanese during their 1910-45 occupation, and nationalized in the 1940s, had grown substantially, using N. Korea's abundant mineral and hydroelectric resources.

Two N. Korean Army officers were sentenced to death by Burmese authorities after they confessed to the October 9, 1983 bombing which killed 17, including 4 S. Korean cabinet ministers, in Rangoon.

South Korea
Republic of Korea
Taehan Min'guk

People: Population (1989 est.): 45 243 000. **Age distrib.** (%): 0–14: 30.6; 15–59: 52.7; 60+: 6.7. **Pop. density:** 459.4 per sq km. **Urban** (1985): 65%. **Ethnic groups:** Korean. **Language:** Korean. **Religions:** Buddhism, Confucianism, Christian.

Geography: Area: 98 477 sq km. **Location:** In Northern E.

Asia. **Neighbors:** N. Korea on N. **Topography:** The country is mountainous, with a rugged east coast. The western and southern coasts are deeply indented, with many islands and harbors. **Capital:** Seoul. **Cities** (1985 est.): Seoul 9 600 000; Pusan 3 500 000; Taegu 2 000 000.

Government: Type: Republic, with power centralized in a strong executive. **Head of state:** Pres. Roh Tae Woo; b. 1932; in office: Feb. 25, 1988. **Head of government:** Prime Min. Lee Hyun Jae; in office: Feb. 18, 1988. **Local divisions:** 9 provinces and Seoul, Pusan, Inchon, and Taegu. **Defence:** 5.5% of GNP (1986).

Economy: Industries: Electronics, ships, textiles, clothing, motor vehicles. **Chief crops:** Rice, barley, vegetables. **Minerals:** Tungsten, coal, graphite. **Arable land:** 22%. **Livestock** (1984): cattle: 2.2 mln.; pigs: 3.6 mln. **Fish catch:** (1985): 3.1 mln. metric tons. **Electricity prod.** (1986): 65.0 bln. kwh. **Crude steel prod.** (1986): 14.5 mln. metric tons. **Labor force:** 30% agric.; 21% manuf. & mining; 47% services.

Finance: Currency: Won (Mar. 1988: 746 = $1 US). **Gross national product** (1986): $90.6 bln. **Per capita income** (1986): $2 180. **Imports** (1987): $33 bln.; partners: Jap. 41%, U.S. 21%. **Exports** (1987): $347 bln.; partners: U.S. 40%, Jap. 15%. **Tourists** (1985): receipts: $673 mln. **National budget** (1987): 18.0 bln. expenditures. **International reserves less gold** (Mar. 1988): $6.9 bln. **Gold:** 320 000 oz t. **Consumer prices** (change in 1987): 3.0%.

Transport: Railway traffic (1986): 21.6 bln. passenger-km; 11.6 bln. net ton-km. **Motor vehicles:** in use (1986): 556 000 passenger cars, 541 000 comm. vehicles. **Civil aviation** (1985): 10.2 bln. passenger-km; 2.0 bln. freight ton-km. **Chief ports:** Pusan, Inchon.

Communications: Television sets: 8.2 mln. in use (1985). **Radios:** 10.2 mln. in use (1984). **Telephones in use** (1985): 6.9 mln. **Daily newspaper circ.** (1986): 24 per 1 000 pop.

Health: Life expectancy at birth (1986): 65.2 male; 71.5 female. **Births** (per 1 000 pop. 1986): 21.8. **Deaths** (per 1 000 pop. 1986): 6.3. **Natural increase** (1986): 1.5%. **Hospital beds** (1985): 74 000. **Physicians** (1985): 29 596. **Infant mortality** (per 1 000 live births 1985): 30.

Education (1987): **Literacy:** 92%. **Attendance:** High school 90%, college 14%.

Canadian Embassy: 10th fl., Kolon Bldg., 45 Mugyo-Dong, Jung-Ku; postal: P.O. Box 6299, Seoul 100; Tel: 753-2605, -06, -07, -08.

Korea, once called the Hermit Kingdom, has a recorded history since the 1st century BC. It was united in a kingdom under the Silla Dynasty, 668 AD. It was at times associated with the Chinese empire; the treaty that concluded the Sino-Japanese war of 1894-95 recognized Korea's complete independence. In 1910 Japan forcibly annexed Korea as Chosun.

At the Potsdam conference, July, 1945, the 38th parallel was designated as the line dividing the Soviet and the American occupation. Russian troops entered Korea Aug. 10, 1945, U.S. troops entered Sept. 8, 1945. The Soviet military organized socialists and communists and blocked efforts to let the Koreans unite their country.

The South Koreans formed the Republic of Korea in May 1948 with Seoul as the capital. Dr. Syngman Rhee was chosen president but a movement spearheaded by college students forced his resignation Apr. 26, 1960.

In an army coup May 16, 1961, Gen. Park Chung Hee became chairman of the ruling junta. He was elected president, 1963; a 1972 referendum allowed him to be reelected for 6 year terms unlimited times. Park was assassinated by the chief of the Korean CIA, Oct. 26, 1979. The calm of the new government was halted by the rise of Gen. Chon Too Hwan, head of the military intelligence, who reinstated martial law, and reverted South Korea to the police state it was under Park.

North Korean raids across the border tapered off in 1971, but incidents occurred in 1973 and 1974. In July 1972 South and North Korea agreed on a common goal of reunifying the 2 nations by peaceful means. But there had been no sign of a thaw in relations between the two regimes until 1985 when they agreed to discuss economic issues. In 1988, radical students demanding reunification clashed with police.

A Korean Air Lines passenger airliner was shot down by a Soviet jet fighter, Sept. 1, 1983, after it strayed into Soviet airspace; all 269 people aboard died.

On June 10, 1987, middle class office workers, shopkeepers and business executives joined students in anti-government protests in Seoul. They were protesting President Chun's decision to choose his successor and not allow the next president to be chosen by direct vote of the people. Following weeks of rioting and violence, Chun agreed July 17 to permit election of the next president by direct popular vote, in addition to other constitutional reforms. Student protest resumed in Sept. in an attempt to gain wage increases for workers. In Dec., Roh Tae Woo was elected president.

South Korea hosted the 1988 summer Olympic games.

Kuwait

State of Kuwait

Dowlat al-Kuwait

People: Population (1989 est.): 1 967 000. **Age distrib.** (%): 0–14: 40.2; 15–59: 57.6; 60+: 2.3. **Pop. density:** 110.4 per sq. km. **Ethnic groups:** Kuwaiti 39%, other Arab 39%, Iranian, Indian, Pakistani. **Languages:** Arabic, others. **Religion:** Moslem 85%.

Geography: Area: 17 817 sq. km. **Location:** In Middle East, at N end of Persian Gulf. **Neighbors:** Iraq on N, Saudi Arabia on S. **Topography:** The country is flat, very dry, and extremely hot. **Capital:** Kuwait. **Cities** (1985 est.): Hawalli 145 000; As-S almiyah 153 000.

Government: Type: Constitutional monarchy. **Head of state:** Emir Shaikh Jabir al-Ahmad al-Jabir as-Sabah; b. 1928; in office: Jan. 1, 1978. **Head of government:** Prime Min. Shaikh Saad Abdulla as-Salim as-Sabah; in office: Feb. 8, 1978. **Local divisions:** 4 governorates. **Defence:** 5.3% of GNP (1984).

Economy: Industries: Oil products. **Minerals:** Oil, gas. **Crude oil reserves** (1987): 94 bln. bbls. **Cultivated land:** 1%. **Electricity prod.** (1986): 16.3 bln. kwh. **Labor force:** social services 45%; construction 20%.

Finance: Currency: Dinar (May 1988: 1.00 = $3.66 US). **Gross national product** (1986): $17.3 bln. **Per capita income** (1975): $11 431. **Imports** (1986): $5.9 bln.; partners: Jap. 21%, Fra. 10%, U.S. 9%. **Exports** (1986): $7.4 bln.; partners: Jap. 16%, It. 10%. **National budget** (1986): $11.1 bln. expenditures **International reserves less gold** (Mar. 1988): $4.3 bln. **Gold:** 2.53 mln. oz t. **Consumer prices** (change in (1987): 0.7%.

Transport: Motor vehicles: in use (1986): 412 000 passenger cars, 145 000 comm. vehicles. **Civil aviation** (1986): 3.7 bln. passenger-km; 343 mln. freight ton-km. **Chief ports:** Mina al-Ahmadi.

Communications: Television sets: 450 000 in use (1986). **Radios:** 500 000 in use (1986). **Telephones in use** (1986): 450 000. **Daily newspaper circ.** (1985): 267 per 1 000 pop.

Health: Life expectancy at birth (1985): 68.0 male; 72.9 female. **Births** (per 1 000 pop. 1986): 29.5. **Deaths** (per 1 000 pop. 1986): 2.4. **Natural increase** (1986): 2.7%. **Hospital beds** (1985): 5 523 plus 232 clinics and health centres. **Physicians** (1984): 2 983. **Infant mortality** (per 1 000 live births 1987): 26.1.

Education (1987): **Literacy:** 71%. **Years compulsory:** 8.

Major International Organizations: UN (World Bank, IMF, GATT), Arab League, OPEC.

Canadian Embassy: 28 Quaraish St., Nuzha District; P.O. Box 25281, 13113 (Safat) Kuwait City; Tel: 251-1451; 255-5754.

Kuwait is ruled by the Al-Sabah dynasty, founded 1759. Britain ran foreign relations and defense from 1899 until independence in 1961. The majority of the population is non-Kuwaiti, with many Palestinians, and cannot vote.

Oil, first exported in 1946, is the fiscal mainstay, providing most of Kuwait's income. Oil pays for free medical care, education, and social security. There are no taxes, except customs duties.

Kuwaiti oil tankers have come under frequent attack by Iran because of Kuwait's support for Iraq in the Iran-Iraq war. In July 1987, U.S. navy warships began escorting Kuwaiti tankers in the Persian Gulf.

In 1988, a Kuwaiti Airways jet was hijacked by pro-Iranian Shiite Moslem terrorists who demanded the release of 17 Shiite terrorists. The ordeal lasted 15 days as Kuwait refused to release the terrorists.

Laos

Lao People's Democratic Republic

Sathalanalat Paxathipatai Paxaxōn Lao

People: Population (1989 est.): 3 923 000. **Pop. density:** 16.6 per sq. km. **Urban** (1985): 15%. **Ethnic groups:** Lao 48%, Mon-Khmer tribes 25%, Thai 14%, Meo and Yao 13%, others. **Languages:** Lao (official), French. **Religions:** Buddhist 50%, tribal 50%.

Geography: Area: 236 780 sq. km. **Location:** In Indochina Peninsula in SE Asia. **Neighbors:** Burma, China on N, Vietnam on E, Cambodia on S, Thailand on W. **Topography:** Landlocked, dominated by jungle. High mountains along the eastern border are the source of the E-W rivers slicing across the country to the Mekong R., which defines most of the western border. **Capital:** Vientiane. **Cities** (1984 est.); Vientiane 120 000.

Government: Type: Communist. **Head of state:** Pres. Phoumi Vonguichit; in office: Oct. 31, 1986. **Head of government:** Prime Min. Kaysone Phomvihan; b. Dec. 13, 1920; in office: Dec. 2, 1975. **Local divisions:** 17 provinces. **Armed forces: Defence:** 10.5% of GNP (1984).

Economy: Industries: Wood products. **Chief crops:** Rice, corn, tobacco, cotton, opium, citrus fruits, coffee. **Minerals:** Tin. **Other resources:** Forests. **Arable land:** 4%. **Livestock** (1985): cattle: 593 mln.; pigs: 1.5 mln. **Fish catch** (1985): 20 000 metric tons. **Electricity prod.** (1986): 900 mln. kwh. **Labor force:** 85% agric.; 6% ind.

Finance: Currency: New kip (Jan. 1988): 35 = $1 US). **Gross national product** (1985): $1.8 bln. **Per capita income** (1985 est.): $500. **Imports** (1985): $163 mln.; partners: Thai. 39%, Jap. 11%, Sing. 14%. **Exports** (1985): $48 mln.; partners: Chi. 43%, U.S. 17%, Thai. 8%.

Transport: Motor vehicles: in use (1982): 15 100 passenger cars, 3 000 comm. vehicles. **Civil Aviation** (1985): 9 mln. passenger km; 100 000 net ton-km.

Communications: Radios: 232 000 in use (1986).

Health: Life expectancy at birth (1986): 45.4 male; 49.3 female. **Births** (per 1 000 pop. 1986): 41.9. **Deaths** (per 1 000 pop. 1986): 17.9. **Natural increase** (1985): 2.4%. **Hospital beds** (1985): 11 650. **Physicians** (1985): 430. **Infant mortality** (per 1 000 live births, 1986): 126.

Education: (1986): **Literacy:** 41%.

Major International Organizations: UN (FAO, IMF, WHO).

Canadian Embassy: c/o P.O. Box 2090, Bangkok 10500, Thailand.

Laos became a French protectorate in 1893, but regained independence as a constitutional monarchy July 19, 1949.

Conflicts among neutralist, communist and conservative factions created a chaotic political situation. Armed conflict increased after 1960.

The 3 factions formed a coalition government in June 1962, with neutralist Prince Souvanna Phouma as premier. A 14-nation conference in Geneva signed agreements, 1962, guaranteeing neutrality and independence. By 1964 the Pathet Lao had withdrawn from the coalition, and, with aid from N. Vietnamese troops, renewed sporadic attacks. U.S. planes bombed the Ho Chi Minh trail, supply line from N. Vietnam to communist forces in Laos and S. Vietnam. An estimated 2.75 million tons of bombs were dropped on Laos during the fighting.

In 1970 the U.S. stepped up air support and military aid. After Pathet Lao military gains, Souvanna Phouma in May 1975 ordered government troops to cease fighting; the Pathet Lao took control. A Lao People's Democratic Republic was proclaimed Dec. 3, 1975; it is strongly influenced by Vietnam.

Lebanon

Republic of Lebanon

al-Jumhouriya al-Lubnaniya

People: Population (1989 est.): 2 852 000. **Age distrib.** (%): 0–14: 35.6; 15–59: 56.4; 60+: 8.0. **Pop. density:** 274.3 per sq. km. **Urban** (1985): 83%. **Ethnic groups:** Lebanese 82%, Armenian 5%, Palestinian 9%. **Languages:** Arabic (official), French, Armenian. **Religions:** Moslem 57%; Christian 42%.

Geography: Area: 10 398 sq. km. **Location:** On Eastern end of Mediterranean Sea. **Neighbors:** Syria on E. Israel on S. **Topography:** There is a narrow coastal strip, and 2 mountain ranges running N-S enclosing the fertile Beqaa Valley. The Litani R. runs S through the valley, turning W to empty into the Mediterranean. **Capital:** Beirut. **Cities** (1985 est.): Beirut 1 500 000; Tripoli 500 000.

Government: Type: Republic. **Head of state:** Pres. Amin Gemayel; in office: Sept. 23, 1982; **Head of government:** Prime Min. Selim al-Hoss; in office: June 1, 1987. **Local divisions:** 4 provinces. **Defence:** 18% of govt. budget (1984).

Economy: Industries: Trade, food products, textiles, cement, oil products. **Chief crops:** Fruits, olives, tobacco, grapes, vegetables, grains. **Minerals:** Iron. **Arable land:** 29%. **Livestock** (1985): goats: 450 000; sheep: 135 000; **Electricity prod.** (1985): 1.3 bln. kwh. **Labor force:** 17% agric.; 75% ind., comm., services.

Finance: Currency: Pound (Mar. 1988: 363 = $1 US). **Gross national product** (1983): $3.0 bln. **Per capita income** (1983): $1 150. **Imports** (1986): $2.2 bln.; partners: It. 15%, Fr. 10%, U.S. 9%, Saudi Ar. 6%. **Exports** (1986): $500 mln.; partners: Saudi Ar. 33%, Syria 8%, Jor. 6%, Kuw. 8%. **National budget** (1985): $1.5 bln. **International reserves less gold** (Mar. 1988): $715 mln. **Gold:** 9.22 mln. oz t.

Transport: Railway traffic (1982): 5.3 mln. passenger-km; 42 mln. net ton-km. **Motor vehicles:** in use (1982): 460 000 passenger cars, 21 000 comm. vehicles. **Civil aviation** (1984): 830 mln. passenger-km; 419 mln. freight ton-km. **Chief ports:** Beirut, Tripoli, Sidon.

Communications: Television sets: 500 000 in use (1986). **Radios:** 2.0 mln. in use (1986). **Telephones:** in use (1978): 231 000. **Daily newspaper circ.** (1985): 228 per 1 000 pop.

Health: Life expectancy at birth (1985): 65.0 male; 68.9 female. **Births** (per 1 000 pop. 1985): 30. **Deaths** (per 1 000 pop. 1985): 8. **Natural increase** (1985): 2.2%. **Hospital beds** (1982): 11 400. **Physicians** (1982): 3 000. **Infant mortality** (per 1 000 live births 1985): 42.

Education: (1984): **Literacy:** 75%. **Years compulsory:** 5; attendance 93%.

Major International Organizations: UN (IMF, ILO, WHO).

Canadian Embassy: c/o P.O. Box 3394, Damascus, Syria.

Formed from 5 former Turkish Empire districts, Lebanon became an independent state Sept. 1, 1920, administered under French mandate 1920-41. French troops withdrew in 1946.

Under the 1943 National Covenant, all public positions were divided among the various religious communities, with Christians in the majority. By the 1970s, Moslems became the majority, and demanded a larger political and economic role.

U.S. Marines intervened, May-Oct. 1958, during a Syrian-aided revolt. Lebanon's efforts to restrain Palestinian commandos caused armed clashes in 1969. Continued raids against Israeli civilians, 1970-75, brought Israeli attacks against guerrilla camps and villages. Israeli troops occupied S. Lebanon, March 1978, and again in Apr. 1980.

An estimated 60 000 were killed and billions of dollars in damage inflicted in a 1975-76 civil war. Palestinian units and leftist Moslems fought against the Maronite militia, the Phalange, and other Christians. Several Arab countries provided political and arms support to the various factions, while Israel aided Christian forces. Up to 15 000 Syrian troops intervened in 1976, and fought Palestinian groups. Arab League troops from several nations tried to impose a cease-fire.

Clashes between Syrian troops and Christian forces erupted, Apr. 1, 1981, near Zahle, Lebanon, bringing to an end the cease-fire that had been in place. By Apr. 22, fighting had broken out not only between Syrians and Christians, but also between two Moslem factions. Israeli commandos attacked Palestinian positions at Tyre and Tulin. In July, Israeli air raids on Beirut killed or wounded some 800 persons. A cease-fire between Israel and the Palestinians was concluded July 24, but hostilities continued.

Israeli forces invaded Lebanon June 6, 1982, in a coordinated land, sea, and air attack aimed at crushing strongholds of the Palestine Liberation Organization (PLO). Israeli and Syrian forces engaged in the Bekka Valley. By June 14, Israeli troops had encircled Beirut. On Aug. 21, the PLO evacuated West Beirut following massive Israeli bombings of the city. The withdrawal was supervised by U.S., French, and Italian troops.

Israeli troops entered West Beirut following the Sept. 14 assassination of newly-elected Lebanese Pres. Bashir Gemayel. On Sept. 16, Lebanese Christian troops entered 2 refugee camps and massacred hundreds of Palestinian refugees.

In 1983, terrorist bombings became a way of life in Beirut as some 50 people were killed in an explosion at the U.S. Embassy, Apr. 18; 241 U.S. servicemen and 58 French soldiers died in separate Moslem suicide attacks, Oct. 23.

PLO leader Yasir Arafat and PLO dissidents backed by Syria fought a 6-week battle in Tripoli until negotiations allowed Arafat and some 4 000 followers to evacuate the city.

On Apr. 26, 1984, pro-Syrian Rashid Karami was appointed premier. The appointment failed to end virtual civil war in Beirut between Christian forces, and Druse and Shiite Moslem militias. There was heavy fighting between Shiite militiamen and Palestinian guerrillas in May 1985. Israeli troops withdrew from Lebanon in June 1985. Also in June, Beirut Airport was the scene of a hostage crisis where Shiite terrorists held U.S. citizens for 17 days.

Kidnapping of foreign nationals by Islamic militants has become common in the 1980s. U.S., British, French, and Soviet citizens have been victims.

Premier Karami was assassinated June 1, 1987, when a bomb exploded aboard a helicopter in which he was travelling.

Lesotho
Kingdom of Lesotho

People: Population (1989 est.): 1 681 000. **Age distrib.** (%): 0–14: 42.3; 15–59: 52.2; 60+: 5.7. **Pop. density:** 55.4 per sq. km. **Ethnic groups:** Sotho 99%. **Languages:** English, Sesotho (official). **Religions:** Roman Catholic 38%, Protestant 42%.

Geography: Area: 30 342 sq. km. **Location:** In Southern Africa. **Neighbors:** Completely surrounded by Republic of South Africa. **Topography:** Landlocked and mountainous, with altitudes ranging from 1 500 to 3 300 m. **Capital:** Maseru. **Cities** (1984 est.): Maseru 80 250.

Government: Type: Constitutional monarchy. **Head of state:** King Moshoeshoe II, b. May 2, 1938; in office: Mar. 12, 1960. **Head of government:** Gen. Justin Lekhanya; b. Apr. 7, 1938; in office: Jan. 20, 1986. **Local divisions:** 10 districts. **Defence:** 6.5% of GNP (1984).

Economy: Industries: Diamond polishing, food processing. **Chief crops:** Corn, grains, peas, beans. **Other resources:** Wool, mohair. **Arable land:** 10%. **Electricity prod.** (1985): 1 mln. kwh. **Labor force:** 31% agric.; 8% ind. and comm., 45% services.

Finance: Currency: Maloti (Mar. 1988: 1.00 = $.47 US). **Gross national product** (1985): $730 mln. **Per capita income** (1984): $520. **Imports** (1985): $326 mln.; partners: Mostly So. Afr. **Exports** (1985): $21 mln.; partners: Mostly So. Afr. **National budget** (1987): $163 mln.

Transport: Motor vehicles: in use (1982): 5 000 passenger cars, 11 000 comm. vehicles.

Communications: Radios: 100 000 in use (1986). **Daily newspaper circ.** (1985): 28 per 1 000 pop.

Health: Life expectancy at birth (1985): 54.2 yrs. **Births** (per 1 000 pop. 1985): 41.7. **Deaths** (per 1 000 pop. 1985): 16.4. **Natural increase** (1985): 2.5%. **Hospital beds** (1982): 2 300. **Physicians** (1982): 114. **Infant mortality** (per 1 000 live births 1985): 98.

Education (1987): **Literacy:** 59%.

Major International Organizations: UN (IMF, UNESCO, WHO), OAU.

Canadian High Commission: c/o The Canadian Embassy, P.O. Box 26006, Arcadia, Pretoria 0007, South Africa.

Lesotho (once called Basutoland) became a British protectorate in 1868 when Chief Moshesh sought protection against the Boers. Independence came Oct. 4, 1966. Elections were suspended in 1970. Over 50% of Lesotho's GNP is provided by citizens working in S. Africa. Livestock raising is the chief industry; diamonds are the chief export.

So. Africa imposed a blockade, Jan. 1, 1986, because Lesotho gave sanctuary to rebel groups fighting to overthrow the So. African Government. The blockade sparked a Jan. 20 military

coup, and was lifted, Jan. 25, when the new leaders agreed to expel the rebels.

Liberia
Republic of Liberia

People: Population (1989 est.): 2 544 000. **Age distrib.** (%): 0–14: 46.8; 15–59: 48.3; 60+: 4.9. **Pop. density:** 25.7 per sq. km. **Urban** (1985): 39.5%. **Ethnic groups:** Americo-Liberian 5%, indigenous tribes 95% **Languages:** English (official), tribal dialects. **Religions:** Moslem 20%, Christian 10%, traditional beliefs 70%.

Geography: Area: 99 060 sq. km. **Location:** On SW coast of W. Africa. **Neighbors:** Sierra Leone on W, Guinea on N, Côte d'Ivoire on E. **Topography:** Marshy Atlantic coastline rises to low mountains and plateaus in the forested interior; 6 major rivers flow in parallel courses to the ocean. **Capital:** Monrovia. **Cities** (1987 est.): Monrovia 400 000.

Government: Type: Civilian republic. **Head of state:** Pres. Samuel K. Doe; in office: Apr. 12, 1980. **Local divisions:** 3 counties. **Defense:** 2.3% of GDP (1984).

Economy: Industries: Food processing, mining. **Chief crops:** Rice, cassava, coffee, cocoa, sugar. **Minerals:** Iron, diamonds, gold. **Other resources:** Rubber, timber. **Arable land:** 4%. **Fish catch** (1984): 13 500 metric tons. **Electricity prod.** (1986): 655 mln. kwh. **Labor force:** 82% agric.

Finance: Currency: Dollar (May 1988: 1.00 = $1 US). **Gross national product** (1984): $1.1 bln. **Per capita income** (1982): $400. **Imports** (1984): $366 mln.; partners: U.S. 27%, W. Ger. 10%, Jap. 6%, Neth. 7%. **Exports** (1984): $432 mln.; partners: W. Ger. 31%, U.S. 17%, It. 14%, Fr. 9%. **National budget** (1986): $380 mln. **International reserves less gold** (Feb. 1988): $750 000. **Consumer prices** (change in 1986): 3.6%.

Transport: Motor vehicles in use (1984): 12 000 passenger cars, 8 000 comm. vehicles. **Chief ports:** Monrovia, Buchanan, Greenville.

Communications: Television sets: 42 000 in use (1986). **Radios:** 500 000 in use (1986). **Telephones in use** (1984): 7 500. **Daily newspaper circ.** (1985): 12 per 1 000 pop.

Health: Life expectancy at birth (1984): 54 yrs.; **Births** (per 1 000 pop. 1985): 48.7. **Deaths** (per 1 000 pop. 1985): 17.2. **Natural increase** (1985): 3.1%. **Hospital beds** (1981): 3 000. **Physicians** (1981): 236. **Infant mortality** (per 1 000 live births 1985): 27.

Education (1987): **Literacy:** 25%; 35% attend primary school.

Major International Organizations: UN and most specialized agencies, OAU.

Canadian Embassy: c/o The Canadian High Commission, P.O. Box 1639, Accra, Ghana.

Liberia was founded in 1822 by U.S. black freedmen who settled at Monrovia with the aid of colonization societies. It became a republic July 26, 1847, with a constitution modeled on that of the U.S. Descendants of freedmen dominated politics.

Charging rampant corruption, an Army Redemption Council of enlisted men staged a bloody predawn coup, April 12, 1980, in which Pres. Tolbert was killed and replaced as head of state by Sgt. Samuel Doe. Doe was chosen president in a disputed election, and survived a subsequent coup, in 1985.

Libya
Socialist People's Libyan Arab Jamahiriya
al-Jamahiriyah al-Arabiya al-Libya al-Shabiya al-Ishtirakiya

People: Population: (1989 est.): 4 271 000. **Age distrib.** (%): 0–14: 45.0; 15–59: 51.2; 60+: 3.8. **Pop. density:** 2.4 per sq. km. **Urban** (1985): 64%. **Ethnic groups:** Arab-Berber 97%. **Language:** Arabic. **Religion:** Sunni Moslem 97%.

Geography: Area: 1 759 404 sq. km. **Location:** On Mediterranean coast of N. Africa. **Neighbors:** Tunisia, Algeria on W,

Niger, Chad on S, Sudan, Egypt on E. **Topography:** Desert and semidesert regions cover 92% of the land, with low mountains in N, higher mountains in S, and a narrow coastal zone. **Capital:** Tripoli. **Cities** (1982 est.): Tripoli 820 000.

Government: Type: Islamic Arabic Socialist "Mass-State." **Head of state:** Col. Muammar al-Qaddafi; b. Sept. 1942; in office: Sept. 1969. **Head of government:** Premier Umar Mustafa al-Muntasir; in office: Mar. 1, 1987. **Local divisions:** 10 regions. **Defence:** 17.8% of GNP (1984).

Economy: Industries: Carpets, textiles, petroleum. **Chief crops:** Dates, olives, citrus and other fruits, grapes, wheat. **Minerals:** Gypsum, oil, gas. **Crude oil reserves** (1987): 22 bln. bbls. **Arable land:** 2%. **Livestock** (1985): sheep: 4.8 mln.; goats: 1.5 mln. **Electricity prod.** (1986): 12.6 bln. kwh. **Labor force:** 18% agric.; 31% ind.; 27% services; 24% govt.

Finance: Currency: Dinar (Feb. 1988: 1.00 = $3.61 US). **Gross domestic product** (1986): $20 bln. **Per capita income** (1984): $7 000. **Imports** (1986): $4.5 bln.; partners: It. 30%, W. Ger. 11%, Fr. 6%, Jap. 8%. **Exports** (1986): $10.9 bln.; partners: It. 24%, W. Ger. 10%, Sp. 7%. **International reserves less gold** (Mar. 1988): $5.5 bln. **Gold:** 3.6 mln. oz t.

Transport: Motor vehicles: in use (1982): 415 000 passenger cars, 334 000 comm. vehicles. **Chief ports:** Tripoli, Benghazi.

Communications: Television sets: 235 000 licensed (1986). **Radios:** 500 000 (1986). **Daily newspaper circ.** (1986): 10 per 1 000 pop.

Health: Life expectancy at birth (1985): 56.1 male; 59.4 female. **Births** (per 1 000 pop. 1985): 46. **Deaths** (per 1 000 pop. 1985): 11.2. **Natural increase** (1985): 3.4%. **Hospital beds** (1982): 16 051. **Physicians** (1982): 5 200. **Infant mortality** (per 1 000 live births 1985): 84.

Education (1985): Literacy: 60%. **Years compulsory:** 7; **Attendance:** 90%.

Major International Organizations: UN, Arab League, OAU, OPEC.

Canadian Embassy: c/o Via G.B. de Rossi 27, 00161 Rome, Italy.

First settled by Berbers, Libya was ruled by Carthage, Rome, and Vandals, the Ottomans, Italy from 1912, and Britain and France after WW II. It became an independent constitutional monarchy Jan. 2, 1952. In 1969 a junta lead by Col. Muammar al-Qaddafi seized power.

In the mid-1970s, Libya helped arm violent revolutionary groups in Egypt and Sudan, and aided terrorists of various nationalities. The USSR sold Libya advanced arms, and established close political ties.

Libya and Egypt fought several air and land battles along their border in July, 1977. Chad charged Libya with military occupation of its uranium-rich northern region in 1977. Libya's 1979 offensive into the Aouzou Strip was repulsed by Chadian forces. Libyan forces withdrew from Chad, Nov. 1981 but later returned and were driven from their last major stronghold by Chad forces in 1987, leaving over $1 billion in military equipment behind.

Widespread nationalization, arrests, imposition of currency regulations, wholesale conscription of civil servants into the army, and the fall in crude oil prices have hurt the economy.

In August, 2, 1981 Libyan jets were shot down by U.S. Navy planes taking part in naval exercises in the Gulf of Sidra which Libya claims as its territory.

The U.S. has accused Libya of masterminding numerous international terrorist actions, including the Dec. 1985 attacks on the Rome and Vienna airports.

The U.S. commenced flight operations over the Gulf of Sidra, Jan. 27, and a U.S. Navy task force began conducting exercises in the Gulf, Mar. 23. When Libya fired antiaircraft missiles at American warplanes during U.S. naval exercises in Jan. 1986 in the Gulf of Sidra, the U.S. responded by sinking 2 Libyan ships and bombing a missile installation in Libya. The U.S. withdrew from the Gulf, Mar. 27.

The U.S. accused Libyan leader Qaddafi of having ordered the Apr. 5 bombing of a West Berlin discotheque which killed 2, including a U.S. serviceman. In retaliation, the U.S. sent warplanes to attack terrorist-related targets in Tripoli and Benghazi, Libya, Apr. 14.

At the economic summit of the 7 major industrial democracies in 1986, a joint statement was issued which condemned terrorism and singled out Libya as a target for action.

Liechtenstein
Principality of Liechtenstein
Fürstentum Liechtenstein

People: Population (1989 est.): 30 000. **Age distrib.** (%): 0–14: 20.1; 15–59: 66.3; 60+: 11.6. **Pop. density:** 186.8 per sq km. **Ethnic groups:** Alemannic 95%, Italian 5%. **Languages:** German (official), Alemannic dialect. **Religions:** Roman Catholic 86%, Protestant 8%.

Geography: Area: 161 sq km. **Neighbors:** Switzerland on W, Austria on E. **Topography:** The Rhine Valley occupies one-third of the country, the Alps cover the rest. **Capital:** Vaduz. **Cities** (1986 cen.): Vaduz 4 920.

Government: Type: Hereditary constitutional monarchy. **Head of state:** Prince Franz Josef II; b. Aug. 16, 1906; in office: Mar. 30, 1938. **Head of government:** Hans Brunhart; b. Mar. 28, 1945; in office: Apr. 26, 1978. **Local divisions:** 2 districts, 11 communities.

Economy: Industries: Machines, instruments, chemicals, furniture, ceramics. **Arable land:** 25%. **Labor force:** 54% industry, trade and building; 41% services; 4% agric., fishing, forestry.

Finance: Currency: Swiss Franc. **Tourists** (1986): 76 000.

Communications: Radios: 9 000 in use (1986). **Telephones in use** (1986): 26 000. **Daily newspaper circ.** (1987): 546 per 1 000 pop.

Health: Births (per 1 000 pop. 1986): 12.80 **Deaths** (per 1 000 pop. 1986): 6.7. **Natural increase** (1986): 0.6%. **Infant mortality** (per 1 000 live births 1985): 6.3

Education (1987): Literacy: 100%. **Years compulsory** 9; attendance: 100%.

Liechtenstein became sovereign in 1866. Austria administered Liechtenstein's ports up to 1920; Switzerland has administered its postal services since 1921. Liechtenstein is united with Switzerland by a customs and monetary union. Taxes are low; many international corporations have headquarters there. Foreign workers comprise a third of the population.

The 1986 general elections were the first in which women were allowed to vote.

Luxembourg
Grand Duchy of Luxembourg
Grand-Duché de Luxembourg

People: Population: (1989 est.): 369 000. **Age distrib.** (%): 0–14: 17.3; 15–59: 64.5; 60+: 18.2. **Pop. density:** 142.8 per sq. km. **Urban** (1985): 81%. **Ethnic groups:** Mixture of French and Germans predominate. **Languages:** French, German, Luxembourgian. **Religion:** Roman Catholic 97%.

Geography: Area: 2 585 sq. km. **Location:** In W. Europe. **Neighbors:** Belgium on W, France on S, W. Germany on E. **Topography:** Heavy forests (Ardennes) cover N, S is a low, open plateau. **Capital:** Luxembourg. **Cities** (1986 est.): Luxembourg 86 000.

Government: Type: Constitutional monarchy. **Head of state:** Grand Duke Jean; b. Jan. 5, 1921; in office: Nov. 12, 1964. **Head of government:** Prime Min. Jacques Santer; in office: July 21, 1984. **Local divisions:** 3 districts, 12 cantons. **Defence:** 0.9% of GNP (1984).

Economy: Industries: Steel, chemicals, beer, tires, tobacco, metal products, cement. **Chief crops:** Corn, wine. **Minerals:** Iron. **Arable land:** 25%. **Electricity prod.** (1986): 1.0 bln kwh. **Crude steel prod.** (1984): 3.9 min. metric tons. **Labor force:** 1% agric.; 42% ind. & comm.; 45% services.

Finance: Currency: Franc (Mar. 1988: 34.72 = $1 US). **Gross national product** (1985): $4.9 bln. **Per capita income** (1981): $10 444. **Note:** trade and tourist data included in Belgian statistics. **Consumer prices** (change in 1987): −0.1%.

Transport: Railway traffic (1986): 276 mln. passenger-km; 600 mln. net ton-km. **Motor vehicles:** in use (1986): 156 000 passenger cars, 13 000 comm. vehicles.

Communications: Television sets: 91 000 in use (1985). **Radios:** 227 000 in use (1985). **Telephones in use** (1985): 151 000. **Daily newspaper circ.** (1985): 365 per 1 000 pop.

Health: Life expectancy at birth (1984): 66.9 male; 73.5 female. **Births** (per 1 000 pop. 1985): 11. **Deaths** (per 1 000 pop. 1985): 11. **Hospital beds** (1985): 4 587. **Physicians** (1985): 663. **Infant mortality** (per 1 000 live births 1983): 11.2.

Education (1983): **Literacy:** 100%. **Years compulsory** 9; attendance 100%.

Major International Organizations: UN, OECD, EC, NATO.

Canadian Embassy: c/o 2, Avenue de Tervuren, 1040 Brussels, Belgium. Luxembourg: Consulate of Canada, c/o Price Waterhouse, 20 Pasteur Ave., 2310 Luxembourg; Tel: (352) 23742.

Luxembourg, founded about 963, was ruled by Burgundy, Spain, Austria, and France from 1448 to 1815. It left the Germanic Confederation in 1866. Overrun by Germany in 2 world wars, Luxembourg ended its neutrality in 1948, when a customs union with Belgium and Netherlands was adopted.

Madagascar

Democratic Republic of Madagascar

Repoblika Demokratika Malagasy

People: Population (1989 est.): 11 148 000. **Pop. density:** 19.0 per sq. km. **Urban** (1985): 21.8%. **Ethnic groups:** 18 Malayan-Indonesian tribes (Merina 26%), with Arab and African presence. **Languages:** Malagasy (official), French. **Religions:** animist 52%, Christian 41%, Moslem 7%.

Geography: Area: 586 996 sq. km. **Location:** In the Indian O., off the SE coast of Africa. **Neighbors:** Comoro Is., Mozambique (across Mozambique Channel). **Topography:** Humid coastal strip in the E, fertile valleys in the mountainous central plateau region, and a wider coastal strip on the W. **Capital:** Antananarivo. **Cities** (1985 est.): Antananarivo 650 000.

Government: Type: Republic strong presidential authority. **Head of state:** Pres. Didier Ratsiraka; b. Nov. 4, 1936; in office: June 15, 1975. **Head of government:** Prime Min. Desire Rakotoarijaona, b. June 19, 1934; in office: Aug. 4, 1977. **Local divisions:** 6 provinces. **Defence:** 9% of govt. budget (1987).

Economy: Industries: Light industry. **Chief crops:** Coffee (over 50% of exports), cloves, vanilla, rice, sugar, sisal, tobacco, peanuts. **Minerals:** Chromium, graphite, coal, bauxite. **Arable land:** 5%. **Livestock** (1985): cattle: 10.8 mln.; pigs: 1.2 mln. **Fish catch** (1985): 56 000 metric tons. **Electricity prod.** (1986): 420 mln. kwh. **Labor force:** 90% agric.

Finance: Currency: Franc (Mar. 1988: 1 266 = $1 US). **Gross national product** (1986): $2.6 bln. **Per capita income** (1986): $255. **Imports** (1986): $438 mln.; partners: Fr. 32%, W. Ger. 6%. **Exports** (1986): $326 mln.; partners: Fr. 34%, U.S. 14%. **National budget** (1986): $770 mln. **International reserves less gold** (June 1987): $156 mln. **Consumer prices** (change in 1987): 15.0%.

Transport: Railway traffic (1984): 205 mln. passenger-km; 222 mln. net ton-km. **Motor vehicles:** in use (1984): 23 000 passenger cars, 14 000 comm. vehicles. **Civil aviation:** (1985): 388 mln. passenger-km; 55 mln. freight ton-km. **Chief ports:** Tamatave, Diego-Suarez, Majunga, Tulear.

Communications: Television sets: 96 000 in use (1986). **Radios:** 2 mln. in use (1986). **Telephones in use** (1983): 37 000.

Health: Life expectancy at birth (1984): 46 years. **Births** (per 1 000 pop. 1985): 45. **Deaths** (per 1 000 pop. 1985): 17. **Natural increase** (1985): 2.8%. **Hospital beds** (1982): 20 800. **Physicians** (1982): 940. **Infant mortality** (per 1 000 live births 1985): 101.

Education (1987): **Literacy:** 53%. **Years compulsory:** 5; attendance 83%.

Major International Organizations: UN (GATT, WHO, IMF), OAU.

Canadian Embassy: c/o The Canadian High Commisson, P.O. Box 1022, Dar-es-Salaam, Tanzania.

Madagascar was settled 2 000 years ago by Malayan-Indonesian people, whose descendants still predominate. A unified kingdom ruled the 18th and 19th centuries. The island became a French protectorate, 1885, and a colony 1896. Independence came June 26, 1960.

Discontentment with inflation and French domination led to a coup in 1972. The new regime nationalized French-owned financial interests, closed French bases and a U.S. space tracking station, and obtained Chinese aid. The government conducted a program of arrests, expulsion of foreigners, and repression of strikes, 1979.

Malawi

Republic of Malawi

People: Population (1989 est.): 8 063 000. **Age distrib.** (%): 0–14: 47.8; 15–59: 48.0; 60+: 4.2. **Pop. density:** 68.1 per sq. km. **Urban** (1985): 12%. **Ethnic groups:** Chewa, 90%, Nyanja, Lomwe, other Bantu tribes. **Languages:** English, Chichewa (both official). **Religions:** Christian 75%, Moslem 20%.

Geography: Area: 118 476 sq. km. **Location:** In SE Africa. **Neighbors:** Zambia on W, Mozambique on SE, Tanzania on N. **Topography:** Malawi stretches 896 km N-S along Lake Malawi (Lake Nyasa), most of which belongs to Malawi. High plateaus and mountains line the Rift Valley the length of the nation. **Capital:** Lilongwe. **Cities** (1986 est.): Blantyre 378 000; Lilongwe 202 000.

Government: Type: One-party state. **Head of state:** Pres. Hastings Kamuzu Banda, b. May 14, 1906; in office: July 6, 1966. **Local divisions:** 24 administrative districts. **Defence:** 1.7% of GNP (1984).

Economy: Industries: Textiles, sugar, farm implements. **Chief crops:** Tea, tobacco, sugar, coffee. **Other resources:** Rubber. **Arable land:** 20%. **Fish catch** (1985): 62 metric tons. **Electricity prod.** (1986): 467 mln. kwh. **Labor force:** 51% agric.; 18% ind. and comm.; 20% govt.; 17% services.

Finance: Currency: Kwacha (Mar. 1988: 2.47 = $1 US). **Gross national product** (1985): $1.1 bln. **Imports** (1985): $291 mln.; partners: So. Afr. 38%, UK 13%, Jap. 6%. **Exports** (1985): $271 mln.; partners: UK 27%, S. Afr. 8%., W. Ger. 7%. **National budget** (1983): $386.4 mln. **International reserves less gold** (Mar. 1988): $55.4 mln. **Gold:** 13 000 oz t. **Consumer prices** (change in 1988): 14%.

Transport: Railway traffic (1986): 122 mln. passenger-km; 111 mln. net ton-km. **Motor vehicles:** in use (1985): 13 000 passenger cars, 14 000 comm. vehicles. **Civil aviation** (1985) 84 mln. passenger-km; 948 000 freight ton-km.

Communications: Radios: 1 mln. in use (1986). **Telephones in use** (1985): 43 000. **Daily newspaper circ.** (1985): 5 per 1 000 pop.

Health: Life expectancy at birth (1981): 42.7 male; 45.4 female. **Births** (per 1 000 pop. 1985): 54.0. **Deaths** (per 1 000 pop. 1985): 21.0. **Natural increase** (1985): 3.2%. **Hospital beds** (1984): 6 596. **Infant mortality** (per 1 000 live births 1985): 170.

Education (1985): **Literacy:** 25%. About 45% attend school.

Major International Organizations: UN (World Bank, IMF), OAU, Commonwealth of Nations.

Canadian High Commission: c/o P.O. Box 31313, Lusaka, Zambia.

Bantus came in the 16th century, Arab slavers in the 19th. The area became the British protectorate Nyasaland, in 1891. It became independent July 6, 1964, and a republic in 1966. It has a pro-West foreign policy and cooperates economically with S. Africa.

Malaysia

People: Population (1989 est.): 16 901 000. **Age distrib.** (%): 0–14: 38.0; 15–59: 56.2; 60+: 5.8. **Pop. density:** 51.3 per sq. km. **Urban** (1985): 38%. **Ethnic groups:** Malay 59%, Chinese 32%, Indian 9%. **Languages:** Malay (official), English, Chinese, Indian languages. **Religions:** Moslem, Hindu, Buddhist, Confucian, Taoist, local religions.

Geography: Area: 329 723 sq. km. **Location:** On the SE tip of Asia, plus the N. coast of the island of Borneo. **Neighbors:** Thailand on N, Indonesia on S. **Topography:** Most of W. Malaysia is covered by tropical jungle, including the central mountain range that runs N-S through the peninsula. The western coast is marshy, the eastern, sandy. E. Malaysia has a wide, swampy coastal plain, with interior jungles and mountains. **Capital:** Kuala Lumpur. **Cities** (1986 est.): Kuala Lumpur 1 mln.

Government: Type: Federal parliamentary democracy with a constitutional monarch. **Head of state:** Paramount Ruler Mahmood Iskander; b. 1932; in office: Apr. 26, 1984. **Head of government:** Prime Min. Datuk Seri Mahathir bin Mohamad; b. Dec. 20, 1925; in office: July 16, 1981. **Local divisions:** 13 states and capital. **Defence:** 3.7% of GNP (1984).

Economy: Industries: Rubber goods, steel, electronics. **Chief crops:** Palm oil, copra, rice, pepper. **Minerals:** Tin (35% world output), iron. **Crude oil reserves** (1987): 3.2 bln. bbls. **Other resources:** Rubber (35% world output). **Arable land:** 13%. **Livestock** (1985): pigs: 2.1 mln. **Fish catch** (1985): 632 000 metric tons. **Electricity prod.** (1985): 14.9 bln. kwh. **Labor force:** 21% agric.; 18% manuf.; 14% tourism.

Finance: Currency: Ringgit (Mar. 1988: 2.56 = $1 US). **Gross national product** (1985): $29.0 bln. **Imports** (1985): $12.3 bln.; partners: Jap. 25%, U.S. 18%, Sing. 14%. **Exports** (1985): $15.4 bln.; partners: Jap. 20%, U.S. 12% Sing. 25%, Neth. 6%. **National budget** (1986): $10.1 bln. **International reserves less gold** (Mar. 1988): $6.9 bln. **Gold:** 2.35 mln. oz t. **Consumer prices** (change in 1987): 1.1%.

Transport: Railway traffic (incl. Singapore) (1983): 1.5 bln. passenger-km; 1.1 bln. net ton-km. **Motor vehicles:** in use (1985): 1.1 mln. passenger cars, 138 000 comm. vehicles. **Civil aviation:** (1985): 6.2 bln. passenger-km; 208 mln. metric ton-km. **Chief ports:** George Town, Kelang, Melaka, Kuching.

Communications: Television sets: 1.6 mln. in use (1985). **Radios:** 2 mln. in use (1985). **Telephones** in use (1983): 976 000. **Daily newspaper circ.** (1985): 133 per 1 000 pop.

Health: Life expectancy at birth (1986): 67.0 male; 71.2 female. **Births** (per 1 000 pop. 1986): 30.6. **Deaths** (per 1 000 pop. 1986): 5.7. **Natural increase** (1986): 2.4%. **Hospital beds** (1983): 34 538. **Physicians** (1983): 4 234. **Infant mortality** (per 1 000 live births 1986): 25.0.

Education (1986): **Literacy:** 80%; 96% attend primary school, 48% attend secondary.

Major International Organizations: UN (World Bank, IMF, GATT), ASEAN.

Canadian High Commission: 7th fl., Plaza MBF, 172 Jalan Ampang, 50540 Kuala Lumpur; P.O. Box 10999, 50732, Kuala Lumpur; Tel: 261-2000.

European traders appeared in the 16th century; Britain established control in 1867. Malaysia was created Sept. 16, 1963. It included Malaya (which had become independent in 1957 after the suppression of Communist rebels), plus the formerly-British Singapore, Sabah (N Borneo), and Sarawak (NW Borneo). Singapore was separated in 1965, in order to end tensions between Chinese, the majority in Singapore, and Malays in control of the Malaysian government. Chinese have charged economic and political discrimination.

A monarch is elected by a council of hereditary rulers of the Malayan states every 5 years.

Abundant natural resources have assured prosperity, and foreign investment has aided industrialization.

Maldives

Republic of Maldives

Divehi Jumhuriya

People: Population (1989 est.): 202 000. **Age distrib.** (%): 0–14: 44.4; 15–59: 51.7; 60+: 3.9. **Pop. density:** 675.6 per sq. km. **Urban** (1985): 26%. **Ethnic groups:** Sinhalese, Dravidian, Arab mixture. **Language:** Divehi (Sinhalese dialect). **Religion:** Sunni Moslem.

Geography: Area: 299 sq. km. **Location:** In the Indian O. SW of India. **Neighbors:** Nearest is India on N. **Topography:** 19 atolls with 1 087 islands, about 200 inhabited. None of the islands are over 13 sq. km in area, and all are nearly flat. **Capital:** Male. **Cities** (1985 est.): Male 46 334.

Government: Type: Republic. **Head of state:** Pres. Maumoon Abdul Gayoom; b. Dec. 29, 1939; in office: Nov. 11, 1978. **Local divisions:** 19 atolls, each with an elected committee and a government-appointed chief.

Economy: Industries: Fish processing, tourism. **Chief crops:** Coconuts, fruit, millet. **Other resources:** Shells. **Arable land:** 10%. **Fish catch** (1985): 61 000 metric tons. **Electricity prod.** (1985): 12.8 mln. kwh. **Labor force:** 80% fishing, agriculture, & manufacturing.

Finance: Currency: Rufiyaa (Mar. 1988: 8.50 = $1 US). **Gross national product** (1985): $50 mln. **Per capita income** (1985): $470. **Imports** (1985): $52 mln.; partners: Sing., Jap., Sri Lan. **Exports** (1985): $22.8 mln.; partners: Jap., Europe. **Tourists** (1985): 50 000.

Transport: Chief ports: Male Atoll.

Communications: Radios: 19 000 in use (1985). **Telephones in use** (1985): 3 000.

Health: Life expectancy at birth (1986): 57.4 male; 58.4 female. **Births** (per 1 000 pop. 1985): 45. **Deaths** (per 1 000 pop. 1985): 14. **Natural increase** (1985): 3.1%. **Infant mortality** (per 1 000 live births 1985): 81.

Education (1987): **Literacy:** 82%. (claimed by govt.). Only 6% of those aged 11-15 attend school.

Major International Organizations: UN.

Canadian High Commission: c/o The Canadian High Commission, P.O. Box 1006, Colombo, Sri Lanka.

The islands had been a British protectorate since 1887. The country became independent July 26, 1965. Long a sultanate, the Maldives became a republic in 1968. Natural resources and tourism are being developed; however, it remains one of the world's poorest countries.

Mali

Republic of Mali

République du Mali

People: Population (1989 est.): 8 460 000. **Age distrib.** (%): 0–14: 46.0; 15–59: 49.4; 60+: 4.6. **Pop. density:** 6.8 per sq. km. **Urban** (1985): 20.8%. **Ethnic groups:** Mande (Bambara, Malinke, Sarakolle) 50%, Peul 17%, Voltaic 12%, Songhai, Tuareg, Moors. **Languages:** French (official), Bambara. **Religion:** Moslem 90%.

Geography: Area: 1 239 903 sq. km. **Location:** In the interior of W. Africa. **Neighbors:** Mauritania, Senegal on W, Guinea, Côte d'Ivoire, Burkina Faso on S, Niger on E, Algeria on N. **Topography:** A landlocked grassy plain in the upper basins of the Senegal and Niger rivers, extending N into the Sahara. **Capital:** Bamako. **Cities** (1986 est.): Bamako (met.) 800 000.

Government: Type: Republic. **Head of state:** Pres. Moussa Traore; b. Sept. 25, 1936; in office: Dec. 6, 1968. **Head of government:** Mamadov Dembele; in office: June 6, 1987. **Local divisions:** 7 regions and a capital district. **Defence:** 3% of GDP (1986).

Economy: Chief crops: Millet, rice, peanuts, cotton. **Other resources:** Bauxite, iron, gold. **Arable land:** 2%. **Livestock** (1985): sheep: 6.4 mln.; cattle: 5.8 mln. **Fish catch** (1985): 33 000 metric tons. **Electricity prod.** (1986): 170 mln. kwh. **Labor force:** 73% agric.; 12% ind. & comm.; 16% services.

Finance: Currency: Franc (Mar. 1988: 281 = $1 US). **Gross national product** (1985): $1.1 bln. **Per capita income** (1984): $190. **Imports** (1985): $294 mln.; partners: Fr. 22%, Côte d'Ivoire 25%. **Exports** (1985): $174 mln.; partners: Belg.-Lux. 25%, Fr. 15%. **Tourists** (1985): $12 mln. receipts. **International reserves less gold** (Feb. 1988): $18.9 mln. **Gold:** 19 000 oz t.

Transport: Railway traffic (1985): 172 mln. passenger-km; 241 mln. net ton-km. **Motor vehicles:** in use (1985): 23 000 passenger cars, 6 000 comm. vehicles.

Communications: Radios: 110 000 in use (1985). **Telephones in use** (1984): 9 500.

Health: Life expectancy at birth (1985): 40.4 male; 43.6 female. **Births** (per 1 000 pop. 1985): 50.2. **Deaths** (per 1 000 pop. 1985): 22.4. **Natural increase** (1985): 2.7%. **Hospital beds** (1983): 4 215. **Physicians** (1983): 283. **Infant mortality** (per 1 000 live births 1985): 173.

Education (1984): **Literacy:** 10%. **Attendance:** 28% under 15 attend school.

Major International Organizations: UN and all of its specialized agencies, OAU, EC.

Canadian Embassy: c/o 01 P.O. Box 4101, Abidjan 01, Côte d'Ivoire.

Until the 15th century the area was part of the great Mali Empire. Timbuktu was a centre of Islamic study. French rule was secured, 1898. The Sudanese Rep. and Senegal became independent as the Mali Federation June 20, 1960, but Senegal withdrew, and the Sudanese Rep. was renamed Mali.

Mali signed economic agreements with France and, in 1963, with Senegal. In 1968, a coup ended the socialist regime. Famine struck in 1973-74, killing as many as 100 000 people. Drought conditions returned in the 1980s.

Mali and Burkina Faso fought a border war in Dec. 1985.

Malta

Repubblika Ta' Malta

People: Population (1989 est.): 358 000. **Age distrib.** (%): 0–14: 24.2; 15–59: 62.5; 60+: 13.3. **Pop. density:** 1 129.3 per sq. km. **Ethnic groups:** Italian, Arab, French. **Languages:** Maltese, English both official. **Religion:** Mainly Roman Catholic.

Geography: Area: 317 sq. km. **Location:** In centre of Mediterranean Sea. **Neighbors:** Nearest is Italy on N. **Topography:** Island of Malta is 247 sq. km; other islands in the group: Gozo, 68 sq. km, Comino, 2.6 sq. km. The coastline is heavily indented. Low hills cover the interior. **Capital:** Valletta. **Cities** (1986 est.): Birkirkara 20 000; Qormi 18 000.

Government: Type: Parlimentary democracy. **Head of state:** Pres. Paul Xuerub; in office: Feb. 15, 1987. **Head of government:** Prime Min. Eddie Fenech Adami; b. Feb 7, 1934; in office: May 12, 1987.

Economy: Industries: Textiles, tourism. **Chief crops:** Potatoes, onions, beans. **Arable land:** 41%. **Electricity prod.** (1986): 825 mln. kwh. **Labor force:** 35% ind. & comm.; 30% services; 22% gov.

Finance: Currency: Pound (Mar. 1988: 1.00 = $3.12 US). **Gross national product** (1985): $1.4 bln. **Per capita income** (1984): $3 660. **Imports** (1985): $756 mln.; partners: UK 18%, It. 23%, W. Ger. 14%, U.S. 7%. **Exports** (1985): $399 mln.; partners: W. Ger. 31%, UK 20%, Libya 8%. **Tourists** (1985): receipts: $149 mln. **National budget** (1984): $483. **International reserves less gold** (Mar. 1988): 1.3 bln. **Gold:** 466 000 oz t. **Consumer prices** (change in 1986): 2.0%.

Transport: Motor vehicles: in use (1985): 82 000 passenger cars, 18 000 comm. vehicles. **Civil aviation** (1986): 744 mln. passenger-km; 4.4 mln. freight ton-km. **Chief ports:** Valletta.

Communications: Television sets: 116 000 licensed (1985). **Radios:** 92 000 in use (1986). **Telephones in use** (1985): 115 000.

Health: Life expectancy at birth (1985): 70.8 male; 76.0 female. **Births** (per 1 000 pop. 1986): 16.5. **Deaths** (per 1 000 pop. 1986): 8.2. **Natural increase** (1986): 0.8%. **Hospital beds** (1984): 3 142. **Physicians** (1984): 413. **Infant mortality** (per 1 000 live births 1985): 13.4.

Education (1985): Literacy: 90%. **Compulsory:** until age 16. **Major International Organizations:** UN (GATT, WHO, IMF), Commonwealth of Nations.

Canadian High Commission: c/o The Canadian Embassy, Via G.B. de Rossi 27, 00161, Rome, Italy.

Malta was ruled by Phoenicians, Romans, Arabs, Normans, the Knights of Malta, France, and Britain (since 1814). It became independent Sept. 21, 1964. Malta became a republic in 1974. The withdrawal of the last of its sailors, Apr. 1, 1979, ended 179 years of British military presence on the island.

With Malta's approval, Egyptian commandos stormed a hijacked EgyptAir passenger plane at Valletta airport Nov. 23, 1985; 57 died in the battle.

Malta is democratic but nonaligned.

Mauritania

Islamic Republic of Mauritania
République Islamique de Mauritanie

People: Population (1989 est.): 1 804 000. **Age distrib.** (%): 0–14: 46.4; 15–59: 49.0; 60+: 4.6. **Pop. density:** 1.8 per sq. km. **Urban** (1983): 25%. **Ethnic groups:** Arab-Berber 80%, Negro 20%. **Languages:** French (official), Hassanya Arabic (national), Toucouleur, Fula, Sarakole, Wolof. **Religion:** Nearly 100% Moslem.

Geography: Area: 1 030 621 sq. km. **Location:** In W. Africa. **Neighbors:** Morocco on N, Algeria, Mali on E, Senegal on S. **Topography:** The fertile Senegal R. valley in the S gives way to a wide central region of sandy plains and scrub trees. The N is arid and extends into the Sahara. **Capital:** Nouakchott. **Cities** (1987 est.): Nouakchott 400 000; Nouadhibou 70 000; Kaedi 22 000.

Government: Type: Military republic. **Head of Government:** President & Premier Maaouya Ould Sidi Ahmed Taya; in office: Apr. 25, 1981. **Local divisions:** 12 regions, one district. **Defence:** 20% of GNP (1986).

Economy: Industries: Iron mining. **Chief crops:** Dates, grain. **Minerals:** Iron, ore, gypsum. **Livestock** (1985): sheep: 5.2 mln.; goats: 3.2 mln.; cattle: 1.3 mln. **Fish catch** (1985): 60 000 metric tons. **Electricity prod.** (1986): 74 mln. kwh. **Labor force:** 47% agric., 14% ind. & comm., 29% services.

Finance: Currency: Ouguiya (Mar. 1988: 73 = $1 US). **Gross national product** (1986): $600 mln. **Per capita income** (1986): $450. **Imports** (1986): $250 mln.; partners: Fr. 29%, Sp. 9%. **Exports** (1986): $340 mln.; partners: Fr. 21%, It. 26%, Jap. 20%. **International reserves less gold** (Feb. 1988): $72.9 mln. **Gold:** 12 000 oz t. **Consumer prices** (change in 1986): 7%.

Transport: Motor vehicles: in use (1985): 15 000 passenger cars, 2 000 comm. vehicles. **Chief ports:** Nouakchott, Nouadhibou.

Communications: Radios: 200 000 in use (1986).

Health: Life expectancy at birth (1987): 46 years. **Births** (per 1 000 pop. 1985): 47. **Deaths** (per 1 000 pop. 1985): 27. **Natural increase** (1985): 2.0%. **Hospital beds** (1984): 1 325. **Physicians** (1984): 170. **Infant mortality** (per 1 000 live births 1985): 138.

Education (1987): Literacy: 17%. **Attendance:** 41% in primary school, 10% in secondary school.

Major International Organizations: UN (GATT, IMF, WHO), OAU, Arab League.

Canadian Embassy: c/o P.O. Box 3373, Dakar, Senegal.

Mauritania became independent Nov. 28, 1960. It annexed the south of former Spanish Sahara in 1976. Saharan guerrillas stepped up attacks in 1977; 8 000 Moroccan troops and French bomber raids aided the government. Mauritania signed a peace treaty with the Polisario Front, 1980, resumed diplomatic relations with Algeria while breaking a defense treaty with Morocco, and renounced sovereignty over its share of former Spanish Sahara. Morocco annexed the territory.

Famine has struck repeatedly during the last decade.

Mauritius

People: Population (1989 est.): 1 047 900. **Age distrib.** (%): 0–14: 36.3; 15–59: 57.2; 60+: 6.4. **Pop. density:** 512.2 per sq. km. **Urban** (1986): 41%. **Ethnic groups:** Indo-Mauritian 68%, Creole 27%, others. **Languages:** English (official), French, Creole. **Religions:** Hindu 51%, Christian 30%, Moslem 16%.

Geography: Area: 2 046 sq. km. **Location:** In the Indian O., 805 km E of Madagascar. **Neighbors:** Nearest is Madagascar on W. **Topography:** A volcanic island nearly surrounded by coral reefs. A central plateau is encircled by mountain peaks. **Capital:** Port Louis. **Cities** (1986 est.): Port Louis 155 000.

Government: Type: Parliamentary democracy. **Head of state:** Queen Elizabeth II, represented by Gov.-Gen. Sir Veerasamy Ringadoo; in office: Jan. 17, 1986. **Head of government:** Prime Min. Aneerood Jugnauth; in office: June 12, 1982. **Local divisions:** 9 administrative divisions.

Economy: Industries: Tourism. **Chief crops:** Sugar cane, tea. **Arable land:** 58%. **Electricity prod.** (1986): 378 mln. kwh. **Labor force:** 27% agric. & fishing; 22% ind. and commerce; 29% govt. services.

Finance: Currency: Rupee (Mar. 1988: 12.78 = $1 US). **Gross national product** (1986): $1.0 bln. **Per capita income** (1982): $1 240. **Imports** (1986): $684 mln.; partners: UK 9%, Fr. 12%, So. Afr. 9%. **Exports** (1986): $676 mln.; partners: UK 50%, Fr. 22%, U.S. 8%. **Tourists** (1985): $65 mln. receipts. **National budget** (1985): $310 mln. **International reserves less gold** (Feb. 1988): $414 mln. **Gold:** 40 000 oz t. **Consumer prices** (change in 1986): 1.9%.

Transport: Motor vehicles: in use (1985): 31 000 passenger cars, 14 000 comm. vehicles. **Chief ports:** Port Louis.

Communications: Television sets: 110 000 in use (1986). **Radios:** 200 000 in use (1986). **Telephones in use** (1985): 64 000. **Daily newspaper circ.** (1985): 75 per 1 000 pop.

Health: Life expectancy at birth (1982): 69 years. **Births** (per 1 000 pop. 1985): 20. **Deaths** (per 1 000 pop. 1985): 6. **Natural increase** (1985): 1.4%. **Hospital beds** (1985): 2 811. **Physicians** (1985): 711. **Infant mortality** (per 1 000 live births 1986): 28.

Education (1986): **Literacy:** 79%. **Attendance:** most children attend school.

Major International Organizations: UN and all of its specialized agencies, OAU, Commonwealth of Nations.

Canadian High Commission: c/o P.O. Box 1022 Dar-es-Salaam, Tanzania.

Mauritius was uninhabited when settled in 1638 by the Dutch, who introduced sugar cane. France took over in 1721, bringing African slaves. Britain ruled from 1810 to Mar. 12, 1968, bringing Indian workers for the sugar plantations.

The economy has suffered in the 1980s because of low world sugar prices.

Mexico

United Mexican States

Estados Unidos Mexicanos

People: Population (1989 est.): 88 087 000. **Age distrib.** (%): 0–14: 39.7; 15–59: 55.0; 60+: 5.3. **Pop. density:** 44.7 per sq. km. **Urban** (1986): 70%. **Ethnic groups:** Mestizo 60%, American Indian 29%, Caucasian 9%. **Language:** Spanish. **Religion:** Roman Catholic 97%.

Geography: Area: 1 972 402 sq. km. **Location:** In southern N. America. **Neighbors:** U.S. on N, Guatemala, Belize on S. **Topography:** The Sierra Madre Occidental Mts. run NW-SE near the west coast; the Sierra Madre Oriental Mts., run near the Gulf of Mexico. They join S of Mexico City. Between the 2 ranges lies the dry central plateau, 1 500 to 2 400 m alt., rising toward the S, with temperate vegetation. Coastal lowlands are tropical. About 45% of land is arid. **Capital:** Mexico City. **Cities** (1985 est.): Mexico City (metro) 18 mln.; Guadalajara (metro) 3 mln.; Monterrey (metro) 2.7 mln.

Government: Type: Federal republic. **Head of state:** Pres. Miguel de la Madrid Hurtado; b. Dec. 12, 1934; in office: Dec. 1, 1982. **Local divisions:** Federal district and 31 states. **Defence:** 0.3% of GNP (1984).

Economy: Industries: Steel, chemicals, electric goods, textiles, rubber, petroleum, tourism. **Chief crops:** Cotton, coffee, sugar cane, vegetables, corn. **Minerals:** Silver, lead, zinc, gold, oil, natural gas. **Crude oil reserves** (1987): 54 bln. bbls. **Arable land:** 13%. **Livestock** (1985): cattle: 31.1 mln.; pigs: 19 mln.; sheep: 6.5 mln. **Fish catch** (1985): 1.5 mln. metric tons. **Electricity prod.** (1986): 90.4 bln. kwh. **Crude steel prod.** (1986): 7.1 mln. metric tons. **Labor force:** 26% agric.; 13% manuf; 31% services; 14% comm.

Finance: Currency: Peso (May 1988: 2 281 = $1 US). **Gross national product** (1987): $126 bln. **Per capita income** (1984): $2 082. **Imports** (1987): $12.7 bln.; partners: U.S. 67%; EC 11%. **Exports** (1987): $20.6 bln.; partners: U.S. 60%, EC 10%. **Tourists** (1985): receipts: $1.7 bln. **National budget** (1985): $86.5 bln. expenditures. **International reserves less gold** (Jan. 1988): $12 bln. **Gold:** 2.5 mln. oz t. **Consumer prices** (change in 1987): 131.8%.

Transport: Railway traffic (1986): 5.8 bln. passenger-km; 48.2 bln. net ton-km. **Motor vehicles:** in use (1985): 5.0 mln. passenger cars, 2.1 mln. comm. vehicles. **Civil aviation** (1986): 16.8 bln. passenger-km; 159 mln. freight ton-km. **Chief ports:** Veracruz, Tampico, Mazatlan, Coatzacoalcos.

Communications: Television sets: 9.4 mln. in use (1986). **Radios:** 25 mln. in use (1986). **Telephones in use** (1985): 7.3 mln. **Daily newspaper circ.** (1982): 130 per 1 000 pop.

Health: Life expectancy at birth (1985): 63.9 male; 68.2 female. **Births** (per 1 000 pop. 1986): 27.3. **Deaths** (per 1 000 pop. 1986): 5.0. **Natural increase** (1986): 2.2%. **Hospital beds** (1984): 72 000. **Physicians** (1980): 53 053. **Infant mortality** (per 1 000 live births 1985): 42.

Education (1986): **Literacy:** 92%. **Years compulsory:** 10. **Major International Organizations:** UN (IMF, GATT), OAS.

Canadian Embassy: Calle Schiller no. 529 (Rincon del Bosque), Colonia Polanco, 11560, Mexico, D.F.; postal: Apartado Postal 105-05, 11580 Mexico, D.F.; Tel: 254-32-88.

Mexico was the site of advanced Indian civilizations. The Mayas, an agricultural people, moved up from Yucatan, built immense stone pyramids, invented a calendar. The Toltecs were overcome by the Aztecs, who founded Tenochtitlan 1325 AD, now Mexico City. Hernando Cortes, Spanish conquistador, destroyed the Aztec empire, 1519-1521.

After 3 centuries of Spanish rule the people rose, under Fr. Miguel Hidalgo y Costilla, 1810, Fr. Morelos y Payon, 1812, and Gen. Agustin Iturbide, who made independence effective Sept. 27, 1821, but made himself emperor as Agustin I. A republic was declared in 1823.

Mexican territory extended into the present American Southwest and California until Texas revolted and established a republic in 1836; the Mexican legislature refused recognition but was unable to enforce its authority there. After numerous clashes, the U.S.-Mexican War, 1846-48, resulted in the loss by Mexico of the lands north of the Rio Grande.

French arms supported an Austrian archduke on the throne of Mexico as Maximilian I, 1864-67, but pressure from the U.S. forced France to withdraw. A dictatorial rule by Porfirio Diaz, president 1877-80, 1884-1911, led to fighting by rival forces until the new constitution of Feb. 5, 1917 provided social reform. Since then Mexico has developed large-scale programs of social security, labor protection, and school improvement. A constitutional provision requires management to share profits with labor.

The Institutional Revolutionary Party has been dominant in politics since 1929. Radical opposition, including some guerrilla activity, has been contained by strong measures.

The presidency of Luis Echeverria, 1970-76, was marked by a more leftist foreign policy and domestic rhetoric. Some land redistribution begun in 1976 was reversed under the succeeding administration.

Some gains in agriculture, industry, and social services have been achieved. The land is rich, but the rugged topography and lack of sufficient rainfall are major obstacles. Crops and farm prices are controlled, as are export and import. Economic prospects brightened with the discovery of vast oil reserves, perhaps the world's greatest. But much of the work force is jobless or underemployed.

Inflation and the drop in world oil prices has caused economic problems in the 1980s. The peso was devalued and private banks were nationalized to restore financial stability.

Many thousands died when a disastrous earthquake struck Mexico City, Sept. 19, 1985.

In 1988, amid charges of election fraud, Carlos Salinas de Gortari was elected president.

Monaco

Principality of Monaco

Principauté de Monaco

People: Population (1989 est.): 29 000. **Age distrib.** (%): 0–14: 12.7; 15–59: 56.3 60+: 30.7. **Pop. density:** 19 333 per sq. km. **Ethnic groups:** French 47%, Italian 16%, Monegasque 16%. **Language:** French (official). **Religion:** Predominantly Roman Catholic.

Geography: Area: 1.5 sq. km. **Location:** On the NW Mediterranean coast. **Neighbors:** France to W, N, E. **Topography:** Monaco-Ville sits atop a high promontory, the rest of the principality rises from the port up the hillside. **Capital:** Monaco-Ville (1985 est.): 1 700.

Government: Type: Constitutional monarchy. **Head of state:** Prince Rainier III; b. May 31, 1923; in office: May 9, 1949. **Head of government:** Min. of State Jean Ausseil; in office: Sept. 1985.

Economy: Industries: Tourism, gambling, chemicals, precision instruments, plastics.

Finance: Currency: French franc or Monégasque franc.

Transport: Chief ports: La Condamine.

Communications: Television sets: 17 000 in use (1984). **Telephones in use** (1984): 18 000.

Health: Births (per 1 000 pop. 1985): 7. **Deaths** (per 1 000 pop. 1985): 10. **Natural increase** (1985): −.3%. **Infant mortality** (per 1 000 live births 1970): 9.3.

Education: (1987): **Literacy:** 99%. **Years compulsory:** 10; attendance 99%.

Canadian Consulate: "Le Continental C", Place des Moulins, 98000 Monte Carlo; Tel: 93-25-58-22.

An independent principality for over 300 years, Monaco has belonged to the House of Grimaldi since 1297 except during the French Revolution. It was placed under the protectorate of Sardinia in 1815, and under that of France, 1861. The Prince of Monaco was an absolute ruler until a 1911 constitution.

Monaco's fame as a tourist resort is widespread. It is noted for its mild climate and magnificent scenery. The area has been extended by land reclamation.

Mongolia

Mongolian People's Republic

Bügd Nayramdakh Mongol Ard Uls

People: Population (1989 est.): 2 093 000. **Pop. density:** 1.3 per sq. km. **Urban** (1985): 52%. **Ethnic groups:** Mongol 90%. **Languages:** Khalkha Mongolian (official, written in Cyrillic letters since 1941), Russian, Chinese. **Religions:** Curbed by govt., traditionally Lama Buddhism prevailed.

Geography: Area: 1 564 879 sq. km. **Location:** In E Central Asia. **Neighbors:** USSR on N, China on S. **Topography:** Mostly a high plateau with mountains, salt lakes, and vast grasslands. Arid lands in the S are part of the Gobi Desert. **Capital:** Ulaanbaatar. **Cities** (1985 est.): Ulaanbaatar 488 000, Darhan 69 000.

Government: Type: Communist state. **Head of state:** Chmn. Zhambyn Batmunkh; b. May 10, 1926; in office: Aug. 23, 1984. **Head of government:** Premier Dumaagiyn Sodnom; in office: Aug. 23, 1984. **Local divisions:** 18 provinces, 3 autonomous municipalities. **Defense:** 11.5% of GNP (1984).

Economy: Industries: Food processing, textiles, chemicals, cement. **Chief crops:** Grain. **Minerals:** Coal, tungsten, copper, molybdenum, gold, tin. **Arable land:** 1%. **Livestock** (1985): sheep: 13.5 mln; cattle: 2.4 mln. **Electricity prod.** (1986): 2.8 bln. kwh. **Labor force:** 52% agric.; 10% manuf.

Finance: Currency: Tugrik (Jan. 1988: 3.36 = $1 US). **Gross national product** (1985): $1.6 bln. **Per capita income** (1984 est.): $1 000. **Imports** (1985): $1 bln.; partners: USSR 91%. **Exports** (1985): $660 mln.; partners: USSR 80%.

Transport: Railway traffic (1985): 436 mln. passenger-km; 5.9 bln. net ton-km.

Communications: Television sets: 88 000 in use (1986). **Radios:** 194 000 in use (1986). **Telephones in use** (1986): 49 000. **Daily newspaper circ.** (1985): 91 per 1 000 pop.

Health: Life expectancy at birth (1986): 61.1 male; 65.2 female. **Births** (per 1 000 pop. 1985): 35. **Deaths** (per 1 000 pop. 1985): 10. **Natural increase** (1985): 2.5%. **Hospital beds** (1986): 21 200. **Physicians** (1986): 4 400. **Infant mortality** (per 1 000 live births 1985): 46.

Major International Organizations: UN (ILO, WHO). **Education** (1985): **Literacy:** 89%. **Years compulsory:** 7 in major population centres.

Canadian Embassy: c/o 23 Starokonyushenny Pereulok, Moscow, U.S.S.R.

One of the world's oldest countries, Mongolia reached the zenith of its power in the 13th century when Genghis Khan and his successors conquered all of China and extended their influence as far W as Hungary and Poland. In later centuries, the empire dissolved and Mongolia came under the suzerainty of China.

With the advent of the 1911 Chinese revolution, Mongolia, with Russian backing, declared its independence. A Mongolian Communist regime was established July 11, 1921.

Mongolia has been changed from a nomadic culture to one of settled agriculture and growing industries with aid from the USSR and East European nations.

Mongolia has sided with the Russians in the Sino-Soviet dispute. A Mongolian-Soviet mutual assistance pact was signed Jan. 15, 1966, and some 60 000 Soviet troops are based in the country.

Morocco

Kingdom of Morocco

al-Mamlaka al-Maghrebia

People: Population (1989 est.): 25 380 000. **Age distrib.** (%): 0–14: 46.4; 15–59: 49.2; 60+: 4.2. **Pop. density:** 56.8 per sq. km. **Urban** (1985): 43%. **Ethnic groups:** Arab-Berber 99%. **Languages:** Arabic (official), with Berber, French, Spanish minorities. **Religion:** Sunni Moslem 99%.

Geography: Area: 446 515 sq. km. **Location:** on NW coast of Africa. **Neighbors:** W. Sahara on S, Algeria on E. **Topography:** Consists of 5 natural regions: mountain ranges (Riff in the N, Middle Atlas, Upper Atlas, and Anti-Atlas); rich plains in the W; alluvial plains in SW; well-cultivated plateaus in the centre; a pre-Sahara arid zone extending from SE. **Capital:** Rabat. **Cities** (1984): Casablanca 2 600 000; Rabat 556 000, Fes 852 000.

Government: Type: Constitutional monarchy. **Head of state:** King Hassan II; b. July 9, 1929; in office: Mar. 3, 1961. **Head of government:** Prime Min. Azzedine Laraki; in office: Sept. 30, 1986. **Local divisions:** 2 prefectures, 36 provinces. **Defence:** 5.0% of GNP (1984).

Economy: Industries: Carpets, clothing, leather goods, tourism. **Chief crops:** Grain, fruits, dates, grapes. **Minerals:** Antimony, cobalt, manganese, phosphates, lead, oil, coal. **Crude oil reserves** (1980): 100 mln. bbls. **Arable land:** 18%. **Livestock** (1985): cattle: 3.3 mln.; sheep: 12 mln.; goats: 4.5 mln. **Fish catch** (1984): 439 000 metric tons. **Electricity prod.** (1986): 6.9 bln. kwh. **Labor force:** 50% agric., 26% services; 15% ind.

Finance: Currency: Dirham (Mar. 1988: 7.93 = $1 US). **Gross national product** (1985): $11.9 bln. **Per capita income** (1984): $630. **Imports** (1986): $3.8 bln.; partners: Fr. 25%, Sp. 7%, Saudi Ar. 15%. **Exports** (1986): $2.4 bln.; partners: Fr. 22%, W. Ger. 7%, Sp. 7%, It. 5%. **Tourists** (1985): $600 mln. receipts. **National budget** (1985): $6.8 bln. expenditures. **International reserves less gold** (Mar. 1988): $277 mln. **Gold:** 704 000 oz t. **Consumer prices** (change in 1987): 2.4%.

Transport: Railway traffic (1985): 1.9 bln. passenger-km; 4.5 bln. net ton-km. **Motor vehicles:** in use (1985): 491 000 passenger cars, 232 000 comm. vehicles. **Civil aviation** (1985): 2.1 bln. passenger-km; 38.7 mln. freight ton-km. **Chief ports:** Tangier, Casablanca, Kenitra.

Communications: Television sets: 1 mln. in use (1986). **Radios:** 3.0 mln. in use (1986). **Telephones in use** (1985): 311 000. **Daily newspaper circ.** (1986): 12 per 1 000 pop.

Health: Life expectancy at birth (1985): 56.1 male; 59.4 female. **Births** (per 1 000 pop. 1985): 44.1. **Deaths** (per 1 000 pop. 1985): 11.7. **Natural increase** (1985): 3.2%. **Hospital beds** (1984): 26 538. **Physicians** (1984): 2 957. **Infant mortality** (per 1 000 live births 1985): 93.

Education (1980): **Literacy:** 70%.

Major International Organizations: UN (ILO, IMF, WHO), OAU, Arab League.

Canadian Embassy: 13, Bis, Rue Jaafar As-Sadik, C.P. 709, Rabat-Agdal; Tel: 713-75, 76, 77.

Berbers were the original inhabitants, followed by Carthaginians and Romans. Arabs conquered in 683. In the 11th and 12th centuries, a Berber empire ruled all NW Africa and most of Spain from Morocco.

Part of Morocco came under Spanish rule in the 19th century; France controlled the rest in the early 20th. Tribal uprisings lasted from 1911 to 1933. The country became independent Mar. 2, 1956. Tangier, an internationalized seaport, was turned over to Morocco, 1956. Ifni, a Spanish enclave, was ceded in 1969.

Morocco annexed over 182 000 sq. km of phosphate-rich land Apr. 14, 1976, two-thirds of former Spanish Sahara, with the remainder annexed by Mauritania. Spain had withdrawn in February. Polisario, a guerrilla movement, proclaimed the region independent Feb. 27, and launched attacks with Algerian support. When Mauritania signed a treaty with the Polisario Front, and gave up its portion of the former Spanish Sahara, Morocco occupied the area, 1980. Morocco accused Algeria of instigating Polisario attacks.

After years of bitter fighting, Morocco controls the main urban areas, but the Polisario Front's guerrillas move freely in the vast, sparsely populated deserts.

Mozambique

People's Republic of Mozambique
República Popular de Moçambique

People: Population (1989 est.): 15 259 000. **Age distrib. (%):** 0–14: 45.3; 15–59: 50.6; 60+: 4.1. **Pop. density:** 19.0 per sq. km. **Ethnic groups:** Bantu tribes. **Languages:** Portuguese (official), Bantu languages predominate. **Religions:** Traditional beliefs 60%, Christian 30%, Moslem 10%.

Geography: Area: 801 528 sq. km. **Location:** On SE coast of Africa. **Neighbors:** Tanzania on N, Malawi, Zambia, Zimbabwe on W, South Africa, Swaziland on S. **Topography:** Coastal lowlands comprise nearly half the country with plateaus rising in steps to the mountains along the western border. **Capital:** Maputo. **Cities:** (1986 est.): Maputo 882 000.

Government: Type: Socialist one-party state. **Head of state:** Pres. Joaquim Chissano; b. Oct. 22, 1939; in office: Oct. 9, 1986. **Head of government:** Mario de Graca Machungo; in office: July 17, 1986. **Local divisions:** 10 provinces. **Defence:** 38% of govt. budget (1986).

Economy: Industries: Cement, alcohol, textiles. **Chief crops:** Cashews, cotton, sugar, copra, tea. **Minerals:** Coal, bauxite. **Arable land:** 4%. **Livestock** (1985): cattle: 1.3 mln. **Fish catch** (1985): 37 000 metric tons. **Electricity prod.** (1986): 1.6 bln. kwh. **Labor force:** 85% agric., 9% ind. & comm., 2% services.

Finance: Currency: Metical (Jan. 1988: 403 = $1 US). **Gross national product** (1986): $1.3 bln. **Per capita income** (1983): $220. **Imports** (1986): $525 mln.; partners: So. Afr. 20%, W. Ger. 15%, Port. 10%. **Exports** (1986): $90 mln.; partners: U.S. 27%, Port. 16%, UK 7%, So. Afr. 7%. **National budget** (1983): $640 mln.

Transport: Railway traffic (1986): 263 mln. passenger-km; 303 mln. net ton-km. **Motor vehicles:** in use (1981): 49 000 passenger cars, 24 700 comm. vehicles. **Chief ports:** Maputo, Beira, Nacala, Quelimane.

Communications: Television sets: 20 000 in use (1986). **Radios:** 500 000 licensed (1986). **Telephones** in use (1985): 60 000. **Daily newspaper circ.** (1986): 5 per 1 000 pop.

Health: Life expectancy at birth (1985): 47 years. **Births** (per 1 000 pop. 1985): 44.6. **Deaths** (per 1 000 pop. 1985): 17.2. **Natural increase** (1985): 2.7%. **Hospital beds** (1986): 12 270. **Physicians** (1986): 279. **Infant mortality** (per 1 000 live births 1985): 158.

Education (1985): **Literacy:** 14%.

Major International Organization: UN (IMF, World Bank), OAU.

Canadian Embassy: c/o The Canadian High Commission, P.O. Box 1430, Harare, Zimbabwe.

The first Portuguese post on the Mozambique coast was established in 1505, on the trade route to the East. Mozambique became independent June 25, 1975, after a ten-year war against Portuguese colonial domination. The 1974 revolution in Portugal paved the way for the orderly transfer of power to Frelimo (Front for the Liberation of Mozambique). Frelimo took over local administration Sept. 20, 1974, over the opposition, in part violent, of some blacks and whites. The new government, led by Maoist Pres. Samora Machel, promised a gradual transition to a communist system. Private schools were closed, rural collective farms organized, and private homes nationalized. Economic problems included the emigration of most of the country's 160 000 whites, a politically untenable economic dependence on white-ruled South Africa, and a large external debt.

In the 1980s, severe drought and civil war has caused famine and heavy loss of life.

Nauru

Republic of Nauru
Naoero

People: Population (1989): 8 100. **Pop density:** 385.7 per sq. km. **Ethnic groups:** Nauruan 57%, Pacific Islanders 26%, Chinese 8%, European 8%. **Languages:** Nauruan (official), English. **Religion:** Predominately Christian.

Geography: Area: 21 sq. km. **Location:** In Western Pacific O. just S of Equator. **Neighbors:** Nearest are Solomon Is. **Topography:** Mostly a plateau bearing high grade phosphate deposits, surrounded by a coral cliff and a sandy shore in concentric rings. **Capital:** Yaren.

Government: Type: Republic. **Head of state:** Pres. Hammer DeRoburt, b. Sept. 25, 1922; in office: May 11, 1978. **Local divisions:** 14 districts.

Economy: Phosphate mining. **Electricity prod.** (1986): 48.00 mln. kwh.

Finance: Currency: Australian dollar. **Gross national product** (1984): $160 mln. **Per capita income** (1984): $21 400. **Imports** (1984): $14 mln. **Exports** (1984): $93 mln.

Communications: Radios: 4 000 in use (1985). **Telephones** in use (1980): 1 500.

Health: Births (per 1 000 pop. 1985): 21. **Deaths** (per 1 000 pop. 1985): 5. **Natural increase** (1985): 1.6%. **Infant mortality** (per 1 000 live births 1985): 26.

Education (1987): Literacy 99%; Compulsory ages 6-16.

The island was discovered in 1798 by the British but was formally annexed to the German Empire in 1886. After World War I, Nauru became a League of Nations mandate administered by Australia. During World War II the Japanese occupied the island and shipped 1 200 Nauruans to the fortress island of Truk as slave laborers.

In 1947 Nauru was made a UN trust territory, administered by Australia. Nauru became an independent republic Jan. 31, 1968.

Phosphate exports provide one of the world's highest per capita revenues for the Nauru people. The deposits are expected to be nearly exhausted by 1990.

Nepal

Kingdom of Nepal
Sri Nepala Sarkar

People: Population (1989 est.): 18 760 000. **Age distrib. (%):** 0–14: 42.2; 15–59: 52.9; 60+: 4.9. **Pop. density:** 129.0 per sq. km. **Urban** (1985): 8%. **Ethnic groups:** The many tribes are descendants of Indian, Tibetan, and Central Asian migrants. **Languages:** Nepali (official) (an Indic language), 12 others. **Religion:** Hindu (official) 90%, Buddhist 7%.

Geography: Area: 145 381 sq. km. **Location:** Astride the Himalaya Mts. **Neighbors:** China on N, India on S. **Topography:** The Himalayas stretch across the N, the hill country with its fertile valleys extends across the centre, while the southern border region is part of the flat, subtropical Ganges Plain. **Capital:** Kathmandu. **Cities** (1987 est.): Kathmandu 422 000, Pokhara, Biratnagar, Birganj.

Government: Type: Constitutional monarchy. **Head of state:** King Birendra Bir Bikram Shah Dev; b. Dec. 28, 1945; in office: Jan. 31, 1972. **Head of government:** Prime Min. Marich Man Singh Shrestha; in office: July 15, 1986. **Local divisions:** 14 zones; 75 districts. **Defence:** 1.3% of GNP (1984).

Economy: Industries: Sugar, jute mills, tourism. **Chief crops:** Jute, rice, grain. **Minerals:** Quartz. **Other resources:** Forests. **Arable land:** 17%. **Livestock** (1986): cattle: 7 mln. **Electricity prod.** (1986): 395 mln. kwh. **Labor force:** 91% agric.

Finance: Currency: Rupee (Mar. 1988: 21.90 = $1 US). **Gross national product** (1986): $2.4 bln. **Per capita income** (1986): $160. **Imports** (1986): $460 mln.; partners: India 47%, Jap. 25%. **Exports** (1986): $162 mln.; partners: India 68%. **Tourists** (1986): receipts: $40 mln. **National budget** (1987): $150 mln. **International reserves less gold** (Mar. 1988): $182 mln. **Gold:** 151 000 oz t. **Consumer prices** (change in 1986): 19.0%.

Communications: Radios: 2 mln. in use (1986). **Telephones** in use (1984): 23 000. **Daily newspaper circ.** (1985): 5 per 1 000 pop.

Health: Life expectancy at birth (1986): 53.4 male; 50.6 female. **Births** (per 1 000 pop. 1986): 42.2. **Deaths** (per 1 000 pop. 1986): 16. **Natural increase** (1986): 2.6%. **Hospital beds** (1986): 3 767. **Physicians** (1986): 692. **Infant mortality** (per 1 000 live births 1985): 313.

Education (1987): **Literacy:** 29%. **Years compulsory:** 3; Attendance: 79% primary, 22% secondary.
Major International Organizations: UN (IMF).
Canadian Embassy: c/o The Canadian High Commission, P.O. Box 5207, New Delhi, India.

Nepal was originally a group of petty principalities, of which, the Gurkhas, became dominant about 1769. In 1951 King Tribhubana Bir Bikram, member of the Shah family, ended the system of rule by hereditary premiers of the Ranas family, who had kept the kings virtual prisoners, and established a cabinet system of government.

Virtually closed to the outside world for centuries, Nepal is now linked to India and Pakistan by roads and air service and to Tibet by road. Polygamy, child marriage, and the caste system were officially abolished in 1963.

Netherlands

Kingdom of the Netherlands

Koningrijk der Nederlanden

People: Population (1989 est.) 14 689 000. **Age distrib. (%):** 0–14: 19.2; 15–60: 64.0; 60+: 18.8. **Pop. density:** 359.7 per sq. km. **Urban** (1986): 88.3%. **Ethnic groups:** Dutch 97%. **Language:** Dutch. **Religions:** Roman Catholic 36%, Dutch Reformed 19.3%.

Geography: Area: 40 841 sq. km. **Location:** In NW Europe on North Sea. **Topography:** The land is flat, an average alt. of 11 m above sea level, with much land below sea level reclaimed and protected by 2 400 km of dikes. Since 1927 the government has been draining the IJsselmeer, formerly the Zuider Zee. By 1972, 166 000 of a planned 222 600 ha had been drained and reclaimed. **Capital:** Amsterdam. **Cities** (1986): Amsterdam 679 000; Rotterdam 571 100; Hague 443 500.

Government: Type: Parliamentary democracy under a constitutional monarch. **Head of state:** Queen Beatrix; b. Jan. 31, 1938; in office: Apr. 30, 1980. **Head of government:** Prime Min. Ruud Lubbers; in office: Nov. 4, 1982. **Seat of govt.:** The Hague. **Local divisions:** 12 provinces. **Defence:** 3.2% of GNP (1987).

Economy: Industries: Metals, machinery, chemicals, oil refinery, diamond cutting, electronics, tourism. **Chief crops:** Grains, potatoes, sugar beets, vegetables, fruits, flowers. **Minerals:** Natural gas, oil. **Crude oil reserves** (1987): 195 mln. bbls. **Arable land:** 26%. **Livestock** (1985): cattle: 5 mln.; pigs: 12.9 mln. **Fish catch** (1985): 480 000 metric tons. **Electricity prod.** (1986): 63.0 bln. kwh. **Crude steel prod.** (1986): 5.2 mln. metric tons. **Labor force:** 1% agric.; 47% ind. and commerce, 44% services, 15% govt.

Finance: Currency: Guilder (June 1988: 1.93 = $1 US). **Gross national product** (1987): $189.8 bln. **Per capita income** (1987): $13 065. **Imports** (1987): $91.4 bln.; partners: W. Ger. 22%, Belg. 11%, U.S. 9%, U.K. 9%. **Exports** (1987): $93.1 bln.; partners : W. Ger. 30%, Belg. 14%, Fr. 10%, UK 9%. **Tourists** (1985): 1.5 mln.; receipts: $1.4 bln. **National budget** (1985): $49 bln. expenditures. **International reserves less gold** (Mar. 1988): $15.4 bln. **Gold:** 43.94 mln. oz t. **Consumer prices** (change in 1987): 0.1%.

Transport: Railway traffic (1985): 9.2 bln. passenger-km; 3.2 bln. net ton-km. **Motor vehicles:** in use (1985): 4.9 mln. passenger cars, 401 000 comm. vehicles. **Civil aviation** (1985): 18.2 bln. passenger-km; 1.2 bln. freight ton-km. **Chief ports:** Rotterdam, Amsterdam, IJmuiden.

Communications: Television sets: 4.6 mln. licensed (1986). **Radios:** 4.8 mln. licensed (1986). **Telephones in use** (1985): 8 mln. **Daily newspaper circ.** (1984): 312 per 1 000 pop.

Health: Life expectancy at birth (1986): 73 male; 79 female. **Births** (per 1 000 pop. 1985): 12. **Deaths** (per 1 000 pop. 1985): 8. **Natural increase** (1985): 0.4%. **Hospital beds** (1985): 68 943. **Physicians** (1985): 31 185. **Infant mortality** (per 1 000 live births 1985): 8.

Education (1985): **Literacy:** 99%. **Years compulsory:** 10; attendance: 100%.

Major International Organizations: UN and all of its specialized agencies, NATO, EC, OECD.

Canadian Embassy: Sophialaan 7, The Hague; Tel: 070-614111.

Julius Caesar conquered the region in 55 BC, when it was inhabited by Celtic and Germanic tribes.

After the empire of Charlemagne fell apart, the Netherlands (Holland, Belgium, Flanders) split among counts, dukes and bishops, passed to Burgundy and thence to Charles V of Spain. His son, Philip II, tried to check the Dutch drive toward political freedom and Protestantism (1568-1573). William the Silent, prince of Orange, led a confederation of the northern provinces, called Estates, in the Union of Utrecht, 1579. The Estates retained individual sovereignty, but were represented jointly in the States-General, a body that had control of foreign affairs and defense. In 1581 they repudiated allegiance to Spain. The rise of the Dutch republic to naval, economic, and artistic eminence came in the 17th century.

The United Dutch Republic ended 1795 when the French formed the Batavian Republic. Napoleon made his brother Louis king of Holland, 1806; Louis abdicated 1810 when Napoleon annexed Holland. In 1813 the French were expelled. In 1815 the Congress of Vienna formed a kingdom of the Netherlands, including Belgium, under William I. In 1830, the Belgians seceded and formed a separate kingdom.

The constitution, promulgated 1814, and subsequently revised, assures a hereditary constitutional monarchy.

The Netherlands maintained its neutrality in World War I, but was invaded and brutally occupied by Germany from 1940 to 1945. After the war, neutrality was abandoned, and the country joined NATO, the Western European Union, the Benelux Union, and, in 1957, became a charter member of the Common Market.

In 1949, after several years of fighting, the Netherlands granted independence to Indonesia, where it had ruled since the 17th century. In 1963, West New Guinea was turned over to Indonesia, after five years of controversy and seizure of Dutch property in Indonesia.

The independence of former Dutch colonies has instigated mass emigrations to the Netherlands, adding to problems of unemployment.

Though the Netherlands has been heavily industrialized, its productive small farms export large quantities of pork and dairy foods.

The Netherlands has agreed to allow NATO to deploy 48 cruise missles on their soil by 1988.

Rotterdam, located along the principal mouth of the Rhine, handles the most cargo of any ocean port in the world. Canals, of which there are 5 565 km, are important in transportation.

Netherlands Antilles

The **Netherlands Antilles,** constitutionally on a level of equality with the Netherlands homeland within the kingdom, consist of 2 groups of islands in the West Indies. **Curacao, Aruba,** and **Bonaire** are near the South American coast; **St. Eustatius, Saba,** and the southern part of **St. Maarten** are SE of Puerto Rico. Northern two-thirds of St. Maarten belong to French Guadeloupe; the French call the island St. Martin. Total area of the 2 groups is 1 001 sq. km, including: Aruba 195, Bonaire 289, Curacao 445, St. Eustatius 29, Saba 13, St. Maarten (Dutch part) 34.

Aruba became independent on Jan. 1, 1986; it is an autonomous member of The Netherlands, the same status as the Netherland Antilles.

Total pop. (est. 1987) was 176 000. Willemstad, on Curacao, is the capital. Chief products are corn, pulse, salt and phosphate; principal industry is the refining of crude oil from Venezuela. Tourism is an important industry, as are electronics and shipbuilding.

New Zealand

People: Population: (1989 est.): 3 397 000. **Age distrib. (%):** 0–14: 23.3; 15–59: 61.1; 60+: 15.6 **Pop. density:** 12.6 per sq. km. **Urban** (1985): 84.0%. **Ethnic groups:** European (mostly British) 87%, Polynesian (mostly Maori) 9%. **Languages:** English (official), Maori. **Religions:** Anglican 29%, Presbyterian 18%, Roman Catholic 15%, others.

Geography: Area: 268 655 sq. km. **Location:** In SW Pacific O. **Neighbors:** Nearest are Australia on W, Fiji, Tonga on N. **Topography:** Each of the 2 main islands (North and South Is.) is mainly hilly and mountainous. The east coasts consist of fertile plains, especially the broad Canterbury Plains on South Is. A volcanic plateau is in centre of North Is. South Is. has glaciers and 15 peaks over 3 000 m. **Capital:** Wellington. **Cities** (1986 met.): Auckland 149 000; Christchurch 168 000; Wellington 137 000; Manakau 177 000

Government: Type: Parliamentary. **Head of state:** Queen Elizabeth II, represented by Gov.-Gen. Paul Reeves. **Head of government:** Prime Min. David Lange; b. Aug. 4, 1942; elected: July 14, 1984. **Local divisions:** 90 counties, 128 boroughs, 10 towns & districts. **Defense:** 1.9% of GNP (1985).

Economy: Industries: Food processing, textiles, machinery, fish, forest prods. **Chief crops:** Grain. **Minerals:** Oil, gas, iron, coal. **Crude oil reserves** (1987): 182 mln. bbls. **Other resources:** Wool, timber. **Arable land:** 2%. **Livestock** (1985): cattle: 8.4 mln.; sheep: 67.2 mln. **Fish catch** (1984): 141 000 metric tons. **Electricity prod.** (1986): 27.0 bln. kwh. **Labor force:** 11% agric. & mining; 21% ind. and commerce, 66% services and gov.

Finance: Currency: Dollar (May 1988: 1.42 = $1 US). **Gross national product** (1986): $23.2 bln. **Per capita income** (1986): $7 282. **Imports** (1987): $7.1 bln.; partners: Austral. 16%, U.S. 16%, Jap. 20%. **Exports** (1987): $7.2 bln.; partners: UK 19%, U.S. 15%, Jap. 15%, Austral. 16%. **Tourists** (1985): receipts $276 mln. **National budget** (1985): $7.4 bln. **International reserves less gold** (Feb. 1988): $3.0 bln. **Gold:** 22 000 oz t. **Consumer prices** (change in 1987): 15.7%.

Transport: Railway traffic (1984): 458 mln. passenger-km; 3.1 bln. net ton-km. **Motor vehicles:** in use (1986): 1.5 mln. passenger cars; 318 000 comm. vehicles. **Civil aviation:** (1986): 8.7 bln. passenger-km, 335 mln. freight ton-km. **Chief ports:** Auckland, Wellington, Lyttleton, Tauranga.

Communications: Television sets: 959 000 in use (1985). **Radios:** 2.7 mln. in use (1984). **Telephones in use** (1985): 2.1 mln. **Daily newspaper circ.** (1985): 323 per 1 000 pop.

Health: Life expectancy at birth (1985): 71.0 male; 76.8 female. **Births** (per 1 000 pop. 1985): 16.2. **Deaths** (per 1 000 pop. 1985): 7.6. **Natural increase** (1985): .8%. **Hospital beds** (1985): 31 273. **Physicians** (1985): 7 750. **Infant mortality** (per 1 000 live births 1985): 10.

Education (1987): Literacy: 99%. Compulsory ages 6-15; attendance: 100%.

Major International Organizations: UN (GATT, World Bank, IMF), Commonwealth of Nations, OECD.

Canadian High Commission: I.C.I. Bldg., Molesworth St., P.O. Box 12-049, Wellington North; Tel: 739-577.

The Maoris, a Polynesian group from the eastern Pacific, reached New Zealand before and during the 14th century. The first European to sight New Zealand was Dutch navigator Abel Janszoon Tasman, but Maoris refused to allow him to land. British Capt. James Cook explored the coasts, 1769-1770.

British sovereignty was proclaimed in 1840, with organized settlement beginning in the same year. Representative institutions were granted in 1853. Maori Wars ended in 1870 with British victory. The colony became a dominion in 1907, and is an independent member of the Commonwealth.

New Zealand fought on the side of the Allies in both world wars, and signed the ANZUS Treaty of Mutual Security with the U.S. and Australia in 1951. New Zealand's refusal to allow U.S. ships with nuclear weapons to use their port facilities caused a strain on the ANZUS alliance in 1985. New Zealand joined with Australia and Britain in a pact to defend Singapore and Malaysia; New Zealand units are stationed in those 2 countries.

In July 1985, the *Rainbow Warrior*, flagship of the Greenpeace organization, was bombed and sunk in Auckland harbour by French secret service agents.

The ANZUS defense alliance ended in 1986 because of differences with the U.S. over the refusal of New Zealand port entry to ships that might be carrying nuclear weapons; defense commitments with the 3d ANZUS partner, Australia, remained.

A labor tradition in politics dates back to the 19th century. Private ownership is basic to the economy, but state ownership or regulation affects many industries. Transportation, broadcasting, mining, and forestry are largely state-owned.

The native Maoris number about 250 000. Four of 92 members of the House of Representatives are elected directly by the Maori people.

New Zealand comprises **North Island,** 114 491 sq. km; **South Island,** 151 590 sq. km; **Stewart Island,** 1 752 sq. km; **Chatham Islands,** 967 sq. km.

In 1965, the **Cook Islands** (pop. 1983 est., 16 900; area 242 sq. km) became self-governing although New Zealand retains

responsibility for defense and foreign affairs. **Niue** attained the same status in 1974; it lies 640 km to W (pop. 1981 est., 3 400; area 260 sq. km). **Tokelau Is.,** (pop. 1981 est., 1 600; area 10 sq. km) are 480 km N of Samoa.

Ross Dependency, administered by New Zealand since 1923, comprises 416 000 sq. km of Antarctic territory.

Nicaragua
Republic of Nicaragua
Republica de Nicaragua

People: Population (1989 est.): 3 692 000. **Age distrib.** (%): 0–14: 46.7; 15–59: 49.2; 60+: 4.1. **Pop. density:** 28.4 per sq. km. **Urban** (1986): 58%. **Ethnic groups:** Mestizo 69%, Caucasian 17%, Black 9%, Indian 5%. **Languages:** Spanish (official), English (on Caribbean coast). **Religion:** Roman Catholic 95%.

Geography: Area: 129 990 sq. km. **Location:** In Central America. **Neighbors:** Honduras on N, Costa Rica on S. **Topography:** Both Atlantic and Pacific coasts are over 320 km long. The Cordillera Mtns., with many volcanic peaks, runs NW-SE through the middle of the country. Between this and a volcanic range to the E lie Lakes Managua and Nicaragua. **Capital:** Managua. **Cities** (1986): Managua 1 mln.

Government: Type: Republic. **Head of Government:** Daniel Ortega Saavedra; in office Jan. 10, 1985. **Local divisions:** 16 departments. **Defence:** 13.4% of GNP (1984).

Economy: Industries: Oil refining, food processing, chemicals, textiles. **Chief crops:** Bananas, cotton, fruit, yucca, coffee, sugar, corn, beans, cocoa, rice, sesame, tobacco, wheat. **Minerals:** Gold, silver, copper, tungsten. **Other resources:** Forests, shrimp. **Arable land:** 10%. **Livestock** (1985): cattle: 1.8 mln.; pigs: 540 000. **Fish catch:** (1985): 4 500 metric tons. **Electricity prod.** (1986): 1.2 bln. kwh. **Labor force:** 41% agric.; 13% ind.; 46% services.

Finance: Currency: Cordoba (Apr. 1988: 70.00 = $1 US). **Gross national product** (1985): $2.8 bln. **Per capita income** (1985): $868. **Imports** (1985): $843 partners: Comecon, CACM, EC. **Exports** (1985): $260 mln.; partners: EC, Japan, Comecon. **National budget** (1984): $1.4 bln. expenditures. **Consumer prices** (change in 1987): 1500%.

Transport: Railway traffic (1984): 20.2 mln. passenger-miles; 13 mln. net ton-miles. **Motor vehicles:** in use (1985): 33 000 passenger cars, 42 000 comm. vehicles. **Chief ports:** Corinto, Puerto Somoza, San Juan del Sur.

Communications: Television sets: 171 000 in use (1986). **Radios:** 300 000 in use (1986). **Telephones in use** (1984): 51 000. **Daily newspaper circ.** (1985): 46 per 1 000 pop.

Health: Life expectancy at birth (1985): 58.7male; 61.0 female. **Births** (per 1 000 pop. 1985): 44. **Deaths** (per 1 000 pop. 1985): 9. **Natural increase** (1985): 3.5%. **Hospital beds** (1985): 5 083. **Physicians** (1985): 2 172. **Infant mortality** (per 1 000 live births 1986): 37.0.

Education (1986): Literacy: 66%. **Years compulsory:** 11 years or 16 years old.

Major International Organizations: UN and all of its specialized agencies, OAS.

Canadian Embassy: c/o Apartado Postal 10303, San José, Costa Rica.

Nicaragua, inhabited by various Indian tribes, was conquered by Spain in 1552. After gaining independence from Spain, 1821, Nicaragua was united for a short period with Mexico, then with the United Provinces of Central America, finally becoming an independent republic, 1838.

U.S. Marines occupied the country at times in the early 20th century, the last time from 1926 to 1933.

Gen. Anastasio Somoza-Debayle was elected president 1967. He resigned 1972, but was elected president again in 1974. Martial law was imposed in Dec. 1974, after officials were kidnapped by the Marxist Sandinista guerrillas. The country's Roman Catholic bishops charged in 1977 that the government had mistreated civilians in its anti-guerrilla campaign. Violent opposition spread to nearly all classes, 1978; a nationwide strike called against the government Aug. 25 touched off a state of civil war at Matagalpa.

Months of simmering civil war erupted when Sandinist guerrillas invaded Nicaragua May 29, 1979, touching off a 7-week-offensive that culminated in the resignation and exile of Somoza, July 17.

In 1983, Nicaragua accused the U.S. of aiding anti-Sandinista contras who were invading from Honduras.

Nicaragua accused the U.S. CIA of directing the mining of its ports, Apr. 6, 1984. It asked the International Court of Justice in The Hague to order the U.S. to halt the mining and cease aiding attacks on its territory. The Court ruled, May 10, that the U.S. should immediately halt any actions to blockade or mine Nicaragua's ports.

In June 1986, the U.S. House of Representatives approved $100 mln. in aid for the contras. It was the first time that the House had granted overt military aid to the contras. The diversion of funds to the contras from the proceeds of a secret arms sale to Iran caused a major scandal in the U.S. during 1987. The plan, masterminded by the U.S. administration's national security advisor and his deputy, took place at a time when military aid to the contras was forbidden by law.

Cease-fire talks between the Sandinista government and the contras were held in 1988.

Niger
Republic of Niger
République du Niger

People: Population (1989 est.): 7 440 000. **Age distrib.** (%): 0–14: 46.7; 15–59: 48.5; 60+: 4.8. **Pop. density:** 5.9 per sq. km. **Urban** (1987): 20%. **Ethnic groups:** Hausa 56%, Djerma 22%, Fulani 8%, Tuareg 8%. **Languages:** French (official), Hausa, Djerma. **Religion:** Sunni Moslem 80%.

Geography: Area: 1 266 902 sq. km. **Location:** In the interior of N. Africa. **Neighbors:** Libya, Algeria on N, Mali, Burkina Faso on W, Benin, Nigeria on S, Chad on E. **Topography:** Mostly arid desert and mountains. A narrow savanna in the S and the Niger R. basin in the SW contain most of the population. **Capital:** Niamey. **Cities** (1987 est.): Niamey 350 000.

Government: Type: Republic; military in power. **Head of state:** Pres. Col. Ali Seibou; in office: Nov. 10, 1987. **Head of government:** Premier Hamid Algabid; in office: Nov. 11, 1983. **Local divisions:** 7 departments. **Defence:** 0.7% of GNP (1984).

Economy: Chief crops: Peanuts, cotton. **Minerals:** Uranium, coal, iron. **Arable land:** 3%. **Livestock** (1985): cattle: 3.5 mln.; sheep: 505 000. **Electricity prod.** (1985): 51 mln. kwh. **Labor force:** 90% agric.

Finance: Currency: CFA franc (Mar. 1988: 281 = $1 US). **Gross domestic product** (1985): $1.6 bln. **Per capita income** (1984): $200. **Imports** (1985): $354 mln.; partners: Fr. 36%, Nig. 13%. **Exports** (1985): $251 mln.; partners: Fr. 36%, Nig. 17%. **National budget** (1986): $317 mln. **International reserves less gold** (Jan. 1988): $244 mln. **Gold:** 11 000 oz t. **Consumer prices** (change in 1987): —6.7%.

Transport: Motor vehicles: in use (1984): 23 000 passenger cars, 9 500 comm. vehicles.

Communications: Radios: 300 000 in use (1986). **Telephones in use** (1985): 11 000. **Daily newspaper circ.** (1986): 1 per 1 000 pop.

Health: Life expectancy at birth (1987): 44 years. **Births** (per 1 000 pop. 1985): 51.0. **Deaths** (per 1 000 pop. 1985): 22.9. **Natural increase** (1985): 2.8%. **Health** (1982): 2 hospitals, 36 medical centres. **Infant mortality** (per 1 000 live births 1986): 145.

Education (1987): **Literacy:** 13%. **Years compulsory:** 6; attendance: 15%.

Major International Organizations: UN (GATT, IMF, WHO, FAO), OAU.

Canadian Embassy: c/o 01 P.O. Box 4101, Abidjan 01, Côte d'Ivoire.

Niger was part of ancient and medieval African empires. European explorers reached the area in the late 18th century. The French colony of Niger was established 1900-22, after the defeat of Tuareg fighters, who had invaded the area from the N a century before. The country became independent Aug. 3, 1960. The next year it signed a bilateral agreement with France retaining close economic and cultural ties, which have continued. Hamani Diori, Niger's first president, was ousted in a 1974 coup. Drought and famine struck in 1973-74, and again in 1975.

Nigeria
Federal Republic of Nigeria

People: Population (1989 est.): 115 152 000. **Pop. density:** 124.7 per sq. km. **Urban** (1985): 23%. **Ethnic groups:** Hausa 21%, Yoruba 20%, Ibo 17%, Fulani 9%, others. **Languages:** English (official), Hausa, Yoruba, Ibo. **Religions:** Moslem 50% (in N), Christian 40% (in S), others.

Geography: Area: 923 696 sq. km. **Location:** On the S coast of W. Africa. **Neighbors:** Benin on W, Niger on N, Chad, Cameroon on E. **Topography:** 4 E-W regions divide Nigeria: a coastal mangrove swamp 16-96 km wide, a tropical rain forest 80-160 km wide, a plateau of savanna and open woodland, and semidesert in the N. **Capital:** Lagos. **Cities** (1983 est.): Lagos 1 097 000; Ibadan 1 060 000.

Government: Type: Military. **Head of state:** Gen. Ibrahim Babangida; b. Aug. 17, 1941; in office: Aug. 30, 1985. **Local divisions:** 21 states plus federal capital territory. **Defence:** 8.2% of govt. budget (1986).

Economy: Industries: Crude oil (95% of export), food processing, assembly of vehicles, textiles. **Chief crops:** Cocoa (main export crop), tobacco, palm products, peanuts, cotton, soybeans. **Minerals:** Oil, gas, coal, iron, limestone, columbium, tin. **Crude oil reserves** (1987): 16.8 bln. bbls. **Other resources:** Timber, rubber, hides. **Arable land:** 34%. **Livestock** (1985): cattle: 12.1 mln.; pigs: 1.3 mln.; sheep 13.1 mln. **Fish catch** (1985): 246 000 metric tons. **Electricity prod.** (1986): 10.7 bln. kwh. **Labor force:** 54% agric., 19% ind., comm. and serv.

Finance: Currency: Naira (Feb. 1988: 1.00 = $.23 US). **Gross national product** (1985): $53 bln. **Per capita income** (1984): $790. **Imports** (1985): $8.8 bln.; partners: U.S., EC. **Exports** (1985): $12.5 bln.; partners: U.S., EC. **Tourist receipts** (1984): $102 mln. **National budget** (1986): $15.6 bln. **International reserves less gold** (Jan. 1988): $1.1 bln. **Gold:** 687 000 oz t. **Consumer prices** (change in 1986): 5.4%.

Transport: Motor vehicles: in use (1981): 262 000 passenger cars, 90 000 comm. vehicles. **Civil aviation** (1986): 2.2 bln. passenger-km; 44 mln. freight ton-km. **Chief ports:** Port Harcourt, Lagos, Warri, Calabar.

Communications: Television sets: 500 000 licensed (1986). **Radios:** 15 mln. licensed (1986). **Telephones in use** (1986): 265 000. **Daily newspaper circ.** (1986): 9 per 1 000 pop.

Health: Life expectancy at birth (1983): 48.3 male; 51.7 female. **Births** (per 1 000 pop. 1985): 46. **Deaths** (per 1 000 pop. 1985): 18. **Natural increase** (1985): 2.8%. **Hospital beds** (1983): 60 840. **Physicians** (1983): 11 294. **Infant mortality:** (per 1 000 live births 1985): 127.

Education (1987): **Literacy:** 42%. **Primary school attendance:** 42%.

Major International Organizations: UN (GATT, IMO, WHO), OPEC, OAU, Commonwealth of Nations.

Canadian High Commission: Committee of Vice-Chancellors Bldg., Plot 8A, 4 Idowu-Taylor St., Victoria Island; Postal: P.O. Box 54506, Ikoyi Station, Lagos. Tel.: 612-382, -383, -384, -385, -386.

Early cultures in Nigeria date back to at least 700 BC. From the 12th to the 14th centuries, more advanced cultures developed in the Yoruba area, at Ife, and in the north, where Moslem influence prevailed.

Portuguese and British slavers appeared from the 15th-16th centuries. Britain seized Lagos, 1861, during an anti-slave trade campaign, and gradually extended control inland until 1900. Nigeria became independent Oct. 1, 1960, and a republic Oct. 1, 1963.

On May 30, 1967, the Eastern Region seceded, proclaiming itself the Republic of Biafra, plunging the country into civil war. Casualties in the war were est. at over 1 million, including many "Biafrans" (mostly Ibos) who died of starvation despite international efforts to provide relief. The secessionists, after steadily losing ground, capitulated Jan. 12, 1970. Within a few years, the Ibos were reintegrated into national life, but mistrust among the regions persists.

Oil revenues have made possible a massive economic development program, largely using private enterprise, but agriculture has lagged. Oil revenues continued to decline in 1987.

After 13 years of military rule, the nation experienced a peaceful return to civilian government, Oct., 1979.

Military rule returned to Nigeria, Dec. 31, 1983 as a coup ousted the democratically-elected government. The government has promised a return to democracy by 1992. Violence erupted between Christians and Moslems in Mar. 1987; 15 died and numerous churches and mosques were torched.

Norway

Kingdom of Norway

Kongeriket Norge

People: Population (1989 est.): 4 204 000. **Age distrib.** (%): 0–14: 19.8; 15–59: 58.9; 60+: 21.3. **Pop. density:** 13.0 per sq. km. **Urban** (1985): 80%. **Ethnic groups:** Germanic (Nordic, Alpine, Baltic), minority Lapps. **Languages:** Norwegian (official), Lappish. **Religion:** Evangelical Lutheran 94%.

Geography: Area: 324 194 sq. km. **Location:** Occupies the W part of Scandinavian peninsula in NW Europe (extends farther north than any European land). **Neighbors:** Sweden, Finland, USSR on E. **Topography:** A highly indented coast is lined with tens of thousands of islands. Mountains and plateaus cover most of the country, which is only 25% forested. **Capital:** Oslo. **Cities** (1987): Oslo 449 000; Bergen 207 000.

Government: Type: Hereditary constitutional monarchy. **Head of state:** King Olav V, b. July 2, 1903; in office: Sept. 21, 1957. **Head of government:** Prime Min. Gro Harlem Brundtland; b. Apr. 20, 1939; in office: May 2, 1986. **Local divisions:** Oslo, Svalbard and 18 fylker (counties). **Defence:** 2.8% of GNP (1984).

Economy: Industries: Paper, shipbuilding, engineering, metals, chemicals, food processing oil, gas. **Chief crops:** Grains, potatoes, fruits. **Minerals:** Oil, copper, pyrites, nickel, iron, zinc, lead. **Crude oil reserves** (1987): 11.1 bln. bbls. **Other resources:** Timber. **Arable land:** 3%. **Livestock** (1986): sheep: 2.3 mln.; cattle: 967 000; pigs: 837 000. **Fish catch** (1986): 1.8 mln. metric tons. **Electricity prod.** (1985): 122.6 bln. kwh. **Crude steel prod.** (1986): 850 000 metric tons. **Labor force:** 7% agric.; 47% ind., 18% services, 26% govt.

Finance: Currency: Kroner (May 1988: 6.27 = $1 US). **Gross national product** (1985): $57 bln. **Per capita income** (1984): $13 790. **Imports** (1987): $22.6 bln.; partners: Swed. 17%, W. Ger. 16%, UK 10%, U.S. 9%. **Exports** (1987): $21.6 bln.; partners: UK 37%, W. Ger. 17%, Swed. 9%. **Tourists** (1986): receipts: $853 mln. **National budget** (1986): $32.5 bln. expenditures. **International reserves less gold** (Mar. 1988): $14.5 bln. **Gold:** 1.18 mln. oz t. **Consumer prices** (change in 1987): 8.7%.

Transport: Railway traffic (1986): 2.2 bln. passenger-km; 2.9 bln. net ton-km. **Motor vehicles:** in use (1986): 1.5 mln. passenger cars, 282 000 comm. vehicles. **Civil aviation:** (1986): 3.9 bln. passenger-km; 137 mln. net ton-km. **Chief ports:** Bergen, Stavanger, Oslo, Tonsberg.

Communications: Television sets: 1.4 mln. licensed (1986). **Radios:** 1.5 mln. in use (1986) **Telephones in use** (1985): 2.5 mln. **Daily newspaper circ.** (1986): 482 per 1 000 pop.

Health: Life expectancy at birth (1986): 72.7 male; 79.5 female. **Births** (per 1 000 pop. 1986): 12.6. **Deaths** (per 1 000 pop. 1986): 10.5. **Natural increase** (1986): 0.2%. **Hospital beds** (1985): 24 776. **Physicians** (1985): 10 110. **Infant mortality** (per 1 000 live births 1985): 8.

Education (1987): Literacy: 100%. **Years Compulsory:** 9.

Major International Organizations: UN and all of its specialized agencies, NATO, OECD.

Canadian Embassy: Oscar's Gate 20, 0352 Oslo 3; Tel: 46-69-55, 59.

The first supreme ruler of Norway was Harald the Fairhaired who came to power in 872 AD. Between 800 and 1000, Norway's Vikings raided and occupied widely dispersed parts of Europe.

The country was united with Denmark 1381-1814, and with Sweden, 1814-1905. In 1905, the country became independent with Prince Charles of Denmark as king.

Norway remained neutral during World War I. Germany attacked Norway Apr. 9, 1940, and held it until liberation May 8, 1945. The country abandoned its neutrality after the war, and

joined the NATO alliance. Norway rejected membership in the Common Market in a 1972 referendum.

Abundant hydroelectric resources provided the base for Norway's industrialization, producing one of the highest living standards in the world.

Norway's merchant marine is one of the world's largest.

Norway and the Soviet Union have disputed their territorial waters boundary in the Barents Sea, north of the 2 countries' common border.

Petroleum output from oil and mineral deposits under the continental shelf has raised state revenues.

Svalbard is a group of mountainous islands in the Arctic O., c. 62 288 sq. km, pop. varying seasonally from 1 500 to 3 600. The largest, Spitsbergen (formerly called West Spitsbergen), 39 156 sq. km. is about 595 km N of Norway. By a treaty signed in Paris, 1920, major European powers recognized the sovereignty of Norway, which incorporated it in 1925. Both Norway and the USSR mine rich coal deposits. Mt. Newton (Spitsbergen) is 1 717 m tall.

Oman

Sultanate of Oman

Saltanat 'Uman

People: Population (1989 est.): 1 389 000. **Pop. density:** 6.5 per sq. km. **Urban** (1985): 8.8%. **Ethnic groups:** Arab 88%, Baluchi 4%, Persian 3%, Indian 2%, African 2%. **Languages:** Arabic (official), English, Urdu, others. **Religions:** Ibadhi Moslem 75%, Sunni Moslem.

Geography: Area: 212 441 sq. km. **Location:** On SE coast of Arabian peninsula. **Neighbors:** United Arab Emirates, Saudi Arabia, South Yemen on W. **Topography:** Oman has a narrow coastal plain up to 16 km wide, a range of barren mountains reaching 3 017 m and a wide, stony, mostly waterless plateau, avg. alt. 305 m. Also the tip of the Ruus-al-Jebal peninsula controls access to the Persian Gulf. **Capital:** Muscat. **Cities** (1982 est.): Muscat 85 000.

Government: Type: Absolute monarchy. **Head of state:** Sultan Qabus bin Said; b. Nov. 18, 1942; in office: July 23, 1970. **Local divisions:** 1 province, numerous districts. **Defence:** 25% of GNP (1985).

Economy: Chief crops: Dates, fruits vegetables, wheat, bananas. **Minerals:** Oil (95% of exports). **Crude oil reserves** (1987): 4.5 bln. bbls. **Fish catch** (1985): 101 000 metric tons. **Electricity prod.** (1986): 2.9 bln. kwh. **Labor force:** 80% agric. & fishing.

Finance: Currency: Rial Omani (Mar. 1988: .38 = $1 US). **Gross national product** (1985): $9.0 bln. **Imports** (1984): $3 bln.; partners: Jap. 21%, UAE 17%, UK 14%. **Exports** (1984): $5 bln.; partners: Jap. 58%, Europe 30%. **National budget** (1985): $4.4 bln. revenues; $5.4 bln. expenditures. **International reserves less gold** (Mar. 1988): $1.3 bln. **Gold:** 289 000 oz t.

Transport: Chief ports: Matrah, Muscat.

Communications: Television sets: 400 000 in use (1986). **Radios:** 500 000 in use (1986). **Telephones in use** (1986): 41 000.

Health: Life expectancy at birth (1986): 48 yrs. **Hospital beds** (1986): 2 861; **Physicians** (1986): 581. **Infant mortality** (per 1 000 live births 1985): 113.4.

Education (1986): Literacy: 20%. **Attendance:** 60% primary, 10% secondary.

Major International Organizations: UN (World Bank, IMF), Arab League.

Canadian Embassy: c/o P.O. Box 25281, 13113 (Safat), Kuwait City, Kuwait.

A long history of rule by other lands, including Portugal in the 16th century, ended with the ousting of the Persians in 1744. By the early 19th century, Muscat and Oman was one of the most important countries in the region, controlling much of the Persian and Pakistan coasts, and ruling far-away Zanzibar, which was separated in 1861 under British mediation.

British influence was confirmed in a 1951 treaty, and Britain helped suppress an uprising by traditionally rebellious interior tribes against control by Muscat in the 1950s. Enclaves on the Pakistan coast were sold to that country in 1958.

On July 23, 1970, Sultan Said bin Taimur was overthrown by his son. The new sultan changed the nation's name to Sultanate of Oman. He launched a domestic development program, and battled leftist rebels in the southern Dhofar area to their defeat, Dec. 1975.

Oil has been the major source of income.

Pakistan
Islamic Republic of Pakistan

People: Population (1989 est.): 110 358 000. **Pop. density:** 137.3 per sq. km. **Urban** (1985): 30%. **Ethnic groups:** Punjabi 66%, Sindhi 13%, Pushtun (Iranian) 8.5%, Urdu 7.6%, Baluchi 2.5%, others. **Languages:** Urdu, English are both official. **Religion:** Moslem 97%.

Geography: Area: 803 882 sq. km. **Location:** In W part of South Asia. **Neighbors:** Iran on W, Afghanistan, China on N, India on E. **Topography:** The Indus R. rises in the Hindu Kush and Himalaya mtns. in the N (highest is K2, or Godwin Austen, 8 610 m, 2d highest in world), then flows over 1 600 km through fertile valley and empties into Arabian Sea. Thar Desert, Eastern Plains flank Indus Valley. **Capital:** Islamabad. **Cities** (1981 cen.): Karachi 5.1 mln.; Lahore 2.9 mln.; Faisalabad 1 mln.; Hyderabad 795 000; Rawalpindi 928 000.

Government: Type: Parliamentary democracy in a federal setting. **Head of government:** Pres. Gulam Ishaq Khan. **Head of state:** vacancy. **Local divisions:** Federal capital, 4 provinces, tribal areas. **Defence:** 5.9% of GNP (1984).

Economy: Industries: Textiles, food processing, chemicals, tobacco, **Chief crops:** Rice, wheat. **Minerals:** Natural gas, iron ore. **Crude oil reserves** (1987): 116 mln. bbls. **Other resources:** Wool. **Arable land:** 26%. **Livestock** (1985): cattle: 16.7 mln.; sheep: 25.8 mln. **Fish catch** (1985): 390 000 metric tons. **Electricity prod.** (1986): 22.5 bln. kwh. **Labor force:** 53% agric.; 19% ind; 28% services.

Finance: Currency: Rupee (June 1988: 17.22 = $1 US). **Gross national product** (1986): $32 bln. **Per capita income** (1984): $360. **Imports** (1987): $5.8 bln.; partners: Sau. Ar. 15%, Jap. 12%, U.S. 9%, Kuwait 10%. **Exports** (1987): $4.1 bln.; partners: China 6%, Jap. 8%, U.S. 7%. **National budget** (1984): $7.2 bln. **International reserves less gold** (Mar. 1988): $555 mln. **Gold:** 1.94 mln. oz t. **Consumer prices** (change in 1987): 4.8%.

Transport: Railway traffic (1986): 168 bln. passenger-km; 8.2 bln. net ton-km. **Motor vehicles:** in use (1985): 248 000 passenger cars, 71 000 comm. vehicles. **Civil aviation** (1986): 7 bln. passenger-km; 309 mln. freight ton-km. **Chief ports:** Karachi.

Communications: Television sets: 1.8 mln. in use (1986). **Radios:** 5.2 mln. in use (1986). **Telephones in use** (1985): 533 000. **Daily newspaper circ.** (1986): 22 per 1 000 pop.

Health: Life expectancy at birth (1986): 52.4 male; 50.6 female. **Births** (per 1 000 pop. 1986): 41.4. **Deaths** (per 1 000 pop. 1986): 14.8. **Natural increase** 1986): 2.6%. **Hospital beds** (1986): 57 709. **Physicians** (1986): 46 494. **Infant mortality** (per 1 000 live births 1985): 125.

Education (1985): **Literacy:** 26%.

Major International Organizations: UN (GATT, ILO, IMF, WHO).

Canadian Embassy: Diplomatic Enclave, Sector G-5, Postal: G.P.O. 1042, Islamabad; Tel: 821101/2/3/4/9, 821302/6 .

Present-day Pakistan shares the 5 000-year history of the India-Pakistan sub-continent. At present day Harappa and Mohenjo Daro, the Indus Valley Civilization, with large cities and elaborate irrigation systems, flourished c. 4000-2500 BC.

Aryan invaders from the NW conquered the region around 1500 BC, forging a Hindu civilization that dominated Pakistan as well as India for 2 000 years.

Beginning with the Persians in the 6th century BC, and continuing with Alexander the Great and with the Sassanians, successive nations to the west ruled or influenced Pakistan, eventually separating the area from the Indian cultural sphere.

The first Arab invasion, 712 AD, introduced Islam. Under the Mogul empire (1526-1857), Moslems ruled most of India, yielding to British encroachment and resurgent Hindus.

After World War I the Moslems of British India began agitation

for minority rights in elections. Mohammad Ali Jinnah (1876-1948) was the principal architect of Pakistan. A leader of the Moslem League from 1916, he worked for dominion status for India; from 1940 he advocated a separate Moslem state.

When the British withdrew Aug. 14, 1947, the Islamic majority areas of India acquired self-government as Pakistan, with dominion status in the Commonwealth. Pakistan was divided into 2 sections, West Pakistan and East Pakistan. The 2 areas were nearly 1 600 km apart on opposite sides of India.

Pakistan became a republic in 1956. Pakistan had a National Assembly (legislature) with equal membership from East and West Pakistan, and 2 Provincial Assemblies. In Oct. 1958, Gen. Mohammad Ayub Khan took power in a coup. He was elected president in 1960, reelected in 1965.

As a member of the Central Treaty Organization, Pakistan had been aligned with the West. Following clashes between India and China in 1962, Pakistan made commercial and aid agreements with China.

Ayub resigned Mar. 25, 1969, after several months of violent rioting and unrest, most of it in East Pakistan, which demanded autonomy. The government was turned over to Gen. Agha Mohammad Yahya Khan and martial law was declared.

The Awami League, which sought regional autonomy for East Pakistan, won a majority in Dec. 1970 elections to a National Assembly which was to write a new constitution. In March, 1971 Yahya postponed the Assembly. Rioting and strikes broke out in the East.

On Mar. 25, 1971, government troops launched attacks in the East. The Easterners, aided by India, proclaimed the independent nation of Bangladesh. In months of widespread fighting, countless thousands were killed. Some 10 million Easterners fled into India.

Full scale war between India and Pakistan had spread to both the East and West fronts by December 3. Pakistan troops in the East surrendered Dec. 16; Pakistan agreed to a cease-fire in the West Dec. 17. On July 3, 1972, Pakistan and India signed a pact agreeing to withdraw troops from their borders and seek peaceful solutions to all problems. Diplomatic relations were resumed in 1976.

Zulfikar Ali Bhutto, leader of the Pakistan People's Party, which had won the most West Pakistan votes in the Dec. 1970 elections, became president Dec. 20.

Bhutto was overthrown in a military coup July, 1977. Convicted of complicity in a 1974 political murder, Bhutto was executed Apr.4, 1979. Benazir Bhutto, his daughter, returned to Pakistan from exile in Europe in 1986. Her efforts to relaunch the Pakistan People's Party sparked violence and antigovernment riots.

There are several million Afghan refugees now in Pakistan.

In Aug. 1988, General Mohammad Zia-ul-Haq was killed when the aircraft he was in exploded shortly after takeoff. Also killed were the U.S. ambassador to Pakistan and many senior officers of Pakistan's armed forces. The death of Zia, who had ruled Pakistan for 11 years, left a power vacuum in the government. Gulam Ishaq Khan, leader of the senate and constitutional successor to Gen. Zia, immediately stepped in to serve as interim leader until elections scheduled for the fall.

Panama
Republic of Panama
República de Panamá

People: Population (1989 est.): 2 370 000. **Age distrib.** (%): 0–14: 37.5; 15–59: 55.8; 60+: 6.7. **Pop. density:** 31.3 per sq. km. **Urban** (1985): 53%. **Ethnic groups:** Mestizo 70%, West Indian 14%, Caucasian 10%, Indian 6%. **Languages:** Spanish (official), English. **Religions:** Roman Catholic 93%, Protestant.

Geography: Area: 75 643 sq. km. **Location:** In Central America. **Neighbors:** Costa Rica on W., Colombia on E. **Topography:** 2 mountain ranges run the length of the isthmus. Tropical rain forests cover the Caribbean coast and eastern Panama. **Capital:** Panama. **Cities** (1987 est.): Panama 439 000.

Government: Type: Constitutional democracy, centralized republic. **Head of state and head of government:** Pres. Eric Arturo Delvalle; b. Feb. 2, 1937; in office: Sept. 28, 1985. **Local divisions:** 9 provinces, 1 territory. **Defence:** 2% of GNP (1985).

Economy: Industries: Oil refining, international banking. **Chief crops:** Bananas, pineapples, cocoa, corn, coconuts, sugar. **Minerals:** Copper. **Other resources:** Forests (mahogany), shrimp. **Arable land:** 8%. **Livestock** (1985): cattle: 1.4 mln.; pigs: 215 000. **Fish catch** (1985): 245 000 metric tons. **Electricity prod.** (1986): 3.1 bln. kwh. **Labor force:** 28% agric., 29.4% ind. and commerce, 30% services.

Finance: Currency: Balboa (Apr. 1988: 1.00 = $1 US). **Gross national product** (1985): $4.4 bln. **Per capita income** (1984): $1 970. **Imports** (1985): $1.3 bln.; partners: U.S. 31%, Mexico 10%. **Exports** (1985): $410 mln.; partners: U.S. 59%, EC 16%. **Tourists** (1985): $200 mln. receipts. **National budget** (1985): $2.7 bln. **International reserves less gold** (Jan. 1988): $84 mln. **Consumer prices** (change in 1986): −0.1%.

Transport: Motor vehicles: in use (1984): 104 000 passenger cars, 35 000 comm. vehicles. **Civil aviation** (1985): 551 mln. passenger-km; 55 mln. net ton-km. **Chief ports:** Balboa, Cristobal.

Communications: Television sets: 300 000 in use (1986). **Radios:** 900 000 in use (1986). **Telephones in use** (1985): 223 000. **Daily newspaper circ.** (1986): 89 per 1 000 pop.

Health: Life expectancy at birth (1985): 69.2 male; 72.9 female. **Births** (per 1 000 pop. 1985): 26. **Deaths** (per 1 000 pop. 1985): 5. **Natural increase** (1985): 2.1%. **Hospital beds** (1985): 7 602. **Physicians** (1985): 2 484. **Infant mortality** (per 1 000 live births 1985): 25.

Education (1985): **Literacy:** 87%. **Primary school attendance:** almost 100%.

Major International Organizations: UN (IMF, IMO, World Bank), OAS.

Canadian Embassy: Consulate of Canada, Calle Roche No. 14, Piso Uno, Officina Una, Apartado Postal 3658, Panama City; Tel.: 62-10-32.

The coast of Panama was sighted by Rodrigo de Bastidas, sailing with Columbus for Spain in 1501, and was visited by Columbus in 1502. Vasco Nunez de Balboa crossed the isthmus and "discovered" the Pacific O. Sept. 13, 1513. Spanish colonies were ravaged by Francis Drake, 1572-95, and Henry Morgan, 1668-71. Morgan destroyed the old city of Panama which had been founded in 1519. Freed from Spain, Panama joined Colombia in 1821.

Panama declared its independence from Colombia Nov. 3, 1903, with U.S. recognition. U.S. naval forces deterred action by Colombia. On Nov. 18, 1903, Panama granted use, occupation and control of the Canal Zone to the U.S. by treaty, ratified Feb. 26, 1904.

New treaties were proposed in 1967 and 1974. In 1978, a new treaty provided for a gradual takeover by Panama of the canal, and withdrawal of U.S. troops, to be completed by 1999. U.S. payments were substantially increased in the interim. The permanent neutrality of the canal was also guaranteed.

Due to easy Panama ship regulations and strictures in the U.S., merchant tonnage registered in Panama since World War II ranks high in size.

President Delvalle was ousted by the National Assembly, Feb. 26, 1988 after he tried to fire the head of the Panama Defence Forces, Gen. Manuel Antonio Noriega. Noriega had been indicted by 2 U.S. Federal Grand Juries on drug charges. A general strike followed. The U.S. imposed economic sanctions and made other efforts to oust Noriega from power.

Papua New Guinea

People: Population (1989 est.): 3 613 000. **Age distrib.** (%): 0–14: 41.6; 15–59: 52.8; 60+: 5.6. **Pop. density:** 7.9 per sq. km. **Urban** (1985): 14%. **Ethnic groups:** Papuans (in S and interior), Melanesian (N,E), pygmies, minorities of Chinese, Australians, Polynesians. **Languages:** English (official), Melanesian Pidgin, Police Motu, numerous local languages. **Religions:** Protestant 63%, Roman Catholic 31%, local religions.

Geography: Area: 456 530 sq. km. **Location:** Occupies eastern half of island of New Guinea. **Neighbors:** Indonesia (West Irian) on W, Australia on S. **Topography:** Thickly forested mtns. cover much of the centre of the country, with lowlands along the coasts. Included are some of the nearby islands of Bismarck and Solomon groups, including Admiralty Is., New Ireland, New Britain, and Bougainville. **Capital:** Port Moresby. **Cities** (1985 est.): Port Moresby 144 000.

Government: Type: Parliamentary democracy. **Head of state:** Queen Elizabeth II, represented by Gov. Gen. Sir Kingsford Dibela; in office: Mar. 1, 1983. **Head of government:** Prime Min. Paias Wingti; in office: Nov. 21, 1985. **Local divisions:** National capital and 19 provinces with elected legislatures. **Defence:** approx. 1.3% of GDP (1984).

Economy: Chief crops: Coffee, coconuts, cocoa. **Minerals:** Gold, copper, silver, gas. **Arable land:** 1%. **Livestock** (1985): pigs: 1.4 mln. **Electricity prod.** (1986): 1.7 bln. kwh. **Labor force:** 75% agric., 8% ind. and commerce, 2% services.

Finance: Currency: Kina (Mar. 1988: 1.00 = $1.13 US). **Gross national product** (1985): $2.2 bln. **Per capita income** (1984): $760. **Imports** (1985): $969 mln.; partners: Austral. 34%, Jap. 14%, Sing. 12%. **Exports** (1985): $920 mln.; partners: Jap. 29%, W. Ger. 21%, Austral. 8%. **National budget** (1986): $976 mln. **International reserves less gold** (Mar. 1988): $509 mln. **Gold:** 63 000 oz t. **Consumer prices** (change in 1986): 5.5%.

Transport: Motor vehicles: in use (1984): 22 000 passenger cars, 39 000 comm. vehicles. **Chief ports:** Port Moresby, Lae.

Communications: Radios: 225 000 in use (1986). **Telephones in use** (1985): 57 000. **Daily newspaper circ.** (1986) 8 per 1 000 pop.

Health: Life expectancy at birth (1986): 52.6 male; 54.2 female. **Births** (per 1 000 pop. 1985): 43. **Deaths** (per 1 000 pop. 1985): 12. **Natural increase** (1985): 3.1%. **Hospital beds** (1984): 14 661. **Physicians** (1984): 280. **Infant mortality** (per 1 000 live births 1985): 91.

Education (1986): **Literacy:** 32%. **Attendance:** 65% primary school; 13% secondary school.

Major International Organizations: UN (GATT), Commonwealth of Nations.

Canadian Embassy: c/o The Canadian High Commission, Commonwealth Ave., Canberra, A.C.T. 2600, Australia.

Human remains have been found in the interior of New Guinea dating back at least 10 000 years and possibly much earlier. Successive waves of peoples probably entered the country from Asia through Indonesia. Europeans visited in the 15th century, but land claims did not begin until the 19th century, when the Dutch took control of the western half of the island.

The southern half of eastern New Guinea was first claimed by Britain in 1884, and transferred to Australia in 1905. The northern half was claimed by Germany in 1884, but captured in World War I by Australia, which was granted a League of Nations mandate and then a UN trusteeship over the area. The 2 territories were administered jointly after 1949, given self-government Dec. 1, 1973, and became independent Sept. 16, 1975.

The indigenous population consists of a huge number of tribes, many living in almost complete isolation with mutually unintelligible languages.

Paraguay
Republic of Paraguay
República del Paraguay

People: Population (1989 est.): 4 518 000. **Age distrib.** (%): 0–14: 41.0; 15–59: 52.0; 60+: 7.0. **Pop. density:** 11.1 per sq. km. **Urban** (1985): 43%. **Ethnic groups:** Mestizo 95%, small Caucasian, Indian, Negro minorities. **Languages:** Spanish (official), Guaraní (used by 90%). **Religion:** Roman Catholic (official) 97%.

Geography: Area: 406 720 sq. km. **Location:** One of the 2 landlocked countries of S. America. **Neighbors:** Bolivia on N, Argentina on S, Brazil on E. **Topography:** Paraguay R. bisects the country. To E are fertile plains, wooded slopes, grasslands. To W is the Chaco plain, with marshes and scrub trees. Extreme W is arid. **Capital:** Asunción. **Cities** (1985 cen.): Asunción 477 000.

Government: Type: Republic; under authoritarian rule. **Head of state:** Pres. Alfredo Stroessner; b. Nov. 3, 1912; in office: Aug. 15, 1954. **Local divisions:** 19 departments. **Defence:** 18.3% of govt. budget (1986).

Economy: Industries: Food processing, wood products, textiles, cement. **Chief crops:** Corn, cotton, beans, sugarcane. **Minerals:** Iron, manganese, limestone. **Other resources:** Forests. **Arable land:** 5%. **Livestock** (1985): cattle: 6.7 mln.; pigs:

1.1 mln. **Electricity prod.** (1986): 1.1 bln. kwh. **Labor force:** 44% agric., 34% ind. and commerce, 18% services.

Finance: Currency: Guarani (Mar. 1988 550.00 = $1 US). **Gross national product** (1986): $3.8 bln. **Per capita income** (1984): $1 260. **Imports** (1985): $478 mln.; partners: Braz. 32%, Arg. 5%, U.S. 8%. **Exports** (1985): $304 mln.; partners: Arg. 12%, Neth. 13%, Braz. 26%. **Tourists** (1985): $80 mln. receipts. **National budget** (1986): $762 mln. **International reserves less gold** (Mar. 1988): $414 mln. **Gold:** 35 000 oz t. **Consumer prices** (change in 1987): 21.8%.

Transport: Railway traffic (1980): 22 mln. passenger-km; 34 mln. net ton-km. **Motor vehicles:** in use (1985): 84 000 passenger cars, 41 000 comm. vehicles. **Civil aviation** (1982): 479 mln. passenger-km; 2.9 mln. net ton-km. **Chief ports:** Asuncion.

Communications: Television sets: 266 000 in use (1986). **Radios:** 624 000 in use (1986). **Telephones in use** (1985): 88 000. **Daily newspaper circ.** (1985): 60 per 1 000 pop.

Health: Life expectancy at birth (1984): 63 yrs. **Births** (per 1 000 pop. 1985): 36.0. **Deaths** (per 1 000 pop. 1985): 7.2. **Natural increase** (1985): 2.8%. **Hospital beds** (1982): 3 345. **Physicians** (1982): 2 201. **Infant mortality** (per 1 000 live births 1985): 52.

Education (1987): **Literacy:** 81%. **Years compulsory:** 7; **Attendance:** 83%.

Major International Organizations: UN (IMF, WHO, ILO), OAS.

Canadian Embassy: c/o The Canadian Embassy, Casilla 27, Santiago, Chile.

The Guarani Indians were settled farmers speaking a common language before the arrival of Europeans.

Visited by Sebastian Cabot in 1527 and settled as a Spanish possession in 1535, Paraguay gained its independence from Spain in 1811. It lost much of its territory to Brazil, Uruguay, and Argentina in the War of the Triple Alliance, 1865-1870. Large areas were won from Bolivia in the Chaco War, 1932-35.

Gen. Alfredo Stroessner has ruled since 1954. Suppression of the opposition and decimation of small Indian groups has been charged by international rights groups.

Peru
Republic of Peru
República del Peru

People: Population (1989 est.): 21 792 000. **Age distrib.** (%): 0–14: 40.5; 15–59: 46.0; 60+: 5.5. **Pop. density:** 17.0 per sq. km. **Urban** (1985): 70%. **Ethnic groups:** Indian 45%, Mestizo 37%, Caucasian 15%. **Languages:** Spanish, Quechua (both official), Aymara; 30% speak no Spanish. **Religion:** 90% Roman Catholic.

Geography: Area: 1 285 116 sq. km. **Location:** On the Pacific coast of S. America. **Neighbors:** Ecuador, Colombia on N, Brazil, Bolivia on E, Chile on S. **Topography:** An arid coastal strip, 16–160 km wide, supports much of the population thanks to widespread irrigation. The Andes cover 27% of land area. The uplands are well-watered, as are the eastern slopes reaching the Amazon basin, which covers half the country with its forests and jungles. **Capital:** Lima. **Cities** (1987 est.): Lima 4 330 000; Arequipa 572 000; Callao 545 000.

Government: Type: Constitutional republic. **Head of state:** Pres. Alan Garcia Perez; b. May 23, 1949; in office: July 28, 1985. **Head of government:** Prime Min. Guillermo Larco Cox; in office: June 26, 1987. **Local divisions:** 24 departments, 1 province. **Defence:** 4.0% of GNP (1987).

Economy: Industries: Fish meal, mineral processing, light industry, textiles. **Chief crops:** Cotton, sugar, coffee, corn. **Minerals:** Copper, lead, molybdenum, silver, zinc, iron, oil. **Crude oil reserves** (1987): 535 mln. bbls. **Other resources:** Wool, sardines. **Arable land:** 3%. **Livestock** (1985): cattle: 3.8 mln.; pigs: 2.1 mln.; sheep: 13.5 mln. **Fish catch** (1985): 3.1 mln. metric tons. **Electricity prod.** (1985): 12.1 bln. kwh. **Labor force:** 38% agric.; 17% ind. and mining; 45% govt. and other services.

Finance: Currency: Intl (Mar. 1988: 33 = $1 US). **Gross national product** (1986): $17.0 bln. **Per capita income** (1984): $940. **Imports** (1986): $2.5 bln.; partners: U.S. 25%, EC 19%. **Exports** (1986): $2.5 bln.; partners: U.S. 6%, EC 23%, Jap. 10%. **Tourists** (1985): $277 mln. receipts. **National budget**

(1987): $3.9 bln. **International reserves less gold** (Mar. 1988): $442 mln. **Gold:** 1.2 mln. oz t. **Consumer prices** (change in 1987): 77.9%.

Transport: Railway traffic (1983): 563 mln. passenger-km; 839 mln. net ton-km. **Motor vehicles:** in use (1982): 359 000 passenger cars, 196 000 comm. vehicles. **Civil aviation** (1985): 1.6 bln. passenger-km; 192 mln. net ton-km. **Chief ports:** Callao, Chimbate, Mollendo.

Communications: Television sets: 1.7 mln. in use (1986). **Oadios:** 3.9 mln. in use (1986). **Telephones in use** (1985): 599 000. **Daily newspaper circ.** (1985): 57 per 1 000 pop.

Health: Life expectancy at birth (1985): 58.3 male; 62.2 female. **Births** (per 1 000 pop. 1985): 36. **Deaths** (per 1 000 pop. 1985): 10. **Natural increase** (1985): 2.6%. **Hospital beds** (1982): 29 991. **Physicians** (1982): 14 751. **Infant mortality** (per 1 000 live births 1985): 82.

Education (1987): **Literacy:** 79%. **Years compulsory:** 10.

Major International Organizations: UN and all of its specialized agencies, OAS.

Canadian Embassy: Federico Gerdes 130 (Ante Calle Libertad) Miraflores, Casilla 1212, Lima; Tel: 44-40-15; 44-38-41; 44-38-93; Night 44-46-88.

The powerful Inca empire had its seat at Cuzco in the Andes covering most of Peru, Bolivia, and Ecuador, as well as parts of Colombia, Chile, and Argentina. Building on the achievements of 800 years of Andean civilization, the Incas had a high level of skill in architecture, engineering, textiles, and social organization.

A civil war had weakened the empire when Francisco Pizarro, Spanish conquistador, began raiding Peru for its wealth, 1532. In 1533 he had the seized ruling Inca, Atahualpa, fill a room with gold as a ransom, then executed him and enslaved the natives.

Lima was the seat of Spanish viceroys until the Argentine liberator, Jose de San Martin, captured it in 1821; Spain was defeated by Simon Bolivar and Antonio J. de Sucre; recognized Peruvian independence, 1824. Chile defeated Peru and Bolivia, 1879-84, and took Tarapaca, Tacna, and Arica; returned Tacna, 1929.

On Oct. 3, 1968, a military coup ousted Pres. Fernando Belaunde Terry. In 1968-74, the military government put through sweeping agrarian changes, and nationalized oil, mining, fish-meal, and banking industries.

Food shortages, escalating foreign debt, and strikes led to another coup, Aug. 29, 1976, and to a slowdown of socialist programs.

After 12 years of military rule, Peru returned to democratic leadership under former Pres. Fernando Belaunde Terry, July 1980. The new government encouraged the return of private enterprise to stimulate the inflation-ridden economy.

There were strikes by police, oil workers, and other labor unions in 1987 and 1988. Terrorist activity, mostly by Maoist groups, has continued.

Philippines
Republic of the Philippines

People: Population (1989 est.): 61 971 000. **Age distrib.** (%): 0–14: 39.0; 15–59: 56.2; 60+: 4.8. **Pop. density:** 206.6 per sq. km. **Urban** (1987): 41%. **Ethnic groups:** Malays the large majority, Chinese, Americans, Spanish are minorities. **Languages:** Pilipino (based on Tagalog), English (both official); numerous others spoken. **Religions:** Roman Catholic 83%, Protestant 9%, Moslem 5%.

Geography: Area: 299 979 sq. km. **Location:** An archipelago off the SE coast of Asia. **Neighbors:** Nearest are Malaysia, Indonesia on S, Taiwan on N. **Topography:** The country consists of some 7 100 islands stretching 1 760 km N-S. About 95% of area and population are on 11 largest islands, which are mountainous, except for the heavily indented coastlines and for the central plain on Luzon. **Capital:** Quezon City (Manila is de facto capital). **Cities** (1985 est.): Manila 1.7 mln.; Quezon City 1.3 mln.; Cebu 552 000.

Government: Type: Republic. **Head of state:** Pres. Corazon C. Aquino; b. 1932; in office: Feb. 25, 1986. **Local divisions:** 12 regions, 74 provinces, 60 cities. **Defence:** 1.2% of GNP (1984).

Economy: Industries: Food processing, textiles, clothing, drugs, wood prods., appliances. **Chief crops:** Sugar, rice, corn, pineapple, coconut. **Minerals:** Cobalt, copper, gold, nickel, silver, iron, petroleum. **Crude oil reserves** (1987): 19 mln. bbls. **Other resources:** Forests (42% of area). **Arable land:** 34%. **Livestock** (1985): cattle: 1.7 mln.; pigs: 7.2 mln. **Fish catch** (1984): 1.8 mln. metric tons. **Electricity prod.** (1986): 22.0 bln. kwh. **Labor force:** 47% agric., 20% ind. and comm., 13% services.

Finance: Currency: Peso (May 1988: 21.01 = $1 US). **Gross national product** (1986): $34.5 bln. **Per capita income** (1985): $598. **Imports** (1986): $5.3 bln.; partners: U.S. 22%, Jap. 16%. **Exports** (1986): $4.7 bln.; partners: U.S. 35%, Jap. 20%. **Tourists** (1985): $507 mln. receipts. **National budget** (1986): $5.7 bln. expenditures. **International reserves less gold** (Mar. 1988): $737 mln. **Gold:** 2.9 mln. oz t. **Consumer prices** (change in 1987): 3.8%.

Transport: Railway traffic (1986): 168 mln. passenger-km; 60 mln. net ton-km. **Motor vehicles:** in use (1985): 753 000 passenger cars, 108 000 comm. vehicles. **Civil aviation** (1985): 7.8 bln. passenger-km; 966 mln. freight ton-km. **Chief ports:** Cebu, Manila, Iloilo, Davao.

Communications: Television sets: 3.9 mln. in use (1986). **Radios:** 7.5 mln. in use (1986). **Telephones in use** (1985): 820 000. **Daily newspaper circ.** (1985): 44 per 1 000 pop.

Health: Life expectancy at birth (1987): 61.9 male; 65.5 female. **Births** (per 1 000 pop. 1986): 33.8. **Deaths** (per 1 000 pop. 1986): 8.2. **Natural increase** (1986): 2.5%. **Hospital beds** (1985): 79 703. **Physicians** (1982): 46 579. **Infant mortality** (per 1 000 live births 1985): 52.5.

Education (1986): **Literacy:** 88%. **Attendance:** 95% in elementary, 57% secondary.

Major International Organizations: UN (World Bank, IMF, GATT), ASEAN.

Canadian Embassy: 9th Floor, Allied Bank Centre, 6754 Ayala Ave., Makati, Metro Manila; P.O. Box 971, Commercial Centre, Makati, Rizal, Manila; Tel: 815-95-36.

The Malay peoples of the Philippine islands, whose ancestors probably migrated from Southeast Asia, were mostly hunters, fishers, and unsettled cultivators when first visited by Europeans.

The archipelago was visited by Magellan, 1521. The Spanish founded Manila, 1571. The islands, named for King Philip II of Spain, were ceded by Spain to the U.S. for $20 million, 1898, following the Spanish-American War. U.S. troops suppressed a guerrilla uprising in a brutal 6-year war, 1899-1905.

Japan attacked the Philippines Dec. 8, 1941 (Far Eastern time). Japan occupied the islands during WW II.

On July 4, 1946, independence was proclaimed in accordance with an act passed by the U.S. Congress in 1934. A republic was established.

A rebellion by Communist-led Huk guerrillas was put down by 1954. But urban and rural political violence periodically reappears.

The Philippines and the U.S. have treaties for U.S. military and naval bases and a mutual defense treaty. Riots by radical youth groups and terrorism by leftist guerrillas and outlaws, increased from 1970. On Sept. 21, 1972, President Marcos declared martial law. Ruling by decree, he ordered some land reform and stabilized prices. But opposition was suppressed, and a high population growth rate aggravated poverty and unemployment. Political corruption was believed to be widespread. On Jan. 17, 1973, Marcos proclaimed a new constitution with himself as president. His wife received wide powers in 1978 to supervise planning and development.

Government troops battled Moslem (Moro) secessionists, 1973-76, in southern Mindanao. Fighting resumed, 1977, after a Libyan-mediated agreement on autonomy was rejected by the region's mainly Christian voters.

Martial law was lifted Jan. 17, 1981. Marcos turned over legislative power to the National Assembly, released political prisoners, and said he would no longer rule by decree. He was reelected to a new 6-year term as president.

The assassination of prominent opposition leader Benigno S. Aquino Jr., Aug. 21, 1983, sparked demonstrations calling for the resignation of Marcos. An independent commission appointed by Marcos concluded that a military conspiracy was responsible for Aquino's death. The May 1984 elections saw Marcos retain his majority in the National Assembly although opponents made a strong showing in key areas like Manila.

A bitter presidential election campaign ended Feb. 7, 1986 as elections were held amid allegations of widespread fraud. On Feb. 16, Marcos was declared the victor over Corazon Aquino,

widow of slain opposition leader Benigno Aquino. Aquino declared herself president and announced a nonviolent "active resistance" to overthrow the Marcos government; the 2 held separate inaugurations on Feb. 25.

On Feb. 22, 2 leading military allies of Marcos quit their posts to protest the rigged elections. Feb. 24, Marcos, declared a state of emergency as his military and religious support continued to erode. That same day U.S. President Ronald Reagan urged Marcos to resign. Marcos ended his 20-year tenure as president Feb. 26 as he fled the country. Aquino was recognized immediately as president by the U.S. and other nations.

In 1987, Aquino announced the start of land reforms. Candidates endorsed by Aquino won large majorities in the legislative elections in May, attesting to her popularity. She is plagued, however, by a weak economy, widespread poverty, communist insurgents and a series of attempted coups.

The archipelago has a coastline of 17 360 km. Manila Bay, with an area of 2 000 sq. km, and a circumference of 192 km., is the finest harbor in the Far East.

All natural resources of the Philippines belong to the state; their exploitation is limited to citizens of the Philippines or corporations of which 60% of the capital is owned by citizens.

Poland
Polish People's Republic
Polska Rzeczpospolita Ludowa

People: Population (1989 est.): 38 389 000. **Age distrib.** (%): 0–14: 25.4; 15–59: 60.8; 60+: 13.8. **Pop. density:** 122.8 per sq. km. **Urban** (1986): 60%. **Ethnic groups:** Polish 98%, German, Ukrainian, Byelorussian. **Language:** Polish. **Religion:** Roman Catholic 94%.

Geography: Area: 122 659 sq. km. **Location:** On the Baltic Sea in E Central Europe. **Neighbors:** E. Germany on W, Czechoslovakia on S, USSR (Lithuania, Byelorussia, Ukraine) on E. **Topography:** Mostly lowlands forming part of the Northern European Plain. The Carpathian Mts. along the southern border rise to 2 460 m. **Capital:** Warsaw. **Cities** (1987 est.): Warsaw 1.6 mln., Lodz 848 000, Kracow 740 000, Wroclaw 631 000, Poznan 570 000.

Government: Type: Communist. **Head of state:** Gen. Wojciech Jaruzelski; in office: Oct. 18, 1981. **Head of government:** Zbigniew Messner. **Local divisions:** 49 provinces. **Defence:** 5.7% of GNP (1984).

Economy: Industries: Shipbuilding, chemicals, metals, autos, food processing. **Chief crops:** Grains, potatoes, sugar beets, tobacco, flax. **Minerals:** Coal, copper, zinc, silver, zinc, sulphur, natural gas. **Arable land:** 49%. **Livestock** (1985): cattle: 10.9 mln.; pigs: 18.9 mln.; sheep: 5 mln. **Fish catch** (1985): 650 000 metric tons. **Electricity prod.** (1986): 141 bln. kwh. **Crude steel prod.** (1986): 17.2 mln. metric tons. **Labor force:** 30% agric.; 44% ind. & comm.; 11% services.

Finance: Currency: Zloty (Mar. 1988: 400 = $1 US). **Gross national product** (1985): $240 bln. **Per capita income** (1986): $2 000. **Imports** (1986): $5.4 bln.; partners: USSR 38%, E. Ger. 7% W. Ger. 7% Czech. 5%. **Exports** (1986): $6.5 bln.; partners: USSR 30%, E. Ger. 6%, Czech. 6%, W. Ger. 10%. **National budget** (1984): $23.3 bln. **Tourists** (1985): $106 mln. receipts. **Consumer prices** (change in 1986): 13.5%.

Transport: Railway traffic (1985): 51 bln. passenger-km; 120 bln. net ton-km. **Motor vehicles:** in use (1985): 3.1 mln. passenger cars, 733 000 comm. vehicles. **Civil aviation** (1985): 2.8 bln. passenger-km; 256 mln. freight ton-km. **Chief ports:** Gdansk, Gdynia, Szczecin.

Communications: Television sets: 10.0 mln. licensed (1986). **Radios:** 9.4 mln. licensed (1986). **Telephones in use** (1986): 4.0 mln. **Daily newspaper circ.** (1982): 215 per 1 000 pop.

Health: Life expectancy at birth (1985): 66.5 74.8; 75.2 female. **Births** (per 1 000 pop. 1985): 19. **Deaths** (per 1 000 pop. 1985): 10. **Natural increase** (1985): 0.9%. **Hospital beds** (1986): 211 000. **Physicians** (1986): 73 000. **Infant mortality** (per 1 000 live births 1985): 18.

Education (1987): **Literacy:** 98%. **Years compulsory:** 8; attendance 97%.

Major International Organizations: UN (GATT, WHO), Warsaw Pact.

Canadian Embassy: Ulica Matejki 1/5, Warsaw 00-481; Tel: 29-80-51.

Slavic tribes in the area were converted to Latin Christianity in the 10th century. Poland was a great power from the 14th to the 17th centuries. In 3 partitions (1772, 1793, 1795) it was apportioned among Prussia, Russia, and Austria. Overrun by the Austro-German armies in World War I, its independence, self-declared on Nov.11, 1918, was recognized by the Treaty of Versailles, June 28, 1919. Large territories to the east were taken in a war with Russia, 1921.

Nazi Germany and the USSR invaded Poland Sept. 1-27, 1939, and divided the country. During the war, some 6 million Polish citizens were killed by the Nazis, half of them Jews. With Germany's defeat, a Polish government-in-exile in London was recognized by the U.S., but the USSR pressed the claims of a rival group. The election of 1947 was completely dominated by the Communists.

In compensation for 181 636 sq. km ceded to the USSR, 1945, Poland received approx. 104 000 sq. km of German territory E of the Oder-Neisse line comprising Silesia, Pomerania, West Prussia, and part of East Prussia.

In 12 years of rule by Stalinists, large estates were abolished, industries nationalized, schools secularized, and Roman Catholic prelates jailed. Farm production fell off. Harsh working conditions caused a riot in Poznan June 28-29, 1956.

A new Politburo, committed to development of a more independent Polish Communism, was named Oct. 1956, with Wladyslaw Gomulka as first secretary of the Communist Party. Collectivization of farms was ended and many collectives were abolished.

In Dec. 1970 workers in port cities rioted because of price rises and new incentive wage rules. On Dec. 20 Gomulka resigned as party leader; he was succeeded by Edward Gierek; the incentive rules were dropped, price rises were revoked.

A law promulgated Feb. 13, 1953, required government consent to high Roman Catholic church appointments. In 1956 Gomulka agreed to permit religious liberty and religious publications, provided the church kept out of politics. In 1961 religious studies in public schools were halted. Government relations with the Church improved in the 1970s. The number of priests and churches was greater in 1971 than in 1939.

After 2 months of labor turmoil had crippled the country, the Polish government, Aug. 30, 1980, met the demands of striking workers at the Lenin Shipyard, Gdansk. Among the 21 concessions granted were the right to form independent trade unions and the right to strike — unprecedented political developments in the Soviet bloc. By 1981, 9.5 mln. workers had joined the independent trade union (Solidarity). Farmers won official recognition for their independent trade union in May. Solidarity leaders proposed, Dec. 12, a nationwide referendum on establishing a non-Communist government if the government failed to agree to a series of demands which included access to the mass media and free and democratic elections to local councils in the provinces.

Spurred by the fear of Soviet intervention, the government, Dec. 13, imposed martial law. Public gatherings, demonstrations, and strikes were banned and an internal and external blackout was imposed. Solidarity leaders called for a nationwide strike, but there were only scattered work stoppages. Lech Walesa and other Solidarity leaders were arrested.

There were widespread labor protests against the government's sharp price increases in 1988. Riot police clashed with strikers at the Lenin steel mill in May.

Portugal
Republic of Portugal
República Portuguesa

People: Population (1989 est.): 10 240 000. **Age distrib. (%):** 0–14: 23.8; 15–59: 59.4; 60+: 16.8. **Pop. density:** 111.2 per sq. km. **Urban** (1983): 30%. **Ethnic groups:** Homogeneous

Mediterranean stock with small African minority. **Language:** Portuguese. **Religion:** Roman Catholic 97%.

Geography: Area: 92 075 sq. km. 94 243 incl. the Azares and Madiera Islands. **Location:** At SW extreme of Europe. **Neighbors:** Spain on N, E. **Topography:** Portugal N of Tajus R, which bisects the country NE-SW, is mountainous, cool and rainy. To the S there are drier, rolling plains, and a warm climate. **Capital:** Lisbon. **Cities** (1987 est.): 2 mln. (met.); Oporto, 1.5 mln. (met.).

Government: Type: Parliamentary democracy. **Head of state:** Pres. Mario Soares; b. Dec. 7, 1924; in office: Mar. 9, 1986. **Head of government:** Prime Min. Anibal Cavaco Silva; in office: Nov. 6, 1985. **Local divisions:** 18 districts, 2 autonomous regions, one dependency. **Defence:** 2.9% of GNP (1987).

Economy: Industries: Textiles, footwear, cork, chemicals, fish canning, wine, paper. **Chief crops:** Grains, potatoes, rice, grapes, olives, fruits. **Minerals:** Tungsten, uranium, copper, iron. **Other resources:** Forests (world leader in cork production). **Arable land:** 39%. **Livestock** (1985): sheep: 5 mln.; pigs: 3.4 mln.; cattle: 1 mln. **Fish catch** (1985): 254 000 metric tons. **Electricity prod.** (1986): 17.2 bln. kwh. **Crude steel prod.** (1985): 420 000 metric tons. **Labor force:** 21% agric.; 34% ind. and comm.; 44% services and govt.

Finance: Currency: Escudo (May 1988: 140.80 = $1 US). **Gross national product** (1986): $28.9 bln. **Per capita income** (1986): $2 970. **Imports** (1986): $9.4 bln.; partners: W. Ger. 12%, U.S. 11%, UK 8%, Fr. 9%. **Exports** (1986): $7.2 bln.; partners: UK 15%, W. Ger. 13%, Fr. 13%, U.S. 6%. **Tourists** (1985): $1.1 bln. receipts. **National budget** (1987): $11.3 bln. expenditures. **International reserves less gold** (Mar. 1988): $5.0 bln. **Gold:** 16.0 mln. oz t. **Consumer prices** (change in 1987): 9.3%.

Transport: Railway traffic (1986): 5.8 bln. passenger-km; 1.4 bln. net ton-km. **Motor vehicles:** in use (1984): 1.6 mln. passenger cars, 103 000 comm. vehicles. **Civil aviation** (1985): 4.2 bln. passenger-km; 142 mln. freight ton-km. **Chief ports:** Lisbon, Setubal, Leixoes.

Communications: Television sets: 1.5 mln. in use (1985). **Radios:** 2.1 mln. in use (1985). **Telephones in use** (1985): 1.8 mln. **Daily newspaper circ.** (1985): 58 per 1 000 pop.

Health: Life expectancy at birth (1985): 67.6 male; 74.1 female. **Births** (per 1 000 pop. 1985): 14. **Deaths** (per 1 000 pop. 1985): 9. **Natural increase** (1985): 0.5%. **Hospital beds** (1986): 53 566. **Physicians** (1986): 24 629. **Infant mortality** (per 1 000 live births 1985): 18.

Education (1985): **Literacy:** 83%, **Years compulsory:** 6; attendance 60%.

Major International Organizations: UN (GATT, IMF, WHO), NATO, EC, OECD.

Canadian Embassy: Rua Rosa Araujo 2, 6th Floor, Lisbon 1200; Tel: 56-38-21.

Portugal, an independent state since the 12th century, was a kingdom until a revolution in 1910 drove out King Manoel II and a republic was proclaimed.

From 1932 a strong, repressive government was headed by Premier Antonio de Oliveira Salazar. Illness forced his retirement in Sept. 1968; he was succeeded by Marcello Caetano.

On Apr. 25, 1974, the government was seized by a military junta led by Gen. Antonio de Spinola, who was named president.

The new government reached agreements providing independence for Guinea-Bissau, Mozambique, Cape Verde Islands, Angola, and Sao Tome and Principe. Spinola resigned Sept. 30, 1974, in face of increasing pressure from leftist officers. Despite a 64% victory for democratic parties in April 1975, the Soviet-supported Communist party increased its influence. Banks, insurance companies, and other industries were nationalized. A countercoup in November halted this trend.

Azores Islands, in the Atlantic, 1 184 km W. of Portugal, have an area of 2 309 sq. km and a pop. (1986) of 252 000. The **Madeira Islands,** 560 km off the NW coast of Africa, have an area of 798 sq. km and a pop. (1986) of 267 000. Both groups were offered partial autonomy in 1976.

Macau, area of 16 sq. km, is an enclave, a peninsula and 2 small islands, at the mouth of the Canton R. in China. Portugal granted broad autonomy in 1976. In 1987, Portugal and China agreed that Macau would revert to China in 1999. Macau, like Hong Kong, was guaranteed 50 years of non-interference in its way of life and capitalist system. Pop. (1986 est.): 433 000.

Qatar

State of Qatar

Dawlet al-Qatar

People: Population (1989 est.): 342 000. **Pop. density:** 31.1 per sq. km. **Ethnic groups:** Arab 45%, Pakistani 15%, Indian 21%, Iranian 6%, others. **Languages:** Arabic (official), English. **Religion:** Moslem 95%.

Geography: Area: 10 999 sq. km. **Location:** Occupies peninsula on W coast of Persian Gulf. **Neighbors:** Saudi Arabia on W, United Arab Emirates on S. **Topography:** Mostly a flat desert, with some limestone ridges, vegetation of any kind is scarce. **Capital:** Doha. **Cities** (1987 est.): Doha 250 000.

Government: Type: Traditional emirate. **Head of state and head of government:** Khalifah ibn Hamad ath-Thani; b. 1932; in office: Feb. 22, 1972 (amir), 1970 (prime min.) **Defence:** 13.1% of GNP (1983).

Economy: Crude oil reserves (1987): 3.3 mln. bbls. **Arable land:** 2.9%. **Electricity prod.** (1984): 3.4 bln. kwh. **Labor force:** 10% agric., 70% ind., services and commerce.

Finance: Currency: Riyal (Mar. 1988: 1.00 = $.27 US). **Gross national product** (1985): $3.8 bln. **Per capita income** (1985): $27 000. **Imports** (1986): $1.1 bln.; partners: Jap. 20%, UK 16%, U.S. 11%. **Exports** (1986): $2.6 bln.; partners: Jap. 52%, Fr. 10%. **National budget** (1987): $3.4 bln. expenditures. **Transport: Chief ports:** Doha, Musayid.

Communications: Radios: 120 000 in use (1986). **Telephones in use** (1985): 110 000.

Health: Life expectancy at birth (1985): 68.2 male; 73.2 female years. **Hospital beds** (1986): 915. **Physicians** (1986): 514.

Education (1987): **Literacy:** 60%. **Compulsory:** ages 6-16; attendance: 98%.

Major International Organizations: UN (FAO, GATT, IMF, World Bank), Arab League, OPEC.

Canadian Embassy: c/o P.O. Box 25281, 13113 (Safat), Kuwait City, Kuwait.

Qatar was under Bahrain's control until the Ottoman Turks took power, 1872 to 1915. In a treaty signed 1916, Qatar gave Great Britain responsibility for its defense and foreign relations. After Britain announced it would remove its military forces from the Persian Gulf area by the end of 1971, Qatar sought a federation with other British protected states in the area; this failed and Qatar declared itself independent, Sept. 1, 1971.

Oil revenues give Qatar a per capita income among the highest in the world, but lack of skilled labor hampers development plans.

Romania

Socialist Republic of Romania

Republica Socialistă România

People: Population (1989 est.): 23 155 000. **Age distrib.** (%): 0–14: 24.6; 15–59: 61.0; 60+: 14.4. **Pop. density:** 97.5 per sq. km. **Urban** (1985): 50%. **Ethnic groups:** Romanian 89%, Hungarian 7.9%, German 1.6%. **Languages:** Romanian, Hungarian, German. **Religions:** Orthodox 80%, Roman Catholic 6%.

Geography: Area: 237 482 sq. km. **Location:** In SE Europe on the Black Sea. **Neighbors:** USSR on E (Moldavia) and N (Ukraine), Hungary, Yugoslavia on W, Bulgaria on S. **Topography:** The Carpathian Mts. encase the north-central Transylvanian plateau. There are wide plains S and E of the mountains, where the lower reaches of the rivers of the Danube system flow. **Capital:** Bucharest. **Cities** (1984 est.): Bucharest 1 900 000, Brasov 346 000, Timisoara 319 000, Constanta 323 000.

Government: Type: Communist. **Head of state:** Pres. Nicolae Ceausescu; b. Jan. 26, 1918; in office; Dec. 9, 1967. **Head of government:** Prime Min. Constantin Dascalescu; in office; May 21, 1982. **Head of Communist Party:** Pres. Nicolae Ceausescu; in office: Mar. 23, 1965. **Local divisions:** Bucharest and 40 counties. **Defence:** 4.4% of GNP (1984).

Economy: Industries: Steel, metals, machinery, oil products, chemicals, textiles, shoes, tourism. **Chief crops:** Corn, wheat, oilseeds, potatoes. **Minerals:** Oil, gas, coal. **Other resources:** Timber. **Arable land:** 45%. **Livestock** (1987): cattle: 7.2 mln.; pigs: 14.7 mln.; sheep: 18.7 mln. **Fish catch** (1986): 293 000 metric tons. **Electricity prod.** (1987): 74.1 bln. kwh. **Crude steel prod.** (1986): 14.3 mln. metric tons. **Labor force:** 28% agric.; 37% ind.

Finance: Currency: Leu (Mar. 1988: 13.96 = $1 US). **Gross national product** (1986): $137 bln. **Per capita income** (1984): $2 020. **Imports** (1984): $8.1 bln.; partners: USSR 22%, Egypt 10%, Iran 8%. **Exports** (1984): $10.7 bln.; partners: USSR 21%, W. Ger. 7%. **Tourists** (1984): $230 mln. receipts. **National budget** (1982): $142 mln. expenditures. **International reserves less gold** (Mar. 1987): $587 mln. **Gold:** 3.3 mln. oz t.

Transport: Railway traffic (1985): 31 bln. passenger-km; 74.2 bln. net ton-km. **Motor vehicles:** in use (1986): 105 000 passenger cars; 100 000 comm. vehicles. **Civil aviation** (1985): 3.4 bln. passenger-km; 73 mln. freight ton-km. **Chief ports:** Constanta, Galati, Braila.

Communications: Television sets: 3.8 mln. licensed (1986). **Radios:** 2.5 mln. in use (1986). **Telephones in use** (1985): 1.9 mln. **Daily newspaper circ.** (1986): 136 per 1 000 pop.

Health: Life expectancy at birth (1984): 67.0 male; 72.6 female. **Births** (per 1 000 pop. 1985): 15. **Deaths** (per 1 000 pop. 1985): 10. **Natural increase** (1985): 0.5%. **Hospital beds** (1986): 212 000. **Physicians** (1986): 40 000. **Infant mortality** (per 1 000 live births 1985): 22.

Education (1986): **Literacy:** 98%. **Years compulsory:** 10; attendance 92%.

Major International Organizations: UN (World Bank, IMF, GATT), Warsaw Pact.

Canadian Embassy: 36 Nicolae Iorga, P.O. Box 2966, Post Office No. 22, 71118 Bucharest; Tel: 50-65-80, 50-62-90, 50-63-30, 50-61-40, 50-64-85, 50-59-56.

Romania's earliest known people merged with invading Proto-Thracians, preceding by centuries the Dacians. The Dacian kingdom was occupied by Rome, 106-271 AD; people and language were Romanized. The principalities of Wallachia and Moldavia, dominated by Turkey, were united in 1859, became Romania in 1861. In 1877 Romania proclaimed independence from Turkey, became an independent state by the Treaty of Berlin, 1878, a kingdom, 1881, under Carol I. In 1886 Romania became a constitutional monarchy with a bicameral legislature.

Romania helped Russia in its war with Turkey, 1877-78. After World War I it acquired Bessarabia, Bukovina, Transylvania, and Banat. In 1940 it ceded Bessarabia and Northern Bukovina to the USSR, part of southern Dobrudja to Bulgaria, and Transylvania to Hungary.

In 1941, Romanian premier Marshal Ion Antonescu led his country in support of Germany against the USSR. In 1944 Antonescu was overthrown by King Michael and Romania joined the Allies.

With occupation by Soviet troops the communist-headed National Democratic Front displaced the National Peasant party. A People's Republic was proclaimed, Dec. 30, 1947; Michael was forced to abdicate. Land owners were dispossessed; most banks, factories and transportation units were nationalized.

On Aug. 22, 1965, a new constitution proclaimed Romania a Socialist, rather than a People's Republic. Since 1959, USSR troops have not been permitted to enter Romania.

Internal policies remain oppressive. Ethnic Hungarians have protested cultural and job discrimination.

Romania has become industrialized, but lags in consumer goods and in personal freedoms. There is strong resistance to the reforms proposed by Soviet leader Gorbachev. All industry is state owned, and state farms and cooperatives own over 90% of arable land.

A major earthquake struck Bucharest in March, 1977, killing over 1 300 people and causing extensive damage to housing and industry.

Rwanda
Republic of Rwanda
Republika y'u Rwanda

People: Population (1989 est.): 7 276 000. **Age distrib.** (%): 0–14: 48.7; 15–59: 47.1; 60+: 4.2. **Pop. density:** 276.3 per sq. km. **Urban** (1985): 5.1%. **Ethnic groups:** Hutu 85%, Tutsi 14%, Twa (pygmies) 1%. **Languages:** French, Kinyarwandu (both official), Swahili. **Religions:** Christian 68%, traditional 23%, Moslem 1%.

Geography: Area: 26 336 sq. km. **Location:** In E central Africa. **Neighbors:** Uganda on N, Zaire on W, Burundi on S, Tanzania on E. **Topography:** Grassy uplands and hills cover most of the country, with a chain of volcanoes in the NW. The source of the Nile R. has been located in the headwaters of the Kagera (Akagera) R., SW of Kigali. **Capital:** Kigali. **Cities** (1983 est.): Kigali 150 000.

Government: Type: Republic. **Head of state:** Pres. Juvenal Habyarimana; b. Mar. 8, 1937; in office: July 5, 1973. **Local divisions:** 10 prefectures, 143 communes. **Defence:** 2.0% of GNP (1984).

Economy: Chief crops: Coffee, tea. **Minerals:** Tin, gold, wolframite. **Arable land:** 48%. **Electricity prod.** (1986): 110 mln. kwh. **Labor force:** 91% agric.

Finance: Currency: Franc (Apr. 1988: 74 = $1 US). **Gross national product** (1985): $1.7 bln. **Per capita income** (1984): $270. **Imports** (1984): $204 mln.; partners: Ken. 21%, Belg. 16%, Jap. 12%, W. Ger. 9%. **Exports** (1984): $147 mln.; partners: Belg.-Lux. 17%, Ugan. 12%. **National budget** (1984): $185 mln. revenues; $208 mln. expenditures. **International reserves less gold** (Mar. 1988): $162 mln. **Consumer prices** (change in 1987): 4.1%.

Transport: Motor vehicles: in use (1986): 7 000 passenger cars, 10 000 comm. vehicles.

Communications: Radios: 250 000 in use (1986). **Telephones in use** (1984): 6 000.

Health: Life expectancy at birth (1985): 48 years. **Births** (per 1 000 pop. 1985): 54.0. **Deaths** (per 1 000 pop. 1985): 16.0. **Natural increase** (1985): 3.8%. **Hospital beds** (1984): 9 000. **Physicians** (1984): 177. **Infant mortality** (per 1 000 live births 1985): 124.

Education (1985): **Literacy:** 37%. **Years compulsory:** 8; **attendance:** 70%.

Major International Organizations: UN (GATT, IMF, WHO), OAU.

Canadian Embassy: Parcel 1534, rue de l'Akagera, P.O. Box 1177, Kigali; Tel: 32.10, 32.78.

For centuries, the Tutsi (an extremely tall people) dominated the Hutus (90% of the population). A civil war broke out in 1959 and Tutsi power was ended. A referendum in 1961 abolished the monarchic system.

Rwanda, which had been part of the Belgian UN trusteeship of Rwanda-Urundi, became independent July 1, 1962. The government was overthrown in a 1973 military coup. Rwanda is one of the most densely populated countries in Africa. All available arable land is being used; erosion is a major problem. The government has carried out economic and social improvement programs, using foreign aid and volunteer labor on public works projects.

St. Christopher (St. Kitts) and Nevis
St. Christopher Nevis

People: Population (1989 est.): 40 000. **Ethnic groups:** black 95%. **Language:** English. **Religion:** Protestant 76%.

Geography: Area: 263 sq. km in the northern part of the Leeward group of the Lesser Antilles in the eastern Caribbean Sea. **Capitol:** Basseterre. (1984 est.): 18 500.

Government: Head of State: Queen Elizabeth II represented by Sir Clement Arrindell. **Head of Government:** Prime Minister Kennedy A. Simmonds; b. Apr. 12, 1936; in office: Sept. 19, 1983.

Economy: Sugar is the principal industry.

Finance: Currency: E. Caribbean Dollar (Mar. 1987: 2.70 = $1 U.S.). **Gross national product** (1986): $66 mln. **Tourists** (1985): 40 000.

Communications: 3 800 telephones (1985).

Health: Infant mortality (per 1 000 live births, 1985): 39.

Education: Literacy (1987): 90%; school compulsory ages 5–14.

Canadian High Commission: c/o P.O. Box 404, Bridgetown, Barbados.

St. Christopher (known by the natives as Liamuiga) and Nevis were discovered and named by Columbus in 1493. They were settled by Britain in 1623, but ownership was disputed with France until 1713. They were part of the Leeward Islands Federation, 1871-1956, and the Federation of the W. Indies, 1958-62. The colony achieved self-government as an Associated State of the UK in 1967, and became fully independent Sept. 19, 1983. Nevis, the smaller of the islands, has the right of secession.

Saint Lucia

People: Population (1989 est.): 128 000. **Age distrib.** (%): 0–20: 43.5; 21–64: 48.3; 65+: 8.2. **Pop. density:** 208 per sq. km. **Ethnic groups:** Predominantly African descent. **Languages:** English (official), French patois. **Religion:** Roman Catholic 90%.

Geography: Area: 616 sq. km. **Location:** In Eastern Caribbean, 2d largest of the Windward Is. **Neighbors:** Martinique to N, St. Vincent to SW. **Topography:** Mountainous, volcanic in origin; Soufriere, a volcanic crater, in the S. Wooded mountains run N-S to Mt. Gimie, 944 m, with streams through fertile valleys. **Capital:** Castries. **City:** Castries (1986 est.): 52 000.

Government: Type: Parliamentary democracy. **Head of state:** Queen Elizabeth II, represented by Gov.-Gen. Vincent Floissac; **Head of government:** Prime Min. John Compton; in office: May 3, 1982. **Local divisions:** 11 quarters.

Economy: Industries: Agriculture, tourism, manufacturing. **Chief crops:** Bananas, coconuts, cocoa, citrus fruits. **Other resources:** Forests. **Arable land:** 28%. **Electricity prod.** (1986): 80 mln. kwh. **Labor force:** 36% agric., 20% ind. & commerce, 18% services.

Finance: Currency: East Caribbean dollar (Mar. 1987: 2.70 = $1 US). **Gross national product** (1985): $146 mln. **Per capita income** (1984): $1 120. **Imports** (1985): $127 mln.; partners: U.S. 36%, UK 12%, Trin./Tob. 11%. **Exports** (1985): $53 mln.; partners: U.S. 28%, UK 25%. **Tourists** (1985): receipts: $69 mln.

Transport: Motor vehicles: in use (1984): 7 000 passenger cars, 2 000 comm. vehicles. **Chief ports:** Castries, Vieux Fort.

Communications: Television sets: 5 000 in use (1985). **Radios:** 92 000 in use (1985). **Telephones in use** (1985): 11 500.

Health: Life expectancy at birth (1987): 70.3 male; 74.9 female. **Births** (per 1 000 pop. 1985): 30. **Deaths** (per 1 000 pop. 1985): 6. **Natural increase** (1985): 2.4%. **Hospital beds** (1984): 522. **Infant mortality** (per 1 000 live births 1985): 20.

Education: Literacy (1987) 78%; **Years compulsory:** ages 5-15; **Attendance:** 80%.

Major International Organizations: UN (IMF, ILO), CARICOM, OAS.

Canadian High Commission: c/o P.O. Box 404, Bridgetown, Barbados.

St. Lucia was ceded to Britain by France at the Treaty of Paris, 1814. Self government was granted with the West Indies Act, 1967. Independence was attained Feb. 22, 1979.

Saint Vincent and the Grenadines

People: Population (1989 est.): 112 000. **Pop. density:** 288.7 per sq. mi. **Ethnic groups:** Mainly of African descent. **Language:** English. **Religions:** Methodist, Anglican, Roman Catholic.

Geography: Area: 388 sq. km. **Location:** In the eastern Caribbean, St. Vincent (346 sq. km) and the northern islets of the Grenadines form a part of the Windward chain. **Neighbors:** St. Lucia to N, Barbados to E, Grenada to S. **Topography:** St. Vincent is volcanic, with a ridge of thickly-wooded mountains running its length; Soufriere, rising in the N, erupted in Apr. 1979. **Capital:** Kingstown. **Cities** (1985 est.): Kingstown 18 378.

Government: Head of state: Queen Elizabeth II, represented by Gov.-Gen. Joseph Lambert Eustace; in office: Feb. 28, 1985. **Head of government:** James Mitchell; in office: July 30, 1984.

Economy: Industries: Agriculture, tourism. **Chief crops:** Bananas (62% of exports), arrowroot, coconuts. **Arable land:** 50%. **Electricity prod.** (1986): 31 mln. kwh. **Labor force:** 30% agric.

Finance: Currency: East Caribbean dollar (Mar. 1987: 2.70 = $1 US). **Gross national product** (1985): $103 mln. **Per capita income** (1984): $920. **Imports** (1981): $60 mln.; partners: UK 17%, Trin./Tob. 14%, U.S. 32%. **Exports** (1981): $12 mln.; partners: UK 45%, Trin./Tob. 23%. **Tourists** (1986): $27 mln. receipts. **National budget** (1982): $34 mln. expenditures.

Transport: Motor vehicles: in use (1984): 4 400 passenger cars, 2 000 comm. vehicles. **Chief port:** Kingstown.

Communications: Telephones in use (1985): 9 000.

Health: Life expectancy at birth (1985): 67.5 male; 71.4 female. **Births** (per 1 000 pop. 1985): 30. **Deaths** (per 1 000 pop. 1985): 7. **Natural increase** (1985): 2.3%. **Infant mortality** (per 1 000 live births 1985): 40.

Education (1984): **Literacy:** 85%.

Canadian High Commission: c/o P.O. Box 404, Bridgetown, Barbados.

Columbus landed on St. Vincent on Jan. 22, 1498 (St. Vincent's Day). Britain and France both laid claim to the island in the 17th and 18th centuries; the Treaty of Versailles, 1783, finally ceded it to Britain. Associated State status was granted 1969; independence was attained Oct. 27, 1979.

The entire economic life of St. Vincent is dependent upon agriculture and tourism.

San Marino

Most Serene Republic of San Marino

Serenissima Repubbica di San Marino

People: Population (1989 est.): 23 000. **Age distrib. (%):** 0–14: 19.0; 15–59: 63.7; 60+: 17.3. **Pop. density:** 368.6 per sq. km. **Urban** (1985): 90.5%. **Ethnic groups:** Sanmarinese 88%, Italian 11%. **Language:** Italian. **Religion:** predominately Roman Catholic.

Geography: Area: 62.4 sq. km. **Location:** In N central Italy near Adriatic coast. **Neighbors:** Completely surrounded by Italy. **Topography:** The country lies on the slopes of Mt. Titano. **Capital:** San Marino. **City** (1987 est.): San Marino 4 179.

Government: Type: Independent republic. **Head of state:** Two co-regents appt. every 6 months. **Local divisions:** 11 districts, 9 sectors.

Economy: Industries: Postage stamps, tourism, woolen goods, paper, cement, ceramics. **Arable land:** 17%.

Finance: Currency: Italian lira. **Tourists** (1986): 2.7 mln; $56 mln. receipts.

Communications: Television sets: 5 000 licensed (1981). **Radios:** 6 000 licensed (1976). **Telephones in use** (1986): 5 000. **Daily newspaper circ.** (1985): 60 per 1 000 pop.

Births (per 1 000 pop. 1985): 11. **Deaths** (per 1 000 pop. 1985): 7. **Natural increase** (1985): 0.4%. **Infant mortality** (per 1 000 live births 1987): 9.6.

Education (1987): **Literacy:** 97%. **Years compulsory:** 8. **Attendance:** 93%.

Canadian Embassy: c/o Via G.B. de Rossi 27, 00161, Rome, Italy.

San Marino claims to be the oldest state in Europe and to have been founded in the 4th century. A communist-led coalition ruled 1947-57; a similar coalition ruled 1978-86. It has had a treaty of friendship with Italy since 1862.

Sao Tome and Principe

Democratic Republic of Sao Tome and Principe

República Democrática de Sao Tome e Principe

People: Population (1989 est.): 114 000. **Pop. density:** 117.9 per sq. km. **Ethnic groups:** Portuguese-African mixture, African minority (Angola, Mozambique immigrants). **Language:** Portuguese. **Religion:** Christian 80%.

Geography: Area: 967 sq. km. **Location:** In the Gulf of Guinea about 200 km off W Central Africa. **Neighbors:** Gabon, Equatorial Guinea on E. **Topography:** Sao Tome and Principe islands, part of an extinct volcano chain, are both covered by lush forests and croplands. **Capital:** Sao Tome. **Cities** (1984 est.): Sao Tome 35 000.

Government: Type: Republic. **Head of state and head of government:** Pres. Manuel Pinto da Costa, b. 1910; in office: July 12, 1975. **Local divisions:** 7 counties.

Economy: Chief crops: Cocoa (82% of exports), coconut products, cinchona. **Arable land:** 38%. **Electricity prod.** (1986): 27 mln. kwh.

Finance: Currency: Dobra (Jan. 1988: 35 = $1 US). **Gross national product** (1984): $34 mln. **Per capita income** (1984): $330. **Imports** (1981): $20 mln.; partners: Port. 61%, Angola 13%. **Exports** (1981): $8 mln.; partners: Neth. 52%, Port. 33%, W. Ger. 8%.

Transport: Motor vehicles: in use (1979): 1 300 passenger cars, 1 900 comm. vehicles. **Chief ports:** Sao Tome, Santo Antonio.

Communications: Radios: 28 000 in use (1986).

Health: Births (per 1 000 pop. 1985): 28. **Deaths** (per 1 000 pop. 1985): 7. **Natural increase** (1985): 2.1%. **Hospital beds** (1978): 665. **Physicians** (1985): 53. **Infant mortality** (per 1 000 live births 1985): 65.

Education (1985): **Literacy:** 50%.

Major International Organizations: UN, OAU.

Canadian Embassy: c/o P.O. Box 4037, Libreville, Gabon.

The islands were uninhabited when discovered in 1471 by the Portuguese, who brought the first settlers — convicts and exiled Jews. Sugar planting was replaced by the slave trade as the chief economic activity until coffee and cocoa were introduced in the 19th century.

Portugal agreed, 1974, to turn the colony over to the Gabon-based Movement for the Liberation of Sao Tome and Principe, which proclaimed as first president its East German-trained leader Manuel Pinto da Costa. Independence came July 12, 1975.

Agriculture and fishing are the mainstays of the economy.

Saudi Arabia

Kingdom of Saudi Arabia

al-Mamlaka al-‘Arabiya as-Sa‘udiya

People: Population (1989 est.): 12 678 000. **Pop. density:** 5.8 per sq. km. **Urban** (1975): 73%. **Ethnic groups:** Arab tribes, immigrants from other Arab and Moslem countries. **Language:** Arabic. **Religion:** Moslem 99%.

Geography: Area: 2 175 422 sq. km. **Location:** Occupies most of Arabian Peninsula in Middle East. **Neighbors:** Kuwait, Iraq, Jordan on N, Yemen, South Yemen, Oman on S, United Arab Emirates, Qatar on E. **Topography:** The highlands on W, up to 2 700 m, slope as an arid, barren desert to the Persian Gulf. **Capital:** Riyadh. **Cities** (1986 est.): Riyadh 1 380 000; Jidda 1 210 000; Mecca 463 000.

Government: Type: Monarchy with council of ministers. **Head of state and head of government:** King Fahd; b. 1922; in office: June 13, 1982. **Local divisions:** 14 provinces. **Defence:** 21.3% of GNP (1984).

Economy: Industries: Oil products. **Chief crops:** Dates, wheat, barley, fruit. **Minerals:** Oil, gas, gold, copper, iron. **Crude oil reserves** (1987): 169 bln. bbls. **Arable land:** 2%. **Livestock** (1985): sheep: 2.2 mln.; goats: 2.4 mln. **Electricity prod.** (1986): 43 bln. kwh. **Labor force:** 14% agric.; 11% ind; 53% serv., comm., & govt.; 20% construction.

Finance: Currency: Riyal (May 1988: 3.74 = $1 US). **Gross national product** (1986): $98.1 bln. **Per capita income** (1979): $11 500. **Imports** (1986): $19.1 bln.; partners: US 18%, Jap. 18%, W. Ger. 17%. **Exports** (1986): $20.0 bln.; partners: US 13%, Jap., 17%, Fr. 10%. **International reserves less gold** (Mar. 1988): $20.2 bln. **Gold:** 4.59 mln. oz t. **Consumer prices** (change in 1986): −3.0%.

Transport: Railway traffic (1987): 70 mln. passenger-km; 321 mln. net ton-km. **Motor vehicles:** in use (1985): 2.1 mln. passenger cars, 1.7 mln. comm. vehicles. **Civil aviation** (1985): 15.0 bln. passenger-km. 437 mln. net ton-km. **Chief ports:** Jidda, Ad-Dammam, Ras Tannurah.

Communications: Television sets: 3.7 mln. in use (1986). **Radios:** 3.2 mln. in use (1986). **Telephones in use** (1986): 980 000. **Daily newspaper circ.** (1986): 41 per 1 000 pop.

Health: Life expectancy at birth (1986): 60 years. **Births** (per 1 000 pop. 1985): 43.7. **Deaths** (per 1 000 pop. 1985): 12.6. **Natural increase** (1985): 3.1%. **Hospital beds** (1986): 23 862. **Physicians** (1986): 13 996. **Infant mortality** (per 1 000 live births 1985): 100.

Education (1986): **Literacy:** 50% (males).

Major International Organizations: UN (IMF, WHO, FAO), Arab League, OPEC.

Canadian Embassy: Diplomatic Quarter, P.O. Box 22593, Riyadh 11416; Tel: 488-2288, 488-0292, 448-0275.

Arabia was united for the first time by Mohammed, in the early 7th century. His successors conquered the entire Near East and North Africa, bringing Islam and the Arabic language. But Arabia itself soon returned to its former status.

Nejd, long an independent state and centre of the Wahhabi sect, fell under Turkish rule in the 18th century, but in 1913 Ibn Saud, founder of the Saudi dynasty, overthrew the Turks and captured the Turkish province of Hasa; took the Hejaz in 1925 and by 1926, most of Asir. The discovery of oil in the 1930s transformed the new country.

Crown Prince Khalid was proclaimed king on Mar. 25, 1975, after the assassination of King Faisal. Fahd became king on June 13, 1982 following Khalid's death. There is no constitution and no parliament. The king exercises authority together with a Council of Ministers. The Islamic religious code is the law of the kingdom.

Saudi units fought against Israel in the 1948 and 1973 Arab-Israeli wars. Many billions of dollars of advanced arms have been purchased from Britain, France, and the U.S., including jet fighters, missiles, and, in 1981, 5 airborne warning and control system (AWACS) aircraft from the U.S., despite strong opposition from Israel. Beginning with the 1967 Arab-Israeli war, Saudi Arabia provided large annual financial gifts to Egypt; aid was later extended to Syria, Jordan, and Palestinian guerrilla groups, as well as to other Moslem countries. The country has aided anti-radical forces in Yemen and Oman.

Faisal played a leading role in the 1973-74 Arab oil embargo against the U.S. and other nations in an attempt to force them to adopt an anti-Israel policy. Saudi Arabia joined most other Arab states, 1979, in condemning Egypt's peace treaty with Israel.

Between 1973 and 1976, Saudi Arabia acquired full ownership of Aramco (Arabian American Oil Co.). In the 1980s, Saudi Arabia's moderate position on crude oil prices has often prevailed at OPEC meetings.

The Hejaz contains the holy cities of Islam — Medina where the Mosque of the Prophet enshrines the tomb of Mohammed, who died in the city June 7, 632, and Mecca, his birthplace. More than 600 000 Moslems from 60 nations make the pilgrimage to Mecca annually. The regime faced its first serious opposition when Moslem fundamentalists seized the Grand Mosque in Mecca, Nov. 20, 1979.

Two Saudi oil tankers were attacked May 1984, as Iran and Iraq began air attacks against shipping in the Persian Gulf.

In 1987, Iranians making a pilgrimage to Mecca clashed with anti-Iranian pilgrims and Saudi police; over 400 were killed. Saudi Arabia broke diplomatic relations with Iran in 1988.

Senegal
Republic of Senegal
République du Sénégal

People: Population (1989 est.): 7 704 000. **Age distrib.** (%): 0–14: 45; 15–59: 50.2; 60+: 4.8. **Pop. density:** 39.3 per sq. km. **Urban** (1986): 30%. **Ethnic groups:** Wolof 36%, Serer 17%, Peulh 17%, Diola 9%, Mandingo 9%. **Languages:** French (official), tribal languages. **Religions:** Moslem 92%, Christian 2%.

Geography: Area: 196 177 sq. km. **Location:** At western extreme of Africa. **Neighbors:** Mauritania on N, Mali on E, Guinea, Guinea-Bissau on S, Gambia surrounded on three sides.

Education (1984): **Literacy:** 10%. **Attendance:** 53% primary, 11% secondary.

Major International Organizations: UN and all of its specialized agencies, OAU.

Canadian Embassy: 45, av. de la République, P.O. Box 3373, Dakar; Tel: 210290.

Portuguese settlers arrived in the 15th century, but French control grew from the 17th century. The last independent Moslem state was subdued in 1893. Dakar became the capital of French West Africa.

Independence as part of the Mali Federation, along with the Sudanese Rep., came June 20, 1960. Senegal withdrew Aug. 20 that year. French political and economic influence is strong.

A long drought brought famine, 1972-73, and again in 1978.

Senegal is recognized as the most democratic of the French-speaking West African nations.

Senegal signed an agreement with The Gambia, Dec. 17, 1981, for confederation of the 2 countries under the name of Senegambia. The confederation began Feb. 1, 1982. The 2 nations retained their individual sovereignty but adopted joint defense and monetary policies.

Seychelles
Republic of Seychelles

People: Population (1989 est.): 70 000. **Age distrib.** (%): 0–14: 36.3; 15–64; 57.3; 65+: 6.4. **Pop. density:** 157 per sq. km. **Urban** (1977): 37.1% **Ethnic groups:** Creoles (mixture of Asians, Africans, and French) predominate. **Languages:** English and French (both official), Creole. **Religion:** Roman Catholic 90%.

Geography: Area: 445 sq. km. **Location:** In the Indian O. 1127 km NE of Madagascar. **Neighbors:** Nearest are Madagascar on SW, Somalia on NW. **Topography:** A group of 86 islands, about half of them composed of coral, the other half granite, the latter predominantly mountainous. **Capital:** Victoria. **Cities** (1986): Victoria 23 000.

Government: Type: Single party republic. **Head of state:** Pres. France-Albert René, b. Nov. 16, 1935; in office: June 5, 1977. **Defence:** 5.6% of GNP (1984).

Economy: Industries: Food processing. **Chief crops:** Coconut products, cinnamon, vanilla, patchouli. **Other resources:** Guano, shark fins, tortoise shells, fish. **Electricity prod.** (1986): 59 mln. kwh. **Labor force:** 18.5% agric.; 19.4% ind. & comm.; 13.5% serv.; 49% govt.

Topography: Low rolling plains cover most of Senegal, rising somewhat in the SE. Swamp and jungles are in SW. **Capital:** Dakar. **Cities** (1984): Dakar 671 000; Thies 126 889; Kaolack 115 679.

Government: Type: Republic. **Head of state:** Pres. Abdou Diouf; b. Sept. 7, 1935; in office: Jan. 1, 1981. **Local divisions:** 10 regions. **Defence:** 2.8% of GNP (1984).

Economy: Industries: Food processing, fishing. **Chief crops:** Peanuts are chief export; millet, rice. **Minerals:** Phosphates. **Arable land:** 27%. **Livestock.** (1985): cattle: 2.2 mln.; sheep: 2.9 mln.; goats: 1 mln. **Fish catch** (1985): 244 000 metric tons. **Electricity prod.** (1986): 737 mln. kwh. **Labor force:** 70% agric.

Finance: Currency: CFA franc (Mar. 1988: 281 = $1 US). **Gross national product** (1985): $2.4 bln. **Per capita income** (1984): $380. **Imports** (1984): $805 mln.; partners Fr. 37%, U.S. 6%. **Exports** (1984): $525 mln.; partners Fr. 25%, UK 6%. **Tourists** (1985): $81 mln. receipts. **International reserves less gold** (Jan. 1988): $14.8 mln. **Gold:** 29 000 oz t. **Consumer prices** (change in 1987): −4.3%.

Transport: Railway traffic (1984): 133 mln. passenger-km; 309 mln. net ton-km. **Motor vehicles:** in use (1984): 73 000 passenger cars, 36 000 comm. vehicles. **Chief ports:** Dakar, Saint-Louis.

Communications: Television sets: 55 000 in use (1986). **Radios:** 450 000 in use (1986). **Telephones in use** (1984): 32 000. **Daily newspaper circ.** (1984): 4 per 1 000 pop.

Health: Life expectancy at birth (1984): 45.0 male, 48.0 female. **Births** (per 1 000 pop. 1985): 47.9. **Deaths** (per 1 000 pop. 1985): 21.1. **Natural increase** (1985): 2.6%. **Hospital beds** (1982): 6 200. **Physicians** (1982): 470. **Infant mortality** (per 1 000 live births 1985): 102.

Finance: Currency: Rupee (Mar. 1988: 5.23 = $1 US). **Gross national product** (1985): $140 mln. **Per capita income** (1985): $2 100. **Imports** (1984): $70.9 mln.; partners: UK 15%, So. Afr. 8%, Bah. 17%. **Exports** (1984): $4.3 mln.; partners: Pak. 38%; Jap. 26%. **National Budget** (1985): $65 mln. **Tourists** (1985): $51 mln. receipts. **International reserves less gold** (Mar. 1988): $13.3 mln. **Consumer prices** (change in 1987): 2.6%.

Transport: Motor vehicles: in use (1984): 3 500 passenger cars, 1 000 comm. vehicles. **Port:** Victoria.

Communications: Radios: 19 000 in use (1986). **Telephones in use** (1985): 11 000. **Daily newspaper circ.** (1986): 48 per 1 000 pop.

Health: Life expectancy at birth (1986): 66 years. **Births** (per 1 000 pop. 1986): 26.2. **Deaths** (per 1 000 pop. 1986): 7.5. **Natural increase** (1986): 1.8%. **Hospital beds** (1986): 331. **Physicians** (1986): 40. **Infant mortality** (per 1 000 live births 1986): 15.

Education (1986): **Literacy:** 80%. **Years compulsory** 9; attendance 95%.

Major International Organizations: UN, OAU, Commonwealth of Nations.

Canadian High Commission: c/o P.O. Box 1022, Dar-es-Salaam, Tanzania.

The islands were occupied by France in 1768, and seized by Britain in 1794. Ruled as part of Mauritius from 1814, the Seychelles became a separate colony in 1903. The ruling party had opposed independence as impractical, but pressure from the OAU and the UN was strong, and independence was declared June 29, 1976. The first president was ousted in a coup a year later by a socialist leader.

A new constitution, announced Mar. 1979, turned the country into a one-party state.

Sierra Leone
Republic of Sierra Leone

People: Population (1989 est.): 4 318 000. **Age distrib.** (%): 0–14: 41.4; 15–59: 53.5; 60+: 5.1. **Pop. density:** 59.7 per sq. km. **Ethnic groups:** Temne 30%, Mende 29%, others. **Languages:** English (official), tribal languages. **Religions:** animist 30%, Moslem 30%, Christian 10%.

Geography: Area: 72 320 sq. km. **Location:** On W coast of W. Africa. **Neighbors:** Guinea on N, E, Liberia on S. **Topography:** The heavily-indented, 336 km coastline has mangrove swamps. Behind are wooded hills, rising to a plateau and mountains in the E. **Capital:** Freetown. **Cities** (1985 est.): Freetown 469 000; Bo, Kenema, Makeni.

Government: Type: Republic. **Head of state and head of government:** Pres. Gen. Joseph Saidu Momoh; b. Jan. 26, 1937; in office: Nov. 28, 1985. **Local divisions:** 12 districts and one region including Freetown.

Economy: Industries: Mining, tourism. **Chief crops:** Cocoa, coffee, palm kernels, rice, ginger. **Minerals:** Diamonds, bauxite. **Arable land:** 25%. **Fish catch** (1984): 52 000 metric tons. **Electricity prod.** (1986): 85 mln. kwh. **Labor force:** 75% agric.; 15% ind. & serv.

Finance: Currency: Leone (Mar. 1988: 1.00 = $.04 US). **Gross national product** (1985): $445 mln. **Per capita income** (1984): $320. **Imports** (1985): $135 mln.; partners: UK 22%, Fr. 11%. **Exports** (1985): $111 mln.; partners: Netherlands 31%; UK 15%, U.S. 9%. **National budget** (1981): $138 mln. expenditures. **International reserves less gold** (Mar. 1988): $11.8 mln. **Consumer prices** (change in 1986): 80.9%.

Transport: Motor Vehicles: in use (1984): 19 000 passenger cars, 30 000 comm. vehicles. **Chief ports:** Freetown, Bonthe.

Communications: Television sets: 25 000 in use (1986). **Radios:** 225 000 in use (1986). **Telephones in use** (1981): 220 000. **Daily newspaper circ.** (1984): 3 per 1 000 pop.

Health: Life expectancy at birth (1986): 46 yrs. **Births** (per 1 000 pop. 1985): 45.3. **Deaths** (per 1 000 pop. 1985): 17.4.

Natural increase (1985): 2.7%. **Hospital beds** (1984): 4 754. **Physicians** (1984): 197. **Infant mortality** (per 1 000 live births 1985): 195.

Education (1986): **Literacy:** 15%.

Major International Organizations: UN (GATT, IMF, WHO), Commonwealth of Nations, OAU.

Canadian High Commission: P.O. Box 54506, Ikoyi Station, Lagos, Nigeria.

Freetown was founded in 1787 by the British government as a haven for freed slaves. Their descendants, known as Creoles, number more than 60 000.

Successive steps toward independence followed the 1951 constitution. Full independence arrived Apr. 27, 1961. Sierra Leone became a republic Apr. 19, 1971. A one-party state approved by referendum 1978, brought political stability, but the economy has been plagued by inflation, corruption, and dependence upon the International Monetary Fund and creditors.

Singapore
Republic of Singapore

People: Population (1989 est.): 2 668 000. **Age distrib.** (%): 0–14: 24.4; 15–59: 67.8; 60+: 7.8. **Pop. density:** 4 584 per sq. km. **Ethnic groups:** Chinese 77%, Malay 15%, Indian 6%. **Languages:** Chinese, Malay, Tamil, English (all official). **Religions:** Buddhism, Taoism, Islam, Hinduism, Christianity.

Geography: Area: 582 sq. km. **Location:** Off tip of Malayan Peninsula in S.E. Asia. **Neighbors:** Nearest are Malaysia on N, Indonesia on S. **Topography:** Singapore is a flat, formerly swampy island. The nation includes 40 nearby islets. **Capital:** Singapore. **Cities** (1978 est.): Singapore 2 334 400.

Government: Type: Parliamentary democracy. **Head of state:** Pres. Wee Kim Wee; in office: Sept. 3, 1985. **Head of government:** Prime Min. Lee Kuan Yew; b. Sept. 16, 1923; in office: June 5, 1959. **Defence:** 6% of GNP (1985).

Economy: Industries: Shipbuilding, oil refining, electronics, banking, textiles, food, rubber, lumber processing, tourism. **Arable land:** 11%. **Livestock** (1984): pigs: 1.3 mln. **Fish catch** (1985): 22 000 metric tons. **Electricity prod.** (1986): 10.0 bln. kwh. **Crude steel prod.** (1981): 350 000 metric tons. **Labor force:** 1% agric.; 58% ind. & comm.; 35% services.

Finance: Currency: Dollar (May 1988: 2.02 = $1 US). **Gross national product** (1985): $16.0 bln. **Per capita income** (1985): $6 200. **Imports** (1987): $32 bln.; partners: Jap. 18%, Malay. 13%, U.S. 13%, Sau. Ar. 9%. **Exports** (1987): $28.6 bln., partners: U.S. 20%, Malay. 16%, Jap. 11%, HK 6%. **Tourists** (1984): $2.0 bln. receipts. **National budget** (1986): $10 bln. expenditures. **Consumer prices** (change in 1987): 0.5%.

Transport: Motor vehicles: in use (1986): 234 000 passenger cars, 114 000 comm. vehicles. **Civil aviation:** (1986) 22.8 bln. passenger-km; 1.1 bln. freight ton-km.

Communications: Television sets: 398 000 (1986). **Radios:** 111 000 in use (1986). **Telephones in use** (1986): 1.0 mln. **Daily newspaper circ.** (1986): 270 per 1 000 pop.

Health: Life expectancy at birth (1986): 69.9 male; 76.2 female. **Births** (per 1 000 pop. 1986): 14.8. **Deaths** (per 1 000 pop. 1986): 5.0. **Natural increase** (1986): .9%. **Hospital beds** (1985): 9 866. **Physicians** (1985): 2 631. **Infant mortality** (per 1 000 live births 1985): 8.9.

Education (1987): **Literacy:** 85%. **Years compulsory:** none; attendance 85%.

Major International Organizations: UN (GATT, IMF, WHO), ASEAN.

Canadian High Commission: IBM Towers, 14th fl., 80 Anson Rd., Singapore 0207; Tel.: 225-6363.

Founded in 1819 by Sir Thomas Stamford Raffles, Singapore was a British colony until 1959 when it became autonomous within the Commonwealth. On Sept. 16, 1963, it joined with Malaya, Sarawak and Sabah to form the Federation of Malaysia.

Tensions between Malayans, dominant in the federation, and ethnic Chinese, dominant in Singapore, led to an agreement under which Singapore became a separate nation, Aug. 9, 1965.

Singapore is one of the world's largest ports. Standards in health, education, and housing are high. International banking has grown.

Solomon Islands

People: Population (1989 est.): 314 000. **Age distrib. (%):** 0–14: 49; 15–59: 45.5; 60+: 5.5. **Pop. density:** 11.4 per sq. km. **Urban** (1986): 15%. **Ethnic groups:** Melanesian 93%, Polynesian 4%. **Languages:** English (official), Pidgin, local languages. **Religions:** Anglican 34%, Roman Catholic 19%, Evangelical 24%, traditional religions.

Geography: Area: 27 555 sq. km. **Location:** Melanesian archipelago in the western Pacific O. **Neighbors:** Nearest is Papua New Guinea on W. **Topography:** 10 large volcanic and rugged islands and 4 groups of smaller ones. **Capital:** Honiara. **Cities:** (1986): Honiara 30 000.

Government: Type: Parliamentary democracy within the Commonwealth of Nations. **Head of state:** Queen Elizabeth II, represented by Gov.-Gen. Baddeley Devesi; b. Oct. 16, 1941; in office: July 7, 1978. **Head of government:** Prime Min. Ezekial Alebua; in office: Dec. 1, 1986. **Local divisions:** 7 provinces and Honiara.

Economy: Industries: Fish canning. **Chief crops:** Coconuts, rice, bananas, yams. **Other resources:** Forests, marine shell. **Arable land:** 2%. **Fish catch** (1984): 35 000 metric tons. **Electricity prod.** (1986): 30.0 mln. kwh. **Labor force:** 32% agric., 32% services, 18% ind. & comm.

Finance: Currency: Dollar (Mar. 1988: 2.03 = $1 US). **Gross national product** (1985): $137 mln. **Per capita income** (1982): $628. **Imports** (1985): $83 mln.; partners: Austral. 31%, Jap. 14%, Sing. 18%. **Exports** (1985): $70 mln.; partners: Jap. 37%, UK 11%.

Communications: Radios: 40 000 in use (1986). **Telephones in use** (1985): 4 000.

Health: Life expectancy at birth: 54 years. **Births:** (per 1 000 pop. 1985): 47. **Deaths** (per 1 000 pop. 1985): 10. **Natural increase** (1985): 3.7%. **Infant mortality** (per 1 000 live births 1985): 46.

Education (1984): **Literacy:** 54%. **Primary school** 73%. **Secondary school:** 13%.

Major International Organizations: UN, Commonwealth of Nations.

Canadian Embassy: c/o The Canadian High Commission, Commonwealth Ave., Canberra A.C.T. 2600, Australia.

The Solomon Islands were sighted in 1568 by an expedition from Peru. Britain established a protectorate in the 1890s over most of the group, inhabited by Melanesians. The islands saw major World War II battles. Self-government came Jan. 2, 1976, and independence was formally attained July 7, 1978.

Somalia

Somali Democratic Republic

Jamhuriyadda Dimugradiga Somaliya

People: Population (1989 est.): 8 552 000. **Pop. density:** 13.4 per sq. km. **Ethnic groups:** mainly Hamitic, others. **Languages:** Somali, Arabic (both official). **Religion:** Sunni Moslem 99%.

Geography: Area: 637 868 sq. km. **Location:** Occupies the eastern horn of Africa. **Neighbors:** Djibouti, Ethiopia, Kenya on W. **Topography:** The coastline extends for 2 720 km. Hills cover the N; the centre and S are flat. **Capital:** Mogadishu. **Cities** (1986 est.): Mogadishu 700 000.

Government: Type: Independent republic. **Head of state:** Pres. Mohammed Siad Barrah; b. 1919; in office: Oct. 21, 1969. **Head of government:** Prime Min. Gen. Muhammad Ali Samatar; in office: Feb. 1, 1987. **Local divisions:** 15 regions. **Defence:** 29% of govt. expenditures (1983).

Economy: Chief crops: Incense, sugar, bananas, sorghum, corn, gum. **Minerals:** Iron, tin, gypsum, bauxite, uranium. **Arable land:** 2%. **Livestock** (1985): cattle: 4 mln.; goats: 18 mln.; sheep: 6 mln. **Fish catch** (1985): 16 000 metric tons. **Electricity prod.** (1986): 137 mln. kwh. **Labor force:** 82% agric.

Finance: Currency: Shilling (Mar. 1988: 100 = $1 US). **Gross national product** (1985): $1.8 bln. **Per capita income** (1985): $300. **Imports** (1985): $470 mln.; partners: It. 35%, UK

8%, U.S. 9%. **Exports** (1985): $110 mln.; partners: Saudi Ar. 66%, It. 12%. **International reserves less gold** (Nov. 1987): $1.3 mln. **Gold:** 19 000 oz t. **Consumer prices** (change in 1986): 35.8%.

Transport: Motor vehicles: in use (1981): 17 200 passenger cars, 9 500 comm. vehicles. **Chief ports:** Mogadishu, Berbera.

Communications: Radios: 250 000 in use (1986).

Health: Life expectancy at birth (1985): 43.9 yrs. **Births** (per 1 000 pop. 1985): 47. **Deaths** (per 1 000 pop. 1985): 17. **Natural increase** (1985): 3.0%. **Hospital beds** (1985): 5 536. **Physicians** (1985): 321. **Infant mortality** (per 1 000 live births 1985): 163.

Education (1986): Literacy: 40%. 50% attend primary school, 7% attend secondary school.

Major International Organizations: UN, OAU, Arab League.

Canadian Embassy: c/o Canadian High Commission, P.O. Box 30481, Nairobi, Kenya.

Arab trading posts developed into sultanates. The Italian Protectorate of Somalia, acquired from 1885 to 1927, extended along the Indian O. from the Gulf of Aden to the Juba R. The UN in 1949 approved eventual creation of Somalia as a sovereign state and in 1950 Italy took over the trusteeship held by Great Britain since World War II.

British Somaliland was formed in the 19th century in the NW. Britain gave it independence June 26, 1960; on July 1 it joined with the former Italian part to create the independent Somali Republic.

On Oct. 21, 1969, a Supreme Revolutionary Council seized power in a bloodless coup, named a Council of Secretaries of State, and abolished the Assembly. In May, 1970, several foreign companies were nationalized.

A severe drought in 1975 killed tens of thousands, and spurred efforts to resettle nomads on collective farms.

Somalia has laid claim to Ogaden, the huge eastern region of Ethiopia, peopled mostly by Somalis. Ethiopia battled Somali rebels and accused Somalia of sending troops and heavy arms in 1977. Russian forces were expelled in 1977 in retaliation for Soviet support of Ethiopia. Some 11 000 Cuban troops with Soviet arms defeated Somali army troops and ethnic Somali rebels in Ethiopia, 1978. As many as 1.5 mln. refugees entered Somalia. Guerrilla fighting in Ogaden has continued, although the Somali government no longer officially supports the Ogaden secessionists.

South Africa

Republic of South Africa

Republiek van Suid-Afrika

People: Population (1989 est.): 35 625 000. **Age distrib. (%):** 0–14: 41.0; 15–59: 52.8; 60+: 6.2. **Pop. density:** 29.1 per sq. km. **Urban** (1985): 55%. **Ethnic groups:** black 68%, white 18%, colored 10%, Asian 3%. **Languages:** Afrikaans, English (both official), Bantu languages predominate. **Religion:** Mainly Christian, Hindu, Moslem minorities.

Geography: Area: 1 223 315 sq. km. **Location:** At the southern extreme of Africa. **Neighbors:** Namibia (SW Africa), Botswana, Zimbabwe on N, Mozambique, Swaziland on E; surrounds Lesotho. **Topography:** The large interior plateau reaches close to the country's 4 320 km coastline. There are few major rivers or lakes; rainfall is sparse in W, more plentiful in E. **Capitals:** Cape Town (legislative), Pretoria (administrative), and Bloemfontein (judicial). **Cities** (1985 met.): Durban 982 000; Cape Town 1 900 000; Johannesburg 1 600 000; Pretoria 822 000.

Government: Type: Tricameral parliament with one chamber each for whites, coloreds, and Asians. **Head of State:** State President Pieter Willem Botha; b. Jan. 12, 1916; in office: Sept. 28, 1978. **Local divisions:** 4 provinces, 10 "homelands" for black Africans. **Defence:** 3.7% of GNP (1986).

Economy: Industries: Steel, tires, motors, textiles, plastics. **Chief crops:** Corn, wool, dairy products, grain, tobacco, sugar, fruit, peanuts, grapes. **Minerals:** Gold (largest producer), chromium, antimony, coal, iron, manganese, nickel, phosphates, tin, uranium, gem diamonds, platinum, copper, vanadium. **Other re-**

sources: Wool. **Arable land:** 12%. **Livestock.** (1984): cattle: 12.7 mln.; pigs: 1.4 mln.; sheep: 30.3 mln. **Fish catch** (1985): 649 000 metric tons. **Electricity prod.** (1986): 148 bln. kwh. **Crude steel prod.** (1986): 9.0 mln. metric tons. **Labor force:** 30% agric.; 29% ind. and commerce; 34% serv.; 7% mining.

Finance: Currency: Rand (May 1988: 2.24 = $1 US). **Gross national product** (1985): $112 bln. **Per capita income** (1985): $4 000. **Imports** (1987): $15.3 bln.; partners: W. Ger. 15%, U.S. 19%, Jap. 13%. **Exports** (1986): $18.4 bln.; partners: U.S. 19%, Jap. 9%. **Tourism** (1982): $630 mln. receipts. **National budget** (1984): $20.7 bln. **International reserves less gold** (Mar. 1988): $475 mln. **Gold:** 5.8 mln. oz t. **Consumer prices** (change in 1987): 16.1%.

Transport: Railway traffic (1986): 17.8 bln. passengers-km.: 92.8 bln. net ton-km. **Motor vehicles:** in use (1985): 2.9 mln. passenger cars, 1.2 mln. comm. vehicles. **Civil aviation:** (1985): 8.7 bln. passenger-km: 397 mln. freight ton-km. **Chief ports:** Durban, Cape Town, East London, Port Elizabeth.

Communications: Television sets (1986): 2.7 mln.; **Radios:** 10 mln. in use (1986). **Telephones** in use (1984): 3.4 mln. **Daily newspaper circ.** (1986): 41 per 1 000 pop.

Health: Life expectancy at birth (1982): White: 70 years; Asians: 65 years; Blacks: 59 years. **Births** (per 1 000 pop. 1985): 33. **Deaths** (per 1 000 pop. 1985): 10. **Natural increase** (1985): 2.3%. **Physicians** (1986): 22 500. **Infant mortality** (per 1 000 live births 1982): Africans 94, Asians 25.3, whites 14.9.

Education (1987): **Literacy:** 99% (whites), 69% (Asians), 62% (coloreds), 50% (Africans).

Major International Organizations: UN (GATT).

Embassy: 5th Floor, Nedbank Plaza, P. O. Box 26006, Arcadia, Pretoria 0007; Tel: 28-7062.

Bushmen and Hottentots were the original inhabitants. Bantus, including Zulu, Xhosa, Swazi, and Sotho, had occupied the area from Transvaal to south of Transkei before the 17th century.

The Cape of Good Hope area was settled by Dutch, beginning in the 17th century. Britain seized the Cape in 1806. Many Dutch trekked north and founded 2 republics, the Transvaal and the Orange Free State. Diamonds were discovered, 1867, and gold, 1886. The Dutch (Boers) resented encroachments by the British and others; the Anglo-Boer War followed, 1899-1902. Britain won and, effective May 31, 1910, created the Union of South Africa, incorporating the British colonies of the Cape and Natal, the Transvaal and the Orange Free State. After a referendum, the Union became the Republic of South Africa, May 31, 1961, and withdrew from the Commonwealth.

With the election victory of Daniel Malan's National party in 1948, the policy of separate development of the races, or apartheid, already existing unofficially, became official. This called for separate development, separate residential areas, and ultimate political independence for the whites, Bantus, Asians, and Coloreds. In 1959 the government passed acts providing the eventual creation of several Bantu nations or Bantustans on 13% of the country's land area, though most black leaders opposed the plan.

In 1963, the Transkei, an area in the SE, became the first of these partially self-governing territories or "Homelands." Transkei was declared independent by the South African government on Oct. 26, 1976, Bophuthatswana on Dec. 6, 1977, and Venda on Sept. 13, 1979; none received international recognition.

Under apartheid, blacks are severely restricted to certain occupations, and are paid far lower wages than are whites for similar work. Only whites may vote or run for public office, and militant white opposition has been curbed. There is an advisory Indian Council, partly elected, partly appointed. In 1969, a Colored People's Representative Council was created. Some liberalization measures were allowed in the 1980s. A new constitution was approved by referendum, Nov. 1983, which extended the parliamentary franchise to the Colored and Asian minorities. Laws banning interracial sex and marriage were repealed in 1985.

In 1986, Nobel Peace Prize winner Bishop Desmond Tutu called for Western nations to apply sanctions against S. Africa to force an end to apartheid. President Botha announced in Apr. the end to the nation's system of racial pass laws and offered blacks an advisory role in government.

On May 19, 1986, S. Africa attacked 3 neighboring countries—Zimbabwe, Botswana, Zambia—to strike at guerrilla strongholds of the AfricanNational Congress.

A nationwide state of emergency was declared June 12, 1986, giving almost unlimited power to the security forces. On Apr. 22, 1987, a 6-week-old walkout by railway workers erupted into violence after the dismissal of 16 000 strikers. As confrontation between blacks and government increased, there waswidespread support in Western nations for a complete trade embargoon S. Africa. Canada applied limited sanctions against S. Africa during 1986. The refusal of England to apply sanctions caused many of the Commonwealth countries to refuse to participate in the XIII Commonwealth Games in Edinburgh.

Some 2 million South African black workers staged a massive strike, June 6-8, 1988, to protest the government's new labor laws and the banning of political activity by trade unions and antiapartheid groups.

Bophuthatswana: Population (1987 est.): 1 606 000. **Area:** 39 997 sq. km, 6 discontinuous geographic units. **Capital:** Mmabatho. **Head of state:** Pres. Kgosi Lucas Manyane Mangope, b. Dec. 27, 1923; in office: Dec. 6, 1977.

Ciskei: Population (1987 est.): 1 140 000. **Area:** 5 387 sq. km. **Capitol:** Bisho. **Head of State:** Pres. Lennox Sebe.

Transkei: Population (1987 est.): 2 832 000. **Area:** 43 722 sq. km., 3 discontinuous geographic units. **Capital:** Umtata. **Head of state:** Pres. Nyangelizwe Vulindlela Ndamase; in office: Feb. 20, 1986. **Head of government:** Gen. Bantu Holomisa; in office: Dec. 30, 1987.

Venda: Population (1987 est.): 516 000. **Area:** 6 214 sq. km, 2 discontinuous geographic units. **Capital:** Thohoyandou. **Head of state:** Patrick Mphephu; in office: Sept. 13, 1979.

Namibia (South-West Africa)

South-West Africa is a sparsely populated land. Made a German protectorate in 1884, it was surrendered to S. Africa in 1915 and was administered by that country under a League of Nations mandate. S. Africa refused to accept UN authority under the trusteeship system.

Other African nations charged S. Africa imposed apartheid, built military bases, and exploited S-W Africa. The UN General Assembly, May 1968, created an 11-nation council to take over administration of S-W Africa and lead it to independence. The council charged that S. Africa had blocked its efforts to visit S-W Africa.

In 1968 the UN General Assembly gave the area the name Namibia. In Jan. 1970 the UN Security Council condemned S. Africa for "illegal" control of the area. In an advisory opinion, June 1971, the International Court of Justice declared S. Africa was occupying the area illegally.

In a 1977 referendum, white voters backed a plan for a multiracial interim government to lead to independence. The Marxist South-West Africa People's Organization (SWAPO) rejected the plan, and launched a guerrilla war. Both S. Africa and Namibian rebels agreed to a UN plan for independence by the end of 1978. S. Africa rejected the plan, Sept. 20, 1978, and held elections, without UN supervision, for Namibia's constituent assembly, Dec., that were ignored by the major black opposition parties.

The UN peace plan, proposed 1980, called for a cease-fire and a demilitarized zone 50 km deep on each side of S-W Africa's borders with Angola and Zambia that would be patrolled by UN peacekeeping forces against guerrilla actions. In 1982, S. African and SWAPO agreed in principle on a cease-fire and the holding of UN-supervised elections. S. Africa, however, insisted on the withdrawal of Cuban forces from Angola as a precondition to Namibian independence. On Jan. 18, 1983, S. Africa dissolved the Namibian National Assembly and resumed direct control of the territory.

In 1988, a U.S.-mediated plan was agreed upon by So. Africa, Angola, and Cuba which called for withdrawal of Cuban troops from Angola and black majority rule in Namibia.

Most of Namibia is a plateau, 1 080 m high, with plains in the N, Kalahari Desert to the E, Orange R. on the S, Atlantic O. on the W. Area is 834 150 sq. km; pop. (1986 est.) 1 203 000; capital, Windhoek.

Products include cattle, sheep, diamonds, copper, lead, zinc, fish. People include Namas (Hottentots), Ovambos (Bantus), Bushmen, and others.

Walvis Bay, the only deepwater port in the country, was turned over to S. African administration in 1922. S. Africa said in 1978 it would discuss sovereignty only after Namibian independence.

Spain
España

People: Population (1989 est.): 39 784 000. **Age distrib.** (%): 0–14: 24.6; 15–59: 59.5; 60+: 15.9. **Pop. density:** 78.8 per sq. km. **Urban** (1987): 79%. **Ethnic groups:** Spanish (Castilian, Valencian, Andalusian, Asturian) 72.8%, Catalan 16.4%, Galician 8.2%, Basque 2.3%. **Languages:** Spanish (official), Catalan, Galician, Basque. **Religion:** Roman Catholic 90%.

Geography: Area: 504 742 sq. km. **Location:** In SW Europe. **Neighbors:** Portugal on W. France on N. **Topography:** The interior is a high, arid plateau broken by mountain ranges and river valleys. The NW is heavily watered, the south has lowlands and a Mediterranean climate. **Capital:** Madrid. **Cities** (1987 est.): Madrid 3 500 000; Barcelona 2 000 000; Valencia 700 000; Seville 580 000.

Government: Type: Constitutional monarchy. **Head of state:** King Juan Carlos I de Borbon y Borbon, b. Jan. 5, 1938; in office: Nov. 22, 1975. **Head of government:** Prime Min. Felipe Gonzalez Marquez; in office: Dec. 2, 1982. **Local divisions:** 50 provinces, 2 territories, 3 islands. **Defence:** 2.2% of GNP (1985).

Economy: Industries: Machinery, steel, textiles, shoes, autos, processed foods. **Chief crops:** Grains, olives, grapes, citrus fruits, vegetables, olives. **Minerals:** Mercury, uranium, lead, iron, copper, zinc, coal. **Crude oil reserves** (1987): 34 mln. bbls. **Other resources:** Forests (cork). **Arable land:** 41%. **Livestock** (1985): cattle: 4.9 mln.; pigs: 11.9 mln.; sheep: 17.3 mln. **Fish catch** (1985): 1.1 mln. tons. **Electricity prod.** (1986): 134.3 bln. kwh. **Crude steel prod.** (1986): 11.9 mln. metric tons. **Labor force:** 16% agric.; 24% ind. and comm.; 52% serv.

Finance: Currency: Peseta (May 1988: 114.30 = $1 US). **Gross national product** (1986): $187.6 bln. **Per capita income** (1984): $4 490. **Imports** (1987): $48.8 bln.; partners: U.S. 11%, EC 33%. **Exports** (1987): $33.9 bln.; partners: EC 49%, U.S. 10%. **Tourists** (1984): $7.7 bln. receipts. **National budget** (1985): $35 bln. expenditures. **International reserves less gold** (Jan. 1988): $31.7 bln. **Gold:** 14.58 min. oz t. **Consumer prices** (change in 1987): 5.3%.

Transport: Railway traffic (1986): 15 bln. passenger-km; 11.2 bln. net ton-km. **Motor vehicles:** in use (1985): 9.2 mln. passenger cars, 1.6 mln. comm. **Civil aviation:** (1986): 19.1 bln. passenger-km; 568 mln. freight ton-km. **Chief ports:** Barcelona, Bilbao, Valencia, Cartagena, Gijon.

Communications: Television sets: 9.9 mln. in use (1986). **Radios:** 10.8 mln. in use (1986). **Telephones in use** (1986): 14.2 mln. **Daily newspaper circ.** (1983): 89 per 1 000 pop.

Health: Life expectancy at birth (1985): 71.3 male; 77.5 female. **Births** (per 1 000 pop. 1985): 11. **Deaths** (per 1 000 pop. 1985): 8. **Natural increase** (1985): 0.3%. **Hospital beds** (1986): 193 000. **Physicians** (1984): 121 362. **Infant mortality** (per 1 000 live births 1985): 9.

Education (1987): Literacy: 97%. **School compulsory:** to age 14.

Major International Organizations: UN and all of its specialized agencies, NATO, OECD, EC.

Canadian Embassy: Edificio Goya, Calle Nunez de Balboa 35; postal: Apartado 587, Madrid 1; Tel: 431-4300.

Spain was settled by Iberians, Basques, and Celts, partly overrun by Carthaginians, conquered by Rome c.200 BC. The Visigoths, in power by the 5th century AD, adopted Christianity but by 711 AD lost to the Islamic invasion from Africa. Christian reconquest from the N led to a Spanish nationalism. In 1469 the kingdoms of Aragon and Castile were united by the marriage of Ferdinand II and Isabella I, and the last Moorish power was broken by the fall of the kingdom of Granada, 1492. Spain became a bulwark of Roman Catholicism.

Spain obtained a colonial empire with the discovery of America by Columbus, 1492, the conquest of Mexico by Cortes, and Peru by Pizarro. It also controlled the Netherlands and parts of Italy and Germany. Spain lost its American colonies in the early 19th century. It lost Cuba, the Philippines, and Puerto Rico during the Spanish-American War, 1898.

Primo de Rivera became dictator in 1923. King Alfonso XIII revoked the dictatorship, 1930, but was forced to leave the country 1931. A republic was proclaimed which disestablished the church, curtailed its privileges, and secularized education. A conservative reaction occurred 1933 but was followed by a Popular Front (1936-1939) composed of socialists, communists, republicans, and anarchists.

Army officers under Francisco Franco revolted against the government, 1936. In a destructive 3-year war, in which some one million died, Franco received massive help and troops from Italy and Germany, while the USSR, France, and Mexico supported the republic. War ended Mar. 28, 1939. Franco was named caudillo, leader of the nation. Spain was neutral in World War II but its relations with fascist countries caused its exclusion from the UN until 1955.

In July 1969, Franco and the Cortes designated Prince Juan Carlos as the future king and chief of state. After Franco's death, Nov. 20, 1975, Juan Carlos was sworn in as king. He presided over the formal dissolution of the institutions of the Franco regime. In free elections June 1977, moderates and democratic socialists emerged as the largest parties.

Catalonia and the Basque country were granted autonomy, Jan. 1980, following overwhelming approval in home-rule referendums. Basque extremists, however, have continued their campaign for independence.

Spain has sought the return of Gibraltar, in British hands since 1704.

The **Balearic Islands** in the western Mediterranean, 5 031 sq. km, are a province of Spain; they include **Majorca** (Mallorca), with the capital, Palma; **Minorca, Cabrera, Ibiza** and **Formentera.** The **Canary Islands,** 7 298 sq. km, in the Atlantic W of Morocco, form 2 provinces, including the islands of **Tenerife, Palma, Gomera, Hierro, Grand Canary, Fuerteventura,** and **Lanzarote** with Las Palmas and Santa Cruz thriving ports. **Ceuta** and **Melilla,** small enclaves on Morocco's Mediterranean coast, are part of Metropolitan Spain.

Sri Lanka
Democratic Socialist Republic of Sri Lanka
Sri Lanka Prajathanthrika Samajavadi Janarajaya

People: Population (1989 est.): 17 541 000. **Age distrib.** (%): 0–14: 35.3; 15–59: 58.1; 60+: 6.6. **Pop. density:** 267.4 per sq. km. **Urban** (1987): 21.5%. **Ethnic groups:** Sinhalese 74%, Tamil 17%, Moor 7%. **Languages:** Sinhala (official), Tamil, English. **Religions:** Buddhist 69%, Hindu 15%, Christian 8%, Moslem 7%.

Geography: Area: 65 605 sq. km. **Location:** In Indian O. off SE coast of India. **Neighbors:** India on NW. **Topography:** The coastal area and the northern half are flat; the S-central area is hilly and mountainous. **Capital:** Colombo. **Cities** (1983): Colombo 1 262 000.

Government: Type: Republic. **Head of state:** Pres. Junius Richard Jayawardene; b. Sept. 17, 1906; in office: Feb. 4, 1978. **Head of government:** Prime Minister Ranasinghe Premadasa, b. June 23, 1924, in office: Feb. 6, 1978. **Local divisions:** 9 provinces, 24 districts. **Defence:** 2.5% of GNP (1984).

Economy: Industries: Plywood, paper, milling, chemicals, textiles. **Chief crops:** Tea, coconuts, rice. **Minerals:** Graphite, limestone, gems, phosphate. **Other resources:** Forests, rubber. **Arable land:** 33%. **Livestock** (1985): cattle: 1.7 mln. **Fish catch** (1985): 140 000 metric tons. **Electricity prod.** (1986): 3.2 bln. kwh. **Labor force:** 46% agric.; 27% ind. and comm.; 26% serv.

Finance: Currency: Rupee (Mar. 1988: 30.89 = $1 US). **Gross national product** (1985): $6.3 bln. **Per capita income** (1984): $340. **Imports** (1987): $2.0 bln.; partners: Jap. 15%, Saudi Ar. 12%, UK 7%. **Exports** (1987): $1.3 bln.; partners: U.S. 22%, UK 7%. **Tourists** (1985): $70 mln. receipts. **National budget** (1984): $1.5 bln. revenues; $1.8 bln. expenditures. **International reserves less gold** (Mar. 1988): $448 mln. **Gold:** 63 000 oz t. **Consumer prices** (change in 1987): 7.7%.

Transport: Railway traffic (1985): 2.1 bln. passenger-km; 247 mln. net ton-km. **Motor vehicles:** in use (1985): 148 000 passenger cars, 137 000 comm. vehicles. **Civil aviation** (1986): 2.1 bln. passenger-km; 56 mln. freight ton-km. **Chief ports:** Colombo, Trincomalee, Galle.

Communications: Radios: 2 mln. in use (1986). **Telephones in use** (1986): 106 000.

Health: Life expectancy at birth (1986): 68.0 male; 71.2 female. **Births** (per 1 000 pop. 1986): 23.9. **Deaths** (per 1 000 pop. 1986): 6.2. **Natural increase** (1986): 1.7%. **Hospital beds** (1985): 45 000. **Physicians** (1985): 2 151. **Infant mortality** (per 1 000 live births 1985): 28.

Education (1985): **Literacy:** 87%. **Years compulsory:** To age 12; attendance 84%.

Major International Organizations: UN (World Bank, IMF), Commonwealth of Nations.

Canadian High Commission: 6 Gregory's Rd., Cinnamon Gardens, Colombo 7; postal: P.O. Box 1006, Colombo; Tel: 59-58-41, -42, -43.

The island was known to the ancient world as Taprobane (Greek for copper-colored) and later as Serendip (from Arabic). Colonists from northern India subdued the indigenous Veddahs about 543 BC; their descendants, the Buddhist Sinhalese, still form most of the population. Hindu descendants of Tamil immigrants from southern India account for one-fifth of the population. Parts were occupied by the Portuguese in 1505 and by the Dutch in 1658. The British seized the island in 1796. As Ceylon it became an independent member of the Commonwealth in 1948. On May 22, 1972, Ceylon became the Republic of Sri Lanka.

Prime Min. W. R. D. Bandaranaike was assassinated Sept. 25, 1959. In new elections, the Freedom Party was victorious under Mrs. Sirimavo Bandaranaike, widow of the former prime minister. In Apr., 1962, the government expropriated British and U.S. oil companies. In Mar. 1965 elections, the conservative United National Party won; the new government agreed to pay compensation for the seized oil companies.

After May 1970 elections, Mrs. Bandaranaike became prime minister again. In 1971 the nation suffered economic problems and terrorist activities by ultra-leftists, thousands of whom were executed. Massive land reform and nationalization of foreign-owned plantations was undertaken in the mid-1970s. Mrs. Bandaranaike was ousted in 1977 elections by the United Nationals. A presidential form of government was installed in 1978 to restore stability.

Tension between the Sinhalese and Tamil separatists has often erupted into violence. Hundreds died in an attack by Tamil rebels Apr. 17, 1987. Sri Lankan forces retaliated in June with attacks on the rebel-held Jaffna Peninsula. India's attempt to mediate a peaceful solution was opposed by both sides.

Sudan

Republic of Sudan

Jamhuryat as-Sudan

People: Population (1989 est.): 25 008 000. **Pop. density:** 10.0 per sq. km. **Urban** (1983): 35%. **Ethnic groups:** black 52%, Arab 39%, Beja 6%. **Languages:** Arabic (official), various tribal languages. **Religions:** Sunni Moslem 70%, animist 18%, Christian 5%.

Geography: Area: 2 503 707 sq. km, the largest country in Africa. **Location:** At the E end of Sahara desert zone. **Neighbors:** Egypt on N, Libya, Chad, Central African Republic on W, Zaire, Uganda, Kenya on S, Ethiopia on E. **Topography:** The N consists of the Libyan Desert in the W, and the mountainous Nubia desert in E, with narrow Nile valley between. The centre contains large, fertile, rainy areas with fields, pasture, and forest. The S has rich soil, heavy rain. **Capital:** Khartoum. **Cities** (1983 est.): Khartoum 476 000; Omdurman 526 000; North Khartoum 341 000; Port Sudan 206 000.

Government: Type: Republic. **Head of government:** Prime Min. Sadiq al Mahdi; b. 1936; in office: May 6, 1986. **Local divisions:** 9 regions. **Defence:** 2.1% of GNP (1984).

Economy: Industries: Textiles, food processing. **Chief crops:** Gum arabic (principal world source), durra (sorghum), cotton (main export), sesame, peanuts, rice, coffee, sugar cane, wheat, dates. **Minerals:** Chrome, copper. **Other resources:** Mahogany. **Arable land:** 5%. **Livestock** (1985): cattle: 20 mln.; sheep: 1.9 mln.; goats: 13 mln. **Electricity prod.** (1986): 1.2. bln. kwh. **Labor force:** 78% agric.; 9% ind., comm.

Finance: Currency: Pound (Mar. 1988: 1.00 = $.22 US). **Gross national product** (1985): $7.3 bln. **Per capita income** (1982 est.): $361. **Imports** (1986): $961 mln.; partners: UK 13%, W. Ger. 8%, Saudi Ar. 11%. **Exports** (1986): $333 mln.; partners: China 6%, It. 9%, Saudi Ar. 21%. **National budget** (1986): $1.0 bln. expenditures. **International reserves less gold** (Mar. 1988): $11.5 mln.

Transport: Railway traffic (1987): 1.6 bln. net ton-km. **Motor vehicles:** in use (1985): 99 000 passenger cars, 17 000 comm. vehicles. **Civil aviation:** (1982): 657 mln. passenger-km; 6.3 mln. freight ton-km. **Chief ports:** Port Sudan.

Communications: Television sets: 250 000 in use (1986). **Radios:** 1.5 mln. (1986). **Telephones in use** (1985): 77 000. **Daily newspaper circ.** (1985): 6 per 1 000 pop.

Health: Life expectancy at birth (1985): 48.0 male; 50.0 female. **Births** (per 1 000 pop. 1985): 45.3. **Deaths** (per 1 000 pop. 1985): 16.6. **Natural increase** (1985): 2.8%. **Hospital beds** (1985): 17 328. **Physicians** (1983): 2 169. **Infant mortality** (per 1 000 live births 1985): 118.

Education (1986): **Literacy:** 20%. **Years compulsory:** 9; attendance 50%.

Major International Organizations: UN (IMF, WHO, FAO), Arab League, OAU.

Canadian Embassy: c/o P.O. 1130, Addis Ababa, Ethiopia.

Northern Sudan, ancient Nubia, was settled by Egyptians in antiquity, and was converted to Coptic Christianity in the 6th century. Arab conquests brought Islam in the 15th century.

In the 1820s Egypt took over the Sudan, defeating the last of earlier empires, including the Fung. In the 1880s a revolution was led by Mohammed Ahmed who called himself the Mahdi (leader of the faithful) and his followers, the dervishes.

In 1898 an Anglo-Egyptian force crushed the Mahdi's successors. In 1951 the Egyptian Parliament abrogated its 1899 and 1936 treaties with Great Britain, and amended its constitution, to provide for a separate Sudanese constitution.

Sudan voted for complete independence as a parliamentary government effective Jan. 1, 1956. Gen. Ibrahim Abboud took power 1958, but resigned under pressure, 1964.

In 1969, in a second military coup, a Revolutionary Council took power, but a civilian premier and cabinet were appointed; the government announced it would create a socialist state. The northern 12 provinces are predominantly Arab-Moslem and have been dominant in the central government. The 3 southern provinces are Negro and predominantly pagan. A 1972 peace agreement gave the South regional autonomy.

The government nationalized a number of businesses in May 1970.

Sudan charged Libya with aiding an unsuccessful coup in Sudan in 1976. Sudan claimed that Libyan planes bombed several border towns, Sept. 1981, and the city of Omdurman, 1984.

Economic problems plagued the nation in the 1980s, aggravated by a hugh influx of refugees from neighboring countries. After 16 years in power, Pres. Nimeiry was overthrown in a bloodless military coup, Apr. 6, 1985.

Suriname

Republic of Suriname

People: Population (1989 est.): 400 000. **Pop. density:** 2.5 per sq. mi. **Ethnic groups** Hindustani 37%, Creole 31%, Javanese 15%. **Languages:** Dutch (official), Sranan (Creole), English, others. **Religions:** Moslem 23%, Hindu 27%, Catholic 25%.

Geography: Area: 163 253 sq. km. **Location:** On N shore of S. America. **Neighbors:** Guyana on W, Brazil on S, French Guiana on E. **Topography:** A flat Atlantic coast, where dikes permit agriculture. Inland is a forest belt; to the S, largely unexplored hills cover 75% of the country. **Capital:** Paramaribo. **Cities** (1984): Paramaribo 180 000.

Government: Type: Republic. **Head of State:** Pres. Ramsewak Shankar, in office: Jan. 25, 1988. **Head of government:** Prime Min. Henck Aaron; in office: Jan. 25, 1988. **Local divisions:** 9 districts.

Economy: Industries: Aluminum. **Chief crops:** Rice, sugar, fruits. **Minerals:** Bauxite. **Other resources:** Forests, shrimp. **Arable land:** 1%. **Electricity prod.** (1986): 1.6 bln. kwh. **Labor force:** 29% agric.; 15% ind. and commerce; 42% govt.

Finance: Currency: Guilder (Mar. 1988: 1.78 = $1 US). **Gross national product** (1985): $1.1 bln. **Per capita income** (1985): $2 920. **Imports** (1985): $299 mln.; partners: U.S. 30%, Neth. 9% Trin./Tob. 21%, Jap. 7%. **Exports** (1985): $314 mln.; partners: U.S. 26%, Neth. 26%. **Tourists** (1983): receipts: $4 mln. **National budget** (1985): $469 mln. **International reserves less gold** (Mar. 1988): $16.2 mln. **Gold:** 54 000 oz t.

Transport: Motor vehicles: in use (1986): 33 000 passenger cars, 14 000 comm. vehicles. **Chief ports:** Paramaribo, Nieuw-Nickerie.

Communications: Television sets: 48 000 in use (1986). **Radios:** 246 000 in use (1986). **Telephones in use** (1985): 36 000. **Daily newspaper circ.** (1987): 80 per 1 000 pop.

Health: Life expectancy at birth (1985): 67.0 male; 71.9 female. **Births** (per 1 000 pop. 1985): 26. **Deaths** (per 1 000 pop. 1985): 8. **Natural increase** (1985): 1.8%. **Infant mortality** (per 1 000 live births 1985): 21.

Education (1984): Literacy: 65%; compulsory ages 6–12.

Major International Organizations: UN (WHO, ILO, FAO, World Bank, IMF), OAS.

Canadian Embassy: c/o Canadian High Commission, P.O. Box 10880, Georgetown, Guyana.

The Netherlands acquired Suriname in 1667 from Britain, in exchange for New Netherlands (New York). The 1954 Dutch constitution raised the colony to a level of equality with the Netherlands and the Netherlands Antilles. In the 1970s the Dutch government pressured for Suriname independence, which came Nov. 25, 1975, despite objections from East Indians. Some 40% of the population (mostly East Indians) emigrated to the Netherlands in the months before independence.

The National Military Council took over control of the government, Feb. 1982. The government came under democratic leadership in 1988.

Swaziland
Kingdom of Swaziland

People: Population (1989 est.): 757 000. **Age distrib.** (%): 0–14: 46.1; 15–59: 48.9; 60+: 5.0. **Pop. density:** 43.6 per sq. km. **Urban** (1985): 26%. **Ethnic groups:** Swazi 90%, Zulu 2.3%, European 2.1%, other African, non-African groups. **Languages:** siSwati, English (both official). **Religions:** Christian 57%, indigenous beliefs 43%.

Geography: Area: 17 362 sq. km. **Location:** In southern Africa, near Indian O. coast. **Neighbors:** South Africa on N, W, S, Mozambique on E. **Topography:** The country descends from W-E in broad belts, becoming more arid in the lowveld region, then rising to a plateau in the E. **Capital:** Mbabane. **Cities** (1986 est.): Mbabane 52 000.

Government: Type: Monarchy. **Head of state:** King Mswati 3d; as of: Apr. 25, 1986. **Head of government:** Prime Min. Sotsha Dlamini; in office: Oct. 6, 1986. **Local divisions:** 4 districts, 2 municipalities, 40 regions.

Economy: Industries: Wood pulp. **Chief crops:** Sugar, corn, cotton, rice, pineapples, sugar, citrus fruits. **Minerals:** Asbestos, iron, coal. **Other resources:** Forests. **Arable land:** 18%. **Electricity prod.** (1986): 120 mln. kwh. **Labor force:** 53% agric.; 9% ind. and commerce; 9% serv.

Finance: Currency: Lilangeni (Mar. 1988: 1.00 = $.47 US). **Gross national product** (1985): $490 mln. **Per capita income** (1983 est.): $790. **Imports** (1985): $322 mln.; partners: S. Afr., 96%. **Exports** (1985): $174 mln.; partners: UK 33%, S. Afr. 20%. **National budget** (1986): $120 mln. **International reserves less gold** (Feb. 1988): $128 mln. **Consumer prices** (change in 1986): 11.8%.

Transport: Motor vehicles: in use (1985): 18 000 passenger cars, 10 000 comm. vehicles.

Communications: Radios: 95 000 in use (1986). **Telephones in use** (1986): 12 000. **Daily newspaper circ.** (1985): 35 per 1 000 pop.

Health: Life expectancy at birth (1983): 46.8 male; 50.0 female. **Births** (per 1 000 pop. 1985): 47.5. **Deaths** (per 1 000 pop. 1985): 17.2. **Natural increase** (1985): 3.0%. **Hospital beds** (1984): 1 608. **Physicians** (1984): 80. **Infant mortality rate** (per 1 000 live births 1985): 156.

Education (1985): **Literacy:** 65%. Almost all attend primary school.

Major International Organizations: UN (IMF, WHO, FAO), OAU, Commonwealth of Nations.

Canadian High Commission: c/o The Canadian Embassy, P.O. Box 26006, Arcadia, Pretoria 0007, South Africa.

The royal house of Swaziland traces back 400 years, and is one of Africa's last ruling dynasties. The Swazis, a Bantu people, were driven to Swaziland from lands to the N by the Zulus in 1820. Their autonomy was later guaranteed by Britain and Transvaal, with Britain assuming control after 1903. Independence came Sept. 6, 1968. In 1973 the king repealed the constitution and assumed full powers.

Under the constitution political parties are forbidden; parliament's role in government is limited to debate and advice.

Sweden
Kingdom of Sweden
Konungariket Sverige

People: Population (1989 est.): 8 371 000. **Age distrib.** (%): 0–14: 18.1; 15–59: 58.8; 60+: 23.1. **Pop. density:** 18.6 per sq. km. **Urban** (1985): 85%. **Ethnic groups:** Swedish 91%, Finnish 3%, Lapps, European immigrants. **Languages:** Swedish, Finnish. **Religion:** Lutheran (official) 95%.

Geography: Area: 449 929 sq. km. **Location:** On Scandinavian Peninsula in N. Europe. **Neighbors:** Norway on W, Denmark on S (across Kattegat), Finland on E. **Topography:** Mountains along NW border cover 25% of Sweden, flat or rolling terrain covers the central and southern areas, which includes several large lakes. **Capital:** Stockholm. **Cities** (1987 est.): Stockholm 663 000; Goteborg 429 000; Malmo 230 000.

Government: Type: Constitutional monarchy. **Head of state:** King Carl XVI Gustaf; b. Apr. 30, 1946; in office: Sept. 19, 1973. **Head of government:** Prime Min. Ingvar Carlsson; b. Nov. 9, 1934; in office: Mar. 1, 1986. **Local divisions:** 24 lan (counties), 284 municipalities. **Defence:** 3.0% of GNP (1985).

Economy: Industries: Steel, machinery, instruments, autos, shipbuilding, shipping, paper. **Chief crops:** Grains, potatoes, sugar beets. **Minerals:** Zinc, iron, lead, copper, gold, silver. **Other resources:** Forests (half the country); yield one fourth exports. **Arable land:** 7%. **Livestock** (1985): cattle: 1.7 mln.; pigs: 2.4 mln. **Fish catch** (1985): 225 000 metric tons. **Electricity prod.** (1985): 136 bln. kwh. **Crude steel prod.** (1986): 4.7 mln. metric tons. **Labor force:** 5% agric.; 30% ind.; 21% commerce & finance; 44% services.

Finance: Currency: Krona (May 1988: 6.00 = $1 US). **Gross national product** (1985): $100 bln. **Per capita income** (1985): $11 989. **Imports** (1987): $40.7 bln.; partners: W. Ger. 17%, UK 13%, U.S. 9%. **Exports** (1987): $44.5 bln.; partners: UK 10%, W. Ger. 10%, Nor. 11%. **Tourists** (1985): $1.3 bln. receipts. **National budget** (1986): $42.9 bln. expenditures. **International reserves less gold** (Mar. 1988): $8.5 bln. **Gold:** 6.06 mln. oz t. **Consumer prices** (change in 1987): 4.2%.

Transport: Railway traffic (1985): 6.5 bln. passenger-km; 17.5 bln. net ton-km. **Motor vehicles:** in use (1985): 3.0 mln. passenger cars, 223 000 comm. vehicles. **Civil aviation** (1985): 5.3 bln. passenger-km: 190 mln. freight ton-km. **Chief ports:** Goteborg, Stockholm, Malmo.

Communications: Television sets: 3.2 mln. licensed (1986). **Radios:** 3.3 mln. (1986). **Telephones in use** (1984): 7.4 mln. **Daily newspaper circ.** (1985): 574 per 1 000 pop.

Health: Life expectancy at birth (1984): 73.1 male; 79.1 female. **Births** (per 1 000 pop. 1986): 12.2. **Deaths** (per 1 000 pop. 1986): 11.2. **Natural increase** (1986): .1%. **Hospital beds** (1985): 115 000. **Physicians** (1984): 20 200. **Infant mortality** (per 1 000 live births (1986): 33.

Education (1987): Literacy: 99%. **Years compulsory:** 9; attendance 100%.

Major International Organizations: UN and all of its specialized agencies, EFTA, OECD.

Canadian Embassy: P.O. Box 16129, S-10323, Stockholm 16; Tel: 23-79-20.

The Swedes have lived in present-day Sweden for at least 5 000 years, longer than nearly any other European people. Gothic tribes from Sweden played a major role in the disintegration of the Roman Empire. Other Swedes helped create the first Russian state in the 9th century.

The Swedes were Christianized from the 11th century, and a strong centralized monarchy developed. A parliament, the Riksdag, was first called in 1435, the earliest parliament on the European continent, with all classes of society represented.

Swedish independence from rule by Danish kings (dating from 1397) was secured by Gustavus I in a revolt, 1521-23; he built up the government and military and established the Lutheran Church. In the 17th century Sweden was a major European power, gaining most of the Baltic seacoast, but its international position subsequently declined.

The Napoleonic wars, in which Sweden acquired Norway (it became independent 1905), were the last in which Sweden participated. Armed neutrality was maintained in both world wars.

Over 4 decades of Social Democratic rule was ended in 1976 parliamentary elections but the party was returned to power in the 1982 elections. Although 90% of the economy is in private hands, the government holds a large interest in hydroelectric production and the railroads are operated by a public agency.

Consumer cooperatives are in extensive operation and also are important in agriculture and housing. Per capita GNP is among the highest in the world.

A labor crisis of strikes locking out more than 800 000 workers, May 1980, brought the country to an industrial standstill.

A Soviet submarine went aground inside Swedish territorial waters near the Karlskrona Naval Base, Oct. 27, 1981. Sweden claimed the submarine was armed with nuclear weapons and the incident a "flagrant violation" of Swedish neutrality. The submarine was towed back to international waters Nov. 6.

Premier Olof Palme was shot and killed on a Stockholm street Feb. 28, 1986.

2.5 mln. (1986). **Telephones in use** (1985): 5.4 mln. **Daily newspaper circ.** (1986): 491 per 1 000 pop.

Health: Life expectancy at birth (1985): 70.3 male; 76.2 female. **Births** (per 1 000 pop. 1986): 11.7. **Deaths** (per 1 000 pop. 1986): 9.2. **Natural increase** (1986): 0.2%. **Hospital beds** (1984): 66 192. **Physicians** (1984): 14 712. **Infant mortality** (per 1 000 live births 1985): 9.

Education (1985): **Literacy:** 99%. **Years compulsory:** 9; attendance 100%.

Major International Organizations: Many UN specialized agencies (though not a member).

Canadian Embassy: Kirchenfeldstrasse 88, 3005 Berne; Postal: P.O. Box 3000 Berne 6, Switzerland; Tel: (031) 44-63-81, -5.

Switzerland, the Roman province of Helvetia, is a federation of 23 cantons (20 full cantons and 6 half cantons), 3 of which in 1291 created a defensive league and later were joined by other districts. Voters in the French-speaking part of Canton Bern voted for self-government, 1978; Canton Jura was created Jan. 1, 1979.

In 1648 the Swiss Confederation obtained its independence from the Holy Roman Empire. The cantons were joined under a federal constitution in 1848, with large powers of local control retained by each canton.

Switzerland has maintained an armed neutrality since 1815, and has not been involved in a foreign war since 1515. Switzerland is a member of several UN agencies and of the European Free Trade Assoc. and has ties with the EC. It is also the seat of many UN and other international agencies.

Switzerland is a leading world banking centre; stability of the currency brings funds from many quarters. In 1984, voters rejected a proposal that would have opened bank records to authorities investigating domestic and foreign tax evasion.

Switzerland
Swiss Confederation

People: Population (1989 est.): 6 485 000. **Age distrib. (%):** 0–14: 17.8; 15–59: 63.2; 60+: 19.0. **Pop. density:** 157.0 per sq. km. **Urban** (1985): 60.4%. **Ethnic groups:** Mixed European stock. **Languages:** German 65%, French 18%, Italian 12%, Romansh 1%. (all official). **Religions:** Roman Catholic 49%, Protestant 48%.

Geography: Area: 41 284 sq. km. **Location:** In the Alps Mts. in Central Europe. **Neighbors:** France on W, Italy on S, Austria on E, W. Germany on N. **Topography:** The Alps cover 60% of the land area, the Jura, near France, 10%. Running between, from NE to SW, are midlands, 30%. **Capital:** Bern. **Cities** (1986 est.): Zurich 351 000; Basel 174 200; Geneva 159 000.

Government: Type: Federal republic. **Head of government:** Pres. Pierre Aubert; in office: Jan. 1, 1986. **Local divisions:** 20 full cantons, 6 half cantons. **Defence:** 2.2% of GNP (1984).

Economy: Industries: Machinery, machine tools, steel, instruments, watches, textiles, foodstuffs (cheese, chocolate), chemicals, drugs, banking, tourism. **Chief crops:** Grains, potatoes, sugar beets, vegetables, tobacco. **Minerals:** Salt. **Other resources:** Hydroelectric potential. **Arable land:** 10%. **Livestock** (1985): cattle: 1.9 mln.; pigs: 1.9 mln. **Electricity prod.** (1985): 57.3 bln. kwh. **Crude steel Prod.** (1986): 1.0 mln. **Labor force:** 39% ind. and commerce, 7% agric., 50% serv.

Finance: Currency: Franc (May 1988: 1.44 = $1 US). **Gross national product** (1985): $97.1 bln. **Per capita income** (1984): $14 408. **Imports** (1987): $50.6 bln.; partners: W. Ger. 30%, Fr. 11%, It. 10%, U.K. 5%. **Exports** (1987): $45.5 bln.; partners: W. Ger. 18%, Fr. 9%, It. 8%, U.S. 8%. **Tourists** (1985): receipts: $3.1 bln. **National budget** (1985): $8.7 bln. **International reserves less gold** (Mar. 1988): $24.1 bln. **Gold:** 83.28 mln. oz t. **Consumer prices** (change in 1987): 1.4%.

Transport: Railway traffic (1986): 9.2 bln. passenger-km; 6.9 bln. net ton-km. **Motor vehicles:** in use (1985): 2.6 mln. passenger cars, 211 000 comm. vehicles. **Civil aviation:** (1986): 12.8 bln. passenger-km; 725 mln. freight ton-km.

Communications: Television sets: 2.2 mln. (1986). **Radios:**

Syria
Syrian Arab Republic
al-jamhouriya al Arabia as-Souriya

People: Population (1989 est.): 12 210 000. **Age distrib. (%):** 0–14: 49.3; 15–59: 44.2; 60+: 6.5. **Pop. density:** 65.9 per sq. km. **Urban** (1986): 49%. **Ethnic groups:** Arab 90%, Others. **Languages:** Arabic (official), Kurdish, Armenian, French, English. **Religions:** Sunni Moslem 74%, Other Moslem 16%, Christian 10%.

Geography: Area: 185 166 sq. km. **Location:** At eastern end of Mediterranean Sea. **Neighbors:** Lebanon, Israel on W, Jordan on S, Iraq on E, Turkey on N. **Topography:** Syria has a short Mediterranean coastline, then stretches E and S with fertile lowlands and plains, alternating with mountains and large desert areas. **Capital:** Damascus. **Cities** (1987 est.): Damascus 1 200 000; Aleppo 1 200 000; Homs 431 000.

Government: Type: Socialist. **Head of state:** Pres. Hafez al-Assad; b. Mar. 1930; in office: Feb. 22, 1971. **Head of government:** Prime Min. Mahmoud Zuabi; in office: Nov. 1, 1987. **Local divisions:** Damascus and 13 provinces. **Defence:** 22.4% of GNP (1984).

Economy: Industries: Oil products, textiles, cement, tobacco, glassware, sugar, brassware. **Chief crops:** Cotton, grain, olives, fruits, vegetables. **Minerals:** Oil, phosphate, gypsum. **Crude oil reserves** (1987): 1.4 bln. bbls. **Other resources:** Wool. **Arable land:** 31%. **Livestock** (1985): sheep: 13 mln.; goats: 1 mln. **Electricity prod.** (1986): 8.0 bln. kwh. **Labor force:** 32% agric.; 29% ind. & comm.; 39% services.

Finance: Currency: Pound (Mar. 1988: 11.22 = $1 US). **Gross national product** (1985): $17.0 bln. **Imports** (1986): $2.7 bln.; partners: Iran, It., W. Ger., Fr. **Exports** (1986): $1.3 bln.; partners: It. 20%, Rom. 28%. **Tourists** (1985): receipts: $154 mln. **Consumer prices** (change in 1986): 36.1%.

Transport: Railway traffic (1985): 944 mln. passenger-km; 1.2 bln. net ton-km. **Motor vehicles:** in use (1985): 108 100 passenger cars, 120 000 comm. vehicles **Civil aviation** (1985): 942 mln. passenger-km; 15.6 mln. net ton-km. **Chief ports:** Latakia, Tartus.

Communications: Television sets: 400 000 in use (1986).

Radios: 2.0 mln. in use (1986). **Telephones in use** (1985): 616 000. **Daily newspaper circ.** (1986): 19 per 1 000 pop.
Health: Life expectancy at birth (1984): 63.3 male; 67.0 female. **Births** (per 1 000 pop. 1985): 44.5. **Deaths** (per 1 000 1985): 7. **Natural increase** (1985): 3.8%. **Hospital beds** (1985): 11 891. **Physicians** (1985): 5 543. **Infant mortality** (per 1 000 live births 1985): 57.
Education (1986): **Literacy:** 78% (males). **Years compulsory:** 6; attendance: 94%.
Major International Organizations: UN (IMF, WHO, FAO), Arab League.
Canadian Embassy: Sheraton Hotel, P.O. Box 3394, Damascus, Syria; Tel: 229300; 716664.

Syria contains some of the most ancient remains of civilization. It was the centre of the Seleucid empire, but later became absorbed in the Roman and Arab empires. Ottoman rule prevailed for 4 centuries, until the end of World War I.

The state of Syria was formed from former Turkish districts, made a separate entity by the Treaty of Sèvres 1920 and divided into the states of Syria and Greater Lebanon. Both were administered under a French League of Nations mandate 1920-1941.

Syria was proclaimed a republic by the occupying French Sept. 16, 1941, and exercised full independence effective Jan. 1, 1944. Syria joined in the Arab invasion of Israel in 1948.

Syria joined with Egypt in Feb. 1958 in the United Arab Republic but seceded Sept. 30, 1961. The Socialist Baath party and military leaders seized power in Mar. 1963. The Baath, a pan-Arab organization, became the only legal party. The government has been dominated by members of the minority Alawite sect.

In the Arab-Israeli war of June 1967, Israel seized and occupied the Golan Heights area inside Syria, from which Israeli settlements had for years been shelled by Syria.

Syria aided Palestinian guerrillas fighting Jordanian forces in Sept. 1970 and, after a renewal of that fighting in July 1971, broke off relations with Jordan. But by 1975 the 2 countries had entered a military coordination pact.

On Oct. 6, 1973, Syria joined Egypt in an attack on Israel. Arab oil states agreed in 1974 to give Syria $1 billion a year to aid anti-Israel moves. Military supplies used or lost in the 1973 war were replaced by the USSR in 1974. Some 30 000 Syrian troops entered Lebanon in 1976 to mediate in a civil war, and fought Palestinian guerrillas and, later, fought Christian militiamen. Syrian troops again battled Christian forces in Lebanon, Apr. 1981, ending a ceasefire that had been in place.

Following the June 6, 1982 Israeli invasion of Lebanon, Israeli planes destroyed 17 Syrian antiaircraft missile batteries in the Bekka Valley, June 9. Some 25 Syrian planes were downed during the engagement. Syrian and Israeli troops exchanged fire in central Lebanon. Israel and Syria agreed to a ceasefire June 11. In 1983, Syria backed the PLO rebels who ousted Yasir Arafat's forces from Tripoli.

In Feb. 1982, an uprising by antigovernment Moslem brotherhood militants brought heavy fighting and caused some 5 000 deaths.

Syria has taken a radical stance in Arab and Middle Eastern affairs. It has led opposition to Arab-Israeli peace initiatives, maintained close ties to Libya and the USSR, and supports Iran in the Gulf war.

Syria's role in promoting acts of international terrorism led to the breaking of diplomatic relations with Great Britain and the implementation of limited sanctions by the European Communities in 1986.

Taiwan
Republic of China
Chung-hua Min-kuo

People: Population (1989 est.): 20 283 000. **Age distrib.** (%): 0-14: 29.6; 15-59: 53.2; 60+: 8.1 **Pop. density:** 564.1 per sq. km. **Ethnic groups:** Taiwanese 85%, Chinese 14%. **Languages:** Mandarin Chinese (official), Taiwan, Hakka dialects. **Religions:** Buddhism, Taoism, Confucianism prevail.
Geography: Area: 35 959 sq. km. **Location:** Off SE coast of

China, between E. and S. China Seas. **Neighbors:** Nearest is China. **Topography:** A mountain range forms the backbone of the island; the eastern half is very steep and craggy, the western slope is flat, fertile, and well-cultivated. **Capital:** Taipei. **Cities** (1986): Taipei 2 534 000; Kaohsiung 1 309 000; Taichung 682 000; Tainan 642 000.
Government: Type: One-party system. **Head of state and Nationalist Party Chmn.:** Pres. Lee Teng-hui; b. Jan. 15, 1923; in office: Jan. 14, 1988. **Head of government:** Prime Min. Yu Kuo-hwa; in office: May 20, 1984. **Local divisions:** 16 counties, 5 cities, Taipei and Kao-Hsiung. **Defence:** 7% of GNP (1987).
Economy: Industries: Textiles, clothing, electronics, processed foods, chemicals, plastics. **Chief crops:** Rice, bananas, pineapples, sugarcane, sweet potatoes, peanuts. **Minerals:** Coal, limestone, marble. **Crude oil reserves** (1987): 10 mln. bbls. **Arable land:** 25%. **Livestock** (1985): pigs: 6.6 mln. **Fish catch** (1985): 1.0 mln. metric tons. **Electricity prod.** (1986): 54.0 bln. kwh. **Crude steel prod.** (1986): 5.5 mln. metric tons. **Labor force:** 17% agric.; 41% ind. & comm.; 42% services.
Finance: Currency: New Taiwan dollar (June 1988: 28.60 = $1 US). **Gross national product** (1986): $72.6 bln. **Per capita income** (1984): $3 000. **Imports** (1986): $24.2 bln.; partners: U.S. 23%, Jap. 27%, Kuw. 6%, Saudi Ar. 10%. **Exports** (1986): $39.8 bln.; partners: U.S. 49%, Jap. 10%, Hong Kong 6%. **Tourists** (1985): $963 mln. receipts. **National budget** (1988): $15.6 bln. **Consumer prices** (change in 1986): 0.7%.
Transport: Motor vehicles: in use (1986): 1.0 mln. passenger cars, 439 000 commercial vehicles. **Civil Aviation** (1986): 12.2 bln. passenger-km; 2.5 mln. net ton-km. **Chief ports:** Kao-Hsiung, Keelung, Hualien, Taichung.
Communications: Television sets: 6 mln. in use (1986). **Radios:** 13 mln. in use (1986). **Telephones in use** (1985): 4.2 mln. **Daily newspaper circ.** (1984): 259 per 1 000 pop.
Health: Life expectancy at birth (1985): 70.8 male; 75.8 female. **Births** (per 1 000 pop. 1986): 15.9. **Deaths** (per 1 000 pop. 1986): 4.9. **Natural increase** (1986): 1.1%. **Physicians** (1985): 16 931. **Hospital beds** (1986): 70 806. **Infant mortality** (per 1 000 live births 1986): 0.7.
Education (1988): **Literacy:** 90%. Years compulsory 9; attendance 99%.

Large-scale Chinese immigration began in the 17th century. The island came under mainland control after an interval of Dutch rule, 1620-62. Taiwan (also called Formosa) was ruled by Japan 1895-1945. Two million Kuomintang supporters fled to Taiwan in 1949. Both the Taipei and Beijing governments consider Taiwan an integral part of China. Taiwan has rejected Beijing's efforts at reunification but unofficial dealings with the mainland are growing.

Land reform, government planning, foreign aid and investment, and free universal education have brought huge advances in industry, agriculture, and mass living standards. In 1987, martial law was lifted after 38 years.

The Penghu (Pescadores), 130 sq. km, pop. 120 000, lie between Taiwan and the mainland. **Quemoy** and **Matsu**, pop. (1980) 61 000 lie just off the mainland.

Tanzania
United Republic of Tanzania
Jamhuri ya Mwungano wa Tanzania

People: Population (1989 est.) 24 746 000. **Pop. density:** 26.2 per sq. km. **Urban** (1987): 18%. **Ethnic groups:** African. **Languages:** Swahili, English (both official). **Religions:** Moslem 35%, Christian 30%, traditional beliefs 35%.
Geography: Area: 944 982 sq. km. **Location:** On coast of E. Africa. **Neighbors:** Kenya, Uganda on N, Rwanda, Burundi, Zaire on W, Zambia, Malawi, Mozambique on S. **Topography:** Hot, arid central plateau, surrounded by the lake region in the W, temperate highlands in N and S, the coastal plains. Mt. Kilimanjaro, 5 895 m, is highest in Africa. **Capital:** Dar-es-Salaam. **Cities** (1986): Dar-es-Salaam 1.4 mln.
Government: Type: Republic. **Head of state:** Pres. Ali Hassan Mwinyi; b. May 8, 1925; in office: Nov. 5, 1985. **Head of government:** Prime Min. Joseph Warioba. **Local divisions:** 25 regions (20 on mainland). **Defence:** 3.4% of GNP (1985).

Economy: Industries: Food processing, clothing. **Chief crops:** Sisal, cotton, coffee, tea, tobacco. **Minerals:** Diamonds, gold, nickel. **Other resources:** Hides. **Arable land:** 16%. **Livestock** (1985): cattle: 14 mln.; goats: 6.4 mln.; sheep : 4.1 mln. **Fish catch** (1985): 272 000 metric **Electricity prod.** (1985): 870 mln. kwh. **Labor force:** 85% agric., 15% ind., comm. & govt.

Finance: Currency: Shilling (Mar. 1988: 93.73 = $1 US). **Gross national product** (1985): $5.8 bln. **Per capita income** (1984): $200. **Imports** (1986): $868 mln. ; partners: UK 14%, Jap. 12%, W. Ger. 10%. **Exports** (1986): $343 mln.; partners: W. Ger. 15%, UK 13%. **Tourists** (1984): $13 mln. receipts. **National budget** (1985): $1.0 bln. expenditures. **International reserves less gold** (Jan. 1988): $248 mln. **Consumer prices** (change in 1987): 29.9%.

Transport: Motor vehicles: in use (1984): 84 000 passenger and comm. vehicles. **Chief ports:** Dar-es-Salaam, Mtwara, Tanga.

Communications: Radios: 2 mln. in use (1986). **Telephones in use** (1985): 113 000. **Daily newspaper circ.** (1984): 5 per 1 000 pop.

Health: Life expectancy at birth (1986): 52 yrs. **Births** (per 1 000 pop. 1984): 49. **Deaths** (per 1 000 pop. 1985): 16.0. **Natural increase** (1985): 3.3%. **Hospital beds** (1984): 22 800. **Physicians** (1984): 1 065. **Infant mortality** (per 1 000 live births 1986): 110.

Education (1987): **Literacy:** 85%. Attendance: 87%.

Major International Organizations: UN and all of its specialized agencies, OAU, Commonwealth of Nations.

Canadian High Commission: Pan African Insurance Bldg., Samora Machel Ave.; Postal: P.O. Box 1022, Dar-es-Salaam; Tel: 20651, -2, -3.

The Republic of Tanganyika in E. Africa and the island Republic of Zanzibar, off the coast of Tanganyika, joined into a single nation, the United Republic of Tanzania, Apr. 26, 1964. Zanzibar retains internal self-government.

Tanganyika. Arab colonization and slaving began in the 8th century AD; Portuguese sailors explored the coast by about 1500. Other Europeans followed.

In 1885 Germany established German East Africa of which Tanganyika formed the bulk. It became a League of Nations mandate and, after 1946, a UN trust territory, both under Britain. It became independent Dec. 9, 1961, and a republic within the Commonwealth a year later.

In 1967 the government set on a socialist course; it nationalized all banks and many industries. The government also ordered that Swahili, not English, be used in all official business. Nine million people have been moved into cooperative villages.

Tanzania exchanged invasion attacks with Uganda, 1978-79. Tanzanian forces drove Idi Amin from Uganda, Mar., 1979.

Zanzibar, the Isle of Cloves, lies 37 km off the coast of Tanganyika; its area is 167 sq. km. The island of **Pemba,** 40 km to the NE, area 988 sq. km, is included in the administration. The total population (1985 est.) is 571 000.

Chief industry is the production of cloves and clove oil of which Zanzibar and Pemba produce the bulk of the world's supply.

Zanzibar was for centuries the centre for Arab slave-traders. Portugal ruled for 2 centuries until ousted by Arabs around 1700. Zanzibar became a British Protectorate in 1890; independence came Dec. 10, 1963. Revolutionary forces overthrew the Sultan Jan. 12, 1964. The new government ousted Western diplomats and newsmen, slaughtered thousands of Arabs, and nationalized farms. Union with Tanganyika followed, 1964. The ruling parties of Tanganyika and Zanzibar were united in 1977, as political tension eased.

Thailand
Kingdom of Thailand
Muang Thai or Prathet Thai

People: Population (1989 est.): 55 017 000. **Age distrib.** (%): 0–14: 36.2; 15–59: 58.1; 60+: 5.7. **Pop. density:** 107.0 per sq. km. **Urban** (1985): 20%. **Ethnic groups:** Thai 84%, Chinese 12%, others 11%. **Languages:** Thai, regional dialects. **Religions:** Buddhist 95%, Moslem 4%.

Geography: Area: 513 961 sq. km. **Location:** On Indochinese and Malayan Peninsulas in S.E. Asia. **Neighbors:** Burma on W. Laos on N, Cambodia on E, Malaysia on S. **Topography:** A plateau dominates the NE third of Thailand, dropping to the fertile alluvial valley of the Chao Phraya R. in the centre. Forested mountains are in N, with narrow fertile valleys. The southern peninsula region is covered by rain forests. **Capital:** Bangkok. **Cities** (1980 est.): Bangkok (met.): 4.7 mln.

Government: Type: Constitutional monarchy. **Head of state:** King Bhumibol Adulyadej; b. Dec. 5, 1927; in office: June 9, 1946. **Head of government:** Prime Min. Prem Tinsulanond; b. 1920; in office: Mar. 3, 1980. **Local divisions:** 73 provinces. **Defence:** 4.2% of GNP (1985).

Economy: Industries: Textiles, mining, wood products. **Chief crops:** Rice (a major export), corn tapioca, sugarcane. **Minerals:** Antimony, tin (among largest producers), tungsten, iron, gas. **Other resources:** Forests (teak is exported), rubber. **Arable land:** 38%. **Livestock** (1985): cattle: 4.8 mln.; pigs: 4.2 mln. **Fish catch** (1983): 2.2 mln. metric tons. **Electricity prod.** (1986): 24.0 bln. kwh. **Labor force:** 59% agric.; 26% ind. & comm.; 10% serv.; 7% govt.

Finance: Currency: Baht (Mar. 1988: 25.15 = $1 US). **Gross national product** (1986): $40 bln. **Per capita income** (1986): $771. **Imports** (1986): $9.1 bln.; partners: Jap. 24%, U.S. 13%, Saudi Ar. 13%. **Exports** (1986): $8.7 bln.; partners: Jap. 14%, U.S. 13%, Sing. 14%. **Tourists** (1985): $1.1 mln. receipts. **National budget** (1988): $9.4 bln. **International reserves less gold** (Mar. 1988): $4.5 bln. **Gold:** 2.47 mln. oz t. **Consumer prices** (change in 1987): 2.5%.

Transport: Railway traffic (1986): 9.2 bln. passenger-km; 2.5 bln. net ton-km. **Motor vehicles:** in use (1983): 411 000 passenger cars, 789 000 comm. vehicles. **Civil aviation** (1986): 11.2 bln. passenger-km; 485 mln. freight ton-km. **Chief ports:** Bangkok, Sattahip.

Communication: Television sets: 3 mln. in use (1985). **Radios:** 7.7 mln. in use (1985). **Telephones in use** (1985): 754 000. **Daily newspaper circ.** (1985): 50 per 1 000 pop.

Health: Life expectancy at birth (1986): 61.3 male; 67.3 female. **Births** (per 1 000 pop. 1986): 25.3. **Deaths** (per 1 000 pop. 1986): 7.4. **Natural increase** (1986): 1.7%. **Hospital beds** (1984): 80 000. **Physicians** (1984): 8 058. **Infant mortality** (per 1 000 live births 1985): 51.

Education (1988): **Literacy:** 89%. **Years compulsory:** 6; attendance 96%.

Major International Organizations: UN (GATT, World Bank).

Canadian Embassy: Boonmitr Bldg., 11th fl., 138 Silom Rd., P.O. Box 2090, Bangkok 10500; Tel: 234-1561, -8.

Thais began migrating from southern China in the 11th century. Thailand is the only country in SE Asia never taken over by a European power, thanks to King Mongkut and his son King Chulalongkorn who ruled from 1851 to 1910, modernized the country, and signed trade treaties with both Britain and France. A bloodless revolution in 1932 limited the monarchy.

Japan occupied the country in 1941. After the war, Thailand followed a pro-West foreign policy.

The military took over the government in a bloody 1976 coup. Kriangsak Chomanan, prime minister resigned, Feb. 1980, under opposition over soaring inflation, oil price increases, labor unrest and growing crime.

Vietnamese troops have crossed the border and been repulsed by Thai forces in the 1980s.

Togo
Republic of Togo
République Togolaise

People: Population (1986 est.): 3 423 000. **Age distrib.** (%): 0-14: 49.8; 15-59: 44.6; 60+:5.6.**Pop. density:** 61.1 per sq. km. **Urban** (1981): 15.2%. **Ethnic groups:** Ewe 35%, Mina 6%, Kabye 22%. **Languages:** French (official), others. **Religions:** Traditional 58%, Christian 22%, Moslem 20%.

Geography: Area: 55 997 sq. km. **Location:** On S coast of W. Africa. **Neighbors:** Ghana on W, Burkina Faso on N, Benin on E. **Topography:** A range of hills running SW-NE splits Togo into 2 savanna plains. **Capital:** Lomé. **Cities** (1985 est.): Lomé 300 000.

Government: Type: Republic; one-party presidential regime. **Head of state:** Pres. Gnassingbe Eyadema; b. Dec. 26, 1937; in office: Apr. 14, 1967. **Local divisions:** 21 prefectures.

Economy: Industries: Textiles, shoes. **Chief crops:** Coffee, cocoa, yams, manioc, millet, rice. **Minerals:** Phosphates. **Arable land:** 26%. **Electricity prod.** (1986): 203 mln. kwh. **Labor force:** 67% agric.; 15% industry.

Finance: Currency: CFA franc (Mar. 1988: 281 = $1 US). **Gross national product** (1985): $696 mln. **Per capita income** (1985): $240. **Imports** (1985): $262 mln.; partners: Fr., U.K., W. Ger. **Exports** (1985): $242 mln.; partners: Neth., Fr., W. Ger. **International reserves less gold** (Jan. 1988): $348.5 mln. **Gold:** 13 000 oz t. **Consumer prices** (change in 1986): 4.1%.

Transport: Railway traffic (1981): 84.5 mln. passenger-km; 37.7 mln. net ton-km. **Motor vehicles** in use (1984): 36 000 passenger cars, 17 000 comm. vehicles. **Chief ports:** Lome.

Communications: Radios: 250 000 in use (1986). **Telephones in use** (1983): 11 000. **Daily newspaper circ.** (1986): 3 per 1 000 pop.

Health: Life expectancy at birth (1984): 47 yrs. **Births** (per 1 000 pop. 1985): 48. **Deaths** (per 1 000 pop. 1985): 17. **Natural increase** (1985): 3.1%. **Hospital beds** (1982): 3 655. **Physicians** (1985): 230. **Infant mortality** (per 1 000 live births 1985): 107.

Education (1985): **Literacy:** 45% (males).

Major International Organizations: UN (GATT, IMF), OAU.

Canadian Embassy: c/o The Canadian High Commission, P.O. Box 1639, Accra, Ghana.

The Ewe arrived in southern Togo several centuries ago. The country later became a major source of slaves. Germany took control in 1884. France and Britain administered Togoland as UN trusteeships. The French sector became the republic of Togo Apr. 27, 1960.

The population is divided between Bantus in the S and Hamitic tribes in the N. Togo has actively promoted regional integration, as a means of stimulating the economy.

Tonga
Kingdom of Tonga
Pule 'anga Tonga

People: Population (1989 est.): 108 000. **Age distrib.** (%): 0–14: 44.4; 15–59: 50.5; 60+:5.1. **Pop. density:** 154.5 per sq. km. **Ethnic groups:** Tongan 98%, other Polynesian, European. **Languages:** Tongan, English. **Religions:** Free Wesleyan 47%, Roman Catholic 14%, Free Church of Tonga 14%, Mormon 9%, Church of Tonga 9%.

Geography: Area: 699 sq. km. **Location:** In western S. Pacific O. **Neighbors:** Nearest is Fiji, on W, New Zealand, on S. **Topography:** Tonga comprises 169 volcanic and coral islands, 45 inhabited. **Capital:** Nuku'alofa. **Cities** (1986): Nuku'alofa (met.) 29 000.

Government: Type: Constitutional monarchy. **Head of state:** King Taufa'ahau Tupou IV; b. July 4, 1918; in office: Dec. 16, 1965. **Head of government:** Prime Min. Fatafehi Tu'ipelehake; b. Jan. 7, 1922; in office: Dec. 16, 1965. **Local divisions:** 3 island districts.

Economy: Industries: Tourism. **Chief crops:** Coconut products, bananas are exported. **Other resources:** Fish. **Arable land:** 77%. **Electricity prod.** (1986): 18 mln. kwh. **Labor force:** 51% agric, 22% services.

Finance: Currency: Pa'anga (Jan. 1988: 1.40 = $1 US). **Gross national product** (1985): $100 mln. **Imports** (1985): $41 mln.; partners: N Z 37%, Austral. 31%, Jap. 6%, Fiji 7%. **Exports** (1985): $7 mln.; partners: Aust. 36%, N Z 34%.

Transport: Motor vehicles: in use (1983): 443 passenger cars, 1 300 comm. vehicles. **Chief ports:** Nuku'alofa.

Communications: Radios: 65 000 in use (1985). **Telephones in use** (1984): 3 996.

Health: Births (per 1 000 pop. 1985): 28. **Deaths** (per 1 000 pop. 1985): 8. **Natural increase** (1985): 2.0%. **Infant mortality** (per 1 000 live births 1985): 45.

Education (1985): **Literacy:** 93%. **Years compulsory:** 8. **Attendance:** 77%.

Canadian High Commission: c/o P.O. Box 12-049, Wellington North, New Zealand.

The islands were first visited by the Dutch in the early 17th century. A series of civil wars ended in 1845 with establishment of the Tupou dynasty. In 1900 Tonga became a British protectorate. On June 4, 1970, Tonga became independent and a member of the Commonwealth.

Trinidad and Tobago
Republic of Trinidad and Tobago

People: Population (1989 est.): 1 261 000. **Age distrib.** (%): 0–14: 32.9; 15–59: 58.7; 60+: 8.4. **Pop. density:** 245.9 per sq. km. **Ethnic groups:** African 43%, East Indian 40%, mixed 14%. **Language:** English (official). **Religions:** Roman Catholic 36%, Protestant 14%, Hindu 24%, Moslem 6%.

Geography: Area: 5 128 sq. km. **Location:** Off eastern coast of Venezuela. **Neighbors:** Nearest is Venezuela on SW. **Topography:** Three low mountain ranges cross Trinidad E-W, with a well-watered plain between N and Central Ranges. Parts of E and W coasts are swamps. Tobago, 302 sq. km, lies 32 km NE. **Capital:** Port-of-Spain. **Cities** (1986 est.): Port-of-Spain 57 000; San Fernando 32 000.

Government: Type: Parliamentary democracy. **Head of state:** Pres. Ellis E. I. Clarke; b. Dec. 28, 1917; in office: July 31, 1976. **Head of government:** Prime Min. A.N.R. Robinson; in office: Dec. 18, 1986. **Local divisions:** 7 counties, Tobago, 4 cities.

Economy: Industries: Oil products, rum, cement, tourism. **Chief crops:** Sugar, cocoa, coffee, citrus fruits, bananas. **Minerals:** Asphalt, oil, **Crude oil reserves** (1987): 567 mln. bbls. **Arable land:** 30%. **Electricity prod.** (1986): 2.7 bln. kwh. **Labor force:** 7% agric., 32% construction, mining, commerce, 47% services.

Finance: Currency: Dollar (Mar. 1988: 3.60 = $1 US). **Gross national product** (1986): $7.8 bln. **Per capita income** (1982): $6 800. **Imports** (1986): $1.3 bln.; partners: U.S. 37%, UK 11%. **Exports** (1986): $1.3 bln.; partners: U.S. 62%. **National budget** (1985): $3.0 bln. expenditures. **International reserves less gold** (Mar. 1988): $148 mln. **Gold:** 54 000 oz t. **Consumer prices** (change in 1986): 7.7%.

Transport: Motor vehicles: in use (1986): 241 000 passenger cars, 82 000 comm. vehicles. **Civil aviation:** (1986): 2.1 bln. passenger-km; 12.5 mln. freight ton-km. **Chief ports:** Port-of-Spain.

Communications: Television sets: 345 000 in use (1986). **Radios:** 552 000 licensed (1986). **Telephones in use** (1984): 109 000. **Daily newspaper circ.** (1984): 151 per 1 000 pop.

Health: Life expectancy at birth (1985): 67.8 male; 72.6 female. **Births** (per 1 000 pop. 1985): 27. **Deaths** (per 1 000 pop. 1985): 7. **Natural increase** (1985): 2.0%. **Hospital beds** (1985): 4 087. **Physicians** (1985): 1 103. **Infant mortality** (per 1 000 pop. 1985): 221.

Education (1984): **Literacy:** 96%. **Years compulsory:** 8.

Major International Organizations: UN (GATT, IMF, WHO), Commonwealth of Nations, OAS.

Canadian High Commission: Huggins Bldg., 72 South Quay, P.O. Box 1246, Port of Spain; Tel: 62-34787, 62-37254, -8.

Columbus sighted Trinidad in 1498. A British possession since 1802, Trinidad and Tobago won independence Aug. 31, 1962. It became a republic in 1976. The People's National Movement party has held control of the government since 1956.

The nation is one of the most prosperous in the Caribbean. Oil production has increased with offshore finds. Middle Eastern oil is refined and exported, mostly to the U.S.

Tunisia
Republic of Tunisia
al Jumhuriyah at-Tunisiyah

People: Population (1989 est.): 7 930 000. **Age distrib.** (%) 0–14: 39.2; 15–59: 54.1; 60+: 6.7. **Pop. density:** 48.5 per sq.

km. **Ethnic groups:** Arab 98%. **Languages:** Arabic (official), French. **Religion:** Moslem 99%.

Geography: Area: 163 598 sq. km. **Location:** On N coast of Africa. **Neighbors:** Algeria on W, Libya on E. **Topography:** The N is wooded and fertile. The central coastal plains are given to grazing and orchards. The S is arid, approaching Sahara Desert. **Capital:** Tunis. **Cities** (1984 est.) Tunis 1 000 000, Sfax 475 000.

Government: Type: Republic. **Head of state:** Pres. Gen. Zine al-Abidine Ben Ami; b. Sept. 3, 1936; in office: July 25, 1957. **Head of government:** Prime Min. Hedi Baccouche; in office: Nov. 17, 1987. **Local divisions:** 21 governorates. **Defence:** 3.2% of GNP (1984).

Economy: Industries: Food processing, textiles, oil products, construction materials, tourism. **Chief crops:** Grains, dates, olives, citrus fruits, figs, vegetables, grapes. **Minerals:** Phosphates, iron, oil, lead, zinc. **Crude oil reserves** (1987): 1.7 bln. bbls. **Arable land:** 30%. **Livestock** (1985): sheep: 5.4 mln.; goats 1 mln. **Fish catch** (1985): 93 000 metric tons. **Electricity prod.** (1984): 3.7 bln. kwh. **Crude steel prod.** (1982): 106 000 metric tons. **Labor force:** 35% agric.; 22% industry; 11% serv.

Finance: Currency: Dinar (Mar. 1988: .80 = $1 US). **Gross national product** (1985): $8.3 bln. **Per capita income** (1986) $1 163. **Imports** (1987): $3.0 bln.; partners: Fr. 26%, It. 12%. **Exports** (1987): $2.1 bln.; partners: It. 17%, Fr. 26%, W. Ger. 10%, U.S. 19%. **Tourists** (1985): $551 mln. receipts. **National budget** (1986): $3.3 bln. expenditures. **International reserves less gold** (Mar. 1988): $394.2 mln. **Gold:** 187 000 oz t. **Consumer prices** (change in 1987): 7.2%.

Transport: Railway traffic (1986): 756 mln. passenger-km; 1.8 bln. net ton-km. **Motor vehicles:** in use (1985): 174 000 passenger cars, 141 000 comm. vehicles; **Civil aviation** (1984): 1.5 bln. passenger-km; 18.3 mln. freight ton-km. **Chief ports:** Tunis, Sfax, Bizerte.

Communications: Television sets: 400 000 in use (1986). **Radios:** 1.1 mln. in use (1986). **Telephones in use** (1985): 297 000. **Daily newspaper circ.** (1986): 36 per 1 000 pop.

Health: Life expectancy at birth (1985): 60.1 male; 61.1 female. **Births** (per 1 000 pop. 1986): 31.1. **Deaths** (per 1 000 pop. 1986): 8.7. **Natural increase** (1985): 2.4%. **Hospital beds** (1986): 15 838. **Physicians** (1986): 3 453. **Infant mortality** (per 1 000 pop. live births 1985): 53.4

Education (1985): **Literacy:** 46%. **Years compulsory:** 8; attendance 85%.

Major International Organizations: UN, Arab League, OAU.

Canadian Embassy: 3, rue du Sénégal, Place Palestine, Tunis; Postal: C.P. 31, Belvédrè, Tunis. Tel: 286-577, -337.

Site of ancient Carthage, and a former Barbary state under the suzerainty of Turkey, Tunisia became a protectorate of France under a treaty signed May 12, 1881. The nation became independent Mar. 20, 1956, and ended the monarchy the following year. Habib Bourguiba has headed the country since independence.

Although Tunisia is a member of the Arab League, Bourguiba in the 1960s urged negotiations to end Arab-Israeli disputes and was denounced by other members.

Tunisia survived a Libyan-engineered raid against the southern mining centre of Gafsa, Jan. 1980.

Turkey
Republic of Turkey
Turkiye Cumhuriyeti

People: Population (1989 est.): 55 377 000. **Age distrib. (%):** 0–14: 38.5; 15–59: 54.9; 60+: 6.6. **Pop. density:** 70.9 per sq. km. **Urban** (1987): 55%. **Ethnic groups:** Turkish 85%, Kurdish 12%. **Languages:** Turkish (official), Kurdish, Arabic. **Religion:** Moslem 98%.

Geography: Area: 780 517 sq. km. **Location:** Occupies Asia Minor, between Mediterranean and Black Seas. **Neighbors:** Bulgaria, Greece on W, USSR (Georgia, Armenia) on N, Iran on E, Iraq, Syria on S. **Topography:** Central Turkey has wide plateaus, with hot, dry summers and cold winters. High mountains ring the interior on all but W, with more than 20 peaks over

3 000 m. Rolling plains are in W; mild, fertile coastal plains are in S, W. **Capital:** Ankara. **Cities** (1988 est.): Istanbul 5 800 000; Ankara 1 700 000; Izmir 2 300 000; Adana 1 700 000.

Government: Type: Republic. **Head of state:** Pres. Kenan Evren; b. 1918; in office: Oct. 27, 1980. **Head of government:** Prime Min. Turgut Ozal; b. 1927; in office: Dec. 13, 1983. **Local divisions:** 67 provinces, with appointed governors. **Defence:** 4.5% of GNP (1986).

Economy: Industries: Iron, steel, machinery, metal prods., cars, processed foods. **Chief crops:** Tobacco (6th largest producer), cereals, cotton, barley, corn, fruits, potatoes, sugar beets. **Minerals:** Antimony, chromium, mercury, borate, copper, coal. **Crude oil reserves** (1987): 139 mln. bbls. **Other resources:** Wool, silk, forests. **Arable land:** 34%. **Livestock** (1985): cattle: 17.4 mln.; sheep: 40.4 mln. **Fish catch** (1985): 567 000 metric tons. **Electricity prod.** (1984): 30.6 bln. kwh. **Crude steel prod.** (1986): 5.9 mln. metric tons. **Labor force:** 58% agric.; 17% ind. and comm.; 25% serv.

Finance: Currency: Lira (Mar. 1988: 1 321 = $1 US). **Gross national product** (1986): $52 bln. **Per capita income** (1986): $1 160. **Imports** (1986): $11.1 bln.; partners: W. Ger. 16%, U.S. 12%. **Exports** (1986): $7.4 bln.; partners: W. Ger. 19%, Iraq 13%, Iran 10%. **Tourists** (1986): 950 mln. receipts. **National budget** (1986): $10.7 bln. expenditures. **International reserves less gold** (Feb. 1988): $1.7 bln. **Gold:** 3.8 mln. oz t. **Consumer prices** (change in 1986): 34.6%.

Transport: Railway traffic (1985): 6.8 bln. passenger-km; 7.7 bln. net ton-km. **Motor vehicles:** in use (1985): 856 000 passenger cars, 553 000 comm. vehicles. **Civil aviation** (1986): 2.6 bln. passenger-km; 45 mln. freight ton-km. **Chief ports:** Istanbul, Izmir, Mersin, Samsun.

Communications: Television sets: 5 mln. in use (1986). **Radios:** 8.2 mln. in use (1986). **Telephones in use** (1986): 2.7 mln.

Health: Life expectancy at birth (1985): 57 years. **Births** (per 1 000 pop. 1985): 33.6. **Deaths** (per 1 000 pop. 1985): 9.3. **Natural increase** (1985): 2.4%. **Hospital beds** (1985): 106 000. **Physicians** (1985): 36 427. **Infant mortality** (per 1 000 live births 1988): 12.3.

Education (1988): **Literacy:** 70%. **Years compulsory:** 8; attendance 95%.

Major International Organizations: UN (GATT, WHO, IMF), NATO, OECD.

Canadian Embassy: Nenehatun Caddesi No. 75, Gaziosmanpasa, Ankara; Tel: 136-1275.

Ancient inhabitants of Turkey were among the worlds first agriculturalists. Such civilizations as the Hittite, Phrygian, and Lydian flourished in Asiatic Turkey (Asia Minor), as did much of Greek civilization. After the fall of Rome in the 5th century, Constantinople was the capital of the Byzantine Empire for 1 000 years. It fell in 1453 to Ottoman Turks, who ruled a vast empire for over 400 years.

Just before World War I, Turkey, or the Ottoman Empire, ruled what is now Syria, Lebanon, Iraq, Jordan, Israel, Saudi Arabia, Yemen, and islands in the Aegean Sea.

Turkey joined Germany and Austria in World War I and its defeat resulted in loss of much territory and fall of the sultanate. A republic was declared Oct. 29, 1923. The Caliphate (spiritual leadership of Islam) was renounced 1924.

Long embroiled with Greece over Cyprus, off Turkey's south coast, Turkey invaded the island July 20, 1974, after Greek officers seized the Cypriot government as a step toward unification with Greece. Turkey sought a new government for Cyprus, with Greek Cypriot and Turkish Cypriot zones.

Religious and ethnic tensions and active left and right extremists have caused endemic violence. Martial law, imposed in 1978, was lifted in 1984. The military formally transferred power to an elected parliament in 1983.

Tuvalu

People: Population (1989 est.): 9 000. **Pop. density:** 346.2 per sq. km. **Ethnic group:** Polynesian. **Languages:** Tuvaluan, English. **Religion:** mainly Protestant.

Geography: Area: 26 sq. km. **Location:** 9 islands forming a NW-SE chain 580 km long in the SW Pacific O. **Neighbors:**

Nearest are Samoa on SE, Fiji on S. **Topography:** The islands are all low-lying atolls, nowhere rising more than 4.5 m above sea level, composed of coral reefs. **Capital:** Funafuti (pop. 1985): 2 800.

Government: Head of state: Queen Elizabeth II, represented by Gov.-Gen. Tupua Leupena; in office: Mar. 1, 1986. **Head of government:** Prime Min. Tomasi Puapua; in office: Sept. 8, 1981. **Local divisions:** 8 island councils on the permanently inhabited islands.

Economy: Industries: Copra. **Chief crops:** Coconuts. **Labor force:** Approx. 1 500 Tuvaluans work overseas in the Gilberts' phosphate industry, or as overseas seamen.

Finance: Currency: Australian dollar.

Transport: Chief port: Funafuti.

Health: (including former Gilbert Is.) **Life expectancy at birth** (1979): 57 male; 60 female. **Births** (per 1 000 pop. 1985): 27. **Deaths** (per 1 000 pop. 1985): 11. **Natural increase** (1985): 1.6%. **Infant mortality** (per 1 000 live births 1985): 35.

Education: Literacy (1985): 96%.

Canadian High Commission: c/o The Canadian High Commission, P.O. Box 12-049, Wellington North, New Zealand.

The Ellice Islands separated from the British Gilbert and Ellice Islands colony, 1975, and became independent Tuvalu Oct. 1, 1978.

Britain and New Zealand provide extensive economic aid.

Uganda

Republic of Uganda

People: Population (1989 est.): 16 811 000. **Age distrib.** (%): 0–14: 48.5%; 15–59: 47.3%; 60+: 4.2. **Pop. density:** 69.5 per sq. km. **Urban** (1980): 8.1%. **Ethnic groups:** Bantu, Nilotic, Nilo-Hamitic, Sudanic tribes. **Languages:** English (official), Luganda, Swahili. **Religions:** Christian 63%, Moslem 6%, traditional beliefs.

Geography: Area: 241 768 sq. km. **Location:** In E. Central Africa. **Neighbors:** Sudan on N, Zaire on W, Rwanda, Tanzania on S, Kenya on E. **Topography:** Most of Uganda is a high plateau 915-1 900 m high, with high Ruwenzori range in W (Mt. Margherita 5 105 m), volcanoes in SW, NE is arid, W and SW rainy. Lakes Victoria, Edward, Albert form much of borders. **Capital:** Kampala. **Cities** (1988): Kampala 331 000.

Government: Type: Military. **Head of state:** Pres. Yoweri Kaguta Museveni; b. 1944; in office: Jan. 29, 1986. **Head of government:** Prime Min. Samson Kisekka; in office: Jan. 3, 1986. **Local divisions:** 10 provinces, 34 districts. **Defence:** 1% of GNP (1983).

Economy: Chief Crops: Coffee, cotton, tea, corn, bananas, sugar. **Minerals:** Copper, cobalt. **Arable land:** 32%. **Meat prod.** (1984): cattle: 5.2 mln.; goats: 2.5 mln.; sheep: 1.3 mln. **Fish catch** (1983): 172 000 metric tons. **Electricity prod.** (1986): 287 mln. kwh. **Labor force:** 90% agric.

Finance: Currency: Shilling (Mar. 1988: 60.00 = $1 US). **Gross national product** (1984): $6.2 bln. **Per capita income** (1976): $240. **Imports** (1985): $323 mln.; partners: Kenya 39%, U.K. 17%. **Exports** (1985): $352 mln.; partners: U.S. 27%, U.K. 9%. **National budget** (1981): $641 mln. revenues; $871 mln. expenditures.

Transport: Motor vehicles: in use (1985): 32 000 passenger cars, 11 000 comm. vehicles.

Communications: Television sets: 90 000 in use (1986). **Radios:** 600 000 in use (1986). **Telephones in use** (1983): 55 000. **Daily newspaper circ.** (1984): 2 per 1 000 pop.

Health: Life expectancy at birth (1985): 49.0 male; 53.0 female. **Births** (per 1 000 pop. 1985): 48. **Deaths** (per 1 000 pop. 1985): 17. **Natural increase** (1985): 3.1%. **Hospital beds** (1983): 19 650. **Physicians** (1983): 665. **Infant mortality** (per 1 000 live births 1985): 113.

Education (1980): **Literacy:** 52%. About 50% attend primary school.

Major International Organizations: UN (GATT, WHO, IMF), OAU, Commonwealth of Nations.

Canadian High Commission: c/o P.O Box 30481, Nairobi, Kenya.

Britain obtained a protectorate over Uganda in 1894. The country became independent Oct. 9, 1962, and a republic within the Commonwealth a year later. In 1967, the traditional kingdoms, including the powerful Buganda state, were abolished and the central government strengthened.

Gen. Idi Amin seized power from Prime Min. Milton Obote in 1971. As many as 300 000 of his opponents were reported killed in subsequent years. Amin was named president for life in 1976.

In 1972 Amin expelled nearly all of Uganda's 45 000 Asians. In 1973 the U.S., Canada, and Norway ended economic aid programs.

A June 1977 Commonwealth conference condemned the Amin government for its "disregard for the sanctity of human life."

Amid worsening economic and domestic crises, Uganda's troops exchanged invasion attacks with long-standing foe Tanzania, 1978 to 1979. Tanzanian forces, coupled with Ugandan exiles and rebels, ended the dictatorial rule of Amin, Apr. 11, 1979.

Union of Soviet Socialist Republics

Soyuz Sovetskykh Sotsialisticheskikh Respublic

People: Population (1989 est.): 287 015 000. **Age distrib.** (%): 0–19: 24.8; 20-59: 62.2; 60+: 13.0. **Pop. density:** 12.8 per sq. km. **Urban** (1986): 66%. **Ethnic groups:** Russian 52% Ukrainian 16%, Uzbek 5%, Byelorussian 4%, many others. **Languages:** Slavic (Russian, Ukrainian, Byelorussian, Polish), Altaic (Turkish, etc.), other Indo-European, Uralian, Caucasian. **Religions:** Russian Orthodox 31%, Moslem 11%, Non-religious or atheist 51%.

Geography: Area: 22 400 464 sq. km. **Location:** Stretches from E. Europe across N Asia to the Pacific O. **Neighbors:** Finland, Poland, Czechoslovakia, Hungary, Norway, Romania on W, Turkey, Iran, Afghanistan, China, Mongolia, N. Korea on S. **Topography:** Covering one-sixth of the earth's land area, the USSR contains every type of climate except the distinctly tropical, and has a varied topography.

The European portion is a low plain, grassy in S, wooded in N with Ural Mtns. on the E. Caucasus Mts. on the S. Urals stretch N-S for 4 025 km. The Asiatic portion is also a vast plain, with mountains on the S and in the E; tundra covers extreme N, with forest belt below; plains, marshes are in W, desert in SW. **Capital:** Moscow. **Cities** (1986 est.): Moscow 8.7 mln.; Leningrad 4.9 mln.; Kiev 2.4 mln.; Tashkent 2.0 mln.; Kharkov 1.5 mln.; Baku 1.7 mln.; Gorky 1.4 mln.; Novosibirsk 1.4 mln.; Minsk 1.5 mln.; Kuibyshev 1.2 mln.; Sverdlovsk 1.3 mln.

Government: Type: Federal Union. **Head of state:** Pres. Andrei Gromyko; b. July 18, 1909; in office: July 27, 1985. **Head of government:** Premier Nikolai I. Ryzhkov; b. 1929; in office: Sept. 27, 1985. **Head of Communist Party:** Mikhail Sergeyvich Gorbachev; b. Mar. 2, 1931; in office: Mar. 11, 1985. **Local divisions:** 15 union republics, within which are 20 autonomous republics, 6 krays (territories), 123 oblasts (regions), 8 autonomous oblasts. **Defence:** 12-15% of GNP (1987).

Economy: Industries: Steel, machinery, machine tools, vehicles, chemicals, cement, textiles, appliances, paper. **Chief crops:** Grain, cotton, sugar beets, potatoes, vegetables, sunflowers. **Minerals:** Iron, manganese, mercury, potash, antimony, bauxite, cobalt, chromium, copper, coal, gold, lead, molybdenum, nickel, phosphates, silver, tin, tungsten, zinc, oil (59%), potassium salts. **Crude oil reserves** (1987): 60 bln. bbls. **Other resources:** Forests (25% of world reserves). **Arable land:** 11%. **Livestock** (1987): cattle: 121 mln.; sheep: 147 000 mln.; pigs: 65 mln. **Fish catch** (1987): 10.7 mln. metric tons. **Electricity prod.** (1986): 1 600 bln. kwh. **Crude steel prod.** (1986): 161 mln. metric tons. **Labor force:** 19% agric.; 29% industry, 26% services.

Finance: Currency: Ruble (Jan. 1988: 1.00 = $1.69 US). **Gross national product** (1985): $734 bln. **Per capita income** (1987): $3 000. **Imports** (1985): $82.9 bln.; partners: E. Ger. 10%, Pol. 7%, Czech. 8%, Bulg. 8%. **Exports** (1985): $86.9 bln.; partners: E. Ger. 10%, Pol. 8%, Bulg. 8%, Czech. 8%. **National budget** (1982): $350 bln. **Tourists** (1984): 7.2 mln.

Transport: Railway traffic (1986): 390 bln. passenger-km; 3.718 bln. net ton-km. **Motor vehicles:** in use (1980): 9.2 mln. passenger cars, 7.9 mln. comm. vehicles; manuf. (1982): 1.3

mln. passenger cars; 874 000 comm. vehicles. **Civil aviation** (1986): 196 bln. passenger-km; 3.3 bln. freight ton-km. **Chief ports:** Leningrad, Odessa, Murmansk, Kaliningrad, Archangelsk, Riga, Vladivostok.

Communications: Television sets: 82 mln. in use (1986). **Radios:** 182 mln. in use (1986). **Telephones in use** (1986): 31.1 mln. **Daily newspaper circ.** (1984): 726 per 1 000 pop.

Health: Life expectancy at birth (1986): 64.0 male; 73.0 female. **Births** (per 1 000 pop. 1986): 19.6. **Deaths** (per 1 000 pop. 1986): 9.7. **Natural increase** (1986): 0.9%. **Hospital beds** (1987): 3.6 mln. **Physicians** (1987): 1.2 mln. **Infant mortality** (per 1 000 live births 1985): 31.

Education (1985): **Literacy:** 99%. Most receive 11 years of schooling.

Major International Organizations: UN (ILO, UNESCO, WHO), Warsaw Pact.

Canadian Embassy: 23 Starokonyushenny Pereulok, Moscow; 241-9155, 241-3067, 241-5070.

The USSR is a federation consisting of 15 union republics, the largest being the Russian Soviet Federated Socialist Republic. Important positions in the republics are filled by centrally chosen appointees, often ethnic Russians.

Beginning in 1939 the USSR by means of military action and negotiation overran contiguous territory and independent republics, including all or part of Lithuania, Latvia, Estonia, Poland, Czechoslovakia, Romania, Germany, Finland, Tannu Tuva, and Japan. The union republics are:

Republic	Area sq. km	Pop. (1985 est.)
Russian SFSR	17 074 033	144 080 000
Ukrainian SSR	603 682	50 994 000
Uzbek SSR	447 458	18 487 000
Kazakh SSR	2 717 218	16 023 000
Byelorussian SSR	207 702	10 008 000
Azerbaijan SSR	86 499	6 708 000
Georgian SSR	69 694	5 234 000
Tadzhik SSR	139 898	4 648 000
Moldavian SSR	33 698	4 147 000
Kirghiz SSR	198 487	4 051 000
Lithuanian SSR	67 782	3 603 000
Armenian SSR	29 280	3 362 000
Turkmen SSR	487 962	3 270 000
Latvian SSR	63 955	2 622 000
Estonian SSR	45 096	1 542 000

The **Russian Soviet Federated Socialist Republic** contains over 50% of the population of the USSR and includes 76% of its territory. It extends from the old Estonian, Latvian, and Finnish borders and the Byelorussian and Ukrainian lines on the W, to the shores of the Pacific, and from the Arctic on the N to the Black and Caspian seas and the borders of Kazakh SSR, Mongolia, and Manchuria on the S. Siberia encompasses a large part of the RSFSR area. Capital: Moscow.

Parts of eastern and western Siberia have been transformed by steel mills, huge dams, oil and gas industries, electric railroads, and highways.

The **Ukraine,** the most densely populated of the republics, borders on the Black Sea, with Poland, Czechoslovakia, Hungary, and Romania on the W and SW. Capital: Kiev.

The Ukraine contains the arable black soil belt, the chief wheat-producing section of the Soviet Union. Sugar beets, potatoes, and livestock are important.

The Donets Basin has large deposits of coal, iron and other metals. There are chemical and machine industries and salt mines.

Byelorussia (White Russia). Capital: Minsk. Chief industries include machinery, tools, appliances, tractors, clocks, cameras, steel, cement, textiles, paper, leather, glass. Main crops are grain, flax, potatoes, sugar beets.

Azerbaijan boasts near Baku, the capital, important oil fields. Its natural wealth includes deposits of iron ore, cobalt, etc. A high-yield winter wheat is grown, as are fruits. It produces iron, steel, cement, fertilizers, synthetic rubber, electrical and chemical equipment. It borders on Iran and Turkey.

In 1988, clashes were reported between Moslem Azerbaijanis and the minority Christian ethnic Armenians.

Georgia, in the western part of Transcaucasia, contains the largest manganese mines in the world. There are rich timber resources and coal mines. Basic industries are food, textiles, iron, steel. Grain, tea, tobacco, fruits, grapes are grown. Capital: Tbilisi (Tiflis). Despite massive party and government purges since 1972, illegal private enterprise and Georgian nationalist feelings persist; attempts to repress them have led to violence.

Armenia is mountainous, sub-tropical, extensively irrigated. Copper, zinc, aluminum, molybdenum, and marble are mined. Instrument making is important. Armenia has sought a reunification with the Nagorno-Karabkh autonomous region of neighboring Azerbaijan. Capital: Erevan.

Uzbekistan, most important economically of the Central Asia republics, produces 67% of USSR cotton, 50% of rice, 33% of silk, 34% of astrakhan, 85% of hemp. Industries include iron, steel, cars, tractors, TV and radio sets, textiles, food. Mineral wealth includes coal, sulphur, copper, and oil. Capital: Tashkent.

Turkmenistan in Central Asia, produces cotton, maize, carpets, chemicals. Minerals: oil, coal, sulphur, barite, lime, salt, gypsum. The Kara Kum desert occupies 80% of the area. Capital: Ashkhabad.

Tadzhikistan borders on China and Afghanistan. Over half the population are Tadzhiks, mostly Moslems, speaking an Iranian dialect. Chief occupations are farming and cattle breeding. Cotton, grain, rice, and a variety of fruits are grown. Heavy industry, based on rich mineral deposits, coal and hydroelectric power, has replaced handicrafts. Capital: Dushanbe.

Kazakhstan extends from the lower reaches of the Volga in Europe to the Altai Mtns. on the Chinese border. It has vast deposits of coal, oil, iron, tin, copper, lead, zinc, etc. Fish for its canning industry are caught in Lake Balkhash and the Caspian and Aral seas. The capital is Alma-Ata. About 50% of the population is Russian or Ukrainian, working in the virgin-grain lands opened up after 1954, and in the growing industries. Capital: Alma-Ata.

Kirghizia is the eastern part of Soviet Central Asia, on the frontier of Xinjiang, China. The people breed cattle and horses and grow tobacco, cotton, rice, sugar beets. Industries include machine and instrument making, chemicals. Capital: Frunze.

Moldavia, in the SW part of the USSR, is a fertile black earth plain bordering Romania and includes Bessarabia. It is an agricultural region that grows grains, fruits, vegetables, and tobacco. Textiles, wine, food and electrical equipment industries have been developed. Capital: Kishinev. The region was taken from Romania in 1940; the people speak Romanian.

Lithuania, on the Baltic, produces cattle, hogs, electric motors, and appliances. The capital is Vilnius (Vilna). **Latvia** on the Baltic and the Gulf of Riga, has timber and peat resources est. at 3 bln. tons. In addition to agricultural products it produces rubber goods, dyes, fertilizers, glassware, telephone apparatus, TV and radio sets, railroad cars. Capital: Riga.

Estonia, also on the Baltic, has textiles, shipbuilding, timber, roadmaking and mining equipment industries and a shale oil refining industry. Capital: Tallinn. The 3 Baltic states were provinces of imperial Russia before World War I, were independent nations between World Wars I and II, but were conquered by Russia in 1940.

Economy. Almost all legal economic enterprises are state-owned.

The USSR is incalculably rich in natural resources; distant Siberian reserves are being exploited with Japanese assistance. Its heavy industry is 2d largest in the world. It leads the world in oil and steel production. Consumer industries have lagged comparatively. Agricultural output has expanded, but in poor crop years the USSR has been forced to make huge grain purchases from the West. Shortages and rationing of basic food products periodically occur.

Industrial growth has dropped, due to shortfalls in oil, coal, and steel industries.

History. Slavic tribes began migrating into Russia from the W in the 5th century AD. The first Russian state, founded by Scandinavian chieftains, was established in the 9th century, centring in Novgorod and Kiev.

In the 13th century the Mongols overran the country. It recovered under the grand dukes and princes of Muscovy, or Moscow, and by 1480 freed itself from the Mongols. Ivan the Terrible was the first to be formally proclaimed Tsar (1547). Peter the Great (1682-1725), extended the domain and in 1721, founded the Russian Empire.

Western ideas and the beginnings of modernization spread through the huge Russian empire in the 19th and early 20th centuries. But political evolution failed to keep pace.

Military reverses in the 1905 war with Japan and in World War I led to the breakdown of the Tsarist regime. The 1917 Revolution began in March with a series of sporadic strikes for higher wages by factory workers. A provisional democratic government under Prince Georgi Lvov was established but was quickly followed in May by the second provisional government, led by Alexander Kerensky. The Kerensky government and the freely-elected Constituent Assembly were overthrown in a communist coup led by Vladimir Ilyich Lenin Nov. 7.

Lenin's death Jan. 21, 1924, resulted in an internal power struggle from which Joseph Stalin eventually emerged the absolute ruler of Russia. Stalin secured his position at first by exiling opponents, but from the 1930s to 1953, he resorted to a series of "purge" trials, mass executions, and mass exiles to work camps. These measures resulted in millions of deaths, according to most estimates.

Germany and the USSR signed a non-aggression pact Aug. 1939; Germany launched a massive invasion of the Soviet Union, June 1941. Notable heroic episode was the "900 days" siege of Leningrad, lasting to Jan. 1944, and causing a million deaths; the city was never taken. Russian winter counterthrusts, 1941-42 and 1942-43, stopped the German advance. Turning point was the failure of German troops to take and hold Stalingrad, Sept. 1942 to Feb. 1943. With British and U.S. Lend-Lease aid and sustaining great casualties, the Russians drove the German forces from eastern Europe and the Balkans in the next 2 years.

After Stalin died, Mar. 5, 1953, Nikita Khrushchev was elected first secretary of the Central Committee. In 1956 he condemned Stalin. "De-Stalinization" of the country on all levels was effected after Stalin's body was removed from the Lenin-Stalin tomb in Moscow.

Under Khrushchev the open antagonism of Poles and Hungarians toward domination by Moscow was brutally suppressed in 1956. He advocated peaceful co-existence with the capitalist countries, but kept apace of the U.S. in arming the USSR with nuclear weapons. He aided the Cuban revolution under Fidel Castro but withdrew Soviet missiles from Cuba during confrontation by U.S. Pres. Kennedy, Sept.-Oct. 1962.

Khrushchev was suddenly deposed, Oct. 1964, and replaced as party first secretary by Leonid I. Brezhnev.

In Aug. 1968 Russian, Polish, East German, Hungarian, and Bulgarian military forces invaded Czechoslovakia to put a curb on liberalization policies of the Czech government.

The USSR in 1971 continued heavy arms shipments to Egypt. In July 1972 Egypt ordered most of the 20 000 Soviet military personnel in that country to leave. When Egypt and Syria attacked Israel in Oct. 1973, the USSR launched huge arms airlifts to the 2 Arab nations. In 1974, the Soviet replenished the arms used or lost by the Syrians in the 1973 war, and continued some shipments to Egypt.

Massive Soviet military assistance aided North Vietnam in the late 1960s and early 1970s. Soviet arms aid and advisers were sent to several African countries in the 1970s, including Algeria, Angola, Somalia, and Ethiopia.

More than 130 000 Jews and over 40 000 ethnic Germans were allowed to emigrate from the USSR in the 1970s, following pressure from the West. Many leading figures in the arts also left the country.

In 1979, Soviet forces entered Afghanistan to support that government against rebels. In 1988, the Soviets announced the withdrawal of their troops.

There were serious food shortages reported in the early 1980s and a new agricultural program, covering 1982-90, was announced amid Soviet fears of becoming dependent on foreign grain imports.

The USSR drew international condemnation on Sept. 1, 1983 when it shot down a Korean 747 commercial airliner, killing 269. The airliner had strayed off course. The Soviets led the Eastern bloc boycott of the 1984 Los Angeles Olympics.

Mikhail Gorbahev was chosen Gen. Secty. of the Communist Party Mar. 1985. He was the youngest member of the Politburo and signalled a change in the attitudes of Soviet leadership. In 1987, Gorbachev initiated a program of reforms, including expanded freedoms and democratization of the political process, and increased openess (*glasnost*).

In June 1988, the first Soviet Communist Party conference since 1941 was held to deal with the economic, political and social reforms initiated by Gorbachev.

The Soviets received worldwide criticism for their secrecy regarding the Apr. 25, 1986 accident at the Chernobyl nuclear plant.

Soviet leader Gorbachev held summit meetings with U.S. Pres. Reagan in 1985, 1986 and in 1987 in Washington, at which time the two powers signed an agreement to ban intermediate-range nuclear weapons.

Government. The Communist Party leadership dominates all areas of national life. A Politburo of 14 full members and 8 candidate members makes all major political, economic, and foreign policy decisions. Party membership in 1978 was reported to be over 16 000 000.

United Arab Emirates
Ittihād al-Imarat al-Arabiyah

People: Population (1989 est.): 1 455 000. **Pop. density:** 17.6 per sq. km. **Ethnic groups:** Arab, Iranian, Pakistani, Indian. **Languages:** Arabic (official), Farsi, English, Hindi, Urdu. **Religions:** Moslem 94%, Christian, Hindu.

Geography: Area: 82 874 sq. km. **Location:** On the S shore of the Persian Gulf. **Neighbors:** Qatar on N, Saudi Ar. on W, S, Oman on E. **Topography:** A barren, flat coastal plain gives way to uninhabited sand dunes on the S. Hajar Mtns. are on E. **Capital:** Abu Dhabi. **Cities** (1984 est.): Abu Dhabi 537 000; Dubai 278 000.

Government: Type: Federation of emirates. **Head of state:** Pres. Zaid ibn Sultan an-Nahayan b. 1923; in office: Dec. 2, 1971. **Head of government:** Prime Min. Rashid ibn Said al-Maktum; in office: June 25, 1979. **Local divisions:** 7 autonomous emirates: Abu Dhabi, Ajman, Dubai, Fujaira, Ras al-Khaimah, Sharjah, Umm al-Qaiwain. **Defense:** 7.4% of GNP (1984).

Economy: Chief crops: Vegetables, dates, limes. **Minerals:** Oil. **Crude oil reserves** (1987): 33 bln. bbls. **Arable land:** 1%. **Electricity prod.** (1986): 5.1 bln. kwh. **Labor force:** 5% agric.; 85% ind. and commerce; 5% serv.; 5% govt.

Finance: Currency: Dirham (Apr. 1988: 3.67 = $1 US). **Gross national product** (1984): $28 bln. **Per capita income** (1983 est.) $23 000. **Imports** (1986): $6.6 bln.; partners: Jap. 18%, UK 11%, W. Ger. 6%. **Exports** (1986): $19.8 bln.; partners: Jap. 36%, U.S. 7%, Fr. 10%. **International reserves less gold** (Feb. 1988): $4.7 bln. **Gold:** 817 000 oz t.

Transport: Chief ports: Dubai, Abu Dhabi.

Communications: Radios: 434 000 in use (1986). **Telephones in use** (1984): 308 000.

Health: Life Expectancy at Birth (1985): 61.6 male, 65.6 female. **Hospital beds** (1984): 4 853. **Physicians** (1984): 1 840.

Education (1985): **Literacy:** 56%. **Years Compulsory:** ages 6-12.

Major International Organizations: UN (World Bank, IMF, ILO), Arab League, OPEC.

Canadian Embassy: c/o P.O. Box 25281, 13113 (SAFAT) Kuwait City, Kuwait.

The 7 "Trucial Sheikdoms" gave Britain control of defense and foreign relations in the 19th century. They merged to become an independent state Dec. 2, 1971.

The Abu Dhabi Petroleum Co. was fully nationalized in 1975. Oil revenues have given the UAE one of the highest per capita GNPs in the world. International banking has grown in recent years.

United Kingdom of Great Britain and Northern Ireland

People: Population (1989 est.): 56 648 000. **Age distrib.** (%): 0–14: 18.8; 15–59: 60.4; 60+: 20.8. **Pop. density:** 232.2 per sq. km. **Urban** (1985): 92.5%. **Ethnic groups:** English 81.5%, Scottish 9.6%, Irish 2.4, Welsh 1.9%, Ulster 1.8%; West Indian, Indian, Pakistani over 2%; others. **Languages:** English, Welsh spoken in western Wales; Gaelic. **Religions:** Church of England, Roman Catholic.

Geography: Area: 244 026 sq. km. **Location:** Off the NW coast of Europe, across English Channel, Strait of Dover, and North Sea. **Neighbors:** Ireland to W, France to SE. **Topography:** England is mostly rolling land, rising to Uplands of southern Scotland; Lowlands are in centre of Scotland, granite Highlands are in N. Coast is heavily indented, especially on W. British Isles have milder climate than N Europe, due to the Gulf Stream, and ample rainfall. Severn, 254 km, and Thames, 346 km, are longest rivers. **Capital:** London. **Cities** (1986 est.): London 6 700 000; Birmingham 1 008 000; Glasgow 733 000; Leeds 710 000; Sheffield 542 000; Liverpool 492 000; Manchester 451 000; Edinburgh 440 000; Bradford 463 000; Bristol 394 000.

Government: Type: Constitutional monarchy. **Head of state:** Queen Elizabeth II; b. Apr. 21, 1926; in office: Feb. 6, 1952. **Head of government:** Prime Min. Margaret Thatcher; b. Oct. 13, 1925; in office: May 4, 1979. **Local divisions:** England and Wales: 47 non-metro counties, 6 metro counties, Greater London; Scotland: 9 regions, 3 island areas; N. Ireland: 26 districts. **Defence:** 5.3% of GDP (1985).

Economy: Type: Industries: Steel, metals, vehicles, shipbuilding, shipping, banking, insurance, textiles, chemicals, electronics, aircraft, machinery, distilling. **Chief crops:** Grains, sugar beets, fruits, vegetables. **Minerals:** Coal, tin, oil, gas, limestone, iron, salt, clay, chalk, gypsum, lead, silica. **Crude oil reserves** (1987): 5.8 bln. bbls. **Livestock** (1985): cattle: 12.6 mln.; pigs: 7.9 mln.; sheep: 25.5 mln. **Fish catch** (1985): 746 000 metric tons. **Electricity prod.** (1986): 312 bln. kwh. **Crude steel prod.** (1986): 14.8 mln. metric tons. **Labor force:** 1.7% agric.; 26% manuf. & eng., 64% services.

Finance: Currency: Pound (June 1988: .55 = $1 US). **Gross national product** (1985): $453 bln. **Per capita income** (1979): $7 216. **Imports** (1987): $154.4 bln.; partners: W. Ger. 13%, U.S. 12%, Fr. 7%, Neth. 8%. **Exports** (1987): $131.2 bln.; partners: U.S. 13%, W. Ger. 10%, Fr. 8%, Neth. 8%. **Tourists** (1985): receipts: $6.2 bln.; **National budget** (1986): $232 bln. expenditures. **International reserves less gold** (Mar. 1988): $41.4 bln. **Gold:** 19.01 mln. oz t. **Consumer prices** (change in 1987): 4.2%.

Transport: Railway traffic (1985): 30.2 bln. passenger-km; 12.7 bln. net ton-km. **Motor vehicles:** in use (1985): 16 mln. passenger cars, 2.7 mln. comm. vehicles. **Civil aviation** (1985): 51.6 bln. passenger-km; 1.5 bln. freight ton-km. **Chief ports:** London, Liverpool, Glasgow, Southampton, Cardiff, Belfast.

Communications: Television sets: 18.7 mln. licensed (1986). **Radios:** 63 mln. licensed (1986). **Telephones in use** (1984): 29 mln. **Daily newspaper circ.** (1984): 538 per 1 000 pop.

Health: Life expectancy at birth: (1983): 70.2 male; 76.2 female. **Births:** (per 1 000 pop. 1986): 13.3. **Deaths:** (per 1 000 pop. 1986): 12.2. **Natural increase:** (1986): 0.1%. **Hospital beds** (1985): 419 000. **Physicians** (1985): 84 700. **Infant mortality:** (per 1 000 live births 1985): 10.

Education (1987): **Literacy:** 99%. **Years compulsory:** 12; attendance 99%.

Major International Organizations: UN all of and its specialized agencies, NATO, EC, OECD.

Canadian High Commission: Macdonald House, 1 Grosvenor Sq., London, WIX OAB, England; Tel: (01) 629-9492.

The United Kingdom of Great Britain and Northern Ireland comprises England, Wales, Scotland, and Northern Ireland.

Queen and Royal Family. The ruling sovereign is Elizabeth II of the House of Windsor, born Apr. 21, 1926, elder daughter of King George VI. She succeeded to the throne Feb. 6, 1952, and was crowned June 2, 1953. She was married Nov. 20, 1947, to Lt. Philip Mountbatten, born June 10, 1921, former Prince of

Greece. He was created Duke of Edinburgh, Earl of Merioneth, and Baron Greenwich, and given the style H.R.H., Nov. 19, 1947; he was given the title Prince of the United Kingdom and Northern Ireland Feb. 22, 1957. Prince Charles Philip Arthur George, born Nov. 14, 1948, is the Prince of Wales and heir apparent. His son, William Philip Arthur Louis, born June 21, 1982, is second in line to the throne.

Parliament is the legislative governing body for the United Kingdom, with certain powers over dependent units. It consists of 2 houses: The **House of Lords** includes 763 hereditary and 314 life peers and peeresses, certain judges, 2 archbishops and 24 bishops of the Church of England. Total membership is over 1 000. The **House of Commons** has 635 members, who are elected by direct ballot and divided as follows: England 516; Wales 36; Scotland 71; Northern Ireland 12.

Resources and Industries. Great Britain's major occupations are manufacturing and trade. Metals and metal-using industries contribute more than 50% of the exports. Of about 60 million acres of land in England, Wales and Scotland, 46 million are farmed, of which 17 million are arable, the rest pastures.

Large oil and gas fields have been found in the North Sea. Commercial oil production began in 1975. There are large deposits of coal.

The railroads, nationalized since 1948, have been reduced in total length, with a basic network, Dec. 1978, of 17 797 km. The merchant marine totaled 126 000 gross registered tons in 1982.

A year-long coal strike costing some $3 bln. ended March 1985. The issue of the closing of uneconomic mines was unresolved.

Britain imports all of its cotton, rubber, sulphur, 80% of its wool, half of its food and iron ore, also certain amounts of paper, tobacco, chemicals. Manufactured goods made from these basic materials have been exported since the industrial age began. Main exports are machinery, chemicals, woollen and synthetic textiles, clothing, autos and trucks, iron and steel, locomotives, ships, jet aircraft, farm machinery, drugs, radio, TV, radar and navigation equipment, scientific instruments, arms, whisky.

Religion and Education. The Church of England is Protestant Episcopal. The Queen is its temporal head, with rights of appointments to archbishoprics, bishoprics, and other offices. There are 2 provinces, Canterbury and York, each headed by an archbishop. Most famous church is Westminster Abbey (1050-1760), site of coronations, tombs of Elizabeth I, Mary of Scots, kings, poets, and of the Unknown Warrior.

The most celebrated British universities are Oxford and Cambridge, each dating to the 13th century. There are about 40 other universities.

History. Britain was part of the continent of Europe until about 6000 BC, but migration of peoples across the English Channel continued long afterward. Celts arrived 2 500 to 3 000 years ago. Their language survives in Welsh and Gaelic enclaves.

England was added to the Roman Empire in 43 AD. The Romans built camps, forts and roads throughout the land and also built Hadrian's Wall as protection against the invasion of the warlike Picts of Scotland. Trade flourished and Christianity was brought to Britain. After the withdrawal of Roman legions in 410, waves of Jutes, Angles, and Saxons arrived from German lands. They contended with Danish raiders for control from the 8th through 11th centuries.

The last successful invasion was by French speaking Normans, led by William, Duke of Normandy, who became William the Conqueror, after defeating the Saxon King Harold in the Battle of Hastings in 1066. William the Conqueror established a strong central government, appointing Norman noblemen to high positions. In time, the Norman and Anglo-Saxon languages and customs merged.

Opposition by nobles to improper use of royal authority forced King John to sign the Magna Carta in 1215, a guarantee of rights and the rule of law. In the ensuing decades, the foundations of the parliamentary system were laid when Edward I called meetings with leading nobles and churchmen. In 1295 the meeting he called was known as the Model Parliament and in 1297 Edward agreed that the Parliament had the right to approve or disapprove taxes proposed by the King.

English dynastic claims to large parts of France led to the Hundred Years War, 1338-1453, and the defeat of England. A long civil war, the War of the Roses, between the House of Lancaster (whose emblem was a white rose) and the House of York (whose emblem was a red rose) lasted 1455-85, and ended with the establishment of the powerful Tudor monarchy. A distinct English civilization flourished. The economy prospered over long periods of domestic peace unmatched in continental Europe. Religious independence from Rome was secured when the Church of England was separated from the authority of the Pope in 1534 by King Henry VIII.

Under Queen Elizabeth I, England became a major naval power, leading to the founding of colonies in the new world and the expansion of trade with Europe and the Orient. In 1588 England defeated the Spanish Armada, a large but cumbersome fleet sent by King Phillip II of Spain to conquer England, and this, together with the explorations carried out by Sir Francis Drake and Sir Walter Raleigh, helped establish her supremacy on the seas. Scotland was united with England when James VI of Scotland was crowned James I of England in 1603.

A struggle between Parliament and the Stuart kings led to a bloody civil war, 1642-49. The country was divided between supporters of Charles I, who wished to rule absolutely, and were known as *Royalists* or *Cavaliers*, and supporters of Parliament, who wanted to limit the King's power and were known as *Roundheads*. Charles did not allow Parliament to meet between 1629 and 1640, and when Parliament did meet in 1640 Charles refused to bow to Parliament's edict that it would only grant him funds if he agreed to limitations of his power. The Puritan leader Oliver Cromwell led his army to a series of victories and established a republic. King Charles I was beheaded. The monarchy was restored in 1660, but the "Glorious Revolution" of 1688 confirmed the sovereignty of Parliament; a Bill of Rights was granted 1689.

In the 18th century, parliamentary rule was strengthened. Technological and entrepreneurial innovations led to the Industrial Revolution. The 13 North American colonies were lost, but replaced by growing empires in Canada and India. Britain's role in the defeat of Napoleon, 1815, strengthened its position as the leading world power.

The extension of the franchise in 1832 and 1867, the formation of trade unions, and the development of universal public education were among the drastic social changes which accompanied the spread of industrialization and urbanization in the 19th century. Large parts of Africa and Asia were added to the empire during the reign of Queen Victoria, 1837-1901.

Though victorious in World War I, Britain suffered huge casualties and economic dislocation. Ireland became independent in 1921, and independence movements became active in India and other colonies.

The country suffered major bombing damage in World War II, but held out against Germany after the fall of France in 1940.

Industrial growth continued in the postwar period, but Britain lost its leadership position to other powers. Labor governments passed programs nationalizing some basic industries and expanding social security. The Thatcher government has however, tried to increase the role of private enterprise. In 1987, Margaret Thatcher became the first British leader in 160 years to be elected to a 3d consecutive term as prime minister.

Britain broke diplomatic relations with Libya, Apr. 22, 1984, 5 days after a policewoman was killed and 10 Libyan exile demonstrators wounded by machine-gun fire from within the Libyan embassy in London. The embassy occupants, including the killer, left Britain, Apr. 27.

Britain joint the NATO alliance and in 1973, the European Communities (Common Market).

Wales

The Principality of Wales in western Britain has an area of 20 768 sq. km and a population (1986 est.) of 2 821 000. Cardiff is the capital, pop. (1981 cen.) 273 856.

Early Anglo-Saxon invaders drove Celtic peoples into the mountains of Wales, terming them Waelise (Welsh, or foreign). There they developed a distinct nationality. Members of the ruling house of Gwynedd in the 13th century fought England but were crushed, 1283. Edward of Caernarvon, son of Edward I of England, was created Prince of Wales, 1301.

England and Wales are administered as a unit. Less than 20% of the population of Wales speak both English and Welsh; about 32 000 speak Welsh solely. Welsh nationalism is advocated by a segment. A 1979 referendum rejected, 4-1, the creation of an elected Welsh Assembly.

Scotland

Scotland, a kingdom now united with England and Wales in Great Britain, occupies the northern 37% of the main British island, and the Hebrides, Orkney, Shetland and smaller islands. Length 443 km, width 241 km, area, 78 743 sq. km, population (1986 est.) 5 121 000.

The Lowlands, a belt of land approximately 100 km wide from the Firth of Clyde to the Firth of Forth, divides the farming region of the Southern Uplands from the granite Highlands of the North, contain 75% of the population and most of the industry. The Highlands, famous for hunting and fishing, have been opened to industry by many hydroelectric power stations.

Edinburgh, pop. (1983 est.) 440 000, is the capital. Glasgow, pop. (1983 est.) 751 000, is Britain's greatest industrial centre. It is a shipbuilding complex on the Clyde and an ocean port. Aberdeen, pop. (1981 cen.) 190 200, NE of Edinburgh, is a major port, centre of granite industry, fish processing, and North Sea oil exploitation. Dundee, pop. (1981 cen.) 174 746, NE of Edinburgh, is an industrial and fish processing centre. About 90 000 persons speak Gaelic as well as English.

History. Scotland was called Caledonia by the Romans who battled early Pict and Celtic tribes and occupied southern areas from the 1st to the 4th centuries. Missionaries from Britain introduced Christianity in the 4th century; St. Columba, an Irish monk, converted most of Scotland in the 6th century.

The Kingdom of Scotland was founded in 1018. William Wallace and Robert Bruce both defeated English armies 1297 and 1314, respectively.

In 1603 James VI of Scotland, son of Mary, Queen of Scots, succeeded to the throne of England as James I, and effected the Union of the Crowns. In 1707 Scotland received representation in the British Parliament, resulting from the union of former separate Parliaments. Its executive in the British cabinet is the Secretary of State for Scotland. The growing Scottish National Party urges independence. A 1979 referendum on the creation of an elected Scotland Assembly was defeated.

There are 8 universities. Memorials of Robert Burns, Sir Walter Scott, John Knox, Mary, Queen of Scots draw many tourists, as do the beauties of the Trossachs, Loch Katrine, Loch Lomond and abbey ruins.

Industries. Engineering products are the most important industry, with growing emphasis on office machinery, autos, electronics and other consumer goods. Oil has been discovered offshore in the North Sea, stimulating on-shore support industries.

Scotland produces fine woollens, worsteds, tweeds, silks, fine linens and jute. It is known for its special breeds of cattle and sheep. Fisheries have large hauls of herring, cod, whiting. Whisky is the biggest export.

The Hebrides are a group of c. 500 islands, 100 inhabited, off the W coast. The Inner Hebrides include **Skye, Mull,** and **Iona,** the last famous for the arrival of St. Columba, 563 AD. The Outer Hebrides include **Lewis** and **Harris.** Industries include sheep raising and weaving. The **Orkney Islands,** c. 90, are to the NE. The capital is Kirkwall, on Pomona Is. Fish curing, sheep raising and weaving are occupations. NE of the Orkneys are the 200 **Shetland Islands,** 24 inhabited, home of Shetland pony. The Orkneys and Shetlands have become centres for the North Sea oil industry.

Northern Ireland

Six of the 9 counties of Ulster, the NE corner of Ireland, constitute Northern Ireland, with the parliamentary boroughs of Belfast and Londonderry. Area 14 148 sq. km, population (1986 est.) 1 568 000, capital and chief industrial centre, Belfast, (1981 cen.) 297 862.

Industries. Shipbuilding, including large tankers, has long been an important industry, centred in Belfast, the largest port. Linen manufacture is also important, along with apparel, rope, and twine. Growing diversification has added engineering products, synthetic fibers, and electronics. They are large numbers of cattle, hogs, and sheep, potatoes, poultry, and dairy foods are also produced.

Government. An act of the British Parliament, 1920, divided Northern from Southern Ireland, each with a parliament and government. When Ireland became a dominion, 1921, and later a republic, Northern Ireland chose to remain a part of the United Kingdom. It elects 12 members to the British House of Commons.

During 1968-69, large demonstrations were conducted by Roman Catholics who charged they were discriminated against in voting rights, housing, and employment. The Catholics, a minority comprising about a third of the population, demanded abolition of property qualifications for voting in local elections. Violence and terrorism intensified, involving branches of the Irish Republican Army (outlawed in the Irish Republic), Protestant groups, police, and British troops.

A succession of Northern Ireland prime ministers pressed reform programs but failed to satisfy extremists on both sides. Over 2 000 were killed in over 13 years of bombings and shootings through 1988, many in England itself. Britain suspended the Northern Ireland parliament Mar. 30, 1972, and imposed direct British rule. A coalition government was formed in 1973 when moderates won election to a new one-house Assembly. But a Protestant general strike overthrew the government in 1974 and direct rule was resumed.

The turmoil and agony of Northern Ireland was dramatized in 1981 by the deaths of 10 imprisoned Irish nationalist hunger strikers in Maze Prison near Belfast. The inmates had starved themselves to death in an attempt to achieve status as political prisoners, but the British government refused to yield to their demands. In 1985, the Hillsborough agreement gave the Rep. of Ireland a voice in the governing of Northern Ireland; the accord was strongly opposed by Ulster loyalists.

Education and Religion. Northern Ireland is 2/3 Protestant, 1/3 Roman Catholic. Education is compulsory through age 15. There are 2 universities and 24 technical colleges.

Channel Islands

The Channel Islands, area 195 sq. km, cen. pop. 1980 130 000, off the NW coast of France, the only parts of the one-time Dukedom of Normandy belonging to England, are **Jersey, Guernsey** and the dependencies of Guernsey — **Alderney, Brechou, Great Sark, Little Sark, Herm, Jethou and Lihou.** Jersey and Guernsey have separate legal existences and lieutenant governors named by the Crown. The islands were the only British soil occupied by German troops in World War II.

Isle of Man

The Isle of Man, area 590 sq. km, 1982 est. pop. 61 000, is in the Irish Sea, 32 km from Scotland, 48 km from Cumberland. It is rich in lead and iron. The island has its own laws and a lieutenant governor appointed by the Crown. The Tynwald (legislature) consists of the Legislative Council, partly elected, and House of Keys, elected. Capital: Douglas. Farming, tourism (413 000 visitors in 1982), fishing (kippers, scallops) are chief occupations. Man is famous for the Manx tailless cat.

Gibraltar

Gibraltar, a dependency on the southern coast of Spain, guards the entrance to the Mediterranean. The Rock has been in British possession since 1704. The Rock is 4.4 km long, 1.2 km wide and 419 m in height; a narrow isthmus connects it with the mainland. Est. pop. 1987, 29 048.

In 1966 Spain called on Britain to give "substantial sovereignty" of Gibraltar to Spain and imposed a partial blockade. In 1967, residents voted for remaining under Britain. A new constitution, May 30, 1969, gave an elected House of Assembly more control in domestic affairs. A UN General Assembly resolution requested Britain to end Gibraltar's colonial status by Oct. 1, 1969. No settlement has been reached.

British West Indies

Swinging in a vast arc from the coast of Venezuela NE, then N and NW toward Puerto Rico are the Leeward Islands, forming a coral and volcanic barrier sheltering the Caribbean from the open Atlantic. Many of the islands are self-governing British possessions. Universal suffrage was instituted 1951-54; ministerial systems were set up 1956-1960.

The **Leeward Islands,** are **Montserrat** (1980 pop. 11 600, area 83 sq. km, capital Plymouth), and **St. Kitts (St. Christopher)-Nevis,** 2 islands which became independent in 1983. Nearby are the small **British Virgin Islands.** (pop. 1987: 12 000).

Anguilla became independent Nov. 1, 1981.

The three **Cayman Islands,** a dependency, lie S of Cuba, NW of Jamaica. Pop. 23 000 (1987), most of it on Grand Cayman. It is a free port; in the 1970s Grand Cayman became a tax-free refuge for foreign funds and branches of many Western banks were opened there. Total area 265 sq. km, capital Georgetown.

The **Turks and Caicos Islands,** at the SE end of the Bahama Islands, are a separate possession. There are about 30 islands, only 6 inhabited, 1987 pop. est. 9 000, area 502 sq. km, capital Grand Turk. Salt, crayfish and conch shells are the main exports.

Bermuda

Bermuda is a British dependency governed by a royal governor and an assembly, dating from 1620, the oldest legislative body among British dependencies. Capital is Hamilton.

It is a group of 360 small islands of coral formation, 20 inhabited, comprising 53.6 sq. km in the western Atlantic, 928 km E of North Carolina. Pop. (1987 est.) was 57 800 (about 61% of African descent). Population density is high.

Tourism is the main industry of the island; Bermuda boasts many resort hotels,. Receipts from tourists totalled $407 mln. In 1986. The government raises most revenue from import duties.

South Atlantic

Falkland Islands and Dependencies, a British dependency, lies 400 km E of the Strait of Magellan at the southern end of South America.

The Falklands or Islas Malvinas include about 200 islands, area 12 220 sq. km, pop. (1980 est.) 1 800. Sheep-grazing is the main industry; wool is the principal export. There are indications of large oil and gas deposits. The islands are also claimed by Argentina though 97% of inhabitants are of British origin. Argentina invaded the islands Apr. 2, 1982. The British responded by sending a task force to the area, landing their main force on the Falklands, May 21, and forcing an Argentine surrender at Port Stanley, June 14. **South Georgia,** area 3 770 sq. km and the uninhabited **South Sandwich Is.** are dependencies of the Falklands.

British Antarctic Territory, south of 60° S lat., was made a separate colony in 1962 and comprises mainly the **South Shetland Islands,** the **South Orkneys** and **Graham's Land.** A chain of meteorological stations is maintained.

St. Helena, an island 1 920 km off the W coast of Africa and 2 900 km E of South America, has 122 sq. km and est. pop., 1981 of 5 300. Flax, lace and rope making are the chief industries. After Napoleon Bonaparte was defeated at Waterloo the Allies exiled him to St. Helena, where he lived from Oct. 16, 1815, to his death, May 5, 1821. Capital is Jamestown.

Tristan da Cunha is the principal of a group of islands of volcanic origin, total area 104 sq. km, half way between the Cape of Good Hope and South America. A volcanic peak 2 028 m high erupted in 1961. The 262 inhabitants were removed to England, but most returned in 1963. The islands are dependencies of St. Helena.

Ascension is an island of volcanic origin, 88 sq. km in area, 1 120 km NW of St. Helena, through which it is administered. It is a communications relay centre for Britain, and has a U.S. satellite tracking centre. Est. pop., 1976, was 1 179, half of them communications workers. The island is noted for sea turtles.

Asia and Indian Ocean

Hong Kong is a Crown Colony at the mouth of the Canton R. in China, 144 km S of Canton. Its nucleus is Hong Kong Is., 92 sq. km, acquired from China 1841, on which is located Victoria, the capital. Opposite is Kowloon Peninsula, 8 sq. km and Stonecutters Is., 0.6 sq. km, added, 1860. An additional 923 sq. km known as the New Territories, a mainland area and islands, were leased from China, 1898, for 99 years. Britain and China, Dec. 19, 1985, signed an agreement under which Hong Kong would be allowed to keep its capitalist system for 50 years after 1997, the year that the 99-year lease will expire. Total area of the colony is 1 063 sq. km, with a population, 1987 est., of

5 608 000 including fewer than 20 000 British. From 1949 to 1962 Hong Kong absorbed more than a million refugees from the mainland.

Hong Kong harbor was long an important British naval station and one of the world's great trans-shipment ports.

Principal industries are textiles and apparel;also tourism, 2.5 mln. visitors, $2.2 bln. expenditures (1986), shipbuilding, iron and steel, fishing, cement, and small manufactures.

Spinning mills, among the best in the world, and low wages compete with textiles elsewhere and have resulted in the protective measures in some countries. Hong Kong also has a booming electronics industry.

British Indian Ocean Territory was formed Nov. 1965, embracing islands formerly dependencies of Mauritius or Seychelles: the Chagos Archipelago (including Diego Garcia), Aldabra, Farquhar and Des Roches. The latter 3 were transferred to Seychelles, which became independent in 1976. Area 57 sq. km. No civilian population remains.

Pacific Ocean

Pitcairn Island is in the Pacific, halfway between South America and Australia. The island was discovered in 1767 by Carteret but was not inhabited until 23 years later when the mutineers of the Bounty landed there. The area is 47 sq. km and pop. 1983, was 61. It is a British colony and is administered by a British Representative in New Zealand and a local Council. The uninhabited islands of **Henderson, Ducie** and **Oeno** are in the Pitcairn group.

United States of America

People: Population (1989 est.): 247 498 000. **Age distrib.(%):** 0–14: 21.6; 15–59: 61.7; 60+: 16.5. **Pop. density:** 26.2 per sq. km. **Urban** (1980): 79.2%.

Geography: Area: 9 428 692 sq. km. **Location:** In southern portion of N. America. **Neighbors:** Canada on N, Mexico on S. **Topography:** Continental: central plains are bounded by Rocky and Coastal Mtns. to W, Appalachian Mtns. to E and alluvial plains around the Gulf of Mexico. **Capital:** Washington, D.C. **Cities:** (1982 est.) New York 7.0 mln; Los Angeles 3.0 mln; Chicago 2.9 mln; Houston 1.7 mln; Philadelphia 1.6 mln; Detroit 1.1 mln.

Government: Type: Republic. **Head of State:** Pres. Ronald Reagan, b. Feb. 6, 1911, in office Jan. 20, 1981. **Local divisions:** 50 states, 1 district, numerous outlying areas.

Defense: 6.4% of GNP (1984).

Economy: Minerals: Coal, copper, lead, molybdenum, phosphates, uranium, bauxite, gold, iron, mercury, nickel, potash, silver, tungsten, zinc. **Crude oil reserves** (1987): 27 bln. bbls. **Arable land:** 21%. **Livestock** (1985): cattle: 105.4 mln.; pigs: 52.2 mln.; sheep: 9.9 mln. **Fish catch** (1985): 2.8 mln. metric tons. **Electricity prod.** (1986): 2 733 bln. kwh. **Crude steel prod.** (1986): 73.7 mln. metric tons.

Finance: Gross national product (1986): $4 235 bln. **Per capita income** (1985): $13 451. **Imports** (1987): $424.0 bln.; partners: Can. 19%, Jap. 20%, Mex. 6%. **Exports** (1987): $250.4 bln.; partners: Can. 22%, Jap. 10%, Mex. 6%, UK 5%. **Tourists** (1986): receipts $12.9 bln. **International reserves less gold** (Mar. 1988): $32.1 bln. **Gold:** 262.0 mln. oz t. **Consumer prices** (change in 1987): 3.7%.

Transport: Railway traffic (1985): 15.5 bln. passenger-km; 1.3 bln. net ton-km. **Motor vehicles:** in use (1986): 135 mln. passenger cars, 40 mln. comm. vehicles. **Civil aviation** (1986): 513 bln. passenger-km; 18.4 bln. freight ton-km.

Communications: Television sets: 145 mln. in use (1985). **Radios:** 480 mln. in use (1986). **Telephones** in use (1984): 134 mln. **Daily newspaper circ.** (1984): 267 per 1 000 pop.

Health: Life expectancy at birth (1986): 71.5 male; 78.5 female. **Births** (per 1 000 pop. 1987): 15.5. **Deaths** (per 1 000 pop. 1987): 8.9. **Natural increase** (1987): 0.6%. **Hospital beds** (1985): 1.3 mln. **Physicians** (1985): 527 900. **Infant mortality** (per 1 000 live births 1986): 10.4.

Major International Organizations: UN (GATT, IMF, WHO, FAO), OAS, NATO, OECD.

Education (1987): **Literacy:** 99%.

Canadian Embassy: 1746 Massachusetts Ave., N.W., Washington, D.C. 20036-1985; Tel: (202) 785-1400.

History: As late as the 1400s, native Indians were the only inhabitants. In the early 1500s, Spaniards moved north from Mexico into what is now the SE and W United States and took control of the Florida peninsula and the land W of the Mississippi R. In 1565, they founded St. Augustine, Florida, the oldest city in the U.S. British settlements were permanently established in the north after 1600. During the 1600s and early 1700s a steady stream of colonists, mostly British but also French, Germans, Dutch, Irish and others, settled in the country, predominantly along the coast. These settlements became the 13 colonies under British rule. The French and Indian War of 1754 led to British control of all territory east of the Mississippi R. except New Orleans, which had belonged to the French, and Florida, which had continued under Spanish control. Policy changes by the British as a result of this war led to the colonial independence movement.

On July 2, 1776 the Declaration of Independence was adopted and the United States of America was formed. A Revolutionary War between the U.S. and Britain raged during the 1770s and in a decisive battle on Oct. 19, 1781 the Americans won their independence. The Treaty of Paris, 1783, officially ended the war.

The War of 1812 between the U.S. and Britain was waged along the Canadian border and in it the Americans did not win the land concessions which they had hoped to gain.

During 1776-1898 the territory of the original States was expanded through purchase of land, treaties and war. By 1898, all of the continental U.S. was established and Alaska and Hawaii were acquired. In this era of expansion, social reforms became increasingly important, especially the abolition of slavery.

By the early 1800s, slavery had been banned in the northern states but not in the South where the plantation system of farming supported the economy. Increased division over this issue led to the secession of southern states and the beginning of the Civil War (Apr. 12). This war, won by the North in 1865, took more American lives than any other, left large parts of the South in ruins and created long-lasting bitterness between the 2 regions.

Industrial growth had started in the early 1800s and large-scale mechanization took place after the Civil War. Major businesses of the time were centred around coal mining, petroleum, railways, and the manufacturing and sale of steel, industrial machinery and clothing. Urbanization was a major trend, particularly in the North. U.S. military strength was also established.

The first full-scale American military mobilization on foreign soil was not until 1917 when the U.S. entered World War I against Germany and helped turn the tide in favor of France and England. U.S. President Woodrow Wilson helped negotiate a peace treaty (1918) and, in the war's aftermath, proposed a League of Nations.

The "Roaring Twenties" brought large-scale, though uneven, economic growth until the Great Depression was triggered by the stock market crash of 1929. For the next decade, unemployment was high and poverty widespread. The Depression lasted until the beginning of World War II. As with the first World War, the U.S. entered several years after the start of the conflict but made a major contribution to the Allied victory. War was declared against Japan, Dec. 8, 1941, immediately following the attack on Pearl Harbor, and against Germany and Italy, Dec. 11. Germany surrendered May 7, 1945, but the war against Japan continued. President Harry Truman ordered the atomic bomb dropped on Hiroshima (Aug. 6) and on Nagasaki 3 days later. Japan surrendered Sept. 2.

The "Cold War" period following World War II saw increasing mistrust between the U.S. and Soviet Union as the Soviets expanded into eastern Europe and encouraged Communist takeover elsewhere while the U.S. tried to contain its spread. In the Korean War (1950-1953), the U.S. successfully helped South Korea defend itself against Communist forces from North Korea. The early 1950s was also a time of internal U.S. "witch hunts" against suspected Communist sympathizers, led by Senator Joseph McCarthy who was later discredited.

The post-war period was a time of economic expansion and further movement of the population from rural areas to the cities. The U.S. continued as a world leader in scientific, medical and technological achievements. Although the Soviet Union was first to put a man in space, the U.S. took the lead in the "space race" in 1969 when, on July 20, U.S. astronaut Neil Armstrong became the first man to walk on the moon.

Th 1960s saw tremendous social change and unrest. American blacks demanded an end to racial discrimination through the civil rights movement; there were protest marches in the South and riots in the cities of the North; civil rights leader Martin Luther King was assassinated in Memphis in 1968. The assasinations of President John Kennedy (1963) and Robert Kennedy (1968) also shocked the world. The Vietnam War brought further internal strife as the nation's population became divided over U.S. involvement in the conflict.

Unrest continued into the 1970s with the political corruption revealed by the Watergate Scandal and the resulting resignation of President Richard Nixon, the first U.S. president to be forced from office. Continued involvement in Vietnam led to increasing protests; U.S. troops were finally withdrawn in 1975 and, shortly afterwards, North Vietnam invaded and took over South Vietnam. Crime and violence in U.S. cities continued during the 1970s and pollution of the environment became an increasing concern.

Economic issues have dominated the 1980s, which began with high unemployment, high inflation and slow economic growth. By the middle of the decade, this recession had ended and the U.S. continues to enjoy one of the highest standards of living in the world.

Internationally, Americans have been the target of hostage-taking (Iran 1979) and terrorist attacks. Suspected Libyan promotion of international terrorism led to the U.S. bombing of that nation in 1986. Attempts to halt the spread of Communism in Central American have led to large military aid packages to the forces trying to overthrow Communist regimes there.

U.S.-Canadian relations have remained strong, especially since the 1984 election of Brian Mulroney as Canadian prime minister. Mulroney stressed the need for closer ties with the U.S., both he and U.S. Pres. Ronald Reagan promoted the free trade agreement reached between the 2 nations in 1987. The U.S. remains Canada's chief foreign ally and trading partner. More than two-thirds of all Canadian exports are purchased by the U.S.; the U.S. in turn sells almost twice as much to Canada as to its next largest trading partner, Japan.

State	Area sq. km	Population
Alabama	134 183	4 053 000
Alaska	1 524 671	534 000
Arizona	294 884	3 317 000
Arkansas	138 070	2 372 000
California	412 602	26 981 000
Colorado	271 042	3 267 000
Connecticut	13 023	3 189 000
Delaware	5 348	633 000
Florida	152 256	11 675 000
Georgia	153 077	5 975 000
Hawaii	16 770	1 062 000
Idaho	222 448	1 003 000
Illinois	146 640	11 553 000
Indiana	943 567	5 504 000
Iowa	146 354	2 851 000
Kansas	213 886	2 461 000
Kentucky	105 063	3 728 000
Louisiana	126 160	4 501 000
Maine	86 359	1 174 000
Maryland	27 500	4 463 000
Massachusetts	21 468	5 832 000
Michigan	151 362	9 145 000
Minnesota	218 577	4 214 000
Mississippi	124 062	2 625 000
Missouri	181 184	5 066 000
Montana	382 559	819 000
Nebraska	200 790	1 598 000
Nevada	287 404	963 000
New Hampshire	24 190	1 027 000
New Jersey	20 374	7 620 000
New Mexico	316 332	1 479 000
New York	128 898	17 772 000
North Carolina	136 724	6 331 000

State	Area sq. km	Population
North Dakota	183 729	679 000
Ohio	107 177	10 752 000
Oklahoma	181 789	3 305 100
Oregon	252 151	2 698 000
Pennsylvania	117 866	11 889 000
Rhode Island	3 156	975 000
South Carolina	80 743	3 378 000
South Dakota	200 322	708 000
Tennessee	109 834	4 803 000
Texas	695 079	16 682 000
Utah	220 782	1 665 000
Vermont	24 983	541 000
Virginia	106 124	5 787 000
Washington	177 299	4 463 000
West Virginia	628 706	1 919 000
Wisconsin	146 000	4 785 000
Wyoming	254 576	507 000
District of Columbia	174	626 000

Outlying U.S. Areas

Commonwealth of Puerto Rico

(Estado Libre Asociado de Puerto Rico)

People. Population (1985): 3 279 231. **Pop. density:** 367.3 per sq. km. **Urban** (1980): 66.8%. **Racial distribution** (1980): 99.9% Hispanic. **Net migration** (1985): −27 691.

Geography. Total area: 8 931 sq. km.

History: Puerto Rico (or Borinquen, after the original Arawak Indian name Boriquen), was discovered by Columbus, Nov. 19, 1493. Ponce de Leon conquered it for Spain, 1509, and established the first settlement at Caparra, across the bay from San Juan.

Sugar cane was introduced, 1515, and slaves were imported 3 years later. Gold mining petered out, 1570. Spaniards fought off a series of British and Dutch attacks; slavery was abolished, 1873. Under the Treaty of Paris, Puerto Rico was ceded to the U.S. after the Spanish-American War, 1898.

Chamber of Commerce: 100 Tetuán P.O.Box. S-3789, San Juan, PR 00904; Ponce & South: El Señorial Bldg., Ponce, PR 00731.

Guam

People. Population (1985): 120 977. **Pop. density:** 1 487.2 per sq. km. **Urban** (1980): 39.5%. **Major ethnic groups** (1980): Chamorro 41.8%, Filipino 21.2%. Native Guamanians, ethnically called Chamorros, are basically of Indonesian stock, with a mixture of Spanish and Filipino. In addition to the offical language, they speak the native Chamorro.

Geography. Total area: 543.4 sq. km. land.

History. Magellan arrived in the Marianas Mar. 6, 1521, and called them the Ladrones (thieves). They were colonized in 1668 by Spanish missionaries who renamed them the Mariana Islands in honor of Maria Anna, Queen of Spain. When Spain ceded Guam to the U.S., it sold the other Marianas to Germany. Japan obtained a League of Nations mandate over the German islands in 1919; in Dec. 1941 it seized Guam; the island was retaken by the U.S. in July 1944.

Guam is a self-governing organized unincorporated U.S. territory. Under the jurisdiction of the Interior Department, it is administered under the Organic Act of 1950, which provides for a governor and a 21-member unicameral legislature, elected biennially by the residents who are American citizens but do not vote for president.

Beginning in Nov., 1970, Guamanians elected their own governor, previously appointed by the U.S. president. He took office in Jan. 1971. In 1972 a U.S. law gave Guam one delegate to the U.S. House of Representatives; the delegate may vote in committee but not on the House floor.

Virgin Islands

St. John, St. Croix, St. Thomas

People. Population (1984): 107 500. **Pop. density:** 313.3 per sq. km. **Urban** (1980): 39%. **Racial distribution:** 15% White; 85% Black. **Major ethnic groups:** West Indian, French, Hispanic.

Geography. Total area: 346 sq. km.

History. The islands were discovered by Columbus in 1493. Spanish forces, 1555, defeated the Caribes and claimed the territory; by 1596 the native population was annihilated. First permanent settlement in the U.S. territory, 1672, by the Danes; U.S. purchased the islands, 1917, for defense purposes.

The inhabitants have been citizens of the U.S. since 1927. Legislation originates in a unicameral house of 15 senators, elected for 2 years. The governor, formerly appointed by the U.S. president, was popularly elected for the first time in Nov. 1970. In 1972 a U.S. law gave the Virgin Islands one delegate to the U.S. House of Representatives; the delegate may vote in committee but not in the House.

Tourist information: Dept. of Commerce, St. Thomas, P.O. Box 6400, St. Thomas, VI 00801; St. Croix, P.O. Box 4535, Chirstiansted, St. Croix 00820.

American Samoa

Capital: Pago Pago, Island of Tutuila. **Area:** 200 sq. km. **Population:** (1985) 34 500.

Blessed with spectacular scenery and delightful South Seas climate, American Samoa is the most southerly of all lands under U. S. ownership. It is an unincorporated territory consisting of 6 small islands of the Samoan group: **Tutuila, Aunu'u, Manu'a Group (Ta'u, Olosega and Ofu),** and **Rose.** Also administered as part of American Samoa is **Swain's Island,** 338 km to the NW, acquired by the U.S. in 1925. The islands are 4 184 km SW of Honolulu.

American Samoa became U. S. territory by a treaty with the United Kingdom and Germany in 1899. The islands were ceded by local chiefs in 1900 and 1904.

Samoa (Western), comprising the larger islands of the Samoan group, was a New Zealand mandate and UN Trusteeship until it became an independent nation Jan. 1, 1962.

Tutuila and Annu'u have an area of 137.8 sq. km. Ta'u has an area of 44 sq. km, and the islets of Ofu and Olosega, 13 sq. km with a population of a few thousand. Swain's Island has nearly 5.2 sq. km and a population of about 100.

About 70% of the land is bush. Chief products and exports are fish products, copra, and handicrafts. Taro, bread-fruit, yams, coconuts, pineapples, oranges, and bananas are also produced.

Formerly under jurisdiction of the Navy, since July 1, 1951, it has been under the Interior Dept. On Jan. 3, 1978, the first popularly elected Samoan governor and lieutenant governor were inaugurated. Previously, the governor was appointed by the Secretary of the Interior. American Samoa has a bicameral legislature and elects its own member of Congress, who enjoys nearly all the privileges and powers as the members from the states.

The American Samoans are of Polynesian origin. They are nationals of the U.S.; there are approximately 20 000 in Hawaii and 65 000 in California and Washington.

Minor Caribbean Islands

Quita Sueño Bank, Roncador and **Serrana,** lie in the Caribbean between Nicaragua and Jamaica. They are uninhabited. U.S. claim to the islands was relinquished in a treaty with Colombia, which entered into force on Sept. 17, 1981.

Navassa lies between Jamaica and Haiti, covers about 5.2 sq. km, is reserved by the U.S. for a lighthouse and is uninhabited.

Wake, Midway, Other Islands

Wake Island, and its sister islands, **Wilkes** and **Peale,** lie in the Pacific Ocean on the direct route from Hawaii to Hong Kong, about 3 700 km W of Hawaii and 2 075 km E of Guam. The group is 7.2 km long, 2.4 km wide, and totals less than 7.8 sq. km.

The U.S. flag was hoisted over Wake Island, July 4, 1898, formal possession taken Jan. 17, 1899; Wake has been administered by the U.S. Air Force since 1972. Population (1983): 1 600.

The **Midway Islands,** acquired in 1867, consist of 2, **Sand** and **Eastern,** in the North Pacific 1 840 km NW of Hawaii, with area of about 5.2 sq. km, administered by the Navy Dept. Population (1983): 2 200.

Johnston Atoll, SW of Hawaii, area 2.6 sq. km, pop. 300 (1978), is operated by Nuclear Defense Agency, and **Kingman Reef,** S of Hawaii, is under Navy control.

Howland, Jarvis, and **Baker Islands,** 2 414-2 665 km southwest of the Hawaiian group, uninhabited since World War II, are under the Interior Dept.

Palmyra is an atoll about 1 600 km south of Hawaii, 10.4 sq. km. Privately owned, it is under the Interior Dept.

Islands Under Trusteeship

The Trust Territory of the Pacific Islands was established in 1947, as the only strategic trusteeship of the 11 trusteeships established by the U.N. The territory has a heterogenous population of about 140 000 people scattrered among more than 2 100 islands and atolls in 3 major archipelagos: the Carolines, the Marshalls and the Marianas. The entire geographic area is sometimes referred to as "Micronesia," meaning "little islands." The area of the Trust Territory covered some 7 769 400 sq. km. of the Pacific Ocean, slightly larger than the continental U.S. However, its islands constituted a land area of only 1 853.8 sq. km. It formerly contained 4 political jurisdictions: The Commonwealth of the Northern Mariana Islands (CNMI), the Federated States of Micronesia (FSM), the Republic of the Marshall Islands (RMI), and the Republic of Palau (RP). As of Oct. 21, 1986, the RMI entered into free association with the U.S., as did the FSM effective Nov. 3, 1986. The CNMI became a commonwealth of the U.S., also effective Nov. 3. Only the RP remains under trusteeship.

Commonwealth of the Northern Mariana Islands

Located in the perpetually warm climes between Guam and the Tropic of Cancer, the 16 islands of the Northern Marianas form a 480 km-long archipelago, comprising a total land area of 475.2 sq. km. The native population, estimated at 20 000, is concentrated on the 3 largest of the 6 inhabited islands: **Saipan,** the seat of government and commerce (16 532), **Rota** (1 484), and **Tinian** (1 012).

The people of the Northern Marianas are predominantly of Chamorro cultural extraction, although numbers of Carolinians and immigrants from other areas of E. Asia and Micronesia have also settled in the islands. Pursuant to the Covenant Agreement, on Nov. 3, 1986, citizens were granted U.S. citizenship. English is among the several languages commonly spoken.

The Northern Mariana Islands has been self-governing since 1978, when both a constitution drafted and adopted by the people became effective, and a bicameral legislature with offices of governor and lieutenant governor was inaugurated. Commercial activity has increased steadily in the last few years, with 1 600 establishments operated in 1985, mostly in tourism, construction, and light industry. In 1986, more than 150 000 tourists visited, an increase of 10% over previous years. An agreement with the U.S. for 1986-92 entitles the Northern Mariana Islands to $228 million for capital development, government operations and special programs.

Federated States of Micronesia

The Federated States of Micronesia extends across the 2 900 km-long Caroline Island archipelago. The 4 states of the FSM are Pohnpei, Kosrae, Truk, and Yap. Each state consists of several islands, except for Kosrae, a single island. The capital of the

FSM is Pohnpei. Populations are: Pohnpei, 26 000; Truk, 43 000; Kosrea, 6 000; Yap, 12 000. Pohnpei is 4 700 km SW of Honolulu and 1 600 km SE of Guam. The islands vary geologically from high, mountainous islands to low, coral atolls. The FSM lies between the equator and 9° N, and 138° E and 168° E. Average year-round temperature is 27°C. Pohnpei gets the highest annual rainfall, averaging up to 635 cm.

The cultures of the FSM are very diverse. Several languages, each with dialects, are spoken: Yapese, Ulithian, Woleasian, Ponapean, Nukuoran, Kapingamarangi, Trukese, and Kosraean. Each state has a constitution and government, headed by a governor. The status of free association recognizes that the FSM is a sovereign-self-governing state, with the U.S. responsible for defense and also extending agreed-upon amounts of economic and service assistance. Each of the state's constitutions recognizes a role for traditional leaders and customs.

Republic of the Marshall Islands

The Republic of the Marshall Islands consists of 2 island/atoll chains, the Ratak (sunrise) Chain, and the Ralik (sunset) Chain, totalling 31 atolls. Each atoll is a cluster of several small islands circling a lagoon. Total land area is 180 sq. km. The capital is **Majuro**, 3 200 km SW of Honolulu and 2 100 km SE of Guam. Population is 35 000, 12 000 in Majuro. Average year-round temperature is 27°C.

Marshallese culture revolves around the complex clan system. Land is owned by each clan and passed down over the generations. In the late 1970s, the U.S. embarked upon an ambitious Capital Improvement Program, with a goal of building a major infrastructure (airport, dock, roads, water-power-sewer system) in Majuro. Funding was completed in 1985.

The Marshall Islands' Constitution includes both American and British concepts. The executive branch is the Nitijela (parliament) and is consulted by a Council of Iroij (local chiefs). The Nitijela elects the president from among its own members. The status of free association recognizes that the Marshall Islands is a sovereign, self-governing state, with the U.S. responsible for defense, and for extending agreed-upon amounts of economic and service assistance. A subsidiary agreement allows the U.S. continued use of Kwajalein Missle Range for 30 years. Another subsidiary agreement provides for settlement of all claims arising out of the nuclear testing programs conducted by the U.S. at Bikini and Enewetak Atolls from 1946 to 1958.

Republic of Palau

Palau consists of more than 200 islands in the Caroline chain, of which 8 are permanently inhabited. The Palau archipelago stretches over 640 km. The capital of Palau, Koror, lies 7 200 km SW of Honolulu and 1 150 km S of Guam. Population of Palau is approximately 14 000, 8 100 in Koror. Average year-round temperature is 27°C, average annual rainfall is 381 cm. The high commissioner of the Trust Territory is appointed by the President of the U.S. Until 1979, the high commissioner appointed a district administrator for Palau to oversee programs and administration there. In support of the evolving political status, the U.S. recognized the Constitution of Palau and the establishment of the Government of Palau. The Constitution became effective in 1980. The president and vice president are elected by popular vote. A council of chiefs advises the president on matters concerning traditional law and custom. Palau has a bicameral national legislature composed of a House of Delegates and a Senate.

Disputed Pacific Islands

In the central Pacific, S and SW of Hawaii lie 25 islands that were claimed by the U.S.; 18 of them were also claimed by the United Kingdom and 7 by New Zealand. **Kiribati** achieved its independence from the U.K. in July, 1979.

The **Tuvalu (Ellice) Islands**, including Funafuti, Nukufetau, Nukulailai, and Nurakita, became independent of the UK, Oct. 1, 1978.

The **Cook Islands**, including Danger, Manahiki, Rakahanga, and Penrhyn (Tongareva), are self-governing in free association with New Zealand. **Tokelau** is a New Zealand territory.

The U.S. signed a treaty with Kiribati on Sept. 20, 1979; with Tuvalu on Feb. 7, 1979; and with the Cook Islands and New Zealand for Tokelau on Dec. 2, 1980. These treaties, which relinquished U.S. claim to the disputed islands, were ratified in August, 1983.

Uruguay
Oriental Republic of Uruguay
República Oriental del Uruguay

People: Population (1989 est.): 2 983 000. **Age distrib.** (%): 0–14: 26.9; 15–59: 57.7; 60+: 15.4. **Pop. density:** 16.9 per sq. km. **Urban** (1985): 86.0%. **Ethnic groups:** Caucasian (Iberian, Italian) 89%, mestizo 10%. **Language:** Spanish. **Religion:** Roman Catholic 66%.

Geography: Area: 176 202 sq. km. **Location:** In southern S. America, on the Atlantic O. **Neighbors:** Argentina on W, Brazil on N. **Topography:** Uruguay is composed of rolling, grassy plains and hills, well-watered by rivers flowing W to Uruguay R. **Capital:** Montevideo. **Cities** (1986 est.): Montevideo 1 246 000.

Government: Type: Republic. **Head of state:** Pres. Julio Maria Sanguinetti Cairolo; b. Jan. 6, 1936; in office: Mar. 1, 1985. **Local divisions:** 19 departments. **Defence:** 2.9% of GNP (1984).

Economy: Industries: Meat-packing, metals, textiles, wine, cement, oil products. **Chief crops:** Corn, wheat, citrus fruits, rice, oats, linseed. **Arable land:** 8%. **Livestock** (1985): cattle: 9.9 mln.; sheep: 20.6 mln. **Fish catch** (1985): 139 000 metric tons. **Electricity prod.** (1984): 3.6 bln. kwh. **Labor force** 16% agric.; 31% ind. and commerce; 12% serv.; 19% govt.

Finance: Currency: New Peso (May. 1988: 330 = $1 US). **Gross national product** (1986): $5.2 bln. **Per capita income** (1985): $1 665. **Imports** (1986): $820 mln.; partners: Nig. 17%, Braz. 12%, Arg. 10%, U.S. 8%. **Exports** (1986): $1.0 bln.; partners: Braz. 14%, U.S. 7%, W. Ger. 9%, Arg. 11%. **Tourists** (1984): $107 mln. receipts. **National budget** (1986): $901 mln. expeditures. **International reserves less gold** (Jan. 1987): $486 mln. **Gold:** 2.60 mln. oz t. **Consumer prices** (change in 1987): 63.6%.

Transport: Railway traffic (1984): 330 mln. passenger-km; 273 mln. net ton-km. **Motor vehicles:** in use (1981): 281 000 passenger cars, 43 000 comm. vehicles. **Civil aviation** (1985): 240 mln. passenger-km; 3.6 mln. freight ton-km. **Chief ports:** Montevideo.

Communications: Television sets: 500 000 in use (1985). **Radios:** 1.7 mln. in use (1985). **Telephones** in use (1985): 374 000. **Daily newspaper circ.** (1985): 185 per 1 000 pop.

Health: Life expectancy at birth (1983): 67.1 male; 73.7 female. **Births** (per 1 000 pop. 1985): 18. **Deaths** (per 1 000 pop. 1985): 10. **Natural increase** (1985): 0.8%. **Hospital beds** (1983): 23 400. **Physicians:** (1984): 5 756. **Infant mortality** (per 1 000 live births 1985): 26.

Education (1984): **Literacy:** 96%.

Major International Organizations: UN (GATT, IMF, WHO), OAS.

Canadian Embassy: c/o Casilla de Correo 1598, Buenos Aires, Argentina.

Spanish settlers did not begin replacing the indigenous Charrua Indians until 1624. Portuguese from Brazil arrived later, but Uruguay was attached to the Spanish Viceroyalty of Rio de la Plata in the 18th century. Rebels fought against Spain beginning in 1810. An independent republic was declared Aug. 25, 1825.

Liberal governments adopted socialist measures as far back as 1911. The state owns the power, telephone, railroad, cement, oil-refining and other industries. Social welfare programs are among the most advanced in the world.

Uruguay's standard of living was one of the highest in South America, and political and labor conditions among the freest. Economic stagnation, inflation, plus floods, drought in 1967 and a general strike in 1968 brought attempts by the government to strengthen the economy through a series of devaluations of the peso and wage and price controls. But inflation continued in the 1980s and the country was forced to ask international creditors to restructure $2.7 billion in debt in 1983.

Tupamaros, leftist guerrillas drawn from the upper classes, increased terrorist actions in 1970. Violence continued and in Feb. 1973 Pres. Juan Maria Bordaberry agreed to military control of his administration. In June he abolished Congress and set up a Council of State in its place. By 1974 the military had apparently defeated the Tupamaros, using severe repressive measures. Bordaberry was removed by the military in a 1976 coup. Civilian government was restored to the country in 1985.

Vanuatu
Republic of Vanuatu
Ripablik Blong Vanuatu

People: Population (1989 est.): 150 000. **Population density:** 10.2 per sq. km. **Ethnic groups:** Mainly Melanesian, some European, Polynesian, Micronesian. **Languages:** Bislama (national), French and English both official. **Religions:** Presbyterian 40%, Anglican 14%, Roman Catholic 16%, animist 15%.
Geography: Area: 14 762 sq. km. **Location:** SW Pacific, 1 920 km NE of Brisbane, Australia. **Topography:** dense forest with narrow coastal strips of cultivated land. **Capital:** Vila. **Cities:** Vila (1987): 15 000.
Government: Type: Republic. **Head of state:** Pres. George Sokomanu; in office: July 30, 1980. **Head of gov't:** Prime Min. Rev. Walter Lini; in office: July 30, 1980.
Economy: Industries: Fish-freezing, meat canneries, tourism. **Chief crops:** Copra (38% of export), cocoa, coffee. **Minerals:** Manganese. **Other resources:** Forests, cattle. **Fish catch** (1984): 2.4 metric tons.
Finance: Currency: Australian dollar and Vanuatu franc (Mar. 1987: 110 vatu = $1 US). **Imports** (1985): $52 mln.; partners: Aus. 36%, Fr. 8%, Japan 13%. **Exports** (1985): $18 mln.; partners: Neth. 48%, Jap. 17%, Fr. 12%, Belg.-Lux. 14%.
Health: Life expectancy at birth (1984): 56.2 male, 53.7 female. **Infant mortality** (per 1 000 live births 1985): 78.
Education: Education not compulsory, but 85-90% of children of primary school age attend primary schools.
Canadian High Commission: c/o Commonwealth Ave, Canberra A.C.T. 2600, Australia.

The Anglo-French condominium of the New Hebrides, administered jointly by France and Great Britain since 1906, became the independent Republic of Vanuatu on July 30, 1980.

Vatican City
State of the Vatican City

People: Population (1989 est.): 1 000. **Ethnic groups:** Italian, Swiss. **Languages:** Italian, Latin.
Geography: Area: 44 ha. **Location:** In Rome, Italy. **Neighbors:** Completely surrounded by Italy.
Currency: Lira.
Canadian Embassy: Via della Conciliazone 4/D, 00193, Rome, Italy; (06) 654-7316, -86, -98. 222-7121.

The popes for many centuries, with brief interruptions, held temporal sovereignty over mid-Italy (the so-called Papal States), comprising an area of some 41 600 sq. km, with a population in the 19th century of more than 3 million. This territory was incorporated in the new Kingdom of Italy, the sovereignty of the pope being confined to the palaces of the Vatican and the Lateran in Rome and the villa of Castel Gandolfo, by an Italian law, May 13, 1871. This law also guaranteed to the pope and his successors a yearly indemnity of over $620 000. The allowance, however, remained unclaimed.
A Treaty of Conciliation, a concordat and a financial convention were signed Feb. 11, 1929, by Cardinal Gasparri and Premier Mussolini. The documents established the independent state of Vatican City, and gave the Catholic religion special status in Italy. The treaty (Lateran Agreement) was made part of the Constitution of Italy (Article 7) in 1947. Italy and the Vatican reached preliminary agreement in 1976 on revisions of the con-

cordat, that would eliminate Roman Catholicism as the state religion and end required religious education in Italian schools.
Vatican City includes St. Peter's, the Vatican Palace and Museum covering over 5 ha, the Vatican gardens, and neighboring buildings between Viale Vaticano and the Church. Thirteen buildings in Rome, outside the boundaries, enjoy extraterritorial rights; these buildings house congregations or officers necessary for the administration of the Holy See.
The legal system is based on the code of canon law, the apostolic constitutions and the laws especially promulgated for the Vatican City by the pope. The Secretariat of State represents the Holy See in its diplomatic relations. By the Treaty of Conciliation the pope is pledged to a perpetual neutrality unless his mediation is specifically requested. This, however, does not prevent the defense of the Church whenever it is persecuted.
The present sovereign of the State of Vatican City is the Supreme Pontiff John Paul II, Karol Wojtyla, born in Wadowice, Poland, May 18, 1920, elected Oct. 16, 1978 (the first non-Italian to be elected Pope in 456 years).

Venezuela
Republic of Venezuela
Republica de Venezuela

People: Population (1989 est.): 19 246 000. **Age distrib.** (%): 0–14: 41.0; 15–59: 54.3; 60+: 4.7. **Pop. density:** 21.1 per sq. km. **Urban** (1985): 85%. **Ethnic groups:** Mestizo 69%, white (Spanish, Portuguese, Italian) 20%, Black 9%, Indian 2%. **Languages:** Spanish (official), Indian languages 2%. **Religion:** Roman Catholic 96%.
Geography: Area: 911 980 sq. km. **Location:** On the Caribbean coast of S. America. **Neighbors:** Colombia on W, Brazil on S, Guyana on E. **Topography:** Flat coastal plain and Orinoco Delta are bordered by Andes Mtns. and hills. Plains, called llanos, extend between mountains and Orinoco. Guyana Highlands and plains are S of Orinoco, which stretches 2 560 km and drains 80% of Venezuela. **Capital:** Caracas. **Cities** (1987 est.): Caracas 3 247 000; Maracaibo 1 295 000; Barquisimeto 718 000; Valencia 1 135 000.
Government: Type: Federal republic. **Head of state:** Pres. Jaime Lusinchi; b. 1924; in office: Feb. 2, 1984. **Local divisions:** 20 states, 2 federal territories, federal district, federal dependency. **Defence:** 1.3% of GNP (1984).
Economy: Industries: Steel, oil products, textiles, containers, paper, shoes. **Chief crops:** Coffee, rice, fruits, sugar. **Minerals:** Oil (5th largest producer), iron (extensive reserves and production), gold. **Crude oil reserves** (1987): 55 bln. bbls. **Arable land:** 4%. **Livestock:** cattle: 12.3 mln.; pigs: 2.8 mln. **Fish catch** (1985): 301 000 metric tons. **Electricity prod.** (1986): 50.2 bln. kwh. **Crude steel prod.** (1986): 3.4 mln. metric tons. **Labor force:** 15% agric.; 28% ind.; 56% services.
Finance: Currency: Bolivar (Apr. 1988: 31.25 = $1 US). **Gross national product** (1986): $57 bln. **Per capita income** (1985): $2 629. **Imports** (1986): $9.5 bln.; partners: U.S. 48%, W. Ger. 6%, Jap. 8%. **Exports** (1986): $10.0 bln.; partners: U.S. 25%, Neth Ant. 21%, Can. 9%. **Tourists** (1984): $343 mln. receipts. **National budget** (1987): $16.6 bln. expenditures. **International reserves less gold** (Mar. 1988): $5.1 bln. **Gold:** 11.46 mln. oz t. **Consumer prices** (change in 1987): 28.1%.
Transport: Railway traffic (1985): 7.9 mln. passenger-km; 13 mln. net ton-km. **Motor vehicles:** in use (1985): 1.5 mln. passenger cars, 763 000 comm. vehicles. **Civil aviation** (1985): 2.4 bln. passenger-km; 215 mln. freight ton-km. **Chief ports:** Maracaibo, La Guaira, Puerto Cabello.
Communications: Television sets: 2.8 mln. in use (1986). **Radios:** 6.7 mln. in use (1986). **Telephones in use** (1985): 1.4 mln. **Daily newspaper circ.** (1982): 120 per 1 000 pop.
Health: Life expectancy at birth (1985): 65 male; 70.6 female. **Births** (per 1 000 pop. 1985): 32. **Deaths** (per 1 000 pop. 1985): 6. **Natural increase** (1985): 2.6%. **Hospital beds** (1978): 41 366. **Physicians** (1983): 21 502. **Infant mortality** (per 1 000 live births 1985): 37.
Education (1987): **Literacy:** 88%. **Years compulsory:** 8; attendance 82%.
Major International Organizations: UN (IMF, WHO, FAO), OAS, OPEC.

Canadian Embassy: Edificio Torre Europa, 7th Floor, Avenida Francisco de Miranda, Chacaito; Postal: Apartado 62302, Caracas 1060A; Tel: 951-6166, 7, 8.

Columbus first set foot on the South American continent on the peninsula of Paria, Aug. 1498. Alonso de Ojeda, 1499, found Lake Maracaibo, called the land Venezuela, or Little Venice, because natives had houses on stilts. Venezuela was under Spanish domination until 1821. The republic was formed after secession from the Colombian Federation in 1830.

Military strongmen ruled Venezuela for most of the 20th century. They promoted the oil industry; some social reforms were implemented. Since 1959, the country has enjoyed progressive, democratically-elected governments.

Venezuela helped found the Organization of Petroleum Exporting States (OPEC). The government, Jan. 1, 1976, nationalized the oil industry with compensation. Development has begun of the Orinoco tar belt, believed to contain the world's largest oil reserves. Oil accounts for much of total export earnings and the economy suffered a severe cash crisis in the mid 1980s as the result of falling oil revenues.

Vietnam
Socialist Republic of Vietnam
Cong Hoa Xa Hoi Chu Nghia Viet Nam

People: Population (1989 est.): 66 708 000. **Age distrib. (%):** 0-14: 48.8; 15-59: 53.6; 60+: 5.6. **Pop. density:** 200.6 per sq. km. **Urban** (1984): 19%. **Ethnic groups:** Vietnamese 84%, Chinese 2%, remainder Muong, Thai, Meo, Khmer, Man, Cham. **Languages:** Vietnamese (official), French, English. **Religions:** Buddhists, Confucians, and Taoists most numerous, Roman Catholics, animists, Moslems, Protestants.

Geography: Area: 332 533 sq. km. **Location:** On the E coast of the Indochinese Peninsula in SE Asia. **Neighbors:** China on N, Laos, Cambodia on W. **Topography:** Vietnam is long and narrow, with a 2 240 km coast. About 24% of country is readily arable, including the densely settled Red R. valley in the N, narrow coastal plains in centre, and the wide, often marshy Mekong R. delta in the S. The rest consists of semi-arid plateaus and barren mountains, with some stretches of tropical rain forest. **Capital:** Hanoi. **Cities** (1981): Ho Chi Minh City 3.5 mln.; Hanoi 2 mln.

Government: Type: Communist. **Head of state:** Pres. Vo Chi Cong; in office: June 18, 1987. **Head of government:** Prime Min. Do Muoi; in office: June 22, 1988. **Head of Communist Party:** Nguyen Van Linh; in office: Dec. 18, 1986. **Local divisions:** 39 provinces. **Defence:** 50% of govt. budget (1982 est.)

Economy: Industries: Food processing, textiles, cement, chemical fertilizers, steel. **Chief crops:** Rice, rubber, fruits and vegetables, corn, manioc, sugarcane. **Minerals:** Phosphates, coal, iron, manganese, bauxite, apatite, chromate. **Other resources:** Forests. **Arable land:** 23%. **Livestock** (1985): cattle: 5 mln,; pigs: 11.7 mln.; sheep & goats: 262 000. **Fish catch** (1984): 765 000 metric tons. **Electricity prod.** (1986): 5.4 bln. kwh. **Labor force:** 70% agric.; 8% ind. and commerce.

Finance: Currency: Dong (Jan. 1988: 80.00 = $1 US). **Gross national product** (1984): $18.1 bln. **Per capita income** (1987): $180. **Imports** (1986): $1.0 bln.; partners: USSR 23%, Jap. 21%. **Exports** (1986): $800 mln.; partners: Hong Kong 31%, USSR 10%, Jap. 18%.

Transport: Motor vehicles: in use (1976): 100 000 passenger cars, 200 000 comm. vehicles. **Chief ports:** Ho Chi Minh City, Haiphong, Da Nang.

Communications: Television sets (1984) 2.2 mln. **Radios:** 6 mln. in use (1984). **Daily newspaper circ.** (1984): 8 per 1 000 pop.

Health: Life expectancy at birth (1985): 57.7 male; 62.1 female. **Births** (per 1 000 pop. 1986): 33.6. **Deaths** (per 1 000 pop. 1986): 10.3. **Natural increase** (1986): 2.3%. **Hospital beds** (1986): 216 000. **Physicians** (1986): 19 100.

Education (1983): **Literacy:** 94%.

Major International Organizations: UN (IMF, WHO).

Canadian Embassy: c/o P.O. Box 2090, Bangkok 10500, Thailand.

Vietnam's recorded history began in Tonkin before the Christian era. Settled by Viets from central China, Vietnam was held by China, 111 BC-939 AD, and was a vassal state during subsequent periods. Vietnam defeated the armies of Kublai Khan, 1288. Conquest by France began in 1858 and ended in 1884 with the protectorates of Tonkin and Annam in the N. and the colony of Cochin-China in the S.

In 1940 Vietnam· was occupied by Japan; nationalist aims gathered force. A number of groups formed the Vietminh (Independence) League, headed by Ho Chi Minh, communist guerrilla leader. In Aug. 1945 the Vietminh forced out Bao Dai, former emperor of Annam, head of a Japan-sponsored regime. France, seeking to reestablish colonial control, battled communist and nationalist forces, 1946-1954, and was finally defeated at Dienbienphu, May 8, 1954. Meanwhile, on July 1, 1949, Bao Dai had formed a State of Vietnam, with himself as chief of state, with French approval. China backed Ho Chi Minh.

A cease-fire accord signed in Geneva July 21, 1954, divided Vietnam along the Ben Hai R. It provided for a buffer zone, withdrawal of French troops from the North and elections to determine the country's future. Under the agreement the communists gained control of territory north of the 17th parallel, 22 provinces with area of 161 200 sq. km and 13 million pop., with its capital at Hanoi and Ho Chi Minh as president. South Vietnam came to comprise the 39 southern provinces with approx. area of 169 000 sq. km and pop. of 12 million. Some 900 000 North Vietnamese fled to South Vietnam. Neither South Vietnam nor the U.S. signed the agreement.

On Oct. 26, 1955, Ngo Dinh Diem, premier of the interim government of South Vietnam, proclaimed the Republic of Vietnam and became its first president.

The Democratic Republic of Vietnam, established in the North, adopted a constitution Dec. 31, 1959, based on communist principles and calling for reunification of all Vietnam. North Vietnam sought to take over South Vietnam beginning in 1954. Fighting persisted from 1956 with the communist Vietcong, aided by North Vietnam, pressing war in the South and South Vietnam receiving U.S. aid. Northern aid to Vietcong guerrillas was intensified in 1959, and large-scale troop infiltration began in 1964, with Soviet and Chinese arms assistance. Large Northern forces were stationed in border areas of Laos and Cambodia.

A serious political conflict arose in the South in 1963 when Buddhists denounced authoritarianism and brutality. This paved the way for a military coup Nov. 1-2, 1963, which overthrew Diem. Several military coups followed. In elections Sept. 3, 1967, Chief of State Nguyen Van Thieu was chosen president.

In 1964, the U.S. began air strikes against North Vietnam. Beginning in 1965, the raids were stepped up and U.S. troops became combatants. U.S. troop strength in Vietnam, which reached a high of 543 400 in Apr. 1969, was ordered reduced by President Nixon in a series of withdrawals, beginning in June 1969. U.S. bombings were resumed in 1972-73.

A ceasefire agreement was signed in Paris Jan. 27, 1973 by the U.S., North and South Vietnam, and the Vietcong. It was never implemented. U.S. aid was curbed in 1974 by the U.S. Congress. Heavy fighting continued for two years throughout Indochina.

North Vietnamese forces launched attacks against remaining government outposts in the Central Highlands in the first months of 1975. Government retreats turned into a rout, and the Saigon regime surrendered April 30. A Provisional Revolutionary Government assumed control, aided by officials and technicians from Hanoi, and first steps were taken to transform society along communist lines. All businesses and farms were collectivized.

Canada accepted over 100 000 Vietnamese refugees, while scores of thousands more sought refuge in other countries.

The war's toll included — Combat deaths: U.S. 47 752; South Vietnam over 200 000; other allied forces 5 225. Civilian casualties were over a million. Displaced war refugees in South Vietnam totaled over 6.5 million.

After the fighting ended, 8 Northern divisions remained stationed in the South. Over 1 million urban residents and 260 000 Montagnards were resettled in the countryside by 1978.

The first National Assembly of both parts of the country met and the country was officially reunited July 2, 1976. The Northern capital, flag, anthem, emblem, and currency were applied to the new state. Nearly all major government posts went to officials of the former Northern government.

Heavy fighting with Cambodia took place, 1977-80, amid mutual charges of aggression and atrocities against civilians. Increasing numbers of Vietnamese civilians, ethnic Chinese, escaped the country, via the sea, or the overland route across

Cambodia. Vietnam launched an offensive against Cambodian refugee strongholds along the Thai-Cambodian border in 1985; they also engaged Thai troops. Vietnam has declared that it will remove its troops from Cambodia by 1990.

Relations with China soured as 140 000 ethnic Chinese left Vietnam charging discrimination; China cut off economic aid. Reacting to Vietnam's invasion of Cambodia, China attacked 4 Vietnamese border provinces, Feb., 1979, instigating heavy fighting.

In 1987, Vietnam announced a package of reforms aimed at reducing central control of the economy as many of the old revolutionary followers of Ho Chi Minh were removed from office.

Western Samoa

Independent State of Western Samoa

Malotuto'atasi o Samoa i Sisifo

People: Population (1989 est.): 169 000. **Age distrib. (%):** 0–14: 50.4; 15–59: 45.4; 60+: 4.3. **Pop. density:** 57.6 per sq. km. **Urban** (1981): 21.2%. **Ethnic groups:** Samoan (Polynesian) 88%, Euronesian (mixed) 10%, European, other Pacific Islanders. **Languages:** Samoan, English both official. **Religions:** Protestant 70%, Roman Catholic 20%.

Geography: Area: 2 934 sq. km. **Location:** In the S. Pacific O. **Neighbors:** Nearest are Fiji on W, Tonga on S. **Topography:** Main islands, Savai'i (1 740 sq. km) and Upolu (1 115 sq. km), both ruggedly mountainous, and small islands Manono and Apolima. **Capital:** Apia. **Cities** (1983 est.): Apia 35 000.

Government: Type: Parliamentary democracy. **Head of state:** King Malietoa Tanumafili II; b. Jan. 4, 1913; in office: Jan. 1, 1962. **Head of government:** Prime Min. Va'ai Kolone: in office: Jan. 1986. **Local divisions:** 24 districts.

Economy: Chief crops: Cocoa, copra, bananas. **Other resources:** Hardwoods, fish. **Arable land:** 43%. **Electricity prod.** (1986): 79 mln. kwh. **Labor force:** 67% agric.

Finance: Currency: Tala (Mar. 1988: 1.00 = $.48 US). **Gross national product** (1985): $86 mln. **Imports** (1985): $63 mln.; partners: NZ 28% Austral. 10%, Jap. 13%, U.S. 30%. **Exports** (1985): $16 mln.; partners: Niger 31%, NZ 26%, U.S. 12%. **International reserves less gold** (Mar. 1988): $35.8 mln. **Consumer prices** (change in 1987): 4.6%.

Transport: Motor vehicles: in use (1984): 2 000 passenger cars, 2 400 comm. vehicles. **Chief ports:** Apia, Asau.

Communications: Radios: 70 000 in use (1985). **Telephones in use** (1984): 6 000.

Health: Life expectancy at birth (1986): 62.6 male; 65.6 female. **Births** (per 1 000 pop. 1985): 38. **Deaths** (per 1 000 pop. 1985): 8. **Natural increase** (1985): 3.0%. **Hospital beds** (1982): 735. **Physicians** (1981): 63. **Infant mortality** (per 1 000 live births 1985): 28.

Education (1983): **Literacy:** 90%. 95% attend elementary school.

Major International Organizations: UN (IMF, World Bank), Commonwealth of Nations.

Canadian High Commission: c/o P.O. Box 12-049, Wellington North, New Zealand.

Western Samoa was a German colony, 1899 to 1914, when New Zealand landed troops and took over. It became a New Zealand mandate under the League of Nations and, in 1945, a New Zealand UN Trusteeship.

An elected local government took office in Oct. 1959 and the country became fully independent Jan. 1, 1962.

North Yemen

Yemen Arab Republic

al-Jumhuriyat al-Arabiyah al-Yamaniyah

People: Population (1989 est.): 6 937 000. **Pop. density:** 35.6 per sq. km. **Ethnic groups:** Arab, some Negroid. **Language:** Arabic. **Religions:** Sunni Moslem 50%, Shiite Moslem 50%.

Geography: Area: 194 986 sq. km. **Location:** On the southern Red Sea coast of the Arabian Peninsula. **Neighbors:** Saudi Arabia on N, South Yemen on S. **Topography:** A sandy coastal strip leads to well-watered fertile mountains in interior. **Capital:** Sanaa. **Cities** (1981 est.): Sanaa 427 000.

Government: Type: Republic; military in power. **Head of state:** Pres. Ali Abdullah Saleh, b. 1942; in office: July 17, 1978. **Head of government:** Prime Min. Abdul Aziz Abdel Ghani; in office: Nov. 13, 1983. **Local divisions:** 10 provinces. **Defence:** 17.8% of GNP (1984).

Economy: Industries: Food processing. **Chief crops:** Wheat, sorghum, qat, fruits, coffee, cotton. **Minerals:** Salt. **Crude oil reserves** (1984): 600 mln. bbls. **Arable land:** 7%. **Livestock** (1985): goats: 2.2 mln.; sheep: 1.8 mln. **Fish catch** (1985): 20 000 metric tons. **Electricity prod.** (1986): 556 mln. kwh. **Labor force:** 64% agric.; 22% ind. and commerce; 14% serv.

Finance: Currency: Rial (Apr. 1988: 9.76 = $1 US). **Gross national product** (1985): $4.1 bln. **Per capita income** (1977-78): $475. **Imports** (1985): $2.9 bln.; partners: Saudi Ar. 20%, Fr. 8%, Jap. 16%. **Exports** (1986): $10 mln.; partners: S. Yemen 23%, Saudi Ar. 8%, Pak. 19%. **National budget** (1985): 946 mln. **International reserves less gold** (Mar. 1988): $416 mln. **Consumer prices** (change in 1985): 20%.

Transport: Chief ports: Al-Hudaydah, Al-Mukha.

Communications: Television sets: (1986): 50 000. **Radios:** 200 000 in use (1986). **Telephones in use** (1984): 63 000.

Health: Life expectancy at birth (1986): 42.7 male; 44.8 female. **Births** (per 1 000 pop. 1985): 53. **Deaths** (per 1 000 pop. 1985): 19. **Natural increase** (1985): 3.4%. **Hospital beds** (1986): 5 900. **Infant mortality** (per 1 000 live births 1985): 137.

Education (1987): **Literacy:** 20%. **Primary school attendance:** 59%.

Major International Organizations: UN (IMF, WHO), Arab League.

Canadian Embassy: c/o P.O. Box 22593, Riyadh 11416, Saudi Arabia.

Yemen's territory once was part of the ancient kingdom of Sheba, or Saba, a prosperous link in trade between Africa and India. A Biblical reference speaks of its gold, spices and precious stones as gifts borne by the Queen of Sheba to King Solomon.

Yemen became independent in 1918, after years of Ottoman Turkish rule, but remained politically and economically backward. Imam Ahmed ruled 1948-1962. The king was reported assassinated Sept. 26, 1962, and a revolutionary group headed by Brig. Gen. Abdullah al-Salal declared the country to be the Yemen Arab Republic.

The Imam Ahmed's heir, the Imam Mohamad al-Badr, fled to the mountains where tribesmen joined royalist forces; internal warfare between them and the republican forces continued. Egypt sent troops and Saudi Arabia military aid to the royalists. About 150 000 people died in the fighting.

There was a bloodless coup Nov. 5, 1967.

In April 1970 hostilities ended with an agreement between Yemen and Saudi Arabia and appointment of several royalists to the Yemen government. There were border skirmishes with forces of South Yemen in 1972-73.

On June 13, 1974, an army group, led by Col. Ibrahim al-Hamidi, seized the government. Hamidi pursued close Saudi and U.S. ties; he was assassinated in 1977.

The People's Democratic Republic of Yemen went to war with Yemen on Feb. 24, 1979. Swift Arab mediation led to a cease-fire and a mutual withdrawal of forces, Mar. 19. An Arab League-sponsored agreement between North and South Yemen on unification of the 2 countries was signed Mar. 29th.

The remittances from 400 000 Yemenis living in Arab oil countries provide most of foreign earnings.

South Yemen

People's Democratic Republic of Yemen

Jumhuriyat al-Yaman ad-Dimuqratiyah ash-Sha'biyan

People: Population (1989 est.): 2 488 000. **Age distrib. (%):** 0–14: 44.4; 15–59: 51.4; 60+: 4.2. **Pop. density:** 7.5 per sq. km. **Urban** (1973): 33.3%. **Ethnic groups:** Arab, 75%, Indian 11%, Somali 8%, others. **Language:** Arabic. **Religions:** Sunni Moslem 91%, Christian 4%, Hindu 3.5%.

Geography: Area: 332 942 sq. km. **Location:** On the southern coast of the Arabian Peninsula. **Neighbors:** Yemen on W, Saudi Arabia on N, Oman on E. **Topography:** The entire country is very hot and very dry. A sandy coast rises to mountains which give way to desert sands. **Capital:** Aden. **Cities** (1985 est.): Aden 318 000.

Government: Type: Republic. **Head of state:** Chairman, Council of Ministers and President: Haidar Abu Bakr Al-Attas; in office: Nov. 6, 1986. **Head of Government:** Prime Min. Yasin Said Numan; in office: Feb. 8, 1986. **Local divisions:** 6 governorates. **Defence:** 17.4% of GNP (1983).

Economy: Industries: Transshipment. **Chief crops:** Cotton (main export), grains. **Arable land:** 1%. **Livestock:** (1984) sheep: 1 mln.; goats: 1.3 mln. **Fish catch** (1983): 74 000 metric tons. **Electricity prod.** (1986) 556 mln. kwh. **Labor force:** 43.8% agric.; 28% ind. and commerce; 28% serv.

Finance: Currency: Dinar (Mar. 1988: 1.00 = $2.98 US). **Gross national product** (1985): $1.1 bln. **Per capita income** (1977): $310. **Imports** (1985) $762 mln.; partners: USSR 14%, Aust. 9%. **Exports** (1985): $316 mln.; partners: Jap. 36%; N. Yem. 23%. **International reserves less gold** (Jan. 1988): $82.9 mln. **Gold:** 42 000 oz t.

Transport: Motor vehicles: in use (1984): 24 000 passenger cars, 27 000 comm. vehicles. **Chief ports:** Aden.

Communications: Television sets: 44 000 in use (1986). **Radios:** 300 000 in use (1986). **Daily newspaper circ.** (1986): 10 per 1 000 pop.

Health: Life expectancy at birth (1985): 45.3 male; 47.7 female. **Births** (per 1 000 pop. 1985): 47.6. **Deaths** (per 1 000 pop. 1985): 18.9. **Natural increase** (1985): 2.8%. **Hospital beds** (1984): 3 805. **Physicians** (1984): 406. **Infant mortality rate** (per 1 000 live births in 1985): 131.

Major International Organizations: UN (IMF, WHO), Arab League.

Education (1980): **Literacy:** 39%. About 90% attend primary school.

Canadian Embassy: c/o P.O. Box 22593, Riyadh 11416, Saudi Arabia.

Aden, mentioned in the Bible, has been a port for trade in incense, spice and silk between the East and West for 2 000 years. British rule began in 1839. Aden provided Britain with a controlling position at the southern entrance to the Red Sea.

A war for independence began in 1963. The National Liberation Front (NLF) and the Egypt-supported Front for the Liberation of Occupied South Yemen, waged a guerrilla war against the British and local dynastic rulers. The 2 groups vied with each other for control. The NLF won out. Independence came Nov. 30, 1967. In 1969, the left wing of the NLF seized power and inaugurated a thorough nationalization of the economy and regimentation of daily life.

The new government broke off relations with the U.S. and nationalized some foreign firms.

In 1972-73 there were border skirmishes with forces of the Yemen Arab Republic. South Yemen aided leftist guerrillas in neighboring Oman. Relations with Saudi Arabia later improved. S. Yemen troops fought in Ethiopia against Eritrean rebels in 1978.

Pres. Salem Robaye Ali, who had tried to improve relations with Yemen, Saudi Arabia, Oman, and the West, was executed after a bloody coup June 1978. The new ruling faction was accused by N. Yemen of the murder of N. Yemen's president 2 days earlier. N. Yemen, Egypt, and Saudi Arabia froze ties with S. Yemen in July.

South Yemen went to war with North Yemen on Feb. 24, 1979. Swift Arab mediation led to a cease-fire and a mutual withdrawal of forces, Mar. 19th. An Arab League-sponsored agreement between North and South Yemen on unification of the 2 countries was signed Mar. 29th.

The government was overthrown in a bloody coup on Jan. 13, 1986, which escalated into civil war. Some 10 000 were killed and 12 000 fled the country before order was restored.

The Port of Aden is the country's most valuable resource.

Socotra, the largest island in the Arabian Sea, Kamaran, an island in the Red Sea near the coast of North Yemen, and Pe-

rim, an island in the strait between the Gulf of Aden and the Red Sea, are controlled by South Yemen.

Yugoslavia

Socialist Federal Republic of Yugoslavia

Socijalistička Federativna Republika Jugoslavija

People: Population (1989 est.): 23 753 000. **Age distrib. (%):** 0–14: 23.5; 15-59: 63.7; 60+: 12.8. **Pop. density:** 92.9 per sq. km. **Urban** (1985): 46.5%. **Ethnic groups:** Serbian 36%, Croatian 20%, Bosnian Moslem 9%, Slovene 8%, Macedonian 6%, Albanian 8%. **Languages:** Serbo-Croatian, Macedonian, Slovenian (all official), Albanian. **Religions:** Eastern Orthodox 50%, Roman Catholic 30%, Moslem 10%.

Geography: Area: 255 784 sq. km. **Location:** On the Adriatic coast of the Balkan Peninsula in SE Europe. **Neighbors:** Italy on W, Austria, Hungary on N, Romania, Bulgaria on E, Greece, Albania on S. **Topography:** The Dinaric Alps run parallel to the Adriatic coast, which is lined by offshore islands. Plains stretch across N and E river basins. S and NW are mountainous. **Capital:** Belgrade. **Cities** (1980 est.): Belgrade 1 300 000; Zagreb 700 000; Skopje 440 000; Sarajevo 400 000; Ljubljana 300 000.

Government: Type: Communist state Federal republic in form. **Head of state:** Pres. Raif Dizdarevic; in office: May 15, 1986. **Head of government:** Prime Min. Branko Mikulic; in office: May 15, 1986. **Head of Communist Party:** Basko Krunic; in office: June 30, 1987. **Local divisions:** 6 republics, 2 autonomous provinces. **Defence:** 3.6% of GNP (1984).

Economy: Industries: Steel, wood products, cement, textiles, tourism. **Chief crops:** Corn, grains, tobacco, sugar beets. **Minerals:** Antimony, bauxite, lead, mercury, coal, iron, copper, chrome, zinc, salt. **Crude oil reserves** (1987): 263 mln. bbls. **Arable land:** 33%. **Livestock** (1985): cattle: 5 mln.; pigs: 7.8 mln.; sheep: 7.6 mln. **Fish catch** (1983): 79 000 metric tons. **Electricity prod.** (1984): 71.5 bln. kwh. **Crude steel prod.** (1986): 4.5 mln. metric tons. **Labor force:** 30% agric.; 70% ind.

Finance: Currency: Dinar (Mar. 1988: 1 532 = $1 US). **Gross national product** (1985): $129.4 bln. **Per capita income** (1985): $3 109. **Imports** (1985): $12.2 bln.; partners: W. Ger. 15%, USSR 19%, It. 8%, U.S. 6%. **Exports** (1985): $10.7 bln.; partners: USSR 27%, It. 9%, W. Ger. 8%, Czech. 7%. **Tourists** (1985): $1 bln. receipts. **National budget** (1987): $4.3 bln. expenditures. **International reserves less gold** (Mar. 1988): $659 mln. **Gold:** 1.87 mln. oz t. **Consumer prices** change in 1986: 89.8%.

Transport: Railway traffic (1986): 12.3 bln. passenger-km; 27.5 bln. net ton-km. **Motor vehicles:** in use (1986): 2.8 mln. passenger cars, 264 000 comm. vehicles. **Civil aviation** (1985): 6.3 bln. passenger-km; 92.5 mln. freight ton-km. **Chief ports:** Rijeka, Split, Koper, Bar, Place.

Communications: Television sets: 4.0 mln. in use (1986). **Radios:** 4.7 mln. licensed (1986). **Telephones in use** (1986): 3.3 mln. **Daily newspaper circ.** (1986): 107 per 1 000 pop.

Health: Life expectancy at birth (1983): 68 male; 73 female. **Births** (per 1 000 pop. 1985): 16. **Deaths** (per 1 000 pop. 1985): 9. **Natural increase** (1985): 0.7%. **Hospital beds** (1985): 139 000. **Physicians** (1985): 38 000. **Infant mortality** (per 1 000 live births 1985): 30.

Education (1985): **Literacy:** 90%. Almost all attend primary school.

Major International Organizations: UN (IMF, World Bank, GATT).

Canadian Embassy: Kneza Milosa 75, 11000 Belgrade; 644-666.

Serbia, which had since 1389 been a vassal principality of Turkey, was established as an independent kingdom by the Treaty of Berlin, 1878. Montenegro, independent since 1389, also obtained international recognition in 1878. After the Balkan wars Serbia's boundaries were enlarged by the annexation of Old Serbia and Macedonia, 1913.

When the Austro-Hungarian empire collapsed after World War I, the Kingdom of the Serbs, Croats, and Slovenes was formed from the former provinces of Croatia, Dalmatia, Bosnia, Herzegovina, Slovenia, Voyvodina and the independent state of Montenegro. The name was later changed to Yugoslavia.

Nazi Germany invaded in 1941. Many Yugoslav partisan troops continued to operate. Among these were the Chetniks led by Draja Mikhailovich, who fought other partisans led by Josip Broz, known as Marshal Tito. Tito, backed by the USSR and Britain from 1943, was in control by the time the Germans had been driven from Yugoslavia in 1945. Mikhailovich was executed July 17, 1946, by the Tito regime.

A constituent assembly proclaimed Yugoslavia a republic Nov. 29, 1945. It became a federated republic Jan. 31, 1946, and Marshal Tito, a communist, became head of the government.

The Stalin policy of dictating to all communist nations was rejected by Tito. He accepted aid and equipment from the U.S., France and Great Britain. Tito also supported the liberal government of Czechoslovakia in 1968 before the Soviet invasion.

A separatist movement among Croatians, 2d to the Serbs in numbers, brought arrests and a change of leaders in the Croatian Republic in Jan. 1972. Violence by extreme Croatian nationalists and fears of Soviet political intervention led to restrictions on political and intellectual dissent. Serbians, Montenegrins, and Macedonians use Cyrillic, Croatians and Slovenians use Latin letters. Croatia and Slovenia have been the most prosperous republics.

Most industry is socialized and private enterprise is restricted to small-scale production. Management of industrial enterprises is handled by workers' councils. Farmland is mostly privately owned but farms are restricted to 10 ha.

Beginning in 1965, reforms designed to decentralize the administration of economic development and to force industries to produce more efficiently in competition with foreign producers were introduced. Yugoslavia has developed considerable trade with the West.

Pres. Tito died May 4, 1980; with his death, the post as head of the Collective Presidency and also that as head of the League of Communists became a rotating system of succession among the members representing each republic and autonomous province.

Zaire
Republic of Zaire
République du Zaïre

People: Population (1989 est.): 33 991 000. **Pop. density:** 14.5 per sq. km. **Urban** (1985): 44.2%. **Ethnic groups:** Bantu tribes 80%, over 200 other tribes. **Languages:** French (official), Bantu dialects. **Religions:** Christian 70%, Moslem 10%.

Geography: Area: 2 345 227 sq. km. **Location:** In central Africa. **Neighbors:** Congo on W, Central African Republic, Sudan on N, Uganda, Rwanda, Burundi, Tanzania on E, Zambia, Angola on S. **Topography:** Zaire includes the bulk of the Zaire (Congo) R. Basin. The vast central region is a low-lying plateau covered by rain forest. Mountainous terraces in the W, savannas in the S and SE, grasslands toward the N, and the high Ruwenzori Mtns. on the E surround the central region. A short strip of territory borders the Atlantic O. The Zaire R. is 4 374 km long. **Capital:** Kinshasa. **Cities** (1985 est.): Kinshasa 3 000 000; Kananga 601 239.

Government: Type: Republic with strong presidential authority. **Head of state:** Pres. Mobutu Sese Seko; b. Oct. 14, 1930; in office: Nov. 25, 1965. **Head of government:** Prime Min. Mabi Mulumba; in office: Jan. 22, 1987. **Local divisions:** 9 regions, Kinshasa. **Defence:** 1.2% of GNP (1984).

Economy: Chief crops: Coffee, rice, sugar cane, bananas, plantains, manioc, mangoes, tea, cocoa, palm oil. **Minerals:** Cobalt (60% of world reserves), copper, cadmium, gold, silver, tin, germanium, zinc, iron, manganese, uranium, radium. **Crude oil reserves** (1987): 111 mln. bbls. **Other resources:** Forests, rubber, ivory. **Arable land:** 5%. **Livestock** (1985): cattle: 1.3 mln.; goats: 2.9 mln. **Fish catch** (1985): 102 000 metric tons. **Electricity prod.** (1986): 5.2 bln. kwh. **Labor force:** 75% agric.

Finance: Currency: Zaire (Mar. 1988: 161 = $1 US). **Gross national product** (1985): $4.7 bln. **Per capita income** (1975): $127. **Imports** (1986): $872 mln.; partners: Belg. 22%, U.S.

10%, W. Ger. 10%, Fra. 13%. **Exports** (1986): $1.0 bln.; partners: Belg.-Lux. 31%, U.S. 36%. **International reserves less gold** (Mar. 1988): $187 mln. **Gold:** 495 000 oz t. **Consumer prices** (change in 1987): 90.4%.

Transport: Railway traffic (1985): 291 mln. passenger-km; 1.9 bln. net ton-km. **Motor vehicles:** in use (1982): 89 000 passenger cars, 16 000 comm. vehicles. **Civil aviation** (1986): 382 mln. passenger-km. 12.1 mln. freight ton-km. **Chief ports:** Matadi, Boma.

Communications: Television sets: 15 000 in use (1986). **Radios:** 500 000 mln. in use (1986). **Telephones in use** (1985): 31 000. **Daily newspaper circ.** (1986): 1 per 1 000 pop.

Health: Life expectancy at birth (1985): 48.3 male; 51.7 female. **Births** (per 1 000 pop. 1985): 45.2. **Deaths** (per 1 000 pop. 1985): 15.8. **Natural increase** (1985): 2.9%. **Hospital beds** (1982): 74 000. **Physicians** (1982): 2 000. **Infant mortality** (per 1 000 live births 1985): 106.

Education (1985): **Literacy:** males 78%, females 44%.

Major International Organizations: UN and all of its specialized agencies, OAU.

Canadian Embassy: 17 Pumbu Ave., P.O. Box 8341, Kinshasa; Tel: 22-706, 24-346.

The earliest inhabitants of Zaire may have been the pygmies, followed by Bantus from the E and Nilotic tribes from the N. The large Bantu Bakongo kingdom ruled much of Zaire and Angola when Portuguese explorers visited in the 15th century.

Leopold II, king of the Belgians, formed an international group to exploit the Congo in 1876. In 1877 Henry M. Stanley explored the Congo and in 1878 the king's group sent him back to organize the region and win over the native chiefs. The Conference of Berlin, 1884-85, organized the Congo Free State with Leopold as king and chief owner. Exploitation of native laborers on the rubber plantations caused international criticism and led to granting of a colonial charter, 1908.

Belgian and Congolese leaders agreed Jan. 27, 1960, that the Congo would become independent June 30. In the first general elections, May 31, the National Congolese movement of Patrice Lumumba won 35 of 137 seats in the National Assembly. He was appointed premier June 21, and formed a coalition cabinet.

Widespread violence caused Europeans and others to flee. The UN Security Council Aug. 9, 1960, called on Belgium to withdraw its troops and sent a UN contingent. President Kasavubu removed Lumumba as premier. Lumumba fought for control backed by Ghana, Guinea and India; he was murdered in 1961.

The last UN troops left the Congo June 30, 1964, and Moise Tshombe became president.

On Sept. 7, 1964, leftist rebels set up a "People's Republic" in Stanleyville. Tshombe hired foreign mercenaries and sought to rebuild the Congolese Army. In Nov. and Dec. 1964 rebels slew scores of white hostages and thousands of Congolese; Belgian paratroops, dropped from U.S. transport planes, rescued hundreds. By July 1965 the rebels had lost their effectiveness.

In 1965 Gen. Joseph D. Mobutu was named president. He later changed his name to Mobutu Sese Seko. The country changed its name to Republic of Zaire on Oct. 27, 1971; in 1972 Zairians with Christian names were ordered to change them to African names.

In 1969-74, political stability under Mobutu was reflected in improved economic conditions. In 1974 most foreign-owned businesses were ordered sold to Zaire citizens, but in 1977 the government asked the original owners to return.

In 1977, a force of Zairians invaded Shaba province (Katanga) from Angola. Zaire repelled the attack, with the aid of Egyptian pilots and Moroccan troops flown in by France. But many European mining experts failed to return after a 2d unsuccessful invasion from Angola in May 1978.

Serious economic difficulties, amid charges of corruption by government officials, have plagued Zaire in the 1980s.

Zambia
Republic of Zambia

People: Population (1989 est.): 7 770 000. **Age distrib. (%):** 0–14: 48.2; 15–59: 47.8; 60+: 4.0. **Pop. density:** 10.3 per sq. km. **Urban** (1985): 49%. **Ethnic groups:** Mostly Bantu tribes. **Languages:** English (official), Bantu dialects. **Religions:** Predominantly animist, Roman Catholic 21%, Protestant, Hindu, Moslem minorities.

Geography: Area: 752 560 sq. km. **Location:** In southern central Africa. **Neighbors:** Zaire on N, Tanzania, Malawi, Mozambique on E, Zimbabwe, Namibia on S, Angola on W. **Topography:** Zambia is mostly high plateau country covered with thick forests, and drained by several important rivers, including the Zambezi. **Capital:** Lusaka. **Cities** (1984 est.): Lusaka 538 000; Kitwe 314 794; Ndola 282 439.

Government: Type: Republic. **Head of state:** Pres. Kenneth David Kaunda; b. Apr. 28, 1924; in office: Oct. 24, 1964. **Head of government:** Prime Min. Kebby Musokotwane; in office: Apr. 24, 1985. **Local divisions:** 9 provinces. **Defence:** 6.6% of GDP (1984 est).

Economy: Chief crops: Corn, tobacco, peanuts, cotton, sugar. **Minerals:** Cobalt, copper, zinc, gold, lead, vanadium, manganese, coal. **Other resources:** Rubber, ivory. **Arable land:** 7%. **Livestock** (1985): cattle: 2.6 mln. **Fish catch** (1985): 64 000 metric tons. **Electricity prod.** (1986): 11.1 bln. kwh. **Labor force:** 60% agric.; 40% ind. and commerce.

Finance: Currency: Kwacha (Mar. 1988: 1.00 = \$.12 US). **Gross national product** (1985): \$2.3 bln. **Per capita income** (1982): \$570. **Imports** (1986): \$714 mln.; partners: UK 26%, Saudi Ar. 18%, W. Ger. 18%, U.S. 9%. **Exports** (1986): \$431 mln.; partners: Jap. 19%, Fr. 15%, UK 13%, U.S. 10%, W. Ger. 9%. **National budget** (1982): \$733 mln. expenditures. **International reserves less gold** (Jan. 1988): \$108.8 mln. **Gold:** 4 000 oz t. **Consumer prices** (change in 1986): 51.6%.

Transport: Motor vehicles: in use (1982): 105 000 passenger cars, 97 000 comm. vehicles. **Civil aviation** (1986): 630 mln. passenger-km.

Communications: Television sets: 66 000 in use (1986). **Radios:** 528 000 in use (1986). **Telephones in use** (1985): 74 000. **Daily newspaper circ.** (1984): 16 per 1 000 pop.

Health: Life expectancy at birth (1984): 47 yrs. **Births** (per 1 000 pop. 1985): 47.4. **Deaths** (per 1 000 pop. 1985): 15.4. **Natural increase** (1985): 3.2%. **Hospital beds** (1982): 21 257. **Physicians** (1982): 839. **Infant mortality** (per 1 000 live births 1985): 107.

Education (1984): **Literacy:** 54%. **Attendance:** less than 50% in grades 1–7.

Major International Organizations: UN (GATT, IMF, WHO), OAU, Commonwealth of Nations.

Canadian High Commission: Barclays Bank North End Branch, Cairo Rd., P.O. Box 31313, Lusaka; Tel: 216161.

As Northern Rhodesia, the country was under the administration of the South Africa Company, 1889 until 1924, when the office of governor was established, and, subsequently, a legislature. The country became an independent republic within the Commonwealth Oct. 24, 1964.

After the white government of Rhodesia declared its independence from Britain Nov. 11, 1965, relations between Zambia and Rhodesia became strained and use of their jointly owned railroad was disputed.

Britain gave Zambia an extra \$12 million aid in 1966 after imposing an oil embargo on Rhodesia, and Zambia set up a temporary airlift to carry copper out from its mines and gasoline in. In Aug. 1968 a 1 703 km pipeline was completed, bringing oil from Tanzania. In 1973 a truck road to carry copper to Tanzania's port of Dar es Salaam was completed. A railroad, built with Chinese aid across Tanzania, reached the Zambian border in 1974.

As part of a program of government participation in major industries, a government corporation in 1970 took over 51% of the ownership of 2 foreign-owned copper mining companies. Privately-held land and other enterprises were nationalized in 1975, as were all newspapers. In the 1980s, decline in copper prices has hurt the economy and severe drought has caused famine.

Zimbabwe

People: Population (1989 est.): 9 987 000. **Age distrib.** (%): 0–14: 44; 15–59: 51.1; 60+: 4.0. **Pop. density:** 25.6 per

sq. km. **Urban** (1985): 25%. **Ethnic groups:** Shona 80%, Ndebele 19%. **Languages:** English (official), Shona, Sindebele. **Religions:** Predominantly traditional tribal beliefs, Christian minority.

Geography: Area: 390 550 sq. km. **Location:** In southern Africa. **Neighbors:** Zambia on N, Botswana on W, S. Africa on S, Mozambique on E. **Topography:** Rhodesia is high plateau country, rising to mountains on eastern border, sloping down on the other borders. **Capital:** Harare. **Cities** (1988 est.): Harare (met.) 730 000; Bulawayo 415 000.

Government: Type: One-party socialist state. **Head of state:** Pres. Robert Mugabe; b. April 14, 1928; in office: Jan. 1, 1988. **Local divisions:** 8 provinces. **Defence:** 6.2% of GNP (1984).

Economy: Industries: Clothing, chemicals, light industries. **Chief crops:** Tobacco, sugar, cotton, corn, wheat. **Minerals:** Chromium, gold, nickel, asbestos, copper, iron, coal. **Arable land:** 7%. **Livestock** (1985): cattle: 5.3 mln.; goats: 1.8 mln. **Electricity prod.** (1986): 4.5 bln. kwh. **Crude steel prod.** (1981): 691 000 metric tons. **Labor force:** 35% agric.; 30% ind. and commerce; 20% serv.; 15% gvt.

Finance: Currency: Dollar (Mar. 1988: 1.00 = \$0.58 US). **Gross domestic product** (1986): \$4.7 bln. **Per capita income** (1986): \$275. **Imports** (1986): \$1.0 bln.; partners: UK 10%, So. Afr. 27%, U.S. 7%, W. Ger. 7%. **Exports** (1986): \$1.3 bln.; partners: UK 7%, So. Afr. 22%, W. Ger. 8%. **Consumer prices** (change in 1986): 14.3%.

Transport: Railway traffic (1984): 6.4 bln. net ton-km. **Motor vehicles:** in use (1985): 253 000 passenger cars, 28 000 comm. vehicles.

Communications: Television sets: 112 000 in use (1986). **Radios:** 315 000 in use (1986). **Telephones in use** (1985): 245 000. **Daily newspaper circ.** (1985): 23 per 1 000 pop.

Health: Life expectancy at birth (1987): 57.9 male; 61.4 female. **Births** (per 1 000 pop. 1985): 53.0. **Deaths** (per 1 000 pop. 1985): 13. **Natural increase** (1985): 4.0%. **Physicians** (1984): 705. **Infant mortality** (per 1 000 live births 1985): 77.

Education (1988): **Literacy:** 50%. **Attendance:** 90% primary, 15% secondary for Africans; higher for whites, Asians.

Major International Organizations: UN (IMF, World Bank), OAU, Commonwealth of Nations.

Canadian High Commission: 45 Baines Ave., P.O. Box 1430, Harare; Tel: 733881/82/83/84/85.

Britain took over the area as Southern Rhodesia in 1923 from the British South Africa Co. (which, under Cecil Rhodes, had conquered the area by 1897) and granted internal self-government. Under a 1961 constitution, voting was restricted to maintain whites in power. On Nov. 11, 1965, Prime Min. Ian D. Smith announced his country's unilateral declaration of independence. Britain termed the act illegal, and demanded Rhodesia broaden voting rights to provide for eventual rule by the majority Africans.

Urged by Britain, the UN imposed sanctions, including embargoes on oil shipments to Rhodesia. Some oil and gasoline reached Rhodesia, however, from South Africa and Mozambique, before the latter became independent in 1975. In May 1968, the UN Security Council ordered a trade embargo.

A new constitution came into effect, Mar. 2, 1970, providing for a republic with a president and prime minister. The election law effectively prevented full black representation through income tax requirements.

A proposed British-Rhodesian settlement was dropped in May 1972 when a British commission reported most Rhodesian blacks opposed it. Intermittent negotiations between the government and various black nationalist groups failed to prevent increasing skirmishes. By mid-1978, over 6 000 soldiers and civilians had been killed. Rhodesian troops battled guerrillas within Mozambique and Zambia. An "internal settlement" signed Mar. 1978 in which Smith and 3 popular black leaders share control until transfer of power to the black majority was rejected by guerrilla leaders.

In the country's first universal-franchise election, Apr. 21, 1979, Bishop Abel Muzorewa's United African National Council gained a bare majority control of the black-dominated parliament. Britain, 1979, began efforts to normalize its relationship with Zimbabwe. A British cease-fire was accepted by all parties, Dec. 5th. Independence was finally achieved Apr. 18, 1980.

World Facts

Area and Population of the World: 1650-1988

Source: Rand McNally & Co.

Continent	Area in sq. km (000s)	% of Earth	Population[1] (thousands)						% World Total, 1988
			1650	1750	1850	1900	1950	1988	
North America	24 350	16.3	5 000	5 000	39 000	106 000	219 000	413 100	8.2
South America	17 870	11.9	8 000	7 000	20 000	38 000	111 000	282 200	5.6
Europe	9 840	6.6	100 000	140 000	265 000	400 000	530 000	684 800	13.5
Asia	44 810	29.9	335 000	476 000	754 000	932 000	1 418 000	3 031 100	60.0
Africa	30 300	20.2	100 000	95 000	95 000	118 000	199 000	615 300	12.2
Australasia	8 550	5.7	2 000	2 000	2 000	6 000	13 000	25 500	0.5
Antarctica	13 990	9.3	uninhabited						
World	149 710	100.0	550 000	725 000	1 175 000	1 600 000	2 490 000	5 052 000	100.0

(1) Estimated.

Population Projections, by Region and for Selected Countries: 1990 to 2025

Source: Population Division of the United Nations

(in millions)

Region and Country	1990	1995	2000	2025
World, total	5 248.5	5 679.3	6 127.1	8 177.1
More developed[1]	1 208.8	1 242.8	1 275.7	1 396.7
Less developed[1]	4 039.7	4 436.4	4 851.5	6 780.4
Africa	645.3	753.2	877.4	1 642.9
Eastern Africa[2]	189.7	224.7	266.2	531.4
Burundi	5.3	6.1	7.0	11.0
Ethiopia	42.7	50.1	58.4	112.0
Kenya	25.4	31.4	38.5	82.9
Madagascar	11.6	13.4	15.6	29.7
Malawi	8.3	9.8	11.7	23.2
Mozambique	16.2	18.8	21.8	39.7
Rwanda	7.3	8.8	10.6	22.2
Somalia	5.9	6.2	7.1	13.2
Uganda	18.8	22.5	26.8	52.3
Tanzania	27.0	32.5	39.1	83.8
Zambia	7.9	9.4	11.2	23.8
Zimbabwe	10.5	12.6	15.1	32.7
Middle Africa[2]	71.9	83.0	96.1	183.5
Angola	10.0	11.5	13.2	24.5
Cameroon	11.1	12.6	14.4	25.2
Cen. African Rep.	2.9	3.3	3.7	6.7
Chad	5.7	6.4	7.3	13.1
Zaire	38.4	44.8	52.4	104.4
Northern Africa[2]	143.8	164.3	185.7	295.0
Algeria	26.0	30.5	35.2	57.3
Egypt	52.7	58.9	65.2	97.4
Libya	4.3	5.2	6.1	11.1
Morocco	27.6	31.9	36.3	59.9
Sudan	24.9	28.7	32.9	55.4
Tunisia	8.1	8.9	9.7	13.6
Southern Af'ca[2]	42.3	48.1	54.5	90.7
South Africa	36.8	41.6	46.9	76.3
Western Africa[2]	197.6	233.1	275.0	542.4
Benin	4.7	5.4	6.4	12.2
Burkina Faso[3]	8.0	9.1	10.5	19.5
Côte d'Ivoire	11.5	13.4	15.6	28.1
Ghana	15.9	18.7	21.9	37.7
Guinea	6.1	7.0	7.9	13.9
Mali	9.3	10.7	12.4	21.4
Niger	7.1	8.3	9.8	18.9
Nigeria	113.3	135.5	161.9	338.1
Senegal	7.5	8.7	10.0	18.9
Togo	3.4	3.9	4.6	9.0
Latin America	453.2	501.3	550.0	786.6
Caribbean[2]	34.6	37.7	40.8	57.7
Cuba	10.5	11.2	11.7	13.6
Dominican Rep.	7.0	7.7	8.4	12.2
Haiti	7.5	8.6	9.9	18.3

Region and Country	1990	1995	2000	2025
Middle America[2]	119.7	134.4	149.6	222.6
El Salvador	6.5	7.5	8.7	15.0
Guatemala	9.7	11.1	12.7	21.7
Honduras	5.1	6.0	7.0	13.3
Mexico	89.0	99.2	109.2	154.1
Nicaragua	3.9	4.5	5.3	9.2
Temperate South America[2]	49.1	52.3	55.5	70.1
Argentina	32.9	35.1	37.2	47.4
Chile	13.1	14.0	14.9	18.8
Uruguay	3.1	3.2	3.4	3.9
Tropical South America[2]	249.8	276.9	304.1	436.3
Bolivia	7.3	8.4	9.7	18.3
Brazil	150.4	165.1	179.5	245.8
Colombia	31.8	34.9	38.0	51.7
Ecuador	10.9	12.7	14.6	25.7
Paraguay	4.2	4.8	5.4	8.6
Peru	22.3	25.1	28.0	41.0
Venezuela	21.3	24.2	27.2	42.8
Northern America[2]	275.2	286.8	297.7	347.3
Canada	27.1	28.3	29.4	34.4
United States	248.0	258.3	268.1	312.7
East Asia[2]	1 317.2	1 390.4	1 470.0	1 696.1
China: Mainland	1 119.6	1 184.2	1 255.7	1 460.1
Hong Kong	6.1	6.6	6.9	7.9
Japan	122.7	125.1	127.7	127.6
Korea, Dem. People's Rep. of	22.4	24.9	27.3	37.6
Korea, Rep. of	43.8	46.8	49.5	58.6
South Asia[2]	1 740.2	1 909.4	2 073.7	2 770.6
Eastern So. Asia[2]	440.4	480.8	519.7	684.7
Burma	44.5	49.8	55.2	82.2
Indonesia	178.4	191.9	204.5	255.3
Kampuchea	8.4	9.2	9.9	12.5
Laos	5.0	5.6	6.2	9.2
Malaysia	17.3	19.1	20.6	26.9
Philippines	61.4	68.3	74.8	102.3
Singapore	2.7	2.9	3.0	3.2
Thailand	56.2	61.1	66.1	86.3
Vietnam	65.4	71.7	78.1	105.1
Middle So. Asia[2]	1 169.9	1 279.9	1 385.7	1 815.9
Afghanistan	19.3	21.7	24.2	35.9
Bangladesh	115.2	130.3	145.8	219.4
India	831.9	899.1	961.5	1 188.5
Iran	51.8	58.7	65.5	96.2
Nepal	18.5	20.7	23.0	33.9
Pakistan	113.3	128.0	142.6	212.8
Sri Lanka	18.0	19.5	20.8	26.2

Region and Country	1990	1995	2000	2025	Region and Country	1990	1995	2000	2025
Western So. Asia[2]. .	129.9	148.7	168.3	270.0	Norway	4.2	4.2	4.2	4.3
Iraq.	18.5	21.6	24.9	42.7	Sweden	8.2	8.2	8.1	7.5
Israel.	4.7	5.0	5.4	7.0	United Kingdom. .	55.8	56.0	56.2	56.4
Jordan.	4.3	5.2	6.4	13.4	Southern Europe[2]. .	146.4	150.0	153.1	162.8
Lebanon.	3.0	3.3	3.6	5.2	Albania	3.4	3.8	4.1	5.8
Saudi Arabia . . .	13.5	16.1	18.9	33.5	Greece	10.2	10.5	10.7	11.8
Syria.	12.8	15.3	18.1	32.3	Italy	57.4	57.9	58.2	56.9
Turkey.	56.0	62.4	68.5	99.3	Portugal	10.4	10.7	11.0	11.9
Yemen Arab Rep.	7.5	8.6	9.9	16.5	Spain	40.5	42.0	43.4	49.2
Europe (excl. Soviet					Yugoslavia	23.9	24.6	25.2	26.6
Union)	499.5	506.5	513.1	526.9	Western Europe[2] . .	154.8	155.3	155.6	149.3
Eastern Europe . . .	115.7	118.2	121.0	131.2	Austria.	7.5	7.5	7.5	7.3
Bulgaria	9.4	9.6	9.7	10.2	Belgium	9.9	9.9	9.9	9.8
Czechoslovakia. .	16.0	16.3	16.8	18.8	France.	55.4	56.3	57.1	58.5
German Dem.					Germany, Fed.				
Rep.	16.6	16.5	16.6	16.1	Rep. of	60.7	60.3	59.8	53.8
Hungary.	10.8	10.8	10.9	10.9	Netherlands	14.7	14.9	15.0	14.6
Poland.	39.0	40.2	41.4	45.9	Switzerland	6.2	6.0	5.9	4.9
Romania.	23.9	24.8	25.6	29.2	Soviet Union	291.3	303.1	314.8	367.1
Northern Europe[2] . .	82.6	83.0	83.4	83.6	Oceania[2]	26.7	28.5	30.4	39.5
Denmark	5.2	5.1	5.1	4.8	Australia	16.7	17.7	18.7	23.5
Finland.	4.9	5.0	5.0	4.8	New Zealand	3.4	3.6	3.7	4.2
Ireland	3.8	4.0	4.2	5.2	Papua New Guinea .	4.2	4.8	5.3	8.2

(1) Regions. (2) Includes countries not shown separately. (3) Formerly Upper Volta.

Population of World's Largest Cities

Source: U.S. Bureau of the Census

The table below represents one attempt at comparing the world's largest cities. The boundary of the city was determined by examining detailed maps of each city in conjunction with the most recent official population statistics. To the extent practical, nonresidential areas such as parks, airports, industrial complexes and water were excluded from the area reported for each city, thus making the population density reflective of the concentrations in the residential portions of the city. By using a consistent definition for the city, it is possible to make comparisons of the cities on the basis of total population, area and population density.

Political and administrative boundaries were disregarded in determining the population of the city; Berlin includes both East and West Berlin, as well as population from East Germany.

The population of each city was projected based on the proportion each city was of its country total at the time of the last 2 censuses and projected country populations. The areal expansion of the city was not projected, hence density figures are valid only for 1985. Figures in the table below may differ from city population figures elsewhere in The Canadian World Almanac because of different methods of determining population.

City, Country	1985 (thousands)	2000 (thousands)	Area (sq. km)	Density (pop per sq. km)	City, Country	1985 (thousands)	2000 (thousands)	Area (sq. km)	Density (pop per sq. km)
Tokyo-Yokahama, Japan	25 434	29 971	420.5	60 485	Bogota, Colombia	4 711	7 935	30.5	154 437
Mexico City, Mexico	16 901	27 872	201.6	83 851	Santiago, Chile	4 700	6 294	49.4	95 094
Sao Paolo, Brazil	14 911	25 354	174.1	85 624	Milan, Italy	4 635	4 839	132.8	34 895
New York, U.S.	14 598	14 648	491.9	29 675	Tianjin, China	4 622	5 298	18.9	244 287
Seoul, South Korea	13 665	21 976	132.1	103 478	Leningrad, USSR	4 569	4 738	53.7	85 128
Osaka-Kobe-Kyoto,					Nagoya, Japan	4 452	5 303	118.5	37 556
Japan	13 562	14 333	191.1	70 955	Manchester, U.K.	4 151	3 827	137.8	30 113
Buenos Aires, Argentina	10 750	12 911	206.6	52 038	Madrid, Spain	4 137	5 104	25.5	162 333
Calcutta, India	10 462	14 088	80.7	129 639	Shenyang, China	4 086	4 684	15.1	271 331
Bombay, India	10 137	15 357	36.7	276 345	Philadelphia, U.S.	4 025	3 979	181.9	22 132
Rio de Janeiro, Brazil . .	10 116	14 169	100.4	100 763	Pusan, S. Korea	3 996	6 700	20.9	191 645
Moscow, USSR	9 873	11 121	146.3	67 465	Barcelona, Spain	3 842	4 834	33.6	114 368
Los Angeles, U.S.	9 638	10 714	428.6	22 487	San Francisco, U.S. . . .	3 790	4 214	165.3	22 933
London, U.K.	9 442	8 574	337.5	27 978	Bangalore, India	3 685	6 764	19.3	190 868
Paris, France	8 633	8 803	166.8	51 754	Lahore, Pakistan	3 603	5 864	22.0	163 703
Cairo, Egypt	8 595	12 512	40.2	214 032	Sydney, Australia	3 396	3 708	130.5	26 021
Manila, Philippines	8 485	12 846	72.6	116 885	Baghdad, Iraq	3 371	5 237	37.5	90 002
Jakarta, Indonesia	8 122	12 804	29.3	276 768	Dhaka, Bangladesh	3 283	6 492	12.4	265 697
Essen, W. Germany	7 604	7 239	271.8	27 973	Athens, Greece	3 252	3 866	44.8	72 604
Teheran, Iran	7 354	14 251	43.2	170 048	Ho Chi Minh City,				
Delhi, India	6 993	11 849	53.3	131 235	Vietnam	3 250	4 481	12.0	271 511
Shanghai, China	6 698	7 540	30.1	222 391	Guangzhou, China	3 248	3 652	30.5	106 477
Chicago, U.S.	6 511	6 568	294.2	22 129	Detroit, U.S.	3 133	2 735	180.7	17 337
Karachi, Pakistan	6 351	11 299	73.4	86 567	Miami, U.S.	3 123	3 894	173.0	18 053
Lagos, Nigeria	6 054	12 528	21.6	279 976	Belo Horizonte, Brazil . .	3 059	5 125	30.5	100 281
Beijing, China	5 608	5 993	58.3	96 183	Wuhan, China	3 048	3 495	25.1	121 442
Taipei, Taiwan	5 550	8 516	53.3	104 155	Ahmadabad, India	3 037	4 837	12.4	245 788
Lima, Peru	5 447	9 241	46.3	117 555	Greater Berlin, Germany	3 033	3 006	105.8	28 667
Hong Kong	5 415	5 956	7.7	701 188	Hyderabad, India	3 022	4 765	34.0	88 936
Istanbul, Turkey	5 389	8 875	63.7	84 584	Caracas, Venezuela	2 993	3 435	20.9	143 542
Bangkok, Thailand	4 998	7 587	39.4	126 900	Toronto, Canada	2 972	3 296	59.5	49 980
Madras, India	4 983	7 384	44.4	112 217					

The World's Refugees in 1987

The following information is from the *World Refugee Survey 1987*, a publication of the U.S. Committee for Refugees, a nonprofit corp. The refugees in this table include only those who are in need of protection and/or assistance, and do not include refugees who have resettled.

In some areas, the United States and Western Europe for example, there are large numbers of undocumented aliens and asylum seekers. These individuals are not included although many might be considered refugees. There is, however, no reliable way to document their number.

Country of Asylum	From	Number
Total Africa	Mostly Western Sahara	**3 574 910**
Algeria	Mostly Western Sahara	167 000[1]
Angola	Namibia, Zaire, S. Africa	92 200
Benin	Chad	3 700
Botswana	Zimbabwe, S. Africa	5 200
Burkina Faso	various	180
Burundi	Rwanda, Zaire	76 000[1]
Cameroon	Chad	7 300
Central African Rep.	Chad	5 100
Congo	various	1 200
Côte d'Ivoire	Ghana, SE Asia	600
Djibouti	Ethiopia	13 500
Egypt	various	1 080
Ethiopia	Sudan, Somalia	220 000
Gabon	various	100
Ghana	Chad	140
Kenya	Ethiopia, Rwanda, Uganda	9 000
Lesotho	South Africa	2 000[1]
Liberia	various	110
Malawi	Mozambique	420 000
Morocco	various	800
Mozambique	S. Africa	500
Nigeria	Chad, others	4 800
Rwanda	Burundi	19 000
Senegal	Guinea Bissau	5 600
Sierra Leone	Namibia	200
Somalia	Ethiopia	430 000[1]
S. Africa	Mozambique	180 000[1]
Sudan	Ethiopia, Uganda, Chad	817 000
Swaziland	South Africa, Mozambique	67 000[1]
Tanzania	Burundi, Zaire, Mozambique	266 000
Togo	Ghana	1 700
Tunisia	various	200
Uganda	Rwanda, Zaire, Sudan	120 400
Zaire	Angola, Rwanda, Burundi	338 000
Zambia	Angola, Mozambique, Zaire	149 000
Zimbabwe	Mozambique	150 500
Total East Asia/Pacific		**560 260**
Burma	China, Bangladesh	1 800
China	Vietnam	100
Hong Kong	Vietnam	9 260
Indonesia	Vietnam	2 490
Japan	Vietnam	590
Korea	Vietnam	80
Macau	Vietnam	550
Malaysia	Philippines, Vietnam	98 220
Papua New Guinea	Indonesia	9 500
Philippines	Vietnam, Cambodia, Laos	11 950
Singapore	Vietnam	200

Country of Asylum	From	Number
Thailand	Burma, Laos, Cambodia	404 500
Vietnam	Cambodia	21 000
Total Europe		**69 200**
Austria	various	18 500
Denmark	various	15 000
Greece	Asia, E. Europe	3 300
Italy	Poland, various	13 000
Portugal	various	800
Spain	Latin Amer., Asia	10 200
Sweden	various	7 000
Yugoslavia	various	1 400
Total Latin America/Caribbean		**290 090**
Argentina	Chile, SE Asia	6 800
Belize	El Salvador, Guatemala	4 300
Bolivia	Guatemala, Chile	220
Brazil	Europe, other	450
Chile	Europe	450
Colombia	Europe	410
Costa Rica	El Salvador, Nicaragua	32 000
Cuba	Haiti	2 000
Dominican Rep.	Haiti	6 000[1]
Ecuador	Chile, various	800
El Salvador	various	200
French Guiana	Suriname	8 000
Guatemala	El Salvador, Nicaragua	400
Honduras	El Salvador, Nicaragua	52 500
Mexico	El Salvador, Guatemala	165 000[1]
Nicaragua	El Salvador, Guatemala	8 200
Panama	El Salvador, others	1 000
Peru	various	700
Uruguay	various	160
Venezuela	Caribbean	500
Total Middle East/South Asia		**8 802 000**
India	Bangladesh, Tibet, Sri Lanka	281 700
Iran	Afghanistan, Iraq	2 600 000
Iraq	Iran	75 000
Kuwait	Afghanistan, others	15 000
Pakistan	Afghanistan	3 545 400
Yemen, North	S. Yemen	61 200
Palestinians		
Gaza Strip		447 850
Jordan		852 750
Lebanon		287 420
Syria		259 850
West Bank		375 830
Total Refugees		**13 296 460**

(1) Significant variance among sources in number reported.

Principal Sources of Refugees

Afghanistan	5 751 000[1]	Burundi	179 000	Namibia	78 000
Palestinians	2 217 805	Western Sahara	165 000	Chad	65 500
Ethiopia	1 122 300[1]	El Salvador	158 900[1]	Yemen (Aden)	61 200
Mozambique	917 000[1]	Sri Lanka	125 000	Nicaragua	55 300[1]
Angola	404 000	Tibet	100 000	Zaire	54 500
Iraq	400 000[1]	Uganda	96 900	Bangladesh	50 000
Cambodia	314 450	Philippines	90 000[1]		
Sudan	205 000	Iran	80 100[1]		
Rwanda	196 700[1]	Laos	78 500		

(1) Significant variance among sources in number reported.

The Principal Languages of the World

Source: Sidney S. Culbert, Guthrie Hall NI-25 — University of Washington, Seattle, Wash. 98195

Total number of speakers (native plus non-native) of languages spoken by at least one million persons (midyear 1988)

Language	Millions
Achinese (N Sumatra, Indonesia)	2
Afrikaans (So. Africa)	10
Akan (or Twi-Fante) Ghana	6
Albanian (Albania; Yugoslavia)	5
Amharic (Ethiopia)	14
Arabic	187
Armenian (USSR)	5
Assamese[1] (Assam, India; Bangladesh)	20
Aymara (Bolivia; Peru)	2
Azerbaijani (Iran; Azer. SSR, USSR)	13
Balinese (Indonesia)	3
Baluchi (Baluchistan, Pakistan)	3
Bashkir (Bashkir ASSR, USSR)	1
Batak (Indonesia) (see also Karo)	4
Baule (Côte d' Ivoire)	2
Beja (Kassala, Sudan; Ethiopia)	1
Bemba (Zambia)	2
Bengali[1]	178
Berber[2]	
Beti (Cameroon; Gabon; Eq. Guinea)	2
Bhili (India)	3
Bikol (SE Luzon, Philippines)	3
Bugis (Suluwesi, Indon; Subah, Malaysia)	3
Bulgarian (Bulgaria)	9
Burmese (Burma)	29
Buyi (S Guizhou, S China)	2
Byelorussian (Byelorussian SSR, USSR)	9
Cantonese (or Yue) (China; Hong-kong)	61
Catalan (NE Spain; S France; Andorra)	9
Cebuano (Bohol Sea area, Philippines)	11
Chagga (Kilimanjaro area, Tanzania)	1
Chiga (Ankole, Uganda)	1
Chinese[3]	
Chuvash (Chuvash ASSR, USSR)	2
Czech (Czechoslovakia)	12
Danish (Denmark)	5
Dogri (Jammu-Kashmir, C and E India)	1
Dong (Guizhou, Hunan, Guangxi, China)	2
Dutch-Flemish (Netherlands; Belgium)	21
Dyerma (SW Niger)	1
Edo (Bendel, S Nigeria)	1
Efik (incl. Ibibio) (SE Nigeria; W. Cam.)	6
English	431
Esperanto	1
Estonian (Estonian SSR, USSR)	1
Ewe (SE Ghana; S Togo)	3
Fang-Bulu (Dialects of Beti, q. v.)	
Farsi (Iranian form of Persian, q. v.)	
Finnish (Finland; Sweden)	5
Flemish (see Dutch-Flemish)	
Fon (SC Benin; S Togo)	1
French	117
Fula (or Peulh) (Cameroon; Nigeria)	12
Fulakunda (Senegambia; Guinea Bissau)	1
Futa Jalon (NW Guinea; Sierra Leone)	1
Galician (Galicia, NW Spain)	3
Galla (see Oromo)	
Ganda (or Luganda) (S Uganda)	3
Georgian (Georgian SSR, USSR)	4
German	118
Gilaki (Gilan, NW Iran)	2
Gondi (Central India)	2
Greek (Greece)	11
Guarani (Paraguay)	4
Gujarati[1] (W and C India; S Pakistan)	37
Gusii (Kisii District, Nyanza, Kenya)	1
Hadiyya (Arusi, Ethiopia)	1
Hakka (or Kejia) (SE China)	29

Language	Millions
Hani (S China)	1
Hausa (N Nigeria; Niger; Cameroon)	31
Hebrew (Israel)	4
Hindi[1,4]	325
Ho (West Bengal, India)	1
Hungarian (or Magyar) (Hungary)	14
Iban (Kalimantan, Indonesia; Malaysia)	1
Ibibio (see Efik)	
Igbo (or Ibo) (lower Niger R., Nigeria)	15
Ijaw (Niger River delta, Nigeria)	2
Ilocano (NW Luzon, Philippines)	6
Indonesian (see Malay-Indonesian)	
Italian (Italy)	63
Japanese	124
Javanese (Java, Indonesia)	55
Kabyle (W Kabylia, N Algeria)	2
Kalenjin (Riff Valley, Kenya)	1
Kamba (E Kenya)	2
Kannada[1] (S India)	40
Kanuri (Nigeria; Niger; Chad; Cam.)	4
Karen, Burmese (SE Burma)	1
Karo-Dairi (N Sumatra, Indonesia)	1
Kashmiri[1] (N India; NE Pakistan)	4
Kazakh (Kazakh SSR, USSR)	8
Kenuzi-Dongola (S Egypt; Sudan)	1
Khalka (see Mongolian)	
Khmer (Kampuchea; Vietnam; Thailand)	7
Khmer, Northern (Thailand)	1
Kikuyu (or Gekoyo) (W and C Kenya)	4
Kirghiz (Kirghiz SSR, USSR)	2
Kituba (Bas-Zaire, Bandundu, Zaire)	3
Kongo (W Zaire; S Congo; NW Angola)	3
Konkani (Maharashtra and SW India)	4
Korean (So., No. Korea; China; Japan)	68
Kurdish (south-west of Caspian Sea)	9
Kurukh (or Oraon) (C and E India)	2
Lao[5] (Laos)	4
Lampung-Komering (Sumatra, Indonesia)	1
Latvian (Latvian SSR, USSR)	2
Lingala (including Bangala) (Zaire)	5
Lithuanian (Lithuanian SSR, USSR)	3
Luba-Lubua (or Chiluba) (Kasai, Zaire)	6
Luba-Shaba (Shaba, Zaire)	1
Lubu (E Sumatra, Indonesia)	1
Luhya (W Kenya)	2
Luo (Kenya; Nyanza, Tanzania)	2
Luri (SW Iran; Iraq)	2
Macedonian (Macedonia, Yugoslavia)	2
Madurese (Madura, Indonesia)	9
Magindanaon (Moro Gulf, S Philippines)	1
Makassar (S Sulawesi, Indonesia)	1
Makua (S Tanzania; N Mozambique)	3
Malagasy (Madagascar)	11
Malay-Indonesian	135
Malay, Pattani (SE coast of Thailand)	1
Malayalam[1] (Kerala, India)	33
Malinke-Bambara-Dyula (W Africa)	7
Mandarin	825
Marathi[1] (Maharashtra, India)	62
Mazandarani (S Mazandaran, N Iran)	2
Mbundu or Umbundu (Benguela, Angola)	3
Mbundu (or Kimbundu) (Luanda, Angola)	2
Meithei (NE India; Bangladesh)	1
Mende (Central, S and E Sierra Leone)	2
Miao (or Hmong) (S China; SE Asia)	5
Min (SE China; Taiwan; Malaysia)	45
Minankabau (W Sumatra, Indonesia)	6

Language	Millions
Moldavian (included with Romanian)	
Mongolian (Mongolia; NE China)	4
Mordvin (in and near Mord. SSR, USSR)	1
Moré (central part of Burkina Faso)	4
Nepali (Nepal; NE India; Bhutan)	12
Ngulu (Zambezia, Mozambique; Malawi)	1
Nkole (Western Prov., Uganda)	1
Norwegian (Norway)	5
Nyamwezi-Sukuma (NW Tanzania)	3
Nyanja (Malawi; Zambia; N Zimbabwe)	4
Oriya[1] (Central and E India)	29
Oromo (W Ethiopia; N Kenya)	9
Pampangan (NW of Manila, Philippines)	1
Panay-Hiligaynon (Philippines)	5
Pangasinan (Lingayen G., Philippines)	1
Pashtu (Pakistan; Afghanistan; Iran)	21
Pedi (see Sotho, Northern)	
Persian (Iran; Afghanistan)	31
Polish (Poland)	42
Portuguese	169
Provençal (S France)	4
Punjabi[1] (Punjab, Pakistan; NW India)	77
Pushto (see Pashtu) (many spellings)	
Quechua (Peru, Bolivia)	7
Riff (N Morocco; Algerian coast)	1
Romanian (Romania; Moldavia, USSR)	25
Ruanda (Rwanda; S Uganda; E Zaire)	7
Rundi (Burundi)	5
Russian	289
Samar-Leyte (Central E Philippines)	3
Sango (Central African Republic)	2
Santali (E India; Nepal)	5
Sasak (Lombok, Alas Strait, Indonesia)	1
Serbo-Croation (Yugoslavia)	20
Shan (Shan, E Burma)	2
Shilha (W Algeria; S Morocco)	3
Sindhi[1] (SE Pakistan; W India)	15
Shona (Zimbabwe)	6
Sidamo (Sidamo, S Ethiopia)	1
Sinhalese (Sri Lanka)	12
Slovak (Czechoslovakia)	5
Slovene (Slovenia, NW Yugoslavia)	2
Soga (Busoga, Uganda)	1
Somali (Somalia; Eth.; Ken.; Djibouti)	7
Sotho, Northern (So. Africa)	3
Sotho, Southern (So. Africa; Lesotho)	4
Spanish	320
Sundanese (Sunda Strait, Indonesia)	21
Swahili (Kenya; Tanz.; Zaire; Uganda)	41
Swati (Swaziland; So. Africa)	1
Swedish (Sweden; Finland)	9
Sylhetti (Bangladesh)	3
Tagalog (Philippines)	33
Tajiki (Tajik Uzbek Kirghiz SSRs, USSR)	4
Tamazight (N Morocco; W Algeria)	3
Tamil[1] (Tamil Nadu, India; Sri Lanka)	63
Tatar (Tatar SSR, USSR)	7
Telugu[1] (Andhra Pradesh, SE India)	65
Temne (central Sierra Leone)	1
Thai[5] (Thailand)	46
Thonga (Mozambique; So. Africa)	4
Tibetan (SW China; N India; Nepal)	5
Tigrinya (S Eritrea, Tigre, Ethiopia)	4
Tiv (SE Nigeria; Cameroon)	2
Tong (see Dong)	
Tonga (SW Zambia; NW Zimbabwe)	1
Tswana (Botswana; So. Africa)	3
Tulu (S India)	2

Language	Millions	Language	Millions	Language	Millions
Tumbuka (N Malawi; NE Zambia) . .	1	Uzbek (Uzbek SSR, USSR)	12	Thailand)	1
Turkish (Turkey)	53	Vietnamese (Vietnam)	54	Yi (S and SW China)	6
Turkmen (S USSR; NE Iran;		Wolaytta (SW Ethiopia)	1	Yiddish[6]	
Afghanistan)	3	Wolof (Senegal)	5	Yoruba (SW Nigeria; Zou, Benin) . .	17
Twi-Fante (see Akan)		Wu (Shanghai and nearby prov.,		Zande (NE Zaire; SW Sudan)	1
Uighur (Xinjiang, NW China; SC		China)	61	Zhuang (S China)	14
USSR)	7	Xhosa (SW Cape Province, So.		Zulu (N Natal, So. Africa; Lesotho) .	7
Ukrainian (Ukraine, USSR; Poland) .	44	Africa)	6		
Urdu[1,4] (Pakistan; India)	88	Yao (China; Vietnam; Laos;			

(1) One of the fifteen languages of the Constitution of India. (2) See Kabyle, Riff, Shilha, and Tamazight. (3) See Mandarin, Cantonese, Wu, Min, and Hakka. The "common speech" (Putonghua) or the "national language" (Guoyu) is a standardized form of Mandarin as spoken in the area of Beijing. (4) Hindi and Urdu are essentially the same language, Hindustani. As the official language of Pakistan it is written in a modified Arabic script and called Urdu. As the official language of India it is written in the Devanagari script and called Hindi. (5) Thai includes Central, Southwestern, Northern and Northeastern Thai. The distinction between Northeastern Thai and Lao is political rather than linguistic. (6) Yiddish is usually considered a variant of German, though it has its own standard grammar, dictionaries, a highly developed literature, and is written in Hebrew characters.

World Exploration

Early Explorers of the Western Hemisphere

The first men to discover the New World or Western Hemisphere are believed to have walked across a "land bridge" from Siberia to Alaska, an isthmus since broken by the Bering Strait. From Alaska, these ancestors of the Indians spread through North, Central and South America. Anthropologists have placed these crossings at between 18000 and 14000 B.C.; but evidence found in 1967 near Puebla, Mex., indicates mankind reached there as early as 35 000-40 000 years ago.

At first, these people were hunters using flint weapons and tools. In Mexico, about 7000-6000 B.C., they founded farming cultures, developing corn, squash, etc. Eventually, they created complex civilizations — Olmec, Toltec, Aztec and Maya and, in South America, Inca. Carbon-14 tests show men lived about 8000 B.C. near what are now Front Royal, Va., Kanawha, W. Va., and Duchess Quarry, N.Y. The Hopewell Culture, based on farming, flourished about 1000 B.C.

Norsemen (Norwegian Vikings sailing out of Iceland and Greenland) are credited by most scholars with being the first Europeans to discover North America, with at least 5 voyages around 1000 A.D. to areas they called Helluland, Markland, Vinland—possibly Labrador, Nova Scotia or Newfoundland and New England.

Christopher Columbus, most famous of the explorers, was born at Genoa, Italy, but made his discoveries sailing for the Spanish rulers Ferdinand and Isabella. Dates of his voyages, places he discovered and other information follow:

1492—First voyage. Left Palos, Spain, Aug. 3 with 88 men (est.). Discovered San Salvador (Guanahani or Watling Is., Bahamas) Oct. 12. Also Cuba, Hispaniola (Haiti-Dominican Republic); built Fort La Navidad on latter.

1493—Second voyage, first part, Sept. 25, with 17 ships, 1500 men. Dominica (Lesser Antilles) Nov. 3; Guadeloupe, Montserrat, Antigua, San Martin, Santa Cruz, Puerto Rico, Virgin Islands. Settled Isabela on Hispaniola. **Second part** (Columbus having remained in Western Hemisphere), Jamaica, Isle of Pines, La Mona Is.

1498—Third voyage. Left Spain May 30, 1498, 6 ships. Discovered Trinidad. Saw South American continent Aug. 1, 1498, but called it Isla Sancta (Holy Island). Entered Gulf of Paria and landed, first time on continental soil. At mouth of Orinoco Aug. 14 he decided this was the mainland.

1502—Fourth voyage, 4 caravels, 150 men. St. Lucia, Guanaja off Honduras; Cape Gracias a Dios, Honduras; San Juan River, Costa Rica; Almirante, Portobelo, and Laguna de Chiriqui, Panama.

Year	Explorer	Nationality and employer	Discovery or exploration
1497	John Cabot	Italian-English	Newfoundland or Nova Scotia
1498	John and Sebastian Cabot	Italian-English	Labrador to Hatteras
1499	Alonso de Ojeda	Spanish	South American coast, Venezuela
1500, Feb.. . .	Vicente y Pinzon	Spanish	South American coast, Amazon River
1500, Apr.. . .	Pedro Alvarez Cabral	Portuguese	Brazil (for Portugal)
1500-02	Gaspar Corte-Real	Portuguese	Labrador
1501	Rodrigo de Bastidas	Spanish	Central America
1513	Vasco Nunez de Balboa	Spanish	Pacific Ocean
1513	Juan Ponce de Leon	Spanish	Florida
1515	Juan de Solis	Spanish	Rio de la Plata
1519	Alonso de Pineda	Spanish	Mouth of Mississippi River
1519	Hernando Cortes	Spanish	Mexico
1520	Ferdinand Magellan	Portuguese-Spanish . .	Straits of Magellan, Tierra del Fuego
1524	Giovanni da Verrazano	Italian-French.	Atlantic coast-New York harbor
1532	Francisco Pizarro	Spanish	Peru
1534	Jacques Cartier	French	Canada, Gulf of St. Lawrence
1536	Pedro de Mendoza	Spanish	Buenos Aires
1536	A.N. Cabeza de Vaca	Spanish	Texas coast and interior

Year	Explorer	Nationality and employer	Discovery or exploration
1539	Francisco de Ulloa	Spanish	California coast
1539-41	Hernando de Soto	Spanish	Mississippi River near Memphis
1539	Marcos de Niza	Italian-Spanish	Southwest (now U.S.)
1540	Francisco V. de Coronado	Spanish	Southwest (now U.S.)
1540	Hernando Alarcon	Spanish	Colorado River
1540	Garcia de L. Cardenas	Spanish	Grand Canyon of the Colorado
1541	Francisco de Orellana	Spanish	Amazon River
1542	Juan Rodriguez Cabrillo	Portuguese-Spanish	San Diego harbor
1565	Pedro Menendez de Aviles	Spanish	St. Augustine
1576	Martin Frobisher	English	Frobisher Bay, Canada
1577-80	Francis Drake	English	California coast
1582	Antonio de Espejo	Spanish	Southwest (named New Mexico)
1584	Amadas & Barlow (for Raleigh)	English	Virginia
1585-87	Sir Walter Raleigh's men	English	Roanoke Is., N.C.
1595	Sir Walter Raleigh	English	Orinoco River
1603-09	Samuel de Champlain	French	Canadian interior, Lake Champlain
1607	Capt. John Smith	English	Atlantic coast
1609-10	Henry Hudson	English-Dutch	Hudson River, Hudson Bay
1634	Jean Nicolet	French	Lake Michigan; Wisconsin
1673	Jacques Marquette, Louis Jolliet	French	Mississippi S to Arkansas
1682	Sieur de La Salle	French	Mississippi S to Gulf of Mexico
1789	Sir Alexander Mackenzie	British	Canadian Northwest

Arctic Exploration

Early Explorers

1587 — John Davis (England). Davis Strait to Sanderson's Hope, 72° 12′ N.

1596 — Willem Barents and Jacob van Heemskerck (Holland). Discovered Bear Island, touched northwest tip of Spitsbergen, 79° 49′ N, rounded Novaya Zemlya, wintered at Ice Haven.

1607 — Henry Hudson (England). North along Greenland's east coast to Cape Hold-with-Hope, 73° 30′, then north of Spitsbergen to 80° 23′. Returning, he discovered Hudson's Touches (Jan Mayen).

1616 — William Baffin and Robert Bylot (England). Baffin Bay to Smith Sound.

1728 — Vitus Bering (Russia). Proved Asia and America were separated by sailing through strait.

1733-40 — Great Northern Expedition (Russia). Surveyed Siberian Arctic coast.

1741 — Vitus Bering (Russia). Sighted Alaska from sea, named Mount St. Elias. His lieutenant, Chirikof, discovered coast.

1771 — Samuel Hearne (Hudson's Bay Co.). Overland from Prince of Wales Fort (Churchill) on Hudson Bay to mouth of Coppermine River.

1778 — James Cook (Britain). Through Bering Strait to Icy Cape, Alaska, and North Cape, Siberia.

1789 — Alexander Mackenzie (North West Co., Britain). Montreal to mouth of Mackenzie River.

1806 — William Scoresby (Britain). N. of Spitsbergen to 81° 30′.

1820-3 — Ferdinand von Wrangel (Russia). Completed a survey of Siberian Arctic coast. His exploration joined that of James Cook at North Cape, confirming separation of the continents.

1845 — Sir John Franklin (Britain) was one of many to seek the Northwest Passage—an ocean route connecting the Atlantic and Pacific via the Arctic. His 2 ships (the *Erebus* and *Terror*) were last seen entering Lancaster Sound July 26.

1881 — The steamer *Jeanette* on an expedition led by Lt. Cmdr. George W. DeLong was trapped in ice and crushed, June 1881. De ˙Long and 11 crewmen died; 12 others survived.

1888 — Fridtjof Nansen (Norway) crossed Greenland's icecap, 1893-96 — Nansen in *Fram* drifted from New Siberian Is. to Spitsbergen; tried polar dash in 1895, reached Franz Josef Land.

1899 — Salomon A. Andree (Sweden) and 2 others started in balloon from Danes, Is., Spitsbergen, on July 11 to drift across pole to America, and disappeared. Over 33 years later, Aug. 6, 1930, their frozen bodies were found on White Is., 82° 57′ N 29° 52′ E.

1903-06 — Roald Amundsen (Norway) first sailed Northwest Passage.

Discovery of North Pole

Robert E. Peary explored Greenland's coast 1891-92, tried for North Pole 1893. In 1900 he reached northern limit of Greenland and 83° 50′ N; in 1902 he reached 84° 06′ N; in 1906 he went from Ellesmere Is. to 87° 06′ N. He sailed in the *Roosevelt*, July, 1908, to winter off Cape Sheridan, Grant Land. The dash for the North Pole began Mar. 1 from Cape Columbia, Ellesmere Land. Peary reached the pole, 90° N, Apr. 6, 1909.

Peary had several supporting groups carrying supplies until the last group turned back at 87° 47′ N. Peary, Matthew Henson and 4 Inuit proceeded with dog teams and sleds. They crossed the pole several times, finally built an igloo at 90°, remained 36 hours. Started south Apr. 7 at 4 p.m. for Cape Columbia. Inuit were Coqueeh, Ootah, Eginwah and Seegloo.

1914 — Donald Macmillan (U.S.). Northwest, 320 km, from Axel Heiberg Island to seek Peary's Crocker Land.

1915-17 — Vihjalmur Stefansson (Canada) discovered Borden, Brock, Meighen and Lougheed Islands.

1918-20 — Roald Amundsen sailed Northeast Passage.

1925 — Amundsen and Lincoln Ellsworth (U.S.) reached 87° 44′ N in attempt to fly to North Pole from Spitsbergen.

1926 — Richard E. Byrd and Floyd Bennett (U.S.) first over North Pole by air, May 9.

1926 — Amundsen, Ellsworth and Umberto Nobile (Italy) flew from Spitsbergen over North Pole May 12, to Teller, Alaska, in dirigible *Norge*.

1928 — Nobile crossed North Pole in airship May 24, crashed May 25. Amundsen lost while trying to effect rescue by plane.

North Pole Exploration Records

On Aug. 3, 1958, the *Nautilus*, under Comdr. William R. Anderson, became the first ship to cross the North Pole beneath the Arctic ice.

The nuclear-powered U.S. submarine *Seadragon*, Comdr. George P. Steele 2d, made the first east-west underwater transit through the Northwest Passage during August, 1960. It sailed from Portsmouth, N.H., headed between Greenland and Labrador through Baffin Bay, then west through Lancaster Sound and McClure Strait to the Beaufort Sea. Traveling submerged for the most part, the submarine made 1360 km from Baffin Bay to the Beaufort Sea in 6 days.

On Aug. 16, 1977, the Soviet nuclear icebreaker *Arktika* reached the North Pole and became the first surface ship to break through the Arctic ice pack to the top of the world.

On April 30, 1978, Naomi Uemura, a Japanese explorer, became the first person to reach the North Pole alone by dog sled. During the 54-day, 960 km trek over the frozen Arctic, Uemura survived attacks by a marauding polar bear.

In April, 1982, Sir Ranulph Fiennes and Charles Burton, British explorers, reached the North Pole and became the first to circle the earth from pole to pole. They had reached the South Pole 16 months earlier. The 83 200 km trek took 3 years, involved 23 people, and cost an estimated $18 million. The expedition was also the first to travel down the Scott Glacier and the first to journey up the Yukon and through the Northwest Passage in a single season.

On May 2, 1986, 6 American and Canadian explorers reached the North Pole assisted only by dogs. They became the first to reach the Pole without mechanical assistance since Robert E. Peary planted a flag there in 1909. The explorers, Americans Will Steger, Paul Schurke, Anne Bancroft, and Geoff Carroll, and Canadians Brent Boddy and Richard Weber completed the 805 km journey in 56 days.

Antarctic Exploration

Early History

Antarctica has been approached since 1773-75, when Capt. James Cook (Britain) reached 71° 10′ S. Many sea and landmarks bear names of early explorers. Bellingshausen (Russia) discovered Peter I and Alexander I Islands, 1819-21. Nathaniel Palmer (U.S.) discovered Palmer Peninsula, 60° W, 1820, without realizing that this was a continent. James Weddell (Britain) found Weddell Sea, 74° 15′ S, 1823.

First to announce existence of the continent of Antarctica was Charles Wilkes (U.S.), who followed the coast for 2 400 km, 1840. Adelie Coast, 140° E, was found by Dumont d'Urville (France), 1840. Ross Ice Shelf was found by James Clark Ross (Britain), 1841-42.

1895 — Leonard Kristensen (Norway) landed a party on the coast of Victoria Land. They were the first ashore on the main continental mass. C.E. Borchgrevink, a member of that party, returned in 1899 with a British expedition, first to winter on Antarctica.

1902-04 — Robert F. Scott (Britain) discovered Edward VII Peninsula. He reached 82° 17′ S, 146° 33′ E from McMurdo Sound.

1908-09 — Ernest Shackleton (Britain) introduced the use of Manchurian ponies in Antarctic sledging. He reached 88° 23′ S, discovering a route on to the plateau by way of the Beardmore Glacier and pioneering the way to the pole.

Discovery of South Pole

1911 — Roald Amundsen (Norway) with 4 men and dog teams reached the pole Dec. 14.

1912 — Capt. Scott reached the pole from Ross Island Jan. 18, with 4 companions. They found Amundsen's tent. None of Scott's party survived. They were found Nov. 12.

1928 — First man to use an airplane over Antarctica was Hubert Wilkins (Britain).

1929 — Richard E. Byrd (U.S.) established Little America on Bay of Whales. On 2 560 km airplane flight begun Nov. 28 he crossed South Pole Nov. 29 with 3 others.

1934-35 — Byrd led 2d expedition to Little America, explored 1 170 000 sq. km, wintered alone at weather station, 80° 08′ S.

1934-37 — John Rymill led British Graham Land expedition; discovered that Palmer Peninsula is part of Antarctic mainland.

1935 — Lincoln Ellsworth (U.S.) flew south along Palmer Peninsula's east coast, then crossed continent to Little America, making 4 landings on unprepared terrain in bad weather.

1939-41 — U.S. Antarctic Service built West Base on Ross Ice Shelf under Paul Siple, and East Base on Palmer Peninsula under Richard Black. U.S. Navy plane flights discovered about 390 000 sq. km of new land.

1940 — Byrd charted most of coast between Ross Sea and Palmer Peninsula.

1946-47 — U.S. Navy undertook Operation High-jump under Byrd. Expedition included 13 ships and 4 000 men. Airplanes photomapped coastline and penetrated beyond pole.

1946-48 — Ronne Antarctic Research Expedition, Comdr. Finn Ronne, determined the Antarctic to be only one continent with no strait between Weddell Sea and Ross Sea; discovered 650 000 sq. km of land by flights to 79° S Lat., and made 14 000 aerial photographs over 1 170 000 sq. km of land. Mrs. Ronne and Mrs. H. Darlington were the first women to winter on Antarctica.

1955-57 — U.S. Navy's Operation Deep Freeze led by Adm. Byrd. Supporting U.S. scientific efforts for the International Geophysical Year, the operation was commanded by Rear Adm. George Dufek. It established 5 coastal stations fronting the Indian, Pacific and Atlantic oceans and also 3 interior stations; explored more than 2 600 000 sq. km in Wilkes Land.

1957-58 — During the International Geophysical year, July 1957 through Dec. 1958, scientists from 12 countries conducted ambitious programs of Antarctic research. A network of some 60 stations on the continent and sub-Arctic islands studied oceanography, glaciology, meteorology, seismology, geomagnetism, the ionosphere, cosmic rays, aurora and airglow.

Dr. V.E. Fuchs led a 12-man Trans-Antarctic Expedition on the first land crossing of Antarctica. Starting from the Weddell Sea, they reached Scott Station Mar. 2, 1958, after traveling 3 453 km in 98 days.

1958 — A group of 5 U.S. scientists led by Edward C. Thiel, seismologist, moving by tractor from Ellsworth Station on Weddell Sea, identified a huge mountain range, 1 500 m above the ice sheet and 2 700 m above sea level. The range, originally seen by a Navy plane, was named the Dufek Massif, for Rear Adm. George Dufek.

1959 — Twelve nations — Argentina, Australia, Belgium, Chile, France, Japan, New Zealand, Norway, South Africa, the Soviet Union, the United Kingdom, and the U.S. — signed a treaty suspending any territorial claims for 30 years and reserving the continent for research.

1961-62 — Scientists discovered a trough, the Bentley Trench, running from Ross Ice Shelf, Pacific, into Marie Byrd Land, around the end of the Ellsworth Mtns., toward the Weddell Sea.

1962 — First nuclear power plant began operation at McMurdo Sound.

1963 — On Feb. 22 a U.S. plane made the longest nonstop flight ever made in the S. Pole area, covering 5 760 km in 10 hours. The flight was from McMurdo Station south past the geographical S. Pole to Shackleton Mtns., southeast to the "Area of Inaccessibility" and back to McMurdo Station.

1964 — A British survey team was landed by helicopter on Cook Island, the first recorded visit since its discovery in 1775.

1964 — New Zealanders completed one of the last and most important surveys when they mapped the mountain area from Cape Adare west some 640 km to Pennell Glacier.

Highest and Lowest Continental Altitudes

Source: National Geographic Society, Washington, D.C.

Continent	Highest point	Metres elevation	Lowest point	Metres below sea level
Asia	Mount Everest, Nepal-Tibet	8 848	Dead Sea, Israel-Jordan	400
South America	Mount Aconcagua, Argentina	6 960	Valdes Peninsula, Argentina	40
North America	Mount McKinley, Alaska	6 194	Death Valley, California	86
Africa	Kilimanjaro, Tanzania	5 895	Lake Assal, Djibouti	156
Europe	Mount El'brus, USSR	5 642	Caspian Sea, USSR	28
Antarctica	Vinson Massif	5 140	Unknown	...
Australia	Mount Kosciusko, New South Wales	2 228	Lake Eyre, South Australia	16

Height of Mount Everest

Mt. Everest was considered to be 8 839.8 m tall when Edmund Hillary and Tenzing Norgay scaled it in 1953. This triangulation figure had been accepted since 1850. In 1954 the Surveyor General of the Republic of India set the height at 8 847.7 m, plus or minus 3 m because of snow. The National Geographic Society accepts the new figure, but many mountaineering groups still use 8 839.8 m.

Mountains

Height of Mount Everest

Mt. Everest was considered to be 8 840 m (29 002 ft.) high when Edmund Hillary and Tenzing Norgay scaled it in 1953. This triangulation figure had been accepted since 1850. In 1954, the Surveyor General of the Republic of India set the height at 8 848 m (29 028 ft.) plus or minus 3 m (10 ft.) because of snow; this new figure was accepted by the National Geographic Society.

In 1987, new calculations based on satellite measurements indicated that the Himalayan peak K-2 rose 8 858 m (29 064 ft) above sea level. In May 1988, a team of U.S., Pakistani and Nepalese scientists monitoring the rising of the Himalayas began work on satellite measurements which were expected to settle the question of which peak, Mt. Everest or K-2, is the world's highest.

High Peaks in United States, Canada, Mexico

Name	Place	Metres	Name	Place	Metres	Name	Place	Metres
McKinley	Alas	6 194	Uncompahgre	Col	4 361	Eolus	Col	4 293
Logan	Yuk	5 951	Crestone	Col	4 357	Missouri	Col	4 290
Citlaltepec (Orizaba)	Mexico	5 700	Lincoln	Col	4 354	Columbia	Col	4 289
St. Elias	Alas-Yuk	5 489	Grays	Col	4 350	Augusta	Alas-Yuk	4 289
Popocatepetl	Mexico	5 452	Antero	Col	4 349	Humboldt	Col	4 287
Foraker	Alas	5 304	Torreys	Col	4 349	Bierstadt	Col	4 285
Iztaccihuatl	Mexico	5 286	Castle	Col	4 348	Sunlight	Col	4 285
Lucania	Yuk	5 226	Quandary	Col	4 348	Split	Cal	4 285
King	Yuk	5 173	Evans	Col	4 348	Nauhcampatepetl		
Steele	Yuk	5 073	Longs	Col	4 345	(Cofre de Perote)	Mexico	4 282
Bona	Alas	5 044	McArthur	Yuk	4 344	Handies	Col	4 282
Blackburn	Alas	4 996	Wilson	Col	4 342	Culebra	Col	4 282
Kennedy	Alas	4 964	White	Cal	4 342	Langley	Cal	4 280
Sanford	Alas	4 949	North Palisade	Cal	4 341	Lindsey	Col	4 280
South Buttress	Alas	4 842	Shavano	Col	4 337	Middle Palisade	Cal	4 279
Wood	Yuk	4 842	Belford	Col	4 327	Little Bear	Col	4 278
Vancouver	Alas-Yuk	4 785	Princeton	Col	4 327	Sherman	Col	4 278
Churchill	Alas	4 766	Crestone Needle	Col	4 327	Redcloud	Col	4 276
Fairweather	Alas-B.C.	4 663	Yale	Col	4 327	Tyndall	Cal	4 273
Macaulay	Yuk	4 663	Bross	Col	4 320	Pyramid	Col	4 272
Zinantecatl (Toluca)	Mexico	4 577	Kit Carson	Col	4 317	Wilson Peak	Col	4 272
Hubbard	Alas-Yuk	4 577	Wrangell	Alas	4 317	Muir	Cal	4 271
Bear	Alas	4 520	Shasta	Cal	4 317	Wetterhorn	Col	4 271
Walsh	Yuk	4 505	Sill	Cal	4 317	North Maroon	Col	4 271
East Buttress	Alas	4 490	El Diente	Col	4 316	San Luis	Col	4 269
Matlalcueyetl	Mexico	4 461	Maroon	Col	4 315	Huron	Col	4 269
Hunter	Alas	4 442	Tabeguache	Col	4 314	Holy Cross	Col	4 268
Alverstone	Alas-Yuk	4 439	Oxford	Col	4 314	Colima	Mexico	4 268
Browne Tower	Alas	4 429	Sneffels	Col	4 313	Sunshine	Col	4 267
Whitney	Cal	4 418	Point Success	Wash	4 313	Grizzly	Col	4 264
Elbert	Col	4 399	Democrat	Col	4 312	Barnard	Col	4 261
Massive	Col	4 396	Capitol	Col	4 307	Stewart	Col	4 260
Harvard	Col	4 395	Liberty Cap	Wash	4 301	Keith	Col	4 258
Rainier	Wash	4 392	Pikes Peak	Col	4 301	Ouray	Col	4 255
Williamson	Cal	4 382	Snowmass	Col	4 295	Le Conte	Cal	4 240
Blanca	Col	4 372	Windom	Col	4 294	Meeker	Col	4 238
La Plata	Col	4 370	Russell	Cal	4 293	Kennedy	Yuk	4 238

South America

Peak, Country	Metres	Peak, Country	Metres	Peak, Country	Metres
Aconcagua, Argentina	6 960	Laudo, Argentina	6 400	Polleras, Argentina	6 235
Ojos del Salado, Arg.-Chile	6 880	Ancohuma, Bolivia	6 388	Pular, Chile	6 225
Bonete, Argentina	6 872	Ausangate, Peru	6 384	Chani, Argentina	6 200
Tupungato, Argentina-Chile	6 800	Toro, Argentina-Chile	6 380	Aucanquilcha, Chile	6 186
Pissis, Argentina	6 780	Illampu, Bolivia	6 362	Juncal, Argentina-Chile	6 180
Mercedario, Argentina	6 770	Tres Cruces, Argentina-Chile	6 356	Negro, Argentina	6 152
Huascaran, Peru	6 768	Huandoy, Peru	6 356	Quela, Argentina	6 135
Llullaillaco, Argentina-Chile	6 723	Parinacota, Bolivia-Chile	6 330	Condoriri, Bolivia	6 125
El Libertador, Argentina	6 720	Tortolas, Argentina-Chile	6 323	Palermo, Argentina	6 120
Cachi, Argentina	6 720	Ampato, Peru	6 310	Solimana, Peru	6 117
Yerupaja, Peru	6 617	Condor, Argentina	6 300	San Juan, Argentina-Chile	6 111
Galan, Argentina	6 660	Salcantay, Peru	6 271	Sierra Nevada, Arg.-Chile	6 103
El Muerto, Argentina-Chile	6 540	Chimborazo, Ecuador	6 267	Antofalla, Argentina	6 100
Sajama, Bolivia	6 520	Huancarhuas, Peru	6 258	Marmolejo, Argentina-Chile	6 075
Nacimiento, Argentina	6 493	Famatina, Argentina	6 250	Chachani, Peru	5 920
Illimani, Bolivia	6 462	Pumasillo, Peru	6 250	Licancabur, Argentina-Chile	5 920
Coropuna, Peru	6 426	Solo, Argentina	6 250		

The highest point in the West Indies is in the Dominican Republic, Pico Duarte (3 175 m).

Antarctica

Peak	Metres	Peak	Metres	Peak	Metres	Peak	Metres
Vinson Massif	5 140	Andrew Jackson	4 191	Shear	3 993	Erebus	3 790
Tyree	4 965	Sidley	4 182	Odishaw	3 965	Don Pedro Christo-	
Shinn	4 801	Ostenso	4 179	Donaldson	3 930	phersen	3 766
Gardner	4 686	Minto	4 166	Ray	3 904	Lysaght	3 757
Epperly	4 602	Miller	4 161	Sellery	3 895	Huggins	3 733
Kirkpatrick	4 528	Long Gables	4 151	Waterman	3 880	Sabine	3 719
Elizabeth	4 480	Dickerson	4 120	Anne	3 872	Astor	3 711
Markham	4 356	Giovinetto	4 088	Press	3 830	Mohl	3 710
Bell	4 303	Wade	4 084	Campbell	3 825	Frankes	3 677
Mackellar	4 297	Fisher	4 080	Falla	3 816	Jones	3 670
Anderson	4 254	Fridtjof Nansen	4 069	Rucker	3 813	Gjelsvik	3 660
Bentley	4 247	Wexler	4 024	Goldthwait	3 810	Coman	3 658
Kaplan	4 230	Lister	4 023	Morris	3 795		

Europe

Alps

Peak, country	Metres
Mont Blanc, Fr. It.	4 807
Monte Rosa (highest peak of group), Switz.	4 634
Dom, Switz.	4 545
Liskamm, It., Switz.	4 527
Weisshorn, Switz.	4 505
Taschhorn, Switz.	4 491
Matterhorn, It., Switz.	4 478
Dent Blanche, Switz.	4 357
Nadelhorn, Switz.	4 327
Grand Combin, Switz.	4 314
Lenzpitze, Switz.	4 294
Finsteraarhorn, Switz.	4 274
Castor, Switz.	4 226
Zinalrothorn, Switz.	4 221
Hohberghorn, Switz.	4 219
Alphubel, Switz.	4 206
Rimptischhorn, Switz.	4 199
Aletschhorn, Switz.	4 195
Strahlhorn, Switz.	4 190
Dent D'Herens, Switz.	4 171

Peak, country	Metres
Breithorn, It., Switz.	4 165
Bishorn, Switz.	4 159
Jungfrau, Switz.	4 158
Ecrins, Fr.	4 103
Monch, Switz.	4 099
Pollux, Switz.	4 091
Schreckhorn, Switz.	4 078
Ober Gabelhorn, Switz.	4 063
Gran Paradiso, It.	4 061
Bernina, It., Switz.	4 049
Fiescherhorn, Switz.	4 049
Grunhorn, Switz.	4 043
Lauteraarhorn, Switz.	4 042
Durrenhorn, Switz.	4 035
Allalinhorn, Switz.	4 027
Weissmies, Switz.	4 023
Lagginhorn, Switz.	4 010
Zupo, Switz.	3 999
Fletschhorn, Switz.	3 996
Adlerhorn, Switz.	3 987
Gletscherhorn, Switz.	3 983
Schalihorn, Switz.	3 975
Scerscen, Switz.	3 971

Peak, country	Metres
Eiger, Switz.	3 970
Jagerhorn, Switz.	3 970
Rottalhorn, Switz.	3 969

Pyrenees

Peak, country	Metres
Aneto, Sp.	3 404
Posets, Sp.	3 375
Perdido, Sp.	3 355
Vignemale, Fr., Sp.	3 298
Long, Sp.	3 194
Estats, Sp.	3 141
Montcalm, Sp.	3 080

Caucasus (Europe-Asia)

Peak, country	Metres
El'brus, USSR.	5 642
Shkara, USSR.	5 201
Dykh Tau, USSR	5 198
Kashtan Tau, USSR	5 144
Dzhangi Tau, USSR	5 049
Kazbek, USSR	5 047

Africa and Australasia

Peak, country	Metres
Kilimanjaro, Tanzania	5 895
Kenya, Kenya	5 199
Margherita Pk., Uganda-Zaire	5 109
Jaja, New Guinea	5 029
Trikora, New Guinea	4 750
Mandala, New Guinea	4 700
Ras Dashan, Ethiopia	4 620

Peak, country	Metres
Meru, Tanzania	4 566
Wilhelm, New Guinea	4 509
Karisimbi, Zaire-Rwanda	4 507
Elgon, Kenya-Uganda	4 321
Batu, Ethiopia	4 307
Guna, Ethiopia	4 231
Gughe, Ethiopia	4 200

Peak, country	Metres
Toubkal, Morocco	4 165
Kinabalu, Malaysia	4 101
Kerinci, Sumatra	3 800
Cook, New Zealand.	3 764
Teide, Canary Islands	3 718
Semeru, Java	3 676
Kosciusko, Australia	2 228

Asia

Peak	Country	Metres
Everest	Nepal-Tibet	8 848[1]
K2 (Godwin Austen)	Kashmir	8 851[1]
Kanchenjunga	India-Nepal	8 598
Lhotse I (Everest)	Nepal-Tibet	8 512
Makalu I	Nepal-Tibet	8 481
Lhotse II (Everest)	Nepal-Tibet	8 400
Dhaulagiri	Nepal	8 172
Manaslu I	Nepal	8 156
Cho Oyu	Nepal-Tibet	8 153
Nanga Parbat	Kashmir	8 126
Annapurna I	Nepal	8 078
Gasherbrum	Kashmir	8 068
Broad	Kashmir	8 047
Gosainthan	Tibet.	8 012
Annapurna II	Nepal	7 937
Gyachung Kang	Nepal	7 897
Disteghil Sar	Kashmir	7 885
Himalchuli	Nepal	7 864
Nuptse (Everest)	Nepal-Tibet	7 841
Masherbrum	Kashmir	7 821
Nanda Devi	India	7 817
Rakaposhi	Kashmir	7 788
Kamet	India-Tibet	7 756
Namcha Barwa	Tibet	7 756
Gurla Mandhata	Tibet	7 728
Ulugh Muz Tagh	Sinkiang-Tibet	7 724

Peak	Country	Metres
Kungur	Sinkiang	7 719
Tirich Mir	Pakistan	7 690
Makalu II	Nepal-Tibet	7 657
Minya Konka	China	7 590
Kula Gangri	Bhutan-Tibet	7 554
Changtzu (Everest)	Nepal-Tibet	7 553
Muz Tagh Ata	Sinkiang	7 546
Skyang Kangri	Kashmir	7 544
Communism Peak	USSR	7 495
Jongsong Peak	India-Nepal	7 459
Pobedy Peak	Sinkiang-USSR	7 439
Sia Kangri	Kashmir	7 422
Haramosh Peak	Pakistan	7 397
Istoro Nal	Pakistan	7 388
Tent Peak	India-Nepal	7 365
Chomo Lhari	Bhutan-Tibet	7 327
Chamlang	Nepal	7 319
Kabru	India-Nepal	7 316
Alung Gangri	Tibet.	7 315
Baltoro Kangri	Kashmir	7 312
Mussu Shan.	Sinkiang	7 282
Mana	India	7 273
Baruntse	Nepal	7 220
Nepal Peak	India-Nepal	7 163
Amne Machin	China	7 160
Gauri Sankar	Nepal-Tibet	7 145

Peak	Country	Metres
Badrinath	India	7 138
Nunkun	Kashmir	7 135
Lenina Peak	USSR	7 134
Pyramid	India-Nepal	7 132
Api	Nepal	7 132
Pauhunri	India-Tibet	7 128
Trisul	India	7 120
Kangto	India-Tibet	7 090
Nyenchhen Thanglha	Tibet	7 088
Trisuli	India	7 074
Pumori	Nepal-Tibet	7 068
Dunagiri	India	7 066
Lombo Kangra	Tibet.	7 060
Saipal	Nepal	7 041
Macha Pucchare	Nepal	6 998
Numbar	Nepal	6 955
Kanjiroba	Nepal	6 882
Ama Dablam	Nepal	6 812
Cho Polu	Nepal	6 734
Lingtren	Nepal-Tibet	6 697
Khumbutse	Nepal-Tibet	6 640
Hlako Gangri	Tibet.	6 482
Mt. Grosvenor	China	6 459
Thagchhab Gangri	Tibet.	6 392
Damavand	Iran	5 671
Ararat	Turkey	5 122

Notable Volcanic Eruptions

Date	Volcano	Deaths	Date	Volcano	Deaths
79 A.D.	Mt. Vesuvius, Italy	16 000	May 8, 1902	Mt. Pelée, Martinique	40 000
1169	Mt. Etna, Sicily	15 000	1911	Mt. Taal, Philippines	1 400
1631	Mt. Vesuvius, Italy	4 000	1919	Mt. Kelud, Java	5 000
1669	Mt. Etna, Sicily	20 000	Jan. 18-21, 1951	Mt. Lamington, New Guinea	3 000
1772	Mt. Papandayan, Java	3 000	Apr. 26, 1966	Mt. Kelud, Java	1 000
1792	Mt. Unzen-Dake, Japan	10 400	May 18, 1980	Mt. St. Helens, U.S.	60
1815	Tamboro, Java	12 000	Nov. 13, 1985	Nevado del Ruiz, Columbia	22 940
Aug. 26-28, 1883	Krakatau, Indonesia	35 000	Aug. 24, 1986	NW Cameroon	1 700 +
Apr. 8, 1902	Santa Maria, Guatemala	1 000			

Notable Active Volcanoes of the World

More than 75 percent of the world's 850 active volcanoes lie within the "Ring of Fire," a zone running along the west coast of the Americas from Chile to Alaska and down the east coast of Asia from Siberia to New Zealand. Twenty percent of these volcanoes are located in Indonesia. Other prominent groupings are located in Japan, the Aleutian Islands and Central America. Almost all active regions are found at the boundaries of the large moving plates which comprise the earth's surface. The "Ring of Fire" marks the boundary between the plates underlying the Pacific Ocean and those underlying the surrounding continents. Other active regions, such as the Mediterranean Sea and Iceland, are located on plate boundaries.

Major Historical Eruptions

Approximately 7 000 years ago, Mazama, a 3 000 m high volcano in southern Oregon, erupted violently, ejecting ash and lava. The ash spread over the entire northwestern United States and as far away as Saskatchewan. During the eruption, the top of the mountain collapsed, leaving a caldera 1.0 km across and about 1 km deep, which filled with rain water to form what is now called Crater Lake.

In 79 A.D., Vesuvio, or Vesuvius, a 1 277 m volcano overlooking Naples Bay became active after several centuries of quiescence. On Aug. 24 of that year, a heated mud and ash flow swept down the mountain engulfing the cities of Pompeii, Herculaneum, and Stabiae with debris over 18 m deep. About 10 percent of the population of the 3 towns was killed.

The largest eruptions in recent centuries have been in Indonesia. In 1883, an eruption similar to the Mazama eruption occurred on the island of Krakatau. On August 27, the 800 m-high peak of the volcano collapsed to 300 m below sea level, leaving only a small portion of the island standing above the sea. Ash from the eruption colored sunsets around the world for 2 years. A tsunami ("tidal wave") generated by the collapse killed 36 000 people in nearby Java and Sumatra and eventually reached England. A similar, but even more powerful, eruption had taken place 68 years earlier at Tambora volcano on the Indonesian island of Sumbawa.

Name, latest activity	Location	Metres
Africa		
Cameroon (1982)	Cameroon	4 070
Nyirangongo (1977)	Zaire	3 475
Nyamuragira (1988)	Zaire	3 057
Karthala (1977)	Comoro Is.	2 438
Piton de la Fournaise (1988)	Reunion Is.	1 823
Erta-Ale (1973)	Ethiopia	503
Antarctica		
Erebus (1988)	Ross Island	3 795
Big Ben (1960)	Heard Island	2 745
Deception Island (1970)	South Shetland Islands	576
Asia-Oceania		
Klyuchevskaya (1985)	USSR	4 750
Kerinci (1987)	Sumatra	3 800
Rindjani (1966)	Indonesia	3 726
Semeru (1988)	Java	3 676
Slamet (1967)	Java	3 428
Raung (1982)	Java	3 332
Shiveluch (1964)	USSR	3 283
Agung (1964)	Bali	3 142
On-Take (1980)	Japan	3 063
Mayon (1978)	Philippines	3 045
Merapi (1988)	Java	2 911
Bezymianny (1986)	USSR	2 900
Marapi (1982)	Sumatra	2 891
Ruapehu (1988)	New Zealand	2 797
Asama (1983)	Japan	2 530
Niigata Yakeyama (1987)	Japan	2 472
Yake Dake (1963)	Japan	2 458
Alaid (1972)	Kuril Is.	2 335
Ulawun (1988)	New Britain	2 296
Ngaurhoe (1975)	New Zealand	2 291
Chokai (1974)	Japan	2 225
Galunggung (1982)	Java	2 168
Amburombu (1969)	Indonesia	2 149
Azuma (1978)	Japan	2 042
Tangkuban Prahu (1967)	Java	2 023
Sangeang Apj (1988)	Indonesia	1 936
Nasu (1977)	Japan	1 893
Tiatia (1973)	Kuril Is.	1 833
Manam (1988)	Papua New Guinea	1 829
Soputan (1984)	Indonesia	1 827
Siau (1976)	Indonesia	1 784
Kelud (1967)	Java	1 731
Batur (1968)	Bali	1 718
Ternate (1963)	Indonesia	1 715
Kirisima (1982)	Japan	1 700
Keli Mutu (1968)	Indonesia	1 664
Akita Komaga Take (1970)	Japan	1 661
Gamkonora (1981)	Indonesia	1 635

Name, latest activity	Location	Metres
Aso (1985)	Japan	1 529
Lewotobi Laki-Laki (1968)	Indonesia	1 590
Lokon-Empung (1988)	Celebes	1 581
Bulusan (1988)	Philippines	1 559
Sarycheva (1976)	Kuril Is.	1 512
Me-akan (1966)	Japan	1 503
Karkar (1981)	Papua New Guinea	1 500
Karymskaya (1985)	USSR	1 484
Lopevi (1982)	New Hebrides	1 449
Ambrym (1979)	New Hebrides	1 334
Awu (1968)	Indonesia	1 326
Sakurajima (1988)	Japan	1 118
Langila (1988)	New Britain	1 093
Dukono (1971)	Indonesia	1 087
Suwanosezima (1987)	Japan	805
Oshima (1988)	Japan	777
Usu (1978)	Japan	732
Pagan (1985)	Mariana Is.	570
White Island (1988)	New Zealand	328
Taal (1987)	Philippines	300
Central America—Caribbean		
Acatenango (1972)	Guatemala	3 960
Fuego (1988)	Guatemala	3 835
Tacana (1986)	Guatemala	3 799
Santiaguito (Santa Maria) (1988)	Guatemala	3 768
Irazu (1987)	Costa Rica	3 432
Poas (1988)	Costa Rica	2 722
Pacaya (1988)	Guatemala	2 544
Izalco (1986)	El Salvador	2 362
San Miguel (1976)	El Salvador	2 132
Rincon de la Vieja (1987)	Costa Rica	1 900
El Viejo (San Cristobal) (1987)	Nicaragua	1 780
Ometepe (Concepcion) (1986)	Nicaragua	1 556
Arenal (1988)	Costa Rica	1 552
Momotombo (1982)	Nicaragua	1 280
Soufriere (1979)	St. Vincent	1 234
Telica (1987)	Nicaragua	1 039
South America		
Guallatiri (1987)	Chile	6 060
Lascar (1986)	Chile	5 990
Cotopaxi (1975)	Ecuador	5 897
Tupungatito (1986)	Chile	5 640
Sangay (1976)	Ecuador	5 230
Guagua Pichincha (1982)	Ecuador	4 784
Purace (1977)	Colombia	4 756
Llaima (1988)	Chile	3 121
Villarica (1984)	Chile	2 840
Hudson (1973)	Chile	2 615
Alcedo (1970)	Galapagos Is.	1 097

Name, latest activity	Location	Metres	Name, latest activity	Location	Metres
North America			**Mid-Pacific**		
Colima (1987)	Mexico	4 268	Mauna Loa (1987)	Hawaii	4 170
Redoubt (1966)	Alaska	3 108	Kilauea (1988)	Hawaii	1 243
Iliamna (1978)	Alaska	3 076			
Shishaldin (1987)	Aleutian Is.	2 861			
Mt. St. Helens (1986)	Washington	2 530			
Veniaminof (1987)	Alaska	2 507			
Pavlof (1988)	Aleutian Is.	2 504	**Mid-Atlantic Ridge**		
El Chichon (1983)	Mexico	2 225	Beerenberg (1985)	Jan Mayen Is.	2 277
Makushin (1987)	Aleutian Is.	2 036	Hekla (1981)	Iceland	1 491
Pogromni (1964)	Alaska	2 002	Leirhnukur (1975)	Iceland	654
Trident (1963)	Alaska	1 832	Krafla (1984)	Iceland	654
Great Sitkin (1974)	Aleutian Is.	1 740	Surtsey (1967)	Iceland	173
Cleveland (1987)	Aleutian Is.	1 730			
Gareloi (1982)	Aleutian Is.	1 626			
Korovin (1987)	Aleutian Is.	1 479			
Akutan (1988)	Aleutian Is.	1 303	**Europe**		
Kiska (1969)	Aleutian Is.	1 303			
Augustine (1986)	Alaska	1 197	Etna (1988)	Italy	3 369
Okmok (1988)	Aleutian Is.	1 073	Stromboli (1986)	Italy	926
Seguam (1977)	Alaska	1 054			

Famous Waterfalls

Source: National Geographic Society; Statistics Canada

The earth has thousands of waterfalls, some of considerable magnitude. Their importance is determined not only by height but volume of flow, steadiness of flow, crest width, whether the water drops sheerly or over a sloping surface, and in one leap or a succession of leaps. A series of low falls flowing over a considerable distance is known as a cascade.

Sete Quedas or Guaira is the world's greatest waterfall when its mean annual flow (estimated at 14 100 cu. m per second) is combined with height. A greater volume of water passes over Boyoma Falls (Stanley Falls), though not one of its seven cataracts, spread over nearly 100 km of the Congo River, exceeds 3 m.

Estimated mean annual flow of other major waterfalls (in cu. m per second) are: Niagara, 6 365; Paulo Afonso, 3 000; Urubupunga, 2 910; Iguazu, 1 830; Patos-Maribondo, 1 590; Victoria, 1 060; and Kaieteur, 700.

Height = total drop in metres in one or more leaps. † = falls of more than one leap; * = falls that diminish greatly seasonally; ** = falls that reduce to a trickle or are dry for part of each year. If river names not shown, they are same as the falls. R. = river; L. = lake; (C) = cascade type.

Name and location	Ht. (m)	Name and location	Ht. (m)	Name and location	Ht. (m)
Africa		Queensland		† Reichenbach	200
		Coomera	64	Rhine	24
Angola		Tully	270	† Simmen	140
Duque de Braganca,		† Wallaman, Stony Cr.	347	Staubbach	300
Lucala R.	104	Highest fall	286	† Trummelbach	400
Ruacana, Cuene R.	124	**New Zealand**			
Ethiopia		Bowen	165	**North America**	
Dal Verme,		Helena	271		
Dorya R.	30	Stirling	154	**Canada**	
Fincha	155	† Sutherland, Arthur R.	580	Alberta	
Tesissat, Blue Nile R.	43	Highest fall	248	Panther, Nigel Cr.	183
Lesotho				British Columbia	
*Maletsunyane	192	**Europe**		† Della	440
Zimbabwe-Zambia				† Takakkaw, Daly Glacier	503
*Victoria, Zambezi R.	105	**Austria**—† Gastein	150	Northwest Territories	
South Africa		Highest fall	85	Virginia, S. Nahanni R.	90
*Augrabies, Orange R.	146	† *Golling, Schwarzbach R.	76	Quebec	
Howick, Umgeni R.	111	† Krimml	400	Montmorency	84
† Tugela	614	**France**—*Gavarnie	422	**Canada—United States**	
Highest fall	182	**Great Britain**—Scotland		Niagara: American	59
Tanzania-Zambia		Glomach	113	Horseshoe	57
*Kalambo	221	Wales		**United States**	
Uganda		Cain	46	California	
Kabalega (Murchison) Victoria		Rhaiadr	73	*Feather, Fall R.	195
Nile R.	40	**Iceland**—Detti	44	Yosemite National Park	
		† Gull, Hvita R.	32	*Bridalveil	189
Asia		**Italy**—Frua, Toce R. (C).	143	*Illilouette	113
		Norway		**Nevada, Merced R.	181
India—*Cauvery	101	Mardalsfossen (Northern)	468	**Ribbon	491
*Gokak, Ghataprabha R.	52	† Mardalsfossen (Southern)	655	**Silver Strand, Meadow Br.	357
*Jog (Gersoppa), Sharavathi R.	253	† **Skjeggedal, Nybuai R.	420	*Vernal, Merced R.	97
Japan		**Skykje	300	† **Yosemite	739
*Kegon, Daiya R.	101	Vetti, Morka-Koldedola R.	274	Yosemite (upper)	436
Laos		Voring, Bjoreio R.	182	Yosemite (lower)	98
Khon Cataracts,		**Sweden**		Yosemite (middle) (C)	206
Mekong R. (C)	21	† Handol	130	Colorado	
		† Tannforsen, Are R.	37	† Seven, South Cheyenne Cr.	91
Australasia		**Switzerland**		Hawaii	
		† Diesbach	120	Akaka, Kolekole Str.	135
Australia		Giessbach (C)	300	Idaho	
New South Wales		Handegg, Aare R.	46	**Shoshone, Snake R.	65
Wentworth	187	Iffigen	37	Twin, Snake R.	37
Highest fall	110	Pissevache, Salanfe R.	65		
Wollomombi	335				

Name and location	Ht.
Kentucky	
Cumberland.	21
Maryland	
*Great, Potomac R. (C)	22
Minnesota	
**Minnehaha	16
New Jersey	
Passaic	21
New York	
*Taughannock	66
Oregon	
† Multnomah	189
Highest fall.	165
Tennessee	
Fall Creek.	78
Washington	
Mt. Rainier Natl. Park	
Narada, Paradise R.	51
Sluiskin, Paradise R.	91

Name and location	Ht.
Palouse	60
**Snoqualmie	82
Wisconsin	
*Big Manitou, Black R. (C)	50
Wyoming	
Yellowstone Natl. Pk. Tower	40
*Yellowstone (upper)	33
*Yellowstone (lower).	94
Mexico	
El Salto	66
**Juanacatlan, Santiago R.	22

South America

Argentina-Brazil	
Iguazu	70
Brazil	
Glass.	404
Patos-Maribondo, Grande R.	35
Paulo Afonso, Sao Francisco R.	84

Name and location	Ht.
Urubupunga, Parana R.	12
Brazil-Paraguay	
Sete Quedas	
Parana R.	40
Colombia	
Catarata de Candelas,	
Cusiana R.	300
*Tequendama, Bogota R.	130
Ecuador	
*Agoyan, Pastaza R.	61
Guyana	
Kaieteur, Potaro R.	226
Great, Kamarang R.	488
† Marina, Ipobe R.	152
Highest fall	91
Venezuela	
† *Angel.	979
Highest fall	807
Cuquenan	610

Notable Deserts of the World

Arabian (Eastern) 181 000 sq. km in Egypt between the Nile River and Red Sea, extending southward into Sudan.

Atacama, 965 km-long area in northern Chile, rich in nitrate and copper deposits.

Chihuahuan, 363 000 sq. km in Texas, New Mexico, Arizona and Mexico.

Death Valley, 8 550 sq. km in eastern California and southwestern Nevada. Contains lowest point below sea level (86m) in Western Hemisphere.

Gibson, 310 000 sq. km in the interior of Western Australia.

Gobi, 1 300 000 sq. km in Mongolia and China.

Great Sandy, 390 000 sq. km in Western Australia.

Great Victoria, 390 000 sq. km in Western and South Australia.

Kalahari, 583 000 sq. km in southern Africa.

Kara-Kum, 311 000 sq. km in Turkmen (USSR).

Kavir (Dasht-e Kavir), great salt waste in central Iran approx. 640 km long.

Kyzyl Kum, 260 000 sq. km in Kazakh and Uzbek (USSR).

Libyan, 1 200 000 sq. km in the Sahara extending from Libya through southwest Egypt into Sudan.

Lut(Dasht-e Lut), 52 000 sq. km in eastern Iran.

Mojave, 39 000 sq. km in southern California.

Nafud (An Nafud), 104 000 sq. km near Jawf in Saudi Arabia.

Namib, long narrow area extending 1 300 km along the southwest coast of Africa.

Nubian, 260 000 sq. km in the Sahara in northeast Sudan.

Painted Desert, section of high plateau in northern Arizona extending 240 km.

Rub al Khali (Empty Quarter), 650 000 sq. km in the south Arabian Peninsula.

Sahara, 9 000 000 sq. km in North Africa extending westward to the Atlantic. Largest desert in the world.

Simpson, 104 000 sq. km in central Australia.

Sonoran, 180 000 sq. km in southwest Arizona and southeast California extending into Mexico.

Syrian, 260 000 sq. km arid wasteland extending over much of northern Saudi Arabia, eastern Jordan, southern Syria and western Iraq.

Taklimakan, 363 000 sq. km in Sinkiang Province, China.

Thar (Great Indian), 260 000 sq. km arid area extending 640 km along India-Pakistan border.

The Great Lakes

Source: Energy, Mines and Resources Canada

The Great Lakes form the largest body of fresh water in the world and with their connecting waterways are the largest inland water transportation unit. Draining a large area of Canada, they enable shipping to reach the Atlantic via their outlet, the St. Lawrence R., and also the Gulf of Mexico via the Illinois Waterway, from Lake Michigan to the Mississippi R. A third outlet connects with the Hudson R. and thence the Atlantic via the N.Y. State Barge Canal System.

Lake Michigan is the only lake wholly in the United States; the others are shared between Canada and the U.S.

	Superior	Michigan	Huron	Erie	Ontario
Length in km	563	494	332	388	311
Breadth in km	257	190	295	92	85
Deepest soundings in metres	405	281	229	64	244
Volume of water in cubic km	12 100	4 920	3 540	484	1 640
Area[1] (sq. km) in U.S.	54 355	57 757	23 623	12 932	8 613
in Canada	29 888	–	39 473	12 880	10 388
Total Area[1] (sq. km) U.S. and Canada	**84 243**	**57 757**	**63 096**	**25 812**	**19 001**
Mean surface above mean water level at Pointe-au-Père, Que., avg. level in metres (1900-1985)	183.1	176.3	176.3	173.9	74.6
Latitude, North	46° 25′	41° 37′	43° 00′	41° 23′	43° 11′
	49° 00′	46° 06′	46° 17′	42° 52′	44° 15′
Longitude, West	84° 22′	84° 45′	79° 43′	78° 51′	76° 03′
	92° 06′	88° 02′	84° 45′	83° 29′	79° 53′
National boundary line in km	461	–	434	405	289

(1) Total area, including islands.
– = zero.

Important World Islands

Source: National Geographic Society; Energy, Mines and Resources, Canada

Figure in parentheses shows rank among the world's 10 largest islands; some islands have not been surveyed accurately; in such cases estimated areas are shown.

Location-Ownership
Area in square kilometres

Arctic Ocean

Canadian

Axel Heiberg (5)	43 178
Baffin (5)	507 451
Banks	70 028
Bathurst	16 042
Devon	55 247
Ellesmere (10)	196 236
Melville	42 149
Prince of Wales	33 339
Somerset	24 786
Southampton	41 214
Victoria (9)	217 291

USSR

Franz Josef Land	20 800
Novaya Zemlya (two is.)	91 000
Wrangel	7 280

Norwegian

Svalbard	62 244
Nordaustlandet	14 066
Spitsbergen	39 156

Atlantic Ocean

Anticosti, Canada	7 941
Ascension, UK	85
Azores, Portugal	2 301
Faial	174
Sao Miguel	757
Bahamas	13 918
Bermuda Is., UK	52
Block, Rhode Island	26
Canary Is., Spain	7 301
Fuerteventura	1 737
Gran Canaria	1 539
Tenerife	2 067
Cape Breton Is.	10 311
Cape Verde Is.	4 550
Faeroe Is., Denmark	1 404
Falkland Is., UK	12 220
Fernando de Noronha Archipelago, Brazil	18
Greenland, Denmark (1)	2 184 000
Iceland	103 399
Long Island, N. Y.	3 630
Bioko Is.	
Equatorial Guinea	2 041
Madeira Is., Portugal	798
Marajo, Brazil	40 373
Martha's Vineyard, Mass.	237
Mount Desert, Me.	281
Nantucket, Mass.	120
Newfoundland	108 860
Prince Edward Is.	5 620
St. Helena, UK	122
South Georgia, UK	3 770
Tierra del Fuego, Chile and Argentina	48 880
Tristan da Cunha, UK	104

British Isles

Great Britain, mainland (8)	218 920
Channel Islands	195
Guernsey	62
Jersey	117
Sark	5
Hebrides	7 134
Ireland	84 757
Irish Republic	70 554
Northern Ireland	14 204
Man	590

Orkney Is.	1 014
Scilly Is.	16
Shetland Is.	1 474
Skye	174
Wight	382

Baltic Sea

Aland Is., Finland	1 511
Bornholm, Denmark	590
Gotland, Sweden	3 026

Caribbean Sea

Antigua	281
Aruba, Netherlands	195
Barbados	432
Cuba	114 967
Isle of Youth	3 073
Curacao, Netherlands	445
Dominica	754
Guadeloupe, France	1 786
Hispaniola, Haiti and Dominican Republic	76 778
Jamaica	11 034
Martinique, France	1 105
Puerto Rico, U.S.	9 139
Tobago	302
Trinidad	4 846
Virgin Is., UK	153
Virgin Is., U.S.	343

Indian Ocean

Andaman Is., India	6 500
Madagascar (4)	589 311
Mauritius	1 872
Pemba, Tanzania	988
Reunion, France	2 519
Seychelles	445
Sri Lanka	65 863
Zanzibar, Tanzania	1 664

Persian Gulf

Bahrain	671

Mediterranean Sea

Balearic Is., Spain	5 034
Corfu, Greece	595
Corsica, France	8 728
Crete, Greece	8 284
Cyprus	9 287
Elba, Italy	224
Euboea, Greece	3 663
Malta	317
Rhodes, Greece	1 409
Sardinia, Italy	24 081
Sicily, Italy	25 537

Pacific Ocean

Aleutian Is., U.S.	17 735
Adak	751
Amchitka	315
Attu	1 009
Kanaga	351
Kiska	286
Tanaga	543
Umnak	1 755
Unalaska	2 766
Unimak	4 160
Canton, Kiribati*	10
Caroline Is., U.S. trust terr.	1 227
Christmas, Kiribati*	244

Diomede, Big, USSR	29
Diomede, Little, U.S.	5
Easter, Chile	179
Fiji	18 346
Vanua Levu	5 829
Viti Levu	10 683
Funafuti, Tuvalu*	5
Galapagos Is., Ecuador	7 912
Graham, Canada	6 361
Guadalcanal, UK	6 500
Guam	543
Hainan, China	33 800
Hawaiian Is., U.S.	16 770
Hawaii	10 496
Oahu	1 542
Hong Kong, UK	75
Japan	379 103
Hokkaido	78 374
Honshu (7)	228 293
Iwo Jima	21
Kyushu	36 696
Okinawa	1 193
Shikoku	18 327
Kodiak, U.S.	9 542
Marquesas Is., France	1 279
Marshall Is., U.S. trust terr.	182
Bikini*	5
Nauru	21
New Caledonia, France	16 978
New Guinea (2)	795 600
New Zealand	270 096
Chatham	967
North	114 491
South	151 593
Stewart	1 752
Northern Mariana Is.	478
Philippines	301 161
Leyte	7 246
Luzon	106 288
Mindanao	95 615
Mindoro	9 854
Negros	12 578
Palawan	11 840
Panay	11 560
Samar	13 130
Quemoy	146
Sakhalin, USSR	76 700
Samoa Is.	3 060
American Samoa	200
Tutuila	135
Samoa (Western)	2 935
Savaii	1 742
Upolu	1 115
Santa Catalina, U.S.	187
Tahiti, France	1 045
Taiwan	35 940
Tasmania, Australia	68 063
Tonga Is.	702
Vancouver Is.	31 285
Vanuatu	14 820

East Indies

Bali, Indonesia	5 582
Borneo, Indonesia-Malaysia, UK (3)	728 260
Celebes, Indonesia	179 400
Java, Indonesia	127 140
Madura, Indonesia	5 494
Moluccas, Indonesia	74 792
New Britain, Papua New Guinea	36 642
New Ireland, Papua New Guinea	9 638
Sumatra, Indonesia (6)	429 000
Timor	30 082

*Atolls: Bikini (lagoon area, 598 sq. km, land area 5.2 sq. km), U.S. Trust Territory of the Pacific Islands; Canton (lagoon 52 sq. km, land 10.4 sq. km), Kiribati; Christmas (lagoon 364 sq. km, land 244 sq. km), Kiribati; Funafuti (lagoon 218 sq. km, land 5.2 sq. km), Tuvalu.

Australia, often called an island, is a continent. Its mainland area is 7 643 935 sq. km.

Islands in minor waters: Manhattan (57 sq km.) Staten (153 sq. km.) and Governors (700 sq. m), all in New York Harbor, U.S.; Isle Royale (543 sq. km), Lake Superior, U.S.; Manitoulin (2 777 sq. km), Lake Huron; Pinang (286 sq. km), Strait of Malacca, Malaysia; Singapore (621 sq. km), Singapore Strait, Singapore; Montreal (482 sq. km), St. Lawrence River.

Ocean Areas and Average Depths

Four major bodies of water are recognized by geographers and mapmakers. They are: the Pacific, Atlantic, Indian and Arctic oceans. The Atlantic and Pacific oceans are considered divided at the equator into the No. and So. Atlantic; the No. and So. Pacific. The Arctic Ocean is the name for waters north of the continental land masses in the region of the Arctic Circle.

	Sq. km	Avg. depth in metres		Sq. km	Avg. depth in metres
Pacific Ocean	166 884 380	3 940	Hudson Bay	732 940	93
Atlantic Ocean	86 892 000	3 575	East China Sea	667 160	189
Indian Ocean	73 711 300	3 840	Andaman Sea	567 060	1 118
Arctic Ocean	13 274 820	1 038	Black Sea	509 860	1 191
South China Sea	2 986 100	1 464	Red Sea	454 740	538
Caribbean Sea	2 525 640	2 575	North Sea	428 740	94
Mediterranean Sea	2 519 660	1 501	Baltic Sea	383 500	55
Bering Sea	2 269 800	1 491	Yellow Sea	295 100	37
Gulf of Mexico	1 513 460	1 615	Persian Gulf	230 880	100
Sea of Okhotsk	1 397 500	973	Gulf of California	153 660	724
Sea of Japan	1 016 860	1 667			

Lakes of the World

Source: U.S. Interior Department; Energy Mines and Resources Canada

A lake is a body of water surrounded by land. Although some lakes are called seas, they are lakes by definition. The Caspian Sea is bounded by the Soviet Union and Iran and is fed by eight rivers.

Name	Continent	Area sq. km	Length km	Depth m	Elev. m
Caspian Sea	Asia-Europe	372 434	1 223	1 025	−28
Superior	North America	84 243	563	405	183
Victoria	Africa	69 748	402	82	1 134
Aral Sea	Asia	64 750	406	67	53
Huron	North America	63 096	332	229	176
Michigan	North America	57 757	494	281	176
Tanganyika	Africa	33 020	676	1 470	772
Baykal	Asia	31 621	636	1 620	455
Great Bear	North America	31 328	309	446	156
Malawi	Africa	28 990	579	695	472
Great Slave	North America	28 568	480	614	156
Erie	North America	25 812	388	64	174
Winnipeg	North America	24 387	428	18	217
Ontario	North America	19 001	311	244	75
Balkhash	Asia	18 499	605	26	340
Ladoga	Europe	17 771	200	225	4
Chad	Africa	16 380	282	7	240
Maracaibo	South America	13 564	214	35	sea level
Onega	Europe	9 640	233	100	33
Eyre	Australia	9 360	145	1	−16
Volta	Africa	8 518	402	n.a.	n.a.
Titicaca	South America	8 320	196	281	3 810
Nicaragua	North America	8 060	164	70	31
Athabasca	North America	7 935	335	124	213
Reindeer	North America	6 650	230	219	337
Turkana	Africa	6 430	248	73	375
Issyk Kul	Asia	6 123	185	702	1 609
Torrens	Australia	5 798	209	n.a.	28
Vanern	Europe	5 605	146	100	45
Nettilling	North America	5 542	108	n.a.	29
Winnipegosis	North America	5 374	227	12	253
Albert	Africa	5 395	161	52	619
Kariba	Africa	5 330	282	119	485
Nipigon	North America	4 848	116	165	261
Gairdner	Australia	4 784	145	n.a.	34
Urmia	Asia	4 719	145	15	1 274
Manitoba	North America	4 624	225	4	248

n.a. not available.

Principal World Rivers

Source: U.S. Interior Department; Energy, Mines and Resources Canada

River	Outflow	Lgth km	River	Outflow	Lgth km	River	Outflow	Lgth km
Albany	James Bay	982	Indus	Arabian Sea	2 897	Rhine	North Sea	1 320
Amazon	Atlantic Ocean	6 437	Irrawaddy	Bay of Bengal	2 152	Rhone	Gulf of Lions	813
Amu	Aral Sea	2 539	Japura	Amazon River	2 816	Rio de la Plata	Atlantic Ocean	241
Amur	Tatar Strait	4 416	Jordan	Dead Sea	322	Rio Grande	Gulf of Mexico	2 832
Angara	Yenisey River	1 852	Kootenay	Columbia River	781	Rio Roosevelt	Aripuana	644
Arkansas	Mississippi	2 348	Lena	Laptev Sea	4 400	Saguenay	St. Lawrence R.	698
Back	Arctic Ocean	974	Liard	Arctic Ocean	1 115	St. John	Bay of Fundy	673
Assiniboine	Hudson Bay	1 070	Loire	Bay of Biscay	1 020	St. Lawrence	Gulf of St. Law.	3 058
Athabasca	Arctic Ocean	1 231	Mackenzie	Arctic Ocean	4 241	Salween	Andaman Sea	2 414
Brahmaputra	Bay of Bengal	2 896	Madeira	Amazon River	3 239	Sao Francisco	Atlantic Ocean	3 099
Bug, Southern	Dnieper River	856	Magdalena	Caribbean Sea	1 538	Saskatchewan	Lake Winnipeg	1 939
Bug, Western	Wisla River	774	Marne	Seine River	525	Seine	English Chan.	798
Canadian	Arkansas River	1 458	Mekong	S. China Sea	4 184	Shannon	Atlantic Ocean	370
Chang Jiang	E. China Sea	6 379	Meuse	North Sea	933	Snake	Columbia River	1 670
Churchill, Man.	Hudson Bay	1 609	Mississippi	Gulf of Mexico	3 779	Sungari	Amur River	1 851
Churchill, Que.	Atlantic Ocean	856	Missouri	Mississippi	4 087	Syr	Aral Sea	2 205
Colorado	Gulf of Calif.	2 333	Murray-Darling	Indian Ocean	3 717	Tajo, Tagus	Atlantic Ocean	1 007
Columbia	Pacific Ocean	2 000	Negro	Amazon	2 253	Tennessee	Ohio River	1 049
Congo	Atlantic Ocean	4 667	Nelson	Hudson Bay	2 575	Thames	North Sea	380
Danube	Black Sea	2 858	Niger	Gulf of Guinea	4 168	Tiber	Tyrrhenian Sea	406
Dnieper	Black Sea	2 285	Nile	Mediterranean	6 695	Tigris	Shatt al-Arab	1 899
Dniester	Black Sea	1 411	Ob-Irtysh	Gulf of Ob	5 410	Tisza	Danube River	966
Don	Sea of Azov	1 970	Oder	Baltic Sea	912	Tocantins	Para River	2 699
Drava	Danube River	719	Ohio	Mississippi	2 108	Ural	Caspian Sea	2 535
Dvina, North	White Sea	1 326	Orange	Atlantic Ocean	2 092	Uruguay	Rio de la Plata	1 609
Dvina, West	Gulf of Riga	1 020	Orinoco	Atantic Ocean	2 575	Volga	Caspian Sea	3 531
Ebro	Mediterranean	909	Ottawa	St. Lawrence R.	1 271	Weser	North Sea	731
Elbe	North Sea	1 165	Paraguay	Parana River	2 549	Wisla	Bay of Danzig	1 086
Euphrates	Shatt al-Arab	2 736	Parana	Rio de la Plata	3 999	Yellow (See Huang)		
Fraser	Str. of Georgia	1 368	Peace	Slave River	1 923	Yenisey	Kara Sea	4 092
Gambia	Atlantic Ocean	1 127	Pilcomayo	Paraguay River	1 609	Yukon	Bering Sea	3 185
Ganges	Bay of Bengal	2 511	Po	Adriatic Sea	652	Zambezi	Indian Ocean	2 736
Garonne	Bay of Biscay	575	Purus	Amazon River	3 380			
Hsi	S. China Sea	1 931	Red	Mississippi	2 076			
Huang	Yellow Sea	4 672	Red River of N.	Lake Winnipeg	877			

International Temperature and Precipitation

Source: Environmental Data Service, U.S. Commerce Department

A standard period of 30 years has been used to obtain the average daily maximum and minimum temperatures and precipitation; length of record of extreme maximum and minimum temperatures includes all available years of data for a given location and is usually a longer period.

Station	Elev. m	Temperature C° Average Daily January Max.	Min.	July Max.	Min.	Extreme Max.	Min.	Average annual precipitation (cm)
Addis Ababa, Ethiopia	2 450	24	6	21	10	34	0	123.7
Algiers, Algeria	59	15	9	28	21	42	0	76.2
Amsterdam, Netherlands	1.5	4	1	21	15	35	−16	65.0
Athens, Greece	107	12	6	32	22	43	−7	40.1
Auckland, New Zealand	7	23	16	13	8	32	1	124.7
Bangkok, Thailand	16	32	19	32	24	40	10	146.8
Beirut, Lebanon	34	17	11	31	23	42	−1	89.2
Belgrade, Yugoslavia	138	3	−3	29	16	42	−26	62.5
Berlin, Germany	57	2	−3	23	13	36	−26	58.7
Bogota, Colombia	2 547	19	9	18	10	24	−1	106.1
Bombay, India	8	31	17	31	24	43	8	180.8
Bucharest, Romania	82	1	−7	30	16	41	−28	57.9
Budapest, Hungary	120	2	−3	28	16	39	−23	61.5
Buenos Aires, Argentina	27	29	17	14	6	40	−6	95.0
Cairo, Egypt	116	18	8	36	21	47	1	2.8
Capetown, South Africa	17	26	16	17	7	39	−2	50.8
Caracas, Venezuela	1 042	24	13	26	16	33	7	83.6
Casablanca, Morocco	50	17	7	26	18	43	−1	40.4
Copenhagen, Denmark	13	2	−2	22	13	33	−19	59.2
Damascus, Syria	720	12	2	36	18	45	−6	21.8
Dublin, Ireland	47	8	2	19	11	30	−13	75.4
Geneva, Switzerland	405	4	−2	25	14	38	−18	86.1
Havana, Cuba	24	26	18	32	24	40	6	122.4

	Elev. m	Temperature C° Average Daily January Max.	January Min.	July Max.	July Min.	Extreme Max.	Extreme Min.	Average annual precipitation (cm)
Hong Kong	33	18	13	31	26	36	0	216.2
Istanbul, Turkey	18	7	2	27	18	38	−8	80.0
Jerusalem, Israel	809	13	5	31	17	42	−3	50.0
Lagos, Nigeria	3	31	23	28	23	40	16	183.6
La Paz, Bolivia	3 658	17	6	17	1	27	−3	57.4
Lima, Peru	120	28	19	19	14	34	9	4.1
London, England	45	7	2	23	13	37	−13	58.2
Madrid, Spain	667	8	1	31	17	39	−10	41.2
Manila, Philippines	15	30	21	31	24	38	14	208.3
Mexico City, Mexico	2 237	19	6	23	12	33	−4	58.4
Moscow, U.S.S.R.	154	−6	−13	24	13	36	−33	63.0
Nairobi, Kenya	1 820	25	12	21	11	31	5	95.8
Oslo, Norway	94	−1	−7	23	13	34	−29	68.3
Paris, France	50	6	0	24	13	41	−17	56.6
Prague, Czechoslovakia	202	1	−4	23	14	37	−27	49.0
Reykjavik, Iceland	28	2	−2	14	9	24	−16	86.1
Rome, Italy	115	12	4	31	18	40	−7	74.9
San Salvador, El Salvador	682	32	16	32	18	41	7	177.8
Santiago, Chile	520	29	12	15	3	37	−4	36.1
Sao Paolo, Brazil	801	25	17	19	12	38	0	145.5
Shanghai, China	5	8	0	33	24	40	−12	114.3
Singapore	10	30	23	31	24	36	19	241.3
Stockholm, Sweden	45	−1	−5	21	13	36	−32	56.9
Sydney, Australia	19	26	18	16	8	46	2	118.1
Teheran, Iran	1 200	7	−3	37	22	43	−21	24.6
Tokyo, Japan	6	8	−2	28	21	38	−8	156.5
Tripoli, Libya	22	16	8	29	22	46	1	38.4
Vienna, Austria	202	1	−3	24	15	37	−26	65.0
Warsaw, Poland	90	−1	−6	24	13	37	−30	55.9

Major Dams of the World

Source: T.W. Mermel, *Intl. Water Power & Dam Construction, Handbook '88.*

World's Highest Dams

Rank order	Name	Country	Height above lowest formation (m)	Rank order	Name	Country	Height above lowest formation (m)
1	Rogun*	USSR	335	14	El Cajón*	Honduras	234
2	Nurek	USSR	300	15	Chirkei	USSR	233
3	Grand Dixence	Switzerland	285	16	Oroville	USA	230
4	Inguri	USSR	272	17	Bhakra	India	226
5	Vaiont	Italy	262	18	Hoover	USA	221
6	Chicoasén	Mexico	261	19	Contra	Switzerland	220
6	Tehri*	India	261	19	Dabaklamm	Austria	220
8	Kishau*	India	253	19	Mratinje	Yugoslavia	220
9	Guavio*	Colombia	246	22	Dworshak	USA	219
10	Sayano-Shushensk*	USSR	245	23	Glen Canyon	USA	216
11	Mica	Canada	242	24	Kumgang	N. Korea	215
12	Mauvoisin	Switzerland	237	24	Toktogue	USSR	215
12	Chivor	Colombia	237				

*Under construction.

World's Largest Volume Dams

Rank order	Name	Country	Dam volume m³ × 10³	Rank Order	Name	Country	Dam volume m³ × 10³
1	Syncrude Tailings*	Canada	540 000	14	Mangla	Pakistan	65 379
2	Chapetón*	Argentina	296 200	15	Afsluitdijk	Netherlands	63 430
3	Pati	Argentina	238 180	16	Yacyretá	Paraguay/Argentina	61 200
4	New Cornelia Tailings	USA	209 500	17	Oroville	USA	59 635
5	Tarbela**	Pakistan	105 570	18	San Luis	USA	59 559
6	Fort Peck	USA	96 050	19	Nurek	USSR	58 000
7	Lower Usuma	Nigeria	93 000	20	Tucuruí	Brazil	55 000
8	Cipasang	Indonesia	90 000	21	Garrison	USA	50 845
9	Atatürk*	Turkey	84 500	22	Cochiti	USA	50 230
10	Guri	Venezuela	77 971	23	Oosterschelde	Netherlands	50 000
11	Rogun*	USSR	75 500	24	Tabqua (Thawra)	Syria	46 000
12	Oahe	USA	66 517	25	Aswan (High)	Egypt	44 300
13	Gardiner	Canada	65 440				

*Under construction. **Includes 352,000m³ of r.c.c. placed in 1974-75.

The World's Largest Nuclear Utilities

Source: Atomic Energy of Canada Ltd

(as of Jan. 1, 1986)

Utility, country	Number of units	MWe[1]	Lifetime output[2] (TWh)
Électricité de France, France	38	34 411	946.8
Central Electricity Generating Board, United Kingdom	23	9 571	553.6
Ontario Hydro, Canada	12	8 113	423.5
Tokyo Electric Power, Japan	9	7 996	284.8
Commonwealth Edison, United States	8	7 746	396.5
Kansai Electric Power, Japan	9	7 408	284.5
Duke Power Co., United States	6	6 423	226.4
Tennessee Valley Authority, United States	5	5 660	211.1
Swedish State Power, Sweden	6	5 492	187.3
Taiwan Power Co., Taiwan	5	4 193	108.7
Dept. of Atomic Energy, India	5	1 095	43.6

(1) MWe = estimated electrical generating capacity in megawatt hours (10^6 watt hours): represents the amount of electricity available at any one moment. (2) Represents the total amount of electricity ever generated, measured in terawatt hours (10^{12} watt hours).

World Nuclear Power

Source: *Nuclear Engineering International*

(as of Jan. 1, 1988)

	Nuclear Reactors				Nuclear electricity generated in 1987	
	Operating		Under Construction			
	number	MWe[1]	number	MWe[1]	TWh[2]	% of total electricity
World total	427	318 612	123	110 474	1660.0	n.a.
Argentina	2	1 005	1	745	6.0	13.4
Belgium	7	5 728	–	–	39.6	66.1
Brazil	1	657	2	2 618	1.0	0.5
Bulgaria	5	2 760	3	3 000	11.5	28.6
Canada	18	12 528	4	3 740	72.9	15.1
China	–	–	3	2 172	–	–
Cuba	2	880	–	–	–	–
Czechoslovakia	8	3 434	8	5 784	20.7	25.9
Finland	4	2 400	–	–	18.5	36.6
France	53	51 602	10	13 568	251.3	69.8
East Germany	5	1 835	6	2 640	10.6	10.0
West Germany	21	19 911	4	4 325	123.2	31.3
Hungary	4	1 760	–	–	10.0	39.2
India	7	1 243	8	1 880	4.7	2.6
Italy	2	1 152	3	2 058	0.1	0.1
Japan	37	28 146	12	11 168	188.5	31.2
Mexico	–	–	2	1 330	–	–
Netherlands	2	540	–	–	3.4	5.2
Pakistan	1	137	–	–	0.3	1.0
Poland	–	–	4	1 860	–	–
Romania	–	–	5	3 395	–	–
South Africa	2	1 930	–	–	6.2	4.5
South Korea	7	5 816	2	1 900	35.1	53.1
Spain	9	6 792	1	1 040	39.5	31.2
Sweden	12	10 030	–	–	69.4	45.3
Switzerland	5	3 065	–	–	21.7	38.3
Taiwan	6	5 144	–	–	31.4	48.5
United Kingdom	38	12 796	5	3 822	48.9	17.5
United States	109	100 323	13	15 809	455.0	17.7
USSR	59	36 334	27	27 620	187.0	11.2
Yugoslavia	1	664	–	–	4.3	5.6

(1) MWe = estimated electrical generating capacity in megawatt hours (10^6 watt hours): represents the amount of electricity available at any one moment. (2) TWh = Terawatt hours (10^{12} watt hours), represents the total amount of electricity generated in the given year. – = zero; n.a. not available.

Major World Gold Producing Countries

(thousands of troy ounces)

	World production	Australia	Canada	China	Colombia	Philippines	South Africa	United States	USSR
1975	38 476	527	1 654	n.a.	309	503	22 938	1 052	n.a.
1980	39 197	548	1 627	n.a.	510	753	21 669	970	8 425
1982	43 083	867	2 081	1 800	473	834	21 355	1 466	8 550
1983	45 163	984	2 363	1 850	427	817	21 847	2 003	8 600
1984	46 827	1 296	2 683	1 900	731	827	21 861	2 085	8 650
1985	49 184	1 881	2 815	1 950	1 142	1 063	21 565	2 427	8 700
1986	51 620	2 414	3 365	2 100	1 286	1 295	20 514	3 739	8 850
1987	52 481	3 472	3 788	2 300	851	1 071	19 228	4 966	8 850

(1) Preliminary estimates.
n.a. not available.

Wheat, Rice and Corn—Exports and Imports of 10 Leading Countries

Source: Economic Research Service, U.S. Agriculture Department

(thousands of metric tons.)

Leading Exporters	Exports[1] 1980	1986	1987p	Leading Importers	Imports[1] 1980	1986	1987p
Wheat				**Wheat**			
United States	41,204	27,324	43,545	Soviet Union	16,000	16,000	21,500
Canada	16,262	20,782	22,500	China, People's Rep	13,789	8,500	14,500
France	13,423	15,604	15,150	Egypt	5,423	6,332	7,073
Australia	9,577	15,650	10,500	Japan	5,840	5,781	5,400
Argentina	3,845	4,430	5,600	Italy	3,028	4,988	4,100
Germany, Fed Rep.	1,502	2,513	3,000	Iran	1,896	2,500	4,000
United Kingdom.	1,100	5,400	3,000	Korea, Rep of	2,095	3,895	3,900
Italy.	1,620	1,832	2,740	Algeria	2,294	3,410	3,800
Saudi Arabia	0	1,000	1,225	Iraq	1,366	2,800	2,700
Hungary	700	1,100	1,050	United Kingdom.	1,882	1,250	2,300
Rice				**Rice**			
Thailand	3,049	4,345	2,700	Bangladesh	84	261	608
United States	3,028	2,719	2,223	India	70	5	600
Pakistan	1,163	1,300	1,100	Iraq	350	550	550
China, People's Rep.	590	1,000	1,000	Saudi Arabia	356	500	500
Italy.	475	524	550	Iran	583	1,000	450
Australia	468	375	400	Nigeria	394	320	400
Korea, DPR	200	250	250	Vietnam	30	450	400
Uruguay	184	230	220	Ivory Coast	275	350	400
Taiwan	159	178	200	Hong Kong	362	375	380
India	900	350	200	Senegal	340	355	335
Corn				**Corn**			
United States	61,163	38,203	43,182	Japan	13,989	15,500	17,130
France	2,380	6,287	6,400	Soviet Union	11,800	7,100	7,300
Argentina	9,098	4,000	4,200	Korea, Rep of	2,355	4,600	5,100
China, People's Rep	125	3,700	3,000	Mexico	3,833	3,400	3,500
Thailand	2,142	2,916	800	Taiwan	2,703	3,707	3,500
Zimbabwe	305	225	700	Spain	4,251	977	2,400
South Africa	4,955	1,800	650	Netherlands	2,638	2,075	2,050
Greece	0	580	630	Egypt	984	2,035	1,500
Spain	1	246	600	Belgium/Luxembourg	2,927	1,642	1,440
Belgium/Luxembourg	1,742	541	390	United Kingdom.	2,349	1,470	1,400

(1) Marketing years; (p) Preliminary

Successful Space Launches: 1957 to 1986

(Criterion of success is attainment of Earth orbit or Earth escape)

Year	Total	USSR	United States	Japan	European Space Agency	India	China
Total	2 866	1 922	867	31	14	3	17
1957-1959	21	6	15	—	—	—	—
1960-1964	268	76	192	—	—	—	—
1965-1969	586	302	279	—	—	—	—
1970-1974	555	405	139	5	—	—	2
1975-1979	607	461	126	10	1	—	6
1980.	105	89	13	2	—	1	—
1981.	123	98	18	3	2	1	1
1982.	121	101	18	1	—	—	1
1983.	127	98	22	3	2	1	1
1984.	129	97	22	3	4	—	3
1985.	121	98	17	2	3	—	1
1986.	103	91	6	2	2	—	2

The World's Largest Banks, 1987[1]

Source: Euromoney Research, London, England

Bank (head office)	Total assets ($billions)	% growth in assets (1986-87)	Net income ($millions)	Shareholders' equity ($millions)
Dai-Ichi Kangyo Bank (Tokyo, Japan)[3]	$289.7	41%	$649.6	$4 846.4
Sumitomo Bank (Osaka, Japan)[3]	271.4	51	364.1	5 262.9
Fuji Bank (Tokyo, Japan)[3]	264.3	43	566.7	5 147.3
Mitsubishi Bank (Tokyo, Japan)[3]	246.5	40	657.8	4 865.8
Mitsubishi Trust and Banking Corp. (Tokyo, Japan)[3]	238.8	64	412.2	2 077.8
Sanwa Bank (Osaka, Japan)[3]	234.7	45	632.7	4 472.5
Sumitomo Trust and Banking Co. (Osaka, Japan)[3]	225.5	63	399.3	2 069.9
Caisse Nationale du Credit Agricole (Paris, France)	214.4	39	404.1	8 741.2
Industrial Bank of Japan (Tokyo, Japan)[3]	205.2	41	384.3	3 530.6
Citicorp (New York, U.S.)	203.6	4	−1 138.0	8 810.0
Yasuda Trust and Banking Co. (Tokyo, Japan)[3]	197.1	64	222.3	1 219.6
Mitsui Trust and Banking Co. (Tokyo, Japan)[3]	196.6	54	288.3	1 673.6
Norinchukin Bank (Tokyo, Japan)[3]	186.2	35	154.0	957.2
Banque Nationale de Paris (Paris, France)	182.7	29	563.5	5 379.4
Tokai Bank (Nagoya, Japan)[3]	170.2	46	309.1	3 021.5
Deutsche Bank (Frankfurt, W. Germany)	169.7	28	423.4	7 111.7
Credit Lyonnais (Paris, France)	168.3	30	416.2	3 501.0
Barclays (London, U.K.)	164.3	41	346.3	7 707.3
Mitsui Bank (Tokyo, Japan)[3]	164.0	44	347.9	2 897.4
National Westminster Bank Group (London, U.K.)	162.9	33	829.1	9 165.3
Toyo Trust & Banking Co. (Tokyo, Japan)[3]	156.2	68	204.6	1 037.0
Société Générale (Paris, France)	153.0	32	444.9	3 182.0
Bank of Tokyo (Tokyo, Japan)[3]	145.2	27	378.3	3 008.3
Long Term Credit Bank of Japan (Tokyo, Japan)[3]	142.6	32	288.2	2 688.1
Dresdner Bank (Frankfurt, W. Germany)	130.5	29	295.1	4 231.9
Union Bank of Switzerland (Zurich, Switzerland)	125.5	34	589.0	7 626.2
Compagnie Financiere de Paribas (Paris, France)	122.3	32	323.0	3 327.0
Swiss Bank Corp. (Basel, Switzerland)	114.4	35	510.4	6 855.1
Industrial & Commercial Bank of China (Beijing, China)[4]	114.4	n.a.	n.a.	4 952.9
Hong Kong and Shanghai Banking Corp. (Hong Kong, H.K.)	107.4	17	460.6	4 269.1
Commerzbank (Dusseldorf, W. Germany)	102.3	34	267.5	2 425.6
Chase Manhattan Corp. (New York, U.S.)	99.1	5	−894.8	3 250.3
Chuo Trust & Banking Co. (Tokyo, Japan)[3]	97.9	71	69.6	372.3
Bayerische Vereinsbank (Munich, W. Germany)	94.6	31	148.6	2 237.1
BankAmerica Corp. (San Francisco, U.S.)	92.8	−11	−955.0	3 259.0
Banca Nazionale del Lavoro Group (Rome, Italy)	92.4	31	115.4	3 009.5
Nippon Credit Bank (Tokyo, Japan)[3]	92.4	41	151.6	1 643.8
Midland Bank Group (London, U.K.)	90.7	16	−735.5	4 840.0
Westdeutsche Landesban Giroz (Dusseldorf, W. Germany)	89.9	26	72.1	2 529.2
Kyowa Bank (Tokyo, Japan)	87.2	41	185.5	1 490.9
Algemene Bank Nederland (Amsterdam, Netherlands)	84.9	27	290.9	3 288.3
Lloyds Bank (London, U.K.)	84.0	19	−424.9	4 475.0
Credit Suisse (Zurich, Switzerland)	83.9	31	430.5	5 174.3
Bayerische Landesbank Girozentrale (Munich, W. Germany)	83.0	40	92.6	1 812.2
Rabobank (Utrecht, Netherlands)	81.9	28	389.3	4 716.2
Daiwa Bank (Osaka, Japan)[3]	81.3	35	185.8	2 005.7
Amsterdam Rotterdam Bank (Amsterdam, Netherlands)	81.0	28	269.5	2 873.1
Deutsche Genossenschaftsbank (Frankfurt, W. Germany)	80.6	40	111.0	1 722.4
Bayerische Hypheken-Und Weschel-Bank (Munich, W. Germany)	79.9	29	153.6	2 437.4
Chemical New York Corp. (New York, U.S.)	78.2	29	−853.7	3 003.0

(1) Data is for year ending Dec. 31, 1987; all figures are in U.S. dollars. (2) Shareholders' equity is the sum of preferred stock, common stock, surplus, undivided profits, capital reserves and current year profit. Does not include subordinated debt and non-capital reserves. (3) Data is for year ending March 31, 1987. (4) Data is for year ending December 31, 1986. n.a. not available.

Third World Debt

Outstanding external debt of Third World nations totaled over $1 trillion at the end of 1986, according to a survey by the World Bank. The following are the leading debtor nations at the beginning of 1987.

Country	Dollars (U.S.)	Country	Dollars (U.S.)	Country	Dollars (U.S.)
Brazil	107.8 billion	Venezuela	34.1 billion	Peru	14.7 billion
Mexico	102.0 billion	Philippines	28.1 billion	Colombia	14.7 billion
Argentina	53.0 billion	Nigeria	22.1 billion	Ecuador	9.1 billion
Indonesia	43.9 billion	Chile	21.2 billion		

United States

Superlative U.S. Statistics

Source: Geological Survey, U.S. Interior Department

Area for 50 states	Total	9 372 614 sq. km
	Land 9 166 759 sq. km—Water 205 856 sq. km	
Largest state	Alaska	1 530 700 sq. km
Smallest state	Rhode Island	3 139 sq. km
Largest county	San Bernardino County, California	52 064 sq. km
Smallest county	New York, New York	57 sq. km
Northernmost city	Barrow, Alaska	71°17′N.
Northernmost point	Point Barrow, Alaska	71°23′N.
Southernmost city	Hilo, Island of Hawaii	19°43′N.
Southernmost town	Naalehu, Island of Hawaii	19°03′N.
Southernmost point	Ka Lae (South Cape), Island of Hawaii	18°56′N. (155°41′W)
Easternmost city	Eastport, Maine	66°59′02″W.
Easternmost town	Lubec, Maine	66°58′49″W.
Easternmost point	West Quoddy Head, Maine	66°57′W.
Westernmost city	Lihue, Island of Kauai, Hawaii	159°22′W.
Westernmost town	Adak, Aleutians, Alaska	176°45′W.
Westernmost point	Cape Wrangell, Attu Island, Aleutians, Alaska	172°27′E.
Highest city	Climax, Colorado	3 551 m
Lowest town	Calipatria, California	−56.1 m
Highest point on Atlantic coast	Cadillac Mountain, Mount Desert Is., Maine	466 m
Oldest national park	Yellowstone National Park (1872), Wyoming, Montana, Idaho.	8 982 sq. km
Largest national park	Wrangell-St. Elias, Alaska	32 971 sq. km
Largest national monument	Death Valley, California, Nevada	8 368 sq. km
Highest waterfall	Yosemite Falls—Total in three sections	739 m
	Upper Yosemite Fall	436 m
	Cascades in middle section	206 m
	Lower Yosemite Fall	97 m
Longest river	Mississippi-Missouri	5 969 km
Highest mountain	Mount McKinley, Alaska	6 194 m
Lowest point	Death Valley, California	−86 m
Deepest lake	Crater Lake, Oregon	589 m
Rainiest spot	Mt. Waialeale, Hawaii	Annual avg. rainfall 1 168 cm
Largest gorge	Grand Canyon, Colorado River, Arizona.	446 km long, 183 m to 29 km wide, 1.6 km deep
Deepest gorge	Hell's Canyon, Snake River, Idaho-Oregon	2 408 m
Strongest surface wind	Mount Washington, New Hampshire recorded 1934	372 km/h
Biggest dam	New Cornelia Tailings, Ten Mile Wash, Arizona.	208 259 760 cu. m material used
Tallest building	Sears Tower, Chicago, Illinois	443 m
Largest building	Boeing 747 Manufacturing Plant, Everett, Washington.	616 800 cu. m; covers 18.8 ha
Tallest structure	TV tower, Blanchard, North Dakota	629 m
Longest bridge span	Verrazano-Narrows, New York	1 298 m
Highest bridge	Royal Gorge, Colorado	321 m above water
Deepest well	Gas well, Washita County, Oklahoma	9 583 m

The 49 States, Including Alaska

Area for 49 states	Total	9 355 855 sq. km
	Land 9 150 118 sq. km—Water 205 737 sq. km	

The 48 Contiguous States

Area for 48 states	Total	7 825 152 sq. km
	Land 7 671 658 sq. km—Water 153 494 sq. km	
Largest state	Texas	691 030 sq. km
Northernmost town	Angle Inlet, Minnesota	49°22′N.
Northernmost point	Northwest Angle, Minnesota	49°23′N.
Southernmost city	Key West, Florida	24°33′N.
Southernmost mainland city	Florida City, Florida	25°27′N.
Southernmost point	Key West, Florida	24°33′N.
Westernmost town	La Push, Washington	124°38′W.
Westernmost point	Cape Alava, Washington	124°44′W.
Highest mountain	Mount Whitney, California	4 348 m

Note to users: The distinction between cities and towns varies from state to state. In this table the U.S. Bureau of the Census usage was followed.

U.S. Area and Population: 1790 to 1980

Source: U.S. Bureau of the Census

Census date	Area (sq.km) Gross	Land	Water	Population Number	Per sq. km of land[1]	Increase over preceding census[2] Number	%
1980 (Apr. 1)	9 371 890	9 166 051	205 840	226 545 518	25.6	23 243 487	11.4
1970 (Apr. 1)	9 371 890	9 159 747	212 143	203 302 031	23.0	23 978 856	13.4
1960 (Apr. 1)	9 371 890	9 170 251	201 639	179 323 175	20.2	27 997 377	18.5
1950 (Apr. 1)	9 371 890	9 199 503	172 387	151 325 798	17.0	19 161 229	14.5
1940 (Apr. 1)	9 371 890	9 205 724	166 167	132 164 569	14.9	8 961 945	7.3
1930 (Apr. 1)	9 371 890	9 197 954	173 936	123 202 624	13.9	17 181 087	16.2
1920 (Jan. 1)	9 371 890	9 185 842	186 049	106 021 537	12.0	13 793 041	15.0
1910 (Apr. 15)	9 371 890	9 186 137	185 753	92 228 496	10.4	16 016 328	21.0
1900 (June 1)	9 371 890	9 186 834	185 057	76 212 168	8.6	13 232 402	21.0
1890 (June 1)	9 355 132	9 169 718	185 414	62 979 766	7.1	12 790 557	25.5
1880 (June 1)	9 355 132	9 169 718	185 414	50 189 209	5.7	11 630 838	30.2
1870 (June 1)[3]	9 355 132	9 169 718	185 414	38 558 371[3]	4.4	7 115 050	22.6
1860 (June 1)	7 824 550	7 690 774	133 776	31 443 321	4.2	8 251 445	35.6
1850 (June 1)	7 747 788	7 614 121	133 667	23 191 876	3.2	6 122 423	35.9
1840 (June 1)	4 642 351	4 530 757	111 594	17 069 453	3.9	4 203 433	32.7
1830 (June 1)	4 642 351	4 530 757	111 594	12 866 020	3.0	3 227 567	33.5
1820 (June 1)	4 642 351	4 530 757	111 594	9 638 453	2.2	2 398 572	33.1
1810 (Aug. 6)	4 461 410	4 355 598	105 811	7 239 881	1.7	1 931 398	36.4
1800 (Aug. 4)	2 308 454	2 239 519	68 935	5 308 483	2.4	1 379 269	35.1
1790 (Aug. 2)	2 308 454	2 239 519	68 935	3 929 214	1.8	–	–

(1) Population density figures given for various years represent the area within the boundaries of the United States which was under the jurisdiction on date in question, including in some cases considerable areas not organized or settled and not covered by the census. In 1870, for example, Alaska was not covered by the census. (2) Percent changes are computed on basis of change in population since preceding census date, and period covered therefore is not always exactly 10 years. (3) Revised figure of 39 818 449 for the 1870 population includes adjustments for undernumeration in the Southern states. On the basis of the revised figure, the population increased by 8 375 128, or 26.6 percent between 1860 and 1870, and by 10 370 760, or 26.1 percent between 1870 and 1880.

States: Settled, Capitals, Entry into Union, Area, Rank

The original 13 states—The 13 colonies that seceded from Great Britain and fought the War of Independence (American Revolution) became the 13 original states. They were: Delaware, Pennsylvania, New Jersey, Georgia, Connecticut, Massachusetts, Maryland, South Carolina, New Hampshire, Virginia, New York, North Carolina, and Rhode Island. The order for the original 13 states is the order in which they ratified the Constitution.

State	Set- tled*	Capital	Entered Union Date	Order	Extent in km (approx. mean) Long	Wide	Area in sq. km[1] Land	Inland water	Total	Rank in area
Ala.	1702	Montgomery	Dec. 14 1819	22	528	304	131 841	2 343	134 184	29
Alas.	1784	Juneau	Jan. 3 1959	49	1 824[2]	1 296[2]	1 480 960	52 408	1 533 368	1
Ariz.	1776	Phoenix	Feb. 14 1912	48	640	496	294 884	1 279	296 163	6
Ark.	1686	Little Rock	June 15 1836	25	416	384	135 057	3 013	138 070	27
Cal.	1769	Sacramento	Sept 9 1850	31	1 232	400	406 539	6 063	412 602	3
Col.	1858	Denver	Aug. 1 1876	38	608	448	269 792	1 251	271 043	8
Conn.	1634	Hartford	Jan. 9 1788	5	176	112	12 642	382	13 024	48
Del.	1638	Dover	Dec. 7 1787	1	160	48	5 153	195	5 348	49
D.C.		Washington			...	...	159	15	174	51
Fla.	1565	Tallahassee	Mar. 3 1845	27	800	256	140 634	11 622	152 256	22
Ga.	1733	Atlanta	Jan. 2 1788	4	480	368	150 990	2 088	153 078	21
Ha.	1820	Honolulu	Aug. 21 1959	50	...	...	16 705	65	16 770	47
Ida.	1842	Boise	July 3 1890	43	912	480	214 960	2 288	217 248	13
Ill.	1720	Springfield	Dec. 3 1818	21	624	336	144 955	1 695	146 640	24
Ind.	1733	Indianapolis	Dec. 11 1816	19	432	224	93 852	504	94 356	38
Ia.	1788	Des Moines	Dec. 28 1846	29	496	320	145 447	907	146 354	25
Kan.	1727	Topeka	Jan. 29 1861	34	640	336	212 646	1 162	213 808	14
Ky.	1774	Frankfort	June 1 1792	15	608	225	103 090	1 937	105 027	37
La.	1699	Baton Rouge	Apr. 30 1812	18	608	209	116 818	9 342	126 160	31
Me.	1624	Augusta	Mar. 15 1820	23	512	304	80 392	5 967	86 359	39
Md.	1634	Annapolis	Apr. 28 1788	7	400	144	25 717	1 784	27 501	42
Mass.	1620	Boston	Feb. 6 1788	6	304	80	20 348	1 121	21 469	45
Mich.	1668	Lansing	Jan. 26 1837	26	784	384	147 724	3 637	151 361	23
Minn.	1805	St. Paul	May 11 1858	32	640	400	206 151	12 425	218 576	12
Miss.	1699	Jackson	Dec. 10 1817	20	544	272	122 970	1 092	124 062	32
Mo.	1735	Jefferson City	Aug. 10 1821	24	480	384	179 387	1 797	181 184	19
Mon.	1809	Helena	Nov. 8 1889	41	1 008	448	378 526	4 033	382 559	4
Neb.	1823	Lincoln	Mar. 1 1867	37	688	336	198 856	1 934	200 790	15
Nev.	1849	Carson City	Oct. 31 1864	36	784	512	285 711	1 693	287 404	7

State	Set-tied*	Capital	Entered Union Date	Order	Extent in km Long	Wide (approx. mean)	Area in sq. km[1] Land	inland water	Total	Rank in area
N.H...	1623	Concord	June 21 1788	9	304	112	23 470	720	24 190	44
N.J. . .	1664	Trenton	Dec. 18 1787	3	240	112	19 555	819	20 374	46
N.M...	1610	Santa Fe	Jan. 6 1912	47	592	549	315 671	660	316 331	5
N.Y...	1614	Albany	July 26 1788	11	528	453	124 361	4 537	128 898	30
N.C...	1660	Raleigh	Nov. 21 1789	12	800	240	126 875	9 849	136 724	28
N.D...	1812	Bismarck . . .	Nov. 2 1889	39	544	338	180 110	3 619	183 729	17
Oh. . .	1788	Columbus . . .	Mar. 1 1803	17	352	352	106 535	642	107 177	35
Okla. .	1889	Oklahoma City.	Nov. 16 1907	46	640	352	178 833	2 956	181 789	18
Ore. . .	1811	Salem.	Feb. 14 1859	33	576	418	250 078	2 072	252 150	10
Pa. . .	1682	Harrisburg . . .	Dec. 12 1787	2	453	256	116 912	954	117 866	33
R.I. . .	1636	Providence . . .	May 29 1790	13	64	48	2 727	429	3 156	50
S.C...	1670	Columbia	May 23 1788	8	416	320	78 585	2 158	80 743	40
S.D...	1859	Pierre	Nov. 2 1889	40	608	336	197 483	2 839	200 322	16
Tenn. .	1769	Nashville	June 1 1796	16	704	192	107 453	2 382	109 835	34
Tex...	1682	Austin	Dec. 29 1845	28	1 264	1 056	681 548	13 530	695 078	2
Ut...	1847	Salt Lake City .	Jan. 4 1896	45	560	432	213 450	7 332	220 782	11
Vt...	1724	Montpelier . . .	Mar. 4 1791	14	256	128	24 094	889	24 983	43
Va. . .	1607	Richmond. . . .	June 25 1788	10	688	320	103 428	2 696	106 124	36
Wash..	1811	Olympia	Nov. 11 1889	42	576	384	173 082	4 217	177 299	20
W.Va..	1727	Charleston . . .	June 20 1863	35	384	208	62 582	289	64 871	41
Wis..	1766	Madison . . .	May 29 1848	30	496	416	141 606	4 394	146 000	26
Wy. . .	1834	Cheyenne . . .	July 10 1890	44	576	448	252 728	1 849	254 577	9

(1) Area is rounded to nearest km. (2) Aleutian Islands and Alexander Archipelago are not considered in these lengths.
* First European permanent settlement.

Metropolitan Statistical Areas: 1980-1985

Source: U.S. Bureau of the Census

(MSAs over 281 000 listed by 1985 population)

By current standards, an area qualifies for recognition as a Metropolitan Statistical Area (MSA) in one of two ways: if there is a city of at least 50 000 population; or a Census Bureau-defined urbanized area of at least 50 000 with a total metropolitan population of at least 100 000 (75 000 in New England). In addition to the county containing the main city, an MSA also includes other counties having strong economic and social ties to the central county. If an area has more than one million population and meets certain other specified requirements, it now is termed a Consolidated Metropolitan Statistical Area (CMSA). MSAs are defined by the Office of Management and Budget as of June 30, 1986.

MSA	Population 1985 (estimate)	1980	Percent change 1980 to 1985
New York-Northern New Jersey-Long Island, NY-NJ-CT CMSA	17 931 100	17 539 532	2.2
Los Angeles-Anaheim-Riverside, CA CMSA . . .	12 738 200	11 497 732	10.8
Chicago-Gary-Lake County, IL-IN-WI CMSA	8 085 200	7 937 307	1.9
San Francisco-Oakland-San Jose, CA CMSA . . .	5 809 300	5 367 900	8.2
Philadelphia-Wilmington-Trenton, PA-NJ-DE-MD CMSA	5 776 500	5 680 509	1.7
Detroit-Ann Arbor, MI CMSA	4 581 200	4 752 764	–3.6
Boston-Lawrence-Salem, MA-NH CMSA	4 051 400	3 971 792	2.0
Houston-Galveston-Brazoria, TX CMSA	3 623 300	3 099 942	16.9
Dallas-Fort Worth, TX CMSA	3 511 600	2 930 539	19.8
Washington, DC-MD-VA . .	3 489 500	3 250 921	7.3
Miami-Fort Lauderdale, FL CMSA	2 878 300	2 643 868	8.9
Cleveland-Akron-Lorain, OH CMSA	2 776 400	2 834 062	–2.0
Atlanta, GA	2 471 700	2 138 143	15.6
St. Louis, MO-IL	2 412 400	2 376 971	1.5
Pittsburgh-Beaver Valley, PA CMSA	2 337 400	2 423 311	–3.5
Minneapolis-St. Paul, MN-WI	2 262 400	2 137 133	5.9
Baltimore, MD	2 252 800	2 199 497	2.4
Seattle-Tacoma, WA CMSA .	2 247 400	2 093 285	7.4
San Diego, CA	2 132 700	1 861 846	14.5
Tampa-St. Petersburg-Clearwater, FL	1 868 700	1 613 621	15.8
Phoenix, AZ	1 846 600	1 509 262	22.4
Denver-Boulder, CO	1 827 100	1 618 461	12.9
Cincinnati-Hamilton, OH-KY-IN CMSA	1 679 900	1 660 258	1.2
Milwaukee-Racine, WI CMSA	1 550 800	1 570 152	–1.3
Kansas City, MO-KS	1 493 900	1 433 464	4.2
Portland-Vancouver, OR-WA CMSA	1 353 800	1 297 977	4.3
New Orleans, LA	1 324 400	1 256 668	5.4
Norfolk-Virginia Beach-Newport News, VA	1 289 500	1 160 311	11.1
Columbus, OH	1 287 600	1 243 827	3.5
Sacramento, CA	1 258 200	1 099 814	14.4
San Antonio, TX	1 235 700	1 072 125	15.3
Indianapolis, IN	1 203 100	1 166 575	3.1
Buffalo-Niagara Falls, NY CMSA	1 187 900	1 242 826	–4.4
Providence-Pawtucket-Fall River, RI-MA CMSA	1 100 900	1 083 139	1.6
Charlotte-Gastonia-Rock Hill, NC-SC	1 049 000	971 447	8.0
Hartford-New Britain-Middletown, CT CMSA	1 035 000	1 013 508	2.1
Salt Lake City-Ogden, UT . .	1 024 800	910 222	12.6
Rochester, NY	982 300	971 230	1.1
Oklahoma City, OK	975 900	860 969	13.3
Louisville, KY-IN	964 300	956 486	0.8

MSA	Population 1985 (estimate)	1980	Percent change 1980 to 1985	MSA	Population 1985 (estimate)	1980	Percent change 1980 to 1985
Memphis, TN-AK-MS	944 700	913 472	3.4	Flint, MI	433 900	450 449	-3.7
Dayton-Springfield, OH ...	931 100	942 083	-1.2	Chattanooga, TN-GA	425 600	426 540	-0.2
Nashville, TN	909 700	850 505	7.0	Lansing-East Lansing, MI .	418 500	419 750	-0.3
Birmingham, AL	903 800	884 014	2.2	Stockton, CA	418 300	347 342	20.4
Greensboro-Winston-Salem-High Point, NC	892 500	851 444	4.8	Saginaw-Bay City-Midland, MI	407 400	421 518	-3.3
Orlando, FL	866 400	699 906	23.8	Worcester, MA	405 000	402 918	0.5
Albany-Schenectady-Troy, NY	841 400	835 880	0.7	Canton, OH	401 200	404 421	-0.8
Jacksonville, FL	823 500	722 252	14.0	York, PA	393 700	381 255	3.3
Honolulu, HI	814 600	762 565	6.8	Lancaster, PA	386 600	362 346	6.7
Richmond-Petersburg, VA .	800 700	761 311	5.2	Jackson, MS	384 700	362 038	6.3
Tulsa, OK	733 100	657 173	11.6	Beaumont-Port Arthur, TX .	381 400	375 497	1.6
Scranton-Wilkes-Barre, PA	723 400	728 796	-0.7	Augusta, GA-SC	380 500	345 923	10.0
West Palm Beach-Boca Raton-Delray Beach, FL .	723 100	576 754	25.4	Davenport-Rock Island-Moline, IA-IL	377 200	384 749	-2.0
Austin, TX	695 500	536 688	29.6	Des Moines, IA	372 100	367 561	1.2
Syracuse, NY	651 200	642 971	1.3	Lakeland-Winter Haven, FL	368 500	321 652	14.6
Allentown-Bethlehem, PA-NJ	650 000	635 481	2.3	Colorado Springs, CO	365 900	309 424	18.3
Grand Rapids, MI	634 900	601 680	5.5	Shreveport, LA	362 400	333 158	8.8
Raleigh-Durham, NC	632 000	560 774	12.7	Corpus Christi, TX	358 800	326 228	10.0
Omaha, NE-IA	611 600	585 122	4.5	Spokane, WA	356 300	341 835	4.2
Toledo, OH	608 100	616 864	-1.4	McAllen-Edinburg-Mission, TX	352 200	283 323	24.3
Greenville-Spartanburg, SC	599 600	570 211	5.2	Fort Wayne, IN	350 900	354 156	-0.9
Knoxville, TN	592 700	565 970	4.7	Peoria, IL	347 700	365 864	-5.0
Tucson, AZ	585 900	531 443	10.2	Melbourne-Titusville-Palm Bay, FL	345 700	272 959	26.6
Fresno, CA	580 000	514 621	12.7	Madison, WI	341 900	323 545	5.7
Harrisburg-Lebanon-Carlisle, PA	572 900	556 242	3.0	Santa Barbara-Santa Maria-Lompoc, CA	332 000	298 694	11.1
Las Vegas, NV	556 700	463 087	20.2	Huntington-Ashland, WVA-KY-OH	331 800	336 410	-1.4
El Paso, TX	545 000	479 899	13.6	Salinas-Seaside-Monterey, CA	329 900	290 444	13.6
Baton Rouge, LA	544 000	494 151	10.1	Lexington-Fayette, KY	329 400	317 548	3.7
Springfield, MA	517 100	515 259	0.4	Pensacola, FL	328 500	289 782	13.4
Youngstown-Warren, OH ..	512 800	531 350	-3.5	Reading, PA	318 100	312 509	1.8
New Haven-Meriden, CT ..	510 100	500 462	1.9	Utica-Rome, NY	317 700	320 180	-0.8
Little Rock-North Little Rock, AR	498 500	474 464	5.1	Daytona Beach, FL	310 600	258 762	20.0
Charleston, SC	481 700	430 346	11.9	Modesto, CA	305 800	265 900	15.0
Bakersfield, CA	480 900	403 089	19.3	Appleton-Oshkosh-Neenah, WI	303 700	291 369	4.2
Mobile, AL	469 100	443 536	5.8	Atlantic City, NJ	292 600	276 385	5.9
Albuquerque, NM	464 300	420 262	10.5	Montgomery, AL	288 700	272 687	5.9
Johnson City-Kingsport-Bristol, TN-VA	442 700	433 638	2.1	Evansville, IN-KY	281 800	276 252	2.0
Columbia, SC	439 400	409 955	7.2	Visalia-Tulare-Porterville, CA	281 100	245 738	14.4
Wichita, KS	435 400	411 870	5.7				

Legal or Public Holidays, 1989

Technically there are no national holidays in the United States; each state has jurisdiction over its holidays, which are designated by legislative enactment or executive proclamation. In practice, however, most states observe the federal legal public holidays, even though the President and Congress can legally designate holidays only for the District of Columbia and for federal employees.

Federal legal public holidays are New Year's Day, Martin Luther King Day, Washington's Birthday, Memorial Day, Independence Day, Labor Day, Columbus Day, Veterans' Day, Thanksgiving, and Christmas.

Chief Legal or Public Holidays

When a holiday falls on a Sunday or a Saturday it is usually observed on the following Monday or preceding Friday. For some holidays, government and business closing practices vary. In most states, the office of the Secretary of State can provide details of holiday closings. In most states, the following will be legal or public holidays in 1989:

Jan. 1 (Sunday) — New Year's Day.

Feb. 12 (Sunday) — Lincoln's Birthday.

Feb. 20 (3d Mon. in Feb.) — Washington's Birthday, or Presidents' Day, or Washington-Lincoln Day.

May 29 (last Mon. in May) — Memorial Day, or Decoration Day.

July 4 (Tuesday) — Independence Day.

Sept. 4 (1st Mon. in Sept.) — Labor Day.

Oct. 9 (2d Mon. in Oct.) — Columbus Day, or Discoverers' Day, or Pioneers' Day.

Nov. 11 (Saturday) — Veterans' Day.

Nov. 23 (4th Thurs. in Nov.) — Thanksgiving Day.

Dec. 25 (Monday) — Christmas Day.

In some states, the following will be legal or public holidays in 1989:

Jan. 15 (Sunday) — Martin Luther King Day. In some states, combined with Robert E. Lee Day and/or observed on Jan. 16, the 3rd Mon. in Jan.

Mar. 24 (Friday) — Good Friday. In some states, observed for half or part of day.

Nov. 8 (1st Tues. after the 1st Mon. in Nov.) — Election Day.

U.S. National Parks and Historic Sites

Figures given are date area initially protected by Congress or presidential proclamation, date given current designation, and gross area in ha Apr. 1, 1987.

National Parks

Acadia, Me. (1916/1929) 16 737. Includes Mount Desert Island, half of Isle au Haut, Schoodic Point on mainland. Highest elevation on Eastern seaboard.

Arches, Ut. (1929/1971) 29 696. Contains giant red sandstone arches and other products of erosion.

Badlands, S.D. (1929/1978) 98 464; eroded prairie, bison, bighorn and antelope. Contains animal fossils of 40 million years ago.

Big Bend, Tex. (1935/1944) 297 623. Rio Grande, Chisos Mts.

Biscayne, Fla. (1968/1980) 70 029. Aquatic park encompasses chain of islands south of Miami.

Bryce Canyon, Ut. (1923/1928) 14 502. Spectacularly colorful and unusual display of erosion effects.

Canyonlands, Ut. (1964) 136 615. At junction of Colorado and Green rivers, extensive evidence of prehistoric Indians.

Capitol Reef, Ut. (1937/1971) 97 898.5. A 96 km uplift of sandstone cliffs dissected by high-walled gorges.

Carlsbad Caverns, N.M. (1923/1930) 18 922. Largest known caverns; not yet fully explored.

Channel Islands, Cal. (1938/1980) 100 914. Seal lion breeding place, nesting sea birds, unique plants.

Crater Lake, Ore. (1902) 74 151. Extraordinary blue lake in crater of extinct volcano encircled by lava walls 152 to 609 m high.

Denali, Alas. (1917/1980) 1 908 859. Name changed from Mt. McKinley NP. Contains highest mountain in U.S.; wildlife.

Everglades, Fla. (1934) 566 150. Largest remaining subtropical wilderness in continental U.S.

Gates of the Arctic, Alas. (1978/1980) 3 044 917. Vast wilderness in north central region.

Glacier, Mon. (1910) 410 193. Superb Rocky Mt. scenery, numerous glaciers and glacial lakes. Part of Waterton-Glacier Intl. Peace Park established by U.S. and Canada in 1932.

Glacier Bay, Alas. (1925/1980) 1 305 272. Great tidewater glaciers that move down mountain sides and break up into the sea; much wildlife.

Grand Canyon, Ariz. (1908/1919) 493 076. Most spectacular part of Colorado River's greatest canyon.

Grand Teton, Wy. (1929) 125 668. Most impressive part of the Teton Mountains, winter feeding ground of largest American elk herd.

Great Basin, Nev. (1922/1986) 30 801. Wide basins and high mountain ranges.

Great Smoky Mountains, N.C.-Tenn. (1926/1934) 210 553. Largest eastern mountain range, magnificent forests.

Guadalupe Mountains, Tex. (1966/1972) 30 876. Extensive Permian limestone fossil reef; tremendous earth fault.

Haleakala, Ha. (1916/1960) 11 597. Dormant volcano on Maui with large colorful craters.

Hawaii Volcanoes, Ha. (1916/1961) 92 748. Contains Kilauea and Mauna Loa, active volcanoes.

Hot Springs, Ark. (1832/1921) 2 363. Government supervised bath houses use waters of 45 of the 47 natural hot springs.

Isle Royale, Mich. (1931) 231 403. Largest island in Lake Superior, noted for its wilderness area and wildlife.

Katmai, Alas. (1918/1980) 1 503 865. Valley of Ten Thousand Smokes, scene of 1912 volcanic eruption.

Kenai Fjords, Alas. (1978/1980) 270 963. Abundant mountain goats, marine mammals, birdlife; the Harding Icefield, one of the major icecaps in U.S.

Kings Canyon, Cal. (1890/1940) 186 931. Mountain wilderness, dominated by Kings River Canyons and High Sierra; contains giant sequoias.

Kobuk Valley, Alas. (1978/1980) 708 395. Broad river is core of native culture.

Lake Clark, Alas. (1978/1980) 1 067 129. Across Cook Inlet from Anchorage. A scenic wilderness rich in fish and wildlife.

Lassen Volcanic, Cal. (1907/1916) 43 049. Contains Lassen Peak, recently active volcano, and other volcanic phenomena.

Mammoth Cave, Ky. (1926/1941) 21 214. 233 km of surveyed underground passages, beautiful natural formations, river 91 m below surface.

Mesa Verde, Col. (1906) 21 079. Most notable and best preserved prehistoric cliff dwellings in the United States.

Mount Rainier, Wash. (1899) 95 268. Greatest single-peak glacial system in the lower 48 states.

North Cascades, Wash. (1968) 204 285. Spectacular mountainous region with many glaciers, lakes.

Olympic, Wash. (1909/1938) 373 107. Mountain wilderness containing finest remnant of Pacific Northwest rain forest, active glaciers, Pacific shoreline, rare elk.

Petrified Forest, Ariz. (1906/1962) 37 852. Extensive petrified wood and Indian artifacts. Contains part of Painted Desert.

Redwood, Cal. (1968) 44 589. Sixty-four km of Pacific coastline, groves of ancient redwoods and world's tallest trees.

Rocky Mountain, Col. (1915) 107 326. On the continental divide, includes 107 named peaks over 3 350 m.

Sequoia, Cal. (1890) 162 884. Groves of giant sequoias, highest mountain in contiguous United States — Mount Whitney (4 417.7 m). World's largest tree.

Shenandoah, Va. (1926/1935) 79 071. Portion of the Blue Ridge Mountains; overlooks Shenandoah Valley; Skyline Drive.

Theodore Roosevelt, N.D. (1947/1978) 28 497. Contains part of T.R.'s ranch and scenic badlands.

Virgin Islands, V.I. (1956) 5 944. Covers 75% of St. John Island, lush growth, lovely beaches, Indian relics, evidence of colonial Danes.

Voyageurs, Minn. (1971/1975) 88 248. Abundant lakes, forests, wildlife, canoeing, boating.

Wind Cave, S.D. (1903) 11 450. Limestone caverns in Black Hills. Extensive wildlife includes a herd of bison.

Wrangell-St. Elias, Alas. (1978/1980) 3 371 800. Largest area in park system, most peaks over 4 875 m, abundant wildlife; day's drive east of Anchorage.

Yellowstone, Ida., Mon., Wy., (1872) 898 347. Oldest national park. World's greatest geyser area has about 3 000 geysers and hot springs; spectacular falls and impressive canyons of the Yellowstone River; grizzly bear, moose, and bison.

Yosemite, Cal. (1890) 308 045. Yosemite Valley, the nation's highest waterfall, 3 groves of sequoias, and mountains.

Zion, Ut. (1909/1919) 59 308. Unusual shapes and landscapes have resulted from erosion and faulting; Zion Canyon, with sheer walls ranging up to 762 m, is readily accessible.

National Historic Sites [*]

Abraham Lincoln Birthplace, Hodgenville, Ky. (1916/1959) 117.

Adams, Quincy, Mass. (1946/1952) 10. Home of Presidents John Adams, John Quincy Adams, and celebrated descendants.

Allegheny Portage Railroad, Pa. (1964) 1 135. Part of the Pennsylvania Canal system.

Andersonville, Andersonville, Ga. (1970) 476. Noted Civil War prison.

Andrew Johnson, Greeneville, Tenn. (1935/1963) 17. Home of the President.

Bent's Old Fort, Col. (1960) 800. Old West fur-trading post.

Carl Sandburg Home, N.C. (1968/1972) 264. Poet's home.

Christiansted, St. Croix; V.I. (1952/1961) 27. Commemorates Danish colony.

Clara Barton, Md. (1974) 9. Home of founder of American Red Cross.

Edgar Allan Poe, Pa. (1978/1980) 1. Poet's home.

Edison, West Orange, N.J. (1955/1962) 21. Home and laboratory.

Eisenhower, Gettysburg, Pa. (1967/1969) 690. Home of 34th president.

Eleanor Roosevelt, Hyde Park, N.Y. (1977) 181. Personal retreat.

Eugene O'Neill, Danville, Cal. (1976) 13. Playwright's home.

Ford's Theatre, Washington, D.C. (1866/1970) 0.29. Includes theater, now restored, where Lincoln was assassinated, house where he died, and Lincoln Museum.

Fort Bowie, Ariz. (1964/1972) 1 000. Focal point of operations against Geronimo and the Apaches.

Fort Davis, Tex. (1961/1963) 460. Frontier outpost battled Comanches and Apaches.

Fort Laramie, Wy. (1938/1960) 833. Military post on Oregon Trail.

Fort Larned, Kan. (1964/1966) 718. Military post on Santa Fe Trail.

Fort Point, San Francisco, Cal. (1970) 29. Largest West Coast fortification.

Fort Raleigh, N.C. (1941) 157. First English settlement.

Fort Scott, Kan. (1965/1978) 17. Commemorates U.S. frontier of 1840-50.

Fort Smith, Ark. (1961) 75. Active post from 1817 to 1890.

Fort Union Trading Post, Mon., N.D. (1966) 434. Principal fur-trading post on upper Missouri, 1829-1867.

Fort Vancouver, Wash. (1948/1961) 209. Hdqts. for Hudson's Bay Company in 1825. Early military and political seat.

Frederick Douglass, D.C. (1962/1988) 8. Home of nation's leading black spokesman.

Frederick Law Olmsted, Mass. (1979) 2. Home of famous park planner (1822-1903).

Friendship Hill, Pa. (1978) 675. Home of Albert Gallatin, Jefferson's Sec'y of Treasury. Not open to public.

Golden Spike, Utah (1957) 2,735. Commemorates completion of first transcontinental railroad in 1869.

Grant-Kohrs Ranch, Mon. (1972) 1,499. Ranch house and part of 19th century ranch.

Hampton, Md. (1948) 59. 18th-century Georgian mansion.

Harry S. Truman, Mo. (1983). 0.78. Home of Pres. Truman after 1919.

Herbert Hoover, West Branch, Ia. (1965) 187. Birthplace and boyhood home of 31st president.

Home of Franklin D. Roosevelt, Hyde Park, N.Y. (1944) 290. Birthplace, home and "Summer White House".

Hopewell Furnace, Pa. (1938/1985) 848. 19th-century iron making village.

Hubbell Trading Post, Ariz. (1965) 160. Indian trading post.

James A. Garfield, Mentor, Oh. (1980) 8. President's home.

Jimmy Carter, Ga. (1987) NA. Birthplace and home of 39th president.

John Fitzgerald Kennedy, Brookline, Mass. (1967) 0.09. Birthplace and childhood home of the President.

John Muir, Martinez, Cal. (1964) 9. Home of early conservationist and writer.

Knife River Indian Villages, N.D. (1974) 1,293. Remnants of 5 Hidatsa villages.

Lincoln Home, Springfield, Ill. (1971) 12. Lincoln's residence when he was elected President, 1860.

Longfellow, Cambridge, Mass. (1972) 2. Longfellow's home, 1837-82, and Washington's hq. during Boston Siege, 1775-76.

Maggie L. Walker, Va. (1978) 1. Richmond home of black leader and 1903 founder of bank.

Martin Luther King, Jr., Atlanta, Ga. (1980) 23. Birthplace, grave.

Martin Van Buren, N.Y. (1974) 40. Lindenwald, home of 8th president, near Kinderhook.

Ninety Six, S.C. (1976) 989. Colonial trading village.

Palo Alto Battlefield, Tex. (1978) 50. One of 2 Mexican War battles fought in U.S.

Pennsylvania Avenue, D.C. (1965) NA. Includes area between Capitol and White House, Ford's Theatre.

Puukohola Heiau, Ha. (1972) 80. Ruins of temple built by King Kamehameha.

Sagamore Hill, Oyster Bay, N.Y. (1962) 83. Home of President Theodore Roosevelt from 1885 until his death in 1919.

Saint-Gaudens, Cornish, N.H. (1964/1977) 148. Home, studio and gardens of American sculptor Augustus Saint-Gaudens.

Saint Paul's Church, N.Y. (1943/1978) 7. Eighteenth Century site of John Peter Zenger's "freedom of press" trial.

Salem Maritime, Mass. (1938) 9. Only port never seized from the patriots by the British. Major fishing and whaling port.

San Juan, P.R. (1949) 75. 16th-century Spanish fortifications.

Saugus Iron Works, Mass. (1968) 9. Reconstructed 17th-century colonial ironworks.

Springfield Armory, Mass. (1974) 55. Small arms manufacturing center for nearly 200 years.

Theodore Roosevelt Birthplace, N.Y., N.Y. (1962) 0.11.

Theodore Roosevelt Inaugural, Buffalo, N.Y. (1966) 1. Wilcox House where he took oath of office, 1901.

Thomas Stone, Md. (1978) 328. Home of signer of Declaration, built in 1771. Not open to public.

Tuskegee Institute, Ala. (1974) 74. College founded by Booker T. Washington in 1881 for blacks, includes student-made brick buildings.

Vanderbilt Mansion, Hyde Park, N.Y. (1940) 212. Mansion of 19th-century financier.

Whitman Mission, Wash. (1936/1963) 98. Site where Dr. and Mrs. Marcus Whitman ministered to the Indians until slain by them in 1847.

William Howard Taft, Cincinnati, Oh. (1969) 3. Birthplace and early home of the 27th president.

Presidents of the U.S.

No.	Name	Politics	Born	in	Inaug.	at age	Died	at age
1	George Washington	Fed.	Feb. 22, 1732	Va.	1789	57	Dec. 14, 1799	67
2	John Adams	Fed.	Oct. 30, 1735	Mass.	1797	61	July 4, 1826	90
3	Thomas Jefferson	Dem.-Rep.	Apr. 13, 1743	Va.	1801	57	July 4, 1826	83
4	James Madison	Dem.-Rep.	Mar. 16, 1751	Va.	1809	57	June 28, 1836	85
5	James Monroe	Dem.-Rep.	Apr. 28, 1758	Va.	1817	58	July 4, 1831	73
6	John Quincy Adams	Dem.-Rep.	July 11, 1767	Mass.	1825	57	Feb. 23, 1848	80
7	Andrew Jackson	Dem.	Mar. 15, 1767	S.C.	1829	61	June 8, 1845	78
8	Martin Van Buren	Dem.	Dec. 5, 1782	N.Y.	1837	54	July 23, 1862	79
9	William Henry Harrison	Whig	Feb. 9, 1773	Va.	1841	68	Apr. 4, 1841	68
10	John Tyler	Whig	Mar. 29, 1790	Va.	1841	51	Jan. 18, 1862	71
11	James Knox Polk	Dem.	Nov. 2, 1795	N.C.	1845	49	June 15, 1849	53
12	Zachary Taylor	Whig	Nov. 24, 1784	Va.	1849	64	July 9, 1850	65
13	Millard Fillmore	Whig	Jan. 7, 1800	N.Y.	1850	50	Mar. 8, 1874	74
14	Franklin Pierce	Dem.	Nov. 23, 1804	N.H.	1853	48	Oct. 8, 1869	64
15	James Buchanan	Dem.	Apr. 23, 1791	Pa.	1857	65	June 1, 1868	77
16	Abraham Lincoln	Rep.	Feb. 12, 1809	Ky.	1861	52	Apr. 15, 1865	56
17	Andrew Johnson	(1)	Dec. 29, 1808	N.C.	1865	56	July 31, 1875	66
18	Ulysses Simpson Grant	Rep.	Apr. 27, 1822	Oh.	1869	46	July 23, 1885	63
19	Rutherford Birchard Hayes	Rep.	Oct. 4, 1822	Oh.	1877	54	Jan. 17, 1893	70
20	James Abram Garfield	Rep.	Nov. 19, 1831	Oh.	1881	49	Sept. 19, 1881	49
21	Chester Alan Arthur	Rep.	Oct. 5, 1829	Vt.	1881	51	Nov. 18, 1886	57
22	Grover Cleveland	Dem.	Mar. 18, 1837	N.J.	1885	47	June 24, 1908	71
23	Benjamin Harrison	Rep.	Aug. 20, 1833	Oh.	1889	55	Mar. 13, 1901	67
24	Grover Cleveland	Dem.	Mar. 18, 1837	N.J.	1893	55	June 24, 1908	71
25	William McKinley	Rep.	Jan. 29, 1843	Oh.	1897	54	Sept. 14, 1901	58
26	Theodore Roosevelt	Rep.	Oct. 27, 1858	N.Y.	1901	42	Jan. 6, 1919	60
27	William Howard Taft	Rep.	Sept. 15, 1857	Oh.	1909	51	Mar. 8, 1930	72
28	Woodrow Wilson	Dem.	Dec. 28, 1856	Va.	1913	56	Feb. 3, 1924	67
29	Warren Gamaliel Harding	Rep.	Nov. 2, 1865	Oh.	1921	55	Aug. 2, 1923	57
30	Calvin Coolidge	Rep.	July 4, 1872	Vt.	1923	51	Jan. 4, 1933	60
31	Herbert Clark Hoover	Rep.	Aug. 10, 1874	Ia.	1929	54	Oct. 20, 1964	90
32	Franklin Delano Roosevelt	Dem.	Jan. 30, 1882	N.Y.	1933	51	Apr. 12, 1945	63
33	Harry S. Truman	Dem.	May 8, 1884	Mo.	1945	60	Dec. 26, 1972	88
34	Dwight David Eisenhower	Rep.	Oct. 14, 1890	Tex.	1953	62	Mar. 28, 1969	78
35	John Fitzgerald Kennedy	Dem.	May 29, 1917	Mass.	1961	43	Nov. 22, 1963	46
36	Lyndon Baines Johnson	Dem.	Aug. 27, 1908	Tex.	1963	55	Jan. 22, 1973	64
37	Richard Milhous Nixon (2)	Rep.	Jan. 9, 1913	Cal.	1969	56		
38	Gerald Rudolph Ford	Rep.	July 14, 1913	Neb.	1974	61		
39	Jimmy (James Earl) Carter	Dem.	Oct. 1, 1924	Ga.	1977	52		
40	Ronald Reagan	Rep.	Feb. 6, 1911	Ill.	1981	69		

(1) Andrew Johnson — a Democrat, nominated vice president by Republicans and elected with Lincoln on National Union ticket. (2) Resigned Aug. 9, 1974.

Marriages, Divorces and Rates in the U.S.

Source: National Center for Health Statistics; U.S. Department of Health and Human Services

Year	Marriages[1] No.	Rate[3]	Divorces[2] No.	Rate[3]	Year	Marriages[1] No.	Rate[3]	Divorces[2] No.	Rate[3]
1895	620 000	8.9	40 387	0.6	1945	1 612 992	12.2	485 000	3.5[4]
1900	709 000	9.3	55 751	0.7	1950	1 667 231	11.1	385 144	2.6
1905	842 000	10.0	67 976	0.8	1955	1 531 000	9.3	377 000	2.3
1910	948 166	10.3	83 045	0.9	1960	1 523 000	8.5	393 000	2.2
1915	1 007 595	10.0	104 298	1.0	1965	1 800 000	9.3	479 000	2.5
1920	1 274 476	12.0	170 505	1.6	1970	2 158 802	10.6	708 000	3.5
1925	1 188 334	10.3	175 449	1.5	1975	2 152 662	10.0	1 036 000	4.8
1930	1 126 856	9.2	195 961	1.6	1980	2 413 000	10.6	1 182 000	5.2
1935	1 327 000	10.4	218 000	1.7	1985	2 425 000	10.2	1 187 000	5.0
1940	1 595 879	12.1	264 000	2.0	1987	2 421 000	9.9	1 157 000	4.8

(1) Includes estimates and marriage licenses for some states for all years. (2) Includes reported annulments. (3) Rate per 1 000 population. (4) Divorce rates for 1945 based on population including armed forces overseas.

Foreign-Born Population in Twelve Metropolitan Areas of the United States: 1980

Source: U.S. Bureau of the Census

Country of origin	New York City	Chicago	Los Angeles	Phila-delphia	Houston	Detroit	Dallas	San Diego	Phoenix	San Antonio	San Fran-cisco	Wash-ington DC
Number of foreign-born persons....	1 946 800	744 930	1 664 793	242 658	220 861	282 766	124 697	235 593	82 536	76 944	509 352	249 994
Percent of population foreign-born.	21.3	10.5	22.3	5.1	7.6	6.5	4.2	12.7	5.5	7.2	15.7	8.2
Europe......	37.7	40.9	13.0	54.8	11.7	47.9	16.4	18.5	30.6	13.8	23.8	26.9
Austria	1.6	1.2	0.4	1.6	0.3	1.2	0.4	0.4	0.9	0.3	0.6	0.8
Czechoslovakia .	1.0	1.4	0.3	0.8	0.3	0.9	0.4	0.3	0.7	0.3	0.4	0.6
France.....	0.8	0.5	0.5	0.9	0.7	0.7	0.9	0.7	1.4	0.8	1.1	1.8
Germany.....	4.3	6.0	2.1	9.4	2.6	6.3	5.0	3.7	7.2	5.8	4.2	6.2
Greece......	2.4	3.2	0.4	2.5	0.7	2.1	0.5	0.5	0.8	0.2	0.8	1.9
Hungary	1.3	0.9	0.7	1.6	0.3	1.6	0.4	0.4	1.2	0.2	0.5	0.7
Ireland	2.7	2.0	0.3	3.8	0.2	1.0	0.4	0.5	0.9	0.5	1.2	0.7
Italy.......	10.5	6.0	1.3	14.9	0.7	8.0	0.7	2.0	3.4	0.6	3.3	2.4
Netherlands ...	0.2	0.5	0.5	0.5	0.5	0.6	0.5	0.7	0.9	0.2	0.8	0.6
Poland	4.6	8.4	1.0	4.7	0.5	7.6	0.6	0.7	1.8	0.5	0.6	1.1
Portugal	0.5	0.1	0.2	0.9	0.1	*	*	0.8	0.1	0.1	1.4	0.6
Sweden	0.2	0.9	0.2	0.3	0.1	0.3	0.2	0.5	0.5	0.1	0.6	0.3
United Kingdom .	2.5	2.5	2.8	7.8	3.2	8.1	4.6	4.7	6.4	3.0	4.1	5.2
England	1.6	1.6	1.9	4.6	2.2	4.4	3.4	3.2	4.3	2.3	2.8	3.6
Northern Ireland....	0.1	0.1	0.1	0.5	*	0.2	0.1	0:1	0.1	0.1	0.1	0.1
Scotland	0.6	0.6	0.5	2.1	0.4	3.0	0.6	1.0	1.4	0.3	0.7	0.7
Wales	*	*	*	0.2	0.1	0.2	0.1	0.1	0.1	*	0.1	0.1
Yugoslavia ...	1.3	3.0	0.6	1.0	0.2	3.7	0.2	0.5	1.1	*	0.5	0.3
U.S.S.R.....	4.9	3.3	2.1	8.9	0.7	3.5	0.9	0.9	2.1	0.5	1.9	1.8
Asia	13.1	17.2	20.4	16.7	21.7	18.3	21.2	27.4	12.7	9.7	42.3	32.0
China......	3.3	1.2	2.0	1.4	2.1	0.9	1.5	1.0	1.6	0.6	11.0	2.8
India	1.4	2.9	0.6	2.8	3.5	2.2	2.4	0.4	0.8	0.6	1.3	3.6
Japan......	0.9	0.8	2.0	0.9	1.1	0.6	1.5	2.8	1.5	1.7	2.7	1.6
Korea......	1.2	2.3	3.0	3.4	1.4	1.1	2.0	0.9	1.6	1.1	1.8	5.9
Philippines ...	1.3	4.3	4.4	2.1	1.9	2.0	1.8	13.0	1.3	1.7	13.2	3.6
Vietnam	0.2	0.6	1.7	1.4	5.3	0.4	3.8	3.3	1.6	1.5	2.2	3.6
North and Central America....	27.4	28.7	54.8	9.5	51.0	23.1	48.5	44.9	44.6	69.4	21.9	17.4
Canada......	1.2	2.2	3.4	3.2	2.3	19.9	3.8	5.9	10.8	1.6	4.1	3.3
Mexico.....	0.4	21.6	41.9	0.6	42.4	1.7	40.0	36.9	31.9	64.9	11.0	0.9
West Indies ...	22.6	3.2	2.7	4.8	3.8	1.2	2.8	0.9	0.8	1.3	1.0	8.4
Cuba.....	2.8	1.9	2.1	1.2	2.0	0.3	2.0	0.3	0.3	0.7	0.6	2.0
Dominican Republic ..	6.6	0.1	0.1	0.3	0.1	0.1	0.1	0.1	0.1	0.1	*	0.5
Jamaica	5.1	0.6	0.2	1.7	0.5	0.4	0.2	0.2	0.1	0.2	0.2	2.8
South America .	8.8	2.5	3.5	2.5	3.9	1.0	2.4	1.7	1.9	1.0	2.5	9.6
North Africa ..	0.6	0.3	0.6	0.5	0.5	0.4	0.6	0.3	0.3	0.3	0.5	1.3
Other Africa. ..	0.7	0.8	0.5	1.1	1.7	0.5	1.5	0.5	0.6	0.3	0.6	3.8
All other countries ...	0.2	0.2	0.5	0.3	0.3	0.2	0.5	1.0	0.6	0.3	1.6	0.8
Country not reported ...	6.5	6.2	4.7	5.6	8.5	5.0	7.9	4.8	6.6	4.8	4.9	6.4

Note: * indicates amount less than 0.1 percent.

Crime Rates by Region, Geographic Division, and State

Source: 1987 Uniform Crime Reports, FBI

(Per 100 000)

Area	Total	Violent Crime[1]	Property crime[2]	Murder	Rape	Robbery	Aggravated Assault	Burglary	Larceny-theft	Motor vehicle theft
United States Total	5 550.0	609.7	4 940.3	8.3	37.4	212.7	351.3	1 329.6	3 081.3	529.4
Northeast	4 838.9	635.4	4 203.5	6.9	29.3	283.7	315.5	1 031.0	2 543.8	628.7
New England	4 598.8	433.0	4 176.8	3.4	27.2	138.9	252.4	1 074.1	2 446.7	656.0
Connecticut	4 995.7	419.0	4 576.7	4.9	24.9	178.1	211.1	1 218.3	2 829.4	529.0
Maine	3 532.3	152.1	3 380.1	2.5	15.7	25.6	108.3	770.7	2 436.1	173.4
Massachusetts	4 733.8	564.6	4'169.2	3.0	31.9	177.3	352.5	1 059.9	2 185.1	924.2
New Hampshire	3 317.7	149.6	3 222.1	3.0	26.6	26.5	93.5	694.8	2 310.9	216.5
Rhode Island	5 285.5	359.7	4 925.8	3.5	24.4	107.7	224.0	1 441.0	2 710.3	783.5
Vermont	4 271.2	136.5	4 134.7	2.7	22.4	16.8	94.5	1 110.4	2 825.7	198.5
Middle Atlantic	4 921.4	708.7	4 212.8	8.0	30.0	333.5	337.2	1 016.2	2 577.1	619.4
New Jersey	5 261.5	541.0	4 720.5	4.6	33.4	232.8	270.3	1 008.8	2 866.3	845.4
New York	5 952.4	1 008.1	4 994.3	11.3	31.1	503.3	462.4	1 216.4	3 024.8	703.1
Pennsylvania	3 163.2	369.4	2 793.9	5.4	26.2	144.4	193.3	722.0	1 722.7	349.2
Midwest	4 907.6	504.3	4 403.3	6.7	37.1	173.2	287.3	1 088.1	2 889.2	426.1
East North Central	5 060.8	571.8	4 524.4	7.6	41.8	206.3	316.1	1 124.5	2 930.1	487.8
Illinois	5 416.5	796.2	4 620.3	8.3	38.4	314.3	435.2	1 123.7	2 957.1	539.5
Indiana	4 119.8	328.5	3 791.3	5.6	29.1	90.0	185.9	886.7	2 332.9	327.5
Michigan	6 456.8	780.1	5 676.7	12.2	67.2	276.5	424.2	1 452.2	3 472.5	752.0
Ohio	4 575.3	421.3	4 154.0	5.8	39.9	153.1	222.5	1 062.5	2 708.6	382.9
Wisconsin	4 169.4	249.9	3 919.5	3.5	20.1	66.4	160.2	842.6	2 830.4	246.5
West North Central	4 416.7	343.8	4 072.9	4.4	26.1	94.6	218.7	1 001.7	2 791.9	279.3
Iowa	4 140.2	231.2	3 909.0	2.1	11.9	36.2	181.1	917.8	2 840.1	151.1
Kansas	4 903.9	36.07	4 543.1	4.4	32.6	82.1	241.6	1 138.0	3 152.0	253.2
Minnesota	4 615.8	285.4	4 330.4	2.6	33.9	102.5	146.3	1 068.9	2 960.1	301.4
Missouri	4 707.5	544.6	4 162.8	8.3	28.9	164.1	343.3	1 111.3	2 625.2	426.3
Nebraska	4 131.6	251.2	3 880.4	3.5	21.6	47.1	179.0	847.9	2 866.5	165.9
North Dakota	2 833.0	56.8	2 776.2	1.5	9.4	7.6	38.4	455.4	2 197.6	123.2
South Dakota	2 678.0	119.0	2 558.3	1.8	20.6	12.3	85.0	534.1	1 928.5	95.6
South	5 893.0	607.1	5 285.9	10.0	39.3	191.9	365.9	1 565.0	3 238.2	482.7
South Atlantic	5 915.5	672.9	5 242.6	10.0	39.6	217.4	405.8	1 513.8	3 276.0	452.8
Delaware	4 938.8	430.7	4 508.1	5.1	68.5	122.5	234.6	1 020.5	3 175.9	311.6
District of Columbia	8 451.6	1 610.3	6 841.3	36.2	39.4	717.4	817.4	1 807.7	4 021.2	1 012.4
Florida	8 503.2	1 024.4	7 478.7	11.4	50.2	356.6	606.3	2 256.9	4 545.2	676.7
Georgia	5 792.0	576.5	5 215.5	11.8	43.1	209.2	312.4	1 552.1	3 171.0	492.4
Maryland	5 477.6	767.8	4 709.8	9.6	39.6	290.3	428.3	1 162.5	2 965.5	581.8
North Carolina	4 649.9	484.0	4 165.0	8.1	29.1	93.9	352.9	1 356.1	2 586.0	223.8
South Carolina	5 161.9	664.9	4 497.0	9.3	43.7	101.1	510.8	1 358.0	2 858.2	280.8
Virginia	3 959.5	295.0	3 664.5	7.4	26.0	105.8	155.8	806.9	2 603.2	254.4
West Virginia	2 190.7	137.3	2 053.4	4.8	22.6	31.2	78.7	603.6	1 288.1	161.7
East South Central	4 057.6	447.4	3 610.2	9.0	31.5	123.3	283.6	1 162.0	2 123.5	324.7
Alabama	4 451.4	559.2	3 892.2	9.3	27.8	112.2	409.9	1 198.3	2 431.1	262.8
Kentucky	3 270.0	337.8	2 932.2	7.5	21.0	90.2	219.1	847.1	1 892.5	192.7
Mississippi	3 438.6	269.8	3 168.8	10.2	29.2	57.0	173.3	1 201.4	1 807.0	160.5
Tennessee	4 665.6	533.5	4 132.2	9.1	43.9	193.8	286.6	1 351.4	2 213.4	566.9
West South Central	6 901.0	596.0	6 305.0	10.7	43.2	191.4	350.7	1 873.3	3 813.0	618.7
Arkansas	4 245.2	312.0	3 833.2	7.6	32.6	79.1	292.6	1 078.0	2 548.7	206.5
Louisiana	5 873.3	693.0	5 180.2	11.1	35.9	179.0	467.0	1 444.5	3 323.2	412.5
Oklahoma	6 025.6	417.6	5 608.0	7.5	35.8	109.5	264.8	1 782.8	3 220.5	604.9
Texas	7 722.4	631.1	7 091.3	11.7	48.1	226.7	344.8	2 118.0	4 238.5	734.8
West	6 460.0	714.3	5 745.7	8.5	233.2	439.7	1 523.5	3 590.4	631.8	
Mountain	6 161.1	464.7	5 696.4	6.2	36.9	109.3	312.3	1 402.2	3 935.4	358.9
Arizona	7 188.6	612.6	6 576.0	7.5	41.2	138.4	425.5	1 626.1	4 527.3	422.6
Colorado	6 451.3	467.5	5 983.8	5.8	40.8	118.8	302.1	1 534.6	4 012.9	436.3
Idaho	4 156.3	214.2	3 942.	3.1	17.5	24.2	169.3	976.8	2 797.9	167.4
Montana	4 599.4	151.2	4 448.2	4.1	19.8	24.2	103.1	806.1	3 404.3	237.8
Nevada	6 371.4	695.7	5 675.7	8.4	61.8	272.5	353.0	1 629.4	3 491.3	555.0
New Mexico	6 546.8	628.5	5 918.3	10.1	43.1	108.3	466.9	1 787.7	3 875.1	345.5
Utah	5 618.6	229.8	5 388.8	3.3	217	52.8	152.0	950.9	4 228.5	209.5
Wyoming	4 031.2	283.1	3 748.2	2.0	31.4	20.	229.6	717.6	2 892.0	138.6
Pacific	6 567.7	804.3	5 673.4	9.4	45.1	264.3	485.6	1 567.3	3 466.0	730.1
Alaska	5 377.5	455.4	4 922.1	10.1	65.0	73.1	307.2	970.1	3 465.7	486.3
California	6 506.4	918.0	5 588.4	6.2	43.8	301.3	562.4	1 518.2	3 240.2	830.1
Hawaii	5 871.0	263.3	5 554.7	4.8	36.3	98.0	124.2	1 155.6	4 033.1	366.0
Oregon	6 969.0	529.5	6 429.4	5.6	45.8	196.0	292.2	1 782.7	4 181.6	465.1
Washington	7 017.1	439.5	6 577.6	5.6	52.2	141.4	240.2	1 904.5	4 277.9	395.2
Puerto Rico	3 358.8	78.2	2,640.7	15.2	14.9	42.4	245.6	1 082.7	996.3	561.7

(1) Violent crimes are murder, rape, robbery and aggravated assault; (2) Property crimes are burglary, larceny-theft, and motor vehicle theft.

The Busiest U.S. Airports in 1987

Source: Air Transport Association of America

(passengers arriving and departing)

Airport	Passengers	Airport	Passengers
Chicago O'Hare	54 543 865	Boston	23 283 047
Atlanta	47 649 470	Honolulu	20 380 282
Los Angeles	44 873 113	St. Louis	20 362 602
Dallas/Ft. Worth	41 875 444	Detroit	19 746 992
Denver	32 355 000	Minneapolis/St. Paul	17 858 986
New York (JFK)	30 192 477	Pittsburgh	17 457 801
San Francisco	29 812 440	Washington, D.C. (DCA)	15 439 860
New York (LGA)	24 225 913	Philadelphia	15 427 317
Miami	24 036 104	Houston	15 388 667
Newark	23 475 254	Orlando	14 781 222

U.S. Industrial Corporations with Largest Sales in 1987[1]

Source: Fortune Magazine

Company	Sales (billions)	Profit (or loss) (millions)	Company	Sales (billions)	Profit (or loss) (millions)
General Motors	$101.7	$3 550	McDonnell Douglas	$13.1	$313
Exxon	76.4	4 840	Rockwell International	12.1	635
Ford	71.6	4 625	Allied-Signal	11.5	656
IBM	54.2	5 258	PepsiCo	11.5	594
Mobil	51.2	1 258	Lockheed	11.3	421
General Electric	39.5	2 915	Kraft	11.0	489
Texaco	34.3	(4 407)	Phillips Petroleum	10.7	35
AT&T	33.5	2 044	Westinghouse Electric	10.6	738
Du Pont	30.4	1 786	Xerox	10.3	578
Chrysler	26.2	1 289	Goodyear Tire & Rubber	10.1	770
Chevron	26.0	1 007	Unisys	9.7	578
Philip Morris	22.2	1 842	3M	9.4	918
Shell Oil	20.8	1 230	Digital Equipment	9.3	1 137
Amoco	20.1	1 360	General Dynamics	9.3	437
United Technologies	17.1	591	Sara Lee	9.1	267
Occidental Petroleum	17.0	240	Conagra	9.0	148
Procter & Gamble	17.0	327	Beatrice	8.9	n.a.
Atlantic Richfield	16.2	1 224	Sun	8.6	348
RJR Nabisco	15.8	1 209	Georgia-Pacific	8.6	458
Boeing	15.3	480	ITT	8.5	1 018
Tenneco	15.0	(218)	Unocal	8.4	181
BP America	14.6	564	Anheuser-Busch	8.2	614
USX	13.8	219	Caterpillar	8.1	350
Dow Chemical	13.3	1 240	Hewlett-Packard	8.0	644
Eastman Kodak	13.3	1 178	Johnson & Johnson	8.0	833

(1) For fiscal year.
n.a. not available.

Employment and Unemployment in the U.S.

Civilian labor force, persons 16 years of age and over (in thousands)

Year*	Employed	Unemployed	Percent unemployed	Year*	Employed	Unemployed	Percent unemployed
1940[1]	47 520	8 120	14.6%	1980	99 303	7 637	7.1%
1950	58 918	3 288	5.0	1981	100 397	8 273	7.6
1960	65 778	3 852	5.5	1982	99 526	10 678	9.7
1965	71 088	3 366	4.5	1983	100 834	10 717	9.6
1970	78 678	4 093	4.9	1984	105 005	8 539	7.5
1975	85 846	7 929	8.5	1985	107 150	8 312	7.2
1976	88 752	7 406	7.7	1986	109 597	8 237	7.0
1977	92 017	6 991	7.1	1987	112 440	7 425	6.2
1978	96 048	6 202	6.1				

(1) Persons 14 years of age and over

*Early unemployment rates: 1915, 9.7; 1916, 4.8; 1917, 4.8; 1918, 1.4; 1919, 2.3; 1920, 4.0; 1921, 11.9; 1922, 7.6; 1923, 3.2; 1924, 5.5; 1925, 4.0; 1926, 1.9; 1927, 4.1; 1928, 4.4; 1929, 3.2; 1930, 8.7; 1931, 15.9; 1932, 23.6; 1933, 24.9; 1934, 21.7; 1935, 20.1; 1936, 16.9; 1937, 14.3; 1938, 19.0; 1939, 17.2.

U.S. Stock Exchanges

N.Y. Stock Exchange Transactions

(U.S. dollars)

Year	Yearly volume Stock shares	Bonds par values	Year	Yearly volume Stock shares	Bonds par values
1900	138 981 000	$579 293 000	1970	2 937 359 448	$4 494 864 600
1905	260 569 000	1 026 254 000	1975	4 693 427 000	5 178 300 000
1910	163 705 000	634 863 000	1980	11 352 294 000	5 190 304 000
1915	172 497 000	961 700 000	1981	11 853 740 659	5 733 071 000
1920	227 636 000	3 868 422 000	1982	16 458 036 768	7 155 443 000
1925	459 717 623	3 427 042 210	1983	21 589 576 997	7 572 315 000
1929	1 124 800 410	2 996 398 000	1984	23 071 031 447	6 982 291 000
1930	810 632 546	2 720 301 800	1985	27 510 706 353	9 046 453 000
1935	81 635 752	3 339 458 000	1986	35 680 016 344	10 475 399 000
1940	207 599 749	1 669 438 000	1987	47 801 314 120	9 726 244 500
1950	524 799 621	1 112 425 170			
1960	766 693 818	1 346 419 750			

American Stock Exchange Transactions

(U.S. dollars)

Year	Yearly volume Stock shares	Bonds[1] princ. amts.	Year	Yearly volume Stock shares	Bonds[1] princ. amts.	Year	Yearly volume Stock shares	Bonds[1] princ. amts.
1929	476 140 375	$513 551 000	1970	843 116 260	$641 270 000	1985	2 100 860 000	$645 182 000
1930	222 270 065	863 541 000	1980	1 626 072 625	355 723 000	1986	2 978 540 000	810 264 000
1940	42 928 337	303 902 000	1981	1 343 400 220	301 226 000	1987	3 505 950 000	686 922 000
1945	143 309 392	167 333 000	1982	1 485 831 536	325 240 000			
1950	107 792 340	47 549 000	1983	2 081 270 000	395 190 000			
1960	286 039 982	32 670 000	1984	1 545 010 000	371 990 000			

(1) Corporate

Components of Dow Jones Industrial Average

Allied-Signal	DuPont	McDonald's	Texaco
Aluminum Co. of Amer.	Eastman Kodak	Merck	Union Carbide
American Express	Exxon	Minn. Mining & Manuf.	United Technologies
AT&T	General Electric	Navistar	USX Corp.
Bethlehem Steel	General Motors	Philip Morris	Westinghouse
Boeing	Goodyear	Primerica	Woolworth
Chevron	IBM	Procter & Gamble	
Coca-Cola	International Paper	Sears Roebuck	

Dow Jones Industrial Average Since 1954

High		Year		Low		High		Year		Low	
Dec.	31	404.39 .... 1954 ... Jan.	11	279.87		Jan.	11	1051.70 .... 1973 ... Dec.	5	788.31	
Dec.	30	488.40 .... 1955 ... Jan.	17	388.20		Mar.	13	891.66 .... 1974 ... Dec.	6	577.60	
Apr.	6	521.05 .... 1956 ... Jan.	23	462.35		July	15	881.81 .... 1975 ... Jan.	2	632.04	
July	12	520.77 .... 1957 ... Oct.	22	419.79		Sept.	21	1014.79 .... 1976 ... Jan.	2	858.71	
Dec.	31	583.65 .... 1958 ... Feb.	25	436.89		Jan.	3	999.75 .... 1977 ... Nov.	2	800.85	
Dec.	31	679.36 .... 1959 ... Feb.	9	574.46		Sept.	8	907.74 .... 1978 ... Feb.	28	742.12	
Jan.	5	685.47 .... 1960 ... Oct.	25	566.05		Oct.	5	897.61 .... 1979 ... Nov.	7	796.67	
Dec.	13	734.91 .... 1961 ... Jan.	3	610.25		Nov.	20	1000.17 .... 1980 ... Apr.	21	759.13	
Jan.	3	726.01 .... 1962 ... June	26	535.76		Apr.	27	1024.05 .... 1981 ... Sept.	25	824.01	
Dec.	18	767.21 .... 1963 ... Jan.	2	646.79		Dec.	27	1070.55 .... 1982 ... Aug.	12	776.92	
Nov.	18	891.71 .... 1964 ... Jan.	2	766.08		Nov.	29	1287.20 .... 1983 ... Jan.	3	1027.04	
Dec.	31	969.26 .... 1965 ... June	28	840.59		Jan.	6	1286.64 .... 1984 ... July	24	1086.57	
Feb.	9	995.15 .... 1966 ... Oct.	7	744.32		Dec.	16	1553.10 .... 1985 ... Jan.	4	1184.96	
Sept.	25	943.08 .... 1967 ... Jan.	3	786.41		Sept.	4	1919.71 .... 1986 ... Jan.	22	1502.29	
Dec.	3	985.21 .... 1968 ... Mar.	21	825.13		Aug.	25	2722.42 .... 1987 ... Oct.	19	1738.74	
May	14	968.85 .... 1969 ... Dec.	17	769.93		July	5	2158.61 .... 1988* ... Jan.	20	1879.14	
Dec.	29	842.00 .... 1970 ... May	6	631.16						*As of Sept. 9	
Apr.	28	950.82 .... 1971 ... Nov.	23	797.97							
Dec.	11	1036.27 .... 1972 ... Jan.	26	889.15							

U.S. Foreign Trade with Leading Countries

Source: Office of Industry and Trade Information, U.S. Commerce Department

(millions of dollars)

Exports from the U.S. to the following areas and countries and imports into the U.S. from those areas and countries:	Exports 1980	1986	1987	Imports 1980	1986	1987
Total	220 705	217 304	252 866	240 834	387 081	424 082
Western Hemisphere	74 114	76 411	94 795	78 489	110 201	120 605
Canada	35 395	45 333	59 814	41 455	68 253	71 510
20 Latin American Republics	36 030	27 969	31 574	29 851	39 541	46 427
Central American Common Market	1 951	1 768	1 873	1 849	2 061	2 158
Dominican Republic	795	921	1 142	786	1 085	1 217
Panama	699	712	743	330	366	402
Bahamas	396	761	782	1 382	442	450
Jamaica	305	457	601	383	299	422
Netherlands Antilles	448	398	507	2 564	471	557
Trinidad and Tobago	680	532	361	2 378	793	859
Western Europe	71 372	61 642	69 718	47 849	89 825	99 934
OECD countries (excludes depend. and Yugo.)	66 654	61 003	69 091	45 952	89 130	98 996
European Economic Community	53 679	53 154	60 575	35 958	75 736	84 876
Belgium and Luxembourg	6 661	5 399	6 189	1 914	4 006	4 359
Denmark	863	758	893	725	1 757	1 882
France	7 485	6 216	7 943	5 247	10 129	11 177
Germany, Federal Republic of	10 960	10 561	11 748	11 681	25 124	28 028
Ireland	836	1 434	1 810	411	1 003	1 155
Italy	5 511	4 838	5 530	4 313	10 607	11 698
Netherlands	8 669	7 848	8 217	1 910	4 066	4 236
United Kingdom	12 694	11 418	14 114	9 755	15 396	17 988
Austria	448	464	549	388	864	979
Finland	505	381	515	439	908	1 085
Iceland	79	80	84	200	238	300
Norway	843	937	842	2 632	1 079	1 514
Portugal	911	638	581	256	552	713
Sweden	1 767	1 871	1 894	1 617	4 420	4 981
Switzerland	3 781	2 977	3 151	2 787	2 787	4 363
Greece	922	430	402	292	395	529
Spain	3 179	2 615	3 148	1 209	2 702	3 101
Turkey	540	1 160	1 483	175	633	897
Yugoslavia	756	528	461	446	646	871
Eastern Europe	3 860	1 900	2 200	1 433	2 001	2 118
USSR	1 513	1 248	1 480	453	558	470
Asia	60 168	64 532	73 268	78 848	153 869	184 195
Near East	11 900	8 415	9 502	17 280	7 890	11 602
Iran	23	34	54	339	569	1 752
Iraq	724	528	683	352	440	526
Israel	2 045	2 239	3 130	943	2 418	2 724
Jordan	407	332	365	3	10	12
Kuwait	886	657	505	472	267	587
Lebanon	303	106	97	33	30	34
Saudi Arabia	5 769	3 449	3 373	12 509	3 612	4 887
Syria	239	59	93	26	8	66
Japan	20 790	26 882	28 249	30 701	81 911	83 074
East and South Asia	27 478	26 099	31 995	30 867	59 296	77 608
Bangladesh	292	165	193	85	230	419
China, People's Republic of	3 755	3 106	3 497	1 054	4 771	6 911
China (Taiwan)	4 337	5 524	7 413	6 850	19 791	26 407
Hong Kong	2 686	3 030	3 983	4 736	12 729	10 490
India	1 689	1 536	1 463	1 098	2 283	2 725
Indonesia	1 545	946	763	5 183	3 112	3 719
Korea, Republic of	4 685	6 355	8 099	4 147	12 729	17 991
Malaysia	1 337	1 730	1 897	2 577	2 421	3 053
Pakistan	642	830	128	733	325	438
Philippines	1 999	1 363	1 599	1 730	1 972	2 481
Singapore	3 033	3 380	4 053	1 920	4 725	6 395
Thailand	1 263	936	1 544	816	1 746	2 387
Oceania	4 876	6 659	6 526	3 392	3 717	4 550
Australia	4 093	5 551	5 495	2 509	2 632	3 287
New Zealand and Samoa	599	883	821	703	984	1 183
Africa	9 060	5 978	6 283	32 251	10 348	12 680
Algeria	542	553	426	6 577	1 831	2 144
Botswana	...	20	29	...	2	7
Egypt	1 874	1 982	2 210	458	112	498
Gabon	48	25	53	278	225	379
Ghana	127	84	115	206	191	260
Ivory Coast	185	60	82	288	425	405
Kenya	141	70	95	54	141	85
Liberia	113	65	70	128	82	101
Libya	509	46	.1	7 124	2	54
Morocco	344	487	383	35	43	54
Nigeria	1 150	409	295	10 905	2 530	3 767
South Africa, Rep. of	2 464	1 159	1 281	3 321	2 365	1 399
Sudan	143	90	152	17	22	23
Tunisia	174	163	119	60	11	73
Zaire	155	105	104	361	221	321

U.S. Exports and Imports of Leading Commodities

Source: Office of Industry and Trade Information, U.S. Commerce Department

(millions of dollars)

Commodity	Exports			Imports		
	1980	1986	1987	1980	1986	1987
Food and live animals	27 744	17 303	19 179	15 763	20 803	20 547
Cattle, except for breeding	...	...	...	228	422	417
Meat and preparations	1 293	1 424	1 768	2 346	2 367	2 786
Dairy products and eggs	255	407	385	318	415	442
Fish	915	1 297	1 588	2 612	4 691	4 788
Grains and preparations	18 079	7 368	8 058	...	...	...
Wheat, including flour	6 586	3 217	3 248	...	...	...
Rice	1 285	621	576	...	...	...
Grains and Animal feed	2 878	2 622	3 907	331	737	815
Vegetables and Fruit	...	2 657	2 956	1 188	4 200	4 476
Sugar	...	...	...	1 988	670	438
Coffee, crude	...	...	...	3 872	4 293	2 706
Cocoa or cacao beans	...	...	...	395	418	504
Tea	...	...	...	131	133	106
Beverages and tobacco	2 663	2 902	3 667	2 772	3 866	4 105
Alcoholic beverages	...	...	...	2 220	3 066	3 268
Tobacco, unmanufactured	2 390	1 210	1 091	422	591	588
Crude materials, inedible, except fuels	23 791	17 324	20 416	10 496	10 432	11 528
Hides and skins	694	1 314	1 450	88	65	82
Oilseeds, oil nuts, oil kernels	5 883	4 334	4 343	...	65	58
Synthetic rubber and rubber latex	695	649	761	...	...	...
Lumber and rough wood	2 675	2 240	3 007	2 134	3 140	3 341
Wood pulp and pulpwood	2 454	2 318	3 084	1 725	1 547	2 110
Textile fibers and wastes	2 864	...	1 631	242	358	438
Ores and metal scrap	4 518	2 802	3 018	3 696	2 148	2 446
Mineral fuels and related materials	7 982	8 115	7 713	9 058	37 310	44 220
Coal	4 523	7 867	6 740	...	...	...
Petroleum and products	2 833	3 640	3 922	73 771	34 140	41 529
Natural gas	...	...	...	5 155	2 994	2 504
Animal and vegetable oils and fats	1 946	1,015	981	533	516	568
Chemicals	20 740	22 766	26 381	8 583	15 001	16 213
Medicines and pharmaceuticals	1 932	3 090	3 782	508	1 240	1 456
Fertilizers, manufactured	2 265	1 935	2 259	1 104	865	795
Plastic materials and resins	3 884	4 301	5 493	...	...	...
Machinery and transport equip.	84 629	95 290	108 596	60 546	161 562	177 809
Machinery	55 790	60 397	69 637	31 904	87 549	99 433
Aircraft engines and parts	1 915	3 729	4 390	...	...	4 475
Auto engines and parts	1 688	2 269	2 406	...	4 495	...
Agricultural machinery	3 104	1 421	1 493	682	1 584	1 836
Tractors and parts	1 809	...	625	...	972	391
Office machines and computers	8 709	15 546	18 692	2 929	14 669	18 462
Transport equipment	28 839	34 893	38 959	28 642	74 013	57 024
Road motor vehicles and parts	14 590	18 575	20 879	24 134	54 661	61 598
Aircraft and parts except engines	12 816	15 106	16 903	1 885	4 494	4 475
Other manufactured goods	42 714	16 629	19 409	55 900	103 559	118 539
Tires and tubes	511	315	514	1 143	1 986	2 271
Wood and manufactures, exc. furniture	2 675	...	...	632	901	...
Paper and manufactures	2 831	2 602	3 180	3 587	6 360	7 310
Glassware and pottery	...	...	...	1 224	2 492	2 871
Diamonds, excl. industrial	...	...	...	2 252	3 459	3 423
Nonmetallic mineral manuf.	2 209	1 886	2 289	...	...	...
Metal manufactures	4 205	3 008	3 534	...	7 129	8 053
Pig iron and ferroalloys	3 123	...	...	...	...	...
Iron and steel-mill products	2 998	1 081	1 229	6 686	8 168	8 490
Nonferrous base metals	2 964	...	1 853	7 623	7 699	7 991
Textiles, other than clothing	3 632	573	677	2 493	9 221	6 511
Clothing	1 203	899	1 156	6 427	17 288	20 491
Footwear	...	...	...	2 808	6 473	7 237
Furniture	521	534	624	...	...	...
Professional, scientific, controlling instruments	6 763	6 733	7 388	...	3 888	4 509
Printed matter	1 097	1 342	1 562	613	1 376	1 494
Clocks and watches	133	83	93	1 097	1 536	1 702
Toys, games, sporting goods	1 012	628	885	1 914	4 728	5 987
Artworks and antiques	...	...	...	2 672	2 092	1 925
Other transactions	8 496	11 011	20 381	7 183	14 914	12 374
Total	220 705	206 376	252 866	240 834	369 961	405 901

U.S. Total Energy Production by Source

Source: Energy Information Administration, Annual Energy Review, 1987

(quadrillion Btu)

Year	Total	Coal	Natural gas[1]	Crude oil[2]	Natural gas plant liquids	Hydroelectric power[3]	Nuclear electric power[4]	Geothermal[4]
1949	30.18	11.97	5.38	10.68	0.71	1.42	–	–
1950	33.98	14.06	6.23	11.45	0.82	1.42	–	–
1955	38.73	12.37	9.34	14.41	1.24	1.36	–	–
1960	41.49	10.82	12.66	14.93	1.46	1.61	0.01	–
1965	49.34	13.06	15.78	16.52	1.88	2.06	0.04	. . .
1970	62.07	14.61	21.67	20.40	2.51	2.63	0.24	0.01
1975	59.86	14.99	19.64	17.73	2.37	3.15	1.90	0.07
1976	59.89	15.65	19.48	17.26	2.33	2.98	2.11	0.08
1977	60.22	15.76	19.57	17.45	2.33	2.33	2.70	0.08
1978	61.10	14.91	19.49	18.43	2.25	2.94	3.02	0.06
1979	63.80	17.54	20.08	18.10	2.29	2.93	2.78	0.08
1980	64.76	18.60	19.91	18.25	2.25	2.90	2.74	0.11
1981	64.42	18.38	19.70	18.15	2.31	2.76	3.01	0.12
1982	63.89	18.64	18.25	18.31	2.19	3.26	3.13	0.10
1983	61.19	17.25	16.53	18.39	2.18	3.50	3.20	0.13
1984	65.81	19.72	17.93	18.85	2.27	3.31	3.55	0.16
1985	64.78	19.33	16.92	18.99	2.24	2.94	4.15	0.20
1986	64.25	19.51	16.47	18.38	2.15	3.03	4.47	0.22
1987[5]	64.55	20.12	16.84	17.59	2.23	2.61	4.92	0.23

(1) Dry natural gas. (2) Includes lease condensate. (3) Electric utility and industrial generation of hydroelectric power. (4) Generated by electric utilities. (5) Preliminary.
. . . = too small to be included; – = zero.

U.S. Total Energy Consumption by Source

Source: Energy Information Administration, Annual Energy Review, 1987

(quadrillion Btu)

Year	Total	Coal	Natural gas	Petroleum[1]	Hydroelectric power[2]	Nuclear electric power[3]	Geothermal[3]
1949	30.46	11.98	5.15	11.88	1.45	–	–
1950	33.08	12.35	5.97	13.32	1.44	–	–
1955	38.82	11.17	9.00	17.25	1.41	–	–
1960	43.80	9.84	12.39	19.92	1.66	0.01	. . .
1965	52.68	11.58	15.77	23.25	2.06	0.04	. . .
1970	66.43	12.26	21.79	29.52	2.65	0.24	0.01
1975	70.55	12.66	19.95	32.73	3.22	1.90	0.07
1976	74.36	13.58	20.35	35.17	3.07	2.11	0.08
1977	76.29	13.92	19.93	37.12	2.51	2.70	0.08
1978	78.09	13.77	20.00	37.97	3.14	3.02	0.06
1979	78.90	15.04	20.67	37.12	3.14	2.78	0.08
1980	75.96	15.42	20.39	34.20	3.12	2.74	0.11
1981	73.99	15.91	19.93	31.93	3.11	3.01	0.12
1982	70.84	15.32	18.51	30.23	3.56	3.13	0.10
1983	70.50	15.90	17.36	30.05	3.87	3.20	0.13
1984	74.06	17.07	18.51	31.05	3.72	3.55	0.16
1985	73.96	17.48	17.85	30.92	3.36	4.15	0.20
1986	74.26	17.26	16.71	32.20	3.40	4.47	0.22
1987[4]	76.01	18.00	17.18	32.63	3.04	4.92	0.23

(1) Petroleum products supplied including natural gas plant liquids and crude oil burned as fuel. (2) Electric utility and industrial generation of hydroelectric power and net electricity imports. (3) Generated by electric utilities. (4) Preliminary.
. . . = too small to be included; – = zero.

Monthly Normal Temperature and Precipitation

Source: NOAA, U.S. Department of Commerce

These normals are based on records for the 30-year period 1951 to 1980 inclusive. For stations that did not have continuous records from the same instrument site for the entire 30 years, the means have been adjusted to the record at the present site.

Airport station; *city office stations. T, temperature in Celsius; P, precipitation in cm.

Station	Jan T	Jan P	Feb T	Feb P	Mar T	Mar P	Apr T	Apr P	May T	May P	June T	June P	July T	July P	Aug T	Aug P	Sept T	Sept P	Oct T	Oct P	Nov T	Nov P	Dec T	Dec P
Albany, N.Y.	-6	6.1	-5	5.8	1	7.6	8	7.4	14	8.4	19	8.4	22	7.6	21	8.4	16	8.1	11	7.4	4	7.6	-3	7.6
Albuquerque, N.M.	2	1.0	4	1.0	8	1.3	13	1.0	18	1.3	24	1.3	25	3.3	24	3.8	21	2.3	14	2.3	7	1.0	2	1.3
Anchorage, Alaska	-11	2.0	-8	2.3	-4	1.8	2	1.8	8	1.5	12	2.8	14	5.1	13	5.3	9	6.4	2	4.3	-6	2.8	-10	2.8
Asheville, N.C.	3	8.9	4	9.1	8	13.0	13	9.7	17	10.7	21	10.7	23	11.2	23	12.2	21	10.2	13	8.4	8	8.4	4	8.9
Atlanta, Ga.	6	12.4	7	11.2	12	15.0	17	11.2	21	10.2	24	8.6	26	11.9	26	8.6	23	8.1	17	6.4	11	8.6	7	10.7
Atlantic City, N.J.	1	8.4	2	8.1	6	9.4	11	7.9	16	7.4	20	7.4	23	9.9	23	11.4	20	6.9	14	7.1	9	8.9	4	8.9
Baltimore, Md.	1	7.6	2	7.6	6	9.4	12	8.6	17	8.6	22	9.7	25	9.9	24	11.7	21	8.9	14	7.9	8	7.9	3	8.6
Barrow, Alaska	-26	0.5	-29	0.5	-27	0.5	-19	0.5	-7	0.5	1	1.0	4	2.3	3	2.5	-1	1.5	-10	1.5	-18	0.8	-25	0.5
Birmingham, Ala.	6	13.2	8	11.9	12	16.8	17	12.7	21	11.4	25	9.4	27	13.7	27	9.9	23	10.9	17	6.9	11	9.1	7	12.7
Bismarck, N.D.	-14	1.3	-9	1.3	-3	1.8	6	3.8	13	5.6	18	7.6	21	5.1	21	4.3	14	3.6	8	2.0	-2	1.3	-9	1.3
Boise, Ida.	-1	4.0	2	2.8	5	2.5	9	3.0	14	3.0	19	2.5	24	0.8	22	1.0	17	1.5	11	2.0	4	3.3	0	3.3
Boston, Mass.	-1	10.2	-1	9.4	3	10.4	9	9.4	15	8.9	20	7.4	23	6.9	22	9.4	18	8.6	13	8.6	7	10.7	1	12.4
Buffalo, N.Y.	-4	7.6	-4	6.1	1	7.6	7	7.6	13	7.4	19	6.9	22	7.6	21	10.7	17	8.6	11	7.4	4	9.1	-2	8.6
Burlington, Vt.	-8	4.8	-8	4.3	-2	5.6	6	7.1	13	7.6	18	9.1	21	8.6	19	9.9	15	8.1	9	7.1	3	7.1	-5	6.1
Caribou, Me.	-12	6.1	-11	5.3	-4	6.1	3	6.6	10	7.4	16	8.1	18	10.2	17	10.2	12	8.9	6	7.9	-1	8.1	-9	7.9
Charleston, S.C.	9	8.4	11	8.6	14	11.2	19	2.6	23	11.2	26	16.5	28	18.5	27	16.5	25	12.4	20	7.4	15	5.6	11	7.9
Chicago, Ill.	-6	4.0	-4	3.3	2	6.6	9	9.4	15	8.1	21	10.4	23	9.1	22	8.9	18	8.6	12	5.8	4	5.3	-2	5.3
Cleveland, Oh.	-3	6.4	-3	5.6	3	7.6	9	8.4	14	8.4	20	8.9	22	8.6	21	8.6	18	7.4	12	6.4	6	7.1	-1	7.1
Columbus, Oh.	-3	7.1	-1	5.6	4	8.1	11	8.6	16	9.7	21	10.2	23	10.2	22	9.4	19	7.1	12	4.8	6	6.6	0	6.6
Dallas-Ft. Worth, Tex.	7	4.3	9	4.8	13	6.1	19	9.1	23	10.9	28	6.6	30	5.1	30	4.6	26	8.4	20	6.4	13	4.6	9	4.3
Denver, Col.	-1	1.3	1	1.8	3	3.0	8	4.6	14	6.4	19	4.1	23	4.8	22	3.8	17	3.0	11	2.5	4	2.0	1	1.5
Des Moines, Ia.	-7	2.5	-4	2.8	2	5.6	11	8.1	17	10.1	22	10.7	24	8.1	23	10.4	18	7.9	12	5.6	4	3.8	-3	3.8
Detroit, Mich.	-5	4.8	-4	4.3	2	6.4	8	6.1	14	7.1	20	8.6	22	7.9	22	8.1	17	5.8	11	5.3	4	5.8	-2	6.4
Dodge City, Kan.	-1	1.3	2	1.3	6	3.8	12	4.6	18	4.4	24	7.6	27	7.9	26	6.6	21	4.8	14	3.3	6	2.0	1	1.3
Duluth, Minn.	-14	3.0	-11	2.3	-5	4.6	3	5.6	10	8.1	15	10.2	18	10.2	17	10.4	12	8.4	7	5.6	-2	4.3	-10	3.3
Eureka, Cal.*	8	17.8	9	13.2	9	13.0	9	7.4	11	4.1	13	1.5	13	0.3	14	1.0	14	2.3	12	6.9	11	15.0	9	15.7
Fairbanks, Alaska	-25	1.3	-20	1.3	-13	1.0	-1	0.8	9	1.5	15	3.3	17	4.6	14	4.8	7	2.8	-4	1.8	-16	1.8	-23	1.8
Fresno, Cal.	8	5.1	11	4.8	12	4.1	16	2.0	20	0.8	24	0.3	27	0.1	26	0.1	23	0.5	18	1.0	12	3.0	7	4.1
Galveston, Tex.	12	7.6	13	5.8	17	5.3	21	6.6	24	8.4	27	8.9	28	9.7	28	11.2	27	14.7	23	6.6	17	8.1	14	9.1
Grand Junction, Col.	-3	1.5	1	1.3	6	2.0	11	1.8	17	2.0	22	1.0	26	1.3	24	2.3	19	1.8	13	2.3	4	1.5	-2	1.5
Gr. Rapids, Mich.	-6	4.8	-4	3.8	1	6.4	8	9.1	14	7.6	19	9.9	22	7.6	21	8.9	17	7.9	11	7.4	4	7.4	-3	6.6
Hartford, Conn.	-4	8.9	-2	8.1	3	10.7	9	10.2	15	8.6	20	8.4	23	7.9	22	10.2	17	9.9	11	8.9	6	10.4	-2	10.7
Helena, Mon.	-8	1.8	-4	1.0	0	1.8	6	2.5	11	4.3	16	5.1	20	2.5	19	3.0	13	2.0	7	1.8	-1	1.3	-5	1.5
Honolulu, Ha.	23	9.7	23	6.9	24	8.9	24	3.0	26	2.5	26	1.3	27	1.3	27	1.5	27	1.5	27	4.8	25	8.1	23	8.6
Houston, Tex.	11	8.1	13	8.4	16	6.9	21	10.7	24	11.9	27	10.1	28	8.4	28	9.9	26	12.4	21	10.4	16	8.6	12	9.4
Huron, S.D.	-12	1.0	-8	2.0	-2	3.0	8	5.1	14	6.9	20	8.4	23	5.1	22	5.1	16	3.6	9	3.6	0	1.8	-7	1.3
Indianapolis, Ind.	-3	6.9	-1	6.4	4	9.1	11	9.4	17	9.4	22	10.2	24	10.9	23	8.9	19	6.9	13	6.4	6	7.6	0	7.6
Jackson, Miss.	8	12.7	9	12.4	13	15.0	18	15.0	23	12.2	26	7.4	28	11.2	27	9.4	24	9.1	18	6.6	13	10.7	9	13.7
Jacksonville, Fla.	12	7.9	13	8.9	16	9.4	20	8.4	23	12.4	26	13.7	27	16.5	27	18.3	26	18.5	21	8.6	16	4.8	13	6.6
Juneau, Alaska	-6	9.4	-2	9.4	-1	8.4	4	7.4	8	8.6	12	7.6	13	10.4	13	12.7	9	16.3	6	19.6	1	13.2	-3	11.9
Kansas City, Mo.	-3	2.5	0	2.5	6	5.3	13	6.6	18	6.6	24	10.4	26	8.9	25	8.1	20	8.4	14	6.4	6	3.0	0	2.8
Knoxville, Tenn.	3	11.9	6	10.7	10	14	16	9.9	19	9.4	23	10.2	26	10.9	25	7.6	22	7.6	16	6.9	9	9.7	5	11.7
Lander, Wyo.	-7	1.3	-3	1.5	0	2.8	6	5.6	12	6.9	17	3.8	22	1.8	21	1.3	14	2.3	8	3.0	-1	2.0	-5	1.3
Lexington, Ky.	0	9.1	2	8.4	7	12.2	13	10.2	18	10.7	22	10.9	24	12.7	24	10.2	21	8.4	14	6.6	8	9.9	2	9.7
Little Rock, Ark.	4	9.9	7	9.7	11	11.9	17	13.7	22	13.5	26	9.4	28	9.1	27	7.9	23	10.9	17	7.1	11	11.2	6	10.7
Los Angeles, Cal.	14	9.4	15	7.6	16	6.1	17	3.0	18	0.5	21	0.1	23	0.1	24	0.3	23	0.8	21	0.5	17	4.8	14	5.1
Louisville, Ky.	1	8.6	2	8.1	7	11.9	14	10.4	18	10.7	23	9.1	26	10.4	24	8.4	21	9.1	14	6.6	8	8.9	3	8.9
Marquette, Mic.*	-11	5.1	-10	4.8	-5	7.1	3	9.1	10	10.2	16	9.9	18	8.1	17	8.4	12	9.9	7	8.4	-1	7.4	-8	6.1
Memphis, Tenn.	4	11.7	7	10.9	11	13.7	17	14.7	22	13.0	26	9.1	28	10.2	27	9.4	23	9.1	17	6.1	11	10.7	6	12.4
Miami, Fla.	19	5.3	20	5.3	22	4.8	24	7.9	26	16.5	27	23.4	28	15.2	28	17.8	28	20.6	26	18.0	23	6.9	21	4.8
Milwaukee, Wis.	-7	4.1	-5	3.3	0	6.6	8	8.6	13	6.6	18	9.1	22	8.9	21	7.9	17	7.4	11	5.8	3	5.1	-4	5.1
Minneapolis, Minn.	-12	2.0	-8	2.3	-2	4.3	8	5.3	15	8.1	20	10.4	23	8.9	22	9.1	16	6.4	10	4.8	1	3.3	-7	2.3
Mobile, Ala.	11	11.7	12	12.4	16	16.5	20	13.7	24	14.0	27	13.0	28	19.6	28	17.3	26	16.8	21	6.6	15	9.4	12	13.7
Moline, Ill.	-7	4.1	-4	3.3	2	7.1	10	10.2	16	10.7	22	10.9	24	12.4	23	9.7	18	9.4	12	6.9	4	5.1	-3	4.8
Nashville, Tenn.	3	11.4	6	10.2	9	14.2	16	12.2	20	11.7	24	9.4	26	9.7	26	8.6	23	9.7	16	6.6	9	8.9	5	11.7
Newark, N.J.	-1	7.9	1	7.9	6	9.1	12	8.9	17	9.1	22	7.4	25	9.9	24	10.9	20	9.4	14	7.9	8	9.1	2	8.6
New Orleans, La.	11	12.7	13	13.2	16	11.9	21	11.4	24	13.0	27	11.7	28	17.0	28	15.2	26	15	21	6.9	16	10.4	13	13.5
New York, N.Y.*	0	8.1	1	7.9	5	10.7	12	9.7	17	9.7	22	8.1	25	9.7	24	10.2	20	9.4	14	8.6	8	10.4	2	9.7
Nome, Alaska	-13	2.0	-16	1.3	-14	1.5	-8	1.5	2	1.3	7	3.0	11	5.6	10	7.9	6	5.8	-2	3.3	-9	2.3	-16	1.8
Norfolk, Va.	4	9.4	5	8.4	9	9.9	14	7.4	19	9.7	24	8.9	26	13.2	26	13.5	22	11.2	16	8.6	11	7.4	7	8.1
Okla. City, Okla.	2	2.5	5	3.0	9	5.3	16	7.4	20	14.0	25	9.9	28	7.6	27	6.1	23	8.1	17	6.9	9	3.8	4	3.0
Omaha, Neb.	-7	2.0	-4	2.9	2	4.8	10	7.4	17	10.9	22	10.4	24	9.1	23	10.4	18	6.4	12	5.3	3	3.3	-3	2.0
Pago Pago, Samoa	27	33.0	27	33.0	27	27.9	27	27.9	27	27.9	27	21.8	26	16.5	26	18.0	27	17.0	27	27.9	27	27.9	27	35.6
Philadelphia, Pa.	-1	8.1	1	7.1	6	9.9	12	8.9	17	8.1	22	9.9	25	9.9	24	10.0	20	8.6	14	7.1	8	8.4	2	8.9
Phoenix, Ariz.	11	1.8	13	1.5	16	2.0	20	0.8	25	0	30	0.5	33	1.8	32	2.5	29	1.5	23	1.5	16	1.3	12	2.0
Pittsburgh, Pa.	-3	7.4	-2	6.1	4	9.1	10	8.4	16	8.9	20	8.4	22	9.7	22	8.4	18	7.1	12	6.4	6	5.8	1	6.6
Portland, Me.	-6	9.7	-5	9.1	0	10.2	6	9.9	12	8.4	17	7.9	20	7.1	19	7.1	15	8.4	9	9.7	3	11.9	-3	11.4
Portland, Ore.	4	15.7	6	9.9	8	9.1	10	5.8	14	5.3	17	3.8	20	1.3	19	2.8	17	4.1	12	7.9	8	13.2	5	16.3
Providence, R.I.	-2	10.4	-2	9.4	3	10.9	9	10.2	14	8.9	19	7.1	23	7.6	22	10.2	18	8.9	12	9.7	6	10.7	0	11.4
Raleigh, N.C.	4	9.1	6	8.6	9	9.4	15	7.4	19	9.9	24	9.4	26	11.2	25	11.2	22	8.4	16	6.9	10	7.4	6	7.9
Rapid City, S.D.	-4	1.0	-3	1.5	0	2.5	7	5.1	13	6.6	18	8.4	23	5.3	22	3.6	16	3.1	10	2.0	2	1.3	-3	1.3
Reno, Nev.	0	3.0	3	2.5	5	1.3	8	1.3	13	1.8	17	0.8	21	0.5	20	0.8	16	0.5	10	0.8	4	1.5	1	3.0
Richmond, Va.	3	8.1	4	7.9	8	9.1	14	7.4	19	9.1	23	9.1	26	13.0	25	12.7	21	8.9	15	9.4	9	8.4	4	8.6
St. Louis, Mo.	-2	4.3	1	5.3	6	8.4	13	9.1	19	9.4	24	9.4	26	9.1	25	6.6	21	6.9	14	5.8	7	6.4	1	5.6

Station	Jan. T.	Jan. P.	Feb. T.	Feb. P.	Mar. T.	Mar. P.	Apr. T.	Apr. P.	May T.	May P.	June T.	June P.	July T.	July P.	Aug. T.	Aug. P.	Sept. T.	Sept. P.	Oct. T.	Oct. P.	Nov. T.	Nov. P.	Dec. T.	Dec. P.
Salt Lake City, Ut.	-2	3.6	1	3.3	5	4.3	9	5.6	15	3.8	20	2.5	26	1.8	24	2.3	18	2.3	12	2.8	4	3.0	-1	3.6
San Antonio, Tex.	10	4.1	12	4.8	17	3.3	21	6.9	24	9.4	28	7.6	29	4.8	29	6.9	26	9.7	21	7.4	16	5.8	12	3.6
San Diego, Cal.	14	5.3	14	3.6	15	4.1	16	2.0	17	0.5	19	0.3	21	0.1	22	0.3	22	0.5	20	0.8	17	2.8	14	3.6
San Francisco, Cal.	9	12.0	11	8.1	12	6.6	13	3.8	14	0.8	16	0.3	17	0.1	17	0.3	18	0.5	16	2.8	13	6.1	9	9.1
San Juan, P.R.	25	7.6	25	5.1	26	5.8	27	9.1	26	14.2	27	11.9	28	12.4	28	15.0	28	15.2	27	15.0	27	14.2	26	11.9
Saulte Ste. Marie, Mich.*	-11	5.6	-10	4.3	-4	5.1	3	6.1	10	7.4	14	8.4	18	7.6	17	8.9	13	9.9	7	7.4	1	8.1	-7	6.6
Savannah, Ga.	9	7.9	11	8.1	14	9.7	19	8.1	23	11.7	26	14.5	27	18.8	27	17.0	25	13.2	19	5.8	14	4.8	11	7.1
Seattle, Wash.	4	15.2	6	10.7	7	9.1	9	6.1	13	4.1	16	3.6	18	1.8	18	3.3	16	5.1	11	8.6	7	14.2	5	16.0
Spokane, Wash.	-2	6.4	0	4.1	3	3.6	8	2.8	12	3.6	17	3.0	21	1.3	20	1.8	16	1.8	9	2.8	2	5.3	-2	6.4
Springfield, Mo.	0	4.1	2	5.3	7	8.6	13	10.2	18	10.9	23	11.9	26	9.1	25	7.1	21	10.7	14	8.1	7	7.4	2	6.6
Syracuse, N.Y.	-5	6.6	-4	6.9	1	7.9	8	8.4	14	8.1	19	9.1	22	9.7	21	9.7	17	8.4	11	7.9	5	8.9	-2	8.1
Tampa, Fla.	16	5.6	16	7.6	19	8.9	22	4.6	25	8.6	27	13.5	28	18.8	28	19.3	27	15.7	23	5.8	19	4.8	16	5.3
Washington, D.C.	-1	7.1	1	6.6	6	8.6	12	7.9	17	9.1	22	10.7	24	9.7	23	10.7	19	8.4	13	7.6	7	7.6	2	8.4
Wilmington, Del.	-1	7.9	1	7.6	6	9.3	11	8.6	17	8.1	22	8.9	24	9.9	24	10.2	20	9.1	13	7.4	8	8.4	2	8.9

Cities of the U.S.

Sources: Bureau of the Census: population (1986 estimates); population growth (1970-1980); population over 65 and under 35 (1980). Geography Division, Bureau of the Census: population density (1980); area (1980), Bureau of Labor Statistics: employment (Jan. 1988), Bureau of Economic Analysis: per capita personal income (MSA, 1986).

(U.S. dollars)

Atlanta, Georgia

Population: 421 910; **Pop. density:** 1 257 per sq. km; **Pop. growth:** −14.1%; **Pop. over 65:** 11.5%; **Pop. under 35:** 60.7%. **Area:** 339 sq. km. **Employment:** 205 829 employed, 8.1% unemployed; **Per capita income:** $16 408.

Transportation: 1 international airport; 7 railroad lines, 2 systems; 2 bus terminals; rapid rail under construction; 6 legs of 3 interstate highways intersecting downtown interchange. **Communications:** 9 TV, 41 radio stations; 21 cable TV companies. **Medical facilities:** 56 hospitals; VA hospital; Natl. Centers for Disease Control; Natl. Cancer Center. **Educational facilities:** 30 colleges, universities, seminaries, junior colleges. **Further information:** Chamber of Commerce, 235 International Blvd., Atlanta, GA 30303.

Baltimore, Maryland

Population: 752 800; **Pop. density:** 3 689 per sq. km; **Pop. growth:** −13.1%; **Pop. over 65:** 12.8%; **Pop. under 35%:** 56.9%. **Area:** 207 sq. km. **Employment:** 312 449 employed, 8.3% unemployed; **Per capita income:** $16 439.

Transportation: 1 major airport; 3 railroads, bus system; subway system; 1 underwater tunnel. **Communications:** 6 TV stations; 33 radio stations. **Medical facilities:** 29 hospitals; 2 major medical centres. **Educational facilities:** 189 public schools; over 30 universities and colleges; major public library system. **Further information:** Greater Baltimore Committee, Suite 900, Two Hopkins Plaza, Baltimore, MD 21202.

Boston, Massachusetts

Population: 573 600; **Pop. density:** 4 678 per sq. km; **Pop. growth:** −12.2%; **Pop. over 65:** 12.7%; **Pop. under 35:** 60.4%. **Area:** 120 sq. km. **Employment:** 288 910 employed, 3.3% unemployed; **Per capita income:** $18 959.

Transportation: 1 major airport; 2 railroads; city rail and subway system; 2 underwater tunnels. **Communications:** 8 TV stations; 33 radio stations. **Medical facilities:** numerous hospitals; 8 major medical research centres. **Educational facilities:** 28 universities and colleges; major public library system. **Further information:** Chamber of Commerce, Federal Reserve Bank, 600 Atlantic Ave., 13th Fl., Boston, MA 02106

Buffalo, New York

Population: 324 820; **Pop. density:** 3 138 per sq. km; **Pop. growth:** −22.7%; **Pop. over 65:** 15.0%; **Pop. under 35:** 55.3%. **Area:** 108 sq. km. **Employment:** 131 038 employed, 8.8% unemployed; **Per capita income:** $14 469.

Transportation: 1 international airport; 6 major railroads, metro rail system; direct highway & rail to all of Canada; water service to Great Lakes-St. Lawrence seaways system, overseas, and Atlantic seaboard. **Communications:** 5 TV, 23 AM & FM radio stations, 5 cable systems. **Medical facilities:** 21 hospitals. **Educational facilities:** 2 universities; 9 colleges, 78 public schools. **Further information:** Greater Buffalo Chamber of Commerce, 107 Delaware Ave., Buffalo, NY 14202.

Chicago, Illinois

Population: 3 009 330; **Pop. density:** 5 072 per sq. km; **Pop. growth:** −10.8%; **Pop. over 65:** 11.4%; **Pop. under 35:** 58.5%. **Area:** 590 sq. km **Employment:** 1 299 291 employed, 7.6% unemployed; **Per capita income:** $16 847.

Transportation: 3 airports; major railroad system; major trucking industry. **Communications:** 9 TV stations; 31 radio stations. **Medical facilities:** over 123 hospitals. **Educational facilities:** 95 institutions of higher learning; major public library system. **Further information:** Association of Commerce and Industry, 200 N. LaSalle St., Chicago, IL 60601.

Cleveland, Ohio

Population: 535 830; **Pop. density:** 2 679 per sq. km; **Pop. growth:** −23.6%; **Pop. over 65:** 13.0%; **Pop. under 35:** 56.7%. **Area:** 204 sq. km. **Employment:** 218 148 employed, 9.3% unemployed; **Per capita income:** $16 238.

Transportation: Hopkin's Intl. airport; rail service; major port; rapid transit system. **Communications:** 7 TV stations; 20 radio stations. **Medical facilities:** numerous hospitals; major medical research centre. **Educational facilities:** 23 universities and colleges; major public library system. **Further information:** Convention & Visitor's Bureau, 1301 E. 6th Street, Cleveland, OH 44114.

Dallas, Texas

Population: 1 003 520; **Pop. density:** 1 130 per sq. km; **Pop. growth:** 7%; **Pop. over 65:** 9.5%; **Pop. under 35:** 61.1%. **Area:** 862 sq. km. **Employment:** 605 275 employed, 7.3% unemployed; **Per capita income:** $17 419.

Transportation: 1 international airport; 6 railroads; major transit system. **Communications:** 9 TV stations; 38 radio stations. **Medical facilities:** 42 hospitals; major medical centre. **Educational facilities:** 37 universities and colleges; major public library system; 186 public schools. **Further information:** Chamber of Commerce, 1507 Pacific Ave., Dallas, TX 75201.

Denver, Colorado

Population: 505 000; **Pop. density:** 1 758 per sq. km; **Pop. growth:** −4.3%; **Pop. over 65:** 12.6%; **Pop. under 35:** 58.9%. **Area:** 287 sq. km. **Employment:** 254 682 employed, 7.5% unemployed (1985); **Per capita income:** $16 986.

Transportation: 1 international airport; 5 major rail freight lines, Amtrak; 2 bus lines; 3 interstate highways intersect city. **Communications:** 7 TV, 35 radio stations. **Medical facilities:** 34 hospitals. **Educational facilities:** 2 universities; 3 colleges. **Further information:** Chamber of Commerce, 1301 Welton St., Denver, CO 80204.

Detroit, Michigan

Population: 1 086 220; **Pop. density:** 3 093 per sq. km; **Pop. growth:** −20.5%; **Pop. over 65:** 11.7%; **Pop. under 35:** 59.5%. **Area:** 352 sq. km. **Employment:** 396 432 employed, 14.5% unemployed (Dec. 1984); **Per capita income:** $16 575.

Transportation: 1 international airport; 10 railroads; major international port; public transit system. **Communications:** 9 TV stations, 37 radio stations. **Medical facilities:** 28 hospitals, major medical centre. **Educational facilities:** 13 universities and colleges; major public library system. **Further information:** Chamber of Commerce, 150 Michigan Avenue, Detroit, MI 48226.

Honolulu Co., Hawaii

Population: 372 330 **Pop. density:** 522 per sq. km. **Pop. growth:** 20.9%; **Pop. over 65:** 7.4%; **Pop. under 35:** 62.4%. **Area:** 1 543 sq. km. **Employment:** 375 832 employed, 3.6% unemployed; **Per capita income:** $15 380.

Transportation: 1 major airport; large, active port for passengers and cargo. **Communications:** 5 TV stations; 23 radio stations. **Medical facilities:** 43 hospitals. **Educational facilities:** 230 public schools (state); 146 private schools (state); 1 university (9 campus centres); major public library system. **Further information:** Visitors Bureau, 2270 Kalakaua Avenue, Honolulu, HI 96815.

Houston, Texas

Population: 1 728 910; **Pop. density:** 1 184 per sq. km; **Pop. growth:** 29.3%; **Pop. over 65:** 6.9%; **Pop. under 35:** 64.4%. **Area:** 1 440 sq. km. **Employment:** 861 953 employed, 8.6% unemployed; **Per capita income:** $15 053.

Transportation: 2 airports; 5 railroads; major bus transit system; major international port. **Communications:** 9 TV stations; 45 radio stations. **Medical facilities:** 59 hospitals; major medical centre. **Educational facilities:** 27 universities and colleges; 7th largest U.S. public school system; major public library system. **Further information:** Chamber of Commerce, 1100 Milam, Houston, TX 77002.

Indianapolis, Indiana

Population: 719 820; **Pop. density:** 779 per sq. km; **Pop. growth:** −4.9%; **Pop. over 65;** 10.3%; **Pop. under 35:** 59.4%. **Area:** 911 sq. km. **Employment:** 365 139 employed, 5.8% unemployed; **Per capita income:** $14 844.

Transportation: 1 international airport; 6 railroads; 3 interstate bus lines. **Communications:** 7 TV stations; 27 radio stations. **Medical facilities:** 17 hospitals; major medical centre. **Educational facilities:** 6 universities and colleges; major public library system. **Further information:** Chamber of Commerce, 320 N. Meridian Street, Indianapolis, IN 46204.

Jacksonville, Florida

Population: 609 860; **Pop. density:** 293 per sq. km; **Pop. growth:** 7.3%; **Pop. over 65:** 9.6%; **Pop. under 35:** 60.0%. **Area:** 1 968 sq. km. **Employment:** 309 051 employed, 5.4% unemployed; **Per capita income:** $13 792.

Transportation: 1 international airport; 3 railroads; 2 interstate bus lines. **Communications:** 6 TV stations; 21 radio stations. **Medical facilities:** 14 hospitals. **Educational facilities:** 5 universities and colleges; major public library system. **Further information:** Chamber of Commerce, 3 Independent Drive, P.O. Box 329, Jacksonville, FL 32201.

Las Vegas, Nevada

Population: 191 510; **Pop. density:** 1 290 per sq. km; **Pop. growth:** 30.9%; **Pop. over 65:** 8.3%; **Pop. under 35:** 58.4%. **Area:** 142 sq. km. **Employment:** 109 984 employed, 7.2% unemployed; **Per capita income:** $14 898.

Transportation: 1 international airport; 2 railroads; bus system. **Communications:** 6 TV and 24 radio stations. **Medical facilities:** 8 hospitals. **Educational facilities:** 116 public schools; Clark Comm. College; Univ. of Nevada. **Further information:** Chamber of Commerce, 2301 E. Sahara Ave., Las Vegas, NV, 89104.

Los Angeles, California

Population: 3 259 340; **Pop. density:** 2 572 per sq. km; **Pop. growth:** +5.5%; **Pop. over 65:** 10.6%; **Pop. under 35:** 58.1%. **Area:** 1 204 sq. km. **Employment:** 1 642 441 employed, 6.3% unemployed; **Per capita income:** $16 988.

Transportation: 1 major airport; 4 railroads; major bus carrier service; major freeway system. **Communications:** 19 TV stations; 71 radio stations. **Medical facilities:** 822 hospitals and clinics; 409 nursing homes. **Educational facilities:** 11 universities and colleges; 1 642 public schools; 800 private schools; 61 public libraries. **Further information:** Chamber of Commerce, P.O. Box 3696, Terminal Annex, Los Angeles, CA 90051.

Memphis, Tennessee

Population: 652 640; **Pop. density:** 949 per sq. km; **Pop. growth:** 3.6%; **Pop. over 65:** 10.4%; **Pop. under 35:** 60.5%. **Area:** 683 sq. km. **Employment:** 325 071 employed, 5.9% unemployed; **Per capita income:** $13 380.

Transportation: 1 major airport; 6 railroads; bus system. **Communications:** 6 TV stations; 26 radio stations. **Medical facilities:** 20 hospitals. **Educational facilities:** 10 universities and colleges; 149 public schools; 76 private schools. **Further information:** Chamber of Commerce, 55 Beale St., Box 224, Memphis TN 38101.

Miami, Florida

Population: 373 940; **Pop. density:** 4 234 per sq. km; **Pop. growth:** 3.6%; **Pop. over 65:** 17.0%; **Pop. under 35:** 46.5%. **Area:** 88 sq. km. **Employment:** 184 264 employed, 6.6% unemployed; **Per capita income:** $14 863.

Transportation: 1 international airport; 2 passenger railroads, 1 all-freight; 2 bus lines; 65 truck lines. **Communications:** 6 commercial, 5 educational TV stations; 31 radio stations. **Medical facilities:** 41 hospitals, 39 nursing homes; VA Hospital. **Educational facilities:** 6 colleges & universities. **Further information:** Metro-Dade Department of Tourism, 234 W. Flagler St., Miami, FL 33130.

Milwaukee, Wisconsin

Population: 605 090; **Pop. density:** 2 503 per sq. km; **Pop. growth:** −11.3%; **Pop. over 65:** 12.5%; **Pop. under 35:** 59.8%. **Area:** 248 sq. km. **Employment:** 286 785 employed, 7.4% unemployed; **Per capita income:** $15 994.

Transportation: 1 international airport; 2 railroads; major port; 4 bus lines. **Communications:** 7 TV stations; 33 radio stations. **Medical facilities:** 29 hospitals; major medical centre. **Educational facilities:** 12 universities and colleges; major public school and library system. **Further information:** Association of Commerce, 756 N. Milwaukee Street, Milwaukee, WI 53202.

New Orleans, Louisiana

Population: 554 500; **Pop. density:** 1 085 per sq. km; **Pop. growth:** −6%; **Pop. over 65:** 11.7%; **Pop. under 35:** 60.1%. **Area:** 515 sq. km. **Employment:** 207 491 employed, 10.3% unemployed; **Per capita income:** $12 838.

Transportation: 2 airports; major railroad centre; major international port. **Communications:** 5 TV stations; 20 radio stations. **Medical facilities:** numerous hospitals; major medical research centre. **Educational facilities:** 13 universities and colleges; major public library system. **Further information:** Chamber of Commerce, 301 Camp Street, New Orleans, LA 70130.

New York City, New York

Population: 7 262 700; **Pop. density:** 9 185 per sq. km; **Pop. growth:** −10.4%; **Pop. over 65:** 13.5%; **Pop. under 35:** 53.7%. **Area:** 780 sq. km. **Employment:** 3 044 000 employed, 5.3% unemployed; **Per capita income:** $18 170.

Transportation: 2 airports; 4 heliports; 2 rail terminals; 40 bus carriers; major subway network; ferry system; 4 underwater tunnels. **Communications:** 17 TV stations, 117 radio stations. **Medical facilities:** over 100 hospitals; 5 medical research centres. **Educational facilities:** 94 universities and colleges; 976 public schools, 914 private schools; 201 public libraries. **Further information:** Convention and Visitors Bureau, 2 Columbus Circle, New York, NY 10019.

Philadelphia, Pennsylvania

Population: 1 642 900; **Pop. density:** 4 678 per sq. km; **Pop. growth:** −13.4%; **Pop. over 65:** 14.1%; **Pop. under 35:** 54.4%. **Area:** 352 sq. km. **Employment:** 696 795 employed, 6.0% unemployed; **Per capita income:** $16 160.

Transportation: 1 major airport; 3 railroads; biggest freshwater port in world; subway, el, rail commuter, bus, and streetcar system. **Communications:** 6 TV stations; 53 radio stations. **Medical facilities:** 124 hospitals. **Educational facilities:** 88 degree-granting institutions; major public library system. **Further information:** Office of City Representative, 1660 Municipal Services Bldg., Philadelphia, PA 19107.

Phoenix, Arizona

Population: 894 070; **Pop. density:** 1 017 per sq. km; **Pop. growth:** 35.1%; **Pop. over 65:** 9.3%; **Pop. under 35:** 60.4%. **Area:** 839 sq. km. **Employment:** 534 017 employed, 7.0% unemployed; **Per capita income:** $15 294.

Transportation: 1 major airport; 2 railroads; 2 transcontinental bus lines; public transit system. **Communications:** 9 TV stations; 38 radio stations. **Medical facilities:** 34 hospitals, 1 medical research centre. **Educational facilities:** 8 universities and colleges; 6 community colleges; major public library system. **Further information:** Chamber of Commerce, 34 W. Monroe, Suite 900, Phoenix, AZ 85003.

St. Louis, Missouri

Population: 426 300; **Pop. density:** 2 717 per sq. km; **Pop. growth:** −27.2%; **Pop. over 65:** 17.6%; **Pop. under 35:** 54%. **Area:** 158 sq. km. **Employment:** 180 217 employed, 8.7% unemployed; **Per capita income:** $15 857.

Transportation: 1 intl. airport; 3d largest rail centre in U.S.; 17 trunk line railroads; 2d largest inland port in U.S.; 9 major highways; 14 bus lines; 350 motor freight lines, 14 barge lines. **Communications:** 6 TV, 35 radio stations. **Medical facilities:** 65 hospitals. **Educational facilities:** 5 universities, 26 colleges and seminaries. **Further information:** Regional Commerce and Association, 10 Broadway, St. Louis, MO 63101.

San Antonio, Texas

Population: 914 350; **Pop. density:** 1 237 per sq. km; **Pop. growth:** 20%; **Pop. over 65:** 9.5%; **Pop. under 35:** 62.1%. **Area:** 681 sq. km. **Employment:** 406 016 employed, 9.0% unemployed; **Per capita income:** $12 709.

Transportation: 1 major airport; 4 railroads; 5 bus lines. **Communications:** 6 TV, 28 radio stations. **Medical facilities:** 26 hospitals; major medical centre. **Educational facilities:** 15 universities and colleges; major public library system. **Further information:** Chamber of Commerce, 602 E. Commerce, P.O. Box 1628, San Antonio, TX 78296.

San Diego, California

Population: 1 015 190; **Pop. density:** 1 160 per sq. km; **Pop. growth:** 25.5%; **Pop. over 65:** 9.7%; **Pop. under 35:** 62.1%. **Area:** 828 sq. km. **Employment:** 491 611 employed, 4.2% unemployed; **Per capita income:** $15 940.

Transportation: 1 major airport; 1 railroad; major freeway system; bus system. **Communications:** 7 TV, 27 radio stations. **Medical facilities:** 18 hospitals; 2 major medical research centres. **Educational facilities:** 8 universities and colleges; major public library system. **Further information:** Chamber of Commerce, 110 West "C," Suite 1600, San Diego, CA 92101.

San Francisco, California

Population: 749 000; **Pop. density:** 5 989 per sq. km; **Pop. growth:** −5.1%; **Pop. over 65:** 15.4%; **Pop. under 35:** 51.7%. **Area:** 119 sq. km. **Employment:** 388 209 employed, 4.2% unemployed; **Per capita income:** $23 542.

Transportation: 1 major airport; intra-city railway system; 2 railway transit systems; bus and railroad service; ferry system; 1 underwater tunnel. **Communications:** 7 TV stations; 27 radio stations. **Medical facilities:** 23 hospitals; 1 major medical centre. **Educational facilities:** 4 universities and colleges; major public library system. **Further information:** Chamber of Commerce, 465 California Street, San Francisco, CA 94104.

Seattle, Washington

Population: 486 200; **Pop. density:** 2 240 per sq. km; **Pop. growth:** −7.0%; **Pop. over 65:** 15.4%; **Pop. under 35:** 54.9%. **Area:** 218 sq. km. **Employment:** 299 141 employed, 6.3% unemployed; **Per capita income:** $17 768.

Transportation: 1 international airport; 3 railroads; ferries serve Puget Sound, Alaska, B.C. **Communications:** 7 TV, 23 AM & 19 FM radio stations. **Medical facilities:** 27 hospitals. **Educational facilities:** 4 colleges; 11 community colleges. **Further information:** Chamber of Commerce, 215 Columbia St., Seattle, WA 98104.

Tampa, Florida

Population: 277 580; **Pop. density:** 1 264 per sq. km; **Pop. growth:** −2.2%; **Pop. over 65:** 14.8%; **Pop. under 35:** 54%. **Area:** 218 sq. km. **Employment:** 167 950 employed, 5.4% unemployed; **Per capita income:** $14 539.

Transportation: 1 international airport; Port of Tampa, 140 steamship lines; 2 bus lines. **Communications:** 7 TV, 27 radio stations. **Medical facilities:** 19 hospitals. **Educational facilities:** 131 public schools; 4 colleges and universities. **Further information:** Chamber of Commerce, 801 E. Kennedy Blvd., P.O. Box 420, Tampa, FL 33601.

Washington, District of Columbia

Population: 626 000; **Pop. density:** 3 281 per sq. km; **Pop. growth:** −15.7%; **Pop. over 65:** 11.6%; **Pop. under 35:** 56.9%. **Area:** 163 sq. km. **Employment:** 303 899 employed, 6.1% unemployed; **Per capita income:** $20 148.

Transportation: 2 airports; rail transit system; extensive local bus service; long distance rail and bus service. **Communications:** 8 TV stations; 40 radio stations. **Medical facilities:** 43 hospitals; major medical research centre. **Educational facilities:** 6 universities and colleges; 24 public libraries. **Further information:** Convention and Visitors Association, 1575 I Street NW, Suite 250, Washington, DC 20005.

Road Distance Between Selected U.S. Cities

(in kilometres)

	Atlanta	Boston	Chicago	Cincinnati	Cleveland	Dallas	Denver	Des Moines	Detroit	Houston
Atlanta, Ga.	—	1 669	1 084	708	1 081	1 279	2 249	1 400	1 125	1 270
Boston, Mass.	1 669	—	1 549	1 352	1 010	2 813	3 136	2 060	1 118	2 903
Chicago, Ill.	1 084	1 549	—	462	539	1 475	1 603	526	428	1 717
Cincinnati, Oh.	708	1 352	462	—	393	1 480	1 873	919	417	1 656
Cleveland, Oh.	1 081	1 010	539	393	—	1 865	2 125	1 049	274	2 048
Dallas, Tex.	1 279	2 813	1 475	1 480	1 865	—	1 257	1 101	1 839	391
Denver, Col.	2 249	3 136	1 603	1 873	2 125	1 257	—	1 076	2 016	1 640
Detroit, Mich.	1 125	1 118	428	417	274	1 839	2 016	940	—	2 035
Houston, Tex.	1 270	2 903	1 717	1 656	2 048	391	1 640	1 456	2 035	—
Indianapolis, Ind.	793	1 458	291	171	473	1 392	1 702	748	447	1 588
Kansas City, Mo.	1 284	2 238	803	951	1 253	787	965	314	1 195	1 142
Los Angeles, Cal.	3 511	4 793	3 305	3 506	3 809	2 232	1 704	2 779	3 718	2 475
Memphis, Tenn.	597	2 085	853	753	1 146	727	1 673	964	1 147	903
Milwaukee, Wis.	1 224	1 689	140	602	679	1 595	1 656	581	568	1 837
Minneapolis, Minn.	1 718	2 201	652	1 113	1 191	1 506	1 353	405	1 080	1 862
New Orleans, La.	771	2 425	1 467	1 265	1 657	798	2 048	1 353	1 681	573
New York, N.Y.	1 353	331	1 290	1 041	761	2 497	2 850	1 800	1 025	2 587
Omaha, Neb.	1 586	2 272	739	1 115	1 261	1 036	864	212	1 152	1 392
Philadelphia, Pa.	1 192	476	1 187	912	665	2 336	2 721	1 691	922	2 426
Pittsburgh, Pa.	1 105	903	727	462	208	1 937	2 270	1 228	462	2 113
Portland, Ore.	4 185	4 901	3 352	3 754	3 891	3 232	1 992	2 874	3 780	3 548
St. Louis, Mo.	870	1 836	465	547	851	1 014	1 379	536	825	1 253
San Francisco	4 016	4 980	3 446	3 800	3 969	2 821	1 987	2 920	3 860	3 076
Seattle, Wash.	4 212	4 788	3 239	3 701	3 778	3 344	2 103	2 814	3 667	3 659
Tulsa, Okla.	1 242	2 473	1 099	1 184	1 488	414	1 096	713	1 463	769
Washington, D.C.	978	690	1 080	774	557	2 122	2 600	1 583	814	2 212

	Indianapolis	Kansas City	Los Angeles	Louisville	Memphis	Milwaukee	Minneapolis	New Orleans	New York	Omaha
Atlanta, Ga.	793	1 284	3 511	615	597	1 224	1 718	771	1 353	1 586
Boston, Mass.	1 458	2 238	4 793	1 514	2 085	1 689	2 201	2 425	331	2 272
Chicago, Ill.	291	803	3 305	470	853	140	652	1 467	1 290	739
Cincinnati, Oh.	171	951	3 506	163	753	602	1 113	1 265	1 041	1 115
Cleveland, Oh.	473	1 253	3 809	555	1 146	679	1 191	1 657	761	1 261
Dallas, Tex.	1 392	787	2 232	1 318	727	1 595	1 506	798	2 497	1 036
Denver, Col.	1 702	965	1 704	1 802	1 673	1 656	1 353	2 048	2 850	864
Detroit, Mich.	447	1 195	3 718	579	1 147	568	1 080	1 681	1 025	1 152
Houston, Tex.	1 588	1 142	2 475	1 493	903	1 837	1 862	573	2 587	1 392
Indianapolis, Ind.	—	780	3 335	179	700	431	943	1 281	1 147	944
Kansas City, Mo.	780	—	2 557	837	726	864	719	1 297	1 928	323
Los Angeles, Cal.	3 335	2 557	—	3 392	2 924	3 358	3 039	3 030	4 483	2 566
Memphis, Tenn.	700	726	2 924	591	—	985	1 329	628	1 770	1 049
Milwaukee, Wis.	431	864	3 358	610	985	—	534	1 599	1 430	793
Minneapolis, Minn.	943	719	3 039	1 121	1 329	534	—	1 953	1 942	574
New Orleans, La.	1 281	1 297	3 030	1 102	628	1 599	1 953	—	2 109	1 620
New York, N.Y.	1 147	1 928	4 483	1 204	1 770	1 430	1 942	2 109	—	2 013
Omaha, Neb.	944	338	2 566	1 105	1 049	793	574	1 620	2 013	—
Philadelphia, Pa.	1 018	1 799	4 354	1 075	1 609	1 327	1 839	1 948	161	1 903
Pittsburgh, Pa.	568	1 348	3 903	624	1 210	867	1 379	1 722	592	1 440
Portland, Ore.	1 974	2 911	1 543	3 733	3 635	3 234	2 700	4 031	4 642	2 661
St. Louis, Mo.	378	414	2 969	423	459	584	888	1 083	1 525	722
San Francisco	3 630	2 953	610	3 780	3 419	3 500	3 121	3 619	4 721	2 708
Seattle, Wash.	3 530	2 959	1 820	3 709	3 685	3 121	2 587	4 142	4 529	2 636
Tulsa, Okla.	1 015	399	2 336	1 060	645	1 218	1 118	1 041	2 162	623
Washington, D.C.	898	1 678	4 233	936	1 395	1 220	1 731	1 735	375	1 796

	Philadelphia	Pittsburgh	Portland	St. Louis	Salt Lake City	San Francisco	Seattle	Toledo	Tulsa	Washington
Atlanta, Ga.	1 192	1 105	4 185	870	3 022	4 016	4 212	1 030	1 242	978
Boston, Mass.	476	903	4 901	1 836	3 770	4 980	4 788	1 189	2 473	690
Chicago, Ill.	1 187	727	3 352	465	2 237	3 446	3 239	373	1 099	1 080
Cincinnati, Oh.	912	462	3 754	547	2 590	3 800	3 701	322	1 184	774
Cleveland, Oh.	665	208	3 891	851	2 759	3 969	3 778	179	1 488	557
Dallas, Tex.	2 336	1 937	3 232	1 014	1 998	2 821	3 344	1 744	414	2 122
Denver, Col.	2 721	2 270	1 992	1 379	811	1 987	2 103	1 960	1 096	2 600
Detroit, Mich.	922	462	3 780	825	2 650	3 860	3 667	95	1 463	814
Houston, Tex.	2 426	2 113	3 548	1 253	2 314	3 076	3 659	1 940	769	2 212
Indianapolis, Ind.	1 018	568	3 583	378	2 420	3 630	3 530	352	1 015	898
Kansas City, Mo.	1 799	1 348	2 911	414	1 747	2 953	2 959	1 105	399	1 678
Los Angeles, Cal.	4 354	3 903	1 543	2 969	1 150	610	1 820	3 662	2 336	4 233
Memphis, Tenn.	1 609	1 210	3 635	459	2 470	3 419	3 685	1 052	645	1 395
Milwaukee, Wis.	1 327	867	3 234	584	2 290	3 500	3 121	513	1 218	1 220
Minneapolis, Minn.	1 840	1 379	2 700	888	1 908	3 121	2 587	1 025	1 118	1 731
New Orleans, La.	1 948	1 721	4 031	1 083	2 796	3 619	4 142	1 586	1 041	1 735
New York, N.Y.	161	592	4 642	1 525	3 511	4 721	4 529	930	2 162	375
Omaha, Neb.	1 904	1 279	2 661	722	1 498	2 708	2 636	1 096	623	1 796
Philadelphia, Pa.	—	463	4 539	1 397	3 401	4 611	4 426	827	2 034	214
Pittsburgh, Pa.	463	—	4 079	946	2 938	4 148	3 966	367	1 583	356
Portland, Ore.	4 539	4 079	—	3 315	1 234	1 023	277	3 725	3 078	4 431
St. Louis, Mo.	1 397	946	3 315	—	2 151	3 361	3 348	730	637	1 276
San Francisco	4 611	4 148	1 023	3 361	1 210	—	1 300	3 804	2 832	4 504
Seattle, Wash.	4 426	3 966	277	3 348	1 345	1 300	—	3 612	3 189	4 319
Tulsa, Okla.	2 034	1 583	3 078	637	1 886	2 832	3 189	1 368	—	1 913
Washington, D.C.	214	356	4 431	1 276	3 294	4 504	4 319	719	1 913	—

Disasters

Canadian Disasters

1583 (Aug. 29): Canada's first recorded marine disaster took 85 lives when the *Delight* was wrecked on Sable Island.

1711 (Aug. 23): As many as 950 drowned when ships attached to the British fleet preparing to attack Quebec were grounded and sank on the rocks of Ile-aux-Oeufs.

1825 (Oct. 5): The Miramichi fire, north of New Brunswick's Miramichi River, destroyed the towns of Newcastle and Douglastown, and killed between 200-500 people.

1841 (May 17): On this date, several large boulders from Cap Diamant tumbled down the precipitous cliffs above the Lower Town of Quebec City and demolished 8 houses—killing 32 people.

1854 (Oct. 27): In one of the earliest Canadian train disasters, a gravel train running near Baptiste Creek, 24 km west of Chatham, Ont., was hit by an express train on the same line. In the collision, 52 persons were killed and 48 seriously injured.

1864 (June 29): Near St. Hilaire, Que., a passenger train was unable to stop for an open draw-bridge at the Beloeil bridge on the Richelieu River. The train plunged through the opening onto passing barges—killing 99 and injuring 100 people.

1873 (Apr. 1): Sailing from Liverpool to New York the steamer *Atlantic* struck Meager's Rock off the coast of Nova Scotia, and sank with the loss of 535 people.

1873 (May 13): Sixty men died when a fire and subsequent explosion in a coal mine at Westville, Pictou County, N.S. trapped firemen and workers. The mine was eventually sealed to starve the fire of oxygen and it was 2 years before all the bodies were recovered.

1891 (Feb. 21): In the first of several major disasters in the coal mines of Springhill, N.S., 125 men were killed in an explosion.

1896 (May 26): Fifty-five people were killed when a bridge at Point Ellice in Victoria, B.C. collapsed while a streetcar was passing over it. The bridge was too weak to support the weight of a recently-built tramline.

1889 (Sept. 19): A massive rockslide from the cliffs above Quebec City's Lower Town demolished most of Champlain St., killing 45 people. The disaster would have been worse except that many people were not in their homes at the time.

1903 (Apr. 29): Parts of the town of Frank, Alta. were obliterated by a sudden landslide when over 50 million tonnes of limestone came crashing down Turtle Mountain, crossed the 4 km wide valley floor and rolled up the other side of the valley. Approximately 50 people were killed. The landslide also sealed a mine entrance at the foot of the mountain and trapped 17 miners inside. The men were able to escape by digging a new tunnel to the surface.

1907 (Aug. 29): The Quebec Bridge, 11 km north of Quebec City, is the largest cantilevered bridge in the world. On Aug. 29, 1907, as the bridge was nearing completion, the southern cantilever span collapsed, killing 75 workmen.

1910 (Mar. 5): A C.P.R. work crew clearing the tracks from a previous snow slide in Rogers Pass, B.C. was hit by an avalanche. 62 men were killed, 1 survived.

1914 (May 29): The Canadian Pacific liner *Empress of Ireland* collided with a Norwegian coal-ship in the St. Lawrence River near Rimouski, Que. and sank in only 14 minutes with the loss of 1 014 lives. This was one of the worst naval disasters in history, with the 8th largest loss of life for a naval accident.

1914 (June 19): The worst coal mine disaster in Canadian history occurred at Hillcrest, Alta. when dust explosions killed 189 men.

1916 (July 29): A forest fire in northern Ontario, thought to have been started by lightning and locomotive sparks, engulfed the towns of Cockrane and Matheson, killing at least 233 persons.

1916 (Sept. 11): The Quebec Bridge was the scene of further tragedy when a new centre span being hoisted into position fell into the river below. This time 13 men were killed—bringing the loss of life during construction of the bridge to 88.

1917 (Dec. 6): Halifax was the scene of Canada's worst single disaster when a French munitions ship filled with explosives collided with a freighter in Halifax Harbor. The French ship, the *Mont Blanc,* was split to the waterline; fuel oil spilled over its explosive cargo and started a fire in the hold. The crew abandoned ship without attempting to extinguish the fire.

In the explosion that followed, the *Mont Blanc* was tossed more than 1 000 m into the air. The explosion levelled homes and businesses in a large part of the city and set off explosives stockpiled on shore. The blast, heard as far away as Prince Edward Island, is thought to be the largest-ever, accidental explosion, and the largest non-nuclear blast in history. More than 1 600 people were killed, 9 000 injured, and 6 000 left homeless. Property damage was estimated at $35 million.

1918 (Oct. 23): The Canadian Pacific Steamship *Princess Sophia* ran onto Vanderbilt Reef while sailing from Alaska to Vancouver. The ship sank 2 days later on Oct. 25. All 343 aboard drowned.

1927 (Jan. 9): A small fire which broke out in Montreal's Laurier Palace Theatre was quickly extinguished, but in the panic that ensued 12 people were crushed to death and 64 were asphyxiated, including many children.

1928 (Apr. 14): The 18-gun sloop *Acorn* sank near Halifax with 115 men on board.

1929 (Nov. 18): Newfoundland's Burin Peninsula was struck by a 4.5 m tidal wave. Property damage was extensive and 27 were killed.

1942 (Dec. 12): An arsonist set fire to the Knights of Columbus hostel in St. John's. Because the hostel had no emergency lighting, the doors opened inwards and exits were restricted, 99 persons died and another 100 were seriously injured.

1949 (Sept. 9): A Quebec Airways DC-3 was sabotaged with a bomb and the plane exploded and crashed near St. Joachim, Que., killing 32 persons. J.A. Guay and 2 accomplices were convicted of the crime and hanged.

1949 (Sept. 17): 700 people were aboard the Great Lakes excursion ship *Noronic* when it caught fire and burned at its pier in Toronto Harbor. The ships' fire hydrants were dry and no alarm was sent to the city fire department until 15 minutes after the blaze was discovered. In the meantime, the single exit became blocked by fire and 118 lives were lost.

1954 (Oct. 15): During the worst inland storm in Canadian history, Hurricane Hazel, over 10 cm of rain fell in Toronto in 12 hours. At that time, many houses in Toronto were built on low-lying flood plains. The storm and resulting floods caused 83 deaths and widespread property damage.

1956 (Nov. 1): A 2d major tragedy struck the coal mines at Springhill, N.S. when an accident killed 39 men.

1958 (June 17): Design errors in Vancouver's Second Narrows Bridge caused one section to collapse. The accident killed 18 men, including the 2 engineers that an investigation later determined were responsible for the errors.

1958 (Oct. 23): A 3d mining accident in Springhill, N.S. killed 75 when a tunnel collapsed.

1963 (Nov. 29): A Trans Canada Airlines DC-8F crashed after take-off from Dorval (Montreal). 118 were killed.

1970 (July 5): At Toronto International Airport, an Air Canada DC-8 lost one starboard engine during a landing attempt. During the pilot's effort to take-off and land again, the remaining starboard engine fell off. The aircraft crashed, killing all 109 persons aboard.

1971 (May 4): During a prolonged rainstorm in St-Jean-Vianney, Que. a giant sink hole appeared in the ground. The hole swallowed 36 houses, several cars and a bus—killing 31 people.

1972 (Sept. 1): The Blue Bird Bar in Montreal was set afire by 3 disgruntled patrons who had been ejected from the bar earlier in the evening. The blaze killed 37.

1975 (Nov. 10): The 218 m ore carrier *Edmond Fitzgerald*, sailing out of Sault Ste. Marie, broke apart during a storm on Lake Superior and sank in 156 m of water with all 29 members of the crew aboard. Two days later only the empty wooden lifeboat and two rubber rafts from the ship were found.

1977 (June 21): A fire which broke out in the cell block of the city police headquarters of St. John, N.B. was so hot that the locks on several cell doors were fused. 20 prisoners were killed and 12 police officers who attempted to rescue the prisoners were injured.

1978 (Aug. 4): The worst bus disaster in North America occurred when the brakes on a chartered bus failed near Eastman, Que. The bus plunged into a lake, and 41 mentally and physically handicapped passengers were killed.

1979 (Dec. 31): 44 persons were killed during New Year's Eve celebrations at a social club in Chapais, Que., in a fire caused by a man playing with a lighter who set New Year's Eve decorations ablaze.

1982 (Feb. 15): The ocean drilling rig, *Ocean Ranger,* overturned and sank during a storm while operating 265 km east of Newfoundland, killing 84 men. Inadequate safety procedures and equipment were later blamed for the accident.

1985 (May 31): A tornado struck Barrie, Ont. mid-afternoon; 12 were killed, 4 of whom were children, and there were hundreds of millions of dollars in property damage.

1985 (June 23): An Air India 747 flying from Toronto never reached its destination of London, England. Wreckage from the plane was found floating in the Atlantic, west of Ireland. The tragedy, thought to be caused by a bomb on board, killed 280 Canadians.

1985 (Dec. 12): In the worst air crash in Canada, an Arrow Airlines DC-8 after refueling in Gander en route to Hopkinsville, Ky. crashed seconds after take-off, killing 256 passengers and crew.

1986 (Feb. 8): A 16-unit VIA Rail passenger train slammed head-on into a 118-unit CN freight train near Hinton, Alta. The freight train was on the wrong track. 26 persons were killed and dozens were seriously injured.

1987 (July 31): A tornado touched down in Edmonton, Alta., killing 26 people, injuring 250 others and causing an estimated $250 million damage. Most of the dead and injured were in a mobile home park that was struck.

Historic Assassinations Since 1865

1865—Apr. 14. U. S. Pres. Abraham Lincoln, shot by John Wilkes Booth in Washington, D. C.; died Apr. 15.

1868—Apr. 7. Canadian Confederationist Thomas D'Arcy McGee shot by a Fenian in Ottawa. This was Canada's first political assassination.

1881—Mar. 13. Alexander II, of Russia—July 2. U. S. Pres. James A. Garfield, shot by Charles J. Guiteau, Washington D.C.; died Sept. 19.

1900—July 29. Umberto I, king of Italy.

1901—Sept. 6. U. S. Pres. William McKinley in Buffalo, N. Y., died Sept. 14. Leon Czolgosz executed for the crime Oct. 29.

1913—Feb. 23. Mexican Pres. Francisco I. Madero and Vice Pres. Jose Pino Suarez.—Mar. 18. George, king of Greece.

1914—June 28. Archduke Francis Ferdinand of Austria-Hungary and his wife in Sarajevo, Bosnia (later part of Yugoslavia), by Gavrilo Princip.

1916—Dec. 30. Grigori Rasputin, politically powerful Russian monk.

1918—July 12. Grand Duke Michael of Russia, at Perm.—July 16. Nicholas II, abdicated as czar of Russia; his wife, the Czarina Alexandra, their son, Czarevitch Alexis, and their daughters, Grand Duchesses Olga, Tatiana, Marie, Anastasia, and 4 members of their household were executed by Bolsheviks at Ekaterinburg.

1920—May 20. Mexican Pres. Gen. Venustiano Carranza in Tlaxcalantongo.

1922—Aug. 22. Michael Collins, Irish revolutionary.—Dec. 16. Polish President Gabriel Narutowicz in Warsaw by an anarchist.

1923—July 20. Gen. Francisco "Pancho" Villa, ex-rebel leader, in Parral, Mexico.

1928—July 17. Gen. Alvaro Obregon, president-elect of Mexico, in San Angel, Mexico.

1933—Feb. 15. In Miami, Fla. Joseph Zangara, anarchist, shot at Pres.-elect Franklin D. Roosevelt, but a woman seized his arm, and the bullet fatally wounded Mayor Anton J. Cermak, of Chicago, who died Mar. 6. Zangara was electrocuted on Mar. 20, 1933.

1934—July 25. In Vienna, Austrian Chancellor Engelbert Dollfuss by Nazis.

1935—Sept. 8. U. S. Sen. Huey P. Long, shot in Baton Rouge, La., by Dr. Carl Austin Weiss, who was slain by Long's bodyguards.

1940—Aug. 20. Leon Trotsky (Lev Bronstein), 63, exiled Russian war minister, near Mexico City. Killer identified as Ramon Mercador del Rio, a Spaniard, served 20 years in Mexican prison.

1948—Jan. 30. Mohandas K. Gandhi, 78, shot in New Delhi, India, by Nathuran Vinayak Godse.—Sept. 17. Count Folke Bernadotte, UN mediator for Palestine, ambushed in Jerusalem.

1951—July 20. King Abdullah ibn Hussein of Jordan.

1956—Sept. 21. Pres. Anastasio Somoza of Nicaragua, in Leon; died Sept. 29.

1957—July 26. Pres. Carlos Castillo Armas of Guatemala, in Guatemala City by one of his own guards.

1958—July 14. King Faisal of Iraq; his uncle, Crown Prince Abdul Illah, and July 15, Premier Nuri as-Said, by rebels in Baghdad.

1959—Sept. 25. Prime Minister Solomon Bandaranaike of Ceylon, by Buddhist monk in Colombo.

1961—Jan. 17. Ex-Premier Patrice Lumumba of the Congo, in Katanga Province—May 30. Dominican dictator Rafael Leonidas Trujillo Molina shot to death by assassins near Ciudad Trujillo.

1963—June 12. Medgar W. Evers, NAACP's Mississippi field secretary, in Jackson, Miss.—Nov. 2. Pres. Ngo Dinh Diem of the Republic of Vietnam and his brother, Ngo Dinh Nhu, in a military coup.—Nov. 22. U. S. Pres. John F. Kennedy fatally shot in Dallas, Tex.; accused Lee Harvey Oswald murdered by Jack Ruby while awaiting trial.

1965—Jan. 21. Iranian premier Hassan Ali Mansour fatally wounded by assassin in Teheran; 4 executed.—Feb. 21. Malcolm X, black nationalist, fatally shot in N. Y. City.

1966—Sept. 6. Prime Minister Hendrik F. Verwoerd of South Africa stabbed to death in parliament at Capetown.

1968—Apr. 4. Rev. Dr. Martin Luther King Jr. fatally shot in Memphis, Tenn. by James Earl Ray.—June 5. Sen. Robert F. Kennedy (D-N. Y.) fatally shot in Los Angeles; Sirhan Sirhan, resident alien, convicted of murder.

1971—Nov. 28. Jordan Prime Minister Wasfi Tal, in Cairo, by Palestinian guerrillas.

1973—Mar. 2. U. S. Ambassador Cleo A. Noel Jr., U. S. Charge d'Affaires George C. Moore and Belgian Charge d'Affaires Guy Eid killed by Palestinian guerrillas in Khartoum, Sudan.

1974—Aug. 15. Mrs. Park Chung Hee, wife of president of So. Korea, hit by bullet meant for her husband.—Aug. 19. U. S. Ambassador to Cyprus, Rodger P. Davies, killed by sniper's bullet in Nicosia.

1975—Feb. 11. Pres. Richard Ratsimandrava, of Madagascar, shot in Tananarive.—Mar. 25. King Faisal of Saudi Arabia shot by nephew Prince Musad Abdel Aziz, in royal palace, Riyadh.—Aug. 15. Bangladesh Pres. Sheik Mujibur Rahman killed in coup.

1976—Feb. 13. Nigerian head of state, Gen. Murtala Ramat Mohammed, slain by self-styled "young revolutionaries."

1977—Mar. 16. Kamal Jumblat, Lebanese Druse chieftain, was shot near Beirut.—Mar. 18. Congo Pres. Marien Ngouabi shot in Brazzaville.

1978—July 9. Former Iraqi Premier Abdul Razak Al-Naif shot in London.

1979—Aug. 27. Lord Mountbatten, WW2 hero, and 2 others were killed when a bomb exploded on his fishing boat off the coast of Co. Sligo, Ire. The IRA claimed responsibility. —Oct. 26. So. Korean President Park Chung Hee and 6 bodyguards fatally shot by Kim Jae Kyu, head of Korean CIA, and 5 aides in Seoul.

1980—Apr. 12. Liberian President William R. Tolbert slain in military coup.—Sept. 17. Former Nicaraguan President Anastasio Somoza Debayle and 2 others shot in Paraguay.

1981—Aug. 30. Iranian President Mohammed Ali Raji and Premier Mohammed Jad Bahonar killed by bomb in Teheran.—Oct. 6. Egyptian President Anwar El-Sadat fatally shot by a band of commandos while reviewing a military parade in Cairo.

1982—Sept. 14. Lebanese President-elect Bishir Gemayel killed by bomb in east Beirut.

1983—Aug. 21. Philippine opposition political leader Benigno Aquino Jr. fatally shot by a gunman at Manila International Airport.—Oct. 9. Four S. Korea cabinet ministers and 15 others killed by bomb blast in Rangoon, Burma.

1984—Oct. 31. Indian Prime Minister Indira Gandhi shot and killed by 2 of her bodyguards, who were members of the minority Sikh sect, in New Delhi.

1986—Feb. 28. Swedish Premier Olof Palme shot and killed by a gunman in Stockholm.

1987—June 1. Lebanese Premier Rashid Karami killed when a bomb exploded aboard a helicopter in which he was traveling.

1988—Apr. 16. PLO military chief Khalil Wazir (Abu Jihad) was gunned down by Israeli commandos in Tunisia.

Major Kidnappings

Edward A. Cudahy Jr., 16, in Omaha, Neb., Dec. 18, 1900. Returned Dec. 20 after $25 000 paid. Pat Crowe confessed.

Robert Franks, 13, in Chicago, May 22, 1924, by 2 youths, Richard Loeb and Nathan Leopold, who killed boy. Demand for $10 000 ignored. Loeb died in prison, Leopold paroled 1958.

Charles A. Lindbergh Jr., 20 mos. old, in Hopewell, N.J., Mar. 1, 1932; found dead May 12. Ransom of $50 000 was paid to man identified as Bruno Richard Hauptmann, 35, paroled German convict who entered U.S. illegally. Hauptmann was convicted after spectacular trial at Flemington, and electrocuted in Trenton, N.J. prison, Apr. 3, 1936.

William A. Hamm Jr., 39, in St. Paul, June 15, 1933. $100 000 paid. Alvin Karpis given life, paroled in 1969.

Charles F. Urschel, in Oklahoma City, July 22, 1933. Released July 31 after $200 000 paid. George (Machine Gun) Kelly and 5 others given life.

Brooke L. Hart, 22, in San Jose, Cal. Thomas Thurmond and John Holmes arrested after demanding $40 000 ransom. When Hart's body was found in San Francisco Bay, Nov. 26, 1933, a mob attacked the jail at San Jose and lynched the 2 kidnappers.

George Weyerhaeuser, 9, in Tacoma, Wash., May 24, 1935. Returned home June 1 after $200 000 paid. Kidnappers given 20 to 60 years.

Charles Mattson, 10, in Tacoma, Wash., Dec. 27, 1936. Found dead Jan. 11, 1937. Kidnapper asked $28 000, failed to contact.

Arthur Fried, in White Plains, N.Y., Dec. 4, 1937. Body not found. Two kidnappers executed.

Robert C. Greenlease, 6, taken from Kansas City, Mo. school Sept. 28, 1953, and held for $600 000. Body found Oct. 7. Mrs. Bonnie Brown Heady and Carl A. Hall pleaded guilty and were executed.

Peter Weinberger, 32 days old, Westbury, N.Y., July 4, 1956, for $2 000 ransom, not paid. Child found dead. Angelo John LaMarca, 31, convicted, executed.

Cynthia Ruotolo, 6 wks old, taken from carriage in front of Hamden, Conn. store Sept. 1, 1956. Body found in lake.

Lee Crary, 8 in Everett, Wash., Sept. 22, 1957, $10 000 ransom, not paid. He escaped after 3 days, led police to George E. Collins, who was convicted.

Eric Peugeot, 4, taken from playground at St. Cloud golf course, Paris, Apr. 12, 1960. Released unharmed 3 days later after payment of undisclosed sum. Two sentenced to prison.

Frank Sinatra Jr., 19, from hotel room in Lake Tahoe, Cal., Dec. 8, 1963. Released Dec. 11 after his father paid $240 000 ransom. Three men sentenced to prison; most of ransom recovered.

Barbara Jane Mackle, 20, abducted Dec. 17, 1968, from Atlanta, Ga., motel, was found unharmed 3 days later, buried in a coffin-like wooden box 18 inches underground, after her father had paid $500 000 ransom; Gary Steven Krist sentenced to life, Ruth Eisenmann-Schier to 7 years; most of ransom recovered.

Anne Katherine Jenkins, 22, abducted May 10, 1969, from her Baltimore apartment, freed 3 days later after her father paid $10 000 ransom.

Mrs. Roy Fuchs, 35, and 3 children held hostage 2 hours, May 14, 1969, in Long Island, N. Y., released after her husband, a bank manager, paid kidnappers $129 000 in bank funds; 4 men arrested, ransom recovered.

C. Burke Elbrick, U.S. ambassador to Brazil, kidnapped by revolutionaries in Rio de Janeiro Sept. 4, 1969; released 3 days later after Brazil yielded to kidnapper's demands to publish manifesto and release 15 political prisoners.

Patrick Dolan, 18, found shot to death near Sao Paulo, Brazil, Nov. 5, 1969, after he was kidnapped and $12 500 paid.

Sean M. Holly, U.S. diplomat, in Guatemala Mar. 6, 1970; freed 2 days later upon release of 3 terrorists from prison.

Lt. Col. Donald J. Crowley, U.S. air attache, in Dominican Republic Mar. 24, 1970; released after government allowed 20 prisoners to leave the country.

Count Karl von Spreti, W. German ambassador to Guatemala, Mar. 31, 1970; slain after Guatemala refused demands for $700 000 and release of 22 prisoners.

Pedro Eugenio Arambaru, former Argentine president, by terrorists May 29, 1970; body found July 17.

Ehrenfried von Holleben, W. German ambassador to Brazil, by terrorists June 11, 1970; freed after release of 40 prisoners.

Daniel A. Mitrione, U.S. diplomat, July 31, 1970, by terrorists in Montevideo, Uruguay; body found Aug. 10 after government rejected demands for release of all political prisoners.

James R. Cross, British trade commissioner, Oct. 5, 1970, by FLQ members in Quebec; freed Dec. 3 after 3 kidnappers and four of their relatives flown to Cuba by government.

Pierre Laporte, Quebec Labor Minister, by FLQ terrorists Oct. 10, 1970; body found Oct. 18. Paul Rose and André Simard were sentenced to life imprisonment for murder; Bernard Lortie was convicted of kidnapping and Jacques Rose was convicted as an accessory. The War Measures Act was declared in force as a response to the Cross and Laporte kidnappings.

Giovanni E. Bucher, Swiss ambassador Dec. 7, 1970, by revolutionaries in Rio de Janeiro; freed Jan. 16, 1971, after Brazil released 70 political prisoners.

Geoffrey Jackson, British ambassador, in Montevideo, Jan. 8, 1971, by Tupamaro terrorists. Held as ransom for release of imprisoned terrorists; released Sept. 9; prisoners escaped.

Ephraim Elrom, Israel consul general in Istanbul, May 17, 1971. Held as ransom for imprisoned terrorists; found dead May 23.

Mrs. Virginia Piper, 49 abducted July 27, 1972, from her home in suburban Minneapolis; found unharmed near Duluth 2 days later after her husband paid $1 million ransom to the kidnappers.

Victor E. Samuelson, Exxon executive, Dec. 6, 1973, in Campana, Argentina, by Marxist guerrillas, freed Apr. 29, 1974, after payment of record $14.2 million ransom.

J. Paul Getty 3d, 17, grandson of the U.S. oil mogul, released Dec. 15, 1973, in southern Italy after $2.8 million ransom paid.

Patricia (Patty) Hearst, 19, taken from her Berkeley, Cal., apartment Feb. 4, 1974. Symbionese Liberation Army demanded her father, Randolph A. Hearst, publisher, give millions to poor. Hearst offered $2 million in food; the Hearst Corp. offered $4 million worth. Patricia said she had joined SLA; she was identified by FBI as taking part in a San Francisco bank holdup, Apr. 15; she claimed she had been coerced. FBI, Sept. 18, 1975, captured Patricia and others in San Francisco; they were indicted on various charges. Patricia for bank robbery. Convicted, Mar. 20, 1976. She was released from prison under executive clemency, Feb. 1, 1979. In 1978, William and Emily Harris were sentenced to 10 years to life for the Hearst kidnapping. Both were paroled in 1983.

J. Reginald Murphy, 40, an editor of *Atlanta* (Ga.) *Constitution,* kidnapped Feb. 20, 1974, freed Feb. 22 after payment of $700 000 ransom by the newspaper. Police arrested William A. H. Williams, a contractor; most of the money was recovered.

J. Guadalupe Zuno Hernandez, 83, father-in-law of Mexican President Luis Echeverria Alvarez, seized by 4 terrorists Aug. 28, 1974; government refused to negotiate; he was released Sept. 8.

E. B. Reville, Hepzibah, Ga., banker, and wife Jean, kidnapped Sept. 30, 1974. Ransom of $30 000 paid. He was found alive; Mrs. Reville was found dead in car trunk Oct. 2.

Jack Teich, Kings Point, N.Y., steel executive, seized Nov. 12, 1974; released Nov. 19 after payment of $750 000.

William F. Niehous, a U.S. businessman, was abducted from his suburban Caracas, Venezuela home, Feb. 27, 1976. He was rescued by police June 29, 1979, ending more than 3 years of captivity.

Hanns-Martin Schleyer, a West German industrialist, was kidnapped in Cologne, Sept. 5, 1977 by armed terrorists. Schleyer was found dead, Oct. 19, in an abandoned car shortly after 3 jailed terrorist leaders of the Baader-Meinhof gang were found dead in their prison cells near Stuttgart, West Germany.

Aldo Moro, former Italian premier, kidnapped in Rome, Mar. 16, 1978, by left-wing terrorists. Five of his bodyguards killed during abduction. Moro's bullet-ridden body was found in a parked car, May 9, in Rome. Six members of the Red Brigades arrested, charged, June 5, with complicity in the kidnapping.

James L. Dozier, a U.S. Army general, kidnapped from his apartment in Verona, Italy, Dec. 17, 1981, by members of the Red Brigades terrorist organization. He was rescued, Jan. 28, 1982.

Enrique Camarena Salazar, and **Alfredo Zavala Avelar,** U.S. Drug Enforcement Agency employees were kidnapped in Guadalajara, Mexico, Feb. 6, 1985. Their bodies were found Mar. 6.

Some Notable Aircraft Disasters Since 1937

Date			Aircraft	Site of accident	Deaths
1937	May	6	German zeppelin Hindenburg	Burned at mooring, Lakehurst, N.J.	36
1944	Aug.	23	U.S. Air Force B-24	Hit school, Freckelton, England	76[1]
1945	July	28	U.S. Army B-25	Hit Empire State bldg., N.Y.C.	14[1]
1947	May	30	Eastern Air Lines DC-4	Crashed near Port Deposit, Md.	53
1952	Dec.	20	U.S. Air Force C-124	Fell, burned, Moses Lake, Wash.	87
1953	Mar.	3	Canadian Pacific Comet Jet	Karachi, Pakistan	11[2]
1953	June	18	U.S. Air Force C-124	Crashed, burned near Tokyo	129
1955	Nov.	1	United Air Lines DC-6B	Exploded, crashed near Longmont, Col.	44[3]
1956	June	20	Venezuelan Super-Constellation	Crashed in Atlantic off Asbury Park, N.J.	74
1956	June	30	TWA Super-Const., United DC-7	Collided over Grand Canyon, Arizona	128
1960	Dec.	16	United DC-8 jet, TWA Super-Const.	Collided over N.Y. City	134[4]
1962	Mar.	16	Flying Tiger Super-Const.	Vanished in Western Pacific	107
1962	June	3	Air France Boeing 707 jet	Crashed on takeoff from Paris	130
1962	June	22	Air France Boeing 707 jet	Crashed in storm, Guadeloupe, W.I.	113
1963	June	3	Chartered Northw. Airlines DC-7	Crashed in Pacific off British Columbia	101
1963	Nov.	29	Trans-Canada Airlines DC-8F	Crashed after takeoff from Montreal	118
1965	May	20	Pakistani Boeing 720-B	Crashed at Cairo, Egypt, airport	121
1966	Jan.	24	Air India Boeing 707 jetliner	Crashed on Mont Blanc, France-Italy	117
1966	Feb.	4	All-Nippon Boeing 727	Plunged into Tokyo Bay	133
1966	Mar.	5	BOAC Boeing 707 jetliner	Crashed on Mount Fuji, Japan	124
1966	Dec.	24	U.S. military-chartered CL-44	Crashed into village in So. Vietnam	129[1]
1967	Apr.	20	Swiss Britannia turboprop	Crashed at Nicosia, Cyprus	126
1967	July	19	Piedmont Boeing 727, Cessna 310	Collided in air, Hendersonville, N.C.	82
1968	Apr.	20	S. African Airways Boeing 707	Crashed on takeoff, Windhoek, SW Africa.	122
1968	May	3	Braniff International Electra	Crashed in storm near Dawson, Tex.	85
1969	Mar.	16	Venezuelan DC-9	Crashed after takeoff from Maracaibo, Venezuela	155[5]
1969	Dec.	8	Olympia Airways DC-6B	Crashed near Athens in storm	93
1970	Feb.	15	Dominican DC-9	Crashed into sea on takeoff from Santo Domingo	102
1970	July	3	British chartered jetliner	Crashed near Barcelona, Spain	112
1970	July	5	Air Canada DC-8	Crashed near Toronto International Airport	108
1970	Aug.	9	Peruvian turbojet	Crashed after takeoff from Cuzco, Peru	101[1]
1970	Nov.	14	Southern Airways DC-9	Crashed in mountains near Huntington, W. Va.	75[6]
1971	July	30	All-Nippon Boeing 727 and Japanese Air Force F-86	Collided over Morioka, Japan	162[7]
1971	Sept.	4	Alaska Airlines Boeing 727	Crashed into mountain near Juneau, Alaska	111
1972	Aug.	14	E. German Ilyushin-62	Crashed on take-off East Berlin.	156
1972	Oct.	13	Aeroflot Ilyushin-62	E. German airline crashed near Moscow	176
1972	Dec.	3	Chartered Spanish airliner	Crashed on take-off, Canary Islands	155
1972	Dec.	29	Eastern Airlines Lockheed Tristar	Crashed on approach to Miami Int'l. Airport	101
1973	Jan.	22	Chartered Boeing 707	Burst into flames during landing, Kano Airport, Nigeria.	176
1973	Feb.	21	Libyan jetliner	Shot down by Israeli fighter planes over Sinai.	108
1973	Apr.	10	British Vanguard turboprop	Crashed during snowstorm at Basel, Switzerland	104
1973	June	3	Soviet Supersonic TU-144	Exploded in air near Goussainville, France	14[8]
1973	July	11	Brazilian Boeing 707	Crashed on approach to Orly Airport, Paris	122
1973	July	31	Delta Airlines jetliner	Crashed, landing in fog at Logan Airport, Boston	89
1973	Dec.	23	French Caravelle jet	Crashed in Morocco	106
1974	Mar.	3	Turkish DC-10 jet	Crashed at Ermenonville near Paris	346
1974	Apr.	23	Pan American 707 jet	Crashed in Bali, Indonesia	107
1974	Dec.	1	TWA-727	Crashed in storm, Upperville, Va.	92
1974	Dec.	4	Dutch-chartered DC-8	Crashed in storm near Colombo, Sri Lanka	191
1975	Apr.	4	Air Force Galaxy C-5B	Crashed near Saigon, So. Vietnam, after takeoff with load of orphans	172
1975	June	24	Eastern Airlines 727 jet	Crashed in storm, JFK Airport, N.Y. City	113
1975	Aug.	3	Chartered 707	Hit mountainside, Agadir, Morocco	168
1976	Sept.	10	British Airways Trident, Yugoslav DC-9	Collided near Zagreb, Yugoslavia	176
1976	Sept.	19	Turkish 727	Hit mountain, southern Turkey	155
1976	Oct.	13	Bolivian 707 cargo jet	Crashed in Santa Cruz, Bolivia	100[9]
1977	Jan.	13	Aeroflot TU-104	Exploded and crashed at Alma-Ata, Central Asia.	90
1977	Mar.	27	KLM 747, Pan American 747	Collided on runway, Tenerife, Canary Islands	581
1977	Nov.	19	TAP Boeing 727	Crashed on Madeira	130
1977	Dec.	4	Malaysian Boeing 737	Hijacked, then exploded in mid-air over Straits of Johore	100
1977	Dec.	13	U.S. DC-3	Crashed after takeoff at Evansville, Ind.	29[10]
1978	Jan.	1	Air India 747	Exploded, crashed into sea off Bombay	213
1978	Sept.	25	Boeing 727, Cessna 172	Collided in air, San Diego, Cal.	150
1978	Nov.	15	Chartered DC-8	Crashed near Colombo, Sri Lanka	183
1979	May	25	American Airlines DC-10	Crashed after takeoff at O'Hare Intl. Airport, Chicago	275[11]
1979	Aug.	17	Two Soviet Aeroflot jetliners	Collided over Ukraine	173
1979	Oct.	31	Western Airlines DC-10	Mexico City Airport	74
1979	Nov.	26	Pakistani Boeing 707	Crashed near Jidda, Saudi Arabia	156
1979	Nov.	28	New Zealand DC-10	Crashed into mountain in Antarctica	257
1980	Mar.	14	Polish Ilyushin 62	Crashed making emergency landing, Warsaw	87[12]
1980	Aug.	19	Saudi Arabian Tristar	Burned after emergency landing, Riyadh	301
1981	Dec.	1	Yugoslavian DC-9	Crashed into mountain in Corsica	174
1982	Jan.	13	Air Florida Boeing 737	Crashed into Potomac River after takeoff	78
1982	July	9	Pan-Am Boeing 727	Crashed after takeoff in Kenner, La.	153[13]
1982	Sept.	11	U.S. Army CH-47 Chinook helicopter	Crashed during air show in Mannheim, W. Germany	46
1983	Sept.	1	S. Korean Boeing 747	Shot down after violating Soviet airspace	269
1983	Nov.	27	Colombian Boeing 747	Crashed near Barajas Airport, Madrid	183
1985	Feb.	19	Spanish Boeing 727	Crashed into Mt. Oiz, Spain	148
1985	June	23	Air-India Boeing 747	Crashed into Atlantic Ocean S. of Ireland	329
1985	Aug.	2	Delta Air Lines jumbo jet	Crashed at Dallas-Ft. Worth Intl. Airport.	133
1985	Aug.	12	Japan Air Lines Boeing 747	Crashed into Mt. Ogura, Japan	520[14]
1985	Dec.	12	Arrow Air DC 8	Crashed after takeoff in Gander, Newfoundland	256[15]
1986	Mar.	31	Mexican Boeing 727	Crashed NW of Mexico City	166

Date			Aircraft	Site of accident	Deaths
1986	Aug.	31	Aeromexico DC-9	Collided with Piper PA-28 over Cerritos, Cal.	82[16]
1987	May	9	Ilyushin 62M	Crashed after takeoff in Warsaw, Poland	183
1987	Aug.	16	Northwest Airlines MD-82	Crashed after takeoff in Romulus, Mich.	156
1988	July	3	Iranian A300 Airbus	Shot down by U.S. Navy warship *Vincennes* over Persian Gulf	290

(1) Including those on the ground and in buildings. (2) First fatal crash of commercial jet plane. (3) Caused by bomb planted by John G. Graham in insurance plot to kill his mother, a passenger. (4) Including all 128 aboard the planes and 6 on ground. (5) Killed 84 on plane and 71 on ground. (6) Including 43 Marshall U. football players and coaches. (7) Airliner-fighter crash, pilot of fighter parachuted to safety, was arrested for negligence. (8) First supersonic plane crash killed 6 crewmen and 8 on the ground; there were no passengers. (9) Crew of 3 killed; 97, mostly children, killed on ground. (10) Including U. of Evansville basketball team. (11) Highest death toll in U.S. aviation history. (12) Including 22 members of U.S. boxing team. (13) Including 8 on ground. (14) Worst single-plane disaster. (15) Incl. 248 members of U.S. 101st Airborne Division. (16) Incl. 15 on the ground.

DISASTERS
Some Notable Shipwrecks Since 1850
(Figures indicate estimated lives lost; as of mid-1988)

1854, Mar.—City of Glasgow; British steamer missing in North Atlantic; 480.

1854, Sept. 27—Arctic; U.S. (Collins Line) steamer sunk in collision with French steamer Vesta near Cape Race; 285-351.

1856, Jan. 23—Pacific; U.S. (Collins Line) steamer missing in North Atlantic; 186-286.

1858, Sept. 23—Austria; German steamer destroyed by fire in North Atlantic; 471.

1863, Apr. 27—Anglo-Saxon; British steamer wrecked at Cape Race; 238.

1865, Apr. 27—Sultana; a Mississippi River steamer blew up near Memphis, Tenn; 1 450.

1869, Oct. 27—Stonewall; steamer burned on Mississippi River below Cairo, Ill.; 200.

1870, Jan. 25—City of Boston; British (Inman Line) steamer vanished between New York and Liverpool; 177.

1870, Oct 19—Cambria; British steamer wrecked off northern Ireland; 196.

1872, Nov. 7—Mary Celeste; U.S. half-brig sailed from New York for Genoa; found abandoned in Atlantic 4 weeks later in mystery of sea; crew never heard from; loss of life unknown.

1873, Jan. 22—Northfleet; British steamer foundered off Dungeness, England; 300.

1873, Apr. 1—Atlantic; British (White Star) steamer wrecked off Nova Scotia; 585.

1873, Nov. 23—Ville du Havre; French steamer, sunk after collision with British sailing ship Loch Earn; 226.

1875, May 7—Schiller; German steamer wrecked off Scilly Isles; 312.

1875, Nov. 4—Pacific; U.S. steamer sunk after collision off Cape Flattery; 236.

1878, Sept. 3—Princess Alice; British steamer sank after collision in Thames River; 700.

1878, Dec. 18—Byzantin; French steamer sank after Dardanelles collision; 210.

1881, May 24—Victoria; steamer capsized in Thames River, Canada; 200.

1883, Jan. 19—Cimbria; German steamer sunk in collision with British steamer Sultan in North Sea; 389.

1887, Nov. 15—Wah Yeung; British steamer burned at sea; 400.

1890, Feb. 17—Duburg; British steamer wrecked, China Sea; 400.

1890, Sept. 19—Ertogrul; Turkish frigate foundered off Japan; 540.

1891, Mar. 17—Utopia; British steamer sank in collision with British ironclad Anson off Gibraltar; 562.

1895, Jan. 30—Elbe; German steamer sank in collision with British steamer Craithie in North Sea; 332.

1895, Mar. 11—Reina Regenta; Spanish cruiser foundered near Gibraltar; 400.

1898, Feb. 15—Maine; U.S. battleship blown up in Havana Harbor; 260.

1898, July 4—La Bourgogne; French steamer sunk in collision with British sailing ship Cromartyshire off Nova Scotia; 549.

1898, Nov. 26—Portland; U.S. steamer wrecked off Cape Cod; 157.

1904, June 15—General Slocum; excursion steamer burned in East River, New York City; 1 030.

1904, June 28—Norge; Danish steamer wrecked on Rockall Island, Scotland; 620.

1906, Aug. 4—Sirio; Italian steamer wrecked off Cape Palos, Spain; 350.

1908, Mar. 23—Matsu Maru; Japanese steamer sank in collision near Hakodate, Japan; 300.

1909, Aug. 1—Waratah; British steamer, Sydney to London, vanished; 300.

1910, Feb. 9—General Chanzy; French steamer wrecked off Minorca, Spain; 200.

1911, Sept. 25—Liberté; French battleship exploded at Toulon; 285.

1912, Mar. 5—Principe de Asturias; Spanish steamer wrecked off Spain; 500.

1912, Apr. 14-15—Titanic; British (White Star) steamer hit iceberg in North Atlantic; 1 503.

1912, Sept. 28—Kichemaru; Japanese steamer sank off Japanese coast; 1 000.

1914, May 29—Empress of Ireland; British (Canadian Pacific) steamer sunk in collision with Norwegian collier in St. Lawrence River; 1 014.

1915, May 7—Lusitania; British (Cunard Line) steamer torpedoed and sunk by German submarine off Ireland; 1 198.

1915, July 24—Eastland; excursion steamer capsized in Chicago River; 812.

1916, Feb. 26—Provence; French cruiser sank in Mediterranean; 3 100.

1916, Mar. 3—Principe de Asturias; Spanish steamer wrecked near Santos, Brazil; 558.

1916, Aug. 29—Hsin Yu; Chinese steamer sank off Chinese coast; 1 000.

1917, Dec. 6—Mont Blanc, Imo; French ammunition ship and Belgian steamer collided in Halifax Harbor; 1 600.

1918, Apr. 25—Kiang-Kwan Chinese steamer sank in collision off Hankow; 500.

1918, July 12—Kawachi; Japanese battleship blew up in Tokayama Bay; 500.

1918, Oct. 25—Princess Sophia; Canadian steamer sank off Alaskan coast; 398.

1919, Jan. 17—Chaonia; French steamer lost in Straits of Messina, Italy; 460.

1919, Sept. 9—Valbanera; Spanish steamer lost off Florida coast; 500.

1921, Mar. 18—Hong Kong; steamer wrecked in South China Sea; 1 000.

1922, Aug. 26—Niitaka; Japanese cruiser sank in storm off Kamchatka, USSR; 300.

1927, Oct. 25—Principessa Mafalda; Italian steamer blew up, sank off Porto Seguro, Brazil; 314.

1928, Nov. 12—Vestris; British steamer sank in gale off Virginia; 113.

1934, Sept. 8—Morro Castle; U.S. steamer, Havana to New York, burned off Asbury Park, N.J.; 134.

1939, May 23—Squalus; U.S. submarine sank off Portsmouth, N.H.; 26.

1939, June 1—Thetis; British submarine, sank in Liverpool Bay; 99.

1942, Feb. 18—Truxtun and Pollux; U.S. destroyer and cargo ship ran aground, sank off Newfoundland; 204.

1942, Oct. 2—Curacao; British cruiser sank after collision with liner Queen Mary; 338.

1944, Dec. 17-18—3 U.S. Third Fleet destroyers sank during typhoon in Philippine Sea; 790.

1947, Jan. 19—Himera; Greek steamer hit a mine off Athens; 392.

1947, Apr. 16—Grandcamp; French freighter exploded in Texas City, Tex., Harbor, starting fires; 510.

1948, Nov.—Chinese army evacuation ship exploded and sunk off S. Manchuria; 6 000.

1948, Dec. 3—Kiangya; Chinese refugee ship wrecked in explosion S. of Shanghai; 1 100+.

1949, Sept. 17—Noronic; Canadian Great Lakes Cruiser burned at Toronto dock; 130.

1952, Apr. 26—Hobson and Wasp; U.S. destroyer and aircraft carrier collided in Atlantic; 176.

1953, Jan. 31—Princess Victoria; British ferry sank in storm off northern Irish coast; 134.

1954, Sept. 26—Toya Maru; Japanese ferry sank in Tsugaru Strait, Japan; 1 172.

1956, July 26—Andrea Doria and Stockholm; Italian liner and Swedish liner collided off Nantucket; 51.

1957, July 14—Eshghabad; Soviet ship ran aground in Caspian Sea; 270.

1961, July 8—Save; Portuguese ship ran aground off Mozambique; 259.

1962, Apr. 8—Dara; British liner exploded and sunk in Persian Gulf; 236.

1964, Feb. 10—Voyager, Melbourne; Australian destroyer sank after collision with Australian aircraft carrier Melbourne off New South Wales; 82.

1965, Nov. 13—Yarmouth Castle; Panamanian registered cruise ship burned and sank off Nassau; 90.

1968, Jan. 25—Dakar; Israeli submarine vanished in Mediterranean Sea; 69.

1968, Jan. 27—Minerve; French submarine vanished in Mediterranean; 52.

1968, late May—Scorpion; U.S. nuclear submarine sank in Atlantic near Azores; 99 (located Oct. 31).

1969, June 2—Evans; U.S. destroyer cut in half by Australian carrier Melbourne, S. China Sea; 74.

1970, Mar. 4—Eurydice; French submarine sank in Mediterranean near Toulon; 57.

1970, Dec. 15—Namyong-Ho; South Korean ferry sank in Korea Strait; 308.

1976, Dec. 25—Patria; Egyptian liner caught fire and sank in the Red Sea; c. 100.

1977, Jan. 11—Grand Zenith; Panamanian-registered tanker sank off Cape Cod, Mass.; 38.

1979, Aug. 14—23 yachts competing in Fastnet yacht race sunk or abandoned during storm in S. Irish Sea; 18.

1981, Jan. 27—Tamponas II; Indonesian passenger ship caught fire and sank in Java Sea; 580.

1981, May 26—Nimitz; U.S. Marine combat jet crashed on deck of U.S. aircraft carrier; 14.

1983, Feb. 12—Marine Electric; coal freighter sank during storm off Chincoteague, Va.; 33.

1983, May 25—10th of Ramadan; Nile steamer caught fire and sank in L. Nassar; 357.

1986, Aug. 31—Admiral Nakhimov; Soviet passenger ship and **Pyotr Vasev,** Soviet freighter, collided in the Black Sea; 398.

1987, Mar. 6—British ferry capsized off Zeebrugge, Belgium; 188.

1987, Dec. 20—Philippine ferry *Dona Paz* and oil tanker *Victor* collided in the Tablas Strait; 3 000+.

Major World Earthquakes

Magnitude of earthquakes (Mag.), distinct from deaths or damage caused, is measured on the Richter scale, on which each higher number represents a tenfold increase in energy measured in ground motion. Adopted in 1935, the scale has been applied in the following table to earthquakes as far back as reliable seismograms are available.

Date		Place	Deaths	Mag.	Date		Place	Deaths	Mag.
526	May 20	Syria, Antioch	250 000	n.a.	1957	Dec. 13	Western Iran	2 000	7.1
856		Greece, Corinth	45 000	n.a.	1960	Feb. 29	Morocco, Agadir	12 000	5.8
1057		China, Chihli	25 000	n.a.	1960	May 21-30	Southern Chile	5 000	8.3
1268		Asia Minor, Cilicia	60 000	n.a.	1962	Sept. 1	Northwestern Iran	12 230	7.1
1290	Sept. 27	China, Chihli	100 000	n.a.	1963	July 26	Yugoslavia, Skopje	1 100	6.0
1293	May 20	Japan, Kamakura	30 000	n.a.	1964	Mar. 27	Alaska	114	8.5
1531	Jan. 26	Portugal, Lisbon	30 000	n.a.	1966	Aug. 19	Eastern Turkey	2 520	6.9
1556	Jan. 24	China, Shaanxi	830 000	n.a.	1968	Aug. 31	Northeastern Iran	12 000	7.4
1667	Nov.	Caucasia, Shemaka	80 000	n.a.	1970	Mar. 28	Western Turkey	1 086	7.4
1693	Jan. 11	Italy, Catania	60 000	n.a.	1970	May 31	Northern Peru	66 794	7.7
1730	Dec. 30	Japan, Hokkaido	137 000	n.a.	1971	Feb. 9	Cal., San Fernando Valley	65	6.5
1737	Oct. 11	India, Calcutta	300 000	n.a.					
1755	June 7	Northern Persia	40 000	n.a.	1972	Apr. 10	Southern Iran	5 057	6.9
1755	Nov. 1	Portugal, Lisbon	60 000	8.75*	1972	Dec. 23	Nicaragua	5 000	6.2
1783	Feb. 4	Italy, Calabria	30 000	n.a.	1974	Dec. 28	Pakistan (9 towns)	5 200	6.3
1797	Feb. 4	Ecuador, Quito	41 000	n.a.	1975	Sept. 6	Turkey (Lice, etc.)	2 312	6.8
1822	Sept. 5	Asia Minor, Aleppo	22 000	n.a.	1976	Feb. 4	Guatemala	22 778	7.5
1828	Dec. 28	Japan, Echigo	30 000	n.a.	1976	May 6	Northeast Italy	946	6.5
1868	Aug. 13-15	Peru and Ecuador	40 000	n.a.	1976	June 26	New Guinea, Irian Jaya.	443	7.1
1875	May 16	Venezuela, Colombia	16 000	n.a.	1976	July 28	China, Tangshan	242 000	8.2
1896	June 15	Japan, sea wave	27 120	n.a.	1976	Aug. 17	Philippines, Mindanao.	8 000	7.8
1906	Apr. 18-19	Cal., San Francisco	503	8.3	1976	Nov. 24	Eastern Turkey	4 000	7.9
1906	Aug. 16	Chile, Valparaiso	20 000	8.6	1977	Mar. 4	Romania, Bucharest, etc.	1 541	7.5
1908	Dec. 28	Italy, Messina	83 000	7.5					
1915	Jan. 13	Italy, Avezzano	29 980	7.5	1977	Aug. 19	Indonesia	200	8.0
1920	Dec. 16	China, Gansu	100 000	8.6	1977	Nov. 23	Northwestern Argentina	100	8.2
1923	Sept. 1	Japan, Yokohama	200 000	8.3	1978	June 12	Japan, Sendai	21	7.5
1927	May 22	China, Nan-Shan	200 000	8.3	1978	Sept. 16	Northeast Iran	25 000	7.7
1932	Dec. 26	China, Gansu	70 000	7.6	1979	Sept. 12	Indonesia	100	8.1
1933	Mar. 2	Japan	2 990	8.9	1979	Dec. 12	Colombia, Ecuador	800	7.9
1934	Jan. 15	India, Bihar-Nepal	10 700	8.4	1980	Oct. 10	Northwestern Algeria	4 500	7.3
1935	May 31	India, Quetta	50 000	7.5	1980	Nov. 23	Southern Italy	4 800	7.2
1939	Jan. 24	Chile, Chillan	28 000	8.3	1982	Dec. 13	North Yemen	2 800	6.0
1939	Dec. 26	Turkey, Erzincan	30 000	7.9	1983	Mar. 31	Southern Colombia	250	5.5
1946	Dec. 21	Japan, Honshu	2 000	8.4	1983	May 26	N. Honshu, Japan	81	7.7
1948	June 28	Japan, Fukui	5 131	7.3	1983	Oct. 30	Eastern Turkey	1 300	7.1
1949	Aug. 5	Ecuador, Pelileo	6 000	6.8	1985	Mar. 3	Chile	146	7.8
1950	Aug. 15	India, Assam	1 530	8.7	1985	Sept. 19, 21	Mexico City	4 200+	8.1
1953	Mar. 18	NW Turkey	1 200	7.2	1987	Mar. 5-6	N.E. Ecuador	4 000+	7.3
1956	June 10-17	N. Afghanistan	2 000	7.7					
1957	July 2	Northern Iran	2 500	7.4					

*estimated from earthquake intensity; n.a. not available.

Some Recent Earthquakes

Source: Scientific Event Alert Network, Smithsonian Institution

Attached is a list of recent earthquakes. Magnitude of earthquakes is measured on the Richter scale, on which each higher number represents a tenfold increase in energy measured in ground motion.

Date	Place	Magnitude	Date	Place	Magnitude
Apr. 12, 1988	Arequipa, Peru	7.0	Oct. 16	Papua New Guinea	7.5
Mar. 10	Trinidad	6.4	Oct. 12	Solomon Islands	6.9
Feb. 29	Komandorski Islands, USSR	6.9	Oct. 5	Tonga Islands	7.3
Feb. 24	Philippines	7.0	Sept. 28	Vanuatu	6.7/6.6
Feb. 5	N. Chile	6.7	Aug. 8	N. Chile	7.0
Jan. 22	Northern Terr., Australia	6.8	July 6	Vanuatu	6.6
Jan. 19	Taltal, Chile	6.8	June 17	Banda Sea, Indonesia	6.7
Dec. 17, 1987	Honshu, Japan	6.4	June 10	S. Illinois	4.9
Nov. 24	S. California	6.2/6.6			
Nov. 17	Gulf of Alaska	7.0			

Notable Nuclear Accidents

1957, Oct. 7 — A fire in the Windscale plutonium production reactor north of Liverpool, England spread radioactive material throughout the countryside. In 1983, the British government said that 39 people probably died of cancer as a result.

1957 — A chemical explosion in Kasli, USSR, in tanks containing nuclear waste, spread radioactive material and forced a major evacuation.

1961, Jan. 3 — An experimental reactor at a federal installation near Idaho Falls, Id., U.S.A. killed 3 workers—the only deaths in U.S. reactor operations. The plant had high radiation levels but damage was contained.

1966, Oct. 5 — A sodium cooling system malfunction caused a partial core meltdown at the Enrico Fermi demonstration breeder reactor near Detroit, Mich., U.S.A. Radiation was contained.

1969, Jan. 21 — A coolant malfunction from an experimental underground reactor at Lucens Vad, Switzerland resulted in the release of a large amount of radiation into a cavern, which was then sealed.

1971, Nov. 19 — The water-storage space at the Northern States Power Co.'s reactor in Monticello, Minn. filled to capacity and spilled over, dumping about 225 000 L of radioactive waste water into the Mississippi River. Some was taken into the St. Paul water system.

1975, Mar. 22 — A technician checking for air leaks with a lighted candle caused a $100 million fire at the Brown's Ferry reactor in Decatur, Ala., U.S.A. The fire burned out electrical controls, cooling the water to dangerous levels.

1979, Mar. 28 — The worst commercial nuclear accident in the U.S. occured as equipment failures and human mistakes led to a loss of coolant, and partial core meltdown at the Three Mile Island reactor in Middletown, Pa.

1979, Aug. 7 — Highly enriched uranium was released from a top-secret nuclear fuel plant near Erwin, Tenn., U.S.A. About 1 000 people were contaminated with up to 5 times as much radiation as would normally be received in a year.

1981, Feb. 11 — Eight workers were contaminated when over 450 000 L of radioactive coolant leaked into the containment building of the TVA's Sequoyah 1 plant in Tennessee.

1981, Apr. 25 — Some 100 workers were exposed to radioactive material during repairs of a nuclear plant at Tsuruga, Japan.

1982, Jan. 25 — A steam-generator pipe broke at the Rochester Gas & Electric Co's Ginna plant near Rochester, N.Y., U.S.A. Small amounts of radioactive steam escaped into the air.

1986, Jan. 6 — A cylinder of nuclear material burst after being improperly heated at a Kerr-McGee plant at Gore, Okla., U.S.A. One worker died and 100 were hospitalized.

1986, Apr. — A serious accident at the Chernobyl nuclear plant about 96 km from Kiev in the Soviet Union spewed clouds of radiation that spread over several European nations.

Record Oil Spills

Name, place	Date	Cause	Tonnes
Ixtoc I oil well, southern Gulf of Mexico	June 3, 1979	Blowout	540 000
Nowruz oil field, Persian Gulf	Feb., 1983	Blowout	540 000 (est.)
Atlantic Empress & Aegean Captain, off Trinidad & Tobago	July 19, 1979	Collision	270 000
Castillo de Bellver, off Cape Town, South Africa	Aug. 6, 1983	Fire	225 000
Amoco Cadiz, near Portsall, France	March 16, 1978	Grounding	200 000
Torrey Canyon, off Land's End, England	March 18, 1967	Grounding	107 100
Sea Star, Gulf of Oman	Dec. 19, 1972	Collision	103 500
Urquiola, La Coruna, Spain	May 12, 1976	Grounding	90 000
Hawaiian Patriot, northern Pacific	Feb. 25, 1977	Fire	89 100
Othello, Tralhavet Bay, Sweden	March 20, 1970	Collision	54 000-90 000

Other Notable Oil Spills

Name, place	Date	Cause	Litres
World Glory, off South Africa	June 13, 1968	Hull failure	51 391 200
Keo, off Massachusetts	Nov. 5, 1969	Hull failure	33 516 000
Storage tank, Sewaren, N.J.	Nov. 4, 1969	Tank rupture	31 920 000
Ekofisk oil field, North Sea	Apr. 22, 1977	Well blowout	31 160 000
Argo Merchant, Nantucket, Mass.	Dec. 15, 1976	Grounding	29 260 000
Pipeline, West Delta, La.	Oct. 15, 1967	Dragging anchor	25 536 000
Tanker off Japan	Nov. 30, 1971	Ship broke in half	23 780 400
Storage tank, Monongahela River	Jan. 2, 1988	Tank collapse	3 268 000

Historical Figures

Greeks

Aeschines, orator, 389-314BC.
Aeschylus, dramatist, 525-456BC.
Aesop, fableist, c620-c560BC.
Alcibiades, politician, 450-404BC.
Anacreon, poet, c582-c485BC.
Anaxagoras, philosopher, c500-428BC.
Anaximander, philosopher, 611-546BC.
Antiphon, speechwriter, c480-411BC.
Apollonius, mathematician, c265-170BC.
Archimedes, math. c287-212BC.
Aristophanes, dramatist, c448-380BC.
Aristotle, philosopher, 384-322BC.
Athenaeus, scholar, fl.c200.
Callicrates, architect, fl.5th cent.BC.
Callimachus, poet, c305-240BC.
Cratinus, comic dramatist, 520-421BC.
Democritus, philosopher, c460-370BC.
Demosthenes, orator, 384-322BC.
Diodorus, historian, fl.20BC.
Diogenes, philosopher, c372-c287BC.

Dionysius, historian, d.c7BC.
Empedocles, philosopher, c490-430BC.
Epicharmus, dramatist, c530-440BC.
Epictetus, philosopher, c55-c135.
Epicurus, philosopher, 341-270BC.
Eratosthenes, scientist, c276-194BC.
Euclid, mathematician, fl.c300BC.
Euripides, dramatist, c484-406BC.
Galen, physician, c129-199.
Heraclitus, philosopher, c535-c475BC.
Herodotus, historian, c484-420BC.
Hesiod, poet, 8th cent. BC.
Hippocrates, physician, c460-377BC.
Homer, poet, believed four c850BC.
Isocrates, orator, 436-338BC.
Menander, dramatist, 342-292BC.
Phidias, sculptor, c500-435BC.
Pindar, poet, c518-c438BC.
Plato, philosopher, c428-c347BC.
Plutarch, biographer, c46-120.

Polybius, historian, c200-c118BC.
Praxiteles, sculptor, 400-330BC.
Pythagoras, phil., math., c580-c500BC.
Sappho, poet, c610-c580BC.
Simonides, poet, 556-c468BC.
Socrates, philosopher, c470-399BC.
Solon, statesman, 640-560BC.
Sophocles, dramatist, c496-406BC.
Strabo, geographer, c63BC-AD24.
Thales, philosopher, c634-c546BC.
Themistocles, politician, c524-c460BC.
Theocritus, poet, c310-250BC.
Theophrastus, phil. c372-c287BC.
Thucydides, historian, fl.5th cent.BC.
Timon, philosopher, c320-c230BC.
Xenophon, historian, c434-c355BC.
Zeno, philosopher, c495-c430BC.

Latins

Ammianus, historian, c330-395.
Apuleius, satirist, c124-c170.
Boethius, scholar, c480-524
Caesar, Julius, general, 100-44BC.
Catilina, politician, c108-62BC.
Carus, poet, c98-55BC.
Cato(Elder), statesman, 234-149BC.
Catullus, poet, c84-54BC.
Cicero, orator, 106-43BC.
Claudian, poet, c370-c404.
Ennius, poet, 239-170BC.
Gellius, author, c130-c165.

Horace, poet, 65-8BC.
Juvenal, satirist, c60-c127.
Livy, historian, 59BC-AD17.
Lucan, poet, 39-65.
Lucilius, poet, c180-c102BC.
Lucretius, poet, c99-c55BC.
Martial, epigrammatist, c38-c103.
Nepos, historian, c100-c25BC.
Ovid,poet, 43BC-AD17.
Persius, satirist, 34-62.
Plautus, dramatist, c254-c184BC.
Pliny, scholar, 23-79.

Pliny(Younger), author, 62-113.
Quintilian, rhetorician, c35-c97.
Sallust, historian, 86-34BC.
Seneca, philosopher, 4BC-AD65.
Silius, poet, c25-101.
Statius, poet, c45-c96.
Suetonius, biographer, c69-c122.
Tacitus, historian, c56-c120.
Terence, dramatist, 185-c159BC.
Tibullus, poet, c55-c19BC.
Virgil, poet, 70-19BC.
Vitruvius, architect, fl.1st cent.BC.

Roman Rulers

BC	Name
	The Kingdom
753	Romulus (Quirinus)
716	Numa Pompilius
673	Tullus Hostilius
640	Ancus Marcius
616	L. Tarquinius Priscus
578	Servius Tullius
534	L. Tarquinius Superbus
	The Republic
509	Consulate established
509	Quaestorship instituted
498	Dictatorship introduced
494	Plebeian Tribunate created
494	Plebeian Aedileship created
444	Consular Tribunate organized
435	Censorship instituted
366	Praetorship established
366	Curule Aedileship created
362	Military Tribunate elected
326	Proconsulate introduced
311	Naval Duumvirate elected
217	Dictatorship of Fabius Maximus
133	Tribunate of Tiberius Gracchus
123	Tribunate of Gaius Gracchus
82	Dictatorship of Sulla
60	First Triumvirate formed (Caesar, Pompeius, Crassus)
46	Dictatorship of Caesar
43	Second Triumvirate formed (Octavianus, Antonius, Lepidus)
	The Empire
27	Augustus (Gaius Julius Caesar Octavianus)
14	Tiberius I
37	Gaius Caesar (Caligula)
41	Claudius I
54	Nero
68	Galba
69	Galba; Otho, Vitellius
69	Vespasianus
79	Titus

AD	Name
81	Domitianus
96	Nerva
98	Trajanus
117	Hadrianus
138	Antoninus Pius
161	Marcus Aurelius and Lucius Verus
169	Marcus Aurelius (alone)
180	Commodus
193	Pertinax; Julianus I
193	Septimius Severus
211	Caracalla and Geta
212	Caracalla (alone)
217	Macrinus
218	Elagabalus (Heliogabalus)
222	Alexander Severus
235	Maximinus I (the Thracian)
238	Gordianus I and Gordianus II; Pupienus and Balbinus
238	Gordianus III
244	Philippus (the Arabian)
249	Decius
251	Gallus and Volusianus
253	Aemilianus
253	Valerianus and Gallienus
258	Gallienus (alone)
268	Claudius Gothicus
270	Quintillus
270	Aurelianus
275	Tacitus
276	Florianus
276	Probus
282	Carus
283	Carinus and Numerianus
284	Diocletianus
286	Diocletianus and Maximianus
305	Galerius and Constantius I
306	Galerius, Maximinus II, Severus I
307	Galerius, Maximinus II, Constantinus I, Licinius, Maxentius
311	Maximinus II, Constantinus I, Licinius, Maxentius
314	Maximinus II, Constantinus I, Licinius

AD	Name
314	Constantinus I and Licinius
324	Constantinus I (the Great)
337	Constantinus II, Constans I, Constantius II
340	Constantius II and Constans I
350	Constantius II
361	Julianus II (the Apostate)
363	Jovianus
	West (Rome) and East (Constantinople)
364	Valentinianus I (West) and Valens (East)
367	Valentinianus I with Gratianus (West) and Valens (East)
375	Gratianus with Valentinianus II (West) and Valens (East)
378	Gratianus with Valentinianus II (West) Theodosius I (East)
383	Valentinianus II (West) and Theodosius I (East)
394	Theodosius I (the Great)
395	Honorius (West) and Arcadius (East)
408	Honorius (West) and Theodosius II (East)
423	Valentinianus III (West) and Theodosius II (East)
450	Valentinianus III (West) and Marcianus (East)
455	Maximus (West), Avitus (West); Marcianus (East)
456	Avitus (West), Marcianus (East)
457	Majorianus (West), Leo I (East)
461	Severus II (West), Leo I (East)
467	Anthemius (West), Leo I (East)
472	Olybrius (West), Leo I (East)
473	Glycerius (West), Leo I (East)
474	Julius Nepos (West), Leo II (East)
475	Romulus Augustulus (West) and Zeno (East)
476	End of Empire in West; Odovacar, King, drops title of Emperor; murdered by King Theodoric of Ostrogoths 493 AD

Rulers of Modern Italy

After the fall of Napoleon in 1814, the Congress of Vienna, 1815, restored Italy as a political patchwork, comprising the Kingdom of Naples and Sicily, the Papal States, and smaller units. Piedmont and Genoa were awarded to Sardinia, ruled by King Victor Emmanuel I of Savoy.

United Italy emerged under the leadership of Camillo, Count di Cavour (1810-1861), Sardinian prime minister. Agitation was led by Giuseppe Mazzini (1805-1872) and Giuseppe Garibaldi (1807-1882), soldier, Victor Emmanuel I abdicated 1821. After a brief regency for a brother, Charles Albert was King 1831-1849, abdicating when defeated by the Austrians at Novara. Succeeded by Victor Emmanuel II, 1849-1861.

In 1859 France forced Austria to cede Lombardy to Sardinia, which gave rights to Savoy and Nice to France. In 1860 Garibaldi led 1000 volunteers in a spectacular campaign, took Sicily and expelled the King of Naples. In 1860 the House of Savoy annexed Tuscany, Parma, Modena, Romagna, the Two Sicilies, the Marches, and Umbria. Victor Emmanuel assumed the title of King of Italy at Turin Mar. 17, 1861. In 1866 he allied with Prussia in the Austro-Prussian War, with Prussia's victory received Venetia. On Sept. 20, 1870, his troops under Gen. Raffaele Cadorna entered Rome and took over the Papal States, ending the temporal power of the Roman Catholic Church.

Succession: Umberto I; 1878, assassinated 1900; Victor Emmanuel III, 1900, abdicated 1946, died 1947; Umberto II, 1946, ruled a month. In 1921 Benito Mussolini (1883-1945) formed the Fascist party and became prime minister Oct. 31, 1922. He made the King Emperor of Ethiopia, 1937; entered World War II as ally of Hitler. He was deposed July 25, 1943.

At a plebiscite June 2, 1946, Italy voted for a republic; Premier Alcide de Gasperi became chief of state June 13, 1946. On June 28, 1946, the Constituent Assembly elected Enrico de Nicola, Liberal, provisional president. Successive presidents: Luigi Einaudi, elected May 11, 1948, Giovanni Gronchi, Apr. 29, 1955; Antonio Segni, May 6, 1962; Giuseppe Saragat, Dec. 28, 1964; Giovanni Leone, Dec. 29, 1971; Alessandro Pertini, July 9, 1978; Francesco Cossiga, July 9, 1985.

Rulers of England and Great Britain

Name	England	Began	Died	Age	Rgd
Saxons and Danes					
Egbert	King of Wessex, won allegiance of all English	829	839	—	10
Ethelwulf	Son, King of Wessex, Sussex, Kent, Essex	839	858	—	19
Ethelbald	Son of Ethelwulf, displaced father in Wessex	858	860	—	2
Ethelbert	2d son of Ethelwulf, united Kent and Wessex	860	866	—	6
Ethelred I	3d son, King of Wessex, fought Danes	866	871	—	5
Alfred	The Great, 4th son, defeated Danes, fortified London	871	899	52	28
Edward	The Elder, Alfred's son, united English, claimed Scotland	899	924	55	25
Athelstan	The Glorious, Edward's son, King of Mercia, Wessex	924	940	45	16
Edmund I	3d son of Edward, King of Wessex, Mercia	940	946	25	6
Edred	4th son of Edward	946	955	32	9
Edwy	The Fair, eldest son of Edmund, King of Wessex	955	959	18	3
Edgar	The Peaceful, 2d son of Edmund, ruled all English	959	975	32	17
Edward	The Martyr, eldest son of Edgar, murdered by stepmother	975	978	17	4
Ethelred II	The Unready, 2d son of Edgar, married Emma of Normandy	978	1016	48	37
Edmund II	Ironside, son of Ethelred II, King of London	1016	1016	27	0
Canute	The Dane, gave Wessex to Edmund, married Emma	1016	1035	40	19
Harold I	Harefoot, natural son of Canute	1035	1040	—	5
Hardecanute	Son of Canute by Emma, Danish King	1040	1042	24	2
Edward	The Confessor, son of Ethelred II (Canonized 1161)	1042	1066	62	24
Harold II	Edward's brother-in-law, last Saxon King	1066	1066	44	0
House of Normandy					
William I	The Conqueror, defeated Harold at Hastings	1066	1087	60	21
William II	Rufus, 3d son of William I, killed by arrow	1087	1100	43	13
Henry I	Beauclerc, youngest son of William I	1100	1135	67	35
House of Blois					
Stephen	Son of Adela, daughter of William I, and Count of Blois	1135	1154	50	19
House of Plantagenet					
Henry II	Son of Geoffrey Plantagenet (Angevin) by Matilda, dau. of Henry I	1154	1189	56	35
Richard I	Coeur de Lion, son of Henry II, crusader	1189	1199	42	10
John	Lackland, son of Henry II, signed Magna Carta, 1215	1199	1216	50	17
Henry III	Son of John, acceded at 9, under regency until 1227	1216	1272	65	56
Edward I	Longshanks, son of Henry III	1272	1307	68	35
Edward II	Son of Edward I, deposed by Parliament, 1327	1307	1327	43	20
Edward III	Of Windsor, son of Edward II	1327	1377	65	50
Richard II	Grandson of Edw. III, minor until 1389, deposed 1399	1377	1400	33	22
House of Lancaster					
Henry IV	Son of John of Gaunt, Duke of Lancaster, son of Edw. III	1399	1413	47	13
Henry V	Son of Henry IV, victor of Agincourt	1413	1422	34	9
Henry VI	Son of Henry V, deposed 1461, died in Tower	1422	1471	49	39
House of York					
Edward IV	Great-great-grandson of Edward III, son of Duke of York	1461	1483	41	22
Edward V	Son of Edward IV, murdered in Tower of London	1483	1483	13	0
Richard III	Crookback, bro. of Edward IV, fell at Bosworth Field	1483	1485	35	2

Name		Began	Died	Age	Rgd
House of Tudor					
Henry VII	Son of Edmund Tudor, Earl of Richmond, whose father had married the widow of Henry V; descended from Edward III through his mother, Margaret Beaufort via John of Gaunt. By marriage with dau. of Edward IV he united Lancaster and York	1485	1509	53	24
Henry VIII	Son of Henry VII by Elizabeth, dau. of Edward IV.	1509	1547	56	38
Edward VI	Son of Henry VIII, by Jane Seymour, his 3d queen. Ruled under regents. Was forced to name Lady Jane Grey his successor. Council of State proclaimed her queen July 10, 1553. Mary Tudor won Council, was proclaimed queen July 19, 1553. Mary had Lady Jane Grey beheaded for treason, Feb., 1554	1547	1553	16	6
Mary I	Daughter of Henry VIII, by Catherine of Aragon	1553	1558	43	5
Elizabeth I	Daughter of Henry VIII, by Anne Boleyn	1558	1603	69	44
Great Britain					
House of Stuart					
James I	James VI of Scotland, son of Mary, Queen of Scots. *First to call himself King of Great Britain. This became official with the Act of Union, 1707*	1603	1625	59	22
Charles I	Only surviving son of James I; beheaded Jan. 30, 1649	1625	1649	48	24
Commonwealth, 1649-1660					
Council of State, 1649; Protectorate, 1653					
The Cromwells	Oliver Cromwell, Lord Protector	1653	1658	59	—
	Richard Cromwell, son, Lord Protector, resigned May 25, 1659	1658	1712	86	—
House of Stuart (Restored)					
Charles II	Eldest son of Charles I, died without issue	1660	1685	55	25
James II	2d son of Charles I. Deposed 1688. Interregnum Dec. 11, 1688, to Feb. 13, 1689	1685	1701	68	3
William III	Son of William, Prince of Orange, by Mary, dau. of Charles I	1689	1702	51	13
and Mary II	Eldest daughter of James II and wife of William III		1694	33	6
Anne	2d daughter of James II	1702	1714	49	12
House of Hanover					
George I	Son of Elector of Hanover, by Sophia, grand-dau. of James I	1714	1727	67	13
George II	Only son of George I, married Caroline of Brandenburg	1727	1760	77	33
George III	Grandson of George II, married Charlotte of Mecklenburg	1760	1820	81	59
George IV	Eldest son of George III, Prince Regent, from Feb., 1811	1820	1830	67	10
William IV	3d son of George III, married Adelaide of Saxe-Meiningen	1830	1837	71	7
Victoria	Dau. of Edward, 4th son of George III; married (1840) Prince Albert of Saxe-Coburg and Gotha, who became Prince Consort	1837	1901	81	63
House of Saxe-Coburg and Gotha					
Edward VII	Eldest son of Victoria, married Alexandra, Princess of Denmark	1901	1910	68	9
House of Windsor					
Name Adopted July 17, 1917					
George V	2d son of Edward VII, married Princess Mary of Teck	1910	1936	70	25
Edward VIII	Eldest son of George V; acceded Jan. 20, 1936, abdicated Dec. 11	1936	1972	77	1
George VI	2d son of George V; married Lady Elizabeth Bowes-Lyon	1936	1952	56	15
Elizabeth II	Elder daughter of George VI, acceded Feb. 6, 1952	1952	—	—	—

Prime Ministers of Great Britain

Served	Prime minister	Served	Prime minister	Served	Prime minister
1721-1742	Robert Walpole	1828-1830	Arthur Wellesley	1902-1905	Arthur J. Balfour
1742-1743	Spencer Compton	1830-1834	Charles Grey	1905-1908	Henry Campbell-Bannerman
1743-1754	Henry Pelham	1834	William Lamb	1908-1916	Herbert H. Asquith
1754-1756	Thomas Pelham-Holles	1834-1835	Robert Peel	1916-1922	David Lloyd George
1756-1757	William Cavendish	1835-1841	William Lamb	1922-1923	Andrew Bonar Law
1757-1762	Thomas Pelham-Holles	1841-1846	Robert Peel	1923-1924	Stanley Baldwin
1762-1763	John Stuart	1846-1852	John Russell	1924	James Ramsay MacDonald
1763-1765	George Grenville	1852	Edward G.G.S. Stanley	1924-1929	Stanley Baldwin
1765-1766	Charles Watson-Wentworth	1852-1855	George H. Gordon	1929-1935	James Ramsay MacDonald
1766-1767	William Pitt	1855-1858	Henry J. Temple	1935-1937	Stanley Baldwin
1767-1770	Augustus Henry Fitzroy	1858-1859	Edward G.G.S. Stanley	1937-1940	Neville Chamberlain
1770-1782	Frederick North	1859-1865	Henry J. Temple	1940-1945	Winston Churchill
1782	Charles Watson-Wentworth	1865-1866	John Russell	1945-1951	Clement Attlee
1782-1783	William Petty	1866-1868	Edward G.G.S. Stanley	1951-1955	Winston Churchill
1783	William H.C. Bentinck	1868	Benjamin Disraeli	1955-1957	Anthony Eden
1783-1801	William Pitt (the Younger)	1868-1874	William E. Gladstone	1957-1963	Harold Macmillan
1801-1804	Henry Addington	1874-1880	Benjamin Disraeli	1963-1964	Alec Douglas-Home
1804-1806	William Pitt (the Younger)	1880-1885	William E. Gladstone	1964-1970	Harold Wilson
1806-1807	William W. Grenville	1885-1886	Robert A.T. Gascoyne-Cecil	1970-1974	Edward Heath
1807-1809	William H.C. Bentinck	1886	William E. Gladstone	1974-1976	Harold Wilson
1809-1812	Spencer Perceval	1886-1892	Robert A.T. Gascoyne-Cecil	1976-1979	James Callaghan
1812-1827	Robert B. Jenkinson	1892-1894	William E. Gladstone	1979-	Margaret Thatcher
1827	George Canning	1894-1895	Archibald Philip Primrose		
1827-1828	Frederick J. Robinson	1895-1902	Robert A.T. Gascoyne-Cecil		

Rulers of Scotland

Kenneth I MacAlpin was the first Scot to rule both Scots and Picts, 846 AD.

Duncan I was the first general ruler, 1034. Macbeth seized the kingdom 1040, was slain by Duncan's son, Malcolm III MacDuncan (Canmore), 1057.

Malcolm married Margaret, Saxon princess who had fled from the Normans. Queen Margaret introduced English language and English monastic customs. She was canonized, 1250. Her son Edgar, 1097, moved the court to Edinburgh. His brothers Alexander I and David I succeeded. Malcolm IV, the Maiden, 1153, grandson of David I, was followed by his brother, William the Lion, 1165, whose son was Alexander II, 1214. The latter's son, Alexander III, 1249, defeated the Norse and regained the Hebrides. When he died, 1286, his granddaughter, Margaret, child of Eric of Norway and grandniece of Edward I of England, known as the Maid of Norway, was chosen ruler, but died 1290, aged 8.

John Baliol, 1292-1296. (Interregnum, 10 years).

Robert Bruce (The Bruce), 1306-1329, victor at Bannockburn, 1314.

David II, only son of Robert Bruce, ruled 1329-1371.

Robert II, 1371-1390, grandson of Robert Bruce, son of Walter, the Steward of Scotland, was called The Steward, first of the so-called Stuart line.

Robert III, son of Robert II, 1390-1406.

James I, son of Robert III, 1406-1437.

James II, son of James I, 1437-1460.

James III, eldest son of James II, 1460-1488.

James IV, eldest son of James III, 1488-1513.

James V, eldest son of James IV, 1513-1542.

Mary, daughter of James V, born 1542, became queen when one week old; was crowned 1543. Married, 1558, Francis, son of Henry II of France, who became king 1559, died 1560. Mary ruled Scots 1561 until abdication, 1567. She also married (2) Henry Stewart, Lord Darnley, and (3) James, Earl of Bothwell. Imprisoned by Elizabeth I, Mary was beheaded 1587.

James VI, 1566-1625, son of Mary and Lord Darnley, became King of England on death of Elizabeth in 1603. Although the thrones were thus united, the legislative union of Scotland and England was not effected until the Act of Union, May 1, 1707.

Rulers of Middle Europe; Rise and Fall of Dynasties

Carolingian Dynasty

Charles the Great, or Charlemagne, ruled France, Italy, and Middle Europe; established Ostmark (later Austria); crowned Roman emperor by pope in Rome, 800 AD; died 814.

Louis I (Ludwig) the Pious, son; crowned by Charlemagne 814, d. 840.

Louis II, the German, son; succeeded to East Francia (Germany) 843-876.

Charles the Fat, son; inherited East Francia and West Francia (France) 876, reunited empire, crowned emperor by pope, 881, deposed 887.

Arnulf, nephew, 887-899. Partition of empire.

Louis the Child, 899-911, last direct descendant of Charlemagne.

Conrad I, duke of Franconia, first elected German king, 911-918, founded House of Franconia.

Saxon Dynasty; First Reich

Henry I, the Fowler, duke of Saxony, 919-936.

Otto I, the Great, 936-973, son; crowned Holy Roman Emperor by pope, 962.

Otto II, 973-983, son; failed to oust Greeks and Arabs from Sicily.

Otto III, 983-1002, son; crowned emperor at 16.

Henry II, the Saint, duke of Bavaria, 1002-1024, great-grandson of Otto the Great.

House of Franconia

Conrad II, 1024-1039, elected king of Germany.

Henry III, the Black, 1039-1056, son; deposed 3 popes; annexed Burgundy.

Henry IV, 1056-1106, son; regency by his mother, Agnes of Poitou. Banned by Pope Gregory VII, he did penance at Canossa.

Henry V, 1106-1125, son; last of Salic House.

Lothair, duke of Saxony, 1125-1137. Crowned emperor in Rome, 1134.

House of Hohenstaufen

Conrad III, duke of Swabia, 1138-1152. In 2d Crusade.

Frederick I, Barbarossa, 1152-1190; Conrad's nephew.

Henry VI, 1190-1196, took lower Italy from Normans. Son became king of Sicily.

Philip of Swabia, 1197-1208, brother.

Otto IV, of House of Welf, 1198-1215; deposed.

Frederick II, 1215-1250, son of Henry VI; king of Sicily; crowned king of Jerusalem; in 5th Crusade.

Conrad IV, 1250-1254, son; lost lower Italy to Charles of Anjou.

Conradin (1252-1268) son, king of Jerusalem and Sicily, beheaded. Last Hohenstaufen.

Interregnum, 1254-1273, Rise of the Electors.

Transition

Rudolph I of Hapsburg, 1273-1291, defeated King Ottocar II of Bohemia. Bequeathed duchy of Austria to eldest son, Albert.

Adolph of Nassau, 1292-1298, killed in war with Albert of Austria.

Albert I, king of Germany, 1298-1308, son of Rudolph.

Henry VII, of Luxemburg, 1308-1313, crowned emperor in Rome. Seized Bohemia, 1310.

Louis IV of Bavaria (Wittelsbach), 1314-1347. Also elected was Frederick of Austria, 1314-1330 (Hapsburg). Abolition of papal sanction for election of Holy Roman Emperor.

Charles IV, of Luxemburg, 1347-1378, grandson of Henry VII, German emperor and king of Bohemia, Lombardy, Burgundy; took Mark of Brandenburg.

Wenceslaus, 1378-1400, deposed.

Rupert, Duke of Palatine, 1400-1410.

Hungary

Stephen I, house of Arpad, 997-1038. Crowned king 1000; converted Magyars; canonized 1083. After several centuries of feuds Charles Robert of Anjou became Charles I, 1308-1342.

Louis I, the Great, son, 1342-1382; joint ruler of Poland with Casimir III, 1370. Defeated Turks.

Mary, daughter, 1382-1395, ruled with husband. Sigismund of Luxemburg, 1387-1437, also king of Bohemia. As bro. of Wenceslaus he succeeded Rupert as Holy Roman Emperor, 1410.

Albert II, 1438-1439, son-in-law of Sigismund; also Roman emperor. (see under Hapsburg.)

Ulaszlo I of Poland, 1440-1444.

Ladislaus V, posthumous son of Albert II, 1444-1457. John Hunyadi (Hunyadi Janos) governor (1446-1452), fought Turks, Czechs; died 1456.

Matthias I (Corvinus) son of Hunyadi, 1458-1490. Shared rule of Bohemia, captured Vienna, 1485, annexed Austria, Styria, Carinthia.

Ladislas II (king of Bohemia), 1490-1516.

Louis II, son, aged 10, 1516-1526. Wars with Suleiman, Turk. In 1527 Hungary was split between Ferdinand I, Archduke of Austria, bro.-in-law of Louis II, and John Zapolya of Transylvania. After Turkish invasion, 1547, Hungary was split between Ferdinand, Prince John Sigismund (Transylvania) and the Turks.

House of Hapsburg

Albert V of Austria, Hapsburg, crowned king of Hungary, Jan. 1438, Roman emperor, March, 1438, as Albert II; died 1439.

Frederick III, cousin, 1440-1493. Fought Turks.

Maximilian I, son, 1493-1519. Assumed title of Holy Roman Emperor (German), 1493.

Charles V, grandson, 1519-1556. King of Spain with mother co-regent; crowned Roman emperor at Aix, 1520. Confronted Luther at Worms; attempted church reform and religious conciliation; abdicated 1556.

Ferdinand I, king of Bohemia, 1526, of Hungary, 1527; disputed. German king, 1531. Crowned Roman emperor on abdication of brother Charles V, 1556.

Maximilian II, son, 1564-1576.

Rudolph II, son, 1576-1612.

Matthias, brother, 1612-1619, king of Bohemia and Hungary.

Ferdinand II of Styria, king of Bohemia, 1617, of Hungary, 1618, Roman emperor, 1619. Bohemian Protestants deposed him, elected Frederick V of Palatine, starting Thirty Years War.

Ferdinand III, son, king of Hungary, 1625, Bohemia, 1627, Roman emperor, 1637. Peace of Westphalia, 1648, ended war. Leopold I, 1658-1705; Joseph I, 1705-1711; Charles VI, 1711-1740.

Maria Theresa, daughter, 1740-1780, Archduchess of Austria, queen of Hungary; ousted pretender, Charles VII, crowned 1742; in 1745 obtained election of her husband Francis I as Roman emperor and co-regent (d. 1765). Fought Seven Years' War with Frederick II (the Great) of Prussia. Mother of Marie Antoinette, Queen of France.

Joseph II, son 1765-1790, Roman emperor, reformer; powers restricted by Empress Maria Theresa until her death, 1780. First partition of Poland. Leopold II, 1790-1792.

Francis II, son, 1792-1835. Fought Napoleon. Proclaimed first hereditary emperor of Austria, 1804. Forced to abdicate as Roman emperor, 1806; last use of title. Ferdinand I, son, 1835-1848, abdicated during revolution.

Austro-Hungarian Monarchy

Francis Joseph I, nephew, 1848-1916, emperor of Austria, king of Hungary. Dual monarchy of Austria-Hungary formed, 1867. After assassination of heir, Archduke Francis Ferdinand, June 28, 1914, Austrian diplomacy precipitated World War I.

Charles I, grand-nephew, 1916-1918, last emperor of Austria and king of Hungary. Abdicated Nov. 11-13, 1918, died 1922.

Rulers of Prussia

Nucleus of Prussia was the Mark of Brandenburg. First margrave was Albert the Bear (Albrecht), 1134-1170. First Hohenzollern margrave was Frederick, burgrave of Nuremberg, 1417-1440.

Frederick William, 1640-1688, the Great Elector. Son, Frederick III, 1688-1713, was crowned King Frederick of Prussia, 1701.

Frederick William I, son, 1713-1740.

Frederick II, the Great, son, 1740-1786, annexed Silesia part of Austria.

Frederick William II, nephew, 1786-1797.

Frederick William III, son, 1797-1840. Napoleonic wars.

Frederick William IV, son, 1840-1861. Uprising of 1848 and first parliament and constitution.

Second and Third Reich

William I, 1861-1888, brother. Annexation of Schleswig and Hanover; Franco-Prussian war, 1870-71, proclamation of German Reich, Jan. 18, 1871, at Versailles; William, German emperor (Deutscher Kaiser), Bismarck, chancellor.

Frederick III, son, 1888.

William II, son, 1888-1918. Led Germany in World War I, abdicated as German emperor and king of Prussia, Nov. 9, 1918. Died in exile in Netherlands June 4, 1941. Minor rulers of Bavaria, Saxony, Wurttemberg also abdicated.

Germany proclaimed a republic at Weimar, July 1, 1919. Presidents: Frederick Ebert, 1919-1925, Paul von Hindenburg-Beneckendorff, 1925, reelected 1932, d. Aug. 2, 1934. Adolf Hitler, chancellor, chosen successor as Leader-Chancellor (Fuehrer & Reichskanzler) of Third Reich. Annexed Austria, March, 1938. Precipitated World War II, 1939-1945. Committed suicide April 30, 1945.

Rulers of France: Kings, Queens, Presidents

Caesar to Charlemagne

Julius Caesar subdued the Gauls, native tribes of Gaul (France) 57 to 52 BC. The Romans ruled 500 years. The Franks, a Teutonic tribe, reached the Somme from the East ca. 250 AD. By the 5th century the Merovingian Franks ousted the Romans. In 451 AD, with the help of Visigoths, Burgundians and others, they defeated Attila and the Huns at Chalons-sur-Marne.

Childeric I became leader of the Merovingians 458 AD. His son Clovis I (Chlodwig, Ludwig, Louis), crowned 481, founded the dynasty. After defeating the Alemanni (Germans) 496, he was baptized a Christian and made Paris his capital. His line ruled until Childeric III was deposed, 751.

The West Merovingians were called Neustrians, the eastern Austrasians. Pepin of Herstal (687-714) major domus, or head of the palace, of Austrasia, took over Neustria as dux (leader) of the Franks. Pepin's son, Charles, called Martel (the Hammer) defeated the Saracens at Tours-Poitiers, 732; was succeeded by his son, Pepin the Short, 741, who deposed Childeric III and ruled as king until 768.

His son, Charlemagne, or Charles the Great (742-814) became king of the Franks, 768, with his brother Carloman, who died 771. He ruled France, Germany, parts of Italy, Spain, Austria, and enforced Christianity. Crowned Emperor of the Romans by Pope Leo III in St. Peter's, Rome, Dec. 25, 800 AD. Succeeded by son, Louis I the Pious, 814. At death, 840, Louis left empire to sons, Lothair (Roman emperor); Pepin I (king of Aquitaine); Louis II (of Germany); Charles the Bald (France). They quarreled and by the peace of Verdun, 843, divided the empire.

AD Name, year of accession

The Carolingians

843 Charles I (the Bald), Roman Emperor, 875
877 Louis II (the Stammerer), son
879 Louis III (died 882) and Carloman, brothers
885 Charles II (the Fat), Roman Emperor, 881
888 Eudes (Odo) elected by nobles
898 Charles III (the Simple), son of Louis II, defeated by
922 Robert, brother of Eudes, killed in war
923 Rudolph (Raoul) Duke of Burgundy
936 Louis IV, son of Charles III
954 Lothair, son, aged 13, defeated by Capet
986 Louis V (the Sluggard), left no heirs

The Capets

987 Hugh Capet, son of Hugh the Great
996 Robert II (the Wise), his son
1031 Henry I, his son
1060 Philip I (the Fair), son
1108 Louis VI (the Fat), son

1137 Louis VII (the Younger), son
1180 Philip II (Augustus), son, crowned at Reims
1223 Louis VIII (the Lion), son
1226 Louis IX, crusader; Louis III (1214-1270) reigned 44 years, arbitrated disputes with English King Henry III; led crusades, 1248 (captured in Egypt 1250) and 1270, when he died of plague in Tunis. Canonized 1297 as St. Louis.
1270 Philip III (the Hardy), son
1285 Philip IV (the Fair), son, king at 17
1314 Louis X (the Headstrong), son. His posthumous son, John I, lived only 7 days
1316 Philip V (the Tall), brother of Louis X
1322 Charles IV (the Fair), brother of Louis X

House of Valois

1328 Philip VI (of Valois), grandson of Philip III
1350 John II (the Good), his son, retired to England
1364 Charles V (the Wise), son
1380 Charles VI (the Beloved), son
1422 Charles VII (the Victorious), son. In 1429 Joan of Arc (Jeanne d'Arc) promised Charles to oust the English, who occupied northern France. Joan won at Orleans and Patay and had Charles crowned at Reims July 17, 1429. Joan was captured May 24, 1430, and executed May 30, 1431, at Rouen for heresy. Charles ordered her rehabilitation, effected 1455.
1461 Louis XI (the Cruel), son, civil reformer
1483 Charles VIII (the Affable), son
1498 Louis XII, great-grandson of Charles V
1515 Francis I, of Angouleme, nephew, son-in-law. Francis I (1494-1547) reigned 32 years, fought 4 big wars, was patron of the arts, aided Cellini, del Sarto, Leonardo da Vinci, Rabelais, embellished Fontainebleau.
1547 Henry II, son, killed at a joust in a tournament. He was the husband of Catherine de Medicis (1519-1589) and the lover of Diane de Poitiers (1499-1566). Catherine was born in Florence, daughter of Lorenzo de Medicis. By her marriage to Henry II she became the mother of Francis II, Charles IX, Henry III and Queen Margaret (Reine Margot) wife of Henry IV. She persuaded Charles IX to order the massacre of Huguenots on the Feast of St. Bartholomew, Aug. 24, 1572, the day her daughter was married to Henry of Navarre.
1559 Francis II, son. In 1548, Mary, Queen of Scots since infancy, was betrothed when 6 to Francis, aged 4. They were married 1558. Francis died 1560, aged 16; Mary ruled Scotland, abdicated 1567.
1560 Charles IX, brother
1574 Henry III, brother, assassinated

House of Bourbon

1589 Henry IV, of Navarre, assassinated. Henry IV made enemies when he gave tolerance to Protestants by Edict of
Nantes, 1598. He was grandson of Queen Margaret of
Navarre, literary patron. He married Margaret of Valois,
daughter of Henry II and Catherine de Medicis; was divorced; in 1600 married Marie de Medicis, who became
Regent of France, 1610-17 for her son, Louis XIII, but
was exiled by Richelieu, 1631.

1610 Louis XIII (the Just), son. Louis XIII (1601-1643) married
Anne of Austria. His ministers were Cardinals Richelieu
and Mazarin.

1643 Louis XIV (The Grand Monarch), son. Louis XIV was king
72 years. He exhausted a prosperous country in wars for
thrones and territory. By revoking the Edict of Nantes
(1685) he caused the emigration of the Huguenots. He
said: "I am the state."

1715 Louis XV, great-grandson. Louis XV married a Polish prin-
cess; lost Canada to the English. His favorites, Mme.
Pompadour and Mme. Du Barry, influenced policies.
Noted for saying "After me, the deluge".

1774 Louis XVI, grandson; married Marie Antoinette, daughter
of Empress Maria Therese of Austria. King and queen
beheaded by Revolution, 1793. Their son, called Louis
XVII, died in prison, never ruled.

First Republic

1792 National Convention of the French Revolution
1795 Directory, under Barras and others
1799 Consulate, Napoleon Bonaparte, first consul. Elected
consul for life, 1802.

First Empire

1804 Napoleon I, emperor. Josephine (de Beauharnais) empress, 1804-09; Marie Louise, empress, 1810-1814. Her
son, Francois (1811-1832), titular King of Rome, later
Duke de Reichstadt and "Napoleon II," never ruled. Napoleon abdicated 1814, died 1821.

Bourbons Restored

1814 Louis XVIII king; brother of Louis XVI.
1824 Charles X, brother; reactionary; deposed by the July
Revolution, 1830.

House of Orleans

1830 Louis-Philippe, the "citizen king."

Second Republic

1848 Louis Napoleon Bonaparte, president, nephew of Napoleon I. He became:

Second Empire

1852 Napoleon III, emperor; Eugenie (de Montijo) empress.
Lost Franco-Prussian war, deposed 1870. Son, Prince
Imperial (1856-79), died in Zulu War. Eugenie died 1920.

Third Republic—Presidents

1871 Thiers, Louis Adolphe (1797-1877)
1873 MacMahon, Marshal Patrice M. de (1808-1893)
1879 Grevy, Paul J. (1807-1891)
1887 Sadi-Carnot, M. (1837-1894), assassinated
1894 Casimir-Perier, Jean P. P. (1847-1907)
1895 Faure, Francois Felix (1841-1899)
1899 Loubet, Emile (1838-1929)
1906 Fallieres, C. Armand (1841-1931)
1913 Poincare, Raymond (1860-1934)
1920 Deschanel, Paul (1856-1922)
1920 Millerand, Alexandre (1859-1943)
1924 Doumergue, Gaston (1863-1937)
1931 Doumer, Paul (1857-1932), assassinated
1932 Lebrun, Albert (1871-1950), resigned 1940
1940 **Vichy govt.** under German armistice: Henri Philippe Pe-
tain (1856-1951) Chief of State, 1940-1944.
Provisional govt. after liberation: Charles de Gaulle
(1890-1970) Oct. 1944-Jan. 21, 1946; Felix Gouin
(1884-1977) Jan. 23, 1946; Georges Bidault (1899-1983)
June 24, 1946.

Fourth Republic—Presidents

1947 Auriol, Vincent (1884-1966)
1954 Coty, Rene (1882-1962)

Fifth Republic—Presidents

1959 de Gaulle, Charles Andre J. M. (1890-1970)
1969 Pompidou, Georges (1911-1974)
1974 Giscard d'Estaing, Valery (1926-   )
1981 Mitterrand, Francois (1916-   )

Rulers of Poland

House of Piasts

Miesko I, 962?-992; Poland Christianized 966. Expansion under 3 Boleslavs: I, 992-1025, son, crowned king 1024; II,
1058-1079, great-grandson, exiled after killing bishop Stanislav
who became chief patron saint of Poland: III, 1106-1138,
nephew, divided Poland among 4 sons eldest suzerain.
1138-1306, feudal division. 1226 founding in Prussia of military
order Teutonic Knights. 1226 invasion by Tartars/Mongols.
Vladislav I, 1306-1333, reunited most Polish territories,
crowned king 1320. Casimir III the Great, 1333-1370, son, developed economic, cultural life, foreign policy.

House of Anjou

Louis I, 1370-1382, nephew/identical with Louis I of Hungary.
Jadwiga, 1384-1399, daughter, married 1386 Jagiello, Grand
Duke of Lituania.

House of Jagelloneans

Vladislav II, 1386-1434, Christianized Lituania, founded per-
sonal union between Poland & Lituania. Defeated 1410 Teutonic
Knights at Grunwald.
Vladislav III, 1434-1444, son, simultaneously king of Hungary.
Fought Turks, killed 1444 in battle of Varna.
Casimir IV, 1446-1492, brother, competed with Hapsburgs,
put son Vladislav on throne of Bohemia, later also of Hungary.
Sigismund I, 1506-1548, brother, patronized science & arts,
his & son's reign "Golden Age."
Sigismund II, 1548-1572, son, established 1569 real union of
Poland and Lituania (lasted until 1795).

Elective kings

Polish nobles proclaimed 1572 Poland a Republic headed by
king to be elected by whole nobility.
Stephen Batory, 1576-1586, duke of Transylvania, married

Ann, sister of Sigismund II August. Fought Russians.
Sigismund III Vasa, 1587-1632, nephew of Sigismund II.
1592-1598 also king of Sweden. His generals fought Russians,
Turks.
Vladislav II Vasa, 1632-1648, son. Fought Russians.
John II Casimir Vasa, 1648-1668, brother. Fought Cossacks,
Swedes, Russians, Turks, Tartars (the "Deluge"). Abdicated
1668.
John III Sobieski, 1674-1696. Won Vienna from Turks, 1683.
Stanislav II, 1764-1795, last king. Encouraged reforms; 1791
1st modern Constitution in Europe. 1772, 1793, 1795 Poland
partitioned among Russia, Prussia, Austria. Unsuccessful insur-
rection against foreign invasion 1794 under Kosciuszko, Amer-
Polish gen.

1795-1918 Poland under foreign rule

1807-1815 Grand Duchy of Warsaw created by Napoleon I,
Frederick August of Saxony grand duke.
1815 Congress of Vienna proclaimed part of Poland "King-
dom" in personal union with Russia.
Polish uprisings: 1830 against Russia, 1846, 1848 against
Austria, 1863 against Russia—all repressed.

1918-1939 Second Republic

1918-1922 Head of State Jozef Pilsudski. Presidents: Gabriel
Narutowicz 1933, assassinated. Stanislav Wojsiechowski
1922-1926, had to abdicate after Pilsudski's coup d'état. Ignacy
Moscicki, 1926-1939, ruled with Pilsudski as (until 1935) virtual
dictator.

1939-1945 Poland under foreign occupation

Nazi aggression Sept. 1939. Polish govt.-in-exile, first in
France, then in England. Vladislav Raczkiewicz pres., Gen. Vladislav Sikorski, then Stanislav Mikolajczyk, prime ministers. Polish Committee of Natl. Liberation proclaimed at Lublin July 1944,
transformed into govt. Jan. 1, 1945.

Rulers of Denmark, Sweden, Norway

Denmark

Earliest rulers invaded Britain; King Canute, who ruled in London 1016-1035, was most famous. The Valdemars furnished kings until the 15th century. In 1282 the Danes won the first national assembly, Danehof, from King Erik V.

Most redoubtable medieval character was Margaret, daughter of Valdemar IV, born 1353, married at 10 to King Haakon VI of Norway. In 1376 she had her first infant son Olaf made king of Denmark. After his death, 1387, she was regent of Denmark and Norway. In 1388 Sweden accepted her as sovereign. In 1389 she made her grand-nephew, Duke Erik of Pomerania, titular king of Denmark, Sweden, and Norway, with herself as regent. In 1397 she effected the Union of Kalmar of the three kingdoms and had Erik VII crowned. In 1439 the three kingdoms deposed him and elected, 1440, Christopher of Bavaria king (Christopher III). On his death, 1448, the union broke up.

Succeeding rulers were unable to enforce their claims as rulers of Sweden until 1520, when Christian II conquered Sweden. He was thrown out 1522, and in 1523 Gustavus Vasa united Sweden. Denmark continued to dominate Norway until the Napoleonic wars, when Frederick VI, 1808-1839, joined the Napoleonic cause after Britain had destroyed the Danish fleet, 1807. In 1814 he was forced to cede Norway to Sweden and Helgoland to Britain, receiving Lauenburg. Successors Christian VIII, 1839; Frederick VII, 1848; Christian IX, 1863; Frederick VIII, 1906; Christian X, 1912; Frederick IX, 1947; Margrethe II, 1972.

Sweden

Early kings ruled at Uppsala, but did not dominate the country. Sverker, c1130-c1156, united the Swedes and Goths. In 1435 Sweden obtained the Riksdag, or parliament. After the Union of Kalmar, 1397, the Danes either ruled or harried the country until Christian II of Denmark conquered it anew, 1520. This led to a rising under Gustavus Vasa, who ruled Sweden 1523-1560, and established an independent kingdom. Charles IX, 1599-1611, crowned 1604, conquered Moscow. Gustavus II Adolphus, 1611-1632, was called the Lion of the North. Later rulers: Christina, 1632; Charles X, Gustavus 1654; Charles XI, 1660; Charles XII (invader of Russia and Poland, defeated at Poltava, June 28, 1709), 1697; Ulrika Eleanora, sister, elected queen 1718; Frederick I (of Hesse), her husband, 1720; Adolphus Frederick, 1751; Gustavus III, 1771; Gustavus IV Adolphus, 1792; Charles XIII, 1809. (Union with Norway began 1814.) Charles XIV John, 1818. He was Jean Bernadotte, Napoleon's Prince of Ponte Corvo, elected 1810 to succeed Charles XIII. He founded the present dynasty: Oscar I, 1844, Charles XV, 1859; Oscar II, 1872; Gustavus V, 1907; Gustav VI Adolf, 1950; Carl XVI Gustaf, 1973.

Norway

Overcoming many rivals, Harald Haarfager, 872-930, conquered Norway, Orkneys, and Shetlands; Olaf I, great-grandson, 995-1000, brought Christianity into Norway, Iceland, and Greenland. In 1035 Magnus the Good also became king of Denmark. Haakon V; 1299-1319, had married his daughter to Erik of Sweden. Their son, Magnus, became ruler of Norway and Sweden at 6. His son, Haakon VI, married Margaret of Denmark; their son Olaf IV became king of Norway and Denmark, followed by Margaret's regency and the Union of Kalmar, 1397.

In 1450 Norway became subservient to Denmark. Christian IV, 1588-1648, founded Christiania, now Oslo. After Napoleonic wars, when Denmark ceded Norway to Sweden, a strong nationalist movement forced recognition of Norway as an independent kingdom united with Sweden under the Swedish kings, 1814-1905. In 1905 the union was dissolved and Prince Carl of Denmark became Haakon VII. He died Sept. 21, 1957, aged 85; succeeded by son, Olav V, b. July 2, 1903.

Rulers of Russia; Premiers of the USSR

First ruler to consolidate Slavic tribes was Rurik, leader of the Russians who established himself at Novgorod, 862 A.D. He and his immediate successors had Scandinavian affiliations. They moved to Kiev after 972 AD and ruled as Dukes of Kiev. In 988 Vladimir was converted and adopted the Byzantine Greek Orthodox service, later modified by Slav influences. Important as organizer and lawgiver was Yaroslav, 1019-1054, whose daughters married kings of Norway, Hungary, and France. His grandson, Vladimir II (Monomakh), 1113-1125, was progenitor of several rulers, but in 1169 Andrew Bogolubski overthrew Kiev and began the line known as Grand Dukes of Vladimir.

Of the Grand Dukes of Vladimir, Alexander Nevsky, 1246-1263, had a son, Daniel, first to be called Duke of Muscovy (Moscow) who ruled 1294-1303. His successors became Grand Dukes of Muscovy. After Dmitri III Donskoi defeated the Tartars in 1380, they also became Grand Dukes of all Russia. Independence of the Tartars and considerable territorial expansion were achieved under Ivan III, 1462-1505.

Tsars of Muscovy—Ivan III was referred to in church ritual as Tsar. He married Sofia, niece of the last Byzantine emperor. His successor, Basil III, died in 1533 when Basil's son Ivan was only 3. He became Ivan IV, "the Terrible"; crowned 1547 as Tsar of all the Russias, ruled till 1584. Under the weak rule of his son, Feodor I, 1584-1598, Boris Godunov had control. The dynasty died, and after years of tribal strife and intervention by Polish and Swedish armies, the Russians united under 17-year-old Michael Romanov, distantly related to the first wife of Ivan IV. He ruled 1613-1645 and established the Romanov line. Fourth ruler after Michael was Peter I.

Tsars, or Emperors of Russia (Romanovs)—Peter I, 1682-1725, known as Peter the Great, took title of Emperor in 1721. His successors and dates of accession were: Catherine, his widow, 1725; Peter II, his grandson, 1727-1730; Anne, Duchess of Courland, 1730, daughter of Peter the Great's brother, Tsar Ivan V; Ivan VI, 1740-1741, great-grandson of Ivan V, child, kept in prison and murdered 1764; Elizabeth, daughter of Peter I, 1741; Peter III, grandson of Peter I, 1761, deposed 1762 for his consort, Catherine II, former princess of Anhalt Zerbst (Germany) who is known as Catherine the Great, 1762-1796; Paul I, her son, 1796, killed 1801; Alexander I, son of Paul, 1801-1825, defeated Napoleon; Nicholas I, his brother, 1825; Alexander II, son of Nicholas, 1855, assassinated 1881 by terrorists; Alexander III, son, 1881-1894.

Nicholas II, son, 1894-1917, last Tsar of Russia, was forced to abdicate by the Revolution that followed losses to Germany in WWI. The Tsar, the Empress, the Tsesarevich (Crown Prince) and the Tsar's 4 daughters were murdered by the Bolsheviks in Ekaterinburg, July 16, 1918.

Provisional Government—Prince Georgi Lvov and Alexander Kerensky, premiers, 1917.

Union of Soviet Socialist Republics

Bolshevik Revolution, Nov. 7, 1917, displaced Kerensky; council of People's Commissars formed, Lenin (Vladimir Ilyich Ulyanov), premier. Lenin died Jan. 21, 1924. Aleksei Rykov (executed 1938) and V. M. Molotov held the office, but actual ruler was Joseph Stalin (Joseph Vissarionovich Djugashvili), general secretary of the Central Committee of the Communist Party. Stalin became president of the Council of Ministers (premier) May 7, 1941, died Mar. 5, 1953. Succeeded by Georgi M. Malenkov, as head of the Council and premier and Nikita S. Khrushchev, first secretary of the Central Committee. Malenkov resigned Feb. 8, 1955, became deputy premier, was dropped July 3, 1957. Marshal Nikolai A. Bulganin became premier Feb. 8, 1955; was demoted and Khrushchev became premier Mar. 27 1958. Khrushchev was ousted Oct. 14-15, 1964, replaced by Leonid I. Brezhnev as first secretary of the party and by Aleksei N. Kosygin as premier. On June 16, 1977, Brezhnev took office as president. Brezhnev died Nov. 10, 1982; 2 days later the Central Committee unanimously elected former KGB head Yuri V. Andropov president. Andropov died Feb. 9, 1984; on Feb. 13, Konstantin U. Chernenko was chosen by Central Committee to succeed Andropov as its general secretary. Chernenko died Mar. 10, 1985. On Mar. 11, he was succeeded as general secretary by Mikhail Gorbachev.

Rulers of Spain

From 8th to 11th centuries Spain was dominated by the Moors (Arabs and Berbers). The Christian reconquest established small competing kingdoms of the Asturias, Aragon, Castile, Catalonia, Leon, Navarre, and Valencia. In 1474 Isabella (Isabel), b. 1451, became Queen of Castile & Leon. Her husband, Ferdinand, b. 1452, inherited Aragon 1479, with Catalonia, Valencia, and the Balearic Islands, became Ferdinand V of Castile. By Isabella's request Pope Sixtus IV established the Inquisition, 1478. Last Moorish kingdom, Granada, fell 1492. Columbus opened New World of colonies, 1492. Isabella died 1504, succeeded by her daughter, Juana "the Mad," but Ferdinand ruled until his death 1516.

Charles I, b. 1500, son of Juana and grandson of Ferdinand and Isabella, and of Maximilian I of Hapsburg; succeeded later as Holy Roman Emperor, Charles V, 1520; abdicated 1556. Philip II, son, 1556-1598, inherited only Spanish throne; conquered Portugal, fought Turks, persecuted non-Catholics, sent Armada against England. Was briefly married to Mary I of England, 1554-1558. Succession: Philip III, 1598-1621; Philip IV, 1621-1665; Charles II, 1665-1700, left Spain to Philip of Anjou, grandson of Louis XIV, who as Philip V, 1700-1746, founded Bourbon dynasty. Ferdinand VI, 1746-1759; Charles III, 1759-1788; Charles IV, 1788-1808, abdicated.

Napoleon now dominated politics and made his brother Joseph King of Spain 1808, but the Spanish ousted him finally in 1813. Ferdinand VII, 1808, 1814-1833, lost American colonies; succeeded by daughter Isabella II, aged 3, with wife Maria Christina of Naples regent until 1843. Isabella

deposed by revolution 1868. Elected king by the Cortes, Amadeo of Savoy, 1870; abdicated 1873. First republic, 1873-1874. Alphonso XII, son of Isabella, 1875-1885. His posthumous son was Alphonso XIII, with his mother, Queen Maria Christina regent; Spanish-American war, Spain lost Cuba, gave up Puerto Rico, Philippines, Sulu Is., Marianas. Alphonso took throne 1902, aged 16, married British Princess Victoria Eugenia of Battenberg. The dictatorship of Primo de Rivera, 1923-30, precipitated the revolution of 1931. Alphonso agreed to leave without formal abdication. The monarchy was abolished and the second republic established, with strong socialist backing. Presidents were Niceto Alcala Zamora, to 1936, when Manuel Azaña was chosen.

In July, 1936, the army in Morocco revolted against the government and General Francisco Franco led the troops into Spain. The revolution succeeded by Feb., 1939, when Azaña resigned. Franco became chief of state, with provisions that if he was incapacitated the Regency Council by two-thirds vote may propose a king to the Cortes, which must have a two-thirds majority to elect him.

Alphonso XIII died in Rome Feb. 28, 1941, aged 54. His property and citizenship had been restored.

A succession law restoring the monarchy was approved in a 1947 referendum. Prince Juan Carlos, son of the pretender to the throne, was designated by Franco and the Cortes in 1969 as the future king and chief of state. Upon Franco's death, Nov. 20, 1975, Juan Carlos was proclaimed king, Nov. 22, 1975.

Rulers of the Netherlands and Belgium

The Netherlands (Holland)

William Frederick, Prince of Orange, led a revolt against French rule, 1813, and was crowned King of the Netherlands, 1815. Belgium seceded Oct. 4, 1830, after a revolt, and formed a separate government. The change was ratified by the two kingdoms by treaty Apr. 19, 1839.

Succession: William II, son, 1840; William III, son, 1849; Wilhelmina, daughter of William III and his 2d wife Princess Emma of Waldeck, 1890; Wilhelmina abdicated, Sept. 4, 1948, in favor of daughter, Juliana. Juliana abdicated Apr. 30, 1980, in favor of daughter, Beatrix.

Belgium

A national congress elected Prince Leopold of Saxe-Coburg King; he took the throne July 21, 1831, as Leopold I. Succession: Leopold II, son 1865; Albert I, nephew of Leopold II, 1909; Leopold III, son of Albert, 1934; Prince Charles, Regent 1944; Leopold returned 1950, yielded powers to son Baudouin, Prince Royal, Aug. 6, 1950, abdicated July 16, 1951. Baudouin I took throne July 17, 1951.

For political history prior to 1830 see articles on the Netherlands and Belgium.

Governments of China

(Until 221 BC and frequently thereafter, China was not a unified state. Where dynastic dates overlap, the rulers or events referred to appeared in different areas of China.)

Hsia	c1994BC	c1523BC	ture; capital: Sian)	618	906
Shang	c1523	c1028	Five Dynasties (Yellow River basin)	902	960
Western Chou	c1027	770	Ten Kingdoms (southern China)	907	979
Eastern Chou	770	256	Liao (Khitan Mongols; capital: Peking)	947	1125
Warring States	403	222			
Ch'in (first unified empire)	221	206	Sung	960	1279
Han	202BC	220AD	Northern Sung (reunified central and southern China)	960	1126
Western Han (expanded Chinese state beyond the Yellow and Yangtze River valleys)	202BC	9AD	Western Hsai (non-Chinese rulers in northwest)	990	1227
Hsin (Wang Mang, usurper)	9AD	23AD	Chin (Tartars; drove Sung out of central China)	1115	1234
Eastern Han (expanded Chinese state into Indo-China and Turkestan)	25	220	Yuan (Mongols; Kublai Khan made Peking his capital in 1267)	1271	1368
Three Kingdoms (Wei, Shu, Wu)	220	265	Ming (China reunified under Chinese rule; capital: Nanking, then Peking in 1420)	1368	1644
Chin (western)	265	317			
(eastern)	317	420	Ch'ing (Manchus, descendents of Tartars)	1644	1911
Northern Dynasties (followed several short-lived governments by Turks, Mongols, etc.)	386	581	Republic (disunity; provincial rulers, warlords)	1912	1949
Southern Dynasties (capital: Nanking)	420	589	People's Republic of China (Nationalist China established on Taiwan)	1949	—
Sui (reunified China)	581	618			
Tang (a golden age of Chinese cul-					

Leaders in the South American Wars of Liberation

Simon Bolivar (1783-1830), Jose Francisco de San Martin (1778-1850), and Francisco Antonio Gabriel Miranda (1750-1816), are among the heroes of the early 19th century struggles of South American nations to free themselves from Spain. All three, and their contemporaries, operated in periods of intense factional strife, during which soldiers and civilians suffered.

Miranda, a Venezuelan, who had served with the French in the American Revolution and commanded parts of the French Revolutionary armies in the Netherlands, attempted to start a revolt in Venezuela in 1806 and failed. In 1810, with British and American backing, he returned and was briefly a dictator, until the British withdrew their support. In 1812 he was overcome by the royalists in Venezuela and taken prisoner, dying in a Spanish prison in 1816.

San Martin was born in Argentina and during 1789-1811 served in campaigns of the Spanish armies in Europe and Africa. He first joined the independence movement in Argentina in 1812 and then in 1817 invaded Chile with 4000 men over the high mountain passes. Here he and General Bernardo O'Higgins (1778-1842) defeated the Spaniards at Chacabuco, 1817, and O'Higgins was named Liberator and became first director of Chile, 1817-1823. In 1821 San Martin occupied Lima and Callao, Peru, and became protector of Peru.

Bolivar, the greatest leader of South American liberation from Spain, was born in Venezuela, the son of an aristocratic family. His organizing and administrative abilities were superior and he foresaw many of the political difficul-

ties of the future. He first served under Miranda in 1812 and in 1813 captured Caracas, where he was named Liberator. Forced out next year by civil strife, he led a campaign that captured Bogota in 1814. In 1817 he was again in control of Venezuela and was named dictator. He organized Nueva Granada with the help of General Francisco de Paula Santander (1792-1840). By joining Nueva Granada, Venezuela, and the present terrain of Panama and Ecuador, the republic of Colombia was formed with Bolivar president. After numerous setbacks he decisively defeated the Spaniards in the second battle of Carabobo, Venezuela, June 24, 1821.

In May, 1822, Gen. Antonio Jose de Sucre, Bolivar's trusted lieutenant, took Quito. Bolivar went to Guayaquil to confer with San Martin, who resigned as protector of Peru and withdrew from politics. With a new army of Colombians and Peruvians Bolivar defeated the Spaniards in a saber battle at Junín in 1824 and cleared Peru.

De Sucre organized Charcas (Upper Peru) as Republica Bolivar (now Bolivia) and acted as president in place of Bolivar, who wrote its constitution. De Sucre defeated the Spanish faction of Peru at Ayacucho, Dec. 19, 1824.

Continued civil strife finally caused the Colombian federation to break apart. Santander turned against Bolivar, but the latter defeated him and banished him. In 1828 Bolivar gave up the presidency he had held precariously for 14 years. He became ill from tuberculosis and died Dec. 17, 1830. He was honored as the great liberator and is buried in the national pantheon in Caracas.

Noted World Political Leaders of the Past

Abu Bakr, 573-634, Mohammedan leader, first caliph, chosen successor to Mohammed.

Dean Acheson, 1893-1971, (U.S.) secretary of state, chief architect of cold war foreign policy.

Konrad Adenauer, 1876-1967, (G.) West German chancellor.

Emilio Aguinaldo, 1869-1964, (Philip.) revolutionary, fought against Spain and the U.S.

Akbar, 1542-1605, greatest Mogul emperor of India.

Salvador Allende Gossens, 1908-1973, (Chil.) president, advocate of democratic socialism.

Herbert H. Asquith, 1852-1928, (Br.) Liberal prime minister, instituted an advanced program of social reform.

Atahualpa, ?-1533, Inca (ruling chief) of Peru.

Kemal Atatürk, 1881-1938, (Turk.) founded modern Turkey.

Clement Attlee, 1883-1967, (Br.) Labour party leader, prime minister, enacted national health, nationalized many industries.

Mikhail Bakunin, 1814-1876, (R.) revolutionary, leading exponent of anarchism.

Arthur J. Balfour, 1848-1930, (Br.) as foreign secretary under Lloyd George issued Balfour Declaration expressing official British approval of Zionism.

Bernard M. Baruch, 1870-1965, (U.S.) financier, gvt. adviser.

Fulgencio Batista y Zaldivar, 1901-1973, (Cub.) ruler overthrown by Castro.

Lord Beaverbrook, 1879-1964, (Br.) financier, statesman, newspaper owner.

Eduard Benes, 1884-1948, (Czech.) president during interwar and post-WW II eras.

David Ben-Gurion, 1886-1973, (Isr.) first premier of Israel.

Lavrenti Beria, 1899-1953, (USSR) Communist leader prominent in political purges under Stalin.

Aneurin Bevan, 1897-1960, (Br.) Labour party leader.

Ernest Bevin, 1881-1951, (Br.) Labour party leader, foreign minister, helped lay foundation for NATO.

Otto von Bismarck, 1815-1898, (G.) statesman known as the Iron Chancellor, uniter of Germany, 1870.

Léon Blum, 1872-1950, (F.) socialist leader, writer, headed first Popular Front government.

Simón Bolivar, 1783-1830, (Venez.) South American revolutionary who liberated much of the continent from Spanish rule.

Cesare Borgia, 1476-1507, (It.) soldier, politician, an outstanding figure of the Italian Renaissance.

Leonid Brezhnev, 1906-1982, (USSR) leader of the Soviet Union, 1964-82.

Aristide Briand, 1862-1932, (F.) foreign minister, chief architect of Locarno Pact and anti-war Kellogg-Briand Pact.

Nikolai Bukharin, 1888-1938, (USSR) communist leader.

Robert Castlereagh, 1769-1822, (Br.) foreign secy, guided Grand Alliance against Napoleon.

Camillo Benso Cavour, 1810-1861, (It.) statesman, largely responsible for uniting Italy under the House of Savoy.

Austen Chamberlain, 1863-1937, (Br.) Conservative party leader, largely responsible for Locarno Pact of 1925.

Neville Chamberlain, 1869-1940, (Br.) Conservative prime minister whose appeasement of Hitler led to Munich Pact.

Winston Churchill, 1874-1965, (Br.) prime minister, soldier, author, guided Britain through WW II.

Galeazzo Ciano, 1903-1944, (It.) fascist foreign minister, helped create Rome-Berlin Axis, executed by Mussolini.

Henry Clay, 1777-1852, (U.S.) "The Great Compromiser," one of most influential pre-Civil War political leaders.

Georges Clemenceau, 1841-1929, (F.) twice premier, Wilson's chief antagonist at Paris Peace Conference after WW I.

Robert Clive, 1725-1774, (Br.) first administrator of Bengal, laid foundation for British Empire in India.

Jean Baptiste Colbert, 1619-1683, (F.) statesman, influential under Louis XIV, created the French navy.

Oliver Cromwell, 1599-1658, (Br.) Lord Protector of England, led parliamentary forces during Civil War.

Curzon of Kedleston, 1859-1925, (Br.) viceroy of India, foreign secretary, major force in dealing with post-WW I problems in Europe and Far East.

Édouard Daladier, 1884-1970, (F.) radical socialist politician, arrested by Vichy, interned by Germans until liberation in 1945.

Georges Danton, 1759-1794, (F.) a leading figure in the French Revolution.

Jefferson Davis, 1808-1889, (U.S.) president of the Confederate States of America.

Alcide De Gasperi, 1881-1954, (It.) premier, founder of the Christian Democratic party.

Charles DeGaulle, 1890-1970, (F.) general, statesman, and first president of the Fifth Republic.

Eamon De Valera, 1882-1975, (Ir.-U.S.) statesman, led fight for Irish independence.

Ngo Dinh Diem, 1901-1963, (Viet.) South Vietnamese president, assassinated in government take-over.

Benjamin Disraeli, 1804-1881, (Br.) prime minister, considered founder of modern Conservative party.

Engelbert Dollfuss, 1892-1934, (Aus.) chancellor, assassinated by Austrian Nazis.

Andrea Doria, 1466-1560, (It.) Genoese admiral, statesman, called "Father of Peace" and "Liberator of Genoa."

John Foster Dulles, 1888-1959, (U.S.) secretary of state under Eisenhower, cold war policy maker.

Friedrich Ebert, 1871-1925, (G.) Social Democratic movement leader, instrumental in bringing about Weimar constitution.

Sir Anthony Eden, 1897-1977, (Br.) foreign secretary, prime minister during Suez invasion of 1956.

Zhou En-lai, 1898-1976, (Chin.) diplomat, prime minister, a leading figure of the Chinese Communist party.

Ludwig Erhard, 1897-1977, (G.) economist, West German chancellor, led nation's economic rise after WW II.

Francisco Franco, 1892-1975, (Sp.) leader of rebel forces during Spanish Civil War and dictator of Spain.

Benjamin Franklin, 1706-1790, (U.S.) printer, publisher, author, inventor, scientist, diplomat.

Louis de Frontenac, 1620-1698, (F.) governor of New France (Canada); encouraged explorations, fought Iroquois.

Hugh Gaitskell, 1906-1963, (Br.) Labour party leader, major force in reversing its stand for unilateral disarmament.

Léon Gambetta, 1838-1882, (F.) statesman, politician, one of the founders of the Third Republic.

Indira Gandhi, 1917-1984, (Ind.) succeeded father, Jawaharlal Nehru, as prime minister, assassinated.

Mohandas K. Gandhi, 1869-1948, (Ind.) political leader, ascetic, led nationalist movement against British rule.

Giuseppe Garibaldi, 1807-1882, (It.) patriot, soldier, a leading figure in the Risorgimento, the Italian unification movement.

Klement Gottwald, 1896-1953 (Czech.) communist leader ushered communism into his country.

Genghis Khan, c. 1167-1227, brilliant Mongol conqueror, ruler of vast Asian empire.

David Lloyd George, 1863-1945, (Br.) Liberal party prime minister, laid foundations for modern welfare state.

William E. Gladstone, 1809-1898, (Br.) prime minister 4 times, dominant force of Liberal party from 1868 to 1894.

Paul Joseph Goebbels, 1897-1945, (G.) Nazi propagandist, master of mass psychology.

Che (Ernesto) Guevara, 1928-1967, (Arg.) guerilla leader, prominent in Cuban revolution, killed in Bolivia.

Dag Hammarskjold, 1905-1961, (Swed.) statesman, UN secretary general.

John Hancock, 1737-1793, (U.S.) revolutionary leader, first signer of Declaration of Independence.

Patrick Henry, 1736-1799, (U.S.) major revolutionary figure, remarkable orator.

Édouard Herriot, 1872-1957, (F.) Radical Socialist leader, twice premier, president of National Assembly.

Theodor Herzl, 1860-1904, (Aus.) founder of modern Zionism.

Heinrich Himmler, 1900-1945, (G.) chief of Nazi SS and Gestapo, primarily responsible for the Holocaust.

Paul von Hindenburg, 1847-1934, (G.) field marshal, president.

Adolf Hitler, 1889-1945, (G.) dictator, founder of National Socialism.

Ho Chi Minh, 1890-1969, (Viet.) North Vietnamese president, Vietnamese Communist leader, national hero.

Samuel Houston, 1793-1893, (U.S.) leader of struggle to win control of Texas from Mexico.

Hubert H. Humphrey, 1911-1978, (U.S.) Minnesota Democrat, senator, vice president, spent 32 years in public service.

Benito Juarez, 1806-1872, (Mex.) rallied countrymen against foreign threats, sought to create democratic, federal republic.

Jiang Kai-shek, 1887-1975, (Chin.) Nationalist Chinese president whose govt. was driven from mainland to Taiwan.

Robert F. Kennedy, 1925-1968, (U.S.) attorney general, senator, assassinated while seeking presidential nomination.

Aleksandr Kerensky, 1881-1970, (R.) revolutionary, served as premier after Feb. 1917 revolution until Bolshevik overthrow.

Nikita Khrushchev, 1894-1971, (USSR) premier, first secretary of Communist party, initiated de-Stalinization.

Lajos Kossuth, 1802-1894, (Hung.) principal figure in 1848 Hungarian revolution.

Kublai Khan, c. 1215-1294, Mongol emperor, founder of Yüan dynasty in China.

Béla Kun, 1886-c.1939, (Hung.) communist, member of 3d International, tried to foment worldwide revolution.

Pierre Laval, 1883-1945, (F.) politician, Vichy foreign minister, executed for treason.

Andrew Bonar Law, 1858-1923, (Br.) Conservative party politician, led opposition to Irish home rule.

Vladimir Ilyich Lenin (Ulyanov), 1870-1924, (USSR) revolutionary, founder of Bolshevism, Soviet leader 1917-1924.

Ferdinand de Lesseps, 1805-1894, (F.) diplomat, engineer, conceived idea of Suez Canal.

Liu Shao-ch'i, c.1898-1974, (Chin.) communist leader, fell from grace during "cultural revolution."

Maxim Litvinov, 1876-1951, (USSR) revolutionary, commissar of foreign affairs, favored cooperation with Western powers.

Henry Cabot Lodge, 1850-1924, (U.S.) Republican senator, led opposition to participation in League of Nations.

Rosa Luxemburg, 1871-1919, (G.) revolutionary leader of the German Social Democratic party and Spartacus party.

J. Ramsay MacDonald, 1866-1937, (Br.) first Labour party prime minister of Great Britain.

Harold MacMillan, 1895-1987 (Br.) prime minister of Great Britain, 1957-63.

Joseph R. McCarthy, 1908-1957, (U.S.) senator notorious for his witch hunt for communists in the government.

Makarios III, 1913-1977, (Cypr.) Greek Orthodox archbishop, first president of Cyprus.

Malcolm X (Malcolm Little), 1925-1965, (U.S.) black separatist leader, assassinated.

Jean Paul Marat, 1743-1793, (F.) revolutionary, politician, identified with radical Jacobins, assassinated.

José Marti, 1853-1895, (Cub.) patriot, poet, leader of Cuban struggle for independence.

Jan Masaryk, 1886-1948, (Czech.) foreign minister, died by mysterious suicide following communist coup.

Thomas G. Masaryk, 1850-1937, (Czech.) statesman, philosopher, first president of Czechoslovak Republic.

Jules Mazarin, 1602-1661, (F.) cardinal, statesman, prime minister under Louis XIII and queen regent Anne of Austria.

Tom Mboya, 1930-1969, (Kenyan) political leader, instrumental in securing independence for his country.

Cosimo I de' Medici, 1519-1574, (It.) Duke of Florence, grand duke of Tuscany.

Lorenzo de' Medici, the Magnificent, 1449-1492, (It.) merchant prince, a towering figure in Italian Renaissance.

Catherine de Medicis, 1519-1589, (F.) queen consort of Henry II, regent of France, influential in Catholic-Huguenot wars.

Golda Meir, 1898-1979, (Isr.) prime minister, 1969-74.

Klemens W.N.L. Metternich, 1773-1859, (Aus.) statesman, arbiter of post-Napoleonic Europe.

Anastas Mikoyan, 1895-1978, (USSR) prominent Soviet leader from 1917; president 1964-65.

Guy Mollet, 1905-1975, (F.) social politician, resistance leader.

Muhammad Ali, 1769?-1849, (Egypt), pasha, founder of dynasty that encouraged emergence of modern Egyptian state.

Benito Mussolini, 1883-1945, (It.) dictator and leader of the Italian fascist state.

Imre Nagy, c. 1895-1958, (Hung.) communist premier, assassinated after Soviets crushed 1956 uprising.

Gamal Abdel Nasser, 1918-1970, (Egypt.) leader of Arab unification, second Egyptian president.

Jawaharlal Nehru, 1889-1964, (Ind.) prime minister, guided India through its early years of independence.

Kwame Nkrumah, 1909-1972 (Ghan.) dictatorial prime minister, deposed in 1966.

Frederick North, 1732-1792, (Br.) prime minister, his inept policies led to loss of American colonies.

Daniel O'Connell, 1775-1847, (Ir.) political leader, known as The Liberator.

Omar, c.581-644, Mohammedan leader, 2d caliph, led Islam to become an imperial power.

Ignace Paderewski, 1860-1941, (Pol.) statesman, pianist, composer, briefly prime minister, an ardent patriot.

Viscount Palmerston, 1784-1865, (Br.) Whig-Liberal prime minister, foreign minister, embodied British nationalism.

George Papandreou, 1888-1968, (Gk.) Republican politician, served three times as prime minister.

Franz von Papen, 1879-1969, (G.) politician, played major role in overthrow of Weimar Republic and rise of Hitler.

Charles Stewart Parnell, 1846-1891, (Ir.) nationalist leader, "uncrowned king of Ireland."

Robert Peel, 1788-1850, (Br.) reformist prime minister, founder of Conservative party.

Juan Perón, 1895-1974, (Arg.) president, dictator.

Joseph Pilsudski, 1867-1935, (Pol.) statesman, instrumental in re-establishing Polish state in the 20th century.

William Pitt, the Elder, 1708-1778, (Br.) statesman, called the "Great Commoner," transformed Britain into imperial power.

William Pitt, the Younger, 1759-1806, (Br.) prime minister during French Revolutionary wars.

Georgi Plekhanov, 1857-1918, (R.) revolutionary, social philosopher, called "father of Russian Marxism."

Raymond Poincaré, 1860-1934, (F.) 9th president of the Republic, advocated harsh punishment of Germany after WW I.

Georges Pompidou, 1911-1974, (F.) Gaullist political leader, president from 1969 to 1974.

Grigori Potemkin, 1739-1791, (R.) field marshal, favorite of Catherine II.

Walter Rathenau, 1867-1922, (G.) industrialist, social theorist, statesman.

Paul Reynaud, 1878-1966, (F.) statesman, premier in 1940 at the time of France's defeat by Germany.

Syngman Rhee, 1875-1965, (Kor.) first president of the Republic of Korea.

Cecil Rhodes, 1853-1902, (Br.) imperialist, industrial magnate, established Rhodes scholarships in his will.

Cardinal de Richelieu, 1585-1642, (F.) statesman, known as "red eminence," chief minister to Louis XIII.

Maximilien Robespierre, 1758-1794, (F.) leading figure of French Revolution, responsible for much of Reign of Terror.

Nelson Rockefeller, 1908-1979, (U.S.) Republican gov. of N.Y., 1959-73; U.S. vice president, 1974-77.

Eleanor Roosevelt, 1884-1962, (U.S.) humanitarian, United Nations diplomat.

John Russell, 1792-1878, (Br.) Liberal prime minister during the Irish potato famine.

Anwar el-Sadat, 1918-1981, (Egypt) president, 1970-1981, promoted peace with Israel.

Antônio de O. Salazar, 1899-1970, (Port.) statesman, longtime dictator.

José de San Martin, 1778-1850, South American revolutionary, protector of Peru.

Eisaku Sato, 1901-1975, (Jap.) prime minister, presided over Japan's post-WW II emergence as major world power.

Ibn Saud, c. 1888-1953, (S. Arab.) founder of Saudi Arabia and its first king.

Philipp Scheidemann, 1865-1939, (G.) Social Democratic leader, first chancellor of the German republic.

Robert Schuman, 1886-1963, (F.) statesman, founded European Coal and Steel Community.

Kurt Schuschnigg, 1897-1977, (Aus.) chancellor, unsuccessful in stopping his country's annexation by Germany.

Haile Selassie, 1891-1975, (Eth.) emperor, maintained monarchy through invasion, occupation, internal resistance.

Carlo Sforza, 1872-1952, (It.) foreign minister, anti-fascist.

Jan C. Smuts, 1870-1950, (S.Af.) statesman, philosopher, soldier, prime minister.

Paul Henri Spaak, 1899-1972, (Belg.) statesman, socialist leader.

Joseph Stalin, 1879-1953, (USSR) Soviet dictator, 1924-53.

Adlai E. Stevenson, 1900-1965, (U.S.) Democratic leader, diplomat, Illinois governor, presidential candidate.

Gustav Stresemann, 1878-1929, (G.) chancellor, foreign minister, dedicated to regaining friendship for post-WW I Germany.

Sukarno, 1901-1970, (Indon.) dictatorial first president of the Indonesian republic.

Sun Yat-sen, 1866-1925, (Chin.) revolutionary, leader of Kuomintang, regarded as the father of modern China.

Robert A. Taft, 1889-1953, (U.S.) conservative Senate leader, called "Mr. Republican."

Charles de Talleyrand, 1754-1838, (F.) statesman, diplomat, the major force of the Congress of Vienna of 1814-15.

U Thant, 1909-1974, (Bur.) statesman, UN secretary-general.

Josip Broz Tito, 1892-1980, (Yug.) president of Yugoslavia from 1953, World War II guerrilla chief, postwar rival of Stalin, leader of 3d world movement.

Hideki Tojo, 1885-1948, (Jap.) statesman, soldier, prime minister during most of WW II.

François Toussaint L'Ouverture, c. 1744-1803, (Hait.) patriot, martyr, thwarted French colonial aims.

Leon Trotsky, 1879-1940, (USSR) revolutionary, founded Red Army, expelled from party in conflict with Stalin.

Rafael L. Trujillo Molina, 1891-1961, (Dom.) absolute dictator, assassinated.

Moise K. Tshombe, 1919-1969, (Cong.) politician, president of secessionist Katanga, premier of Republic of Congo (Zaire).

Walter Ulbricht, 1893-1973, (G.) communist leader of German Democratic Republic.

Eleutherios Venizelos, 1864-1936, (Gk.) most prominent Greek statesman in early 20th century; expanded territory.

Hendrik F. Verwoerd, 1901-1966, (S.Af.) prime minister, rigorously applied apartheid policy despite protest.

Robert Walpole, 1676-1745, (Br.) statesman, generally considered Britain's first prime minister.

Chaim Weizmann, 1874-1952, Zionist leader, scientist, first Israeli president.

Emiliano Zapata, c. 1879-1919, (Mex.) revolutionary, major influence on modern Mexico.

Mao Zedong, 1893-1976, (Chin.) chief Chinese Marxist theorist, soldier, led Chinese revolution establishing his nation as an important communist state.

Notable Military and Naval Leaders of the Past

Creighton Abrams, 1914-1974, (U.S.) commanded forces in Vietnam, 1968-72.

Harold Alexander, 1891-1969, (Br.) led Allied invasion of Italy, 1943.

Ethan Allen, 1738-1789, (U.S.) headed Green Mountain Boys; captured Ft. Ticonderoga, 1775.

Edmund Allenby, 1861-1936, (Br.) in Boer War, WW1; led Egyptian expeditionary force, 1917-18.

Benedict Arnold, 1741-1801, (U.S.) victorious at Saratoga; tried to betray West Point to British.

Henry "Hap" Arnold, 1886-1950, (U.S.) commanded Army Air Force in WW2.

Petr Bagration, 1765-1812, (R.) hero of Napoleonic wars.

John Barry, 1745-1803, (U.S.) won numerous sea battles during revolution.

Pierre Beauregard, 1818-1893, (U.S.) Confederate general ordered bombardment of Ft. Sumter that began the Civil War.

Gebhard v. Blücher, 1742-1819, (G.) helped defeat Napoleon at Waterloo.

Napoleon Bonaparte, 1769-1821, (F.) defeated Russia and Austria at Austerlitz, 1805; invaded Russia, 1812; defeated at Waterloo, 1815.

Edward Braddock, 1695-1755, (Br.) commanded forces in French and Indian War.

Omar N. Bradley, 1893-1981, (U.S.) headed U.S. ground troops in Normandy invasion, 1944.

John Burgoyne, 1722-1792, (Br.) defeated at Saratoga.

Claire Chennault, 1890-1958, (U.S.) headed Flying Tigers in WW2.

Mark Clark, 1896-1984, (U.S.) led forces in WW2 and Korean War.

Karl v. Clausewitz, 1780-1831, (G.) wrote books on military theory.

Henry Clinton, 1738-1795, (Br.) commander of forces in America, 1778-81.

Lucius D. Clay, 1897-1978, (U.S.) led Berlin airlift, 1948-49.

Charles Cornwallis, 1738-1805, (Br.) victorious at Brandywine, 1777; surrendered at Yorktown.

Crazy Horse, 1849-1877, (U.S.) Sioux war chief victorious at Little Big Horn.

George A. Custer, 1839-1876, (U.S.) defeated and killed at Little Big Horn.

Moshe Dayan, 1915-1981, (Isr.) directed campaigns in the 1967, 1973 wars.

Stephen Decatur, 1779-1820, (U.S.) naval hero of Barbary wars, War of 1812.

Anton Denikin, 1872-1947, (R.) led White forces in Russian civil war.

George Dewey, 1837-1917, (U.S.) destroyed Spanish fleet at Manila, 1898.

Hugh C. Dowding, 1883-1970, (Br.) headed RAF, 1936-40.

Jubal Early, 1816-1894, (U.S.) Confederate general led raid on Washington, 1864.

Dwight D. Eisenhower, 1890-1969, (U.S.) commanded Allied forces in Europe, WW2.

David Farragut, 1801-1870, (U.S.) Union admiral captured New Orleans, Mobile Bay.

Ferdinand Foch, 1851-1929, (F.) headed victorious Allied armies, 1918.

Nathan Bedford Forrest, 1821-1877, (U.S.) Confederate general led cavalry raids against Union supply lines.

Frederick the Great, 1712-1786, (G.) led Prussia in The Seven Years War.

Nathanael Greene, 1742-1786, (U.S.) defeated British in Southern campaign, 1780-81.

Charles G. Gordon, 1833-1885, (Br.) led forces in China; killed at Khartoum.

Horatio Gates, 1728-1806, (U.S.) commanded army at Saratoga.

Ulysses S. Grant, 1822-1885, (U.S.) headed Union army, 1864-65; forced Lee's surrender, 1865.

Heinz Guderian, 1888-1953, (G.) tank theorist led panzer forces in Poland, France, Russia.

Douglas Haig, 1861-1928, (Br.) led British armies in France, 1915-18.

William F. Halsey, 1882-1959, (U.S.) defeated Japanese fleet at Leyte Gulf, 1944.

Sir Arthur Travers Harris, 1895-1984, (Br.) led Britain's WWII bomber command.

Richard Howe, 1726-1799, (Br.) commanded navy in America, 1776-78; first of June victory against French, 1794.

William Howe, 1729-1814, (Br.) commanded forces in America, 1776-78.

Isaac Hull, 1773-1843, (U.S.) sunk British frigate Guerriere, 1812.

Thomas (Stonewall) Jackson, 1824-1863, (U.S.) Confederate general led forces in the Shenandoah Valley campaign.

Joseph Joffre, 1852-1931, (F.) headed Allied armies, won Battle of the Marne, 1914.

John Paul Jones, 1747-1792, (U.S.) raided British coast; commanded *Bonhomme Richard* in victory over Serapis, 1779.

Stephen Kearny, 1794-1848, (U.S.) headed Army of the West in Mexican War.

Ernest J. King, 1878-1956, (U.S.) chief naval strategist in WW2.

Horatio H. Kitchener, 1850-1916, (Br.) led forces in Boer War; victorious at Khartoum; organized army in WW1.

Lavrenti Kornilov, 1870-1918, (R.) Commander-in-Chief, 1917; led counter-revolutionary march on Petrograd.

Thaddeus Kosciusko, 1746-1817, (P.) aided American cause in revolution.

Mikhail Kutuzov, 1745-1813, (R.) fought French at Borodino, 1812; abandoned Moscow; forced French retreat.

Marquis de Lafayette, 1757-1834, (F.) aided American cause in the revolution.

Thomas E. Lawrence (of Arabia), 1888-1935, (Br.) organized revolt of Arabs against Turks in WW1.

Henry (Light-Horse Harry) Lee, 1756-1818, (U.S.) cavalry officer in revolution.

Robert E. Lee, 1807-1870, (U.S.) Confederate general defeated at Gettysburg; surrendered to Grant, 1865.

James Longstreet, 1821-1904, (U.S.) aided Lee at Gettysburg.

Douglas MacArthur, 1880-1964, (U.S.) commanded forces in SW Pacific in WW2; headed occupation forces in Japan, 1945-51; UN commander in Korean War.

Francis Marion, 1733-1795, (U.S.) led guerrilla actions in S.C. during revolution.

Duke of Marlborough, 1650-1722, (Br.) led forces against Louis XIV in War of the Spanish Sucession.

George C. Marshall, 1880-1959, (U.S.) chief of staff in WW2; authored Marshall Plan.

George B. McClellan, 1826-1885, (U.S.) Union general commanded Army of the Potomac, 1861-62.

George Meade, 1815-1872; (U.S.) commanded Union forces at Gettysburg.

Billy Mitchell, 1879-1936, (U.S.) air-power advocate; court-martialed for insubordination, later vindicated.

Helmuth v. Moltke, 1800-1891; (G.) victorious in Austro-Prussian, Franco-Prussian wars.

Louis de Montcalm, 1712-1759, (F.) headed troops in Canada; defeated at Quebec, 1759.

Bernard Law Montgomery, 1887-1976, (Br.) stopped German offensive at Alamein, 1942; helped plan Normandy invasion.

Daniel Morgan, 1736-1802, (U.S.) victorious at Cowpens, 1781.

Louis Mountbatten, 1900-1979, (Br.) Supreme Allied Commander of SE Asia, 1943-46.

Joachim Murat, 1767-1815, (F.) leader of cavalry at Marengo, 1800; Austerlitz, 1805; and Jena, 1806.

Horatio Nelson, 1758-1805, (Br.) naval commander destroyed French fleet at Trafalgar.

Michel Ney, 1769-1815, (F.) commanded forces in Switzerland, Austria, Russia; defeated at Waterloo.

Chester Nimitz, 1885-1966, (U.S.) commander of naval forces in Pacific in WW2.

George S. Patton, 1885-1945, (U.S.) led assault on Sicily, 1943; headed 3d Army invasion of German-occupied Europe.

Oliver Perry, 1785-1819, (U.S.) won Battle of Lake Erie in War of 1812.

John Pershing, 1860-1948, (U.S.) commanded Mexican border campaign, 1916; American expeditionary forces in WW1.

Henri Philippe Pétain, 1856-1951, (F.) defended Verdun, 1916; headed Vichy government in WW2.

George E. Pickett, 1825-1875, (U.S.) Confederate general famed for "charge" at Gettysburg.

Hyman Rickover, 1900-1986 (U.S.) father of the nuclear navy.

Erwin Rommel, 1891-1944, (G.) headed Afrika Korps.

Karl v. Rundstedt, 1875-1953, (G.) supreme commander in West, 1943-45.

Aleksandr Samsonov, 1859-1914, (R.) led invasion of E. Prussia, defeated at Tannenberg, 1914.

Winfield Scott, 1786-1866, (U.S.) hero of War of 1812; headed forces in Mexican war, took Mexico City.

Philip Sheridan, 1831-1888, (U.S.) Union cavalry officer headed Army of the Shenandoah, 1864-65.

William T. Sherman, 1820-1891, (U.S.) Union general sacked Atlanta during "march to the sea," 1864.

Carl Spaatz, 1891-1974, (U.S.) directed strategic bombing against Germany, later Japan, in WW2.

Raymond Spruance, 1886-1969, (U.S.) victorious at Midway Island, 1942.

Joseph W. Stilwell, 1883-1946, (U.S.) headed forces in the China, Burma, India theater in WW2.

J.E.B. Stuart, 1833-1864, (U.S.) Confederate cavalry commander.

George H. Thomas, 1816-1870, (U.S.) saved Union army at Chattanooga, 1863; victorious at Nashville, 1864.

Semyon Timoshenko, 1895-1970, (USSR) defended Moscow, Stalingrad; led winter offensive, 1942-43.

Alfred v. Tirpitz, 1849-1930, (G.) responsible for submarine blockade in WW1.

Jonathan M. Wainwright, 1883-1953, (U.S.) forced to surrender on Corregidor, 1942.

George Washington, 1732-1799, (U.S.) led Continental army, 1775-83.

Archibald Wavell, 1883-1950, (Br.) commanded forces in N. and E. Africa, and SE Asia in WW2.

Anthony Wayne, 1745-1796, (U.S.) captured Stony Point, 1779; defeated Indians at Fallen Timbers, 1794.

Duke of Wellington, 1769-1852, (Br.) defeated Napoleon at Waterloo.

James Wolfe, 1727-1759, (Br.) captured Quebec from French, 1759.

Georgi Zhukov, 1895-1974, (USSR) defended Moscow, 1941; led assault on Berlin.

Noted World Historians, Economists, and Social Reformers of the Past

Francis Bacon, 1561-1626, (Br.) philosopher, essayist, and statesman.

Thomas Barnardo, 1845-1905, (Br.) social reformer, pioneered in the care of destitute children.

Bede (the Venerable), c.673-735, (Br.) scholar, historian.

Louis Blanc, 1811-1882, (F.) Socialist leader and historian whose ideas were a link between utopian and Marxist socialism.

Van Wyck Brooks, 1886-1963, (U.S.) cultural historian, critic.

Edmund Burke, 1729-1797, (Ir.) British parliamentarian and political philosopher; influenced many Federalists.

Thomas Carlyle, 1795-1881, (Sc.) philosopher, historian, and critic.

Benedetto Croce, 1866-1952, (It.) philosopher, statesman, and historian.

Emile Durkheim, 1858-1917, (F.) a founder of modern sociology.

Friedrich Engels, 1820-1895, (G.) political writer, with Marx wrote the *Communist Manifesto*.

Irving Fisher, 1867-1947, (U.S.) economist, contributed to the development of modern monetary theory.

Charles Fourier, 1772-1837, (F.) utopian socialist.

Henry George, 1839-1897, (U.S.) economist, reformer, led single-tax movement.

Edward Gibbon, 1737-1794, (Br.) historian, wrote *The History of the Decline and Fall of the Roman Empire.*

Francesco Guicciardini, 1483-1540, (It.) historian, wrote *Storia d'Italia*, principal historical work of the 16th-century.

Thomas Hobbes, 1588-1679, (Br.) social philosopher.

Helen Keller, 1980-1968, (U.S.) crusader for better treatment for the handicapped.

John Maynard Keynes, 1883-1946, (Br.) economist, principal advocate of deficit spending.

Martin Luther King Jr., 1929-1964; (U.S.) civil rights leader; won Nobel Peace Prize, 1964.

Lucien Lévy-Bruhl, 1857-1939, (F.) philosopher, studied the psychology of primitive societies.

Kurt Lewin, 1890-1947, (U.S.) German-born psychologist, studied human motivation and group dynamics.

John Locke, 1632-1704, (Br.) political philosopher.

Thomas B. Macauley, 1800-1859, (Br.) historian, statesman.

Bronislaw Malinowski, 1884-1942, (Pol.) anthropologist, considered the father of social anthropology.

Thomas R. Malthus, 1766-1834, (Br.) economist, famed for *Essay on the Principle of Population.*

Karl Mannheim, 1893-1947, (Hung.) sociologist, historian.

Karl Marx, 1818-1883, (G.) political philosopher, proponent of modern communism.

Giuseppe Mazzini, 1805-1872, (It.) political philosopher.

George H. Mead, 1863-1931, (U.S.) philosopher and social psychologist.

Margaret Mead, 1901-1978, (U.S.) cultural anthropologist, popularized field.

James Mill, 1773-1836, (Sc.) philosopher, historian, and economist; a proponent of Utilitarianism.

John Stuart Mill, 1806-1873, (Br.) philosopher, political economist.

Theodor Mommsen, 1817-1903, (G.) historian, wrote *The History of Rome.*

Charles-Louis Montesquieu, 1689-1755, (F.) social philosopher.

Florence Nightingale, 1820-1910, (Br.) founder of modern nursing.

Jose Ortega y Gasset, 1883-1955, (Sp.) philosopher and humanist; advocated control by an elite.

Robert Owen, 1771-1858, (Br.) political philosopher, reformer.

Emmeline Pankhurst, 1858-1928, (Br.) woman suffragist.

Vilfredo Pareto, 1848-1923, (It.) economist, sociologist.

Marco Polo, c.1254-1324, (It.) narrated an account of his travels to China.

William Prescott, 1796-1859, (U.S.) early American historian.

Pierre Joseph Proudhon, 1809-1865, (F.) social theorist, regarded as the father of anarchism.

Francois Quesnay, 1694-1774, (F.) economic theorist, demonstrated circular flow of economic activity through society.

David Ricardo, 1772-1823, (Br.) economic theorist, advocated free international trade.

Jean-Jacques Rousseau, 1712-1778, (F.) social philosopher, author.

Ferdinand de Saussure, 1857-1913, (Swiss) a founder of modern lingustics.

Hjalmar Schacht, 1877-1970, (G.) economist.

Albert Schweitzer, 1875-1965, (Alsatian) social philosopher, theologian, and humanitarian.

Earl of Shaftesbury (A.A. Cooper), 1801-1885, (Br.) social reformer.

Joseph Schumpeter, 1883-1950, (U.S.) Czech.-born economist, championed big business, capitalism.

George Simmel, 1858-1918, (G.) sociologist, philosopher.

Adam Smith, 1723-1790, (Br.) economist, advocated laissez-faire economy and free trade.

Oswald Spengler, 1880-1936, (G.) philosopher and historian, wrote *The Decline of the West.*

William G. Sumner, 1840-1910, (U.S.) social scientist, economist; championed laissez-faire economy, Social Darwinism.

Hippolyte Taine, 1828-1893, (F.) historian.

Alexis de Tocqueville, 1805-1859, (F.) political scientist, historian.

Arnold Toynbee, 1889-1975, (Br.) historian, wrote 10-volume *A Study of History.*

Heinrich von Treitschke, 1834-1896, (G.) historian, political writer.

George Trevelyan, 1838-1928, (Br.) historian, statesman.

Harriet Tubman, c.1820-1913, (U.S.) abolitionist, ran Underground Railroad.

Giovanni Vico, 1668-1744, (It.) historian, philosopher.

Voltaire (F.M. Arouet), 1694-1778, (F.) philosopher, historian, and poet.

Izaak Walton, 1593-1683, (Br.) author, wrote first biographical works in English literature.

Booker T. Washington, 1856-1915, (U.S.) educator, reformer; championed vocational training for blacks.

Sidney J., 1859-1947, and wife **Beatrice,** 1858-1943, **Webb** (Br.) leading figures in Fabian Society and British Labour Party.

Max Weber, 1864-1920, (G.) sociologist.

Noted World Philosophers and Religionists of the Past

Pierre Abelard, 1079-1142, (F.) philosopher, theologian, and teacher, used dialectic method to support Christian dogma.

Felix Adler, 1851-1933, (U.S.) German-born founder of the Ethical Culture Society.

Thomas Aquinas, 1225-1274, (It.) theologian, philosopher.

St. Augustine, 354-430, Latin bishop considered the founder of formalized Christian theology.

Averroes, 1126-1198, (Sp.) Islamic philosopher.

Roger Bacon, c.1214-1294, (Br.) philosopher and scientist.

Karl Barth, 1886-1968, (Sw.) theologian, a leading force in 20th-century Protestantism.

Thomas à Becket, 1118-1170, (Br.) archbishop of Canterbury, opposed Henry II.

St. Benedict, c.480-547, (It.) founded the Benedictines.

Jeremy Bentham, 1748-1832, (Br.) philosopher, reformer, founder of Utilitarianism.

Henri Bergson, 1859-1941, (F.) philosopher of evolution.

George Berkeley, 1685-1753, (Ir.) philosopher, churchman.

John Biddle, 1615-1662, (Br.) founder of English Unitarianism.

Jakob Boehme, 1575-1624, (G.) theosophist and mystic.

William Brewster, 1567-1644, (Br.) headed pilgrims, signed Mayflower Compact.

Emil Brunner, 1889-1966, (Sw.) theologian.

Giordano Bruno, 1548-1600, (It.) philosopher.

Martin Buber, 1878-1965, (G.) Jewish philosopher, theologian, wrote *I and Thou.*

Buddha (Siddhartha Gautama), c.563-c.483 BC, (Ind.) philosopher, founded Buddhism.

John Calvin, 1509-1564, (F.) theologian, a key figure in the Protestant Reformation.

Auguste Comte, 1798-1857, (F.) philosopher, the founder of positivism.

Confucius, 551-479 BC, (Chin.) founder of Confucianism.

John Cotton, 1584-1652, (Br.) Puritan theologian.

Thomas Cranmer, 1489-1556, (Br.) churchman, wrote much of *Book of Common Prayer;* promoter of English Reformation.

René Descartes, 1596-1650, (F.) philosopher, mathematician.

Denis Diderot, 1713-1784, (F.) philosopher, creator of first modern encyclopedia.

Mary Baker Eddy, 1821-1910, (U.S.) founder of Christian Science.

(Desiderius) Erasmus, c.1466-1536, (Du.) Renaissance humanist.

Johann Fichte, 1762-1814, (G.) philosopher, the first of the Transcendental Idealists.

George Fox, 1624-1691, (Br.) founder of Society of Friends.

St. Francis of Assisi, 1182-1226, (It.) founded Franciscans.

al Ghazali, 1058-1111, Islamic philosopher.

Georg W. Hegel, 1770-1831, (G.) Idealist philosopher.

Martin Heidegger, 1889-1976, (G.) existentialist philosopher, affected fields ranging from physics to literary criticism.

Johann G. Herder, 1744-1803, (G.) philosopher, cultural historian; a founder of German Romanticism.

David Hume, 1711-1776, (Sc.) philosopher, historian.

Jan Hus, 1369-1415, (Czech.) religious reformer.

Edmund Husserl, 1859-1938, (G.) philosopher, founded the Phenomenological movement.

Thomas Huxley, 1825-1895, (Br.) philosopher, educator.

Thomas à Kempis, c.1380-1471, (G.) theologian probably wrote *Imitation of Christ.*

Ignatius of Loyola, 1491-1556, (Sp.) founder of the Jesuits.

William Inge, 1860-1954, (Br.) theologian, explored the mystic aspects of Christianity.

William James, 1842-1910, (U.S.) philosopher, psychologist; advanced theory of the pragmatic nature of truth.

Karl Jaspers, 1883-1969, (G.) existentialist philosopher.

Immanuel Kant, 1724-1804, (G.) metaphysician, preeminent founder of modern critical philosophy.

Soren Kierkegaard, 1813-1855, (Den.) philosopher, considered the father of Existentialism.

John Knox, 1505-1572, (Sc.) leader of the Protestant Reformation in Scotland.

Lao-Tzu, 604-531 BC, (Chin.) philosopher, considered the founder of the Taoist religion.

Gottfried von Leibniz, 1646-1716, (G.) philosopher, mathematician.

Martin Luther, 1483-1546, (G.) leader of the Protestant Reformation, founded Lutheran church.

Maimonides, 1135-1204, (Sp.) Jewish philosopher.

Jacques Maritain, 1882-1973, (F.) Neo-Thomist philosopher.

Aimee Semple McPherson, 1890-1944, (U.S.) Canadian-born evangelist.

Philipp Melanchthon, 1497-1560, (G.) theologian, humanist; an important voice in the Reformation.

Mohammed, c.570-632, Arab prophet of the religion of Islam.

George E. Moore, 1873-1958, (Br.) ethical theorist.

Elijah Muhammad, 1897-1975, (U.S.) leader of the Black Muslim sect.

Heinrich Muhlenberg, 1711-1787, (G.) organized the Lutheran Church in America.

John H. Newman, 1801-1890, (Br.) Roman Catholic cardinal, led Oxford Movement.

Friedrich Nietzsche, 1844-1900, (G.) moral philosopher.

Blaise Pascal, 1623-1662, (F.) philosopher and mathematician.

St. Patrick, c.389-c.461, brought Christianity to Ireland.

St. Paul, ?-c.67, a founder of the Christian religion.

Charles S. Peirce, 1839-1914, (U.S.) philosopher, logician; originated concept of Pragmatism, 1878.

Josiah Royce 1855-1916, (U.S.) Idealist philosopher.

Charles T. Russell, 1852-1916, (U.S.) founder of Jehovah's Witnesses.

Fredrich von Schelling, 1775-1854, (G.) philosopher.

Friedrich Schleiermacher, 1768-1834, (G.) theologian, a founder of modern Protestant theology.

Arthur Schopenhauer, 1788-1860, (G.) philosopher.

Joseph Smith, 1805-1844, (U.S.) founded Latter Day Saints (Mormon) movement, 1830.

Herbert Spencer, 1820-1903, (Br.) philosopher of evolution.

Baruch Spinoza, 1632-1677, (Du.) rationalist philosopher.

Daisetz Teitaro Suzuki, 1870-1966, (Jap.) Buddhist scholar.

Emanuel Swedenborg, 1688-1722, (Swed.) philosopher, mystic.

Paul Tillich, 1886-1965, (U.S.) German-born philosopher and theologian.

John Wesley, 1703-1791, (Br.) theologian, evangelist; founded Methodism.

Alfred North Whitehead, 1861-1947, (Br.) philosopher, mathematician.

William of Occam, c.1285-c.1349 (Br.) philosopher.

Ludwig Wittgenstein, 1889-1951, (Aus.) philosopher.

John Wycliffe, 1320-1384, (Br.) theologian, reformer.

Brigham Young, 1801-1877, (U.S.) Mormon leader, colonized Utah.

Huldrych Zwingli, 1484-1531, (Sw.) theologian, led Swiss Protestant Reformation.

Noted Artists and Sculptors of the Past

Artists are painters unless otherwise indicated.

Washington Allston, 1779-1843, (U.S.) landscapist. Belshazzar's Feast.

Albrecht Altdorfer, 1480-1538, (Ger.) landscapist. Battle of Alexander.

Andrea del Sarto, 1486-1530, frescoes. Madonna of the Harpies.

Fra Angelico, c. 1400-1455, (It.) Renaissance muralist. Madonna of the Linen Drapers' Guild.

Alexsandr Archipenko, 1887-1964, (U.S.) sculptor. Boxing Match, Medranos.

John James Audubon, 1785-1851, (U.S.) Birds of America.

Hans Baldung Grien, 1484-1545, (Ger.) Todentanz.

Ernst Barlach, 1870-1938, (Ger.) Expressionist sculptor. Man Drawing a Sword.

Frederic-Auguste Bartholdi, 1834-1904, (Fr.) Liberty Enlightening the World, Lion of Belfort.

Fra Bartolommeo, 1472-1517, (It.) Vision of St. Bernard.

Aubrey Beardsley, 1872-1898, (Br.) illustrator. Salome, Lysistrata.

Max Beckmann, 1884-1950, (Ger.) Expressionist. The Descent from the Cross.

Gentile Bellini, 1426-1507, (It.) Renaissance. Procession in St. Mark's Square.

Giovanni Bellini, 1428-1516, (It.) St. Francis in Ecstasy.

Jacopo Bellini, 1400-1470, (It.) Crucifixion.

George Wesley Bellows, 1882-1925, (U.S.) sports artist. Stag at Sharkey's.

Thomas Hart Benton, 1889-1975, (U.S.) American regionalist. Threshing Wheat, Arts of the West.

Gianlorenzo Bernini, 1598-1680, (It.) Baroque sculpture. The Assumption.

Albert Bierstadt, 1830-1902, (U.S.) landscapist. The Rocky Mountains, Mount Corcoran.

George Caleb Bingham, 1811-1879, (U.S.) Fur Traders Descending the Missouri.

William Blake, 1752-1827, (Br.) engraver. Book of Job, Songs of Innocence, Songs of Experience.

Rosa Bonheur, 1822-1899, (Fr.) The Horse Fair.

Pierre Bonnard, 1867-1947, (Fr.) Intimist. The Breakfast Room.

Gutzon Borglum, 1871-1941, (U.S.) sculptor. Mt. Rushmore Memorial.

Hieronymus Bosch, 1450-1516, (Flem.) religious allegories. The Crowning with Thorns.

Sandro Botticelli, 1444-1510, (It.) Renaissance. Birth of Venus.

Constantin Brancusi, 1876-1957, (Rum.) Nonobjective sculptor. Flying Turtle, The Kiss.

Georges Braque, 1882-1963, (Fr.) Cubist. Violin and Palette.

Pieter Bruegel the Elder, c. 1525-1569, (Flem.) The Peasant Dance.

Pieter Bruegel the Younger, 1564-1638, (Flem.) Village Fair, The Crucifixion.

Edward Burne-Jones, 1833-1898, (Br.) Pre-Raphaelite artist-craftsman. The Mirror of Venus.

Alexander Calder, 1898-1976, (U.S.) sculptor. Lobster Trap and Fish Tail.

Michelangelo Merisi da Caravaggio, 1573-1610, (It.) Baroque. The Supper at Emmaus.

Emily Carr, 1871-1945, (Can.) landscapist. Blunden Harbour, Big Raven.

Carlo Carra, 1881-1966, (It.) Metaphysical school. Lot's Daughters.

Mary Cassatt, 1845-1926, (U.S.) Impressionist. Woman Bathing.

George Catlin, 1796-1872, (U.S.) American Indian life. Gallery of Indians.

Benvenuto Cellini, 1500-1571, (It.) Mannerist sculptor, goldsmith. Perseus.

Paul Cezanne, 1839-1906, (Fr.) Card Players, Mont-Sainte-Victoire with Large Pine Trees.

Marc Chagall, 1898-1985, (Rus.) Jewish life and folklore. I and the Village.

Jean Simeon Chardin, 1699-1779, (Fr.) still lifes. The Kiss, The Grace.

Frederic Church, 1826-1900, (U.S.) Hudson River school. Niagara, Andes of Ecuador.

Giovanni Cimabue, 1240-1302, (It.) Byzantine mosaicist. Madonna Enthroned with St. Francis.

Claude Lorrain, 1600-1682, (Fr.) ideal-landscapist. The Enchanted Castle.

Thomas Cole, 1801-1848, (U.S.) Hudson River school. The Ox-Bow.

John Constable, 1776-1837, (Br.) landscapist. Salisbury Cathedral from the Bishop's Grounds.

John Singleton Copley, 1738-1815, (U.S.) portraitist. Samuel Adams, Watson and the Shark.

Lovis Corinth, 1858-1925, (Ger.) Expressionist. Apocalypse.

Jean-Baptiste-Camille Corot, 1796-1875, (Fr.) landscapist. Souvenir de Mortefontaine, Pastorale.

Correggio, 1494-1534, (It.) Renaissance muralist. Mystic Marriages of St. Catherine.

Gustave Courbet, 1819-1877, (Fr.) Realist. The Artist's Studio.

Lucas Cranach the Elder, 1472-1553, (Ger.) Protestant Reformation portraitist. Luther.

Nathaniel Currier, 1813-1888, and **James M. Ives,** 1824-1895, (both U.S.) lithographers. A Midnight Race on the Mississippi.

John Steuart Curry, 1897-1946, (U.S.) Americana, murals. Baptism in Kansas.

Honore Daumier, 1808-1879, (Fr.) caricaturist. The Third-Class Carriage.

Jacques-Louis David, 1748-1825, (Fr.) Neoclassicist. The Oath of the Horatii.

Arthur Davies, 1862-1928, (U.S.) Romantic landscapist. Unicorns.

Edgar Degas, 1834-1917, (Fr.) The Ballet Class.

Eugene Delacroix, Co. 1789-1863, (Fr.) Romantic. Massacre at Chios.

Paul Delaroche, 1797-1856, (Fr.) historical themes. Children of Edward IV.

Luca Della Robbia, 1400-1482, (It.) Renaissance terracotta artist. Cantoria (singing gallery), Florence cathedral.

Donatello, 1386-1466, (It.) Renaissance sculptor. David, Gattamelata.

Jean Dubuffet, 1902-1985, (Fr.) painter, sculpter, printmaker. Group of Four Trees.

Marcel Duchamp, 1887-1968, (Fr.) Nude Descending a Staircase.

Raoul Dufy, 1877-1953, (Fr.) Fauvist. Chateau and Horses.

Asher Brown Durand, 1796-1886, (U.S.) Hudson River school. Kindred Spirits.

Albrecht Durer, 1471-1528, (Ger.) Renaissance engraver, woodcuts. St. Jerome in His Study, Melancholia I, Apocalypse.

Anthony van Dyck, 1599-1641, (Flem.) Baroque portraitist. Portrait of Charles I Hunting.

Thomas Eakins, 1844-1916, (U.S.) Realist. The Gross Clinic.

Jacob Epstein, 1880-1959, (Br.) religious and allegorical sculptor. Genesis, Ecce Homo.

Jan van Eyck, 1380-1441, (Flem.) naturalistic panels. Adoration of the Lamb.

Anselm Feuerbach, 1829-1880, (Ger.) Romantic Classicism. Judgement of Paris, Iphigenia.

John Bernard Flannagan, 1895-1942, (U.S.) animal sculptor. Triumph of the Egg.

Jean-Honore Fragonard, 1732-1806, (Fr.) Rococo. The Swing.

Daniel Chester French, 1850-1931, (U.S.) The Minute Man of Concord; seated Lincoln, Lincoln Memorial, Washington, D.C.

Caspar David Friedrich, 1774-1840, (Ger.) Romantic landscapes. Man and Woman Gazing at the Moon.

Thomas Gainsborough, 1727-1788, (Br.) portraitist. The Blue Boy.

Paul Gauguin, 1848-1903, (Fr.) Post-impressionist. The Tahitians.

Lorenzo Ghiberti, 1378-1455, (It.) Renaissance sculptor. Gates of Paradise baptistry doors, Florence.

Alberto Giacometti, 1901-1966, (It.) attenuated sculptures of solitary figures. Man Pointing.

Giorgione, c. 1477-1510, (It.) Renaissance. The Tempest.

Giotto di Bondone, 1267-1337, (It.) Renaissance. Presentation of Christ in the Temple.

Francois Girardon, 1628-1715, (Fr.) Baroque sculptor of classical themes. Apollo Tended by the Nymphs.

Vincent van Gogh, 1853-1890, (Dutch) The Starry Night, L'Arlesienne.

Arshile Gorky, 1905-1948, (U.S.) Surrealist. The Liver Is the Cock's Comb.

Francisco de Goya y Lucientes, 1746-1828, (Sp.) The Naked Maja, The Disasters of War (etchings).

El Greco, 1541-1614, View of Toledo.

Horatio Greenough, 1805-1852, (U.S.) Neo-classical sculptor. George Washington.

Matthias Grünewald, 1480-1528, (Ger.) mystical religious themes. The Resurrection.

Frans Hals, c. 1580-1666, (Dutch) portraitist. Laughing Cavalier, Gypsy Girl.

Childe Hassam, 1859-1935, (U.S.) Impressionist. Southwest Wind.

Edward Hicks, 1780-1849, (U.S.) folk painter. The Peaceable Kingdom.

Hans Hofmann, 1880-1966, (U.S.) early Abstract Expressionist. Spring. The Gate.

William Hogarth, 1697-1764, (Br.) caricaturist. The Rake's Progress.

Katsushika Hokusai, 1760-1849, (Jap.) printmaker. Crabs.

Hans Holbein the Elder, 1460-1524, (Ger.) late Gothic. Presentation of Christ in the Temple.

Hans Holbein the Younger, 1497-1543, (Ger.) portraitist. Henry VIII.

Winslow Homer, 1836-1910, (U.S.) marine themes. Marine Coast, High Cliff.

Edward Hopper, 1882-1967, (U.S.) realistic urban scenes. Sunlight in a Cafeteria.

Jean-Auguste-Dominique Ingres, 1780-1867, (Fr.) Classicist. Valpincon Bather.

George Inness, 1825-1894, (U.S.) luminous landscapist. Delaware Water Gap.

Vasily Kandinsky, 1866-1944, (Rus.) Abstractionist. Capricious Forms.

Paul Klee, 1879-1940, (Swiss) Abstractionist. Twittering Machine.

Oscar Kokoschka, 1886-1980, (Aus.) Expressionist. View of Prague.

Kathe Kollwitz, 1867-1945, (Ger.) printmaker, social justice themes. The Peasant War.

Gaston Lachaise, 1882-1935, (U.S.) figurative sculptor. Standing Woman.

John La Farge, 1835-1910, (U.S.) muralist. Red and White Peonies.

Fernand Leger, 1881-1955, (Fr.) machine art. The Cyclists.

Leonardo da Vinci, 1452-1519, (It.) Mona Lisa, Last Supper, The Annunciation.

Emanuel Leutze, 1816-1868, (U.S.) historical themes. Washington Crossing the Delaware.

Jacques Lipchitz, 1891-1973, (Fr.) Cubist sculptor. Harpist.

Filippino Lippi, 1457-1504, (It.) Renaissance. The Vision of St. Bernard.

Fra Filippo Lippi, 1406-1469, (It.) Renaissance. Coronation of the Virgin.

Morris Louis, 1912-1962, (U.S.) Abstract Expressionist. Signa, Stripes.

Aristide Maillol, 1861-1944, (Fr.) sculptor. The Mediterranean.

Edouard Manet, 1832-1883, (Fr.) forerunner of Impressionism. Luncheon on the Grass, Olympia.

Andrea Mantegna, 1431-1506, (It.) Renaissance frescoes. Triumph of Caesar.

Franz Marc, 1880-1916, (Ger.) Expressionist. Blue Horses.

John Marin, 1870-1953, (U.S.) expressionist seascapes. Maine Island.

Reginald Marsh, 1898-1954, (U.S.) satirical artist. Tattoo and Haircut.

Masaccio, 1401-1428, (It.) Renaissance. The Tribute Money.

Henri Matisse, 1869-1954, (Fr.) Fauvist. Woman with the Hat.

Michelangelo Buonarroti, 1475-1564, (It.) Pieta, David, Moses, The Last Judgment, Sistine Ceiling.

Jean-Francois Millet, 1814-1875, (Fr.) painter of peasant subjects. The Gleaners, The Man with a Hoe.

Amedeo Modigliani, 1884-1920, (It.) Reclining Nude.

Piet Mondrian, 1872-1944, (Dutch) Abstractionist. Composition.

Claude Monet, 1840-1926, (Fr.) Impressionist. The Bridge at Argenteuil, Haystacks.

Henry Moore, 1898-1986, (Br.) sculptor of large-scale, abstract works. Reclining Figure (several).

Gustave Moreau, 1826-1898, (Fr.) Symbolist. The Apparition, Dance of Salome.

James Wilson Morrice, 1865-1924, (Can.) landscapist. The Ferry, Quebec, Venice, Looking Over the Lagoon.

Grandma Moses, 1860-1961, (U.S.) folk painter. Out for the Christmas Trees.

Edvard Munch, 1863-1944, (Nor.) Expressionist. The Cry.

Bartolome Murillo, 1618-1682, (Sp.) Baroque religious artist. Vision of St. Anthony. The Two Trinities.

Barnett Newman, 1905-1970, (U.S.) Abstract Expressionist. Stations of the Cross.

Georgia O'Keeffe, 1887-1986, (U.S.) Southwest motifs. Cow's Skull.

Jose Clemente Orozco, 1883-1949, (Mex.) frescoes. House of Tears.

Charles Willson Peale, 1741-1827, (U.S.) American Revolutionary portraitist. Washington, Franklin, Jefferson, John Adams.

Rembrandt Peale, 1778-1860, (U.S.) portraitist. Thomas Jefferson.

Pietro Perugino, 1446-1523, (It.) Renaissance. Delivery of the Keys to St. Peter.

Pablo Picasso, 1881-1973, (Sp.) Guernica, Dove, Head of a Woman.

Piero della Francesca, c. 1415-1492, (It.) Renaissance. Duke of Urbino, Flagellation of Christ.

Camille Pissarro, 1830-1903, (Fr.) Impressionist. Morning Sunlight.

Jackson Pollock, 1912-1956, (U.S.) Abstract Expressionist. Autumn Rhythm.

Nicolas Poussin, 1594-1665, (Fr.) Baroque pictorial classicism. St. John on Patmos.

Maurice B. Prendergast, c. 1860-1924, (U.S.) Post-impressionist water colorist. Umbrellas in the Rain.

Pierre-Paul Prud'hon, 1758-1823, (Fr.) Romanticist. Crime pursued by Vengeance and Justice.

Pierre Cecile Puvis de Chavannes, 1824-1898, (Fr.) muralist. The Poor Fisherman.

Raphael Sanzio, 1483-1520, (It.) Renaissance. Disputa, School of Athens, Sistine Madonna.

Man Ray, 1890-1976, (U.S.) Dadaist. Observing Time, The Lovers.

Odilon Redon, 1840-1916, (Fr.) Symbolist lithographer. In the Dream.

Rembrandt van Rijn, 1606-1669, (Dutch) The Bridal Couple, The Night Watch.

Frederic Remington, 1861-1909, (U.S.) painter, sculptor, portrayer of the American West. Bronco Buster.

Pierre-Auguste Renoir, 1841-1919, (Fr.) Impressionist. The Luncheon of the Boating Party.

Joshua Reynolds, 1723-1792, (Br.) portraitist. Mrs. Siddons as the Tragic Muse.

Diego Rivera, 1886-1957, (Mex.) frescoes. The Fecund Earth.

Norman Rockwell, 1894-1978, (U.S.) illustrator. Saturday Evening Post covers.

Auguste Rodin, 1840-1917, (Fr.) sculptor. The Thinker, The Burghers of Calais.

Mark Rothko, 1903-1970, (U.S.) Abstract Expressionist. Light, Earth and Blue.

Georges Rouault, 1871-1958, (Fr.) Expressionist. The Old King.

Henri Rousseau, 1844-1910, (Fr.) primitive exotic themes. The Snake Charmer.

Theodore Rousseau, 1812-1867, (Swiss-Fr.) landscapist. Under the Birches, Evening.

Peter Paul Rubens, 1577-1640, (Flem.) Baroque. Mystic Marriage of St. Catherine.

Jacob van Ruisdael, c. 1628-1682, (Dutch) landscapist. Jewish Cemetery.

Salomon van Ruysdael, c. 1600-1670, (Dutch) landscapist. River with Ferry-Boat.

Albert Pinkham Ryder, 1847-1917, (U.S.) seascapes and allegories. Toilers of the Sea.

Augustus Saint-Gaudens, 1848-1907, (U.S.) memorial statues. Farragut, Mrs. Henry Adams (Grief).

Andrea Sansovino, 1460-1529, (It.) Renaissance sculptor. Baptism of Christ.

Jacopo Sansovino, 1486-1570, (It.) Renaissance sculptor. St. John the Baptist.

John Singer Sargent, 1856-1925, (U.S.) Edwardian society portraitist. The Wyndham Sisters, Madam X.

Georges Seurat, 1859-1891, (Fr.) Pointillist. Sunday Afternoon on the Island of Grande Jatte.

Gino Severini, 1883-1966, (It.) Futurist and Cubist. Dynamic Hieroglyph of the Bal Tabarin.

Ben Shahn, 1898-1969, (U.S.) social and political themes. Sacco and Vanzetti series, Seurat's Lunch, Handball.

Charles Sheeler, 1883-1965, (U.S.) Abstractionist. Upper Deck.

David Alfaro Siqueiros, 1896-1974, (Mex.) political muralist. March of Humanity.

John F. Sloan, 1871-1951, (U.S.) depictions of New York City. Wake of the Ferry.

David Smith, 1906-1965, (U.S.) welded metal sculpture. Hudson River Landscape, Zig, Cubi series.

Gilbert Stuart, 1755-1828, (U.S.) portraitist. George Washington.

Thomas Sully, 1783-1872, (U.S.) portraitist. Col. Thomas Handasyd Perkins, The Passage of the Delaware.

Yves Tanguy, 1900-1955, (Fr.) Surrealist. Rose of the Four Winds.

Giovanni Battista Tiepolo, 1696-1770, (It.) Rococo frescoes. The Crucifixion.

Jacopo Tintoretto, 1518-1594, (It.) Mannerist. The Last Supper.

Titian, c. 1485-1576, (It.) Renaissance. Venus and the Lute Player, The Bacchanal.

Henri de Toulouse-Lautrec, 1864-1901, (Fr.) At the Moulin Rouge.

John Trumbull, 1756-1843, (U.S.) historical themes. The Declaration of Independence.

Joseph Mallord William Turner, 1775-1851, (Br.) Romantic landscapist. Snow Storm.

Paolo Uccello, 1397-1475, (It.) Gothic-Renaissance. The Rout of San Romano.

Maurice Utrillo, 1883-1955, (Fr.) Impressionist. Sacre-Coeur de Montmartre.

John Vanderlyn, 1775-1852, (U.S.) Neo-classicist. Ariadne Asleep on the Island of Naxos.

Diego Velazquez, 1599-1660, (Sp.) Baroque. Las Meninas, Portrait of Juan de Pareja.

Jan Vermeer, 1632-1675, (Dutch) interior genre subjects. Young Woman with a Water Jug.

Paolo Veronese, 1528-1588, (It.) devotional themes, vastly peopled canvases. The Temptation of St. Anthony.

Andrea del Verrocchio, 1435-1488, (It.) Florentine sculptor. Colleoni.

Maurice de Vlaminck, 1876-1958, (Fr.) Fauvist landscapist. The Storm.

Andy Warhol, 1928-1987 (U.S.) Pop Art, Campbell's Soup Cans.

Antoine Watteau, 1684-1721, (Fr.) Rococo painter of "scenes of gallantry". The Embarkation for Cythera.

George Frederic Watts, 1817-1904, (Br.) painter and sculptor of grandiose allegorical themes. Hope, Physical Energy.

Benjamin West, 1738-1820, realistic historical themes. Death of General Wolfe.

James Abbott McNeill Whistler, 1834-1903, (U.S.) Arrangement in Grey and Black, No. 1: The Artist's Mother.

Archibald M. Willard, 1836-1918, (U.S.) The Spirit of '76.

Grant Wood, 1891-1942, (U.S.) Midwestern regionalist. American Gothic, Daughters of Revolution.

Ossip Zadkine, 1890-1967, (Rus.) School of Paris sculptor. The Destroyed City, Musicians, Christ.

Noted World Writers of the Past

Conrad Aiken, 1889-1973, (U.S.) poet, critic.

Louisa May Alcott, 1832-1888, (U.S.) novelist. Little Women.

Sholom Aleichem, 1859-1916, (R.) Yiddish writer. Tevye's Daughter, The Great Fair.

Vicente Aleixandre, 1898-1984, (Sp.) poet. 1977 Nobel Prize winner.

Horatio Alger, 1832-1899, (U.S.) "rags to riches" books.

Hans Christian Andersen, 1805-1875, (Den.) author of fairy tales. The Princess and the Pea, The Ugly Duckling.

Sherwood Anderson, 1876-1941, (U.S.) author. Winesburg, Ohio.

Matthew Arnold, 1822-1888, (Br.) poet, critic. "Thrysis," "Dover Beach."

Jane Austen, 1775-1817, (Br.) novelist. Pride and Prejudice, Sense and Sensibility, Emma, Mansfield Park.

Isaac Babel, 1894-1941, (R.) short-story writer, playwright. Odessa Tales, Red Cavalry.

Enid Bagnold, 1890-1981, (Br.) playwright, novelist. National Velvet.

James M. Barrie, 1860-1937, (Br.) playwright, novelist. Peter Pan, Dear Brutus, What Every Woman Knows.

Honoré de Balzac, 1799-1850, (Fr.) novelist. Le Père Goriot, Cousine Bette, Eugénie Grandet, The Human Comedy.

Charles Baudelaire, 1821-1867, (Fr.) symbolist poet. Les Fleurs du Mal.

L. Frank Baum, 1856-1919, (U.S.) children's author. Wizard of Oz series.

Simone de Beauvoir, 1908-1986, (Fr.) novelist, essayist. The Second Sex.

Brendan Behan, 1923-1964, (Ir.) playwright. The Quare Fellow, The Hostage, Borstal Boy.

Robert Benchley, 1889-1945, (U.S.) humorist. From Bed to Worse, My Ten Years in a Quandary.

Stephen Vincent Benét, 1898-1943, (U.S.) poet, novelist. John Brown's Body.

John Berryman, 1914-1972, (U.S.) poet. Homage to Mistress Bradstreet.

William Blake, 1757-1827, (Br.) poet, mystic, artist. Songs of Innocence, Songs of Experience.

Giovanni Boccaccio, 1313-1375, (It.) poet, storyteller. Decameron, Filostrato.

Jorge Luis Borges, 1900-1986, (Arg.) short story writer, poet, essayist. Labyrinth.

James Boswell, 1740-1795, (Sc.) author. The Life of Samuel Johnson.

Bertolt Brecht, 1898-1956, (G.) dramatist, poet. The Threepenny Opera, Mother Courage and Her Children.

Charlotte Brontë, 1816-1855, (Br.) novelist. Jane Eyre.

Emily Brontë, 1818-1848, (Br.) novelist. Wuthering Heights.

Elizabeth Barrett Browning, 1806-1861, (Br.) poet. Sonnets from the Portuguese.

Robert Browning, 1812-1889, (Br.) poet. "My Last Duchess," "Soliloquy of the Spanish Cloister."

Pearl Buck, 1892-1973, (U.S.) novelist. The Good Earth.

Mikhail Bulgakov, 1891-1940, (R.) novelist, playwright. The Heart of a Dog, The Master and Margarita.

John Bunyan, 1628-1688, (Br.) writer. Pilgrim's Progress.

Robert Burns, 1759-1796, (Sc.) poet. "Flow Gently, Sweet Afton," "My Heart's in the Highlands," "Auld Lang Syne."

Edgar Rice Burroughs, 1875-1950, (U.S.) novelist. Tarzan of the Apes.

George Gordon Lord Byron, 1788-1824, (Br.) poet. *Don Juan, Childe Harold.*

Italo Calvino, 1923-1985 (It.) novelist, short story writer. *If on a Winter's Night a Traveler . . .*

Albert Camus, 1913-1960, (F.) novelist. *The Plague, The Outsider, Caligula, The Fall.*

Lewis Carroll, 1832-1898, (Br.) writer, mathematician. *Alice's Adventures in Wonderland, Through the Looking Glass.*

Karel Capek, 1890-1938, (Czech.) playwright, novelist, essayist. *R.U.R. (Rossum's Universal Robots).*

Giacomo Casanova, 1725-1798, (It.) Venetian adventurer, author, world famous for his memoirs.

Willa Cather, 1876-1947, (U.S.) novelist, essayist. *O Pioneers!, My Antonia.*

Miguel de Cervantes Saavedra, 1547-1616, (Sp.) novelist, dramatist, poet. *Don Quixote de la Mancha.*

Raymond Chandler, 1889-1959, (U.S.) writer of detective fiction. Philip Marlowe series.

Geoffrey Chaucer, c. 1340-1400, (Br.) poet. *The Canterbury Tales.*

John Cheever, 1912-1983, (U.S.) short story writer, novelist. *The Wapshot Scandal.*

Anton Chekhov, 1860-1904, (R.) short-story writer, dramatist. *Uncle Vanya, The Cherry Orchard, The Three Sisters.*

G.K. Chesterton, 1874-1936, (Br.) author, Fr. Brown series.

Agatha Christie, 1891-1976, (Br.) mystery writer. *And Then There Were None, Murder on the Orient Express.*

Jean Cocteau, 1889-1963, (F.) writer, visual artist, filmmaker. *The Beauty and the Beast, Enfants Terribles.*

Samuel Taylor Coleridge, 1772-1834, (Br.) poet, man of letters. "Kubla Khan," "The Rime of the Ancient Mariner."

Sidonie Colette, 1873-1954, (F.) novelist. *Claudine, Gigi.*

Joseph Conrad, 1857-1924, (Br.) novelist. *Lord Jim, Heart of Darkness, The Nigger of the Narcissus.*

James Fenimore Cooper, 1789-1851, (U.S.) novelist. Leather-Stocking Tales.

Pierre Corneille, 1606-1684, (F.) Dramatist. *Medeé, Le Cid, Horace, Cinna, Polyeucte.*

Stephen Crane, 1871-1900, (U.S.) novelist. *The Red Badge of Courage.*

e.e. cummings, 1894-1962, (U.S.) poet. *Tulips and Chimneys.*

Gabriele d'Annunzio, 1863-1938, (It.) poet, novelist, dramatist. *The Child of Pleasure, The Intruder, The Victim.*

Dante Alighieri, 1265-1321, (It.) poet. *The Divine Comedy.*

Daniel Defoe, 1660-1731, (Br.) writer. *Robinson Crusoe, Moll Flanders, Journal of the Plague Year.*

Charles Dickens, 1812-1870, (Br.) novelist. *David Copperfield, Oliver Twist, Great Expectations, The Pickwick Papers.*

Emily Dickinson, 1830-1886, (U.S.) poet.

Isak Dinesen (Karen Blixen), 1885-1962, (Dan.) author. *Out of Africa, Seven Gothic Tales, Winter's Tales.*

John Donne, 1573-1631, (Br.) poet. *Songs and Sonnets, Holy Sonnets,* "Death Be Not Proud."

John Dos Passos, 1896-1970, (U.S.) author. *U.S.A.*

Fyodor Dostoyevsky, 1821-1881, (R.) author. *Crime and Punishment, The Brothers Karamazov, The Idiot.*

Arthur Conan Doyle, 1859-1930, (Br.) author, created Sherlock Holmes.

Theodore Dreiser, 1871-1945, (U.S.) novelist. *An American Tragedy, Sister Carrie.*

John Dryden, 1631-1700, (Br.) poet, dramatist, critic. *Fables, Ancient and Modern.*

Alexandre Dumas, 1802-1870, (F.) novelist, dramatist. *The Three Musketeers, The Count of Monte Cristo.*

Alexandre Dumas (fils), 1824-1895, (F.) dramatist, novelist. *La Dame aux camélias, Le Demi-Monde.*

Ilya G. Ehrenburg, 1891-1967, (R.) novelist, journalist. *The Thaw.*

George Eliot, 1819-1880, (Br.) novelist. *Adam Bede, Silas Marner, The Mill on the Floss.*

T.S. Eliot, 1888-1965, (Br.) poet, critic. *The Waste Land,* "The Love Song of J. Alfred Prufrock," *Murder in the Cathedral.*

Ralph Waldo Emerson, 1803-1882, (U.S.) poet, essayist. "The Concord Hymn," "Brahma," *Nature.*

James T. Farrell, 1904-1979, (U.S.) novelist. Studs Lonigan trilogy.

William Faulkner, 1897-1962, (U.S.) novelist. *Sanctuary, Light in August, The Sound and the Fury, Absalom, Absalom!*

Edna Ferber, 1885-1968, (U.S.) novelist, dramatist. *Show Boat, Saratoga Trunk, Giant, Dinner at Eight.*

Henry Fielding, 1707-1754, (Br.) novelist. *Tom Jones.*

F. Scott Fitzgerald, 1896-1940, (U.S.) short-story writer, novelist. *The Great Gatsby, Tender is the Night.*

Gustave Flaubert, 1821-1880, (F.) novelist. *Madame Bovary.*

C.S. Forester, 1899-1966, (Br.) novelist. Horatio Hornblower series.

E.M. Forster, 1879-1970, (Br.) novelist. *A Passage to India, Where Angels Fear to Tread, Maurice.*

Anatole France, 1844-1924. (F.) writer. *Penguin Island, My Friend's Book, Le Crime de Sylvestre Bonnard.*

Robert Frost, 1874-1963, (U.S.) poet. "Birches," "Fire and Ice," "Stopping by Woods on a Snowy Evening."

John Galsworthy, 1867-1933, (Br.) novelist, dramatist. *The Forsyte Saga, A Modern Comedy.*

Jean Genet, 1911-1986, (Fr.) playwright, novelist. "The Blacks."

André Gide, 1869-1951, (F.) writer, *The Immoralist, The Pastoral Symphony, Strait is the Gate.*

Jean Giraudoux, 1882-1944, (F.) novelist, dramatist. *Electra, The Madwoman of Chaillot, Ondine, Tiger at the Gate.*

Johann W. von Goethe, 1749-1832, (G.) poet, dramatist, novelist. *Faust.*

Nikolai Gogol, 1809-1852, (R.) short-story writer, dramatist, novelist. *Dead Souls, The Inspector General.*

Oliver Goldsmith, 1730?-1774, (Br.-Ir.) writer. *The Vicar of Wakefield, She Stoops to Conquer.*

Maxim Gorky, 1868-1936, (R.) writer, founder of Soviet realism. *Mother, The Lower Depths.*

Robert Graves, 1895-1985, (Br.) poet, classical scholar, novelist. *The White Goddess.*

Thomas Gray, 1716-1771, (Br.) poet. "Elegy Written in a Country Churchyard."

Zane Grey, 1875-1939, (U.S.) writer of western stories.

Jakob Grimm, 1785-1863, (G.) philologist, folklorist. *German Methodology, Grimm's Fairy Tales.*

Wilhelm Grimm, 1786-1859, (G.) philologist, folklorist. *Grimm's Fairy Tales.*

Knute Hamsun, 1859-1952 (Nor.) novelist. *Hunger.*

Dashiell Hammett, 1894-1961, (U.S.) writer of detective fiction, created Sam Spade series.

Thomas Hardy, 1840-1928, (Br.) novelist, poet. *The Return of the Native, Tess of the D'Urbervilles, Jude the Obscure.*

Joel Chandler Harris, 1848-1908, (U.S.) short-story writer. Uncle Remus series.

Moss Hart, 1904-1961, (U.S.) playwright. *Once in a Lifetime, You Can't Take It With You.*

Jaroslav Hasek, 1883-1923, (Czech.) writer. *The Good Soldier Schweik.*

Nathaniel Hawthorne, 1804-1864, (U.S.) novelist, short story writer. *The Scarlet Letter, The House of the Seven Gables.*

Heinrich Heine, 1797-1856, (G.) poet. *Book of Songs.*

Lillian Hellman, 1907-1984, (U.S.) playwright, author of memoirs, "The Little Foxes," *An Unfinished Woman.*

Ernest Hemingway, 1899-1961, (U.S.) novelist, short-story writer. *A Farewell to Arms, For Whom the Bell Tolls.*

O. Henry (W.S. Porter), 1862-1910, (U.S.) short-story writer. "The Gift of the Magi."

Hermann Hesse, 1877-1962, (G.) novelist, poet. *Death and the Lover, Steppenwolf, Siddhartha.*

Oliver Wendell Holmes, 1809-1894, (U.S.) poet, novelist. *The Autocrat of the Breakfast-Table.*

Alfred E. Housman, 1859-1936, (Br.) poet. *A Shropshire Lad.*

Victor Hugo, 1802-1885, (F.) poet, dramatist, novelist. *Notre Dame de Paris, Les Misérables.*

Aldous Huxley 1894-1963, (Br.) author. *Point Counter Point, Brave New World.*

Henrik Ibsen, 1828-1906, (Nor.) dramatist, poet. *A Doll's House, Ghosts, The Wild Duck, Hedda Gabler.*

William Inge, 1913-1973, (U.S.) playwright. *Come Back Little Sheba, Bus Stop, The Dark at the Top of the Stairs, Picnic.*

Washington Irving, 1783-1859, (U.S.) essayist, author. "Rip Van Winkle," "The Legend of Sleepy Hollow."

Shirley Jackson, 1919-1965, (U.S.) writer. "The Lottery."

Henry James, 1843-1916, (U.S.) novelist, critic. *Washington Square, Portrait of a Lady, The American.*

Samuel Johnson, 1709-1784, (Br.) author, scholar, critic. *Dictionary of the English Language.*

Ben Jonson, 1572-1637, (Br.) dramatist, poet. *Volpone.*

James Joyce, 1882-1941, (Ir.) novelist. *Ulysses, A Portrait of the Artist as a Young Man, Finnegans Wake.*

Franz Kafka, 1883-1924, (G.) novelist, short-story writer. *The Trial, Amerika, The Castle.*

George S. Kaufman, 1889-1961, (U.S.) playwright. *The Man Who Came to Dinner, You Can't Take It With You, Stage Door.*

Nikos Kazantzakis, 1883?-1957, (Gk.) novelist. *Zorba the Greek, A Greek Passion.*

John Keats, 1795-1821, (Br.) poet. "On a Grecian Urn," *La Belle Dame Sans Merci.*

Joyce Kilmer, 1886-1918, (U.S.) poet, "Trees."

Rudyard Kipling, 1865-1936, (Br.) author, poet. "The White Man's Burden," "Gunga Din," *The Jungle Book.*

Jean de la Fontaine, 1621-1695, (F.) poet. *Fables choisies.*

Pär Lagerkvist, 1891-1974, (Swed.) poet, dramatist, novelist. *Barabbas, The Sybil.*

Selma Lagerlöf, 1858-1940, (Swed.) novelist. *Jerusalem, The Ring of the Lowenskolds.*

Alphonse de Lamartine, 1790-1869, (F.) poet, novelist, statesman. *Méditations poétiques.*

Charles Lamb, 1775-1834, (Br.) essayist. *Specimens of English Dramatic Poets, Essays of Elia.*

Giuseppe di Lampedusa, 1896-1957, (It.) novelist. *The Leopard.*

Ring Lardner, 1885-1933, (U.S.) short story writer, humorist. *You Know Me, Al.*

D. H. Lawrence, 1885-1930, (Br.) novelist. *Women in Love, Lady Chatterley's Lover, Sons and Lovers.*

Mikhail Lermontov, 1814-1841, (R.) novelist, poet. *"Demon," Hero of Our Time.*

Alain-René Lesage, 1668-1747, (F.) novelist. *Gil Blas de Santillane.*

Gotthold Lessing, 1729-1781, (G.) dramatist, philosopher, critic. *Miss Sara Sampson, Minna von Barnhelm.*

Sinclair Lewis, 1885-1951, (U.S.) novelist, playwright. *Babbitt, Arrowsmith, Dodsworth, Main Street.*

Vachel Lindsay, 1879-1931, (U.S.) poet. *General William Booth Enters into Heaven, The Congo.*

Hugh Lofting, 1886-1947, (Br.) Dr. Doolittle series.

Jack London, 1876-1916, (U.S.) novelist, journalist. *Call of the Wild, The Sea-Wolf.*

Henry Wadsworth Longfellow, 1807-1882, (U.S.) poet. *Evangeline, The Song of Hiawatha.*

Amy Lowell, 1874-1925, (U.S.) poet, critic. *A Dome of Many-Colored Glass,* "Patterns," "Lilacs."

Robert Lowell, 1917-1977, (U.S.) poet. "Lord Weary's Castle," "For the Union Dead."

Emil Ludwig, 1881-1948, (G.) biographer. *Goethe, Beethoven, Napoleon, Bismarck.*

Niccolò Machiavelli, 1469-1527, (It.) author, statesman. *The Prince, Discourses on Livy.*

Bernard Malamud, 1915-1986, (U.S.) short story writer, novelist, *"The Magic Barrel," The Assistant, The Fixer.*

Stéphane Mallarmé, 1842-1898, (F.) poet. *The Afternoon of a Faun.*

Thomas Malory, ?-1471, (Br.) writer. *Morte d'Arthur.*

Andre Malraux, 1901-1976, (F.) novelist. *Man's Fate, The Voices of Silence.*

Osip Mandelstam, 1891-1938, (R.) Acmeist poet.

Thomas Mann, 1875-1955, (G.) novelist, essayist. *Buddenbrooks, Death in Venice, The Magic Mountain.*

Katherine Mansfield, 1888-1923, (Br.) short story writer. "Bliss," "The Garden Party."

Christopher Marlowe, 1564-1593, (Br.) dramatist, poet. *Tamburlaine the Great, Dr. Faustus, The Jew of Malta.*

John Masefield, 1878-1967, (Br.) poet. "Sea Fever," "Cargoes," *Salt Water Ballads.*

W. Somerset Maugham, 1874-1965, (Br.) author. *Of Human Bondage, The Razor's Edge, The Moon and Sixpence.*

Guy de Maupassant, 1850-1893, (F.) novelist, short-story writer. "A Life," "Bel-Ami," "The Necklace."

François Mauriac, 1885-1970, (F.) novelist, dramatist. *Viper's Tangle, The Kiss to the Leper.*

Vladimir Mayakovsky, 1893-1930, (R.) poet, dramatist. *The Cloud in Trousers.*

Carson McCullers, 1917-1967, (U.S.) novelist. *The Heart is a Lonely Hunter, Member of the Wedding.*

Herman Melville, 1819-1891, (U.S.) novelist, poet. *Moby Dick, Typee, Billy Budd, Omoo.*

H.L. Mencken, 1880-1956, (U.S.) author, critic, editor. *Prejudices, The American Language.*

George Meredith, 1828-1909, (Br.) novelist, poet. *The Ordeal of Richard Feverel, The Egoist.*

Prosper Mérimée, 1803-1870, (F.) author. *Carmen.*

Edna St. Vincent Millay, 1892-1950, (U.S.) poet. *The Harp Weaver and Other Poems, A Few Figs from Thistles.*

A.A. Milne, 1882-1956, (Br.) author. *Winnie-the-Pooh.*

John Milton, 1608-1674, (Br.) poet. *Paradise Lost.*

Gabriela Mistral, 1889-1957, (Chil.) poet. *Sonnets of Death, Desolación, Tala, Lagar.*

Jean Baptiste Molière, 1622-1673, (F.) dramatist. *Le Tartuffe, Le Misanthrope, Le Bourgeois Gentilhomme.*

Ferenc Molnár, 1878-1952, (Hung.) dramatist, novelist. *Liliom, The Guardsman, The Swan.*

Michel de Montaigne, 1533-1592, (F.) essayist. *Essais.*

Eugenio Montale, 1896-1981, (It.) poet.

Marianne Moore, 1887-1972, (U.S.) poet. *O to Be a Dragon.*

Thomas More, 1478-1535, (Br.) author. *Utopia.*

H.H. Munro (Saki), 1870-1916, (Br.) author. *Reginald, The Chronicles of Clovis, Beasts and Super-Beasts.*

Alfred de Musset, 1810-1857, (F.) poet, dramatist. *Confession d'un enfant du siècle.*

Vladimir Nabokov, 1899-1977, (Rus.-U.S.) author. *Lolita, Ada, Pale Fire.*

Ogden Nash, 1902-1971, (U.S.) poet. *Hard Lines, I'm a Stranger Here Myself, The Private Dining Room.*

Pablo Neruda, 1904-1973, (Chil.) poet. *Twenty Love Poems and One Song of Despair, Toward the Splendid City.*

Sean O'Casey, 1884-1964, (Ir.) dramatist. *Juno and the Paycock, The Plough and the Stars.*

Flannery O'Connor, 1925-1964, (U.S.) novelist, short story writer. *Wise Blood,* "A Good Man Is Hard to Find."

Clifford Odets, 1906-1963, (U.S.) playwright. *Waiting for Lefty, Awake and Sing, Golden Boy, The Country Girl.*

John O'Hara, 1905-1970, (U.S.) novelist. *Butterfield 8, From the Terrace, Appointment in Samarra.*

Omar Khayyam, c. 1028-1122, (Per.) poet. *Rubaiyat.*

Eugene O'Neill, 1888-1953, (U.S.) playwright. *Emperor Jones, Anna Christie, Long Day's Journey into Night.*

George Orwell, 1903-1950, (Br.) novelist, essayist. *Animal Farm, Nineteen Eighty-Four.*

Thomas (Tom) Paine, 1737-1809, (U.S.) author, political theorist. *Common Sense.*

Dorothy Parker, 1893-967, (U.S.) poet, short-story writer. *Enough Rope, Laments for the Living.*

Boris Pasternak, 1890-1960, (R.) poet, novelist. *Doctor Zhivago, My Sister, Life.*

Samuel Pepys, 1633-1703, (Br.) public official, author of the greatest diary in the English language.

S. J. Perelman, 1904-1979, (U.S.) humorist. *The Road to Miltown, Under the Spreading Atrophy.*

Francesco Petrarca, 1304-1374, (It.) poet, humanist. *Africa, Trionfi, Canzoniere, On Solitude.*

Luigi Pirandello, 1867-1936, (It.) novelist, dramatist. *Six Characters in Search of an Author.*

Edgar Allan Poe, 1809-1849, (U.S.) poet, short-story writer, critic. "Annabel Lee," "The Raven," "The Fall of the House of Usher."

Alexander Pope, 1688-1744, (Br.) poet. *The Rape of the Lock, An Essay on Man.*

Katherine Anne Porter, 1890-1980, (U.S.) novelist, short story writer. *Ship of Fools.*

Ezra Pound, 1885-1972, (U.S.) poet. *Cantos.*

Marcel Proust, 1871-1922, (F.) novelist. *A la recherche du temps perdu (Remembrance of Things Past).*

Aleksandr Pushkin, 1799-1837, (R.) poet, prose writer. *Boris Godunov, Eugene Onegin, The Bronze Horseman.*

François Rabelais, 1495-1553, (F.) writer, physician. *Gargantua, Pantagruel.*

Jean Racine, 1639-1699, (F.) dramatist. *Andromaque, Phèdre, Bérénice, Britannicus.*

Ayn Rand, 1905-1982 (Rus.-U.S.) novelist, philosopher. *The Fountainhead, Atlas Shrugged.*

Erich Maria Remarque, 1898-1970, (Ger.-U.S.) novelist. *All Quiet on the Western Front.*

Samuel Richardson, 1689-1761, (Br.) novelist. *Clarissa Harlowe, Pamela; or, Virtue Rewarded.*

Rainer Maria Rilke, 1875-1926, (G.) poet. *Life and Songs, Divine Elegies, Sonnets to Orpheus.*

Arthur Rimbaud, 1854-1891, (F.) *A Season in Hell,* "Le Bateau ivre."

Theodore Roethke, 1908-1963, (U.S.) poet. *Open House, The Waking, The Far Field.*

Romain Rolland, 1866-1944, (F.) novelist, biographer. *Jean-Christophe.*

Pierre de Ronsard, 1524-1585, (F.) poet. *Sonnets pour Hélène.*

Edmond Rostand, 1868-1918, (F.) poet, dramatist. *Cyrano de Bergerac.*

Damon Runyon, 1880-1946, (U.S.) short-story writer, journalist. *Guys and Dolls, Blue Plate Special.*

John Ruskin, 1819-1900, (Br.) critic, social theorist. *Modern Painters, The Seven Lamps of Architecture.*

Antoine de Saint-Exupery, 1900-1944, (F.) writer, aviator. *Wind, Sand and Stars, Le Petit Prince.*

George Sand, 1804-1876, (F.) novelist. *Consuelo, The Haunted Pool, Les Maitres sonneurs.*

Carl Sandburg, 1878-1967, (U.S.) poet. *Chicago Poems, Smoke and Steel, Harvest Poems.*

George Santayana, 1863-1952, (U.S.) poet, essayist, philosopher. *The Sense of Beauty, The Realms of Being.*

William Saroyan, 1908-1981, (U.S.) playwright, novelist. *The Time of Your Life, The Human Comedy.*

Jean-Paul Sartre, 1905-1980, (Fr.) philosopher, novelist, playwright, *Nausea, No Exit, On Being and Nothingness.*

Friedrich von Schiller, 1759-1805, (G.) dramatist, poet, historian. *Don Carlos, Maria Stuart, Wilhelm Tell.*

Sir Walter Scott, 1771-1832, (Sc.) novelist, poet. *Ivanhoe, Rob Roy, The Bride of Lammermoor.*

Jaroslav Seifert, 1902-1986, (Cz.) poet.

William Shakespeare, 1564-1616, (Br.) dramatist, poet. *Romeo and Juliet, Hamlet, King Lear, The Merchant of Venice.*

George Bernard Shaw, 1856-1950, (Ir.) playwright, critic. *St. Joan, Pygmalion, Major Barbara, Man and Superman.*

Mary Wollstonecraft Shelley, 1797-1851, (Br.) author. *Frankenstein.*

Percy Bysshe Shelley, 1792-1822, (Br.) poet. *Prometheus Unbound, Adonais,* "Ode to the West Wind," "To a Skylark."

Richard B. Sheridan, 1751-1816, (Br.) dramatist. *The Rivals, School for Scandal.*

Mikhail Sholokhov, 1906-1984 (U.S.S.R.) author, 1965 Nobel laureate. *And Quiet Flows the Don.*

Upton Sinclair, 1878-1968, (U.S.) novelist. *The Jungle.*

Edmund Spenser, 1552-1599, (Br.) poet. *The Faerie Queen.*

Christina Stead, 1903-1983 (Austral.) novelist, short-story writer. *The Man Who Loved Children.*

Richard Steele, 1672-1729, (Br.) essayist, playwright, began the Tatler and Spectator. *The Conscious Lovers.*

Gertrude Stein, 1874-1946, (U.S.) author. *Three Lives, The Autobiography of Alice B. Toklas.*

John Steinbeck, 1902-1968, (U.S.) novelist. *Grapes of Wrath, Of Mice and Men, Winter of Our Discontent.*

Stendhal (Marie Henri Beyle), 1783-1842, (F.) poet, novelist. *The Red and the Black, The Charterhouse of Parma.*

Laurence Sterne, 1713-1768, (Br.) novelist. *Tristram Shandy.*

Wallace Stevens, 1879-1955, (U.S.) poet. *Harmonium, The Man With the Blue Guitar, Transport to Summer.*

Robert Louis Stevenson, 1850-1894, (Br.) novelist, poet, essayist. *Treasure Island, A Child's Garden of Verses.*

Rex Stout, 1886-1975, (U.S.) novelist, created Nero Wolfe.

Harriet Beecher Stowe, 1811-1896, (U.S.) novelist. *Uncle Tom's Cabin.*

Lytton Strachey, 1880-1932, (Br.) biographer, critic. *Eminent Victorians, Queen Victoria, Elizabeth and Essex.*

August Strindberg, 1849-1912, (Swed.) dramatist, novelist. *The Father, Miss Julie, The Creditors.*

Jonathan Swift, 1667-1745, (Br.) author. *Gulliver's Travels.*

Algernon C. Swinburne, 1837-1909, (Br.) poet, critic. *Songs Before Sunrise.*

John M. Synge, 1871-1909, (Ir.) poet, dramatist. *Riders to the Sea, The Playboy of the Western World.*

Rabindranath Tagore, 1861-1941, (Ind.), author, poet. *Sadhana, The Realization of Life, Gitanjali.*

Sara Teasdale, 1884-1933, (U.S.) poet. *Helen of Troy and Other Poems, Rivers to the Sea, Flame and Shadow.*

Alfred Lord Tennyson, 1809-1892, (Br.) poet. *Idylls of the King, In Memoriam,* "The Charge of the Light Brigade."

William Makepeace Thackeray, 1811-1863, (Br.) novelist. *Vanity Fair.*

Dylan Thomas, 1914-1953, (Welsh) poet. *Under Milk Wood, A Child's Christmas in Wales.*

Henry David Thoreau, 1817-1862, (U.S.) transcendentalist thinker, writer. *Walden.*

James Thurber, 1894-1961, (U.S.) humorist, artist. *The New Yorker, The Owl in the Attic, Thurber Carnival.*

J.R.R. Tolkien, 1892-1973, (Br.) author. *The Hobbit, Lord of the Rings.*

Leo Tolstoy, 1828-1910, (R.) novelist. *War and Peace, Anna Karenina.*

Anthony Trollope, 1815-1882, (Br.) novelist. *The Warden, Barchester Towers,* The Palliser novels.

Ivan Turgenev, 1818-1883, (R.) novelist, short-story writer. *Fathers and Sons, First Love, A Month in the Country.*

Mark Twain (Samuel Clemens), 1835-1910, (U.S.) novelist, humorist. *The Adventures of Huckleberry Finn, Tom Sawyer.*

Sigrid Undset, 1881-1949, (Nor.) novelist, poet. *Kristin Lavransdatter.*

Paul Valéry, 1871-1945, (F.) poet, critic. *La Jeune Parque, The Graveyard by the Sea.*

Jules Verne, 1828-1905, (F.) novelist, originator of modern science fiction. *Twenty Thousand Leagues Under the Sea.*

François Villon, 1431-1463?, (F.) poet. *Le petit et le Grand, Testament.*

Evelyn Waugh, 1903-1966, (Br.) satirist. *The Loved One, Brideshead Revisited.*

H.G. Wells, 1866-1946, (Br.) author. *The Time Machine, The Invisible Man, The War of the Worlds.*

Rebecca West, 1893-1983 (Br.) author. *Black Lamb and Grey Falcon.*

Edith Wharton, 1862-1937, (U.S.) novelist. *The Age of Innocence, The House of Mirth.*

E.B. White, 1899-1985 (U.S.), essayist, children's book author. *Here is New York, Charlotte's Web.*

T.H. White, 1906-1964, (Br.) author. *The Once and Future King.*

Walt Whitman, 1819-1892, (U.S.) poet. *Leaves of Grass.*

John Greenleaf Whittier, 1807-1892, (U.S.) poet, journalist. *Snow-bound.*

Oscar Wilde, 1854-1900, (Ir.) author, wit. *The Picture of Dorian Gray, The Importance of Being Earnest.*

Thornton Wilder, 1897-1975, (U.S.) playwright. *Our Town, The Skin of Our Teeth, The Matchmaker.*

Tennessee Williams, 1912-1983 (U.S.) playwright. *A Streetcar Named Desire, Cat on a Hot Tin Roof, The Glass Menagerie.*

William Carlos Williams, 1883-1963, (U.S.) poet, physician. *Tempers, Al Que Quiere!, Paterson.*

Edmund Wilson, 1895-1972, (U.S.) author, literary and social critic. *Axel's Castle, To the Finland Station.*

P.G. Wodehouse, 1881-1975, (U.S.) poet, dramatist. The "Jeeves" novels, *Anything Goes.*

Thomas Wolfe, 1900-1938, (U.S.) novelist. *Look Homeward, Angel, You Can't Go Home Again, Of Time and the River.*

Virginia Woolf, 1882-1941, (Br.) novelist, essayist. *Mrs. Dalloway, To the Lighthouse, The Waves.*

William Wordsworth, 1770-1850, (Br.) poet. "Tintern Abbey," "Ode: Intimations of Immortality."

William Butler Yeats, 1865-1939, (Ir.) poet, playwright. *The Wild Swans at Coole, The Tower, Last Poems.*

Émile Zola, 1840-1902, (F.) novelist. *Nana, The Dram Shop.*

Poets Laureate of England

There is no authentic record of the origin of the office of Poet Laureate of England. According to Warton, there was a Versificator Regis, or King's Poet, in the reign of Henry III (1216-1272), and he was paid 100 shillings a year. Geoffrey Chaucer (1340-1400) assumed the title of Poet Laureate, and in 1389 got a royal grant of a yearly allowance of wine. In the reign of Edward IV (1461-1483), John Kay held the post. Under Henry VII (1485-1509), Andrew Bernard was the Poet Laureate, and was succeeded under Henry VIII (1509-1547) by John Skelton. Next came Edmund Spenser, who died in 1599; then Samuel Daniel, appointed 1599, and then Ben Jonson, 1619. Sir William D'Avenant was appointed in 1637. He was a godson of William Shakespeare.

Others were John Dryden, 1670; Thomas Shadwell, 1688; Nahum Tate, 1692; Nicholas Rowe, 1715; the Rev. Laurence Eusden, 1718; Colley Cibber, 1730; William Whitehead, 1757, on the refusal of Gray; Rev. Thomas Warton, 1785, on the refusal of Mason; Henry J. Pye, 1790; Robert Southey, 1813, on the refusal of Sir Walter Scott; William Wordsworth, 1843; Alfred, Lord Tennyson, 1850; Alfred Austin, 1896; Robert Bridges, 1913; John Masefield, 1930; Cecil Day Lewis, 1967; Sir John Betjeman, 1972; Ted Hughes, 1984.

Noted Scientists of the Past

Howard H. Aiken, 1900-1973, (U.S.) mathematician, credited with designing forerunner of the digital computer.

Albertus Magnus, 1193-1280, (G.) theologian, philosopher, scientist, established medieval Christian study of natural science.

Andre-Marie Ampère, 1775-1836, (F.) scientist known for contributions to electrodynamics.

Amedeo Avogadro, 1776-1856, (It.) chemist, physicist, advanced important theories on properties of gases.

A.C. Becquerel, 1788-1878, (F.) physicist, pioneer in electrochemical science.

A.H. Becquerel, 1852-1908, (F.) physicist, discovered radioactivity in uranium.

Alexander Graham Bell, 1847-1922, (U.S.) inventor, first to patent and commercially exploit the telephone, 1876.

Daniel Bernoulli, 1700-1782, (Swiss) mathematician, advanced kinetic theory of gases and fluids.

Jöns Jakob Berzelius, 1779-1848, (Swed.) chemist, developed modern chemical symbols and formulas.

Henry Bessemer, 1813-1898, (Br.) engineer, invented Bessemer steel-making process.

Louis Blériot, 1872-1936, (F.) engineer, pioneer aviator, invented and constructed monoplanes.

Niels Bohr, 1885-1962, (Dan.) physicist, leading figure in the development of quantum theory.

Max Born, 1882-1970, (G.) physicist known for research in quantum mechanics.

Satyendranath Bose, 1894-1974, (In.) physicist, chemist, mathematician known for Bose statistics, forerunner of modern quantum theory.

Walter Brattain, 1902-1988, (U.S.) inventor, worked on invention of transistor.

Louis de Broglie, 1893-1987, (F.) physicist, best known for wave theory.

Robert Bunsen, 1811-1899, (G.) chemist, invented Bunsen burner.

Luther Burbank, 1849-1926, (U.S.) plant breeder whose work developed plant breeding into a modern science.

Vannevar Bush, 1890-1974, (U.S.) electrical engineer, developed differential analyzer, first electronic analogue computer.

Alexis Carrel, 1873-1944, (F.) surgeon, biologist, developed methods of suturing blood vessels and transplanting organs.

George Washington Carver, 1860?-1943, (U.S.) agricultural chemist, experimenter, benefactor of South, a black hero.

Henry Cavendish, 1731-1810, (Br.) chemist, physicist, discovered hydrogen.

James Chadwick, 1891-1974, (Br.) physicist, discovered the neutron.

Jean M. Charcot, 1825-1893, (F.) neurologist known for work on hysteria, hypnotism, sclerosis.

Albert Claude, 1899-1983, (Belg.) a founder of modern cell biology.

John D. Cockcroft, 1897-1967, (Br.) nuclear physicist, constructed first atomic particle accelerator with E.T.S. Walton.

William Crookes, 1832-1919, (Br.) physicist, chemist, discovered thallium, invented a cathode-ray tube, radiometer.

Marie Curie, 1867-1934, (Pol.-F.) physical chemist known for work on radium and its compounds.

Pierre Curie, 1859-1906, (F.) physical chemist known for work with his wife on radioactivity.

Gottlieb Daimler, 1834-1900, (G.) engineer, inventor, pioneer automobile manufacturer.

John Dalton, 1766-1844, (Br.) chemist, physicist, formulated atomic theory, made first table of atomic weights.

Charles Darwin, 1809-1882, (Br.) naturalist, established theory of organic evolution.

Humphry Davy, 1778-1829, (Br.) chemist, research in electrochemistry led to isolation of potassium, sodium, calcium, barium, boron, magnesium, and strontium.

Lee De Forest, 1873-1961, (U.S.) inventor, pioneer in development of wireless telegraphy, sound pictures, television.

Max Delbruck, 1907-1981, (U.S.) pioneer in modern molecular genetics.

Rudolf Diesel, 1858-1913, (G.) mechanical engineer, patented Diesel engine.

Thomas Dooley, 1927-1961, (U.S.) "jungle doctor," noted for efforts to supply medical aid to underdeveloped countries.

Christian Doppler, 1803-1853, (Aus.) physicist, demonstrated Doppler effect (change in energy wavelengths caused by motion).

Thomas A. Edison, 1847-1931, (U.S.) inventor, held over 1,000 patents, including incandescent electric lamp, phonograph.

Paul Ehrlich, 1854-1915, (G.) bacteriologist, pioneer in modern immunology and bacteriology.

Albert Einstein, 1879-1955, (Ger.-U.S.) theoretical physicist, known for formulation of relativity theory.

John F. Enders, 1897-1985, (U.S.) virologist who helped discover vaccines against polio, measles, and mumps.

Leonhard Euler, 1707-1783, (Swiss) mathematician, physicist, authored first calculus book.

Gabriel Fahrenheit, 1686-1736, (G.) physicist, introduced Fahrenheit scale for thermometers.

Michael Faraday, 1791-1867, (Br.) chemist, physicist, known for work in field of electricity.

Pierre de Fermat, 1601-1665, (F.) mathematician, discovered analytic geometry, founded modern theory of numbers and calculus of probabilities.

Enrico Fermi, 1901-1954, (It.) physicist, one of chief architects of the nuclear age.

Galileo Ferraris, 1847-1897, (It.) physicist, electrical engineer, discovered principle of rotary magnetic field.

Richard Feynman, 1919-1988, (U.S.) a leading theoretical physicist of the postwar generation.

Camille Flammarion, 1842-1925, (F.) astronomer, popularized study of astronomy.

Alexander Fleming, 1881-1955, (Br.) bacteriologist, discovered penicillin.

Jean B.J. Fourier, 1768-1830, (F.) mathematician, discovered theorem governing periodic oscillation.

James Franck, 1882-1964, (G.) physicist, proved value of quantum theory.

Sigmund Freud, 1856-1939, (Aus.) psychiatrist, founder of psychoanalysis.

Galileo Galilei, 1564-1642, (It.) astronomer, physicist, a founder of the experimental method.

Luigi Galvani, 1737-1798, (It.) physician, physicist, known as founder of galvanism.

Carl Friedrich Gauss, 1777-1855, (G.) mathematician, astronomer, physicist, made important contributions to almost every field of physical science, founded a number of new fields.

Joseph Gay-Lussac, 1778-1850, (F.) chemist, physicist, investigated behavior of gases, discovered law of combining volumes.

Josiah W. Gibbs, 1839-1903, (U.S.) theoretical physicist, chemist, founded chemical thermodynamics.

Robert H. Goddard, 1882-1945 (U.S.) physicist, father of modern rocketry.

George W. Goethals, 1858-1928, (U.S.) army engineer, built the Panama Canal.

William C. Gorgas, 1854-1920, (U.S.) sanitarian, U.S. army surgeon-general, his work to prevent yellow fever, malaria helped insure construction of Panama Canal.

Ernest Haeckel, 1834-1919, (G.) zoologist, evolutionist, a strong proponent of Darwin.

Otto Hahn, 1879-1968, (G.) chemist, worked on atomic fission.

J.B.S. Haldane, 1892-1964, (Sc.) scientist, known for work as geneticist and application of mathematics to science.

James Hall, 1761-1832, (Br.) geologist, chemist, founded experimental geology, geochemistry.

Edmund Halley, 1656-1742, (Br.) astronomer, calculated the orbits of many planets.

William Harvey, 1578-1657, (Br.) physician, anatomist, discovered circulation of the blood.

Hermann v. Helmholtz, 1821-1894, (G.) physicist, anatomist, physiologist, made fundamental contributions to physiology, optics, electrodynamics, mathematics, meteorology,

William Herschel, 1738-1822, (Br.) astronomer, discovered Uranus.

Heinrich Hertz, 1857-1894, (G.) physicist, his discoveries led to wireless telegraphy.

David Hilbert, 1862-1943, (G.) mathematician, formulated first satisfactory set of axioms for modern Euclidean geometry.

Edwin P. Hubble, 1889-1953, (U.S.) astronomer, produced first observational evidence of expanding universe.

Alexander v. Humboldt, 1769-1859, (G.) explorer, naturalist, propagator of earth sciences, originated ecology, geophysics.

Julian Huxley, 1887-1975, (Br.) biologist, a gifted exponent and philosopher of science.

Edward Jenner, 1749-1823, (Br.) physician, discovered vaccination.

William Jenner, 1815-1898, (Br.) physician, pathological anatomist.

Frederic Joliot-Curie, 1900-1958, (F.) physicist, with his wife continued work of Curies on radioactivity.

Irene Joliot-Curie, 1897-1956, (F.) physicist, continued work of Curies in radioactivity.

James P. Joule, 1818-1889, (Br.) physicist, determined relationship between heat and mechanical energy (conservation of energy).

Carl Jung, 1875-1961, (Sw.) psychiatrist, founder of analytical psychology.

Wm. Thomson Kelvin, 1824-1907, (Br.) mathematician, physicist, known for work on heat and electricity.

Sister Elizabeth Kenny, 1886-1952, (Austral.) nurse, developed method of treatment for polio.

Johannes Kepler, 1571-1630, (G.) astronomer, discovered important laws of planetary motion.

Joseph Lagrange, 1736-1813, (F.) geometer, astronomer, worked in all fields of analysis, and number theory, and analytical and celestial mechanics.

Jean B. Lamarck, 1744-1829, (F.) naturalist, forerunner of Darwin in evolutionary theory.

Irving Langmuir, 1881-1957, (U.S.) physical chemist, his studies of molecular films on solid and liquid surfaces opened new fields in colloid research and biochemistry.

Pierre S. Laplace, 1749-1827, (F.) astronomer, physicist, put forth nebular hypothesis of origin of solar system.

Antoine Lavoisier, 1743-1794, (F.) chemist, founder of modern chemistry.

Ernest O. Lawrence, 1901-1958, (U.S.) physicist, invented the cyclotron.

Louis Leakey, 1903-1972, (Br.) anthropologist, discovered important fossils, remains of early hominids.

Anton van Leeuwenhoek, 1632-1723, (Du.) microscopist, father of microbiology.

Gottfried Wilhelm Leibniz, 1646-1716, (G.) mathematician, developed theories of differential and integral calculus.

Justus von Liebig, 1803-1873, (G.) chemist, established quantitative organic chemical analysis.

Joseph Lister, 1827-1912, (Br.) pioneer of antiseptic surgery.

Percival Lowell, 1855-1916, (U.S.) astronomer, predicted the existence of Pluto.

Guglielmo Marconi, 1874-1937, (It.) physicist, known for his development of wireless telegraphy.

James Clerk Maxwell, 1831-1879, (Sc.) physicist, known especially for his work in electricity and magnetism.

Maria Goeppert Mayer, 1906-1972, (G.-U.S.) physicist, independently developed theory of structure of atomic nuclei.

Lise Meitner, 1878-1968, (Aus.) physicist whose work contributed to the development of the atomic bomb.

Gregor J. Mendel, 1822-1884, (Aus.) botanist, known for his experimental work on heredity.

Franz Mesmer, 1734-1815, (G.) physician, developed theory of animal magnetism.

Albert A. Michelson, 1852-1931, (U.S.) physicist, established speed of light as a fundamental constant.

Robert A. Millikan, 1868-1953, (U.S.) physicist, noted for study of elementary electronic charge and photoelectric effect.

Thomas Hunt Morgan, 1866-1945, (U.S.) geneticist, embryologist, established chromosome theory of heredity.

Isaac Newton, 1642-1727, (Br.) natural philosopher, mathematician, discovered law of gravitation, laws of motion.

J. Robert Oppenheimer, 1904-1967, (U.S.) physicist, director of Los Alamos during development of the atomic bomb.

Wilhelm Ostwald, 1853-1932, (G.) physical chemist, philosopher, chief founder of physical chemistry.

Louis Pasteur, 1822-1895, (F.) chemist, originated process of pasteurization.

Max Planck, 1858-1947, (G.) physicist, originated and developed quantum theory.

Henri Poincaré, 1854-1912, (F.) mathematician, physicist, influenced cosmology, relativity, and topology.

Joseph Priestley, 1733-1804, (Br.) chemist, one of the discoverers of oxygen.

Rabi, Isidor Isaac, 1899-1988 (U.S.) physicist, pioneered atom exploration.

Walter S. Reed, 1851-1902, (U.S.) army pathologist, bacteriologist, proved mosquitos transmit yellow fever.

Bernhard Riemann, 1826-1866, (G.) mathematician, contributed to development of calculus, complex variable theory, and mathematical physics.

Wilhelm Roentgen, 1845-1923, (G.) physicist, discovered X-rays.

Bertrand Russell, 1872-1970, (Br.) logician, philosopher, one of the founders of modern logic, wrote *Principia Mathematica.*

Ernest Rutherford, 1871-1937, (Br.) physicist, discovered the atomic nucleus.

Giovanni Schiaparelli, 1835-1910, (It.) astronomer, hypothesized canals on the surface of Mars.

Angelo Secchi, 1818-1878, (It.) astronomer, pioneer in classifying stars by their spectra.

Harlow Shapley, 1885-1972, (U.S.) astronomer, noted for his studies of the galaxy.

Charles P. Steinmetz, 1865-1923, (G.-U.S.) electrical engineer, developed basic ideas on alternating current systems.

Leo Szilard, 1898-1964, (Hung.-U.S.) physicist, helped create first sustained nuclear reaction.

Nikola Tesla, 1856-1943, (Croatia-U.S.) electrical engineer, contributed to most developments in electronics.

Rudolf Virchow, 1821-1902, (G.) pathologist, a founder of cellular pathology.

Alessandro Volta, 1745-1827, (It.) physicist, pioneer in electricity.

Alfred Russell Wallace, 1823-1913, (Br.) naturalist, proposed concept of evolution similar to Darwin.

August v. Wasserman, 1866-1925, (G.) bacteriologist, discovered reaction used as test for syphilis.

James E. Watt, 1736-1819, (Sc.) mechanical engineer, inventor, invented modern steam condensing engine.

Alfred L. Wegener, 1880-1930, (G.) meteorologist, geophysicist, postulated theory of continental drift.

Norbert Wiener, 1894-1964, (U.S.) mathematician, founder of the science of cybernetics.

Sweall Wright, 1890-1988 (U.S.) a leading evolutionary theorist.

Ferdinand v. Zeppelin, 1838-1917 (G.) soldier, aeronaut, airship designer.

Noted Business Leaders, Industrialists, and Philanthropists of the Past

Elizabeth Arden (F.N. Graham), 1884-1966, (U.S.) Canadian-born businesswoman founded and headed cosmetics empire.

John Jacob Astor, 1763-1848, (U.S.) German-born fur trader, banker, real estate magnate; at death, richest in U.S.

Adolphus Busch, 1839-1913, (U.S.) German-born businessman, established brewery empire.

Asa Candler, 1851-1929, (U.S.) founded Coca-Cola Co.

Andrew Carnegie, 1835-1919, (U.S.) Scots-born industrialist, founded U.S. Steel; financed over 2,800 libraries.

William Colgate, 1783-1857, (U.S.) British-born businessman, philanthropist; founded soap-making empire.

Samuel Cunard, 1787-1865, (Can.) pioneered trans-Atlantic steam navigation.

Walt Disney, 1901-1966, (U.S.) pioneer in cinema animation, built entertainment empire.

Herbert H. Dow, 1866-1930, (U.S.) Canadian-born founder of chemical co.

Eleuthere I. du Pont, 1771-1834, (U.S.) French-born gunpowder manufacturer; founded one of world's largest business empires.

William C. Durant, 1861-1947, (U.S.) industrialist, formed General Motors.

George Eastman, 1854-1932, (U.S.) inventor, manufacturer of photographic equipment.

Henry M. Flagler, 1830-1913, (U.S.) financier, helped form Standard Oil; developed Florida as resort state.

Henry Ford, 1867-1947, (U.S.) automaker, developed first popular low-priced car.

Alfred C. Fuller, 1885-1973, (U.S.) Canadian-born businessman, founded brush co.

Jean Paul Getty, 1892-1976, (U.S.) founded oil empire.

Meyer Guggenheim, 1828-1905, (U.S.) Swiss-born merchant, philanthropist; built merchandising, mining empires.

William Randolph Hearst, 1863-1951, (U.S.) a dominant figure in American journalism; built vast publishing empire.

Henry J. Heinz, 1844-1919, (U.S.) founded food empire.

James J. Hill, 1838-1916, (U.S.) Canadian-born railroad magnate, financier; founded Great Northern Railway.

Conrad N. Hilton, 1888-1979, (U.S.) intl. hotel chain founder.

Howard Hughes, 1905-1976, (U.S.) industrialist, financier, movie maker.

H.L. Hunt, 1889-1974, (U.S.) oil magnate.

Henry J. Kaiser, 1882-1967, (U.S.) industrialist, built empire in steel, aluminum.

Will K. Kellogg, 1860-1951, (U.S.) businessman, philanthropist, founded breakfast food co.

Ray A. Kroc, 1902-1984, (U.S.) builder of McDonald's fast food empire; owner, San Diego Padres baseball team.

Alfred Krupp, 1812-1887, (G.) armaments magnate.

John Pierpont Morgan, 1837-1913, (U.S.) most powerful figure in U.S. finance and industry at the turn-of-the-century.

Aristotle Onassis, 1900-1975, (Gr.) shipping magnate.

John D. Rockefeller, 1839-1937, (U.S.) industrialist, established Standard Oil; became world's wealthiest person.

John D. Rockefeller Jr., 1874-1960, (U.S.) philanthropist, established foundation; provided land for United Nations.

Meyer A. Rothschild, 1743-1812, (G.) founded international banking house.

(Ernst) Werner von Siemens, 1816-1892 (G.) industrialist, inventor.

Cornelius Vanderbilt, 1794-1877, (U.S.) financier, established steamship, railroad empires.

History of the World

Prehistory: Our Ancestors Take Over

Homo sapiens. The precise origins of *homo sapiens,* the species to which all humans belong, are subject to broad speculation based on a small number of fossils, genetic and anatomical studies, and the geological record. But most scientists agree that we evolved from ape-like primate ancestors in a process that began millions of years ago.

Current theories say the first hominid (human-like primate) was *Ramapithecus,* who emerged 12 million years ago. Its remains have been found in Asia, Europe, and Africa. Further development was apparently limited to Africa, where 2 lines of hominids appeared some 5 or 6 million years ago. One was *Australopithecus,* a tool-maker and social animal, who lived from perhaps 4 to 3 million years ago, and then apparently became extinct.

The 2nd was a human line, *Homo habillus,* a large-brained specimen that walked upright and had a dextrous hand. *Homo habillus* lived in semi-permanent camps and had a food-gathering and sharing economy.

Homo erectus, our nearest ancestor, appeared in Africa perhaps 1.75 million years ago, and began spreading into Asia and Europe soon after. It had a fairly large brain and a skeletal structure similar to ours. *Homo erectus* learned to control fire, and probably had primitive language skills. The final brain development to *Homo sapiens* and then to our sub-species *Homo sapiens sapiens* occurred between 500 000 and 50 000 years ago, over a wide geographic area and in many different steps and recombinations. All humans of all races belong to this sub-species.

Earliest cultures. A variety of cultural modes — in tool-making, diet, shelter, and possibly social arrangements and spiritual expression, arose as early mankind adapted to different geographic and climatic zones.

Three basic tool-making traditions are recognized by archeologists as arising and often coexisting from one million years ago to the near past: the *chopper tradition,* found largely in E. Asia, with crude chopping tools and simple flake tools; the *flake tradition,* found in Africa and W. Europe, with a variety of small cutting and flaking tools, and the *biface tradition,* found in all of Africa, W. and S. Europe, and S. Asia, producing pointed hand axes chipped on both faces. Later biface sites yield more refined axes and a variety of other tools, weapons, and ornaments using bone, antler, and wood as well as stone.

Only sketchy evidence remains for the di⁣fferent stages in man's increasing control over the environment. Traces of 400 000-year-old covered wood shelters have been found at Nice, France. Scraping tools at Neanderthal sites (200 000-30 000 BC in Europe, N. Africa, the Middle East and Central Asia) suggest the treatment of skins for clothing. Sites from all parts of the world show seasonal migration patterns and exploitation of a wide range of plant and animal food sources.

Painting and decoration, for which there is evidence at the Nice site, flourished along with stone and ivory sculpture after 30 000 years ago; 60 caves in France and 30 in Spain show remarkable examples of wall painting. Other examples have been found in Africa. Proto-religious rites are suggested by these works, and by evidence of ritual cannibalism by Peking Man, 500 000 BC, and of ritual burial with medicinal plants and flowers by Neanderthals at Shanidar in Iraq.

The Neolithic Revolution. Sometime after 10 000 BC, among widely separated human communities, a series of dramatic technological and social changes occurred that are summed up as the Neolithic Revolution. The cultivation of previously wild plants encouraged the growth of permanent settlements. Animals were domesticated as a work force and food source. The manufacture of pottery and cloth began. These techniques permitted a huge increase in world population and in human control over the earth.

No region can safely claim priority as the "inventor" of these techniques. Dispersed sites in Cen. and S. America, S.E. Asia, and the Middle East show roughly contemporaneous (10000-8000 BC) evidence of one or another "neolithic" trait. Dates near 6000-3000 BC have been given for E. and S. Asian, W. European, and sub-Saharan African neolithic remains. The variety of crops — field grains, rice, maize, and roots, and the varying mix of other traits suggest that the revolution occurred independently in all these regions.

History Begins: 4000 - 1000 BC

Near Eastern cradle. If history began with writing, the first chapter opened in Mesopotamia, the Tigris-Euphrates river valley. Clay tablets with pictographs were used by the Sumerians to keep records after 4000 BC. A **cuneiform** (wedge shaped) script evolved by 3000 BC as a full syllabic alphabet. Neighboring peoples adapted the script to their own language.

Sumerian life centred, from 4000 BC, on large cities (Eridu, Ur, Uruk, Nippur, Kish, Lagash) organized around temples and priestly bureaucracies, with the surrounding plains watered by vast irrigation works and worked with traction plows. Sailboats, wheeled vehicles, potters wheels, and kilns were used. Copper was smelted and tempered in Sumeria from c4000 BC and bronze was produced not long after. Ores, as well as precious stones and metals were obtained through long-distance ship and caravan trade. Iron was used from c2000 BC. Improved ironworking, developed partly by the **Hittites**, became widespread by 1200 BC.

Sumerian political primacy passed among cities and their kingly dynasties. Semitic-speaking peoples, with cultures derived from the Sumerian, founded a succession of dynasties that ruled in Mesopotamia and neighboring areas for most of 1 800 years; among them the **Akkadians** (first under Sargon c2350 BC), the Amorites (whose laws, codified by **Hammurabi**, c1792-1750 BC, have Biblical parallels), and the Assyrians, with interludes of rule by the Hittites, Kassites, and Mitanni, all possibly Indo-Europeans. The political and cultural centre of gravity shifted northwest with each successive empire.

Mesopotamian learning, maintained by scribes and preserved by successive rulers in vast libraries, was not abstract or theoretical. Algebraic and geometric problems could be solved on a practical basis in construction, commerce, or administration. Systematic lists of astronomical phenomena, plants, animals and stones were kept; medical texts listed ailments and their herbal cures.

The Sumerians worshipped anthropomorphic gods representing natural forces — Anu, god of heaven; Enlil (Ea), god of water. Epic poetry related these and other gods in a hierarchy. Sacrifices were made at **ziggurats** — huge stepped temples. Gods were thought to control all events, which could be foretold using oracular materials. This religious pattern persisted into the first millenium BC.

The Syria-Palestine area, site of some of the earliest urban homes (Jericho, 7000 BC), and of the recently uncovered **Ebla** civilization (fl. 2500 BC), experienced Egyptian cultural and political influence along with Mesopotamian. The **Phoenician** coast was an active commercial centre. A phonetic alphabet

Thai bronzes

3500

Bronze Age begins

Sumerian cities

1st pyramids

Egypt unified

Indus Valley civilization

2500

was invented here before 1600 BC. It became the ancestor of all European, Middle Eastern, Indian, S.E. Asian, Ethiopian, and Korean alphabets.

Regional commerce and diplomacy were aided by the use of Akkadian as a *lingua franca*, later replaced by Aramaic.

Egypt. Agricultural villages along the Nile were united by 3300 BC into two kingdoms, Upper and Lower Egypt, unified under the Pharaoh Menes c3100 BC; Nubia to the south was added 2600 BC. A national bureaucracy supervised construction of canals and monuments (**pyramids** starting 2700 BC). Brilliant First Dynasty achievements in architecture, sculpture and painting, set the standards and forms for all subsequent Egyptian civilization and are still admired. **Hieroglyphic writing** appeared by 3400 BC, recording a sophisticated literature including romantic and philosophical modes after 2300 BC.

An ordered hierarchy of gods, including totemistic animal elements, was served by a powerful priesthood in Memphis. The pharaoh was identified with the falcon god Horus. Later trends were the belief in an afterlife, and the quasi-monotheistic reforms of **Akhenaton** (c1379-1362 BC).

After a period of conquest by Semitic Hyksos from Asia (c1700-1500 BC), the New Kingdom established an empire in Syria. Egypt became increasingly embroiled in Asiatic wars and diplomacy. Eventually it was conquered by Persia in 525 BC, and it faded away as an independent culture.

India. An urban civilization with a so-far-undeciphered writing system stretched across the Indus Valley and along the Arabian Sea c3000-1500 BC. Major sites are Harappa and **Mohenjo-Daro** in Pakistan, well-planned geometric cities with underground sewers and vast granaries. The entire region (1 560 000 sq. km) may have been ruled as a single state. Bronze was used, and arts and crafts were highly developed. Religious life apparently took the form of fertility cults.

Indus civilization was probably in decline when it was destroyed by **Aryan invaders** from the northwest, speaking an Indo-European language from which all the languages of Pakistan, north India and Bangladesh descend. Led by a warrior aristocracy whose legendary deeds are recorded in the **Rig Veda**, the Aryans spread east and south, bringing their pantheon of sky gods, elaborate priestly (Brahmin) ritual, and the beginnings of the caste system; local customs and beliefs were assimilated by the conquerors.

Europe. On Crete, the bronze-age **Minoan civilization** emerged c2500 BC. A prosperous economy and richly decorative art (e.g. at Knossos palace) was supported by seaborne commerce. Mycenae and other cities in Greece and Asia Minor (e.g. **Troy**) preserved elements of the culture to c1100 BC. Cretan Linear A script, c2000-1700 BC, is undeciphered; Linear B, c1300-1200 BC, records a Greek dialect.

Possible connection between Minoan-Mycenaean monumental stonework, and the great megalithic monuments and tombs of W. Europe, Iberia, and Malta (c4000-1500 BC) is unclear.

China. Proto-Chinese neolithic cultures had long covered northern and southeastern China when the first large political state was organized in the north by the **Shang dynasty** c1500 BC. Shang kings called themselves Sons of Heaven, and presided over a cult of human and animal sacrifice to ancestors and nature gods. The Chou dynasty, starting c1100 BC, expanded the area of the Son of Heaven's dominion, but feudal states exercised most temporal power.

A writing system with 2 000 different characters was already in use under the Shang, with **pictographs** later supplemented by phonetic characters. The system, with modifications, is still in use, despite changes in spoken Chinese.

Technical advances allowed urban specialists to create fine ceramic and jade products, and bronze casting after 1500 BC was the most advanced in the world.

Bronze artifacts have recently been discovered in northern Thailand dating to 3600 BC, hundreds of years before similar Middle Eastern finds.

Americas. Olmecs settled on the Gulf coast of Mexico, 1500 BC, and soon developed the first civilization in the Western Hemisphere. Temple cities and huge stone sculpture date to 1200 BC. A rudimentary calendar and writing system existed. Olmec religion, centring on a jaguar god, and art forms influenced all later Meso-American cultures.

Neolithic ceremonial centres were built on the Peruvian desert coast, c2000 BC.

Classical Era of Old World Civilizations

Greece. After a period of decline during the Dorian Greek invasions (1200-1000 BC), Greece and the Aegean area developed a unique civilization. Drawing upon Mycenaean traditions, Mesopotamian learning (weights and measures, lunisolar calendar, astronomy, musical scales), the Phoenician alphabet (modified for Greek), and Egyptian art, the revived **Greek city-states** saw a rich elaboration of intellectual life. Long-range commerce was aided by metal coinage (introduced by the Lydians in Asia Minor before 700 BC); colonies were founded around the Mediterranean and Black Sea shores (Cumae in Italy 760 BC, Massalia in France c600 BC).

. **Philosophy**, starting with Ionian speculation on the nature of matter and the universe (Thales c634-546), and including mathematical speculation (Pythagoras c580-c500), culminated in Athens in the rationalist idealism of **Plato** (c428-347) and **Socrates** (c470-399); the latter was executed for alleged impiety. Aristotle (384-322) united all fields of study in his system. The arts were highly valued. Architecture culminated in the **Parthenon** in Athens (438, sculpture by Phidias); poetry and drama (Aeschylus 525-456) thrived. Male beauty and strength, a chief artistic theme, were enhanced at the gymnasium and the national games at Olympia.

Ruled by local tyrants or oligarchies, the Greeks were never politically united, but managed to resist inclusion in the Persian Empire (Darius defeated at Marathon 490 BC, Xerxes at Salamis, Plataea 479 BC). Local warfare was common; the **Peloponnesian Wars**, 431-404 BC, ended in Sparta's victory over Athens. Greek political power waned, but classical Greek cultural forms spread throughout the ancient world from the Atlantic to India.

Hebrews. Nomadic Hebrew tribes entered Canaan before 1200 BC, settling among other Semitic peoples speaking the same language. They brought from the desert a **monotheistic faith** said to have been revealed to Abraham in Canaan c1800 BC and to Moses at Mt. Sinai c1250 BC, after the Hebrews' escape from bondage in Egypt. David (ruled 1000-961 BC) and Solomon (ruled 961-922 BC) united the

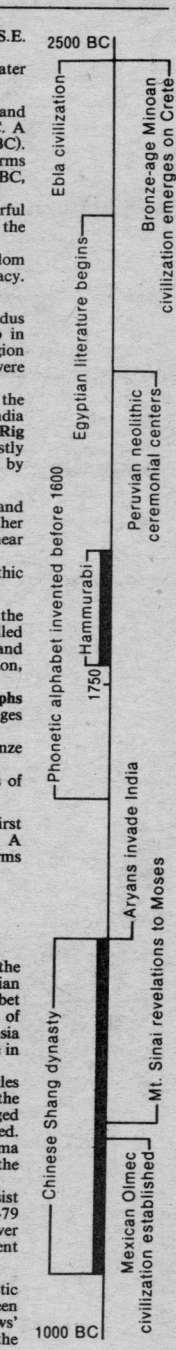

2500 BC

Ebla civilization

Bronze-age Minoan civilization emerges on Crete

Egyptian literature begins

Peruvian neolithic ceremonial centers

Phonetic alphabet invented before 1600

Hammurabi

1750

Aryans invade India

Mt. Sinai revelations to Moses

Chinese Shang dynasty

Mexican Olmec civilization established

1000 BC

Paleontology: The History of Life

All dates are approximate, and are subject to change based on new fossil finds or new dating techniques; but the sequence of events is generally accepted. Dates are in years before the present.

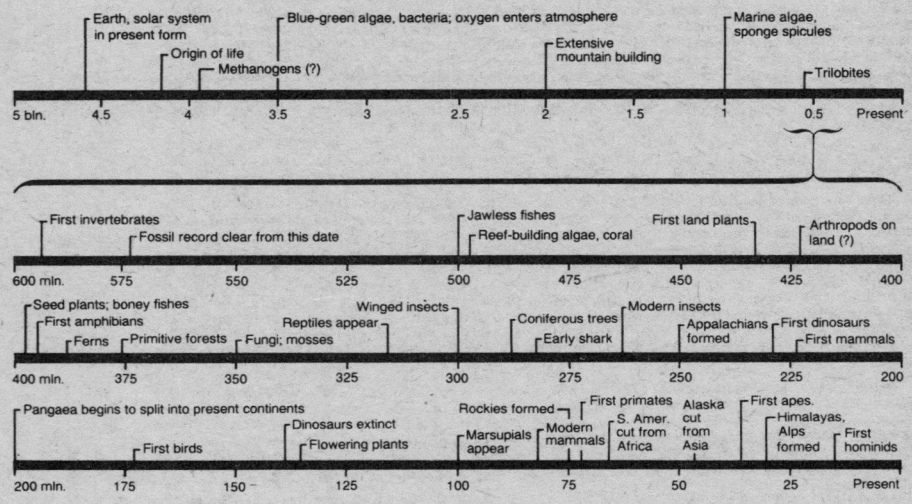

Earth, solar system in present form
Origin of life
Methanogens (?)
Blue-green algae, bacteria; oxygen enters atmosphere
Extensive mountain building
Marine algae, sponge spicules
Trilobites
5 bln.
4.5
4
3.5
3
2.5
2
1.5
1
0.5
Present
First invertebrates
Fossil record clear from this date
Jawless fishes
Reef-building algae, coral
First land plants
Arthropods on land (?)
600 mln.
575
550
525
500
475
450
425
400
Seed plants; boney fishes
First amphibians
Ferns
Primitive forests
Fungi; mosses
Reptiles appear
Winged insects
Coniferous trees
Early shark
Modern insects
Appalachians formed
First dinosaurs
First mammals
400 mln.
375
350
325
300
275
250
225
200
Pangaea begins to split into present continents
First birds
Dinosaurs extinct
Flowering plants
Rockies formed
Marsupials appear
Modern mammals
First primates
S. Amer. cut from Africa
Alaska cut from Asia
First apes.
Himalayas, Alps formed
First hominids
200 mln.
175
150
125
100
75
50
25
Present

Ancient Near Eastern Civilizations 4000 B.C.-500 B.C.

Scythians
Danube R.
Black Sea
MACEDON
LYDIA
PHRYGIA
Sardis
HITTITES
Halys R.
Kushshar
MINOANS
Mediterranean Sea
CILICIA
ASSYRIA
ARMENIA
PHOENICIANS
ARAM
Ebla
Damascus
Mari
Sidon
Tyre
Jerusalem
HEBREWS
ARABS
Nineveh
Ashur
MEDES
Ecbatana
Euphrates R.
BABYLONIA
Tigris R.
ELAM
Susa
Babylon
SUMER
Ur
Memphis
EGYPT
Tel el Amarna
Nile
Thebes
Red Sea
NUBIA
SABAEANS
Persian Empire c. 500 B.C.
Caspian Sea
Aral Sea
Jaxartes River
Oxus River
Samarkand
SOGDIANA
BACTRIA
PARTHIA
Persepolis
PERSIS
Persian Gulf
Sutkagen Dor
INDUS VALLEY CIV.
Taxila
Harappa
Mohenjo-Daro
Arabian Sea

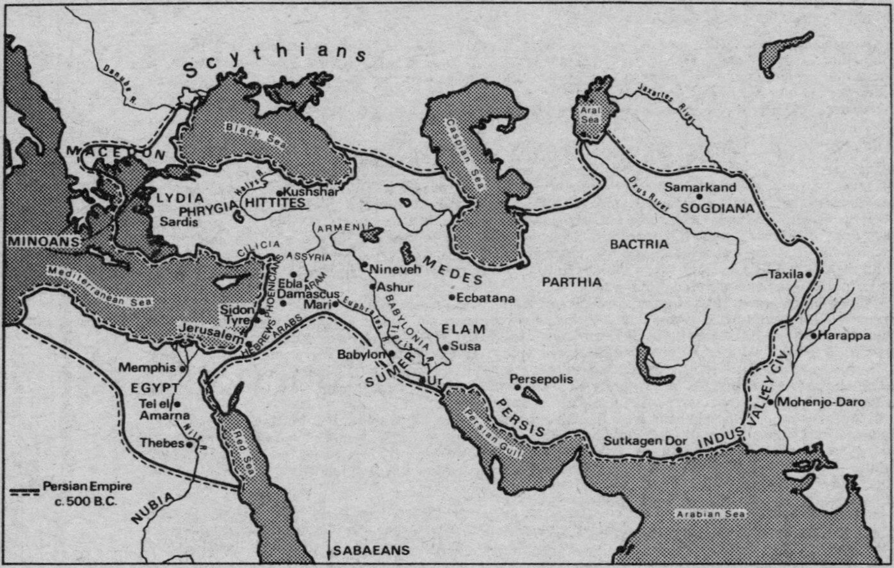

Hebrews in a kingdom that briefly dominated the area. Phoenicians to the north established colonies around the E. and W. Mediterranean (**Carthage** c814 BC) and sailed into the Atlantic.

A temple in Jerusalem became the national religious centre, with sacrifices performed by a hereditary priesthood. Polytheistic influences, especially of the fertility cult of Baal, were opposed by **prophets** (Elijah, Amos, Isaiah).

Divided into **two kingdoms** after Solomon, the Hebrews were unable to resist the revived Assyrian empire, which conquered Israel, the northern kingdom in 722 BC. Judah, the southern kingdom, was conquered in 586 BC by the Babylonians under Nebuchadnezzar II. But with the fixing of most of the Biblical canon by the mid-fourth century BC, and the emergence of rabbis, arbiters of law and custom, Judaism successfully survived the loss of Hebrew autonomy. A Jewish kingdom was revived under the Hasmoneans (168-42 BC).

China. During the **Eastern Chou** dynasty (770-256 BC), Chinese culture spread east to the sea and south to the Yangtze. Large feudal states on the periphery of the empire contended for pre-eminence, but continued to recognize the Son of Heaven (king), who retained a purely ritual role enriched with courtly music and dance. In the Age of Warring States (403-221 BC), when the first sections of the **Great Wall** were built, the Ch'in state in the West gained supremacy, and finally united all of China.

Iron tools entered China c500 BC, and casting techniques were advanced, aiding agriculture. Peasants owned their land, and owed civil and military service to nobles. Cities grew in number and size, though barter remained the chief trade medium.

Intellectual ferment among noble scribes and officials produced the Classical Age of Chinese literature and philosophy. **Confucius** (551-479 BC) urged a restoration of a supposedly harmonious social order of the past through proper conduct in accordance with one's station and through filial and ceremonial piety. The *Analects*, attributed to him, are revered throughout East Asia. **Mencius** (d. 289 BC) added the view that the Mandate of Heaven can be removed from an unjust dynasty. The Legalists sought to curb the supposed natural wickedness of people through new institutions and harsh laws; they aided the Ch'in rise to power. The Naturalists emphasized the balance of opposites — yin, yang — in the world. **Taoists** sought mystical knowledge through meditation and disengagement.

India. The political and cultural centre of India shifted from the Indus to the Ganges River Valley. Buddhism, Jainism, and mystical revisions of orthodox Vedism all developed around 500-300 BC. The *Upanishads*, last part of the *Veda*, urged escape from the illusory physical world. Vedism remained the preserve of the priestly Brahmin caste. In contrast, **Buddhism**, founded by Siddarta Gautama (c563-c483 BC), appealed to merchants in the growing urban centres, and took hold at first (and most lastingly) on the geographic fringes of Indian civilization. The classic Indian epics were composed in this era: The *Ramayana* around 300 BC, the *Mahabharata* over a period starting 400 BC.

Northern India was divided into a large number of monarchies and aristocratic republics, probably derived from tribal groupings, when the Magadha kingdom was formed in Bihar c542 BC. It soon became the dominant power. The **Maurya dynasty**, founded by Chandragupta c321 BC, expanded the kingdom, uniting most of N. India in a centralized bureaucratic empire. The third Mauryan king, **Asoka** (ruled c274-236) conquered most of the subcontinent: he converted to Buddhism, and inscribed its tenets on pillars throughout India. He downplayed the caste system and tried to end expensive sacrificial rites.

Before its final decline in India, Buddhism developed the popular worship of heavenly Bodhisatvas (enlightened beings), and produced a refined architecture (stupa—shrine—at Sanchi 100 AD) and sculpture (Gandhara reliefs 1-400 AD).

Persia. Aryan peoples (Persians, Medes) dominated the area of present Iran by the beginning of the first millenium BC. The prophet **Zoroaster** (born c628 BC) introduced a dualistic religion in which the forces of good (Ahura Mazda, Lord of Wisdom) and evil (Ahiram) battle for dominance; individuals are judged by their actions and earn damnation or salvation. Zoroaster's hymns (*Gathas*) are included in the *Avesta*, the Zoroastrian scriptures. A version of this faith became the established religion of the Persian Empire, and probably influenced later monotheistic religions.

Africa. Nubia, periodically occupied by Egypt since the third millenium, ruled Egypt c750-661, and survived as an independent Egyptianized kingdom (**Kush**; capital Meroe) for 1 000 years.

The Iron Age Nok culture flourished c500 BC-200 AD on the Benue Plateau of **Nigeria.**

Americas. The Chavin culture controlled north Peru from 900-200 BC. Its ceremonial centres, featuring the jaguar god, survived long after. Chavin architecture, ceramics, and textiles influenced other Peruvian cultures.

Mayan civilization began to develop in Central America in the 5th century BC.

Great Empires Unite the Civilized World: 400 BC - 400 AD

Persia and Alexander. Cyrus, ruler of a small kingdom in Persia from 559 BC, united the Persians and Medes within 10 years, conquered Asia Minor and Babylonia in another 10. His son Cambyses and grandson **Darius** (ruled 522-486) added vast lands to the east and north as far as the Indus Valley and Central Asia, as well as Egypt and Thrace. The whole empire was ruled by an international bureaucracy and army, with Persians holding the chief positions. The resources and styles of all the subject civilizations were exploited to create a rich syncretic art.

The Hellenized kingdom of Macedon, which under Phillip II dominated Greece, passed to his son **Alexander** in 336 BC. Within 13 years, Alexander conquered all the Persian dominions. Imbued by his tutor Aristotle with Greek ideals, Alexander encouraged Greek colonization, and Greek-style cities were founded throughout the empire (e.g. Alexandria, Egypt). After his death in 323 BC, wars of succession divided the empire into three parts — Macedon, Egypt (ruled by the **Ptolemies**), and the **Seleucid** Empire.

In the ensuing 300 years (the **Hellenistic Era**), a cosmopolitan Greek-oriented culture permeated the ancient world from W. Europe to the borders of India, absorbing native elites everywhere.

Hellenistic philosophy stressed the private individual's search for happiness. The Cynics followed Diogenes (c372-287), who stressed satisfaction of animal needs and contempt for social convention. Zeno (c335-c263) and the Stoics exalted reason, identified it with virtue, and counseled an ascetic disregard for misfortune. The Epicureans tried to build lives of moderate pleasure without political or emotional

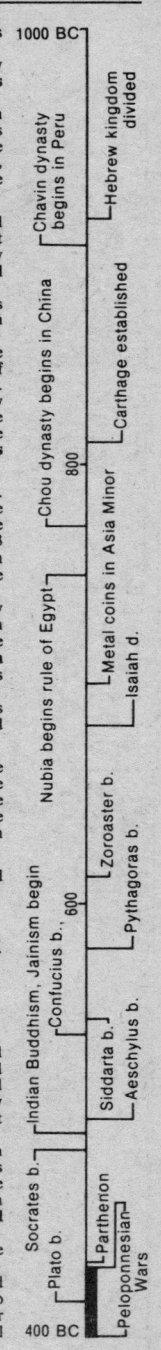

1000 BC

Chavin dynasty begins in Peru

Hebrew kingdom divided

Chou dynasty begins in China

800

Carthage established

Nubia begins rule of Egypt

Metal coins in Asia Minor

Isaiah d.

Indian Buddhism, Jainism begin

Confucius b.

600

Zoroaster b.

Pythagoras b.

Socrates b.

Siddarta b.

Aeschylus b.

Plato b.

Parthenon

Peloponnesian Wars

400 BC

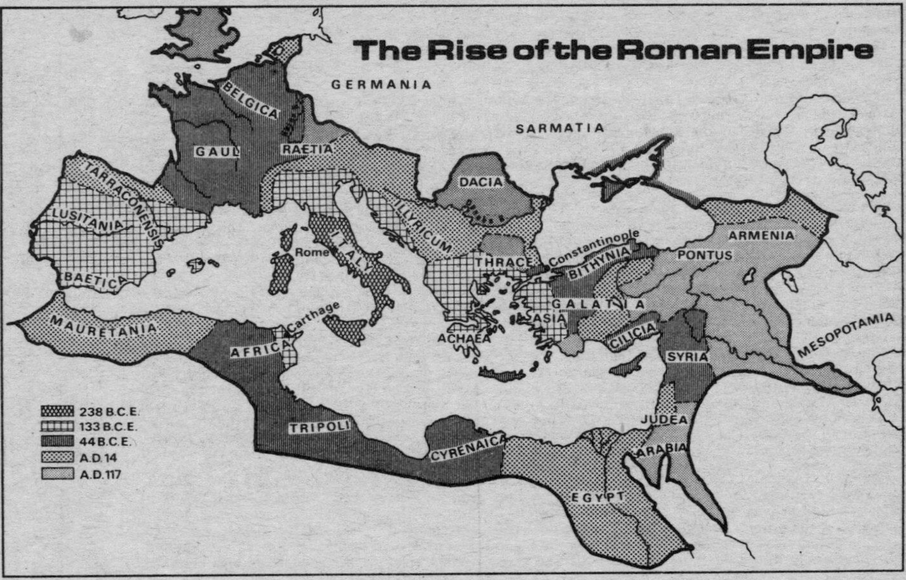

The Rise of the Roman Empire

GERMANIA

BELGICA

GAUL

RAETIA

SARMATIA

TARRACONENSIS

LUSITANIA

DACIA

ILLYRICUM

ITALY

THRACE   Constantinople

BITHYNIA

ARMENIA

PONTUS

BAETIC

Rome

GALATIA

ASIA

ACHAEA

CILICIA

MAURETANIA

Carthage

AFRICA

SYRIA

MESOPOTAMIA

JUDEA

ARABIA

TRIPOLI

238 B.C.E.
133 B.C.E.
44 B.C.E.
A.D. 14
A.D. 117

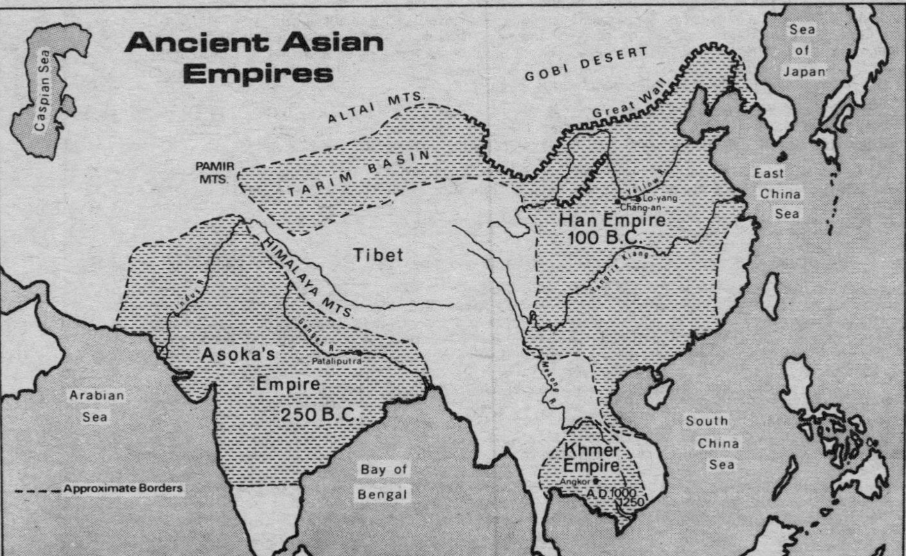

CYRENAICA

EGYPT

Ancient Asian Empires

Caspian Sea

GOBI DESERT

Sea of Japan

ALTAI MTS.

Great Wall

PAMIR MTS.

TARIM BASIN

HIMALAYA MTS.

Tibet

Han Empire 100 B.C.

Chang-an   Lo-yang

East China Sea

Arabian Sea

Asoka's Empire 250 B.C.

Pataliputra

Bay of Bengal

Khmer Empire

Angkor   A.D. 1000 1250

South China Sea

- - - Approximate Borders

involvement. Hellenistic arts imitated life realistically, especially in sculpture and literature (comedies of Menander, 342-292).

The sciences thrived, especially at Alexandria, where the Ptolemies financed a great library and museum. Fields of study included mathematics (**Euclid's** geometry, c300 BC; Menelaus' non-Euclidean geometry, c100 AD); astronomy (heliocentric theory of Aristarchus, 310-230 BC; Julian calendar 45 BC; Ptolemy's *Almagest*, c150 AD); geography (world map of Eratosthenes, 276-194 BC); hydraulics (**Archimedes**, 287-212 BC); medicine (Galen, 130-200 AD), and chemistry. Inventors refined uses for siphons, valves, gears, springs, screws, levers, cams, and pulleys.

A restored Persian empire under the **Parthians** (N. Iranian tribesmen) controlled the eastern Hellenistic world 250 BC-229 AD. The Parthians and the succeeding Sassanian dynasty (229-651) fought with Rome periodically. The **Sassanians** revived Zoroastrianism as a state religion, and patronized a nationalistic artistic and scholarly renaissance.

Rome. The city of Rome was founded, according to legend, by Romulus in 753 BC. Through military expansion and colonization, and by granting citizenship to conquered tribes, the city annexed all of Italy south of the Po in the 100-year period before 268 BC. The Latin and other Italic tribes were annexed first, followed by the Etruscans (a civilized people north of Rome) and the Greek colonies in the south. With a large standing army and reserve forces of several hundred thousand, Rome was able to defeat Carthage in the 3 **Punic Wars**, 264-241, 218-201, 149-146 (despite the invasion of Italy by Hannibal, 218), thus gaining Sicily and territory in Spain and North Africa.

New provinces were added in the East, as Rome exploited local disputes to conquer Greece and Asia Minor in the 2d century BC, and Egypt in the first (after the defeat and suicide of **Antony and Cleopatra**, 30 BC). All the Mediterranean civilized world up to the disputed Parthian border was now Roman, and remained so for 500 years. Less civilized regions were added to the Empire: Gaul (conquered by Julius Caesar, 56-49 BC), Britain (43 AD) and Dacia NE of the Danube (117 AD).

The original aristocratic republican government, with democratic features added in the fifth and fourth centuries BC, deteriorated under the pressures of empire and class conflict (**Gracchus** brothers, social reformers, murdered 133, 121; slave revolts 135, 73). After a series of civil wars (Marius vs. Sulla 88-82, Caesar vs. Pompey 49-45, triumvirate vs. Caesar's assassins 44-43, Antony vs. Octavian 32-30), the empire came under the rule of a deified monarch (first emperor, **Augustus**, 27 BC-14 AD). Provincials (nearly all granted citizenship by Caracalla, 212 AD) came to dominate the army and civil service. Traditional Roman law, systematized and interpreted by independent jurists, and local self-rule in provincial cities were supplanted by a vast tax-collecting bureaucracy in the 3d and 4th centuries. The legal rights of women, children, and slaves were strengthened.

Roman innovations in **civil engineering** included water mills, windmills, and rotary mills, and the use of cement that hardened under water. Monumental architecture (baths, theaters, apartment houses) relied on the arch and the dome. The network of roads (some still standing) stretched 84 800 km, passing through mountain tunnels as long as 5.6 km. Aqueducts brought water to cities, underground sewers removed waste.

Roman art and literature were derivative of Greek models. Innovations were made in sculpture (naturalistic busts and equestrian statues), decorative wall painting (as at Pompeii), satire (Juvenal, 60-127), history (Tacitus 56-120), prose romance (Petronius, d. 66 AD). Violence and torture dominated mass public amusements, which were supported by the state.

India. The **Gupta** monarchs reunited N. India c320 AD. Their peaceful and prosperous reign saw a revival of Hindu religious thought and Brahmin power. The old Vedic traditions were combined with devotion to a plethora of indigenous deities (who were seen as manifestations of Vedic gods). **Caste lines** were reinforced, and Buddhism gradually disappeared. The art (often erotic), architecture, and literature of the period, patronized by the Gupta court, are considered to be among India's finest achievements (Kalidasa, poet and dramatist, fl. c400). Mathematical innovations included the use of zero and decimal numbers. Invasions by White Huns from the NW destroyed the empire c550.

Rich cultures also developed in S. India in this era. Emotional Tamil religious poetry aided the Hindu revival. The Pallava kingdom controlled much of S. India c350-880, and helped spread Indian civilization to S.E. Asia.

China. The Ch'in ruler Shih Huang Ti (ruled 221-210 BC), known as the First Emperor, centralized political authority in China, standardized the written language, laws, weights, measures, and coinage, and conducted a census, but tried to destroy most philosophical texts. The **Han dynasty** (206 BC-220 AD) instituted the Mandarin bureaucracy, which lasted for 2 000 years. Local officials were selected by examination in the Confucian classics and trained at the imperial university and at provincial schools. The invention of **paper** facilitated this bureaucratic system. Agriculture was promoted, but the peasants bore most of the tax burden. Irrigation was improved; water clocks and sundials were used; astronomy and mathematics thrived; landscape painting was perfected.

With the expansion south and west (to nearly the present borders of today's China), trade was opened with India, S.E. Asia, and the Middle East, over sea and caravan routes. Indian missionaries brought Mahayana Buddhism to China by the first century AD, and spawned a variety of sects. Taoism was revived, and merged with popular superstitions. Taoist and Buddhist monasteries and convents multiplied in the turbulent centuries after the collapse of the Han dynasty.

Christianity is Founded: 1-750 AD

Christianity. Religions indigenous to particular Middle Eastern nations became international in the first 3 centuries of the Roman Empire. Roman citizens worshipped **Isis** of Egypt, **Mithras** of Persia, **Demeter** of Greece, and the great mother **Cybele** of Phrygia. Their cults centred on mysteries (secret ceremonies) and the promise of an afterlife, symbolized by the death and rebirth of the god. Judaism, which had begun as the national cult of Judea, also spread by emigration and conversion. It was the only ancient religion west of India to survive.

Christians, who emerged as a distinct sect in the second half of the 1st century AD, revered **Jesus**, a Jewish preacher said to have been killed by the Romans at the request of Jewish authorities in Jerusalem c30 AD. They considered him the Savior (Messiah, or Christ) who rose from the dead and could grant eternal life to the faithful, despite their sinfulness. They believed he was an incarnation of the one god

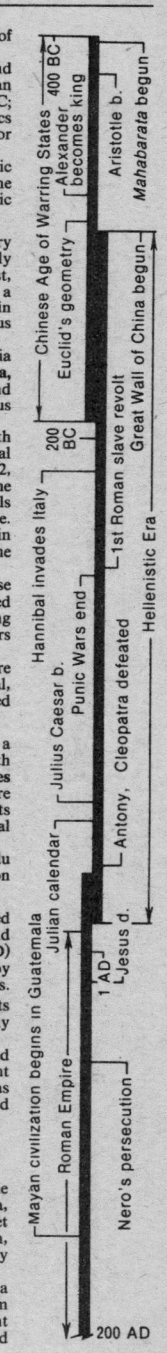

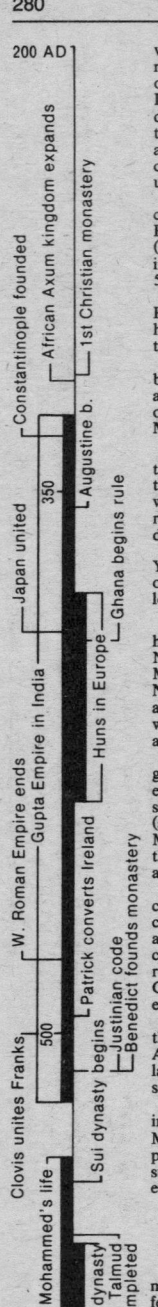

Timeline labels (left margin, top to bottom): 200 AD, Constantinople founded, African Axum kingdom expands, 1st Christian monastery, Japan united, Augustine b., Ghana begins rule, 350, W. Roman Empire ends, Gupta Empire in India, Huns in Europe, Patrick converts Ireland, Justinian code, Benedict founds monastery, Sui dynasty begins, 500, Clovis unites Franks, Mohammed's life, Tang dynasty, Talmud completed, 650 AD.

worshipped by the Jews, and that he would return soon to pass final judgment on the world. The missionary activities of such early leaders as **Paul of Tarsus** spread the faith, at first mostly among Jews or among quasi-Jews attracted by the Pauline rejection of such difficult Jewish laws as circumcision. Intermittent persecution, as in Rome under Nero in 64 AD, on grounds of suspected disloyalty, failed to disrupt the Christian communities. Each congregation, generally urban and of plebeian character, was tightly organized under a leader (bishop), elders (presbyters or priests), and assistants (deacons). Stories about Jesus (the Gospels) and the early church (Acts) were written down in the late first and early 2d centuries, and circulated along with letters of Paul. An authoritative canon of these writings was not fixed until the 4th century.

A school for priests was established at Alexandria in the second century. Its teachers (**Origen** c182-251) helped define Christian doctrine and promote the faith in Greek-style philosophical works. Pagan Neoplatonism was given Christian coloration in the works of Church Fathers such as Augustine (354-430). Christian hermits, often drawn from the lower classes, began to associate in monasteries, first in Egypt (St. Pachomius c290-345), then in other eastern lands, then in the West (**St. Benedict's rule,** 529). Popular devotion to saints, especially Mary, mother of Jesus, spread.

Under **Constantine** (ruled 306-337), Christianity became in effect the established religion of the Empire. Pagan temples were expropriated, state funds were used to build huge churches and support the hierarchy, and laws were adjusted in accordance with Christian notions. Pagan worship was banned by the end of the fourth century, and severe restrictions were placed on Judaism.

The newly established church was rocked by doctrinal disputes, often exacerbated by regional rivalries both within and outside the Empire. Chief heresies (as defined by church councils backed by imperial authority) were **Arianism,** which denied the divinity of Jesus; **Donatism,** which rejected the convergence of church and state and denied the validity of sacraments performed by sinful clergy; and the **Monophysite** position denying the dual nature of Christ.

Judaism. First century Judaism embraced several sects, including: the **Sadducees,** mostly drawn from the Temple priesthood, who were culturally Hellenized; the **Pharisees,** who upheld the full range of traditional customs and practices as of equal weight to literal scriptural law, and elaborated synagogue worship; and the **Essenes,** an ascetic, millenarian sect. Messianic fervor led to repeated, unsuccessful rebellions against Rome (66-70, 135). As a result, the Temple was destroyed, and the population decimated.

To avoid the dissolution of the faith, a program of codification of law was begun at the academy of Yavneh. The work continued for some 500 years in Palestine and Babylonia, ending in the final redaction of the **Talmud** (c600), a huge collection of legal and moral debates, rulings, liturgy, Biblical exegesis, and legendary materials.

Islam. The earliest Arab civilization emerged by the end of the 2d millenium BC in the watered highlands of Yemen. Seaborne and caravan trade in frankincense and myrrh connected the area with the Nile and Fertile Crescent. The Minaean, Sabean (Sheba), and Himyarite states successively held sway. By Mohammed's time (7th century AD), the region was a province of Sassanian Persia. In the North, the **Nabataean kingdom** at Petra and the kingdom of Palmyra were first Aramaicized and then Romanized, and finally absorbed like neighboring Judea into the Roman Empire. Nomads shared the central region with a few trading towns and oases. Wars between tribes and raids on settled communities were common, and were celebrated in a poetic tradition that by the 6th century helped establish a classic literary Arabic.

In 611 **Mohammed,** a wealthy 40-year-old Arab of Mecca, had a revelation from Allah, the one true god, calling on him to repudiate pagan idolatry. Drawing on elements of Judaism and Christianity, and eventually incorporating some Arab pagan traditions (such as reverence for the black stone at the kaaba shrine in Mecca), Mohammed's teachings, recorded in the **Koran,** forged a new religion, Islam (submission to Allah). Opposed by the leaders of Mecca, Mohammed made a *hejira* (migration) to Medina to the north in 622, the beginning of the Moslem lunar calendar. He and his followers defeated the Meccans in 624 in the first *jihad* (holy war), and by his death (632), nearly all the Arabian peninsula accepted his religious and secular leadership.

Under the first two **caliphs** (successors) Abu Bakr (632-34) and Oman (634-44), Moslem rule was confirmed over Arabia. Raiding parties into Byzantine and Persian border areas developed into campaigns of conquest against the two empires, which had been weakened by wars and by disaffection among subject peoples (including Coptic and Syriac Christians opposed to the Byzantine orthodox church). Syria, Palestine, Egypt, Iraq, and Persia all fell to the inspired Arab armies. The Arabs at first remained a distinct minority, using non-Moslems in the new administrative system, and tolerating Christians, Jews, and Zoroastrians as self-governing "Peoples of the Book," whose taxes supported the empire.

Disputes over the succession, and puritan reaction to the wealth and refinement that empire brought to the ruling strata, led to the growth of schismatic movements. The followers of Mohammed's son-in-law Ali (assassinated 661) and his descendants became the founders of the more mystical **Shi'ite** sect, still the largest non-orthodox Moslem sect. The Karijites, puritanical, militant, and egalitarian, persist as a minor sect to the present.

Under the **Ummayad** caliphs (661-750), the boundaries of Islam were extended across N. Africa and into Spain. Arab armies in the West were stopped at Tours in 732 by the Frank **Charles Martel.** Asia Minor, the Indus Valley, and Transoxiana were conquered in the East. The vast majority of the subject population gradually converted to Islam, encouraged by tax and career privileges. The Arab language supplanted the local tongues in the central and western areas, but Arab soldiers and rulers in the East eventually became assimilated to the indigenous languages.

New Peoples Enter History: 400-900

Barbarian invasions. Germanic tribes infiltrated S and E from their Baltic homeland during the 1st millenium BC, reaching S. Germany by 100 BC and the Black Sea by 214 AD. Organized into large federated tribes under elected kings, most resisted Roman domination and raided the empire in time of civil war (Goths took Dacia 214, raided Thrace 251-269). German troops and commanders came to dominate the Roman armies by the end of the 4th century. **Huns,** invaders from Asia, entered Europe 372, driving more Germans into the western empire. Emperor Valens allowed Visigoths to cross the Danube 376. Huns under Attila (d. 453) raided Gaul, Italy, Balkans. The western empire, weakened by overtaxation and social stagnation, was overrun in the 5th century. Gaul was effectively lost 406-7, Spain 409, Britain 410, Africa 429-39. Rome itself was sacked 410 by Visigoths under Alaric, 455 by Vandals. The last western emperor, Romulus Augustulus, was deposed 476 by the Germanic chief Odoacer.

Celts. Celtic cultures, which in pre-Roman times covered most of W. Europe, were confined almost entirely to the British Isles after the Germanic invasions. **St. Patrick** completed the conversion of Ireland (c457-92). A strong monastic tradition took hold. Irish monastic missionaries in Scotland, England, and the continent (Columba c521-597; Columban c543-615) helped restore Christianity after the Germanic invasions. The monasteries became renowned centres of classic and Christian learning, and presided over the recording of a Christianized Celtic mythology, elaborated by secular writers and bards. An intricate decorative art style developed, especially in book illumination (Lindisfarne Gospels, c700, Book of Kells, 8th century).

Successor states. The Visigoth kingdom in Spain (from 419) and much of France (to 507) saw a continuation of much Roman administration, language, and law (Breviary of Alaric 506), until its destruction by the Moslems, 711. The Vandal kingdom in Africa, from 429, was conquered by the Byzantines, 533. Italy was ruled in succession by an Ostrogothic kingdom under Byzantine suzerainty 489-554, direct Byzantine government, and the German Lombards (568-774). The latter divided the peninsula with the Byzantines and the papacy under the dynamic reformer Pope Gregory the Great (590-604) and his successors.

King Clovis (ruled 481-511) united the Franks on both sides of the Rhine, and after his conversion to orthodox Christianity, defeated the Arian Burgundians (after 500) and Visigoths (507) with the support of the native clergy and the papacy. Under the **Merovingian** kings a feudal system emerged: power was fragmented among hierarchies of military landowners. Social stratification, which in late Roman times had acquired legal, hereditary sanction, was reinforced. The Carolingians (747-987) expanded the kingdom and restored central power. **Charlemagne** (ruled 768-814) conquered nearly all the Germanic lands, including Lombard Italy, and was crowned Emperor by Pope Leo III in Rome in 800. A centuries-long decline in commerce and the arts was reversed under Charlemagne's patronage. He welcomed Jews to his kingdom, which became a centre of Jewish learning (Rashi 1040-1105). He sponsored the "Carolingian Renaissance" of learning under the Anglo-Latin scholar Alcuin (c732-804), who reformed church liturgy.

Byzantine Empire. Under Diocletian (ruled 284-305) the empire had been divided into 2 parts to facilitate administration and defense. Constantine founded **Constantinople**, 330, (at old Byzantium) as a fully Christian city. Commerce and taxation financed a sumptuous, orientalized court, a class of hereditary bureaucratic families, and magnificent urban construction (Hagia Sophia, 532-37). The city's fortifications and naval innovations (Greek fire) repelled assaults by Goths, Huns, Slavs, Bulgars, Avars, Arabs, and Scandinavians. Greek replaced Latin as the official language by c700. Byzantine art, a solemn, sacral, and stylized variation of late classical styles (mosaics at S. Vitale, Ravenna, 526-48) was a starting point for medieval art in E. and W. Europe.

Justinian (ruled 527-65) reconquered parts of Spain, N. Africa, and Italy, codified Roman law (*codex Justinianus*, 529, was medieval Europe's chief legal text), closed the Platonic Academy at Athens and ordered all pagans to convert. Lombards in Italy, Arabs in Africa retook most of his conquests. The Isaurian dynasty from Anatolia (from 717) and the Macedonian dynasty (867-1054) restored military and commercial power. The Iconoclast controversy (726-843) over the permissibility of images, helped alienate the Eastern Church from the papacy.

Arab Empire. Baghdad, founded 762, became the seat of the **Abbasid** Caliphate (founded 750), while Ummayads continued to rule in Spain. A brilliant cosmopolitan civilization emerged, inaugurating an Arab-Moslem golden age. Arab lyric poetry revived; Greek, Syriac, Persian, and Sanskrit books were translated into Arabic, often by Syriac Christians and Jews, whose theology and Talmudic law, respectively, influenced Islam. The arts and music flourished at the court of **Harun al-Rashid** (786-809), celebrated in *The Arabian Nights.* The sciences, medicine, and mathematics were pursued at Baghdad, Cordova, and Cairo (founded 969). Science and Aristotelian philosophy culminated in the systems of Avicenna (980-1037), Averroes (1126-98), and Maimonides (1135-1204), a Jew; all influenced later Christian scholarship and theology. The Islamic ban on images encouraged a sinuous, geometric decorative tradition, applied to architecture and illumination. A gradual loss of Arab control in Persia (from 874) led to the capture of Baghdad by Persians, 945. By the next century, Spain and N. Africa were ruled by Berbers, while Turks prevailed in Asia Minor and the Levant. The loss of political power by the caliphs allowed for the growth of non-orthodox trends, especially the mystical **Sufi** tradition (theologian Ghazali, 1058-1111).

Africa. Immigrants from Saba in S. Arabia helped set up the **Axum** kingdom in Ethiopia in the 2d century (their language, Ge'ez, is preserved by the Ethiopian Church). In the 4th century, when the kingdom became Christianized, it defeated Kushite Meroe and expanded into Yemen. Axum was the centre of a vast ivory trade; it controlled the Red Sea coast until c1100. Arab conquest in Egypt cut Axum's political and economic ties with Byzantium.

The Iron Age entered W. Africa by the end of the 1st millenium BC. **Ghana,** the first known sub-Saharan state, ruled in the upper Senegal-Niger region c400-1240, controlling the trade of gold from mines in the S to trans-Sahara caravan routes to the N. The **Bantu** peoples, probably of W. African origin, began to spread E and S perhaps 2 000 years ago, displacing the Pygmies and Bushmen of central and southern Africa over a 1 500-year period.

Japan. The advanced Neolithic Yayoi period, when irrigation, rice farming, and iron and bronze casting techniques were introduced from China or Korea, persisted to c400 AD. The myriad Japanese states were then united by the **Yamato** clan, under an emperor who acted as the chief priest of the animistic **Shinto** cult. Japanese political and military intervention in Korea by the 6th century quickened a Chinese cultural invasion, bringing Buddhism, the Chinese language (which long remained a literary and governmental medium), Chinese ideographs and Buddhist styles in painting, sculpture, literature, and architecture (7th c. Horyu-ji temple at Nara). The Taika Reforms, 646, tried to centralize Japan

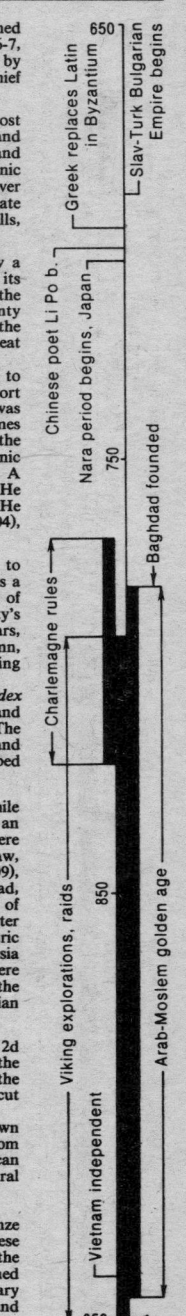

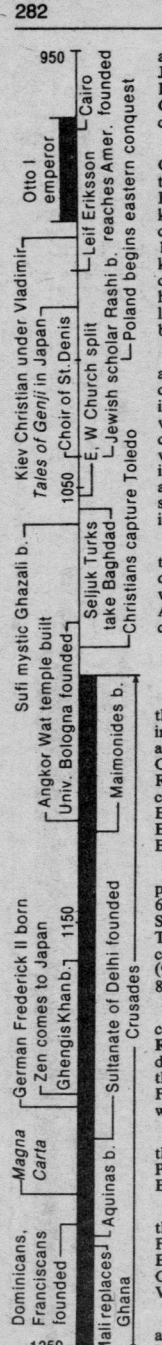

according to Chinese bureaucratic and Buddhist philosophical values, but failed to curb traditional Japanese decentralization. A nativist reaction against the Buddhist **Nara period** (710-94) ushered in the Heian period (794-1185) centred at the new capital, Kyoto. Japanese elegance and simplicity modified Chinese styles in architecture, scroll painting, and literature; the writing system was also simplified. The courtly novel *Tale of Genji* (1010-20) testifies to the enhanced role of women.

Southeast Asia. The historic peoples of southeast Asia began arriving some 2 500 years ago from China and Tibet, displacing scattered aborigines. Their agriculture relied on rice and tubers (yams), which they may have introduced to Africa. Indian cultural influences were strongest; literacy and Hindu and Buddhist ideas followed the southern India-China trade route. From the southern tip of Indochina, the kingdom of **Funan** (1st-7th centuries) traded as far west as Persia. It was absorbed by Chenla, itself conquered by the **Khmer Empire** (600-1300). The Khmers, under Hindu god-kings (Suryavarman II, 1113-c1150), built the monumental Angkor Wat temple centre for the royal phallic cult. The **Nam-Viet** kingdom in Annam, dominated by China and Chinese culture for 1 000 years, emerged in the 10th century, growing at the expense of the Khmers, who also lost ground in the NW to the new, highly-organized **Thai** kingdom. On Sumatra, the **Srivijaya** Empire at Palembang controlled vital sea lanes (7th to 10th centuries). A Buddhist dynasty, the Sailendras, ruled central **Java** (8th-9th centuries), building at Borobudur one of the largest stupas in the world.

China. The short-lived Sui dynasty (581-618) ushered in a period of commercial, artistic, and scientific achievement in China, continuing under the **T'ang** dynasty (618-906). Such inventions as the magnetic compass, gunpowder, the abacus, and printing were introduced or perfected. Medical innovations included cataract surgery. The state, from the cosmopolitan capital, Ch'ang-an, supervised foreign trade which exchanged Chinese silks, porcelains, and art works for spices, ivory, etc., over Central Asian caravan routes and sea routes reaching Africa. A golden age of poetry bequeathed tens of thousands of works to later generations (Tu Fu 712-70, Li Po 701-62). Landscape painting flourished. Commercial and industrial expansion continued under the **Northern Sung** dynasty (960-1126), facilitated by paper money and credit notes. But commerce never achieved respectability; government monopolies expropriated successful merchants. The population, long stable at 50 million, doubled in 200 years with the introduction of early-ripening rice and the double harvest. In art, native Chinese styles were revived.

Americas. An Indian empire stretched from the Valley of Mexico to Guatemala, 300-600, centring on the huge city **Teotihuacan** (founded 100 BC). To the S, in Guatemala, a high **Mayan** civilization developed, 150-900, around hundreds of rural ceremonial centres. The Mayans improved on Olmec writing and the calendar, and pursued astronomy and mathematics (using the idea of zero). In S. America, a widespread pre-Inca culture grew from **Tiahuanaco** near Lake Titicaca (Gateway of the Sun, c700).

Christian Europe Regroups and Expands: 900-1300

Scandinavians. Pagan Danish and Norse (**Viking**) adventurers, traders, and pirates raided the coasts of the British Isles (Dublin founded c831), France, and even the Mediterranean for over 200 years beginning in the late 8th century. Inland settlement in the W was limited to Great Britain (King Canute, 994-1035) and Normandy, settled under Rollo, 911, as a fief of France. Other Vikings reached Iceland (874), Greenland (c986), and probably N. America (Leif Eriksson c1000). Norse traders (**Varangians**) developed Russian river commerce from the 8th-11th centuries, and helped set up a state at Kiev in the late 9th century. Conversion to Christianity occurred during the 10th century, reaching Sweden 100 years later. Eleventh century Norman bands conquered S. Italy and Sicily. Duke **William of Normandy** conquered England, 1066, bringing continental feudalism and the French language, essential elements in later English civilization.

East Europe. Slavs inhabited areas of E. Central Europe in prehistoric times, and reached most of their present limits by c850. The first Slavic states were in the Balkans (Slav-Turk **Bulgarian Empire**, 680-1018) and Moravia (628). Missions of St. Cyril (whose Greek-based Cyrillic alphabet is still used by S. and E. Slavs) converted Moravia, 863. The Eastern Slavs, part-civilized under the overlordship of the Turkish-Jewish **Khazar** trading empire (7th-10th centuries), gravitated toward Constantinople by the 9th century. The **Kievan state** adopted Eastern Christianity under Prince Vladimir, 989. King Boleslav I (992-1025) began **Poland's** long history of eastern conquest. The Magyars (**Hungarians**) in Europe since 896, accepted Latin Christianity, 1001.

Germany. The German kingdom that emerged after the breakup of Charlemagne's Empire remained a confederation of largely autonomous states. The Saxon Otto I, king from 936, established the **Holy Roman Empire** of Germany and Italy in alliance with Pope John XII, who crowned him emperor, 962; he defeated the Magyars, 955. Imperial power was greatest under the **Hohenstaufens** (1138-1254), despite the growing opposition of the papacy, which ruled central Italy, and the Lombard League cities. Frederick II (1194-1250) improved administration, patronized the arts; after his death German influence was removed from Italy.

Christian Spain. From its northern mountain redoubts, Christian rule slowly migrated south through the 11th century, when Moslem unity collapsed. After the capture of **Toledo** (1085), the kingdoms of Portugal, Castile, and Aragon undertook repeated crusades of reconquest, finally completed in 1492. Elements of Islamic civilization persisted in recaptured areas, influencing all W. Europe.

Crusades. Pope Urban II called, 1095, for a crusade to restore Asia Minor to Byzantium and conquer the Holy Land from the Turks. Some 10 crusades (to 1291) succeeded only in founding 4 temporary Frankish states in the Levant. The 4th crusade sacked Constantinople, 1204. In Rhineland (1096), England (1290), France (1306), Jews were massacred or expelled, and wars were launched against Christian heretics (**Albigensian** crusade in France, 1229). Trade in eastern luxuries expanded, led by the Venetian naval empire.

Economy. The agricultural base of European life benefitted from improvements in **plow design** c1000, and by draining of lowlands and clearing of forests, leading to a rural population increase. Towns grew in N. Italy, Flanders, and N. Germany (Hanseatic League). Improvements in **loom design** permitted factory textile production. **Guilds** dominated urban trades from the 12th century. Banking (centred in Italy, 12th-15th century) facilitated long-distance trade.

The Church. The split between the Eastern and Western churches was formalized in 1054. W. and Central Europe was divided into 500 bishoprics under one united hierarchy, but conflicts between secular and church authorities were frequent (German **Investiture Controversy,** 1075-1122). Clerical power was first strengthened through the international monastic reform begun at Cluny, 910. Popular religious enthusiasm often expressed itself in heretical movements (Waldensians from 1173), but was channelled by the **Dominican** (1215) and **Franciscan** (1223) friars into the religious mainstream.

Arts. Romanesque architecture (11th-12th centuries) expanded on late Roman models, using the rounded arch and massed stone to support enlarged basilicas. Painting and sculpture followed Byzantine models. The literature of **chivalry** was exemplified by the epic (Chanson de Roland, c1100) and by courtly love poems of the troubadours of Provence and minnesingers of Germany. **Gothic architecture** emerged in France (choir of St. Denis, c1040) and spread as French cultural influence predominated in Europe. Rib vaulting and pointed arches were used to combine soaring heights with delicacy, and freed walls for display of stained glass. Exteriors were covered with painted relief sculpture and elaborate architectural detail.

Learning. Law, medicine, and philosophy were advanced at independent **universities** (Bologna, late 11th century), originally corporations of students and masters. Twelfth century translations of Greek classics, especially Aristotle, encouraged an analytic approach. Scholastic philosophy, from Anselm (1033-1109) to Aquinas (1225-74) attempted to reconcile reason and revelation.

Apogee of Central Asian Power; Islam Grows: 1250-1500

Turks. Turkic peoples, of Central Asian ancestry, were a military threat to the Byzantine and Persian Empires from the 6th century. After several waves of invasions, during which most of the Turks adopted Islam, the **Seljuk Turks** took Baghdad, 1055. They ruled Persia, Iraq, and, after 1071, Asia Minor, where massive numbers of Turks settled. The empire was divided in the 12th century into smaller states ruled by Seljuks, Kurds (**Saladin** c1137-93), and Mamelukes (a military caste of former Turk, Kurd, and Circassian slaves), which governed Egypt and the Middle East until the Ottoman era (c1290-1922).

Osman I (ruled c1290-1326) and succeeding sultans united Anatolian Turkish warriors in a militaristic state that waged holy war against Byzantium and Balkan Christians. Most of the Balkans had been subdued, and Anatolia united, when **Constantinople fell,** 1453. By the mid-16th century, Hungary, the Middle East, and North Africa had been conquered. The Turkish advance was stopped at Vienna, 1529, and at the naval battle of Lepanto, 1571, by Spain, Venice, and the papacy.

The Ottoman state was governed in accordance with orthodox Moslem law. Greek, Armenian, and Jewish communities were segregated, and ruled by religious leaders responsible for taxation; they dominated trade. State offices and most army ranks were filled by slaves through a system of child conscription among Christians.

India. Mahmud of Ghazni (971-1030) led repeated Turkish raids into N. India. Turkish power was consolidated in 1206 with the start of the **Sultanate at Delhi.** Centralization of state power under the early Delhi sultans went far beyond traditional Indian practice. Moslem rule of most of the subcontinent lasted until the British conquest some 600 years later.

Mongols. Genghis Khan (c1162-1227) first united the feuding Mongol tribes, and built their armies into an effective offensive force around a core of highly mobile cavalry. He and his immediate successors created the largest land empire in history; by 1279 it stretched from the east coast of Asia to the Danube, from the Siberian steppes to the Arabian Sea. East-West trade and contacts were facilitated (Marco Polo c1254-1324). The western Mongols were Islamized by 1295; successor states soon lost their Mongol character by assimilation. They were briefly reunited under the Turk Tamerlane (1336-1405).

Kublai Khan ruled China from his new capital Peking (founded 1264). Naval campaigns against Japan (1274, 1281) and Java (1293) were defeated, the latter by the Hindu-Buddhist maritime kingdom of Majapahit. The **Yuan** dynasty made use of Mongols and other foreigners (including Europeans) in official posts, and tolerated the return of Nestorian Christianity (suppressed 841-45) and the spread of Islam in the South and West. A native reaction expelled the Mongols, 1367-68.

Russia. The Kievan state in Russia, weakened by the decline of Byzantium and the rise of the Catholic Polish-Lithuanian state, was overrun by the Mongols, 1238-40. Only the northern trading republic of Novgorod remained independent. The grand dukes of Moscow emerged as leaders of a coalition of princes that eventually defeated the Mongols, by 1481. With the fall of Constantinople, the **Tsars** (Caesars) at Moscow (from Ivan III, ruled 1462-1505) set up an independent Russian Orthodox Church. Commerce failed to revive. The isolated Russian state remained agrarian, with the peasant class falling into serfdom.

Persia. A revival of Persian literature, using the Arab alphabet and literary forms, began in the 10th century (epic of Firdausi, 935-1020). An art revival, influenced by Chinese styles, began in the 12th. Persian cultural and political forms, and often the Persian language, were used for centuries by Turkish and Mongol elites from the Balkans to India. Persian mystics from Rumi (1207-73) to Jami (1414-92) promoted **Sufism** in their poetry.

Africa. Two Berber dynasties, imbued with Islamic militance, emerged from the Sahara to carve out empires from the Sahel to central Spain — the **Almoravids,** c1050-1140, and the fanatical **Almohads,** c1125-1269. The Ghanaian empire was replaced in the upper Niger by Mali, c1230-c1340, whose Moslem rulers imported Egyptians to help make **Timbuktu** a centre of commerce (in gold, leather, slaves) and learning. The Songhay empire (to 1590) replaced Mali. To the S, forest kingdoms produced refined art works (Ife terra cotta, **Benin** bronzes). Other Moslem states in Nigeria (Hausas) and Chad originated in the 11th century, and continued in some form until the 19th century European conquest. Less developed Bantu kingdoms existed across central Africa.

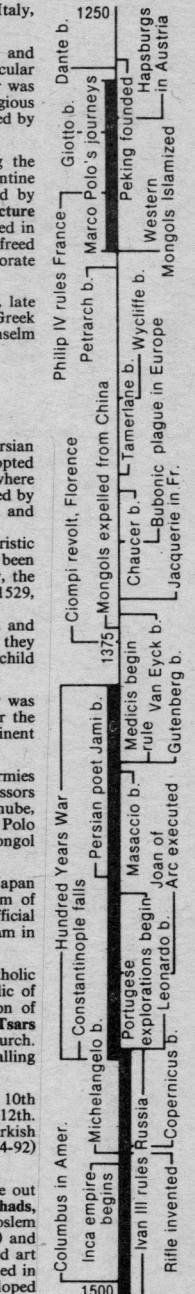

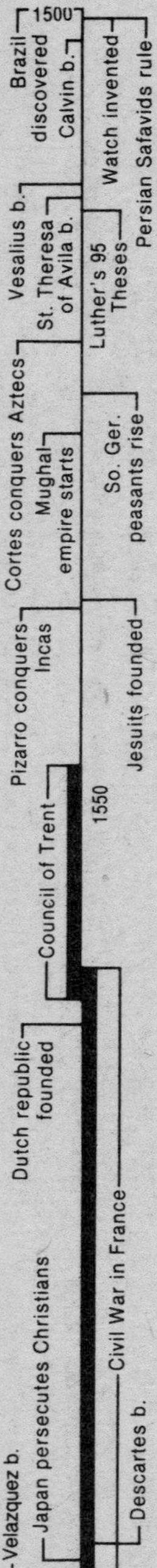
1500
Brazil discovered
Calvin b.
Watch invented
Persian Safavids rule
Vesalius b.
St. Theresa of Avila b.
Luther's 95 Theses
Cortes conquers Aztecs
Mughal empire starts
So. Ger. peasants rise
Pizarro conquers Incas
Jesuits founded
Council of Trent
1550
Dutch republic founded
Civil War in France
Japan persecutes Christians
Velazquez b.
Descartes b.
1600

Some 40 Moslem Arab-Persian trading colonies and city-states were established all along the E. African coast from the 10th century (Kilwa, Mogadishu). The interchange with Bantu peoples produced the **Swahili** language and culture. Gold, palm oil, and slaves were brought from the interior, stimulating the growth of the Monamatapa kingdom of the Zambezi (15th century). The Christian Ethiopian empire (from 13th century) continued the traditions of Axum.

Southeast Asia. Islam was introduced into Malaya and the Indonesian islands by Arab, Persian, and Indian traders. Coastal Moslem cities and states (starting before 1300), enriched by trade, soon dominated the interior. Chief among these was the **Malacca** state, on the Malay peninsula, c1400-1511.

Arts and Statecraft Thrive in Europe: 1350-1600

Italian Renaissance & humanism. Distinctive Italian achievements in the arts in the late Middle Ages (Dante, 1265-1321, Giotto, 1276-1337) led to the vigorous new styles of the Renaissance (14th-16th centuries). Patronized by the rulers of the quarreling petty states of Italy (Medicis in Florence and the papacy, c1400-1737), the plastic arts perfected realistic techniques, including **perspective** (Masaccio, 1401-28, Leonardo 1452-1519). Classical motifs were used in architecture and increased talent and expense were put into secular buildings. The Florentine dialect was refined as a national literary language (Petrarch, 1304-74). Greek refugees from the E strengthened the respect of humanist scholars for the classic sources (Bruni 1370-1444). Soon an international movement aided by the spread of **printing** (Gutenberg c1400-1468), **humanism** was optimistic about the power of human reason (Erasmus of Rotterdam, 1466-1536, Thomas More's *Utopia,* 1516) and valued individual effort in the arts and in politics (Machiavelli, 1469-1527).

France. The French monarchy, strengthened in its repeated struggles with powerful nobles (Burgundy, Flanders, Aquitaine) by alliances with the growing commercial towns, consolidated bureaucratic control under Philip IV (ruled 1285-1314) and extended French influence into Germany and Italy (popes at Avignon, France, 1309-1417). The **Hundred Years War,** 1338-1453, ended English dynastic claims in France (battles of Crécy, 1346, Poitiers, 1356; Joan of Arc executed, 1431). A French Renaissance, dating from royal invasions of Italy, 1494, 1499, was encouraged at the court of Francis I (ruled 1515-47), who centralized taxation and law. French vernacular literature consciously asserted its independence (La Pleiade, 1549).

England. The evolution of England's unique political institutions began with the Magna Carta, 1215, by which King John guaranteed the privileges of nobles and church against the monarchy and assured jury trial. After the Wars of the Roses (1455-85), the **Tudor dynasty** reasserted royal prerogatives (Henry VIII, ruled 1509-47), but the trend toward independent departments and ministerial government also continued. English trade (wool exports from c1340) was protected by the nation's growing maritime power (**Spanish Armada** destroyed, 1588).

English replaced French and Latin in the late 14th century in law and literature (Chaucer, 1340-1400) and English translation of the Bible began (Wycliffe, 1380s). Elizabeth I (ruled 1558-1603) presided over a confident flowering of poetry (Spenser, 1552-99), drama (**Shakespeare,** 1564-1616), and music.

German Empire. From among a welter of minor feudal states, church lands, and independent cities, the **Hapsburgs** assembled a far-flung territorial domain, based in Austria from 1276. The family held the title Holy Roman Emperor from 1452 to the Empire's dissolution in 1806, but failed to centralize its domains, leaving Germany disunited for centuries. Resistance to Turkish expansion brought Hungary under Austrian control from the 16th century. The Netherlands, Luxembourg, and Burgundy were added in 1477, curbing French expansion.

The Flemish painting tradition of naturalism, technical proficiency, and bourgeois subject matter began in the 15th century (Jan Van Eyck, 1366-1440), the earliest northern manifestation of the Renaissance. **Durer** (1471-1528) typified the merging of late Gothic and Italian trends in 16th century German art. Imposing civic architecture flourished in the prosperous commercial cities.

Spain. Despite the unification of Castile and Aragon in 1479, the 2 countries retained separate governments, and the nobility, especially in Aragon and Catalonia, retained many privileges. Spanish lands in Italy (Naples, Sicily) and the Netherlands entangled the country in European wars through the mid-17th century, while explorers, traders, and conquerors built up a Spanish empire in the Americas and the Philippines.

From the late 15th century, a **golden age** of literature and art produced works of social satire (plays of Lope de Vega, 1562-1635; Cervantes, 1547-1616), as well as spiritual intensity (El Greco, 1541-1614; Velazquez, 1599-1660).

Black Death. The bubonic plague reached Europe from the E in 1348, killing as much as half the population by 1350. Labor scarcity forced a rise in wages and brought greater freedom to the peasantry, making possible **peasant uprisings** (Jacquerie in France, 1358, Wat Tyler's rebellion in England, 1381). In the *ciompi* revolt, 1378, Florentine wage earners demanded a say in economic and political power.

Explorations. Organized European maritime exploration began, seeking to evade the Venice-Ottoman monopoly of eastern trade and to promote Christianity. Expeditions from Portugal beginning 1418 explored the west coast of Africa, until **Vasco da Gama** rounded the Cape of Good Hope in 1497 and reached India. A Portuguese trading empire was consolidated by the seizure of Goa, 1510, and Malacca, 1551. Japan was reached in 1542. Spanish voyages (**Columbus,** 1492-1504) uncovered a new world, which Spain hastened to subdue. Navigation schools in Spain and Portugal, the development of large sailing ships (carracks), and the invention of the rifle, c1475, aided European penetration.

Mughals and Safavids. East of the Ottoman empire, two Moslem dynasties ruled unchallenged in the 16th and 17th centuries. The Mughal empire in India, founded by Persianized Turkish invaders from the NW under Babur, dates from their 1526 conquest of Delhi. The dynasty ruled most of India for over 200 years, surviving nominally until 1857. **Akbar** (ruled 1556-1605) consolidated administration at his glorious court, where Urdu (Persian-influenced Hindi) developed. Trade relations with Europe increased. Under Shah Jahan (1629-58), a secularized art fusing Hindu and Moslem elements flourished in miniature painting and architecture (**Taj Mahal**). Sikhism, founded c1519, combined elements of both faiths.

Suppression of Hindus and Shi'ite Moslems in S India in the late 17th century weakened the empire.

Fanatical devotion to the Shi'ite sect characterized the Safavids of Persia, 1502-1736, and led to hostilities with the Sunni Ottomans for over a century. The prosperity and strength of the empire are evidenced by the mosques at its capital, **Isfahan**. The dynasty enhanced Iranian national consciousness.

China. The Ming emperors, 1368-1644, the last native dynasty in China, wielded unprecedented personal power, while the Confucian bureaucracy began to suffer from inertia. European trade (Portugese monopoly through **Macao** from 1557) was strictly controlled. Jesuit scholars and scientists (Matteo Ricci 1552-1610) introduced some Western science; their writings familiarized the West with China. Chinese technological inventiveness declined from this era, but the arts thrived, especially painting and ceramics.

Japan. After the decline of the first hereditary shogunate (chief generalship) at **Kamakura** (1185-1333), fragmentation of power accelerated, as did the consequent social mobility. Under Kamakura and the Ashikaga shogunate, 1338-1573, the daimyos (lords) and samurai (warriors) grew more powerful and promoted a martial ideology. Japanese pirates and traders plied the China coast. Popular Buddhist movements included the nationalist Nichiren sect (from c1250) and **Zen** (brought from China, 1191), which stressed meditation and a disciplined esthetic (tea ceremony, landscape gardening, judo, Noh drama).

Reformed Europe Expands Overseas: 1500-1700

Reformation begun. Theological debate and protests against real and perceived clerical corruption existed in the medieval Christian world, expressed by such dissenters as Wycliffe (c1320-84) and his followers, the Lollards, in England, and **Huss** (burned as a heretic, 1415) in Bohemia.

Luther (1483-1546) preached that only faith could lead to salvation, without the mediation of clergy or good works. He attacked the authority of the Pope, rejected priestly celibacy, and recommended individual study of the Bible (which he translated, c1525). His 95 Theses (1517) led to his excommunication (1520). **Calvin** (1509-64) said God's elect were predestined for salvation; good conduct and success were signs of election. Calvin in Geneva and Knox (1505-72) in Scotland erected theocratic states.

Henry VIII asserted English national authority and secular power by breaking away from the Catholic church, 1534. Monastic property was confiscated, and some Protestant doctrines given official sanction.

Religious wars. A century and a half of religious wars began with a South German peasant uprising, 1524, repressed with Luther's support. Radical sects—democratic, pacifist, millennarian—arose (Anabaptists ruled Muenster, 1534-35), and were suppressed violently. Civil war in France from 1562 between **Huguenots** (Protestant nobles and merchants) and Catholics ended with the 1598 Edict of Nantes tolerating Protestants (revoked 1685). Hapsburg attempts to restore Catholicism in Germany were resisted in 25 years of fighting; the 1555 Peace of Augsburg guarantee of religious independence to local princes and cities was confirmed only after the **Thirty Years War**, 1618-48, when much of Germany was devastated by local and foreign armies (Sweden, France).

A Catholic Reformation, or **counter-reformation**, met the Protestant challenge, clearly defining an official theology at the Council of Trent, 1545-63. The **Jesuit** order, founded 1534 by Loyola (1491-1556), helped reconvert large areas of Poland, Hungary, and S. Germany and sent missionaries to the New World, India, and China, while the Inquisition helped suppress heresy in Catholic countries. A revival of piety appeared in the devotional literature (Theresa of Avila, 1515-82) and the grandiose Baroque art (Bernini, 1598-1680) of Roman Catholic countries.

Scientific Revolution. The late nominalist thinkers (Ockham, c1300-49) of Paris and Oxford challenged Aristotelian orthodoxy, allowing for a freer scientific approach. But metaphysical values, such as the Neoplatonic faith in an orderly, mathematical cosmos, still motivated and directed subsequent inquiry. **Copernicus** (1473-1543) promoted the heliocentric theory, which was confirmed when Kepler (1571-1630) discovered the mathematical laws describing the orbits of the planets. The Christian-Aristotelian belief that heavens and earth were fundamentally different collapsed when Galileo (1564-1642) discovered moving sunspots, irregular moon topography, and moons around Jupiter. He and **Newton** (1642-1727) developed a mechanics that unified cosmic and earthly phenomena. To meet the needs of the new physics, Newton and Leibnitz (1646-1716) invented calculus, Descartes (1596-1650) invented analytic geometry.

An explosion of observational science included the discovery of blood circulation (Harvey, 1578-1657) and microscopic life (Leeuwenhoek, 1632-1723), and advances in anatomy (Vesalius, 1514-64, dissected corpses) and chemistry (Boyle, 1627-91). Scientific research institutes were founded: Florence, 1657, London (**Royal Society**), 1660, Paris, 1666. Inventions proliferated (Savery's steam engine, 1696).

Arts. Mannerist trends of the high Renaissance (**Michelangelo**, 1475-1564) exploited virtuosity, grace, novelty, and exotic subjects and poses. The notion of artistic genius was promoted, in contrast to the anonymous medieval artisan. Private connoisseurs entered the art market. These trends were elaborated in the 17th century **Baroque** era, on a grander scale. Dynamic movement in painting and sculpture was emphasized by sharp lighting effects, use of rich materials (colored marble, gilt), realistic details. Curved facades, broken lines, rich, deep-cut detail, and ceiling decoration characterized Baroque architecture, especially in Germany. Monarchs, princes, and prelates, usually Catholic, used Baroque art to enhance and embellish their authority, as in royal portraits by Velazquez (1599-1660) and Van Dyck (1599-1641).

National styles emerged. In France, a taste for rectilinear order and serenity (Poussin, 1594-1665), linked to the new rational philosophy, was expressed in classical forms. The influence of **classical values** in French literature (tragedies of Racine, 1639-99) gave rise to the "battle of the Ancients and Moderns." New forms included the essay (Montaigne, 1533-92) and novel (*Princesse de Cleves*, La Fayette, 1678).

Dutch painting of the 17th century was unique in its wide social distribution. The Flemish tradition of undemonstrative realism reached its peak in **Rembrandt** (1606-69) and Vermeer (1632-75).

Economy. European economic expansion was stimulated by the new trade with the East, New World gold and silver, and a doubling of population (50 mln. in 1450, 100 mln. in 1600). New business and financial techniques were developed and refined, such as joint-stock companies, insurance, and letters of credit and exchange. The Bank of Amsterdam, 1609, and the Bank of England, 1694, broke the old monopoly of private banking families. The rise of a business mentality was typified by the spread of clock

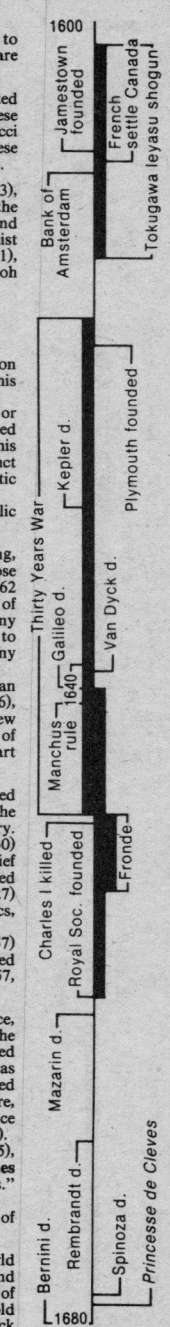

1600

Jamestown founded

French settle Canada

Tokugawa Ieyasu shogun

Bank of Amsterdam

Kepler d.

Plymouth founded

Thirty Years War

Galileo d.

1640

Van Dyck d.

Manchu rule

Charles I killed

Royal Soc. founded

Fronde

Mazarin d.

Rembrandt d.

Bernini d.

Spinoza d.

Princesse de Cleves

1680

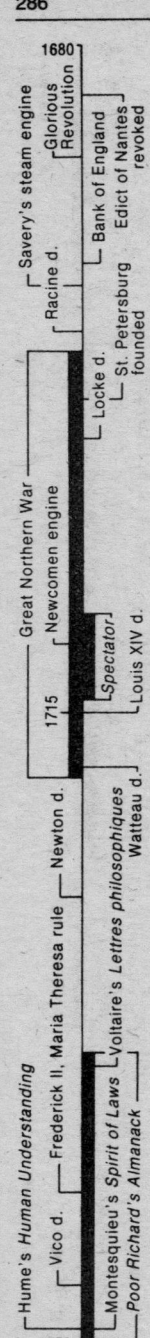

towers in cities in the 14th century. By the mid-15th century, portable clocks were available; the first watch was invented in 1502.

By 1650, most governments had adopted the **mercantile system,** in which they sought to amass metallic wealth by protecting their merchants' foreign and colonial trade monopolies. The rise in prices and the new coin-based economy undermined the craft guild and feudal manorial systems. Expanding industries, such as clothweaving and mining, benefitted from technical advances. Coal replaced disappearing wood as the chief fuel; it was used to fuel new 16th century blast furnaces making cast iron.

New World. The **Aztecs** united much of the Mesoamerican culture area in a militarist empire by 1519, from their capital, Tenochtitlan (pop. 300 000), which was the centre of a cult requiring enormous levels of ritual human sacrifice. Most of the civilized areas of S. America were ruled by the centralized **Inca Empire** (1476-1534), stretching 3 200 km from Ecuador to N.W. Argentina. Lavish and sophisticated traditions in pottery, weaving, sculpture, and architecture were maintained in both regions.

These empires, beset by revolts, fell in 2 short campaigns to gold-seeking Spanish forces based in the Antilles and Panama. **Cortes** took Mexico, 1519-21; **Pizarro** Peru, 1531-35. From these centres, land and sea expeditions claimed most of N. and S. America for Spain. The Indian high cultures did not survive the impact of Christian missionaries and the new upper class of whites and mestizos. In turn, New World silver, and such Indian products as potatoes, tobacco, corn, peanuts, chocolate, and rubber exercised a major economic influence on Europe. While the Spanish administration intermittently concerned itself with the welfare of Indians, the population remained impoverished at most levels, despite the growth of a distinct South American civilization. European diseases reduced the native population.

Brazil, which the Portuguese discovered in 1500 and settled after 1530, and the Caribbean colonies of several European nations developed a plantation economy where sugar cane, tobacco, cotton, coffee, rice, indigo, and lumber were grown commercially by slaves. From the early 16th to the late 19th centuries, some 10 million Africans were transported to **slavery** in the New World.

Netherlands. The urban, Calvinist northern provinces of the Netherlands rebelled against Hapsburg Spain, 1568, and founded an oligarchic mercantile republic. Their strategic control of the Baltic grain market enabled them to exploit Mediterranean food shortages. Religious refugees — French and Belgian Protestants, Iberian Jews — added to the cosmopolitan commercial talent pool. After Spain absorbed Portugal in 1580, the Dutch seized Portuguese possessions and created a vast, though generally short-lived commercial empire in Brazil, the Antilles, Africa, India, Ceylon, Malacca, Indonesia, and Taiwan, and challenged or supplanted Portuguese traders in China and Japan.

England. Anglicanism became firmly established under Elizabeth I after a brief Catholic interlude under "Bloody Mary," 1553-58. But religious and political conflicts led to a rebellion by Parliament, 1642. Roundheads (Puritans) defeated Cavaliers (Royalists); Charles I was beheaded, 1649. The new **Commonwealth** was ruled as a military dictatorship by Cromwell, who also brutally crushed an Irish rebellion, 1649-51. Conflicts within the Puritan camp (democratic Levelers defeated 1649) aided the Stuart restoration, 1660, but Parliament was permanently strengthened and the peaceful **"Glorious Revolution",** 1688, advanced political and religious liberties (writings of Locke, 1632-1704). British privateers (Drake, 1540-96) challenged Spanish control of the New World, and penetrated Asian trade routes (Madras taken, 1639). N. American colonies (Jamestown, 1607, Plymouth, 1620) provided an outlet for religious dissenters.

France. Emerging from the religious civil wars in 1628, France regained military and commercial great power status under the ministries of **Richelieu** (1624-42), **Mazarin** (1643-61), and **Colbert** (1662-83). Under **Louis XIV** (ruled 1643-1715) royal absolutism triumphed over nobles and local *parlements* (defeat of Fronde, 1648-53). Permanent colonies were founded in Canada (1608), the Caribbean (1626), and India (1674).

Sweden. Sweden seceded from the Scandinavian Union in 1523. The thinly-populated agrarian state (with copper, iron, and timber exports) was united by the Vasa kings, whose conquests by the mid-17th century made Sweden the dominant Baltic power. The empire collapsed in the Great Northern War (1700-21).

Poland. After the union with Lithuania in 1447, Poland ruled vast territories from the Baltic to the Black Sea, resisting German and Turkish incursions. Catholic nobles failed to gain the loyalty of the Orthodox Christian peasantry in the East; commerce and trades were practiced by German and Jewish immigrants. The bloody 1648-49 cossack uprising began the kingdom's dismemberment.

China. A new dynasty, the **Manchus,** invaded from the NE and seized power in 1644, and expanded Chinese control to its greatest extent in Central and Southeast Asia. Trade and diplomatic contact with Europe grew, carefully controlled by China. New crops (sweet potato, maize, peanut) allowed an economic and population growth (300 million pop. in 1800). Traditional arts and literature were pursued with increased sophistication (*Dream of the Red Chamber*, novel, mid-18th century).

Japan. Tokugawa Ieyasu, shogun from 1603, finally unified and pacified feudal Japan. Hereditary daimyos and samurai monopolized government office and the professions. An urban merchant class grew, literacy spread, and a cultural renaissance occurred (haiku of Basho, 1644-94). Fear of European domination led to persecution of Christian converts from 1597, and stringent isolation from outside contact from 1640.

Philosophy, Industry, and Revolution: 1700-1800

Science and Reason. Faith in human reason and science as the source of truth and a means to improve the physical and social environment, espoused since the Renaissance (Francis Bacon, 1561-1626), was bolstered by scientific discoveries in spite of theological opposition (**Galileo's forced retraction,** 1633). Descartes applied the logical method of mathematics to discover "self-evident" scientific and philosophical truths, while Newton emphasized induction from experimental observation.

The challenge of reason to traditional religious and political values and institutions began with Spinoza (1632-77), who interpreted the Bible historically and called for political and intellectual freedom. French philosophes assumed leadership of the **"Enlightenment"** in the 18th century. Montesquieu

(1689-1755) used British history to support his notions of limited government. Voltaire's (1694-1778) diaries and novels of exotic travel illustrated the intellectual trends toward secular ethics and relativism. Rousseau's (1712-1778) radical concepts of the **social contract** and of the inherent goodness of the common man gave impetus to anti-monarchical republicanism. The *Encyclopedia*, 1751-72, edited by Diderot and d'Alembert, designed as a monument to reason, was largely devoted to practical technology.

In England, ideals of political and religious liberty were connected with empiricist philosophy and science in the followers of Locke. But the extreme **empiricism of Hume** (1711-76) and Berkeley (1685-1753) posed limits to the identification of reason with absolute truth, as did the evolutionary approach to law and politics of Burke (1729-97) and the utilitarianism of Bentham (1748-1832). Adam Smith (1723-90) and other **physiocrats** called for a rationalization of economic activity by removing artificial barriers to a supposedly natural free exchange of goods.

Despite the political disunity and backwardness of most of Germany, German writers participated in the new philosophical trends popularized by Wolff (1679-1754). **Kant's** (1724-1804) **idealism**, unifying an empirical epistemology with *a priori* moral and logical concepts, directed German thought away from skepticism. Italian contributions included work on electricity by Galvani (1737-98) and Volta (1745-1827), the pioneer **historiography of Vico** (1668-1744), and writings on penal reform by Beccaria (1738-94). The American Franklin (1706-90) was celebrated in Europe for his varied achievements.

The growth of the **press** (*Spectator*, 1711-14) and the wide distribution of realistic but sentimental **novels** attested to the increase of a large bourgeois public.

Arts. Rococo art, characterized by extravagant decorative effects, asymmetries copied from organic models, and artificial pastoral subjects, was favored by the continental aristocracy for most of the century (Watteau, 1684-1721), and had musical analogies in the ornamentalized polyphony of late Baroque. The **Neoclassical** art after 1750, associated with the new scientific archeology, was more streamlined, and infused with the supposed moral and geometric rectitude of the Roman Republic (David, 1748-1825). In England, **town planning** on a grand scale began (Edinburgh, 1767).

Industrial Revolution in England. Agricultural improvements, such as the sowing drill (1701) and livestock breeding, were implemented on the large fields provided by enclosure of common lands by private owners. Profits from agriculture and from colonial and foreign trade (1800 volume, £ 54 million) were channelled through hundreds of banks and the **Stock Exchange** (founded 1773) into new industrial processes.

The Newcomen steam pump (1712) aided coal mining. Coal fueled the new efficient steam engines patented by Watt in 1769, and coke-smelting produced cheap, sturdy iron for machinery by the 1730s. The **flying shuttle** (1733) and **spinning jenny** (1764) were used in the large new cotton textile factories, where women and children were much of the work force. Goods were transported cheaply over **canals** (3 200 km built 1760-1800).

Central and East Europe. The monarchs of the three states that dominated eastern Europe — Austria, Prussia, and Russia — accepted the advice and legitimation of philosophes in creating more modern, centralized institutions in their kingdoms, enlarged by the division of Poland (1772-95).

Under **Frederick II** (ruled 1740-86) Prussia, with its efficient modern army, doubled in size. State monopolies and tariff protection fostered industry, and some legal reforms were introduced. Austria's heterogeneous realms were legally unified under **Maria Theresa** (ruled 1740-80) and **Joseph II** (1780-90). Reforms in education, law, and religion were enacted, and the Austrian serfs were freed (1781). With its defeat in the Seven Years' War in 1763, Austria lost Silesia and ceased its active role in Germany, but was compensated by expansion to the E and S (Hungary, Slavonia, 1699, Galicia, 1772).

Russia, whose borders continued to expand in all directions, adopted some Western bureaucratic and economic policies under Peter I (ruled 1682-1725) and Catherine II (ruled 1762-96). Trade and cultural contacts with the West multiplied from the new Baltic Sea capital, **St. Petersburg** (founded 1703).

American Revolution. The British colonies in N. America attracted a mass immigration of religious dissenters and poor people throughout the 17th and 18th centuries, coming from all parts of the British Isles, Germany, the Netherlands, and other countries. The population reached 3 million whites and blacks by the 1770s. The small native population was decimated by European diseases and wars with and between the various colonies. British attempts to control colonial trade, and to tax the colonists to pay for the costs of colonial administration and defense clashed with traditions of local self government, and eventually provoked the colonies to rebellion.

French Revolution. The growing French middle class lacked political power, and resented aristocratic tax privileges, especially in light of liberal political ideals popularized by the American Revolution. Peasants lacked adequate land and were burdened with feudal obligations to nobles. Wars with Britain drained the treasury, finally forcing the king to call the **Estates-General** in 1789 (first time since 1614) in an atmosphere of food riots (poor crop in 1788).

Aristocratic resistance to absolutism was soon overshadowed by the reformist Third Estate (middle class), which proclaimed itself the **National Constituent Assembly** June 17 and took the "Tennis Court oath" on June 20 to secure a constitution. The storming of the **Bastille** July 14 by Parisian artisans was followed by looting and seizure of aristocratic property throughout France. Assembly reforms included abolition of class and regional privileges, a Declaration of Rights, suffrage by taxpayers (75% of males), and the **Civil Constitution of the Clergy** providing for election and loyalty oaths for priests. A republic was declared Sept. 22, 1792, in spite of royalist pressure from Austria and Prussia, which had declared war in April (joined by Britain the next year). Louis XVI was beheaded Jan. 21, 1793, Queen Marie Antoinette was beheaded Oct. 16, 1793.

Royalist uprisings in La Vendee and the S and military reverses led to a **reign of terror** in which tens of thousands of opponents of the Revolution and criminals were executed. Radical reforms in the **Convention** period (Sept. 1793-Oct. 1795) included the abolition of colonial slavery, economic measures to aid the poor, support of public education, and a short-lived de-Christianization.

Division among radicals (execution of Hebert, March 1794, Danton, April, and Robespierre, July) aided the ascendance of a moderate **Directory**, which consolidated military victories. **Napoleon Bonaparte** (1769-1821), a popular young general, exploited political divisions and participated in a coup Nov. 9, 1799, making himself first consul (dictator).

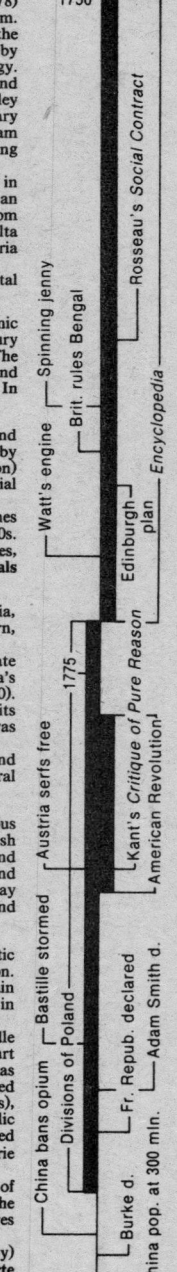

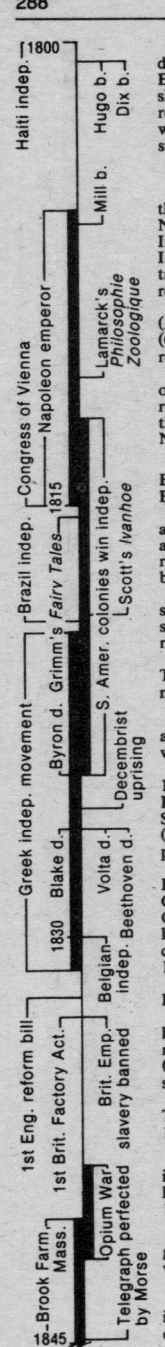

India. Sikh and Hindu rebels (Rajputs, Marathas) and Afghans destroyed the power of the Mughals during the 18th century. After France's defeat in the Seven Years War, 1763, Britain was the chief European trade power in India. Its control of inland **Bengal and Bihar** was recognized by the Mughal shah in 1765, who granted the **British East India Co.** (under Clive, 1727-74) the right to collect land revenue there. Despite objections from Parliament (1784 India Act) the company's involvement in local wars and politics led to repeated acquisitions of new territory. The company exported Indian textiles, sugar, and indigo.

Change Gathers Steam: 1800-1840

French ideals and empire spread. Inspired by the ideals of the French Revolution, and supported by the expanding French armies, new republican regimes arose near France: the **Batavian** Republic in the Netherlands (1795-1806), the **Helvetic** Republic in Switzerland (1798-1803), the **Cisalpine** Republic in N. Italy (1797-1805), the **Ligurian** Republic in Genoa (1797-1805), and the **Parthenopean** Republic in S. Italy (1799). A Roman Republic existed briefly in 1798 after Pope Pius VI was arrested by French troops. In Italy and Germany, new nationalist sentiments were stimulated both in imitation of and reaction to France (anti-French and anti-Jacobin peasant uprisings in Italy, 1796-9).

From 1804, when Napoleon declared himself emperor, to 1812, a succession of military victories (Austerlitz, 1805, Jena, 1806) extended his control over most of Europe, through puppet states (**Confederation of the Rhine** united W. German states for the first time and **Grand Duchy of Warsaw** revived Polish national hopes), expansion of the empire, and alliances.

Among the lasting reforms initiated under Napoleon's absolutist reign were: establishment of the Bank of France, centralization of tax collection, codification of law along Roman models (*Code Napoleon*), and reform and extension of secondary and university education. In an 1801 concordat, the papacy recognized the effective autonomy of the French Catholic Church. Some 400 000 French soldiers were killed in the Napoleonic Wars, along with 600 000 foreign troops.

Last gasp of old regime. France's coastal blockade of Europe (**Continental System**) failed to neutralize Britain. The disastrous 1812 invasion of Russia exposed Napoleon's overextension. After an 1814 exile at Elba, Napoleon's armies were defeated at **Waterloo**, 1815, by British and Prussian troops.

At the **Congress of Vienna**, the monarchs and princes of Europe redrew their boundaries, to the advantage of Prussia (in Saxony and the Ruhr), Austria (in Illyria and Venetia), and Russia (in Poland and Finland). British conquest of Dutch and French colonies (S. Africa, Ceylon, Mauritius) was recognized, and France, under the restored Bourbons, retained its expanded 1792 borders. The settlement brought 50 years of international peace to Europe.

But the Congress was unable to check the advance of liberal ideals and of nationalism among the smaller European nations. The 1825 **Decembrist** uprising by liberal officers in Russia was easily suppressed. But an independence movement in **Greece**, stirred by commercial prosperity and a cultural revival, succeeded in expelling Ottoman rule by 1831, with the aid of Britain, France, and Russia.

A constitutional monarchy was secured in France by an **1830 revolution**; Louis Philippe became king. The revolutionary contagion spread to **Belgium**, which gained its independence from the Dutch monarchy, 1830; to **Poland**, whose rebellion was defeated by Russia, 1830-31; and to Germany.

Romanticism. A new style in intellectual and artistic life began to replace Neo-classicism and Rococo after the mid-18th century. By the early 19th, this style, Romanticism, had prevailed in the European world.

Rousseau had begun the reaction against excessive rationalism and skepticism; in education (*Emile*, 1762) he stressed subjective spontaneity over regularized instruction. In Germany, Lessing (1729-81) and Herder (1744-1803) favorably compared the German folk song to classical forms, and began a cult of Shakespeare, whose passion and "natural" wisdom was a model for the Romantic *Sturm und Drang* (storm and stress) movement. Goethe's *Sorrows of Young Werther* (1774) set the model for the tragic, passionate genius.

A new interest in **Gothic architecture** in England after 1760 (Walpole, 1717-97) spread through Europe, associated with an aesthetic Christian and mystic revival (Blake, 1757-1827). Celtic, Norse, and German mythology and folk tales were revived or imitated (Macpherson's Ossian translation, 1762, Grimm's *Fairy Tales*, 1812-22). The medieval revival (Scott's *Ivanhoe*, 1819) led to a new interest in history, stressing national differences and organic growth (Carlyle, 1795-1881; Michelet, 1798-1874), corresponding to theories of natural evolution (Lamarck's *Philosophie zoologique*, 1809, Lyell's *Geology*, 1830-33).

Revolution and war fed an obsession with freedom and conflict, expressed by poets (**Byron**, 1788-1824, **Hugo**, 1802-85) and philosophers (**Hegel**, 1770-1831).

Wild gardens replaced the formal French variety, and painters favored rural, stormy, and mountainous landscapes (**Turner**, 1775-1851; **Constable**, 1776-1837). Clothing became freer, with wigs, hoops, and ruffles discarded. Originality and genius were expected in the life as well as the work of inspired artists (Murger's *Scenes from Bohemian Life*, 1847-49). Exotic locales and themes (as in "Gothic" horror stories) were used in art and literature (Delacroix, 1798-1863, **Poe**, 1809-49).

Music exhibited the new dramatic style and a breakdown of classical forms (Beethoven, 1770-1827). The use of folk melodies and modes aided the growth of distinct national traditions (Glinka in Russia, 1804-57).

Latin America. Haiti, under the former slave **Toussaint L'Ouverture**, was the first Latin American independent state, 1800. All the mainland Spanish colonies won their independence 1810-24, under such leaders as **Bolivar** (1783-1830). Brazil became an independent empire under the Portuguese prince regent, 1822. A new class of military officers divided power with large landholders and the church.

United States. Heavy immigration and exploitation of ample natural resources fueled rapid economic growth. The spread of the franchise, public education, and antislavery sentiment were signs of a widespread democratic ethic.

China. Failure to keep pace with Western arms technology exposed China to greater European influence, and hampered efforts to bar imports of opium, which had damaged Chinese society and drained wealth overseas. In the **Opium War**, 1839-42, Britain forced China to expand trade opportunities and to cede Hong Kong.

Triumph of Progress: 1840-80

Idea of Progress. As a result of the cumulative scientific, economic, and political changes of the preceding eras, the idea took hold among literate people in the West that continuing growth and improvement was the usual state of human and natural life.

Darwin's statement of the **theory of evolution** and survival of the fittest (*Origin of Species*, 1859), defended by intellectuals and scientists against theological objections, was taken as confirmation that progress was the natural direction of life. The controversy helped define popular ideas of the dedicated scientist and ever-expanding human knowledge of and control over the world (Foucault's demonstration of earth's rotation, 1851, Pasteur's germ theory, 1861).

Liberals following Ricardo (1772-1823) in their faith that unrestrained competition would bring continuous economic expansion sought to adjust political life to the new social realities, and believed that unregulated competition of ideas would yield truth (Mill, 1806-73). In England, successive reform bills (1832, 1867, 1884) gave representation to the new industrial towns, and extended the franchise to the middle and lower classes and to Catholics, Dissenters and Jews. On both sides of the Atlantic, reformists tried to improve conditions for the mentally ill (Dix, 1802-87), women (Anthony, 1820-1906), and prisoners. Slavery was barred in the British Empire, 1833; the United States, 1865; and Brazil, 1888.

Socialist theories based on ideas of human perfectibility or historical progress were widely disseminated. Utopian socialists like Saint-Simon (1760-1825) envisaged an orderly, just society directed by a technocratic elite. A model factory town, New Lanark, Scotland, was set up by utopian Robert Owen (1771-1858), and utopian communal experiments were tried in the U.S. (Brook Farm, Mass., 1841-7). Bakunin's (1814-76) anarchism represented the opposite utopian extreme of total freedom. Marx (1818-83) posited the inevitable triumph of socialism in the industrial countries through a historical process of class conflict.

Spread of industry. The technical processes and managerial innovations of the English industrial revolution spread to Europe (especially Germany) and the U.S., causing an explosion of industrial production, demand for raw materials, and competition for markets. Inventors, both trained and self-educated, provided the means for larger-scale production (Bessemer steel, 1856, sewing machine, 1846). Many inventions were shown at the 1851 London Great Exhibition at the Crystal Palace, whose theme was universal prosperity.

Local specialization and long-distance trade were aided by a revolution in transportation and communication. Railroads were first introduced in the 1820s in England and the U.S. Over 240 000 km of track had been laid worldwide by 1880, with another 160 000 km laid in the next decade. Steamships were improved (*Savannah* crossed Atlantic, 1819). The telegraph, perfected by 1844 (Morse), connected the Old and New Worlds by cable in 1866, and quickened the pace of international commerce and politics. The first commercial telephone exchange went into operation in the U.S. in 1878.

The new class of industrial workers, uprooted from their rural homes, lacked job security, and suffered from dangerous overcrowded conditions at work and at home. Many responded by organizing trade unions (legalized in England, 1824; France, 1884). The U.S. Knights of Labor had 700 000 members by 1886. The First International, 1864-76, tried to unite workers internationally around a Marxist program. The quasi-Socialist Paris Commune uprising, 1871, was violently suppressed. Factory Acts to reduce child labor and regulate conditions were passed (1833-50 in England). Social security measures were introduced by the Bismarck regime in Germany, 1883-89.

Revolutions of 1848. Among the causes of the continent-wide revolutions were an international collapse of credit and resulting unemployment, bad harvests in 1845-7, and a cholera epidemic. The new urban proletariat and expanding bourgeoisie demanded a greater political role. Republics were proclaimed in France, Rome, and Venice. Nationalist feelings reached fever pitch in the Hapsburg empire, as Hungary declared independence under Kossuth, a Slav Congress demanded equality, and Piedmont tried to drive Austria from Lombardy. A national liberal assembly at Frankfurt called for German unification.

But riots fueled bourgeois fears of socialism (Marx and Engels' 1848 *Communist Manifesto*) and peasants remained conservative. The old establishment — The Papacy, the Hapsburgs (using Croats and Romanians against Hungary), the Russian army — was able to rout the revolutionaries by 1849. The French Republic succumbed to a renewed monarchy by 1852 (Emperor Napoleon III).

Great nations unified. Using the "blood and iron" tactics of Bismarck from 1862, Prussia controlled N. Germany by 1867 (war with Denmark, 1864, Austria, 1866). After defeating France in 1870 (loss of Alsace-Lorraine), it won the allegiance of S. German states. A new **German Empire** was proclaimed, 1871. **Italy**, inspired by Mazzini (1805-72) and Garibaldi (1807-82), was unified by the reformed Piedmont kingdom through uprisings, plebiscites, and war.

The **U.S.**, its area expanded after the 1846-47 Mexican War, defeated a secession attempt by slave states, 1861-65. Britain's North American colonies (Ontario, Quebec, New Brunswick and Nova Scotia) were united to form the **Dominion of Canada, 1867.** Control in **India** was removed from the East India Co. and centralized under British administration after the 1857-58 Sepoy rebellion, laying the groundwork for the modern Indian State. Queen Victoria was named Empress of India, 1876.

Europe dominates Asia. The Ottoman Empire began to collapse in the face of Balkan nationalisms and European imperial incursions in N. Africa (Suez Canal, 1869). The Turks had lost control of most of both regions by 1882. Russia completed its expansion south by 1884 (despite the temporary setback of the Crimean War with Turkey, Britain, and France, 1853-56) taking Turkestan, all the Caucasus, and Chinese areas in the East and sponsoring Balkan Slavs against the Turks. A succession of reformist and reactionary regimes presided over a slow modernization (serfs freed, 1861). Persian independence suffered as Russia and British India competed for influence.

China was forced to sign a series of unequal treaties with European powers and Japan. Overpopulation and an inefficient dynasty brought misery and caused rebellions (Taiping, Moslems) leaving tens of millions dead. Japan was forced by the U.S. (Commodore Perry's visits, 1853-54) and Europe to end its isolation. The Meiji restoration, 1868, gave power to a Westernizing oligarchy. Intensified empire-building gave Burma to Britain, 1824-86, and Indo-China to France, 1862-95. Christian missionary activity followed imperial and trade expansion in Asia.

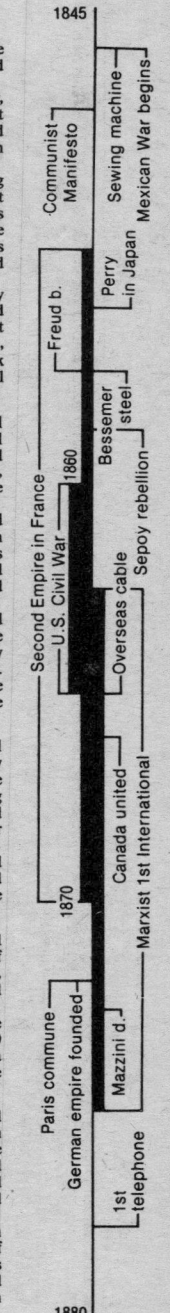

Timeline (1845–1880): 1845 · Communist Manifesto · Sewing machine · Mexican War begins · Freud b. · Perry in Japan · Bessemer steel · 1860 · Second Empire in France · U.S. Civil War · Overseas cable · Sepoy rebellion · Marxist 1st International · 1870 · Canada united · Paris commune · German empire founded · Mazzini d. · 1st telephone · 1880

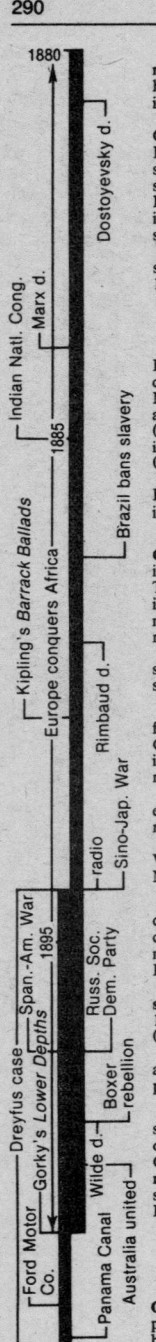

Respectability. The fine arts were expected to reflect and encourage the progress of morals and manners among the different classes. "Victorian" prudery, exaggerated delicacy, and familial piety were heralded by **Bowdler's** expurgated edition of Shakespeare (1818). Government-supported mass education inculcated a work ethic as a means to escape poverty (Horatio Alger, 1832-99).

The official **Beaux Arts** school in Paris set an international style of imposing public buildings (Paris Opera, 1861-74, Vienna Opera, 1861-69) and uplifting statues (Bartholdi's *Statue of Liberty*, 1885). Realist painting, influenced by photography (Daguerre, 1837), appealed to a new mass audience with social or historical narrative (Wilkie, 1785-1841, Poynter, 1836-1919) or with serious religious, moral, or social messages (pre-Raphaelites, Millet's *Angelus*, 1858) often drawn from ordinary life. The **Impressionists** (Pissarro, 1830-1903, Renoir, 1841-1919) rejected the central role of serious subject matter in favor of a colorful and sensual depiction of a moment, but their sunny, placid depictions of bourgeois scenes kept them within the respectable consensus.

Realistic **novelists** presented the full panorama of social classes and personalities, but retained sentimentality and moral judgment (Dickens, 1812-70, Eliot, 1819-80, Tolstoy, 1828-1910, Balzac, 1799-1850).

Veneer of Stability: 1880-1900

Imperialism triumphant. The vast **African** interior, visited by European explorers (Barth, 1821-65, Livingstone, 1813-73) was conquered by the European powers in rapid, competitive thrusts from their coastal bases after 1880, mostly for domestic political and international strategic reasons. W. African Moslem kingdoms (Fulani), Arab slave traders (Zanzibar), and Bantu military confederations (Zulu) were alike subdued. Only Christian Ethiopia (defeat of Italy, 1896) and Liberia resisted successfully. France (W. Africa) and Britain ("Cape to Cairo", Boer War, 1899-1902) were the major beneficiaries. The ideology of "the white man's burden" (Kipling, *Barrack Room Ballads*, 1892) or of a "civilizing mission" (France) justified the conquests.

West European foreign capital investments soared to nearly $40 billion by 1914, but most was in E. Europe (France, Germany) the Americas (Britain) and the white colonies. The foundation of the modern interdependent world economy was laid, with cartels dominating raw material trade.

An industrious world. Industrial and technological proficiency characterized the 2 new great powers — **Germany** and the U.S. Coal and iron deposits enabled Germany to reach second or third place status in iron, steel, and shipbuilding by the 1900s. German electrical and chemical industries were world leaders. The U.S. post-civil war boom (interrupted by "panics," 1884, 1893, 1896) was shaped by massive immigration from S. and E. Europe from 1880, government subsidy of railroads, and huge private monopolies (Standard Oil, 1870, U.S. Steel, 1901). The **Spanish-American War,** 1898 (Philippine rebellion, 1899-1901) and the Open Door policy in China (1899) made the U.S. a world power.

England led in **urbanization** (72% by 1890), with **London** the world capital of finance, insurance, and shipping. Electric subways (London, 1890), sewer systems (Paris, 1850s), parks, and bargain department stores helped improve living standards for most of the urban population of the industrial world.

Asians assimilate. Asian reaction to European economic, military, and religious incursions took the form of imitation of Western techniques and adoption of Western ideas of progress and freedom. The Chinese "self-strengthening" movement of the 1860s and 1870s included rail, port, and arsenal improvements and metal and textile mills. Reformers like **K'ang Yu-wei** (1858-1927) won liberalizing reforms in 1898, right after the European and Japanese "scramble for concessions."

A universal education system in Japan and importation of foreign industrial, scientific, and military experts aided Japan's unprecedented rapid modernization after 1868, under the authoritarian Meiji regime. Japan's victory in the **Sino-Japanese War,** 1894-95, put Formosa and Korea in its power.

In India, the British alliance with the remaining princely states masked reform sentiment among the Westernized urban elite; higher education had been conducted largely in English for 50 years. The **Indian National Congress,** founded in 1885, demanded a larger government role for Indians.

"Fin-de-siecle" sophistication. Naturalist writers pushed realism to its extreme limits, adopting a quasi-scientific attitude and writing about formerly taboo subjects like sex, crime, extreme poverty, and corruption (Flaubert, 1821-80, Zola, 1840-1902, Hardy, 1840-1928). Unseen or repressed psychological motivations were explored in the clinical and theoretical works of **Freud** (1856-1939) and in the fiction of Dostoevsky (1821-81), James (1843-1916), Schnitzler (1862-1931) and others.

A contempt for bourgeois life or a desire to shock a complacent audience was shared by the French **symbolist** poets (Verlaine, 1844-96, Rimbaud, 1854-91), neo-pagan English writers (Swinburne, 1837-1909), continental dramatists (Ibsen, 1828-1906) and satirists (Wilde, 1854-1900). Nietzsche (1844-1900) was influential in his elitism and pessimism.

Post-impressionist art neglected long-cherished conventions of representation (Cezanne, 1839-1906) and showed a willingness to learn from primitive and non-European art (Gauguin, 1848-1903, Japanese prints).

Racism. Gobineau (1816-82) gave a pseudo-biological foundation to modern racist theories, which spread in the latter 19th century along with **Social Darwinism,** the belief that societies are and should be organized as a struggle for survival of the fittest. The Medieval period was interpreted as an era of natural Germanic rule (Chamberlain, 1855-1927) and notions of superiority were associated with German national aspirations (Treitschke, 1834-96). **Anti-Semitism,** with a new racist rationale, became a significant political force in Germany (Anti-Semitic Petition, 1880), Austria (Lueger, 1844-1910), and France (Dreyfus case, 1894-1906).

Last Respite: 1900-1909

Alliances. While the peace of Europe (and its dependencies) continued to hold (1907 **Hague Conference** extended the rules of war and international arbitration procedures), imperial rivalries, protectionist trade practices (in Germany and France), and the escalating arms race (British *Dreadnought* battleship launched, Germany widens Kiel canal, 1906) exacerbated minor disputes (German-French Moroccan "crises", 1905, 1911).

Security was sought through alliances: **Triple Alliance** (Germany, Austria-Hungary, Italy) renewed 1902, 1907; Anglo-Japanese Alliance, 1902; Franco-Russian Alliance, 1899; **Entente Cordiale** (Britain, France) 1904; Anglo-Russian Treaty, 1907; German-Ottoman friendship.

Ottomans decline. The inefficient, corrupt Ottoman government was unable to resist further loss of territory. Nearly all European lands were lost in 1912 to Serbia, Greece, Montenegro, and Bulgaria. Italy took Libya and the Dodecanese islands the same year, and Britain took Kuwait, 1899, and the Sinai, 1906. The **Young Turk** revolution in 1908 forced the sultan to restore a constitution, introduced some social reform, industrialization, and secularization.

British Empire. British trade and cultural influence remained dominant in the empire, but constitutional reforms presaged its eventual dissolution: the colonies of **Australia** were united in 1901 under a self-governing commonwealth. **New Zealand** acquired dominion status in 1907. The old Boer republics joined Cape Colony and Natal in the self-governing **Union of South Africa** in 1910.

The 1909 Indian Councils Act enhanced the role of elected province legislatures in **India.** The Moslem League, founded 1906, sought separate communal representation.

East Asia. Japan exploited its growing industrial power to expand its empire. Victory in the 1904-05 war against Russia (naval battle of Tsushima, 1905) assured Japan's domination of **Korea** (annexed 1910) and Manchuria (took Port Arthur 1905).

In China, central authority began to crumble (empress died, 1908). Reforms (Confucian exam system ended 1905, modernization of the army, building of railroads) were inadequate and secret societies of reformers and nationalists, inspired by the Westernized **Sun Yat-sen** (1866-1925) fomented periodic uprisings in the south.

Siam, whose independence had been guaranteed by Britain and France in 1896, was split into spheres of influence by those countries in 1907.

Russia. The population of the Russian Empire approached 150 million in 1900. Reforms in education, law, and local institutions (*zemstvos*), and an industrial boom starting in the 1880s (oil, railroads) created the beginnings of a modern state, despite the autocratic czarist regime. Liberals (1903 Union of Liberation), Socialists (Social Democrats founded 1898, Bolsheviks split off 1903), and populists (Social Revolutionaries founded 1901) were periodically repressed, and national minorities persecuted (anti-Jewish pogroms, 1903, 1905-6).

An industrial crisis after 1900 and harvest failures aggravated poverty in the urban proletariat, and the 1904-05 defeat by Japan (which checked Russia's Asian expansion) sparked the revolution of 1905-06. A **Duma** (parliament) was created, and an agricultural reform (under Stolypin, prime minister 1906-11) created a large class of landowning peasants (kulaks).

The world shrinks. Developments in transportation and communication and mass population movements helped create an awareness of an interdependent world. Early **automobiles** (Daimler, Benz, 1885) were experimental, or designed as luxuries. Assembly-line mass production (Ford Motor Co., 1903) made the invention practicable, and by 1910 nearly 500 000 motor vehicles were registered in the U.S. alone. **Heavier-than-air flights** began in 1903 in the U.S. (Wright brothers), preceded by glider, balloon, and model plane advances in several countries. Trade was advanced by improvements in **ship design** (gyrocompass, 1907), speed (Lusitania crossed Atlantic in 5 days, 1907), and reach (Panama Canal begun, 1904).

The first transatlantic **radio** telegraphic transmission occurred in 1901, 6 years after Marconi discovered radio. Radio transmission of human speech had been made in 1900. Telegraphic transmission of photos was achieved in 1904, lending immediacy to news reports. **Phonographs,** popularized by Caruso's recordings (starting 1902) made for quick international spread of musical styles (ragtime). **Motion pictures,** perfected in the 1890s (Dickson, Lumiere brothers), became a popular and artistic medium after 1900; newsreels appeared in 1909.

Emigration from crowded European centres soared in the decade: 9 million migrated to the U.S., and millions more went to Canada, Argentina, Australia, Siberia, South Africa, and Algeria. Some 70 million Europeans emigrated in the century before 1914. Several million Chinese, Indians, and Japanese migrated to Southeast Asia, where their urban skills often enabled them to take a predominant economic role.

Social reform. The social and economic problems of the poor were kept in the public eye by realist fiction writers (Dreiser's *Sister Carrie,* 1900; Gorky's *Lower Depths,* 1902; Sinclair's *Jungle,* 1906), journalists (U.S. **muckrakers** — Steffens, Tarbell) and artists (Ashcan school). Frequent labor strikes and occasional assassinations by anarchists or radicals (Austrian Empress, 1898; King Umberto I of Italy, 1900; U.S. Pres. McKinley, 1901; Russian Interior Minister Plehve, 1904; Portugal's King Carlos, 1908) added to social tension and fear of revolution.

But democratic reformism prevailed. In Germany, Bernstein's (1850-1932) **revisionist Marxism,** downgrading revolution, was accepted by the powerful Social Democrats and trade unions. The British Fabian Society (the Webbs, Shaw) and the Labour Party (founded 1906) worked for reforms such as social security and union rights (1906), while women's suffragists grew more militant. U.S. **progressives** fought big business (Pure Food and Drug Act, 1906). In France, the 10-hour work day (1904) and separation of church and state (1905) were reform victories, as was universal suffrage in Austria (1907).

Arts. An unprecedented period of experimentation, centred in France, produced several new **painting** styles: fauvism exploited bold color areas (Matisse, *Woman with Hat,* 1905); expressionism reflected powerful inner emotions (the Brücke group, 1905); cubism combined several views of an object on one flat surface (Picasso's *Demoiselles,* 1906-07); futurism tried to depict speed and motion (Italian Futurist Manifesto, 1910). **Architects** explored new uses of steel structures, with facades either neo-classical (Adler and Sullivan in U.S.); curvilinear Art Nouveau (Gaudi's Casa Mila, 1905-10); or functionally streamlined (Wright's Robie House, 1909).

Music and Dance shared the experimental spirit. Ruth St. Denis (1877-1968) and Isadora Duncan (1878-1927) pioneered modern dance, while Diaghilev in Paris revitalized classic ballet from 1909. Composers explored atonal music (Debussy, 1862-1918) and dissonance (Schönberg, 1874-1951), or revolutionized classical forms (Stravinsky, 1882-71), often showing jazz or folk music influences.

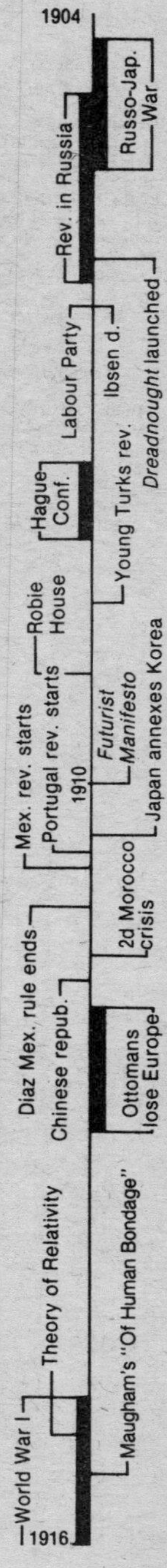

Timeline (right margin, 1904–1916):

- 1904
- Rev. in Russia
- Russo-Jap. War
- Labour Party
- Ibsen d.
- Dreadnought launched
- Hague Conf.
- Young Turks rev.
- Robie House
- Futurist Manifesto
- Japan annexes Korea
- Mex. rev. starts
- Portugal rev. starts
- 1910
- 2d Morocco crisis
- Diaz Mex. rule ends
- Chinese repub.
- Ottomans lose Europe
- Theory of Relativity
- Maugham's "Of Human Bondage"
- World War I
- 1916

The Seven Wonders of the World

These ancient works of art and architecture were considered awe-inspiring in splendor and/or size by the Greek and Roman world of the Alexandrian epoch and later. Classical writers disagreed as to which works made up the list of Wonders, but the following were usually included:

The Pyramids of Egypt: The only surviving Wonder, these monumental structures of masonry located on the west bank of the Nile River above Cairo were built from 3000 to 1800 B.C. as royal tombs. Three—Khufu, Khafra, and Menkaura—were often grouped as the first Wonder of the World. The largest, **The Great Pyramid of Khufu**, or Cheops, is a solid mass of limestone blocks covering 5.2 ha. It is estimated to contain 2.3 million blocks of stone, the stones themselves averaging 2¼ tonnes and some weighing 27 tonnes. Its construction reputedly took 100 000 laborers 20 years.

The Hanging Gardens of Babylon: These gardens were laid out on a brick terrace about 37 sq m and 23 m above the ground. To irrigate the trees, shrubs, and flowers, screws were turned to lift water from the Euphrates River. The gardens were probably built by King Nebuchandnezzar II around 600 B.C. **The Walls of Babylon**, long, thick, and made of colorfully glazed brick, were considered by some to be among the Seven Wonders.

The Statue of Zeus (Jupiter) at Olympia: This statue of the king of the gods showed him seated on a throne. His flesh was made of ivory, his robe and ornaments of gold. Reputedly 12 m high, the statue was made by Phidias and was placed in the great temple of Zeus in the sacred grove of Olympia around 457 B.C.

The Colossus of Rhodes: A bronze statue of the sun god Helios, the Colossus was worked on for 12 years in the early 2nd century B.C. by the sculptor Chares. It was probably 36.5 m high. A symbol of the city of Rhodes at its height, the statue stood on a promontory overlooking the harbor.

The Temple of Artemis (Diana) at Ephesus: This largest and most complex temple of ancient times was built around 550 B.C. and was made of marble except for its tile-covered wooden roof. It was begun in honor of a non-Hellenic goddess who later became identified with the Greek goddess of the same name. Ephesus was one of the greatest of the Ionian cities.

The Mausoleum at Halicarnassus: The source of our word "mausoleum," this marble tomb was built in what is now southeastern Turkey by Artemisia for her husband Mausolus, an official of the Persian Empire who died in 353 B.C. About 41 m high, it was adorned with the works of 4 sculptors.

The Pharos (Lighthouse) of Alexandria: This sculpture was designed around 270 B.C., during the reign of King Ptolemy II, by the Greek architect Sostratos. Estimates of its height range from 60 to 180 m.

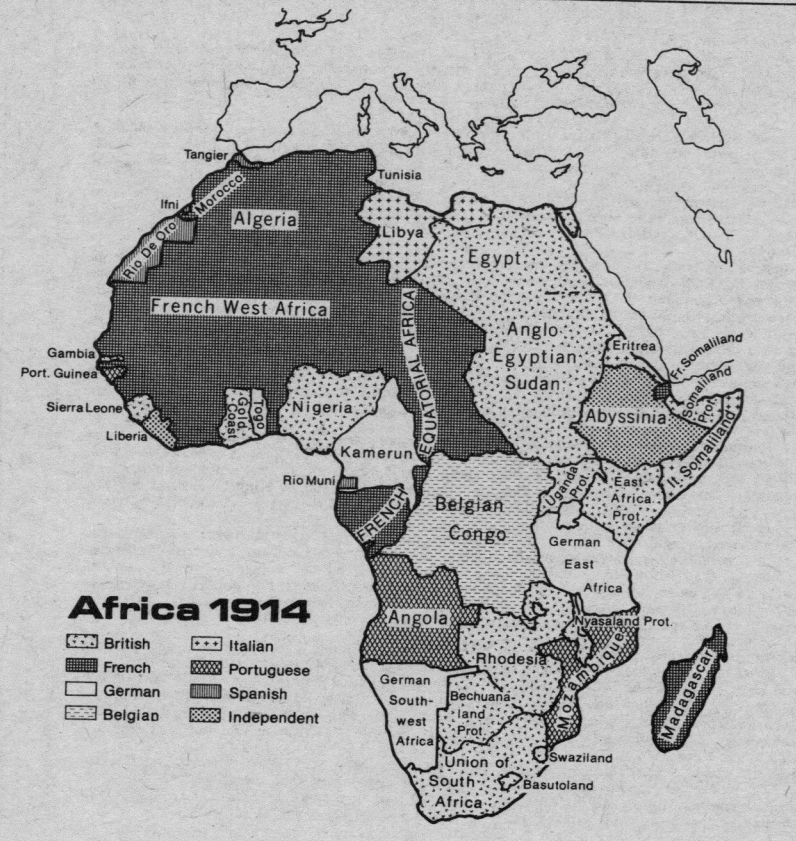

Africa 1914

British · French · German · Belgian · Italian · Portuguese · Spanish · Independent

War and Revolution: 1910-1919

War threatens. Germany under Wilhelm II sought a political and imperial role consonant with its industrial strength, challenging Britain's world supremacy and threatening France, still resenting the loss of Alsace-Lorraine. Austria wanted to curb an expanded Serbia (after 1912) and the threat it posed to its own Slav lands. Russia feared Austrian and German political and economic aims in the Balkans and Turkey. An accelerated arms race resulted: the German standing army rose to over 2 million men by 1914. Russia and France had over a million each, Austria and the British Empire nearly a million each. Dozens of enormous battleships were built by the powers after 1906.

The **assassination of Austrian Archduke Ferdinand** by a Serbian, June 28, 1914, was the pretext for war. The system of alliances made the conflict Europe-wide; Germany's invasion of Belgium to outflank France forced Britain to enter the war. Patriotic fervor was nearly unanimous among all classes in most countries.

World War I. German forces were stopped in France in one month. The rival armies dug **trench networks**. Artillery and improved machine guns prevented either side from any lasting advance despite repeated assaults (600 000 dead at **Verdun**, Feb.-July 1916). Poison gas, used by Germany in 1915, proved ineffective. Over one million U.S. troops tipped the balance after mid-1917, forcing Germany to sue for peace.

In the East, the Russian armies were thrown back (battle of **Tannenberg**, Aug. 20, 1914) and the war grew unpopular. An Allied attempt to relieve Russia through Turkey failed (**Gallipoli** 1916). The new Bolshevik regime signed the capitulatory Brest-Litovsk peace in March, 1918. Italy entered the war on the Allied side, Apr. 1915, but was pushed back by Oct. 1917. A renewed offensive with Allied aid in Oct.-Nov. 1918 forced Austria to surrender.

The British Navy successfully blockaded Germany, which responded with submarine U-boat attacks; **unrestricted submarine warfare** against neutrals after Jan. 1917 helped bring the U.S. into the war. Other battlefields included Palestine and Mesopotamia, both of which Britain wrested from the Turks in 1917, and the African and Pacific colonies of Germany, most of which fell to Britain, France, Australia, Japan, and South Africa.

From 1916, the civilian population and economy of both sides were mobilized to an unprecedented degree. Over 10 million soldiers died (May 1917 French mutiny crushed).

Settlement. At the **Versailles conference** (Jan.-June 1919) and in subsequent negotiations and local wars (Russian-Polish War 1920), the map of Europe was redrawn with a nod to U.S. Pres. Wilson's principle of self-determination. Austria and Hungary were separated and much of their land was given to Yugoslavia (formerly Serbia), Romania, Italy, and the newly independent Poland and Czechoslovakia. Germany lost territory in the West, North, and East, while Finland and the Baltic states were detached from Russia. Turkey lost nearly all its Arab lands to British-sponsored Arab states or to direct French and British rule.

A huge **reparations** burden and partial demilitarization were imposed on Germany. The League of Nations was formed founded on the principles of collective security and the preservation of peace through arbitration of international disputes.

Russian revolution. Military defeats and high casualties caused a contagious lack of confidence in Czar Nicholas, who was forced to abdicate, Mar. 1917. A liberal provisional government failed to end the war, and massive desertions, riots, and fighting between factions followed. A moderate socialist government under Kerensky was overthrown in a violent **coup by the Bolsheviks** in Petrograd under Lenin, who disbanded the elected Constituent Assembly, Nov. 1917.

The Bolsheviks suppressed all opposition and ended the war with Germany, Mar. 1918. **Civil war** broke out in the summer between the Red Army, including the Bolsheviks and their supporters, and monarchists, anarchists, nationalities (Ukrainians, Georgians, Poles) and others. Small U.S., British, French and Japanese units also opposed the Bolsheviks, 1918-19 (Japan in Vladivostok to 1922). The civil war, anarchy, and pogroms devastated the country until the 1920 Red Army victory. The wartime total monopoly of political, economic, and police power by the Communist Party leadership was retained.

Other European revolutions. An unpopular monarchy in **Portugal** was overthrown in 1910. The new republic took severe anti-clerical measures, 1911.

After a century of Home Rule agitation, during which **Ireland** was devastated by famine (one million dead, 1846-47) and emigration, republican militants staged an unsuccessful uprising in Dublin, Easter 1916. The execution of the leaders and mass arrests by the British won popular support for the rebels. The Irish Free State, comprising all but the 6 northern counties, achieved dominion status in 1922.

In the aftermath of the world war, radical revolutions were attempted in Germany (**Spartacist** uprising Jan. 1919), **Hungary** (Kun regime 1919), and elsewhere. All were suppressed or failed for lack of support.

Chinese revolution. The Manchu Dynasty was overthrown and a republic proclaimed, Oct. 1911. First president Sun Yat-sen resigned in favor of strongman Yuan Shih-k'ai. Sun organized the parliamentarian **Kuomintang** party.

Students launched protests May 4, 1919 against League of Nations concessions in China to Japan. Nationalist, liberal, and socialist ideas and political groups spread. The **Communist Party** was founded 1921. A communist regime took power in Mongolia with Soviet support in 1921.

India restive. Indian objections to British rule erupted in nationalist riots as well as in the non-violent tactics of Gandhi (1869-1948). Nearly 400 unarmed demonstrators were shot at **Amritsar**, Apr. 1919. Britain approved limited self-rule that year.

Mexican revolution. Under the long Diaz dictatorship (1876-1911) the economy advanced, but Indian and mestizo lands were confiscated, and concessions to foreigners (mostly U.S.) damaged the middle class. A **revolution in 1910** led to civil wars and U.S. intervention (1914, 1916-17). Land reform and a more democratic constitution (1917) were achieved.

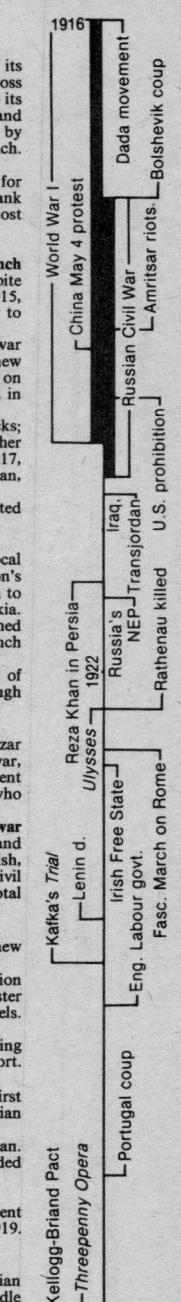

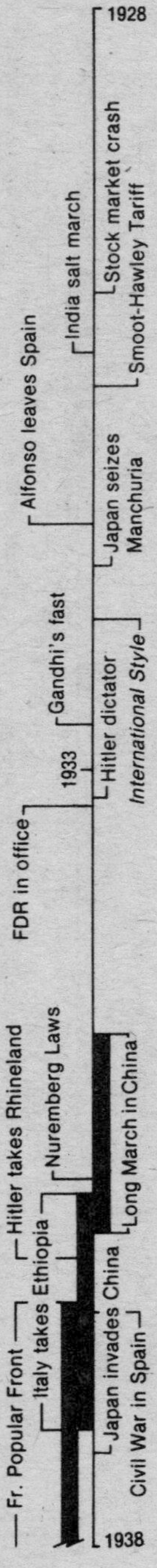

The Aftermath of War: 1920-29

N. America. Easy credit, technological ingenuity, and war-related industrial decline in Europe caused a long economic boom, in which ownership of the new products — autos, phones, radios — became democratized. Prosperity, and drastic change in fashion, created a wide perception of social change, despite prohibition of alcoholic beverages (1919-33). Union membership and strikes increased.

Europe sorts itself out. Germany's liberal **Weimar constitution** (1919) could not guarantee a stable government in the face of rightist violence (Rathenau assassinated 1922) and Communist refusal to cooperate with Socialists. Reparations and Allied occupation of the Rhineland caused staggering inflation which destroyed middle class savings, but economic expansion resumed after mid-decade, aided by U.S. loans. A sophisticated, innovative culture developed in architecture and design (Bauhaus, 1919-28), film (Lang, *M,* 1931), painting (Grosz), music (Weill, *Threepenny Opera,* 1928), theater (Brecht, *A Man's a Man,* 1926), criticism (Benjamin), philosophy (Jung), and fashion. This culture was considered decadent and socially disruptive by rightists.

England elected its first labor governments (Jan. 1924, June 1929). A 10-day general strike in support of coal miners failed, May 1926. In **Italy,** strikes, political chaos and violence by small Fascist bands culminated in the Oct. 1922 Fascist March on Rome, which established Mussolini's dictatorship. Strikes were outlawed (1926), and Italian influence was pressed in the Balkans (Albania a protectorate 1926). A conservative dictatorship was also established in **Portugal** in a 1926 military coup.

Czechoslovakia, the only stable democracy to emerge from the war in Central or East Europe, faced opposition from Germans (in the Sudetenland), Ruthenians, and some Slovaks. As the industrial heartland of the old Hapsburg empire, it remained fairly prosperous. With French backing, it formed the Little Entente with Yugoslavia (1920) and **Romania** (1921) to block Austrian or Hungarian irredentism. **Hungary** remained dominated by the landholding classes and expansionist feeling. Croats and Slovenes in **Yugoslavia** demanded a federal state until King Alexander proclaimed a dictatorship (1929). Poland faced nationality problems as well (Germans, Ukrainians, Jews); Pilsudski ruled as dictator from 1926. The Baltic states were threatened by traditionally dominant ethnic Germans and by Soviet-supported communists.

An economic collapse and famine in **Russia,** 1921-22, claimed 5 million lives. The New Economic Policy (1921) allowed land ownership by peasants and some private commerce and industry. Stalin was absolute ruler within 4 years of Lenin's 1924 death. He inaugurated a collectivization program 1929-32, and used foreign communist parties for Soviet state advantage.

Internationalism. Revulsion against World War I led to pacifist agitation, the Kellogg-Briand Pact renouncing aggressive war (1928), and **naval disarmament** pacts (Washington, 1922, London, 1930). But the League of Nations was able to arbitrate only minor disputes (Greece-Bulgaria, 1925).

Middle East. Mustafa Kemal (Ataturk) led **Turkish** nationalists in resisting Italian, French, and Greek military advances, 1919-23. The sultanate was abolished 1922, and elaborate reforms passed, including secularization of law and adoption of the Latin alphabet. Ethnic conflict led to persecution of **Armenians** (over 1 million dead in 1915, 1 million expelled), Greeks (forced Greek-Turk population exchange, 1923), and Kurds (1925 uprising).

With evacuation of the Turks from **Arab** lands, the puritanical Wahabi dynasty of eastern Arabia conquered present Saudi Arabia, 1919-25. British, French, and Arab dynastic and nationalist manoeuvering resulted in the creation of two more Arab monarchies in 1921: Iraq and Transjordan (both under British control), and two French mandates: Syria and Lebanon. Jewish immigration into British-mandated **Palestine,** inspired by the Zionist movement, was resisted by Arabs, at times violently (1921, 1929 massacres).

Reza Khan ruled **Persia** after his 1921 coup (shah from 1925), centralized control, and created the trappings of a modern state.

China. The Kuomintang under **Chiang Kai-shek** (1887-1975) subdued the warlords by 1928. The Communists were brutally suppressed after their alliance with the Kuomintang was broken in 1927. Relative peace thereafter allowed for industrial and financial improvements, with some Russian, British, and U.S. cooperation.

Arts. Nearly all bounds of subject matter, style, and attitude were broken in the arts of the period. Abstract art first took inspiration from natural forms or narrative themes (Kandinsky from 1911), then worked free of any representational aims (Malevich's suprematism, 1915-19, Mondrian's geometric style from 1917). The **Dada** movement from 1916 mocked artistic pretension with absurd collages and constructions (Arp, Tzara, from 1916). Paradox, illusion, and psychological taboos were exploited by **surrealists** by the latter 1920s (Dali, Magritte). Architectural schools celebrated industrial values, whether vigorous abstract constructivism (Tatlin, *Monument to 3rd International,* 1919) or the machined, streamlined **Bauhaus** style, which was extended to many design fields (Helvetica type face).

Prose writers explored revolutionary narrative modes related to dreams (Kafka's *Trial,* 1925), internal monologue (Joyce's *Ulysses,* 1922), and word play (Stein's *Making of Americans,* 1925). Poets and novelists wrote of modern alienation (Eliot's *Waste Land,* 1922) and aimlessness (Lost Generation).

Sciences. Scientific specialization prevailed by the 20th century. Advances in knowledge and technological aptitude increased with the geometric increase in the number of practitioners. Physicists challenged common-sense views of causality, observation, and a mechanistic universe, putting science further beyond popular grasp (Einstein's general theory of relativity, 1915; Bohr's quantum mechanics, 1913; Heisenberg's uncertainty principle, 1927).

Rise of the Totalitarians: 1930-39

Depression. A worldwide financial panic and economic depression began with the Oct. 1929 U.S. stock market crash and the May 1931 failure of the Austrian Credit-Anstalt. A credit crunch caused international bankruptcies and **unemployment:** 12 million jobless by 1932 in the U.S., 5.6 million in Germany, 2.7 million in England. Governments responded with **tariff restrictions** (Smoot-Hawley Act

Timeline (left margin, 1928–1938):
- 1928
- India salt march
- Stock market crash
- Smoot-Hawley Tariff
- Alfonso leaves Spain
- Japan seizes Manchuria
- Gandhi's fast
- Hitler dictator
- International Style
- 1933
- FDR in office
- Nuremberg Laws
- Long March in China
- Hitler takes Rhineland
- Italy takes Ethiopia
- Fr. Popular Front
- Japan invades China
- Civil War in Spain
- 1938

1930; Ottawa Imperial Conference, 1932) which dried up world trade. Government public works programs were vitiated by deflationary budget balancing.

Germany. Years of agitation by violent extremists was brought to a head by the Depression. Nazi leader **Hitler** was named chancellor by Pres. Hindenburg Jan. 1933, and given dictatorial power by the Reichstag in Mar. Opposition parties were disbanded, strikes banned, and all aspects of economic, cultural, and religious life brought under central government and Nazi party control and manipulated by sophisticated propaganda. Severe persecution of Jews began (**Nuremberg Laws** Sept. 1935). Many Jews, political opponents and others were sent to concentration camps (Dachau, 1933) where thousands died or were killed. Public works, renewed conscription (1935), arms production, and a 4-year plan (1936) ended unemployment.

Hitler's expansionism started with reincorporation of the Saar (1935), occupation of the **Rhineland** (Mar. 1936), and annexation of Austria (Mar. 1938). At **Munich**, Sept. 1938, an indecisive Britain and France sanctioned German dismemberment of Czechoslovakia.

Russia. Urbanization and education advanced. Rapid industrialization was achieved through successive **5-year-plans** starting 1928, using labor discipline and mass forced labor. Industry was financed by a decline in living standards and exploitation of agriculture, which was almost totally collectivized by the early 1930s (*kolkhoz*, collective farm; *sovkhoz*, state farm, often in newly-worked lands). Successive **purges** increased the role of professionals and management at the expense of workers. Millions perished in a series of man-made disasters: elimination of kulaks (peasant land-owners), 1929-34; severe famine, 1932-33; party purges (Great Purge, 1936-38); suppression of nationalities; and poor conditions in labor camps.

Spain. An industrial revolution during World War I created an urban proletariat, which was attracted to socialism and anarchism; Catalan nationalists challenged central authority. The 5 years after King Alfonso left Spain, Apr. 1931, were dominated by tension between intermittent leftist and anti-clerical governments and clericals, monarchists and other rightists. Anarchist and communist rebellions were crushed, but a July, 1936, extreme right rebellion led by Gen. Francisco Franco and aided by Nazi Germany and Fascist Italy succeeded, after a 3-year **civil war** (over 1 million dead in battles and atrocities). The war polarized international public opinion.

Italy. Despite propaganda for the ideal of the Corporate State, few domestic reforms were attempted. An entente with Hungary and Austria, Mar. 1934, a pact with Germany and Japan, Nov. 1937, and intervention by 50-75 000 troops in Spain, 1936-39, sealed Italy's identification with the fascist bloc (anti-Semitic laws after Mar. 1938). Ethiopia was conquered, 1935-37, and **Albania** annexed, Jan. 1939, in conscious imitation of ancient Rome.

East Europe. Repressive regimes fought for power against an active opposition (liberals, socialists, communists, peasants, Nazis). Minority groups and Jews were restricted within national boundaries that did not coincide with ethnic population patterns. In the destruction of **Czechoslovakia, Hungary** occupied southern Slovakia (Mar. 1938) and Ruthenia (Mar. 1939), and a pro-Nazi regime took power in the rest of Slovakia. Other boundary disputes (e.g. Poland-Lithuania, Yugoslavia-Bulgaria, Romania-Hungary) doomed attempts to build joint fronts against Germany or Russia. Economic depression was severe.

East Asia. After a period of liberalism in **Japan**, nativist militarists dominated the government with peasant support. Manchuria was seized, Sept. 1931-Feb. 1932, and a puppet state set up (Manchukuo). Adjacent Jehol (inner Mongolia) was occupied in 1933. China proper was invaded July 1937; large areas were conquered by Oct. 1938.

In **China** Communist forces led by Mao Zedong left Kuomintang-besieged strongholds in the South in The Long March (1934-35) to the North. The Kuomintang-Communist civil war was suspended Jan. 1937 in the face of threatening Japan.

The democracies. The Roosevelt Administration, in office Mar. 1933, embarked on an extensive program of social reform and economic stimulation, including protection for labor unions (heavy industries organized), social security, public works, wages and hours laws, assistance to farmers. Isolationist sentiment (1937 Neutrality Act) prevented U.S. intervention in Europe, but military expenditures were increased in 1939.

French political instability and polarization prevented resolution of economic and international security questions. The **Popular Front** government under Blum (June 1936-Apr. 1938) passed social reforms (40-hour week) and raised arms spending. National coalition governments ruled Britain from Aug. 1931, brought some economic recovery, but failed to define a consistent foreign policy until Chamberlain's government (from May 1937), which practiced deliberate **appeasement** of Germany and Italy.

India. Twenty years of agitation for autonomy and then for independence (Gandhi's **salt march,** 1930) achieved some constitutional reform (extended provincial powers, 1935) despite Moslem-Hindu strife. Social issues assumed prominence with peasant uprisings (1921), strikes (1928), Gandhi's efforts for untouchables (1932 "fast unto death"), and social and agrarian reform by the provinces after 1937.

Arts. The streamlined, geometric design motifs of Art Deco (from 1925) prevailed through the 1930s. Abstract art flourished (Moore sculptures from 1931) alongside a new realism related to social and political concerns (**Socialist Realism** the official Soviet style from 1934; Mexican muralists Rivera, 1886-1957, and Orozco, 1883-1949), which was also expressed in fiction and poetry (Steinbeck's *Grapes of Wrath,* 1939; Sandburg's *The People, Yes,* 1936). Modern architecture (*International Style,* 1932) was unchallenged in its use of man-made materials (concrete, glass), lack of decoration, and monumentality (Rockefeller Center, 1929-40). U.S.-made films captured a world-wide audience with their larger-than-life fantasies (*Gone with the Wind,* 1939).

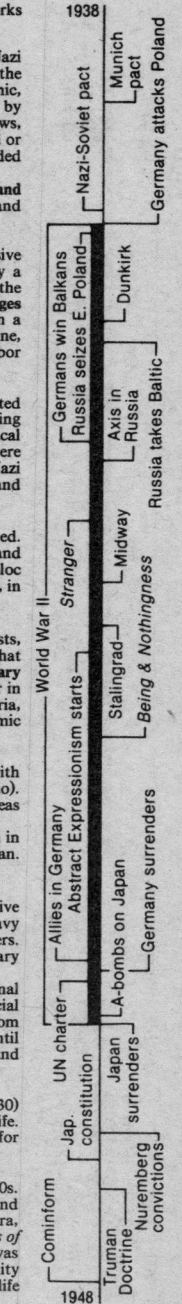

1938

1948

Nazi-Soviet pact
Munich pact
Germany attacks Poland
Germans win Balkans
Russia seizes E. Poland
Dunkirk
Axis in Russia
Russia takes Baltic
Stranger
Midway
Stalingrad
Being & Nothingness
World War II
Abstract Expressionism starts
Germany surrenders
Allies in Germany
A-bombs on Japan
Japan surrenders
UN charter
Jap. constitution
Popular Front
Nuremberg convictions
Truman Doctrine
Cominform

Timeline (left margin, 1948–1958): Israel indep.; China People's Rep.; Gandhi killed; Burma independent; *Lonely Crowd*; Ger. Dem. Rep.; Indonesia indep.; Indochina War; Egypt rev.; H-bomb; Stalin d.; Korean War; McCarthy censured; Peron ousted; Bandung conf.; SEATO founded; Hungary rev.; Suez War; *On the Road*; Ghana indep.; Sputnik; EEC Treaty

War, Hot and Cold: 1940-49

War in Europe. The Nazi-Soviet non-agression pact (Aug. 1939) freed Germany to attack Poland (Sept.). Britain and France, who had guaranteed Polish independence, declared war on Germany. Russia seized East Poland (Sept.), attacked Finland (Nov.) and took the Baltic states (July 1940). Mobile German forces staged "**blitzkrieg**" attacks Apr.-June, 1940, conquering neutral Denmark, Norway, and the low countries and defeating France; 350 000 British and French troops were evacuated at **Dunkirk** (May). The Battle of Britain, June-Dec. 1940, denied Germany air superiority. German-Italian campaigns won the Balkans by Apr. 1941. Three million Axis troops **invaded Russia** June 1941, marching through the Ukraine to the Caucasus, and through White Russia and the Baltic republics to Moscow and Leningrad.

Russian winter counterthrusts, 1941-1942 and 1942-1943 stopped the German advance (Stalingrad Sept. 1942-Feb. 1943). With British and U.S. Lend-Lease aid and sustaining great casualties, the Russians drove the Axis from all E. Europe and the Balkans in the next 2 years. Invasions of N. Africa (Nov. 1942), Italy (Sept. 1943), and Normandy (June 1944) brought U.S., British, Free French and Allied troops to Germany by spring 1945. Germany surrendered May 7, 1945.

War in Asia-Pacific. Japan occupied Indochina Sept. 1940, dominated Thailand Dec. 1941, attacked Hawaii, the Philippines, Hong Kong, Malaya Dec. 7, 1941. Indonesia was attacked Jan. 1942, Burma conquered Mar. 42. Battle of **Midway** (June 1942) turned back the Japanese advance. "Island-hopping" battles (Guadalcanal Aug. 1942-Jan. 1943, **Leyte Gulf** Oct. 1944, Iwo Jima Feb.-Mar. 1945, Okinawa Apr. 1945) and massive bombing raids on Japan from June 1944 wore out Japanese defenses. Two U.S. atom bombs, dropped Aug. 6 and 9, forced Japan to surrender Aug. 14, 1945.

Atrocities. The war brought 20th-century cruelty to its peak. Nazi murder camps (Auschwitz) systematically killed 6 million Jews. Gypsies, political opponents, sick and retarded people, and others deemed undesirable were murdered by the Nazis, as were vast numbers of Slavs, especially leaders.

Civilian deaths. German bombs killed 70 000 English civilians. Some 100 000 Chinese civilians were killed by Japanese forces in the capture of Nanking. Severe retaliation by the Soviet army, E. European partisans, Free French and others took a heavy toll. U.S. and British bombing of Germany killed hundreds of thousands, as did U.S. bombing of Japan (80-200 000 at Hiroshima alone). Some 45 million people lost their lives in the war.

Settlement. The United Nations charter was signed in San Francisco June 26, 1945 by 50 nations. The International Tribunal at Nuremberg convicted 22 German leaders for war crimes Sept. 1946, 23 Japanese leaders were convicted Nov. 1948. Postwar border changes included large gains in territory for the USSR, losses for Germany, a shift westward in Polish borders, and minor losses for Italy. Communist regimes, supported by Soviet troops, took power in most of E. Europe, including Soviet-occupied Germany (GDR proclaimed Oct. 1949). Japan lost all overseas lands.

Recovery. Basic political and social changes were imposed on Japan and W. Germany by the western allies (Japan constitution Nov. 1946, W. German basic law May 1949). U.S. Marshall Plan aid ($12 billion 1947-1951) spurred W. European economic recovery after a period of severe inflation and strikes in Europe and the U.S. The British Labour Party introduced a national health service and nationalized basic industries in 1946.

Cold War. Western fears of further Soviet advances (Cominform formed Oct. 1947, Czechoslovakia coup, Feb. 1948, Berlin blockade Apr. 1948-Sept. 1949) led to formation of NATO. Civil War in Greece and Soviet pressure on Turkey led to U.S. aid under the Truman Doctrine (Mar. 1947). Other anti-communist security pacts were the Org. of American States (Apr. 1948) and Southeast Asia Treaty Org. (Sept. 1954). A new wave of Soviet purges and repression intensified in the last years of Stalin's rule, extending to E. Europe (Slansky trial in Czechoslovakia, 1951). Only Yugoslavia resisted Soviet control (expelled by Cominform, June 1948; U.S. aid, June 1949).

China, Korea. Communist forces emerged from World War II strengthened by the Soviet takeover of industrial Manchuria. In 4 years of fighting, the Kuomintang, or Nationalists, withdrew to Taiwan; the People's Republic of China was proclaimed Oct. 1, 1949. Korea was divided by Russian and U.S. occupation forces. Separate republics were proclaimed in the 2 zones Aug.-Sept. 1948.

India. India and Pakistan became independent dominions Aug. 15, 1947. Millions of Hindu and Moslem refugees were created by the partition; riots, 1946-47, took hundreds of thousands of lives; Gandhi himself was assassinated Jan. 1948. Burma became completely independent Jan. 1948; Ceylon achieved dominion status in Feb.

Middle East. The UN approved partition of Palestine into Jewish and Arab states. Israel was proclaimed May 14, 1948. Arabs rejected partition, but failed to defeat Israel in war, May 1948-July 1949. Immigration from Europe and the Middle East swelled Israel's Jewish population. British and French forces left Lebanon and Syria, 1946. Transjordan occupied most of Arab Palestine.

Southeast Asia. Communists and others fought against restoration of French rule in Indochina from 1946; a non-communist government was recognized by France Mar. 1949, but fighting continued. Both Indonesia and the Philippines became independent, the former in 1949 after 4 years of war with Netherlands, the latter in 1946. Philippine economic and military ties with the U.S. remained strong; a communist-led peasant rising was checked in 1948.

Arts. New York became the centre of the world art market; abstract expressionism was the chief mode (Pollock from 1943, de Kooning from 1947). Literature and philosophy explored existentialism (Camus' *Stranger*, 1942, Sartre's *Being and Nothingness*, 1943). Non-western attempts to revive or create regional styles (Senghor's Negritude, Mishima's novels) only confirmed the emergence of a universal culture.

Post WW II: 1950-59

Polite decolonization. The peaceful decline of European political and military power in Asia and Africa accelerated in the 1950s. Nearly all of N. Africa was freed by 1956, but France fought a bitter war to retain Algeria, with its large European minority, until 1962. **Ghana**, independent 1957, led a parade of new black African nations (over 2 dozen by 1962) which altered the political character of the UN. Ethnic disputes often exploded in the new nations after decolonization (UN troops in Cyprus 1964; **Nigeria** civil war 1967-70). Leaders of the new states, mostly sharing socialist ideologies, tried to create an Afro-Asian bloc (Bandung Conf. 1955), but Western economic influence and U.S. political ties remained strong (Baghdad Pact, 1955).

Trade. World trade volume soared, in an atmosphere of monetary stability assured by international accords (**Bretton Woods** 1944). In Europe, economic integration advanced (**European Economic Community** 1957, European Free Trade Association 1960). Comecon (1949) coordinated the economies of Soviet-bloc countries.

U.S. Economic growth produced an abundance of consumer goods (9.3 million motor vehicles sold, 1955). Suburban housing tracts changed life patterns for middle and working classes (Levittown 1946-51). **Eisenhower's** landside election victories (1952, 1956) reflected consensus politics. Censure of McCarthy (Dec. '54) curbed the political abuse of anti-communism. A system of alliances and military bases bolstered U.S. influence on all continents. Trade and payments surpluses were balanced by overseas investments and foreign aid ($50 billion, 1950-59).

USSR. In the "thaw" after Stalin's death in 1953, relations with the West improved (evacuation of Vienna, Geneva summit conf., both 1955). Repression of scientific and cultural life eased, and many prisoners were freed or rehabilitated culminating in **de-Stalinization** (1956). Khrushchev's leadership aimed at consumer growth, but farm production lagged, despite the virgin lands program (from 1954). The 1956 Hungarian revolution, the 1960 U-2 spy plane episode, and other incidents renewed East-West tension.

East Europe. Resentment of Russian domination and Stalinist repression combined with nationalist, economic and religious factors to produce periodic violence. East Berlin workers rioted in 1953, Polish workers rioted in Poznan, June 1956, and a broad-based revolution broke out in Hungary, Oct. 1956. All were suppressed by Soviet force or threats (at least 7 000 dead in Hungary). But Poland was allowed to restore private ownership of farms, and a degree of personal and economic freedom returned to Hungary. Yugoslavia experimented with worker self-management and a market economy.

Korea. The 1945 division of Korea left industry in the North, which was organized into a militant regime and armed by Russia. The South was politically disunited. Over 60 000 North Korean troops invaded the South June 25, 1950. The U.S., backed by the UN Security Council, sent troops. UN troops reached the Chinese border in Nov. Some 200 000 Chinese troops crossed the Yalu River and drove back UN forces. Cease-fire in July 1951 found the opposing forces near the original 38th parallel border. After 2 years of sporadic fighting, an armistice was signed July 27, 1953. U.S. troops remained in the South, and U.S. economic and military aid continued. The war stimulated rapid economic recovery in Japan.

China. Starting in 1952, industry, agriculture, and social institutions were collectivized. As many as several million people were executed as Kuomintang supporters or as class and political enemies. The Great Leap Forward, 1958-60, unsuccessfully tried to force the pace of development by substituting labor for investment.

Indochina. Ho's forces, aided by Russia and the new Chinese Communist government, fought French and pro-French Vietnamese forces to a standstill, and captured the strategic Dienbienphu camp in May, 1954. The Geneva Agreements divided Vietnam in half pending elections (never held), and recognized Laos and Cambodia as independent. The U.S. aided the anti-Communist Republic of Vietnam in the South.

Middle East. Arab revolutions placed leftist, militantly nationalist regimes in power in Egypt (1952) and Iraq (1958). But Arab unity attempts failed (United Arab Republic joined Egypt, Syria, Yemen 1958-61). Arab refusal to recognize Israel (Arab League economic blockade began Sept. 1951) led to a permanent state of war, with repeated incidents (Gaza, 1955). Israel occupied Sinai, Britain and France took the Suez Canal, Oct. 1956, but were replaced by the UN Emergency Force. The Mossadegh government in Iran nationalized the British-owned oil industry May 1951, but was overthrown in a U.S.-aided coup Aug. 1953.

Latin America. Dictator Juan Peron, in office 1946, enforced land reform, some nationalization, welfare state measures, and curbs on the Roman Catholic Church, but crushed opposition. A Sept. 1955 coup deposed Peron. The 1952 revolution in Bolivia brought land reform, nationalization of tin mines, and improvement in the status of Indians, who nevertheless remained poor. The Batista regime in Cuba was overthrown, Jan. 1959, by Fidel Castro, who imposed a communist dictatorship, aligned Cuba with Russia, improved education and health care. A U.S.-backed anti-Castro invasion (Bay of Pigs, Apr. 1961) was crushed. Self-government advanced in the British Caribbean.

Technology. Large outlays on research and development in the U.S. and USSR focussed on military applications (H-bomb in U.S. 1952, USSR 1953, Britain 1957, intercontinental missiles late 1950s). Soviet launching of the Sputnik satellite, Oct. 1957, spurred increases in U.S. science education funds (National Defense Education Act).

Literature and letters. Alienation from social and literary conventions reached an extreme in the theater of the absurd (Beckett's *Waiting for Godot* 1952), the "new novel" (Robbe-Grillet's *Voyeur* 1955), and avant-garde film (Antonioni's *L'Avventura* 1960).

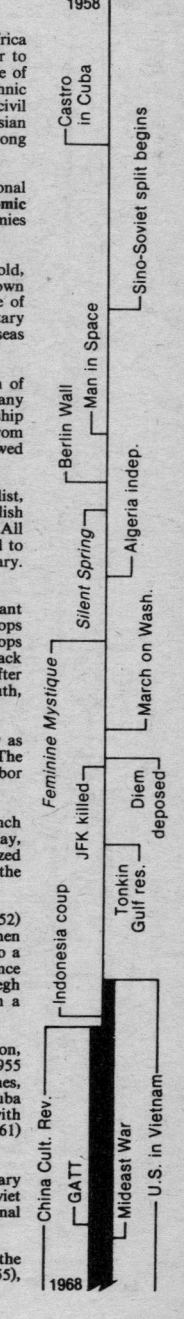

1958 · Castro in Cuba · Sino-Soviet split begins · Berlin Wall · Man in Space · Algeria indep. · Silent Spring · March on Wash. · Feminine Mystique · JFK killed · Diem deposed · Tonkin Gulf res. · Indonesia coup · China Cult. Rev. · GATT · Mideast War · U.S. in Vietnam · 1968

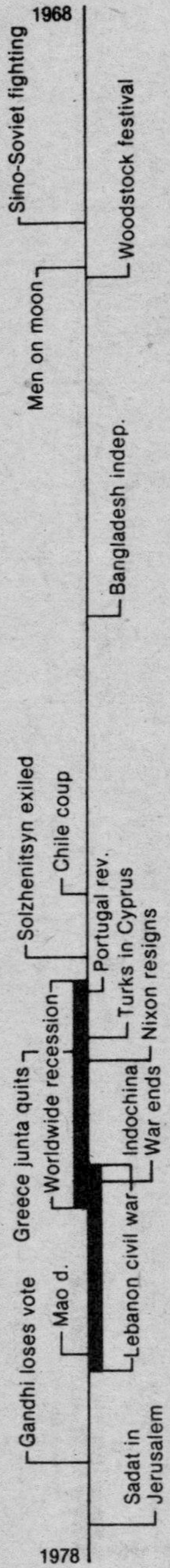
1968
Sino-Soviet fighting
Woodstock festival
Men on moon
Bangladesh indep.
Solzhenitsyn exiled
Chile coup
Portugal rev.
Turks in Cyprus
Nixon resigns
Worldwide recession
Greece junta quits
Indochina
War ends
Lebanon civil war
Mao d.
Gandhi loses vote
Sadat in
Jerusalem
1978

Rising Expectations: 1960-69

Economic boom. The longest sustained economic boom on record spanned almost the entire decade in the capitalist world; the closely-watched GNP figure doubled in the U.S. 1960-70, fueled by Vietnam War-related budget deficits. The **General Agreement on Tariffs and Trade,** 1967, stimulated West European prosperity, which spread to peripheral areas (Spain, Italy, E. Germany). Japan became a top economic power ($20 billion exports 1970). Foreign investment aided the industrialization of Brazil. Soviet 1965 economic reform attempts (decentralization, material incentives) were limited; but growth continued.

Reform and radicalization. A series of political and social reform movements took root in the U.S., later spreading to other countries with the help of ubiquitous U.S. film and television programs and heavy overseas travel. Blacks agitated peaceably and with partial success against segregation and poverty (1963 March on Washington, 1964 **Civil Rights Act**); but some urban ghettos erupted in extensive riots (Watts, 1965; Detroit, 1967; King assassination, Apr. 4, 1968). New concern for the poor (Harrington's *Other America,* 1963) led to Pres. Johnson's **"Great Society"** programs (Medicare, Water Quality Act, Higher Education Act, all 1965). Concern with the **environment** surged (Carson's *Silent Spring,* 1962). **Feminism** revived as a cultural and political movement (Friedan's *Feminine Mystique,* 1963, National Organization for Women founded 1966) and a movement for homosexual rights emerged (Stonewall riot, in NYC, 1969).

Opposition to U.S. involvement in Vietnam, especially among university students (**Moratorium** protest Nov. 1969) turned violent (Weatherman Chicago riots Oct. 1969). New Left and Marxist theories became popular, and membership in radical groups swelled (Students for a Democratic Society, Black Panthers). Maoist groups, especially in Europe, called for total transformation of society. In France, students sparked a nationwide strike affecting 10 million workers May-June 1968, but an electoral reaction barred revolutionary change.

Arts and styles. The boundary between fine and popular arts were blurred by Pop Art (Warhol) and rock musicals (Hair, 1968). Informality and exaggeration prevailed in fashion (beards, miniskirts). A non-political "counterculture" developed, rejecting traditional bourgeois life goals and personal habits, and use of marijuana and hallucinogens spread (Woodstock festival Aug. 1969). Indian influence was felt in music (Beatles), religion (Ram Dass), and fashion.

Science. Achievements in space (men on moon July 1969) and electronics (lasers, integrated circuits) encouraged a faith in scientific solutions to problems in agriculture ("green revolution"), medicine (heart transplants 1967) and other areas. The harmful effects of science, it was believed, could be controlled (1963 nuclear weapon test ban treaty, 1968 non-proliferation treaty).

China. Mao's revolutionary militance caused disputes with Russia under "revisionist" Khrushchev, starting 1960. The two powers exchanged fire in 1969 border disputes. China used force to capture areas disputed with India, 1962. The "Great Proletarian Cultural Revolution" tried to impose a utopian egalitarian program in China and spread revolution abroad; political struggle, often violent, convulsed China 1965-68.

Indochina. Communist-led guerrillas aided by N. Vietnam fought from 1960 against the S. Vietnam government of Ngo Dinh Diem (killed 1963). The U.S. military role increased after the 1964 Tonkin Gulf incident. U.S. forces peaked at 543 400, Apr. 1969. Massive numbers of N. Viet troops also fought. Laotian and Cambodian neutrality were threatened by communist insurgencies, with N. Vietnamese aid, and U.S. intrigues.

Third World. A bloc of authoritarian leftist regimes among the newly independent nations emerged in political opposition to the U.S.-led Western alliance, and came to dominate the conference of nonaligned nations (Belgrade 1961, Cairo 1964, Lusaka 1970). Soviet political ties and military bases were established in Cuba, Egypt, Algeria, Guinea, and other countries, whose leaders were regarded as revolutionary heros by opposition groups in pro-Western or colonial countries. Some leaders were ousted in coups by pro-Western groups—Zaire's Lumumba (killed 1961), Ghana's Nkrumah (exiled 1966), and Indonesia's Sukarno (effectively ousted 1965 after a Communist coup failed).

Middle East. Arab-Israeli tension erupted into a brief war June 1967. Israel emerged as a major regional power. Military shipments before and after the war brought much of the Arab world into the Soviet political sphere. Most Arab states broke U.S. diplomatic ties, while Communist countries cut their ties to Israel. Intra-Arab disputes continued: Egypt and Saudi Arabia supported rival factions in a bloody Yemen civil war 1962-70; Lebanese troops fought Palestinian commandos in 1969.

East Europe. To stop the large-scale exodus of citizens, E. German authorities built a fortified wall across Berlin Aug. 1961. Soviet sway in the Balkans was weakened by Albania's support of China (USSR broke ties Dec. 1961) and Romania's assertion of industrial and foreign policy autonomy in 1964. Liberalization in Czechoslovakia, spring 1968, was crushed by troops of 5 Warsaw Pact countries. West German treaties with Russia and Poland, 1970, facilitated the transfer of German technology and confirmed post-war boundaries.

Disillusionment: 1970-79

U.S.: Caution and neoconservatism. A relatively sluggish economy, energy and resource shortages (natural gas crunch 1975, gasoline shortage 1979), and environmental problems contributed to a **"limits of growth"** philosophy that affected politics (Cal. Gov. Brown). Suspicion of science and technology killed or delayed major projects (supersonic transport dropped 1971, DNA recombination curbed 1976, Seabrook A-plant protests 1977-78) and was fed by the Three Mile Island nuclear reactor accident in Mar. 1979.

Mistrust of big government weakened support for government reform plans among liberals. School busing and racial quotas were opposed (**Bakke decision** June 1978); the Equal Rights Amendment for women languished; civil rights for homosexuals were opposed (Dade County referendum June 1977).

U.S. defeat in **Indochina** (evacuation Apr. 1975), revelations of Central Intelligence Agency misdeeds (Rockefeller Commission report June 1975), and the **Watergate** scandals (Nixon quit Aug. 1974) reduced faith in U.S. moral and material capacity to influence world affairs. Revelations of Soviet crimes (Solzhenitsyn's *Gulag Archipelago* from 1974) and Russian intervention in Africa aided a revival of anti-Communist sentiment.

Economy sluggish. The 1960s boom faltered in the 1970s; a severe recession in the U.S. and Europe 1974-75 followed a huge oil price hike Dec. 1973. Monetary instability (U.S. cut ties to gold Aug. 1971), the decline of the dollar, and **protectionist** moves by industrial countries (1977-78) threatened trade. Business investment and spending for research declined. Severe inflation plagued many countries (25% in Britain, 1975; 18% in U.S., 1979).

China picks up pieces. After the 1976 deaths of Mao and Zhou, a power struggle for the leadership succession was won by pragmatists. A nationwide purge of orthodox Maoists was carried out, and the "Gang of Four", led by Mao's widow Jiang Qing, was arrested.

The new leaders, led by Hua Guofeng, freed over 100 000 political prisoners, and reduced public adulation of Mao. Political and trade ties were expanded with Japan, Europe, and the U.S. in the late 1970s, as relations worsened with Russia, Cuba, and Vietnam (4-week invasion by China in 1979). Ideological guidelines in industry, science, education, and the armed forces, which the ruling faction said had caused chaos and decline, were reversed (bonuses to workers, Dec. 1977; exams for college entrance, Oct. 1977). Severe restrictions on cultural expression were eased (Beethoven ban lifted Mar. 1977).

Europe. European unity moves (EEC-EFTA trade accord 1972) faltered as economic problems appeared (Britain floated pound 1972; France floated franc 1974). Germany and Switzerland curbed guest workers from S. Europe. Greece and Turkey quarrelled over Cyprus (Turks intervened 1974) and Aegean oil rights.

All of non-Communist Europe was under democratic rule after free elections were held in **Spain** June 1976, 7 months after the death of Franco. The conservative, colonialist regime in **Portugal** was overthrown Apr. 1974. In **Greece**, the 7-year-old military dictatorship yielded power in 1974. Northern Europe, though ruled mostly by Socialists (**Swedish** Socialists unseated 1976, after 44 years in power), turned conservative. The **British** Labour government imposed wage curbs 1975, and suspended nationalization schemes. Terrorism in **Germany** (1972 Munich Olympics killings) led to laws curbing some civil liberties. **French** "new philosophers" rejected leftist ideologies, and the shaky Socialist-Communist coalition lost a 1978 election bid.

Religion back in politics. The improvement in Moslem countries' political fortunes by the 1950s (with the exception of Central Asia under Soviet and Chinese rule), and the growth of Arab oil wealth, was followed by a resurgence of traditional piety. **Libyan** dictator Qaddafi mixed strict Islamic laws with socialism in his militant ideology and called for an eventual Moslem return to Spain and Sicily. The illegal Moslem Brotherhood in **Egypt** was accused of violence, while extreme Moslem groups bombed theatres, 1977, to protest secular values.

In **Turkey**, the National Salvation Party was the first Islamic group to share power (1974) since secularization in the 1920s. Religious authorities, such as Ayatollah Ruholla Khomeini, led the **Iranian** revolution and religiously motivated Moslems took part in the insurrection in Saudi Arabia that briefly seized the Grand Mosque in Mecca in 1979. Moslem puritan opposition to **Pakistan** Pres. Bhutto helped lead to his overthrow July 1977. However, Moslem solidarity could not prevent Pakistan's eastern province (**Bangladesh**) from declaring independence, Dec. 1971, after a bloody civil war.

Moslem and Hindu resentment against coerced sterilization in **India** helped defeat the Gandhi government, which was replaced Mar. 1977 by a coalition including religious Hindu parties and led by devout Hindu Desai. Moslems in the southern **Philippines**, aided by Libya, conducted a long rebellion against central rule from 1973.

Evangelical Protestant groups grew in numbers and prosperity in the U.S. ("**born again**" Pres. Carter elected 1976), and the Catholic charismatic movement obtained respectability. A revival of interest in Orthodox Christianity occurred among **Russian** intellectuals (Solzhenitsyn). The secularist **Israeli** Labor party, after decades of rule, was ousted in 1977 by conservatives led by Begin, an observant Jew; religious militants founded settlements on the disputed West Bank, part of Biblically-promised Israel. U.S. Reform Judaism revived many previously discarded traditional practices.

The Buddhist Soka Gakkai movement launched the Komeito party in Japan, 1964, which became a major opposition party in 1972 and 1976 elections.

Old-fashioned religious wars raged intermittently in **N. Ireland** (Catholic vs. Protestant, 1969-) and **Lebanon** (Christian vs. Moslem, 1975-), while religious militancy complicated the Israel-Arab dispute (1973 Israel-Arab war). In spite of a **1979 peace treaty between Egypt and Israel** which looked forward to a resolution of the Palestinian issue, increased religious militancy on the West Bank made such a resolution seem unlikely.

Latin America. Repressive conservative regimes strengthened their hold on most of the continent, with the violent coup against the elected Allende government in Chile, Sept. 1973, the 1976 military coup in **Argentina**, and coups against reformist regimes in **Bolivia**, 1971 and 1979, and **Peru**, 1976. In Central America, increasing liberal and leftist militancy led to the ouster of the Somoza regime of Nicaragua in 1979 and civil conflict in El Salvador.

Indochina. Communist victory in Vietnam, Cambodia, and Laos by May 1975 did not bring peace. Attempts at radical social reorganization left over one million dead in Cambodia during 1975-78 and caused hundreds of thousands of ethnic Chinese and others to flee Vietnam ("boat people," 1979). The Vietnamese invasion of Cambodia swelled the refugee population and contributed to widespread starvation in that devastated country.

Russian expansion. Soviet influence, checked in some countries (troops ousted by Egypt 1972) was projected further afield, often with the use of Cuban troops (Angola 1975-, Ethiopia 1977-), and aided by a growing navy, merchant fleet, and international banking ability. Detente with the West — 1972 Berlin pact, 1972 strategic arms pact (**SALT**) — gave way to a more antagonistic relationship in the late 1970s, exacerbated by the Soviet invasion of Afghanistan in 1979.

Africa. The last remaining European colonies were granted independence (**Spanish Sahara** 1976, **Djibouti** 1977) and, after 10 years of civil war and many negotiation sessions, a black government took over Zimbabwe (Rhodesia) in 1979; white domination remained in **S. Africa**. Great power involvement in local wars (Russia in **Angola, Ethiopia**; France in **Chad, Zaire, Mauritania**) and the use of tens of thousands of Cuban troops was denounced by some African leaders as neocolonialist. Ethnic or tribal clashes made Africa the chief world locus of sustained warfare in the late 1970s.

Arts. Traditional modes in painting, architecture, and music, pursued in relative obscurity for much of the 20th century, returned to popular and critical attention in the 1970s. The pictorial emphasis in neorealist and photorealist painting, the return of many architects to detail, decoration, and traditional natural materials, and the concern with ordered structure in musical composition were, ironically, novel experiences for artistic consumers after the exhaustion of experimental possibilities. However, these more conservative styles coexisted with modernist works in an atmosphere of variety and tolerance.

1980-85

(For Canadian events see Notable Dates in Canadian History, page 21)

United States. Double-digit inflation, high unemployment, a severe drop in industrial output and the government's tight money policy strongly influenced the defeat of Pres. Jimmy Carter and election of former Calif. Gov. Ronald Reagan as U.S. President, 1980. With Reagan's supply-side economic program, interest rates and inflation decreased by 1983. The economic recovery was largely responsible for Reagan's landslide re-election, 1984, but as of the next year the deficit was more than $200 billion, and U.S. debt had doubled under Reagan to $2 trillion. Congress approved a balanced-budget proposal, forcing deficit reductions (Dec. 1985).

U.S.S.R. 1980-85 were troublesome years, with 3 consecutive heads of state dying in office (Brezhnev, 1982; Andropov, 1984; Chernenko, 1985); a sluggish domestic economy, dissent dealt with harshly (Nobel Peace Prize winner Sakharov's exile to Gorky, 1980); restricted emigration for Jews and others. With invasion of Afghanistan (Dec. 1979), U.S. Pres. Carter embargoed grain sales, led boycott of Moscow Olympics (1980); Pres. Reagan lifted embargo (1981), but mutual mistrust and recrimination continued, climaxing with 1983 Soviet shooting of an unarmed South Korean commercial airliner, killing 260, and worldwide condemnation. Soviets led most Eastern European nations in boycott of L.A. Olympics (1984). In 1985, the economy improved slightly and Chernenko's successor, Mikhail Gorbachev, a relatively young and energetic 54, met with Pres. Reagan, the 2 pledging "a fresh start."

Poland. 17 000 Polish workers, embittered by food shortages, insufficient housing and public transport, went on strike at Gdansk's Lenin Shipyard (Aug. 1980). They were joined by another 120 000 and won the right to strike, to form independent trade unions, the release of political prisoners, and the end of government censorship. The unions formed a national body headed by Lech Walesa and, by 1981, 1 million of 2.9 million Polish Communist Party members joined the 9.5-million-member Solidarity. But the union's call (Dec. 1981) for a referendum on establishing a non-Communist government, and demand for access to mass media, brought government imposition of martial law and detention of Walesa. Parliament dissolved the unions (Oct. 1982), Walesa was released as a "private person" (Nov. 1982) and martial law was ended (July 1982). Walesa was awarded the Nobel Peace Prize. (Oct. 1983).

The Middle East. This remained the world's most militarily-unstable area, with sharp divisions on economic, political, racial and religious issues.

In **Iran,** the revolution (1979-80) and the violent political upheavals afterward brought virtual civil war. A dispute with Iraq over the Shatt al-Arab waterway between the 2 countries became open warfare, Sept. 1980, with no end in sight in 1985.

Libya's support for international terrorism caused the U.S. to order their diplomatic mission in Washington closed (May 1981). American jets shot down 2 Libyan warplanes off Libya after being fired on (Aug. 1981). Pres. Reagan embargoed Libyan oil (Mar. 1982). The U.S. accused Libya of aiding terrorists who staged Dec. 1985 attacks at the Rome and Vienna airports.

Israel affirmed the entire city of Jerusalem as its capital (July 1980); destroyed an Iraqi atomic reactor, stating that it could produce nuclear weapons to be used against Israel (1981); invaded Lebanon (1982), bringing the PLO to agree to withdraw peacefully. Christian militia killed more than 600 Palestinians at refugee camps in West Beirut (1982); a 1983 Israeli commission criticized Defence Minister Ariel Sharon for "blunders" and "non-fulfillment of duty," recommending his resignation or dismissal. Israel and **Lebanon** formally ended their war, May 1983; the Israeli withdrawal began in Feb. 1985 and ended in June 1985.

South Africa. Anti-apartheid sentiment gathered force. In 1981, the U.N. General Assembly voted against allowing South Africa to re-occupy the seat it was denied in 1974 because its delegation was not thought to represent South African blacks. In South Africa, anti-apartheid demonstrations grew, as did a violent response from the police. From 1983, anti-apartheid protests increased in the U.S. and Europe. South African white voters approved a constitution (Nov. 1983) that for the first time gave "Coloureds" and Asians a limited voice in the government, while still excluding Blacks—70% of the population. Bishop Desmond Tutu, a South African black, was awarded the Nobel Peace Prize (Oct. 1984). The South African government declared a state of emergency in July 1985. Pres. Reagan imposed economic sanctions, Aug. 1985, and in Sept., 11 Western European nations imposed sanctions.

China. From 1980-85 the new pragmatic leadership of the Chinese Communist Party, under Chairman Deng Xiaoping, pursued far-reaching changes in political and economic institutions and expanded China's commercial and technical ties to the industrialized world. The administrative structure was streamlined; the promotion of younger officials accelerated; the revised constitution re-established the old township and district rural governments while retaining the people's communes as economic organizations only; a major effort was made to increase the role of market forces in stimulating urban economic development. Relations with other countries improved.

Central America. In **Nicaragua,** the leftist Sandinista National Liberation Front, in power after the 1979 civil war, faced increasing problems because of Nicaragua's military aid to leftist guerrillas in El Salvador and the U.S. backing of anti-government forces, or "contras," based in Honduras and Costa Rica. The U.S. said the aid was needed to halt the export of the revolution to other parts of Central America. In response to an accusation by Nicaragua, the U.S. CIA admitted directing the mining of Nicaraguan ports (1984), the U.S. Senate responded by adopting a nonbinding resolution condemning U.S. participation. In 1985, the House rejected Pres. Reagan's request for military aid to the contras, but in June approved $26 million in humanitarian aid.

In **El Salvador,** a military coup (Oct. 1979) failed to halt right-wing violence and left-wing activity. Archbishop Oscar Romero was assassinated (Mar. 1980), allegedly by rightists, and from Jan. to June 1980 some 4 000 civilians reportedly were killed. From 1981, right-wing activity was increasingly directed not only against the left but against the junta, which received increasing U.S. military and economic aid. In 1984, the newly elected pres., José Napoleón Duarte, a moderate, issued more humane codes of conduct to the Army, set up a commission to investigate alleged human rights abuses, and disbanded the military police's intelligence unit; the U.S. then approved $126 million in military aid.

Japan. Relations with the U.S., Western Europe, and the Association of Southeast Asian Nations, 1980-85, were dominated by trade imbalances favoring Japan. Japanese automakers heeded U.S. criticism by agreeing to voluntary restraints (1984), but negotiations over tariff reductions on imports, purchases of satellite equipment, and liberalization of financial markets were postponed. In 1984, Japan achieved a record annual trade surplus, with exports to the U.S. rising 40% to a record high of $60 billion.

Britain. In 1980, the British economy experienced its worst recession since the 1930s. A 13-week strike in the nationalized steel industry—the first in that economic sector since a general strike in 1926—ended with a 15.5% wage increase. Prime Minister Margaret Thatcher trusted the British economy to the discipline of market forces, while unemployment continued to rise and black and white inner-city youths rioted (1981). Britain went to war in 1982, quickly fighting off Argentina's seizure of the British-administered Falkland Islands. The National Union of Mineworkers year-long strike (1984-85) ended with the National Coal Board's plan to close 20 "uneconomic" pits, ending jobs for some 20 000 of the industry's 186 000 workers.

Astronomy, Calendars and Time

Planets and the Sun

The planets of the solar system, in order of their mean distance from the sun, are Mercury, Venus, Earth, Mars, Jupiter, Saturn, Uranus, Neptune and Pluto. Both Uranus and Neptune are visible through good field glasses, but Pluto is so distant and so small that only large telescopes or long exposure photographs can make it visible.

Since Mercury and Venus are nearer to the sun than is the Earth, their motions about the sun are seen from the Earth as wide swings first to one side of the sun and then to the other, although they are both passing continuously around the sun in orbits that are almost circular. When their passage takes them either between the Earth and the sun, or beyond the sun as seen from the Earth, they are invisible to us. Because of the laws which govern the motions of planets about the sun, both Mercury and Venus require much less time to pass between the Earth and the sun than around the far side of the sun, so their periods of visibility and invisibility are unequal.

The planets that lie farther from the sun than does the Earth may be seen for longer periods of time and are invisible only when they are so located in our sky that they rise and set about the same time as the sun when, of course, they are overwhelmed by the sun's great brilliance. None of the planets has any light of its own but each shines only by reflecting sunlight from its surface. Mercury and Venus, because they are between the Earth and the sun, show phases very much as the moon does. The planets farther from the sun are always seen as full, although Mars does occasionally present a slightly gibbous phase — like the moon when not quite full.

The planets move rapidly among the stars because they are very much nearer to us. The stars are also in motion, some of them at tremendous speeds, but they are so far away that their motion does not change their apparent positions in the heavens sufficiently for anyone to perceive that change in a single lifetime. The very nearest star is about 7 000 times as far away as the most distant planet.

The Sun

The sun, the controlling body of our solar system, is a star whose dimensions cause it to be classified among stars as average in size, temperature, and brightness. Its proximity to the Earth makes it appear to us as tremendously large and bright. A series of thermo-nuclear reactions involving the atoms of the elements of which it is composed produces the heat and light that make life possible on Earth.

The sun has a diameter of 1 382 400 km and is distant, on the average, 1 486 400 000 km from the Earth. It is 1.41 times as dense as water. The light of the sun reaches the Earth in 499.012 seconds or slightly more than 8 minutes. The average solar surface temperature has been measured by several indirect methods which agree closely on a value of 6,000° Kelvin or about 5 500°C. The interior temperature of the sun is about 19 500 000°C.

When sunlight is analyzed with a spectroscope, it is found to consist of a continuous spectrum composed of all the colors of the rainbow in order, crossed by many dark lines. The "absorption lines" are produced by gaseous materials in the atmosphere of the sun. More than 60 of the natural terrestrial elements have been identified in the sun, all in gaseous form because of the intense heat of the sun.

Spheres and Corona

The radiating surface of the sun is called the **photosphere,** and just above it is the **chromosphere.** The chromosphere is visible to the naked eye only at times of total solar eclipses, appearing then to be a pinkish-violet layer with occasional great prominences projecting above its general level. With proper instruments the chromosphere can be seen or photographed whenever the sun is visible without waiting for a total eclipse. Above the chromosphere is the **corona,** also visible to the naked eye only at times of total eclipse. Instruments also permit the brighter portions of the corona to be studied whenever conditions are favorable. The pearly light of the corona surges millions of miles from the sun. Iron, nickel, and calcium are believed to be principal contributors to the composition of the corona, all in a state of extreme attenuation and high ionization that indicates temperatures on the order of over half a million degrees Celsius.

Sunspots

There is an intimate connection between sunspots and the corona. At times of low sunspot activity, the fine streamers of the corona will be much longer above the sun's equator than over the polar regions of the sun, while during high sunspot activity, the corona extends fairly evenly outward from all regions of the sun, but to a much greater distance in space. Sunspots are dark, irregularly-shaped regions whose diameters may reach tens of thousands of kilometres. The average life of a sunspot group is from 2 to 3 weeks, but there have been groups that have lasted for more than a month, being carried repeatedly around as the sun rotated upon its axis. The record for the duration of a sunspot is 18 months. Sunspots reach a low point every 11.3 years, with a peak of activity occurring irregularly between 2 successive minima.

The sun is 400 000 times as bright as the full moon and gives the Earth 6 million times as much light as do all the other stars put together. Actually, most of the stars that can be easily seen on any clear night are brighter than the sun.

Planets of the Solar System

Mercury

Mercury, nearest planet to the sun, is the 2d smallest of the 9 planets known to be orbiting the sun. Its diameter is 4 960 km and its mean distance from the sun is 57 600 000 km.

Mercury moves with great speed in its journey about the sun, averaging about 48 km a second to complete its circuit in 88 of our days. Mercury rotates upon its axis over a period of nearly 59 days, thus exposing all of its surface periodically to the sun. It is believed that the surface passing before the sun may have a temperature of about 427°C, while the temperature on the side turned temporarily away from the sun does not fall as low as might be expected. This night temperature has been described by Russian astronomers as "room temperature" — possibly about 21°C. This would contradict the former belief that Mercury did not possess an atmosphere, for some sort of atmosphere would be needed to retain the fierce solar radiation that strikes Mercury. A shallow but dense layer of carbon dioxide would produce the "greenhouse" effect, in which heat accumulated during exposure to the sun would not completely escape at night. The actual presence of a carbon dioxide atmosphere is in dispute. Other research, however, has indicated a nighttime temperature approaching −184°.

This uncertainty about conditions upon Mercury and its motion arise from its shorter angular distance from the sun as seen from the Earth, for Mercury is always too much in line with the sun to be observed against a dark sky, but is always seen during either morning or evening twilight.

Mariner 10 made 3 passes by Mercury in 1974 and 1975. A large fraction of the surface was photographed from varying distances, revealing a degree of cratering similar to that of the moon. An atmosphere of hydrogen and helium may be made up of gases of the solar wind temporarily concentrated by the presence of Mercury. The discovery of a weak but permanent magnetic field was a surprise. It has been held that both a fluid core and rapid rotation were necessary for the generation of a planetary magnetic field. Mercury may demonstrate these conditions to be unnecessary, or the field may reveal something about the history of Mercury.

Venus

Venus, slightly smaller than the Earth, moves about the sun at a mean distance of 107 200 000 km in 225 of our days. Its synodical revolution — its return to the same relationship with the Earth and the sun, which is a result of the combination of its own motion and that of the Earth — is 584 days. Every 19 months, then, Venus will be nearer to the Earth than any other planet of the solar system. The planet is covered with a dense, white, cloudy atmosphere that conceals whatever is below it. This same cloud reflects sunlight efficiently so that when Venus is favorably situated, it is the 3d brightest object in the sky, exceeded only by the sun and the moon.

Spectral analysis of sunlight reflected from Venus' cloud tops has shown features that can best be explained by identifying the material of the clouds as sulphuric acid (oil of vitriol). Infrared spectroscopy from a balloon-borne telescope nearly 32 km above the Earth's surface gave indications of a small amount of water vapor present in the same region of the atmosphere of Venus. In 1956, radio astronomers at the Naval Research Laboratories in Washington, D. C., found a temperature for Venus of about 316°C, in marked contrast to −87°C, previously found at the cloud tops. Subsequent radio work confirmed a high temperature and produced evidence for this temperature to be associated with the solid body of Venus. With this peculiarity in mind, space scientists devised experiments for the U.S. space probe Mariner 2 to perform when it flew by in 1962. Mariner 2 confirmed the high temperature and the fact that it pertained to the ground rather than to some special activity of the atmosphere. In addition, Mariner 2 was unable to detect any radiation belts similar to the Earth's so-called Van Allen belts. Nor was it able to detect the existence of a magnetic field even as weak as 1/100 000 of that of the Earth.

In 1967, a Russian space probe, Venera 4, and the American Mariner 5 arrived at Venus within a few hours of each other. Venera 4 was designed to allow an instrument package to land gently on the planet's surface via parachute. It ceased transmission of information in about 75 minutes when the temperature it read went above 260°C. After considerable controversy, it was agreed that it still had 32 km to go to reach the surface. The U.S. probe, Mariner 5, went around the dark side of Venus at a distance of about 9 600 km. Again, it detected no significant magnetic field but its radio signals passed to Earth through Venus' atmosphere twice — once on the night side and once on the day side. The results are startling. Venus' atmosphere is nearly all carbon dioxide and must exert a pressure at the planet's surface of up to 100 times the Earth's normal sea-level pressure of one atmosphere. Since the Earth and Venus are about the same size, and were presumably formed at the same time by the same general process from the same mixture of chemical elements, one is faced with the question: which is the planet with the unusual history — Earth or Venus?

Radar astronomers using powerful transmitters as well as sensitive receivers and computers have succeeded in determining the rotation period of Venus. It turns out to be 243

days clockwise — in other words, contrary to the spin of most of the other planets and to its own motion around the sun. If it were exactly 243.16 days, Venus would always present the same face toward the Earth at every inferior conjunction. This rate and sense of rotation allows a "day" on Venus of 117.4 Earth days. Any part of Venus will receive sunlight on its clouds for over 58 days and will be in darkness for 58 days. Recent radar observations have shown surface features below the clouds. Large craters, continent-sized highlands, and extensive, dry "ocean" basins have been identified.

Mariner 10 passed Venus before traveling on to Mercury in 1974. The carbon dioxide molecule found in such abundance in the atmosphere is rather opaque to certain ultraviolet wavelengths, enabling sensitive television cameras to take pictures of the Venusian cloud cover. Photos radioed to Earth show a spiral pattern in the clouds from equator to the poles.

In Dec. 1978, 2 U.S. Pioneer probes arrived at Venus. One went into orbit about Venus, the other split into 5 separate probes targeted for widely-spaced entry points to sample different conditions. The instrumentation ensemble was selected on the basis of previous missions that had shown the range of conditions to be studied. The probes confirmed expected high surface temperatures and high winds aloft. Winds of about 320 km per hour, there, may account for the transfer of heat into the night side in spite of the low rotation speed of the planet. Surface winds were light at the time, however. Atmosphere and cloud chemistries were examined in detail, providing much data for continued analysis. The probes detected 4 layers of clouds and more light on the surface than expected solely from sunlight. This light allowed Russian scientists to obtain at least 2 photos showing rocks on the surface. Sulphur seems to play a large role in the chemistry of Venus, and reactions involving sulphur may be responsible for the glow. To learn more about the weather and atmospheric circulation on Venus, the orbiter takes daily photos of the daylight side cloud cover. It confirms the cloud pattern and its circulation shown by Mariner 10. The ionosphere shows large variability. The orbiter's radar operates in 2 modes: one, for ground elevation variability, and the 2d for ground reflectivity in 2 dimensions, thus "imaging" the surface. Radar maps of the entire planet that show the features mentioned above have been produced.

Mars

Mars is the first planet beyond the Earth, away from the sun. Mars' diameter is about 6 720 km, although a determination of the radius and mass of Mars by the space-probe, Mariner 4, which flew by Mars on July 14, 1965 at a distance of less than 9 600 km, indicated that these dimensions were slightly larger than had been previously estimated. While Mars' orbit is also nearly circular, it is somewhat more eccentric than the orbits of many of the other planets, and Mars is more than 48 million km farther from the sun in some parts of its year than it is at others. Mars takes 687 of our days to make one circuit of the sun, traveling at about 24 km a second. Mars rotates upon its axis in almost the same period of time that the Earth does — 24 hours and 37 minutes. Mars' mean distance from the sun is 226 million km, so that the temperature on Mars would be lower than that on the Earth even if Mars' atmosphere were about the same as ours. The atmosphere is not, however, for Mariner 4 reported that atmospheric pressure on Mars is between 1% and 2% of the Earth's atmospheric pressure. This thin atmosphere appears to be largely carbon dioxide. No evidence of free water was found.

There appears to be no magnetic field about Mars. This would eliminate the previous conception of a dangerous radiation belt around Mars. The same lack of a magnetic field would expose the surface of Mars to an influx of cosmic radiation about 100 times as intense as that on Earth.

Deductions from years of telescopic observation indicate that 5/8ths of the surface of Mars is a desert of reddish rock, sand, and soil. The rest of Mars is covered by irregular patches that appear generally green in hues that change through the Martian year. These were formerly held to be some sort of primitive vegetation, but with the findings of Mariner 4 of a complete lack of water and oxygen, such growth does not appear possible. The nature of the green areas is now unknown. They may be regions covered with volcanic salts whose color changes with changing temperatures and atmospheric conditions, or they may be gray, rather than green. When large gray areas are placed beside large red areas, the gray areas will appear green to the eye.

Mars' axis of rotation is inclined from a vertical to the plane of its orbit about the sun by about 25° and therefore Mars has seasons as does the Earth, except that the Martian seasons are longer because Mars' year is longer. White caps form about the winter pole of Mars, growing through the winter and shrinking in summer. These polar caps are now believed to be both water ice and carbon dioxide ice. It is the carbon dioxide that is seen to come and go with the seasons. The water ice is apparently in many layers with dust between them, indicating climatic cycles.

The canals of Mars have become more of a mystery than they were before the voyage of Mariner 4. Markings forming a network of fine lines crossing much of the surface of Mars have been seen there by men who have devoted much time to the study of the planet, but no canals have shown clearly enough in previous photographs to be universally accepted. A few of the 21 photographs sent back to Earth by Mariner 4 covered areas crossed by canals. The pictures show faint, ill-defined, broad, dark markings, but no positive identification of the nature of the markings.

Mariners 6 & 7 in 1969 sent back many more photographs of higher quality than those of the pioneering Mariner 4. These pictures showed cratering similar to the earlier views, but in addition showed 2 other types of terrain. Some regions seemed featureless for many square kilometres, but others were chaotic, showing high relief without apparent organization into mountain chains or craters.

Mariner 9, the first artificial body to be placed in an orbit about Mars, has transmitted over 10 000 photographs covering 100% of the planet's surface. Preliminary study of these photos and other data shows that Mars resembles no other planet we know. Using terrestrial terms, however, scientists describe features that seem to be clearly of volcanic origin. One of these features is Nix Olympica, (now called Olympus Mons), apparently a shield volcano whose caldera is over 80 km wide, and whose outer slopes are over 480 km in diametre, and which stands about 27 000 m above the surrounding plain. Some features may have been produced by cracking (faulting) of the surface and the sliding of one region over or past another. Many craters seem to have been produced by impacting bodies such as may have come from the nearby asteroid belt. Features near the south pole may have been produced by glaciers that are no longer present. Flowing water, non-existent on Mars at the present time, probably carved canyons, one 10 times longer and 3 times deeper than the Grand Canyon.

Although the Russians landed a probe on the Martian surface, it transmitted for only 20 seconds. In 1976, the U.S. landed 2 Viking spacecraft on the Martian surface. The landers had devices aboard to perform chemical analyses of the soil in search of evidence of life. The results have been inconclusive. The 2 Viking orbiters have returned the best pictures yet of Martian topographic features. Many features can be explained only if Mars once had large quantities of flowing water.

Mars' position in its orbit and its speed around that orbit in relation to the Earth's position and speed bring Mars fairly close to the Earth on occasions about 2 years apart and then move Mars and the Earth too far apart for accurate observation and photography. Every 15-17 years, the close approaches are especially favorable to close observation.

Mars has 2 satellites, discovered in 1877 by Asaph Hall. The outer satellite, Deimos, revolves around Mars in about 31 hours. The inner satellite, Phobos, whips around Mars in a little more than 7 hours, making 3 trips around the planet each Martian day. Mariner and Viking photos show these bodies to be irregularly shaped and pitted with numerous craters. Phobos also shows a system of linear grooves, each about 528 km across and roughly parallel. Phobos measures about 13 by 19 km and Deimos about 8 by 12 km in size.

Jupiter

Jupiter is the largest of the planets. Its equatorial diameter is 140 800 km, 11 times the diameter of the Earth. Its polar diameter is about 9 600 km shorter. This is an equilibrium condition resulting from the liquidity of the planet and its extremely rapid rate of rotation: a Jupiter day is only 10 Earth hours long. For a planet this size, this rotational speed is amazing, and it moves a point on Jupiter's equator at a speed of 35 200 km an hour, as compared with 1 600 km an hour for a point on the Earth's equator. Jupiter is at an average distance of 768 million km from the sun and takes almost 12 of our years to make one complete circuit of the sun.

The only directly observable chemical constituents of Jupiter's atmosphere are methane (CH_4) and ammonia (NH_3), but it is reasonable to assume the same mixture of elements available to make Jupiter as to make the sun. This would mean a large fraction of hydrogen and helium must be present also, as well as water (H_2O). The temperature at the tops of the clouds may be about $-162°$. The clouds are probably ammonia ice crystals, becoming ammonia droplets lower down. There may be a space before water ice crystals show up as clouds: in turn, these become water droplets near the bottom of the entire cloud layer. The total atmosphere may be only a few hundred kilometres in depth, pulled down by the surface gravity (= 2.64 times Earth's) to a relatively thin layer. Of course, the gases become denser with depth until they may turn into a slush or a slurry. Perhaps there is no surface — no real interface between the gaseous atmosphere and the body of Jupiter. Pioneers 10 and 11 provided evidence for considering Jupiter to be almost entirely liquid hydrogen. Long before a rocky core about the size of the Earth is reached, hydrogen mixed with helium becomes a liquid metal at very high temperature and pressure. Jupiter's cloudy atmosphere is a fairly good reflector of sunlight and makes it appear far brighter than any of the stars.

Fourteen of Jupiter's 17 or more satellites have been found through Earth-based observations. Four of the moons are large and bright, rivaling our own moon and the planet Mercury in diameter and may be seen through a field glass. They move rapidly around Jupiter and their change of position from night to night is extremely interesting to watch. The other satellites are much smaller and in all but one instance much farther from Jupiter and cannot be seen except through powerful telescopes. The 4 outermost satellites are revolving around Jupiter clockwise as seen from the north, contrary to the motions of the great majority of the satellites in the solar system and to the direction of revolution of the planets around the sun. The reason for this retrograde motion is not known, but one theory is that Jupiter's tremendous gravitational power may have captured 4 of the minor planets or asteroids that move about the sun between Mars and Jupiter, and that these would necessarily revolve backward. At the great distance of these bodies from Jupiter — some 22.4 million km — direct motion would result in decay of the orbits, while retrograde orbits would be stable. Jupiter's mass is more than twice the mass of all the other planets put together, and accounts for Jupiter's tremendous gravitational field and so, probably, for its numerous satellites and its dense atmosphere.

In December, 1973, Pioneer 10 passed about 128 000 km from the equator of Jupiter and was whipped into a path taking it out of our solar system in about 50 years, and beyond the system of planets, on June 13, 1983. In December, 1974, Pioneer 11 passed within 48 000 km of Jupiter, moving roughly from south to north, over the poles.

Photographs from both encounters were useful at the time but were far surpassed by those of Voyagers I and II. Thousands of high resolution multi-color pictures show rapid variations of features both large and small. The Great Red Spot exhibits internal counterclockwise rotation. Much turbulence is seen in adjacent material passing north or south of it. The satellites Amalthea, Io, Europa, Ganymede, and Callisto were photographed, some in great detail. Each is individual and unique, with no similarities to other known planets or satellites. Io has active volcanoes that probably have ejected material into a doughnut-shaped ring enveloping its orbit about Jupiter. This is not to be confused with the thin, flat, disk-like ring closer to Jupiter's surface. Now that such a ring has been seen by the Voyagers, older uncertain observations from Earth can be reinterpreted as early sightings of this structure.

Saturn

Saturn, last of the planets visible to the unaided eye, is almost twice as far from the sun as Jupiter, almost 1 440 million km. It is 2d in size to Jupiter but its mass is much smaller. Saturn's specific gravity is less than that of water. Its diameter is about 113 600 km at the equator; its rotational speed spins it completely around in a little more than 10 hours, and its atmosphere is much like that of Jupiter, except that its temperature at the top of its cloud layer is at least 38° lower. At about − 184°C, the ammonia would be frozen out of Saturn's clouds. The theoretical construction of Saturn resembles that of Jupiter; it is either all gas, or it has a small dense centre surrounded by a layer of liquid and a deep atmosphere.

Until Pioneer 11 passed Saturn in September 1979 only 10 satellites of Saturn were known. Since that time, the situation is quite confused. Added to data interpretations from the fly-by are Earth-based observations using new techniques while the rings were edge-on and virtually invisible. It was hoped that the Voyager I and II fly-bys would help sort out the system. It is now believed that Saturn has at least 22 satellites, some sharing orbits. The Saturn satellite system is still confused.

Saturn's ring system begins about 11 200 km above the visible disk of Saturn, lying above its equator and extending about 56 000 km into space. The diameter of the ring system visible from Earth is about 272 000 km; the rings are estimated to be no thicker than 16 km. In 1973, radar observation showed the ring particles to be large chunks of material averaging a metre on a side.

Voyager I and II observations showed the rings to be considerably more complex than had been believed, so much so that interpretation will take much time. To the untrained eye, the Voyager photographs could be mistaken for pictures of a colorful phonograph record.

Uranus

Voyager II, after passing Saturn in Aug. 1981, headed for a rendezvous with Uranus culminating in a fly-by Jan. 24, 1986. This encounter answered many questions, and raised others.

Uranus, discovered by Sir William Herschel on Mar. 13, 1781, lies at a distance of 2.8 billion km from the sun, taking 84 years to make its circuit around our star. Uranus has a diameter of about 51 200 km and spins once in some 16.8 hours, according to fly-by data. One of the most fascinating features of Uranus is how far it is tipped over. Its north pole lies 98° from being directly up and down to its orbit plane. Thus, its seasons are extreme. When the sun rises at the north pole, it stays up for 42 years; then it sets and the north pole will be in darkness (and winter) for 42 years.

The satellite system of Uranus, consisting of at least 15 moons, (the 5 largest having been known before the fly-by) have orbits lying in the plane of the planet's equator. In that plane there is also a complex of rings, 9 of which were discovered in 1978. Invisible from Earth, the 9 original rings were found by observers watching Uranus pass before a star. As they waited, they saw their photoelectric equipment register several short eclipses of the star. Then the planet occulted the star as expected. After the star came out from behind Uranus, the star winked out several more times. Subsequent observations and analyses indicated the 9 narrow, nearly opaque rings circling Uranus. Evidence from the Voyager II fly-by has shown the ring particles to be predominantly a metre or so in diameter.

In addition to the 10 new, very small satellites, Voyager II returned detailed photos of the 5 large satellites. As in the case of other satellites newly observed in the Voyager program, these bodies proved to be entirely different from each other and any others. Miranda has grooved markings, reminiscent of Jupiter's Ganymede, but often arranged in a chevron pattern. Ariel shows rifts and channels. Umbriel is extremely dark, prompting some observers to regard its surface as among the oldest in the system. Titania has rifts and fractures, but not the evidence of flow found on Ariel. Oberon's main feature is its surface saturated with craters, unrelieved by other formations.

The structure of Uranus is subject to some debate. Basically, however, it may have a rocky core surrounded by a thick icy mantle on top of which is a crust of hydrogen and helium that gradually becomes an atmosphere. Perhaps continued analysis of the wealth of data returned by Voyager II will shed some light on this problem.

Neptune

Neptune, currently the most distant planet from the sun (until 1999), lies at an average distance of 4.5 billion km. Having a diameter of about 49 600 km and a rotation period of 18.2 hours, it is a virtual twin of Uranus. It is significantly more dense than Uranus, however, and this increases the debate over its internal structure. Neptune circles the sun in 164 years in a nearly circular orbit.

Neptune has 3 satellites, the 3d being found in 1981. The largest, Triton, is in a retrograde orbit suggesting that it was captured rather than being co-eval with Neptune. Triton is sufficiently large to raise significant tides on Neptune which will one day, say 100 million years from now, cause Triton to come close enough to Neptune for it to be torn apart. Nereid was found in 1949, and is in a long looping orbit suggesting it, too, was captured. The orbit of the 3d body is under analysis at this writing. Observations made in 1968 but not interpreted until 1982 suggest that Neptune, too, has a ring system.

As with the other giant planets, Neptune is emitting more energy than it receives from the sun. These excesses are thought to be cooling from internal heat sources and from the heat of the formation of the planets.

Little is known of Neptune beyond its distance, but Voyager II, if all continues to operate, will send us pictures and observations in 1989.

Pluto

Although Pluto on the average stays about 5.7 billion km from the sun, its orbit is so eccentric that it is now approaching its minimum distance of 4.3 billion km, less than the current distance of Neptune. Thus Pluto, until 1999, is temporarily planet number 8 from the sun. At its mean distance, Pluto takes 247.7 years to circumnavigate the sun. Until recently that was about all that was known of Pluto.

About a century ago, a hypothetical planet was believed to lie beyond Neptune and Uranus. Little more than a guess, a mass of one Earth was assigned to the mysterious body and mathematical searches were begun. Amid some controversy about the validity of the predictive process, Pluto was found nearly where it was predicted to be. It was found by Clyde Tombaugh at the Lowell Observatory in Flagstaff, Ariz., in 1930.

At the U.S. Naval Observatory, also in Flagstaff, on July 2, 1978, James Christy obtained a photograph of Pluto that was distinctly elongated. Repeated observations of this shape and its variation were convincing evidence of the discovery of a satellite of Pluto. Now named Charon, it may be 800 km across, at a distance of over 16 000 km, and taking 6.4 days to move around Pluto, the same length of time Pluto takes to rotate once. Gravitational laws allow these interactions to give us the mass of Pluto as 0.0017 of the Earth and a diameter of 2 400 km. This makes the density about the same as that of water.

It is now clear that Pluto, the body found by Tombaugh, could not have influenced Neptune and Uranus to go astray. Theorists are again at work looking for a new planet X.

The Planets and the Solar System

Planet	Mean daily motion "	Orbital velocity Km per sec.	Sidereal revolution days	Synodical revolution days	Dist. from sun in millions of Km Max.	Min.	Dist. from Earth in millions of Km Max.	Min.	Light at perihelion	aphelion
Mercury ..	14732	47.88	88.0	115.9	69.8	46.0	219	80	10.58	4.59
Venus ...	5768	35.02	224.7	583.9	108.9	107.5	259	40	1.94	1.89
Earth	3548	29.79	365.3	—	152.2	147.1	—	—	1.03	0.97
Mars	1886	24.12	687.0	779.9	249.4	206.8	399	56	0.524	0.360
Jupiter ...	299	13.07	4332.1	398.9	815.9	741.2	966	592	0.0408	0.0336
Saturn ...	120	9.64	10825.9	378.1	1 508.7	1 349.2	1 659	1 199	0.01230	0.00984
Uranus...	42	6.81	30676.1	369.7	2 992.8	2 686.4	3 143	2 585	0.00300	0.00250
Neptune ..	21	5.44	59911.1	367.5	4 541.0	4 442.3	4 691	4 292	0.00114	0.00109
Pluto	14	4.75	90824.2	366.7	7 324.6	4 435.9	7 474	4 286	0.00114	0.00042

1. Light at perihelion and aphelion is solar illumination in units of mean illumination at Earth.

Planet	Mean longitude of:* ascending node ° ' "	perihelion ° ' "	Inclination* of orbit to ecliptic ° ' "	Mean* distance**	Eccentricity* of orbit	Mean longitude at the epoch* ° ' "
Mercury....	48 11 46	77 16 48	7 00 17	0.387099	0.205629	211 23 37
Venus.....	76 34 37	131 37 12	3 23 41	0.723327	0.006792	21 47 25
Earth.....	—	102 45 25	—	0.999999	0.016732	335 27 03
Mars.....	49 28 23	335 51 43	1 50 59	1.523652	0.093273	343 25 58
Jupiter	100 22 23	15 30 22	1 18 18	5.20316	0.048191	49 52 10
Saturn.....	113 33 25	91 42 43	2 29 13	9.52355	0.054690	271 13 10
Uranus.....	73 58 52	169 15 36	0 46 21	19.1690	0.047313	264 35 32
Neptune	131 40 48	43 57 36	1 46 13	30.0468	0.010382	280 07 11
Pluto	110 07 08	223 57 04	17 08 44	39.3395	0.246171	222 18 01

*Consistent for the standard Epoch: 1988 Aug. 27 Ephemeris Time **Astronomical units

Sun and planets	Semi-diameter at unit distance ' "	at mean least dist. ' "	in Km mean s.d.	Volume ⊕=1.	Mass. ⊕=1.	Density ⊕=1.	Sidereal period of rotation d.	h.	m.	s.	Gravity at surface ⊕=1.	Reflecting power Pct.	Probable temperature °F.
Sun	959.62	—	696 119	1303730	332830	0.26	24	16	48		27.9	—	+10,000
Mercury ...	3.37	5.5	2 438	0.0559	0.0553	0.99	58	21	58		0.37	0.06	+ 620
Venus ...	8.34	30.1	6 051	0.8541	0.8150	0.95	243	R			0.88	0.72	+ 900
Earth	—		6 378	1.000	1.000	1.00		23	56	4.1	1.00	0.39	+ 72
Moon	2.40	932.4	1 738	0.020	0.0123	0.62	27		43		0.17	0.07	+ 10
Mars	4.69	8.95	3 393	0.1506	0.1074	0.71		24	37	23	0.38	0.16	— 10
Jupiter ...	98.35	23.4	71 392	1403	317.83	0.23		9	3	30	2.64	0.70	— 240
Saturn ...	82.83	9.7	59 995	832	95.16	0.11		10	30		1.15	0.75	— 300
Uranus ...	35.4	1.9	25 427	63	14.50	0.23		15	36	R	1.15	0.90	— 340
Neptune ...	33.4	1.2	24 300	55	17.20	0.31		18	26		1.12	0.82	— 370
Pluto*.....	1.9	0.05	1 497	0.01	0.0025	0.25	6	9	17		0.04	0.14	?	?

*Observers at the U.S. Naval Observatory have derived values similar to these after having discovered that Pluto has a satellite. It apparently revolves about Pluto in a period equal to Pluto's rotation period. (R) retrograde of Venus and Uranus.

Notable U.S. Unmanned and Planetary Missions

Spacecraft	Launch date (GMT)	Mission	Remarks
Mariner 2	Aug. 27, 1962	Venus	Passed within 34 405 km from Venus Dec. 14, 1962; contact lost Jan. 3, 1963 at 87 million km
Ranger 7	July 28, 1964	Moon	Yielded over 4 000 photos
Mariner 4	Nov. 28, 1964	Mars	Passed behind Mars July 14, 1965; took 22 photos from 9 650 km
Ranger 8	Feb. 17, 1965	Moon	Yielded over 7 000 photos
Surveyor 3	Apr. 17, 1967	Moon	Scooped and tested lunar soil
Mariner 5	June 14, 1967	Venus	In solar orbit; closest Venus fly-by Oct. 19, 1967
Mariner 6	Feb. 25, 1969	Mars	Came within 3 200 km of Mars July 31, 1969; sent back data, photos
Mariner 7	Mar. 27, 1969	Mars	Came within 3 200 km of Mars 8, 195, 1969
Mariner 9	May 30, 1971	Mars	First craft to orbit Mars Nov. 13, 1971; sent back over 7 000 photos
Pioneer 10	Mar. 3, 1972	Jupiter	Passed Jupiter Dec. 3, 1973; exited the solar system June 14, 1983
Mariner 10	Nov. 3, 1973	Venus, Mercury	Passed Venus Feb. 5, 1974; arrived Mercury Mar. 29, 1974. First time gravity of one planet (Venus) used to whip spacecraft toward another (Mercury)
Viking 1	Aug. 20, 1975	Mars	Landed on Mars July 20, 1976; did scientific research, sent photos; functioned 6 1/2 years
Viking 2	Sept. 9, 1975	Mars	Landed on Mars Sept. 3, 1976; functioned 3 1/2 years
Voyager 1	Sept. 5, 1977	Jupiter, Saturn	Encountered Jupiter Mar. 5, 1979; Saturn Nov. 13, 1980
Voyager 2	Aug. 20, 1987	Jupiter, Saturn, Uranus	Encountered Jupiter July 9, 1979; Saturn Aug. 26, 1981; Uranus Jan. 8 and Jan. 27, 1986
Pioneer 12	May 20, 1978	Venus	Entered Venus orbit Dec. 4, 1978
Pioneer 13	Aug. 8, 1978	Venus	Encountered Venus Dec. 9, 1978

Celestial Events Highlights, 1989

Edited by Dr. Kenneth L. Franklin, Astronomer Emeritus
American Museum-Hayden Planetarium

(Greenwich Mean Time, or as indicated)

The planets this year will not disappoint us for a bit of showmanship, taking over the whole sky rather than crowding into a small space. Jupiter and Mars begin the year in our evening sky, Mars fading rapidly to near obscurity by the beginning of Summer. As Jupiter descends into the evening twilight, Saturn begins to be prominent in the late evening in the southeast. It takes charge of the night sky by the first of July, as Venus begins to take over the western horizon at dusk. Saturn joins Venus in the fall as Jupiter takes over first the eastern sky, then the whole dome overhead at year's end, only Venus outshining it before rapidly setting in the southwest. Several times in the last half of the year, Venus and the crescent moon will be quite near, forming a beautiful sight in the deepening blue of evening twilight. Watch the listings for close approaches of Saturn to Uranus and Neptune; these will afford the opportunity of finding these elusive planets with the aid of binoculars.

Of the nearly 30 occultations of bright objects this year, Mercury and Venus each are hidden twice, the remaining events being of Antares and Regulus. The last in the series of Regulus occultations occurs on the 24th of October. Of all the events this year, only the first occultation of Regulus, Jan. 24 (the evening of Jan. 23, EST), has any good chance of being seen by some U.S. observers. As usual, use the announcement of an occultation or close approach between objects to signal an opportunity to find them approximately within the field of view of binoculars. Consider some to be good opportunities for photography.

January

Mercury begins the month and year in the evening sky, achieves greatest elongation, 19 degrees east of the sun, and is 1.7 degrees north of the moon on the 9th, is stationary on the 15th, and moves through inferior conjunction on the 25th to become a morning star, never very convenient for observation.

Venus rises before the sun all month, but gets too close to the morning twilight for sighting by month's end after passing 0°.6 south of Saturn on the 16th, and 0°.9 south of Neptune on the 19th.

Mars, beginning the month in Pisces, is south at sunset, setting about midnight, still bright from its recent favorable opposition, but fading rapidly, already much fainter than nearby Jupiter.

Jupiter, in Taurus, is south about 9 pm, much brighter than Mars to the west, and is stationary on the 20th, resuming its direct, eastward motion.

Saturn starts the year in the morning glow of the rising sun as it leaves conjunction last month, appearing as a bright star in Sagittarius all year, passed by Venus within a degree on the 16th.

Moon occults Antares on the 5th, passes Venus on the 6th, Mercury on the 9th, Mars on the 14th, Jupiter on the 17th, and occults Regulus on the 24th.

Jan. 1—Earth at perihelion, 147.1 million km from the sun.

Jan. 3—The Quadrantid meteor shower is not hurt by the waning crescent moon, which rises about 3 am.

Jan. 5—The moon's occultation of Antares this month may be observed from the Indian Ocean.

Jan. 12—Venus passes 0°.5 south of Uranus; using binoculars, look for Venus and Uranus close in this morning's dawn.

Jan. 19—With a telescope or luck with binoculars, find Neptune, about 8th magnitude, near Venus in this morning's dawn sky; the sun enters Capricorn.

Jan. 24—After the moon rises this Monday evening, about 8 pm, watch the moon move over to Regulus; observers in the eastern U.S. may see the moon occult Leo's bright star before midnight, the rest will watch the moon move away from the star.

Jan. 25—Mercury is in inferior conjunction, between the earth and the sun.

February

Mercury is in the morning sky all month, being 26° west of the sun on the 18th, becoming lost in the dawn twilight during the last week.

Venus, although bright, dips into the ever-brightening dawn, effectively lost by month's end.

Mars rapidly fades to first magnitude by month's end having nearly traversed Aries in its approach to Jupiter.

Jupiter, in western Taurus, is the brightest planet in the evening sky, although it is fading almost imperceptibly, a half magnitude since the first of the year.

Saturn continues to mount the eastern morning sky, easily seen even at its faintest this season.

Moon occults Antares on the 1st, passes Uranus, Saturn, and Neptune on the 3rd, Mercury on the 4th, Mars on the 12th, Jupiter on the 13th, occults Regulus and is in total eclipse on the 20th, and occults Antares again on the 28th.

Feb. 1—Mercury is 4°N of Venus in the early dawn, but is fainter than 1st magnitude, while Venus is −3.9.; Antares is occulted by the waning crescent moon.

Feb. 5—Mercury is stationary, resuming its direct, eastward motion.

Feb. 16—Sun enters Aquarius.

Feb. 18—Mercury is at greatest elongation, 26° west of the sun.

Feb. 20—Regulus is occulted by the full moon; Pluto stationary, beginning retrograde motion; the moon is totally immersed in the earth's shadow, i.e., totally eclipsed.

Feb. 28—Antares is occulted by the third quarter moon.

March

Mercury is occulted by the very thin crescent moon on the 6th, but too early for the U.S.

Venus is too close to the sun all month for viewing.

Mars, somewhat fainter than 1st magnitude, passes 2°N of Jupiter on the 12th, both south of the Pleiades, and is still in Taurus at month's end.

Jupiter is still prominent in Taurus as it is passed by Mars on the 12th.

Saturn continues its patient stay in Sagittarius, is passed by the moon twice, on the 3rd and the 30th, and is 0°.2 south of Neptune about 9 pm EST on the 2nd, but it won't rise in the U.S. for another 6 hours.

Moon passes Uranus on the 2nd, Neptune and Saturn on the 3rd, occults Mercury on the 6th, partially eclipses the sun on the 7th, passes Mars and Jupiter on the 12th, occults Regulus on the 19th, and again passes Uranus, Neptune, and Saturn, on the 30th.

Mar. 3—Saturn passes 0°.2 S of Neptune.

Mar. 6—Mercury is occulted by the moon.

Mar. 7—Partial solar eclipse.

Mar. 11—Sun enters Pisces.

Mar. 12—Mars passes Jupiter; note the fat crescent moon north of the pair this evening.

Mar. 19—Regulus is occulted by the moon.

Mar. 20—Vernal equinox at 15:28 GMT, when the sun moves north over the earth's equator; Spring begins in the northern hemisphere and Autumn in the southern.

Mar. 28—Antares is occulted by the moon; Mars is 7°N of Aldebaran.

April

Mercury is in superior conjunction, beyond the sun, on the 4th just 9 hours before the conjunction of Venus, lost to view until the 2nd half of the month when determined observers may be able to glimpse it low in the evening twilight.

Venus is in superior conjunction, beyond the sun, on the 4th just 9 hours after Mercury is, but, slower moving, Venus won't be viewable this month.

Mars nearly completes its transit of Taurus this month, and continues to fade.

Jupiter continues to remain prominent between the head of Taurus and the Pleiades.

Saturn begins its retrograde, western motion on the 23rd, preparing for its July opposition; this reversal of direction occurs when the earth is moving directly toward it in our mutual orbiting of the sun.

Moon passes Jupiter on the 9th, Mars on the 10th, occults Regulus on the 15th, Antares on the 24th, and passes Uranus, Neptune, and Saturn on the 28th.

Apr. 4—Mercury, and Venus, in superior conjunction, beyond the sun.

Apr. 9—Uranus stationary, beginning retrograde motion.

Apr. 13—Neptune stationary, beginning retrograde motion.

Apr. 15—Regulus is occulted by the moon.

Apr. 18—Sun enters Aries.

Apr. 22—Lyrid meteor shower washed out by the full moon.

Apr. 23—Saturn stationary, beginning retrograde motion.

Apr. 24—Antares is occulted by the moon.

May

Mercury is at greatest elongation, 21° east of the sun on the 1st, is stationary on the 12th, passes 0.°6 N of Venus on the 16th, and inferior conjunction, between the earth and the sun, on the 23rd, possibly visible only the first week.

Venus remains in the western twilight until the end of the month, but is still not noticeable by then; binoculars may help see it pass Jupiter by 0°.8 on the 23rd (evening of the 22nd, EST).

Mars leaves Taurus to get about 1.°5 north of delta Geminorum on the 28th, which is about 1.5 magnitudes fainter than the planet.

Jupiter, after passing close to Venus on the evening of the 22nd (EST), loses itself in the evening twilight by the end of the month, leaving our evening sky until the final nights of the year.

Saturn remains the brightest object in Sagittarius.

Moon passes Mercury on the 6th, Jupiter on the 7th, Mars on the 9th, occults Regulus on the 13th, Antares on the 21st, and passes Uranus on the 23rd, Neptune and Saturn on the 24th.

May 1—Mercury at greatest elongation, 21° east of the sun.

May 4—Pluto in opposition.

May 12—Mercury stationary beginning its retrograde motion.

May 13—Regulus occulted by the moon; sun enters Taurus.

May 21—Antares occulted by the moon.

May 23—Venus passes 0°.8 N of Jupiter; Mercury in inferior conjunction, between the earth and the sun.

June

Mercury is stationary on the 5th, resuming its direct motion, reaches greatest elongation, 23° west of the sun, on the 18th, technically visible in the dawn sky all month.

Venus is increasingly visible in the evening sky all month; look for it 3° south of the very thin crescent moon low in the bright evening twilight of the 4th (EST).

Mars, about as faint as it will be, nearly 2nd magnitude, enters Cancer near the middle of the month.

Jupiter is in conjunction with the sun on the 9th, barely emerging into the dawn twilight before July.

Saturn passes 0°.3 south of Neptune on the 24th, both in Sagittarius.

Moon passes Venus on the 5th, Mars on the 6th, occults Regulus on the 9th, Antares on the 17th, passes Uranus on the 19th, and Neptune and Saturn on the 20th.

Jun. 5—Mercury stationary, resuming direct motion.

Jun. 9—Jupiter in conjunction with the sun; Regulus occulted by the moon.

Jun. 17—Antares occulted by the moon.

Jun. 20—Sun enters Gemini.

Jun. 21—At 9:53 GMT the sun reaches its most northerly position above the earth, and seems to stand still in its north-south journey, thus the solstice; Summer begins in the northern hemisphere, Winter in the south.

Jun. 24—Saturn passes 0°.3 S south of Neptune; Uranus in opposition.

July

Mercury in superior conjunction at mid-month passing beyond the sun, swings from the morning to the evening sky, but is mostly unobservable the whole time; a chance to find it might be on the morning of the 2nd when it and Jupiter are 0°.6 apart.

Venus, increasingly prominent in the western evening twilight, is very close to the thin crescent moon the evening of 4th (EST), passes a half degree from Mars on the 12th, and 1°.2 N of Regulus on the 23rd.

Mars, nearly 2nd magnitude, moving into Leo from Cancer about mid-month, may be found by looking close to Venus on the 12th.

Jupiter, becoming more prominent in the morning sky, moves to the eastern edge of Taurus this month.

Saturn, riding just above the Teapot of Sagittarius, is the bright southern planet that rises about sunset, remains in the sky all night, to set about sunset, a phenomenon associated with its position just opposite the sun in the sky, on the 2nd.

Moon passes Mercury and Jupiter on the 5th, occults Venus and passes Mars on the 5th, occults Regulus on the 6th and Antares on the 15th, passes Uranus on the 16th, Saturn and Neptune on the 17th, and Jupiter again on the 29th.

Jul. 2—Saturn at opposition; Mercury 0.°6 S of Jupiter; Neptune at opposition.

Jul. 4—Earth at aphelion, its most distant point from the sun this year, 151.9 million km away.

Jul. 5—Venus occulted by the moon.

Jul. 6—Regulus occulted by the moon.

Jul. 12—Venus passes 0°.5 N of Mars.

Jul. 15—Antares occulted by the moon.

Jul. 18—Mercury in superior conjunction.

Jul. 20—Sun enters Cancer.

Jul. 23—Venus 1°.2 N of Regulus.

Jul. 25—Pluto is stationary in Virgo, resuming direct motion.

August

Mercury is in the evening twilight all month, at its greatest elongation, 27° east of the sun on the 29th, perhaps the best month for an attempted sighting; with binoculars, try for the evening of the 5th when it will be 0°.1 N of fainter Mars.

Venus is easily recognized as the evening star.

Mars has a last fling of prominence as it passes 0°.7 north of brighter Regulus on the 2nd, and has a near miss with Mercury on the 5th, before descending into the evening twilight.

Jupiter, is clearly the brightest "star" in the morning sky, this month approaches the foot of the western twin whose "head" star is Castor.

Saturn continues to point out Sagittarius, the archer, being the brightest point in that part of the sky.

Moon passes Mercury, occults Regulus, and passes Mars on the 3rd, Venus on the 4th, occults Antares on the 11th, passes Uranus, Saturn, and Neptune on the 13th, is totally eclipsed on the 17th, passes Jupiter on the 26th, and partially eclipses the sun on the 31st.

Aug. 2—Mars 0°.7 N of Regulus.
Aug. 3—Regulus occulted by the moon.
Aug. 4—Mercury 0°.8 N of Regulus.
Aug. 5—Mercury 0°.01 N of Mars.
Aug. 10—Sun enters Leo.
Aug. 11—Antares occulted by the moon; just past 1st quarter, the moon will set a little after midnight to give watchers of the Perseid meteor shower a chance for a good show tonight, tomorrow morning, and tomorrow night, too.
Aug. 17—Total lunar eclipse.
Aug. 29—Mercury at greatest elongation, 27° east of the sun.

September

Mercury, possibly visible this 1st week, seeks seclusion in the evening twilight, anticipating inferior conjunction on the 24th.

Venus clearly outshines Spica, which it passes by nearly 2° on the 6th.

Mars is not even a glimmer in the western twilight, as it is totally lost from view for 2 months.

Jupiter wanders slowly among the feet of the twins as it shines in the high southeast by dawn.

Saturn is stationary in Sagittarius on the 11th, resuming its direct, easterly motion, a condition that prevails when the earth is moving directly away from Saturn in our mutual journeys around the sun.

Moon occults Mercury on the 2nd, passes Venus on 6th, occults Antares on the 7th, passes Uranus on the 9th, Saturn and Neptune on the 10th, Jupiter on the 22nd, and occults Regulus on the 26th.

Sep. 2—Mercury occulted by the moon.
Sep. 6—Venus passes 1°.9 N of Spica.
Sep. 7—Antares occulted by the moon.
Sep. 10—Uranus stationary, resuming direct motion.
Sep. 11—Saturn and Mercury stationary, Saturn resuming direct motion, Mercury beginning retrograde.
Sep. 16—Sun enters Virgo.
Sep. 21—Neptune stationary, resuming direct motion.
Sep. 23—Autumnal equinox occurs at 1:20 GMT (8:20 pm on the 22nd EST), as the sun crosses the equator to enter the southern hemisphere: Autumn begins in the northern hemisphere; Spring in the south.
Sep. 24—Mercury in inferior conjunction, between the earth and the sun.
Sep. 26—Regulus occulted by the moon.
Sep. 29—Mars in conjunction.

October

Mercury is in the morning twilight, too immersed for even difficult viewing, and is stationary on the 3rd, before its greatest elongation, 18° west of the sun on the 10th.

Venus, shining brightly, low in the southwest, is near the broad crescent moon the evening of the 3rd, and just 1°.9 north of Antares the evening of the 16th (4th, and 17th, respectively in Greenwich Mean Time).

Mars is still out of sight in the sun's glare.

Jupiter slows its eastward progress all month, coming to a halt as it becomes stationary on the 29th, beginning its retrograde motion.

Saturn resolutely approaches Venus in the southwestern evening sky.

Moon passes Venus on the 4th, occults Antares on the 5th, passes Uranus, Saturn and Neptune on the 7th, Jupiter on the 20th, and occults Regulus on the 24th.

Oct. 3—Mercury stationary, resuming its direct motion.
Oct. 5—Antares occulted by the moon.
Oct. 10—Mercury at greatest elongation, 18° west of the sun.
Oct. 17—Venus 1°.8 N of Antares.
Oct. 24—Regulus occulted by the moon.

Oct. 29—Jupiter stationary, beginning its retrograde motion.
Oct. 30—Sun enters Libra.

November

Mercury is lost to view all month, passing superior conjunction on the 10th.

Venus is very close to the crescent moon in the twilight sky of the evening of the 2nd, the moon occulting the planet for observers in most of Asia; the planet outshines Saturn over a hundredfold this month, a comparison easily made as they pass in Sagittarius within 4° of each other on the 15th; Jupiter in Gemini, half a sky away from Venus, is 2 magnitudes fainter than the dazzling evening star.

Mars, still nearly as faint as a 2nd magnitude star, emerges from the dawn twilight by month's end, streaking eastward through Libra.

Jupiter, prominent in Gemini, rises shortly after sunset to dominate the sky almost all night.

Saturn, passing 4° north of Venus on the 15th, is low in the southwest after sunset.

Moon occults Antares on the 1st, Venus on the 2nd, passes Uranus, Saturn and Neptune on the 3rd, Jupiter on the 16th, Mars on the 26th, and Uranus again on the 30th.

Nov. 1—Antares occulted by the moon.
Nov. 2—Venus occulted by the moon.
Nov. 7—Pluto in conjunction.
Nov. 8—Venus 3° S of Uranus; Venus at greatest elongation, 47° east of sun.
Nov. 10—Mercury in superior conjunction.
Nov. 12—Saturn 0°.5 S of Neptune.
Nov. 15—Venus 4° S of Neptune and Saturn.
Nov. 18—Leonid meteor shower is hurt somewhat by the waning gibbous moon, but it is always worth a look.
Nov. 22—Sun enters Scorpius.
Nov. 29—Sun enters Ophiuchus.

December

Mercury is in the evening sky this month, but very poorly placed for easy observation from the northern hemisphere.

Venus, although low in the southwest, puts on its holiday star show; notice it and the crescent moon the evenings of the 1st and the 2nd, Venus first higher then lower than the moon; continuing the show by coming to greatest brilliancy on the 14th, it fades only slightly by year's end; then watch how quickly it disappears from our sky in the new year.

Mars, dimly seen in the dawn sky, makes it into Scorpius by the end of the month.

Jupiter is the undisputed lord of the entire night sky (after Venus sets), coming to opposition on the 27th.

Saturn, still in Sagittarius, descends into the evening twilight by month's end to vanish from our view, completing the year as far east of the sun as it began the year to the west of the sun.

Moon passes Neptune and Saturn on the 1st, occults Venus on the 2nd, passes Jupiter on the 13th, Mars on the 25th, occults Antares on the 26th, passes Mercury on the 29th, and Venus on the 30th.

Dec. 2—Venus occulted by the moon.
Dec. 10—Mercury 2° S of Uranus.
Dec. 14—Venus at greatest brilliancy.
Dec. 15—Mercury 3° S of Neptune.
Dec. 16—Mercury 2° S of Saturn; sun enters Sagittarius.
Dec. 21—Solstice at 21:22 GMT (16:22 EST), when the sun reaches its most southerly point in the sky; Winter begins in the northern hemisphere, Summer in the south.
Dec. 23—Mercury at greatest elongation, 20° east of the sun.
Dec. 26—Antares occulted by the moon.
Dec. 27—Uranus in conjunction; Jupiter in opposition; Venus stationary, beginning retrograde motion.
Dec. 30—Mercury stationary, beginning retrograde motion.

The Earth: Size, Computation of Time, Seasons

Size and Dimensions

The Earth is the 5th largest planet and the 3d from the sun. Its mass is 6 sextillion, 588 quintillion short tons. Using the parameters of an ellipsoid adopted by the International Astronomical Union in 1964 and recognized by the International Union of Geodesy and Geophysics in 1967, the length of the equator is 40 074.06 km, the length of a meridian is 40 006.9 km, the equatorial diameter is 12 755.97 km, and the area of this reference ellipsoid is approximately 512 040 880 sq. km.

The Earth is considered a solid, rigid mass with a dense core of magnetic, probably metallic, material. The outer part of the core is probably liquid. Around the core is a thick shell or mantle of heavy crystalline rock which in turn is covered by a thin crust forming the solid granite and basalt base of the continents and ocean basins. Over broad areas of the Earth's surface the crust has a thin cover of sedimentary rock such as sandstone, shale, and limestone formed by weathering of the Earth's surface and deposition of sands, clays, and plant and animal remains.

The temperature in the Earth increases about 1°C. with every 30–60 m in depth, in the upper 100 km of the Earth, and the temperature near the core is believed to be near the melting point of the core materials under the conditions at that depth. The heat of the Earth is believed to be derived from radioactivity in the rocks, pressures developed within the Earth, and original heat (if the Earth, in fact, was formed at high temperatures).

Atmosphere of the Earth

The Earth's atmosphere is a blanket composed of nitrogen, oxygen, and argon, in amounts of about 78, 21, and 1% by volume. Also present in minute quantities are carbon dioxide, hydrogen, neon, helium, krypton and xenon.

Water vapor displaces other gases and varies from nearly zero to about 4% by volume. The height of the ozone layer varies from approximately 19 to 33.6 km above the Earth. Traces exist as low as 9.6 km and as high as 56 km. Traces of methane have been found.

The atmosphere rests on the Earth's surface with the weight equivalent to a layer of water 10.2 m deep. For about 90 000 m upward the gases remain in the proportions stated. Gravity holds the gases to the Earth. The weight of the air compresses it at the bottom, so that the greatest density is at the Earth's surface. Pressure, as well as density, decreases as height increases because the weight pressing upon any layer is always less than that pressing upon the layers below.

The temperature of the air drops with increased height until the **tropopause** is reached. This may vary from 7 500 to 18 000 km. The atmosphere below the tropopause is the **troposphere**; the atmosphere for about 32 km above the tropopause is the **stratosphere**, where the temperature generally increases with height except at high latitudes in winter. A temperature maximum near the 48 km level is called the **stratopause**. Above this boundary is the **mesosphere** where the temperature decreases with height to a minimum, the **mesopause**, at a height of 80 km. Extending above the mesosphere to the outer fringes of the atmosphere is the **thermosphere**, a region where temperature increases with height to a value measured in thousands of degrees. The lower portion of this region, extending from 80 to about 640 km in altitude, is characterized by a high ion density, and is thus called the **ionosphere**. The outer region is called **exosphere**; this is the region where gas molecules traveling at high speed may escape into outer space, above 960 km.

Latitude, Longitude

Position on the globe is measured by means of meridians and parallels. Meridians, which are imaginary lines drawn around the Earth through the poles, determine **longitude**. The meridian running through Greenwich, England, is the **prime meridian of longitude**, and all others are either east or west. Parallels, which are imaginary circles parallel with the equator, determine **latitude**. The length of a degree of longi-

tude varies as the cosine of the latitude. At the equator a degree is 111.31 km; this is gradually reduced toward the poles. Value of a longitude degree at the poles is zero.

Latitude is reckoned by the number of degrees north or south of the equator, an imaginary circle on the Earth's surface everywhere equidistant between the two poles. According to the IAU Ellipsoid of 1964, the length of a degree of latitude is 110.571 km at the equator and varies slightly north and south because of the oblate form of the globe; at the poles it is 111.69 km.

Computation of Time

The Earth rotates on its axis and follows an elliptical orbit around the sun. The rotation makes the sun appear to move across the sky from East to West. It determines day and night and the complete rotation, in relation to the sun, is called the **apparent** or **true solar day**. This varies but an average determines the **mean solar day** of 24 hours.

The mean solar day is in universal use for civil purposes. It may be obtained from apparent solar time by correcting observations of the sun for the equation of time, but when high precision is required, the mean solar time is calculated from its relation to sidereal time. These relations are extremely complicated, but for most practical uses, they may be considered as follows:

Sidereal time is the measure of time defined by the diurnal motion of the vernal equinox, and is determined from observation of the meridian transits of stars. One complete rotation of the Earth relative to the equinox is called the **sidereal day**. The **mean sidereal day** is 23 hours, 56 minutes, 4.091 seconds of mean solar time.

The **Calendar Year** begins at 12 o'clock midnight precisely local clock time, on the night of Dec. 31-Jan. 1. The day and the calendar month also begin at midnight by the clock. The interval required for the Earth to make one absolute revolution around the sun is a **sidereal year**; it consisted of 365 days, 6 hours, 9 minutes, and 9.5 seconds of mean solar time (approximately 24 hours per day) in 1900, and is increasing at the rate of 0.0001-second annually.

The **Tropical Year**, on which the return of the seasons depends, is the interval between two consecutive returns of the sun to the vernal equinox. The tropical year consists of 365 days, 5 hours, 48 minutes, and 46 seconds in 1900. It is decreasing at the rate of 0.530 seconds per century.

In 1956, the unit of time interval was defined to be identical with the second of **Ephemeris Time**, 1/31 556 925.9747 of the tropical year for 1900 January 0d 12th hour E.T. A physical definition of the second based on a quantum transition of cesium (atomic second) was adopted in 1964. The atomic second is equal to 9 192 631 770 cycles of the emitted radiation. In 1967, this atomic second was adopted as the unit of time interval for the International System of Units.

The Zones and Seasons

The five zones of the Earth's surface are Torrid, lying between the Tropics of Cancer and Capricorn; North Temperate, between Cancer and the Arctic Circle; South Temperate, between Capricorn and the Antarctic Circle; The Frigid Zones, between the polar Circles and the Poles.

The inclination or tilt of the Earth's axis with respect to the sun determines the seasons. These are commonly marked in the North Temperate Zone, where spring begins at the vernal equinox, summer at the summer solstice, autumn at the autumnal equinox and winter at the winter solstice.

In the South Temperate Zone, the seasons are reversed. Spring begins at the autumnal equinox, summer at the winter solstice, etc.

If the Earth's axis were perpendicular to the plane of the Earth's orbit around the sun there would be no change of seasons. Day and night would be of nearly constant length and there would be equable conditions of temperature. But the axis is tilted 23° 27' away from a perpendicular to the orbit and only in March and September is the axis at right angles to the sun.

The points at which the sun crosses the equator are the equinoxes, when day and night are most nearly equal. The points at which the sun is at a maximum distance from the equator are the solstices. Days and nights are then most unequal.

In June, the North Pole is tilted 23° 27' toward the sun and the days in the northern hemisphere are longer than the nights, while the days in the southern hemisphere are shorter than the nights. In December, the North Pole is tilted 23° 27' away from the sun and the situation is reversed.

The Seasons in 1989

In 1989 the 4 seasons will begin as follows: add one hour to EST for Atlantic Time; subtract one hour for Central, two hours for Mountain, 3 hours for Pacific, 4 hours for Yukon, 5 hours for Alaska-Hawaii and six hours for Bering Time. Also shown in Greenwich Mean Time.

		Date	GMT	EST
Vernal Equinox	Spring	Mar. 20	15:28	10:28
Summer Solstice	Summer	June 21	09:53	04:53
Autumnal Equinox	Autumn	Sept. 23	01:20	20:20*
Winter Solstice	Winter	Dec. 21	21:22	16:22
*Previous Day				

Poles of The Earth

The geographic (rotation) poles, or points where the Earth's axis of rotation cuts the surface, are not absolutely fixed in the body of the Earth. The pole of rotation describes an irregular curve about its mean position.

Two periods have been detected in this motion: (1) an annual period due to seasonal changes in barometric pressure, load of ice and snow on the surface and to other phenomena of seasonal character; (2) a period of about 14 months due to the shape and constitution of the Earth.

In addition there are small but as yet unpredictable irregularities. The whole motion is so small that the actual pole at any time remains within a circle of 9 to 12 km in radius centred at the mean position of the pole.

The pole of rotation for the time being is of course the pole having a latitude of 90° and an indeterminate longitude.

Magnetic Poles

The north magnetic pole of the Earth is that region where the magnetic force is vertically downward and the south magnetic pole that region where the magnetic force is vertically upward. A compass placed at the magnetic poles experiences no directive force in azimuth.

There are slow changes in the distribution of the Earth's magnetic field. These changes were at one time attributed in part to a periodic movement of the magnetic poles around the geographical poles, but later evidence refutes this theory and points, rather, to a slow migration of "disturbance" foci over the Earth.

There appear shifts in position of the magnetic poles due to the changes in the Earth's magnetic field. The centre of the area designated as the north magnetic pole was estimated to be in about latitude 70.5° N and longitude 96° W in

1905; from recent nearby measurements and studies of the secular changes, the position in 1970 is estimated as latitude 76.2° N and longitude 101° W. Improved data rather than actual motion account for at least part of the change.

The position of the south magnetic pole in 1912 was near 71° S and longitude 150° E; the position in 1970 is estimated at latitude 66° S and longitude 139.1° E.

The direction of the horizontal components of the magnetic field at any point is known as magnetic north at that point, and the angle by which it deviates east or west of true north is known as the magnetic declination, or in the mariner's terminology, the variation of the compass.

A compass without error points in the direction of magnetic north. (In general, this is not the direction of the magnetic north pole.) If one follows the direction indicated by the north end of the compass, this person will travel along a rather irregular curve which eventually reaches the north magnetic pole (though not usually by a great-circle route). However, the action of the compass should not be thought of as due to any influence of the distant pole, but simply as an indication of the distribution of the Earth's magnetism at the place of observation.

Rotation of The Earth

The speed of rotation of the Earth about its axis has been found to be slightly variable. The variations may be classified as:

(A) Secular. Tidal friction acts as a brake on the rotation and causes a slow secular increase in the length of the day, about 1 millisecond per century.

(B) Irregular. The speed of rotation may increase for a number of years, about 5 to 10, and then start decreasing. The maximum difference from the mean in the length of the day during a century is about 5 milliseconds. The accumulated difference in time has amounted to approximately 44 seconds since 1900. The cause is probably motion in the interior of the Earth.

(C) Periodic. Seasonal variations exist with periods of one year and six months. The cumulative effect is such that each year the Earth is late about 30 milliseconds near June 1 and is ahead about 30 milliseconds near Oct. 1. The maximum seasonal variation in the length of the day is about 0.5 millisecond. It is believed that the principal cause of the annual variation is the seasonal change in the wind patterns of the Northern and Southern Hemispheres. The semiannual variation is due chiefly to tidal action of the sun, which distorts the shape of the Earth slightly.

The secular and irregular variations were discovered by comparing time based on the rotation of the Earth with time based on the orbital motion of the moon about the Earth and of the planets about the sun. The periodic variation was determined largely with the aid of quartz-crystal clocks. The introduction of the cesium-beam atomic clock in 1955 made it possible to determine in greater detail than before the nature of the irregular and periodic variations.

The Moon

The moon completes a circuit around the earth in a period whose mean or average duration is 27 days, 7 hours, 43.2 minutes. This is the moon's sidereal period. Because of the motion of the moon in common with the earth around the sun, the mean duration of the lunar month — the period from one new moon to the next new moon — is 29 days 12 hours 44.05 minutes. This is the moon's synodical period.

The mean distance of the moon from the earth according to the American Ephemeris is 384 392 km. Because the orbit of the moon about the earth is not circular but elliptical, however, the maximum distance from the earth that the moon may reach is 406 686 km and the least distance is 356 400 km. All distances are from the centre of one object to the centre of the other.

The moon's diameter is 3 476 km. If we deduct the radius of the moon, 1 738 km, and the radius of the earth, 6 377 km from the minimum distance or perigee, given above, we

shall have for the nearest approach of the bodies' surfaces 348 285 km.

The moon rotates on its axis in a period of time exactly equal to its sidereal revolution about the earth — 27.321666 days. The moon's revolution about the earth is irregular because of its elliptical orbit. The moon's rotation, however, is regular and this, together with the irregular revolution, produces what is called "libration in longitude" which permits us to see first farther around the east side and then farther around the west side of the moon. The moon's variation north or south of the ecliptic permits us to see farther over first one pole and then the other of the moon and this is "libration in latitude." These two libration effects permit us to see a total of about 60% of the moon's surface over a period of time. The hidden side of the moon was photographed in 1959 by the Soviet space vehicle Lunik III. Since then many excellent pictures of nearly all of the moon's surface have been transmitted to earth by Lunar Orbiters launched by the U.S.

The tides are caused mainly by the moon, because of its proximity to the earth. The ratio of the tide-raising power of the moon to that of the sun is 11 to 5.

Harvest Moon and Hunter's Moon

The Harvest Moon, the full moon nearest the Autumnal Equinox, ushers in a period of several successive days when the moon rises soon after sunset. This phenomenon gives farmers in temperate latitudes extra hours of light in which to harvest their crops before frost and winter come. The 1989 Harvest Moon falls on Sept. 15 GMT. Harvest moon in the south temperate latitudes falls on Apr. 21.

The next full moon after Harvest Moon is called the Hunter's Moon, accompanied by a similar phenomenon but less marked; — Oct. 14, northern hemisphere; May 20, southern hemisphere.

Moon's Perigee and Apogee, 1989

Perigee

Date		GMT	EST		Date	GMT	EST
Jan. .	10	23	18	July .	23	7	2
Feb. .	7	22	17	Aug. .	19	12	7
Mar. .	8	8	3	Sept. .	16	15	10
Apr. .	5	20	15	Oct. .	15	1	20*
May .	4	5	0	Nov .	12	13	8
June .	1	5	0	Dec. .	10	23	18
June .	28	4	11*				

*Previous day

Apogee

Date	GMT	EST		Date	GMT	EST
Jan. .	27	0	19*	Aug. .	7	15	10
Feb. .	23	14	9	Sept. .	4	8	3
Mar. .	22	18	13	Oct. .	1	20	15
Apr. .	16	9	4	Oct. .	28	22	17
May .	16	9	4	Nov. .	25	4	23*
June .	13	2	21*	Dec. .	22	19	14
July .	10	21	16				

Eclipses, 1989
(E.S.T.)

There are four eclipses in 1989, two of the moon and two of the sun.

1. A total eclipse of the moon, February 20, the beginning of the umbral phase visible in the western half of North America, the Pacific Ocean, Australia, New Zealand, and Asia. The end of the umbral phase is visible in the western Pacific Ocean, New Zealand, Australia, Asia, Europe except the Iberian peninsula, Africa except the West, and the Indian Ocean.

Circumstances of the Eclipse

Moon enters penumbra	February 20 7:30	am E.S.T.
Moon enters umbra	8:43	
Moon enters totality	9:56	
Middle of eclipse	10:35	
Moon leaves totality	11:15	
Moon leaves umbra	12:27	pm
Moon leaves penumbra	1:41	

Magnitude of the eclipse: 1.279

2. A partial eclipse of the sun, March 7, visible in part of North America west of the line from Chicago, Illinois, to Del Rio, Texas, past the southern end of Baja California, Mexico.

Circumstances of the Eclipse

Eclipse begins	March 7 11:17	am E.S.T.
Greatest eclipse	1:08	pm
Eclipse ends	2:58	

Magnitude of greatest eclipse: 0.827

3. A total eclipse of the moon, August 16. The beginning of the umbral phase is visible in Europe, the Middle East, Africa, Antarctica, the Atlantic Ocean, South and Central America, eastern half of North America, and the eastern half of the South Pacific Ocean. The ending is visible in West Africa, western Europe, Antarctica, the Atlantic Ocean, South, Central and North America except Alaska, and the eastern half of the Pacific Ocean.

Circumstances of the Eclipse

Moon enters penumbra	August 16 7:23	pm E.S.T.
Moon enters umbra	8:21	
Moon enters totality	9:20	
Middle of eclipse	10:08	
Moon leaves totality	10:56	
Moon leaves umbra	11:56	
Moon leaves penumbra	August 17 12:53	am

Magnitude of the eclipse: 1.604

4. A partial eclipse of the sun visible in Madagascar, parts of South Africa, and parts of Antarctica.

Circumstances of the Eclipse

Eclipse begins	August 30 10:34	pm E.S.T.
Greatest eclipse	August 31 12:31	am
Eclipse ends	2:28	

Magnitude of greatest eclipse: 0.635

Aurora Borealis and Aurora Australis

The Aurora Borealis, also called the Northern Lights, is a broad display of rather faint light in the northern skies at night. The Aurora Australis, a similar phenomenon, appears at the same time in southern skies. The aurora appears in a wide variety of forms. Sometimes it is seen as a quiet glow, almost foglike in character; sometimes as vertical streamers in which there may be considerable motion; sometimes as a series of luminous expanding arcs. There are many colors, with white, yellow and red predominating.

The auroras are most vivid and most frequently seen at about 20 degrees from the magnetic poles, along the northern coast of the North American continent and the eastern part of the northern coast of Europe. They have been seen as far south as Key West and as far north as Australia and New Zealand, but rarely.

While the cause of the auroras is not known beyond question, there seems to be a correlation between auroral displays and sun-spot activity. It is thought that atomic particles expelled from the sun by the forces that cause solar flares speed through space at velocities of 640 to 965 km per second. These particles are entrapped by the earth's magnetic field, forming what are termed the Van Allen belts. The encounter of these clouds of the solar wind with the earth's magnetic field weakens the field so that previously trapped particles are allowed to impact the upper atmosphere. The collisions between solar and terrestrial atoms result in the glow in the upper atmosphere called the aurora. The glow may be vivid

where the lines of magnetic force converge near the magnetic poles.

The auroral displays appear at heights ranging from 80 to about 1 000 km and have given us a means of estimating the extent of the earth's atmosphere.

The auroras are often accompanied by magnetic storms whose forces, also guided by the lines of force of the earth's magnetic field, disrupt electrical communication.

Constellations

Culturally, constellations are imagined patterns among the stars that, in some cases, have been recognized through millenia of tradition. In the early days of astronomy, knowledge of the constellations was necessary in order to function as an astronomer. For today's astronomers, constellations are simply areas on the entire sky in which interesting objects await observation and interpretation.

Because western culture has prevailed in establishing modern science, equally viable and interesting constellations and celestial traditions of other cultures (of Asia or Africa, for example) are not well known outside of their regions of origin. Even the patterns with which we are most familiar today have undergone considerable change over the centuries, because the western heritage embraces teachings of cultures disparate in time as well as place.

Today, students of the sky the world over recognize 88 constellations that cover the entire celestial sphere. Many of these have their origins in ancient days; many are "modern," contrived out of unformed stars by astronomers a few centuries ago. Unformed stars were those usually too faint or inconveniently placed to be included in depicting the more prominent constellations. When astronomers began to travel to South Africa in the 16th and 17th centuries, they found a sky that itself was unformed, and showing numerous brilliant stars. Thus, we find constellations in the southern hemisphere like the "air pump," the "microscope," the "furnace," and other technological marvels of the time, as well as some arguably traditional forms, such as the "fly."

Many of the commonly recognized constellations had their origins in ancient Asia Minor—Syria, Babylon, etc. These were adopted by the Greeks and Romans who translated their names and stories into their own languages, some details being modified in the process. After the declines of these cultures, most such knowledge entered oral tradition, or remained hidden in monastic libraries. Beginning in the 8th century, the Moslem explosion spread through the Mediterranean world. Wherever possible, everything was translated into Arabic to be taught in the universities the Moslems established all over their new-found world.

In the 13th century, Alphonsus XX of Spain, an avid student of astronomy, succeeded in having Claudius Ptolemy's

Almagest, as its Arabian title was known, translated into Latin. It thus became widely available to European scholars. In the process, the constellation names were translated, but the star names were retained in their Arabic forms. Transliterating Arabic into the Roman alphabet has never been an exact art, so many of the star names we use today only "seem" Arabic to all but scholars.

Names of stars often indicated what parts of the traditional figures they represented: Deneb, the tail of the swan; Betelgeuse, the armpit of the giant. Thus, the names were an indication of the position in the sky of a particular star, provided one recognized the traditional form of the mythic figure.

In English, usage of the Latin names for the constellations couples often inconceivable creatures, represented in unimaginable configurations, with names that often seem unintelligible. Avoiding traditional names, astronomers may designate the brighter stars in a constellation with Greek letters, usually in order of brightness. Thus, the "alpha star" is often the brightest star of that constellation. The "of" implies possession, so the genetive (possessive) form of the constellation name is used, as in Alpha Orionis, the first star of Orion (Betelgeuse). Astronomers usually use a 3-letter form for the constellation name, understanding it to be read as either the nominative or genitive case of the name.

Until the 1920's, astronomers used curved boundaries for the constellation areas. As these were rather arbitrary at best, the International Astronomical Union adopted boundaries that ran due north-south and east-west, filling the sky much as the contiguous states fill up the area of the "lower 48" United States.

Within these boundaries, and occasionally crossing them, popular "asterisms" are recognized: the Big Dipper is a small part of Ursa Major, the big bear; the Sickle is the traditional head and mane of Leo, the lion; one of the horntips of Taurus, the bull, properly belongs to Auriga, the charioteer; the northeast star of the Great Square of Pegasus is Alpha Andromedae.

It is unlikely that further change will occur in the realm of the celestial constellations.

Name	Genitive	Abbreviation	Meaning	Name	Genitive	Abbreviation	Meaning
Andromeda	Andromedae	And	Chained Maiden	Circinus	Circini	Cir	Compasses (art)
Antlia	Antliae	Ant	Air Pump	Columba	Columbae	Col	Dove
Apus	Apodis	Aps	Bird of Paradise	Coma Berenices	Comae Berenices	Com	Berenice's Hair
Aquarius	Aquarii	Aqr	Water Bearer	Corona Australis	Coronae Australis	CrA	Southern Crown
Aquila	Aquilae	Aql	Eagle	Corona Borealis	Coronae Borealis	CrB	Northern Crown
Ara	Arae	Ara	Altar	Corvus	Corvi	Crv	Crow
Aries	Arietis	Ari	Ram	Crater	Crateris	Crt	Cup
Auriga	Aurigae	Aur	Charioteer	Crux	Crucis	Cru	Cross (southern)
Bootes	Bootis	Boo	Herdsmen	Cygnus	Cygni	Cyg	Swan
Caelum	Caeli	Cae	Chisel	Delphinus	Delphini	Del	Dolphin
Camelopardalis	Camelopardalis	Cam	Giraffe	Dorado	Doradus	Dor	Goldfish
Cancer	Cancri	Cnc	Crab	Draco	Draconis	Dra	Dragon
Canes Venatici	Canum Venaticorum	CVn	Hunting Dogs	Equuleus	Equulei	Equ	Little Horse
				Eridanus	Eridani	Eri	River
Canis Major	Canis Majoris	CMa	Great Dog	Fornax	Fornacis	For	Furnace
Canis Minor	Canis Minoris	CMi	Little Dog	Gemini	Geminorum	Gem	Twins
Capricornus	Capricorni	Cap	Sea-goat	Grus	Gruis	Gru	Crane (bird)
Carina	Carinae	Car	Keel	Hercules	Herculis	Her	Hercules
Cassiopeia	Cassiopeiae	Cas	Queen	Horologium	Horologii	Hor	Clock
Centaurus	Centauri	Cen	Centaur	Hydra	Hydrae	Hya	Water Snake (female)
Cepheus	Cephei	Cep	King				
Cetus	Ceti	Cet	Whale	Hydrus	Hydri	Hyi	Water Snake (male)
Chamaeleon	Chamaeleontis	Cha	Chameleon				

Name	Genitive	Abbreviation	Meaning	Name	Genitive	Abbreviation	Meaning
Indus	Indi	Ind	Indian	Piscis Austrinis	Piscis Austrini	PsA	Southern Fish
Lacerta	Lacertae	Lac	Lizard	Puppis	Puppis	Pup	Stern (deck)
Leo	Leonis	Leo	Lion	Pyxis	Pyxidis	Pyx	Compass (sea)
Leo Minor	Leonis Minoris	LMi	Little Lion	Reticulum	Reticuli	Ret	Reticle
Lepus	Leporis	Lep	Hare	Sagitta	Sagittae	Sge	Arrow
Libra	Librae	Lib	Balance	Sagittarius	Sagittarii	Sgr	Archer
Lupus	Lupi	Lup	Wolf	Scorpius	Scorpii	Sco	Scorpion
Lynx	Lyncis	Lyn	Lynx	Sculptor	Sculptoris	Scl	Sculptor
Lyra	Lyrae	Lyr	Lyre	Scutum	Scuti	Sct	Shield
Mensa	Mensae	Men	Table Mountain	Serpens	Serpentis	Ser	Serpent
Microscopium	Microscopii	Mic	Microscope	Sextans	Sextantis	Sex	Sextant
Monoceros	Monocerotis	Mon	Unicorn	Taurus	Tauri	Tau	Bull
Musca	Muscae	Mus	Fly	Telescopium	Telescopii	Tel	Telescope
Norma	Normae	Nor	Square (rule)	Triangulum	Trianguli	Tri	Triangle
Octans	Octantis	Oct	Octant	Tringulum Australe	Trianguli Australis	TrA	Southern Triangle
Ophiuchus	Ophiuchi	Oph	Serpent Bearer	Tucana	Tucanae	Tuc	Toucan
Orion	Orionis	Ori	Hunter	Ursa Major	Ursae Majoris	UMa	Great Bear
Pavo	Pavonis	Pav	Peacock	Ursa Minor	Ursae Minoris	UMi	Little Bear
Pegasus	Pegasi	Peg	Flying Horse	Vela	Velorum	Vel	Sail
Perseus	Persei	Per	Hero	Virgo	Virginis	Vir	Maiden
Phoenix	Phoenicis	Phe	Phoenix	Volans	Volantis	Vol	Flying Fish
Pictor	Pictoris	Pic	Painter	Vulpecula	Vulpeculae	Vul	Fox
Pisces	Piscium	Psc	Fishes				

The Zodiac

The sun's apparent yearly path among the stars is known as the **ecliptic**. The zone 16° wide, 8° on each side of the ecliptic, is known as the **zodiac**. Inside of this zone are the apparent paths of the sun, moon, earth, and major planets. Beginning at the point on the ecliptic which marks the position of the sun at the vernal equinox, and thence proceeding eastward, the zodiac is divided into 12 signs of 30° each, as shown herewith.

These signs are named from the 12 constellations of the zodiac with which the signs coincided in the time of the astronomer Hipparchus, about 2 000 years ago. Owing to the precession of the equinoxes, that is to say, to the retrograde motion of the equinoxes along the ecliptic, each sign in the zodiac has, in the course of 2 000 years, moved backward 30° into the constellation west of it; so that the sign Aries is now in the constellation Pisces, and so on. The vernal equinox will move from Pisces into Aquarius about the middle of the 26th century. The signs of the zodiac with their Latin and English names are as follows:

Spring	1.	♈	Aries.	The Ram.
	2.	♉	Taurus.	The Bull.
	3.	♊	Gemini.	The Twins.
Summer	4.	♋	Cancer.	The Crab.
	5.	♌	Leo.	The Lion.
	6.	♍	Virgo.	The Virgin.
Autumn	7.	♎	Libra.	The Balance.
	8.	♏	Scorpio.	The Scorpion.
	9.	♐	Sagittarius.	The Archer.
Winter	10.	♑	Capricorn.	The Goat.
	11.	♒	Aquarius.	The Water Bearer.
	12.	♓	Pisces.	The Fishes.

Largest Telescopes

Most of the world's major astronomical installations are in the northern hemisphere, while many of astronomy's major problems are found in the southern sky. This imbalance has long been recognized and is being remedied.

In the northern hemisphere the largest reflector is the 599 cm mirror at the Special Astrophysical Observatory in the Caucasus in the Soviet Union. The largest reflectors in the U.S. include 3 in California: at Palomar Mtn., 508 cm; at Lick Observatory, Mt. Hamilton, 305 cm; and at Mt. Wilson Observatory, 254 cm. Also in the U.S. are a 401 cm reflector at Kitt Peak, Arizona, dedicated in June 1973, and a 272 cm telescope at the McDonald Observatory on Mt. Locke in Texas. A telescope at the Crimean Astrophysical Observatory in the Soviet Union has a 264 cm mirror.

Placed in service in 1975 were three large reflectors for the southern hemisphere. Associated Universities for Research in Astronomy (AURA), the operating organization of Kitt Peak National Observatory, dedicated the 401 cm reflector (twin of the telescope on Kitt Peak) at Cerro Tololo International Observatory, Chile; the European Southern Observatory has a 358 cm reflector at La Silla, Chile; and the Anglo-Australian telescope, 386 cm in diameter, is at Siding Spring Observatory in Australia.

Optical Telescopes

Optical astronomical telescopes are of two kinds, refracting and reflecting. In the first, light passes through a lens which brings the light rays into focus, where the image may be examined after being magnified by a second lens, the eyepiece, or directly photographed.

The reflector consists of a concave parabolic mirror, generally of Pyrex or now of a relatively heat insensitive material, cervit, coated with silver or aluminum, which reflects the light rays back toward the upper end of the telescope, where they are either magnified and observed by the eyepiece or, as in the case of the refractors, photographed. In most reflecting telescopes, the light is reflected again by a secondary mirror and comes to a focus after passing through a hole in the side of the telescope, where the eye-piece or camera is located, or after passing through a hole in the centre of the primary mirror.

World's Largest Refractors

Location and diameter in centimeters

Yerkes Obs., Williams Bay, Wis.	102
Lick Obs., Mt. Hamilton, Cal.	91
Astrophys. Obs., Potsdam, E. Germany	81
Paris Observatory, Meudon, France	81
Allegheny Obs., Pittsburgh, Pa.	76
Univ. of Paris, Nice, France	76
Royal Greenwich Obs., Herstmonceux, England	71
Union Obs., Johannesburg, South Africa	67
Universitats-Sternwarte, Vienna, Austria	67
Leander McCormick Obs., Univ. of Virginia, Charlottesville, Va.	66
Obs., Academy of Sciences, Pulkova, USSR	66
Astronomical Obs., Belgrade, Yugoslavia	66
Obs. Mitaka, Tokyo-to, Japan	66
US Naval Obs., Washington, D.C.	66
Mt. Stromlo Obs., Canberra, Australia	66

Chronological Eras, 1989

Era	Year	Begins in 1989		Era	Year	Begins in 1989	
Byzantine	7498	Sept.	14	Grecian	2306	Sept.	14
Jewish	5750	Sept.	29	(Seleucidae)		or Oct.	14
		(sunset)		Diocletian	1706	Sept.	11
Roman (Ab Urbe Condita)	2741	Jan.	14	Indian (Saka)	1911	Mar.	22
Nabonassar (Babylonian)	2738	Apr.	26	Mohammedan (Hegira)	1410	Aug.	3
Japanese	2649	Jan.	1				

Chronological Cycles, 1989

Dominical Letter .... A	Golden Number (Lunar Cycle) . XIV	Roman Indication 12
Epact 32	Solar Cycle 10	Julian Period (year of) 6702

Julian and Gregorian Calendars; Leap Year

Calendars based on the movements of sun and moon have been used since ancient times, but none has been perfect. The Julian calendar, under which western nations measured time until 1582 A.D., was authorized by Julius Caesar in 46 B.C., the year 709 of Rome. His éxpert was a Greek, Sosigenes. The Julian calendar, on the assumption that the true year was 365 1/4 days long, gave every fourth year 366 days. The Venerable Bede, an Anglo-Saxon monk, announced in 730 A.D. that the 365 1/4-day Julian year was 11 min., 14 sec. too long, making a cumulative error of about a day every 128 years, but nothing was done about it for over 800 years.

By 1582 the accumulated error was estimated to have amounted to 10 days. In that year Pope Gregory XIII decreed that the day following Oct. 4, 1582, should be called Oct. 15, thus dropping 10 days.

However, with common years 365 days and a 366-day leap year every fourth year, the error in the length of the year would have recurred at the rate of a little more than 3 days every 400 years. So 3 of every 4 centesimal years (ending in 00) were made common years, not leap years. Thus 1600 was a leap year, 1700, 1800 and 1900 were not, but 2000 will be. Leap years are those divisible by 4 except centesimal years, which are common unless divisible by 400.

The Gregorian calendar was adopted at once by France, Italy, Spain, Portugal and Luxembourg. Within 2 years most German Catholic states, Belgium and parts of Switzerland and the Netherlands were brought under the new calendar, and Hungary followed in 1587. The rest of the Netherlands, along with Denmark and the German Protestant states made the change in 1699-1700 (German Protestants retained the old reckoning of Easter until 1776).

The British Government imposed the Gregorian calendar on all its possessions, including the American colonies, in 1752. The British decreed that the day following Sept. 2,

1752, should be called Sept. 14, a loss of 11 days. All dates preceding were marked O.S., for Old Style. In addition New Year's Day was moved to Jan. 1 from Mar. 25. (e.g., under the old reckoning, Mar. 24, 1700 had been followed by Mar. 25, 1701.) In 1753 Sweden too went Gregorian, retaining old Easter rules until 1844.

In 1793 the French Revolutionary Government adopted a calendar of 12 months of 30 days each with 5 extra days in September of each common year and a 6th extra day every 4th year. Napoleon reinstated the Gregorian calendar in 1806.

The Gregorian system later spread to non-European regions, first in the European colonies, then in the independent countries, replacing traditional calendars at least for official purposes. Japan in 1873, Egypt in 1875, China in 1912 and Turkey in 1917 made the change, usually in conjunction with political upheavals. In China, the republican government began reckoning years from its 1911 founding — e.g., 1948 was designated the year 37. After 1949, the Communists adopted the Common, or Christian Era year count, even for the traditional lunar calendar.

In 1918 the revolutionary government in Russia decreed that the day after Jan. 31, 1918, Old Style, would become Feb. 14, 1918, New Style. Greece followed in 1923. (In Russia the Orthodox Church has retained the Julian calendar, as have various Middle Eastern Christian sects.) For the first time in history, all major cultures have one calendar.

To change from the Julian to the Gregorian calendar, add 10 days to dates Oct. 5, 1582, through Feb. 28, 1700; after that date add 11 days through Feb. 28, 1800; 12 days through Feb. 28, 1900; and 13 days through Feb. 28, 2100.

A century consists of 100 consecutive calendar years. The 1st century consisted of the years 1 through 100. The 20th century consists of the years 1901 through 2000 and will end Dec. 31, 2000. The 21st century will begin Jan. 1, 2001.

Gregorian Calendar

Pick desired year from table below or on page 316 (for years 1821 to 2080). The number shown with each year shows which calendar to use for that year, as shown on pages 316-317. (The Gregorian calendar was inaugurated Oct. 15, 1582. From that date to Dec. 31, 1582, use calendar 6.)

1583-1802

1583 . . 7	1603 . . 4	1623 . . 1	1643 . . 5	1663 . . 2	1683 . . 6	1703 . . 2	1723 . . 6	1743 . . 3	1763 . . 7	1783 . . 4
1584 . . 8	1604 . . 12	1624 . . 9	1644 . . 13	1664 . . 10	1684 . . 14	1704 . . 10	1724 . . 14	1744 . . 11	1764 . . 8	1784 . . 12
1585 . . 3	1605 . . 7	1625 . . 4	1645 . . 1	1665 . . 5	1685 . . 2	1705 . . 5	1725 . . 2	1745 . . 6	1765 . . 3	1785 . . 7
1586 . . 4	1606 . . 1	1626 . . 5	1646 . . 2	1666 . . 6	1686 . . 3	1706 . . 6	1726 . . 3	1746 . . 7	1766 . . 4	1786 . . 1
1587 . . 5	1607 . . 2	1627 . . 6	1647 . . 3	1667 . . 7	1687 . . 4	1707 . . 7	1727 . . 4	1747 . . 1	1767 . . 5	1787 . . 2
1588 . . 13	1608 . . 10	1628 . . 14	1648 . . 11	1668 . . 8	1688 . . 12	1708 . . 8	1728 . . 12	1748 . . 9	1768 . . 13	1788 . . 10
1589 . . 1	1609 . . 5	1629 . . 2	1649 . . 6	1669 . . 3	1689 . . 7	1709 . . 3	1729 . . 7	1749 . . 4	1769 . . 1	1789 . . 5
1590 . . 2	1610 . . 6	1630 . . 3	1650 . . 7	1670 . . 4	1690 . . 1	1710 . . 4	1730 . . 1	1750 . . 5	1770 . . 2	1790 . . 6
1591 . . 3	1611 . . 7	1631 . . 4	1651 . . 1	1671 . . 5	1691 . . 2	1711 . . 5	1731 . . 2	1751 . . 6	1771 . . 3	1791 . . 7
1592 . . 11	1612 . . 8	1632 . . 12	1652 . . 9	1672 . . 13	1692 . . 10	1712 . . 13	1732 . . 10	1752 . . 14	1772 . . 11	1792 . . 8
1593 . . 6	1613 . . 3	1633 . . 7	1653 . . 4	1673 . . 1	1693 . . 5	1713 . . 1	1733 . . 5	1753 . . 2	1773 . . 6	1793 . . 3
1594 . . 7	1614 . . 4	1634 . . 1	1654 . . 5	1674 . . 2	1694 . . 6	1714 . . 2	1734 . . 6	1754 . . 3	1774 . . 7	1794 . . 4
1595 . . 1	1615 . . 5	1635 . . 2	1655 . . 6	1675 . . 3	1695 . . 7	1715 . . 3	1735 . . 7	1755 . . 4	1775 . . 1	1795 . . 5
1596 . . 9	1616 . . 13	1636 . . 10	1656 . . 14	1676 . . 11	1696 . . 8	1716 . . 11	1736 . . 8	1756 . . 12	1776 . . 9	1796 . . 13
1597 . . 4	1617 . . 1	1637 . . 5	1657 . . 2	1677 . . 6	1697 . . 3	1717 . . 6	1737 . . 3	1757 . . 7	1777 . . 4	1797 . . 1
1598 . . 5	1618 . . 2	1638 . . 6	1658 . . 3	1678 . . 7	1698 . . 4	1718 . . 7	1738 . . 4	1758 . . 1	1778 . . 5	1798 . . 2
1599 . . 6	1619 . . 3	1639 . . 7	1659 . . 4	1679 . . 1	1699 . . 5	1719 . . 1	1739 . . 5	1759 . . 2	1779 . . 6	1799 . . 3
1600 . . 14	1620 . . 11	1640 . . 8	1660 . . 12	1680 . . 9	1700 . . 6	1720 . . 9	1740 . . 13	1760 . . 10	1780 . . 14	1800 . . 4
1601 . . 2	1621 . . 6	1641 . . 3	1661 . . 7	1681 . . 4	1701 . . 7	1721 . . 4	1741 . . 1	1761 . . 5	1781 . . 2	1801 . . 5
1602 . . 3	1622 . . 7	1642 . . 4	1662 . . 1	1682 . . 5	1702 . . 1	1722 . . 5	1742 . . 2	1762 . . 6	1782 . . 3	1802 . . 6

Julian Calendar

To find which of the 14 calendars printed on pages 326-327 applies to any year, starting Jan. 1, under the Julian system, find the century for the desired year in the three left-hand columns below; read across. Then find the year in the four top rows; read down. The number in the intersection is the calendar designation for that year.

Year (last two figures of desired year)

Century	00	01 02 03 04 / 29 30 31 32 / 57 58 59 60 / 85 86 87 88	05 06 07 08 / 33 34 35 36 / 61 62 63 64 / 89 90 91 92	09 10 11 12 / 37 38 39 40 / 65 66 67 68 / 93 94 95 96	13 14 15 16 / 41 42 43 44 / 69 70 71 72 / 97 98 99	17 18 19 20 / 45 46 47 48 / 73 74 75 76	21 22 23 24 / 49 50 51 52 / 77 78 79 80	25 26 27 28 / 53 54 55 56 / 81 82 83 84
0 700 1400	12	7 1 2 10	5 6 7 8	3 4 5 13	1 2 3 11	6 7 1 9	4 5 6 14	2 3 4 12
100 800 1500	11	6 7 1 9	4 5 6 14	2 3 4 12	7 1 2 10	5 6 7 8	3 4 5 13	1 2 3 11
200 900 1600	10	5 6 7 8	3 4 5 13	1 2 3 11	6 7 1 9	4 5 6 14	2 3 4 12	7 1 2 10
300 1000 1700	9	4 5 6 14	2 3 4 12	7 1 2 10	5 6 7 8	3 4 5 13	1 2 3 11	6 7 1 9
400 1100 1800	8	3 4 5 13	1 2 3 11	6 7 1 9	4 5 6 14	2 3 4 12	7 1 2 10	5 6 7 8
500 1200 1900	14	2 3 4 12	7 1 2 10	5 6 7 8	3 4 5 13	1 2 3 11	6 7 1 9	4 5 6 14
600 1300 2000	13	1 2 3 11	6 7 1 9	4 5 6 14	2 3 4 12	7 1 2 10	5 6 7 8	3 4 5 13

Lunar Calendar, Chinese New Year, Vietnamese Tet

The ancient Chinese lunar calendar is divided into 12 months of either 29 or 30 days (compensating for the fact that the mean duration of the lunar month is 29 days, 12 hours, 44.05 minutes). The calendar is synchronized with the solar year by the addition of extra months at fixed intervals.

The Chinese calendar runs on a sexagenary cycle, i.e., 60 years. The cycles 1876-1935 and 1936-1995, with the years grouped under their twelve animal designations, are printed below. The year 1989 (Lunar Year 4687) is found in the sixth column, under Snake, and is known as a "Year of the Snake." Readers can find the animal name for the year of their birth, marriage, etc., in the same chart. (Note: the first 3-7 weeks of each of the western years belong to the previous Chinese year and animal designation.)

Both the western (Gregorian) and traditional lunar calendars are used publicly in China, and two New Year's celebrations are held. On Taiwan, in overseas Chinese communities, and in Vietnam, the lunar calendar has been used only to set the dates for traditional festivals, with the Gregorian system in general use.

The four-day Chinese New Year, Hsin Nien, and the three-day Vietnamese New Year festival, Tet, begin at the first new moon after the sun enters Aquarius. The day may fall, therefore, between Jan. 21 and Feb. 19 of the Gregorian calendar. Feb. 6, 1989 marks the start of the new Chinese year. The date is fixed according to the date of the new moon in the Far East. Since this is west of the International Date Line the date may be one day later than that of the new moon in the United States.

Rat	Ox	Tiger	Hare (Rabbit)	Dragon	Snake	Horse	Sheep (Goat)	Monkey	Rooster	Dog	Pig
1900	1901	1902	1903	1904	1905	1906	1907	1908	1909	1910	1911
1912	1913	1914	1915	1916	1917	1918	1919	1920	1921	1922	1923
1924	1925	1926	1927	1928	1929	1930	1931	1932	1933	1934	1935
1936	1937	1938	1939	1940	1941	1942	1943	1944	1945	1946	1947
1948	1949	1950	1951	1952	1953	1954	1955	1956	1957	1958	1959
1960	1961	1962	1963	1964	1965	1966	1967	1968	1969	1970	1971
1972	1973	1974	1975	1976	1977	1978	1979	1980	1981	1982	1983
1984	1985	1986	1987	1988	1989	1990	1991	1992	1993	1994	1995

Days Between Two Dates

Table covers period of two ordinary years. Example—Days between Feb. 10, 1988 and Dec. 15, 1989; subtract 41 from 714; answer is 673 days. For leap year, such as 1989, one day must be added: final answer is 674.

Date	Jan.	Feb.	Mar.	April	May	June	July	Aug.	Sept.	Oct.	Nov.	Dec.
1	1	32	60	91	121	152	182	213	244	274	305	335
2	2	33	61	92	122	153	183	214	245	275	306	336
3	3	34	62	93	123	154	184	215	246	276	307	337
4	4	35	63	94	124	155	185	216	247	277	308	338
5	5	36	64	95	125	156	186	217	248	278	309	339
6	6	37	65	96	126	157	187	218	249	279	310	340
7	7	38	66	97	127	158	188	219	250	280	311	341
8	8	39	67	98	128	159	189	220	251	281	312	342
9	9	40	68	99	129	160	190	221	252	282	313	343
10	10	41	69	100	130	161	191	222	253	283	314	344
11	11	42	70	101	131	162	192	223	254	284	315	345
12	12	43	71	102	132	163	193	224	255	285	316	346
13	13	44	72	103	133	164	194	225	256	286	317	347
14	14	45	73	104	134	165	195	226	257	287	318	348
15	15	46	74	105	135	166	196	227	258	288	319	349
16	16	47	75	106	136	167	197	228	259	289	320	350
17	17	48	76	107	137	168	198	229	260	290	321	351
18	18	49	77	108	138	169	199	230	261	291	322	352
19	19	50	78	109	139	170	200	231	262	292	323	353
20	20	51	79	110	140	171	201	232	263	293	324	354
21	21	52	80	111	141	172	202	233	264	294	325	355
22	22	53	81	112	142	173	203	234	265	295	326	356
23	23	54	82	113	143	174	204	235	266	296	327	357
24	24	55	83	114	144	175	205	236	267	297	328	358
25	25	56	84	115	145	176	206	237	268	298	329	359
26	26	57	85	116	146	177	207	238	269	299	330	360
27	27	58	86	117	147	178	208	239	270	300	331	361
28	28	59	87	118	148	179	209	240	271	301	332	362
29	29	—	88	119	149	180	210	241	272	302	333	363
30	30	—	89	120	150	181	211	242	273	303	334	364
31	31	—	90	—	151	—	212	243	—	304	—	365

Date	Jan.	Feb.	Mar.	April	May	June	July	Aug.	Sept.	Oct.	Nov.	Dec.
1	366	397	425	456	486	517	547	578	609	639	670	700
2	367	398	426	457	487	518	548	579	610	640	671	701
3	368	399	427	458	488	519	549	580	611	641	672	702
4	369	400	428	459	489	520	550	581	612	642	673	703
5	370	401	429	460	490	521	551	582	613	643	674	704
6	371	402	430	461	491	522	552	583	614	644	675	705
7	372	403	431	462	492	523	553	584	615	645	676	706
8	373	404	432	463	493	524	554	585	616	646	677	707
9	374	405	433	464	494	525	555	586	617	647	678	708
10	375	406	434	465	495	526	556	587	618	648	679	709
11	376	407	435	466	496	527	557	588	619	649	680	710
12	377	408	436	467	497	528	558	589	620	650	681	711
13	378	409	437	468	498	529	559	590	621	651	682	712
14	379	410	438	469	499	530	560	591	622	652	683	713
15	380	411	439	470	500	531	561	592	623	653	684	714
16	381	412	440	471	501	532	562	593	624	654	685	715
17	382	413	441	472	502	533	563	594	625	655	686	716
18	383	414	442	473	503	534	564	595	626	656	687	717
19	384	415	443	474	504	535	565	596	627	657	688	718
20	385	416	444	475	505	536	566	597	628	658	689	719
21	386	417	445	476	506	537	567	598	629	659	690	720
22	387	418	446	477	507	538	568	599	630	660	691	721
23	388	419	447	478	508	539	569	600	631	661	692	722
24	389	420	448	479	509	540	570	601	632	662	693	723
25	390	421	449	480	510	541	571	602	633	663	694	724
26	391	422	450	481	511	542	572	603	634	664	695	725
27	392	423	451	482	512	543	573	604	635	665	696	726
28	393	424	452	483	513	544	574	605	636	666	697	727
29	394	—	453	484	514	545	575	606	637	667	698	728
30	395	—	454	485	515	546	576	607	638	668	699	729
31	396	—	455	—	516	—	577	608	—	669	—	730

Perpetual Calendar

The number shown for each year indicates which Gregorian calendar to use. For 1583-1802, or for Julian calendar, see page 306. For years 1803-1820, use numbers for 1983-2000, respectively.

The page is a perpetual calendar consisting of fourteen numbered year-type blocks (7, 8, 9, 10, 11, 12, 13, 14) and the year 1988, each containing twelve monthly calendar grids.

Block 7

JANUARY, FEBRUARY, MARCH, APRIL, MAY, JUNE, JULY, AUGUST, SEPTEMBER, OCTOBER, NOVEMBER, DECEMBER

Block 8

JANUARY, FEBRUARY, MARCH, APRIL, MAY, JUNE, JULY, AUGUST, SEPTEMBER, OCTOBER, NOVEMBER, DECEMBER

Block 9

JANUARY, FEBRUARY, MARCH, APRIL, MAY, JUNE, JULY, AUGUST, SEPTEMBER, OCTOBER, NOVEMBER, DECEMBER

Block 10

JANUARY, FEBRUARY, MARCH, APRIL, MAY, JUNE, JULY, AUGUST, SEPTEMBER, OCTOBER, NOVEMBER, DECEMBER

Block 11

JANUARY, FEBRUARY, MARCH, APRIL, MAY, JUNE, JULY, AUGUST, SEPTEMBER, OCTOBER, NOVEMBER, DECEMBER

Block 12

JANUARY, FEBRUARY, MARCH, APRIL, MAY, JUNE, JULY, AUGUST, SEPTEMBER, OCTOBER, NOVEMBER, DECEMBER

Block 13

JANUARY, FEBRUARY, MARCH, APRIL, MAY, JUNE, JULY, AUGUST, SEPTEMBER, OCTOBER, NOVEMBER, DECEMBER

Block 14

JANUARY, FEBRUARY, MARCH, APRIL, MAY, JUNE, JULY, AUGUST, SEPTEMBER, OCTOBER, NOVEMBER, DECEMBER

1988

JANUARY, FEBRUARY, MARCH, APRIL, MAY, JUNE, JULY, AUGUST, SEPTEMBER, OCTOBER, NOVEMBER, DECEMBER

Each month grid is headed by the weekday columns S M T W T F S.

Holidays in Canada

Source: Labour Canada

Federal legislation provides paid holidays for all federal employees on New Year's Day, Good Friday, Easter Monday, Victoria Day, Canada Day, Labour Day, Thanksgiving Day, Remembrance Day, Christmas Day and Boxing Day. Other employees are covered by legislation which differs in each province. The chart below shows the dates of paid holidays, and the provinces in which employees are entitled to them, for 1988. Some employers provide additional paid holidays voluntarily or through contractual agreements with their employees.

Paid Public Holidays,[1] 1988

Jan. 1 (Friday)—**New Year's Day.** All provinces and territories.

Apr. 1—Good Friday. All provinces[2] and territories.

Apr. 4—Easter Monday. Businesses remain open in all provinces.[2]

May 23 (Monday preceding May 25)—**Victoria Day.** All provinces and territories except Nfld., N.S. and N.B.

June 24 (Friday)—**Fête nationale/National Holiday,** Que.

July 1 (Friday)—**Canada Day.** All provinces except Que. In Nfld., known as **Memorial Day** and observed on the Monday nearest July 1.

Aug. 1 (1st Monday in Aug.)—**Civic Holiday.** Alta. (**Heritage Day**), B.C. (**B.C. Day**), Man.*, N.B. (**N.B. Day**), N.S.*, N.W.T., Ont.* (**Simcoe Day**), Sask. (**Sask. Day**).

Aug. 15 (3d Monday in Aug.)—**Discovery Day,** Yukon.

Sept. 5 (1st Monday in Sept.)—**Labour Day.** All provinces and territories.

Oct. 10 (2nd Monday in Oct.)—**Thanksgiving Day.** All provinces except Nfld., N.S. and N.B.

Nov. 11 (Friday)—**Remembrance Day.** Alta., B.C., Man.*, N.S.*, Sask., Yukon, N.W.T.

Dec. 25 (Sunday)—**Christmas Day.** All provinces and territories.

Dec. 26 (Monday)—**Boxing Day.** Although not designated as a paid holiday, many employers grant their employees the day off with pay. Retail stores remain open in most provinces.

Other General or Public Holidays, 1988

Jan. 11 (Monday)—**Sir John A. Macdonald's Birthday.** Schools in some provinces close when anniversary falls on a weekday.

Mar. 14 (Monday nearest Mar. 17)—**St. Patrick's Day.** Nfld.

Apr. 25 (Monday nearest Apr. 23)—**St. George's Day.** Nfld.

June 27 (Monday nearest June 24)—**Discovery Day.** Nfld.

July 11 (Monday nearest July 12)—**Orangemen's Day.** Nfld.

(1) Known as "general" or as "public" holidays depending upon the province, these holidays entitle the employee to the day off with pay. Provincial specifications as to the number of hours or days an employee must have worked prior to the holiday for entitlement to the holiday with pay, and exceptions to the laws that apply to employees in service industries, emergency services or health care, are available from the provincial Ministry or Department of Labor. (2) In Quebec, certain businesses can choose either Good Friday or Easter Monday as a holiday for their employees.
* Employers are not required by provincial law to provide paid holidays on these days in the provinces indicated although many do so voluntarily or because of contractual agreements.

Standard Time Differences—World Cities

The time indicated in the table is fixed by law and is called the legal time, or, more generally, Standard Time. Use of Daylight Saving Time varies widely. *Indicates morning of the following day. At 12:00 noon, Eastern Standard Time, the standard time (in 24-hour time) in foreign cities is as follows:

City	Time	City	Time	City	Time	City	Time
Addis Ababa	20 00	Cape Town	19 00	Leningrad	20 00	Santiago (Chile)	13 00
Alexandria	19 00	Caracas	13 00	Lima	12 00	Seoul	2 00*
Amsterdam	18 00	Casablanca	17 00	Lisbon	17 00	Shanghai	1 00*
Athens	19 00	Copenhagen	18 00	Liverpool	17 00	Singapore	1 00*
Auckland	5 00*	Dacca	23 00	London	17 00	Stockholm	18 00
Baghdad	20 00	Delhi	22 30	Madrid	18 00	Sydney (Australia)	3 00*
Bangkok	0 00	Dublin	17 00	Manila	1 00*	Tashkent	23 00
Beijing	1 00*	Gdansk	18 00	Mecca	20 00	Teheran	20 30
Belfast	17 00	Geneva	18 00	Melbourne	3 00*	Tel Aviv	19 00
Berlin	18 00	Havana	12 00	Mexico City	11 00	Tokyo	2 00*
Bogota	12 00	Helsinki	19 00	Montevideo	14 00	Valparaiso	13 00
Bombay	22 30	Ho Chi Minh City	1 00*	Moscow	20 00	Vladivostok	3 00*
Bremen	18 00	Hong Kong	1 00*	Nagasaki	2 00*	Vienna	18 00
Brussels	18 00	Istanbul	19 00	Oslo	18 00	Warsaw	18 00
Bucharest	19 00	Jakarta	0 00	Paris	18 00	Wellington (N.Z.)	5 00*
Budapest	18 00	Jerusalem	19 00	Prague	18 00	Yokohama	2 00*
Buenos Aires	14 00	Johannesburg	19 00	Rangoon	23 30	Zurich	18 00
Cairo	19 00	Karachi	22 00	Rio De Janeiro	14 00		
Calcutta	22 30	Le Havre	18 00	Rome	18 00		

Standard Time Differences — North American Cities

Standard Time, whereby the world is divided into 24 time zones, was invented by Sir Sandford Fleming, in 1878. Canada is divided into 6 Standard Time Zones: Newfoundland, Atlantic, Eastern, Central, Mountain and Pacific. At 12 o'clock noon, Eastern Standard Time, the standard time in N.A. cities is as follows:

City	Time	City	Time	City	Time
Albuquerque, N.M. . .	10.00 A.M.	*Honolulu, Ha.	7.00 A.M.	Prince George, B.C..	9.00 A.M.
Atlanta, Ga.	12.00 Noon	Houston, Tex.	11.00 A.M.	Providence, R.I. . .	12.00 Noon
Austin, Tex.	11.00 A.M.	*Indianapolis, Ind. . .	12.00 Noon	*Regina, Sask. . . .	11.00 A.M.
Baltimore, Md. . . .	12.00 Noon	Jacksonville, Fla. . .	12.00 Noon	Quebec, Que.	12.00 Noon
Birmingham, Ala. . .	11.00 A.M.	Juneau, Alas. . . .	8.00 A.M.	Reno, Nev.	9.00 A.M.
Boston, Mass.	12.00 Noon	Kansas City, Mo. . .	11.00 A.M.	Richmond, Va. . . .	12.00 Noon
Buffalo, N.Y.	12.00 Noon	Knoxville, Tenn. . .	12.00 Noon	Rochester, N.Y. . .	12.00 Noon
Butte, Mon.	10.00 A.M.	Lethbridge, Alta. . .	10.00 A.M.	Sacramento, Cal. . .	9.00 A.M.
Calgary, Alta. . . .	10.00 A.M.	Lexington, Ky. . . .	12.00 Noon	Saint John, N.B. . .	1.00 P.M.
Charleston, S.C. . .	12.00 Noon	Little Rock, Ark. . .	11.00 A.M.	St. John's, Nfld. . .	1.30 P.M.
Charleston, W.Va. . .	12.00 Noon	Los Angeles, Cal. .	9.00 A.M.	St. Louis, Mo. . . .	11.00 A.M.
Charlottetown, P.E.I.	1.00 P.M.	Louisville, Ky. . . .	12.00 Noon	St. Paul, Minn. . . .	11.00 A.M.
Chicago, Ill.	11.00 A.M.	*Mexico City	11.00 A.M.	Salt Lake City, Ut. .	10.00 A.M.
Cleveland, Oh.. . . .	12.00 Noon	Memphis, Tenn. . . .	11.00 A.M.	San Diego, Cal. . .	9.00 A.M.
Colorado Spr., Col. .	10.00 A.M.	Miami, Fla.	12.00 Noon	San Francisco, Cal. .	9.00 A.M.
Dallas, Tex.	11.00 A.M.	Milwaukee, Wis. . .	11.00 A.M.	Saskatoon, Sask. . .	11.00 A.M.
Dartmouth, N.S. . . .	1.00 P.M.	Minneapolis, Minn. . .	11.00 A.M.	Seattle, Wash. . . .	9.00 A.M.
*Dawson, Yuk.	9.00 A.M.	Montreal, Que.. . . .	12.00 Noon	Sherbrooke, Que. . .	12.00 Noon
Dayton, Oh.	12.00 Noon	Nashville, Tenn. . .	11.00 A.M.	Tampa, Fla.	12.00 Noon
Denver, Col.	10.00 A.M.	New Haven, Conn. . .	12.00 Noon	Thunder Bay, Ont.. .	12.00 Noon
Des Moines, Ia. . . .	11.00 A.M.	New Orleans, La. . .	11.00 A.M.	Toledo, Oh.	12.00 Noon
Detroit, Mich.	12.00 Noon	New York, N.Y. . . .	12.00 Noon	Topeka, Kan.	11.00 A.M.
Duluth, Minn.	11.00 A.M.	Norfolk, Va.	12.00 Noon	Toronto, Ont.	12.00 Noon
Edmonton, Alta. . . .	10.00 A.M.	Okla. City, Okla. . .	11.00 A.M.	*Tucson, Ariz.. . . .	10.00 A.M.
El Paso, Tex.	10.00 A.M.	Omaha, Neb.	11.00 A.M.	Vancouver, B.C. . . .	9.00 A.M.
Fairbanks, Alas. . . .	8.00 A.M.	Ottawa, Ont.	12.00 Noon	Victoria, B.C.	9.00 A.M.
*Fort Wayne, Ind. . .	12.00 Noon	Philadelphia, Pa. . .	12.00 Noon	Washington, D.C.. . .	12.00 Noon
Fredericton, N.B. . .	1.00 P.M.	*Phoenix, Ariz. . . .	10.00 A.M.	Winnipeg, Man. . . .	11.00 A.M.
Galveston, Tex. . . .	11.00 A.M.	Pittsburgh, Pa. . . .	12.00 Noon	Yellowknife, NWT . .	10.00 A.M.
Grand Rapids, Mich. .	12.00 Noon	Portland, Me.	12.00 Noon		
Halifax, N.S.	1.00 P.M.	Portland, Ore.	9.00 A.M.		

*Cities with an asterisk do not observe daylight saving time. During much of the year, it is necessary to add one hour to the cities which do observe daylight savings time to get the proper time relation.

Latitude, Longitude, Elevation of Canadian Cities

City	Lat. N ° '	Long. W ° '	Elev. (m)	City	Lat. N ° '	Long. W ° '	Elev. (m)
Alert, N.W.T.	83 31	62 17	31	Niagara Falls, Ont. . .	43 06	79 03	180
Belleville, Ont.	44 09	77 23	78	North Bay, Ont.	46 18	79 27	204
Brandon, Man.	49 51	99 57	386	Oshawa, Ont.	43 53	78 51	107
Brantford, Ont.	43 08	80 15	215	Ottawa, Ont.	45 26	75 41	56
Burlington, Ont.	43 19	79 47	87	Peterborough, Ont.	44 18	78 19	205
Calgary, Alta.	51 02	114 03	1 045	Prince Rupert, B.C.	54 19	130 19	38
Charlottetown, P.E.I.	46 14	63 07	9	Quebec, Que.	46 48	71 12	50
Churchill, Man.	58 45	94 10	29	Regina, Sask.	50 26	104 36	577
Dartmouth, N.S.	44 39	63 34	7	St. Catharines, Ont.	43 09	79 14	110
Dawson, Yukon	64 03	139 26	369	Saint John, N.B.	45 16	66 03	8
Edmonton, Alta.	53 32	113 29	666	St. John's, Nfld.	47 33	52 42	61
Fredericton, N.B.	45 57	66 38	9	Saskatoon, Sask.	52 07	106 39	484
Guelph, Ont.	43 32	80 14	325	Sault Ste. Marie, Ont.	46 30	84 20	180
Halifax, N.S.	44 38	63 34	18	Sherbrooke, Que.	45 24	71 51	152
Hamilton, Ont.	43 15	79 52	100	Sudbury, Ont.	46 29	80 59	259
Hull, Que.	45 25	75 42	56	Sydney, N.S.	46 08	60 11	5
Kingston, Ont.	44 13	76 28	80	Thunder Bay, Ont.	48 22	89 14	188
Kitchener, Ont.	43 26	80 29	335	Toronto, Ont.	43 39	79 23	91
LaSalle, Que.	45 25	73 39	34	Trois-Rivières, Que.	46 20	72 32	35
Laval, Que.	45 33	73 44	43	Vancouver, B.C.	49 18	123 04	43
Lethbridge, Alta.	49 41	112 49	910	Victoria, B.C.	48 25	123 21	17
London, Ont.	42 59	81 14	251	Whitehorse, Yukon	60 43	135 03	703
Mississauga, Ont.	43 33	79 35	79	Windsor, Ont.	42 18	83 02	184
Moncton, N.B.	46 05	64 46	12	Winnipeg, Man.	49 53	97 08	232
Montreal, Que.	45 30	73 33	27	Yellowknife, N.W.T.	62 27	114 22	205
Moose Jaw, Sask.	50 23	105 32	544				

Weights and Measures

Ancient Measures

Biblical
Cubit	=	21.8 inches
Omer	=	0.45 peck
		3.964 litres
Ephah =		10 omers
Shekel	=	0.497 ounce
		14.1 grams

Greek
Cubit	=	18.3 inches
Stadion	=	607.2 or 622 feet
Obolos	=	715.38 milligrams
Drachma	=	4.2923 grams
Mina	=	0.9463 pounds
Talent	=	60 mina

Roman
Cubit	=	17.5 inches
Stadium	=	202 yards
As, libra,	=	325.971 grams,
pondus		.71864 pounds

Roman Numerals

I	–	1	VI	–	6	XI	–	11	L	–	50	CD	–	400	X	–	10 000
II	–	2	VII	–	7	XIX	–	19	LX	–	60	D	–	500	L	–	50 000
III	–	3	VIII	–	8	XX	–	20	XC	–	90	CM	–	900	C	–	100 000
IV	–	4	IX	–	9	XXX	–	30	C	–	100	M	–	1 000	D	–	500 000
V	–	5	X	–	10	XL	–	40	CC	–	200	V	–	5 000	M	–	1 000 000

Large Numbers

Canada, U.S.	Number of zeros	French British, German	Canada, U.S.	Number of zeros	French British, German
million	6	million	septillion	24	quadrillion
billion	9	milliard	octillion	27	1 000 quadrillion
trillion	12	billion	nonillion	30	quintillion
quadrillion	15	1 000 billion	decillion	33	1 000 quintillion
quintillion	18	trillion			
sextillion	21	1 000 trillion			

The International System of Units

Seven units have been adopted to serve as the base for the International System as follows: **length**—metre; **mass**—kilogram; **time**—second; **electric current**—ampere; **thermodynamic temperature**—kelvin; **amount of substance**—mole; and **luminous intensity**—candela.

Prefixes

The following prefixes, in combination with the basic unit names, provide the multiples and submultiples in the International System. For example, the unit name "metre," with the prefix "kilo" added, produces "kilometre," meaning "1 000 metres."

Prefix	Symbol	Multiples	Equivalent	Prefix	Symbol	Multiples	Equivalent
exa	E	10^{18}	quintillionfold	centi	c	10^{-2}	hundredth part
peta	P	10^{15}	quadrillionfold	milli	m	10^{-3}	thousandth part
tera	T	10^{12}	trillionfold	micro	μ	10^{-6}	millionth part
giga	G	10^{9}	billionfold	nano	n	10^{-9}	billionth part
mega	M	10^{6}	millionfold	pico	p	10^{-12}	trillionth part
kilo	k	10^{3}	thousandfold	femto	f	10^{-15}	quadrillionth part
hecto	h	10^{2}	hundredfold	atto	a	10^{-18}	quintillionth part
deka	da	10	tenfold				
deci	d	10^{-1}	tenth part				

Common Units of the International System Used in Canada

litre	=	L	=	volume or capacity		metre	=	m	=	length
degree Celsius	=	°C	=	temperature		kilogram	=	kg	=	mass
hectare	=	ha	=	area		second	=	s	=	time
tonne	=	t	=	mass		ampere	=	A	=	electric current
electron volt	=	eV	=	energy		kelvin	=	K	=	thermodynamic temperature
nautical mile	=	M	=	distance (navigation)		mole	=	mol	=	amount of substance
knot	=	kn	=	speed (navigation)		candela	=	cd	=	luminous intensity
standard atmosphere	=	atm	=	atmospheric pressure		newton	=	N	=	force
hertz	=	Hz	=	frequency		joule	=	J	=	energy, work
pascal	=	Pa	=	pressure, stress		coulomb	=	C	=	electric change
watt	=	W	=	power, radiant flux		ohm	=	Ω	=	electric resistance
volt	=	V	=	electric potential, electromotive force		farad	=	F	=	electric capacitance

Tables of Metric Weights and Measures

Linear Measure

10 millimetres (mm)	= 1 centimetre (cm)
10 centimetres	= 1 decimetre (dm) = 100 millimetres
10 decimetres	= 1 metre (m) = 1 000 millimetres
10 metres	= 1 dekametre (dam)
10 dekametres	= 1 hectometre (hm) = 100 metres
10 hectometres	= 1 kilometre (km) = 1 000 metres

Area Measure

100 square millimetres (mm²)	= 1 square centimetre (cm²)
10 000 square centimetres	= 1 square metre (m²) = 1 000 000 square millimetres
10 000 square metres	= 1 hectare (ha)
100 hectares	= 1 square kilometre (km²) = 1 000 000 square metres

Volume Measure

10 millilitres (mL)	= 1 centilitre (cL)

10 centilitres	= 1 decilitre (dL) = 100 millilitres
10 decilitres	= 1 litre (L) = 1 000 millilitres
10 litres	= 1 dekalitre (daL)
10 dekalitres	= 1 hectolitre (hL) = 100 litres
10 hectolitres	= 1 kilolitre (kL) = 1 000 litres
1 000 cubic millimetres (mm³)	= 1 cubic centimetre (cm³)
1 000 cubic centimetres	= 1 cubic decimetre (dm³) = 1 000 000 cubic millimetres
1 000 cubic decimetres	= 1 cubic metre (m³) = 1 stere = 1 000 000 cubic centimetres = 1 000 000 000 cubic millimetres

Weight

10 milligrams (mg)	= 1 centigram (cg)
10 centigrams	= 1 decigram (dg) = 100 milligrams
10 decigrams	= 1 gram (g) = 1 000 milligrams
10 grams	= 1 dekagram (dag)
10 dekagrams	= 1 hectogram (hg) = 100 grams
10 hectograms	= 1 kilogram (kg) = 1 000 grams
1 000 kilograms	= 1 metric ton (t)

Traditional Canadian Measures

Linear Measure

12 inches (in)	= 1 foot (ft)
3 feet	= 1 yard (yd)
5 ½ yards	= 1 rod (rd), pole, or perch (16 ½ feet)
40 rods	= 1 furlong (fur)=220 yards=660 feet
8 furlongs	= 1 statute mile (mi) = 1 760 yards = 5,280 feet
3 miles	= 1 league = 5 280 yards = 15 840 feet
6076.11549 feet	= 1 International Nautical Mile

Volume or Capacity Measure

When necessary to distinguish the liquid pint or quart from the dry pint or quart, the word "liquid" or the abbreviation "liq" should be used in combination with the name or abbreviation of the liquid unit.

4 gills	= 1 pint (pt) = 20 fl. oz.; 34.7 cubic in.
2 pints	= 1 quart (qt) = 40 fl. oz.; 69.4 cubic in.
4 quarts	= 1 gallon (gal) = 277 cubic in. = 8 pints = 32 gills

When necessary to distinguish the dry pint or quart from the liquid pint or quart, the word "dry" should be used in combination with the name or abbreviation of the dry unit.

2 pints (pt)	= 1 quart (qt) = 69.375 cubic in.
8 quarts	= 1 peck (pk) = 555 cubic in. = 16 pints
4 pecks	= 1 bushel (bu) = 2 219 cubic in. = 32 quarts
1 cubic foot (ft³)	= 1 728 cubic inches (in³)
27 cubic feet	= 1 cubic yard (yd³)

Area Measure

Squares and cubes of units are sometimes abbreviated by using "superior" figures. For example. ft² means square foot, and ft³ means cubic foot.

144 square inches	= 1 square foot (ft²)
9 square feet	= 1 square yard (yd²) = 1 296 square inches
30 ¼ square yards	= 1 square rod (rd²) = 272 ¼ square feet
160 square rods	= 1 acre = 4 840 square yards = 43 560 square feet

640 acres	= 1 square mile (mi²)
1 mile square	= 1 section (of land)
6 miles square	= 1 township = 36 sections = 36 square miles

Gunter's or Surveyors' Chain Measure

7.92 inches (in)	= 1 link
100 links	= 1 chain (ch) = 4 rods = 66 feet
80 chains	= 1 survey mile (mi) = 320 rods = 5 280 feet

Troy Weight

24 grains	= 1 pennyweight (dwt)
20 pennyweights	= 1 ounce troy (oz t) = 480 grains
12 ounces troy	= 1 pound troy (lb t) = 240 pennyweights = 5 760 grains

Avoirdupois Weight

When necessary to distinguish the avoirdupois ounce or pound from the troy ounce or pound, the word "avoirdupois" or the abbreviation "avdp" should be used in combination with the name or abbreviation of the avoirdupois unit.

(The "grain" is the same in avoirdupois and troy weight.)

27 ¹¹/₃₂ grains	= 1 dram (dr) = .22 cubic in.
16 drams	= 1 ounce (oz) = 437 ½ grains
16 ounces	= 1 pound (lb) = 256 drams = 7 000 grains
100 pounds	= 1 hundredweight (cwt)*
20 hundredweights	= 1 ton = 2 000 pounds*

In "gross" or "long" measure, the following values are recognized.

112 pounds	= 1 gross or long hundredweight*
20 gross or long hundredweights	= 1 gross or long ton = 2 240 pounds*

*When the terms "hundredweight" and "ton" are used unmodified, they are commonly understood to mean the 100-pound hundredweight and the 2 000-pound ton, respectively: these units may be designated "net" or "short" when necessary to distinguish them from the corresponding units in gross or long measure.

Tables of Equivalents

In this table it is necessary to distinguish between the "international" and the "survey" foot. The international foot, defined in 1959 as exactly equal to 0.3048 metre, is shorter than the old survey foot by exactly 2 parts in one million. In this table the survey foot is italicized.

When the name of a unit is enclosed in brackets thus, [1 hand], this indicates (1) that the unit is not in general current use or (2) that the unit is believed to be based on "custom and usage" rather than on formal definition.

Equivalents involving decimals are, in most instances, rounded off to the third decimal place except where they are exact, in which cases these exact equivalents are so designated.

Lengths

1 angstrom (A)	0.1 nanometre (exactly)
	0.000 1 micrometre (exactly)
	0.000 000 1 millimetre (exactly)
	0.000 000 004 inch
1 cable's length	120 fathoms (exactly)
	720 *feet* (exactly)
	219 metres
1 centimetre (cm)	0.3937 inch
1 chain (ch) (Gunter's or surveyors)	66 feet (exactly)
	20.1168 metres
1 chain (engineers)	100 feet
	30.48 metres (exactly)
1 decimetre (dm)	3.937 inches
1 degree (geographical)	364 566.929 feet
	69.047 miles (avg.)
	111.123 kilometres (avg.)
-of latitude	68.708 miles at equator
	69.403 miles at poles
-of longitude	69.171 miles at equator
1 dekametre (dam)	32.808 feet
1 fathom	6 feet (exactly)
	1.8288 metres (exactly)
1 foot (ft)	0.3048 metres (exactly)
1 furlong (fur)	10 chains (surveyors) (exactly)
	660 *feet* (exactly)
	⅛ statute mile (exactly)
	201.168 metres
[1 hand] (height measure for horses from ground to top of shoulders)	4 inches
1 inch (in)	2.54 centimetres (exactly)
1 kilometre (km)	0.621 mile
	3 281.5 feet
1 league (land)	3 survey miles (exactly)
	4.828 kilometres
1 link (Gunter's or surveyors)	7.92 inches (exactly)
	0.201 metre
1 link engineers	1 foot
	0.305 metre
1 metre (m)	39.37 inches
	1.094 yards
1 micrometre (μm) [the Greek letter mu]	0.001 millimetre (exactly)
	0.000 039 37 inch
1 mil	0.001 inch (exactly)
	0.025 4 millimetre (exactly)
1 mile (mi) (statute or land)	5 280 *feet* (exactly)
	1.609 kilometres
1 international nautical mile (nmi)	1.852 kilometres (exactly)
	1.150779 survey miles
	6 076.11549 feet
1 millimetre (mm)	0.039 37 inch
1 nanometre (nm)	0.001 micrometre (exactly)
	0.000 000 039 37 inch
1 pica (typography)	12 points
1 point (typography)	0.013 837 inch (exactly)
	0.351 millimetre
1 rod (rd), pole, or perch	16 ½ *feet* (exactly)
	5.029 metres
1 yard (yd)	0.9144 metre (exactly)

Areas or Surfaces

1 acre	43 560 square *feet* (exactly)
	4 840 square yards
	0.405 hectare
1 are (a)	119.599 square yards
	0.025 acre
1 bolt (cloth measure):	
length	100 yards (on modern looms)
width	42 inches (usually, for cotton)
	60 inches (usually, for wool)
1 hectare (ha)	2.471 acres

[1 square (building)]	100 square feet
1 square centimetre (cm²)	0.155 square inch
1 square decimetre (dm²)	15.500 square inches
1 square foot (ft²)	929.030 square centimetres
1 square inch (in²)	6.4516 square centimetres (exactly)
1 square kilometre (km²)	247.104 acres
	0.386 square mile
1 square metre (m²)	1.196 square yards
	10.764 square feet
1 square mile (mi²)	258.999 hectares
1 square millimetre (mm²)	0.002 square inch
1 square rod (rd²) sq. pole, or sq. perch	25.293 square metres
1 square yard (yd²)	0.836 square metre

Capacities or Volumes

1 barrel (bbl) liquid	35 gallons
1 bushel (bu) (British Imperial) (struck measure)	1.032 U.S. bushels struck measure
	2 219.36 cubic inches
1 cord (cd) firewood	128 cubic feet (exactly)
1 cubic centimetre (cm³)	0.061 cubic inch
1 cubic decimetre (dm³)	61.024 cubic inches
1 cubic inch (in³)	0.554 fluid ounce
	4.433 fluid drams
	16.387 cubic centimetres
1 cubic foot (ft³)	7.481 gallons
	28.317 cubic decimetres
1 cubic metre (m³)	1.308 cubic yards
1 cubic yard (yd³)	0.765 cubic metre
1 cup, measuring	8 fluid ounces (exactly)
	½ liquid pint (exactly)
1 dram, fluid (fl dr)	0.961 U.S. fluid dram
	0.217 cubic inch
	3.552 millilitres
1 dekalitre (daL)	2.642 gallons
	1.135 pecks
1 gallon (gal) (U.S.)	231 cubic inches (exactly)
	3.785 litres
	0.833 Canadian gallon
	128 U.S. fluid ounces (exactly)
1 gallon (gal) (British Imperial)	277.42 cubic inches
	1.201 U.S. gallons
	4.546 litres
	160 fluid ounces (exactly)
1 gill (gi)	7.219 cubic inches
	4 fluid ounces (exactly)
	0.118 litre
1 hectolitre (hL)	26.418 gallons
	2.838 bushels
1 litre (L) (1 cubic decimetre exactly)	1.057 liquid quarts
	0.908 dry quart
	61.025 cubic inches
1 millilitre (mL) (1 cu cm exactly)	0.271 fluid dram
	16.231 minims
	0.061 cubic inch
1 ounce, fluid (fl oz)	0.961 U.S. fluid ounce
	1.734 cubic inches
	28.412 millilitres
1 peck (pk)	8.810 litres
1 pint (pt), dry	33.600 cubic inches
	0.551 litre
1 pint (pt), liquid	28.875 cubic inches (exactly)
	0.473 litre
1 quart (qt) (British)	69.354 cubic inches
	1.032 U.S. dry quarts
	1.201 U.S. liquid quarts
1 tablespoon	3 teaspoons*(exactly)
	4 fluid drams
	½ fluid ounce (exactly)
1 teaspoon	⅓ tablespoon*(exactly)
	1⅓ fluid drams*

*The equivalent "1 teaspoon—1⅓ fluid drams" has been found to correspond more closely with the actual capacities of "measuring" and silver teaspoons than the equivalent "1 teaspoon—1 fluid dram" which is given by many dictionaries.

Weights or Masses

1 assay ton™ (AT) . . . . 29.167 grams

™Used in assaying. The assay ton bears the same relation to the milligram that a ton of 2 000 pounds avoirdupois bears to the ounce troy; hence the weight in milligrams of precious metal obtained from one assay ton of ore gives directly the number of troy ounces to the net ton.

1 bale (cotton measure). . . . $\begin{cases} 500 \text{ pounds in U.S.} \\ 750 \text{ pounds in Egypt} \end{cases}$

1 carat (c) . . . . $\begin{cases} 200 \text{ milligrams (exactly)} \\ 3.086 \text{ grains} \end{cases}$

1 dram avoirdupois (dr avdp) $\begin{cases} 27^{11}/_{32} (=27.344) \text{ grains} \\ 1.772 \text{ grams} \end{cases}$
gamma, see microgram

1 grain . . . . 64.799 milligrams

1 gram . . . . $\begin{cases} 15.432 \text{ grains} \\ 0.035 \text{ ounce, avoirdupois} \end{cases}$

1 hundredweight, gross or $\begin{cases} 112 \text{ pounds (exactly)} \\ 50.802 \text{ kilograms} \end{cases}$
long™ (gross cwt) . . . .

1 hundredweight, net or short . . . $\begin{cases} 100 \text{ pounds (exactly)} \\ 45.359 \text{ kilograms} \end{cases}$
(cwt. or net cwt.)

1 kilogram (kg) . . . . 2.205 pounds

1 microgram (μg [The Greek letter mu in combination with the letter g]) . . . . . 0.000001 gram (exactly)

1 milligram (mg) . . . . 0.015 grain

1 ounce, avoirdupois (oz avdp) . . . . $\begin{cases} 437.5 \text{ grains (exactly)} \\ 0.911 \text{ troy ounce} \\ 28.350 \text{ grams} \end{cases}$

1 ounce, troy (oz t) . . . . . $\begin{cases} 480 \text{ grains (exactly)} \\ 1.097 \text{ avoirdupois ounces} \\ 31.103 \text{ grams} \end{cases}$

1 pennyweight (dwt) . . . . . 1.555 grams

1 pound, avoirdupois (lb avdp) . . . . $\begin{cases} 7 \text{ 000 grains (exactly)} \\ 1.215 \text{ troy pounds} \\ 453.592 \text{ 37 grams (exactly)} \end{cases}$

1 pound, troy (lb t) . . . . . . $\begin{cases} 5 \text{ 760 grains (exactly)} \\ 0.823 \text{ avoirdupois pound} \\ 373.242 \text{ grams} \end{cases}$

1 ton, gross or long™™ (gross ton) . . . . $\begin{cases} 2 \text{ 240 pounds (exactly)} \\ 1.12 \text{ net tons (exactly)} \\ 1.016 \text{ metric tons} \end{cases}$

™™The gross or long ton and hundredweight are used commercially in the United States only a limited extent, usually in restricted industrial fields. These units are the same as British "ton" and "hundredweight."

1 ton, metric (t) . . . . $\begin{cases} 2 \text{ 204.623 pounds} \\ 0.984 \text{ gross ton} \\ 1.102 \text{ net tons} \end{cases}$

1 ton, net or short (sh ton). . $\begin{cases} 2 \text{ 000 pounds (exactly)} \\ 0.893 \text{ gross ton} \\ 0.907 \text{ metric ton} \end{cases}$

Tables of Interrelation of Units of Measurement

Units of length and area of the international and survey measures are included in the following tables. Units unique to the survey measure are italicized. See pg 302, Tables of Equivalents, 1st para.

1 international foot	= 0.999 998 survey foot (exactly)
1 survey foot	= 1200/3937 metre (exactly)
1 international foot	= 12 × 0.0254 metre (exactly)

Bold face type indicates exact values

Units of Length

Units	Inches	Links	Feet	Yards	Rods	Chains	Miles	cm	Meters
1 inch=	1	0.126 263	0.083 333	0.027 778	0.005 051	0.001 263	0.000 016	2.54	0.025 4
1 link=	7.92	1	0.66	0.22	0.04	0.01	0.000 125	20.117	0.201 168
1 foot=	12	1.515 152	1	0.333 333	0.060 606	0.015 152	0.000 189	30.48	0.304 8
1 yard=	36	4.545 45	3	1	0.181 818	0.045 455	0.000 568	91.44	0.914 4
1 rod=	198	25	16.5	5.5	1	0.25	0.003 125	502.92	5.029 2
1 chain=	792	100	66	22	4	1	0.012 5	2011.68	20.116 8
1 mile=	63 360	8000	5280	1760	320	80	1	160 934.4	1609.344
1 cm=	0.3937	0.049 710	0.032 808	0.010 936	0.001 988	0.000 497	0.000 006	1	0.01
1 metre=	39.37	4.970 960	3.280 840	1.093 613	0.198 838	0.049 710	0.000 621	100	1

Units of Area

Units	Sq. inches	Sq. links	Sq. feet	Sq. yards	Sq. rods	Sq. chains
1 sq. inch=	1	.015 942 3	0.006 944	0.000 771 605	0.000 025 5	0.000 001 594
1 sq. link=	62.726 4	1	0.435 6	0.0484	0.0016	0.000 1
1 sq. foot=	144	2.295 684	1	0.111 111 1	0.003 673 09	0.000 229 568
1 sq. yard=	1296	20.661 16	9	1	0.033 057 85	0.002 066 12
1 sq. rod=	39 204	625	272.25	30.25	1	0.062 5
1 sq. chain=	627 264	10 000	4 356	484	16	1
1 acre=	6 272 640	100 000	43 560	4 840	160	10
1 sq. mile=	4 014 489 600	64 000 000	27 878 400	3 097 600	102 400	6400
1 sq. cm=	0.155 000 3	0.002 471 05	0.001 076	0.000 119 599	0.000 003 954	0.000 000 247
1 sq. metre=	1550.003	24.710 44	10.763 91	1.195 990	0.039 536 70	0.002 471 044
1 hectare=	15 500 031	247 104	107 639.1	11 959.90	395.367 0	24.710 44

Units	Acres	Sq. miles	Sq. cm	Sq. metres	Hectares
1 sq. inch=	0.000 000 159 423	0.000 000 000 249 10	6.451 6	0.000 645 16	0.000 000 065
1 sq. link=	0.000 01	0.000 000 015 625	404.685 642 24	0.040 468 56	0.000 004 047
1 sq. foot=	0.000 022 956 84	0.000 000 035 870 06	929.034 1	0.092 903 41	0.000 009 290
1 sq. yard=	0.000 206 611 6	0.000 000 322 830 6	8 361.273 6	0.836 127 36	0.000 083 613
1 sq. rod=	0.006 25	0.000 009 765 625	252 929.5	25.292 95	0.002 529 295
1 sq. chain=	0.1	0.000 156 25	4 046 873	404.687 3	0.040 468 73
1 acre=	1	0.001 562 5	40 468 73	4 046.873	0.404 687 3
1 sq. mile=	640	1	25 899 881 103	2 589 988.11	258.998 811 034
1 sq. cm=	0.000 000 024 711	0.000 000 000 038 610	1	0.000 1	0.000 000 01
1 sq. metre=	0.000 247 104 4	0.000 000 386 102 2	10 000	1	0.0001
1 hectare=	2.471 044	0.003 861 006	100 000 000	10 000	1

Units of Mass Not Less than Avoirdupois Ounces

Units	Avdp oz	Avdp lb	Short cwt	Short tons	Long tons	Kilograms	Metric tons
1 oz av=	1	0.0625	0.000 625	0.000 031 25	0.000 027 902	0.028 349 523	0.000 028 350
1 lb av=	16	1	0.01	0.000 5	0.000 446 429	0.453 592 37	0.000 453 592
1 sh cwt=	1 600	100	1	0.05	0.044 642 86	45.359 237	0.045 359 237
1 sh ton=	32 000	2000	20	1	0.892 857 1	907.184 74	0.907 184 74
1 long ton=	35 840	2240	22.4	1.12	1	1016.046 908 8	1.016 046 909
1 kg=	35.273 96	2.204 623	0.022 046 23	0.001 102 311	0.000 984 207	1	0.001
1 metric ton=	35 273.96	2 204.623	22.046 23	1.102 311	0.984 206 5	1000	1

Units of Mass Not Greater than Pounds and Kilograms

Units	Grains	Pennyweights	Avdp drams	Avdp ounces
1 grain=	1	0.041 666 67	0.036 571 43	0.002 285 71
1 pennyweight=	24	1	0.877 714 3	0.054 857 14
1 dram avdp=	27.343 75	1.139 323	1	0.062 5
1 ounce avdp=	437.5	18.229 17	16	1
1 ounce troy=	480	20	17.554 29	1.097 143
1 pound troy=	5760	240	210.651 4	13.165 71
1 pound avdp=	7000	291.666 7	256	16
1 milligram=	0.015 432	0.000 643 015	0.000 564 383	0.000 035 274
1 gram=	15.432 36	0.643 014 9	0.564 383 4	0.035 273 96
1 kilogram=	15 432.36	643.014 9	564.383 4	35.273 96

Units	Troy ounces	Troy pounds	Avdp pounds	Milligrams	Grams	Kilograms
1 grain=	0.002 083 33	0.000 173 611	0.000 142 857	64.798 91	0.064 798 91	0.000 064 799
1 pennyw't.=	0.05	0.004 166 667	0.003 428 571	1555.173 84	1.555 173 84	0.001 555 174
1 dram avdp=	0.056 966 15	0.004 747 179	0.003 906 25	1771.845 195	1.771 845 195	0.001 771 845
1 oz avdp=	0.911 458 3	0.075 954 86	0.062 5	28 349.523 125	28.349 523 125	0.028 349 52
1 oz troy=	1	0.083 333 333	0.068 571 43	31 103.476 8	31.103 476 8	0.031 103 48
1 lb troy=	12	1	0.822 857 1	373 241.721 6	373.241 721 6	0.373 241 722
1 lb avdp=	14.583 33	1.215 278	1	453 592.37	453.592 37	0.453 592 37
1 milligram=	0.000 032 151	0.000 002 679	0.000 002 205	1	0.001	0.000 001
1 gram=	0.032 150 75	0.002 679 229	0.002 204 623	1000	1	0.001
1 kilogram=	32.150 75	2.679 229	2.204 623	1 000 000	1000	1

Units of Volume

Units	Cubic inches	Cubic feet	Cubic yards	Cubic cm	Cubic dm	Cubic metres
1 cubic inch=	1	0.000 578 704	0.000 021 433	16.387 064	0.016 387	0.000 016 387
1 cubic foot=	1728	1	0.037 037 04	28 316.846 592	28.316 847	0.028 316 847
1 cubic yard=	46 656	27	1	764 554.857 984	764.554 858	0.764 554 858
1 cubic cm=	0.061 023 74	0.000 035 315	0.000 001 308	1	0.001	0.000 001
1 cubic dm=	61.023 74	0.035 314 67	0.001 307 951	1 000	1	0.001
1 cubic metre=	61 023.74	35.314 67	1.307 951	1 000 000	1000	1

U.S. Units of Volume (Liquid Measure)

Units	Minims	Fluid drams	Fluid ounces	Gills	Liquid pt
1 minim=	1	0.016 666 7	0.002 083 33	0.000 520 833	0.000 130 208
1 fluid dram=	60	1	0.125	0.031 25	0.007 812 5
1 fluid ounce=	480	8	1	0.25	0.062 5
1 gill=	1920	32	4	1	0.25
1 liquid pint=	7680	128	16	4	1
1 liquid quart=	15 360	256	32	8	2
1 gallon=	61 440	1024	128	32	8
1 cubic inch=	265.974	4.432 900	0.554 112 6	0.138 528 1	0.034 632 03
1 cubic foot=	459 603.1	7 660.052	957.506 5	239.376 6	59.844 16
1 millilitre=	16.230 73	0.270 512 18	0.033 814 02	0.008 453 506	.002 113 376
1 litre=	16 230.73	270.512 18	33.814 02	8.453 506	2.113 376

Units	Liquid quarts	Gallons	Cubic inches	Cubic feet	Litres
1 minim=	0.000 065 104 17	0.000 016 276 04	0.003 759 766	0.000 002 175 790	0.000 061 611 52
1 flu. dram=	0.003 906 25	0.000 976 562 5	0.225 585 9	0.000 130 547 4	0.003 696 691
1 fluid oz=	0.031 25	0.007 812 5	1.804 687 5	0.001 044 379	0.029 573 53
1 gill=	0.125	0.031 25	7.218 75	0.004 177 517	0.118 294 118
1 liquid pt=	0.5	0.125	28.875	0.016 710 07	0.473 176 473
1 liquid qt=	1	0.25	57.75	0.033 420 14	0.946 352 946
1 gallon=	4	1	231	0.133 680 6	3.785 411 784
1 cubic in.=	0.017 316 02	0.004 329 004	1	0.000 578 703 7	0.016 387 064
1 cubic foot=	29.922 08	7.480 519	1728	1	28.316 846 592
1 litre=	1.056 688	0.264 172 05	61.023 74	0.035 314 67	1

U.S. Units of Volume (Dry Measure)

Units	Dry pints	Dry quarts	Pecks	Bushels	Cubic in.	Litres
1 dry pint=	1	0.5	0.062 5	0.015 625	33.600 312 5	0.550 610 47
1 dry quart=	2	1	0.125	0.031 25	67.200 625	1.101 220 9
1 peck=	16	8	1	0.25	537.605	8.809 767 5
1 bushel=	64	32	4	1	2150.42	35.239 07
1 cubic inch=	0.029 761 6	0.014 880 8	0.001 860 10	0.000 465 025	1	0.016 387 06
1 litre=	1.816 166	0.908 083	0.113 510 37	0.028 377 59	61.023 74	1

Weight of Water

1	cubic inch	.0360	pound	1	imperial gallon	10.0	pounds
12	cubic inches	.433	pound	11.2	imperial gallons	112.0	pounds
1	cubic foot	62.4	pounds	224	imperial gallons	2240.0	pounds
1	cubic foot	7.48052	U.S. gal	1	U.S. gallon	8.33	pounds
1.8	cubic feet	112.0	pounds	13.45	U.S. gallons	112.0	pounds
35.96	cubic feet	2240.0	pounds	269.0	U.S. gallons	2240.0	pounds

Temperature Conversion Table

The numbers in **bold face type** refer to the temperature either in degrees Celsius or Fahrenheit which are to be converted. If converting from degrees Fahrenheit to Celsius, the equivalent will be found in the column on the left, while if converting from degrees Celsius to Fahrenheit the answer will be found in the column on the right.

For temperatures not shown. To convert Fahrenheit to Celsius subtract 32 degrees and multiply by 5, divide by 9; to convert Celsius to Fahrenheit, multiply by 9, divide by 5 and add 32 degrees.

Celsius		Fahrenheit	Celsius		Fahrenheit	Celsius		Fahrenheit
− 273.2	− **459.7**	....	− 17.8	**0**	32	35.0	**95**	203
− 184	− **300**	....	− 12.2	**10**	50	36.7	**98**	208.4
− 169	− **273**	− 459.4	− 6.67	**20**	68	37.8	**100**	212
− 157	− **250**	− 418	− 1.11	**30**	86	43	**110**	230
− 129	− **200**	− 328	4.44	**40**	104	49	**120**	248
− 101	− **150**	− 238	10.0	**50**	122	54	**130**	266
− 73.3	− **100**	− 148	15.6	**60**	140	60	**140**	284
− 45.6	− **50**	− 58	21.1	**70**	158	66	**150**	302
− 40.0	− **40**	− 40	23.9	**75**	167	93	**200**	392
− 34.4	− **30**	− 22	26.7	**80**	176	121	**250**	482
− 28.9	− **20**	− 4	29.4	**85**	185	149	**300**	572
− 23.3	− **10**	14	32.2	**90**	194			

Miscellaneous Measures

Caliber—the diameter of a gun bore. In the U.S., caliber is traditionally expressed in hundredths of inches, eg. .22 or .30. In Britain, caliber is often expressed in thousandths of inches, eg. .270 or .465. Now, it is commonly expressed in millimetres, eg. the 7.62 mm M14 rifle and the 5.56 mm M16 rifle. Heavier weapons' caliber has long been expressed in millimetres, eg. the 81 mm mortar, the 105 mm. howitzer (light), the 155 mm howitzer (medium or heavy).

Naval guns' caliber refers to the barrel length as a multiple of the bore diameter. A 5-inch, 50-caliber naval gun has a 5-inch bore and a barrel length of 250 inches.

Carat, karat—a measure of the amount of alloy per 24 parts in gold. Thus 24-carat gold is pure; 18-carat gold is one-fourth alloy.

Decibel (dB)—a measure of the relative loudness or intensity of sound. A 20-decibel sound is 10 times louder than a 10-decibel sound; 30 decibels is 100 times louder; 40 decibels is 1 000 times louder, etc. One decibel is the smallest difference between sounds detectable by the human ear. A 140-decibel sound is painful.

10 decibels	– a light whisper
20	– quiet conversation
30	– normal conversation
40	– light traffic
50	– typewriter, loud conversation
60	– noisy office
70	– normal traffic, quiet train
80	– rock music, subway
90	– heavy traffic, thunder
100	– jet plane at takeoff

Em—a printer's measure designating the square width of any given type size. Thus, an em of 10-point type is 10 points. An en is half an em.

Gauge—a measure of shotgun bore diameter. Gauge numbers originally referred to the number of lead balls of the gun barrel diameter in a pound. Thus, a 16 gauge shotgun's bore was smaller than a 12-gauge shotgun's. Today, an international agreement assigns millimeter measures to each gauge, eg:

Gauge	Bore diameter in mm
6	23.34
10	19.67
12	18.52
14	17.60
16	16.81
20	15.90

Horsepower—the power needed to lift 550 pounds one foot in one second, or to lift 33 000 pounds one foot in one minute. Equivalent to 746 watts or 2 546.0756 Btu/h.

Quire—25 sheets of paper

Ream—500 sheets of paper

Compound Interest

Compounded Annually

Principal	Period	4%	5%	6%	7%	8%	9%	10%	12%	14%	16%
$100	1 day	0.011	0.014	0.016	0.019	0.022	0.025	0.027	0.033	0.038	0.044
	1 week	0.077	0.096	0.115	0.134	0.153	0.173	0.192	0.230	0.268	0.307
	6 mos.	2.00	2.50	3.00	3.50	4.00	4.50	5.00	6.00	7.00	8.00
	1 year	4.00	5.00	6.00	7.00	8.00	9.00	10.00	12.00	14.00	16.00
	2 years	8.16	10.25	12.36	14.49	16.64	18.81	21.00	25.44	29.96	34.56
	3 years	12.49	15.76	19.10	22.50	25.97	29.50	33.10	40.49	48.15	56.09
	4 years	16.99	21.55	26.25	31.08	36.05	41.16	46.41	57.35	68.90	81.06
	5 years	21.67	27.63	33.82	40.26	46.93	53.86	61.05	76.23	92.54	110.03
	6 years	26.53	34.01	41.85	50.07	58.69	67.71	77.16	97.38	119.50	143.64
	7 years	31.59	40.71	50.36	60.58	71.38	82.80	94.87	121.07	150.23	182.62
	8 years	36.86	47.75	59.38	71.82	85.09	99.26	114.36	147.60	185.26	227.84
	9 years	42.33	55.13	68.95	83.85	99.90	117.19	135.79	177.31	225.19	280.30
	10 years	48.02	62.89	79.08	96.72	115.89	136.74	159.37	210.58	270.72	341.14
	12 years	60.10	79.59	101.22	125.22	151.82	181.27	213.84	289.60	381.79	493.60
	15 years	80.09	107.89	139.66	175.90	217.22	264.25	317.72	447.36	613.79	826.55
	20 years	119.11	165.33	220.71	286.97	366.10	460.44	572.75	864.63	1 274.35	1 846.08

Playing Cards and Dice Chances

Hand	Poker Hands Number possible		Odds against
Royal flush	4	649	739 to 1
Other straight flush	36	72	192 to 1
Four of a kind	624	4	164 to 1
Full house	3 744		693 to 1
Flush	5 108		508 to 1
Straight	10 200		254 to 1
Three of a kind	54 912		46 to 1
Two pairs	123 552		20 to 1
One pair	1 098 240		4 to 3 (1.37 to 1)
Nothing	1 302 540		1 to 1
Total	**2 598 960**		

Dice
(probabilities on 2 dice)

Total	Odds against (Single toss)	Total	Odds against (Single toss)
2	35 to 1	8	31 to 5
3	17 to 1	9	8 to 1
4	11 to 1	10	11 to 1
5	8 to 1	11	17 to 1
6	31 to 5	12	35 to 1
7	5 to 1		

Dice
(Probabilities of consecutive winning plays)

No. consecutive wins	By 7 11 or point	No. consecutive wins	By 7 11 or point
1	244 in 495	6	1 in 70
2	6 in 25	7	1 in 141
3	3 in 25	8	1 in 287
4	1 in 17	9	1 in 582
5	1 in 34		

Pinochle Auction
(Odds against finding in "widow" of 3 cards)

Open places	Odds against	Open places	Odds against
1	5 to 1	4	3 to 2 for
2	2 to 1	5	2 to 1 for
3	Even		

Bridge

0 The odds—against suit distribution in a hand of 4-4-3-2 are about 4 to 1, against 5-4-2-2 about 8 to 1, against 6-4-2-1 about 20 to 1, against 7-4-1-1 about 254 to 1, against 8-4-1-0 about 2 211 to 1, and against 13-0-0-0 about 158 753 389 899 to 1.

Mathematical Formulas

To find the CIRCUMFERENCE of a:

Circle — Multiply the diameter by 3.14159265 (usually 3.1416).

To find the AREA of a:

Circle — Multiply the square of the diameter by .785398 (usually .7854).
Rectangle — Multiply the length of the base by the height.
Sphere (surface) — Multiply the square of the radius by 3.1416 and multiply by 4.

Square — Square the length of one side.
Trapezoid — Add the two parallel sides, multiply by height and divide by 2.
Triangle — Multiply the base by the height and divide by 2.

To find the VOLUME of a:

Cone — Multiply the square of the radius of the base by 3.1416, multiply by the height, and divide by 3.
Cube — Cube the length of one edge.
Cylinder — Multiply the square of the radius of the base by 3.1416 and multiply by the height.
Pyramid — Multiply the area of the base by the height and divide by 3.

Rectangular Prism — Multiply the length by the width by the height.
Sphere — Multiply the cube of the radius by 3.1416, multiply by 4 and divide by 3.

Measures of Force and Pressure

Dyne = force necessary to accelerate a 1-gram mass 1 centimetre per second squared = 0.000072 poundal
Poundal = force necessary to accelerate a 1-pound mass 1 foot per second squared = 13 825.5 dynes = 0.138255 newtons
Newton = force needed to accelerate a 1-kilogram mass 1 metre per second squared

Pascal (pressure) = 1 newton per square metre = 0.020885 pound per square foot
Atmosphere (air pressure at sea level) = 2 116.102 pounds per square foot = 14.6952 pounds per square inch = 1.0332 kilograms per square centimetre = 101 323 newtons per square metre.

Electrical Units

The **watt** is the unit of power (electrical, mechanical, thermal, etc.). Electrical power is given by the product of the voltage and the current.

Energy is sold by the **joule**, but in common practice the billing of electrical energy is expressed in terms of the **kilowatt-hour**, which is 3 600 000 joules or 3.6 megajoules.

The **horsepower** is a non-metric unit sometimes used in mechanics. It is equal to 746 watts.

The **ohm** is the unit of electrical resistance and represents the physical property of a conductor that offers a resistance to the flow of electricity, permitting just 1 ampere to flow at 1 volt of pressure.

Colors of the Spectrum

Color, an electromagnetic wave phenomenon, is a sensation produced through the excitation of the retina of the eye by rays of light. The colors of the spectrum may be produced by viewing a light beam refracted by passage through a prism, which breaks the light into its wave lengths.

Customarily, the primary colors of the spectrum are thought of as those 6 monochromatic colors that occupy relatively large areas of the spectrum: red, orange, yellow, green, blue, and violet. However, Sir Isaac Newton named a 7th, indigo, situated between blue and violet on the spectrum. Aubert estimated (1865) the solar spectrum to contain approximately 1 000 distinguishable hues of which according to Rood (1881) 2 million tints and shades can be distinguished; Luckiesh stated (1915) that 55 distinctly different hues have been seen in a single spectrum.

Many physicists recognize only 3 primary colors: red, yellow, and blue (Mayer, 1775); red, green, and violet (Thomas Young, 1801); red, green, and blue (Clerk Maxwell, 1860).

The color sensation of black is due to complete lack of stimulation of the retina, that of white to complete stimulation. The infra-red and ultra-violet rays, below the red (long) end of the spectrum and above the violet (short) end respectively, are invisible to the naked eye. Heat is the principal effect of the infra-red rays and chemical action that of the ultra-violet rays.

Chemical Elements, Discoverers, Atomic Weights

Atomic weights, based on the exact number 12 as the assigned atomic mass of the principal isotope of carbon, carbon 12, are provided through the courtesy of the International Union of Pure and Applied Chemistry and Butterworth Scientific Publications.

For the radioactive elements, with the exception of uranium and thorium, the mass number of either the isotope of longest half-life (*) or the better known isotope (**) is given.

Chemical element	Symbol	Atomic number	Atomic weight	Year discov.	Discoverer
Actinium	Ac	89	227*	1899	Debierne
Aluminum	Al	13	26.9815	1825	Oersted
Americium	Am	95	243*	1944	Seaborg, et al.
Antimony	Sb	51	121.75	1450	Valentine
Argon	Ar	18	39.948	1894	Rayleigh, Ramsay
Arsenic	As	33	74.9216	13th c.	Albertus Magnus
Astatine	At	85	210*	1940	Corson, et al.
Barium	Ba	56	137.34	1808	Davy
Berkelium	Bk	97	249**	1949	Thompson, Ghiorso, Seaborg
Beryllium	Be	4	9.0122	1798	Vauquelin
Bismuth	Bi	83	208.980	15th c.	Valentine
Boron	B	5	10.811a	1808	Gay-Lussac, Thenard
Bromine	Br	35	79.904b	1826	Balard
Cadmium	Cd	48	112.40	1817	Stromeyer
Calcium	Ca	20	40.08	1808	Davy
Californium	Cf	98	251*	1950	Thompson, et al.
Carbon	C	6	12.01115a	B.C.	
Cerium	Ce	58	140.12	1803	Klaproth
Cesium	Cs	55	132.905	1860	Bunsen, Kirchhoff
Chlorine	Cl	17	35.453b	1774	Scheele
Chromium	Cr	24	51.996b	1797	Vauquelin
Cobalt	Co	27	58.9332	1735	Brandt
Copper	Cu	29	63.546b	B.C.	
Curium	Cm	96	247*	1944	Seaborg, James, Ghiorso
Dysprosium	Dy	66	162.50	1886	Boisbaudran
Einsteinium	Es	99	254*	1952	Ghiorso, et al.
Erbium	Er	68	167.26	1843	Mosander
Europium	Eu	63	151.96	1901	Demarcay
Fermium	Fm	100	257*	1953	Ghiorso, et al.
Fluorine	F	9	18.9984	1771	Scheele
Francium	Fr	87	223*	1939	Perey
Gadolinium	Gd	64	157.25	1886	Marignac
Gallium	Ga	31	69.72	1875	Boisbaudran
Germanium	Ge	32	72.59	1886	Winkler
Gold	Au	79	196.967	B.C.	
Hafnium	Hf	72	178.49	1923	Coster, Hevesy
Hahnium	Ha	105	262*	1970	Ghiorso, et al.
Helium	He	2	4.0026	1868	Janssen, Lockyer
Holmium	Ho	67	164.930	1878	Soret, Delafontaine
Hydrogen	H	1	1.00797a	1766	Cavendish
Indium	In	49	114.82	1863	Reich, Richter
Iodine	I	53	126.9044	1811	Courtois
Iridium	Ir	77	192.2	1804	Tennant
Iron	Fe	26	55.847b	B.C.	
Krypton	Kr	36	83.80	1898	Ramsay, Travers
Lanthanum	La	57	138.91	1839	Mosander
Lawrencium	Lr	103	262*	1961	Ghiorso, T. Sikkeland, A.E. Larsh, and R.M. Latimer
Lead	Pb	82	207.19	B.C.	
Lithium	Li	3	6.939	1817	Arfvedson
Lutetium	Lu	71	174.97	1907	Welsbach, Urbain
Magnesium	Mg	12	24.312	1829	Bussy
Manganese	Mn	25	54.9380	1774	Gahn
Mendelevium	Md	101	258*	1955	Ghiorso, et al.
Mercury	Hg	80	200.59	B.C.	
Molybdenum	Mo	42	95.94	1782	Hjelm
Neodymium	Nd	60	144.24	1885	Welsbach
Neon	Ne	10	20.183	1898	Ramsay, Travers
Neptunium	Np	93	237*	1940	McMillan, Abelson
Nickel	Ni	28	58.71	1751	Cronstedt
Niobium[1]	Nb	41	92.906	1801	Hatchett
Nitrogen	N	7	14.0067	1772	Rutherford
Nobelium	No	102	259*	1958	Ghiorso, et al.
Osmium	Os	76	190.2	1804	Tennant
Oxygen	O	8	15.9994a	1774	Priestley, Scheele
Palladium	Pd	46	106.4	1803	Wollaston
Phosphorus	P	15	30.9738	1669	Brand
Platinum	Pt	78	195.09	1735	Ulloa
Plutonium	Pu	94	242**	1940	Seaborg, et al.
Polonium	Po	84	210**	1898	P. and M. Curie
Potassium	K	19	39.102	1807	Davy
Praseodymium	Pr	59	140.907	1885	Welsbach
Promethium	Pm	61	147**	1945	Glendenin, Marinsky, Coryell
Protactinium	Pa	91	231*	1917	Hahn, Meitner
Radium	Ra	88	226*	1898	P. & M. Curie, Bemont
Radon	Rn	86	222*	1900	Dorn
Rhenium	Re	75	186.2	1925	Noddack, Tacke, Berg
Rhodium	Rh	45	102.905	1803	Wollaston

Chemical element	Symbol	Atomic number	Atomic weight	Year discov.	Discoverer
Rubidium	Rb	37	85.47	1861	Bunsen, Kirchhoff
Ruthenium	Ru	44	101.07	1845	Klaus
Rutherfordium	Rf	104	261*	1969	Ghiorso, et al.
Samarium	Sm	62	150.35	1879	Boisbaudran
Scandium	Sc	21	44.956	1879	Nilson
Selenium	Se	34	78.96	1817	Berzelius
Silicon	Si	14	28.086a	1823	Berzelius
Silver	Ag	47	107.868b	B.C.	
Sodium	Na	11	22.9898	1807	Davy
Strontium	Sr	38	87.62	1790	Crawford
Sulfur	S.	16	32.064a	B.C.	
Tantalum	Ta	73	180.948	1802	Ekeberg
Technetium	Tc	43	99**	1937	Perrier and Segre
Tellurium	Te	52	127.60	1782	Von Reichenstein
Terbium	Tb	65	158.924	1843	Mosander
Thallium	Tl	81	204.37	1861	Crookes
Thorium	Th	90	232.038	1828	Berzelius
Thulium	Tm.	69	168.934	1879	Cleve
Tin	Sn	50	118.69	B.C.	
Titanium	Ti	22	47.90	1791	Gregor
Tungsten (Wolfram)	W	74	183.85	1783	d'Elhujar
Uranium	U.	92	238.03	1789	Klaproth
Vanadium	V.	23	50.942	1830	Sefstrom
Xenon	Xe	54	131.30	1898	Ramsay, Travers
Ytterbium	Yb	70	173.04	1878	Marignac
Yttrium	Y.	39	88.905	1794	Gadolin
Zinc	Zn	30	65.37	B.C.	
Zirconium	Zr	40	91.22	1789	Klaproth

(1) Formerly Columbium. (a) Atomic weights so designated are known to be variable because of natural variations in isotopic composition. The observed ranges are: hydrogen±0.0001; boron±0.003; carbon±0.005; oxygen±0.0001; silicon±0.001; sulfur±0.003. (b) Atomic weights so designated are believed to have the following experimental uncertainties: chlorine±0.001; chromium±0.001; iron±0.003; bromine±0.001; silver±0.001; copper±0.001.

Density of Gases and Vapors
at 0°C and 760 mmHg
Source: National Bureau of Standards (kilograms per cubic meter)

Gas	Wgt.	Gas	Wgt.	Gas	Wgt.
Acetylene	1.171	Ethylene	1.260	Methyl fluoride	1.545
Air	1.293	Fluorine	1.696	Mono methylamine	1.38
Ammonia	.759	Helium	.178	Neon	.900
Argon	1.784	Hydrogen	.090	Nitric oxide	1.341
Arsene	3.48	Hydrogen bromide	3.50	Nitrogen	1.250
Butane-iso.	2.60	Hydrogen chloride	1.639	Nitrosyl chloride	2.99
Butane-n	2.519	Hydrogen iodide	5.724	Nitrous oxide	1.997
Carbon dioxide	1.977	Hydrogen selenide	3.66	Oxygen	1.429
Carbon monoxide	1.250	Hydrogen sulfide	1.539	Phosphine	1.48
Carbon oxysulfide	2.72	Krypton	3.745	Propane	2.020
Chlorine	3.214	Methane	.717	Silicon tetrafluoride	4.67
Chlorine monoxide	3.89	Methyl chloride	2.25	Sulfur dioxide	2.927
Ethane	1.356	Methyl ether	2.091	Xenon	5.897

Inventions and Discoveries

Invention	Date	Inventor	Nation.	Invention	Date	Inventor	Nation.
Adding machine	1642	Pascal	French	Babbitt metal	1839	Babbitt	U.S.
Adding machine	1885	Burroughs	U.S.	Bakelite	1907	Baekeland	Belg., U.S.
Addressograph	1892	Rotheim	Norwegian	Balloon	1783	Montgolfier	French
Aerosol spray	1926	Goodhue	U.S.	Barometer	1643	Torricelli	Italian
Air brake	1868	Westinghouse	U.S.	Basketball	1891	Naismith	Canadian
Air conditioning	1911	Carrier	U.S.	Bicycle, modern	1885	Starley	English
Air pump	1654	Guericke	German	Bifocal lens	1780	Franklin	U.S.
Airplane, automatic pilot	1912	Sperry	U.S.	Block signals, railway	1867	Hall	U.S.
Airplane, experimental	1896	Langley	U.S.	Bomb, depth	1916	Tait	U.S.
Airplane jet engine	1939	Ohain	German	Bottle machine	1895	Owens	U.S.
Airplane with motor	1903	Wright bros.	U.S.	Braille printing	1829	Braille	French
Airplane, hydro.	1911	Curtiss	U.S.	Burner, gas	1855	Bunsen	German
Airship	1852	Giffard	French				
Airship, rigid dirigible.	1900	Zeppelin	German				
Apple, McIntosh	1811	McIntosh	Canadian				
Arc welder	1919	Thomson	U.S.	Calculating machine	1833	Babbage	English
Autogyro	1920	de la Cierva	Spanish	Camera—see also Photography			
Automobile, differ-				Camera, Kodak	1888	Eastman, Walker.	U.S.
ential gear.	1885	Benz	German				
Automobile, electric	1892	Morrison	U.S.	Camera, Polaroid Land	1948	Land	U.S.
Automobile, exp'mtl	1864	Marcus	Austrian	Car coupler	1873	Janney	U.S.
Automobile, gasoline	1889	Daimler	German	Carburetor, gasoline	1893	Maybach	German
Automobile, gasoline	1892	Duryea	U.S.	Card record recorder	1894	Cooper	U.S.
Automobile magneto	1897	Bosch	German	Carding machine	1797	Whittemore	U.S.
Automobile muffler	...	Maxim, H.P.	U.S.	Carpet sweeper	1876	Bissell	U.S.
Automobile self-starter	1911	Kettering	U.S.	Cash register	1879	Ritty	U.S.

Invention	Date	Inventor	Nation.
Cathode ray tube	1878	Crookes	English
Cellophane	1908	Brandenberger	Swiss
Celluloid	1870	Hyatt	U.S.
Cement, Portland	1824	Aspdin	English
Chronometer	1761	Harrison	English
Circuit breaker	1925	Hilliard	U.S.
Clock, pendulum	1657	Huygens	Dutch
Coaxial cable system	1929	Affel, Espensched	U.S.
Coke oven	1893	Hoffman	Austrian
Compressed air rock drill	1871	Ingersoll	U.S.
Comptometer	1887	Felt	U.S.
Computer, automatic sequence	1944	Aiken et al	U.S.
Condenser microphone (telephone)	1916	Wente	U.S.
Corn, hybrid	1917	Jones	U.S.
Cotton gin	1793	Whitney	U.S.
Cream separator	1878	DeLaval	Swedish
Cultivator, disc	1878	Mallon	U.S.
Cystoscope	1878	Nitze	German
Diesel engine	1895	Diesel	German
Dynamite	1866	Nobel	Swedish
Dynamo, continuous current	1871	Gramme	Belgian
Dynamo, hydrogen cooled	1915	Schuler	U.S.
Electric battery	1800	Volta	Italian
Electric fan	1882	Wheeler	U.S.
Electrocardiograph	1903	Einthoven	Dutch
Electroencephalograph	1929	Berger	German
Electromagnet	1824	Sturgeon	English
Electron spectrometer	1944	Deutsch, Elliott, Evans	U.S.
Electron tube multigrid	1913	Langmuir	U.S.
Electroplating	1805	Brugnatelli	Italian
Electrostatic generator	1929	Van de Graaff	U.S.
Elevator brake	1852	Otis	U.S.
Elevator, push button	1922	Larson	U.S.
Engine, coal-gas 4-cycle	1876	Otto	German
Engine, compression ignition	1883	Daimler	German
Engine, electric ignition	1883	Benz	German
Engine, gas, compound	1926	Eickemeyer	U.S.
Engine, gasoline	1872	Brayton, Geo.	U.S.
Engine, gasoline	1889	Daimler	German
Engine, steam, piston	1705	Newcomen	English
Engine, steam, piston	1769	Watt	Scottish
Engraving, half-tone	1852	Talbot	English
Filament, tungsten	1913	Coolidge	U.S.
Fish, frozen	1928	Huntsman	Canadian
Flanged rail	1831	Stevens	U.S.
Flatiron, electric	1882	Seely	U.S.
Foghorn, steam-operated	1859	Foulis	Canadian
Furnace (for steel)	1858	Siemens	German
Galvanometer	1820	Sweigger	German
Gas discharge tube	1922	Hull	U.S.
Gas lighting	1792	Murdoch	Scottish
Gas mantle	1885	Welsbach	Austrian
Gas mask	1915	McPherson	Canadian
Gasoline (lead ethyl)	1922	Midgley	U.S.
Gasoline, cracked	1913	Burton	U.S.
Gasoline, high octane	1930	Ipatieff	Russian
Geiger counter	1913	Geiger	German
Glass, laminated safety	1909	Benedictus	French
Glider	1853	Cayley	English
Gun, breechloader	1811	Thornton	U.S.
Gun, Browning	1897	Browning	U.S.
Gun, magazine	1875	Hotchkiss	U.S.
Gun, silencer	1908	Maxim, H.P.	U.S.
Guncotton	1847	Schoenbein	German
Gyrocompass	1911	Sperry	U.S.
Gyroscope	1852	Foucault	French
Harvester, combine	1937	Carroll	Canadian
Harvester-thresher	1818	Lane	U.S.
Helicopter	1939	Sikorsky	U.S.
Hydrometer	1768	Baume	French
Ice-making machine	1851	Gorrie	U.S.

Invention	Date	Inventor	Nation.
Insulin	1922	Banting/Best	Canadian
Iron lung	1928	Drinker, Slaw.	U.S.
Kaleidoscope	1817	Brewster	Scottish
Kerosene oil	1853	Gesner	Canadian
Kinetoscope	1889	Edison	U.S.
Lacquer, nitrocellulose	1921	Flaherty	U.S.
Lamp, arc	1847	Staite	English
Lamp, incandescent	1879	Edison	U.S.
Lamp, incand., frosted	1924	Pipkin	U.S.
Lamp, incand., gas	1913	Langmuir	U.S.
Lamp, Klieg	1911	Kliegl, A.&J.	U.S.
Lamp, mercury vapor	1912	Hewitt	U.S.
Lamp, miner's safety	1816	Davy	English
Lamp, neon	1909	Claude	French
Lathe, turret	1845	Fitch	U.S.
Lens, achromatic	1758	Dollond	English
Lens, fused bifocal	1908	Borsch	German
Leydenjar (condenser)	1745	von Kleist	German
Lightning rod	1752	Franklin	U.S.
Linoleum	1860	Walton	U.S.
Linotype	1884	Mergenthaler	U.S.
Lock, cylinder	1851	Yale	U.S.
Locomotive, electric	1851	Vail	U.S.
Locomotive, exp'mtl	1802	Trevithick	English
Locomotive, exp'mtl	1812	Fenton et al.	English
Locomotive, exp'mtl	1813	Hedley	English
Locomotive, exp'mtl	1814	Stephenson	English
Locomotive practical	1829	Stephenson	English
Locomotive, 1st U.S.	1830	Cooper, P.	U.S.
Loom, power	1785	Cartwright	English
Loudspeaker, dynamic	1924	Rice, Kellogg	U.S.
Machine gun	1861	Gatling	U.S.
Machine gun, improved	1872	Hotchkiss	U.S.
Machine gun (Maxim)	1883	Maxim, H.S.	U.S., Eng.
Magnet, electro	1828	Henry	U.S.
Mantle, gas	1885	Welsbach	Austrian
Mason jar	1858	Mason, J.	U.S.
Match, friction	1827	John Walker	English
Mercerized textiles	1843	Mercer, J.	English
Meter, induction	1888	Shallenberg	U.S.
Metronome	1816	Malezel	German
Micrometer	1636	Gascoigne	English
Microphone	1877	Berliner	U.S.
Microscope, compound	1590	Janssen	Dutch
Microscope, electronic	1931	Knoll, Ruska	German
Microscope, field ion	1951	Mueller	German
Monitor, warship	1861	Ericsson	U.S.
Monotype	1887	Lanston	U.S.
Motor, AC	1892	Tesla	U.S.
Motor, DC	1837	Davenport	U.S.
Motor, induction	1887	Tesla	U.S.
Motorcycle	1885	Daimler	German
Movie machine	1894	Jenkins	U.S.
Movie, panoramic	1952	Waller	U.S.
Movie, talking	1927	Warner Bros.	U.S.
Mower, lawn	1831	Budding, Ferrabee	English
Mowing machine	1822	Bailey	U.S.
Neoprene	1930	Carothers	U.S.
Newsprint	1838	Fenerty	Canadian
Nylon synthetic	1930	Carothers	U.S.
Nylon	1937	Du Pont lab	U.S.
Oil cracking furnace	1891	Gavrilov	Russian
Oil extraction (from tar sands)	1920	Clark	Canadian
Oil filled power cable	1921	Emanueli	Italian
Oleomargarine	1869	Mege-Mouries	French
Ophthalmoscope	1851	Helmholtz	German
Pablum	1930	Brown/Drake/Tisdall	Canadian
Paint roller	1940	Breakey	Canadian
Paper machine	1809	Dickinson	U.S.
Parachute	1785	Blanchard	French
Pen, ballpoint	1888	Loud	U.S.
Pen, fountain	1884	Waterman	U.S.
Pen, steel	1780	Harrison	English
Pendulum	1583	Galileo	Italian
Percussion cap	1807	Forsythe	Scottish
Phonograph	1877	Edison	U.S.

Invention	Date	Inventor	Nation.
Photo, color	1892	Ives	U.S.
Photo film, celluloid	1893	Reichenbach	U.S.
Photo film, transparent	1884	Eastman, Goodwin	U.S.
Photoelectric cell	1895	Elster	German
Photographic paper	1835	Talbot	U.S.
Photography	1835	Talbot	English
Photography	1835	Daguerre	French
Photography	1816	Niepce	French
Photophone	1880	Bell	U.S.-Scot.
Phototelegraphy	1925	Bell Labs	U.S.
Piano	1709	Cristofori	Italian
Piano, player	1863	Fourneaux	French
Pin, safety	1849	Hunt	U.S.
Pistol (revolver)	1836	Colt	U.S.
Plow, cast iron	1785	Ransome	English
Plow, disc.	1896	Hardy	U.S.
Pneumatic hammer	1890	King	U.S.
Potatoes, instant mashed	1961	Asselbergs	Canadian
Powder, smokeless	1884	Vieille	French
Printing press, rotary	1845	Hoe	U.S.
Printing press, web	1865	Bullock	U.S.
Propeller, screw	1804	Stevens	U.S.
Propeller, screw	1837	Ericsson	Swedish
Propeller, variable pitch	1927	Turnball	Canadian
Punch card accounting	1889	Hollerith	U.S.
Radar	1940	Watson-Watt	Scottish
Radio amplifier	1906	De Forest	U.S.
Radio beacon	1928	Donovan	U.S.
Radio crystal oscillator	1918	Nicolson	U.S.
Radio receiver, cascade tuning	1913	Alexanderson	U.S.
Radio receiver, heterodyne	1913	Fessenden	U.S.
Radio transmitter triode modulation	1914	Alexanderson	U.S.
Radio tube, alternating current	1925	Samuel	Canadian
Radio tube-diode	1905	Fleming	English
Radio tube oscillator	1915	De Forest	U.S.
Radio tube triode	1906	De Forest	U.S.
Radio, signals	1895	Marconi	Italian
Radio, magnetic detector	1902	Marconi	Italian
Radio FM 2-path	1933	Armstrong	U.S.
Railway sleeping car	1857	Sharp	Canadian
Rayon	1883	Swan	English
Razor, electric	1928	Schick	U.S.
Razor, safety	1895	Gillette	U.S.
Reaper	1834	McCormick	U.S.
Record, cylinder	1887	Bell, Tainter	U.S.
Record, disc	1887	Berliner	U.S.
Record, long playing	1947	Goldenmark	U.S.
Record, wax cylinder	1888	Edison	U.S.
Refrigerants, low-boiling fluorine compound	1930	Midgely and co-workers	U.S.
Refrigerator car	1868	David	U.S.
Resin, synthetic	1931	Hill	English
Rifle, repeating	1860	Spencer	U.S.
Rocket engine	1926	Goddard	U.S.
Rubber, vulcanized	1839	Goodyear	U.S.
Saw, band	1808	Newberry	English
Saw, circular	1777	Miller	English
Searchlight, arc	1915	Sperry	U.S.
Sewing machine	1846	Howe	U.S.
Shoe-sewing machine	1860	McKay	U.S.
Shrapnel shell	1784	Shrapnel	English
Shuttle, flying	1733	Kay	English
Slide rule	1620	Oughtred	English
Snowmobile	1937	Bombadier	Canadian
Soap, hardwater	1928	Bertsch	German
Space Arm (Canadarm)	1981	Spar Aerospace	Canadian
Spectroscope	1859	Kirchoff, Bunsen	German
Spectroscope (mass)	1918	Dempster	U.S.
Spinning jenny	1767	Hargreaves	English
Spinning mule	1779	Crompton	English
Standard Time	1878	Fleming	Canadian
Steamboat, exp'mtl	1778	Jouffroy	French
Steamboat, exp'mtl	1785	Fitch	U.S.
Steamboat, exp'mtl	1787	Rumsey	U.S.
Steamboat, exp'mtl	1788	Miller	Scottish
Steamboat, exp'mtl	1803	Fulton	U.S.
Steamboat, exp'mtl	1804	Stevens	U.S.

Invention	Date	Inventor	Nation.
Steamboat, practical	1802	Symington	Scottish
Steamboat, practical	1807	Fulton	U.S.
Steam car	1770	Cugnot	French
Steam turbine	1884	Parsons	English
Steel (converter)	1856	Bessemer	English
Steel alloy	1891	Harvey	U.S.
Steel alloy, high-speed	1901	Taylor, White	U.S.
Steel, electric	1900	Heroult	French
Steel, manganese	1884	Hadfield	English
Steel, stainless	1916	Brearley	English
Stereoscope	1838	Wheatstone	English
Stethoscope	1819	Laennec	French
Stethoscope, binaural	1840	Cammann	U.S.
Stock ticker	1870	Edison	U.S.
Storage battery, rechargeable	1859	Plante	French
Stove, electric	1896	Hadaway	U.S.
Submarine	1891	Holland	U.S.
Submarine, even keel	1894	Lake	U.S.
Submarine, torpedo	1776	Bushnell	U.S.
Table hockey	1932	Munro	Canadian
Tank, military	1914	Swinton	English
Tape recorder, magnetic	1899	Poulsen	Danish
Telegraph, magnetic	1837	Morse	U.S.
Telegraph, quadruplex	1864	Edison	U.S.
Telegraph, railroad	1887	Woods	U.S.
Telegraph, wireless high frequency	1895	Marconi	Italian
Telephone	1876	Bell	U.S.-Scot.
Telephone amplifier	1912	De Forest	U.S.
Telephone, automatic	1891	Stowger	U.S.
Telephone, radio	1900	Poulsen, Fessenden	Danish
Telephone, radio	1906	De Forest	U.S.
Telephone, radio, l. d	1915	AT&T	U.S.
Telephone, recording	1898	Poulsen	Danish
Telephone, wireless	1899	Collins	U.S.
Telescope	1608	Lippershey	Neth.
Telescope	1609	Galileo	Italian
Telescope, astronomical	1611	Kepler	German
Teletype	1928	Morkrum, Kleinschmidt	U.S.
Television, iconoscope	1923	Zworykin	U.S.
Television, electronic	1927	Farnsworth	U.S.
Television, (mech. scanner)	1923	Baird	Scottish
Thermometer	1593	Galileo	Italian
Thermometer	1730	Reaumur	French
Thermometer, mercury	1714	Fahrenheit	German
Time recorder	1890	Bundy	U.S.
Time, self-regulator	1918	Bryce	U.S.
Tire, double-tube	1845	Thomson	Scottish
Tire, pneumatic	1888	Dunlop	Scottish
Toaster, automatic	1918	Strite	U.S.
Tool, pneumatic	1865	Law	English
Torpedo, marine	1804	Fulton	U.S.
Tractor, crawler	1904	Holt	U.S.
Transformer A.C.	1885	Stanley	U.S.
Transistor	1947	Shockley, Brattain, Bardeen	U.S.
Trolley car, electric	1884 -87	Van DePoele, Sprague	U.S.
Tungsten, ductile	1912	Coolidge	U.S.
Turbine, gas	1849	Bourdin	French
Turbine, hydraulic	1848	Francis	U.S.
Turbine, steam	1884	Parsons	English
Type, movable	1447	Gutenberg	German
Typewriter	1867	Sholes, Soule, Glidden	U.S.
Vacuum cleaner, electric	1907	Spangler	U.S.
Washer, electric	1901	Fisher	U.S.
Welding, atomic hydrogen	1924	Langmuir, Palmer	U.S.
Welding, electric	1877	Thomson	U.S.
Wind tunnel	1912	Eiffel	French
Wire, barbed	1874	Glidden	U.S.
Wire, barbed	1875	Haisn	U.S.
Wrench, double-acting	1913	Owen	U.S.
X-ray tube	1913	Coolidge	U.S.
Zipper	1891	Judson	U.S.

Associations and Societies

Names and addresses of labor, religious, sports and women's organizations are contained in their own sections elsewhere in this book.

Academy of Canadian Cinema and Television: 653 Yonge St., 2nd fl., Toronto, Ont. M4Y 1Z9

Action League of Physically Handicapped Adults: 627 Maitland St., London, Ont. N5Y 2V7

Air Cadets League of Canada: 424 Metcalfe St., Ste. 124, Ottawa, Ont. K2P 2C3

Air Transport Association of Canada: 99 Bank St., Ste. 747, Ottawa, Ont. K1P 6B9

Alcoholics Anonymous: 234 Eglinton Ave. E., Ste. 502, Toronto, Ont. M4R 1K5

Alcoholism and Drug Addiction Research Foundation: 33 Russell St., Toronto, Ont. M5S 2S1

Allergy Information Association: 65 Tromley Ave., Ste. 10, Islington, Ont. M9B 5Y7

Alzheimer Society of Canada: 1320 Yonge St., Ste. 302, Toronto, Ont. M4T 1X2

Amnesty International: 130 Slater St., Ste. 800, Ottawa, Ont. K1P 6E2

Amyotrophic Lateral Sclerosis Society of Canada: 250 Rogers Rd., Toronto, Ont. M6E 1R1

Animal Defence League: P.O. Box 3880, Stn. C, Ottawa, Ont. K1Y 4M5

Antique and Classic Boat Society Inc., The: P.O. Box 305, Islington, Ont. M9A 3X4

Antique and Classic Car Club of Canada—Maple Leaf Region: 7013 Cadiz Cr., Mississauga, Ont. L5N 1Y3

Aquatic Hall of Fame and Museum of Canada: 436 Main St., Winnipeg, Man. R3B 1B2

Army Cadet League of Canada: 4 Queen Elizabeth Dr., Ottawa, Ont. K2P 2H9

Army, Navy and Air Force Veterans Association: 275 Slater St., Ste. 1502, Ottawa, Ont. K1P 5H9

Arthritis Society, The: 250 Bloor St. E., Ste. 401, Toronto, Ont. M4W 3P2

Artists in Stained Glass: 367 Dundas St. W., Toronto, Ont. M5B 1Z9

Assembly of First Nations: 47 Clarence St., Ste. 300, Ottawa, Ont. K1N 9K1

Association of Student Councils: 171 College St., Toronto, Ont. M5T 1P7

Association of Universities and Colleges of Canada: 151 Slater St., Ste. 1200, Ottawa, Ont. K1P 5N1

Autism Society Canada: 20 College St., Ste. 2, Toronto, Ont. M5G 1K2

Automobile Protection Association: 292 St.-Joseph Blvd. W., Montreal, Que. H2V 2N7

B'Nai B'rith Canada: 15 Hove St., Downsview, Ont. M3H 4Y8

Barber Shop Harmony Society: 16222–114-A St., Edmonton, Alta. T5X 2M4

Benevolent and Protective Order of Elks of Canada: 438 Victoria Ave. E., Regina, Sask. S4N 0P6

Better Business Bureaus, Canadian Council of: 2180 Steeles Ave. W., Ste. 219, Concord, Ont. L4K 2Z5

Big Brothers of Canada: 3019 Harvester Rd., Burlington, Ont. L7N 3G4

Birthright: 777 Coxwell Ave., Toronto, Ont. M4C 3C6

Boy Scouts of Canada: P.O. Box 5151, Station F, Ottawa, Ont. K2C 3G7

Boys and Girls Clubs of Canada: 250 Consumers Rd., Ste. 505, Willowdale, Ont. M2J 4V6

British Pensioners Association (Canada): 411 Clendenan Ave., Toronto, Ont. M6P 2X7

C.D. Howe Institute: 125 Adelaide St. E., Toronto, Ont. M5C 1L7

Canada Council, The: 99 Metcalfe St., P.O. Box 1047, Ottawa, Ont. K1P 5V8

Canada Student Exchange Program: 1117 St. Catherine St. W., Ste. 312, Montreal, Que. H3B 1H9

Canada World Youth: 2330 Notre-Dame O., 3e étage, Montreal, Que. H3J 1N4

Canada's Aviation Hall of Fame: 9797 Jasper Ave., P.O. Box 118, Edmonton, Alta. T5J 1N9

Canadian Abortion Rights Action League: 344 Bloor St. W., Ste. 306, Toronto, Ont. M5S 3A7

Canadian Academy of Bridge, The: 444 Yonge St., Toronto, Ont. M5B 2H4

Canadian Amateur Backgammon Association: 2070 Dugald Rd., Winnipeg, Man. R2C 3G7

Canadian Amateur Musicians: P.O. Box 353, Montreal, Que. H3Z 2T5

Canadian Amphibian and Reptile Conservation Society: 9 Mississauga Rd. N., Ste. 1, Mississauga, Ont. L5H 2H5

Canadian Association for Community Living: Kinsmen Bldg., York University Campus, 4700 Keele St., Ste. 311, Downsview, Ont. M3J 1P3

Canadian Association for Free Expression Inc.: 3232 Bloor St. W., Ste. 102, Toronto, Ont. M8X 1E4

Canadian Association for Narcolepsy: P.O. Box 223, Stn. S, Toronto, Ont. M5M 4L7

Canadian Association of Sexual Assault Centres: 77 E. 20th Ave., Vancouver, B.C. V5V 1L7

Canadian Association of the Deaf: 271 Spadina Rd., Ste. 311, Toronto, Ont. M5R 2V3

Canadian Astronomical Society: 5071 W. Saanich Rd., R.R. #5, Victoria, B.C. V8X 4M6

Canadian Authors Association, The: 121 Avenue Rd., Ste. 104, Toronto, Ont. M5R 2G3

Canadian Automobile Association: 1775 Courtwood Cr., Ottawa, Ont. K2C 3J2

Canadian Bankers' Association, The: 2 First Canadian Pl., P.O. Box 348, Toronto, Ont. M5X 1E1

Canadian Bar Association, The: 130 Albert St., Ste. 1700, Ottawa, Ont. K1P 5G4

Canadian Book Publishers' Council: 45 Charles St. E., 7th fl., Toronto, Ont. M4Y 1S2

Canadian Cancer Society: 77 Bloor St. W., Ste. 1702, Toronto, Ont. M5S 3A1

Canadian Cardiovascular Society: 360 Victoria Ave., Rm. 401, Westmount, Que. H3Z 2N4

Canadian Cat Association: 52 Dean St., Brampton, Ont. L6W 1M6

Canadian Centre for Arms Control and Disarmament: 151 Slater St., Ste. 710, Ottawa, Ont. K1P 5H3

Canadian Ceramic Society: 2175 Sheppard Ave. E., Ste. 110, Willowdale, Ont. M2J 1W8

Canadian Cerebral Palsy Association: 40 Dundas St. W., Ste. 222, P.O. Box 110, Toronto, Ont. M5G 2C2

Canadian Chamber of Commerce, The: 55 Metcalfe St., Ste. 1160, Ottawa, Ont. K1P 6N4

Canadian Chiropractic Association: 290 Lawrence Ave. W., 2nd fl., Toronto, Ont. M5M 1B3

Canadian Civil Liberties Association: 229 Yonge St., Ste. 403, Toronto, Ont. M5B 1N9

Canadian Coalition on Acid Rain, The: 112 St. Clair Ave. W., Ste. 401, Toronto, Ont. M4V 2Y3

Canadian Committee for Soviet Jewry: 1590 ave. Dr. Penfield, Montreal, Que. H3G 1C5

Canadian Construction Association: 85 Albert St., 2nd fl., Ottawa, Ont. K1P 6A4

Canadian Correspondence Chess Association: 4745 W. 6th Ave., Vancouver, B.C. V6T 1C4

Canadian Council of Better Business Bureaus: 2180 Steeles Ave. W., Ste. 219, Concord, Ont. L4K 2Z4

Canadian Council of Professional Engineers: 116 Albert St., Ste. 401, Ottawa, Ont. K1P 4G3

Canadian Council of War Veterans Associations Inc.: 16 Kingslake Rd., Willowdale, Ont. M2J 3C9

Canadian Country Vacations Association: P.O. Box 2580, Winnipeg, Man. R3B 4C3

Canadian Craft and Hobby Association: 3640-26th St., N.E., Calgary, Alta. T1Y 4T7

Canadian Credit Institute, The: P.O. Box 500, Station F, Toronto, Ont. M4Y 2L8

Canadian Cystic Fibrosis Foundation: 2221 Yonge St., Ste. 601, Toronto, Ont. M4S 2B4

Canadian Diabetes Association: 78 Bond St., Toronto, Ont. M5B 2J8

Canadian Direct Marketing Association: 1 Concord Gate, Ste. 607, Don Mills, Ont. M3C 3N6

Canadian Donkey and Mule Association: R.R.1, Bowden, Alta, T0M 0K0

Canadian Esperanto Association: 6358 de Bordeaux, Montreal, Que. H2G 2R8

Canadian Federation of Independent Business: 4141 Yonge St., Ste. 401, Willowdale, Ont. M2P 2A6

Canadian Federation of Students: 126 York St., Ste. 300, Ottawa, Ont. K1N 5T5

Canadian Film and Television Association: 663 Yonge St., Ste. 401, Toronto, Ont. M4Y 2A4

Canadian Forestry Association: 185 Somerset St. W., Ste. 203, Ottawa, Ont. K2P 0J2

Canadian Foundation for Children and the Law: 720 Spadina Ave., Ste. 105, Toronto, Ont. M5S 2T9

Canadian Foundation for Ileitis and Colitis: 21 St. Clair Ave. E., Ste. 301, Toronto, Ont. M4T 1L9

Canadian 4-H Council: 1690 Woodward Dr., Ste. 208, Ottawa, Ont. K2C 3R9

Canadian Gas Association: 55 Scarsdale Rd., Don Mills, Ont. M3B 2R3

Canadian Goat Society: P.O. Box 399, New Hamburg, Ont. N0B 2G0

Canadian Graphic Arts Institute: 19 Duncan St., Toronto, Ont. M5H 3H1

Canadian Hearing Society Foundation: 271 Spadina Rd., Toronto, Ont. M5R 2V3

Canadian Heart Foundation: One Nicholas St., Ste. 1200, Ottawa, Ont. K1N 7B7

* Canadian Hemophilia Society, The: 100 King St. W., Ste. 210, Hamilton, Ont. L8P 1A2

Canadian Historical Association, The: 395 Wellington St., Ottawa, Ont. K1A 0N3

Canadian Home and School and Parent-Teacher Federation Inc.: 323 Chapel St., Ottawa, Ont. K1N 7Z2

Canadian Home Builders' Association: 200 Elgin St., Ste. 502, Ottawa, Ont. K2P 1L5

Canadian Hospital Association: 17 York St., Ste. 100, Ottawa, Ont. K1N 9J6

Canadian Hostelling Association: 333 River Rd., Vanier, Ont. K1L 8H9

Canadian Human Rights Foundation: 1980 Sherbrooke St. W., Ste. 340, Montreal, Que. H3H 1E8

Canadian Hypnotherapy Association: 1538 Sherbrooke St. W., Ste. 710, Montreal, Que. H3G 1L5

Canadian Importers' Association Inc.: 210 Dundas St. W., Ste. 210, Toronto, Ont. M5G 2E8

Canadian Institute of Chartered Accountants: 150 Bloor St. W., Toronto, Ont. M5S 2Y2

Canadian Institute of International Affairs: 15 King's College Circle, Toronto, Ont. M5S 2V9

Canadian Institute of Management: 2175 Sheppard Ave. E., Ste. 110, Willowdale, Ont. M2J 1W8

Canadian Institute of Planners: 46 Elgin St., Ste. 30, Ottawa, Ont. K1P 5K6

Canadian International DX Radio Club: P.O. Box 61, 52152 Range Rd., Sherwood Park, Alta. T8G 1A5

Canadian Junior Chamber—Jaycees: 39 Leacock Way, Kanata, Ont. K2K 1T1

Canadian Kennel Club: 2150 Bloor St. W., Toronto, Ont. M6S 4V7

Canadian Library Association: 200 Elgin St., Ste. 602, Ottawa, Ont. K2P 1L5

Canadian Liver Foundation: 1320 Yonge St., Ste. 301, Toronto, Ont. M4T 1X2

Canadian Lung Association: 75 Albert St., Ste. 908, Ottawa, Ont. K1P 5E7

Canadian Manufacturers' Association, The: One Yonge St., 14th fl., Toronto, Ont. M5E 1J9

Canadian Medic-Alert Foundation Inc.: 293 Eglinton Ave. E., Toronto, Ont. M4P 2Z8

Canadian Medical Association: P.O. Box 8650, Ottawa, Ont. K1G 0G8

Canadian Mental Health Association: 2160 Yonge St., 3rd fl., Toronto, Ont. M4S 2Z3

Canadian Metric Association: P.O. Box 35, Fonthill, Ont. L0S 1E0

Canadian Motorcycle Association Inc.: P.O. Box 448, Stn. B, Hamilton, Ont. L8L 8C4

Canadian Museums Association: 280 Metcalfe St., Ste. 202, Ottawa, Ont. K2P 1R7

Canadian National Institute for the Blind, The: 1931 Bayview Ave., Toronto, Ont. M4G 3E8

Canadian Nature Federation: 453 Sussex Dr., Ottawa, Ont. K1N 6Z4

Canadian Nuclear Association: 111 Elizabeth St., 11th fl., Toronto, Ont. M5G 1P7

Canadian Numismatic Association, The: c/o Ross Irwin, P.O. Box 1263, Guelph, Ont. N1H 6N6

Canadian Nurses Association: 50 The Driveway, Ottawa, Ont. K2P 1E2

Canadian Olympic Association: Olympic House, Cité du Havre, Montreal, Que. H3C 3R4

Canadian Owners and Pilots Association: P.O. Box 734, Stn. B, Ottawa, Ont. K1P 5S4

Canadian Paediatric Society: Children's Hospital of Eastern Ontario, 401 Smyth Rd., Ottawa, Ont. K1H 8L1

Canadian Paraplegic Association: 520 Sutherland Dr., Toronto, Ont. M4G 3V9

Canadian Parents for French: 309 Cooper St., Ste. 210, Ottawa, Ont. K6P 0G5

Canadian Peace Congress: 300 Bathurst St., Toronto, Ont. M5T 2S3

Canadian Pensioners Concerned Incorporated: 51 Bond St., Toronto, Ont. M5B 1X1

Canadian Petroleum Association: 150-6th Ave., S.W., Ste. 3800, Calgary, Alta. T2P 3Y7

Canadian Pharmaceutical Association: 1785 Alta Vista Dr., 2nd fl., Ottawa, Ont. K1G 3Y6

Canadian Physiotherapy Association: 890 Yonge St., 9th fl., Toronto, Ont. M4W 3P4

Canadian Pony Society: P.O. Box 173, Okotoks, Alta. T0L 1T0

Canadian Power Squadrons: 26 Golden Gate Ct., Scarborough, Ont. M1P 3A5

Canadian Progress Club: 2395 Bayview Ave., Willowdale, Ont. M2L 1A2

Canadian Psoriasis Foundation: P.O. Box 5036, Armdale Stn., Halifax, N.S. B3L 4M6

Canadian Psychiatric Association: 225 Lisgar St., Ste. 103, Ottawa, Ont. K2P 0C6

Canadian Public Health Association: 1335 Carling Ave., Ste. 210, Ottawa, Ont. K1Z 8N8

Canadian Public Relations Society: 720-220 Laurier Ave. W., Ottawa, Ont. K1P 5Z9

Canadian Railroad Historical Association: P.O. Box 148, St. Constant, Que. J0L 1X0

Canadian Real Estate Association: 320 Queen St., Place de Ville, Tower A, Ste. 2100, Ottawa, Ont. K1R 5A3

Canadian Red Cross Society, The: 1800 Alta Vista Dr., Ottawa, Ont. K1G 4J5

Canadian Rheumatism Association: c/o The Arthritis Centre, 895 West 10th Ave., Vancouver, B.C. V5Z 1L7

Canadian Rose Society: 686 Pharmacy Ave., Scarborough, Ont. M1L 3H8

Canadian Save the Children Fund: 3080 Yonge St., Ste. 6020, Toronto, Ont. M4N 3P4

Canadian Schizophrenia Foundation: 7375 Kingsway, Burnaby, B.C. V3N 3B5

Canadian Sickle Cell Society: 1801 Eglinton Ave. W., Ste. 204A, Toronto, Ont. M6E 2H8

Canadian Society for the Prevention of Cruelty to Animals, The: 5215 rue Jean-Talon O., Montreal, Que. H4P 1X4

Canadian Standardbred Horse Society: 233 Evans Ave., Toronto, Ont. M8Z 1J6

Canadian Stroke Recovery Association: 170 The Donway W., Ste. 122A, Don Mills, Ont. M3C 2G3

Canadian Thoroughbred Horse Society: P.O. Box 172, Rexdale, Ont. M9W 5L1

Canadian Turtle Derby: P.O. Box 122, Boissevain, Man. R0K 0E0

Canadian Veterinary Medical Association: 339 Booth St., Ottawa, Ont. K1R 7K1

Canadian Warplane Heritage Inc.: P.O. Box 35, Mount Hope, Ont. L0R 1W0

Canadian Wild Horse Society: 3660-40th St. S.E., Salmon Arm, B.C. V1E 4M3

Canadian Wildlife Federation: 1673 Carling Ave., Ottawa, Ont. K2A 3Z1

Canadian Wolf Defenders Association: P.O. Box 3480, Stn. D, Edmonton, Alta. T5L 4J3

Canadians Concerned About Southern Africa (Toronto): 555 Bloor St. W., 3rd fl., Toronto, Ont. M5S 1Y6

Canadians for Decency: P.O. Box 637, Stn. B, Willowdale, Ont. M2K 2P9

Canadians for One Canada: 55 University Ave., Ste. 600, Toronto, Ont. M5J 2H7

CARE Canada: 1550 Carling Ave., P.O. Box 9000, Stn. T, Ottawa, Ont. K1G 4X6

Certified General Accountants Association of Canada: 1176 W. Georgia St., Ste. 740, Vancouver, B.C. V6E 4A2

Chess Federation of Canada, The: P.O. Box 7339, Ottawa, Ont. K1L 8E4

Child Find: 345 Lakeshore Rd. E., Ste. 314, Oakville, Ont. L6J 1J5

Clans and Scottish Societies of Canada: 3546 Autumn Harvest Dr., Mississauga, Ont. L4Y 3S1

College of Family Physicians of Canada, The: 4000 Leslie St., Willowdale, Ont. M2K 2R9

Commonwealth Parliamentary Association: Parliament Buildings, P.O. Box 950, Ottawa, Ont. K1A 0X2

Conference Board of Canada: 255 Smyth Rd., Ottawa, Ont. K1H 8M7

Consumers' Association of Canada: 49 Auriga Dr., Nepean, Ont. K2E 8A1

Couchiching Institute of Public Affairs: 2200 Lakeshore Blvd. W., Ste. 102, Toronto, Ont. M8V 1A4

CUSO: 135 Rideau St., Ottawa, Ont. K1N 9K7

Dairy Bureau of Canada: 20 Holly St., Ste. 400, Toronto, Ont. M4S 3B1

Ducks Unlimited Canada: 1190 Waverley St., Winnipeg, Man. R3T 2E2

Dying With Dignity: 175 St. Clair Ave. W., Toronto, Ont. M4V 1P7

Easter Seal Society: 24 Ferrand Dr., Don Mills, Ont. M3C 3N2

Electric Vehicle Association of Canada: 275 Slater St., Ste. 500, Ottawa, Ont. K1P 5H9

Empire Club of Canada: 100 Front St. W., Toronto, Ont. M5J 1E3

Energy Probe Research Foundation: 100 College St., Toronto, Ont. M5G 1L5

Epilepsy Canada: 2099 Alexandre DeSéve, Ste. 27, Montreal, Que. H2L 4K8

Farm Safety Association: 340 Woodlawn Rd. W., Ste. 22, Guelph, Ont. N1H 7K6

Fraser Institute, The: 626 Bute St., Vancouver, B.C. V6E 3M1

Girl Guides of Canada: 50 Merton St., Toronto, Ont. M4S 1A3

Greenpeace Foundation of Canada: 2623 W. 4th Ave., Vancouver, B.C. V6K 1P8

Heritage Canada Foundation: P.O. Box 1358, Station B, Ottawa, Ont. K1P 5R4

Huntington Society of Canada: P.O. Box 333, Cambridge, Ont. N1R 5T8

Information Technology Association of Canada: 211 Consumers Rd., Ste. 300, Willowdale, Ont. M2J 4G8

Institute for Research on Public Policy: 3771 Haro Rd., Victoria, B.C. V8P 5C3

Insurance Institute of Canada: 481 University Ave., Toronto, Ont. M5G 2E9

International Air Transport Association: 2000 Peel St., Montreal, Que. H3A 2R4

International Churchill Society: 20 Burbank Dr., Willowdale, Ont. M2K 1M8

International Civil Aviation Organization: 1000 Sherbrooke St. W., Montreal, Que. H3A 2R2

International Development and Refugee Foundation: 1521 Trinity Dr., Unit 16, Mississauga, Ont. L5T 1P6

International Save the Pun Foundation: P.O. Box 5040, Stn. A, Toronto, Ont. M5W 1N4

Inuit Tapirisat of Canada: 176 Gloucester St., 3rd fl., Ottawa, Ont. K2P 0A6

Inventors Association of Canada: P.O. Box 281, Swift Current, Sask. S9H 3V6

Investment Funds Institute of Canada, The: 70 Bond St., Ste. 400, Toronto, Ont. M5B 1X2

John Howard Society of Canada: 55 Parkdale Ave., Ottawa, Ont. K1Y 1E5

Juvenile Diabetes Foundation: 4632 Yonge St., Ste. 100, Willowdale, Ont. M2N 5M1

Kidney Foundation of Canada: 4060 Ste-Catherine St. W., Ste. 555, Montreal, Que. H3Z 2Z3

Kiwanis International: Casa Loma, 1 Austin Terrace, Toronto, Ont. M5R 1X8

Knights of Columbus: P.O. Drawer 1670, New Haven, C.T. 06507

Learning Disabilities Association of Canada: 323 Chapel St., Ste. 200, Ottawa, Ont. K1N 7Z2

Leprosy Mission Canada: 40 Wynford Dr., Ste. 216, Don Mills, Ont. M3C 1J5

Lions Club International: 6 Lansing Sq., Ste. 227, Willowdale, Ont. M2J 1T5

Loyal Orange Association: 94 Sheppard Ave. W., Willowdale, Ont. M2N 1M5

Lung Association, The: 573 King St. E., Ste. 201, Toronto, Ont. M5A 1M5

Mariposa Folk Foundation: Swansea Town Hall, 95 Livinia Ave., Toronto, Ont. M6S 3H9

Media Watch: 250-1820 Fir St., Vancouver, B.C. V6K 3B1

Métis National Council: 501-45th St. W., Ste. 5, Saskatoon, Sask. S7L 5Z9

Memorial Society Association of Canada: P.O. Box 96, Station A, Weston, Ont. M9N 3M6

Monarchist League of Canada, The: 2 Wedgewood Cr., Ottawa, Ont. K1B 4B4

Multiple Sclerosis Society of Canada: 250 Bloor St. E., Ste. 820, Toronto, Ont. M4W 3P9

Muscular Dystrophy Association of Canada: 150 Eglinton Ave. E., Ste. 400, Toronto, Ont. M4P 1E8

National Darts Federation of Canada: 362 The East Mall, Ste. 1610, Islington, Ont. M9B 6C4

National Research Council of Canada: Montreal Rd., Building M-58, Ottawa, Ont. K1A 0R6

Nature Conservancy of Canada: 794A Broadview Ave., Toronto, Ont. M4K 2P7

Navy League of Canada: 4 Queen Elizabeth Dr., Ste. 409, Ottawa, Ont. K2P 2H9

Non-Smokers Rights Association: 344 Bloor St. W., Ste. 308, Toronto, Ont. M5S 1W9

Olympic Trust of Canada: 2 St. Clair Ave. W., Ste. 606, Toronto, Ont. M4V 1L5

One Parent Families Association of Canada: 6979 Yonge St., Ste. 203, Willowdale, Ont. M2M 3X9

Organ Donors Canada: 5326 Ada Blvd., Edmonton, Alta. T5W 4N7

Outdoors Unlittered: 455 Granville St., Ste. 502, Vancouver, B.C. V6C 1V2

Oxfam Canada: 251 Laurier Ave. W., Ste. 301, Ottawa, Ont. K1P 5J6

Palliative Care Foundation: 33 Prince Arthur Ave., Toronto, Ont. M5R 1B2

Parental Stress Services—Parents Anonymous: P.O. Box 843, Burlington, Ont. L7R 3X2

Parents Against Drugs: 70 Maxome Ave., Willowdale, Ont. M2M 3K1

Parents Without Partners, Inc.: 205 Yonge St., Ste. 13, Toronto, Ont. M5B 1N2

Parkinson Foundation of Canada: 55 Bloor St. W., Ste. 232, Toronto, Ont. M4W 1A5

PARTICIPaction: 40 Dundas St. W., P.O. Box 64, Ste. 220, Toronto, Ont. M5G 2C2

Patients Rights Association: 40 Homewood Ave., Ste. 315, Toronto, Ont. M4Y 2K2

People Against Impaired Drivers: P.O. Box 7244, Stn M, Edmonton, Alta. T5E 6C8

Pioneer Clubs Canada, Inc.: 2320 Fairview Ave., P.O. Box 447, Burlington, Ont. L7R 3Y3

Planetary Association for Clean Energy, Inc.: 191 Promenade du Portage, Ste. 600, Hull, Que. J8X 2K6

Planned Parenthood Federation of Canada: 323 Chapel St., 3rd fl., Ottawa, Ont. K1N 7Z2

Pollution Probe Foundation, The: 12 Madison Ave., Toronto, Ont. M5R 2S1

Reye's Syndrome Foundation of Canada: c/o Children's Hospital of Western Ontario, Dept. of Pediatrics, P.O. Box 5375, London, Ont. N6A 4G5

Right to Life Association: 144A Yonge St., Toronto, Ont. M5C 1X6

Royal Life Saving Society of Canada, The: 191 Church St., Toronto, Ont. M5B 1Y7

Royal Philatelic Society, The: P.O. Box 5320, Stn. F, Ottawa, Ont. K2C 3J1

Simplified Speling Sosiety of Canada: 22 Montrose Ave., Toronto, Ont. M6J 2T7

St. John Ambulance: 312 Laurier Ave. E., Ottawa, Ont. K1N 8V4

Society of St. Vincent de Paul: 835 Brown Ave., Quebec, Que. G1S 4S1

Standards Council of Canada: 350 Sparks St., Ste. 1200, Ottawa, Ont. K1P 6N7

Telephone Pioneers of America: 483 Bay St., 6th fl., S. Tower, Toronto, Ont. M5G 2E1

Television Bureau of Canada Inc.: 890 Yonge St., Ste. 700, Toronto, Ont. M4W 3P4

Thyroid Foundation of Canada: P.O. Box 1643, Kingston, Ont. K7L 5C8

Trust Companies Association of Canada: 50 O'Connor St., Ste. 720, Ottawa, Ont. K1P 6L2

United Nations Association in Canada: 63 Sparks St., Ste. 808, Ottawa, Ont. K1P 5A6

United Way: 150 Kent St., Ste. 600, Ottawa, Ont. K1P 5P4

Victorian Order of Nurses for Canada: 5 Blackburn Ave., Ottawa, Ont. K1N 8A2

Vintage Car Club of Canada: 2618 Patricia Ave., Port Coquitlam, B.C. V3B 2H4

War Amputations of Canada, The: 2827 Riverside Dr., Ottawa, Ont. K1V 0C4

World Federalists of Canada: 46 Elgin St., Ste. 32, Ottawa, Ont. K1P 5K6

World Literacy of Canada: 692 Coxwell Ave., Toronto, Ont. M4C 3B6

World Vision Canada: 6630 Turner Valley Rd., Mississauga, Ont. L5N 2S4

World Wildlife Fund Canada: 60 St. Clair Ave. E., Ste. 201, Toronto, Ont. M4T 1N5

How to Burglar-Proof Your Home and Car

Your Home

- Don't let mail or newspapers collect outside.
- Don't leave windows unlocked.
- Make sure shrubbery around the house is trimmed back from windows and doors.
- Install deadbolt or interlocking bolt rim locks on all doors and insert a metal rod, or a suitable length of wooden dowel or 2 × 4, along the inside track of a sliding door.
- Install an automatic timer to turn lights on during the evening.
- Leave drapes parted.
- Leave a car parked in the driveway or ask a neighbor to park there.
- Make sure the grass is cut during the summer and snow is shovelled during the winter.
- Lock the garage door or park close enough to prevent the door from being opened.
- Never "hide" a key outside.

- Chain and padlock the gas barbeque.
- Don't leave cash or credit cards within sight, and always have the numbers of the cards recorded for reference.
- Don't leave ladders outside, unless secured.
- Consider installing metal window bars over basement windows.
- Alert neighbors to your absence and ask them to keep an eye on your property.

Your Car

- Never leave your car unattended with the engine running.
- Lock the car at all times.
- Lock all valuables in the trunk, out of sight.
- Don't leave credit cards or cash in the vehicle.
- Don't leave the ownership papers in the car.
- Don't hide a spare key under the hood.
- Drive with the doors locked.

Poison-Proofing Your Home

The average household contains as many as 250 poisons and, each year in Canada, hundreds of fatalities are caused by poisoning. There are 2 key steps to poison-proofing your home: identify the common household poisons and then store these potentially-dangerous products out of the reach of children.

Common Household Poisons

- Cleaners and bleaches—including detergents, ammonia, naphtha, oven cleaner and bleach
- Solvents—including paint remover, kerosene and turpentine
- Polishes and waxes—including paint, car and furniture wax, silver polish
- Herbicides, insecticides and insect repellants
- Mercury (from a thermometer)
- Cosmetics and toiletries—including after shave, bubble bath, nail polish, hair lotions
- Drugs and medicines—including both prescription and non-prescription drugs, such as vitamins, ASA, cough medicines and cold medications
- House plants, ornamental plants and flower and vegetable garden plants

How to Store Them:

- Keep products in their original containers and be certain all containers are clearly labelled.

- Prescription drugs should be stored out of the reach of children and in containers with safety lids.
- Household cleaners should be stored on high shelves, not underneath the sink.
- Return medication or cleaning products to a safe place after using them.
- Keep all poisonous liquids and solids out of the reach of children; if possible, install child-proof locking cabinets.
- Never call medicine "candy"; it gives children a distorted idea.
- Warn children at an early age not to eat household plants or wild plants and berries.
- Never keep food and household cleaners next to each other.
- Don't continue to store old products around the house.
- Don't leave a purse or handbag where a child can reach it since there are often prescription drugs inside.
- Should poisoning occur, identify the suspected poison and immediately seek medical help. Many areas have poison information centres. Never attempt to induce vomiting without medical advice.

Women in Canada

The Women's Movement in Canada

The organized women's movement in Canada developed in the late nineteenth century when women began working together to gain voting rights, access to higher education and equality in the workplace.

In the nineteenth century, women property owners were able to vote in many municipal elections but the male establishment strongly resisted wider suffrage. Opponents of equal voting rights claimed that women, by nature, were unsuited to vote or to hold political office.

The Dominion Women's Enfranchisement Association was formed in 1889 to promote the cause of female voting rights in Canada. In the 1890s, the Women's Christian Temperance Union called for female voting as a means to gain its primary goal, the prohibition of alcohol. Other groups, such as the National Council of Women, the Political Equality League and the National Union of Women's Suffrage Societies, added their voices to the call for female voting rights.

The first breakthroughs took place in western Canada, where Nellie McClung's effective campaign led to Manitoba becoming the first province to grant women the right to vote and hold office in January 1916. By 1918, Saskatchewan, Alberta, British Columbia, Ontario and Nova Scotia had followed.

The focus of the campaign then shifted to the federal franchise. Women serving as nurses and ambulance drivers overseas and working in essential industries at home were making important contributions to Canada's effort in the First World War (1914-18). The federal government first recognized this contribution by giving female members of the armed forces and female relatives of soldiers the right to vote in the election of 1917. The following year, all women were given the same right. By 1920, federal legislation had made these rights permanent and also had made women eligible to sit in the House of Commons.

In the post-war years, more provinces extended the franchise to women. New Brunswick granted women the right to vote in provincial elections in 1919; but the corresponding right to hold office was not granted until 1934. Prince Edward Island in 1922 enacted legislation to allow women both to vote and to hold provincial office. In 1925, the then-separate colony of Newfoundland extended voting and office-holding rights to its female citizens. Only Quebec, with its conservative traditions, resisted this reform beyond the 1920s. But after a concerted campaign led by Thérèse Casgrain, the women of Quebec finally won the right to vote and hold provincial office in 1940.

Soon after their suffrage victories, women began to fill public offices. Louise McKinney, who won a seat in the Alberta legislature in 1917, became the first Canadian woman (and the first woman anywhere in the British Commonwealth) to hold such an office. In 1921, Agnes MacPhail became the first Canadian woman elected to the House of Commons.

Women also began to fill appointed positions. Emily Murphy became the first woman magistrate in 1916 and Helen MacGill the first judge in 1917. But these achievements did not give women complete legal equality. Lawyers challenged the right of women to hold office because they were not "persons" as defined by the British North America Act. Emily Murphy and 4 other prominent Alberta women (called "the Alberta Five") petitioned the Supreme Court of Canada to rule on this matter. In 1928, the Supreme Court agreed that women were not "persons" in this legal sense. Next, the Alberta Five appealed the case to the British Privy Council which ruled, in 1929, that women were indeed persons and thus, qualified to hold office. This decision paved the way for the appointment in 1931 of Canada's first woman senator, Cairine Wilson.

There have been a number of milestones in Canadian women's involvement in politics in the years since the 1920s. Thérèse Casgrain was the first woman to lead a political party (the Quebec CCF 1951-57). Ellen Fairclough became Canada's first woman cabinet minister in 1957. In 1982, Iona Campagnolo became the first woman president of a federal political party (the Liberals). Jeanne Sauvé was the first female speaker of the House of Commons before being appointed Canada's first female governor-general. In 1984, more women (28) were elected to the House of Commons than in any previous election.

While women fought for political equality, they also struggled for educational rights and equality in the workplace. The first woman graduated from a Canadian university (Mount Allison) in 1875, and other universities opened their doors to women students over the next 20 years. By the end of the 1920s, about 25% of university students were women. Access to university education gradually opened up occupations previously reserved for men. Women began to practise medicine and law before the turn of the century and accountancy by the 1920s. By 1930, there were enough business and professional organizations for women to support an umbrella organization, the Canadian Federation of Business and Professional Women's Clubs.

Outside of the professions, many more women entered the workforce. Frequently they took jobs that were traditionally considered "women's work". By 1921, about two-thirds of women in the labor force worked in clerical jobs, as domestics, or as teachers and nurses. Most of these female workers were unmarried, due to the prevailing view of the husband as breadwinner and the wife as housemaker. This situation changed during the labor shortage of the Second World War (1939-45). Women, both married and single, worked in a wide range of jobs so that, by 1945, 33% of Canadian women held jobs.

Over the last 40 years, the number of working women has risen dramatically so that females now make up more than 40% of the workforce. But despite these rising numbers, women still tend to earn less than men. In the first years of this century, the average woman's wage was about 55% of a man's. Even in the same jobs, women were paid substantially less than male co-workers who were viewed as breadwinners for the family. In response, the National Council of Women demanded in 1907 "equal pay for equal work". In 1981 the average female wage was still only 64% of that paid the average male worker. Today, the National Action Committee on the Status of Women and many other contemporary womens' groups are campaigning for pay equity, equal pay for work of equal value.

In June 1987, Ontario passed North America's first pay equity legislation, requiring employers to end wage discrimination between men and women doing different jobs deemed to be of comparable value to the employer.

Canadian Women's Firsts ·

Name	First Canadian woman to:	Year	Comment
Bell, Marilyn	swim across L. Ontario	1954	1st person to complete the crossing
Bird, Florence	head a royal commission	1967	The Royal Commission on the Status of Women
Bondar, Roberta	become an astronaut	1983	one of 6 scientists chosen as Canada's original astronauts

Name	First Canadian woman to:	Year	Comment
Bourgeoys, Mother Marguerite	become a saint	1982	born in France 1620; sailed for Canada 1657
Brooke, Francis	write a novel	1769	the novel was *The History of Emily Montegue*
Bryant, Alys	pilot an aircraft in Canada	1913	
Campagnolo, Iona	become president of the Liberal Party of Canada	1982	
Casgrain, Thérèse	lead, provincially, a major political party	1951	the party was the Quebec Co-operative Commonwealth Federation, 1951-57
Crehan, Mercy Ellen	become a chartered accountant	1921	
Dobson, Melanie	become a Rhodes Scholar	1977	amongst the 1st female Rhodes Scholars in the world, she was one of 4 Canadian women: Ellen Gillespie, Mary Sheppard, and Jessie Sloan
Fairclough, Ellen	become a federal cabinet minister	1957	her appointment was as secretary of state
Ferguson, Muriel	become speaker of the Senate	1972	
Glube, Constance	be appointed a chief justice	1982	in Nova Scotia's trial division
Hartman, Grace	lead a major national union	1975	as President, The Canadian Union of Public Employees, 1975-83
Hellstrom, Sheila A.	become a general in the Canadian Armed Forces	1987	as a one-star brigadier-general
Heggtveit, Anne	win a gold medal in Olympic skiing	1960	this was the 1st gold gained by a Canadian
Hubou, Marie	become a nurse	1617	
Hogg, Helen Battles	receive the Klumpke-Roberts Award	1983	in recognition of her contribution to astronomy
Jewett, Pauline	become president of a university	1974	at Simon Fraser U.
Keith, Vicki	swim across L. Ontario twice	1987	1st person to complete the two-way crossing
Lockhart, Grace A.	graduate from university	1875	received B.Sc. from Mount Allison U.
MacGill, Helen G.	become a judge	1917	appointed to the juvenile court
MacPhail, Agnes	be elected to the House of Commons	1921	an Independent who represented the constituency of Grey-Bruce in Ont.
Maillet, Antonine	win the Prix Goncourt	1979	for her novel *Pelagie-la-Charrette*
McGibbon, Pauline	be appointed a lieutenant-governor	1974	in Ont.; also the 1st female lieutenant-governor in the British Commonwealth
McKinney, Louise	become a member of a legislature in the British Commonwealth	1917	elected to the Alberta Legislature
Meagher, Blanche	become an ambassador	1958	to Israel, 1958-61
Martin, Clara Brett	become a lawyer	1897	admitted to the bar of Ont.
Milner, Brenda	receive the Izaak Walton Killam prize	1983	for her work in neuropsychology at the Montreal Neurological Institute
Murphy, Emily Gowan	become a magistrate in the British Empire	1916	appointed police magistrate, Edmonton; with Henrietta Edwards, Louise McKinney, Nellie McClung and I. Parlby carried the Persons Case to the British Privy Council which ruled in 1929 that women were persons
Nicholas, Cindy	complete a 2-way swim across the English Channel	1977	1st woman in the world to do so
Pickford, Mary	win an Academy Award	1928-29	for her role in Coquette
Salverson, Laura	receive a Governor General's Literary Award	1937	for her novel *The Dark Weaver*
Sauvé, Jeanne	become Governor General of Canada	1984	was also 1st woman speaker of the House of Commons, 1980
Saver, Marion	win the title of Miss Canada	1946	as Miss Stayner, Ont.
Stowe, Emily	become a doctor	1880	began practising medicine in 1867
Smith, Cecil	compete at the Olympic Games	1924	in Chamonix, she placed 6th in women's figure skating
Whitton, Charlotte	become mayor of a large city	1951	as mayor of Ottawa, Ont.
Wilson, Alice	be elected a fellow of the Royal Society of Canada	1937	for her work in paleontology
Wilson, Bertha	be appointed to the Supreme Court of Canada	1982	from Ont. Court of Appeal
Wilson, Cairine	become a senator	1930	in 1949, she became Canada's first woman delegate to the U.N.
Wood, Sharon	scale the summit of Mt. Everest	1986	

Selected Canadian Women's Organizations

(with membership of 500 or more)

Source: Canadian World Almanac Survey
(date founded in parentheses)

B'nai B'rith Women of Canada (1964)—638A Sheppard Ave. W., Ste. 210, Downsview, Ont. M3H 2S1, (416) 630-9313. Pres. Ruth Rose; 3 500 members. Goals: a Jewish women's organization to provide service, develop leadership, engender personal growth and support B'nai B'rith women's agencies.

Canadian Advisory Council on the Status of Women[1] (1973)—P.O. Box 1541, Stn. B, Ottawa, Ont. K1P 5R5, (613) 992-4975. Pres. Sylvia Gold. Goals: to advise the federal government on issues of interest and concern to women and to inform and educate the public on these issues.

Canadian Association of Elizabeth Fry Societies (1969)—251 Bank St., Ste. 600, Ottawa, Ont. K2P 1X3, (613) 238-2422. Pres. Felicity Hawthorn; 19 member societies. Goals: to work with, and on behalf of, women involved with the justice system, particularly women in conflict with the law; to encourage reform and develop public awareness of justice issues affecting women.

Canadian Federation of Business and Professional Women's Clubs (1930)—56 Sparks St., Ste. 308, Ottawa, Ont. K1P 5A9, (613) 234-7619. Pres. Gertrude Demecha; 4 000 members. Goals: to promote the interests of gainfully-employed women, to eliminate discrimination and to improve their professional status.

Canadian Federation of University Women (1919)—55 Parkdale Ave., Ste. 105, Ottawa, Ont. K1Y 1E5, (613) 722-8732. Pres. Linda Souter; 12 000 members. Goals: to provide an opportunity for educated women to keep up with developments in their own and other fields of endeavor.

Canadian Research Institute for the Advancement of Women (1976)—151 Slater St., Ste. 408, Ottawa, Ont. K1P 5H3, (613) 563-0681. Pres. Marilyn Porter, 1 025 members. Goals: to encourage, co-ordinate and disseminate research into women's experience.

Catholic Women's League of Canada (1921)—3081 Ness Ave., Winnipeg, Man. R2Y 2G3, (204) 885-4856. Pres. Evelyn Wryzykowski; 130 000 members. Goals: to promote the teachings of the Catholic Church; to exemplify the Christian ideal in family life; to protect the sanctity of life; to enhance the role of women; to recognize the dignity of people everywhere; to uphold Christian education and values; to contribute to the understanding and growth of religious freedom, social justice, peace and harmony.

Federated Women's Institutes of Canada (1919)—251 Bank St., Ste. 606, Ottawa, Ont. K2P 1X3, (613) 234-1090. Pres. Mrs. Jennie McInnes; 40 000 members. Goals: to provide opportunities for the personal development of women in agriculture, citizenship, culture, education and health.

Federation of Junior Leagues of Canada (1972)—610-235 Keith Road, West Vancouver, B.C. V7T 1L5, (604) 926-0094. Administrative Co-Chair Heather D. Farrell; 3 000 members. Goals: to improve the community through effective action and leadership of trained volunteers and to promote voluntarism.

Hadassah-Wizo Organization of Canada (1917)—1310 Greene Ave., Ste. 900, Montreal, Que. H3Z 2B8, (514) 937-9431. Pres. Naomi Frankenburg; 17 000 members. Goals: to assist indigent women and children in schools in Israel and to maintain health, social and welfare projects and institutions.

IODE National Chapter of Canada (1900)—40 Orchard View Blvd., #254, Toronto, Ont. M4R 1B9, (416) 487-4416. Pres. Mrs. A.R. Dick; 14 000 members. Goals: to promote education, particularly the study of history and current issues; to work for the relief of those in poverty or distress irrespective of race, color, creed or sex; to assist in the progress of the arts; to give donations for charitable purposes.

Ladies Orange Benevolent Association of Canada—101-6831 Arcola St., Burnaby, B.C. V5E 1H4, (604) 526-6847. Pres. Mrs. Edith Halliday. Goals: to unite Protestant women, pre-

serve and develop Protestantism, maintain the laws and constitution of Canada and practise charitable works.

MATCH International Centre (1976)—1102-200 Elgin St., Ottawa, Ont. K2P 1L5, (613) 238-1312. Pres. Macha MacKay; 3 000 members. Goals: to support progressive and innovative projects in Latin America, Africa, Asia and the Caribbean that involve women organizing for better health care, improved working conditions in factories and as domestics, more child care options, access to literacy, and to oppose violence against women; to establish the link between the similarities of women's experiences globally while encouraging an appreciation of the way women's lives differ because of factors such as class, race, nationality and ethnicity.

Na'amat Canada (1925)—7005 Kildare Rd., Ste. 6, Montreal, Que. H4W 1C1, (514) 488-0792. Pres. Tillie Margolis; 4 000 members. Goals: to train Canadian Jewish women to be committed citizens, actively involved in local, provincial and national affairs; to instill knowledge of and pride in their heritage; to preserve their ethnic singularity; to raise funds for the care and education of needy women and children in Israel.

National Action Committee on the Status of Women (1972)—344 Bloor St. W., Ste. 505, Toronto, Ont. M5S 1W9, (416) 922-3246. Pres. Louise Dulude; 570 member-organizations. Goals: to initiate and work for improvements in the status of women by actions designed to change legislation, attitudes, customs and practices; to evaluate and advocate changes to benefit women; to encourage the formation of organizations interested in improving the status of women; to exchange information with member organizations.

National Council of Jewish Women of Canada (1897)—1110 Finch Ave. W., Ste. 518, Downsview, Ont. M3J 2T2, (416) 665-8251. Pres. Mrs. Penny Yellen; 4 000 members. Goals: to train volunteers to be professional and leaders to be effective; concern for: the community, women's issues, Jewish issues, human rights, the disabled, the aged, the health and strength of the peoples of Israel.

National Council of Women of Canada (1893)—270 MacLaren St., Ste. 20, Ottawa, Ont. K2P 0M3, (613) 233-4953. Executive Director Pearl Dobson; 750 000 members. Goals: to advocate improved social conditions for women, the family and the nation.

R.E.A.L. Women (Realistic Equal Active for Life Women) (1983)—Box 8813, Stn. T, Ottawa, Ont. K1G 3J1, (613) 738-1213. Pres. Mrs. Lettie Morse; 45 000 members. Goals: to advance the equality of women and to lobby for the integration of issues concerning the preservation of traditional family life in all government policies and legislation.

Women's Canadian O.R.T. (Organization for Educational Research and Technological Training) (1948)—3101 Bathurst St., Ste. 604, Toronto, Ont. M6A 2A6, (416) 787-0339. Pres. Harriet Morton; 5 000 members. Goals: to help fund O.R.T.'s global network of schools where students are taught a wide range of marketable skills.

Women's Inter-Church Council of Canada (1918)—77 Charles St. W., Toronto, Ont. M5S 1K5, (416) 922-6177. Pres. Jean Gordon; represents network of 50 000 members. Goals: to challenge Christian women to grow in ecumenism; to share spirituality; to dialogue about concerns as women; to take action for human rights by responding to national and international issues.

YWCA of/du Canada (1870)—80 Gerrard St. E., Toronto, Ont. M5B 1G6, (416) 593-9886. Pres. Mae Boa; 350 000 members. Goals: to develop and improve the status of women; to foster a network for business women and homemakers; to provide a haven for women in trouble and a focus for women working together to benefit all women.

---

(1) The Advisory Council is composed of a small membership, appointed by the federal government, that reports to parliament through the minister responsible for the status of women.

Canadian Social Trends

Canadian Population Density

Source: Censuses of Canada

(population per sq. km)

	Canada	Nfld	PEI	NS	NB	Que	Ont	Man	Sask	Alta	BC	YT	NWT
1871	0.4	n.a.	16.7	7.2	4.0	0.9	1.7	...	n.a.	n.a.	...	n.a.	n.a.
1881	0.5	n.a.	19.3	8.2	4.5	1.0	2.1	0.1	n.a.	n.a.	0.1	n.a.	n.a.
1891	0.6	n.a.	19.3	8.4	4.5	1.1	2.3	0.3	n.a.	n.a.	0.1	n.a.	n.a.
1901	0.6	n.a.	18.3	8.6	4.6	1.2	2.3	0.4	0.1	0.1	0.2	0.05	...
1911	0.8	n.a.	16.6	9.2	4.9	1.5	2.7	0.8	0.8	0.6	0.4	0.02	...
1921	1.0	n.a.	15.7	9.8	5.4	1.7	3.1	1.1	1.2	0.9	0.6	0.01	...
1931	1.2	n.a.	15.6	9.6	5.7	2.1	3.7	1.2	1.5	1.1	0.7	0.01	...
1941	1.3	n.a.	16.8	10.8	6.4	2.5	4.0	1.3	1.5	1.2	0.9	0.01	...
1951	1.5	0.9	17.4	12.0	7.3	2.8	4.9	1.4	1.4	1.5	1.3	0.02	...
1961	2.0	1.2	18.5	14.0	8.3	3.9	7.0	1.7	1.6	2.1	1.8	0.03	0.01
1971	2.3	1.4	19.7	14.9	8.8	4.4	8.6	1.8	1.6	2.5	2.4	0.03	0.01
1981	2.6	1.5	21.7	16.0	9.7	4.7	9.4	1.9	1.7	3.5	3.1	0.04	0.01
1988[1]	2.8	1.5	22.6	16.7	9.9	4.9	10.5	2.0	1.8	3.7	3.2	0.05	0.02

(1) Estimate as of Jan. 1.
. . . = too small to be included; n.a. not available.

Canadian Urban and Rural Population

Source: Censuses of Canada

(thousands)

	Urban Total	Urban %	Non-Farm	%	Rural Farm	%	Total	%
1871	722	19.6	n.a.	n.a.	n.a.	n.a.	2 967	80.4
1881	1 110	25.7	n.a.	n.a.	n.a.	n.a.	3 215	74.3
1891	1 537	31.8	n.a.	n.a.	n.a.	n.a.	3 296	68.2
1901	2 014	37.5	n.a.	n.a.	n.a.	n.a.	3 357	62.5
1911	3 273	45.4	n.a.	n.a.	n.a.	n.a.	3 934	54.6
1921	4 352	49.5	n.a.	n.a.	n.a.	n.a.	4 436	50.5
1931	5 469	52.7	1 670	16.1	3 238	31.2	4 908	47.3
1941	6 271	54.5	2 123	18.4	3 113	27.1	5 236	45.5
1951	8 817	62.9	2 423	17.3	2 769	19.8	5 192	37.1
1956	10 715	66.6	2 734	17.0	2 632	16.4	5 366	33.4
1961	12 700	69.6	3 465	19.0	2 073	11.4	5 538	30.4
1966	14 727	73.6	3 374	16.9	1 914	9.6	5 288	26.4
1971	16 410	76.1	3 738	17.3	1 420	6.6	5 158	23.9
1976	17 367	75.5	4 591	20.0	1 035	4.5	5 626	24.5
1981	18 436	75.7	4 867	20.0	1 040	4.3	5 907	24.3
1986	19 352	76.5	5 067	20.0	890	3.5	5 957	23.5

n.a. not available.

Urban and Rural Population by Province, 1986

Source: Census of Canada

	Urban Total	Urban %	Non-Farm	%	Rural Farm	%	Total	%
Canada	19 352 085	76.5	5 066 760	20.0	890 490	3.5	5 957 245	23.5
Newfoundland	334 730	58.9	231 930	40.8	1 685	0.3	233 615	41.1
Prince Edward Island .	48 290	38.1	68 085	53.8	10 275	8.1	78 355	61.9
Nova Scotia	471 130	54.0	387 875	44.4	14 175	1.6	402 045	46.0
New Brunswick	350 300	49.4	347 025	48.9	12 110	1.7	359 135	50.6
Quebec	5 088 995	77.9	1 300 085	19.9	143 380	2.2	1 443 465	22.1
Ontario	7 469 420	82.1	1 399 485	15.4	232 790	2.6	1 632 275	17.9
Manitoba	766 855	72.1	211 475	19.9	84 690	8.0	296 160	27.9
Saskatchewan	620 200	61.4	227 920	22.6	161 495	16.0	389 420	38.6
Alberta	1 877 755	79.4	309 950	13.1	178 115	7.5	488 065	20.6
British Columbia	2 285 005	79.2	546 590	19.0	51 775	1.8	598 360	20.8
Yukon	15 195	64.6	8 305	35.3	–	–	8 305	35.3
Northwest Territories ..	24 210	46.3	28 025	53.6	–	–	28 025	53.6

– = zero.

Size of Families in Canada

Source: Censuses of Canada

(thousands of families)

	1951		1961		1971		1981		1986	
	Families	Avg. size	Families	Avg. size	Families	Avg. size	Families	Avg. size	Families	Avg. size
Canada	3 287	3.7	4 147	3.9	5 071	3.7	6 325	3.3	6 735[2]	3.1
Newfoundland	75	4.4	89	4.7	108	4.4	135	3.8	142	3.6
Prince Edward Island .	21	4.0	22	4.2	24	4.0	30	3.5	32	3.4
Nova Scotia	145	3.9	162	4.0	181	3.8	216	3.3	230[2]	3.2
New Brunswick	112	4.1	125	4.3	140	4.0	177	3.4	187[2]	3.3
Quebec	856	4.2	1 104	4.2	1 357	3.9	1 672	3.3	1 752[2]	3.1
Ontario	1 163	3.4	1 511	3.6	1 882	3.6	2 279	3.2	2 446[2]	3.1
Manitoba	191	3.6	216	3.7	236	3.6	262	3.2	276[2]	3.2
Saskatchewan	196	3.7	212	3.8	216	3.7	246	3.3	261[2]	3.2
Alberta	223	3.7	306	3.8	382	3.7	566	3.3	616[2]	3.2
British Columbia	300	3.3	394	3.6	534	3.5	728	3.1	776[2]	3.0
Yukon	5[1]	3.9[1]	7[1]	4.3[1]	11[1]	4.3[1]	6	3.3	6	3.2
Northwest Territories .	5[1]	3.9[1]	7[1]	4.3[1]	11[1]	4.3[1]	9	4.0	11	3.9

(1) Includes the Yukon and Northwest Territories. (2) Excludes incompletely enumerated Indian reserves and settlements.

Composition of Canadian Families

Source: Censuses of Canada

(thousands)

	1961		1971		1981		1986	
	No. of families	%	No. of families	%	No. of families	%	No. of families	%
Total families[1]	4 147	100.0	5 071	100.0	6 325	100.0	6 735	100.0
Without children at home . . .	1 217	29.3	1 545	30.5	2 013	31.8	2 201	32.7
With children at home	2 930	70.7	3 526	69.5	4 312	68.2	4 533	67.3
one child	839	20.2	1 045	20.6	1 580	25.0	1 770	26.2
two children	855	20.6	1 077	21.2	1 648	26.1	1 821	27.0
three children	557	13.4	677	13.4	730	11.5	699	10.4
four children	312	7.5	367	7.2	243	3.8	182	2.7
five children	162	3.9	186	3.7	70	1.1	41	0.6
six children	206[2]	5.0[2]	84	1.7	25	0.4	12	0.2
seven children	206[2]	5.0[2]	43	0.8	10	0.2	4	0.1
eight or more	206[2]	5.0[2]	47	0.9	7	0.1	3	0.1
Lone parent families	385	9.3	471	9.3	653	10.3	854	12.7
lone female parent	305	7.4	371	7.3	541	8.6	702	10.4
lone male parent	80	1.9	100	2.0	112	1.8	152	2.3

(1) Based on the census family definition: a husband and wife (without children or with children who never married) or a parent with one or more children who never married, living together in the same home. (2) Includes six or more children.

Single Parents in Canada, 1981

Source: Census of Canada

(thousands)

	Total	With 1 child		With 2 children		With 3 children		With 4 children		With 5 or more children	
		Number	%	Number	%	Number	%	Number	%	Number	%
Total Single Mothers[1]	589	315	53.5	173	29.4	66	11.2	22	3.7	12	2.0
under 35 years . . .	185	99	53.5	61	33.0	18	9.7	5	2.7	2	1.1
35-44 years	140	49	35.0	51	36.4	25	17.9	9	6.4	5	3.6
45-54 years	116	55	47.4	35	30.2	16	13.8	6	5.2	4	3.4
55 years and over .	149	112	75.2	26	17.4	7	4.7	2	1.3	1	0.7
Total Single Fathers[2]	124	70	56.5	34	27.4	13	10.5	5	4.0	3	2.4
under 35 years . . .	17	10	58.8	5	29.4	1	5.9	. . .	. . .	. . .	. . .
35-44 years	32	15	46.9	10	31.3	4	12.5	1	3.1	1	3.1
45-54 years	35	17	48.6	10	28.6	5	14.3	2	5.7	1	2.9
55 years and over .	40	28	70.0	8	20.0	3	7.5	1	2.5	1	2.5

(1) In 1981, of all single mothers, 11% were not married, 29% were separated, 26% were divorced and 33% were widowed. (2) In 1981, of all single fathers, 4% were not married, 40% were separated, 26% were divorced and 30% were widowed.
. . . = too small to be included.

Births by Unmarried Women in Canada[1]

Source: Statistics Canada

	All Ages		Under 20 Years		20-24 Years		25 Years and Over	
	No. of births	% of all births[2]	No. of births	% of all births[2]	No. of births	% of all births[2]	No. of births	% of all births[2]
1974	20 455	9.3	10 569	36.3	6 096	8.2	3 790	3.2
1975	25 735	10.1	13 159	39.9	7 640	8.8	4 936	3.7
1976	26 529	10.5	13 420	43.0	8 105	9.5	5 004	3.7
1977	39 707	11.3	17 554	48.4	12 857	11.1	9 296	4.6
1978	40 870	11.7	17 507	51.4	13 782	12.2	9 581	4.7
1979	43 492	12.2	17 349	54.3	15 225	13.5	10 918	5.2
1980	47 624	13.2	17 777	56.8	16 981	15.1	12 866	5.9
1981	51 215	14.2	17 745	60.5	18 798	17.0	14 672	6.6
1982	56 286	15.5	18 311	64.2	21 193	19.3	16 782	7.4
1983	58 972	16.2	16 889	66.0	22 682	21.2	19 401	8.4
1984	61 821	16.8	16 445	68.9	23 773	23.0	19 396	8.9
1985	65 584	17.9	15 975	71.6	25 008	25.4	24 601	10.0
1986	68 760	18.8	16 194	74.8	25 922	27.9	26 644	10.6

(1) Excludes Newfoundland. (2) Births by unmarried women as a percentage of all births for the age group indicated.

Day Care Spaces in Canada[1]

Source: Health and Welfare Canada

	1980	1985	1986	1987		1980	1985	1986	1987
Canada	109 141	192 374	220 517	243 545					
Newfoundland	491	804	922	1 318	Manitoba	4 941	9 153	9 731	10 526
Prince Edward Island	620	1 036	1 319	1 264	Saskatchewan	3 495	5 463	5 524	5 720
Nova Scotia	2 675	4 463	4 865	5 397	Alberta	16 404	32 473	37 984	43 082
New Brunswick	2 649	3 035	3 482	4 503	British Columbia	13 268	18 498	19 800	18 595
Quebec	23 793	45 472	52 530	58 425	Yukon	160	339	362	457
Ontario	40 545	71 314	83 663	94 018	Northwest Territories	100	324	335	240

(1) Licensed or provincially-approved centres or private homes which provide care for children, outside of their own home, for 8-10 hrs. per day; as of Mar. 31.

Marital Status of the Canadian Population, 1986

Source: Census of Canada

	Total Population (Thousands)		Single		Married		Widowed		Divorced	
Age groups	male	female	male	female	male	female	male	female	male	female
15 years and over	9 721	10 196	30.7	23.9	64.3	61.8	2.2	10.2	2.8	4.1
15-19 years	985	940	98.7	95.3	1.2	4.6	...	0.1	...	...
20-24 years	1 131	1 122	79.2	60.2	20.6	39.1	...	0.1	0.2	0.6
25-29 years	1 165	1 177	39.6	25.7	59.0	71.4	...	0.2	1.3	2.7
30-34 years	1 084	1 102	19.6	13.3	77.2	81.0	0.1	0.5	3.1	5.2
35-39 years	1 011	1 015	11.4	8.6	84.0	83.5	0.2	0.9	4.4	7.0
40-44 years	811	804	8.3	6.7	86.2	83.6	0.4	1.8	5.2	7.9
45-49 years	660	656	7.2	5.8	86.8	83.2	0.7	3.5	5.3	7.5
50-54 years	616	613	7.1	5.6	86.5	81.2	1.4	6.6	5.1	6.7
55-59 years	594	610	7.4	5.9	85.5	76.8	2.5	11.8	4.6	5.6
60-64 years	530	595	7.4	6.2	84.8	69.9	4.1	19.6	3.7	4.4
65-69 years	415	497	7.0	7.0	83.5	59.6	6.5	30.1	2.9	3.3
70-74 years	324	414	7.4	8.4	80.0	46.8	10.3	42.5	2.3	2.3
75-79 years	210	300	7.8	9.6	74.2	33.0	16.3	55.8	1.8	1.6
80-84 years	115	194	8.6	10.2	64.7	20.4	25.3	68.4	1.4	1.0
85-89 years	49	104	8.7	10.2	52.1	10.5	38.2	78.7	1.0	0.6
90 years and over	21	55	8.4	10.6	36.8	4.6	54.0	84.4	0.7	0.4

... = too small to be included.

Marriages and Divorces in Canada

Source: Statistics Canada

	Marriages				Divorces		
	Total	Rate[1]	Average age at marriage brides	grooms	Total	Rate[1]	Average length of marriage[2]
1925	66 378	6.9	25.3	29.8	550	0.06	n.a.
1930	73 341	7.0	25.0	29.2	875	0.09	n.a.
1935	78 908	7.1	25.0	29.0	1 431	0.13	n.a.
1940	125 797	10.8	25.2	28.9	2 416	0.21	n.a.
1945	111 376	9.0	25.5	29.0	5 101	0.42	n.a.
1950	125 083	9.1	25.3	28.5	5 386	0.39	n.a.
1955	128 029	8.2	25.1	28.0	6 053	0.39	n.a.
1960	130 338	7.3	24.7	27.7	6 980	0.39	n.a.
1965	145 519	7.4	24.5	27.2	8 974	0.46	n.a.
1970	188 428	8.8	24.9	27.3	29 775	1.40	n.a.
1975	197 585	8.7	25.0	27.6	50 611	2.22	n.a.
1980	191 069	8.0	25.9	28.5	62 019	2.59	12.0
1981	190 082	7.8	26.2	28.8	67 671	2.78	12.1
1982	188 360	7.6	26.4	29.0	70 436	2.86	12.0
1983	184 675	7.4	26.8	29.4	68 567	2.76	12.0
1984	185 597	7.4	27.2	29.8	65 172	2.60	12.4
1985	184 096	7.3	27.4	30.0	61 980	2.44	12.5

(1) Rate per 1 000 population. (2) Refers to the average length (in years) of those marriages ending in divorce during the year stated. n.a. not available.

Marriages and Divorces by Province, 1985

Source: Statistics Canada

	Marriages				Divorces		
	Total	Rate[1]	Average age at marriage brides	grooms	Total	Rate[1]	Average length of marriage[2]
Canada	**184 096**	**7.3**	**27.4**	**30.0**	**61 980**	**2.44**	**12.5**
Newfoundland	3 220	5.5	25.1	27.7	561	0.97	12.7
Prince Edward Island	956	7.5	26.1	28.7	213	1.68	13.6
Nova Scotia	6 807	7.7	27.3	29.9	2 337	2.65	12.4
New Brunswick	5 312	7.4	26.2	28.8	1 360	1.89	13.2
Quebec	37 026	5.6	27.3	29.8	15 814	2.40	13.1
Ontario	72 891	8.0	27.6	30.2	20 854	2.30	12.8
Manitoba	8 296	7.8	27.0	29.5	2 314	2.16	11.8
Saskatchewan	7 132	7.2	25.9	28.6	1 927	1.89	12.2
Alberta	19 750	8.5	27.2	29.9	8 102	3.45	10.7
British Columbia	22 292	8.1	28.6	31.6	8 330	2.88	12.4
Yukon	185	9.7	28.8	32.2	96	4.21	11.3
Northwest Territories	229	5.2	25.1	29.2	72	1.41	10.8

(1) Rate per 1 000 population. (2) Refers to the average length of those marriages ending in divorce during 1985.

Marriage and Divorce Rates by Country

Source: United Nations Statistics

	Marriage rate[1] (1984)	Divorce rate[1] (1984)	Divorces per 1 000 marriages (1984)		Marriage rate[1] (1984)	Divorce rate[1] (1984)	Divorces per 1 000 marriages (1984)
Canada	7.4	2.6	351.1	Italy	5.2[2]	0.3[5]	50.4[5]
Australia	7.0	2.8	395.9	Japan	6.2	1.5	241.6
Belgium	6.0[2]	1.9[2]	316.2[2]	Mexico	7.2[4]	0.4[4]	49.0[4]
Czechoslovakia	7.8	2.4	308.4	Netherlands	5.7	2.4	417.2
Denmark	5.6	2.8	506.2	New Zealand	7.8	2.8	362.7
England[6]	7.0	2.9	411.7	Norway	5.0	1.9	388.3
West Germany	6.0	2.1	359.0	Poland	7.7	1.4	185.6
Finland	5.8	2.0	337.8	Scotland	7.0	2.3	328.7
France	5.1[2]	1.9[2]	369.1[2]	Sweden	4.4	2.4	553.0
Greece	6.1[2]	0.6[3]	83.0[3]	Switzerland	5.9[2]	1.8[4]	313.2[4]
Hungary	7.0	2.7	382.9	United States	10.5[2]	4.9[2]	464.4[2]
Israel	7.2	1.2	161.8	USSR	9.6	3.4	353.9

(1) Rate per 1 000 population. (2) Preliminary figure. (3) 1983 statistics. (4) 1982 statistics. (5) Figure less reliable. (6) Includes Wales.

Ages of Brides and Grooms in Canadian Marriages, 1985

Source: Statistics Canada

This table compares the number of brides and grooms, by age category, for 1985. It shows, for example, that 79 836 brides aged 20-24 were married; 343 of them married men aged 40-44.

					Age of Groom[1]					
Age of Bride	15-19 years	20-24 years	25-29 years	30-34 years	35-39 years	40-44 years	45-49 years	Over 50 years	Not stated	Total marriages
Under 15 years	2	2	–	–	–	–	–	–	–	4
15-19 years	2 093	10 383	2 435	390	112	26	11	4	25	15 479
20-24 years	938	42 252	28 858	5 732	1 431	343	97	83	102	79 836
25-29 years	101	6 344	22 831	10 924	3 786	1 094	338	209	58	45 685
30-34 years	15	799	4 163	6 646	4 174	1 812	711	431	31	18 782
35-39 years	4	189	869	1 895	2 658	1 920	797	10	9 382	
40-44 years	5	30	180	423	847	1 244	1 080	1 299	9	5 117
45-49 years	1	15	36	82	216	427	733	1 610	4	3 124
Over 50 years	1	13	16	24	70	178	353	5 844	30	6 529
Not stated	1	21	35	10	5	5	–	6	75	158
Total marriages	3 161	60 048	59 423	26 126	13 299	7 049	4 363	10 283	344	184 096

(1) There were no grooms under the age of 15 who married in 1985.
– = zero.

Canadian Marriage Information

Source: Canadian World Almanac Questionnaire

Province	Marriage-able age	With consent[1]	Wait for licence (days)	Wait after licence (days)	Women's legal name after marriage		
					husband's surname	maiden name	hyphenation or combination
Newfoundland	19	16	4	4	yes	yes	yes
Prince Edward Island[2]	18	16[3]	5	0	yes	yes	yes
Nova Scotia	19	16[4]	5	0	yes	yes	yes
New Brunswick	18	16[4]	5	0	yes[6]	yes[6]	yes[6]
Quebec	18	14(m); 12(f)	20	5	no[5]	yes[5]	no[5]
Ontario	18	16	0	3	yes[6]	yes[6]	yes[6]
Manitoba	18	16[4]	0	1	yes	yes	*
Saskatchewan	18	16[4]	1	0	yes	yes	*
Alberta[2]	18	16[7]	0	0	yes	yes	yes
British Columbia	19	16[4]	0	2	yes	yes	*
Yukon	19[8]	16[4]	0	1	yes	yes	*
Northwest Territories	19[8]	15[9]	0	0	yes	yes	yes

(1) Of parent or guardian. (2) Blood test required. (3) Females under 16 years of age can be married if they have a child or are pregnant, with confirmation from a doctor. (4) Any person under age 16 can marry with the authorization of an appropriate judge (Family Court, Provincial Court, Supreme Court, County Court or Court of Queen's Bench; depending on the province). (5) Since Apr. 1, 1981, women married in Quebec legally maintain their maiden names. (6) After marriage, either spouse may use his/her surname prior to marriage, their spouse's surname, or a combination or hyphenation of both. (7) Females under 16 years of age can be married if they have a child or are pregnant, with confirmation from a doctor and parental consent. (8) Age 18 if person has been living away from parent's home for more than 6 months and has not received financial aid from parents. (9) Any person under 15 years of age can be married with the consent of the Commissioner of the Northwest Territories.
* Requires legal name change; m = male, f = female.

How to Obtain Birth, Death or Marriage Certificates

To obtain application forms and fee information, write to **Vital Statistics,** in whichever province or territory the birth, death or marriage occurred, at the address below:

Newfoundland: . . . .
Dept. of Health, Ground Floor, Confederation Building, St. John's, Nfld. A1C 5T7.

Prince Edward Island: . . . .
P.O. Box 2000, Charlottetown, P.E.I. C1A 7N8.

Nova Scotia: . . . .
P.O. Box 157, Halifax, N.S. B3J 2M9.

New Brunswick: . . . .
Department of Health and Community Services, Vital Statistics, P.O. Box 6000, Fredericton, N.B. E3B 5H1.

Quebec: . . . .
Archives civiles, Palais de Justice of the judicial district in which the marriage, birth or death took place.

Ontario: . . . .
  Registrar General, Macdonald Block, Queen's Park, Toronto, Ont. M7A 1Y5.
Manitoba: . . . .
  Manitoba Community Services, Vital Statistics, 254 Portage Ave., Winnipeg, Man. R3C 0B6.
Saskatchewan: . . . .
  3475 Albert St., Regina, Sask. S4S 6X6.
Alberta: . . . .
  Texaco Building, 10130-112 St., Edmonton, Alta. T4K 2P2; or McDougall Centre, 455-6th Street S.W., Calgary, Alta. T2N 2A1
British Columbia: . . . .
  1515 Blanshard St., Victoria, B.C. V8W 3C8.
Yukon: . . . .
  Registrar Deputy, P.O. Box 2703, Whitehorse, Yukon Y1A 2C6.
Northwest Territories: . . . .
  Dept. of Justice, Government of the N.W.T., P.O. Box 1320, Yellowknife, N.W.T. X1A 2L9.

Canadian Divorce Legislation

Source: Dept. of Justice

Under Canada's new divorce law, which took effect June 1, 1986, the only ground for divorce is marriage breakdown. Previously, separation had to be at least 3 years unless other grounds such as adultery could be proven. The new legislation also changes factors affecting child custody and support payment. The court now bases decisions on these matters on what is reasonable and best for the parties concerned, regardless of who is responsible for the end of the marriage.

Grounds for divorce
The sole basis for divorce is marriage breakdown, which is considered to have occurred if:
• spouses have lived apart for one year with the idea that the marriage is over, or
• adultery has been committed, or
• physical or mental abuse has been committed.
If a divorce is sought on the grounds that the spouses live apart and the marriage is over, neither spouse has to prove that the other is at fault, and either or both spouses may ask for the divorce. A court appearance at a trial may not be necessary if both spouses agree to the terms of the divorce. Proof will be required if the basis of the marriage breakdown is adultery or mental or physical cruelty, in which case the court may grant the divorce before the spouses have lived apart for one year.

Reconciliation
Spouses may live together again, either before or after a divorce action has been initiated, for up to 90 days without affecting the continuation of the divorce action if the reconciliation attempt fails.

Finalization
After a court grants a divorce, the decision is subject to appeal for 30 days. If no appeal is made during that time the divorce is final and the divorced parties are free to marry on the 31st day. Custody, access and support arrangements can still be changed after a divorce is final.

Spousal support
Depending on the needs, income and resources of each spouse, the court may order one spouse to pay support to the other. Spousal support is intended to give value to the contributions made during the marriage, to make sure that one spouse doesn't endure economic hardship, and to make sure that the spouse who lives with the children is not at a financial disadvantage. The law also says that the judge must structure the support order in a way that will promote the economic self-sufficiency of the spouse who is entitled to support.

Child support
One parent may be granted custody of the child with responsibility for making major decisions about the child's upbringing and education; however, the court considers that children should have contact with both parents provided that this is in the child's best interests. The child usually lives with the parent who has custody, but the other parent has the right to spend time with the child and to information about the child's well-being. Parents who have joint custody share in major decisions concerning the child. When parents have joint custody the child may have alternating living arrangements, living with one parent for one week and with the other the next, or one parent may take care of the child on weekdays and the other on weekends.

Financial responsibilities
Regardless of whether a parent has sole or joint custody, both parents are financially responsible for the child and are expected to contribute to the child's upbringing according to their individual income and resources. One parent may still be ordered to make child support payments to the other even if parents have joint custody.
Legislation proclaimed in the fall of 1987 calls for the federal government to release information about a spouse's whereabouts to help locate defaulting spouses or to trace children taken in contravention of a custody order. This information may be released to a court, police force, or to an enforcement agency. A second service which allows the garnishment of designated federal moneys such as income tax refunds was proclaimed in force in May 1988.

Enforcement Services
Some provinces and territories have automatic enforcement services to enforce custody, access, child or spousal support orders. Support is paid directly to the service, which then pays the money to the recipient. In the event of non-payment, the enforcement service initiates legal action free of charge to make sure that court orders are fulfilled. In other provinces, the service is not automatic and the enforcement service is not involved in the collection of support payments until their help is requested when court orders are not met. In those provinces or territories that do not have an enforcement service, legal action to enforce divorce orders must be initiated by the individual.
As of mid 1988, Ontario, Manitoba, Saskatchewan, Alberta, Yukon, Northwest Territories, and New Brunswick had automatic enforcement services. The remaining provinces have other forms of enforcement.

Divorce by Length of Marriage, 1985

Source: Statistics Canada

Length of Marriage	Canada													Yukon and
	Divorces	%	Nfld	PEI	NS	NB	Que	Ont	Man	Sask	Alta	BC	NWT
Less than one year .	177	0.3	1	–	7	–	32	41	7	9	55	23	2
1-4 years	9 676	15.6	65	22	386	160	2 295	2 703	372	330	1 986	1 331	26
5-9 years	18 312	29.5	172	58	674	378	4 184	6 367	755	585	2 530	2 546	63
10-14 years	13 439	21.7	152	48	499	335	3 508	4 695	524	411	1 490	1 738	39
15-19 years	8 413	13.6	65	37	307	205	2 390	2 906	283	229	858	1 120	13
20-24 years	5 156	8.3	50	22	210	113	1 467	1 772	148	141	540	681	12
25-29 years	3 396	5.5	24	18	132	86	939	1 203	114	102	325	446	7
30 years and over ..	3 343	5.4	32	8	119	82	991	1 143	109	118	295	440	6
Not stated	68	0.1	–	–	3	1	8	24	2	2	23	5	–
Total divorces	61 980	100.0	561	213	2 337	1 360	15 814	20 854	2 314	1 927	8 102	8 330	168

– = zero.

Canada's Official Languages

Canada's official bilingualism continues a tradition that predates Confederation. Beginning in 1849, all bills of the United Canada Parliament (governing what is now Ontario and Quebec) were given assent in both English and French.

Constitutional protection was given to certain language rights in the *Constitution Act, 1867* (formerly the *B.N.A. Act*). According to that Act, both English and French could be used in the debates of both houses of Parliament or the Federal Courts, and all federal statutes were to be published in both languages. The *Constitution Act* also provided that the provincial legislature, statutes and provincial courts of Quebec were to be bilingual.

During the 1960s, in addition to its legal status in Quebec, French was recognized by law as a language of instruction at the elementary and secondary levels in the schools of New Brunswick, Ontario, and Manitoba. Legislation was subsequently extended in the 1970s and the early 1980s to provide for French elementary or secondary programs in Saskatchewan, Alberta, Nova Scotia and Prince Edward Island. Other provinces established various administrative arrangements to meet local requirements. In 1969, New Brunswick adopted a provincial *Official Languages Act* granting equal status to both English and French.

In 1969, the federal government passed the *Official Languages Act*, a statute which provided detailed rules for the use of English and French by federal institutions and which created the office of Commissioner of Official Languages for Canada. The Commissioner's duty is to ensure that the Act is complied with and to investigate any complaints that the status of an official language is not being respected by federal institutions.

Parliament passed a strengthened version of its *Official Languages Act* in July 1988. The new Act continued the same themes established by the 1969 Act but added provisions designed to increase the use of both languages in the justice system and to provide greater opportunity for federal employees to work in the official language of their choice. As well, the Act now states that anyone who has made a complaint to the Commissioner and is not satisfied with the outcome may apply to the Federal Court for an order remedying the alleged breach of statutory duty.

Language rights received further constitutional protection in 1982 with the passage of the *Constitution Act, 1982*. This constitutional document states that French and English are the official languages of Canada and have equal status in all federal institutions. At the request of New Brunswick, the constitution also entrenches the equal status of both official languages in that province's institutions. The *Constitution Act, 1982* also provides for minority language educational rights throughout Canada.

At the provincial level, Quebec, Manitoba, Ontario, New Brunswick, Saskatchewan and Alberta have their own language legislation. The *Manitoba Act* of 1870, through which Manitoba entered Confederation, permitted the use of both English and French in the provincial legislature and required government records and journals to be in both languages. However, in 1890 Manitoba passed the *Official Language Act* making English the only language of Manitoba's legislature, courts and official records. Two Manitoba court decisions—one in 1892, the 2d in 1909—held that this English language law was unconstitutional, but these decisions were ignored by the Manitoba legislature.

In 1979, however, the Supreme Court of Canada ruled the Act unconstitutional. Manitoba responded in 1980 passing a statute *permitting*, but not requiring, statutes to be enacted in, or translated into, French. This new statute still fell short of Manitoba's constitutional obligations. In 1985, the Supreme Court of Canada held that most of the 1980 Act was unconstitutional, and further ruled that every statute of Manitoba that had been enacted in English only was unconstitutional and therefore invalid. To prevent the chaos that would result from a full-scale repeal of provincial laws, the Court agreed to allow the province time to re-enact legislation in both official languages. Most laws must be re-enacted by Dec. 31, 1988; all others must be re-enacted by Dec. 31, 1990.

Since 1974, with the passing in Quebec's legislature of the *Official Language Act*, French has been Quebec's official language. Further Quebec legislation was enacted in 1977 by the *Charter of the French Language*. The intention of the Charter, according to its wording, is to make French "the normal and everyday language of work, instruction, communication, commerce and business." It includes such provisions as a requirement that public signs and commercial advertising be solely in French, except in special circumstances.

In a court challenge in 1979, the Supreme Court of Canada ruled that those parts of the statute relating to the legislature and the courts were invalid. Similarly in 1984, the Supreme Court of Canada declared that certain sections on the language of instruction were invalid because of their inconsistency with provisions of the *Constitution Act, 1982* pertaining to minority language educational rights. While in other respects French remains Quebec's official language, the province enacted legislation in 1987 recognizing that, subject to resource constraints, "every English-speaking person is entitled to receive health services and social services in the English language".

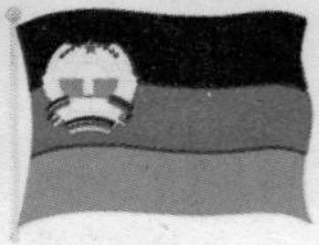

AFGHANISTAN	 ALBANIA	 ALGERIA	 ANGOLA	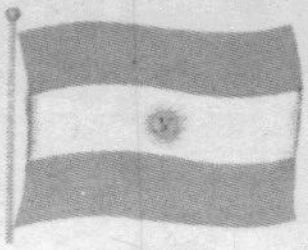 ARGENTINA
 AUSTRALIA	 AUSTRIA	 BAHAMAS	 BAHRAIN	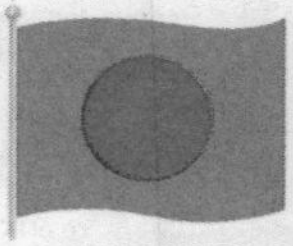 BANGLADESH
 BARBADOS	 BELGIUM	 BELIZE	 BENIN	 BHUTAN
 BOLIVIA	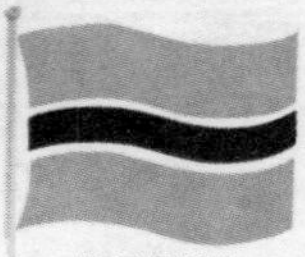 BOTSWANA	 BRAZIL	 BRUNEI	 BULGARIA
 BURKINA FASO	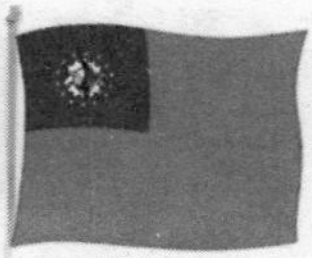 BURMA	 BURUNDI	 CAMBODIA (Kampuchea)	 CAMEROON
 CANADA	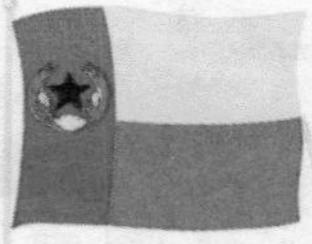 CAPE VERDE	 CENTRAL AFRICAN REPUBLIC	 CHAD	 CHILE
 CHINA	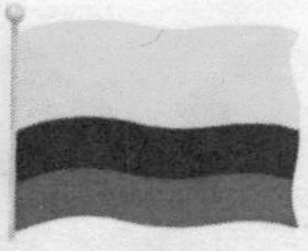 COLOMBIA	 COMOROS	 CONGO	 COSTA RICA

CUBA

CYPRUS

CZECHOSLOVAKIA

DENMARK

DJIBOUTI

F2

DOMINICA	 DOMINICAN REPUBLIC	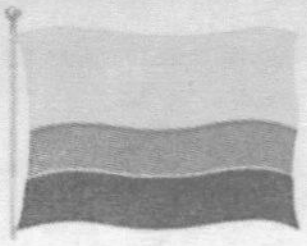 ECUADOR	 EGYPT	 EL SALVADOR
 EQUATORIAL GUINEA	 ETHIOPIA	 FIJI	 FINLAND	 FRANCE
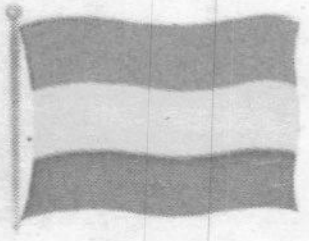 GABON	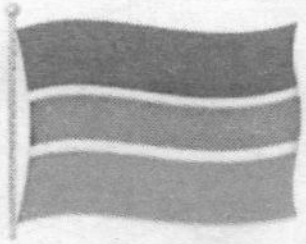 GAMBIA	 GERMANY (EAST)	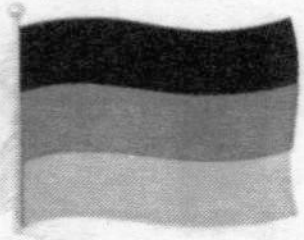 GERMANY (WEST)	 GHANA
 GREECE	 GRENADA	 GUATEMALA	 GUINEA	 GUINEA-BISSAU
 GUYANA	 HAITI	 HONDURAS	 HUNGARY	 ICELAND
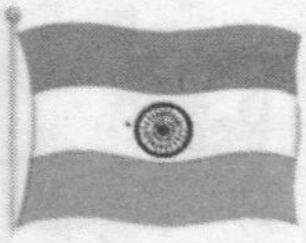 INDIA	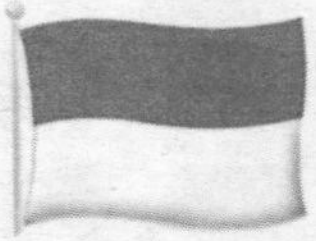 INDONESIA	 IRAN	 IRAQ	 IRELAND
 ISRAEL	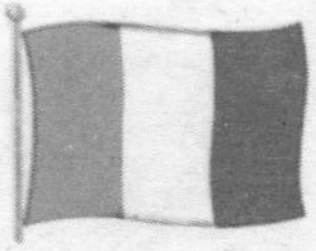 ITALY	 IVORY COAST	 JAMAICA	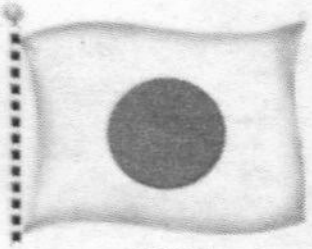 JAPAN
 JORDAN	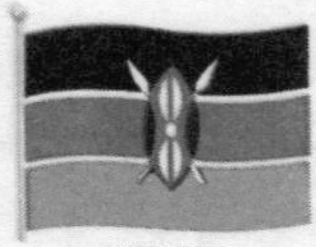 KENYA	 KOREA (NORTH)	KOREA (SOUTH)	KUWAIT

F3

LAOS

LEBANON

LESOTHO

LIBERIA

LIBYA

LIECHTENSTEIN

LUXEMBOURG

MADAGASCAR

MALAWI

MALAYSIA

MALI

MALTA

MAURITANIA

MAURITIUS

MEXICO

MONACO

MONGOLIA

MOROCCO

MOZAMBIQUE

NEPAL

NETHERLANDS

NEW ZEALAND

NICARAGUA

NIGER

NIGERIA

NORWAY

OMAN

PAKISTAN

PANAMA

PAPUA-NEW GUINEA

PARAGUAY

PERU

PHILIPPINES

POLAND

PORTUGAL

QATAR

ROMANIA

RWANDA

SAINT LUCIA

ST. VINCENT AND
THE GRENADINES

SAN MARINO

SAO TOME
AND PRINCIPE

SAUDI ARABIA

SENEGAL

SIERRA LEONE

SINGAPORE

SOLOMON ISLANDS

SOMALIA

SOUTH AFRICA

SPAIN

SRI LANKA

SUDAN

SURINAME

SWAZILAND

SWEDEN

SWITZERLAND

SYRIA

TAIWAN

TANZANIA

THAILAND

TOGO

TRINIDAD AND TOBAGO

TUNISIA

TURKEY

UGANDA

UNION OF SOVIET
SOCIALIST REPUBLICS

UNITED ARAB EMIRATES

UNITED KINGDOM

UNITED STATES

URUGUAY

VATICAN CITY

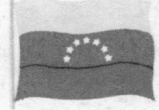

VENEZUELA

VIETNAM

WESTERN SAMOA

YEMEN

PEOPLE'S DEMOCRATIC
REPUBLIC OF YEMEN

YUGOSLAVIA

ZAIRE

ZAMBIA

ZIMBABWE

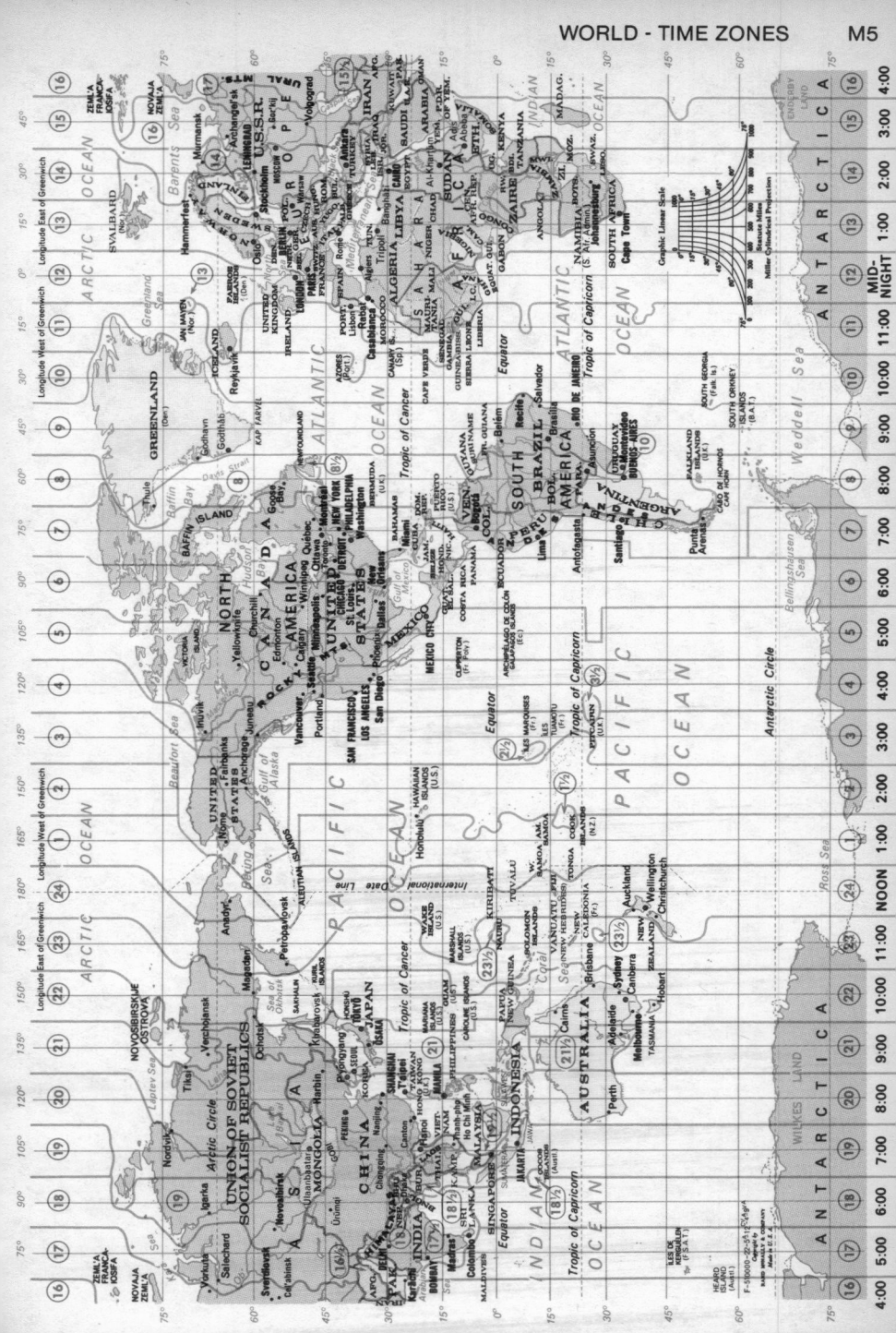

Kilometres 0　200　400　600 Km.
Miles 0　200　400　600 Mi.

National capitals are shown
with a solid underscore.
Secondary capitals are shown
with a dashed underscore.
PARIS　National capital
Tallinn　Secondary capital

Miller Oblated Stereographic Projection

ATLANTIC OCEAN

NORWEGIAN SEA

NORTH SEA

Barents Sea

Baltic Sea

BLACK SEA

CASPIAN SEA

MEDITERRANEAN SEA

Adriatic Sea

Tyrrhenian Sea

Ionian Sea

Aegean Sea

URAL MOUNTAINS

URAL SKI JEGORY

UNION OF SOVIET SOCIALIST REPUBLICS

NORWAY　SWEDEN　FINLAND　LAPLAND

DENMARK

UNITED KINGDOM

IRELAND

ICELAND

FRANCE　SPAIN　PORTUGAL

GERMANY　POLAND　HUNGARY　ROMANIA　YUGOSLAVIA　BULGARIA

ITALY　GREECE

TURKEY　SYRIA　IRAQ　IRAN

ALGERIA　MOROCCO　TUNISIA

Moscow　Leningrad　Kiev　Minsk　Paris　London　Berlin　Rome　Madrid　Lisbon　Oslo　Stockholm　Helsinki　Copenhagen　Warsaw　Budapest　Bucharest　Sofija　Athens　Ankara　Tehran　Baghdad　Rabat　Casablanca

FAEROE ISLANDS (Den.)

SHETLAND ISLANDS

HEBRIDES

CYPRUS

CRETE

CORSE (Fr.)　SARDEGNA　SICILIA

Kilometres 0 200 400 600 Km.
Miles 0 200 400 600 Mi.

PACIFIC OCEAN

SEA OF JAPAN

JAPAN

HOKKAIDO

Sapporo

HONSHU

TOKYO
Yokohama
OSAKA
Nagoya
KYOTO

SHIKOKU

KYUSHU

Nagasaki
Kagoshima

NANSEI-SHOTO (RYUKYU ISLANDS) (Jap.)

OSUMI-SHOTO

Tropic of Cancer

EAST CHINA SEA

PHILIPPINE SEA

SEA OF OKHOTSK

SAKHALIN
U.S.S.R.

SIKHOTE ALIN

Khabarovsk

Vladivostok

MANCHURIA

NORTH KOREA

Pyongyang

SEOUL
SOUTH KOREA

Pusan

Taegu

Hiroshima

Kitakyushu

YELLOW SEA

Changchun

SHENYANG

Fushun

PEKING
TIANJIN

Shijiazhuang

Qingdao

SHANGHAI
Hangzhou

Ningbo

Wenzhou

Fuzhou

TAIPEI
TAIWAN

Kaohsiung

NEI MONGGOL ZIZHIQU
INNER MONGOLIA

Hohhot
Datong

Baotou

Taiyuan

Xi'an

WUHAN
Changsha

CHONGQING

Chengdu

Kunming

Guiyang

CANTON
HONG KONG (U.K.)
Macau

SOUTH CHINA SEA

C H I N A

Lanzhou

Yinchuan

G O B I

M O N G O L I A

Ulaanbaatar

UNION OF SOVIET SOCIALIST REPUBLICS

KAZAKHSKAJA S.S.R.

Alma-Ata

TIEN SHAN

XINJIANG UYGUR ZIZHIQU
SINKIANG

TARIM PENDI

TAKLIMAKAN SHAMO

Urumqi

ALTUN SHAN

QAIDAM PENDI

QINGHAI

NAN SHAN

XIZANG ZIZHIQU
TIBET

KUNLUN SHAN

H I M A L A Y A S

NEPAL

BHUTAN

BANGLADESH

I N D I A

CALCUTTA

BAY OF BENGAL

B U R M A

Mandalay

THAILAND

LAOS

Chiang Mai

VIETNAM

Hanoi

Nanning

Haikou

HAINAN DAO

PHILIPPINES
LUZON

BATAN ISLANDS

BABUYAN ISLANDS

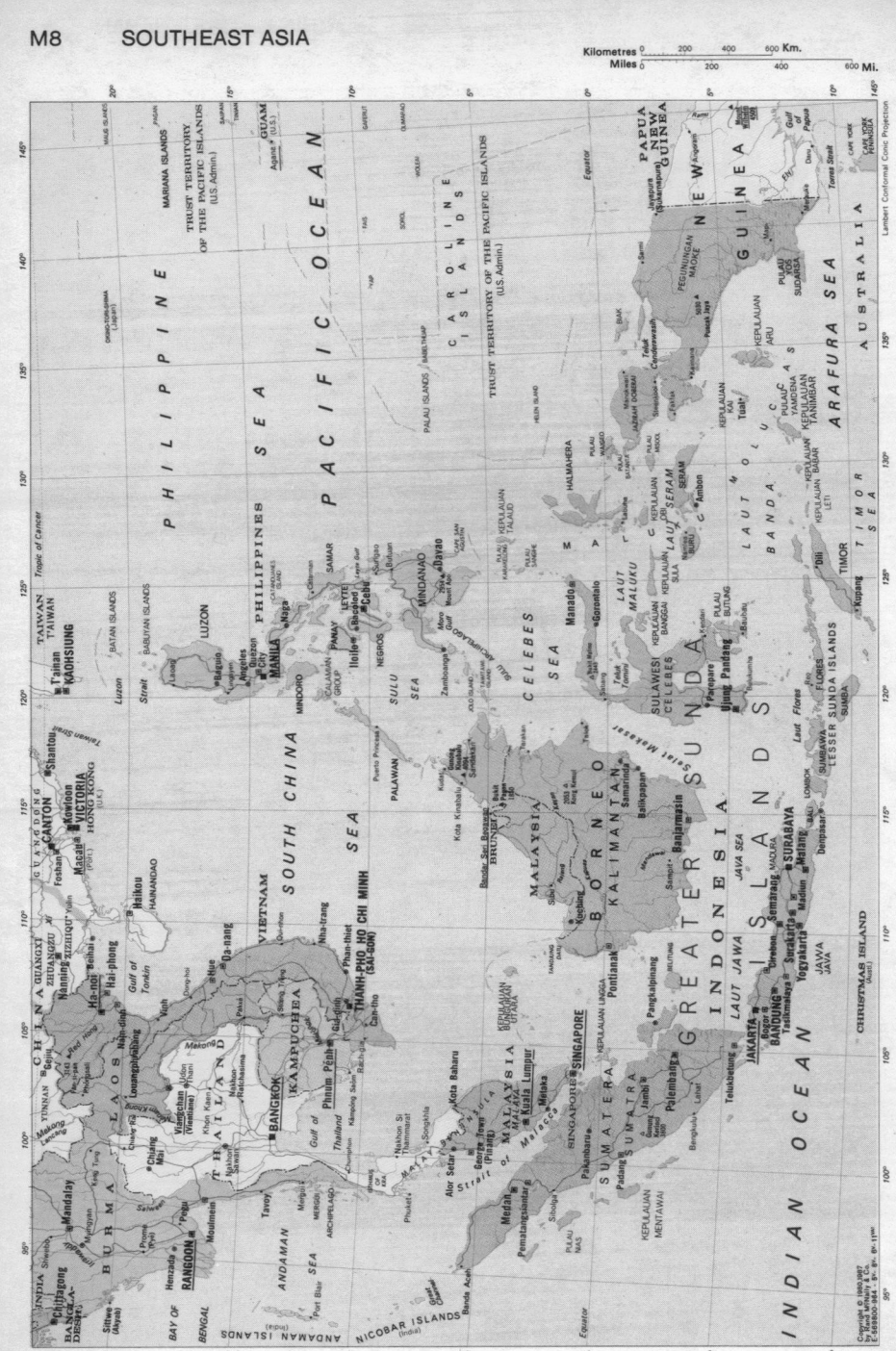

Kilometres 0   200   400   600 Km.
Miles 0   200   400   600 Mi.

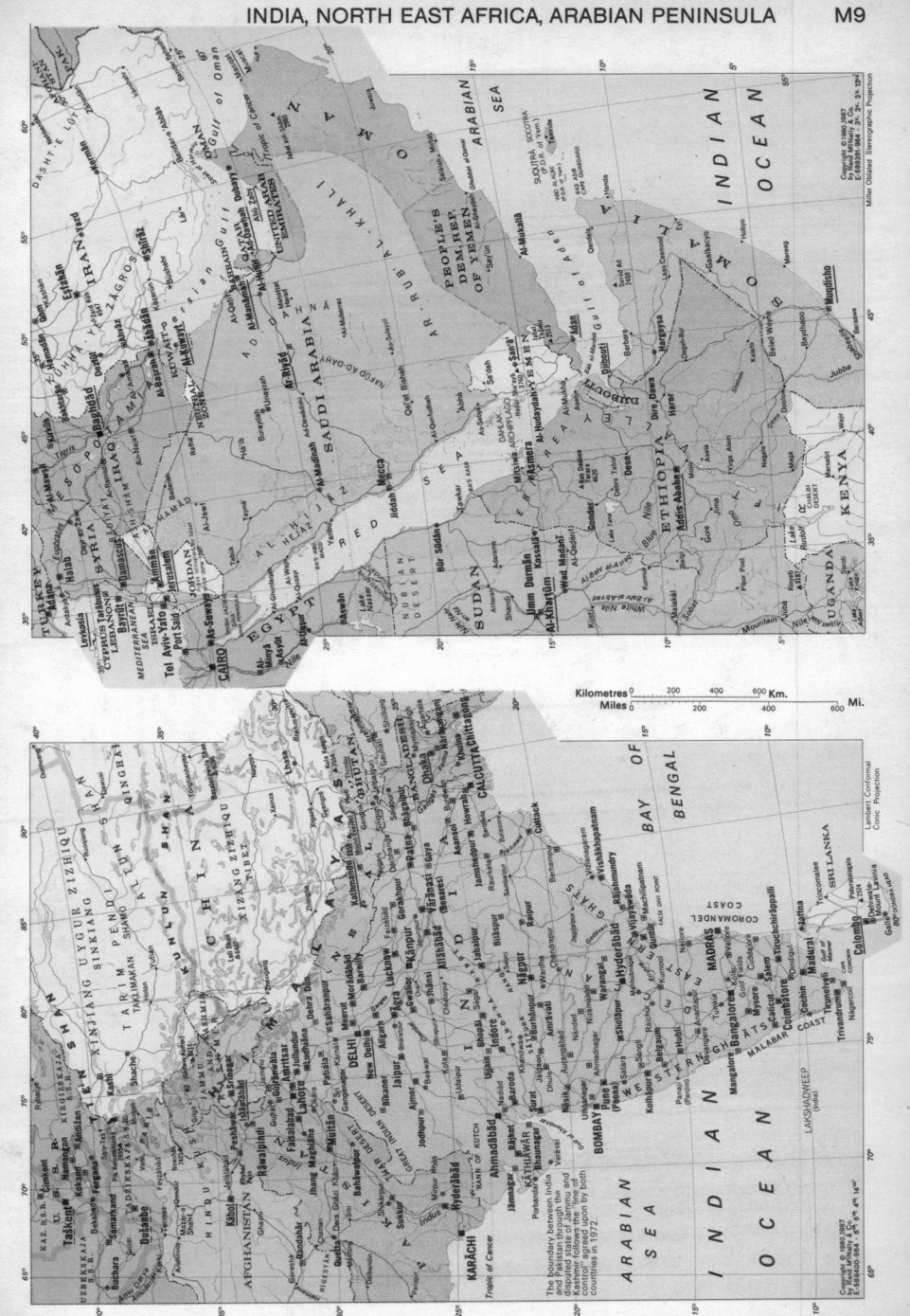

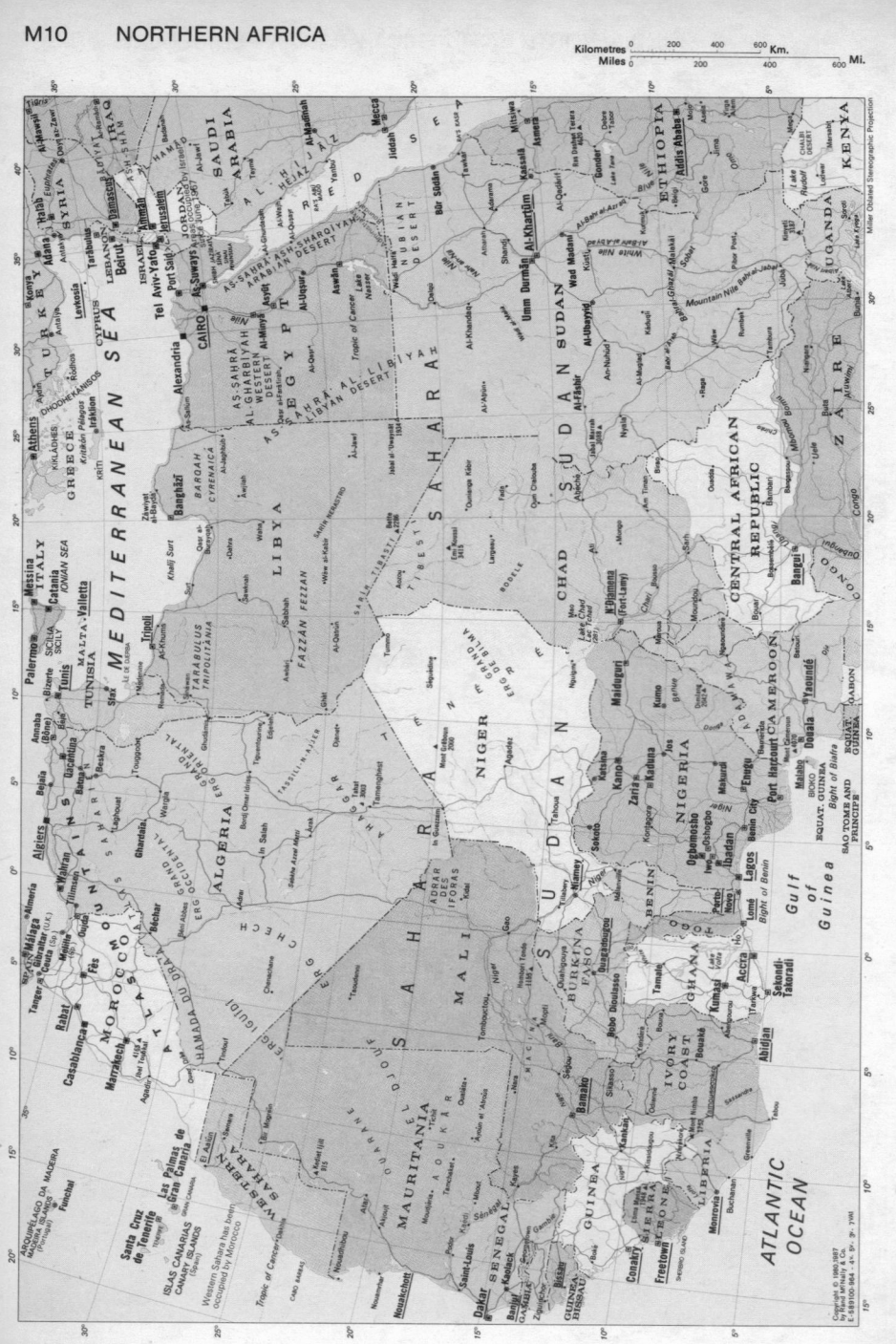

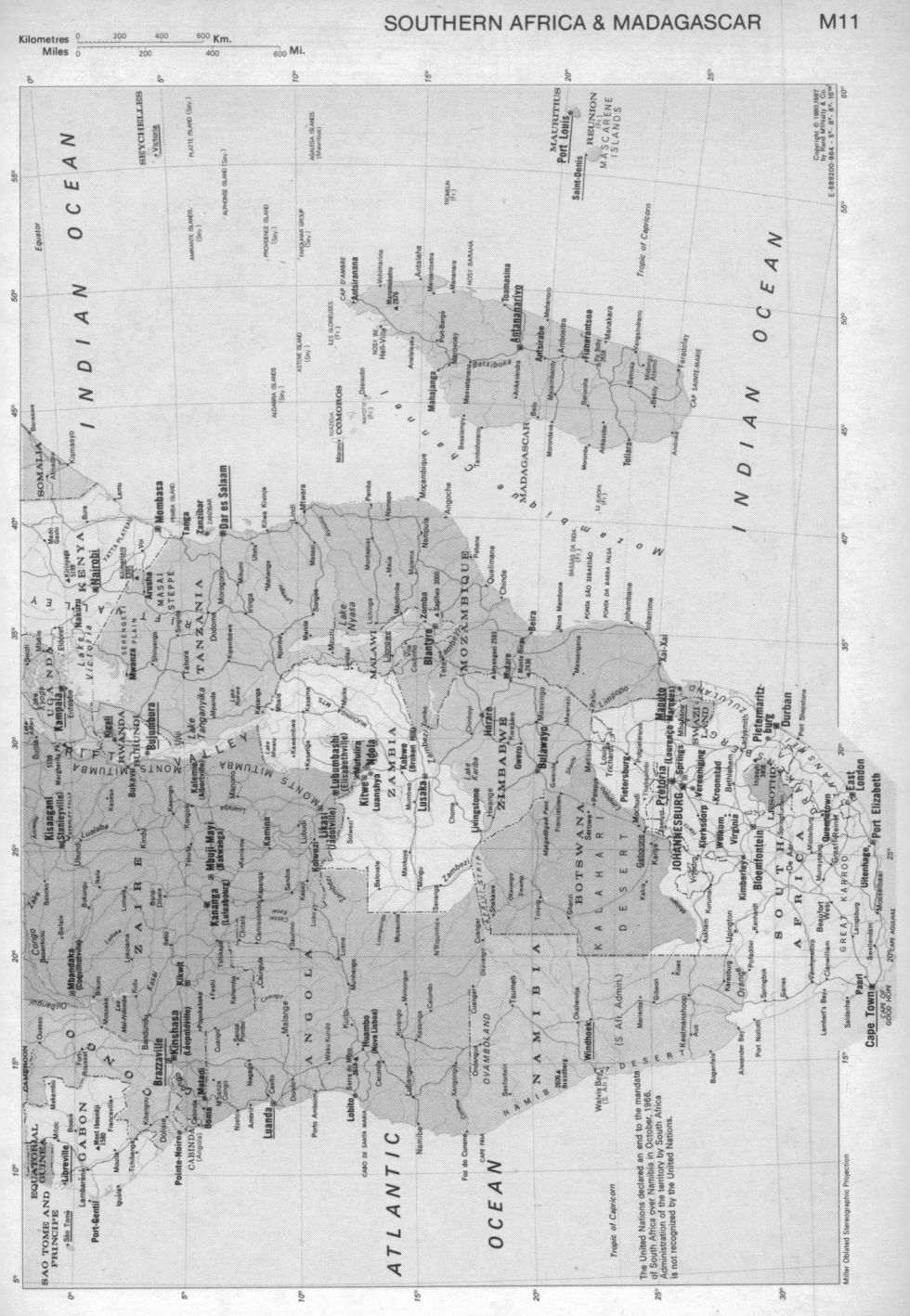

Kilometres
Miles

The United Nations declared an end to the mandate
of South Africa over Namibia in October, 1966.
Administration of the territory by South Africa
is not recognized by the United Nations.

Copyright © 1980-1987
by Rand McNally & Co.
E-9882200-364

Miller Oblated Stereographic Projection

Kilometres 0 200 400 600 Km.
Miles 0 200 400 600 Mi.

Lambert Conformal Conic Projection

ATLANTIC OCEAN

GREENLAND

Labrador Sea

Davis Strait

Baffin Bay

NORTHWEST TERRITORIES

Hudson Bay

QUEBEC

ONTARIO

MANITOBA

SASKATCHEWAN

ALBERTA

BRITISH COLUMBIA

YUKON

UNITED STATES

CANADA

ROCKY MOUNTAINS

COAST MOUNTAINS

MACKENZIE MTS

SELWYN MOUNTAINS

PELLY MOUNTAINS

BROOKS RANGE

ALASKA RANGE

PACIFIC OCEAN

Beaufort Sea

Gulf of Alaska

Baffin Island

Victoria Island

Banks Island

Devon Island

Somerset Island

Prince of Wales Island

Bathurst Island

Melville Island

Southampton Island

Vancouver Island

James Bay

Ungava Peninsula

CASCADE RANGE

SIERRA NEVADA

GREAT BASIN

MONTREAL

TORONTO

OTTAWA

Québec

DETROIT

CHICAGO

Winnipeg

Edmonton

Calgary

Saskatoon

Regina

Vancouver

Seattle

Portland

SAN FRANCISCO

Anchorage

Fairbanks

BOSTON

NEW YORK

PHILADELPHIA

Duluth

Minneapolis

St. Paul

Milwaukee

Buffalo

Cleveland

Halifax

Kilometres 0   200   400   600 Km.
Miles 0   200   400   600 Mi.

ATLANTIC OCEAN

PACIFIC OCEAN

GULF OF MEXICO

CARIBBEAN SEA

WEST INDIES

BAHAMA

BERMUDA

CANADA

UNITED STATES

BRITISH COLUMBIA

ALBERTA

SASKATCHEWAN

MANITOBA

ONTARIO

QUEBEC

VANCOUVER ISLAND

Edmonton
Calgary
Winnipeg
Seattle
Tacoma
Spokane
Portland
Salem
Vancouver
Victoria
Boise
Butte
Helena
Great Falls
Billings
Salt Lake City
Provo
Ogden
Sacramento
San Francisco
Oakland
San Jose
Fresno
Las Vegas
Los Angeles
Long Beach
San Diego
Tijuana
Phoenix
Tucson
Albuquerque
Santa Fe
El Paso
Denver
Colorado Springs
Pueblo
Amarillo
Lubbock
Midland
Odessa
San Angelo
Abilene
Wichita Falls
Fort Worth
Dallas
Waco
Austin
San Antonio
Houston
Galveston
Beaumont
Port Arthur
Corpus Christi
Laredo
Brownsville
Oklahoma City
Tulsa
Wichita
Kansas City
Topeka
Lincoln
Omaha
Des Moines
Sioux City
Sioux Falls
Rapid City
Bismarck
Fargo
Grand Forks
Duluth
Minneapolis
St. Paul
Madison
Milwaukee
CHICAGO
Rockford
Peoria
Springfield
St. Louis
Little Rock
Fort Smith
Memphis
Nashville
Knoxville
Chattanooga
Atlanta
Birmingham
Montgomery
Mobile
New Orleans
Baton Rouge
Shreveport
Monroe
Jackson
Louisville
Lexington
Cincinnati
Indianapolis
Columbus
Cleveland
Detroit
Flint
Grand Rapids
TORONTO
Hamilton
Buffalo
Rochester
Syracuse
Pittsburgh
NEW YORK
PHILADELPHIA
WASHINGTON
Baltimore
Richmond
Norfolk
Raleigh
Charlotte
Columbia
Charleston
Savannah
Jacksonville
Daytona Beach
Orlando
Tampa
St. Petersburg
Sarasota
Fort Lauderdale
West Palm Beach
Miami
BOSTON
Providence
Hartford
QUEBEC
Montreal
Ottawa

MEXICO

SIERRA MADRE ORIENTAL
SIERRA MADRE OCCIDENTAL

Ciudad Juarez
Chihuahua
Hermosillo
Mazatlan
Durango
Torreon
Saltillo
Monterrey
Reynosa
Matamoros
Ciudad Victoria
Tampico
San Luis Potosi
Aguascalientes
Leon
Guadalajara
Queretaro

Golfo de California

BAJA CALIFORNIA

La Paz
San Jose del Cabo

ROCKY MOUNTAINS
GREAT BASIN
COAST RANGES
SIERRA NEVADA

Rio Grande

Lake Superior
Lake Michigan
Lake Huron
Lake Erie
Lake Ontario

Tropic of Cancer

Havana
Nassau
Santa Clara
Camaguey
Holguin
Santiago de Cuba
CUBA
HAITI
DOMINICAN REPUBLIC
Port-au-Prince
Santo Domingo
HISPANIOLA
PUERTO RICO
San Juan
TURKS AND CAICOS ISLANDS

YUCATAN PENINSULA
Merida

Copyright © 1980,1987
by Rand McNally & Co.

ATLANTIC

OCEAN

Tropic of Cancer

GULF OF MEXICO

PACIFIC OCEAN

CARIBBEAN SEA

WEST INDIES

GREATER ANTILLES

LESSER ANTILLES

BAHAMAS

CUBA

JAMAICA

HAITI

DOMINICAN REPUBLIC

HISPANIOLA

PUERTO RICO (U.S.)

VIRGIN ISLANDS

TURKS AND CAICOS ISLANDS (U.K.)

CAYMAN ISLANDS (U.K.)

NETHERLANDS ANTILLES

ANGUILLA (U.K.)

SAINT CHRISTOPHER-NEVIS-ANTIGUA AND BARBUDA

GUADELOUPE

DOMINICA

MARTINIQUE

SAINT LUCIA

SAINT VINCENT AND THE GRENADINES

BARBADOS

GRENADA

TRINIDAD AND TOBAGO

UNITED STATES

MEXICO

YUCATAN PENINSULA

BELIZE

GUATEMALA

EL SALVADOR

HONDURAS

NICARAGUA

COSTA RICA

PANAMA

COLOMBIA

VENEZUELA

Miami
Key West
Fort Myers
West Palm Beach
Fort Lauderdale
Havana
Nassau
Kingston
Santiago de Cuba
Camagüey
Holguín
Port-au-Prince
Santo Domingo
San Juan
Ponce
Fort-de-France
Bridgetown
Port of Spain
Caracas
Maracaibo
Barranquilla
Cartagena
Santa Marta
Colón
Panamá
San José
Managua
Tegucigalpa
San Salvador
Santa Ana
Guatemala
San Pedro Sula
Belize City
Belmopan
Mérida
Cancún

Kilometres
Miles
Lambert Conformal Conic Projection

Copyright © 1980,1987
by RAND MCNALLY & CO.

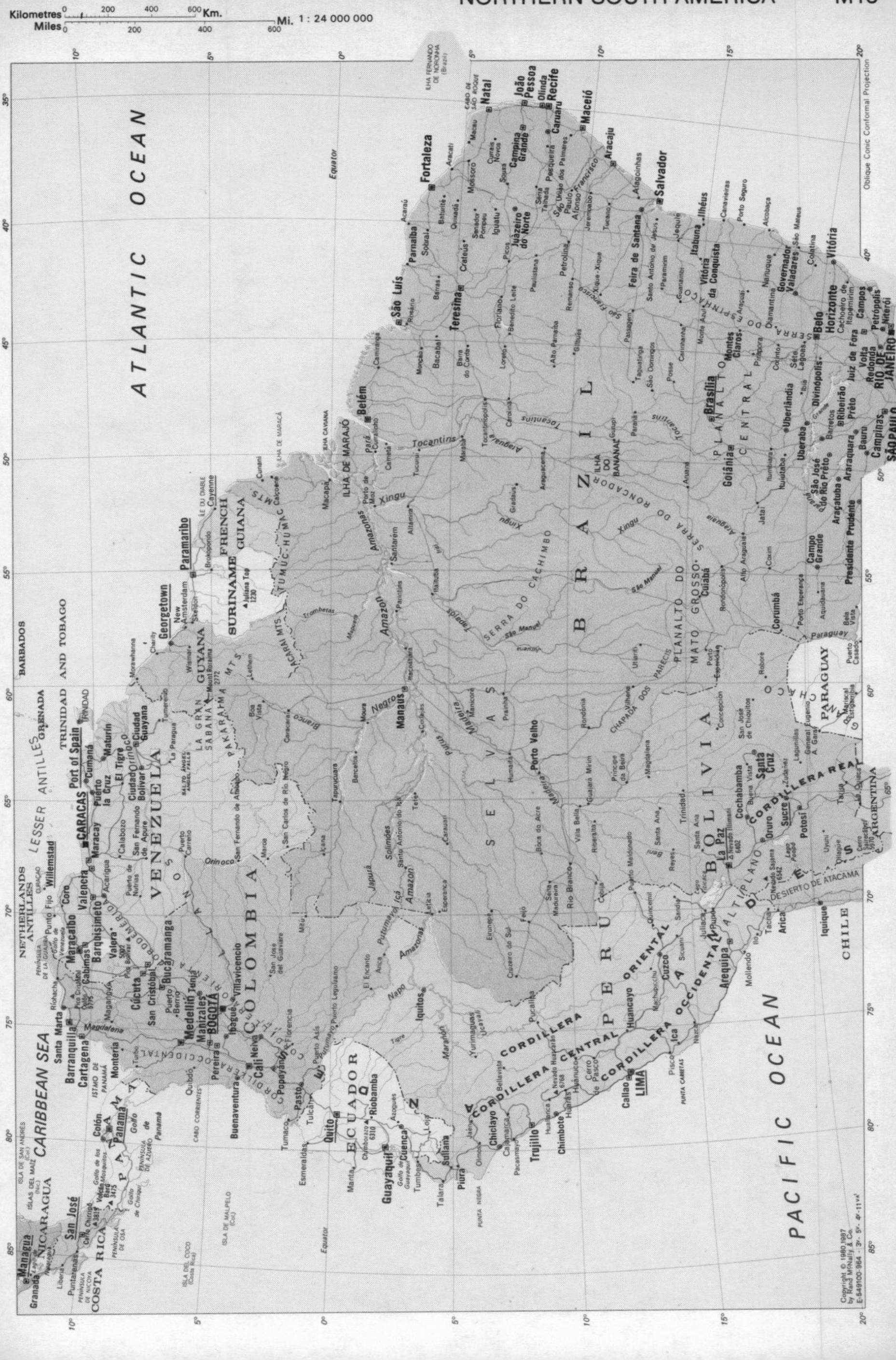

Kilometres 0 200 400 600 Km.
Miles 0 200 400 600
Mi. 1 : 24 000 000

ATLANTIC OCEAN

PACIFIC OCEAN

CARIBBEAN SEA

B R A Z I L

VENEZUELA

COLOMBIA

ECUADOR

PERU

BOLIVIA

PARAGUAY

GUYANA

SURINAME

FRENCH GUIANA

CHILE

LESSER ANTILLES

NETHERLANDS ANTILLES

TRINIDAD AND TOBAGO

BARBADOS

GRANADA

COSTA RICA

NICARAGUA

Equator

Tropic of Capricorn

CARACAS
BOGOTÁ
Quito
LIMA
La Paz
Sucre
Paramaribo
Georgetown
Cayenne
BRASÍLIA

RIO DE JANEIRO
SÃO PAULO
Salvador
Recife
João Pessoa
Natal
Fortaleza
São Luís
Belém
Manaus
Teresina
Maceió
Aracaju
Vitória
Belo Horizonte
Campinas
Santos
Niterói

Medellín
Cali
Barranquilla
Cartagena
Maracaibo
Valencia
Barquisimeto
Bucaramanga
Cúcuta
Villavicencio
Guayaquil
Chiclayo
Trujillo
Piura
Arequipa
Cuzco
Santa Cruz
Cochabamba
Potosí
Oruro

Amazonas
Tocantins
Xingu
Orinoco
São Francisco

SERRA DO RONCADOR
MATO GROSSO
PLANALTO
CORDILLERA ORIENTAL
CORDILLERA CENTRAL
CORDILLERA OCCIDENTAL
CORDILLERA REAL
ALTIPLANO
DESIERTO DE ATACAMA
SELVAS
LA GRAN SABANA
PARIMA
ACARAI MTS.
TUMUC-HUMAC MTS.
ILHA DE MARAJÓ

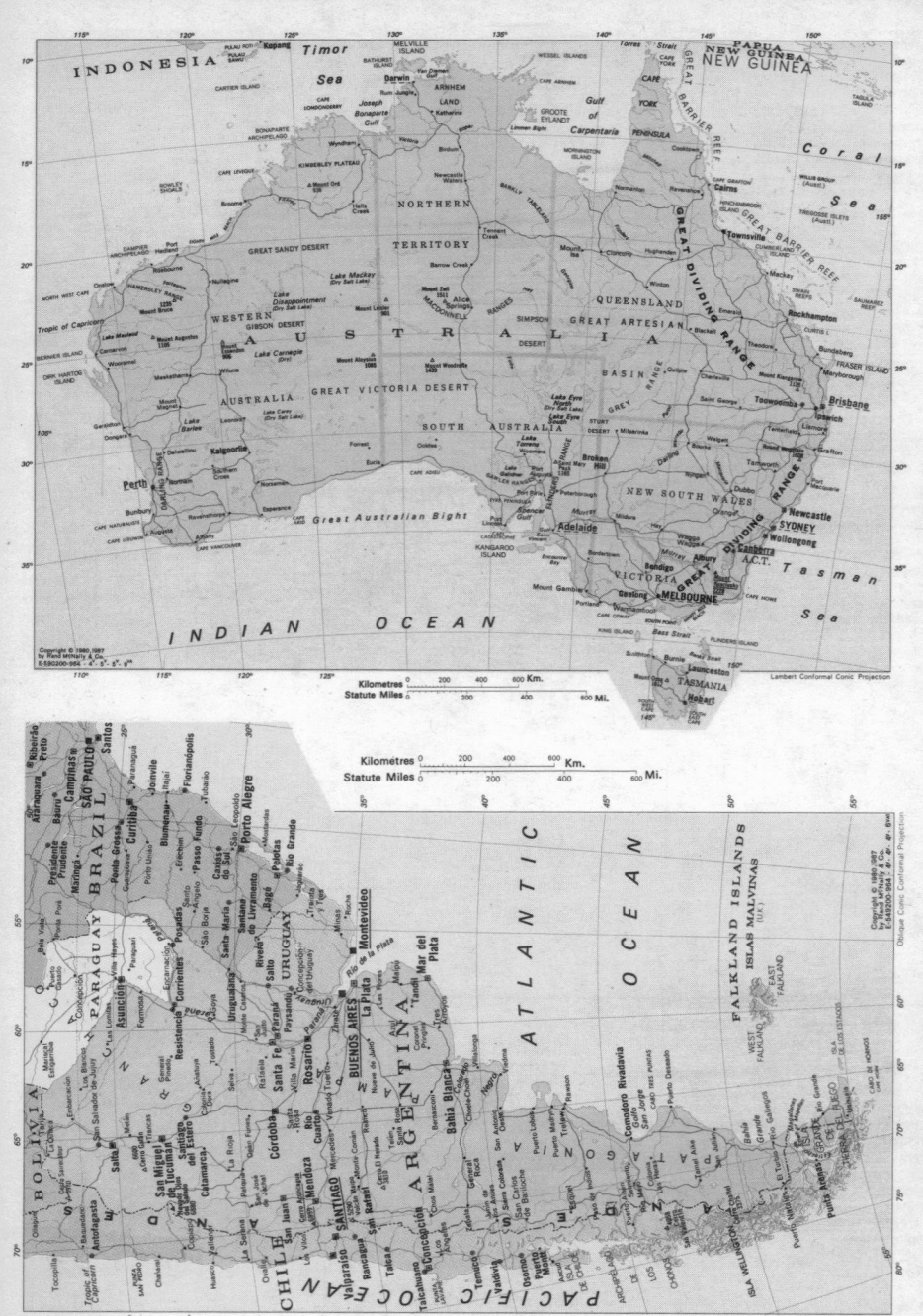

In 1984, the Council for the Northwest Territories adopted legislation which recognized and provided for the use of aboriginal languages and which established English and French as official languages of the territories. Ontario enacted legislation in 1986 to provide for French language services in the provincial government. In 1988, the legislature of the Yukon Territories passed a *Languages Act* recognizing French and English as languages of the Legislative Assembly, laws and courts; it also provided for French services and recognized the significance of aboriginal languages in the Yukon.

In a 1988 ruling, the Supreme Court of Canada declared that the *Northwest Territories Act of 1891* required Saskatchewan and Alberta to provide bilingual legislatures, bilingual legislation and bilingual court systems. But the Court also declared that the law was not "entrenched" and that the provinces could

therefore amend it unilaterally, as part of their own provincial constitutions. Both provinces then enacted legislation declaring that the law did not apply to their respective jurisdictions and validating earlier unilingual English laws.

The Saskatchewan Act, however, provides for the use of French and English in the Legislature and in 6 provincial courts; it also gives the government authority to determine which present or future laws ought to be enacted, printed and published in both languages. Alberta's Act makes provision for the use of French and English by members of the Legislature and in 4 provincial courts.

As of mid-1988, several cases concerning language matters were pending before Canadian courts.

Population by Official Languages

Source: Censuses of Canada

(percentage distribution)

	1961 English[1]	1961 French[1]	1961 Bilingual[2]	1981 English[1]	1981 French[1]	1981 Bilingual[2]	1986 English[1]	1986 French[1]	1986 Bilingual[2]
Canada	67.4	19.1	12.2	67.0	16.6	15.3	66.8	15.8	16.2
Newfoundland	98.5	0.1	1.2	97.6	...	2.3	97.2	...	2.6
Prince Edward Island	91.1	1.2	7.6	91.7	0.2	8.1	90.3	0.2	9.4
Nova Scotia	92.9	0.8	6.1	92.3	0.2	7.4	91.5	0.2	8.1
New Brunswick	62.0	18.7	19.0	60.5	13.0	26.5	58.6	12.1	29.1
Quebec	11.6	61.9	25.5	6.7	60.1	32.4	5.7	59.0	34.5
Ontario	89.0	1.5	7.9	86.7	0.7	10.8	86.1	0.6	11.7
Manitoba	89.6	0.9	7.4	90.3	0.3	7.9	89.7	0.2	8.8
Saskatchewan	93.6	0.4	4.5	94.6	0.1	4.6	94.6	0.1	4.7
Alberta	94.1	0.4	4.3	92.4	0.2	6.4	92.4	0.1	6.4
British Columbia	95.3	0.2	3.5	92.8	0.1	5.7	92.3	...	6.2
Yukon	93.5	0.3	5.6	91.9	...	7.9	91.2	...	8.6
Northwest Territories	58.9	0.5	7.0	79.9	0.1	6.0	80.9	0.1	6.7

(1) Refers to persons who speak either English or French, but not both. (2) Refers to persons who speak both English and French.
. . . = too small to be included.

Unemployment Rates[1] by Age, 1987

Source: Statistics Canada

	All ages[2]	Age Groups 15-19	Age Groups 20-24	Age Groups 25-34	Age Groups 35-44	Age Groups 45-54	Age Groups 55-64
Canada	8.9	15.1	12.9	9.0	6.9	6.5	7.1
Newfoundland	18.6	32.2	28.3	19.5	13.2	11.8	n.a.
Prince Edward Island	13.3	n.a.	n.a.	n.a.	n.a.	n.a.	n.a.
Nova Scotia	12.5	19.9	19.7	13.6	9.2	8.1	n.a.
New Brunswick	13.2	19.9	20.3	14.2	9.7	9.0	n.a.
Quebec	10.3	16.0	14.3	10.6	8.4	8.2	8.6
Ontario	6.1	12.0	8.4	6.2	4.5	4.3	5.1
Manitoba	7.4	13.9	11.0	7.2	5.1	5.3	n.a.
Saskatchewan	7.3	13.9	12.3	7.6	5.3	n.a.	n.a.
Alberta	9.6	16.9	14.0	8.8	7.3	7.9	9.1
British Columbia	12.0	18.6	18.6	11.8	9.9	8.7	10.5

(1) The number of unemployed as a percentage of the labor force. (2) 15 years of age and over.
n.a. = not available

Poverty in Canada

Source: Statistics Canada

The low-income cut-off level (commonly referred to as the "poverty line") is set by Statistics Canada, using a standard that families or individuals who spend 58.5% or more of their pre-tax income on food, clothing and shelter are in financial difficulty.

The table below shows the income level establishing the poverty line in 1986. It varies according to changes in the cost of living, family size and place of residence. For instance, in 1986 the poverty line for a family of 4 living in Vancouver was $21 663; for a family of 4 living in a rural area it was $15 936.

In 1986, some 3 689 000 Canadians, one in every 7, had incomes below the poverty line. This includes some 1 016 000 children under 16 years of age, or one child in every 6. There were wide regional variations in poverty rates. Newfoundland had the highest poverty rate, 22.8% of its population. Ontario had the lowest poverty rate, 10.8% of its population.

Family size[1]	Urban areas				Rural areas
	Less than 30 000 persons	30 000 to 99 999 persons	100 000 to 499 999 persons	500 000 persons or more	
1 person	$ 8 774	$ 9 490	$10 116	$10 651	$ 7 877
2 persons	11 546	12 445	13 339	14 053	10 295
3 persons	15 488	16 650	17 815	18 799	13 785
4 persons	17 903	19 246	20 588	21 663	15 936
5 persons	20 768	22 290	23 902	25 243	18 531
6 persons	22 647	24 349	26 049	27 571	20 231
7 or more persons	24 975	26 856	28 735	30 347	22 290

(1) Does not distinguish between adults and children as family members.

Canadian Residents Living Below the Poverty Line

Source: Statistics Canada

(thousands of persons and families)

	1972	1975	1980	1984	1985	1986
Single persons	642	832	1 041	1 026	1 009	982
Males	234	295	345	394	377	377
Females	408	537	696	632	632	605
Families	707	661	745	972	908	851
2 persons	275	266	291	351	338	337
3 persons	131	136	181	250	234	214
4 persons	118	117	145	210	184	174
5 or more persons	184	143	128	161	152	127
With children under 16 years	418	397	461	633	590	539
1 child	124	132	181	259	232	225
2 children	128	127	177	233	226	196
3 children	78	73	69	141[1]	132[1]	118[1]
4 or more children	88	66	34	141[1]	132[1]	118[1]
Lone parent families	n.a.	218[2]	252	318	323	291
lone male parent	n.a.	13[2]	15	23	21	19
lone female parent	n.a.	205[2]	237	295	302	272

(1) 3 or more children. (2) 1976 data.
n.a. not available.

Average Family[1] Income

Source: Statistics Canada

	1971	1975	1980	1984	1985	1986
Canada	$10 113	$16 368	$26 913	$35 092	$37 368	$39 589
Newfoundland	6 855	12 359	19 781	26 187	27 746	27 687
Prince Edward Island	6 669	12 032	21 683	28 134	29 738	31 097
Nova Scotia	7 721	13 068	21 252	29 833	33 376	33 480
New Brunswick	7 882	13 283	20 501	29 247	30 710	31 811
Quebec	9 713	15 273	25 073	33 561	34 582	36 759
Ontario	11 154	17 772	28 270	37 721	40 949	44 098
Manitoba	9 083	14 869	24 528	33 269	34 319	35 990
Saskatchewan	7 762	15 784	25 479	32 487	34 558	35 779
Alberta	10 107	16 878	30 665	37 062	40 384	41 794
British Columbia	10 989	17 520	30 191	35 248	36 980	39 083

(1) Based on the census family definition: a husband and wife (with or without children who have never married) or a parent with one or more children who have never married, living together in the same home.

Average Income by Age, Male and Female,[1] 1986

Source: Statistics Canada

	Canada		Atlantic Provinces		Quebec		Ontario		Prairie Provinces		British Columbia	
Age Groups	Male	Female	Male	Female	Male	Female	Male	Female	Male	Female	Male	Female
15 yrs and over	$23 855	$13 233	$19 233	$10 600	$22 211	$12 766	$26 017	$14 047	$23 368	$13 415	$24 830	$13 228
15-19 yrs.	4 490	3 901	3 895	2 881	3 960	3 846	4 639	3 997	5 023	4 757	4 570	3 028
20-24 yrs.	13 153	10 426	11 182	8 549	12 585	9 919	13 235	10 656	13 586	11 391	15 363	10 974
25-34 yrs.	24 812	15 596	21 077	12 721	22 405	15 213	26 735	16 664	25 755	15 766	25 773	14 898
35-44 yrs.	31 883	17 220	25 655	13 645	29 649	16 743	34 675	18 585	32 076	16 687	32 806	17 138
45-54 yrs.	32 749	15 690	26 612	12 272	29 164	14 426	36 289	16 758	31 844	15 964	34 962	16 516
55-59 yrs.	29 830	13 811	23 266	11 347	27 878	12 670	34 542	14 041	25 435	14 179	29 096	16 376
60-64 yrs.	25 135	10 729	20 661	9 619	22 868	10 424	28 247	11 260	23 381	10 770	25 312	10 326
65-69 yrs.	18 982	10 880	15 034	9 299	17 145	9 137	21 025	12 372	19 324	10 915	18 860	11 073
70 yrs. and over	15 378	10 344	11 874	8 597	13 913	9 446	17 709	11 347	14 690	10 593	14 998	10 041

(1) Represents all individuals who earned income of one or more dollars.

Percentage of Households Owning Major Retail Items

Source: Statistics Canada

	1960	1965	1970	1975	1980	1985	1986	1987
Air conditioners	n.a.	2.2	4.3	12.4	16.7	17.8	18.1	19.6
Automobiles	66.6	75.0	77.7	78.9	79.8	77.1	77.4	78.3
Clothes dryers	12.2	25.2	40.8	48.1	63.2	68.6	68.6	69.5
Dishwashers	n.a.	2.7	7.5	15.2	28.6	37.0	37.9	39.4
Electric refrigerators	90.3	95.8	98.4	99.3	99.6	99.2	99.3	99.1
Electric stoves	56.2	69.0	78.6	85.1	89.4	92.3	92.6	93.0
Electric washers	86.8	86.2	83.7	76.9	77.3	77.4	76.4	76.5
Freezers	11.5	22.6	33.2	41.8	51.0	57.0	57.7	57.3
Microwave ovens	n.a.	n.a.	n.a.	0.8	n.a.	22.9	33.6	43.2
Radios	96.2	96.1	97.2	98.3	98.7	98.7	99.1	98.8
Telephones	83.3	89.4	93.9	96.4	97.6	98.2	98.1	98.5
Television, cable	n.a.	n.a.	n.a.	40.4	54.8	62.4	64.9	67.2
Televisions	80.6	92.6	96.0	96.8	97.7	98.4	98.6	98.5
Televisions, color	n.a.	n.a.	12.1	53.4	81.1	91.4	93.2	94.4
Video recorders	n.a.	n.a.	n.a.	n.a.	n.a.	23.4	35.1	45.0
Number of households[1]	4 404	5 000	5 784	6 721	7 787	9 079	9 331	9 556

(1) In thousands.
n.a. not available.

Personal Expenditure on Consumer Goods and Services

Source: Statistics Canada

(per capita expenditure in dollars)

	1966	%	1975	%	1980	%	1987	%
Total	$1 896	100.0	$4 299	100.0	$7 171	100.0	$12 604	100.0
Rent and fuel	337	17.8	773	18.0	1 452	20.2	2 663	21.1
Food	331	17.5	641	14.9	970	13.5	1 478	11.7
Restaurants and hotels	110	5.8	294	6.8	500	7.0	797	6.3
Recreation equipment and services	70	3.7	245	5.7	401	5.6	791	6.3
Clothing	157	8.3	307	7.2	485	6.8	759	6.0
New and used cars	118	6.2	241	5.6	348	4.8	696	5.5
Financial, legal and other services	81	4.3	193	4.5	318	4.4	675	5.4
Household furnishings and supplies	82	4.3	213	5.0	358	5.0	598	4.7
Gas and oil	51	2.7	130	3.0	244	3.4	397	3.0
Car repairs, parts and services	48	2.5	116	2.7	202	2.8	380	3.0
Alcohol	68	3.6	155	3.6	230	3.2	372	3.0
Medical care	62	3.3	93	2.2	186	2.6	341	2.7
Education	44	2.3	124	2.9	209	2.9	336	2.7
Tobacco	53	2.8	90	2.1	134	1.9	263	2.1
Purchased transportation	31	1.6	78	1.8	150	2.1	246	2.0
Reading and entertainment supplies	31	1.6	74	1.7	127	1.8	225	1.8
Communications	27	1.4	62	1.4	115	1.6	203	1.6
Household appliances	30	1.6	77	1.8	112	1.6	203	1.6
Furniture	34	1.8	92	2.1	131	1.8	192	1.5
Drugs	22	1.2	47	1.1	77	1.1	178	1.4
Domestic, childcare and other household services	23	1.2	41	1.0	73	1.0	161	1.3
Toilet articles	18	0.9	36	0.8	62	0.9	119	0.9
Personal care	19	1.0	33	0.8	55	0.8	116	0.9
Jewellery, watches and repairs	11	0.6	36	0.8	63	0.9	87	0.7
Laundry and dry cleaning	13	0.7	15	0.3	22	0.3	36	0.3

Type of Housing by Metropolitan[1] Areas, 1986

Source: Census of Canada

(percentage of all dwellings)

	No. of dwellings[2]	Housing Type single-detached	hi-rise apartments[3]	mobile homes[4]	other dwellings[5]	Ownership[6] owner-occupied	rental
Canada[6]	8 991 670	57.5%	8.9%	1.3%	32.3%	62.4%	37.6%
Calgary, Alta.[6]	248 590	55.9	8.3	0.6	35.1	57.9	42.1
Chicoutimi-Jonquière, Que.	51 305	49.5	1.0	1.3	48.2	61.5	38.5
Edmonton, Alta.[6]	283 365	57.7	7.1	1.4	33.8	57.1	42.9
Halifax, N.S.	103 830	51.6	10.8	1.8	35.8	58.3	41.7
Hamilton, Ont.	201 330	59.8	19.0	. . .	21.2	64.6	35.4
Kitchener, Ont.	110 155	55.4	9.9	. . .	34.6	61.9	38.1
London, Ont.	129 385	56.3	16.5	0.2	26.9	57.8	42.2
Montreal, Que.[6]	1 115 380	28.0	8.4	0.2	63.4	44.7	55.3
Oshawa, Ont.	68 010	61.8	10.1	0.2	27.9	70.2	29.8
Ottawa-Hull, Ont.-Que.	302 335	43.3	19.0	0.5	37.1	54.1	45.9
Quebec, Que.	218 425	41.5	5.7	0.7	52.1	53.0	47.0
Regina, Sask.	67 680	69.6	5.0	0.7	24.6	65.7	34.3
St. Catharines-Niagara, Ont.	124 575	71.6	6.0	0.2	22.1	72.0	28.0
Saint John, N.B.	41 720	53.3	4.3	3.2	39.2	61.6	38.4
St. John's, Nfld.	47 905	55.9	1.2	0.9	42.0	68.3	31.7
Saskatoon, Sask.	73 960	62.9	5.3	1.1	30.6	59.9	40.1
Sherbrooke, Que.	48 530	41.6	1.8	0.4	56.2	50.1	49.9
Sudbury, Ont.	51 600	60.9	7.1	0.8	31.2	64.5	35.5
Thunder Bay, Ont.	43 665	69.5	5.2	0.4	25.0	69.3	30.7
Toronto, Ont.	1 199 800	43.1	28.2	. . .	28.6	58.3	41.7
Trois-Rivières, Que.	47 475	45.7	2.1	0.4	51.8	55.4	44.6
Vancouver, B.C.	532 220	53.3	9.9	0.6	36.3	56.5	43.5
Victoria, B.C.[6]	105 445	56.6	5.2	0.9	37.2	67.2	32.8
Windsor, Ont.	91 615	68.4	11.2	0.4	19.9	60.8	39.2
Winnipeg, Man.	236 325	59.8	12.7	0.1	27.4	59.7	40.3

(1) For census metropolitan areas, which include neighboring municipalities from which the major urban centre draws its work force. (2) A dwelling represents a home where a person or persons may be able to reside. (3) Building with 5 or more stories. (4) Includes houseboats and railway cars. (5) Includes semi-detached houses, row houses and apartment buildings with less than 5 stories. (6) Excludes dwellings on Indian reserves.
. . . = too small to be included.

Apartment Rents and Vacancy Rates for Metropolitan[1] Areas

Source: Canada Mortgage and Housing Corporation

Metropolitan Area	Vacancy rate[2] 1975	1980	1985	1986	1987	Average rent[2] (2 bedroom apt.) 1986	1987
Calgary, Alta	0.4	0.4	2.7	3.9	4.3	$509	$510
Chicoutimi-Jonquière, Que.	1.1	1.4	3.2	9.0	10.5	403	399
Edmonton, Alta.	0.3	1.1	4.4	4.1	5.6	457	472
Halifax, N.S.	1.8	1.2	0.6	2.3	4.4	528	541
Hamilton, Ont.	3.0	1.3	0.4	0.3	0.3	412	436
Kitchener, Ont.	2.3	1.1	0.4	0.2	0.2	421	440
London, Ont.	2.2	4.1	0.4	0.7	1.0	439	477
Montreal, Que.	0.7	3.4	1.6	1.8	3.6	425	470
Oshawa, Ont.	n.a.	2.4	0.1	0.2	0.3	476	504
Ottawa, Ont.	2.3	3.5	0.8	1.9	1.6	539	570
Quebec, Que.	1.4	2.8	1.5	3.2	5.6	449	450
Regina, Sask.	. . .	0.7	3.1	3.4	2.6	470	477
St. Catharines-Niagara, Ont.	2.9	1.8	0.3	0.8	0.5	422	438
Saint John, N.B.	0.6	3.6	3.1	4.8	4.2	377	379
St. John's, Nfld.	3.7	0.1	2.0	4.9	10.1	522	539
Saskatoon, Sask.	. . .	0.5	2.5	2.8	4.3	442	441
Sudbury, Ont.	1.2	1.9	0.6	0.9	1.0	409	482
Thunder Bay, Ont.	0.5	1.0	0.6	2.4	2.1	490	510
Toronto, Ont.	1.8	0.5	0.4	0.1	0.1	550	569
Trois-Rivières, Que.	n.a.	n.a.	2.1	6.7	9.0	350	362
Vancouver, B.C.	0.1	0.1	2.2	0.9	1.1	583	588
Victoria, B.C.	0.1	0.1	1.9	0.6	0.4	472	489
Windsor, Ont.	3.9	6.1	0.7	1.0	0.7	520	527
Winnipeg, Man.	2.1	5.1	0.9	1.6	2.8	483	496

(1) For census metropolitan areas, which include neighboring municipalities from which the major urban centre draws its work force. (2) As of each Oct., in a CMHC survey of privately-initiated apartments of 6 units and over.
. . . = less than 0.1% vacancy rate; n.a. not available.

Average Resale Value of Canadian Homes[1]

Source: The Canadian Real Estate Association

	1975	1980	1981	1983	1984	1985	1986	1987
Canada	$47 201	$67 072	$77 056	$76 761	$76 544	$80 778	$94 940	$111 431
Calgary, Alta.	48 341	93 977	107 739	98 792	86 723	80 462	86 482	93 102
Edmonton, Alta.	43 846	84 622	91 393	85 792	79 214	74 309	74 626	77 373
Halifax, N.S.	38 326	53 160	59 365	70 251	78 473	79 350	85 037	89 013
Hamilton, Ont.	45 103	54 834	58 508	64 015	65 995	72 972	89 079	114 625
Mississauga, Ont.	61 977	80 340	83 559	93 797	93 596	99 674	126 863	169 469
Montreal, Que.	35 266	49 194	55 003	63 676	64 361	70 563	78 135	92 292
Ottawa, Ont.	49 633	63 177	64 853	86 608	102 083	107 640	111 925	119 612
Regina, Sask.	33 880	48 628	54 915	59 053	58 889	61 403	63 941	65 078
Saint John, N.B.	35 884	45 170	48 572	47 136	53 256	57 088	63 441	69 145
St. John's, Nfld.	n.a.	53 246	55 789	58 455	61 537	66 642	70 554	73 745
Toronto, Ont.	57 583	75 620	90 925	101 631	102 318	109 093	138 301	189 105
Vancouver, B.C.	57 763	100 065	148 860	115 818	113 722	112 852	120 035	132 658
Victoria, B.C.	n.a.	85 066	121 648	97 515	90 970	88 451	95 633	102 040
Winnipeg, Man.	33 463	50 490	52 655	55 335	58 754	62 478	71 000	78 286

(1) Average price of all homes sold on the Multiple Listing Service.
n.a. not available.

Canadian Lotteries

(as of May 1, 1988)

Source: Canadian World Almanac Questionnaire

	Lottery name	Ticket cost	Tickets issued per draw[1]	Jackpot winnings	Chances of winning[2] jackpot	Chances of winning[2] any prize	% of prize return[3]
Nationally	Loto 6/49	$ 1.00	varies	$1 000 000[4]	1: 13 983 816	1: 53	45
	The Provincial	5.00	1 000 000	1 000 000	1: 1 000 000	1: 5	45
Atlantic Canada ...	Auto-Plus	1.00	1 000 000	100 000	1: 1 000 000	1: 10	47
	Tag	1.00	600 000	100 000	1: 600 000	1: 10	47
	Pik 4	1.00/2.00/5.00	varies	10 000	1: 14 125	1: 14	47
	Instant	1.00/2.00	varies	25 000	1: 240 000	1: 5	47
Quebec	Inter Plus	2.00	1 000 000	250 000	1: 1 000 000	1: 57	50
	Mini Loto	.50	2 700 000	50 000	1: 900 000	1: 90	44
	Sélect 42	1.00	varies	500 000	1: 5 245 786	1: 34	48
	La Quotidienne	0.50	varies	varies	1: 10 000	1:167	45
	Instant	1.00/2.00	varies	100 000	1: 1 440 000	1: 4.3	50
Ontario	Wintario	1.00	4 000 000	200 000	1: 4 000 000	1: 5.9	40
	Lottario	1.00	3 000 000	varies	1: 3 260 000	1: 27	50
	Instant	2.00	varies	varies	1: 480 000	1: 4.3	42
Western Canada ...	Western Express	1.00	1 230 000	100 000	1: 1 221 759	1: 4.17	50
	Lotto 6/36	1.00	varies	varies	1: 1 947 792	1: 22.2	50
	Instant	1.00/2.00	varies	varies	varies	varies	45-50
	The Plus	1.00	varies	100 000	1: 1 000 000	1: 5.26	53
British Columbia ...	The Express	1.00	1 000 000	100 000	1: 333 333	1: 8	62
	The Pick	1.00	varies	200 000	1: 1 159 600	1: 7	50
	Lotto BC	1.00	varies	150 000[4]	1: 628 000	1: 54	46
	Instant	1.00	varies	10 000	1: 240 000	1: 7.8	45
	Punto	1.00	varies	100 000	1:116 640 000	1: 81	50
	Extra	1.00	varies	500 000	1: 3 764 376	1: 6.8	40

(1) All tickets issued may or may not be sold by draw date. (2) The mathematical chances of winning a prize. (3) The portion of the lottery game's gross sales which is offered as cash prizes. (4) This is a minimum amount which may increase depending on the pool.
n.a. not available.

Income and Taxation

Canadian Income Tax

Income tax was introduced in Canada in 1917 as a temporary measure to help finance the war effort. The law introducing the tax (the *Income War Tax Act*) was shorter and much simpler than our current legislation. It imposed tax at graduated rates, ranging from 4% on the first $1 500 of income to 25% for any income above $100 000.

This "temporary" war tax was not repealed when the war ended. But in 1948 the federal government removed "war" from the title and gave the statute the name it has today—the *Income Tax Act*. This act has been amended many times—most notably in 1972 when a major overhaul of the tax system broadened the tax base slightly and introduced a tax on capital gains—but is still the basis of our federal income tax laws.

In June 1987, the government announced major tax changes which took effect in 1988. Among the changes: the establishment of only 3 federal tax brackets (17% on income up to $27 500, 26% on income between $27 501 and $55 000, 29% on income above $55 000); the elimination of the $1 000 interest and dividend deduction and the $500 employment expense deduction; the replacement of several deductions with tax credits.

Provincial Income Tax

Every province except Quebec collects income tax from its residents by "piggy-backing" on the federal tax. Each province imposes tax of a fixed percentage based on the amount of income tax an individual must pay to the federal government. The federal government collects the tax, then remits the appropriate amounts to the provincial governments.

Quebec, however, chooses to collect its own provincial income tax, so Quebec residents must file two income tax forms: the federal form filed by all Canadian taxpayers, and the Quebec income tax form.

Filing Tax Returns

Though corporations must file tax returns each year, individuals need only file if they owe taxes. Persons owing money must file a return by Apr. 30 of the year following the taxation year. Failure to do so makes you liable to an administrative penalty of 5% of unpaid tax plus an additional penalty of one percent per month on the amount outstanding, to a maximum of 12 months.

Individual Income Tax Rates–1988
Source: Coopers & Lybrand

Federal

Taxable Income	Basic federal tax	Marginal Rate on excess[1]
$ 1 ..... $ 0		17%
27 500 ..... 4 675		26%
55 000 ..... 11 825		29%

Quebec[1]

Taxable Income	Tax	Marginal Rate on excess
$ 1	–	16.0%
7 000	1 120	19.5%
14 000	2 485	21.5%
23 000	4 420	24.5%
50 000	11 035	26.0%

(1) The Quebec government collects its own taxes and does not charge a specific rate of tax based on what its residents owe the federal government in income tax. Quebec residents, therefore, must file 2 tax forms, one each for the federal and Quebec governments.

Provincial Tax Rates
(rates applied to basic federal tax)

Newfoundland	60 %
Prince Edward Island	56 %[1]
Nova Scotia	56.5%
New Brunswick	60 %
Ontario	51 %[2]
Manitoba	54 %[3]
Saskatchewan	50 %[4]
Alberta	46.5%[5]
British Columbia	51.5%
Northwest Territories	43 %
Yukon Territory	45 %
Non residents	47 %[6]

(1) To be increased by 5% (10% in 1989) of basic provincial tax in excess of $12 500. (2) To be increased by 10% of basic provincial tax in excess of $10 000. (3) To be increased by a net income tax of 2% of net income, plus a surtax equal to a maximum of the 2% net income tax less $600. (4) To be increased by a net income tax of 2%, plus a surtax of 12% of provincial tax (including the 2% tax) in excess of $4 000. (5) To be increased by 8% of basic provincial tax in excess of $3 500, plus an additional tax equal to 0.5% of taxable income. (6) Non residents are subject to additional federal tax in lieu of provincial tax.

1988 Individual Tax Tables¹

Source: Coopers & Lybrand

Taxable Income	Que.² Prov.	Fed.	Ont.	BC.	Alta.	Sask.³	Man.⁴	NS.	Nfld.	NB.	PEI
$ 6 000	$ –	$ –	$ –	$ –	$ –	$ –	$ –	$ –	$ –	$ –	$ –
7 000	64	147	175	263	175	200	175	271	277	277	270
8 000	259	294	420	525	350	480	424	542	554	554	541
9 000	454	441	785	788	525	760	731	813	831	831	811
10 000	649	588	1 047	1 051	800	1 040	1 038	1 085	1 108	1 108	1 081
11 000	844	735	1 309	1 313	1 101	1 370	1 344	1 356	1 385	1 385	1 351
12 000	1 039	882	1 571	1 576	1 402	1 701	1 651	1 627	1 663	1 663	1 622
13 000	1 234	1 029	1 833	1 839	1 703	2 031	1 958	1 898	1 940	1 940	1 892
14 000	1 429	1 176	2 094	2 101	2 004	2 361	2 265	2 169	2 217	2 217	2 162
15 000	1 644	1 323	2 356	2 364	2 306	2 641	2 572	2 440	2 494	2 494	2 433
16 000	1 859	1 470	2 618	2 626	2 607	2 921	2 879	2 711	2 771	2 771	2 703
17 000	2 074	1 618	2 880	2 889	2 881	3 201	3 186	2 983	3 048	3 048	2 973
18 000	2 289	1 765	3 142	3 152	3 140	3 481	3 493	3 254	3 325	3 325	3 244
19 000	2 504	1 912	3 403	3 414	3 399	3 761	3 800	3 525	3 602	3 602	3 514
20 000	2 719	2 059	3 665	3 677	3 658	4 041	4 107	3 796	3 879	3 879	3 784
21 000	2 934	2 206	3 927	3 940	3 917	4 321	4 413	4 067	4 156	4 156	4 054
22 000	3 149	2 353	4 189	4 202	4 176	4 602	4 710	4 338	4 434	4 434	4 325
23 000	3 364	2 500	4 451	4 465	4 436	4 882	4 997	4 610	4 711	4 711	4 595
24 000	3 609	2 647	4 712	4 728	4 695	5 162	5 284	4 881	4 988	4 988	4 865
25 000	3 854	2 794	4 974	4 990	4 954	5 442	5 571	5 152	5 265	5 265	5 136
26 000	4 099	2 941	5 236	5 253	5 213	5 722	5 858	5 423	5 542	5 542	5 406
27 000	4 344	3 088	5 498	5 516	5 472	6 002	6 145	5 694	5 819	5 819	5 676
28 000	4 589	3 274	5 829	5 848	5 799	6 351	6 502	6 037	6 170	6 170	6 018
29 000	4 834	3 499	6 229	6 250	6 192	6 769	6 931	6 452	6 593	6 593	6 432
30 000	5 079	3 724	6 630	6 651	6 586	7 187	7 359	6 866	7 017	7 017	6 845
31 000	5 324	3 949	7 030	7 053	6 980	7 604	7 807	7 281	7 441	7 441	7 258
32 000	5 569	4 174	7 430	7 455	7 373	8 022	8 255	7 696	7 865	7 865	7 672
33 000	5 814	4 399	7 831	7 856	7 767	8 440	8 703	8 111	8 289	8 289	8 085
34 000	6 059	4 623	8 231	8 258	8 161	8 858	9 152	8 525	8 712	8 712	8 499
35 000	6 304	4 848	8 632	8 660	8 554	9 276	9 600	8 940	9 136	9 136	8 912
36 000	6 549	5 073	9 032	9 061	8 948	9 693	10 048	9 355	9 560	9 560	9 325
37 000	6 794	5 298	9 432	9 463	9 342	10 111	10 496	9 769	9 984	9 984	9 739
38 000	7 039	5 523	9 833	9 865	9 736	10 529	10 944	10 184	10 408	10 408	10 152
39 000	7 284	5 748	10 233	10 267	10 129	10 959	11 393	10 599	10 831	10 831	10 566
40 000	7 529	5 973	10 634	10 668	10 523	11 395	11 841	11 013	11 255	11 255	10 979
41 000	7 774	6 198	11 034	11 070	10 917	11 831	12 289	11 428	11 679	11 679	11 392
42 000	8 019	6 423	11 434	11 472	11 310	12 267	12 737	11 843	12 103	12 103	11 806
43 000	8 264	6 648	11 835	11 873	11 710	12 702	13 185	12 258	12 527	12 527	12 219
44 000	8 509	6 872	12 235	12 275	12 113	13 138	13 634	12 672	12 950	12 950	12 633
45 000	8 754	7 097	12 636	12 677	12 517	13 574	14 082	13 087	13 374	13 374	13 046
46 000	8 999	7 322	13 036	13 078	12 920	14 010	14 530	13 502	13 798	13 798	13 459
47 000	9 244	7 547	13 436	13 480	13 323	14 446	14 978	13 916	14 222	14 222	13 873
48 000	9 489	7 772	13 837	13 882	13 727	14 881	15 426	14 331	14 646	14 646	14 286
49 000	9 734	7 997	14 237	14 284	14 130	15 317	15 875	14 746	15 069	15 069	14 700
50 000	9 979	8 222	14 638	14 685	14 534	15 753	16 323	15 160	15 493	15 493	15 113
51 000	10 239	8 447	15 038	15 087	14 937	16 189	16 771	15 575	15 917	15 917	15 526
52 000	10 499	8 672	15 438	15 489	15 340	16 625	17 219	15 990	16 341	16 341	15 940
53 000	10 759	8 897	15 839	15 890	15 744	17 060	17 667	16 405	16 765	16 765	16 353
54 000	11 019	9 121	16 239	16 292	16 147	17 496	18 116	16 819	17 188	17 188	16 767
55 000	11 279	9 346	16 640	16 694	16 550	17 932	18 564	17 234	17 612	17 612	17 180
56 000	11 539	9 597	17 086	17 142	17 000	18 415	19 059	17 697	18 085	18 085	17 641
57 000	11 799	9 848	17 533	17 590	17 449	18 899	19 554	18 159	18 558	18 558	18 102
58 000	12 059	10 099	17 979	18 038	17 898	19 382	20 050	18 622	19 030	19 030	18 563
59 000	12 319	10 350	18 426	18 486	18 348	19 866	20 545	19 084	19 503	19 503	19 024
60 000	12 579	10 601	18 873	18 934	18 797	20 349	21 040	19 547	19 976	19 976	19 485
61 000	12 839	10 851	19 319	19 382	19 246	20 833	21 536	20 009	20 448	20 448	19 947
62 000	13 099	11 102	19 766	19 830	19 696	21 316	22 031	20 472	20 921	20 921	20 408
63 000	13 359	11 353	20 212	20 278	20 145	21 800	22 526	20 934	21 394	21 394	20 869
64 000	13 619	11 604	20 659	20 726	20 594	22 283	23 022	21 397	21 866	21 866	21 330
65 000	13 879	11 855	21 106	21 174	21 044	22 767	23 517	21 859	22 339	22 339	21 791

(1) Amounts shown reflect a claim for only the basic personal tax credit. Where other personal credits apply these amounts can be reduced by the value of the additional credits. The amounts shown also reflect the Federal and provincial surtaxes (and, in Alberta, the 0.5% flat tax on taxable income) and tax reductions where appropriate. Home owners, renter assistance, child sales tax, political contribution, venture capital and cost of living credits available in certain provinces have not been taken into account. Where taxable income includes the grossed-up amount of taxable Canadian dividends the amounts of tax shown should be reduced by the combined Dividend Tax Credit to approximate the amount of tax payable. For 1988, dividends are to be grossed-up by one-quarter (as opposed to 33⅓% in 1987) and the Dividend Tax Credit is roughly equal to the amount of the gross-up. (2) Because taxable income differs for Federal and Quebec purposes, Quebec taxpayers may have to determine the tax payable to each jurisdiction on separate lines of the table before totalling. (3) The tax payable for Saskatchewan includes the flat tax of 2% on the assumption that net income is the same as taxable income. Where net income exceeds taxable income, the tax payable should be increased by 2% of the excess to more accurately approximate the liability. (4) The tax payable for Manitoba includes the additional tax of 2% of net income on the assumption that net income is the same as taxable income. Where net income exceeds taxable income the tax payable should be increased by 2% of the excess to more accurately approximate the liability.
– = zero.

Taxable Income	Que.[2] Prov.	Que.[2] Fed.	Ont.	BC.	Alta.	Sask.[3]	Man.[4]	NS.	Nfld.	NB.	PEI
$ 66 000	$14 139	$12 106	$21 552	$21 622	$21 493	$23 250	$24 012	$22 322	$22 812	$22 812	$22 252
67 000	14 399	12 357	21 999	22 070	21 942	23 734	24 507	22 785	23 285	23 285	22 713
68 000	14 659	12 607	22 445	22 518	22 392	24 217	25 003	23 247	23 757	23 757	23 174
69 000	14 919	12 858	22 892	22 966	22 841	24 701	25 498	23 710	24 230	24 230	23 635
70 000	15 179	13 109	23 339	23 414	23 290	25 184	25 993	24 172	24 703	24 703	24 096
71 000	15 439	13 360	23 785	23 863	23 740	25 668	26 489	24 635	25 175	25 175	24 558
72 000	15 699	13 611	24 232	24 311	24 189	26 151	26 984	25 097	25 648	25 648	25 019
73 000	15 959	13 862	24 678	24 759	24 638	26 635	27 479	25 560	26 121	26 121	25 480
74 000	16 219	14 112	25 125	25 207	25 088	27 118	27 975	26 022	26 593	26 593	25 941
75 000	16 479	14 363	25 572	25 655	25 537	27 602	28 470	26 485	27 066	27 066	26 402
76 000	16 739	14 614	26 018	26 103	25 987	28 085	28 965	26 948	27 539	27 539	26 863
77 000	16 999	14 865	26 465	26 551	26 436	28 569	29 460	27 410	28 012	28 012	27 324
78 000	17 259	15 116	26 911	26 999	26 885	29 052	29 956	27 873	28 484	28 484	27 785
79 000	17 519	15 367	27 358	27 447	27 335	29 536	30 451	28 335	28 957	28 957	28 246
80 000	17 779	15 618	27 805	27 895	27 784	30 019	30 946	28 798	29 430	29 430	28 707
81 000	18 039	15 868	28 251	28 343	28 233	30 503	31 442	29 260	29 902	29 902	29 169
82 000	18 299	16 119	28 698	28 791	28 683	30 986	31 937	29 723	30 375	30 375	29 630
83 000	18 559	16 370	29 114	29 239	29 132	31 470	32 432	30 185	30 848	30 848	30 091
84 000	18 819	16 621	29 591	29 687	29 581	31 953	32 928	30 648	31 320	31 320	30 552
85 000	19 079	16 872	30 038	30 135	30 031	32 437	33 423	31 110	31 793	31 793	31 013
86 000	19 339	17 123	30 494	30 583	30 480	32 920	33 918	31 573	32 266	32 266	31 474
87 000	19 599	17 374	30 955	31 031	30 929	33 404	34 413	32 036	32 739	32 739	31 935
88 000	19 859	17 624	31 417	31 479	31 379	33 887	34 909	32 498	33 211	33 211	32 396
89 000	20 119	17 875	31 878	31 927	31 828	34 371	35 404	32 961	33 684	33 684	32 857
90 000	20 379	18 126	32 339	32 375	32 277	34 854	35 899	33 423	34 157	34 157	33 318
91 000	20 639	18 377	32 801	32 824	32 727	35 338	36 395	33 886	34 629	34 629	33 780
92 000	20 899	18 628	33 262	33 272	33 176	35 821	36 890	34 348	35 102	35 102	34 241
93 000	21 159	18 879	33 724	33 720	33 625	36 305	37 385	34 811	35 575	35 575	34 702
94 000	21 419	19 129	34 185	34 168	34 075	36 788	37 881	35 273	36 047	36 047	35 163
95 000	21 679	19 380	34 646	34 616	34 524	37 272	38 376	35 736	36 520	36 520	35 626
96 000	21 939	19 631	35 108	35 064	34 973	37 755	38 871	36 199	36 993	36 993	36 095
97 000	22 199	19 882	35 569	35 512	35 423	38 239	39 366	36 661	37 466	37 466	36 565
98 000	22 459	20 133	36 031	35 960	35 872	38 722	39 862	37 124	37 938	37 938	37 034
99 000	22 719	20 384	36 492	36 408	36 321	39 206	40 357	37 586	38 411	38 411	37 503
100 000	22 979	20 635	36 953	36 856	36 771	39 689	40 852	38 049	38 884	38 884	37 972

Canadian Minimum Wages

Source: Labour Canada

(hourly rate for experienced adult workers)

	Federal[1]	Nfld	PEI	NS	NB	Que	Ont	Man	Sask	Alta	BC	YT	NWT
1965	1.25	.70(m) .50(f)	1.00	1.05(m) .80(f)	.80	.85	1.00	.85	$38/wk	1.00	1.00	n.a.	n.a.
1970	1.65	1.25(m) 1.00(f)	1.25(m) .95(f)	1.25(m) 1.00(f)	1.15	1.40	1.50	1.50	1.25	1.55	1.50	1.50	1.50
1975	2.60	2.20	2.30	2.25	2.30	2.80	2.40	2.60	2.50	2.50	2.75	2.70	2.50
1980	3.25	3.15	3.00	3.00	3.05	3.65	3.00	3.15	3.65	3.50	3.65	3.35	3.50
1985	3.50	4.00	4.00	4.00	3.80	4.00	4.00	4.30	4.50	3.80	3.65	4.25	4.25
1986	4.00	4.00	4.00	4.00	4.00	4.35	4.35	4.30	4.50	3.80	3.65	4.25	5.00
1987	4.00	4.00	4.00	4.00	4.00	4.55	4.55	4.70	4.50	3.80	4.00	4.75	5.00
1988	4.00	4.25[2]	4.25[3]	4.00[4]	4.00	4.75[3]	4.75[3]	4.70	4.50	4.50[5]	4.50[6]	5.39[7]	5.00

Minimum wage rates (1988) for other categories are: **Nfld.:** domestics, $2.75; **PEI:** under 18, $3.75[3]; **NS:** 14-18, $3.55; **NB:** for those whose hours cannot be determined and are not paid by commission, $176/wk; **Que.:** hotel, restaurant and similar workers, $4.03[3]; live-in domestics, $172/wk[3]; **Ont.:** students under 18, $3.90[3]; serving alcohol, $4.25[3]; domestics who work more than 24 hours a week, $4.75/hr.[3]; **Alta.:** under 18, attending school, $4.00; salespersons, $150/wk; **B.C.:** under 18, $4.00[6]; domestics, farm workers, $32.00 per day or part day; superintendent of building with less than 60 units $240/month and $9.00 per unit; superintendent of building with more than 60 units, $816/month; farm workers paid by weight or volume picked, $816/month.

(1) Applies to work under federal government jurisdiction as defined by the Constitution Act, 1867, Sections 91 and 92. (2) As of Apr. 1, 1988. (3) As of Oct. 1, 1988. (4) $4.50 as of Jan. 1, 1989. (5) As of Sept. 1, 1988. (6) As of July 1, 1988. (7) As of May 1, 1988. n.a. not available; m = male; f = female.

Average Income in Canada

Source: Statistics Canada

This table shows actual average income from 1969 to 1986 in addition to average income in constant dollars over the same period. Constant dollars are adjusted to remove the effects of inflation, thereby providing a realistic way of comparing incomes for different years. An increase in constant dollar income means that incomes have increased faster than the cost of living; a decrease in constant dollar income means that incomes have not kept pace with inflation.

	Families[1]				Individuals			
	Female Head		Male Head		Females		Males	
	actual	constant[2]	actual	constant[2]	actual	constant[2]	actual	constant[2]
1969	$ 4 892	$16 316	$ 9 013	$30 060	$ 3 256	$10 859	$ 4 746	$15 829
1971	5 486	17 214	10 486	32 904	3 597	11 287	5 136	16 116
1973	6 687	18 601	12 910	35 912	4 267	11 870	6 206	17 263
1975	8 528	19 296	16 993	38 450	5 450	12 332	7 964	18 020
1977	10 691	20 850	20 544	40 066	6 923	13 502	9 919	19 345
1979	12 663	20 773	24 946	40 922	8 754	14 360	12 427	20 386
1980	13 561	20 199	28 295	42 145	9 776	14 561	13 461	20 050
1981	16 161	21 397	31 364	41 526	11 430	15 133	16 239	21 500
1982	17 004	20 319	34 222	40 893	12 964	15 491	17 250	20 613
1983	17 249	19 486	36 015	40 686	12 981	14 665	17 629	19 915
1984	19 000	20 569	37 098	40 162	13 617	14 742	18 186	19 688
1985	19 827	20 638	39 550	41 167	12 378	12 884	22 689	23 617
1986	21 015	21 015	41 816	41 816	13 233	13 233	23 855	23 855

(1) Based on the Census family definition: a husband and wife (without children or with children who never married) or a parent with one or more children who never married, living together in the same home. (2) Converted to 1986 dollars.

Average Canadian Income and Taxes by Occupation, 1985

Source: Revenue Canada Taxation Statistics

Occupation	Average income[1]	Average federal tax	Number[2]	Occupation	Average income[1]	Average federal tax	Number[2]
Self-employed doctors and surgeons	103 096	20 424	35 260	Municipal government employees	24 694	2 921	625 153
Self-employed dentists ..	86 670	16 034	8 680	Investors	22 344	2 037	1 076 587
Self-employed lawyers and notaries	68 820	12 537	20 163	Business employees ...	21 332	2 579	7 089 255
Self-employed accountants	60 272	9 494	11 528	Institutional employees ..	20 745	2 215	957 625
Self-employed engineers and architects	43 325	6 740	4 837	Property owners	19 288	2 210	130 737
Teachers and professors .	35 488	4 715	230 023	Self-employed salespeople	18 423	2 017	38 073
Provincial crown corp. employees	33 104	4 550	149 823	Fishermen	17 235	1 557	35 609
Federal crown corp. employees	31 312	4 046	200 259	Farmers	15 634	993	265 694
Federal government employees	28 880	3 678	327 449	Business proprietors	13 999	1 261	528 095
Armed forces employees	27 422	3 381	87 303	Pensioners	13 467	776	1 247 934
Other self-employed professionals	25 829	3 361	58 321	Self-employed entertainers and artists	12 846	1 289	22 971
Provincial government employees	25 175	2 978	391 339	Unclassified employees	12 819	1 145	523 127
				Unclassified	4 722	297	1 798 641
				All occupations	19 386	2 181	15 864 486

(1) Average total income after business expense deductions but before personal deductions. (2) Based on number of tax returns.

Income by Family,[1] 1986

Source: Statistics Canada

(percentage distribution of families by income groups)

Income groups	Canada	Nfld	PEI	NS	NB	Que	Ont	Man	Sask	Alta	BC
Less than $5 000	1.4	2.6	1.0	1.7	1.1	1.2	1.1	2.3	2.6	1.5	1.7
$ 5 000– 9 999	4.2	8.4	4.0	6.2	7.9	5.2	3.1	4.4	5.6	3.1	3.7
$10 000–12 499	3.5	7.2	4.5	4.6	4.7	4.3	2.3	3.2	4.2	2.8	4.7
$12 500–14 999	4.6	8.3	6.9	7.2	5.8	5.3	3.3	6.2	7.0	4.1	4.2
$15 000–17 499	4.8	7.4	6.5	6.0	5.8	4.9	4.0	5.6	5.3	5.0	5.4
$17 000–19 999	4.1	6.0	8.3	5.6	5.0	4.4	3.5	5.4	5.4	3.4	4.1

Income groups	Canada	Nfld	PEI	NS	NB	Que	Ont	Man	Sask	Alta	BC
Less than $20 000[2]	22.6	39.9	31.2	31.3	30.3	25.3	17.3	27.1	30.1	19.9	23.8
$20 000–24 999	8.6	13.3	12.9	10.1	11.1	9.8	7.0	9.6	9.5	8.9	7.7
$25 000–29 999	8.9	9.3	12.2	10.2	11.5	9.6	8.1	10.4	8.3	8.5	8.4
Less than $30 000[2]	40.1	62.5	56.3	51.6	52.9	44.7	32.4	47.1	47.9	37.3	39.9
$30 000–34 999	9.2	8.5	12.7	10.8	10.1	9.7	9.1	8.7	9.2	8.2	8.8
$35 000–39 999	9.0	7.8	8.2	8.8	9.7	8.7	9.1	8.8	7.7	9.0	9.5
Less than $40 000[2]	58.3	78.8	77.2	71.2	72.7	63.1	50.6	64.6	64.8	54.5	58.2
$40 000–44 999	8.1	6.7	5.3	5.7	7.2	7.5	8.9	8.0	7.3	7.2	9.3
$45 000–49 999	6.8	4.2	6.0	4.8	5.0	6.5	7.3	5.6	6.1	7.6	7.1
Less than $50 000[2]	73.2	89.7	88.5	81.7	84.9	77.1	66.8	78.2	78.2	69.3	74.6
$50 000–54 999	6.0	2.6	3.7	5.6	5.1	5.6	7.1	4.6	4.1	5.5	5.8
$55 000–$59 999	4.7	1.8	1.6	2.8	3.0	4.0	5.6	3.9	3.6	5.5	5.2
Less than $60 000[2]	83.9	94.1	93.8	90.1	93.0	86.7	79.5	86.7	85.9	80.3	85.6
$60 000–$64 999	3.7	1.8	1.1	3.1	2.3	3.9	4.1	3.0	3.1	4.5	3.1
$65 000–$69 999	2.8	1.2	1.7	1.3	1.5	2.3	3.7	2.7	2.9	3.1	2.6
Less than $70 000[2]	90.4	97.1	96.6	94.5	96.8	92.9	87.3	92.4	91.9	87.9	91.3
$70 000–$74 999	2.2	0.9	0.6	1.5	1.0	1.9	2.7	1.7	1.8	2.9	1.9
$75 000 and over	7.3	1.9	2.7	4.3	2.2	5.4	9.7	6.0	6.5	9.3	6.6
Number of families (000s)[3]	6 834	147	34	226	189	1 838	2 461	277	256	616	791
Average family income ...	$39 589	$27 687	$31 097	$33 480	$31 811	$36 759	$44 098	$35 990	$35 779	$41 794	$39 083

(1) Based on the census family definition: a husband and wife (with or without children who never married) or a parent with one or more children who never married, living together in the same home. (2) Cumulative totals so that, for instance, 73.2% of Canadian families had incomes of less than $50 000. (3) Estimates.

Income by Educational Level: Male and Female, 1986

Source: Statistics Canada

(percentage distribution of individual income earners)

Males

Income groups	Elementary	Some high school	Some post-secondary	College diploma	University degree
Less than $ 2 000	3.7	7.2	6.0	2.1	1.2
Less than $ 5 000	9.2	14.0	17.9	6.7	4.0
Less than $10 000	33.4	26.6	31.7	17.0	9.8
Less than $15 000	53.2	39.4	43.0	28.2	17.1
Less than $20 000	64.7	51.8	53.1	38.8	23.7
Less than $25 000	74.8	63.5	61.9	49.7	29.0
Less than $30 000	82.8	73.8	71.1	60.2	36.7
Less than $40 000	93.8	89.2	86.3	81.6	56.0
Less than $50 000	97.6	95.8	94.2	93.5	74.5
$50 000 and over	2.3	4.1	5.8	6.5	25.5
Total persons (000s)[1]	1 640	4 447	897	1 076	1 202
Average income	$18 064	$21 253	$22 455	$26 457	$40 097

Females

Income groups	Elementary	Some high school	Some post-secondary	College diploma	University degree
Less than $ 2 000	7.5	12.6	11.2	7.0	3.7
Less than $ 5 000	23.4	26.8	27.5	16.6	9.5
Less than $10 000	70.5	51.9	48.9	33.6	22.0
Less than $15 000	87.7	69.8	65.1	50.4	34.0
Less than $20 000	94.0	82.1	77.9	65.5	45.9
Less than $25 000	97.3	91.4	87.2	79.0	57.1
Less than $30 000	98.6	95.7	93.5	88.1	67.4
Less than $40 000	99.6	99.0	97.6	97.3	86.1
Less than $50 000	99.8	99.7	98.8	99.1	94.1
$50 000 and over	0.1	0.4	1.1	1.0	5.9
Total persons (000s)[1]	1 416	4 209	849	1 229	880
Average income	$ 8 894	$11 649	$12 827	$16 391	$23 770

(1) Estimated.

Income Comparison by Type of Job: Male and Female, 1986

Source: Statistics Canada

(percentage distribution of income earners)

Males

Income[1]	Man-agers	Profes-sionals	Clerks	Sales-persons	Services	Farmers	Manu-facturing	Construc-tion	Trans-port
Less than $2 000[2] ..	0.5	1.4	4.0	6.9	9.6	8.5	2.3	2.2	3.8
$2 000–4 999	1.1	2.7	7.0	7.4	10.3	9.2	3.6	4.1	4.5
Less than $5 000[2] ..	1.6	4.1	11.0	14.3	19.9	17.7	5.9	6.3	8.3
$5 000–7 499	1.8	2.6	4.6	5.9	9.8	8.3	3.7	4.2	5.0
$7 500–9 999	2.4	2.9	4.9	4.7	7.6	9.2	3.5	6.2	4.4
Less than $10 000[2] .	5.8	9.6	20.5	24.9	37.3	35.2	13.1	16.7	17.7
$10 000–12 499 .	2.3	4.5	4.8	7.2	6.1	11.5	5.1	6.8	5.9
$12 500–14 999 .	2.9	3.2	4.8	5.7	6.2	8.8	4.6	7.4	6.1
Less than $15 000[2] .	11.0	17.3	30.1	37.8	49.6	55.5	22.8	30.9	29.7
$15 000–17 499 .	4.0	3.3	6.4	6.7	5.9	7.7	6.0	6.7	6.6
$17 500–19 999 .	3.3	4.2	4.8	4.5	5.7	5.2	6.5	7.7	5.6
Less than $20 000[2] .	18.3	24.8	41.3	49.0	61.2	68.4	35.3	45.3	41.9
$20 000–22 499 .	4.0	3.9	7.6	5.6	6.4	5.4	7.6	5.8	6.5
$22 500–$24 999 .	4.6	4.0	7.7	3.9	4.1	4.3	6.5	6.6	6.0
Less than $25 000[2] .	26.9	32.7	56.6	58.5	71.7	78.1	49.4	57.7	54.4
$25 000–29 999 .	9.7	9.0	12.6	10.5	8.1	6.0	14.0	11.2	14.0
Less than $30 000[2] .	36.6	41.7	69.2	69.0	79.8	84.1	63.4	68.9	68.4
$30 000–39 999 .	24.5	22.0	21.6	14.2	10.8	8.1	24.0	18.5	19.2
Less than $40 000[2] .	61.1	63.7	90.8	83.2	90.6	92.2	87.4	87.5	87.6
$40 000–$49 999 .	16.9	18.1	6.3	8.1	6.9	3.5	8.9	9.6	7.6
Less than $50 000[2] .	78.0	81.8	97.1	91.3	97.5	95.7	96.3	97.0	95.2
$50 000 and over ..	21.8	18.2	3.0	8.6	2.5	4.7	3.7	3.1	4.9
Total males[3] (000s) ..	962	947	437	645	753	456	775	715	833
Average earnings ..	**$38 834**	**$36 141**	**$22 900**	**$25 361**	**$18 064**	**$18 055**	**$25 372**	**$23 628**	**$23 961**

Females

Income[1]	Man-agers	Profes-sionals	Clerks	Sales-persons	Services	Farmers	Manu-facturing	Trans-port
Less than $2 000[2] ..	1.6	2.6	3.7	11.8	14.8	12.8	3.3	6.5
$2 000–4 999	3.0	6.2	8.5	18.5	17.7	15.1	6.0	7.6
Less than $5 000[2] ..	4.6	8.8	12.2	30.3	32.5	27.9	9.3	14.1
$5 000–7 499	4.0	5.0	7.3	12.2	16.2	11.2	10.0	8.3
$7 500–9 999	4.0	6.2	8.5	11.4	12.6	14.6	14.1	15.3
Less than $10 000[2] .	12.6	20.0	28.0	53.9	61.3	53.7	33.4	37.7
$10 000–12 499 .	6.7	7.3	10.1	11.3	10.9	15.3	17.7	10.9
$12 500–14 999 .	6.1	7.4	9.2	7.3	6.6	10.6	12.8	13.1
Less than $15 000[2] .	25.4	34.7	47.3	72.5	78.8	79.6	63.9	61.7
$15 000–17 499 .	8.4	6.7	10.4	5.1	4.5	8.1	10.6	7.5
$17 500–19 999 .	9.9	6.9	10.6	4.7	5.3	3.2	7.7	7.5
Less than $20 000[2] .	43.7	48.3	68.3	82.3	88.6	90.9	82.2	76.7
$20 000–22 499 .	11.0	7.7	10.9	4.5	4.2	2.2	5.9	8.0
$22 500–24 999 .	6.8	6.1	7.0	3.7	1.7	3.8	2.1	4.4
Less than $25 000[2] .	61.5	62.1	86.2	90.5	94.5	96.9	90.2	89.1
$25 000–29 999 .	13.5	11.9	7.6	3.8	2.4	0.4	4.6	6.1
Less than $30 000[2] .	75.0	74.0	93.8	94.3	96.9	97.3	94.8	95.2
$30 000–39 999 .	14.3	17.6	4.9	3.3	2.9	1.9	3.9	3.8
Less than $40 000[2] .	89.3	91.6	98.7	97.6	99.8	99.2	98.7	99.0
$40 000–49 999 .	4.7	5.9	1.0	0.6	0.2	0.2	0.6	0.9
Less than $50 000[2] .	94.0	97.5	99.7	98.2	100.0	99.4	99.3	99.9
$50 000 and over ..	6.1	2.4	0.5	1.7	0.1	0.8	0.5	—
Total females[3] (000s)	516	1 140	1 658	513	948	84	219	137
Average earnings ..	**$24 172**	**$21 671**	**$15 956**	**$11 693**	**$9 695**	**$10 041**	**$13 920**	**$13 870**

(1) Includes both full and part-time workers. (2) Cumulative totals so that, for instance, 68.3% of females in clerical jobs earned less than $20 000. (3) Estimates.
— = zero.

Average Income in Selected Canadian Cities, 1985

Source: Revenue Canada Taxation Statistics

City	Average income[1]	Total income ($000)	No. of tax returns	City	Average income[1]	Total income ($000)	No. of tax returns
West Vancouver, B.C. .	32 760	782 415	23 883	Burlington, Ont.	24 501	1 835 956	74 931
Markham, Ont.	28 458	2 383 688	83 760	Nepean, Ont.	24 127	1 312 841	54 413
Oakville, Ont.	27 702	1 552 602	56 045	Ottawa, Ont.	23 672	5 505 812	233 023
Woodbridge, Ont.	24 616	638 005	25 918	Richmond Hill, Ont. ...	23 666	771 494	32 599

City	Average income[1]	Total income ($000)	No. of tax returns	City	Average income[1]	Total income ($000)	No. of tax returns
North York, Ont.	23 659	6 750 162	285 305	London, Ont.	20 037	3 607 994	180 058
Etobicoke, Ont.	23 151	2 858 503	123 469	Thunder Bay, Ont.	19 979	1 571 074	78 635
North Vancouver, B.C.	23 094	1 559 827	67 540	Kingston, Ont.	19 731	1 202 259	60 930
Mississauga, Ont.	22 927	5 424 602	236 595	St. Catharines, Ont.	19 660	1 577 264	80 226
Calgary, Alta.	22 334	9 918 566	425 056	Saskatoon, Sask.	19 625	2 206 422	112 425
Toronto, Ont.	22 220	16 260 109	731 747	Dartmouth, N.S.	19 190	1 058 636	55 165
Richmond, B.C.	21 837	1 500 587	68 716	Laval, Que.	19 142	3 462 349	180 873
Vancouver, B.C.	21 758	6 416 766	294 913	Kitchener, Ont.	19 014	1 894 574	99 637
Brampton, Ont.	21 479	2 517 104	117 187	Surrey, B.C.	18 770	1 889 448	100 659
Regina, Sask.	20 729	2 306 762	111 280	Fredericton, N.B.	18 392	723 815	39 354
Oshawa, Ont.	20 698	1 665 670	80 472	Hamilton, Ont.	18 321	3 724 106	203 268
Halifax, N.S.	20 659	1 603 158	77 600	St. John's, Nfld.	17 933	1 059 433	50 075
Windsor, Ont.	20 637	2 781 224	134 764	Quebec, Que.	17 862	1 911 711	107 021
Edmonton, Alta.	20 465	7 722 863	377 367	Montreal, Que.	17 813	11 976 242	672 296
Scarborough, Ont.	20 316	6 297 166	309 956	Winnipeg, Man.	17 622	7 755 578	434 426
York, Ont.	20 201	1 359 642	67 303	Sherbrooke, Que.	17 080	862 786	50 512
Victoria, B.C.	20 108	2 922 420	145 336	Longueuil, Que.	17 001	1 324 132	77 885

(1) Average total income after business deductions but before personal deductions.

Individual and Corporate Income Tax, 1950-1986

Source: Revenue Canada

(millions of dollars)

Year[1]	Total tax collected[2]	Individual income tax	% of total	Corporate income tax	% of total	Cost of collecting tax
1950	1 300.8	622.0	47.8	603.2	46.4	28.1
1955	2 457.0	1 284.0	52.3	1 066.5	43.4	25.7
1960	3 148.2	1 752.2	55.7	1 234.2	39.2	31.8
1965	4 940.7	2 903.9	58.8	1 804.5	36.5	42.7
1970	10 988.4	7 661.9	69.7	3 080.0	28.0	82.5
1975	23 275.0	17 436.9	74.9	5 386.4	23.1	226.7
1980	37 328.7	27 935.1	74.8	8 511.6	22.8	388.8
1981	44 417.1	33 888.2	76.3	9 537.5	21.5	455.0
1982	53 316.8	41 998.4	78.8	9 316.7	17.5	545.6
1983	56 946.4	46 263.7	81.2	7 593.7	13.3	606.7
1984	61 196.1	50 093.6	81.9	7 963.9	13.0	665.6
1985	66 884.0	53 148.0	79.5	10 046.7	15.0	729.0
1986	72 857.7	59 658.9	81.9	9 983.0	13.7	774.7

(1) For fiscal year ending Mar. 31. (2) Includes non-resident tax, excess profits and special taxes, miscellaneous tax revenue, Canada Pension Plan contributions and Unemployment Insurance premiums.

Historical Purchasing Power of a Dollar in Canada

This table shows how many current (1988) dollars it would take to equal the purchasing power of a single dollar in earlier years. For example, the amount listed beside 1970 ($3.50) means that, in 1970, $1 bought the same amount of goods that cost $3.50 in 1988—or that $10 000 in 1970 bought you the same package of goods and services that cost $35 000 in 1988.

If you lived on $50 a week in 1950 and wanted to know what that would be by today's standards, multiply $50 times the relative value of a 1950 dollar ($5.70) and you have your answer: $285.00.

The relative value of a dollar for the years listed was calculated according to changes in the cost of living in Canada as measured by the Consumer Price Index.

1915	$11.58	1955	$5.04	1967	$3.93	1979	$1.78
1920	6.27	1956	4.97	1968	3.78	1980	1.62
1925	7.80	1957	4.82	1969	3.62	1981	1.44
1930	7.80	1958	4.69	1970	3.50	1982	1.30
1935	9.77	1959	4.63	1971	3.40	1983	1.23
1940	8.92	1960	4.57	1972	3.25	1984	1.17
1945	7.80	1961	4.53	1973	3.02	1985	1.13
1950	5.70	1962	4.49	1974	2.72	1986	1.08
1951	5.15	1963	4.40	1975	2.45	1987	1.04
1952	5.04	1964	4.33	1976	2.28	1988[1]	1.00
1953	5.07	1965	4.22	1977	2.11		
1954	5.04	1966	4.08	1978	1.94		

(1) Based on June Consumer Price Index.

Health

Health Care in Canada

Under the Canadian Constitution, health care is primarily the responsibility of the provinces. However, through its role in supplying needed funds for health programs and setting national standards, the federal government has maintained a major role in Canada's health care system. The result is a national system in which care is delivered mainly by the provinces but is overseen and partly funded by Ottawa.

Publicly-sponsored health care is universal in Canada, with more than 90% of hospital and doctor's care costs paid by provincially-administered plans. The present medicare system evolved slowly, beginning with government-sponsored hospital insurance programs operated by British Columbia and Saskatchewan in the late 1940s and early 1950s. In 1957 Ottawa officially adopted the medicare concept with the *Hospital Insurance and Diagnostic Services Act*. This paved the way for publicly-covered hospital, radiology and laboratory services across Canada. Doctor's care was added under the *Medical Care Act* of 1966, which saw Ottawa assume 50% of the program's cost in each province. That changed in 1977, when the *Established Programs Financing Act* introduced a more complicated funding arrangement based on Gross National Product and a per-capita calculation. This act also loosened restrictions on how provinces could spend federal contributions.

Each province is responsible for building and operating hospitals, the accessibility of medical facilities and services, and the administration of the provincial health insurance plan. Doctors are paid by the province for services delivered under medicare, with money collected from the public through general taxation or government health insurance premiums. Every province now prohibits doctors from charging direct health care fees in addition to those covered by medicare.

The *Medical Care Act* of 1966 required that provincial health programs meet 5 criteria to qualify for funding: universality, comprehensiveness, portability, accessibility and public administration. Seeing extra-billing as a threat to accessibility, the federal government in 1984 passed the *Canada Health Act*, allowing it to withhold transfer payments of tax revenues to provinces which persist in permitting direct fees.

Not all health care costs are covered by provincial health plans. Those not covered typically include dental care, most prescriptions, eye glasses and a portion of long-term care facility costs. Many Canadians have dental insurance through personal or employment-sponsored plans, and some extend medicare coverage through private insurance plans. However, most provinces will provide some of these services for senior citizens and those on social assistance.

The total cost of health services provided across Canada in 1985 was $40 billion, with public funding accounting for 76%. Provincial and local governments are estimated to have spent approximately $1 150 that year on every man, woman and child in Canada. Health spending is around 8.6% of Gross National Product, which compares favorably with other western industrial nations. This may be a factor in Canada's high life expectancy at birth: 71.9 years for males and 79 years for females (1982 figures).

The federal government provides health care for a number of groups traditionally under its jurisdiction. These include Indians, Inuit, northern residents, the military, veterans, the RCMP and inmates of federal prisons.

As well, Ottawa regulates the quality and safety of food and drugs, deals with some environmental hazards, administers quarantine regulations and certifies medical exams for the licensing of pilots. It collects and distributes health data through the Dept. of National Health and Welfare and Statistics Canada, and operates preventive care and fitness programs through the Health Promotion Directorate and Fitness Canada.

Immediate and future issues in Canadian health care include the rising cost of services and the aging of the population. Partly due to high technology, hospital expenditures increased 240% from 1970 to 1980, far in excess of inflation. As well, those 65 years of age and over are projected to make up approximately 15% of the population by the year 2006, up from 9.7% in 1981; those 85 or older are increasing in numbers at an even faster rate. This may lead to greater use of lower-cost community care to reduce high-cost hospital care.

Canadian Public Hospitals, 1987

Source: Statistics Canada

	General				Specialty[1]			
	Hospitals[2]	Beds[2]	Admissions[3] (000s)	Occupancy[3]	Hospitals[2]	Beds[2]	Admissions[3] (000s)	Occupancy[3]
Canada	848	128 206	3 475 154	81.5	212	42 531	202 162	91.0
Newfoundland	31	2 857	83 025	74.6	11	756	7 666	75.4
Prince Edward Island	7	690	24 431	78.4	1	43	34	96.7
Nova Scotia	44	4 807	131 921	75.1	5	941	17 258	72.6
New Brunswick	32	4 302	120 018	81.6	3	860	1 487	82.6
Quebec	119	30 469	684 171	84.5	74	20 336	68 464	93.0
Ontario	189	42 263	1 250 721	83.9	39	8 332	60 204	89.2
Manitoba	78	5 976	167 172	75.8	8	497	1 580	84.4
Saskatchewan	132	6 824	204 546	74.6	3	535	1 169	88.3
Alberta	119	12 728	400 647	73.1	41	5 579	19 737	91.9
British Columbia	93	17 108	402 367	84.3	26	4 636	24 563	93.4
Northwest Territories	4	182	6 135	61.3	1	16	–	–

(1) Comprises pediatric, psychiatric, rehabilitation and extended care hospitals, and nursing stations. (2) As of Jan. 1, 1987. (3) Based on reporting hospitals for year ending April 1, 1986. Occupancy rate represents the average percentage of beds occupied.
– = zero; n.a. not available.

Canadian Health Expenditure

Source: Statistics Canada

(millions of dollars)

	Canada	Nfld	PEI	NS	NB	Que	Ont	Man	Sask	Alta	BC	Yukon and NWT
1960	2 137	31	10	72	62	530	819	113	116	163	218	3
1965	3 415	52	14	116	87	952	1 291	167	157	265	308	5
1970	6 256	97	26	195	144	1 708	2 438	295	238	486	618	11
1975	12 239	239	55	393	275	3 286	4 567	545	459	1 013	1 370	37
1980	22 719	452	116	670	552	5 951	7 970	990	853	2 157	2 923	86
1981	26 643	527	125	815	667	6 855	9 244	1 174	989	2 633	3 506	107
1982	31 173	603	138	953	802	7 813	10 816	1 336	1 174	3 422	3 953	164
1983	34 697	684	145	1 051	875	8 642	12 282	1 477	1 359	3 708	4 295	181
1984[1] ...	37 420	714	152	1 168	936	9 242	13 541	1 612	1 471	3 847	4 547	190
1985[1] ...	39 793	745	163	1 259	975	9 877	14 539	1 730	1 551	4 062	4 680	213

(1) Preliminary.

Number of Medical Professionals[1], 1971-1986

Source: Health and Welfare Canada

	Physicians[2]		Dentists		Optometrists		Pharmacists[5]	
	number	persons per physician	number	persons per dentist	number	persons per optometrist	number	persons per pharmacist
1971	32 942	659	7 453	2 913	1 511	14 368	11 330	1 916
1976	40 130	577	9 401	2 463	1 764	13 128	14 687[4]	1 578
1977	41 398	566	10 058	2 328	1 841	12 720	15 328	1 529
1978	42 238	560	10 451	2 262	1 869	12 651	15 709	1 507
1979	43 192	554	10 763	2 222	1 919	12 461	16 052	1 491
1980	44 275	547	11 095	2 183	1 916[3]	12 642	16 588	1 461
1981	45 542	538	11 484	2 134	2 070	11 841	17 039	1 438
1982	47 384	523	11 880	2 086	2 180[4]	11 368	14 704	1 685
1983	48 860	512	12 271	2 039	2 250	11 121	15 337	1 631
1984	49 916	506	12 624	2 001	2 287	11 047	15 734	1 606
1985	51 966	491	13 027	1 958	2 386	10 688	15 957	1 598
1986	53 207	479	13 164	1 937	2 585	9 865	16 448	1 550

(1) Represents actively practising civilian physicians, dentists and optometrists and licensed pharmacists; data as of Dec. (2) Includes interns and residents. (3) As of June, 1980. (4) Estimate. (5) Excludes honorary and non-practising pharmacists for 1982-1986.

Leading Causes of Death Among Canadian Males, 1986

Source: Statistics Canada

Age Group	Heart Disease number	rate[1]	Cancer number	rate[1]	Stroke number	rate[1]	Respiratory Disease number	rate[1]	Accidents number	rate[1]
less than 1 yr. ...	12	6.3	8	4.2	1	0.5	42	22.0	45	23.6
1-4 yrs.	8	1.1	40	5.4	2	0.3	20	2.7	167	22.5
5-9 yrs.	4	0.4	50	5.4	4	0.4	5	0.5	133	14.5
10-14 yrs.	7	0.8	31	3.4	2	0.2	14	1.5	146	15.9
15-19 yrs.	15	1.5	45	4.6	2	0.2	20	2.0	837	84.9
20-24 yrs.	40	3.5	85	7.5	10	0.9	19	1.7	1 245	110.0
25-29 yrs.	49	4.2	106	9.1	17	1.5	25	2.1	1 043	89.5
30-34 yrs.	98	9.0	175	16.1	27	2.4	25	2.3	882	81.4
35-39 yrs.	230	22.7	276	27.3	52	5.1	26	2.6	730	72.2
40-44 yrs.	469	57.8	399	49.2	48	5.9	45	5.5	617	76.1
45-49 yrs.	746	113.0	746	113.0	84	12.7	62	9.4	456	69.1
50-54 yrs.	1 498	243.1	1 324	214.9	114	18.5	132	21.4	484	78.5
55-59 yrs.	2 276	383.4	2 421	407.9	235	39.6	270	45.5	537	90.5
60-64 yrs.	3 348	631.1	3 520	663.5	355	66.9	507	95.6	435	82.0
65-69 yrs.	4 266	1 029.2	4 042	975.2	538	129.8	838	202.2	378	91.2
70-74 yrs.	5 286	1 630.0	4 375	1 349.1	873	269.2	1 306	402.7	388	119.6
75-79 yrs.	5 252	2 502.1	3 832	1 825.6	1 122	534.5	1 710	814.7	337	160.6
80-84 yrs.	4 337	3 761.5	2 728	2 366.0	1 093	948.0	1 735	1 504.8	293	254.1
85 yrs. and over .	4 703	6 796.2	1 981	2 862.7	1 306	1 887.3	2 046	2 956.6	378	546.2
All ages	32 646[2]	261.5	26 184	209.7	5 885	47.1	8 847	70.9	9 532[2]	76.3

(1) Deaths per 100 000 population. (2) Includes cases in which age was not specified.

Leading Causes of Death Among Canadian Females, 1986

Source: Statistics Canada

Age Group	Heart Disease number	Heart Disease rate[1]	Cancer number	Cancer rate[1]	Stroke number	Stroke rate[1]	Respiratory Disease number	Respiratory Disease rate[1]	Accidents number	Accidents rate[1]
less than 1 yr. . . .	6	3.3	6	3.3	1	0.6	28	15.4	39	21.5
1-4 yrs.	7	1.0	41	5.8	3	0.4	18	2.6	99	14.0
5-9 yrs.	5	0.6	28	3.2	2	0.2	5	0.6	72	8.2
10-14 yrs.	4	0.5	24	2.8	3	0.3	10	1.1	77	8.9
15-19 yrs.	10	1.1	41	4.4	6	0.6	9	1.0	251	26.7
20-24 yrs.	18	1.6	39	3.5	10	0.9	17	1.5	276	24.6
25-29 yrs.	16	1.4	107	9.1	13	1.1	10	0.8	251	21.3
30-34 yrs.	33	3.0	190	17.2	24	2.2	19	1.7	252	22.9
35-39 yrs.	53	5.2	363	35.8	40	3.9	21	2.1	221	21.8
40-44 yrs.	87	10.8	554	68.9	59	7.3	37	4.6	207	25.8
45-49 yrs.	189	28.8	822	125.3	82	12.5	44	6.7	181	27.6
50-54 yrs.	333	54.3	1 299	211.9	115	18.8	80	13.0	201	32.8
55-59 yrs.	665	109.1	1 801	295.4	191	31.3	131	21.5	177	29.0
60-64 yrs.	1 249	210.0	2 482	417.4	272	45.7	271	45.6	202	34.0
65-69 yrs.	2 025	407.3	2 841	571.4	415	83.5	417	83.9	196	39.4
70-74 yrs.	3 294	795.7	3 029	731.6	804	194.2	723	174.6	235	56.8
75-79 yrs.	4 253	1 415.3	2 844	946.4	1 225	407.7	882	293.5	252	83.9
80-84 yrs.	4 987	2 570.6	2 273	1 171.6	1 661	856.2	972	501.0	318	163.9
85 yrs. and over .	8 936	5 634.3	2 480	1 563.7	3 218	2 029.0	2 390	1 506.9	702	442.6
All ages	26 170	204.1	21 264	165.8	8 144	63.5	6 084	47.4	4 209	32.8

(1) Deaths per 100 000 population.

AIDS

AIDS (Acquired Immunodeficiency Syndrome) is caused by a virus (HIV) which attacks the body's natural defence mechanism, making a person vulnerable to illnesses that a healthy immune system could prevent. Infection with the HIV virus does not always lead to AIDS; the amount of virus, in addition to infection by other viruses, may influence its development.

According to recent estimates, between 30 and 50 percent of individuals with HIV will have developed AIDS within 5 years of infection, and another 20 to 25 percent will experience AIDS-related illness. Of those diagnosed as having AIDS in Canada and the United States, over 90 percent have died within 5 years and 80 percent within 3 years.

AIDS was first identified in the United States in 1981. Canada's first reported case was in 1982. The World Health Organization estimates that more than 200 000 AIDS cases had occurred worldwide by 1988 and that between 500 000 and 3 million new cases will be identified by 1991 from among persons who have already been infected. The ultimate health impact of the HIV infection, including effects on future generations, is unknown.

The AIDS virus is transmitted in 4 known ways: through sexual contact with an infected person; through sharing contaminated needles; through transfusion of infected blood or blood products; from an infected mother to an infant in the womb or during breast feeding. AIDS cannot be transmitted through casual or social contact, through food or water, or by insects.

AIDS in Canada

Source: Federal Centre for AIDS

(as of mid-August 1988)

	No. of Reported Cases[1] Males	Females	Total	%	No. of Deaths	Rate (per million population[2])
Canada	1 800	118	1 918	100.0	1 062	74.3
Newfoundland	n.a.	n.a.	8	0.4	6	13.8
Prince Edward Island . . .	2	–	2	0.1	1	15.6
Nova Scotia	28	2	30	1.6	12	33.8
New Brunswick	7	1	8	0.4	6	11.1
Quebec	490	78	568	29.6	284	85.2
Ontario	732	21	753	39.3	462	80.9
Manitoba	26	–	26	1.4	14	24.0
Saskatchewan	n.a.	n.a.	23	1.2	16	22.5
Alberta	105	8	113	5.9	68	47.2
British Columbia	377	8	385	20.1	193	131.2
Yukon	n.a.	n.a.	1	0.1	–	43.1
Northwest Territories	n.a.	n.a.	1	0.1	–	19.6

(1) Cases are attributed to the province where onset of the illness occurred. (2) Based on April 1987 population estimates.
– = zero; n.a. not available.

Reported[1] Cases of AIDS

(as of August 1988)

Source: The World Health Organization and Federal Centre for AIDS, Canada

	Number of cases	Rate (per million population[2])		Number of cases	Rate (per million population[2])
World total	**104 098**	n.a.	Tanzania	1 608	68.4
North America	**72 214**	n.a.	Togo	2	. . .
Canada	1 896	73.5	Tunisia	19	2.5
Mexico	1 233	15.1	Uganda	2 369	149.0
United States	69 085	276.3	Zaire	335	10.5
Europe	**12 414**	n.a.	Zambia	754	106.2
Austria	176	23.2	Zimbabwe	119	12.7
Belgium	340	34.3	**Central and South America**	**6 699**	n.a.
Bulgaria	3	0.3	Antigua & Barbuda	3	3.8
Czechoslovakia	10	0.6	Argentina	163	5.3
Denmark	263	51.6	Bahamas	188	940.0
Finland	27	5.5	Barbados	55	275.0
France	3 628	66.0	Belize	7	70.0
East Germany	6	0.4	Bermuda	75	1 071.4
West Germany	1 973	32.3	Bolivia	6	1.0
Greece	106	10.6	Brazil	2 956	219.0
Hungary	12	1.1	Cayman Islands	3	150.0
Iceland	5	25.0	Chile	69	5.8
Ireland	37	10.3	Colombia	174	6.1
Italy	1 865	32.5	Costa Rica	43	16.5
Luxembourg	10	25.0	Cuba	27	2.7
Malta	10	25.0	Dominica	4	57.1
Netherlands	501	34.3	Dominican Republic	504	81.3
Norway	81	19.3	Ecuador	52	5.6
Poland	3	0.1	El Salvador	23	4.2
Portugal	125	12.1	French Guyana	113	1 412.5
Romania	4	0.2	Grenada	8	80.0
Spain	1 126	28.9	Guadeloupe	74	246.7
Sweden	192	22.9	Guatemala	34	4.3
Switzerland	439	66.5	Guyana	14	1.6
United Kingdom	1 429	25.2	Haiti	1 374	211.4
USSR	4	. . .	Honduras	109	25.3
Yugoslavia	38	1.6	Jamaica	56	24.3
Africa	**11 530**	n.a.	Martinique	38	126.7
Algeria	13	0.6	Panama	30	14.3
Angola	6	0.7	Paraguay	8	2.2
Benin	9	2.1	Peru	69	3.5
Botswana	16	13.3	St. Lucia	10	100.0
Burkina Faso	960	192.0	St. Vincent & the Grena-		
Burundi	26	3.6	dines	8	80.0
Cameroon	25	2.4	Suriname	9	30.0
Cape Verde	4	13.3	Trinidad & Tobago	227	206.4
Central African Rep.	254	94.1	Turks & Caicos Islands	5	625.0
Congo	1 250	595.2	Uruguay	20	6.7
Côte d'Ivoire	250	23.1	Venezuela	140	8.1
Egypt	5	0.1	**Australasia**	**951**	n.a.
Ethiopia	21	0.5	Australia	872	53.8
Gabon	18	15.0	New Zealand	77	23.3
Gambia	35	43.8	Tonga	1	10.0
Ghana	145	10.4	**Asia**	**292**	n.a.
Guinea	4	0.6	China	2	. . .
Guinea-Bissau	16	17.8	Cyprus	3	4.3
Kenya	1 497	66.8	Hong Kong	12	2.1
Lesotho	2	1.2	India	9	. . .
Liberia	2	0.8	Israel	58	13.2
Malawi	583	78.8	Japan	66	0.5
Mali	29	3.4	Jordan	3	0.8
Morocco	9	0.4	Lebanon	5	1.5
Mozambique	9	0.6	Malaysia	3	0.2
Niger	9	. . .	Philippines	13	0.2
Nigeria	11	0.1	Qatar	32	106.7
Reunion	2	3.3	South Korea	2	. . .
Rwanda	901	132.5	Singapore	4	1.5
Senegal	66	9.3	Sri Lanka	2	0.1
South Africa	114	3.3	Syria	3	0.3
Sudan	23	1.0	Thailand	12	0.2
Swaziland	7	10.0	Turkey	21	0.4

(1) As reported to the World Health Organization; the actual number of cases may be much higher. (2) Based on 1987 population estimates. n.a. not available; . . . = too small to be included.

Cancer Information

Source: Canadian Cancer Society

Site	Warning Signs	Comments
Lung	Chronic cough; blood may appear in sputum. Fever and chest pains may also occur.	Lung cancer is largely preventable; it is the leading cause of cancer death among men and increasing at a tremendous rate for women. Don't smoke.
Intestine and Rectum	Bleeding from the rectum; persistent indigestion; a change in bowel habits; vague, dull, or annoying abdominal pains.	A balanced, low-fat diet with adequate amounts of green and yellow vegetables, i.e. cabbage, cauliflower, broccoli or brussel sprouts and foods containing Vitamin C and E is recommended. Checkup should include bowel examination.
Mouth and Pharynx	Unusual conditions in the mouth; sores that don't heal; trouble swallowing.	Ask your dentist to check unusual conditions. Cytological smears of suspicious areas will detect the presence of many cancers.
Stomach	Indigestion; pain in upper abdomen; persistent loss of appetite; vomitting of blood; unexplained weight loss.	Mortality has declined 50% in the past 20 years. Avoid highly spiced foods.
Skin	A pearly nodule that may grow larger or a red, scaly, sharply outlined patch or a mole-like growth which is dark brown mixed with areas of white, blue, pink or grey. May change shape or color.	Most common of all cancers and is usually caused by over-exposure to the sun. Most cases are simple to treat, but early treatment is important.
Breast	Puckered or dimpled skin; bleeding or discharge from the nipples; lump or thickening in the breast.	Practise monthly breast self-examination. Reduce fat in diet. 85% of lumps are benign, but early detection and treatment is essential.
Cervix and Uterus	Unusual bleeding or discharge.	The Pap test has made cervical cancer preventable.
Prostate	Pain in the lower back or during urination or ejaculation. Problems during urination; urine may contain blood.	More than half the men over 50 in N. America develop a growth in the prostate gland; in most cases the growth is benign. Doctor should give a digital examination during checkup.
Bladder	Blood in urine; frequent urination, strong urges to urinate and discomfort or burning during urination.	Most common in men aged 45-80. Avoid smoking and cancer-causing industrial compounds; limit use of saccharin and coffee.
Leukemia	No distinctive early warning signs. Symptoms ressemble those of common less serious diseases (e.g., fatigue, pallor, overall feeling of ill health).	Commonest type of cancer in children. Unlike other cancers, there is no tumor instead countless immature white blood cells spill into bloodstream from bone marrow and travel throughout body.

The Canadian Cancer Society suggests all Canadians follow the Seven Steps to Health: have a medical and dental checkup; watch for any change in your normal state of health; find out about any lump or sore that doesn't heal; protect yourself against too much sunlight; do not smoke; have a Pap test; do a monthly breast self-examination.

Estimated New Cases and Deaths from Cancer in Canada, 1988

Source: Canadian Cancer Statistics 1988, Canadian Cancer Society

Site	Number of new cases			Number of deaths		
	Total	Male	Female	Total	Male	Female
All cancers[1]	96 300	50 600	45 700	50 800	28 000	22 800
Brain	1 850	1 000	850	1 300	720	580
Bladder	4 700	3 500	1 200	1 080	760	320
Breast	11 500	n.a.	11 500	4 600	n.a.	4 600
Cervix & uterus	4 300	n.a.	4 300	890	n.a.	890
Intestine & rectum	14 000	7 100	6 900	5 700	2 900	2 800
Kidney	2 190	1 400	790	1 000	620	380
Leukemia	3 000	1 700	1 300	1 770	1 000	770
Lung	15 400	11 200	4 200	13 400	9 300	4 100
Lymphoma	5 600	3 000	2 600	2 600	1 400	1 200
Mouth & pharynx	2 670	1 900	770	950	680	270
Ovary	1 900	n.a.	1 900	1 200	n.a.	1 200
Pancreas	2 700	1 400	1 300	2 600	1 400	1 200
Prostate	8 400	8 400	n.a.	3 000	3 000	n.a.
Skin (Melanoma)[1]	2 200	1 000	1 200	500	290	210
Stomach	3 000	1 900	1 100	1 950	1 200	750
All other sites[1]	12 890	7 100	5 790	8 260	4 730	3 530

(1) Excludes non-melanoma skin cancer.
n.a. not available or not applicable.

Heart Disease Warning Signs

Source: Heart and Stroke Foundation of Ontario

Heart Attack

- prolonged heavy pressure, or squeezing pain in the centre of the chest, behind the breastbone
- pain may spread to the shoulder, arm, neck or jaw
- pain or discomfort is often accompanied by sweating
- nausea, vomiting or shortness of breath may occur
- symptoms may subside and return.

Stroke

- a sudden temporary weakness or numbness in the face, leg or arm

- temporary loss of speech or trouble speaking or understanding speech.
- Episodes of double vision
- Unexplained dizziness, headaches, etc. in conjunction with other symptoms.

What to do?

Act immediately. Have the victim stop activity and sit or lie down. Get to a hospital emergency room at once; 50% of all heart attack deaths occur before the victim gets to the hospital. **Keep a list** of emergency telephone numbers near the telephone. **Don't rely** on the victim's opinion of whether medical help is required.

Stress: How Much Can Affect Your Health?

Source: Reprinted with permission from the *Journal of Psychosomatic Research*, Vol. 11, pp. 213-218, T.H. Holmes, M.D., R.H. Rahe, M.D.; The Social Readjustment Rating Scale © 1967, Pergamon Press, Ltd.

Change, both good and bad, can create stress and stress, if sufficiently severe, can lead to illness. Drs. Thomas Holmes and Richard Rahe, psychiatrists at the University of Washington in Seattle, have developed the Social Readjustment Rating Scale. In their study, they gave a point value to stressful events. The psychiatrists discovered that in 79 percent of the persons studied, major illness followed the accumulation of stress-related changes totaling over 300 points in one year.

The Social Readjustment Rating Scale

Life Event	Value	Life Event	Value
Death of Spouse	100	In-law troubles	29
Divorce	73	Outstanding personal achievement	28
Marital separation from mate	65	Wife beginning or ceasing work outside the home	26
Detention in jail or other institution	63	Beginning or ceasing formal schooling	26
Death of a close family member	63	Major change in living conditions (e.g., building a new home, remodeling, deterioration of home or neighborhood)	25
Major personal injury or illness	53		
Marriage	50		
Being fired at work	47	Revision of personal habits (dress, manners, association, etc.)	24
Marital reconciliation with mate	45	Troubles with the boss	23
Retirement from work	45	Major change in working hours or conditions	20
Major change in the health or behavior of a family member	44	Change in residence	20
		Changing to a new school	20
Pregnancy	40	Major change in usual type and/or amount of recreation	19
Sexual difficulties	39		
Gaining a new family member (e.g., through birth, adoption, moving in, etc.)	39	Major change in church activities (e.g., a lot more or a lot less than usual)	19
Major business readjustment (e.g., merger, reorganization, bankruptcy, etc.)	39	Major change in social activities (e.g., clubs, dancing, movies, visiting, etc.)	18
Major change in financial state (e.g., a lot worse off or a lot better off than usual)	38	Taking out a mortgage or loan for a lesser purchase (e.g., for a car, TV, freezer, etc.)	17
Death of a close friend	37	Major change in sleeping habits (a lot more or a lot less sleep, or change in part of day when asleep)	16
Changing to a different line of work	36		
Major change in the number of arguments with spouse (e.g., either a lot more or a lot less than usual regarding child-rearing, personal habits, etc.)	35	Major change in number of family get-togethers (e.g., a lot more or a lot less than usual)	15
Taking out a mortgage or loan for a major purchase (e.g. for a home, business, etc.)	31	Major change in eating habits (a lot more or a lot less food intake, or very different meal hours or surroundings)	15
Foreclosure on a mortgage or loan	30	Vacation	13
Major change in responsibilities at work (e.g., promotion, demotion, lateral transfer)	29	Christmas	12
Son or daughter leaving home (e.g., marriage, attending college, etc.)	29	Minor violations of the law (e.g., traffic tickets, jaywalking, disturbing the peace, etc.)	11

Fitness

Source: Participaction

Only a century ago, more than half the population got enough exercise from work to stay in shape. Today, less than 1% of all energy expended in North American factories, workshops and farms comes from human muscles. In order to lead full and healthy lives most people must turn to recreational activities to provide fitness.

Physical fitness is comprised of 4 elements: muscular strength, flexibility, an efficient cardiovascular system and low body fat content. Of these, the improvements to the cardiovascular system which come from physical activity are the most important part of getting into shape.

The Cardiovascular System

The heart, lungs and the network of blood vessels form the cardiovascular system. Its function is to carry oxygen to the more than 300 trillion cells of the body. In each of these cells, oxygen combined with fuel from food produces energy.

When the cardiovascular system hasn't been exercised through aerobic activity—that is, activity that places increased demands for oxygen on the body, such as walking, jogging, bike riding—it becomes weak. This can make even simple tasks difficult. A lack of cardiovascular fitness is at the root of many common health problems such as nagging aches and pains, stress and breathlessness after a basic activity such as climbing 2 flights of stairs.

One way of measuring the fitness of your cardiovascular system is through your heart rate. The average heart rate is 70 beats/minute while at rest. Fitness reduces the resting heart rate; conditioned athletes have resting heart rates of only 40-45 beats/minute. A reduction of 10 beats/minute in the resting heart rate will save the heart over 18 days of work during one year. Over 35 years, the heart will be spared about 2 years of work!.

Cardiovascular fitness also strengthens the heart muscle and increases the power of the heart beat. This improved distribution of blood through the body makes work easier and gives the fit person more energy. Also, a person with a fit heart can resist disease more easily and can recover from sickness faster. Fitness can also reduce blood cholesterol by circulating more oxygen through the body. In some people, high blood pressure may be reduced.

The Fitness Formula

Fitness can be achieved no matter what your age or what kind of shape you're in.

The fitness formula is expressed as:

F—Frequency
To build fitness, you should pursue your chosen activity a minimum of 3 times/week. After 48 hours, the benefits gained from an activity session start to fade. But activities undertaken more than 5 times/week can lead to stress and exhaustion.

I-Intensity
Activity intensity is measured by the heart rate in beats/minute. The heart rate must be in the "target zone" for your age to produce fitness benefits. The lower end of the zone is 170 beats/minute minus your age, the upper end of the zone is 200 minus your age.
This "target zone" does not change with greater fitness; it stays constant for your age.

T-Time
To maximize the fitness value of your activity, you must keep your heart rate in its "target zone" for at least 15 continuous minutes.

Body Measurements

Exercise can change the shape of your body but only within the limits imposed by the type of body you have. There are 3 basic body types:

endomorph: round and soft-looking with the torso roughly the same girth from shoulders to hips

mesomorph: muscular and large-boned, with broad shoulders and narrow waist

ectomorph: thin, small-boned and lightly muscled with long limbs

Given the limits of body type, the amount of fat and muscle tone will also affect your body shape and measurements. Increasing the amount and strength of muscle will improve posture and bone alignment. However, for most people, reducing fat is the most important factor in shaping up.

A simple formula, called the Body Mass Index (BMI), will help you find out if your weight is within a healthy range for your height and body type. The BMI recognizes that there are many healthy body shapes and sizes, so within the healthy range there are many acceptable weights for your height. The BMI can be used for men and women aged 20 to 65 years old. It should not be used for children, adolescents, pregnant or lactating women, adults over 65 years old and muscular athletes.

To determine your BMI you need to know your weight in kilograms and your height in metres. Simply divide your weight by your height multiplied by itself.

For example, if you weigh 70 kg and are 1.75 m tall, your BMI would be:

$$\text{weight} \div (\text{height} \times \text{height}) = 70 \div (1.75 \times 1.75)$$
$$= 22.9$$

Check below to determine the meaning of your BMI:

Under 20: may be associated with health problems for some individuals. Consult a dietician and physician for advice.

20 to 25: associated with the lowest risk of illness for most people. This is the healthy range you want to stay in.

25 to 27: may be associated with health problems for some people. Caution is suggested if your BMI is in this zone.

over 27: associated with increased risk of health problems such as heart disease, high blood pressure and diabetes. Consult a dietician or physician for advice.

Energy Expenditure by Activity

Source: Participation

The following table shows the number of kilojoules[1] (kJ) burned by body weight for 15 minutes of each activity. For example, if you weigh 50 kg you will burn 450 kJ in 15 minutes of downhill skiing. An expenditure of 32 000 kJ is required to burn 1 kg of fat. You would have to ski almost 18 hours to burn off 1 kg of fat!

Body Weight in kilograms (kg)

Activity	20	25	30	35	40	45	50	55	60	70	80	90	100
Baseball	90	110	130	150	170	200	220	240	260	300	340	390	430
Basketball	130	160	200	230	260	290	320	360	390	450	520	580	650
Bicycling (20 km/h)	200	250	300	350	400	450	490	540	590	690	790	890	990
Canoeing	130	160	200	230	260	290	320	360	390	450	520	580	650
Dancing	80	100	120	140	150	170	190	210	220	270	310	350	380
Field hockey	230	290	340	400	450	510	570	630	690	800	910	1030	1140
Football	150	190	230	270	310	340	380	420	460	540	610	690	770

Activity	\multicolumn{12}{c}{Body Weight in kilograms (kg)}
	20	25	30	35	40	45	50	55	60	70	80	90	100
Hiking	150	190	220	260	300	330	370	410	440	520	590	670	740
Hockey	260	330	390	460	520	590	660	720	790	920	1050	1180	1310
Horseback riding (trot)	130	160	190	220	250	280	310	340	370	440	500	560	620
Roller skating	110	130	160	180	210	240	260	290	310	370	420	470	520
Racquetball	180	230	270	320	360	410	450	490	540	630	720	810	900
Running (11 km/h)	260	320	390	450	520	580	640	710	770	900	1030	1160	1290
Sailing	60	70	80	100	110	120	140	150	170	190	220	250	280
Skating	110	130	160	180	210	240	260	290	310	370	420	470	520
Skiing, cross-country	220	270	320	380	430	490	540	590	650	750	860	970	1080
Skiing, downhill	180	220	270	310	360	400	450	490	530	620	710	800	890
Skipping	260	320	390	450	520	580	640	710	780	900	1030	1160	1290
Snowshoeing	120	170	220	260	310	350	400	440	490	580	670	760	850
Snow shovelling	140	180	210	250	290	320	360	390	430	500	570	650	720
Soccer	170	210	250	290	330	370	410	450	490	580	660	740	820
Swimming (40 m/min)	160	200	240	280	320	360	400	440	480	560	640	720	800
Tennis	130	160	190	220	260	290	320	350	380	450	510	570	640
Volleyball	110	130	160	180	210	240	260	290	310	370	420	470	520

(1) 1 kJ equals about ¼ Calorie.

Food and Nutrition

Food contains proteins, carbohydrates, fats, water, vitamins and minerals. Nutrition is the way your body takes in and uses these ingredients to maintain proper functioning. If you aren't eating foods that your body needs, you suffer from poor nutrition and, sooner or later, your health will deteriorate.

Protein

Proteins are composed of amino acids and are indispensable in the diet. They build, maintain, and repair the body. Best sources: eggs, milk, fish, meat, poultry, soybeans, nuts. High quality proteins such as eggs, meat, or fish supply all 8 amino acids needed in the diet. Low quality proteins such as nuts and grain do not.

Fats

Fats provide energy by furnishing calories to the body, and by carrying vitamins A, D, E, and K. They are the most concentrated source of energy in the diet. Best sources: butter, margarine, salad oils, nuts, cream, egg yokes, most cheeses, lard, meat.

Carbohydrates

Carbohydrates provide energy for body function and activity by supplying immediate calories. The carbohydrate group includes sugars, starches, fiber, and starchy vegetables. Best sources: grains, legumes, nuts, potatoes, fruits.

Fibre

Fibre is the part of the plant the body cannot digest. It is a natural laxative that helps prevent constipation and hemorrhoids, and possibly colon and rectal cancers. Best sources are bran, whole grains, fresh fruit, vegetables and legumes.

Salt

Salt draws extra water into the blood vessels, which causes extra pressure on the artery walls leading to high blood pressure. Best to avoid prepared, highly processed foods and use herbs, spices and lemon juice instead of high-salt condiments like catsup or relishes.

Water

Water dissolves and transports other nutrients throughout the body aiding the process of digestion, absorption, circulation, and excretion. It also helps regulate body temperature. We get water from all foods.

Vitamins

Vitamin A—promotes good eyesight and helps keep the skin and mucous membranes resistant to infection. Best sources: liver, carrots, sweet potatoes, kale, collard greens, turnips, fortified milk.

Vitamin B₁ (thiamine)—prevents beriberi. Essential to carbohydrate metabolism and health of nervous system. Best sources: pork, legumes, enriched bread.

Vitamin B₂ (riboflavin)—protects skin, mouth, eye, eyelids, and mucous membranes. Essential to protein and energy metabolism. Best sources: liver, milk, meat, poultry, broccoli, mushrooms.

Vitamin B₆ (pyridoxine)—important in the regulation of the central nervous system and in protein metabolism. Best sources: whole grains, meats, nuts, brewers' yeast.

Vitamin B₁₂ (cobalamin)—necessary for the formation of red blood cells. Best sources: liver, meat, fish, eggs, soybeans.

Niacin—maintains the health of skin, tongue, and digestive system. Best sources: poultry, peanuts, fish, organ meats, enriched flour and bread.

Other B vitamins are—biotin, choline, folic acid (folacin), inositol, PABA (para-aminobenzoic acid), and pantothenic acid.

Vitamin C (ascorbic acid)—maintains collagen, a protein necessary for the formation of skin, ligaments, and bones. It helps heal wounds and mend fractures, and aids in resisting some types of virus and bacterial infections. Best sources: citrus fruits and juices, turnips, broccoli, Brussels sprouts, potatoes and sweet potatoes, tomatoes, cabbage.

Vitamin D—important for bone development. Best sources: sunlight, fortified milk and milk products, fish-liver oils, egg yolks, organ meats.

Vitamin E (tocopherol)—helps protect red blood cells. Best sources: vegetable oils, wheat germ, whole grains, eggs, peanuts, organ meats, margarine, green leafy vegetables.

Vitamin K—necessary for formation of prothrombin, which helps blood to clot. Also made by intestinal bacteria. Best dietary sources: green leafy vegetables, tomatoes.

Folacin (folic acid)—aids in red blood cell formation. Best sources: liver, green leafy vegetables, legumes.

Minerals

Calcium—the most abundant mineral in the body, works with phosphorus in building and maintaining bones and teeth. Best sources: milk and milk products, cheese, and blackstrap molasses.

Phosphorus—the 2d most abundant mineral, performs more functions than any other mineral, and plays a part in nearly every chemical reaction in the body. Best sources: whole grains, cheese, milk.

Iron—necessary for the formation of myoglobin, which transports oxygen to muscle tissue, and hemoglobin, which transports oxygen in the blood. Best sources: organ meats, beans, green leafy vegetables, and shellfish.

Iodine—aids in function of the thyroid gland. Best sources: iodized salt, fish, seafoods, kelp.

Magnesium—aids in formation and maintenance of strong bones and teeth; aids in energy metabolism and tissue formation. Best sources: nuts, whole grains, dairy products, peanut butter.

Zinc—aids in energy metabolism and tissue formation. Best sources: oysters, liver, meats, egg yolks.

Other minerals—chromium, cobalt, copper, fluorine, manganese, molybdenum, potassium, selenium, sodium and sulfur.

Nutritive Value of Food

Source: Health and Welfare Canada

Food	Measure	Food Energy (calories)	Protein (g)	Fat (g)	Carbohydrate (g)	Calcium (mg)	Iron (mg)	Vitamin A (RE')	Cholesterol (mg)	Sodium (mg)	Vitamin C (mg)
Dairy Products											
Cheese, cheddar	45 g	181	11	15	1	324	0.3	136	47	279	0
cottage, creamed	250 ml	244	30	11	6	142	0.3	114	36	960	tr
cream	15 ml	49	1	5	tr	11	0.2	61	15	41	0
swiss	45 g	169	13	12	2	432	0.1	114	41	117	0
pasteurized, processed, cheese spread	15 ml	41	2	3	1	79	tr	42	8	188	0
Cream, half and half	15 ml	20	tr	2	1	16	tr	16	6	6	tr
sour	15 ml	16	tr	1	1	12	tr	13	5	5	tr
whipping	15 ml	52	tr	6	tr	10	tr	63	21	6	tr
Ice cream, vanilla, hardened	125 ml	141	3	8	17	92	0.1	70	32	61	tr
Milk, whole	250 ml	157	8	9	12	306	0.1	106	36	126	2
2%	250 ml	129	9	5	12	315	0.1	106	21	129	2
skim	250 ml	90	9	tr	13	317	0.1	106	5	134	3
Shake, thick, vanilla	250 ml	306	11	8	48	399	0.3	76	33	259	0
Sherbet, orange	125 ml	97	1	1	21	37	0.1	14	5	32	1
Yogurt, fruit flavored	125 g	128	6	3	19	179	tr	16	5	73	tr
Eggs											
Cooked in shell	1	79	6	6	1	28	1.1	78	274	69	0
Fried	1	83	5	6	1	26	0.9	83	246	144	0
Scrambled with milk and butter	1	95	6	7	1	47	0.9	89	248	155	tr
Fats & Oils											
Butter	15 ml	100	tr	11	tr	3	tr	106	31	116	0
Margarine	15 ml	100	tr	12	tr	3	0	139[2]	—	138	0
Mayonnaise	15 ml	100	tr	11	tr	3	0.1	12	10	84	0
Salad dressing, French	15 ml	65	tr	6	2	3	tr	5	—	202	tr
Meat, Poultry, Fish											
Bacon, side (fried crisp)	2 slices	92	5	9	tr	2	0.4	—	—	153	—
Beef, ground, med. fat	1 pattie	257	22	18	0	10	2.9	11	85	42	—
roast, relatively fat	2 pieces	375	19	33	0	8	2.4	19	85	43	—
steak, broiled, relatively fat	1 piece	318	22	25	0	10	2.8	14	85	51	—
stewing beef or pot roast	1 piece	339	22	27	0	9	2.8	16	82	44	—
Bologna	1 slice	40	2	4	tr	1	0.2	1	—	169	—
Chicken, fried, breast, flesh & skin	½ breast	154	25	5	1	9	1.3	21	61	—	—
roasted	4 pieces	122	21	3	—	8	1.5	24	71	59	—
Cod, panfried	1½ fillets	229	23	15	—	27	0.8	180	80	222	—
Crab, canned	½ can	91	16	2	1	41	0.7	—	91	900	—
Fish sticks, breaded, cooked, frozen	3	170	11	8	12	6	—	—	—	473	—
Ham, roasted	2 pieces	337	21	28	0	9	2.7	—	79	674	—
Lamb, chops, broiled, lean and fat	1	400	25	33	0	10	1.5	—	110	78	—
Liver, beef, fried	3 slices	206	24	10	5	10	8.0	418	394	166	24
Lobster, boiled	454 g	419	27	34	1	109	0.9	376	456	285	—
Pork chop, thick with bone	1	260	16	21	0	8	2.2	0	59	43	—
Salmon, canned	100 ml	183	20	11	—	100[3]	0.8	63	32	—	—
fresh	⅔ steak	164	24	7	—	—	1.1	43	42	104	—
Sausages, pork	1 link	95	4	8	—	1	0.5	—	—	192	—
Scallops	6	112	23	1	—	115	3.0	—	53	265	—
Shrimp, raw	20 small	91	18	1	2	63	1.6	—	150	140	—

Food	Measure	Food Energy (calories)	Protein (g)	Fat (g)	Carbohydrate (mg)	Calcium (mg)	Iron (mg)	Vitamin A (RE[1])	Cholesterol (mg)	Sodium (mg)	Vitamin C (mg)
Sole, steamed	1 fillet	58	13	1	0	14	0.4	tr	45	74	—
Spareribs, pork	6 pieces	198	9	18	0	4	1.1	—	—	16	—
Tuna, canned	125 ml	177	26	7	—	7	1.7	72	59	—	—
Turkey, roast	3 pieces	171	28	5	—	7	1.6	—	84	117	—
Veal, cutlet or chop (no bone)	1	211	24	12	—	10	3.0	—	91	58	—
Wieners	1	124	7	10	1	3	0.6	—	31	542	—
Combination Meat											
Beef pot pie, baked (10 cm diam.)	1 pie	560	23	33	43	32	4.1	356	48	645	7
Chili con carne (canned with beans)	250 ml	351	20	16	32	48	4.5	16	—	1402	—
Egg rolls, pork	2 rolls	479	7	42	18	28	1.5	24	—	—	10
Lasagna, frozen, cooked	1 serving	132	10	7	9	108	0.8	23	—	455	1
Meat loaf (10 cm × 8 cm × 9 mm)	1 slice	264	10	19	11	26	1.7	15	—	—	—
Spaghetti, meat and sauce (tomato)	125 ml	136	6	6	11	17	2.5	133	—	—	—
Tortière, (pork pie) ⅛ of 23 cm pie	1 sector	451	15	34	21	18	2.7	3	—	—	—
Fruits & Products											
Apples	1	70	tr	tr	18	8	0.4	5	0	2	3
Apple juice	250 ml	130	tr	tr	32	16	1.6	—	0	3	93[2]
Avocados, Florida	1	390	4	33	27	30	1.8	88	0	18	43
Bananas, med.	1	100	1	tr	26	10	0.8	23	0	2	12
Blueberries	250 ml	90	1	1	22	22	1.4	15	0	1	21
Cherries, sweet	250 ml	96	2	tr	24	30	0.5	15	0	3	14
Fruit Cocktail	250 ml	206	1	tr	53	24	1.0	38	0	14	5
Grapefruit, white	½	45	1	tr	12	19	0.5	1	0	2	44
Grapes, Canadian	30	65	2	2	24	24	0.6	15	0	5	6
Oranges	1	65	1	tr	16	54	0.5	26	0	2	66
Orange juice, frozen, diluted	250 ml	127	2	tr	31	26	0.2	58	0	3	127
Peaches, whole	1	35	1	tr	10	9	0.5	132	0	1	7
Pears	1	100	1	1	25	13	0.5	3	0	4	7
Pineapple, canned, water pack	250 ml	101	1	tr	26	31	0.8	13	0	3	18
Plums	1	25	tr	tr	7	7	0.3	14	0	1	3
Raisins, seedless	250 ml	506	4	1	135	108	6.1	3	0	47	2
Rhubarb, cooked, sugar added	250 ml	406	1	tr	103	224	1.6	23	0	6	18
Strawberries	250 ml	58	1	1	14	33	1.5	9	0	2	93
Watermelon	1 slice	115	2	1	27	30	2.1	251	0	9	30
Breads, Cereals & Products											
Baked goods, date square	1	226	2	5	45	24	1.3	1	—	135	0
doughnuts	1	125	1	6	16	13	0.4	9	—	160	0
Breads, Melba	1 slice	15	tr	tr	3	—	—	—	—	29	0
enriched white	1 slice	82	2	1	15	20	0.5	0	—	152	0
rye, light	1 slice	73	3	—	16	22	0.5	0	—	167	0
wheat, cracked	1 slice	77	3	1	15	25	0.3	0	—	159	0
whole wheat, 100%	1 slice	73	3	1	14	50	0.7	0	—	158	0
Cakes, devil's food	1 piece	235	3	9	40	41	0.6	30	33	181	0
fruit, dark	1 slice	55	1	2	9	11	0.4	3	7	24	0
plain, sheet	1 piece	315	4	12	48	55	0.3	45	—	258	0
Cereals, bran flakes	200 ml	98	3	tr	25	15	5.6	0	—	216	0
corn flakes	200 ml	67	1	tr	15	1	3.4	0	—	151	0
granola	125 ml	288	6	16	34	34	1.8	—	—	—	0
oatmeal, cooked, rolled oats	125 ml	69	3	1	12	11	0.8	0	—	273	0
Rice Krispies	250 ml	61	1	tr	—	14	2.3	0	—	149	0
wheat, shredded	1 biscuit	80	3	tr	18	10	0.8	0	—	—	0
Cookies, brownies with nuts	1	95	1	6	10	8	0.4	12	17	50	0
chocolate chip	1	50	1	3	6	4	0.2	3	—	35	0
oatmeal	1	86	1	3	13	—	—	—	—	31	0
Crackers, graham	4	110	2	3	21	11	0.4	0	—	188	0
saltines	4	50	1	1	8	2	0.1	0	—	121	0
Muffins, bran	1	86	3	3	14	35	1.3	18	21	157	0
plain	1	120	3	4	17	42	0.6	12	21	176	tr
Pasta, cooked macaroni or spaghetti	250 ml	164	5	1	34	12	2.4	0	—	2	0
pizza, cheese	1 sector	177	9	6	21	—	0.8	43	—	351	4
Pies, apple	1 sector	410	3	18	61	1	0.5	5	0	482	2
pumpkin	1 sector	317	6	17	37	76	0.8	370	92	321	tr
cherry, 2 crusts	1 sector	387	4	18	62	22	0.5	71	0	486	tr
lemon meringue	1 sector	357	5	14	53	20	0.7	114	131	395	4
Rice, cooked, brown	250 ml	209	4	1	—	19	0.9	0	—	477	0
cooked, white	250 ml	226	4	1	—	15	0.4	0	—	670	0

Food	Measure	Food Energy (calories)	Protein (g)	Fat (g)	Carbohydrate (g)	Calcium (mg)	Iron (mg)	Vitamin A (RE[1])	Cholesterol (mg)	Sodium (mg)	Vitamin C (mg)
Sugars & Sweets											
Candies, hard 1-5 g	6	110	0	tr	28	6	0.5	0	—	9	0
Chocolate bars	30 g	134	3	6	17	25	0.7	—	—	26	0
Chocolate, plain milk	30 g	145	2	9	16	65	0.3	24	—	26	tr
coated peanuts	30 g	160	5	12	11	33	0.4	tr	—	17	tr
Jelly beans	30 g	103	0	tr	26	3	0.3	0	—	3	0
Honey	15 ml	65	tr	0	17	1	0.1	0	0	1	tr
Sugar, granulated	15 ml	40	0	0	11	0	tr	0	0	tr	0
Syrup, maple	15 ml	50	0	0	13	33	0.6	0	0	tr	0
Vegetables & Related Products											
Asparagus, 1 cm diam.	4 spears	10	1	tr	2	13	0.4	54	0	1	16
Beans, snap	250 ml	32	2	tr	—	67	0.8	72	0	5	16
Beets, cooked, diced or sliced	250 ml	58	2	tr	13	25	0.9	3	0	77	11
Broccoli, 1 cm pcs.	250 ml	45	6	1	8	158	1.4	450	0	18	162
Cabbage, cooked	250 ml	37	2	tr	6	68	0.4	20	0	25	51
Carrots, cooked, diced	250 ml	47	1	tr	11	51	0.9	1606	0	50	9
Cauliflower, cooked	250 ml	26	3	tr	5	26	0.8	7	0	11	70
Celery, stalk (large)	1 stalk	5	tr	tr	2	16	0.1	10	0	50	4
Corn, canned, drained	250 ml	148	4	tr	34	8	0.8	61	0	413	8
Cucumber, raw, pared	6 slices	5	tr	tr	1	9	0.2	tr	0	3	6
Fiddlehead, frozen, cooked	250 ml	33	4	tr	5	8	1.3	—	0	3	25
Lettuce, raw, iceberg	250 ml	10	1	tr	2	16	0.4	26	0	7	5
Mushrooms, fresh sautéed	4 avg.	78	2	7	3	8	0.7	17	—	11	tr
Onions, raw	1 onion	40	2	tr	10	30	0.6	4	0	11	11
Peas, green, cooked	250 ml	121	10	1	20	39	3.0	91	0	2	35
Potatoes, boiled	1	105	3	tr	23	10	0.8	tr	0	4	22
french fried	10	155	2	7	20	9	0.7	tr	—	3	12
Spinach, cooked	250 ml	42	5	1	6	176	4.2	1539	0	95	53
Squash, cooked, summer	250 ml	32	2	tr	7	55	0.8	87	0	2	22
Tomatoes, raw	1	35	2	tr	7	20	0.8	135	0	5	34
Turnips, raw, yellow	250 ml	42	1	tr	9	55	0.7	81	0	69	28
Vegetable juice	250 ml	47	2	tr	9	32	1.2	184	0	512	24
Zucchini, cooked	250 ml	27	2	tr	—	55	0.9	66	0	2	35
Dry Beans, Peas											
Lentils, cooked, drained	250 ml	69	12	tr	30	40	3.3	3	0	—	0
Red kidney, cooked, drained	250 ml	76	16	1	44	78	4.9	1	0	8	—
Split peas, dry, cooked	250 ml	302	21	1	55	29	4.5	11	0	34	—
Miscellaneous											
Beer (1 bottle = 341 ml)	1 bottle	150	1	0	14	18	tr	—	0	25	—
Gin, rum, vodka, whiskey	50 ml	117	—	—	—	—	—	—	—	tr	—
Wine, table	105 ml	85	—	0	4	9	—	—	—	5	—
Cola-type beverage	200 ml	77	0	0	20	—	—	0	0	—	0
Gingerale	200 ml	61	0	0	15	—	—	0	0	—	0
Ketchup	15 ml	15	tr	tr	4	4	0.1	24	—	156	3
Lemonade, diluted with 4⅓ parts water	250 ml	116	tr	tr	30	2	tr	1	0	2	18
Meat gravy, brown	15 ml	41	tr	4	2	tr	0.1	—	—	—	—
Olives, black (large)	2	15	tr	2	tr	9	0.1	1	0	81	—
green (med)	4	15	tr	2	tr	8	0.2	4	0	384	—
Peanut butter	15 ml	95	4	8	3	9	0.3	—	—	97	—
Peanuts, roasted	125 ml	438	19	38	14	56	1.4	—	—	314	0
Pickles, assorted, sweet	2 pieces	6	tr	tr	1	6	0.5	—	0	—	1
dill	1	15	1	tr	3	35	1.4	14	0	1928	8
Popcorn, popped with oil & salt	250 ml	40	1	2	5	1	0.2	—	—	175	0
Popsicle	1	70	1	0	17	tr	tr	0	—	tr	—
Potato chips	10 chips	115	1	8	10	8	0.4	tr	—	—	3
Pretzels, stick, 8 cm	5 sticks	10	tr	tr	2	1	tr	0	—	50	0
Relish	15 ml	14	tr	tr	3	2	0.2	1	0	93	1
Sesame seeds	125 ml	338	11	31	10	64	1.4	—	—	—	—
Soup, cream of tomato	250 ml	185	7	6	24	177	0.8	164	—	1114	16

(1) RE = Retinol Equivalent. (2) Added by manufacturers. (3) Value will be greatly reduced if bones are discarded. tr = trace. — = no value found but measurable amount may be present.

Canada's Food Guide

Source: Health and Welfare Canada

Canada's Food Guide is the key to good nutrition through sensible eating. The Guide divides the more than 50 nutrients found in food into 4 basic groups: milk and milk products; meat, fish, poultry and alternates; breads and cereals; and fruits and vegetables. Food eaten from these groups daily, in the servings specified, will provide all the nutrients the body needs. A 5th category, called extras, exists but is not essential because these foods, such as potato chips, gravy and candy, have little nutritional value.

Canada's Food Guide recommends, every day:

2 servings from the milk and milk products group; examples of one serving: 250 ml milk; 175 ml yogurt; 45 g cheese

2 servings from the meat, fish, poultry and alternates group: examples of one serving: 60-90 g meat, fish or poultry; 60 ml peanut butter; 250 ml cooked dried beans; 2 eggs; 60 g cheddar cheese

3 servings from the breads and cereals group: examples of one serving: 1 slice bread; 1 small roll or muffin; 125 ml cooked cereal; 175 ml ready-to-eat cereal; 125-175 cooked rice or pasta

4 servings from the fruits and vegetables group: examples of one serving: 125 ml raw or cooked fruits or vegetables; 125 ml fruit or vegetable juice; 1 med. potato, apple, carrot or peach

Recommended Daily Nutrient Intakes for Canadians

Source: Health and Welfare Canada

This table shows recommended nutrient and energy intakes necessary to maintain proper health. Recommended nutrient intakes have been set high enough to meet the requirements of most individuals. Recommended energy intakes are average requirements; individual needs will vary directly with a person's body size and level of physical activity.

	Age (years)	Average Weight (kg)	Megajoules	Calories	Vitamin A (RE)[4]	Vitamin D (µg)[5]	Vitamin E (mg)[6]	Vitamin C (mg)	Folacin (µg)[7]	Vitamin B₁₂ (µg)	Calcium (mg)	Magnesium (mg)	Iron (mg)[8]	Iodine (µg)	Zinc (mg)[9]	Protein (g)[3]
Infants	0-2 mos.	4.5	2.0	500	400	10	3	20	50	0.3	350	30	0.4	25	2	11
	3-5 mos.	7.0	2.8	700	400	10	3	20	50	0.3	350	40	5	35	3	14
	6-8 mos.	8.5	3.4	800	400	10	3	20	50	0.3	400	50	7	40	3	17
	9-11 mos.	9.5	3.8	950	400	10	3	20	55	0.3	400	50	7	45	3	18
Children	1	11	4.8	1100	400	10	3	20	65	0.3	500	55	6	55	4	19
	2-3	14	5.6	1300	400	5	4	20	80	0.4	500	70	6	65	4	22
	4-6	18	7.6	1800	500	5	5	25	90	0.5	600	90	6	85	5	26
Males	7-9	25	9.2	2200	700	2.5	7	35	125	0.8	700	110	7	110	6	31
	10-12	34	10.4	2500	800	2.5	8	40	170	1.0	900	150	10	125	7	38
	13-15	50	12.0	2800	900	2.5	9	50	150	1.5	1100	210	12	160	9	50
	16-18	62	13.2	3200	1000	2.5	10	55	185	1.9	900	250	10	160	9	55
	19-24	71	12.4	3000	1000	2.5	10	60	220	2.0	800	240	8	160	9	58
	25-49	74	11.2	2700	1000	2.5	9	60	220	2.0	800	250	8	160	9	61
	50-74	73	9.6	2300	1000	2.5	7	60	205	2.0	800	250	8	160	9	60
	75+	69	8.4	2000	1000	2.5	6	60	210	2.0	800	230	8	160	9	57
Females	7-9	25	8.0	1900	700	2.5	6	30	125	0.8	700	110	7	95	6	30
	10-12	36	9.2	2200	800	2.5	7	40	180	1.0	1000	160	10	110	7	40
	13-15	48	9.2	2200	800	2.5	7	45	145	1.5	800	200	13	160	8	42
	16-18	53	8.8	2100	800	2.5	7	45	160	1.9	700	215	14	160	8	43
	19-24	58	8.8	2100	800	2.5	6	45	175	2.0	700	200	14	160	8	43
	25-49	59	8.0	1900	800	2.5	6	45	175	2.0	700	200	14	160	8	44
	50-74	63	7.6	1800	800	2.5	6	45	190	2.0	800	210	7	160	8	47
	75+	64	6.0	1500	800	2.5	5	45	190	2.0	800	220	7	160	8	47
Pregnancy	1st trimester		+0.4	+100	+100	+2.5	+2	+ 0	+305	+1.0	+500	+15	+6	+25	+0	+15
	2d trimester		+1.3	+300	+100	+2.5	+2	+20	+305	+1.0	+500	+20	+6	+25	+1	+20
	3d trimester		+1.3	+300	+100	+2.5	+2	+20	+305	+1.0	+500	+25	+6	+25	+2	+25
Lactation			+1.9	+450	+400	+2.5	+3	+30	+120	+0.5	+500	+80	+0	+50	+6	+20

(1) For other water soluble vitamins, the following intakes are recommended: thiamin, 0.48 mg/5 MJ (0.4 mg/1000 Cal.); riboflavin, 0.6 mg/5 MJ (0.5 mg/1000 Cal.); niacin, 8.6 NE/5 MJ (7.2 NE/1000 Cal.), NE = niacin equivalents; vitamin B₆, 15 µg, as pyridoxine, per gram of protein. (2) Recommended intake for phosphorus is same as calcium. (3) Assumed that breast milk or protein of the same quality is the source for the first 2 months. (4) RE = retinol equivalents. (5) Expressed as cholecalciferol or ergocalciferol. Recommended intakes assume normal amounts of exposure to sunlight; may be less if exposure to sunlight is greater than usual. (6) Expressed as d-α-tocopherol equivalents. (7) Expressed as total folate. (8) Assumed that breast milk is the source up to 2 months of age. After menopause, recommended intake is 7 mg/day. (9) Assumed that breast milk is the source for the first 2 months.

Basic First Aid

First aid experts stress that knowing what to do for an injured person until a doctor or trained person gets to an accident scene can save a life, especially in cases of stoppage of breath, severe bleeding, and shock.

People with special medical problems, such as diabetes, cardiovascular disease, epilepsy, or allergy, are also urged to wear some sort of emblem identifying it, as a safeguard against use of medication that might be injurious or fatal in an emergency. Emblems may be obtained from Canadian Medic Alert Foundation Inc., 293 Eglinton Ave. E., Toronto, Ont. M4P 2Z8.

Most accidents occur in homes. National Safety Council figures show that home accidents annually far outstrip those in other locations, such as in autos, at work, or in public places.

In all cases, get medical assistance as soon as possible.

Animal bites — Wounds should be washed with soap under running water and animal should be caught alive for rabies test.

Asphyxiation — Start mouth-to-mouth resuscitation immediately after getting patient to fresh air.

Bleeding — Elevate the wound above the heart if possible. Press hard on wound with sterile compress until bleeding stops. Send for doctor if it is severe.

Burns — If mild, with skin unbroken and no blisters, plunge into ice water until pain subsides. Apply a dry dressing if necessary. Send for physician if burn is severe. Apply sterile compresses and keep patient quiet and comfortably warm until doctor's arrival. Do not try to clean burn, or to break blisters.

Chemicals in eye — With patient lying down, pour cupfuls of water immediately into corner of eye, letting it run to other side to remove chemicals thoroughly. Cover with sterile compress. Get medical attention immediately .

Choking — Do not use back slaps to dislodge obstruction. (See Abdominal Thrust)

Convulsions — Place person on back on bed or rug so he can't hurt himself. Loosen clothing. Turn head to side. Do not place a blunt object between the victim's teeth. If convulsions do not stop, get medical attention immediately.

Cuts (minor) — Apply mild antiseptic and sterile compress after washing with soap under warm running water.

Drowning — (See Mouth-to-Mouth Resuscitation) Artificial breathing must be started at once, before victim is out of the water, if possible. If the victim's stomach is bloated with water, put victim on stomach, place hands under stomach, and lift. If no pulse is felt, begin cardiopulmonary resuscitation. This should only be done by those professionally trained. If necessary, treat for shock. (See Shock)

Foreign body in eye — Touch object with moistened corner of handkerchief if it can be seen. If it cannot be seen or does not come out after a few attempts, take patient to doctor. Do not rub eye.

Fainting — If victim feels faint, lower head to knees. Lay him down with head turned to side if he becomes unconscious. Loosen clothing and open windows. Keep patient lying quietly for at least 15 minutes after he regains consciousness. Call doctor if faint lasts for more than a few minutues.

Falls — Send for physician if patient has continued pain. Cover wound with sterile dressing and stop any severe bleeding. Do not move patient unless absolutely necessary — as in case of fire — if broken bone is suspected. Keep patient warm and comfortable.

Loss of Limb — If a limb is severed, it is important to properly protect the limb so that it can possibly be reattached to the victim. After the victim is cared for, the limb should be placed in a clean plastic bag, garbage can or other suitable container. Pack ice around the limb on the OUTSIDE of the bag to keep the limb cold. Call ahead to the hospital to alert them of the situation.

Poisoning — Call doctor. Use antidote listed on label if container is found. Except for lye, other caustics, and petroleum products, induce vomiting unless victim is unconscious. Give milk if poison or antidote is unknown.

Shock (electric) — If possible, turn off power. Don't touch victim until contact is broken; pull from contact with electrical source using rope, wooden pole, or loop of dry cloth. Start mouth-to-mouth resuscitation if breathing has stopped.

Shock (injury-related) — Keep the victim lying down; if uncertain as to his injuries, keep the victim flat on his back. Maintain the victim's normal body temperature; if the weather is cold or damp, place blankets or extra clothing over and under the victim; if weather is hot, provide shade.

Snakebites — Immediately get victim to a hospital. If there is mild swelling or pain, apply a consticting band 2 to 4 inches above the bite.

Stings from insects — If possible, remove stinger and apply solution of ammonia and water, or paste of baking soda. Call physician immediately if body swells or patient collapses.

Unconsciousness — Send for doctor and place person on his back. Start resuscitation if he stops breathing. Never give food or liquids to an unconscious person.

Abdominal Thrust

Recommended first aid for choking victims is the abdominal thrust, also known as the Heimlich maneuver, after its creator, Dr. Henry Heimlich. Slaps on the back are no longer advised and may even prove detrimental in an attempt to assist a choking victim.

- Get behind the victim and wrap your arms around him above his waist.
- Make a fist with one hand and place it, with the thumb knuckle pressing inward, just below the point of the "v" of the rib cage.
- Grasp the wrist with the other hand and give one or more upward thrusts or hugs.
- Start mouth-to-mouth resuscitation if breathing stops.

Mouth-to-Mouth Resuscitation

Use the following directions for mouth-to-mouth resuscitation if the victim is not breathing:

- Determine consciousness by tapping the victim on the shoulder and asking loudly, "Are you okay?"
- Tilt the victim's head back so that his chin is pointing upward. Do not press on the soft tissue under the chin, as this might obstruct the airway. If you suspect that an accident victim might have neck or back injuries, open the airway by placing the tips of your index and middle fingers on the corners of the victim's jaw to lift it forward without tilting the head.
- Place your cheek and ear close to the victim's mouth and nose. Look at the victim's chest to see if it rises and falls. Listen and feel for air to be exhaled for about 5 seconds.
- If there is no breathing, pinch the victim's nostrils shut with the thumb and index finger of your hand that is pressing on the victim's forehead. Another way to prevent leakage of air when the lungs are inflated is to press your cheek against the victim's nose.
- Blow air into victim's mouth by taking a deep breath and then sealing your mouth tightly around the victim's mouth. Initially, give four, quick, full breaths without allowing the lungs to deflate completely between each breath.
- Watch the victim's chest to see if it rises.
- Stop blowing when the victim's chest is expanded. Raise your mouth; turn your head to the side and listen for exhalation.

Health Insurance

	Eligibility	Costs (as of Sept 1988)	Hospital Insurance Plan Coverage[1] for In-Patient and Out-Patient Services
Common to all prov. plans	All residents[2] and their depend-ants (spouse and children as specified below). Excludes tourists, transients and visitors. Members of Canadian Armed Forces, R.C.M.P., and inmates of federal penitentiaries are covered by other federal plans. Students are covered under plan of home province.		**In:** all medically required hospital services including ward accommodation and meals; nursing, lab, radiological and diagnostic services; drugs, biologicals and supplies; oper-ating and caserooms; anaesthetic equipment; radio-therapy; physiotherapy. **Out:** most services provided by out-patient depts. including lab, radiological and diagnostic services; emergency services and supplies. **Exclusions:** private or semi-private room and special nursing unless medically required; bedside t.v.'s, radios, telephones; take-home drugs and appliances.
Nfld.	Unmarried, dependent children.	No premiums.	**Out:** physiotherapy, radiotherapy, plaster casts. **Excl.:** ambulance and transportation services.
P.E.I.	Unmarried, dependent children.	No premiums.	**In and Out:** physiotherapy, other services rendered by persons paid by hospital. **Excl.:** ambulance services.
N.S.	Unmarried, unemployed children to age 18.	No premiums.	**Out:** diabetic care, haemo-dialysis, inhalation therapy, home parental nutrition, radiotherapy, physiotherapy, services at NS Hearing and Speech Clinic and NS Tumor Clinic, erythromelalgia care.
N.B.	Unmarried, dependent children to age 19.	No premiums.	**Excl.:** ambulance services, visits solely for administration of drugs.
Que.	Unmarried, dependent children to age 18 if perma-nently living with resident.	No premiums.	**In:** implanted prostheses and devices, other services rendered by persons paid by hospital. **Out:** physiotherapy; radiotherapy; inhalation, speech and hearing and ergotherapy; clinical psychology services; orthoptic services for visual defects; services and exams required under Que. legislation.
Ont.	Unmarried, unemployed, dependent children to age 21. Disabled, dependent children to any age, if disabled prior to age 21.	Monthly premiums ($29.75-59.50). No premiums for seniors and social aid recipients. Premium assistance available.	**In:** mental health and approved ambulance services. **Out:** occupational, speech, psychological, audiological and physiotherapy; diet counselling; home renal dialysis and hyper-alimentation; hemophiliacs program. **Excl.:** visits solely for drug administration.
Man.	Unmarried, dependent children to age 19. Disabled, dependent children to any age.	No premiums.	**In:** physiotherapy; occupational and speech therapy, dietetic counselling. **Excl.:** ambulance and transportation services, acupuncture.
Sask.	Unmarried, dependent children to age 18.	No premiums.	**In:** other services rendered by persons paid by hospital. **Excl.:** custodial care; care in mental health institutions; services in approved physiotherapy and osteopathy clinics; ambulance services except between hospitals in same Sask. city.
Alta.	Unmarried, dependent children to age 21 (to age 25 if student). Single, dis-abled, dependent children to any age.	Monthly premiums ($18-36). No pre-miums for seniors and those receiving Alta. Widows' Pension. Subsidy for low income residents.	**In:** between hospital transportation; valve implants, pace-makers, steel pins, joint prostheses; other services rendered by persons paid by hospital. **Out:** occupational, speech, respiratory, psychiatric and physiotherapy; special orthopedic & diabetic clinics. **Excl.:** transportation services.
B.C.	Unmarried, dependent children to age 19 (to age 25 if student).	Monthly premiums ($29-58). Subsidy for low income residents.	**In:** ambulance services (nominal charge), cosmetic surgery hospital costs if it must be done in hospital, other services rendered by persons paid by hospital. **Out:** renal dialysis; cancer, psychiatric and physiotherapy; cytology, rehabilitive, diabetic, arthritis and psoriasis services, dietetic counselling.
Y.T.	Unmarried, dependent children to age 19 (to age 25 if student). Single, dis-abled, dependent children to any age.	No premiums.	**In and Out:** other services rendered by persons paid by hospital. **Excl.:** custodial care, transportation unless medically required service is unavailable locally.
N.W.T.	Unmarried, dependent children.	No premiums.	**In:** occupational and speech therapy, psychiatric and psychological services, approved detoxification prog. **Out:** occupational, speech and physiotherapy, approved psychiatrist and psychologist services.

(1) Excludes services covered under Workers' Compensation, Veterans Affairs and other federal or provincial legislation. (2) Residents are persons legally entitled to be or remain in Canada, who make their home and are ordinarily present in the province or territory. New residents from other provinces are eligible on the first day of their 3d month of residence and are covered by the plan of their old province until that time.

by Province

Health Insurance Plan Coverage		
Physician Services	**Other Medical Services**	**Drugs, Supplies and Aids**
All medically required services in office, home or hospital; surgical procedures; anaesthesia; lab, radiological and diagnostic services; specialist services if referred, otherwise G.P. rates. **Excludes:** pre-school, insurance and employment exam, cosmetic surgery not medically required, prep. of reports, phone advice, mileage and travel, medical-legal services.	**Dental:** specified oral-dental surgical procedures performed in a hospital by dental surgeon (or by dentist in Nfld., N.B. and Que.); some prov. offer additional coverage as specified below. **Other:** services by health care professionals in private practice as specified below (services may be restricted to certain groups and/or amount of cost covered limited).	**Drugs:** covers full cost (unless otherwise specified) of specified prescribed drugs for groups as specified below. **Excludes:** patent drugs, vitamins, cold and cough remedies, expectorants, analgesics, soap. **Other Supplies and Aids:** coverage may be limited to special needs groups and/or amount of cost covered may be limited.
Authorized group immunizations. **Excl.:** annual health exam, vaccinations for travel, acupuncture.	**Dental:** limited service under 13 yrs.; comprehensive coverage for children of social aid recipients and special needs groups, incl. cleft palate/lip. **Other:** optometrist.	**Drugs:** ingredient cost (not dispensing fee) of prescribed drugs covered for seniors receiving Guaranteed Income Supplement and social aid recipients.
Maternity care, approved group innoculations and immunizations. **Excl.:** acupuncture.	**Dental:** routine dental care for children aged 4 to 16 years.	**Drugs:** for social assistance recipients.
Maternity care, well-baby care, sterilization for men and women, approved group immunizations. **Excl.:** acupuncture, ambulance.	**Dental:** all required services to age 16; services for those with special needs including cleft palate/lip. **Other:** optometrist.	**Drugs:** for seniors, those with Cystic Fibrosis, Diabetes Insipidus. **Other:** ostomy equipment, diabetic supplies, prostheses.
Innoculations. **Excl.:** physical exam, vaccinations for travel, psychoanalysis, trans-sexual surgery, acupuncture.	**Other:** optometrist for under 19 or seniors; podiatrist, chiropodist, chiropractor for seniors.	**Drugs:** seniors (co-pay charge), those with Cystic Fibrosis, bone marrow/organ transplant. **Other:** seniors: injection, ostomy and diabetic supplies; foot care, hearing and visual aids; prosthetics and orthotics; rehabilitative equipment.
Physical exam, psychiatric treatment, sterilization, approved grp. immunization. Specialist services without referral. **Excl.:** acupuncture, psychoanalysis unless institution authorized.	**Dental:** specified dental care under 16. Dental care and prostheses for social aid recipients. **Other:** optometrist.	**Drugs:** for seniors, social aid or income supplement recipients. **Other:** prostheses, orthopedic and other devices/supplies; ostomy appliances; hearing aids; aids for physically and visually handicapped.
Physical exam; vasectomy; maternity care; immunizations, injections and tests. Specialist services without referral. **Excl.:** acupuncture, psych. tests.	**Dental:** special care for those with cleft palate/lip. **Other:** optometrist, chiropractor, osteopath, chiropodist, podiatrist, approved physiotherapy facilities.	**Drugs:** for seniors, provincial social aid recipients. **Other:** assistive devices program for those disabled prior to age 21; home dialysis.
Maternity care; physical exams; immunizations, injections and tests. **Excl.:** unauthorized group immunizations.	**Dental:** specified preventive care for 6 to 14 yrs. living in rural area; special services for those with cleft palate/lip. **Other:** optometrist, chiropractor.	**Drugs:** for all residents 80% costs over $125 deductible (except seniors $75). **Other:** prosthetic and orthotic devices; aids for the deaf; orthopedic shoes and hearing aids for children under 18; eyeglasses for seniors.
Physical exams, immunizations, maternity care, well-baby care, exams and reports for adoption. Specialist services without referral.	**Dental:** preventive and treatment services for children; services for those with cleft palate/lip. **Other:** optometrist, chiropractor, audiologist.	**Drugs:** ingredient cost of drug (not prescription charge) for all residents. **Other:** prosthetics, orthotic and other aids for disabled; special needs phone services; aids for the blind; ostomy supplies. Program for social aid clients.
Medical exams for driver's licence for those over 68 yrs. **Excl.:** unauthorized group immunizations, experimental medical services.	**Dental:** dental services and dentures for seniors, widows and their dependants (also clinical psychologist, naturopath, home nursing services).[3] **Other:** chiropractor, physiotherapist, optometrist, podiatrist.	**Drugs:** 80% cost for seniors, widows and their dependants (also hearing aids, eyeglasses, surgical and medical supplies/equipment).[3] **Other:** foot care and podiatric appliances.
Physical exams, maternity care. **Excl.:** acupuncture, preventive medical counselling.	**Dental:** cleft palate/lip, severe congenital facial abnormalities only. **Other:** chiropractor, optometrist, physiotherapist, podiatrist, naturopath, masseur; mental health, speech and hearing, alcohol and drug services.	**Drugs:** full cost for seniors, the handicapped and welfare recipients; all others 80% cost over $200 deductible per family or person.
Maternity care. **Excl.:** ambulance and transportation services, experimental medical services.	**Dental:** limited dental services and dentures for seniors. **Other:** optometrist and home nursing for seniors.	**Drugs:** seniors; chronic disease program. **Other:** seniors: hearing aids, surgical and medical supplies, eyeglasses; under 16: prostheses, hearing aids, orthopedic shoes.
Maternity care, specialist rates without referral.	**Other:** eye exam by opthomologist but not optometrist.	**Drugs:** seniors.

Landed immigrants are eligible from the day of their arrival (except B.C. where there is a 3 month residence requirement and Ontario where there is a one month residence requirement). (3) Services covered under Alberta Blue Cross which is premium free for seniors, their spouses, those between 55-64 receiving Alberta Widow's Pension and their dependants.

Phobias

Phobia is defined as "an irrational, exaggerated fear of or aversion to a particular thing or situation". Listed below are the terms for some common phobias.

Fear of

air	aerophobia
animals	zoophobia
beards	pogonophobia
bees	apiphobia
being afraid	phobophobia
being alone	monophobia
being beaten	rhabdophobia
being buried alive	taphophobia
being stared at	scopophobia
blood	hematophobia
blushing	ereuthophobia
books	bibliophobia
cancer	cancerophobia
cats	gatophobia
chickens	alektorophobia
children	pediophobia
choking	pnigophobia
churches	ecclesiaphobia
cold	frigophobia
corpse	necrophobia
crossing a bridge	gephyrophobia
crowds	ochlophobia
darkness	nyctophobia
daylight	phengophobia
death	necrophobia
deformity	dysmorphophobia
demons	demonophobia
dirt	mysophobia
disease	nosophobia
disorder	ataxiophobia
dogs	cynophobia
dreams	oneirophobia
drinking	dipsophobia

Fear of

drugs	pharmacophobia
dust	amathophobia
electricity	electrophobia
empty rooms	kenophobia
enclosed space	claustrophobia
everything	panophobia
eyes	ommatophobia
fire	pyrophobia
fish	ichthyophobia
flying	aerophobia
fog	homichlophobia
food	sitophobia
germs	spermophobia
ghosts	phasmophobia
god	theophobia
going to bed	clinophobia
heart disease	cardiophobia
heights	acrophobia
horses	hippophobia
human beings	anthropophobia
injections	trypanophobia
insanity	maniaphobia
insects	entomophobia
lightning	astrapophobia
making false statements	mythophobia
marriage	gamophobia
men	androphobia
meteors	meteorophobia
mice	musophobia
mirrors	eisoptrophobia
missiles	ballistophobia
money	chrometophobia
nakedness	gymnophobia

Fear of

night	nyctophobia
noise	phonophobia
open spaces	agoraphobia
pain	algophobia
pleasure	hedonophobia
pregnancy	maieusiophobia
rain	ombrophobia
reptiles	batrachophobia
ridicule	katagelophobia
school	scholionophobia
sex	genophobia
sleep	hypnophobia
slime	blennophobia
smothering	pnigerophobia
snakes	ophodiophobia
speaking aloud	phonophobia
speed	tachophobia
spiders	arachnophobia
stings	cnidophobia
strangers	xenophobia
surgical operations	ergasiophobia
thirteen	triskaidekaphobia
thunder	tonitrophobia
touching	haphephobia
travel	hodophobia
trees	dendrophobia
vehicles	amaxophobia
wasps	spheksophobia
water	hydrophobia
women	gynophobia
worms	helminthophobia

Effects of Commonly Abused Drugs

Source: Addiction Research Foundation

The effects of any drug depend on the amount taken at one time, the past drug experience of the user, the circumstances in which the drug is taken (the place, the feelings and activities of the user, the presence of other people, the simultaneous use of alcohol or other drugs, etc.), and the manner in which the drug is taken.

Depressants

Depressants, also known as sedative/hypnotics, slow down or depress the central nervous system, producing a calming effect and inducing sleep. Effects can range from mild sedation to general anesthesia and, in extreme cases, death by respiratory arrest. In general, depressants promote a feeling of well-being and a releasing of one's inhibitions. Some drugs classified as depressants include alcohol, barbiturates, most sleeping pills and sedatives and inhalants.

Most Commonly Abused Depressants
Alcohol

The main type of alcohol found in alcoholic beverages is ethyl alcohol or ethanol, produced both naturally and synthetically by the fermentation of fruits, vegetables and grains.

Effects: At low to moderate doses, alcohol promotes a relaxation of inhibitions and a general feeling of well-being. As doses increase, intoxication causes cognitive, perceptual and motor impairment. At very high doses severe respiratory depression may cause death. Approximately 8 to 12 hours after a short period of heavy drinking, physical effects of a "hangover" occur, including headache, nausea, vomiting and shakiness. The long-term effects of repeated alcohol use include a loss of appetite, vitamin deficiencies, stomach ailments, skin problems and sexual impotence. More severe effects are damage to the liver, heart and central nervous system and memory loss.

Dangers: Because tolerance to alcohol increases through regular use, increased doses are necessary to achieve the desired effects. Psychological and physical dependence can occur with both regular and irregular use. Through chronic use, symptoms of withdrawal will occur if alcohol is no longer available. Withdrawal symptoms depend on the duration and frequency of alcohol abuse. They range from agitation, insomnia, perspiring, shakiness and loss of appetite to tremors, seizures, hallucinations and sometimes death.

Alcohol and Pregnancy: Risks to the fetus increase with the amount of alcohol consumed by the mother. One danger is fetal alcohol syndrome and deformities in the newborn child.

Barbiturates

Barbiturates are central nervous system depressants. Some types include amobarbital (Sodium Amytal), butabarbital (Butisol Sodium), pentobarbital (Nembutal), phenobarbital (Luminal) and secobarbital (Seconal). Barbiturates are used clinically as an anesthetic and sedative and to control epileptic seizures.

Effects: Low dosage, short-term use will result in the relief of anxiety and tension. Larger doses can be sleep-inducing or can produce similar effects to alcohol, including physical impairment, a feeling of euphoria, slurred speech, slowed reactions and relaxation of emotional inhibitions. Long-term use causes disruptions of normal sleep patterns, impaired memory, judgment and thinking, feelings of hostility, depression and general moodiness. Physical manifestations of prolonged use are chronic fatigue, reduced sexual desire, impaired fine and gross motor coordination and respiratory disorders.

Dangers: Barbiturates are extremely hazardous when abused. Tolerance results from regular use, necessitating an increasing dosage in order to produce the same effects. Rapid tolerance occurs with frequent use to induce sleep. Regular barbiturate users risk a psychological dependence. Characteristic withdrawal symptoms are restlessness, anxiety, insomnia and irritability. In extreme cases, delirium, convulsions and death have occurred.

Barbiturates and Pregnancy: Research studies have concluded that the use of certain sedative hypnotic drugs during pregnancy is associated with various congenital defects. Behavioral abnormalities are also symptomatic. Newborns can exhibit withdrawal symptoms such as respiratory distress, irritability, fever, and sleeping and feeding problems.

Inhalants

Inhalants, including solvents and aerosols, are volatile hydrocarbons (organic chemicals) produced from petroleum and natural gas, that evaporate quickly at room temperature. Solvents include plastic cement, model airplane glue, lacquer thinners, nail polish remover, lighter fluid, cleaning fluid and gasoline. Aerosols include deodorants, hairsprays, insecticides, paint, and cookware coating products. Children and young adults are the primary group abusing these chemicals.

Effects: Solvents and aerosols produce an extremely rapid effect by quickly entering the bloodstream and flowing to the brain. These chemicals cause a depression of the central nervous system, slowing down both the heart rate and the rate of breathing. The user feels euphoric very quickly and may experience graphic imaginings which occasionally result in quite bizarre behavior. Short-term effects include loss of coordination and self-control, disorientation, red eyes, bad breath and mouth and nose sores. "Sudden sniffing death" can occur because of an abnormal reaction of the heart to strenuous activity and stress. Suffocation deaths may also occur when the user places a plastic bag over the head to intensify or speed up the effects. Long-term effects include fatigue, depression, tremors, irritability, hostility and confusion.

Dangers: The regular use of inhalants induces tolerance, necessitating increased doses to produce the desired effects. Psychological and physical dependence can occur from repeated use. Withdrawal symptoms including chills, hallucinations, abdominal pains, headaches and muscular cramps can occur when regular use of these chemicals is stopped. Residual damage to the brain and other organs has been reported in heavy users.

Minor Tranquillizers

The benzodiazepines (eg. Valium, Librium, Serax) are the most widely prescribed psychotherapeutic drugs. They are effective in controlling anxiety and producing sleep with a lower risk of producing physical dependence than barbiturates. Women are the primary users of minor tranquillizers.

Effects: Minor tranquillizers produce a calming effect, sedation and sleep, but do not produce the major side effects characteristic of barbiturate use. Increased doses cause loss of muscular co-ordination and mental confusion, and eventually disruption of psycho-motor skills. Long-term effects after repeated use include chronic intoxication and physical dependence.

Dangers: Even low daily dosages on a regular basis induces tolerance. Psychological and physical dependence is also a danger, resulting in withdrawal symptoms when the use of the drug ceases. Withdrawal symptoms include restlessness, anxiety, insomnia, muscle twitching, loss of appetite, nausea and vomiting.

Minor Tranquillizers and Pregnancy: Mothers using minor tranquillizers during pregnancy may have an increased risk of bearing children with minor congenital malformations. Some minor tranquillizers may also cause withdrawal symptoms in newborns.

Hallucinogens

Hallucinogen literally means hallucination-producing, though because hallucinogens include a wide variety of drugs and because the effects can differ significantly among individual users, it is difficult to generalize about common effects of their use. Some drugs classified as hallucinogens are LSD, MDA, mescaline, PCP, marijuana and hashish.

Most Commonly Abused Hallucinogens

LSD

Lysergic acid diethylamide, commonly known as LSD or "acid" is a semi-synthetic drug produced from lysergic acid. It is derived from ergot, a fungus produced from grains such as rye.

Effects: The user will feel the effects of LSD in less than an hour. The experience will last between 2 and 12 hours. Physiological effects include increased heart rate, blood pressure and body temperature, dilated pupils, muscular weakness and incoordination, nausea, chills and hyperventilation. Psychological effects include changes in perception, and thought and mood swings, from pleasant to fearful, can occur in rapid succession. The sensations experienced depend on the user, the circumstances under which the drug was taken, past experience with LSD and the size of the dose. Increasing doses produce quantitative rather than qualitative changes. Sensory distortions such as seeing a kaleidoscope of color or experiencing a blending of two senses (eg. music is "seen") are common occurrences. Also, matters of insignificance are assigned a profound importance; thus, some LSD users feel that they have had mystical experiences when the drug is used.

Dangers: Although physical dependence on LSD does not occur, the effects of the drug are unpredictable. The possibility of having a "bad trip" is one of the dangers. Experiencing a "flashback", a spontaneous recurrence of the sensations produced by the drug, is a possible after-effect which can produce extreme anxiety. LSD-associated suicide attempts are related to the heavy use of this drug.

LSD and Pregnancy: There may be a relationship between the use of LSD and an increased risk of spontaneous abortion, and between LSD and a higher incidence of congenital abnormalities.

Cannabis

Marijuana and hashish are produced from the dried leaves and flowering tops of the hemp plant (cannabis sativa), THC (tetrahydrocannabinol) is the substance in cannabis which produces the effects of this drug.

Effects: Low to moderate use of cannabis produces fairly mild effects such as a slight increase in heart rate, mild muscle weakness and lack of coordination, red eyes, increased appetite, and a dry mouth. Psychological experiences are generally euphoric, including such effects as a relaxation of one's inhibitions, increased calmness, drowsiness and sedation. Mood and perceptual changes can also occur with high doses. Effects of long-term use include chronic bronchitis and a probable greater risk of cancer because of the high tar yield of marijuana cigarettes. Heavy use also can result in a user experiencing "chronic intoxication syndrome" characterized by a loss of energy and drive, confused thinking and impaired memory.

Dangers: Tolerance results from regular use, making increased doses necessary to produce the same desired effects. Regular use may also cause psychological and mild physical dependence. Abrupt abstinence after long-term and regular high-dose use can result in a withdrawal syndrome which includes sleep disturbances, anxiety, restlessness, sweating, loss of appetite and upset stomach.

PCP (Phencyclidine)

PCP is a dissociative anesthetic originally used for human anesthesia, but later limited to veterinary medicine because of its extremely undesirable side effects. It possesses both stimulant and depressive properties. Common street names for PCP are "angel dust", "crystal", "hog", "peace pill" and "horse tranquillizer". PCP can be administered orally, sniffed or injected.

Effects: The effects of PCP vary widely between users and from one drug experience to the next. Effects include euphoria, relaxation and sedation, distortions of body image, time/space and visual/auditory exaggeration. The user experiences difficulties with speech and articulation, and motor skills, as well as constriction of pupils, blurred vision, and sometimes dizziness and drowsiness. Adverse effects such as anxiety, paranoia and terror can occur even at low doses because of the unpredictable nature of PCP. Moderately higher doses generally result in the manifestation of the analgesic properties of the drug, causing a decrease in pain and increased sleep. Higher doses result in an intensification of the lower dose effects plus a greater degree of hallucinogenic experiences, disorientation, bizarre behavior and a fear of imminent death, which may last for days. The user can experience high blood pressure, a fever, irregular breathing, nausea and vomiting. High doses can cause a coma, convulsions and death due to respiratory arrest. Effects caused by long-term use result in thinking and memory impairment, LSD-like "flashbacks", persistent speech problems, severe anxiety and depression and social withdrawal and isolation. Regular PCP users may develop toxic psychosis resulting in aggressive, assaultive behavior, paranoia, delusions and hallucinations.

Dangers: The unpredictability of PCP makes it an extremely dangerous drug. Furthermore, because PCP is often misrepresented as other substances, unsuspecting users who are not prepared for its effects may have a terrifying experience. Physical dependence has not yet been clearly established, but the intense euphoria caused by PCP can lead to repeated use of this drug.

Narcotic Analgesics

Narcotic analgesics can be derived from natural (eg. morphine and codeine), semi-synthetic (eg. heroin) or synthetic (eg. methadone) sources. Narcotic means "to benumb", thus relief from pain is a major reason for the use of these drugs. Clinical use of narcotic analgesics is prescribed for pain, cough suppression and the control of severe diarrhea. Some of these drugs are prescribed in order to manage the physical dependence on other narcotic analgesics.

Narcotics and Pregnancy: Tests have proven that approximately 50 percent of all narcotic-dependent women experience complications during pregnancy and childbirth. The most common medical problems include anemia, cardiac disease, diabetes, pneumonia and hepatitis. Also, there is an abnormally high rate of spontaneous abortion, breech births, caesarean sections and premature deliveries. Infants are often smaller than average and most will experience withdrawal symptoms.

Most Commonly Abused Narcotic Analgesics
Heroin

Heroin is a semi-synthetic narcotic analgesic produced by chemical modification of morphine. The drug is extremely powerful in both its euphoric and analgesic qualities. It can be injected, sniffed, smoked and swallowed, though injection, or "mainlining", is the most popular method practised by regular users because it produces the quickest and most potent results. Common street names are "H", "horse", "junk", "smack", and "scag".

Effects: Short-term effects at low doses of nausea and vomiting are tolerated very quickly. Regular use produces euphoria and relaxation and the user often goes "on the nod", meaning that alternating states of wakefulness and drowsiness are experienced. Physical reactions include decreased physical activity, visual impairment, loss of appetite, constipation, reduced libido, increased urination and an itchy and burning skin sensation. Higher doses produce an intensification of the effects as well as a decreased sensitivity to pain, poor concentration, sleepiness and depression of breathing, heart rate and blood pressure. Very high doses will cause deep sleep, coma and a further lowering of blood pressure, respiration, heart rate and body temperature. Effects of long-term use are mainly associated with the lifestyle of the user and the adverse effects of using a needle to inject the drug. Contracting AIDS, tetanus, viral hepatitis, endocarditis and pneumonia are some of the common risks taken by heroin-dependent users. Severe overdose can cause death due to respiratory arrest.

Dangers: Heroin is one of the most addictive narcotic analgesics. Regular users eventually reach a plateau where high

doses of the drug are necessary to produce the desired effects. Continued use at this stage is mainly to avoid withdrawal. Withdrawal begins 8 to 12 hours after the last dose of heroin, resulting in symptoms which are fairly similar to a severe case of the flu (eg. shivering, runny nose, cramps, diarrhea, tears). Although physical withdrawal can be reached within 7 to 10 days, psychological dependence continues long afterwards. The user will feel depressed, anxious, will experience insomnia and a loss of appetite, but most importantly, will continue to crave the effects that heroin produces. This intense craving results in many users returning to the drug.

Stimulants

Although drugs included in this class vary widely in their common properties, all produce increased activity of the central and autonomic nervous systems. Stimulants can cause heightened feelings of well-being in some users, but with others they can be anxiety-producing. In addition to increasing the user's heart rate, blood pressure and rate of respiration, stimulants can increase wakefulness to the point of insomnia, and can act as appetite suppressants. Chronic use can result in stimulant psychosis which resembles acute paranoia. Drugs classified as stimulants are amphetamines, caffeine, cocaine, diethylpropion, methylphenidate, and nicotine.

Most Commonly Abused Stimulants
Amphetamines

Benzadrine, Dexedrine, Methedrine and Ritalin are some trade names of amphetamines. Common street names are "uppers" and "speed". Illegal use of amphetamines is based on a variety of non-therapeutic reasons such as the desire to enhance moods, to avoid sleep or to improve athletic performance. Medical use of amphetamines has been greatly reduced to include only a few relatively uncommon conditions for which these drugs can be legally prescribed.

Effects: Common physical short-term effects of amphetamines include appetite suppression, increased rate of breathing, heart rate and blood pressure and dilated pupils. Psychological effects are greater alertness and energy, and a general feeling of well-being. At larger doses, amphetamines cause fever, headaches, blurred vision and dizziness. The user becomes very excited, talkative, aggressive, hostile and feels superior. Very high doses result in further physical deterioration, sometimes to the point of collapse. The user becomes flushed, the heart rate is both rapid and irregular and tremors and a loss of coordination are experienced. Long-term effects due to extensive use of amphetamines produce an exaggeration of the short-term effects. The user is often susceptible to disease because of a failure to meet an acceptable level of nutrient intake. Psychosis can also be an effect, often leading to acts of sudden violence.

Dangers: Amphetamine users often turn to depressant drugs to counter the effects of amphetamines. Also, regular use leads to both physical and psychological dependence. Withdrawal symptoms include fatigue, long but disturbed sleep, hunger and moderate to severe depression.

Cocaine

Cocaine is procured from the leaves of the *Erythroxylon coca* bush which grows mainly in Peru and Bolivia. Although cocaine has been in use for centuries, its popularity has risen greatly since the late 1960s. Common street names for cocaine are "coke", "snow", "leaf", or "blow". The drug is most often "snorted" into the nostrils but is also injected.

Effects: In general, the effects of cocaine are almost identical to those produced by amphetamines. However, cocaine is also a very strong local anesthetic. Therefore, large doses of the drug can produce a marked depression of the central nervous system which can result in respiratory arrest. Chronic cocaine snorting causes stuffiness and a runny nose, eczema around the nostrils, and perforation of the nasal septum.

Dangers: Cocaine is highly addictive. There is a compelling need for regular users to maintain and gradually increase their dosage. Symptoms of dependence include fatigue, long but erratic sleep, hunger, irritability and depression.

Cocaine and Pregnancy:
Little research has been done on the effects of cocaine on pregnant women or the fetus. Preliminary reports indicate that cocaine use by pregnant women

may result in a greater risk of spontaneous abortion, still birth and congenital malformations and neurobehavioural impairments in the infant.

Another form of cocaine known as **crack** ("rock" or "crystal") is created by mixing cocaine with baking soda and water into a paste, which, when hardened, is cut into chips that resemble soap or whitish gravel. The drug is usually smoked in a water pipe. Virtually unknown until 1985, crack is now widespread throughout the U.S. and its availability and use are growing in Canada.

Effects: Same as cocaine but intensified. The rapid constriction of the blood vessels which happens when the vapors of the burning drug are inhaled affects the entire cardiovascular system. Respiratory failure, coronary arrest (heart attack) and convulsions of the brain may occur. Appetite suppression caused by the use of crack leads to weight loss and eventually malnutrition.

Dangers: Crack puts its users at an extremely high risk of addiction. The 4 stages of cocaine addiction—euphoria, depression, sleeplessness and a schizophrenic-like psychosis, complete with delusions and hallucinations—can be experienced in one single use of the drug by heavy users. A common nightmare of addicts is that bugs are crawling over the skin.

The deep depression experienced by a crack addict often leads to accidents, drug overdose or suicide.

Tobacco (Nicotine)

Nicotine, derived from the tobacco plant *Nicotiana tabacum*, is an extremely toxic drug and mild stimulant. There are 15 to 20 mg of nicotine in a typical cigarette, but less than 1 mg reaches the bloodstream when it is smoked. Nicotine causes many of the negative effects of smoking and is primarily responsible for the addictive nature of this habit.

Effects: Short-term effects include an increase in heart rate, blood pressure and respiration and a slight decrease in skin temperature. Although smoking stimulates the central nervous system, it can also cause relaxation in some regular smokers. Long-term effects, including those caused by tar, are mainly on the bronchio-pulmonary and cardiovascular systems. Smoking is the major cause of lung cancer, and increases susceptibility of the smoker to bronchitis and emphysema. Smoking increases the risk of blocked blood vessels in the heart, the brain and the limbs. It also increases the chance of developing stomach ulcers and pneumonia.

Dangers: Both physical and psychological dependence occurs, generally when use exceeds 10 cigarettes per day. Craving a cigarette is a powerful urge among heavy smokers.

Tobacco and Pregnancy: Tests have proven that women who smoke bear smaller babies, have more premature births and a greater incidence of miscarriage and stillbirth. There is also evidence that the mental and physical development of their children is impaired.

Tobacco Use by Canadians, 1985

Source: Statistics Canada

(percentage of population)

| | Non-Smokers | | | Smokers | | | |
| | | | | | Cigarettes | | |
	Total	Never smoked	Former smokers	Total[1]	Occasional	Daily	Pipe or cigar only
Males							
All[2] ages	58.9	33.9	25.0	41.1	4.4	33.1	2.5
15-19 years	71.9	66.3	5.6	28.1	6.0	19.5	...
20-24 years	58.2	49.4	8.8	41.8	6.8	32.2	...
25-44 years	53.6	32.2	21.3	46.4	4.8	38.0	2.8
45-64 years	57.7	21.4	36.4	42.3	2.4	35.6	3.0
65 years and over	70.4	21.0	49.4	29.4	3.1	22.7	3.6
Females							
All[2] ages	66.7	50.3	16.4	33.2	4.3	27.8	...
15-19 years	70.9	64.9	6.0	29.1	6.8	20.8	...
20-24 years	52.6	42.1	10.5	47.4	6.9	37.9	...
25-44 years	64.5	44.3	20.2	35.3	3.9	30.7	...
45-64 years	66.0	48.8	17.2	33.8	4.1	28.6	...
65 years and over	83.2	67.3	15.9	16.7	1.9	14.8	...

(1) Includes individuals who did not specify type of smoker. (2) 15 years of age and over.
. . . = too small to be included.

Canadian Per Capita Alcohol Consumption[1]

Source: Brewers Association of Canada

(litres per person per year)

| | Beer[2] | | | Wine[2] | | | Spirits[2] | | |
	1975	1980	1985[3]	1975	1980	1985[3]	1975	1980	1985[3]
Canada	118.07	113.55	105.65	8.11	11.00	12.40	10.75	10.51	8.53
Newfoundland	129.26	135.33	118.37	3.10	3.78	4.26	9.20	10.28	7.54
Prince Edward Island	88.28	100.59	94.42	4.78	5.35	5.49	12.76	12.33	9.03
Nova Scotia	98.10	99.88	95.22	6.19	6.74	7.79	10.90	11.37	9.12
New Brunswick	97.92	105.46	96.05	5.45	5.25	5.92	8.68	8.73	6.41
Quebec	127.75	120.50[4]	108.75	8.95	11.79	12.66	7.05	5.71[4]	4.74
Ontario	120.01	113.41	108.41	7.31	10.59	12.02	11.54	11.27	9.17
Manitoba	110.39	102.04	107.99	6.65	8.14	8.68	12.56	12.25	9.91
Saskatchewan	92.80	95.73[4]	89.66	4.91	6.03[4]	6.87	12.91	11.74[4]	10.25
Alberta	107.51	108.73[5]	99.93	8.84	12.25[5]	13.10	13.69	16.21[5]	13.15
British Columbia	116.63	113.66	101.72	12.32	16.68	20.35	14.41	14.16	10.79
Yukon	208.33	203.21	195.26	14.39	20.93	19.53	23.22	22.59	17.09
Northwest Territories	132.11	107.71	121.73	11.85	9.20	8.22	18.85	17.00	15.69

(1) Adult population 15 years of age and older; for the fiscal year ending Mar. 31. (2) Includes domestic and imported. (3) Estimates. (4) Strike in liquor distribution system. (5) Strike in brewing industry.

Child Abuse Alert List

Source: Ontario Centre for the Prevention of Child Abuse

The Parent

- Expresses fear of/shows evidence of losing control
- Shows detachment from child
- Gives indication of abuse of alcohol or drugs
- States child is "always injuring self"
- Complains that there is no one to "bail him/her out" when "uptight" with child
- Reluctant to answer questions, defensive, becomes angry with questions
- Indicates he/she was raised in a "motherless", harsh way
- Shows unrealistic expectations of baby or child, indicating lack of knowledge of normal development
- Shows marked lack of concern for child's welfare, and little or no remorse
- Treats siblings differently, with obvious preferences, and dislike for one child
- Appears to be under considerable stress, but does not seek help. Seems sad

The Child

- Has an injury or marks which are unexplained or inadequately explained
- Has received no apparent medical attention for an injury
- Shows evidence of repeated injury
- Is unusually fearful of adults, perhaps of one sex more than other
- If a baby, shows a "frozen watchfulness" with adults; shows a failure to thrive
- Unusual apprehension when an adult approaches a crying child
- Is frequently over-tired and/or inappropriately dressed for the weather
- Unusually aggressive or disruptive or nervous
- Arrives early at school, leaves late, indicates parent(s) won't care about absence
- Difficulty in sitting, genital-area discomfort, resistance to being touched at all by an adult
- Craves attention and affection but easily hurt and untrustful

Physical Signs

- Unexplained bruises and welts, especially those:
  —on face, back, buttocks, thighs
  —in stages of simultaneous healing
  —in the shape of an instrument such as belt, hair brush, etc.
  —appearing after the child's absence, weekend, vacation
- Unexplained burns:
  —cigarette burns (hands, feet, back, buttocks)
  —immersion burns (sock-like or glove-like in shape)
  —burns patterned like electric burner, iron, etc.
  —rope burns (arms, legs, torso)
- Unexplained fractures, especially:
  —to skull or facial structure
  —in stages of simultaneous healing
  —multiple or spiral fractures
- Inappropriate dress, especially long sleeved clothing in hot weather (guardian may be concealing marks)

Behavioral Signs

- reports of injury by parents
- extreme wariness of parents
- extreme wariness of adults in general
- wariness of physical contact, especially when initiated by an adult
- resistance to being touched
- extreme watchfulness, sometimes described as "frozen watchfulness"
- apprehensiveness when other children cry
- fear of going home
- unexplained prolonged absence (guardian may keep child at home while injury heals)
- unlikely or inconsistent explanations for bruises, etc.
  —denial that bruises exist
- extremes of behavior:
  —extreme aggressiveness/withdrawal
  —extreme fearfulness/fearlessness (recklessness)
  —extreme attention seeking/attention avoidance
  —extreme tearfulness/tearlessness; no expectation of comfort

Signs of Sexual Abuse of Children

- Dramatic change in school behavior/performance
- Inability to concentrate
- Arriving early at school and leaving late, with few absences, or opposite extreme—truancy
- Non-participation in school and extra-curricular activities
- Chronic depression and/or anxiety
- Excessive fear of males, being touched, going home
- Evidence of "bribes"
- Indication of age-inappropriate sexual knowledge and behavior (may be reflected in drawings, verbal statements, play with peers or toys)

- Hints of sexual activity
- Repressive or pseudomature behavior
- Withdrawal
- Self-destructive behavior such as alcohol/drug abuse, self-mutilation, being accident-prone
- Suicide threats or attempts
- Running away from home
- Unfounded physical complaints
- Pregnancy
- Promiscuity
- Adolescent promiscuity

Communicable Diseases of Childhood

Source: Health and Welfare Canada

Disease	Cause	How spread	Incubation period[1]	Time when contagious	Prevention	Control
Chickenpox	A virus: Present in secretions from nose, throat and mouth of infected people.	Contact with infected people or articles used by them. Very contagious.	13 to 17 days. Sometimes 3 weeks.	1-2 days before to 5 or 6 days after first appearance of skin blisters.	None	Exclusion from school for 1 wk. after eruption appears. Avoid contact with susceptibles. Long-lasting immunity usual after one attack.

Disease	Cause	How spread	Incubation period[1]	Time when contagious	Prevention	Control
Diphtheria	Diphtheria bacillus: Present in secretions from nose and throat or in skin lesions of infected people and carriers.	Contact with infected people and carriers or articles used by them.	Usually 2 to 5 days.	About 2 to 4 weeks after onset of disease.	Vaccination with diphtheria toxoid administered first at 2 mo. of age, then at 4 mo. and 6 mo. Boosters required at 18 mo. and before school entrance.	Antitoxin and antibiotics used in treatment and for protection after exposure. One attack does not necessarily give lasting immunity.
Measles	A virus: Present in secretions from nose and mouth of infected people.	Contact with infected people or articles used by them.	10-12 days	4 days before until about 5 days after rash appears.	Measles vaccine administered once at 12-15 mo. of age. Usually given in combination with rubella or mumps vaccines.	Measles vaccination within 3 days of exposure will prevent disease in susceptible contacts. Immunity usual after one attack.
Mumps	A virus: Present in saliva of infected people.	Contact with infected people or articles used by them.	12 to 26 (commonly 18) days.	About 6 days before symptoms to 9 days after. Principally about time swelling of parotid glands starts.	Mumps vaccine, administered once, not earlier than 12 mo. of age. Usually given in combination with rubella or measles vaccines.	Isolation usually not practical. Immunity usual after one attack but second attack can occur.
Polio	3 strains of polio virus identified: Present in discharges from nose, throat, bowels of infected people.	Primarily, contact with infected people.	Usually 7 to 12 days.	Greatest in late incubation and first few days of illness.	Polio vaccine; administered early in the first year of life.	Ensure vaccination of all susceptible contacts. Immunity to infecting strain of virus usual after one attack.
Rubella	A virus: Present in secretions from nose and mouth of infected people.	Contact with infected people or articles used by them. Very contagious.	14 to 21 (usually 18) days.	From 7 days before to 5 days after onset of rash.	Rubella (German measles) vaccine, administered 12-15 mo. of age. Usually combined with measles and mumps vaccines.	Important to identify pregnant female contacts. Immunity usual after one attack.
Strep Infections	Streptococci of several strains cause scarlet fever and strep sore throats: Present in secretions from mouth, nose, ears of infected people.	Contact with infected people, rarely from contaminated articles.	2 to 5 days.	Greatest during acute illness (about 10 days).	No prevention. Antibiotic treatment for those who have had rheumatic fever.	Isolation for about 1 day after start of treatment with antibiotics—used for about 10 days. One attack does not necessarily give immunity.
Tetanus	Tetanus bacilli: Found in soil.	Contracted through soil—contaminated wounds.	4 days to 3 weeks. Sometimes longer. Average about 10 days.	Not directly communicable from person to person.	Immunization with tetanus toxoid, administered first at 2 mo. of age, then at 4 mo. and 6 mo. Boosters required at 18 mo. and before school entrance.	If necessary, booster dose of tetanus toxoid for protection given on day of injury. Antitoxin used in treatment and for temporary protection for person not immunized. One attack does not necessarily give immunity.
Whooping Cough	Pertussis bacillus: Present in secretions from mouth and nose of infected people.	Contact with infected people and articles used by them.	From 7 to 10 days.	From onset of first symptoms to about 3d week of the disease.	Immunization with whooping cough vaccine, administered first at 2 mo. of age, then at 4 mo. and 6 mo. Boosters required at 18 mo. and before school school entrance. Repeated as recommended by physician.	Special antibiotics may help to lighten attack for child not immunized. Isolation from susceptible infants for about 3 wks. from onset or until cough stops. Immunity usual after one attack.

(1) From date of exposure to first signs of the disease.

Education

Educational Attainment in Canada

Source: Censuses of Canada

(percentages)

| | 1971[1] | | 1976[1] | | 1981[1] | |
	males	females	males	females	males	females
Less than grade 9	33.2	31.4	25.8	24.9	20.8	20.6
High school	43.5	48.2	41.9	46.1	41.8	45.4
Some post-secondary	16.7	17.5	23.8	24.5	27.5	27.8
University degree	6.6	3.0	8.5	4.4	9.9	6.2
Bachelor	4.9	2.6	6.5	3.8	7.7	5.3
Master's or doctorate	1.7	0.4	2.0	0.6	2.2	0.8
Total Population[1] (000s)	7 474	7 579	8 342	8 548	9 152	9 458

(1) Population 15 years and over.

Enrolment and Teachers in Canadian Schools, 1987-88[1]

Source: Statistics Canada

| | Elementary and Secondary[2] | | | Community Colleges | | | Universities | | |
	enrolment[3]	teachers[3]	schools	enrolment[3]	teachers[3]	schools	enrolment[3]	teachers[3]	schools
Canada[4]	4 961 600	273 905	15 553	320 550	24 315	198	474 820	35 800	68
Newfoundland	136 140	8 000	583	3 000	220	10	11 610	1 000	1
Prince Edward Island	24 660	1 285	74	950	60	2	2 000	140	1
Nova Scotia	172 400	10 210	580	2 500	310	13	23 730	1 980	12
New Brunswick	139 400	7 560	468	2 300	260	8	15 060	1 150	4
Quebec	1 154 720	70 865	2 852	162 600	11 900	79	116 200	8 000	8
Ontario	1 876 560	99 040	5 391	92 300	6 600	31	184 300	13 750	21
Manitoba	219 500	12 375	838	3 900	360	10	19 530	1 700	6
Saskatchewan	215 470	11 460	1 034	3 700	500	4	21 470	1 710	3
Alberta	475 300	25 505	1 715	25 700	2 250	20	45 130	3 330	5
British Columbia	525 700	26 345	1 889	23 300	1 820	19	35 790	3 040	7
Yukon	4 900	300	25	50	5	1	–	–	–
Northwest Territories	13 100	700	75	250	30	1	–	–	–

(1) Estimates. (2) Includes public, private and federal schools and schools for the blind and deaf. (3) Full-time. (4) Includes Dept. of National Defence schools stationed overseas.
— = zero.

Education Spending[1] in Canada, 1960-1988

Source: Statistics Canada

(millions of dollars)

	1960	1965	1970	1975	1980	1984	1985	1986	1987[2]	1988[2]
Canada[3]	1 706	3 400	6 624	11 061	19 975	30 183	31 993	33 896	36 276	37 819
Newfoundland	23	41	104	234	411	714	653	721	760	819
Prince Edward Island	6	11	26	53	85	119	127	150	152	160
Nova Scotia	57	103	230	363	629	975	1 020	1 121	1 195	1 239
New Brunswick	43	73	172	261	464	773	803	837	929	968
Quebec	448	981	1 700	3 222	6 114	8 228	8 797	9 232	9 817	10 286
Ontario	609	1 239	2 669	3 995	6 883	10 291	11 023	11 928	12 837	13 588
Manitoba	81	147	272	467	760	1·221	1 338	1 409	1 493	1 562
Saskatchewan	95	155	262	399	722	1 204	1 293	1 364	1 457	1 452
Alberta	157	285	535	875	1 712	3 113	3 339	3 530	3 774	3 694
British Columbia	166	313	561	1 042	1 931	3 067	3 093	3 163	3 369	3 530
Yukon and NWT	11	20	33	49	90	150	164	176	184	192

(1) From all sources of funding for academic years ending in the spring. (2) Estimates. (3) Provinces may not add up to Canadian total due to overseas and undistributed funds.

Public and Private School Enrolment[1] in Canada, 1960–1987

Source: Statistics Canada

(thousands of students and percentages)

	1960	1965	1970	1975	1980	1985	1986	1987
Canada								
No. of students	4 011	4 997	5 775	5 633	5 185	4 946	4 928	4 938
% public	94.8	94.9	96.6	96.2	95.4	94.3	94.3	94.4
% private	4.1	4.1	2.7	3.1	3.8	4.8	4.8	4.6
Newfoundland								
No. of students	125	145	161	159	151	146	143	140
% public	100.0	99.6	99.6	99.7	99.7	99.7	99.7	99.7
% private	–	0.4	0.3	0.2	0.2	0.2	0.2	0.2
Prince Edward Island								
No. of students	25	28	30	28	27	25	25	25
% public	97.0	98.1	99.5	99.7	99.8	99.6	99.6	99.5
% private	2.8	1.8	0.2	–	–	0.2	0.2	0.3
Nova Scotia								
No. of students	184	205	216	207	192	179	176	174
% public	96.2	96.4	98.6	98.8	98.6	98.1	98.0	98.0
% private	3.4	3.0	1.0	0.7	0.7	1.0	1.1	1.1
New Brunswick								
No. of students	151	167	175	167	158	145	143	141
% public	97.9	98.5	99.4	99.5	98.9	98.7	98.7	98.7
% private	1.7	1.1	0.2	0.1	0.5	0.8	0.8	0.8
Quebec								
No. of students	1 138	1 437	1 658	1 513	1 266	1 154	1 141	1 139
% public	91.6	92.6	95.3	93.9	92.8	91.5	91.3	91.1
% private	8.2	7.1	4.3	5.7	6.9	8.1	8.4	8.5
Ontario								
No. of students	1 352	1 726	2 038	2 054	1 942	1 855	1 854[2]	1 867[2]
% public	97.6	96.9	97.5	97.1	96.1	94.9	95.4	96.0
% private	1.9	2.6	2.1	2.5	3.5	4.7	4.1	3.6
Manitoba								
No. of students	194	236	260	244	225	219	219	219
% public	91.8	92.6	94.5	94.1	92.6	90.9	90.9	90.8
% private	5.4	4.8	3.1	2.8	3.6	4.2	4.3	4.4
Saskatchewan								
No. of students	211	243	255	231	217	213	214	215
% public	95.7	95.9	97.9	96.8	95.8	94.7	94.7	94.5
% private	2.2	1.8	0.7	0.8	1.0	1.3	1.4	1.4
Alberta								
No. of students	289	361	423	441	445	464	467	472
% public	96.2	97.2	97.9	97.9	97.7	96.2	96.0	95.7
% private	2.2	1.7	1.3	1.3	1.3	2.7	2.8	3.0
British Columbia								
No. of students	328	432	539	566	539	525	524	525
% public	93.3	92.6	95.2	95.7	94.9	93.6	92.9	92.7
% private	4.9	5.9	4.1	3.7	4.6	5.8	6.4	6.5

(1) For academic years ending in the spring; public schools include Protestant and Roman Catholic separate schools unless otherwise indicated.
(2) Prior to 1986, students enrolled in Ontario Roman Catholic separate schools were categorized as public up to grade 10 and private for grades 11, 12 and 13. In 1986, public funding was extended to grade 11, and, in 1987, to grade 12.
– = zero.

French Immersion Enrolment in Canada

Source: Statistics Canada

	1980-81		1984-85		1985-86		1986-87	
	No. of Fr. imm. students	% of total enrol- ment[2]	No. of Fr. imm. students	% of total enrol- ment[2]	No. of Fr. imm. students	% of total enrol- ment[2]	No. of Fr. imm. students	% of total enrol- ment[2]
Canada[1]	64 761	1.7	139 835	3.7	162 339	4.3	184 345	4.9
Newfoundland	392	0.3	1 437	1.0	2 015	1.4	2 621	1.9
Prince Edward Island	1 280	4.7	2 181	8.6	2 492	9.9	2 514	10.1
Nova Scotia	590	0.3	1 099	0.6	1 859	1.1	2 421	1.4
New Brunswick	5 532	3.6	12 820	8.8	14 530	10.1	15 368	10.9
Ontario	46 638	2.4	76 527	4.1	87 819	4.7	98 809	5.3
Manitoba	4 286	1.9	11 043	5.0	12 581	5.7	14 619	6.7
Saskatchewan	1 603	0.7	4 735	2.4	5 965	2.8	7 503	3.5
Alberta	n.a.	n.a.	16 983	3.7	19 017	4.1	21 194	4.5
British Columbia	4 368	0.8	12 632	2.4	15 590	3.0	18 744	3.6
Yukon	35	0.7	186	4.0	247	5.4	291	6.1
Northwest Territories	37	0.3	192	1.5	224	1.7	261	2.0

(1) Excludes Quebec. (2) Includes elementary and secondary.
n.a. not available.

Largest School Boards in Canada

Source: Canadian Education Association[1]

	1969-70	1974-75	1979-80	1984-85	1986-87	1987-88
Toronto Metropolitan Separate School Board	77 752	92 599	92 297	94 288	102 893	104 611
Commission des Écoles Catholiques de Montréal	227 147	173 945	128 489	103 314	98 110	94 800
Calgary Board of Education	79 655	85 047	83 456	82 499	84 820	85 120
Peel Board of Education	61 859	78 137	82 854	83 064	83 334	83 443
Scarborough Board of Education	83 566	86 928	83 007	77 968	72 993	75 544
Toronto Board of Education	109 881	97 819	83 743	75 374	72 978	71 986
Edmonton Public School Board	76 944	72 937	65 150	68 905	70 403	70 403
North York Board of Education	104 351	99 894	80 130	64 998	61 229	58 605
York Region Board of Education	24 516	44 758	43 184	45 381	50 843	54 409
The Dufferin-Peel Roman Catholic School Board	n.a.	n.a.	29 983	40 668	48 277	52 714
Waterloo County Board of Education	48 267	50 017	49 650	50 328	50 514	51 119
Vancouver School Board	75 126	66 526	56 865	51 354	48 884	50 960
Durham Board of Education	47 580	47 785	48 857	48 098	49 408	50 692
Halton Board of Education	n.a.	52 372	49 448	43 564	41 854	43 256
Carleton Board of Education	n.a.	37 800	39 673	39 986	41 315	42 887
London Board of Education	47 506	46 780	43 256	41 420	40 782	42 630
Simcoe County Board of Education	n.a.	43 637	42 596	39 993	39 144	40 440
Hamilton Board of Education	55 175	49 333	42 791	40 778	39 224	39 247
Surrey School District No. 36	28 107	29 412	29 465	33 906	34 789	36 313
Winnipeg School Division No. 1	48 387	39 789	34 192	35 515	35 283	33 906

(1) From an annual survey conducted each September.
n.a. not available.

University Degrees[1] Awarded in Canada: Male and Female, 1970-1985

Source: Statistics Canada

(percentage distribution)

	1970 males	1970 females	1975 males	1975 females	1980 males	1980 females	1985 males	1985 females
Total Degrees	61.7	38.3	55.7	44.3	50.4	49.6	48.1	51.9
Education	46.6	53.4	39.6	60.4	31.9	68.8	28.7	71.3
Fine Arts	40.6	59.4	44.1	55.9	35.3	64.7	35.7	64.3
Humanities	n.a.	n.a.	n.a.	n.a.	39.9	60.1	38.9	61.1
English	n.a.	n.a.	n.a.	n.a.	29.0	71.0	26.8	73.2
History	n.a.	n.a.	n.a.	n.a.	54.3	45.7	55.7	44.3
Journalism	43.2	56.8	55.6	44.4	33.5	66.5	33.7	66.3
Theology	74.3	25.7	76.3	23.7	64.7	35.3	62.8	37.2
Social Sciences	n.a.	n.a.	n.a.	n.a.	57.2	42.8	50.1	49.9
Commerce	93.5	6.5	83.3	16.7	72.1	27.9	59.1	40.9
Economics	n.a.	n.a.	n.a.	n.a.	75.4	24.6	65.7	34.3
Geography	n.a.	n.a.	n.a.	n.a.	63.2	36.8	60.3	39.7
Law	92.9	7.1	79.2	20.8	65.0	35.0	55.4	44.6
Political Science	n.a.	n.a.	n.a.	n.a.	65.0	35.0	61.5	38.5
Psychology	n.a.	n.a.	n.a.	n.a.	31.0	69.0	26.6	73.4
Social Work	55.9	44.1	32.4	67.6	25.5	74.5	20.5	79.5
Sociology	n.a.	n.a.	n.a.	n.a.	32.7	67.3	27.7	72.3
Biological Sciences	n.a.	n.a.	n.a.	n.a.	49.5	50.5	44.0	56.0
Agriculture	93.6	6.4	81.4	18.6	65.7	34.3	58.0	42.0
Biology	n.a.	n.a.	n.a.	n.a.	55.0	45.0	49.6	50.4
Veterinary Medicine	94.0	6.0	79.0	21.0	60.5	39.5	48.2	51.8
Applied Sciences	n.a.	n.a.	n.a.	n.a.	92.4	7.6	88.4	11.6
Architecture	92.6	7.4	89.1	10.9	59.6	20.4	73.0	27.0
Engineering	98.9	1.1	98.2	1.8	94.3	5.7	90.4	9.6
Chemical	n.a.	n.a.	n.a.	n.a.	86.9	13.1	78.8	21.2
Civil	n.a.	n.a.	n.a.	n.a.	93.4	6.6	88.6	11.4
Electrical	n.a.	n.a.	n.a.	n.a.	96.5	3.5	94.3	5.7
Mechanical	n.a.	n.a.	n.a.	n.a.	97.5	2.5	94.5	5.5
Forestry	97.8	2.2	99.5	0.5	87.4	12.6	79.5	20.5
Health Sciences	n.a.	n.a.	n.a.	n.a.	40.7	59.3	34.4	65.6
Dentistry	94.9	5.1	90.4	9.6	83.3	16.7	77.2	22.8
Medicine	89.7	10.3	75.3	24.7	66.4	33.6	59.0	41.0
Nursing	2.7	97.3	2.7	97.3	4.9	95.1	3.3	96.7
Rehabilitation	2.2	97.8	7.4	92.6	8.8	91.2	10.4	89.6
Pure Sciences	n.a.	n.a.	n.a.	n.a.	71.6	28.4	70.7	29.3
Chemistry	n.a.	n.a.	n.a.	n.a.	69.4	30.6	64.2	35.8
Computer Sciences	n.a.	n.a.	n.a.	n.a.	75.2	24.8	72.9	27.1
Geology	n.a.	n.a.	n.a.	n.a.	78.5	21.5	78.8	21.2
Mathematics	n.a.	n.a.	n.a.	n.a.	63.4	36.6	62.2	37.8
Physics	n.a.	n.a.	n.a.	n.a.	89.0	11.0	84.5	15.5

(1) Bachelor's and first professional degrees.
n.a. not available.

Number of University Degrees Awarded in Canada, 1985

Source: Statistics Canada

	Males			Females		
	Bachelors	Masters	Doctoral	Bachelors	Masters	Doctoral
Total Degrees	46 864	8 813	1 472	50 610	6 381	528
Education	4 426	1 223	132	10 987	1 696	82
Fine Arts	1 084	126	7	1 952	166	5
Humanities	3 835	885	147	6 027	1 136	105
English	732	123	26	2 001	172	32
History	1 064	149	28	845	88	16
Journalism	105	23	–	207	19	–
Theology	706	216	14	419	114	4
Social Studies	17 122	3 603	281	17 032	2 273	137
Commerce	7 057	1 972	25	4 890	757	6
Economics	2 606	322	47	1 361	101	8
Geography	1 016	134	20	670	64	5
Law	1 742	55	2	1 403	32	2
Political Science	1 475	224	31	924	113	8
Psychology	1 330	179	98	3 669	354	71
Social Work	323	140	1	1 250	387	5
Sociology	636	70	29	1 658	101	17
Biological Sciences	2 224	432	186	2 836	270	61
Agriculture	450	130	56	326	69	12
Biology	1 204	163	70	1 225	91	24
Veterinary Medicine	123	30	11	132	14	4
Applied Sciences	7 388	1 442	259	969	169	18
Architecture	373	48	1	138	14	1
Engineering	6 682	1 330	246	706	136	14
Chemical	629	143	23	169	38	4
Civil	1 021	309	47	132	37	2
Electrical	1 805	325	73	110	12	4
Mechanical	1 771	244	44	103	14	2
Forestry	276	56	12	71	12	3
Health Sciences	2 146	283	130	4 093	442	46
Dentistry	390	15	2	115	6	–
Medicine	1 291	189	110	896	126	42
Nursing	63	4	–	1 820	113	–
Rehabilitation	90	2	–	776	85	1
Pure Sciences	5 352	805	318	2 216	224	68
Chemistry	513	101	108	286	46	30
Computer Sciences	2 278	206	28	847	48	5
Geology	764	167	45	206	48	8
Mathematics	1 283	135	31	781	62	15
Physics	486	169	92	89	12	8

– = zero.

Tuition Fees[1] for 1988-1989 at Canada's 20 Largest Universities

Source: Canadian World Almanac Questionnaire

University	Arts/Science/Business[2]	Engineering	Law	Medicine
Alberta, Univ. of	985	1 252	985	1 494
British Columbia, Univ. of	1 455	1 884	1 946	2 511
Calgary, Univ. of	972	1 216	972	1 944
Carleton Univ.	1 411	1 531	n.o.	n.o.
Concordia Univ.	450	510	n.o.	n.o.
Guelph, Univ. of	1 249	1 355	n.o.	n.o.
Laval, Univ.	546/596/596	596	546	546
Manitoba, Univ. of	1 179/1 412/1 366	1 427	1 457	2 133
McGill Univ.	570	570	570	719
McMaster Univ.	1 410	1 531	n.o.	2 691[3]
Memorial Univ.	1 164	1 164	n.o.	1 164
Montréal, Univ. de	540	647	540	740
Ottawa, Univ. of/du	1 411	1 532	1 411	1 796
Québec, Univ. du	500	500	500	n.o.
Queen's Univ.	1 411	1 531	1 411	1 794
Saskatchewan, Univ. of	1 280	1 390	1 390	1 890
Toronto, Univ. of	1 410	1 531	1 410	1 794
Waterloo, Univ. of	1 411	1 511	n.o.	n.o.
Western Ontario, Univ. of	1 584.65	1 704.65	1 584.65	1 967.65
York Univ.	1 665	n.o.	1 665	n.o.

(1) Fees are for Canadian students, based on a full course load; does not include incidental fees, which may vary depending on the faculty or college concerned. Fees for universities on a trimester system have been doubled. (2) Undergraduate tuition fees for the faculties of Arts, Science and Business are the same unless more than one amount is shown. (3) First and second year fees; third year fees are $1 794.00.
n.o. not offered.

Canadian Universities and Colleges

Source: Canadian World Almanac Questionnaire

(degree-granting institutions with enrolment of 450 or more full-time students)

Institution and address[1]	Established	Students[2]	Teachers[3]
Acadia Univ., Wolfville, N.S. B0P 1X0	1838	3 349	230
Alberta, Univ. of, Edmonton, Alta. T6G 2E2	1906	25 210	1 760
Bishop's Univ., Lennoxville, Que. J1M 1Z7	1843	1 496	95
Brandon Univ., Brandon, Man. R7A 6A9	1899	1 500	170
British Columbia, Univ. of, Vancouver, B.C. V6T 1W5	1908	25 376	1 792
Brock Univ., St. Catharines, Ont. L2S 3A1	1964	4 917	310
Calgary, Univ. of, Calgary, Alta. T2N 1N4	1945	16 842	1 272
Camrose Lutheran Coll., 4901-46 Ave., Camrose, Alta. T4V 2R3	1910	741	50
Cape Breton, Univ. Coll. of, Box 5300, Sydney, N.S. B1P 6L2	1974	1 796	152
Carleton Univ., Ottawa, Ont. K1S 5B6	1942	12 475	670
Concordia Univ., Montreal, Que. H3G 1M8	1974	13 279	770
Dalhousie Univ., Halifax, N.S. B3H 3J5	1818	8 236	922
King's Coll., Univ. of, Halifax, N.S. B3H 2A1	1789	609	19
Guelph, Univ. of, Guelph, Ont. N1G 2W1	1964	11 281	706
Lakehead Univ., Thunder Bay, Ont. P7B 5E1	1965	3 357	260
Laurentian Univ./Univ. Laurentian, Sudbury, Ont. P3E 2C6	1960	4 794	299
Laval, Université, Quebec, Que. G1K 7P4	1852	21 839[4]	1 492[4]
Lethbridge, Univ. of, Lethbridge, Alta. T1K 3M4	1967	2 717	200[4]
Manitoba, Univ. of, Winnipeg, Man. R3T 2N2	1877	16 193[4]	1 325[4]
McGill Univ., Montreal, Que. H3A 2T5	1821	18 099	1 439
McMaster Univ., Hamilton, Ont., L8S 4L8	1887	11 534	1 007
Memorial Univ. of Newfoundland, St. John's, Nfld. A1C 5S7	1925	11 990	997
Moncton, Univ. de, Moncton, N.B. E1A 3E9	1963	4 235	411
Montréal, Univ. de, C.P. 6128, Succ. A., Montreal, Que. H3C 3J7	1920	18 144	1 427
École des Hautes Études Commerciales, Montreal, Que. H3T 1V6	1907	2 227	152
École Polytechnique de Montréal, C.P. 6079, Montreal, Que. H3C 3A7	1865	3 832	219
Mount Allison Univ., Sackville, N.B. E0A 3C0	1840	1 798	148
Mount Saint Vincent Univ., Halifax, N.S. B3M 2J6	1925	2 143	149
New Brunswick, Univ. of, Box 4400, Fredericton, N.B. E3B 5A3	1785	7 779	671
Nova Scotia Agricultural Coll., Truro, N.S. B2N 5E3	1905	514	66
Nova Scotia Coll. of Art & Design, Halifax, N.S. B3J 3J6	1887	476	43
Ottawa, Univ. of/Univ. d'Ottawa, Ottawa, Ont. K1N 6N5	1848	13 351	1 055
Prince Edward Island, Univ. of, Charlottetown, P.E.I. C1A 4P3	1969	2 029	145
Québec, Univ. du, Sainte-Foy, Que. G1V 2M3	1968	27 223	1 824
Queen's Univ., Kingston, Ont. K7L 3N6	1841	11 706	859
Regina, Univ. of, Regina, Sask. S4S 0A2	1974	4 321[4]	385[4]
Campion Coll., 3769 Winnipeg St., Regina, Sask. S4S 0A2	1917	563[4]	18[4]
Luther Coll., Regina, Sask. S4S 0A2	1913	480[4]	11[4]
Royal Military Coll. of Canada, Kingston, Ont. K7K 5L0	1876	769	170
Ryerson Polytech. Inst., 350 Victoria St., Toronto, Ont. M5B 2K3	1948	11 400	650
Saint Mary's Univ., Halifax, N.S. B3H 3C3	1802	3 660	225
Saskatchewan, Univ. of, Saskatoon, Sask. S7N 0W0	1907	12 607[4]	1 100[4]
St. Thomas More Coll., Saskatoon, Sask. S7N 0W0	1936	1 024[4]	35[4]
Sherbrooke, Univ. de, Sherbrooke, Que. J1K 2R1	1954	8 893	562
Simon Fraser Univ., Burnaby, B.C. V5A 1S6	1965	7 575	486
St. Francis Xavier Univ., Antigonish, N.S. B2G 1C0	1853	2 600	175
St. Thomas Univ., Box 4569, Fredericton, N.B. E3B 5G3	1910	1 350	80
Technical Univ. of Nova Scotia, Box 1000, Halifax, N.S. B3J 2X4	1907	1 269	100[4]
Toronto, Univ. of, Toronto, Ont. M5S 1A1	1827	35 619	2 897
Trent Univ., Box 4800, Peterborough, Ont. K9J 7B8	1963	3 275	225
Trinity Western Univ., 7600 Glover Rd., Langley, B.C. V3A 4R9	1962	1 201	54
Victoria, Univ. of, Box 1700, Victoria, B.C. V8W 2Y2	1963	7 580	554
Waterloo, Univ. of, Waterloo, Ont. N2L 3G1	1957	15 501	828
Western Ontario, Univ. of, London, Ont. N6A 5B8	1878	18 007	1 434
Brescia Coll., 1285 Western Rd., London, Ont. N6G 1H2	1919	589	23
Huron Coll., London, Ont. N6G 1H3	1863	722	34
King's Coll., 266 Epworth Ave., London, Ont. N6A 2M3	1912	1 364	54
Wilfrid Laurier Univ., Waterloo, Ont. N2L 3C5	1911	4 975	289
Windsor, Univ. of, Windsor, Ont. N9B 3P4	1857	8 483	510
Winnipeg, Univ. of, Winnipeg, Man. R3B 2E9	1871	2 960	250
York Univ., 4700 Keele St., North York, Ont. M3J 1P3	1959	20 281	1 168

(1) Indented colleges are degree-granting affiliates of the university preceding them. (2) Enrolments for 1987-1988, full-time undergraduate and graduate students, all faculties and campuses, excluding indented colleges. (3) Total full-time teaching staff, 1987-1988. (4) 1986-1987 data.

Canadian Colleges

(with 200 or more full-time students[1])

Atlantic Provinces

Bay St. George Community College, Box 540, Stephenville, Nfld. A2N 2Z6

Canadian Coast Guard College, Box 4500, Sydney, N.S. B1P 6L7

University College of Cape Breton, (Technology Programs), Sydney, N.S. B1P 6L2

College of Trades & Technology, Box 1693, St. John's, Nfld. A1C 5P7

Holland College, Weymouth St., Charlottetown, P.E.I. C1A 4Z1

New Brunswick Community College, Bathurst, Box 1, Bathurst, N.B. E2A 3Z2

New Brunswick Community College, Moncton, Box 2100, Stn. A, Moncton, N.B. E1C 8H9

New Brunswick Community College, Saint John, Box 2270, Saint John, N.B. E2L 3V1

Newfoundland & Labrador Institute of Fisheries and Marine Technology, Box 4920, St. John's, Nfld. A1C 5R3

Nova Scotia Institute of Technology, Box 2210, Halifax, N.S. B3J 3C4

Nova Scotia Nautical Institute, (Pier 21), Box 578, Halifax, N.S. B3J 2S9

Nova Scotia Teachers College, Box 810, Truro, N.S. B2N 5G5

Saint John School of Nursing, Box 187, Saint John, N.B. E2L 3X8

Victoria General Hospital, School of Nursing, Nurse's Residence, 1240 Tower Rd., Halifax, N.S. B3H 2Y9

Quebec

Cegep de l'Abitibi-Témiscamingue, (425 boul. du College), C.P. 1500, Rouyn, Que. J9X 5E5

Cegep Ahuntsic, 9155 rue St-Hubert, Montréal, Que. H2M 1Y8

Cegep d'Alma, 675 boul. Auger ouest, Alma, Que. G8B 2B7

Cegep André-Laurendeau, 1111 rue Lapierre, Lasalle, Que. H8N 2J4

College de Bois-de-Boulogne, 10555 ave. de Bois-de-Boulogne, Montréal, Que. H4N 1L4

College Régional Champlain, 554 Ontario, C.P. 5000, Sherbrooke, Que. J1J 3R6

Cegep de Chicoutimi, 534 rue Jacques-Cartier est, Chicoutimi, Que. G7H 1Z6

Cegep Dawson, 485 rue McGill, Montréal, Que. H2Y 2H4

Cegep de Drummondville, 960 rue St-Georges, Drummondville, Que. J2C 6A2

Cegep Edouard Montpetit, 945 chemin de Chambly, Longueuil, Que. J4H 3M6

Cegep François-Xavier-Garneau, (1660 boul. de l'Entente), C.P. 6300, Québec, Que. G1T 2S5

Cegep de la Gaspésie, et des Îles, (96 rue Jacques Cartier), C.P. 590, Gaspé Sud, Que. G0C 1R0

Cegep de Granby, 235 St-Jacques, Granby, Que. J2G 3N1

Cegep de Hauterive, 537 boul. Blanche, Baie-Comeau, Que. G5C 2B2

Cegep John Abbott, C.P. 2000, Ste-Anne de Bellevue, Que. H9X 3L9

Cegep de Joliette, (20 rue St-Charles sud), C.P. 130, Joliette, Que. J6E 4T1

Cegep de Jonquière, 2505 rue St-Hubert, C.P. 340, Jonquière, Que. G7X 7W2

Cegep de La Pocatière, 140 4e ave., La Pocatière, Que.G0R 1Z0

Cegep de Lévis-Lauzon, 205 rue Mgr-Bourget, Lauzon, Que. G6V 6Z9

Cegep de Limoilou, 1300 8e ave., C.P. 1400, Québec, Que. G1K 7H3

Cegep Lionel-Groulx, 100 rue Duquet, Ste-Thérèse, Que. J7E 3G6

Cegep de Maisonneuve, 3800 rue Sherbrooke est, Montréal, Que. H1X 2A2

Cegep de Matane, 616 ave. St-Rédempteur, Matane, Que. G4W 3P7

Cegep Montmorency, 475 boul. de L'Avenir, Laval, Que. H7N 5H9

Cegep de l'Outaouais, (333 boul. Cité des Jeunes), C.P. 5220, Succ. A, Hull, Que. J8Y 6M5

Cegep de la Région de l'Amiante, 671 boul. Smith sud, Thetford Mines, Que. G6G 1N1

Cegep de Rimouski, 60 rue de l'Evêché ouest, Rimouski, Que. G5L 4H6

Cegep de Rivière-du-Loup, 80 rue Frontenac, Rivière-du-Loup, Que. G5R 1S8

Cegep de Rosemont, 6400 16e ave., Montréal, Que. H1X 2S9

Cegep de St-Félicien, (1105 boul. Hamel), C.P. 5000, St-Félicien, Que. G0W 2N0

Cegep de Ste-Foy, 2410 chemin Ste-Foy, Ste-Foy, Que. G1V 1T3

Cegep de St-Hyacinthe, 3000 rue Boullé, St-Hyacinthe (Douville), Que. J2S 1H9

Cegep St-Jean sur Richelieu, (30 boul. du Séminaire), C.P. 1018, St-Jean sur Richelieu, Que. J3B 7B1

Cegep de St-Jérôme, 455 rue Fournier, St-Jérôme, Que. J7Z 4V2

Cegep de St-Laurent, 625 boul. Ste-Croix, Ville St-Laurent, Que. H4L 3X7

Cegep de Sept-Îles, 175 rue de la Vérendrye, Sept-Îles, Que. G4R 5B7

Cegep de Shawinigan, 2263 boul. du Collège, Shawinigan, Que. G9N 6V8

Cegep de Sherbrooke, 475 rue Parc, Sherbrooke, Que. J1H 5M7

Cegep de Sorel-Tracy, 3000 boul. de la Mairie, Tracy, Que. J3R 5B9

Cegep de Trois-Rivières, 3500 rue de Courval, Trois-Rivières, Que. G9A 5E6

Cegep de Valleyfield, 169 rue Champlain, Valleyfield, Que. J6T 1X6

Cegep Vanier, 821 boul. Ste-Croix, Ville St-Laurent, Que. H4L 3X9

Cegep de Victoriaville, 475 rue Notre-Dame est, Victoriaville, Que. G6P 4B3

Cegep du Vieux-Montréal, 255 rue Ontario est, C.P. 1444, Succ N, Montréal, Que. H2X 3M8

Ontario

Algonquin College of Applied Arts & Technology, 1385 Woodroffe Ave., Nepean, Ont. K2G 1V8

Cambrian College of Applied Arts & Technology, 1400 Barrydowne Rd., Sudbury, Ont. P3A 3V8

Canadian Memorial Chiropractic College, 1900 Bayview Ave., Toronto, Ont. M4G 3E6

Canadore College of Applied Arts & Technology, Box 5001, North Bay, Ont. P1B 8K9

Centennial College of Applied Arts & Technology, Box 631, Stn. A, Scarborough, Ont. M1K 5E9

Centralia College of Agricultural Technology, Huron Park, Ont. N0M 1Y0

Conestoga College of Applied Arts & Technology, 299 Doon Valley Dr., Kitchener, Ont. N2G 4M4

Confederation College of Applied Arts & Technology, Box 398, Stn. F, Thunder Bay, Ont. P7C 4W1

Durham College of Applied Arts & Technology, (Simcoe St. N.), Box 385, Oshawa, Ont. L1H 7L7

Fanshawe College of Applied Arts & Technology, Box 4005, London, Ont. N5W 5H1

George Brown College of Applied Arts & Technology, Box 1015, Stn. B, Toronto, Ont. M5T 2T9

Georgian College of Applied Arts & Technology, One Georgian Dr., Barrie, Ont. L4M 3X9

Humber College of Applied Arts & Technology, Box 1900, Rexdale, Ont. M9W 5L7

Kemptville College of Agricultural Technology, Kemptville, Ont. K0G 1J0

Lambton College of Applied Arts & Technology, 1457 London Rd., Box 969, Sarnia, Ont. N7T 7K4

Loyalist College of Applied Arts & Technology, Wallbridge-Loyalist Rd., Box 4200, Belleville, Ont. K8N 5B9

Mohawk College of Applied Arts & Technology, Fennell Ave. and West 5th, Box 2034, Hamilton, Ont. L8N 3T2

Niagara College of Applied Arts & Technology, (Woodlawn Rd.), Box 1005, Welland, Ont. L3B 5S2

Northern College of Applied Arts & Technology, Box 2002, South Porcupine, Ont. P0N 1H0

Ontario College of Art, 100 McCaul St., Toronto, Ont. M5T 1W1

Ridgetown College of Agricultural Technology, Ridgetown, Ont. N0P 2C0

St. Clair College of Applied Arts & Technology, 2000 Talbot Rd. W., Windsor, Ont. N9A 6S4

St. Lawrence College: Brockville Campus, 2288 Parkedale Ave., Brockville, Ont. K6V 5X3; Cornwall Campus, Windmill Point, Cornwall, Ont. K6H 4Z1; Kingston Campus, King & Portsmouth, Kingston, Ont. K7L 5A6

The Sault College of Applied Arts & Technology, Box 60, Sault Ste. Marie, Ont. P6A 5L3

Seneca College of Applied Arts & Technology, 1750 Finch Ave. E., North York, Ont. M2J 2X5

Sheridan College of Applied Arts & Technology, 1430 Trafalgar Rd., Oakville, Ont. L6H 2L1

Sir Sandford Fleming College of Applied Arts & Technology, 526 McDonnel St., Box 653, Peterborough, Ont. K9J 7B1

Toronto Institute of Medical Technology, 222 St. Patrick St., Toronto, Ont. M5T 1V4

Prairies

Alberta College of Art, 1407-14th Ave. N.W., Calgary, Alta. T2N 4R3

Assiniboine Community College, 1430 Victoria Ave. E., Brandon, Man. R7A 5Z9

Concordia College, 7128 Ada Blvd., Edmonton, Alta. T5B 4E4

Foothills Provincial General Hospital, School of Nursing, 1403-29 St. N.W., Calgary, Alta. T2N 2T9

Grande Prairie Regional College, 10726-106 Ave., Grande Prairie, Alta. T8V 4C4

Grant MacEwan Community College, Box 1796, Edmonton, Alta. T5J 2P2

Health Sciences Centre, School of Nursing, 700 McDermot Ave., Winnipeg, Man. R3E 0T2

Kesley Institute of Applied Arts & Sciences, Box 1520, Idylwyld Dr. & 33rd St., Saskatoon, Sask. S7K 3R5

Keyano College, 8115 Franklin Ave., Fort McMurray, Alta. T9H 2H7

Lakeland College, Vermillion Campus, Vermillion, Alta. T0B 4M0.

Lethbridge Community College, 3000 College Dr. S., Lethbridge, Alta. T1K 1L6

Medicine Hat College, 299 College Dr. S.E., Medicine Hat, Alta. T1A 3Y6

Misericordia Hospital, School of Nursing, 16940-87 Ave., Edmonton, Alta. T5R 4H5

Mount Royal College, 4825 Richard Rd. S.W., Calgary, Alta. T3E 6K6

The Northern Alberta Institute of Technology, 11762-106 St., Edmonton, Alta. T5G 2R1

Olds College, Olds, Alta. T0M 1P0

Red Deer College, 56 Ave. & 32 St., Box 5005, Red Deer, Alta. T4N 5H5

Red River Community College, 2055 Notre Dame Ave., Winnipeg, Man. R3H 0J9

Royal Alexandria Hospital, School of Nursing, 10240 Kingsway Ave., Edmonton, Alta. T5H 3V9

Saskatchewan Technical Institute, Saskatchewan St. & 6th Ave. N.W., Moose Jaw, Sask. S6H 4R4

The Southern Alberta Institute of Technology, 1301-16th Ave. N.W., Calgary, Alta. T2M 0L4

University of Alberta Hospital, School of Nursing, 84 Ave. & 112 St., Edmonton, Alta. T6G 1K6

Wascana Institute of Applied Arts & Sciences, Box 556, Regina, Sask. S4P 3A3

British Columbia and Territories

Arctic College, Thebacha Campus, Box 600, Fort Smith, N.W.T. X0E 0P0

B.C. Institute of Technology, 3700 Willingdon Ave., Burnaby, B.C. V5G 3H2

Camosun College, 3100 Foul Bay Rd., Victoria, B.C. V8P 4X8

Capilano College, 2055 Purcell Way, North Vancouver, B.C. V7J 3H5

Cariboo College, Box 3010, Kamloops, B.C. V2C 5N3

College of New Caledonia, 3330-22 Ave., Prince George, B.C. V2N 1P8

Douglas College, Box 2503, New Westminster, B.C. V3L 5B2

Emily Carr College of Art & Design, 1399 Johnston St., Granville Island, Vancouver, B.C. V6H 3R9

Fraser Valley College: East Campus, 45600 Airport Rd., Chilliwack, B.C. V2P 6T4; West Campus, 33844 King Rd., Abbotsford, B.C. V2S 4N2

Kwantlen College, Box 9030, Surrey, B.C. V3T 5H8

Malaspina College, 900-5th St., Nanaimo, B.C. V9R 5S5

Okanagan College, 1000 KLO Rd., Kelowna, B.C. V1Y 4X8

Selkirk College, Castlegar Campus, Box 1200, Castlegar, B.C. V1N 3J1

Vancouver Community College, (1155 E. Broadway), Box 24700, Stn. C, Vancouver, B.C. V5T 4N4

Vancouver General Hospital School of Nursing, 835 W. 10th Ave., Vancouver, B.C. V5Z 4E8

Yukon College, 1000 Lewes Blvd., Whitehorse, Y.T. Y1A 3H9

(1) Based on Statistics Canada 1985 figures.

Social Security

Federal Government Benefits—How to Apply

Death and Survivors' Benefits
- applications available at the Income Security Programs office
- file separately for both death and survivors' claims
- deceased's S.I.N., birth or baptism certificate and death certificate required
- the individual responsible for the deceased's estate should apply as soon as possible

Disability Benefits
- forms available at the Income Security Programs office
- proof of age, S.I.N. and information on your medical condition required
- apply immediately after the disability occurs, or, if unable, someone may apply on your behalf
- amount of payment determined according to earnings and C.P.P. contributions.

Family Allowance
- applications available at hospitals, post offices or Income Security Programs office; any Canadian citizen or permanent legal resident may receive payment for each child under 18
- birth certificate or other acceptable proof required for children born outside Canada

Guaranteed Income Supplement
- application forwarded once Old Age Security application has been approved
- all incomes, single or combined, must be declared
- a form requiring annual statement of income must be completed and returned each year or further payments will be discontinued

Old Age Security
- applications may be obtained from the Income Security Programs office
- apply in person at least 6 months prior to your 65th birthday; if you are ill, someone may apply on your behalf
- applicant must be 65 years of age, possess legal Canadian residence status, and meet residence requirements
- proof of age, such as a birth or baptism certificate, is necessary

Unemployment Insurance
- application available at Canada Employment Centres
- S.I.N. and Record of Employment (which should be given to you by your employer, proving time worked and amount earned, upon release from employment) are required
- if you do not have a Record of Employment you must indicate why on the application form
- once approved, other forms will be sent periodically for completion and return

Canada Assistance Plan
(welfare assistance)
- applications are available at community services departments in municipalities throughout Canada
- claimants and dependents must supply birth certificates and other documents as required to establish identity
- welfare assistance payments will vary depending on individual circumstances and claimant's place of residence
- any changes in income must be reported immediately

Family Allowances

Under the family allowances program, established by the federal government in 1945, monthly payments are made to the parents or guardians of dependent children who are under 18 years of age and living in Canada. To qualify, a parent or guardian who lives in Canada must be a Canadian citizen or a permanent legal resident of Canada or a visitor who has been legally admitted to Canada for at least one year. Parents or guardians living outside the country may receive allowances for children in their care if they are paying Canadian income tax.

Family allowance payments are adjusted each January to reflect increases in the cost of living; the 1988 allowance was $32.81 per child per month. Provinces may vary this rate according to the age or number of children in a family; only Quebec and Alberta have done so.

Family allowance payments usually begin the month after the child is born or the month after the child arrives in Canada. Payments stop when a child reaches 18, if the parents leave Canada and stop paying Canadian income tax, if parents cease caring for the child, or if the child earns enough money to pay income tax.

Application forms are available at hospitals, post offices or at Health and Welfare Canada income security program offices.

Government Spending on Family Allowances

Sources: Statistics Canada and Health and Welfare Canada

	Number of Recipients[1] families	children[3]	Total payments[2] ($000)	Avg. monthly payments[1] per child
1951	1 910 192	4 367 391	$ 309 465	$ 6.00
1961	2 602 930	6 397 134	506 192	6.68
1966	2 785 636	6 865 057	551 735	6.73
1971	3 024 423	6 824 479	557 878	6.81
1976	3 509 746	7 311 884	1 957 513	22.08
1981	3 645 009	6 826 071	1 850 907	23.96

	Number of Recipients[1] families	children[3]	Total payments[2] ($000)	Avg. monthly payments[1] per child
1982	3 641 791	6 732 593	2 019 520	26.91
1983	3 641 998	6 671 966	2 230 595	28.52
1984	3 637 616	6 621 965	2 326 572	29.95
1985	3 634 510	6 586 042	2 417 755	31.27
1986	3 644 829	6 584 620	2 500 561	31.58
1987	3 659 017	6 591 974	2 534 420	31.95
1988	3 666 262	6 596 745	2 564 458	32.81

(1) As of March. (2) For fiscal years ending Mar. 31. (3) Prior to 1974, eligibility age was 15 years and under; since 1974 it has been 17 years and under.
n.a. not available.

Veterans Allowances and Disability Pensions

The *War Veterans Allowances Act*, approved in 1930, gives benefits to Canadian veterans who suffered disabilities or are unable to work as a result of injuries sustained in World War I, World War II or the Korean War. To qualify, the veteran must have lived in Canada for at least 10 years, be 60 years or older (younger if medical reasons warrant), and have little or no income. In Apr. 1988, the maximum monthly allowance was $748.51 for a single veteran and $1 136.48 for a married veteran.

Allowances are also paid to civilians who served alongside the armed forces during a war; these include firefighters and the merchant marine. Counselling services, treatment services and emergency funds are also available to veterans and their spouses and children.

The *Pension Act, 1919*, gives compensation to armed forces personnel for disability or death related to military service. Since 1962, benefits have also been paid to civilians working with the armed forces during wartime. In some cases, benefits are paid to veterans of Commonwealth forces. The amount of the monthly pension varies according to the disability.

Veterans Benefits, Selected Years, 1946–1988

Source: Veterans Affairs Canada

Year[1]	Total pensioners	Disability Pensions[2] (by period of service) World War I	World War II	Korean War	Peacetime service	Surviving dependants	Veterans Allowances Total allowances	Veterans	Veterans' surviving dependants	Civilians[3]
1946	142 671	72 396	36 454	–	–	33 821	28 312	25 030	3 282	n.a.
1951	195 660	66 001	95 650	–	–	34 009	38 600	30 608	7 992	n.a.
1961	186 665	45 588	105 338	1 651	1 389	32 699	69 546	47 865	21 681	n.a.
1966	174 567	33 688	106 191	1 843	2 133	30 712	87 153	55 947	29 888	1 318
1971	159 126	22 298	102 666	2 010	3 344	28 808	83 955	48 384	32 749	2 822
1976	142 254	12 404	96 776	2 084	4 106	26 884	89 371	47 999	37 297	4 075
1981	130 494	6 581	90 840	2 139	5 793	25 141	94 518	51 175	38 897	4 446
1982	131 890	5 178	88 141	2 125	6 291	30 155	90 804	49 533	36 927	4 344
1983	138 705	4 400	86 596	2 125	6 891	38 693	87 051	48 650	34 095	4 306
1984	139 813	3 691	84 946	2 142	7 383	41 651	88 638	50 177	34 048	4 413
1985	138 661	3 036	82 638	2 133	7 631	43 223	88 357	49 990	33 882	4 485
1986	140 962	2 669	84 237	2 204	8 883	42 969	83 826	47 455	31 852	4 519
1987	141 024	2 123	83 153	2 125	9 842	43 691	82 400	47 101	30 891	4 408
1988	141 023	1 672	81 705	2 225	10 848	44 573	72 643	40 383	28 091	4 169

(1) As of March. (2) Includes recipients of Civilian War Disability pensions. (3) Includes surviving dependants.
— = zero; n.a. not available.

Old Age Security and Guaranteed Income Supplement

Source: Health and Welfare Canada

The Old Age Security (OAS) program, introduced in 1952, provides pensions to persons 65 years and older who meet Canadian residence requirements. Full monthly pensions ($315.97 per month as of July 1988) are given to persons who have lived in Canada for 40 years since the age of 18; some persons who have lived in Canada for 10 consecutive years are also eligible for full pensions. Partial pensions, introduced in 1977, are based on the number of years a pensioner has lived in Canada.

The Guaranteed Income Supplement (GIS) was introduced in 1966 to assist those with little or no income other than their OAS pension. The amount of income supplement depends upon the pensioner's income, marital status and spouse's income. Generally, the maximum GIS payment is reduced by $1 for every $2 of income a pensioner has above his/her old age security pension. For example, in July 1988 a single pensioner with no personal income received OAS benefits of $315.97 per month and an income supplement of $375.51 per month. If this person had a private pension of $400 per month, the GIS would be reduced $200 to $175.51 per month.

Government Spending on Old Age Security, 1952-1988

Source: Statistics Canada and Health and Welfare Canada

	Number of Recipients[1]		Net Payments[2] ($000)		Average Yearly[3] payment per pensioner	
	OAS	GIS	OAS	GIS	OAS	GIS
1952	643 013	n.a.	76 067	n.a.	n.a.	n.a.
1961	904 906	n.a.	592 413	n.a.	n.a.	n.a.
1966	1 105 776	n.a.	927 299	n.a.	n.a.	n.a.
1971	1 720 128	860 392	1 627 219	280 005	956.22	n.a.
1976	1 957 288	1 087 113	2 975 788	923 251	1 534.08	863.05
1980	2 236 049	1 190 579	4 679 002	1 494 447	2 119.95	1 274.78
1981	2 302 841	1 245 188	5 322 086	1 918 067	2 331.15	1 592.29
1982	2 368 569	1 256 813	6 140 552	2 241 914	2 617.59	1 815.58
1983	2 425 685	1 250 852	7 005 302	2 416 263	2 911.22	1 969.61
1984	2 490 881	1 246 119	7 648 959	2 524 450	3 105.30	2 056.06
1985	2 569 488	1 296 545	8 215 898	2 952 921	3 245.97	2 348.36
1986	2 652 234	1 329 886	8 857 668	3 319 428	3 374.46	2 555.33
1987	2 748 504	1 345 391	9 520 047	3 451 376	3 514.95	2 614.56
1988	2 835 107	1 356 672	10 250 544	3 618 244	3 668.49	2 702.00

(1) As of March. (2) For fiscal years ending Mar. 31. (3) For fiscal years ending Mar. 31 using annual average number of recipients. n.a. not available or not applicable.

Canada and Quebec Pension Plans

Source: Health and Welfare Canada

The Canada and Quebec Pension Plans were instituted in 1966 to provide benefits to Canadians who have contributed to the plan during their working lives. Both plans pay a monthly retirement benefit in addition to a one-time death benefit, survivor benefits for the spouse and dependent children of a deceased contributor, and benefits to the severely disabled and their families.

Payments to the plan are made by all workers aged 18 to 70 based on a contribution rate, which in 1988 is 4 percent of "pensionable earnings". This payment is shared equally by employers and employees; self-employed persons must pay the entire amount themselves. The contribution rate is scheduled to increase over a 25-year period, reaching 7.6 percent in 2011. Contributions are not paid if income falls below an annual minimum ($2 600 in 1988) or on income above an annual maximum ($26 500 in 1988).

Retirement benefits from the plan are based on lifetime earnings and generally amount to 25 percent of average annual income, adjusted for inflation. The maximum monthly benefit in 1988 was $543.06.

Since Jan. 1987, Canadians eligible for CPP benefits who retire before age 65 can receive partial pensions beginning as early as age 60. Those who begin collecting at 60 receive 70 percent of the amount they would be entitled to at age 65. For each month past age 60 that a person delays retirement, an additional half a percentage point is added—so that someone retiring at age 61 would receive 76 of their full (age 65) pension while someone postponing retirement to age 70 would receive 130 percent.

The Canada Pension Plan is administered by the federal government while the Quebec Pension Plan is administered by the Government of Quebec's Pension Board. The same rules and benefits apply to each.

Government Spending on Pension Plans

Source: Health and Welfare Canada, Régie des Rentes du Québec and Statistics Canada

	Canada Pension Plan				Quebec Pension Plan			
	Benefi-ciaries[1]	Benefits paid[2] ($000)	Contrib-utors[4] (000s)	Avg. monthly retirement payments[1]	Benefi-ciaries[1]	Benefits paid[2] ($000)	Contrib-utors[4] (000s)	Avg. monthly retirement payments[1]
1971	251 853	$ 89 236	6 755	$ 23	79 649	$ 47 576	2 053	$ 25
1976	774 890	587 834	7 561	67	232 815	266 181	2 601	66
1977	894 177	833 251	7 667	81	269 681	351 360	2 658	80
1978	989 707	1 059 068	7 779	94	314 743	446 659	2 718	98
1979	1 080 277	1 328 410	8 161	109	345 741	n.a.	2 743	113
1980	1 182 564	1 635 072	8 198	125	375 730	709 069	2 745	129
1981	1 274 306	2 010 924	8 626	144	406 069	704 798	2 793	148
1982	1 359 861	2 455 571	8 485	168	434 342	856 418	2 683	172
1983	1 455 953	3 035 824	8 406	193	463 470	1 052 564	2 724	197
1984	1 547 253	3 656 841	8 589	212	518 241	1 281 327	2 736	215
1985	1 633 037	4 223 311	8 721	229	577 695	1 629 052	2 850	230
1986	1 741 170	4 887 134	n.a.	247	627 317	1 899 730	n.a.	243
1987	1 941 898	5 721 315	n.a.	270	666 847	2 132 658	n.a.	258
1988	2 114 217	7 367 269	n.a.	289	702 141	2 406 453	n.a.	276

(1) As of March. (2) For fiscal years ending Mar. 31. (3) From 1971 to 1978, data is for calendar years; Jan. 1979 to Mar. 1980, data is for 15 months; from 1981 to 1988, data is for fiscal years ending Mar. 31. (4) Calendar years.
n.a. not available.

Unemployment Insurance

Source: Health and Welfare Canada

The Unemployment Insurance program, introduced by the federal government in 1940, has 2 objectives: to provide income protection for workers suffering temporary income interruptions and to facilitate the best possible match between unemployed workers and available jobs. The program covers most workers in Canada, major exclusions being those 65 years of age and over, the self-employed (except fishermen who are covered by special arrangement), and those who work less than 15 hours per week and earn less than 20 percent of the maximum insurable earnings ($113.00 per week in 1988).

To qualify for benefits, claimants must have suffered an interruption of earnings from employment and accumulated a specified number of weeks of insurable employment. This varies from 10 to 14 weeks, depending on the unemployment rate in the region where the claimant lives. To receive benefits, a person must file a claim stating that they are without work, are willing to work, and are registered at the Canada Employment Centre. Following a 2-week waiting period, claimants are eligible to receive 60% of their average weekly insured earnings up to a

maximum of $339.00 per week in 1988. The longest period for which benefits can be claimed is 50 weeks, but this period varies, depending on the length of previous employment as well as the national and regional unemployment rate.

Maternity benefits are payable to persons who prove pregnancy with a medical certificate and who have 20 weeks of insurable employment. A maximum of 15 consecutive weeks of maternity benefits are payable as part of initial benefits; they may start as early as 8 weeks before the expected week of confinement for birth and as late as 17 weeks after birth.

The Unemployment Insurance program is financed through contributions from employer and employee premiums and by the federal government. The basic employee premium rate for 1988 was $2.35 for each $100 of weekly insurable earnings. The employer premium is 1.4 times the employee rate ($3.29 per $100 in 1988). The maximum weekly insurable earnings in 1988 was $565.00. This amount is adjusted in accordance with the rate of increase in wages and salaries averaged over the most recent 8-year period.

Unemployment Insurance Payments, 1943-1987

Source: Statistics Canada

	Claims[1] (000s)	Benefit payments ($000)	Weeks paid (000s)	Maximum weekly payment[2]	Average weekly payment[2]
1943	36.7	941	85	$14.40	$ 11.12
1944	90.9	3 277	283	14.40	11.57
1945	296.4	14 576	1 224	14.40	11.91
1946	488.7	51 085	4 245	14.40	12.03
1947	442.9	32 039	2 756	14.40	11.62
1948	649.1	40 258	3 390	18.30	11.88
1949	933.9	69 351	5 148	18.30	13.47
1950	1 150.2	98 994	6 980	21.00	14.18
1951	1 144.1	75 996	5 165	21.00	14.71
1952	1 391.3	118 112	7 199	24.00	16.41
1953	1 679.7	157 779	8 718	24.00	18.10
1954	2 102.2	240 722	13 095	24.00	18.38
1955	1 929.8	228 865	12 375	30.00	18.49
1956	1 625.4	210 330	11 177	30.00	18.82
1957	2 373.2	305 076	14 572	30.00	20.94
1958	2 780.5	492 901	23 152	30.00	21.29
1959	2 428.3	406 097	19 170	36.00	21.18
1960	2 700.4	481 836	21 592	36.00	22.32
1961	2 460.5	493 971	20 735	36.00	23.82
1962	2 192.2	409 208	16 928	36.00	24.17
1963	2 038.0	394 163	16 122	36.00	24.45
1964	1 859.9	344 390	14 017	36.00	24.57
1965	1 628.2	312 110	12 718	36.00	24.54
1966	1 547.7	295 301	12 041	36.00	24.52
1967	1 817.0	352 645	13 852	36.00	25.46
1968	1 928.1	438 128	16 488	53.00	26.57
1969	1 855.1	498 992	15 735	53.00	31.71
1970	2 260.8	695 222	19 817	53.00	35.08
1971	2 371.0	890 594	22 634	100.00	39.35
1972	2 469.9	1 871 802	30 461	100.00	61.79
1973	2 237.5	2 004 212	29 537	107.00	68.45
1974	2 410.4	2 119 213	28 461	113.00	74.89
1975	2 857.2	3 144 022	37 327	123.00	84.64
1976	2 678.2	3 342 247	36 190	133.00	92.89
1977	2 806.0	3 884 969	38 702	147.00	101.00
1978	2 808.5	4 536 910	41 355	160.00	109.71
1979	2 600.1	4 008 001	36 896	159.00	108.63
1980	2 762.2	4 393 308	36 333	174.00	120.92
1981	2 947.4	4 828 273	37 011	189.00	130.45
1982	3 919.2	8 575 445	60 441	210.00	141.88
1983	3 434.2	10 169 063	66 585	231.00	152.72
1984	3 492.5	9 985 625	61 862	255.00	161.42
1985	3 312.4	10 266 888	59 788	276.00	171.05
1986	3 353.1	10 513 557	58 063	297.00	181.07
1987	3 220.8	10 439 361	54 864	318.00	190.28

(1) Initial and renewal. (2) Excludes work-sharing and job creation benefits to maintain comparability.

Unemployment Insurance Payments, by Province, 1987

Source: Statistics Canada

	Beneficiaries[1]	Claims received	No. of weeks paid (000s)	Total payments ($000)	Avg. weekly benefit
Canada[2]	1 032 970	3 220 800	54 864	10 439 361	$190.28
Newfoundland	67 670	134 800	3 573	651 198	182.23
Prince Edward Island	12 610	26 800	665	123 179	185.22
Nova Scotia	51 230	130 600	2 733	498 037	182.23
New Brunswick	56 850	129 200	3 013	564 170	187.28
Quebec	315 820	940 600	16 871	3 135 712	185.86
Ontario	231 050	958 900	12 238	2 385 253	194.90
Manitoba	33 380	119 500	1 762	331 196	187.96
Saskatchewan	28 990	95 900	1 520	287 081	188.84
Alberta	89 790	275 200	4 753	950 978	200.08
British Columbia	141 930	398 900	7 548	1 470 032	194.76
Yukon	1 700	4 600	87	19 912	230.10
Northwest Territories	1 760	5 200	92	20 592	223.45

(1) 12-month averages. (2) Includes beneficiaries residing outside Canada.

Canada Assistance Plan

Source: Health and Welfare Canada; National Council of Welfare

The Canada Assistance Plan (CAP), introduced in 1966, is a cost-shared program in which the federal government pays 50 percent of the costs incurred by provinces, territories, and municipalities in providing social assistance and welfare services. The provinces are responsible for the design and administration of social assistance programs. While all these programs have key features in common, each is governed by its own set of regulations and these vary from province to province.

The primary objectives of the CAP are: 1) to support the provision by provinces of adequate assistance and institutional care for persons in need; 2) to support the provinces' ability to provide welfare services which aim to lessen or prevent the causes and effects of poverty, child neglect, or dependence on public assistance.

The principal eligibility criterion for all welfare programs throughout the country is that applicants must be in need of social assistance. "Need" is determined on the basis of a test to ensure that individuals have sufficient means to support themselves and their dependents. The needs test takes into account budgetary requirements as well as the resources available to meet those needs.

Persons who benefit from assistance and welfare services include: one-parent families; mentally and physically disabled persons; the aged; children who are in care or who are in need of protection because of abuse or neglect; the unemployed; families/individuals in crisis; low-income workers; and battered women.

The Plan also provides for the federal government to pay half the cost of work activity projects. Such agreements have been signed with all the provinces but not with the territories. Work activity projects are designed to improve the employability of persons who have difficulty finding or retaining jobs or in undertaking job training.

Government Spending on the Canada Assistance Plan[1]

Source: Health and Welfare Canada

	Recipients[2]				Expenditures[3] ($000)			
	1970	1980	1985	1987	1970	1980	1985	1987
Canada	1 346 009	1 505 481	2 070 439	1 904 900	449 937	1 904 101	3 990 500	4 003 044
Newfoundland	85 698	53 003	53 306	50 500	20 289	43 187	74 035	85 480
Prince Edward Island	9 404	10 070	10 217	9 300	3 293	10 268	17 575	19 780
Nova Scotia	51 814	56 125	78 855	73 000	15 246	53 670	104 672	127 099
New Brunswick	54 343	71 952	73 939	73 700	11 795	66 403	126 175	145 108
Quebec	477 440	562 960	742 503	649 600	155 677	747 814	1 503 106	1 107 757
Ontario	354 913	404 516	532 347	518 400	132 257	472 570	943 523	1 132 209
Manitoba	58 667	53 439	71 916	60 600	19 260	60 181	132 178	154 581
Saskatchewan	55 578	46 990	69 807	62 100	17 233	60 060	143 512	160 705
Alberta	84 386	94 585	138 178	150 500	31 441	127 388	334 286	426 265
British Columbia	113 766	144 454	289 735	247 700	43 086	255 602	598 787	632 056
Yukon	n.a.	7 387[4]	1 805	1 200	360	1 093	10 227	n.a.
Northwest Territories	n.a.	7 387[4]	7 831	8 300	n.a.	5 865	2 424	12 004

(1) Expenditures shown are from the federal government only. (2) As of March. (3) For fiscal years ending Mar. 31. Federal government payments are shown for the years in which they were made to the provinces. Some payments include reimbursements to the provinces for expenditures made during previous fiscal years. (4) Includes Yukon and Northwest Territories.
n.a. not available or not applicable.

Crime and Justice

The Canadian Judiciary

The Supreme Court of Canada This is the highest court in the land. Its function is to hear appeals from all the provincial appellate courts and the Federal Court of Appeal. The 9 justices of the Supreme Court, including the Chief Justice, are appointed and paid by the federal government.

Federal Court This Court consists of a trial division and a court of appeal and has jurisdiction over a small range of specialized areas such as admiralty law, income tax, patents and customs. Once called the Exchequer Court, the Federal Court is administered totally by the federal government.

Appellate Courts When a decision of the provincial superior courts is to be appealed, these courts hear the appeal and decide upon it. An appeal is not a new trial; there are almost never any witnesses and the judges do not rehear the whole case. Instead, they examine written transcripts of the trial and listen to legal arguments presented by the parties' lawyers. The appellate courts are provincial institutions and are called either the Court of Appeal, the Supreme Court Appeal Division or Appellate Division; the judges are appointed by the federal government.

Superior Court of Original Jurisidiction This is the highest court at the provincial level, with jurisdiction to hear all civil and criminal cases, unless a statute specifically says otherwise. The name of the superior court differs among provinces. It can be called either the Court of Queen's Bench, the High Court of Justice or the Supreme Court Trial Division. The judges of these courts are appointed and paid by the federal government.

District or County Courts These trial courts hear all but the most serious criminal matters and civil matters up to a certain dollar value. The judges of these courts are also appointed by the federal government.

Provincial Courts This is the lowest rung of the judicial ladder. The jurisdiction of the provincial courts is limited by statute to the less serious criminal matters and civil cases involving relatively small sums of money. These judges are appointed and paid by the province in which they serve.

The Supreme Court of Canada

The Supreme Court of Canada is Canada's highest court of law. It was created by federal statute in 1875. Originally, Supreme Court decisions could be appealed to a special tribunal in England, but such appeals were abolished for criminal cases in 1933 and for civil cases in 1949. Since then, the Supreme Court of Canada has been the court of last resort for every case—criminal or civil—commenced in a Canadian court.

The Supreme Court has jurisdiction to hear appeals from the courts of appeal of each province, as well as from the Federal Court of Appeal. The Court is also empowered to consider questions referred to it by the federal cabinet, and to rule on the legality of bills submitted by the government.

The *Constitution Act, 1982*, with its new Canadian Charter of Rights and Freedoms, has expanded the role of the courts in general, and of the Supreme Court in particular. Though it has always been within the power of Canadian courts to declare laws or other government actions invalid, this power had narrow limits prior to 1982. Legislation could only be struck down if the government introducing it had exceeded its legislative authority as defined in the *Constitution Act, 1867* (the BNA Act). In other words, the federal government was not permitted to legislate on matters within provincial legislative authority, and the provincial governments were not permitted to legislate on matters within federal legislative authority. As long as the legislation satisfied that test, it was valid no matter how objectionable it might otherwise seem to be.

But since the *Constitution Act* became law in 1982, the courts have had the power to strike down legislation or invalidate other government actions if they infringe or deny any of the fundamental rights and freedoms recognized by the Charter of Rights and Freedoms. This new power has made our judges the watchdogs of Parliament and, ultimately, the guardians of our constitutionally-guaranteed rights. As the highest court in the land, it is the Supreme Court of Canada that has the final word on whether laws violate the Constitution.

The Supreme Court consists of 9 judges, including the Chief Justice. Three of the judges must be appointed from Quebec. By convention (although it is not legally required) 3 have usually been appointed from Ontario, 2 from the West and one from Atlantic Canada. All judges are appointed and paid by the federal government, and may hold office until age 75.

Supreme Court Justices of Canada

(as of mid 1988)

Name	Date of Birth	Date Appointed	Appointed from
Brian Dickson	May 25,1916	Mar. 26, 1973[1]	Court of Queen's Bench of Manitoba
Jean Beetz	Mar. 27, 1927	Jan. 1, 1974	Quebec Court of Appeal
William R. McIntyre	Mar. 15, 1918	Jan. 1, 1979	Court of Appeal of B.C.
Antonio Lamer	July 8, 1933	Mar. 28, 1980	Quebec Court of Appeal
Bertha Wilson	Sept. 18, 1923	Mar. 4, 1982	Ontario Court of Appeal
Gerald E. Le Dain	Nov. 27, 1924	May 29, 1984	Federal Court of Appeal and of Court Martial Appeal
Gerard V. La Forest	Apr. 1,.1926	Jan. 16, 1985	Court of Appeal of New Brunswick
Claire L'Heureux Dubé	Sept. 7, 1927	Apr. 15, 1987	Quebec Court of Appeal
John Sopinka	Mar. 19, 1933	May 24, 1988	private law practice

(1) Appointed Chief Justice Apr. 18, 1984.

Some Landmark Canadian Supreme Court Decisions

Roncarelli vs. Duplessis (1959)

In 1946, Premier Maurice Duplessis, who was also attorney general of Quebec, ordered the liquor commission to revoke the liquor licence of Montreal restauranteur Frank Roncarelli. Roncarelli's business was ruined. Duplessis ordered the action not because of any misconduct on Roncarelli's part but because Roncarelli was a Jehovah's Witness who was active in bailing out fellow Witnesses when they were arrested for passing out literature on street corners. The Supreme Court ruled that Duplessis had committed a civil wrong and held him personally responsible for compensating Roncarelli for $46 132.

This is one of the most powerful statements by the court on the importance of the "rule of law" in the Canadian constitutional environment. The decision stood for the idea that no person is above the law and that members of the executive branch of government do not make the law but only administer it.

Anti-Inflation Act Reference (1976)

In 1975 the government of Prime Minister Pierre Trudeau passed the *Anti-Inflation Act*, a series of extraordinary temporary measures aimed at controlling the rampant inflation of the day.

Several provincial governments felt this legislation represented an unconstitutional interference with provincial regulatory authority and contractual rights. To settle the matter, the federal government asked the Court to rule on the constitutional validity of the *Anti-Inflation Act*. The federal government and Ontario argued before the Court that the Act was constitutional. Presenting the case against the Act were Quebec, Saskatchewan, British Columbia, Alberta, the Canadian Labor Congress and a number of other individual trade unions.

The Court ruled that even though the Act involved actions by the federal government that infringed on the exclusive realms of the provinces, it was justified under the "emergency powers" which the federal government has under the constitution. Chief Justice Bora Laskin defined the test for determining whether the use of the emergency power was justified as being whether the federal government had a "rational basis" for perceiving a crisis of emergency proportions. If the rational basis existed, then the Court was willing to defer to the judgement of the government.

This decision modified the law as it had been established in the early part of the century by such cases as the Board of Commerce case (1922) and the Fort Frances case (1923). In these, the federal government was held to a much stricter standard before courts were willing to accept that a specific situation was grave enough to justify invocation of federal emergency power. The Anti-Inflation Reference effectively enhanced the power of the federal government at the expense of the provinces.

"The Damage Trilogy"

(Andrews v. Grand & Toy Alta. Ltd. (1978); Arnold v. Teno (1978); Thornton v. School Dist. No. 57 Bd. of School Trustees (1978))

These 3 cases revolutionized the method used by Canadian courts in calculating damage awards to those who are successful in law suits for injury. Prior to the "damage trilogy,"—as these cases which appeared before the Supreme Court in rapid succession are commonly known—Canadian courts calculated damages using a "global approach". This involved simply picking a single amount to compensate the person for all of his or her injuries. Under this global approach, awards varied greatly for similar cases, it was difficult for higher courts to review the award on appeal, and, generally, the awards were quite low in value.

The damage trilogy established that each aspect of the injured person's loss should be assessed separately based on the available evidence. For example, in the Andrews case involving a young man who was rendered a quadriplegic in a traffic accident for which an employee of Grand & Toy was partially responsible, the court listed 14 major categories of compensation including cost of future care, loss of prospective earnings, loss of expectation of life. The court also considered technical details such as allowances for inflation, tax and rate of return on investment. The final result was that Andrews was awarded $817 344 and received 75% of that amount to account for the fact that the court found him to be 25% responsible for his injuries.

"The Patriation Reference" (1981)

In the fall of 1980, after federal-provincial conferences failed to come to a consensus on how to patriate the constitution, Prime Minister Pierre Trudeau decided to proceed without provincial consent and parliament passed a constitutional amendment package in April 1981. Only Ontario and New Brunswick agreed with the federal package and the other 8 provinces asked the Supreme Court to rule on the legality of the federal move. The Court said that, although the federal action was technically legal, the government would breach a constitutional convention if it proceeded with the constitutional change without having first secured a "substantial degree" of provincial consent. The result made it politically impossible for Ottawa to proceed. A new round of federal-provincial discussions resulted in agreement on a revised package of constitutional changes.

With this decision and the introduction of the *Charter of Rights and Freedoms*, the Court is firmly established as the third branch of government with its own claim to full constitutional status. This status would become entrenched if the Meech Lake Accord is approved.

The Queen vs. Big M Drug Mart Ltd. (1985)

This case was the first major test of how the Supreme Court would interpret the freedom of religion provisions in the new *Charter of Rights and Freedoms*.

Big M Drug Mart was prosecuted for violating the federal *Lord's Day Act*, a 1907 law prohibiting any person from carrying on business or labor activities on a Sunday or, as the Act phrased it, "the Lord's Day". The Court ruled that, by forcing all members of society to observe the Christian Sabbath, the law infringed on the guarantee of freedom of conscience and religion in the *Charter of Rights and Freedoms*. In this way the Charter has increased the importance of protecting the rights of minorities, superseding the previous standard of majority rule when defining the rights of individuals.

The Big M Drug Mart case involved a second precedent, establishing that, under the Charter, corporations have rights similar to individuals.

Big M Drug Mart Ltd. is a corporation and, although corporations have always been considered to be 'persons' before the law, it could not be said to have a conscience or any religious belief. The Court ruled that it was irrelevant "whether a corporation could enjoy or exercise freedom of religion". If a law is constitutionally invalid because it impairs freedom of religion, the Court decided, then a corporation should be as free as an individual person to make this argument in court.

Operation Dismantle Inc. vs. The Queen (1985)

Operation Dismantle, a disarmament lobby group, challenged a federal Cabinet decision to permit United States testing of the cruise missile in Canadian territory. The challenge was based on the *Charter of Rights and Freedoms* guarantee of the right to life, liberty and security of the person.

The significance of the case lies not in its outcome (Operation Dismantle lost and the testing went forward) but rather in the unanimous ruling by the Court that decisions made by Cabinet are subject to review under the Charter, even when there is no particular legislation passed. This case illustrated a dramatic change under the Charter: prior to its introduction, Cabinet decisions were not subject to judicial review.

The Right to Strike (1987)

In a reference involving the *Public Service Employee Relations Act*, the *Labour Relations Act* and *the Police Officers Collective Bargaining Act*, the Supreme Court was asked to decide if the workers' right to strike was protected by the section of the *Charter of Rights and Freedoms* which guarantees freedom of association.

The Court held that, although the right of individuals to organize into collective bargaining units (unions) was protected by the constitution, the actions of the union (e.g., a strike) were not as a result also protected.

If the Court had ruled that the right to strike was protected by the constitution, that decision would have removed the government's right to end strikes by enacting back-to-work legislation. The outcome of this case was a serious blow to the power of labor unions in Canada.

The Queen vs. Vaillancourt (1987)

In this case, the Supreme Court struck down an entire section of the criminal code, in effect wiping out an entire category of murder in Canadian law.

The law was known as the provision for "constructive murder". Section 213 of the criminal code said that if a person caused a death while in the process of committing certain serious offences and they had a weapon with them during the commission of the offence, then that person was guilty of murder. It was therefore not necessary that the accused had any intention to cause the death or even knew that his actions were likely to cause death. It was a strictly technical definition that held that if the serious offence was committed, the weapon was present, and a death resulted, then the accused was guilty of murder.

Yvan Vaillancourt was convicted under this law. He and an accomplice robbed a poolroom. He did not have a weapon, but his accomplice had a gun which Vaillancourt thought was not loaded. In the course of the robbery, the accomplice shot and killed a customer of the poolroom.

The Supreme Court declared that the constructive murder law was invalid because it violated 2 sections of the *Charter of Rights and Freedoms*. According to the Court, it was contrary to the principles of fundamental justice to convict a person of murder when there was no intention to kill anyone. Secondly, by dispensing with the duty of the crown to prove that the accused had a guilty mind, the law infringed on the right of the accused to be presumed innocent until proven guilty.

The decision was widely welcomed because, until the Supreme Court acted, Canada was one of the few countries in the western world to still have the harsh constructive murder provision in its law.

The Abortion Ruling (1988)

The increased power granted to the Supreme Court of Canada by the 1982 *Charter of Rights and Freedoms* was dramatically demonstrated by the 1988 Court decision to declare Canada's abortion law unconstitutional.

Section 251 of the Criminal Code, passed by Parliament in 1969, allowed abortions to be performed only in accredited hospitals and only after a committee of doctors had determined that the continued pregnancy would be a threat to the woman's life or health.

For 20 years, Dr. Henry Morgentaler (see p. 398) had openly performed "illegal" abortions in clinics, ignoring the Criminal Code requirement. In 1983, after opening a clinic in Toronto, Morgentaler was charged with performing illegal abortions. He was acquitted by a jury in 1984 but, in 1985, the Ontario Court of Appeal overturned that acquittal. Morgentaler appealed that decision to the Supreme Court in 1986, arguing that the 1969 law violated clauses in the *Charter of Rights and Freedoms*.

In a 5-2 decision handed down in Jan. 1988, the Court found that the abortion law violated the Charter's guarantee of life, liberty and security of the person.

"Forcing a woman by threat of criminal sanction to carry a fetus to term unless she meets certain criteria unrelated to her own priorities and aspirations is a profound interference with a woman's body," wrote Chief Justice Brian Dickson.

Although the decision left Canada without an abortion law, it did leave open the possibility of Parliament enacting new legislation which would protect the fetus after a certain stage of pregnancy.

"The value to be placed on the fetus as potential life is directly related to the stage of its development during gestation," wrote Madam Justice Bertha Wilson. "The undeveloped fetus starts out as a newly fertilized ovum; the fully developed fetus emerges ultimately as an infant. Accordingly, the fetus should be viewed in developmental terms. This view of the fetus supports a permissive approach to abortion in the early stages where the woman's autonomy would be absolute and a restrictive approach in the later stages where the state's interest in protecting the fetus would justify its prescribing conditions."

Legal Aid

Legal aid exists to provide representation to people who could not otherwise afford to retain a lawyer. Each province has its own legal aid system, but all of the plans in Canada follow one of 3 models:

Judicare system: Under a judicare system, legal services are provided by lawyers in private practice. The government pays some or all of the legal fees but employs no lawyers of its own to do exclusively legal aid work. New Brunswick, Alberta and Yukon Territory have judicare systems.

Staff system: In some provinces, the legal aid plan employs its own staff lawyers to act for clients on legal aid. Except in special circumstances when outside counsel are retained, all legal aid work is done by these staff lawyers. Provinces with a staff system are Prince Edward Island, Nova Scotia and Saskatchewan.

Combined Services: In some provinces, legal aid work is done by both staff lawyers and lawyers in private practice. This system is used in Newfoundland, Quebec, Manitoba and British Columbia. Ontario's system, though primarily judicare, also employs lawyers at community legal services clinics and is therefore considered a combined system. British Columbia also employs clinics, but to a much lesser extent than Ontario. In the Northwest Territories the primary base for service is the judicare system, but some clinics are used.

The cost of legal aid in criminal matters has been shared by the federal and provincial governments since 1972. In civil matters there has been some federal assistance since about 1980. Other sources for funding legal aid include interest from lawyers' trust accounts (contributed by the law societies of B.C., Man., Nfld. and Ont.), court costs awarded to legal aid clients at trial, and other contributions by legal aid clients.

Canadian Law Enforcement

Policing in most Canadian provinces is carried out by municipal police forces and the Royal Canadian Mounted Police (R.C.M.P.). In addition, Ontario, Quebec, New Brunswick, and Newfoundland have their own provincial forces.

Municipal Police Forces

Each city and town is required by provincial law to have enough police to maintain law and order. Municipalities will either operate their own police forces, or contract with the R.C.M.P. or the provincial police force to provide the necessary police.

Royal Canadian Mounted Police

The R.C.M.P. was founded as the North-West Mounted Police in 1873. The force is maintained by the federal government, and is the responsibility of the federal solicitor general. The R.C.M.P. has contracts with every province except Ontario and Quebec to provide police services to communities that do

not maintain their own police forces. In those communities, the R.C.M.P. enforces all laws—federal, provincial and municipal.

Ontario Provincial Police

The Ontario Provincial Police force is operated by the provincial government, and is the responsibility of Ontario's solicitor general. The O.P.P. enforces both federal and provincial laws in those parts of Ontario where provincial law does not require municipal police forces. The force also maintains a traffic patrol on many of the province's highways, and enforces the Liquor Licence Act. As well, the O.P.P. provides municipal policing under contract.

Quebec Police Force

The Quebec Police Force is similar to the O.P.P. in that it is a provincial force, with jurisdiction throughout the province. The force is responsible to Quebec's attorney general, and has a mandate to maintain peace, order and public safety throughout Quebec. It enforces criminal and provincial laws.

Police in Canada by Type of Force, 1965-1987

Source: Canadian Centre for Justice Statistics

	Total[1]	RCMP	Municipal	Ontario Provincial	Quebec Provincial	New Brunswick Highway Patrol	Royal Newfoundland Constabulary
1965	32 010	7 398	18 488	2 797	2 163	n.a.	n.a.
1970	40 295	9 498	22 437	3 755	3 354	n.a.	n.a.
1975	50 663	14 072	27 430	4 042	4 107	n.a.	n.a.
1980	52 922	13 879	29 493	4 000	4 585	n.a.	n.a.
1985	53 464	14 271	29 636	4 345	4 248	113	n.a.
1986	54 604	15 206	29 415	4 484	4 158	114	442
1987	52 510	13 483	30 122	4 227	4 165	114	399

(1) Until 1986, includes police officers from CN Railways, CP Railways, and Ports Canada. Beginning in 1987, statistics are no longer kept on numbers of CN, CP, and Ports Canada officers.
n.a. not applicable.

Number of Police[1] by Province, 1965-1987

Source: Canadian Centre for Justice Statistics

	1965 Police officers	1965 Population per police officer	1975 Police officers	1975 Population per police officer	1985 Police officers	1985 Population per police officer	1987 Police officers	1987 Population per police officer
Canada[2]	32 010	620	50 663	452	53 464	477	52 510	488
Newfoundland ...	521	940	777	714	927	626	916	620
Prince Edward Is. .	104	1 038	198	596	180	711	184	692
Nova Scotia	889	848	1 197	690	1 439	614	1 450	606
New Brunswick ...	582	1 058	1 105	610	1 175	613	1 201	593
Quebec	9 531	602	14 526	428	13 893	476	13 801	478
Ontario[3]	10 773	639	17 439	472	18 461	495	18 836	492
Manitoba	1 184	813	2 036	500	2 086	516	2 095	515
Saskatchewan[4] ...	1 114	855	1 846	497	1 964	519	1 939	523
Alberta	1 956	744	3 362	540	4 245	559	4 305	553
British Columbia ..	2 599	711	4 728	520	5 784	501	5 544	528
Yukon	56	268	83	263	116	196	101	242
Northwest Terr. ...	128	219	185	229	232	219	202	256

(1) Full-time police officers. (2) Until 1985, this total included RCMP officers from HQ, N, and Depot Divisions, and police officers from CN Railways, CP Railways and Ports Canada. Beginning in 1987, officers from CN, CP, and Ports Canada were no longer included in this total.

Number of Inmates in Canadian Prisons[1]

Source: Canadian Centre for Justice Statistics

Year	Federal prisons	Provincial prisons	Year	Federal prisons	Provincial prisons
1960	6 738	10 896	1983	10 438	17 157
1965	7 518	12 627	1984	10 857	16 242
1970	7 375	12 124	1985	11 214	16 358
1975	8 456	11 277	1986	11 106	15 657
1980	8 651	13 851			

(1) Average number of offenders in custody daily during the fiscal year.

Canadian Criminal Offences and Crime Rate

Source: Canadian Centre for Justice Statistics

	1986					1987				
	No. of offences[3]	Adults Charged male	female	Young offenders	Crime rate[4]	No. of offences[3]	Adults Charged male	female	Young offenders	Crime rate[4]
Total Offences[2]	2 374 251	367 819	70 184	178 634	9 365	2 454 118	381 681	75 725	170 380	9 577
Total crimes of violence	204 917	71 082	7 600	14 744	808	218 652	77 986	8 545	15 629	853
Homicide	569	458	67	38	2	646	490	83	37	3
First degree murder	261	209	27	14	1	307	235	30	13	1
Second degree murder	261	213	33	19	1	281	208	42	20	1
Manslaughter	44	36	5	5	...	52	44	10	3	...
Infanticide	3	–	2	–	–	6	3	1	1	...
Attempted murder	880	577	69	70	3	914	619	90	59	4
Assault	176 305	63 012	6 883	12 992	695	191 163	70 311	7 747	14 023	746
Aggravated sexual assault	429	218	7	42	2	414	197	3	20	2
Sexual assault with weapon	910	379	8	72	4	929	427	12	65	4
Sexual assault	19 191	5 964	69	1 526	76	20 960	6 652	86	1 780	82
Assault, common	111 757	34 533	4 365	7 921	441	123 378	39 804	4 894	8 650	481
Assault with weapon or causing bodily harm	29 013	13 891	1 441	2 417	114	29 876	14 860	1 658	2 471	117
Aggravated assault	2 722	1 444	225	212	11	2 502	1 430	226	183	10
Causing bodily harm	2 947	1 546	136	206	12	2 957	1 587	118	206	12
Abduction	892	202	60	9	4	965	192	66	16	4
Robbery	23 268	5 823	464	1 478	92	22 340	5 565	502	1 315	87
Total property crimes	1 448 550	148 201	41 180	115 441	5 714	1 460 536	146 742	42 647	108 602	5 700
Breaking and entering	365 140	37 169	1 635	34 779	1 440	361 538	36 890	1 645	32 631	1 411
Theft—motor vehicles	85 585	8 744	485	7 507	338	86 609	8 827	513	7 331	338
Theft over $1 000	68 024	5 480	961	2 184	268	71 285	4 866	905	1 609	278
Theft $1 000 and under	773 257	56 435	26 401	61 881	3 050	788 927	57 289	28 138	58 163	3 079
Have stolen goods	25 985	12 030	1 702	5 590	102	26 923	11 837	1 577	5 595	105
Frauds	130 559	28 343	9 996	3 500	515	125 254	27 033	9 869	3 273	489
Other crimes	624 282	108 493	16 186	42 295	2 462	673 215	115 666	18 842	40 088	2 627
Prostitution	7 426	2 939	3 863	880	29	10 440	5 329	4 922	548	41
Gaming and betting	1 372	1 311	144	13	5	1 592	1 487	183	67	6
Offensive weapons	17 022	7 695	533	2 488	67	17 006	7 631	584	2 166	66
Arson	7 550	745	121	934	30	8 145	732	120	879	32
Counterfeiting currency	2 044	184	22	42	8	1 557	75	19	17	7
Disturbing the peace	50 755	8 881	1 186	4 912	200	53 993	8 898	1 215	3 158	211
Indecent acts	11 187	2 756	288	362	44	10 935	2 504	196	280	43
Kidnapping	580	285	25	28	2	641	281	30	30	3
Mischief (property damage) over $1 000	121 208	7 817	654	5 962	478	69 029	4 918	453	3 139	269
Mischief (property damage) $1 000 and under	206 436	11 500	1 096	11 654	814	279 607	14 915	1 488	13 760	1 091
Total drugs	56 251	32 611	4 228	4 767	222	61 406	34 220	4 799	4 108	240
Heroin	914	439	112	9	4	774	391	102	11	3
Possession	302	157	65	1	1	312	162	71	7	1
Trafficking	357	197	32	4	1	363	194	29	4	1
Importation	255	85	15	4	1	99	35	2	–	–
Cocaine	6 729	3 928	706	93	27	8 190	5 146	887	100	32
Possession	3 117	2 231	403	69	12	3 647	2 725	481	69	14
Trafficking	3 326	1 636	282	24	13	4 228	2 335	389	30	16
Importation	286	61	21	–	1	315	86	17	1	1
Cannabis	41 514	25 401	2 834	4 179	164	43 062	25 789	3 057	3 653	168
Possession	31 766	19 597	1 983	3 614	125	30 886	19 144	2 026	2 991	121
Trafficking	8 645	5 414	744	559	34	10 558	6 038	877	647	41
Importation	427	139	28	1	2	574	235	43	5	2
Cultivation	676	251	79	5	3	1 044	372	111	10	4

(1) Preliminary data. (2) Offences under the Criminal Code or federal statutes; does not include offences under provincial statutes or municipal by-laws. (3) The number of offences is greater than the number of persons charged because some persons are charged with several offences, or with the same offence more than once and because no charges are laid for some offences. (4) Per 100 000 population.
. . . = too small to be included; – = zero.

Police Murders[1] in Canada, 1961-1987

Source: Canadian Centre for Justice Statistics

1961 ... .2 ... .(both in Que.)	1975 ... .2 ... .(N.S. 1, Que. 1)
1962 ... .11 ... .(Que. 4, B.C. 4, Ont. 3)	1976 ... .3 ... .(Que. 2, Alta. 1)
1963 ... .none	1977 ... .5 ... .(Que. 2, Ont. 2, Alta. 1)
1964 ... .2 ... .(Nfld. 1, Que. 1)	1978 ... .6 ... .(N.B. 2, Ont. 2, Man. 1, Sask. 1)
1965 ... .2 ... .(Ont. 1, B.C. 1)	1979 ... .1 ... .(Que. 1)
1966 ... .3 ... .(Ont. 1, Sask. 1, Alta. 1)	1980 ... .3 ... .(Ont. 2, B.C. 1)
1967 ... .3 ... .(Que. 1, Ont. 1, Alta. 1)	1981 ... .5 ... .(Que. 2, Ont. 2, Sask. 1)
1968 ... .5 ... .(Ont. 3, Que. 2)	1982 ... .1 ... .(Ont. 1)
1969 ... .5 ... .(Que. 2, Ont. 2, Man. 1)	1983 ... .1 ... .(Ont. 1)
1970 ... .3 ... .(Sask. 2, Man. 1)	1984 ... .6 ... .(Ont. 5, Que. 1)
1971 ... .3 ... .(Que. 2, Man. 1)	1985 ... .6 ... .(Ont. 5, Que. 1)
1972 ... .3 ... .(Ont. 2, Que. 1)	1986 ... .4 ... .(Que. 3, Man. 1)
1973 ... .5 ... .(Ont. 4, Que. 1)	1987[2] ... .3 ... .(N.B. 1, Alta. 1, B.C. 1)
1974 ... .6 ... .(N.B. 2, B.C. 2, Que. 1, Alta. 1)	

(1) Includes police officers murdered while on duty only. (2) Preliminary data.

Capital Punishment in Canada

Capital punishment was abolished in Canada in 1976 but there has not been an execution since Dec. 11, 1962. Up to then there were 643 executions, all by hanging.

At the time of Confederation, murder, treason and rape were punishable by death. The first bill proposing abolition of capital punishment was introduced in Parliament in 1914. It was defeated, as were other abolitionist bills between 1915 and 1917, in 1924 and in 1950.

In 1954, the death penalty was repealed for rape and, in 1961, Parliament amended the criminal code to create 2 classes of murder: capital murder (punishable by death) and non-capital murder (punishable by life imprisonment).

The Cabinet commuted all death sentences to life imprisonment between 1962 and 1967 when, on a trial basis, capital punishment was abolished for all crimes except the murder of police officers or prison guards. The trial period was to last for 5 years but, in 1973, it was extended until the death penalty was formally abolished in 1976, by a vote of 130-124, in a free vote in Parliament. In Feb. 1987, the Progressive Conservative government, in response to the demands of Conservative backbenchers, announced that it would hold a free vote on whether the death penalty should be restored. The motion to reinstate capital punishment was defeated 148-127 in June 1987.

Executions in Canada

Year	Executions	Year	Executions	Year	Executions	Year	Executions
1879	5	1900	6	1921	8	1942	6
1880	6	1901	4	1922	9	1943	7
1881	3	1902	9	1923	13	1944	6
1882	4	1903	5	1924	13	1945	6
1883	5	1904	6	1925	6	1946	14
1884	6	1905	5	1926	9	1947	10
1885	12	1906	2	1927	9	1948	12
1886	2	1907	7	1928	7	1949	13
1887	3	1908	7	1929	11	1950	13
1888	7	1909	13	1930	10	1951	6
1889	1	1910	13	1931	22	1952	12
1890	10	1911	7	1932	16	1953	11
1891	2	1912	8	1933	16	1954	4
1892	4	1913	9	1934	12	1955	8
1893	1	1914	13	1935	17	1956	4
1894	4	1915	14	1936	8	1957	4
1895	3	1916	8	1937	12	1958	2
1896	–	1917	7	1938	7	1959	–
1897	3	1918	6	1939	7	1960	–
1898	8	1919	19	1940	8	1961	1
1899	9	1920	7	1941	9	1962	2[1]

(1) The last execution in Canada was the double hanging on Dec. 11, 1962 of Ronald Turpin and Arthur Lucas, both convicted of killing police officers.
– = zero.

Homicides[1] in Canada, 1961-1987

Source: Canadian Centre for Justice Statistics

	Canada		Nfld		PEI		NS		NB		Que		Ont	
	No.	Rate[2]	No.	Rate[2]	No.	Rate[2]	No.	Rate[2]	No.	Rate[2]	No.	Rate[2]	No.	Rate[2]
1961	233	1.3	1	0.2	1	1.0	6	0.8	2	0.3	52	1.0	89	1.4
1966	250	1.3	3	0.6	1	0.9	9	1.2	6	1.0	56	1.0	71	1.0
1971	473	2.2	2	0.4	–	–	16	2.0	10	1.6	124	2.1	151	2.0
1975	701	3.1	4	0.7	–	–	14	1.7	12	1.8	226	3.7	206	2.5
1976	668	2.9	6	1.1	2	1.7	25	3.0	14	2.0	205	3.3	183	2.2
1977	711	3.1	8	1.4	1	0.8	14	1.7	38	5.6	197	3.1	192	2.3
1978	661	2.8	9	1.6	4	3.3	13	1.6	27	3.9	180	2.9	182	2.2
1979	631	2.7	5	0.9	–	–	17	2.0	11	1.6	186	2.9	175	2.1
1980	593	2.5	3	0.5	1	0.8	12	1.4	9	1.3	181	2.8	159	1.9
1981	648	2.7	4	0.7	1	0.8	11	1.3	17	2.4	186	2.9	170	2.0
1982	668	2.7	6	1.1	–	–	12	1.4	13	1.9	191	3.0	184	2.1
1983	682	2.7	6	1.0	–	–	13	1.5	11	1.6	190	2.9	202	2.3
1984	667	2.7	6	1.0	–	–	15	1.7	14	2.0	198	3.0	190	2.1
1985	704	2.8	5	0.9	1	0.8	26	3.0	14	2.0	219	3.3	193	2.1
1986	569	2.2	4	0.7	–	–	15	1.7	12	1.7	156	2.4	139	1.5
1987[3]	651	2.5	4	0.7	–	–	12	1.4	22	3.1	170	2.6	217	2.3

	Man		Sask		Alta		BC		Yukon		NWT	
	No.	Rate[2]	No.	Rate[2]	No.	Rate[2]	No.	Rate[2]	No.	Rate[2]	No.	Rate[2]
1961	15	1.6	14	1.5	18	1.4	34	2.1	1	6.9	–	–
1966	17	1.8	12	1.3	27	1.9	48	2.6	–	–	–	–
1971	33	3.3	29	3.1	45	2.8	61	2.8	–	–	2	5.8
1975	37	3.7	36	4.0	57	3.2	98	4.0	6	28.2	5	12.1
1976	31	3.0	34	3.7	68	3.7	88	3.6	4	18.4	8	18.8
1977	44	4.3	46	4.9	70	3.7	91	3.6	6	27.5	4	9.3
1978	39	3.8	32	3.4	84	4.2	85	3.3	2	8.9	4	9.2
1979	44	4.3	36	3.8	56	2.7	90	3.5	4	17.9	7	15.9
1980	31	3.0	31	3.2	55	2.6	105	3.9	2	9.0	4	9.0
1981	41	4.0	29	3.0	73	3.3	110	4.0	1	4.3	5	10.9
1982	35	3.4	39	4.0	70	3.0	109	3.9	2	8.4	7	14.8
1983	40	3.8	33	3.3	75	3.2	108	3.8	1	4.5	3	6.2
1984	43	4.1	30	3.0	54	2.3	110	3.9	2	8.9	5	10.1
1985	26	2.4	28	2.8	63	2.7	113	3.9	6	25.9	10	19.6
1986	47	4.4	26	2.6	64	2.7	89	3.1	3	13.1	14	27.5
1987[3]	43	4.0	29	2.9	75	3.2	76	2.6	–	–	3	5.8

(1) Includes offences of murder, manslaughter and infanticide. One "offence" is counted for each victim. (2) The number of homicides per 100 000 population. (3) Preliminary data.
– = zero.

Famous Canadian Court Cases

The "Black" Donnellys

The murder of the "Black" Donnellys in 1880 ended a bloody 30-year feud that had terrorized the villagers of Lucan, Ont.

The Donnellys were a family to whom violence—often irrational violence—had become an accepted way of life. Avenging every slight, real or imagined, with ruthless attacks against person and property, the Donnellys exhibited an almost inhuman capacity to inflict suffering. They were particularly fond of arson; any farmer who crossed a Donnelly could soon expect to see his barn in flames, his animals butchered.

The head of the clan, James Donnelly, was sentenced to 7 years in prison in 1857 for killing a man in a brawl. The barns of all 3 principal witnesses at Donnelly's trial were later burned to the ground.) But, for the most part, the Donnellys' long series of crimes went unpunished because no one dared testify against them.

However, the community's hatred and fear of the Donnellys finally reached a breaking point. On Feb. 4, 1880, some 30 men stormed the Donnelly farm house, killing and beheading James Donnelly and one of his sons, beating to death the elder Donnelly's wife and a visiting niece, then setting fire to the house. Later that same night, another Donnelly son was shot and killed.

Six men were eventually charged with the murder of James Donnelly and his family. The prosecution relied on the eye-witness evidence of a 12-year-old boy who—unknown to Donnelly's killers—watched the attack while hiding in the Donnelly home.

James Carroll, the alleged "ringleader" of the vigilante group that had killed the Donnellys, was tried first. His trial resulted in a hung jury (i.e., the jury members could not agree on a verdict). At a 2d trial Carroll was acquitted. Because the evidence against all 6 men was identical, the charges against the other accused were dropped following Carroll's acquittal.

No one was ever convicted for the murder of the "Black Donnellys". James Carroll and the other alleged murderers become local heroes.

Louis Riel

In what is still Canada's best known political trial, more than 100 years after it took place, Métis leader Louis Riel was convicted of treason and sentenced to death.

The story of Riel, one of the most controversial figures in Canadian history, begins in 1869 when the Red River Colony (in what is now Manitoba), was about to be released from control of the Hudson's Bay Company and brought into the new Canadian Confederation. The Métis, French-speaking Roman Catholics of mixed European and Indian blood, wanted no such transfer to occur until specific consideration was given to their property and cultural rights. Louis Riel, educated as a priest and trained as a lawyer, became the Métis spokesman.

Opposition soon led to rebellion. Riel and his followers seized Fort Garry from the Hudson's Bay Company and successfully defended their position against an armed Canadian force.

While negotiations between the Métis and the Canadian government were being planned, a 2d Canadian force was captured by the Métis and imprisoned in Fort Garry. Thomas Scott, one of the military leaders, was court martialled by the Métis and put to death.

Agreements were finally reached between Riel and the Canadian government, and the terms were embodied in the *Manitoba Act, 1870*, the statute by which Manitoba entered Confederation. But through the course of the uprisings, Riel had aroused strong feelings both in Ontario, where he was condemned for the murder of Thomas Scott, and in Quebec, where he was revered for his defence of Roman Catholicism and the French language.

In 1884, Riel was approached by Métis seeking his help to protect their rights in Saskatchewan. At first, Riel sought peaceful negotiation with the federal government. Eventually, however, he took more drastic measures, and on Mar. 19, 1885 formed a provisional government in Batoche, Sask. The federal government retaliated. A battle ensued and Riel soon surrendered.

He was tried for treason in Regina. Rejecting his lawyer's advice to plead not guilty by reason of insanity, Riel was convicted. He was hanged at Regina on Nov. 16, 1885.

Evelyn Dick

A grisly murder, an accused woman with a scandalous past, apparently overwhelming evidence of guilt, and the skillful advocacy of a man destined to become Canada's most prominent courtroom advocate are only some of the elements that made the Evelyn Dick case a headline writer's dream.

The victim was John Dick, whose dismembered torso was discovered in Hamilton, Ont., in Mar., 1946. The police questioned Dick's estranged wife, Evelyn, a beautiful 25-year-old who estimated she had slept with 150 different men—including many prominent members of Hamilton society. Evelyn provided a series of statements to the police, often contradictory, often more bizarre than the plots of cheap detective novels. But this much was clear: Evelyn knew something about the death of John Dick.

Her statements, along with some physical evidence found at the homes of Evelyn and her father, Donald MacLean, led to charges of murder against Evelyn Dick, her parents, and Bill Bohuzuk—a man with whom John Dick once caught his wife. The case took another strange twist when Evelyn's mother, Alexandra MacLean, had the charges against her dropped at the preliminary inquiry and subsequently testified for the Crown in the case against her daughter.

But there were still more surprises. While investigating the John Dick murder, police discovered the body of a murdered baby encased in cement in Evelyn Dick's home. The baby was identified as Evelyn's son, Peter David White, and she was later charged with the murder of the baby as well.

In Oct., 1946, Evelyn Dick was sentenced to death for the murder of her husband. But the conviction was appealed, and Evelyn hired lawyer J.J. Robinette, whose skillful advocacy in the face of apparently overwhelming odds brought him to the forefront of the Canadian legal profession. The Court of Appeal set aside Evelyn's conviction, and ordered a new trial. At that 2d trial, she was acquitted of John Dick's murder.

But the story did not end there. Less than 3 weeks later, Evelyn Dick was back in court to face a charge of killing Peter David White. This time, she was convicted of manslaughter and sentenced to life imprisonment. She was paroled in 1958.

No one was ever convicted for the brutal murder of John Dick.

Steven Truscott

A 14-year-old boy was sentenced to hang on the basis of circumstantial evidence, and doubts about the 1959 trial of Steven Truscott remain 30 years later.

In June 1959, the body of 12-year-old Lynne Harper was found in the woods near Clinton, Ont. The girl had been raped and strangled. Truscott, a classmate who was the last person known to have seen Harper alive, was arrested and charged with her murder. On Sept. 30, 1959, the jury returned a verdict of guilty with a recommendation for mercy. The judge, however, sentenced the boy to death.

Truscott's appeal to the Ontario Court of Appeal failed, and he was denied permission to bring his case before the Supreme Court of Canada. His death sentence, however, was commuted by Cabinet to life imprisonment, and in 1969 he was paroled and began living under an assumed name.

The case against Truscott had been based largely on circumstantial evidence. In 1966, following public pressure to re-open the Truscott matter, the federal government referred a question to the Supreme Court of Canada asking whether or not Truscott's appeal would have been successful had it been allowed 15 years earlier. By an 8-1 majority, the Supreme Court found that the original jury verdict should stand.

But the Supreme Court decision did not end the matter. Truscott continued to proclaim his innocence, and doubts remain about whether Lynne Harper's real murderer has ever been brought to justice.

Colin Thatcher

Colin Thatcher, a wealthy rancher, former Saskatchewan energy minister, and the son of a former provincial premier, was arrested in 1984 for the murder of his ex-wife, JoAnn Wilson.

Wilson's body had been found 15 months earlier in the garage of her Regina home; her head had been battered with a sharp, heavy object. Thatcher and Wilson had divorced in 1979, after 17 years of marriage. The divorce was bitter, and was followed by a protracted dispute over the custody of one of their 3 children.

Thatcher's controversial personality as well as his political and financial prominence, made his trial a sensational media event. The jury found Thatcher guilty on Nov. 6, 1984, and he was sentenced to life imprisonment. The conviction was upheld by the Saskatchewan Court of Appeal in 1986 and the Supreme Court of Canada in 1987.

Baby Deaths at the Hospital for Sick Children

An alarming increase in deaths in the cardiac unit of Toronto's Hospital for Sick Children during 1980 and 1981 led the police, and much of the public, to conclude that someone in the hospital was murdering babies.

Between July 1, 1980 and Mar. 31, 1981, 36 children (33 babies and 3 older children) died in cardiac wards 4A and 4B. Twenty-five of these deaths occurred between midnight and 6 a.m.; and although there were 4 nursing teams per ward, in all cases except one, the babies began to show critical symptoms when only one of these teams was on duty.

One member of that nursing team, Susan Nelles, was arrested and charged with the murder of 4 of the infants in Mar. 1981. But Nelles was never tried. After her preliminary inquiry (a hearing to determine if there is enough evidence to proceed to a trial) the judge concluded that the Crown did not have a case, and Nelles was immediately discharged. No other arrests were made.

In Apr. 1983 the Ontario government appointed a Royal Commission, led by Mr. Justice Samuel Grange of Ontario's Supreme Court, to investigate the deaths. In its report, presented in Dec. 1984 after months of public hearings, the Commission concluded that 8 of the children had died from overdoses of digoxin, a drug used to treat congestive heart failure.

Were they murdered? The Commission did not specifically say so; but the report clearly dismissed the possibility of accidental overdoses. The Commission also concluded that 6 of the other deaths were from natural causes, 7 from unknown causes, and that the remainder looked suspiciously like digoxin poisoning.

Despite the Grange Commission's findings, no new charges have been laid against anyone, and the children's deaths remain a mystery.

Clifford Olson

The horror of mass murder was coupled with the outrage of a criminal profiting from his crime in the 1982 case of Clifford Olson.

Olson, a Coquitlam, B.C. construction worker who had spent almost 25 of his 42 years behind bars, was convicted Jan. 14, 1982 of the brutal murders of 11 children aged 9 to 18. The murders had all taken place within 150 km of Vancouver.

Great controversy surrounded the investigation of the case when it was disclosed that the R.C.M.P. had paid $100 000 to a trust fund for Olson's family in return for information concerning the location of some of the victims' bodies. Parents of several of the victims successfully sued to have the money placed instead in a fund for the benefit of the victims' families. But the British Columbia Court of Appeal later decided that the parents had no claim to the money and that Olson's ex-wife would be allowed to keep it. In July 1986, the Supreme Court of Canada ruled that the families had no right to appeal the lower court ruling.

Olson was sentenced to 11 concurrent life terms, with no eligibility for parole for at least 25 years.

Peter Demeter

In July 1973, the body of Christine Demeter was found bludgeoned to death and lying in a pool of blood on the garage floor of the Mississauga, Ont. home she shared with her husband. Peter Demeter, who had been some 30 km from their home at the time of the killing, was accused of arranging his wife's murder.

According to the prosecution, Demeter had 2 motives: money and another woman. He held a million-dollar insurance policy on his wife's life; and, shortly before the murder, Demeter had spent a week in Montreal with his Austrian mistress, 29-year-old model Marina Hundt.

When the case came to trial in the fall of 1974, it attracted public attention because of the brutality of the murder, the accused's stature as a wealthy real estate developer, and the presence of "the other woman", Hundt, who had come to live with Demeter 5 months earlier and read their loveletters as evidence at the trial.

The case against Demeter was based mainly on the testimony of a witness who said Demeter had discussed Christine's murder with him, on tape recordings in which Demeter appeared to implicate himself in the killing, and on phone tap evidence which contradicted some of his statements. Demeter's behavior on the day of the murder, when he did not appear distraught at his wife's savage killing, was also an issue.

Several weeks into the proceedings the trial took a strange twist when police arrested a man named Joe Dinardo on an unrelated arson charge. Dinardo told police that Christine Demeter had been killed by a man named Laszlo Eper, who had been killed by police in a shootout earlier that year. Dinardo also claimed that Christine had hired Eper to kill her husband, but that he killed her instead after she changed her mind and called off the deal. The jury heard only part of Dinardo's story because the judge ruled that most of it was hearsay and inadmissible as evidence.

On December 5, 1974, the jury found Peter Demeter guilty of murder. He was sentenced to life imprisonment. He appealed

to the Ontario Court of Appeal, and again to the Supreme Court of Canada, but without success.

Demeter made headlines again in recent years. In 1985, while still in prison for his wife's murder, he was convicted twice for counselling 2 convicts to kidnap and murder the son of his cousin. In 1988, a jury found him guilty of conspiring to kidnap and murder the daughter of his former lawyer.

This latest conviction raises the number of life sentences received by Demeter to 5: one for his wife's murder, 2 for the 1985 counselling convictions and 2 from his 1988 trial. In handing down the latest sentences, Mr. Justice John O'Driscoll recommended that Demeter never be released on parole.

Henry Morgentaler

Despite openly performing numerous illegal abortions, Dr. Henry Morgentaler was never convicted of this offence by a jury, in a series of court battles spanning 3 provinces and more than a decade. Morgentaler's battle against Canada's abortion law eventually led to a Supreme Court decision that the law was unconstitutional.

Before Jan. 1988, Canada's Criminal Code permitted a doctor to perform an abortion only at approved hospitals and only when a hospital committee had certified that the abortion was necessary to protect the life or health of the pregnant woman. Morgentaler, who opposed the law, regularly performed abortions in private clinics and without the required committee certification.

Morgentaler was first tried for performing illegal abortions in Quebec in 1973. On Nov. 13 of that year he was acquitted by a jury. But the Quebec Court of Appeal overturned the jury's acquittal and substituted a conviction. The Supreme Court of Canada upheld that conviction, and Morgentaler was sentenced to 18 months in prison.

In 1975, while still serving his sentence, Morgentaler was tried on a 2d charge and was again acquitted by a jury. The acquittal was again appealed, but this time the Quebec Court of Appeal affirmed the jury's verdict.

Following Morgentaler's acquittal on the 2d charge, federal Justice Minister Ron Basford ordered that he be retried on the first charge, for which he was already serving a jail sentence. This peculiar order of events occurred because Parliament had responded to the Morgentaler case by amending the law on appeals so that it was no longer possible for an appeal court to substitute a conviction after an accused had been acquitted by a jury. Morgentaler's retrial took place in Sept. 1976, and once again he was acquitted by the jury.

On Oct. 29, 1976, he was ordered to stand trial on yet another charge of performing an illegal abortion. But the Quebec government intervened, and on Dec. 10 all remaining charges against Morgentaler were dropped.

The next round of Morgentaler's fight began in Winnipeg. On June 3, 1983, police raided Morgentaler's clinic and charged him and 7 employees. The Winnipeg clinic was raided again later that month and additional charges were laid.

Meanwhile, Morgentaler had opened a clinic in Toronto. On July 5, 1983, 3 weeks after the clinic opened, police raided the building and charged Morgentaler and 2 associates. The 3 were tried in Toronto and, on Nov. 8, 1984, were acquitted by a jury.

In Oct. 1985, the Ontario Court of Appeal overturned Morgentaler's acquittal and ordered a new trial. Morgentaler appealed this decision to the Supreme Court of Canada. On Jan. 28, 1988, the Supreme Court restored Morgentaler's acquittal on the ground that the abortion law was not valid. The court struck out the law because it violated a woman's constitutional right to life, liberty and security of the person as stated in section 7 of the Charter of Rights and Freedoms.

In addition to exonerating Morgentaler, the decision left Canada without any law regulating abortion until Parliament approves new legislation.

Jim Keegstra

Once the mayor of Eckville, Alta., and vice-president of Alberta's Social Credit party, high school teacher Jim Keegstra was convicted on July 20, 1985 of promoting hatred against an identifiable group (the Jewish people) and fined $5 000.

The case began when parents of students in Keegstra's class at Eckville High School complained that he was teaching pupils that there was an international Jewish conspiracy. School board officials warned Keegstra to stop, and eventually he was dismissed.

The R.C.M.P. conducted an investigation into allegations that Keegstra was promoting hatred, and this investigation led to the charge which was the basis of Keegstra's conviction.

Keegstra, who was mayor of Eckville from 1979 until 1983 when he was not re-elected, appealed the case. On June 6, 1988, the Alberta Court of Appeal quashed Keegstra's conviction. In the judgment, the 3 man court did not address the facts surrounding Keegstra's case but rather ruled that the law under which he was charged was not valid.

The court held that the Criminal Code section which prohibits promoting hatred against identifiable groups is a violation of the freedom of speech guarantees in the *Charter of Rights and Freedoms*. The court also said that the wording of the law failed to protect an individual's right to be convicted only when a crime is established beyond a reasonable doubt.

In Aug. 1988, the Alberta government announced that it will appeal the decision to the Supreme Court of Canada.

Ernst Zundel

The 1985 trial of Ernst Zundel demonstrated that freedom of speech in Canada is not an absolute right if the statements made are against the public interest.

Zundel, a citizen of West Germany who had lived in Canada for 20 years, published a pamphlet, "Did Six Million Really Die?", which claimed that the Nazi extermination of millions of Jews during World War II was a hoax. He was convicted of publishing a statement known to be false and that was likely to cause injury or mischief to a public interest.

Zundel's trial attracted widespread public attention largely because part of his defence consisted of disputing the historical validity of the Holocaust. This evidence was said to be relevant to the charge against him.

Zundel was sentenced to 15 months imprisonment plus 15 months probation and ordered not to publish anything about the Holocaust. But the Ontario Court of Appeal quashed the conviction in Jan. 1987, citing errors in law made by the judge during his trial.

The Ontario government attempted to have that decision overturned by the Supreme Court of Canada, which refused to hear an appeal. Ontario then ordered a new trial. At this 2d trial, the judge ruled that the Holocaust was a fact that the prosecution did not need to prove. In May 1988, Zundel was convicted again and this time sentenced to 9 months in jail.

Zundel is appealing the verdict from the 2d trial; it is likely that the case will eventually be heard in the Supreme Court of Canada where the issue will not be Zundel's guilt or innocence but rather the constitutional validity of the law under which he was charged.

Donald Marshall

Canada's most famous wrongful murder conviction gave rise to a spectacular commission of inquiry that began in September 1987 and which has subjected the entire Nova Scotia justice system to harshly critical scrutiny.

On the night of May 28, 1971, Donald Marshall Jr. and Sandy Seale, both 17, were drunk and on their way to a dance in Sydney, N.S. They never got there. On their way through a small mid-town park they encountered 2 men. It still is not clear exactly what took place, but shortly thereafter Sandy Seale lay on the ground dying from a knife wound to his stomach and Donald Marshall had suffered a gash to his arm. The man who inflicted the wounds was Roy Ebsary, an eccentric 59-year-old war veteran and former psychiatric patient who was accompanied by a friend, Jimmy MacNeil. Both men fled. Marshall, in a state of shock, also ran away looking for help. Sandy Seale died in hospital 20 hours later.

The Sydney police were under extreme pressure to solve the Seale murder because the previous murder in the city, a few years earlier, remained unsolved; it would be embarrassing for the police to be stymied again. When a preliminary investigation of Marshall's story produced no immediate results, the police began to focus on him as their prime suspect, even though Seale was one of Marshall's best friends and he had no apparent

motive for the killing. They found 3 local teenagers who had seen the 2 youths together earlier in the evening. After a hasty investigation, Marshall was charged with the murder.

The most damning evidence at the trial came from the 3 teenage witnesses who, years later, all complained that they had been bullied by police into giving false testimony. There was also some irrelevant evidence which should not have been admissible but was heard, such as a nurse's testimony about Marshall's tattoo that read "I hate cops". In spite of numerous loopholes in the case (such as no murder weapon, no autopsy report, no photographs of the crime scene, no convincing motive for the murder) and the accused's unwavering protests of innocence, Marshall was found guilty of second-degree murder and was sentenced to life in prison.

Within days of Marshall's conviction, Jimmy MacNeil, Ebsary's companion who was present at the murder, came forward and confessed to police. The police dismissed his story and, incredibly, Marshall's lawyer wasn't notified of this crucial new information, even though he was preparing an appeal. Without this and other new evidence that pointed to the real killer, Marshall's January 1972 appeal failed and he began serving his life sentence in Dorchester Penitentiary.

Over the next 10 years, Marshall was repeatedly denied day passes and parole consideration because of his refusal to admit responsibility for Seale's death. Finally, on August 26, 1981, Donald Marshall learned from a visiting friend that a man named Roy Ebsary had been bragging around town about Seale's killing. Marshall and his lawyer again attempted to initiate a new investigation; this time, they were able to provoke an RCMP review of the case.

On June 16, 1982, federal Justice Minister Jean Chrétien formally referred Marshall's case to the Nova Scotia Court of Appeals, observing that this was not "the first error the judicial system in Canada has been confronted with". On May 10, 1983, the Court of Appeals acquitted Marshall of the murder. Two days later, Ebsary was charged with second-degree murder. After a preliminary hearing, the court found that Ebsary, who confessed to the killing, had acted on impulse when the 2 youths asked for money. He was eventually tried and convicted of manslaughter. After numerous appeals, Ebsary, now 71, served a one-year sentence in 1985. He died in February 1988.

Following intense pressure from the public and from Marshall's lawyer, the Nova Scotia government reluctantly agreed to compensate Marshall and, in September 1984, he received $270 000 for his lost years. He also received $45 000 from a trust fund established by concerned citizens. After paying his lawyers, he was left with $215 000. The federal government refused to pay Marshall's legal bills.

The Inquiry

The Royal Commission on the Donald Marshall, Jr. Prosecution is investigating the incident that cost Marshall the first 11 years of his adult life and has spawned 4 trials, 2 appeals and a review by the Nova Scotia Supreme Court.

This commission, which began hearings in September 1987 and is expected to cost $7-million, has a 2-fold mandate. First, it will investigate why the justice system failed Marshall at his 1971 trial. This will involve numerous delicate questions such as whether racism played a role in the arrest and conviction (Marshall is a Micmac Indian and Sandy Seale was black), whether the police pressured teenage witnesses to lie, and whether the authorities withheld evidence that might have prevented Marshall's conviction. The commission's 2d task is to determine whether Marshall was treated fairly in his efforts to exonerate himself and later in his attempts to obtain compensation for his years in prison.

As of mid-1988 the inquiry had investigated charges of misconduct in all levels of the Nova Scotia justice system. It had probed the actions of the Sydney police department, the provincial attorney general's office and the Nova Scotia Court of Appeals. The inquiry may set dramatic legal precedents relating to cabinet confidentiality (Ronald Giffin, former Nova Scotia Attorney General, is appealing a ruling by the inquiry that he must disclose details of cabinet discussions regarding the Marshall case) and judicial immunity (the Supreme Court of Canada will decide whether the Commission has the power to compel 5 Nova Scotia Appeal Court justices to testify regarding their deliberations in Marshall's 1983 acquittal).

Although the injustice suffered by Donald Marshall was the incident which instigated this inquiry, the result of the hearings has put the entire Nova Scotia justice system on trial.

National Defence

Canadian Regular Armed Forces Strength

Source: Department of National Defence

Canada has an all-volunteer Armed Forces which, since 1968, has been a
single body composed of what had been a separate army, navy and air force.

	Navy	Army	Air Force	Total Armed Forces		Navy	Army	Air Force	Total Armed Forces
1914 ...	379	3 000	–	3 379	1944 ...	81 582	495 804	210 089	787 475
1915 ...	1 255	81 195	–	82 450	1945 ...	92 529	494 258	174 254	761 041
1916 ...	1 557	274 194	–	275 751	1950 ...	9 259	20 652	17 274	47 185
1917 ...	2 220	304 585	–	306 805	1951 ...	11 082	34 986	22 359	68 427
1918 ...	4 792	326 258	–	331 050	1952 ...	13 505	49 278	32 611	95 394
1919 ...	5 495	228 292	–	233 787	1953 ...	15 546	48 458	40 423	104 427
1920 ...	1 048	4 684	–	5 732	1955 ...	19 207	49 409	49 461	118 077
1925 ...	496	3 410	384	4 290	1960 ...	20 675	47 185	51 737	119 597
1930 ...	783	3 510	844	5 137	1965 ...	19 756	46 264	48 144	114 164
1935 ...	860	3 509	794	5 163	1970 ...	–	–	–	93 353
1939 ...	1 585	4 169	2 191	7 945	1975 ...	–	–	–	79 817
1940 ...	6 135	76 678	9 483	92 296	1980 ...	–	–	–	80 166
1941 ...	17 036	194 774	48 743	260 553	1985 ...	–	–	–	83 740
1942 ...	32 067	311 118	111 223	454 408	1987 ...	–	–	–	85 804
1943 ...	56 259	460 387	176 307	692 953	1988 ...	–	–	–	87 448

(1) As of Apr. 1.

Senior Canadian Military Personnel

(as of March 31, 1988)

Chief of the Defence Staff—Gen. Paul D. Manson
Vice-Chief of the Defence Staff—Lt. Gen. J.E. Vance
Deputy Chief of the Defence Staff—
  Vice-Admiral H.M.D. MacNeil
Maritime Command—Vice-Admiral C.M. Thomas
Mobile Command—Lt. Gen. James A. Fox

Air Command—Lt. Gen. Larry A. Ashley
Communications Command—Brig. Gen. W.H. Batt
Canadian Forces Europe—Maj. Gen. John L. Sharpe
Training Systems—Brig. Gen. A.C. Brown
Northern Region Headquarters—Brig. Gen. P.J. O'Donnell

Canadian Defence Spending

Source: Statistics Canada

(millions of dollars; fiscal years ending Mar. 31)

	Spending	% of Govt. spending		Spending	% of Govt. spending		Spending	% of Govt. spending
1910	6	7.4	1940	126	18.5	1965	1 582	19.5
1914	14	7.6	1941	730	58.4	1970	1 791	11.9
1915	72	29.3	1942	1 268	67.3	1975	2 361	10.7
1916	173	51.2	1943	2 563	58.4	1980	4 375	8.6
1917	312	62.3	1944	4 242	79.7	1981	5 049	8.7
1918	344	59.9	1945	4 000	76.2	1982	5 907	9.2
1919	439	63.1	1950	387	15.8	1983	7 041	9.7
1920	347	46.9	1951	787	27.1	1984	7 840	9.2
1925	13	3.7	1952	1 447	38.5	1985	8 767	9.3
1930	22	5.4	1953	1 959	42.2	1986	9 383	9.2
1935	14	2.9	1955	1 762	37.8	1987	9 955	9.3
1939	35	6.3	1960	1 537	24.5	1988[1]	10 340	n.a.

(1) Budget estimate.
n.a. not available.

Canadians Killed in Major Military Conflicts

Source: Dept. of Veteran's Affairs

Conflict	Date	Participants	Number killed
Northwest Rebellion[1]	1885	3 323	38
Boer War (South African War)	1899-1902	7 368[2]	89
World War I	1914-1918	626 636[3]	68 300[4]
World War II	1939-1945	1 086 343[5]	46 542[4]
Korean War	1950-1953	25 583	516[4]

(1) First battle in history to be fought entirely by Canadian troops. (2) Includes Canadians in the South African police force and 8 nursing sisters. (3) Includes 2 854 nursing sisters. (4) Based on the Book of Remembrance which includes all Canadians killed while serving in the Canadian Armed Forces and Allied Forces. (5) Includes 45 423 women.

Canadian Military Participation in Major Conflicts

The Boer War, 1899-1902

When war between Britain and the 2 Afrikaner republics of South Africa (Transvaal and the Orange Free State) began on Oct. 11, 1899, Prime Minister Wilfrid Laurier was reluctant to enter the conflict because public opinion on the issue was divided. French Canadians tended to be sympathetic to the Afrikaners while most English Canadians supported Britain. Reluctantly, Laurier sent 1 000 troops to aid Britain on Oct. 30, 1899. Another 6 300 volunteers followed later.

Paardeberg

At the battle of Paardeberg, Feb. 27, 1900, 2 Maritime companies failed to observe an order to retreat during an Afrikaner counter-attack. Soon afterwards, 4 000 exhausted Afrikaners surrendered. Thirty-one Canadians were killed in the battle.

Leliefontein

On Nov. 7, 1900, while covering the retreat of the British infantry near Leliefontein, 90 men of the Royal Canadian Dragoons were surrounded by several hundred Boer horsemen. In the ensuing battle 3 Canadians lost their lives; the British managed to gain safe ground.

The First World War, 1914-1918

Canada officially entered the First World War on Aug. 4, 1914 when Britain declared war on Germany and Austro-Hungary. Britain's declaration automatically involved Canada as a member of the Empire. By Oct. 3, 1914, the first contingent of Canadian troops, mostly volunteers, had sailed for England.

Second Battle of Ypres

On Apr. 22, 1915, French and Algerian troops were forced to retreat from their positions near Ypres, Belgium, after the Germans unleashed a new, deadly weapon: chlorine gas. However, the 1st Canadian Division, in its first major battle of the war, held on under heavy fire and gas attacks. After a week and 6 000 Canadian casualties, the German advance was stopped. Then, on May 8, 1915, the Germans launched another major attack at nearby Frezenberg Ridge. The Princess Patricia's Canadian Light Infantry managed to halt the offensive, suffering 392 casualties out of 546 men.

The Battle of the Somme

On the 1st day of the Battle of the Somme, July 1, 1916, the 1st Newfoundland Regiment was annihilated. This marked the beginning of 5 months of futile and bloody fighting. By the time the battle was called off in Nov., the Allies had lost 623 907 troops, of which 24 713 were Canadians and Newfoundlanders. Only 13 km of mud-filled trenches had been gained.

Vimy Ridge

On Easter weekend, 1917, Canada's 4 divisions captured Vimy Ridge. Following this victory, the British commander, Lt. Gen. Sir Julian Byng, was promoted and replaced by a Canadian, Lt. Gen. Sir Arthur Currie, who successfully repelled German counter-attacks on the strategically important

Passchendaele

In Oct., 1917, Currie was called upon to complete a failed British offensive at Passchendaele, Belgium. After 2 weeks of fighting, his Canadian troops seized Passchendaele on Nov. 7. As Currie had feared, Canadian losses were high: of some 20 000 initial troops, 15 654 were either killed or wounded.

Amiens

Using airplanes, tanks, artillery, infantry and cavalry, Canadian and Australian troops led a major assault on German positions near Amiens, France on Aug. 8, 1918 (later known as the "black day of the German Army"). The attack and ensuing victories initiated the "100 days" of the German retreat leading to the Nov. 11, 1918 armistice.

The Second World War, 1939-1945

After approval in Parliament, Canada declared war on Germany, Sept. 10, 1939, 9 days after Germany's invasion of Poland and 7 days after Britain and France entered the conflict.

Canadian forces spent the first years of the war training in England. A few fought in the Battle of Britain, July-Oct., 1940, the first battle waged entirely in the air. Others, acting as spies behind enemy lines in France, supplied vital information on German activities and formed networks of resistance groups.

As the war progressed, thousands of Canadian airmen flew nighttime raids over Germany; approximately 10 000 never returned. Others provided naval support for the Atlantic defence and supply convoys. Of over one million Canadian troops, 42 042 were killed; another 4 500 Canadians died while serving with other Allied forces.

Hong Kong

On Dec. 18, 1941, the Royal Rifles of Canada and the Winnipeg Grenadiers were overpowered by Japanese forces on Hong Kong. Of the 1 975 Canadians, 557 were killed or died in prison camps. The remaining prisoners were not liberated until the summer of 1945.

Dieppe

In the early morning of Aug. 19, 1942, a major offensive against the Germans, Operation Jubilee, was launched. In this test-run raid on the French coastal town of Dieppe, the Allies intended to march inland, disrupt German defences and retreat back to the beaches for evacuation. The raid was a major disaster. The 2nd Canadian Infantry Division, landing at Puys and Pourville, failed to make any headway. Half the Canadian troops were evacuated, 900 were killed and 1 300 taken prisoner.

Sicily

The 1st Canadian Division took part in the Allied invasion of Sicily in July 1943. Canadian troops, moving up mainland Italy, were instrumental in breaking through major German defence lines. In 1944, these troops were withdrawn from

Italy to aid in the northwest European campaign, following the Normandy invasion.

D-Day

On June 6, 1944 (D-Day), the 3rd Canadian Infantry Division and the 2nd Canadian Armoured Brigade took part in the Allied invasion of Normandy, the largest amphibious assault in history. Canadian troops advanced 9 km the first day, leading the breakout from the Normandy beaches. In order for the Americans to push east into Germany, the First Canadian Army drove north towards Holland to head off the infamous German Panzer Tank Division. By the following spring, the Canadians had liberated Holland and were marching towards Germany. On May 5, 1945, Germany surrendered.

The Korean War, 1950-1953

On June 25, 1950, the United Nations was informed that North Korea had attacked South Korea. On July 7, the UN Security Council, with its Soviet member absent, accepted a U.S. proposal for a UN multilateral force to aid South Korea. Initially, Canada contributed 3 destroyers and an air-transport squadron, but later sent a Canadian Army unit.

Two months after arriving, the Princess Patricia's Canadian Light Infantry encountered heavy fighting along the Kap'Yong River valley on the night of Apr. 24, 1951. Though 10 were killed and 23 wounded, the Canadians, with the Australians, managed to halt the offensive, and were awarded Distinguished Unit Citations from the U.S. government.

Armed Forces Personnel, 1985

Source: U.S. Arms Control and Disarmament Agency, *World Military Expenditures and Arms Transfers*

Armed forces refer to active-duty military personnel, including paramilitary forces where those forces resemble regular units in their organization, equipment, training or mission. Reserve forces are not included.

	Number (000s)	Rate[1]		Number (000s)	Rate[1]		Number (000s)	Rate[1]
Argentina	129	4.3	Germany, West	495	8.1	Nigeria	144	1.4
Brazil	496	3.5	Greece	206	20.7	Pakistan	644	6.5
Bulgaria	177	19.8	India	1 515	2.0	Poland	432	11.6
Canada	84	3.3	Indonesia	281	1.6	Romania	244	10.7
Chile	124	10.3	Iran	345	7.3	Soviet Union	4 500	16.1
China	4 100	3.9	Iraq	788	49.9	Syria	402	38.8
Cuba	297	29.5	Israel	195	47.8	Taiwan	440	22.8
Czechoslovakia	214	13.8	Italy	531	9.3	Thailand	270	5.2
Egypt	466	9.5	Japan	241	2.0	Turkey	825	16.3
El Salvador	48	9.6	Korea, North	784	38.5	United Kingdom	335	5.9
France	563	10.2	Korea, South	600	14.6	United States	2 289	9.6
Germany, East	240	14.4	Nicaragua	74	23.4	Vietnam	1 000	16.5

(1) Rate per 1 000 population.

Leading Arms Exporting Countries, 1985

Source: U.S. Arms Control and Disarmament Agency, *World Military Expenditures and Arms Transfers, 1987*

(millions of dollars)

Soviet Union	$15 300	Germany, East	$550
United States	12 300	Spain	500
France	4 600	Bulgaria	470
Czechoslovakia	1 400	Romania	430
Poland	1 100	Yugoslavia	400
Italy	975	Korea, North	380
United Kingdom	825	Brazil	330
Germany, West	625		
China	575		

Leading Arms Importing Countries, 1985

(millions of dollars)

Iraq	$4 000	Soviet Union	$1 100
Saudi Arabia	3 700	Vietnam	1 100
India	2 300	Israel	1 000
Cuba	2 100	Japan	1 000
Germany, West	1 700	Australia	925
Iran	1 700	Germany, East	825
Libya	1 600	Ethiopia	800
Syria	1 500		
Egypt	1 400		

Nuclear Arms Treaties and Negotiations: An Historical Overview

Aug. 4, 1963—Nuclear Test Ban Treaty, signed in Moscow by the U.S., USSR, and Great Britain, prohibited testing of nuclear weapons in space, above ground, and under water.

Jan. 1967—Outer Space Treaty banned the introduction of nuclear weapons into space.

1968—Non-proliferation of Nuclear Weapons Treaty, with U.S., USSR, and Great Britain as major signers, limited the spread of military nuclear technology by agreement not to assist nonnuclear nations in getting or making nuclear weapons.

May 26, 1972—SALT I (Strategic Arms Limitations Talks) agreement, in negotiation since Nov. 17, 1969, signed in Moscow by U.S. and USSR. In the area of defensive nuclear weapons, the treaty limited antiballistic missiles to 2 sites of 100 antiballistic missile launchers in each country (amended in 1974 to one site in each country). The treaty also imposed a 5-year freeze on testing and deployment of intercontinental ballistic missiles and submarine-launched ballistic missiles. An interim short-term agreement putting a ceiling on numbers of offensive nuclear weapons was also signed. SALT I was in effect until Oct. 3, 1977.

July 3, 1974—Protocol on antiballistic missile systems and a treaty and protocol on limiting underground testing of nuclear weapons was signed by U.S. and USSR in Moscow.

Nov. 24, 1974—Vladivostok Agreement announced establishing the framework for a more comprehensive agreement on offensive nuclear arms, setting the guidelines of a second SALT treaty.

Sept. 1977—U.S. and USSR agreed to continue to abide by SALT I, despite its expiration date.

June 18, 1979—SALT II, signed in Vienna by the U.S. and USSR, constrained offensive nuclear weapons, limiting each side to 2 400 missile launchers and heavy bombers with that ceiling to apply until Jan. 1, 1985. The treaty also set a combined total of 1 320 ICBMs and SLBMs with multiple warheads on each side. Although approved by the U.S. Senate Foreign Relations Committee, the treaty never reached the Senate floor because Pres. Jimmy Carter withdrew his support for the treaty following the December 1979 invasion of Afghanistan by Soviet troops.

Nov. 18, 1981—U.S. Pres. Ronald Reagan proposed his controversial "zero option" to cancel deployment of new U.S. intermediate-range missiles in Western Europe in return for Soviet dismantling of comparable forces (600 SS-20, SS-4, and SS-5 missiles already stationed in the European part of its territory).

Nov. 30, 1981—Geneva talks on limiting intermediate nuclear forces based in and around Europe began.

May 9, 1982—U.S. Pres. Ronald Reagan proposed 2-step plan for strategic arms reductions and announced that he had proposed to the USSR that START (Strategic Arms Reduction Talks) begin in June.

May 18, 1982—Soviet Pres. Leonid Brezhnev rejected Reagan's plan as one-sided, but responded positively to the call for arms reduction talks.

June 29, 1982—START (Strategic Arms Reduction Talks) began in Geneva.

1985-1987—Disarmament talks between the U.S. and the USSR began in Geneva, Switzerland on March 12, 1985.

Dec. 8, 1987—I.N.F. (Intermediate-Range Nuclear Forces) Treaty signed in Washington, D.C. by USSR leader Mikhail Gorbachev and U.S. Pres. Ronald Reagan eliminating all medium- and shorter-range nuclear missiles; ratified with conditions by U.S. Senate on May 27, 1988.

Nuclear Weapon Tests

Source: Natural Resources Defense Council

(Known nuclear tests, 1945-1987)

	United States	Soviet Union	Britain	France	China		United States	Soviet Union	Britain	France	China
1945-49	8	1	0	0	0	1980-87	125	157	11	70	6
1950-59[1]	188	89	21	0	0	**Total**	**827**	**626**	**41**	**157**	**31**
1960-69[2]	344	168	4	30	10						
1970-79[3]	162	198	5	57	5						

(1) Stockholm International Peace Research Institute and the Swedith National Defense Research Institute report 18 additional Soviet tests conducted between 1956 and 1958. (2) Since 1962, British underground nuclear tests have been conducted jointly with the United States in Nevada. (3) French Ministry of Defense reports 16 additional Soviet tests conducted between 1963 and 1977. India reported one test in 1974.

U.S. Military Personnel Strengths—Worldwide

(As of March 31, 1987)

Source: U.S. Department of Defense

U.S. Territories & Special Locations		Netherlands	3 130	British Indian Ocean Terr.	1 280
Continental U.S.	1 340 674	Norway	219	Egypt	1 368
Alaska	21 510	Portugal	1 645	Saudi Arabia	439
Hawaii	46 900	Spain	9 027	Afloat	10 369
Guam	8 970	Turkey	4 964	**Total¹**	**14 357**
Johnston Atoll	142	United Kingdom	29 669	**Other Western Hemisphere**	
Puerto Rico	3 652	Afloat	19 020	Bermuda	1 139
Transients	47 703	**Total¹**	**343 423**	Canada	540
Afloat	190 622	**East Asia & Pacific**		Cuba (Guantanamo)	2 497
Total¹	**1 660 306**	Australia	753	Honduras	1 072
Western & Southern Europe		Japan	47 204	Panama	10 386
		Philippines	16 290	Afloat	2 139
Belgium	3 418	Rep. of Korea	43 886	**Total¹**	**18 524**
W. Germany	250 168	Thailand	115	**Total Worldwide**	**2 167 723**
Greece	3 490	Afloat	22 637	Ashore	1 922 936
Greenland	305	**Total¹**	**131 113**	Afloat	244 787
Iceland	3 161	**Africa, Near East & South Asia**			
Italy	14 911	Bahrain	120		

(1) Area totals include countries with less than 100 assigned U.S. military members.

Religious Information

Estimated Religious Population of the World

Source: The 1988 Encyclopaedia Britannica Book of the Year

Religionists	Africa	East Asia	Europe	Latin America	Northern America	Oceania	South Asia	U.S.S.R.	World	%
Christians	271 035 700	78 100 000	413 920 700	399 554 500	232 048 400	21 287 100	129 076 700	103 373 400	1,644 396 500	32.9
Roman Cath.	102 522 200	9 204 000	257 155 000	371 863 600	91 209 800	7 434 000	81 694 100	5 111 900	926 194 600	18.5
Protestants	71 883 000	32 100 000	76 652 000	13 960 000	94 965 500	7 510 000	26 142 100	8 803 800	332 016 400	6.6
Orthodox	24 746 700	81 000	35 606 100	570 000	5 910 000	507 400	3 200 000	89 442 300	160 063 500	3.2
Anglicans	22 389 900	334 000	32 886 200	1 210 000	7 511 000	5 350 000	290 000	400	69 971 500	1.4
Other	49 493 900	36 381 000	11 621 400	7 950 900	32 452 100	485 700	17 750 500	15 000	156 150 500	3.1
Moslems	245 110 500	23 795 000	8 901 500	645 000	2 682 600	96 000	547 350 500	31 807 200	860 388 300	17.2
Nonreligious	1 495 000	641 756 600	50 923 940	13 237 000	21 047 700	2 884 400	20 651 100	84 332 030	836 327 770	16.7
Hindus	1 410 000	10 100	590 000	660 000	810 000	295 000	651 918 900	1 200	655 695 200	13.1
Buddhists	12 800	154 796 300	216 000	490 000	190 000	16 000	153 585 000	320 000	309 626 100	6.2
Atheists	240 000	136 886 000	17 803 000	2 538 000	1 073 000	512 000	5 300 000	60 774 500	225 126 500	4.5
Chinese folk religionists	9 500	179 103 100	49 000	60 000	110 000	16 000	8 169 400	100	187 517 100	3.7
New Religionists	13 000	42 217 200	34 000	370 000	1 075 600	6 100	66 990 000	200	110 706 100	2.2
Tribal religionists	68 219 450	730 000	100	1 160 000	60 000	81 000	24 508 200	0	94 758 750	1.9
Jews	257 000	1 800	1 483 600	990 000	8 084 000	86 000	4 050 000	3 123 000	18 075 400	0.4
Sikhs	26 000	1 000	215 000	6 000	9 500	6 600	16 340 000	50	16 604 150	0.3
Shamanists	1 000	12 500 000	400	400	200	200	10 000	250 000	12 762 200	0.2
Confucians	500	5 900 000	1 000	500	10 000	200	2 000	200	5 914 400	0.1
Baha'is	1 265 000	48 400	70 500	570 000	310 000	59 000	2 300 000	5 000	4 627 900	0.1
Jains	47 500	500	9 900	2 000	2 000	900	3 400 000	20	3 462 820	0.1
Shintoists	50	3 400 000	360	800	1 000	500	200	100	3 403 010	0.1
Other religionists	65 000	62 000	310 000	6 768 800	750 000	25 000	230 000	6 000	8 216 800	0.2
World Pop.	589 208 000	1,279 308 000	494 529 000	423 053 000	268 264 000	25 372 000	1,633 882 000	283 993 000	4,997 609 000	100.0

Canadian Population by Religious Denominations

Source: Censuses of Canada

(thousands of persons)

	1931	%	1941	%	1951	%	1961	%	1971	%	1981	%
Total population ..	10 377	100.0	11 507	100.0	14 009	100.0	18 238	100.0	21 568	100.0	24 083	100.0
Adventist	16	0.2	18	0.2	21	0.1	26	0.1	29	0.1	42	0.2
Anglican	1 639	15.8	1 754	15.2	2 061	14.7	2 409	13.2	2 543	11.8	2 436	10.1
Bahai	n.a.	n.a.	n.a.	n.a.	n.a.	n.a.	n.a.	n.a.	n.a.	n.a.	8	...
Baptist	444	4.3	484	4.2	520	3.7	594	3.3	667	3.1	697	2.9
Buddhist	16	0.2	16	0.1	8	0.1	12	0.1	16	0.1	52	0.2
Christian and Missionary Alliance	4	...	4	...	6	...	18	0.1	24	0.1	34	0.1
Christian Reformed[1]	n.a.	n.a.	n.a.	n.a.	n.a.	n.a.	62	0.3	83	0.4	77	0.3
Churches of Christ, Disciples	16	0.2	21	0.2	15	0.1	20	0.1	16	0.1	15	0.1
Confucian	24	0.2	22	0.2	6	...	5	...	2	...	n.a.	n.a.
Doukhobor	15	0.1	17	0.1	13	0.1	13	0.1	9	...	7	...
Free Methodist	8	0.1	9	0.1	9	0.1	14	0.1	19	0.1	12	0.1
Greek Orthodox ...	103	1.0	140	1.2	172	1.2	240	1.3	317	1.5	315	1.3
Hindu	n.a.	n.a.	n.a.	n.a.	n.a.	n.a.	n.a.	n.a.	n.a.	n.a.	70	0.3
Hutterite[2]	n.a.	n.a.	n.a.	n.a.	n.a.	n.a.	n.a.	n.a.	14	0.1	17	0.1
Islam	n.a.	n.a.	n.a.	n.a.	n.a.	n.a.	n.a.	n.a.	n.a.	n.a.	98	0.4
Jehovah's Witnesses	14	0.1	7	0.1	35	0.2	68	0.4	175	0.8	143	0.6
Jewish	156	1.5	169	1.5	205	1.5	254	1.4	276	1.3	296	1.2
Latter Day Saints ..	n.a.	n.a.	n.a.	n.a.	n.a.	n.a.	n.a.	n.a.	n.a.	n.a.	90	0.4
Lutheran	395	3.8	402	3.5	445	3.2	663	3.6	716	3.3	703	2.9
Mennonite[3]	89	0.9	112	1.0	126	0.9	152	0.8	168	0.8	189	0.8
Mormon	22	0.2	25	0.2	33	0.2	50	0.3	67	0.3	n.a.	n.a.

	1931	%	1941	%	1951	%	1961	%	1971	%	1981	%
Pentecostal	26	0.3	58	0.5	95	0.7	144	0.8	220	1.0	339	1.4
Presbyterian	872	8.4	831	7.2	782	5.6	819	4.5	872	4.0	812	3.4
Roman Catholic . . .	4 103	39.5	4 806	41.8	6 069	43.3	8 343	45.7	9 975	46.2	11 210	46.5
Salvation Army	31	0.3	34	0.3	70	0.5	92	0.5	120	0.6	125	0.5
Sikh	n.a.	n.a.	n.a.	n.a.	n.a.	n.a.	n.a.	n.a.	n.a.	n.a.	68	0.3
Ukrainian Catholic[4] .	187	1.8	186	1.6	191	1.4	190	1.0	228	1.1	191	0.8
Unitarian	4	. . .	6	0.1	4	. . .	15	0.1	21	0.1	15	0.1
United Church[5]	2 021	19.5	2 209	19.2	2 867	20.5	3 664	20.1	3 769	17.5	3 758	15.6
No religion	21	0.2	19	0.2	60	0.4	95	0.5	930	4.3	1 752	7.3

(1) Included with United Church 1931-51. (2) Included with Mennonite 1931-61. (3) Includes Hutterite 1931-61. (4) Includes Greek Catholic 1931-71. (5) Includes Christian Reformed 1931-1951.
. . . = too small to be included; n.a. not available

Religious Denominations by Province, 1981

Source: Census of Canada

Religion	Canada	Nfld	PEI	NS	NB	Que	Ont	Man	Sask	Alta	BC	Yukon and NWT
Total population	24 083 495	563 750	121 225	839 800	689 370	6 369 070	8 534 265	1 013 705	956 440	2 213 650	2 713 615	68 615
Catholic	11 402 605	204 470	56 450	310 725	371 245	5 618 360	3 036 245	318 815	310 005	613 930	538 430	23 925
Roman Catholic	11 210 390	204 430	56 415	310 140	371 100	5 609 685	2 986 170	269 070	279 840	573 495	526 355	23 680
Ukrainian Catholic . .	190 590	40	25	565	135	8 615	49 310	49 350	30 090	40 280	11 940	240
Eastern non-Christian .	305 890	675	230	3 030	1 175	34 330	137 115	7 790	4 190	38 195	78 640	530
Baha'i	7 960	40	30	415	100	645	3 250	165	460	780	1 815	265
Buddhist	51 955	135	50	420	240	12 000	18 595	2 010	985	6 205	11 190	125
Hindu	69 500	315	75	1 025	470	6 695	41 660	1 750	1 155	7 360	8 975	20
Islam	98 160	95	65	795	315	12 120	52 110	1 920	1 125	16 865	12 715	35
Sikh	67 710	65	–	275	50	1 785	16 645	1 685	220	5 985	40 940	60
Eastern Orthodox	361 560	65	55	2 345	575	73 275	167 320	21 135	22 495	49 275	24 640	385
Armenian Orthodox . . .	9 430	–	–	15	–	4 625	4 360	–	–	65	360	–
Greek Orthodox	314 875	50	40	2 020	535	62 250	140 610	19 785	21 065	46 505	21 640	360
Serbian Orthodox	5 410	–	–	–	20	330	4 405	95	30	180	340	5
Ukrainian Orthodox . . .	7 200	–	–	20	–	475	3 225	930	805	1 115	620	5
Jewish	296 425	220	80	2 010	845	102 355	148 255	15 670	1 580	10 650	14 680	85
Protestant	9 914 580	352 695	61 170	487 255	295 785	407 070	4 418 960	573 420	557 315	1 240 000	1 484 925	35 985
Adventist	41 605	775	100	1 375	985	2 420	16 265	1 075	2 210	7 320	9 015	80
Anglican	2 436 375	153 530	6 810	131 130	66 260	132 115	1 164 315	108 220	77 725	202 265	374 055	19 960
Associated Gospel . . .	7 895	–	–	65	25	130	5 755	105	975	565	280	–
Baptist	696 850	1 200	6 055	101 590	88 520	25 050	288 465	19 260	16 785	66 370	81 850	1 695
Brethren in Christ	22 260	360	230	425	240	565	15 540	490	845	1 040	2 525	10
Christian and Missionary Alliance . .	33 895	–	–	70	55	230	7 220	2 015	6 110	10 090	7 975	135
Churches of Christ, Disciples	15 350	5	845	1 035	715	185	6 545	925	1 525	2 440	1 115	30
Church of God	10 035	5	30	55	25	470	3 435	440	1 000	3 070	1 505	–
Church of Nazarene . .	13 360	115	715	745	560	120	3 760	280	860	4 540	1 610	65
Doukhobors	6 700	–	–	5	–	45	135	165	1 065	215	5 065	5
Evangelical Free Church	5 780	–	–	20	–	60	335	395	1 935	2 905	–
Hutterites	16 530	–	–	–	–	5	105	5 940	2 980	7 395	100	–
Jehovah's Witnesses	143 480	2 015	430	4 920	3 530	19 850	48 465	6 425	9 815	16 195	31 515	320
Latter Day Saints	89 870	200	140	1 570	810	2 150	20 095	1 840	3 080	42 980	16 740	270
Lutheran	702 905	455	205	12 310	1 810	17 660	254 180	58 830	88 785	144 680	122 395	1 575
Mennonite	189 370	90	5	220	180	1 075	46 485	63 490	26 265	20 540	30 895	125
Methodist	47 840	55	60	300	135	1 615	25 360	2 085	4 425	7 360	6 340	95
Missionary Church	7 940	15	25	–	–	5	6 000	90	150	1 395	260	10
Pentecostal	338 785	37 450	1 310	10 695	21 450	17 420	119 530	15 830	16 435	41 485	55 095	2 090
Plymouth Brethren	8 060	35	155	225	40	895	3 275	610	315	550	1 960	5
Presbyterian	812 105	2 700	12 620	38 280	12 070	34 620	517 020	23 910	16 070	63 890	89 810	1 115
Reformed, Canadian	10 560	–	20	–	10	–	6 215	495	–	1 685	2 140	–
Reformed, Christian	77 370	5	220	885	80	280	50 670	1 390	465	13 460	9 890	20
Salvation Army	125 085	45 115	315	4 900	1 960	1 440	45 065	3 695	3 050	7 020	12 270	250
Unitarian	14 505	35	45	325	285	1 330	6 120	800	325	1 210	3 960	65
United Church	3 758 015	104 835	29 645	169 605	87 460	126 275	1 655 555	240 400	263 375	525 480	548 360	7 035
Wesleyan	7 770	–	10	1 220	4 265	185	1 995	–	–	40	50	–
Worldwide Church of God	8 130	160	10	235	140	690	1 780	620	1 125	1 825	1 525	20

– = zero or too few to be included.

Major Christian Denominations:

Italics indicate that area which, generally speaking, most

Denomination	Origins	Organization	Authority	Special rites
Anglicans	Henry VIII separated English Catholic Church from Rome, 1534, for political reasons.	*Bishops, in apostolic succession, are elected by diocesan representatives; part of Anglican Communion, symbolically headed by Archbishop of Canterbury.*	Scripture as interpreted by tradition, esp. *39 Articles* (1563); not dogmatic. Tri-annual convention of bishops, priests, and laymen.	Infant baptism, Holy Communion, others. Sacrament is symbolic, but has real spiritual effect.
Baptists	In radical Reformation objections to infant baptism, demands for church-state separation; John Smyth, English Separatist in 1609; Roger Williams, 1638, Providence, R.I.	Congregational, *i.e.,* each local church is autonomous.	Scripture; some Baptists, particularly in the South, interpret the Bible literally.	Baptism, after about age 12, by total immersion; Lord's Supper.
Church of Christ (Disciples)	Among evangelical Presbyterians in Ky. (1804) and Penn. (1809), in distress over Protestant factionalism and decline of fervor. Organized 1832.	Congregational.	*"Where the Scriptures speak, we speak; where the Scriptures are silent, we are silent."*	Adult baptism, Lord's Supper (weekly).
Lutherans	Martin Luther in Wittenberg, Germany, 1517, objected to Catholic doctrine of salvation by merit and sale of indulgences; break complete by 1519.	Varies from congregational to episcopal.	*Scripture, and tradition as spelled out in Augsburg Confession (1530) and other creeds. These confessions of faith are binding although interpretations vary.*	Infant baptism, Lord's Supper. Christ's true body and blood present "in, with, and under the bread and wine."
Methodists	Rev. John Wesley began movement, 1738, within Church of England.	Conference and superintendent system. *In United Methodist Church, general superintendents are bishops—not a priestly order, only an office—who are elected for life.*	Scripture as interpreted by tradition, reason, and experience.	Baptism of infants or adults, Lord's Supper commanded. Other rites, inc. marriage, ordination, solemnize personal commitments.
Mormons	In visions of the Angel Moroni by Joseph Smith, 1827, in New York, in which he received a new revelation on golden tablets: *The Book of Mormon.*	Theocratic; all male adults are in priesthood which culminates in Council of 12 Apostles and 1st Presidency (1st President, 2 counselors).	*The Bible, Book of Mormon and other revelations to Smith, and certain pronouncements of the 1st Presidency.*	Adult baptism, laying on of hands (which confers the gift of the Holy Spirit), Lord's Supper. Temple rites: baptism for the dead, marriage for eternity, others.
Orthodox	Original Christian proselytizing in 1st century; broke with Rome, 1054, after centuries of doctrinal disputes and diverging traditions.	Synods of bishops in autonomous, usually national, churches elect a patriarch, archbishop or metropolitan. These men, as a group, are the heads of the church.	Scripture, tradition, and the first 7 church councils up to Nicaea II in 787. Bishops in council have authority in doctrine and policy.	Seven sacraments: infant baptism and anointing, Eucharist (both bread and wine), ordination, penance, anointing of the sick, marriage.
Pentecostal	In Topeka, Kansas (1901), and Los Angeles (1906) in reaction to loss of evangelical fervor among Methodists and other denominations.	Originally a movement, not a formal organization, Pentecostalism now has a variety of organized forms and continues also as a movement.	Scripture, individual charismatic leaders, the teachings of the Holy Spirit.	*Spirit baptism, esp. as shown in "speaking in tongues"; healing and sometimes exorcism; adult baptism, Lord's Supper.*
Presbyterians	In Calvinist Reformation in 1500s; differed with Lutherans over sacraments, church government. John Knox founded Scotch Presbyterian church about 1560.	*Highly structured representational system of ministers and laypersons (presbyters) in local, regional and national bodies. (synods).*	Scripture.	Infant baptism, Lord's Supper; bread and wine symbolize Christ's spiritual presence.
Roman Catholics	Traditionally, by Jesus who named St. Peter the 1st Vicar; historically, in early Christian proselytizing and the conversion of imperial Rome in the 4th century.	Hierarchy with supreme power vested in Pope elected by cardinals. Councils of Bishops advise on matters of doctrine and policy.	*The Pope, when speaking for the whole church in matters of faith and morals, and tradition, which is partly recorded in scripture and expressed in church councils.*	Seven sacraments: baptism, contrition and penance, confirmation, Eucharist, marriage, ordination, and anointing of the sick (unction).
United Church of Christ	*By ecumenical union, 1957, of Congregationalists and Evangelical & Reformed, representing both Calvinist and Lutheran traditions.*	Congregational; a General Synod, representative of all congregations, sets general policy.	Scripture.	Infant baptism, Lord's Supper.

How Do They Differ?

distinguishes that denomination from any other.

Practice	Ethics	Doctrine	Other	Denomination
Formal, based on *Book of Common Prayer* (1549); services range from austerely simple to highly elaborate.	Tolerant; sometimes permissive; some social action programs.	*Apostles' Creed* is basic; otherwise, considerable variation ranges from rationalist and liberal to acceptance of most Roman Catholic dogma.	Strongly ecumenical, holding talks with all other branches of Christendom.	Anglicans
Worship style varies from staid to evangelistic. Extensive missionary activity.	Usually opposed to alcohol and tobacco; sometimes tends toward a perfectionist ethical standard.	*No creed; true church is of believers only, who are all equal.*	Since no authority can stand between the believer and God, the Baptists are strong supporters of church-state separation.	Baptists
Tries to avoid any rite or doctrine not explicitly part of the 1st century church. Some congregations may reject instrumental music.	Some tendency toward perfectionism; increasing interest in social action programs.	Simple New Testament faith; avoids any elaboration not firmly based on Scripture.	Highly tolerant in doctrinal and religious matters; strongly supportive of scholarly education.	Church of Christ (Disciples)
Relatively simple formal liturgy with emphasis on the sermon.	Generally, conservative in personal and social ethics; doctrine of "2 kingdoms" (worldly and holy) supports conservatism in secular affairs.	Salvation by faith alone through grace. Lutheranism has made major contributions to Protestant theology.	Though still somewhat divided along ethnic lines (German, Swede, etc.), main divisions are between funamentalists and liberals.	Lutherans
Worship style varies widely by denomination, local church, geography.	Originally pietist and perfectionist; always strong social activist elements	No distinctive theological development; 25 Articles abriged from Church of England's 39 not binding.	In 1968, United Methodist Church joined pioneer English- and German-speaking groups. UMs leaders in ecumenical movement.	Methodists
Staid service with hymns, sermon. Secret temple ceremonies may be more elaborate. Strong missionary activity.	Temperance; strict tithing. Combine a strong work ethic with communal self-reliance.	God is a material being; he created the universe out of pre-existing matter; all persons can be saved and many will become divine. Most other beliefs are traditionally Christian.	Mormons regard mainline churches as apostate, corrupt. Reorganized Church (founded 1860) rejects most Mormon doctrine and practice except Book of Mormon.	Mormons
Elaborate liturgy, usually in the vernacular, though extremely traditional. The liturgy is the essence of Orthodoxy. Veneration of icons.	Tolerant; very little social action; divorce, remarriage permitted in some cases. Priests need not be celibate; bishops are.	Emphasis on Christ's resurrection, rather than crucifixion; the Holy Spirit proceeds from God the Father only.	Orthodox Church in America, originally under Patriarch of Moscow, was granted autonomy in 1970. Greek Orthodox do not recognize this autonomy.	Orthodox
Loosely structured service with rousing hymns and sermons, culminating in spirit baptism.	Usually, emphasis on perfectionism with varying degrees of tolerance.	Simple traditional beliefs, usually Protestant, with emphasis on the immediate presence of God in the Holy Spirit	Once confined to lower-class "holy rollers," Pentecostalism now appears in mainline churches and has established middle-class congregations.	Pentecostal
A simple, sober service in which the sermon is central.	Traditionally, a tendency toward strictness with firm church- and self-discipline; otherwise tolerant.	Emphasizes the sovereignty and justice of God; no longer doctrinaire.	While traces of belief in predestination (that God has foreordained salvation for the "elect") remain, this idea is no longer a central element in Presbyterianism.	Presbyterians
Relatively elaborate ritual; wide variety of public and private rites, eg., rosary recitation, processions, novenas.	Theoretically very strict; tolerant in practice on most issues. Divorce and remarriage not accepted. Celibate clergy, except in Eastern rite.	Highly elaborated. Salvation by merit gained through faith. Unusual development of doctrines surrounding Mary. Dogmatic.	Roman Catholicism is presently in a period of relatively rapid change as a result of Vatican Councils I and II.	Roman Catholics
Usually simple services with emphasis on the sermon.	Tolerant; some social action emphasis.	Standard Protestant; *Statement of Faith* (1959) is not binding.	The 2 main churches in the 1957 union represented earlier unions with small groups of almost every Protestant denomination.	United Church of Christ

The Major World Religions

Buddhism

Founded: About 525 BC, reportedly near Benares, India.

Founder: Gautama Siddhartha (ca. 563-480), the Buddha, who achieved enlightenment through intense meditation.

Sacred Texts: The *Tripitaka*, a collection of the Buddha's teachings, rules of monastic life, and philosophical commentaries on the teachings; also a vast body of Buddhist teachings and commentaries, many of which are called *sutras*.

Organization: The basic institution is the *sangha* or monastic order through which the traditions are passed to each generation. Monastic life tends to be democratic and anti-authoritarian. Large lay organizations have developed in some sects.

Practice: Varies widely according to the sect and ranges from austere meditation to magical chanting and elaborate temple rites. Many practices, such as exorcism of devils, reflect pre-Buddhist beliefs.

Divisions: A wide variety of sects grouped into 3 primary branches: Therevada (sole survivor of the ancient Hinayana schools) which emphasizes the importance of pure thought and deed; Mahayana, which includes Zen and Soka-gakkai, ranges from philosophical schools to belief in the saving grace of higher beings or ritual practices, and to practical meditative disciplines; and Tantrism, an unusual combination of belief in ritual magic and sophisticated philosophy.

Location: Throughout Asia, from Ceylon to Japan. Zen and Soka-gakkai have several thousand adherents in the U.S.

Beliefs: Life is misery and decay, and there is no ultimate reality in it or behind it. The cycle of endless birth and rebirth continues because of desire and attachment to the unreal "self". Right meditation and deeds will end the cycle and achieve Nirvana, the Void, nothingness.

Judaism

Founded: About 1300 BCE.

Founder: Abraham is regarded as the founding patriarch, but the Torah of Moses is the basic source of the teachings.

Sacred Texts: The five books of Moses constitute the written Torah. Special sanctity is also assigned other writings of the Hebrew Bible—the teachings of oral Torah are recorded in the Talmud, the Midrash, and various commentaries.

Organization: Originally theocratic, Judaism has evolved a congregational polity. The basic institution is the local synagogue, operated by the congregation and led by a rabbi of their choice. Chief Rabbis in France and Great Britain have authority only over those who accept it; in Israel, the 2 Chief Rabbis have civil authority in family law.

Practice: Among traditional practitioners, almost all areas of life are governed by strict religious discipline. Sabbath and holidays are marked by special observances, and attendance at public worship is regarded as especially important then. The chief annual observances are Passover, celebrating the liberation of the Israelites from Egypt and marked by the ritual Seder meal in the home, and the 10 days from Rosh Hashana (New Year) to Yom Kippur (Day of Atonement), a period of fasting and penitence.

Divisions: Judaism is an unbroken spectrum from ultra conservative to ultra liberal, largely reflecting different points of view regarding the binding character of the prohibitions and duties—particularly the dietary and Sabbath observations—prescribed in the daily life of the Jew.

Location: Almost worldwide, with concentrations in Israel and the U.S.

Beliefs: Strictly monotheistic. God is the creator and absolute ruler of the universe. Men are free to choose to rebel against God's rule. God established a particular relationship with the Hebrew people: by obeying a divine law God gave them they would be a special witness to God's mercy and justice. The emphasis in Judaism is on ethical behavior (and, among the traditional, careful ritual obedience) as the true worship of God.

Hinduism

Founded: Ca. 1500 BC by Aryan invaders of India where their Vedic religion intermixed with the practices and beliefs of the natives.

Sacred texts: The *Veda*, including the *Upanishads*, a collection of rituals and mythological and philosophical commentaries; a vast number of epic stories about gods, heroes and saints, including the *Bhagavadgita*, a part of the *Mahabharata*, and the *Ramayana;* and a great variety of other literature.

Organization: None, strictly speaking. Generally, rituals should be performed or assisted by Brahmins, the priestly caste, but in practice simpler rituals can be performed by anyone. Brahmins are the final judges of ritual purity, the vital element in Hindu life. Temples and religious organizations are usually presided over by Brahmins.

Practice: A variety of private rituals, primarily passage rites (eg. initiation, marriage, death, etc.) and daily devotions, and a similar variety of public rites in temples. Of the latter, the *puja*, a ceremonial dinner for a god, is the most common.

Divisions: There is no concept of orthodoxy in Hinduism, which presents a bewildering variety of sects, most of them devoted to the worship of one of the many gods. The 3 major living traditions are those devoted to the gods Vishnu and Shiva and to the goddess Shakti; each of them divided into further sub-sects. Numerous folk beliefs and practices, often in amalgamation with the above groups, exist side-by-side with sophisticated philosophical schools and exotic cults.

Location: Confined to India, except for the missionary work of Vedanta, the Krishna Consciousness society, and individual *gurus* (teachers) in the West.

Beliefs: There is only one divine principle; the many gods are only aspects of that unity. Life in all its forms is an aspect of the divine, but it appears as a separation from the divine, a meaningless cycle of birth and rebirth (*samsara*) determined by the purity or impurity of past deeds (*karma*). To improve one's *karma* or escape *samsara* by pure acts, thought, and/or devotion is the aim of every Hindu.

Islam

Founded: 622 AD in Medina, Arabian peninsula.

Founder: Mohammed (ca. 570-632), the Prophet.

Sacred texts: *Koran*, the words of God. *Hadith*, collections of the sayings of the Prophet.

Organization: Theoretically the state and religious community are one, administered by a caliph. In practice, Islam is a loose collection of congregations united by a very conservative tradition. Islam is basically egalitarian and non-authoritarian.

Practice: Every Moslem has 5 duties: to make the profession of faith ("There is no god but Allah ..."), pray 5 times a day, give a regular portion of his goods to charity, fast during the day in the month of Ramadan, and make at least one pilgrimage to Mecca if possible.

Divisions: The 2 major sects of Islam are the Sunni (orthodox) and the Shi'ah. The Shi'ah believe in 12 *imams*, perfect teachers, who still guide the faithful from Paradise. Shi'ah practice tends toward the ecstatic, while the Sunni is staid and simple. The Shi'ah sect affirms man's free will; the Sunni is deterministic. The mystic tradition in Islam is Sufism. A Sufi adept believes he has acquired a special inner knowledge direct from Allah.

Location: From the west coast of Africa to the Philipines across a broad band that includes Tanzania, southern USSR and western China, India, Malaysia and Indonesia. Islam claims over 2 million adherents in North America.

Beliefs: Strictly monotheistic. God is creator of the universe, omnipotent, just, and merciful. Man is God's highest creation, but limited and commits sins. He is misled by Satan, an evil spirit. God revealed the *Koran* to Mohammed to guide men to the truth. Those who repent and sincerely submit to God return to a state of sinlessness. In the end, the sinless go to Paradise, a place of physical and spiritual pleasure, and the wicked burn in Hell.

Greek Orthodox Church Calendar, 1989

Source: Greek Orthodox Diocese of Toronto

Date	Holy Days	Date	Holy Days
Jan. 1	Circumcision of Jesus Christ; feast day of St. Basil	June 8	Ascension of Jesus Christ
		June 18	Sunday of Pentecost
Jan. 6	Epiphany: Baptism of Jesus Christ—Sanctification of the Waters	June 25	All Saints' Day
		June 29	Feast day of Sts. Peter and Paul
Jan. 7	Feast day of St. John the Baptist	June 30	Feast day of the Twelve Apostles of Jesus Christ
Jan. 30	Feast day of the Three Hierarchs: St. Basil the Great, St. Gregory the Theologian, and St. John Chrysostom	Aug. 6	Transfiguration of Jesus Christ
		Aug. 15	Dormition of the Virgin Mary
		Aug. 29	Beheading of St. John the Baptist
Feb. 2	Presentation of Jesus Christ to the Temple	Sept. 1	Beginning of the Church Year
Mar. 13	Great Lent begins	Sept. 14	Adoration of the Holy Cross
Mar. 19	Sunday of Orthodoxy (1st Sunday of Lent)	Oct. 23	Feast day of St. James (St. Iakovos)
Mar. 25	Annunciation of the Virgin Mary	Oct. 26	Feast day of St. Demetrios the Martyr
Apr. 23	Palm Sunday	Nov. 15	Christmas Lent begins
Apr. 23–29	Holy Week	Nov. 21	Presentation of the Virgin Mary to the Temple
Apr. 28	Holy (Good) Friday: Burial of Jesus Christ	Nov. 30	Feast day of St. Andrew the Apostle
Apr.[1] 30	Easter Sunday: Resurrection of Jesus Christ	Dec. 6	Feast day of St. Nicholas, Bishop of Myra
May[2] 1	Feast of St. George	Dec. 25	Christmas Day; Nativity of Jesus Christ
May 21	Feast days of Sts. Constantine and Helen		

(1) The date of Pascha (Easter) varies annually in accordance with the ancient formula of the Church (i.e., the first Sunday following the full moon after the vernal equinox, but always after the Jewish Passover). Some Eastern Orthodox Churches still adhere to the Julian (old) Calendar and observe the holy days (with the exception of the Easter cycle) 13 days later. The Greek Orthodox Church celebrates holy days in accordance with the Gregorian (new) Calendar, except for the Paschal (Easter) cycle of holy days, which is calculated in accordance with the Julian (old) calendar so that all Orthodox Churches can celebrate Pascha (Easter) on the same day. (2) The feast day of St. George is normally celebrated Apr. 23. If this day arrives during Lent, it is then celebrated the day after Easter.

Islamic (Moslem) Calendar 1988–1989

Source: Canadian Islamic Organization

The Islamic Calendar is a lunar reckoning from the year of the *hegira*, 622 A.D., when Muhammed moved from Mecca to Medina. It runs in cycles of 30 years, of which the 2d, 5th, 7th, 10th, 13th, 16th, 18th, 21st, 24th, 26th, and 29th are leap years; 1408 is the 29th year, 1410 is the 30th year of the cycle. Common years have 354 days, leap years 355, the extra day being added to the last month, Zu'lhijjah. Except for this case, the 12 months beginning with Muharram have alternately 30 and 29 days.

Year	Name of month	Month begins	Year	Name of Month	Month begins
1409	Muharram (New Year)	Aug. 14, 1988	1409	Shawwai	May 7, 1989
1409	Safar	Sept. 13, 1988	1409	Zu'lkadah	June 5, 1989
1409	Rabia I	Oct. 12, 1988	1409	Zu'lhijjah	July 4, 1989
1409	Rabia II	Nov. 11, 1988	1410	Muharram (New Year)	Aug. 2, 1989
1409	Jumada I	Dec. 11, 1988	1410	Safar	Sept. 1, 1989
1409	Jumada II	Jan. 9, 1989	1410	Rabia I	Sept. 30, 1989
1409	Rajab	Feb. 8, 1989	1410	Rabia II	Oct. 30, 1989
1409	Shaban	Mar. 9, 1989	1410	Jumada I	Nov. 28, 1989
1409	Ramadan	Apr. 7, 1989			

Jewish Holy Days, Festivals, and Fasts

	1988 (5747–48)		1989 (5748–49)		1990 (5749–50)		1991 (5750–52)		1992 (5752–53)	
Tu B'Shvat	Feb. 3	Wed	Jan. 21	Sat	Feb. 10	Sat	Jan. 30	Wed	Jan. 20	Mon
Ta'anis Esther (Fast of Esther)	Mar. 2	Wed	Mar. 20	Mon	Mar. 8	Thu*	Feb. 27	Wed	Mar. 18	Wed
Purim	Mar. 3	Thu	Mar. 21	Tue	Mar. 11	Sun	Feb. 28	Thu	Mar. 19	Thu
Passover	April 2	Sat	April 20	Thu	April 10	Tue	Mar. 30	Sat	April 18	Sat
	April 8	Sat	April 27	Thu	April 17	Tue	April 6	Sat	April 25	Sat
Lag B'Omer	May 5	Thu	May 23	Tue	May 13	Sun	May 2	Thu	May 21	Thu
Shavuot	May 22	Sun	June 9	Fri	May 30	Wed	May 19	Sun	June 7	Sun
	May 28	Mon	June 10	Sat	May 31	Thu	May 20	Mon	June 8	Mon
Fast of the 17th Day of Tammuz	July 3	Sun	July 20	Thu	July 10	Tue	June 30	Sun*	July 19	Sun*
Fast of the 9th Day of AV	July 24	Sun	Aug. 10	Thu	July 31	Tue	July 21	Sun*	Aug. 9	Sun*
Rosh Hashanah	Sep. 12	Mon	Sep. 30	Sat	Sep. 20	Thu	Sep. 9	Mon	Sep. 28	Mon
	Sep. 13	Tue	Oct. 1	Sun	Sep. 21	Fri	Sep. 10	Tue	Sep. 29	Tue
Fast of Gedalya	Sep. 14	Wed	Oct. 2	Mon	Sep. 23	Sun*	Sep. 11	Wed	Sep. 30	Wed
Yom Kippur	Sep. 21	Wed	Oct. 9	Mon	Sep. 29	Sat	Sep. 18	Wed	Oct. 7	Wed
Sukkot	Sep. 26	Mon	Oct. 14	Sat	Oct. 4	Thu	Sep. 23	Mon	Oct. 12	Mon
	Oct. 2	Sun	Oct. 20	Fri	Oct. 10	Wed	Sep. 29	Sun	Oct. 18	Sun
Shmini Atzeret	Oct. 3	Sun	Oct. 21	Sat	Oct. 11	Thu	Sep. 30	Sun	Oct. 19	Sun
	Oct. 4	Tue	Oct. 22	Sun	Oct. 12	Fri	Oct. 1	Tue	Oct. 20	Tue
Chanukah	Dec. 4	Sun	Dec. 23	Sat	Dec. 12	Wed	Dec. 2	Mon	Dec. 20	Sun
	Dec. 11	Sun	Dec. 30	Sat	Dec. 19	Wed	Dec. 9	Mon	Dec. 27	Sun
Fast of the 10th of Tevet	Dec. 18	Sun	Jan. 7	Sun	Dec. 27	Thu	Dec. 17	Tue	Jan. 3, 1993	Sun

The months of the Jewish year are: 1) Tishri; 2) Cheshvan (also Marcheshvan); 3) Kislev; 4) Tebet (also Tebeth); 5) Shebat (also Shebhat); 6) Adar; 6a) Adar Sheni (II) added in leap years; 7) Nisan; 8) Iyar; 9) Sivan; 10) Tammuz; 11) Av (also Abh); 12) Elul. All Jewish holy days, etc., begin at sunset on the day previous. *Date changed to avoid Sabbath.

Anglican Church Calendar and and Liturgical Colors

Source: The Anglican Church in Canada

White—from Christmas Day through the First Sunday after Epiphany; Maundy Thursday (as an alternative to crimson at the Eucharist); from the Vigil of Easter to the Day of Pentecost (Whitsunday); Trinity Sunday; Feasts of the Lord (except Holy Cross Day); the Confession of St. Peter; the Conversion of St. Paul; St. Joseph; St. Mary Magdalene; St. Mary the Virgin; St. Michael and All Angels; All Saints' Day; St. John the Evangelist; memorials of other saints who were not martyred; weddings and funerals. **Red**—the Day of Pentecost; Holy Cross Day; feasts of apostles and evangelists (except those listed above); feasts and memorials of martyrs (including Holy Innocents' Day). **Violet**—Advent and Lent. **Crimson**—Holy Week. **Green**—the seasons after Epiphany and after Pentecost. **Black**—optional alternative for funerals. Alternative colors used in some churches: **Blue**—Advent. **Lenten White**—Ash Wednesday to Palm Sunday.

	1988	1989	1990	1991	1992
The Epiphany	Jan. 3	Jan. 8	Jan. 7	Jan. 6	Jan. 5
Ash Wednesday	Feb. 17	Feb. 8	Feb. 28	Feb. 13	Mar. 4
First Sunday in Lent	Feb. 21	Feb. 12	Mar. 4	Feb. 17	Mar. 8
Palm/Passion Sunday	Mar. 27	Mar. 19	Apr. 8	Mar. 24	Apr. 12
Good Friday	Apr. 1	Mar. 24	Apr. 13	Mar. 29	Apr. 17
Easter Sunday	Apr. 3	Mar. 26	Apr. 15	Mar. 31	Apr. 19
Ascension Day	May 12	May 4	May 24	May 9	May 28
Day of Pentecost	May 22	May 14	June 3	May 19	June 7
Trinity Sunday	May 29	May 21	June 10	May 26	June 14
All Saints' Day	Nov. 1	Nov. 1	Nov. 1	Nov. 1	Nov. 1
First Sunday of Advent	Nov. 27	Dec. 3	Dec. 2	Dec. 1	Nov. 29
Christmas Day	Dec. 25	Dec. 25	Dec. 25	Dec. 25	Dec. 25

In the Anglican Church the days of fasting are Ash Wednesday and Good Friday. Other days of special devotion (abstinence) are the 40 days of Lent and all Fridays of the year, except those in Christmas and Easter seasons and any Feasts of the Lord which occur on a Friday or during Lent. Ember Days (optional) are days of prayer for the Church's ministry. They fall on the Wednesday, Friday and Saturday after the first Sunday in Lent, the Day of Pentecost, Holy Cross Day, and the Third Sunday of Advent. Rogation Days (also optional) are the 3 days before Ascension Day, and are days of prayer for God's blessing on the crops, on commerce and industry, and for the conservation of the Earth's resources.

Roman Catholic Church Calendar and Liturgical Colors

Source: Canadian Conference of Catholic Bishops

White—Christmas; Easter Season; feasts of the Lord; feasts and memorials of Mary, the angels and saints who were not martyrs. **Red**—Palm (Passion) Sunday; Good Friday; Pentecost; celebrations of the Lord's Passion; feast of apostles and evangelists; celebration of martyrs. **Violet**—During Advent and Lent. **Green**—During Ordinary time. **Rose**—May be used on the Third Sunday of Advent and Fourth Sunday of Lent.

	1988	1989	1990	1991	1992
Feast of Mary, Mother of God	Jan. 1	Jan. 1	Jan. 1	Jan. 1	Jan. 1
The Epiphany	Jan. 3	Jan. 8	Jan. 7	Jan. 6	Jan. 5
St. Marguerite Bourgeoys[1]	Jan. 12	Jan. 12	Jan. 12	Jan. 12	Jan. 12
Ash Wednesday[2]	Feb. 17	Feb. 8	Feb. 28	Feb. 13	Mar. 4
Saint Joseph, patron saint of Canada	Mar. 19	Mar. 18	Mar. 19	Mar. 19	Mar. 19
Annunciation of the Lord	Mar. 25	Apr. 3	Mar. 25	Mar. 25	Mar. 25
Palm/Passion Sunday	Mar. 27	Mar. 19	Apr. 8	Mar. 24	Apr. 12
Good Friday[2]	Apr. 1	Mar. 24	Apr. 13	Mar. 29	Apr. 11
Easter Sunday	Apr. 3	Mar. 26	Apr. 15	Mar. 31	Apr. 19
Ascension of the Lord	May 15	May 7	May 27	May 12	May 31
Pentecost	May 22	May 14	June 3	May 19	June 7
Trinity Sunday	May 29	May 21	June 10	May 26	June 14
Corpus Christi	June 5	May 28	June 17	June 2	June 21
Birth of John the Baptist	June 24	June 24	June 24	June 24	June 24
Sacred Heart	June 10	June 3	June 22	June 7	June 26
Assumption of Mary	Aug. 15	Aug. 15	Aug. 15	Aug. 15	Aug. 15
Canadian Martyrs[1]	Oct. 19	Oct. 19	Oct. 19	Oct. 19	Oct. 19
All Saint's Day	Nov. 1	Nov. 1	Nov. 1	Nov. 1	Nov. 1
Christ the King	Nov. 20	Nov. 26	Nov. 25	Nov. 24	Nov. 22
Immaculate Conception	Dec. 8	Dec. 8	Dec. 8	Dec. 8	Dec. 8
Christmas Day	Dec. 25	Dec. 25	Dec. 25	Dec. 25	Dec. 25

(1) Memorials of special significance for the Roman Catholic Church in Canada. (2) Days of abstinence and fasting.

Chronological List of Popes

Source: Annuario Pontificio. Table lists year of accession of each Pope.

The Roman Catholic Church names the Apostle Peter as founder of the Church in Rome. He arrived there c. 42, was martyred there c. 67, and raised to sainthood.
The Pope's temporal title is: Sovereign of the State of Vatican City.
The Pope's spiritual titles are: Bishop of Rome, Vicar of Jesus Christ, Successor of St. Peter, Prince of the Apostles, Supreme Pontiff of the Universal Church, Patriarch of the West, Primate of Italy, Archbishop and Metropolitan of the Roman Province.
Anti-Popes are in *Italics*. Anti-Popes were illegitimate claimants of or pretenders to the papal throne.

Year	Name of Pope	Year	Name of Pope	Year	Name of Pope	Year	Name of Pope
See above.	St. Peter	615	St. Deusdedit	974	Benedict VII	1305	Clement V
67	St. Linus		or Adeodatus	983	John XIV	1316	John XXII
76	St. Anacletus	619	Boniface V	985	John XV	*1328*	*Nicholas V*
	or Cletus	625	Honorius I	996	Gregory V	1334	Benedict XII
88	St. Clement I	640	Severinus	*997*	*John XVI*	1342	Clement VI
97	St. Evaristus	640	John IV	999	Sylvester II	1352	Innocent VI
105	St. Alexander I	642	Theodore I	1003	John XVII	1362	Bl. Urban V
115	St. Sixtus I	649	St. Martin I, Martyr	1004	John XVIII	1370	Gregory XI
125	St. Telesphorus	654	St. Eugene I	1009	Sergius IV	1378	Urban VI
136	St. Hyginus	657	St. Vitalian	1012	Benedict VIII	*1378*	*Clement VII*
140	St. Pius I	672	Adeodatus II	*1012*	*Gregory*	1389	Boniface IX
155	St. Anicetus	676	Donus	1024	John XIX	*1394*	*Benedict XIII*
166	St. Soter	678	St. Agatho	1032	Benedict IX	1404	Innocent VII
175	St. Eleutherius	682	St. Leo II	1045	Sylvester III	1406	Gregory XII
189	St. Victor I	684	St. Benedict II	1045	Benedict IX	*1409*	*Alexander V*
199	St. Zephyrinus	685	John V	1045	Gregory VI	*1410*	*John XXIII*
217	St. Callistus I	686	Conon	1046	Clement II	1417	Martin V
217	*St. Hippolytus*	*687*	*Theodore*	1047	Benedict IX	1431	Eugene IV
222	St. Urban I	*687*	*Paschal*	1048	Damasus II	*1439*	*Felix V*
230	St. Pontian	687	St. Sergius I	1049	St. Leo IX	1447	Nicholas V
235	St. Anterus	701	John VI	1055	Victor II	1455	Callistus III
236	St. Fabian	705	John VII	1057	Stephen IX (X)	1458	Pius II
251	St. Cornelius	708	Sisinnius	*1058*	*Benedict X*	1464	Paul II
251	*Novatian*	708	Constantine	1059	Nicholas II	1471	Sixtus IV
253	St. Lucius I	715	St. Gregory II	1061	Alexander II	1484	Innocent VIII
254	St. Stephen I	731	St. Gregory III	*1061*	*Honorius II*	1492	Alexander VI
257	St. Sixtus II	741	St. Zachary	1073	St. Gregory VII	1503	Pius III
259	St. Dionysius	752	Stephen II (III)	*1080*	*Clement III*	1503	Julius II
269	St. Felix I	757	St. Paul I	1086	Bl. Victor III	1513	Leo X
275	St. Eutychian	*767*	*Constantine*	1088	Bl. Urban II	1522	Adrian VI
283	St. Caius	768	*Philip*	1099	Paschal II	1523	Clement VII
296	St. Marcellinus	768	Stephen III (IV)	*1100*	*Theodoric*	1534	Paul III
308	St. Marcellus I	772	Adrian I	*1102*	*Albert*	1550	Julius III
309	St. Eusebius	795	St. Leo III	*1105*	*Sylvester IV*	1555	Marcellus II
311	St. Melchiades	816	Stephen IV (V)	1118	Gelasius II	1555	Paul IV
314	St. Sylvester I	817	St. Paschal I	*1118*	*Gregory VIII*	1559	Pius IV
336	St. Marcus	824	Eugene II	1119	Callistus II	1566	St. Pius V
337	St. Julius I	827	Valentine	*1124*	*Celestine II*	1572	Gregory XIII
352	Liberius	827	Gregory IV	1124	Honorius II	1585	Sixtus V
355	*Felix II*	*844*	*John*	1130	Innocent II	1590	Urban VII
366	St. Damasus I	844	Sergius II	*1130*	*Anacletus II*	1590	Gregory XIV
366	*Ursinus*	847	St. Leo IV	*1138*	*Victor IV*	1591	Innocent IX
384	St. Siricius	855	Benedict III	1143	Celestine II	1592	Clement VIII
399	St. Anastasius I	*855*	*Anastasius*	1144	Lucius II	1605	Leo XI
401	St. Innocent I	858	St. Nicholas I	1145	Bl. Eugene III	1605	Paul V
417	St. Zosimus	867	Adrian II	1153	Anastasius IV	1621	Gregory XV
418	St. Boniface I	872	John VIII	1154	Adrian IV	1623	Urban VIII
418	*Eulalius*	882	Marinus I	1159	Alexander III	1644	Innocent X
422	St. Celestine I	884	St. Adrian III	*1159*	*Victor IV*	1655	Alexander VII
432	St. Sixtus III	885	Stephen V (VI)	*1164*	*Paschal III*	1667	Clement IX
440	St. Leo I	891	Formosus	*1168*	*Callistus III*	1670	Clement X
461	St. Hilary	896	Boniface VI	*1179*	*Innocent III*	1676	Bl. Innocent XI
468	St. Simplicius	896	Stephen VI (VII)	1181	Lucius III	1689	Alexander VIII
483	St. Felix III (II)	897	Romanus	1185	Urban III	1691	Innocent XII
492	St. Gelasius I	897	Theodore II	1187	Gregory VIII	1700	Clement XI
496	St. Anastasius II	898	John IX	1187	Clement III	1721	Innocent XIII
498	St. Symmachus	900	Benedict IV	1191	Celestine III	1724	Benedict XIII
498	*Lawrence*	903	Leo V	1198	Innocent III	1730	Clement XII
	(501-505)	*903*	*Christopher*	1216	Honorius III	1740	Benedict XIV
514	St. Hormisdas	904	Sergius III	1227	Gregory IX	1758	Clement XIII
523	St. John I, Martyr	911	Anastasius III	1241	Celestine IV	1769	Clement XIV
526	St. Felix IV (III)	913	Landus	1243	Innocent IV	1775	Pius VI
530	Boniface II	914	John X	1254	Alexander IV	1800	Pius VII
530	*Dioscorus*	928	Leo VI	1261	Urban IV	1823	Leo XII
533	John II	928	Stephen VII (VIII)	1265	Clement IV	1829	Pius VIII
535	St. Agapitus I	931	John XI	1271	Bl. Gregory X	1831	Gregory XVI
536	St. Silverius, Martyr	936	Leo VII	1276	Bl. Innocent V	1846	Pius IX
537	Vigilius	939	Stephen VIII (IX)	1276	Adrian V	1878	Leo XIII
556	Pelagius I	942	Marinus II	1276	John XXI	1903	St. Pius X
561	John III	946	Agapitus II	1277	Nicholas III	1914	Benedict XV
575	Benedict I	955	John XII	1281	Martin IV	1922	Pius XI
579	Pelagius II	963	Leo VIII	1285	Honorius IV	1939	Pius XII
590	St. Gregory I	964	Benedict V	1288	Nicholas IV	1958	John XXIII
604	Sabinian	965	John XIII	1294	St. Celestine V	1963	Paul VI
608	Boniface III	973	Benedict VI	1294	Boniface VIII	1978	John Paul I
608	St. Boniface IV	*974*	*Boniface VII*	1303	Bl. Benedict XI	1978	John Paul II

The Papal Visit, 1984 and 1987

Pope John Paul II visited Canada from Sept. 9 to Sept. 20, 1984. The itinerary for the visit—the first to Canada by a Pope—is listed below.

Sept. 9: The Pope arrived in Quebec, where the first Christians had landed in Canada over 450 years earlier. In Quebec City the Pope prayed at the tomb of Monseigneur François de Laval, the first bishop in North America, and founder of the Séminaire du Québec, a college that eventually became Laval University. Later the Pope celebrated an open-air mass at the university.

Sept. 10: The Pope visited the Quebec Museum and the François-Charon Centre for the Handicapped. A celebration with native people was then held at Ste-Anne-de-Beaupré, a well-known site of pilgrimage. The Pope flew to Trois-Rivières in the afternoon, where missionaries had first persuaded an Indian tribe to establish a permanent settlement. At Cap-de-Madeleine, the Pope celebrated an open-air mass with the theme of "Love and Devotion to the Virgin Mary" at the Marian Shrine.

Sept. 11: The day was spent in Montreal, beginning with a visit to the tomb of Brother André, builder of a shrine dedicated to St. Joseph. After meeting with priests at St. Joseph's Oratory, the Pope visited the tomb of Mother Marguerite Bourgeoys, founder of the Congregation of Notre-Dame and of several schools. Mother Marguerite Bourgeoys was canonized in 1982 and is Canada's first female saint. The afternoon began with a visit to the 160-year-old Église Notre Dame, followed by a youth rally at Olympic Stadium.

Sept. 12: The visit to St. John's, Nfld. had for its theme "The Role of the Family". In the afternoon, an open-air mass was held. The Pope made an address to teachers at the Basilica in the evening, then attended a youth rally at Memorial University.

Sept. 13: Before leaving Newfoundland, the Pope blessed the fishing fleet at Flatrock, where he spoke of the need to put people above profits. He travelled next to Moncton, for a celebration at Moncton Cathedral. An open air mass held at Front Mountain Road continued the Moncton theme of "The Church as Community". Travelling next to Halifax, the Pope was met by Micmac Indian elders at CFB Shearwater. Afterwards, he took a "popemobile" tour to Central Commons, then met with clergy at St. Mary's Basilica, where the theme was "The Church's World Mission".

Sept. 14: The Pope visited with sick children and the handicapped, then attended an open air mass at Central Commons. Arriving in Toronto in the afternoon, the Pope began his visit by meeting with clergy at St. Michael's Cathedral. An ecumenical service was then held at St. Paul's Anglican Church, with representatives from 37 different churches and faith groups in Canada in attendance. At the request of the Canadian Council of Churches, the Pope met privately after the service with 17 representatives from the Anglican Church, the Armenian Church of Canada, the Coptic Orthodox Church, The Greek Orthodox Church and the Protestant denominations. At a rally sponsored by the Canadian-Polish Congress, the Polish-Canadian audience greeted the Pope with thunderous applause upon his entrance to Varsity Stadium. In a spontaneous departure from his prepared text, the Pope pleaded dramatically in Polish for increased freedom in his homeland. Then he returned to his address on the need to preserve the family, culture, and Christian ideals and virtues.

Sept. 15: The Pope travelled by helicopter to Midland, Ont. to visit the shrine of Ste-Marie-Among-the-Hurons. He met with the sick and elderly at Martyrs' Shrine Church, then visited the graves of Jesuit martyrs, Father Brébeuf and Father Lalement. A mass was then held at Shrine Field. In the afternoon the Pontiff returned to Toronto, for an open-air eucharist celebration at Downsview Airport in the City of North York. The crowd was estimated to have been the largest of the papal tour.

Sept. 16: The Pope travelled to Winnipeg and visited the Ukrainian Cathedral of St. Vladimir and Olga, where the theme was "Faith and Culture in a Multicultural Society". He received the St. Boniface Hospital's 1984 Research Foundation Award, given annually for distinction in health care or humanitarianism, in a ceremony held at St. Mary's Cathedral. Before leaving for Edmonton, the Pope held a mass at Bird's Hill Park. In Edmonton the Pope participated in evening prayers at Edmonton's Cathedral.

Sept. 17: The Pope celebrated an open air mass at CFB Nameo.

Sept. 18: A planned meeting with Métis and Dene People at Fort Simpson, N.W.T. was delayed and eventually cancelled due to heavy fog making air travel impossible. In the afternoon the Pope arrived in Vancouver, attended a mass at Pacific National Exhibition Park, and then met with youth, the elderly and handicapped at B.C. Place in the evening.

Sept. 19: The Pope's theme for his Ottawa addresses was the need to pursue world peace. He attended mass in Hull, Que. and then visited Rideau Hall, the Governor General's residence, for a civic reception.

Sept. 20: The Pope met with Canadian bishops, then travelled by helicopter to an open air mass at Equestrian Park, Nepean. After an afternoon tour of downtown Ottawa, the Pope attended farewell ceremonies on Parliament Hill, then departed for Rome.

1987

Keeping a promise he had made 3 years earlier when poor weather forced cancellation of a visit, Pope John Paul II travelled to Fort Simpson, N.W.T. Sept. 20, 1987. During his half-day stay, the Pope said mass and told a crowd of 3 000 that Canada's native people deserved a "just and equitable degree" of self-government.

Headquarters of Religious Organizations in Canada

(year organized in parentheses)

Anglican Church of Canada—(creation of General Synod 1893)–600 Jarvis St., Toronto, Ont. M4Y 2J6; Primate, Most Rev. Michael G. Peers.

Apostolic Church in Canada—27 Castlefield Ave., Toronto, Ont. M4R 1G3; Pres., Rev. David E.S. Morris.

Apostolic Church of Pentecost of Canada Inc. (1921)—105-807 Manning Rd. N.E., Calgary, Alta. T2E 7M9; Mod., Wesley S. Schindel.

Baha'i Community Canada (organized 1844, first Canadian community est. 1902)—7200 Leslie St., Thornhill, Ont. L3T 2A1; Gen. Sec., Dr. Hossain B. Danesh.

Bible Holiness Movement, The (1949)—P.O. Box 223, Stn. A, Vancouver, B.C. V6C 2M3; Evangelist Wesley H. Wakefield, Bishop-General.

Brethren in Christ Church—2519 Stevensville Rd., Stevensville, Ont. L0S 1S0; Gen. Sec., Donald Shafer; Bishop, Canadian Conference, Rev. Harvey R. Sider.

Buddhist Council of Canada (1979)—c/o Toronto Buddhist Church, 918 Bathurst St., Toronto, Ont. M5R 3G5; Pres., Dr. Suwanda Sugunasiri.

Canadian Baptist Federation—7185 Millcreek Dr., Mississauga, Ont., L5N 5R4; Pres., Robert MacQuade; Gen. Sec. Treas., Dr. Richard C. Coffin.

Canadian Council of Christians and Jews (1947)—49 Front St. E., Toronto, Ont. M5E 1B3; Exec. Dir., Elizabeth Loweth.

Canadian Council of Churches, The (1944)—40 St. Clair Ave. E., Suite 201, Toronto, Ont. M4T 1M9; Gen. Sec., Dr. Stuart E. Brown.

Canadian Jewish Congress (1919)—1590 Avenue Docteur Penfield, Montreal, Que. H3G 1C5; Pres., Dorothy Reitman.

Christian Church (Disciples of Christ) in Canada (1830)—55 Cork St. E., Guelph, Ont. N1H 2W7; Exec. Regional Minister, Dr. Robert W. Steffer.

Christian and Missionary Alliance in Canada, The (1889)—105 Gordon Baker Rd., Suite 510, North York, Ont. M2H 3P8; Pres., Dr. Melvin P. Sylvester.

Christian Reformed Church in North America—P.O. Box 5070, 3475 Mainway, Burlington, Ont. L7R 1Y8.

Christian Science Church in Canada—Committee on Publication, 339 Bloor St. W., Suite 214, Toronto, Ont. M5S 1W7; J. Don Fulton.

Church of God—P.O. Box 2036, Bramalea, Ont. L6T 3S3; Supt., Rev. S.A. Lankford.

Church of Jesus Christ of Latter-day Saints (Mormons) (1830)—Public Communications and Special Affairs, 7181 Woodbine Ave., Suite 234, Markham, Ont. L3R 1A3; Pres., North America North West, Elder Rex C. Reeve, Sr.; Pres., North America North East, Elder John K. Carmack; Pres. North America Central, Elder, Lorne C. Dunn.

Church of the Nazarene (1908)—P.O. Box 30080, Stn. B., Calgary, Alta. T2M 4N7; Canadian Exec. Board, Rev. Rudolf Pedersen.

Evangelical Baptist Churches in Canada, The Fellowship of (1953)—3034 Bayview Ave., Willowdale, Ont. M2N 6J5; Gen. Sec., Dr. Roy W. Lawson.

Evangelical Lutheran Church in Canada (1986)—1512 St. James St., Winnipeg, Man. R3H 0L2; Bishop, The Rev. Dr. Donald W. Sjoberg.

Foursquare Gospel Church of Canada—7895 Welsley Dr., Burnaby, B.C. V5E 3X4; Pres., Dr. Victor F. Gardner.

Free Methodist Church in Canada (1880)—4315 Village Centre Court, Mississauga, Ont. L4Z 1S2; Pres., Bishop D.N. Bastian.

Greek Orthodox Church in Canada—40 Donlands Ave., Toronto, Ont. M4J 3N6; Bishop of Toronto, Rt. Rev. Sotirios Athanassoulas.

Islamic Society of North America (1981, formerly Muslim Student Association of United States and Canada est. 1963)—Canadian Zonal Office, P.O. Box 160, Station P, Toronto, Ont. M5S 2S7.

Jehovah's Witnesses (Branch Office est. in Winnipeg 1918)—P.O. Box 4100, Georgetown, Ont. L7G 4Y4; Exec. Dir., Kenneth Little.

Lutheran Council in Canada (agency for Evangelical Lutheran Church in Canada and Lutheran Church-Canada)—25 Old York Mills Rd., Toronto, Ont. M2P 1B5; Exec. Dir., Rev. Lawrence R. Likness.

Lutheran Church-Canada (1989)—P.O. Box 55, Stn. A., Winnipeg, Man. T5K 1C5; Exec. Dir., William Buller.

Mennonite Brethren Churches of North America, Canadian Conference (inc. 1945)—3-169 Riverton Ave., Winnipeg, Man. R2L 2E5; Mod., H. Neufeld.

Orthodox Church in America (Diocese of Canada, 1897)—55 Clarey Ave., Ottawa, Ont. K1S 2R6; Administrator, Bishop Seraphim (Storheim).

Pentecostal Assemblies of Canada, The (inc. 1919)—10 Overlea Blvd., Toronto, Ont. M4H 1A5; Gen. Supt., Rev. James M. MacKnight.

Pentecostal Holiness Church of Canada—P.O. Box 442, Waterloo, Ont. N2J 4A9; Gen. Supt., Dr. G.H. Nunn.

Presbyterian Church in Canada, The (1875)—50 Wynford Dr., Don Mills, Ont. M3C 1J7; Mod. Rev. Dr. Bruce Miles; Gen. Sec. of Administrative Council, Dr. Earle F. Roberts.

Religious Society of Friends (Quakers) (Canadian Yearly Meeting formed 1955)—60 Lowther Ave., Toronto, Ont. M5R 1C7; Canadian Yearly Meeting Clerk, Edward S. Bell.

Reorganized Church of Jesus Christ of Latter-day Saints, The (1830)—390 Speedvale Ave. E., Guelph, Ont. N1E 1N5; Bishop of Canada and Ont. Region, A.K. Bennett.

Roman Catholic Church in Canada—There is no headquarters for the Roman Catholic Church in Canada. Each diocese is under the jurisdiction of a bishop who is under the jurisdiction of the Pope.

Salvation Army, The (1882)—Territorial Headquarters, 20 Salvation Square, P.O. Box 4021, Stn. A, Toronto, Ont. M5W 2B1; Territorial Commander, Canadian and Bermuda Territory, Commissioner Will Pratt.

Seventh-Day Adventist Church in Canada—1148 King St. E., Oshawa, Ont. L1H 1H8; Pres., James W. Wilson.

Sikh Foundation (1984)—1 Yonge Street, Suite 1801, Toronto, Ont. M5E 1E5.

Ukrainian Orthodox Church of Canada (1918)—9 St. Johns Ave., Winnipeg, Man. R2W 1G8; Primate, His Eminence, Most Rev. Archbishop Wasyly (Fedak); Chmn. Exec. Comm., Consistory, Very Rev. Stephan Jarmus.

Unitarian Council, Canadian (Unitarian Universalist Denomination in Canada) (1961)—175 St. Clair Ave. W., Toronto, Ont. M4V 1P7; Pres., Elinor R. Knight; Exec. Dir., Kathleen D. Hunter.

United Church of Canada, The (1925)—85 St. Clair Ave. E., Toronto, Ont. M4T 1M8; Mod., Rt. Rev. Anne Squire.

Birthstones

The origin of birthstones can be traced back to the jewelled breastplate worn by Aaron, the High Priest of the Israelites and brother of Moses, which was described in *Exodus*, Chapter 39. The 12 stones in the breastplate became symbolically associated with the 12 months of the year and the 12 signs of the zodiac. Birthstones are believed to bring good luck or health to the wearer.

January	Garnet	July	Ruby
February	Amethyst	August	Sardonyx or Peridot
March	Aquamarine or Bloodstone	September	Sapphire
April	Diamond	October	Opal or Tourmaline
May	Emerald	November	Topaz
June	Pearl, Moonstone or Alexandrite	December	Turquoise, Zircon, or Lapis Lazuli

Canada's Economy

Canadian Gross Domestic Product

Source: Statistics Canada

The gross domestic product (GDP) measures the value of all goods and services produced in Canada. The real (adjusted for inflation) change in the GDP shows year-to-year changes in economic activity and is considered a prime indicator of how well the nation's economy is performing.

(millions of dollars)

	Current Dollars		Constant (1981) Dollars			Current Dollars		Constant (1981) Dollars	
	GDP	annual % change	Real GDP	annual % change		GDP	annual % change	Real GDP	annual % change
1926	5 354	n.a.	35 578	n.a.	1957	34 467	4.8	121 471	2.5
1927	5 777	7.9	38 912	9.4	1958	35 689	3.5	124 108	2.2
1928	6 279	8.7	42 486	9.2	1959	37 877	6.1	128 998	3.9
1929	6 400	1.9	42 866	0.9	1960	39 448	4.1	132 752	2.9
1930	6 009	−6.1	41 463	−3.3	1961	40 886	3.6	136 914	3.1
1931	4 975	−17.2	36 819	−11.2	1962	44 408	8.6	146 614	7.1
1932	4 079	−18.0	33 407	−9.3	1963	47 678	7.4	154 224	5.2
1933	3 723	−8.7	31 004	−7.2	1964	52 191	9.5	164 504	6.7
1934	4 186	12.4	34 229	10.4	1965	57 523	10.2	175 359	6.6
1935	4 514	7.8	36 687	7.2	1966	64 388	11.9	187 263	6.8
1936	4 879	8.1	38 369	4.6	1967	69 064	7.3	192 752	2.9
1937	5 477	12.3	41 765	8.9	1968	75 418	9.2	203 072	5.4
1938	5 523	0.8	42 346	1.4	1969	83 026	10.1	213 946	5.4
1939	5 880	6.5	45 510	7.5	1970	89 116	7.3	219 498	2.6
1940	6 987	18.8	51 541	13.3	1971	97 290	9.2	232 137	5.8
1941	8 532	22.1	58 410	13.3	1972	108 629	11.7	245 441	5.7
1942	10 497	23.0	68 691	17.6	1973	127 372	17.3	264 369	7.7
1943	11 282	7.5	71 311	3.8	1974	152 111	19.4	276 006	4.4
1944	12 068	7.0	73 916	3.7	1975	171 540	12.8	283 187	2.6
1945	12 063	0.0	72 125	−2.4	1976	197 924	15.4	300 638	6.2
1946	12 167	0.9	70 513	−2.2	1977	217 879	10.1	311 504	3.6
1947	13 940	14.6	74 143	5.1	1978	241 604	10.9	325 751	4.6
1948	15 969	14.6	75 268	1.5	1979	276 096	14.3	338 362	3.9
1949	17 347	8.6	78 647	4.5	1980	309 891	12.2	343 384	1.5
1950	19 125	10.2	84 784	7.8	1981	355 994	14.9	355 994	3.7
1951	22 280	16.5	88 562	4.5	1982	374 442	5.2	344 543	−3.2
1952	25 170	13.0	95 951	8.3	1983	405 717	8.4	355 445	3.2
1953	26 395	4.9	100 722	5.0	1984	444 735	9.6	377 865	6.3
1954	26 531	0.5	99 620	−1.1	1985	478 765	7.7	395 217	4.6
1955	29 250	10.2	109 104	9.5	1986	506 483	5.8	407 736	3.2
1956	32 902	12.5	118 514	−8.6	1987	549 692	8.5	424 136	4.0

Value of Production in Canadian Industry

Source: Statistics Canada

(millions of dollars)

	1960	%	1970	%	1975	%	1980	%	1983	%	1984	%
All industries ..	32 336	100.0	75 427	100.0	150 726	100.0	278 083	100.0	360 888	100.0	392 953	100.0
Agriculture	1 745	5.4	2 472	3.3	6 147	4.1	9 268	3.3	10 165	2.8	10 984	2.8
Communications .	744	2.3	2 105	2.8	3 738	2.5	7 580	2.7	10 544	2.9	11 714	3.0
Construction	1 745	5.4	4 748	6.3	11 729	7.8	16 369	5.9	18 637	5.2	28 273	4.7
Finance	3 383	10.5	8 497	11.3	17 313	11.5	31 301	11.3	51 183	14.2	56 280	14.3
Fishing and trapping	91	0.3	132	0.2	198	0.1	601	0.2	726	0.2	673	0.2
Forestry	403	1.2	622	0.8	1 092	0.7	2 433	0.9	2 412	0.7	2 674	0.4
Manufacturing ...	8 427	26.1	17 606	23.3	32 035	21.3	57 227	20.6	63 465	17.6	71 939	18.3
Mining	1 433	4.4	3 040	4.0	6 157	4.1	18 877	6.8	22 443	6.2	25 934	6.6
Public administration .	2 342	7.2	5 530	7.3	11 707	7.8	20 541	7.4	29 830	8.3	31 809	8.1
Retail trade	3 016	9.3	5 383	7.1	10 440	6.9	17 432	6.3	21 208	5.9	23 112	5.9
Services	4 239	13.1	14 508	19.2	29 973	19.9	57 931	20.8	79 085	21.9	84 284	21.4
Storage	89	0.3	187	0.2	352	0.2	700	0.3	901	0.2	957	0.2
Transportation ...	2 105	6.5	4 434	5.9	8 023	5.3	15 044	5.4	19 385	5.4	21 396	5.4
Utilities	1 070	3.3	2 198	2.9	4 071	2.7	9 665	3.5	15 128	4.2	15 999	4.1
Wholesale trade	1 506	4.7	3 965	5.3	7 751	5.1	13 114	4.7	15 776	4.4	16 925	4.3

Canadian Inflation Rate, by Year

Source: Statistics Canada

Year	Rate	Year	Rate	Year	Rate	Year	Rate
1915	1.7	1955	0.0	1967	3.6	1979	9.2
1920	5.8	1956	1.5	1968	4.0	1980	10.2
1925	0.9	1957	3.1	1969	4.5	1981	12.5
1930	-0.7	1958	2.5	1970	3.4	1982	10.8
1935	0.6	1959	1.1	1971	2.8	1983	5.8
1940	4.1	1960	1.3	1972	4.8	1984	4.4
1945	0.5	1961	1.0	1973	7.6	1985	4.0
1950	3.0	1962	1.2	1974	10.9	1986	4.1
1951	10.6	1963	1.7	1975	10.8	1987	4.4
1952	2.3	1964	1.8	1976	7.5		
1953	-0.8	1965	2.4	1977	8.0		
1954	0.6	1966	3.7	1978	8.9		

Canadian Consumer Price Index, by Year

Source: Statistics Canada

1981 = 100

Year	Index	Year	Index	Year	Index	Year	Index
1915	12.4	1955	28.5	1967	36.5	1979	80.7
1920	22.9	1956	28.9	1968	38.0	1980	88.9
1925	18.4	1957	29.8	1969	39.7	1981	100.0
1930	18.4	1958	30.6	1970	41.0	1982	110.8
1935	14.7	1959	31.0	1971	42.2	1983	117.2
1940	16.1	1960	31.4	1972	44.2	1984	122.3
1945	18.4	1961	31.7	1973	47.6	1985	127.2
1950	25.2	1962	32.0	1974	52.8	1986	132.4
1951	27.9	1963	32.6	1975	58.5	1987	138.2
1952	28.5	1964	33.2	1976	62.9		
1953	28.3	1965	34.0	1977	67.9		
1954	28.5	1966	35.2	1978	73.9		

Consumer Price Index, by Item

Source: Statistics Canada

1981 = 100

This table shows the relative costs, as far back as 1950, of categories of purchases made by Canadian consumers. To compare today's (1987) costs with those of another year, divide the 1987 index by the index for the year you wish to compare it with; then multiply that by your actual cost in the year for which you are making the comparison.

Example: you spent $40 per week on family food purchases in 1960. To calculate what that would be in today's dollars divide the 1987 food index (132.4) by the 1960 food index (25.8). Now multiply the result by $40. The answer, $205.27, is what you now must spend to buy the same package of groceries that cost $40 in 1960.

	All items	Food	Housing	Clothing	Trans-portation	Health and personal care	Recreation and education	Tobacco and alcohol
1950	25.2	21.6	25.3	35.9	24.3	20.8	27.0	32.8
1955	24.5	23.7	29.7	38.9	27.3	25.9	32.4	34.3
1960	31.4	25.8	32.2	40.0	32.3	31.6	38.2	37.0
1965	34.0	28.7	34.2	43.7	34.0	35.9	40.8	39.1
1970	41.0	34.1	42.3	51.5	40.4	44.3	50.7	47.0
1975	58.5	55.8	58.9	65.4	54.4	60.2	67.3	59.9
1976	62.9	57.3	65.4	69.0	60.3	65.3	71.3	64.2
1977	67.9	62.0	71.5	73.7	64.6	70.2	74.7	68.7
1978	73.9	71.6	76.9	76.5	68.3	75.2	77.6	74.3
1979	80.7	81.0	82.3	83.6	74.9	82.0	82.9	79.6
1980	88.9	89.8	89.0	93.4	84.5	90.2	90.8	88.6
1981	100.0	100.0	100.0	100.0	100.0	100.0	100.0	100.0
1982	110.8	107.2	112.5	105.6	114.1	110.6	108.7	115.5
1983	117.2	111.2	120.2	109.8	119.8	118.2	115.8	130.0
1984	122.3	117.4	124.7	112.5	124.8	122.8	119.7	140.6
1985	127.2	120.8	129.0	115.6	130.8	127.2	124.5	154.0
1986	132.4	126.8	132.9	118.8	135.0	132.6	130.3	172.3
1987	138.2	132.4	138.3	123.8	139.9	139.2	137.3	183.9

Canadian Interest Rates, 1974-1988

Source: Bank of Canada

(average annual)

	Bank rate	Prime rate	Savings rate[1]	Conventional 5 yr. mortgage	Govt.of Canada average bond yield (10 yrs.and over)
1974	8.50	10.75	8.50	11.24	8.90
1975	8.50	9.42	7.00	11.43	9.04
1976	9.38	10.08	7.81	11.78	9.18
1977	7.79	8.50	6.00	10.36	8.70
1978	8.98	9.69	7.06	10.57	9.27
1979	12.10	12.90	10.13	11.98	10.21
1980	12.89	14.25	11.15	14.32	12.48
1981	17.93	19.29	15.42	18.15	15.22
1982	13.96	15.81	11.50	17.89	14.26
1983	9.55	11.17	6.85	13.29	11.79
1984	11.31	12.06	7.69	13.59	12.75
1985	9.65	10.58	6.08	12.13	11.04
1986	9.21	10.52	6.02	11.21	9.52
1987	8.40	9.52	4.81	11.17	9.95
1988, Jan.	8.63	9.75	4.75	11.75	9.74
Feb.	8.58	9.75	4.75	11.50	9.61
Mar.	8.78	9.75	4.75	11.00	10.13
Apr.	9.06	10.25	5.25	11.25	10.36
May	9.12	10.25	5.25	11.25	10.38
June	9.44	10.75	5.50	11.25	10.13

(1) Non-chequable savings account.

Value of the Canadian Dollar Compared to Foreign Currencies

Source: Bank of Canada

	Canadian dollar in US dollars			Foreign Currency Units Per Canadian Dollar (annual averages)						
	High	Low	Average	British pound	French franc	German mark	Swiss franc	Japanese yen	Italian lira	Mexican peso
1965	n.a.	n.a.	0.9276	0.3318	4.5454	3.7051	4.0144	333.8898	579.3743	11.5942
1966	n.a.	n.a.	0.9282	0.3323	4.6000	3.7120	4.0161	336.1345	579.7101	11.6023
1967	n.a.	n.a.	0.9270	0.3372	4.6000	3.6955	4.0112	335.6831	578.3690	11.5875
1968	n.a.	n.a.	0.9281	0.3877	4.5956	3.7051	4.0064	334.5601	580.3831	11.5996
1969	n.a.	n.a.	0.9287	0.3885	4.8123	3.6417	4.0048	332.7787	582.4112	11.6090
1970	n.a.	n.a.	0.9579	0.3997	5.2938	3.4928	4.1288	342.9355	600.6006	11.9717
1971	n.a.	n.a.	0.9903	0.4051	5.4555	3.4483	4.0717	343.4066	611.9951	12.3747
1972	n.a.	n.a.	1.0096	0.4033	5.0891	3.2175	3.8551	305.8104	588.9282	12.6183
1973	1.0127	0.9885	0.9999	0.4076	4.4307	2.6441	3.1496	270.5628	581.3954	12.4984
1974	1.0443	1.0044	1.0225	0.4370	4.9140	2.6420	3.0349	298.1515	664.8936	12.7812
1975	1.0095	0.9615	0.9830	0.4426	4.2070	2.4131	2.5368	291.5452	641.0256	12.2865
1976	1.0389	0.9588	1.0141	0.5615	4.8379	2.5510	2.5336	300.5711	840.3361	14.6477
1977	0.9985	0.8963	0.9403	0.5385	4.6189	2.1805	2.2502	251.2563	829.8755	21.2134
1978	0.9170	0.8363	0.8770	0.4568	3.9448	1.7572	1.5547	182.4818	743.4944	19.9681
1979	0.8778	0.8320	0.8536	0.4023	3.6311	1.5640	1.4192	186.0465	709.2199	19.4628
1980	0.8767	0.8249	0.8554	0.3677	3.6088	1.5518	1.4314	192.9385	730.9942	19.6309
1981	0.8506	0.8031	0.8340	0.4117	4.3346	1.8804	1.6335	183.4862	942.5071	20.4248
1982	0.8446	0.7680	0.8103	0.4634	5.3050	1.9662	1.6418	201.3693	1 094.0919	44.6828
1983	0.8208	0.7990	0.8114	0.5352	6.1576	2.0687	1.7027	192.6782	1 228.5012	124.8440
1984	0.8038	0.7486	0.7723	0.5780	6.7250	2.1911	1.8093	183.2509	1 351.3514	146.7782
1985	0.7587	0.7107	0.7325	0.5649	6.5232	2.1381	1.7809	173.4004	1 392.7577	222.1235
1986	0.7332	0.6913	0.7197	0.4905	4.9751	1.5564	1.2872	120.5400	1 069.5187	430.6632
1987	0.7721	0.7248	0.7541	0.4603	4.5290	1.3543	1.1230	108.8376	997.5171	994.0358
1988, Jan. . . .	0.7846	0.7688	0.7780	0.4322	4.3440	1.2870	1.0482	99.4036	946.9697	1 736.1111
Feb. . . .	0.7949	0.7828	0.7887	0.4486	4.5208	1.3382	1.0977	101.8849	985.2217	1 788.9088
Mar. . .	0.8109	0.7944	0.8006	0.4367	4.5537	1.3423	1.1096	101.7398	993.0487	1 841.6206
Apr. . .	0.8147	0.8003	0.8120	0.4311	4.5914	1.3530	1.1192	101.1225	1 005.0251	1 862.1974
May . .	0.8139	0.8019	0.8085	0.4327	4.6361	1.3699	1.1414	100.8776	1 018.3299	1 858.7361
June . .	0.8322	0.8096	0.8214	0.4622	4.8662	1.4432	1.2008	104.6463	1 071.8114	1 886.7925

n.a. not available.

Foreign Control[1] of Canadian Industries, 1985

Source: Statistics Canada

	Share of Sales[2]				Total	
	Foreign-controlled			Canadian controlled	sales (millions)	Number of corporations[4]
	Total	U.S.	other			
Total[3]	**29.0%**	**21.9%**	**7.1%**	**71.0%**	**$805 273**	**413 444**
Tobacco	98.0	31.5	66.5	2.0	1 424	12
Transport Equipment	88.3	84.8	3.5	11.7	55 653	1 594
Rubber products	88.1	67.4	20.7	11.9	4 145	156
Chemicals and chemical products	76.0	56.9	19.1	24.0	19 015	1 160
Electrical products	60.8	46.7	14.1	39.2	14 745	1 303
Mining, mineral fuels	58.0	49.4	8.6	42.0	32 181	2 453
Petroleum and coal products	57.4	39.6	17.8	42.6	35 703	131
Non-metallic mineral products	54.9	27.8	27.1	45.1	6 697	1 587
Textile mills	52.3	43.2	9.1	47.7	5 798	1 142
Machinery	52.0	43.3	8.7	48.0	8 485	1 993
Beverages	36.6	n.a.	n.a.	63.4	5 259	264
Food	26.4	20.9	5.5	73.6	35 825	3 906
Paper and allied industries	26.1	16.9	9.2	73.9	21 868	676
Metal mining	26.0	13.4	12.6	74.0	10 089	225
Wholesale trade	25.8	12.6	13.2	74.2	150 153	49 799
Services	15.4	14.0	1.4	84.6	57 026	120 965
Furniture	13.6	12.9	0.7	86.4	3 211	2 536
Printing and publishing	12.6	8.9	3.7	87.4	10 003	6 042
Retail trade	12.0	10.0	2.0	88.0	131 213	85 890
Communications	11.1	11.1	–	88.9	12 770	960
Clothing	9.2	8.6	0.6	90.8	5 338	2 803
Construction	6.9	4.2	2.6	93.1	41 248	59 286
Transportation	5.4	3.4	2.0	94.6	40 396	22 239
Public utilities	3.2	3.0	0.2	96.8	24 893	1 053
Agriculture, fishing and forestry	2.9	2.1	0.8	97.1	9 854	23 030

(1) A corporation is usually considered to be foreign-controlled if 50% or more of its voting rights are known to be held outside Canada or by a Canadian-resident corporation that is itself foreign-controlled. (2) Based on gross revenues from Canadian operations. (3) Excludes financial industries. (4) Includes all corporations operating in Canada whose gross revenues exceeded $15 million or whose assets exceeded $10 million. n.a. not available; – = zero.

Foreign Direct Investment in Canada[1]

Source: Statistics Canada

(millions of dollars)

	1970	%	1975	%	1980	%	1984	%	1985	%
Total	**26 358**	**100.0**	**37 392**	**100.0**	**61 707**	**100.0**	**79 589**	**100.0**	**83 474**	**100.0**
United States	21 403	81.2	29 666	79.3	48 686	78.9	60 393	75.9	63 096	75.6
United Kingdom	2 503	9.5	3 629	9.7	5 333	8.6	7 534	9.5	7 899	9.5
West Germany	240	0.9	592	1.6	1 698	2.8	2 110	2.7	2 376	2.8
Netherlands	446	1.7	671	1.8	1 189	1.9	2 018	2.5	2 060	2.5
Japan	103	0.4	257	0.7	605	1.0	1 750	2.2	1 877	2.2
Switzerland	322	1.2	555	1.5	816	1.3	1 263	1.6	1 377	1.6
France	405	1.5	531	1.4	824	1.3	1 175	1.5	1 250	1.5
Bermuda	29	0.1	243	0.6	762	1.2	766	1.0	810	1.0
Belgium-Luxembourg	255	1.0	313	0.8	481	0.8	317	0.4	323	0.4
Sweden	126	0.5	228	0.6	322	0.5	297	0.4	310	0.4
Panama	17	0.1	67	0.2	99	0.2	261	0.3	227	0.3
Italy	68	0.3	83	0.2	62	0.1	139	0.2	192	0.2
Ireland	6	...	12	...	81	0.1	131	0.2	163	0.2
Hong Kong	20	0.1	34	0.1	51	0.1	146	0.2	148	0.2
Bahamas	84	0.3	114	0.3	122	0.2	129	0.2	131	0.2
Australia	12	...	37	0.1	74	0.1	102	0.1	116	0.1
Netherlands Antilles	7	...	15	...	30	...	70	0.1	85	0.1
Austria	3	...	4	...	18	...	31	...	39	...
Norway	5	...	13	...	20	...	28	...	34	...
Denmark	14	0.1	17	...	31	...	26	...	29	...
Africa	180	0.7	72	0.2	138	0.2	8	...	12	...
Mexico	5	...	9	...	...	...	6	...	6	...
Venezeula	3	...	1	...	3	...	5	...	5	...

(1) Represents long-term foreign investment in Canadian businesses; only those businesses with at least 10% foreign ownership are identified. ... = too small to be included.

Canadian Direct Investment Abroad[1]

Source: Statistics Canada

(millions of dollars)

	1970	%	1975	%	1980	%	1984	%	1985	%
All Countries	6 188	100.0	10 526	100.0	26 967	100.0	44 225	100.0	49 909	100.0
United States	3 251	52.5	5 559	52.8	16 781	62.2	30 778	69.6	35 521	71.2
United Kingdom	586	9.5	1 019	9.7	2 860	10.6	3 277	7.4	3 627	7.3
Bermuda	136	2.2	462	4.4	959	3.6	1 314	3.0	1 451	2.9
Indonesia	...	...	98	0.9	590	2.2	1 051	2.4	1 091	2.2
Brazil	...	...	1 039	9.9	691	2.6	938	2.1	1 036	2.1
Australia	246	4.0	453	4.3	694	2.6	1 034	2.3	987	2.0
Ireland	43	0.7	64	0.6	233	0.9	565	1.3	786	1.6
Switzerland	21	0.3	72	0.7	291	1.1	407	0.9	542	1.1
West Germany	77	1.2	156	=1.5	276	1.0	426	1.0	529	1.1
Netherlands	52	0.9	72	0.7	300	1.1	350	0.8	449	0.9
Spain	...	...	35	0.3	168	0.6	283	0.6	290	0.6
Japan	48	0.8	74	0.7	109	0.4	229	0.5	230	0.5
France	82	1.3	215	2.0	289	1.1	111	0.3	214	0.4
Mexico	45	0.7	75	0.7	165	0.6	269	0.6	208	0.4
Italy	53	0.9	36	0.3	125	0.5	141	0.3	189	0.4
Jamaica	109	1.8	118	1.1	159	0.6	161	0.4	153	0.3
Belgium/Luxembourg	40	0.6	36	0.3	74	0.3	97	0.2	145	0.3
South Africa	73	1.2	126	1.2	159	0.6	139	0.3	105	0.2
Bahamas	151	2.4	147	1.4	266	1.0	150	0.3	84	0.2
Argentina	...	...	39	0.4	23	0.1	69	0.2	61	0.1
Norway	...	...	56	0.5	64	0.2	59	0.1	60	0.1
Venezuela	12	0.2	19	0.2	59	0.2	53	0.1	56	0.1
Denmark	...	...	54	0.5	80	0.3	39	0.1	48	0.1
Trinidad and Tobago .	n.a.	n.a.	24	0.2	19	0.1	13	...	13	...

(1) Represents long-term Canadian investment in businesses operating outside Canada; only those businesses with at least 10% Canadian ownership are identified.
... = too small to be included.

Understanding the Economy: A Glossary of Terms

Appreciation: the increase in the value of a currency relative to other currencies under free market conditions.

Balanced budget: when the federal government's budget is balanced, all revenues equal expenditures in a budget year. Thus there is no surplus or deficit, but a national debt may still exist.

Balance of payments: a measure of all yearly business transactions between one country and the rest of the world. It is the difference between the value of exports and imports, as well as the difference between investment money coming into and leaving the country.

Bank of Canada: the sole money-issuing bank in Canada, acting as banker to all other financial institutions and the government. It is responsible for Canada's banking system, sets interest rates and regulates the money supply.

Bank rate: the interest rate at which the Bank of Canada is prepared to lend money to the chartered banks.

Cartel: a group of companies in a specific industry which band together to restrict output and increase prices in order to get higher profits. In Canada, cartels are illegal. The best known international cartel is the Organization of Petroleum Exporting Countries (OPEC).

Consumer price index: an indexed measure of the average prices of household goods to show inflationary trends; compiled monthly by Statistics Canada.

Cost of living: the cost of maintaining a particular standard of living measured in terms of purchased goods and services. The rise in the cost of living is the same as the rate of inflation.

Deficit spending: the practice whereby a government goes into debt to finance some of its expenditures.

Demand-side economics: a school of thinking which states that an economy can prosper through policies which tend to increase public and private spending on goods and services.

Depreciation: the decrease in the value of a currency relative to other currencies under free market conditions. This differs from a devaluation.

Depression: a long period of little business activity when prices are low, unemployment is high, and purchasing power decreases sharply.

Devaluation: the official lowering of the value of a nation's currency relative to foreign currencies.

Disposable income: income after taxes which is available to persons for spending and saving.

Equalization payments: transfers of tax revenues from the Canadian government to provinces with a higher proportion of lower income earners, to compensate them for their lower per capita tax revenues.

Exchange rate: the price of one currency relative to another country's currency.

Fiscal policy: the deliberate use of government budget measures—i.e., tax and spending policies—to alleviate economic problems such as low GNP, high unemployment and inflation.

Free trade: a system whereby the free movement of all goods and services, investment money and workers between countries is neither restricted nor encouraged by governments.

Gross domestic product (GDP): the value of all goods and services produced in a country.

Gross national product (GNP): the value of all goods and services produced by citizens of a country both inside and outside the country.

Inflation: a steady rise in the average level of prices in an economy.

Less developed countries (LDCs): also known as Third World countries, these are countries considered economically-underdeveloped relative to the western industrialized nations.

Lockout: action taken by an employer to shut down operations because of a labor dispute.

Minimum wage: a minimum hourly wage as set by federal or provincial legislation.

Monetary policy: the government's manipulation of interest rates and the money supply to achieve economic growth, employment and price stability.

Money supply: the amount of money in an economy, with money defined as all currency in circulation and chequing accounts.

National debt: the debt of the central government—in Canada's case, the federal government.

Per capita GNP: also known as per capita income, it is the nation's gross national product divided by its population.

Prime interest rate: the rate charged by chartered banks on short-term loans to large commercial customers with the highest credit rating.

Protectionism: government policies designed to restrict imports in order to protect domestic industries. These policies include customs duties (tariffs) and restrictions on the quantity of imports (quotas).

Real GNP: gross national product adjusted for inflation.

Recession: not as severe or as long-lasting as a depression but with the same general characteristics: a decline in real GNP, unemployment and widespread decline in many sectors of the economy.

Stagflation: a high inflation rate combined with a high unemployment rate.

Strike: an organized refusal to work by employees.

Supply-side economics: a school of thinking which states that an economy can prosper through policies affecting costs of production—that is, by giving production incentives to labor and greater financial rewards to investors.

Trade balance: the difference between the value of exports and imports.

Transfer payments: government payments where no productive return is provided, such as old age pensions, unemployment insurance and welfare.

Wage-price controls: legislation whereby the government sets wage, salary and price increases in order to curb inflation.

Wage-price spiral: inflation brought about by increased wages which increase costs to the producers, who in turn increase prices. The increase in prices would cause labor to bargain for higher wages, resulting in a spiralling inflation.

Economic Comparison of Canada and Other Countries

Source: *World Development Report 1988*, World Bank

	GNP per capita (1986)[1]	Avg. annual real GNP growth per capita[2]	Avg. annual rate of inflation[3]	Energy use per capita (kg of oil equivalent)[4]	Population per physician[5]	Daily calorie supply per capita[6]
Australia	$11 920	1.7	8.2	4 710	520	3 302
Brazil	1 810	4.3	157.1	830	1 300	2 657
Canada	14 120	2.6	5.5	8 945	550	3 443
China	300	5.1	3.8	532	1 730	2 620
Egypt	760	3.1	12.4	577	760	3 275
France	10 720	2.8	8.8	3 640	460	3 358
Greece	3 680	3.3	20.3	1 932	390	3 637
Hong Kong	6 910	6.2	6.9	1 260	1 290	2 692
Hungary	2 020	3.9	5.4	2 985	390	3 544
India	290	1.8	7.8	208	3 700	2 126
Israel	6 210	2.6	182.9	1 944	400	3 019
Italy	8 550	2.6	13.2	2 539	750	3 493
Jamaica	840	−1.4	19.8	844	2 830	2 578
Japan	12 840	4.3	1.6	3 186	740	2 695
Libya	n.a.	n.a.	n.a.	2 259	620	3 585
Mexico	1 860	2.6	63.7	1 235	1 210	3 126
Nicaragua	790	−2.2	56.5	259	2 230	2 464
Pakistan	350	2.4	7.5	205	2 910	2 180
Peru	1 090	0.1	100.1	478	1 440[7]	2 120
Poland	2 070	n.a.	31.2	3 369	550	3 224
South Africa	1 850	0.4	13.6	2 470	n.a.	2 926
South Korea	2 370	6.7	5.4	1 408	1 390	2 806
Sweden	13 160	1.6	8.2	6 374	410	3 007
Uganda	230	−2.6	74.9	26	21 270	2 483
United Kingdom ..	8 870	1.7	6.0	3 802	680	3 148
United States	17 480	1.6	4.4	7 193	500	3 682
USSR	n.a.	n.a.	n.a.	4 949	270	3 332
Vietnam	n.a.	n.a.	n.a.	87	4 110	2 281
West Germany ...	12 080	2.5	3.0	4 464	420	3 519
Yugoslavia	2 300	3.9	51.8	2 041	700	3 499

(1) In U.S. dollars. (2) From 1965-1986. (3) 1980-1986; the inflation rate is calculated using Gross Domestic Product price indices for each country. (4) For 1986. (5) As of 1981. (6) For 1985. (7) As of 1982.
n.a. not available.

Federal Government Surplus or Deficit,[1] 1957-1987

Source: Finance Canada

(millions of dollars; fiscal year ending Mar. 31)

	Surplus or deficit	% of GDP[2]		Surplus or deficit	% of GDP[2]		Surplus or deficit	% of GDP[2]
1957	− 325	1.0[3]	1968	− 711	− 1.0	1979	− 12 617	− 5.2
1958	− 196	− 0.6[3]	1969	− 400	− 0.5	1980	− 11 501	− 4.2
1959	− 877	− 2.5[3]	1970	332	0.4	1981	− 13 522	− 4.4
1960	− 600	− 1.7[3]	1971	− 780	− 0.9	1982	− 14 872	− 4.2
1961	− 529	− 1.4[3]	1972	− 1 542	− 1.6	1983	− 27 816	− 7.4
1962	− 948	− 2.3	1973	− 1 675	− 1.5	1984	− 32 399	− 8.0
1963	− 833	− 1.9	1974	− 1 999	− 1.6	1985	− 38 324	− 8.6
1964	− 1 169	− 2.5	1975	− 2 009	− 1.3	1986	− 34 404	− 7.2
1965	− 315	− 0.6	1976	− 5 737	− 3.3	1987	− 30 605	− 6.0
1966	303	0.5	1977	− 6 297	− 3.2			
1967	− 187	− 0.3	1978	− 10 426	− 4.8			

(1) A minus (−) sign indicates a deficit. (2) GDP (Gross Domestic Product) represents the value of all goods and services produced in Canada. (3) Represents percentage of GNP.

Per Capita National Debt, 1940-1987

Source: Statistics Canada

	millions of dollars		dollars			millions of dollars		dollars	
Year[1]	Net debt[2]	Interest on debt	Net debt per capita	Interest per capita	Year[1]	Net debt[2]	Interest on debt	Net debt per capita	Interest per capita
1940 ..	3 271.3	139.2	287	12	1976 ..	23 296.4	3 908.5	1 013	170
1945 ..	11 298.4	409.1	936	34	1977 ..	29 585.9	4 714.2	1 270	202
1950 ..	11 644.6	439.8	849	32	1978 ..	39 621.8	5 540.7	1 687	236
1955 ..	11 263.1	477.9	718	30	1979 ..	55 806.2	7 026.2	2 358	297
1960 ..	12 089.2	735.6	677	41	1980 ..	72 159.0	8 494.0	2 999	353
1965 ..	15 504.4	1 012.1	789	52	1981 ..	85 681.0	10 658.0	3 520	438
1970 ..	16 943.3	1 675.9	796	79	1982 ..	100 553.0	15 114.0	4 082	614
1971 ..	17 322.4	1 779.6	803	83	1983 ..	128 369.0	16 903.0	5 158	679
1972 ..	17 936.7	1 963.6	823	90	1984 ..	160 768.0	18 077.0	6 399	720
1973 ..	17 455.8	2 104.5	792	96	1985 ..	199 092.0	22 445.0	7 850	885
1974 ..	18 128.4	2 548.8	811	114	1986 ..	233 496.0	25 441.0	9 209	1 003
1975 ..	19 275.6	3 164.1	849	139	1987 ..	264 101.0	26 658.0	10 356	1 045

(1) As of Mar. 31, on a public accounts basis. (2) Accumulated budgetary deficit (net recorded assets minus gross liabilities) since Confederation.

Provincial Government Net Liabilities and Assets[1]

Source: Statistics Canada

(millions of dollars; fiscal years ending Mar. 31)

	Nfld	PEI	NS	NB	Que	Ont	Man	Sask	Alta	BC	Yukon	NWT
1975	− 612	− 81	− 376	− 409	+ 354	− 2 845	+ 35	+ 479	+ 1 331	+ 1 328	− 37	− 96
1976	− 715	− 91	− 424	− 502	+ 79	− 4 235	− 96	+ 597	+ 1 994	+ 897	− 33	− 92
1977	− 929	− 80	− 480	− 601	− 336	− 5 195	− 208	+ 648	+ 2 922	+ 1 064	− 27	− 83
1978	− 1 094	− 105	− 566	− 760	− 778	− 6 613	− 657	+ 713	+ 4 841	+ 1 443	− 20	− 76
1979	− 1 365	− 114	− 731	− 815	− 1 132	− 7 840	− 707	+ 837	+ 7 656	+ 1 648	− 14	− 77
1980	− 1 541	− 119	− 812	− 813	− 1 655	− 8 533	− 652	+ 913	+ 9 418	+ 1 962	− 26	− 66
1981	− 1 533	− 135	− 966	− 925	− 3 211	− 9 378	− 730	+ 1 050	+ 12 153	+ 2 144	+ 15	+ 52
1982	− 1 699	− 135	− 1 439	− 1 079	− 17	− 10 528	− 970	+ 1 176	+ 14 939	+ 1 948	+ 25	+ 71
1983	− 1 866	− 165	− 1 822	− 1 476	− 2 069	− 13 055	− 1 375	+ 884	+ 15 119	+ 811	+ 33	+ 68
1984	− 2 118	− 161	− 2 148	− 1 751	− 3 931	− 15 529	− 1 916	+ 599	+ 16 071	− 204	+ 50	+ 112
1985	− 2 415	− 164	− 2 594	− 1 983	− 5 924	− 17 161	− 2 373	+ 131	+ 18 194	− 1 012	+ 63	+ 115
1986	− 2 616	− 169	− 3 010	− 2 232	− 9 997	− 21 164	− 3 288	− 631	+ 18 686	− 1 700	+ 87	+ 149

(1) A minus sign (−) represents a net liability (debt); a plus sign (+) represents a net asset (i.e. assets are greater than liabilities).

Canadian Manufacturing Industries, 1985

Source: Statistics Canada

	No. of Employees			Value of manufacturing	Value added[1]	Businesses[2]
	Total	Male	Female		(millions of dollars)	
Total Manufacturing	1 766 763	1 303 066	463 697	$248 493	$95 875	36 854
Transportation industries	210 984	174 966	36 018	43 182	14 089	1 471
Food industries	192 000	130 977	61 023	32 793	9 738	3 228
Metal products	139 698	119 020	20 678	13 971	6 638	5 537
Electrical products	137 165	90 779	46 386	13 270	6 677	1 379
Printing and publishing	117 062	72 101	44 961	9 535	5 983	5 443
Paper industries	114 187	99 821	14 366	18 075	7 555	688
Clothing industries	110 910	27 059	83 851	5 543	2 808	2 497
Wood products	107 560	97 499	10 061	11 122	4 624	3 476
Primary metal industries	106 808	99 650	7 158	16 971	7 006	435
Chemical products	87 224	63 621	23 603	18 269	7 625	1 256
Machinery industries	74 732	64 829	9 903	7 451	3 635	1 815
Miscellaneous	67 676	41 591	26 085	5 065	2 541	3 280
Mineral products[3]	50 605	43 986	6 619	5 879	3 047	1 532
Furniture	49 868	39 351	10 517	3 399	1 797	1 727
Plastic products	38 182	25 676	12 506	3 861	1 749	1 091
Beverage industries	31 903	27 503	4 400	4 864	2 736	304
Textile industries	31 110	16 646	14 464	2 650	1 146	802
Primary textiles	26 758	18 939	7 819	2 670	1 157	215
Rubber industries	25 366	21 341	4 025	2 554	1 268	148
Leather industries	23 129	9 866	13 263	1 308	634	384
Oil and coal	16 739	13 261	3 478	24 421	2 614	121
Tobacco industries	7 097	4 584	2 513	1 641	809	25

(1) The value of shipments of manufactured goods minus the cost of producing these shipments. (2) Based on the number of business locations. (3) Excludes metallic mineral products.

Manufacturing by Metro Areas[1], 1984

Source: Statistics Canada

	Employees	%	Businesses[12]	%	Value of goods ($millions)	%
Canada	1 722 044	100.0	36 464	100.0	$230 070	100.0
Toronto, Ont.	345 760	20.1	7 608	20.9	42 010	18.3
Montreal, Que.	241 596	14.0	5 628	15.4	29 415	12.8
Hamilton, Ont.	62 660	3.6	784	2.2	8 703	3.8
Vancouver, BC	61 952	3.6	2 283	6.3	9 073	3.9
Kitchener, Ont.	48 029	2.8	744	2.0	4 588	2.0
Winnipeg, Man.	39 698	2.3	897	2.5	3 657	1.6
Windsor, Ont.	35 630	2.1	484	1.3	8 388	3.6
St. Catharines-Niagara, Ont.	33 397	1.9	420	1.2	4 778	2.1
Edmonton, Alta.	25 952	1.5	852	2.3	7 794	3.4
London, Ont.	20 916	1.2	387	1.1	2 427	1.1
Calgary, Alta.	20 397	1.2	776	2.1	3 035	1.3
Ottawa-Hull, Ont.-Que.	19 056	1.1	452	1.2	2 727	1.2
Quebec, Que.	18 860	1.1	575	1.6	3 180	1.4
Chicoutimi-Jonquière, Que.	10 161	0.6	86	0.2	1 661	0.7
Trois Rivières, Que.	9 474	0.6	123	0.3	1 114	0.5
Halifax, NS	7 224	0.4	215	0.6	2 077	0.9
Thunder Bay, Ont.	6 893	0.4	108	0.3	1 033	0.4
Saskatoon, Sask.	6 336	0.4	204	0.6	784	0.3
Sudbury, Ont.	5 844	0.3	81	0.2	404	0.2
Saint John, NB	5 078	0.3	77	0.2	1 906	0.8
Regina, Sask.	4 675	0.3	163	0.4	1 068	0.5
Victoria, BC	3 853	0.2	234	0.6	323	0.1
St. John's, Nfld.	3 036	0.2	96	0.3	302	0.1

(1) For census Metropolitan areas, which include neighboring municipalities from which the major urban centre draws its work force. (2) Based on the number of locations.

Manufacturing by Province

Source: Statistics Canada

(millions of dollars)

	1920	1933	1944	1953	1960	1965	1970	1975	1980	1985
Canada	3 707	1 954	9 074	17 785	23 280	33 889	46 381	88 427	168 014	248 493
Newfoundland	n.a.	n.a.	n.a.	107	127	175	263	650	1 097	1 224
Prince Edward Island	6	3	11	23	28	43	63	109	234	297
Nova Scotia	147	48	204	320	388	563	758	1 819	3 454	4 635
New Brunswick	107	41	152	296	369	513	730	1 669	3 561	4 243
Quebec	1 053	604	2 930	5 387	7 076	9 492	13 084	23 967	44 599	60 460
Ontario	1 864	959	4 340	8 877	11 479	17 676	24 010	44 389	82 150	131 988
Manitoba	156	84	352	585	711	913	1 260	2 581	4 357	5 549
Saskatchewan	58	32	175	267	330	421	545	1 176	2 118	2 983
Alberta	86	49	253	556	860	1 283	1 900	4 726	10 521	17 192
British Columbia	230[1]	134[1]	656	1 367	1 909	2 806	3 761	7 326	15 893	19 863
Yukon and Northwest Territories	n.a.	n.a.	n.a.	3	3	4	7	14	30	59

(1) Includes the Yukon.
n.a. not available.

Value of Canadian Building Construction

Source: Statistics Canada

(millions of dollars)

	1960		1970		1980		1985		1987[1]	
	Value	%	Value	%	Value	%	Value	%	Value	%
Total Construction	4 051	100.0	8 098	100.0	26 540	100.0	41 459	100.0	57 228	100.0
Residential	1 913	47.2	4 009	49.5	13 872	52.3	24 145	58.2	36 003	62.9
single detached	n.a.	n.a.	1 367	16.9	5 016	18.9	7 153	17.3	13 277	23.2
semi-detached	n.a.	n.a.	141	1.7	569	2.1	346	0.8	536	0.9
apartments	n.a.	n.a.	1 250	15.4	2 432	9.2	2 627	6.3	5 255	9.2
other	n.a.	n.a.	1 251	15.4	5 855	22.1	14 019	33.8	16 935	29.6
Industrial	452	11.2	1 000	12.3	3 025	11.4	3 470	8.4	3 189	5.6
factories	366	9.0	848	10.5	2 500	9.4	2 935	7.1	2 855	5.0
Commercial	738	18.2	1 287	15.9	5 912	22.3	8 697	21.0	12 068	21.1
hotels[2]	48	1.2	93	1.1	475	1.8	722	1.7	946	1.7
office buildings	310	7.7	617	7.6	2 610	9.8	3 937	9.5	5 494	9.6
stores	188	4.6	273	3.4	1 410	5.3	2 037	4.9	3 131	5.5
theatres[3]	32	0.8	86	1.1	461	1.7	818	2.0	847	1.5
Institutional	615	15.2	1 330	16.4	2 172	8.2	3 119	7.5	4 172	7.3
schools	347	8.6	890	11.0	942	3.5	1 292	3.1	2 084	3.6
churches	70	1.7	29	0.4	117	0.4	151	0.4	129	0.2
hospitals	154	3.8	263	3.2	777	2.9	1 009	2.4	1 038	1.8
Other	333	8.2	473	5.8	1 560	5.9	2 028	4.9	1 796	3.1
farm buildings	168	4.1	208	2.6	887	3.3	756	1.8	640	1.1
airports, bus and train stations	26	0.6	27	0.3	88	0.3	187	0.5	137	0.2

(1) Preliminary. (2) Includes clubs, restaurants, cafeterias and tourist cabins. (3) Includes arenas, amusement and recreation buildings.
n.a. not available.

Value of Retail Sales by Type of Business

Source: Statistics Canada

(millions of dollars)

	1965		1970		1975		1980		1985		1986	
	Retail sales	%	Retail sales	%	Retail sales	%	Retail sales	%	Retail sales	%	Retail sales	%
Total	21 155	100.0	28 034	100.0	51 200	100.0	83 889	100.0	129 446	100.0	140 009	100.0
Food stores	5 494	26.0	7 489	26.7	12 881	25.2	21 529	25.7	32 258	24.9	34 630	24.7
Car dealers	4 175	19.7	4 197	15.0	10 184	19.9	16 170	19.3	26 682	20.6	29 487	21.1
Department stores	2 010	9.5	2 852	10.2	5 786	11.3	9 373	11.2	12 039	9.3	12 728	9.1
Service stations/garages	1 778	8.4	2 531	9.0	3 857	7.5	6 996	8.3	12 585	9.7	12 308	8.8
Clothing	1 112	5.3	1 405	5.0	2 267	4.4	3 727	4.4	5 168	4.6	6 553	4.7
women's clothing	392	1.9	561	2.0	863	1.7	1 578	1.9	2 777	2.1	3 036	2.2
family clothing	357	1.7	398	1.4	740	1.4	1 180	1.4	1 867	1.4	2 079	1.5
men's clothing	363	1.7	446	1.6	664	1.3	969	1.2	1 324	1.0	1 438	1.0

	1965 Retail sales	%	1970 Retail sales	%	1975 Retail sales	%	1980 Retail sales	%	1985 Retail sales	%	1986 Retail sales	%
Drugstores	610	2.9	840	3.0	1 488	2.9	2 728	3.3	5 357	4.1	6 064	4.3
Furniture and appliances	678	3.2	847	3.0	1 372	2.7	2 039	2.4	3 214	2.5	3 659	2.6
Auto parts	n.a.	n.a.	n.a.	n.a.	n.a.	n.a.	1 735	2.1	2 802	2.2	3 068	2.2
General merchandise	n.a.	n.a.	n.a.	n.a.	n.a.	n.a.	1 894	2.3	2 699	2.1	2 858	2.0
General stores	510	2.4	575	2.1	995	1.9	1 556	1.9	1 983	1.5	2 097	1.5
Personal goods	n.a.	n.a.	n.a.	n.a.	n.a.	n.a.	1 201	1.4	1 719	1.3	2 049	1.5
Sporting goods	n.a.	n.a.	n.a.	n.a.	n.a.	n.a.	1 009	1.2	1 868	1.4	2 029	1.4
Hardware	332	1.6	383	1.4	581	1.1	787	0.9	1 158	0.9	1 432	1.0
Shoe stores	248	1.2	328	1.2	474	0.9	868	1.0	1 288	1.0	1 425	1.0
Variety stores	521	2.5	553	2.0	819	1.6	996	1.2	1 267	1.0	1 247	0.9
Jewellery	186	0.9	219	0.8	427	0.8	749	0.9	932	0.7	1 042	0.7
Books and stationery	n.a.	n.a.	n.a.	n.a.	n.a.	n.a.	415	0.5	715	0.6	786	0.6
Florists	n.a.	n.a.	n.a.	n.a.	n.a.	n.a.	312	0.4	472	0.4	516	0.4

n.a. not available.

New Passenger Car Sales in Canada, by Company, 1987

Source: Member companies of the Motor Vehicle Manufacturers' Association and the Automobile Importers of Canada

BMW	4 864	Hyundai	50 648	Nissan	36 416	Toyota	68 753
Chrysler	156 078	Jaguar	2 660	Saab	1 639	Volkswagen ...	41 470
Ford	193 000	Lada	1 054	Skocar	625	Volvo	7 415
General Motors	379 159	Mazda	26 635	Subaru	8 447		
Honda	72 976	Mercedes Benz	4 403	Suzuki	3 808		

Sales of Foreign and Domestic Passenger Cars in Canada

Source: Statistics Canada

(thousands of cars)

	Total cars sold	Domestic[1] total	%	Foreign total	%	Japanese	%	other	%
1950	325	262	80.6	63	19.4	n.a.	n.a.	n.a.	n.a.
1955	387	365	94.3	22	5.7	n.a.	n.a.	n.a.	n.a.
1960	448	322	71.9	126	28.1	n.a.	n.a.	n.a.	n.a.
1965	709	634	89.4	75	10.6	n.a.	n.a.	n.a.	n.a.
1970	640	497	77.7	143	22.3	n.a.	n.a.	n.a.	n.a.
1975	989	835	84.4	154	15.6	96	9.7	58	5.9
1980	932	741	79.5	191	20.5	138	14.8	53	5.7
1981	904	647	71.6	258	28.5	208	23.0	50	5.5
1982	713	489	68.6	224	31.4	178	25.0	46	6.5
1983	843	625	74.1	218	25.9	177	21.0	42	5.0
1984	971	725	74.7	246	25.3	171	17.6	75	7.7
1985	1 137	795	69.9	342	30.1	199	17.5	143	12.6
1986	1 091	762	69.8	329	30.2	198	18.1	131	12.0
1987	1 065	701	65.8	364	34.2	243	22.8	121	11.3

(1) North American.
n.a. not available.

Canadian Motor Vehicle Production

Source: Statistics Canada

	Total	Passenger cars	Commercial vehicles	% for export		Total	Passenger cars	Commercial vehicles	% for export
1961	386 923	323 638	63 285	3.3	1980	1 323 999	820 114	503 885	70.0
1965	846 609	706 810	139 799	10.3	1981	1 289 231	796 378	492 853	75.3
1970	1 159 504	923 437	236 067	75.1	1982	1 293 417	851 431	441 986	86.8
1975	1 385 137	1 027 242	357 895	68.1	1983[1]	1 524 413	968 867	555 546	83.3
1976	1 527 852	1 119 005	408 847	71.4	1984[1]	1 829 384	1 180 085	649 299	83.9
1977	1 691 084	1 120 157	570 927	73.1	1985[1]	1 932 738	1 077 935	854 803	81.5
1978	1 741 966	1 107 874	634 092	72.4	1986[1]	1 854 125	1 061 365	792 760	83.2
1979	1 586 238	960 614	625 624	65.2	1987[1]	1 635 681	810 086	825 595	81.4

(1) Only includes member companies of the Motor Vehicle Manufacturers' Association, not comparable to previous years which include other non-member companies. Members include American Motors Canada Inc., Chrysler Canada Ltd., Ford Motor Co. of Canada, Ltd., General Motors of Canada Ltd., Mack Canada Inc., Navistar International Corp. Canada, Paccar of Canada Ltd., Volvo Canada Ltd., Western Star Trucks Inc.

Canadian Paper Money

Source: Bank of Canada

Denomination	Dominant color	Face (Portrait)	Back (Vignette)		No. in Circulation[1] (000s)
			Old	New	
$1[2]	Green	H.M. Queen Elizabeth II	Parliament Hill across Ottawa R.	–	329 776
$2	Terra Cotta	H.M. Queen Elizabeth II	Inuit hunting scene on Baffin Island	Robin	149 782
$5	Blue	Sir Wilfrid Laurier	Salmon seiner, Johnson Strait, Vancouver Island	Belted Kingfisher	120 586
$10	Purple	Sir John A. Macdonald	Industrial scene, Sarnia, Ont.	Osprey	126 645
$20	Olive Green	H.M. Queen Elizabeth II	Moraine Lake, Alta.	Common Loon	352 580
$50	Red	William Lyon Mackenzie King	Dome Formation, RCMP Musical Ride	Snowy Owl	55 474
$100	Brown	Sir Robert Borden	Waterfront scene, Lunenburg, N.S.	Canada Goose	60 388
$1 000	Rose	H.M. Queen Elizabeth II	Anse St. Jean, Saguenay R., Que.	undecided[3]	1 072

(1) As of Dec. 31, 1987. (2) Has not been redesigned because a new $1 coin was introduced in July, 1987. (3) As of 1988.

Money Facts

- Bank of Canada notes are printed at 2 security printers in Ottawa.
- the paper is manufactured in Canada of cotton fibres.
- in 1987, 800 million new notes were issued at an average cost to the Bank of $0.06 each or $48 million.
- the stated dimensions of a bank note are 152.4 × 69.85 mm, though the actual size may vary slightly.
- the average circulation life is approximately one year for smaller denominations but more than 8 years for a $100 bill.

Canadian Gold Coins

Source: The Royal Canadian Mint

Year	Denomination	Design	Quantity	Price
1912-14	$ 5.00	Coat of Arms	277 614	face value
	$ 10.00	Coat of Arms	348 380	face value
1967	$ 20.00	Coat of Arms	337 512	issued with PR sets
1976	$100.00 (14 k)	Athena & Athlete	650 000	$105.00
	$100.00 (22 k)	Athena & Athlete	350 000	$150.00
1977	$100.00	Flowers of Canada	182 838	$140.00
1978	$100.00	12 Canada Geese	200 000	$150.00
1979	$100.00	Children dancing around the world	250 000	$185.00
1979-81	$ 50.00	Maple Leaf	3 078 000	market price of gold plus premium
1980	$100.00	Inuk in a kayak	130 275	$430.00
1981	$100.00	Musical notes of 'O Canada' on a map of Canada	100 950	$300.00
1982-84[1]	$ 5.00	Maple Leaf	648 000	
	$ 10.00	Maple Leaf	720 800	
	$ 50.00	Maple Leaf	2 927 000	
1982	$100.00	An open book with the coat of arms on one page and a maple leaf on the other	121 706	$290.00
1983	$100.00	A ship, Cabot Tower and an anchor	83 200	$310.00
1984	$100.00	Jacques Cartier and ship	69 874	$325.00
1985	$ 5.00	Maple Leaf	398 000	
	$ 10.00	Maple Leaf	620 000	
	$ 50.00	Maple Leaf	1 908 000	
	$100.00	Bighorn sheep	61 332	$325.00
1986	$ 5.00	Maple Leaf	529 516	
	$ 10.00	Maple Leaf	915 200	
	$ 20.00	Maple Leaf	529 200	
	$ 50.00	Maple Leaf	779 115	
	$100.00	Intertwined olive branch and Maple Leaf	76 409	$325.00
1987	$ 5.00	Maple Leaf	459 000	
	$ 10.00	Maple Leaf	376 800	
	$ 20.00	Maple Leaf	332 800	
	$ 50.00	Maple Leaf	978 000	
	$100.00	Hand holding Olympic torch	n.a.	$255.00

(1) Between 1982-84, the Royal Canadian mint began producing Maple Leaf gold bullion coins in the following weights: 1/10 oz., $5; 1/4 oz., $10; 1 oz., $50. In 1986, a 1/2 oz., $20 coin was added. Each coin is worth the market price of gold plus a premium.
n.a. not available.

Canada's Labor Force

Canadian Labor Force by Province, 1987

Source: Statistics Canada

(thousands)

	Population 15 years and over	Labor force[1]	Partici- pation rate[2]	Employed	% Employed[3]	Unem- ployed	% Unem- ployed[4]
Newfoundland	430	228	53.1	186	43.2	42	18.6
Prince Edward Island	97	61	62.8	53	54.5	8	13.3
Nova Scotia	677	405	59.8	354	52.3	51	12.5
New Brunswick	546	319	58.3	277	50.7	42	13.2
Quebec	5 210	3 306	63.5	2 966	56.9	341	10.3
Ontario	7 279	5 013	68.9	4 706	64.7	307	6.1
Manitoba	809	537	66.4	497	61.5	40	7.4
Saskatchewan	742	495	66.7	458	61.8	36	7.3
Alberta	1 768	1 274	72.0	1 151	65.1	123	9.6
British Columbia	2 267	1 484	65.5	1 306	57.6	178	12.0
Canada	**19 825**	**13 121**	**66.2**	**11 955**	**60.3**	**1 167**	**8.9**

(1) The labor force consists of employed workers and those who are unemployed but actively seeking work. (2) Participation rate is the percent of the total population aged 15 and over that makes up the labor force. (3) The percent of the total population aged 15 and over that is employed. (4) The percent of the labor force that is unemployed.

Labor Force of Canadian Metropolitan[1] Areas, 1987

Source: Statistics Canada

(thousands)

	Population 15 years and over	Labor force[2]	Partici- pation rate[3]	Employed	% Em- ployed[4]	Unem- ployed	% Unem- ployed[5]
Toronto, Ont.	2 608	1 874	71.9	1 790	68.6	85	4.5
Montreal, Que.	2 348	1 555	66.2	1 400	59.6	155	10.0
Vancouver, B.C.	1 112	757	68.1	670	60.3	86	11.4
Ottawa-Hull, Ont.-Que.	616	445	72.2	412	66.8	33	7.4
Edmonton, Alta.	563	410	72.8	364	64.6	46	11.3
Winnipeg, Man.	494	333	67.5	307	62.1	26	7.9
Calgary, Alta.	468	349	74.6	317	67.8	32	9.0
Quebec, Que.	458	291	63.5	266	58.0	25	8.6
Hamilton, Ont.	451	315	69.9	295	65.5	20	6.3
St. Catharines-Niagara, Ont. . .	248	156	63.0	142	57.1	15	9.3
Kitchener-Waterloo, Ont.	241	172	71.5	162	67.4	10	5.6
London, Ont.	235	165	70.0	153	65.1	12	7.0
Halifax, N.S.	220	155	70.1	141	63.9	14	8.9
Victoria, B.C.	199	122	61.2	108	54.5	13	11.0
Windsor, Ont.	192	125	65.2	114	59.2	12	9.2
Regina, Sask.	141	100	70.8	93	65.9	7	6.9
Saskatoon, Sask.	133	91	68.3	82	61.6	9	9.9
Oshawa, Ont.	133	98	73.4	91	68.7	6	6.4
Chicoutimi-Jonquière, Que. . . .	117	68	57.8	60	51.1	8	11.6
St. John's, Nfld.	113	72	63.1	63	55.2	9	12.6
Sudbury, Ont.	111	68	61.3	60	54.3	8	11.4
Thunder Bay, Ont.	97	66	68.2	61	62.6	5	8.2
Trois-Rivières, Que.	95	59	61.7	52	55.0	6	11.0
Saint John, N.B.	87	53	61.6	47	53.8	7	12.7

(1) For census metro areas, which include neighboring municipalities from which the major urban centre draws its work force. (2) The labor force consists of employed workers and those who are unemployed but actively seeking work. (3) Participation rate is the percent of the total population aged 15 and over that makes up the labor force. (4) The percent of the total population aged 15 and over that is employed. (5) The percent of the labor force that is unemployed.

Employment by Industry

Source: Statistics Canada

(thousands and percentage of workers)

	1960	%	1970	%	1975	%	1980	%	1985	%	1987	%
Agriculture	683	11.5	491	6.3	483	5.2	479	4.5	488	4.3	475	4.0
Forestry	97	1.6	71	0.9	60	0.6	71	0.7	68	0.6	70	0.6
Fishing and trapping .	17	0.3	20	0.3	21	0.2	33	0.3	34	0.3	38	0.3
Mining	93	1.6	125	1.6	139	1.5	196	1.8	191	1.7	182	1.5
Manufacturing	1 471	24.7	1 768	22.7	1 871	20.2	2 111	19.7	1 981	17.5	2 044	17.1
Construction	418	7.0	467	6.0	603	6.5	624	5.8	587	5.2	680	5.7
Utilities[1]	513	8.6	687	8.8	812	8.7	906	8.5	884	7.8	906	7.6
Trade[2]	982	16.5	1 303	16.8	1 637	17.6	1 837	17.2	2 001	17.7	2 116	17.7
Finance[3]	227	3.8	364	4.8	474	5.1	611	5.7	629	5.6	695	5.8
Services[4]	1 464	24.5	2 000	25.7	2 520	27.1	3 096	28.9	3 648	32.3	3 934	32.9
Government[5]	n.a.	n.a.	482	6.2	665	7.2	744	6.9	802	7.1	814	6.8
Total Employment ..	**5 965**	**100.0**	**7 778**	**100.0**	**9 284**	**100.0**	**10 708**	**100.0**	**11 311**	**100.0**	**11 955**	**100.0**

(1) Utilities comprise transportation, communications, electricity, gas and waterworks. (2) Trade is the sales and distribution network of merchandise. (3) Finance includes insurance, real estate, banking and related activities. (4) Services refers to occupations in which a service is provided but no goods are produced—e.g. teaching, health care. (5) Government includes municipal, provincial and federal levels. n.a. not available.

Employment in Canada's Industries, by Province, 1987

Source: Statistics Canada

(thousands)

	Canada	Nfld	PEI	NS	NB	Que	Ont	Man	Sask	Alta	BC
Agriculture	475	...	6	9	6	76	122	41	92	90	31
Primary	291	19	...	19	12	42	60	8	11	66	53
Manufacturing	2 044	21	4	45	37	573	1 038	57	24	87	157
Construction	680	12	...	22	16	160	274	25	24	72	72
Utilities[1]	906	16	...	27	24	232	316	47	33	88	119
Trade[2]	2 116	35	9	67	54	521	806	89	80	209	246
Finance[3]	695	5	...	18	12	169	302	29	21	57	80
Service[4]	3 934	58	17	117	92	984	1 504	161	141	399	462
Government[5]	814	18	5	31	24	209	285	40	32	84	87
All Industries	**11 955**	**186**	**53**	**354**	**277**	**2 966**	**4 706**	**497**	**458**	**1 151**	**1 306**

(1) Utilities comprise transportation, communications, electricity, gas and waterworks. (2) Trade is the sales and distribution network of merchandise. (3) Finance includes insurance, real estate, banking and related activities. (4) Services refers to occupations in which a service is provided but no goods are produced—e.g. teaching, health care. (5) Government includes municipal, provincial and federal levels. . . . = too small to be included.

Unemployment By Industry

Source: Statistics Canada

(thousands of persons and percent unemployed[1])

	1965	%	1970	%	1975	%	1980	%	1985	%	1986	%	1987	%
Agriculture	8	1.3	13	2.5	14	2.8	21	4.2	37	7.1	34	6.6	33	6.6
Primary[2]	28	10.7	30	12.3	26	10.6	30	9.1	51	14.7	51	15.0	46	13.7
Manufacturing	57	3.4	112	6.0	149	7.4	181	7.9	223	10.1	195	8.8	187	8.4
Construction	53	10.3	84	15.3	80	11.8	100	13.8	147	20.0	134	17.6	120	15.0
Utilities[3]	25	3.9	35	4.8	42	4.9	48	5.0	68	7.2	67	6.9	58	6.0
Trade[4]	30	2.6	57	4.2	96	5.6	132	6.7	195	8.9	192	8.5	176	7.7
Finance[5]	n.a.	n.a.	10	2.6	14	2.9	22	3.4	42	6.2	32	4.7	33	4.6
Services[6]	53	2.4	69	3.3	145	5.4	218	6.6	386	9.6	367	8.8	354	8.3
Government[7]	n.a.	n.a.	16	3.3	29	4.2	45	5.7	72	8.3	67	7.7	63	7.2
Total[8]	**280**	**3.9**	**486**	**5.9**	**690**	**6.9**	**865**	**7.5**	**1˙328**	**10.5**	**1 236**	**9.6**	**1 167**	**8.9**

(1) The number of unemployed as a percentage of each industry's labor force. (2) Primary industries are fishing, trapping, forestry and mining. (3) Utilities comprise transportation, communications, electricity, gas and waterworks. (4) Trade is the sales and distribution of merchandise. (5) Finance includes insurance, real estate, banking and related activities. (6) Services refers to occupations in which a service is provided but no goods are produced—e.g. teaching, health care. (7) Government includes federal, provincial and municipal levels. (8) Includes unclassified workers. n.a. not available.

Canadian Unemployment Rates

Source: Statistics Canada

	Canada	Nfld	PEI	NS	NB	Que	Ont	Man	Sask	Alta	BC
1966	3.4	5.8	n.a.	4.7	5.3	4.1	2.6	2.8	1.5	2.5	4.6
1970	5.7	7.3	n.a.	5.3	6.3	7.0	4.4	5.3	4.2	5.1	7.7
1975	6.9	14.0	8.0	7.7	9.8	8.1	6.3	4.5	2.9	4.1	8.5
1976	7.1	13.3	9.6	9.5	11.0	8.7	6.2	4.7	3.9	4.0	8.6
1977	8.1	15.5	9.8	10.6	13.2	10.3	7.0	5.9	4.5	4.5	8.5
1978	8.3	16.2	9.8	10.5	12.5	10.9	7.2	6.5	4.9	4.7	8.3
1979	7.4	15.1	11.2	10.1	11.1	9.6	6.5	5.3	4.2	3.9	7.6
1980	7.5	13.3	10.6	9.7	11.0	9.8	6.8	5.5	4.4	3.7	6.8
1981	7.5	13.9	11.2	10.2	11.5	10.3	6.6	5.9	4.7	3.8	6.7
1982	11.0	16.8	12.9	13.2	14.0	13.8	9.8	8.5	6.2	7.7	12.1
1983	11.9	18.8	12.2	13.2	14.8	13.9	10.4	9.4	7.4	10.8	13.8
1984	11.3	20.5	12.8	13.1	14.9	12.8	9.1	8.3	8.0	11.2	14.7
1985	10.5	21.3	13.2	13.8	15.2	11.8	8.0	8.1	8.1	10.1	14.2
1986	9.6	20.0	13.4	13.4	14.4	11.0	7.0	7.7	7.7	9.8	12.6
1987	8.9	18.6	13.3	12.5	13.2	10.3	6.1	7.4	7.3	9.6	12.0

n.a. not available.

Future Employment Opportunities

Source: Employment and Immigration Canada

Job Title	New Job Openings[1] (1985-1992)	% change in employment[2]	Job Title	New Job Openings[1] (1985-1992)	% change in employment[2]
Accountants	42 300	28.3	Managers, production	6 200	24.7
Administrators, health	4 800	39.7	Managers, sales	40 100	22.2
Administrators, teaching	6 900	19.9	Managers, senior officials	28 200	33.9
Aircraft pilots	900	13.4	Managers, services	21 100	43.0
Architects	2 300	30.3	Mathematicians	1 500	26.8
Artists, illustrating	5 200	14.4	Mechanics, motor vehicle	27 000	9.8
Barbers/hairdressers	28 300	23.7	Metal casting jobs	2 100	15.4
Biologists	1 700	23.9	Nurses	64 900	16.6
Bookkeepers	126 100	12.6	Nutritionists	1 300	17.1
Brick and stone masons	2 600	14.2	Optometrists	1 200	24.0
Brokers, financial	6 700	14.3	Painters, building	5 300	16.4
Bus drivers	21 400	43.4	Personnel	9 400	29.8
Carpenters	20 300	18.9	Pharmacists	4 600	9.7
Cashiers and tellers	64 600	12.5	Photographers	2 800	19.8
Chefs and cooks	62 200	21.6	Physicians	14 100	31.8
Chemists	2 000	22.7	Physicists	300	23.1
Chiropractors	1 000	41.7	Physio/occupational therapists	5 100	16.6
Clerks, bank	13 700	14.1	Plumbers	7 800	18.0
Clerks, general office	46 100	12.7	Police officers	11 800	15.2
Clerks, shipping and receiving	20 700	10.8	Psychologists	2 300	26.1
Clerks, stock	23 100	10.3	Radio and T.V. announcers	1 400	13.8
Coaches, sports	6 100	23.0	Radio and T.V. repairers	2 500	9.3
Community workers	17 100	38.3	Receptionists	31 800	13.9
Computer programmers	11 800	19.8	Roofers	1 000	11.0
Data processing operators	19 100	12.5	Sales, clerks	69 700	8.4
Dental assistants	12 900	31.4	Sales, insurance	16 100	14.1
Dentists	2 900	25.7	Sales, real estate	23 100	14.0
Designers, product/interior	6 300	12.3	Sales, technical	2 500	10.7
Directors/Producers, arts	3 200	20.8	Secretaries	117 900	12.8
Drafters	9 500	23.2	Sheet metal workers	4 400	9.9
Ecologists	500	16.7	Social workers	10 600	32.2
Economists	3 100	25.8	Sociologists	300	23.1
Electricians, construction	7 200	15.8	Surveyors	3 400	20.9
Electricians, equipment	8 000	10.4	Teachers, community college[4]	–	–
Engineers, chemical	600[3]	10.9	Teachers, grade school	30 300	17.8
Engineers, civil	4 100[3]	14.0	Teachers, high school	8 500	6.5
Engineers, electrical	3 500[3]	13.5	Teachers, university	1 600	4.6
Engineers, industrial	1 900[3]	11.9	Tool and die makers	2 900	10.6
Engineers, mechanical	2 200[3]	12.2	Translators	2 000	15.0
Funeral directors	1 800	23.5	Truck drivers	69 300	28.0
Geologists	1 600	21.9	Typists	31 600	13.3
Janitors	94 800	14.5	Veterinarians	700	20.0
Lawyers	10 700	31.0	Waiters/waitresses	90 500	23.7
Librarians	5 200	33.3	Watch and clock repairers	900	8.7
Machinists	9 100	10.1	Welders	16 400	11.3
Managers, farm	11 000	38.1	Wood furniture makers	5 600	10.8
Managers, financial	15 700	25.7	Writers/editors	9 600	14.2
Managers, industrial relations	6 900	27.0			

(1) New job openings refers to both an increase in the total number of job positions and job openings due to people leaving the work force between 1985 and 1992. (2) % change in employment refers to the number of new job openings between 1985 and 1992 as a percentage of the number of jobs in 1985. (3) Does not include new job openings due to people leaving the work force. (4) No new job openings expected for community college teachers.

Labor Force by Age (Both Sexes)

Source: Statistics Canada

(thousands)[1]

Age		1960[2]	1965[2]	1970	1975	1980	1984	1985	1986	1987
15 years and over	Population	11 831	13 128	14 528	16 323	18 053	19 148	19 372	19 594	19 825
	Labor Force[3]	6 411	141	8 265	9 974	11 573	12 399	12 629	12 870	13 121
	Participation Rate[4]	54.2	54.4	56.9	61.1	64.1	64.8	65.2	65.7	66.2
	Employed	5 965	6 862	7 778	9 284	10 708	11 000	11 311	11 634	11 955
	% Employed[5]	50.4	52.3	53.5	56.9	59.3	57.4	58.4	59.4	60.3
	Unemployed	446	280	486	690	865	1 399	1 328	1 236	1 167
	% Unemployed[6]	7.0	3.9	5.9	6.9	7.5	11.3	10.5	9.6	8.9
15-19 years	Population	1 661	2 139	2 018	2 258	2 302	1 996	1 926	1 887	1 859
	Labor Force[3]	627	738	791	1 153	1 267	1 042	1 019	1 025	1 041
	Participation Rate[4]	37.7	34.5	39.2	51.1	55.0	52.2	52.9	54.3	56.0
	Employed	545	673	678	981	1 061	834	828	853	884
	% Employed[5]	32.8	31.5	33.6	43.4	46.1	41.8	43.0	45.2	47.5
	Unemployed	82	65	112	172	206	208	191	172	157
	% Unemployed[6]	13.1	8.8	14.2	14.9	16.2	19.9	18.8	16.8	15.1
20-24 years	Population	1 128	1 339	1 788	2 039	2 253	2 336	2 319	2 269	2 198
	Labor Force[3]	777	935	1 268	1 548	1 794	1 850	1 843	1 825	1 768
	Participation Rate[4]	68.9	69.8	70.9	75.9	79.6	79.2	79.5	80.4	80.4
	Employed	705	892	1 164	1 395	1 596	1 540	1 561	1 564	1 539
	% Employed[5]	62.5	66.6	65.1	68.4	70.8	65.9	67.3	68.9	70.0
	Unemployed	72	44	104	153	198	310	282	261	229
	% Unemployed[6]	9.3	4.7	8.2	9.9	11.0	16.8	15.3	14.3	12.9
25-34 years	Population	2 413	2 341	2 735	3 428	3 987	4 339	4 410	4 482	4 556
	Labor Force[3]	1 506	1 496	1 847	2 537	3 148	3 527	3 626	3 744	3 816
	Participation Rate[4]	62.4	63.9	67.5	74.0	78.9	81.3	82.2	83.6	83.8
	Employed	1 408	1 450	1 760	2 382	2 940	3 117	3 233	3 374	3 471
	% Employed[5]	58.4	61.9	64.4	69.5	73.7	71.8	73.3	75.3	76.2
	Unemployed	98	47	87	155	208	410	393	371	345
	% Unemployed[6]	6.5	3.1	4.7	6.1	6.6	11.6	10.8	9.9	9.0
35-44 years	Population	2 295	2 461	2 477	2 516	2 794	3 362	3 488	3 608	3 730
	Labor Force[3]	1 445	1 611	1 703	1 859	2 201	2 758	2 885	3 013	3 146
	Participation Rate[4]	63.0	65.5	68.7	73.9	78.8	82.0	82.7	83.5	84.4
	Employed	1 369	1 564	1 633	1 777	2 091	2 528	2 659	2 795	2 929
	% Employed[5]	59.7	63.6	65.9	70.6	74.9	75.2	76.2	77.5	78.5
	Unemployed	76	46	69	82	110	230	226	217	217
	% Unemployed[6]	5.3	2.9	4.1	4.4	5.0	8.3	7.8	7.2	6.9
45-54 years	Population	1 798	2 007	2 222	2 420	2 432	2 484	2 498	2 525	2 565
	Labor Force[3]	1 152	1 331	1 499	1 672	1 782	1 864	1 904	1 920	2 001
	Participation Rate[4]	64.1	66.3	67.5	69.1	73.3	75.1	76.2	76.1	78.0
	Employed	1 088	1 292	1 440	1 597	1 695	1 719	1 768	1 795	1 870
	% Employed[5]	60.5	64.4	64.8	66.0	69.7	69.2	70.8	71.1	72.9
	Unemployed	64	40	59	75	87	145	136	125	131
	% Unemployed[6]	5.6	3.0	3.9	4.5	4.9	7.8	7.2	6.5	6.5
55-64 years	Population	1 237	1 422	1 671	1 854	2 075	2 269	2 294	2 313	2 325
	Labor Force[3]	674	808	947	1 005	1 119	1 167	1 176	1 163	1 165
	Participation Rate[4]	54.5	56.8	56.7	54.2	53.9	51.4	51.3	50.3	50.1
	Employed	631	778	900	963	1 068	1 074	1 080	1 078	1 082
	% Employed[5]	51.0	54.7	53.9	51.9	51.5	74.3	47.1	46.6	46.5
	Unemployed	43	30	47	42	51	93	96	85	83
	% Unemployed[6]	6.4	3.7	5.0	4.3	4.5	8.0	8.2	7.3	7.1

(1) Except where percentages are indicated. (2) For 1960 and 1965 the working population was considered to be 14 years and over. (3) The labor force consists of employed workers and those who are unemployed but actively seeking work. (4) Participation rate is the percent of the total population aged 15 and over that makes up the labor force. (5) The percent of the total population 15 and over that is employed. (6) The percent of the labor force that is unemployed.

Foreign Trade

Canadian Balance of International Payments

Source: Statistics Canada

The Canadian balance of payments is a measure of all yearly business transactions between Canada and the rest of the world. These transactions are listed in 2 accounts: current account and capital account. The current account keeps track of all Canadian payments for imported goods and services and of all money received for Canadian exports of goods and services. The capital account records all investment transactions (stocks, bonds, real estate, new companies, loans, foreign currency trading, interest payments) between Canada and other countries.

The balance of payments, the sum of the 2 accounts, shows whether Canada is experiencing a surplus (more money flowing into the country than out) or a deficit (more money leaving the country than coming in). In the short run, neither a deficit nor a surplus is necessarily bad or good. However, a persistent deficit might cause inflation by depreciating the Canadian dollar, or could lead to higher interest rates by forcing Canada to borrow from foreign countries. A prolonged surplus might contribute to an increase in the value of the Canadian dollar, reducing foreign demand for Canadian exports and causing unemployment.

(millions of dollars)

Year	Balance of payments[1]	Current Account			Capital Account		
		Receipts[2]	Payments	Balance[3]	Investment inflow[4]	Investment outflow[5]	Total investment balance[6]
1961	− 167	7 892	8 830	− 938	n.a.	n.a.	771
1965	271	11 693	12 792	− 1 098	n.a.	n.a.	1 369
1970	316	21 907	20 874	1 033	1 860	2 577	− 717
1975	1 326	42 076	46 707	− 4 631	7 202	1 245	5 957
1976	3 779	47 440	51 536	− 4 096	11 349	3 473	7 876
1977	2 225	54 544	58 866	− 4 322	7 615	1 068	6 546
1978	3 146	65 098	70 001	− 4 903	13 493	5 444	8 049
1979	2 507	79 725	84 590	− 4 864	12 974	5 602	7 372
1980	1 176	93 893	95 024	− 1 130	9 861	7 555	2 306
1981	8 457	103 931	110 061	− 6 131	33 033	18 446	14 587
1982	2 111	105 556	102 732	2 824	5 929	6 642	− 713
1983	5 692	112 244	109 177	3 066	11 237	8 611	2 626
1984	7 051	136 061	132 624	3 437	15 730	12 115	3 615
1985	5 805	146 535	147 721	− 1 186	11 757	4 766	6 991
1986	3 951	149 872	159 140	− 9 268	25 279	12 060	13 219
1987	4 692	156 339	165 940	− 9 601	27 016	12 723	14 293

(1) Sum of the current and capital account balances. (2) Money received for Canadian exports of goods and services. (3) Receipts minus payments. (4) Represents net foreign investment to Canada. (5) Represents net Canadian investment to other countries. (6) Investment inflow minus investment outflow.

Canada's Official Monetary Reserves

Source: Bank of Canada

(millions of U.S. dollars)

	Total reserves	U.S. dollars	Other foreign currencies	Gold	IMF reserves[1]	Special drawing rights[2]
1965	3 036.9	1 519.9	12.8	1 150.8	353.4	–
1966	2 701.9	1 195.4	12.4	1 045.6	448.5	–
1967	2 716.9	1 255.2	13.4	1 014.9	433.4	–
1968	3 045.8	1 964.9	11.6	863.1	206.2	–
1969	3 106.3	1 743.6	12.3	872.3	478.1	–
1970	4 679.0	3 022.1	14.5	790.7	669.6	182.1
1971	5 570.4	4 060.6	13.6	791.8	332.6	371.9
1972	6 049.9	4 355.0	12.6	834.1	342.9	505.2
1973	5 768.2	3 927.2	12.2	926.9	338.9	563.7
1974	5 825.3	3 767.7	12.9	940.7	529.7	574.3
1975	5 325.6	3 207.1	15.7	899.4	648.0	555.4

	Total reserves	U.S. dollars	Other foreign currencies	Gold	IMF reserves[1]	Special drawing rights[2]
1976	5 843.4	3 446.3	15.8	879.0	944.5	557.8
1977	4 607.5	2 298.7	15.8	935.6	852.1	505.3
1978	4 566.2	2 459.5	18.4	1 009.1	556.8	522.4
1979	3 886.9	1 863.9	23.9	1 022.6	390.6	585.9
1980	4 029.6	2 037.6	23.1	936.6	579.0	453.2
1981	4 371.1	2 865.3	95.8	833.7	402.4	174.0
1982	3 793.2	2 454.9	120.1	782.3	365.0	70.8
1983	4 205.4	2 373.8	368.2	739.1	703.3	−21.0
1984	3 182.1	1 692.1	48.6	690.8	678.4	72.2
1985	3 275.6	1 523.9	50.1	773.0	710.8	217.9
1986	4 095.6	2 274.1	43.4	844.5	686.3	247.4
1987	8 203.2	6 163.3	54.5	919.5	660.6	405.2

(1) Canada, as a participating member, is required to hold reserves (primarily in Canadian dollars) with the International Monetary Fund (IMF). This pool of foreign currencies can be used by any member country to alleviate international trade balance problems. (2) Special Drawing Rights (SDRs) serve the same purpose as regular IMF reserves but are allocated differently and each country does not require IMF approval to use them. − = zero.

Canadian Trade with the United States, 1987

Source: Statistics Canada

(thousands of dollars)

Canadian Imports from the U.S.

Commodity	Value	%
Total Imports	79 069 318	100.0
Motor vehicle parts	15 276 032	19.3
Automobiles	8 690 625	11.0
Chemicals	4 742 387	6.0
plastics	1 637 729	2.1
organic	1 003 419	1.3
inorganic	399 532	0.5
fertilizers	177 161	0.2
Special purpose machinery	4 524 769	5.7
Computers	4 344 807	5.5
Food	3 419 741	4.3
fruits and vegetables	1 617 317	2.0
meat and fish	627 250	0.8
grain	234 950	0.3
coffee	77 858	0.1
sugar	74 086	0.1
dairy produce, eggs & honey ..	56 665	0.1
alcohol	12 903	...
Telecommunications equipment .	3 294 233	4.2
Trucks	2 993 503	3.8
Aircraft and parts	2 442 951	3.1
General purpose machinery	1 758 245	2.2
Wood and paper	1 552 918	2.0
paper	742 206	0.9
lumber	406 509	0.5
pulp	118 697	0.2
Farm machinery	1 264 238	1.6
Newspapers and books	1 228 772	1.6
Metal ores	982 377	1.2
iron	248 499	0.3
aluminum	164 072	0.2
Textiles	963 688	1.2
Precious metals	910 599	1.2
Iron and steel	843 632	1.1
Coal	724 122	0.9
Aluminum alloys	740 055	0.9
Photographic supplies	626 778	0.8
Air conditioners	440 507	0.6
Medical equipment	388 847	0.5
Copper alloys	166 442	0.2
Live animals	155 713	0.2
Sports equipment	153 801	0.2
Crude petroleum	138 006	0.2
Tobacco	15 098	...

Canadian Exports to the U.S.

Commodity	Value	%
Total Exports[1]	91 756 404	100.0
Wood and paper	14 272 289	15.6
newsprint	5 084 171	5.5
lumber	4 231 989	4.6
wood pulp	2 461 357	2.7
paper	1 561 233	1.7
shingles and shakes	212 226	0.2
Automobiles	14 021 174	15.3
Motor vehicle parts	11 162 825	12.2
Metal ores and alloys	8 231 317	9.0
iron and steel	2 882 036	3.1
aluminum	2 288 960	2.5
precious metals	1 118 407	1.2
copper	677 296	0.7
nickel	451 792	0.5
zinc	405 206	0.4
radioactive ores	226 596	0.2
Trucks	5 963 370	6.5
Crude petroleum	4 819 759	5.3
Food	4 185 661	4.6
meat and fish	2 414 761	2.6
grains	356 095	0.4
whiskey	306 105	0.3
fruits and vegetables	267 806	0.3
sugar	199 366	0.2
dairy produce, eggs & honey ..	40 635	...
Chemicals	3 890 613	4.2
rubber and plastics	1 065 941	1.2
inorganic	1 039 124	1.1
fertilizers	742 727	0.8
organic	697 230	0.8
Industrial machinery	2 550 745	2.8
Natural gas	2 527 254	2.8
Oil products	2 095 887	2.3
Aircraft and parts	1 950 522	2.1
Telecommunications equipment .	1 813 653	2.0
Office machines	1 583 902	1.7
Electricity	1 199 764	1.3
Newspapers and books	547 237	0.6
Farm machinery	508 691	0.6
Live animals	318 819	0.3
Textiles	251 883	0.3
Tobacco	74 404	0.1
Sulphur	70 173	0.1

(1) Excludes re-exports of $2.7 billion.
. . . = too small to be included.

Canadian Exports by Country

Source: Statistics Canada

(millions of dollars)

	1960	%	1970	%	1980	%	1985	%	1986	%
Total Exports	5 386	100.0	16 820	100.0	76 159	100.0	119 475	100.0	125 087	100.0
United States	3 036	56.4	10 900	64.8	48 173	63.3	93 059	77.9	94 506	75.6
Asia	299	5.6	1 299	7.7	7 480	9.8	10 146	8.5	12 407	9.9
China	9	0.2	142	0.8	874	1.1	1 297	1.1	1 438	1.1
Hong Kong	22	0.4	21	0.1	199	0.3	346	0.3	491	0.4
India	37	0.7	131	0.8	359	0.5	496	0.4	275	0.2
Japan	179	3.3	813	4.8	4 374	5.7	5 737	4.8	7 074	5.7
Malaysia	5[2]	0.1	14	0.1	95	0.1	209	0.2	121	0.1
Philippines	17	0.3	31	0.2	86	0.1	46	...	123	0.1
Singapore	5[2]	0.1	11	0.1	202	0.3	120	0.1	178	0.1
South Korea	...	...	19	0.1	512	0.7	786	0.7	1 178	0.9
Taiwan	3	0.1	18	0.1	254	0.3	434	0.4	766	0.6
Western Europe	1 525	28.3	3 133	18.6	11 292	14.8	8 191	6.9	10 788	8.6
Belgium[1]	70	1.3	192	1.1	1 002	1.3	722	0.6	1 167	0.9
France	74	1.4	157	0.9	1 017	1.3	743	0.6	1 087	0.9
West Germany	168	3.1	388	2.3	1 668	2.2	1 233	1.0	1 606	1.3
Italy	69	1.3	187	1.1	1 004	1.3	542	0.5	869	0.7
Netherlands	63	1.2	281	1.7	1 442	1.9	956	0.8	1 072	0.9
Spain	10	0.2	67	0.4	235	0.3	134	0.1	218	0.2
Sweden	21	0.4	49	0.3	286	0.4	199	0.2	267	0.2
Switzerland	27	0.5	41	0.2	387	0.5	324	0.3	437	0.3
United Kingdom	925	17.2	1 501	8.9	3 245	4.3	2 482	2.1	3 030	2.4
Eastern Europe	39	0.7	170	1.0	2 148	2.8	1 910	1.6	1 013	0.8
Czechoslovakia	7	0.1	7	...	128	0.2	23	...	15	...
East Germany	1	...	...	...	11	...	112	0.1	56	...
Hungary	1	...	7	...	11	...	16	...	17	...
Poland	17	0.3	15	0.1	357	0.5	36	...	15	...
Romania	1	...	4	...	23	...	39	...	54	...
USSR	8	0.1	102	0.6	1 540	2.0	1 612	1.3	801	0.6
Yugoslavia	4	0.1	27	0.2	70	0.1	43	...	18	...
Central America	133	2.5	387	2.3	1 592	2.1	1 471	1.2	1 633	1.3
Cuba	13	0.2	59	0.4	425	0.6	330	0.3	274	0.2
El Salvador	2	...	3	...	16	...	15	...	16	...
Jamaica	18	0.3	48	0.3	66	0.1	55	...	99	0.1
Mexico	39	0.7	96	0.6	495	0.6	399	0.3	530	0.4
Nicaragua	1	...	2	...	15	...	19	...	10	...
Puerto Rico	11	0.2	49	0.3	95	0.1	213	0.2	237	0.2
South America	123	2.3	374	2.2	2 414	3.2	1 446	1.2	1 719	1.4
Argentina	20	0.4	60	0.4	232	0.3	64	0.1	102	0.1
Brazil	20	0.4	93	0.6	962	1.3	686	0.6	645	0.5
Chile	7	0.1	23	0.1	112	0.1	82	0.1	101	0.1
Colombia	17	0.3	25	0.1	236	0.3	163	0.1	270	0.2
Peru	9	0.2	36	0.2	57	0.1	49	...	123	0.1
Venezuela	36	0.7	112	0.7	680	0.9	333	0.3	389	0.3
Middle East	26	0.5	126	0.7	1 146	1.5	1 259	1.1	1 275	1.0
Egypt	2	...	38	0.2	130	0.2	193	0.2	85	0.1
Iran	3	0.1	8	...	42	0.1	65	0.1	170	0.1
Iraq	3	0.1	4	...	153	0.2	72	0.1	120	0.1
Israel	6	0.1	15	0.1	115	0.2	144	0.1	161	0.1
Lebanon	3	0.1	5	...	41	0.1	11	...	10	...
Libya	...	...	3	...	73	0.1	95	0.1	30	...
Saudi Arabia	3	0.1	7	...	313	0.4	235	0.2	273	0.2
Turkey	2	...	22	0.1	41	0.1	221	0.2	267	0.2
United Arab Emirates	...	...	...	...	46	0.1	20	...	23	...
Africa	77	1.4	176	1.0	1 074	1.4	1 079	0.9	852	0.7
Algeria	5	...	19	0.1	394	0.5	332	0.3	202	0.2
Kenya	1	...	2	...	15	...	18	...	10	...
Morocco	...	...	5	...	71	0.1	170	0.1	204	0.2
Nigeria	2	...	8	...	105	0.1	70	0.1	23	...
South Africa	53	1.0	105	0.6	206	0.3	155	0.1	116[3]	0.1[3]
Australasia	126	2.3	249	1.5	808	1.1	878	0.7	856	0.7
Australia	100	1.9	202	1.2	679	0.9	676	0.6	702	0.6
New Zealand	24	0.4	44	0.3	115	0.2	193	0.2	140	0.1

(1) Includes Luxembourg. (2) Includes Malaysia and Singapore. (3) Includes Botswana, Lesotho, Swaziland and Namibia.
. . . = too small to be included.

Canadian Imports by Country

Source: Statistics Canada

(millions of dollars)

	1960	%	1970	%	1980	%	1985	%	1987	%
Total Imports	5 483	100.0	13 952	100.0	69 274	100.0	104 355	100.0	116 239	100.0
United States	3 687	67.2	9 917	71.1	48 614	70.2	73 817	70.7	79 069	68.0
Asia	211	3.8	865	6.2	5 031	7.3	11 219	10.8	14 572	12.5
China	6	0.1	19	0.1	155	0.2	403	0.4	771	0.7
Hong Kong	16	0.3	78	0.6	574	0.8	887	0.8	1 138	1.0
India	29	0.5	40	0.3	168	0.1	168	0.2	171	0.1
Japan	110[2]	2.0	582	4.2	2 796	4.0	6 115	5.9	7 551	6.5
Malaysia	28[2]	0.5	34	0.2	83	0.1	146	0.1	187	0.2
Philippines	2	. . .	4	. . .	101	0.1	109	0.1	107	0.1
Singapore	28[2]	0.5	20	0.1	150	0.2	210	0.2	262	0.2
South Korea	. . .	. . .	15	0.1	414	0.6	1 607	1.5	1 844	1.6
Taiwan	1	. . .	52	0.4	558	0.8	1 286	1.2	2 023	1.7
Western Europe	961	17.5	1 948	14.0	7 007	10.1	12 553	12.0	15 793	13.6
Belgium[1]	41	0.8	52	0.4	251	0.4	530	0.5	619	0.5
France	50	0.9	158	1.1	773	1.1	1 373	1.3	1 489	1.3
West Germany	127	2.3	370	2.7	1 455	2.1	2 716	2.6	3 534	3.0
Italy	43	0.8	145	1.0	611	0.9	1 331	1.3	1 703	1.5
Netherlands	31	0.6	79	0.6	264	0.4	623	0.6	750	0.6
Spain	7	0.1	34	0.2	187	0.3	366	0.4	485	0.4
Sweden	20	0.4	106	0.8	416	0.6	683	0.7	884	0.8
Switzerland	24	0.4	81	0.6	522	0.8	489	0.5	587	0.5
United Kingdom	589	10.7	738	5.3	1 974	2.8	3 281	3.1	4 339	3.7
Eastern Europe	14	0.3	75	0.5	307	0.4	296	0.3	387	0.3
Czechoslovakia	7	0.1	27	0.2	63	0.1	67	0.1	64	0.1
East Germany	1	. . .	4	0.1	10	. . .	12	. . .	34	. . .
Hungary	. . .	. . .	9	0.1	26	. . .	34	. . .	47	. . .
Poland	2	. . .	12	0.1	72	0.1	58	0.1	69	0.1
Romania	. . .	. . .	5	. . .	38	0.1	45	. . .	57	. . .
USSR	3	0.1	9	0.1	59	0.1	28	. . .	36	. . .
Yugoslavia	. . .	. . .	7	0.1	33	. . .	43	. . .	71	0.1
Central America	144	2.6	214	1.5	1 035	1.5	2 062	2.0	2 007	1.7
Cuba	7	0.1	9	0.1	163	0.2	45	. . .	52	. . .
El Salvador	. . .	. . .	4	. . .	27	. . .	36	. . .	43	. . .
Jamaica	38	0.7	27	0.2	50	0.1	155	0.1	114	0.1
Mexico	21	0.4	47	0.3	345	0.5	1 331	1.3	1 170	1.0
Nicaragua	. . .	. . .	1	. . .	32	. . .	26	. . .	29	. . .
Puerto Rico	3	0.1	7	0.1	103	0.1	199	0.2	227	0.2
South America	277	5.1	447	3.2	3 015	4.4	2 395	2.3	2 143	1.8
Argentina	4	0.1	9	0.1	36	0.1	91	0.1	112	0.1
Brazil	25	0.5	49	0.4	348	0.5	809	0.8	851	0.7
Chile	1	. . .	3	. . .	97	0.1	130	0.1	153	0.1
Colombia	13	0.2	27	0.2	101	0.1	89	0.1	133	0.1
Peru	3	0.1	4	. . .	96	0.1	68	0.1	75	0.1
Venezuela	195	3.6	339	2.4	2 217	3.2	1 092	1.0	551	0.5
Middle East	104	1.9	104	0.7	3 027	4.4	371	0.4	705	0.6
Egypt	1	. . .	. . .	. . .	11	. . .	31	. . .	34	. . .
Iran	31	0.6	34	0.2	3	. . .	143	0.1	110	0.1
Iraq	1	. . .	14	0.1	281	0.4	. . .	. . .	81	0.1
Israel	2	. . .	14	0.1	55	0.1	93	0.1	116	0.1
Lebanon	. . .	. . .	1	. . .	1	. . .	1	. . .	2	. . .
Libya	. . .	. . .	. . .	. . .	. . .	. . .	38	. . .	–	–
Saudi Arabia	37	0.7	24	0.2	2 452	3.5	24	. . .	175	0.2
Turkey	. . .	. . .	1	. . .	11	. . .	36	. . .	78	0.1
United Arab Emirates	8	0.1	7	0.1	62	0.1	2	. . .	49	. . .
Africa	33	0.6	153	1.1	538	0.8	1 034	1.0	760	0.7
Algeria	. . .	. . .	. . .	. . .	12	. . .	322	0.3	22	. . .
Kenya	3	0.1	6	. . .	18	. . .	14	. . .	13	. . .
Morocco	. . .	. . .	. . .	. . .	11	. . .	14	. . .	29	. . .
Nigeria	4	0.1	45	0.3	42	0.1	230	0.2	252	0.2
South Africa	11	0.2	46	0.3	356	0.5	228	0.2	155[3]	0.1[3]
Australasia	52	0.9	199	1.4	699	1.0	605	0.6	784	0.7
Australia	36	0.7	146	1.0	517	0.7	387	0.4	564	0.5
New Zealand	10	0.2	43	0.3	147	0.2	160	0.2	200	0.2

(1) Includes Luxembourg. (2) Includes Malaysia and Singapore. (3) Includes Botswana, Lesotho, Swaziland and Namibia.
. . . = too small to be included.

Canadian Trade Balance[1]

Source: Statistics Canada

(millions of dollars)

	1960	1970	1980	1985	1986	1987
All Countries	− 97	2 868	6 885	15 119	8 158	8 848
United States	− 651	983	− 441	19 234	16 083	15 436
Asia	88	434	2 449	− 1 073	− 3 493	− 2 165
China	3	123	719	893	561	667
Hong Kong	6	− 57	− 375	− 541	− 708	− 647
India	8	91	264	328	192	104
Japan	69	231	1 578	− 378	− 1 664	− 477
Malaysia	− 13[3]	− 20	12	63	− 41	− 66
Philippines	15	27	− 15	− 63	− 60	16
Singapore	− 13[3]	− 9	52	− 90	− 55	− 84
South Korea	. . .	19	98	− 821	− 773	− 666
Taiwan	2	18	− 304	− 852	− 1 129	− 1 257
Western Europe	564	1 185	4 285	− 4 362	− 5 596	− 5 005
Belgium[2]	29	140	751	192	238	549
France	24	− 1	244	− 629	− 573	− 402
West Germany	41	18	213	− 1 483	− 2 144	− 1 928
Italy	26	42	393	− 789	− 960	− 834
Netherlands	32	202	1 178	333	315	322
Spain	3	33	48	− 232	− 303	− 268
Sweden	1	− 57	− 130	− 484	− 541	− 617
Switzerland	3	40	− 135	− 165	− 238	− 150
United Kingdom	336	763	1 271	− 799	− 1 004	− 1 309
Eastern Europe	25	95	1 841	1 614	1 278	626
Czechoslovakia	. . .	− 20	65	− 44	− 48	− 49
East Germany	. . .	− 4	1	100	91	22
Hungary	1	− 2	− 15	− 18	− 31	− 31
Poland	15	3	285	− 22	− 48	− 54
Romania	1	− 1	− 15	− 6	75	− 3
USSR	5	93	1 481	1 584	1 196	766
Yugoslavia	4	20	37	− 1	− 3	− 52
Central America	− 11	173	557	− 591	− 518	− 374
Cuba	6	50	262	286	297	223
El Salvador	1	− 1	− 11	− 20	− 53	− 27
Jamaica	− 20	21	16	− 100	− 77	− 14
Mexico	18	49	150	− 932	− 773	− 639
Nicaragua	1	1	− 17	− 7	− 11	− 18
Puerto Rico	8	42	− 8	14	13	10
South America	− 154	− 73	− 601	− 949	− 111	− 424
Argentina	16	51	196	− 27	− 16	− 9
Brazil	− 5	44	614	− 123	− 30	− 205
Chile	6	20	15	− 48	− 34	− 52
Colombia	4	− 2	135	74	66	137
Peru	6	32	− 39	− 19	46	48
Venezuela	− 159	− 227	− 1 537	− 759	− 107	− 162
Middle East	− 78	22	− 1 881	888	459	570
Egypt	1	38	119	162	130	51
Iran	− 28	− 26	39	− 78	− 199	60
Iraq	2	− 10	− 128	71	105	39
Israel	4	1	60	51	9	45
Lebanon	3	4	40	10	17	9
Libya	. . .	3	73	58	52	30
Saudi Arabia	− 34	− 17	− 2 139	212	29	97
Turkey	2	21	30	186	146	188
United Arab Emirates	− 8	− 7	− 16	18	23	− 26
Africa	44	23	536	46	− 117	92
Algeria	. . .	19	382	10	182	180
Kenya	− 2	− 4	− 3	4	34	− 3
Morocco	. . .	5	60	156	135	174
Nigeria	− 2	− 37	63	− 159	− 342	− 228
South Africa	42	59	− 150	− 73	− 219	− 39[4]
Australasia	74	50	109	273	148	72
Australia	64	56	162	289	148	138
New Zealand	14	1	− 32	33	− 23	− 59

(1) The trade balance is the value of merchandise exports minus the value of merchandise imports; it does not include services. (2) Includes Luxembourg. (3) Includes Malaysia and Singapore. (4) Includes Botswana, Lesotho, Swaziland and Namibia.
. . . = too small to be included.

Canadian Imports of Leading Commodities

Source: Statistics Canada

(millions of dollars)

	1975	%	1980	%	1985	%	1987	%
All Imports	34 668	100.0	69 274	100.0	104 355	100.0	116 239	100.0
Motor vehicle engines[1]	4 528	13.1	7 638	11.0	17 617	16.9	16 956	14.6
Automobiles	2 528	7.3	4 416	6.4	10 774	10.3	12 346	10.6
Food	2 582	7.4	4 633	6.7	5 767	5.5	6 602	5.7
fruits and vegetables	780	2.2	1 498	2.2	2 208	2.1	2 501	2.2
meat and fish	343	1.0	622	0.9	921	0.9	1 234	1.1
coffee	169	0.5	488	0.7	478	0.5	462	0.4
sugar	521	1.5	563	0.8	222	0.2	256	0.2
tea	35	0.1	65	0.1	88	0.1	75	0.1
Chemicals	1 477	4.3	3 354	4.8	5 443	5.2	6 233	5.4
Special industrial machinery .	1 874	5.4	4 330	6.3	4 974	4.7	6 147	5.3
Computers	343	1.0	1 653	2.4	3 937	3.8	5 093	4.4
General purpose machinery .	1 353	3.9	2 421	3.5	2 953	2.8	3 481	3.0
Trucks	810	2.3	1 135	1.6	2 559	2.5	3 293	2.8
Crude petroleum	3 299	9.5	6 919	10.0	3 695	3.5	3 179	2.7
Aircraft, engines and parts ..	696	2.0	1 826	2.6	2 778	2.6	2 759	2.4
Iron and steel[2]	1 116	3.2	1 771	2.6	2 435	2.3	2 412	2.1
Textiles	745	2.1	1 276	1.8	1 886	1.8	2 261	1.9
Wood and paper	644	1.9	919	1.3	1 483	1.4	1 975	1.7
Farm machinery	1 239	3.6	2 092	3.0	1 739	1.7	1 658	1.4
Precious metals	76	0.2	1 739	2.5	1 466	1.4	1 139	1.0
Televisions	221	0.6	443	0.6	831	0.8	879	0.8
Coal	576	1.6	811	1.2	887	0.8	725	0.6
Live animals	75	0.2	113	0.2	109	0.1	162	0.1

(1) Includes motor vehicle parts. (2) Includes ores, scrap metal and iron and steel products.

Canadian Exports[1] of Leading Commodities

Source: Statistics Canada

(millions of dollars)

	1975	%	1980	%	1985	%	1987	%
All Exports	32 466	100.0	74 446	100.0	116 145	100.0	121 462	100.0
Wood and paper	5 019	15.5	12 629	17.0	15 686	13.5	20 383	16.8
newsprint	1 744	5.4	3 684	4.9	5 412	4.7	6 029	5.0
lumber	973	3.0	2 989	4.0	4 595	4.0	5 859	4.8
wood pulp	1 831	5.6	3 873	5.2	3 405	2.9	5 473	4.5
Automobiles	3 069	9.5	4 687	6.3	15 921	13.7	14 092	11.6
Motor vehicle engines[2]	2 138	6.6	3 466	4.7	10 919	9.4	11 535	9.5
Food	3 955	12.2	7 925	10.6	9 085	7.8	10 103	8.3
grains	2 708	8.3	4 834	6.5	4 538	3.9	4 131	3.4
meat and fish	579	1.8	1 773	2.4	2 658	2.3	3 812	3.1
fruits and vegetables	116	0.4	295	0.4	427	0.4	580	0.5
whisky	243	0.7	309	0.4	352	0.3	338	0.3
Chemicals	1 025	3.2	4 056	5.4	5 475	4.7	6 136	5.1
Trucks	1 080	3.3	2 445	3.3	5 818	5.0	6 010	4.9
Crude petroleum	3 052	9.4	2 899	3.9	5 972	5.1	4 855	4.0
Iron and steel[3]	1 467	4.5	3 385	4.5	3 663	3.2	3 788	3.1
Industrial machinery	928	2.9	2 181	2.9	3 059	2.6	3 459	2.8
Telecommunications equip. ..	323	1.0	932	1.3	2 743	2.4	2 557	2.1
Aircraft, engines and parts ..	422	1.3	1 404	1.9	2 096	1.8	2 540	2.1
Natural gas	1 092	3.4	3 984	5.4	4 011	3.5	2 527	2.1
Office machines	272	0.8	739	1.0	1 364	1.2	2 031	1.7
Coal	494	1.5	934	1.3	2 010	1.7	1 670	1.4
Sulphur	113	0.3	534	0.7	1 289	1.1	885	0.7
Copper ores	331	1.0	601	0.8	552	0.5	721	0.6
Farm machinery	542	1.7	876	1.2	524	0.5	551	0.5
Nickel ores	516	1.6	447	0.6	580	0.5	510	0.4
Textiles	100	0.3	243	0.3	283	0.2	425	0.3
Live animals	83	0.3	254	0.3	467	0.4	366	0.3
Tobacco	73	0.2	82	0.1	105	0.1	139	0.1

(1) Excludes re-exports, i.e., goods imported into Canada and then re-exported without any alterations done to them. (2) Includes motor vehicle parts. (3) Includes ores, scrap metal and iron and steel products.

Business and Labor

Canada's Largest Corporations, 1987

Source: The Financial Post 500

Company	Sales or operating revenue ($ millions)	Assets ($ millions)	Profit or loss(−) ($ millions)	Employees	% Foreign-owned	Major Shareholders
General Motors of Canada Ltd.	$16 884	$ 5 917	$ 5	44 749	100%	General Motors, Detroit
BCE Inc.[1]	14 649	26 025	1 087	117 000	8	Wide distribution
Ford Motor Co. of Canada Ltd.	13 977	3 622	124	27 200	97	Ford Motor, Detroit 94%
Canadian Pacific Ltd.	12 209	18 001	637	85 400	29	Wide distribution
George Weston Ltd.	11 035	3 546	134	67 300	1	Wittington Investments 58%
Alcan Aluminium Ltd.	9 013	9 953	574	63 000	57	Wide distribution
Imperial Oil Ltd.	7 562	9 478	716	11 627	79	Exxon, New York 70%
Noranda Inc.	7 344	9 596	343	44 000	—	Brascade Resources 35%, Brascan 12%
Chrysler Canada Ltd.	7 247	2 949	99	15 677	100	Chrysler, Detroit
Provigo Inc.[2]	6 418	1 555	67	21 000	—	Unigesco 21%, Sobeys 20%, Caisse de dépôt 11%
Ontario Hydro	5 280	32 657	271	32 147	—	Ontario govt. 100%
PetroCanada	5 194	8 453	213	7 204	—	Federal govt. 100%
Brascan Ltd.	5 178	5 158	175	22	15	Brascan Holdings 49%
Hydro-Québec	5 095	31 659	509	18 933	—	Quebec govt. 100%
Hudson's Bay Co.[2]	4 845	3 614	−78	38 000	3	Woodbridge 74%
Shell Canada Ltd.	4 819	5 509	350	6 913	71	Shell, Neth./Britain
Imasco Ltd.	4 815	5 650	283	92 353	40	B.A.T. Industries, Britain
Canadian National Railway Co.	4 784	7 594	107	48 252	—	Federal govt. 100%
International Thomson Organization Ltd.	4 690	4 442	277	23 200	10	Woodbridge 74%
Steinberg Inc.[3]	4 491	1 469	58	34 000	—	Steinberg family 87%
Campeau Corp.[2]	4 264[7]	n.a.	n.a.	38 000	—	R. Campeau
Sears Canada Inc.	4 035	2 622	82	50 000	60	Sears, Roebuck Chicago
Canada Safeway Ltd.[2]	3 872	966	9	22 000	100	Kohlberg, Kravis, Roberts, New York
Oshawa Group Ltd.[2]	3 804	673	50	19 000	—	Wolfe family 100%
John Labatt Ltd.[4]	3 782	2 355	125	16 200	—	Brascan 37%, Caisse de dépôt 10%
Seagram Co.[2]	3 694	9 616	688	14 400	46	Bronfman family 38%
TransCanada PipeLines Ltd.	3 355	6 669	160	2 207	3	BCE Inc. 49%
Canadian Wheat Board[3]	3 208	4 836	n.a.	504	—	Federal govt. 100%
Canada Packers Inc.[5]	3 205	675	37	12 500	—	Cedcasac Holdings 11% company pension plan 11%
MacMillan Bloedel Ltd.	3 135	2 516	281	15 226	19	Noranda Forest 50%
Air Canada	3 131	3 085	46	22 000	—	Federal govt. 100%
IBM Canada Ltd.	3 104	2 380	231	12 147	100	IBM, Armonk, N.Y.
Moore Corp.	3 025	2 520	194	26 480	18	Royal Trustco 14%
Abitibi-Price Inc.	2 988	2 550	126	16 300	—	Olympia & York 75%
Canada Post Corp.[5]	2 970	2 629	−130	61 640	—	Federal govt. 100%
Polysar Energy & Chemical Corp.[6]	2 869	5 446	228	6 900	—	Nova 25%
Texaco Canada Inc.	2 649	3 873	320	3 288	78	Texaco, White Plains, N.Y.
Mitsui & Co. (Canada)[6]	2 609	213	4	130	100	Mitsui, Japan
Varity Corp.[2]	2 572	2 070	67	16 330	70	Wide distribution
Domtar Inc.	2 568	2 855	161	15 871	19	Dofor 28%, Caisse de dépôt 16%
Stelco Inc.	2 546	2 804	63	16 960	4	Wide distribution
Canadian Tire Corp.	2 484	1 431	99	n.a.	—	Billes family 61%, C.T.C. Dealer Holdings 17%
Inco Ltd.	2 373	3 891	166	18 706	55	Wide distribution
Nova Corp.	2 322	4 686	179	7 100	4	Wide distribution
Total Petroleum (North America) Ltd.	2 317	1 318	−36	4 800	79	Total Compagnie Françasie des Petroles, France 50%
Consolidated-Bathurst Inc.	2 261	2 265	182	15 026	15	Associated Newspapers, Britain, Power Corp. 40%
Ivaco Inc.	2 175	1 767	38	12 170	—	Ivanier family 37%, R. Klein 13%, M. Herling 12%
Dofasco Inc.	2 163	3 060	154	13 400	—	Ivaco 11%
F.W. Woolworth Co.[2]	2 026	666	33	26 500	100	Woolworth World Trade, New York
British Columbia Hydro & Power Authority[6]	1 987	9 802	67	6 393	—	British Columbia govt. 100%

(1) Name changed from Bell Canada Enterprises Inc. (2) For fiscal year ending Jan. 1988. (3) For fiscal year ending July 1987. (4) For fiscal year ending Apr. 1987. (5) For fiscal year ending Mar. 1987. (6) Name changed from Canada Development Corp. (7) Estimate. n.a. not available; — = zero.

Tops in Their Fields, 1987

Source: The Financial Post 500

(thousands of dollars)

Agriculture

Company	Sales or operating revenue
Canadian Wheat Board	$3 208 000
Saskatchewan Wheat Pool	1 804 275
James Richardson & Sons	1 255 583
Co-opérative fédérée de Québec	1 243 656
Cargill	1 113 828
Alberta Wheat Pool	1 012 517
United Grain Growers	905 941
Agropur	821 297
Manitoba Pool Elevators	492 307
Xcan Grain	448 197

Food & Beverage Makers

Company	Sales or operating revenue
John Labatt	$3 782 234
Seagram	3 693 615
Canada Packers	3 205 281
Molson	1 858 168
McCain Foods	1 500 000
Unilever Canada	910 406
Maple Leaf Mills	864 000
Kraft	823 790
Nabisco Brands	822 015
Burns Foods	800 000

Communications

Company	Sales or operating revenue
BCE	$14 649 000
International Thomson	4 690 062
Anglo-Canadian Telephone	1 781 548
Southam	1 451 971
Maclean Hunter	1 125 000
Thomson Newspapers	1 095 849
Alberta Government Telephones	1 071 661
Torstar	903 583
Quebecor	682 632
Hollinger	525 000

Forestry

Company	Sales or operating revenue
MacMillan Bloedel	$3 134 500
Abitibi-Price	2 988 000
Domtar	2 567 800
Consolidated-Bathurst	2 261 430
B. C. Forest Products	1 400 427
Canfor	1 244 925
Crown Forest	1 029 885
Repap Enterprises	926 955
Weldwood of Canada	741 035
Q & O Paper	561 964

Automotive Products

Company	Sales or operating revenue
General Motors of Canada	$16 884 371
Ford Motor Co. of Canada	13 976 800
Chrysler Canada	7 246 800
Magna International	1 152 463
Goodyear Canada	695 534
Hayes-Dana	501 063
Paccar of Canada	487 249
Uniroyal Goodrich Canada	372 557
Firestone Canada	364 105
Derlan Industries	269 376

Energy

Company	Sales or operating revenue
Imperial Oil	$7 562 000
Ontario Hydro	5 280 000
PetroCanada	5 194 000
Hydro-Québec	5 095 319
Shell Canada	4 819 000
TransCanada Pipelines	3 355 400
Texaco Canada	2 649 000
Nova	2 322 438
Total Petroleum	2 316 534
British Columbia Hydro	1 987 000

Mining

Company	Sales or operating revenue
Alcan Aluminium	$9 012 822
Inco	2 372 836
Rio Algom	1 532 556
Falconbridge	1 339 825
Cominco	1 306 101
Placer Dome	833 900
QIT Fer et Titane	503 000
Denison Mines	442 220
Eldorado Nuclear	335 015
Hudson Bay Mining	324 367

Other Manufacturing

Company	Sales or operating revenue
Moore	$3 025 260
Polysar Energy	2 868 500
Varity	2 571 963
Stelco	2 546 378
Ivaco	2 174 976
Dofasco	2 163 071
General Electric Canada	1 689 345
Dow Chemical Canada	1 550 000
Bombardier	1 456 400
Du Pont Canada	1 340 977

Merchandising

Company	Sales or operating revenue
George Weston	$11 034 800
Provigo	6 418 100
Hudson's Bay	4 845 178
Steinberg	4 491 355
Sears Canada	4 035 098
Canada Safeway	3 872 368
Oshawa Group	3 804 015
Canadian Tire	2 483 822
F.W. Woolworth	2 025 969
Groupe Metro-Richelieu	1 915 417

Real Estate & Construction

Company	Sales or operating revenue
PCL Construction	$1 259 986
Trizec	1 049 000
Lavalin	1 024 000
Ellis-Don	756 000
Cadillac Fairview	680 651
SNC Group	440 779
Tridel Enterprises	410 435
George Wimpey Canada	361 139
Coscan Development	341 681
Lundrigans-Comstock	340 300

Transportation

Company	Sales or operating revenue
Canadian National Railway	$4 784 129
Air Canada	3 131 100
PWA	1 870 946
Laidlaw Transportation	1 205 902
Via Rail Canada	712 315
Wardair	518 654
CSL Group	409 600
Fednav	407 082
British Columbia Rail	321 842
Trimac	291 320

Conglomerates

Company	Sales or operating revenue
Canadian Pacific	$12 208 600
Noranda	7 343 566
Brascan	5 178 000
Imasco	4 814 556
Campeau	4 263 646
Federal Industries	1 631 527
Jim Pattison Group	1 627 502
Unicorp Canada	1 441 100
Federated Co-operatives	1 427 997
Onex	1 194 550

Canada's Largest Corporate Employers, 1987

Source: The Financial Post 500

Company	Employees	Sales per employee	Company	Employees	Sales per employee
BCE	117 000	$125 205	Provigo	21 000	$305 624
Imasco	92 353	52 132	Dylex	21 000	61 898
Canadian Pacific	85 400	142 958	Société générale de financement	20 190	24 404
George Weston	67 300	163 964	Onex	20 000	59 728
Alcan Aluminium	63 000	143 061	Oshawa Group	19 000	200 211
Canada Post	61 640	48 184	Hydro-Québec	18 933	269 124
McDonald's Restaurants	54 000	21 511	Inco	18 706	126 849
Sears Canada Inc.	50 000	80 702	Cara Operations	18 000	15 189
Canadian National Railway	48 252	99 149	Anglo-Canadian Telephone	17 457	102 054
General Motors of Canada	44 749	377 313	Stelco	16 960	150 140
Noranda Inc.	44 000	166 899	Varity	16 330	157 499
Hudson's Bay	38 000	127 505	Abitibi-Price	16 300	183 313
Campeau	38 000	112 201	John Labatt	16 200	233 471
Steinberg	36 000	124 760	Domtar	15 871	161 792
K-Mart Canada	32 510	46 217	Chrysler Canada	15 677	462 257
Ontario Hydro	32 147	164 245	MacMillan Bloedel	15 226	205 865
Crownx	29 900	22 310	Consolidated-Bathurst	15 026	150 501
Ford Motor Co. of Canada	27 200	513 853	Southam	14 954	97 096
F.W. Woolworth	26 500	76 452	Seagram	14 400	256 501
Moore	26 480	114 247	Dofasco	13 400	161 423
Laidlaw Transportation	24 000	50 246	PWA	13 097	142 853
International Thomson	23 200	202 158	Canada Packers	12 500	256 422
Canada Safeway	22 000	176 017	Thomson Newspapers	12 500	87 668
Air Canada	22 000	142 323	Cineplex Odeon	12 500	55 178
Scott's Hospitality	21 900	39 888	Magna International	12 218	94 325

Largest Canadian Exporters, 1987

Source: The Financial Post 500

(thousands of dollars)

Company	Total Canadian exports	Exports as % of total sales	Company	Total Canadian exports	Exports as % of total sales
General Motors of Canada	$9 395 861	56%	Canfor	$763 000	61%
Ford Motor Co. of Canada	6 744 800	48	Cominco	735 000	56
Chrysler Canada	4 375 700	60	Cargill	728 705	65
Noranda	3 171 562	43	Falconbridge	772 031	54
Canadian Pacific	2 886 500	24	Consolidated-Bathurst	681 700	30
Canadian Wheat Board	2 664 000	83	Repap Enterprises	574 833	62
Alcan Aluminium	2 165 358	24	Mobil Oil Canada	558 355	35
MacMillan Bloedel	1 793 200	57	Rio Algom	525 187	34
Inco	1 221 246	51	Stelco	520 000	20
Abitibi-Price	1 133 100	38	Crown Forest	506 149	49
Mitsui & Co. (Canada)	1 038 000	40	Seaboard Lumber	503 286	100
Bombardier	1 031 400	71	Amoco Canada Petroleum	484 540	33
IBM Canada	993 000	32	George Weston	466 000	4
Nova	927 768	40	Allied-Signal Canada	450 252	68
B.C. Forest Products	828 600	59	Hydro-Québec	445 666	9
Royal Canadian Mint	826 225	80	Domtar	433 000	17
Mitsubishi Canada	807 740	71	TransCanada PipeLines	407 700	12
Pratt & Whitney Canada	807 729	82	McDonnell Douglas Canada	386 846	100
Canada Commercial	774 789	100	Canpotex	380 299	100
Magna International	772 000	67	Donohue	379 980	74

Canadian Corporate Profits and Losses, 1987

Source: The Financial Post 500

Largest Profits		Largest Losses	
(thousands of dollars)		(thousands of dollars)	
BCE	$1 087 000	Dome Petroleum	$401 000
Imperial Oil	716 000	Canada Post	128 981
Seagram	687 680	Dylex	117 821
Canadian Pacific	636 700	Hudson's Bay	78 474
Alcan Aluminium	574 158	Ocelot Industries	60 636

Business Turnarounds, 1987

Some Good Turnarounds (from a 1986 loss to a 1987 profit)		
	1986 loss	1987 profit
Polysar Energy	$283 200 000	$227 500 000
CN Railway	86 280 000	107 293 000
Cominco	48 251 000	80 650 000
Varity	32 284 000	66 777 000
Hudson Bay Mining	20 225 000	39 250 000

Some Wrong Turns (from a 1986 profit to a 1987 loss)		
	1986 profit	1987 loss
Dylex	$25 118 000	$117 821 000
Hudson's Bay	32 978 000	78 474 000
Total Petroleum	52 735 000	35 567 000
National Business Systems	6 456 000	26 277 000
Potash Corp. of Saskatchewan	7 984 000	20 712 000

Largest Foreign-Owned Companies in Canada, 1987

Source: The Financial Post 500

(thousands of dollars)

Company	1987 Sales	% Foreign-owned	Parent
General Motors of Canada Ltd.	$16 884 371	100	General Motors (U.S.)
Ford Motor Co. of Canada	13 976 800	94	Ford Motor (U.S.)
Imperial Oil	7 562 000	70	Exxon (U.S.)
Chrysler Canada	7 246 800	100	Chrysler (U.S.)
Shell Canada Ltd.	4 819 000	71	Shell (Neth./Brit.)
Sears Canada	4 035 098	60	Sears, Roebuck (U.S.)
Canada Safeway	3 872 368	100	Kohlberg, Kravis, Roberts (U.S.)
IBM Canada	3 104 000	100	IBM (U.S.)
Texaco Canada	2 649 000	78	Texaco (U.S.)
Mitsui (Canada)	2 608 542	100	Mitsui (Japan)
Total Petroleum	2 316 534	50	Total Petroles (France)
F.W. Woolworth	2 025 969	100	Woolworth World Trade (U.S.)
Anglo-Canadian Telephone	1 781 548	86	GTE (U.S.)
United Westburne	1 728 266	70	Dumez SA (France)
General Electric Canada	1 689 345	92	General Electric (U.S.)
Mobil Oil Canada	1 586 133	100	Mobil Oil (U.S.)
Dow Chemical Canada	1 550 000	100	Dow Chemical (U.S)
Rio Algom	1 532 556	53	RTZ (Britain)
K-Mart Canada	1 502 523	100	K-Mart (U.S.)
Amoco Canada Petroleum	1 480 389	100	Amoco (U.S.)

Largest Canadian Subsidiaries, 1987

Source: The Financial Post 500

(thousands of dollars)

Company (head office)	Sales	Assets	Major shareholder
Loblaw Cos. (Toronto)	$8 630 700	$ 2 213 500	George Weston 78%
Northern Telecom Ltd. (Mississauga)	6 435 741	6 326 292	BCE Inc. 53%
Bell Canada (Montreal)	6 377 500	13 507 500	BCE Inc. 100%
Noranda Forest Inc. (Toronto)	4 314 700	3 927 700	Noranda Inc. 81%
Polysar Ltd. (Sarnia, Ont.)	2 474 190	2 369 872	Polysar Energy & Chemical 100%
Kelly, Douglas & Co. (Vancouver)	2 099 736	475 712	Loblaw Cos. 85%
Imperial Tobacco Ltd. (Montreal)	1 925 987	n.a.	Imasco 100%
CIP Inc. (Montreal)	1 925 821	1 861 290	Canadian Pacific 100%
Zeller's Inc.[1] (Toronto)	1 844 965	700 217	Hudson's Bay 100%
Consumers' Gas Co.[2] (Toronto)	1 619 155	1 861 791	GW Utilities 83%
British Columbia Telephone Co. (Vancouver)	1 581 000	3 111 700	Anglo-Canadian Telephone 50%
Amca International Ltd. (Toronto)	1 472 564	1 117 444	Canadian Pacific 51%
Westfair Foods Ltd. (Winnipeg)	1 444 453	333 893	Kelly, Douglas 100%
Union Gas Ltd.[3] (Chatham, Ont.)	1 342 698	1 355 942	Union Enterprises 100%
Union Enterprises Ltd.[3] (Toronto)	1 338 122	1 501 527	Unicorp Canada 60%
Algoma Steel Corp. (Sault Ste. Marie)	1 227 952	1 571 510	Canadian Pacific 54%
Canadian Utilities Ltd. (Edmonton)	1 135 230	2 624 302	Atco 65%
Sobeys Stores Ltd.[4] (Stellarton, N.S.)	1 056 323	239 952	Empire Co. 100%
Consumers Distributing[1] (Toronto)	1 000 000	395 000	Provigo 100%
Gaz Metropolitain Inc.[2] (Montreal)	929 152	1 160 956	Noverco 100%

(1) For fiscal year ending Jan. 1988. (2) For fiscal year ending Sept. 1987. (3) For fiscal year ending Mar. 1987. (4) For fiscal year ending April 1987.
n.a. not available.

Largest Canadian Financial Institutions, 1987

Source: The Financial Post 500

(thousands of dollars)

Company (head office)	Assets	Revenue	Employees	Major Shareholders
Royal Bank of Canada[1] (Montreal)	$102 170 201	$9 498 149	42 839	Wide distribution
Canadian Imperial Bank of Commerce[1] (Toronto)	88 374 898	8 019 776	33 874	Wide distribution
Bank of Montreal[1] (Montreal)	84 227 721	8 019 496	34 482	Wide distribution
Bank of Nova Scotia[1] (Halifax)	71 429 739	6 396 467	26 187	Wide distribution
Toronto Dominion Bank[1] (Toronto)	54 525 475	5 140 533	21 710	Wide distribution
National Bank of Canada[1] (Montreal)	29 978 043	2 782 241	11 550	Wide distribution
La confédération des caisses populaires Desjardins du Québec (Quebec City)	29 574 500	2 877 717	23 968	Member federations
Caisse de dépôt et placement du Québec (Quebec City)	27 459 000	2 885 000	195	Quebec govt. 100%
Trilon Financial Corp. (Toronto)	27 254 000	3 236 000	n.a.	Brascan 47%; Olympia & York 14%
CT Financial Services Inc. (London, Ont.)	25 538 135	2 904 400	11 368	Imasco 99%
Central Capital Corp. (Halifax)	12 530 910	1 042 741	5 000	L. Ellen, H.R. Cohen 55% combined
National Victoria & Grey Trustco Ltd.[1] (Stratford, Ont.)	10 934 278	1 116 995	4 235	E-L Financial 20%; NVG Holdings 19%
Laurentian Group Corp. (Quebec City)	9 699 036	1 660 396	7 500	Groupe Victoire, France, Laurentian Mutual 63%, Eaton's 11%
Canada Mortgage and Housing Corp. (Ottawa)	9 540 117	891 600	3 100	Federal govt. 100%
Montreal Trustco Inc. (Montreal)	7 662 264	898 844	4 050	Power Financial 61%
Export Development Corp. (Ottawa)	6 932 700	664 900	496	Federal govt. 100%
General Motors Acceptance Corp. of Canada (Toronto)	6 417 133	704 462	563	General Motors Acceptance, Detroit
Province of Alberta Treasury Branches[2] (Edmonton)	5 519 593	523 329	2 981	Alberta govt. 100%
Lloyds Bank Canada (Toronto)	5 389 728	489 549	1 600	Lloyds Bank PLC, Britain
Farm Credit Corp.[2] (Ottawa)	4 914 482	482 992	573	Federal govt. 100%

(1) For fiscal year ending Oct. 1987. (2) For fiscal year ending Mar. 1987.
n.a. not available.

Top Canadian Acquisitions Abroad, 1977–1987

Source: The Financial Post 500

(millions of dollars)

Acquiring Company	Acquired or Merged company (head office)	1987 value[1]	Purchase price	Year acquired	% of stock acquired
Campeau Corp.	Allied Stores Corp. (New York)	$5 187	$5 004	1986	100
Seagram Co.	du Pont (Wilmington, Del.)	3 899	3 120	1981	20
Northern Telecom Ltd.	STC PLC (Britain)	1 099	1 099	1987	28
Olympia & York Developments	Santa Fe Southern Pacific Corp. (Chicago)	914	914	1987	10
Hiram Walker Resources Ltd.	Davis Oil Co. (Denver)	868	737	1982	100
Peoples Jewellers Ltd.	Zale Corp. (Irving, Tex.)	864	834	1986	100
Bank of Montreal	Harris Bankcorp Inc. (Chicago)	785	718	1984	100
First City Financial Corp.	Scovill Inc. (Stamford, Conn.)	781	740	1985	100
Genstar Corp.	Flinkote Co. (Stamford, Conn.)	699	447	1979	100
Alcan Aluminium Ltd.	Aluminum assets, Arco (Los Angeles)	692	655	1985	100

(1) U.S. consumer price index used for conversion to 1987 dollars for American assets acquired.

Top Foreign Acquisitions in Canada, 1977–1987

Source: The Financial Post 500

(millions of dollars)

Acquiring Company (head office)	Acquired or merged company	1987 value[1]	Purchase price	Year acquired	% of stock acquired
Allied Lyons PLC. (Britain)	Hiram Walker—Gooderham & Worts	$2 714	$2 600	1986	100
CFCL Acquisitions Corp.[2]	Cadillac Fairview Corp.	2 600	2 600	1987	100
Superior Oil Co. (Houston)	Canadian Superior Oil Ltd.	919	537	1979	51
Fletcher Challenge Ltd. (New Zealand)	British Columbia Forest Products Ltd.	753	753	1987	69
Union Faith Co. (Hong Kong)	Husky Oil Ltd.	484	484	1987	43
Elders IXL (Australia)	Carling O'Keefe Ltd.	396	396	1987	100
British Telecom (Britain)	Mitel Corp.	348	320	1985	51
Lloyds Bank (Britain)	Continental Bank of Canada	209	200	1986	90
Boeing Co. (Seattle)	de Havilland Aircraft of Canada	162	155	1986	100
Ford Motor Co. (Detroit)	Versatile Farm Equipment Corp.	126	126	1987	100

(1) Canadian consumer price index used for conversion to 1987 dollars for Canadian assets acquired. (2) Formed by JMB Realty Corp. as holding company for Cadillac Fairview and almost entirely owned by U.S. institutional investors.

Largest Crown Corporations

Source: *The Globe and Mail, Report on Business*, July 1988

Federal

Company	Revenue ($000)	Profit ($000)	Assets ($000)	Employees
Petro-Canada[1]	5 079 000	213 000	8 453 000	10 565
Canadian National Railway[1]	4 597 889	107 293	7 593 649	61 124
Air Canada[1]	3 212 500	45 700	3 084 800	22 134
Canada Post Corp.[2]	2 970 056	− 128 981	2 628 521	61 640
Canadian Broadcasting Corp.[2]	1 048 982	− 57 803	754 574	11 130
Canada Mortgage and Housing[1]	900 625	35 036	9 540 117	3 200
Teleglobe Canada[3]	831 652	62 950	502 413	1 166
Via Rail Canada[1]	714 669	6 021	953 921	4 178
Export Development Corp.[1]	664 867	1 498	6 932 728	527
Farm Credit Corp.[2]	482 992	− 132 490	4 914 084	579
Eldorado Nuclear[1]	339 386	− 5 237	901 212	1 013
Atomic Energy of Canada[2]	306 171	17 599	1 018 115	5 007
Federal Business Devel. Bank[2]	238 878	6 728	1 920 224	n.a.
Marine Atlantic[1]	210 128	3 119	334 990	2 416
Northern Canada Power Comm.[2]	101 749	− 2 604	142 919	270
St. Lawrence Seaway Authority[2]	62 083	− 6 562	652 758	1 053
Canada Ports[3]	20 108	− 1 740	100 041	1 517
Canada Development Investment[1]	17 803	− 3 932	284 497	n.a.

Provincial

Company	Revenue ($000)	Profit ($000)	Assets ($000)	Employees
Ontario Hydro[1]	5 367 000	271 000	32 657 000	32 147
Hydro-Quebec[1]	5 343 000	508 000	31 659 000	n.a.
Caisse de Dépôt et Placement[1]	2 885 000	2 852 000	27 459 000	195
B.C. Hydro[2]	2 097 000	67 000	9 802 000	6 508
Alberta Government Telephones[1]	1 131 978	53 169	2 360 120	11 477
Insurance Corp. of B.C.[1]	1 000 995	− 57 793	1 957 449	2 415
Saskatchewan Power Corp.[1]	899 000	36 000	2 939 000	3 064
N.B. Electric Power Comm.[2]	866 621	29 304	2 829 712	2 500
Régie de l'assur. automobile[3]	825 144	16 687	3 392 557	1 763
Manitoba Hydro-Electric Board[2]	614 035	13 448	3 240 128	3 853
Sidbec Dosco[1]	567 904	8 547	491 967	3 300
Treasury Branches Deposits	523 329	− 32 455	5 519 593	3 500
Nova Scotia Power Corp.[2]	509 345	− 9 277	1 474 803	2 383
Manitoba Telephone System[2]	393 624	− 19 991	920 084	4 660
Groupe SGP[3]	359 166	39 369	853 462	21 239
Newfoundland & Labrador Hydro[1]	353 507	43 409	2 146 520	1 309
B.C. Transit[2]	352 588	77	1 363 193	3 124
B.C. Railway[1]	322 214	54 255	1 310 870	2 660
Manitoba Public Insurance[4]	320 378	− 67 230	414 708	1 100
Potash Corp. of Saskatchewan[1]	257 473	− 20 712	1 314 872	1 756
B.C. Ferry Corp.[2]	223 573	− 11 601	372 523	2 700
Saskatchewan Housing Corp.[1]	204 270	− 1 771	371 431	n.a.
Sask. Mining Development[1]	203 715	60 279	914 051	175
Rexfor[2]	163 721	4 916	187 118	2 251
Sask. Government Insurance[3]	128 544	3 865	182 531	1 300
Ont. Northland Transportation[3]	110 649	17 776	232 856	1 300
Soquip[2]	61 077	1 628	360 250	n.a.
Soquem[2]	53 872	− 1 422	114 491	76
Industrial Estates[2]	8 494	− 5 796	83 525	n.a.
Nova Scotia Resources[2]	5 037	− 195	133 063	5

(1) Year ending Dec. 1987. (2) Year ending Mar. 1987. (3) Year ending Dec. 1986. (4) Year ending Oct. 1987.
n.a. not available.

Investment: A Glossary of Terms

Annual report: A report issued by a company to its shareholders at the end of the fiscal year. It contains a report on company operations and formal financial statements.

Bear market: A market in which prices are falling.

Bid and ask: The bid price is the highest price anyone is willing to pay to buy a stock; the ask is the lowest price anyone will accept to sell a stock. Together, the bid and ask prices are a "quote."

Blue chip stocks: Stocks with good investment qualities, usually common shares of well-established companies with good earnings records and long-time dividend payments.

Bond: A written promise or IOU by the issuer to repay a fixed amount of borrowed money on a specified date, and to pay a set annual rate of interest in the meantime, generally at semi-annual intervals. Bonds are usually considered a safe investment because the borrower (whether a company or the government) must make interest payments before its money is spent on anything else.

Bull market: A market in which prices are rising.

Canada Savings Bonds: These are issued each fall, and are popular with small investors, because they come in denominations starting at $100. They are not traded. They have a term of several years, and a minimum guaranteed rate of interest. However, the government sets an effective rate during the issuing period each year, and adjusts it when necessary to conform with interest rate trends. Interest can be awarded yearly or compounded, depending upon which type of bond the purchaser buys.

Capital gain or loss: Profit or loss resulting from the sale of a security. The gain or loss is the difference between the buying and selling price of the security, with commissions figured in.

Common shares: Securities issued by the company which represent part-ownership in the company. Common shares sometimes carry a voting privilege and entitle the holder to a share in the company's profits, usually issued in the form of dividends.

Convertible bond: A corporate bond (see below) which may be converted into a stated number of shares of the corporation's common stock. Its price tends to fluctuate with the price of the stock, as well as with changes in interest rates.

Corporate bonds: Evidence of debt by a corporation. The bond bears interest much like a government bond, and matures at a certain date in the future. Considered safer than the common or preferred stock of the same company.

Dividend: A portion of a company's profit paid to the common and preferred shareholders. The amount is decided upon by the company's board of directors, and may be paid in cash or stock.

Futures: Contracts to buy or sell specific quantities of a commodity or financial instrument with delivery delayed until some agreed-upon time in the future.

Government of Canada Bonds: These bear a fixed rate of interest and a maturation date in the future, and are traded on the market, with the price rising and falling in response to interest rate trends. Long-term government bonds are considered a safe investment. Provinces and municipalities may also issue long-term bonds.

Money market: Part of the capital market established for short-term borrowing and lending of funds. Money market dealers conduct business over the telephone, and trade securities such as short-term (3 years and less) government bonds, government treasury bills and commercial paper.

Mutual fund: A portfolio, or selection, of professionally bought and managed stocks in which you pool your money, along with thousands of other people. A share price is based on net asset value, or the value of all the investments owned by the fund, less any debt, and divided by the total number of shares. The major advantage is less risk—your investment is spread out over many stocks, and if one or 2 do badly, the remainder may shield you from the losses. Bond funds are mutual funds that deal in the bond market exclusively. Money market mutual funds concentrate on debt instruments sold on the money market. Equity mutual funds place their investments in the common shares of companies.

Options: Contracts which give the holder the right to buy ("call" options) or sell ("put" options) a fixed amount of a certain stock within a specified time, at a specific price.

Penny stock: Low-priced, often speculative issues selling at less than $1 a share.

Price/earnings ratio: A common stock's current market price, divided by the company's annual per-share earnings.

Preferred shares: Shares issued by a company to raise additional capital, after the issuance of common shares. Preferred shares carry dividends at predetermined rates, which must be paid before any dividends are paid to common shareholders.

Stock yield: The percentage of the dividend paid in relation to the price of the stock. For example, a stock selling at $40 a share with an annual dividend of $2 a share yields 5%.

TSE 300 Index: A composite index of 300 leading stocks on the Toronto Stock Exchange, chosen from 14 major groups in the economy, each of which is given a proportionate weighting. The rise and fall of the 300 Index figure is an indication of the overall trend in the stock market.

Treasury bills: These are short-term government obligations, which are sold at a discount and redeemed at face value at maturity. Three-month (91-day) and 6-month treasury bills are sold at weekly auctions, usually on Thursday, and the average yield of 91-day bills purchased helps determine the Bank Rate of the Bank of Canada. One-year trasury bills are sold at auctions every 2 weeks. Treasury bills can be resold on the money market. Provinces also issue these bills.

Warrant: A certificate giving the holder the right to purchase securities at a stipulated price within a specified period of time. Warrants are usually attached to a new issue of securities to assist the initial sale. They are often detachable and may be traded separately; however, they expire after a certain length of time.

How to Buy Stocks

Canada has 5 stock exchanges, located in Toronto, Montreal, Vancouver, Calgary and Winnipeg. The largest is the Toronto Stock Exchange, established in 1852, which accounts for about 75% of the total value of shares traded in the country. Each exchange serves its geographical area and has its own emphasis in stocks and transactions; the Vancouver Stock Exchange is the biggest market for the volatile shares of small mining stocks, while the Winnipeg Stock Exchange is active in commodities trading.

The basis of the stock market system is the need for companies to raise money for expansion or other ventures. One way to do this is to offer common or preferred shares to the public. To execute a share offering, the company places the shares with one or more brokerage houses, which act as underwriters, selling them to their clients. When the shares are sold, they can be listed on a stock exchange, where their owners can trade them freely with other investors.

Anyone can buy shares in a public company if he or she has the money. All transactions, however, must be executed through a licensed broker who has access to the stock market trading floor. Brokerage houses can be found listed in the Yellow Pages, or in the advertisements in the financial section. Most are "full-service" brokers, who will supply the investor with background data and investment advice. For this, they charge a fee of 2% or more for each "buy" and "sell" transaction. There are also, however, discount brokers, who provide only the basic buy and sell services and charge a proportionately lower fee.

To buy stocks, the investor must first find a broker who suits his needs and level of sophistication, and open an account. That done, he can place an order for a specific number of a chosen stock, often with a specified price he is willing to pay. The broker then places a "buy" order by telephone with his trader on the floor of the stock exchange on which those shares are listed. The trader takes the order, goes to the post where that stock is traded and calls out the order until he finds another trader willing to sell at that price. When he does, the trade is completed. It is then listed on the nationwide stock ticker used by brokerage firms, but no public record is kept of the names of the buyer and seller. The successful trade is reported to the broker, who advises the buyer. He will also get a written confirmation in a few days.

In some cases, the buyer will want to purchase stocks which, although traded publicly, are not listed formally on a stock exchange. These stocks are said to trade "over the counter," and are bought directly from securities dealers who act as a secondary market for them.

Besides buying shares, or equities, in a company, an investor can trade options, which are also listed on the stock exchanges. These are contracts allowing the purchaser to buy or sell a stock at a specified price during a specified time period. A "put" option entitles the purchaser to sell the stock for that price; a "call" option entitles him to buy it. Options allow the investor to profit from expected changes in the market or in the company which he thinks will affect the stock prices. He can make money by exercising the option, if the stock price performs as he predicted, or by selling the option itself, which may rise in price if market conditions make it look like a good investment.

A third option is to buy futures, which are contracts to buy or sell a specified amount of a commodity, like wheat or pork bellies, or a financial instrument, like a government treasury bill, for a particular price in the future. Again, this allows the investor to profit from expected developments in the market, but commodities futures, especially, are known as a relatively high-risk venture.

The price of a stock or option purchased must be paid to the broker within 5 working days of the transaction. However, some investors seek to gain "leverage" in the trade by borrowing some of the money from the broker, thus allowing them to buy more stock and realize a greater profit, repaying the broker when they resell the stock. This is known as buying on margin.

Most Actively Traded Stocks in Canada, 1987

Source: Toronto Stock Exchange

Company	Shares traded (millions)	Value of trading ($ millions)	Company	Shares traded (millions)	Value of trading ($ millions)
Canadian Pacific	138.8	3 266	B.C. Forest Products	64.4	1 242
Nova Alta (Class A, non-voting)	101.8	894	Bank of Nova Scotia	62.0	1 037
Falconbridge Ltd.	84.9	1 942	BCE Inc.	54.5	2 157
Laidlaw (Class B, non-voting)	83.2	1 682	Royal Bank	51.6	1 708
Noranda Inc.	77.9	2 179	Cominco Ltd.	49.0	866
Dome Petroleum	76.9	96	Consolidated Carma (Class A)	48.7	13
Alcan Aluminium	73.9	3 069	Royex Gold	46.8	293
C. I. B. C.	65.9	1 386	International Pagurian	46.1	114
Inco Ltd.	65.3	1 549	Encor Energy	45.7	373
Canadian Development	65.1	724	Toronto Dominion Bank	44.2	1 259

Winners and Losers on the Canadian Stock Exchanges, 1987

Source: Financial Post 500

Top Industrial Winners	Closing price	Change in year	Biggest Industrial Losers	Closing price	Change in year
Memotec Data	$28.50	+185%	United Bison Resources	$0.50	−98%
American Barrick Resources	14.25	+160	Consolidated Boulder Mountain Resources	0.46	−95
Cal Graphite	16.00	+151	Skyhigh Resources	0.65	−95
Crown Forest Industries A	80.00	+142	International Daleco Technologies	0.35	−94
British Gas ADR 2nd installment	30.50	+126	Pacific Star Communications	0.70	−92
Potash Co. of America $2.50 pfd.	19.25	+114	Praxis Technologies	0.75	−89
Prenor Group	35.00	+94	L.E.V. Scientific Industries	1.05	−86
Echo Bay Mines	30.63	+94	Amcan Cyphermaster	0.72	−85
Brenda Mines	16.75	+94	Challenger International	1.25	−85
Pine Point Mines	14.50	+93	Pacific Aqua Foods	0.75	−85

Canadian Stock Exchange Trading, 1987

Source: Toronto Stock Exchange

	Value Traded	%	Volume Traded	%
Toronto	$100 224 304 252	77.3	7 393 698 717	49.4
Montreal	21 875 596 915	16.9	2 022 147 963	13.5
Vancouver	6 650 301 038	5.1	4 795 142 825	32.1
Alberta	971 991 022	0.7	740 753 453	5.0
Winnipeg	426 776	. . .	150 032	. . .

. . . = too small to be included.

Toronto Stock Exchange (TSE) Price Index,[1] 1956-87

Source: Toronto Stock Exchange

	High[2]	Date	Low[2]	Date	Year end	Net Change	Percent change
1956	617.67	July 31	524.63	Nov. 30	564.97	n.a.	n.a.
1957	606.14	May 31	432.11	Dec. 31	432.11	−132.86	−23.52
1958	547.72	Dec. 31	444.10	Feb. 28	547.72	115.61	26.75
1959	598.96	July 31	538.37	Nov. 30	555.09	7.37	1.35
1960	544.74	Dec. 31	494.06	July 31	544.74	−10.35	−1.86
1961	700.85	Dec. 31	575.60	Jan. 31	700.85	156.11	28.66
1962	686.81	Feb. 28	571.84	Sept. 30	628.99	−71.86	−10.25
1963	702.71	Dec. 31	638.45	Feb. 28	702.71	73.72	11.72
1964	853.53	Dec. 31	715.36	Feb. 29	853.53	150.82	21.46
1965	911.26	Apr. 30	838.42	July 31	881.14	27.61	3.23
1966	917.75	Jan. 31	761.11	Sept. 30	789.51	−91.63	−10.40
1967	922.50	Sept. 30	843.44	Jan. 31	899.20	109.69	13.89
1968	1 062.88	Dec. 31	814.79	Mar. 31	1 062.88	163.68	18.20
1969	1 131.04	May 31	950.75	July 31	1 019.77	−43.11	−4.06
1970	1 006.40	Feb. 28	810.78	June 30	947.54	−72.23	−7.08
1971	1 036.09	Apr. 16	879.80	Nov. 12	990.54	43.00	4.54
1972	1 226.58	Dec. 29	1 044.60	Jan. 7	1 226.58	236.04	23.83
1973	1 329.28	Oct. 31	1 122.34	May 18	1 193.56	−33.02	−2.69
1974	1 276.81	Mar. 15	821.10	Dec. 6	844.48	−349.08	−29.25
1975	1 081.96	July 18	862.74	Jan. 3	953.54	109.06	12.91
1976	1 106.17	May 13	920.15	Nov. 30	1 011.52	57.98	6.08
1977	1 068.53	July 20	957.58	Oct. 26	1 059.59	48.07	4.75
1978	1 336.34	Oct. 12	996.88	Jan. 30	1 309.99	250.40	23.63
1979	1 813.48	Dec. 31	1 310.31	Jan. 2	1 813.17	503.18	38.41
1980	2 405.65	Dec. 1	1 670.89	Mar. 27	2 268.70	455.53	25.12
1981	2 393.33	July 17	1 752.70	Sept. 28	1 954.24	−314.46	−13.86
1982	1 958.08	Dec. 31	1 332.22	July 8	1 958.08	3.84	0.20
1983	2 611.79	Sept. 12	1 926.44	Jan. 4	2 552.35	594.27	30.35
1984	2 594.59	Jan. 9	2 077.36	July 25	2 400.33	−152.02	−5.96
1985	2 902.17	Dec. 31	2 347.49	Jan. 7	2 900.60	500.27	20.84
1986	3 134.50	Apr. 29	2 744.00	Jan. 23	3 066.18	165.58	5.71
1987	4 118.94	Aug. 13	2 783.25	Nov. 10	3 160.05	93.87	3.06

(1) A composite index of 300 leading stocks. The rise or fall of the index shows stock market trends. (2) High and low values are selected from the following time frames: 1958-70, month-end; 1971-75, month-end or weekly; 1976, daily close; 1977 on, intra-day values.
n.a. not available.

Canadian Labor Unions Directory

Source: Labour Canada

(with membership of 30 000 or more; as of Jan. 1, 1988)

Alberta Teachers' Association (Ind.), 11010-142 St., Edmonton, Alta. T5N 2R1; pres., Brendan Dunphy; 39 372 members.

Amalgamated Clothing and Textile Workers Union (AFL-CIO/CLC), 601-15 Gervais Dr., Don Mills, Ont. M3C 1Y8; Cdn. Dir., John Alleruzzo; 30 000 members.

British Columbia Teachers' Federation (Ind.), 2235 Burrard St., Vancouver, B.C. V6J 3H9; pres., Elsie McMurphy; 30 200 members.

Canadian Auto Workers (CLC), 205 Placer Court, North York, Ont. M2H 3H9; nat. pres. Robert (Bob) White; 143 000 members.

Canadian Brotherhood of Railway, Transport and General Workers (CLC), 2300 Carling Ave., Ottawa, Ont. K2B 7G1; pres., James D. Hunter; 39 900 members.

Canadian Paperworkers Union (CLC), 255 rue SaintJacques, Montreal, Que. H2Y 1M6; pres., James M. Buchanan; 69 000 members.

Canadian Union of Public Employees (CLC), 21 Florence St., Ottawa, Ont. K2P 0W6; nat. pres., Jeff Rose; 342 000 members.

Commission des enseignantes et enseignants des commissions scolaires (CEQ), 2336 chemin Sainte-Foy, C.P. 5800, Sainte-Foy, Qué. G1V 4E5; prés., Hervé Bergeron; 75 000 members.

Communications and Electrical Workers of Canada (CLC), Suite 906, 141 Laurier Ave. W., Ottawa, Ont. K1P 5J3; pres., Fred W. Pomeroy; 40 000 members.

Energy and Chemical Workers Union (CLC), No. 202, 9940-106 St., Edmonton, Alta. T5K 2N2; nat. dir., Reginald C. Basken; 35 000 members.

Fédération des infirmières et infirmiers du Québec (Ind.), 5e étage, 1425 boul. Dorchester, ouest, Montréal, Qué. H3G 1T7; prés. Diane Lavallée; 37 000 members.

Fédération des affaires sociales inc. (CSN), 1601 ave. de Lorimier, Montréal, Qué. H2K 4M5; prés., Catherine Loumède; 96 585 members.

Federation of Women Teachers' Associations of Ontario (Ind.), 3rd Fl., 1260 Bay St., Toronto, Ont. M5R 2B8; pres., Elaine Cline; 31 110 members.

Hotel Employees and Restaurant Employees International Union (AFL-CIO/CLC), Eastern Canada, bureau 500, 1410, rue Stanley, Montreal, Que. H3A 1P8; v.pres. James Stamos; Western Canada, 4853 E. Hastings St., Burnaby, B.C. V5C 2L1; v.pres. Ron Bonar; 30 000 members.

International Association of Machinists and Aerospace Workers (AFL-CIO/CLC), Suite 300, 100 Metcalfe St., Ottawa, Ont. K1P 5M1; general v.pres., Valerié E. Bourgeois; 58 members.

International Brotherhood of Electrical Workers (AFL-CIO/CFL), Suite 401, 45 Sheppard Ave. E., Willowdale, Ont. M2N 5Y1; int.v.pres., Ken Woods; 64 480 members.

International Brotherhood of Teamsters, Chauffeurs, Warehousemen and Helpers of America (Ind.), 8 000 boul. Langelier, suite 404, St. Léonard, Que; int. dir. Cdn. Conference of Teamsters, Louis Lacroix; 91 500 members.

International Union of Operating Engineers (AFL-CIO/CLC), Suite 105, 17704-103 Ave., Edmonton, Alta. T5S 1J9; Cdn. general v.pres., N. Budd Coutts; 36 000 members.

IWA-Canada (CLC), 500-1285 West Pender St., Vancouver, B.C. V6E 4B2; pres. J.J. Munro; 45 000 members.

Labourers' International Union of North America (AFL-CIO), 1177 Bélanger Ave., Suite 101, Ottawa, Ont. K1H 8N7; dir. Cdn. Research and Services, Nello Scipioni; 46 715 members.

National Union of Provincial Government Employees (CLC), Suite 204, 2841 Riverside Dr., Ottawa, Ont. K1V 8N4; nat. pres., John L. Flyer; 292 359 members.

Ontario Nurses Association (Ind.), 600-85 Grenville St., Toronto, Ont. M5S 1B3; pres., Monica Lesley; 46 680 members.

Ontario Secondary School Teachers' Federation (Ind.), 60 Mobile Dr., Toronto, Ont. M4A 2P3; pres., Jim Head; 35 722 members.

Public Service Alliance of Canada (CLC), 233 Gilmour St., Ottawa, Ont. K2P 0P1; nat. pres., Daryl T. Beam, 175 759 members.

Service Employees International Union (AFL-CIO/CLC), 1 Credit Union Dr., Toronto, Ont. M4A 2S6; Cdn. v.pres., S.E. (Ted) Roscoe and Aimé Gohier; 70 000 members.

Syndicat des fonctionnaires provinciaux du Québec inc. (Ind.), Bureau 200, 214, ave. Saint-Sacrement, Québec, Qué. G1N 4N9; pres. gen., Jean-Louis Harguindeguy; 40 000 members.

United Association of Journeymen and Apprentices of the Plumbing and Pipe Fitting Industry of the United States and Canada (AFL-CIO/CFL), 702-310 Broadway Ave., Winnipeg, Man. R3C 0S6; Cdn dir., J. Russ St. Eloi; 40 000 members.

United Brotherhood of Carpenters and Joiners of America (AFL-CIO), Suite 807, 5799 Yonge St., Willowdale, Ont. M2M 3V3; Cdn. off., John Carruthers and Ronald J. Dancer; 66 000 members.

United Food and Commercial Workers International Union (AFL-CIO/CLC), Suite 300, 61 International Blvd., Rexdale, Ont. M9W 6K4; Cdn. Dir., Clifford Evans; 170 000 members.

United Steelworkers of America (AFL-CIO/CLC), 7th Fl., 234 Eglinton Ave. E., Toronto, Ont. M4P 1K7; Nat. dir., E. Gerard Docquier; 160 000 members.

Ind = Independent; CLC = Canadian Labour Congress; CFL = Canadian Federation of Labour; AFL-CIO = American Federation of Labor-Congress of Industrial Organizations; CEQ = Centrale de l'Enseignement du Québec; CSN = Confédération des Syndicats Nationaux.

Union Membership and Work Stoppages in Canada

Source: Labour Canada

	Union Membership		Strikes and Lockouts			
	Total (000s)	% civilian labor force	Number	Workers involved	Work-days lost	Percent days lost[1]
1960	1 459	23.5	274	49 408	738 700	0.06
1961	1 447	22.6	287	97 959	1 335 080	0.11
1962	1 423	22.2	311	74 332	1 417 900	0.11
1963	1 449	22.3	332	83 428	917 140	0.07
1964	1 493	22.3	343	100 535	1 580 550	0.11
1965	1 589	23.2	501	171 870	2 349 870	0.17
1966	1 736	24.5	617	411 459	5 178 170	0.34
1967	1 921	26.1	522	252 018	3 974 760	0.25
1968	2 010	26.6	582	223 562	5 082 732	0.32
1969	2 075	26.3	595	306 799	7 751 880	0.46
1970	2 173	27.2	542	261 706	6 539 560	0.39
1971	2 231	26.8	569	239 631	2 866 590	0.16
1972	2 388	27.8	598	706 474	7 753 530	0.43
1973	2 591	29.2	724	348 470	5 776 080	0.30
1974	2 732	29.4	1 218	580 912	9 221 890	0.46
1975	2 884	29.8	1 171	506 443	10 908 810	0.53
1976	3 042	30.6	1 039	1 570 940	11 609 890	0.55
1977	3 149	31.0	803	217 557	3 307 880	0.15
1978	3 278	31.3	1 058	401 688	7 392 820	0.34
1979	n.a.	n.a.	1 050	462 504	7 834 230	0.34
1980	3 397	30.5	1 028	441 025	8 975 390	0.38
1981	3 487	30.6	1 048	338 548	8 878 490	0.37
1982	3 617	31.4	677	444 302	5 795 420	0.25
1983	3 563	30.6	645	329 309	4 443 960	0.19
1984	3 651	30.6	717	186 755	3 871 820	0.16
1985	3 666	30.2	825	159 727	3 180 710	0.13
1986	3 730	29.7	735	483 615	7 106 425	0.28
1987	3 781	29.8	658	582 679	3 984 369	0.15

(1) Percent of total labor force working time.
n.a. not available.

Transportation

Automobile Registrations in Canada
Source: Statistics Canada

(thousands of passenger cars)

	Canada	Nfld	PEI	NS	NB	Que	Ont	Man	Sask	Alta	BC	Yukon and NWT
1920	252	n.a.	1	11	10	36	156	37	60	38	28	n.a.
1925	641	n.a.	3	20	17	81	304	47	72	51	46	n.a.
1930	1 062	n.a.	7	36	30	148	497	68	109	86	81	n.a.
1935	992	n.a.	7	36	26	139	492	59	76	77	79	n.a.
1940	1 236	n.a.	7	45	31	181	612	73	93	93	101	n.a.
1945	1 161	n.a.	7	40	29	171	557	69	96	92	99	n.a.
1950	1 913	11	10	62	49	303	888	111	129	151	198	1
1955	2 961	27	13	107	75	549	1 318	162	167	336	303	3
1960	4 104	46	19	140	106	844	1 733	213	213	340	446	5
1965	5 279	70	26	178	137	1 146	2 140	260	268	424	624	7
1970	6 602	90	30	202	159	1 602	2 576	307	284	530	812	10
1975	8 693	127	41	262	219	2 189	3 225	395	349	716	1 157	13
1980	10 256	147	48	364	253	2 548	3 709	458	393	1 142	1 181	13
1985	11 118	168	55	366	278	2 483	4 094	513	387	1 289	1 468	16
1986	11 477	176	56	337	286	2 614	4 244	527	389	1 296	1 527	25

n.a. not available.

Fuel Consumption of 1988 Automobiles
Source: 1988 Fuel Consumption Guide, Transport Canada

Automobile type	Engine size[1]	Cylinders[2]	Transmission[3]	Litres per 100 km city	Litres per 100 km highway	Miles per gallon city	Miles per gallon highway
Acura Integra	1.6	4	M5	8.8	7.0	32	40
Audi 90 Quattro	2.3	5	M5	13.0	8.9	22	32
Audi 5000S	2.3	5	A3	12.6	9.5	22	30
BMW 325	2.7	6	M5	11.5	8.2	25	34
BMW 735i	3.4	6	M5	16.0	10.4	18	27
Buick Century	3.8	6	A4	12.3	7.3	23	39
Buick Lesabre	3.8	6	A4	12.3	7.3	23	39
Buick Regal	2.8	6	A4	11.7	7.4	24	38
Buick Skyhawk	2.0	4	A3	9.4	6.6	30	43
Cadillac Seville	4.5	8	A4	14.2	9.1	20	31
Chevrolet Camaro	2.8	6	A4	12.3	7.7	23	37
Chevrolet Camaro	5.0	8	A4	13.8	8.3	20	34
Chevrolet Cavalier	2.8	6	A3	11.8	8.2	24	34
Cherolet Celebrity	2.5	4	A3	10.0	7.0	28	40
Chevrolet Corvette	5.7	8	A4	17.0	10.8	17	26
Chevrolet Monte Carlo ...	5.0	8	A4	14.2	9.0	20	31
Chevrolet Nova	1.6	4	M5	7.7	5.6	37	50
Chevrolet Sprint	1.0	3	M5	5.3	4.4	53	64
Chrysler Daytona Turbo ..	2.2	4	M5	10.3	6.6	27	43
Chrysler Fifth Avenue	5.2	8	A3	14.6	10.1	19	28
Chrysler Lebaron GTS ...	2.2	4	A3	10.3	7.4	27	38
Chrysler New Yorker	3.0	6	A3	12.4	8.4	23	34
Dodge Aries	2.2	4	M5	9.4	6.4	30	44
Dodge Colt	1.5	4	M5	7.8	5.8	36	49
Dodge Shadow	2.2	4	M5	9.4	6.4	30	44
Dodge 600	2.5	4	A3	10.8	8.0	26	35
Ford Escort	1.9	4	M5	8.5	5.9	33	48
Ford Crown Victoria	5.0	8	A4	14.3	9.8	20	29
Ford Mustang	2.3	4	A4	10.8	7.8	26	36
Ford Mustang	5.0	8	M5	14.1	8.8	20	32
Ford Taurus	2.5	4	M5	10.3	6.7	27	42
Ford Tempo	2.3	4	M5	11.2	7.6	25	37
Ford Thunderbird	3.8	6	A4	12.2	8.4	23	34
Honda Accord	2.0	4	M5	8.7	6.3	32	45
Honda Civic	1.5	4	M5	8.3	6.5	34	43
Honda Prelude S	2.0	4	M5	10.5	8.0	27	35
Hyundai Excel	1.5	4	M5	8.5	5.9	33	48

445

Automobile type	Engine size[1]	Cylinders[2]	Transmission[3]	Litres per 100 km city	Litres per 100 km highway	Miles per gallon city	Miles per gallon highway
Hyundai Stellar	2.0	4	M5	9.8	7.2	29	39
Jaguar XJ-S V12	5.3	12	A3	17.6	12.6	16	22
Lincoln Continental	3.8	6	A4	13.8	8.7	20	32
Mazda RX-7	1.3	R2	M5	14.4	9.2	20	31
Mazda 626	2.2	4	M5	10.2	7.1	28	40
Mercedes Benz 300E	3.0	6	A4	13.5	9.8	21	29
Mercedes Benz 420 SEL	4.2	8	A4	16.0	12.0	18	24
Mercury Cougar	3.8	6	A4	12.2	8.4	23	34
Mercury Grand Marquis	5.0	8	A4	14.3	9.8	20	29
Mercury Topaz	2.3	4	A3	10.7	8.1	26	35
Mercury Tracer	1.6	4	M5	8.3	6.2	34	46
Merkur Scorpio	2.9	6	M5	13.5	9.2	21	31
Nissan Maxima	3.0	6	M5	13.1	8.5	22	33
Nissan Micra	1.2	4	M5	6.4	4.7	44	60
Nissan Pulsar NX	1.6	4	M5	9.0	6.4	31	44
Nissan Sentra	1.6	4	M5	8.3	6.1	34	46
Nissan 200SX	2.0	4	M5	10.3	7.8	27	36
Nissan 300ZX	3.0	6	M5	13.5	8.6	21	33
Oldsmobile Cutlass Ciera	2.8	6	A4	11.5	7.4	25	38
Peugot 505	2.2	4	M5	13.1	9.2	22	31
Plymouth Colt	1.5	4	M5	7.8	5.8	36	49
Plymouth Reliant	2.2	4	A3	9.7	7.0	29	40
Plymouth Sundance	2.2	4	M5	9.4	6.4	30	44
Pontiac Fiero	2.8	6	M5	13.5	7.9	21	36
Pontiac Firebird	2.8	6	A4	12.3	7.7	23	37
Pontiac Firebird	5.0	8	A4	13.8	8.3	20	34
Pontiac Grand Am	2.5	4	A3	10.1	7.0	28	40
Pontiac Grand Prix	2.8	6	A4	11.7	7.4	24	38
Pontiac Sunbird	2.0	4	A3	9.4	6.6	30	43
Pontiac Tempest	2.0	4	S5	9.4	6.0	30	47
Pontiac 6000	2.8	6	A4	11.6	7.4	24	38
Porsche 911 Carrera	3.2	6	M5	13.5	8.6	21	33
Porsche 944S Turbo	2.5	4	M5	12.2	8.1	23	35
Rolls-Royce Silver Spirit	6.8	8	A3	24.9	18.7	11	15
Saab 900 Turbo	2.0	4	M5	11.6	8.1	24	35
Saab 9000S	2.0	4	M5	11.6	7.9	24	36
Subaru GL	1.8	4	M5	9.0	6.9	31	41
Toyota Camry	2.0	4	M5	9.1	6.7	31	42
Toyota Celica	2.0	4	M5	9.1	6.7	31	42
Toyota Corrola	1.6	4	M5	7.9	6.1	36	46
Toyota Supra	3.0	6	M5	13.1	9.4	22	30
Toyota MR2	1.6	4	M5	9.0	6.9	31	41
Toyota Tercel	1.5	4	M5	7.5	5.7	38	50
Volkswagen Cabriolet	1.8	4	M5	9.9	7.9	29	36
Volkswagon Fox	1.8	4	M4	9.3	7.3	30	39
Volkswagen Golf	1.8	4	M5	9.4	6.7	30	42
Volkswagen Jetta	1.8	4	M5	9.3	6.4	30	44
Volkswagen Scirocco	1.8	4	M5	9.6	7.2	29	39
Volvo 240 DL	2.3	4	M5	10.7	7.7	26	37
Volvo 760 Turbo	2.3	4	A4	12.5	9.7	23	29

(1) Displacement measured in litres. (2) R = rotary. (3) A = automatic; M = manual; S = manual with shift indicator light; the number beside the letter refers to the gears, for instance:, M5 = 5 speed manual, A3 = 3 speed automatic.

Canadian Motor Vehicle Traffic Deaths

Source: Statistics Canada

	1960	1965	1970	1975	1980	1984	1985	1986
Canada	2 763	4 070	4 264	5 109	5 397	3 973	4 099	3 922
Newfoundland	43	64	61	97	93	52	63	58
Prince Edward Island	13	24	28	38	36	28	37	26
Nova Scotia	139	186	182	202	205	157	153	127
New Brunswick	141	182	183	190	216	161	131	133
Quebec	727	1 318	1 411	1 623	1 468	1 049	1 276	973
Ontario	987	1 318	1 300	1 520	1 527	1 203	1 239	1 083
Manitoba	104	132	132	167	189	126	141	162
Saskatchewan	126	166	159	229	246	222	209	245
Alberta	224	252	320	435	649	454	414	534
British Columbia	252	421	471	593	745	499	413	557
Yukon	7[1]	7[1]	17[1]	8	13	9	9	12
Northwest Territories	7[1]	7[1]	17[1]	7	10	13	14	12

(1) Includes Yukon and Northwest Territories.

Canada's Busiest Ports, 1986

Source: Statistics Canada

(thousands of tonnes of cargo)

	No. of vessels	Total cargo	%	Domestic shipping	%	International shipping	%
All Ports	107 303	327 585	100.0	121 012	100.0	206 573	100.0
Vancouver, BC	12 072	57 215	17.5	4 451	3.7	52 764	25.5
Sept Iles, Que	1 405	22 594	6.9	4 068	3.4	18 526	9.0
Montreal, Que	5 805	21 274	6.5	6 597	5.5	14 677	7.1
Port Cartier, Que	878	19 338	5.9	4 046	3.3	15 292	7.4
Thunder Bay, Ont	2 119	17 687	5.4	14 685	12.1	3 002	1.5
Halifax, NS	3 222	13 485	4.1	3 325	2.7	10 160	4.9
Quebec, Que	1 866	12 052	3.7	4 548	3.8	7 504	3.6
Saint John, NB	1 955	11 940	3.6	1 449	1.2	10 491	5.1
Prince Rupert, B.C.	1 741	10 578	3.2	596	0.5	9 982	4.8
Hamilton, Ont	1 223	10 413	3.2	4 693	3.9	5 720	2.8
Busiest 10 ports	32 286	196 576	60.0	48 458	40.0	148 118	71.7

Principal Commodities Handled at Canadian Ports, 1986

Source: Statistics Canada

(thousands of tonnes of cargo)

	Total cargo	%	Domestic shipping	%	International shipping	%
All Commodities	327 585	100.0	121 012	100.0	206 573	100.0
Iron Ores	47 718	14.6	11 052	9.1	36 666	17.7
Coal	44 124	13.5	4 548	3.8	39 576	19.2
Wheat	35 073	10.7	18 390	15.2	16 683	8.1
Logs	20 435	6.2	17 416	14.4	3 019	1.5
Fuel oil	17 877	5.5	11 663	9.6	6 214	3.0
Crude petroleum	14 236	4.3	512	0.4	13 724	6.6
Limestone	11 403	3.5	9 056	7.5	2 347	1.1
Barley	11 312	3.5	5 098	4.2	6 214	3.0
Pulpwood	10 715	3.3	8 699	7.2	2 016	1.0
Salt	9 152	2.8	5 701	4.7	3 451	1.7
Principal 10 commodities	222 045	67.8	92 135	76.1	129 910	62.9

Canada's Busiest Airports[1], 1986

Source: Statistics Canada

Airport	Flights[2]	Passengers No.	%	Airport	Flights[2]	Passengers No.	%
Toronto/Pearson Intl., Ont.	170 872	15 154 248	31.0	Windsor, Ont.	5 151	246 661	0.5
Vancouver Intl., B.C.	76 832	7 247 743	14.8	Prince George, B.C.	5 076	215 338	0.4
Montreal/Dorval Intl., Que.	74 713	5 440 674	11.1	Sault Ste. Marie, Ont.	4 642	176 523	0.4
Calgary Intl., Alta.	62 054	3 814 607	7.8	Fort St. John, B.C.	3 968	137 042	0.3
Winnipeg Intl., Man.	35 637	2 177 925	4.5	Mont Joli, Que.	3 861	77 182	0.2
Ottawa Intl., Ont.	32 488	1 936 707	4.0	Val D'Or, Que.	3 850	90 203	0.2
Edmonton Intl., Alta.	32 109	1 964 657	4.0	Yellowknife, N.W.T.	3 790	100 039	0.2
Halifax Intl., N.S.	30 546	1 710 750	3.5	Sydney, N.S.	3 768	113 356	0.2
Montreal/Mirabel Intl., Que.	18 960	1 393 393	2.9	Charlottetown, P.E.I.	3 539	142 637	0.3
Regina, Sask.	14 402	610 890	1.3	Moncton, N.B.	3 514	193 299	0.4
Saskatoon, Sask.	14 227	574 217	1.2	Fredericton, N.B.	3 409	160 350	0.3
Quebec, Que.	12 540	472 938	1.0	Cranbrook, B.C.	3 388	91 677	0.2
Edmonton Municipal, Alta.	11 668	692 443	1.4	Penticton, B.C.	3 347	82 380	0.2
Thunder Bay, Ont	9 348	417 059	0.9	North Bay, Ont.	3 122	62 245	0.1
Kelowna, B.C.	9 185	355 742	0.7	Kamloops, B.C.	3 027	90 459	0.2
St. Johns, Nfld.	8 325	500 680	1.0	Sudbury, Ont.	2 929	129 884	0.3
Saint John, N.B.	6 420	188 954	0.4	Dryden Municipal, Ont.	2 648	40 021	0.1
Sept-Iles, Que	5 192	136 498	0.3	All Airports	762 048	48 824 952	100.0

(1) Scheduled services only. (2) Takeoffs and landings.

Air Passenger Traffic[1] Between Canadian and U.S. Cities

Source: Statistics Canada

(thousands of passengers)

City-pair	1970	1980	1985	1986	City-pair	1970	1980	1985	1986
Toronto–New York	450	683	637	747	Toronto–Boston	63	137	171	200
Montreal–New York	382	354	410	461	Toronto–Los Angeles	70	188	162	198
Toronto–Chicago	140	210	228	260	Montreal–Miami	80	240	166	172
Vancouver–Los Angeles	61	197	184	253	Montreal–Boston	89	134	129	161
Vancouver–San Francisco	81	145	133	211	Toronto–Miami	80	157	134	155

(1) Scheduled transborder flights of the top 10 city-pairs, ranked in order of passenger traffic.

Air Passenger Traffic[1] Between Canadian Cities

Source: Statistics Canada

(thousands of passengers)

City-pair	1970	1980	1985	1986	City-pair	1970	1980	1985	1986
Montreal–Toronto	675	1 127	1 198	1 221	Thunder Bay–Toronto	85	192	196	206
Toronto–Vancouver	163	532	458	785	Vancouver–Winnipeg	90	192	173	188
Ottawa–Toronto	306	575	633	635	Montreal–Vancouver	78	169	147	184
Calgary–Vancouver	166	455	430	493	Ottawa–Vancouver	32	94	108	136
Calgary–Toronto	83	397	400	427	Kelowna–Vancouver	48	149	152	135
Edmonton–Vancouver	139	377	349	401	Sault Ste. Marie–Toronto	61	115	116	127
Toronto–Winnipeg	171	316	322	347	Halifax–Montreal	90	116	118	120
Calgary–Edmonton	235	723	351	312	Prince George–Vancouver	58	177	115	119
Edmonton–Toronto	70	298	270	308	Calgary–Winnipeg	61	136	120	117
Halifax–Toronto	99	220	260	283	Toronto–Windsor	93	108	104	112

(1) Scheduled domestic flights of the top 20 city-pairs ranked in order of passenger traffic.

Road Distance Between Canadian Cities

Source: Statistics Canada

(in kilometres)

	Calgary	Charlottetown	Edmonton	Fredericton	Halifax	Montreal	Ottawa	Quebec	Regina	St. John's	Saskatoon	Thunder Bay	Toronto	Vancouver	Victoria	Whitehorse	Winnipeg	Yellowknife
Calgary	●	4 917	299	4 558	5 042	3 743	3 553	4 014	764	6 183	620	2 050	3 434	1 057	1 123	2 385	1 336	1 811
Charlottetown	4 917	●	4 949	359	232	1 184	1 374	945	4 163	1 294	4 421	2 878	1 724	5 985	6 051	7 034	3 592	6 460
Edmonton	299	4 949	●	4 598	5 082	3 764	3 574	4 035	785	6 212	528	2 071	3 455	1 244	1 310	2 086	1 357	1 511
Fredericton	4 558	359	4 598	●	346	834	1 024	586	3 813	1 622	4 070	2 527	1 373	5 634	5 700	6 684	3 241	6 109
Halifax	5 042	232	5 082	346	●	1 318	1 508	912	4 297	1 349	4 554	3 011	1 857	6 119	6 185	7 168	3 726	6 593
Montreal	3 743	1 184	3 764	834	1 318	●	190	270	2 979	2 448	3 236	1 693	539	4 801	4 867	5 850	2 408	5 275
Ottawa	3 553	1 374	3 574	1 024	1 508	190	●	460	2 789	2 638	3 046	1 503	399	4 611	4 677	5 660	2 218	5 086
Quebec	4 014	945	4 035	586	912	270	460	●	3 249	2 208	3 507	1 963	810	5 071	5 137	6 120	2 678	5 546
Regina	764	4 163	785	3 813	4 297	2 979	2 789	3 249	●	5 427	257	1 286	2 670	1 822	1 888	2 871	571	2 297
St. John's	6 183	1 294	6 212	1 622	1 349	2 448	2 638	2 208	5 427	●	5 684	4 141	2 987	7 248	7 314	8 298	4 855	7 723
Saskatoon	620	4 421	528	4 070	4 554	3 236	3 046	3 507	257	5 684	●	1 543	2 927	1 677	1 743	2 614	829	2 039
Thunder Bay	2 050	2 878	2 071	2 527	3 011	1 693	1 503	1 963	1 286	4 141	1 543	●	1 384	3 108	3 174	4 157	715	3 582
Toronto	3 434	1 724	3 455	1 373	1 857	539	399	810	2 670	2 987	2 927	1 384	●	4 492	4 558	5 528	2 099	4 966
Vancouver	1 057	5 985	1 244	5 634	6 119	4 801	4 611	5 071	1 822	7 248	1 677	3 108	4 492	●	66	2 697	2 232	2 411
Victoria	1 123	6 051	1 310	5 700	6 185	4 867	4 677	5 137	1 888	7 314	1 743	3 174	4 558	66	●	2 763	2 298	2 477
Whitehorse	2 385	7 034	2 086	6 684	7 168	5 850	5 660	6 120	2 871	8 298	2 614	4 157	5 528	2 697	2 763	●	3 524	2 704
Winnipeg	1 336	3 592	1 357	3 241	3 726	2 408	2 218	2 678	571	4 855	829	715	2 099	2 232	2 298	3 524	●	2 868
Yellowknife	1 811	6 460	1 511	6 109	6 593	5 275	5 086	5 546	2 297	7 723	2 039	3 582	4 966	2 411	2 477	2 704	2 868	●

Air Distances Between Selected World Cities

(in kilometres)

	Bangkok	Beijing	Berlin	Cairo	Cape Town	Caracas	Chicago	Hong Kong	Hono-lulu	Lima
Bangkok	...	3 292	8 611	7 278	10 137	16 983	13 789	1 733	10 634	19 701
Beijing	3 292	...	7 376	7 559	12 943	14 401	10 626	1 958	8 169	16 652
Berlin	8 611	7 376	...	2 891	9 591	8 428	7 102	8 758	11 778	11 094
Cairo	7 278	7 559	2 891	...	7 208	10 204	9 881	8 183	14 236	12 431
Cape Town	10 137	12 943	9 591	7 208	...	10 243	13 662	11 868	18 560	9 770
Caracas	16 983	14 401	8 428	10 204	10 243	...	4 014	16 355	9 688	2 747
Chicago	13 789	10 626	7 102	9 881	13 662	4 014	...	12 545	6 848	6 074
Hong Kong	1 733	1 958	8 758	8 183	11 868	16 355	12 545	...	8 940	18 372
Honolulu	10 634	8 169	11 778	14 236	18 560	9 688	6 848	8 940	...	9 569
London	9 564	8 164	938	3 516	9 636	7 490	6 368	9 638	11 649	10 162
Los Angeles	12 288	10 056	9 303	12 100	16 040	5 844	2 808	11 649	4 114	6 711
Madrid	10 196	9 244	1 874	3 358	8 541	6 993	6 740	10 552	12 666	9 504
Melbourne	7 350	9 080	15 958	13 958	10 338	15 635	15 564	7 393	8 858	12 967
Mexico City	15 757	12 475	9 744	12 389	13 707	3 595	2 719	14 140	6 097	4 246
Montreal	13 416	10 489	6 018	8 732	12 746	3 923	1 199	12 447	7 913	6 388
Moscow	7 062	5 804	1 619	2 901	10 103	9 939	8 024	7 139	11 339	12 650
New York	13 948	11 012	6 402	9 041	12 555	3 411	1 149	12 969	7 995	5 855
Paris	9 456	8 238	882	3 215	9 310	7 614	6 666	9 638	11 985	10 249
Rio de Janeiro	16 080	17 326	9 990	9 884	6 084	4 512	8 499	17 713	13 335	3 768
Rome	8 840	8 146	1 186	2 134	8 417	8 359	7 762	9 290	12 936	10 861
San Francisco	12 761	9 522	9 126	12 013	16 489	6 278	2 991	11 110	3 858	7 269
Singapore	1 421	4 459	9 918	8 265	9 667	18 346	15 080	2 582	10 822	18 808
Stockholm	8 188	6 650	850	3 372	10 335	8 803	6 969	8 146	11 062	11 530
Tokyo	4 610	2 103	8 941	9 586	14 729	14 172	10 159	2 882	6 209	15 496
Warsaw	8 098	6 959	518	2 605	9 549	8 944	7 529	8 282	11 852	11 609
Washington, D.C.	14 170	11 170	6 727	9 368	12 703	3 294	959	13 121	7 784	5 646

	London	Los Angeles	Madrid	Mel-bourne	Mexico City	Montreal	Moscow	New Delhi	New York	Paris
Bangkok	9 564	12 288	10 196	7 350	15 757	13 416	7 062	2 917	13 948	9 456
Beijing	8 164	10 056	9 244	9 080	12 475	10 489	5 804	3 786	11 012	8 238
Berlin	938	9 303	1 874	15 958	9 744	6 018	1 619	5 789	6 402	882
Cairo	3 516	12 100	3 358	13 958	12 389	8 732	2 901	4 438	9 041	3 215
Cape Town	9 636	16 040	8 541	10 338	13 707	12 746	10 103	9 282	12 555	9 310
Caracas	7 490	5 844	6 993	15 635	3 595	3 923	9 939	14 212	3 411	7 614
Chicago	6 368	2 808	6 740	15 564	2 719	1 199	8 024	12 045	1 149	6 666
Hong Kong	9 638	11 649	10 552	7 393	14 140	12 447	7 139	3 763	12 969	9 638
Honolulu	11 649	4 114	12 666	8 858	6 097	7 913	11 339	11 926	7 995	11 985
London	...	8 751	1 263	16 895	8 943	5 236	2 516	6 727	5 582	344
Los Angeles	8 751	...	9 409	12 761	2 481	3 905	9 763	11 281	3 944	9 012
Madrid	1 263	9 409	...	17 310	9 080	5 548	3 455	7 289	5 781	1 054
Melbourne	16 895	12 761	17 310	...	13 557	16 726	14 401	10 183	16 668	16 782
Mexico City	8 943	2 481	9 080	13 557	...	3 728	10 742	14 674	3 363	9 212
Montreal	5 236	3 905	5 548	16 726	3 728	...	7 081	11 282	533	5 522
Moscow	2 516	9 763	3 455	14 401	10 742	7 081	...	4 341	7 535	2 500
New York	5 582	3 944	5 781	16 668	3 363	533	7 535	11 775	...	5 850
Paris	344	9 012	1 054	16 782	9 212	5 522	2 500	6 600	5 850	...
Rio de Janeiro	9 252	10 185	8 117	13 236	7 665	8 171	11 537	14 084	7 725	9 146
Rome	1 440	10 179	1 369	15 976	10 261	6 603	2 386	5 928	6 907	1 110
San Francisco	8 636	558	9 337	12 640	3 036	4 092	9 469	12 375	4 138	8 973
Singapore	10 856	14 106	11 392	6 048	16 616	14 808	8 412	4 137	15 340	10 737
Stockholm	1 516	8 775	2 660	15 495	9 673	5 976	1 152	5 493	6 413	1 614
Tokyo	9 588	8 801	10 790	8 145	11 319	10 412	7 498	5 854	10 872	9 739
Warsaw	1 456	9 528	2 296	15 443	10 196	6 471	1 160	5 273	6 870	1 371
Washington, D.C.	5 911	3 701	6 101	16 380	3 033	787	7 845	12 068	330	6 179

	Rio de Janeiro	Rome	San Fran-cisco	Singa-pore	Stock-holm	Teheran	Tokyo	Vienna	Warsaw	Wash. D.C.
Bangkok	16 080	8 840	12 761	1 421	8 188	5 456	4 610	8 450	8 098	14 170
Beijing	17 326	8 146	9 522	4 459	6 650	5 615	2 103	7 479	6 959	11 170
Berlin	9 990	1 186	9 126	9 918	850	3 516	8 941	525	518	6 727
Cairo	9 884	2 134	12 013	8 265	3 372	1 986	9 586	2 383	2 605	9 368
Cape Town	6 084	8 417	16 489	9 667	10 335	8 433	14 729	9 101	9 549	12 703
Caracas	4 512	8 359	6 278	18 346	8 803	11 778	14 172	8 644	8 944	3 294
Chicago	8 467	7 762	2 991	15 080	6 969	10 462	10 159	7 559	7 529	959
Hong Kong	17 713	9 290	11 110	15 080	8 146	6 183	2 882	8 738	8 282	13 121
Honolulu	13 335	12 936	3 858	2 582	11 062	12 985	6 209	12 280	11 852	7 784
London	9 252	1 440	8 636	10 822	1 516	4 413	9 588	1 241	1 456	5 911
Los Angeles	10 185	10 179	558	14 106	8 775	12 360	8 801	9 828	9 528	3 701
Madrid	8 117	1 369	9 337	11 392	2 660	4 792	10 790	1 815	2 296	6 101
Melbourne	13 236	15 976	12 640	6 048	15 495	12 592	8 145	15 752	15 443	16 380

	Rio de Janeiro	Rome	San Francisco	Singapore	Stockholm	Teheran	Tokyo	Vienna	Warsaw	Wash. D.C.
Mexico City	7 665	10 261	3 036	16 616	9 673	13 168	11 319	10 169	10 196	3 033
Montreal	8 171	6 603	4 092	14 808	5 976	9 461	10 412	6 450	6 471	787
Moscow	11 537	2 386	9 469	8 412	1 152	2 465	7 498	1 678	1 160	7 845
New York	7 725	6 907	4 138	15 340	6 413	9 881	10 872	6 813	6 870	330
Paris	9 146	1 110	8 973	10 737	1 624	4 224	9 739	1 038	1 371	6 179
Rio de Janeiro	...	9 183	10 640	15 744	10 753	11 865	18 555	9 858	10 386	7 689
Rome	9 183	...	10 071	10 022	2 003	3 422	9 882	767	1 319	7 236
San Francisco	10 640	10 071	...	13 593	8 687	11 845	8 286	9 644	9 419	3 928
Singapore	15 744	10 022	13 593	...	9 551	6 602	5 310	9 710	9 401	15 546
Stockholm	10 753	2 003	8 687	9 551	...	3 496	8 130	1 255	795	6 730
Tokyo	18 555	9 882	8 286	5 310	8 130	7 683	...	9 154	8 603	10 927
Warsaw	10 386	1 319	9 419	9 401	795	3 023	9 154	558	...	7 195
Washington, D.C. ...	7 689	7 236	3 928	15 546	6 730	10 203	10 927	7 141	7 195	...

Breaking the Sound Barrier; Speed of Sound

The prefix Mach is used to describe supersonic speed. It derives from Ernst Mach, a Czech-born German physicist, who contributed to the study of sound. When a plane moves at the speed of sound it is Mach 1. When twice the speed of sound it is Mach 2. When it is near but below the speed of sound its speed can be designated at less than Mach 1, for example, Mach .90. Mach is defined as "in jet propulsion, the ratio of the velocity of a rocket or a jet to the velocity of sound in the medium being considered."

When a plane passes the sound barrier—flying faster than sound travels—listeners in the area hear thunderclaps, but pilots do not hear them.

Sound is produced by vibrations of an object and is transmitted by alternate increase and decrease in pressures that radiate outward through a material media of molecules —somewhat like waves spreading out on a pond after a rock has been tossed into it.

The frequency of sound is determined by the number of times the vibrating waves undulate per second, and is measured in cycles per second. The slower the cycle of waves, the lower the frequency. As frequencies increase, the sound is higher in pitch.

Sound is audible to human beings only if the frequency falls within a certain range. The human ear is usually not sensitive to frequencies of less than 20 vibrations per second, or more than about 20 000 vibrations per second—although this range varies among individuals. Anything at a pitch higher than the human ear can hear is termed ultrasonic.

Intensity or loudness is the strength of the pressure of these radiating waves, and is measured in decibels. The human ear responds to intensity in a range from zero to 120 decibels. Any sound with pressure over 120 decibels is painful.

The speed of sound is generally placed at 331 m per second at sea level at 0°C. It varies in other temperatures and in different media. Sound travels faster in water than in air, and even faster in iron and steel. If in air it travels a km in 3 seconds, it does a km under water in .6 of a second, and through iron in .2 of a second. It travels through ice cold vapor at approximately 1 412 m per second, ice-cold water, 1 481; granite, 3 888; hardwood, 3 786; brick, 3 576; glass, 4 923 to 5 907; silver, 2 597; gold, 1 715.

International Aeronautical Records

Source: The National Aeronautic Association, 1763 R St. NW, Washington, DC 20005, representative of the Federation Aeronautique Internationale, certifying agency for world aviation and space records. The International Aeronautical Federation was formed in 1905 by representatives from Belgium, France, Germany, Great Britain, Spain, Italy, Switzerland, and the United States, with headquarters in Paris. Regulations for the control of official records were signed Oct. 14, 1905. World records are defined as maximum performance, regardless of class or type of aircraft used. Records to mid 1988.

World Absolute Records—Maximum Performance in Any Class

Speed over a straight course — 3 529.56 km/h — Capt. Elden W. Joersz, USAF, Lockheed SR-71; Beale AFB, Cal., July 28, 1976.
Speed over a closed circuit — 3 367.221 km/h — Maj. Adolphus H. Bledsoe Jr., USAF, Lockheed SR-71; Beale AFB, Cal., July 27, 1976.
Speed around the world, non-stop, non-refueled — 186.11 kph — Richard Rutan & Jeana Yeager, U.S., Voyager, Edwards AFB, Cal., Dec. 14-23, 1986.
Altitude — 37 650 m — Alexander Fedotov, USSR, E-266M; Podmoskovnoye, USSR, Aug. 31, 1977.
Altitude in horizontal flight — 25 929.031 m — Capt. Robert C. Helt, USAF, Lockheed SR-71; Beale AFB, Cal., July 28, 1976.

Class K Spacecraft

Duration — 326 days — Col. Yuri V. Ramanenko, USSR space station *Mir;* Dec. 29, 1987.
Altitude — 377 668.9 km — Frank Borman, James A. Lovell Jr., William Anders, Apollo 8; Dec. 21-27, 1968.
Greatest mass lifted — 127 980 kg — Frank Borman, James A. Lovell Jr., William Anders, Apollo 8; Dec. 21-27, 1968.
Distance — 140 800 200 km — Anatoly Beresovoy & Valentin Lebedev, USSR, Salyut 7, Soyuz T5, Soyuz T7; May 13-Dec. 10, 1982.

World "Class" Records

All other records, international in scope, are termed World "Class" records and are divided into classes: airships, free balloons, airplanes, seaplanes, amphibians, gliders, and rotorplanes. Airplanes (Class C) are sub-divided into four groups: Group 1 — piston engine aircraft, Group II — turboprop aircraft, Group III — jet aircraft, Group IV — rocket powered aircraft. A partial listing of world records follows:

Airplanes (Class C-I, Group I—piston engine)

Distance, closed circuit without landing — 40 212 139 km — Richard Rutan and Jeana Yeager, U.S., Voyager; Edwards AFB; Dec. 14-23, 1986.

Distance, straight line — 18 081.99 km — Cmdr. Thomas D. Davies, USN; Cmdr. Eugene P. Rankin, USN; Cmdr. Walter S. Reid, USN, and Lt. Cmdr. Ray A. Tabeling, USN; Lockheed P2V-1; from Pearce Field, Perth, Australia to Columbus, Oh., Sept. 29-Oct. 1, 1946.

Speed for 100 km without payload — 755.668 km/h — Jacqueline Cochran, U.S.; North American P-51; Coachella Valley, Cal., Dec. 10, 1947.

Speed for 1 000 km without payload — 693.78 km/h — Jacqueline Cochran, U.S.; North American P-51; Santa Rosasummit, Cal. — Flagstaff, Ariz. course, May 24, 1948.

Speed for 5 000 km without payload — 544.59 km/h — Capt. James Bauer, USAF, Boeing B-29; Dayton, Oh., June 28, 1946.

Speed around the world — 327.73 km/h — D.N. Dalton, Australia; Beechcraft Duke; Brisbane, Aust., July 20-25, 1975. Time: 5 days, 2 hours, 19 min., 57 sec.

Light Airplanes—(Class C-1.d)

Great circle distance without landing — 12 760 km — Peter Wilkins, Australia, Piper Malibu, Sydney, Aust. to Phoenix, Ariz., Mar. 30-Apr. 1, 1987.

Speed for 100 km — in a closed circuit — 519.480 km/h — Ms. R. M. Sharpe, Great Britain; Vickers Supermarine Spitfire 5-B; Wolverhampton, June 17, 1950.

Helicopters (Class E-1)

Great circle distance without landing — 3 561.55 km — Robert G. Ferry, U.S.; Hughes YOH-6A helicopter; Culver City, Cal., to Ormond Beach, Fla., Apr. 6-7, 1966.

Speed around the world —56.97 km/h — H. Ross Perot Jr.; Bell 206 L-11 Long Ranger N39112; Dallas, Tex.–Dallas, Tex.; Sept. 1-30, 1982; 29 days, 3 hrs., 8 min., 13 sec.

Gliders (Class D-I—single seater)

Distance, straight line — 1 460.8 km — Hans Werner Grosse, West Germany; ASK12 sailplane; Luebeck to Biarritz, Apr. 25, 1972.
Distance to a goal and return — 1 646.68 km — Thomas Knauff; U.S., Nimbus III; Williamsport, Pa., Apr. 15, 1983.

Airplanes (Class C-I, Group II—Turboprop)

Great circle distance without landing — 14 052.95 km — Lt. Col. Edgar L. Allison Jr., USAF, Lockheed HC-130 Hercules aircraft; Taiwan to Scott AFB, Ill.; Feb. 20, 1972.

Altitude — 15 549 m — Donald R. Wilson, U.S.; LTV L450F aircraft; Greenville, Tex., Mar. 27, 1972.

Speed for 1 000 km without payload — 871.38 km/h — Ivan Soukhomline, USSR; TU-114 aircraft; Sternberg, USSR; Mar. 24, 1960.

Speed for 5 000 km without payload — 877.212 km/h — Ivan Soukhomline, USSR; TU-114 aircraft; Sternberg, USSR; Apr. 9, 1960.

Airplanes (Class C-1, Group III—Jet Engine)

Great circle distance without landing — 20 168.78 km — Maj. Clyde P. Evely, USAF, Boeing B-52-H, Kadena, Okinawa to Madrid, Spain, Jan. 10-11, 1962.

Distance in a closed circuit — 18 245.05 km — Capt. William Stevenson, USAF, Boeing B-52-H, Seymour-Johnson, N.C., June 6-7, 1962.

Altitude — 36 650 m — Alexander Fedotov, USSR; E-226M airplane; Podmoskovnoye, USSR, Aug. 31, 1977.

Speed for 100 km in a closed circuit — 2 605 km/h — Alexander Fedotov, USSR; E-266 airplane, Apr. 8, 1973.

Speed for 500 km in a closed circuit — 2 981.5 km/h — Mikhail Komarov, USSR; E-266 airplane, Oct. 5, 1967.

Speed for 1 000 km in a closed circuit — 3 367.221 km/h — Maj. Adolphus H. Bledsoe Jr., USAF; Lockheed SR-71; Beale AFB, Cal., July 27, 1976.

Speed for 2 000 km without payload — 2 012.257 km/h — S. Agapov, USSR; Podmoscovnde, USSR; July 20, 1983.

Speed around the world — 825.32 km/h — Brooke Knapp, U.S., Gulfstream III; Washington, D.C., Feb. 13-15, 1984.

Balloons-Class A

Altitude — 34 668 m — Cmdr. Malcolm D. Ross, USNR; Lee Lewis Memorial Winzen Research Balloon; Gulf of Mexico, May 4, 1961.

Distance —8 382.4 km — Ben Abruzzo; Raven Experimental; Nagashima, Japan to Covello, Cal., Nov. 9-12, 1981.

Duration — 137 hr., 5 min., 50 sec. — Ben Abruzzo and Maxie Anderson; Double Eagle II; Presque Isle, Maine to Miserey, France 4 972.18 km; Aug. 12-17, 1978.

Speed — 51 hr., 14 min. — Evelien Brink, Willhem Hageman, Henk Brink; Dutch Viking; Atlantic crossing to Almere, Netherlands.

FAI Course Records

Los Angeles to New York — 1 954.79 km/h — Capt. Robert G. Sowers, USAF; Convair B-58 Hustler; elapsed time: 2 hrs. 58.71 sec., Mar. 5, 1962.

New York to Los Angeles — 1 741 km/h — Capt. Robert G. Sowers, USAF; Convair B-58 Hustler; elapsed time: 2 hrs. 15 min. 50.08 sec., Mar. 5, 1962.

New York to Paris — 1 753.068 km/h — Maj. W. R. Payne, U.S.; Convair B-58 Hustler; elapsed time: 3 hrs 19 min. 44 sec., May 26, 1961.

London to New York — 945.423 km/h — Maj. Burl Davenport, USAF; Boeing KC-135; elapsed time: 5 hrs. 53 min. 12.77 sec.; June 27, 1958.

Baltimore to Moscow, USSR — 906.64 km/h — Col. James B. Swindal, USAF; Boeing VC-137 (707); elapsed time: 8 hrs. 33 min. 45.4 sec., May 19, 1963.

New York to London — 2 908.026 km/h — Maj. James V. Sullivan, USAF; Lockheed SR-71; elapsed time 1 hr. 54 min. 56.4 sec., Sept. 1, 1974.

London to Los Angeles — 2 310.353 km/h — Capt. Harold B. Adams, USAF; Lockheed SR-71; elapsed time: 3 hrs. 47 min. 39 sec., Sept. 13, 1974.

Notable Around the World and Intercontinental Trips

	From/To	Kilometres	Time	Date
Nellie Bly	New York/New York		72d 06h 11m	1889
George Francis Train	New York/New York		67d 12h 03m	1890
Charles Fitzmorris	Chicago/Chicago		60d 13h 29m	1901
J. W. Willis Sayre	Seattle/Seattle		54d 09h 42m	1903
J. Alcock-A.W. Brown[1]	Newfoundland/Ireland	3 136	16h 12m	June 14-15, 1919
Two U.S. Army airplanes	Seattle/Seattle	41 765	35d 01h 11m	1924
Richard E. Byrd[2]	Spitsbergen/N. Pole	2 472	15h 30m	May 9, 1926
Amundsen-Ellsworth-Nobile Expedition	Spitsbergen/Teller, Alaska		80h	May 11-14,1926
E.S. Evans and L. Wells (N. Y.World)	New York/New York	29 440	28d 14h 36m 05s	June 16-July 14, 1926
Charles Lindbergh[4]	New York/Paris	5 776	33h 29m 30s	May 20-21, 1927
Amelia Earhart, W. Stultz, L. Gordon	Newfoundland/Wales		20h 40m	June 17-18, 1928
Graf Zeppelin	Friedrichshafen, Ger./Lakehurst, N.J.	10 608	4d 15h 46m	Oct. 11-15, 1928
Graf Zeppelin	Friedrichshafen, Ger./Lakehurst, N.J.	34 720	20d 04h	Aug. 14-Sept. 4, 1929
Wiley Post and Harold Gatty (Monoplane Winnie Mae)	New York/New York	24 758	8d 15h 51m	July 1, 1931
C. Pangborn-H. Herndon Jr.[5]	Tokyo/Wenatchee, Wash.	7 133	41h 34m	Oct. 3-5, 1931
Amelia Earhart[6]	Newfoundland/Ireland	3 242	14h 56m	May 20-21, 1932
Wiley Post (Monoplane Winnie Mae)[7]	New York/New York	24 954	115h 36m 30s	July 15-22, 1933
Hindenburg Zeppelin	Lakehurst, N.J./Frankfort, Ger.		42h 53m	Aug. 9-11, 1936
H. R. Ekins (Scripps-Howard Newspapers in race) (Zeppelin Hindenburg to Germany air planes from Frankfurt)	Lakehurst, N.J./Lakehurst, N.J.	41 046	18d 11h 14m 33s	Sept. 30-Oct. 19, 1936
Howard Hughes and 4 assistants	New York/New York	23 718	3d 19h 08m 10s	July 10-13, 1938
Douglas Corrigan	New York/Dublin		28h 13m	July 17-18, 1938
Mrs. Clara Adams (Pan American Clipper)	Port Washington, N.Y./Newark, N.J.		16d 19h 04m	June 28-July 15, 1939
Globester, U.S. Air Transport Command	Wash., D.C./Wash., D.C.	37 246	149h 44m	Oct. 4, 1945
Capt. William P. Odom (A-26 Reynolds Bombshell)	New York/New York	32 000	78h 55m 12s	Apr. 12-16, 1947
America, Pan American 4-engine Lockheed Constellation[8]	New York/New York	35 500	101h 32m	June 17-30, 1947
Col. Edward Eagan	New York/New York	32 894	147h 15m	Dec. 13, 1948
USAF B-50 Lucky Lady II (Capt. James Gallagher)[9]	Ft. Worth, Tex./Ft. Worth, Tex.	37 523	94h 01m	Feb. 26-Mar. 2, 1949
Col. D. Schilling, USAF[10]	England/Limestone, Me.	5 280	10h 01m	Sept. 22, 1950
C.F. Blair Jr.	Norway/Alaska	5 280	10h 29m	May 29, 1951
Two U.S. S-55.	Massachusetts/Scotland	5 456	42h 30m	July 15-31, 1952
Canberra Bomber[11]	N. Ireland/Newfoundland	3 317	04h 34m	Aug. 26, 1952
	Newfoundland/N. Ireland	3 317	03h 25m	Aug. 26, 1952
Three USAF B-52 Stratofortresses[12]	Merced, Cal./Cal.	238 920	45h 19m	Jan. 15-18, 1957
Max Conrad	Chicago/Rome	8 000	34h 03m	Mar. 5-6, 1959
USSR TU-114[13]	Moscow/New York	8 147.2	11h 06m	June 28, 1959
Boeing 707-320	New York/Moscow	8 144	08h 54m	July 23, 1959
Peter Gluckmann (solo)	San Francisco/San Francisco	36 480	29d	Aug. 22-Sept. 20, 1959
Sue Snyder	Chicago/Chicago	33 950.4	62h 59m	June 22-24, 1960
Max Conrad (solo)	Miami/Miami	41 513.6	8d 18h 35m 57s	Feb. 28-Mar. 8, 1961
Sam Miller & Louis Fodor	New York/New York		46h 28m	Aug. 3-4, 1963
Robert & Joan Wallick	Manila/Manila	37 006.4	05d 06h 17m 10s	June 2-7, 1966
Arthur Godfrey, Richard Merrill Fred Austin, Karl Keller	New York/New York	37 332.8	86h 9m 01s	June 4-7, 1966
Trevor K. Brougham	Darwin, Australia/Darwin	39 680	5d 05h 57m	Aug. 5-10, 1972
Walter H. Mullikin, Albert Frink, Lyman Watt, Frank Cassaniti, Edward Shields	New York/New York	37 019.2	1d 22h 50s	May 1-3,1976
David Kunst[14]	Waseca, Minn./Waseca, Minn.	23 335	4yrs 3mos 16d	June 10, 1970-Oct. 5, 1974
Arnold Palmer	Denver/Denver	36 776	57h 25m 42s	May 17-19, 1976
Boeing 747[15]	San Francisco/San Francisco	42 211.2	54h 7m 12s	Oct. 28-31, 1977
Concorde	London/Wash., D.C.	1 636.8 Km/h	03h 34m 48s	May 29, 1976
Concorde	Paris/New York	1 660 Km/h	03h 30m 11s	Aug. 22, 1978
Richard Rutan and Jeana Yeager[16]	Edwards AFB, Cal.	40 244	09d 03m 44s	Dec. 14-23, 1986

(1) Non-stop transtlantic flight. (2) Polar flight. (3) Distance by train and auto, 6 614 km; by plane, 10 138 km; by steamship, 12 874 km. (4) Solo transatlantic flight in the Ryan monoplane the "Spirit of St. Louis". (5) First to fly solo around Pacific flight. (6) Woman's transoceanic solo flight. (7) First to fly solo around northern circumference of the world, also first to fly twice around the world. (8) Inception of regular commercial global air service. (9) First non-stop round-the-world flight, refueled 4 times in flight. (10) Non-stop jet transatlantic flight. (11) Transatlantic round trip on same day. (12) First non-stop global flight by jet planes; refueled in flight by KC-97 aerial tankers; average speed approx. 844 Km/h. (13) Non-stop between Moscow and New York. (14) First to circle the earth on foot. (15) Speed record around the world over both the earth's poles. (16) Circled the world non-stop without refueling.

Memorable Manned Space Flights

Sources: National Aeronautics and Space Administration and The World Almanac.

Crew, date	Mission name	Orbits[1]	Duration	Remarks
Yuri A. Gagarin (4/12/61)	Vostok 1	1	1h 48m.	First manned orbital flight.
Alan B. Shepard Jr. (5/5/61)	Mercury-Redstone 3	(2)	15m 22s . .	First American in space.
Virgil I. Grissom (7/21/61)	Mercury-Redstone 4	(2)	15m 37s . .	Spacecraft sank. Grissom rescued.
Gherman S. Titov (8/6-7/61)	Vostok 2	16	25h 18m.	First space flight of more than 24 hrs.
John H. Glenn Jr. (2/20/62)	Mercury-Atlas 6	3	4h 55m 23s . .	First American in orbit.
M. Scott Carpenter (5/24/62)	Mercury-Atlas 7	3	4h 56m 05s . .	Manual retrofire error caused 250 mi. landing overshoot.
Andrian G. Nikolayev (8/11-15/62)	Vostok 3	64	94h 22m.	Vostok 3 and 4 made first group flight.
Pavel R. Popovich (8/12-15/62)	Vostok 4	48	70h 57m.	On first orbit it came within 3 miles of Vostok 3.
Walter M. Schirra Jr. (10/3/62)	Mercury-Atlas 8	6	9h 13m 11s . .	Closest splashdown to target to date (4.5 mi.).
L. Gordon Cooper (5/15-16/63)	Mercury-Atlas 9	22	34h 19m 49s . .	First U.S. evaluation of effects on man of one day in space.
Valery F. Bykovsky (6/14-6/19/63)	Vostok 5	81	119h 06m.	Vostok 5 and 6 made 2d group flight.
Valentina V. Tereshkova (6/16-19/63)	Vostok 6	48	70h 50m.	First woman in space.
Vladimir M. Komarov, Konstantin P. Feoktistov, Boris B. Yegorov (10/12/64)	Voskhod 1	16	24h 17m.	First 3-man orbital flight: first without space suits.
Pavel I. Belyayev, Aleksei A. Leonov (3/18/65)	Voskhod 2	17	26h 02m.	Leonov made first "space walk" (10 min.)
Virgil I. Grissom, John W. Young (3/23/65)	Gemini-Titan 3	3	4h 53m 00s . .	First manned spacecraft to change its orbital path.
James A. McDivitt, Edward H. White 2d, (6/3-7/65)	Gemini-Titan 4	62	97h 56m 11s . .	White was first American to "walk in space" (20 min.).
L. Gordon Cooper Jr., Charles Conrad Jr. (8/21-29/65)	Gemini-Titan 5	120	190h 55m 14s . .	First use of fuel cells for electric power; evaluated guidance and navigation system.
Frank Borman, James A. Lovell Jr. (12/4-18/65) . .	Gemini-Titan 7	206	330h 35m 31s . .	Longest duration Gemini flight
Walter M. Schirra Jr., Thomas P. Stafford (12/15-16/65)	Gemini-Titan 6-A	16	25h 51m 24s . .	Completed world's first space rendezvous with Gemini 7.
Neil A. Armstrong, David R. Scott (3/16-17/66)	Gemini-Titan 8	6.5	10h 41m 26s . .	First docking of one space vehicle with another; mission aborted, control malfunction.
John W. Young, Michael Collins (7/18-21/66)	Gemini-Titan 10	43	70h 46m 39s . .	First use of Agena target vehicle's propulsion systems.
Charles Conrad Jr., Richard F. Gordon Jr. (9/12-15/66)	Gemini-Titan 11	44	71h 17m 08s . .	Docked, made 2 revolutions of earth tethered; set Gemini altitude record (739.2 mi.).
James A. Lovell Jr., Edwin E. Aldrin Jr. (11/11-15/66)	Gemini-Titan 12	59	94h 34m 31s . .	Final Gemini mission; record 5½ hrs. of extravehicular activity.
Vladimir M. Komarov (4/23/67)	Soyuz 1	17	26h 40m.	Crashed after re-entry killing Komarov.
Walter M. Schirra Jr., Donn F. Eisele, R. Walter Cunningham (10/11-22/68)	Apollo-Saturn 7	163	260h 09m 03s . .	First manned flight of Apollo spacecraft command-service module only.
Georgi T. Beregovoi (10/26-30/68)	Soyuz 3	64	94h 51m.	Made rendezvous with unmanned Soyuz 2.
Frank Borman, James A. Lovell Jr., William A. Anders (12/21-27/68) .	Apollo-Saturn 8	10[3]	147h 00m 42s	First flight to moon (command-service module only); views of lunar surface televised to earth.
Vladimir A. Shatalov (1/14-17/69)	Soyuz 4	45	71h 14m.	Docked with Soyuz 5.
Boris V. Volyanov, Aleksei S. Yeliseyev, Yevgeny V. Khrunov (1/15-18/69)	Soyuz 5	46	72h 46m.	Docked with Soyuz 4; Yeliseyev and Khrunov transferred to Soyuz 4.

Crew, date	Mission name	Orbits[1]	Duration	Remarks
James A. McDivitt, David R. Scott, Russell L. Schweickart (3/3-13/69) . Thomas P. Stafford, Eugene	Apollo-Saturn 9	151	241h 00m 54s . .	First manned flight of lunar module.
A. Cernan, John W. Young (5/18-26/69). . . . Neil A. Armstrong, Edwin E. Aldrin Jr., Michael Collins	Apollo-Saturn 10	31[4]	192h 03m 23s . .	First lunar module orbit of moon. First lunar landing made by Armstrong and Aldrin; collected 48.5 lbs. of soil, rock samples; lunar stay time 21 h, 36m, 21 s.
(7/16-24/69) . . . . . . Georgi S. Shonin, Valery	Apollo-Saturn 11	30[3]	195h 18m 35s . .	
N. Kubasov (10/11-16/69) Anatoly V. Filipchenko, Vladislav N. Volkov, Viktor V. Gorbatko	Soyuz 6	79	118h 42m.	First welding of metals in space. Space lab construction tests made; Soyuz 6, 7 and 8 — first time 3 spacecraft 7 crew orbited earth at once.
(10/12-17/69)	Soyuz 7	79	118h 41m.	
Charles Conrad Jr., Richard F. Gordon, Alan L. Bean				Conrad and Bean made 2d moon landing; collected 74.7 lbs. of samples, lunar stay time 31 h, 31 m.
(11/14-24/69)	Apollo-Saturn 12	45[3]	244h 36m 25s . .	
James A. Lovell Jr., Fred W. Haise Jr., John L. Swigart Jr.				Aborted after service module oxygen tank ruptured; crew returned safely using lunar module oxygen and power.
(4/11-17/70)	Apollo-Saturn 13	. . .	142h 54m 41s . .	
Alan B. Shepard Jr., Stuart A. Roosa, Edgar D. Mitchell				Shepard and Mitchell made 3d moon landing, collected 96 lbs. of lunar samples; lunar stay 33 h, 31 m.
(1/31-2/9/71).	Apollo-Saturn 14	34[3]	216h 01m 57s . .	
Georgi T. Dobrovolsky, Vladislav N. Volkov, Viktor I. Patsayev				Docked with Salyut space station; and orbited in Salyut for 23 days; crew died during re-entry from loss of pressurization.
(6/6-30/71)	Soyuz 11	360	569h 40m.	
David R. Scott, Alfred M. Worden, James B. Irwin				Scott and Irwin made 4th moon landing; first lunar rover use; first deep space walk; 170 lbs. of samples; 66 h, 55 m, stay.
(7/26-8/7/71).	Apollo-Saturn 15	74[3]	295h 11m 53s . .	
Charles M. Duke Jr., Thomas K. Mattingly, John W. Young				Young and Duke made 5th moon landing; collected 213 lbs. of lunar samples; lunar stay line 71 h, 2 m.
(4/16-27/72)	Apollo-Saturn 16	64[3]	265h 51m 05s . .	
Eugene A. Cernan, Ronald E. Evans, Harrison H. Schmitt				Cernan and Schmitt made 6th manned lunar landing; collected 243 lbs. of samples; record lunar stay of 75 h.
(12/7-19/72)	Apollo-Saturn 17	75[3]	301h 51m 59s . .	
Charles Conrad Jr., Joseph P. Kerwin, Paul J. Weitz				First American manned orbiting space station; made long-flights tests, crew repaired damage caused during boost.
(5/25-6/22/73)	Skylab 2	. . .	672h 49m 49s . .	
Alan L. Bean, Jack R. Lousma, Owen K. Garriott				Crew systems and operational tests, exceeded pre-mission plans for scientific activities; space walk total 13h, 44 m.
(7/28-9/25/73)	Skylab 3	. . .	1,427h 09m 04s . .	
Gerald P. Carr, Edward G. Gibson, William Pogue				Final Skylab mission; record space walk of 7 h, 1 m., record space walks total for a mission 22 h, 21 m.
(11/16/73-2/8/74). . .	Skylab 4	. . .	2,017h 16m 30s . .	
Alexi Leonov, Valeri Kubason (7/15-7/21/75) .	Soyuz 19	96	143h 31m	
Vance Brand, Thomas P. Stafford, Donald K. Slayton				U.S.-USSR joint flight. Crews linked-up in space, conducted experiments, shared meals, and held a joint news conference.
(7/15-7/24/75).	Apollo 18	136	217h 30m.	
Leonid Kizim, Vladmir Solovyov, Oleg Atkov (2/8-10/2/84).	Salyut 7	. . .	237 days.	Set space endurance record.

(1) The U.S. measures orbital flights in revolutions while the Soviets use "orbits." (2) Suborbital. (3) Moon orbits in command module. (4) Moon orbits.
Fire aboard spacecraft Apollo I on the ground at Cape Kennedy, Fla. killed Virgil I. Grissom, Edward H. White and Roger B. Chaffee on Jan. 27, 1967. They were the only U.S. astronauts killed in space tests.

U.S. Space Shuttles

Name, date	Crew	Name, date	Crew
Columbia (4/12-14/81) . . .	Robert L. Crippen, John W. Young.	Discovery (4/12-19/85) . . .	Karol J. Bobko, Donald E. Williams, Sen. Jake Garn, Charles D. Walker, Jeffrey A. Hoffman, S. David Griggs, M. Rhea Seddon.
Columbia (11/12-14/81) . .	Joe Engle, Richard Truly.		
Columbia (3/22-30/82) . . .	Jack Lousma, C. Gordon Fullerton.	Challenger (4/29-5/6/85). .	Robert F. Overmyer, Frederick D. Gregory, Don L. Lind, Taylor G. Wang, Lodewijk van den Berg, Norman Thagard, William Thornton.
Columbia (6-27/7-4/82) . . .	Thomas Mattingly 2d, Henry Hartsfield Jr.		
Columbia (11/11-16/82) . .	Vance Brand, Robert Overmyer, William Lenoir, Joseph Allen.	Discovery (6/17-6/24/85). .	John O. Creighton, Shannon W. Lucid, Steven R. Nagel, Daniel C. Brandenstein, John W. Fabian, Prince Sultan Salman al-Saud (first Arab), Patrick Baudry.
Challenger (4/4-9/83)	Paul Weitz, Karol Bobko, Story Musgrave, Donald Peterson.		
Challenger (6/18-24/83) . .	Robert L. Crippen, Norman Thagard, John Fabian, Frederick Hauck, Sally K. Ride (1st U.S. woman in space).	Challenger (7/29-8/6/85). .	Roy D. Bridges Jr., Anthony W. England, Karl G. Henize, F. Story Musgrave, C. Gordon Fullerton, Loren W. Acton, John-David F. Bartoe.
Challenger (8/30-9/5/83). .	Richard Truly, Daniel Brandenstein, William Thornton, Guion Bluford (1st U.S. black in space), Dale Gardner.	Discovery (8/27-9/3/85) . .	John M. Lounge, James D. van Hoften, William F. Fisher, Joe H. Engle, Richard O. Covey.
Columbia (11/28-12/8/83) .	John Young, Brewster Shaw Jr., Robert Parker, Owen Garriott, Byron Lichtenberg, Ulf Merbold.	Atlantis (10/4-10/7/85) . . .	Karol J. Bobko, Ronald J. Grabe, David C. Hilmers, William A. Pailes, Robert C. Stewart.
Challenger (2/3-11/84) . . .	Vance Brand, Robert Gibson, Ronald McNair, Bruce McCandless, Robert Stewart.	Challenger (10/30-11/6/85)	Henry W. Hartsfield Jr., Steven R. Nagel, Bonnie J. Dunbar, James F. Buchli, Guion S. Bluford Jr., Ernst Messerschmid, Reinhard Furrer, Wubbo J. Ockels.
Challenger (4/6-13/84) . . .	Robert L. Crippen, Francis R. Scobee, George D. Nelson, Terry J. Hart, James D. Van Hoften.		
Discovery (8/30-9/5/84) . .	Henry W. Hartsfield Jr., Michael L. Coats, Steven A. Hawley, Judith A. Resnik, Richard M. Mullane, Charles D. Walker.	Atlantis (11/26-12/3/85) . .	Brewster H. Shaw Jr., Bryan D. O'Connor, Charles Walker, Rodolfo Neri (first Mexican), Jerry L. Ross, Sherwood C. Spring, Mary L. Cleave.
Challenger (10/5-13/84) . .	Robert L. Crippen, Jon A. McBride, Kathryn D. Sullivan, Sally K. Ride, Marc Garneau (first Canadian), David C. Leestma, Paul D. Scully-Power.	Columbia (1/12-1/18/86) . .	Robert L. Gibson, Charles F. Bolden Jr., George D. Nelson, Bill Nelson (first congressman), Franklin R. Chang-Diaz, Steven A. Hawley, Robert J. Cenker.
Discovery (11/8-16/84) . . .	Frederick H. Hauck, David M. Walker, Dr. Anna L. Fisher, Joseph P. Allen, Dale A. Gardner.	Challenger (1/28/86- exploded after takeoff) . .	Francis R. Scobee, Michael J. Smith, Robert E. McNair, Ellison S. Onizuka, Judith A. Resnik, Gregory B. Jarvis, Sharon Christa McAuliffe
Discovery (1/24-27/85) . . .	Thomas K. Mattingly, Loren J. Shriver, James F. Buchli, Ellison S. Onizuka, Gary E. Payton.	Discovery (9/29/88)	5-man crew led by navy captain Rick Hauck

Major World Navigational Waterways

Inland waterways and canals have been built since ancient times for such purposes as irrigation, drainage, water supply and hydroelectric power as well as for navigation. Below are descriptions of some of the world's most commercially-significant navigational waterways.

Grand Canal (China)

Construction was begun in approximately the 4th century B.C. on the Grand Canal which today runs for 1 600 km and is the world's oldest and longest man-made waterway. A decline in the state of the canal was reversed between 1958 and 1964 when it was dredged and widened. It now runs from Hangzhou and the Yangtze River in south China to Tianjin (the port for Beijing) in the north.

Kiel Canal (West Germany)

The Kiel Canal is 98 km long and was dug through a spit of land in northern West Germany from 1887 to 1895. It was modernized between 1907 and 1914 and cuts travel distance between the North Sea and the Baltic Sea by several hundred km. It crosses fairly level terrain, and therefore has locks at either end of the canal: at Brunsbuttel on the North Sea and at Kiel on the Baltic Sea. In 1984, 50 920 vessels of 53 million net tons passed through the canal, making it one of the busiest man-made waterways in Europe.

Volga-Don Canal (Soviet Union)

In the 19th century, Russia concentrated on making connections between the heads of navigation of its great rivers, the Volga, Dnieper, Don, Dvina, and Vistula. The resulting network made navigation possible from the Baltic to both the Black and Caspian seas.

The Volga-Don canal was completed in 1952 and makes up 101 km of the 540 km Volga-Don waterway from Volgograd to Rostov. Because of the canal, the White, Baltic, Caspian, Azov, and Black seas are now part of a single water transportation system.

Panama Canal (Panama)

The Panama Canal is 82 km long and connects Limon Bay on the Caribbean Sea to Balboa Harbor on the Pacific Ocean. It rises through a series of locks to over 22 m above sea level at the Gatun Lake (450 sq. km) which is an important part of the waterway and the principal source of its water. The minimum channel depth throughout the length of the canal is 11.3 m and its width 91 m. In 1985, 11 513 ships passed through the canal.

In 1903, Panama granted use, occupation and control of the Canal Zone to the U.S. by treaty. In 1978, a new treaty provided for a gradual Panamanian takeover of the Canal and the withdrawal of U.S. troops, to be completed by 1999. U.S. payments to Panama were substantially increased in the interim. Another 1978 treaty between Panama and the U.S. also guarantees the permanent neutrality of the canal.

Suez Canal (Egypt)

The Suez Canal is a lockless 173 km-long sea-level waterway connecting the Mediterranean Sea and the Red Sea. The main channel is 13 m deep, enabling ships of a maximum draft of 11.3 m to navigate the channel. In 1983, 22 224 vessels of 378.2 million tons went through the canal.

The canal was built by a French corporation, but Britain obtained controlling interest in 1875. The last British troops were removed June 13, 1956. The following month, on July 26, Egypt nationalized the canal. French and British stockholders eventually received some compensation. In 1948, Egypt barred Israeli ships and cargoes destined for Israel. After the 1967 Arab-Israeli War, the canal was closed to all shipping. It was reopened in 1975 and Egypt agreed to allow passage to Israeli cargo in 3d party ships. In May 1979, Egypt began allowing Israeli ships through the canal.

St. Lawrence Seaway—Great Lakes Waterway

The Great Lakes form the largest body of fresh water in the world and with their connecting waterways are the largest inland water transportation unit.

The St. Lawrence & Great Lakes Waterway, the largest inland navigation system on the North American continent, extends from the Atlantic Ocean to Duluth, Minnesota at the western end of Lake Superior, a distance of 3 747 km. With the deepening of channels and locks to 8 m, ocean carriers are able to penetrate to ports in the Canadian interior and the American midwest.

Shallow canals were dug as early as 1783 in the St. Lawrence River; by 1900 a canal system was in place from Montreal to Lake Superior. In 1954, the U.S. and Canada agreed to cooperate in developing the St. Lawrence Seaway which was built at a cost of $460 million, $130 million of which was contributed by the U.S. government. The Seaway was opened to navigation on Apr. 1, 1959.

The St. Lawrence–Great Lakes Waterway contains many major canals: the 3 new canals of the Seaway, with their 7 locks, providing navigation for vessels of 8 m draught from Montreal to Lake Ontario; the Welland Ship Canal by-passing the Niagara River between Lake Ontario and Lake Erie with its 8 locks; and the Sault Ste. Marie Canal and lock between Lake Huron and Lake Superior. These 16 locks overcome a drop of 174 m from the head of the lakes to Montreal. From Montreal to Lake Ontario the former bottleneck of narrow, shallow canals and of slow passage through 22 locks has been overcome, giving faster and safer movement for larger vessels. The new locks and linking channels now accommodate all but the largest ocean-going vessels and the upper St. Lawrence and Great Lakes are open to 80% of the world's saltwater fleet.

Subsidiary Canadian canals or branches include the St. Peters Canal between Bras d'or Lakes and the Atlantic Ocean in Nova Scotia; the St. Ours and Chambly Canals on the Richelieu River, Quebec; the Ste. Anne and Carillon Canals on the Ottawa River; the Rideau Canal between the Ottawa River and Lake Ontario, the Trent and Murray Canals between Lake Ontario and Georgian Bay in Ontario and the St. Andrew's Canal on the Red River. The commercial value of these canals is not great but they are maintained to control water levels and permit the passage of small vessels and pleasure craft. The Canso Canal, completed in 1957, permits shipping to pass through the causeway connecting Cape Breton Island with the Nova Scotia mainland.

The Welland Canal overcomes the 98 m drop of Niagara Falls and the rapids of the Niagara River. It has 8 locks, each 258 m long, 24 m wide and 9 m deep. Regulations permit ships of 219 m length and 23 m beam to transit.

The Illinois Waterway (US) was built in 1933 and is 526 km long. It is composed of a series of artificial and natural channels linking Lake Michigan to the Mississippi River via the Illinois River.

The New York State Barge Canal (US) was built between 1903–18 and is 837 km long. It includes 580 km of the old Erie Canal that was constructed 1813–25. The Erie Canal cuts travel time by 30 percent and shipping costs by 90 percent. Its success made New York City the chief Atlantic port in the U.S. The present-day canal connects Lake Erie to New York City via the Hudson River.

Energy

Consumer Cost of Fuel

Source: Energy, Mines and Resources Canada

(annual averages)

	Regular Leaded Gasoline		Heating Oil[1]		Natural Gas[1]	Electricity[1]
	cents per litre	cents per gallon	cents per litre	cents per gallon	cents per cubic metre	cents per kilowatt hour
1971	11.2	50.9	4.7	21.4	3.6	n.a.
1975	15.9	72.3	8.2	37.3	4.8	n.a.
1980	25.9	117.7	16.9	76.8	10.6	3.3
1981	35.3	160.5	24.4	110.9	13.2	3.7
1982	42.9	195.0	30.1	136.8	15.4	4.1
1983	45.9	208.7	33.3	151.4	18.0	4.2
1984	48.4	220.0	35.5	161.4	18.5	4.8
1985	51.1	232.3	38.3	174.1	19.4	5.0
1986	44.8	203.7	30.9	140.5	19.3	5.2
1987	47.3	215.0	29.1	132.3	18.6	5.4

(1) Residential sales.
n.a. not available.

Consumer Cost of Fuel by Province, 1987

Source: Energy, Mines and Resources Canada

(annual average)

	Gasoline				Heating oil[1]	Natural gas[1]	Electricity[1]
	Regular leaded cents per litre	Regular unleaded cents per litre	Premium unleaded cents per litre	Diesel cents per litre	cents per litre	cents per cubic metre	cents per kilowatt hour
Canada	47.3	50.1	51.6	46.7	29.1	18.6	5.4
Newfoundland	53.2	56.3	57.4	58.8	32.5	n.a.	7.0
Prince Edward Island	51.6	53.7	54.7	58.5	32.3	n.a.	8.3
Nova Scotia	48.7	50.3	51.3	50.2	28.5	n.a.	7.3
New Brunswick	45.7	48.8	50.9	51.7	33.0	34.1	6.5
Quebec	53.1	57.0	58.7	51.6	26.6	25.1	4.7
Ontario	45.1	48.2	49.8	47.1	30.9	21.5	5.6
Manitoba	46.7	47.8	49.1	46.5	31.1	18.5	4.6
Saskatchewan	42.5	44.6	46.0	43.0	29.0	14.1	6.1
Alberta	41.4	43.8	45.0	37.9	n.a.	16.0	5.1
British Columbia	49.7	50.3	51.8	44.0	29.3	17.6	5.5

(1) Residential sales.
n.a. = not applicable.

Household Heating, by Province

Source: Statistics Canada

(percentage of households)

	Oil		Gas		Electricity		Wood	
	1977	1987	1977	1987	1977	1987	1977	1987
Canada	45.1	19.3	38.5	45.0	14.4	31.0	1.5	4.3
Newfoundland	66.9	32.1	n.a.	...	27.8	41.7	4.5	26.8
Prince Edward Island	90.6	81.4	n.a.	...	...	...	...	18.6
Nova Scotia	83.4	64.2	...	1.6	9.4	17.6	4.3	15.0
New Brunswick	76.9	37.4	n.a.	...	17.6	42.3	4.9	19.5
Quebec	65.7	22.7	7.6	9.6	24.1	63.6	2.1	3.6
Ontario	40.2	18.6	47.3	59.4	11.5	19.7	0.8	2.2
Manitoba	19.8	6.2	60.4	57.0	17.3	33.8	...	3.0
Saskatchewan	24.3	10.6	71.8	80.2	2.1	5.6	...	2.6
Alberta	3.5	n.a.	94.8	95.4	...	1.9	...	n.a.
British Columbia	36.0	14.4	49.1	54.3	13.0	24.0	1.5	6.4

n.a. not available; ... = too small to be included.

Natural Gas Production[1] by Province

Source: Statistics Canada

(millions of cubic metres and millions of dollars)

	1960		1970		1980		1985		1986	
	Quantity	Value	Quantity	Value	Quantity	Value	Quantity	Value	Quantity	Value
Canada	14 814	53	52 432	292	69 820	5 737	77 128	7 335	71 896	5 623
New Brunswick	3	. . .	3		2	. . .	1	. . .	1	. . .
Ontario	481	7	483	6	363	27	521	65	504	65
Saskatchewan	1 036	4	1 522	7	1 203	20	1 614	93	1 814	130
Alberta	10 869	34	42 743	250	60 517	5 370	67 481	6 681	62 556	5 049
British Columbia	2 424	8	7 679	29	7 374	276	7 282	476	6 820	366
Northwest Territories	1	. . .	2	. . .	361	44	229	20	201	13

(1) Marketable natural gas.
. . . = too small to be included.

Coal Production by Province

Source: Statistics Canada

(thousands of tonnes and millions of dollars)

	1960		1970		1980		1985		1986	
	Quantity	Value	Quantity	Value	Quantity	Value	Quantity	Value	Quantity	Value
Canada	9 989	75	15 063	86	36 688	932	60 436	1 845	57 811	1 726
Nova Scotia	4 146	45	1 925	22	2 726	133	2 810	167	2 955	178
New Brunswick	933	9	359	3	439	17	557	32	485	28
Saskatchewan	1 969	4	3 465	7	5 971	34	9 672	108	8 280	101
Alberta	2 170	12	6 154	28	17 396	302	24 730	448	24 950	446
British Columbia	766	6	3 160	26	10 156	445	22 667	1 090	21 141	973

Nuclear Generating Stations in Canada

Source: Atomic Energy of Canada Limited

Reactor	Province	Installed Capacity (MW)	Approved	Operational	Energy Produced in 1987 (MWh)
NPD (Nuclear Power Demonstration Station)[1]	Ontario	25	1955	1962	n.a.[2]
Pickering A	Ontario	2 × 542	1964	1971	23 700 814[3]
		2 × 542	1967	1972-73	
Pickering B	Ontario	4 × 540	1974	1983-86	
Bruce A	Ontario	2 × 815	1969	1977-78	42 006 479[4]
		2 × 825	1969	1977-79	
Bruce B	Ontario	2 × 885	1975	1984-85	
		2 × 890	1975	1986-87	
Darlington	Ontario	4 × 935	1977	1988-92	n.a.[5]
Gentilly 2	Quebec	685	1973	1983	4 658 470
Point Lepreau	New Brunswick	680	1974	1983	5 107 728

(1) Located near Chalk River, Ont. (2) Shut down in May 1987. (3) Data applies to all reactors at Pickering A and B. (4) Data applies to all reactors at Bruce A and B. (5) Under construction.
MWh = megawatt hours; n.a. = not applicable.

Electricity Production in Canada

Source: Statistics Canada

(percentage distribution of electricity production by type)

	1960	1965	1970	1975	1980	1985	1987
Hydro	92.6%	81.1%	76.5%	74.0%	68.4%	67.4%	65.0%
Steam[1]	6.7	18.0	22.1	20.8	21.4	19.1	19.1
Nuclear	–	0.1	0.5	4.3	9.8	12.8	15.1
Internal combustion[2]	0.5	0.5	0.4	0.4	0.3	0.2	0.1
Gas turbine[3]	0.3	0.2	0.5	0.5	0.2	0.6	0.6
Total production, MWh[4](000s)	114 378	144 274	204 723	273 392	367 306	447 182	482 108

(1) Powered by natural gas and heavy fuel oil. (2) Produced from diesel fuel powering an internal-combustion engine. (3) Produced primarily from natural gas powering a turbine generator. (4) MWh = megawatt hours.
– = zero.

Electricity Production by Province, 1986

Source: Statistics Canada

(Megawatt hours)

	Canada	Nfld	PEI	NS	NB	Que
Hydro	307 644 677	39 129 120	–	1 001 244	3 145 913	144 328 170
Steam[1]	77 567 410	1 277 253	10 054	6 408 719	3 818 688	–56 286
Nuclear	67 233 013	–	–	–	5 227 106	3 792 441
Internal combustion[2]	725 948	562	–	–	21	200 870
Gas turbine[3]	2 662 878	239	1 814	1 435	–5	–4 286
Total production	455 833 926	40 407 174	11 868	7 411 398	12 191 723	148 260 909
% by province	100.0	8.9	...	1.6	2.7	32.5

	Ont	Man	Sask	Alta	BC	Yukon and NWT
Hydro	41 050 255	23 840 289	3 764 093	1 800 102	48 923 364	662 127
Steam[1]	25 075 541	159 108	8 143 996	31 090 873	1 639 464	–
Nuclear	58 213 466	–	–	–	–	–
Internal combustion[2]	372	52 474	–	50 752	210 588	210 309
Gas turbine[3]	884 647	36	5 273	1 774 626	–901	–
Total production	125 224 281	24 051 907	11 913 362	34 716 353	50 772 515	872 436
% by province	27.5	5.3	2.6	7.6	11.1	0.2

(1) Powered by natural gas and heavy fuel oil. (2) Produced from diesel fuel powering an internal-combustion engine. (3) Produced primarily from natural gas powering a turbine generator.
– = zero.

Oil Production[1] by Province

Source: Statistics Canada

(thousands of cubic metres and millions of dollars)

	1960 Quantity	1960 Value	1970 Quantity	1970 Value	1980 Quantity	1980 Value	1985 Quantity	1985 Value	1986 Quantity	1986 Value
Canada	30 120	423	80 009	1 269	89 531	9 639	91 256	19 653	91 406	10 342
Ontario	160	3	167	3	93	10	112	25	136	17
Manitoba	757	11	939	15	564	55	821	181	823	95
Saskatchewan	8 249	104	14 256	200	9 368	866	11 614	2 375	11 717	1 175
Alberta	20 739	302	60 312	987	77 163	8 491	75 566	16 432	75 040	8 688
British Columbia	138	2	4 201	63	2 182	206	1 993	439	2 162	260
Northwest Territories	77	1	134	1	161	11	1 150	201	1 528	107

(1) Marketable crude oil and equivalent.

Canadian Oil Imports

Source: Statistics Canada

(thousands of cubic metres and millions of dollars)

	1970 Quantity	1970 Value	1975 Quantity	1975 Value	1980 Quantity	1980 Value	1985 Quantity	1985 Value	1987 Quantity	1987 Value
All Countries	33 012	415	47 417	3 298	32 542	6 877	15 856	3 695	21 767	3 179
Algeria	–	–	22	2	60	12	1 162	284	–	–
Egypt	–	–	–	–	–	–	116	27	140	20
Gabon	–	–	262	20	–	–	98	24	–	–
Iran	3 046	33	10 950	756	–	–	601	138	617	94
Iraq	1 427	14	1 943	133	1 152	253	–	–	525	79
Kuwait	841	7	1 679	111	852	167	–	–	–	–
Libya	–	–	472	36	–	–	166	38	–	–
Mexico	–	–	–	–	553	130	2 118	471	949	134
Nigeria	2 881	34	1 028	77	153	41	969	229	1 642	250
Norway	–	–	–	–	–	–	379	91	505	80
Saudi Arabia	2 183	24	10 996	747	12 022	2 445	–	–	1 106	156
Tunisia	–	–	–	–	–	–	424	98	–	–
United Arab Emirates	776	7	2 016	141	265	62	–	–	348	44
United Kingdom	–	–	–	–	301	70	4 899	1 172	11 538	1 724
United States	–	–	1	...	7 196	1 686	1 314	290	1 000	138
Venezuela	20 690	281	14 815	1 054	9 881	1 987	3 541	813	1 916	252
South Yemen	–	–	2 848	197	–	–	–	–	–	–
Other countries	1 168	15	384	26	107	24	68	21	1 481	208

... = too small to be included; – = zero.

Canadian Energy Imports and Exports

Source: Statistics Canada

	Crude Oil		Natural Gas		Coal		Electricity		Radioactive ores[1]
	Quantity cu.m (000s)	Value ($ million)	Quantity cu.m (millions)	Value ($ million)	Quantity tonnes (000s)	Value ($ million)	Quantity KWh (millions)	Value ($ million)	Value ($ million)
1960 Imports	19 953	280	158	2	12 320	77	116	...	–
Exports	6 712	94	2 579	18	774	7	5 639	16	264
1965 Imports	22 912	312	444	6	15 063	126	3 405	14	–
Exports	17 164	280	11 442	104	1 119	13	3 379	15	54
1970 Imports	32 995	415	336	5	17 122	151	2 882	12	–
Exports	38 280	649	21 759	206	4 004	30	5 147	34	26
1975 Imports	47 422	3 302	296	8	15 272	576	2 940	13	–
Exports	41 707	3 052	26 896	1 092	11 697	478	7 216	104	51
1980 Imports	32 694	6 919	3	...	16 067	811	154	3	–
Exports	12 426	2 899	22 972	3 984	14 311	794	28 323	773	231
1983 Imports	14 603	3 319	1	...	14 727	841	117	3	–
Exports	16 778	3 457	19 297	3 847	16 974	1 232	36 742	1 228	63
1984 Imports	14 850	3 376	1	...	19 061	1 094	373	13	–
Exports	20 874	4 404	21 427	3 923	24 355	1 820	37 544	1 378	334
1985 Imports	15 856	3 695	1	...	15 022	887	206	8	–
Exports	27 886	5 972	26 155	4 011	27 572	1 996	41 531	1 425	232
1986 Imports	20 167	2 885	2	...	13 369	744	231	9	–
Exports	33 617	3 775	21 389	2 524	25 900	1 851	35 271	1 086	167
1987 Imports	21 767	3 179	1	...	14 150	725	375	9	–
Exports	35 776	4 855	27 672	2 527	25 466	1 670	45 318	1 200	278

(1) Quantity figures not available.
– = zero; . . . = too small to be included.

World Oil Reserves

Source: Energy, Mines and Resources Canada

(millions of cubic metres)

	1975	%	1980	%	1985	%	1987	%
Total World Reserves	104 672	100.0	102 970	100.0	111 142	100.0	141 009	100.0
Africa[1]	1 464	1.4	1 080	1.0	1 508	1.4	1 451	1.0
Asia[1]	1 149	1.1	1 610	1.6	1 645	1.5	1 741	1.2
Canada	1 057	1.0	930	0.9	916	0.8	1 085	0.8
Central & South America[1]	980	0.9	1 024	1.0	1 224	1.1	1 237	0.9
China	3 178	3.0	3 258	3.2	2 927	2.6	2 924	2.1
Western Europe[2]	1 507	1.4	1 316	1.3	2 131	1.9	2 741	1.9
Mexico	1 510	1.4	6 992	6.8	7 834	7.0	7 725	5.5
Middle East[1]	1 358	1.3	735	0.7	937	0.8	1 241	0.9
OPEC[3]	71 492	68.3	69 023	67.0	75 501	67.9	106 360	75.4
Algeria	1 171	1.1	1 303	1.3	1 402	1.3	1 351	1.0
Ecuador	389	0.4	175	0.2	262	0.2	257	0.2
Gabon	350	0.3	72	0.1	83	0.1	102	0.1
Indonesia	2 225	2.1	1 510	1.5	1 351	1.2	1 335	0.9
Iran	10 250	9.8	9 137	8.9	7 608	6.8	14 755	10.5
Iraq	5 451	5.2	4 767	4.6	7 010	6.3	15 891	11.3
Kuwait	10 806	10.3	10 313	10.0	14 266	12.8	14 607	10.4
Libya	4 148	4.0	3 655	3.5	3 385	3.0	3 337	2.4
Neutral Zone	1 017	1.0	963	0.9	855	0.8	828	0.6
Nigeria	3 210	3.1	2 654	2.6	2 638	2.4	2 539	1.8
Qatar	930	0.9	570	0.6	524	0.5	501	0.4
Saudi Arabia	23 614	22.6	26 220	25.5	26 824	24.1	26 535	18.8
United Arab Emirates	5 118	4.9	4 832	4.7	5 226	4.7	15 375	10.9
Venezuela	2 813	2.7	2 852	2.8	4 067	3.7	8 947	6.3
United Kingdom	2 543	2.4	2 352	2.3	2 066	1.9	826	0.6
United States	5 244	5.0	4 195	4.1	4 449	4.0	4 016	2.8
USSR	12 776	12.2	10 011	9.7	9 694	8.7	9 376	6.6

(1) Excludes OPEC. (2) Excludes United Kingdom. (3) OPEC: Organization of Petroleum Exporting Countries.

World Energy Consumption, 1986

Source: British Petroleum Company

(millions of tonnes of oil equivalent)

	Oil		Natural gas		Coal		Hydro-electricity		Nuclear	
	total	%	total	%	total	%	total	%	total	%
World total	2 881.0	100.0	1 507.1	100.0	2 309.1	100.0	519.4	100.0	372.7	100.0
Africa	81.7	2.8	28.5	1.9	66.2	2.9	16.1	3.1	1.0	0.3
Australasia	27.4	1.0	13.8	0.9	39.8	1.7	4.1	0.8	–	–
Austria	10.2	0.4	4.5	0.3	3.3	0.1	7.7	1.5	–	–
Belgium[2]	23.3	0.8	7.6	0.5	9.4	0.4	0.1	...	9.0	2.4
Canada	67.1	2.3	43.0	2.9	34.6	1.5	69.0	13.3	16.9	4.5
China	99.2	3.4	12.1	0.8	531.2	23.0	28.2	5.4	–	–
Denmark	10.5	0.4	1.1	0.1	7.2	0.3	–	–	–	–
Finland	11.3	0.4	1.0	0.1	3.0	0.1	3.1	0.6	4.5	1.2
France	85.5	3.0	23.4	1.6	19.4	0.8	13.1	2.5	51.5	13.8
Greece	12.2	0.4	0.1	...	5.8	0.3	1.2	0.2	–	–
Iceland	0.5	...	–	–	0.1	...	1.0	0.2	–	–
Ireland	4.4	0.2	1.4	0.1	2.5	0.1	0.2	...	–	–
Italy	86.5	3.0	28.1	1.9	13.6	0.6	11.1	2.1	2.2	0.6
Japan	204.4	7.1	36.4	2.4	70.2	3.0	19.6	3.8	41.4	11.1
Latin America[3]	215.4	7.5	71.2	4.7	22.1	1.0	82.2	15.8	1.5	0.4
Middle East[4]	108.3	3.8	48.0	3.2	2.2	0.1	2.6	0.5	–	–
Netherlands	32.0	1.1	32.2	2.1	6.7	0.3	–	–	1.1	0.3
New Zealand	3.9	0.1	4.1	0.3	0.9	...	5.8	1.1	–	–
Norway	9.4	0.3	–	–	0.5	...	21.7	4.2	–	–
Portugal	9.5	0.3	–	–	0.8	...	1.2	0.2	–	–
Spain	43.2	1.5	2.4	0.2	19.3	0.8	6.6	1.3	8.3	2.2
South Asia[5]	56.3	2.0	17.2	1.1	111.7	4.8	20.0	3.9	1.3	0.3
South East Asia[6]	117.3	4.1	18.6	1.2	39.1	1.7	7.3	1.4	12.0	3.2
Sweden	18.0	0.6	0.2	...	3.3	0.1	15.0	2.9	16.5	4.4
Switzerland	13.2	0.5	0.9	0.1	0.5	...	8.7	1.7	5.5	1.5
Turkey	18.8	0.7	0.3	...	10.4	0.5	4.0	0.8	–	–
United Kingdom	77.0	2.7	49.1	3.3	67.1	2.9	1.4	0.3	12.7	3.4
United States	746.8	25.9	416.5	27.6	436.5	18.9	88.2	17.0	112.8	30.3
USSR	445.0	15.4	505.3	33.5	376.2	16.3	52.5	10.1	35.2	9.4
West Germany	119.6	4.2	40.2	2.7	77.1	3.3	5.0	1.0	27.3	7.3

(1) All energy sources have been converted to an "oil equivalent"—i.e. the amount of oil required to fuel an oil-fired plant in order to generate the same amount of electricity. (2) Includes Luxembourg. (3) Mexico, Caribbean (including Puerto Rico but excluding Cuba), Central and South America. (4) Arabian Peninsula, Iran, Iraq, Israel, Jordon, Lebanon, Syria. (5) Afghanistan, Bangladesh, Burma, India, Nepal, Pakistan, Sri Lanka. (6) Brunei, Hong Kong, Indonesia, Malaysia, Philippines, Singapore, South Korea, Taiwan, Papua New Guinea and the South West Pacific Islands.
– = zero; ... = too small to be included.

World Oil Production

Source: Energy, Mines and Resources Canada

(thousands of cubic metres per day)

	1975	%	1980	%	1985	%	1987	%
Total World Production	8 402	100.0	9 411	100.0	8 413	100.0	8 851	100.0
Canada	227	2.7	228	2.4	234	2.8	243	2.7
China	237	2.8	336	3.6	398	4.7	427	4.8
Mexico	112	1.3	308	3.3	434	5.2	404	4.6
OPEC[1]	4 315	51.4	4 273	45.4	2 554	30.4	2 883	32.6
Algeria	156	1.9	161	1.7	102	1.2	101	1.1
Indonesia	208	2.5	251	2.7	201	2.4	208	2.4
Iran	850	10.1	264	2.8	350	4.2	385	4.3
Iraq	359	4.3	399	4.2	228	2.7	330	3.7
Kuwait	331	3.9	263	2.8	163	1.9	216	2.4
Libya	235	2.8	284	3.0	168	2.0	154	1.7
Nigeria	283	3.4	327	3.5	234	2.8	205	2.3
Qatar	70	0.8	75	0.8	48	0.6	47	0.5
Saudi Arabia	1 124	13.4	1 573	16.7	539	6.4	667	7.5
United Arab Emirates	264	3.1	272	2.9	190	2.3	236	2.7
Venezuela	373	4.4	345	3.7	266	3.2	277	3.1
other	61	0.7	60	0.6	67	0.8	57	0.6
United Kingdom	2	...	258	2.7	402	4.8	393	4.4
United States	1 331	15.8	1 366	14.5	1 417	16.8	1 320	14.9
USSR	1 530	18.2	1 821	19.3	1 788	21.3	1 874	21.2

(1) OPEC: Organization of Petroleum Exporting Countries.
... = too small to be included.

Agriculture

As recently as 1931, approximately 30 percent of the Canadian population lived on farms. By 1986, that percentage had dropped to less than 4 percent. But Canada's farms are now larger, technology has reduced labor while increasing production, and agriculture remains one of the country's most important industries.

The money received by farmers for their products now totals about $20 billion annually. When wholesale, processing and retail activities are included, agriculture accounts for more than 25 percent of Canada's economy. In 1987, food and agricultural products made up about 17 percent of Canadian exports. Canada is the world's 5th largest producer of wheat—behind the Soviet Union, the United States, China and India—and the 2d largest wheat exporter, surpassed only by the United States.

There are 4 main types of farms in Canada: livestock farms, grain farms producing such crops as wheat and oats, combination farms producing both grain and livestock, and special crop farms producing vegetables, fruits, tobacco and other products. Both the type and amount of farming within Canada is affected by climate and location.

The Atlantic Region

The Atlantic Region is an area of diverse agricultural activity. Newfoundland, because of poorly-developed soils and a difficult climate, has a very limited agricultural industry supplying only local markets. But farming is the leading industry on Prince Edward Island; potatoes are the main PEI crop, encouraged by a moist climate and silty, stone-free soils. The land also supports mixed grains and dairy farms.

Nova Scotia's main agricultural areas surround the Bay of Fundy and Northumberland Strait where they are protected from Atlantic gales; dairy farming and poultry production is common. Nova Scotia's Annapolis Valley is famous for fruit, mainly apples. In New Brunswick, potatoes and livestock are produced in the Saint John River Valley, and there is mixed farming in the northwest of the province.

The Central Region

In Canada's central region, the fertile soils and moist climate of southern Ontario and Quebec support a thriving agricultural industry. While these growing conditions allow a variety of crops, the population concentration in this area encourages specialization in products with high transportation costs. Dairy farms are concentrated around Montreal and in southwestern Ontario, supplying milk, butter and cheese to the major centres, such as London, Hamilton, Toronto, Kingston, Montreal and Quebec City. Vegetable crops are also grown near these centres. Farms specializing in poultry and egg production, sheep and hogs are also common.

The Niagara Peninsula, squeezed between Lakes Ontario and Erie, is a major fruit-growing centre. The moderating effects of the lakes delay the growth of the fruit trees in the spring until danger of frost is past. Tender fruit crops—peaches, pears, plums and cherries—as well as grapes thrive in these conditions. Tobacco grows well on the glacially-created sand plains of southwestern Ontario.

The Prairies

The Prairie provinces of Manitoba, Saskatchewan and Alberta contain 80 percent of Canada's farmland. Here, a combination of flat, easily-worked land, fertile soils, long sunny summer days and sufficient precipitation encourages the healthy growth of high-quality grains. This area grows almost all of Canada's wheat, about 90 percent of its barley and rye, and more than 75 percent of its oats.

Manitoba grows canola/rapeseed and flax in addition to wheat and other grains; there is also considerable mixed farming in the province, with an emphasis on beef cattle; dairy farms are common around Winnipeg. Saskatchewan grows approximately 60 percent of Canada's wheat and large quantities of other grains, but mixed farming as well as poultry, egg and livestock production also contributes to the provincial economy. Alberta, also a major grain producer, has more beef cattle ranches than any other province. They are located mainly in the south of the

province and in the foothills of the Rocky Mountains where the steep slopes and dry land is unsuited to the cultivation of crops.

The Pacific Region

In the Pacific region, only 2 percent of British Columbia is agricultural land. But the pockets of farmland are extremely productive. The lower mainland and the southern tip of Vancouver Island comprise the Georgia Strait agricultural region, an area concentrating on dairy farming and poultry raising to supply the province's population centres. Other crops include raspberries, strawberries, peas, tomatoes and flowers.

The Okanagan Valley contains 90 percent of British Columbia's orchards, producing grapes, apples and tender fruit such as peaches, plums, apricots and cherries. Here, local climatic and physiographic characteristics have resulted in conditions suitable for the orchard industry, although irrigation is often necessary and frost damage is a hazard. Beef cattle and sheep are raised in the interior of the province, where growing conditions are not suitable for crops requiring cultivation but grazing can be carried out.

The North

Canada's north generally has soil and climatic conditions unsuited to agriculture. A small number of farms produce some dairy products, beef cattle and vegetables for the local market, and vegetables for the local market.

Government Programs

Government has traditionally played a strong role in Canada's agricultural industry. Agriculture Canada, a federal department, provides income security for farmers through programs established to ensure stable farm prices and income security in case of crop failure. The department also supports scientific research aimed at solving problems in soil management, agricultural engineering and soil and crop production.

Canagrex is a federal Crown corporation established in 1983 to promote the export of agricultural products. It provides consulting and counselling services as well as marketing and promotion assistance to agriculture and food industry firms wishing to expand markets outside Canada.

Provincial programs are also available to support agriculture. These often focus on aspects of the farm and community by providing advice on farm management, home economics or crop and livestock improvements. Other programs have provided loans and grants to encourage farmers to upgrade their operations by enlarging their holdings and buying new equipment. In several provinces, irrigation or drainage programs have been sponsored by the provincial government.

Among the measures taken by both the federal and provincial governments to encourage a stable agricultural industry is the establishment of marketing boards to exert some control over agricultural production and prices.

The Canadian Wheat Board, established in 1935, was the first marketing board. It is the sole agency handling wheat, oats and barley sold from one province to another, and from Canada to other countries. Producers deliver their grain to a local elevator under a quota system which spreads delivery opportunities among all producers. The farmers are paid a government-guaranteed "floor" price upon delivery. Should the Wheat Board sell the grain for more than the floor price, the additional revenues are distributed to producers after the Board has sold all the crop. The Wheat Board also co-ordinates the movement of grain from local elevators to large terminals at ports such as Thunder Bay, Churchill, Montreal and Vancouver. The grain leaves from these terminals to customers around the world.

The Canadian Dairy Commission is another national marketing agency that uses quotas to balance supply with demand. In order to keep consumer prices at levels that provide reasonable returns to dairy operators, the commission will also buy dairy products at predetermined prices.

As well as wheat and dairy products, hogs, eggs, turkeys, chickens, tobacco, soybeans and other products are sold through marketing boards. Co-operatives have also been established that attempt, through voluntary means, to accomplish the same ends as marketing boards.

Farm Population in Canada

Source: Censuses of Canada

	Canada[1]	Nfld	PEI	NS	NB	Que	Ont	Man	Sask	Alta	BC
1931	3 289 214	n.a.	55 478	177 690	180 214	777 017	800 960	256 305	564 012	375 097	102 367
1941	3 152 491	n.a.	51 067	143 709	163 706	838 861	704 420	249 599	514 677	383 964	102 446
1951	2 911 996	19 975	46 855	115 414	149 916	792 756	702 778	219 233	399 473	345 222	120 292
1956	2 746 755	13 055	43 296	98 944	128 978	765 459	683 148	206 729	362 231	332 191	112 668
1961	2 128 400	11 090	34 753	58 020	63 334	585 485	524 490	172 946	305 740	287 814	84 655
1966	1 960 365	9 236	31 041	46 283	52 042	507 869	498 025	161 662	281 089	281 583	91 443
1971	1 489 565	5 156	21 338	26 997	27 453	334 579	391 713	131 202	233 792	237 924	79 353
1976	1 056 571	1 452	12 279	12 479	12 184	198 195	286 415	101 904	193 068	190 785	47 791
1981	1 039 851	1 925	12 015	17 681	14 972	186 362	279 826	96 394	180 255	190 755	59 655
1986	890 490	1 685	10 275	14 175	12 110	143 380	232 790	84 690	161 495	178 115	51 775

(1) Includes Yukon and Northwest Territories.
n.a. not available.

Number of Farms in Canada by Size, 1986

Source: Census of Canada

	Canada	Nfld	PEI	NS	NB	Que	Ont	Man	Sask	Alta	BC
Total Farms	293 089	651	2 833	4 283	3 554	41 448	72 713	27 336	63 431	57 777	19 063
Less than 3 acres		74	100	192	124	837	1 638				830
3- 9 acres	14 679[1]	106	80	195	146	1 230	2 752	766[1]	593[1]	1 031[1]	3 985
10- 69 acres	35 561	271	380	720	382	6 016	14 684	1 710	1 107	3 365	6 926
70- 129 acres		71	558	676	527	7 901	17 406				1 476
130- 179 acres	86 955[2]	32	383	456	342	5 806	8 799	4 881[2]	7 017[2]	12 588[2]	1 562
180- 239 acres		34	381	504	458	6 003	8 632				462
240- 399 acres	42 799	27	512	764	771	8 182	10 872	4 270	7 505	8 726	1 170
400- 559 acres	25 193	10	231	395	402	3 205	4 140	3 429	6 514	6 267	600
560- 759 acres	21 897	10	101	196	199	1 372	1 974	3 484	7 939	6 103	519
760-1 119 acres	26 294	6	67	120	122	661	1 206	3 914	12 323	7 341	534
1 120-1 599 acres	18 637	1	20	38	49	174	414	2 493	9 892	5 164	392
1 600 acres and over	21 074	9	20	27	32	61	196	2 389	10 541	7 192	607

(1) Number of farms less than 10 acres. (2) Number of farms between 70 and 239 acres.

Types of Farms[1] in Canada, 1986

Source: Census of Canada

	Canada	Nfld	PEI	NS	NB	Que	Ont	Man	Sask	Alta	BC
Total Farms	260 745	415	2 458	3 170	2 776	37 160	63 253	25 262	60 809	51 743	13 699
Cattle	59 262	45	652	979	739	5 763	17 160	4 682	7 866	17 110	4 266
Small grains	58 595	—	90	62	62	2 922	13 693	8 758	16 942	15 403	663
Wheat	46 857	—	4	1	7	217	733	6 272	30 968	8 504	151
Dairy	34 186	68	584	698	631	15 906	11 028	1 412	881	1 828	1 150
Miscellaneous specialty	14 449	75	149	481	313	4 051	4 203	731	609	1 944	1 893
Hogs	12 026	17	221	132	125	2 749	4 840	1 111	906	1 635	290
Fruits and vegetables	10 377	94	60	457	252	2 250	4 089	100	36	119	2 920
Other mixed farms	8 850	37	69	146	122	1 256	2 223	810	1 086	2 081	1 020
Field crops	5 918	13	474	45	384	771	1 988	415	285	1 187	356
Mixed livestock	5 577	12	127	42	45	382	1 653	615	1 064	1 399	238
Poultry	4 648	54	28	127	96	893	1 643	356	166	533	752

(1) Farms with sales of $2 500 or more.
— = zero.

Farmland Use in Canada

Source: Censuses of Canada

(millions of hectares)

	Total farmland	Improved farmland				Unimproved farmland		Total farms	Average farm size
		cropland	improved pasture	summer fallow	other	wood-land	other	(000s)	(hectares)
1901	25.7	8.1	—	n.a.	n.a.	6.8	6.7	511	50.3
1911	44.1	14.4	—	1.0	n.a.	7.1	17.3	683	64.5
1921	57.0	20.2	3.1	4.8	0.4	9.6	18.7	711	80.2
1931	66.0	23.6	3.2	6.8	1.0	10.8	20.5	729	90.6
1941	70.2	22.8	3.4	9.5	1.3	9.0	24.1	733	95.8

	Total farmland	cropland	improved pasture	summer fallow	other	wood-land	other	Total farms (000s)	Average farm size (hectares)
			Improved farmland			**Unimproved farmland**			
1951	**70.4**	25.2	4.0	8.9	1.1	9.2	22.0	623	113.1
1961	**69.8**	25.3	4.1	11.4	1.0	6.8	21.0	481	145.2
1971	**68.7**	27.8	4.1	10.8	1.0	4.6	20.2	366	187.5
1976	**68.4**	28.3	4.1	10.9	0.9	4.4	19.8	339	202.6
1981	**65.9**	30.9	4.4	9.7	1.0	3.5	16.2	318	207.0
1986	**67.8**	33.1	3.6	8.5	0.8	2.8	19.0	293	231.4

– = zero; n.a. not available.

Canadian Farm Cash Receipts[1] by Commodity, 1987

Source: Statistics Canada

(thousands of dollars)

	Canada	Nfld	PEI	NS	NB	Que
Total Cash Receipts[2]	**19 965 571**	**47 386**	**204 625**	**285 981**	**241 619**	**3 232 772**
Barley	480 534	–	2 372	177	1 011	21 803
Calves	375 848	101	72	3 046	1 811	93 574
Canola-rapeseed	699 617	–	–	–	–	–
Cattle	3 401 849	1 285	29 013	26 697	20 719	229 052
Corn	468 734	–	–	–	–	95 955
Dairy products	2 877 695	12 203	32 029	81 991	54 471	1 047 184
Eggs	498 187	8 711	2 947	19 522	13 795	91 300
Flaxseed	109 493	–	–	–	–	–
Forest and maple products	133 962	131	490	6 539	7 627	81 470
Fruits	332 494	714	2 187	21 142	9 592	50 982
Fur farming	74 865	639	2 500	16 337	3 034	7 129
Honey	49 842	–	88	430	369	8 998
Nurseries	444 299	2 310	1 250	12 675	6 165	62 523
Oats	47 275	–	346	154	894	8 990
Pigs	2 117 647	4 423	26 748	34 383	20 762	649 686
Potatoes	347 299	1 235	81 039	7 166	53 353	45 989
Poultry	996 699	12 547	1 189	32 904	26 702	281 150
Rye	20 503	–	–	–	–	–
Sheep and lambs	34 146	125	246	1 606	526	7 012
Soybeans	256 343	–	–	–	–	–
Sugar beets	21 467	–	–	–	–	–
Tobacco	257 178	–	8 728	1 922	962	25 563
Vegetables	632 118	2 231	4 604	9 663	8 382	124 860
Wheat	2 529 089	–	516	743	417	11 419

	Ont	Man	Sask	Alta	BC
Total Cash Receipts[2]	**5 520 302**	**1 850 286**	**3 824 314**	**3 707 533**	**1 050 753**
Barley	14 160	59 587	154 520	223 145	3 759
Calves	103 437	36 186	71 246	9 437	56 938
Canola-rapeseed	–	105 691	289 370	300 704	3 852
Cattle	1 035 499	230 539	503 260	1 206 301	119 484
Corn	366 841	5 938	–	–	–
Dairy products	997 729	110 247	89 355	221 107	231 379
Eggs	191 147	47 247	18 619	47 319	57 580
Flaxseed	–	63 591	40 062	5 915	–
Forest and maple products	17 520	1 489	1 332	2 334	15 030
Fruits	128 182	–	–	–	119 695
Fur farming	29 498	2 488	196	1 842	11 202
Honey	8 202	8 319	7 623	11 937	3 876
Nurseries	243 983	13 299	4 429	27 150	70 515
Oats	1 403	7 229	7 977	19 419	863
Pigs	684 468	252 893	113 417	281 905	48 962
Potatoes	51 795	43 369	7 948	34 343	21 062
Poultry	349 225	51 294	34 667	95 245	111 776
Rye	309	4 828	10 719	4 604	43
Sheep and lambs	11 084	1 658	2 233	7 737	1 919
Soybeans	256 343	–	–	–	–
Sugar beets	–	8 787	–	12 680	–
Tobacco	220 003	–	–	–	–
Vegetables	358 842	16 588	–	31 836	75 112
Wheat	62 673	394 215	1 494 737	559 132	5 237

(1) Gross cash receipts to farmers from the sale of agricultural products. (2) Excludes supplementary payments.
– = zero.

Value[1] of Canadian Agricultural Products

Source: Statistics Canada

(millions of dollars)

	Canada[2]	PEI	NS	NB	Que	Ont	Man	Sask	Alta	BC
1930	642	8	16	14	92	213	47	124	97	30
1935	533	5	15	11	71	161	36	110	99	23
1940	731	7	15	16	110	216	63	150	124	31
1945	1 656	16	27	33	217	443	151	406	291	72
1950	2 122	21	35	41	321	650	199	410	354	90
1955	2 239	24	41	37	360	724	173	416	357	107
1960	2 734	28	44	45	403	850	223	543	471	128
1965	3 818	41	51	60	507	1 102	342	887	664	164
1970	4 193	45	68	58	667	1 411	336	686	705	217
1975	10 119	86	114	99	1 355	2 689	942	2 512	1 899	422
1980	15 821	139	197	151	2 280	4 388	1 475	3 291	3 130	770
1985	19 733	178	259	225	3 078	5 146	1 993	4 050	3 782	1 022
1986	20 073	182	265	227	3 228	5 508	2 072	4 006	3 567	1 019
1987	19 918	205	286	242	3 233	5 520	1 850	3 824	3 708	1 051

(1) Based on the gross cash returns to farmers from the sale of all agricultural products; excludes supplementary payments. (2) Excludes Newfoundland, Yukon and Northwest Territories.

Number of Livestock by Province, 1987[1]

Source: Statistics Canada

(thousands)

	Canada	Nfld	PEI	NS	NB	Que	Ont	Man	Sask	Alta	BC
All cattle	10 492.7	7.2	93.0	135.0	98.5	1 429.0	2 370.0	890.0	1 790.0	3 075.0	605.0
beef cows	2 974.5	0.8	11.3	26.7	17.7	170.0	340.0	325.0	765.0	1 130.0	188.0
beef heifers[2]	517.3	0.2	2.7	7.2	4.7	39.5	100.0	55.0	125.0	145.0	38.0
bulls	192.9	0.2	1.1	1.8	1.8	27.0	30.0	18.0	38.0	63.0	12.0
calves	3 179.9	1.5	25.0	34.0	24.4	255.0	635.0	280.0	595.0	1 125.0	205.0
dairy heifers	622.1	1.0	7.6	14.9	10.6	230.0	240.0	26.0	17.0	43.0	32.0
milk cows	1 646.9	3.4	22.3	35.6	28.6	650.0	510.0	78.0	79.0	152.0	88.0
slaughter heifers	396.6	—	4.5	3.8	3.8	10.5	165.0	33.0	45.0	125.0	6.0
steers	962.5	0.1	18.5	11.0	6.9	47.0	350.0	75.0	126.0	292.0	36.0
All sheep and lambs	498.8	3.4	5.0	25.0	7.0	79.0	170.0	18.7	36.7	124.0	30.0
lambs	127.5	0.6	1.3	6.0	2.2	9.5	49.3	2.2	13.2	36.0	7.2
sheep	371.3	2.8	3.7	19.0	4.8	69.5	120.7	16.5	23.5	88.0	22.8
Pigs	10 825.5	16.5	125.0	147.0	116.0	3 305.0	3 480.0	1 216.0	685.0	1 480.0	255.0

(1) As of Jan. 1. (2) For breeding.
— = zero.

Fruit Production and Value, 1985

Source: Statistics Canada

(thousands of dollars)

	Canada tonnes	Canada value	Nova Scotia tonnes	Nova Scotia value	New Brunswick tonnes	New Brunswick value	Quebec tonnes	Quebec value	Ontario tonnes	Ontario value	British Columbia tonnes	British Columbia value
Apples	478 605	115 598	58 105	9 136	7 620	2 749	91 825	24 057	182 697	44 250	138 358	35 406
Delicious	n.a.	n.a.	6 287	n.a.	–	–	–	–	39 230	10 394	63 757	16 088
McIntosh	n.a.	n.a.	17 908	n.a.	4 096	n.a.	n.a.	n.a.	64 965	14 529	44 135	12 609
Spy	43 608	n.a.	6 001	n.a.	–	–	–	–	37 607	7 584	–	–
Cortland	n.a.	n.a.	5 144	n.a.	1 810	n.a.	n.a.	n.a.	–	–	–	–
Spartan	27 491	6 211	–	–	–	–	–	–	3 452	1 046	24 039	5 165
Blueberries[1]	22 431	20 312	8 763	5 326	2 359	1 300	3 965	2 772	–	–	6 859	10 662
Cherries	16 039	15 069	–	–	–	–	–	–	7 783	7 432	8 256	7 637
sweet	8 690	8 891	–	–	–	–	–	–	1 571	2 162	7 119	6 729
sour	7 349	6 178	–	–	–	–	–	–	6 212	5 270	1 137	908
Cranberries[2]	8 185	13 847	227	350	–	–	–	–	–	–	7 942	13 483
Grapes	76 636	36 430	–	–	–	–	–	–	62 901	27 388	13 735	9 042
Peaches	42 204	22 033	–	–	–	–	–	–	31 758	17 814	10 446	4 219
Pears	28 217	11 845	1 814	685	–	–	–	–	12 749	6 405	13 654	4 755
Plums, prunes	5 485	3 938	295	194	–	–	–	–	2 413	2 951	2 777	793
Raspberries	15 263	26 887	34	114	27	58	1 147	3 640	621	2 274	13 434	20 801
Strawberries[3]	38 301	46 355	2 835	3 520	1 451	2 739	13 491	15 728	12 854	15 773	6 831	7 077

(1) Includes Nfld.: 145 tonnes, $64 000; PEI: 340 tonnes, $188 000. (2) Includes PEI: 16 tonnes, $14 000. (3) Includes Nfld.: 113 tonnes, $430 000; PEI: 726 tonnes, $1.1 million.
— = zero; n.a. not available.

Canadian Milk, Butter and Cheese Sales, 1986

Source: Statistics Canada

	Milk and cream[1] (kL)	Homogenized milk[2] (kL)	2% milk[2] (kL)	Skim milk[2] (kL)	Cereal cream[2] (kL)	Ice cream[3] (kL)	Butter[3] (tonnes)	Cheddar cheese[3] (tonnes)
Canada	7 283 222	760 798	1 595 950	123 036	75 383[4]	319 331[4]	97 067[4]	111 613[4]
Newfoundland	17 129	10 254	13 045	406	n.a.	–	–	–
Prince Edward Island.	99 927	6 263	5 817	544	n.a.	n.a.	1 270	5 683[5]
Nova Scotia	181 117	42 646	49 422	7 253	2 345	11 067	1 695	5 683[5]
New Brunswick	133 169	30 673	31 871	4 068	1 357	n.a.	2 601	5 683[5]
Quebec	2 830 479	283 177	337 076	16 334	17 395	70 867	45 928	52 422
Ontario	2 433 043	191 512	703 435	39 705	30 538	128 976	29 056	34 290
Manitoba	291 317	30 302	63 514	9 163	2 117	16 961	3 859	5 859
Saskatchewan	218 052	22 787	63 736	6 236	1 945	n.a.	n.a.	n.a.
Alberta	589 715	57 218	160 122	18 766	7 047	39 640	7 323	7 310
British Columbia	489 274	85 966	167 912	20 561	12 400	32 719	n.a.	n.a.

(1) Farm sales. (2) Sales by dairies. (3) Dairy manufacturers production. (4) Includes confidential provincial figures listed as not available. (5) Includes PEI, NS and NB.
kL = kilolitres; – = zero; n.a. not available.

Vegetable Production and Value, 1985

Source: Statistics Canada

Production
(tonnes)

	Canada	Nfld	PEI	NS	NB	Que	Ont	Man	Alta	BC
Asparagus ..	3 070	–	–	–	–	635	2 074	54	–	307
Beans	45 570[1]	–	23	n.a.	n.a.	22 149	15 038	–	n.a.	4 482
Beets	21 588	–	1 090	274	254	11 020	6 861	127	926	1 036
Cabbage	156 202	1 138	1 568	5 024	3 054	58 890	72 423	3 189	4 534	6 382
Carrots	264 562	306	3 720	20 685	3 057	102 065	119 746	2 087	5 481	7 415
Cauliflower ..	48 011	–	157	588	4 325	10 730	27 650	n.a.	226	4 335
Celery	31 600	–	–	–	–	11 020	16 450	735	–	3 395
Corn	279 057	–	139	1 170	1 219	66 981	167 957	20 493[2]	20 493[2]	21 098
Cucumbers ..	54 387	–	314	218	500	13 263	37 451	431	819	1 391
Lettuce	51 497	–	122	252	316	31 900	10 689	–	–	8 218
Mushrooms ..	45 093	–	1 899[3]	1 899[3]	1 899[3]	1 899[3]	23 062	5 438[2]	20 493[2]	14 694
Onions	147 956	–	–	–	–	34 930	101 166	3 837	1 234	6 789
Parsnips	2 924	–	88	80	58	–	1 952	451	–	295
Peas	80 651[1]	–	17 506[4]	17 506[4]	17 506[4]	18 949	29 270	–	n.a.	n.a.
Peppers	22 916	–	–	–	–	5 485	17 144	–	–	287
Potatoes	3 029 636[5]	4 082	799 049	36 197	698 532	460 000	347 441	340 421	217 724	99 065
Radishes	5 167	–	–	–	–	2 230	2 172	–	–	765
Rutabagas ...	92 584	4 164	5 103	4 572	4 137	26 870	43 486	953	1 402	1 897
Spinach	3 882	–	–	–	–	1 275	2 235	–	–	372
Tomatoes ...	545 410[1]	–	22	n.a.	n.a.	21 948	520 744	41	–	n.a.

Value
(thousands of dollars)

	Canada	Nfld	PEI	NS	NB	Que	Ont	Man	Alta	BC
Asparagus ..	6 852	–	–	–	–	1 440	4 579	114	–	719
Beans	14 656[1]	–	30	n.a.	n.a.	5 782	5 704	–	n.a.	1 453
Beets	4 007	–	134	84	143	1 369	1 372	50	324	531
Cabbage	29 427	432	252	968	740	10 614	11 732	703	1 628	2 358
Carrots	39 490	126	694	1 739	182	17 670	13 166	690	2 067	3 156
Cauliflower ..	23 804	–	109	439	2 392	4 555	12 685	n.a.	289	3 335
Celery	8 861	–	–	–	–	3 580	3 684	308	–	1 289
Corn	41 749	–	70	493	572	11 046	22 669	3 152[2]	3 152[2]	3 747
Cucumbers ..	17 784	–	137	74	237	3 442	11 479	190	1 210	1 015
Lettuce	19 377	–	81	183	188	11 243	4 571	–	–	3 111
Mushrooms ..	124 259	–	7 185[3]	7 185[3]	7 185[3]	7 185[3]	60 910	19 208[2]	19 208[2]	36 956
Onions	19 620	–	–	–	–	4 829	11 187	1 015	579	2 010
Parsnips	1 388	–	54	41	36	–	687	318	–	252
Peas	28 775[1]	–	5 147[4]	5 147[4]	5 147[4]	7 404	10 331	–	n.a.	n.a.
Peppers	10 903	–	–	–	–	2 858	7 754	–	–	291
Potatoes	236 900[5]	964	44 300	3 942	39 012	35 591	40 280	35 082	22 800	12 059
Radishes	3 448	–	–	–	–	1 247	1 619	–	–	582
Rutabagas ...	15 106	1 377	671	871	880	4 394	5 297	231	645	740
Spinach	1 973	–	–	–	–	641	998	–	–	334
Tomatoes ...	87 353[1]	–	24	n.a.	n.a.	7 474	78 324	45	–	n.a.

(1) Includes confidential provincial figures listed as not available. (2) Includes Man., Alta. and Sask. (3) Includes PEI, NS, NB and Que. (4) Includes PEI, NS and NB. (5) Includes Sask. production of 27 125 tonnes valued at $2.9 million.
– = zero; n.a. not available.

Egg Production in Canada, 1986

Source: Statistics Canada

	Production[1]		Sales[1]		Number of layers (000s)	Eggs per layer
	dozens (000s)	value ($000)	dozens (000s)	value ($000)		
Canada	491 493	512 027	444 593	408 688	23 485	251
Newfoundland	8 338	8 634	8 324	8 620	407	246
Prince Edward Island	3 176	3 102	3 112	3 043	149	255
Nova Scotia	17 917	19 079	16 919	16 457	867	248
New Brunswick	10 239	13 587	8 198	7 912	525	234
Quebec	79 224	91 455	68 299	64 187	3 804	250
Ontario	195 648	198 638	180 514	164 644	9 040	260
Manitoba	52 837	47 996	50 110	42 657	2 514	252
Saskatchewan	21 196	20 792	17 991	16 285	1 127	226
Alberta	44 491	48 779	38 086	34 821	2 298	232
British Columbia	58 427	59 965	53 040	50 062	2 754	255

(1) Includes exports.

Harvested Area of Principal Canadian Crops

Source: Statistics Canada

(thousands of hectares)

	1940	1950	1960	1970	1975	1980	1985	1987
Barley for grain	1 757	2 635	2 775	4 004	4 468	4 574	4 773	5 046
Beans, dry	39	27	27	33	59	38	36	57
Buckwheat	132	47	29	62	19	48	21	34
Canola-rapeseed	n.a.	8[2]	309	1 639	1 627	2 080	2 803	2 671
Corn for grain	75	126	185	459	633	964	1 197	998
Corn, fodder	201	187	148	294	393	480	342	250
Flaxseed	159	238	1 017	1 341	567	575	740	615
Mixed grains	494	575	553	793	743	579	513	391
Oats for grain	4 977	4 526	3 893	2 785	2 411	1 514	1 411	1 263
Peas, dry	33	16	25	35	30	49	77	255
Potatoes	221	150	118	128	106	107	115	113
Rye	419	460	227	337	333	310	372	313
Soybeans	4[1]	57	92	136	158	283	425	460
Sugar beets	32	41	35	28	32	27	12	23
Tame hay	3 983	4 139	4 899	5 252	5 267	5 477	5 394	5 752
Wheat	11 625	11 052	9 930	5 052	9 479	11 097	13 729	13 508

(1) Data is for 1941. (2) Data is for 1949.
n.a. not available.

Harvested Area of Principal Field Crops, by Province, 1987

Source: Statistics Canada

(thousands of hectares)

	Canada	PEI	NS	NB	Que	Ont	Man	Sask	Alta	BC
Barley for grain	5 046	27	5	11	174	239	688	1 538	2 307	57
Beans, dry	57	–	–	–	–	57	–	–	–	–
Buckwheat	34	–	–	–	11	6	16	–	–	–
Canola-rapeseed ...	2 671	–	–	–	–	16	405	1 052	1 153	45
Corn, fodder	250	–	2	–	58	162	10	–	7	11
Corn for grain	998	–	1	–	228	745	20	–	4	–
Flaxseed	615	–	–	–	–	–	336	251	28	–
Mixed grains	391	25	–	–	28	219	32	24	61	–
Oats for grain	1 263	10	7	12	103	111	182	324	486	28
Peas, dry	255	–	–	–	–	–	73	154	28	–
Rye	313	–	–	–	–	20	26	174	89	4
fall rye	277[1]	–	–	–	–	20[1]	n.a.	154	73	4[1]
spring rye	36	–	–	–	–	–	n.a.	20	16	–
Soybeans	460	–	–	–	7	453	–	–	–	–
Sugar beets	23	–	–	–	–	–	11	–	12	–
Tame hay	5 752[2]	55	69	70	986	1 032	627	809	1 760	340
Wheat	13 508	5	3	4	65	191	1 977	8 276	2 942	45
durum wheat	2 186	–	–	–	–	–	142	1 720	324	–
spring wheat	10 790[3]	5[3]	3[3]	4[3]	57	53	1 821	6 374	2 428	45[3]
winter wheat	532	–	–	–	8	138	14	182	190	–

(1) Includes small quantities of spring rye. (2) Includes Nfld.: 4 hectares. (3) Includes relatively small estimates of winter wheat.
– = zero; n.a. not available.

Production and Use of Canadian Wheat[1]

Source: Statistics Canada

(millions of tonnes)

	Total production[2]	Exports Wheat grain	Exports Wheat flour	Exports Total	Domestic Consumption Human food	Domestic Consumption Animal feed	Domestic Consumption Other uses	Domestic Consumption Total
1870	0.5	...	...	0.1	n.a.	n.a.	n.a.	0.6
1875	0.7	0.2	...	0.2	n.a.	n.a.	n.a.	0.7
1880	0.9	0.1	...	0.1	n.a.	n.a.	n.a.	0.8
1885	1.2	0.1	...	0.1	n.a.	n.a.	n.a.	1.0
1890	1.1	0.1	...	0.1	n.a.	n.a.	n.a.	1.1
1895	1.5	0.3	...	0.3	n.a.	n.a.	n.a.	1.2
1900	1.5	0.3	0.1	0.4	n.a.	n.a.	n.a.	1.1
1905	2.9	1.1	0.2	1.3	n.a.	n.a.	n.a.	1.6
1910	3.6	1.3	0.4	1.7	n.a.	n.a.	n.a.	1.9
1915	10.7	6.4	0.9	7.3	n.a.	n.a.	n.a.	3.4
1920	7.2	3.7	0.8	4.5	1.1	0.5	1.1	1.6
1925	7.7	7.5	1.3	8.8	1.2	0.5	1.1	1.7
1930	11.4	6.2	0.8	7.0	1.1	1.4	1.1	4.1
1935	7.7	6.3	0.6	6.9	1.2	0.9	0.9	3.1
1940	14.7	5.0	1.3	6.3	1.3	1.3	0.9	3.5
1945	8.6	7.6	1.8	9.4	1.5	1.7	1.0	4.3
1950	12.7	5.0	1.5	6.6	1.4	1.6	1.0	4.0
1955	14.1	7.4	1.1	8.5	1.5	2.1	0.9	4.5
1960	17.7	8.6	1.0	9.6	1.5	1.7	1.0	4.3
1965	9.0	14.9	1.0	15.9	1.7	1.4	1.3	4.3
1970	17.1	11.2	0.7	11.9	1.8	2.2	0.7	4.6
1975	13.3	10.2	0.5	10.7	1.9	1.7	1.0	4.6
1980	17.2	15.2	0.7	15.9	2.0	2.4	1.2	5.5
1981	19.3	15.6	0.7	16.3	1.9	2.1	1.2	5.2
1982	24.8	18.0	0.5	18.4	2.0	2.0	1.2	5.2
1983	26.7	21.0	0.4	21.4	2.0	1.8	1.3	5.1
1984	26.5	21.3	0.5	21.8	2.0	1.2	2.3	5.5
1985	21.2	17.1	0.5	17.6	2.0	2.0	1.3	5.3
1986	24.3	17.3	0.4	17.7	2.1	2.1	1.4	5.6
1987	31.4	20.4	0.4	20.8	2.1	2.9	1.3	6.3

(1) For crop year ending July 31. (2) Export and consumption totals may not equal total production because some wheat is stored.
. . . = too small to be included; n.a. not available.

Canada's Share of the World Wheat Market[1]

Source: Statistics Canada

(thousands of metric tonnes)

	1980 World wheat imports	1980 Canadian Total	1980 Canadian Share(%)	1985 World wheat imports	1985 Canadian Total	1985 Canadian Share(%)	1987 World wheat imports	1987 Canadian Total	1987 Canadian Share(%)
All Countries	86 000	14 993	17.4	113 466	19 406	17.1	99 754	20 762	20.8
Algeria	1 959	497	25.4	2 800	473	16.9	3 500	448	12.8
Bangladesh	2 055	395	19.2	1 898	56	3.0	1 500	409	27.3
Belgium/Luxembourg	1 213	12	1.0	1 403	125	8.9	1 231	75	6.1
Brazil	4 769	1 033	21.7	4 690	1 192	25.4	2 800	885	31.6
China	8 865	2 647	29.9	7 400	2 801	37.9	8 500	3 611	42.5
Colombia	649	–	–	600	2	0.3	625	202	32.3
Cuba	n.a.	n.a.	n.a.	1 300	795	61.2	1 300	1 253	96.4
Czechoslovakia	700	6	0.9	200	5	2.5	200	11	5.4
Egypt	5 200	31	0.6	6 944	462	6.7	6 332	234	3.7
France	505	4	0.8	375	107	28.5	281	1	0.4
East Germany	500	26	5.2	426	181	42.5	800	199	24.9
West Germany	1 336	12	0.9	2 570	18	0.7	1 773	24	1.4
Iceland	15	3	20.0	20	4	20.0	25	8	31.2
India	2	1	50.0	700	5	0.7	15	–	–
Indonesia	1 295	–	–	1 436	401	27.9	1 600	141	8.8
Iran	1 187	42	3.5	3 200	24	0.8	2 500	128	5.1
Iraq	2 300	488	21.2	3 000	367	12.2	2 800	691	24.7

	1980			1985			1987		
	World wheat imports	Canadian Total	Share(%)	World wheat imports	Canadian Total	Share(%)	World wheat imports	Canadian Total	Share(%)
Israel	524	–	–	587	74	12.6	670	79	11.8
Italy	3 395	682	20.1	4 475	235	5.3	4 988	693	13.9
Japan	5 599	1 290	23.0	5 603	1 185	21.1	5 781	1 351	23.4
Libya	424	14	3.3	400	103	25.8	600	166	27.7
Mexico	1 005	60	6.0	491	–	–	500	236	47.2
Netherlands	1 600	65	4.1	1 670	126	7.5	1 578	78	4.9
Nigeria	1 350	28	2.1	1 750	24	1.4	1 000	–	–
Norway	301	137	45.5	110	72	65.5	230	89	38.9
Pakistan	554	34	6.1	1 042	33	3.2	374	51	13.6
Peru	853	–	–	974	76	7.8	1 150	288	25.0
Poland	3 122	1 518	48.6	1 602	73	4.6	2 300	32	1.4
Portugal	742	17	2.3	545	–	–	573	268	46.8
South Korea	1 845	2	0.1	3 111	–	–	3 895	1 800	27.7
Sri Lanka	753	8	1.1	571	100	17.5	675	–	–
Sudan	340	7	2.1	600	23	3.8	600	31	5.2
Switzerland	233	63	27.0	245	18	7.3	286	...	0.1
Syria	521	20	3.8	1 280	656	51.3	600	5	0.8
Taiwan	703	79	11.2	780	110	14.1	866	82	9.4
United Kingdom	2 490	1 376	55.3	992	677	68.2	1 250	527	42.2
United States	n.a.	n.a.	n.a.	256	183	71.5	572	428	74.8
USSR	12 125	2 044	16.9	28 100	7 619	27.1	16 000	5 948	37.2
Venezuela	860	4	0.5	1 028	323	31.4	1 050	171	16.3

(1) For the crop year ending June 30.
. . . = too small to be included; – = zero; n.a. not available.

World Wheat, Rice and Corn Production, 1986

Source: UN Food and Agriculture Organization

(thousands of tonnes)

Country	Wheat	Rice	Corn	Country	Wheat	Rice	Corn
World total	535 842	475 533	480 609	Japan	876	14 559	1[1]
Afghanistan	2 500[1]	454[2]	750[1]	Kampuchea	n.a.	2 000[1]	92[1]
Argentina	8 900	405	12 400	Korea, North	710[1]	6 000[1]	2 700[1]
Australia	17 356	687	228	Korea, South	5[2]	n.a.	113
Austria	1 415	n.a.	1 740	Laos	n.a.	1 490	37[1]
Bangladesh	1 042	24 247	1[1]	Madagascar	n.a.	2 138[2]	153[2]
Belgium[2]	1 265[2]	n.a.	58[2]	Malaysia	n.a.	1 860[2]	25[1]
Brazil	5 433	10 399	20 510	Mexico	4 772	523	12 154
Bulgaria	4 000[2]	69[2]	2 750[1]	Nepal	598	2 350	880
Burma	246	15 000[1]	350	Netherlands	940	n.a.	2[1]
Canada	31 850	n.a.	6 694	New Zealand	424	n.a.	227
Chile	1 626	127	721	Pakistan	13 923	5 241	1 067
China	89 002[1]	177 000[1]	65 560[1]	Panama	n.a.	172[2]	75[2]
Colombia	82	1 632	788	Peru	121	745	864
Cuba	n.a.	540[1]	95[2]	Philippines	n.a.	9 350	4 155[2]
Czechoslovakia	5 035	n.a.	992	Poland	7 390[2]	n.a.	86[2]
Denmark	2 177	n.a.	n.a.	Portugal	463	153	607
Ecuador	24	393[2]	309	Romania	7 900[2]	150[2]	20 000[2]
Egypt	1 929	2 450[2]	3 801[2]	South Africa	2 034	3[1]	8 077
Ethiopia	700[1]	n.a.	1 500[1]	Soviet Union	92 300	2 600	12 500
Finland	529	n.a.	n.a.	Spain	n.a.	494	3 451
France	26 587	60	10 792	Sri Lanka	n.a.	2 594	46[1]
Germany, East	4 193	n.a.	1[1]	Sweden	n.a.	n.a.	n.a.
Germany, West	10 406	n.a.	1 302	Switzerland	497	n.a.	180
Greece	2 200	102	2 070	Syria	1 969	n.a.	67
Hungary	5 803	44	7 214	Thailand	n.a.	19 100	4 197
India	46 885	90 000[1]	8 000[1]	Turkey	19 000	275	2 300
Indonesia	n.a.	39 275	5 767	United Kingdom	13 874	n.a.	1[1]
Iran	7 128	1 569	50[1]	United States	56 792	6 097	209 632
Iraq	1 100[2]	145[2]	36[2]	Uruguay	234	421	92
Ireland	475[2]	n.a.	n.a.	Venezuela	n.a.	322	1 300[2]
Israel	169	n.a.	8[2]	Vietnam	n.a.	16 197	600[1]
Italy	9 070	1 082	6 560	Yugoslavia	4 776	48	12 502

(1) FAO estimate. (2) Unofficial figure. (3) Includes Luxembourg.
n.a. = not available.

Primary Industries

Canadian Mineral Reserves

Source: Energy, Mines and Resources Canada

(as of 1987)

	Copper (tonnes)	Nickel (tonnes)	Lead (tonnes)	Zinc (tonnes)	Molyb-denum (tonnes)	Silver (tonnes)	Gold (kg)
Canada	13 331 000	6 704 000	7 167 000	22 423 000	346 000	26 694	1 496 358
Newfoundland	–	–	–	58 000	–	–	42 971
New Brunswick	62 000	–	–	104 000	–	–	–
Nova Scotia	330 000	–	3 648 000	8 964 000	–	9 759	72 251
Quebec	623 000	–	–	987 000	1 000	1 506	229 387
Ontario	6 260 000	4 908 000	133 000	3 972 000	13 000	6 893	881 898
Manitoba	492 000	1 796 000	25 000	641 000	–	721	40 478
Saskatchewan	5 000	–	–	1 000	–	2	2 283
British Columbia	5 560 000	–	1 256 000	2 516 000	333 000	5 838	162 528
Yukon	–	–	1 275 000	1 958 000	–	1 849	7 065
N.W.T.	–	–	831 000	3 222 000	–	126	57 496

– = zero.

Minerals

Source: Bureau of Mines, U.S. Interior Department

Aluminum: The most abundant mineral element in the Earth's crust. Bauxite is the main source of aluminum. Guinea and Australia have about 46 percent of the world's reserves. It is used in packaging 28%, transportation 19% and building 19%. Canada accounts for over 5% of world production.

Asbestos: Composed of 6 minerals, mainly chrysotile, amosite and crocidolite. Of high tensile strength and resistant to heat and chemical attack, asbestos is used primarily in the construction, transportation and electrical appliance industries. Canada (with 25% of world production) is the 2d largest producer after the USSR (approx. 50% of world production).

Chromium: Some 99 percent of the world's chromite is found in South Africa and Zimbabwe. The chemical and metallurgical industries are major chromite consumers. Its most important use is in the manufacture of stainless steel.

Coal: A combustible sedimentary rock formed from the remains of plant life, coal is ranked in 4 classes: anthracite, bituminous, subbituminous and lignite. Anthracite, the most valuable, is mixed with bituminous coal to make coke for use in the iron and steel industry. Subbituminous and lignite act as thermal power fuel and steam for industrial use. It is found throughout the world.

Cobalt: Used in jet-engine parts, cutting tools, electronic devices, pigments for paints and allied products and in the treatment of cancer. Principal cobalt-producing countries include Zaire, Zambia, Canada and the USSR. The U.S. uses about one-third of total world consumption.

Columbium: Used in pipeline steels for transporting oil and gas and in structural steels in the aerospace industry. Brazil and Canada are the world's leading producers.

Copper: Main uses of copper are in building construction, electrical and electronic products, industrial machinery and equipment and transportation. The leading producer is Chile, followed by the U.S., USSR, Canada (Montreal has the world's largest copper refinery), Zambia, and Zaire.

Gold: Used in jewellery and arts, industry (mainly electronic) and dentistry. South Africa has about half of the world's resources and is the world's leading producer. The USSR ranks 2d; Canada is 4th in world production.

Gypsum: A low-cost, high-bulk mineral used in the construction industry (as plaster, dry-wall, stucco and for other applications) and in the chemical industry. Canada ranks 2d in the world, after the U.S., in crude gypsum production.

Iron ore: The source of primary iron for the world's iron and steel industries. Major iron ore producers include the USSR, Brazil, Australia, China and Canada.

Lead: The U.S. is the world's largest producer and consumer of lead. Transportation accounts for the major end use, mainly in batteries, gasoline additives and other applications. Other uses include ammunition and TV tubes. Other major producers are Australia, Canada and the USSR.

Manganese: Essential to iron and steel production. The U.S., Japan, and Western Europe are all deficient in economically-minable manganese. South Africa and the USSR have over 90% of the world's reserves.

Molybdenum: Because of its very high melting point (2610°C), it is an important alloying element in iron, steels and specialty alloys. It is also used in catalysts, dyes and pigments. The U.S. is the world's largest producer, with Canada 2d.

Nickel: Vital to the iron and steel industry and plays a key role in the development of the chemical and aerospace industries. Leading producers include the USSR, Canada, Australia, Indonesia and New Caledonia.

Platinum-Group Metals: The platinum group comprises 6 closely-related metals: platinum, palladium, rhodium, ruthenium, iridium, and osmium. They commonly occur together in nature and are among the scarcest of the metallic elements. They are consumed by the automotive, electrical and electronic industries, and are used in dentistry and medicine. The USSR and South Africa have over 90% of the world's reserves.

Potash: Over 90% of potash use is in fertilizers; other uses include soaps, glass, ceramics, chemical dyes, drugs, synthetic rubber and explosives. Canada and the USSR each account for about 25% of the world's potash. Approximately 40% of world potash supplies come from Canadian sources.

Silica: Occurring as quartz, silica is the most abundant rock-forming compound, making up 60% of the Earth's crust. It is used in the manufacture of all types of glass, for sandblasting and other construction applications, and in the production of transistors and computer chips.

Silver: Used in the following industries: photography, electrical and electronic products, sterlingware, electroplated ware, and jewellery. Silver is mined in over 55 countries; major producers are Mexico, the USSR, Peru, the U.S., Canada, Australia and Poland.

Sulphur: Used primarily in fertilizers, and in the pulp and paper, metal refining and petrochemical industries. Major producers are the U.S., the USSR and Canada (the world's largest exporter of elemental sulphur).

Tantalum: A refractory metal with unique electrical, chemical, and physical properties. It is used in electrical components and machinery. Thailand, Australia, and Brazil are the leading producers.

Tatanium: A sponge metal which is mostly used in jet engines, airframes, and space and missile applications. It is produced in the USSR, Japan, and the western U.S.

Uranium: Used in the production of nuclear energy and weapons. The U.S., Canada and South Africa account for the majority of the western world's production of uranium. Other important producing countries are Australia, France, Zaire, Niger and Gabon.

Vanadium: Used as an alloying element in steel. The USSR and South Africa are the world's largest producers.

Zinc: Used as protective coating on steel, as diecastings, as an alloying metal with copper to make brass, and as chemical compounds in rubber and paints. It is mined in over 50 countries with Canada the leading producer, followed by the USSR, Australia, Peru and the U.S.

Canadian Mining by Province, 1987[1]

Source: Statistics Canada

Production

(millions of units)

	Unit of weight	Canada	Nfld	NS	NB	Que	Ont	Man	Sask	Alta	BC	Yukon	NWT
Asbestos	t	0.7	0.1	–	–	0.5	–	–	–	–	0.1	–	–
Cement	t	12.2	n.a.	n.a.	n.a.	3.6	5.2	0.5	n.a.	1.1	1.2	–	–
Coal	t	59.8	–	2.8	0.6	–	–	–	9.9	25.1	21.4	–	–
Cobalt	kg	2.9	–	–	–	–	2.5	0.4	–	–	–	–	–
Copper	kg	767.3	–	–	7.8	56.4	280.6	71.8	2.5	–	348.3	. . .	–
Gold	g	117.8	n.a.	n.a.	0.4	29.2	54.1	3.8	0.9	. . .	11.9	5.1	11.8
Gypsum	t	8.8	0.4	6.0	–	–	1.4	0.4	–	–	0.5	–	–
Iron Ore	t	37.6	18.8	–	–	15.5	3.2	–	–	–	0.1	–	–
Lead	kg	390.5	–	–	79.4	–	8.5	0.6	–	–	67.2	100.3	134.5
Lime	t	2.3	–	–	n.a.	n.a.	1.5	n.a.	–	0.2	0.1	–	–
Natural Gas ..	cu. m	72.0	–	–	. . .	–	0.5	–	1.7	62.2	7.4	–	0.2
Nickel	kg	187.8	–	–	–	–	131.5	56.3	–	–	–	–	–
Oil	cu. m	87.1	–	. . .	. . .	–	0.1	0.8	11.7	70.8	2.1	–	1.5
Potash	t	7.5	–	–	n.a.	–	–	–	n.a.	–	–	–	–
Salt	t	10.3	–	n.a.	n.a.	n.a.	5.7	–	0.5	1.5	–	–	–
Sand & gravel[2]	t	260.3	2.7	7.6	9.7	31.9	94.5	13.0	13.9	44.4	38.6	2.4	1.3
Silver	g	1.3	–	–	0.2	0.1	0.3	–	–	–	0.4	0.1	–
Stone	t	105.7	0.5	4.8	2.5	37.9	51.0	4.1	–	0.3	4.1	0.1	0.3
Sulphur	t	6.9	–	–	–	–	. . .	. . .	–	6.6	0.3	–	–
Uranium	kg	13.2	–	–	–	–	4.4	–	8.8	–	–	–	–
Zinc	kg	1 329.4	13.4	–	231.4	93.2	323.1	66.2	1.4	–	118.7	154.5	327.7

Value

(millions of dollars)

	Canada	Nfld	NS	NB	Que	Ont	Man	Sask	Alta	BC	Yukon	NWT
Asbestos	235.2	21.0	–	–	166.4	–	–	–	–	47.8	–	–
Cement	976.0	9.5	39.5	9.3	216.9	413.7	48.9	17.9	132.1	88.3	–	–
Coal	1 635.0	–	170.7	32.8	–	–	–	111.5	396.2	923.8	–	–
Cobalt	54.5	–	–	–	–	47.0	7.4	–	–	–	–	–
Copper	1 844.6	–	–	18.7	135.5	674.6	172.6	5.9	–	837.2	. . .	–
Gold	2 242.9	7.8	3.0	8.4	555.8	1 029.2	71.4	18.0	0.3	227.0	97.2	224.8
Gypsum	87.9	4.7	51.0	–	–	18.7	8.2	–	–	5.3	–	–
Iron Ore	1 254.2	685.4	–	–	n.a.	n.a.	–	–	–	2.3	–	–
Lead	412.8	–	–	84.0	–	9.0	0.6	–	–	71.0	106.0	142.2
Lime	177.9	–	–	n.a.	n.a.	116.2	5.3	–	17.7	9.8	–	–
Natural Gas	4 310.7	–	–	. . .	–	62.1	–	100.9	3 843.6	292.6	–	11.5
Nickel	1 288.5	–	–	–	–	902.4	386.1	–	–	–	–	–
Oil	11 992.7	–	0.4	. . .	–	18.9	112.8	1 417.5	10 003.9	312.9	–	126.2
Potash	705.8	–	–	n.a.	–	–	–	n.a.	–	–	–	–
Salt	235.4	–	n.a.	n.a.	n.a.	140.5	–	24.5	15.4	–	–	–
Sand & gravel[2]	729.1	13.3	22.7	n.a.	n.a.	289.2	36.8	29.8	141.0	102.3	7.0	4.2
Silver	373.7	–	–	62.2	36.9	100.5	11.3	0.5	. . .	118.8	39.7	3.8
Stone	547.5	3.0	26.0	13.8	189.6	260.8	28.0	–	1.5	23.7	0.4	0.8
Sulphur	650.8	–	–	–	–	–	0.2	1.1	604.8	44.6	–	–
Uranium	1 121.1	–	–	–	–	509.2	–	611.9	–	–	–	–
Zinc	1 693.7	17.0	–	294.8	118.7	411.6	84.3	1.8	–	151.2	196.8	417.4
All Mining	36 038.6	767.8	390.1	700.7	2 527.8	5 656.6	1 022.5	2 996.8	17 148.1	3 429.0	447.2	950.1

(1) Preliminary data. (2) Includes P.E.I. production of 540 000 tonnes valued at $1.9 million.
– = zero; . . . = too small to be included; n.a. not available.

Production of Leading Canadian Minerals, 1950–1987

Source: Statistics Canada

(thousands of units)

	Unit of weight	1950	1960	1970	1980	1985	1986[1]	1987[1]
Cement	t	15 188	5 250	7 208	10 270	10 192	10 611	12 205
Coal	t	17 363	9 989	15 063	36 677	60 436	57 811	59 790
Copper	kg	239 685	398 490	610 275	716 352	738 637	698 527	767 299
Gold	g	138 151	143 999	74 939	55 092	87 562	102 899	117 834
Iron ore	t	3 270	19 551	47 458	49 054	39 502	36 167	37 553
Nickel	kg	112 181	194 596	277 489	184 799	169 971	163 639	187 805
Potash	t	n.a.	n.a.	3 103	7 198	6 661	6 752	7 465
Sand and gravel	t	66 310	174 246	183 845	276 452	256 183	257 971	260 265
Uranium	kg	n.a.	11 564	3 724	6 739	10 441	11 502	13 202
Zinc	kg	284 154	369 107	1 135 708	883 683	1 049 275	988 173	1 329 408

(1) Preliminary data.
n.a. not available.

Canadian Mineral Exports[1]

Source: Statistics Canada

	Unit of weight	1975		1985	
		Quantity	Value ($000)	Quantity	Value ($000)
Aluminum	t	24 004	$ 4 347	52 573	$ 25 568
Asbestos	t	1 085 598	304 817	721 517	446 350
Coal	t	11 694 658	477 899	27 572 019	1 996 429
Copper	t	314 517	299 745	296 928	431 393
Gold	kg	6 543	30 773	5 969	64 714
Gypsum	t	3 691 677	11 381	5 880 430	49 866
Iron	t	36 059 829	686 356	32 216 269	1 172 888
Lead	t	211 908	53 643	62 606	12 040
Molybdenum	t	15 710	73 412	5 635	49 543
Nickel	t	84 391	355 222	59 950	409 657
Platinum metals	kg	13 471	43 443	7 174	52 171
Radioactive ores[2]	—	n.a.	51 101	n.a.	231 896
Salt	t	1 423 848	5 185	2 263 075	29 272
Silver	kg	471 403	56 102	331 341	61 584
Sulphur[3]	t	3 284 246	113 036	7 848 378	1 290 800
Zinc	t	705 084	293 581	409 741	217 754

(1) Domestic exports of mineral ores and concentrates only, unless otherwise specified. (2) Primarily uranium. (3) Ores and crude or refined minerals.
n.a. not available.

Canada's Logging Industry,[1] 1985

Source: Statistics Canada

	Employees[2]		Businesses[3]		Value of shipments		Value added[4]
	No.	%	No.	%	($000)	%	($000)
Canada[5]	40 733	100.0	3 739	100.0	5 461 527	100.0	2 167 249
Newfoundland	1 048	2.6	61	1.6	97 881	1.8	41 422
Nova Scotia	1 289	3.2	180	4.8	152 525	2.8	50 380
New Brunswick	2 334	5.7	255	6.8	351 137	6.4	129 531
Quebec	9 494	23.3	721	19.3	957 749	17.5	441°933
Ontario	7 313	18.0	518	13.9	949 222	17.4	387 901
Manitoba	348	0.9	40	1.1	50 927	0.9	19 147
Saskatchewan	446	1.1	74	2.0	69 622	1.3	24 477
Alberta	603	1.5	110	2.9	94 992	1.7	32 675
British Columbia	17 845	43.8	1 772	47.4	2 736 956	50.1	1 039 517

(1) Includes primarily businesses involved in felling and bucking, bunching, yarding, forwarding, decking and loading of round wood, and in the recovery of lost logs, as well as businesses engaged in transporting primary wood products with specialized logging equipment. Also included are barking mills. (2) Production and related workers only. (3) Based on the number of business locations. (4) The value of shipments minus the cost of producing them. (5) Includes 7 businesses located in P.E.I. and 1 business in the Yukon and Northwest Territories.
. . . = too small to be included.

Canada's Pulp and Paper Industry,[1] 1985

Source: Statistics Canada

	Employees[2]		Businesses[3]		Value of shipments ($000)		Value added[4] ($000)
	No.	%	No.	%	($000)	%	($000)
Canada[5]	86 477	100.0	688	100.0	18 074 629	100.0	7 555 162
Nova Scotia	2 385	2.8	14	2.0	476 180	2.6	225 910
New Brunswick	4 313	5.0	18	2.6	958 227	5.3	317 337
Quebec	31 121	36.0	212	30.8	6 054 234	33.5	2 720 839
Ontario	31 251	36.1	317	46.1	6 036 236	33.4	2 468 039
Manitoba	1 199	1.4	23	3.3	238 661	1.3	97 529
Alberta	1 711	2.0	31	4.5	462 272	2.6	204 694
British Columbia	12 452	14.4	60	8.7	3 437 486	19.0	1 359 229

(1) Includes pulp and paper, asphalt roofing, paper box and bag, and other paper products industries. (2) Production and related workers only. (3) Based on the number of business locations. (4) The value of shipments minus the cost of producing them. (5) Includes 8 businesses located in Nfld. and 5 businesses in Sask.

Canada's Wood Industries,[1] 1985

Source: Statistics Canada

	Employees[2]		Businesses[3]		Value of shipments ($000)		Value added[4] ($000)
	No.	%	No.	%	($000)	%	($000)
Canada	90 976	100.0	3 476	100.0	11 121 616	100.0	4 623 796
Newfoundland	349	0.4	68	2.0	25 521	0.2	9 492
Prince Edward Island	147	0.2	25	0.7	10 299	0.1	3 299
Nova Scotia	1 734	1.9	142	4.1	137 766	1.2	59 959
New Brunswick	3 273	3.6	145	4.2	343 702	3.1	122 795
Quebec	24 521	27.0	1 101	31.7	2 565 728	23.1	1 085 450
Ontario	19 777	21.7	851	24.5	2 103 431	18.9	902 792
Manitoba	1 781	2.0	96	2.8	162 054	1.5	75 435
Saskatchewan	1 049	1.2	63	1.8	125 533	1.1	50 817
Alberta	4 441	4.9	222	6.4	555 886	5.0	242 177
British Columbia	33 904	37.3	763	22.0	5 091 676	45.8	2 071 578

(1) Includes sawmills, planing and shingle mills, veneer and plywood industries, and other millwork industries producing lumber for the manufacturing industry. (2) Production and related workers only. (3) Based on the number of business locations. (4) The value of shipments minus the cost of producing them.

Canada's Fishing Industry, 1984

Source: Dept. of Fisheries and Oceans

	Registered fishermen	Fish processing industry employees	businesses	tonnes	Catches landed value ($000)	marketed value ($000)
Canada	83 791	24 372	397	1 277 797	903 541	1 971 444[1]
Newfoundland	27 617	8 637	99	449 316	163 389	449 793
Prince Edward Island	3 399	712	19	38 521	38 301	59 507
Nova Scotia	13 235	5 793	100	394 504	265 280	525 489
New Brunswick	6 665	3 829	74	100 012	75 567	293 710
Quebec	8 500	1 859	39	84 478	58 153	107 977
Ontario	1 588	n.a.	15	22 667	35 105	70 210
Manitoba	*	n.a.	1	13 040	18 106	34 756
Saskatchewan	*	n.a.	1	3 508	3 998	7 922
Alberta	*	n.a.	n.a.	1 420	1 248	2 476
British Columbia	17 187	2 972	49	169 168	242 935	119 676
Northwest Territories	*	n.a.	n.a.	1 163	1 459	2 723

1) The sum of the provincial totals differs from the Canada total due to removal of inter-provincial shipments.
* There were 5 600 registered fishermen in the Prairie provinces and N.W.T. in 1984.
n.a. not available.

Canadian Commercial Fishing, 1984

Source: Dept. of Fisheries and Oceans

Atlantic Coast	Tonnes	Landed value ($000)	Inland Waters	Tonnes	Landed value ($000)	Pacific Coast	Tonnes	Landed value ($000)
Total	1 065 205	599 101	Total	43 424	61 505	Total	169 168	242 935
Capelin	43 608	9 723	Alewife	987	195	Clams	6 105	5 700
Catfish	3 597	822	Bass, Rock	25	27	Cod, Black	3 852	6 998
Clam	6 624	5 896	Bass, White	2 009	1 878	Cod, Grey	3 459	1 672
Cod	474 925	171 278	Carp	757	169	Cod, Ling	3 707	2 183
Crab, Queen	42 710	49 884	Catfish	381	394	Crabs	1 155	4 558
Cusk	3 126	1 296	Char, Arctic	62	380	Dogfish	2 441	551
Eel	623	1 295	Eel	249	542	Flounder	169	53
Flatfishes, small	79 990	25 563	Perch	5 412	19 324	Hake	33 596	5 213
Haddock	32 654	22 641	Pickerel, Yellow	7 123	18 368	Halibut	5 364	9 419
Hake	13 993	3 411	Pike	3 233	2 395	Herring	33 703	39 857
Halibut	3 155	9 599	Salmon	3	5	Herring roe	172	4 508
Herring	130 293	19 748	Sauger	2 069	3 173	Oysters	2 897	2 109
Lobster	28 701	152 821	Smelt	7 490	1 608	Pollock	596	136
Mackerel	17 331	3 935	Sturgeon	145	412	Rockfish	14 695	7 052
Oyster	2 249	3 456	Sucker	1 450	276	Salmon, Chum	9 003	14 938
Pollock	35 217	8 357	Sunfish	110	115	Salmon, Coho	10 089	35 532
Redfish	65 110	14 481	Tomcod	87	57	Salmon, Pink	12 058	10 742
Salmon	894	3 584	Trout, Lake	679	1 040	Salmon, Sockeye	12 877	45 976
Scallop	36 474	56 385	Tullibee	1 803	1 915	Salmon, Spring	6 254	37 318
Shrimp	11 727	16 277	Whitefish	8 352	8 602	Shrimp and prawn	914	4 284
Smelt	1 016	491				Smelt	2	4
Squid	398	128				Sole	3 225	2 072
Swordfish	572	2 695				Steelhead	150	292
Trout and char	254	517				Tuna	47	113
Tuna	249	1 203				Turbot	360	75
Turbot	21 745	6 794						

Trapping in Canada, 1987[1]

Source: Statistics Canada

	Pelts	Value	Avg. value per pelt[2]		Pelts	Value	Avg. value per pelt[2]
All furs	3 200 000	$75 265 071	$ n.a.				
Badger	2 298	56 026	24.38	Lynx	6 951	$3 693 771	$530.35
Bear, black	2 668	148 329	55.60	Marten	222 674	21 595 583	96.98
Bear, grizzly	–	–		Mink	101 561	4 381 486	43.14
Bear, white	274	226 623	827.09	Muskrat	1 675 243	7 684 301	4.59
Beaver	505 833	20 277 637	40.09	Otter	20 668	979 199	47.38
Cougar	–	–		Raccoon	139 221	3 151 968	22.64
Coyote	78 941	5 385 231	68.22	Skunk	306	950	3.10
Fisher	15 021	3 533 712	235.25	Squirrel	255 955	194 244	0.76
Fox, blue	269	5 398	20.07	Weasel	85 025	192 705	2.27
Fox, red	72 378	2 683 685	37.08	Wildcat	1 748	377 119	220.85
Fox, silver or black	801	33 820	42.22	Wolf	3 316	374 430	112.92
Fox, white	8 055	138 749	17.22	Wolverine	744	149 834	201.39

(1) For trapping season ending in the spring; excludes ranch-raised animals. (2) Average value is the price paid to trapper.
– = zero; n.a. not available.

Canadian Exports and Imports of Furs[1]

Source: Statistics Canada

(thousands of dollars)

	Exports					Imports			
	1975	1980	1985	1986		1975	1980	1985	1986
Total Exports	40 966	178 574	101 548	97 091	Total Imports	55 903	140 236	195 417	179 367
Beaver	6 356	27 444	6 984	7 509	Asian mink	402	10	–	11
Chinchilla	246	159	210	201	Fox	7 397	21 374	37 658	34 508
Weasel	112	277	185	84	Kolinsky	88	11	–	–
Fisher	665	2 113	3 229	2 877	Mink	20 316	38 137	61 625	62 038
Fox	5 021	15 350	11 078	11 763	Muskrat	8 627	9 641	5 972	5 830
Lynx	2 537	8 882	4 893	4 397	Persian lamb	135	241	–	3
Marten	509	5 068	8 663	8 624	Rabbit	223	176	77	34
Mink	11 439	43 820	31 535	31 308	Raccoon	11 752	45 536	59 349	46 336
Muskrat	3 603	16 984	8 007	7 908					
Otter	164	781	122	135					
Rabbit	22	521	134	225					
Seal	4 464	5 081	446	235					
Squirrel	337	1 736	257	190					
Wolf	1 569	6 326	3 366	3 588					

(1) Undressed pelts.
– = zero.

Environment

Environment Report, 1989

The air, the soil and the water of the Earth have all been polluted to varying degrees by human activity. Pollutants have altered the Earth's atmosphere to a degree that will, in the near future, dramatically affect the world's climate. Localized cases of contamination by pollution, such as the Bhopal disaster, have killed thousands of people. Yet, because pollution is not seen to be directly killing people on a daily, large-scale basis, the efforts being made to control this poisoning of the planet have been few and largely ineffective.

According to Environment Canada, pollution is such a threat to life on Earth that only a nuclear world war poses a greater danger.

On April 27, 1987 the United Nations World Commission on Environment and Development issued *Our Common Future*, a report which conveys an urgent warning: the future of our planet and humanity itself is at risk. Rapid population growth coupled with the consumer-oriented habits of developed nations are exhausting the natural resources that support life. By the end of this century, one million species of plants and animals will have vanished from the Earth forever.

The primary factors contributing to the degradation of the environment are:

Atmospheric Pollution

During June 1988 more than 300 scientists and policy makers from 46 countries, U.N. organizations and other bodies met in Toronto to discuss the implications of change caused by pollution in the atmosphere. The issues they identified as major concerns included global warming, depletion of the ozone layer and acid rain.

Global Warming: The Greenhouse Effect

Deforestation, the burning of fossil fuels and poor agricultural practices have significantly increased carbon dioxide and other "greenhouse gases" in the atmosphere. The scientific community now agrees that the increasing concentrations of these gases will change the global climate.

Canada, through the burning of fossil fuels, is one of the world's largest per capita producers of greenhouse gases.

Evidence suggests that over the next few decades the global mean temperature will rise 1.5 to 4.5°C and up to twice the global average in the Arctic as a result of greenhouse gases accumulating in the atmosphere.

Scientists agree that this warming will be accompanied by changes in the amount and distribution of precipitation. In Canada, rainfall patterns are expected to move northwards and agriculture in the southern prairies will be seriously affected. Water levels in the Great Lakes will fall substantially and contaminants which pollute the water will be further concentrated. Lower water levels will seriously affect the generation of hydroelectric power and interfere with shipping.

Another direct effect of global warming will be a rise in the level of the oceans as mountain glaciers located in the mid-latitudes melt. Though ocean levels will probably only increase by 30 cm, by 2050 the rise could be as much as 1.5 m.

Such an increase will inundate low-lying coastal lands and islands and reduce coastal fresh water supplies through increased saltwater intrusion. In Canada, the loss of land in areas such as the Hudson Bay coastline and PEI will be significant. Many river deltas and neighbouring agricultural lands, such as lower Vancouver and the Mackenzie delta, will be threatened. However, Canada would not be as severely affected as many other regions such as Florida, Bangladesh and the low countries of western Europe.

Ozone Layer Depletion

The layer of ozone in our atmosphere absorbs most of the sun's damaging ultraviolet radiation.

Over the last 10 years, the ozone layer has declined by 3% at mid-latitudes in the southern hemisphere. There are indications that a smaller decline has occurred in the northern hemisphere.

Every 1% decline in the ozone layer is expected to increase some kinds of skin cancer by 4-6%. Ozone depletion will also lead to increased eye disease, such as cataracts, and could adversely affect the body's immune system.

Increased ultraviolet light resulting from a depleted ozone layer will reduce crop yields worldwide and damage small organisms at the base of the aquatic food chain, affecting fisheries.

The depletion of ozone in the atmosphere has been linked to the chemicals in a group of synthetic compounds known as chlorofluorocarbons (CFCs) and halons.

At ground level, CFCs are non-toxic and extremely stable. They are used in refrigeration and air-conditioning products, as blowing agents in the manufacture of hard and soft foam products such as furniture padding, as propellants in spray cans and as cleaning solvents.

Halons are used in firefighting equipment.

In the upper atmosphere, under the sun's powerful ultraviolet rays, the CFC and halon molecules break down, releasing chlorine and bromine which attack the ozone.

Nearly one million tons of CFCs and halons are released annually into the atmosphere. Because these chemicals can be active for 100 years, the ozone layer would continue to deplete for at least 100 years after the use of CFCs and halons was stopped.

CFCs and halons also contribute to global warming.

Acid Rain

When sulphur dioxide and nitrogen oxide are released into the atmosphere, they combine with water vapour and return to the earth in the form of acid rain, snow, fog or dust.

Acid rain—the name given to both wet and dry acidic deposits—is of particular concern in Europe and North America where it is causing billions of dollars in damage annually.

In 1980, Canadian sulphur dioxide emissions were 4.7 million tonnes; the U.S. emitted 24.1 million tonnes. Nitrogen oxide emissions for 1980 were 1.8 million tonnes in Canada and 20 million tonnes in the U.S.

Nearly 50% of the acid rain affecting eastern Canada originates in the U.S.; in regions of particular concern, such as the Muskoka area of southern Ontario, over 65% of the acid rain comes from the U.S.

In North America the main sources of sulphur dioxide emissions are coal-fired power generating stations and non-ferrous ore smelters. Diesel engines, marine and rail transport are also significant sources. Nitrogen oxide comes primarily from the transportation sector (cars, trucks, planes etc.) electric utilities and fuel combustion facilities.

Acid rain is depleting aquatic life in lakes and streams in eastern Canada and is increasing the acidity of soil water and shallow groundwater.

Acid rain adversely affects our forests: 40% of the productive forest area in Canada is located in areas that receive moderate to high levels of acid deposition. Symptoms of high acidity in forests include discolored and falling leaves, poor rates of growth and dying and dead trees.

Acid rain also erodes stonework and concrete in buildings, monuments, bridges and other structures and is suspected of contributing to respiratory problems in people. It may also cause indirect health effects through contamination of drinking water and accumulation in foodstuffs.

Economically, acid rain endangers the fishery, tourism, agriculture and forestry resources in Canada that make up about 8% of Canada's GNP.

Water Pollution

Two of the basic requirements to sustain human life are fresh air to breathe and clean water to drink. Scientists are now beginning to see the effects of water pollution on marine life. The dangers to human health are potentially devastating. The basic sources of water pollution are:

Industrial effluents

Over 100 000 chemicals are in commercial use worldwide and about 1000 new chemicals enter the market every year. Most of those chemicals have the potential to enter national water systems.

Like air pollution, water pollution does not respect political boundaries. So, water pollution in Lake Michigan can produce problems in the St. Lawrence River which in turn are passed into the Atlantic Ocean. Though the pollutants become progressively more diluted as they enter larger bodies of water such as the world's oceans, their eventual accumulation will pose world-wide pollution problems which will require international cooperation to solve.

Municipal sewage
Canada is one of the most developed nations of the world yet more than 30% of Canadian urban sewage is not treated.

Waterways polluted by sewage threaten marine life. The potential for using the water for recreational purposes, and therefore tourism, is also greatly diminished.

Municipal sewage pollutes by increasing the growth of algae in the water. The nutrients, such as phosphorus and nitrogen, in the sewage cause the algal growth. Algae uses oxygen, and without oxygen in the water, waste can't decompose. Low levels of oxygen can also cause bottom sediments to be released, causing additional pollution.

Sewage treatment plants can eliminate pollution of water by municipal sewage.

In 1988, the federal government pledged $110 million to clean up the St. Lawrence River. This program includes protection to save the St. Lawrence beluga whale which has been described by one scientist as "the most polluted mammal on earth."

Solid Wastes
For years waterways and the oceans in particular have served as convenient dumping grounds for a wide variety of wastes.

In addition to the human health risks created by solid waste dumping, the effects on wildlife, sea life and to beaches and coastlines from oil spills is well-documented. In 1988, medical waste was washed ashore along beaches in the northeastern U.S.

Hazardous Wastes
Canada produces approximately 3 million tonnes of hazardous waste per year. There are 4 categories of hazardous waste:
1) by-products of industrial manufacturing
2) discarded consumer products that have become useless or contaminated
3) residues of hazardous materials which accidentally spill in storage or during transportation
4) discarded products and residues from laboratories and institutions.

The more common hazardous wastes are acids from metallurgical processes, spent caustic from the pulp and paper industry and the leftovers from oil refining.

Improper disposal of hazardous wastes can cause air, water, and soil pollution detrimental to human, animal and plant life.

The practice of some European nations of shipping their hazardous wastes to less developed countries where storage and treatment facilities are non-existant was brought to the world's attention in 1988. This form of disposal will cause environmental problems in those countries which can least afford to deal with them.

Pollutants in the News
PCBs
PCBs are synthetic chemical compounds consisting of chlorine, carbon and hydrogen known as polychlorinated biphenyls.

First synthesized in 1881, PCBs were desirable components in a wide range of industrial and consumer products because they are relatively fire-resistant, very stable, do not conduct electricity and have low volatility at normal temperatures.

PCBs are extremely resistant to chemical and biological breakdown by natural processes.

Approximately 635 000 tonnes of PCBs were produced in North America before their manufacture was banned in 1977. Of the 40 000 tonnes of PCBs that entered Canada 24 000 tonnes were used or recorded as being in storage. The remainder, 16 000 tonnes, is dispersed in the environment. PCBs are hazardous because they accumulate in living organisms. They move up through the food chain through aquatic plants, fish and birds and eventually to humans.

Public attention wasn't focussed on PCBs until 1968 when 1200 people in Yusho, Japan were poisoned by eating fish oil that had become contaminated by PCBs.

The full extent of human health implications is not known. The most common effect is chloracne, a painful and disfiguring skin condition. Liver damage can also result.

Dioxins
Dioxins are chemical by-products formed during the production of other chemicals or during combustion processes. There are 75 known members of the dioxins family including one chemical considered to be the most toxic substance on earth.

The herbicide 2,4,5-T which contains dioxins is used in Canada in forestry and along rights of way such as hydro transmission lines.

Another herbicide, 2,4-D, contains various dioxins and approximately 4.5 million kg are used annually in the Canadian prairies to control broadleaf weeds.

Another group of chemicals containing dioxins are used as wood preservatives. In Canada, about 3 million kg are used this way each year.

Even some minor ingredients of health-care products, such as triclosan and hexachlorophene are known to contain dioxins.

Waste dumps can be sources of dioxins; in Canada, the area of greatest concern is Lake Ontario where dioxins enter the Niagara River from U.S. landfill sites.

Finally, incineration, particularly of municipal garbage and industrial waste, but also automobile exhaust and cigarette smoke, produces dioxins.

The precise long-term effects of dioxins on humans and the environment are not known, but there is widespread agreement that long-term exposure should be avoided. People exposed to even moderate levels develop chloracne and, occasionally, nervous disorders.

Canadian Efforts
Canadian Environmental Protection Act
The *Canadian Environmental Protection Act* of 1988 sets environmental quality objectives, guidelines and regulations to prevent the contamination of our water, soil and air.

The Act regulates emissions, such as those that cause acid rain, and allows for import and export restrictions or limits on the use of substances, such as chlorofluorocarbons.

Through managing the entire life cycle of toxic substances, from their development and manufacture, to transport, distribution, use and storage, CEPA includes tough sanctions to deal with those who disobey regulations. Punishment includes fines, imprisonment and the cost of cleanup. Also, for the first time, corporate officials can be prosecuted and punished for violations of CEPA that they authorized or participated in on behalf of their companies.

Montreal Protocol on Substances that Deplete the Ozone Layer
Actually an international treaty, the Montreal Protocol establishes a timetable to control major industrial substances that deplete the ozone layer.

Before it can come into effect, the treaty must be ratified by 11 countries accounting for at least two-thirds of the 1986 global consumption of CFCs and halons.

The initial objective of the Protocol is to limit consumption of CFCs and halons at 1986 levels. Within 10 years, consumption will be reduced to 50% of 1986 levels.

In the long term, a review of the science and the control measures taken to date is scheduled. If necessary, the parties who sign the treaty can agree on more stringent controls to reflect the latest scientific findings.

Canada ratified the Montreal Protocol in June 1988.

The Canadian Acid Rain Control Program
In 1985 Canada began a program to substantially reduce it's acid rain emissions.

Its goal is to reduce acid deposition to less than 20 kg per hectare per year. This is a level that most lakes and rivers can tolerate without damage.

To reach this target, Canada will reduce sulphur dioxide emissions from sources east of the Saskatchewan-Manitoba border to 2.3 million tonnes by 1994. This is a 50% reduction from 1980 levels.

This program is expected to cost $500 million annually.

The federal government has also cut allowable motor vehicle nitrogen oxide emissions by 60% for cars and light trucks and 50% for heavy trucks.

Canada has also made direct approaches to the president of the U.S. and members of Congress to obtain a 50% reduction in the flow of acid rain-causing emissions from the U.S. into Canada. So far, Canada has been unsuccessful in its attempts to obtain concessions from the U.S.

Canadian Normal Temperatures, Highs, Lows, Precipitation

Source: Environment Canada

These normals are based on varying periods of record over the thirty-year period 1951 to 1980 inclusive. Extreme temperatures are based on varying periods of record for each station through 1986. Airport station unless * designates city office station. Celsius thermometer registration.

Province	Station	Temperature						Precipitation normal annual (millimetres)
		Normal				Extreme		
		January		July				
		Max.	Min.	Max.	Min.	Highest	Lowest	
Alberta	Calgary	−6	−18	23	9	36	−45	424
Alberta	Edmonton (Industrial Airport)	−11	−19	23	12	34	−48	466
British Columbia	Prince George	−8	−17	22	18	34	−50	628
British Columbia	Victoria	6	0	22	11	36	−16	873
British Columbia	Vancouver	5	0	22	13	33	−18	1 113
Manitoba	Churchill	−24	−31	17	7	34	−45	402
Manitoba	Winnipeg	−14	−24	26	13	41	−45	526
Newfoundland	Gander	−2	−10	22	11	36	−31	1 130
Newfoundland	St. John's	−1	−7	20	11	31	−24	1 514
New Brunswick	Fredericton	−4	−15	26	13	37	−37	1 109
New Brunswick	Moncton	−3	−13	24	13	37	−31	1 174
New Brunswick	Saint John	−3	−13	22	12	35	−37	1 444
Nova Scotia	Halifax	−2	−10	23	13	35	−26	1 491
Nova Scotia	Sydney	−1	−9	23	12	35	−27	1 400
Ontario	Ottawa	−6	−15	26	15	38	−36	879
Ontario	Sudbury	−9	−19	24	13	38	−38	861
Ontario	Toronto*	−1	−8	27	17	41	−33	801
Ontario	Windsor	−1	−9	28	17	38	−26	849
Prince Edward Island	Charlottetown	−3	−11	23	14	34	−28	1 169
Quebec	Montreal	−6	−15	26	16	38	−38	946
Quebec	Quebec	−8	−17	25	13	36	−36	1 174
Quebec	Val-d'Or	−11	−23	23	11	36	−44	920
Saskatchewan	Prince Albert	−16	−27	24	11	38	−50	398
Saskatchewan	Regina	−13	−23	26	12	43	−50	384
Northwest Territories	Alert*	−28	−36	6	1	20	−50	154
Northwest Territories	Yellowknife	−25	−33	21	12	32	−51	267
Yukon	Dawson*	−27	−34	22	9	35	−58	306
Yukon	Whitehorse	−16	−25	20	8	34	−52	261

Weather Data for Canadian Cities, 1987

Source: Environment Canada

Station	Temperature		Precipitation						Fastest wind (km/h)
	High	Low	Total (mm)[1]	Greatest in 24 hrs.	No. of days	Total snowfall (cm)	Greatest in 24 hrs. (cm)	No. of days	
Calgary, Alta.	31.8 (June 14)	−23.7 (Dec. 6)	35.1	23.0 (Aug. 4)	87	66.6	12.4 (Apr. 18)	33	98 (Jan. 11)
Charlottetown, P.E.I.	32.1 (Aug. 18)	−22.7 (Feb. 15)	1 187.5	65.4 (Sept. 9)	169	417.8	30.0 (Feb. 1)	71	93 (Jan. 23/Feb. 1)
Churchill, Man.	30.2 (July 31)	−37.9 (Jan. 24)	431.1	24.2 (May 13)	159	247.6	18.8 (Feb. 21)	108	89 (Apr. 28)
Edmonton, Alta.	31.7 (July 27)	−19.1 (Dec. 30)	455.5	52.0 (July 31)	96	135.7	10.2 (May 19)	31	85 (July 31)
Fredericton, N.B.	33.3 (Aug. 17)	−31.2 (Jan. 28)	979.8	51.2 (Sept. 9)	145	372.2	37.7 (Jan. 11)	56	89 (Oct. 25)
Halifax, N.S.	28.5 (Aug. 15)	−18.0 (Feb. 11)	1 238.8	41.0 (Mar. 21)	158	245.6	28.4 (Jan. 26)	62	102 (Jan. 23)
Hamilton, Ont.	33.5 (June 19)	−23.5 (Feb. 15)	947.8	n.a.	155	166.6	n.a.	55	91 (Dec. 9)
Iqaluit, N.W.T.[1]	18.3 (July 17)	−44.3 (Feb. 9)	428.7	21.2 (July 25)	155	249.0	12.4 (Apr. 13)	97	83 (Apr. 14)
Moncton, N.B.	33.5 (Aug. 18)	−27.0 (Jan. 28)	1 205.3	54.7 (Sept. 9)	156	537.5	45.8 (Jan. 11-12)	61	104 (Jan. 23)
Montreal, Que.	33.9 (Aug. 17)	−30.6 (Feb. 14)	901.1	61.6 (June 8)	136	201.5	21.8 (Feb. 8)	43	87 (July 24)
Ottawa, Ont.	34.3 (July 12)	−27.4 (Jan. 24)	913.5	59.0 (July 24)	153	207.0	30.2 (May 25–26)	59	78 (Apr. 27/June 8)
Quebec, Que.	33.1 (July 13)	−27.5 (Jan. 7)	n.a.	73.2 (June 27)	n.a.	n.a.	18.0 (Dec. 20)	n.a.	n.a.
Regina, Sask.	37.2 (June 15)	−27.5 (Dec. 31)	341.9	44.0 (May 27)	108	72.8	10.0 (Mar. 14)	46	98 (May 12)
Saint John, N.B.	28.1 (July 25)	−26.9 (Mar. 4)	1 177.8	54.2 (Sept. 14)	149	400.8	31.0 (Jan. 31)	59	100 (Jan. 23)
St. John's, Nfld.	28.6 (July 15)	−18.7 (Mar. 11)	1 364.1	46.8 (Mar. 16)	226	427.9	45.8 (Feb. 14–15)	90	113 (Dec. 30)
Saskatoon, Sask.	38.7 (June 15)	−26.5 (Dec. 30)	228.9	14.8 (July 19)	93	61.0	9.4 (Feb. 14)	40	78 (June 1/June 23)
Sault Ste. Marie, Ont.	31.7 (Aug. 3)	−30.0 (Feb. 28)	910.0	40.4 (Sept. 19)	160	253.3	30.2 (Dec. 2)	62	109 (July 11)
Thunder Bay, Ont.	33.2 (June 18)	−33.7 (Jan. 23)	555.8	48.2 (Aug. 11-12)	119	92.9	17.0 (Jan. 19–20)	44	80 (Feb. 7/July 29)
Toronto, Ont.	34.2 (June 14)	−20.9 (Feb. 15)	764.0	29.4 (Nov. 25)	137	125.6	21.8 (Jan. 19)	36	111 (July 24)
Vancouver, B.C.	28.9 (June 30)	−4.4 (Jan. 8)	937.5	43.8 (Dec. 9)	141	8.0	2.6 (Dec. 20)	5	78 (Nov. 30)
Victoria, B.C.	30.3 (Sept. 1)	−3.5 (Jan. 8)	656.7	70.4 (Dec. 9)	119	6.2	5.2 (Feb. 28)	2	74 (Nov. 30/Dec. 1)
Waterloo, Ont	32.6 (June 14)	−26.7 (Feb. 15)	946.1	65.4 (Aug. 2)	155	135.4	14.6 (Jan. 19)	46	82 (June 1)
Whitehorse, Yukon	27.4 (July 21)	−38.0 (Mar. 3)	170.4	15.2 (July 19)	109	106.0	8.6 (Feb. 10)	58	91 (Mar. 30)
Windsor, Ont.	34.5 (July 20)	−19.4 (Jan. 25)	1 063.3	55.5 (Aug. 26–27)	148	145.8	18.0 (Dec. 28)	38	109 (Aug. 2)
Winnipeg, Man.	35.0 (June 15)	−35.4 (Jan. 23)	458.5	57.3 (Aug. 14)	111	87.4	13.0 (Feb. 25)	42	96 (Oct. 1)
Yellowknife, N.W.T.	27.5 (July 30)	−36.3 (Jan. 13)	295.3	15.4 (June 23/Sept. 30)	129	196.7	11.8 (Nov. 14)	91	89 (June 13)

(1) Name changed from Frobisher Bay.
n.a. not available.

Canadian Normal Temperatures and Precipitation

Source: Environment Canada

Normal refers to the mean daily temperature and total monthly precipitation based on varying periods of record over the thirty-year period 1951 to 1980 inclusive. Airport station unless * designates city office station. T, Temperature in Celsius; P, precipitation in millimetres.

Station	Jan. T	Jan. P	Feb. T	Feb. P	Mar. T	Mar. P	Apr. T	Apr. P	May T	May P	June T	June P	July T	July P	Aug. T	Aug. P	Sept. T	Sept. P	Oct. T	Oct. P	Nov. T	Nov. P	Dec. T	Dec. P
Calgary, Alta.	-12	16	-7	16	-4	16	3	33	9	49	14	89	16	65	15	55	11	38	6	18	-3	13	-8	16
Charlottetown, P.E.I.	-7	117	-8	97	-3	95	2	82	9	84	15	80	18	84	18	88	14	86	8	106	3	121	-4	129
Churchill, Man.	-28	15	-26	13	-20	18	-11	23	-2	32	6	44	12	46	11	58	5	51	-2	43	-12	39	-22	21
Dawson, Yukon*	-31	17	-24	16	-15	10	-2	10	8	21	14	39	16	47	13	44	7	28	-4	29	-17	22	-26	25
Edmonton, Alta.	-15	25	-10	19	-5	19	4	22	11	43	15	77	17	89	16	78	11	39	6	17	-4	16	-10	25
Fredericton N.B.	-9	103	-8	90	-2	85	4	80	11	83	16	85	19	89	18	87	13	87	8	97	1	106	-7	118
Frobisher Bay, N.W.T.	-26	26	-26	23	-23	23	-14	26	-3	25	3	39	8	63	7	59	2	46	-5	44	-13	34	-22	22
Halifax, N.S.	-6	153	-6	134	-2	128	3	115	9	106	15	90	18	94	18	111	14	94	9	134	3	153	-3	180
Hamilton, Ont.	-6	63	-6	53	-1	71	6	79	13	66	18	65	21	71	20	75	16	74	9	61	3	68	-3	78
Kitchener, Ont.*	-7	60	-6	57	-1	72	6	75	13	77	18	86	21	84	20	89	16	72	10	69	3	80	-4	76
London, Ont.	-7	75	-6	61	-1	75	6	81	12	67	18	74	20	72	20	80	15	79	9	73	3	85	-4	88
Moncton, N.B.	-8	125	-8	99	-3	112	3	90	9	84	15	90	19	95	18	79	13	76	8	99	2	110	-5	121
Montreal, Que.	-10	72	-9	65	-3	74	6	74	13	66	18	82	21	90	20	92	15	88	9	76	2	81	-7	87
Ottawa, Ont.	-11	61	-10	60	-3	68	6	69	13	68	18	73	21	86	19	88	14	79	8	68	1	78	-9	80
Quebec, Que.	-12	90	-11	78	-5	82	3	73	11	87	16	110	19	117	18	117	13	119	7	61	0	97	-9	114
Regina, Sask.	-18	17	-14	16	-8	18	3	24	11	44	16	80	19	53	18	45	12	37	5	19	-5	14	-13	17
Saint John, N.B.	-8	149	-8	116	-3	114	3	107	9	108	14	94	17	103	17	102	13	112	8	128	2	146	-5	166
St. John's, Nfld.	-4	156	-5	140	-2	132	1	116	5	102	11	86	16	75	15	122	12	117	7	146	3	163	-2	161
Saskatoon, Sask.	-19	18	-15	16	-9	18	3	21	11	40	16	59	19	54	17	38	11	32	5	17	-6	15	-14	20
Sault Ste. Marie, Ont.	-10	74	-10	68	-5	60	3	64	9	84	15	74	17	56	17	83	13	95	8	74	1	86	-7	80
Toronto, Ont.*	-5	61	-4	52	1	70	8	73	14	66	19	64	22	74	21	73	17	66	11	61	5	68	-2	73
Vancouver, B.C.	3	154	5	115	6	101	9	60	12	52	15	45	17	32	17	41	14	67	10	114	6	150	4	182
Victoria, B.C.	3	154	5	99	6	72	8	39	12	29	14	29	16	18	16	27	14	40	10	78	6	131	4	157
Whitehorse, Yukon	-21	18	-13	13	-8	14	0	10	7	13	12	31	14	34	13	38	8	30	1	22	-9	20	-17	20
Windsor, Ont.	-5	55	-4	50	1	72	8	83	14	70	20	89	22	83	21	84	17	67	11	57	4	65	-2	73
Winnipeg, Man.	-19	21	-16	18	-8	23	3	39	11	66	17	80	20	76	18	75	12	53	6	31	-5	25	-14	19
Yellowknife, N.W.T.	-29	13	-25	11	-19	12	-7	10	5	17	13	17	16	34	14	44	7	31	-2	35	-14	25	-24	18

Provincial Temperature Records

Source: Environment Canada

	Warmest				Coldest		
	°C	Date	Weather station		°C	Date	Weather station
British Columbia	44.4	July 16, 1941	Lillooet		-58.9	Jan. 31, 1947	Smith River
Alberta	43.3	July 21, 1931	Bassano Dam		-61.1	Jan. 11, 1911	Fort Vermilion
Saskatchewan	45.0	July 5, 1937	Midale		-56.7	Feb. 1, 1893	Prince Albert
Manitoba	44.4	July 11, 1936	St. Albans		-52.8	Jan. 9, 1899	Norway House
Ontario	42.2	July 20, 1919	Biscotasing		-58.3	Jan. 23, 1935	Iroquois Falls
Quebec	40.0	July 6, 1921	Ville Marie		-54.4	Feb. 5, 1923	Doucet
Nova Scotia	38.3	Aug. 19, 1935	Collegeville		-41.1	Jan. 31, 1920	Upper Stewiacke
New Brunswick	39.4	Aug. 18, 1935	Nepisiguit Falls		-47.2	Feb. 2, 1955	Sisson Dam
Prince Edward Is.	36.7	Aug. 19, 1935	Charlottetown		-37.2	Jan. 26, 1884	Kilmahumaig
Newfoundland	41.7	Aug. 11, 1914	Northwest River		-51.1	Feb. 17, 1973	Esker
Northwest Terr.	39.4	July 18, 1941	Fort Smith		-57.2	Dec. 26, 1917	Fort Smith
Yukon	36.1	June 14, 1969	Mayo		-63.0	Feb. 3, 1947	Snag

Speed of Winds in Canada

Source: Environment Canada

Kilometres-per-hour average is for the period of record 1951 to 1980. High is for gust wind speed based on varying periods of record, depending on the origin of the station, through 1987.

Station	Avg.	High	Station	Avg.	High	Station	Avg.	High
Calgary, Alta.	16.2	127	London, Ont.	16.0	128	Sault Ste. Marie, Ont.	15.1	119
Charlottetown, P.E.I.	19.3	177	Moncton, N.B.	18.1	161	Thunder Bay, Ont.	13.4	122
Churchill, Man.	22.7	151	Montreal, Que.	15.6	161	Toronto, Ont.	18.0	126
Dawson, Yukon	3.7	59	Ottawa, Ont.	14.6	135	Vancouver, B.C.	12.0	129
Edmonton, Alta.	14.1	117	Quebec, Que.	16.0	177	Victoria, B.C.	11.1	109
Fredericton, N.B.	13.8	132	Regina, Sask.	20.8	153	Whitehorse, Yukon	14.1	106
Frobisher Bay, N.W.T.	16.7	156	Saint John, N.B.	18.5	146	Windsor, Ont.	17.0	148
Halifax, N.S.	18.2	132	St. John's, Nfld.	24.3	193	Winnipeg, Man.	18.6	129
Hamilton, Ont.	17.7	133	Saskatoon, Sask.	17.5	151	Yellowknife, N.W.T.	15.5	105

Wind Chill Factor

Source: Environment Canada

(watts per square metre)

This graph shows the combined chilling effect of low temperature and wind, and represents the real rate at which an object cools. Watts per square metre has replaced the use of an equivalent temperature as being a more accurate indicator of the wind chill factor.

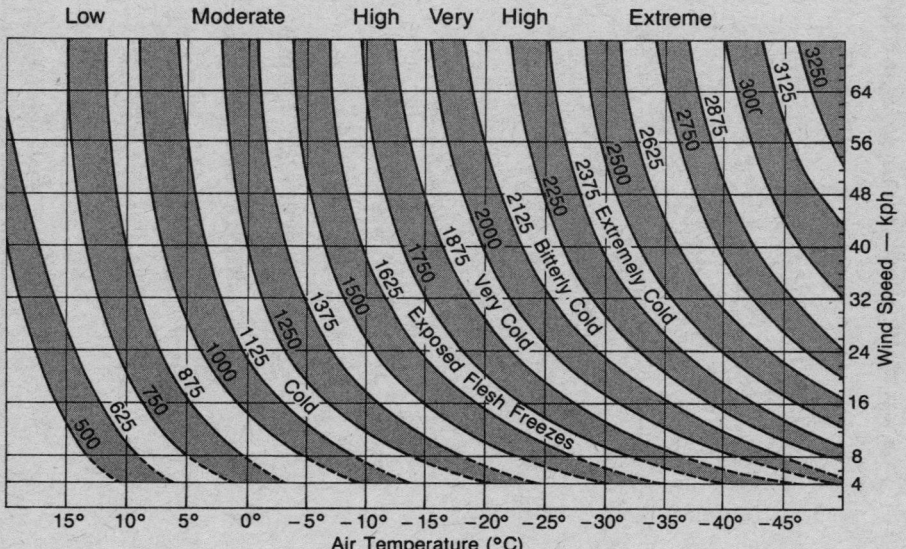

To determine the **wind chill factor** follow the temperature across and the wind speed up until the two lines intersect. For example, at −10°C with a wind speed of 32 km/h the point of intersection lies between 1500 and 1625, or approximately 1570.

Examples of Wind Chill Factor

Wind Chill Factor	Comments
700	Conditions considered comfortable when dressed for outdoor winter activities.
1200	Conditions no longer pleasant for outdoor activities on overcast days.
1400	Conditions no longer pleasant for outdoor activities on sunny days.
1600	Freezing of exposed skin begins for most people depending on the degree of activity and the amount of sunshine.
2300	Conditions for outdoor travel such as walking become dangerous. Exposed areas of the face freeze in less than 1 minute for the average person.
2700	Exposed flesh will freeze within half a minute for the average person.

Cold Wave or Wind Chill Warning[1]

Issued in	When wind chill factor measures	Issued in	When wind chill factor measures
Newfoundland	2 100	Ontario	1 625
Maritimes	2 000	Manitoba	1 600
Quebec	2 000 for 12 hours or more	Saskatchewan	1 600
	2 375 for 6 hours or more	Yukon	2 500

(1) Issued by Atmospheric Environment Service. No specific warning issued in Alberta, Pacific or Arctic regions.

Humidex

Source: Environment Canada

This humidity index shows what the actual temperature combined with the relative humidity feels like in degrees celsius. For instance, when the temperature is 26° and the humidity is 80%, the temperature feels like 35°C. At 46° and over on the Humidex many types of labor must be restricted and virtually everyone will feel discomfort.

Relative Humidity (%)

Temp (°C)	100	95	90	85	80	75	70	65	60	55	50	45	40	35	30	25
43													56°	54°	51°	49°
42												56°	54°	52°	50°	48°
41											56°	54°	52°	50°	48°	46°
40										57°	54°	52°	51°	49°	47°	44°
39									56°	54°	53°	51°	49°	47°	45°	43°
38							57°	56°	54°	52°	51°	49°	47°	46°	43°	42°
37					58°	57°	55°	53°	51°	50°	49°	47°	45°	43°	42°	40°
36			58°	57°	56°	54°	53°	51°	50°	48°	47°	45°	43°	42°	40°	38°
35		58°	57°	56°	54°	52°	51°	49°	48°	47°	45°	43°	42°	41°	38°	37°
34	58°	57°	55°	53°	52°	51°	49°	48°	47°	45°	43°	42°	41°	39°	37°	36°
33	55°	54°	52°	51°	50°	48°	47°	46°	44°	43°	42°	40°	38°	37°	36°	34°
32	52°	51°	50°	49°	47°	46°	45°	43°	42°	41°	39°	38°	37°	36°	34°	33°
31	50°	49°	48°	46°	45°	44°	43°	41°	40°	39°	38°	36°	35°	34°	33°	31°
30	48°	47°	46°	44°	43°	42°	41°	40°	38°	37°	36°	36°	34°	33°	31°	31°
29	46°	45°	44°	43°	42°	41°	39°	38°	37°	36°	34°	33°	32°	31°	30°	
28	43°	42°	41°	41°	39°	38°	37°	36°	35°	34°	33°	32°	31°	29°	28°	
27	41°	40°	39°	38°	37°	36°	35°	34°	33°	32°	31°	30°	29°	28°	28°	
26	39°	38°	37°	36°	35°	34°	33°	32°	31°	31°	29°	28°	28°	27°		
25	37°	36°	35°	34°	33°	32°	31°	30°	29°	28°	27°	27°	26°			
24	35°	34°	33°	33°	32°	31°	30°	29°	28°	28°	27°	26°	26°	25°		
23	33°	32°	32°	31°	30°	29°	28°	27°	27°	26°	25°	24°	23°			
22	31°	29°	29°	28°	28°	27°	26°	26°	24°	24°	23°	23°				
21	29°	29°	28°	27°	27°	26°	26°	24°	24°	24°	23°	23°	23°	22°		

Weather Terms

Public Weather Forecasts and Outlooks

Weather forecasts are issued at 05:30, 11:30, 16:30 and 21:00 h daily by Environment Canada on a regional basis. Forecasts, which describe expected weather conditions until midnight of the next day, are updated throughout the day as required. **Outlooks**, which are not as detailed as forecasts, are issued 3 to 5 days in advance and are updated each afternoon. **Weather warnings** are issued whenever weather conditions are expected to endanger the public welfare. **Severe weather watch** bulletins provide an alert to the *potential* for severe summer storms, such as thunderstorms or tornadoes. **Severe weather warning** bulletins provide an alert to an *impending* weather event.

Marine Weather Forecasts

Public weather forecasts are not intended to be used for marine purposes. Marine forecasts are issued by Environment Canada 4 times daily to those using the coastal waters of B.C., the Maritime provinces, Newfoundland and Labrador.

Mountain Weather Forecasts

When B.C. is on Standard Time, special weather forecasts are issued for mountain areas.

Weatheradio Canada

Environment Canada broadcasts weather information continu-ously on one of 3 VHF/FM frequencies: 162:40, 162:475 or 162:55 megahertz.

Weather Terms

Precipitation—"showers", "snowflurries", "thundershow-ers" and "thunderstorms" are used only when precipitation is expected to last usually less than half an hour and to occur in some, but not all, localities. If the precipitation is expected to be general throughout the forecast period the terms "rain"or "snow" will normally be used.

Sky condition—"sunny", "clear" or "a few clouds" will be used to describe skies less than half covered by clouds; "cloudy" will be used if the sky is more than half covered by clouds and "overcast" describes a totally cloudy sky.

Winds—if not mentioned, are expected to be below 30 km/h.

Probability of precipitation—describes the chance of experi-encing precipitation during a specific time period. "Chance of/ risk of precipitation, rain, hail, fog, frost, etc.)" indicates there is less than a 50% chance of occurrence.

Temperature trend—will be given only when a marked or unseasonable change in temperature is expected.

Canada's National Parks

Park	Location	Size (sq.km)	Year est.	1987 Visitors	Description
Auyuittuq	north shore of Baffin Is., N.W.T.	21 471	1972	467	Located on the Arctic Circle; an isolated and very rugged wilderness area with mountains, fjords, tundra and permafrost.
Banff	Banff, Alta.	6 641	1885	3 329 230	Canada's oldest national park is noted for its ice-capped peaks, glaciers, hot springs, wildlife and skiing.
Bruce Peninsula	299 km northwest of Toronto, between Lake Huron and Georgian Bay	138	1987	n.a.	Niagara Escarpment, limestone cliffs on Georgian Bay. Includes Fathom Five National Marine Park which has 19 islands, more than 20 shipwrecks, clear water and distinctive underwater geological features.
Cape Breton Highlands	across northern Cape Breton Is., N.S.	951	1936	914 595	The scenic Cabot Trail is characterized by a rugged shoreline with plunging cliffs.
Elk Island	45 km east of Edmonton, Alta.	194	1913	363 335	A large population of plains and wood bison, elk and moose inhabit the rolling woodlands and lakes.
Forillon	northeast tip of Gaspé Peninsula, Que.	240	1970	735 752	A rich variety of bird and animal life, limestone cliffs, and the highest mountains in the inhabited eastern Canadian region.
Fundy	southeastern shore on the Bay of Fundy, N.B.	207	1948	776 886	The giant tides of the Bay of Fundy, among the highest in the world, and a bold, irregular coastline.
Georgian Bay Islands	160 km northwest of Toronto, Ont.	24	1929	135 333	Endangered species, limestone cliffs, caves and archaeological sites are preserved on 77 islands.
Glacier	45 km east of Revelstoke, B.C.	1 349	1886	1 306 826	Glaciers, snowy peaks, avalanche slopes, turbulent rivers and grizzly bears are the main features.
Pukaskwa	northeastern shore of Lake Superior	1 878	1978	9 926	Impressive shoreline with 60 km of coastal hiking and white water canoe routes.
Grasslands	100 km south of Swift Current, Sask.	260	1981	n.a.	The unique natural habitat of short-grass prairie is preserved. Colonies of blacktailed prairie dogs, pronghorn antelope and the prairie falcon are found.
Gros Morne	west coast of Nfld.	1 813	1973	261 874	Offers Nfld's 2d highest mountain—Gros Morne, spectacular fjords, and the Long Range Mountains.
Jasper	340 km west of Edmonton, Alta.	10 878	1907	1 933 475	Contains the largest and most accessible icefield in the Canadian Rockies—Columbia Icefield—and preserves the headwaters of many major rivers, particularly the Athabasca.
Kejimkujik	central southwestern N.S.	382	1967	217 245	Gently rolling country with many lakes and rivers—provides good canoeing and camping.
Kluane	southwest corner of Yukon	22 015	1972	87 194	Features Mount Logan, Canada's highest peak, grizzly bears, dall sheep and whitewater rivers.
Kootenay	1 km east of Radium Hot Springs, B.C.	1 406	1920	2 166 528	Hot springs, alpine lakes, canyons, glaciers and 2 river valleys, inhabited by big horn sheep and mountain goats.

Park	Location	Size (sq.km)	Year est.	1987 Visitors	Description
Kouchibouguac	eastern N.B.	244	1969	537 265	Excellent swimming and sunbathing along the many beaches and sand dunes; cycling and hiking trails; windsurfing.
La Mauricie	55 km north of Trois-Rivières, Que.	549	1970	266 190	Hilly terrain at the edge of the Canadian shield provides a view of transitional forest vegetation, from northern evergreens to St. Lawrence deciduous.
Mingan Archipelago Reserve	north of Anticosti Is. along the shore of St. Lawrence, Que.	97	1984	19 803	Interesting rock formations, plant species, nesting seabirds and whales, seals and porpoises.
Mount Revelstoke	Revelstoke, B.C.	263	1914	1 316 408	Dense rain forests, colorful alpine vegetation, lakes, and deep snow country.
Nahanni	southwestern N.W.T.	4 766	1972	810	Accessible only by air; site of Virginia Falls, twice the height of Niagara Falls, whirlpools, hot springs, canyons and rapids.
Northern Yukon	northern tip of Yukon	6 050	1984	n.a.	Important migration route for the Porcupine herd of caribou; a major North American waterfowl area; home to the grizzly, the black bear and the polar bear.
Pacific Rim	west coast of Vancouver Island	389	1970	511 206	Divided in 3 sections—Long Beach, the Broken Group Islands and the West Coast Trail; offers rain forest, beaches and scenic, rugged hiking.
Point Pelee	southernmost point of Ont.	16	1918	529 822	Extensive marshlands and beaches provide refuge for many migratory birds and butterfiles.
Prince Albert	200 km north of Saskatoon, Sask.	3 875	1927	210 381	This mixture of forest land and lakes is home to woodland caribou, bison and a pelican nesting colony.
Prince Edward Island	north shore of P.E.I.	32	1937	1 521 691	Beautiful salt water beaches, sweeping sand dunes, high coastal cliffs, marshes, ponds and woodlands
Riding Mountain	270 km northwest of Winnipeg, Man.	2 978	1933	921 908	Wildlife—wolf, elk, moose, black bear and beaver— abound.
St. Lawrence Islands	on the Thousand Island Parkway, Ont.	3	1904	194 558	Thousand Islands landscape and the St. Lawrence River.
South Moresby	southern part of Queen Charlotte Islands, B.C.	1 470	1988	n.a.	Called Canada's "Galapagos", home to 39 unique plants and animals, features rugged coastline, rain forests. Heartland of Haida Indian culture.
Terra Nova	east coast of Nfld. on Bonavista Bay	400	1957	434 128	Rolling forested hills, spongy bogs and inland ponds are bordered by a rugged coastline.
Waterton Lakes	southwest corner of Alta.	526	1895	602 045	Provides a spectacular transition from prairie grasslands to Rocky Mountains, giving rise to a rich variety of wildlife.
Wood Buffalo	straddles the Alta.-N.W.T. border	44 807	1922	3 398	Second largest national park in the world is home to the largest free-roaming herd of bison, the only naturally nesting whooping cranes, peregrine falcons and red-sided garter snakes.
Yoho	25 km east of Golden, B.C.	1 313	1886	1 354 954	Contains several of the highest peaks in the Rocky Mountains, icefields, waterfalls and a varied plant and animal life.

n.a. not available.

Provincial Parks

Source: Canadian World Almanac Questionnaire

(area in sq. km)

	Number of parks	Total area	Developed area	Camping Number	Fee[2]
Newfoundland[1]	85	1 497	n.a.	42	$6–$9
Prince Edward Island	32	15	12	14	$8.25–11.50
Nova Scotia	115	124	75	21	$7
New Brunswick	105	252	n.a.	28	$6.50–10.50
Quebec	16	4 000	3 000	11	$7.50–13.50
Ontario	217	56 274	42 343	96	$9.25–$12
Manitoba	164	14 254	n.a.	105	$7–$14
Saskatchewan	31	9 080	30	21	$8–$12
Alberta	61	1 258	n.a.	52	$7–$11
British Columbia	388	53 616	n.a.	136	$6–$12

(1) Includes Labrador. (2) Per night.
n.a. not available.

A Collection of Animal Collectives

The English language boasts an abundance of names to describe groups of things, particularly pairs or aggregations of animals. Some of these words have fallen into comparative disuse, but many of them are still in service, helping to enrich the vocabularies of those who like their language to be precise, who tire of hearing a group referred to as "a bunch of," or who enjoy the sound of words that aren't overworked.

band of gorillas	**crash** of rhinoceri	**knot** of toads	**shoal** of fish, pilchards
bed of clams, oysters	**cry** of hounds	**leap** of leopards	**skein** of geese
bevy of quail, swans	**down** of hares	**leash** of greyhounds, foxes	**skulk** of foxes
brace of ducks	**drift** of swine	**litter** of pigs	**sloth** of bears
brood of chicks	**drove** of cattle, sheep	**mob** of kangaroos	**sounder** of swine
cast of hawks	**exaltation** of larks	**murder** of crows	**span** of mules
cete of badgers	**flight** of birds	**muster** of peacocks	**spring** of teals
charm of goldfinches	**flock** of sheep, geese	**mute** of hounds	**swarm** of bees
chattering of choughs	**gaggle** of geese	**nest** of vipers	**team** of ducks, horses
cloud of gnats	**gam** of whales	**nest, nide** of pheasants	**tribe** or **trip** of goats
clowder of cats	**gang** of elks	**pack** of hounds, wolves	**troop** of kangaroos,
clutch of chicks	**grist** of bees	**pair** of horses	monkeys
clutter of cats	**herd** of elephants	**pod** of whales, seals	**volery** of birds
colony of ants	**horde** of gnats	**pride** of lions	**watch** of nightingales
congregation of plovers	**husk** of hares	**school** of fish	**wing** of plovers
covey of quail, partridge	**kindle** or **kendle** of kittens	**sedge** or **siege** of herons	**yoke** of oxen

Some Endangered Species in the World

Source: U.S. Fish and Wildlife Service, U.S. Interior Department; as of mid-May, 1988

Common name	Scientific name	Historic range
Mammals		
Asian wild ass	Equus hemianus	Southwestern & Central Asia
Bobcat	Felis rufus escuinapae	Central Mexico
Cheetah	Acinonyx jubatus	Africa to India
Asian elephant..................	Elephas maximas.	S. Central & E. Africa
Bactrian camel..................	Camelus bactrianus	Mongolia, China
Gorilla	Gorilla gorilla	Central & W. Africa
Leopard	Panthera pardus	Africa, Asia
Asiatic lion	Panthera leo persica	Turkey to India
Howler monkey..................	Alouatta pigra	Mexico to S. America
Giant panda	Ailuropoda melanoleuca.	China
Black rhinoceros.................	Diceros bicornis	Sub-Saharan Africa
Tiger	Panthera tigris	Asia
Gray whale	Eschrichtius robustus	N. Pacific Ocean
Wild yak	Bos grunniens	China (Tibet), India
Mountain zebra	Equus zebra zebra	South Africa

Birds

Hooded crane	Grus monacha	Japan, USSR
Indigo macaw	Anodorhynchus leari.	Brazil
West African ostrich	Struthio camelus spatzi	Spanish Sahara
Golden parakeet	Aratinga guarouba	Brazil
Australian parrot	Geopsittacus occidentalis	Australia

Endangered Species in Canada[1]

Source: Committee on the Status of Endangered Wildlife in Canada

An endangered species is any native species of plant or animal whose existence in Canada is threatened with imminent extinction due to the action of humans.

Species	Critical habitat	Comments	Reasons why endangered
		Birds	
Eskimo Curlew	for breeding: tundra and lichen woodland	nearly disappeared between 1880 and 1895	human disturbance; hunting; loss of habitat
Greater Prairie Chicken	open, undisturbed native grasslands	virtually no longer existing in the wild	loss of habitat
Kirtland's Warbler	dense jack-pine stands	a long population decline now seems stabilized	loss of habitat; nest parasitism
Mountain Plover	flat, heavily grazed grasslands of southern Alta. and Sask.	small population	loss of habitat; predation; human disturbance
Peregrine Falcon (*anatum*)	for breeding: taiga region; for nesting: cliffs	virtually no longer existing in the wild	human disturbance—egg collecting, taking of young for falconry, hunting; loss of habitat
Piping Plover	along beaches, close to the water	steadily declining numbers throughout its range and continuing threats to habitat	water level manipulation; human disturbance
Spotted Owl	old growth timber in B.C.	very few remain	loss of habitat
Whooping Crane	breeding: generally Wood Buffalo National Park	long-term population has stabilized, leaving a small population	hunting: accidental shooting; loss of habitat
		Fish	
Acadian Whitefish	Tusket and Petit rivers in southern N.S.	less than 500 in Petit R.	were commercially fished; human development, such as hydro dams and fish ladders made capture easier; pollution of habitat (acid rain)
Aurora Trout	small lakes; however, no species left in wild	wild species have disappeared and subspecies maintained entirely in hatcheries	low food availability; effects of acid rain
Salish Sucker	Campbell and Salmon rivers headwaters, B.C.	last seen in Campbell R. 1976; uncommon in the Salmon R.	loss of habitat in headwater areas due to urbanization; human disturbance
		Mammals	
Beluga (White Whale) St. Lawrence River stock	St. Lawrence estuary	long-term declining population	hunting; human disturbance through shipping and commercial fishing; loss of habitat through dredging, port development, dam construction, dumping and resource exploration; pollution and contaminants
Ungava Bay stock	Ungava Bay, northern Quebec	long-term declining population	overhunted
Bowhead Whale	winter; southern edge of pack ice	long-term population decline; only 2 300 remain	animal has been commercially overhunted
Eastern Cougar (Mountain lion)	mixed and coniferous forest	long-term population decline	hunting; human disturbance; loss of food through limited deer population

Right Whale	coasts of N. America, both Atlantic and Pacific, from tropics to sub-arctic	long-term population decline, only 100–200 remain	overhunted
Sea Otter	Pacific Coast	wiped out in Canada by the 1930s, re-introduced to coastal waters of Vancouver Is.; population now stable	overhunted
Vancouver Island Marmot	alpine and subalpine areas, steep slopes, talus debris and open meadows	long-term population decline; total population between 50 and 100 animals	loss of habitat

Reptile

Leatherback Turtle	nesting: beaches	Canadian designation based on international status	predation

Plants

Cucumber Tree	9 sites in southwestern Ont.	only a few seed-bearing trees remain	human disturbance through lumbering and forest clearing
Eastern Mountain Avens	generally in the Maritime provinces	very restricted distribution	threatened by expanding man-induced gull colony; recreational development
Eastern Prickly Pear Cactus	southwestern Ont.	only 4 confirmed locations remain	loss of habitat; human disturbance (collecting)
Furbish's Lousewort (herb)	banks of the upper Saint John R., N.B.	about 600 plants remain	loss of habitat from destruction of riverside areas by farming, forestry, industry, flooding and hydro projects
Gattinger's Agalinis	delta islands of St. Clair river in southwestern Ont.	only small populations at 4 sites remain	loss of habitat through road and building construction and agricultural expansion
Heart-Leaved Plantain	one site remains on the eastern shore of L. Huron; moist depressions in undisturbed deciduous woodland	about 300 plants on Canadian site; reduced population throughout N. American range	loss of habitat and collecting by natives for medicinal purposes
Hoary Mountain Mint	one site in Ont.	remaining number unknown	human disturbance
Large Whorled Pogonia	only 2 known locations in Ont.	population is declining at one site	human disturbance
Pink Coreopsis (herb)	only in the Tusket R. valley, N.S.	range has decreased significantly since the 1930s	human disturbance through increased cottage development and use of off-road vehicles
Pink Milkwort (herb)	2 sites only in Lambton County, Ont.	only about 100 plants remain	loss of habitat from expanded agricultural land use
Slender Bush Clover	one site in Windsor, Ont.	population is located in urban area; less than 200 plants remain	human disturbance; loss of habitat through urban and commercial development
Small White Lady Slipper (orchid)	tall grass prairie, bogs, swampy meadows, remnant prairies, edge of thickets	long-term decline throughout range	loss of habitat through agricultural and urban development
Small Whorled Pogonia (orchid)	one site Elgin County, Ont.	only 2 plants in Ont. as of 1980	human disturbance; loss of habitat
Skinner's Agalinis	delta islands of St. Clair river in southwestern Ont.	only small populations at 2 sites remain	loss of suitable habitat through road and building construction
Southern Maidenhair Fern	Fairmont Hot Springs, B.C.	plant size, number of plants and number of sites decreasing	loss of habitat
Spotted Wintergreen	St. Williams and Wasaga areas in S. Ont.	only 3 genetic clonal populations in existence	no variation in the genetic make-up of existing populations
Water Pennywort	only found at Wilson's Lake and Kejimkujik Lake in southeastern N.S.	Canada is the northern limit of its range	loss of habitat through cottage development and aquatic recreational activities

(1)Status as of Apr. 1988.

Animal Superlatives

Source: *The Kid's World Almanac and Books of Facts*, 2nd edition, Pharos Book, NY

Mammals

Largest	Blue Whale	30 m long, 150 tonnes
Largest land	African Bush Elephant	3.2 m tall, 6 tonnes
Smallest	Kitti's Hog-nosed Bat	1.5 to 3 g
Fastest	Cheetah	112 km/h
Slowest	Three-toed Sloth	2 m/minute
Best jumper	Kangaroo	3.2 m high, 9 m in distance
Longest breathholder	Bottle-nosed Whale	2 hours

Birds

Largest	Ostrich	2.4 m tall, 136 kg
Largest flying	Wandering Albatross	4 m wingspan, 12 kg
Smallest	Bee Hummingbird	5 cm, 3 g
Highest flying	Bar-headed Goose	9 000 m
Fastest flying	Indian Swift	320 km/h
Fastest gliding	Vulture	145 km/h
Deepest diver	Emperor Penguin	270 m

Fish

Largest	Whale Shark	30 m long, 13 tonnes
Largest freshwater	Pirarucu	4.5 m long, 226 kg
Smallest	Dwarf Goby	less than 1.5 cm
Fastest	Sailfish	110 km/h
Slowest	Seahorse	27 cm/minute
Most electric	Electric Eel	400 volts

Reptiles

Largest	Saltwater Crocodile	4.8 m long, 520 kg
Smallest	Gecko	less than 2 cm
Fastest	Leatherback Turtle	35 km/h
Slowest	Tortoise	4.5 m/minute
Largest snake	Anaconda	11.3 m long, 450 kg
Largest poisonous snake	King Cobra	5.5 m
Fastest snake	Black Mamba	11 km/h

Insects

Largest	Atlas Moth	25 cm wingspan
Heaviest	Goliath Beetle	110 g
Fastest	Dragon Fly	58 km/h
Best jumper	Flea	20 cm high, 33 cm in distance

Some Wildlife Species Introduced to Canada

Source: Human Activity and the Environment, Statistics Canada: Reproduced with permission of the Minister of Supply and Services Canada.

Species	Where—When introduced	Origin	Status	Release
Birds				
Rock Dove (Pigeon)	1906	Europe	very common across southern Canada, mainly around human settlements	intentional
Crested Mynah ...	Vancouver, 1897	Orient	established in the Vancouver area	accidental
Gray Partridge	1904-1930, various provinces	Czechoslovakia; Hungary	generally successful, except in N.B.	intentional
Ring-Necked Pheasant	1882-1950s, various provinces and Yukon 1950s, St. John's, Nfld.	Asia	successfully established, except in Yukon	Newfoundland— accidental (from a commercial poultry establishment), remainder—intentional
Mountain Quail ...	Victoria, B.C. 1860, 1870s; Fraser Valley and Vancouver Island 1870-1880s	western U.S.A.	small populations established on Vancouver Is.	intentional
English Skylark ...	near Victoria, B.C. 1903, 1913	Europe	well established	intentional
House Sparrow ...	New York, 1850; then Quebec and Halifax	England	established across Canada by 1890	intentional
Common Starling .	New York, 1890, spread to Canada by 1914	Europe	established across Canada by 1950	intentional

Species	Where–When introduced	Origin	Status	Release
Fish				
Common Carp	Ont. 1880, 1891; Man. 1885-6; B.C. 1970s	Asia and Europe	established, abundant and competes with native species	intentional and accidental
European Flounder .	Lakes Erie and Superior	Europe	unknown	accidentally released from ballast water of European ships
Goldfish	throughout Canada	eastern Asia	surviving, and in some areas, common; hybridization with carp	deliberate illegal introductions and accidental releases
Mosquito fish	Alta. 1924; B.C. 1928; Man. 1958	U.S.A.	established in Alberta; unsuccessful elsewhere	intentional as a mosquito control experiment
Brown Trout	various provinces since 1884	Europe	established, and in some cases have replaced native trout	intentional for sport fishing
Mammals				
Fallow Deer	B.C. 1895	Mediterranean Asia	successful; flourishing on James, Saltspring and Sidney Islands, B.C.	intentional
European Hare ...	Brantford, Ont. 1912; Fort William, Ont. 1940s	Germany	well established in southern Ont., unsuccessful in northern areas	accidental at Brantford when 9 animals escaped from captivity; intentional at Fort William
House Mouse	arrived with first Europeans	Europe; Asia	found in most settled areas of Canada	accidental
Reindeer	Nfld. 1907, (mainland in 1918) Rocky Bay, Que., 1918, later to Anticosti Is., Great Slave Lake area, N.W.T. 1911, Mackenzie R. delta, 1935	Norway, Alaska	unsuccessful on Anticosti Is. and in Great Slave Lake area, Mackenzie delta herd remains strong	intentional
Eastern Fox Squirrel .	Pelee Island, Ont. 1890	Ohio	firmly established and common in areas of suitable habitat	intentional

Gestation, Longevity, and Incubation of Animals

Longevity figures were supplied by Ronald T. Reuther. They refer to animals in captivity; the potential life span of animals is rarely attained in nature. Maximum longevity figures are from the Biology Data Book, 1972. Figures on gestation and incubation are averages based on estimates by leading authorities.

Animal	Gestation (day)	Average longevity (years)	Maximum longevity (yrs., mos.)	Animal	Gestation (day)	Average longevity (years)	Maximum longevity (yrs., mos.)
Ass	365	12	35-10	Leopard	98	12	19-4
Baboon	187	20	35-7	Lion	100	15	25-1
Bear: Black	219	18	36-10	Monkey (rhesus)	164	15	—
Grizzly	225	25	—	Moose	240	12	—
				Mouse (meadow)	21	3	—
Polar	240	20	34-8	Mouse (dom. white)	19	3	3-6
Beaver	122	5	20-6	Opossum (American)	14-17	1	—
Buffalo (American)	278	15	—	Pig (domestic)	112	10	27
Bactrian camel	406	12	29-5	Puma	90	12	19
Cat (domestic)	63	12	28	Rabbit (domestic)	31	5	13
Chimpanzee	231	20	44-6	Rhinoceros (black)	450	15	—
Chipmunk	31	6	8	Rhinoceros (white)	—	20	—
Cow	284	15	30	Sea lion (California)	350	12	28
Deer (white-tailed)	201	8	17-6	Sheep (domestic)	154	12	20
Dog (domestic)	61	12	20	Squirrel (gray)	44	10	—
Elephant (African)	—	35	60	Tiger	105	16	26-3
Elephant (Asian)	645	40	70	Wolf (maned)	63	5	—
Elk	250	15	26-6	Zebra (Grant's)	365	15	—
Fox (red)	52	7	14				
Giraffe	425	10	33-7	**Incubation time (days)**			
Goat (domestic)	151	8	18	Chicken 21			
Gorilla	257	20	39-4	Duck 30			
Guinea pig	68	4	7-6	Goose 30			
Hippopotamus	238	25	—	Pigeon 18			
Horse	330	20	46	Turkey 26			
Kangaroo	42	7	—				

Major Venomous Animals

Snakes

Coral snake - 60 to 120 cm long, in Americas south of Canada; bite is nearly painless; very slow onset of paralysis, difficulty breathing; mortality high without antivenin.

Rattlesnake - 60 to 240 cm long, throughout W. Hemisphere. Rapid onset of symptoms of severe pain, swelling; mortality low, but amputation of affected limb is sometimes necessary; antivenin. Probably higher mortality rate for Mojave rattler.

Cottonmouth water moccasin - up to 150 cm long, wetlands of southern U.S. from Virginia to Texas. Rapid onset of symptoms of severe pain, swelling; mortality low, but tissue destruction can be extensive; antivenin.

Copperhead - less than 120 cm long, from New England to Texas; pain and swelling; very seldom fatal; antivenin seldom needed.

Bushmaster - up to 270 cm long, wet tropical forests of C. and S. America; few bites occur, but mortality rate is high.

Barba Amarilla or **Fer-de-lance** - up to 210 cm long, from tropical Mexico to Brazil; severe tissue damage common; moderate mortality; antivenin.

Asian pit vipers - from 60 to 150 cm long throughout Asia; reactions and mortality vary but most bites cause tissue damage and mortality is generally low.

Sharp-nosed pit viper or **One Hundred Pace Snake** - up to 150 cm long, in southern Vietnam and Taiwan, China; the most toxic of Asian pit vipers; very rapid onset of swelling and tissue damage, internal bleeding; moderate mortality; antivenin.

Boomslang - under 180 cm long, in African savannahs; rapid onset of nausea and dizziness, often followed by slight recovery and then sudden death from internal hemorrhaging; bites rare, mortality high; antivenin.

European vipers - from 30 to 90 cm long; bleeding and tissue damage; mortality low; antivenins.

Puff adder - up to 150 cm long, fat; south of the Sahara and throughout the Middle East; rapid large swelling, great pain, dizziness; moderate mortality often from internal bleeding; antivenin.

Gaboon viper - over 180 cm long, fat; 5 cm fangs; south of the Sahara; massive tissue damage, internal bleeding; few recorded bites.

Saw-scaled or carpet viper - up to 60 cm long, in dry areas from India to Africa; severe bleeding, fever; high mortality, causes more human fatalities than any other snake; antivenin.

Desert horned viper - in dry areas of Africa and western Asia; swelling and tissue damage; low mortality.

Russell's viper or tic-palonga - over 150 cm long, throughout Asia; internal bleeding; moderate mortality rate; bite reports common; antivenin.

Black mamba - up to 420 cm long, fast-moving; S. and C. Africa; rapid onset of dizziness, difficulty breathing, erratic heartbeat; mortality high, nears 100% without antivenin.

Kraits - in S. Asia; rapid onset of sleepiness; numbness; up to 50% mortality even with antivenin treatment.

Common or Asian cobra - 120 to 240 cm long, throughout S. Asia; considerable tissue damage, sometimes paralysis; mortality probably not more than 10%; antivenin.

King cobra - up to 480 cm long, throughout S. Asia; rapid swelling, dizziness, loss of consciousness, difficulty breathing, erratic heart-beat; mortality varies sharply with amount of venom involved; most bites involve non-fatal amounts; antivenin.

Yellow or Cape cobra - 210 cm long, in southern Africa; most toxic venom of any cobra; rapid onset of swelling, breathing and cardiac difficulties; mortality high without treatment; antivenin.

Ringhals, or spitting, cobra - 150 cm to 210 cm long; southern Africa; squirt venom through holes in front of fangs as a defense; venom is severely irritating and can cause blindness.

Australian brown snakes - very slow onset of symptoms of cardiac or respiratory distress; moderate mortality; antivenin.

Tiger snake - 60 to 180 cm long, S. Australia; pain, numbness, mental disturbances with rapid onset of paralysis; may be the most deadly of all land snakes though antivenin is quite effective.

Death adder - has over 90 cm long, Australia; rapid onset of faintness, cardiac and respiratory distress; at least 50% mortality without antivenin.

Taipan - up to 330 cm long, in Australia and New Guinea; rapid paralysis with severe breathing difficulty; mortality nears 100% without antivenin.

Sea snakes - throughout Pacific, Indian oceans except NE Pacific; almost painless bite, variety of muscle pain, paralysis; mortality rate low, many bites are not envenomed; some antivenins.

> *Note:* Not all snake bites by venomous snakes are actually envenomed. Any animal bite, however, carries the danger of tetanus and anyone suffering a venomous snake bite should seek medical attention. Antivenins are not certain cures; they are only an aid in the treatment of bites. Mortality rates above are for envenomed bites; low mortality, up to 2% result in death; moderate, 2-5%; high, 5-15%. Even when the victim recovers fully, prolonged hospitalization and extensive medical procedures are usually required.

Lizards

Gila monster - up to 61 cm long with heavy body and tail, in high desert in southwest U.S. and N. Mexico; immediate severe pain followed by vomiting, thirst, difficulty swallowing, weakness approaching paralysis; no recent mortality.

Mexican beaded lizard - similar to Gila monster, Mexican west-coast; reaction and mortality rate similar to Gila monster.

Insects

Ants, bees, wasps, hornets, etc. Global distribution. Usual reaction is piercing pain in area of sting. Not directly fatal, except in cases of massive multiple stings. Many people suffer allergic reactions - swelling, rashes, partial paralysis –and a few may die within minutes from severe sensitivity to the venom (anaphylactic shock).

Spiders, scorpions

Black widow - small, round-bodied with hour-glass marking; the widow and its relatives are found around the world in tropical and temperate zones; sharp pain, weakness, clammy skin, muscular rigidity, breathing difficulty and, in small children, convulsions; low mortality; antivenin.

Recluse or fiddleback and brown spiders - small, oblong body; throughout U.S.; pain with later ulceration at place of bite; in severe cases fever, nausea, and stomach cramps; ulceration may last months; very low mortality.

Atrax **spiders** - several varieties, often large, in Australia; slow onset of breathing, circulation difficulties; low mortality.

Tarantulas - large, hairy spiders found around the world; American tarantulas, and probably all others, are **harmless**, though their bite may cause some pain and swelling.

Scorpions - crab-like body with stinger in tail, various sizes, many varieties throughout tropical and subtropical areas; various symptoms may include severe pain spreading from the wound, numbness, severe emotional agitation, cramps; severe reactions include vomiting, diarrhea, respiratory failure; low mortality, usually in children; antivenins.

Sea Life

Sea wasps - jellyfish, with tentacles up to 900 cm long, in the S. Pacific; very rapid onset of circulatory problems; high mortality largely because of speed of toxic reaction; antivenin.

Portuguese man-of-war - jellyfish-like, with tentacles up to 21 m long, in most warm water areas; immediate severe pain; not fatal, though shock may cause death in a rare case.

Octopi - global distribution, usually in warm waters; all varieties produce venom but only a few can cause death; rapid onset of paralysis with breathing difficulty.

Stingrays - several varieties of differing sizes, found in tropical and temperate seas and some fresh water; severe pain, rapid onset of nausea, vomiting, breathing difficulties; wound area may ulcerate, gangrene may appear; seldom fatal.

Stonefish - brownish fish which lies motionless as a rock on bottom in shallow water; throughout S. Pacific and Indian oceans; extraordinary pain, rapid paralysis; low mortality.

Cone-shells - molluscs in small, beautiful shells in the S. Pacific and Indian oceans; shoot barbs into victims; paralysis; low mortality.

Canadian Cities

Calgary, Alta.

Year incorporated: 1893. **Population** (1986): 636 104; 50.9% male, 49.1% female. **Area:** 535 sq. km. **Pop. density:** 1 189 per sq. km. **Pop. growth** (annual avg. 1981-1986): 1.5%. **Pop. over 65:** 14 790 males; 21 575 females. **Pop. under 35:** 203 520 males; 188 730 females. **Pop. married:** 48.1%. **Pop. divorced:** 3.4%.

Mother tongue: 83.0% English; 2.2% French; 14.8% other. **Foreign born:** 125 525, 21.2%. **Religious breakdown:** 54.6% Protestant; 25.6% Catholic; 2.8% Eastern non-Christian; 1.2% Eastern Orthodox; 0.9% Jewish.

Avg. income (1981): $20 854 males; $9 812 females; $33 462 families. **Below poverty line:** 10.4% of families; 29.4% of individuals. **Avg. family size:** 3.1. **Single parent families:** 11.1%.

Climate: Avg. temps. −12° (Jan.); 16° (July). **Avg. annual precip.** 300 mm. **Avg. annual snowfall:** 153 cm.

Charlottetown, P.E.I.

Year incorporated: 1855. **Population** (1986): 15 776; 44.2% male, 55.8% female. **Area:** 7 sq. km. **Pop. density:** 2 257 per sq. km. **Pop. growth** (annual avg. 1981-1986): 0.6%. **Pop. over 65:** 1 045 males; 2 035 females. **Pop. under 35:** 3 590 males; 3 890 females. **Pop. married:** 39.9%. **Pop. divorced:** 2.6%.

Mother tongue: 96.0% English; 2.1% French; 1.9% other. **Foreign born:** 745, 4.9%. **Religious breakdown:** 46.5% Protestant; 46.5% Catholic.

Avg. income (1981): $13 393 males; $7 462 females; $23 392 families. **Below poverty line:** 15.9% of families; 43.8% of individuals. **Avg. family size:** 3.1. **Single parent families:** 23.7%.

Climate: Avg. temps. −7° (Jan.); 18° (July). **Avg. annual precip.** 841 mm. **Avg. annual snowfall:** 331 cm.

Edmonton, Alta.

Year incorporated: 1904. **Population** (1986): 573 982; 50.4% male, 49.6% female. **Area:** 670 sq. km. **Pop. density:** 857 per sq. km. **Pop. growth** (annual avg. 1981-1986): 1.6%. **Pop. over 65:** 16 305 males; 22 590 females. **Pop. under 35:** 177 505 males; 166 915 females. **Pop. married:** 47.3%. **Pop. divorced:** 3.3%.

Mother tongue: 75.6% English; 3.2% French; 21.1% other. **Foreign born:** 113 810, 21.4%. **Religious breakdown:** 47.0% Protestant; 31.5% Catholic; 4.0% Eastern Orthodox; 2.8% Eastern non-Christian; 0.8% Jewish.

Avg. income (1981): $19 090 males; $9 657 females; $31 177 families. **Below poverty line:** 11.9% of families; 32.2% of individuals. **Avg. family size:** 3.1. **Single parent families:** 12.9%.

Climate: Avg. temps. −15° (Jan.); 17° (July). **Avg. annual precip.** 353 mm. **Avg. annual snowfall:** 138 cm.

Fredericton, N.B.

Year incorporated: 1848. **Population** (1986): 44 352; 47.7% male, 52.3% female. **Area:** 130 sq. km. **Pop. density:** 342 per sq. km. **Pop. growth** (annual avg. 1981-1986): 0.3%. **Pop. over 65:** 1 765 males; 2 665 females. **Pop. under 35:** 12 510 males; 13 025 females. **Pop. married:** 48.5%. **Pop. divorced:** 2.6%.

Mother tongue: 91.0% English; 6.0% French; 3.0% other. **Foreign born:** 3 015, 6.9%. **Religious breakdown:** 65.5% Protestant; 27.1% Catholic; 0.5% Jewish.

Avg. income (1981): $15 876 males; $8 061 females; $25 032 families. **Below poverty line:** 13.9% of families; 37.1% of individuals. **Avg. family size:** 3.1. **Single parent families:** 14.1%.

Climate: Avg. temps. −9° (Jan.); 19° (July). **Avg. annual precip.** 825 mm. **Avg. annual snowfall:** 290 cm.

Halifax, N.S.

Year incorporated: 1841. **Population** (1986): 113 577; 47.3% male, 52.4% female. **Area:** 80 sq. km. **Pop. density:** 1 424 per sq. km. **Pop. growth** (annual avg. 1981-1986): −0.2%. **Pop. over 65:** 5 180 males; 8 400 females. **Pop. under 35:** 32 480 males; 33 425 females. **Pop. married:** 44.8%. **Pop. divorced:** 3.3%.

Mother tongue: 92.7% English; 3.1% French; 4.2% other. **Foreign born:** 10 730, 9.4%. **Religious breakdown:** 49.2% Protestant; 40.4% Catholic; 1.2% Eastern Orthodox; 1.0% Eastern non-Christian; 0.9% Jewish.

Avg. income (1981): $16 240 males; $8 732 females; $26 671 families. **Below poverty line:** 14.9% of families; 35.2% of individuals. **Avg. family size:** 3.2. **Single parent families:** 15.5%.

Climate: Avg. temps. −6° (Jan.); 18° (July). **Avg. annual precip.** 1 224 mm. **Avg. annual snowfall:** 271 cm.

Hamilton, Ont.

Year incorporated: 1846. **Population** (1986): 306 728; 48.6% male, 51.4% female. **Area:** 123 sq. km. **Pop. density:** 2 500 per sq. km. **Pop. growth** (annual avg. 1981-1986): 0.02%. **Pop. over 65:** 14 685 males; 21 700 females. **Pop. under 35:** 84 690 males; 83 980 females. **Pop. married:** 49.9%. **Pop. divorced:** 2.7%.

Mother tongue: 75.4% English; 1.9% French; 22.8% other. **Foreign born:** 87 735, 28.6%. **Religious breakdown:** 48.5% Protestant; 38.6% Catholic; 2.9% Eastern Orthodox; 1.3% Eastern non-Christian; 0.9% Jewish.

Avg. income (1981): $16 379 males; $7 981 females; $25 202 families. **Below poverty line:** 16.1% of families; 42.7% of individuals. **Avg. family size:** 3.1. **Single parent families:** 13.4%.

Climate: Avg. temps. −6° (Jan.); 21° (July).

Laval, Que.

Year incorporated: 1965. **Population** (1986): 284 164; 50.0% male, 50.0% female. **Area:** 245 sq. km. **Pop. density:** 1 158 per sq. km. **Pop. growth** (annual avg. 1981-1986): 1.2%. **Pop. over 65:** 6 160 males; 9 235 females. **Pop. under 35:** 81 100 males; 78 195 females. **Pop. married:** 50.9%. **Pop. divorced:** 1.9%.

Mother tongue: 10.6% English; 80.8% French; 8.6% other. **Foreign born:** 26 850, 10.0%. **Religious breakdown:** 85.7% Catholic; 4.3% Protestant; 3.7% Jewish; 3.1% Eastern Orthodox.

Avg. income (1981): $17 877 males; $8 810 females; $28 587 families. **Below poverty line:** 12.0% of families; 41.7% of individuals. **Avg. family size:** 3.3. **Single parent families:** 10.6%.

London, Ont.

Year incorporated: 1855. **Population** (1986): 269 140; 48.0% male, 52.0% female. **Area:** 162 sq. km. **Pop. density:** 1 659 per sq. km. **Pop. growth** (annual avg. 1981-1986): 1.2%. **Pop. over 65:** 10 095 males; 15 785 females. **Pop. under 35:** 73 565 males; 75 255 females. **Pop. married:** 50.1%. **Pop. divorced:** 2.5%.

Mother tongue: 86.6% English; 1.2% French; 12.2% other. **Foreign born:** 52 630, 20.7%. **Religious breakdown:** 60.3% Protestant; 26.3% Catholic; 1.7% Eastern Orthodox; 1.3% Eastern non-Christian; 0.8% Jewish.

Avg. income (1981): $17 013 males; $8 814 females; $26 888 families. **Below poverty line:** 12.2% of families; 37.6% of individuals. **Avg. family size:** 3.1. **Single parent families:** 12.5%.

Climate: Avg. temps. −7° (Jan.); 20° (July). **Avg. annual precip.** 726 mm. **Avg. annual snowfall:** 209 cm.

Mississauga, Ont.

Year incorporated: 1974. **Population** (1986): 374 005; 49.9% male, 50.1% female. **Area:** 274 sq. km. **Pop. density:** 1 366 per sq. km. **Pop. growth** (annual avg. 1981-1986): 3.7%. **Pop. over 65:** 6 180 males; 9 200 females. **Pop. under 35:** 98 820 males; 99 640 females. **Pop. married:** 51.6%. **Pop. divorced:** 1.7%.

Mother tongue: 75.4% English; 1.8% French; 22.8% other. **Foreign born:** 108 715, 34.5%. **Religious breakdown:** 45.8% Protestant; 39.6% Catholic; 3.6% Eastern non-Christian; 2.1% Eastern Orthodox; 0.4% Jewish.

Avg. income (1981): $20 624 males; $9 528 females; $32 684 families. **Below poverty line:** 8.4% of families; 25.9% of individuals. **Avg. family size:** 3.3. **Single parent families:** 9.4%.

Moncton, N.B.

Year incorporated: 1973. **Population** (1986): 55 468; 47.0% male, 53.0% female. **Area:** 141 sq. km. **Pop. density:** 393 per sq. km. **Pop. growth** (annual avg. 1981-1986): 0.3%. **Pop. over 65:** 2 510 males; 4 230 females. **Pop. under 35:** 15 210 males; 15 730 females. **Pop. married:** 47.1%. **Pop. divorced:** 2.5%.

Mother tongue: 65.7% English; 32.8% French; 1.5% other. **Foreign born:** 2 500, 4.6%. **Religious breakdown:** 53.4% Catholic; 40.9% Protestant; 0.6% Jewish.

Avg. income (1981): $14 369 males; $7 198 females; $22 061 families. **Below poverty line:** 17.3% of families; 44.6% of individuals. **Avg. family size:** 3.2. **Single parent families:** 15.7%.

Climate: Avg. temps. −8° (Jan.); 19° (July). **Avg. annual precip.** 794 mm. **Avg. annual snowfall:** 341 cm.

Montreal, Que.

Year incorporated: 1832. **Population** (1986): 1 015 420; 47.6% male, 52.4% female. **Area:** 177 sq. km. **Pop. density:** 5 740 per sq. km. **Pop. growth** (annual avg. 1981-1986): 0.7%. **Pop. over 65:** 48 645 males; 80 210 females. **Pop. under 35:** 255 725 males; 250 040 females. **Pop. married:** 45.0%. **Pop. divorced:** 3.4%.

Mother tongue: 15.0% English; 65.6% French; 19.4% other. **Foreign born:** 210 500, 21.5%. **Religious breakdown:** 78.2% Catholic; 7.6% Protestant; 3.8% Eastern Orthodox; 3.7% Jewish; 1.3% Eastern non-Christian.

Avg. income (1981): $14 057 males; $8 774 females; $23 171 families. **Below poverty line:** 22.9% of families; 48.1% of individuals. **Avg. family size:** 3.0. **Single parent families:** 17.8%.

Climate: Avg. temps. −10° (Jan.); 21° (July). **Avg. annual precip.** 723 mm. **Avg. annual snowfall:** 235 cm.

North York, Ont.

Year incorporated: 1979. **Population** (1986): 556 297; 48.4% male, 51.6% female. **Area:** 177 sq. km. **Pop. density:** 3 145 per sq. km. **Pop. growth** (annual avg. 1981-1986): −0.1. **Pop. over 65:** 22 680 males; 31 815 females. **Pop. under 35:** 154 405 males; 155 110 females. **Pop. married:** 50.4%. **Pop. divorced:** 2.2%.

Mother tongue: 65.2% English; 1.5% French; 33.3% other. **Foreign born:** 243 330, 43.5%. **Religious breakdown:** 35.6% Catholic; 35.0% Protestant; 13.7% Jewish; 3.8% Eastern non-Christian; 3.6% Eastern Orthodox.

Avg. income (1981): $19 200 males; $9 859 females; $31 847 families. **Below poverty line:** 12.9% of families; 31.9% of individuals. **Avg. family size:** 3.2. **Single parent families:** 13.0%.

Ottawa, Ont.

Year incorporated: 1854. **Population** (1986): 300 763; 47.0% male, 53.0% female. **Area:** 110 sq. km. **Pop. density:** 2 730 per sq. km. **Pop. growth** (annual avg. 1981-1986): 0.4%. **Pop. over 65:** 13 050 males; 23 770 females. **Pop. under 35:** 79 245 males; 80 260 females. **Pop. married:** 46.9%. **Pop. divorced:** 2.9%.

Mother tongue: 68.6% English; 19.3% French; 2.9% other. **Foreign born:** 55 390, 18.8%. **Religious breakdown:** 48.3% Catholic; 36.4% Protestant; 1.8% Eastern non-Christian; 1.8% Jewish; 1.6% Eastern Orthodox.

Avg. income (1981): $18 925 males; $10 607 females; $31 106 families. **Below poverty line:** 14.0% of families; 32.3% of individuals. **Avg. family size:** 3.0. **Single parent families:** 15.6%.

Climate: Avg. temps. −11° (Jan.); 21° (July). **Avg. annual precip.** 663 mm. **Avg. annual snowfall:** 227 cm.

Quebec, Que.

Year incorporated: 1832. **Population** (1986): 164 580; 46.3% male, 53.7% female. **Area:** 89 sq. km. **Pop. density:** 1 852 per sq. km. **Pop. growth** (annual avg. 1981-1986): −0.2%. **Pop. over 65:** 7 330 males; 14 230 females. **Pop. under 35:** 29 345 males; 44 365 females. **Pop. married:** 42.6%. **Pop. divorced:** 2.9%.

Mother tongue: 2.7% English; 96.0% French; 1.3% other. **Foreign born:** 4 070, 2.4%. **Religious breakdown:** 94.5% Catholic; 1.7% Protestant.

Avg. income (1981): $14 433 males; $8 626 females; $23 467 families. **Below poverty line:** 21.6% of families; 49.5% of individuals. **Avg. family size:** 3.1. **Single parent families:** 18.5%.

Climate: Avg. temps. −12° (Jan.); 19° (July). **Avg. annual precip.** 836 mm. **Avg. annual snowfall:** 343 cm.

Regina, Sask.

Year incorporated: 1903. **Population** (1986): 175 064; 48.7% male, 51.3% female. **Area:** 110 sq. km. **Pop. density:** 1 591 per sq. km. **Pop. growth** (annual avg. 1981-1986): 1.5%. **Pop. over 65:** 6 080 males; 8 910 females. **Pop. under 35:** 50 690 males; 50 860 females. **Pop. married:** 47.6%. **Pop. divorced:** 2.2%.

Mother tongue: 84.4% English; 1.5% French; 14.1% other. **Foreign born:** 17 265, 10.6%. **Religious breakdown:** 53.3% Protestant; 34.1% Catholic; 2.3% Eastern Orthodox; 0.8% Eastern non-Christian; 0.4% Jewish.

Avg. income (1981): $18 321 males; $9 166 females; $29 357 families. **Below poverty line:** 11.5% of families; 35.1% of individuals. **Avg. family size:** 3.2. **Single parent families:** 12.2%.

Climate: Avg. temps. −18° (Jan.); 19° (July). **Avg. annual precip.** 287 mm. **Avg. annual snowfall:** 116 cm.

St. Catharines, Ont.

Year incorporated: 1876. **Population** (1986): 123 455; 48.5% male, 51.5% female. **Area:** 94 sq. km. **Pop. density:** 1 307 per sq. km. **Pop. growth** (annual avg. 1981-1986): −0.1%. **Pop. over 65:** 6 080 males; 8 540 females. **Pop. under 35:** 33 800 males; 33 745 females. **Pop. married:** 51.5%. **Pop. divorced:** 2.2%.

Mother tongue: 79.7% English; 3.1% French; 17.2% other. **Foreign born:** 28 940, 23.3%. **Religious breakdown:** 56.8% Protestant; 33.7% Catholic; 1.1% Eastern Orthodox; 0.4% Jewish.

Avg. income (1981): $17 644 males; $7 415 females; $26 086 families. **Below poverty line:** 13.3% of families; 42.6% of individuals. **Avg. family size:** 3.1. **Single parent families:** 12.2%.

Saint John, N.B.

Year incorporated: 1785. **Population** (1986): 76 381; 47.9% male, 52.1% female. **Area:** 323 sq. km. **Pop. density:** 237 per sq. km. **Pop. growth** (annual avg. 1981-1986): –1.0%. **Pop. over 65:** 3 715 males; 6 150 females. **Pop. under 35:** 23 355 males; 23 105 females. **Pop. married:** 44.9%. **Pop. divorced:** 2.4%.

Mother tongue: 92.1% English; 6.2% French; 1.7% other. **Foreign born:** 3 765, 4.7%. **Religious breakdown:** 51.0% Protestant; 43.3% Catholic.

Avg. income (1981): $15 274 males; $7 529 females; $23 759 families. **Below poverty line:** 16.8% of families; 37.9% of individuals. **Avg. family size:** 3.3. **Single parent families:** 17.9%.

Climate: Avg. temps. –8° (Jan.); 17° (July). **Avg. annual precip.** 1 152 mm. **Avg. annual snowfall:** 293 cm.

St. John's, Nfld.

Year incorporated: 1888. **Population** (1986): 96 216; 47.6% male, 52.4% female. **Area:** 102 sq. km. **Pop. density:** 947 per sq. km. **Pop. growth** (annual avg. 1981-1986): 3.0%. **Pop. over 65:** 3 355 males; 5 525 females. **Pop. under 35:** 24 755 males; 25 600 females. **Pop. married:** 42.7% **Pop. divorced:** 1.4%.

Mother tongue: 98.0% English; 0.4% French; 1.6% other. **Foreign born:** 3 510, 4.2%. **Religious breakdown:** 50.1% Catholic; 44.8% Protestant; 0.2% Jewish.

Avg. income (1981): $15 912 males; $7 995 females; $26 806 families. **Below poverty line:** 17.9% of families; 43.3% of individuals. **Avg. family size:** 3.5. **Single parent families:** 15.4%.

Climate: Avg. temps. –4° (Jan.); 16° (July). **Avg. annual precip.** 1 089 mm. **Avg. annual snowfall:** 359 cm.

Saskatoon, Sask.

Year incorporated: 1906. **Population** (1986): 177 641; 48.2% male, 51.8% female. **Area:** 132 sq. km. **Pop. density:** 1 343 per sq. km. **Pop. growth** (annual avg. 1981-1986): 3.0%. **Pop. over 65:** 6 000 males; 8 665 females. **Pop. under 35:** 48 085 males; 49 690 females. **Pop. married:** 47.1%. **Pop. divorced:** 2.3%.

Mother tongue: 82.1% English; 2.1% French; 15.8% other. **Foreign born:** 17 785, 11.5%. **Religious breakdown:** 55.6% Protestant; 30.9% Catholic; 2.0% Eastern Orthodox; 0.8% Eastern non-Christian; 0.4% Jewish.

Avg. income (1981): $17 726 males; $8 195 females; $28 093 families. **Below poverty line:** 13.8% of families; 41.4% of individuals. **Avg. family size:** 3.2. **Single parent families:** 12.4%.

Climate: Avg. temps. –19° (Jan.); 19° (July). **Avg. annual precip.** 245 mm. **Avg. annual snowfall:** 113 cm.

Sherbrooke, Que.

Year incorporated: 1875. **Population** (1986): 74 438; 46.8% male, 53.2% female. **Area:** 55 sq. km. **Pop. density:** 1 343 per sq. km. **Pop. growth** (annual avg. 1981-1986): 0.1%. **Pop. over 65:** 3 180 males; 5 465 females. **Pop. under 35:** 20 730 males; 20 985 females. **Pop. married:** 45.4%. **Pop. divorced:** 3.5%.

Mother tongue: 6.0% English; 92.2% French; 1.8% other. **Foreign born:** 3 230, 4.4%. **Religious breakdown:** 90.9% Catholic; 3.9% Protestant.

Avg. income (1981): $14 834 males; $7 588 females; $23 654 families. **Below poverty line:** 21.5% of families; 51.9% of individuals. **Avg. family size:** 3.1. **Single parent families:** 16.5%.

Climate: Avg. annual precip. 697 mm. **Avg. annual snowfall:** 323 cm.

Toronto, Ont.

Year incorporated: 1834. **Population** (1986): 612 289; 48.5% male, 51.5% female. **Area:** 97 sq. km. **Pop. density:** 6 303 per sq. km. **Pop. growth** (annual avg. 1981-1986): 0.4%. **Pop. over 65:** 28 710 males; 46 115 females. **Pop. under 35:** 162 690 males; 163 885 females. **Pop. married:** 43.8%. **Pop. divorced:** 3.6%.

Mother tongue: 62.1% English; 1.7% French; 36.2% other. **Foreign born:** 257 575, 43.0%. **Religious breakdown:** 39.1% Catholic; 34.4% Protestant; 4.4% Eastern Orthodox; 4.1% Jewish; 2.9% Eastern non-Christian.

Avg. income (1981): $17 601 males; $10 820 females; $29 794 families. **Below poverty line:** 17.2% of families; 34.3% of individuals. **Avg. family size:** 3.1. **Single parent families:** 14.9%.

Climate: Avg. temps. –5° (Jan.); 22° (July). **Avg. annual precip.** 664 mm. **Avg. annual snowfall:** 139 cm.

Trois-Rivières, Que.

Year incorporated: 1857. **Population** (1986): 50 122; 46.7% male, 53.3% female. **Area:** 78 sq. km. **Pop. density:** 644 per sq. km. **Pop. growth** (annual avg. 1981-1986): –0.2%. **Pop. over 65:** 2 180 males; 3 825 females. **Pop. under 35:** 13 395 males; 13 495 females. **Pop. married:** 45.7%. **Pop. divorced:** 3.0%.

Mother tongue: 2.8% English; 96.3% French; 0.9% other. **Foreign born:** 1 075, 2.1%. **Religious breakdown:** 95.1% Catholic; 2.3% Protestant; 0.2% Eastern non-Christian.

Avg. income (1981): $14 825 males; $7 445 females; $22 855 families. **Below poverty line:** 24.4% of families; 56.2% of individuals. **Avg. family size:** 3.1. **Single parent families:** 17.3%.

Whitehorse, Yukon

Year incorporated: 1950. **Population** (1986): 15 199; 52.0% male, 48.0% female. **Area:** 413 sq. km. **Pop. density:** 37 per sq. km. **Pop. growth** (annual avg. 1981-1986): 0.5%. **Pop. over 65:** 225 males; 170 females. **Pop. under 35:** 5 245 males; 5 065 females. **Pop. married:** 47.7%. **Pop. divorced:** 2.8%.

Mother tongue: 89.9% English; 2.7% French; 7.4% other. **Foreign born:** 1 825, 12.3%. **Religious breakdown:** 53.1% Protestant; 23.6% Catholic; 1.2% Eastern non-Christian; 1.0% Eastern Orthodox.

Avg. income (1981): $20 510 males; $11 365 females; $34 038 families. **Avg. family size:** 3.2. **Single parent families:** 12.9%.

Climate: Avg. temps. –21° (Jan.); 14° (July). **Avg. annual precip.** 146 mm. **Avg. annual snowfall:** 137 cm.

Windsor, Ont.

Year incorporated: 1892. **Population** (1986): 193 111; 48.3% male, 51.7% female. **Area:** 120 sq. km. **Pop. density:** 1 611 per sq. km. **Pop. growth** (annual avg. 1981-1986): 0.1%. **Pop. over 65:** 9 255 males; 13 990 females. **Pop. under 35:** 53 590 males; 62 580 females. **Pop. married:** 48.3%. **Pop. divorced:** 2.8%.

Mother tongue: 74.1% English; 5.6% French; 20.3% other. **Foreign born:** 45 850, 23.9%. **Religious breakdown:** 53.3% Catholic; 34.8% Protestant; 3.6% Eastern Orthodox; 1.4% Eastern non-Christian; 1.0% Jewish.

Avg. income (1981): $17 095 males; $8 281 females; $25 924 families. **Below poverty line:** 16.6% of families; 42.9% of individuals. **Avg. family size:** 3.2. **Single parent families:** 14.4%.

Climate: Avg. temps. –5° (Jan.); 22° (July). **Avg. annual precip.** 738 mm. **Avg. annual snowfall:** 117 cm.

Winnipeg, Man.

Year incorporated: 1873. **Population** (1986): 594 551; 48.2% male, 51.8% female. **Area:** 572 sq. km. **Pop density:** 1 040 per sq. km. **Pop. growth** (annual avg. 1981-1986): 1.1%. **Pop. over 65:** 26 500 males; 39 210 females. **Pop. under 35:** 161 125 males; 162 025 females. **Pop. married:** 48.7%. **Pop. divorced:** 2.4%.

Mother tongue: 73.5% English; 4.9% French; 21.6% other. **Foreign born:** 110 015, 19.5%. **Religious breakdown:** 49.7% Protestant; 33.8% Catholic; 2.7% Jewish; 2.2% Eastern Orthodox; 1.2% Eastern non-Christian.

Avg. income (1981): $16 612 males; $8 254 females; $26 669 families. **Below poverty line:** 14.5% of families; 40.3% of individuals. **Avg. family size:** 3.1. **Single parent families:** 13.0%.

Climate: Avg. temps. −19° (Jan.); 20° (July). **Avg. annual precip.** 411 mm. **Avg. annual snowfall:** 126 cm.

Vancouver, B.C.

Year incorporated: 1886. **Population** (1986): 431 147; 48.6% male, 51.4% female. **Area:** 113 sq. km. **Pop. density:** 3 817 per sq. km. **Pop. growth** (annual avg. 1981-1986): 0.8%. **Pop. over 65:** 25 910 males; 37 320 females. **Pop. under 35:** 106 805 males; 105 920 females. **Pop. married:** 45.1%. **Pop. divorced:** 4.4%.

Mother tongue: 66.2% English; 1.7% French; 32.1% other. **Foreign born:** 160 610, 38.8%. **Religious breakdown:** 39.7% Protestant; 22.5% Catholic; 5.5% Eastern non-Christian; 2.1% Jewish; 1.9% Eastern Orthodox.

Avg. income (1981): $17 636 males; $10 227 females; $30 252 families. **Below poverty line:** 14.3% of families; 35.9% of individuals. **Avg. family size:** 3.0. **Single parent families:** 14.1%.

Climate: Avg. temps. 3° (Jan.); 16° (July). **Avg. annual precip.** 1 055 mm. **Avg. annual snowfall:** 60 cm.

Victoria, B.C.

Year incorporated: 1862. **Population** (1986): 66 303; 44.1% male, 55.9% female. **Area:** 19 sq. km. **Pop. density:** 3 531 per sq. km. **Pop. growth** (annual avg. 1981-1986): 0.6%. **Pop. over 65:** 5 850 males; 10 740 females. **Pop. under 35:** 14 710 males; 15 755 females. **Pop. married:** 46.6%. **Pop. divorced:** 5.5%.

Mother tongue: 86.7% English; 1.7% French; 11.6% other. **Foreign born:** 17 500, 27.2%. **Religious breakdown:** 55.9% Protestant; 16.1% Catholic; 1.7% Eastern non-Christian; 0.8% Eastern Orthodox; 0.4% Jewish.

Avg. income (1981): $15 130 males; $9 279 females; $23 906 families. **Below poverty line:** 12.6% of families; 36.2% of individuals. **Avg. family size:** 2.6. **Single parent families:** 14.8%.

Climate: Avg. temps. 3° (Jan.); 16° (July). **Avg. annual precip.** 823 mm. **Avg. annual snowfall:** 50 cm.

Yellowknife, N.W.T.

Year incorporated: 1970. **Population** (1986): 11 753; 52.4% male, 47.6% female. **Area:** 102 sq. km. **Pop. density:** 115 per sq. km. **Pop. growth** (annual avg. 1981-1986): 4.8%. **Pop. over 65:** 80 males; 60 females. **Pop. under 35:** 3 605 males; 3 390 females. **Pop. married:** 46.9%. **Pop. divorced:** 2.2%.

Mother tongue: 83.4% English; 4.1% French; 12.5% other. **Foreign born:** 1 310, 13.8%. **Religious breakdown:** 46.8% Protestant; 35.9% Catholic; 1.0% Eastern Orthodox; 0.9% Eastern non-Christian.

Avg. income (1981): $21 605 males; $12 057 females; $36 134 families. **Below poverty line:** 10.6%. **Avg. family size:** 3.3. **Single parent families:** 10.6%.

Climate: Avg. temps. −29° (Jan.); 16° (July). **Avg. annual precip.** 150 mm. **Avg. annual snowfall:** 135 cm.

Immigrant Population by City

Source: Censuses of Canada

(number and percent born outside Canada)

	1941	%	1951	%	1961	%	1971	%	1981	%
Toronto, Ont.	209 691	31.4	208 952	30.9	281 877	41.9	310 595	43.6	257 575	43.0
North York, Ont.	n.a.	n.a.	n.a.	n.a.	79 152	29.3	179 475	35.6	243 339	43.5
Montreal, Que.	125 856	13.9	126 136	12.3	204 282	17.2	228 400	18.8	210 500	21.5
Vancouver, B.C.	108 259	39.3	112 242	32.6	132 835	34.5	146 715	34.4	160 610	38.8
Calgary, Alta.	31 199	35.1	35 944	27.9	62 671	25.1	82 595	20.5	125 525	21.2
Edmonton, Alta.	30 040	32.0	39 598	24.8	68 835	24.5	82 800	19.1	113 810	21.4
Winnipeg, Man.	77 523	34.9	71 252	30.2	75 715	28.5	61 295	24.9	110 015	19.5
Mississauga, Ont. . . .	n.a.	n.a.	n.a.	n.a.	n.a.	n.a.	40 005	25.6	108 715	34.5
Hamilton, Ont.	51 582	31.0	58 712	28.2	85 738	31.3	93 375	30.2	87 735	28.6
Ottawa, Ont.	19 382	12.5	23 889	11.8	41 754	15.6	49 195	16.3	55 390	18.8
London, Ont.	18 761	24.0	18 796	19.7	36 522	21.5	48 175	21.6	52 630	20.7
Brampton, Ont.	n.a.	n.a.	n.a.	n.a.	4 593	24.9	10 405	25.3	47 105	31.6
Windsor, Ont.	30 812	29.3	30 507	25.4	31 161	27.2	48 815	24.0	45 850	23.9
Kitchener, Ont.	6 336	17.8	7 969	17.8	16 688	22.4	24 940	22.3	31 720	22.7
St. Catharines, Ont. .	8 824	29.1	9 652	25.4	21 560	25.5	25 535	23.3	28 940	23.3
Burlington, Ont.	n.a.	n.a.	n.a.	n.a.	10 338	22.0	18 900	21.7	26 945	23.5
Laval, Que.	n.a.	n.a.	n.a.	n.a.	1 320	6.9	18 630	8.2	26 850	10.0
Thunder Bay, Ont. . .	17 200	31.3	16 876	25.5	23 595	26.1	23 045	21.3	19 375	17.2
Saskatoon, Sask. . . .	12 933	30.1	12 305	23.1	17 190	18.0	17 595	13.9	17 785	11.5
Victoria, B.C.	19 395	44.0	18 461	36.0	19 751	35.9	19 550	31.7	17 500	27.2
Regina, Sask.	16 474	28.3	15 424	21.6	19 562	17.4	18 365	13.2	17 265	10.6
Halifax, N.S.	8 234	11.7	5 669	6.6	6 510	7.0	9 850	8.1	10 730	9.4
Quebec, Que.	3 096	2.1	2 655	1.6	3 687	2.1	3 730	2.0	4 070	2.4
Saint John, N.B.	3 901	7.5	2 721	5.4	2 859	5.2	4 030	4.5	3 765	4.7
St. John's, Nfld.	n.a.	n.a.	1 148	2.2	1 768	2.8	3 160	3.6	3 510	4.2
Fredericton, N.B. . . .	1 094	10.9	1 171	7.3	1 540	7.8	2 230	9.2	3 015	6.9
Charlottetown, P.E.I. .	844	5.7	603	3.8	656	3.6	815	4.3	745	4.9

n.a. not available.

Tourism

Passports and Visas

Source: Department of External Affairs

Passports

Passport applications may be obtained at post offices, travel agencies and passport offices. Applications may be submitted in person at a regional passport office or mailed to: The Passport Office, Department of External Affairs, Ottawa, Ont. K1A 0G3.

How long is the wait?

Regional offices are located in: Calgary, Edmonton, Fredericton, Halifax, Hamilton, London, Montreal, North York, Ottawa, Hull, Quebec, St. John's, Saint-Laurent, Saskatoon, Scarborough, Toronto, Vancouver, Victoria, Windsor and Winnipeg. If the application is in order, a passport may usually be obtained from a regional office within 3 working days from the date submitted. Applications submitted by mail are usually forwarded from Ottawa by mail within 2 weeks of the day the application was received.

Requirements

With your application you must:
• Submit evidence of Canadian citizenship. If you were born in Canada, you must submit a birth certificate or a certificate of Canadian citizenship. (Large certificates of Canadian citizenship issued after Feb. 14, 1977, are not acceptable). If you were born abroad you must submit either a certificate of Canadian citizenship or naturalization, or a certificate of registration of birth abroad, or a certificate of retention of citizenship.[1]
• Have your application signed by a guarantor who is a Canadian citizen residing in Canada, who has known you for at least 2 years, and who is included in one of the following groups: minister of a religion authorized by law to perform marriages; signing officer of a bank, trust company or full-time manager of a credit union; judge, magistrate or police officer; person occupying a senior administrative position or teaching appointment in a university; head of a community college; principal of a secondary or primary school; professional accountant; professional engineer; mayor; lawyer; notary public; medical doctor, dentist; veterinarian; postmaster; chiropractor.
• Complete and submit a "Declaration in Lieu of Guarantor" if you do not know an eligible guarantor.
• Provide 2 signed photographs that fall within the photograph specifications, one of which is signed on the back by your guarantor or by the official who signed the "Declaration in Lieu of Guarantor".
• Submit any Canadian passport, certificate of identity or refugee travel document issued to you within the last 5 years.
• Submit a fee of $25 in cash, money order or cheque payable to the Receiver General for Canada.

Children

Although children under the age of 16 may be included on one of their parent's passports, External Affairs recommends that individual passports for children be obtained. If the parents are separated or divorced, only the parent having custody of the child may apply for the child's passport, although both parents are requested to sign the application. The parent who has custody of the child must provide all legal documents referring to custody of or access to the child. Children 16 years of age and over must have their own passport. The requirements and fee for a child's passport are the same as for an adult.

Visas

Visas are documents or endorsements on your passport, issued by the country you wish to visit, that permit entry into that country. Because visas often cannot be obtained at a country's border, you should consult your travel agent or write to the diplomatic or consular mission in Canada of the country being visited, prior to departure. The same applies for information on entry and exit permits, vaccinations or other requirements.[2] Submit visa applications to the appropriate foreign mission well in advance of your planned departure to allow sufficient time for processing and handling.

Canadians do not require visas or passports to enter the United States, Mexico and some Caribbean countries. Evidence of travel to Israel on your passport may prohibit entry into Arab states and some African countries. To avoid this problem it is sometimes possible to arrange to have Israeli visas, entry and exit stamps placed on a separate piece of paper. Certain African states may refuse you admittance if your passport contains evidence of travel in the Republic of South Africa. Admissability should be verified with the diplomatic mission of each African state concerned.[2] Information on entry requirements can also be found in the monthly publication, *Travel Information Manual (TIM)*, which may be found at airline ticket offices, travel agencies and in major public libraries.

(1) For children born abroad of Canadian parents. (2) See page 108 for addresses of foreign missions in Canada.

Canadian Travel Balance of Trade

Source: Statistics Canada

	Receipts[1]	Payments[2]	Balance[3]		Receipts[1]	Payments[2]	Balance[3]
1930	180	92	88	1977	2 025	3 666	− 1 641
1935	117	64	53	1978	2 378	4 084	− 1 706
1940	105	43	62	1979	2 887	3 955	− 1 068
1945	166	83	83	1980	3 349	4 577	− 1 228
1950	275	226	49	1981	3 760	4 876	− 1 116
1955	328	449	− 121	1982	3 724	5 008	− 1 284
1960	420	627	− 207	1983	3 841	6 045	− 2 204
1965	747	796	− 49	1984	4 416	6 542	− 2 126
1970	1 234	1 460	− 226	1985	5 006	7 110	− 2 104
1975	1 815	2 542	− 727	1986	6 333	7 499	− 1 166
1976	1 930	3 121	− 1 191	1987[4]	6 289	8 762	− 2 473

(1) Spending by foreign travellers in Canada. (2) Spending by Canadian travellers in other countries. (3) Receipts minus payments. (4) Preliminary.

Canadian Customs Regulations[1]

Source: Revenue Canada

Personal Exemption

Canadian residents returning from another country can bring goods into Canada, free of duty and taxes, if they qualify for a personal exemption under conditions listed below. Goods brought in under personal exemption must be for personal or household use, and your exemption cannot be pooled with, or transferred to, other people. A parent or guardian may make a customs declaration on behalf of an infant but the goods declared in the child's name must be for his or her use only.

After 24 hours' absence or more: any number of times a year, you are allowed to bring back goods to the value of $20 (excluding tobacco products and alcoholic beverages). Only an oral statement is necessary.

After 48 hours' absence or more: any number of times a year, you may bring back goods to the value of $100. A written declaration may be required.

After 7 days' absence or more: once every calendar year, you may bring in goods to the value of $300. A written declaration will be required. Seven-day periods are determined by dates rather than hours—for example, if you leave on Monday the 7th and return on Monday the 14th.

Tobacco Products and Alcoholic Beverages

You may bring in alcoholic beverages and tobacco products free of duty and taxes after a 48-hour or 7-day absence, but not under the 24-hour exemption. The dollar value of these items will form part of your exemption. All tobacco products and alcoholic beverages must accompany you upon return. Any person aged 16 or over is entitled to bring in 200 cigarettes and 50 cigars and 0.91 kg of tobacco. If you meet the age requirements set by the province or territory through which you re-enter Canada, you may bring in 1.1 litres (40 imperial oz.) of wine or liquor or 24 cans or bottles (355 ml or 12 fl. oz.) of beer or ale or its equivalent (totalling 8.5 litres).

Your Declaration

Upon returning to Canada, you must declare to Customs all goods you have acquired abroad, whether or not you paid for them yourself. This includes goods purchased at a Canadian or foreign duty free store. If goods are not declared, or are falsely declared, they may be seized and forfeited and the traveller may face severe penalties.

Goods brought in under the $20 or $100 exemption must accompany you. Under the $300 yearly exemption, goods must also accompany you if they were purchased in continental North America, including Panama and the islands of St. Pierre and Miquelon. Beyond these areas, goods acquired may follow you by mail or other means of transportation.

Special Tax Rate

After any trip abroad for 48 hours or more, you are entitled to a special 20% tax rate on goods valued up to $300 over and above your $100 or $300 personal exemption. This special tax rate applies only to goods which accompany you and may not include alcohol or tobacco products. Any value of goods imported above this limit are subject to regular duty and taxes.

Agricultural Goods

Upon returning to Canada you are required to declare all plant or animal products. The Customs officer will decide whether or not the item should be inspected. Items which do not meet the requirements of the Animal Health Division or the Plant Health Division may be detained or refused entry. It is recommended that you consult Agriculture Canada regarding specific restrictions on animal or plant importation.

Other Restrictions

Canadian travellers abroad should be aware of restrictions placed on the import of certain goods, such as agricultural produce, live animals, firearms, motor vehicles, CB radios, explosives, fireworks and ammunition. Prior to purchasing any of these items abroad you should consult your nearest Canadian Customs office to determine whether a permit may be required.

If your pet is to accompany you on your trip, it is recommended that you first check for restrictions which may apply in the country you will be visiting.

(1) For Canadian residents travelling abroad; figures are in Canadian dollars.

Travel Destinations of Canadians

Source: Statistics Canada

(thousands of visits[1])

	1980	1985	1986		1980	1985	1986
Total Visits	27 402	28 118	28 729	Netherlands	120	187	187
United States	24 594	23 886	24 721	Portugal	35	62	75
California	826	763	789	Spain	39	98	85
Florida	1 482	1 536	1 572	Switzerland	117	200	170
Maine	1 098	974	970	United Kingdom	446	644	540
Michigan	2 099	2 052	1 685	Yugoslavia	13	25	25
New Hampshire	778	708	658	**Caribbean**	621	776	750
New York	3 623	3 700	4 176	Bahamas	125	100	73
Ohio	815	757	762	Barbados	110	87	58
Pennsylvania	873	867	1 020	Bermuda	42	40	50
Vermont	1 273	1 189	1 102	Cuba	33	60	62
Washington	1 833	1 642	1 708	Jamaica	70	77	103
Europe	1 591	2 578	2 269	Puerto Rico	39	40	n.a.
Austria	75	130	103	**Central America**	236	290	306
Belgium	74	107	108	Mexico	220	264	282
Denmark	28	29	35	**Asia**	159	274	315
France	205	377	346	Hong Kong	24	53	63
West Germany	169	259	235	Japan	27	47	43
Greece	38	72	42	**Australasia**	66	108	138
Ireland	29	53	38	**Africa**	66	86	72
Italy	105	190	151	**South America**	56	108	148

(1) Includes visits which lasted less than one day.
n.a. not available.

Tourist Visits[1] to Canada

Source: Statistics Canada

	1975	1980	1985	1987
Total Tourists[2]	13 663 000	12 785 000	13 171 000	14 975 000
United States[3]	12 499 000	10 963 000	11 558 000	12 720 000
Europe	892 322	1 377 852	1 042 188	1 564 236
Austria	8 244	15 498	16 518	23 599
Belgium	15 806	26 435	16 700	29 255
Czechoslovakia	4 046	4 109	4 292	5 562
Denmark	11 770	18 342	16 766	25 654
Finland	7 986	11 689	12 152	14 855
France	82 509	134 309	116 617	210 039
West Germany	138 030	237 532	181 998	298 670
Greece	13 165	16 806	15 571	19 750
Hungary	4 720	6 406	6 219	7 586
Iceland	n.a.	1 230	1 216	1 625
Ireland	8 683	15 776	12 856	16 606
Italy	45 380	65 782	65 121	103 459
Malta	1 102	1 750	1 142	1 138
Netherlands	65 347	98 020	63 921	88 490
Norway	8 546	12 037	10 068	14 359
Poland	6 370	13 598	29 757	26 241
Portugal	13 690	13 620	14 344	16 332
Romania	495	1 423	1 547	1 533
Spain	11 589	17 109	13 688	22 159
Sweden	19 659	34 043	22 119	31 207
Switzerland	28 418	53 650	49 028	70 234
Turkey	1 862	3 521	3 148	3 356
United Kingdom	379 657	553 225	345 054	506 626
USSR	2 957	5 642	8 962	6 993
Yugoslavia	8 798	12 348	9 713	12 991
Asia	196 439	384 829	420 592	648 310
China	200	7 048	11 134	18 666
Hong Kong	20 778	30 839	43 272	66 694
India	22 023	48 547	34 553	53 031
Iran	n.a.	1 658	3 323	2 800
Israel	20 644	45 820	37 546	65 175
Japan	90 411	162 253	174 503	311 687
South Korea	3 942	8 125	14 860	17 264
Lebanon	2 892	4 126	3 424	3 433
Malaysia	n.a.	12 497	13 994	14 709
Pakistan	4 504	5 937	7 360	8 420
Philippines	6 456	14 295	13 281	16 330
Singapore	n.a.	7 746	10 168	12 049
Taiwan	5 299	10 164	15 903	19 956
Caribbean[3]	110 721	173 046	146 852	171 477
Bahamas	4 084	4 753	4 568	5 311
Barbados	4 944	8 192	7 756	9 144
Bermuda	6 788	8 143	10 645	11 767
Cuba	722	1 592	1 494	1 404
Dominican Republic	n.a.	2 497	2 985	2 708
Haiti	3 528	8 438	7 268	5 819
Jamaica	25 049	27 276	15 222	18 242
Mexico	34 796	58 317	42 136	56 427
St. Pierre & Miquelon	2 616	6 724	6 401	8 582
Trinidad and Tobago	16 807	28 896	29 850	27 603
Australasia	55 508	90 020	96 766	133 626
Australia	41 487	65 967	76 028	89 686
New Zealand	11 701	20 117	15 682	35 067
South America	46 370	91 907	59 805	82 261
Argentina	7 378	18 209	10 970	24 877
Brazil	10 740	16 684	13 683	23 495
Colombia	3 956	7 732	6 881	7 554
Guyana	6 363	8 452	3 059	3 187
Venezuela	7 130	23 558	7 760	7 086
Africa	26 196	45 359	41 835	42 726
Algeria	792	2 106	1 858	1 532
Egypt	2 491	5 549	5 795	5 515
Nigeria	329	3 775	2 661	1 926
South Africa	9 253	15 332	11 163	11 204

(1) Includes visits which lasted less than one day. (2) Does not include visitors entering and leaving Canada the same day. (3) Includes Central America, Greenland and St. Pierre & Miquelon.
n.a. not available.

Canada's National Historic Parks and Sites*

Source: Parks Canada

Atlantic Region

Alexander Graham Bell: Baddeck, N.S. Museum of the telephone and medical aeronautical inventions.

Ardgowan: Parkdale, P.E.I. Former home of William Henry Pope, one of Prince Edward Island's Fathers of Confederation.

The Bank Fishery—Age of Sail: Lunenburg, N.S. Fisheries museum of the Atlantic.

Beaubears Island: Newcastle, N.B. Former Acadian settlement, dating back to 1755.

Cape Spear: St. John's, Nfld. Oldest existing lighthouse in Newfoundland.

Carleton Martello Tower: Saint John, N.B. Circular stone tower built during the war of 1812 to guard against an American attack.

Castle Hill: Placentia, Nfld. Fortifications built in the late 1600s.

Fort Amherst/Port La Joye: Rocky Point, P.E.I. Museum on early French colonization.

Fort Anne: Annapolis Royal, N.S. 4-bastioned earthenworks fort, built between 1702 and 1708.

Fort Beauséjour: Aulac, N.B. Former Acadian and British settlements, built in 1751.

Fort Edward*: Windsor, N.S. Oldest wooden blockhouse in Canada.

Fort McNab*: McNab's Island, Halifax Harbor, N.S. Played a major role in protecting the British naval station in Halifax.

Fortress of Louisbourg: Louisbourg, N.S. Once the largest fortress and naval base in North America.

Grand Pré: Grand Pré, N.S. Exhibits on Acadian history.

Halifax Citadel: Halifax, N.S. Fortifications of the city and harbor.

Halifax Waterfront Buildings*: Halifax, N.S. Recreation of the early 19th Century waterfront.

L'Anse-aux-Meadows: Great Northern Peninsula, Nfld. Site of the oldest known European settlement in the New World.

Port-au-Choix: Port-au-Choix, Nfld. Archaic Indian burial site.

Port Royal: Port Royal, N.S. First permanent settlement in North America, north of Florida.

Prince of Wales Martello Tower: Halifax, N.S. Former defence post.

Province House*: Charlottetown, P.E.I. Birthplace of Canadian Confederation.

St. Andrews Blockhouse*: St. Andrews, N.B. Defensive fortification of New Brunswick during the War of 1812.

St. Peter's Canal: 50 km northeast of Port Hawkesbury, N.S. Canal constructed between 1854 and 1869.

Signal Hill: St. John's, Nfld. Site of the final battle of the Seven Year's War and the first trans-Atlantic radio signal transmission (1901).

Survival of the Acadians*: St. Joseph, N.B. Exhibit on Acadian history.

York Redoubt*: Halifax, N.S. 200-year-old fortification and war post.

Quebec

Artillery Park: Quebec, Que. Played a major political and military role during a 250-year period of French, English and Canadian governments.

Battle of the Châteauguay: Ormstown, Que. Location of the historic Battle of 1813.

Battle of the Ristigouche: Pointe-à-la-Croix, Que. Site of the 1760 Battle of Ristigouche.

Cartier-Brébeuf: Quebec, Que. Commemorative Park to Jacques Cartier.

Coteau-du-Lac: Coteau-du-Lac, Que. First canal lock built in Canada.

Forges du Saint-Maurice: Trois-Rivières, Que. Remains of various iron-making forges.

Fort Chambly: Chambly, Que. Former military establishment, dating from 1665.

Fort Lennox: Saint-Paul-de-L'Ile-aux-Noix, Que. Fort dating back to early 19th Century.

Fort Témiscamingue*: Lake Témiscamingue, Que. Old Hudson's Bay Company trading post.

Fortifications of Quebec*: Quebec, Que. Vast defence system of walls and gates surrounding the old city.

Jacques Cartier Monument*: Gaspé, Que. Distinctive monument commemorating the 16th Century explorer.

Lachine Canal: Montreal, Que. Canal used between 1825 and 1959 in order to bypass the Lachine Rapids on the St. Lawrence.

Louis S. St-Laurent: Compton, Que. Former residence of Canada's 12th prime minister.

National Battlefields of Quebec: Quebec, Que. Better known as "The Plains of Abraham", this is the site of the historic battle between generals Wolfe and Montcalm (1759).

Pointe-au-Père: Quebec, Que. Restored lighthouse.

Point Lévis Fort No. I: Lauzon, Que. Defensive fort erected to counter the threat of American invasions in the 1860s.

Quebec Canals: Quebec. A system of heritage canals linking thousands of km of inland waterways.

Shipbuilding in Quebec: Old Port of Quebec, Que. Highlights of the timber trade and shipbuilding in 19th Century Quebec.

Sir George-Étienne Cartier House: Montreal, Que. Former residence of Sir George-Étienne Cartier, lawyer, railway promoter and Father of Confederation.

Sir Wilfrid Laurier House: Ville des Laurentides, Que. Onetime residence of Canada's 7th prime minister.

Ontario

Battle of the Windmill*: Hwy 2, Near Prescott, Ont. Site of an American attempt to capture Fort Wellington in 1838.

Bellevue House: Kingston, Ont. Residence of Canada's first prime minister, Sir John A. Macdonald.

Bethune Memorial House: Gravenhurst, Ont. Birthplace of Norman Bethune, known for his work in China as a field surgeon and medical educator.

Brown's Bay Wreck: Mallorytown Landing, Ont. Display of gunboat wreck.

Fort Malden: Amherstberg, Ont. Once a major base for defence of the Detroit frontier during the War of 1812 and the rebellion of 1837.

Fort St. Joseph: St. Joseph Island, Ont. Location of former military post built by the British in order to defend the western frontier of British North America.

Fort Wellington, Ontario: Prescott, Ont. Built during the War of 1812 to defend the navigation route along the St. Lawrence.

Laurier House: Ottawa, Ont. Residence of prime ministers: Sir Wilfrid Laurier and William Lyon Mackenzie King.

Murney Martello Tower: Kingston, Ont. The 11-m limestone structure was built for defence in 1846.

Niagara: Niagara-on-the-Lake, Ont. A number of forts and monuments strategically important to the survival of Upper Canada during the War of 1812; Fort George, Butler's Barracks, Fort Mississauga, Queenston Heights and Brock's Monument are all located here.

Rideau Canal: Ont. Constructed by the British military after the War of 1812 to provide Upper Canada with an alternate transportation route to avoid American attacks.

Southwold Prehistoric Earthworks: Leamington, Ont. A Neutral Indian village, dating back to around 1500.

Woodside: Kitchener, Ont. Boyhood home of William Lyon Mackenzie King, Canada's 10th prime minister.

Prairies

Batoche*: 88 km northeast of Saskatoon, Sask. Site encompasses battlefield of the North West Rebellion, 1885.

Battleford: Battleford, Sask. Former Northwest Mounted Police post.

Cypress Hills Massacre*: Maple Creek, Sask. Site of the 1873 Indian massacre by American frontier traders.

Fort Esperance*: 222 km east of Regina, Sask. First North West Company post on the Qu'Appelle River.

Fort Prince of Wales: Churchill, Man. Hudson's Bay Company stone fort on Hudson Bay.

Fort Walsh: Maple Creek, Sask. Reconstructed NWMP post of 1870s.
Lower Fort Garry: Selkirk, Man. Former supply depot of the Hudson's Bay Company.
Motherwell Homestead: Abernethy, Sask. Former homestead of William Richard Motherwell, political activist and agrarian reformer.
Riel House: St. Vital, Man. Residence of Louis Riel's family in the late 19th century.
Rocky Mountain House: Rocky Mountain House, Alta. Location of 4 fur trading sites dating from 1799 to 1875.
St. Andrews Rectory: Man. Rectory of early church mission.
York Factory*: 241 km southeast of Churchill, Man. Hudson's Bay fur trading post during the 18th and 19th centuries.

Western Region

Chilkoot Trail: northwestern B.C. Historic travel route of the Klondike Gold Rush.

* = National Historic Site

Fisgard Light House*: Victoria, B.C. In 1860, this site became the first permanent navigational aid to be located on the west coast.
Fort Langley: Fort Langley, B.C. Former Hudson's Company trading post and supply depot.
Fort Rodd Hill: Victoria, B.C. Defensive fort dating back to 1893.
Fort St. James: 161 km northwest of Prince George, B.C. Late 19th Century trading post.
Kitwanga*: 120 km northeast of Terrace, B.C. Hilltop stronghold called Battle Hill commemorating native culture.
Klondike*: Dawson City, Yukon Territory. Site of the Klondike Gold Rush, includes attractions reminiscent of the era: the Old Post Office, Sternwheeler Keno, Harrington's Store and Robert Service's rustic cabin. .
St. Roch*: Vancouver, B.C. Restored RCMP World War II Arctic patrol and supply ship that circumnavigated North America.
Yukon*: Whitehorse, Yukon. This sternwheeler commemorates the importance of river transport in Yukon's development.

Provincial Attractions

Source: Canadian World Almanac Questionnaire/
The Official Directory of Canadian Museums, Canadian Museum's Association

Canada has a wealth of attractions for both tourists and residents. The following listing is meant to provide an overview of the highlights with each province, major cities and territories. It is by no means a complete listing; for a thorough guide to events and sites contact the provincial agencies responsible for tourism at the addresses given. For a complete listing of National Parks, see page 481. Also see National Historic Sites, page 496.

Newfoundland

(Contact: Department of Development and Tourism, P.O. Box 2016, St. John's, Nfld. A1C 5R8)

Region	Site/Address	Admission	Hours	Description
Corner Brook	Captain James Cook Monument	free	n.a.	This site includes a monument displaying copies of the original charts of Captain Cook who surveyed and charted the Bay of Islands area about 1764.
St. John's	Newfoundland Museum, Duckworth St. and The Murray Premises, Water St.	free	daily	The Duckworth St. museum houses collections and exhibitions reflecting the 7 000 year history of Nfld. and Labrador. The new museum on Water St. contains the Maritime History Gallery and highlights underwater archaelogy, navigation, cartography, and sea disasters.
	Quidi Vidi Battery, Quidi Vidi Village	free	summer: daily	Originally erected by the French in 1762 and later rebuilt by the British, the battery has been restored to the 1812 period. This battery is manned by guides in period uniforms of the Royal Artillery.
	Signal Hill National Historic Park, Signal Hill	free	daily summer: 9 a.m.-8 p.m. winter: 8:30-4:30	Used as a signalling centre and later to defend the harbor and the city, the English and French sought control of the Hill over the centuries. The last battle of the Seven Years War was fought here (1762) and this is where Marconi received the first transatlantic wireless signal.
	The Anglican Cathedral of St. John the Baptist	free	daily	One of the finest examples of ecclesiastical Gothic architecture in N. America. Precious religious objects are kept in the Chapter House.
	The Basilica of St. John the Baptist	free	daily	Completed in 1850 and holds 2 000 worshippers. Houses rare sculptures and religious symbols.
	St. John's Regatta, Lakeside	free	early Aug.	One of the oldest annual sporting events in N. America has been held since 1826. Features a rowing competition and carnival atmosphere. .
	Cape Spear National Historic Park, 16 km South of St. John's, Route 11	free	daily	Situated on the most easterly point of North America, the Cape Spear Lighthouse is the oldest (1835) existing lighthouse in Nfld. The 2 storey, wooden structure served as a beacon for the guidance and safety of mariners from 1836-1955.

Region	Site/Address	Admission	Hours	Description
Southern Shore	Witless Bay Bird Sanctuary (restricted) Witless Bay, via Route 10	free	daily	The seabird sanctuary located on these islands is situated approximately 5 km off the coast from the community of Witless Bay, 32 km south of St. John's on Route 10. A boat tour around the islands is available.
	Cape St. Mary's Sea-bird Sanctuary, Cape St. Mary's, off Route 100	free	daily	The 2d largest gannetry in North America is approximately 200 km southeast of St. John's and offers an excellent opportunity to photograph the seabirds.
Bonavista Peninsula	Dugeon Provincial Park, Bonavista, off Rte. 238	free	daily	A collapsed sea cave with a natural archway carved out by tidal action highlights this site. A restored 19th century lighthouse is nearby, at Cape Bonavista.
	The Hiscock House Trinity, off Route 230	free	summer: daily	Hiscock House, located in historic Trinity and restored to the 1910 period, represents a typical local merchant's household in rural Nfld. in the early 20th century.
Burin Peninsula	Southern Newfound-land Seaman's Museum, Grand Bank, off Rte. 220	free	daily	This museum offers a vivid contrast between its modern design and the starkness of the surround-ing landscape. Features historical fishing artifacts.
Grand Falls	Mary March Museum and National Exhibi-tion Centre, Grand Falls, off Route 1	n.a.	daily	The museum offers exhibits dealing with the natu-ral and human history of Central Newfoundland, particularly relating to the Beothuk culture.
Great Northern Peninsula	Port au Choix National Historic Park, off Rte. 430	free	summer: daily	The site of a burial ground of the Maritime Archaic Indians who inhabited this area 5 000 years ago. Artifacts and remains can be seen.
Labrador	Basque Whaling Archaeological Site, Rte. 510, Red Bay	free	summer: Mon.-Sat.	Research has revealed evidence of a settlement established in the 16th century by Basque whalers. There are 2 projects: the underwater excavation of a shipwreck and the excavation of a land site.

Prince Edward Island

(Contact: Department of Finance and Tourism, P.O. Box 2000, Charlottetown, Prince Edward Island C1A 7N8)

Region	Site/Address	Admission	Hours	Description
Cavendish	Green Gables House, Rte. 6	free	May-Oct.: daily	The setting for Anne of Green Gables is furnished to depict the period setting of the novel.
Charlottetown	Confederation Centre Art Gallery and Museum, Confedera-tion Centre	$1; Family $2; Seniors; $.50	all year: daily	One of Canada's leading art museums hosts major touring exhibitions and a large collection of works by Robert Harris.
	Province House National Historic Site	free	all year: daily	The birthplace of the Canadian nation and today, the legislative centre of the province.
The Charlottetown Festival	Charlottetown Festi-val Theatre	$12-$19.75	June-Oct. 10: evening perform-ances daily; matinees Wed. and Sat.	Home to more than 40 original Canadian produc-tions; the main presentation, Anne of Green Gables, has played for almost 25 years.
New London	Lucy Maud Mont-gomery's Birthplace	Adults $.75; Children $.25	June-Sept.: daily	Birthplace of the esteemed author includes a rep-lica of the old blue chest made famous in her books, personal belongings and scrapbooks.
Park Corner	Anne of Green Gables Museum at Silver Bush, Rte. 20	Adults $1; Children $.50	June-Oct.: daily	Lucy Maud Montgomery was married here in 1911; displays include autographed first editions, and handcrafts belonging to the author.
P.E.I. National Park	12 miles from Char-lottetown on N. shore	park fees	all year	42 km of ocean beach, including the beautiful Cavendish Beach, with campgrounds and resorts. Many of the islands famous lobster suppers are served in church or community halls nearby.
Woodleigh	Rte. 234 Northeast of Kensington	Adults: $5; Children: $2.50; Under 6 yr: $1; Seniors: $4.50; Season Pass: $20.	July 4-Oct. 10: daily	Large scale models of York Minster, the Tower of London and Scotland's Dunvegan Castle are among the group of historic and legendary struc-tures which have been recreated in this English garden setting.

Nova Scotia

(Contact: Department of Tourism, P.O. Box 456, Halifax, N.S. B3J 2R5)

Region	Site/Address	Admission	Hours	Description
Halifax	St. Paul's Church, Barrington St.	free	summer & fall: daily, except for Sunday services	Canada's oldest Protestant church, St. Paul's, opened in 1750 and is of wooden construction with classical, somewhat Georgian, design.
	Province House, Prince and Granville Sts.	free	summer: Mon-Sat. winter: Mon-Fri.	Canada's oldest British colonial parliament building, Province House was built between 1811 and 1819, and is still home to the N.S. Legislature.
	Nova Scotia Museum, 1747 Summer St.	free	summer: daily winter: closed Mon.	Exhibits on people and the environment and on natural history. The museum features an extensive collection of Micmac Indian artifacts.
	Maritime Museum of the Atlantic, Lower Water St.	free	summer: daily winter: closed Mon.	Exhibits focus on the region's maritime history. A restored 19th century ship chandler's shop, Days of Sail Gallery, ship models, Titanic exhibit, small craft and naval artifacts are displayed. The C.S.S. Acadia is permanently docked at the wharf and is open in summer.
	Bluenose II, Privateer's Wharf, Upper Water St.	n.a.	For public sailings contact Bluenose II info office (902) 422-2678	A replica of the Bluenose, the famous racing schooner; cruises available July and Aug. when not on charters or promotions.
	Historic Properties, Privateer's Wharf and Granville St.	free	daily	Restored 19th century waterfront buildings have been declared a National Historic Site.
	Halifax Citadel National Historic Park, Sackville St.	small fee during summer	daily	This fort was built between 1829 and 1856. Made of ironstone and granite, the star-shaped fort was manned by the British Army until 1906, and by Canadian forces during World Wars I and II. The colorful 78th Highlanders drill inside the citadel.
	Art Gallery of Nova Scotia, 6152 Cobourg Rd.	free	daily	Home of the main provincial fine art collection; a diverse group of historic and contemporary paintings are exhibited.
Annapolis Royal	The Habitation, Port-Royal National Historic Park	free	May 15-Oct. 15: daily	The earliest permanent European settlement (founded 1605) north of Florida. The settlement was looted and burnt by an English expedition in 1613. The site now has a bakeshop, kitchen, blacksmith shop, community room, chapel and other rooms as in the days of Samuel de Champlain.
	Fort Anne National Historic Park	free	daily	Building began on this French fort in the 1700s to protect Port-Royal's inhabitants from attacks by New England troops. The storehouse and the power magazine are surviving original buildings.
Louisbourg	Fortress of Louisbourg National Historic Park	Adults $4; Children $1; Family $8	June-Oct.	Approximately 20% of this French fortress of 1744 has been reconstructed to now contain more than 40 stone and wooden buildings, furnished to the period.
Baddeck	Alexander Graham Bell National Historic Park, Chebucto St.	free	daily	Bell's experiments including the development of the telephone, discoveries in medicine, work on early aircraft engines, as well as mementos of Bell's personal life are displayed.
Cabot Trail	Cape Breton Highlands National Park, between Ingonish and Cheticamp	vehicle permit required	daily	The Cabot Trail is a modern 303 km highway running along 3 sides of the park. Spectacular views on the coast and park abound. The area offers saltwater swimming, sandy beaches, picnicking, and hiking.
	Halifax Public Gardens	free	daily	Canada's first (established 1830s) public garden; considered one of North America's finest surviving examples of a Victorian Garden.
Dartmouth	Dartmouth Heritage Museum, 100 Wyse Rd.	free	summer: daily winter: afternoons	The museum collection exhibits Micmac Indian artifacts, the founding of Dartmouth in 1750, the military era, the whalers, the building of Shubenacadie Canal, and a display of N.S. patriot James Howe's re-created study.
Sherbrooke	Sherbrooke Village	Adults $2; Children $.50	May 15-Oct. 15: daily	The restored buildings of Sherbrooke Village reflect the village's boom town when gold was struck in 1831. Weaving, quilting, boatbuilding, and blacksmithing are demonstrated by costumed staff.

Region	Site/Address	Admission	Hours	Description
Grand Pré	Grand Pré National Historic Park	free	daily	Site of the largest Acadian settlement in the Minas Basin area, this village was home to Acadians from 1680 until their deportation in 1755, when the settlement was burned by New England and British troops. Acquired by the federal government in 1957, the park now exhibits artifacts representing the Acadian way of life.
Peggy's Cove	Rte. 333	free	daily	One of the most photographed sites in Canada, the Cove is a rugged fishing community.

New Brunswick

(Contact: Tourism New Brunswick, P.O. Box 12345, Fredericton, N.B. E3B 5C3)

Region	Site/Address	Admission	Hours	Description
Saint John	New Brunswick Museum, 277 Douglas Ave.	Adults $2; Students $.50; Family $4; Seniors free	daily winter: closed Mondays	Canada's first natural history museum, founded in 1842, offers paintings by New Brunswick artists of the 19th and 20th centuries and historic displays.
	Carleton Martello Tower, Fundy Dr. at Whipple St.	free	May 15-Oct. 15; daily	A National Historic Park. Built for the War of 1812, the Tower commands an impressive view of the city and environs. Includes a restored powder magazine of the 1840s and 1866 barrack room and an exhibit explaining the role of martello towers.
	Fort Howe, Magazine St.	free	all year outside viewing only	A replica of a 1777 blockhouse provides outstanding photo opportunities.
	Barbour's General Store/Little Red Schoolhouse, Market Slip (foot of King St.)	free	May-Oct: daily	The General Store is restored and stocked to the year 1867 with authentic merchandise in original packaging. The Little Red Schoolhouse is a furnished rural one-room schoolhouse.
	Loyalist House, 120 Union St.	Adults $2; Children $.25	July and Aug.: daily	An 1817 Georgian mansion of a successful Loyalist family presenting a memorial to the first 50 years of the Loyalists in Canada.
Shediac	Parlée Beach Provincial Park	park fees $3 per car	n.a.	A fine, sandy, salt-water beach is found here, and there is also a popular waterslide park.
Hopewell Cape	Flower Pot Rocks, Rte. 114	$2	n.a.	These are curious rock formations that have been sculpted by the famous Fundy tides.
Moncton	Magnetic Hill, Trans Canada Hwy., ext 488B	free	all year	Where cars seems to coast uphill backwards; attracts over 500 000 visitors annually.
	Magic Mountain Water Park	Adults $13.96 Children $9.95 Family (four) $44.00	Summer Season: 10:00-8:00 p.m.	Adjacent to Magnetic Hill, a water theme park, with water slides, a lazy river for tube rides, a wave pool, shops and restaurant facilities.
Campobello Island	Roosevelt International Park, Campobello Island	free	May-Oct: daily	The summer home and furnishings of F.D. Roosevelt.
Fredericton	Kings Landing Historical Settlement, Trans Canada Hwy., exit 259	Adults $6; Youths $3; Seniors $4; Family $13	June 1-Thanksgiving: daily; Oct & Nov. by appointment	A living and working settlement restored to reflect the United Empire Loyalists arrival in the early 1800s. Includes 12 homes, school, church, forge, working saw mill, and grist mill and a costumed staff of over 100.
	Fredericton Military Compound, Carleton St.	free	daily	Restored guard house of 1828-32; officers' quarters now house a museum and guided tours are offered.
	Christ Church Cathedral, Queen St.	free	daily	A beautiful example of decorated Gothic architecture, noted throughout N. America.
	Beaverbrook Art Gallery, 703 Queen St.	Adults $2; Seniors $1; Students $.50	daily	Paintings by the Group of Seven and other Canadian artists, and by Dali, Reynolds, Turner and Hogarth. Sculpture and English porcelains are also on display.
Acadian Coast	Acadian Historical Village, Caraquet	Adults $6 Children $3; Children under 6 free; Family $13	June 1-Sept. 1: daily	A village reminiscent of local Acadian life between 1780-1880: includes residences, school, chapel, fish house, general store, tavern, blacksmith shop, cobbler shop, printing shop, cabinet maker, and other buildings.

Region	Site/Address	Admission	Hours	Description
Grande-Anse	Pope's Museum, 184 rue Acadie	Adults $3; Children $1.50; Seniors $2; Family $7	June 7-Sept 7: daily; Off season: by appointment	Presents a history of the Popes since St. Peter. The museum offers an art gallery, a liturgical treasures hall and a showcase of Pope John Paul II.
Hillsborough	Salem and Hillsborough Railway, Main St., Hillsborough	Adults $6; Seniors $5.50; Children $3; Family $18	mid May-mid June: 1:30pm, 3:00pm mid June-Sept.: 1:30pm, 3:00pm, 4:30pm Oct.: 2:15 pm	Equipment in use or on display includes 1913 Steam Crane, 1940 CN Caboose, 1946 CN Diesel Switcher, Steam locomotives, and assorted passenger and freight cars. Train rides available along retired CNR track across Hiram Creek trestle bridge.
St. Andrews	St. Andrews Blockhouse National Historic Site, Joe's Point Rd.	free	June-mid Sept: daily	War of 1812 restored blockhouse fortification, interpretive displays and guided tours.
	The Huntsman Marine Laboratory and Aquarium	Adults $3; Students & Seniors $2 Family $8	Mid May-Oct: daily	Provides insight into life in the depths of the Bay of Fundy through live specimens, displays, and A/V presentations. A "please touch tank" and playful Harbour Seals have special appeal for children.
Shippagan	Marine Centre, Rte. 113	Adults $3; Children $1.50; Students $2; Seniors $2; Family $9	May-Sept.: daily	The Centre's aquarium, museum and theatre provide an in-depth study of the Gulf of St. Lawrence's marine life, fishing industry and fishermen.

Quebec

(Contact: Tourisme Québec, C.P. 20 000, Quebec, Que, G1K 7X2)

Region	Site/Address	Admission	Hours	Description
Quebec City (a world heritage site)	Place Royale, 25, rue St. Pierre	free	daily	Champlain founded the 1st permanent settlement here in 1608.
	Hôtel du Parlement, Parliament Hill	free	Tours: Mon-Fri. 24 June-1 Sept: daily no tours: June & Dec.	Built between 1877-86, the National Assembly sits in the Blue Chamber. The public may attend debates.
	Fortifications of Quebec, 100, rue St. Louis	free	May-Sept: Wed.-Sun.	The oldest walls of their kind in N. America.
	The Citadel, 1, Côte de la citadelle, Quebec	Adults $3; Children $1	Tel.: 648-3563 for hours	Made up of 25 buildings, including the Governor General's residence and regimental museum. Changing of the guard mid-June to Labour Day, 10:00.
	Martello Towers, 390, rue de Bernières	free	closed Wed. Open June 1-Sept. 1	Built before 1796 to protect the western approach to the city.
	Basilique Notre-Dame de Quebec, 16, rue Buade	free	daily	Richly decorated, historical basilica.
	Holy Trinity Anglican Cathedral, 31 rue des Jardins	free	daily	Modelled on the Church of St. Martin-in-the-Fields of London; contains priceless treasures.
	Basilique Sainte-Anne-de-Beaupré, 10 018 ave. Royale, Sainte-Anne-de-Beaupré	free	daily masses at hours which vary according to the seasons	Includes an historical cyclorama, and several chapels in addition to the shrine. A site of pilgrimage since 1658.
	Galarie du Musée, 24, blvd. Champlain	free	Closed Mon.-Tue.	Focus on contemporary art with works by Quebec and other artists.
	Musée du Quebec, 1, ave. Wolfe-Montcalm	free	daily, except closed Mon., Sept. 15-June 14.	Collection highlights Quebec art from the 17th century to present day.

Region	Site/Address	Admission	Hours	Description
	Musée et archives du seminaire de Quebec, 9, rue de l'Université	Adults $2; Students and seniors $1; Children $.50;	closed Mon. summer hours: call 692-2843	Each of its 8 rooms centres around a different theme; Quebec art, European secular and religious art, Oriental art, jewellery, stamps, etc.
	Musée de la civilisation, 85, rue Dalhousie Quebec	Adults $4; Students $2; Seniors $3; Under 17 free	daily	Collection of Amerindian-Inuit and Euro-Québécoise art. Including beautiful furniture, pewter, ceramics and glass; tools and instruments; antique toys. Opened Oct. 1988.
	Quebec Winter Carnival, 290, rue Joly	–	Feb. 2-12, 1989	The famous Carnival is known for its spirit of fun which pervades the city. There are many events; the canoe race across the frozen St. Lawrence R. is a highlight. There are also ice sculptures, games and "Bonhomme Carnaval".
Gaspé Peninsula	Percé Rock, 357, route de la mer, Ste. Flavie	free	daily	One of the most photographed landmarks in Canada.
Charlevoix	Le Massif de-Petite-Rivière-Saint-François, Hwy. 138	$27	On reservation (418) 435-3593	800 m vertical drop is the highest in Quebec for skiing.
Montreal	Festival international de Jazz de Montreal, 355 o, rue Ste. Catherine	n.a.	July, 1989	Parades, street entertainers, free concerts each day.
	Le Vieux Montreal	free	daily	Charming, restored old city of Montreal.
	Notre-Dame Basilica, Place d'Armes, 116, rue Notre-Dame Ouest	free	daily	One of the most beautiful and one of the largest churches in N. America. Built 1824-29.
	The Sulpician Seminary, Notre-Dame	–	tours every 30 mins. daily	Montreal's oldest building, constructed 1685. The clock is the oldest public time-piece in N. America (1700).
	Notre-Dame-de-Bonsecours Chapel, 440 St. Paul St. E.	free	daily	The "sailors's church", built in 1772, houses numerous objet d'art.
	Montreal City Hall, 275 Notre-Dame St. E.	–	–	Re-built in 1922; fine example of public architecture.
	Mount Royal, Belvedere, Look-Out, Mount Royal Park	free	always open	Enjoy a fine view of the city of Montreal and the St. Lawrence R.
	Musée d'art contemporain de Montréal, Cité du Havre	free	Tues.-Sun.	Various exhibits and retrospectives.
	Musée des beaux arts de Montréal/Montréal Museum of Fine Arts, 1379, rue Sherbrooke Ouest	free	Tues.-Sun. and Thurs.	Sculpture, paintings, furniture, porcelain, ceramics, fabrics and tapestry, stained glass, Historic and contemporary Canadian, Quebec, Inuit, and Indian art, and representations from: ancient Egypt, Greece and Rome; Middle Ages to current Europe; China, Japan, Africa, etc.
	McCord Museum, 690 Sherbrooke St. W.	Family $2; Adults $1; Students and seniors $.75; Children $.50	Wed.-Sun.	A museum of social history with the only comprehensive collection of Canadian ethnology in Quebec; a collection of costumes and textiles; extensive collection of paintings, prints, and drawings and the Notman Photographic Archives, consisting of 700 000 negatives and prints from the early days of photography.
	St-Joseph's Oratory, 3800 Queen Mary Road	free	daily	A world renowned landmark; attracts millions of pilgrims because of the miraculous healings said to have occurred here.
	Olympic Park, 4545 Pierre de Coubertin Ave.	Guided tours: Adults $4; Children $2.50	guided tours daily; check events at (514) 252-4737	Includes the Stadium, Velodrome and swimming pools all built for the Olympics of 1976.

Ontario

(Contact: Ministry of Tourism and Recreation, Queen's Park, Toronto, Ont. M7A 2E5)

Region	Site/Address	Admission	Hours	Description
Elora	Elora Gorge	n.a.	daily	A spectacular limestone canyon with many caves, waterfalls and rapids.
Hamilton	Art Gallery of Hamilton, 123 King St. W.	n.a.	daily except Mon.	A collection of paintings, sculptures and graphics by Canadian, European and American artists.
	Dundurn Castle, Dundurn Park	n.a.	daily, afternoons only	The home of Sir Allan Napier McNab, prime minister of the United Provinces of Canada, 1854-56, has been restored to its former splendor.
	Royal Botanical Gardens Plains Rd., west of Hamilton	free	daily	The gardens contain a wide variety of natural areas over 1 000 ha. Colorful displays of famous plant collections run all year in the Mediterranean Greenhouse Complex ($1 adults; $.75 children & seniors). A teahouse overlooks the rock garden.
Kitchener/Waterloo	Oktoberfest, various festival halls	varies	9 days, early-mid. Oct.	One of the largest Bavarian festivals in N. America.
	Farmer's Market, Kitchener	free	every Sat. May-Dec.: Wed. 7h-14h	Features local produce and handicrafts from the area's Mennonite farmers and craftspeople.
Niagara Falls	Niagara Falls	free	all year	One of the natural wonders of the world; equally spectacular summer and winter. Illumination makes the falls a great attraction at night.
The Shaw Festival	P.O. Box 774, Niagara-on-the-Lake, Ont. L0S 1J0	check with theatre	early April-mid-Oct.	The only festival in the world devoted to the production of plays written by George Bernard Shaw. Numerous plays are staged during the season, including both evening and matinee performances.
The Stratford Shakespearean Festival	55 Queen St., P.O. Box 520, Stratford M5A 6V2	check with theatre	May-Oct.	During each season performances are held at the 3 theatres of the Festival: the Festival Theatre, the Avon Theatre and the Third Stage. The Festival is internationally acclaimed and features both classical and modern plays and musicals.
Algonquin Park	Highway 60	check with park	all year	A well-known provincial park; 7 511 sq. km, crisscrossed with canoe routes and hiking trails. Excellent fishing and canoeing.
Midland	Sainte-Marie among the Hurons, Highway 12	n.a.	mid May-Thanksgiving: daily	A reconstruction of the Jesuit mission that was the only inland European settlement north of Mexico in the 17th century.
	Martyr's Shrine, opposite Sainte-Marie	n.a.	Victoria Day weekend-Thanksgiving: daily	Attracts many pilgrims each year. Six of N. America's 8 martyred saints were missionaries here.
Toronto	Provincial Parliament Building, Queen's Park	free	summer: daily; fall and winter: weekdays	Built in the late 1800s, this imposing edifice of pink sandstone and granite is the seat of Ontario's government and home to the Legislature.
	Casa Loma, 1 Austin Terrace	Adults $5; Children & Seniors $2	all year: daily except Jan.-Feb.: weekends only	A fairytale castle in the centre of the city, built in 1911 at a cost of $3 million.
	City Hall, Queen and Bay Sts.	free	all year: daily guided tours	A Toronto landmark. At Nathan Phillips Square there are summers arts and crafts shows, ethnic festivals and concerts; in winter, the reflecting pool becomes a skating rink.
	Ontario Place, 955 Lakeshore Blvd. W.	Adults $6 Children $2; 65 and over $3	mid-May to mid-Sept.	A waterfront development of islands and futuristic buildings featuring entertainment for all ages and theme pavilions.
	Harbourfront, Queen's Quay	free	daily	Waterfront redevelopment stretches 4 km along Lake Ontario and includes an antique market, theatre, films, concerts, etc. and the ferry to the Toronto Islands.
	Canada's Wonderland 9580 Jane St., Maple	Adults $19.75; Children $9.95; less than 3 years free	end of May to Labour Day: daily May, June, Sept. Oct.: weekends	A large theme park, featuring Hanna-Barbera Land, The Smurfs and exciting rides.
	CN Tower, 301 Front St. W.	Adults $8; Youth $4.50; Children $4; Seniors $4.50	daily	The world's tallest free-standing structure, with indoor and outdoor observation decks, including the highest observation deck in the world at 457 m.

Region	Site/Address	Admission	Hours	Description
	Royal Ontario Museum, 100 Queen's Park	Adults $5; Seniors and children $3 Family $10	daily	Canada's largest public museum with galleries featuring life sciences, fossils, art, and archeology collections.
	Eaton Centre, Dundas and Yonge Sts.	free	all year: daily	Toronto's largest downtown, indoor shopping complex with stores; restaurants and theatres on 3 levels.
	Exhibition Stadium, Exhibition Place at Lakeshore Blvd. W.	varies	varies	Home of the Blue Jays and Argonauts, check with stadium for ticket availability.
	Art Gallery of Ontario, 317 Dundas St. W.	Adults $3.50; All others $1.50; Children under 12 free	daily	One of Canada's most important fine arts museums, the Gallery houses a collection of 11 000 works including the world's largest collection of Henry Moore sculpture.
	Ontario Science Centre, 770 Don Mills Rd.	Adults $5.50; Youth $4.50 Children $1.75	daily	Based on the concept that science and technology are an engrossing part of our lives, visitors are encouraged to touch, feel and experiment with exhibits.
	Canadian National Exhibition, Exhibition Place, Lakeshore Blvd. W.	Adults $5; Children $2; Seniors, before 1h free, after $1.50	mid-Aug. to Labour Day	The oldest and largest annual exhibition in the world with agricultural and technical exhibits, a large midway, a spectacular airshow and grandstand show.
	Metro Toronto Zoo, Meadowvale Rd.	Adults $7; Students and seniors $4; Children $2; less than 5 yrs. free	daily	One of the largest, most comprehensive and enlightened zoos in the world. Herds and species of animals roam freely across its 5 major zoological preserves: Africa, Australia, Eurasia, Indo-Malaya and the Americas.
	Old Fort York, Garrison Rd.	Adults $3; Children and seniors $1.50	daily	Rebuilt in 1813 and now restored with 8 original log, stone and brick buildings. Marches of the Fort York Guard.
Kleinburg	McMichael Canadian Collection	Adults $2.50; Seniors $1.50; Students and children up to 15 $1; less than 5 yrs. free; Family $6	daily	One of the most important collections of paintings by the Group of Seven and Tom Thomson.
Kingston	Old Fort Henry, junction of Hwys. 2 and 15	n.a.	mid-May to mid-Oct.: daily	A living museum of military life, architecture, and artifacts of the 1800s complete with colorful guardsmen, thundering cannons and military drills.
Maxville	Glengarry Highland Games	n.a.	Saturday before first Monday in Aug.	Pipe bands, pipers and Scottish dancers from all over N. America gather to compete in one of Canada's largest Highland gatherings.
Morrisburg	Upper Canada Village, Hwy. 2	n.a.	mid-May to mid-Oct.: daily	A composite pre-1867 town that recreates the period with working woollen mill, sawmill and blacksmith's shop. There are 35 buildings which can be seen on foot, by horse-drawn cart or "bateau".
Ottawa	Parliament Buildings, Parliament Hill	free	tours daily	Canada's seat of government crowned by the Peace Tower. Changing of the Governor General's Foot Guards can be seen during July and Aug. daily at 10:00 a.m. When House of Commons is in session, visitors may sit in the gallery.
	Canadian War Museum, 330 Sussex Dr.	free	daily	National collection of art, artifacts, and hardware related to Canada's military past.
	National Aviation Museum, Rockcliffe Airport	free	May-Labour Day: daily; Sept.-May: Tues.-Sun.	Housed in World War II hangars, a collection of 105 aircraft, engines and aviation artifacts, from pioneering days of aviation to the present.
	Canadian Museum of Civilization, relocating to Hull in July 1989.	free	closed until July 1989	The first of its kind in N. America, dealing with Canadian history and heritage. A wide range of exhibition techniques are used, from models and films to electronic games.

Region	Site/Address	Admission	Hours	Description
	National Museum of Science and Technology, 1867 St.-Laurent Blvd.	free	May-Labour Day: daily; Labour Day-Apr.: Tues.-Sun.	Displays of locomotives and vintage cars to the most recent technological advances; participation and testing of skills are encouraged.
	National Gallery of Canada, 380 Sussex Dr.	free	daily except Christmas and Mondays, Sept.-Apr.	National collection of art, both large and varied, from Europe and Canada.
	National Arts Centre, Confederation Square	grounds are free; theatre prices vary	daily	An opera house, 2 theatres, sculpture, flowers and terraces on the banks of the Rideau Canal. Home of the National Arts Centre Symphony Orchestra.
	National Museum of Natural Sciences, McLeod St. at Elgin St.	free	May-Labour Day: daily Closed Mon. rest of the year.	Housed in a beautiful and historic building, the museum illustrates the wonderful world of nature.
	Rideau Canal, throughout Ottawa city centre	free	daily	Used for pleasure-boat cruising in summer and for Winterlude: a 10-day carnival during early Feb. with ice sculptures, sporting events, skating and entertainment.
	Festival of Spring throughout Ottawa	free	2d or 3d wk. of May	Over 4 million tulips bloom during this Spring Festival; also includes outdoor beer gardens, flea markets, fireworks and other events.
Sudbury	Science North, 100 Ramsey Lake Rd.	Adults $5; Children and seniors $3; Family $14	daily	In the shape of 2 giant snowflakes on a rocky outcrop, this centre is a place for discovery and exploration of the dynamics of science.
Sault Ste. Marie	Agawa Canyon	Adults $34; Children $17 ($12 in June, July, Aug.)	check with railway	The Algoma Central Railway is the only way to visit this scenic wilderness area, with its waterfalls, mountains, ravines and forests. The foliage is spectacular in the fall; the Snow Train runs during the winter.

Manitoba

(Contact: Travel Manitoba, Dept. 9254, 7th Floor-155 Carlton St., Winnipeg, Man. R3C 3H8)

Region	Site/Address	Admission	Hours	Description
Winnipeg	Red and Assiniboine River boat tours along river front	ticket prices and operating hours vary		M.S. Lord Selkirk, M.S. River Rouge, and M.S. Paddlewheel Queen paddlewheel boats and cruise ships provide trips on the 2 rivers.
	Manitoba Museum of Man and Nature, 190 Rupert St.	Adults $2.50; Students, Seniors, Children 12 and under $1.50; less than 3 years free	daily	Has 7 major galleries: Orientation, Grasslands, Earth History, Arctic-Subarctic, Boreal Forest, the Nonsuch (full-scale replica of 17th century ketch), Urban Gallery.
	Winnipeg Art Gallery, 300 Memorial Blvd.	free but fees may be charged for special exhibits	daily except Mon. and holidays	Contemporary Canadian paintings, prints, drawings and sculpture with focus on Manitoba artists. Historical Canadian works, contemporary American prints, a collection of Gothic panel paintings, Decorative Arts and a large collection of contemporary Inuit Art.
	IMAX Theatre, Portage Place Mall, Level 3–393 Portage	varies reserved seats only	daily	Offers the viewer the world's largest movie format: 55 feet high and 71 feet wide.
	Folklorama: pavilions and activities located throughout the city	varies	first 2 wks. in Aug.	Approximately 40 cultures are represented in different pavilions. Cuisine, performances of singing and dancing, artwork and handicraft displays, parades and ceremonies characterize the festival.
Churchill	Polar Bear Tours and Beluga Whale Tours	varies	summer and fall	All-terrain vehicles take you to the tundra to view polar bears that congregate when the ice first freezes. In early summer, the gentle Beluga whales enter Churchill Harbour and boat tours take the tourist to within 15 m of the whales. Churchill is also noted for spectacular sights of Aurora Borealis, fishing, hunting and bird-watching.

Saskatchewan

(Contact: Tourism Saskatchewan, 1919 Saskatchewan Dr., Regina, Sask. S4P 3V7)

Region	Site/Address	Admission	Hours	Description
Maple Creek	Fort Walsh National Historic Park	free	Mid-May to mid-Oct.	Early North-West Mounted Police post reconstructed to 1882; trading post restored to 1872.
Moose Jaw	Kinsmen International Band Festival, Moose Jaw Civic Centre	n.a.	mid-May	Largest annual event of its kind in N. America; 7 000 musicians, 110 bands, and 50 choral groups compete for awards.
	Saskatchewan Air Show, CFB Moose Jaw	n.a.	mid-July	Largest annual air show on the prairies with military and civil aeronautics and stunts, featuring the Snowbirds.
Craven	Big Valley Jamboree, 37 km N.W. of Regina	n.a.	mid-July	Leading country music stars featured with Canadian and U.S. talent.
Regina	Legislative Building, Legislative Dr.	free	daily	Built 1908-12 and designed to reflect the architecture of English renaissance and Louis XVI of France. With 265 rooms.
	Legislative Building Art Gallery, Legislative Dr.	free	daily	Portraits, photographs and artwork exhibited, with displays on Saskatchewan history.
	Saskatchewan Museum of Natural History, College Ave. and Albert St.	free	daily	Large diorama showcases provide views of wildlife in natural environments, also features geology, paleontology, archaeology, conservation and zoology displays.
	Canadian Western Agribition, Exhibition grounds	n.a.	end Nov.-early Dec.	Top rated N. American livestock show with annual sales of $2.5 million. Indoor rodeo, horserama, pedigreed grain show and Mexabition.
	Plains Historical Museum, 1801 Scarth St.	Adults $1; Seniors and students $.50; less than 6 yrs. free	Mon.-Fri.: 11:30 am to 5 pm Wknds:afternoons	A human history museum which tells the story of the Plains People. Includes Indian, Métis, and pioneer artifacts, period rooms: a sod hut, school room, kitchen and parlor.
	Wascana Centre	free	daily	Includes a magnificent park, marina, museum of natural history and bird sanctuary in the centre of the city.
Battleford	Battleford National Historic Park, 4.8 km S.E. of North Battleford on Central Ave.	free	May-mid-Oct.: daily	Original North-West Mounted Police post with 4 period-furnished barracks and reconstructed stockade/bastions.
Meadow Lake	Meadow Lake Provincial Park, N.W. of Meadow Lake	park fees	daily	Includes excellent beaches, and over 150 000 ha of forest and waterways.
Saskatoon	Western Development Museum, 2610 Lorne Ave. S.	Adults $2.50; Seniors $1.50; Children $.75; Under 6 free	daily	A living museum which preserves the history of western Canada. Includes Boom Town (1910) and old-time shops.
	Mendel Art Gallery, 950 Spadina Cr. E.	free	daily	Features permanent art collection and changing exhibitions of international, national and regional artwork.
	Ukrainian Museum of Canada, 910 Spadina Cr. E.	Adults $1; Seniors and children: $.50	daily	Features displays on Ukrainian culture in Canada, family life, immigration history, etc. Also folk art workshops, travelling exhibits and tours.

Alberta

(Contact: Travel Alberta, 15th Floor, 10025 Jasper Ave., Edmonton, Alta. T5J 3Z3)

Region	Site/Address	Admission	Hours	Description
Calgary	Glenbow Museum, 130-9th Ave. S.E.	Adults $2; Students and children $1; less than 12 yrs. free; Seniors $.50	Tues.-Sun.: daily	The history of western Canada is interpreted through displays of art and lifestyle. The museum has an extensive collection of western Cree and Plains Indians artifacts and one of the best gun collections in the country.

Region	Site/Address	Admission	Hours	Description
	Calgary Exhibition and Stampede, Stampede Park and throughout the city	1-800-661-1260 (toll free) for information	July 7-16 (1989)	The famous Stampede features the Half Million Dollar Rodeo, Chuckwagon Racing, stage shows, Indian Village, Western Village, Midway, agricultural and art exhibits, parades and pancake breakfasts.
	Heritage Park, West of 14th St. and Heritage Dr., S.W.	Adult $5; Senior $4.50; Youth (12-17) $3.50; Child (3-11) $2.50; under 3 free	May 21-Labour Day: daily	Over 100 exhibits and restored buildings, antique railway cars and a sternwheeler represent prairie town life in the early 1900s.
	Calgary Zoo, Botanical Gardens/ Prehistoric Park, St. George's Island	Adults $5.50; Youth $2.75; Children $1.50; Seniors $2.75	daily	The 2d largest zoo in Canada, with a large lowland gorilla display, a diverse collection of animals in natural settings, and the Prehistoric Park (life-size dinosaur sculptures).
	Fort Calgary, 750-9 Ave. S.E.	free	daily (summer)	The original site of Fort Calgary has historical exhibits, audio-visual displays and artifacts of the early settlers.
	Dinosaur Provincial Park, 40 km N.E. of Brooks	park fees	daily	Proclaimed a World Heritage Site in 1980, the park has dinosaur fields and interpretive programs; admittance to park areas is restricted.
Fort Macleod	Fort Macleod Museum	Adults $3; Seniors $2.50; Students $1; Children $.50	May-Oct.; daily	A representation of the original North-West Mounted Police fort (built 1874). A mounted patrol ride entertains July-Aug., daily.
	Head-Smashed-In Buffalo Jump, 16 km W. of Hwy. 2 on Secondary Hwy. 785	free; donations accepted	daily	The largest and best preserved buffalo jump in North America was used for more than 5 600 years by the Plains people to drive Bison to their death. Declared a World Heritage Site by UNESCO. Interpretive Centre explains area's history.
Drumheller	Dinosaur Trail	free	daily	A 40 km loop west of Drumheller, the trail offers views of Red Deer River Badlands, Homestead Antique Museum, and Horsethief Canyon Viewpoint.
	Tyrrell Museum of Paleontology, Dinosaur Trail	free; donations accepted	daily	The world's most extensive display of dinosaurs, a wide variety of fossils, computers, videos and interactive displays are highlights of this museum.
Icefields Parkway (Hwy. 93)	Columbia Icefields Tours, 105 km S. of Jasper	Adults $13; Children $7; less than 5 yrs. free	last week in May to Sept.	View the Athabasca and Dome glaciers and Mount Athabasca. Ice-walk tours are also available.
Lake Louise	Victoria Glacier, Moraine Lake, Valley of the Ten Peaks, 13 km E. of Lake Louise	n.a.	seasonal	The Lake Louise Gondola Lift offers spectacular views of Lake Louise, Victoria Glacier and the Bow Range. The emerald-colored Moraine Lake is surrounded by the 10 Wenkchemna Peaks.
Banff	Sunshine Village, 8 km W of Banff/ Mount Norquay, 5 km from Banff	n.a.	seasonal	Two renowned downhill ski resorts where a Winter Festival and ski events are held annually. The Sunshine gondola operates in the summer late June to early Sept.
Jasper	Marmot Basin	n.a.	seasonal	Marmot Basin has recreational skiing, ski races, an Ice Sculpting Contest in Jan. and Winter Carnival in Feb.
Edmonton	Provincial Museum, 12845-102 Ave.	free	daily	Alberta's heritage and history represented in 4 major galleries: paleontology, zoology, Indian artifacts, settlers and fur traders.
	Klondike Days, Northlands Coliseum and throughout city	varies	July 19-28 (1989)	Gambling casinos, gold-panning, Sourdough River Raft Race, Sunday Promenade, pancake breakfasts and all day entertainment are featured.
	Fort Edmonton Park, Whitemud Dr. and Fox. Dr.	Adults $4.50; Seniors $3.25; Children 13-17 $3.25; 6-12 $2.25	summer: daily winter: Sat., Sun., holidays	As well as a full-scale replica of Fort Edmonton, the park has a historical village with 1885 Street, 1905 Street, 1920 Street, and the George McDougall Shrine.

Region	Site/Address	Admission	Hours	Description
	West Edmonton Mall, 170 St. and 87 Ave.	varies	open daily	The world's largest shopping and recreation mall has aquaria, aviaries, shopping, entertainment, a water park, dolphin shows, submarine rides, the Ice Palace skating rink and an indoor amusement park.
	Edmonton Art Gallery, 2 Sir Winston Churchill Sq.	Adults $2; Students/ Seniors $1; Under 12 free	daily	Contemporary and historical Canadian and international art is exhibited in this collection of over 1 200 works; also has a children's gallery.
	Edmonton Space Sciences Centre, Coronation Park, 142 St. and 111 Ave.	exhibits free; admission for shows	daily	The largest planetarium in Canada features hands-on exhibits, the Devonian IMAX Theatre, Margaret Zeidler Theatre, films on space, flying and other topics.
	Strathcona Archaeological Centre, Strathcona Science Park, between Hwys. 16 and 16A	free; donations accepted	Victoria Day-Labour Day: daily	An ongoing archaeological excavation of a 5 000 year old site, with a display centre and guided tours through the excavation site.

(See Banff and Jasper National Parks p. 481)

British Columbia

(Contact: Tourism British Columbia, Parliament Buildings, Victoria, B.C. V8V 1X4)

Region	Site/Address	Admission	Hours	Description
Vancouver	Arts, Sciences and Technology Centre, 1455 Quebec St.	Adults $5; Seniors $4; Children $3	daily	Features participatory science demonstrations, exhibits, special live performances, arts workshops, and an electricity show each weekend. Located in Expo Centre.
	The Dr. Sun Yat-Sen Classical Chinese Garden, Chinatown	Adults $3; Seniors and students $2 Children (6-15) $1.50; Family $6	daily	Situated in the heart of Chinatown, the Garden is the first authentic classical Chinese garden ever built outside of China. The Garden is also the site of a gallery displaying items from the Ming Dynasty.
	Chinatown, Pender St.	free	daily	One of the largest Chinatowns in N. America with many restaurants, shops and a food market.
	Canada Pavilion, entrance at north end of Howe St.	n.a.	n.a.	Designed like an ocean-going vessel with five soaring white sails that form the roofline. Facilities include a cruise-ship dock, luxury hotel, CN IMAX Theatre, amphitheatre, restaurant and promenades.
	B.C. Pavilion, near B.C. Place Stadium Gate	n.a.	n.a.	These 3 buildings surround the glass-covered Plaza of Nations on the site of Expo 86 and showcase B.C.'s people, their cultures, the landscapes and achievements in technology.
	Gastown, Water St.	free	daily	A scenic area with 1880s-style architecture, cobblestone streets, restored buildings, a steam clock, antique stores, wax museum, art shops, restaurants and boutiques.
	Granville Island, south end of Granville St. bridge	free	market open Tues. to Sun. (winter) daily (summer)	This restored site now offers a public market, live theatre, restaurants, artisan shops, art galleries, a playground, water park, and Granville Island brewery.
	Grouse Mountain aerial tramway, 6400 Nancy Green Way	Adults $8.50; Seniors $6; Children (6-16) $5; less than 6 yrs. free; family $20	daily	The tramway rises to an elevation of 1 100 m giving spectacular views of the city and mountains. Grouse Mountain has hiking and nature trails, an adventure playground, chairlift rides and skiing 7 days a week in winter.
	Stanley Park, Georgia St.	free	daily	400 ha peninsula located near the city centre noted for its beaches, playgrounds, swimming pools, golf, tennis courts, forest walks, Park Zoo, Totem Poles, Lions Gate Bridge, Siwash Rock, Prospect Point, and the seawall promenade.

Region	Site/Address	Admission	Hours	Description
	Vancouver Public Aquarium, Stanley Park	Adults $5.50; Seniors $4.25; Children (5-12) $3; Family $14; Youth (13-18) $4.25; less than 5 yrs. free	daily	Over 8 000 aquatic animals, 3 Killer whales, dolphins and Beluga whales, an underwater viewing gallery, sea otters, harbor seals, sharks, native fish and exotic fish from around the world.
	Vancouver Art Gallery, 750 Hornby St.	Adults $2.50; Seniors and students $1; less than 12 yrs free	closed Mon.	The major works of Emily Carr, works by Canadian, British, Dutch, French and American artists from the 17th century to the present in painting, sculpture, graphic arts and photography are on display.
	Royal Hudson Steam Train (T) and Brittania Boat/Train Tours (B/T), Train depot: 1311 W. 1st St. N. Vancouver; Boat Dock: foot of Denman St., Vancouver	Adults $20 (T), $38 (B/T); Youth and Seniors $16 (T), $34 (B/T); Children (5-11) $12 (T), $23 (B/T); less than 5 yrs. free	May to Sept., Wed.-Sun. monthly except Aug.: daily	A trip by steam train to the old logging town of Squamish, with scenic mountain and ocean views. The Royal Hudson Train/MV Brittania excursion takes you by boat to Howe Sound and then to Squamish.
North Vancouver	Capilano Suspension Bridge and Park, 3735 Capilano Rd.	Adults $4; Seniors $3.50; Students $3; Children $1; less than 6 yrs. free	daily	70 m above Capilano River, the bridge is 137 m across; the park has gardens, waterfalls, and mountain scenery, picnicking and hiking.
Barkerville	Barkerville 1870s Goldrush Town	Adults $5; Seniors and Youth $3; Children (6-12) $1; Children under 5 free; Family $10	daily	An 1860s to 1870s gold rush town brought back to life with a live theatre show, gold panning, displays, and tours. The museum and Theatre Royal are open only in summer.
Duncan	B.C. Forest Museum	n.a.	May to Sept.	A park setting with indoor/outdoor exhibits depicting the theme of "Man in the Forest"; walking trails guide you through the history of the forest industry.
Port Alberni	Cathedral Grove, Hwy. 4 through MacMillan Provincial Park	free	daily	West coast cedars and Douglas Fir soar above the forest floor in one of the few accessible examples of virgin forest.
Victoria	Royal B.C. Provincial Museum, 675 Belleville St.	Adults $5; Seniors and Youth $3; Children (6-12) $1; Children under 5 free; Family $10	daily (closed Christmas and New Year's)	B.C. history, coastal and interior Indian artifacts and natural history are recounted and displayed in guided tours, lectures and films.
	Parliament Buildings, 501 Belleville St.	free	all year: daily guided tours	B.C. history, architecture and history of buildings, legislative information and procedure, and a visit to the Legislative Chamber are featured.
	Butchart Gardens, 22 km N. of Victoria on Hwy. 17	Adults $8; Children (13-17) $4; (5-12) $1	daily	Famous for the beautiful Italian, English Rose, Japanese, and Sunken Gardens, Star Pond, Concert Lawn, Ross Fountain, Fireworks Basin and Show Greenhouse. The gardens are illuminated at dusk May to Sept.: fireworks and stage shows take place in July and Aug.
	Empress Hotel, 721 Government St.	free to hotel	daily	Facing the harbor, the hotel is a landmark in Victoria where high tea is a major attraction.
	Craigdarroch Castle, Joan Cr.	Adults $3; Seniors/Students $2.50	daily	A castle built during the second half of the 1880s.

Yukon

(Contact: Tourism Yukon, P.O. Box 2703, Whitehorse, Yukon Y1A 2C6)

Region	Site/Address	Admission	Hours	Description
Whitehorse	MacBride Museum, 1st Ave. and Wood St.	$3	May-Sept.: daily	The memorabilia of early life in the frontier offers a glimpse into the history of the city and the Territory.
	Frantic Follies Vaudeville Revue, Sheffield Hotel	$14	June-mid-Sept.: nightly	Includes songs and skits from the gold rush, can-can dancers and the poetry of Robert Service.
	S.S. Klondike Riverboat, Yukon R. at Robert Campbell Bridge	free	mid-May-mid-Sept.: daily	One of the largest sternwheelers to ply Yukon waters has been fully fitted, furnished and restored as a National Historic Site.
	Old Log Church, 3rd Ave. and Elliot St.	n.a.	June-Sept.: daily	First opened in 1900 as an Anglican Church, the log church was reopened as a museum in 1962. The museum, now officially designated as an historical site, display documents, artifacts and photographs related to early missionary work.
	Yukon Gardens, top of south access rd. to Alaska Hwy.	$4.75	daily	The only northern show garden in the western world. Features wild and domestic fruit, flora, and vegetables.
Dawson City	Ft. Herchmer Tour, St. Paul's Anglican Church	free	daily except Sun.	Tours at 11 h and 16 h daily of the historic buildings, barracks and churches.
	Steamer *Keno*, Front St.	free	June 1-Sept. 15: daily	One of the last riverboats on the Yukon and Stewart rivers, the *Keno* is now a National Historic Site.
	Dawson City Museum, 5th Ave.	$3	daily	Local history with emphasis on the Klondike gold rush is featured.
	Gaslight Follies Theatre, 3rd Ave. and King St.	$8-10	nightly except Tues.	The performance in the authentically reconstructed Palace Grand Theatre is a 2 hour show with live entertainment in turn-of-the-century music-hall style with music, songs and dancing, featuring spectacular costumes.
	Diamond Tooth Gertie's Gambling Casino	$3	May-Sept.: nightly	Operated by the Klondike Visitors Association, Gertie's provides frolicking adult entertainment reminiscent of the '98 gold rush.
	Discovery Days, throughout the city	–	mid-Aug.	Gold was discovered Aug. 17, 1896 in the Klondike and each year Dawson City remember the occasion with a parade, raft and canoe races, dances and other events.
Kluane	Silver City Ghost Town, Kluane Lake	free	Tues.-Fri. and Sun.	Once an important settlement, now abandoned; a trading post, road-house and North-West Mounted Police barracks can still be seen.
	Kluane Park Interpretive Centre	free	daily	The Centre features an arrangement of internationally acclaimed audio-visual displays focussing on the grandeur of Kluane—the largest Canadian park with the highest mountain range in North America and largest non-polar ice fields in the world. The Centre also arranges guided hikes through the park for groups of 20 or more.
	Sheep Mountain Interpretive Area	free	daily	Information focusses on the Dall sheep, who live here year-round.

(See Kluane National Park, page 481)

Northwest Territories

(Contact: TravelArctic, Yellowknife, N.W.T. X1A 2L9 or Arctic Hotline 1-800-661-0788)

Region	Site/Address	Admission	Hours	Description
Yellowknife	Prince of Wales Northern Heritage Centre, Frame Lake North	free	summer: daily winter: closed Wed., Christmas and New Year's Day	Focusses on Canadian Arctic and Subarctic archaeology, ethnology, history and the natural sciences. Local fine and decorative arts are also on display.
	Midnight Sun Tournament, Yellowknife Golf Club	n.a.	3d weekend in June	Tee-off is at midnight in this tournament held over the solstice weekend. It is open to individuals and to small groups.

(See Nahanni, Wood Buffalo and Auyuittuq National Parks on pages 481–482.)

n.a. not available; – not applicable.

Awards, Medals and Prizes

The Governor General's Literary Awards, 1976–1987

The Governor General's Literary Awards, Canada's foremost literary prizes, are presented annually to recognize and reward Canadian writers. The awards were initiated in 1937 by the Canadian Author's Association with the agreement of Governor General Baron Tweedsmuir (novelist John Buchan), and were administered by the Association until 1958.

The Awards are now administered by the Canada Council which appoints juries composed of literary specialists who select the best English and French-language works in each of 6 best categories: drama, fiction, poetry, non-fiction, and beginning in 1987, children's literature (text and illustration) and translation. The juries review all books by Canadian authors, illustrators and translators published in Canada or abroad during the previous year (Dec. 1—Nov. 30). In the case of translation, the original work must also be a Canadian-authored title. Winners receive a medal from the Governor General, $5 000 and a specially-bound copy of their award-winning book.

English	Year and Category	French
	1976	
Bear, Marion Engel	**Fiction**	*Les rescapés*, André Major
The Writing of Canadian History, Carl Berger	**Non-fiction**	*Les Bas Canada 1791-1840 changements structuraux et crise*, Fernand Ouellet
Top Soil, Joe Rosenblatt	**Poetry or Drama**	*Poèmes 1946-1968*, Alphonse Piché
	1977	
The Wars, Timothy Findley	**Fiction**	*Ces enfants de ma vie*, Gabrielle Roy
Essays on the Constitution, Frank Scott	**Non-fiction**	*Le développement des idéologies au Québec des origines à nos jours*, Denis Monière
Under the Thunder the Flowers Light up the Earth, D.G. Jones	**Poetry or Drama**	*Les Célébrations et Adidou Adidouce*, Michel Garneau[1]
	1978	
Who Do You Think You Are?, Alice Munro	**Fiction**	*Les grandes marées*, Jacques Poulin
Go Boy, Roger Caron	**Non-fiction**	*Paul-Emile Borduas: Biographie critique et analyse de l'œuvre*, François-Marc Gagnon
Poems New and Selected, Patrick Lane	**Poetry or Drama**	*Mon refuge est un volcan*, Gilbert Langevin
	1979	
The Resurrection of Joseph Bourne, Jack Hodgins	**Fiction**	*Le Sourd dans la ville*, Marie-Claire Blais
Emily Carr: A Biography, Maria Tippett	**Non-fiction**	*Le fait anglais au Quebec*, Dominique Clift et Sheila McLeod Arnopoulos
There's a Trick with a Knife I'm Learning to Do, Michael Ondaatje	**Poetry or Drama**	*Peinture aveugle*, Robert Melançon
	1980	
Burning Water, George Bowering	**Fiction**	*La première personne*, Pierre Turgeon
Discipline of Power: The Conservative Interlude and the Liberal Restoration, Jeffrey Simpson	**Non-fiction**	*La famille et l'homme à délivrer du pouvoir*, Maurice Champagne-Gilbert.
McAlmon's Chinese Opera, Stephen Scobie	**Poetry or Drama**	*De l'œil et de l'écoute*, Michel Van Schendel
	1981	
Home Truths: Selected Canadian Stories, Mavis Gallant	**Fiction**	*La province lunaire*, Denys Chabot
Caribou and the barren-lands, George Calef	**Non-fiction**	*L'échappée des discours de l'œil*, Madeleine Ouellette-Michalska
The Collected Poems of F.R. Scott, F.R. Scott	**Poetry**	*Visages*, Michel Beaulieu
Blood Relations, Sharon Pollack	**Drama**	*C'était avant la guerre à l'Anse à Gilles*, Marie Laberge
	1982	
Man Descending, Guy Vanderhaeghe	**Fiction**	*Le cercle des arènes*, Roger Fournier
Louisbourg Portraits: Life in an Eighteenth-Century Garrison Town, Christopher Moore	**Non-fiction**	*Le marxisme des années soixante: une saison dans l'histoire de la pensée critique*, Maurice Lagueux
The Vision Tree: Selected Poems, Phyllis Webb	**Poetry**	*Forages*, Michel Savard
Billy Bishop Goes To War, a play by John Gray with Eric Peterson, John Gray	**Drama**	*HA ha!. . .*, Réjean Ducharme
	1983	
Shakespeare's Dog, Leon Rooke	**Fiction**	*Laura Laur*, Suzanne Jacob
Byng of Vimy: General and Governor General, Jeffrey Williams	**Non-fiction**	*Le contrôle social du crime*, Maurice Cusson
Settlements, David Donnell	**Poetry**	*Un goût de sel*, Suzanne Paradis
Quiet in the Land, Anne Chislett	**Drama**	*Syncope*, René Gingras

English	Year and Category	French
	1984	
The Engineer of Human Souls, Josef Skvorecky	**Fiction**	*Agonie*, Jacques Brault
The Private Capital: Ambition and Love in the Age of Macdonald and Laurier, Sandra Gwyn	**Non-fiction**	*Le XXᵉ siècle: Histoire du catholicisme québecois*, Jean Hamelin et Nicole Gagnon
Celestial Navigation, Paulette Jiles	**Poetry**	*Double Impression*, Nicole Brossard
White Biting Dog, Judith Thompson	**Drama**	*Ne blâmez jamais les Bédouins*, René-Daniel Dubois
	1985	
The Handmaid's Tale, Margaret Atwood	**Fiction**	*Lucie ou un midi en novembre*, Fernand Ouellette
The Regenerators: Social Criticism in Late Victorian English Canada, Ramsay Cook	**Non-fiction**	*La littérature contre elle-même*, François Ricard
Waiting for Saskatchewan, Fred Wah	**Poetry**	*Action Writing*, André Roy
Criminals in Love, George F. Walker	**Drama**	*Duo pour voix obstinées*, Maryse Pelletier
	1986	
The Progress of Love, Alice Munro	**Fiction**	*Les silences du corbeau*, Yvon Rivard
Northrop Frye on Shakespeare, Northrop Frye	**Non-fiction**	*Le réalism socialiste: une esthétique impossible*, Régine Robin
The Collected Poems of Al Purdy, Al Purdy	**Poetry**	*L'écouté*, Cecile Cloutier
Doc, Sharon Pollack	**Drama**	*La visite des sauvages*, Anne Legault
	1987	
A Dream Like Mine, M.T. Kelly	**Fiction**	*L'Obsédante Obèse et autres agressions*, Gilles Archambault
The Russian Album, Michael Ignatieff	**Non-fiction**	*La Petite Noirceur*, Jean Larose
Afterworlds, Gwendolyn MacEwen	**Poetry**	*Les Heures*, Fernand Ouellette
Prague, John Krizanc	**Drama**	*Un oiseau vivant dans la gueule*, Jeanne-Mance Delisle
Rainy Day Magic, Marie-Louise Gay	**Children's Literature (Illustration)**	*Venir au monde*, Darcia Labrosse
Galahad Schwartz and the Cockroach Army, Morgan Nyberg	**Children's Literature (Text)**	*Le Don*, David Schinkel and Yves Beauchesne
Enchantment and Sorrow: The Autobiography of Gabrielle Roy, Patricia Claxton	**Translation**	*L'homme qui se croyait aimé, ou La vie secrete d'un premier ministre*, Ivan Steenhout and Christiane Teasdale

(1) Award declined by the recipient.

The Izaak Walton Killam Memorial Prize

Source: Canada Council

The Izaak Walton Killam Memorial Prizes, inaugurated in 1981, are awarded each March in recognition of distinguished lifetime achievement and outstanding contributions to the advancement of knowledge in the natural sciences, engineering and health sciences. The three $50 000 prizes, administered by the Canada Council, are financed through a donation by Mrs. Dorothy J. Killam, reflecting the intentions of her husband an outstanding Canadian industrialist and philanthropist. A 15-member committee of scholars from various academic disciplines is responsible for selecting the winners.

	Winners	Institution	Research field
1981¹	Feroze Ghadially	University of Saskatchewan	pathology
	Raymond Lemieux	University of Alberta	chemistry
	Louis Siminovitch	University of Toronto/Hospital for Sick Children	medical genetics
1982	William Tutte	University of Waterloo	mathematics
1983	Brenda Milner	McGill University/Montreal Neurological Institute	neuropsychology
1984	Werner Israel	University of Alberta	physics
1985²	Pierre Dansereau	Université de Québec	ecology
	Phil Gold	McGill University	medicine
	Ralph Gordon Stanton	University of Manitoba	mathematics
	Raymond N. Yong	McGill University	engineering
1986	Jacques Genest	Clinical Research Institute of Montreal/ University of Montreal/McGill University	medicine
	Howard Rapson	University of Toronto	engineering
	Karel Wiesner	University of New Brunswick	chemistry
1987	Ronald James Gillespie	McMaster University	chemistry
	James Fraser Mustard	McMaster University	medicine
	Ashok Vijh	Quebec Hydro Research Institute	engineering
1988	Henry J.M. Barnett	John P. Robarts Research Institute	neurology
	William Gauvin	McGill University	engineering
	John Polanyi	University of Toronto	chemistry

(1) For the inaugural year, 3 prizes were awarded. (2) Owing to the number of outstanding nominees, the Canada Council decided to award 4 prizes in 1985.

The Booker Prize

Source: Book Trust Book House

The Booker Prize for Fiction was established in 1968 in response to the need for a significant British literary award. The intention of the prize is to reward merit, raise the stature of the author in the eyes of the public and increase the sales of the books. Booker, an international food and agriculture business, provides the financial backing, and Book Trust, an educational charity subsidized by the Arts Council of Great Britain, administers the prize. The value of the Booker Prize, since 1984, is £15 000. (The short list of authors for each year appears below with winners in **boldface**.)

1970
Bernice Rubens, *The Elected Member*
A.L. Barker, *John Brown's Body*
Elizabeth Bowen, *Eva Trout*
Iris Murdoch, *Bruno's Dream*
William Trevor, *Mrs Eckdorf in O'Neill's Hotel*
T. Wheeler, *The Conjunction*

1971
V.S. Naipaul, *In a Free State*
Thomas Kilroy, *The Big Chapel*
Doris Lessing, *Briefing for a Descent into Hell*
Mordecai Richler, *St. Urbain's Horseman*
Derek Robinson, *Goshawk Squadron*
Elizabeth Taylor, *Mrs Palfrey at the Claremont*

1972
John Berger, *G*
Susan Hill, *Bird of Night*
Thomas Keneally, *The Chant of Jimmy Blacksmith*
David Storey, *Pasmore*

1973
J.G. Farrell, *The Siege of Krishnapur*
Beryl Bainbridge, *The Dressmaker*
Elizabeth Mavor, *The Green Equinox*

1974
Nadine Gordimer, *The Conservationist*
Kingsley Amis, *Ending Up*
Beryl Bainbridge, *The Bottle Factory Outing*
Stanley Middleton, *Holiday*
C.P. Snow, *In Their Wisdom*

1975
Ruth Prawer Jhabvala, *Heat and Dust*
Thomas Keneally, *Gossip from the Forest*

1976
David Storey, *Saville*
Andre Brink, *An Instant in the Wind*
R.C. Hutchinson, *Rising*
Brian Moore, *The Doctor's Wife*
Julian Rathbone, *King Fisher Lives*
William Trevor, *The Children of Dynmouth*

1977
Paul Scott, *Staying On*
Paul Bailey, *Peter Smart's Confessions*
Caroline Blackwood, *Great Granny Webster*
Jennifer Johnston, *Shadows on Our Skin*
Penelope Lively, *The Road to Lichfield*
Barbara Pym, *Quartet in Autumn*

1978
Iris Murdoch, *The Sea*
Kingsley Amis, *Jake's Thing*
Andre Brink, *Rumours of Rain*
Penelope Fitzgerald, *The Bookshop*
Jane Gardam, *God on the Rocks*
Bernice Rubens, *A Five-Year Sentence*

1979
Penelope Fitzgerald, *Offshore*
Thomas Keneally, *Confederates*
V.S. Naipaul, *A Bend in the River*
Julian Rathbone, *Joseph*
Fay Weldon, *Praxis*

1980
William Golding, *Rites of Passage*
Anthony Burgess, *Earthly Powers*
J.L. Carr, *A Month in the Country*
Anita Desai, *Clear Light of Day*
Alice Munro, *The Beggar Maid*
Julia O'Faolain, *No Country for Young Men*
Barry Unsworth, *Pascali's Island*

1981
Salman Rushdie, *Midnight's Children*
Molly Keane, *Good Behaviour*
Doris Lessing, *The Sirian Experiments*
Ian McEwan, *The Comfort of Strangers*
Anne Schlee, *Rhine Journey*
Muriel Spark, *Loitering with Intent*
D.M. Thomas, *The White Hotel*

1982
Thomas Keneally, *Schindler's Ark*
John Arden, *Silence Among the Weapons*
William Boyd, *An Ice-Cream War*
Lawrence Durrell, *Constance or Solitary Practices*
Alice Thomas Ellis, *The 27th Kingdom*
Timothy Mo, *Sour Sweet*

1983
J.M. Coetzee, *Life & Times of Michael K*
Malcolm Bradbury, *Rates of Exchange*
John Fuller, *Flying to Nowhere*
Anita Mason, *The Illusionist*
Salman Rushdie, *Shame*
Graham Swift, *Waterland*

1984
Anita Brookner, *Hotel du Lac*
J.G. Ballard, *Empire of the Sun*
Julian Barnes, *Flaubert's Parrot*
Anita Desai, *In Custody*
Penelope Lively, *According to Mark*
David Lodge, *Small World*

1985
Keri Hulme, *The Bone People*
Peter Carey, *Illywhacker*
J.L. Carr, *The Battle of Pollocks Grossing*
Doris Lessing, *The Good Terrorist*
Jan Morris, *Last Letters from Hav*
Iris Murdoch, *The Good Apprentice*

1986
Kingsley Amis, *The Old Devils*
Margaret Atwood, *The Handmaid's Tale*
Paul Bailey, *Gabriel's Lament*
Robertson Davies, *What's Bred in the Bone*
Kazuo Ishiguro, *An Artist of the Floating World*
Timothy Mo, *An Insular Possession*

1987
Penelope Lively, *Moon Tiger*
Chinua Achebe, *Anthills of the Savannah*
Peter Ackroyd, *Chatterton*
Nina Bawden, *Circles of Deceit*
Brian Moore, *The Colour of Blood*
Iris Murdoch, *The Book and the Brotherhood*

The Alfred B. Nobel Prize Winners

Alfred B. Nobel, inventor of dynamite, bequeathed $9 000 000 U.S., the interest to be distributed yearly to those who had most benefited mankind in physics, chemistry, medicine-physiology, literature, and peace. The first Nobel Memorial Prize in Economics was awarded in 1969. No awards given for years omitted. In 1987, each prize was worth approximately $442 000 Canadian.

Peace

1988 U.N. Peacekeeping Force
1987 Oscar Arias Sanchez, Costa Rica
1986 Elie Wiesel, U.S.
1985 Intl. Physicians for the Prevention of Nuclear War, U.S.
1984 Bishop Desmond Tutu, So. African
1983 Lech Walesa, Polish
1982 Alva Myrdal, Swedish; Alfonso Garcia Robles, Mexican
1981 Office of U.N. High Commissioner for Refugees
1980 Adolfo Perez Esquivel, Argentine
1979 Mother Teresa of Calcutta, Albanian-Indian
1978 Anwar Sadat, Egyptian Menachem Begin, Israeli
1977 Amnesty International
1976 Mairead Corrigan, Betty Williams, N. Irish
1975 Andrei Sakharov, USSR
1974 Eisaku Sato, Japanese, Sean MacBride, Irish
1973 Henry Kissinger, U.S. Le Duc Tho, N. Vietnamese (Tho declined)
1971 Willy Brandt, W. German
1970 Norman E. Borlaug, U.S.
1969 Intl. Labor Organization
1968 Rene Cassin, French
1965 U.N. Children's Fund (UNICEF)
1964 Martin Luther King Jr., U.S.
1963 International Red Cross, League of Red Cross Societies
1962 Linus C. Pauling, U.S.

1961 Dag Hammarskjold, Swedish
1960 Albert J. Luthuli, South African
1959 Philip J. Noel-Baker, British
1958 Georges Pire, Belgian
1957 Lester B. Pearson, Canadian
1954 Office of the UN High Commissioner for Refugees
1953 George C. Marshall, U.S.
1952 Albert Schweitzer, French
1951 Leon Jouhaux, French
1950 Ralph J. Bunche, U.S.
1949 Lord John Boyd Orr of Brechin Mearns, British
1947 Friends Service Council, Brit. Amer. Friends Service Com.
1946 Emily G. Balch, John R. Mott, both U.S.
1945 Cordell Hull, U.S.
1944 International Red Cross
1938 Nansen International Office for Refugees
1937 Viscount Cecil of Chelwood, Brit.
1936 Carlos de Saavedra Lamas, Arg.
1935 Carl von Ossietzky, German
1934 Arthur Henderson, British
1933 Sir Norman Angell, British
1931 Jane Addams, U.S. Nicholas Murray Butler, U.S.
1930 Nathan Soderblom, Swedish
1929 Frank B. Kellogg, U.S.
1927 Ferdinand E. Buisson, French Ludwig Quidde, German

1926 Aristide Briand, French Gustav Stresemann, German
1925 Sir J. Austen Chamberlain, Brit. Charles G. Dawes, U.S.
1922 Fridtjof Nansen, Norwegian
1921 Karl H. Branting, Swedish Christian L. Lange, Norwegian
1920 Leon V.A. Bourgeois, French
1919 Woodrow Wilson, U.S.
1917 International Red Cross
1913 Henri La Fontaine, Belgian
1912 Elihu Root, U.S.
1911 Tobias M.C. Asser, Dutch Alfred H. Fried, Austrian
1910 Permanent Intl. Peace Bureau
1909 Auguste M. F. Beernaert, Belg. Paul H. B. B. d'Estournelles de Constant, French
1908 Klas P. Arnoldson, Swedish Fredrik Bajer, Danish
1907 Ernesto T. Moneta, Italian Louis Renault, French
1906 Theodore Roosevelt, U.S.
1905 Baroness Bertha von Suttner, Austrian
1904 Institute of International Law
1903 Sir William R. Cremer, British
1902 Elie Ducommun, Charles A. Gobat, both Swiss
1901 Jean H. Dunant, Swiss Frederic Passy, French

Literature

1987 Joseph Brodsky, Russ.-U.S.
1986 Wole Soyinka, Nigerian
1985 Claude Simon, French
1984 Jaroslav Siefert, Czech.
1983 William Golding, British
1982 Gabriel Garcia Marquez, Colombian-Mex.
1981 Elias Cenetti, Bulgarian-British
1980 Czeslaw Milosz, Polish-U.S.
1979 Odysseus Elytis, Greek
1978 Isaac Bashevis Singer, U.S. (Yiddish)
1977 Vicente Aleixandre, Spanish
1976 Saul Bellow, U.S.
1975 Eugenio Montale, Ital.
1974 Eyvind Johnson, Harry Edmund Martinson, both Swedish
1973 Patrick White, Australian
1972 Heinrich Boll, W. German
1971 Pablo Neruda, Chilean
1970 Aleksandr I. Solzhenitsyn, Russ.
1969 Samuel Beckett, Irish
1968 Yasunari Kawabata, Japanese
1967 Miguel Angel Asturias, Guate.
1966 Samuel Joseph Agnon, Israeli Nelly Sachs, Swedish
1965 Mikhail Sholokhov, Russian
1964 Jean Paul Sartre, French (Prize declined)
1963 Giorgos Seferis, Greek

1962 John Steinbeck, U.S.
1961 Ivo Andric, Yugoslavian
1960 Saint-John Perse, French
1959 Salvatore Quasimodo, Italian
1958 Boris L. Pasternak, Russian (Prize declined)
1957 Albert Camus, French
1956 Juan Ramon Jimenez, Puerto Rican-Span.
1955 Halldor K. Laxness, Icelandic
1954 Ernest Hemingway, U.S.
1953 Sir Winston Churchill, British
1952 Francois Mauriac, French
1951 Par F. Lagerkvist, Swedish
1950 Bertrand Russell, British
1949 William Faulkner, U.S.
1948 T.S. Eliot, British
1947 Andre Gide, French
1946 Hermann Hesse, Swiss
1945 Gabriela Mistral, Chilean
1944 Johannes V. Jensen, Danish
1939 Frans E. Sillanpaa, Finnish
1938 Pearl S. Buck, U.S.
1937 Roger Martin du Gard, French
1936 Eugene O'Neill, U.S.
1934 Luigi Pirandello, Italian
1933 Ivan A. Bunin, French
1932 John Galsworthy, British
1931 Erik A. Karlfeldt, Swedish
1930 Sinclair Lewis, U.S.

1929 Thomas Mann, German
1928 Sigrid Undset, Norwegian
1927 Henri Bergson, French
1926 Grazia Deledda, Italian
1925 George Bernard Shaw, British
1924 Wladyslaw S. Reymont, Polish
1923 William Butler Yeats, Irish
1922 Jacinto Benavente, Spanish
1921 Anatole France, French
1920 Knut Hamsun, Norwegian
1919 Carl F. G. Spitteler, Swiss
1917 Karl A. Gjellerup, Danish Henrik Pontoppidan, Danish
1916 Verner von Heidenstam, Swed.
1915 Romain Rolland, French
1913 Rabindranath Tagore, Indian
1912 Gerhart Hauptmann, German
1911 Maurice Maeterlinck, Belgian
1910 Paul J. L. Heyse, German
1909 Selma Lagerlof, Swedish
1908 Rudolf C. Eucken, German
1907 Rudyard Kipling, British
1906 Giosue Carducci, Italian
1905 Henryk Sienkiewicz, Polish
1904 Frederic Mistral, French Jose Echegaray, Spanish
1903 Bjornsterne Bjornson, Norw.
1902 Theodor Mommsen, German
1901 Rene F. A Sully Prudhomme, French

Physiology or Medicine

1987 Susumu Tonegawa, Jap.
1986 Stanley Cohen, U.S.;
Rita Levi-Montalcini, Ital.-U.S.
1985 Michael S. Brown, Joseph L.
Goldstein, both U.S.
1984 Cesar Milstein, Brit.-Argentina;
Georges J. F. Koehler, German;
Niels K. Jerne, Brit.-Danish
1983 Barbara McClintock, U.S.
1982 Sune Bergstrom, Bengt
Samuelsson, both Swedish;
John R. Vane, British.
1981 Roger W. Sperry,
David H. Hubel, Tosten N. Wiesel,
all U.S.
1980 Baruj Benacerraf, George Snell,
both U.S.; Jean Dausset, France
1979 Alian M. Cormack, U.S.
Geoffrey N. Hounsfield, British
1978 Daniel Nathans, Hamilton O. Smith,
both U.S.; Werner Arber, Swiss
1977 Rosalyn S. Yalow, Roger C.L.
Guillemin, Andrew V. Schally, all
U.S.
1976 Baruch S. Blumberg, U.S.
Daniel Carleton Gajdusek, U.S.
1975 David Baltimore, Howard Temin,
both U.S.; Renato Dulbecco,
Ital.-U.S.
1974 Albert Claude, Lux.-U.S.; George
Emil Palade, Rom.-U.S.; Christian
Rene de Duve, Belg.
1973 Karl von Frisch, Ger.; Konrad
Lorenz, Ger.-Austrian; Nikolaas
Tinbergen, Brit.
1972 Gerald M. Edelman, U.S.
Rodney R. Porter, British
1971 Earl W. Sutherland Jr., U.S.
1970 Julius Axelrod, U.S.
Sir Bernard Katz, British
Ulf von Euler, Swedish
1969 Max Delbruck,
Alfred D. Hershey,
Salvador Luria, all U.S.
1968 Robert W. Holley,
H. Gobind Khorana,
Marshall W. Nirenberg, all U.S.

1967 Ragnar Granit, Swedish
Haldan Keffer Hartline, U.S.
George Wald, U.S.
1966 Charles B. Huggins,
Francis Peyton Rous, both U.S.
1965 Francois Jacob, Andre Lwoff,
Jacques Monod, all French
1964 Konrad E. Bloch, U.S.
Feodor Lynen, German
1963 Sir John C. Eccles, Australian
Alan L. Hodgkin, British
Andrew F. Huxley, British
1962 Francis H. C. Crick, British
James D. Watson, U.S.
Maurice H. F. Wilkins, British
1961 Georg von Bekesy, U.S.
1960 Sir F. MacFarlane Burnet,
Australian
Peter B. Medawar, British
1959 Arthur Kornberg, U.S.
Severo Ochoa, U.S.
1958 George W. Beadle, U.S.
Edward L. Tatum, U.S.
Joshua Lederberg, U.S.
1957 Daniel Bovet, Italian
1956 Andre F. Cournand, U.S.
Werner Forssmann, German
Dickinson W. Richards, Jr., U.S.
1955 Alex H. T. Theorell, Swedish
1954 John F. Enders,
Frederick C. Robbins,
Thomas H. Weller, all U.S.
1953 Hans A. Krebs, British
Fritz A. Lipmann, U.S.
1952 Selman A. Waksman, U.S.
1951 Max Theiler, U.S.
1950 Philip S. Hench,
Edward C. Kendall, both U.S.
Tadeus Reichstein, Swiss
1949 Walter R. Hess, Swiss
Antonio Moniz, Portuguese
1948 Paul H. Müller, Swiss
1947 Carl F. Cori,
Gerty T. Cori, both U.S.
Bernardo A. Houssay, Arg.
1946 Hermann J. Muller, U.S.
1945 Ernst B. Chain, British

Sir Alexander Fleming, British
Sir Howard W. Florey, British
1944 Joseph Erlanger, U.S.
Herbert S. Gasser, U.S.
1943 Henrik C. P. Dam, Danish
Edward A. Doisy, U.S.
1939 Gerhard Domagk, German
1938 Corneille J. F. Heymans, Belg.
1937 Albert Szent-Gyorgyi, Hung.-U.S.
1936 Sir Henry H. Dale, British
Otto Loewi, U.S.
1935 Hans Spemann, German
1934 George R. Minot, Wm. P. Murphy,
G. H. Whipple, all U.S.
1933 Thomas H. Morgan, U.S.
1932 Edgar D. Adrian, British
Sir Charles S. Sherrington, Brit.
1931 Otto H. Warburg, German
1930 Karl Landsteiner, U.S.
1929 Christiaan Eijkman, Dutch
Sir Frederick G. Hopkins, British
1928 Charles J. H. Nicolle, French
1927 Julius Wagner-Jauregg, Aus.
1926 Johannes A. G. Fibiger, Danish
1924 Willem Einthoven, Dutch
1923 Frederick G. Banting, Canadian
John J. R. Macleod, Scottish
1922 Archibald V. Hill, British
Otto F. Meyerhof, German
1920 Schack A. S. Krogh, Danish
1919 Jules Bordet, Belgian
1914 Robert Barany, Austrian
1913 Charles R. Richet, French
1912 Alexis Carrel, French
1911 Allvar Gullstrand, Swedish
1910 Albrecht Kossel, German
1909 Emil T. Kocher, Swiss
1908 Paul Ehrlich, German
Elie Metchnikoff, French
1907 Charles L. A. Laveran, French
1906 Camillo Golgi, Italian
Santiago Ramon y Cajal, Sp.
1905 Robert Koch, German
1904 Ivan P. Pavlov, Russian
1903 Niels R. Finsen, Danish
1902 Sir Ronald Ross, British
1901 Emil A. von Behring, German

Chemistry

1987 Donald J. Cram, Charles J. Pederson,
both U.S.; Jean-Marie Lehn, France.
1986 John Polanyi, Canadian; Dudley
Herschback, Yuan Tseh Lee, both U.S.
1985 Herbert A. Hauptman, Jerome
Karle, both U.S.
1984 Bruce Merrifield, U.S.
1983 Henry Taube, Canadian
1982 Aaron Klug, S. African
1981 Kenichi Fukui, Japan.,
Roald Hoffmann, U.S.
1980 Paul Berg., U.S.
Walter Gilbert, U.S.,
Frederick Sanger, U.K.
1979 Herbert C. Brown, U.S.
George Wittig, German
1978 Peter Mitchell, British
1977 Ilya Prigogine, Belgian
1976 William N. Lipscomb, U.S.
1975 John Cornforth, Austral.-Brit.,
Vladimir Prelog, Yugo.-Switz.
1974 Paul J. Flory, U.S.
1973 Ernst Otto Fischer, W. German
Geoffrey Wilkinson, British
1972 Christian B. Anfinsen, U.S.
Stanford Moore, U.S.
William H. Stein, U.S.

1971 Gerhard Herzberg, Canadian
1970 Luis F. Leloir, Arg.
1969 Derek H. R. Barton, British
Odd Hassel, Norwegian
1968 Lars Onsager, U.S.
1967 Manfred Eigen, German
Ronald G. W. Norrish, British
George Porter, British
1966 Robert S. Mulliken, U.S.
1965 Robert B. Woodward, U.S.
1964 Dorothy C. Hodgkin, British
1963 Giulio Natta, Italian
Karl Ziegler, German
1962 John C. Kendrew, British
Max F. Perutz, British
1961 Melvin Calvin, U.S.
1960 Willard F. Libby, U.S.
1959 Jaroslav Heyrovsky, Czech
1958 Frederick Sanger, British
1957 Sir Alexander R. Todd, British
1956 Sir Cyril N. Hinshelwood, British
Nikolai N. Semenov, USSR
1955 Vincent du Vigneaud, U.S.
1954 Linus C. Pauling, U.S.
1953 Hermann Staudinger, German
1952 Archer J. P. Martin, British

Richard L. M. Synge, British
1951 Edwin M. McMillan, U.S.
Glenn T. Seaborg, U.S.
1950 Kurt Alder, German
Otto P. H. Diels, German
1949 William F. Giauque, U.S.
1948 Arne W. K. Tiselius, Swedish
1947 Sir Robert Robinson, British
1946 James B. Sumner, John H.
Northrop, Wendell M. Stanley, all
U.S.
1945 Artturi I. Virtanen, Finnish
1944 Otto Hahn, German
1943 Georg de Hevesy, Hungarian
1939 Adolf F. J. Butenandt, German
Leopold Ruzicka, Swiss
1938 Richard Kuhn, German
1937 Walter N. Haworth, British
Paul Karrer, Swiss
1936 Peter J. W. Debye, Dutch
1935 Frederic Joliot-Curie, French
Irene Joliot-Curie, French
1934 Harold C. Urey, U.S.
1932 Irving Langmuir, U.S.
1931 Friedrich Bergius, German
Karl Bosch, German

1930 Hans Fischer, German
1929 Sir Arthur Harden, British
     Hans von Euler-Chelpin, Swed.
1928 Adolf O. R. Windaus, German
1927 Heinrich O. Wieland, German
1926 Theodor Svedberg, Swedish
1925 Richard A. Zsigmondy, German
1923 Fritz Pregl, Austrian
1922 Francis W. Aston, British
1921 Frederick Soddy, British

1920 Walther H. Nernst, German
1918 Fritz Haber, German
1915 Richard M. Willstatter, German
1914 Theodore W. Richards, U.S.
1913 Alfred Werner, Swiss
1912 Victor Grignard, French
     Paul Sabatier, French
1911 Marie Curie, Polish-French
1910 Otto Wallach, German
1909 Wilhelm Ostwald, German

1908 Ernest Rutherford, British
1907 Eduard Buchner, German
1906 Henri Moissan, French
1905 Adolf von Baeyer, German
1904 Sir William Ramsay, British
1903 Svante A. Arrhenius, Swedish
1902 Emil Fischer, German
1901 Jacobus H. van't Hoff, Dutch

Physics

1987 J. Georg Bednorz, W. German;
     K. Alex Müller, Swiss
1986 Ernst Ruska (W. Germ),
     Gerd Bennig (W. Germ.),
     Heinrich Rohrer (Swiss)
1985 Klaus von Klitzing, W. German
1984 Carlo Rubbia, Italian, Simon van
     der Meere, Dutch
1983 Subrahmanyan Chandrasekhar,
     William A. Fowler, both U.S.
1982 Kenneth G. Wilson, U.S.
1981 Nicolass Boembergen, Arthur
     Schlawlow, both U.S.; Kai M.
     Siegbahn, Swedish
1980 James W. Cronin, Val L. Fitch, both
     U.S.
1979 Steven Weinberg, Sheldon L.
     Glashow, both U.S.; Abdus Salam,
     Pakistani
1978 Pyotr Kapitsa, USSR; Arno
     Penzias, Robert Wilson, both U.S.
1977 John H. Van Vleck, Philip W.
     Anderson, both U.S.; Nevill F. Mott,
     British
1976 Burton Richter, U.S.
     Samuel C.C. Ting, U.S.
1975 James Rainwater, U.S.
     Ben Mottelson, U.S.-Danish,
     Aage Bohr, Danish
1974 Martin Ryle, British
     Antony Hewish, British
1973 Ivar Giaever, U.S.
     Leo Esaki, Japan
     Brian D. Josephson, British
1972 John Bardeen, U.S.
     Leon N. Cooper, U.S.
     John R. Schrieffer, U.S.
1971 Dennis Gabor, British
1970 Louis Neel, French
     Hannes Alfven, Swedish
1969 Murray Gell-Mann, U.S.
1968 Luis W. Alvarez, U.S.
1967 Hans A. Bethe, U.S.
1966 Alfred Kastler, French

1965 Richard P. Feynman, U.S.
     Julian S. Schwinger, U.S.
     Shinichiro Tomonaga, Japanese
1964 Nikolai G. Basov, USSR
     Aleksander M. Prochorov, USSR
     Charles H. Townes, U.S.
1963 Maria Goeppert-Mayer, U.S.
     J. Hans D. Jensen, German
     Eugene P. Wigner, U.S.
1962 Lev. D. Landau, USSR
1961 Robert Hofstadter, U.S.
     Rudolf L. Mossbauer, German
1960 Donald A. Glaser, U.S.
1959 Owen Chamberlain, U.S.
     Emilio G. Segre, U.S.
1958 Pavel Cherenkov, Ilya Frank,
     Igor Y. Tamm, all USSR
1957 Tsung-dao Lee,
     Chen Ning Yang, both U.S.
1956 John Bardeen, U.S.
     Walter H. Brattain, U.S.
     William Shockley, U.S.
1955 Polykarp Kusch, U.S.
     Willis E. Lamb, U.S.
1954 Max Born, British
     Walter Bothe, German
1953 Frits Zernike, Dutch
1952 Felix Bloch, U.S.
     Edward M. Purcell, U.S.
1951 Sir John D. Cockcroft, British
     Ernest T. S. Walton, Irish
1950 Cecil F. Powell, British
1949 Hideki Yukawa, Japanese
1948 Patrick M. S. Blackett, British
1947 Sir Edward V. Appleton, British
1946 Percy Williams Bridgman, U.S.
1945 Wolfgang Pauli, U.S.
1944 Isidor Isaac Rabi, U.S.
1943 Otto Stern, U.S.
1939 Ernest O. Lawrence, U.S.
1938 Enrico Fermi, Italian
1937 Clinton J. Davisson, U.S.
     Sir George P. Thomson, British
1936 Carl D. Anderson, U.S.

     Victor F. Hess, Austrian
1935 Sir James Chadwick, British
1933 Paul A. M. Dirac, British
     Erwin Schrodinger, Austrian
1932 Werner Heisenberg, German
1930 Sir Chandrasekhara V. Raman,
     Indian
1929 Prince Louis-Victor de Broglie,
     French
1928 Owen W. Richardson, British
1927 Arthur H. Compton, U.S.
     Charles T. R. Wilson, British
1926 Jean B. Perrin, French
1925 James Franck,
     Gustav Hertz, both German
1924 Karl M. G. Siegbahn, Swedish
1923 Robert A. Millikan, U.S.
1922 Niels Bohr, Danish
1921 Albert Einstein, Ger.-U.S.
1920 Charles E. Guillaume, French
1919 Johannes Stark, German
1918 Max K. E. L. Planck, German
1917 Charles G. Barkla, British
1915 Sir William H. Bragg, British
     Sir William L. Bragg, British
1914 Max von Laue, German
1913 Heike Kamerlingh-Onnes, Dutch
1912 Nils G. Dalen, Swedish
1911 Wilhelm Wien, German
1910 Johannes D. van der Waals, Dutch
1909 Carl F. Braun, German
     Guglielmo Marconi, Italian
1908 Gabriel Lippmann, French
1907 Albert A. Michelson, U.S.
1906 Sir Joseph J. Thomson, British
1905 Philipp E. A. von Lenard, Ger.
1904 John W. Strutt, Lord Rayleigh,
     British
1903 Antoine Henri Becquerel, French
     Marie Curie, Polish-French
     Pierre Curie, French
1902 Hendrik A. Lorentz,
     Pieter Zeeman, both Dutch
1901 Wilhelm C. Roentgen, German

Nobel Memorial Prize in Economics

1987 Robert Solow, U.S.
1986 James Buchanan, U.S.
1985 Franco Modigliani, It.-U.S.
1984 Richard Stone, British
1983 Gerard Debreu, Fr.-U.S.
1982 George J. Stigler, U.S.
1981 James Tobin, U.S.
1980 Lawrence R. Klein, U.S.
1979 Theodore W. Schultz, U.S.,

     Sir Arthur Lewis, British
1978 Herbert A. Simon, U.S.
1977 Bertil Ohlin, Swedish
     James E. Meade, British
1976 Milton Friedman, U.S.
1975 Tjalling Koopmans, Dutch-U.S.,
     Leonid Kantorovich, USSR
1974 Gunnar Myrdal, Swed.,
     Friedrich A. von Hayek, Austrian

1973 Wassily Leontief, U.S.
1972 Kenneth J. Arrow, U.S.
     John R. Hicks, British
1971 Simon Kuznets, U.S.
1970 Paul A. Samuelson, U.S.
1969 Ragnar Frisch, Norwegian
     Jan Tinbergen, Dutch

Noted Canadians

Widely-Known Canadians of the Present

Biographies of Canadian prime ministers are found on pages 35-39; authors are on pages 560-61; sports personalities are on pages 648-651; entertainers are listed on pages 528-539.

Harold Ballard, b. July 30, 1905, Toronto, Ont.: principal owner Toronto Maple Leafs and Maple Leaf Gardens; owner Hamilton Tiger-Cats.

William Bennett, b. Kelowna, B.C., Apr. 14, 1932: former British Columbia premier (1975-86).

Conrad Black, b. Montreal, Que., Aug. 25, 1944: chairman of Argus Corporation Ltd., one of Canada's largest conglomerates.

Robert Bourassa, b. Montreal, Que., July 14, 1933: Quebec premier since 1985 and from 1970-76.

Ed Broadbent, b. Oshawa, Ont., Mar. 21, 1936: national leader of the New Democratic party since 1975.

Charles Bronfman, b. Montreal, Que. June 27, 1931: chairman of Cemp Investments Ltd. and of the Montreal Expos.

John Buchanan, b. Sydney, N.S., Apr. 22, 1931: Nova Scotia premier since 1978 and provincial P.C. leader since 1971.

Shirley Carr, b. Niagara Falls, Ont.: president of the Canadian Labor Congress since 1986.

Jean Chrétien, b. Shawinigan, Que., Jan. 11, 1934: finished 2d in 1984 Liberal leadership contest; member of Parliament (1965-86) and prominent member of federal Cabinet in Trudeau government.

Alex Colville, b. Toronto, Ont., Aug. 24, 1920: artist and lecturer: represented in permanent collections of the National Gallery and Museum of Modern Art (N.Y.).

David Crombie, b. Toronto, Ont., Apr. 24, 1936: federal cabinet minister, 1979-80 and 1984-88; mayor of Toronto (1973-78).

John Crosbie, b. St. John's, Nfld., Jan. 30, 1931: minister of international trade; justice minister (1984-86).

John Crow, b. 1937, London, England: Governor of the Bank of Canada since 1987.

Ken Danby, b. Sault Ste. Marie, Ont., Mar. 6, 1940: artist, known for realistic paintings.

Bill Davis, b. Brampton, Ont., July 30, 1929: former Ontario premier (1971-84).

Paul Desmarais, b. Sudbury, Ont., Jan. 4, 1927: chairman of Power Corporation of Canada.

Grant Devine, b. Regina, Sask., July 5, 1944: Saskatchewan premier since 1982 and provincial P.C. leader since 1979.

Brian Dickson, b. Yorkton, Sask., July 25, 1916: chief justice of the Supreme Court of Canada since 1984.

Jean Drapeau, b. Montreal, Que., Feb. 18, 1916: former mayor of Montreal (1954-57 and 1960-86).

Gary Filmon, b. Aug. 24, 1942, Winnipeg, Man. Manitoba premier since 1988 and provincial P.C. leader since 1983.

Maureen Forrester, b. Montreal, Que., July 25, 1930: contralto; chairman of the Canada Council since 1984.

John Fraser, b. Yokohama, Japan, Dec. 15, 1931: speaker of the House of Commons (1986-88).

Barbara Frum, b. Niagara Falls, Ont., Sept. 8, 1938: broadcaster and announcer, CBC "The Journal".

Marc Garneau, b. Quebec, Que., Feb. 23, 1949: first Canadian astronaut (U.S. space shuttle Oct. 1984).

Don Getty, b. Westmount, Que., Aug. 30, 1933: Alberta premier and provincial P.C. leader since 1985.

Joe Ghiz, b. Charlottetown, P.E.I., Jan. 27, 1945: Prince Edward Island premier since 1985 and provincial Liberal leader since 1981.

Peter Gzowski, b. Toronto, Ont., July 13, 1934: radio host and author, *The Game of Our Lives* (1981).

Richard Hatfield, b. Hartland, N.B., Apr. 9, 1931: former New Brunswick premier (1970-1987).

Mel Hurtig, b. Edmonton, Alta., June 24, 1932: Canadian nationalist and publisher, *The Canadian Encyclopedia* (1985).

K.C. Irving, b. Buctouche, N.B., Mar. 4, 1899: industrialist, established Irving Oil and other major businesses in New Brunswick.

Norman Jewison, b. July 21, 1926, Toronto, Ont.: film director; many Academy Award nominations including best director for *Moonstruck* (1987); founder and co-chairman of the Canadian Centre for Advanced Film Studies.

Karen Kain, b. Hamilton, Ont., Mar. 28, 1951: principal dancer with the National Ballet of Canada.

Yousuf Karsh, b. Mardin, Armenia-in-Turkey, Dec. 23, 1908: photographer, renowned for portraits of international personalities.

Stephen Lewis, b. Ottawa, Ont., Nov. 11, 1937: Canadian Ambassador to the United Nations (1984-88); Ontario NDP leader (1970-78).

Peter Lougheed, b. Calgary, Alta., July 26, 1928: former Alberta premier (1971-85).

Peter Mansbridge, b. July 6, 1948, London, England: chief correspondent, anchor of The National and all CBC television news specials.

Don Mazankowski, b. Viking, Alta., July 27, 1931: deputy prime minister since 1986; transport minister (1984-86).

Frank McKenna, b. Apolaqui, N.B., Jan. 19, 1948: New Brunswick premier since 1987 and provincial Liberal leader since 1985.

Henry Morgentaler, b. Lodz, Poland, Mar. 19, 1923: doctor whose challenge of Canada's abortion law led to a Supreme Court ruling that the law was unconstitutional.

Mila Mulroney (née Pivnicki), b. Sarajevo, Yugoslavia, July 13, 1953: married Brian Mulroney May 26, 1973; honorary chairperson Cystic Fibrosis Foundation.

Knowlton Nash, b. Toronto, Ont., Nov. 18, 1927: CBC news broadcaster.

Jim Pattison, b. Saskatoon, Sask., Oct. 1, 1928: businessman, owns the Jim Pattison Group; chairman of Expo '86.

Brian Peckford, b. Whitbourne, Nfld., Aug. 27, 1942: Newfoundland premier and provincial P.C. leader since 1979.

David Peterson, b. Toronto, Ont., Dec. 28, 1943: Ontario premier since 1985 and provincial Liberal leader since 1982.

Peter Pocklington, b. Regina, Sask., Nov. 18, 1941: entrepreneur; owner of the Edmonton Oilers.

Christopher Pratt, b. St. John's, Nfld., Dec. 9, 1935: artist; has developed style known as "conceptual realism."

Lloyd Robertson, b. Jan. 19, 1934, Stratford, Ont.: chief anchor and senior news editor for CTV news.

J.J. Robinette, b. Toronto, Ont., Nov. 20, 1906: lawyer, gained his reputation in several renowned criminal cases; recently counsel in the Supreme Court of Canada.

Jeanne Sauvé, b. Prud'homme, Sask., Apr. 26, 1922: Governor General of Canada since 1984.

Edward Schreyer, b. Beausejour, Man., Dec. 21, 1935: Governor General of Canada (1979-84); Manitoba premier (1969-77).

Joey Smallwood, b. Gambo, Nfld., Dec. 24, 1900: led Newfoundland into Confederation and was the province's first premier (1949-72).

David Suzuki, b. Vancouver, B.C., Mar. 24, 1936: scientist, educator, television personality.

E.P. Taylor, b. Ottawa, Ont., Jan. 29, 1901: financier, industrialist, founded Argus Corporation Ltd.

Ken Thomson, b. Toronto, Ont., Sept. 1, 1923: businessman, chairman of Thomson Newspapers Ltd.

Bill Vander Zalm, b. Noordwykerhout, Holland, May 29, 1934: British Columbia premier and leader of B.C. Social Credit party since 1986.

Galen Weston, b. England, Oct. 29, 1940: chairman and president of George Weston Ltd.

Bob White, b. Ireland, Apr. 28, 1935: national president of the Canadian Auto Workers union.

Michael Wilson, b. Toronto, Ont., Nov. 4, 1937: finance minister since 1984.

Widely-Known Canadians of the Past

William Aberhart (1978-1943), b. Hibbard Twp., Ont.: founded the Social Credit party in Canada; Alberta premier (1935-43).

Frederick G. Banting (1891-1941), b. Alliston, Ont.: co-discoverer of insulin for which he was awarded the Nobel prize in medicine (1923).

W. "Max" Aitken (Baron Beaverbrook) (1879-1964), b. Maple, Ont.: Canadian publisher and philanthropist; minister in British Cabinet up to 1945.

W.A.C. Bennett (1900-1979), b. Hastings, N.B.: British Columbia premier (1952-72).

Charles H. Best (1899-1978), b. West Pembroke, Me.: co-discoverer of insulin with Banting.

Norman Bethune (1890-1939), b. Gravenhurst, Ont.: surgeon, died while assisting the Chinese revolutionary army.

Billy Bishop (1894-1956), b. Owen Sound, Ont.: WWI flying ace, shot down 72 enemy aircraft, including 25 in a 10-day period in 1918.

Samuel Bronfman (1891-1971), b. Brandon, Man.: industrialist, established the success of the Seagram Company Limited.

Jack Bush (1909-1977), b. Toronto, Ont.: abstract artist.

Frank Carmichael (1890-1945), b. Orillia, Ont.: artist, founding member of the Group of Seven.

Emily Carr (1871-1945), b. Victoria, B.C.: artist and writer, best known for her paintings of native Indian life.

George-Étienne Cartier (1814-1873), b. St. Antoine, Upper Canada: leading French-Canadian Father of Confederation; joint premier of United Canada (1857-62).

Maurice Duplessis (1890-1959), b. Trois-Rivières, Que.: Quebec premier (1936-39) and (1944-59).

Timothy Eaton (1834-1907), b. Ballymena, Ireland: founded the T. Eaton Co. in 1869.

Sir Sandford Fleming (1827-1915), b. Kirkcaldy, Scotland: engineer, chief surveyor of the Canadian Northern Railway route; developed the system of international Standard Time and designed Canada's first postage stamp.

Glenn Gould (1932-1982), b. Toronto, Ont.: classical pianist and composer.

Joseph Howe (1804-1873), b. Halifax, N.S.: politician and journalist, led fight against Nova Scotia entry into Confederation but later accepted post in federal Cabinet.

Alexander Y. (A.Y.) Jackson (1882-1974), b. Montreal, Que.: artist, best known for his paintings of the Canadian landscape, member and promoter of the Group of Seven.

Paul Kane (1810-1871), b. Mallow, Ireland: artist and explorer, best known for paintings of the Canadian West and native Indians.

Izaak Walton Killam (1885-1955), b. Yarmouth, N.S.: industrialist and philanthropist, built international investment empire.

Cornelius Krieghoff (1815-1872), b. Amsterdam, Holland: artist, best known for paintings of Quebec habitant life.

René Lévesque (1922-1987), b. New Carlisle, Que.: led separatist Parti Québécois to power in 1976; Quebec premier (1976-85).

William Lyon Mackenzie (1795-1861), b. Dundee, Scotland: organized 1837 rebellion for political reform in Upper Canada; first mayor of Toronto (1935).

Hart Massey (1823-1896), b. Haldemand Twp., Ont.: developed the family farm implement business which became Massey-Ferguson Ltd.

Vincent Massey (1887-1967), b. Toronto, Ont.: first Canadian-born Governor General (1952-59).

Nellie McClung (1873-1951), b. Chatsworth, Ont.: feminist and social reformer, fought for female suffrage and prohibition.

Thomas D'Arcy McGee (1825-1868), b. Carlingford, Ireland: eloquent advocate of Confederation; assassinated Apr. 7, 1868.

Col. Robert Samuel McLaughlin (1871-1972), b. Enniskillen, Ont.: developed a carriage and motor car company which became General Motors of Canada.

Marshall McLuhan (1911-1980), b. Edmonton, Alta.: communications theorist, *The Gutenberg Galaxy* (1962), *Understanding Media: The Extensions of Man* (1964) *The Medium is the Massage* (1967).

Sir William Osler (1849-1919), b. Bond Head, Upper Canada: physician and author, built an international reputation through his wide-ranging abilities as a practitioner and educator.

Louis Joseph Papineau (1786-1871), b. Montreal, Lower Canada: led movement for political reform in Lower Canada.

Wilder Penfield (1891-1976), b. Spokane, Washington: neurosurgeon, a pioneer in mapping the parts of the human brain according to their function.

Louis Riel (1844-1885), b. St. Boniface, Man.: led Metis in North West rebellions of 1870 and 1885; hung for treason in Regina, Nov. 16, 1885.

Hans Selye (1907-1982), b. Vienna, Austria: discovered that mental stress affects physical health (1936).

Roy Thomson (Lord Thomson of Fleet) (1894-1976), b. Toronto, Ont.: newspaper publisher, owned major newspapers in Canada, the U.S. and Britain.

W. Garfield Weston (1893-1978), b. Toronto, Ont.: industrialist, a pioneer in supermarket food retailing in Canada.

James S. Woodsworth (1874-1942), b. Etobicoke, Ont.: founded the Co-operative Commonwealth Federation (later the NDP).

Entertainment, Arts and Media

Best-Selling Records in Canada, 1987[1]

Source: THE RECORD

Singles

1. "La Bamba," Los Lobos
2. "I Wanna Dance . . .," Whitney Houston
3. "Lean On Me," Club Nouveau
4. "Livin' On A Prayer," Bon Jovi
5. "I Want Your Sex," George Michael
6. "Nothing's Gonna . . .," Glenn Medeiros
7. "Nothing's Gonna Stop Us Now," Starship
8. "You Keep Me Hangin' On," Kim Wilde
9. "Funky Town," Pseudo Echo
10. "Boom Boom," Paul Lekakis
11. "With Or Without You," U2
12. "La Isla Bonita," Madonna
13. "Mony Mony," Billy Idol
14. "Walk Like an Egyptian," The Bangles
15. "I Just Died In Your Arms," Cutting Crew
16. "Alone," Heart
17. "Always," Atlantic Starr
18. "Who's That Girl," Madonna
19. "Head to Toe," Lisa Lisa & Cult Jam
20. "At This Moment," Billy Vera & The Beaters
21. "Heart & Soul," T'Pau
22. "The Final Countdown," Europe
23. "Lessons In Love," Level 42
24. "Bad," Michael Jackson
25. "Heat of the Night," Bryan Adams
26. "Together," Joey Gregorash

Albums[1]

1. *Slippery When Wet*, Bon Jovi
2. *The Joshua Tree*, U2
3. *Whitney*, Whitney Houston
4. *Bad*, Michael Jackson
5. *True Blue*, Madonna
6. *La Bamba* (soundtrack)
7. *Graceland*, Paul Simon
8. *Whitesnake*, Whitesnake
9. *Hysteria*, Def Leppard
10. *Into The Fire*, Bryan Adams
11. *Lonesome Jubilee*, John Cougar Mellencamp
12. *Bad Animals*, Heart
13. *Tunnel Of Love*, Bruce Springsteen
14. *Dirty Dancing* (soundtrack)
15. *Tango In The Night*, Fleetwood Mac
16. *A Momentary Lapse of Reason*, Pink Floyd
17. *Who's That Girl* (soundtrack)
18. *The Final Countdown*, Europe
19. *Nothing Like The Sun*, Sting
20. *Always And Forever*, Randy Travis
21. *A Very Special Christmas*, various artists
22. *Vital Idol*, Billy Idol
23. *Girls Girls Girls*, Motley Crue
24. *Licensed to Ill*, The Beastie Boys
25. *Solitude Standing*, Suzanne Vega
26. *Beverly Hills Cop II* (soundtrack)

(1) Based on sales information provided by the record companies.

Top-Selling[1] Canadian Record Singles, 1975-1988

Source: Canadian Recording Industry Association

Artist	Record Title	Canadian Sales
Northern Lights	*Tears Are Not Enough*	300 000 +
The Rovers	*Wasn't That a Party*	200 000 +
Irish Rovers	*The Unicorn*	100 000 +
Alain Barrière	*Tue T'en Vas*	100 000 +
Claudja Barry	*Boogie Woogie Dancin' Shoes*	100 000 +
J & R Williams	*La Danse des Canards*	100 000 +
Anne Murray	*You Needed Me*	100 000 +
Corey Hart	*Never Surrender*	100 000 +
Platinum Blonde	*Crying Over You*	100 000 +
Bryan Adams	*Diana*[2]	100 000 +
Glass Tiger	*Someday*	50 000 +
Corey Hart	*Can't Help Falling In Love*	50 000 +
Bryan Adams	*Heat of the Night*	50 000 +
Nuance	*Vivre Dans La Nuit*	50 000 +
Bryan Adams	*Christmas Time*	50 000 +
Corey Hart	*Everything In My Heart*	50 000 +
Martine St-Clair	*Ce Soir L'Amour Est Dans Tes Yeux*	50 000 +
Glass Tiger	*Don't Forget Me (When I'm Gone)*	50 000 +
Corey Hart	*Boy in the Box*	50 000 +
Heart	*What About Love*	50 000 +
The Bat Boys	*OK Blue Jays*	50 000 +
Bryan Adams	*Heaven*	50 000 +
Fondation Québec Afrique	*Les yeux de la faim*	50 000 +
Gino Vannelli	*Black Cars*	50 000 +
Gowan	*A Criminal Mind*	50 000 +

Artist	Record Title	Canadian Sales
Celine Dion	D'amour et d'amitié	50 000+
Bryan Adams	Run To You	50 000+
Luba	Let It Go	50 000+
Homemade Theatre	Sant Jaws	50 000+
Celine Dion	Une colombe	50 000+
Martine St-Clair	Il y a de l'amour	50 000+
Réné Simard	Comment ça va	50 000+
Men Without Hats	Safety Dance	50 000+
Payola$	Eyes of a Stranger	50 000+
Voggue	Love Buzz	50 000+
Claude Dubois	Femme de Société	50 000+
Straight Lines	Letting Go	50 000+
Chilliwack	My Girl (Gone Gone Gone)	50 000+
Francesca	Il est parti	50 000+
Loverboy	Turn Me Loose	50 000+
Martha & The Muffins	Echo Beach	50 000+
Daniel Hetu	Je t'Attendais	50 000+
Freddie James	Everybody Get Up and Boogie	50 000+
Streetheart	Under My Thumb	50 000+
Nick Gilder	Hot Child In The City	50 000+
Claude Dubois	Le Blues Du Businessman	50 000+
Zachary Richard	L'Arbe Ex Dans Ses Feuilles	50 000+
Martin Stevens	Love Is In The Air	50 000+
Shake	Rien N'est Plus Beau Que L'Amour	50 000+
Patrick Juvet	Ou Sont Les Femmes	50 000+
Dan Hill	Sometimes When We Touch	50 000+
Patsy Gallant	Sugar Daddy	50 000+
April Wine	You Won't Dance With Me	50 000+
Burton Cummings	Stand Tall	50 000+
Réné Simard	Fernando	50 000+
André Gagnon	Wow	50 000+
Sweeney Todd	Roxy Roller	50 000+
Hagood Hardy	The Homecoming	50 000+
Blue Rodeo	Try	50 000+
Luba	When a Man Loves a Woman	50 000+

(1) Includes only Canadian sales of over 50 000, based on certification by the Canadian Recording Industry Association, as of July 1988, of recordings that meet Canadian content standards by satisfying 3 of the following 4 criteria: music by a Canadian; performed by a Canadian artist; Canadian production; lyrics by a Canadian. (2) An extended play single.

Top-Selling[1] Canadian Record Albums, 1975-1988

Source: Canadian Recording Industry Association

Artist	Album Title	Canadian Sales
Bryan Adams	Reckless	1 million+
Corey Hart	Boy In The Box	1 million+
Anne Murray	Greatest Hits	600 000+
Loverboy	Loverboy	500 000+
Zamfir	The Lonely Shepherd	500 000+
Platinum Blonde	Alien Shores	500 000+
Glass Tiger	The Thin Red Line	400 000+
Bryan Adams	Into The Fire	300 000+
Bryan Adams	Cuts Like a Knife	300 000+
Rush	Moving Pictures	300 000+
Corey Hart	First Offense	300 000+
Anne Murray	Christmas Wishes	300 000+
Loverboy	Get Lucky	300 000+
Bob & Doug McKenzie	The Great White North	300 000+
Raffi	Singable Songs For The Very Young	300 000+
Ginette Reno	Je Ne Suis Qu'une Chanson	300 000+
Honeymoon Suite	Honeymoon Suite	200 000+
Gowan	Strange Animal	200 000+
Dan Hill	Longer Fuse	200 000+
Burton Cummings	Dream of a Child	200 000+
Heart	Dreamboat Annie	200 000+
Kim Mitchell	Shakin' Like a Human Being	200 000+
Bryan Adams	Into The Night	200 000+
Platinum Blonde	Standing in the Dark	200 000+
Honeymoon Suite	The Big Prize	200 000+
Sharon, Lois and Bram	One Elephant, Deux Elephants	200 000+
Corey Hart	Fields of Fire	200 000+
Raffi	More Singable Songs	200 000+
Prism	Armageddon	200 000+
Angele Arsenault	Libre	200 000+
Harmonium	Harmonium	200 000+

Artist	Album Title	Canadian Sales
April Wine	*The Nature of The Beast*	200 000+
Powder Blues	*Uncut*	200 000+
Aldo Nova	*Aldo Nova*	200 000+
Chilliwack	*Hit Express*	200 000+
The Emeralds	*Bird Dance*	200 000+
Gordon Lightfoot	*Gord's Gold*	200 000+
The Rovers	*The Rovers' 20th Anniversary*	200 000+
Loverboy	*Keep it Up*	200 000+
Headpins	*Turn it Loud*	200 000+
April Wine	*Greatest Hits*	200 000+
Burton Cummings	*Best of Burton Cummings*	200 000+
Showdown	*Welcome to the Rodeo*	200 000+
Marjo	*Celle Qui Va*	200 000+

(1) Includes only Canadian sales of over 200 000, based on certification by the Canadian Recording Industry Association, as of July 1988, of recordings that meet Canadian content standards by satisfying 3 of the following 4 criteria: music by a Canadian; performed by a Canadian artist; Canadian production; lyrics by a Canadian.

Best-Selling Compact Discs in Canada, 1987[1]

1. *The Joshua Tree*, U2
2. *Sgt. Pepper's*, The Beatles
3. *Bad*, Michael Jackson
4. *Graceland*, Paul Simon
5. *Slippery When Wet*, Bon Jovi
6. *Tunnel Of Love*, Bruce Springsteen
7. *Into The Fire*, Bryan Adams
8. *Lonesome Jubilee*, John Cougar Mellencamp
9. *A Momentary Lapse of Reason*, Pink Floyd
10. *Whitney*, Whitney Houston
11. *Tango In The Night*, Fleetwood Mac
12. *Abbey Road*, The Beatles
13. *Dark Side Of The Moon*, Pink Floyd
14. *A Hard Day's Night*, The Beatles
15. *Brothers in Arms*, Dire Straits
16. *Please Please Me*, The Beatles
17. *Bad Animals*, Heart
18. *La Bamba* (soundtrack)
19. *With The Beatles*, The Beatles
20. *Rubber Soul*, The Beatles
21. *For Sale*, The Beatles
22. *So*, Peter Gabriel
23. *Revolver*, The Beatles
24. *Back In The High Life*, Steve Winwood
25. *Invisible Touch*, Genesis
26. *White Album*, The Beatles

(1) Based on sales information provided by the record companies.

The Juno Awards

The Juno Awards were established in 1975 to honor achievement in the Canadian recording industry. The name was chosen to honor Pierre Juneau, former head of the Canadian Radio-television and Telecommunications Commission (CRTC) which instituted "Canadian content" requirements in the nation's broadcast industry.

Nominations for most major Juno categories are determined by record sales, although the actual winners are selected by a vote of members of the Canadian Academy of Recording Arts and Sciences.

Album of the Year[1]		International Album of the Year[3]	
1975	*Four Wheel Drive*, Bachman-Turner Overdrive	1975	*Elton John's Greatest Hits*, Elton John
1976	*Neiges*, Andre Gagnon	1976	*Frampton Comes Alive*, Peter Frampton
1977	*Longer Fuse*, Dan Hill	1977	*Rumours*, Fleetwood Mac
1978	*Dream of a Child*, Burton Cummings	1978	*Saturday Night Fever*, Bee Gees
1979	*New Kind of Feeling*, Anne Murray	1979	*Breakfast In America*, Supertramp
1980	*Greatest Hits*, Anne Murray	1980	*The Wall*, Pink Floyd
1981	*Loverboy*, Loverboy	1981	*Double Fantasy*, John Lennon
1982	*Get Lucky*, Loverboy	1982	*Business As Usual*, Men At Work
1983-84	*Cuts Like a Knife*, Bryan Adams	1983-84	*Synchronicity*, The Police
1985	*Reckless*, Bryan Adams		*Eliminator*, ZZ Top
1986	*The Thin Red Line*, Glass Tiger	1985	*Born in the U.S.A.*, Bruce Springsteen
1987	*Shakin' Like A Human Being*, Kim Mitchell	1986	*Brothers in Arms*, Dire Straits
		1987	*True Blue*, Madonna

Single of the Year[2]

1975	"You Ain't Seen Nothing Yet", Bachman-Turner Overdrive
1976	"Roxy-Roller", Sweeney Todd
1977	"Sugar Daddy", Patsy Gallant
1978	"Hot Child In The City", Nick Gilder
1979	"I Just Fall In Love Again", Anne Murray
1980	"Could I Have This Dance", Anne Murray "Echo Beach", Martha & The Muffins
1981	"Turn Me Loose", Loverboy
1982	"Eyes of a Stranger", Payola$
1983-84	"Rise Up", The Parachute Club
1985	"Never Surrender", Corey Hart
1986	"Don't Forget Me (When I'm Gone)", Glass Tiger
1987	"Someday", Glass Tiger

International Single of the Year[4]

1975	"Love Will Keep Us Together", Captain & Tennille
1976	"I Love To Love", Tina Charles
1977	"When I Need You", Leo Sayer
1978	"You're The One That I Want", John Travolta/Olivia Newton-John
1979	"Heart of Glass", Blondie
1980	"Another Brick In The Wall", Pink Floyd
1981	"Bette Davis Eyes", Kim Carnes
1982	"Eye Of The Tiger", Survivor
1983-84	"Billie Jean", Michael Jackson
1985	"I Want To Know What Love Is", Foreigner
1986	"Life Is Life", Opus
1987	"Venus", Bananarama

Group of the Year

1975	Bachman-Turner Overdrive
1976	Heart
1977	Rush
1978	Rush
1979	Trooper
1980	Prism
1981	Loverboy
1982	Loverboy
1983-84	Loverboy
1985	The Parachute Club
1986	Honeymoon Suite
1987	Tom Cochrane & Red Rider

Country Group of the Year

1975	The Mercey Brothers
1976	The Good Brothers
1977	The Good Brothers
1978	The Good Brothers
1979	The Good Brothers
1980	The Good Brothers
1981	The Good Brothers
1982	The Good Brothers
1983-84	The Good Brothers
1985	The Family Brown
1986	Prairie Oyster
1987	Prairie Oyster

Male Vocalist of the Year

1975	Gino Vannelli
1976	Burton Cummings
1977	Dan Hill
1978	Gino Vannelli
1979	Burton Cummings
1980	Bruce Cockburn
1981	Bruce Cockburn
1982	Bryan Adams
1983-84	Bryan Adams
1985	Bryan Adams
1986	Bryan Adams
1987	Bryan Adams

Female Vocalist of the Year

1975	Joni Mitchell
1976	Patsy Gallant
1977	Patsy Gallant
1978	Anne Murray
1979	Anne Murray
1980	Anne Murray
1981	Anne Murray
1982	Carole Pope
1983-84	Carole Pope
1985	Luba
1986	Luba
1987	Luba

Country Male Vocalist of the Year

1975	Murray McLauchlan
1976	Murray McLauchlan
1977	Ronnie Prophet
1978	Ronnie Prophet
1979	Murray McLauchlan
1980	Eddie Eastman
1981	Ronnie Hawkins
1982	Eddie Eastman
1983-84	Murray McLauchlan
1985	Murray McLauchlan
1986	Murray McLauchlan
1987	Ian Tyson

Country Female Vocalist of the Year

1975	Anne Murray
1976	Carroll Baker
1977	Carroll Baker
1978	Carroll Baker
1979	Anne Murray
1980	Anne Murray
1981	Anne Murray
1982	Anne Murray
1983-84	Anne Murray
1985	Anne Murray
1986	Anne Murray
1987	K.D. Lang

Most Promising Group of the Year

1975	Myles & Lenny
1976	T.H.P. Orchestra
1977	Hometown Band
1978	Doucette
1979	Streetheart
1980	Powder Blues
1981	Saga
1982	Payola$
1983-84	The Parachute Club
1985	Idle Eyes
1986	Glass Tiger
1987	Frozen Ghost

Instrumental Artist(s) of the Year

1975	Hagood Hardy
1976	Hagood Hardy
1977	André Gagnon
1978	Liona Boyd
1979	Frank Mills
1980	Frank Mills
1981	Liona Boyd
1982	Liona Boyd
1983-84	Liona Boyd
1985	The Canadian Brass
1986	David Foster
1987	David Foster

Most Promising Male Vocalist of the Year
1975	Dan Hill
1976	Burton Cummings
1977	David Bradstreet
1978	Nick Gilder
1979	Walter Rossi
1980	Graham Shaw
1981	Eddie Schwartz
1982	Kim Mitchell
1983-84	Zappacosta
1985	Paul Janz
1986	Billy Newton-Davis
1987	Tim Feehan

Most Promising Female Vocalist of the Year
1975	Patricia Dahlquist
1976	Colleen Peterson
1977	Lisa Dal Bello
1978	Claudja Barry
1979	France Joli
1980	Carole Pope
1981	Shari Ulrich
1982	Lydia Taylor
1983-84	Sherry Kean
1985	K.D. Lang
1986	Kim Richardson
1987	Rita MacNeil

Producer of the Year
1975	Peter Anastasoff, *The Homecoming*
1976	Mike Flicker, *Dreamboat Annie*—Heart
1977	McCauley & Mollin, *Longer Fuse*—Dan Hill
1978	Gino, Joe and Ross Vannelli, *Brother to Brother*—Gino Vannelli
1979	Bruce Fairbairn, *Armageddon*—Prism
1980	Gene Martynec "Tokyo"—Bruce Cockburn, "High School Confidential"—Rough Trade
1981	Paul Dean/Bruce Fairbairn, "Working for the Weekend" and "It's Over"—Loverboy
1982	Bill Henderson/Brian McLeod, "Watcha Gonna Do", "Secret Information"—Chilliwack
1983-84	Bryan Adams, *Cuts Like A Knife*—Bryan Adams
1985	David Foster, *Chicago 17*—Chicago
1986	David Foster, *St. Elmo's Fire*
1987	Daniel Lanois, *So*—Peter Gabriel, *The Joshua Tree*—U2

Composer of the Year
1975	Hagood Hardy, "The Homecoming"
1976	Gordon Lightfoot, "Wreck Of The Edmund Fitzgerald"
1977	Dan Hill, "Sometimes When We Touch"
1978	Dan Hill, "Sometimes When We Touch"
1979	Frank Mills, "Peter Piper"
1980	Eddie Schwartz, "Hit Me With Your Best Shot" Mike Reno & Paul Dean, "Turn Me Loose"
1981	Payola$, Bob Rock & Paul Hyde, "Eyes of a Stranger"
1982	Bryan Adams/Jim Vallance, "Cuts Like A Knife"
1985	Bryan Adams/Jim Vallance
1986	Jim Vallance
1987	Jim Vallance

Best Classical Recording
1976	*Beethoven Vol. 1-2-3*, Anton Kuerti
1977	*Three Borodin Symphonies*, Toronto Symphony Orchestra
1978	*Roxalana Raslack*, Glenn Gould
1979	*The Crown of Ariadne*, Judy Loman; R. Murray Schafer, Composer
1980	*Stravinsky—Chopin Ballads*, Arthur Ozolins
1981	*Ravel: Daphnis et Chloe* (Complete ballet), l'Orchestre Symphonique de Montréal, conducted by Charles Dutoit
1982	*The Goldberg Variations*, Glenn Gould, Bach
1983-84	*Ballades op. 10, Rhapsodies op. 79*, Glenn Gould, A. Brahms

Best Classical Album
(solo or chamber ensemble)
1985	*W.A. Mozart—String Quartets*, The Orford String Quartet
1986	*Stolen Gems*, James Campbell and Eric Robertson
1987	*Schubert, Quintet in C*, The Orford String Quartet, Ofra Harnoy

(large ensemble)
1985	*Ravel: Ma Mère L'oye/Pavane Pour Une Infante Defunte/Valses Nobles et Sentimentales*, l'Orchestre Symphonique de Montréal, Charles Dutoit
1986	*Holst: The Planets*, Toronto Symphony, Andrew Davis
1987	*Holst: The Planets*, l'Orchestre Symphonique de Montréal, Charles Dutoit

Best R&B/Soul
1985	*Lost Somewhere Inside Your Love*, Liberty Silver
1986	"Love Is a Contact Sport", Billy Newton-Davis
1987	"Peek-A-Boo", Kim Richardson

Best Jazz Album
1976	*Nimmons 'N Nine Plus Six*, Phil Nimmons
1977	*Big Band Jazz*, Rob McConnell and The Boss Brass
1978	*Jazz Canada Montreux*, Tommy Banks Big Band
1979	*Sackville 4005*, Ed Bickert/Don Thompson
1980	*Present Perfect*, Rob McConnell and The Boss Brass
1981	*The Brass Connection*, The Brass Connection
1982	*I Didn't Know About You*, Fraser MacPherson/Oliver Gannon
1983-84	*All In Good Time*, Rob McConnell and The Boss Brass
1985	*A Beautiful Friendship*, Don Thompson
1986	*Lights of Burgundy*, Oliver Jones
1987	*If You Could See Me Now*, The Oscar Peterson Four

Best Reggae/Calypso Recording
1985	*Heaven Must Have Sent You*, Liberty Silver & Otis Gayle
1986	*Revolutionary Tea Party*, Lillian Allen
1987	*Mean While*, Leroy Sibbles

Best Video of the Year

1983-84	*Sunglasses At Night*—Corey Hart, Rob Quartly
1985	*A Criminal Mind*—Gowan, Rob Quartly
1986	*How Many (Rivers to Cross)*—Luba, Greg Masvak
1987	*Love Is Fire*—The Parachute Club, Ron Berti

Best Children's Album

1978	*There's A Hippo in My Tub*, Anne Murray
1979	*Smorgasbord*, Sharon, Lois & Bram
1980	*Singing'n Swinging*, Sharon, Lois & Bram
1981	*Inch By Inch*, Sandra Beech
1982	*When You Dream A Dream*, Bob Schneider
1983-84	*Rugrat Rock*, Rugrats
1985	*Murmel Murmel Munsch*, Robert Munsch
1986	*10 Carrot Diamond*, Charlotte Diamond
1987	*Drums*, Bill Usher

(1) Prior to 1979 was Best Selling Album. (2) Prior to 1979 was Best Selling Single. (3) Prior to 1979 was Best Selling International Album. (4) Prior to 1979 was Best Selling International Single.

Grammy Awards

Source: National Academy of Recording Arts & Sciences

1962
Record: Tony Bennett, *I Left My Heart in San Francisco.*
Album: Vaughn Meader, *The First Family.*

1963
Record: Henry Mancini, *The Days of Wine and Roses.*
Album: *The Barbra Streisand Album.*

1964
Record: Stan Getz and Astrud Gilberto, *The Girl From Ipanema.*
Album: *Getz/Gilberto.*

1965
Record: Herb Alpert, *A Taste Of Honey.*
Album: Frank Sinatra, *September of My Years.*

1966
Record: Frank Sinatra, *Strangers in the Night.*
Album: Frank Sinatra, *A Man and His Music.*

1967
Record: 5th Dimension, *Up, Up and Away.*
Album: The Beatles, *Sgt. Pepper's Lonely Hearts Club Band.*

1968
Record: Simon & Garfunkel, *Mrs. Robinson.*
Album: Glen Campbell, *By the Time I Get to Phoenix.*

1969
Record: 5th Dimension, *Aquarius/Let the Sunshine In.*
Album: *Blood, Sweat and Tears.*

1970
Record: Simon & Garfunkel, *Bridge Over Troubled Waters.*
Album: *Bridge Over Troubled Waters.*

1971
Record: Carole King, *It's Too Late.*
Album: Carole King, *Tapestry.*

1972
Record: Roberta Flack, *The First Time Ever I Saw Your Face.*
Album: *The Concert For Bangla Desh.*

1973
Record: Roberta Flack, *Killing Me Softly with His Song.*
Album: Stevie Wonder, *Innervisions.*

1974
Record: Olivia Newton-John, *I Honestly Love You.*
Album: Stevie Wonder, *Fulfullingness' First Finale.*

1975
Record: Captain & Tennille, *Love Will Keep Us Together.*
Album: Paul Simon, *Still Crazy After All These Years.*

1976
Record: George Benson, *This Masquerade.*
Album: Stevie Wonder, *Songs in the Key of Life.*

1977
Record: Eagles, *Hotel California.*
Album: Fleetwood Mac, *Rumours.*

1978
Record: Billy Joel, *Just the Way You Are.*
Album: Bee Gees, *Saturday Night Fever.*

1979
Record: The Doobie Brothers, *What a Fool Believes.*
Album: Billy Joel, *52nd Street.*

1980
Record: Christopher Cross, *Sailing.*
Album: Christopher Cross, *Christopher Cross.*

1981
Record: Kim Carnes, *Bette Davis Eyes.*
Album: John Lennon, Yoko Ono, *Double Fantasy.*

1982
Record: Toto, *Rosanna.*
Album: Toto, *Toto IV.*

1983
Record: Michael Jackson, *Beat It.*
Album: Michael Jackson, *Thriller.*

1984
Record: Tina Turner, *What's Love Got to Do With It.*
Album: Lionel Richie, *Can't Slow Down.*

1985
Record: USA for Africa, *We Are the World.*
Album: Phil Collins, *No Jacket Required.*

1986
Record: Steve Winwood, *Higher Love.*
Album: Paul Simon, *Graceland.*

1987
Record: Paul Simon, *Graceland.*
Album: U2, *The Joshua Tree.*

Most Popular Radio Stations in Canada

Source: BBM Bureau of Measurement Radio Survey, Fall, 1987

Station	City	Reach[1] (000s)	Station	City	Reach[1] (000s)
CHUM-FM	Toronto	1 094	CJCL	Toronto	616
CFTR	Toronto	1 056	CHFI-FM	Toronto	610
CFRB	Toronto	985	CKMF-FM*	Montreal	584
CKAC*	Montreal	925	CFGL-FM*	Montreal	576
CKOI-FM*	Montreal	821	CJMS*	Montreal	541
CILQ-FM	Toronto	791	CFNY-FM	Toronto	510
CHOM-FM	Montreal	719	CJMF-FM*	Quebec	464
CBL	Toronto	696	CBL-FM	Toronto	462
CHUM	Toronto	664	CKLG	Vancouver	461
CKFM-FM	Toronto	654	CITE-FM*	Montreal	420

Station	City	Reach[1]	Station	City	Reach[1]
		(000s)			(000s)
CBF*	Montreal	408	VOCM	St. John's, Nfld.	278
CKVL*	Montreal	408	CKY	Winnipeg	276
CJFM-FM	Montreal	406	CFGM	Toronto	273
CFQR-FM	Montreal	403	CFCW	Camrose	262
CKNW	Vancouver	403	CIEL-FM*	Montreal	254
CBU	Vancouver	390	CKDS-FM	Hamilton	252
CJAD	Montreal	386	CJCA	Edmonton	248
CHED	Edmonton	363	CHAY-FM	Barrie	247
CHRC*	Quebec	361	CHML	Hamilton	245
CFOX-FM	Vancouver	341	CBF-FM*	Montreal	238
CHAM	Hamilton	337	CKGM	Montreal	232
CKEY	Toronto	332	CIRK-FM	Edmonton	210
CFMI-FM	Vancouver	314	CFQC	Saskatoon	191
CFRA	Ottawa/Hull	301	CKRC	Winnipeg	191
CJOB	Winnipeg	292	CFRN	Edmonton	180
CFUN	Vancouver	289	C100	Halifax	173
CJEZ-FM	Toronto	280	CHOZ-FM	St. John's, Nfld.	157
CKOC	Hamilton	280	CFCY	Charlottetown	126
CKO-TO	Toronto	279	CKCW	Moncton	111
CHEZ-FM	Ottawa/Hull	278	CFBC	Saint John, N.B.	97

(1) Reach represents the total number of persons, 7 years of age and over, who listened to each station for at least one quarter-hour during an average survey week.
* Indicates French-language station.

Canadian Rock and
Popular Music Notables

(singles for which the artists are known are listed in quotes; albums are in italics; date is year of release)

Bryan Adams, b. Kingston, Ont., Nov. 11, 1959: singer-songwriter; *Reckless* (1984), "Straight from the Heart" (1983), "Run to You" (1984), "Heaven" (1985).

Alta Moda, Toronto-based group formed in 1981: "Julian" (1987).

Paul Anka, b. Ottawa, Ont., July 30, 1941: singer-songwriter; wrote "My Way" to melody of French song "Comme d'habitude" for Frank Sinatra; "Diana" (1957), "Lonely Boy" (1959), "(You're) Having My Baby" (1974).

April Wine, originally Waverly, N.S.-based quartet formed in 1969: "You Could Have Been a Lady" (1972), *The Nature of the Beast* (1981).

Bachman-Turner Overdrive, Vancouver-based quartet formed in early 1970s; featured Randy Bachman: *Not Fragile* (1974), "You Ain't Seen Nothing Yet" (1974), "Takin' Care of Business" (1974).

The Band, Toronto-based sextet formed in the late 1960s as back-up band for Ronnie Hawkins and later Bob Dylan: *Music From Big Pink* (1968), "Up on Cripple Creek" (1969).

The Beaumarks, Montreal-based quartet formed in the 1950s: "Clap Your Hands" (1960).

The Bells, Montreal-based sextet formed in the late 1960s: "Stay Awhile" (1971).

Blue Rodeo, Toronto-based group founded in 1984: *Outskirts* (1987), "Try" (1987).

The Box, Montreal-based quintet formed in the early 1980s: "Closer Together" (1987).

Chalk Circle, Toronto-based quartet formed in early 1980s: "This Mourning" (1987).

Robert Charlebois, b. Montreal, Que., June 25, 1945: singer-songwriter; "Lindberg" (1968), *Solidaritude* (1973).

Chilliwack, Vancouver-based quartet formed in 1969: "My Girl (Gone Gone Gone)" (1981).

David Clayton-Thomas, b. Surrey, England, Sept. 13, 1941: singer; member of Blood, Sweat & Tears and later a solo artist; "Spinning Wheel" (1969).

Bruce Cockburn, b. Ottawa, Ont., May 27, 1945: singer-songwriter; "Wondering Where the Lions Are" (1979), "Waiting For A Miracle" (1987).

Leonard Cohen, b. Montreal, Que., Sept. 21, 1934: *Songs of Leonard Cohen* (1968), "Suzanne" (1968).

Tom Cochrane & Red Rider, Toronto-based quintet formed in 1976; formerly known as Red Rider: "White Hot" (1980), *Neruda* (1983), "The Untouchable One" (1986).

The Crew Cuts, Toronto-based vocal quartet formed in 1952: "Sh-Boom" (1954).

Burton Cummings, b. Montreal, Que., Dec. 31, 1947: singer-songwriter; lead singer of The Guess Who; as solo artist *My Own Way to Rock* (1977), "Stand Tall" (1976).

Bobby Curtola, b. Thunder Bay, Ont., Apr. 17, 1944: singer; Canada's first "teen idol"; "Fortune Teller" (1962).

The Diamonds, Toronto-based vocal quartet formed in 1954: "Little Darlin'" (1957), "The Stroll" (1957).

Denny Doherty, b. Halifax, N.S., Nov. 29, 1941: singer-songwriter; founding member of The Mamas & The Papas.

Doug & The Slugs, Vancouver-based sextet formed in late 1970s: "Too Bad" (1980), "Makin' It Work" (1983).

Downchild, Toronto-based blues septet formed in early 1970s: "Flip, Flop and Fly" (1973).

Edward Bear, Toronto-based trio formed in late 1960s; led by Larry Evoy: "Last Song" (1972).

Five Man Electrical Band, Ottawa-based rock quintet formed in 1963 as The Staccatos: "Signs" (1971).

David Foster, b. Victoria, B.C.: singer-songwriter, producer; "Love Theme from *St. Elmo's Fire*" (1985), "The Best of Me" (1986), with Olivia Newton-John.

The Four Lads, Toronto-based vocal quartet formed in 1952: "Moments to Remember" (1955), "No, Not Much!" (1956).

Nick Gilder, b. London, England, 1951: singer-songwriter; "Hot Child in the City" (1978).

Glass Tiger, Newmarket, Ont.-based quintet formed in early 1980s: *The Thin Red Line* (1986), "Don't Forget Me (When I'm Gone)" (1986), "I'm Still Searching" (1988).

Gowan, b. Larry Gowan: singer-songwriter; *Strange Animal* (1985), "A Criminal Mind" (1985).

The Guess Who, Winnipeg-based quartet formed in 1965; also known as Al & the Silvertones and Chad Allen & the Expressions; featured Burton Cummings and Randy Bachman: "Shakin' All Over" (1965), "These Eyes" (1968), "American Woman" (1970).

Corey Hart, b. Montreal, Que., May 31, 1962: singer-songwriter; "Sunglasses at Night" (1984), *Boy in the Box*, (1985), "Never Surrender" (1985), "In Your Soul" (1988).

Ronnie Hawkins, b. Huntsville, Ark., Jan. 10, 1935: singer; pioneer of Canadian rock music; "Mary Lou" (1959), "Forty Days" (1959).

Dan Hill, b. Toronto, Ont., June 3, 1954: singer-songwriter; "Sometimes When We Touch" (1977), "Can't We Try" (1987).

Honeymoon Suite, Toronto-based quintet formed in early 1980s: "New Girl Now" (1984), "Feel It Again" (1986).

Ian & Sylvia, Toronto-based husband-wife performing/song-writing duo formed in 1960: "Four Strong Winds" (1963), "The Lovin' Sound" (1967).

Terry Jacks, b. Winnipeg, Man., Mar. 29, 1944: singer-song-writer; founding member of The Poppy Family; "Seasons in the Sun" (1973).

Kensington Market, Toronto-based rock group formed in 1967: "I Would Be the One" (1968).

Andy Kim, b. Andrew Youakim, Montreal, Que., Dec. 5, 1946: singer-songwriter; "Rock Me Gently" (1974).

k.d. lang, b. Consort, Alta., Nov. 2, 1961: singer; "Down to My Last Cigarette" (1988), *Shadowland* (1988).

Gordon Lightfoot, b. Orillia, Ont., Nov. 17, 1938: singer-songwriter; "Sundown" (1974), "The Wreck of the Edmund Fitzgerald" (1976), "Anything for Love" (1986).

Lighthouse, Toronto-based 13-piece rock ensemble formed in 1969: "One Fine Morning" (1971), "Sunny Days" (1972).

Loverboy, Vancouver-based quintet formed in 1981: "Working for the Weekend" (1981), "Heaven in Your Eyes" (1986).

Luba, b. Luba Kowalchyk, Montreal, Que., Apr. 24: singer-songwriter; "Let It Go" (1984), "How Many (Rivers to Cross)" (1986), *Between The Earth and The Sky* (1986).

M + M, Toronto-based quartet formed as Martha & The Muffins in 1978: "Echo Beach" (1980).

Mandala, Toronto-based R&B quintet formed as The Five Rogues in 1964: "Opportunity" (1967), "Loveitis" (1968).

Mashmakhan, Montreal-based rock quartet formed in late 1960s: "As the Years Go By" (1970).

Murray McLauchlan, b. Paisley, Scotland, June 30, 1948: singer-songwriter; "Farmer's Song" (1973).

Men Without Hats, Montreal-based trio: "Safety Dance" (1983), "Pop Goes the World" (1988).

Joni Mitchell, b. Fort Macleod, Alta., Nov. 7, 1943: singer-songwriter; "Both Sides Now" (1969), "Big Yellow Taxi" (1970), "Help Me" (1974), *Miles of Isles* (1974).

Kim Mitchell, b. Sarnia, Ont.: singer-songwriter; former lead singer of Max Webster; *Shakin' Like a Human Being* (1986), "Patio Lanterns" (1987), "Easy To Tame" (1987).

Motherlode, Toronto-based R&B quartet formed in late 1960s: "When I Die" (1969).

Anne Murray, b. Springhill, N.S., June 20, 1945: singer; "Snowbird" (1970), "You Needed Me" (1978), "I Just Fall In Love Again" (1979).

The Northern Pikes, Saskatoon-based quartet formed in 1983: *Big Blue Sky* (1987), "Teenland" (1987).

The Nylons, Toronto-based *a cappella* group formed in late 1970s: "Kiss Him Goodbye" (1987).

Ocean, Toronto-based pop quintet formed in late 1960s: "Put Your Hand in the Hand" (1971).

Offenbach, Montreal-based quintet formed in 1969: "Caline de Blues" (1976).

Michel Pagliaro, b. Montreal, Que., Nov. 9, 1948: singer-songwriter, producer; former lead singer of Les Chanceliers: "What the Hell I Got" (1975).

The Parachute Club, Toronto-based group formed in early 1980s: *At the Feet of the Moon* (1984), "Rise Up" (1983).

The Payola$, Vancouver-based quintet formed in the late 1970s: "Eyes of a Stranger" (1982).

Platinum Blonde, Toronto-based quartet formed in early 1980s: *Alien Shores* (1985), "Crying Over You" (1985).

The Poppy Family, Vancouver-based group formed in 1968; featured husband and wife Terry and Susan Jacks: "Which Way You Goin' Billy" (1969).

The Powder Blues Band, Vancouver-based 9-piece blues band formed in mid 1970s: "Doin' It Right" (1980).

Prism, Vancouver-based sextet formed in 1976: *Armageddon* (1979), "Spaceship Superstar" (1977).

Robbie Robertson, b. July 5, 1943, Montreal, Que.: founding member of The Band; "Showdown At Big Sky" (1988).

Rock & Hyde, Vancouver-based duo formed in 1986; members Bob Rock and Paul Hyde were with The Payola$: *Under the Volcano* (1987), "Dirty Water" (1987).

Rough Trade, Toronto-based sextet formed in early 1970s; fronted by Carole Pope and Kevan Staples: *Avoid Freud* (1981), "High School Confidential" (1981).

Rush, Toronto-based trio formed in 1968 by Geddy Lee, Neil Peart and Alex Lifeson: *Permanent Waves* (1980), *Moving Pictures* (1981), "Limelight" (1981).

Jack Scott, b. Jack Scafone Jr., Windsor, Ont., Jan. 24, 1936: singer; "What in the World's Come Over You" (1960).

Jane Siberry, b. Toronto, Ont., Oct. 13, 1955: singer-song-writer; *The Speckless Sky* (1985), "One More Colour" (1985).

Skylark, Vancouver-based group led by David Foster: "Wild-flower" (1973).

The Stampeders, Toronto-based sextet formed in mid 1960s in Calgary: "Sweet City Woman" (1971).

Lucille Starr, b. St. Boniface, Man., May 13, 1938: singer; she and Bob Regan were together known as The Canadian Sweethearts; "The French Song" (1964).

Steppenwolf, late 1960s rock group formed from Toronto band Sparrow: "Born to be Wild" (1968), "Magic Carpet Ride" (1968).

Streetheart, Regina-based quintet formed in 1976: "Under My Thumb" (1979).

Sweeney Todd, originally Vancouver-based sextet formed in mid 1970s; included Nick Gilder and Bryan Adams: "Roxy Roller" (1976).

Ian Thomas, b. Hamilton, Ont., July 23, 1950: singer-song-writer; "Painted Ladies" (1973); "Hold On" (1981).

Toronto, Toronto-based sextet formed in late 1970s: *Looking for Trouble* (1980), "Your Daddy Don't Know" (1982).

Triumph, Toronto-based trio formed in 1975 by Gil Moore, Mike Levine and Rik Emmett: "Hold On" (1979), *Allied Forces* (1981).

Trooper, Vancouver-based quintet formed in 1972: *Thick As Thieves* (1978) "Raise a Little Hell" (1978).

The Ugly Ducklings, Toronto-based group formed in early 1960s; part of Yorkville Village scene: "Gas Light" (1967).

Valdy, b. Valdemar Horsdal, Ottawa, Ont., 1946: singer-song-writer; "Rock and Roll Song" (1952).

Gino Vanelli, b. Montreal, Que., June 16, 1952: singer-song-writer; "I Just Wanna Stop" (1978), "Living Inside Myself" (1981), "Wild Horses" (1987).

Neil Young, b. Toronto, Ont., Nov. 12, 1945: singer-song-writer; member of Buffalo Springfield and Crosby, Stills, Nash and Young; *After the Goldrush* (1970), "Only Love Can Break Your Heart" (1970), "Heart of Gold" (1972).

Original Names of Selected Entertainers

Edie Adams: Elizabeth Edith Enke
Eddie Albert: Edward Albert Heimberger
Alan Alda: Alphonso D'Abruzzo
Jane Alexander: Jane Quigley
Fred Allen: John Sullivan
Woody Allen: Allen Konigsberg
Julie Andrews: Julia Wells
Eve Arden: Eunice Quedens
Beatrice Arthur: Bernice Frankel
Jean Arthur: Gladys Greene
Fred Astaire: Frederick Austerlitz

Lauren Bacall: Betty Joan Perske
Anne Bancroft: Anna Maria Italiano
Brigitte Bardot: Camille Javal
Gene Barry: Eugene Klass
Orson Bean: Dallas Burrows
Pat Benatar: Patricia Andrejewski
Robbie Benson: Robert Segal
Tony Bennett: Anthony Benedetto
Busby Berkeley: William Berkeley Enos
Jack Benny: Benjamin Kubelsky
Joey Bishop: Joseph Gottlieb

Robert Blake: Michael Gubitosi
Victor Borge: Borge Rosenbaum
David Bowie: David Robert Jones
Boy George: George Alan O'Dowd
Fanny Brice: Fanny Borach
Morgan Brittany: Suzanne Cupito
Charles Bronson: Charles Buchinski
Albert Brooks: Albert Einstein
Mel Brooks: Melvin Kaminsky
George Burns: Nathan Birnbaum
Ellen Burstyn: Edna Gilhooley
Richard Burton: Richard Jenkins
Red Buttons: Aaron Chwatt
Nicolas Cage: Nicholas Coppola
Michael Caine: Maurice Micklewhite
Maria Callas: Maria Kalogeropoulos
Diahann Carroll: Carol Diahann Johnson
Cyd Charisse: Tula Finklea
Ray Charles: Ray Charles Robinson
Cher: Cherilyn Sarkisian
Patsy Cline: Virginia Patterson Hensley
Lee J. Cobb: Leo Jacoby
Claudette Colbert: Lily Chauchoin
Michael Connors: Kreker Ohanian
Robert Conrad: Conrad Robert Falk
Alice Cooper: Vincent Furnier
Howard Cosell: Howard Cohen
Elvis Costello: Declan Patrick McManus
Lou Costello: Louis Cristillo
Joan Crawford: Lucille Le Sueur
Tony Curtis: Bernard Schwartz

Vic Damone: Vito Farinola
Rodney Dangerfield: Jacob Cohen
Bobby Darin: Walden Waldo Cassotto
Doris Day: Doris von Kappelhoff
Yvonne De Carlo: Peggy Middleton
Sandra Dee: Alexandra Zuck
John Denver: Henry John Deutschendorf Jr.
Bo Derek: Cathleen Collins
John Derek: Derek Harris
Angie Dickinson: Angeline Brown
Phyllis Diller: Phyllis Driver
Diana Dors: Diana Fluck
Melvyn Douglas: Melvyn Hesselberg
Bob Dylan: Robert Zimmerman

Sheena Easton: Sheena Shirley Orr
Barbara Eden: Barbara Huffman
Ron Ely: Ronald Pierce
Chad Everett: Raymond Cramton
Tom Ewell: S. Yewell Tompkins

Douglas Fairbanks: Douglas Ullman
Morgan Fairchild: Patsy McClenny
Alice Faye: Ann Leppert
Stepin Fetchit: Lincoln Perry
W.C. Fields: William Claude Dukenfield
Peter Finch: William Mitchell
Barry Fitzgerald: William Joseph Shields
Joan Fontaine: Joan de Havilland
John Ford: Sean O'Fearna
John Forsythe: John Freund
Redd Foxx : John Sanford
Anthony Franciosa: Anthony Papaleo
Arlene Francis: Arlene Kazanjian
Connie Francis: Concetta Franconero

Greta Garbo: Greta Gustafsson
Vincent Gardenia: Vincent Scognamiglio
John Garfield: Julius Garfinkle
Judy Garland: Frances Gumm
James Garner: James Baumgardner
Crystal Gayle: Brenda Gayle Webb
Eydie Gorme: Edith Gormezano
Stewart Granger: James Stewart
Cary Grant: Archibald Leach
Lee Grant: Lyova Rosenthal
Joel Grey: Joe Katz

Buddy Hackett: Leonard Hacker
Jean Harlow: Harlean Carpentier
Rex Harrison: Reginald Carey
Laurence Harvey: Larushka Skikne
Helen Hayes: Helen Brown
Susan Hayward: Edythe Marriner
Rita Hayworth: Margarita Cansino
Pee-Wee Herman: Paul Rubenfeld
Barbara Hershey: Barbara Herzstine

William Holden: William Beedle
Judy Holliday: Judith Tuvim
Harry Houdini: Ehrich Weiss
Leslie Howard: Leslie Stainer
Moe Howard: Moses Horowitz
Rock Hudson: Roy Scherer Jr. (later Fitzgerald)
Engelbert Humperdinck: Arnold Dorsey
Kim Hunter: Janet Cole
Mary Beth Hurt: Mary Supinger
Betty Hutton: Betty Thornberg

David Janssen: David Meyer
Elton John: Reginald Dwight
Don Johnson: Donald Wayne
Jennifer Jones: Phyllis Isley
Tom Jones: Thomas Woodward
Louis Jourdan: Louis Gendre

Boris Karloff: William Henry Pratt
Danny Kaye: David Kaminsky
Diane Keaton: Diane Hall
Michael Keaton: Michael Douglas
Howard Keel: Harold Leek
Chaka Khan: Yvette Stevens
Carole King: Carole Klein
Ben Kingsley: Krishna Banji
Nastassja Kinski: Nastassja Naksyznyski
Ted Knight: Tadeus Wladyslaw Konopka

Cheryl Ladd: Cheryl Stoppelmoor
Veronica Lake: Constance Ockleman
Dorothy Lamour: Mary Kaumeyer
Michael Landon: Eugene Orowitz
Mario Lanza: Alfredo Cocozza
Stan Laurel: Arthur Jefferson
Steve Lawrence: Sidney Leibowitz
Brenda Lee: Brenda Mae Tarpley
Bruce Lee: Lee Yuen Kam
Gypsy Rose Lee: Rose Louise Hovick
Michelle Lee: Michelle Dusiak
Peggy Lee: Norma Egstrom
Janet Leigh: Jeanette Morrison
Vivien Leigh: Vivien Hartley
Huey Lewis: Hugh Cregg
Jerry Lewis: Joseph Levitch
Hal Linden: Harold Lipshitz
Carole Lombard: Jane Peters
Jack Lord: John Joseph Ryan
Sophia Loren: Sophia Scicoloni
Peter Lorre: Laszio Lowenstein
Myrna Loy: Myrna Williams
Bela Lugosi: Bela Ferenc Blasko

Moms Mabley: Loretta Mary Aitken
Shirley MacLaine: Shirley Beaty
Madonna: Madonna Louise Ciccone
Lee Majors: Harvey Lee Yeary 2d
Karl Malden: Malden Sekulovich
Jayne Mansfield: Vera Jane Palmer
Fredric March: Frederick Bickel
Peter Marshall: Pierre LaCock
Dean Martin: Dino Crocetti
Ethel Merman: Ethel Zimmerman
Ray Milland: Reginald Truscott-Jones
Ann Miller: Lucille Collier
Joni Mitchell: Roberta Joan Anderson
Marilyn Monroe: Norma Jean Mortenson, (later) Baker
Yves Montand: Ivo Levi
Ron Moody: Ronald Moodnick
Demi Moore: Demi Guynes
Garry Moore: Thomas Garrison Morfit
Rita Moreno: Rosita Alverio
Harry Morgan: Harry Bratsburg
Paul Muni: Muni Weisenfreund

Mike Nichols: Michael Igor Peschowsky
Sheree North: Dawn Bethel

Hugh O'Brian: Hugh Krampke
Maureen O'Hara: Maureen Fitzsimmons

Patti Page: Clara Ann Fowler
Jack Palance: Walter Palanuik
Lilli Palmer: Lilli Peiser
Bert Parks: Bert Jacobson
Minnie Pearl: Sarah Ophelia Cannon
Bernadette Peters: Bernadette Lazzaro
Edith Piaf: Edith Gassion
Slim Pickens: Louis Lindley

Mary Pickford: Gladys Smith
Stephanie Powers: Stefania Federkiewcz
Paula Prentiss: Paula Ragusa
Robert Preston: Robert Preston Meservey
Prince: Prince Rogers Nelson

Tony Randall: Leonard Rosenberg
Martha Raye: Margaret O'Reed
Donna Reed: Donna Belle Mullenger
Della Reese: Delloreese Patricia Early
Joan Rivers: Joan Sandra Molinsky
Edward G. Robinson: Emanual Goldenberg
Ginger Rogers: Virginia McMath
Roy Rogers: Leonard Slye
Mickey Rooney: Joe Yule Jr.
Lillian Russell: Helen Leonard

Susan St. James: Susan Miller
Soupy Sales: Milton Hines
Susan Sarandon: Susan Tomaling
Randolph Scott: George Randolph Crane
Jane Seymour: Joyce Frankenberg
Omar Sharif: Michael Shalhoub
Martin Sheen: Ramon Estevez
Beverly Sills: Belle Silverman
Talia Shire: Talia Coppola
Phil Silvers: Philip Silversmith

Suzanne Somers: Suzanne Mahoney
Ann Sothern: Harriette Lake
Barbara Stanwyck: Ruby Stevens
Jean Stapleton: Jeanne Murray
Ringo Starr: Richard Starkey
Connie Stevens: Concetta Ingolia
Sting: George Sumner
Donna Summers: LaDonna Gaines

Robert Taylor: Spangler Arlington Brugh
Danny Thomas: Amos Jacobs
Sophie Tucker: Sophia Kalish
Tina Turner: Annie Mae Bullock
Conway Twitty: Harold Lloyd Jenkins
Rudolph Valentino: Rudolpho D'Antonguolla
Frankie Valli: Frank Castelluccio

David Wayne: Wayne McMeekan
John Wayne: Marion Morrison
Clifton Webb: Webb Parmalee Hollenbeck
Raquel Welch: Raquel Tejada
Gene Wilder: Jerome Silberman
Shelly Winters: Shirley Schrift
Stevie Wonder: Stevland Morris
Natalie Wood: Natasha Gurdin
Jane Wyman: Sarah Jane Fulks
Gig Young: Byron Barr

Entertainment Personalities — Where and When Born

Actors, Actresses, Dancers, Musicians, Producers, Radio-TV Performers, Singers
(As of July, 1988)

Name	Birthplace	Born	Name	Birthplace	Born
Abbado, Claudio	Milan, Italy	6/26/33	Anderson, Harry	Newport, R.I.	10/14/52
Abraham, F. Murray	Pittsburgh, Pa.	10/24/40	Anderson, Ian	Dunfermline, Scotland	8/10/47
Acuff, Roy	Maynardville, Tenn.	9/15/03	Anderson, Judith	Adelaide, Australia	2/10/98
Adams, Bryan	Kingston, Ont.	11/5/59	Anderson, Loni	St. Paul, Minn.	8/7/44
Adams, Don	New York, N.Y.	4/19/26	Anderson, Lynn	Grand Forks, N.D.	9/26/47
Adams, Edie	Kingston, Pa.	4/16/29	Anderson, Marian	Philadelphia, Pa.	2/17/02
Adams, Joey	New York, N.Y.	1/6/11	Anderson, Melissa Sue	Berkeley, Cal.	9/26/62
Adams, Mason	New York, N.Y.	2/26/19	Anderson, Richard	Long Branch, N.J.	8/8/26
Adams, Maud	Lulea, Sweden	2/12/45	Anderson, Richard Dean	Minneapolis, Minn.	1/23/53
Adler, Larry	Baltimore, Md.	2/10/14	Andersson, Bibi	Stockholm, Sweden	11/11/35
Agutter, Jenny	London, England	12/20/52	Andress, Ursula	Bern, Switzerland	3/19/36
Aiello, Danny	New York, N.Y.	6/20/33	Andrews, Anthony	London, England	1948
Ailey, Alvin	Rogers, Tex.	1/5/31	Andrews, Dana	Collins, Miss.	1/1/09
Aimee, Anouk	Paris, France	4/27/32	Andrews, Julie	Walton, England	10/1/35
Akins, Claude	Nelson, Ga.	5/25/18	Andrews, Maxene	Minneapolis, Minn.	1/3/18
Albanese, Licia	Bari, Italy	7/22/13	Andrews, Patty	Minneapolis, Minn.	2/16/20
Alberghetti, Anna Maria	Pesaro, Italy	5/15/36	Anka, Paul	Ottawa, Ont.	7/30/41
Albert, Eddie	Rock Island, Ill.	4/22/08	Ann-Margret	Stockholm, Sweden	4/28/41
Albert, Edward	Los Angeles, Cal.	2/20/51	Anspach, Susan	New York, N.Y.	11/23/45
Albright, Lola	Akron, Oh.	7/20/24	Ant, Adam	London, England	11/3/54
Alda, Alan	New York, N.Y.	1/28/36	Archer, Anne	Los Angeles, Cal.	8/25/50
Alexander, Jane	Boston, Mass.	10/28/39	Arden, Eve	Mill Valley, Cal.	4/30/12
Allen, Debbie	Houston, Tex.	1/16/53	Arkin, Alan	New York, N.Y.	3/26/34
Allen, Karen	Carrollton, Ill.	10/5/51	Arnaz, Desi Jr.	Los Angeles, Cal.	1/19/53
Allen, Mel	Birmingham, Ala.	2/14/13	Arnaz, Lucie	Hollywood, Cal.	7/17/51
Allen, Nancy	New York, N.Y.	6/24/50	Arness, James	Minneapolis, Minn.	5/26/23
Allen, Peter	Tenderfield, Australia	2/10/44	Arnold, Eddy	Henderson, Tenn.	5/15/18
Allen, Steve	New York, N.Y.	12/26/21	Arquette, Rosanna	New York, N.Y.	8/10/59
Allen, Woody	Brooklyn, N.Y.	12/1/35	Arrau, Claudio	Chillau, Chile	2/6/03
Alley, Kirstie	Wichita, Kan.	1/12/55	Arroyo, Martina	New York, N.Y.	2/2/37
Allman, Gregg	Nashville, Tenn.	12/7/47	Arthur, Beatrice	New York, N.Y.	5/13/23
Allyson, June	New York, N.Y.	10/7/17	Arthur, Jean	New York, N.Y.	10/17/05
Alonso, Maria Conchita	Cuba	1957	Ashcroft, Peggy	Croydon, England	12/22/07
Alpert, Herb	Los Angeles, Cal.	3/31/35	Ashley, Elizabeth	Ocala, Fla.	8/30/39
Altman, Robert	Kansas City, Mo.	2/20/25	Asner, Ed	Kansas City, Mo.	11/15/29
Ameche, Don	Kenosha, Wis.	5/31/08	Assante, Armand	New York, N.Y.	10/4/49
Ames, Ed	Boston, Mass.	7/9/27	Astin, John	Baltimore, Md.	3/30/30
Ames, Leon	Portland, Ind.	1/20/03	Atherton, William	New Haven, Conn.	7/30/47
Amos, John	Newark, N.J.	12/27/39	Atkins, Chet	Luttrell, Tenn.	6/20/24
Amsterdam, Morey	Chicago, Ill.	12/14/14	Atkins, Christopher	Rye, N.Y.	2/21/61
			Attenborough, Richard	Cambridge, England	8/29/23

Name	Birthplace	Born
Auberjonois, Rene	New York, N.Y.	6/1/40
Aumont, Jean-Pierre	Paris, France	1/5/09
Autry, Gene	Tioga, Tex.	9/29/11
Avalon, Frankie	Philadelphia, Pa.	9/8/40
Ax, Emmanuel	Lvov, USSR	6/8/49
Aykroyd, Dan	Ottawa, Ont.	7/1/52
Ayres, Lew	Minneapolis, Minn.	12/28/08
Aznavour, Charles	Paris, France	5/22/24
Bacall, Lauren	New York, N.Y.	9/16/24
Backus, Jim	Cleveland, Oh.	2/25/13
Bacon, Kevin	Philadelphia, Pa.	1958
Baez, Joan	Staten Island, N.Y.	1/9/41
Bailey, Pearl	Newport News, Va.	3/29/18
Bain, Conrad	Lethbridge, Alta.	2/4/23
Baio, Scott	Brooklyn, N.Y.	9/22/61
Baker, Anita	Detroit, Mich.	1957
Baker, Carroll	Johnstown, Pa.	5/28/31
Baker, Joe Don	Groesbeck, Tex.	2/12/36
Ball, Lucille	Jamestown, N.Y.	8/6/11
Ballard, Kaye	Cleveland, Oh.	11/20/26
Balsam, Martin	New York, N.Y.	11/4/19
Bancroft, Anne	New York, N.Y.	9/17/31
Bardot, Brigitte	Paris, France	9/28/34
Bari, Lynn	Roanoke, Va.	12/18/15
Barker, Bob	Darrington, Wash.	12/12/23
Barkin, Ellen	New York, N.Y.	1959
Barnes, Priscilla	Ft. Dix, N.J.	12/7/56
Barrault, Jean-Louis	Vesinet, France	9/8/10
Barrie, Barbara	Chicago, Ill.	5/23/31
Barry, Gene	New York, N.Y.	6/4/22
Bartholomew, Freddie	London, England	3/28/24
Bartok, Eva	Budapest, Hungary	6/18/26
Baryshnikov, Mikhail	Riga, Latvia	1/28/48
Basinger, Kim	Athens, Ga.	12/8/54
Bassey, Shirley	Cardiff, Wales	1/8/37
Bateman, Jason	Rye, N.Y.	1/14/69
Bateman, Justine	Rye, N.Y.	2/19/66
Bates, Alan	Allestree, England	2/17/34
Baxter-Birney, Meredith	Los Angeles, Cal.	6/21/47
Beal, John	Joplin, Mo.	8/13/09
Bean, Orson	Burlington, Vt.	7/22/28
Beasley, Allyce	New York, N.Y.	1/6/54
Beatty, Ned	Louisville, Ky.	7/6/37
Beatty, Robert	Hamilton, Ont.	10/19/09
Beatty, Warren	Richmond, Va.	3/30/37
Beck, John	Chicago, Ill.	1/28/43
Bedelia, Bonnie	New York, N.Y.	3/25/46
Bee Gees		
Gibb, Barry	Manchester, England	9/1/46
Gibb, Robin	" "	12/22/49
Gibb, Maurice	" "	12/22/49
Beery, Noah Jr.	New York, N.Y.	8/10/13
Begley, Ed Jr.	Los Angeles, Cal.	9/16/49
Belafonte, Harry	New York, N.Y.	3/1/27
Belafonte-Harper, Shari	New York, N.Y.	9/22/54
Bel Geddes, Barbara	New York, N.Y.	10/31/22
Bellamy, Ralph	Chicago, Ill.	6/17/04
Belmondo, Jean-Paul	Neuilly-sur-Seine, France	4/9/33
Belushi, Jim	Chicago, Ill.	6/15/54
Benatar, Pat	Brooklyn, N.Y.	1/10/53
Benedict, Dirk	Helena, Mont.	3/1/45
Benjamin, Richard	New York, N.Y.	5/22/38
Bennett, Joan	Palisades, N.J.	2/27/10
Bennett, Tony	New York, N.Y.	8/3/26
Benson, George	Pittsburgh, Pa.	3/22/43
Benson, Robby	Dallas, Tex.	1/21/55
Beradino, John	Los Angeles, Cal.	5/8/17
Berenger, Tom	Chicago, Ill.	5/31/50
Bergen, Candice	Beverly Hills, Cal.	5/9/46
Bergen, Polly	Knoxville, Tenn.	7/14/30
Bergerac, Jacques	Biarritz, France	5/26/27
Bergman, Ingmar	Uppsala, Sweden	7/14/18
Berle, Milton	New York, N.Y.	7/12/08
Berlinger, Warren	Brooklyn, N.Y.	8/31/37
Berman, Lazar	Leningrad, USSR	2/26/30
Berman, Shelley	Chicago, Ill.	2/3/26
Bernsen, Corbin	No. Hollywood, Cal.	9/7/54
Bernstein, Leonard	Lawrence, Mass.	8/25/18
Berry, Chuck	St. Louis, Mo.	1/15/26
Berry, Ken	Moline, Ill.	11/3/33
Bertinelli, Valerie	Wilmington, Del.	4/23/60
Bikel, Theodore	Vienna, Austria	5/2/24
Birney, David	Washington, D.C.	4/23/39
Bishop, Joey	Bronx, N.Y.	2/3/18
Bisoglio, Val	New York, N.Y.	5/7/26
Bisset, Jacqueline	Weybridge, England	9/13/44
Bixby, Bill	San Francisco, Cal.	1/22/34
Black, Karen	Park Ridge, Ill.	7/1/42
Blackstone Jr., Harry	Three Rivers, Mich.	6/30/34
Blaine, Vivian	Newark, N.J.	11/21/21
Blair, Linda	St. Louis, Mo.	1/22/59
Blake, Amanda	Buffalo, N.Y.	2/20/29
Blake, Robert	Nutley, N.J.	9/18/33
Blanc, Mel	San Francisco, Cal.	5/30/08
Bledsoe, Tempestt	Chicago, Ill.	8/1/73
Bloom, Claire	London, England	2/15/31
Blyth, Ann	Mt. Kisco, N.Y.	8/16/28
Bogarde, Dirk	London, England	3/28/20
Bogdanovich, Peter	Kingston, N.Y.	7/30/39
Bonet, Lisa	San Francisco, Cal.	11/16/67
Bono, Sonny	Detroit, Mich.	2/16/40
Booke, Sorrell	Buffalo, N.Y.	1/4/30
Boone, Debby	Hackensack, N.J.	9/22/56
Boone, Pat	Jacksonville, Fla.	6/1/34
Booth, Shirley	New York, N.Y.	8/30/07
Borge, Victor	Copenhagen, Denmark	1/3/09
Borgnine, Ernest	Hamden, Conn.	1/24/17
Bosley, Tom	Chicago, Ill.	10/1/27
Bosson, Barbara	Charleroi, Pa.	11/1/39
Bostwick, Barry	San Mateo, Cal.	2/24/46
Bottoms, Joseph	Santa Barbara, Cal.	4/22/54
Bottoms, Timothy	Santa Barbara, Cal.	8/30/51
Bowie, David	London, England	1/8/47
Boxleitner, Bruce	Elgin, Ill.	5/12/50
Boy George	London, England	6/14/61
Boyd, Liona	London, England	7/11/50
Boyle, Peter	Philadelphia, Pa.	10/18/33
Bracken, Eddie	New York, N.Y.	2/7/20
Brand, Neville	Kewanee, Ill.	8/13/21
Brando, Marlon	Omaha, Neb.	4/3/24
Brazzi, Rossano	Bologna, Italy	9/18/16
Brendel, Alfred	Wiesenberg, Austria	1/5/31
Brennan, Eileen	Los Angeles, Cal.	9/3/35
Brenner, David	Philadelphia, Pa.	2/4/45
Brewer, Teresa	Toledo, Oh.	5/7/31
Brian, David	New York, N.Y.	8/5/14
Bridges, Beau	Hollywood, Cal.	12/9/41
Bridges, Jeff	Los Angeles, Cal.	12/4/49
Bridges, Lloyd	San Leandro, Cal.	1/15/13
Bridges, Todd	San Francisco, Cal.	5/27/65
Brimley, Wilford	Salt Lake City, Ut.	9/27/34
Broderick, Matthew	New York, N.Y.	3/21/61
Brolin, James	Los Angeles, Cal.	7/18/40
Bronson, Charles	Ehrenfeld, Pa.	11/3/22
Brooks, Albert	Beverly Hills, Cal.	7/22/47
Brooks, Avery	Evansville, Ind.	10/2/-
Brooks, Mel	New York, N.Y.	6/28/26
Brooks, Stephen	Columbus, Oh.	1942
Brosnan, Pierce	Co. Meath, Ireland	5/16/52
Brown, Blair	Washington, D.C.	1948
Brown, James	Pulaski, Tenn.	6/17/28
Brown, Jim	St. Simons Island, Ga.	2/17/36
Brown, Les	Reinerton, Pa.	3/14/12
Brown, Ray	Pittsburgh, Pa.	10/13/26
Browne, Roscoe Lee	Woodbury, N.J.	5/2/25
Bruce, Carol	Great Neck, N.Y.	11/15/19
Bryant, Anita	Barnsdall, Okla.	3/25/40
Bujold, Genevieve	Montreal, Que.	7/1/42
Bumbry, Grace	St. Louis, Mo.	1/4/37
Burghoff, Gary	Bristol, Conn.	5/24/40
Burke, Paul	New Orleans, La.	7/21/26
Burnett, Carol	San Antonio, Tex.	4/26/36
Burns, George	New York, N.Y.	1/20/96
Burr, Raymond	New Westminster, B.C.	5/21/17
Burstyn, Ellen	Detroit, Mich.	12/7/32
Burton, LeVar	Landsthul, W. Germany	2/16/57
Busey, Gary	Goose Creek, Tex.	6/29/44
Buttons, Red	New York, N.Y.	2/5/19
Buzzi, Ruth	Westerly, R.I.	7/24/36
Byrne, David	Dumbarton, Scotland	5/14/52
Caan, James	New York, N.Y.	3/26/39
Caballe, Montserrat	Barcelona, Spain	4/12/33
Caesar, Sid	Yonkers, N.Y.	9/8/22
Cage, Nicolas	Long Beach, Cal.	1964
Caine, Michael	London, England	3/14/33
Caldwell, Sarah	Maryville, Mo.	3/6/24
Caldwell, Zoe	Melbourne, Australia	9/14/33
Calhoun, Rory	Los Angeles, Cal.	8/8/22
Callas, Charlie	Brooklyn, N.Y.	12/20/-
Calloway, Cab	Rochester, N.Y.	12/25/07

Name	Birthplace	Born
Cameron, Kirk	Panorama City, Cal.	10/12/70
Camp, Hamilton	London, England	10/30/34
Campanella, Joseph	New York, N.Y.	11/21/27
Campbell, Glen	Billstown, Ark.	4/22/36
Candy, John	Toronto, Ont.	10/11/50
Cannon, Dyan	Tacoma, Wash.	1/4/37
Cantrell, Lana	Sydney, Australia	8/7/43
Capra, Frank	Palermo, Italy	5/18/97
Cara, Irene	New York, N.Y.	3/18/58
Carey, Macdonald	Sioux City, Ia.	3/15/13
Carey, Phil	Hackensack, N.J.	7/15/25
Carey, Ron	Newark, N.J.	12/11/35
Cariou, Len	Winnipeg, Man.	9/30/39
Carle, Frankie	Providence, R.I.	3/25/03
Carlin, George	New York, N.Y.	5/12/38
Carlisle, Kitty	New Orleans, La	9/3/15
Carmen, Eric	Cleveland, Oh.	8/11/49
Carmichael, Ian	Hull, England	6/18/20
Carnes, Kim	California	1948
Carney, Art	Mt. Vernon, N.Y.	11/4/18
Caron, Leslie	Boulogne, France	7/1/31
Carpenter, John	Carthage, N.Y.	1/16/48
Carr, Vikki	El Paso, Tex.	7/19/41
Carradine, David	Hollywood, Cal.	10/8/36
Carradine, John	New York, N.Y.	2/5/06
Carradine, Keith	San Mateo, Cal.	8/8/50
Carreras, Jose	Barcelona, Spain	12/5/47
Carroll, Diahann	Bronx, N.Y.	7/17/35
Carroll, Pat	Shreveport, La.	5/5/27
Carson, Johnny	Corning, Ia.	10/23/25
Carter, Dixie	McLemoresville, Tenn.	5/25/39
Carter, Jack	New York, N.Y.	6/24/23
Carter, June	Maces Spring, Va.	6/23/29
Carter, Lynda	Phoenix, Ariz.	7/24/51
Carter, Nell	Birmingham, Ala.	9/13/48
Carvey, Dana	Missoula, Mont.	4/2/55
Cash, Johnny	Kingsland, Ark.	2/26/32
Cash, Rosanne	Memphis, Tenn.	5/24/55
Cass, Peggy	Boston, Mass.	5/21/24
Cassavetes, John	New York, N.Y.	12/9/29
Cassidy, David	New York, N.Y.	4/12/50
Cassidy, Shaun	Los Angeles, Cal.	9/27/58
Castellano, Richard	New York, N.Y.	9/4/33
Cates, Phoebe	New York, N.Y.	1963
Caulfield, Joan	West Orange, N.J.	6/1/22
Cavallaro, Carmen	New York, N.Y.	5/6/13
Cavett, Dick	Gibbon, Neb.	11/19/36
Chamberlain, Richard	Beverly Hills, Cal.	3/31/35
Champion, Marge	Los Angeles, Cal.	9/2/23
Channing, Carol	Seattle, Wash.	1/31/23
Channing, Stockard	New York, N.Y.	2/13/44
Chaplin, Geraldine	Santa Monica, Cal.	7/31/44
Chaplin, Sydney	Beverly Hills, Cal.	3/31/26
Charisse, Cyd	Amarillo, Tex.	3/8/21
Charles, Ray	Albany, Ga.	9/23/30
Charo	Murcia, Spain	1/15/51
Chase, Chevy	New York, N.Y.	10/8/43
Checker, Chubby	Philadelphia, Pa.	10/3/41
Cher	El Centro, Cal.	5/20/46
Chong, Tommy	Edmonton, Alta.	5/24/38
Christie, Julie	Assam, India	4/14/40
Christopher, William	Evanston, Ill.	10/20/32
Christy, June	Springfield, Ill.	11/20/25
Clapton, Eric	Surrey, England	3/30/45
Clark, Dane	New York, N.Y.	2/18/13
Clark, Dick	Mt. Vernon, N.Y.	11/30/29
Clark, Petula	Ewell, Surrey, England	11/15/32
Clark, Roy	Meherrin, Va.	4/5/33
Clark, Susan	Sarma, Ont.	3/8/40
Clary, Robert	Paris, France	3/1/26
Clayburgh, Jill	New York, N.Y.	4/30/44
Clayton-Thomas, David	Surrey, England	9/13/41
Cleese, John	England	10/24/39
Cliburn, Van	Shreveport, La.	7/12/34
Clooney, Rosemary	Maysville, Ky.	5/23/28
Close, Glenn	Greenwich, Conn.	3/19/47
Coburn, James	Laurel, Neb.	8/31/28
Coca, Imogene	Philadelphia, Pa.	11/18/08
Cockburn, Bruce	Ottawa, Ont.	5/27/45
Cohn, Mindy	Los Angeles, Cal.	5/20/66
Colbert, Claudette	Paris, France	9/18/05
Cole, Natalie	Los Angeles, Cal.	2/6/50
Cole, Olivia	Memphis, Tenn.	11/26/42
Coleman, Dabney	Austin, Tex.	1/3/32
Coleman, Gary	Zion, Ill.	2/8/68
Collins, Dorothy	Windsor, Ont.	11/18/26

Name	Birthplace	Born
Collins, Joan	London, England	5/23/33
Collins, Judy	Seattle, Wash.	5/1/39
Collins, Phil	London, England	1/30/51
Comden, Betty	Brooklyn, N.Y.	5/3/19
Como, Perry	Canonsburg, Pa.	5/18/12
Connery, Sean	Edinburgh, Scotland	8/25/30
Conniff, Ray	Attleboro, Mass.	11/6/16
Conner, Nadine	Compton, Cal.	2/20/13
Connors, Chuck	Brooklyn, N.Y.	4/10/21
Connors, Mike	Fresno, Cal.	8/15/25
Conrad, Robert	Chicago, Ill.	3/1/35
Conrad, William	Louisville, Ky.	9/27/20
Constantine, Michael	Reading, Pa.	5/22/27
Conti, Tom	Paisley, Scotland	11/22/41
Convy, Bert	St. Louis, Mo.	6/23/33
Conway, Tim	Willoughby, Oh.	12/15/33
Cook, Barbara	Atlanta, Ga.	10/25/27
Cook, Peter	Torquay, England.	11/17/37
Cooke, Alistair	Manchester, England.	11/20/08
Coolidge, Rita	Nashville, Tenn.	5/1/45
Cooper, Alice	Detroit, Mich.	2/4/48
Cooper, Jackie	Los Angeles, Cal.	9/15/22
Coppola, Francis	Detroit, Mich.	4/7/39
Corby, Ellen	Racine, Wis.	6/3/13
Cord, Alex	New York, N.Y.	8/3/31
Corea, Chick	Chelsea, Mass.	6/12/41
Corelli, Franco	Ancona, Italy	4/8/23
Corey, Jeff	New York, N.Y.	8/10/14
Cosby, Bill	Philadelphia, Pa.	7/12/37
Costello, Elvis	London, England	8/25/54
Cotten, Joseph	Petersburg, Va.	5/15/05
Cougar, John	Seymour, Ind.	10/7/51
Courtenay, Tom	Hull, England	2/25/37
Cox, Ronny	Cloudcroft, N.M.	8/23/38
Craddock, Crash	Greensboro, N.C.	6/16/40
Crain, Jeanne	Barstow, Cal.	5/25/25
Crenna, Richard	Los Angeles, Cal.	11/30/26
Crespin, Regine	Marseilles, France	2/23/29
Cronyn, Hume	London, Ont.	7/18/11
Crosby, Bob	Spokane, Wash.	8/25/13
Crosby, Cathy Lee	Los Angeles, Cal.	12/2/48
Crosby, David	Los Angeles, Cal.	8/14/41
Crosby, Norm	Boston, Mass.	9/15/27
Cross, Christopher	San Antonio, Tex.	5/3/51
Cruise, Tom	Syracuse, N.Y.	1962
Crystal, Billy	Long Beach, N.Y.	3/14/47
Cugat, Xavier	Barcelona, Spain	1/1/00
Cullen, Bill	Pittsburgh, Pa.	2/18/20
Cullum, John	Knoxville, Tenn.	3/2/30
Culp, Robert	Oakland, Cal.	8/16/30
Cummings, Burton	Montreal, Que.	12/31/47
Cummings, Constance	Seattle, Wash.	5/15/10
Cummings, Robert	Joplin, Mo.	6/9/10
Curtin, Jane	Cambridge, Mass.	9/6/47
Curtin, Phyllis	Clarksburg, W.Va.	12/3/30
Curtis, Jamie Lee	Los Angeles, Cal.	11/22/58
Curtis, Keene	Salt Lake City, Ut.	2/15/23
Curtis, Ken	Lamar, Col.	7/2/16
Curtis, Tony	New York, N.Y.	6/3/25
Curtola, Bobby	Port Arthur, Ont.	4/17/44
Cusack, Cyril	Durban, S. Africa	11/26/10
Cushing, Peter	Surrey, England	5/26/13
Dafoe, Willem	Milwaukee, Wis.	1955
Dahl, Arlene	Minneapolis, Minn.	8/11/28
Dailey, Irene	New York, N.Y.	9/12/20
Dale, Jim	Rothwell, England	8/15/35
Dalton, Abby	Las Vegas, Nev.	8/15/32
Dalton, Timothy	Wales	3/21/44
Daly, John	Johannesberg, S. Africa	2/20/14
Daly, Tyne	Madison, Wis.	2/21/47
Damone, Vic	Brooklyn, N.Y.	6/12/28
D'Angelo, Beverly	Columbus, Oh.	1954
Dangerfield, Rodney	Babylon, N.Y.	11/22/21
Daniels, Charlie	Wilmington, N.C.	10/28/36
Daniels, William	Brooklyn, N.Y.	3/31/27
Danner, Blythe	Philadelphia, Pa.	2/3/43
Danson, Ted	San Diego, Cal.	12/29/47
Danza, Tony	New York, N.Y.	4/21/50
Darby, Kim	Hollywood, Cal.	7/8/48
Darren, James	Philadelphia, Pa.	6/8/36
Davidson, John	Pittsburgh, Pa.	12/13/41
Davis, Ann B.	Schenectady, N.Y.	5/5/26
Davis, Bette	Lowell, Mass.	4/5/08
Davis, Clifton	Chicago, Ill.	10/4/45
Davis, Geena	Ware, Mass.	1/21/57
Davis, Judy	Perth, Australia	1956

Name	Birthplace	Born	Name	Birthplace	Born
Davis, Mac	Lubbock, Tex.	1/21/42	Dylan, Bob	Duluth, Minn.	5/24/41
Davis, Ossie	Cogdell, Ga.	12/18/17	Dysart, Richard	Brighton, Mass.	3/30/-
Davis, Sammy Jr.	New York, N.Y.	12/8/25	Easton, Sheena	Bellshill, Scotland.	4/27/59
Davis, Skeeter	Dry Ridge, Ky.	12/30/31	Eastwood, Clint	San Francisco, Cal.	5/31/30
Dawber, Pam	Farmington Hills, Mich.	10/18/51	Ebert, Roger	Urbana, Ill.	6/18/42
Dawn, Hazel	Ogden, Ut.	3/23/98	Ebsen, Buddy	Belleville, Ill.	4/2/08
Dawson, Richard	Hampshire, England	11/20/32	Eckstine, Billy	Pittsburgh, Pa.	7/8/14
Day, Dennis	New York, N.Y.	5/21/17	Edelman, Herb	Brooklyn, N.Y.	11/5/33
Day, Doris	Cincinnati, Oh.	4/3/24	Eden, Barbara	Tucson, Ariz.	8/23/34
Day, Laraine	Roosevelt, Ut.	10/13/20	Edwards, Blake	Tulsa, Okla.	7/26/22
Dean, Jimmy	Plainview, Tex.	8/10/28	Edwards, Ralph	Merino, Col.	6/13/13
DeCarlo, Yvonne	Vancouver, B.C.	9/1/22	Edwards, Vincent	Brooklyn, N.Y.	7/7/28
De Camp, Rosemary	Prescott, Ariz.	11/14/10	Eggar, Samantha	London, England	3/5/39
Dee, Frances	Los Angeles, Cal.	11/26/07	Eichhorn, Lisa	Reading, Pa.	2/4/52
Dee, Ruby	Cleveland, Oh.	10/27/23	Eikenberry, Jill	New Haven, Conn.	2/21/47
Dee, Sandra	Bayonne, N.J.	4/23/42	Ekberg, Anita	Malmo, Sweden	9/29/31
Defore, Don	Cedar Rapids, Ia.	8/25/17	Ekland, Britt	Stockholm, Sweden	10/6/42
DeHaven, Gloria	Los Angeles, Cal.	7/23/25	Elam, Jack	Miami, Arizona	11/13/16
De Havilland, Olivia	Tokyo, Japan	7/1/16	Eldridge, Florence	Brooklyn, N.Y.	9/5/01
Della Chiesa, Vivienne	Chicago, Ill.	10/9/20	Elliott, Bob	Boston, Mass.	3/26/23
Delon, Alain	Sceaux, France	11/8/35	Elliott, Denholm	London, England	5/31/22
DeLuise, Dom	Brooklyn, N.Y.	8/1/33	Elliott, Sam	Sacramento, Cal.	8/9/44
De Mille, Agnes	New York, N.Y.	1905	Estevez, Emelio	New York, N.Y.	1963
De Mornay, Rebecca	California	1962	Estrada, Erik	New York, N.Y.	3/16/49
Deneuve, Catherine	Paris, France	10/22/43	Evans, Dale	Uvalde, Tex.	10/31/12
De Niro, Robert	New York, N.Y.	8/17/45	Evans, Gene	Holbrook, Ariz.	7/11/24
Dennehy, Brian	Bridgeport, Conn.	1940	Evans, Linda	Hartford, Conn.	11/18/42
Denning, Richard	Poughkeepsie, N.Y.	3/27/14	Evans, Maurice	Dorchester, England	6/3/01
Dennis, Sandy	Hastings, Neb.	4/27/37	Evans, Robert	New York, N.Y.	6/29/30
Denver, Bob	New Rochelle, N.Y.	1/9/35	Everett, Chad	South Bend, Ind.	6/11/36
Denver, John	Roswell, N.M.	12/31/43	Everly, Don	Brownie, Ky.	2/1/37
DePalma, Brian	Newark, N.J	9/11/40	Everly, Phil	Brownie, Ky.	1/19/38
Derek, Bo	Long Beach, Cal.	11/20/56	Ewell, Tom	Owensboro, Ky.	4/29/09
Derek, John	Hollywood, Cal.	8/12/26	Fabares, Shelley	Santa Monica, Cal.	1/19/42
Dern, Bruce	Chicago, Ill.	6/4/36	Fabian (Forte)	Philadelphia, Pa.	2/6/43
Devane, William	Albany, N.Y.	9/5/37	Fabray, Nanette	San Diego, Cal.	10/27/20
DeVito, Danny	Neptune, N.J.	11/17/44	Fairbanks, Douglas Jr.	New York, N.Y.	12/9/09
Dewhurst, Colleen	Montreal, Que.	6/3/26	Fairchild, Morgan	Dallas, Tex.	2/3/50
DeWitt, Joyce	Wheeling, W.Va.	4/23/49	Falana, Lola	Philadelphia, Pa.	9/11/46
Dey, Susan.	Pekin, Ill.	12/10/52	Falk, Peter	New York, N.Y.	9/16/27
Diamond, Neil	Brooklyn, N.Y.	1/24/41	Farentino, James	Brooklyn, N.Y.	2/24/38
Dickinson, Angie	Kulm, N.D.	9/30/31	Fargo, Donna	Mt. Airy, N.C.	11/10/45
Dietrich, Marlene	Berlin, Germany	12/27/01	Farr, Jamie	Toledo, Oh.	7/1/34
Diller, Phyllis	Lima, Oh.	7/17/17	Farrell, Charles	Onset Bay, Mass.	8/9/01
Dillman, Bradford	San Francisco, Cal.	4/14/30	Farrell, Eileen	Willimantic, Conn.	2/13/20
Dillon, Matt	New Rochelle, N.Y.	2/18/64	Farrell, Mike	St. Paul, Minn.	2/6/39
Dixon, Ivan	New York, N.Y.	4/6/31	Farrow, Mia	Los Angeles, Cal.	2/9/45
Dobson, Kevin	New York, N.Y.	3/18/44	Fawcett, Farrah	Corpus Christi, Tex.	2/2/47
Domingo, Placido	Madrid, Spain	1/21/41	Faye, Alice	New York, N.Y.	5/5/12
Domino, Fats	New Orleans, La.	2/26/28	Feld, Fritz	Berlin, Germany	10/15/00
Donahue, Phil	Cleveland, Oh.	12/21/35	Feldon, Barbara	Pittsburgh, Pa.	3/12/41
Donahue, Troy	New York, N.Y.	1/27/36	Feldshuh, Tovah	New York, N.Y.	12/27/52
Donald, James	Aberdeen, Scotland	5/18/17	Feliciano, Jose	Lares, Puerto Rico	9/10/45
Donovan	Glasgow, Scotland	5/10/43	Fell, Norman	Philadelphia, Pa.	3/24/24
Dorati, Antal	Budapest, Hungary	4/9/06	Fellini, Federico	Rimini, Italy	1/20/20
Douglas, Kirk	Amsterdam, N.Y.	12/9/18	Fellows, Edith	Boston, Mass.	5/20/23
Douglas, Michael	New Brunswick, N.J.	9/25/44	Fender, Freddy	San Benito, Tex.	6/4/37
Douglas, Mike	Chicago, Ill.	8/11/25	Ferrell, Conchata	Charleston, W. Va.	3/28/43
Down, Leslie-Ann	London, England	3/17/54	Ferrer, Jose	Santurce, P.R.	1/8/12
Downs, Hugh	Akron, Oh.	2/14/21	Ferrer, Mel	Elberon, N.J.	8/25/17
Doyle, David	Lincoln, Neb.	12/1/29	Ferrigno, Lou.	Brooklyn, N.Y.	11/9/52
Dragon, Daryl	Los Angeles, Cal.	8/27/42	Field, Sally	Pasadena, Cal.	11/6/46
Drake, Alfred.	Bronx, N.Y.	10/7/14	Fields, Kim	Los Angeles, Cal.	5/12/69
Drew, Ellen	Kansas City, Mo.	11/23/15	Finney, Albert	Salford, England	5/9/36
Dreyfuss, Richard	Brooklyn, N.Y.	10/29/47	Firkusny, Rudolf	Napajedla, Czech.	2/11/12
Dru, Joanne	Logan, W.Va.	1/31/23	Firth, Peter	Yorkshire, England	10/27/53
Dryer, Fred.	Hawthorne, Cal.	7/6/46	Fischer-Dieskau, Dietrich	Berlin, Germany	5/28/25
Duchin, Peter	New York, N.Y.	7/28/37	Fisher, Carrie	Beverly Hills, Cal.	10/21/56
Duff, Howard.	Bremerton, Wash.	11/24/17	Fisher, Eddie	Philadelphia, Pa.	8/10/28
Duffy, Julia	Minneapolis, Minn.	6/27/52	Fitzgerald, Ella.	Newport News, Va.	4/25/18
Duffy, Patrick	Townsend, Mont.	3/17/49	Fitzgerald, Geraldine	Dublin, Ireland.	11/24/13
Dufour, Val	New Orleans, La.	2/5/27	Flack, Roberta.	Black Mountain, N.C.	2/10/39
Dukakis, Olympia	Massachusetts	1932	Flanders, Ed	Minneapolis, Minn.	12/29/34
Duke, Patty.	New York, N.Y.	12/14/46	Fleming, Rhonda	Hollywood, Cal.	8/10/23
Dullea, Keir.	Cleveland, Oh.	5/30/36	Fletcher, Louise	Birmingham, Ala.	1936
Dunaway, Faye	Bascom, Fla.	1/14/41	Foch, Nina	Leyden, Netherlands.	4/20/24
Duncan, Sandy	Henderson, Tex.	2/20/46	Fogelberg, Dan	Peoria, Ill.	8/13/51
Dunham, Katherine	Joliet, Ill.	6/22/10	Fonda, Jane	New York, N.Y.	12/21/37
Dunn, Nora	Chicago, Ill.	4/29/52	Fonda, Peter	New York, N.Y.	2/23/39
Dunne, Irene	Louisville, Ky.	12/20/98	Fontaine, Joan	Tokyo, Japan	10/22/17
Dunnock, Mildred	Baltimore, Md.	1/25/04	Fonteyn, Margot	Reigate, England	5/18/19
Durbin, Deanna	Winnipeg, Man.	12/4/21	Ford (Tenn.), Ernie	Bristol, Tenn.	2/13/19
Durning, Charles.	Highland Falls, N.Y.	2/28/23	Ford, Glenn	Quebec, Que.	5/1/16
Dussault, Nancy	Pensacola, Fla.	6/30/36	Ford, Harrison	Chicago, Ill.	7/13/42
Duvall, Robert	San Diego, Cal.	1/5/31	Forrest, Steve	Huntsville, Tex.	9/29/24
Duvall, Shelley	Houston, Tex.	1949	Forrester, Maureen	Montreal, Que.	7/25/30

Name	Birthplace	Born	Name	Birthplace	Born
Forsythe, Henderson	Macon, Mo.	9/11/17	Goldsboro, Bobby	Marianna, Fla.	1/11/41
Forsythe, John	Penns Grove, N.J.	1/29/18	Goldthwait, Bob	Syracuse, N.Y.	1962
Foster, Jodie	Los Angeles, Cal.	11/19/62	Gordon, Gale	New York, N.Y.	2/2/06
Fox, James	London, England	5/19/39	Gorman, Cliff	New York, N.Y.	10/13/36
Fox, Michael J.	Edmonton, Alta.	6/9/61	Gorme, Eydie	Bronx, N.Y.	8/16/32
Foxworth, Robert	Houston, Tex.	11/1/41	Gorshin, Frank	Pittsburgh, Pa.	4/5/34
Foxx, Redd	St. Louis, Mo.	12/9/22	Gossett Jr., Louis	Brooklyn, N.Y.	5/27/36
Frampton, Peter	Kent, England	4/22/50	Gould, Elliott	Brooklyn, N.Y.	8/29/38
Francescatti, Zino	Marseilles, France	8/9/05	Gould, Harold	Schenectady, N.Y.	12/10/23
Franciosa, Anthony	New York, N.Y.	10/25/28	Gould, Morton	Richmond Hill, N.Y.	12/10/13
Francis, Anne	Ossining, N.Y.	9/16/30	Goulding, Ray	Lowell, Mass.	3/20/22
Francis, Arlene	Boston, Mass.	10/20/08	Goulet, Robert	Lawrence, Mass.	11/26/33
Francis, Connie	Newark, N.J.	12/12/38	Gowdy, Curt	Green River, Wyo.	7/31/19
Francis, Genie	Los Angeles, Cal.	5/26/62	Graham, Martha	Pittsburgh, Pa.	5/11/94
Frankenheimer, John	Malba, N.Y.	2/19/30	Grammer, Kelsey	Virgin Islands	2/20/-
Franklin, Aretha	Memphis, Tenn.	3/25/42	Graham, Virginia	Chicago, Ill.	7/4/12
Franklin, Bonnie	Santa Monica, Cal.	1/6/44	Granger, Farley	San Jose, Cal.	7/1/25
Franklin, Joe	New York, N.Y.	1929	Granger, Stewart	London, England	5/6/13
Frann, Mary	St. Louis, Mo.	2/27/43	Granville, Bonita	New York, N.Y.	2/2/23
Franz, Dennis	Chicago, Ill.	10/28/44	Grant, Lee	New York, N.Y.	10/31/29
Freed, Bert	New York, N.Y.	11/3/19	Graves, Peter	Minneapolis, Minn.	3/18/25
Freeman Jr., Al	San Antonio, Tex.	3/21/34	Gray, Coleen	Staplehurst, Neb.	10/23/22
French, Victor	Santa Barbara, Cal.	12/4/34	Gray, Erin	Honolulu, Ha.	1/7/52
Frick, Mr. (W. Groebli)	Basel, Switzerland	4/21/15	Gray, Linda	Santa Monica, Cal.	9/12/40
Friedkin, William	Chicago, Ill.	8/29/39	Grayson, Kathryn	Winston52Salem, N.C.	2/9/22
Frost, David	Tenterden, England	4/7/39	Greco, Buddy	Philadelphia, Pa.	8/14/26
Funicello, Annette	Utica, N.Y.	10/22/42	Greco, Jose	Abruzzi, Italy	12/23/18
Funt, Allen	New York, N.Y.	9/16/14	Green, Adolph	New York, N.Y.	12/2/15
			Green, Al	Forest City, Ark.	4/13/46
Gabor, Eva	Hungary	1921	Greene, Ellen	New York, N.Y.	1950
Gabor, Zsa Zsa	Hungary	—	Greene, Michelle	Las Vegas, Nev.	2/3/-
Gabriel, John	Niagara Falls, N.Y.	5/25/31	Greene, Shecky	Chicago, Ill.	4/8/26
Gail, Max	Detroit, Mich.	4/5/43	Gregory, Cynthia	Los Angeles, Cal.	7/8/46
Gallagher, Megan	Reading, Pa.	2/6/-	Gregory, Dick	St. Louis, Mo.	10/12/32
Galloway, Don	Brooksville, Ky.	7/27/37	Gregory, James	Bronx, N.Y.	12/23/11
Galway, James	Belfast, Ireland	12/8/39	Grey, Joel	Cleveland, Oh.	4/11/32
Garagiola, Joe	St. Louis, Mo.	2/12/26	Griffin, Merv	San Mateo, Cal.	7/6/25
Garbo, Greta	Stockholm, Sweden	9/18/05	Griffith, Andy	Mount Airy, N.C.	6/1/26
Gardenia, Vincent	Naples, Italy	1/7/22	Griffith, Melanie	New York, N.Y.	8/9/57
Gardner, Ava	Smithfield, N.C.	12/24/22	Grimes, Tammy	Lynn, Mass.	1/30/36
Garfunkel, Art	New York, N.Y.	10/13/41	Grizzard, George	Roanoke Rapids, N.C.	4/1/28
Garland, Beverly	Santa Cruz, Cal.	10/17/29	Grodin, Charles	Pittsburgh, Pa.	4/21/35
Garner, James	Norman, Okla.	4/7/28	Groh, David	New York, N.Y.	5/2/41
Garr, Terri	Lakewood, Oh.	12/11/49	Grosbard, Ulu	Antwerp, Belgium	1/19/29
Garrett, Betty	St. Joseph, Mo.	5/23/19	Gross, Michael	Chicago, Ill.	6/21/47
Garson, Greer	Co. Down, N. Ireland	9/29/08	Grouch, Andrea	Los Angeles, Cal.	7/1/42
Gatlin, Larry	Seminole, Tex.	5/2/48	Guardino, Harry	New York, N.Y.	12/23/25
Gavin, John	Los Angeles, Cal.	4/8/32	Guillaume, Robert	St. Louis, Mo.	11/30/28
Gayle, Crystal	Paintsville, Ky.	1/9/51	Guinness, Alec	London, England	4/2/14
Gaynor, Mitzi	Chicago, Ill.	9/4/30	Gunn, Moses	St. Louis, Mo.	10/2/29
Gazzara, Ben	New York, N.Y.	8/28/30	Guthrie, Arlo	New York, N.Y.	7/10/47
Geary, Anthony	Coalsville, Ut.	5/29/47	Guttenberg, Steve	New York, N.Y.	8/24/58
Gedda, Nicolai	Stockholm, Sweden	7/11/25	Gwynne, Fred	New York, N.Y.	7/10/26
Geldof, Bob	Co. Dublin, Ire.	10/5/51			
Gennaro, Peter	Metairie, La.	1924	Hackett, Buddy	Brooklyn, N.Y.	8/31/24
Gentry, Bobbie	Chickasaw Co., Miss.	7/27/44	Hackman, Gene	San Bernardino, Cal.	1/30/30
George, Phyllis	Denton, Tex.	6/25/49	Hagen, Uta	Gottingen, Germany	6/12/19
Gerard, Gil	Little Rock, Ark.	1/23/43	Haggard, Merle	Bakersfield, Cal.	4/6/37
Gere, Richard	Philadelphia, Pa.	8/31/49	Haggerty, Dan	Hollywood, Cal.	11/19/41
Getty, Estelle	New York, N.Y.	7/25/-	Hagman, Larry	Weatherford, Tex.	9/21/31
Ghostley, Alice	Eve, Mo.	8/14/26	Hague, Albert	Belin, Germany	10/13/20
Giannini, Giancarlo	Spezia, Italy	8/1/42	Haid, Charles	San Francisco, Cal.	6/2/43
Gibb, Cynthia	Bennington, Vt.	12/14/63	Hale, Barbara	DeKalb, Ill.	4/18/22
Gibbs, Marla	Chicago, Ill.	6/14/31	Hall, Daryl	Pottstown, Pa.	10/11/49
Gibson, Henry	Germantown, Pa.	9/21/35	Hall, Deidre	Milwaukee, Wis.	10/3/48
Gibson, Mel	Peerskill, N.Y.	1/3/51	Hall, Huntz	New York, N.Y.	8/15/19
Gielgud, John	London, England	4/14/04	Hall, Monty	Winnipeg, Man.	8/25/23
Gilbert, Melissa	Los Angeles, Cal.	5/8/64	Hall, Tom T.	Olive Hill, Ky.	5/25/36
Gilberto, Astrud	Salvador, Brazil	3/30/40	Hamel, Veronica	Philadelphia, Pa.	11/20/43
Gilford, Jack	New York, N.Y.	7/25/07	Hamill, Mark	Oakland, Cal.	9/25/52
Gillette, Anita	Baltimore, Md.	8/16/36	Hamilton, George	Memphis, Tenn.	8/12/39
Gilley, Mickey	Natchez, Miss.	3/9/36	Hamilton, Linda	Salisbury, Md.	9/26/-
Ginty, Robert	New York, N.Y.	11/14/48	Hamlin, Harry	Pasadena, Cal.	10/30/51
Gish, Lillian	Springfield, Oh.	10/14/96	Hampshire, Susan	London, England	5/12/38
Glaser, Paul Michael	Cambridge, Mass.	3/25/43	Hampton, Lionel	Birmingham, Ala.	4/12/13
Glass, Ron	Evansville, Ind.	7/10/45	Hancock, Herbie	Chicago, Ill.	4/12/40
Glenn, Scott	Pittsburgh, Pa.	1939	Hanks, Tom	Oakland, Cal.	1957
Gless, Sharon	Los Angeles, Cal.	5/31/43	Hannah, Daryl	Chicago, Ill.	1961
Glover, Danny	San Francisco, Cal.	1948	Harmon, Mark	Burbank, Cal.	9/2/51
Glynn, Carlin	Cleveland, Oh.	2/19/40	Harper, Jessica	Chicago, Ill.	1949
Gobel, George	Chicago, Ill.	5/20/19	Harper, Tess	Mommoth Springs, Ark.	1952
Godard, Jean Luc	Paris, France	12/3/30	Harper, Valerie	Suffern, N.Y.	8/22/40
Goddard, Paulette	Great Neck, N.Y.	6/3/11	Harrelson, Woody	Midland, Tex.	7/23/-
Godunov, Alexander	Sakhalin Is., USSR	11/28/49	Harrington, Pat Jr.	New York, N.Y.	8/13/29
Goldberg, Whoopi	New York, N.Y.	1949	Harris, Barbara	Evanston, Ill.	7/25/35
Goldblum, Jeff	Pittsburgh, Pa.	10/22/53	Harris, Ed	Tenafly, N.J.	1950

Name	Birthplace	Born
Harris, Emmylou	Birmingham, Ala.	4/2/47
Harris, Julie	Grosse Pte. Park, Mich.	12/2/25
Harris, Phil	Linton, Ind.	6/24/04
Harris, Richard	Co. Limerick, Ireland	10/1/33
Harris, Rosemary	Ashby, England	9/19/30
Harrison, George	Liverpool, England	2/25/43
Harrison, Gregory	Avalon, Cal.	5/31/50
Harrison, Rex	Huyton, England	3/5/08
Harron, Don	Toronto, Ont.	9/19/24
Harry, Deborah	Miami, Fla.	7/1/45
Harry, Jackee	Winston-Salem, N.C.	8/14/-
Hart, Mary	Sioux Falls, S.D.	1951
Hart, Corey	Montreal, Que.	5/31/62
Hartley, Mariette	New York, N.Y.	6/21/40
Hartman, David	Pawtucket, R.I.	5/19/35
Hartman, Lisa	Houston, Tex.	6/1/56
Hasselhoff, David	Baltimore, Md.	7/17/52
Hasso, Signe	Stockholm, Sweden	8/15/15
Hauer, Rutger	Netherlands	1/23/44
Haver, June	Rock Island, Ill.	6/10/26
Havoc, June	Seattle, Wash.	11/8/16
Hawkins, Ronnie	Huntsville, Ark.	1/19/35
Hawn, Goldie	Washington, D.C.	11/21/45
Hayden, Melissa	Toronto, Ont.	4/25/23
Hayes, Helen	Washington, D.C.	10/10/00
Hayes, Isaac	Covington, Tenn.	8/20/42
Hayes, Peter Lind	San Francisco, Cal.	6/25/15
Hays, Robert	Bethesda, Md.	7/24/47
Healy, Mary	New Orleans, La.	4/14/18
Heatherton, Joey	Rockville Centre, N.Y.	9/14/44
Heckart, Eileen	Columbus, Oh.	3/29/19
Helmond, Katherine	Galveston, Tex.	7/5/34
Hemingway, Margaux	Portland, Ore.	2/19/55
Hemingway, Mariel	Ketchum, Ida.	11/22/61
Hemmings, David	Guildford, England	11/18/41
Hemsley, Sherman	Philadelphia, Pa.	2/1/38
Henderson, Florence	Dale, Ind.	2/14/34
Henderson, Skitch	Halstad, Minn.	1/27/18
Henner, Marilu	Chicago, Ill.	4/6/52
Henning, Doug	Fort Garry, Man.	5/3/47
Henreid, Paul	Trieste, Austria	1/10/08
Hensley, Pamela	Los Angeles, Cal.	10/3/50
Henson, Jim	Greenville, Miss.	9/24/36
Hepburn, Audrey	Brussels, Belgium	5/4/29
Hepburn, Katharine	Hartford, Conn.	11/8/09
Herman, Pee-Wee	Peerskill, N.Y.	1952
Herrmann, Edward	Washington, D.C.	7/21/43
Hershey, Barbara	Los Angeles, Cal.	2/5/48
Hesseman, Howard	Lebanon, Ore.	2/27/40
Heston, Charlton	Evanston, Ill.	10/4/23
Higgins, Joel	Bloomington, Ill.	9/28/46
Hildegarde	Adell, Wis.	2/1/06
Hill, Arthur	Melfort, Sask.	8/1/22
Hill, Benny	Southampton, England	1/21/25
Hill, Dan	Toronto, Ont.	6/3/54
Hill, George Roy	Minneapolis, Minn.	12/20/22
Hiller, Wendy	Stockport, England	8/15/12
Hillerman, John	Denison, Tex.	12/30/32
Hines, Gregory	New York, N.Y.	2/14/46
Hines, Jerome	Hollywood, Cal.	11/8/21
Hingle, Pat	Denver, Col.	7/19/23
Hirsch, Judd	Bronx, N.Y.	3/15/35
Hirt, Al	New Orleans, La.	11/7/22
Ho, Don	Kakaako, Oahu, Ha.	8/13/30
Hoffman, Dustin	Los Angeles, Cal.	8/8/37
Hogan, Paul	New South Wales, Australia	1941
Holbrook, Hal	Cleveland, Oh.	2/17/25
Holder, Geoffrey	Trinidad	8/1/30
Holliday, Polly	Jasper, Ala.	7/2/37
Holliman, Earl	Delhi, La.	9/11/28
Holloway, Sterling	Cedartown, Ga.	1/4/05
Holm, Celeste	New York, N.Y.	4/29/19
Hooks, Robert	Washington, D.C.	4/18/37
Hope, Bob	London, England	5/29/03
Hopkins, Anthony	Wales	12/31/37
Hopkins, Telma	Louisville, Ky.	10/28/48
Hopper, Dennis	Dodge City, Kan.	5/17/36
Horne, Lena	Brooklyn, N.Y.	6/30/17
Horne, Marilyn	Bradford, Pa.	1/16/34
Horowitz, Vladimir	Kiev, Russia	10/1/04
Horsley, Lee	Muleshoe, Tex.	5/15/55
Horton, Robert	Los Angeles, Cal.	7/29/24
Hoskins, Bob	Suffolk, England	10/26/42
Houseman, John	Bucharest, Romania	9/22/02
Houston, Whitney	Newark, N.J.	1963
Howard, Ken	El Centro, Cal.	3/28/44
Howard, Ron	Duncan, Okla.	3/1/54
Howell, C. Thomas	Los Angeles, Cal.	12/7/66
Howes, Sally Ann	London, England	7/20/30
Hughes, Barnard	Bedford Hills, N.Y.	7/16/15
Hulce, Tom	White Water, Wis.	1953
Humperdinck, Engelbert	Madras, India	5/3/36
Hunt, Linda	Morristown, N.J.	1945
Hunter, Holly	Conyers, Ga.	1959
Hunter, Kim	Detroit, Mich.	11/12/22
Hunter, Ross	Cleveland, Oh.	5/6/21
Hunter, Tab	New York, N.Y.	7/11/31
Hunter, Tommy	London, Ont.	3/10/37
Hurt, John	Chesterfield, England	1/22/40
Hurt, Mary Beth	Marshalltown, Ia.	9/26/48
Hurt, William	Washington, D.C.	3/20/50
Hussey, Olivia	Buenos Aires, Argentina	4/17/51
Hussey, Ruth	Providence, R.I.	10/30/14
Huston, Anjelica	Ireland	1952
Hutchinson, Josephine	Seattle, Wash.	10/12/-
Hutton, Betty	Battle Creek, Mich.	2/26/21
Hutton, Lauren	Charleston, S.C.	11/17/43
Hutton, Timothy	Malibu, Cal.	8/16/60
Hyde-White, Wilfrid	Gloucester, England	5/12/03
Hyman, Earle	Rocky Mount, N.C.	11/11/26
Ian, Janis	New York, N.Y.	4/7/50
Iglesias, Julio	Spain	9/23/43
Ireland, Jill	London, England	4/24/36
Ireland, John	Vancouver, B.C.	1/30/15
Irons, Jeremy	Cowes, England	9/19/48
Irving, Amy	Palo Alto, Cal.	9/10/53
Irving, George S.	Springfield, Mass.	11/1/22
Ives, Burl	Hunt Township, Ill.	6/14/09
Ivey, Judith	El Paso, Tex.	9/4/51
Jacks, Terry	Winnipeg, Man.	3/29/44
Jackson, Anne	Allegheny, Pa.	9/3/26
Jackson, Glenda	Liverpool, England	5/9/38
Jackson, Jermaine	Gary, Ind.	12/11/54
Jackson, Kate	Birmingham, Ala.	10/29/48
Jackson, Michael	Gary, Ind.	8/29/58
Jackson, Victoria	Miami, Fla.	8/2/59
Jacobi, Derek	London, England	10/22/38
Jaeckel, Richard	Long Beach, Cal.	10/10/26
Jagger, Dean	Lima, Oh.	11/7/03
Jagger, Mick	Dartford, England	7/26/43
James, Dennis	Jersey City, N.J.	8/24/17
James, John	Minneapolis, Minn.	4/18/56
Janis, Conrad	New York, N.Y.	2/11/28
Jarreau, Al	Milwaukee, Wis	3/12/40
Jeffreys, Anne	Goldsboro, N.C.	1/26/23
Jeffries, Fran	San Jose, Cal.	1939
Jenner, Bruce	Mt. Kisco, N.Y.	10/28/49
Jennings, Waylon	Littlefield, Tex.	6/15/37
Jett, Joan	Philadelphia, Pa.	9/22/60
Jillian, Ann	Cambridge, Mass.	1/29/51
Joel, Billy	Bronx, N.Y.	5/9/49
John, Elton	Middlesex, England	3/25/47
Johns, Glynis	Durban, S. Africa	10/5/23
Johnson, Arte	Benton Harbor, Mich.	1/20/29
Johnson, Ben	Foeaker, Okla.	6/13/18
Johnson, Don	Flatt Creek, Mo.	12/15/49
Johnson, Van	Newport, R.I.	8/25/16
Jones, Allan	Scranton, Pa.	10/14/07
Jones, Dean	Morgan City, Ala.	1/25/35
Jones, George	Saratoga, Tex.	9/12/31
Jones, Grace	Spanishtown, Jamaica	5/19/52
Jones, Grandpa	Niagara, Ky.	10/20/13
Jones, Henry	Philadelphia, Pa.	8/1/12
Jones, Jack	Hollywood, Cal.	1/14/38
Jones, James Earl	Tate Co., Miss.	1/17/31
Jones, Jennifer	Tulsa, Okla.	3/2/19
Jones, Shirley	Smithton, Pa.	3/31/34
Jones, Tom	Pontypridd, Wales	6/7/40
Jones, Tommy Lee	San Saba, Tex.	9/15/46
Jordan, Richard	New York, N.Y.	7/19/38
Jourdan, Louis	Marseilles, France	6/19/19
Julia, Raul	San Juan, P.R.	1940
Jump, Gordon	Dayton, Oh.	4/1/32
Jurado, Katy	Guadalajara, Mexico	1/16/24
Kahn, Madeline	Boston, Mass.	9/29/42
Kanaly, Steve	Burbank, Cal.	3/14/46
Kane, Carol	Cleveland, Oh.	6/18/52
Kaplan, Gabe	Brooklyn, N.Y.	3/31/45
Karlen, John	New York, N.Y.	5/28/-
Karras, Alex	Gary, Ind.	7/15/35

Name	Birthplace	Born	Name	Birthplace	Born
Katt, William	Los Angeles, Cal.	2/16/55	Lasser, Louise	New York, N.Y.	4/11/39
Kavner, Julie	Los Angeles, Cal.	9/7/51	Lauper, Cyndi	New York, N.Y.	6/20/53
Kazan, Elia	Constantinople, Turkey	9/7/09	Laurie, Piper	Detroit, Mich.	1/22/32
Kazan, Lainie	New York, N.Y.	5/15/42	Lauter, Ed	Long Beach, N.Y.	10/30/40
Keach, Stacy	Savannah, Ga.	6/2/41	Lavin, Linda	Portland, Me.	10/15/37
Keaton, Diane	Santa Ana, Cal.	1/5/46	Lawrence, Carol	Melrose Park, Ill.	9/5/34
Keaton, Michael	Pittsburgh, Pa.	9/9/51	Lawrence, Steve	Brooklyn, N.Y.	7/8/35
Keel, Howard	Gillespie, Ill.	4/13/17	Lawrence, Vicki	Inglewood, Cal.	3/26/49
Keeler, Ruby	Halifax, N.S.	8/25/09	Leach, Robin	London, England	1941
Keeshan, Bob	Lynbrook, N.Y.	6/27/27	Leachman, Cloris	Des Moines, Ia.	4/4/26
Keitel, Harvey	Brooklyn, N.Y.	1947	Lean, David	Croydon, England	3/25/08
Keith, Brian	Bayonne, N.J.	11/14/21	Lear, Norman	New Haven, Conn.	7/27/22
Keith, David	Knoxville, Tenn.	5/8/54	Learned, Michael	Washington, D.C.	4/9/39
Kellerman, Sally	Long Beach, Cal.	6/2/37	LeBon, Simon	Bushey, England	10/27/58
Kelley, DeForest	Atlanta, Ga.	1/20/20	Lederer, Francis	Prague, Czechoslovakia	11/6/06
Kelly, Gene	Pittsburgh, Pa.	8/23/12	Lee, Brenda	Atlanta, Ga.	12/11/44
Kelly, Jack	Astoria, N.Y.	9/16/27	Lee, Christopher	London, England	5/27/22
Kelly, Nancy	Lowell, Mass.	3/25/21	Lee, Michele	Los Angeles, Cal.	6/24/42
Kennedy, Arthur	Worcester, Mass.	2/17/14	Lee, Peggy	Jamestown, N.D.	5/26/20
Kennedy, George	New York, N.Y.	2/18/26	Le Gallienne, Eva	London, England	1/11/99
Kennedy, Jayne	Washington, D.C.	11/27/51	Legrand, Michel	Paris, France	2/24/32
Kennedy, Tom	Louisville, Ky.	2/26/27	Leibman, Ron	New York, N.Y.	10/11/37
Kent, Allegra	Los Angeles, Cal.	8/11/37	Leifer, Carol	E. Williston, N.Y.	1956
Kercheval, Ken	Wolcottville, Ind.	7/15/35	Leigh, Janet	Merced, Cal.	7/6/27
Kerns, Joanna	San Francisco, Cal.	2/12/55	Leinsdorf, Erich	Vienna, Austria	2/4/12
Kerr, Deborah	Helensburgh, Scotland.	9/30/21	Lemmon, Jack	Boston, Mass.	2/8/25
Kerr, John	New York, N.Y.	11/15/31	Lennon, Julian	Liverpool, England	4/8/63
Khan, Chaka	Great Lakes, Ill.	3/23/53	Lennon Sisters		
Kidder, Margot	Yellowknife, N.W.T.	10/17/48	Dianne	Los Angeles, Cal.	12/1/39
Kiley, Richard	Chicago, Ill.	3/31/22	Janet	Culver City, Cal.	11/15/46
King, Alan	Brooklyn, N.Y.	12/26/27	Kathy	Santa Monica, Cal.	8/22/42
King, B. B.	Itta Bena, Miss.	9/16/25	Peggy	Los Angeles, Cal.	4/8/41
King, Carole	Brooklyn, N.Y.	2/9/42	Leno, Jay	New Rochelle, N.Y.	4/28/50
King, Perry	Alliance, Oh.	4/30/48	Leonard, Sheldon	New York, N.Y.	2/22/07
Kingsley, Ben	Yorkshire, England	12/31/43	Leontovich, Eugenie	Moscow, Russia	3/21/00
Kinski, Klaus	Berlin, Germany	1926	Leslie, Joan	Detroit, Mich.	1/26/25
Kinski, Nastassia	Berlin, W. Germany	1/24/60	Lester, Jerry	Chicago, Ill.	1911
Kirby, Durward	Covington, Ky.	8/24/12	Letterman, David	Indianapolis, Ind.	4/12/47
Kirkland, Gelsey	Bethlehem, Pa.	12/29/52	Levine, James	Cincinnati, Oh.	6/23/43
Kirsten, Dorothy	Montclair, N.J.	7/6/19	Lewis, Emmanuel	New York, N.Y.	3/9/71
Kitt, Eartha	North, S.C.	1/26/28	Lewis, Huey	New York, N.Y,	1952
Klein, Robert	New York, N.Y.	2/8/42	Lewis, Jerry	Newark, N.J.	3/16/26
Klemperer, Werner	Cologne, Germany	3/22/19	Lewis, Jerry Lee	Ferriday, La.	9/29/35
Kline, Kevin	St. Louis, Mo.	10/24/47	Lewis, Shari	New York, N.Y.	1/17/34
Klugman, Jack	Philadelphia, Pa.	4/27/22	Light, Judith	Trenton, N.J.	2/9/49
Knight, Gladys	Atlanta, Ga.	5/28/44	Lightfoot, Gordon	Orillia, Ont.	11/17/38
Knotts, Don	Morgantown, W. Va.	7/21/24	Lillie, Beatrice	Toronto, Ont.	5/29/94
Knox, Alexander	Strathroy, Ont.	1/16/07	Linden, Hal	New York, N.Y.	3/20/31
Kopell, Bernie	New York, N.Y.	6/21/33	Lindfors, Viveca	Uppsala, Sweden.	12/29/20
Korman, Harvey	Chicago, Ill.	2/15/27	Lindsey, Mort	Newark, N.J.	3/21/23
Kotero, Apollonia	Santa Monica, Cal.	8/2/56	Linkletter, Art	Sask.	7/17/12
Kotto, Yaphet	New York, N.Y.	11/15/37	Linn-Baker, Mark	St. Louis, Mo.	6/17/53
Kramer, Stanley	New York, N.Y.	9/29/13	Lithgow, John	Rochester, N.Y.	10/19/45
Kramer, Stephanie	Los Angeles, Cal.	8/6/56	Little, Cleavon	Chickasha, Okla.	6/1/39
Kristofferson, Kris	Brownsville, Tex.	6/22/36	Little, Rich	Ottawa, Ont.	11/26/38
Kubelik, Rafael	Bychori, Czechoslovakia.	6/29/14	Little Richard	Macon, Ga.	12/25/35
Kubrick, Stanley	Bronx, N.Y.	7/26/28	Lloyd, Christopher	Stamford, Conn.	10/22/38
Kulp, Nancy	Harrisburg, Pa.	8/28/21	Lloyd, Emily	England	9/29/70
Kurtz, Swoosie	Omaha, Neb.	9/6/44	Locke, Sondra	Shelbyville, Tenn.	5/28/47
			Lockhart, June	New York, N.Y.	6/25/25
LaBelle, Patti	Philadelphia, Pa.	10/4/44	Locklear, Heather	Los Angeles, Cal.	9/25/61
Ladd, Cheryl	Huron, S.D.	7/12/51	Lockwood, Margaret	Karachi, India	9/15/16
Ladd, Diane	Meridian, Mass.	11/29/39	Loder, John	London, England	1/3/98
Lahti, Christine	Detroit, Mich.	4/4/50	Loggia, Robert	New York, N.Y.	1/3/30
Laine, Frankie	Chicago, Ill.	3/30/13	Loggins, Kenny	Everett, Wash.	1/7/48
Lamarr, Hedy	Vienna, Austria	11/9/13	Lollobrigida, Gina	Subiaco, Italy	7/4/28
Lamas, Lorenzo	Los Angeles, Cal.	1/20/58	Lom, Herbert	Prague, Czechoslovakia	1/9/17
Lamb, Gil	Minneapolis, Minn.	6/14/06	London, Julie	Santa Rosa, Cal.	9/26/26
Lamour, Dorothy	New Orleans, La.	12/10/14	Long, Shelley	Ft. Wayne, Ind.	8/23/49
Lancaster, Burt	New York, N.Y.	11/2/13	Lopez, Priscilla	New York, N.Y.	2/26/48
Landau, Martin	New York, N.Y.	1933	Lopez, Trini	Dallas, Tex.	5/15/37
Landesberg, Steve	New York, N.Y.	11/23/–	Lord, Jack	New York, N.Y.	—
Landis, John	Chicago, Ill.	8/30/50	Loren, Sophia	Rome, Italy	9/20/34
Landon, Michael	Forest Hills, N.Y.	10/21/37	Loring, Gloria	New York, N.Y.	12/10/46
Lane, Abbe	Brooklyn, N.Y.	12/14/32	Loudon, Dorothy	Boston, Mass.	9/17/33
Lane, Diane	New York, N.Y.	1963	Louise, Tina	New York, N.Y.	3/11/34
Lane, Priscilla	Indianola, Ia.	6/12/17	Lovitz, John	Tarzana, Cal.	7/21/57
lang, k.d.	Consort, Alberta	11/2/61	Lowe, Rob	Charlottesville, Va.	3/17/64
Lange, Hope	Redding Ridge, Conn.	11/28/31	Loy, Myrna	Helena, Mon.	8/2/05
Lange, Jessica	Cloquet, Minn.	4/20/49	Lucas, George	Modesto, Cal.	5/14/44
Langella, Frank	Bayonne, N.J.	1/1/40	Lucci, Susan	Westchester Co., N.Y.	12/23/49
Langford, Frances	Lakeland, Fla.	4/4/13	Luckinbill, Laurence	Ft. Smith, Ark.	11/21/34
Lansbury, Angela	London, England	10/16/25	Ludwig, Christa	Berlin, Germany	3/16/28
Lansing, Robert	San Diego, Cal.	6/5/29	Luke, Keye	Canton, China.	1904
Laredo, Ruth	Detroit, Mich.	11/20/37	Lumet, Sidney	Philadelphia, Pa.	6/25/24
Larroquette, John	New Orleans, La.	11/25/47	Lund, John	Rochester, N.Y.	2/6/13

Name	Birthplace	Born
Lupino, Ida	London, England	2/4/18
LuPone, Patti	Northport, N.Y.	4/21/49
Lynley, Carol	New York, N.Y.	2/13/42
Lynn, Jeffrey	Auburn, Mass.	2/16/09
Lynn, Loretta	Butcher Hollow, Ky.	4/14/35
Maazel, Lorin	Paris, France	3/6/30
MacArthur, James	Los Angeles, Cal.	12/8/37
MacCorkindale, Simon	Cambridge, England	2/12/53
MacGraw, Ali	Pound Ridge, N.Y.	4/1/39
MacKenzie, Gisele	Winnipeg, Man.	1/10/27
MacLaine, Shirley	Richmond, Va.	4/24/34
MacLeod, Gavin	Mt. Kisco, N.Y.	2/28/30
MacMurray, Fred	Kankakee, Ill.	8/30/08
MacNee, Patrick	London, England	2/6/22
MacNeil, Cornell	Minneapolis, Minn.	9/24/22
Macchio, Ralph	Long Island, N.Y.	11/4/62
Macy, Bill	Revere, Mass.	5/18/22
Madden, John	Austin, Minn.	4/10/36
Madonna (Ciccone)	Bay City, Mich.	8/16/58
Majors, Lee	Wyandotte, Mich.	4/23/40
Makarova, Natalia	Leningrad, USSR	11/21/40
Malbin, Elaine	New York, N.Y.	5/24/32
Malden, Karl	Chicago, Ill.	3/22/13
Malfitano, Catherine	New York, N.Y.	4/18/48
Malkovich, John	Christopher, Ill.	12/9/54
Malle, Louis	Thumeries, France	10/30/32
Malone, Dorothy	Chicago, Ill.	1/30/25
Manchester, Melissa	Bronx, N.Y.	2/15/51
Mancini, Henry	Cleveland, Oh.	4/16/24
Mandel, Howie	Toronto, Ont.	11/29/-
Mandrell, Barbara	Houston, Tex.	12/25/48
Mangione, Chuck	Rochester, N.Y.	11/29/40
Manilow, Barry	New York, N.Y.	6/17/46
Mann, Herbie	New York, N.Y.	4/16/30
Marceau, Marcel	Strasbourg, France	3/22/23
Marchand, Nancy	Buffalo, N.Y.	6/19/28
Margolin, Janet	New York, N.Y.	7/25/43
Marin, Cheech	Los Angeles, Cal.	7/13/46
Markova, Alicia	London, England	12/1/10
Marriner, Neville	Lincoln, England	4/15/24
Marsh, Jean	London, England	7/1/34
Marshall, E. G.	Owatonna, Minn.	6/18/10
Marshall, Penny	New York, N.Y.	10/15/43
Marshall, Peter	Huntington, W.Va.	3/30/27
Martin, Dean	Steubenville, Oh.	6/17/17
Martin, Dick	Detroit, Mich.	1/30/23
Martin, Mary	Weatherford, Tex.	12/1/13
Martin, Pamela Sue	Westport, Conn.	1/5/54
Martin, Steve	Waco, Tex.	1945
Martin, Tony	San Francisco, Cal.	12/25/13
Martins, Peter	Copenhagen, Denmark	10/27/46
Martino, Al	Philadelphia, Pa.	10/7/27
Mason, Jackie	Sheboygan, Wis.	1931
Mason, Marsha	St. Louis, Mo.	4/3/42
Mason, Pamela	London, England	3/10/22
Mastroianni, Marcello	Rome, Italy	9/28/24
Matheson, Tim	Glendale, Cal.	12/31/47
Mathis, Johnny	San Francisco, Cal.	9/30/35
Matthau, Walter	New York, N.Y.	10/1/20
Mature, Victor	Louisville, Ky.	1/29/16
May, Elaine	Philadelphia, Pa.	4/21/32
Mayo, Virginia	St. Louis, Mo.	11/30/20
Mazurki, Mike	Austria	12/25/09
Mazursky, Paul	Brooklyn, N.Y.	4/25/30
McArdle, Andrea	Philadelphia, Pa.	11/5/63
McBride, Patricia	Teaneck, N.J.	8/23/42
McCallum, David	Glasgow, Scotland	9/19/33
McCambridge, Mercedes	Joliet, Ill.	3/17/18
McCarthy, Andrew	New York, N.Y.	1963
McCarthy, Kevin	Seattle, Wash.	2/15/14
McCartney, Paul	Liverpool, England	6/18/42
McClanahan, Rue	Healdton, Okla.	2/21/36
McClure, Doug	Glendale, Cal.	5/11/38
McCoo, Marilyn	Jersey City, N.J.	9/30/45
McCord, Kent	Los Angeles, Cal.	9/26/42
McCrea, Joel	Los Angeles, Cal.	11/5/05
McDowall, Roddy	London, England	9/17/28
McDowell, Malcolm	Leeds, England	6/19/43
McEntire, Reba	Chockie, Okla.	3/28/54
McFarland, Spanky	Dallas, Tex.	10/2/28
McGavin, Darren	San Joaquin, Cal.	5/7/22
McGoohan, Patrick	New York, N.Y.	3/19/28
McGovern, Elizabeth	Evanston, Ill.	7/18/61
McGovern, Maureen	Youngstown, Oh.	7/27/49
McGuire, Dorothy	Omaha, Neb.	6/14/19
McIntire, John	Spokane, Wash.	6/27/07
McKechnie, Donna	Pontiac, Mich.	11/16/42
McKee, Lonette	Detroit, Mich.	1954
McKellen, Ian	Burnley, England	5/25/39
McKeon, Nancy	Westbury, N.Y.	4/4/66
McLauchlan, Murray	Paisley, Scotland	6/30/48
McLean, Don	New Rochelle, N.Y.	10/2/45
McLerie, Allyn	Grand Mere, Que.	12/1/26
McMahon, Ed	Detroit, Mich.	3/6/23
McMillan, Kenneth	New York, N.Y.	7/2/32
McNair, Barbara	Racine, Wis.	3/4/39
McNichol, Jimmy	Los Angeles, Cal.	7/2/61
McNichol, Kristy	Los Angeles, Cal.	9/11/62
McQueen, Butterfly	Tampa, Fla.	1/7/11
McRaney, Gerald	Collins, Miss.	8/19/47
Meadows, Audrey	Wu Chang, China.	2/8/24
Meadows, Jayne	Wu Chang, China.	9/27/20
Meara, Anne	New York, N.Y.	9/20/29
Meeker, Ralph	Minneapolis, Minn.	11/21/20
Mehta, Zubin	Bombay, India.	4/29/36
Melanie	New York, N.Y.	2/3/47
Mellencamp, John Cougar	Seymour, Ind.	10/7/51
Mendes, Sergio	Nitero, Brazil	2/11/41
Menuhin, Yehudi	New York, N.Y.	4/22/16
Mercer, Marian	Akron, Oh.	11/26/35
Mercouri, Melina	Athens, Greece	10/18/25
Meredith, Burgess	Cleveland, Oh.	11/16/08
Merrick, David	Hong Kong	11/27/12
Merrill, Dina	New York, N.Y.	12/9/25
Merrill, Gary	Hartford, Conn.	8/2/15
Merrill, Robert	Brooklyn, N.Y.	6/4/19
Messina, Jim	Maywood, Cal.	12/5/47
Meyers, Ari	San Juan, Puerto Rico	4/6/69
Midler, Bette	Paterson, N.J.	12/1/45
Milanov, Zinka	Zagreb, Yugoslavia.	5/17/08
Miles, Joanna	Nice, France	3/6/40
Miles, Sarah	Ingatestone, England.	12/31/41
Miles, Vera	near Boise City, Okla.	8/23/30
Miller, Ann	Houston, Tex.	4/12/23
Miller, Mitch	Rochester, N.Y.	7/4/11
Miller, Roger	Ft. Worth, Tex.	1/2/36
Mills, Donna	Chicago, Ill.	12/11/43
Mills, Hayley	London, England	4/18/46
Mills, John	Suffolk, England	2/22/08
Mills, Juliet	London, England	11/21/41
Mills Brothers:		
Mills, Herbert	Piqua, Oh.	4/12/12
Mills, Donald	Piqua, Oh.	4/29/15
Milner, Martin	Detroit, Mich.	12/28/31
Milnes, Sherrill	Downers Grove, Ill.	1/10/35
Milsap, Ronnie	Robinsville, N.C.	1/16/43
Milstein, Nathan	Odessa, Russia.	12/31/04
Mimieux, Yvette	Hollywood, Cal.	1/8/39
Minnelli, Liza	Los Angeles, Cal.	3/12/46
Mitchell, Cameron	Dallastown, Pa.	4/11/18
Mitchell, James	Sacramento, Cal.	2/29/20
Mitchell, Joni	Fort Macleod, Alta.	11/7/43
Mitchum, Robert	Bridgeport, Conn.	8/6/17
Moffat, Donald	Plymouth, England	12/26/30
Moffo, Anna	Wayne, Pa.	6/27/34
Molinaro, Al	Kenosha, Wis.	6/24/19
Moll, Richard	Pasadena, Cal.	1/13/-
Montalban, Ricardo	Mexico City, Mexico	11/25/20
Montand, Yves	Monsumagno, Italy	10/13/21
Montgomery, Elizabeth	Hollywood, Cal.	4/15/33
Montgomery, George	Brady, Mon.	8/29/16
Moody, Ron	London, England	1/8/24
Moore, Clayton	Chicago, Ill.	9/14/14
Moore, Constance	Sioux City, Ia.	1/18/22
Moore, Demi	Roswell, N.M.	11/11/62
Moore, Dudley	London, England	4/19/35
Moore, Garry	Baltimore, Md.	1/31/15
Moore, Mary Tyler	Brooklyn, N.Y.	12/29/37
Moore, Melba	New York, N.Y.	10/29/45
Moore, Roger	London, England	10/14/27
Moore, Terry	Los Angeles, Cal.	1/1/32
Moran, Erin	Los Angeles, Cal.	10/18/61
Moranis, Rick	Toronto, Ont.	1953
Moreau, Jeanne	Paris, France	1/23/28
Moreno, Rita	Humacao, P.R.	12/11/31
Morgan, Dennis	Prentice, Wis.	12/10/10
Morgan, Harry	Detroit, Mich.	4/10/15
Morgan, Henry	New York, N.Y.	3/31/15
Morgan, Jane	Boston, Mass.	1920

Name	Birthplace	Born	Name	Birthplace	Born
Morgan, Jaye P.	Mancos, Col.	12/3/31	Opatoshu, David	New York, N.Y.	1/30/18
Moriarty, Michael	Detroit, Mich.	4/5/41	Orbach, Jerry	New York, N.Y.	10/20/35
Morini, Erika	Vienna, Austria	1/5/10	Orlando, Tony	New York, N.Y.	4/3/44
Morita, Pat	Berkeley, Cal.	6/28/30	Osbourne, Ozzy	Birmingham, England.	12/3/48
Morley, Robert	Wiltshire, England	5/26/08	Osmond, Donny	Ogden, Ut.	12/9/57
Morris, Greg	Cleveland, Oh.	9/27/34	Osmond, Marie	Ogden, Ut.	10/13/59
Morris, Howard	New York, N.Y.	9/4/25	O'Sullivan, Maureen	Boyle, Ireland	5/17/11
Morse, Robert	Newton, Mass.	5/18/31	O'Toole, Annette	Houston, Tex.	4/1/52
Moses, William	Los Angeles, Cal.	11/17/59	O'Toole, Peter	Connemara, Ireland	8/2/32
Mulgrew, Kate	Dubuque, Ia.	4/29/55	Owens, Buck	Sherman, Tex.	8/12/29
Mulhare, Edward	Ireland	4/8/23	Owens, Gary	Mitchell, S.D.	5/10/36
Mull, Martin	Chicago, Ill.	8/18/43	Ozawa, Seiji	Shenyang, China	9/1/35
Mulligan, Richard	New York, N.Y.	11/13/32			
Munsel, Patrice	Spokane, Wash.	5/14/25	Paar, Jack	Canton, Oh.	5/1/18
Murphy, Ben	Jonesboro, Ark.	3/6/42	Pacino, Al	New York, N.Y.	4/25/40
Murphy, Eddie	Brooklyn, N.Y.	4/3/61	Page, LaWanda	Cleveland, Oh.	10/19/20
Murphy, George	New Haven, Conn.	7/4/02	Page, Patti	Claremore, Okla.	11/8/27
Murphy, Michael	Los Angeles, Cal.	5/5/38	Paige, Janis	Tacoma, Wash.	9/16/22
Murray, Anne	Springhill, N.S.	6/20/45	Palance, Jack	Lattimer, Pa.	2/18/20
Murray, Arthur	New York, N.Y.	4/4/95	Palin, Michael	England	1943
Murray, Bill	Evanston, Ill.	9/21/50	Palmer, Betsy	East Chicago, Ind.	11/1/29
Murray, Don	Hollywood, Cal.	7/31/29	Papas, Irene	Greece	3/9/26
Murray, Kathryn	Jersey City, N.J.	9/15/06	Papp, Joseph	Brooklyn, N.Y.	6/22/21
Murray, Ken	New York, N.Y.	7/14/03	Parker, Alan	London, England	2/14/44
Musante, Tony	Bridgeport, Conn.	6/30/36	Parker, Eleanor	Cedarville, Oh.	6/26/22
Musburger, Brent	Portland, Ore.	5/26/39	Parker, Fess	Ft. Worth, Tex.	8/16/25
Muti, Ricardo	Naples, Italy	7/28/41	Parker, Jameson	Baltimore, Md.	11/18/50
			Parker, Jean	Deer Lodge, Mon.	8/11/12
Nabors, Jim	Sylacauga, Ala.	6/12/33	Parks, Bert	Atlanta, Ga.	12/30/14
Nash, Graham	Blackpool, England	2/2/42	Parsons, Estelle	Lynn, Mass.	11/20/27
Natwick, Mildred	Baltimore, Md.	6/19/08	Parton, Dolly	Sevierville, Tenn.	1/19/46
Neal, Patricia	Packard, Ky.	1/20/26	Pasternak, Joseph	Hungary	9/19/01
Neff, Hildegarde	Ulm, Germany	12/28/25	Patane, Giuseppe	Napoli, Italy	1/1/32
Nelligan, Kate	London, Ont.	3/16/51	Patinkin, Mandy	Chicago, Ill.	11/30/52
Nelson, Barry	San Francisco, Cal.	4/16/20	Pavarotti, Luciano	Modena, Italy	10/12/35
Nelson, Craig T.	Spokane, Wash.	4/4/46	Paycheck, Johnny	Greenfield, Oh.	5/31/38
Nelson, David	New York, N.Y.	10/24/36	Payne, John	Roanoke, Va.	5/23/12
Nelson, Ed	New Orleans, La.	12/21/28	Pearl, Minnie	Centerville, Tenn.	10/25/12
Nelson, Gene	Seattle, Wash.	3/24/20	Peck, Gregory	La Jolla, Cal.	4/5/16
Nelson, Harriet (Hilliard)	Des Moines, Ia.	7/18/14	Pendergrass, Teddy	Philadelphia, Pa.	3/26/50
Nelson, Judd	Portland, Me.	1959	Penn, Arthur	Philadelphia, Pa.	9/27/22
Nelson, Tracy	Santa Monica, Cal.	10/25/63	Penn, Sean	Santa Monica, Cal.	8/17/60
Nelson, Willie	Abbott, Tex.	4/30/33	Penny, Joe	London, England	9/14/56
Nero, Peter	New York, N.Y.	5/22/34	Peppard, George	Detroit, Mich.	10/1/28
Newhart, Bob	Oak Park, Ill.	9/5/29	Perkins, Anthony	New York, N.Y.	4/4/32
Newley, Anthony	Hackney, England	9/24/31	Perlman, Itzhak	Tel Aviv, Israel	8/31/45
Newman, Barry	Boston, Mass.	11/7/38	Perlman, Rhea	Brooklyn, N.Y.	3/31/48
Newman, Laraine	Los Angeles, Cal.	3/2/52	Perrine, Valerie	Galveston, Tex.	9/3/43
Newman, Paul	Cleveland, Oh.	1/26/25	Persoff, Nehemiah	Jerusalem, Palestine	8/14/20
Newman, Phyllis	Jersey City, N.J.	3/19/35	Peters, Bernadette	New York, N.Y.	2/28/48
Newman, Randy	Los Angeles, Cal.	11/28/43	Peters, Brock	New York, N.Y.	7/2/27
Newton, Wayne	Norfolk, Va.	4/3/42	Peters, Jean	Canton, Oh.	10/15/26
Newton-John, Olivia	Cambridge, England	9/26/48	Peters, Roberta	New York, N.Y.	5/4/30
Nichols, Mike	Berlin, Germany	11/6/31	Peterson, Oscar	Montreal, Que.	8/15/25
Nicholson, Jack	Neptune, N.J.	4/28/37	Petit, Pascale	Paris, France	2/27/38
Nicks, Stevie	California	5/26/48	Pfeiffer, Michelle	Santa Ana, Cal.	4/29/57
Neilsen, Leslie	Regina, Sask.	2/12/26	Phillips, MacKenzie	Alexandria, Va.	11/10/59
Nilsson, Birgit	Karup, Sweden	5/17/18	Phillips, Michelle	Long Beach, Cal.	4/6/44
Nimoy, Leonard	Boston, Mass.	3/26/31	Pickett, Cindy	Norman, Okla.	4/18/47
Noble, James	Dallas, Tex.	3/5/22	Picon, Molly	New York, N.Y.	6/1/98
Nolte, Nick	Omaha, Neb.	2/8/40	Pinchot, Bronson	New York, N.Y.	5/20/59
Norman, Jessye	Augusta, Ga.	9/15/45	Piscopo, Joe	Passaic, N.J.	6/17/51
Norris, Chuck	Ryan, Okla.	1939	Pleasence, Donald	Worksop, England	10/5/19
North, Sheree	Los Angeles, Cal.	1/17/33	Pleshette, Suzanne	New York, N.Y.	1/31/37
Novak, Kim	Chicago, Ill.	2/18/33	Plowright, Joan	Brigg, England	10/28/29
Novello, Don	Ashabula, Oh.	1/1/43	Plummer, Amanda	New York, N.Y.	3/23/57
Nureyev, Rudolf	Russia	3/17/38	Plummer, Christopher	Toronto, Ont.	12/13/27
			Poitier, Sidney	Miami, Fla.	2/20/27
Oates, John	New York, N.Y.	4/7/48	Polanski, Roman	Paris, France	8/18/33
O'Brian, Hugh	Rochester, N.Y.	4/19/30	Ponti, Carlo	Milan, Italy	12/11/13
O'Brien, Margaret	San Diego, Cal.	1/15/37	Post, Markie	Palo Alto, Cal.	11/4/50
O'Connell, Helen	Lima, Oh.	5/23/20	Poston, Tom	Columbus, Oh.	10/17/27
O'Connor, Carroll	New York, N.Y.	8/2/24	Potts, Annie	Nashville, Tenn.	10/28/--
O'Connor, Donald	Chicago, Ill.	8/28/25	Powell, Jane	Portland, Ore.	4/1/28
Odetta	Birmingham, Ala.	12/31/30	Powers, Stefanie	Hollywood, Cal.	11/12/43
O'Hara, Maureen	Dublin, Ireland	8/17/21	Prentiss, Paula	San Antonio, Tex.	3/4/39
O'Herlihy, Dan	Wexford, Ireland	5/1/19	Presley, Priscilla	New York, N.Y.	5/24/45
O'Keefe, Michael	Paulland, N.J.	1955	Preston, Billy	Houston, Tex.	9/9/46
Olin, Ken	Chicago, Ill.	7/30/54	Previn, Andre	Berlin, Germany	4/6/29
Olivier, Laurence	Dorking, England	5/22/07	Price, Leontyne	Laurel, Miss.	2/10/27
Olmos, Edward James	E. Los Angeles, Cal.	2/24/47	Price, Ray	Perryville, Tex.	1/12/26
Olsen, Merlin	Logan, Ut.	9/15/40	Price, Vincent	St. Louis, Mo.	5/27/11
O'Neal, Patrick	Ocala, Fla.	9/26/27	Pride, Charlie	Sledge, Miss.	3/18/39
O'Neal, Ryan	Los Angeles, Cal.	4/20/41	Prince	Minneapolis, Minn.	6/7/58
O'Neal, Tatum	Los Angeles, Cal.	11/5/63	Principal, Victoria	Japan	1/30/46
O'Neill, Jennifer	Brazil	2/20/48	Prosky, Robert	Philadelphia, Pa.	12/13/30
Ontkean, Michael	Vancouver, B.C.	1/24/46			

Name	Birthplace	Born
Prowse, Juliet	Bombay, India	9/25/37
Pryor, Richard	Peoria, Ill.	12/1/40
Pulliam, Keshia Knight	Newark, N.J.	4/9/79
Pyle, Denver	Bethune, Col.	5/11/20
Quaid, Dennis	Houston, Tex.	4/9/54
Quaid, Randy	Houston, Tex.	10/1/50
Quayle, Anthony	Lancashire, England	9/7/13
Quinlan, Kathleen	Pasadena, Cal.	11/19/54
Quinn, Anthony	Chihuahua, Mexico	4/21/15
Rabb, Ellis	Memphis, Tenn.	6/20/30
Rabbitt, Eddie	Brooklyn, N.Y.	11/27/41
Rachins, Alan	Cambridge, Mass.	10/10/-
Radner, Gilda	Detroit, Mich.	6/28/46
Rae, Charlotte	Milwaukee, Wis.	4/22/26
Raffin, Deborah	Los Angeles, Cal.	3/13/53
Rainer, Luise	Vienna, Austria	1/12/09
Raines, Ella	Snoqualmie Falls, Wash.	8/6/21
Raitt, John	Santa Ana, Cal.	1/19/17
Ralston, Esther	Bar Harbor, Me.	9/17/02
Ralston, Vera Hruba	Prague, Czechoslovakia	6/12/19
Rambo, Dack	Delano, Cal.	11/13/41
Rampal, Jean41Pierre	Marseilles, France	1/7/22
Randall, Tony	Tulsa, Okla.	2/26/20
Randolph, John	New York, N.Y.	1/1/15
Rashad, Phylicia	Houston, Tex.	6/17/48
Ratzenberger, John	Bridgeport, Conn.	4/6/47
Rawls, Lou	Chicago, Ill.	12/1/36
Ray, Aldo	Pen Argyl, Pa.	9/25/26
Ray, Gene Anthony	New York, N.Y.	5/24/63
Ray, Johnnie	Dallas, Ore.	1/10/27
Rayburn, Gene	Christopher, Ill.	12/22/17
Raye, Martha	Butte, Mon.	8/27/16
Raymond, Gene	New York, N.Y.	8/13/08
Reddy, Helen	Melbourne, Australia	10/25/41
Redford, Robert	Santa Monica, Cal.	8/18/37
Redgrave, Lynn	London, England	3/8/43
Redgrave, Vanessa	London, England	1/30/37
Reed, Jerry	Atlanta, Ga.	3/20/37
Reed, Oliver	London, England	2/13/38
Reed, Rex	Ft. Worth, Tex.	10/2/38
Reed, Robert	Highland Park, Ill.	10/19/32
Reese, Della	Detroit, Mich.	7/6/31
Reeve, Christopher	New York, N.Y.	9/25/52
Reeves, Dell	Sparta, N.C.	7/14/33
Reid, Kate	London, England	11/4/30
Reid, Tim	Norfolk, Va.	12/19/44
Reilly, Charles Nelson	New York, N.Y.	1/13/31
Reiner, Carl	Bronx, N.Y.	3/20/22
Reiner, Rob	Bronx, N.Y.	3/6/45
Reinhold, Judge	Wilmington, Del.	1956
Reinking, Ann	Seattle, Wash.	11/10/49
Remick, Lee	Quincy, Mass.	12/14/35
Resnik, Regina	New York, N.Y.	8/30/24
Reynolds, Burt	Waycross, Ga.	2/11/36
Reynolds, Debbie	El Paso, Tex.	4/1/32
Reynolds, Marjorie	Buhl, Ida.	8/12/21
Rich, Charlie	Forest City, Ark.	12/14/32
Richards, Keith	Kent, England	12/18/43
Richardson, Tony	Shipley, England	6/5/28
Richie, Lionel	Tuskegee, Ala.	6/20/50
Rickles, Don	New York, N.Y.	5/8/26
Rigg, Diana	Doncaster, England	7/20/38
Ringwald, Molly	Rosewood, Cal.	2/14/68
Ritter, John	Burbank, Cal.	9/17/48
Rivera, Chita	Washington, D.C.	1/23/33
Rivers, Joan	Brooklyn, N.Y.	6/8/33
Robards, Jason Jr.	Chicago, Ill.	7/26/22
Robbins, Jerome	New York, N.Y.	10/11/18
Roberts, Doris	St. Louis, Mo.	11/4/30
Roberts, Eric	Biloxi, Miss.	4/18/56
Roberts, Pernell	Waycross, Ga.	5/18/30
Roberts, Tony	New York, N.Y.	10/22/39
Robertson, Cliff	La Jolla, Cal.	9/9/25
Robertson, Dale	Harrah, Okla.	7/14/23
Robinson, Charles	Houston, Tex.	11/9/-
Robinson, Smokey	Detroit, Mich.	2/19/40
Roche, Eugene	Boston, Mass.	9/22/28
Rodgers, Jimmie	Camas, Wash.	1933
Rodriquez, Johnny	Sabinal, Tex.	12/10/51
Rogers, Chas. (Buddy)	Olathe, Kan.	8/13/04
Rogers, Fred	Latrobe, Pa.	3/20/28
Rogers, Ginger	Independence, Mo.	7/16/11
Rogers, Kenny	Houston, Tex.	8/21/38
Rogers, Mimi	Coral Gables, Fla.	1/27/-
Rogers, Roy	Cincinnati, Oh.	11/5/12
Rogers, Wayne	Birmingham, Ala.	4/7/-
Roland, Gilbert	Juarez, Mexico	12/11/05
Rolle, Esther	Pompano Beach, Fla.	11/8/33
Romero, Cesar	New York, N.Y.	2/15/07
Ronstadt, Linda	Tucson, Ariz.	7/15/46
Rooney, Mickey	Brooklyn, N.Y.	9/23/20
Rose Marie	New York, N.Y.	8/15/25
Ross, Diana	Detroit, Mich.	3/26/44
Ross, Katharine	Hollywood, Cal.	1/29/43
Ross, Marion	Albert Lea, Minn.	10/25/28
Rostropovich, Mstislav	Baku, USSR	3/12/27
Roth, David Lee	Bloomington, Ind.	10/10/55
Rowlands, Gena	Cambria, Wis.	6/19/34
Rubinstein, John	Los Angeles, Cal.	12/8/46
Rudolf, Max	Frankfurt, Germany	6/15/02
Rule, Janice	Norwood, Oh.	8/15/31
Rush, Barbara	Denver, Col.	1/4/30
Russell, Jane	Bemidji, Minn.	6/21/21
Russell, Ken	Southampton, England	7/3/27
Russell, Kurt	Springfield, Mass.	3/17/51
Russell, Mark	Buffalo, N.Y.	8/23/32
Russell, Nipsey	Atlanta, Ga.	10/13/24
Russell, Theresa	San Diego, Cal.	1957
Rutherford, Ann	Toronto, Ont.	11/2/20
Ryan, Peggy	Long Beach, Cal.	8/28/24
Ryan, Roz	Detroit, Mich.	7/7/51
Rydell, Bobby	Philadelphia, Pa.	4/26/42
Sahl, Mort	Montreal, Que.	5/11/27
Saint, Eva Marie	Newark, N.J.	7/4/24
St. James, Susan	Los Angeles, Cal.	8/14/46
St. John, Jill	Los Angeles, Cal.	8/19/40
Sainte-Marie, Buffy	Graven, Sask.	2/20/41
Sajac, Pat	Chicago, Ill.	10/26/-
Saks, Gene	New York, N.Y.	11/8/21
Sales, Soupy	Franklinton, N.C.	1/8/26
Samms, Emma	London, England	8/28/61
Sanderson, William	Memphis, Tenn.	1/10/48
Sandy, Gary	Dayton, Oh.	12/25/45
Sanford, Isabel	New York, N.Y.	8/29/17
Santana, Carlos	Mexico	7/20/47
Sarandon, Chris	Beckley, W.Va.	7/24/42
Sarandon, Susan	New York, N.Y.	10/4/46
Sarnoff, Dorothy	New York, N.Y.	5/25/17
Sarrazin, Michael	Quebec, Que.	5/22/40
Savalas, Telly	Garden City, N.Y.	1/21/24
Saxon, John	Brooklyn, N.Y.	8/5/35
Scaggs, Boz	Dallas, Tex.	6/8/44
Schallert, William	Los Angeles, Cal.	7/6/22
Scheider, Roy	Orange, N.J.	11/10/32
Schell, Maria	Vienna, Austria	1/15/26
Schell, Maximilian	Vienna, Austria	12/8/30
Schell, Ronnie	Richmond, Cal.	12/23/31
Schenkel, Chris	Bippus, Ind.	8/21/23
Schnabel, Stefan	Berlin, Germany	2/2/12
Schneider, Alexander	Vilna, Poland	10/21/08
Schneider, John	Mt. Kisco, N.Y.	4/8/54
Schreiber, Avery	Chicago, Ill.	4/9/35
Schroder, Ricky	Staten Island, N.Y.	4/13/70
Schwarzenegger, Arnold	Braz, Austria	7/30/47
Schwarzkopf, Elisabeth	Jarotschin, Poland	12/9/15
Scofield, Paul	Hurst, Pierpont, England	1/21/22
Scolari, Peter	New Rochelle, Ill.	9/12/54
Scorsese, Martin	New York, N.Y.	11/17/42
Scott, George C.	Wise, Va.	10/18/27
Scott, Lizabeth	Scranton, Pa.	9/29/22
Scott, Martha	Jamesport, Mo.	9/22/14
Scotto, Renata	Savona, Italy	2/24/35
Scully, Vin	New York, N.Y.	11/29/27
Sebastian, John	New York N.Y.	3/17/44
Sedaka, Neil	New York, N.Y.	3/13/39
Seeger, Pete	New York, N.Y.	5/3/19
Segal, George	Great Neck, N.Y.	2/13/34
Segal, Vivienne	Philadelphia, Pa.	4/19/97
Seinfeld, Gerry	New York, N.Y.	1954
Sellacca, Connie	New York, N.Y.	5/25/55
Selleck, Tom	Detroit, Mich.	1/29/45
Serkin, Rudolf	Eger, Austria	3/28/03
Severinsen, Doc	Arlington, Ore.	7/7/27
Seymour, Jane	Middlesex, England	2/15/51
Shackelford, Ted	Oklahoma City, Okla.	6/23/46
Shandling, Garry	Tucson, Ariz.	1950
Shankar, Ravi	India	4/7/20
Sharif, Omar	Alexandria, Egypt	4/10/32

Name	Birthplace	Born
Shatner, William	Montreal, Que.	3/22/31
Shearer, Moira	Scotland	1/17/26
Sheedy, Ally	New York, N.Y.	6/12/62
Sheen, Charlie	Santa Monica, Cal.	1966
Sheen, Martin	Dayton, Oh.	8/3/40
Sheldon, Jack	Jacksonville, Fla.	11/30/31
Shelley, Carole	London, England	8/16/39
Shepard, Sam	Ft. Sheridan, Ill.	11/5/43
Shepherd, Cybill	Memphis, Tenn.	2/18/50
Shera, Mark	Bayonne, N.J.	7/10/49
Shields, Brooke	New York, N.Y.	5/31/65
Shire, Talia	New York, N.Y.	4/25/46
Shirley, Ann	New York, N.Y.	4/17/18
Shore, Dinah	Winchester, Tenn.	3/1/17
Short, Bobby	Danville, Ill.	9/15/24
Short, Martin	Hamilton, Ont.	3/26/-
Shull, Richard	Evanston, Ill.	2/24/29
Shuster, Frank	Toronto, Ont.	9/5/16
Siberry, Jane	Toronto, Ont.	10/13/55
Sidney, Sylvia	New York, N.Y.	8/8/10
Siepi, Cesare	Milan, Italy	2/10/23
Sikking, James B.	Los Angeles, Cal.	3/5/34
Sills, Beverly	Brooklyn, N.Y.	5/25/29
Silver, Ron	New York, N.Y.	7/2/46
Simmons, Gene	Haifa, Israel	8/25/49
Simmons, Jean	London, England	1/31/29
Simon, Carly	New York, N.Y.	6/25/45
Simon, Paul	Newark, N.J.	11/5/42
Simone, Nina	Tyron, N.C.	2/21/33
Sinatra, Frank	Hoboken, N.J.	12/12/15
Sinatra, Nancy	Jersey City, N.J.	6/8/40
Singer, Lori	Corpus Christie, Tex.	11/6/62
Singer, Marc	Vancouver, B.C.	1/29/-
Siskel, Gene	Chicago, Ill.	1/26/46
Skelton, Red (Richard)	Vincennes, Ind.	7/18/10
Skerritt, Tom	Detroit, Mich.	8/25/33
Slater, Helen	Massapequa, N.Y.	1965
Slezak, Erika	Hollywood, Cal.	8/5/-
Slick, Grace	Chicago, Ill.	10/30/39
Smith, Allison	New York, N.Y.	12/9/69
Smith, Alexis	Penticton, B.C.	6/8/21
Smith, Buffalo Bob	Buffalo, N.Y.	11/27/17
Smith, Connie	Elkhart, Ind.	8/14/41
Smith, Jaclyn	Houston, Tex.	10/26/48
Smith, Keely	Norfolk, Va.	3/9/35
Smith, Maggie	Ilford, England.	12/28/34
Smith, Roger	South Gate, Cal.	12/18/32
Smits, Jimmy	New York, N.Y.	7/9/58
Smothers, Dick	New York, N.Y.	11/20/39
Smothers, Tom	New York, N.Y.	2/2/37
Snodgress, Carrie	Park Ridge, Ill.	10/27/45
Snow, Hank	Liverpool, N.S.	5/9/14
Snyder, Tom	Milwaukee, Wis.	5/12/36
Solti, Georg	Budapest, Hungary.	10/21/12
Somers, Suzanne	San Bruno, Cal.	10/16/46
Somes, Michael	nr. Stroud, England.	9/28/17
Sommer, Elke	Berlin, Germany	11/5/40
Sorvino, Paul	New York, N.Y.	1939
Sothern, Ann	Valley City, N.D.	1/22/09
Soul, David	Chicago, Ill.	8/28/43
Spacek, Sissy	Quitman, Tex.	12/25/49
Spano, Joe	San Francisco, Cal.	7/7/46
Spelling, Aaron	Dallas, Tex.	4/22/28
Spielberg, Steven	Cincinnati, Oh.	12/18/47
Springfield, Dusty	London, England	4/16/39
Springfield, Rick	Sydney, Australia.	8/23/49
Springsteen, Bruce	Freehold, N.J.	9/23/49
Stack, Robert	Los Angeles, Cal.	1/13/19
Stafford, Jo	Coalinga, Cal.	11/12/18
Stahl, Richard	Detroit, Mich.	1/4/32
Stallone, Sylvester	New York, N.Y.	7/6/46
Stamos, John	Cypress, Cal.	8/19/63
Stamp, Terence	Stepney, England.	7/22/39
Stander, Lionel	New York, N.Y.	1/11/08
Stang, Arnold	Chelsea, Mass.	9/28/25
Stanley, Kim	Tularosa, N.M.	2/11/25
Stanton, Harry Dean	Kentucky	7/14/26
Stanwyck, Barbara	Brooklyn, N.Y.	7/16/07
Stapleton, Jean	New York, N.Y.	1/19/23
Stapleton, Maureen	Troy, N.Y.	6/21/25
Starr, Kay	Dougherty, Okla.	7/21/22
Starr, Ringo	Liverpool, England	7/7/40
Steber, Eleanor	Wheeling, W. Va.	7/17/16
Steenburgen, Mary	Newport, Ark.	1953
Steiger, Rod	W. Hampton, N.Y.	4/14/25
Steinberg, David	Winnipeg, Man.	8/29/42

Name	Birthplace	Born
Stephens, James	Mt. Kisco, N.Y.	5/18/51
Sterling, Jan	New York, N.Y.	4/3/23
Sterling, Robert	New Castle, Pa.	11/13/17
Stern, Isaac	Kreminiecz, Russia	7/21/20
Sternhagen, Frances	Washington, D.C.	1/13/30
Stevens, Andrew	Memphis, Tenn.	6/10/55
Stevens, Cat	London, England	7/21/48
Stevens, Connie	Brooklyn, N.Y.	8/8/38
Stevens, Kaye	E. Cleveland, Oh.	7/21/35
Stevens, Rise	New York, N.Y.	6/11/13
Stevens, Stella	Yazoo City, Miss.	10/1/36
Stevenson, McLean	Normal, Ill.	11/14/29
Stevenson, Parker	Philadelphia, Pa.	6/4/52
Stewart, James	Indiana, Pa.	5/20/08
Stewart, Rod	London, England	1/10/45
Stickney, Dorothy	Dickinson, N.D.	6/21/00
Stiers, David Ogden	Peoria, Ill.	10/31/42
Stiller, Jerry	New York, N.Y.	6/8/29
Stills, Stephen	Dallas, Tex.	1/3/45
Sting (G. Sumner)	Newcastle, England	10/2/51
Stockwell, Dean	Hollywood, Cal.	3/5/36
Stookey, Paul	Baltimore, Md.	12/30/37
Storch, Larry	New York, N.Y.	1/8/23
Storm, Gale	Bloomington, Tex.	4/5/22
Straight, Beatrice	Old Westbury, N.Y.	8/2/18
Strasberg, Susan	New York, N.Y.	5/22/38
Strasser, Robin	New York, N.Y.	5/7/45
Stratas, Teresa	Toronto, Ont.	5/26/38
Strauss, Peter	New York, N.Y.	2/20/47
Streep, Meryl	Summit, N.J.	6/22/49
Streisand, Barbra	Brooklyn, N.Y.	4/24/42
Stritch, Elaine	Detroit, Mich.	2/2/26
Struthers, Sally	Portland, Ore.	7/28/48
Stuarti, Enzo	Rome, Italy	3/3/25
Sullivan, Barry	New York, N.Y.	8/29/12
Sullivan, Susan	New York, N.Y.	11/18/44
Sullivan, Tom	Boston, Mass.	3/27/47
Sumac, Yma	Ichocan, Peru	9/10/27
Summer, Donna	Boston, Mass.	12/31/48
Sutherland, Donald	St. John, N.B.	7/17/34
Sutherland, Joan	Sydney, Australia.	11/7/26
Swayze, Patrick	Houston, Tex.	8/18/54
Swenson, Inga	Omaha, Neb.	12/29/34
Swit, Loretta	Passaic, N.J.	11/4/37
Mr. T (Lawrence Tero)	Chicago, Ill.	5/21/52
Talbot, Lyle	Pittsburgh, Pa.	2/8/02
Tallchief, Maria	Fairfax, Okla.	1/24/25
Tambor, Jeffrey	San Francisco, Cal.	7/8/-
Tandy, Jessica	London, England	6/7/09
Tarkenton, Fran	Richmond, Va.	2/3/40
Tayback, Vic	New York, N.Y.	1/6/29
Taylor, Elizabeth	London, England	2/27/32
Taylor, James	Boston, Mass.	3/12/48
Taylor, Rod	Sydney, Australia.	1/11/29
Te Kanawa, Kiri	Gisborne, New Zealand	3/6/44
Tebaldi, Renata	Pesaro, Italy.	2/1/22
Temple, Shirley	Santa Monica, Cal.	4/23/28
Tennille, Toni	Montgomery, Ala.	5/8/43
Terry-Thomas	London, England	7/14/11
Tharp, Twyla	Portland, Ind.	7/1/41
Thaxter, Phyllis	Portland, Me.	11/20/21
Thicke, Alan	Kirkland Lake, Ont.	3/1/47
Thomas, B.J.	Houston, Tex.	8/7/42
Thomas, Betty	St. Louis, Mo.	7/27/48
Thomas, Danny	Deerfield, Mich.	1/6/14
Thomas, Heather	Greenwich, Conn.	9/8/57
Thomas, Ian	Hamilton, Ont.	7/23/50
Thomas, Marlo	Detroit, Mich.	11/21/43
Thomas, Philip Michael	Columbus, Oh.	5/26/49
Thomas, Richard	New York, N.Y.	6/13/51
Thompson, Jack	Sydney, Australia.	8/31/40
Thompson, Lea	Minneapolis, Minn.	1962
Thompson, Sada	Des Moines, Ia.	9/27/29
Thulin, Ingrid	Sweden	1/27/29
Tiegs, Cheryl	Minnesota	9/27/47
Tierney, Gene	Brooklyn, N.Y.	11/20/20
Tiffany	Norwalk, Cal.	1972
Tillis, Mel	Tampa, Fla.	8/8/32
Tiny Tim	New York, N.Y.	4/12/23
Todd, Richard	Dublin, Ireland.	6/11/19
Tomlin, Lily	Detroit, Mich.	9/1/39
Tomlinson, David	Scotland	5/7/17
Toomey, Regis	Pittsburgh, Pa.	8/13/02
Torme, Mel	Chicago, Ill.	9/13/25
Torn, Rip	Temple, Tex.	2/6/31
Tracy, Arthur	Russia	6/25/03

Name	Birthplace	Born
Travanti, Daniel J.	Kenosha, Wis.	3/7/40
Travers, Mary	Louisville, Ky.	11/9/36
Travis, Randy	No. Carolina.	1963
Travolta, John	Englewood, N.J.	2/18/54
Trevor, Claire	New York, N.Y.	3/8/09
Troyanos, Tatiana	New York, N.Y.	9/12/38
Tucker, Michael	Baltimore, Md.	2/6/44
Tucker, Tanya	Seminole, Tex.	10/10/58
Tune, Tommy	Wichita Falls, Tex.	2/28/39
Turner, Ike	Clarksdale, Miss.	11/5/31
Turner, Kathleen.	Springfield, Mo.	6/19/54
Turner, Lana	Wallace, Ida.	2/8/20
Turner, Tina	Nutbush, Tenn.	11/26/38
Tushingham, Rita	Liverpool, England	3/14/40
Twiggy (Leslie Hornby)	London, England	9/19/49
Twitty, Conway	Friar's Point, Miss.	9/1/33
Tyson, Cicely	New York, N.Y.	12/19/33
Uecker, Bob	Milwaukee, Wis.	1/26/35
Uggams, Leslie	New York, N.Y.	5/25/43
Ullman, Tracey	Slough, England	1960
Ullmann, Liv	Tokyo, Japan	12/16/39
Urich, Robert.	Toronto, Oh.	12/19/47
Ustinov, Peter	London, England	4/16/21
Vaccaro, Brenda	Brooklyn, N.Y.	11/18/39
Vale, Jerry	New York, N.Y.	7/8/31
Valente, Caterina	Paris, France	1/14/31
Valentine, Karen.	Santa Rosa, Cal.	5/25/47
Valli, Frankie	Newark, N.J.	5/3/37
Vanelli, Gino	Montreal, Que.	6/16/52
Van Ark, Joan	New York, N.Y.	6/16/46
Van Cleef, Lee.	Somerville, N.J.	1/9/25
Van Doren, Mamie	Rowena, S.D.	2/6/33
Van Dyke, Dick	West Plains, Mo.	12/13/25
Van Dyke, Jerry	Danville, Ill.	7/27/32
Van Fleet, Jo.	Oakland, Cal.	12/30/19
Van Pallandt, Nina.	Copenhagen, Denmark	7/15/32
Van Patten, Dick.	New York, N.Y.	12/9/28
Vaughan, Sarah	Newark, N.J.	3/27/24
Vaughn, Robert	New York, N.Y.	11/22/32
Venuta, Benay	San Francisco, Cal.	1/27/11
Verdon, Gwen	Los Angeles, Cal.	1/13/25
Vereen, Ben	Miami, Fla.	10/10/46
Verrett, Shirley.	New Orleans, La.	5/31/31
Vickers, Jon	Prince Albert, Sask.	10/26/26
Vigneault, Gilles	Natashquan, Que.	10/27/28
Vigoda, Abe	New York, N.Y.	2/24/21
Villella, Edward	Long Island, N.Y.	10/1/36
Vincent, Jan-Michael	Denver, Col.	7/15/44
Vinson, Helen	Beaumont, Tex.	9/17/07
Vinton, Bobby	Canonsburg, Pa.	4/16/35
Voight, Jon	Yonkers, N.Y.	12/29/38
Von Stade, Frederica	Somerville, N.J.	6/1/45
Von Sydow, Max	Lund, Sweden.	4/10/29
Voorhees, Donald	Allentown, Pa.	7/26/03
Waggoner, Lyle	Kansas City, Kan.	4/13/35
Wagner, Lindsay.	Los Angeles, Cal.	6/22/49
Wagner, Robert	Detroit, Mich.	2/10/30
Wagoner, Porter.	West Plains, Mo.	8/12/27
Wahl, Ken	Chicago, Ill.	1956
Wain, Bea	Bronx, N.Y.	4/30/17
Waite, Ralph	White Plains, N.Y.	6/22/29
Walden, Robert	New York, N.Y.	9/25/43
Walken, Christopher	New York, N.Y.	3/31/43
Walker, Clint.	Hartford, Ill.	5/30/27
Walker, Nancy.	Philadelphia, Pa.	5/10/21
Wallach, Eli.	Brooklyn, N.Y.	12/7/15
Walston, Ray	Laurel, Miss.	12/2/14
Walter, Jessica	New York, N.Y.	1/31/44
Wanamaker, Sam.	Chicago, Ill.	6/14/19
Ward, Rachel	London, England	1958
Ward, Simon.	London, England	10/19/41
Warden, Jack	Newark, N.J.	9/18/20
Warfield, William.	W. Helena, Ark.	1/22/20
Warner, Malcolm-Jamal	Jersey City, N.J.	8/18/70
Warren, Leslie Ann	New York, N.Y.	8/16/46
Warren, Michael	So. Bend, Ind.	3/5/46
Warrick, Ruth	St. Joseph, Mo.	6/29/15
Warwick, Dionne.	E. Orange, N.J.	12/12/41
Washington, Denzel.	Mt. Vernon, N.Y.	12/28/54
Waterston, Sam.	Cambridge, Mass.	11/15/40
Watson, Mills.	Oakland, Cal.	7/10/40
Watts, Andre.	Nuremberg, Germany	6/20/46
Waxman, Al	Toronto, Ont.	3/2/35
Wayne, David	Traverse City, Mich.	1/30/14
Wayne, Johnny	Toronto, Ont.	5/28/18
Weaver, Dennis	Joplin, Mo.	6/4/24
Weaver, Fritz.	Pittsburgh, Pa.	1/19/26
Weaver, Sigourney	New York, N.Y.	10/8/49
Webber, Robert	Santa Ana, Cal.	10/14/28
Weir, Peter.	Sydney, Australia.	8/8/44
Welch, Raquel	Chicago, Ill.	9/5/40
Weld, Tuesday	New York, N.Y.	8/27/43
Welk, Lawrence	nr. Strasburg, N.D.	3/11/03
Wells, Kitty	Nashville, Tenn.	8/30/19
Wendt, George	Chicago, Ill.	10/17/48
Weston, Jack	Cleveland, Oh.	1925
Wheichel, Lisa	Ft. Worth, Tex.	5/29/63
White, Barry	Galveston, Tex.	9/12/44
White, Betty	Oak Park, Ill.	1/17/24
White, Jesse	Buffalo, N.Y.	1/3/19
White, Vanna.	N. Myrtle Beach, S.C.	2/18/57
Whiting, Margaret.	Detroit, Mich.	7/22/24
Whitmore, James	White Plains, N.Y.	10/1/21
Widmark, Richard	Sunrise, Minn.	12/26/14
Wiest, Dianne	Kansas City, Mo.	—
Wilde, Cornel	New York, N.Y.	10/13/15
Wilder, Billy	Vienna, Austria	6/22/06
Wilder, Gene.	Milwaukee, Wis.	6/11/35
Williams, Andy	Wall Lake, Ia.	12/3/30
Williams, Billy Dee.	New York, N.Y.	4/6/37
Williams, Cindy	Van Nuys, Cal.	8/22/47
Williams, Emlyn	Mostyn, Wales	11/26/05
Williams, Esther	Los Angeles, Cal.	8/8/23
Williams, Hal	Columbus, Oh.	12/14/38
Williams Jr., Hank	Shreveport, La.	5/26/49
Williams, Joe.	Cordele, Ga.	12/12/18
Williams, JoBeth	Houston, Tex.	1953
Williams, Paul	Omaha, Neb.	9/19/40
Williams, Robin	Chicago, Ill.	7/21/52
Williams, Roger	Omaha, Neb.	1926
Williams, Treat.	Rowayton, Conn.	12/1/51
Williamson, Nicol	Hamilton, Scotland	9/14/38
Willis, Bruce	Penns Grove, N.J.	3/19/55
Wilson, Demond	Valdosta, Ga.	10/13/46
Wilson, Dolores	Philadelphia, Pa.	1929
Wilson, Elizabeth	Grand Rapids, Mich.	4/4/25
Wilson, Flip	Jersey City, N.J.	12/8/33
Wilson, Nancy	Chillicothe, Oh.	2/20/37
Windom, William.	New York, N.Y.	9/28/23
Winfield, Paul	Los Angeles, Cal.	5/22/41
Winfrey, Oprah	Kosciusko, Miss.	11/29/54
Winger, Debra	Columbus, Oh.	5/16/55
Winkler, Henry	New York, N.Y.	10/30/45
Winters, Jonathan	Dayton, Oh.	11/11/25
Winters, Shelley	St. Louis, Mo.	8/18/22
Wiseman, Joseph	Montreal, Que.	5/15/18
Withers, Jane	Atlanta, Ga.	4/12/26
Wonder, Stevie	Saginaw, Mich.	5/13/50
Woodard, Alfre	Tulsa, Okla.	11/2/53
Woods, James.	Vernal, N.U.	4/18/47
Woodward, Edward	Croyden, England	6/1/30
Woodward, Joanne	Thomasville, Ga.	2/27/30
Wopat, Tom	Lodi, Wis.	9/9/51
Worth, Irene	Nebraska	6/23/16
Wray, Fay	Alberta.	9/10/07
Wright, Martha.	Seattle, Wash.	3/23/26
Wright, Max	Detroit, Mich.	8/2/–
Wright, Teresa	New York, N.Y.	10/27/18
Wrightson, Earl	Baltimore, Md.	11/1/16
Wyatt, Jane	Campgaw, N.J.	8/10/11
Wyman, Jane	St. Joseph, Mo.	1/4/14
Wynette, Tammy	Red Bay, Ala.	5/5/42
Yarborough, Glenn	Milwaukee, Wis.	1/12/30
Yarrow, Peter	New York, N.Y.	5/31/38
York, Michael	Fulmer, England	3/27/42
York, Susannah	London, England	1/9/41
Yothers, Tina.	Whittier, Cal.	9/5/73
Young, Alan	Northumberland, England	11/19/19
Young, Burt	New York, N.Y.	4/30/40
Young, Loretta	Salt Lake City, Ut.	1/6/12
Young, Neil.	Toronto, Ont.	11/12/45
Young, Robert	Chicago, Ill.	2/22/07
Youngman, Henny	Liverpool, England	1/12/06
Zadora, Pia.	Hoboken, N.J.	1957
Zappa, Frank	Baltimore, Md.	12/21/40
Zeffirelli, Franco	Florence, Italy.	2/12/23
Zeman, Jacklyn	Englewood, N.J.	3/6/–
Zimbalist, Efrem Jr.	New York, N.Y.	11/30/23
Zimbalist, Stephanie	New York, N.Y.	10/6/56
Zmed, Adrian	Chicago, Ill.	3/14/54
Zukerman, Pinchas	Tel Aviv, Israel	7/16/48

World Entertainment Personalities of the Past

(as of July, 1988)

Born	Died	Name	Born	Died	Name	Born	Died	Name
1895	1974	Abbott, Bud	1882	1951	Blaney, Charles E.	1942	1981	Chapin, Harry
1872	1953	Adams, Maude	1900	1943	Bledsoe, Jules	1889	1977	Chaplin, Charles
1855	1926	Adler, Jacob P.	1928	1972	Blocker, Dan	1893	1940	Chase, Charlie
1903	1985	Adler, Luther	1909	1979	Blondell, Joan	1893	1961	Chatterton, Ruth
1898	1933	Adoree, Renee	1888	1959	Blore, Eric	1888	1972	Chevalier, Maurice
1902	1986	Aherne, Brian	1901	1975	Blue, Ben	1888	1960	Clark, Bobby
1909	1964	Albertson, Frank	1899	1957	Bogart, Humphrey	1914	1968	Clark, Fred
1907	1981	Albertson, Jack	1880	1965	Boland, Mary	1887	1950	Clayton, Lou
1885	1952	Alda, Frances	1895	1969	Boles, John	1920	1966	Clift, Montgomery
1894	1956	Allen, Fred	1904	1987	Bolger, Ray	1932	1963	Cline, Patsy
1906	1964	Allen, Gracie	1903	1960	Bond, Ward	1898	1937	Clive, Colin
1883	1950	Allgood, Sara	1892	1981	Bondi, Beulah	1892	1967	Clyde, Andy
1886	1954	Anderson, John Murray	1917	1981	Boone, Richard	1911	1976	Cobb, Lee J.
1915	1967	Andrews, Laverne	1833	1893	Booth, Edwin	1877	1961	Coburn, Charles
1876	1958	Anglin, Margaret	1796	1852	Booth, Junius Brutus	1887	1934	Cody, Lew
1887	1933	Arbuckle, Fatty (Roscoe)	1894	1953	Bordoni, Irene	1878	1942	Cohan, George M.
1900	1976	Arlen, Richard	1888	1960	Bori, Lucrezia	1919	1965	Cole, Nat (King)
1868	1946	Arliss, George	1905	1965	Bow, Clara	1878	1955	Collier, Constance
1888	1945	Armetta, Henry	1874	1946	Bowes, Maj. Edward	1890	1965	Collins, Ray
1900	1971	Armstrong, Louis	1928	1977	Boyd, Stephen	1891	1958	Colman, Ronald
1917	1986	Arnaz, Desi	1898	1972	Boyd, William	1908	1934	Columbo, Russ
1890	1956	Arnold, Edward	1899	1978	Boyer, Charles	1907	1944	Compton, Betty
1905	1974	Arquette, Cliff	1893	1939	Brady, Alice	1887	1940	Connolly, Walter
1899	1987	Astaire, Fred	1871	1936	Breese, Edmund	1917	1982	Conried, Hans
1906	1987	Astor, Mary	1898	1964	Brendel, El	1855	1909	Conried, Henrich
1885	1946	Atwill, Lionel	1894	1974	Brennan, Walter	1914	1975	Conte, Richard
1845	1930	Auer, Leopold	1904	1979	Brent, George	1914	1984	Coogan, Jackie
1905	1967	Auer, Mischa	1875	1948	Brian, Donald	1935	1964	Cooke, Sam
1900	1972	Austin, Gene	1891	1951	Brice, Fanny	1901	1961	Cooper, Gary
1898	1940	Ayres, Agnes	1891	1959	Broderick, Helen	1888	1971	Cooper, Gladys
			1904	1951	Bromberg, J. Edward	1896	1973	Cooper, Melville
			1892	1973	Brown, Joe E.	1914	1968	Corey, Wendell
1864	1922	Bacon, Frank	1926	1966	Bruce, Lenny	1893	1974	Cornell, Katherine
1892	1968	Bainter, Fay	1895	1953	Bruce, Nigel	1890	1972	Correll, Charles (Andy)
1895	1957	Baker, Belle	1910	1982	Bruce, Virginia	1905	1979	Costello, Dolores
1906	1975	Baker, Josephine	1920	1985	Brynner, Yul	1904	1957	Costello, Helene
1904	1983	Balanchine, George	1903	1979	Buchanan, Edgar	1908	1959	Costello, Lou
1882	1956	Bancroft, George	1891	1957	Buchanan, Jack	1877	1950	Costello, Maurice
1903	1968	Bankhead, Tallulah	1885	1957	Buck, Gene	1899	1973	Coward, Noel
1890	1952	Banks, Leslie	1938	1982	Buono, Victor	1890	1950	Cowl, Jane
1890	1955	Bara, Theda	1885	1970	Burke, Billie	1924	1973	Cox, Wally
1810	1891	Barnum, Phineas T.	1912	1967	Burnette, Smiley	1908	1983	Crabbe, Buster
1912	1978	Barrie, Wendy	1896	1956	Burns, Bob	1847	1924	Crabtree, Lotta
1879	1959	Barrymore, Ethel	1902	1971	Burns, David	1928	1978	Crane, Bob
1882	1942	Barrymore, John	1882	1941	Burr, Henry	1911	1986	Crawford, Broderick
1878	1954	Barrymore, Lionel	1925	1984	Burton, Richard	1908	1977	Crawford, Joan
1848	1905	Barrymore, Maurice	1897	1946	Busch, Mae	1916	1944	Cregar, Laird
1897	1963	Barthelmess, Richard	1883	1966	Bushman, Francis X.	1880	1942	Crews, Laura Hope
1890	1962	Barton, James	1896	1946	Butterworth, Charles	1880	1974	Crisp, Donald
1914	1984	Basehart, Richard	1893	1971	Byington, Spring	1942	1973	Croce, Jim
1904	1984	Basie, Count				1910	1960	Cromwell, Richard
1873	1951	Bauer, Harold				1903	1977	Crosby, Bing
1923	1985	Baxter, Anne	1904	1972	Cabot, Bruce	1897	1975	Cross, Milton
1889	1951	Baxter, Warner	1918	1977	Cabot, Sebastian	1910	1986	Crothers, Scatman
1880	1928	Bayes, Nora	1899	1986	Cagney, James	1878	1968	Currie, Finlay
1904	1965	Beatty, Clyde	1895	1956	Calhern, Louis	1816	1876	Cushman, Charlotte
1902	1962	Beavers, Louise	1923	1977	Callas, Maria			
1884	1946	Beery, Noah	1853	1942	Calve, Emma			
1889	1949	Beery, Wallace	1933	1976	Cambridge, Godfrey	1914	1978	Dailey, Dan
1901	1970	Begley, Ed	1865	1940	Campbell, Mrs. Patrick	1899	1981	Chief Dan George
1854	1931	Belasco, David	1892	1964	Cantor, Eddie	1923	1965	Dandridge, Dorothy
1949	1982	Belushi, John	1878	1947	Carey, Harry	1869	1941	Danforth, William
1906	1968	Benaderet, Bea	1950	1983	Carpenter, Karen	1894	1963	Daniell, Henry
1906	1964	Bendix, William	1880	1961	Carrillo, Leo	1901	1971	Daniels, Bebe
1904	1965	Bennett, Constance	1892	1972	Carroll, Leo G.	1860	1935	Daniels, Frank
1943	1987	Bennett, Michael	1905	1965	Carroll, Nancy	1936	1973	Darin, Bobby
1873	1944	Bennett, Richard	1910	1963	Carson, Jack	1921	1965	Darnell, Linda
1894	1974	Benny, Jack	1862	1937	Carter, Mrs. Leslie	1879	1967	Darwell, Jane
1924	1970	Benzell, Mimi	1873	1921	Caruso, Enrico	1909	1986	Da Silva, Howard
1899	1966	Berg, Gertrude	1876	1973	Casals, Pablo	1866	1949	Davenport, Harry
1903	1978	Bergen, Edgar	1927	1976	Cassidy, Jack	1897	1961	Davies, Marion
1915	1982	Bergman, Ingrid	1893	1969	Castle, Irene	1907	1961	Davis, Joan
1895	1976	Berkeley, Busby	1887	1918	Castle, Vernon	1931	1955	Dean, James
1863	1927	Bernard, Sam	1889	1960	Catlett, Walter	1905	1968	Dekker, Albert
1923	1986	Bernardi, Herschel	1887	1950	Cavanaugh, Hobart	1908	1983	Del Rio, Dolores
1844	1923	Bernhardt, Sarah	1873	1938	Chaliapin, Feodor	1892	1983	Demarest, William
1893	1943	Bernie, Ben	1919	1980	Champion, Gower	1881	1959	DeMille, Cecil B.
1889	1967	Bickford, Charles	1918	1961	Chandler, Jeff	1891	1967	Denny, Reginald
1911	1960	Bjoerling, Jussi	1883	1930	Chaney, Lon	1901	1974	DeSica, Vittorio
1895	1973	Blackmer, Sidney	1905	1973	Chaney Jr., Lon	1905	1977	Devine, Andy

Born	Died	Name	Born	Died	Name	Born	Died	Name
1942	1972	De Wilde, Brandon	1857	1928	Foy, Eddie	1879	1942	Herbert, Henry
1907	1974	De Wolfe, Billy	1903	1968	Francis, Kay	1887	1951	Herbert, Hugh
1865	1950	De Wolfe, Elsie	1887	1966	Frawley, William	1886	1956	Hersholt, Jean
1921	1985	Diamond, Selma	1885	1938	Frederick, Pauline	1895	1942	Hibbard, Edna
1879	1947	Digges, Dudley	1870	1955	Friganza, Trixie	1899	1980	Hitchcock, Alfred
1901	1966	Disney, Walt	1890	1958	Frisco, Joe	1914	1955	Hodiak, John
1894	1949	Dix, Richard	1860	1915	Frohman, Charles	1894	1973	Holden, Fay
1856	1924	Dockstader, Lew	1851	1940	Frohman, Daniel	1918	1981	Holden, William
1892	1941	Dolly, Jennie	1885	1947	Fyffe, Will	1922	1965	Holliday, Judy
1892	1970	Dolly, Rosie				1936	1959	Holly, Buddy
1905	1958	Donat, Robert				1888	1951	Holt, Jack
1889	1972	Donlevy, Brian	1901	1960	Gable, Clark	1918	1973	Holt, Tim
1901	1981	Douglas, Melvyn	1889	1963	Galli-Curci, Amelita	1871	1947	Homer, Louise
1907	1959	Douglas, Paul	1877	1967	Garden, Mary	1898	1978	Homolka, Oscar
—	1980	Dragonette, Jessica	1913	1952	Garfield, John	1902	1972	Hopkins, Miriam
1889	1956	Draper, Ruth	1922	1969	Garland, Judy	1858	1935	Hopper, DeWolf
1881	1965	Dresser, Louise	1939	1984	Gaye, Marvin	1874	1959	Hopper, Edna Wallace
1869	1934	Dressler, Marie	1906	1984	Gaynor, Janet	1915	1969	Hopper, William
1820	1897	Drew, Mrs. John	1902	1978	Geer, Will	1888	1970	Horton, Edward Everett
1853	1927	Drew, John (son)	1900	1954	George, Gladys	1874	1926	Houdini, Harry
1909	1951	Duchin, Eddy	1892	1962	Gibson, Hoot	1881	1965	Howard, Eugene
1890	1974	Dumbrille, Douglas	1890	1957	Gigli, Beniamino	1867	1961	Howard, Joe
1889	1965	Dumont, Margaret	1894	1971	Gilbert, Billy	1893	1943	Howard, Leslie
1878	1927	Duncan, Isadora	1895	1936	Gilbert, John	1885	1955	Howard, Tom
1905	1967	Dunn, James	1855	1937	Gillette, William	1916	1988	Howard, Trevor
1935	1973	Dunn, Michael	1867	1943	Gillmore, Frank	1885	1949	Howard, Willie
1893	1980	Durante, Jimmy	1879	1939	Gilpin, Charles	1925	1985	Hudson, Rock
1907	1968	Duryea, Dan	1897	1987	Gingold, Hermione	1890	1977	Hull, Henry
1858	1924	Duse, Eleanora	1898	1968	Gish, Dorothy	1886	1957	Hull, Josephine
			1916	1987	Gleason, Jackie	1895	1958	Humphrey, Doris
1894	1929	Eagels, Jeanne	1886	1959	Gleason, James	1895	1945	Hunter, Glenn
1896	1930	Eames, Clare	1884	1938	Gluck, Alma	1927	1969	Hunter, Jeffrey
1865	1952	Eames, Emma	1903	1983	Godfrey, Arthur	1901	1962	Husing, Ted
1901	1967	Eddy, Nelson	1874	1955	Golden, John	1906	1987	Huston, John
1897	1971	Edwards, Cliff	1882	1974	Goldwyn, Samuel	1884	1950	Huston, Walter
1879	1945	Edwards, Gus	1915	1969	Gorcey, Leo			
1899	1974	Ellington, Duke	1884	1940	Gordon, C. Henry	1892	1950	Ingram, Rex
1941	1974	Elliot, Cass	1896	1985	Gordon, Ruth	1895	1969	Ingram, Rex
1871	1940	Elliott, Maxine	1899	1982	Gosden, Freeman (Amos)	1895	1980	Iturbi, Jose
1891	1967	Elman, Mischa	1869	1944	Gottschalk, Ferdinand	1838	1905	Irving, Henry
1881	1951	Errol, Leon	1829	1869	Gottschalk, Louis	1871	1944	Irving, Isabel
1903	1967	Erwin, Stuart	1916	1973	Grable, Betty	1872	1914	Irving, Laurence
1888	1976	Evans, Edith	1925	1981	Grahame, Gloria			
1913	1967	Evelyn, Judith	1904	1986	Grant, Cary	1875	1942	Jackson, Joe
			1915	1987	Greene, Lorne	1911	1972	Jackson, Mahalia
1883	1939	Fairbanks, Douglas	1879	1954	Greenstreet, Sydney	1891	1984	Jaffe, Sam
1914	1970	Farmer, Frances	1893	1978	Greenwood, Charlotte	1916	1983	James, Harry
1870	1929	Farnum, Dustin	1874	1948	Griffith, David Wark	1889	1956	Janis, Elsie
1876	1953	Farnum, William	1912	1980	Griffith, Hugh	1886	1950	Jannings, Emil
1882	1967	Farrar, Geraldine	1912	1967	Guthrie, Woody	1930	1980	Janssen, David
1904	1971	Farrell, Glenda	1875	1959	Gwenn, Edmund	1829	1905	Jefferson, Joseph
1868	1940	Faversham, William				1859	1923	Jefferson, Thomas
1861	1939	Fawcett, George	1888	1942	Hackett, Charles	1900	1974	Jenkins, Allen
1897	1961	Fay, Frank	1902	1958	Hackett, Raymond	1898	1981	Jessel, George
1895	1962	Fazenda, Louise	1870	1943	Haines, Robert T.	1862	1930	Jewett, Henry
1933	1982	Feldman, Marty	1892	1950	Hale, Alan	1892	1962	Johnson, Chic
1898	1985	Fetchit, Stepin	1927	1981	Haley, Bill	1878	1952	Johnson, Edward
1894	1979	Fiedler, Arthur	1899	1979	Haley, Jack	1886	1950	Jolson, Al
1918	1973	Field, Betty	1902	1985	Hamilton, Margaret	1889	1942	Jones, Buck
1898	1979	Fields, Gracie	1847	1919	Hammerstein, Oscar	1933	1983	Jones, Carolyn
1867	1941	Fields, Lew	1879	1955	Hampden, Walter	1911	1965	Jones, Spike
1879	1946	Fields, W.C.	1924	1964	Haney, Carol	1943	1970	Joplin, Janis
1931	1978	Fields, Totie	1893	1964	Hardwicke, Cedric	1896	1988	Jordan, Jim
1916	1977	Finch, Peter	1892	1957	Hardy, Oliver	1897	1961	Jordan, Marian
1865	1932	Fiske, Minnie Maddern	1883	1939	Hare, T.E. (Ernie)			(Molly McGee)
1888	1961	Fitzgerald, Barry	1911	1937	Harlow, Jean	1902	1982	Jory, Victor
1895	1962	Flagstad, Kirsten	1872	1946	Harned, Virginia	1905	1981	Joslyn, Allyn
1900	1971	Flippen, Jay C.	1844	1911	Harrigan, Edward			
1909	1959	Flynn, Errol	1870	1946	Hart, William S.	1910	1966	Kane, Helen
1925	1974	Flynn, Joe	1907	1955	Hartman, Grace	1887	1969	Karloff, Boris
1880	1942	Fokine, Michel	1928	1973	Harvey, Laurence	1893	1970	Karns, Roscoe
1910	1968	Foley, Red	1910	1973	Hawkins, Jack	1913	1987	Kaye, Danny
1905	1982	Fonda, Henry	1890	1973	Hayakawa, Sessue	1913	1987	Kaye, Sammy
1920	1978	Fontaine, Frank	1885	1969	Hayes, Gabby	1811	1868	Kean, Charles
1887	1983	Fontanne, Lynn	1918	1980	Haymes, Dick	1806	1880	Kean, Mrs. Charles
1853	1937	Forbes-Robertson, J.	1902	1971	Hayward, Leland	1787	1833	Kean, Edmund
1895	1973	Ford, John	1917	1975	Hayward, Susan	1895	1966	Keaton, Buster
1901	1976	Ford, Paul	1918	1987	Hayworth, Rita	1858	1929	Keenan, Frank
1899	1966	Ford, Wallace	1896	1937	Healy, Ted	1830	1873	Keene, Laura
1806	1872	Forrest, Edwin	1910	1971	Heflin, Van	1841	1893	Keene, Thomas W.
1927	1987	Fosse, Bob	1901	1987	Heifetz, Jascha	1899	1960	Keith, Ian
1901	1970	Foster, Preston	1873	1918	Held, Anna	1894	1973	Kellaway, Cecil
			1942	1970	Hendrix, Jimi	1898	1979	Kelly, Emmett
			1910	1969	Henie, Sonja			

Born	Died	Name	Born	Died	Name	Born	Died	Name
1929	1982	Kelly, Grace	1892	1977	Lunt, Alfred	1901	1970	Morris, Chester
1910	1981	Kelly, Patsy	1853	1932	Lupino, George	1849	1925	Morris, Clara
1899	1956	Kelly, Paul	1893	1942	Lupino, Stanley	1914	1959	Morris, Wayne
1873	1939	Kelly, Walter C.	1897	1957	Lyman, Abe	1943	1971	Morrison, Jim
1907	1968	Kelton, Pert	1926	1982	Lynde, Paul	1932	1982	Morrow, Vic
1823	1895	Kemble, Agnes	1926	1971	Lynn, Diana	1915	1977	Mostel, Zero
1775	1854	Kemble, Charles	1885	1954	Lytell, Bert	1897	1969	Mowbray, Alan
1809	1893	Kemble, Fannie	1867	1936	Lytton, Henry	1895	1967	Muni, Paul
1848	1935	Kendal, Madge				1894	1953	Munn, Frank
1843	1917	Kendal, William H.				1915	1970	Munshin, Jules
1926	1959	Kendall, Kay	1907	1965	MacDonald, Jeanette	1924	1971	Murphy, Audie
1890	1948	Kennedy, Edgar	1902	1969	MacLane, Barton	1885	1965	Murray, Mae
1886	1945	Kent, William	1921	1986	MacRae, Gordon			
			1909	1973	Macready, George			
			1861	1946	Macy, George Carleton			
1880	1947	Kerrigan, J. Warren	1908	1973	Magnani, Anna	1896	1970	Nagel, Conrad
1886	1956	Kibbee, Guy	1896	1967	Mahoney, Will	1900	1973	Naish, J. Carroll
1902	1966	Kiepura, Jan	1890	1975	Main, Marjorie	1898	1961	Naldi, Nita
1888	1964	Kilbride, Percy	1933	1967	Mansfield, Jayne	1888	1950	Nash, Florence
1863	1933	Kilgour, Joseph	1854	1907	Mansfield, Richard	1865	1945	Nash, George
1894	1944	King, Charles	1905	1980	Mantovani, Annunzio	1879	1945	Nazimova, Alla
1897	1971	King, Dennis	1897	1975	March, Fredric	1899	1987	Negri, Pola
1923	1986	Knight, Ted	1945	1981	Marley, Bob	1846	1905	Neilson, Ada
1901	1980	Kostelanetz, Andre	1865	1950	Marlowe, Julia	1848	1880	Neilson, Adelaide
1919	1962	Kovacs, Ernie	1890	1966	Marshall, Herbert	1868	1957	Neilson-Terry, Julia
1885	1974	Kruger, Otto	1864	1943	Marshall, Tully	1906	1975	Nelson, Ozzie
			1920	1981	Martin, Ross	1940	1985	Nelson, Rick
1913	1964	Ladd, Alan	1885	1969	Martinelli, Giovanni	1885	1967	Nesbit, Evelyn
1895	1967	Lahr, Bert	1924	1987	Marvin, Lee	1870	1951	Nethersole, Olga
1919	1973	Lake, Veronica	1888	1964	Marx, Arthur (Harpo)	1910	1983	Niven, David
1925	1982	Lamas, Fernando	1890	1977	Marx, Julius (Groucho)	1874	1948	Niblo, Fred
1902	1986	Lancaster, Elsa	1887	1961	Marx, Leonard (Chico)	1890	1950	Nijinsky, Vaslav
1919	1948	Landis, Carole	1909	1984	Mason, James	1893	1974	Nilsson, Anna Q.
1904	1972	Landis, Jessie Royce	1896	1983	Massey, Raymond	1902	1985	Nolan, Lloyd
1884	1944	Langdon, Harry	1862	1951	Maude, Cyril	1898	1930	Normand, Mabel
1853	1929	Langtry, Lillie	1879	1948	May, Edna	1879	1959	Norworth, Jack
1921	1959	Lanza, Mario	1885	1957	Mayer, Louis B.	1899	1968	Novarro, Ramon
1870	1950	Lauder, Harry	1895	1973	Maynard, Ken	1893	1951	Novello, Ivor
1899	1962	Laughton, Charles	1884	1945	McCormack, John			
1890	1965	Laurel, Stan	1907	1962	McCormick, Myron			
1923	1984	Lawford, Peter	1888	1931	McCoy, Bessie	1903	1978	Oakie, Jack
1898	1952	Lawrence, Gertrude	1891	1978	McCoy, Tim	1860	1926	Oakley, Annie
1890	1929	Lawrence, Margaret	1895	1952	McDaniel, Hattie	1928	1982	Oates, Warren
1940	1973	Lee, Bruce	1924	1965	McDonald, Marie	1911	1979	Oberon, Merle
1907	1952	Lee, Canada	1913	1975	McGiver, John	1915	1985	O'Brien, Edmond
1914	1970	Lee, Gypsy Rose	1899	1981	McHugh, Frank	1899	1983	O'Brien, Pat
1848	1929	Lehmann, Lilli	1879	1949	McIntyre, Frank J.	1908	1981	O'Connell, Arthur
1888	1976	Lehmann, Lotte	1857	1937	McIntyre, James	1898	1943	O'Connell, Hugh
1896	1950	Lehr, Lew	1879	1937	McKinley, Mabel	1880	1959	O'Connor, Una
1913	1967	Leigh, Vivien	1883	1959	McLaglen, Victor	1878	1945	O'Hara, Fiske
1852	1908	Leighton, Margaret	1907	1971	McMahon, Horace	1908	1968	O'Keefe, Dennis
1922	1976	Leighton, Margaret	1930	1980	McQueen, Steve	1880	1938	Oland, Warner
1894	1931	Leitzel, Lillian	1920	1980	Medford, Kay	1860	1932	Olcott, Chauncey
1940	1980	Lennon, John	1880	1946	Meek, Donald	1883	1942	Oliver, Edna May
1900	1981	Lenya, Lotte	1879	1936	Meighan, Thomas	1892	1963	Olsen, Ole
1870	1941	Leonard, Eddie	1861	1931	Melba, Nellie	1849	1920	O'Neill, James
1911	1973	Leonard, Jack E.	1890	1973	Melchior, Lauritz	1899	1985	Ormandy, Eugene
1900	1987	LeRoy, Mervyn	1904	1961	Melton, James	1876	1949	Ouspenskaya, Maria
1906	1972	Levant, Oscar	1890	1963	Menjou, Adolphe	1887	1972	Owen, Reginald
1905	1980	Levene, Sam	1902	1966	Menken, Helen			
1911	1980	Levenson, Sam	1908	1984	Merman, Ethel			
1881	1955	Levy, Ethel	1905	1986	Milland, Ray	1860	1941	Paderewski, Ignace
1902	1971	Lewis, Joe E.	1904	1944	Miller, Glenn	1924	1987	Page, Geraldine
1892	1971	Lewis, Ted	1860	1926	Miller, Henry	1889	1954	Pallette, Eugene
1874	1944	Lhevinne, Josef	1898	1936	Miller, Marilyn	1914	1986	Palmer, Lilli
1919	1987	Liberace	1895	1927	Mills, Florence	1894	1958	Pangborn, Franklin
1889	1952	Lincoln, Elmo	1939	1976	Mineo, Sal	1914	1975	Parks, Larry
1820	1887	Lind, Jenny	1903	1955	Minnevitch, Borrah	1881	1940	Pasternack, Josef A.
1889	1968	Lindsay, Howard	1913	1955	Miranda, Carmen	1837	1908	Pastor, Tony
1869	1952	Lipman, Clara	1892	1962	Mitchell, Thomas	1843	1919	Patti, Adelina
1893	1971	Lloyd, Harold	1880	1940	Mix, Tom	1840	1889	Patti, Carlotta
1870	1922	Lloyd, Marie	1845	1909	Modjeska, Helena	1885	1931	Pavlova, Anna
1891	1957	Lockhart, Gene	1926	1962	Monroe, Marilyn	1900	1973	Paxinou, Katina
1913	1969	Logan, Ella	1911	1973	Monroe, Vaughn	1904	1984	Peerce, Jan
1909	1942	Lombard, Carole	1875	1964	Monteux, Pierre	1885	1950	Pemberton, Brock
1902	1977	Lombardo, Guy	1917	1951	Montez, Maria	1899	1967	Pendleton, Nat
1927	1974	Long, Richard	1904	1981	Montgomery, Robert	1905	1941	Penner, Joe
1903	1983	Loo, Richard	1901	1947	Moore, Grace	1892	1937	Perkins, Osgood
1895	1975	Lopez, Vincent	1885	1955	Moore, Tom	1893	1956	Peters, Brandon
1888	1968	Lorne, Marion	1876	1962	Moore, Victor	1915	1963	Piaf, Edith
1904	1964	Lorre, Peter	1906	1974	Moorehead, Agnes	1893	1979	Pickford, Mary
1912	1962	Lovejoy, Frank	1882	1949	Moran, George	1897	1984	Pidgeon, Walter
1890	1971	Lowe, Edmund	1884	1952	Moran, Polly	1892	1957	Pinza, Ezio
1892	1947	Lubitsch, Ernst	1890	1949	Morgan, Frank	1898	1963	Pitts, Zasu
1882	1956	Lugosi, Bela	1900	1941	Morgan, Helen	1904	1976	Pons, Lily
1894	1971	Lukas, Paul	1888	1956	Morgan, Ralph	1897	1981	Ponselle, Rosa

Born	Died	Name
1904	1963	Powell, Dick
1912	1982	Powell, Eleanor
1892	1984	Powell, William
1913	1958	Power, Tyrone
1872	1983	Powers, Eugene
1905	1986	Preminger, Otto
1935	1977	Presley, Elvis
1918	1987	Preston, Robert
1911	1978	Prima, Louis
1856	1919	Primrose, George
1954	1977	Prinze, Freddie
1879	1956	Prouty, Jed
1871	1942	Pryor, Arthur
1895	1980	Raft, George
1890	1967	Rains, Claude
1889	1970	Rambeau, Marjorie
1900	1947	Rankin, Arthur
1892	1967	Rathbone, Basil
1897	1960	Ratoff, Gregory
1883	1953	Rawlinson, Herbert
1891	1943	Ray, Charles
1941	1967	Redding, Otis
1908	1985	Redgrave, Michael
1921	1986	Reed, Donna
1914	1959	Reeves, George
1923	1964	Reeves, Jim
1860	1916	Rehan, Ada
1892	1923	Reid, Wallace
1873	1943	Reinhardt, Max
1909	1971	Rennie, Michael
1902	1983	Richardson, Ralph
1870	1940	Richman, Charles
1895	1972	Richman, Harry
1921	1985	Riddle, Nelson
1872	1961	Ring, Blanche
1898	1977	Ritchard, Cyril
1907	1974	Ritter, Tex
1905	1969	Ritter, Thelma
1901	1965	Ritz, Al
1906	1986	Ritz, Harry
1903	1985	Ritz, Jim
1925	1982	Robbins, Marty
1898	1976	Robeson, Paul
1878	1949	Robinson, Bill
1893	1973	Robinson, Edward G.
1865	1942	Robson, May
1905	1977	Rochester (E. Anderson)
1897	1933	Rodgers, Jimmy
1894	1958	Rodzinsky, Artur
1879	1935	Rogers, Will
1880	1962	Rooney, Pat
1899	1966	Rose, Billy
1910	1980	Roth, Lillian
1922	1987	Rowan, Dan
1887	1982	Rubinstein, Artur
1878	1953	Ruffo, Titta
1886	1970	Ruggles, Charles
1864	1936	Russell, Annie
1924	1961	Russell, Gail
1861	1922	Russell, Lillian
1911	1976	Russell, Rosalind
1892	1972	Rutherford, Margaret
1903	1973	Ryan, Irene
1909	1973	Ryan, Robert
1924	1963	Sabu (Dastagir)
1877	1968	St. Denis, Ruth
1884	1955	Sakall, S.Z.
1885	1936	Sale (Chic), Charles
1906	1972	Sanders, George
1934	1973	Sands, Diana
1896	1960	Savo, Jimmy
1879	1954	Scheff, Fritzi
1892	1930	Schenck, Joe
1895	1964	Schildkraut, Joseph
1865	1930	Schildkraut, Rudolph
1889	1965	Schipa, Tito
1882	1951	Schnabel, Artur
1938	1982	Schneider, Romy
1910	1949	Schumann, Henrietta
1861	1936	Schumann-Heink, E.
1866	1945	Scott, Cyril
1920	1983	Scott, Hazel

Born	Died	Name
1898	1987	Scott, Randolph
1914	1965	Scott, Zachary
1843	1896	Scott-Siddons, Mrs.
1938	1979	Seberg, Jean
1892	1974	Seeley, Blossom
1893	1987	Segovia, Andres
1925	1980	Sellers, Peter
1902	1965	Selznick, David O.
1858	1935	Sembrich, Marcella
1880	1960	Sennett, Mack
1881	1951	Shattuck, Arthur
1860	1929	Shaw, Mary
1927	1978	Shaw, Robert
1891	1972	Shawn, Ted
1868	1949	Shean, Al
1902	1983	Shearer, Norma
1915	1967	Sheridan, Ann
1885	1934	Sherman, Lowell
1918	1970	Shriner, Herb
1875	1953	Shubert, Lee
1755	1831	Siddons, Mrs. Sarah
1921	1985	Signoret, Simone
1882	1930	Sills, Milton
1912	1985	Silvers, Phil
1919	1980	Silverheels, Jay
1900	1976	Sim, Alastair
1891	1934	Skelly, Hal
1858	1942	Skinner, Otis
1863	1948	Smith, C. Aubrey
1907	1986	Smith, Kate
1917	1979	Soo, Jack
1826	1881	Sothern, Edward A.
1859	1933	Sothern, Edward H.
1884	1957	Sothern, Harry
1854	1932	Sousa, John Philip
1884	1957	Sparks, Ned
1876	1948	Speaks, Oley
1890	1970	Spitalny, Phil
1873	1937	Standing, Guy
1900	1941	Stephenson, James
1883	1939	Sterling, Ford
1882	1928	Stevens, Emily A.
1934	1970	Stevens, Inger
1882	1977	Stokowski, Leopold
1873	1959	Stone, Fred
1879	1961	Stone, Lewis
1904	1980	Stone, Milburn
1898	1959	Sturges, Preston
1911	1960	Sullavan, Margaret
1902	1974	Sullivan, Ed
1903	1956	Sullivan, Francis L.
1892	1946	Summerville, Slim
1899	1983	Swanson, Gloria
1904	1969	Swarthout, Gladys
1893	1957	Talmadge, Norma
1899	1972	Tamiroff, Akim
1878	1947	Tanguay, Eva
1899	1934	Tashman, Lilyan
1885	1966	Taylor, Deems
1899	1958	Taylor, Estelle
1887	1946	Taylor, Laurette
1911	1969	Taylor, Robert
1878	1938	Tearle, Conway
1884	1953	Tearle, Godfrey
1892	1937	Tell, Alma
1864	1942	Tempest, Marie
1910	1963	Templeton, Alec
1847	1928	Terry, Ellen
1871	1940	Tetrazzini, Luisa
1899	1936	Thalberg, Irving
1857	1914	Thomas, Brandon
1892	1960	Thomas, John Charles
1882	1976	Thorndike, Sybil
1902	1975	(Three Stooges) Fine, Larry
1906	1952	Howard, Curly
1897	1975	Howard, Moe
1869	1936	Thurston, Howard
1896	1960	Tibbett, Lawrence
1887	1940	Tinney, Frank
1909	1958	Todd, Michael
1874	1947	Toler, Sidney
1905	1968	Tone, Franchot
1867	1957	Toscanini, Arturo

Born	Died	Name
1898	1968	Tracy, Lee
1900	1967	Tracy, Spencer
1903	1972	Traubel, Helen
1894	1975	Treacher, Arthur
1853	1917	Tree, Herbert Beerbohm
1890	1973	Truex, Ernest
1932	1984	Truffaut, Francois
1919	1986	Tucker, Forest
1915	1975	Tucker, Richard
1884	1966	Tucker, Sophie
1874	1940	Turpin, Ben
1908	1959	Twelvetrees, Helen
1894	1970	Ulric, Lenore
1933	1975	Ure, Mary
1895	1926	Valentino, Rudolph
1901	1986	Vallee, Rudy
1870	1950	Van, Billy B.
1911	1979	Vance, Vivian
1893	1943	Veidt, Conrad
1926	1981	Vera-Ellen
1885	1957	Von Stroheim, Erich
1906	1981	Von Zell, Harry
1887	1969	Walburn, Raymond
1874	1946	Waldron, Charles D.
1904	1966	Walker, June
1914	1951	Walker, Robert
1898	1983	Wallenstein, Alfred
1887	1980	Walsh, Raoul
1876	1962	Walter, Bruno
1878	1936	Walthall, Henry B.
1872	1952	Ward, Fannie
1866	1951	Warfield, David
1900	1984	Waring, Fred
1876	1958	Warner, H. B.
1878	1964	Warwick, Robert
1924	1963	Washington, Dinah
1900	1977	Waters, Ethel
1867	1945	Watson, Billy
1907	1979	Wayne, John
1891	1966	Webb, Clifton
1920	1982	Webb, Jack
1867	1942	Weber, Joe
1905	1973	Webster, Margaret
1915	1985	Welles, Orson
1896	1975	Wellman, William
1922	1984	Werner, Oskar
1892	1980	West, Mae
1895	1968	Wheeler, Bert
1889	1938	White, Pearl
1891	1967	Whiteman, Paul
1865	1948	Whitty, May
1912	1979	Wilding, Michael
1895	1948	William, Warren
1877	1922	Williams, Bert
1867	1918	Williams, Evan
1923	1953	Williams, Hank
1905	1975	Wills, Bob
1903	1978	Wills, Chill
1894	1953	Wilson, Dooley
1917	1972	Wilson, Marie
1884	1969	Winninger, Charles
1904	1959	Withers, Grant
1881	1931	Wolheim, Louis
1907	1961	Wong, Anna May
1938	1981	Wood, Natalie
1892	1978	Wood, Peggy
1888	1963	Woolley, Monty
1881	1956	Wycherly, Margaret
1902	1981	Wyler, William
1886	1966	Wynn, Ed
1916	1986	Wynn, Keenan
1890	1960	Young, Clara Kimball
1917	1978	Young, Gig
1887	1953	Young, Roland
1902	1979	Zanuck, Darryl F.
1869	1932	Ziegfeld, Florenz
1873	1976	Zukor, Adolph

Composers of Popular Music

Milton Ager, 1893-1979 (U.S.): "I Wonder What's Become of Sally", "Hard Hearted Hannah", "Ain't She Sweet?".

Paul Anka, b. 1941 (Can.): "Put Your Head On My Shoulder", "My Way", "She's a Lady", the Tonight Show theme.

Harold Arlen, 1905-1986 (U.S.): "Stormy Weather", "Over the Rainbow", "Blues in the Night", "That Old Black Magic".

Burt Bacharach, b. 1928 (U.S.): "Raindrops Keep Fallin' on My Head", "Walk on By", "What the World Needs Now is Love".

Ernest Ball, 1878-1927 (U.S.): "Mother Machree", "When Irish Eyes Are Smiling".

Irving Berlin, b. 1888 (U.S.): "Alexander's Ragtime Band", "Puttin' on the Ritz", "Easter Parade", "God Bless America", "White Christmas", "There's no Business Like Show Business".

Chuck Berry, b. 1926 or 1931 (U.S.): "Johnny B. Goode", "Roll Over Beethoven", "Rock and Roll Music", "Sweet Little Sixteen".

Eubie Blake, 1883-1983 (U.S.): "I'm Just Wild About Harry".

Carrie Jacobs Bond, 1862-1946 (U.S.): "I Love You Truly".

Nacio Herb Brown, 1896-1964 (U.S.): "Singing in the Rain", "You Were Meant for Me", "All I Do Is Dream of You".

Hoagy Carmichael, 1899-1981 (U.S.): "Stardust", "Georgia on My Mind", "Old Buttermilk Sky".

George M. Cohan, 1878-1942 (U.S.): "Give My Regards to Broadway", "Over There".

Leonard Cohen, b. 1934 (Can.): "Suzanne", "Bird On The Wire".

Phil Collins, b. 1951 (Br.): "Against All Odds", "One More Night".

Sam Cooke, 1935-1964 (U.S.): "You Send Me", "Cupid", "Wonderful World".

Noel Coward, 1899-1973 (Br.): "Mad Dogs and Englishmen", "Mad About the Boy".

John Denver, b. 1943 (U.S.): "Annie's Song", "Rocky Mountain High", "Sunshine on My Shoulders".

Neil Diamond, b. 1941 (U.S.): "I'm a Believer", "Sweet Caroline".

Walter Donaldson, 1893-1947 (U.S.): "Carolina in the Morning", "You're Driving Me Crazy", "Makin' Whoopee".

Vernon Duke, 1903-1969 (U.S.): "April in Paris".

Bob Dylan, b. 1941 (U.S.): "Blowin' in the Wind", "Mr. Tambourine Man".

Gus Edwards, 1879-1945 (U.S.): "School Days", "By the Light of the Silvery Moon".

Sherman Edwards, b. 1919 (U.S.): "See You in September", "Wonderful Wonderful!".

Duke Ellington, 1899-1974 (U.S.): "Sophisticated Lady", "Satin Doll", "It Don't Mean a Thing", "Solitude".

Sammy Fain, b. 1902: "I'll Be Seeing You", "Love Is a Many-Splendored Thing".

Fred Fisher, 1875-1942 (U.S.): "Peg O' My Heart", "Chicago".

Stephen Collins Foster, 1826-1864 (U.S.): "My Old Kentucky Home", "Old Folks At Home".

George Gershwin, 1898-1937 (U.S.): "Someone to Watch Over Me", "I've Got a Crush on You", "Embraceable You", "I've Got Rhythm".

W.C. Handy, 1873-1958 (U.S.): "St. Louis Blues".

Ray Henderson, 1896-1970 (U.S.): "That Old Gang of Mine", "Five Foot Two, Eyes of Blue".

Brian Holland, b. 1941, **Lamont Dozier,** b. 1941, **Eddie Holland,** b. 1939 (all U.S.): co-wrote a string of Motown hits, including "Heat Wave", "Where Did Our Love Go", "Baby, I Need Your Loving", "Stop! In the Name of Love".

Billy Joel, b. 1949 (U.S.): "Just the Way You Are", "Tell Her About It", "Leave a Tender Moment Alone".

Carole King, b. 1942 (U.S.): "Will You Love Me Tomorrow?", "Natural Woman", "Up on the Roof", "You've Got a Friend".

Jerry Leiber, Mike Stoller, both b. 1942 (U.S.): "Hound Dog", "Don't Be Cruel", "Jailhouse Rock", "Yakety Yak".

John Lennon, 1940-1980 (Br.): "Help!", "Nowhere Man", "All You Need Is Love", "Imagine".

Gordon Lightfoot, b. 1938 (Can.): "Early Morning Rain", "If You Could Read My Mind", "Sundown".

Henry Mancini, b. 1924 (U.S.): "Moon River", "Days of Wine and Roses".

Barry Mann, b. 1939 and **Cynthia Weil,** b. 1937 (U.S): "You've Lost That Loving Feelin' ", "(You're My) Soul and Inspiration".

Paul McCartney, b. 1942 (Br.): "Yesterday", "And I Love Her", "Hey Jude", "Let It Be", "My Love".

Jimmy McHugh, 1894-1969 (U.S.): "Don't Blame Me", "I'm In the Mood for Love", "I Feel a Song Coming On".

Joseph Meyer, b. 1894 (U.S.): "If You Knew Susie", "California, Here I Come", "Crazy Rhythm".

Joni Mitchell, b. 1943 (Can.): "Both Sides Now", "Woodstock", "Circle Game", "Big Yellow Taxi".

Cole Porter, 1893-1964 (U.S.): "Anything Goes", "I Get a Kick Out of You".

Lionel Richie, b. 1949 (U.S.): "Three Times a Lady", "Still", "Lady", "Truly".

Smokey Robinson, b. 1940 (U.S.): "My Girl", "The Tracks of My Tears", "Ooh Baby Baby".

Vincent Rose, 1880-1944 (U.S.): "Whispering", "Blueberry Hill".

Harry Ruby, 1895-1974 (U.S.): "Three Little Words", "Who's Sorry Now?".

Neil Sedaka, b. 1939 (U.S.): "Breaking Up Is Hard To Do", "Love Will Keep Us Together".

Paul Simon, b. 1942 (U.S.): "The Sounds of Silence", "Bridge Over Troubled Water", "Still Crazy After All These Years", *Graceland*.

James Van Heusen, b. 1913 (U.S.): "Swinging on a Star", "All the Way", "Love and Marriage".

Albert von Tilzer, 1878-1956 (U.S.): "I'll Be With You In Apple Blossom Time", "Take Me Out To the Ball Game".

Fats Waller, 1904-1943 (U.S.): "Honeysuckle Rose", "Ain't Misbehavin' ".

Harry Warren, 1893-1981 (U.S.): "We're in the Money", "I Only Have Eyes for You".

Jimmy Webb, b. 1946 (U.S.): "By the Time I Get to Phoenix", "Didn't We?", "Wichita Lineman".

Percy Wenrich, 1887-1952 (U.S.): "When You Wore a Tulip", "Moonlight Bay", "Put On Your Old Gray Bonnet".

Richard A. Whiting, 1891-1938 (U.S.): "Till We Meet Again", "Beyond the Blue Horizon", "My Ideal".

Stevie Wonder, b. 1950 (U.S.): "You Are the Sunshine of My Life", "I Just Called to Say I Love You".

Neil Young, b. 1945 (Can.): "Helpless", "Southern Man", "Only Love Can Break Your Heart", "Heart of Gold".

Lyricists

Johnny Burke, 1908-1974, (U.S.) What's New?; Misty; Imagination; Polka Dots and Moonbeams.

Sammy Cahn, b. 1913, (U.S.) High Hopes; Love and Marriage; The Second Time Around; It's Magic.

Betty Comden, b. 1919 (U.S.) and **Adolph Green,** b. 1915 (U.S.) The Party's Over; Just in Time; New York, New York.

Hal David, b. 1921 (U.S.) What the World Needs Now Is Love; Close to You.

Buddy De Sylva, 1895-1950, (U.S.) When Day is Done; Look for the Silver Lining; April Showers.

Howard Dietz, 1896-1983, (U.S.) Dancing in the Dark; You and the Night and the Music; That's Entertainment.

Al Dubin, 1891-1945, (U.S.) Tiptoe Through the Tulips; Anniversary Waltz; Lullaby of Broadway.

Fred Ebb, b. 1936 (U.S.) *Cabaret, Zorba, Woman of the Year.*

Dorothy Fields, 1905-1974, (U.S.) On the Sunny Side of the Street; Don't Blame Me; The Way You Look Tonight.

Ira Gershwin, 1896-1983, (U.S.) The Man I Love; Fascinating Rhythm; S'Wonderful; Embraceable You.

Wm. S. Gilbert, 1836-1911, (Br.) *The Mikado; H.M.S. Pinafore.*

Mack Gordon, 1905-1959, (Pol.-U.S.) You'll Never Know; The More I See You; Chattanooga Choo-Choo; You Make Me Feel So Young.

Oscar Hammerstein II, 1895-1960, (U.S.) Ol' Man River; Oklahoma; Carousel.

E. Y. (Yip) Harburg, 1898-1981, (U.S.) Brother, Can You Spare a Dime; April in Paris; Over the Rainbow.

Lorenz Hart, 1895-1943, (U.S.) Isn't It Romantic; Blue Moon; Lover; Manhattan; My Funny Valentine; Mountain Greenery.

DuBose Heyward, 1885-1940, (U.S.) Summertime; A Woman Is A Sometime Thing.

Gus Kahn, 1886-1941, (U.S.) Memories; Ain't We Got Fun.

Alan J. Lerner, 1918-1986, (U.S.) Brigadoon; My Fair Lady; Camelot; Gigi.; On a Clear Day You Can See Forever.

Johnny Mercer, 1909-1976, (U.S.) Blues in the Night; Come Rain or Come Shine; Laura; That Old Black Magic.

Bob Merrill, b. 1921, (U.S.) People; Don't Rain on My Parade.

Jack Norworth, 1879-1959, (U.S.) Take Me Out to the Ball Game; Shine On Harvest Moon.

Mitchell Parish, b. 1901, (U.S.) Stairway to the Stars; Stardust.

Andy Razaf, 1895-1973, (U.S.) Honeysuckle Rose, Ain't Misbehavin', S'posin'.

Leo Robin, 1900-1984, (U.S.) Thanks for the Memory; Hooray for Love; Diamonds are a Girl's Best Friend.

Jack Yellen, b. 1892, (U.S.) Down by the O-Hi-O; Ain't She Sweet; Happy Days Are Here Again.

Composers of Musicals and Operettas

Richard Adler, b. 1921 (U.S.): *Pajama Game, Damn Yankees.*

Irving Berlin, b. 1888 (U.S.): *This is the Army, Annie Get Your Gun, Call Me Madam.*

Leonard Bernstein, b. 1918 (U.S.): *On the Town, Wonderful Town, West Side Story.*

Jerry Bock, b. 1928 (U.S.): *Mr. Wonderful, Fiorello, Fiddler on the Roof, The Rothschilds.*

Noel Coward, 1899-1973 (Br.): *Bitter Sweet.*

Rudolf Friml, 1879-1972 (U.S.): *The Firefly, Rose Marie, Vagabond King, Bird of Paradise.*

John Gay, 1685-1732 (Br.): *The Beggar's Opera.*

Victor Herbert, 1859-1924 (Ir.-U.S.): *Mlle. Modiste, Babes in Toyland, The Red Mill, Naughty Marietta, Sweethearts.*

Jerry Herman, b. 1932 (U.S.): *Hello Dolly, Mame.*

Scott Joplin, 1868-1917 (U.S.): *Treemonisha.*

John Kander, b. 1927 (U.S.): *Cabaret, Chicago, Funny Lady.*

Jerome Kern, 1885-1945 (U.S.): *Sally, Sunny, Show Boat.*

Burton Lane, b. 1912 (U.S.): *Finian's Rainbow, On a Clear Day You Can See Forever.*

Franz Lehar, 1870-1948 (Hung.): *Merry Widow.*

Mitch Leigh, b. 1928 (U.S.): *Man of La Mancha.*

Frank Loesser, 1910-1969 (U.S.): *Guys and Dolls, Where's Charley?, The Most Happy Fella, How to Succeed. . .*

Frederick Loewe, b. 1901 (Aust.-U.S.): *The Day Before Spring, Brigadoon, Paint Your Wagon, My Fair Lady, Camelot.*

Cole Porter, 1893-1964 (U.S.): *Anything Goes, Kiss Me Kate, Can Can, Silk Stockings.*

Richard Rogers, 1902-1979 (U.S.): *Oklahoma!, Carousel, South Pacific, The King and I, Flower Drum Song, The Sound of Music.*

Sigmund Romberg, 1887-1951 (Hung.): *Maytime, The Student Prince, Desert Song, Blossom Time.*

Harry Rome, b. 1908 (U.S.): *Pins and Needles, Call Me Mister, Wish You Were Here, Fanny, Destry Rides Again.*

Stephen Sondheim, b. 1930 (U.S.): *A Little Night Music, Sunday in the Park with George, Sweeney Todd.*

John Philip Sousa, 1854-1932 (U.S.): *El Capitan, Stars and Stripes Forever.*

Oskar Straus, 1870-1954 (Aus.): *Chocolate Soldier.*

Johann Strauss, 1825-1899 (Aus.): *Gypsy Baron, Die Fledermaus.*

Charles Strouse, b. 1928 (U.S.): *Bye Bye Birdie, Annie.*

Jule Styne, b. 1905 (Br.-U.S.): *Gentlemen Prefer Blondes, Bells Are Ringing, Gypsy, Funny Girl.*

Arthur S. Sullivan, 1842-1900 (Br.): *H.M.S. Pinafore, Pirates of Penzance, The Mikado.*

Deems Taylor, 1885-1966 (U.S.): *Peter Ibbetson.*

Andrew Lloyd Webber, b. 1948 (Br.): *Jesus Christ Superstar, Cats.*

Kurt Weill, 1900-1950 (G.-U.S.): *Threepenny Opera, Lady in the Dark, Knickerbocker Holiday, One Touch of Venus.*

Meredith Willson, 1902-1984 (U.S.): *The Music Man.*

Vincent Youmans, 1898-1946 (U.S.): *Wildflower, No No Nanette, Hit the Deck, Rainbow, Smiles.*

Composers of Classical Music

Carl Philipp Emanuel Bach, 1714-1788, (G.) Prussian and Wurtembergian Sonatas.

Johann Christian Bach, 1735-1782, (G.) Concertos; sonatas.

Johann Sebastian Bach, 1685-1750, (G.) St. Matthew Passion, The Well-Tempered Clavichord.

Samuel Barber, 1910-1981, (U.S.) Adagio for Strings, Vanessa.

Bela Bartok, 1881-1945, (Hung.) Concerto for Orchestra, The Miraculous Mandarin.

Ludwig Van Beethoven, 1770-1827, (G.) Concertos (Emperor); sonatas (Moonlight, Pastorale, Pathetique); symphonies (Eroica).

Vincenzo Bellini, 1801-1835, (It.) La Sonnambula, Norma, I Puritani.

Alban Berg, 1885-1935, (Aus.) Wozzeck, Lulu.

Hector Berlioz, 1803-1869, (F.) Damnation of Faust, Symphonie Fantastique, Requiem.

Georges Bizet, 1838-1875, (F.) Carmen, Pearl Fishers.

Ernest Bloch, 1880-1959, (Swiss) Schelomo, Voice in the Wilderness, Sacred Service.

Luigi Boccherini, 1743-1805, (It.) Cello Concerto in B Flat, Symphony in C.

Alexander Borodin, 1833-1887, (R.) Prince Igor, In the Steppes of Central Asia.

Johannes Brahms, 1833-1897, (G.) Liebeslieder Waltzes, Rhapsody in E Flat Major, Opus 119 for Piano, Academic Festival Overture; symphonies; quartets.

Benjamin Britten, 1913-1976, (Br.) Peter Grimes, Turn of the Screw, Ceremony of Carols, War Requiem.

Anton Bruckner, 1824-1896, (Aus.) Symphonies (Romantic), Intermezzo for String Quintet.

Ferruccio Busoni, 1866-1924, (It.) Doctor Faust, Comedy Overture.

Dietrich Buxtehude, 1637-1707, (D.) Cantatas, trio sonatas.

William Byrd, 1543-1623, (Br.) Masses, sacred songs.

(Alexis-) Emmanuel Chabrier, 1841-1894, (Fr.) Le Roi Malgre Lui, Espana.

Gustave Charpentier, 1860-1956, (F.) Louise.

Frederic Chopin, 1810-1849, (P.) Polonaises, mazurkas, waltzes, etudes, nocturnes. Polonaise No. 6 in A Flat Major (Heroic); sonatas.

Aaron Copland, b. 1900, (U.S.) Appalachian Spring.

(Achille-) Claude Debussy, 1862-1918, (F.) Pelleas et Melisande, La Mer, Prelude to the Afternoon of a Faun.

C.P. Leo Delibes, 1836-1891, (F.) Lakme, Coppelia, Sylvia.

Norman Dello Joio, b. 1913, (U.S.), Triumph of St. Joan, Psalm of David.

Gaetano Donizetti, 1797-1848, (It.) Elixir of Love, Lucia Di Lammermoor, Daughter of the Regiment.

Paul Dukas, 1865-1935, (Fr.) Sorcerer's Apprentice.

Antonin Dvorak, 1841-1904, (C.) Symphony in E Minor (From the New World).

Edward Elgar, 1857-1934, (Br.) Pomp and Circumstance.

Manuel de Falla, 1876-1946, (Sp.) La Vide Breve, El Amor Brujo.

Gabriel Faure, 1845-1924, (Fr.) Requiem, Ballade.

Friedrich von Flotow, 1812-1883, (G.) Martha.

Cesar Franck, 1822-1890, (Belg.) D Minor Symphony.

Umberto Giordano, 1867-1948, (It.) Andrea Chenier.

Alexander K. Glazunoff, 1865-1936, (R.) Symphonies, Stenka Razin.

Mikhail Glinka, 1804-1857, (R.) Ruslan and Ludmilla.

Christoph W. Gluck, 1714-1787, (G.) Alceste, Iphigenie en Tauride.

Charles Gounod, 1818-1893, (F.) Faust, Romeo and Juliet.

Edvard Grieg, 1843-1907, (Nor.) Peer Gynt Suite, Concerto in A Minor.

George Frederick Handel, 1685-1759, (G., Br.) Messiah, Xerxes, Berenice.

Howard Hanson, 1896-1981, (U.S.) Symphonies No. 1 (Nordic) and 2 (Romantic).

Roy Harris, 1898-1979, (U.S.) Symphonies, Amer. Portraits.

Joseph Haydn, 1732-1809, (Aus.) Symphonies (Clock); oratorios; chamber music.

Paul Hindemith, 1895-1963, (U.S.) Mathis Der Maler.

Gustav Holst, 1874-1934, (Br.) The Planets.

Arthur Honegger, 1892-1955, (Swiss) Judith, Le Roi David, Pacific 231.

Alan Hovhaness, b. 1911, (U.S.) Symphonies, Magnificat.

Engelbert Humperdinck, 1854-1921, (G.) Hansel and Gretel.

Charles Ives, 1874-1954, (U.S.) Third Symphony.

Aram Khachaturian, 1903-1978, (Armen.) Gayane (ballet), symphonies.

Zoltan Kodaly, 1882-1967, (Hung.) Hary Janos, Psalmus Hungaricus.

Fritz Kreisler, 1875-1962, (Aus.) Caprice Viennois, Tambourin Chinois.

Rodolphe Kreutzer, 1766-1831, (F.) 40 etudes for violin.

Edouard V.A. Lalo, 1823-1892, (F.) Symphonie Espagnole.

Ruggiero Leoncavallo, 1857-1919, (It.) Pagliacci.

Franz Liszt, 1811-1886, (Hung.) 20 Hungarian rhapsodies; symphonic poems.

Edward MacDowell, 1861-1908, (U.S.) To a Wild Rose.

Gustav Mahler, 1860-1911, (Aus.) Lied von der Erde.

Pietro Mascagni, 1863-1945, (It.) Cavalleria Rusticana.

Jules Massenet, 1842-1912, (F.) Manon, Le Cid, Thais.

Felix Mendelssohn, 1809-1847, (G.) Midsummer Night's Dream, Songs Without Words.

Gian-Carlo Menotti, b. 1911, (It.-U.S.) The Medium, The Consul, Amahl and the Night Visitors.

Giacomo Meyerbeer, 1791-1864, (G.) Robert le Diable, Les Huguenots.

Claudio Monteverdi, 1567-1643, (It.) Opera; masses; madrigals.

Wolfgang Amadeus Mozart, 1756-1791, (Aus.) Magic Flute, Marriage of Figaro; concertos; symphonies, etc.

Modest Moussorgsky, 1835-1881, (R.) Boris Godunov, Pictures at an Exhibition.

Jacques Offenbach, 1819-1880, (F.) Tales of Hoffmann.

Carl Orff, 1895-1982, (G.) Carmina Burana.

Ignace Paderewski, 1860-1941, (P.) Minuet in G.

Giovanni P. da Palestrina, c. 1525-1594, (It.) Masses; madrigals.

Amilcare Ponchielli, 1834-1886, (It.) La Gioconda.

Francis Poulenc, 1899-1963, (F.) Dialogues des Carmelites.

Serge Prokofiev, 1891-1953, (R.) Love for Three Oranges, Lt. Kije, Peter and the Wolf.

Giacomo Puccini, 1858-1924, (It.) La Boheme, Manon Lescaut, Tosca, Madame Butterfly.

Sergei Rachmaninov, 1873-1943, (R.) 24 preludes, E concerti, 4 symphonies. Prelude in C Sharp Minor.

Maurice Ravel, 1875-1937, (Fr.) Bolero, Daphnis et Chloe, Rapsodie Espagnole.

Nikolai Rimsky-Korsakov, 1844-1908, (R.) Golden Cockerel, Capriccio Espagnol, Scheherazade, Russian Easter Overture.

Gioacchino Rossini, 1792-1868, (It.) Barber of Seville, Semiramide, William Tell.

Chas. Camille Saint-Saens, 1835-1921, (F.) Samson and Delilah, Danse Macabre.

Alessandro Scarlatti, 1660-1725, (It.) Cantatas; concertos.

Domenico Scarlatti, 1685-1757, (It.) Harpsichord sonatas.

Arnold Schoenberg, 1874-1951, (Aus.) Pelleas and Melisande, Transfigured Night, De Profundis.

Franz Schubert, 1797-1828, (A.) Lieder; symphonies (Unfinished); overtures (Rosamunde).

William Schuman, b. 1910, (U.S.) Credendum, New England Triptych.

Robert Schumann, 1810-1856, (G.) Symphonies, songs.

Aleksandr Scriabin, 1872-1915, (R.) Prometheus.

Dimitri Shostakovich, 1906-1975, (R.) Symphonies, Lady Macbeth of Mzensk, The Nose.

Jean Sibelius, 1865-1957, (Finn.) Finlandia, Karelia.

Bedrich Smetana, 1824-1884, (Cz.) The Bartered Bride.

Karlheinz Stockhausen, b. 1928, (G.) Kontrapunkte, Kontakte.

Richard Strauss, 1864-1949, (G.) Salome, Elektra, Der Rosenkavalier, Thus Spake Zarathustra.

Igor F. Stravinsky, 1882-1971, (R.-U.S.) Oedipus Rex, Le Sacre du Printemps, Petrushka.

Peter I. Tchaikovsky, 1840-1893, (R.) Nutcracker Suite, Swan Lake, Eugene Onegin.

Ambroise Thomas, 1811-1896, (F.) Mignon.

Virgil Thomson, b. 1896, (U.S.) Opera, ballet; Four Saints in Three Acts.

Ralph Vaughan Williams, 1872-1958, (Br.) Job, London Symphony, Symphony No. 7 (Antartica).

Giuseppe Verdi, 1813-1901, (It.) Aida, Rigoletto, Don Carlo, Il Trovatore, La Traviata, Falstaff, Macbeth.

Heitor Villa-Lobos, 1887-1959, (Brazil) Choros.

Antonio Vivaldi, 1678-1741, (It.) Concerti, The Four Seasons.

Richard Wagner, 1813-1883, (G.) Rienzi, Tannhauser, Lohengrin, Tristan und Isolde.

Carl Maria von Weber, 1786-1826, (G.) Der Freischutz.

Noted Jazz Artists

Jazz has been called America's only completely unique contribution to Western culture. The following individuals have made major contributions in this field:

Julian "Cannonball" Adderley, 1928-1975: alto sax.

Louis "Satchmo" Armstrong, 1900-1971: trumpet, singer; originated the "scat" vocal.

Mildred Bailey, 1907-1951: blues singer.

Chet Baker, 1929-1988: trumpet.

Count Basie, 1904-1964: orchestra leader, piano.

Sidney Bechet, 1897-1950: early innovator, soprano sax.

Bix Beiderbecke, 1903-1931: cornet, piano, composer.

Bunny Berrigan, 1909-1942: trumpet, singer.

Barney Bigard, 1906-1980: clarinet.

Art Blakey, b. 1919: drums, leader.

Jimmy Blanton, 1921-1942: bass.

Charles "Buddy" Bolden, 1868-1931: cornet; formed the first jazz band in the 1890s.

Big Bill Broonzy, 1893-1958: blues singer, guitar.

Clifford Brown, 1930-1956: trumpet.

Ray Brown, b. 1926: bass.

Dave Brubeck, b. 1920: piano, combo leader.

Don Byas, b. 1912: tenor sax.

Harry Carney, 1910-1974: baritone sax.

Benny Carter, b. 1907: alto sax, trumpet, clarinet.

Ron Carter, b. 1937: bass, cello.

Sidney Catlett, 1910-1951: drums.

Charlie Christian, 1919-1942: guitar.

Kenny Clarke, 1914-1985: pioneer of modern drums.

Buck Clayton, b. 1911: trumpet, arranger.

Al Cohn, b. 1925: tenor sax, composer.

Cozy Cole, 1909-1981: drums.

Ornette Coleman, b. 1930: saxophone; unorthodox style.

John Coltrane, 1926-1967: tenor sax innovator.

Eddie Condon, 1904-1973: guitar, band leader; promoter of Dixieland.

Chick Corea, b. 1941: pianist, composer.

Tadd Dameron, 1917-1965: piano, composer.

Eddie "Lockjaw" Davis, 1922-1987: tenor sax.

Miles Davis, b. 1926: trumpet; pioneer of cool jazz.

Wild Bill Davison, b. 1906: cornet, leader; prominent in early Chicago jazz.

Buddy De Franco, b. 1933: clarinet.

Paul Desmond, 1924-1977: alto sax.

Vic Dickenson, 1906-1984: trombone, composer.

Warren "Baby" Dodds, 1898-1959: Dixieland drummer.

Johnny Dodds, 1892-1940: clarinet.

Eric Dolphy, 1928-1964: alto sax, composer.

Jimmy Dorsey, 1904-1957: clarinet, alto sax; band leader.

Tommy Dorsey, 1905-1956: trombone; band leader.

Roy Eldridge, b. 1911: trumpet, drums, singer.

Duke Ellington, 1899-1974: piano, band leader, composer.

Bill Evans, 1929-1980: piano.

Gil Evans, 1912-1988: composer, arranger, piano.

Ella Fitzgerald, b. 1918: singer.

"Red" Garland, 1923-1984: piano.

Erroll Garner, 1921-1977: piano, composer, "Misty."

Stan Getz, b. 1927: tenor sax.

Dizzy Gillespie, b. 1917: trumpet, composer; bop developer.

Benny Goodman, 1909-1986: clarinet, band and combo leader.

Dexter Gordon, b. 1923: tenor sax; bop-derived style.

Stephane Grappelli, b. 1908: violin.

Bobby Hackett, 1915-1976: trumpet, cornet.

Lionel Hampton, b. 1913: vibes, drums, piano, combo leader.
Herbie Hancock, b. 1940: piano, composer.
W. C. Handy, 1873-1958: composer, "St. Louis Blues."
Coleman Hawkins, 1904-1969: tenor sax; 1939 recording of "Body and Soul", a classic.
Roy Haynes, b. 1926: drums.
Fletcher Henderson, 1898-1952: orchestra leader, arranger; pioneered jazz and dance bands of the 30s.
Woody Herman, b. 1913: clarinet, alto sax, band leader.
Jay C. Higginbotham, 1906-1973: trombone.
Earl "Fatha" Hines, 1905-1983: piano, songwriter.
Johnny Hodges, 1906-1971: alto sax.
Billie Holiday, 1915-1959: blues singer, "Strange Fruit."
Sam "Lightnin' " Hopkins, 1912-1982: blues singer, guitar.
Mahalia Jackson, 1911-1972: gospel singer.
Milt Jackson, b. 1923: vibes, piano, guitar.
Illinois Jacquet, b. 1922: tenor sax.
Keith Jarrett, b. 1945: technically phenomenal pianist.
Blind Lemon Jefferson, 1897-1930: blues singer, guitar.
Bunk Johnson, 1879-1949: cornet, trumpet.
James P. Johnson, 1891-1955: piano, composer.
J. J. Johnson, b. 1924: trombone, composer.
Elvin Jones, b. 1927: drums.
Jo Jones, 1911-1985: drums.
Philly Joe Jones, 1923-1985: drums.
Quincy Jones, b. 1933: arranger.
Thad Jones, 1923-1986: trumpet, cornet.
Scott Joplin, 1868-1917: composer; "Maple Leaf Rag."
Stan Kenton, 1912-1979: orchestra leader, composer, piano.
Barney Kessel, b. 1923: guitar.
Lee Konitz, b. 1927: alto sax.
Gene Krupa, 1909-1973: drums, band and combo leader.
Scott LaFaro, 1936-1961: bass.
Huddie Ledbetter (Leadbelly), 1888-1949: blues singer, guitar.
John Lewis, b. 1920: composer, piano, combo leader.
Jimmie Lunceford, 1902-1947: band leader, sax.
Herbie Mann, b. 1930: flute.
Wynton Marsalis, b. 1961: trumpet.
Jimmy McPartland, b. 1907: trumpet.
Marian McPartland, b. 1920: piano.
Glenn Miller, 1904-1944: trombone, dance band leader.
Charles Mingus, 1922-1979: bass, composer, combo leader.
Thelonious Monk, 1920-1982: piano, composer, combo leader; a developer of bop.
Wes Montgomery, 1925-1968: guitar.
"Jelly Roll" Morton, 1885-1941: composer, piano, singer.
Bennie Moten, 1894-1935: piano; an early organizer of large jazz orchestras.
Gerry Mulligan, b. 1927: baritone sax, arranger, leader.
Turk Murphy, 1915-1987: trombone, band leader.
Theodore "Fats" Navarro, 1923-1950: trumpet.
Red Nichols, 1905-1965: cornet, combo leader.
Red Norvo, b. 1908: vibes, band leader.
Anita O'Day, b. 1919: singer.
King Oliver, 1885-1938: cornet, band leader; teacher of Louis Armstrong.
Kid Ory, 1886-1973: trombone, "Muskrat Ramble".

Charlie "Bird" Parker, 1920-1955: alto sax, composer; rated by many as the greatest jazz improviser.
Art Pepper, 1925-1983: alto sax.
Oscar Peterson, b. 1925: piano, composer, combo leader.
Oscar Pettiford, 1922-1960: a leading bassist in the bop era.
Bud Powell, 1924-1966: piano; modern jazz pioneer.
Sun Ra, b. 1915?: big band leader, pianist, composer.
Gertrude "Ma" Rainey, 1886-1939: blues singer.
Don Redman, 1900-1964: composer, arranger; pioneer in the evolution of the large orchestra.
Django Reinhardt, 1910-1953: guitar; Belgian gypsy, first European to influence American jazz.
Buddy Rich, 1917-1987: drums, band leader.
Max Roach, b. 1925: drums.
Sonny Rollins, b. 1929: tenor sax.
Frank Rosollino, 1926-1978: trombone.
Jimmy Rushing, 1903-1972: blues singer.
George Russell, b. 1923: composer, piano.
Pee Wee Russell, 1906-1969: clarinet.
Artie Shaw, b. 1910: clarinet, combo leader.
George Shearing, b. 1919: piano, composer, "Lullaby of Birdland."
Horace Silver, b. 1928: piano, combo leader.
Zoot Sims, 1925-1985: tenor, alto sax; clarinet.
Zutty Singleton, 1898-1975: Dixieland drummer.
Bessie Smith, 1894-1937: blues singer.
Clarence "Pinetop" Smith, 1904-1929: piano, singer; pioneer of boogie woogie.
Willie "The Lion" Smith, 1897-1973: stride style pianist.
Muggsy Spanier, 1906-1967: cornet, band leader.
Billy Strayhorn, 1915-67: composer, piano.
Sonny Stitt, 1924-1982: alto, tenor sax.
Art Tatum, 1910-1956: piano; technical virtuoso.
Billy Taylor, b. 1921: piano, composer.
Cecil Taylor, b. 1933: piano, composer.
Jack Teagarden, 1905-1964: trombone, singer.
Dave Tough, 1908-1948: drums.
Lennie Tristano, 1919-1978: piano, composer.
Joe Turner, 1911-1985: blues singer.
McCoy Tyner, b. 1938: piano, composer.
Sarah Vaughan, b. 1924: singer.
Joe Venuti, 1904-1978: first great jazz violinist.
Thomas "Fats" Waller, 1904-1943: piano, singer, composer. "Ain't Misbehavin' ".
Dinah Washington, 1924-1963: singer.
Chick Webb, 1902-1939: band leader, drums.
Ben Webster, 1909-1973: tenor sax.
Paul Whiteman, 1890-1967: orchestra leader; a major figure in the introduction of jazz to a large audience.
Charles "Cootie" Williams, 1908-1985: trumpet, band leader.
Mary Lou Williams, 1914-1981: piano, composer.
Teddy Wilson, 1912-1986: piano, composer.
Kai Winding, 1922-1983: trombone, composer.
Jimmy Yancey, 1894-1951: piano.
Lester "Pres" Young, 1909-1959: tenor sax, composer: a bop pioneer.

Top Prices for Artworks

Source: Christie's International PLC

The following are the ten most expensive works of art sold at auction as of Jan. 1988:

Work of Art, Artist	Year sold	Price (millions)	Work of Art, Artists	Year sold	Price (millions)
"Irises", van Gogh	1987	$53.9	"Adoration of the Magi", Mantegna	1985	$10.4
"Sunflowers", van Gogh	1987	39.9	"Portrait of a Young Girl Wearing a Gold-Trimmed Cloak", Rembrandt	1986	10.3
"The Bridge of Trinquetaille", van Gogh	1987	20.2	"Seascape: Folkestone", Turner	1984	10.0
"The Gospels of Henry the Lion", 12th-century manuscript	1983	11.9	"Landscape With Rising Sun", van Gogh	1985	9.9
"Rue Mosnier With Street Pavers", Manet	1966	11.0	"Woman Reading", Braque	1986	9.5

All-Time Top 50 Films

Source: *Variety*, January, 1988

Rental figures are in absolute dollars, reflecting actual amounts received by the distributors (estimated for movies in current release). Ticket price inflation favors recent films, but older films have the advantage of numerous reissues adding to their totals.

Title	Total Rentals
1. E.T. The Extra-Terrestrial; 1982	$ 228 379 346
2. Star Wars; 1977	193 500 000
3. Return of the Jedi; 1983	168 002 414
4. The Empire Strikes Back; 1980	141 600 000
5. Jaws; 1975	129 549 242
6. Ghostbusters; 1984	128 264 005
7. Raiders of the Lost Ark; 1981	115 598 000
8. Indiana Jones and the Temple of Doom; 1984	109 000 000
9. Beverly Hills Cop; 1984	108 000 000
10. Back to the Future; 1985	104 237 346
11. Grease; 1978	96 300 000
12. Tootsie; 1982	95 268 806
13. The Exorcist; 1973	89 000 000
14. The Godfather; 1972	86 275 000
15. Superman; 1978	82 800 000
16. Close Encounters of the Third Kind; 1977/1981	82 750 000
17. Beverly Hills Cop II; 1987	80 857 776
18. The Sound of Music; 1965	$ 79 748 000
19. Gremlins; 1984	79 500 000
20. Top Gun; 1986	79 400 000
21. Rambo Part II: First Blood; 1985	78 919 250
22. Gone With the Wind; 1939	77 612 077
23. Rocky IV; 1985	75 974 593
24. Saturday Night Fever; 1977	74 100 000
25. The Sting; 1973	71 366 309
26. Crocodile Dundee; 1986	70 227 000
27. Platoon; 1986	69 742 143
28. Rocky III; 1982	66 235 909
29. Superman II; 1981	65 100 000
30. Snow White & the Seven Dwarfs; 1937	62 750 000
31. National Lampoon's Animal House; 1978	62 400 928
32. On Golden Pond; 1981	61 174 744
33. Kramer vs. Kramer; 1979	59 986 335
34. One Flew Over the Cuckoo's Nest; 1975	$ 59 930 732
35. Nine To Five; 1980	59 100 100
36. Smokey and the Bandit; 1977	59 949 900
37. Stir Crazy; 1980	58 364 420
38. The Karate Kid Part II; 1986	57 700 000
39. Star Trek IV: The Voyage Home; 1986	56 820 071
40. Rocky; 1976	56 521 647
41. Star Trek; 1979	56 000 000
42. An Officer and a Gentleman; 1982	55 223 000
43. American Graffiti; 1973	55 128 252
44. Porky's; 1982	54 000 000
45. The Towering Inferno; 1975	52 000 000
46. Every Which Way But Loose; 1978	51 900 000
47. Jaws; 1978	50 431 964
48. Terms of Endearment; 1983	50 250 000
49. Love Story; 1970	50 000 000
50. The Color Purple; 1985	49 000 000

Motion Picture Academy Awards (Oscars)

1927-28
Actor: Emil Jannings, *The Way of All Flesh.*
Actress: Janet Gaynor, *Seventh Heaven.*
Director: Frank Borzage, *Seventh Heaven;* Lewis Milestone, *Two Arabian Knights.*
Picture: *Wings,* Paramount.

1928-29
Actor: Warner Baxter, *In Old Arizona.*
Actress: Mary Pickford, *Coquette.*
Director: Frank Lloyd, *The Divine Lady.*
Picture: *Broadway Melody,* MGM.

1929-30
Actor: George Arliss, *Disraeli.*
Actress: Norma Shearer, *The Divorcee.*
Director: Lewis Milestone, *All Quiet on the Western Front.*
Picture: *All Quiet on the Western Front,* Univ.

1930-31
Actor: Lionel Barrymore, *Free Soul.*
Actress: Marie Dressler, *Min and Bill.*
Director: Norman Taurog, *Skippy.*
Picture: *Cimarron,* RKO.

1931-32
Actor: Fredric March, *Dr. Jekyll and Mr. Hyde;* Wallace Beery, *The Champ* (tie).
Actress: Helen Hayes, *Sin of Madelon Claudet.*
Director: Frank Borzage, *Bad Girl.*
Picture: *Grand Hotel,* MGM.
Special: Walt Disney, *Mickey Mouse.*

1932-33
Actor: Charles Laughton, *Private Life of Henry VIII.*
Actress: Katharine Hepburn, *Morning Glory.*
Director: Frank Lloyd, *Cavalcade.*
Picture: *Cavalcade,* Fox.

1934
Actor: Clark Gable, *It Happened One Night.*
Actress: Claudette Colbert, same.
Director: Frank Capra, *It Happened One Night.*
Picture: *It Happened One Night,* Columbia.

1935
Actor: Victor McLaglen, *The Informer.*
Actress: Bette Davis, *Dangerous.*
Director: John Ford, *The Informer.*
Picture: *Mutiny on the Bounty,* MGM.

1936
Actor: Paul Muni, *Story of Louis Pasteur.*
Actress: Luise Rainer, *The Great Ziegfeld.*
Sup. Actor: Walter Brennan, *Come and Get It.*
Sup. Actress: Gale Sondergaard, *Anthony Adverse.*
Director: Frank Capra, *Mr. Deeds Goes to Town.*
Picture: *The Great Ziegfeld,* MGM.

1937
Actor: Spencer Tracy, *Captains Courageous.*
Actress: Luise Rainer, *The Good Earth.*
Sup. Actor: Joseph Schildkraut, *Life of Emile Zola.*
Sup. Actress: Alice Brady, *In Old Chicago.*
Director: Leo McCarey, *The Awful Truth.*
Picture: *Life of Emile Zola,* Warner.

1938
Actor: Spencer Tracy, *Boys Town.*
Actress: Bette Davis, *Jezebel.*
Sup. Actor: Walter Brennan, *Kentucky.*
Sup. Actress: Fay Bainter, *Jezebel.*
Director: Frank Capra, *You Can't Take It With You.*
Picture: *You Can't Take It With You,* Columbia.

1939
Actor: Robert Donat, *Goodbye Mr. Chips.*
Actress: Vivien Leigh, *Gone With the Wind.*
Sup. Actor: Thomas Mitchell, *Stage Coach.*
Sup. Actress: Hattie McDaniel, *Gone With the Wind.*
Director: Victor Fleming, *Gone With the Wind.*
Picture: *Gone With the Wind,* Selznick International.

1940
Actor: James Stewart, *The Philadelphia Story.*
Actress: Ginger Rogers, *Kitty Foyle.*
Sup. Actor: Walter Brennan, *The Westerner.*
Sup. Actress: Jane Darwell, *The Grapes of Wrath.*
Director: John Ford, *The Grapes of Wrath.*
Picture: *Rebecca,* Selznick International.

1941
Actor: Gary Cooper, *Sergeant York.*
Actress: Joan Fontaine, *Suspicion.*
Sup. Actor: Donald Crisp, *How Green Was My Valley.*
Sup. Actress: Mary Astor, *The Great Lie.*
Director: John Ford, *How Green Was My Valley.*
Picture: *How Green Was My Valley,* 20th Cent.-Fox.

1942
Actor: James Cagney, *Yankee Doodle Dandy*.
Actress: Greer Garson, *Mrs. Miniver*.
Sup. Actor: Van Heflin, *Johnny Eager*.
Sup. Actress: Teresa Wright, *Mrs. Miniver*.
Director: William Wyler, *Mrs. Miniver*.
Picture: *Mrs. Miniver*, MGM.

1943
Actor: Paul Lukas, *Watch on the Rhine*.
Actress: Jennifer Jones, *The Song of Bernadette*.
Sup. Actor: Charles Coburn, *The More the Merrier*.
Sup. Actress: Katina Paxinou, *For Whom the Bell Tolls*.
Director: Michael Curtiz, *Casablanca*.
Picture: *Casablanca*, Warner.

1944
Actor: Bing Crosby, *Going My Way*.
Actress: Ingrid Bergman, *Gaslight*.
Sup. Actor: Barry Fitzgerald, *Going My Way*.
Sup. Actress: Ethel Barrymore, *None But the Lonely Heart*.
Director: Leo McCarey, *Going My Way*.
Picture: *Going My Way*, Paramount.

1945
Actor: Ray Milland, *The Lost Weekend*.
Actress: Joan Crawford, *Mildred Pierce*.
Sup. Actor: James Dunn, *A Tree Grows in Brooklyn*.
Sup. Actress: Anne Revere, *National Velvet*.
Director: Billy Wilder, *The Lost Weekend*.
Picture: *The Lost Weekend*, Paramount.

1946
Actor: Fredric March, *Best Years of Our Lives*.
Actress: Olivia de Havilland, *To Each His Own*.
Sup. Actor: Harold Russell, *The Best Years of Our Lives*.
Sup. Actress: Anne Baxter, *The Razor's Edge*.
Director: William Wyler, *The Best Years of Our Lives*.
Picture: *The Best Years of Our Lives*, Goldwyn, RKO.

1947
Actor: Ronald Colman, *A Double Life*.
Actress: Loretta Young, *The Farmer's Daughter*.
Sup. Actor: Edmund Gwenn, *Miracle on 34th Street*.
Sup. Actress: Celeste Holm, *Gentleman's Agreement*.
Director: Elia Kazan, *Gentleman's Agreement*.
Picture: *Gentleman's Agreement*, 20th Cent.-Fox.

1948
Actor: Laurence Olivier, *Hamlet*.
Actress: Jane Wyman, *Johnny Belinda*.
Sup. Actor: Walter Huston, *Treasure of Sierra Madre*.
Sup. Actress: Claire Trevor, *Key Largo*.
Director: John Huston, *Treasure of Sierra Madre*.
Picture: *Hamlet*, Two Cities Film, Universal International.

1949
Actor: Broderick Crawford, *All the King's Men*.
Actress: Olivia de Havilland, *The Heiress*.
Sup. Actor: Dean Jagger, *Twelve O'Clock High*.
Sup. Actress: Mercedes McCambridge, *All the King's Men*.
Director: Joseph L. Mankiewicz, *Letter to Three Wives*.
Picture: *All the King's Men*, Columbia.

1950
Actor: Jose Ferrer, *Cyrano de Bergerac*.
Actress: Judy Holliday, *Born Yesterday*.
Sup. Actor: George Sanders, *All About Eve*.
Sup. Actress: Josephine Hull, *Harvey*.
Director: Joseph L. Mankiewicz, *All About Eve*.
Picture: *All About Eve*, 20th Century-Fox.

1951
Actor: Humphrey Bogart, *The African Queen*.
Actress: Vivien Leigh, *A Streetcar Named Desire*.
Sup. Actor: Karl Malden, *A Streetcar Named Desire*.
Sup. Actress: Kim Hunter, *A Streetcar Named Desire*.
Director: George Stevens, *A Place in the Sun*.
Picture: *An American in Paris*, MGM.

1952
Actor: Gary Cooper, *High Noon*.
Actress: Shirley Booth, *Come Back, Little Sheba*.
Sup. Actor: Anthony Quinn, *Viva Zapata!*
Sup. Actress: Gloria Grahame, *The Bad and the Beautiful*.
Director: John Ford, *The Quiet Man*.
Picture: *Greatest Show on Earth*, C.B. DeMille, Paramount.

1953
Actor: William Holden, *Stalag 17*.
Actress: Audrey Hepburn, *Roman Holiday*.
Sup. Actor: Frank Sinatra, *From Here to Eternity*.
Sup. Actress: Donna Reed, *From Here to Eternity*.
Director: Fred Zinnemann, *From Here to Eternity*.
Picture: *From Here to Eternity*, Columbia.

1954
Actor: Marlon Brando, *On the Waterfront*.
Actress: Grace Kelly, *The Country Girl*.
Sup. Actor: Edmond O'Brien, *The Barefoot Contessa*.
Sup. Actress: Eva Marie Saint, *On the Waterfront*.
Director: Elia Kazan, *On the Waterfront*.
Picture: *On the Waterfront*, Horizon-American, Colum.

1955
Actor: Ernest Borgnine, *Marty*.
Actress: Anna Magnani, *The Rose Tattoo*.
Sup. Actor: Jack Lemmon, *Mister Roberts*.
Sup. Actress: Jo Van Fleet, *East of Eden*.
Director: Delbert Mann, *Marty*.
Picture: *Marty*, Hecht and Lancaster's Steven Prods., U.A.

1956
Actor: Yul Brynner, *The King and I*.
Actress: Ingrid Bergman, *Anastasia*.
Sup. Actor: Anthony Quinn, *Lust for Life*.
Sup. Actress: Dorothy Malone, *Written on the Wind*.
Director: George Stevens, *Giant*.
Picture: *Around the World in 80 Days*, Michael Todd, U.A.

1957
Actor: Alec Guinness, *The Bridge on the River Kwai*.
Actress: Joanne Woodward, *The Three Faces of Eve*.
Sup. Actor: Red Buttons, *Sayonara*.
Sup. Actress: Miyoshi Umeki, *Sayonara*.
Director: David Lean, *The Bridge on the River Kwai*.
Picture: *The Bridge on the River Kwai*, Columbia.

1958
Actor: David Niven, *Separate Tables*.
Actress: Susan Hayward, *I Want to Live*.
Sup. Actor: Burl Ives, *The Big Country*.
Sup. Actress: Wendy Hiller, *Separate Tables*.
Director: Vincente Minnelli, *Gigi*.
Picture: *Gigi*, Arthur Freed Production, MGM.

1959
Actor: Charlton Heston, *Ben-Hur*.
Actress: Simone Signoret, *Room at the Top*.
Sup. Actor: Hugh Griffith, *Ben-Hur*.
Sup. Actress: Shelley Winters, *Diary of Anne Frank*.
Director: William Wyler, *Ben-Hur*.
Picture: *Ben-Hur*, MGM.

1960
Actor: Burt Lancaster, *Elmer Gantry*.
Actress: Elizabeth Taylor, *Butterfield 8*.
Sup. Actor: Peter Ustinov, *Spartacus*.
Sup. Actress: Shirley Jones, *Elmer Gantry*.
Director: Billy Wilder, *The Apartment*.
Picture: *The Apartment*, Mirisch Co., U.A.

1961
Actor: Maximilian Schell, *Judgment at Nuremberg*.
Actress: Sophia Loren, *Two Women*.
Sup. Actor: George Chakiris, *West Side Story*.
Sup. Actress: Rita Moreno, *West Side Story*.
Director: Jerome Robbins, Robert Wise, *West Side Story*.
Picture: *West Side Story*, United Artists.

1962
Actor: Gregory Peck, *To Kill a Mockingbird*.
Actress: Anne Bancroft, *The Miracle Worker*.
Sup. Actor: Ed Begley, *Sweet Bird of Youth*.
Sup. Actress: Patty Duke, *The Miracle Worker*.
Director: David Lean, *Lawrence of Arabia*.
Picture: *Lawrence of Arabia*, Columbia.

1963
Actor: Sidney Poitier, *Lilies of the Field*.
Actress: Patricia Neal, *Hud*.
Sup. Actor: Melvyn Douglas, *Hud*.
Sup. Actress: Margaret Rutherford, *The V.I.P.s*.
Director: Tony Richardson, *Tom Jones*.
Picture: *Tom Jones*, Woodfall Prod., UA-Lopert Pictures.

1964
Actor: Rex Harrison, *My Fair Lady*.
Actress: Julie Andrews, *Mary Poppins*.
Sup. Actor: Peter Ustinov, *Topkapi*.
Sup. Actress: Lila Kedrova, *Zorba the Greek*.
Director: George Cukor, *My Fair Lady*.
Picture: *My Fair Lady*, Warner Bros.

1965
Actor: Lee Marvin, *Cat Ballou*.
Actress: Julie Christie, *Darling*.
Sup. Actor: Martin Balsam, *A Thousand Clowns*.
Sup. Actress: Shelley Winters, *A Patch of Blue*.
Director: Robert Wise, *The Sound of Music*.
Picture: *The Sound of Music*, 20th Century-Fox.

1966
Actor: Paul Scofield, *A Man for All Seasons.*
Actress: Elizabeth Taylor, *Who's Afraid of Virginia Woolf?*
Sup. Actor: Walter Matthau, *The Fortune Cookie.*
Sup. Actress: Sandy Dennis, *Who's Afraid of Virginia Woolf?*
Director: Fred Zinnemann, *A Man for All Seasons.*
Picture: *A Man for All Seasons,* Columbia.

1967
Actor: Rod Steiger, *In the Heat of the Night.*
Actress: Katharine Hepburn, *Guess Who's Coming to Dinner.*
Sup. Actor: George Kennedy, *Cool Hand Luke.*
Sup. Actress: Estelle Parsons, *Bonnie and Clyde.*
Director: Mike Nichols, *The Graduate.*
Picture: *In the Heat of the Night.*

1968
Actor: Cliff Robertson, *Charly.*
Actress: Katharine Hepburn, *The Lion in Winter;* Barbra
    Streisand, *Funny Girl* (tie).
Sup. Actor: Jack Albertson, *The Subject Was Roses.*
Sup. Actress: Ruth Gordon, *Rosemary's Baby.*
Director: Sir Carol Reed, *Oliver!*
Picture: *Oliver!*

1969
Actor: John Wayne, *True Grit.*
Actress: Maggie Smith, *The Prime of Miss Jean Brodie.*
Sup. Actor: Gig Young, *They Shoot Horses, Don't They?*
Sup. Actress: Goldie Hawn, *Cactus Flower.*
Director: John Schlesinger, *Midnight Cowboy.*
Picture: *Midnight Cowboy.*

1970
Actor: George C. Scott, *Patton* (refused).
Actress: Glenda Jackson, *Women in Love.*
Sup. Actor: John Mills, *Ryan's Daughter.*
Sup. Actress: Helen Hayes, *Airport.*
Director: Franklin Schaffner, *Patton.*
Picture: *Patton.*

1971
Actor: Gene Hackman, *The French Connection.*
Actress: Jane Fonda, *Klute.*
Sup. Actor: Ben Johnson, *The Last Picture Show.*
Sup. Actress: Cloris Leachman, *The Last Picture Show.*
Director: William Friedkin, *The French Connection.*
Picture: *The French Connection.*

1972
Actor: Marlon Brando, *The Godfather* (refused).
Actress: Liza Minnelli, *Cabaret.*
Sup. Actor: Joel Grey, *Cabaret.*
Sup. Actress: Eileen Heckart, *Butterflies are Free.*
Director: Bob Fosse, *Cabaret.*
Picture: *The Godfather.*

1973
Actor: Jack Lemmon, *Save the Tiger.*
Actress: Glenda Jackson, *A Touch of Class.*
Sup. Actor: John Houseman, *The Paper Chase.*
Sup. Actress: Tatum O'Neal, *Paper Moon.*
Director: George Roy Hill, *The Sting.*
Picture: *The Sting.*

1974
Actor: Art Carney, *Harry and Tonto.*
Actress: Ellen Burstyn, *Alice Doesn't Live Here Anymore.*
Sup. Actor: Robert DeNiro, *The Godfather, Part II.*
Sup. Actress: Ingrid Bergman, *Murder on the Orient Express.*
Director: Francis Ford Coppola, *The Godfather, Part II.*
Picture: *The Godfather, Part II.*

1975
Actor: Jack Nicholson, *One Flew Over the Cuckoo's Nest.*
Actress: Louise Fletcher, *One Flew Over the Cuckoo's Nest.*
Sup. Actor: George Burns, *The Sunshine Boys.*
Sup. Actress: Lee Grant, *Shampoo.*
Director: Milos Forman, *One Flew Over the Cuckoo's Nest.*
Picture: *One Flew Over the Cuckoo's Nest.*

1976
Actor: Peter Finch, *Network.*
Actress: Faye Dunaway, *Network.*
Sup. Actor: Jason Robards, *All the President's Men.*
Sup. Actress: Beatrice Straight, *Network.*
Director: John G. Avildsen, *Rocky.*
Picture: *Rocky.*

1977
Actor: Richard Dreyfuss, *The Goodbye Girl.*
Actress: Diane Keaton, *Annie Hall.*
Sup. Actor: Jason Robards, *Julia.*
Sup. Actress: Vanessa Redgrave, *Julia.*
Director: Woody Allen, *Annie Hall.*
Picture: *Annie Hall.*

1978
Actor: Jon Voight, *Coming Home.*
Actress: Jane Fonda, *Coming Home.*
Sup. Actor: Christopher Walken, *The Deer Hunter.*
Sup. Actress: Maggie Smith, *California Suite.*
Director: Michael Cimino, *The Deer Hunter.*
Picture: *The Deer Hunter.*

1979
Actor: Dustin Hoffman, *Kramer vs. Kramer.*
Actress: Sally Field, *Norma Rae.*
Sup. Actor: Melvyn Douglas, *Being There.*
Sup. Actress: Meryl Streep, *Kramer vs. Kramer.*
Director: Robert Benton, *Kramer vs. Kramer.*
Picture: *Kramer vs. Kramer.*

1980
Actor: Robert DeNiro, *Raging Bull.*
Actress: Sissy Spacek, *Coal Miner's Daughter.*
Sup. Actor: Timothy Hutton, *Ordinary People.*
Sup. Actress: Mary Steenburgen, *Melvin & Howard.*
Director: Robert Redford, *Ordinary People .*
Picture: *Ordinary People.*

1981
Actor: Henry Fonda, *On Golden Pond.*
Actress: Katharine Hepburn, *On Golden Pond.*
Sup. Actor: John Gielgud, *Arthur.*
Sup. Actress: Maureen Stapleton, *Reds.*
Director: Warren Beatty, *Reds.*
Picture: *Chariots of Fire.*

1982
Actor: Ben Kingsley, *Gandhi.*
Actress: Meryl Streep, *Sophie's Choice.*
Sup. Actor: Louis Gossett, Jr., *An Officer and a Gentleman.*
Sup. Actress: Jessica Lange, *Tootsie.*
Director: Richard Attenborough, *Gandhi.*
Picture: *Gandhi.*

1983
Actor: Robert Duvall, *Tender Mercies.*
Actress: Shirley MacLaine, *Terms of Endearment.*
Supporting Actor: Jack Nicholson, *Terms of Endearment.*
Supporting Actress: Linda Hunt, *The Year of Living Dangerously.*
Director: James L. Brooks, *Terms of Endearment.*
Picture: *Terms of Endearment.*

1984
Actor: F. Murray Abraham, *Amadeus.*
Actress: Sally Field, *Places in the Heart.*
Supporting Actor: Haing S. Ngor, *The Killing Fields.*
Supporting Actress: Peggy Ashcroft, *A Passage to India.*
Director: Milos Forman, *Amadeus.*
Picture: *Amadeus.*

1985
Actor: William Hurt, *Kiss of the Spider Woman.*
Actress: Geraldine Page, *The Trip to Bountiful.*
Supporting Actor: Don Ameche, *Cocoon.*
Supporting Actress: Anjelica Huston, *Prizzi's Honor.*
Director: Sydney Pollack, *Out of Africa.*
Picture: *Out of Africa.*

1986
Actor: Paul Newman, *The Color of Money.*
Actress: Marlee Matlin, *Children of a Lesser God.*
Supporting Actor: Michael Caine, *Hannah and Her Sisters.*
Supporting Actress: Dianne Wiest, *Hannah and Her Sisters.*
Director: Oliver Stone, *Platoon.*
Picture: *Platoon.*

1987
Picture: *The Last Emperor.*
Actor: Michael Douglas, *Wall Street.*
Actress: Cher, *Moonstruck.*
Supporting Actress: Olympia Dukakis, *Moonstruck.*
Supporting Actor: Sean Connery, *The Untouchables.*
Director: Bernardo Bertolucci, *The Last Emperor.*
Foreign Film: *Babette's Feast.*
Original Screenplay: John Patrick Shanley, *Moonstruck.*
Screenplay Adaptation: Mark Peploe, Bernarndo Bertolucci, *The Last Emperor.*
Cinematography: Vittorio Storaro: *The Last Emperor.*
Original Song: "(I've Had) The Time of My Life," *Dirty Dancing,* music Frankie Previte, John DeNicola, Donald Markowitz, lyrics Frankie Previte.
Short Film, Animated: *The Man Who Planted Trees.*
Short Film, Live: *Ray's Male Heterosexual Dance Hall.*
Documentary, Feature: *The 10-Year-Lunch.*
Documentary, Short Subject: *Young at Heart.*
Thalberg Award, to film maker, for body of work: Billy Wilder.

1987 Oscar Nominations

Picture: *Broadcast News; Fatal Attraction; Hope and Glory; The Last Emperor; Moonstruck.*

Actor: Michael Douglas, *Wall Street*; William Hurt, *Broadcast News*; Marcello Mastroianni, *Dark Eyes*; Jack Nicholson, *Ironweed*; Robin Williams, *Good Morning, Vietnam.*

Actress: Cher, *Moonstruck*; Glenn Close, *Fatal Attraction*; Holly Hunter, *Broadcast News*; Sally Kirkland, *Anna*; Meryl Streep, *Ironweed.*

Supporting Actor: Albert Brooks, *Broadcast News*; Sean Connery, *The Untouchables*; Morgan Freeman, *Street Smart*; Vincent Gardenia, *Moonstruck*; Denzel Washington, *Cry Freedom.*

Supporting Actress: Norma Aleandro, *Gaby—A True Story*; Anne Archer, *Fatal Attraction*; Olympia Dukakis, *Moonstruck*; Anne Ramsey, *Throw Momma From The Train*; Ann Sothern, *The Whales of August.*

Director: Norman Jewison, *Moonstruck*; Adrian Lyne, *Fatal Attraction*; John Boorman, *Hope and Glory*; Bernardo Bertolucci, *The Last Emperor*; Lasse Hallstrom, *My Life As A Dog.*

Foreign Film: *Au revoir les enfants* (France); *Babette's Feast* (Denmark); *Course Completed* (Spain); *The Family* (Italy); *Pathfinder* (Norway).

Original Screenplay: Louis Malle, *Au revoir les enfants*; James L. Brooks, *Broadcast News*; John Patrick Shanley, *Moonstruck*; Woody Allen, *Radio Days*; John Boorman, *Hope and Glory.*

Screenplay Adaptation: Tony Huston, *The Dead*; James Dearden, *Fatal Attraction*; Stanley Kubrick, Michael Herr and Gustav Hasford, *Full Metal Jacket*; Mark Peploe and Bernardo Bertolucci, *The Last Emperor*; Lasse Hallstrom, Reidar Jonsson, Brasse Brannstrom and Per Berglund, *My Life As A Dog.*

Cinematography: *Broadcast News; Empire of the Sun; Hope and Glory; The Last Emperor; Matewan.*

Original Song: "Cry Freedom" (*Cry Freedom*) by George Fenton and Jonas Gangwa; "(I've Had) The Time Of My Life" (*Dirty Dancing*) music by Franke Previte, John DeNicola, Donald Markowitz, lyric by Franke Previte; "Nothing's Gonna Stop Us Now" (*Mannequin*) by Albert Hammond and Diane Warren; "Shakedown" (*Beverly Hills Cop II*) music by Harold Faltermeyer, Keith Forsey, lyric by Harold Faltermeyer, Keith Forsey, Bob Seger; "Storybook Love" (*The Princess Bride*) Willy DeVille.

The Cannes Film Festival Awards, 1970-1988

1970
Best Film: *M*A*S*H** (U.S.A.)
Special Grand Jury Prize: *Investigation of a Citizen Above Suspicion* (Italy)
Best Director: John Boorman, *Leo the Last*
Best Actor: Marcello Mastroianni, *Drama of Jealousy*
Best Actress: Ottavia Piccolo, *Metello*

1971
Best Film: *The Go-Between* (Great Britain)
Special Grand Jury Prize: *Taking Off* (U.S.A.); *Johnny Got His Gun* (U.S.A.)
Best Director: (Not Awarded)[1]
Best Actor: Riccardo Cucciola, *Sacco and Vanzetti*
Best Actress: Kitty Winn, *Panic in Needle Park*

1972
Best Film: *The Working Class Goes to Paradise* (Italy); *The Mattei Affair* (Italy)
Special Grand Jury Prize: *Solaris* (U.S.S.R.)
Best Director: Miklos Jancso, *The Red Psalm*
Best Actor: Jean Yanne, *We Will Not Grow Old Together*
Best Actress: Susannah York, *Images*

1973
Best Film: *Scarecrow* (U.S.A.); *The Hireling* (Great Britain)
Special Grand Jury Prize: *The Mother and the Whore* (France)
Best Director: (Not Awarded)[1]
Best Actor: Giancarlo Giannini, *Love and Anarchy*
Best Actress: Joanne Woodward, *The Effect of Gamma Rays on Man-in-the-Moon Marigolds*

1974
Best Film: *The Conversation* (U.S.A.)
Special Jury Prize: *Il Fiore delle Mille e una Notte* (Italy)
Best Director: (Not Awarded)[1]
Best Actor: Jack Nicholson, *The Last Detail*
Best Actress: Marie-José Nat, *Les Violons du bal*

1975
Best Film: *Chronicle of the Burning Years* (Algeria)
Special Grand Jury Prize: *The Enigma of Kaspar Hauser* (W. Germany)
Best Director: Costa Gavras, *Section Spéciale*; Michel Brault, *Les Ordres*
Best Actor: Vittorio Gassman, *Scent of Woman*
Best Actress: Valerie Perrine, *Lenny*

1976
Best Film: *Taxi Driver* (U.S.A.)
Special Grand Jury Prize: *Cria Cuervos* (Spain); *The Marquise of O* (W. Germany)
Best Director: Ettore Scola, *Brutti, Sporchi, Cattivi . . .*
Best Actor: José-Luis Gómez, *La Familia de Pascual Duarte*
Best Actress: Mari Torocsik, *Deryne, hol van?*; Dominique Sanda, *L'Eredita Ferramonti*

1977
Best Film: *Padre Padrone* (Italy)
Best Director: (Not Awarded)[1]
Best Actor: Fernando Rey, *Elisa My Love*
Best Actress: Shelley Duvall, *Three Women*; Monique Mercure, *J.A. Martin, Photographe*

1978
Best Film: *The Tree of Wooden Clogs* (Italy)
Special Jury Prize: *Bye Bye Monkey* (Italy); *The Shout* (Great Britain)
Best Director: Nagisa Oshima, *Empire of Passion*
Best Actor: Jon Voight, *Coming Home*
Best Actress: Jill Clayburgh, *An Unmarried Woman*; Isabelle Huppert, *Violette Nozière*

1979
Best Film: *Apocalypse Now* (U.S.A.); *The Tin Drum* (W. Germany)
Special Jury Prize: *Siberiade* (U.S.S.R.)
Best Director: Terrance Malick, *Days of Heaven*
Best Actor: Jack Lemmon, *The China Syndrome*
Best Actress: Sally Field, *Norma Rae*

1980
Best Film: *All That Jazz* (U.S.A.); *Kagemusha* (Japan)
Special Jury Prize: *Mon Oncle d'Amérique* (France)
Best Director: Krzysztof Zanussi, *Constans*
Best Actor: Michel Piccoli, *A Leap Into The World*
Best Actress: Anouk Aimée, *A Leap Into The World*

1981
Best Film: *Man of Iron* (Poland)
Special Jury Prize: *Les années lumière* (Switzerland)
Best Director: (Not Awarded)[1]
Best Actor: Ugo Tognazzi, *A Ridiculous Man*
Best Actress: Isabelle Adjani, *Possession; Quartet*

1982
Best Film: *Missing* (U.S.A.); *Yol* (Turkey)
Special Grand Jury Prize: *The Night of San Lorenzo* (Italy)
Best Director: Werner Herzog, *Fitzcarraldo*
Best Actor: Jack Lemmon, *Missing*
Best Actress: Jadwiga Jankowska-Cieslak, *Another Way*

1983
Best Film: *The Ballad of Narayama* (Japan)
Special Grand Jury Prize: *Monty Python, The Meaning of Life* (Great Britain)
Best Director: (Not Awarded)[1]
Best Actor: Gian Maria Volonte, *The Death of Mario Ricci*
Best Actress: Hanna Schygulla, *The Story of Piera*

1984
Best Film: *Paris, Texas* (International Collaboration)
Special Grand Jury Prize: *Diary For My Children* (Hungary)
Best Director: Bertrand Tavernier, *A Sunday in the Country*
Best Actor: Francisco Rabal, Alfredo Landa, *Los Santos Innocentes*
Best Actress: Helen Mirren, *Cal*

1985	1987

Best Film: *Father's Gone on a Business Trip* (Yugoslavia)
Special Grand Jury Prize: *Birdy* (U.S.A.)
Best Director: André Techine, *Rendez-vous*
Best Actor: William Hurt, *Kiss of the Spider Woman*
Best Actress: Cher, *Mask;* Norma Aleandro, *Official Version*

Best Film: *Under Satan's Sun* (France)
Special Grand Jury Prize: *Repent* (U.S.S.R.)
Best Director: Wim Wenders, *The Wings of Desire*
Best Actor: Marcello Mastroianni, *Black Eyes*
Best Actress: Barbara Hershey, *The Bayou*

1986	1988

Best Film: *The Mission* (Great Britain)
Special Grand Jury Prize: *The Sacrifice* (Sweden)
Best Director: Martin Scorsese, *After Hours*
Best Actor: Michel Blanc, *Tenue de Soirée;* Bob Hoskins, *Mona Lisa*
Best Actress: Barbara Sukowa, *Rosa Luxemburg;* Fernanda Torres, *Speak to Me of Love*

Best Film: *Pelle The Conqueror* (Denmark)
Special Grand Jury Prize: *A World Apart* (Great Britain)
Best Director: Fernando E. Solanas, *The South*
Best Actor: Forest Whitaker, *Bird*
Best Actress: Barbara Hershey, Jodhi May and Linda Mvusi, *A World Apart*

(1) The Cannes Festival Jury is not obliged to select a winner in any category except that of Best Film.

Genie (Canadian Film) Awards, 1975-1987

Source: Academy of Canadian Cinema

The Genie Awards (known as the Canadian Film Awards from 1949 to 1978) have been presented since 1980 by the Academy of Canadian Cinema to honor achievement in the Canadian film industry. Awards apply to films released in the previous year. Voting is conducted in a 2-step process whereby the winners are chosen by all academy members from among the 5 nominees selected in each category by their respective craft branches. Winners receive a statue first known as the "Etrog" (after its sculptor, Sorel Etrog), but renamed the Genie because the name is bilingual and symbolizes the magic and creative expression of filmmaking.

Year	Best Picture	Best Actor	Best Actress
1975	*The Apprenticeship of Duddy Kravitz*	Stuart Gillard (*Why Rock the Boat?*)	Margot Kidder (*Black Christmas* and *A Quiet Day in Belfast*)
1976	*Lies My Father Told Me*	André Melançon (*Partis pour la gloire*)	Marilyn Lightstone (*Lies My Father Told Me*)
1977	*J.A. Martin photographe*	Len Cariou (*One Man*)	Monique Mercure (*J.A. Martin photographe*)
1978	*The Silent Partner*	Richard Gabourie (*Three Card Monte*)	Helen Shaver (*In Praise of Older Women*)
1980[1]	*The Changeling*	Christopher Plummer (*Murder By Decree*)	Kate Lynch (*Meatballs*)
1981	*Les Bons Débarras*	Thomas Peacocke (*The Hounds of Notre Dame*)	Marie Tifo (*Les Bons Débarras*)
1982	*Ticket to Heaven*	Nick Mancuso (*Ticket to Heaven*)	Margot Kidder (*Heartaches*)
1983	*The Grey Fox*	Donald Sutherland (*Threshold*)	Rae Dawn Chong (*Quest for Fire*)
1984	*The Terry Fox Story*	Eric Fryer (*The Terry Fox Story*)	Martha Henry (*The Wars*)
1985	*The Bay Boy*	Gabriel Arcand (*Le Crime d'Ovide Plouffe*)	Louise Marleau (*La femme de l'hotel*)
1986	*My American Cousin*	John Wildman (*My American Cousin*)	Margaret Langrick (*My American Cousin*)
1987	*The Decline Of The American Empire*	Gordon Pinsent (*John And The Missus*)	Martha Henry (*Dancing In The Dark*)

(1) No awards given in 1979.

The Genie Awards, 1988

Source: Academy of Canadian Cinema and Television

Picture: *Un Zoo la nuit/Night Zoo*
Actor: Roger Le Bel, *Un Zoo la nuit/Night Zoo*
Actress: Sheila McCarthy, *I've Heard the Mermaids Singing*
Supporting Actor: Germain Houde, *Un Zoo la nuit/Night Zoo*
Supporting Actress: Paule Baillargeon, *I've Heard the Mermaids Singing*
Director: Jean-Claude Lauzon, *Un Zoo la nuit/Night Zoo*
Screenplay: Jean-Claude Lauzon, *Un Zoo la nuit/Night Zoo*

Cinematography: Guy Dufaux, *Un Zoo la nuit/Night Zoo*
Art Direction: Jean-Baptiste Tard, *Un Zoo la nuit/Night Zoo*
Film Editing: Michel Arcand, *Un Zoo la nuit/Night Zoo*
Costume Design: Andrée Morin, *Un Zoo la nuit/Night Zoo*
Music Score: Jean Corriveau, *Un Zoo la nuit/Night Zoo*
Original Song: "Lost in a Hurricane", *Un Zoo la nuit/Night Zoo*
Documentary: *God Rides a Harley*
Short Film: *George and Rosemary*

The Gemini Awards, 1987

Source: Academy of Canadian Cinema and Television

The Gemini Awards were established in 1986 to honor outstanding contributions to the Canadian television industry. The 59 Gemini Awards, given out annually by the Academy of Canadian Cinema and Television, grew out of the former ACTRA Awards, last presented in 1985.

Best continuing drama series	"Night Heat"
Best dramatic mini-series	"Ford: The Man and the Machine"
Best TV movie	"The Marriage Bed"
Best comedy series	"Seeing Things"
Best variety series	"S & M Comic Book"
Best documentary series	"The Nature of Things"
Best children's series	"Degrassi Junior High"
Best information series	"The Journal"
Best short drama	"The Truth About Alex"
Best variety program	"The Ian & Sylvia Reunion"
Best documentary program	"The Champions Part III: The Final Battle"
Best performing arts program	"A Moving Picture"
Best animated program or series	"Babar And Father Christmas"
Best children's program	"Down at Fraggle Rock: Behind The Scenes"
Best sports program or series	"The Race Is On!"
Best special event coverage	"Royal Wedding"
Best pay TV dramatic program or series	"Daughters Of The Country"
Best performance by a lead actor in a continuing dramatic role	Eric Peterson—"Street Legal" (Even Lawyers Sing the Blues) and Winston Rekert—"Adderly" (Adderly With Eggroll)
Best performance by a lead actress in a continuing dramatic role	Dixie Seatle—"Adderly" (A Matter of Discretion)
Best performance by a lead actor in a single dramatic program or mini-series	Booth Savage—"The Last Season"
Best performance by a lead actress in a single dramatic program or mini-series	Victoria Snow—"Daughters Of The Country" (The Wake)
Best performance by a lead actor in a continuing role in a comedy series	Louis Del Grande—"Seeing Things" (Here's Looking At You)
Best performance by a lead actress in a continuing role in a comedy series	Dinah Christie—"Check It Out!" (Love and Marriage)
Best performance by a supporting actor	Eugene Clark—"Night Heat" (Fire and Ice)
Best performance by a supporting actress	Vivian Reis—"The Marriage Bed"

The Emmy Awards, 1987-88

Drama series	*thirtysomething*, ABC
Comedy series	*The Wonder Years*, ABC
Mini-series	*The Murder of Mary Phagan*, NBC
Variety (music or comedy)	*Irving Berlin's 100th Birthday Celebration*, CBS
Drama-comedy special	*Inherit the Wind*, NBC
Actor (drama series)	Richard Kiley, *A Year in The Life*, NBC
Actor (comedy series)	Michael J. Fox, *Family Ties*, NBC
Actor (mini-series or special)	Jason Robards, *Inherit the Wind*, NBC
Actress (drama series)	Tyne Daly, *Cagney & Lacey*, CBS
Actress (comedy series)	Beatrice Arthur, *The Golden Girls*, NBC
Actress (mini-series or special)	Jessica Tandy, *Foxfire: Hallmark Hall of Fame*, CBS
Supporting actress (drama series)	Patricia Wettig, *thirtysomething*, ABC
Supporting actress (comedy series)	Estelle Getty, *The Golden Girls*, NBC
Supporting actress (mini-series or special)	Jane Seymour, *Onassis: The Richest Man in The World*, ABC
Supporting actor (drama series)	Larry Drake, *L.A. Law*, NBC
Supporting actor (comedy series)	John Larroquette, *Night Court*, NBC
Supporting actor (mini-series or special)	John Shea, *Baby M*, ABC
Individual performance (variety or music)	Robin Williams, *ABC Presents A Royal Gala*, ABC
Writing (drama series)	*thirtysomething: Business as Usual*, ABC
Writing (comedy series)	*Frank's Place: The Bridge*, CBS
Writing (mini-series or special)	*The Attic: The Hiding of Anne Frank, General Foods Golden Showcase*, CBS
Writing (variety or music)	*Jackie Mason On Broadway*, HBO
Directing (drama series)	*St. Elsewhere: Weigh In, Way Out*, NBC
Directing (comedy series)	*Hooperman: Pilot*, ABC
Directing (mini-series or special)	*Gore Vidal's Lincoln*, NBC
Directing (variety or music)	*Celebrating Gershwin: Great Performances*, PBS
Music direction	*Julie Andrews. . .The Sound of Christmas*, ABC
Costume design (variety or music)	*Las Vegas: An All Star 75th Anniversary Special*, ABC

Longest-Running Canadian TV Shows

Source: CBC; CTV

(up to the end of the 1987-88 season)

Program	Seasons	Program	Seasons
Hockey Night in Canada	36 (1952-)	Expos Baseball	17 (1971-)
CFL Football	36 (1952-)	Canada AM	16 (1972-)
Country Canada/Country Calendar	34 (1954-)	The Beachcombers	16 (1972-)
Front Page Challenge	31 (1957-)	Market Place	16 (1972-)
The Nature of Things	28 (1960-)	Meeting Place	16 (1972-)
The Friendly Giant	27 (1958-85)	What's New	16 (1972-)
Hymn Sing	23 (1965-)	Definition	14 (1974-)
The Tommy Hunter Show	23 (1965-)	the fifth estate	13 (1975-)
Wide World of Sports	23 (1965-)	Live It Up	11 (1977-)
Romper Room	22 (1966-)	What's Cooking	11 (1977-)
W-5	22 (1966-)	Headline Hunters	11 (1972-83)
Mr. Dressup	21 (1967-)	The Littlest Hobo	10 (1978-)
Man Alive	21 (1967-)	Don Messer's Jubilee	10 (1959-69)
Question Period	20 (1968-)	Juliette	10 (1956-66)
This Land	20 (1967-86)		

Top Television Programs, 1950-1988

Source: A.C. Nielsen Company of Canada Limited

Top ten television series in North America for each season, based on average A.C. Nielsen ratings representing the percentage of households watching a program. Programs are listed in order of popularity.

1950-51

1. Texaco Star Theater
2. Fireside Theatre
3. Philco TV Playhouse
4. Your Show of Shows
5. The Colgate Comedy Hour
6. Gillette Cavalcade of Sports
7. The Lone Ranger
8. Arthur Godfrey's Talent Scouts
9. Hopalong Cassidy
10. Mama

1951-52

1. Arthur Godfrey's Talent Scouts
2. Texaco Star Theater
3. I Love Lucy
4. The Red Skelton Show
5. The Colgate Comedy Hour
6. Arthur Godfrey and His Friends
7. Fireside Theatre
8. Your Show of Shows
9. The Jack Benny Show
10. You Bet Your Life

1952-53

1. I Love Lucy
2. Arthur Godfrey's Talent Scouts
3. Arthur Godfrey and His Friends
4. Dragnet
5. Texaco Star Theater
6. The Buick Circus Hour
7. The Colgate Comedy Hour
8. Gangbusters
9. You Bet Your Life
10. Fireside Theatre

1953-54

1. I Love Lucy
2. Dragnet
3. Arthur Godfrey's Talent Scouts
4. You Bet Your Life
5. The Chevy Show (Bob Hope)
6. The Milton Berle Show
7. Arthur Godfrey and His Friends
8. The Ford Show
9. The Jackie Gleason Show
10. Fireside Theatre

1954-55

1. I Love Lucy
2. The Jackie Gleason Show
3. Dragnet
4. You Bet Your Life
5. The Toast of the Town
6. Disneyland
7. The Chevy Show (Bob Hope)
8. The Jack Benny Show
9. The Martha Raye Show
10. The George Gobel Show

1955-56

1. The $64,000 Question
2. I Love Lucy
3. The Ed Sullivan Show
4. Disneyland
5. The Jack Benny Show
6. December Bride
7. You Bet Your Life
8. Dragnet
9. The Millionaire
10. I've Got a Secret

1956-57

1. I Love Lucy
2. The Ed Sullivan Show
3. General Electric Theater
4. The $64,000 Question
5. December Bride
6. Alfred Hitchcock Presents
7. I've Got a Secret
8. Gunsmoke
9. The Perry Como Show
10. The Jack Benny Show

1957-58

1. Gunsmoke
2. The Danny Thomas Show
3. Tales of Wells Fargo
4. Have Gun Will Travel
5. I've Got a Secret
6. The Life and Legend of Wyatt Earp
7. General Electric Theater
8. The Restless Gun
9. December Bride
10. You Bet Your Life

1958-59

1. Gunsmoke
2. Wagon Train
3. Have Gun Will Travel
4. The Rifleman
5. The Danny Thomas Show
6. Maverick
7. Tales of Wells Fargo
8. The Real McCoys
9. I've Got a Secret
10. The Life and Legend of Wyatt Earp

1959-60

1. Gunsmoke
2. Wagon Train
3. Have Gun Will Travel
4. The Danny Thomas Show
5. The Red Skelton Show
6. Father Knows Best
7. 77 Sunset Strip
8. The Price is Right
9. Wanted: Dead or Alive
10. Perry Mason

1960-61

1. Gunsmoke
2. Wagon Train
3. Have Gun Will Travel
4. The Andy Griffith Show
5. The Real McCoys
6. Rawhide
7. Candid Camera
8. The Untouchables
9. The Price is Right
10. The Jack Benny Show

1961-62

1. Wagon Train
2. Bonanza
3. Gunsmoke
4. Hazel
5. Perry Mason
6. The Red Skelton Show
7. The Andy Griffith Show
8. The Danny Thomas Show
9. Dr. Kildare
10. Candid Camera

1962-63

1. The Beverly Hillbillies
2. Candid Camera
3. The Red Skelton Show
4. Bonanza
5. The Lucy Show
6. The Andy Griffith Show
7. Ben Casey
8. The Danny Thomas Show
9. The Dick Van Dyke Show
10. Gunsmoke

1963-64

1. The Beverly Hillbillies
2. Bonanza
3. The Dick Van Dyke Show
4. Petticoat Junction
5. The Andy Griffith Show
6. The Lucy Show
7. Candid Camera
8. The Ed Sullivan Show
9. The Danny Thomas Show
10. My Favorite Martian

1964-65

1. Bonanza
2. Bewitched
3. Gomer Pyle, U.S.M.C
4. The Andy Griffith Show
5. The Fugitive
6. The Red Skelton Hour
7. The Dick Van Dyke Show
8. The Lucy Show
9. Peyton Place II
10. Combat

1965-66

1. Bonanza
2. Gomer Pyle, U.S.M.C
3. The Lucy Show
4. The Red Skelton Hour
5. Batman (Thurs.)
6. The Andy Griffith Show
7. Bewitched
8. The Beverly Hillbillies
9. Hogan's Heroes
10. Batman (Wed.)

1966-67

1. Bonanza
2. The Red Skelton Hour
3. The Andy Griffith Show
4. The Lucy Show
5. The Jackie Gleason Show
6. Green Acres
7. Daktari
8. Bewitched
9. The Beverly Hillbillies
10. Gomer Pyle, U.S.M.C

1967-68

1. The Andy Griffith Show
2. The Lucy Show
3. Gomer Pyle, U.S.M.C
4. Gunsmoke
5. Family Affair
6. Bonanza
7. The Red Skelton Hour
8. The Dean Martin Show
9. The Jackie Gleason Show
10. Saturday Night at the Movies

1968-69

1. Rowan & Martin's Laugh-In
2. Gomer Pyle, U.S.M.C
3. Bonanza
4. Mayberry R.F.D.
5. Family Affair
6. Gunsmoke
7. Julia
8. The Dean Martin Show
9. Here's Lucy
10. The Beverly Hillbillies

1969-70

1. Rowan & Martin's Laugh-In
2. Gunsmoke
3. Bonanza
4. Mayberry R.F.D.
5. Family Affair
6. Here's Lucy
7. The Red Skelton Hour
8. Marcus Welby, M.D.
9. Walt Disney's Wonderful World of Color
10. The Doris Day Show

1970-71

1. Marcus Welby, M.D.
2. The Flip Wilson Show
3. Here's Lucy
4. Ironside
5. Gunsmoke
6. ABC Movie of the Week
7. Hawaii Five-O
8. Medical Center
9. Bonanza
10. The F.B.I.

1971-72

1. All in the Family
2. The Flip Wilson Show
3. Marcus Welby, M.D.
4. Gunsmoke
5. ABC Movie of the Week
6. Sanford and Son
7. Mannix
8. Funny Face
9. Adam 12
10. The Mary Tyler Moore Show

1972-73

1. All in the Family
2. Sanford and Son
3. Hawaii Five-O
4. Maude
5. Bridget Loves Bernie
6. Sunday Mystery Movie
7. The Mary Tyler Moore Show
8. Gunsmoke
9. The Wonderful World of Disney
10. Ironside

1973-74

1. All in the Family
2. The Waltons
3. Sanford and Son
4. M*A*S*H
5. Hawaii Five-O
6. Maude
7. Kojak
8. The Sonny and Cher Comedy Hour
9. The Mary Tyler Moore Show
10. Cannon

1974-75

1. All in the Family
2. Sanford and Son
3. Chico and The Man
4. The Jeffersons
5. M*A*S*H
6. Rhoda
7. Good Times
8. The Waltons
9. Maude
10. Hawaii Five-O

1975-76

1. All in the Family
2. Rich Man, Poor Man
3. Laverne & Shirley
4. Maude
5. The Bionic Woman
6. Phyllis
7. Sanford and Son
8. Rhoda
9. The Six Million Dollar Man
10. ABC Monday Night Movie

1976-77

1. Happy Days
2. Laverne & Shirley
3. ABC Monday Night Movie
4. M*A*S*H
5. Charlie's Angels
6. The Big Event
7. The Six Million Dollar Man
8. ABC Sunday Night Movie
9. Baretta
10. One Day at a Time

1977-78

1. Laverne & Shirley
2. Happy Days
3. Three's Company
4. 60 Minutes
5. Charlie's Angels
6. All in the Family
7. Little House on the Prairie
8. Alice
9. M*A*S*H
10. One Day at a Time

1978-79

1. Laverne & Shirley
2. Three's Company
3. Happy Days
4. Mork & Mindy
5. Angie
6. Ropers[1]
6. M*A*S*H[1]
8. All in the Family
9. 60 Minutes
10. Taxi

1979-80

1. 60 Minutes
2. Three's Company
3. Flo
4. That's Incredible
5. Alice[1]
5. M*A*S*H[1]
7. Dallas
8. Jeffersons
9. Dukes of Hazzard
10. One Day at a Time

1980-81

1. Dallas
2. 60 Minutes
3. Dukes of Hazzard
4. Private Benjamin
5. M*A*S*H
6. Love Boat
7. NBC Tuesday Night Movie
8. House Calls
9. Jeffersons[1]
9. Little House on the Prairie[1]

1981-82

1. Dallas
2. 60 Minutes
3. Three's Company
4. Jeffersons[1]
4. Joanie Loves Chachi[1]
6. Dukes of Hazzard
7. Too Close For Comfort
8. Alice
9. ABC Monday Night Movie
10. M*A*S*H

1982-83

1. 60 Minutes
2. Dallas
3. Magnum, P.I.[1]
3. M*A*S*H[1]
5. Dynasty
6. Three's Company
7. Simon & Simon
8. Falcon Crest
9. Love Boat
10. NFL Monday Night Football[1]
10. Jeffersons[1]
10. A Team[1]

1983-84

1. Dallas
2. 60 Minutes
3. Dynasty
4. A Team
5. Simon & Simon
6. Magnum, P.I.
7. Falcon Crest
8. Kate & Allie
9. Hotel
10. Cagney & Lacey

1984-85

1. Dynasty
2. Dallas
3. Bill Cosby Show
4. 60 Minutes
5. Family Ties
6. Simon & Simon[1]
6. A Team[1]
8. Knots Landing
9. Murder, She Wrote
10. Crazy Like a Fox[1]
10. Falcon Crest[1]

1985-86

1. Bill Cosby Show
2. Family Ties
3. Murder, She Wrote
4. 60 Minutes
5. Cheers
6. Dallas[1]
6. Dynasty[1]
6. The Golden Girls[1]
9. Miami Vice
10. Who's The Boss?

(1) Tied

1986-87

1. The Cosby Show
2. Family Ties
3. Cheers
4. Murder, She Wrote
5. The Golden Girls
6. 60 Minutes
7. Night Court
8. Growing Pains
9. Moonlighting
10. Who's the Boss?

1987-88

1. Bill Cosby Show
2. A Different World
3. Cheers
4. Growing Pains
5. Night Court
6. The Golden Girls
7. Who's The Boss?
8. 60 Minutes
9. Murder, She Wrote
10. Wonder Years

All-time Top Television Programs

Source: A.C. Nielsen estimates, Jan. 25, 1987-Mar. 6, 1988, excluding unsponsored or joint network telecasts or programs under 30 minutes long.
Ranked by percent of average audience in the United States.

Program	Telecast Date	Network	Households (000s)
M*A*S*H Special	Feb. 28, 1983	CBS	50 150
Dallas	Nov. 21, 1980	CBS	41 470
Roots Pt. VIII	Jan. 30, 1977	ABC	36 380
Super Bowl XVI	Jan. 24, 1982	CBS	40 020
Super Bowl XVII	Jan. 30, 1983	NBC	40 480
Super Bowl XX	Jan. 26, 1986	NBC	41 490
Gone With The Wind—Pt. 1	Nov. 7, 1976	NBC	33 960
Gone With The Wind—Pt. 2	Nov. 8, 1976	NBC	33 750
Super Bowl XII	Jan. 15, 1978	CBS	34 410
Super Bowl XIII	Jan. 21, 1979	NBC	35 090
Bob Hope Christmas Show	Jan. 15, 1970	NBC	27 260
Super Bowl XVIII	Jan. 22, 1984	CBS	38 800
Super Bowl XIX	Jan. 20, 1985	ABC	39 390
Super Bowl XIV	Jan. 20, 1980	CBS	35 330
The Day After	Nov. 20, 1983	ABC	38 550
Roots Pt. VI	Jan. 28, 1977	ABC	32 680
The Fugitive	Aug. 29, 1967	ABC	25 700
Super Bowl XXI	Jan. 25, 1987	CBS	40 030
Roots Pt. V	Jan. 27, 1977	ABC	32 540
Ed Sullivan	Feb. 9, 1964	CBS	23 240
Bob Hope Christmas Show	Jan. 14, 1971	NBC	27 050
Roots Pt. III	Jan. 25, 1977	ABC	31 900
Super Bowl XI	Jan. 9, 1977	NBC	31 610
Super Bowl XV	Jan. 25, 1981	NBC	34 540
Super Bowl VI	Jan. 16, 1972	CBS	27 450
Roots Pt. II	Jan. 24, 1977	ABC	31 400
Beverly Hillbillies	Jan. 8, 1964	CBS	22 570
Roots Pt. IV	Jan. 26, 1977	ABC	31 190
Ed Sullivan	Feb. 16, 1964	CBS	22 445
Academy Awards	Apr. 7, 1970	ABC	25 390
Thorn Birds Pt. III	Mar. 29, 1983	ABC	35 990
Thorn Birds Pt. IV	Mar. 30, 1983	ABC	35 900
NFC Championship Game	Jan. 10, 1982	CBS	34 960
Beverly Hillbillies	Jan. 15, 1964	CBS	21 960
Super Bowl VII	Jan. 14, 1973	NBC	27 670

Average Television Viewing Time

Source: Nielsen Media Research, Nov. 1987 (hours: minutes, per week)

		Total	Mon.-Fri. 10am-4:30pm	Mon.-Fri. 4:30pm-7:30pm	Mon.-Sun. 8-11pm	Sat. 7am-1pm	Mon.-Fri. 11:30pm-1am
Average all persons		29:40	4:23	4:25	8:46	:47	1:07
Women	Total 18 +	33:42	6:05	4:59	9:56	:36	1:19
	18-24	24:35	4:49	3:16	6:58	:37	1:06
	55 +	41:17	7:48	7:07	12:06	:32	1:24
Men	Total 18 +	28:58	3:17	3:52	9:02	:35	1:19
	18-24	23:45	3:29	2:51	6:26	:35	1:15
	55 +	37:07	5:06	6:09	11:19	:34	1:17
Teens[1]	Female	23:13	2:30	4:12	7:16	1:00	:38
	Male	24:16	2:22	3:54	7:40	:59	:41
Kids	2-5	25:26	5:26	4:19	5:05	1:43	:19
	6-11	22:46	2:22	4:25	6:07	1:43	:23

(1) Ages 12-17

Television Network Addresses and Phone Numbers

American Broadcasting Company (ABC)
1330 Avenue of Americas
New York, NY 10019
U.S.A.
(212) 887-7777

Atlantic Television System (ATV)
2885 Robie St.
Halifax, N.S.
B3J 2Z4
(902) 453-4000

British Columbia Television (BCTV)
Box 4700
Vancouver, B.C.
V6B 4A3
(604) 420-2288

CBS, Inc.
51 W. 52nd St.
New York, NY 10019
U.S.A.
(212) 975-4321

CTV Television Network Ltd.
42 Charles St. E.
Toronto, Ont.
M4Y 1T4
(416) 928-6000

Canadian Broadcasting Corp. (CBC)
Box 8478
Ottawa, Ont.
K1G 3J5
(613) 724-1200

Global Television Network
81 Barber Greene Rd.
Don Mills, Ont.
M3C 2A2
(416) 446-5311

National Broadcasting Company (NBC)
30 Rockefeller Plaza
New York, NY 10112
U.S.A.
(212) 664-4444

Newfoundland Broadcasting Co. Ltd. (NTV)
Box 2020
St. John's, Nfld.
A1C 5S2
(709) 579-5015

Public Broadcasting Service (PBS)
609 Fifth Ave.
New York, NY 10017
U.S.A.
(212) 753-7373

TVA Television Network
1600 de Maisonneuve Blvd. E
Ste. D-360
Montreal, Que.
H2L 4P2
(514) 526-0476

Westinghouse Broadcasting (Group W)
888 7th Ave.
10th Fl.
New York, NY 10106
U.S.A.
(212) 307-3000

WNYW
205 E. 67 St.
New York, NY 10021
U.S.A.
(212) 535-1000

Canadian Cable Networks

Allarcom Pay TV Ltd.
#200, 5324 Calgary Trail
Edmonton, Alta.
T6H 4J8
(403) 437-7744

Cathay International TV Inc.
494 W. 39th Ave.
Vancouver, B.C.
V5Y 2P7
(604) 321-5266

Chinavision Canada Corp.
160 Duncan Mill Rd.
Don Mills, Ont.
M3B 1Z5
(416) 391-3388

First Choice Canadian Communications Corp.
98 Queen St. E.
Suite 300
Toronto, Ont.
M5C 1S6
(416) 364-9115

MuchMusic Network
299 Queen St. W.
Toronto, Ont.
M5V 2Z5
(416) 591-5757

Super Ecran
666 ouest rue Sherbrooke
15e étage
Montreal, Que.
H3A 1E7
(514) 288-2188

Telelatino Network
105 Carlton St.
3rd fl.
Toronto, Ont.
M5B 1M2
(416) 591-6846

TSN—The Sports Network
1155 Leslie St.
Don Mills, Ont.
M3C 2J6
(416) 449-2244

Longest Running Broadway Plays[1]

Chorus Line*	5 369	Hair	1 750	Oh! Calcutta! (original)	1 314
Oh, Calcutta (revival)*	5 357	La Cage aux Folles	1 743	Angel Street	1 295
Grease	3 388	The Wiz	1 672	Lightnin'	1 291
42d Street*	3 262	Born Yesterday	1 642	Promises, Promises	1 281
Fiddler on the Roof	3 242	Ain't Misbehavin'	1 604	The King and I	1 246
Life With Father	3 224	Best Little Whorehouse in Texas	1 584	Cactus Flower	1 234
Tobacco Road	3 182	Mary, Mary	1 572	Sleuth	1 222
Hello Dolly	2 844	Evita	1 567	"1776"	1 217
My Fair Lady	2 717	Voice of the Turtle	1 557	Equus	1 209
Cats*	2 390	Barefoot in the Park	1 530	Sugar Babies	1 208
Annie	2 377	Dreamgirls	1 522	Guys and Dolls	1 200
Man of La Mancha	2 328	Mame	1 508	Torch Song Trilogy	1 166
Abie's Irish Rose	2 327	Same Time, Next Year	1 453	Cabaret	1 165
Oklahoma!	2 212	Arsenic and Old Lace	1 444	Mister Roberts	1 157
Pippin	1 994	The Sound of Music	1 443	Amadeus	1 155
South Pacific	1 925	How To Succeed in Business Without Really Trying	1 417	Annie Get Your Gun	1 147
Magic Show	1 920			Seven Year Itch	1 141
Deathtrap	1 792	Hellzapoppin	1 404	Butterflies Are Free	1 128
Gemini	1 788	The Music Man	1 375	Pins and Needles	1 108
Harvey	1 775	Funny Girl	1 348	Plaza Suite	1 097
Dancin'	1 774	Mumenschanz	1 326		

(1) Number of performances as of June 30, 1988. *Still running July 1, 1988.

Canadian Dance Companies

Company	Founded	Artistic Director	Address
Alberta Ballet	1966	Ali Pourfarrokh	10645 63 Ave., Edmonton, Alta. T6H 1P7
Canadian Children's Dance Theatre	1981	Michael Smith/ Deborah Lundmark	429 Melita Cr., Toronto, Ont. M6G 3X5
Contemporary Dancers	1964	Tedd Robinson	109 Pulford St., Winnipeg, Man. R3L 1X8
Dancemakers	1974	Bill James	927 Dupont St., Toronto, Ont. M6H 1Z1
Desrosiers Dance Theatre	1980	Robert Desrosiers	95 Trinity St., Toronto, Ont. M5A 3C7
EDAM	1982	Peter Bingham/ Lola MacLaughlin/ Jennifer Mascall/ Peter Ryan	303 East 8th Ave., Vancouver, B.C. V5T 1S1
Ensemble national de folklore Les Sortilèges	1966	Jimmy DiGenova	6560 rue Chambord, Montreal, Que. H2G 3B9
Formolo Dance Image Maker	1981	Maria Formolo	804-10136 100th St., Edmonton, Alta. T5J 0P1
Margie Gillis Dance Foundation	1981	Margie Gillis	3575 Blvd. St. Laurent, #501, Montreal, Que. H2X 2T3
Les Grands Ballets Canadiens	1958	Linda Stearns	4816 rue Rivard, Montreal, Que. H2J 2N6
Danny Grossman Dance Company	1975	Danny Grossman	511 Bloor St. W., Toronto, Ont. M5S 1Y4
Jumpstart Performance Society	1984	Lee Eisler/ Nelson Gray	6450 Deer Lake Ave., Burnaby, B.C. V5G 2J3
Kokoro Dance	1986	Barbara Bourget/ Jay Hirabayashi	2910 West 5th Ave., Vancouver, B.C. V6K 1T6
Kompany Dance and Affiliated Artists Society	1979	Ron Schuster/ Darold Roles/ Vanessa Harris	810-10136 100 St., Edmonton, Alta. T5J 0P1
Le Groupe de la Place Royale	1966	Peter Boneham	130 Sparks St., Ottawa, Ont. K1P 5B6
The Paula Moreno Spanish Dance Co. Inc.	1977	Paula Moreno	121 Avenue Rd., Toronto, Ont. M5R 2G3
The National Ballet of Canada	1951	Valerie Wilder/ Lynn Wallis	157 King St. E., Toronto, Ont. M5C 1G9
The National Tap Dance Company of Canada	1976	William Orlowski/ Stephan Dymond	63 Madison Ave., Toronto, Ont. M5R 2S3
O Vertigo Danse	1984	Ginette Laurin	403-3575 St. Laurent, Montreal, Que. H2X 2T7
Gina Lori Riley Dance Enterprises	1979	Gina Lori Riley	201-384 Pitt St. E., Windsor, Ont. N9A 2V7
Paula Ross Dance Co.	1965	Paula Ross	P.O. Box 429, Ucluelet, B.C. V0R 3A0
Royal Winnipeg Ballet	1939	Henry Jurriens	380 Graham Ave., Winnipeg, Man. R3C 4K2
Theatre Ballet of Canada	1971	Lawrence Gradus	P.O. Box 366, Stn. A, Ottawa, Ont. K1N 8V3
Toronto Dance Theatre	1968	David Earle	80 Winchester St., Toronto, Ont. M4X 1B2
Toronto Independent Dance Enterprise (T.I.D.E.)	1978	Denise Fujiwara/ Sallie Lyons	45 Bellwoods Ave., Toronto, Ont. M6J 3N4
Trickster	1980	David Chantler/ Sheryl Simmons	#701, 339-10 Ave. S.E. Calgary, Alta. T2G 0W2
Ukrainian Shumka Dancers	1959	John Pichlyk	P.O. Box 342, Edmonton, Alta. T5J 2J6
The Brian Webb Dance Company	1979	Brian Webb	P.O. Box 1796, Edmonton, Alta. T5J 2P2
Anna Wyman Dance Theatre	1971	Anna Wyman	927 Granville St., 3rd fl., Vancouver, B.C. V6Z 1L3

Canadian Symphony Orchestras

Orchestra	Conductor	Address
Calgary Philharmonic Orchestra	Mario Bernardi	205-8th Ave. S.E., Calgary, Alta. T2G 0K9
Edmonton Symphony Orchestra	Uri Mayer	10010-109th St., Edmonton, Alta. T5J 1M4
Hamilton Philharmonic Orchestra	Boris Brott	P.O. Box 2080, Station A, Hamilton, Ont. L8N 3Y7
International Symphony Orchestra of Sarnia and Port Huron	Zdzislaw Kopac	180½ Christina St. N., Sarnia, Ont. N7T 5T9
Kingston Symphony	Brian Jackson	P.O. Box 1616, Kingston, Ont. K7L 5C8
Kitchener-Waterloo Symphony Orchestra	Raffi Armenian	101 Queen St. N., Kitchener, Ont. N2H 6P7
Lethbridge Symphony Orchestra	Stewart Grant	P.O. Box 1101, Lethbridge, Alta. T1J 4A2
Mississauga Symphony Orchestra	John Barnum	161 Lakeshore Rd. West, Mississauga, Ont. L5H 1G3
National Arts Centre Orchestra	Gabriel Chmura	P.O. Box 1534, Station B, Ottawa, Ont. K1P 5W1
National Youth Orchestra of Canada	Gabriel Chmura/ Simon Streatfield[1]	1032 Bathurst St., Toronto, Ont. M5R 3G7
Newfoundland Symphony Orchestra	Mario Duschenes	Arts and Culture Centre, Prince Philip Dr., St. John's, Nfld. A1C 5P9
Niagara Symphony Orchestra	Ermanno Florio	P.O. Box 401, St. Catharines, Ont. L2R 6V9
North York Symphony	Kerry Stratton	1210 Sheppard Ave. E., Ste. 109, North York, Ont. M2K 1E3
Okanagan Symphony Orchestra	Leonard Camplin	P.O. Box 1120, Kelowna, B.C. V1Y 7P8
Orchestra London Canada	Uri Mayer	520 Wellington St., London, Ont. N6A 3P9
l'Orchestre symphonique de Montréal	Charles Dutoit	85 St. Catherine St. W., Ste. 900, Montreal, Que. H2X 3P4
l'Orchestre symphonique de Québec	Simon Streatfield	580 Grande-Allée est., Ste. 150, Quebec, Que. G1R 2K2
l'Orchestre symphonique de Trois-Rivières	Gilles Bellemare	P.O. Box 1281, Trois-Rivières, Que. G9A 5K8
Ottawa Symphony Orchestra	Brian Law	P.O. Box 3644, Station C, Ottawa, Ont. K1Y 4J7
Prince George Symphony Orchestra	William Janzen	Studio 2880, 15th Ave., Prince George, B.C. V2M 1T1
Regina Symphony Orchestra	Derrick Inouye	200 Lakeshore Dr., Regina, Sask. S4P 3V7
Saskatoon Symphony	Daniel Swift	P.O. Box 1361, Saskatoon, Sask. S7K 3N9
Symphony Hamilton	Roberto DeClara	1280 Main St. West, Hamilton, Ont. L8S 4M2
Thunder Bay Symphony Orchestra	Dwight Bennett	P.O. Box 2004, Thunder Bay, Ont. P7B 5E7
Toronto Symphony Orchestra	Gunther Herbig	60 Simcoe St., Ste. C116, Toronto, Ont. M5J 2H5
Vancouver Symphony Orchestra	Peter McCoppin	601 Smithe St., Vancouver, B.C. V6B 5G1
Victoria Symphony	Glen Fast	846 Broughton St., Victoria, B.C. V8W 1E4
Winnipeg Symphony Orchestra	Kazuhiro Koizumi	555 Main St., Rm. 101, Winnipeg, Man. R3B 1C3
Windsor Symphony Orchestra	Dwight Bennett	545 Ouellette Ave., 2nd fl., Windsor, Ont. N9A 4J3

(1) 1988 summer season.

Canadian Opera Companies

Calgary Opera Association: 306-1011-1st St. S.W., Calgary, Alta. T2R 1J2. David Speers, gen. mgr.

Canadian Opera Co.: 227 Front St. E., Toronto, Ont., M5A 1E8. Lotfi Mansouri, gen. dir. (until Jan. 1989).

Edmonton Opera Association: 202-11456 Jasper Ave., Edmonton, Alta. T5K 0M1. Robert Hallam, gen. mgr.

Manitoba Opera Association: Rm. 121, 555 Main St., Winnipeg, Man. R3B 1C3. Bruce Lang, adm. dir.

L'Opéra de Montréal: 1157 Ste-Catherine St. E., Montreal, Que. H2L 2G8. Bernard S. Creighton, dir., admin & finance.

Vancouver Opera Association: 1132 Hamilton St., Vancouver, B.C. V6B 2S2. Beverly Trifonidis, gen. mgr.

Noted Canadian Authors

Hubert Aquin (1929-1977), b. Montreal, Que.: novelist, *Trou de mémoire* (1962), *Prochain épisode* (1965), Neige noire (1974).

Margaret Atwood. b. Ottawa, Ont., Nov. 18, 1939: poet, novelist, *The Circle Game* (1966), *Surfacing* (1972), *Lady Oracle* (1976), *The Handmaid's Tale* (1985).

Pierre Berton, b. Whitehorse, Yukon, July 12, 1920: popular historian, *The National Dream* (1970), *The Last Spike* (1971)

Earle Birney, b. Calgary Alta., May 13, 1904: poet, novelist, *David* (1943), *Now is Time* (1946), *Turvey* (1949).

Marie-Claire Blais, b. Quebec City, Que., Oct. 5, 1939: novelist, *La Belle Bête* (1959), *Une Saison dans la vie d'Emmanuel* (1965), *Le Sourd dans la ville* (1979).

Morley Callaghan, b. Toronto, Ont., Feb. 22, 1903: novelist, *The Loved and the Lost* (1951), *Our Lady of the Snows* (1985).

Roch Carrier b. Beauce, Que., 13 May 1937: poet, novelist, playwright, *Jolis deuils* (1964), *La Guerre, Yes Sir!* (1968).

Leonard Cohen, b. Montreal, Que., Sept. 21, 1934: poet, novelist, songwriter, *Beautiful Losers* (1966), *The Energy of Slaves* (1972), *Death of a Lady's Man* (1978).

Octave Crémazie (1827-1879), b. Quebec City, Que.: poet, "Le vieux soldat canadien" (1855), *Le Drapeau de Carillon* (1858).

Robertson Davies, b. Thamesville, Ont., Aug. 28, 1913: novelist, *Fifth Business* (1970), *The Rebel Angels* (1981), *What's Bred in the Bone* (1985), *The Lyre of Orpheus* (1988).

Mazo De la Roche (1879-1961), b. Newmarket, Ont.: novelist, playwright, *Jalna* (1927), *Young Renny* (1935).

Marian Engel (1933-1985), b. Toronto, Ont., novelist, *No Clouds of Glory* (1968), *Bear* (1976), *Lunatic Villas* (1981).

Brian Fawcett, b. Prince George, B.C., 1944: novelist, short story writer, *My Career with the Leafs and Other Stories* (1982), *The Secret Journal of Alexander Mackenzie* (1986), *Cambodia: A Book for People Who Find Television Too Slow* (1986).

Northrop Frye, b. Sherbrooke, Que., July 14, 1912: literary critic and novelist, *The Bush Garden* (1971), *The Great Code* (1982).

Mavis Gallant, b. Montreal, Que., Aug. 11, 1922: short story writer, novelist, *My Heart is Broken* (1964), *A Fairly Good Time* (1970), *Home Truths: Selected Canadian Stories* (1982).

François-Xavier Garneau (1809-1866), b. Quebec City, Que.: poet, historian, *Histoire du Canada* (1845-1848).

Gratien Gélinas, b. St-Tite, Que., Dec. 8, 1909: playwright, *Tit-Coq* (1948), *Bousille et les justes* (1959).

Frederick Philip Grove, (1879-1948) b. Randomno, E. Prussia: novelist, *Settlers of the Marsh* (1925), *Fruits of the Earth* (1933), *In Search of Myself* (1946).

Anne Hébert, b. Ste-Catherine-de-Fossambault, Que., Aug. 1, 1916: poet, playwright, novelist, *Le Torrent* (1960), *Kamouraska* (1970), *Les Fous de Bassan* (1982).

Jack Hodgins, b. Comox, B.C., Oct. 3, 1938: novelist, short story writer, *Spit Delaney's Island* (1976), *The Invention of the World* (1977), *The Resurrection of Joseph Bourne* (1979), *The Barclay Family Theatre* (1981).

Pauline Johnson (1861-1913), b. Six Nations Indian Reserve, Upper Canada: poet, *Canadian Born* (1903), *Flint and Feather* (1912).

Robert Kroetsch, b. Heisler, Alta., June 26, 1927: novelist, *The Studhorse Man* (1965), *Badlands* (1975), *Sketches of a Lemon* (1981).

Margaret Laurence, (1926-1987), b. Neepawa, Man.: novelist, *The Stone Angel* (1964), *A Jest of God* (1966), *The Diviners* (1974).

Irving Layton. b. Neamtz, Romania, Mar. 12, 1912: poet, *Here and Now* (1945), *A Red Carpet for the Sun* (1959), *The Gucci Bag* (1983).

Stephen Leacock (1869-1944), b. Swanmore, England: humorist and essayist, *Sunshine Sketches of a Little Town* (1912), *Arcadian Adventures With the Idle Rich* (1914).

Dennis Lee, b. Toronto, Ont., Aug. 31, 1939: poet, author of children's books, *Civil Elegies* (1968, rev. 1982), *Alligator Pie* (1974), *Jelly Belly* (1983), *The Difficulty of Living on Other Planets* (1987).

Roger Lemelin, b. Quebec, Que., Apr. 7, 1919: novelist, scriptwriter, *Au pied de la pente douce* (1944; tr. *The Town Below*, 1948), *Les Plouffe* (1948; tr. *The Plouffe Family*, 1950).

Malcom Lowry (1909-1957), b. New Brighton, Eng.: novelist, *Under the Volcano* (1946).

Antonine Maillet, b. Buctouche, N.B., May 10, 1929: novelist, *La Sagouine* (1974), *Pélagie-la-Charrette* (1979).

John McCrae (1872-1918), b. Guelph, Ont.: poet, best known for "In Flanders Fields".

Hugh MacLennan, b. Glace Bay, N.S., Mar. 20, 1907: novelist, *Two Solitudes* (1945), *Voices in Time* (1980).

W.O. Mitchell, b. Weyburn, Sask., Mar. 13, 1914: novelist, *Who Has Seen the Wind* (1947), *Since Daisy Creek* (1984).

Lucy Maud Montgomery (1874-1942), b. Clifton, P.E.I.: novelist, *Anne of Green Gables* (1908).

Susanna Moodie (1803-1885), b. Bungay, England: novelist, *Roughing It in the Bush* (1852).

Brian Moore, b. Belfast, N. Ire., Aug. 25, 1921: novelist, *The Lonely Passion of Judith Hearne* (1955), *The Luck of Ginger Coffey* (1960), *The Mangan Inheritance* (1979).

Farley Mowat, b. Belleville, Ont., May 12, 1921: writer of "subjective nonfiction", *Lost in the Barrens* (1956), *Never Cry Wolf* (1963), *A Whale for the Killing* (1972), *Sea of Slaughter* (1984).

Alice Munro, b. Wingham, Ont., July 10, 1931: novelist, *Dance of the Happy Shades* (1968), *The Moons of Jupiter* (1982).

Emile Nelligan (1879-1941), b. Montreal, Que.: poet, "Romance du vin", "Vaisseau d'or".

Peter C. Newman, b. Vienna, Austria, May 10, 1929: popular historian, journalist, *The Canadian Establishment* (1975, 1981), *Company of Adventurers* (1986).

Michael Ondaatje, b. Colombo, Sri Lanka, Sept. 12, 1943: poet, *The Dainty Monsters* (1967), *The Collected Works of Billy the Kid* (1970), *Rat Jelly* (1973), *There's a Trick with a Knife I'm Learning to Do* (1979).

Edwin J. Pratt (1883-1964), b. Western Bay, Nfld.: poet, *Newfoundland Verse* (1923), *Brebeuf and his Brethren* (1940).

Al Purdy, b. Wooler, Ont., Dec. 30, 1918: poet, *The Enchanted Echo* (1944), *The Crafte So Longe to Lerne* (1959), *The Cariboo Horses* (1965), *The Stone Bird* (1981).

James Reaney, b. Easthope, Ont., Sept. 1, 1926: playwright and poet, *The Killdeer and Other Plays* (1962), *Masks of Childhood* (1972), *Poems* (1972).

Mordecai Richler, b. Montreal, Que., Jan. 27, 1931: novelist, *The Apprenticeship of Duddy Kravitz* (1959), *Cocksure* (1968) *Joshua Then and Now* (1980).

Gabrielle Roy (1909-1983), b. St. Boniface, Man.: novelist, *Bonheur d'occasion* (1945), *La Montagne secrète* (1961), *Ces enfants de ma vie* (1977).

F.R. Scott (1899-1985), b. Quebec City, Que.: poet, lawyer, *Essays on the Constitution* (1977), *Collected Poems* (1981).

Robert Service (1874-1958), b. Preston, England: poet, *Songs of a Sourdough* (1907), *Rhymes of a Rolling Stone* (1912), *Rhymes of a Roughneck* (1950).

Josef Skvorecky, b. Nachod, Czech., 1924: novelist, *The Bass Saxophone* (1963), *The Engineer of Human Souls* (1983).

Yves Thériault (1915-1983), b. Quebec City, Que.: novelist, *Contes pour un homme seul* (1944), *Agaguk* (1958).

Michel Tremblay, b. Montreal, Que., June 25, 1942: playwright, novelist, *Le Train* (1959), *Contes pour buveurs attardés* (1966), *Les Belles-Soeurs* (1968).

Sheila Watson, b. New Westminster, B.C., Oct. 24, 1909: novelist, critic, *The Double Hook* (1959), *Four Stories* (1979), *And the Four Animals* (1980).

Rudy Wiebe, b. Speedwell, Sask., Oct. 4, 1934: novelist, short story writer, *The Temptations of Big Bear* (1973), *The Scorched-Wood People* (1977), *My Lovely Energy* (1983).

George Woodcock, b. Winnipeg, May 8, 1912: literary journalist, historian, *The Centre Cannot Hold* (1943), *Anarchism* (1962), *Odysseus Ever Returning* (1970), *Letters to the Past* (1982).

Canadian Daily Newspaper Circulation[1]

Source: Audit Bureau of Circulation; FAS-FAX Report

(for newspapers with 25 000 or more circulation)

Newspaper	Daily[2]	Weekend	
Toronto Star (all day)	519 320[3]	806 327 (Sat.)	532 697 (Sun.)
Le Journal de Montréal (m)	327 502[3]	355 145 (Sat.)	347 778 (Sun.)
Toronto: Globe and Mail (m)	326 462[4]	335 345 (Sat.)	
Toronto Sun (m)	289 707[3]	186 452 (Sat.)	460 599 (Sun.)
Vancouver Sun (e)	227 106[5]	276 585 (Fri.)	281 102 (Sat.)
Montreal: La Presse (m)	207 296[3]	326 988 (Sat.)	183 719 (Sun.)
Montreal Gazette (m)	192 309[3]	272 139 (Sat.)	197 971 (Sun.)
Ottawa Citizen (all day)	192 070[3]	248 979 (Sat.)	
Vancouver Province (m)	180 087		222 616 (Sun.)
Winnipeg Free Press (e)	170 199[3]	234 562 (Sat.)	145 854 (Sun.)
Edmonton Journal (m)	166 857[6]	203 533 (Fri.)	149 037 (Sun.)
Calgary Herald (m)	138 464[6]	180 211 (Fri.)	124 370 (Sun.)
London Free Press (m)	131 308		

Newspaper	Daily[2]	Weekend	
Hamilton Spectator (e)	119 947[7]		
Quebec: Le Soleil (m)	120 156[3]	153 353 (Sat.)	98 610 (Sun.)
Quebec: Le Journal (m)	108 797[3]	109 990 (Sat.)	97 717 (Sun.)
Edmonton Sun (m)	92 265		130 920 (Sun.)
Windsor Star (e)	87 740		
Halifax Chronicle-Herald (m)	87 194		
Victoria Times-Colonist (all day)	80 878		78 164 (Sun.)
Kitchener-Waterloo Record (e)	78 561		
Regina Leader-Post (e)	74 285		
Calgary Sun (m)	73 083		97 867 (Sun.)
Saskatoon Star-Phoenix (e)	65 893		
Halifax Mail-Star (e)	59 591		
Trois-Rivières: Le Nouvelliste (m)	57 410		
Winnipeg Sun (m)	48 492[3]		60 076 (Sun.)
Moncton Times-Transcript (e)	44 267	56 630 (Sat.)	
St. Catharines Standard (e)	43 804[7]		
Sherbrooke: La Tribune (m)	42 076[3]	47 950 (Sat.)	
Ottawa: Le Droit (all day)	40 090[8]	45 988 (Sat.)	
St. John's Telegram (e)	38 531[3]	54 959 (weekend)	
Kingston Whig-Standard (e)	35 848[7]		
Chicoutimi: Le Quotidien de Saguenay—Lac St-Jean (m)	34 868		
Brantford Expositor (e)	33 505[7]		
Saint John Times-Globe (e)	32 656[3]		
Sydney Post (e)	32 050		
Saint John Telegraph-Journal (m)	30 752[3]	60 476 (Sat.)	
Thunder Bay Chronicle Journal (e)	30 712		
Fredericton Gleaner (e)	29 359		
Sudbury Star (e)	29 139		
Montreal: Le Devoir (m)	29 018[6]	33 497 (Sat.)	
Peterborough Examiner (e)	27 295		
Sault Ste. Marie Star (e)	27 211		
Lethbridge Herald (e)	26 327[7]		
North Bay Nugget (e)	25 263		

(1) Average paid daily circulation for 6 months ending Mar. 31, 1988, unless otherwise indicated. (2) Monday to Saturday unless otherwise indicated. (3) Monday to Friday. (4) Average paid circulation for 5 months ending May 31, 1988. Figures supplied by publisher. (5) Monday through Thursday. (6) Monday to Thursday plus Saturday. (7) Average for 3 months. (8) Average paid daily circulation for 6 months ending Mar. 31, 1987.

(m) morning; (e) evening.

Leading Canadian Paid-Circulation Magazines[1]

Source: Audit Bureau of Circulations; CARD

Magazine	Circulation[2]	Magazine	Circulation[2]
Reader's Digest (Canadian English edition)	1 300 421	Almanach Moderne	150 000[8]
Chatelaine	1 029 807	Almanach du Peuple	141 442
TV Guide	808 353	Outdoor Canada	140 533
Maclean's	649 562	Coupe de Pouce	137 438
Leisure Ways	576 600[3]	Toronto Life Fashion	137 003
Canadian Living	539 835	Select Home Magazine	122 902
Legion Magazine	538 982	Saturday Night	121 055
Time (Canadian edition)	345 198	Hockey News	115 346
Sélection du Reader's Digest (Canadian French edition)	343 425	Rock Express	115 000[4]
Châtelaine (French language edition)	294 116	Travel a la Carte	110 794[2]
Canadian Churchman	271 663[4]	Financial Times of Canada	110 385
L'Actualité	264 265	Your Money	106 964
Touring	263 364[5]	Le Lundi	106 035
United Church Observer	251 705[6]	Toronto Life	98 041
Flare	224 936	Les Idées de Ma Maison	96 335
The Financial Post (weekly edition)	198 985[7]	City & Country Home	87 181
Canadian Geographic	181 095	Canadian Workshop	87 081
Equinox	161 597	Canadian Business	84 052
Harrowsmith	156 189	Croc	81 800
		Sentier Chasse-Pêche	68 939

(1) Paid circulation magazines are sold by subscription and delivered through the mail and/or sold at newsstands. (2) Average paid circulation for 6 months ending Dec. 31, 1987. (3) 4 months ending Mar. 1987. (4) Average paid circulation for 6 months ending June 1987. (5) 6 months ending Sept. 1987. (6) Indicates total average paid circulation for 6 months ending June 1987. (7) 7 months ending Jan. 1988. (8) As of Mar. 1988 for 1987 edition.

Sports

Baseball

National League Final Standings, 1988

Eastern Division

Club	W	L	Pct	GB
New York	100	60	.625	—
Pittsburgh	85	75	.531	15
Montreal	81	81	.500	20
Chicago	77	85	.475	24
St. Louis	76	86	.469	25
Philadelphia	65	96	.404	35½

Western Division

Club	W	L	Pct	GB
Los Angeles	94	67	.584	—
Cincinnati	87	74	.540	7
San Diego	83	78	.516	11
San Francisco	83	79	.512	11½
Houston	82	80	.506	12½
Atlanta	54	106	.338	39½

Individual Batting (at least 115 at-bats); Individual Pitching (at least 50 innings)

Chicago Cubs

Batting	Avg	AB	R	H	HR	RBI
Palmeiro	.307	580	75	178	8	53
Dawson	.303	591	78	179	24	79
Grace	.296	486	65	144	7	57
Law	.293	556	73	163	11	78
Jackson	.266	188	29	50	6	20
Sandberg	.264	618	77	163	19	69
Webster	.260	523	69	136	6	39
Berryhill	.259	309	19	80	7	38
Trillo	.250	164	15	41	1	14
Dunston	.249	575	69	143	9	56

Pitching	W	L	ERA	IP	BB	SO	Sv
Nipper	2	4	3.04	80	34	27	1
Maddux	18	8	3.18	249	81	140	
Moyer	9	15	3.48	202	55	121	
Lancaster	4	6	3.78	85	34	36	5
Sutcliffe	13	14	3.86	226	70	144	
Perry	4	4	4.14	58	16	35	1
Pico	6	7	4.15	112	37	57	1
Schiraldi	9	13	4.38	166	63	140	1
DiPino	2	3	4.98	90	32	69	6
Coffman	2	6	5.78	67	54	24	

New York Mets

Batting	Avg	AB	R	H	HR	RBI
Backman	.303	294	44	89	0	17
Wilson	.296	378	61	112	8	41
McReynolds	.288	552	82	159	27	99
Sasser	.285	123	9	35	1	17
Magaden	.277	314	39	87	1	35
Hernandez	.276	348	43	96	11	55
Dykstra	.270	429	57	116	8	33
Strawberry	.269	543	101	146	39	101
Carter	.242	455	39	110	11	46
Teufel	.334	273	35	64	4	31
Johnson	.230	495	85	114	24	68
Elster	.214	406	41	87	9	37
Mazzilli	.147	116	9	17	0	12

Pitching	W	L	ERA	IP	BB	SO	Sv
Myers	7	3	1.72	68	17	69	26
Cone	20	3	2.22	231	80	213	
Leach	7	2	2.54	92	24	51	3
McDowell	5	5	2.63	89	31	46	16
Ojeda	10	13	2.88	190	33	133	
Fernandez	12	10	3.03	187	70	189	
Gooden	18	9	3.19	248	57	175	
Darling	17	9	3.25	240	60	161	

Montreal Expos

Batting	Avg	AB	R	H	HR	RBI
Galarraga	.302	609	99	184	29	92
Jones	.295	224	29	66	3	24
Brooks	.279	588	61	164	20	90
Hudler	.273	216	38	59	4	14
Fitzgerald	.271	155	17	42	5	23
Raines	.270	429	66	116	12	48
Foley	.265	377	33	100	5	43
Wallach	.257	592	52	152	12	69
Martinez	.255	447	51	114	6	46
Nixon	.244	271	47	66	0	15
Santovenia	.236	309	26	73	8	41
Rivera	.224	371	35	83	4	30

Pitching	W	L	ERA	IP	BB	SO	Sv
Perez	12	8	2.44	188	44	131	
Parrett	12	4	2.65	91	45	62	6
Martinez	15	13	2.72	235	55	120	
McGaffigan	6	0	2.76	91	37	71	4
Hesketh	4	3	2.85	72	35	64	9
B. Smith	12	10	3.00	198	32	122	
Dopson	3	11	3.04	168	58	101	
Holman	4	8	3.23	100	34	58	
Burke	3	5	3.40	82	25	42	18
Heaton	3	10	4.99	97	43	43	2

St. Louis Cardinals

Batting	Avg	AB	R	H	HR	RBI
McGee	.292	562	73	164	3	50
Guerrero	.286	364	40	104	10	65
Pagnozzi	.282	195	17	55	0	15
Oquendo	.277	451	36	125	7	46
Smith	.270	575	80	155	3	51
Pena	.263	505	55	133	10	51
Coleman	.260	616	77	160	3	38
Horner	.257	206	15	53	3	33
Pendleton	.253	391	44	99	6	53
Brunansky	.245	523	69	128	22	79
Walling	.239	234	22	56	1	21
Alicea	.212	297	20	63	1	24
Ford	.195	128	11	25	1	18

Pitching	W	L	ERA	IP	BB	SO	Sv
Magrane	5	9	2.18	165	51	100	
Dayley	2	7	2.77	55	19	38	5
Terry	9	6	2.92	129	34	65	3
Worrell	5	9	3.00	90	34	78	32
DeLeon	13	10	3.67	225	86	298	
McWilliams	6	9	3.90	136	45	70	1
Cox	3	8	3.98	86	25	47	
Mathews	4	6	4.24	68	33	31	
O'Neal	2	3	4.58	53	10	20	

Philadelphia Phillies

Batting	Avg	AB	R	H	HR	RBI
Jordan	.308	273	41	84	11	43
Jones	.290	124	15	36	8	26
Dernier	.289	166	19	48	1	10
Thompson	.288	378	53	109	2	33
Hayes	.272	367	43	100	6	45
Bradley	.264	569	77	150	11	56
Schmidt	.249	390	52	97	12	62
Samuel	.243	629	68	153	12	67
James	.242	566	57	137	19	66
Parrish	.215	424	44	91	15	60
Daulton	.208	144	13	30	1	12
G. Gross	.203	133	10	27	0	5
Jeltz	.187	379	39	71	0	27

Pitching	W	L	ERA	IP	BB	SO	Sv
Harris	4	6	2.36	107	52	71	1
Tekulve	3	7	3.60	80	22	43	4
Gross	12	14	3.69	231	89	162	
Bedrosian	6	6	3.75	74	27	61	28
Maddux	4	3	3.76	88	34	59	
Rawley	8	16	4.18	198	78	87	
Carman	10	14	4.29	201	70	116	
Ruffin	6	10	4.43	144	80	82	3
Palmer	7	9	4.47	129	48	85	
Freeman	2	3	6.10	51	43	37	

Pittsburgh Pirates

Batting	Avg	AB	R	H	HR	RBI
Van Slyke	.288	587	101	169	25	100
Bonds	.283	538	97	152	24	58
Ortiz	.280	118	8	33	2	18
Bonilla	.274	584	87	160	24	100
Oberkfell	.271	476	49	129	3	42
Wilson	.270	126	11	34	2	15
Bream	.264	462	50	122	10	65
Lind	.262	611	82	160	2	49
LaValliere	.261	352	24	92	2	47
Cangelosi	.254	118	18	30	0	8
Reynolds	.248	323	35	80	6	51
Belliard	.213	286	28	61	0	11
Pedrique	.180	128	7	23	0	4

Pitching	W	L	ERA	IP	BB	SO	Sv
Walk	12	10	2.71	212	65	81	
LaPoint	4	2	2.77	52	10	19	
Robinson	11	5	3.03	124	39	87	9
Drabek	15	7	3.08	219	50	127	
Smiley	13	11	3.25	205	46	129	
Gott	6	6	3.49	77	22	76	34
Kipper	2	6	3.74	65	26	39	
Dunne	7	11	3.92	170	88	70	
Fisher	8	10	4.61	146	57	66	1

San Diego Padres

Batting	Avg	AB	R	H	HR	RBI
Gwynn	.313	521	64	163	7	70
Alomar	.266	545	85	145	9	41
Ready	.266	331	43	88	7	39
Flannery	.265	170	16	45	0	19
Wynne	.264	333	37	88	11	42
Thon	.264	258	36	68	1	18
Moreland	.256	511	40	131	5	64
Templeton	.249	362	35	90	3	36
Santiago	.248	492	49	122	10	46
Kruk	.241	378	54	91	9	44
Martinez	.236	365	48	86	18	65
Brown	.235	247	14	58	2	19
Parent	.195	118	9	23	6	15

Pitching	W	L	ERA	IP	BB	SO	Sv
Davis	5	10	2.01	98	42	102	28
Leiper	3	0	2.17	54	14	33	1
McCullers	3	6	2.49	97	55	81	10
Show	16	11	3.26	234	53	144	
Hawkins	14	11	3.35	217	76	91	
Booker	2	2	3.39	63	19	43	
Rasmussen	16	10	3.43	204	58	112	
Grant	2	8	3.69	97	36	61	
Whitson	13	11	3.77	205	45	118	
Jones	9	14	4.12	179	44	82	

Atlanta Braves

Batting	Avg	AB	R	H	HR	RBI
Perry	.300	547	61	164	8	74
Gant	.259	563	85	146	19	60
James	.256	386	46	99	3	30
Virgil	.256	320	23	82	9	31
Thomas	.252	606	54	153	13	68
Hall	.247	231	27	57	1	15
Benedict	.242	236	11	57	0	19
Davis	.230	257	21	59	7	36
Murphy	.226	592	77	134	24	77
Blocker	.212	198	13	42	2	10

Pitching	W	L	ERA	IP	BB	SO	Sv
Alvarez	5	6	2.99	102	53	81	3
Assenmacher	8	7	3.06	79	32	71	5
Puleo	5	5	3.47	106	47	70	1
P. Smith	7	15	3.69	195	88	124	
Mahler	9	16	3.69	249	42	131	
Z. Smith	5	10	4.30	140	44	59	
Glavine	7	17	4.56	195	63	84	
Jiminez	1	6	5.01	55	12	26	

Cincinnati Reds

Batting	Avg	AB	R	H	HR	RBI
Larkin	.296	588	91	174	12	56
Daniels	.291	495	95	144	18	64
Oester	.280	150	20	42	0	10
Davis	.273	472	81	129	26	93
Sabo	.271	538	74	146	11	44
Griffey	.255	243	26	62	4	23
Treadway	.252	301	30	76	2	23
O'Neill	.252	485	58	122	16	73
Esasky	.243	391	40	95	15	62
Collins	.236	174	12	41	0	14
Winningham	.232	203	16	47	0	21
Reed	.226	265	20	60	1	16
Diaz	.219	315	26	69	10	35
McClendon	.219	137	9	30	3	14
Durham	.218	124	14	27	4	8
Concepcion	.198	197	11	39	0	8

Pitching	W	L	ERA	IP	BB	SO	Sv
Franco	6	6	1.57	86	27	46	39
Dibble	1	1	1.82	59	21	59	0
Rijo	13	8	2.39	162	63	160	
Williams	3	2	2.59	62	35	43	1
Jackson	23	8	2.73	260	71	161	
Murphy	0	6	3.08	84	38	74	3
Browning	18	5	3.41	250	64	124	
Charlton	4	5	3.96	61	20	39	
Robinson	3	7	4.12	78	26	38	
Birtsas	1	3	4.20	64	24	38	
Armstrong	4	7	5.79	65	38	45	

San Francisco Giants

Batting	Avg	AB	R	H	HR	RBI
Riles	.294	187	26	55	3	28
Butler	.287	568	109	163	6	43
Clark	.282	575	102	162	29	109
Aldrete	.267	389	44	104	3	50
Thompson	.264	477	66	126	7	48
Maldonado	.255	499	53	127	12	68
Youngblood	.252	123	12	31	0	16
Uribe	.252	493	47	124	3	35
Mitchell	.251	505	60	127	19	80
Manwaring	.250	116	12	29	1	15
Melvin	.234	273	23	64	8	27
Speier	.216	171	26	37	3	18
Williams	.205	156	17	32	8	19
Brenly	.189	206	13	39	5	22

Pitching	W	L	ERA	IP	BB	SO	Sv
Robinson	10	5	2.45	176	49	122	6
Lefferts	3	8	2.92	92	23	58	11
Reuschel	19	11	3.12	245	42	92	
Downs	13	9	3.32	168	47	118	
Krukow	7	4	3.54	124	31	75	
Garrelts	5	9	3.58	98	46	86	13
LaCoss	7	7	3.62	114	47	70	
Hammaker	9	9	3.73	144	41	65	5
Price	1	6	3.94	61	27	49	4

Los Angeles Dodgers

Batting	Avg	AB	R	H	HR	RBI
Hatcher	.293	191	22	56	1	25
Gibson	.290	542	106	157	25	76
Sax	.277	632	70	175	5	57
Marshall	.277	542	63	150	20	82
Shelby	.263	494	65	130	10	64
Scioscia	.257	408	29	105	3	35
Dempsey	.251	167	25	42	7	30
Anderson	.249	285	31	71	2	20
Woodson	.249	173	15	43	3	15
Heep	.242	149	14	36	0	11
Hamilton	.236	309	34	73	6	33
Stubbs	.223	242	30	54	8	34
Griffin	.199	316	39	63	1	27
Davis	.196	281	29	55	2	17

Pitching	W	L	ERA	IP	BB	SO	Sv
Holton	7	3	1.70	84	26	49	1
Pena	6	7	1.91	94	27	83	12
Howell	5	3	2.08	65	21	70	21
Hershiser	23	8	2.26	267	73	178	1
Tudor	10	8	2.32	197	41	87	
Orosco	3	2	2.72	53	30	43	9
Belcher	12	6	2.91	179	51	152	4
Leary	17	11	2.91	228	56	180	
Crews	4	0	2.91	71	16	45	
Valenzuela	5	8	4.24	142	76	64	1
Soto	3	7	4.66	87	28	34	

Houston Astros

Batting	Avg	AB	R	H	HR	RBI
Puhl	.303	234	42	71	3	19
Ramirez	.276	566	51	156	6	59
Davis	.271	561	78	152	30	99
Hatcher	.268	530	79	142	7	52
Young	.257	576	79	148	0	37
Bass	.255	541	57	138	14	72
C. Reynolds	.255	161	20	41	1	14
Trevino	.249	193	19	48	2	13
Doran	.248	480	66	119	7	53
Bell	.241	323	27	78	7	40
Ashby	.238	227	19	54	7	33
Pankovits	.221	140	13	31	2	12
Biggio	.211	123	14	26	3	5
Candaele	.170	147	11	25	0	5

Pitching	W	L	ERA	IP	BB	SO	Sv
Agosto	10	2	2.26	91	30	33	4
Smith	4	5	2.67	57	19	38	27
Scott	14	8	2.92	218	53	190	
Andersen	2	4	2.94	82	20	66	5
Deshaies	11	14	3.00	207	72	127	
Knepper	14	5	3.14	175	67	103	
Meads	3	1	3.18	39	14	27	
Ryan	12	11	3.52	220	87	228	
Darwin	8	13	3.84	192	48	129	3
Andujar	2	5	4.00	78	21	35	
Forsch	10	8	4.29	136	44	54	

American League Final Standings, 1988

Eastern Division

Club	W	L	Pct	GB
Boston	89	73	.549	—
Detroit	88	74	.543	1
Milwaukee	87	75	.537	2
Toronto	87	75	.537	2
New York	85	76	.528	3½
Cleveland	78	84	.481	11
Baltimore	54	107	.335	34½

Western Division

Club	W	L	Pct	GB
Oakland	104	58	.642	—
Minnesota	91	71	.562	13
Kansas City	84	77	.522	19½
California	75	87	.463	29
Chicago	71	90	.441	32½
Texas	70	91	.435	33½
Seattle	68	93	.422	35½

Individual Batting (at least 115 at-bats); Individual Pitching (at least 50 innings)

Baltimore Orioles

Batting	Avg	AB	R	H	HR	RBI
Orsulak	.288	379	48	109	8	27
Murray	.284	603	75	171	28	84
C. Ripkin	.264	575	87	152	23	81
Tettleton	.261	283	31	74	11	37
Schu	.256	270	22	69	4	20
Sheets	.230	452	38	104	10	47
Stanicek	.230	261	29	60	4	17
Kennedy	.226	265	20	60	3	16
Traber	.222	352	25	78	10	45
Gonzales	.215	237	13	51	2	15
Anderson	.212	325	31	69	1	21
B. Ripkin	.207	512	52	106	2	34
Gerhart	.195	262	27	51	9	23

Pitching	W	L	ERA	IP	BB	SO	Sv
Schmidt	8	5	3.40	129	38	67	2
Neidenfuer	3	4	3.51	59	19	40	18
Sisk	3	3	3.72	94	45	26	
Bautista	6	15	4.30	171	45	76	
Ballard	8	12	4.40	153	42	41	
Thurmond	1	8	4.58	74	27	29	3
Williamson	5	8	4.90	117	40	69	2
Tibbs	4	15	5.39	158	63	82	
Morgan	1	6	5.43	71	23	29	1

Boston Red Sox

Batting	Avg	AB	R	H	HR	RBI
Boggs	.366	584	128	214	5	58
Greenwell	.325	590	86	192	22	119
Burks	.294	540	93	159	18	92
Evans	.293	559	96	164	21	111
Reed	.293	338	60	99	1	28
Barrett	.283	612	83	173	1	65
Carone	.269	264	31	71	3	27
Rice	.264	485	57	128	15	72
Benzinger	.254	405	47	103	13	70
Owen	.249	257	40	64	5	18
Gedman	.231	299	33	69	9	39
Parrish	.217	406	32	88	14	52

Pitching	W	L	ERA	IP	BB	SO	Sv
Smith	4	5	2.80	83	37	96	29
Clemens	18	12	2.93	264	62	291	
Stanley	6	4	3.19	101	29	57	5
Boddicker	13	15	3.39	236	77	156	
Lamp	7	6	3.48	82	19	49	
Gardner	8	6	3.50	149	64	109	2
Hurst	18	6	3.66	216	65	166	
Sellers	1	7	4.83	85	56	70	
Boyd	9	7	5.34	129	41	71	
Smithson	9	6	5.97	126	37	73	

Detroit Tigers

Batting	Avg	AB	R	H	HR	RBI
Trammell	.311	466	73	145	15	69
Bergman	.294	289	37	85	5	35
Whitaker	.275	403	54	111	12	55
Salazar	.270	452	61	122	12	62
Lemon	.264	512	67	135	17	64
Sheridan	.254	347	47	88	11	47
Nokes	.251	382	53	96	16	53
Murphy	.250	144	16	36	4	19
Heath	.247	219	24	54	5	18
Lynn	.246	391	46	96	25	56
Brookens	.243	441	62	107	5	38
Herndon	.224	174	16	39	4	20
Knight	.217	299	34	65	3	33
Walewander	.211	175	23	37	0	6
Pettis	.210	458	65	96	3	36
Evans	.208	437	48	91	22	64

Pitching	W	L	ERA	IP	BB	SO	Sv
Henneman	9	6	1.87	91	24	58	22
Gibson	4	2	2.93	92	34	50	
Robinson	13	6	2.98	172	72	114	
Hernandez	6	5	3.06	67	31	59	10
King	4	1	3.41	68	34	45	3
Morris	15	13	3.94	235	83	168	
Terrell	7	16	3.97	206	78	84	
Tanana	14	11	4.21	203	64	127	
Alexander	14	11	4.32	229	46	126	
Power	6	7	5.91	99	38	57	

New York Yankees

Batting	Avg	AB	R	H	HR	RBI
Winfield	.322	559	96	180	25	107
Mattingly	.311	599	94	186	18	88
Washington	.308	455	62	140	11	64
Henderson	.305	554	118	169	6	50
Slaught	.283	322	33	91	9	43
Phelps	.263	297	54	78	24	54
Aguayo	.250	140	12	35	3	8
Clark	.242	496	81	120	27	93
Santana	.240	480	50	115	4	38
Randolph	.230	404	43	93	2	34
Skinner	.227	251	23	57	4	23
Ward	.225	231	26	52	4	24
Meacham	.217	115	18	25	0	7
Pagliarulo	.216	444	46	96	15	67
Velarde	.174	115	18	20	5	12

Pitching	W	L	ERA	IP	BB	SO	Sv
Candelaria	13	7	3.38	157	23	121	1
Righetti	5	4	3.52	87	37	70	25
Allen	5	3	3.84	117	37	61	
Leiter	4	4	3.92	57	33	60	
Guidry	2	3	4.18	56	15	32	
Rhoden	12	12	4.20	197	56	94	
Mohorcic	4	8	4.22	74	29	44	6
Shields	5	5	4.37	82	30	55	
Hudson	6	6	4.49	106	36	58	2
John	9	8	4.49	176	46	81	

Toronto Blue Jays

Batting	Avg	AB	R	H	HR	RBI
Mulliniks	.300	337	49	101	12	48
Lee	.291	381	38	111	2	38
Fernandez	.287	648	76	186	5	70
McGriff	.282	536	100	151	34	82
Gruber	.278	569	75	158	16	81
Leach	.276	199	21	55	0	23
Borders	.273	154	15	42	5	21
Bell	.269	614	78	165	24	97
Liriano	.264	276	36	73	3	23
Whitt	.251	398	63	100	16	70
Barfield	.244	468	62	114	18	56
Moseby	.239	472	77	113	10	42
Fielder	.230	174	24	40	9	23
Campusano	.218	142	14	31	2	12

Pitching	W	L	ERA	IP	BB	SO	Sv
Henke	4	4	2.91	68	24	66	25
Stieb	16	8	2.04	207	79	147	
Cerutti	6	7	3.13	123	42	65	1
Musselman	8	5	3.18	85	30	39	
Key	12	5	3.29	131	30	65	
Ward	9	3	3.30	111	60	91	15
Flanagan	13	13	4.18	211	80	99	
Eichhorn	0	3	4.18	66	27	28	1
Clancy	11	13	4.49	196	47	118	1
Wells	3	5	4.62	64	31	56	4

Cleveland Indians

Batting	Avg	AB	R	H	HR	RBI
Francona	.311	212	34	66	1	12
Franco	.303	613	88	186	10	54
Hall	.280	515	69	144	6	71
Castillo	.273	176	12	48	4	14
Snyder	.272	511	71	139	26	75
Carter	.271	621	85	168	27	98
Clark	.263	156	11	41	3	18
Allanson	.263	434	44	114	5	50
Kittle	.258	225	31	58	18	43
Washington	.256	223	30	57	2	21
Upshaw	.245	493	58	121	11	50
Jacoby	.241	552	59	133	9	49
Zuvella	.231	130	9	30	0	7
Bell	.218	211	23	46	2	21

Pitching	W	L	ERA	IP	BB	SO	Sv
Jones	3	4	2.27	83	16	72	37
Havens	2	3	3.14	57	17	30	1
Swindell	18	14	3.20	242	45	180	
Candiotti	14	8	3.28	216	53	137	
Farrell	14	10	4.24	210	67	92	
Gordon	3	4	4.40	59	19	20	1
Yett	9	6	4.62	134	55	71	
Bailes	9	14	4.90	145	46	53	
Black	4	4	5.00	81	34	63	1
Nichols	1	7	5.06	69	23	31	

Kansas City Royals

Batting	Avg	AB	R	H	HR	RBI
Brett	.306	589	90	180	24	103
Seitzer	.304	559	90	170	5	60
Tabler	.282	444	53	125	2	66
Tartabull	.274	507	80	139	26	102
Wilson	.262	591	81	155	1	37
Stillwell	.251	459	63	115	10	53
Buckner	.249	285	19	71	3	43
Jackson	.246	439	63	108	25	68
Quirk	.240	196	22	47	8	25
White	.235	537	48	126	8	58
Eisenreich	.218	202	26	44	1	19
Pecota	.208	178	29	37	1	15

Pitching	W	L	ERA	IP	BB	SO	Sv
Farr	5	4	2.50	82	30	72	20
Gubicza	20	8	2.70	269	83	183	
Leibrandt	13	12	3.19	243	62	125	
Montgomery	7	2	3.45	62	30	47	1
Saberhagen	14	16	3.80	260	59	171	
Bannister	12	13	4.33	189	68	113	

Seattle Mariners

Batting	Avg	AB	R	H	HR	RBI
Davis	.295	478	67	141	18	69
Coles	.292	195	32	57	10	34
Reynolds	.283	598	61	169	4	41
Brantley	.263	577	76	152	15	56
Cotto	.259	386	50	100	8	33
Bradley	.257	335	45	86	4	33
Quinones	.248	499	63	124	12	52
Balboni	.235	413	46	97	23	66
Valle	.231	290	29	67	10	50
Presley	.230	544	50	125	14	62
Buhner	.215	261	36	56	13	38
Kingery	.203	123	21	25	1	9

Pitching	W	L	ERA	IP	BB	SO	Sv
Jackson	6	5	2.63	99	43	76	4
Bankhead	7	9	3.07	135	38	102	
Langston	15	11	3.34	261	110	235	
Moore	9	15	3.78	228	63	182	1
Reed	1	1	3.96	86	33	48	1
Swift	8	12	4.59	174	65	47	
Campbell	6	10	5.89	114	43	63	
Trout	4	7	7.83	56	31	14	

Minnesota Twins

Batting	Avg	AB	R	H	HR	RBI
Puckett	.356	657	109	234	24	121
Moses	.316	206	33	65	2	12
Hrbek	.312	510	75	159	25	76
Gaetti	.301	468	66	141	28	88
Harper	.295	166	15	49	3	20
Gladden	.269	576	91	155	11	62
Larkin	.267	505	56	135	8	70
Herr	.263	304	42	80	1	21
Bush	.261	394	51	103	14	51
Laudner	.251	375	38	94	13	54
Gagne	.236	461	70	109	14	48
Newman	.223	260	35	58	0	19
Lombardozzi	.209	287	34	60	3	27

Pitching	W	L	ERA	IP	BB	SO	Sv
Anderson	16	9	2.45	202	37	83	
Reardon	2	4	2.47	73	15	56	42
Viola	24	7	2.64	255	54	193	
Atherton	7	5	3.41	74	22	43	3
Straker	2	5	3.92	82	25	23	1
Berenguer	8	4	3.96	100	61	99	2
Toliver	7	6	4.24	114	52	69	
Portugal	3	3	4.53	57	17	31	3
Lea	7	7	4.85	130	50	72	
Blyleven	10	17	5.43	207	51	145	

Chicago White Sox

Batting	Avg	AB	R	H	HR	RBI
Gallagher	.303	347	59	105	5	31
Baines	.277	599	55	166	13	81
Fisk	.277	253	37	70	19	50
Lyons	.269	472	59	127	5	45
Guillen	.261	566	58	148	0	39
Salas	.250	196	17	49	3	9
Walker	.247	377	45	93	8	42
Diaz	.237	152	12	36	3	12
Manrique	.235	345	43	81	5	37
Pasqua	.227	422	48	96	20	50
Hill	.217	221	17	48	2	20
Boston	.217	281	37	61	15	31
Calderon	.212	264	40	56	14	35
Johnson	.185	124	11	23	0	6
Williams	.159	220	18	35	8	28

Pitching	W	L	ERA	IP	BB	SO	Sv
Thigpen	5	8	3.30	90	33	62	34
Reuss	13	9	3.44	183	43	73	
Perez	12	10	3.79	197	72	138	
McDowell	5	10	3.97	158	68	84	
Long	8	11	4.03	174	43	77	2
Bittiger	2	4	4.23	61	29	33	
Patterson	0	2	4.79	20	7	8	1
Davis	2	5	6.64	63	50	37	1

Milwaukee Brewers

Batting	Avg	AB	R	H	HR	RBI
Molitor	.312	609	115	190	13	60
Yount	.306	621	92	190	13	91
Gantner	.276	539	67	149	0	47
Meyer	.263	327	22	86	11	45
Braggs	.261	272	30	71	10	42
Deer	.252	492	71	124	23	85
Surhoff	.245	493	47	121	5	38
Sveum	.242	467	41	113	9	51
Leonard	.235	374	45	88	8	44
O'Brien	.220	118	12	26	2	9
Brock	.212	364	53	77	6	50
Schroeder	.156	122	9	19	5	10

Pitching	W	L	ERA	IP	BB	SO	Sv
Mirabella	2	2	1.65	60	21	33	4
Plesac	1	2	2.41	52	12	52	30
Higuera	16	9	2.45	227	59	192	
Crim	7	6	2.91	105	28	58	9
August	13	7	3.09	148	48	66	
Bosio	7	15	3.36	182	38	84	6
Nieves	7	5	4.08	110	50	73	1
Wegman	13	13	4.12	199	50	84	
Jones	5	0	4.35	80	29	48	1
Filer	5	8	4.43	101	33	39	
Birkbeck	10	8	4.72	124	37	64	

Oakland A's

Batting	Avg	AB	R	H	HR	RBI
Canseco	.307	610	129	187	42	124
Henderson	.304	507	100	154	24	94
Polonia	.292	288	51	84	2	27
Lansford	.279	556	80	155	7	57
Steinbach	.265	351	42	93	9	51
McGwire	.260	550	87	143	32	99
Parker	.257	377	43	97	12	55
Hassey	.257	323	32	83	7	45
Javier	.257	397	49	102	2	35
Hubbard	.255	294	35	75	3	33
Weiss	.250	452	44	113	3	39
Baylor	.220	264	28	58	7	34
Galiego	.209	277	38	58	2	20

Pitching	W	L	ERA	IP	BB	SO	Sv
Eckersley	4	2	2.35	72	11	70	45
Cadaret	5	2	2.89	71	36	65	3
Plunk	7	2	3.00	78	39	79	5
Nelson	9	6	3.06	111	38	67	3
Burns	8	2	3.16	102	34	57	1
Stewart	21	12	3.23	275	110	192	
Honeycutt	3	2	3.50	79	25	47	7
Welch	17	9	3.64	244	81	158	
Davis	16	7	3.70	201	91	127	
Young	11	8	4.14	156	50	69	
Ontiveros	3	4	4.61	54	21	30	

Texas Rangers

Batting	Avg	AB	R	H	HR	RBI
Wilkerson	.293	338	41	99	0	28
Petralli	.282	351	35	99	7	36
Fletcher	.276	515	59	142	0	47
O'Brien	.272	547	57	149	16	71
Sierra	.254	615	77	156	23	91
Buechele	.250	503	68	126	16	58
Incaviglia	.249	418	59	104	22	54
Espy	.248	347	46	86	2	39
McDowell	.247	437	55	108	6	37
Browne	.229	214	26	49	1	17
Stanley	.229	249	21	57	3	27
Kunkel	.227	154	14	35	2	15
Brower	.224	201	29	45	1	11

Pitching	W	L	ERA	IP	BB	SO	Sv
McMurtry	3	3	2.25	60	24	35	3
Guante	5	6	2.82	79	26	65	12
Hough	15	16	3.32	252	126	174	
Guzman	11	13	3.70	206	82	157	
Russell	10	9	3.82	188	66	88	
Witt	8	10	3.92	174	101	148	
Kilgus	12	15	4.16	203	71	88	
Williams	2	7	4.63	68	47	61	18
Hayward	4	6	5.46	62	35	37	

California Angels

Batting	Avg	AB	R	H	HR	RBI
Ray	.306	602	75	184	6	83
Boone	.295	352	38	104	5	39
Joyner	.295	597	81	176	13	85
Armas	.272	368	42	100	13	49
Davis	.268	600	81	161	21	93
White	.259	455	76	118	11	51
Howell	.254	500	59	127	16	63
Hendrick	.244	127	12	31	3	19
Downing	.242	484	80	117	25	64
McLemore	.240	233	38	56	2	16
Schofield	.239	527	61	126	6	34
Miller	.221	140	21	31	2	7

Pitching	W	L	ERA	IP	BB	SO	Sv
Harvey	7	5	2.13	76	20	67	17
Minton	4	5	2.85	79	34	46	7
Cliburn	4	2	4.07	84	32	42	
Witt	13	16	4.15	249	87	133	
Finley	9	15	4.17	194	82	111	
McCaskill	8	6	4.31	146	61	98	
Petry	3	9	4.38	139	59	64	
Clark	6	6	5.07	94	31	39	
Fraser	12	13	5.41	194	80	86	

World Series Results, 1903-1987

1903 Boston AL 5, Pittsburgh NL 3
1904 No series
1905 New York NL 4, Philadelphia AL 1
1906 Chicago AL 4, Chicago NL 2
1907 Chicago NL 4, Detroit AL 0, 1 tie
1908 Chicago NL 4, Detroit AL 1
1909 Pittsburgh NL 4, Detroit AL 3
1910 Philadelphia AL 4, Chicago NL 1
1911 Philadelphia AL 4, New York NL 2
1912 Boston AL 4, New York NL 3, 1 tie
1913 Philadelphia AL 4, New York NL 1
1914 Boston NL 4, Philadelphia AL 0
1915 Boston AL 4, Philadelphia NL 1
1916 Boston AL 4, Brooklyn NL 1
1917 Chicago AL 4, New York NL 2
1918 Boston AL 4, Chicago NL 2
1919 Cincinnati NL 5, Chicago AL 3
1920 Cleveland AL 5, Brooklyn NL 2
1921 New York NL 5, New York AL 3
1922 New York NL 4, New York AL 0, 1 tie
1923 New York AL 4, New York NL 2
1924 Washington AL 4, New York NL 3
1925 Pittsburgh NL 4, Washington AL 3
1926 St. Louis NL 4, New York AL 3
1927 New York AL 4, Pittsburgh NL 0
1928 New York AL 4, St. Louis NL 0
1929 Philadelphia AL 4, Chicago NL 1
1930 Philadelphia AL 4, St. Louis NL 2
1931 St. Louis NL 4, Philadelphia AL 3

1932 New York AL 4, Chicago NL 0
1933 New York NL 4, Washington AL 1
1934 St. Louis NL 4, Detroit AL 3
1935 Detroit AL 4, Chicago NL 2
1936 New York AL 4, New York NL 2
1937 New York AL 4, New York NL 1
1938 New York AL 4, Chicago NL 0
1939 New York AL 4, Cincinnati NL 0
1940 Cincinnati NL 4, Detroit AL 3
1941 New York AL 4, Brooklyn NL 1
1942 St. Louis NL 4, New York AL 1
1943 New York AL 4, St. Louis NL 1
1944 St. Louis NL 4, St. Louis AL 2
1945 Detroit AL 4, Chicago NL 3
1946 St. Louis NL 4, Boston AL 3
1947 New York AL 4, Brooklyn NL 3
1948 Cleveland AL 4, Boston NL 2
1949 New York AL 4, Brooklyn NL 1
1950 New York AL 4, Philadelphia NL 0
1951 New York AL 4, New York NL 2
1952 New York AL 4, Brooklyn NL 3
1953 New York AL 4, Brooklyn NL 2
1954 New York NL 4, Cleveland AL 0
1955 Brooklyn NL 4, New York AL 3
1956 New York AL 4, Brooklyn NL 3
1957 Milwaukee NL 4, New York AL 3
1958 New York AL 4, Milwaukee NL 3
1959 Los Angeles NL 4, Chicago AL 2
1960 Pittsburgh NL 4, New York AL 3
1961 New York AL 4, Cincinnati NL 1

1962 New York AL 4, San Francisco NL 3
1963 Los Angeles NL 4, New York AL 0
1964 St. Louis NL 4, New York AL 3
1965 Los Angeles NL 4, Minnesota AL 3
1966 Baltimore AL 4, Los Angeles NL 0
1967 St. Louis NL 4, Boston AL 3
1968 Detroit AL 4, St. Louis NL 3
1969 New York NL 4, Baltimore AL 1
1970 Baltimore AL 4, Cincinnati NL 1
1971 Pittsburgh NL 4, Baltimore AL 3
1972 Oakland AL 4, Cincinnati NL 3
1973 Oakland AL 4, New York NL 3
1974 Oakland AL 4, Los Angeles NL 1
1975 Cincinnati NL 4, Boston AL 3
1976 Cincinnati NL 4, New York AL 0
1977 New York AL 4, Los Angeles NL 2
1978 New York AL 4, Los Angeles NL 2
1979 Pittsburgh NL 4, Baltimore AL 3
1980 Philadelphia NL 4, Kansas City AL 2
1981 Los Angeles NL 4, New York AL 2
1982 St. Louis NL 4, Milwaukee AL 3
1983 Baltimore AL 4, Philadelphia NL 1
1984 Detroit AL 4, San Diego NL 1
1985 Kansas City AL 4, St. Louis NL 3
1986 New York NL 4, Boston AL 3
1987 Minnesota AL 4, St. Louis NL 3

World Series MVPs

1955 Johnny Podres, Brooklyn (NL)
1956 Don Larsen, New York (AL)
1957 Lew Burdette, Milwaukee (NL)
1958 Bob Turley, New York (AL)
1959 Larry Sherry, Los Angeles (NL)
1960 Bobby Richardson, New York (AL)
1961 Whitey Ford, New York (AL)
1962 Ralph Terry, New York (AL)
1963 Sandy Koufax, Los Angeles (NL)
1964 Bob Gibson, St. Louis (NL)
1965 Sandy Koufax, Los Angeles (NL)
1966 Frank Robinson, Baltimore (AL)

1967 Bob Gibson, St. Louis (NL)
1968 Mickey Lolich, Detroit (AL)
1969 Donn Clendenon, New York (NL)
1970 Brooks Robinson, Baltimore (AL)
1971 Roberto Clemente, Pittsburgh (NL)
1972 Gene Tenace, Oakland (AL)
1973 Reggie Jackson, Oakland (AL)
1974 Rollie Fingers, Oakland (AL)
1975 Pete Rose, Cincinnati (NL)
1976 Johnny Bench, Cincinnati (NL)
1977 Reggie Jackson, New York (AL)
1978 Bucky Dent, New York (AL)

1979 Willie Stargell, Pittsburgh (NL)
1980 Mike Schmidt, Philadelphia (NL)
1981 Ron Cey, Pedro Guerrero, Steve Yeager, Los Angeles (NL)
1982 Darrell Porter, St. Louis (NL)
1983 Rick Dempsey, Baltimore (AL)
1984 Alan Trammell, Detroit (AL)
1985 Bret Saberhagen, Kansas City (AL)
1986 Ray Knight, New York (NL)
1987 Frank Viola, Minnesota (AL)

Major League Pennant Winners, 1901–1988

National League   American League

Year	Winner	Won	Lost	Pct	Manager	Year	Winner	Won	Lost	Pct	Manager
1901	Pittsburgh	90	49	.647	Clarke	1901	Chicago	83	53	.610	Griffith
1902	Pittsburgh	103	36	.741	Clarke	1902	Philadelphia	83	53	.610	Mack
1903	Pittsburgh	91	49	.650	Clarke	1903	Boston	91	47	.659	Collins
1904	New York	106	47	.693	McGraw	1904	Boston	95	59	.617	Collins
1905	New York	105	48	.686	McGraw	1905	Philadelphia	92	56	.622	Mack
1906	Chicago	116	36	.763	Chance	1906	Chicago	93	58	.616	Jones
1907	Chicago	107	45	.704	Chance	1907	Detroit	92	58	.613	Jennings
1908	Chicago	99	55	.643	Chance	1908	Detroit	90	63	.588	Jennings
1909	Pittsburgh	110	42	.724	Clarke	1909	Detroit	98	54	.645	Jennings
1910	Chicago	104	50	.675	Chance	1910	Philadelphia	102	48	.680	Mack
1911	New York	99	54	.647	McGraw	1911	Philadelphia	101	50	.669	Mack
1912	New York	103	48	.682	McGraw	1912	Boston	105	47	.691	Stahl
1913	New York	101	51	.664	McGraw	1913	Philadelphia	96	57	.627	Mack
1914	Boston	94	59	.614	Stallings	1914	Philadelphia	99	53	.651	Mack
1915	Philadelphia	90	62	.592	Moran	1915	Boston	101	50	.669	Carrigan
1916	Brooklyn	94	60	.610	Robinson	1916	Boston	91	63	.591	Carrigan
1917	New York	98	56	.636	McGraw	1917	Chicago	100	54	.649	Rowland
1918	Chicago	84	45	.651	Mitchell	1918	Boston	75	51	.595	Barrow
1919	Cincinnati	96	44	.686	Moran	1919	Chicago	88	52	.629	Gleason
1920	Brooklyn	93	60	.604	Robinson	1920	Cleveland	98	56	.636	Speaker
1921	New York	94	56	.614	McGraw	1921	New York	98	55	.641	Huggins
1922	New York	93	61	.604	McGraw	1922	New York	94	60	.610	Huggins
1923	New York	95	58	.621	McGraw	1923	New York	98	54	.645	Huggins
1924	New York	93	60	.608	McGraw	1924	Washington	92	62	.597	Harris
1925	Pittsburgh	95	58	.621	McKechnie	1925	Washington	96	55	.636	Harris
1926	St. Louis	89	65	.578	Hornsby	1926	New York	91	63	.591	Huggins
1927	Pittsburgh	94	60	.610	Bush	1927	New York	110	44	.714	Huggins
1928	St. Louis	95	59	.617	McKechnie	1928	New York	101	53	.656	Huggins
1929	Chicago	98	54	.645	McCarthy	1929	Philadelphia	104	46	.693	Mack
1930	St. Louis	92	62	.597	Street	1930	Philadelphia	102	52	.662	Mack

National League

Year	Winner	Won	Lost	Pct	Manager
1931	St. Louis	101	53	.656	Street
1932	Chicago	90	64	.584	Grimm
1933	New York	91	61	.599	Terry
1934	St. Louis	95	58	.621	Frisch
1935	Chicago	100	54	.649	Grimm
1936	New York	91	62	.597	Terry
1937	New York	95	57	.625	Terry
1938	Chicago	89	63	.586	Hartnett
1939	Cincinnati	97	57	.630	McKechnie
1940	Cincinnati	100	53	.654	McKechnie
1941	Brooklyn.	100	54	.649	Durocher
1942	St. Louis	106	48	.688	Southworth
1943	St. Louis	105	49	.682	Southworth
1944	St. Louis	105	49	.682	Southworth
1945	Chicago	98	56	.636	Grimm
1946	St. Louis	98	58	.628	Dyer
1947	Brooklyn	94	60	.610	Shotton
1948	Boston	91	62	.595	Southworth
1949	Brooklyn	97	57	.630	Shotton
1950	Philadelphia . . .	91	63	.591	Sawyer
1951	New York	98	59	.624	Durocher
1952	Brooklyn	96	57	.627	Dressen
1953	Brooklyn	105	49	.682	Dressen
1954	New York	97	57	.630	Durocher
1955	Brooklyn	98	55	.641	Alston
1956	Brooklyn	93	61	.604	Alston
1957	Milwaukee. . . .	95	59	.617	Haney
1958	Milwaukee. . . .	92	62	.597	Haney
1959	Los Angeles. . .	88	68	.564	Alston
1960	Pittsburgh	95	59	.617	Murtaugh
1961	Cincinnati	93	61	.604	Hutchinson
1962	San Francisco. .	103	62	.624	Dark
1963	Los Angeles. . .	99	63	.611	Alston
1964	St. Louis	93	69	.574	Keane
1965	Los Angeles. . .	97	65	.599	Alston
1966	Los Angeles. . .	95	67	.586	Alston
1967	St. Louis	101	60	.627	Schoendienst
1968	St. Louis	97	65	.599	Schoendienst

American League

Year	Winner	Won	Lost	Pct	Manager
1931	Philadelphia . . .	107	45	.704	Mack
1932	New York.	107	47	.695	McCarthy
1933	Washington. . . .	99	53	.651	Cronin
1934	Detroit.	101	53	.656	Cochrane
1935	Detroit.	93	58	.616	Cochrane
1936	New York	102	51	.667	McCarthy
1937	New York	102	52	.662	McCarthy
1938	New York.	99	53	.651	McCarthy
1939	New York.	106	45	.702	McCarthy
1940	Detroit.	90	64	.584	Baker
1941	New York	101	53	.656	McCarthy
1942	New York	103	51	.669	McCarthy
1943	New York	98	56	.636	McCarthy
1944	St. Louis	89	65	.578	Sewell
1945	Detroit.	88	65	.575	O'Neill
1946	Boston	104	50	.675	Cronin
1947	New York	97	57	.630	Harris
1948	Cleveland.	97	58	.626	Boudreau
1949	New York	97	57	.630	Stengel
1950	New York	98	56	.636	Stengel
1951	New York	98	56	.636	Stengel
1952	New York	95	59	.617	Stengel
1953	New York	99	52	.656	Stengel
1954	Cleveland.	111	43	.721	Lopez
1955	New York	96	58	.623	Stengel
1956	New York	97	57	.630	Stengel
1957	New York	98	56	.636	Stengel
1958	New York	92	62	.597	Stengel
1959	Chicago	94	60	.610	Lopez
1960	New York	97	57	.630	Stengel
1961	New York	109	53	.673	Houk
1962	New York	96	66	.593	Houk
1963	New York	104	57	.646	Houk
1964	New York	99	63	.611	Berra
1965	Minnesota	102	60	.630	Mele
1966	Baltimore	97	63	.606	Bauer
1967	Boston	92	70	.568	Williams
1968	Detroit.	103	59	.636	Smith

National League

	East				West					Playoff
Year	Winner	W	L	Pct	Manager	Winner	W	L	Pct	Manager	winner
1969	N.Y. Mets. . .	100	62	.617	Hodges	Atlanta	93	69	.574	Harris	New York
1970	Pittsburgh. . .	89	73	.549	Murtaugh	Cincinnati.	102	60	.630	Anderson	Cincinnati
1971	Pittsburgh. . .	97	65	.599	Murtaugh	San Francisco . .	90	72	.556	Fox	Pittsburgh
1972	Pittsburgh. . .	96	59	.619	Virdon	Cincinnati. . . .	95	59	.617	Anderson	Cincinnati
1973	N.Y. Mets. . .	82	79	.509	Berra	Cincinnati. . . .	99	63	.611	Anderson	New York
1974	Pittsburgh. . .	88	74	.543	Murtaugh	Los Angeles . .	102	60	.630	Alston	Los Angeles
1975	Pittsburgh. . .	92	69	.571	Murtaugh	Cincinnati. . . .	108	54	.667	Anderson	Cincinnati
1976	Philadelphia .	101	61	.623	Ozark	Cincinnati. . . .	102	60	.630	Anderson	Cincinnati
1977	Philadelphia .	101	61	.623	Ozark	Los Angeles . .	98	64	.605	Lasorda	Los Angeles
1978	Philadelphia .	90	72	.556	Ozark	Los Angeles . .	95	67	.586	Lasorda	Los Angeles
1979	Pittsburgh. . .	98	64	.605	Tanner	Cincinnati. . . .	90	71	.559	McNamara	Pittsburgh
1980	Philadelphia .	91	71	.562	Green	Houston	93	70	.571	Virdon	Philadelphia
1981(a)	Philadelphia .	34	21	.618	Green	Los Angeles . . .	36	21	.632	Lasorda	(c)
1981(b)	Montreal . . .	30	23	.566	Williams, Fanning	Houston	33	20	.623	Virdon	Los Angeles
1982	St. Louis . . .	92	70	.568	Herzog	Atlanta	89	73	.549	Torre	St. Louis
1983	Philadelphia .	90	72	.556	Corrales, Owens	Los Angeles . . .	91	71	.562	Lasorda	Philadelphia
1984	Chicago. . . .	96	65	.596	Frey	San Diego	92	70	.568	Williams	San Diego
1985	St. Louis . . .	101	61	.623	Herzog	Los Angeles . . .	95	67	.586	Lasorda	St. Louis
1986	N.Y. Mets. . .	108	54	.667	Johnson	Houston	96	66	.593	Lanier	New York
1987	St. Louis . . .	95	67	.586	Herzog	San Francisco . .	90	72	.556	Craig	St. Louis
1988	N.Y. Mets. . .	100	60	.625	Johnson	Los Angeles. . .	94	67	.584	Lasorda	Los Angeles

American League

	East				West					Playoff
Year	Winner	W	L	Pct	Manager	Winner	W	L	Pct	Manager	winner
1969	Baltimore . . .	109	53	.673	Weaver	Minnesota	97	65	.599	Martin	Baltimore
1970	Baltimore . . .	108	54	.667	Weaver	Minnesota	98	64	.605	Rigney	Baltimore
1971	Baltimore . . .	101	57	.639	Weaver	Oakland	101	60	.627	Williams	Baltimore
1972	Detroit.	86	70	.551	Martin	Oakland	93	62	.600	Williams	Oakland
1973	Baltimore . . .	97	65	.599	Weaver	Oakland	94	68	.580	Williams	Oakland
1974	Baltimore . . .	91	71	.562	Weaver	Oakland	90	72	.556	Dark	Oakland
1975	Boston	95	65	.594	Johnson	Oakland	98	64	.605	Dark	Boston
1976	New York . . .	97	62	.610	Martin	Kansas City . . .	90	72	.556	Herzog	New York
1977	New York . . .	100	62	.617	Martin	Kansas City . . .	102	60	.630	Herzog	New York
1978	New York . . .	100	63	.613	Martin, Lemon	Kansas City . . .	92	70	.568	Herzog	New York
1979	Baltimore . . .	102	57	.642	Weaver	California.	88	74	.543	Fregosi	Baltimore

	East					West					Playoff
Year	Winner	W	L	Pct	Manager	Winner	W	L	Pct	Manager	winner
1980	New York . . .	103	59	.636	Howser	Kansas City	97	65	.599	Frey	Kansas City
1981(a)	New York . . .	34	22	.607	Michael	Oakland	37	23	.617	Martin	(d)
1981(b)	Milwaukee	31	22	.585	Rodgers	Kansas City	30	23	.566	Frey, Howser	New York
1982	Milwaukee	95	67	.586	Rodgers, Kuenn	California.	93	69	.574	Mauch	Milwaukee
1983	Baltimore	98	64	.605	Altobelli	Chicago	99	63	.611	LaRussa	Baltimore
1984	Detroit	104	58	.642	Anderson	Kansas City	84	78	.519	Howser	Detroit
1985	Toronto	99	62	.615	Cox	Kansas City	91	71	.562	Howser	Kansas City
1986	Boston.	95	66	.590	McNamara	California.	92	70	.568	Mauch	Boston
1987	Detroit	98	64	.605	Anderson	Minnesota	85	77	.525	Kelly	Minnesota
1988	Boston.	89	73	.549	Morgan	Oakland	104	58	.642	La Russa	Oakland

(a) First half; (b) Second half; (c) Montreal and L.A. won the divisional playoffs; (d) N.Y. and Oakland won the divisional playoffs.

Most Valuable Player

Baseball Writers' Association

National League

Year	Player, team	Year	Player, team	Year	Player, team
1931	Frank Frisch, St. Louis	1951	Roy Campanella, Brooklyn	1971	Joe Torre, St. Louis
1932	Charles Klein, Philadelpha	1952	Hank Sauer, Chicago	1972	Johnny Bench, Cincinnati
1933	Carl Hubbell, New York	1953	Roy Campanella, Brooklyn	1973	Pete Rose, Cincinnati
1934	Dizzy Dean, St. Louis	1954	Willie Mays, New York	1974	Steve Garvey, Los Angeles
1935	Gabby Hartnett, Chicago	1955	Roy Campanella, Brooklyn	1975	Joe Morgan, Cincinnati
1936	Carl Hubbell, New York	1956	Don Newcombe, Brooklyn	1976	Joe Morgan, Cincinnati
1937	Joe Medwick, St. Louis	1957	Henry Aaron, Milwaukee	1977	George Foster, Cincinnati
1938	Ernie Lombardi, Cincinnati	1958	Ernie Banks, Chicago	1978	Dave Parker, Pittsburgh
1939	Bucky Walters, Cincinnati	1959	Ernie Banks, Chicago	1979	(tie) Willie Stargell, Pittsburgh
1940	Frank McCormick, Cincinnati	1960	Dick Groat, Pittsburgh		Keith Hernandez, St. Louis
1941	Dolph Camilli, Brooklyn	1961	Frank Robinson, Cincinnati	1980	Mike Schmidt, Philadelphia
1942	Mort Cooper, St. Louis	1962	Maury Wills, Los Angeles	1981	Mike Schmidt, Philadelphia
1943	Stan Musial, St. Louis	1963	Sandy Koufax, Los Angeles	1982	Dale Murphy, Atlanta
1944	Martin Marion, St. Louis	1964	Ken Boyer, St. Louis	1983	Dale Murphy, Atlanta
1945	Phil Cavarretta, Chicago	1965	Willie Mays, San Francisco	1984	Ryne Sandberg, Chicago
1946	Stan Musial, St. Louis	1966	Roberto Clemente, Pittsburgh	1985	Willie McGee, St. Louis
1947	Bob Elliott, Boston	1967	Orlando Cepeda, St. Louis	1986	Mike Schmidt, Philadelphia
1948	Stan Musial, St. Louis	1968	Bob Gibson, St. Louis	1987	André Dawson, Chicago
1949	Jackie Robinson, Brooklyn	1969	Willie McCovey, San Francisco		
1950	Jim Konstanty, Philadelphia	1970	Johnny Bench, Cincinnati		

American League

Year	Player, team	Year	Player, team	Year	Player, team
1931	Lefty Grove, Philadelphia	1951	Yogi Berra, New York	1971	Vida Blue, Oakland
1932	Jimmy Foxx, Philadelphia	1952	Bobby Shantz, Philadelphia	1972	Dick Allen, Chicago
1933	Jimmy Foxx, Philadelphia	1953	Al Rosen, Cleveland	1973	Reggie Jackson, Oakland
1934	Mickey Cochrane, Detroit	1954	Yogi Berra, New York	1974	Jeff Burroughs, Texas
1935	Henry Greenberg, Detroit	1955	Yogi Berra, New York	1975	Fred Lynn, Boston
1936	Lou Gehrig, New York	1956	Mickey Mantle, New York	1976	Thurman Munson, New York
1937	Charley Gehringer, Detroit	1957	Mickey Mantle, New York	1977	Rod Carew, Minnesota
1938	Jimmy Foxx, Boston	1958	Jackie Jensen, Boston	1978	Jim Rice, Boston
1939	Joe DiMaggio, New York	1959	Nellie Fox, Chicago	1979	Don Baylor, California
1940	Hank Greenberg, Detroit	1960	Roger Maris, New York	1980	George Brett, Kansas City
1941	Joe DiMaggio, New York	1961	Roger Maris, New York	1981	Rollie Fingers, Milwaukee
1942	Joe Gordon, New York	1962	Mickey Mantle, New York	1982	Robin Yount, Milwaukee
1943	Spurgeon Chandler, New York	1963	Elston Howard, New York	1983	Cal Ripken Jr., Baltimore
1944	Hal Newhouser, Detroit	1964	Brooks Robinson, Baltimore	1984	Willie Hernandez, Detroit
1945	Hal Newhouser, Detroit	1965	Zoilo Versalles, Minnesota	1985	Don Mattingly, New York
1946	Ted Williams, Boston	1966	Frank Robinson, Baltimore	1986	Roger Clemens, Boston
1947	Joe DiMaggio, New York	1967	Carl Yastrzemski, Boston	1987	George Bell, Toronto
1948	Lou Boudreau, Cleveland	1968	Denny McLain, Detroit		
1949	Ted Williams, Boston	1969	Harmon Killebrew, Minnesota		
1950	Phil Rizzuto, New York	1970	John (Boog) Powell, Baltimore		

Batting Champions

National League

Year	Player	Club	Pct.
1924	Rogers Hornsby	St. Louis	.424
1925	Rogers Hornsby	St. Louis	.403
1926	Eugene Hargrave	Cincinnati . . .	.353
1927	Paul Waner	Pittsburgh . . .	.380
1928	Rogers Hornsby	Boston.	.387
1929	Lefty O'Doul	Philadelphia . . .	.398
1930	Bill Terry	New York . . .	.401
1931	Chick Hafey.	St. Louis	.349
1932	Lefty O'Doul	Brooklyn	.368
1933	Charles Klein	Philadelphia . . .	.368
1934	Paul Waner	Pittsburgh . . .	.362
1935	Arky Vaughan	Pittsburgh . . .	.385
1936	Paul Waner	Pittsburgh . . .	.373
1937	Joe Medwick	St. Louis	.374
1938	Ernie Lombardi	Cincinnati . . .	.342

American League

Year	Player	Club	Pct.
1924	Babe Ruth	New York . . .	.378
1925	Harry Heilmann	Detroit	.393
1926	Henry Manush.	Detroit	.378
1927	Harry Heilmann	Detroit	.398
1928	Goose Goslin	Washington . .	.379
1929	Lew Fonseca	Cleveland . . .	.369
1930	Al Simmons	Philadelphia . . .	.381
1931	Al Simmons	Philadelphia . . .	.390
1932	Dale Alexander	Detroit-Boston . .	.367
1933	Jimmy Foxx	Philadelphia . . .	.356
1934	Lou Gehrig	New York . . .	.363
1935	Buddy Myer	Washington . .	.349
1936	Luke Appling.	Chicago	.388
1937	Charlie Gehringer	Detroit	.371
1938	Jimmy Foxx	Boston	.349

National League

Year	Player	Club	Pct.
1939	John Mize	St. Louis	.349
1940	Debs Garms	Pittsburgh	.355
1941	Pete Reiser	Brooklyn	.343
1942	Ernie Lombardi	Boston	.330
1943	Stan Musial	St. Louis	.357
1944	Dixie Walker	Brooklyn	.357
1945	Phil Cavarretta	Chicago	.355
1946	Stan Musial	St. Louis	.365
1947	Harry Walker	Philadelphia	.363
1948	Stan Musial	St. Louis	.376
1949	Jackie Robinson	Brooklyn	.342
1950	Stan Musial	St. Louis	.346
1951	Stan Musial	St. Louis	.355
1952	Stan Musial	St. Louis	.336
1953	Carl Furillo	Brooklyn	.344
1954	Willie Mays	New York	.345
1955	Richie Ashburn	Philadelphia	.338
1956	Hank Aaron	Milwaukee	.328
1957	Stan Musial	St. Louis	.351
1958	Richie Ashburn	Philadelphia	.350
1959	Hank Aaron	Milwaukee	.355
1960	Dick Groat	Pittsburgh	.325
1961	Roberto Clemente	Pittsburgh	.351
1962	Tommy Davis	Los Angeles	.346
1963	Tommy Davis	Los Angeles	.326
1964	Roberto Clemente	Pittsburgh	.339
1965	Roberto Clemente	Pittsburgh	.329
1966	Matty Alou	Pittsburgh	.342
1967	Roberto Clemente	Pittsburgh	.357
1968	Pete Rose	Cincinnati	.335
1969	Pete Rose	Cincinnati	.348
1970	Rico Carty	Atlanta	.366
1971	Joe Torre	St. Louis	.363
1972	Billy Williams	Chicago	.333
1973	Pete Rose	Cincinnati	.338
1974	Ralph Garr	Atlanta	.353
1975	Bill Madlock	Chicago	.354
1976	Bill Madlock	Chicago	.339
1977	Dave Parker	Pittsburgh	.338
1978	Dave Parker	Pittsburgh	.334
1979	Keith Hernandez	St. Louis	.344
1980	Bill Buckner	Chicago	.324
1981	Bill Madlock	Pittsburgh	.341
1982	Al Oliver	Montreal	.331
1983	Bill Madlock	Pittsburgh	.323
1984	Tony Gwynn	San Diego	.351
1985	Willie McGee	St. Louis	.353
1986	Tim Raines	Montreal	.334
1987	Tony Gwynn	San Diego	.369
1988	Tony Gwynn	San Diego	.313

American League

Year	Player	Club	Pct.
1939	Joe DiMaggio	New York	.381
1940	Joe DiMaggio	New York	.352
1941	Ted Williams	Boston	.406
1942	Ted Williams	Boston	.356
1943	Luke Appling	Chicago	.328
1944	Lou Boudreau	Cleveland	.327
1945	George Stirnweiss	New York	.309
1946	Mickey Vernon	Washington	.353
1947	Ted Williams	Boston	.343
1948	Ted Williams	Boston	.369
1949	George Kell	Detroit	.343
1950	Billy Goodman	Boston	.354
1951	Ferris Fain	Philadelphia	.344
1952	Ferris Fain	Philadelphia	.327
1953	Mickey Vernon	Washington	.337
1954	Roberto Avila	Cleveland	.341
1955	Al Kaline	Detroit	.340
1956	Mickey Mantle	New York	.353
1957	Ted Williams	Boston	.388
1958	Ted Williams	Boston	.328
1959	Harvey Kuenn	Detroit	.353
1960	Pete Runnels	Boston	.320
1961	Norm Cash	Detroit	.361
1962	Pete Runnels	Boston	.326
1963	Carl Yastrzemski	Boston	.321
1964	Tony Oliva	Minnesota	.323
1965	Tony Oliva	Minnesota	.321
1966	Frank Robinson	Baltimore	.316
1967	Carl Yastrzemski	Boston	.326
1968	Carl Yastrzemski	Boston	.301
1969	Rod Carew	Minnesota	.332
1970	Alex Johnson	California	.328
1971	Tony Oliva	Minnesota	.337
1972	Rod Carew	Minnesota	.318
1973	Rod Carew	Minnesota	.350
1974	Rod Carew	Minnesota	.364
1975	Rod Carew	Minnesota	.359
1976	George Brett	Kansas City	.333
1977	Rod Carew	Minnesota	.388
1978	Rod Carew	Minnesota	.333
1979	Fred Lynn	Boston	.333
1980	George Brett	Kansas City	.390
1981	Carney Lansford	Boston	.336
1982	Willie Wilson	Kansas City	.332
1983	Wade Boggs	Boston	.361
1984	Don Mattingly	New York	.343
1985	Wade Boggs	Boston	.368
1986	Wade Boggs	Boston	.357
1987	Wade Boggs	Boston	.363
1988	Wade Boggs	Boston	.366

Home Run Leaders

National League

Year		HR
1925	Rogers Hornsby, St. Louis	39
1926	Hack Wilson, Chicago	21
1927	Hack Wilson, Chicago; Cy Williams, Philadelphia	30
1928	Hack Wilson, Chicago; Jim Bottomley, St. Louis	31
1929	Charles Klein, Philadelphia	43
1930	Hack Wilson, Chicago	56
1931	Charles Klein, Philadelphia	31
1932	Charles Klein, Philadelphia, Mel Ott, New York	38
1933	Charles Klein, Philadelphia	28
1934	Collins, St. Louis; Mel Ott, New York	35
1935	Walter Berger, Boston	34
1936	Mel Ott, New York	33
1937	Mel Ott, New York; Joe Medwick, St. Louis	31
1938	Mel Ott, New York	36
1939	John Mize, St. Louis	28
1940	John Mize, St. Louis	43
1941	Dolph Camilli, Brooklyn	34
1942	Mel Ott, New York	30
1943	Bill Nicholson, Chicago	29
1944	Bill Nicholson, Chicago	33
1945	Tommy Holmes, Boston	28
1946	Ralph Kiner, Pittsburgh	23
1947	Ralph Kiner, Pittsburgh; John Mize, New York	51
1948	Ralph Kiner, Pittsburgh; John Mize, New York	40
1949	Ralph Kiner, Pittsburgh	54
1950	Ralph Kiner, Pittsburgh	47
1951	Ralph Kiner, Pittsburgh	42
1952	Ralph Kiner, Pittsburgh; Hank Sauer, Chicago	37

American League

Year		HR
1925	Bob Meusel, New York	33
1926	Babe Ruth, New York	47
1927	Babe Ruth, New York	60
1928	Babe Ruth, New York	54
1929	Babe Ruth, New York	46
1930	Babe Ruth, New York	49
1931	Babe Ruth, Lou Gehrig, New York	46
1932	Jimmy Foxx, Philadelphia	58
1933	Jimmy Foxx, Philadelphia	48
1934	Lou Gehrig, New York	49
1935	Jimmy Foxx, Philadelphia, Hank Greenberg, Detroit	36
1936	Lou Gehrig, New York	49
1937	Joe DiMaggio, New York	46
1938	Hank Greenberg, Detroit	58
1939	Jimmy Foxx, Boston	35
1940	Hank Greenberg, Detroit	41
1941	Ted Williams, Boston	37
1942	Ted Williams, Boston	36
1943	Rudy York, Detroit	34
1944	Nick Etten, New York	22
1945	Vern Stephens, St. Louis	24
1946	Hank Greenberg, Detroit	44
1947	Ted Williams, Boston	32
1948	Joe DiMaggio, New York	39
1949	Ted Williams, Boston	43
1950	Al Rosen, Cleveland	37
1951	Gus Zernial, Chicago-Philadelphia	33
1952	Larry Doby, Cleveland	32

National League

Year		HR
1953	Ed Mathews, Milwaukee	47
1954	Ted Kluszewski, Cincinnati	49
1955	Willie Mays, New York	51
1956	Duke Snider, Brooklyn	43
1957	Hank Aaron, Milwaukee	44
1958	Ernie Banks, Chicago	47
1959	Ed Mathews, Milwaukee	46
1960	Ernie Banks, Chicago	41
1961	Orlando Cepeda, San Francisco	46
1962	Willie Mays, San Francisco	49
1963	Hank Aaron, Milwaukee; Willie McCovey, San Francisco	44
1964	Willie Mays, San Francisco	47
1965	Willie Mays, San Francisco	52
1966	Hank Aaron, Atlanta	44
1967	Hank Aaron, Atlanta	39
1968	Willie McCovey, San Francisco	36
1969	Willie McCovey, San Francisco	45
1970	Johnny Bench, Cincinnati	45
1971	Willie Stargell, Pittsburgh	48
1972	Johnny Bench, Cincinnati	40
1973	Willie Stargell, Pittsburgh	44
1974	Mike Schmidt, Philadelphia	36
1975	Mike Schmidt, Philadelphia	38
1976	Mike Schmidt, Philadelphia	38
1977	George Foster, Cincinnati	52
1978	George Foster, Cincinnati	40
1979	Dave Kingman, Chicago	48
1980	Mike Schmidt, Philadelphia	48
1981	Mike Schmidt, Philadelphia	31
1982	Dave Kingman, New York	37
1983	Mike Schmidt, Philadelphia	40
1984	Mike Schmidt, Phil.; Dale Murphy, Atlanta	36
1985	Dale Murphy, Atlanta	37
1986	Mike Schmidt, Philadelphia	37
1987	Andre Dawson, Chicago	49
1988	Darryl Strawberry, New York	39

American League

Year		HR
1953	Al Rosen, Cleveland	43
1954	Larry Doby, Cleveland	32
1955	Mickey Mantle, New York	37
1956	Mickey Mantle, New York	52
1957	Roy Sievers, Washington	42
1958	Mickey Mantle, New York	42
1959	Rocky Colavito, Cleveland, Harmon Killebrew, Washington	42
1960	Mickey Mantle, New York	40
1961	Roger Maris, New York	61
1962	Harmon Killebrew, Minnesota	48
1963	Harmon Killebrew, Minnesota	45
1964	Harmon Killebrew, Minnesota	49
1965	Tony Conigliaro, Boston	32
1966	Frank Robinson, Baltimore	49
1967	Carl Yastrzemski, Boston, Harmon Killebrew, Minn.	44
1968	Frank Howard, Washington	44
1969	Harmon Killebrew, Minnesota	49
1970	Frank Howard, Washington	44
1971	Bill Melton, Chicago	33
1972	Dick Allen, Chicago	37
1973	Reggie Jackson, Oakland	32
1974	Dick Allen, Chicago	32
1975	George Scott, Milwaukee; Reggie Jackson, Oakland	36
1976	Graig Nettles, New York	32
1977	Jim Rice, Boston	39
1978	Jim Rice, Boston	46
1979	Gorman Thomas, Milwaukee	45
1980	Reggie Jackson, New York; Ben Oglivie, Milwaukee	41
1981	Bobby Grich, California; Tony Armas, Oakland; Dwight Evans, Boston; Eddie Murray, Baltimore	22
1982	Gorman Thomas, Milwaukee; Reggie Jackson, California	39
1983	Jim Rice, Boston	39
1984	Tony Armas, Boston	43
1985	Darrell Evans, Detroit	40
1986	Jesse Barfield, Toronto	40
1987	Mark McGwire, Oakland	49
1988	Jose Conseco, Oakland	42

Runs Batted In Leaders

National League

Year		RBI
1952	Hank Sauer, Chicago	121
1953	Roy Campanella, Brooklyn	142
1954	Ted Kluszewski, Cincinnati	141
1955	Duke Snider, Brooklyn	136
1956	Stan Musial, St. Louis	109
1957	Hank Aaron, Milwaukee	132
1958	Ernie Banks, Chicago	129
1959	Ernie Banks, Chicago	143
1960	Hank Aaron, Milwaukee	126
1961	Orlando Cepeda, San Francisco	142
1962	Tommy Davis, Los Angeles	153
1963	Hank Aaron, Milwaukee	130
1964	Ken Boyer, St. Louis	119
1965	Deron Johnson, Cincinnati	130
1966	Hank Aaron, Atlanta	127
1967	Orlando Cepeda, St. Louis	111
1968	Willie McCovey, San Francisco	105
1969	Willie McCovey, San Francisco	126
1970	Johnny Bench, Cincinnati	148
1971	Joe Torre, St. Louis	137
1972	Johnny Bench, Cincinnati	125
1973	Willie Stargell, Pittsburgh	119
1974	Johnny Bench, Cincinnati	129
1975	Greg Luzinski, Philadelphia	120
1976	George Foster, Cincinnati	121
1977	George Foster, Cincinnati	149
1978	George Foster, Cincinnati	120
1979	Dave Winfield, San Diego	118
1980	Mike Schmidt, Philadelphia	121
1981	Mike Schmidt, Philadelphia	91
1982	Dale Murphy, Atlanta; Al Oliver, Montreal	109
1983	Dale Murphy, Atlanta	121
1984	Mike Schmidt, Phil.; Gary Carter, Montreal	106
1985	Dave Parker, Cincinnati	125
1986	Mike Schmidt, Philadelphia	119
1987	Andre Dawson, Chicago	137
1988	Will Clark, San Francisco	109

American League

Year		RBI
1952	Al Rosen, Cleveland	105
1953	Al Rosen, Cleveland	145
1954	Larry Doby, Cleveland	126
1955	Ray Boone, Detroit, Jack Jensen, Boston	116
1956	Mickey Mantle, New York	130
1957	Roy Sievers, Washington	114
1958	Jack Jensen, Boston	122
1959	Jack Jensen, Boston	112
1960	Roger Maris, New York	112
1961	Roger Maris, New York	142
1962	Harmon Killebrew, Minnesota	126
1963	Dick Stuart, Boston	118
1964	Brooks Robinson, Baltimore	118
1965	Rocky Colavito, Cleveland	108
1966	Frank Robinson, Baltimore	122
1967	Carl Yastrzemski, Boston	121
1968	Ken Harrelson, Boston	109
1969	Harmon Killebrew, Minnesota	140
1970	Frank Howard, Washington	126
1971	Harmon Killebrew, Minnesota	119
1972	Dick Allen, Chicago	113
1973	Reggie Jackson, Oakland	117
1974	Jeff Burroughs, Texas	118
1975	George Scott, Milwaukee	109
1976	Lee May, Baltimore	109
1977	Larry Hisle, Minnesota	119
1978	Jim Rice, Boston	139
1979	Don Baylor, California	139
1980	Cecil Cooper, Milwaukee	122
1981	Eddie Murray, Baltimore	78
1982	Hal McRae, Kansas City	133
1983	Cecil Cooper, Milwaukee; Jim Rice, Boston	126
1984	Tony Armas, Boston	123
1985	Don Mattingly, New York	145
1986	Joe Carter, Cleveland	121
1987	George Bell, Toronto	134
1988	Jose Conseco, Oakland	124

Earned-Run Average Leaders

Year	National League — Player, club	G	IP	ERA	Year	American League — Player, club	G	IP	ERA
1969	Juan Marichal, San Francisco	37	300	2.10	1969	Dick Bosman, Washington	31	193	2.19
1970	Tom Seaver, New York	37	291	2.81	1970	Diego Segui, Oakland	47	162	2.56
1971	Tom Seaver, New York	36	286	1.76	1971	Vida Blue, Oakland	39	312	1.82
1972	Steve Carlton, Philadelphia	41	346	1.98	1972	Luis Tiant, Boston	43	179	1.91
1973	Tom Seaver, New York	36	290	2.07	1973	Jim Palmer, Baltimore	38	296	2.40
1974	Buzz Capra, Atlanta	39	217	2.28	1974	Catfish Hunter, Oakland	41	318	2.49
1975	Randy Jones, San Diego	37	285	2.24	1975	Jim Palmer, Baltimore	39	323	2.09
1976	John Denny, St. Louis	30	207	2.52	1976	Mark Fidrych, Detroit	31	250	2.34
1977	John Candelaria, Pittsburgh	33	231	2.34	1977	Frank Tanana, California	31	241	2.54
1978	Craig Swan, New York	29	207	2.43	1978	Ron Guidry, New York	35	274	1.74
1979	J. R. Richard, Houston	38	292	2.71	1979	Ron Guidry, New York	33	236	2.78
1980	Don Sutton, Los Angeles	32	212	2.21	1980	Rudy May, New York	41	175	2.47
1981	Nolan Ryan, Houston	21	149	1.69	1981	Steve McCatty, Oakland	22	186	2.32
1982	Steve Rogers, Montreal	35	277	2.40	1982	Rick Sutcliffe, Cleveland	34	216	2.96
1983	Atlee Hammaker, San Fran.	23	172	2.25	1983	Rick Honeycutt, Texas	25	174	2.42
1984	Alejandro Pena, Los Angeles	28	199	2.48	1984	Mike Boddicker, Baltimore	34	261	2.79
1985	Dwight Gooden, New York	35	276	1.53	1986	Dave Stieb, Toronto	36	265	2.48
1986	Mike Scott, Houston	37	275	2.22	1986	Roger Clemens, Boston	33	254	2.48
1987	Nolan Ryan, Houston	34	211	2.76	1987	Jimmy Key, Toronto	36	261	2.76

ERA is computed by multiplying earned runs allowed by 9, then dividing by innings pitched.

Pitchers with 300 Major League Wins

Pitcher	Wins	Pitcher	Wins
Cy Young	511	Eddie Plank	325
Walter Johnson	416	Phil Niekro	318
Grover C. Alexander	373	Gaylord Perry	314
Christy Mathewson	373	Tom Seaver	311
Pud Galvin	365	Charles Radbourn	308
Don Sutton	363	Lefty Grove	300
Warren Spahn	363	Early Wynn	300
Kid Nichols	360		
Tim Keefe	346		
Steve Carlton	329		
John Clarkson	328		

All-Time Home Run Leaders

Player	HR	Player	HR	Player	HR	Player	HR
Hank Aaron	755	Ernie Banks	512	Frank Howard	382	Lee May	354
Babe Ruth	714	Mel Ott	511	Orlando Cepeda	379	Dick Allen	351
Willie Mays	660	Lou Gehrig	493	Tony Perez	379	George Foster	348
Frank Robinson	586	Stan Musial	475	Norm Cash	377	Dwight Evans	346
Harmon Killebrew	573	Willie Stargell	475	Jim Rice	376	Ron Santo	342
Reggie Jackson	563	Carl Yastrzemski	452	Rocky Colavito	374	John (Boog) Powell	339
Mike Schmidt	552	Dave Kingman	442	Gil Hodges	370	Don Baylor	338
Mickey Mantle	536	Billy Williams	426	Ralph Kiner	369	Joe Adcock	336
Jimmy Foxx	534	Duke Snider	407	Joe DiMaggio	361	Dale Murphy	334
Ted Williams	521	Darrell Evans	403	John Mize	359	Eddie Murray	333
Willie McCovey	521	Al Kaline	399	Yogi Berra	358	Bobby Bonds	332
Ed Mathews	512	Graig Nettles	390	Dave Winfield	357	Hank Greenburg	331
		Johnny Bench	389			Willie Horton	325

Cy Young Award Winners

Year	Player, club	Year	Player, club	Year	Player, club
1956	Don Newcombe, Dodgers	1970	(NL) Bob Gibson, Cardinals	1979	(NL) Bruce Sutter, Cubs
1957	Warren Spahn, Braves		(AL) Mike Cuellar, Orioles		(AL) Mike Flanagan, Orioles
1958	Bob Turley, Yankees	1971	(NL) Ferguson Jenkins, Cubs	1980	(NL) Steve Carlton, Phillies
1959	Early Wynn, White Sox		(AL) Vida Blue, A's		(AL) Steve Stone, Orioles
1960	Vernon Law, Pirates	1972	(NL) Steve Carlton, Phillies	1981	(NL) Fernando Valenzuela, Dodgers
1961	Whitey Ford, Yankees		(AL) Gaylord Perry, Indians		(AL) Rollie Fingers, Brewers
1962	Don Drysdale, Dodgers	1973	(NL) Tom Seaver, Mets	1982	(NL) Steve Carlton, Phillies
1963	Sandy Koufax, Dodgers		(AL) Jim Palmer, Orioles		(AL) Pete Vuckovich, Brewers
1964	Dean Chance, Angels	1974	(NL) Mike Marshall, Dodgers	1983	(NL) John Denny, Phillies
1965	Sandy Koufax, Dodgers		(AL) Jim (Catfish) Hunter, A's		(AL) LaMarr Hoyt, White Sox
1966	Sandy Koufax, Dodgers	1975	(NL) Tom Seaver, Mets	1984	(NL) Rick Sutcliffe, Cubs
1967	(NL) Mike McCormick, Giants		(AL) Jim Palmer, Orioles		(AL) Willie Hernandez, Tigers
	(AL) Jim Lonborg, Red Sox	1976	(NL) Randy Jones, Padres	1985	(NL) Dwight Gooden, Mets
1968	(NL) Bob Gibson, Cardinals		(AL) Jim Palmer, Orioles		(AL) Bret Saberhagen, Royals
	(AL) Dennis McLain, Tigers	1977	(NL) Steve Carlton, Phillies	1986	(NL) Mike Scott, Astros
1969	(NL) Tom Seaver, Mets		(AL) Sparky Lyle, Yankees		(AL) Roger Clemens, Red Sox
	(AL) (tie) Dennis McLain, Tigers	1978	(NL) Gaylord Perry, Padres	1987	(NL) Steve Bedrosian, Phillies
	Mike Cuellar, Orioles		(AL) Ron Guidry, Yankees		(AL) Roger Clemens, Red Sox

Rookie of the Year
Baseball Writers' Association

1947—Combined selection—Jackie Robinson, Brooklyn, 1b
1948—Combined selection—Alvin Dark, Boston, N.L. ss

National League

Year	Player, team	Year	Player, team	Year	Player, team
1949	Don Newcombe, Brooklyn, p	1963	Pete Rose, Cincinnati, 2b		Pat Zachry, Cincinnati, p
1950	Sam Jethroe, Boston, of	1964	Richie Allen, Philadelphia, 3b	1977	Andre Dawson, Montreal, of
1951	Willie Mays, New York, of	1965	Jim Lefebvre, Los Angeles, 2b	1978	Bob Horner, Atlanta, 3b
1952	Joe Black, Brooklyn, p	1966	Tommy Helms, Cincinnati, 2b	1979	Rick Sutcliffe, Los Angeles, p
1953	Jim Gilliam, Brooklyn, 2b	1967	Tom Seaver, New York, p	1980	Steve Howe, Los Angeles, p
1954	Wally Moon, St. Louis, of	1968	Johnny Bench, Cincinnati c	1981	Fernando Valenzuela, Los
1955	Bill Virdon, St. Louis, of	1969	Ted Sizemore, Los Angeles, 2b		Angeles, p
1956	Frank Robinson, Cincinnati, of	1970	Carl Morton, Montreal, p	1982	Steve Sax, Los Angeles, 2b
1957	Jack Sanford, Philadelphia, p	1971	Earl Williams, Atlanta, c	1983	Darryl Strawberry, New York, of
1958	Orlando Cepeda, S.F., 1b	1972	Jon Matlack, New York, p	1984	Dwight Gooden, New York, p
1959	Willie McCovey, S.F., 1b	1973	Gary Matthews, S.F., of	1985	Vince Coleman, St. Louis, of
1960	Frank Howard, Los Angeles, of	1974	Bake McBride, St. Louis, of	1986	Todd Worrell, St. Louis, p
1961	Billy Williams, Chicago, of	1975	John Montefusco, S.F., p	1987	Benito Santiago, San Diego, c
1962	Ken Hubbs, Chicago, 2b	1976	(tie) Butch Metzger, San Diego, p		

American League

Year	Player, team	Year	Player, team	Year	Player, team
1949	Roy Sievers, St. Louis, of	1963	Gary Peters, Chicago, p	1977	Eddie Murray, Baltimore, dh
1950	Walt Dropo, Boston, 1b	1964	Tony Oliva, Minnesota, of	1978	Lou Whitaker, Detroit, 2b
1951	Gil McDougald, New York, 3b	1965	Curt Blefary, Baltimore, of	1979	(tie) John Castino, Minnesota, 3b
1952	Harry Byrd, Philadelphia, p	1966	Tommie Agee, Chicago, of		Alfredo Griffin, Toronto, ss
1953	Harvey Kuenn, Detroit, ss	1967	Rod Carew, Minnesota, 2b	1980	Joe Charboneau, Cleveland, of
1954	Bob Grim, New York, p	1968	Stan Bahnsen, New York, p	1981	Dave Righetti, New York, p
1955	Herb Score, Cleveland, p	1969	Lou Piniella, Kansas City, of	1982	Cal Ripken Jr., Baltimore, ss, 3b
1956	Luis Aparicio, Chicago, ss	1970	Thurman Munson, New York, c	1983	Ron Kittle, Chicago, of
1957	Tony Kubek, New York, if-of	1971	Chris Chambliss, Cleveland, 1b	1984	Alvin Davis, Seattle, 1b
1958	Albie Pearson, Washington, of	1972	Carlton Fisk, Boston, c	1985	Ozzie Guillen, Chicago, ss
1959	Bob Allison, Washington, of	1973	Al Bumbry, Baltimore, of	1986	Jose Canseco, Oakland, of
1960	Ron Hansen, Baltimore, ss	1974	Mike Hargrove, Texas, 1b	1987	Mark McGwire, Oakland, 1b
1961	Don Schwall, Boston, p	1975	Fred Lynn, Boston, of		
1962	Tom Tresh, New York, if-of	1976	Mark Fidrych, Detroit, p		

Montreal Expos Opening-Day Lineups

(listed by batting order)

1969		1970		1971		1972		1973	
Maury Willis	SS	Gary Sutherland	2B	Boots Day	CF	Ron Hunt	2B	Ron Hunt	2B
Gary Sutherland	2B	Rusty Staub	RF	Ron Hunt	2B	Bob Bailey	3B	Tim Foli	SS
Rusty Staub	RF	Ron Fairly	1B	Rusty Staub	RF	Mike Jorgensen	1B	Mike Jorgensen	1B
Mack Jones	LF	Bob Bailey	LF	Bob Bailey	3B	Ron Fairly	RF	Ron Fairly	LF
Bob Bailey	1B	Coco Laboy	3B	Ron Fairly	1B	Ken Singleton	LF	Ken Singleton	RF
John Bateman	C	Adolfo Philips	CF	Mack Jones	LF	Boots Day	CF	Bob Bailey	3B
Coco Laboy	3B	John Boccabella	C	John Bateman	C	Terry Humphrey	C	Jorge Roque	CF
Don Hahn	CF	Bobby Wine	SS	Bobby Wine	SS	Tim Foli	SS	John Boccabella	C
Jim Grant	P	Joe Sparma	P	Carl Morton	P	Bill Stoneman	P	Mike Torrez	P

1974		1975		1976		1977		1978	
Ron Hunt	3B	Tony Scott	LF	Pepe Mangual	CF	Dave Cash	2B	Ellis Valentine	RF
Willie Davis	CF	Tim Foli	SS	Larry Biittner	LF	Tim Foli	SS	Dave Cash	2B
Bob Bailey	LF	Pepe Mangual	CF	Mike Jorgensen	1B	Ellis Valentine	RF	André Dawson	CF
Hal Breeden	1B	Mike Jorgensen	1B	Larry Parrish	3B	Tony Perez	1B	Gary Carter	C
Ken Singleton	RF	Barry Foote	C	Barry Foote	C	Larry Parrish	3B	Tony Perez	1B
Jim Cox	2B	Gary Carter	RF	Gary Carter	RF	Gary Carter	C	Warren Cromartie	LF
Barry Foote	C	Pete Mackanin	2B	Pete Mackanin	2B	André Dawson	CF	Larry Parrish	3B
Tim Foli	SS	Larry Parrish	3B	Tim Foli	SS	Warren Cromartie	LF	Chris Speier	SS
Steve Renko	P	Dave McNally	P	Steve Rogers	P	Steve Rogers	P	Steve Rogers	P

1979		1980		1981		1982		1983	
André Dawson	CF	Ron LeFlore	LF	Tim Raines	LF	Tim Raines	LF	Tim Raines	LF
Rodney Scott	2B	Rodney Scott	2B	Rodney Scott	2B	Wallace Johnson	2B	Bryan Little	SS
Warren Cromartie	LF	André Dawson	CF	André Dawson	CF	André Dawson	CF	André Dawson	CF
Ellis Valentine	RF	Ellis Valentine	RF	Ellis Valentine	RF	Al Oliver	1B	Al Oliver	1B
Tony Perez	1P	Larry Parrish	3B	Gary Carter	C	Gary Carter	C	Gary Carter	C
Gary Carter	C	Larry Parrish	3B	Larry Parrish	3B	Warren Cromartie	RF	Tim Wallach	3B
Larry Parrish	3B	Warren Cromartie	1B	Warren Cromartie	1B	Tim Wallach	3B	Warren Cromartie	RF
Chris Speier	SS	Chris Speier	SS	Chris Speier	SS	Chris Speier	SS	Doug Flynn	2B
Steve Rogers	P	Steve Rogers	P	Steve Rogers	P	Steve Rogers	P	Steve Rogers	P

1984		1985		1986		1987		1988	
Pete Rose	LF	Tim Raines	LF	Tim Raines	LF	Alonzo Powell	LF	Tim Raines	LF
Bryan Little	2B	Herm Winningham	CF	Vance Law	2B	Mitch Webster	RF	Mitch Webster	CF
Tim Raines	CF	André Dawson	RF	André Dawson	RF	Andrés Galarraga	1B	Hubie Brooks	RF
André Dawson	RF	Dan Driessen	1B	Jason Thompson	1B	Hubie Brooks	SS	Tim Wallach	3B
Gary Carter	C	Hubie Brooks	SS	Hubie Brooks	SS	Tim Wallach	3B	Andrés Galarraga	1B
Tim Wallach	3B	Vance Law	2B	Tim Wallach	3B	Vance Law	2B	Tom Foley	2B
Terry Francona	1B	Tim Wallach	3B	Mitch Webster	RF	Jeff Reed	C	Louis Rivera	SS
Argenis Salazer	SS	Mike Fitzgerald	C	Dann Bilardello	C	Reid Nichols	CF	Jeff Reed	C
Charlie Lea	P	Steve Rogers	P	Bryn Smith	P	Floyd Youmans	P	Dennis Martinez	P

Montreal Expos Year-By-Year Record

Year	Won	Lost	Avg.	Pos	Games behind	Home attendance	Manager
1969	52	110	.321	6th	48	1 212 608	Gene Mauch
1970	73	89	.451	6th	16	1 424 683	Gene Mauch
1971	71	90	.441	5th	25½	1 290 963	Gene Mauch
1972	70	86	.449	5th	26½	1 142 145	Gene Mauch
1973	79	83	.488	4th	3½	1 246 863	Gene Mauch
1974	79	82	.491	4th	8½	1 019 134	Gene Mauch
1975	75	87	.463	5th	17½	908 292	Gene Mauch
1976	55	107	.340	6th	46	646 704	K. Kuehl/C. Fox
1977	75	87	.463	5th	26	1 433 757	Dick Williams
1978	76	86	.469	4th	14	1 427 007	Dick Williams
1979	95	65	.594	2d	8	2 102 173	Dick Williams
1980	90	72	.556	2d	1	2 208 175	Dick Williams
1981	60	48	.556	—	—	1 534 564	Williams/Fanning
1st half	30	25	.545	3d	4	—	
2nd half	30	23	.566	1st	+ ½		
1982	86	76	.531	3d	6	2 318 292	Jim Fanning
1983	82	80	.506	3d	8	2 320 651	Bill Virdon
1984	78	83	.484	5th	18	1 606 531	Virdon/Fanning
1985	84	77	.522	3d	16½	1 502 494	Buck Rodgers
1986	78	83	.484	4th	29½	1 128 981	Buck Rodgers
1987	91	71	.562	3d	4	1 850 324	Buck Rodgers
1988	81	81	.500	3d	20	1 478 659	Buck Rodgers

Montreal Expos Year-by-Year Batting Leaders

Source: Montreal Expos

	Average (350 ABs)	At Bats	Runs	Hits	Doubles
1969	Rusty Staub, .302	Coco Laboy, 562	Rusty Staub, 89	Rusty Staub, 166	Coco Laboy, 29
1970	Ron Fairly, .288	Rusty Staub, 569	Rusty Staub, 98	Rusty Staub, 156	Coco Laboy, 26
1971	Rusty Staub, .311	Rusty Staub, 599	Rusty Staub, 94	Rusty Staub, 186	Rusty Staub, 34
1972	Tim Foli, .278	Tim Foli, 540	Ron Hunt, 56	Ken Singleton, 139	Ken Singleton, 23
1973	Ron Hunt, .309	Ken Singleton, 560	Ken Singleton, 100	Ken Singleton, 169	Ken Singleton, 26
1974	Willie Davis, .295	Willie Davis, 611	Willie Davis, 86	Willie Davis, 180	Willie Davis, 27
1975	Larry Parrish, .274	Tim Foli, 572	Pepe Mangual, 84	Larry Parrish, 145	Larry Parrish, 32
1976	Tim Foli, .264	Tim Foli, 546	Larry Parrish, 65	Tim Foli, 144	Tim Foli, 36
1977	Ellis Valentine, .293	Dave Cash, 650	Dave Cash, 91	Dave Cash, 188	Dave Cash, 42
1978	Warren Cromartie, .297	Dave Cash, 658	André Dawson, 84	Warren Cromartie, 180	Larry Parrish, 39
1979	Larry Parrish, .307	Warren Cromartie, 659	Warren Cromartie, 90	Warren Cromartie, 181	Warren Cromartie, 46
1980	André Dawson, .308	Warren Cromartie, 597	André Dawson, 96	André Dawson, 178	André Dawson, 41
1981	Warren Cromartie, .304 Tim Raines, .304	André Dawson, 394	André Dawson, 71	André Dawson, 119	André Dawson, 21
1982	Al Oliver, .331*	Tim Raines, 647	André Dawson, 107	Al Oliver, 204	Al Oliver, 43
1983	Al Oliver, .300	André Dawson, 633	Tim Raines, 133	André Dawson, 189	Al Oliver, 38
1984	Tim Raines, .309	Tim Raines, 622	Tim Raines, 106	Tim Raines, 192	Tim Raines, 38
1985	Tim Raines, .320	Hubie Brooks, 605	Tim Raines, 115	Tim Raines, 184	Tim Wallach, 36
1986	Tim Raines, .334*	Tim Raines, 580	Tim Raines, 91	Tim Raines, 194	Tim Raines, 35
1987	Tim Raines, .330	Tim Wallach, 593	Tim Raines, 123	Tim Wallach, 177	Tim Wallach, 42
1988	Andrés Galarraga, .302	Andrés Galarraga, 609	Andrés Galarraga, 99	Andrés Galarraga, 184	Andrés Galarraga, 42

	Triples	Home Runs	Runs Batted In	Walks	Strike-outs
1969	Bob Bailey, 6	Rusty Staub, 29	Coco Laboy, 83	Rusty Staub, 110	Mack Jones, 110
1970	Rusty Staub, 7	Rusty Staub, 30	Rusty Staub, 94	Rusty Staub, 112	Rusty Staub, 93
1971	Rusty Staub, 6	Rusty Staub, 19	Rusty Staub, 97	Bob Bailey, 97	Bob Bailey, 105
1972	Bailey/Day, 4	Ron Fairly, 17	Ron Fairly, 68	Ken Singleton, 70	Bob Bailey, 112
1973	Bob Bailey, 4	Bob Bailey, 26	Ken Singleton, 103	Ken Singleton, 123	Bob Bailey, 99
1974	Willie Davis, 9	Bob Bailey, 20	Willie Davis, 89	Bob Bailey, 100	Bob Bailey, 107
1975	Pete Mackanin, 6	Mike Jorgensen, 18	Gary Carter, 68	Mike Jorgensen, 79	Pepe Mangual, 115
1976	Larry Parrish, 5	Larry Parrish, 11	Larry Parrish, 61	Mike Jorgensen, 52	Pete Mackanin, 66
1977	Cash/Cromartie, 7	Gary Carter, 31	Tony Perez, 91	Chris Speier, 67	Tony Perez, 111
1978	André Dawson, 8	André Dawson, 25 Ellis Valentine, 25	Tony Perez, 78	Gary Carter, 68	André Dawson, 128
1979	André Dawson, 12	Larry Parrish, 30	André Dawson, 92	Rodney Scott, 66	André Dawson, 115
1980	Rodney Scott, 13	Gary Carter, 29	Gary Carter, 101	Rodney Scott, 70	Ron LeFlore, 89
1981	Tim Raines, 7*	André Dawson, 24	Gary Carter, 68	Rodney Scott, 50	Larry Parrish, 73
1982	Tim Raines, 8	Gary Carter, 29	Al Oliver, 109*	Gary Carter, 78	André Dawson, 96
1983	André Dawson, 10	André Dawson, 32	André Dawson, 113	Tim Raines, 97	Tim Wallach, 97
1984	Tim Raines, 9	Gary Carter, 27	Gary Carter, 106	Tim Raines, 87	Tim Wallach, 101
1985	Tim Raines, 13	André Dawson, 23	Hubie Brooks, 100	Vance Law, 86	Tim Wallach, 96
1986	Mitch Webster, 13*	André Dawson, 20	André Dawson, 78	Tim Raines, 78	André Dawson, 79
1987	Raines/Webster, 8	Tim Wallach, 26	Tim Wallach, 123	Tim Raines, 90	Andrés Galarraga, 127
1988	Andrés Galarraga, 8	Andrés Galarraga, 29	Andrés Galarraga, 92	Tim Raines, 53	Andrés Galarraga, 153

	Slugging %[1] (350 ABs)	On Base %[2] (350 ABs)	Stolen Bases	Sacrifice Hits	Sacrifice Flies
1969	Rusty Staub, .526	n.a.	Maury Wills, 15	n.a.	n.a.
1970	Bob Bailey, .596	n.a.	Rusty Staub, 12	n.a.	n.a.
1971	Rusty Staub, .482	n.a.	Bob Bailey, 13	n.a.	n.a.
1972	Ron Fairly, .430	n.a.	Mike Jorgensen, 12	n.a.	n.a.
1973	Bob Bailey, .489	n.a.	Mike Jorgensen, 16	n.a.	n.a.
1974	Bob Bailey, .446	n.a.	Larry Lintz, 50	n.a.	n.a.
1975	Mike Jorgensen, .422	n.a.	Pepe Mangual, 33	n.a.	n.a.
1976	Tim Foli, .366	n.a.	Pepe Mangual, 17	n.a.	n.a.
1977	Gary Carter, .529	n.a.	Cash/Dawson, 21		
1978	Ellis Valentine, .489	n.a.	André Dawson, 28	n.a.	n.a.
1979	Larry Parrish, .551	n.a.	Rodney Scott, 39	n.a.	n.a.
1980	André Dawson, .492	n.a.	Ron LeFlore, 97*	n.a.	n.a.
1981	André Dawson, .553*	n.a.	Tim Raines, 71*	n.a.	n.a.
1982	Al Oliver, .514	n.a.	Tim Raines, 78*	n.a.	n.a.
1983	André Dawson, .539	Tim Raines, .392	Tim Raines, 90*	Flynn/Little, 5	André Dawson, 18
1984	Gary Carter, .487	Tim Raines, .391	Tim Raines, 75*	Bryan Little, 8	André Dawson, 6
1985	Tim Raines, .475	Tim Raines, .405	Tim Raines, 70	Bryn Smith, 11	Hubie Brooks, 8
1986	André Dawson, .478	Tim Raines, .413*	Tim Raines, 70	Dann Bilardello, 7	André Dawson, 6
1987	Tim Raines, .526	Tim Raines, .429	Tim Raines, 50	Mitch Webster, 8	Tim Wallach, 7
1988	Andrés Galarraga, .540	Andrés Galarraga, .352	Otis Nixon, 46	Dennis Martinez, 10	Tim Wallach, 7

(1) The total number of bases of all base hits divided by the number of times of bat. (2) The total number of hits plus walks plus times hit by pitcher divided by the number of times at bat plus walks plus sacrifice flies plus times hit by the pitcher.
*League leader; n.a. not available.

Montreal Expos Career Batting Leaders

Source: Montreal Expos

(up to the end of the 1988 season)

Games		At Bats		Hits		Runs Batted in	
André Dawson	1 443	André Dawson	5 628	André Dawson	1 575	André Dawson	838
Gary Carter	1 408	Gary Carter	5 018	Gary Carter	1 365	Gary Carter	794
Tim Wallach	1 151	Tim Raines	4 331	Tim Raines	1 319	Tim Wallach	598
Tim Raines	1 130	Tim Wallach	4 216	Tim Wallach	1 100	Bob Bailey	466
Warren Cromartie	1 038	Warren Cromartie	3 796	Warren Cromartie	1 063	Larry Parrish	444

Doubles		Triples		Home Runs		Total Bases	
André Dawson	295	Tim Raines	70	André Dawson	225	André Dawson	2 679
Gary Carter	256	André Dawson	67	Gary Carter	215	Gary Carter	2 312
Tim Raines	233	Warren Cromartie	30	Tim Wallach	148	Tim Raines	1 926
Tim Wallach	230	Mitch Webster	25	Bob Bailey	118	Tim Wallach	1 822
Warren Cromartie	222	Larry Parrish	24	Larry Parrish	100	Warren Cromartie	1 525
		Tim Wallach	24				

Runs		Walks		Average[1]			
André Dawson	828	Tim Raines	612	Al Oliver	.315	Ellis Valentine	.288
Tim Raines	793	Gary Carter	549	Tim Raines	.305	Ken Singleton	.285
Gary Carter	683	Bob Bailey	502	Rusty Staub	.295	Tony Perez	.281
Tim Wallach	479	Ron Fairly	370	Andrés Galarraga	.291	Warren Cromartie	.280
Warren Cromartie	446	André Dawson	354	Hubie Brooks	.290	André Dawson	.280

(1) Minimum 1 000 at bats.

Montreal Expos Year-by-Year Pitching Leaders

Source: Montreal Expos

	Wins	Losses	ERA (Min. 140 inn.)	Games
1969	Bill Stoneman, 11	Bill Stoneman, 19	Jerry Robertson, 3.95	Dan McGinn, 74
1970	Carl Morton, 18	Bill Stoneman, 15	Carl Morton, 3.60	Claude Raymond, 59
1971	Bill Stoneman, 17	Carl Morton, 18	Ernie McAnally, 2.90	Mike Marshall, 66
1972	Mike Torrez, 16	Ernie McAnally, 15	Bill Stoneman, 2.98	Mike Marshall, 65
1973	Steve Renko, 15	Balor Moore, 16	Mike Marshall, 2.66	Mike Marshall, 92
1974	Rogers/Torrez, 15	Steve Rogers, 22	Dennis Blair, 3.27	Chuck Taylor, 61
1975	Dale Murray, 15	Dennis Blair, 15	Dan Warthen, 3.11	Dale Murray, 63
1976	Woodie Fryman, 13	Steve Rogers, 17	Steve Rogers, 3.21	Dale Murray, 81
1977	Steve Rogers, 17	Steve Rogers, 14	Steve Rogers, 3.10	Will McEnaney, 69
1978	Ross Grimsley, 20	Ross Grimsley, 11	Steve Rogers, 2.47	Darold Knowles, 60
1979	Bill Lee, 16	Steve Rogers, 12	Dan Schatzeder, 2.83	Elias Sosa, 62
1980	Steve Rogers, 16 Scott Sanderson, 16	Steve Rogers, 11 Scott Sanderson, 11	Steve Rogers, 2.98	Elias Sosa, 67
1981	Steve Rogers, 12	Bill Gullickson, 9	Bill Gullickson, 2.81	Woodie Fryman, 35
1982	Steve Rogers, 19	Ray Burris, 14 Bill Gullickson, 14	Steve Rogers, 2.40*	Jeff Reardon, 75
1983	Bill Gullickson, 17 Steve Rogers, 17	Bill Gullickson, 12 Steve Rogers, 12	Bryn Smith, 2.49	Jeff Reardon, 66

	Wins	**Losses**	**ERA** (Min. 140 inn.)	**Games**
1984	Charlie Lea, 15	Steve Rogers, 15	Charlie Lea, 2.80	Jeff Reardon, 68
1985	Bryn Smith, 18	Bill Gullickson, 12	Joe Hesketh, 2.49	Tim Burke, 78*
1986	Floyd Youmans, 13	Floyd Youmans, 12	Andy McGaffigan, 2.65	Tim Burke, 68
1987	Neal Heaton, 13	Bob Sebra, 15	Dennis Martinez, 3.30	Andy McGaffigan, 69
1988	Dennis Martinez, 15	Dennis Martinez, 13	Pascual Perez, 2.44	Andy McGaffigan, 63

	Games started	**Innings Pitched**	**Strikeouts**	**Walks**
1969	Bill Stoneman, 36	Bill Stoneman, 235.2	Bill Stoneman, 185	Bill Stoneman, 123
1970	Carl Morton, 37	Carl Morton, 284.2	Bill Stoneman, 176	Carl Morton, 125
1971	Bill Stoneman, 39	Bill Stoneman, 294.2	Bill Stoneman, 251	Bill Stoneman, 146
1972	Bill Stoneman, 35	Bill Stoneman, 250.2	Bill Stoneman, 171	Mike Torrez, 103
1973	Steve Renko, 35	Steve Renko, 249.2	Steve Renko, 164	Mike Torrez, 115
1974	Steve Rogers, 38	Steve Rogers, 252.3	Steve Rogers, 154	Mike Torrez, 84
1975	Steve Rogers, 35	Steve Rogers, 251.2	Steve Rogers, 137	Dennis Blair, 106
1976	Rogers/Fryman, 32	Steve Rogers, 230	Steve Rogers, 150	Don Stanhouse, 92
1977	Steve Rogers, 40	Steve Rogers, 301.2	Steve Rogers, 206	Don Stanhouse, 84
1978	Ross Grimsley, 36	Ross Grimsley, 263	Steve Rogers, 126	Dan Schatzeder, 68
1979	Steve Rogers, 37	Steve Rogers, 248.2	Steve Rogers, 143	Steve Rogers, 78
1980	Steve Rogers, 37	Steve Rogers, 281	Steve Rogers, 147	Steve Rogers, 85
1981	Gullickson/Rogers/ Sanderson, 22	Steve Rogers, 161	Bill Gullickson, 115	Ray Burris, 41 Steve Rogers, 41
1982	Steve Rogers, 35	Steve Rogers, 277	Steve Rogers, 179	Steve Rogers, 65
1983	Steve Rogers, 36	Steve Rogers, 273	Steve Rogers, 146	Charlie Lea, 84
1984	Bill Gullickson, 32	Bill Gullickson, 226.2	Charlie Lea, 123	Steve Rogers, 83
1985	Bryn Smith, 32	Bryn Smith, 222.1	Bryn Smith, 127	David Palmer, 67
1986	Jay Tibbs, 31	Floyd Youmans, 219	Floyd Youmans, 202	Floyd Youmans, 118
1987	Neal Heaton, 32	Neal Heaton, 193.1	Bob Sebra, 156	Bob Sebra, 67
1988	Dennis Martinez, 34	Dennis Martinez, 235.1	Pascual Perez, 131	John Dopson, 58

* League leader.

Montreal Expos Career Pitching Leaders

Source: Montreal Expos

(up to the end of the 1988 season)

Games		**Innings**		**Wins**		**Losses**	
Steve Rogers	399	Steve Rogers	2 839	Steve Rogers	158	Steve Rogers	152
Jeff Reardon	359	Steve Renko	1 359	Bill Gullickson	72	Steve Renko	82
Woodie Fryman	297	Bill Gullickson	1 186	Bryn Smith	71	Bill Stoneman	72
Bryn Smith	251	Bryn Smith	1 185	Steve Renko	68	Bill Gullickson	61
Mike Marshall	247	Bill Stoneman	1 085	Scott Sanderson	56	Bryn Smith	60

Games Started		**Complete Games**		**Saves**		**Walks**	
Steve Rogers	393	Steve Rogers	129	Jeff Reardon	152	Steve Rogers	876
Steve Renko	192	Bill Stoneman	46	Mike Marshall	75	Steve Renko	624
Bill Gullickson	170	Steve Renko	40	Woodie Fryman	52	Bill Stoneman	535
Bryn Smith	161	Bill Gullickson	31	Tim Burke	48	Mike Torrez	303
Bill Stoneman	157	Bill Stoneman	24	Dale Murray	33	Charlie Lea	291

Strikeouts		**Shutouts**		**No Hit Games**
Steve Rogers	1 621	Steve Rogers	37	Bill Stoneman, Apr. 17, 1969, at Phil., 7-0
Bill Stoneman	831	Bill Stoneman	15	Bill Stoneman, Oct. 2, 1972, at Montreal, 7-0
Steve Renko	810	Woodie Fryman	8	Charlie Lea, May 10, 1981, at Montreal, 4-0
Bryn Smith	709	Charlie Lea	8	David Palmer, Apr. 21, 1984, at St. Louis, 4-0
Bill Gullickson	678	Scott Sanderson	8	Pascual Perez, Sept. 24, 1988, at Philadelphia, 1-0

Montreal Expos Individual Statistics, 1988

Batters

	AVG	OBA	AB	R	H	2B	3B	HR	RBI	BB	SO	SB	CS	E
Huson	.310	.370	42	7	13	2	0	0	3	4	3	2	1	4
W. Johnson ..	.309	.387	94	7	29	5	1	0	3	12	15	0	2	1
Galarraga	.302	.352	609	99	184	42	8	29	92	39	153	13	4	15
Jones	.295	.358	224	29	66	6	1	3	24	20	18	18	6	2
Brooks	.279	.318	588	61	164	35	2	20	90	35	108	7	3	9
Hudler	.273	.303	216	38	59	14	2	4	14	10	34	29	7	10
Fitzgerald	.271	.347	155	17	42	6	1	5	23	19	22	2	2	6
Raines	.270	.350	429	66	116	19	7	12	48	53	44	33	7	3
Tejada	.267	.250	15	1	4	2	0	0	2	0	4	0	0	0
Foley	.265	.319	377	33	100	21	3	5	43	30	49	2	7	15

Batters

	AVG	OBA	AB	R	H	2B	3B	HR	RBI	BB	SO	SB	CS	E
O'Malley	.259	.323	27	3	7	0	0	0	2	3	4	0	0	2
Wallach	.257	.302	592	52	152	32	5	12	69	38	88	2	6	18
DeMartinez	.255	.313	447	51	114	13	6	6	46	38	94	23	9	6
Webster	.255	.354	259	33	66	5	2	2	13	36	37	12	10	1
Nixon	.244	.312	271	47	66	8	2	0	15	28	42	46	13	1
Santovenia	.236	.294	309	26	73	20	2	8	41	24	77	2	3	9
Winningham	.233	.320	90	10	21	2	1	0	6	12	18	4	5	1
Rivera	.224	.271	371	35	83	17	3	4	30	24	69	3	4	18
Reed	.220	.292	123	10	27	3	2	0	9	13	22	1	0	1
Engle	.216	.310	37	4	8	3	0	1	1	5	5	0	0	0
Paredes	.187	.282	91	6	17	2	0	1	10	9	17	5	2	3
Candaele	.172	.238	116	9	20	5	1	0	4	10	11	1	0	2
Nettles	.172	.240	93	5	16	4	0	1	14	9	19	0	0	5
Team Totals	.251	.309	5 573	628	1 400	260	48	107	575	454	1 053	189	89	142

AVG = batting average; OBA = on base average; AB = times at bat; R = runs; H = hits; 2B = doubles; 3B = triples; HR = home runs; RBI = runs batted in; BB = walks; SO = strikeouts; SB = stolen bases; CS = caught stealing; E = errors.

Pitchers

	W	L	ERA	G	GS	SV	IP	H	R	HR	BB	SO
R. Johnson	3	0	2.42	4	4	0	26.0	23	8	3	7	25
Perez	12	8	2.44	27	27	0	188.0	133	59	15	44	131
Parrett	12	4	2.65	61	0	6	91.2	66	29	8	45	62
DeMartinez	15	13	2.72	34	34	0	235.1	215	94	21	55	120
McGaffigan	6	0	2.76	63	0	4	91.1	81	31	4	37	71
Hesketh	4	3	2.85	60	0	9	72.2	63	30	1	35	64
B. Smith	12	10	3.00	32	32	0	198.0	179	79	15	32	122
Dopson	3	11	3.04	26	26	0	168.2	150	69	15	58	101
M. Smith	0	0	3.12	5	0	1	8.2	6	3	0	5	4
Youmans	3	6	3.21	14	13	0	84.0	64	35	8	41	54
Holman	4	8	3.23	18	16	0	100.1	101	39	3	34	58
Burke	3	5	3.40	61	0	18	82.0	84	36	7	25	42
Heaton	3	10	4.99	32	11	2	97.1	98	54	14	43	43
Pacillo	1	0	5.06	6	0	0	10.2	14	7	2	4	11
Barrett	0	0	5.79	4	0	1	9.1	10	6	2	2	5
Sauveur	0	0	6.00	4	0	0	3.0	3	2	1	2	3
St. Claire	0	0	6.14	6	0	0	7.1	11	5	2	5	6
McClure	1	3	6.16	19	0	0	19.0	23	13	3	6	12
Team Totals	81	81	3.08	163	163	43	1 482.2	1 310	592	122	476	923

W = games won; L = games lost; ERA = earned run average; G = games played in; GS = games started; SV = saves; IP = innings pitched; H = hits allowed; R = runs allowed; HR = home runs allowed; BB = walks allowed; SO = strikeouts.

Toronto Blue Jays Opening-Day Lineups

(listed by batting order)

1977

John Scott	LF
Hector Torres	SS
Doug Ault	1B
Otto Velez	DH
Gary Woods	CF
Steve Bowling	RF
Pedro Garcia	2B
Dave McKay	3B
Rick Cerone	C
Bill Singer	P

1978

Rick Bosetti	CF
Al Woods	LF
Roy Howell	3B
Rico Carty	DH
John Mayberry	1B
Tommy Hutton	RF
Dave McKay	2B
Luis Gomez	SS
Alan Ashby	C
Dave Lemanczyk	P

1979

Alfredo Griffin	SS
Bobby Bailor	RF
Roy Howell	3B
Rico Carty	DH
John Mayberry	1B
Rick Bosetti	CF
Bobby Brown	LF
Dave McKay	2B
Rick Cerone	C
Tom Underwood	P

1980

Alfredo Griffin	SS
Bob Bailor	RF
John Mayberry	1B
Otto Velez	DH
Roy Howell	3B
Barry Bonnell	LF
Rick Bosetti	CF
Damaso Garcia	2B
Ernie Whitt	C
Dave Lemanczyk	P

1981

Alfredo Griffin	SS
Lloyd Moseby	CF
Otto Velez	DH
John Mayberry	1B
Willie Upshaw	LF
Damaso Garcia	2B
Barry Bonnell	RF
Danny Ainge	3B
Ernie Whitt	C
Jim Clancy	P

1982

Alfredo Griffin	SS
Al Woods	LF
Lloyd Moseby	CF
Willie Upshaw	1B
John Mayberry	DH
Jesse Barfield	RF
Ernie Whitt	C
Damaso Garcia	2B
Rance Mulliniks	3B
Mark Bomback	P

1983

Damaso Garcia	2B
Dave Collins	LF
Willie Upshaw	1B
Cliff Johnson	DH
Jesse Barfield	RF
Ernie Whitt	C
Lloyd Moseby	CF
Rance Mulliniks	3B
Alfredo Griffin	SS
Dave Stieb	P

1984

Damaso Garcia	2B
Rance Mulliniks	3B
Lloyd Moseby	CF
Willie Upshaw	1B
Cliff Johnson	DH
George Bell	LF
Jesse Barfield	RF
Ernie Whitt	C
Alfredo Griffin	SS
Jim Clancy	P

1985		1986		1987		1988	
Damaso Garcia	2B	Lloyd Moseby	CF	Tony Fernandez	SS	Nelson Liriano	2B
Lloyd Moseby	CF	Tony Fernandez	SS	Rance Mulliniks	3B	Lloyd Moseby	LF
George Bell	LF	Rance Mulliniks	3B	Lloyd Moseby	CF	Tony Fernandez	SS
Jesse Barfield	RF	Willie Upshaw	1B	George Bell	LF	George Bell	DH
Jeff Burroughs	DH	George Bell	LF	Jesse Barfield	RF	Rance Mulliniks	3B
Willie Upshaw	1B	Jesse Barfield	RF	Willie Upshaw	1B	Ernie Whitt	C
Buck Martinez	C	Ernie Whitt	C	Ernie Whitt	C	Jesse Barfield	RF
Garth Iorg	3B	Cecil Fielder	DH	Fred McGriff	DH	Fred McGriff	1B
Tony Fernandez	SS	Damaso Garcia	2B	Mike Sharperson	2B	Sil Campusano	CF
Dave Stieb	P	Dave Stieb	P	Jimmy Key	P	Jimmy Key	P

Toronto Blue Jays Year-By-Year Record

Year	Won	Lost	Avg.	Pos	Games behind	Home attendance	Manager
1977	54	107	.335	7th	45½	1 701 052	Roy Hartsfield
1978	59	102	.366	7th	50	1 562 585	Roy Hartsfield
1979	53	109	.327	7th	50½	1 431 651	Roy Hartsfield
1980	67	95	.414	7th	36	1 400 327	Bob Mattick
1981	37	69	.349	–	–	755 083	Bob Mattick
1st half	16	42	.276	7th	19	—	
2d half	21	27	.438	7th	7½	—	
1982	78	84	.481	6th[1]	17	1 275 978	Bobby Cox
1983	89	73	.549	4th	9	1 930 415	Bobby Cox
1984	89	73	.549	2d	15	2 110 009	Bobby Cox
1985	99	62	.615	1st	+ 2	2 468 925	Bobby Cox
1986	86	76	.531	4th	9½	2 455 477	Jimy Williams
1987	96	66	.593	2d	2	2 778 459	Jimy Williams
1988	87	75	.537	3d	2	2 595 175	Jimy Williams

(1) Tied.

Toronto Blue Jays Year-by-Year Batting Leaders

Source: Toronto Blue Jays

	Average (350 ABs)	At Bats	Runs	Hits	Doubles
1977	Roy Howell, .316	Bob Bailor, 496	Bob Bailor, 62	Bob Bailor, 154	Ron Fairley, 24
1978	Roy Howell, .270	Bob Bailor, 621	Bob Bailor, 74	Bob Bailor, 164	Bob Bailor, 29
1979	Alfredo Griffin, .287	Alfredo Griffin, 624	Alfredo Griffin, 81	Alfredo Griffin, 179	Rick Bosetti, 35
1980	Al Woods, .300	Alfredo Griffin, 653	Alfredo Griffin, 63	Alfredo Griffin, 166	Damaso Garcia, 30
1981	Domaso Garcia, .252[1]	Alfredo Griffin, 388	Lloyd Moseby, 36	Lloyd Moseby, 88	Alfredo Griffin, 19
1982	Domaso Garcia, .310	Willie Upshaw, 580	Domaso Garcia, 89	Domaso Garcia, 185	Damaso Garcia, 32
1983	Lloyd Moseby, .315	Willie Upshaw, 579	Lloyd Moseby, 104	Willie Upshaw, 177	Rance Mulliniks, 34
1984	Dave Collins, .308	Domaso Garcia, 633	Lloyd Moseby, 97	Domaso Garcia, 180	George Bell, 39
1985	Rance Mulliniks, .295	George Bell, 607	Jesse Barfield, 94	George Bell, 167	Jesse Barfield, 34
1986	Tony Fernandez, .310	Tony Fernandez, 687	Jesse Barfield, 107	Tony Fernandez, 213	George Bell, 38
1987	Tony Fernandez, .322	George Bell, 610	George Bell, 111	George Bell, 188	George Bell, 32
1988	Tony Fernandez, .287	Tony Fernandez, 648	Fred McGriff, 100	Tony Fernandez, 186	Tony Fernandez, 41

	Triples	Home Runs	Runs batted in	Walks	Strike-outs
1977	Steve Staggs, 6	Ron Fairly, 19	Fairly/Ault, 64	Otto Velez, 65	Otto Velez, 87
1978	Dave McKay, 8	John Mayberry, 22	John Mayberry, 70	John Mayberry, 61	Roy Howell, 90
1979	Alfredo Griffin, 10	John Mayberry, 21	John Mayberry, 74	John Mayberry, 69	Roy Howell, 91
1980	Alfredo Griffin, 15*	John Mayberry, 30	John Mayberry, 82	John Mayberry, 77	Roy Howell, 92
1981	Alfredo Griffin, 6	John Mayberry, 17	Moseby/Mayberry, 43	Otto Velez, 55	Lloyd Moseby, 86
1982	Lloyd Moseby, 9*	Willie Upshaw, 21	Willie Upshaw, 75	Willie Upshaw, 52	Lloyd Moseby, 106
1983	Alfredo Griffin, 9	Barfield/Upshaw, 27	Willie Upshaw, 104	Cliff Johnson, 67	Jesse Barfield, 110
1984	Collins/Moseby, 15*	George Bell, 26	Lloyd Moseby, 92	Lloyd Moseby, 78	Lloyd Moseby, 122
1985	Tony Fernandez, 10	George Bell, 28	George Bell, 95	Lloyd Moseby, 76	Jesse Barfield, 143
1986	Tony Fernandez, 9	Jesse Barfield, 40*	Bell/Barfield, 108	Willie Upshaw, 78	Jesse Barfield, 146
1987	Tony Fernandez, 8	George Bell, 47	George Bell, 134*	Lloyd Moseby, 70	Jesse Barfield, 141
1988	Lloyd Moseby, 7	Fred McGriff, 34	George Bell, 97	Fred McGriff, 79	Fred McGriff, 149

	Slugging%[2] (350 ABs)	On base%[3] (350 ABs)	Stolen Bases	Sacrifice Hits	Sacrifice Flies
1977	Ron Fairly, .465	Roy Howell, .370	Bob Bailor, 15	Alan Ashby, 10	Otto Velez, 6
1978	John Mayberry, .416	John Mayberry, .330	Rick Bosetti, 9	Luis Gomez, 19	John Mayberry, 7
1979	John Mayberry, .461	John Mayberry, .374	Alfredo Griffin, 21	Alfredo Griffin, 16	Rick Bosetti, 7
1980	Otto Velez, .487	Otto Velez, .368	Alfredo Griffin, 18	Griffin/Moseby, 10	Griffin/Howell, 5
1981	John Mayberry, .452[1]	Otto Velez, .366[1]	Damaso Garcia, 13	Al Woods, 8	Lloyd Moseby, 4
1982	Willie Upshaw, .443	Barry Bonnell, .345	Damaso Garcia, 54	Alfredo Griffin, 11	Garth Iorg, 7
1983	Willie Upshaw, .515	Lloyd Moseby, .380	Collins/Garcia, 31	Alfredo Griffin, 11	Willie Upshaw, 7
1984	Cliff Johnson, .507	Cliff Johnson, .393	Dave Collins, 60	Alfredo Griffin, 13	Buck Martinez, 9
1985	Jesse Barfield, .536	Rance Mulliniks, .387	Lloyd Moseby, 37	Tony Fernandez, 7	George Bell, 8
1986	Jesse Barfield, .559	Jesse Barfield, .368	Lloyd Moseby, 32	Tony Fernandez, 5	Leach/Moseby, 7
1987	George Bell, .606	Tony Fernandez, .379	Lloyd Moseby, 39	Garth Iorg, 5	George Bell, 9
1988	Fred McGriff, .552	Tony Fernandez, .386	Lloyd Moseby, 31	Kelly Gruber, 5	George Bell, 8

(1) Based on 250 ABs. (2) The total number of bases of all base hits divided by the number of times at bat. (3) The total number of hits plus walks plus times hit by pitcher divided by the number of times at bat plus walks plus sacrifice flies plus times hit by the pitcher.
* Indicates league leader.

Toronto Blue Jays Career Batting Leaders

Source: Toronto Blue Jays

(up to the end of the 1988 season)

Games		At Bats		Runs		Hits	
Lloyd Moseby	1 257	Lloyd Moseby	4 622	Lloyd Moseby	696	Lloyd Moseby	1 208
Willie Upshaw	1 115	Willie Upshaw	3 710	Willie Upshaw	538	Damaso Garcia	1 028
Ernie Whitt	1 089	Damaso Garcia	3 572	Jesse Barfield	522	Willie Upshaw	982
Jesse Barfield	1 010	Jesse Barfield	3 383	George Bell	486	George Bell	963
Garth Iorg	931	George Bell	3 353	Damaso Garcia	453	Jesse Barfield	903
Damaso Garcia	902	Afredo Griffin	3 151	Ernie Whitt	382	Tony Fernandez	820
George Bell	886	Ernie Whitt	3 129	Tony Fernandez	362	Alfredo Griffin	789
Alfredo Griffin	873	Tony Fernandez	2 744	Rance Mulliniks	318	Ernie Whitt	787
Rance Mulliniks	736	Garth Iorg	2 450	Garth Iorg	251	Rance Mulliniks	689
Tony Fernandez	727	Rance Mulliniks	2 401	Bob Bailor	230	Garth Iorg	633

Toronto Blue Jays Individual Career Batting

Source: Toronto Blue Jays

(up to end of 1988 season)

Player	Avg	G	AB	R	H	2B	3B	HR	RBI	BB	SO	SB/CS
Jesse Barfield	.267	1 010	3 383	522	903	158	27	174	516	337	827	55/38
George Bell	.287	886	3 353	486	963	171	30	163	550	190	423	52/22
Juan Beniquez	.288	86	139	15	40	7	1	6	29	13	19	0/0
Pat Borders	.273	56	154	15	42	6	3	5	21	3	24	5/7
Sil Campusano	.218	73	142	14	31	10	2	2	12	9	23	0/0
Rob Ducey	.255	61	102	27	26	6	1	1	12	13	17	2/0
Tony Fernandez	.299	727	2 744	362	820	140	35	25	274	185	223	84/43
Sal Butera	.233	23	60	3	14	2	1	1	6	1	9	0/0
Cecil Fielder	.243	218	506	67	123	19	2	31	84	46	144	0/2
Kelly Gruber	.250	403	1 082	146	270	51	9	34	135	60	197	37/12
Alexis Infante	.200	20	15	7	3	0	0	0	0	2	4	0/0
Rick Leach	.283	376	763	95	216	46	6	8	95	67	76	0/2
Manny Lee	.268	271	620	69	166	18	7	4	56	38	96	6/8
Nelson Liriano	.256	136	434	65	111	12	4	5	33	27	62	25/7
Fred McGriff	.269	264	836	159	225	41	4	54	125	139	255	9/3
Lloyd Moseby	.261	1 257	4 622	696	1 208	217	57	150	608	491	914	231/79
Rance Mulliniks	.287	855	2 401	318	689	177	31	61	319	313	362	10/9
Lou Thornton	.237	79	76	24	18	1	1	1	8	3	24	1/1
Ernie Whitt	.252	1 089	3 129	382	787	140	14	120	465	351	398	17/20

Avg. = batting average, the number of base hits divided by the number of times at bat; G = games; AB = times at bat; R = runs; H = hits; 2B = doubles; 3B = triples; HR = home runs; RBI = runs batted in; BB = walks; SO = strikeouts; SB/CS = stolen bases/caught stealing.

Toronto Blue Jays Individual Career Pitching

Source: Toronto Blue Jays

(up to end of 1988 season)

Pitcher	Won	Lost	ERA	G	GS	CG	SV	SHO	IP	HR	HB	BB	SO
Doug Bair	0	0	4.05	10	0	0	0	0	13.1	2	0	3	8
Tony Castillo	1	0	3.00	14	0	0	0	0	15.0	2	0	2	14
John Cerutti	26	17	3.96	128	54	4	2	1	427.0	68	6	152	251
Jim Clancy	128	140	4.10	352	345	73	1	11	2 204.1	219	28	814	1 237
Mark Eichhorn	24	18	2.98	202	7	0	15	0	389.1	29	19	138	306
Mike Flanagan	16	15	3.84	41	41	2	0	1	260.1	26	6	95	142
Tom Henke	16	18		215	0	0	99	0	293.1	26	3	89	354
Jimmy Key	61	35	3.23	191	124	17	10	5	898.2	91	13	252	496
Jeff Musselman	20	10	3.86	89	16	0	3	0	179.1	12	6	89	97
Jose Nunez	5	3	4.56	50	11	0	0	0	126.1	15	1	75	117
Mark Ross	0	0	4.91	3	0	0	0	0	7.1	0	0	4	4
Dave Stieb	131	109	3.37	324	316	96	1	26	2 251.2	182	95	797	1 331
Todd Stottlemyre	4	8	5.69	28	16	0	0	0	98.0	15	4	46	67
Duane Ward	10	4	3.81	78	2	0	15	0	125.1	7	5	84	110
David Wells	7	8	4.42	59	0	0	5	0	93.2	15	6	76	102
Frank Wills	0	0	5.23	10	0	0	0	0	20.2	2	0	6	19

ERA = earned run average, the number of earned runs multiplied by 9 and divided by the number of innings pitched; G = games; GS = games started; CG = complete games; SV = saves; SHO = shutouts; IP = innings pitched; HR = home runs against; HB = hit batters; BB = walks; SO = strikeouts.

Toronto Blue Jays Year-by-Year Pitching Leaders

Source: Toronto Blue Jays

	Wins	Losses	ERA (Min. 140 inn.)	Games
1977	Dave Lemanczyk, 13	Jerry Garvin, 18	Pete Vuckovich, 3.47	Pete Vuckovich, 53
1978	Jim Clancy, 10	Jesse Jefferson, 16	Jim Clancy, 4.09	Tom Murphy, 50
1979	Tom Underwood, 9	Phil Huffman, 18	Tom Underwood, 3.69	Tom Buskey, 44
1980	Jim Clancy, 13	Jim Clancy, 16	Jim Clancy, 3.30	Jerry Garvin, 61
1981	Dave Stieb, 11	Luis Leal, 13	Dave Stieb, 3.19	Joey McLaughlin, 40
1982	Dave Stieb, 17	Luis Leal, 15	Dave Stieb, 3.25	Dale Murray, 56
1983	Dave Stieb, 17	Jim Gott, 14	Dave Stieb, 3.04	Joey McLaughlin, 50
1984	Doyle Alexander, 17	Jim Clancy, 15	Dave Stieb, 2.83	Jimmy Key, 63
1985	Doyle Alexander, 17	Dave Stieb, 13	Dave Stieb, 2.48*	Gary Lavelle, 69
1986	Clancy/Key/Eichhorn, 14	Jim Clancy, 14	Mark Eichhorn, 1.72	Mark Eichhorn, 69
1987	Jimmy Key, 17	Jim Clancy, 11	Jimmy Key, 2.76*	Mark Eichhorn, 89
1988	Dave Stieb, 16	Clancy/Flanagan, 13	Dave Stieb, 3.04	Duane Ward, 64

	Games started	Complete games	Saves
1977	Jerry Garvin, 34 Dave Lemanczyk, 34	Jerry Garvin, 12	Pete Vuckovich, 8
1978	Clancy/Jefferson/Underwood, 30	Jesse Jefferson, 9	Victor Cruz, 9
1979	Tom Underwood, 32	Tom Underwood, 12	Tom Buskey, 7
1980	Jim Clancy, 34	Jim Clancy, 15	Jerry Garvin, 8
1981	Dave Stieb, 25	Dave Stieb, 11	Joey McLaughlin, 10
1982	Jim Clancy, 40*	Dave Stieb, 19	Dale Murray, 11
1983	Dave Stieb, 36	Dave Stieb, 14	Randy Moffitt, 10
1984	Jim Clancy, 36*	Stieb/Alexander, 11	Key/Jackson, 10
1985	Stieb/Alexander, 36	Dave Stieb, 8	Bill Caudill, 14
1986	Jimmy Key, 35	Jim Clancy, 6	Tom Henke, 27
1987	Jim Clancy, 37	Jimmy Key, 8	Tom Henke, 34*
1988	Mike Flanagan, 34	Dave Stieb, 8	Tom Henke, 25

	Shutouts	Innings pitched	Strikeouts	Walks
1977	Garvin/Clancy/Vuckovich, 1	Dave Lemanczyk, 252.0	Jerry Garvin, 127	Dave Lemanczyk, 87
1978	Jesse Jefferson, 2	Jesse Jefferson, 211.1	Tom Underwood, 140	Jim Clancy, 91
1979	Dave Lemanczyk, 3	Tom Underwood, 227.0	Tom Underwood, 127	Tom Underwood, 95
1980	Dave Stieb, 4	Jim Clancy, 250.2	Jim Clancy, 152	Jim Clancy, 128
1981	Dave Stieb, 2	Dave Stieb, 183.2	Dave Stieb, 89	Jim Clancy, 64
1982	Dave Stieb, 5	Dave Stieb, 288.1	Dave Stieb, 149	Luis Leal, 79
1983	Dave Stieb, 4	Dave Stieb, 278.0	Dave Stieb, 187	Dave Stieb, 83
1984	Leal/Stieb/Alexander, 2	Dave Stieb, 267.0*	Dave Stieb, 198	Clancy/Stieb, 88
1985	Dave Stieb, 2	Dave Stieb, 265.0	Dave Stieb, 167	Dave Stieb, 96
1986	Jim Clancy, 3	Jimmy Key, 232.0	Mark Eichhorn, 166	Dave Stieb, 87
1987	Clancy/Key/Stieb, 1	Jimmy Key, 261.0	Jim Clancy, 180	Dave Stieb, 87
1988	Dave Stieb, 4	Mike Flanagan, 211.0	Dave Stieb, 147	Mike Flanagan, 80

* League leader.

Toronto Blue Jays Career Pitching Leaders

Source: Toronto Blue Jays

(up to the end of the 1988 season)

Wins		Losses		Games Started		Complete Games	
Dave Stieb	131	Jim Clancy	140	Jim Clancy	345	Dave Stieb	96
Jim Clancy	128	Dave Stieb	109	Dave Stieb	316	Jim Clancy	73
Jimmy Key	61	Luis Leal	58	Luis Leal	151	Luis Leal	27
Luis Leal	51	Jesse Jefferson	56	Jimmy Key	124	Doyle Alexander	25
Doyle Alexander	46	Dave Lemanczyk	45	Doyle Alexander	103	Dave Lemanczyk	25
Dave Lemanczyk	27	Jerry Garvin	41	Dave Lemanczyk	82	Jesse Jefferson	21
John Cerutti	26	Jimmy Key	35	Jerry Garvin	65	Tom Underwood	19
Mark Eichhorn	24	Tom Underwood	30	Jim Gott	65	Jimmy Key	17
Roy Lee Jackson	24	Jim Gott	30	Tom Underwood	62	Jerry Garvin	15
Jesse Jefferson	22	Doyle Alexander	26			Jim Gott	8

Saves		Walks		Strikeouts		Shutouts	
Tom Henke	99	Jim Clancy	814	Dave Stieb	1 331	Dave Stieb	26
Joey McLaughlin	31	Dave Stieb	797	Jim Clancy	1 237	Jim Clancy	11
Roy Lee Jackson	30	Luis Leal	320	Jimmy Key	496	Jimmy Key	5
Bill Caudill	16	Jesse Jefferson	266	Luis Leal	491	Jesse Jefferson	4
Mark Eichhorn	16	Jimmy Key	252	John Cerutti	427	Doyle Alexander	3
Duane Ward	15	Jerry Garvin	219	Doyle Alexander	392	Jim Gott	3
Mike Willis	15	Dave Lemanczyk	212	Mark Eichhorn	389	Dave Lemanczyk	3
Dennis Lamp	13	Jim Gott	183	Jerry Garvin	320	Tom Underwood	2
Jim Acker	12	Tom Underwood	182	Jesse Jefferson	307	Mike Flanagan	1
Dale Murray	11	Doyle Alexander	172	Tom Henke	293	Jerry Garvin	1

Hit Batsmen		Wild Pitches		HR's Allowed		ERA	
Dave Stieb	95	Jim Clancy	82	Jim Clancy	213	Jimmy Key	3.23
Jim Clancy	28	Dave Stieb	39	Dave Stieb	182	Dave Stieb	3.37
Luis Leal	22	Dave Lemanczyk	36	Luis Leal	101	Doyle Alexander	3.56
Mark Eichhorn	19	Luis Leal	23	Jimmy Key	91	Tom Underwood	3.88
Jim Acker	19	John Cerutti	21	Jesse Jefferson	82	John Cerutti	3.96
Balor Moore	19	Jimmy Key	21	Doyle Alexander	81	Jim Clancy	4.10
Doyle Alexander	14	Tom Underwood	18	Jerry Garvin	74	Luis Leal	4.14
Jimmy Key	13	Jerry Garvin	17	John Cerutti	68	Jim Gott	4.25
Jerry Garvin	13	Doyle Alexander	16	Dave Lemanczyk	52	Jerry Garvin	4.46
Dave Lemanczyk	13	Pete Vuckovich	12	Tom Underwood	46	Dave Lemanczyk	4.68

Toronto Blue Jays Individual Statistics, 1988

Batters

	AVG	OBA	AB	R	H	2B	3B	HR	RBI	BB	SO	SB	CS	E
Ducey	.315	.361	54	15	17	4	1	0	6	5	7	1	0	0
Mulliniks	.300	.395	337	49	101	21	1	12	48	56	57	1	0	0
Beniquez	.293	.373	58	9	17	2	0	1	8	8	6	0	0	0
Lee	.291	.333	381	38	111	16	3	2	38	26	64	3	3	12
Fernandez	.287	.335	648	76	186	41	4	5	70	45	65	15	5	14
McGriff	.282	.376	536	100	151	35	4	34	82	79	149	1	5	5
Gruber	.278	.328	569	75	158	33	5	16	81	38	92	23	5	16
Leach	.276	.336	199	21	55	13	1	0	23	18	27	0	1	0
Borders	.273	.285	154	15	42	6	3	5	21	3	24	0	0	7
Bell	.269	.304	614	78	165	27	5	24	97	34	66	4	2	5
Liriano	.264	.297	276	36	73	6	2	3	23	11	40	12	5	2
Whitt	.251	.348	398	63	100	11	2	16	70	61	38	4	2	4
Barfield	.244	.302	468	62	114	21	5	18	56	41	108	7	3	5
Moseby	.239	.343	472	77	113	17	7	10	42	70	93	31	8	5
Butera	.233	.246	60	3	14	2	1	1	6	1	9	0	0	1
Fielder	.230	.289	174	24	40	6	1	9	23	14	53	0	1	1
Campusano	.218	.282	142	14	31	10	2	2	12	9	33	0	0	0
Infante	.200	.294	15	7	3	0	0	0	0	2	4	0	0	8
Thornton	.000	.000	2	1	0	0	0	0	0	0	0	0	0	1
Team Totals	**.268**	**.332**	**5 557**	**763**	**1 491**	**271**	**47**	**158**	**706**	**521**	**935**	**107**	**36**	**110**

AVG = batting average; OBA = on base average; AB = times at bat; R = runs; H = hits; 2B = doubles; 3B = triples; HR = home runs; RBI = runs batted in; BB = walks; SO = strikeouts; SB = stolen bases; CS = caught stealing; E = errors.

Pitchers

	W	L	ERA	G	GS	SV	IP	H	R	HR	BB	SO
Henke	4	4	2.91	52	0	25	68.0	60	23	6	24	66
Castillo	1	0	3.00	14	0	0	15.0	10	5	2	2	14
Stieb	16	8	3.04	32	31	0	207.1	157	76	15	79	147
Nunez	0	1	3.07	13	2	0	29.1	28	11	3	17	18
Cerutti	6	7	3.13	46	12	1	123.2	120	56	12	42	65
Musselman	8	5	3.18	15	15	0	85.0	80	34	4	30	39
Key	12	5	3.29	21	21	0	131.1	127	55	13	30	65
Ward	9	3	3.30	64	0	15	111.2	101	46	5	60	91
Bair	0	0	4.05	10	0	0	13.1	14	6	1	3	8
Flanagan	13	13	4.18	34	34	0	211.0	220	106	22	80	99
Eichhorn	0	3	4.18	37	0	1	66.2	79	32	3	27	28
Clancy	11	13	4.49	36	31	1	196.1	207	106	26	47	118
Wells	3	5	4.62	41	0	4	64.1	65	36	12	31	56
Ross	0	0	4.91	3	0	0	7.1	5	6	0	4	4
Wills	0	0	5.23	10	0	0	20.2	22	12	2	6	19
Stottlemyre	4	8	5.69	28	16	0	98.0	109	70	15	46	67
Team Totals	**87**	**75**	**3.80**	**162**	**162**	**47**	**1 449.0**	**1 404**	**680**	**143**	**528**	**904**

W = games won; L = games lost; ERA = earned run average; G = games played in; GS = games started; SV = saves; IP = innings pitched; H = hits allowed; R = runs allowed; HR = home runs allowed; BB = walks allowed; SO = strikeouts.

Hockey

The Greatest Imaginary NHL Team of All Time

(listed by position in order in which they were selected through a Canadian World Almanac survey of NHL coaches and general managers)

Goal – Jacques Plante, Terry Sawchuk. **Defence** – Bobby Orr, Doug Harvey, Larry Robinson, Denis Potvin, Eddie Shore, Paul Coffey. **Centre:** Wayne Gretzky, Jean Béliveau, Stan Mikita, Phil Esposito. **Left Wing:** Bobby Hull, Frank Mahovlich, Ted Lindsay. **Right Wing:** Gordie Howe, Maurice "Rocket" Richard, Mike Bossy.

We asked the NHL coaches and general managers to choose an all-time "dream team" made up of 2 goaltenders, 6 defencemen, 4 centres, 3 left wingers and 3 right wingers. The final selections at each position are based on total points received; highest points were awarded to 1st choices with less points given, in descending order, to lower selections.

The only unanimous 1st choice was Bobby Orr on defence, followed by a near-unanimous 2d choice, Doug Harvey. Filling the remaining 4 defence positions are Larry Robinson, Denis Potvin, Eddie Shore and Paul Coffey. They were followed in the voting by Red Kelly, Tim Horton, Raymond Bourque, Brad Park, Pierre Pilote, Jean-Guy Talbot and "Black Jack" Stewart.

Jacques Plante and Terry Sawchuk tied in the voting for the greatest goaltender. Others who received votes were Ken Dryden, Bernie Parent, Glenn Hall, Turk Broda, Gump Worsley and Georges Vézina.

Although a majority of votes for greatest all-time centre went to Wayne Gretzky, several experts preferred Jean Béliveau. Stan Mikita and Phil Esposito were frequent choices as the 3d and 4th best centres, followed by Bobby Clarke, Bryan Trottier, Henri Richard, Marcel Dionne, Mario Lemieux, Peter Stastny, Gilbert Perreault and Bob Pulford.

Bobby Hull was a run-away winner as top choice at left wing, followed by Frank Mahovlich and Ted Lindsay who edged out Dickie Moore for 3d spot. Others receiving mention were Claude Provost, Bert Olmstead, Johnny Bucyk, Bob Gainey, Michel Goulet, Bill Barber and Gilles Tremblay.

At right wing, Gordie Howe was picked ahead of Rocket Richard, although the choice was not unanimous. Mike Bossy finished a strong 3d, ahead of Guy Lafleur, Jari Kurri, Boom Boom Geoffrion and Andy Bathgate.

The Greatest Stanley Cup Winning Team of All Time

(selected in a survey of NHL coaches and managers)

The Montreal Canadiens, 1959 – 1960

Goal – Jacques Plante, Charlie Hodge; **Defence** – Doug Harvey, Tom Johnson, Bob Turner, Jean-Guy Talbot, Albert Langois; **Forwards** – Ralph Backstrom, Jean Béliveau, Marcel Bonin, Bernie Geoffrion, Phil Goyette, Bill Hicke, Don Marshall, Ab McDonald, Dickie Moore, André Pronovost, Claude Provost, Henri Richard, Maurice Richard; **Coach** – Toe Blake; **Manager** – Frank Selke.

In a Canadian World Almanac survey of coaches and general managers of the 21 NHL teams, the 1959-60 Montreal Canadiens were selected the greatest Stanley Cup winning team of all time. The consensus of the hockey experts is that this team, which includes 8 Hall of Fame members – Jacques Plante, Doug Harvey, Tom Johnson, Jean Béliveau, Boom Boom Geoffrion, Dickie Moore, Henri Richard and Maurice "Rocket" Richard – would defeat any other team of any era if such an imaginary contest were possible.

Finishing a close 2d in the balloting was another great Montreal team, the 1976-77 Canadiens, which included Ken Dryden, Larry Robinson, Serge Savard, Guy Lapointe, Yvan Cournoyer, Guy Lafleur, Jacques Lemaire and Steve Shutt. The 3d pick of the coaches and managers was the 1951–52 Detroit Red Wings whose stars included Terry Sawchuk, Red Kelly, Marcel Pronovost, Sid Abel, Alex Delvecchio, Gordie Howe and Ted Lindsay.

Stanley Cup Champions, 1918-1988

Source: National Hockey League

The Stanley Cup, the oldest trophy competed for by professional athletes in North America, was donated by Frederick Arthur, Lord Stanley of Preston, in 1893. Originally presented to the amateur hockey champions of Canada, it has been awarded to the top professional team since 1910 and, since 1926, has been competed for only by NHL teams.

Year	Champion	Final opponent	Series result	Winning coach	Winning manager
1918	Toronto Arenas	Vancouver	3-2	Dick Carroll	Charlie Querrie
1919	No decision[1]				
1920	Ottawa Senators	Seattle	3-2	Pete Green	Tommy Gorman
1921	Ottawa Senators	Vancouver	3-2	Pete Green	Tommy Gorman
1922	Toronto St. Pats	Vancouver	3-2	Eddie Powers	Charlie Querrie
1923	Ottawa Senators	Vancouver; Edm.[2]	3-1; 2-0	Pete Green	Tommy Gorman
1924[3]	Montreal Canadiens	Vancouver; Calgary	2-0; 2-0	Leo Dandurand	Leo Dandurand
1925	Victoria Cougars	Montreal	3-1	Lester Patrick	Lester Patrick
1926	Montreal Maroons	Victoria	3-1	Eddie Gerard	Eddie Gerard
1927	Ottawa Senators	Boston	2-0	Dave Gill	Dave Gill
1928	New York Rangers	Montreal	3-2	Lester Patrick	Lester Patrick
1929	Boston Bruins	New York	2-0	Cy Denneny	Art Ross
1930	Montreal Canadiens	Boston	2-0	Cecil Hart	Cecil Hart
1931	Montreal Canadiens	Chicago	3-2	Cecil Hart	Cecil Hart
1932	Toronto Maple Leafs	New York	3-0	Dick Irvin	Conn Smythe
1933	New York Rangers	Toronto	3-1	Lester Patrick	Lester Patrick
1934	Chicago Black Hawks	Detroit	3-1	Tommy Gorman	Tommy Gorman
1935	Montreal Maroons	Toronto	3-0	Tommy Gorman	Tommy Gorman
1936	Detroit Red Wings	Toronto	4-0	Jack Adams	Jack Adams

1937	Detroit Red Wings	New York	3-2	Jack Adams	Jack Adams
1938	Chicago Black Hawks	Toronto	4-1	Bill Stewart	Bill Stewart
1939	Boston Bruins	Toronto	4-1	Art Ross	Art Ross
1940	New York Rangers	Toronto	4-2	Frank Boucher	Lester Patrick
1941	Boston Bruins	Detroit	4-0	Cooney Weiland	Art Ross
1942	Toronto Maple Leafs	Detroit	4-3	Hap Day	Conn Smythe
1943	Detroit Red Wings	Boston	4-0	Jack Adams	Jack Adams
1944	Montreal Canadiens	Chicago	4-0	Dick Irvin	Tommy Gorman
1945	Toronto Maple Leafs	Detroit	4-3	Hap Day	Conn Smythe
1946	Montreal Canadiens	Boston	4-1	Dick Irvin	Tommy Gorman
1947	Toronto Maple Leafs	Montreal	4-2	Hap Day	Conn Smythe
1948	Toronto Maple Leafs	Detroit	4-0	Hap Day	Conn Smythe
1949	Toronto Maple Leafs	Detroit	4-0	Hap Day	Conn Smythe
1950	Detroit Red Wings	New York	4-3	Tommy Ivan	Jack Adams
1951	Toronto Maple Leafs	Montreal	4-1	Joe Primeau	Conn Smythe
1952	Detroit Red Wings	Montreal	4-0	Tommy Ivan	Jack Adams
1953	Montreal Canadiens	Boston	4-1	Dick Irvin	Frank Selke
1954	Detroit Red Wings	Montreal	4-3	Tommy Ivan	Jack Adams
1955	Detroit Red Wings	Montreal	4-3	Jimmy Skinner	Jack Adams
1956	Montreal Canadiens	Detroit	4-1	Toe Blake	Frank Selke
1957	Montreal Canadiens	Boston	4-1	Toe Blake	Frank Selke
1958	Montreal Canadiens	Boston	4-2	Toe Blake	Frank Selke
1959	Montreal Canadiens	Toronto	4-1	Toe Blake	Frank Selke
1960	Montreal Canadiens	Toronto	4-0	Toe Blake	Frank Selke
1961	Chicago Black Hawks	Detroit	4-2	Rudy Pilous	Tommy Ivan
1962	Toronto Maple Leafs	Chicago	4-2	Punch Imlach	Punch Imlach
1963	Toronto Maple Leafs	Detroit	4-1	Punch Imlach	Punch Imlach
1964	Toronto Maple Leafs	Detroit	4-3	Punch Imlach	Punch Imlach
1965	Montreal Canadiens	Chicago	4-3	Toe Blake	Sam Pollock
1966	Montreal Canadiens	Detroit	4-2	Toe Blake	Sam Pollock
1967	Toronto Maple Leafs	Montreal	4-2	Punch Imlach	Punch Imlach
1968	Montreal Canadiens	St. Louis	4-0	Toe Blake	Sam Pollock
1969	Montreal Canadiens	St. Louis	4-0	Claude Ruel	Sam Pollock
1970	Boston Bruins	St. Louis	4-0	Harry Sinden	Milt Schmidt
1971	Montreal Canadiens	Chicago	4-3	Al MacNeil	Sam Pollock
1972	Boston Bruins	New York	4-2	Tom Johnson	Milt Schmidt
1973	Montreal Canadiens	Chicago	4-2	Scotty Bowman	Sam Pollock
1974	Philadelphia Flyers	Boston	4-2	Fred Shero	Keith Allen
1975	Philadelphia Flyers	Buffalo	4-2	Fred Shero	Keith Allen
1976	Montreal Canadiens	Philadelphia	4-0	Scotty Bowman	Sam Pollock
1977	Montreal Canadiens	Boston	4-0	Scotty Bowman	Sam Pollock
1978	Montreal Canadiens	Boston	4-2	Scotty Bowman	Sam Pollock
1979	Montreal Canadiens	New York	4-1	Scotty Bowman	Irving Grundman
1980	N.Y. Islanders	Philadelphia	4-2	Al Arbour	Bill Torrey
1981	N.Y. Islanders	Minnesota	4-1	Al Arbour	Bill Torrey
1982	N.Y. Islanders	Vancouver	4-0	Al Arbour	Bill Torrey
1983	N.Y. Islanders	Edmonton	4-0	Al Arbour	Bill Torrey
1984	Edmonton Oilers	New York	4-1	Glen Sather	Glen Sather
1985	Edmonton Oilers	Philadelphia	4-1	Glen Sather	Glen Sather
1986	Montreal Canadiens	Calgary	4-1	Jean Perron	Serge Savard
1987	Edmonton Oilers	Philadelphia	4-3	Glen Sather	Glen Sather
1988	Edmonton Oilers	Boston	4-0	Glen Sather	Glen Sather

(1) The series between Montreal Canadiens and Seattle Metropolitans was halted by Spanish influenza epidemic with the series tied at 2 wins each.   (2) Ottawa also met and defeated Edmonton Eskimos, champions of the WCHL.   (3) Because of an agreement between the NHL and the 2 western leagues (WCHL and PCHA), Canadiens had to play the champions of each league.

Top 25 All-Time NHL Goal Scoring Leaders

Source: National Hockey League

(up to the end of the 1987-88 season)

Player	Team(s)	Seasons	Games	Goals	Goals per game
Gordie Howe	Detroit	25	1 687	786	.466
	Hartford	1	80	15	.188
	Total	**26**	**1 767**	**801**	**.453**
Marcel Dionne	Detroit	4	309	139	.450
	Los Angeles	11¾	921	550	.597
	NY Rangers	1¼	81	35	.432
	Total	**17**	**1 311**	**724**	**.552**
Phil Esposito	Chicago	4	235	74	.315
	Boston	8¼	625	459	.734
	NY Rangers	5¾	422	184	.436
	Total	**18**	**1 282**	**717**	**.572**

Bobby Hull	Chicago	15	1 036	604	.583
	Winnipeg	2/3	18	4	.222
	Hartford	1/3	9	2	.222
	Total	**16**	**1 063**	**610**	**.574**
Wayne Gretzky	Edmonton	9	696	583	.838
Mike Bossy	NY Islanders	10	752	573	.762
John Bucyk	Detroit	2	104	11	.106
	Boston	21	1 436	545	.380
	Total	**23**	**1 540**	**556**	**.361**
Maurice Richard	Montreal	18	978	544	.556
Stan Mikita	Chicago	22	1 394	541	.388
Frank Mahovlich	Toronto	11 2/3	720	296	.411
	Detroit	2 2/3	198	108	.545
	Montreal	3 2/3	263	129	.490
	Total	**18**	**1 181**	**533**	**.451**
Guy Lafleur	Montreal	14	961	518	.539
Gilbert Perreault	Buffalo	17	1 191	512	.430
Jean Béliveau	Montreal	18	1 125	507	.451
Jean Ratelle	NY Rangers, Bost.	21	1 281	491	.383
Norm Ullman	Detroit, Toronto	20	1 410	490	.348
Lanny McDonald	Tor., Col., Cgy.	15	1 060	489	.461
Darryl Sittler	Tor., Phil., Det.	15	1 096	484	.442
Bryan Trottier	NY Islanders	13	991	470	.474
Alex Delvecchio	Detroit	23	1 549	456	.294
Rick Middleton	NY Rangers, Bost.	14	1 005	448	.446
Yvan Cournoyer	Montreal	16	968	428	.442
Steve Shutt	Montreal, Los Angeles	13	930	424	.456
Bill Barber	Philadelphia	12	903	420	.465
Michel Goulet	Quebec	9	687	414	.603
Garry Unger	Tor., Det., St. L., Atl., L.A., Edm.	16	1 105	413	.374

Top 25 All-Time NHL Point-Scoring Leaders

Source: National Hockey League

(up to the end of the 1987-88 season)

Player	Team(s)	Seasons	Games	Goals	Assists	Points	Points per game
Gordie Howe	Detroit	25	1 687	786	1 023	1 809	1.072
	Hartford	1	80	15	26	41	.513
	Total	**26**	**1 767**	**801**	**1 049**	**1 850**	**1.047**
Marcel Dionne	Detroit	4	309	139	227	366	1.184
	Los Angeles	11 3/4	921	550	757	1 307	1.419
	NY Rangers	1 1/4	81	35	40	75	.926
	Total	**17**	**1 311**	**724**	**1 024**	**1 748**	**1.333**
Wayne Gretzky	Edmonton	9	696	583	1 086	1 669	2.398
Phil Esposito	Chicago	4	235	74	100	174	.740
	Boston	8 1/4	625	459	553	1 012	1.619
	NY Rangers	5 3/4	422	184	220	404	.957
	Total	**18**	**1 282**	**717**	**873**	**1 590**	**1.240**
Stan Mikita	Chicago	22	1 394	541	926	1 467	1.052
John Bucyk	Detroit	2	104	11	19	30	.288
	Boston	21	1 436	545	794	1 339	.932
	Total	**23**	**1 540**	**556**	**813**	**1 369**	**.889**
Gilbert Perreault	Buffalo	17	1 191	512	814	1 326	1.113
Bryan Trottier	NY Islanders	13	991	470	814	1 284	1.296
Alex Delvecchio	Detroit	24	1 549	456	825	1 281	.827
Jean Ratelle	NY Rangers	15 1/4	862	336	481	817	.948
	Boston	5 3/4	419	155	295	450	1.074
	Total	**21**	**1 281**	**491**	**776**	**1 267**	**.989**
Guy Lafleur	Montreal	14	961	518	728	1 246	1.296
Norm Ullman	Det., Tor.	20	1 410	490	739	1 229	.872
Jean Béliveau	Montreal	20	1 125	507	712	1 219	1.084
Bobby Clarke	Philadelphia	15	1 144	358	852	1 210	.105
Bobby Hull	Chi., Wpg., Hart.	16	1 063	610	560	1 710	1.100
Mike Bossy	NY Islanders	10	752	573	553	1 126	1.497
Darryl Sittler	Tor., Phil.	15	1 096	484	637	1 121	1.023
Frank Mahovlich	Tor., Det., Mont.	18	1 181	533	570	1 103	.934
Denis Potvin	NY Islanders	15	1 060	310	742	1 052	.992
Henri Richard	Montreal	20	1 256	358	688	1 046	.833
Rod Gilbert	NY Rangers	18	1 065	406	615	1 021	.959
Bernie Federko	St. Louis	12	861	330	676	1 006	1.168
Rick Middleton	N.Y. Rang., Bost.	14	1 005	448	540	988	.983
Lanny McDonald	Tor., Col., Cgy.	15	1 060	489	499	988	.932
Dave Keon	Tor., Hart.	18	1 296	396	590	986	.761

Regular Season NHL Scoring Champions, 1917-1988

Source: National Hockey League

Season	Player and Team	Games Played	Goals	Assists	Points
1987-88	Mario Lemieux, Pittsburgh	77	70	98	168
1986-87	Wayne Gretzky, Edmonton	79	62	121	183
1985-86	Wayne Gretzky, Edmonton	80	52	163	215
1984-85	Wayne Gretzky, Edmonton	80	73	135	208
1983-84	Wayne Gretzky, Edmonton	74	87	118	205
1982-83	Wayne Gretzky, Edmonton	80	71	125	196
1981-82	Wayne Gretzky, Edmonton	80	92	120	212
1980-81	Wayne Gretzky, Edmonton	80	55	109	164
1979-80	Marcel Dionne, Los Angeles	80	53	84	137
1978-79	Bryan Trottier, NY Islanders	76	47	87	134
1977-78	Guy Lafleur, Montreal	78	60	72	132
1976-77	Guy Lafleur, Montreal	80	56	80	136
1975-76	Guy Lafleur, Montreal	80	56	69	125
1974-75	Bobby Orr, Boston	80	46	89	135
1973-74	Phil Esposito, Boston	78	68	77	145
1972-73	Phil Esposito, Boston	78	55	75	130
1971-72	Phil Esposito, Boston	76	66	67	133
1970-71	Phil Esposito, Boston	78	76	76	152
1969-70	Bobby Orr, Boston	76	33	87	120
1968-69	Phil Esposito, Boston	74	49	77	126
1967-68	Stan Mikita, Chicago	72	40	47	87
1966-67	Stan Mikita, Chicago	70	35	62	97
1965-66	Bobby Hull, Chicago	65	54	43	97
1964-65	Stan Mikita, Chicago	70	28	59	87
1963-64	Stan Mikita, Chicago	70	39	50	89
1962-63	Gordie Howe, Detroit	70	38	48	86
1961-62	Bobby Hull, Chicago	70	50	34	84
1960-61	Bernie Geoffrion, Montreal	64	50	45	95
1959-60	Bobby Hull, Chicago	70	39	42	81
1958-59	Dickie Moore, Montreal	70	41	55	96
1957-58	Dickie Moore, Montreal	70	36	48	84
1956-57	Gordie Howe, Detroit	70	44	45	89
1955-56	Jean Béliveau, Montreal	70	47	41	88
1954-55	Bernie Geoffrion, Montreal	70	38	37	75
1953-54	Gordie Howe, Detroit	70	33	48	81
1952-53	Gordie Howe, Detroit	70	49	46	95
1951-52	Gordie Howe, Detroit	70	47	39	86
1950-51	Gordie Howe, Detroit	70	43	43	86
1949-50	Ted Lindsay, Detroit	69	23	55	78
1948-49	Roy Conacher, Chicago	60	26	42	68
1947-48	Elmer Lach, Montreal	60	30	31	61
1946-47	Max Bentley, Chicago	60	29	43	72
1945-46	Max Bentley, Chicago	47	31	30	61
1944-45	Elmer Lach, Montreal	50	26	54	80
1943-44	Herbie Cain, Boston	48	36	46	82
1942-43	Doug Bentley, Chicago	50	33	40	73
1941-42	Bryan Hextall, NY Rangers	48	24	32	56
1940-41	Bill Cowley, Boston	46	17	45	62
1939-40	Milt Schmidt, Boston	48	22	30	52
1938-39	Toe Blake, Montreal	48	24	23	47
1937-38	Gordie Drillon, Toronto	48	26	26	52
1936-37	Dave Schriner, NY Americans	48	21	25	46
1935-36	Dave Schriner, NY Americans	48	19	26	45
1934-35	Charlie Conacher, Toronto	48	36	21	57
1933-34	Charlie Conacher, Toronto	42	32	20	52
1932-33	Bill Cook, NY Rangers	48	28	22	50
1931-32	Harvey Jackson, Toronto	48	28	25	53
1930-31	Howie Morenz, Montreal	39	28	23	51
1929-30	Cooney Weiland, Boston	44	43	30	73
1928-29	Ace Bailey, Toronto	44	22	10	32
1927-28	Howie Morenz, Montreal	43	33	18	51
1926-27	Bill Cook, NY Rangers	44	33	4	37
1925-26	Nels Stewart, Mtl. Maroons	36	34	8	42
1924-25	Babe Dye, Toronto	29	38	6	44
1923-24	Cy Denneny, Ottawa	21	22	1	23
1922-23	Babe Dye, Toronto	22	26	11	37
1921-22	Punch Broadbent, Ottawa	24	32	14	46
1920-21	Newsy Lalonde, Montreal	24	33	8	41
1919-20	Joe Malone, Quebec	24	39	6	45
1918-19	Newsy Lalonde, Montreal	17	23	9	32
1917-18	Joe Malone, Montreal	20	44	*	44

* Number of assists not recorded

Stanley Cup Playoff Scoring Leaders, 1940–1988

Year	Player and Team	Games played	Goals	Assists	Points
1940	Phil Watson, NY Rangers	12	3	6	9
	Neil Colville, NY Rangers	12	2	7	9
1941	Milt Schmidt, Boston	11	5	6	11
1942	Don Grosso, Detroit	12	8	6	14
1943	Carl Liscombe, Detroit	10	6	8	14
1944	Toe Blake, Montreal	9	7	11	18
1945	Joe Carveth, Detroit	14	5	6	11
1946	Elmer Lach, Montreal	9	5	12	17
1947	Maurice Richard, Montreal	10	6	5	11
1948	Ted Kennedy, Toronto	9	8	6	14
1949	Gordie Howe, Detroit	11	8	3	11
1950	Pentti Lund, NY Rangers	12	6	5	11
1951	Maurice Richard, Montreal	11	9	4	13
	Max Bentley, Toronto	11	2	11	13
1952	Ted Lindsay, Detroit	8	5	2	7
	Floyd Curry, Montreal	11	4	3	7
	Metro Prystai, Detroit	8	2	5	7
	Gordie Howe, Detroit	8	2	5	7
1953	Ed Sanford, Boston	11	8	3	11
1954	Dickie Moore, Montreal	11	5	8	13
1955	Gordie Howe, Detroit	11	9	11	20
1956	Jean Beliveau, Montreal	10	12	7	19
1957	Bernie Geoffrion, Montreal	11	11	7	18
1958	Fleming Mackell, Boston	12	5	14	19
1959	Dickie Moore, Montreal	11	5	12	17
1960	Henri Richard, Montreal	8	3	9	12
	Bernie Geoffrion, Montreal	8	2	10	12
1961	Gordie Howe, Detroit	11	4	11	15
	Pierre Pilote, Chicago	12	3	12	15
1962	Stan Mikita, Chicago	12	6	15	21
1963	Gordie Howe, Detroit	11	7	9	16
	Norm Ullman, Detroit	11	4	12	16
1964	Gordie Howe, Detroit	14	9	10	19
1965	Bobby Hull, Chicago	14	10	7	17
1966	Norm Ullman, Detroit	12	6	9	15
1967	Jim Pappin, Toronto	12	7	8	15
1968	Bill Goldsworthy, Minnesota	14	8	7	15
1969	Phil Esposito, Boston	10	8	10	18
1970	Phil Esposito, Boston	14	13	14	27
1971	Frank Mahovlich, Montreal	20	14	13	27
1972	Phil Esposito, Boston	15	9	15	24
	Bobby Orr, Boston	15	5	19	24
1973	Yvan Cournoyer, Montreal	17	15	10	25
1974	Rick MacLeish, Philadelphia	17	13	9	22
1975	Rick MacLeish, Philadelphia	17	11	9	20
1976	Reggie Leach, Philadelphia	16	19	5	24
1977	Guy Lafleur, Montreal	14	9	17	26
1978	Guy Lafleur, Montreal	15	10	11	21
	Larry Robinson, Montreal	15	4	17	21
1979	Jacques Lemaire, Montreal	16	11	12	23
	Guy Lafleur, Montreal	16	10	13	23
1980	Bryan Trottier, NY Islanders	21	12	17	29
1981	Mike Bossy, NY Islanders	18	17	18	35
1982	Bryan Trottier, NY Islanders	19	6	23	29
1983	Wayne Gretzky, Edmonton	16	12	26	38
1984	Wayne Gretzky, Edmonton	19	13	22	35
1985	Wayne Gretzky, Edmonton	18	17	30	47
1986	Doug Gilmour, St. Louis	19	9	12	21
	Bernie Federko, St. Louis	19	7	14	21
1987	Wayne Gretzky, Edmonton	21	5	29	34
1988	Wayne Gretzky, Edmonton	19	12	31	43

NHL Individual Records

(up to the end of the 1987-88 season)

Most seasons: 26—Gordie Howe, Detroit Red Wings, 1946-47 through 1970-71; Hartford Whalers, 1979-80.
Most games: 1 767—Gordie Howe, Detroit Red Wings, 1946-47 through 1970-71; Hartford Whalers, 1979-80.
Most goals: 801—Gordie Howe, Detroit Red Wings, Hartford Whalers, in 26 seasons and 1 767 games.
Most assists: 1 086—Wayne Gretzky, Edmonton Oilers in 9 seasons, 696 games.
Most points: 1 850—Gordie Howe, Detroit Red Wings, Hartford Whalers, in 26 seasons, 1 767 games (801 goals, 1 049 assists).

Most penalty minutes: ..... 3 966—**Dave Williams**, Toronto, Vancouver, Detroit, Los Angeles, Hartford in 13 seasons, 962 games.
Most consecutive games: .... 962—**Doug Jarvis**, Montreal, Washington, Hartford from Oct. 8, 1975 through Apr. 5, 1987.
Most games appeared in by a goaltender, career: ....971—**Terry Sawchuk**, Detroit, Boston, Toronto, Los Angeles, New York Rangers (1949-70).
Most consecutive complete games by a goaltender: .... 502—**Glenn Hall**, Detroit, Chicago. Played 502 games from beginning of 1955-56 season through first 12 games of 1962-63. In his 503rd straight game, Nov. 7, 1962, at Chicago, Hall was removed from the game against Boston with a back injury in the first period.
Most shutouts by a goaltender, career: .... 103—**Terry Sawchuk**, Detroit, Boston, Toronto, Los Angeles, New York Rangers in 20 seasons.
Most 50-or-more goal seasons: .... 9—**Mike Bossy**, New York Islanders, in 9 seasons.
Most goals, one season: .... 92—**Wayne Gretzky**, Edmonton Oilers, 1981-82. (80 games)
Most assists, one season: .... 163—**Wayne Gretzky**, Edmonton Oilers, 1985-86. (80 games)
Most goals, one season, by a defenceman: .... 48—**Paul Coffey**, Edmonton Oilers, 1985-86. (79 games)
Most goals, one season, by a centre: .... 92—**Wayne Gretzky**, Edmonton Oilers, 1981-82. (80 games)
Most goals, one season, by a right winger: .... 71—**Jari Kurri**, Edmonton Oilers, 1984-85. (80 games)
Most goals, one season, by a left winger: .... 60—**Steve Shutt**, Montreal Canadiens, 1976-77. (80 games)
Most goals, one season, by a rookie: .... 53—**Mike Bossy**, New York Islanders, 1977-78. (80 games)
Most points, one season, by a defenceman: .... 139—**Bobby Orr**, Boston Bruins, 1970-71. (78 games)
Most points, one season, by a centre: .... 215—**Wayne Gretzky**, Edmonton Oilers, 1985-86. (80 games)
Most points, one season, by a right winger: ...... 147—**Mike Bossy**, New York Islanders, 1981-82. (80 games)
Most points, one season, by a left winger: ...... 121—**Michel Goulet**, Quebec Nordiques, 1983-84. (80 games)
Most points, one season, by a rookie: .... 109—**Peter Stastny**, Quebec Nordiques, 1980-81. (80 games)
Most power-play goals, one season: .... 34—**Tim Kerr**, Philadelphia Flyers, 1985-86. (76 games)
Most penalty minutes, one season: .... 472—**Dave Schultz**, Philadelphia Flyers, 1974-75. (80 games)
Most shutouts, one season: .... 22—**George Hainsworth**, Montreal Canadiens, 1928-29. (44 games)

NHL Individual Award Winners, 1950–1988

	Hart Trophy (most valuable player)[1]	Calder Trophy (best rookie)[1]	Norris Trophy (best defenceman)[1]
1988	Mario Lemieux, Pittsburgh	Joe Nieuwendyk, Calgary	Raymond Bourque, Boston
1987	Wayne Gretzky, Edmonton	Luc Robitaille, Los Angeles	Raymond Bourque, Boston
1986	Wayne Gretzky, Edmonton	Gary Suter, Calgary	Paul Coffey, Edmonton
1985	Wayne Gretzky, Edmonton	Mario Lemieux, Pittsburgh	Paul Coffey, Edmonton
1984	Wayne Gretzky, Edmonton	Tom Barrasso, Buffalo	Rod Langway, Washington
1983	Wayne Gretzky, Edmonton	Steve Larmer, Chicago	Rod Langway, Washington
1982	Wayne Gretzky, Edmonton	Dale Hawerchuk, Winnipeg	Doug Wilson, Chicago
1981	Wayne Gretzky, Edmonton	Peter Stastny, Quebec	Randy Carlyle, Pittsburgh
1980	Wayne Gretzky, Edmonton	Raymond Bourque, Boston	Larry Robinson, Montreal
1979	Bryan Trottier, N.Y. Islanders	Bobby Smith, Minnesota	Denis Potvin, N.Y. Islanders
1978	Guy Lafleur, Montreal	Mike Bossy, N.Y. Islanders	Denis Potvin, N.Y. Islanders
1977	Guy Lafleur, Montreal	Willi Plett, Atlanta	Larry Robinson, Montreal
1976	Bobby Clarke, Philadelphia	Bryan Trottier, N.Y. Islanders	Denis Potvin, N.Y. Islanders
1975	Bobby Clarke, Philadelphia	Eric Vail, Atlanta	Bobby Orr, Boston
1974	Phil Esposito, Boston	Denis Potvin, N.Y. Islanders	Bobby Orr, Boston
1973	Bobby Clarke, Philadelphia	Steve Vickers, N.Y. Rangers	Bobby Orr, Boston
1972	Bobby Orr, Boston	Ken Dryden, Montreal	Bobby Orr, Boston
1971	Bobby Orr, Boston	Gilbert Perreault, Buffalo	Bobby Orr, Boston
1970	Bobby Orr, Boston	Tony Esposito, Chicago	Bobby Orr, Boston
1969	Phil Esposito, Boston	Danny Grant, Minnesota	Bobby Orr, Boston
1968	Stan Mikita, Chicago	Derek Sanderson, Boston	Bobby Orr, Boston
1967	Stan Mikita, Chicago	Bobby Orr, Boston	Harry Howell, N.Y. Rangers
1966	Bobby Hull, Chicago	Brit Selby, Toronto	Jacques Laperrière, Montreal
1965	Bobby Hull, Chicago	Roger Crozier, Detroit	Pierre Pilote, Chicago
1964	Jean Béliveau, Montreal	Jacques Laperrière, Montreal	Pierre Pilote, Chicago
1963	Gordie Howe, Detroit	Kent Douglas, Toronto	Pierre Pilote, Chicago
1962	Jacques Plante, Montreal	Bobby Rousseau, Montreal	Doug Harvey, N.Y. Rangers
1961	Bernie Geoffrion, Montreal	Dave Keon, Toronto	Doug Harvey, Montreal
1960	Gordie Howe, Detroit	Bill Hay, Chicago	Doug Harvey, Montreal
1959	Andy Bathgate, N.Y. Rangers	Ralph Backstrom, Montreal	Tom Johnson, Montreal
1958	Gordie Howe, Detroit	Frank Mahovlich, Toronto	Doug Harvey, Montreal
1957	Gordie Howe, Detroit	Larry Regan, Boston	Doug Harvey, Montreal
1956	Jean Béliveau, Montreal	Glenn Hall, Detroit	Doug Harvey, Montreal
1955	Ted Kennedy, Toronto	Ed Litzenberger, Chicago	Doug Harvey, Monreal
1954	Al Rollins, Chicago	Camille Henry, N.Y. Rangers	Red Kelly, Detroit
1953	Gordie Howe, Detroit	Lorne Worsley, N.Y. Rangers	—
1952	Gordie Howe, Detroit	Bernie Geoffrion, Montreal	—
1951	Milt Schmidt, Boston	Terry Sawchuk, Detroit	—
1950	Charlie Rayner, N.Y. Rangers	Jack Gelineau, Boston	—

	Vezina Trophy (best goalkeeper)[2]	Lady Byng Trophy (most sportsmanlike)[1]	Conn Smythe Trophy (most valuable in playoffs)[3]
1988	.... Grant Fuhr, Edmonton	Mats Naslund, Montreal	Wayne Gretzky, Edmonton
1987	.... Ron Hextall, Philadelphia	Joe Mullen, Calgary	Ron Hextall, Philadelphia
1986	.... John Vanbiesbrouck, N.Y. Rangers	Mike Bossy, N.Y. Islanders	Patrick Roy, Montreal
1985	.... Pelle Lindbergh, Philadelphia	Jari Kurri, Edmonton	Wayne Gretzky, Edmonton
1984	.... Tom Barrasso, Buffalo	Mike Bossy, N.Y. Islanders	Mark Messier, Edmonton
1983	.... Pete Peeters, Boston	Mike Bossy, N.Y. Islanders	Bill Smith, N.Y. Islanders
1982	.... Bill Smith, N.Y. Islanders	Rick Middleton, Boston	Mike Bossy, N.Y. Islanders
1981	.... Richard Sevigny, Montreal Denis Herron, Montreal Michel Larocque, Montreal	Rick Kehoe, Pittsburgh	Butch Goring, N.Y. Islanders
1980	.... Bob Suavé, Buffalo Don Edwards, Buffalo	Wayne Gretzky, Edmonton	Bryan Trottier, N.Y. Islanders
1979	.... Ken Dryden, Montreal Michel Larocque, Montreal	Bob MacMillan, Atlanta	Bob Gainey, Montreal
1978	.... Ken Dryden, Montreal Michel Larocque, Montreal	Butch Goring, Los Angeles	Larry Robinson, Montreal
1977	.... Ken Dryden, Montreal Michel Larocque, Montreal	Marcel Dionne, Los Angeles	Guy Lafleur, Montreal
1976	.... Ken Dryden, Montreal	Jean Ratelle, N.Y./Bost.	Reggie Leach, Philadelphia
1975	.... Bernie Parent, Philadelphia	Marcel Dionne, Detroit	Bernie Parent, Philadelphia
1974	.... Bernie Parent, Philadelphia Tony Esposito, Chicago	John Bucyk, Boston	Bernie Parent, Philadelphia
1973	.... Ken Dryden, Montreal	Gilbert Perreault, Buffalo	Yvan Cournoyer, Montreal
1972	.... Tony Esposito, Chicago Gary Smith, Chicago	Jean Ratelle, N.Y. Rangers	Bobby Orr, Boston
1971	... Ed Giacomin, N.Y. Rangers Gilles Villemure, N.Y. Rangers	John Bucyk, Boston	Ken Dryden, Montreal
1970	.... Tony Esposito, Chicago	Phil Goyette, St. Louis	Bobby Orr, Boston
1969	.... Jacques Plante, St. Louis Glenn Hall, St. Louis	Alex Delvecchio, Detroit	Serge Savard, Montreal
1968	.... Lorne Worsley, Montreal Rogie Vachon, Montreal	Stan Mikita, Chicago	Glenn Hall, St. Louis
1967	.... Glenn Hall, Chicago Denis Dejordy, Chicago	Stan Mikita, Chicago	Dave Keon, Toronto
1966	.... Lorne Worsley, Montreal Charlie Hodge, Montreal	Alex Delvecchio, Detroit	Roger Crozier, Detroit
1965	.... Terry Sawchuk, Toronto Johnny Bower, Toronto	Bobby Hull, Chicago	Jean Béliveau, Montreal

1964	.... Charlie Hodge, Montreal	Ken Wharram, Chicago	**Frank J. Selke Trophy** (best defensive forward)[1]
1963	.... Glenn Hall, Chicago	Dave Keon, Toronto	
1962	.... Jacques Plante, Montreal	Dave Keon, Toronto	1988 Guy Carbonneau, Montreal
1961	.... Johnny Bower, Toronto	Red Kelly, Toronto	1987 Dave Poulin, Philadelphia
1960	.... Jacques Plante, Montreal	Don McKenney, Boston	1986 Troy Murray, Chicago
1959	.... Jacques Plante, Montreal	Alex Delvecchio, Detroit	1985 Craig Ramsay, Buffalo
1958	.... Jacques Plante, Montreal	Camille Henry, N.Y. Rangers	1984 Doug Jarvis, Washington
1957	.... Jacques Plante, Montreal	Andy Hebenton, N.Y. Rangers	1983 Bobby Clarke, Philadelphia
1956	.... Jacques Plante, Montreal	Earl Reibel, Detroit	1982 Steve Kasper, Boston
1955	.... Terry Sawchuk, Detroit	Sid Smith, Toronto	1981 Bob Gainey, Montreal
1954	.... Harry Lumley, Toronto	Red Kelly, Detroit	1980 Bob Gainey, Montreal
1953	.... Terry Sawchuk, Detroit	Red Kelly, Detroit	1979 Bob Gainey, Montreal
1952	.... Terry Sawchuk, Detroit	Sid Smith, Toronto	1978 Bob Gainey, Montreal
1951	.... Al Rollins, Toronto	Red Kelly, Detroit	
1950	.... Bill Durnan, Montreal	Edgar Laprade, N.Y. Rangers	

(1) As selected at the end of the regular season by members of the Professional Hockey Writers' Association in the 21 NHL cities. (2) Since the 1981-82 season, Vezina Trophy winners have been selected by general managers of the 21 NHL clubs. In earlier seasons the trophy was awarded to the goalkeeper(s) of the team allowing the fewest goals during the regular season. (3) As selected by members of the Professional Hockey Writers' Association at the end of the last game of the Stanley Cup finals.

NHL All-Star Teams[1]

First Team	Position	Second Team
	1988	
Grant Fuhr, Edmonton	Goal	Patrick Roy, Montreal
Raymond Bourque, Boston	Defence	Gary Suter, Calgary
Scott Stevens, Washington	Defence	Brad McCrimmon, Calgary
Mario Lemieux, Pittsburgh	Centre	Wayne Gretzky, Edmonton
Hakan Loob, Calgary	Right Wing	Cam Neely, Boston
Luc Robitaille, Los Angeles	Left Wing	Michel Goulet, Quebec

First Team	Position	Second Team
	1987	
Ron Hextall, Philadelphia	Goal	Mike Liut, Hartford
Raymond Bourque, Boston	Defence	Larry Murphy, Washington
Mark Howe, Philadelphia	Defence	Al MacInnis, Calgary
Wayne Gretzky, Edmonton	Centre	Mario Lemieux, Pittsburgh
Jari Kurri, Edmonton	Right Wing	Tim Kerr, Philadelphia
Michel Goulet, Quebec	Left Wing	Luc Robitaille, Los Angeles
	1986	
John Vanbiesbrouck, N.Y. Rangers	Goal	Bob Froese, Philidelphia
Paul Coffey, Edmonton	Defence	Larry Robinson, Montreal
Mark Howe, Philadelphia	Defence	Raymond Bourque, Boston
Wayne Gretzky, Edmonton	Centre	Mario Lemieux, Pittsburgh
Mike Bossy, N.Y. Islanders	Right Wing	Jari Kurri, Edmonton
Michel Goulet, Quebec	Left Wing	Mats Naslund, Montreal
	1985	
Pelle Lindbergh, Philadelphia	Goal	Tom Barrasso, Buffalo
Paul Coffey, Edmonton	Defence	Rod Langway, Washington
Raymond Bourque, Boston	Defence	Doug Wilson, Chicago
Wayne Gretzky, Edmonton	Centre	Dale Hawerchuk, Winnipeg
Jari Kurri, Edmonton	Right Wing	Mike Bossy, N.Y. Islanders
John Ogrodnick, Detroit	Left Wing	John Tonelli, N.Y. Islanders
	1984	
Tom Barrasso, Buffalo	Goal	Pat Riggin, Washington
Rod Langway, Washington	Defence	Paul Coffey, Edmonton
Raymond Bourque, Boston	Defence	Denis Potvin, N.Y. Islanders
Wayne Gretzky, Edmonton	Centre	Bryan Trottier, N.Y. Islanders
Mike Bossy, N.Y. Islanders	Right Wing	Jari Kurri, Edmonton
Michel Goulet, Quebec	Left Wing	Mark Messier, Edmonton

(1) As selected by members of the Professional Hockey Writers' Association at the end of the season.

Top Ten NHL Draft Selections, 1983–1988

(Teams selected by in parentheses)

Selection	1988	1987	1986
1	Mike Modano (Minnesota)	Pierre Turgeon (Buffalo)	Joe Murphy (Detroit)
2	Trevor Linden (Vancouver)	Brendan Shanahan (New Jersey)	Jimmy Carson (Los Angeles)
3	Curtis Leschyshyn (Quebec)	Glen Wesley (Boston)	Neil Brady (New Jersey)
4	Darrin Shannon (Pittsburgh)	Wayne McBean (Los Angeles)	Zarley Zalapski (Pittsburgh)
5	Daniel Doré (Quebec)	Chris Joseph (Pittsburgh)	Shawn Anderson (Buffalo)
6	Scott Pearson (Toronto)	Dave Archibald (Minnesota)	Vincent Damphousse (Toronto)
7	Martin Gelinas (Los Angeles)	Luke Richardson (Toronto)	Dan Woodley (Vancouver)
8	Jeremy Roenick (Chicago)	Jimmy Waite (Chicago)	Pat Elynuik (Winnipeg)
9	Rod Brind'Amour (St. Louis)	Bryan Fogarty (Quebec)	Brian Leetch (N.Y. Rangers)
10	Teemu Selanne (Winnipeg)	Jayson More (N.Y. Rangers)	Jocelyn Lemieux (St. Louis)

Selection	1985	1984	1983
1	Wendel Clark (Toronto)	Mario Lemieux (Pittsburgh)	Brian Lawton (Minnesota)
2	Craig Simpson (Pittsburgh)	Kirk Muller (New Jersey)	Sylvain Turgeon (Hartford)
3	Craig Wolanin (New Jersey)	Ed Olczyk (Chicago)	Pat Lafontaine (N.Y. Islanders)
4	Jim Sandlak (Vancouver)	Al Iafrate (Toronto)	Steve Yzerman (Detroit)
5	Dana Murzyn (Hartford)	Petr Svoboda (Montreal)	Tom Barrasso (Buffalo)
6	Brad Dalgarno (N.Y. Islanders)	Craig Redmond (Los Angeles)	John MacLean (New Jersey)
7	Ulf Dahlen (N.Y. Rangers)	Shawn Burr (Detroit)	Russ Courtnall (Toronto)
8	Brent Fedyk (Detroit)	Shayne Corson (Montreal)	Andrew McBain (Winnipeg)
9	Craig Duncanson (Los Angeles)	Dodge Bodger (Pittsburgh)	Cam Neely (Vancouver)
10	Dan Gratton (Los Angeles)	J.J. Daigneault (Vancouver)	Normand Lacombe (Buffalo)

Year-by-Year Record of Canadian Teams in the NHL

Source: National Hockey League

Quebec Nordiques

Season	GP	W	L	T	GF	GA	Pts.	Finished	Playoff Result
1979-80	80	25	44	11	248	313	61	5th, Adams Div.	Out of playoffs
1980-81	80	30	32	18	314	318	78	4th, Adams Div.	Lost prelim. round
1981-82	80	33	31	16	356	345	82	4th, Adams Div.	Lost conf. champ.
1982-83	80	34	34	12	343	336	80	4th, Adams Div.	Lost div. semi-final
1983-84	80	42	28	10	360	278	94	3d, Adams Div.	Lost div. final
1984-85	80	41	30	9	323	275	91	2d, Adams Div.	Lost conf. final
1985-86	80	43	31	6	330	289	92	1st, Adams Div.	Lost div. semi-final
1986-87	80	31	39	10	267	276	72	4th, Adams Div.	Lost div. final
1987-88	80	32	43	5	271	306	69	5th, Adams Div.	Out of playoffs

Montreal Canadiens

Season	GP	W	L	T	GF	GA	Pts.	Finished[1]	Playoff Result
1950-51	70	25	30	15	173	184	65	third	Lost final
1951-52	70	34	26	10	195	164	78	second	Lost final
1952-53	70	28	23	19	155	148	75	second	Won Stanley Cup
1953-54	70	35	24	11	195	141	81	second	Lost final
1954-55	70	41	18	11	228	157	93	second	Lost final
1955-56	70	45	15	10	222	131	100	first	Won Stanley Cup
1956-57	70	35	23	12	210	155	82	second	Won Stanley Cup
1957-58	70	43	17	10	250	158	96	first	Won Stanley Cup
1958-59	70	39	18	13	258	158	91	first	Won Stanley Cup
1959-60	70	40	18	12	255	178	92	first	Won Stanley Cup
1960-61	70	41	19	10	254	188	92	first	Lost semi-final
1961-62	70	42	14	14	259	166	98	first	Lost semi-final
1962-63	70	28	19	23	225	183	79	third	Lost semi-final
1963-64	70	36	21	13	209	167	85	first	Lost semi-final
1964-65	70	36	23	11	211	185	83	second	Won Stanley Cup
1965-66	70	41	21	8	239	173	90	first	Won Stanley Cup
1966-67	70	32	25	13	202	188	77	second	Lost final
1967-68	74	42	22	10	236	167	94	1st, East Div.	Won Stanley Cup
1968-69	76	46	19	11	271	202	103	1st, East Div.	Won Stanley Cup
1969-70	76	38	22	16	244	201	92	5th, East Div.	Out of playoffs
1970-71	78	42	23	13	291	216	97	3d, East Div.	Won Stanley Cup
1971-72	78	46	16	16	307	205	108	3d, East Div.	Lost quarter-final
1972-73	78	52	10	16	329	184	120	1st, East Div.	Won Stanley Cup
1973-74	78	45	24	9	293	240	99	2d, East Div.	Lost quarter-final
1974-75	80	47	14	19	374	225	113	1st, Norris Div.	Lost semi-final
1975-76	80	58	11	11	337	174	127	1st, Norris Div.	Won Stanley Cup
1976-77	80	60	8	12	387	171	132	1st, Norris Div.	Won Stanley Cup
1977-78	80	59	10	11	359	183	129	1st, Norris Div.	Won Stanley Cup
1978-79	80	52	17	11	337	204	115	1st, Norris Div.	Won Stanley Cup
1979-80	80	47	20	13	328	240	107	1st, Norris Div.	Lost quarter-final
1980-81	80	45	22	13	332	232	103	1st, Norris Div.	Lost prelim. round
1981-82	80	46	17	17	360	223	109	1st, Adams Div.	Lost div. semi-final
1982-83	80	42	24	14	350	286	98	2d, Adams Div.	Lost div. semi-final
1983-84	80	35	40	5	286	295	75	4th, Adams Div.	Lost conf. champ.
1984-85	80	41	27	12	309	262	94	1st, Adams Div.	Lost div. final
1985-86	80	40	33	6	330	280	87	2d, Adams Div.	Won Stanley Cup
1986-87	80	41	29	10	277	241	92	2d, Adams Div.	Lost conf. champ.
1987-88	80	45	22	13	298	238	103	1st, Adams Div.	Lost div. final

(1) Prior to 1967-68, the NHL was a 6-team league.

Toronto Maple Leafs

Season	GP	W	L	T	GF	GA	Pts.	Finished[1]	Playoff Result
1950-51	70	41	16	13	212	138	95	second	Won Stanley Cup
1951-52	70	29	25	16	168	157	74	third	Lost Semi-final
1952-53	70	27	30	13	156	167	67	fifth	Out of playoffs
1953-54	70	32	24	14	152	131	78	third	Lost semi-final
1954-55	70	24	24	22	147	135	70	third	Lost semi-final
1955-56	70	24	33	13	153	181	61	fourth	Lost semi-final
1956-57	70	21	34	15	174	192	57	fifth	Out of playoffs
1957-58	70	21	38	11	192	226	53	sixth	Out of playoffs
1958-59	70	27	32	11	189	201	65	fourth	Lost final
1959-60	70	35	26	9	199	195	79	second	Lost final
1960-61	70	39	19	12	234	176	90	second	Lost semi-final

Season	GP	W	L	T	GF	GA	Pts.	Finished[1]	Playoff Result
1961-62	70	37	22	11	232	180	85	second	Won Stanley Cup
1962-63	70	35	23	12	221	180	82	first	Won Stanley Cup
1963-64	70	33	25	12	192	172	78	third	Won Stanley Cup
1964-65	70	30	26	14	204	173	74	fourth	Lost semi-final
1965-66	70	34	25	11	208	187	79	third	Lost semi-final
1966-67	70	32	27	11	204	211	75	third	Won Stanley Cup
1967-68	74	33	31	10	209	176	76	5th, East Div.	Out of playoffs
1968-69	76	35	26	15	234	217	85	4th, East Div.	Lost quarter-final
1969-70	76	29	34	13	222	242	71	6th, East Div.	Out of playoffs
1970-71	78	37	33	8	248	211	82	4th, East Div.	Lost quarter-final
1971-72	78	33	31	14	209	208	80	4th, East Div.	Lost quarter-final
1972-73	78	27	41	10	247	279	64	6th, East Div.	Out of playoffs
1973-74	78	35	27	16	274	230	86	4th, East Div.	Lost quarter-final
1974-75	80	31	33	16	280	309	78	3d, Adams Div.	Lost quarter-final
1975-76	80	34	31	15	294	276	83	3d, Adams Div.	Lost quarter-final
1976-77	80	33	32	15	301	285	81	3d, Adams Div.	Lost quarter-final
1977-78	80	41	29	10	271	237	92	3d, Adams Div.	Lost semi-final
1978-79	80	34	33	13	267	252	81	3d, Adams Div.	Lost quarter-final
1979-80	80	35	40	5	304	327	75	4th, Adams Div.	Lost prelim. round
1980-81	80	28	37	15	322	367	71	5th, Adams Div.	Lost prelim. round
1981-82	80	20	44	16	298	380	56	5th, Norris Div.	Out of playoffs
1982-83	80	28	40	12	293	330	68	3d, Norris Div.	Lost div. semi-final
1983-84	80	26	45	9	303	287	61	5th, Norris Div.	Out of playoffs
1984-85	80	20	52	8	253	358	48	5th, Norris Div.	Out of playoffs
1985-86	80	25	48	7	311	386	57	4th, Norris Div.	Lost div. final
1986-87	80	32	42	6	286	319	70	4th, Norris Div.	Lost div. final
1987-88	80	21	49	10	283	345	52	4th, Norris Div.	Lost div. semi-final

(1) Prior to 1967-68, the NHL was a 6-team league.

Winnipeg Jets

Season	GP	W	L	T	GF	GA	Pts.	Finished	Playoff Result
1979-80	80	20	49	11	214	314	51	5th, Smythe Div.	Out of playoffs
1980-81	80	9	57	14	246	400	32	6th, Smythe Div.	Out of playoffs
1981-82	80	33	33	14	319	332	80	2d, Norris Div.	Lost div. semi-final
1982-83	80	33	39	8	311	333	74	4th, Smythe Div.	Lost div. semi-final
1983-84	80	31	38	11	340	374	73	4th, Smythe Div.	Lost div. semi-final
1984-85	80	43	27	10	358	332	96	2d, Smythe Div.	Lost div. final
1985-86	80	26	47	7	295	372	59	3d, Smythe Div.	Lost div. semi-final
1986-87	80	40	32	8	279	271	88	3d, Smythe Div.	Lost div. final
1987-88	80	33	36	11	292	310	77	3rd, Smythe Div.	Lost div. semi-final

Calgary Flames[1]

Season	GP	W	L	T	GF	GA	Pts.	Finished	Playoff Result
1972-73	78	25	38	15	191	239	65	7th, West Div.	Out of playoffs
1973-74	78	30	34	14	214	238	74	4th, West Div.	Lost quarter-final
1974-75	80	34	31	15	243	233	83	4th, Patrick Div.	Out of playoffs
1975-76	80	35	33	12	262	237	82	3d, Patrick	Lost prelim. round
1976-77	80	34	34	12	264	265	80	3d, Patrick Div.	Lost prelim. round
1977-78	80	34	27	19	274	252	87	3d, Patrick Div.	Lost prelim. round
1978-79	80	41	31	8	327	280	90	4th, Patrick Div.	Lost prelim. round
1979-80	80	35	32	13	282	269	83	4th, Patrick Div.	Lost prelim. round
1980-81	80	39	27	14	329	298	92	3d, Patrick Div.	Lost semi-final
1981-82	80	29	34	17	334	345	75	3d, Smythe Div.	Lost div. semi-final
1982-83	80	32	34	14	321	317	78	2d, Smythe Div.	Lost div. final
1983-84	80	34	32	14	311	314	82	2d, Smythe Div.	Lost div. final
1984-85	80	41	27	12	363	302	94	3d, Smythe Div.	Lost div. final
1985-86	80	40	31	9	354	315	89	2d, Smythe Div.	Lost Cup final
1986-87	80	46	31	3	318	289	95	2d, Smythe Div.	Lost div. semi-final
1987-88	80	48	23	9	397	305	105	1st, Smythe Div.	Lost div. final

(1) Franchise was transferred from Atlanta June 24, 1980.

Edmonton Oilers

Season	GP	W	L	T	GF	GA	Pts.	Finished	Playoff Result
1979-80	80	28	39	13	301	322	69	4th, Smythe Div.	Lost prelim. round
1980-81	80	29	35	16	328	327	74	4th, Smythe Div.	Lost quarter final
1981-82	80	48	17	15	417	295	111	1st, Smythe Div.	Lost div. semi-final
1982-83	80	47	21	12	424	315	106	1st, Smythe Div.	Lost final
1983-84	80	57	18	5	446	314	119	1st, Smythe Div.	Won Stanley Cup
1984-85	80	49	20	11	401	298	109	1st, Smythe Div.	Won Stanley Cup
1985-86	80	56	17	7	426	310	119	1st, Smythe Div.	Lost div. final
1986-87	80	50	24	6	372	284	106	1st, Smythe Div.	Won Stanley Cup
1987-88	80	44	25	11	363	288	99	2d, Smythe Div.	Won Stanley Cup

Vancouver Canucks

Season	GP	W	L	T	GF	GA	Pts.	Finished	Playoff Result
1970-71	78	24	46	8	229	296	56	6th, East Div.	Out of playoffs
1971-72	78	20	50	8	203	297	48	7th, East Div.	Out of playoffs
1972-73	78	22	47	9	233	339	53	7th, East Div.	Out of playoffs
1973-74	78	24	43	11	224	296	59	7th, East Div.	Out of playoffs
1974-75	80	38	32	10	271	254	86	1st, Smythe Div.	Lost quarter-final
1975-76	80	33	32	15	271	272	81	2d, Smythe Div.	Lost prelim. round
1976-77	80	25	42	13	235	294	63	4th, Smythe Div.	Out of playoffs
1977-78	80	20	43	17	239	320	57	3d, Smythe Div.	Out of playoffs
1978-79	80	25	42	13	217	291	63	2d, Smythe Div.	Lost prelim. round
1979-80	80	27	37	16	256	281	70	3d, Smythe Div.	Lost prelim. round
1980-81	80	28	32	20	289	301	76	3d, Smythe Div.	Lost prelim. round
1981-82	80	30	33	17	290	286	77	2d, Smythe Div.	Lost Cup final
1982-83	80	30	35	15	303	309	75	3d, Smythe Div.	Lost div. semi-final
1983-84	80	32	39	9	306	328	73	3d, Smythe Div.	Lost div. semi-final
1984-85	80	25	46	9	284	401	59	5th, Smythe Div.	Out of playoffs
1985-86	80	23	44	13	282	333	59	4th, Smythe Div.	Lost div. semi-final
1986-87	80	29	43	8	282	314	66	5th, Smythe Div.	Out of playoffs
1987-88	80	25	46	9	272	320	59	5th, Smythe Div.	Out of playoffs

National Hockey League, 1987–1988

Prince of Wales Conference

Adams Division

	W	L	T	GF	GA	Pts
Montreal	45	22	13	298	238	103
Boston	44	30	6	300	251	94
Buffalo	37	32	11	283	305	85
Hartford	35	38	7	249	267	77
Quebec	32	43	5	271	306	69

Patrick Division

	W	L	T	GF	GA	Pts
NY Islanders .	39	31	10	308	267	88
Washington ..	38	33	9	281	249	85
Philadelphia ..	38	33	9	292	292	85
New Jersey ..	38	36	6	293	296	82
NY Rangers ..	36	34	10	300	285	82
Pittsburgh	36	35	9	319	316	81

Clarence Campbell Conference

Norris Division

	W	L	T	GF	GA	Pts
Detroit	41	28	11	322	269	93
St. Louis	34	38	8	278	294	76
Chicago	30	41	9	284	328	69
Toronto	21	49	10	273	345	52
Minnesota	19	48	13	242	349	51

Smythe Division

	W	L	T	GF	GA	Pts
Calgary	48	23	9	397	305	105
Edmonton	44	25	11	363	288	99
Winnipeg	33	36	11	292	310	77
Los Angeles ..	30	42	8	318	359	68
Vancouver ...	25	46	9	272	320	59

NHL Playoff Results, 1988

Prince of Wales Conference

Division Semi Finals

Hartford 3 at Montreal 4
Hartford 3 at Montreal 7
Montreal 4 at Hartford 3
Montreal 5 at Hartford 7
Hartford 3 at Montreal 1
Montreal 2 at Hartford 1
Montreal defeated Hartford 4-2

Buffalo 3 at Boston 7
Buffalo 1 at Boston 4
Boston 2 at Buffalo 6
Boston 5 at Buffalo 6*
Buffalo 4 at Boston 5
Boston 5 at Buffalo 2
Boston defeated Buffalo 4-2

New Jersey 3 at NY Islanders 4*
New Jersey 3 at NY Islanders 2
NY Islanders 0 at New Jersey 3
NY Islanders 5 at New Jersey 4*
New Jersey 4 at NY Islanders 2
NY Islanders 5 at New Jersey 6
New Jersey defeated NY Islanders 4-2

Clarence Campbell Conference

Toronto 6 at Detroit 2
Toronto 2 at Detroit 6
Detroit 6 at Toronto 3
Detroit 8 at Toronto 0
Toronto 6 at Detroit 5*
Detroit 5 at Toronto 3
Detroit defeated Toronto 4-2

Chicago 1 at St. Louis 4
Chicago 2 at St. Louis 3
St. Louis 3 at Chicago 6
St. Louis 6 at Chicago 5
Chicago 3 at St. Louis 5
St. Louis defeated Chicago 4-1

Los Angeles 2 at Calgary 9
Los Angeles 4 at Calgary 6
Calgary 2 at Los Angeles 5
Calgary 7 at Los Angeles 3
Los Angeles 4 at Calgary 6
Calgary defeated Los Angeles 4-1

Philadelphia 4 at Washington 2
Philadelphia 4 at Washington 5
Washington 3 at Philadelphia 4
Washington 4 at Philadelphia 5*
Philadelphia 2 at Washington 5
Washington 7 at Philadelphia 2
Philadelphia 4 at Washington 5*
Washington defeated Philadelphia 4-3

Winnipeg 4 at Edmonton 7
Winnipeg 2 at Edmonton 3
Edmonton 4 at Winnipeg 6
Edmonton 5 at Winnipeg 3
Winnipeg 2 at Edmonton 6
Edmonton defeated Winnipeg 4-1

Division Finals

Boston 2 at Montreal 5
Boston 4 at Montreal 3
Montreal 1 at Boston 3
Montreal 0 at Boston 2
Boston 4 at Montreal 1
Boston defeated Montreal 4-1

St. Louis 4 at Detroit 5
St. Louis 0 at Detroit 6
Detroit 3 at St. Louis 6
Detroit 3 at St. Louis 1
St. Louis 3 at Detroit 4
Detroit defeated St. Louis 4-1

New Jersey 1 at Washington 3
New Jersey 5 at Washington 2
Washington 4 at New Jersey 10
Washington 4 at New Jersey 1
New Jersey 3 at Washington 1
Washington 7 at New Jersey 2
New Jersey 3 at Washington 2
New Jersey defeated Washington 4-3

Edmonton 3 at Calgary 1
Edmonton 5 at Calgary 4*
Calgary 2 at Edmonton 4
Calgary 4 at Edmonton 6
Edmonton defeated Calgary 4-0

Conference Champions

New Jersey 3 at Boston 5
New Jersey 3 at Boston 2*
Boston 6 at New Jersey 1
Boston 1 at New Jersey 3
New Jersey 1 at Boston 7
Boston 3 at New Jersey 6
New Jersey 2 at Boston 6
Boston defeated New Jersey 4-3

Detroit 1 at Edmonton 4
Detroit 3 at Edmonton 5
Edmonton 2 at Detroit 5
Edmonton 4 at Detroit 3*
Detroit 4 at Edmonton 8
Edmonton defeated Detroit 4-1

Stanley Cup Championship

Boston 1 at Edmonton 2
Boston 2 at Edmonton 4

Edmonton 6 at Boston 3
Boston 3 at Edmonton 6

Edmonton defeated Boston 4-0

* overtime

NHL Scoring Leaders, 1987–88

Player	GP	G	A	Pts	+/–	PIM	PP	SH	S	Pct
Mario Lemieux, Pittsburgh	77	70	98	168	23	92	22	10	382	18.3
Wayne Gretzky, Edmonton	64	40	109	149	39	24	9	5	211	19.0
Denis Savard, Chicago	80	40	87	131	4	95	14	7	270	16.3
Dale Hawerchuk, Winnipeg	80	44	77	121	– 9	59	20	3	292	15.1
Luc Robitaille, Los Angeles	80	53	58	111	– 9	82	17	0	220	24.1
Peter Stastny, Quebec	76	46	65	111	2	69	20	0	199	23.1
Mark Messier, Edmonton	77	37	74	111	21	103	12	3	182	20.3
Jimmy Carson, Los Angeles	80	55	52	107	– 19	45	22	0	264	20.8
Hakan Loob, Calgary	80	50	56	106	41	47	9	4	198	25.3
Michel Goulet, Quebec	80	48	58	106	– 31	56	29	1	284	16.9
Mike Bullard, Calgary	79	48	55	103	25	68	21	0	230	20.9
Steve Yzerman, Detroit	64	50	52	102	30	44	10	6	242	20.7
Jari Kurri, Edmonton	80	43	53	96	25	30	10	3	207	20.8
Kirk Muller, New Jersey	80	37	57	94	19	114	17	2	215	17.2
Bobby Smith, Montreal	78	27	66	93	14	78	8	0	198	13.6
Joe Nieuwendyk, Calgary	75	51	41	92	20	23	31	3	212	24.1
Pat Lafontaine, NY Islanders	75	47	45	92	12	52	15	0	242	19.4
Gary Suter, Calgary	75	21	70	91	39	124	6	1	204	10.3
Craig Simpson, Pittsburgh/Edmonton	80	56	34	90	20	77	22	0	177	31.6
Steve Larmer, Chicago	80	41	48	89	– 5	42	21	7	245	16.7
Bernie Federko, St. Louis	79	20	69	89	– 12	52	9	0	119	16.8

GP = Games played; G = Goals; A = Assists; Pts = Points; +/– = Plus/minus statistic, which shows the number of even-strength and shorthanded goals scored by a player's team, minus those scored against it, while he is on the ice; PIM = Penalties in minutes; PP = Power play goals; SH = Shorthanded goals; S = Shots on goal; Pct = Percentage of shots that score goals.

NHL Individual Leaders 1987–1988

Goals

Lemieux, Pittsburgh, 70; Simpson, Pittsburgh/Edmonton, 56; Carson, Los Angeles, 55; Robitaille, Los Angeles, 53; Nieuwendyk, Calgary, 51.

Assists

Gretzky, Edmonton, 109; Lemieux, Pittsburgh, 98; Savard, Chicago, 87; Hawerchuk, Winnipeg, 77; Messier, Edmonton, 74.

Power Play Goals

Nieuwendyk, Calgary, 31; Goulet, Quebec, 29; Dionne, NY Rangers, 22; Lemieux, Pittsburgh, 22; MacLean, Winnipeg, 22; Carson, Los Angeles, 22; Simpson, Edmonton, 22.

Shorthanded Goals

Lemieux, Pittsburgh, 10; Loob, Calgary, 8; Nicholls, Los Angeles, 7; Larmer, Chicago, 7; Savard, Chicago, 7; Yzerman, Detroit, 6.

Game-Winning Goals

Richer, Montreal, 11; Wilson, Hartford, 9; Verbeek, New Jersey, 8; Nieuwendyk, Calgary, 8; Simpson, Edmonton, 8.

Goals by Rookies

Nieuwendyk, Calgary, 51; Sheppard, Buffalo, 38; Hull, Calgary/St. Louis, 32; Dahlen, NY Rangers, 29; Brown, Pittsburgh, 24.

Shots

Lemieux, Pittsburgh, 382; Bourque, Boston, 344; Gartner, Washington, 316; Hawerchuk, Winnipeg, 292; Goulet, Quebec, 284.

Shooting Percentage (min. 80 shots)

Simpson, Edmonton, 31.6; Brown, Pittsburgh, 30.0; Verbeek, New Jersey, 25.7; Makela, NY Islanders, 25.4; Loob, Calgary, 25.3.

Plus/Minus

McCrimmon, Calgary, 48; Svoboda, Montreal, 46; Loob, Calgary, 41; Smith, Edmonton, 40; Gretzky, Edmonton, 39; Suter, Calgary, 39.

Goals–Against Average (min. 25 games)

Peeters, Washington, 2.78; Hayward, Montreal, 2.86; Roy, Montreal, 2.90; Lemelin, Boston, 2.93; Stefan, Detroit, 3.11.

Wins

Fuhr, Edmonton, 40; Vernon, Calgary, 39; Hextall, Philadelphia, 30; Vanbiesbrouck, NY Rangers, 27; Barrasso, Buffalo, 25; Liut, Hartford, 25.

Save Percentage

Roy, Montreal, .900; Peeters, Washington, .898; Barrasso, Buffalo, .896; Hrudey, NY Islanders, .896; Hayward, Montreal, .896.

Shutouts

Hanlon, Detroit, 4; Malarchuk, Washington, 4; Fuhr, Edmonton, 4; Roy, Montreal, 3; Hrudey, NY Islanders, 3; Lemelin, Boston, 3.

Major League Arenas and Stadiums in Canada

Hockey		Football/Baseball	
Name, location	**Seating capacity**	**Name, location**	**Seating capacity**
Le Collisée, Quebec	15 434	B.C. Place, Vancouver	59 478
Maple Leaf Gardens, Toronto	16 182	Commonwealth Stadium, Edmonton	60 081
Montreal Forum	16 074	Exhibition Stadium, Toronto	54 545[1]
Northlands Coliseum, Edmonton	17 312	Ivor Wynne Stadium, Hamilton	29 195
Olympic Saddledome, Calgary	16 833	Landsdowne Park, Ottawa	34 838
Pacific Coliseum, Vancouver	16 553	McMahon Stadium, Calgary	38 408
Winnipeg Arena	15 250	Olympic Stadium, Montreal	59 149[2]
		Taylor Field, Regina	27 637
		Winnipeg, Stadium	32 946
		SkyDome, Toronto	56 000[3]

(1) 43 737 seats for baseball. (2) 58 643 seats for football. (3) The SkyDome, scheduled to open in 1989, will have a seating capacity of approximately 56 000 for football and 54 000 for baseball.

Individual Scoring

(40 or more games played)

Boston Bruins

	GP	G	A	Pts	+/−	PIM
Ray Bourque	78	17	64	81	34	72
Ken Linseman	77	29	45	74	36	167
Steve Kasper	79	26	44	70	1−	35
Cam Neely	69	42	27	69	30	175
Randy Burridge	79	27	28	55	0	105
Bob Sweeney	80	22	23	45	11	73
Keith Crowder	68	17	26	43	14	173
Glen Wesley	79	7	30	37	21	69
Gord Kluzak	66	6	31	37	18	135
Reed Larson	62	10	24	34	3	93
Rick Middleton	59	13	19	32	3	11
Michael Thelven	67	6	25	31	12	57
Lyndon Byers	53	10	14	24	10	236
Jay Miller	78	7	12	19	5−	304
Bill O'Dwyer	77	7	10	17	3−	83
Allen Pedersen	78	0	6	6	6	90
Willi Plett	65	2	3	5	10−	170
Rejean Lemelin	49	0	0	0	0	2

Buffalo Sabres

	GP	G	A	Pts	+/−	PIM
Dave Andreychuk	80	30	48	78	1	112
Christian Ruuttu	73	26	45	71	3−	85
Phil Housley	74	29	37	66	17−	96
Ray Sheppard	74	38	27	65	6−	14
Mike Foligno	74	29	28	57	11−	220
Pierre Turgeon	76	14	28	42	8−	34
Calle Johansson	71	4	38	42	12	37
Scott Arniel	73	17	23	40	8	61
John Tucker	45	19	19	38	4	20
Doug Smith	70	9	19	28	10−	117
Lindy Ruff	77	2	23	25	9−	179
Mike Ramsey	63	5	16	21	6	77
Mark Napier	47	10	8	18	3−	8
Mike Donnelly	57	8	10	18	6−	52
Uwe Krupp	75	2	9	11	1−	151
Kevin Maguire	46	4	6	10	1−	162
Ed Hospodar	42	0	1	1	1−	98
Tom Barrasso	54	0	1	1	0	50

Calgary Flames

	GP	G	A	Pts	+/−	PIM
Hakan Loob	80	50	56	106	41	47
Mike Bullard	79	48	55	103	25	68
Joe Nieuwendyk	75	51	41	92	20	23
Gary Suter	75	21	70	91	39	124
Joe Mullen	80	40	44	84	28	30
Al MacInnis	80	25	58	83	13	114
John Tonelli	74	17	41	58	10	84
Joel Otto	62	13	39	52	16	194
Jim Peplinski	75	20	31	51	20	234
Rob Ramage	79	9	40	49	4−	164
Brad McCrimmon	80	7	35	42	48	98
Gary Roberts	74	13	15	28	24	282
Lanny McDonald	60	10	13	23	2	57
Craig Coxe	71	7	15	22	2	218
Brian Glynn	67	5	14	19	2−	87
Dana Murzyn	74	7	11	18	1	139
Ric Nattress	63	2	13	15	14	37
Tim Hunter	68	8	5	13	8−	337
Mike Vernon	64	0	7	7	0	47

Chicago Black Hawks

	GP	G	A	Pts	+/−	PIM
Denis Savard	80	44	87	131	4	95
Steve Larmer	80	41	48	89	5−	42
Rick Vaive	76	43	26	69	20−	108
Troy Murray	79	22	36	58	17−	96
Dirk Graham	70	24	24	48	7−	71
Brian Noonan	77	10	20	30	27−	44
Behn Wilson	58	6	23	29	19−	166
Bob Murray	62	6	20	26	7−	44
Wayne Presley	42	12	10	22	13−	52
Steve Ludzik	73	6	15	21	14−	40
Everett Sanipass	57	8	12	20	9−	126
Gary Nylund	76	4	15	19	9−	208
Dan Vincelette	69	6	11	17	15−	109

Detroit Red Wings

	GP	G	A	Pts	+/−	PIM
Steve Yzerman	64	50	52	102	30	44
Gerard Gallant	73	34	39	73	24	242
Petr Klima	78	37	25	62	4	46
Bob Probert	74	29	33	62	16	398
John Chabot	78	13	44	57	12	10
Adam Oates	63	14	40	54	16	20
Brent Ashton	73	26	27	53	10	50
Shawn Burr	78	17	23	40	7	97
Dave Barr	51	14	26	40	20	58
Darren Veitch	63	7	33	40	10	45
Jeff Sharples	56	10	25	35	13	42
Lee Norwood	51	9	22	31	4	131
Doug Halward	70	5	21	26	6	130
Tim Higgins	62	12	13	25	5	94
Joe Murphy	50	10	9	19	4−	37
Mike O'Connell	48	6	13	19	24	38
Mel Bridgman	57	6	11	17	4	42
Rick Zombo	62	3	14	17	24	96
Jim Nill	60	3	12	15	5−	99
Joey Kocur	64	7	7	14	11−	263
Gilbert Delorme	55	2	8	10	9	81
Glen Hanlon	47	0	1	1	0	30

Edmonton Oilers

	GP	G	A	Pts	+/−	PIM
Wayne Gretzky	64	40	109	149	39	24
Mark Messier	77	37	74	111	21	103
Jari Kurri	80	43	53	96	25	30
Craig Simpson	80	56	34	90	20	77
Glenn Anderson	80	38	50	88	5	58
Esa Tikkanen	80	23	51	74	21	153
Geoff Courtnall	74	36	30	66	25	123
Steve Smith	79	12	43	55	40	286
Mike Krushelnyski	76	20	27	47	26	64
Charlie Huddy	77	13	28	41	23	71
Craig MacTavish	80	15	17	32	3−	47
Keith Acton	72	11	17	28	19−	95
Dave Hannan	72	13	14	27	10	66
Marty McSorley	60	9	17	26	23	223
Jeff Beukeboom	73	5	20	25	27	201
Kevin Lowe	70	9	15	24	18	89
Craig Muni	72	4	15	19	32	77
Normand Lacombe	53	8	9	17	3−	36
Kevin McClelland	74	10	6	16	1	281
Grant Fuhr	75	0	8	8	0	16
Steve Dykstra	42	3	4	7	1	130

Hartford Whalers

	GP	G	A	Pts	+/−	PIM
Ron Francis	80	25	50	75	8−	89
Carey Wilson	70	27	41	68	3−	40
Kevin Dineen	74	25	25	50	14−	219
Ray Ferraro	68	21	29	50	1	83
Dave Babych	71	14	36	50	25−	54
Sylvain Turgeon	71	23	26	49	5−	71
John Anderson	63	17	32	49	5−	20
Ulf Samuelsson	76	8	34	42	9−	159
Dave Tippett	80	16	21	37	4−	30
Paul MacDermid	80	20	14	34	2	139
Dean Evason	77	10	18	28	29−	117
Sylvain Cote	67	7	21	28	8−	30
Stewart Gavin	56	11	10	21	17−	59
Lindsay Carson	63	7	11	18	4−	67
Neil Sheehy	62	3	10	13	13	189
Torrie Robertson	63	2	8	10	0	293
Scot Kleinendorst	44	3	6	9	5−	86
Brent Peterson	52	2	7	9	9−	44
Joel Quenneville	77	1	8	9	13−	44
Randy Ladouceur	68	1	7	8	7	91
Mike Liut	60	0	1	1	0	4

(Boston Bruins, continued)

	GP	G	A	Pts	+/−	PIM
Bob Mogill	67	4	7	11	19−	131
Mike Stapleton	53	2	9	11	10−	59
Glen Cochrane	73	1	8	9	7−	204
Dave Mason	54	1	6	7	12−	185
Mark Bergevin	58	1	6	7	19−	85
Darren Pang	45	0	6	6	0	2

Los Angeles Kings

	GP	G	A	Pts	+/-	PIM
Luc Robitaille	80	53	58	111	9—	82
Jimmy Carson	80	55	52	107	19—	45
Bernie Nicholls	65	32	46	78	2—	114
Dave Taylor	68	26	41	67	4—	129
Steve Duchesne	71	16	39	55	0	109
Bob Carpenter	71	19	33	52	21—	84
Jim Fox	68	16	35	51	7—	18
Paul Fenton	71	20	23	43	14—	46
Mike Allison	52	16	15	31	3	67
Jay Wells	58	2	23	25	3—	159
Craig Laughlin	59	9	13	22	16—	32
Phil Sykes	40	9	12	21	5	82
Chris Kontos	42	3	17	20	2—	14
Bob Bourne	72	7	11	18	31—	28
Ken Hammond	46	7	9	16	1—	69
Ron Duguay	63	6	10	16	14—	40
Tom Laidlaw	57	1	12	13	3	47
Dean Kennedy	58	1	11	12	22—	158
Larry Playfair	54	0	7	7	13—	197
Roland Melanson	47	0	0	0	0	16

Minnesota North Stars

	GP	G	A	Pts	+/-	PIM
Dino Ciccarelli	67	41	45	86	29—	79
Brian Bellows	77	40	41	81	8—	81
Brian Maclellan	75	16	32	48	44—	74
Brian Lawton	74	17	24	41	10—	71
Neal Broten	54	9	30	39	23—	32
Moe Mantha	76	11	27	38	1—	53
David Archibald	78	13	20	33	17—	26
Bob Brooke	77	5	20	25	6—	108
Dave Gagner	51	8	11	19	14—	55
Gord Dineen	70	5	13	18	4	83
Frantisek Musil	80	9	8	17	2—	213
Terry Ruskowski	47	5	12	17	15—	76
Basil McRae	80	5	11	16	28—	378
Curt Giles	72	1	12	13	33—	76
Bob Rouse	74	0	12	12	30—	168
Richard Zemlak	54	1	4	5	15—	307
Don Beaupre	43	0	0	0	0	8

Montreal Canadiens

	GP	G	A	Pts	+/-	PIM
Bobby Smith	78	27	66	93	14	78
Mats Naslund	78	24	59	83	17	14
Stephane Richer	72	50	28	78	12	72
Claude Lemieux	78	31	30	61	16	137
Chris Chelios	71	20	41	61	15	172
Mike McPhee	77	23	20	43	19	53
Larry Robinson	53	6	34	40	26	30
Shayne Corson	71	12	27	39	22	152
Guy Carbonneau	80	17	21	38	14	61
Ryan Walter	61	13	23	36	12	39
Brian Skrudland	79	12	24	36	14	112
Petr Svoboda	69	7	22	29	46	149
Kjell Dahlin	48	13	12	25	5	6
Bob Gainey	78	11	11	22	8	14
Sergio Momesso	53	7	14	21	9	91
Craig Ludwig	74	4	10	14	17	69
Rick Green	59	2	11	13	21	33
Mike Lalor	66	1	10	11	4	113
John Kordic	60	2	6	8	0	159
Patrick Roy	45	0	2	2	0	14

New Jersey Devils

	GP	G	A	Pts	+/-	PIM
Kirk Muller	80	37	57	94	19	114
Aaron Broten	80	26	57	83	20	80
Pat Verbeek	73	46	31	77	29	227
Bruce Driver	74	15	40	55	7	68
Patrik Sundstrom	78	15	36	51	16—	42
John MacLean	76	23	16	39	10—	145
Joe Cirella	80	8	31	39	15	191
Claude Loiselle	68	17	18	35	7	118
Tom Kurvers	56	5	29	34	6	46
Mark Johnson	54	14	19	33	10—	14
Craig Wolanin	78	6	25	31	0	170
Doug Sulliman	59	16	14	30	8—	25
Jack O'Callahan	50	7	19	26	3—	97
Brendan Shanahan	65	7	19	26	20—	131
Doug Brown	70	14	11	25	7	20

New York Islanders (continued)

	GP	G	A	Pts	+/-	PIM
Andy Brickley	45	8	14	22	1	14
Jim Korn	52	8	13	21	22—	140
Ken Daneyko	80	5	7	12	3—	239
Randy Velischek	51	3	9	12	13—	66
Perry Anderson	60	4	6	10	8—	222
David Maley	44	4	2	6	13—	65
Alain Chevrier	45	0	1	1	0	8

New York Islanders

	GP	G	A	Pts	+/-	PIM
Pat LaFontaine	75	47	45	92	12	52
Bryan Trottier	77	30	52	82	10	48
Mikko Makela	73	36	40	76	14	22
Brent Sutter	70	29	31	60	13	55
Alan Kerr	80	24	34	58	30	198
Denis Potvin	72	19	32	51	26	112
Tomas Jonsson	72	6	41	47	6	115
Greg Gilbert	76	17	28	45	14	46
Randy Wood	75	22	16	38	2—	80
Derek King	55	12	24	36	7	30
Brad Lauer	69	17	18	35	13	67
Patrick Flatley	40	9	15	24	7	28
Bob Bassen	77	6	16	22	8	99
Dale Henry	48	5	15	20	8	115
Gerald Diduck	68	7	12	19	22	113
Ken Leiter	51	4	13	17	18	24
Steve Konroyd	62	2	15	17	16	99
Rich Kromm	71	5	10	15	2	20
Ken Morrow	53	1	4	5	0	40
Kelly Hrudey	47	0	2	2	0	20

New York Rangers

	GP	G	A	Pts	+/-	PIM
Walt Poddubny	77	38	50	88	2	76
Kelly Kisio	77	23	55	78	8	88
Tomas Sandstrom	69	28	40	68	6—	95
Marcel Dionne	67	31	34	65	14—	54
James Patrick	70	17	45	62	16	52
Brian Mullen	74	25	29	54	2—	42
John Ogrodnick	64	22	32	54	3	16
Ulf Dahlen	70	29	23	52	5	26
Michel Petit	74	9	27	36	1—	258
Don Maloney	66	12	21	33	12	60
Mark Hardy	80	8	24	32	32—	130
David Shaw	68	7	25	32	8—	100
Lucien Deblois	74	9	21	30	3—	103
Jan Erixon	70	7	19	26	3	33
Chris Nilan	72	10	10	20	2—	305
Paul Cyr	60	5	14	19	7—	79
Jari Gronstrand	62	3	11	14	8	63
Joe Paterson	53	2	6	8	14—	178
Ron Greschner	51	1	5	6	9—	82
John Vanbiesbrouck	56	0	5	5	0	46

Philadelphia Flyers

	GP	G	A	Pts	+/-	PIM
Murray Craven	72	30	46	76	25	58
Brian Propp	74	27	49	76	8	76
Rick Tocchet	65	31	33	64	3	301
Mark Howe	75	19	43	62	23	62
Peter Zezel	69	22	35	57	7	42
Scott Mellanby	75	25	26	51	7—	185
Dave Poulin	68	19	32	51	17	32
Ilkka Sinisalo	68	25	17	42	2	30
Per-Erik Eklund	71	10	32	42	6—	12
Doug Crossman	76	9	29	38	1—	43
Ron Sutter	69	8	25	33	9—	146
Willie Huber	56	9	22	31	16—	70
Kjell Samuelsson	74	6	24	30	28	184
Derrick Smith	76	16	8	24	20—	104
Kerry Huffman	52	6	17	23	11—	34
Dave Brown	47	12	5	17	10	114
Brad Marsh	70	3	9	12	13—	57
Greg Smyth	47	1	6	7	2—	192
Ron Hextall	62	1	6	7	0	104

Pittsburgh Penguins

	GP	G	A	Pts	+/−	PIM
Mario Lemieux	77	70	98	168	23	92
Dan Quinn	70	40	39	79	8—	50
Randy Cunneyworth	71	35	39	74	13	141
Paul Coffey	46	15	52	67	1—	93
Doug Bodger	69	14	31	45	3—	103
Rob Brown	51	24	20	44	8	56
Dave Hunter	80	14	21	35	9	83
Charlie Simmer	50	11	17	28	6	24
John Callander	41	11	16	27	13—	45
Bryan Erickson	53	7	19	26	12—	20
Ville Siren	58	1	20	21	14	62
Dave McLlwain	66	11	8	19	1—	40
Troy Loney	65	5	13	18	3—	151
Dan Frawley	47	6	8	14	0	152
Randy Hillier	55	1	12	13	6—	144
Jim Johnson	55	1	12	13	5—	87
Rod Buskas	76	4	8	12	6	206
Chris Dahlquist	44	3	6	9	3	69

Quebec Nordiques

	GP	G	A	Pts	+/−	PIM
Peter Stastny	76	46	65	111	2	69
Michel Goulet	80	48	58	106	31—	56
Anton Stastny	69	27	45	72	9—	14
Alan Haworth	72	23	34	57	5—	112
Jeff Brown	78	16	37	53	25—	64
Gaetan Duchesne	80	24	23	47	8	83
Lane Lambert	61	13	27	40	0	98
Jason LaFreniere	40	10	19	29	1—	4
Jeff Jackson	68	9	18	27	5—	103
Terry Carkner	63	3	24	27	8—	159
Tommy Albelin	60	3	23	26	7—	47
Randy Moller	66	3	22	25	11—	169
Alain Cote	76	4	18	22	3	26
Mike Eagles	76	10	10	20	18—	74
Paul Gillis	80	7	10	17	29—	164
Robert Picard	65	3	13	16	1—	103
Normand Rochefort	46	3	10	13	2—	49
Steven Finn	75	3	7	10	4—	198
Gord Donnelly	63	4	3	7	16—	301
Mario Gosselin	54	0	0	0	0	8

St. Louis Blues

	GP	G	A	Pts	+/−	PIM
Bernie Federko	79	20	69	89	12—	52
Doug Gilmour	72	36	50	86	13—	59
Tony McKegney	80	40	38	78	10	82
Brett Hull	65	32	32	64	14	16
Mark Hunter	66	32	31	63	6—	136
Tony Hrkac	67	11	37	48	5	22
Brian Sutter	76	15	22	37	16—	147
Brian Benning	77	8	29	37	5—	107
Rick Meagher	76	18	16	34	0	76
Gino Cavallini	64	15	17	32	4—	62
Gaston Gingras	70	7	23	30	1	18
Herb Raglan	73	10	15	25	10—	190
Robert Nordmark	67	3	18	21	6—	60
Perry Turnbull	51	10	9	19	8	82
Tim Bothwell	78	6	13	19	6	76
Gordie Roberts	70	3	15	18	10—	143
Paul Cavallini	72	6	10	16	7	152
Doug Evans	41	5	7	12	7—	49
Todd Ewen	64	4	2	6	5—	227
Greg Millen	48	0	0	0	0	4

Toronto Maple Leafs

	GP	G	A	Pts	+/−	PIM
Ed Olczyk	80	42	33	75	22—	55
Gary Leeman	80	30	31	61	6—	62
Mark Osborne	79	23	37	60	3—	102
Al Iafrate	77	22	30	52	21—	80
Tom Fergus	63	19	31	50	5	81
Russ Courtnall	65	23	26	49	16—	47
Vincent Damphousse	75	12	36	48	2	40
Al Secord	74	15	27	42	21—	221

	GP	G	A	Pts	+/−	PIM
Peter Ihnacak	68	10	20	30	6—	41
Rick Lanz	75	6	22	28	12—	65
Borje Salming	66	2	24	26	7	82
Todd Gill	65	8	17	25	20—	131
Dale Degray	56	6	18	24	4	63
Greg Terrion	59	4	16	20	6—	65
Dan Daoust	67	9	8	17	7—	57
Sean McKenna	70	8	7	15	25—	24
Luke Richardson	78	4	6	10	25—	90
Dave Semenko	70	2	3	5	8—	107
Ken Wregget	56	0	5	5	0	40

Vancouver Canucks

	GP	G	A	Pts	+/−	PIM
Tony Tanti	73	40	37	77	1—	90
Greg Adams	80	36	40	76	24—	30
Barry Pederson	76	19	52	71	2	92
Petri Skriko	73	30	34	64	12—	32
Stan Smyl	57	12	25	37	5—	110
Doug Lidster	64	4	32	36	19—	105
Jim Benning	77	7	26	33	0	58
Jim Sandlak	49	16	15	31	9—	81
Rich Sutter	80	15	15	30	4—	165
Doug Wickenheiser	80	7	19	26	15—	36
Randy Boyd	60	7	16	23	9—	64
Garth Butcher	80	6	17	23	14—	285
John LeBlanc	41	12	10	22	12—	18
Steve Tambellini	41	11	10	21	17—	8
David Saunders	56	7	13	20	15—	10
Paul Lawless	48	4	11	15	11—	16
Daryl Stanley	57	2	7	9	12—	151
Dave Richter	49	2	4	6	5—	224
Larry Melnyk	63	2	4	6	19—	107
Kirk McLean	41	0	2	2	0	8

Washington Capitals

	GP	G	A	Pts	+/−	PIM
Mike Gartner	80	48	33	81	20	73
Scott Stevens	80	12	60	72	14	184
Larry Murphy	79	8	53	61	2	72
Mike Ridley	70	28	31	59	1	22
Dale Hunter	79	22	37	59	7	238
Dave Christian	80	37	21	58	14—	26
Bengt Gustafsson	78	18	36	54	2	29
Kevin Hatcher	71	14	27	41	1	137
Michal Pivonka	71	11	23	34	1	28
Kelly Miller	80	9	23	32	9	35
Garry Galley	58	7	23	30	11	44
Greg Adams	78	15	12	27	3—	153
Bob Gould	72	12	14	26	1—	56
Peter Sundstrom	76	8	17	25	2—	34
Yvon Corriveau	44	10	9	19	17	84
Rod Langway	63	3	13	16	1	28
Grant Ledyard	44	5	10	15	11—	46
Lou Franceschetti	59	4	8	12	2	113
Greg Smith	54	1	6	7	5	67
Clint Malarchuk	54	0	2	2	0	10

Winnipeg Jets

	GP	G	A	Pts	+/−	PIM
Dale Hawerchuk	80	44	77	121	9—	59
Paul MacLean	77	40	39	79	16—	76
Andrew McBain	74	32	31	63	10—	145
Randy Carlyle	78	15	44	59	20—	210
Dave Ellett	68	13	45	58	8—	106
Thomas Steen	76	16	38	54	12—	53
Mario Marois	79	7	44	51	5	111
Laurie Boschman	80	25	23	48	24—	227
Iain Duncan	62	19	23	42	2—	73
Ray Neufeld	78	18	18	36	29—	167
Doug Smail	71	15	16	31	5	34
Peter Taglianetti	70	6	17	23	13—	182
Gilles Hamel	63	8	11	19	16—	35
Hannu Jarvenpaa	41	6	11	17	0	34
Steve Rooney	56	7	6	13	2	217
Ron Wilson	69	5	8	13	1—	75
Mark Kimpel	45	4	6	10	4	23
Brad Berry	48	0	6	6	11—	75
Jim Kyte	51	1	3	4	1	128
Daniel Berthiaume	56	0	2	2	0	10

Team Canada in International Hockey Competition

The 1972 Series
(an 8-game series)

Team Canada: Goal – Ken Dryden, Tony Esposito; **Defence** – Don Awrey, Gary Bergman, Guy Lapointe, Brad Park, Serge Savard, Rod Seiling, Pat Stapleton, Bill White; **Forwards** – Red Berenson, Wayne Cashman, Bobby Clarke, Yvan Cournoyer, Ron Ellis, Phil Esposito, Rod Gilbert, Bill Goldsworthy, Vic Hadfield, Paul Henderson, Dennis Hull, Frank Mahovlich, Peter Mahovlich, Stan Mikita, Jean-Paul Parise, Gilbert Perreault, Jean Ratelle.

Date	Location	Score	Date	Location	Score
Sept. 2	Montreal	Soviets 7, Team Canada 3	Sept. 22	Moscow	Soviets 5, Team Canada 4
Sept. 4	Toronto	Team Canada 4, Soviets 1	Sept. 24	Moscow	Team Canada 3, Soviets 2
Sept. 6	Winnipeg	Soviets 4, Team Canada 4	Sept. 26	Moscow	Team Canada 4, Soviets 3
Sept. 8	Vancouver	Soviets 5, Team Canada 3	Sept. 28	Moscow	Team Canada 6, Soviets 5

Canada won the series 4 games to 3, with 1 game tied.

The Canada Cup, 1976

Team Canada: Goal – Gerry Cheevers, Ken Dryden, Chico Resch, Rogatien Vachon; **Defence** – Guy Lapointe, Denis Potvin, Larry Robinson, Serge Savard, Jimmy Watson; **Forwards** – Bill Barber, Bobby Clarke, Marcel Dionne, Phil Esposito, Bob Gainey, Danny Gare, Bobby Hull, Guy Lafleur, Reggie Leach, Richard Martin, Lanny McDonald, Bobby Orr, Gilbert Perreault, Steve Shutt, Darryl Sittler.

Final-Round Results
Canada 6, Czechoslovakia 0   Canada 5, Czechoslovakia 4*
* – Darryl Sittler scored at 11:33 overtime.

Canada won best 2-out-of-3 final series 2 games to 0.

The Canada Cup, 1981

Team Canada: Goal – Don Edwards, Mike Liut; **Defence** – Barry Beck, Raymond Bourque, Brian Engblom, Craig Hartsburg, Denis Potvin, Paul Reinhart, Larry Robinson; **Forwards** – Mike Bossy, Marcel Dionne, Ron Duguay, Bob Gainey, Danny Gare, Clark Gillies, Butch Goring, Wayne Gretzky, Guy Lafleur, Ken Linsemen, Rick Middleton, Gilbert Perreault, Bryan Trottier.

Semi-Final Results
Soviet Union 4, Czechoslovakia 1   Canada 4, United States 1

Final Game Score
Soviet Union 8, Canada 1

The Soviet Union won the series.

The Canada Cup, 1984

Team Canada: Goal – Grant Fuhr, Reggie Lemelin, Pete Peeters; **Defence** – Raymond Bourque, Paul Coffey, Randy Gregg, Charlie Huddy, Kevin Lowe, Larry Robinson, Doug Wilson; **Forwards** – Glenn Anderson, Brian Bellows, Mike Bossy, Bob Bourne, Mike Gartner, Michel Goulet, Wayne Gretzky, Mark Messier, Rick Middleton, Peter Stastny, Brent Sutter, John Tonelli, Steve Yzerman.

Playoff Results
Canada 3, Soviet Union 2   Sweden 9, United States, 2

Final Results
Canada 5, Sweden 2   Canada 6, Sweden 5

Canada won best-2-out-of-3 series 2 games to 0.

The Canada Cup, 1987

Team Canada: Goal—Grant Fuhr, Ron Hextall, Kelly Hrudey; **Defence**—Raymond Bourque, Paul Coffey, Doug Crossman, Craig Hartsburg, Larry Murphy, James Patrick, Normand Rochefort; **Forwards**—Glenn Anderson, Kevin Dineen, Mike Gartner, Doug Gilmour, Michel Goulet, Wayne Gretzky, Dale Hawerchuk, Claude Lemieux, Mario Lemieux, Mark Messier, Brian Propp, Brent Sutter, Rick Tocchet.

Semi-Final Results
Canada 5, Czechoslovakia 3   Soviet Union 4, Sweden 2

Final Results
Soviet Union 6, Canada 5*
Canada 6, Soviet Union 5*
Canada 6, Soviet Union 5

Canada won the best-2-out-of-3 series 2 games to 1.

*overtime.

The Hockey Hall of Fame and Museum

(Toronto, Ont.)

(year of election to the Hall indicated in brackets)

Abel, Sid (1969)
Adams, Jack (1959)
Apps, Syl (1961)
Armstrong, George (1975)

Bailey, Ace (1975)
Bain, Dan (1945)
Baker, Hobey (1945)
Barry, Marty (1965)
Bathgate, Andy (1978)
Béliveau, Jean (1972)
Benedict, Clinton (1965)
Bentley, Doug (1964)
Bentley, Max (1966)
Blake, Toe (1966)
Boivin, Leo (1986)
Boon, Dickie (1952)
Bouchard, Butch (1966)
Boucher, Frank (1958)
Boucher, Buck (1960)
Bower, Johnny (1976)
Bowie, Russell (1945)
Brimsek, Frank (1966)
Broadbent, Punch (1962)
Broda, Turk (1967)
Bucyk, Johnny (1981)
Burch, Billy (1974)

Cameron, Harry (1962)
Cheevers, Gerry (1985)
Clancy, King (1958)
Clapper, Dit (1945)
Clarke, Bob (1987)
Cleghorn, Sprague (1958)
Colville, Neil (1967)
Conacher, Charlie (1961)
Connell, Alex (1958)
Cook, Bill (1952)
Coulter, Art (1974)
Cournoyer, Yvan (1982)
Cowley, William (1968)
Crawford, Rusty (1962)

Darragh, Jack (1962)
Davidson, Scotty (1950)
Day, Hap (1961)
Delvecchio, Alex (1977)
Denneny, Cy (1959)
Drillon, Gordie (1975)
Drinkwater, Charles (1950)
Dryden, Ken (1983)
Dunderdale, Thomas (1974)
Durnan, Bill (1964)
Dutton, Red (1958)
Dye, Babe (1970)

Esposito, Phil (1984)
Esposito, Tony (1988)

Farrell, Arthur (1965)
Foyston, Frank (1958)
Frederickson, Frank (1958)

Gadsby, Bill (1970)
Gardiner, Chuck (1945)
Gardiner, Herb (1958)
Gardner, Jimmy (1962)
Geoffrion, Bernie "Boom Boom" (1972)

Gerard, Eddie (1945)
Giacomin, Ed (1987)
Gilbert, Rod (1982)
Gilmour, Billy (1962)
Goheen, Moose (1952)
Goodfellow, Ebbie (1963)
Grant, Mike (1950)
Green, Shorty (1962)
Griffis, Si (1950)

Hainsworth, George (1961)
Hall, Glenn (1975)
Hall, Joe (1961)
Harvey, Doug (1973)
Hay, George (1958)
Hern, Riley (1962)
Hextall, Bryan (1969)
Holmes, Hap (1972)
Hooper, Tom (1962)
Horner, Red (1965)
Horton, Tim (1977)
Howe, Gordie (1972)
Howe, Syd (1965)
Howell, Harry (1979)
Hull, Bobby (1983)
Hutton, Bouse (1962)
Hyland, Harry (1962)

Irvin, Dick (1958)

Jackson, Busher (1971)
Johnson, Moose (1952)
Johnson, Ching (1958)
Johnson, Tom (1970)
Joliat, Aurel (1947)
Keats, Duke (1958)
Kelly, Red (1969)
Kennedy, Teeder (1966)
Keon, Dave (1986)

Lach, Elmer (1966)
Lafleur, Guy (1988)
Lalonde, Newsy (1950)
Laperrière, Jacques (1987)
Laviolette, Jack (1962)
Lehman, Hugh (1958)
Lemaire, Jacques (1984)
LeSueur, Percy (1961)
Lindsay, Ted (1966)
Lumley, Harry (1980)

Mackay, Mickey (1952)
Mahovlich, Frank (1981)
Malone, Joe (1950)
Mantha, Sylvio (1960)
Marshall, Jack (1965)
Maxwell, Steamer (1962)
McGee, Frank (1945)
McGimsie, Billy (1962)
McNamara, George (1958)
Mikita, Stan (1983)
Moore, Dickie (1974)
Moran, Paddy (1958)
Morenz, Howie (1945)
Mosienko, Bill (1965)

Nighbor, Frank (1945)
Noble, Reg (1962)

O'Connor, Buddy (1988)
Oliver, Harry (1967)
Olmstead, Bert (1985)
Orr, Bobby (1979)

Parent, Bernie (1984)
Park, Brad (1988)
Patrick, Lynn (1980)
Patrick, Lester (1945)
Phillips, Tommy (1945)
Pilote, Pierre (1975)
Pitre, Didier "Pit" (1962)
Plante, Jacques (1978)
Pratt, Babe (1966)
Primeau, Joe (1963)
Pronovost, Marcel (1978)
Pulford, Harvey (1945)

Quackenbush, Bill (1976)

Rankin, Frank (1961)
Ratelle, Jean (1985)
Rayner, Chuck (1973)
Reardon, Ken (1966)
Richard, Henri (1979)
Richard, Maurice "Rocket" (1961)
Richardson, George (1950)
Roberts, Gordon (1971)
Ross, Art (1945)
Russel, Blair (1965)
Russell, Ernest (1965)
Ruttan, Jack (1962)

Savard, Serge (1986)
Sawchuk, Terry (1971)
Scanlan, Fred (1965)
Schmidt, Milt (1961)
Schriner, Sweeney (1962)
Seibert, Earl (1963)
Seibert, Oliver (1961)
Shore, Eddie (1945)
Siebert, Babe (1964)
Simpson, Bullet Joe (1962)
Smith, Alfred (1962)
Smith, Hooley (1972)
Smith, Thomas (1973)
Stanley, Allan (1981)
Stanley, Barney (1962)
Stewart, Black Jack (1964)
Stewart, Nels (1962)
Stuart, Bruce (1961)
Stuart, Hod (1945)

Taylor, Cyclone (1945)
Thompson, Tiny (1959)
Trihey, Harry (1950)

Ullman, Norm (1982)

Vezina, Georges (1945)

Walker, Jack (1960)
Walsh, Marty (1962)
Watson, Moose (1962)
Welland, Cooney (1971)
Westwick, Harry (1962)
Whitcroft, Fred (1962)
Wilson, Phat (1962)
Worsley, Lorne "Gump" (1980)
Worters, Roy (1969)

Football

The Grey Cup

The Grey Cup was donated in 1909 by Governor General Earl Grey for the ''Rugby Football Championship of Canada.'' Since 1954, only teams in the Canadian Football League have challenged for the trophy, with the winners of the East and West divisions meeting in the championship game.

1909 .... U. of Toronto 26, Parkdale 6	1950 .... Toronto 13, Winnipeg 0
1910 .... U. of Toronto 16, Ham. Tigers 7	1951 .... Ottawa 21, Saskatchewan 14
1911 .... U. of Toronto 14, Toronto 7	1952 .... Toronto 21, Edmonton 11
1912 .... Ham. Alerts 11, Toronto 4	1953 .... Hamilton 12, Winnipeg 6
1913 .... Ham. Tigers 44, Parkdale 2	1954 .... Edmonton 26, Montreal 25
1914 .... Toronto 14, U. of Toronto 2	1955 .... Edmonton 34, Montreal 19
1915 .... Ham. Tigers 13, Tor. R.A.A. 7	1956 .... Edmonton 50, Montreal 27
1916–19 .... No games held.	1957 .... Hamilton 32, Winnipeg 7
1920 .... U. of Toronto 16, Toronto 3	1958 .... Winnipeg 35, Hamilton 28
1921 .... Toronto 23, Edmonton 0	1959 .... Winnipeg 21, Hamilton 7
1922 .... Queen's U. 13, Edmonton 1	1960 .... Ottawa 16, Edmonton 6
1923 .... Queen's U. 54, Regina 0	1961 .... Winnipeg 21, Hamilton 14
1924 .... Queen's U. 11, Balmy Beach 3	1962 .... Winnipeg 28, Hamilton 27
1925 .... Ott. Senators 24, Winnipeg 1	1963 .... Hamilton 21, British Columbia 10
1926 .... Ott. Senators 10, U. of Toronto 7	1964 .... British Columbia 34, Hamilton 24
1927 .... Balmy Beach 9, Ham. Tigers 6	1965 .... Hamilton 22, Winnipeg 16
1928 .... Ham. Tigers 30, Regina 0	1966 .... Saskatchewan 29, Ottawa 14
1929 .... Ham. Tigers 14, Regina 3	1967 .... Hamilton 24, Saskatchewan 1
1930 .... Balmy Beach 11, Regina 6	1968 .... Ottawa 24, Calgary 21
1931 .... Mtl. A.A.A. 22, Regina 0	1969 .... Ottawa 29, Saskatchewan 11
1932 .... Ham. Tigers 25, Regina 6	1970 .... Montreal 23, Calgary 10
1933 .... Toronto 4, Sarnia 3	1971 .... Calgary 14, Toronto 11
1934 .... Sarnia 20, Regina 12	1972 .... Hamilton 13, Saskatchewan 10
1935 .... Winnipeg 18, Ham. Tigers 12	1973 .... Ottawa 22, Edmonton 18
1936 .... Sarnia 26, Ott. R.R. 20	1974 .... Montreal 20, Edmonton 7
1937 .... Toronto 4, Winnipeg 3	1975 .... Edmonton 9, Montreal 8
1938 .... Toronto 30, Winnipeg 7	1976 .... Ottawa 23, Saskatchewan 20
1939 .... Winnipeg 8, Ottawa 7	1977 .... Montreal 41, Edmonton 6
1940[1] ...... Ottawa 12, Balmy Beach 5	1978 .... Edmonton 20, Montreal 13
Ottawa 8, Balmy Beach 2	1979 .... Edmonton 17, Montreal 9
1941 .... Winnipeg 18, Ottawa 16	1980 .... Edmonton 48, Hamilton 10
1942 .... Tor. R.C.A.F. 8, Win. R.C.A.F. 5	1981 .... Edmonton 26, Ottawa 23
1943 .... Ham. F. Wild 23, Win. R.C.A.F. 14	1982 .... Edmonton 32, Toronto 16
1944 .... Mtl. St. H.D. Navy 7, Ham. F. Wild 6	1983 .... Toronto 18, B.C. 17
1945 .... Toronto 35, Winnipeg 0	1984 .... Winnipeg 47, Hamilton 17
1946 .... Toronto 28, Winnipeg 6	1985 .... B.C. 37, Hamilton 24
1947 .... Toronto 10, Winnipeg 9	1986 .... Hamilton 39, Edmonton 15
1948 .... Calgary 12, Ottawa 7	1987 .... Edmonton 38, Toronto 36
1949 .... Mtl. Als. 28, Calgary 15	

(1) A 2-game total point series.

Canadian Football League

Final 1987 Standings

Source: Canadian Football League

Eastern Division

	W	L	T	F	A	Pts	Pct
Winnipeg	12	6	0	554	409	24	.667
Toronto	11	6	1	484	427	23	.639
Hamilton	7	11	0	470	509	14	.389
Ottawa	3	15	0	377	598	6	.167

Western Division

	W	L	T	F	A	Pts	Pct
B.C.	12	6	0	502	370	24	.667
Edmonton	11	7	0	617	462	22	.611
Calgary	10	8	0	453	517	20	.556
Saskatchewan .	5	12	1	364	529	11	.306

Playoff Results

Division Semifinals

East: Toronto 29, Hamilton 13
West: Edmonton 30, Calgary 16

Division Finals

East: Toronto 19, Winnipeg 3
West: Edmonton 31, B.C. 7

Grey Gup Championship—Edmonton 38, Toronto 36

1987 CFL Individual Leaders

Source: Canadian Football League

Passing

	Comp	Ptc. comp	Yds	TDs
Clements, Winnipeg ...	336	56.8	4 686	35
Dewalt, B.C.	303	57.1	3 855	19
Porras, Hamilton	242	59.6	3 293	18
Worman, Calgary	179	50.3	3 021	16
Dillon, Ottawa	222	55.2	2 901	14
Dunigan, Edmonton ...	175	53.7	2 823	21
Allen, Edmonton	150	52.3	2 670	17
Burgess, Saskatchewan	127	52.3	1 691	7
Renfroe, Toronto	111	47.8	1 686	9
Paopao, Ottawa	147	51.6	1 629	7

Pass Receiving

	No	Yds	Avg	TDs
Kelly, Edmonton	68	1 626	23.9	13
Stapler, Hamilton	85	1 516	17.8	13
Willis, Calgary	74	1 477	20.0	10
Sandusky, B.C.	80	1 437	18.0	12
Smith, Toronto	79	1 392	17.6	10
Tuttle, Winnipeg	75	1 310	17.5	8
Lewis, Ottawa	94	1 195	12.7	3
Jones, Edmonton	55	1 147	20.9	8
Murphy, Winnipeg	84	1 130	13.5	5
Boyd, Winnipeg	57	1 039	18.2	9
Alphin, Ottawa	67	1 029	15.4	8

Rushing

	Yds	Carries	Avg	TDs
Reaves, Winnipeg	1 471	271	5.4	9
Fenerty, Toronto	879	178	4.9	12
Allen, Calgary	857	165	5.2	5
Parker, B.C.	635	157	4.0	1
Minter, Ottawa	627	150	4.2	7
Allen, Edmonton	562	66	8.5	6
Crouse, B.C.	531	108	4.9	5
Bender, Saskatchewan .	525	148	3.5	5
Petros, Calgary	467	95	4.9	5
McCray, Saskatchewan	457	86	5.3	1

Scoring

	Pts	TDs	Con	FG	S
Passaglia, B.C.	214	0	47	52	11
Chomyc, Toronto	193	0	44	47	8
Kennerd, Winnipeg ...	177	0	59	35	13
Ridgway, Saskatchewan	174	0	23	49	4
Hay, Calgary	172	0	42	39	13
Kauric, Edmonton	145	0	47	28	14
Dorsey, Ottawa	141	0	28	36	5
Ruoff, Hamilton	115	0	29	26	8
Fenerty, Toronto	90	15	0	0	0
Stapler, Hamilton	81	13	1	0	1

CFL Individual Player Records

Source: Canadian Football League

(up to the end of the 1987 season)

Most points one season: .... 214—Lui Passaglia, B.C., 1987
Most points one game: .... 36—Bob McNamara, Wpg., Wpg. at B.C., Oct. 13, 1956
Most touchdowns one season: .... 20—Pat Abbruzzi, Mtl., 1956
Most touchdowns one game: .... 6—Bob McNamara, Wpg., Wpg. at B.C., Oct. 13, 1956
Most touchdown passes one season: .... 40—Peter Liske, Cal., 1967
Most touchdown passes one game: .... 8—Joe Zuger, Ham., Sask. at Mtl., Oct. 15, 1962
Most touchdowns scored rushing one season: ...... 18—Gerry James, Wpg., 1957; Jim Germany, Edm., 1981
Most touchdowns scored rushing one game: .... 5—Earl Lunsford, Cal., Edm. at Cal., Sept. 3, 1962
Most touchdowns on pass receptions one season: .... 18—Brian Kelly, Edm., 1984
Most touchdowns on pass receptions one game: .... 5—Ernie Pitts, Wpg., Wpg. at Sask., Aug. 29, 1959
Most passes thrown one season: .... 664—Warren Moon, Edm., 1983
Most passes thrown one game: .... 62—Joe Adams, Sask., Tor. at Sask., July 29, 1983
Most passes completed one season: .... 380—Warren Moon, Edm., 1983
Most passes completed one game: .... 41—Dieter Brock, Wpg., Wpg. at Ott., Oct. 3, 1981
Most yards passed one season: .... 5 648—Warren Moon, Edm., 1983
Most yards passed one game: .... 586—Sam Etcheverry, Mtl., Ham. at Mtl., Oct. 16, 1954
Most consecutive pass completions: .... 18—Joe Paopao, B.C., Tor. at B.C., Sept. 22, 1979
The longest completed pass: .. 109 yds.—Sam Etcheverry to Hal Patterson, Mtl., Ham. at Mtl., Sept. 22, 1956;
                                      —Jerry Keeling to Terry Evanshen, Cal., Cal. at Wpg., Sept. 27, 1966
Most yards rushing one season: .... 1 896—Willie Burden, Cal., 1975
Most yards rushing one game: .... 287—Ron Stewart, Ott., Ott. at Mtl., Oct. 10, 1960
Longest rushing plays: .... 109 yds—George Dixon, Mtl., Ott. at Mtl., Sept. 2, 1963;
                                      Willie Fleming, B.C., B.C. at Edm., Oct. 17, 1964
Most carries one season: .... 332—Willie Burden, Cal., 1975
Most carries one game: .... 37—Doyle Orange, Tor., Ham. at Tor., Aug. 13, 1975
Most pass reception yardage one season: .... 2 003—Terry Greer, Tor., 1983
Most pass reception yardage one game: .... 338—Hal Patterson, Mtl., Mtl. at Ham., Sept. 29, 1956
Most pass receptions one season: .... 116—James Murphy, Wpg., 1986
Most pass receptions one game: .... 16—Terry Greer, Tor., Tor. at Ott., Aug. 19, 1983
Most consecutive games catching passes: .... 137—Tony Gabriel, Ham./Ott., 1973-81
Most field goals one season: .... 52—Lui Passaglia, B.C., 1987
Most field goals one game: .... 8—Dave Ridgway, Sask., Sask. at Ott., July 29, 1984
Longest field goals: .... 60 yds—Dave Ridgway, Sask., Wpg. at Sask., Oct. 8, 1987
Longest punts: .... 108 yds—Zenon Andrusyshyn, Tor., Tor. at Edm., Oct. 23, 1977
Most interceptions one season: .... 15—Al Brenner, Ham., 1972
Most quarterback sacks one season: .... 26.5—James Parker, B.C., 1984

All-Time Leading CFL Players

(up to the end of the 1987 season)

Source: Canadian Football League

Touchdowns

Player	TDs	Season		Player	TDs	Season
George Reed, Sask.	137 13	(1963-75)		Ron Stewart, Ott.	67 12	(1959-70)
Brian Kelly, Edm.	97 9	(1979-87)		Tommy Joe Coffey, Edm./Ham./Tor.	65 14	(1959-73)
Dick Shatto, Tor.	91 12	(1954-65)		Gerry James, Wpg./Sask.	63 11	(1952-64)
Tom Scott, Wpg./Edm./Cal.	91 11	(1974-84)		Lovell Coleman, Cal./Ott./B.C.	62 10	(1960-70)
Jackie Parker, Edm./Tor./B.C.	88 13	(1954-68)		Tom Forzani, Cal.	62 11	(1973-83)
Willie Fleming, B.C.	86 8	(1959-68)		Hugh Campbell, Sask.	60 6	(1963-69)
Normie Kwong, Cal./Edm.	83 13	(1948-60)		George Dixon, Mtl.	59 7	(1959-65)
Terry Evanshen, Mtl./Cal./Ham./Tor.	80 14	(1965-78)		Earl Lunsford, Cal.	56 6	(1956-63)
Virgil Wagner, Mtl.	79 9	(1946-54)		Dave Thelen, Ott./Tor.	56 9	(1958-66)
Leo Lewis, Wpg.	75 12	(1955-66)		Garney Henley, Ham.	56 16	(1960-75)
Hal Patterson, Mtl./Ham.	75 14	(1954-67)		Ken Carpenter, Sask.	55 5	(1954-59)
Tony Gabriel, Ham./Ott.	72 11	(1971-81)		Ernie Pitts, Wpg./B.C.	55 14	(1957-70)
Johnny Bright, Cal./Edm.	71 13	(1952-64)		Russ Jackson, Ott.	55 12	(1958-69)
Jim Germany, Edm.	71 7	(1977-83)		Peter Dalla Riva, Mtl.	55 14	(1968-81)
Bob Simpson, Ott.	70 13	(1950-62)		Larry Key, B.C.	55 5	(1978-82)
Jim Young, B.C.	68 13	(1967-79)				

Points

Player	Points	TDs	Con	FGs	Sing	Seasons
Dave Cutler, Edm.	2 237	0	627	464	218	16 (1969-84)
Lui Passaglia, B.C.	1 938	1	461	427	190	12 (1976-87)
Bernie Ruoff, Wpg./Ham.	1 742	0	393	378	215	13 (1975-87)
Gerry Organ, Ott.	1 462	2	391	318	105	12 (1971-83)
John T. Hay, Ott./Cal.	1 365	0	344	300	121	10 (1978-87)
Don Sweet, Mtl./Ham.	1 342	0	327	314	73	14 (1972-85)
Trevor Kennerd, Wpg.	1 274	0	363	265	116	8 (1980-87)
Larry Robinson, Cal.	1 030	9	362	171	101	14 (1961-74)
Zenon Andrusyshyn, Tor./Ham./Edm./Mtl.	1 010	0	222	215	143	12 (1971-86)
Tommy Joe Coffey, Edm./Ham./Tor.	971	65	204	108	53	14 (1959-73)
Jack Abendschan, Sask.	863	0	312	59	74	11 (1965-75)
Dave Ridgway, Sask.	837	0	177	197	69	6 (1982-87)
George Reed, Sask.	823	137	0	0	1	13 (1963-75)
Jackie Parker, Edm./Tor./B.C.	750	88	103	40	19	13 (1954-68)
Don Sutherin, Ham./Ott./Tor.	714	4	270	114	78	12 (1958-70)
Gerry James, Wpg./Sask.	645	63	143	40	21	11 (1952-64)
Ian Hunter, Ham./Tor.	626	0	155	135	66	6 (1972-79)
Brian Kelly, Edm.	586	97	2	0	0	9 (1979-87)
Cyril McFall, Cal.	578	0	131	134	45	5 (1974-78)
Bob Macoritti, Wpg./Sask.	576	0	145	122	65	6 (1975-80)
Dean Dorsey, Tor./Ott.	572	0	132	135	35	5 (1982-87)
Ted Gerela, B.C.	570	0	132	123	69	7 (1967-73)
Tommy Scott, Wpg./Edm./Cal.	546	91	0	0	0	11 (1974-84)
Dick Shatto, Tor.	542	91	3	0	1	12 (1954-65)
Willie Fleming, B.C.	517	86	1	0	0	8 (1959-68)
Peter Kempf, B.C./Mtl./Edm.	502	5	167	92	29	6 (1963-68)
Terry Evanshen, Mtl./Cal./Ham./Tor.	484	80	2	0	0	14 (1965-78)
Normie Kwong, Cal./Edm.	460	83	0	0	0	13 (1948-60)
Leo Lewis, Wpg.	450	75	5	0	1	12 (1955-66)
Dave Mann, Tor.	435	33	73	22	98	12 (1958-70)
Tony Gabriel, Ham./Ott.	434	72	1	0	0	11 (1971-81)
Hal Patterson, Mtl./Ham.	432	75	0	0	0	14 (1954-67)
Jim Germany, Edm.	426	71	0	0	0	7 (1977-83)

Rushing

Player	Yards	Carries	Avg	Long	TDs	Seasons
George Reed, Sask.	16 116	3 243	5.0	71	134	13 (1963-75)
Johnny Bright, Cal./Edm.	10 909	1 969	5.5	90	69	13 (1952-64)
Normie Kwong, Cal./Edm.	9 022	1 745	5.2	60	78	13 (1948-60)
Leo Lewis, Wpg.	8 861	1 351	6.5	92	48	11 (1955-66)
Dave Thelen, Ott./Tor.	8 463	1 530	5.5	77	47	9 (1958-66)
Jim Evenson, B.C./Ott.	7 060	1 460	4.8	68	37	7 (1968-74)

Player	Yards	Carries	Avg	Long	TDs	Seasons
Earl Lunsford, Cal.	6 994	1 199	5.8	85	55	6	(1956-63)
Dick Shatto, Tor.	6 958	1 322	5.3	67	39	12	(1954-65)
Lovell Coleman, Cal./Ott./B.C.	6 566	1 135	5.8	85	42	10	(1960-70)
Willie Burden, Cal.	6 234	1 242	5.0	71	32	8	(1974-81)
Jim Thomas, Edm.	6 160	1 111	5.5	104	37	10	(1962-71)
Jim Washington, Wpg./Sask.	6 127	1 206	5.1	68	31	7	(1974-80)
Willie Fleming, B.C.	6 125	868	7.1	109	37	8	(1959-68)
Jim Germany, Edm.	5 730	1 082	5.3	96	65	7	(1977-83)
Ron Stewart, Ott.	5 690	983	5.8	72	42	13	(1958-70)
George Dixon, Mt.	5 615	896	6.3	109	42	7	(1959-65)
Gerry James, Wpg./Sask.	5 554	995	5.6	74	57	11	(1952-64)
Dave Raimey, Wpg./Tor.	5 528	886	6.2	100	25	7	(1965-74)

Pass Receivers

Player	Receptions	Yards	Avg	TDs	Seasons
Tommy Joe Coffey, Edm./Ham./Tor.	650	10 320	15.9	63	14	(1959-73)
Tom Scott, Wpg./Edm./Cal.	649	10 837	16.7	88	11	(1974-84)
Tony Gabriel, Ham./Ott.	614	9 832	16.0	69	11	(1971-81)
Terry Evanshen, Mtl./Cal./Ham./Tor.	600	9 697	16.2	80	14	(1965-78)
Brian Kelly, Edm.	575	11 169	19.4	97	9	(1979-87)
Tom Forzani, Cal.	553	8 285	15.0	62	11	(1973-83)
Joe Poplawski, Wpg.	549	8 341	15.2	48	9	(1978-86)
Rocky DiPietro, Ham.	547	7 450	13.6	34	10	(1978-87)
Jim Young, B.C.	522	9 248	17.7	65	13	(1967-79)
Bobby Taylor, Cal./Tor./Ham./Edm.	521	8 223	15.8	50	14	(1961-74)
Dick Shatto, Tor.	466	6 684	14.3	52	12	(1954-65)
Hal Patterson, Mtl./Ham.	460	9 473	20.6	64	14	(1954-67)
Peter Dalla Riva, Mtl.	450	6 413	14.3	54	14	(1968-81)
Herman Harrison, Cal.	443	6 693	15.1	43	9	(1964-72)
George McGowan, Edm.	424	6 356	15.0	42	8	(1971-78)
Terry Greer, Tor.	404	6 817	15.9	47	6	(1980-85)
James Murphy, Wpg	387	5 971	15.4	41	5	(1983-87)
Red O'Quinn, Mtl.	377	5 679	15.1	34	6	(1954-59)
Rudy Linterman, Cal./Tor.	376	4 908	13.1	18	10	(1968-77)

Passing

Player	Pass Attempts	Comp	Yds	Pct	Avg	Int	TDs	Seasons
Ron Lancaster, Ott./Sask.	6 233	3 384	50 535	54.3	14.9	396	333	19	(1960-78)
Tom Clements, Ott./Sask./Ham./Wpg.	4 657	2 602	34 830	60.3	13.9	214	252	12	(1975-87)
Dieter Brock, Wpg./Ham.	4 535	2 602	34 830	57.4	13.4	158	210	11	(1974-84)
Sam Etcheverry, Mtl.	2 829	1 630	25 582	57.6	15.7	163	174	7	(1953-60)
Condredge Holloway, Ott./Tor.	2 985	1 696	24 982	56.8	14.7	93	154	12	(1975-86)
Russ Jackson, Ott.	2 530	1 356	24 592	53.6	18.1	125	185	12	(1958-69)
Bernie Faloney, Edm./Ham./Mtl./B.C.	2 876	1 493	24 264	51.9	16.3	201	151	12	(1954-66)
Roy Dewalt, B.C.	2 898	1 705	22 863	58.8	13.4	86	129	8	(1980-87)
Joe Kapp, Cal./B.C.	2 709	1 476	22 725	54.5	15.4	130	136	8	(1959-67)
Tom Wilkinson, Tor./B.C./Edm.	2 662	1 613	22 579	60.6	14.0	126	154	15	(1967-81)
John Hufnagel, Cal./Sask./Wpg.	2 665	1 475	21 370	55.4	14.5	128	126	11	(1976-86)
Peter Liske, Tor./Cal./B.C.	2 571	1 449	21 266	56.4	14.7	133	130	7	(1965-75)
Warren Moon, Edm.	2 382	1 369	21 228	57.5	15.5	77	144	6	(1978-83)
Joe Paopao, B.C./Sask.	2 784	1 584	20 622	56.9	13.0	150	103	10	(1976-87)
Joe Barnes, Mtl./Sask./Tor./Cal.	2 454	1 350	18 491	55.0	13.7	117	94	11	(1976-86)
Jerry Keeling, Cal./Ott./Ham.	2 477	1 302	18 239	52.6	14.0	158	119	15	(1961-75)
Jackie Parker, Edm./Tor./B.C.	2 061	1 089	16 476	52.8	15.1	123	88	13	(1954-68)
Kenny Ploen, Wpg.	1 916	1 084	16 470	56.6	15.2	106	119	11	(1957-67)
Frank Tripucka, Sask./Ott.	1 930	1 090	15 506	56.5	14.2	136	87	8	(1953-63)
Don Jonas, Tor./Wpg./Ham.	1 930	977	15 064	51.7	15.4	130	98	5	(1970-74)
Sonny Wade, Mtl.	2 097	1 083	15 014	51.6	13.9	169	89	10	(1969-78)
Eagle Day, Wpg./Cal./Tor.	1 753	1 015	14 405	57.9	14.2	71	74	7	(1956-66)
Chuck Ealey, Ham./Wpg./Tor.	1 726	955	13 326	55.3	14.0	69	82	7	(1972-78)
Wally Gabler, Tor./Wpg./Ham.	1 690	854	13 080	50.5	15.3	118	61	7	(1966-72)
Joe Zuger, Ham.	1 618	814	12 676	50.3	15.6	95	76	10	(1962-71)
Jimmy Jones, Mtl./Ham.	1 721	950	12 405	55.2	13.1	84	72	7	(1973-79)
Jack Jacobs, Wpg.	1 330	710	11 094	53.4	15.6	53	104	5	(1950-54)

CFL All-Canadian All-Star Teams

Source: Canadian Football League

1987

Offence	Defence
Quarterback—Tom Clements, Winnipeg	End—Gregg Stumon, B.C.
Running Back—Willard Reaves, Winnipeg	End—Bobby Jurasin, Saskatchewan
Running Back—Gill Fenerty, Toronto	Tackle—Mike Walker, Hamilton
Slotback—Darrell Smith, Toronto	Tackle—Jearld Baylis, Toronto
Slotback—Perry Tuttle, Winnipeg	Middle Linebacker—James West, Winnipeg
Wide Receiver—Brian Kelly, Edmonton	Outside Linebacker—Tyron Jones, Winnipeg
Wide Receiver—Jim Sandusky, B.C.	Outside Linebacker—Kevin Konar, B.C.
Centre—Rod Connop, Edmonton	Cornerback—Roy Bennett, Winnipeg
Guard—Roger Aldag, Saskatchewan	Cornerback—James Jefferson, Winnipeg
Guard—Dan Ferrone, Toronto	Halfback—Larry Crawford, B.C.
Tackle—Chris Walby, Winnipeg	Halfback—Ken Hailey, Winnipeg
Tackle—Chris Schultz, Toronto	Safety—Scott Flagel, Winnipeg
Punter—Hank Ilesic, Toronto	
Kicker—Dave Ridgway, Saskatchewan	
Specialty Teams—Henry Williams, Edmonton	

1986

Offence	Defence
Quarterback—Rick Johnson, Calgary	End—James Parker, B.C.
Running Back—Gary Allen, Calgary	End—Grover Covington, Hamilton
Running Back—Bobby Johnson, Saskatchewan	Tackle—Harold Hallman, Calgary
Slotback—Joe Poplawski, Winnipeg	Tackle—Brett Williams, Montreal
Slotback—Rocky DiPietro, Hamilton	Middle Linebacker—Dan Bass, Edmonton
Wide Receiver—James Murphy, Winnipeg	Outside Linebacker—Tyrone Jones, Winnipeg
Wide Receiver—James Hood, Montreal	Outside Linebacker—Willie Pless, Toronto
Centre—Bob Poley, Calgary	Cornerback—Roy Bennett, Winnipeg
Guard—Roger Aldag, Saskatchewan	Cornerback—Less Browne, Hamilton
Tackle—Chris Walby, Winnipeg	Defensive Back—Larry Crawford, B.C.
Tackle—Rudy Phillips, Edmonton	Defensive Back—Mark Streeter, Hamilton
Punter—Hank Ilesic, Toronto	Safety—Scott Flagel, Winnipeg
Kicker—Lance Chomyc, Toronto	
Specialty Teams—Gary Allen, Calgary	

The Schenley Awards[1]

	Outstanding player	Outstanding Canadian	Outstanding defensive player
1987	Tom Clements, Winnipeg	Scott Flagel, Winnipeg	Gregg Stumon, B.C.
1986	James Murphy, Winnipeg	Joe Poplawski, Winnipeg	James Parker, B.C.
1985	Mervyn Fernandez, B.C.	Paul Bennett, Hamilton	Tyrone Jones, Winnipeg
1984	Willard Reaves, Winnipeg	Nick Arakgi, Montreal	James Parker, B.C.
1983	Warren Moon, Edmonton	Paul Bennett, Winnipeg	Greg Marshall, Ottawa
1982	Condredge Holloway, Toronto	Rocky DiPietro, Hamilton	James Parker, Edmonton
1981	Deiter Brock, Winnipeg	Joe Poplawski, Winnipeg	Dan Kepley, Edmonton
1980	Deiter Brock, Winnipeg	Gerry Dattilio, Montreal	Dan Kepley, Edmonton
1979	David Green, Montreal	Dave Fennell, Edmonton	Ben Zambiasi, Hamilton
1978	Tony Gabriel, Ottawa	Tony Gabriel, Ottawa	Dave Fennell, Edmonton
1977	Jimmy Edwards, Hamilton	Tony Gabriel, Ottawa	Dan Kepley, Edmonton
1976	Ron Lancaster, Saskatchewan	Tony Gabriel, Ottawa	Bill Baker, B.C.
1975	Willie Burden, Calgary	Jim Foley, Ottawa	Jim Corrigall, Toronto
1974	Tom Wilkinson, Edmonton	Tony Gabriel, Hamilton	John Helton, Calgary
1973	George McGowan, Edmonton	Gerry Organ, Ottawa	Ray Nettles, B.C.
1972	Garney Henley, Hamilton	Jim Young, B.C.	John Helton, Calgary
1971	Don Jonas, Winnipeg	Terry Evanshen, Montreal	Wayne Harris, Calgary
1970	Ron Lancaster, Saskatchewan	Jim Young, B.C.	Wayne Harris, Calgary
1969	Russ Jackson, Ottawa	Russ Jackson, Ottawa	John LaGrone, Edmonton
1968	Bill Symons, Toronto	Ken Nielson, Winnipeg	Ken Lehmann, Ottawa
1967	Peter Liske, Calgary	Terry Evanshen, Calgary	Ed McQuarters, Saskatchewan
1966	Russ Jackson, Ottawa	Russ Jackson, Ottawa	Wayne Harris, Calgary
1965	George Reed, Saskatchewan	Zeno Karcz, Hamilton	Wayne Harris, Calgary
1964	Lovell Coleman, Calgary	Tommy Grant, Hamilton	Tom Brown, B.C.
1963	Russ Jackson, Ottawa	Russ Jackson, Ottawa	Tom Brown, B.C.
1962	George Dixon, Montreal	Harvey Wylie, Calgary	John Barrow, Hamilton
1961	Bernie Faloney, Hamilton	Tony Pajaczkowski, Calgary	Frank Rigney, Winnipeg
1960	Jackie Parker, Edmonton	Ron Stewart, Ottawa	Herb Gray, Winnipeg
1959	Johnny Bright, Edmonton	Russ Jackson, Ottawa	Roger Nelson, Edmonton
1958	Jackie Parker, Edmonton	Ron Howell, Hamilton	Don Luzzi, Calgary
1957	Jackie Parker, Edmonton	Gerry James, Winnipeg	Kaye Vaughan, Ottawa
1956	Hal Patterson, Montreal	Normie Kwong, Edmonton	Kaye Vaughan, Ottawa
1955	Pat Abbruzzi, Montreal	Normie Kwong, Edmonton	Tex Coulter, Montreal
1954	Sam Etcheverry, Montreal	Gerry James, Winnipeg	
1953	Bill Vessels, Edmonton		

(1) Winners are chosen by a vote of the Football Reporters of Canada.

National Football League Champions

Year	East Winner (W-L-T)	West Winner (W-L-T)	Playoff
1933	New York Giants (11-3-0)	Chicago Bears (10-2-1)	Chicago Bears 23, New York 21
1934	New York Giants (8-5-0)	Chicago Bears (13-0-0)	New York 30, Chicago Bears 13
1935	New York Giants (9-3-0)	Detroit Lions (7-3-2)	Detroit 26, New York 7
1936	Boston Redskins (7-5-0)	Green Bay Packers (10-1-1)	Green Bay 21, Boston 6
1937	Washington Redskins (8-3-0)	Chicago Bears (9-1-1)	Washington 28, Chicago Bears 21
1938	New York Giants (8-2-1)	Green Bay Packers (8-3-0)	New York 23, Green Bay 17
1939	New York Giants (9-1-1)	Green Bay Packers (9-2-0)	Green Bay 27, New York 0
1940	Washington Redskins (9-2-0)	Chicago Bears (8-3-0)	Chicago Bears 73, Washington 0
1941	New York Giants (8-3-0)	Chicago Bears (10-1-1)(a)	Chicago Bears 37, New York 9
1942	Wash. Redskins (10-1-1)	Chicago Bears (11-0-0)	Washington 14, Chicago Bears 6
1943	Wash. Redskins (6-3-1)(a)	Chicago Bears (8-1-1)	Chicago Bears, 41, Washington 21
1944	New York Giants (8-1-1)	Green Bay Packers (8-2-0)	Green Bay 14, New York 7
1945	Wash. Redskins (8-2-0)	Cleveland Rams (9-1-0)	Cleveland 15, Washington 14
1946	New York Giants (7-3-1)	Chicago Bears (8-2-1)	Chicago Bears 24, New York 14
1947	Philadelphia Eagles (8-4-0)(a)	Chicago Cardinals (9-3-0)	Chicago Cardinals 28, Philadelphia 21
1948	Philadelphia Eagles (9-2-1)	Chicago Cardinals (11-1-0)	Philadelphia 7, Chicago Cardinals 0
1949	Philadelphia Eagles (11-1-0)	Los Angeles Rams (8-2-2)	Philadelphia 14, Los Angeles 0
1950	Cleveland Browns (10-2-0)(a)	Los Angeles Rams (9-3-0)(a)	Cleveland 30, Los Angeles 28
1951	Cleveland Browns (11-1-0)	Los Angeles Rams (8-4-0)	Los Angeles 24, Cleveland 17
1952	Cleveland Browns (8-4-0)	Detroit Lions (9-3-0)(a)	Detroit 17, Cleveland 7
1953	Cleveland Browns (11-1-0)	Detroit Lions (10-2-0)	Detroit 17, Cleveland 16
1954	Cleveland Browns (9-3-0)	Detroit Lions (9-2-1)	Cleveland 56, Detroit 10
1955	Cleveland Browns (9-2-1)	Los Angeles Rams (8-3-1)	Cleveland 38, Los Angeles 14
1956	New York Giants (8-3-1)	Chicago Bears (9-2-1)	New York 47, Chicago Bears 7
1957	Cleveland Browns (9-2-1)	Detroit Lions (8-4-0)(a)	Detroit 59, Cleveland 14
1958	New York Giants (9-3-0)(a)	Baltimore Colts (9-3-0)	Baltimore 23, New York 17(b)
1959	New York Giants (10-2-0)	Baltimore Colts (9-3-0)	Baltimore 31, New York 16
1960	Philadelphia Eagles (10-2-0)	Green Bay Packers (8-4-0)	Philadelphia 17, Green Bay 13
1961	New York Giants (10-3-1)	Green Bay Packers (11-3-0)	Green Bay 37, New York 0
1962	New York Giants (12-2-0)	Green Bay Packers (13-1-0)	Green Bay 16, New York 7
1963	New York Giants (11-3-0)	Chicago Bears (11-1-2)	Chicago 14, New York 10
1964	Cleveland Browns (10-3-1)	Baltimore Colts (12-2-0)	Cleveland 27, Baltimore 0
1965	Cleveland Browns (11-3-0)	Green Bay Packers (10-3-1)(a)	Green Bay 23, Cleveland 12
1966	Dallas Cowboys (10-3-1)	Green Bay Packers (12-2-0)	Green Bay 34, Dallas 27

(a) Won divisional playoff. (b) Won at 8:15 sudden death overtime period.

Year	Conference	Division	Winner (W-L-T)	Playoff
1967	East	Century	Cleveland (9-5-0)	Dallas 52, Cleveland 14
		Capitol	Dallas (9-5-0)	
	West	Central	Green Bay (9-4-1)	Green Bay 28, Los Angeles 7
		Coastal	Los Angeles (11-1-2)(a)	Green Bay 21, Dallas 17
1968	East	Century	Cleveland (10-4-0)	Cleveland 31, Dallas 20
		Capitol	Dallas (12-2-0)	
	West	Central	Minnesota (8-6-0)	Baltimore 24, Minnesota 14
		Coastal	Baltimore (13-1-0)	Baltimore 34, Cleveland 0
1969	East	Century	Cleveland (10-3-1)	Cleveland 38, Dallas 14
		Capitol	Dallas (11-2-1)	
	West	Central	Minnesota (12-2-0)	Minnesota 23, Los Angeles 20
		Coastal	Los Angeles (11-3-0)	Minnesota 27, Cleveland 7
1970	American	Eastern	Baltimore (11-2-1)	Baltimore 17, Cincinnati 0
		Central	Cincinnati (8-6-0)	Oakland 21, Miami 14
		Western	Oakland (8-4-2)	Baltimore 27, Oakland 17
	National	Eastern	Dallas (10-4-0)	Dallas 5, Detroit 0
		Central	Minnesota (12-2-0)	San Francisco 17, Minnesota 14
		Western	San Francisco (10-3-1)	Dallas 17, San Francisco 10
1971	American	Eastern	Miami (10-3-1)	Miami 27, Kansas City 24
		Central	Cleveland (9-5-0)	Baltimore 20, Cleveland 3
		Western	Kansas City (10-3-1)	Miami 21, Baltimore 0
	National	Eastern	Dallas (11-3-0)	Dallas 20, Minnesota 12
		Central	Minnesota (11-3-0)	San Francisco 24, Washington 20
		Western	San Francisco (9-5-0)	Dallas 14, San Francisco 3
1972	American	Eastern	Miami (14-0-0)	Miami 20, Cleveland 14
		Central	Pittsburgh (11-3-0)	Pittsburgh 13, Oakland 7
		Western	Oakland (10-3-1)	Miami 21, Pittsburgh 17
	National	Eastern	Washington (11-3-0)	Washington 16, Green Bay 3
		Central	Green Bay (10-4-0)	Dallas 30, San Francisco 28
		Western	San Francisco (8-5-1)	Washington 26, Dallas 3
1973	American	Eastern	Miami (12-2-0)	Miami 34, Cincinnati 16
		Central	Cincinnati (10-4-0)	Oakland 33, Pittsburgh 14
		Western	Oakland (9-4-1)	Miami 27, Oakland 10
	National	Eastern	Dallas (10-4-0)	Dallas 27, Los Angeles 16
		Central	Minnesota (12-2-0)	Minnesota 27, Washington 20
		Western	Los Angeles (12-2-0)	Minnesota 27, Dallas 10
1974	American	Eastern	Miami (11-3-0)	Oakland 28, Miami 26
		Central	Pittsburgh (10-3-1)	Pittsburgh 32, Buffalo 14
		Western	Oakland (12-2-0)	Pittsburgh 24, Oakland 13
	National	Eastern	St. Louis (10-4-0)	Minnesota 30, St. Louis 14
		Central	Minnesota (10-4-0)	Los Angeles 19, Washington 10
		Western	Los Angeles (10-4-0)	Minnesota 14, Los Angeles 10

Year	Conference	Division	Winner (W-L-T)	Playoff
1975	American	Eastern	Baltimore (10-4-0)	Pittsburgh 28, Baltimore 10
		Central	Pittsburgh (12-2-0)	Oakland 31, Cincinnati 28
		Western	Oakland (11-3-0)	Pittsburgh 16, Oakland 10
	National	Eastern	St. Louis (11-3-0)	Dallas 17, Minnesota 14
		Central	Minnesota (12-2-0)	Los Angeles 35, St. Louis 23
		Western	Los Angeles (12-2-0)	Dallas 37, Los Angeles 7
1976	American	Eastern	Baltimore (11-3-0)	Pittsburgh 40, Baltimore 14
		Central	Pittsburgh (10-4-0)	Oakland 24, New England 21
		Western	Oakland (13-1-0)	Oakland 24, Pittsburgh 7
	National	Eastern	Dallas (11-3-0)	Minnesota 35, Washington 20
		Central	Minnesota (11-2-1)	Los Angeles 14, Dallas 12
		Western	Los Angeles (10-3-1)	Minnesota 24, Los Angeles 13
1977	American	Eastern	Baltimore (10-4-0)	Oakland 37, Baltimore 31
		Central	Pittsburgh (9-5-0)	Denver 34, Pittsburgh 21
		Western	Denver (12-2-0)	Dallas 37, Chicago 7
	National	Eastern	Dallas (12-2-0)	Minnesota 14, Los Angeles 7
		Central	Minnesota (9-5-0)	Denver 20, Oakland 17
		Western	Los Angeles (10-4-0)	Dallas 23, Minnesota 6
1978	American	Eastern	New England (11-5-0)	Pittsburgh 33, Denver 10
		Central	Pittsburgh (14-2-0)	Houston 31, New England 14
		Western	Denver (10-6-0)	Pittsburgh 34, Houston 5
	National	Eastern	Dallas (12-4-0)	Dallas 27, Atlanta 20
		Central	Minnesota (8-7-1)	Los Angeles 34, Minnesota 10
		Western	Los Angeles (12-4-0)	Dallas 28, Los Angeles 0
1979	American	Eastern	Miami (10-6-0)	Houston 17, San Diego 14
		Central	Pittsburgh (12-4-0)	Pittsburgh 34, Miami 14
		Western	San Diego (12-4-0)	Pittsburgh 27, Houston 13
	National	Eastern	Dallas (11-5-0)	Tampa Bay 24, Philadelphia 17
		Central	Tampa Bay (10-6-0)	Los Angeles 21, Dallas 19
		Western	Los Angeles (9-7-0)	Los Angeles 9, Tampa Bay 0
1980	American	Eastern	Buffalo (11-5-0)	San Diego 20, Buffalo 14
		Central	Cleveland (11-5-0)	Oakland 14, Cleveland 12
		Western	San Diego (11-5-0)	Oakland 34, San Diego 27
	National	Eastern	Philadelphia (12-4-0)	Philadelphia 31, Minnesota 16
		Central	Minnesota (9-7-0)	Dallas 30, Atlanta 27
		Western	Atlanta (12-4-0)	Philadelphia 20, Dallas 7
1981	American	Eastern	Miami (11-4-1)	San Diego 41, Miami 38
		Central	Cincinnati (12-4-0)	Cincinnati 28, Buffalo 21
		Western	San Diego (10-6-0)	Cincinnati 27, San Diego 7
	National	Eastern	Dallas (12-4-0)	Dallas 38, Tampa Bay 0
		Central	Tampa Bay (9-7-0)	San Francisco 38, N.Y. Giants 24
		Western	San Francisco (13-3-0)	San Francisco 28, Dallas 27
1982(1)	American		L.A. Raiders (8-1-0)	
	National		Washington (8-1-0)	

AFC playoffs—Miami 28, New England 13; L.A. Raiders 27, Cleveland 10; N.Y. Jets 44, Cincinnati 17; San Diego 31, Pittsburgh 28; N.Y. Jets 17, L.A. Raiders 14; Miami 34, San Diego 13; Miami 14, N.Y. Jets 0. **NFC playoffs**—Washington 31, Detroit 7; Green Bay 41, St. Louis 16; Dallas 30, Tampa Bay 17; Minnesota 30, Atlanta 24; Washington 21, Minnesota 7; Dallas 37, Green Bay 26; Washington 31, Dallas 17.

Year	Conference	Division	Winner (W-L-T)	Playoff
1983	American	Eastern	Miami (12-4-0)	Seattle 27, Miami 20
		Central	Pittsburgh (10-6-0)	L.A. Raiders 38, Pittsburgh 10
		Western	L.A. Raiders (12-4-0)	L.A. Raiders 30, Seattle 14
	National	Eastern	Washington (14-2-0)	Washington 51, L.A. Rams 7
		Central	Detroit (9-7-0)	San Francisco 24, Detroit 23
		Western	San Francisco (10-6-0)	Washington 24, San Francisco 21
1984	American	Eastern	Miami (14-2-0)	Miami 31, Seattle 10
		Central	Pittsburgh (9-7-0)	Pittsburgh 24, Denver 17
		Western	Denver (13-3-0)	Miami 45, Pittsburgh 28
	National	Eastern	Washington (11-5-0)	Chicago 23, Washington 19
		Central	Chicago (10-6-0)	San Francisco 21, N.Y. Giants 10
		Western	San Francisco (15-1-0)	San Francisco 23, Chicago 0
1985	American	Eastern	Miami (12-4-0)	New England 27, L.A. Raiders 20
		Central	Cleveland (8-8-0)	Miami 24, Cleveland 21
		Western	L.A. Raiders (12-4-0)	New England 31, Miami 14
	National	Eastern	Dallas (10-6-0)	Chicago 21, N.Y. Giants 0
		Central	Chicago (15-1-0)	L.A. Rams 20, Dallas 0
		Western	L.A. Rams (11-5-0)	Chicago 24, L.A. Rams 0
1986	American	Eastern	New England (11-5-0)	Denver 22, New England 17
		Central	Cleveland (12-4-0)	Cleveland 23, N.Y. Jets 20
		Western	Denver (11-5-0)	Denver 23, Cleveland 20
	National	Eastern	N.Y. Giants (14-2-0)	N.Y. Giants 49, San Francisco 3
		Central	Chicago (14-2-0)	Washington 27, Chicago 13
		Western	San Francisco (10-5-1)	N.Y. Giants 17, Washington 0
1987	American	Eastern	Indianapolis (9-6-0)	Cleveland 38, Indianapolis 21
		Central	Cleveland (10-5-0)	Denver 34, Houston 21
		Western	Denver (10-4-1)	Denver 38, Cleveland 33
	National	Eastern	Washington (11-4-0)	Washington 21, Chicago 7
		Central	Chicago (11-4-0)	Minnesota 36, San Francisco 24
		Western	San Francisco (13-2-0)	Washington 17, Minnesota 10

(1) Strike-shortened season

Super Bowl

Year	Winner	Loser	Winning Coach	Site
1967	Green Bay Packers, 35	Kansas City Chiefs, 10	Vince Lombardi	Los Angeles Coliseum
1968	Green Bay Packers, 33	Oakland Raiders, 14	Vince Lombardi	Orange Bowl, Miami
1969	New York Jets, 16	Baltimore Colts, 7	Weeb Ewbank	Orange Bowl, Miami
1970	Kansas City Chiefs, 23	Minnesota Vikings, 7	Hank Stram	Tulane Stadium, New Orleans
1971	Baltimore Colts, 16	Dallas Cowboys, 13	Don McCafferty	Orange Bowl, Miami
1972	Dallas Cowboys, 24	Miami Dolphins, 3	Tom Landry	Tulane Stadium, New Orleans
1973	Miami Dolphins, 14	Washington Redskins, 7	Don Shula	Los Angeles Coliseum
1974	Miami Dolphins, 24	Minnesota Vikings, 7	Don Shula	Rice Stadium, Houston
1975	Pittsburgh Steelers, 16	Minnesota Vikings, 6	Chuck Noll	Tulane Stadium, New Orleans
1976	Pittsburgh Steelers, 21	Dallas Cowboys, 17	Chuck Noll	Orange Bowl, Miami
1977	Oakland Raiders, 32	Minnesota Vikings, 14	John Madden	Rose Bowl, Pasadena
1978	Dallas Cowboys, 27	Denver Broncos, 10	Tom Landry	Superdome, New Orleans
1979	Pittsburgh Steelers, 35	Dallas Cowboys, 31	Chuck Noll	Orange Bowl, Miami
1980	Pittsburgh Steelers, 31	Los Angeles Rams, 19	Chuck Noll	Rose Bowl, Pasadena
1981	Oakland Raiders, 27	Philadelphia Eagles, 10	Tom Flores	Superdome, New Orleans
1982	San Francisco 49ers, 26	Cincinatti Bengals, 21	Bill Walsh	Silverdome, Pontiac, Mich.
1983	Washington Redskins, 27	Miami Dolphins, 17	Joe Gibbs	Rose Bowl, Pasadena
1984	Los Angeles Raiders, 38	Washington Redskins, 9	Tom Flores	Tampa Stadium
1985	San Francisco 49ers, 38	Miami Dolphins, 16	Bill Walsh	Stanford Stadium, Palo Alto, Cal.
1986	Chicago Bears, 46	New England Patriots, 10	Mike Ditka	Superdome, New Orleans
1987	New York Giants, 39	Denver Broncos, 20	Bill Parcells	Rose Bowl, Pasadena
1988	Washington Redskins, 42	Denver Broncos, 10	Joe Gibbs	San Diego Stadium

Redskins Defeat Broncos in Super Bowl

The Washington Redskins won the 1988 Super Bowl championship by crushing the Denver Broncos 42-10 at Jack Murphy San Diego Stadium. It was the Redskins' second Super Bowl title; they defeated the Miami Dolphins in the 1983 Super Bowl game. Quarterback Doug Williams of the Redskins, who passed for a Super Bowl-record 340 yards, was chosen the game's most valuable player.

Scoring

Denver—Nattiel 56 yd. pass from Elway (Karlis kick)
Denver—Karlis 24 yd. field goal
Washington—Sanders 80 yd. pass from Williams (Haji-Sheikh kick)
Washington—Clark 37 yd. pass from Williams (Haji-Sheikh kick)
Washington—Smith 58 yd. run (Haji-Sheikh kick)
Washington—Sanders 50 yd. pass from Williams (Haji-Sheikh kick)
Washington—Didier 8 yd. pass from Williams (Haji-Sheikh kick)
Washington—Smith 4 yd. run (Haji-Sheikh kick)

Individual Statistics

Rushing — Washington, T.Smith 22-204, Bryant 8-38, G.Clark 1-25, Rogers 5-17, Griffin 1-2, Williams 2-(2), Sanders 1-(-4). Denver, Lang 5-38, Elway 3-32, Winder, 8-30, Sewell 1-(-3).

Passing — Washington, Williams 18-29-340-1, Schroeder 0-1-0-0. Denver, Elway 14-38-257-3, Sewell 1-1-23-0.

Receiving — Washington, Sanders 9-193, G.Clark 3-55, Warren 2-15, Monk 1-40, Bryant 1-20, T.Smith 1-9, Didier 1-8. Denver, Jackson 4-76, Sewell 4-41, Nattiel 2-69, Kay 2-38, Winder 1-26, Elway 1-23, Lang 1-7.

Score by Quarters

Washington	0	35	0	7	42
Denver	10	0	0	0	10

Team Statistics

	Washington	Denver
First downs	25	18
Total net yards	602	327
Rushing yards	280	97
Passing yards	322	230
Yards per pass play	10.1	5.2
Punts-average	4-37	7-36
Penalties-yards	6-65	5-26
Fumbles-lost	1-0	0-0
Time of possession	35:15	24:45

Super Bowl MVPs

1967 Bart Starr, Green Bay	1975 Franco Harris, Pittsburgh	1983 John Riggins, Washington
1968 Bart Starr, Green Bay	1976 Lynn Swann, Pittsburgh	1984 Marcus Allen, L.A. Raiders
1969 Joe Namath, N.Y. Jets	1977 Fred Biletnikoff, Oakland	1985 Joe Montana, San Francisco
1970 Len Dawson, Kansas City	1978 Randy White, Harvey Martin, Dallas	1986 Richard Dent, Chicago
1971 Chuck Howley, Dallas	1979 Terry Bradshaw, Pittsburgh	1987 Phil Simms, N.Y. Giants
1972 Roger Staubach, Dallas	1980 Terry Bradshaw, Pittsburgh	1988 Doug Williams, Washington
1973 Jake Scott, Miami	1981 Jim Plunkett, Oakland	
1974 Larry Csonka, Miami	1982 Joe Montana, San Francisco	

National Football League

Final 1987 Standings

National Conference

Eastern Division

	W	L	T	Pct	Pts	Opp
Washington	11	4	0	.733	379	285
Dallas	7	8	0	.467	340	348
St. Louis	7	8	0	.467	362	368
Philadelphia	7	8	0	.467	337	380
New York Giants	6	9	0	.400	280	312

Central Division

	W	L	T	Pct	Pts	Opp
Chicago	11	4	0	.733	356	282
Minnesota	8	7	0	.533	336	335
Green Bay	5	9	1	.367	255	300
Detroit	4	11	0	.267	269	384
Tampa Bay	4	11	0	.267	286	360

Western Division

	W	L	T	Pct	Pts	Opp
San Francisco	13	2	0	.867	459	253
New Orleans	12	3	0	.800	422	283
Los Angeles Rams	6	9	0	.400	317	361
Atlanta	3	12	0	.200	205	436

American Conference

Eastern Division

	W	L	T	Pct	Pts	Opp
Indianapolis	9	6	0	.600	300	238
New England	8	7	0	.533	320	293
Miami	8	7	0	.533	362	335
Buffalo	7	8	0	.467	270	305
New York Jets	6	9	0	.400	334	360

Central Division

	W	L	T	Pct	Pts	Opp
Cleveland	10	5	0	.667	390	239
Houston	9	6	0	.600	345	349
Pittsburgh	8	7	0	.533	285	299
Cincinnati	4	11	0	.267	285	370

Western Division

	W	L	T	Pct	Pts	Opp
Denver	10	4	1	.700	379	288
Seattle	9	6	0	.600	371	314
San Diego	8	7	0	.533	253	317
Los Angeles Raiders	5	10	0	.333	301	289
Kansas City	4	11	0	.267	273	388

NFC playoffs—Minnesota 44, New Orleans 10; Washington 21, Chicago 7; Minnesota 36, San Francisco 24; Washington 17, Minnesota 10.

AFC playoffs—Houston 23, Seattle 20; Cleveland 38, Indianapolis 21; Denver 34, Houston 10; Denver 38, Cleveland 33.

National Football Conference Leaders

Passing

Player, team	Atts	Com	YG	TD	Year
John Brodie, San Francisco	378	223	2 941	24	1970
Roger Staubach, Dallas	211	126	1 882	15	1971
Norm Snead, N.Y. Giants	325	196	2 307	17	1972
Roger Staubach, Dallas	286	179	2 428	23	1973
Sonny Jurgensen, Washington	167	107	1 185	11	1974
Fran Tarkenton, Minnesota	425	273	2 294	25	1975
James Harris, Los Angeles	158	91	1 460	8	1976
Roger Staubach, Dallas	361	210	2 620	18	1977
Roger Staubach, Dallas	413	231	3 190	25	1978
Roger Staubach, Dallas	461	267	3 586	27	1979
Ron Jaworski, Philadelphia	451	257	3 529	27	1980
Joe Montana, San Francisco	488	311	3 565	19	1981
Joe Thiesmann, Washington	252	161	2 033	13	1982
Steve Bartkowski, Atlanta	423	274	3 167	22	1983
Joe Montana, San Francisco	432	279	3 630	28	1984
Joe Montana, San Francisco	494	303	3 653	27	1985
Tommy Kramer, Minnesota	372	208	3 000	24	1986
Joe Montana, San Francisco	398	266	3 054	31	1987

Pass-Receiving

Player, team	Ct	YG	TD
Dick Gordon, Chicago	71	1 026	13
Bob Tucker, Giants	59	791	4
Harold Jackson, Philadelphia	62	1 048	4
Harold Carmichael, Philadelphia	67	1 116	9
Charles Young, Philadelphia	63	696	3
Chuck Foreman, Minnesota	73	691	9
Drew Pearson, Dallas	58	806	6
Ahmad Rashad, Minnesota	51	681	2
Rickey Young, Minnesota	88	704	5
Ahmad Rashad, Minnesota	80	1 156	9
Earl Cooper, San Francisco	83	567	4
Dwight Clark, San Francisco	85	1 105	4
Dwight Clark, San Francisco	60	913	5
Roy Green, St. Louis	78	1 227	14
Charlie Brown, Washington	78	1 225	8
Earnest Gray, N.Y. Giants	78	1 139	5
Art Monk, Washington	106	1 372	7
Roger Craig, San Francisco	92	1 016	6
Jerry Rice, San Francisco	86	1 570	15
J.T. Smith, St. Louis	91	1 117	8

Scoring

Player, team	TD	PAT	FG	Pts	Year
Fred Cox, Minnesota	0	35	30	125	1970
Curt Knight, Washington	0	27	29	114	1971
Chester Marcol, Green Bay	0	29	33	128	1972
David Ray, Los Angeles	0	40	30	130	1973
Chester Marcol, Green Bay	0	19	25	94	1974
Chuck Foreman, Minnesota	22	0	0	132	1975
Mark Moseley, Washington	0	31	22	97	1976
Walter Payton, Chicago	16	0	0	96	1977
Frank Corrall, Los Angeles	0	31	29	118	1978
Mark Moseley, Washington	0	39	25	114	1979
Ed Murray, Detroit	0	35	27	116	1980
Ed Murray, Detroit	0	46	25	121	1981
Wendell Tyler, L.A. Rams	13	0	0	78	1982
Mark Moseley, Washington	0	62	33	161	1983
Ray Wersching, San Francisco	0	56	25	131	1984
Kevin Butler, Chicago	0	51	31	144	1985
Kevin Butler, Chicago	0	36	28	120	1986
Jerry Rice, San Francisco	23	0	0	138	1987

Rushing

Player, team	Yds	Atts	TD
Larry Brown, Washington	1 125	237	5
John Brockington, Green Bay	1 105	216	4
Larry Brown, Washington	1 216	285	8
John Brockington, Green Bay	1 144	265	3
Larry McCutcheon, Los Angeles	1 109	236	3
Jim Otis, St. Louis	1 076	269	5
Walter Payton, Chicago	1 390	311	13
Walter Payton, Chicago	1 852	339	14
Walter Payton, Chicago	1 395	333	11
Walter Payton, Chicago	1 610	369	14
Walter Payton, Chicago	1 460	317	15
George Rogers, New Orleans	1 674	378	13
Tony Dorsett, Dallas	745	177	5
Eric Dickerson, L.A. Rams	1 808	390	18
Eric Dickerson, L.A. Rams	2 105	379	14
Gerald Riggs, Atlanta	1 719	397	10
Eric Dickerson, L.A. Rams	1 821	404	11
Charles White, L.A. Rams	1 374	324	11

American Football Conference Leaders

Passing

Player, team	Atts	Com	YG	TD	Year
Daryle Lamonica, Oakland	356	179	2 516	22	1970
Bob Griese, Miami	263	145	2 089	19	1971
Earl Morrall, Miami	150	83	1 360	11	1972
Ken Stabler, Oakland	260	163	1 997	14	1973
Ken Anderson, Cincinnati	328	213	2 667	18	1974
Ken Anderson, Cincinnati	377	228	3 169	21	1975
Ken Stabler, Oakland	291	194	2 737	27	1976
Bob Griese, Miami	307	180	2 252	22	1977
Terry Bradshaw, Pittsburgh	368	207	2 915	28	1978
Dan Fouts, San Diego	530	332	4 082	24	1979
Brian Sipe, Cleveland	554	337	4 132	30	1980
Ken Anderson, Cincinnati	479	300	3 754	29	1981
Ken Anderson, Cincinnati	309	218	2 495	12	1982
Dan Marino, Miami	296	173	2 210	20	1983
Dan Marino, Miami	564	362	5 084	48	1984
Ken O'Brien, N.Y. Jets	488	297	3 888	25	1985
Dan Marino, Miami	623	378	4 746	44	1986
Bernie Kosar, Cleveland	389	241	3 033	22	1987

Pass-Receiving

Player, team	Ct	YG	TD	Year
Marlin Briscoe, Buffalo	57	1 036	8	1970
Fred Biletnikoff, Oakland	61	929	9	1971
Fred Biletnikoff, Oakland	58	802	7	1972
Fred Willis, Houston	57	371	1	1973
Lydell Mitchell, Baltimore	72	544	2	1974
Reggie Rucker, Cleveland	60	770	3	1975
Lydell Mitchell, Baltimore	60	554	4	
MacArthur Lane, Kansas City	66	686	1	1976
Lydell Mitchell, Baltimore	71	620	4	1977
Steve Largent, Seattle	71	1 168	8	1978
Joe Washington, Baltimore	82	750	3	1979
Kellen Winslow, San Diego	89	1 290	9	1980
Kellen Winslow, San Diego	88	1 075	10	1981
Kellen Winslow, San Diego	54	721	6	1982
Todd Christensen, L.A. Raiders	92	1 247	12	1983
Ozzie Newsome, Cleveland	89	1 001	5	1984
Lionel James, San Diego	86	1 027	6	1985
Todd Christensen, L.A. Raiders	95	1 153	8	1986
Al Toon, N.Y. Jets	68	976	5	1987

Scoring

Player, team	TD	PAT	FG	Pts	Year
Jan Stenerud, Kansas City	0	26	30	116	1970
Garo Yepremian, Miami	0	33	28	117	1971
Bobby Howfield, N.Y. Jets	0	40	27	121	1972
Roy Gerela, Pittsburgh	0	36	29	123	1973
Roy Gerela, Pittsburgh	0	33	20	93	1974
O.J. Simpson, Buffalo	23	0	0	138	1975
Toni Linhart, Baltimore.	0	49	20	109	1976
Errol Mann, Oakland.	0	39	20	99	1977
Pat Leahy, N.Y. Jets	0	41	22	107	1978
John Smith, New England.	0	46	23	115	1979
John Smith, New England.	0	51	26	129	1980
Jim Breech, Cincinnati	0	49	22	115	1981
Marcus Allen, L.A. Raiders	14	0	0	84	1982
Gary Anderson, Pittsburgh	0	38	27	119	1983
Gary Anderson, Pittsburgh	0	45	24	117	1984
Gary Anderson, Pittsburgh	0	40	33	139	1985
Tony Franklin, New England . . .	0	44	32	140	1986
Jim Breech, Cincinnati	0	25	24	97	1987

Rushing

Player, team	Yds	Atts	TD
Floyd Little, Denver	901	209	3
Floyd Little, Denver	1 133	284	6
O.J. Simpson, Buffalo	1 251	292	6
O.J. Simpson, Buffalo	2 003	332	12
Otis Armstrong, Denver	1 407	263	9
O.J. Simpson, Buffalo	1 817	329	16
O.J. Simpson, Buffalo	1 503	290	8
Mark van Eeghen, Oakland	1 273	324	7
Earl Campbell, Houston.	1 450	302	13
Earl Campbell, Houston.	1 697	368	19
Earl Campbell, Houston.	1 934	373	13
Earl Campbell, Houston.	1 376	361	10
Freeman McNeil, N.Y. Jets	786	151	6
Curt Warner, Seattle	1 446	335	13
Earnest Jackson, San Diego	1 179	296	8
Marcus Allen, L.A. Raiders	1 759	380	11
Curt Warner, Seattle	1 481	319	13
Eric Dickerson, L.A. Rams/Indianapolis	1 288	283	6

All-Time Football Records

NFL, AFL, and All-American Football Conference

(at start of 1988 season)

Leading Lifetime Scorers

Player	League	Yrs	TD	PAT	FG	Total	Player	League	Yrs	TD	PAT	FG	Total
George Blanda	NFL-AFL	26	9	943	335	2 002	Chris Bahr	NFL	12	0	424	218	1 042
Jan Stenerud	AFL-NFL	19	0	580	373	1 699	Bruce Gossett	NFL	11	0	374	219	1 031
Lou Groza	AAFC-NFL	21	1	810	264	1 608	Pat Leahy	NFL	14	0	424	218	1 078
Jim Turner	AFL-NFL	16	1	521	304	1 439	Sam Baker	NFL	15	2	428	179	977
Mark Moseley	NFL	16	0	482	300	1 382	Rafael Septien	NFL	10	0	420	180	960
Jim Bakken	NFL	17	0	534	282	1 380	Lou Michaels	NFL	13	1	386	187	955*
Fred Cox	NFL	15	0	519	282	1 365	Roy Gerela	AFL-NFL	11	0	351	184	903
Gino Cappelletti	AFL	11	42	350	176	1 130	Bobby Walston	NFL	12	46	365	80	881
Ray Wersching	NFL	15	0	456	222	1 122	Pete Gogolak	AFL-NFL	10	0	344	173	863
Don Cockroft	NFL	13	0	432	216	1 080	*Includes safety.						
Garo Yepremian	AFL-NFL	14	0	444	210	1 074							

Most Points, Season — 176, Paul Hornung, Green Bay Packers, 1960 (15 TD's, 41 PAT's, 15 FG's).
Most Points, Game — 40, Ernie Nevers, Chicago Cardinals vs. Chicago Bears, Nov. 28, 1929 (6 TD's, 4 PAT's).
Most Touchdowns, Season — 24, John Riggins, Washington Redskins, 1984 (24 rushing).
Most Touchdowns, Game — 6, Ernie Nevers, Chicago Cardinals vs. Chicago Bears, Nov. 28, 1929 (6 rushing); Dub Jones, Cleveland Browns vs. Chicago Bears, Nov. 25, 1951 (4 rushing, 2 pass receptions); Gale Sayers, Chicago Bears vs. San Francisco 49ers, Dec. 12, 1965 (4 rushing, 1 pass reception, 1 punt return).
Most Points After Touchdown, Season — 66, Uwe von Schamann, Miami Dolphins, 1984.
Most Consecutive Points After Touchdown — 234, Tommy Davis, San Francisco 49ers, 1959-1969.
Most Field Goals, Game — 7, Jim Bakken, St. Louis Cardinals vs. Pittsburgh Steelers, Sept. 24, 1967.
Most Field Goals, Season — 35, Ali Haji-Sheikh, N.Y. Giants, 1983.
Most Field Goals Attempted, Season — 49, Bruce Gossett, Los Angeles Rams, 1966; Curt Knight, Washington Redskins, 1971.
Most Field Goals Attempted, Game — 9, Jim Bakken, St. Louis Cardinals vs. Pittsburgh Steelers, Sept. 24, 1967 (7 successful).
Most Consecutive Field Goals — 23, Mark Moseley, Washington Redskins, 1981-1982.
Most Consecutive Games, Field Goal — 31, Fred Cox, Minnesota Vikings, 1968-1970.
Longest Field Goal — 63 yds., Tom Dempsey, New Orleans Saints vs. Detroit Lions, Nov. 8, 1970.
Highest Field Goal Completion Percentage, Season (20 attempts) — 95.24 Mark Moseley, Washington Redskins, 1982 (20 FG's in 21 attempts).

Leading Lifetime Receivers

Player	League	Yrs	No	Yds	Avg	Player	League	Yrs	No	Yds	Avg
Steve Largent	NFL	12	752	12 041	16.0	Wes Chandler	NFL	10	555	8 933	16.1
Charlie Joiner	NFL	18	750	12 146	16.2	Lance Alworth	AFL-NFL	11	542	10 266	18.9
Charley Taylor	NFL	13	649	9 110	14.0	Kellen Winslow	NFL	11	521	7 954	15.3
Don Maynard	AFL-NFL	15	633	11 834	18.7	John Stallworth	NFL	14	537	8 723	16.2
Raymond Berry	NFL	13	631	9 275	14.7	Bobby Mitchell	NFL	11	521	7 954	15.3
Harold Carmichael	NFL	14	590	8 985	15.2	Nat Moore	NFL	13	510	7 546	14.8
Fred Biletnikoff	AFL-NFL	14	589	8 974	15.2	Dwight Clark	NFL	9	506	6 750	13.3
Harold Jackson	NFL	16	579	10 372	17.9	Art Monk	NFL	8	504	7 033	14.0
Ozzie Newsome	NFL	10	575	7 073	12.3	Billy Howton	NFL	12	503	8 459	16.8
James Lofton	NFL	10	571	10 536	18.4						
Lionel Taylor	AFL	10	567	7 195	12.7						

Most Yards Gained, Season — 1 746, Charley Hennigan, Houston Oilers, 1961.
Most Yards Gained, Game — 309, Stephone Paige, Kansas City Chiefs vs. San Diego Chargers, Dec. 22, 1985.
Most Pass Receptions, Season — 106, Art Monk, Washington Redskins, 1984.
Most Pass Receptions, Game — 18, Tom Fears, Los Angeles Rams vs. Green Bay Packers, Dec. 3, 1950 (189 yards).
Most Consecutive Games, Pass Receptions — 152, Steve Largent, Seattle Seahawks, 1976-1987.
Most Touchdown Passes, Career — 99, Don Hutson, Green Bay Packers, 1935-1945.
Most Touchdown Passes, Season — 22, Jerry Rice, San Francisco 49ers, 1987.
Most Touchdown Passes, Game — 5, Bob Shaw, Chicago Cardinals vs. Baltimore Colts, Oct. 2, 1950; Kellen Winslow, San Diego vs. Oakland, Nov. 22, 1981.

Leading Lifetime Passers
(Minimum 1 500 attempts)

Player	League	Yrs	Att	Comp	Yds	Pts*	Player	League	Yrs	Att	Comp	Yds	Pts*
Dan Marino	NFL	5	2 494	1 512	19 422	94.1	Bart Starr	NFL	16	3 149	1 808	24 718	80.5
Joe Montana	NFL	9	3 276	2 084	24 552	92.5	Fran Tarkenton	NFL	18	6 467	3 686	47 003	80.4
Ken O'Brien	NFL	5	1 566	947	11 676	86.8	Dan Fouts	NFL	15	5 604	3 294	43 040	80.2
Otto Graham	AAFC-NFL	10	2 626	1 464	23 584	86.6	Bill Kenney	NFL	9	2 316	1 272	16 728	78.4
Dave Krieg	NFL	8	2 116	1 224	15 808	84.5	Johnny Unitas	NFL	18	5 186	2 830	40 239	78.2
Roger Staubach	NFL	11	2 958	1 685	22 700	83.4	Bert Jones	NFL	10	2 551	1 430	18 190	78.2
Sonny Jurgensen	NFL	18	4 262	2 433	32 224	82.6	Frank Ryan	NFL	13	2 133	1 090	16 042	77.6
Len Dawson	NFL-AFL	19	3 741	2 136	28 711	82.6	Joe Theismann	NFL	12	3 602	2 044	25 206	77.4
Danny White	NFL	12	2 908	1 732	21 685	82.0	Bob Griese	AFL-NFL	14	3 429	1 926	25 092	77.1
Ken Anderson	NFL	15	4 452	2 643	32 667	82.0							
Neil Lomax	NFL	7	2 710	1 562	19 376	82.0							

*Rating points based on performances in the following categories: Percentage of completions, percentage of touchdown passes, percentage of interceptions, and average gain per pass attempt.

Most Yards Gained, Season — 5 084, Dan Marino, Miami Dolphins, 1984.
Most Yards Gained, Game — 554, Norm Van Brocklin, Los Angeles Rams vs. New York Yankees, Sept. 18, 1951 (27 completions in 41 attempts).
Most Touchdowns Passing, Career — 342, Fran Tarkenton, Minnesota Vikings, 1961-66; N.Y. Giants, 1967-71; Vikings, 1972-78.
Most Touchdown Passing, Season — 48, Dan Marino, Miami Dolphins, 1984.
Most Touchdown Passing, Game — 7, Sid Luckman, Chicago Bears vs. New York Giants, Nov. 14, 1943; Adrian Burk, Philadelphia Eagles vs. Washington Redskins, Oct. 17, 1954; George Blanda, Houston Oilers vs. New York Titans, Nov. 19, 1961; Y.A. Tittle, New York Giants vs. Washington Redskins, Oct. 28, 1962; Joe Kapp, Minnesota Vikings vs. Baltimore Colts, Sept. 28, 1969.
Most Passing Attempts, Season — 623, Dan Marino, Miami Dolphins, 1986.
Most Passing Attempts, Game — 68, George Blanda, Houston Oilers vs. Buffalo Bills, Nov. 1, 1964 (37 completions).
Most Passes Completed, Season — 378, Dan Marino, Miami Dolphins, 1986.
Most Passes Completed, Game — 42, Richard Todd, N.Y. Jets vs. San Francisco 49ers, Sept. 21, 1980.
Most Consecutive Passes Completed — 22, Joe Montana, S.F. vs. Cleveland, (5), Nov. 29, & Green Bay (17), Dec. 6, 1987.
Most Consecutive Games, Touchdown Passes — 47, John Unitas, Baltimore Colts, 1956-1960.

Leading Lifetime Rushers

Player	League	Yrs	Att	Yards	Avg	Player	League	Yrs	Att	Yards	Avg
Walter Payton	NFL	13	3 838	16 726	4.4	Larry Csonka	AFL-NFL	11	1 891	8 081	4.3
Jim Brown	NFL	9	2 359	12 312	5.2	Mike Pruitt	NFL	11	1 844	7 378	4.0
Franco Harris	NFL	13	2 949	12 120	4.1	Leroy Kelly	NFL	10	1 727	7 274	4.2
Tony Dorsett	NFL	11	2 755	12 036	4.4	George Rogers	NFL	7	1 692	7 176	4.2
John Riggins	NFL	14	2 916	11 352	3.9	John Henry Johnson	NFL-AFL	13	1 571	6 803	4.3
O.J. Simpson	AFL-NFL	11	2 404	11 236	4.7	Wilbert Montgomery	NFL	9	1 540	6 789	4.4
Joe Perry	AAFC-NFL	16	1 929	9 723	5.0	Chuck Muncie	NFL	9	1 561	6 702	4.3
Earl Campbell	NFL	8	2 187	9 407	4.3	Mark van Eeghen	NFL	10	1 652	6 651	4.0
Jim Taylor	NFL	10	1 941	8 597	4.4	Lawrence McCutcheon	NFL	10	1 521	6 578	4.3
Eric Dickerson	NFL	5	1 778	8 256	4.6						
O.J. Anderson	NFL	9	1 884	8 086	4.3						

Most Yards Gained, Season — 2,105, Eric Dickerson, Los Angeles Rams, 1984.
Most Yards Gained, Game — 275, Walter Payton, Chicago Bears vs. Minnesota Vikings, Nov. 20, 1977.
Most Games, 100 Yards or more, Season — 12, Eric Dickerson, Los Angeles Rams, 1984.
Most Games, 100 Yards or more, Career — 77, Walter Payton, Chicago Bears, 1975-87.
Most Touchdowns Rushing, Career — 110, Walter Payton, Chicago Bears, 1975-1987.
Most Touchdowns Rushing, Season — 24, John Riggins, Washington Redskins, 1983.
Most Touchdowns Rushing, Game — 6, Ernie Nevers, Chicago Cardinals vs. Chicago Bears, Nov. 8, 1929.
Most Rushing Attempts, Season — 407, James Wilder, Tampa Bay Buccaneers, 1984.
Most Rushing Attempts, Game — 43, Butch Woolfolk, N.Y. Giants vs. Philadelphia, Nov. 20, 1983; James Wilder, Tampa Bay Buccaneers vs. Pittsburgh, Sept. 30, 1984.
Longest run from Scrimmage — 99 yds., Tony Dorsett, Dallas vs. Minnesota, Jan. 3, 1983 (scored touchdown).

Pass Interceptions

Most Passes Had Intercepted, Game — 8, Jim Hardy, Chicago Cardinals vs. Philadelphia Eagles, Sept. 24, 1950 (39 attempts)
Most Passes Had Intercepted, Season — 42, George Blanda, Houston Oilers, 1962 (418 attempts).
Most Passes Had Intercepted, Career — 277, George Blanda, Chicago Bears, 1949-1958; Houston Oilers, 1960-1966; Oakland Raiders, 1967-1975 (4 000 attempts).
Most Consecutive Passes Attempted Without Interception — 294, Bart Starr, Green Bay Packers, 1964-1965.
Most Interceptions By, Season — 14, Dick Lane, Los Angeles Rams, 1952.
Most Interceptions By, Career — 81, Paul Krause, Washington Redskins, 1964-67; Minnesota Vikings, 1968-79.
Most Consecutive Games, Passes Intercepted By — 8, Tom Morrow, Oakland Raiders, 1962 (4), 1963 (4).

Punting

Most Punts, Game — 15, John Teltschick, Philadelphia Eagles vs. N.Y. Giants, Dec. 6, 1987.
Most Punts, Career — 1 154, Dave Jennings, N.Y. Giants 1974-1984; N.Y. Jets, 1985-1987.
Most Punts, Season — 114, Bob Parsons, Chicago Bears, 1981.
Highest Punting Average, Season (20 punts) — 51.40, Sam Baugh, Washington Redskins, 1940 (35 punts).
Longest Punt — 98 yds., Steve O'Neal, New York Jets vs. Denver Broncos, Sept. 21, 1969.

Kickoff Returns

Most Yardage Returning Kickoffs, Career — 6 922, Ron Smith, Chicago Bears, 1965; Atlanta Falcons, 1966-67; Los Angeles Rams, 1968-69; Chicago Bears, 1970-72; San Diego Chargers, 1973; Oakland Raiders, 1974.
Most Yardage Returning Kickoffs, Season — 1 345, Buster Rhymes, Minnesota Vikings, 1985.
Most Yardage Returning Kickoffs, Game — 294, Wally Triplett, Detroit Lions vs. Los Angeles Rams, Oct. 29, 1950 (4 returns).
Most Touchdowns Scored via Kickoff Returns, Career — 6, Ollie Matson, Chicago Cardinals, 1952 (2), 1954, 1956, 1958 (2); Gale Sayers, Chicago Bears, 1965, 1966 (2), 1967 (3); Travis Williams, Green Bay Packers, 1967 (4), 1969; Los Angeles Rams, 1971.
Most Touchdowns Scored via Kickoff Returns, Season — 4, Travis Williams, Green Bay Packers, 1967; Cecil Turner, Chicago Bears, 1970.
Most Touchdowns Scored via Kickoff Returns, Game — 2, Tim Brown, Philadelphia Eagles vs. Dallas Cowboys, Nov. 6, 1966; Travis Williams, Green Bay Packers vs. Cleveland Browns, Nov. 12, 1967; Ron Brown, Los Angeles Rams vs. Green Bay Packers, Nov. 24, 1985.
Most Kickoff Returns, Career — 275, Ron Smith, Chicago Bears, 1965; Atlanta Falcons, 1966-67; Los Angeles Rams, 1968-69; Chicago Bears, 1970-72; San Diego Chargers, 1973; Oakland Raiders, 1974.
Most Kickoff Returns, Season — 60, Drew Hill, Los Angeles Rams, 1981.
Longest Kickoff Return — 106 yds., Al Carmichael, Green Bay Packers vs. Chicago Bears, October 7, 1956; Noland Smith, Kansas City vs. Denver, Dec. 17, 1967; Roy Green, St. Louis Cardinals vs. Dallas Cowboys, Oct. 21, 1979 (all scored TD).

Punt Returns

Most Yardage Returning Punts, Career — 3 291, Billy Johnson, Houston, 1974-80, Atlanta, 1982-87.
Most Yardage Returning Punts, Season — 692, Fulton Walker, Miami-L.A. Raiders, 1985.
Most Yardage Returning Punts, Game — 207, Leroy Irvin, Los Angeles Rams vs. Atlanta Falcons, Oct. 11. 1981.
Most Touchdowns Scored via Punt Returns, Career — 8, Jack Christiansen, Detroit Lions, 1951-1958; Rick Upchurch, Denver Broncos, 1975-83.
Most Punt Returns, Career — 279, Billy Johnson, Houston Oilers, 1974-1980; Atlanta Falcons, 1982-1987.
Most Punt Returns, Season — 70, Danny Reece, Tampa Bay Buccaneers, 1979.

Miscellaneous Records

Most Fumbles, Season — 17, Dan Pastorini, Houston Oilers, 1973; Warren Moon, Houston Oilers, 1984.
Most Fumbles, Game — 7, Len Dawson, Kansas City Chiefs vs. San Diego Chargers, Nov. 15, 1964.
Winning Streak (Regular Season) — 17 games, Chicago Bears, 1933-34.
Most Seasons, Active Player — 26, George Blanda, Chicago Bears, 1949-1958; Houston Oilers, 1960-1966 and Oakland, 67-75.
Most Consecutive Games Played, Career — 282, Jim Marshall, Cleveland Browns, 1960; Minnesota Vikings, 1961-1979.

First-Round Picks in the 1988 NFL Draft

Team	Player	Pos.	College	Team	Player	Pos.	College
1—Atlanta	Aundray Bruce	LB	Auburn	15—San Diego	Anthony Miller	WR	Tennessee
2—Kansas City	Neil Smith	DE	Nebraska	16—Miami	Eric Kumerow	LB	Ohio State
3—Detroit	Bennie Blades	FS	Miami	17—New England	John Stephens	RB	NW Louisiana
4—Tampa Bay	Paul Gruber	OT	Wisconsin	18—Pittsburgh	Aaron Jones	DT	E. Kentucky
5—Cincinnati	Rickey Dixon	FS	Oklahoma	19—Minnesota	Randall McDaniel	OG	Arizona State
6—L.A. Raiders	Tim Brown	WR	Notre Dame	20—L.A. Rams	Aaron Cox	WR	Arizona State
7—Green Bay	Sterling Sharpe	WR	South Carolina	21—Cleveland	Clifford Charlton	LB	Florida
8—N.Y. Jets	Dave Cadigan	OT	USC	22—Houston	Lorenzo White	RB	Michigan State
9—L.A. Raiders	Terry McDaniel	DB	Tennessee	23—Chicago	Brad Muster	RB	Stanford
10—N.Y. Giants	Eric Moore	OT	Indiana	24—New Orleans	Craig Heyward	RB	Pittsburgh
11—Dallas	Michael Irvin	WR	Miami	25—L.A. Raiders	Scott Davis	DE	Illinois
12—Phoenix	Ken Harvey	LB	California	26—Denver	Ted Gregory	NT	Syracuse
13—Philadelphia	Keith Jackson	TE	Oklahoma	27—Chicago	Wendell Davis	WR	Louisiana State
14—L.A. Rams	Gaston Green	RB	UCLA				

U.S. College Football

Rose Bowl (Pasadena)

1970 Southern Cal 10, Michigan 3
1971 Stanford 27, Ohio State 17
1972 Stanford 13, Michigan 12
1973 So. California 42, Ohio State 17
1974 Ohio State 42, So. California 21
1975 So. California 18, Ohio State 17
1976 UCLA 23, Ohio State 10
1977 So. California 14, Michigan 6
1978 Washington 27, Michigan 20
1979 So. California 17, Michigan 10
1980 So. California 17, Ohio State 16
1981 Michigan 23, Washington 6
1982 Washington 28, Iowa 0
1983 UCLA 24, Michigan 14
1984 UCLA 45, Illinois 9
1985 So. California 20, Ohio State 17
1986 UCLA 45, Iowa 28
1987 Arizona St. 22, Michigan 15
1988 Michigan St. 20, USC 17

Orange Bowl (Miami)

1970 Penn State 10, Missouri 3
1971 Nebraska 17, Louisiana St. 12
1972 Nebraska 38, Alabama 6
1973 Nebraska 40, Notre Dame 6
1974 Penn State 16, Louisiana St. 9
1975 Notre Dame 13, Alabama 11
1976 Oklahoma 14, Michigan 6
1977 Ohio State 27, Colorado 10
1978 Arkansas 31, Oklahoma 6
1979 Oklahoma 31, Nebraska 24
1980 Oklahoma 24, Florida St. 7
1981 Oklahoma 18, Florida St. 17
1982 Clemson 22, Nebraska 15
1983 Nebraska 21, Louisiana St. 20
1984 Miami (Fla.) 31, Nebraska 30
1985 Washington 28, Oklahoma 17
1986 Oklahoma 25, Penn State 10
1987 Oklahoma 42, Arkansas 8
1988 Miami (Fla.) 20, Oklahoma 14

Sugar Bowl (New Orleans)

1970 Mississippi 27, Arkansas 22
1971 Tennessee 34, Air Force 13
1972 Oklahoma 40, Auburn 22
*1972 (Dec.) Oklahoma 14, Penn State 0
1973 Notre Dame 24, Alabama 23
1974 Nebraska 13, Florida 10
1975 Alabama 13, Penn State 6
1977 (Jan.) Pittsburgh 27, Georgia 3
1978 Alabama 35, Ohio State 6
1979 Alabama 14, Penn State 7
1980 Alabama 24, Arkansas 9
1981 Georgia 17, Notre Dame 10
1982 Pittsburgh 24, Georgia 20
1983 Penn State 27, Georgia 23
1984 Auburn 9, Michigan 7
1985 Nebraska 28, Louisiana St. 10
1986 Tennessee 35, Miami (Fla.) 7
1987 Nebraska 30, Louisiana St. 15
1988 Syracuse 16, Auburn 16
*Penn St. awarded game by forfeit

Cotton Bowl (Dallas)

1970 Texas 21, Notre Dame 17
1971 Notre Dame 24, Texas 11
1972 Penn State 30, Texas 6
1973 Texas 17, Alabama 13
1974 Nebraska 19, Texas 3
1975 Penn State 41, Baylor 20
1976 Arkansas 31, Georgia 10
1977 Houston 30, Maryland 21
1978 Notre Dame 38, Texas 10
1979 Notre Dame 35, Houston 34
1980 Houston 17, Nebraska 14
1981 Alabama 30, Baylor 2
1982 Texas 14, Alabama 12
1983 SMU 7, Pittsburgh 3
1984 Georgia 10, Texas 9
1985 Boston Coll. 45, Houston 28
1986 Texas A&M 36, Auburn 16
1987 Ohio St. 28, Texas A&M 12
1988 Texas A&M 35, Notre Dame 10

Heisman Trophy Winners

Awarded annually to the outstanding U.S. college football player.

1935 Jay Berwanger, Chicago, HB
1936 Larry Kelley, Yale, E
1937 Clinton Frank, Yale, HB
1938 David O'Brien, Tex. Christian, QB
1939 Nile Kinnick, Iowa, HB
1940 Tom Harmon, Michigan, HB
1941 Bruce Smith, Minnesota, HB
1942 Frank Sinkwich, Georgia, HB
1943 Angelo Bertelli, Notre Dame, QB
1944 Leslie Horvath, Ohio State, QB
1945 Felix Blanchard, Army, FB
1946 Glenn Davis, Army, HB
1947 John Lujack, Notre Dame, QB
1948 Doak Walker, SMU, HB
1949 Leon Hart, Notre Dame, E
1950 Vic Janowicz, Ohio State, HB
1951 Richard Kazmaier, Princeton, HB
1952 Billy Vessels, Oklahoma, HB

1953 John Lattner, Notre Dame, HB
1954 Alan Ameche, Wisconsin, FB
1955 Howard Cassady, Ohio St., HB
1956 Paul Hornung, Notre Dame, QB
1957 John Crow, Texas A & M, HB
1958 Pete Dawkins, Army, HB
1959 Billy Cannon, La. State, HB
1960 Joe Bellino, Navy, HB
1961 Ernest Davis, Syracuse, HB
1962 Terry Baker, Oregon State, QB
1963 Roger Staubach, Navy, QB
1964 John Huarte, Notre Dame, QB
1965 Mike Garrett, USC, HB
1966 Steve Spurrier, Florida, QB
1967 Gary Beban, UCLA, QB
1968 O. J. Simpson, USC, RB
1969 Steve Owens, Oklahoma, RB
1970 Jim Plunkett, Stanford, QB

1971 Pat Sullivan, Auburn, QB
1972 Johnny Rodgers, Nebraska, RB-R
1973 John Cappelletti, Penn State, RB
1974 Archie Griffin, Ohio State, RB
1975 Archie Griffin, Ohio State, RB
1976 Tony Dorsett, Pittsburgh, RB
1977 Earl Campbell, Texas, RB
1978 Billy Sims, Oklahoma, RB
1979 Charles White, USC, RB
1980 George Rogers, So. Carolina, RB
1981 Marcus Allen, USC, RB
1982 Herschel Walker, Georgia, RB
1983 Mike Rozier, Nebraska, RB
1984 Doug Flutie, Boston College, QB
1985 Bo Jackson, Auburn, RB
1986 Vinny Testaverde, Miami, QB
1987 Tim Brown, Notre Dame, WR

NATIONAL BASKETBALL ASSOCIATION, 1987-88

Final Standings

Eastern Conference

Atlantic Division

Club	W	L	Pct	GB
Boston	57	25	.695	...
Washington	38	44	.463	19
New York	38	44	.463	19
Philadelphia	36	46	.439	21
New Jersey	19	63	.232	38

Central Division

Club	W	L	Pct	GB
Detroit	54	28	.659	...
Atlanta	50	32	.610	4
Chicago	50	32	.610	4
Cleveland	42	40	.512	12
Milwaukee	42	40	.512	12
Indiana	38	44	.463	16

Western Conference

Midwest Division

Club	W	L	Pct	GB
Denver	54	28	.659	...
Dallas	53	29	.646	1
Utah	47	35	.573	7
Houston	46	36	.561	8
San Antonio	31	51	.378	23
Sacramento	24	58	.293	30

Pacific Division

Club	W	L	Pct	GB
L.A. Lakers	62	20	.756	...
Portland	53	29	.646	9
Seattle	44	38	.537	18
Phoenix	28	54	.341	34
Golden State	20	62	.244	42
L.A. Clippers	17	65	.207	45

NBA Playoff Results

Eastern Division

Boston defeated New York 3 games to 1.
Detroit defeated Washington 3 games to 2.
Chicago defeated Cleveland 3 games to 2.
Atlanta defeated Milwaukee 3 games to 2.
Detroit defeated Chicago 4 games to 1.
Boston defeated Atlanta 4 games to 3.
Detroit defeated Boston 4 games to 2.

Western Division

L.A. Lakers defeated San Antonio 3 games to 0.
Dallas defeated Houston 3 games to 1.
Denver defeated Seattle 3 games to 2.
Utah defeated Portland 3 games to 1.
Dallas defeated Denver 4 games to 2.
L.A. Lakers defeated Utah 4 games to 3.
L.A. Lakers defeated Dallas 4 games to 3.

Championship

L.A. Lakers defeated Detroit 4 games to 3.

NBA Champions 1950-1988

	Regular season				Playoffs	
Year	Eastern Conference	Western Conference			Winner	Runner-up
1950	Syracuse	Minneapolis			Minneapolis	Syracuse
1951	Philadelphia	Minneapolis			Rochester	New York
1952	Syracuse	Rochester			Minneapolis	New York
1953	New York	Minneapolis			Minneapolis	New York
1954	New York	Minneapolis			Minneapolis	Syracuse
1955	Syracuse	Ft. Wayne			Syracuse	Ft. Wayne
1956	Philadelphia	Ft. Wayne			Philadelphia	Ft. Wayne
1957	Boston	St. Louis			Boston	St. Louis
1958	Boston	St. Louis			St. Louis	Boston
1959	Boston	St. Louis			Boston	Minneapolis
1960	Boston	St. Louis			Boston	St. Louis
1961	Boston	St. Louis			Boston	St. Louis
1964	Boston	Los Angeles			Boston	Los Angeles
1963	Boston	Los Angeles			Boston	Los Angeles
1964	Boston	San Francisco			Boston	San Francisco
1965	Boston	Los Angeles			Boston	Los Angeles
1966	Philadelphia	Los Angeles			Boston	Los Angeles
1967	Philadelphia	San Francisco			Philadelphia	San Francisco
1968	Philadelphia	St. Louis			Boston	Los Angeles
1969	Baltimore	Los Angeles			Boston	Los Angeles
1970	New York	Atlanta			New York	Los Angeles
	Atlantic	Central	Midwest	Pacific	Winner	Runner-up
1971	New York	Baltimore	Milwaukee	Los Angeles	Milwaukee	Baltimore
1972	Boston	Baltimore	Milwaukee	Los Angeles	Los Angeles	New York
1973	Boston	Baltimore	Milwaukee	Los Angeles	New York	Los Angeles
1974	Boston	Capital	Milwaukee	Los Angeles	Boston	Milwaukee
1975	Boston	Washington	Chicago	Golden State	Golden State	Washington
1976	Boston	Cleveland	Milwaukee	Golden State	Boston	Phoenix
1977	Philadelphia	Houston	Denver	Los Angeles	Portland	Philadelphia
1978	Philadelphia	San Antonio	Denver	Portland	Washington	Seattle
1979	Washington	San Antonio	Kansas City	Seattle	Seattle	Washington
1980	Boston	Atlanta	Milwaukee	Los Angeles	Los Angeles	Philadelphia
1981	Boston	Milwaukee	San Antonio	Phoenix	Boston	Houston
1982	Boston	Milwaukee	San Antonio	Los Angeles	Los Angeles	Philadelphia
1983	Philadelphia	Milwaukee	San Antonio	Los Angeles	Philadelphia	Los Angeles
1984	Boston	Milwaukee	Utah	Los Angeles	Boston	Los Angeles
1985	Boston	Milwaukee	Denver	L.A. Lakers	L.A. Lakers	Boston
1986	Boston	Milwaukee	Houston	L.A. Lakers	Boston	Houston
1987	Boston	Atlanta	Dallas	L.A. Lakers	L.A. Lakers	Boston
1988	Boston	Detroit	Denver	L.A. Lakers	L.A. Lakers	Detroit

MVP in Playoffs

1969	Jerry West, Los Angeles	1977	Bill Walton, Portland	1985	Kareem Abdul-Jabbar, L.A.
1970	Willis Reed, New York	1978	Wes Unseld, Washington		Lakers
1971	Lew Alcindor, Milwaukee	1979	Dennis Johnson, Seattle	1986	Larry Bird, Boston
1972	Wilt Chamberlain, Los Angeles	1980	Magic Johnson, Los Angeles	1987	Magic Johnson, L.A. Lakers
1973	Willis Reed, New York	1981	Cedric Maxwell, Boston	1988	James Worthy, L.A. Lakers
1974	John Havlicek, Boston	1982	Magic Johnson, Los Angeles		
1975	Rick Barry, Golden State	1983	Moses Malone, Philadelphia		
1976	Jo Jo White, Boston	1984	Larry Bird, Boston		

Statistical Leaders, 1987-1988

Individual Scoring

(Minimum: 70 games played or 1400 points)

	G	Pts	Avg
Jordan, Chicago	82	2868	35.0
Wilkins, Atlanta	78	2397	30.7
Bird, Boston	76	2275	29.9
Barkley, Philadelphia	80	2264	28.3
Malone, Utah	82	2268	27.7
Drexler, Portland	81	2185	27.0
Ellis, Seattle	75	1938	25.8
Aguirre, Dallas	77	1932	25.1
English, Denver	80	2000	25.0
Olajuwon, Houston	79	1805	22.8
McHale, Boston	64	1446	22.6
Scott, L.A. Lakers	81	1754	21.7
Theus, Sacramento	73	1574	21.6
McDaniel, Seattle	78	1669	21.4
Cummings, Milwaukee	76	1621	21.3
Thorpe, Sacramento	82	1704	20.8
J. Malone, Washington	80	1641	20.5
Chambers, Seattle	82	1674	20.4
M. Malone, Washington	79	1607	20.3
Ewing, New York	82	1653	20.2

Field Goal Percentage

(Minimum: 300 field goals)

	FG	FGA	Pct
McHale, Boston	550	911	.604
Parish, Boston	442	750	.589
Barkley, Philadelphia	753	1283	.587
Stockton, Utah	454	791	.574
Berry, San Antonio	540	960	.563
Rodman, Detroit	398	709	.561
Williams, New Jersey	466	832	.560
Levingston, Atlanta	314	564	.557
Ewing, New York	656	1183	.555
West, Phoenix	316	573	.551

Free Throw Percentage

(Minimum: 125 made)

	FT	FTA	Pct
Sikma, Milwaukee	321	348	.922
Bird, Boston	415	453	.916
Long, Indiana	166	183	.907
Gminski, Philadelphia	355	392	.906
Dawkins, San Antonio	198	221	.896
Davis, Phoenix	205	231	.887
Mullin, Golden State	239	270	.885
J. Malone, Washington	335	380	.882
Garland, Golden State	138	157	.879
Vandeweghe, Portland	159	181	.878

3-Pt. Field Goal Leaders

(Minimum: 25 made)

	FG	FGA	Pct
Hodges, Phoenix	86	175	.491
Price, Cleveland	72	148	.486
Long, Indiana	34	77	.442
G. Henderson, Philadelphia	69	163	.423
Tripucka, Utah	31	74	.419
Ainge, Boston	148	357	.414

Bird, Boston	98	237	.414
Tucker, New York	69	167	.413
Ellis, Seattle	107	259	.413

Assists Per Game

(Minimum: 70 games or 400 assists)

	G	No	Avg
Stockton, Utah	82	1128	13.8
Johnson, L.A. Lakers	72	858	11.9
Jackson, New York	82	868	10.6
Porter, Portland	82	831	10.1
Rivers, Atlanta	80	747	9.3
McMillan, Seattle	82	702	8.6
Thomas, Detroit	81	678	8.4
Cheeks, Philadelphia	79	635	8.0
Lever, Denver	82	639	7.8
Johnson, Boston	77	598	7.8

Rebounds

(Minimum: 70 games or 800 rebounds)

	G	Tot	Avg
Cage, L.A. Clippers	72	938	13.03
Oakley, Chicago	82	1066	13.00
Olajuwon, Houston	79	959	12.1
Malone, Utah	82	986	12.0
Williams, New Jersey	70	834	11.9
Barkley, Philadelphia	80	951	11.9
Tarpley, Dallas	81	959	11.8
M. Malone, Washington	79	884	11.2
Thorpe, Sacramento	82	837	10.2
Laimbeer, Detroit	82	832	10.1

Steals Per Game

(Minimum: 70 games or 125 steals)

	G	No	Avg
Jordan, Chicago	82	259	3.16
Robertson, San Antonio	82	243	2.96
Stockton, Utah	82	242	2.95
Lever, Denver	82	223	2.72
Drexler, Portland	81	203	2.51
Jackson, New York	82	205	2.50
Cheeks, Philadelphia	79	167	2.11
McMillan, Seattle	82	169	2.06
Olajuwon, Houston	79	162	2.05

Blocked Shots Per Game

(Minimum: 70 games or 100 blocked shots)

	G	No	Avg
Eaton, Utah	82	304	3.71
Benjamin, L.A. Clippers	66	225	3.41
Ewing, New York	82	245	2.99
Olajuwon, Houston	79	214	2.71
Bol, Washington	77	208	2.70
Nance, Cleveland	67	159	2.37
Oldham, Sacramento	54	110	2.04
Williams, Indiana	75	146	1.95
Williams, Cleveland	77	145	1.88
Hinson, New Jersey	77	140	1.82

All-Time NBA Statistical Leaders

(at the start of the 1987-88 season unless otherwise noted)

Scoring Average
(400 games or 10 000 Points Minimum)

	G	Pts.	Avg
Wilt Chamberlain	1 045	31 419	30.1
Elgin Baylor	846	23 149	27.4
Jerry West	932	25 192	27.0
Bob Pettit	792	20 880	26.4
George Gervin	791	20 708	26.2
*Dominique Wilkins	479	12 458	26.0
Oscar Robertson	1 040	26 710	25.7
*Adrian Dantley	827	21 058	25.4
*Kareem Abdul-Jabbar	1 408	37 639	25.3
*Larry Bird	711	17 783	25.0

Field Goal Percentage
(2 000 FGM Minimum)

	FGA	FGM	Pct.
Artis Gillmore	9 389	5 633	.600
Steve Johnson	3 757	2 205	.587
Darryl Dawkins	6 051	3 466	.573
James Worthy	5 021	2 832	.564
Larry Nance	5 486	3 098	.564
Jeff Ruland	3 685	2 080	.564
Kevin McHale	6 836	3 846	.563
Kareem Abdul-Jabbar	26 745	15 044	.562
Bill Cartwright	5 277	2 920	.553
Buck Williams	5 700	3 142	.551

Free Throw Percentage
(1 200 FTM Minimum)

	FTA	FTM	Pct.
Rick Barry	4 243	3 818	.900
*Larry Bird	3 726	3 348	.898
Calvin Murphy	3 864	3 445	.892
Bill Sharman	3 357	3 143	.884
Mike Newlin	3 456	3 005	.870
*Kiki Vandeweghe	2 823	2 455	.869
Fred Brown	2 211	1 869	.858
*John Long	1 920	1 649	.854
Larry Siegfried	1 945	1 662	.854
James Silas	1 690	1 440	.852

Points

	Pts.
*Kareem Abdul-Jabbar	37 639
Wilt Chamberlain	31 419
Elvin Hayes	27 313
Oscar Robertson	26 710
John Havlicek	26 395
Jerry West	25 192
Elgin Baylor	23 149
*Moses Malone	21 703
Hal Greer	21 586
*Alex English	21 242

Games Played

*Kareem Abdul-Jabbar	1 486
Elvin Hayes	1 303
John Havlicek	1 270
Paul Silas	1 254
Hal Greer	1 122
Len Wilkens	1 077
Dolph Schayes	1 059
Johnny Green	1 057
Don Nelson	1 053
Leroy Ellis	1 048

Assists

Oscar Robertson	9 887
Len Wilkens	7 211
*Magic Johnson	7 037
Bob Cousy	6 955
Guy Rodgers	6 917
Nate Archibald	6 476
Jerry West	6 238
John Havlicek	6 114
Norm Nixon	6 047
*John Lucas	5 956

Field Goals Made

*Kareem Abdul-Jabbar	15 524
Wilt Chamberlain	12 681
Elvin Hayes	10 976
John Havlicek	10 513
Oscar Robertson	9 508
Jerry West	9 016
*Alex English	8 778
Elgin Baylor	8 693
Hal Greer	8 504
George Gervin	8 045

Rebounds

Wilt Chamberlain	23 924
Bill Russell	21 620
*Kareem Abdul-Jabbar	17 106
Elvin Hayes	16 279
Nate Thurmond	14 464
Walt Bellamy	14 241
Wes Unseld	13 769
Jerry Lucas	12 942
Bob Pettit	12 849
Paul Silas	12 357

*Includes 1987-88 season.

NBA Scoring Leaders

Year	Scoring champion	Pts	Avg	Year	Scoring champion	Pts	Avg
1960	Wilt Chamberlain, Philadelphia	2 707	37.9	1975	Bob McAdoo, Buffalo	2 831	34.5
1961	Wilt Chamberlain, Philadelphia	3 033	38.4	1976	Bob McAdoo, Buffalo	2 427	31.1
1962	Wilt Chamberlain, Philadelphia	4 029	50.4	1977	Pete Maravich, New Orleans	2 273	31.1
1963	Wilt Chamberlain, San Francisco	3 586	44.8	1978	George Gervin, San Antonio	2 232	27.2
1964	Wilt Chamberlain, San Francisco	2 948	36.5	1979	George Gervin, San Antonio	2 365	29.6
1965	Wilt Chamberlain, San Fran., Phila.	2 534	34.7	1980	George Gervin, San Antonio	2 585	33.1
1966	Wilt Chamberlain, Philadelphia	2 649	33.5	1981	Adrian Dantley, Utah	2 452	30.7
1967	Rick Barry, San Francisco	2 775	35.6	1982	George Gervin, San Antonio	2 551	32.3
1968	Dave Bing, Detroit	2 142	27.1	1983	Alex English, Denver	2 326	28.4
1969	Elvin Hayes, San Diego	2 327	28.4	1984	Adrian Dantley, Utah	2 418	30.6
1970	Jerry West, Los Angeles	2 309	31.2	1985	Bernard King, New York	1 809	32.9
1971	Lew Alcindor, Milwaukee	2 596	31.7	1986	Dominique Wilkins, Atlanta	2 366	30.3
1972	Kareem Abdul-Jabbar (Alcindor), Milwaukee	2 822	34.8	1987	Michael Jordan, Chicago	3 041	37.1
1973	Nate Archibald, Kansas City-Omaha	2 719	34.0	1988	Michael Jordan, Chicago	2 868	35.0
1974	Bob McAdoo, Buffalo	2 261	30.6				

NBA Most Valuable Player

1956	Bob Pettit, St. Louis	1973	Dave Cowens, Boston
1957	Bob Cousy, Boston	1974	Kareem Abdul-Jabbar, Milwaukee
1958	Bill Russell, Boston	1975	Bob McAdoo, Buffalo
1959	Bob Pettit, St. Louis	1976	Kareem Abdul-Jabbar, Los Angeles
1960	Wilt Chamberlain, Philadelphia	1977	Kareem Abdul-Jabbar, Los Angeles
1961	Bill Russell, Boston	1978	Bill Walton, Portland
1962	Bill Russell, Boston	1979	Moses Malone, Houston
1963	Bill Russell, Boston	1980	Kareem Abdul-Jabbar, Los Angeles
1964	Oscar Robertson, Cincinnati	1981	Julius Erving, Philadelphia
1965	Bill Russell, Boston	1982	Moses Malone, Houston
1966	Wilt Chamberlain, Philadelphia	1983	Moses Malone, Philadelphia
1967	Wilt Chamberlain, Philadelphia	1984	Larry Bird, Boston
1968	Wilt Chamberlain, Philadelphia	1985	Larry Bird, Boston
1969	Wes Unseld, Baltimore	1986	Larry Bird, Boston
1970	Willis Reed, New York	1987	Magic Johnson, L.A. Lakers
1971	Lew Alcindor, Milwaukee	1988	Michael Jordan, Chicago
1972	Kareem Abdul-Jabbar (Alcindor), Milwaukee		

NBA Rookie of the Year

1970	Lew Alcindor, Milwaukee	1980	Larry Bird, Boston
1971	Dave Cowens, Boston;	1981	Darrell Griffith, Utah
	Geoff Petrie, Portland (tie)	1982	Buck Williams, New Jersey
1972	Sidney Wicks, Portland	1983	Terry Cummings, San Diego
1973	Bob McAdoo, Buffalo	1984	Ralph Sampson, Houston
1974	Ernie DiGregorio, Buffalo	1985	Michael Jordan, Chicago
1975	Keith Wilkes, Golden State	1986	Patrick Ewing, New York
1976	Alvan Adams, Phoenix	1987	Chuck Person, Indiana
1977	Adrian Dantley, Buffalo	1988	Mark Jackson, New York
1978	Walter Davis, Phoenix		
1979	Phil Ford, Kansas City		

NBA All League Team in 1988

First team	Position	Second team
Larry Bird, Boston	Forward	Karl Malone, Utah
Charles Barkley, Philadelphia	Forward	Dominique Wilkins, Atlanta
Akeem Olajuwon, Houston	Centre	Patrick Ewing, New York
Magic Johnson, L.A. Lakers	Guard	John Stockton, Utah
Michael Jordan, Chicago	Guard	Clyde Drexler, Portland

NBA All-Defensive Team in 1988

First team	Position	Second team
Rodney McCray, Houston	Forward	Buck Williams, New Jersey
Kevin McHale, Boston	Forward	Karl Malone, Utah
Akeem Olajuwon, Houston	Centre	Mark Eaton, Utah
		Patrick Ewing, New York
Michael Jordan, Chicago	Guard	Alvin Robertson, San Antonio
Michael Cooper, L.A. Lakers	Guard	Lafayette Lever, Denver

1988 NBA Player Draft

The following are the first round picks of the National Basketball Assn.

L.A Clippers—Danny Manning, Kansas
Indiana—Rik Smits, Marist
Philadelphia—Charles Smith, Pittsburgh
New Jersey—Chris Morris, Auburn
Golden State—Mitch Richmond, Kansas St.
L.A. Clippers—Hersey Hawkins, Bradley
Phoenix—Tim Perry, Temple
Charlotte—Rex Chapman, Kentucky
Miami—Rony Seikaly, Syracuse
San Antonio—Willie Anderson, Georgia
Chicago—Will Purdue, Vanderbilt
Washington—Harvey Grant, Oklahoma
Milwaukee—Jeff Grayer, Iowa St.

Phoenix—Dan Majerle, Central Michigan
Seattle—Gary Grant, Michigan
Houston—Derrick Chievous, Missouri
Utah—Eric Leckner, Wyoming
Sacramento—Ricky Berry, San Jose
New York—Rod Strickland, DePaul
Miami—Kevin Edwards, DePaul
Portland—Mark Bryant, Seton Hall
Cleveland—Randolph Keys, S. Mississippi
Denver—Jerome Lane, Pittsburgh
Boston—Brian Shaw, Cal-Santa Barbara
L.A. Lakers—David Rivers, Notre Dame

NCAA Division I Champions

Year	Champion	Coach	Final opponent	Score	MVP	Site
1970	UCLA	John Wooden	Jacksonville	80-69	Sidney Wicks, UCLA	College Park, Md.
1971	UCLA	John Wooden	Villanova[1]	68-62	Howard Porter, Villanova[1]	Houston, Tex.
1972	UCLA	John Wooden	Florida St.	81-76	Bill Walton, UCLA	Los Angeles, Cal.
1973	UCLA	John Wooden	Memphis St.	87-66	Bill Walton, UCLA	St. Louis, Mo.
1974	N. Carolina St.	Norm Sloan	Marquette	76-64	David Thompson, N.C. St.	Greensboro, N.C.
1975	UCLA	John Wooden	Kentucky	92-85	Richard Washington, UCLA	San Diego, Cal.
1976	Indiana	Bob Knight	Michigan	86-68	Kent Benson, Indiana	Philadelphia, Pa.
1977	Marquette	Al McGuire	N. Carolina	67-59	Butch Lee, Marquette	Atlanta, Ga.
1978	Kentucky	Joe Hall	Duke	94-88	Jack Givens, Kentucky	St. Louis, Mo.
1979	Michigan St.	Jud Heathcote	Indiana St.	75-64	Magic Johnson, Michigan St.	Salt Lake City, Ut.
1980	Louisville	Denny Crum	UCLA[1]	59-54	Darrell Griffith, Louisville	Indianapolis, Ind.
1981	Indiana	Bob Knight	N. Carolina	63-50	Isiah Thomas, Indiana	Philadelphia, Pa.
1982	N. Carolina	Dean Smith	Georgetown	63-62	James Worthy, No. Carolina	New Orleans, La.
1983	N. Carolina St.	Jim Valvano	Houston	54-52	Akeem Olajuwon, Houston	Albuquerque, N.M.
1984	Georgetown	John Thompson	Houston	84-75	Patrick Ewing, Georgetown	Seattle, Wash.
1985	Villanova	Rollie Massimino	Georgetown	66-64	Ed Pinckney, Villanova	Lexington, Ky.
1986	Louisville	Denny Crum	Duke	72-69	Pervis Ellison, Louisville	Dallas, Tex.
1987	Indiana	Bob Knight	Syracuse	74-73	Keith Smart, Indiana	New Orleans, La.
1988	Kansas	Larry Brown	Oklahoma	83-79	Danny Manning, Kansas	Kansas City, Mo.

(1) Declared ineligible subsequent to the tournament.

Horse Racing

Canada's Triple Crown

Canada's Triple Crown series – the Queen's Plate, the Prince of Wales Stakes and the Breeders Stakes – was inaugurated in 1959. The Queen's Plate is run on a dirt track at a distance of one mile and a quarter; the other 2 races are one mile and a half on turf. The 3-sided gold trophy that goes with the Triple Crown has been won only twice: by New Providence in 1959 and by Canebora in 1963.

The Queen's Plate, 1915–1988
Source: The Ontario Jockey Club

The Queen's Plate, first run in 1860, is North America's oldest annual sports event. The race for 3-year-olds foaled in Canada, is run at Toronto's Woodbine Race Track in late June or July.

Year	Winner	Jockey	Trainer	Second	Time[1]	Odds[2]
1915	Tartarean	Harry Watts	John Nixon	Fair Montague	2:09.1	3.80
1916	Mandarin	Arthur Pickens	Barry T. Littlefield	Gala Water	2:12	.20
1917	Belle Mahone	Frank Robinson	Barry T. Littlefield	Tarahera	2:08.4	.40
1918	Springside	Lee Mink	Ed Whyte	Ladder of Light	2:08.4	1.00
1919	Ladder of Light	Larry Lyke	Joe Doane	Doleful	2:09.2	2.50
1920	St. Paul	Roxy Romanelli	Harry Giddings Jr.	Bugle March	2:09	1.70
1921	Herendesy	Jimmy Burton	George Walker	Royal Visitor	2:10	.87
1922	South Shore	Kenny Parrington	Fred Schelke	Paddle	2:12	2.37
1923	Flowerful	Terry Wilson	William H. Bringloe	Cheechako	2:11	9.50
1924	Maternal Pride	George Walls	William G. Wilson	Thorndyke	1:57.3	95.67
1925	Fairbank	Chick Lang	Jack Givens	Duchess	1:56.2	4.87
1926	Haplite	Henry Erickson	William H. Bringloe	Attack	1:59.3	.65
1927	Troutlet	Francis Horn	John Nixon	Mr. Gaiety	1:55.4	2.80
1928	Young Kitty	Lester Pichon	William H. Bringloe	Bonnington	1:57	.50
1929	Shorelint	Jaydee Mooney	Fred Schelke	Ichitaro	1:57.3	13.15
1930	Aymond	Henry Little	Jack Hutton	Whale Oil	1:57.1	14.10
1931	Froth Blower	Frank Mann	Harry Giddings Jr.	Bronze	1:59.1	1.62
1932	Queensway	Frank Mann	Harry Giddings Jr.	King O'Connor	1:55.1	3.00
1933	King O'Connor	Eddie Legere	William H. Bringloe	Easter Hatter	1:56.2	2.75
1934	Horometer	Frank Mann	Harry Giddings Jr.	Speyhold	1:54.1	.05
1935	Sally Fuller	Herb Lindberg	Johnny Thorpe	Chickpen	1:55.1	4.07
1936	Monsweep	Danny Brammer	William H. Bringloe	Stormblown	1:55	3.07
1937	Goldlure	Sterling Young	William H. Bringloe	Cease Fire	1:55.2	4.27
1938	Bunty Lawless	John Bailey	Jack Anderson	Mona Bell	1:54.2	2.97
1939	Archworth	Sydney D. Birley	Mark Cowell	Sea General	1:54.2	1.70
1940	Willie the Kid	Ronnie Nash	Pete McCann	Curwen	1:55.4	3.35
1941	Budpath	Bobby Watson	Lloyd Gentry	Undisturbed	1:56.4	3.25
1942	Ten to Ace	Charlie Smith	Harry Giddings Jr.	Cossack Post	1:57.4	.27
1943	Paolita	Pat Remillard	Willie Thurner	Arbor Vita	2:02.3	37.25
1944	Acara	Bobby Watson	Cecil Howard	Ompalo	1:54.4	2.42
1945	Uttermost	Bobby Watson	Cecil Howard	Tarian	1:53.4	.55
1946	Kingarvie	Johnny Dewhurst	Arthur Brent	David T.	1:55.3	.50
1947	Moldy	Colin McDonald	Arthur Brent	Burboy	1:54.1	17.25
1948	Last Mark	Howard Bailey	James G. Fair	Lord Fairmond	1:52	2.52
1949	Epic	Chris Rogers	Bert Alexandra	Speedy Irish	1:52.1	1.40
1950	McGill	Chris Rogers	Pete Keiser	Sir Strome	1:52.2	2.10
1951	Major Factor	Alf Bavington	Pete McCann	Libertine	1:53	3.15
1952	Epigram	Gil Robillard	Rip Bowden	Genthorn	1:58.3	11.52
1953	Canadiana	Eddie Arcaro	Pete McCann	Blue Scooter	1:52.1	.60
1954	Collisteo	Chris Rogers	Dick Townrow	Queen's Own	1:52	11.10
1955	Ace Marine	George Walker	Yonnie Starr	Baffin Bay	1:52.2	5.60
1956	Canadian Champ	Dave Stevenson	John Passero	Argent	1:55	.30
1957	Lyford Cay	Avelino Gomez	Pete McCann	Chopadette	2:02.3	.55
1958	Calendon Beau	Al Coy	Yonnie Starr	White Apache	2:04.1	2.90
1959	New Providence	Robert Ussery	Pete McCann	Major Flight	2:04.4	6.55
1960	Victoria Park	Avelino Gomez	Horatio A. Luro	Quintain	2:02	.05
1961	Blue Light	Hugo Dittfach	Patrick MacMurchy	Just Don't Shove	2:05	18.75
1962	Flaming Page	Jim Fitzsimmons	Horatio A. Luro	Choperion	2:04.3	1.10
1963	Canebora	Manuel Ycaza	Pete McCann	Son Blue	2:04	3.20
1964	Northern Dancer	Bill Hartack	Horatio Luro	Langcrest	2:02.1	.15
1965	Whistling Sea	Tak Inouye	Roy Johnson	Flyalong	2:03.4	7.20
1966	Titled Hero	Avelino Gomez	Patrick MacMurchy	Bye and Near	2:03.3	.25
1967	Jammed Lovely	Jim Fitzsimmons	Yonnie Starr	Pine Point	2:03	11.45
1968	Merger	Wayne Harris	Roy Johnson	Big Blunder	2:05.2	3.20
1969	Jumpin Joseph	Avelino Gomez	Bobby Bateman	Fanfaron	2:04.1	1.05
1970	Almoner	Sandy Hawley	Jerry Lavigne	Fanfreluche	2:04.4	2.85
1971	Kennedy Road	Sandy Hawley	James C. Bentley	Fabe Count	2:03	.45
1972	Victoria Song	Robin Platts	Larry Grant	Barachois	2:03.1	6.30
1973	Royal Chocolate	Ted Colangelo	Gil Rowntree	Sinister Purpose	2:08	23.05
1974	Amber Herod	Robin Platts	Gil Rowntree	Native Aid	2:09.1	9.75
1975	L'Enjoleur	Sandy Hawley	Yonnie Starr	Near the High Sea	2:02.3	1.15

Year	Winner	Jockey	Trainer	Second	Time[1]	Odds[2]
1976	Norcliffe	Jeffrey Fell	Roger Attfield	Military Bearing	2:05	1.60
1977	Sound Reason	Robin Platts	Gil Rowntree	Northernette	2:06.3	1.55
1978	Regal Embrace	Sandy Hawley	Mac Benson	Overskate	2:02	2.55
1979	Steady Growth	Brian Swatuk	John Tammaro	Bold Regent	2:06.3	1.65
1980	Driving Home	Bill Parsons	Glenn Magnusson	Someolio Man	2:04.1	20.95
1981	Fiddle Dancer Boy	David Clark	James C. Bentley	Wayover	2:04.4	8.45
1982	Son of Briartic	John-Paul Souter	J.C. Lavigne	Runaway Groom	2:04.3	8.75
1983	Bompago	Larry Attard	John Cardella	Sir Khaled	2:04.1	2.45
1984	Key to the Moon	Robin Platts	Gil H. Rowntree	Let's Go Blue	2:03.4	2.90
1985	La Lorgnette	David Clark	Macdonald Benson	Imperial Choice	2:04.3	3.80
1986	Golden Choice	Vince Bracciale	Mike Tammaro	Cool Halo	2:07.1	11.60
1987	Market Control	Ken Skinner	Roger Attfield	Afleet	2:03.2	9.30
1988	Regal Intention	Jack Lauzon	Jim Day	Regal Classic	2:06.1	.55

(1) Fractions of a second are in fifths. (2) Amount of winnings for each $1 wagered to win.

Prince of Wales Stakes

Year	Winner	Jockey	Time[1]	Year	Winner	Jockey	Time[1]
1959	New Providence	Avelino Gomez	2:18	1974	Rushton's Corsair	Jim Kelly	2:23.2
1960	Bulpamiru	Hugo Dittfach	2:19.4	1975	L'Enjoleur	Sandy Hawley	2:32.2
1961	Song of Even	Jim Fitzsimmons	2:29	1976	Norcliffe	Jeff Fell	2:30.1
1962	King Gorm	Hugo Dittfach	2:21.1	1977	Dance in Time	Gary Stahlbaum	2:31.4
1963	Canebora	Hugo Dittfach	2:30.3	1978	Overskate	Robin Platts	2:34.2
1964	Canadillis	Avelino Gomez	2:35	1979	Mass Rally	George Ho Sang	2:33.2
1965	Good Old Mort	S. McComb	2:22.4	1980	Allan Blue	Joe Belowus	2:34.4
1966	He's A Smoothie	Hugo Dittfach	2:19	1981	Cadet Corps	Robin Platts	2:34.4
1967	Battling	Hugo Dittfach	2:21.1	1982	Runaway Groom	Robin Platts	2:38.2
1968	Rouletabille	Richard Grubb	2:18.3	1983	Archdeacon	Vince Bracciale	2:32
1969	Sharp-Eyed Quillo	H. Gustines	2:16.3	1984	Val Dansant	John LeBlanc	2:48.3
1970	Almoner	Sandy Hawley	2:19.4	1985	Imperial Choice	Irwin Driedger	2:34.3
1971	New Pro	Jim Kelly	2:15.1	1986	Golden Choice	Vince Bracciale	2:44.2
1972	Presidial	John LeBlanc	2:16.3	1987	Coryphee	Brian Swatuk	2:39.3
1973	Tara Road	Sandy Hawley	2:16.4	1988	Regal Classic	Sandy Hawley	2:00.1[2]

(1) Fractions of a second are in fifths. (2) In 1988 the race was changed to 1 3/16 miles on dirt from 1 1/2 miles on turf.

Breeders Stakes

Year	Winner	Jockey	Time[1]	Year	Winner	Jockey	Time[1]
1959	New Providence	Avelino Gomez	2:39.4	1974	Haymaker's Jig	Robin Platts	2:30.4
1960	Hidden Treasure	Al Coy	2:34.2	1975	Momigi	Gary Melanson	2:38.1
1961	Song of Even	Jim Fitzsimmons	2:31.3	1976	Tiny Tinker	Sandy Hawley	2:31.1
1962	Crafty Lace	Ron Turcotte	2:52	1977	Dance in Time	Gary Stahlbaum	3:01.3
1963	Canebora	Manuel Ycaza	2:32.1	1978	Overskate	Robin Platts	2:29.2
1964	Artic Hills	R. Armstrong	2:33.3	1979	Bridle Path	Sandy Hawley	2:29.3
1965	Good Old Mort	P. Kallai	2:43	1980	Ben Fab	Gary Stahlbaum	2:31.3
1966	Titled Hero	Avelino Gomez	2:31.2	1981	Social Wizard	George Ho Sang	2:48.4
1967	Pine Point	Avelino Gomez	2:32.1	1982	Runaway Groom	Robin Platts	2:32.1
1968	No Parando	John LeBlanc	2:30	1983	Kingsbridge	Robin Platts	2:32.2
1969	Grey Whiz	John LeBlanc	2:29	1984	Bounding Away	David Clark	2:32.3
1970	Mary of Scotland	Richard Grubb	2:38.2	1985	Crowning Honors	Brian Swatuk	2:50
1971	Belle Geste	Noel Turcotte	2:28	1986	Carotene	Richard Dos Ramos	2:32.3
1972	Nice Dancer	Sandy Hawley	2:35.4	1987	Hangin On a Star	Dave Penna	2:30
1973	Come In Dad	Wayne Green	2:33.3	1988	King's Deputy	Sandy Hawley	2:30.3

(1) Fractions of a second are in fifths.

Leading Jockeys in Canada, 1973–1987

Source: Daily Racing Form of Canada

(by money won)

Year	Jockey	Mounts	1st	Win %	2d	3d	Earnings
1973	Sandy Hawley	1 370	379	27.7	248	204	n.a.
1974	Sandy Hawley	1 004	297	29.6	192	115	$1 497 891
1975	Jeff Fell	1 220	272	22.3	217	117	1 490 508
1976	Jeff Fell	1 204	255	21.2	194	143	1 709 797
1977	Gary Stahlbaum	1 180	191	17.2	169	145	1 294 763
1978	Sandy Hawley	1 087	314	28.9	209	139	1 981 614
1979	George HoSang	854	159	18.6	115	108	1 167 115
1980	Gary Stahlbaum	901	173	19.2	162	116	1 558 911
1981	Gary Stahlbaum	826	148	17.9	145	101	1 447 055
1982	Gary Stahlbaum	856	152	17.8	111	106	1 820 055
1983	Robin Platts	802	141	17.6	123	97	2 593 620
1984	Gary Stahlbaum	903	139	15.4	131	131	2 252 409
1985	Irwin Driedger	963	125	13.0	127	116	2 517 690
1986	Larry Attard	1 128	171	15.1	156	150	2 526 339
1987	Dave Penna	504	84	16.7	70	80	2 507 574

n.a. not available.

Queen's Plate Chart

EIGHTH RACE
Woodbine
JULY 10, 1988

1 ¼ MILES. (2.01⅕) 129th Running QUEENS PLATE (Grade I–C). Purse $225,000 Added. 3–year–olds foaled in Canada. (Closed). Scale Weight: Colts and geldings 126 lbs. Fillies, 121 lbs. By subscription of $35 each to accompany the nomination by December 15, 1986 (597 nominated); second subscription of $100 by December 15, 1987 (284 remained eligible); third subscription of $200 by May 1, 1988 (126 remained eligible); and an additional $3,000 when making final entry two days prior to the race. In order to remain eligible each subcription or payment must be paid on or before due date. The owner of the first horse receives the Guineas. The added money and all fees to be divided; 60% to the winner, 20% to second, 11% to third, 6% to fourth and 3% to fifth. Final entries to be made through the entry box on a date and time to be determined by the Racing Secretary.
Value of race $332,495; value to winner $199,497; second $66,499; third $36,574; fourth $19,950; fifth $9,975. Mutuel pool $665,948. Exactor Pool $348,071.

Last Raced	Horse	Eqt.	A.	Wt	PP	¼	½	¾	1	Str	Fin	Jockey	Odds $1
2Jly88 ^{8}WO^{1}	Regal Intention		3	126	6	2^{1}	2^{3}	2^{1}	$1^{2\frac{1}{2}}$	$1^{3\frac{1}{2}}$	$1^{3\frac{1}{4}}$	Lauzon J M	a-.55
26Jun88 ^{7}WO^{1}	Regal Classic		3	126	3	4^{1}	3^{hd}	4^{hd}	$3^{1\frac{1}{2}}$	2^{2}	$2^{2\frac{1}{2}}$	Hawley S	a-.55
26Jun88 ^{7}WO^{2}	Granacus		3	126	8	$8^{\frac{1}{2}}$	8^{hd}	7^{2}	$4^{1\frac{1}{2}}$	3^{4}	$3^{1\frac{1}{4}}$	Vasquez J	2.40
29Jun88 ^{8}WO^{1}	Grey Skelly		3	121	1	$10^{1\frac{1}{2}}$	$10^{\frac{1}{2}}$	$10^{\frac{1}{2}}$	$8^{2\frac{1}{2}}$	$5^{1\frac{1}{2}}$	4^{nk}	Swatuk B	38.00
26Jun88 ^{7}WO^{4}	No Malice		3	126	10	$3^{1\frac{1}{2}}$	$4^{\frac{1}{2}}$	$6^{1\frac{1}{2}}$	$5^{\frac{1}{2}}$	4^{hd}	5^{nk}	Krone J A	36.10
26Jun88 ^{7}WO^{3}	Tejabo		3	126	9	9^{3}	9^{7}	$8^{1\frac{1}{2}}$	9^{3}	$7^{4\frac{1}{2}}$	$6^{3\frac{1}{2}}$	Clark D	b-11.95
2Jly88 ^{8}WO^{3}	Sweeping Change	b	3	126	2	6^{hd}	5^{hd}	$5^{\frac{1}{2}}$	$6^{1\frac{1}{2}}$	6^{3}	7^{4}	Seymour D J	34.30
2Jly88 ^{8}WO^{2}	Rather Theatrical	b	3	126	5	11	11	11	11	9^{3}	8^{4}	Penna D	b-11.95
26Jun88 ^{7}WO^{5}	Lucky J. W.		3	126	4	$7^{\frac{1}{2}}$	7^{hd}	$9^{4\frac{1}{2}}$	$10^{\frac{1}{2}}$	11	$9^{\frac{1}{2}}$	Ravera P P	108.80
26Jun88 ^{7}WO^{7}	Plate Dancer	b	3	126	11	$5^{\frac{1}{2}}$	$6^{3\frac{1}{2}}$	$3^{\frac{1}{2}}$	7^{hd}	10^{hd}	10^{nk}	Ward W	97.05
9Jun88 ^{7}WO^{1}	Baldski's Prize		3	126	7	$1^{2\frac{1}{2}}$	1^{5}	$1^{1\frac{1}{2}}$	2^{hd}	$8^{\frac{1}{2}}$	11	Platts R	9.85

a–Coupled: Regal Intention and Regal Classic; b–Tejabo and Rather Theatrical.
OFF AT 5:13 Start good, Won handily. Time, :24, :48, 1:13⅖, 1:39, 2:06⅕ Track fast.

$2 Mutuel Prices:			
1–REGAL INTENTION (a–entry)	3.10	3.00	2.10
1–REGAL CLASSIC (a–entry)	3.10	3.00	2.10
7–GRANACUS			2.50

$2 EXACTOR 1–1 PAID $12.80.

Dk. b. or br. c, by Vice Regent—Tiffany Tam, by Tentam. Trainer Day James E. Bred by Sam–Son Farms (Ont–C).

REGAL INTENTION was well placed early in behind the early leader, was outrun around the clubhouse turn, moved up on the leader approaching the far turn, took command around the turn to open up, had a clear advantage in midstretch and retained it with authority. REGAL CLASSIC was unhurried early when between rivals, advanced around the far turn, was just outside into the home lane then closed evenly off the rail. GRANACUS was well back early, lodged his bid around the final turn but never threatening in the run for the wire. GREY SKELLY was far back early then finished with determination. NO MALICE showed little. SWEEPING CHANGE was within striking distance around the far turn but could not menace. BALDSKI'S PRIZE moved quickly to the fore, set the early pace then tired badly.

Owners— 1, Sam-Son Farm; 2, Sam-Son Fm & Windfields Fm; 3, Knob Hill Stable ; 4, Kellier E; 5, Marcello R; 6, Kepburn Stables; 7, Kinghaven Farms; 8, Burnett M; 9, Good M & W L; 10, Irish Acres Farm; 11, Huntington Stud Farm.

Trainers— 1, Day James E; 2, Day James E; 3, Collins Patrick J; 4, Kovatsh A; 5, Marko Bill; 6, Mattine M; 7, Attfield Roger; 8, Mattine M; 9, Dwyer David; 10, Hickey P Noel; 11, O'Callaghan Daniel M.

©Copyright Daily Racing Form of Canada Ltd.
Reproduced with permission of copyright owner.

Kentucky Derby

Churchill Downs, Louisville, Ky.; inaugurated 1875; distance 1¼ miles; 1½ miles until 1896. 3-year olds.

The Kentucky Derby has been won five times by two jockeys, Eddie Arcaro, 1938, 1941, 1945, 1948 and 1952; and Bill Hartack, 1957, 1960, 1962, 1964 and 1969; four times by Willie Shoemaker, 1955, 1959, 1965, and 1986; and three times by each of three jockeys, Isaac Murphy, 1884, 1890, and 1891; Earle Sande, 1923, 1925 and 1930, and Angel Cordero in 1974, 1976 and 1985.

Year	Winner	Jockey	Trainer	Wt.[1]	Second	Winner's share[2]	Time[3]
1920	Paul Jones	T. Rice	W. Garth	126	Upset	30 375	2:09.
1921	Behave Yourself	C. Thompson	H. J. Thompson	126	Black Servant	38 450	2:04.1
1922	Morvich	A. Johnson	F. Burlew	126	Bet Mosie	46 775	2:04.3
1923	Zev	E. Sande	D. J. Leary	126	Martingale	53 600	2:05.2
1924	Black Gold	J. D. Mooney	H. Webb	126	Chilhowee	52 775	2:05.1
1925	Flying Ebony	E. Sande	W. B. Duke	126	Captain Hal	52 950	2:07.3
1926	Bubbling Over	A. Johnson	H. J. Thompson	126	Bagenbaggage	50 075	2:03.4
1927	Whiskery	L. McAtee	F. Hopkins	126	Osmand	51 000	2:06.
1928	Reigh Count	C. Lang	B. S. Michell	126	Misstep	55 375	2:10.2
1929	Clyde Van Dusen	L. McAtee	C. Van Dusen	126	Naishapur	53 950	2:10.4
1930	Gallant Fox	E. Sande	J. Fitzsimmons	126	Gallant Knight	50 725	2:07.3
1931	Twenty Grand	C. Kurtsinger	J. Rowe Jr.	126	Sweep All	48 725	2:01.4
1932	Burgoo King	E. James	H. J. Thompson	126	Economic	52 350	2:05.1
1933	Brokers Tip	D. Meade	H. J. Thompson	126	Head Play	48 925	2:06.4
1934	Cavalcade	M. Garner	R. A. Smith	126	Discovery	28 175	2:04.
1935	Omaha	W. Saunders	J. Fitzsimmons	126	Roman Soldier	39 525	2:05.
1936	Bold Venture	I. Hanford	M. Hirsch	126	Brevity	37 725	2:03.3
1937	War Admiral	C. Kurtsinger	G. Conway	126	Pompoon	52 050	2:03.1
1938	Lawrin	E. Arcaro	B. A. Jones	126	Dauber	47 050	2:04.4
1939	Johnstown	J. Stout	J. Fitzsimmons	126	Challedon	46 350	2:03.2
1940	Gallahadion	C. Bierman	R. Waldron	126	Bimelech	60 150	2:05.
1941	Whirlaway	E. Arcaro	B. A. Jones	126	Staretor	61 275	2:01.2
1942	Shut Out	W. D. Wright	J. M. Gaver	126	Alsab	64 225	2:04.2
1943	Count Fleet	J. Longden	G. D. Cameron	126	Blue Swords	60 275	2:04.
1944	Pensive	C. McCreary	B. A. Jones	126	Broadcloth	64 675	2:04.1
1945	Hoop, Jr.	E. Arcaro	I. H. Parke	126	Pot o'Luck	64 850	2:07.
1946	Assault	W. Mehrtens	M. Hirsch	126	Spy Song	96 400	2:06.3
1947	Jet Pilot	E. Guerin	T. Smith	126	Phalanx	92 160	2:06.3
1948	Citation	E. Arcaro	B. A. Jones	126	Coaltown	83 400	2:05.2
1949	Ponder	S. Brooks	B. A. Jones	126	Capot	91 600	2:04.1
1950	Middleground	W. Boland	M. Hirsch	126	Hill Prince	92 650	2:01.3
1951	Count Turf	C. McCreary	S. Rutchick	126	Royal Mustang	98 050	2:02.3
1952	Hill Gail	E. Arcaro	B. A. Jones	126	Sub Fleet	96 300	2:01.3
1953	Dark Star	H. Moreno	E. Hayward	126	Native Dancer	90 050	2:02.
1954	Determine	R. York	W. Molter	126	Hasty Road	102 050	2:03.
1955	Swaps	W. Shoemaker	M. A. Tenney	126	Nashua	108 400	2:01.4
1956	Needles	D. Erb	H. L. Fontaine	126	Fabius	123 450	2:03.2
1957	Iron Liege	W. Hartack	H. A. Jones	126	Gallant Man	107 950	2:02.1
1958	Tim Tam	I. Valenzuela	H. A. Jones	126	Lincoln Road	116 400	2:05.
1959	Tomy Lee	W. Shoemaker	F. Childs	126	Sword Dancer	119 650	2:02.1
1960	Venetian Way	W. Hartack	V. Sovinski	126	Bally Ache	114 850	2:02.2
1961	Carry Back	J. Sellers	J. A. Price	126	Crozier	120 500	2:04.
1962	Decidedly	W. Hartack	H. Luro	126	Roman Line	119 650	2:00.2
1963	Chateaugay	B. Baeza	J. Conway	126	Never Bend	108 900	2:01.4
1964	Northern Dancer	W. Hartack	H. Luro	126	Hill Rise	114 300	2:00.
1965	Lucky Debonair	W. Shoemaker	F. Catrone	126	Dapper Dan	112 000	2:01.1
1966	Kauai King	D. Brumfield	H. Forrest	126	Advocator	120 500	2:02.
1967	Proud Clarion	R. Ussery	L. Gentry	126	Barbs Delight	119 700	2:00.3
1968	Dancer's Image[5]	R. Ussery	H. Forrest	126	Forward Pass	122 600	2:02.1
1969	Majestic Prince	W. Hartack	J. Longden	126	Arts and Letters	113 200	2:01.4
1970	Dust Commander	M. Manganello	D. Combs	126	My Dad George	127 800	2:03.2
1971	Canonero II	G. Avila	J. Arias	126	Jim French	145 500	2:03.1
1972	Riva Ridge	R. Turcotte	L. Laurin	126	No Le Hace	140 300	2:01.4
1973	Secretariat	R. Turcotte	L. Laurin	126	Sham	155 050	1:59.2
1974	Cannonade	A. Cordero	W. Stephens	126	Hudson County	274 000	2:04.
1975	Foolish Pleasure	J. Vasquez	L. Jolley	126	Avatar	209 611	2:02.
1976	Bold Forbes	A. Cordero	L. Barrera	126	Honest Pleasure	165 200	2:01.3
1977	Seattle Slew	J. Cruguet	W. H. Turner Jr.	126	Run Dusty Run	214 700	2:02.1
1978	Affirmed	S. Cauthen	L. Barrera	126	Alydar	186 900	2:01.1
1979	Spectacular Bid	R. Franklin	G. Delp	126	General Assembly	228 650	2:02.2
1980	Genuine Risk[4]	J. Vasquez	L. Jolley	121	Rumbo	250 550	2:02
1981	Pleasant Colony	J. Velasquez	J. Campo	126	Woodchopper	317 200	2:02
1982	Gato del Sol	E. Delahoussaye	E. Gregson	126	Laser Light	428 850	2:02.2
1983	Sunny's Halo	E. Delahoussaye	D. Cross	126	Desert Wine	426 000	2:02.1
1984	Swale	L. Pincay	W. Stephens	126	Coax Me Chad	537 000	2:02.2
1985	Spend a Buck	A. Cordero	C. Gambolati	126	Stephan's Odyssey	406 800	2:00.1
1986	Ferdinand	W. Shoemaker	C. Whittingham	126	Bold Arrangement	609 400	2:02.4
1987	Alysheba	C. McCarron	J. Van Berg	126	Bet Twice	618 600	2:03.2
1988	Winning Colors[4]	G. Stevens	D. W. Lukas	126	Forty Niner	611 200	2:02.1

(1) Weight in lbs. (2) Winner's share in U.S. dollars. (3) Fractions of a second are in fifths. (4) Regret, Genuine Risk and Winning Colors are the only fillies to win the Derby. (5) Dancer's Image was disqualified from purse money after tests disclosed that he had run with a pain-killing drug, phenylbutazone, in his system. All wagers were paid on Dancer's Image. Forward Pass was awarded first place money.

Preakness

Pimlico, Baltimore, Md.; inaugurated 1873; 1 3-16 miles, 3 yr. olds.

Year	Winner	Jockey	Trainer	Second	Winner's share[1]	Time[2]
1955	Nashua	E. Arcaro	J. Fitzsimmons	Saratoga	$67 550	1:54.3
1956	Fabius	W. Hartack	H.A. Jones	Needles	84 250	1:58.2
1957	Bold Ruler	E. Arcaro	J. Fitzsimmons	Iron Liege	65 250	1:56.1
1958	Tim Tam	I. Valenzuela	H.A. Jones	Lincoln Road	97 900	1:57.1
1959	Royal Orbit	W. Harmatz	R. Cornell	Sword Dancer	136 200	1:57
1960	Bally Ache	R. Ussery	H.J. Pitt	Victoria Park	121 000	1:57.3
1961	Carry Back	J. Sellers	J.A. Price	Globemaster	126 200	1:57.3
1962	Greek Money	J.L. Rotz	V.W. Raines	Ridan	135 800	1:56.1
1963	Candy Spots	W. Shoemaker	M.A. Tenney	Chateaugay	127 500	1:56.1
1964	Northern Dancer	W. Hartack	H. Luro	The Scoundrel	124 200	1:56.4
1965	Tom Rolfe	R. Turcotte	F.Y. Whiteley Jr.	Dapper Dan	128 100	1:56.1
1966	Kauai King	D. Brumfield	H. Forrest	Stupendous	129 000	1:55.2
1967	Damascus	W. Shoemaker	F.Y. Whiteley Jr.	In Reality	141 500	1:55.1
1968	Forward Pass	I. Valenzuela	H. Forrest	Out of the Way	142 700	1:56.4
1969	Majestic Prince	W. Hartack	J. Longden	Arts and Letters	129 500	1:55.3
1970	Personality	E. Belmonte	J.W. Jacobs	My Dad George	151 300	1:56.1
1971	Canonero II	G. Avila	J. Arias	Eastern Fleet	137 400	1:54
1972	Bee Bee Bee	E. Nelson	D.W. Carroll	No Le Hace	135 300	1:55.3
1973	Secretariat	R. Turcotte	L. Laurin	Sham	129 900	1:54.2
1974	Little Current	M. Rivera	L. Rondinello	Neopolitan Way	156 000	1:54.3
1975	Master Derby	D. McHargue	W.E. Adams	Foolish Pleasure	158 100	1:56.2
1976	Elocutionist	J. Lively	P.T. Adwell	Play The Red	129 700	1:55
1977	Seattle Slew	J. Cruguet	W.H. Turner Jr.	Iron Constitution	138 600	1:54.2
1978	Affirmed	S. Cauthen	L. Barrera	Alydar	136 200	1:54.2
1979	Spectacular Bid	R. Franklin	G. Delp	Golden Act	165 300	1:54.1
1980	Codex	A. Cordero	D.W. Lukas	Genuine Risk	180 600	1:54.1
1981	Pleasant Colony	J. Velasquez	J. Campo	Bold Ego	270 800	1:54.3
1982	Aloma's Ruler	J. Kaenel	J. Lenzini	Linkage	209 990	1:55.2
1983	Deputed Testamony	D. Miller	J.W. Boniface	Desert Wine	251 200	1:55.2
1984	Gate Dancer	A. Cordero	J. Van Berg	Play On	243 600	1:53.3
1985	Tank's Prospect	P. Day	D.W. Lukas	Chief's Crown	423 200	1:53.2
1986	Snow Chief	A. Solis	M.F. Stute	Ferdinand	411 900	1:54.4
1987	Alysheba	C. McCarron	J. Van Berg	Bet Twice	421 100	1:55.4
1988	Risen Star	E. Delahoussaye	L. Roussel 3d	Brian's Time	413 700	1:56.1

(1) Winner's share in U.S. dollars. (2) Fractions of a second are in fifths.

Belmont Stakes

Elmont, N.Y.; inaugurated 1867; 1 ½ miles, 3 year olds.

Year	Winner	Jockey	Trainer	Second	Winner's share[1]	Time[2]
1955	Nashua	E. Arcaro	J. Fitzsimmons	Blazing Count	$83 700	2:29
1956	Needles	D. Erb	H. Fontaine	Career Boy	83 600	2:29.4
1957	Gallant Man	W. Shoemaker	J. Nerud	Inside Tract	77 300	2:26.3
1958	Cavan	P. Anderson	T.J. Barry	Tim Tam	73 440	2:30.1
1959	Sword Dancer	W. Shoemaker	J.E. Burch	Bagdad	93 525	2:28.2
1960	Celtic Ash	W. Hartack	T.J. Barry	Venetian Way	96 785	2:29.3
1961	Sherluck	B. Baeza	H. Young	Globemaster	104 900	2:29.1
1962	Jaipur	W. Shoemaker	W.F. Mulholland	Admiral's Voyage	109 550	2:28.4
1963	Chateaugay	B. Baeza	J.P. Conway	Candy Spots	101 700	2:30.1
1964	Quadrangle	M. Ycaza	J.E. Burch	Roman Brother	110 850	2:28.2
1965	Hail to All	J. Sellers	E. Yowell	Tom Rolfe	104 150	2:28.2
1966	Amberoid	W. Boland	L. Laurin	Buffle	117 700	2:29.3
1967	Damascus	W. Shoemaker	F.Y. Whiteley Jr.	Cool Reception	104 950	2:28.4
1968	Stage Door Johnny	H. Gustines	J.M. Gaver	Forward Pass	117 700	2:27.1
1969	Arts and Letters	B. Baeza	J.E. Burch	Majestic Prince	104 050	2:28.4
1970	High Echelon	J.L. Rotz	J.W. Jacobs	Needles N Pens	115 000	2:34
1971	Pass Catcher	W. Blum	E. Yowell	Jim French	97 710	2:30.2
1972	Riva Ridge	R. Turcotte	L. Laurin	Ruritania	93 950	2:28
1973	Secretariat	R. Turcotte	L. Laurin	Twice A Prince	90 120	2:24
1974	Little Current	M. Rivera	L. Rondinello	Jolly Johu	101 970	2:29.1
1975	Avatar	W. Shoemaker	A.T. Doyle	Foolish Pleasure	116 160	2:28.1
1976	Bold Forbes	A. Cordero	Laz Barrera	McKenzie Bridge	116 850	2:29
1977	Seattle Slew	J. Cruguet	W.H. Turner Jr.	Run Dusty Run	109 080	2:29.3
1978	Affirmed	S. Cauthen	Laz Barrera	Alydar	110 580	2:26.4
1979	Coastal	R. Hernandez	D.A. Whiteley	Golden Act	161 400	2:28.3
1980	Temperence Hill	E. Maple	J. Cantey	Genuine Risk	176 220	2:29.4
1981	Summing	G. Martens	Luis Barrera	Highland Blade	170 580	2:29
1982	Conquistador Cielo	L. Pincay	W. Stephens	Gato Del Sol	159 720	2:28.1
1983	Caveat	L. Pincay	W. Stephens	Slew o'Gold	215 100	2:27.4
1984	Swale	L. Pincay	W. Stephens	Pine Circle	310 020	2:27.1
1985	Creme Fraiche	E. Maple	W. Stephens	Stephan's Odyssey	307 740	2:27
1986	Danzig Connection	C. McCarron	W. Stephens	John's Treasure	338 640	2:29.4
1987	Bet Twice	C. Perret	W.A. Croll Jr.	Crypto Clearance	329 160[3]	2:28.1
1988	Risen Star	E. Delahoussaye	L. Roussel 3d	King Post	303 720	2:26.3

(1) Winner's share in U.S. dollars. (2) Fractions of a second are in fifths. (3) Does not include $1 million bonus for upsetting potential Triple Crown winner Alysheba.

Triple Crown Winners, Jockeys, and Trainers

(Kentucky Derby, Preakness, and Belmont Stakes)

Year	Horse	Jockey	Trainer	Year	Horse	Jockey	Trainer
1919	Sir Barton	J. Loftus	H. G. Bedwell	1946	Assault	Mehrtens	M. Hirsch
1930	Gallant Fox	E. Sande	J. Fitzsimmons	1948	Citation	E. Arcaro	H.A. Jones
1935	Omaha	W. Sanders	J. Fitzsimmons	1973	Secretariat	R. Turcotte	L. Laurin
1937	War Admiral	C. Kurtsinger	G. Conway	1977	Seattle Slew	J. Cruguet	W.H. Turner Jr.
1941	Whirlaway	E. Arcaro	B.A. Jones	1978	Affirmed	S. Cauthen	L.S. Barrera
1943	Count Fleet	J. Longden	G.D. Cameron				

Annual Leading North American Money-Winning Jockeys

Year	Jockey	Dollars[1]	Year	Jockey	Dollars[1]	Year	Jockey	Dollars[1]
1956	Bill Hartack	2 343 955	1967	Braulio Baeza	3 088 888	1978	Darrel McHargue	6 029 885
1957	Bill Hartack	3 060 501	1968	Braulio Baeza	2 835 108	1979	Laffit Pincay Jr.	8 193 535
1958	Willie Shoemaker	2 961 693	1969	Jorge Velasquez	2 542 315	1980	Chris McCarron	7 663 300
1959	Willie Shoemaker	2 843 133	1970	Laffit Pincay Jr.	2 626 526	1981	Chris McCarron	8 397 604
1960	Willie Shoemaker	2 123 961	1971	Laffit Pincay Jr.	3 784 377	1982	Angel Cordero Jr.	9 483 590
1961	Willie Shoemaker	2 690 819	1972	Laffit Pincay Jr.	3 225 827	1983	Angel Cordero Jr.	10 116 697
1962	Willie Shoemaker	2 916 844	1973	Laffit Pincay Jr.	4 093 492	1984	Chris McCarron	12 045 813
1963	Willie Shoemaker	2 526 925	1974	Laffit Pincay Jr.	4 251 060	1985	Laffit Pincay Jr.	13 353 299
1964	Willie Shoemaker	2 649 553	1975	Braulio Baeza	3 695 198	1986	Jose Santos	11 329 297
1965	Braulio Baeza	2 582 702	1976	Angel Cordero Jr.	4 709 500	1987	Jose Santos	12 375 433
1966	Braulio Baeza	2 951 022	1977	Steve Cauthen	6 151 750			

(1) U.S. dollars.

Annual Leading North American Money-Winning Horses

Year	Horse	Dollars[1]	Year	Horse	Dollars[1]	Year	Horse	Dollars[1]
1947	Armed	376 325	1961	Carry Back	565 349	1975	Foolish Pleasure	716 278
1948	Citation	709 470	1962	Never Bend	402 969	1976	Forego	491 701
1949	Ponder	321 825	1963	Candy Spots	604 481	1977	Seattle Slew	641 370
1950	Noor	346 940	1964	Gun Bow	580 100	1978	Affirmed	901 541
1951	Counterpoint	250 525	1965	Buckpasser	568 096	1979	Spectacular Bid	1 279 334
1952	Crafty Admiral	277 255	1966	Buckpasser	669 078	1980	Temperence Hill	1 130 452
1953	Native Dancer	513 425	1967	Damascus	817 941	1981	John Henry	1 148 800
1954	Determine	328 700	1968	Forward Pass	546 674	1982	Perrault	1 197 400
1955	Nashua	752 550	1969	Arts and Letters	555 604	1983	All Along	2 138 963
1956	Needles	440 850	1970	Personality	444 049	1984	Slew O'Gold	2 627 944
1957	Round Table	600 383	1971	Riva Ridge	503 263	1985	Spend a Buck	3 552 704
1958	Round Table	662 780	1972	Droll Roll	471 633	1986	Snow Chief	1 875 200
1959	Sword Dancer	537 004	1973	Secretariat	860 404	1987	Alysheba	2 511 156
1960	Bally Ache	455 045	1974	Chris Evert	551 063			

(1) U.S. dollars.

Harness Racing

Source: U.S. Trotting Assn.; records to Oct. 7, 1988

Trotting Records

(Times in fifths of seconds)

One mile records (mile track)

All-age—1:51.1—Mack Lobell, Springfield, Ill., Aug. 21, 1987.

Two-year-old—1:55.3—Mack Lobell, Lexington, Ky., Oct. 3, 1986.

Three-year-old—1:51.1—Mack Lobell, Springfield, Ill., Aug. 21, 1987.

(Half-mile track)

All-age—1:56.1—Mack Lobell, Saratoga Springs, N.Y., Aug. 5, 1988.

Two-year old—1:58.0—Tarpart Ramey, Indianapolis, IN., Aug. 22, 1986.

Three-year-old—1:56.1—Mack Lobell, Saratoga Springs, N.Y., Aug. 5, 1988.

Pacing Records

One mile records (mile track)

All-age—148.2—Matts Scotter, Lexington, Ky., Sept. 25, 1988.

Two-year-old—152.1—Raque Bogart, Lexington, Ky., Sept. 30, 1988.

Three-year-old—148.2—Matts Scotter, Lexington, Ky., Sept. 25, 1988.

(Half-mile track)

All-age—1:51—Falcon Seelster, Delaware, Oh., Sept. 19, 1985.

Two-year-old—1:55.1—Kentucky Spur, Louisville, Ky., Aug. 10, 1988.

Three-year-old—1:51—Falcon Seelster, Delaware, Oh., Sept. 19, 1985.

Harness Horse of the Year

(Chosen by the U.S. Trotting Assn. and the U.S. Harness Writers Assn.)

1948	Rodney	1958	Emily's Pride	1968	Nevele Pride	1978	Abercrombie
1949	Good Time	1959	Bye Bye Byrd	1969	Nevele Pride	1979	Niatross
1950	Proximity	1960	Adios Butler	1970	Fresh Yankee	1980	Niatross
1951	Pronto Don	1961	Adios Butler	1971	Albatross	1981	Fan Hanover
1952	Good Time	1962	Su Mac Lad	1972	Albatross	1982	Cam Fella
1953	Hi Lo's Forbes	1963	Speedy Scot	1973	Sir Dalrae	1983	Cam Fella
1954	Stenographer	1964	Bret Hanover	1974	Delmonica Hanover	1984	Fancy Crown
1955	Scott Frost	1965	Bret Hanover	1975	Savior	1985	Nihilator
1956	Scott Frost	1966	Bret Hanover	1976	Keystone Ore	1986	Forrest Skipper
1957	Torpid	1967	Nevele Pride	1977	Green Speed	1987	Mack Lobell

Annual Leading Money-Winning Horses

Trotters

Year	Horse	Dollars[1]	Year	Horse	Dollars[1]	Year	Horse	Dollars[1]
1962	Duke Rodney	206 113	1971	Fresh Yankee	293 960	1980	Classical Way	350 410
1963	Speedy Scot	144 403	1972	Super Bowl	437 108	1981	Shiaway St. Pat	480 095
1964	Speedy Scot	235 710	1973	Spartan Hanover	262 023	1982	Speed Bowl	672 084
1965	Dartmouth	252 348	1974	Delmonica Hanover	252 165	1983	Joie De Vie	1 007 705
1966	Noble Victory	210 696	1975	Savoir	351 385	1984	Baltic Speed	1 062 611
1967	Carlisle	231 243	1976	Steve Lobell	338 770	1985	Prakis	1 610 608
1968	Nevele Pride	427 440	1977	Green Speed	584 405	1986	Royal Prestige	1 052 114
1969	Lindy's Pride	323 997	1978	Speedy Somolli	362 404	1987	Mack Lobell	1 878 798
1970	Fresh Yankee	359 002	1979	Chiola Hanover	553 058			

Pacers

Year	Horse	Dollars[1]	Year	Horse	Dollars[1]	Year	Horse	Dollars[1]
1962	Henry T. Adios	220 302	1971	Albatross	558 009	1980	Niatross	1 414 313
1963	Overtrick	208 833	1972	Albatross	459 921	1981	McKinzie Almahurst	936 418
1964	Race Time	199 292	1973	Sir Dalrae	307 354	1982	Fortune Teller	1 313 175
1965	Bret Hanover	341 784	1974	Armbro Omaha	345 146	1983	Ralph Hanover	1 711 990
1966	Bret Hanover	407 534	1975	Silk Stockings	336 312	1984	On The Road Again	1 751 695
1967	Romulus Hanover	277 636	1976	Keystone Ore	539 762	1985	Nihilator	1 864 286
1968	Rum Customer	355 618	1977	Governor Skipper	522 148	1986	Redskin	1 407 263
1969	Overcall	373 150	1978	Abercrombie	703 260	1987	Jate Lobell	1 645 598
1970	Most Happy Fella	387 239	1979	Hot Hitter	826 542			

(1) U.S. dollars.

Leading Drivers

Races Won

Year	Driver		Year	Driver		Year	Driver		Year	Driver	
1968	Herve Filion. . .	407	1973	Herve Filion. . .	445	1978	Herve Filion. . .	423	1982	Herve Filion. . .	495
1969	Herve Filion. . .	394	1974	Herve Filion. . .	637	1979	Ron Waples . . .	443	1983	Eddie Davis. . .	470
1970	Herve Filion. . .	486	1975	Daryl Buse . . .	360	1980	Herve Filion. . .	474	1984	Michel Lachance	466
1971	Herve Filion. . .	543	1976	Herve Filion. . .	445	1981	Eddie Davis. . .	404	1985	Michel Lachance	592
1972	Herve Filion. . .	605	1977	Herve Filion. . .	441		Herve Filion. . .	404	1986	Michel Lachance	770
									1987	Michel Lachance	715

Money Won

Year	Driver	Dollars[1]	Year	Driver	Dollars[1]	Year	Driver	Dollars[1]
1962	Stanley Dancer. . .	760 343	1971	Herve Filion.	1 915 945	1980	John Campbell . . .	3 732 306
1963	Bill Haughton	790 086	1972	Herve Filion.	2 473 265	1981	Bill O'Donnell. . . .	4 065 608
1964	Stanley Dancer. . .	1 051 538	1973	Herve Filion.	2 233 302	1982	Bill O'Donnell. . . .	5 755 067
1965	Bill Haughton	889 943	1974	Herve Filion.	3 474 315	1983	John Campbell . . .	6 104 082
1966	Stanley Dancer. . .	1 218 403	1975	Carmine Abbatiello	2 275 093	1984	Bill O'Donnell. . . .	9 059 184
1967	Bill Haughton	1 305 773	1976	Herve Filion.	2 241 045	1985	Bill O'Donnell. . . .	10 207 372
1968	Bill Haughton	1 654 172	1977	Herve Filion.	2 551 058	1986	John Campbell . . .	9 515 055
1969	Del Insko	1 635 463	1978	Carmine Abbatiello	3 344 457	1987	John Campbell . . .	10 186 495
1970	Herve Filion.	1 647 837	1979	John Campbell . . .	3 308 984			

(1) U.S. dollars.

Boxing

Boxing Champions by Classes

As of Sept. 15, 1988 the only generally accepted title holder was in the heavyweight division. There are numerous governing bodies in boxing including the World Boxing Council, the World Boxing Assn., the International Boxing Federation, the United States Boxing Assn., the North American Boxing Federation, and the European Boxing Union. Other organizations are recognized by TV networks and the print media. All the governing bodies have their own champions and assorted boxing divisions. The following are the recognized champions in the principal divisions of the World Boxing Association and the World Boxing Council.

	WBA	WBC
Heavyweight	Mike Tyson, U.S.	Mike Tyson, U.S.
Cruiserweight (not over 195 lbs.)	Evander Holyfield, U.S.	Evander Holyfield, U.S.
Light Heavyweight (not over 175 lbs.) . . .	Virgil Hill, U.S.	Don Lalonde, Canada
Middleweight (not over 160 lbs.)	Sumbu Kalambay, Italy	Iran Barkley, U.S.
Jr. Middleweight (not over 154 lbs.)	Julian Jackson, Virgin Islands	Donald Curry, U.S.
Welterweight (not over 147 lbs.)	Tomas Molinares, Colombia	Lloyd Honeyghan, England
Jr. Welterweight (not over 140 lbs.)	Juan Coggi, Argentina	Roger Mayweather, U.S.
Lightweight (not over 135 lbs.)	Julio Cesar Chavez, Mexico	Jose Luis Ramirez, Mexico
Jr. Lightweight (not over 130 lbs.)	Brian Mitchell, So. Africa	Azumah Nelson, Ghana
Featherweight (not over 126 lbs.)	Antonio Esparragoza, Venezuela	Jeff Fenech, Australia
Jr. Featherweight (not over 122 lbs.). . . .	Juan Jose Estrada, Mexico	Daniel Zaragoza, Mexico
Bantamweight (not over 118 lbs.)	Khaokar Galazy, Thailand	Miguel Lora, Colombia
Flyweight (not over 112 lbs.)	Fidel Bassa, Colombia	Kim Young Kang, So. Korea

Ring Champions by Years

*Abandoned title

Heavyweights

1882-1892	John L. Sullivan[1]	1959-1960	Ingemar Johansson
1892-1897	James J. Corbett[2]	1960-1962	Floyd Patterson
1897-1899	Robert Fitzsimmons	1962-1964	Sonny Liston
1899-1905	James J. Jeffries[3]	1964-1967	Cassius Clay* (Muhammad Ali)[4]
1905-1906	Marvin Hart	1970-1973	Joe Frazier
1906-1908	Tommy Burns	1973-1974	George Foreman
1908-1915	Jack Johnson	1974-1978	Muhammad Ali
1915-1919	Jess Willard	1978-1979	Leon Spinks[5],Muhammad Ali*
1919-1926	Jack Dempsey	1978	Ken Norton (WBC), Larry Holmes (WBC)[6]
1926-1928	Gene Tunney*	1979	John Tate (WBA)
1928-1930	vacant	1980	Mike Weaver (WBA)
1930-1932	Max Schmeling	1982	Michael Dokes (WBA)
1932-1933	Jack Sharkey	1983	Gerrie Coetzee (WBA)
1933-1934	Primo Carnera	1984	Tim Witherspoon (WBC); Pinklon Thomas (WBC); Greg Page (WBA)
1934-1935	Max Baer	1985	Tony Tubbs (WBA); Michael Spinks (IBF)
1935-1937	James J. Braddock	1986	Tim Witherspoon (WBA); Trevor Berbick (WBC); Mike Tyson (WBC); James (Bone-crusher) Smith (WBA)
1937-1949	Joe Louis*		
1949-1951	Ezzard Charles	1987	Mike Tyson (WBA)
1951-1952	Joe Walcott		
1952-1956	Rocky Marciano*		
1956-1959	Floyd Patterson		

(1) London Prize Ring (bare knuckle champion). (2) First Marquis of Queensberry champion. (3) Jeffries abandoned the title (1905) and designated Marvin Hart and Jack Root as logical contenders and agreed to referee a fight between them, the winner to be declared champion. Hart defeated Root in 12 rounds (1905) and in turn was defeated by Tommy Burns (1906) who immediately laid claim to the title. Jack Johnson defeated Burns (1908) and was recognized as champion. He clinched the title by defeating Jeffries in an attempted comeback (1910). (3) Title declared vacant by the World Boxing Assn. and other groups in 1967 after Clay's refusal to fulfill his military obligation. Joe Frazier was recognized as champion by New York, 5 other states, Mexico, and So. America. Jimmy Ellis was declared champion by the World Boxing Assn. Frazier KOd Ellis, Feb. 16, 1970. (5) After Spinks defeated Ali, the WBC recognized Ken Norton as champion. Norton subsequently lost his title to Larry Holmes. (6) Holmes was stripped of his WBC title in 1984. He was the International Boxing Federation champion when he lost to Michael Spinks.

Light Heavyweights

1903	Jack Root, George Gardner	1920-1922	George Carpentier
1903-1905	Bob Fitzsimmons	1922-1923	Battling Siki
1905-1912	Philadelphia Jack O'Brien*	1923-1925	Mike McTigue
1912-1916	Jack Dillon	1925-1926	Paul Berlenbach
1916-1920	Battling Levinsky	1926-1927	Jack Delaney*

1927-1929	Tommy Loughran*	1966-1968	Dick Tiger
1930-1934	Maxey Rosenbloom	1968-1974	Bob Foster*, John Conteh (WBA)
1934-1935	Bob Olin	1975-1977	John Conteh (WBC), Miguel Cuello (WBC), Victor Galindez (WBA)
1935-1939	John Henry Lewis*		
1939	Melio Bettina	1978	Mike Rossman (WBA), Mate Parlov (WBC), Marvin Johnson (WBC)
1939-1941	Billy Conn*		
1941	Anton Christoforidis (won NBA title)	1979	Victor Galindez (WBA), Matthew Saad Muhammad (WBC)
1941-1948	Gus Lesnevich, Freddie Mills		
1948-1950	Freddie Mills	1980	Eddie Mustava Muhammad (WBA)
1950-1952	Joey Maxim	1981	Michael Spinks (WBA), Dwight Braxton (WBC)
1952-1960	Archie Moore	1983	Michael Spinks
1961-1962	vacant	1986	Marvin Johnson (WBA), Dennis Andries (WBC)
1962-1963	Harold Johnson	1987	Thomas Hearns (WBC); Leslie Stewart (WBA); Virgil Hill; Donny Lalonde (WBC)
1963-1965	Willie Pastrano		
1965-1966	Jose Torres		

Middleweights

1884-1891	Jack "Nonpareil" Dempsey	1958	Ray Robinson
1891-1897	Bob Fitzsimmons*	1959	Gene Fullmer (NBA); Ray Robinson (N.Y.)
1897-1907	Tommy Ryan*	1960	Gene Fullmer (NBA); Paul Pender (New York and Mass.)
1907-1908	Stanley Ketchel, Billy Papke		
1908-1910	Stanley Ketchel	1961	Gene Fullmer (NBA); Terry Downes (New York, Mass., Europe)
1911-1913	vacant		
1913	Frank Klaus, George Chip	1962	Gene Fullmer, Dick Tiger (NBA), Paul Pender (New York and Mass.)*
1914-1917	Al McCoy		
1917-1920	Mike O'Dowd	1963	Dick Tiger (universal).
1920-1923	Johnny Wilson	1963-1965	Joey Giardello
1923-1926	Harry Greb	1965-1966	Dick Tiger
1926-1931	Tiger Flowers, Mickey Walker	1966-1967	Emile Griffith
1931-1932	Gorilla Jones (NBA)	1967	Nino Benvenuti
1932-1937	Marcel Thil	1967-1968	Emile Griffith
1938	Al Hostak (NBA), Solly Krieger (NBA)	1968-1970	Nino Benvenuti
1939-1940	Al Hostak (NBA)	1970-1977	Carlos Monzon*
1941-1947	Tony Zale	1977-1978	Rodrigo Valdez
1947-1948	Rocky Graziano	1978-1979	Hugo Corro
1948	Tony Zale, Marcel Cerdan	1979-1980	Vito Antuofermo
1949-1951	Jake LaMotta	1980	Alan Minter, Marvin Hagler
1951	Ray Robinson, Randy Turpin, Ray Robinson*	1981-1986	Marvin Hagler
1953-1955	Carl (Bobo) Olson	1987	Ray Leonard* (WBC); Thomas Hearns (WBC); Sumbu Kalambay (WBA).
1955-1957	Ray Robinson		
1957	Gene Fullmer, Ray Robinson, Carmen Basilio	1988	Iran Barkley (WBC).

Welterweights

1892-1894	Mysterious Billy Smith	1954-1955	Johnny Saxton
1894-1896	Tommy Ryan	1955	Tony De Marco, Carmen Basilio
1896	Kid McCoy*	1956	Carmen Basilio, Johnny Saxton, Basilio
1900	Rube Ferns, Matty Matthews	1957	Carmen Basilio*
1901	Rube Ferns	1958-1960	Virgil Akins, Don Jordan
1901-1904	Joe Walcott	1960	Benny Paret
1904-1906	Dixie Kid, Joe Walcott, Honey Mellody	1961	Emile Griffith, Benny Paret
1907-1911	Mike Sullivan	1962	Emile Griffith
1911-1915	vacant	1963	Luis Rodriguez, Emile Griffith
1915-1919	Ted Lewis	1964-1966	Emile Griffith*
1919-1922	Jack Britton	1966-1969	Curtis Cokes
1922-1926	Mickey Walker	1969-1970	Jose Napoles, Billy Backus
1926	Pete Latzo	1971-1975	Jose Napoles
1927-1929	Joe Dundee	1975-1976	John Stracey (WBC), Angel Espada (WBA)
1929	Jackie Fields	1976-1979	Carlos Palomino (WBC), Jose Cuevas (WBA)
1930	Jack Thompson, Tommy Freeman	1979	Wilfredo Benitez (WBC), Sugar Ray Leonard (WBC)
1931	Freeman, Thompson, Lou Brouillard		
1932	Jackie Fields	1980	Roberto Duran (WBC), Thomas Hearns (WBA), Sugar Ray Leonard (WBC)
1933	Young Corbett, Jimmy McLarnin		
1934	Barney Ross, Jimmy McLarnin	1981-1982	Sugar Ray Leonard*
1935-1938	Barney Ross	1983	Donald Curry (WBA); Milton McCrory (WBC)
1938-1940	Henry Armstrong	1985	Donald Curry
1940-1941	Fritzie Zivic	1986	Lloyd Honeyghan (WBC)
1941-1946	Fred Cochrane	1987	Mark Breland (WBA); Marlon Starling (WBA); Jorge Vaca (WBC).
1946-1946	Marty Servo*; Ray Robinson[1]		
1946-1950	Ray Robinson*	1988	Thomas Molinares (WBA); Lloyd Honeyghan (WBC).
1951	Johnny Bratton (NBA)		
1951-1954	Kid Gavilan		

(1) Robinson gained the title by defeating Tommy Bell in an elimination agreed to by the NY Commission and the NBA. Both claimed Robinson waived his title when he won the middleweight crown from LaMotta in 1951.

Lightweights

1896-1899	Kid Lavigne		1956-1962	Joe Brown
1899-1902	Frank Erne		1962-1965	Carlos Ortiz
1902-1908	Joe Gans		1965	Ismael Laguna
1908-1910	Battling Nelson		1965-1968	Carlos Ortiz
1910-1912	Ad Wolgast		1968-1969	Teo Cruz
1912-1914	Willie Ritchie		1969-1970	Mando Ramos
1914-1917	Freddie Welsh		1970	Ismael Laguna, Ken Buchanan (WBA)
1917-1925	Benny Leonard*		1971	Mando Ramos (WBC), Pedro Carrasco (WBC)
1925	Jimmy Goodrich, Rocky Kansas		1972-1979	Roberto Duran* (WBA)
1926-1930	Sammy Mandell		1972	Pedro Carrasco, Mando Ramos, Chango Carmona, Rodolfo Gonzalez (all WBC)
1930	Al Singer, Tony Canzoneri			
1930-1933	Tony Canzoneri		1974-1976	Guts Ishimatsu (WBC)
1933-1935	Barney Ross*		1976-1977	Esteban De Jesus (WBC)
1935-1936	Tony Canzoneri		1979	Jim Watt (WBC), Ernesto Espana (WBA)
1936-1938	Lou Ambers		1980	Hilmer Kenty (WBA)
1938	Henry Armstrong		1981	Alexis Arguello (WBC), Sean O'Grady (WBA), Arturo Frias (WBA)
1939	Lou Ambers			
1940	Lew Jenkins		1982-1984	Ray Mancini (WBA)
1941-1943	Sammy Angott		1983	Edwin Rosario (WBC)
1944	S. Angott (NBA), J. Zurita (NBA)		1984	Livingstone Bramble (WBA); Jose Luis Ramirez (WBC)
1945-1951	Ike Williams (NBA: later universal)			
1951-1952	James Carter		1985	Hector (Macho) Camacho (WBC)
1952	Lauro Salas, James Carter		1986	Edwin Rosario (WBA); Jose Luis Ramirez (WBC)
1953-1954	James Carter			
1954	Paddy De Marco; James Carter		1987	Julio Cesar Chavez (WBA)
1955	James Carter; Bud Smith			
1956	Bud Smith, Joe Brown			

Featherweights

1892-1900	George Dixon (disputed)		1964-1967	Vicente Saldivar*
1900-1901	Terry McGovern, Young Corbett*		1968-1971	Paul Rojas (WBA), Sho Saijo (WBA)
1901-1912	Abe Attell		1971	Antonio Gomez (WBA), Kuniaki Shibada (WBC)
1912-1923	Johnny Kilbane			
1923	Eugene Criqui, Johnny Dundee		1972	Ernesto Marcel* (WBA), Clemente Sanchez* (WBC), Jose Legra (WBC)
1923-1925	Johnny Dundee*			
1925-1927	Kid Kaplan*		1973	Eder Jofre (WBC)
1927-1928	Benny Bass, Tony Canzoneri		1974	Ruben Olivares (WBA), Alexis Arguello (WBA), Bobby Chacon (WBC)
1928-1929	Andre Routis			
1929-1932	Battling Battalino*		1975	Ruben Olivares (WBC), David Kotey (WBC)
1932-1934	Tommy Paul (NBA)		1976	Danny Lopez (WBC)
1933-1936	Freddie Miller		1977	Rafael Ortega (WBA)
1936-1937	Petey Sarron		1978	Cecilio Lastra (WBA), Eusebio Pedrosa (WBA)
1937-1938	Henry Armstrong*		1980	Salvador Sanchez (WBC)
1938-1940	Joey Archibald[1]		1982	Juan LaPorte (WBC)
1942-1948	Willie Pep		1984	Wilfredo Gomez (WBC); Azumah Nelson (WBC)
1948-1949	Sandy Saddler			
1949-1950	Willie Pep		1985	Barry McGuigan (WBA)
1950-1957	Sandy Saddler*		1986	Steve Cruz (WBA)
1957-1959	Hogan (Kid) Bassey		1987	Antonio Esparragoza (WBA)
1959-1963	Davey Moore		1988	Jeff Fenech (WBC)
1963-1964	Sugar Ramos			

(1) After Petey Scalzo knocked out Archibald in an overweight match and was refused a title bout, the NBA named Scalzo champion. The NBA title succession: Scalzo, 1938-1941; Richard Lemos, 1941; Jackie Wilson, 1941-1943; Jackie Callura, 1943; Phil Terranova, 1943-1944; Sal Bartolo, 1944-1946.

History of Heavyweight Championship Bouts

(numbers indicate how many rounds the bout lasted)

1889—July 8—John L. Sullivan def. Jake Kilrain, 75, Richburg, Miss. Last championship bare knuckles bout.

*1892—Sept. 7—James J. Corbett def. John L. Sullivan, 21, New Orleans. Big gloves used for first time.

1894—Jan. 25—James J. Corbett KOd Charley Mitchell, 3, Jacksonville, Fla.

*1897—Bob Fitzsimmons def. James J. Corbett, 14, Carson City, Nev.

*1899—June 9—James J. Jeffries def. Bob Fitzsimmons, 11, Coney Island, N.Y.

1899—Nov. 3—James J. Jeffries def. Tom Sharkey, 25, Coney Island, N.Y.

1900—May 11—James J. Jeffries KOd James J. Corbett, 23, Coney Island, N.Y.

1901—Nov. 15—James J. Jeffries KOd Gus Ruhlin, 5, San Francisco.

1902—July 25—James J. Jeffries KOd Bob Fitzsimmons, 8, San Francisco.

1903—Aug. 14—James J. Jeffries KOd James J. Corbett, 10, San Francisco.

1904—Aug. 26—James J. Jeffries KOd Jack Monroe, 2, San Francisco.

*1905—James J. Jeffries retired, July 3—Marvin Hart KOd Jack Root, 12, Reno. Jeffries refereed and presented the title to the victor. Jack O'Brien also claimed the title.

*1906—Feb. 23—Tommy Burns def. Marvin Hart, 20, Los Angeles.

1906—Nov. 28—Philadelphia Jack O'Brien and Tommy Burns, 20, draw, Los Angeles.

1907—May 8—Tommy Burns def. Jack O'Brien, 20, Los Angeles.

1907—July 4—Tommy Burns KOd Bill Squires, 1, Colma, Cal.

1907—Dec. 2—Tommy Burns KOd Gunner Moir, 10, London.

1908—Feb. 10—Tommy Burns KOd Jack Palmer, 4, London.

1908—March 17—Tommy Burns KOd Jem Roche, 1, Dublin.

1908—April 18—Tommy Burns KOd Jewey Smith, 5, Paris.

1908—June 13—Tommy Burns KOd Bill Squires, 8, Paris.

1908—Aug. 24—Tommy Burns KOd Bill Squires, 13, Sydney, New South Wales.

1908—Sept. 2—Tommy Burns KOd Bill Lang, 2, Melbourne, Australia.

*1908—Dec. 26—Jack Johnson KOd Tommy Burns, 14, Sydney, Australia. Police halted contest.

1909—May 19—Jack Johnson and Jack O'Brien, 6, draw, Philadelphia.

1909—June 30—Jack Johnson and Tony Ross, 6, draw, Pittsburgh.

1909—Sept. 9—Jack Johnson and Al Kaufman, 10, draw, San Francisco.

1909—Oct. 16—Jack Johnson KOd Stanley Ketchel, 12, Colma, Cal.

1910—July 4—Jack Johnson KOd Jim Jeffries, 15, Reno, Nev. Jeffries came back from retirement.

1912—July 4—Jack Johnson def. Jim Flynn, 9, Las Vegas, N.M. Contest stopped by police.

1913—Nov. 28—Jack Johnson KOd Andre Spaul, 2, Paris.

1913—Dec. 9—Jack Johnson and Jim Johnson, 10, draw, Paris. Bout called a draw when Jack Johnson declared he had broken his arm.

1914—June 27—Jack Johnson def. Frank Moran, 20, Paris.

*1915—April 5—Jess Willard KOd Jack Johnson, 26, Havana. Cuba.

1916—March 25—Jess Willard and Frank Moran, 10, draw, New York.

*1919—July 4—Jack Dempsey KOd Jess Willard, Toledo, Oh. Willard failed to answer bell for 4th round.

1920—Sept. 6—Jack Dempsey KOd Billy Miske, 3, Benton Harbor, Mich.

1920—Dec. 14—Jack Dempsey KOd Bill Brennan, 12, New York.

1921—July 2—Jack Dempsey KOd George Carpentier, 4, Boyle's Thirty Acres, Jersey City, N.J. Carpentier had held the so-called white heavyweight title since July 16, 1914, in a series established in 1913, after Jack Johnson's exile in Europe late in 1912.

1923—July 4—Jack Dempsey def. Tom Gibbons, 15, Shelby, Mont.

1923—Sept. 14—Jack Dempsey KOd Luis Firpo, 2, New York.

*1926—Sept. 23—Gene Tunney def. Jack Dempsey, 10, Philadelphia.

1927—Sept. 22—Gene Tunney def. Jack Dempsey, 10, Chicago.

1928—July 26—Gene Tunney KOd Tom Heeney, 11, New York; soon afterward he announced his retirement.

*1930—June 12—Max Schmeling def. Jack Sharkey, 4, New York. Sharkey fouled Schmeling in a bout which was generally considered to have resulted in the election of a successor to Gene Tunney, New York.

1931—July 3—Max Schmeling KOd Young Stribling, 15, Cleveland.

*1932—June 21—Jack Sharkey def. Max Schmeling, 15, New York.

*1933—June 29—Primo Carnera KOd Jack Sharkey, 6, New York.

1933—Oct. 22—Primo Carnera def. Paulino Uzcudun, 15, Rome.

1934—March 1—Primo Carnera def. Tommy Loughran, 15, Miami.

*1934—June 14—Max Baer KOd Primo Carnera, 11, New York.

*1935—June 13—James J. Braddock def. Max Baer, 15, New York.

*1937—June 22—Joe Louis KOd James J. Braddock, 8, Chicago.

1937—Aug. 30—Joe Louis def. Tommy Farr, 15, New York.

1938—Feb. 23—Joe Louis KOd Nathan Mann, 3, New York.

1938—April 1—Joe Louis KOd Harry Thomas, 5, New York.

1938—June 22—Joe Louis KOd Max Schmeling, 1, New York.

1939—Jan. 25—Joe Louis KOd John H. Lewis, 1, New York.

1939—April 17—Joe Louis KOd Jack Roper, 1, Los Angeles.

1939—June 28—Joe Louis KOd Tony Galento, 4, New York.

1939—Sept. 20—Joe Louis KOd Bob Pastor, 11, Detroit.

1940—February 9—Joe Louis def. Arturo Godoy, 15, New York.

1940—March 29—Joe Louis KOd Johnny Paycheck, 2, New York.

1940—June 20—Joe Louis KOd Arturo Godoy, 8, New York.

1940—Dec. 16—Joe Louis KOd Al McCoy, 6, Boston.

1941—Jan. 31—Joe Louis KOd Red Burman, 5, New York.

1941—Feb. 17—Joe Louis KOd Gus Dorzaio, 2, Philadelphia.

1941—March 21—Joe Louis KOd Abe Simon, 13, Detroit.

1941—April 8—Joe Louis KOd Tony Musto, 9, St. Louis.

1941—May 23—Joe Louis def. Buddy Baer, 7, Washington, D.C., on a disqualification.

1941—June 18—Joe Louis KOd Billy Conn, 13, New York.

1941—Sept. 29—Joe Louis KOd Lou Nova, 6, New York.

1942—Jan. 9—Joe Louis KOd Buddy Baer, 1, New York.

1942—March 27—Joe Louis KOd Abe Simon, 6, New York.

1946—June 19—Joe Louis KOd Billy Conn, 8, New York.

1946—Sept. 18—Joe Louis KOd Tami Mauriello, 1, New York.

1947—Dec. 5—Joe Louis def. Joe Walcott, 15, New York.

1948—June 25—Joe Louis KOd Joe Walcott, 11, New York.

*1949—June 22—Following Joe Louis' retirement Ezzard Charles def. Joe Walcott, 15, Chicago, NBA recognition only.

1949—Aug. 10—Ezzard Charles KOd Gus Lesnevich, 7, New York.

1949—Oct. 14—Ezzard Charles KOd Pat Valentino, 8, San Francisco; clinched American title.

1950—Aug. 15—Ezzard Charles KOd Freddy Beshore, 14, Buffalo.

1950—Sept. 27—Ezzard Charles def. Joe Louis in latter's attempted comeback, 15, New York; universal recognition.

1950—Dec. 5—Ezzard Charles KOd Nick Barone, 11, Cincinnati.

1951—Jan. 12—Ezzard Charles KOd Lee Oma, 10, New York.

1951—March 7—Ezzard Charles def. Joe Walcott, 15, Detroit.

1951—May 30—Ezzard Charles def. Joey Maxim, light heavyweight champion, 15, Chicago.

*1951—July 18—Joe Walcott KOd Ezzard Charles, 7, Pittsburgh.

1952—June 5—Joe Walcott def. Ezzard Charles, 15, Philadelphia.

*1952—Sept. 23—Rocky Marciano KOd Joe Walcott, 13, Philadelphia.

1953—May 15—Rocky Marciano KOd Joe Walcott, 1, Chicago.

1953—Sept. 24—Rocky Marciano KOd Roland LaStarza, 11, New York.

1954—June 17—Rocky Marciano def. Ezzard Charles, 15, New York.

1954—Sept. 17—Rocky Marciano KOd Ezzard Charles, 8, New York.

1955—May 16—Rocky Marciano KOd Don Cockell, 9, San Francisco.

1955—Sept. 21—Rocky Marciano KOd Archie Moore, 9, New York. Marciano retired undefeated, Apr. 27, 1956.

*1956—Nov. 30—Floyd Patterson KOd Archie Moore, 5, Chicago.

1957—July 29—Floyd Patterson KOd Hurricane Jackson, 10, New York.

1957—Aug. 22—Floyd Patterson KOd Pete Rademacher, 6, Seattle.

1958—Aug. 18—Floyd Patterson KOd Roy Harris, 12, Los Angeles.

1959—May 1—Floyd Patterson KOd Brian London, 11, Indianapolis.

*1959—June 26—Ingemar Johansson KOd Floyd Patterson, 3, New York.

*1960—June 20—Floyd Patterson KOd Ingemar Johansson, 5, New York. First heavyweight in boxing history to regain title.

1961—Mar. 13—Floyd Patterson KOd Ingemar Johansson, 6, Miami Beach.

1961—Dec. 4—Floyd Patterson KOd Tom McNeeley, 4, Toronto.

*1962—Sept. 25—Sonny Liston KOd Floyd Patterson, 1, Chicago.

1963—July 22—Sonny Liston KOd Floyd Patterson, 1, Las Vegas.

*1964—Feb. 25—Cassius Clay KOd Sonny Liston, 7, Miami Beach.

1965—May 25—Cassius Clay KOd Sonny Liston, 1, Lewiston, Maine.

1965—Nov. 11—Cassius Clay KOd Floyd Patterson, 12, Las Vegas.

1966—Mar. 29—Cassius Clay def. George Chuvalo, 15, Toronto.

1966—May 21—Cassius Clay KOd Henry Cooper, 6, London.

1966—Aug. 6—Cassius Clay KOd Brian London, 3, London.

1966—Sept. 10—Cassius Clay KOd Karl Mildenberger, 12, Frankfurt, Germany.

1966—Nov. 14—Cassius Clay KOd Cleveland Williams, 3, Houston.
1967—Feb. 6—Cassius Clay def. Ernie Terrell, 15, Houston.
1967—Mar. 22—Cassius Clay KOd Zora Folley, 7, New York. Clay was stripped of his title by the WBA and others for refusing military service.
*1970—Feb. 16—Joe Frazier KOd Jimmy Ellis, 5, New York.
1970—Nov. 18—Joe Frazier KOd Bob Foster, 2, Detroit.
1971—Mar. 8—Joe Frazier def. Cassius Clay (Muhammad Ali), 15, New York.
1972—Jan. 15—Joe Frazier KOd Terry Daniels, 4, New Orleans.
1972—May 25—Joe Frazier KOd Ron Stander, 5, Omaha.
*1973—Jan. 22—George Foreman KOd Joe Frazier, 2, Kingston, Jamaica.
1973—Sept. 1—George Foreman KOd Joe Roman, 1, Tokyo.
1974—Mar. 3—George Foreman KOd Ken Norton, 2, Caracas.
*1974—Oct. 30—Muhammad Ali KOd George Foreman, 8, Zaire.
1975—Mar. 24—Muhammad Ali KOd Chuck Wepner, 15, Cleveland.
1975—May 16—Muhammad Ali KOd Ron Lyle, 11, Las Vegas.
1975—June 30—Muhammad Ali def. Joe Bugner, 15, Malaysia.
1975—Oct. 1—Muhammad Ali KOd Joe Frazier, 14, Manila.
1976—Feb. 20—Muhammad Ali KOd Jean-Pierre Coopman, 5, San Juan.
1976—Apr. 30—Muhammad Ali def. Jimmy Young, 15, Landover, Md.
1976—May 25—Muhammad Ali KOd Richard Dunn, 5, Munich.
1976—Sept. 28—Muhammad Ali def. Ken Norton, 15, New York.
1977—May 16—Muhammad Ali def. Alfredo Evangelista, 15, Landover, Md.

1977—Sept. 29—Muhammad Ali def. Earnie Shavers, 15, New York.
*1978—Feb. 15—Leon Spinks def. Muhammad Ali, 15, Las Vegas.
*1978—Sept. 15—Muhammad Ali def. Leon Spinks, 15, New Orleans. Ali retired in 1979.

(Bouts when title changed hands only)

*1978—June 9—(WBC) Larry Holmes def. Ken Norton, 15, Las Vegas.
*1980—Mar. 31—(WBA) Mike Weaver KOd John Tate, 15, Knoxville.
*1982—Dec. 10—(WBA) Michael Dokes KOd Mike Weaver, 1, Las Vegas.
*1983—Sept. 23—(WBA) Gerrie Coetzee KOd Michael Dokes, 10, Richfield, Oh.
*1984—Mar. 10—(WBC) Tim Witherspoon def. Greg Page, 12, Las Vegas, Nev.
*1984—Aug. 31—(WBC) Pinklon Thomas def. Tim Witherspoon, 12, Las Vegas, Nev.
*1984—Dec. 2—(WBA) Greg Page KOd Gerrie Coetzee, 8, Sun City, Bophuthatswana
*1985—Apr. 29—(WBA) Tony Tubbs def. Greg Page, 15, Buffalo, N.Y.
*1985—Sept. 21—(IBF) Michael Spinks def. Larry Holmes, 15, Las Vegas, Nev.
*1986—Jan. 17—(WBA) Tim Witherspoon def. Tony Tubbs, 15, Atlanta, Ga.
*1986—Mar. 23—(WBC) Trevor Berbick def. Pinklon Thomas, 12, Miami, Fla.
1986—Nov. 22—(WBC) Mike Tyson KOd Trevor Berbick, 2, Las Vegas.
1986—Dec. 12—(WBA) James (Bonecrusher) Smith KOd Tim Witherspoon, 1, New York.
1987—Mar. 7—(WBA) Mike Tyson def. James (Bonecrusher) Smith, 12, Las Vegas.

*Title Changed Hands

Canadian Boxing Champions, 1950–1988

Source: Canadian Boxing Federation

Heavyweight
(79.379 kg and over)

1950–51	Vern Escoe (Edmonton)	1979–85	Trevor Berbick (Halifax)
1952–56	Earl Walls (Toronto)	1986	Ken Lakusta (Edmonton)
1958–59	George Chuvalo (Toronto)	1986–87	Willie de Wit (Grand Prairie, Alta.)
1960–62	Robert Cleroux (Montreal)	1988	Donovan "Razor" Ruddock (Toronto)
1964–77	George Chuvalo (Toronto)		

Light Heavyweight
(79.379 kg max.)

1950–51	Tiger Warrington (Liverpool, N.S.)	1968–72	Al Sparks (Winnipeg)
1952	Eddie Zastre (Winnipeg)	1973–80	Gary Summerhays (Brantford)
1953	Yvon Durelle (Baie Ste. Anne)	1981–82	Roddie McDonald (Toronto)
1954	Doug Harper (Winnipeg)	1983–85	Donnie Lalonde (Winnipeg)
1955–59	Yvon Durelle (Baie Ste. Anne)	1986	Roddie McDonald (Toronto)
1960–61	Burke Emery (Sherbrooke)	1986–88	Willie Featherstone (Toronto)
1964–67	Leslie Borden (Montreal)		

Middleweight
(72.575 kg max.)

1950–51	Roy Wouters (Vancouver)	1970	Gary Broughton (Brantford)
1953	Yvon Durelle (Baie Ste. Anne)	1971–72	Dave Downey (Halifax)
1954	Charlie Chase (Montreal)	1975	Lawrence Hafey (New Glasgow)
1955	Lou Lawrence (Vancouver)	1976–79	Fernand Marcotte (Quebec)
1958–61	Wilf Greaves (Edmonton)	1980–82	Ralph Hollett (Halifax)
1962–65	Blair Richardson (Sydney, N.S.)	1983–84	Alex Hilton (Montreal)
1966–69	Dave Downey (Halifax)	1985–88	Michael Olajide (Vancouver)

Welterweight
(66.678 kg max.)

1950–51	Johnny Greco (Montreal)	1971–76	Clyde Gray (Toronto)
1952–53	Marcel Brisebois (Montreal)	1977	Guerrero Chavex (Montreal)
1954	Claude Fortin (Montreal)	1978–79	Clyde Gray (Toronto)
1955	Tony Percy (Montreal)	1980	Chris Clarke (Halifax)
1956–57	Johnny Salkeld (Calgary)	1981–83	Mario Cusson (Montreal)
1958	Gale Kerwin (Ottawa)	1984	Dave Hilton (Montreal)
1960–61	Gale Kerwin (Ottawa)	1985	Donnie Poole (Toronto)
1962–63	Peter Schmidt (Toronto)	1986–87	Ricky Anderson (Halifax)
1964–68	Joey Durelle (Baie Ste. Anne)	1987–88	Donovan Boucher (Toronto)
1969–70	Donato Paduano (Montreal)		

Lightweight
(61.235 kg max.)

1950	Arthur King (Toronto)	1976	Barry Sponagle (New Glasgow, N.S.)
1951–52	Armond Savoie (Montreal)	1977	Cleveland Denny (Montreal)
1953	Arthur King (Toronto)	1978	Gaeton Hart (Buckingham, Que.)
1954–59	Richard Howard (Halifax)	1979	Nicky Furlano (Toronto)
1960–61	Eddie Beatie (Hamilton)	1980	Gaeton Hart (Buckingham, Que.)
1963–65	Tyrone Gardner (Sydney, N.S.)	1981	Michael Lalonde (Hull)
1966	Ronnie Sampson (Sydney, N.S.)	1982	Johnny Summerhays (Brantford)
1967–73	Al Ford (Edmonton)	1983–87	Remo DiCarlo (Toronto)
1974–75	Johnny Summerhays (Brantford)	1987–88	Mark Adams (Parrsboro, N.S.)

Featherweight
(57.153 kg max.)

1950–51	Frankie Almond (Vancouver)	1966–68	Billy McGrandle (Edmonton)
1954	Mike Garlash (Kitchener)	1969–70	Rocky McDougall (Sydney, N.S.)
1955–57	Gaby Palotti (Montreal)	1983–84	Tony Salvatore (Montreal)
1958	Gerry Simpson (Montreal)	1985–87	Tony Pep (Vancouver)
1959–62	Dave Hilton (Montreal)	1988	Barrington Francis (Montreal)
1965	Rocky McDougall (Sydney, N.S.)		

Canadian Interuniversity Athletic Union Champions

Men

	Basketball	Football	Ice Hockey	Soccer	Swimming & Diving	Volleyball
1975-76	Manitoba	Ottawa	Toronto	Alberta	Toronto	British Columbia
1976-77	Acadia	Western Ontario	Toronto	Concordia	Waterloo	Winnipeg
1977-78	St. Mary's	Western Ontario	Alberta	York	Waterloo	Manitoba
1978-79	St. Mary's	Queen's	Alberta	Manitoba	Waterloo	Saskatchewan
1979-80	Victoria	Acadia	Alberta	Alberta	Toronto	Manitoba
1980-81	Victoria	Alberta	Moncton	New Brunswick	Toronto	Alberta
1981-82	Victoria	Acadia	Moncton	McGill	Calgary	Calgary
1982-83	Victoria	British Columbia	Saskatchewan	McGill	Calgary	British Columbia
1983-84	Victoria	Calgary	Toronto	Laurentian	Calgary	Manitoba
1984-85	Victoria	Guelph	York	British Columbia	Calgary	Manitoba
1985-86	Victoria	Calgary	Alberta	British Columbia	Toronto	Winnipeg
1986-87	Brandon	British Columbia	Trois-Rivières	British Columbia	Calgary	Winnipeg
1987-88	Brandon	McGill	York	Victoria	Calgary	Manitoba

Women

	Basketball	Field Hockey	Swimming & Diving	Track & Field	Volleyball
1975-76	Laurentian	Toronto	–	–	Western Ontario
1976-77	Laurentian	Dalhousie	Acadia	–	British Columbia
1977-78	Laurentian	Toronto	Acadia	–	British Columbia
1978-79	Laurentian	British Columbia	Toronto	–	Saskatchewan
1979-80	Victoria	Toronto	Toronto	–	Saskatchewan
1980-81	Victoria	British Columbia	Toronto	Western Ontario	Saskatchewan
1981-82	Victoria	Toronto	Toronto	Western Ontario	Dalhousie
1982-83	Bishop's	British Columbia	Toronto	Western Ontario	Winnipeg
1983-84	Bishop's	British Columbia	Toronto	York	Winnipeg
1984-85	Victoria	Victoria	British Columbia	Alta. & Sask.	Winnipeg
1985-86	Toronto	Toronto	British Columbia	Saskatchewan	Winnipeg
1986-87	Victoria	Toronto	Toronto	Calgary	Winnipeg
1987-88	Manitoba	Victoria	Toronto	York	Winnipeg

Golf

Canadian Open Golf Champions

Source: The Royal Canadian Golf Association

Year	Winner	Year	Winner	Year	Winner	Year	Winner
1961	Jacky Cupit	1968	Bob Charles	1975	Tom Weiskopf	1982	Bruce Lietzke
1962	Ted Kroll	1969	Tommy Aaron	1976	Jerry Pate	1983	John Cook
1963	Doug Ford	1970	Kermit Zarley	1977	Lee Trevino	1984	Greg Norman
1964	Kel Nagle	1971	Lee Trevino	1978	Bruce Lietzke	1985	Curtis Strange
1965	Gene Littler	1972	Gay Brewer	1979	Lee Trevino	1986	Bob Murphy
1966	Don Massengale	1973	Tom Weiskopf	1980	Bob Gilder	1987	Curtis Strange
1967	Billy Casper	1974	Bobby Nichols	1981	Peter Oosterhuis	1988	Ken Green

Masters Golf Tournament Champions

Year	Winner	Year	Winner	Year	Winner	Year	Winner
1961	Gary Player	1968	Bob Goalby	1975	Jack Nicklaus	1982	Craig Stadler
1962	Arnold Palmer	1969	George Archer	1976	Ray Floyd	1983	Severiano Ballesteros
1963	Jack Nicklaus	1970	Billy Casper	1977	Tom Watson	1984	Ben Crenshaw
1964	Arnold Palmer	1971	Charles Coody	1978	Gary Player	1985	Bernhard Langer
1965	Jack Nicklaus	1972	Jack Nicklaus	1979	Fuzzy Zoeller	1986	Jack Nicklaus
1966	Jack Nicklaus	1973	Tommy Aaron	1980	Severiano Ballesteros	1987	Larry Mize
1967	Gay Brewer Jr.	1974	Gary Player	1981	Tom Watson	1988	Sandy Lyle

U.S. Men's Open Golf Champions

Year	Winner	Year	Winner	Year	Winner	Year	Winner
1961	Gene Littler	1968	Lee Trevino	1975	Lou Graham	1982	Tom Watson
1962	Jack Nicklaus	1969	Orville Moody	1976	Jerry Pate	1983	Larry Nelson
1963	Julius Boros	1970	Tony Jacklin	1977	Hubert Green	1984	Fuzzy Zoeller
1964	Ken Venturi	1971	Lee Trevino	1978	Andy North	1985	Andy North
1965	Gary Player	1972	Jack Nicklaus	1979	Hale Irwin	1986	Ray Floyd
1966	Billy Casper	1973	Johnny Miller	1980	Jack Nicklaus	1987	Scott Simpson
1967	Jack Nicklaus	1974	Hale Irwin	1981	David Graham	1988	Curtis Strange

Professional Golfer's Association Championships

Year	Winner	Year	Winner	Year	Winner	Year	Winner
1961	Jerry Barber	1968	Julius Boros	1975	Jack Nicklaus	1982	Ray Floyd
1962	Gary Player	1969	Ray Floyd	1976	Dave Stockton	1983	Hal Sutton
1963	Jack Nicklaus	1970	Dave Stockton	1977	Lanny Wadkins	1984	Lee Trevino
1964	Bob Nichols	1971	Jack Nicklaus	1978	John Mahaffey	1985	Hubert Green
1965	Dave Marr	1972	Gary Player	1979	David Graham	1986	Bob Tway
1966	Al Geiberger	1973	Jack Nicklaus	1980	Jack Nicklaus	1987	Larry Nelson
1967	Don January	1974	Lee Trevino	1981	Larry Nelson	1988	Jeff Sluman

British Open Golf Champions

Year	Winner	Year	Winner	Year	Winner	Year	Winner
1961	Arnold Palmer	1968	Gary Player	1975	Tom Watson	1982	Tom Watson
1962	Arnold Palmer	1969	Tony Jacklin	1976	Johnny Miller	1983	Tom Watson
1963	Bob Charles	1970	Jack Nicklaus	1977	Tom Watson	1984	Seve Ballesteros
1964	Tony Lema	1971	Lee Trevino	1978	Jack Nicklaus	1985	Sandy Lyle
1965	Peter Thomson	1972	Lee Trevino	1979	Seve Ballesteros	1986	Greg Norman
1966	Jack Nicklaus	1973	Tom Weiskopf	1980	Tom Watson	1987	Nick Faldo
1967	Roberto de Vicenzo	1974	Gary Player	1981	Bill Rogers	1988	Seve Ballesteros

PGA Leading Money Winners

Year	Player	Dollars	Year	Player	Dollars	Year	Player	Dollars
						1978	Tom Watson	362 429
1960	Arnold Palmer	75 262	1969	Frank Beard	175 223	1979	Tom Watson	462 636
1961	Gary Player	64 540	1970	Lee Trevino	157 037	1980	Tom Watson	530 808
1962	Arnold Palmer	81 448	1971	Jack Nicklaus	244 490	1981	Tom Kite	375 699
1963	Arnold Palmer	128 230	1972	Jack Nicklaus	320 542	1982	Craig Stadler	446 462
1964	Jack Nicklaus	113 284	1973	Jack Nicklaus	308 362	1983	Hal Sutton	426 668
1965	Jack Nicklaus	140 752	1974	Johnny Miller	353 201	1984	Tom Watson	476 260
1966	Billy Casper	121 944	1975	Jack Nicklaus	323 149	1985	Curtis Strange	542 321
1967	Jack Nicklaus	188 988	1976	Jack Nicklaus	266 438	1986	Greg Norman	653 296
1968	Billy Casper	205 168	1977	Tom Watson	310 653	1987	Curtis Strange	925 941

(1) U.S. dollars

Professional Golf Tournaments in 1988

Men

Date	Event	Winner	Score	Prize
Jan. 17	MONY Tournament of Champions, Carlsbad, Cal.	Steve Pate	202	$90 000
Jan. 24	Bob Hope Chrysler Classic, Indian Wells, Cal.	Jay Haas	338	180 000
Jan. 31	Phoenix Open, Ariz.	Sandy Lyle	269	117 000
Feb. 7	A.T.&T. National Pro-Am, Pebble Beach, Cal.	Steve Jones	280	126 000
Feb. 8	Hawaiian Open, Honolulu	Lanny Wadkins	271	108 000
Feb. 14	Andy Williams Open, La Jolla, Cal.	Steve Pate	269	117 000
Feb. 28	Los Angeles Open	Chip Beck	267	135 000
Mar. 6	Doral Ryder Open, Miami, Fla.	Ben Crenshaw	274	180 000
Mar. 13	Honda Classic, Coral Springs, Fla.	Joey Sidelar	276	126 000
Mar. 20	Bay Hill Classic, Orlando, Fla.	Paul Azinger	271	135 000
Mar. 27	Tournament Players Championship, Ponte Vedra, Fla.	Mark McCumber	273	205 000
Apr. 3	Greater Greensboro Open, N.C.	Sandy Lyle	271	180 000
Apr. 10	Masters Tournament, Augusta, Ga.	Sandy Lyle	281	183 000
Apr. 17	Heritage Classic, Hilton Head, S.C.	Greg Norman	271	126 000
Apr. 24	U.S.F.&G. Classic, New Orleans, La.	Chip Beck	262	135 000
May 1	Independent Insurance AgentOpen, The Woodlands, Tex.	Curtis Strange	270	126 000
May 8	Las Vegas Invitational	Gary Koch	274	250 000
May 15	Byron Nelson Classic, Irving, Tex.	Bruce Lietzke	271	135 000
May 22	Colonial National Tournament, Ft. Worth, Tex.	Lanny Wadkins	270	135 000
May 29	Memorial Tournament, Dublin, Oh.	Curtis Strange	274	160 000
June 5	Kemper Open, Potomac, Md.	Morris Hatalsky	*274	144 000
June 12	Westchester Classic, Harrison, N.Y.	Seve Ballesteros	276	126 000
June 20	U.S. Open, Brookline, Mass.	Curtis Strange	*278	180 000
June 26	Atlanta Classic, Marietta, Ga.	Larry Nelson	268	126 000
July 3	Western Open, Oak Brook, Ill.	Jim Benepe	278	162 000
July 10	Anheuser-Busch Classic, Williamsburg, Va.	Tom Sieckmann	*270	117 000
July 24	Greater Hartford Open, Conn.	Mark Brooks	269	126 000
July 31	Buick Open, Grand Blanc, Mich.	Scott Verplank	268	126 000
Aug. 7	St. Jude Classic, Tenn.	Jodie Mudd	273	171 000
Aug. 14	PGA Championship, Palm Beach Gardens, Fla.	Jeff Sluman	272	160 000
Aug. 21	The International, Castle Rock, Col.	Joey Sindelar	+17 pts.	180 000
Aug. 28	World Series of Golf, Akron, Oh.	Mike Reid	*275	162 000
	Canadian Open, Oakville, Ont.	Curtis Strange	276	108 000
Sept. 11	Greater Milwaukee Open	Ken Green	268	126 000
Sept. 25	Southwest Classic, Abilene, Tex.		272	72 000
Sept. 18	Bank of Boston Classic, Sutton, Mass.	Mark Calcavecchia	274	108 000

Women

Date	Event	Winner	Score	Prize
Feb. 8	Mazda Classic, Boca Raton, Fla.	Nancy Lopez	283	$30 000
Feb. 28	Hawaiian Open, Honolulu	Ayako Okamota	213	45 000
Mar. 6	Kemper Open, Princeville, Ha.	Betsy King	280	45 000
Mar. 20	Tucson Open, Tucson, Ariz.	Laura Davis	278	45 000
Mar. 27	Turquoise Classic, Phoenix, Ariz.	Ok-Hee Ku	281	52 000
Apr. 3	Dinah Shore Invitational, Rancho Mirage, Cal.	Amy Alcott	274	80 000
Apr. 17	All Star-Centinela Open, Los Angeles	Nancy Lopez	*210	60 000
May 18	Crestar Classic, Suffolk, Va.	Juli Inkster	209	45 000
May 15	Chrysler-Plymouth Classic, Middletown, N.J.	Nancy Lopez	204	37 000
May 29	Corning Classic, Corning, N.Y.	Sherri Turner	273	48 000
June 5	Jamie Farr Toledo Classic, Oh.	Laura Davies	277	41 000
June 12	Rochester International, N.Y.	Mei-chi Cheng	*287	45 000
June 7	McDonald's Classic, Wilmington, Del.	Betsy King	278	75 000
June 14	Mayflower Classic, Indianapolis, Ind.	Colleen Walker	278	52 500
June 19	Lady Keystone Open, Hershey, Pa.	Sherley Furlong	205	45 000
July 3	Du Maurier Classic, British Columbia	Sally Little	279	75 000
July 10	Mayflower Classic, Indianapolis	Terry-Jo Myers	276	60 000
July 17	Boston Five Classic, Danvers, Mass.	Colleen Walker	274	45 000
July 24	U.S. Women's Open, Edison, N.J.	Liselotte Neumann	277	70 000
July 31	Greater Washington Open, Bethesda, Md.	Ayako Okamoto	206	33 000
Aug. 7	Pat Bradley International, High Point, N.C.	Martha Nause	14pts	62 500
Aug. 23	Atlantic City Classic, Somers Pt., N.J.	Juli Inkster	*206	33 750
Aug. 28	World Championship of Women's Golf, Buford, Ga.	Rosie Jones	279	81 500
Sept. 5	Rail Charity Classic, Springfield, Ill.	Betsy King	207	37 000
Sept. 11	Cellular One-Ping Championship, Portland, Ore.	Betsy King	213	33 750
Sept. 18	Safeco Classic, Kent, Wash.	Juli Inkster	277	33 750
Sept. 25	San Jose Classic, Cal.		205	45 000

*Won playoff.

(1) U.S. dollars

U.S. Women's Open Golf Champions

Year	Winner	Year	Winner	Year	Winner	Year	Winner
1957	Betsy Rawls	1965	Carol Mann	1973	Susie Maxwell Berning	1981	Pat Bradley
1958	Mickey Wright	1966	Sandra Spuzich	1974	Sandra Haynie	1982	Janet Alex
1959	Mickey Wright	1967	Catherine Lacoste*	1975	Sandra Palmer	1983	Jan Stephenson
1960	Betsy Rawls	1968	Susie Maxwell Berning	1976	JoAnne Carner	1984	Hollis Stacy
1961	Mickey Wright	1969	Donna Caponi	1977	Hollis Stacy	1985	Kathy Baker
1962	Murle Lindstrom	1970	Donna Caponi	1978	Hollis Stacy	1986	Jane Geddes
1963	Mary Mills	1971	JoAnne Carner	1979	Jerilyn Britz	1987	Laura Davies
1964	Mickey Wright	1972	Susie Maxwell Berning	1980	Amy Alcott	1988	Liselotte Neumann

*Amateur

Tennis

U.S. Open Champions

Men's Singles

Year	Champion	Final opponent	Year	Champion	Final opponent
1920	Bill Tilden	William Johnston	1955	Tony Trabert	Ken Rosewall
1921	Bill Tilden	Wallace Johnson	1956	Ken Rosewall	Lewis Hoad
1922	Bill Tilden	William Johnston	1957	Malcolm Anderson	Ashley Cooper
1923	Bill Tilden	William Johnston	1958	Ashley Cooper	Malcolm Anderson
1924	Bill Tilden	William Johnston	1959	Neale A. Fraser	Alejandro Olmedo
1925	Bill Tilden	William Johnston	1960	Neale A. Fraser	Rod Laver
1926	Rene Lacoste	Jean Borotra	1961	Roy Emerson	Rod Laver
1927	Rene Lacoste	Bill Tilden	1962	Rod Laver	Roy Emerson
1928	Henri Cochet	Francis Hunter	1963	Rafael Osuna	F. A. Froehling 3d
1929	Bill Tilden	Francis Hunter	1964	Roy Emerson	Fred Stolle
1930	John Doeg	Francis Shields	1965	Manuel Santana	Cliff Drysdale
1931	H. Ellsworth Vines	George Lott	1966	Fred Stolle	John Newcombe
1932	H. Ellsworth Vines	Henri Cochet	1967	John Newcombe	Clark Graebner
1933	Fred Perry	John Crawford	1968	Arthur Ashe	Tom Okker
1934	Fred Perry	Wilmer Allison	1969	Rod Laver	Tony Roche
1935	Wilmer Allison	Sidney Wood	1970	Ken Rosewall	Tony Roche
1936	Fred Perry	Don Budge	1971	Stan Smith	Jan Kodes
1937	Don Budge	Baron G. von Cramm	1972	Ilie Nastase	Arthur Ashe
1938	Don Budge	C. Gene Mako	1973	John Newcombe	Jan Kodes
1939	Robert Riggs	S. Welby Van Horn	1974	Jimmy Connors	Ken Rosewall
1940	Don McNeill	Robert Riggs	1975	Manuel Orantes	Jimmy Connors
1941	Robert Riggs	F. L. Kovacs	1976	Jimmy Connors	Bjorn Borg
1942	F. R. Schroeder Jr.	Frank Parker	1977	Guillermo Vilas	Jimmy Connors
1943	Joseph Hunt	Jack Kramer	1978	Jimmy Connors	Bjorn Borg
1944	Frank Parker	William Talbert	1979	John McEnroe	Vitas Gerulaitis
1945	Frank Parker	William Talbert	1980	John McEnroe	Bjorn Borg
1946	Jack Kramer	Thomas Brown Jr.	1981	John McEnroe	Bjorn Borg
1947	Jack Kramer	Frank Parker	1982	Jimmy Connors	Ivan Lendl
1948	Pancho Gonzales	Eric Sturgess	1983	Jimmy Connors	Ivan Lendl
1949	Pancho Gonzales	F. R. Schroeder Jr.	1984	John McEnroe	Ivan Lendl
1950	Arthur Larsen	Herbert Flam	1985	Ivan Lendl	John McEnroe
1951	Frank Sedgman	E. Victor Seixas Jr.	1986	Ivan Lendl	Miroslav Mecir
1952	Frank Sedgman	Gardnar Mulloy	1987	Ivan Lendl	Mats Wilander
1953	Tony Trabert	E. Victor Seixas Jr.	1988	Mats Wilander	Ivan Lendl
1954	E. Victor Seixas Jr.	Rex Hartwig			

Women's Singles

Year	Champion	Final opponent	Year	Champion	Final opponent
1936	Alice Marble	Helen Jacobs	1963	Maria Bueno	Margaret Smith
1937	Anita Lizana	Jadwiga Jedrzejowska	1964	Maria Bueno	Carole Graebner
1938	Alice Marble	Nancye Wynne	1965	Margaret Smith	Billie Jean Moffitt
1939	Alice Marble	Helen Jacobs	1966	Maria Bueno	Nancy Richey
1940	Alice Marble	Helen Jacobs	1967	Billie Jean King	Ann Haydon Jones
1941	Sarah Palfrey Cooke	Pauline Betz	1968	Virginia Wade	Billie Jean King
1942	Pauline Betz	Louise Brough	1969	Margaret Court	Nancy Richey
1943	Pauline Betz	Louis Brough	1970	Margaret Court	Rosemary Casals
1944	Pauline Betz	Margaret Osborne	1971	Billie Jean King	Rosemary Casals
1945	Sarah P. Cooke	Pauline Betz	1972	Billie Jean King	Kerry Melville
1946	Pauline Betz	Doris Hart	1973	Margaret Court	Evonne Goolagong
1947	Louise Brough	Margaret Osborne	1974	Billie Jean King	Evonne Goolagong
1948	Margaret Osborne duPont	Louise Brough	1975	Chris Evert	Evonne Goolagong
1949	Margaret Osborne duPont	Doris Hart	1976	Chris Evert	Evonne Goolagong
1950	Margaret Osborne duPont	Doris Hart	1977	Chris Evert	Wendy Turnbull
1951	Maureen Connolly	Shirley Fry	1978	Chris Evert	Pam Shriver
1952	Maureen Connolly	Doris Hart	1979	Tracy Austin	Chris Evert Lloyd
1953	Maureen Connolly	Doris Hart	1980	Chris Evert Lloyd	Hana Mandlikova
1954	Doris Hart	Louise Brough	1981	Tracy Austin	Martina Navratilova
1955	Doris Hart	Patricia Ward	1982	Chris Evert Lloyd	Hana Mandlikova
1956	Shirley Fry	Althea Gibson	1983	Martina Navratilova	Chris Evert Lloyd
1957	Althea Gibson	Louise Brough	1984	Martina Navratilova	Chris Evert Lloyd
1958	Althea Gibson	Darlene Hard	1985	Hana Mandlikova	Martina Navratilova
1959	Maria Bueno	Christine Truman	1986	Martina Navratilova	Helena Sukova
1960	Darlene Hard	Maria Bueno	1987	Martina Navratilova	Steffi Graf
1961	Darlene Hard	Ann Haydon	1988	Steffi Graf	Gabriela Sabatini
1962	Margaret Smith	Darlene Hard			

Mixed Doubles

Year	Champions	Year	Champions
1974	Pam Teeguarden—Geoff Masters	1982	Anne Smith—Kevin Curren
1975	Rosemary Casals—Dick Stockton	1983	Elizabeth Sayers—John Fitzgerald
1976	Billie Jean King—Phil Dent	1984	Manuela Maleeva—Tom Gullikson
1977	Betty Stove—Frew McMillan	1985	Martina Navratilova—Heinz Gunthardt
1978	Betty Stove—Frew McMillan	1986	Raffaella Reggi—Sergio Casal
1979	Greer Stevens—Bob Hewitt	1987	Martina Navratilova—Emilio Sanchez
1980	Wendy Turnbull—Marty Riessen	1988	Jana Novotna—Jim Pugh
1981	Anne Smith—Kevin Curren		

Men's Doubles

Year	Champions
1973	John Newcombe—Owen Davidson
1974	Bob Lutz—Stan Smith
1975	Jimmy Connors—Ilie Nastase
1976	Marty Riessen—Tom Okker
1977	Bob Hewitt—Frew McMillan
1978	Stan Smith—Bob Lutz
1979	John McEnroe—Peter Fleming
1980	Bob Lutz—Stan Smith
1981	John McEnroe—Peter Fleming
1982	Kevin Curren—Steve Denton
1983	John McEnroe—Peter Fleming
1984	Tomas Smid—John Fitzgerald
1985	Ken Flach—Robert Seguso
1986	Andres Gomez—Slobodan Zivolinovic
1987	Stefan Edberg—Anders Jarryd
1988	Sergio Casal—Emilio Sanchez

Women's Doubles

Year	Champions
1973	Margaret S. Court—Virginia Wade
1974	Billie Jean King—Rosemary Casals
1975	Margaret Court—Virginia Wade
1976	Linky Boshoff—Ilana Kloss
1977	Betty Stove—Martina Navratilova
1978	Martina Navratilova—Billie Jean King
1979	Betty Stove—Wendy Turnbull
1980	Billie Jean King—Martina Navratilova
1981	Anne Smith—Kathy Jordan
1982	Rosemary Casals—Wendy Turnbull
1983	Martina Navratilova—Pam Shriver
1984	Martina Navratilova—Pam Shriver
1985	Claudia Kohde-Kilsch—Helena Sukova
1986	Martina Navratilova—Pam Shriver
1987	Martina Navratilova—Pam Shriver
1988	Gigi Fernandez—Robin White

Davis Cup Challenge Round

Year	Result	Year	Result	Year	Result
1900	United States 5, British Isles 0	1930	France 4, United States 1	1962	Australia 5, Mexico 0
1901	(not played)	1931	France 3, Great Britain 2	1963	United States 3, Australia 2
1902	United States 3, British Isles 2	1932	France 3, United States 2	1964	Australia 3, United States 2
1903	British Isles 4, United States 1	1933	Great Britain 3, France 2	1965	Australia 4, Spain 1
1904	British Isles 5, Belgium 0	1934	Great Britain 4, United States 1	1966	Australia 4, India 1
1905	British Isles 5, United States 0	1935	Great Britain 5, United States 0	1967	Australia 4, Spain 1
1906	British Isles 5, United States 0	1936	Great Britain 3, Australia 2	1968	United States 4, Australia 1
1907	Australia 3, British Isles 2	1937	United States 4, Great Britain 1	1969	United States 5, Romania 0
1908	Australasia 3, United States 2	1938	United States 3, Australia 2	1970	United States 5, W. Germany 0
1909	Australasia 5, United States 0	1939	Australia 3, United States 2	1971	United States 3, Romania 2
1910	(not played)	1940-45	(not played)	1972	United States 3, Romania 2
1911	Australasia 5, United States 0	1946	United States 5, Australia 0	1973	Australia 5, United States 0
1912	British Isles 3, Australasia 2	1947	United States 4, Australia 1	1974	South Africa (default by India)
1913	United States 3, British Isles 2	1948	United States 5, Australia 0	1975	Sweden 3, Czech. 2
1914	Australasia 3, United States 2	1949	United States 4, Australia 1	1976	Italy 4, Chile 1
1915-18	(not played)	1950	Australia 4, United States 1	1977	Australia 3, Italy 1
1919	Australasia 4, British Isles 1	1951	Australia 3, United States 2	1978	United States 4, Great Britain 1
1920	United States 5, Australasia 0	1952	Australia 4, United States 1	1979	United States 5, Italy 0
1921	United States 5, Japan 0	1953	Australia 3, United States 2	1980	Czechoslovakia 4, Italy 1
1922	United States 4, Australasia 1	1954	United States 3, Australia 2	1981	United States 3, Argentina 1
1923	United States 4, Australasia 1	1955	Australia 5, United States 0	1982	United States 3, France, 0
1924	United States 5, Australasia 0	1956	Australia 5, United States 0	1983	Australia 3, Sweden 1
1925	United States 5, France 0	1957	Australia 3, United States 2	1984	Sweden 3, United States 0
1926	United States 4, France 1	1958	United States 3, Australia 2	1985	Sweden 3, W. Germany 2
1927	France 3, United States 2	1959	Australia 3, United States 2	1986	Australia 3, Sweden 2
1928	France 4, United States 1	1960	Australia 4, Italy 1	1987	Sweden 5, India 0
1929	France 3, United States 2	1961	Australia 5, Italy 0		

All-England Champions, Wimbledon

Men's Singles

Year	Champion	Final opponent	Year	Champion	Final opponent
1957	Lew Hoad	Ashley Cooper	1973	Jan Kodes	Alex Metreveli
1958	Ashley Cooper	Neale Fraser	1974	Jimmy Connors	Ken Rosewall
1959	Alex Olmedo	Rod Laver	1975	Arthur Ashe	Jimmy Connors
1960	Neale Fraser	Rod Laver	1976	Bjorn Borg	Ilie Nastase
1961	Rod Laver	Chuck McKinley	1977	Bjorn Borg	Jimmy Connors
1962	Rod Laver	Martin Mulligan	1978	Bjorn Borg	Jimmy Connors
1963	Chuck McKinley	Fred Stolle	1979	Bjorn Borg	Roscoe Tanner
1964	Roy Emerson	Fred Stolle	1980	Bjorn Borg	John McEnroe
1965	Roy Emerson	Fred Stolle	1981	John McEnroe	Bjorn Borg
1966	Manuel Santana	Dennis Ralston	1982	Jimmy Connors	John McEnroe
1967	John Newcombe	Wilhelm Bungert	1983	John McEnroe	Chris Lewis
1968	Rod Laver	Tony Roche	1984	John McEnroe	Jimmy Connors
1969	Rod Laver	John Newcombe	1985	Boris Becker	Kevin Curren
1970	John Newcombe	Ken Rosewall	1986	Boris Becker	Ivan Lendl
1971	John Newcombe	Stan Smith	1987	Pat Cash	Ivan Lendl
1972	Stan Smith	Ilie Nastase	1988	Stefan Edberg	Boris Becker

Women's Singles

Year	Champion	Year	Champion	Year	Champion	Year	Champion
1957	Althea Gibson	1965	Margaret Smith	1973	Billie Jean King	1981	Chris Evert Lloyd
1958	Althea Gibson	1966	Billie Jean King	1974	Chris Evert	1982	Martina Navratilova
1959	Maria Bueno	1967	Billie Jean King	1975	Billie Jean King	1983	Martina Navratilova
1960	Maria Bueno	1968	Billie Jean King	1976	Chris Evert	1984	Martina Navratilova
1961	Angela Mortimer	1969	Ann Haydon-Jones	1977	Virginia Wade	1985	Martina Navratilova
1962	Karen Hantze-Susman	1970	Margaret Court	1978	Martina Navratilova	1986	Martina Navratilova
1963	Margaret Smith	1971	Evonne Goolagong	1979	Martina Navratilova	1987	Martina Navratilova
1964	Maria Bueno	1972	Billie Jean King	1980	Evonne Goolagong	1988	Steffi Graf

Auto Racing

World Grand Prix Champions

Year	Driver	Year	Driver	Year	Driver
1950	Nino Farina, Italy	1963	Jim Clark, Scotland	1976	James Hunt, England
1951	Juan Fangio, Argentina	1964	John Surtees, England	1977	Niki Lauda, Austria
1952	Alberto Ascari, Italy	1965	Jim Clark, Scotland	1978	Mario Andretti, U.S.
1953	Alberto Ascari, Italy	1966	Jack Brabham, Australia	1979	Jody Scheckter, So. Africa
1954	Juan Fangio, Argentina	1967	Denis Hulme, New Zealand	1980	Alan Jones, Australia
1955	Juan Fangio, Argentina	1968	Graham Hill, England	1981	Nelson Piquet, Brazil
1956	Juan Fangio, Argentina	1969	Jackie Stewart, Scotland	1982	Keke Rosberg, Finland
1957	Juan Fangio, Argentina	1970	Jochen Rindt, Austria	1983	Nelson Piquet, Brazil
1958	Mike Hawthorne, England	1971	Jackie Stewart, Scotland	1984	Niki Lauda, Austria
1959	Jack Brabham, Australia	1972	Emerson Fittipaldi, Brazil	1985	Alain Prost, France
1960	Jack Brabham, Australia	1973	Jackie Stewart, Scotland	1986	Alain Prost, France
1961	Phil Hill, United States	1974	Emerson Fittipaldi, Brazil	1987	Nelson Piquet, Brazil
1962	Graham Hill, England	1975	Niki Lauda, Austria		

Auto Racing

Indianapolis 500 Winners

Year	Winner	Chassis	Engine	Avg[1] km/h	Purse	Runner up
1970	Al Unser	P.J. Colt	Ford	250.647	$1 000 002	Mark Donohue
1971	Al Unser	P.J. Colt	Ford	253.843	1 001 604	Peter Revson
1972	Mark Donohue	McLaren	Offenhauser	263.064	1 011 846	Al Unser
1973	Gordon Johncock	Eagle	Offenhauser	255.901[2]	1 011 846	Billy Vukovich
1974	Johnny Rutherford	McLaren	Offenhauser	255.217	1 015 686	Bobby Unser
1975	Bobby Unser	Eagle	Offenhauser	240.128[3]	1 101 322	Johnny Rutherford
1976	Johnny Rutherford	McLaren	Offenhauser	239.343[4]	1 037 775	A.J. Foyt
1977	A.J. Foyt	Coyote	Ford	259.630	1 116 807	Tom Sneva
1978	Al Unser	Lola	Cosworth	259.681	1 145 225	Tom Sneva
1979	Rick Mears	Penske	Cosworth	255.716	1 271 954	A.J. Foyt
1980	Johnny Rutherford	Chaparral	Cosworth	229.908	1 502 425	Tom Sneva
1981	Bobby Unser	Penske	Cosworth	223.829	1 609 375	Mario Andretti
1982	Gordon Johncock	Wildcat	Cosworth	260.748	2 067 475	Rick Mears
1983	Tom Sneva	March	Cosworth	260.895	2 411 450	Al Unser
1984	Rick Mears	March	Cosworth	263.315	2 795 399	Roberto Guerrero
1985	Danny Sullivan	March	Cosworth	246.194	3 261 025	Mario Andretti
1986	Bobby Rahal	March	Cosworth	274.743	4 001 450	Kevin Cogan
1987	Al Unser	March	Cosworth	260.988	4 490 375	Roberto Guerrero
1988	Rick Mears	Penske	ChevyV8	144.809	5 000 016	Emerson Fittipaldi

(1) Averages are for the entire race. (2) 332.5 miles. (3) 435 miles. (4) 255 miles. Race record—274.743 km/h, Bobby Rahal, 1986.

Daytona 500 Winners

Year	Driver, car	Avg. km/h	Year	Driver, car	Avg. km/h
1970	Pete Hamilton, Plymouth	240.753	1980	Buddy Baker, Oldsmobile	285.815
1971	Richard Petty, Plymouth	232.473	1981	Richard Petty, Buick	273.019
1972	A. J. Foyt, Mercury	259.982	1982	Bobby Allison, Buick	247.818
1973	Richard Petty, Dodge	252.990	1983	Cale Yarborough, Pontiac	251.017
1974	Richard Petty, Dodge[2]	226.741	1984	Cale Yarborough, Chevrolet	242.995
1975	Benny Parsons, Chevrolet	247.267	1985	Bill Elliott, Ford	277.226
1976	David Pearson, Mercury	244.908	1986	Geoff Bodine, Chevrolet	238.376
1977	Cale Yarborough, Chevrolet	246.574	1987	Bill Elliott, Ford	176.263
1978	Bobby Allison, Ford	257.083	1988	Bobby Allison, Buick	137.531
1979	Richard Petty, Oldsmobile	231.702			

(1) Averages are for the entire race. (2) 450 miles.

Notable One-Mile Speed Records

Date	Driver	Car	Km/h	Date	Driver	Car	Km/h
1/26/06	Marriott	Stanley (Steam)	205.442	9/ 3/35	Campbell	Bluebird Special	484.61
3/16/10	Oldfield	Benz	211.983	11/19/37	Eyston	Thunderbolt 1	501.17
4/23/11	Burman	Benz	228.089	9/16/38	Eyston	Thunderbolt 1	575.3
2/12/19	DePalma	Packard	241.194	8/23/39	Cobb	Railton	593.7
4/27/20	Milton	Dusenberg	249.816	9/16/47	Cobb	Railton-Mobil	634.4
4/28/26	Parry-Thomas	Thomas Spl.	274.585	8/ 5/63	Breedlove	Spirit of America	655.71
3/29/27	Seagrave	Sunbeam	327.959	10/27/64	Arfons	Green Monster	863.73
4/22/28	Keech	White Triplex	334.013	11/15/65	Breedlove	Spirit of America	966.547
3/11/29	Seagrave	Irving-Napier	372.466	10/23/70	Gabelich	Blue Flame	1 001.640
2/ 5/31	Campbell	Napier-Campbell	396.026	10/9/79	Barrett	Budweiser Rocket	1 027.759*-
2/24/32	Campbell	Napier-Campbell	408.70	10/4/83	Noble	Thrust 2	1 019.7
2/22/33	Campbell	Napier-Campbell	437.905				

*not recognized as official by sanctioning bodies.

Canadian Alpine Skiing Champions

Source: Ski Canada

Men

	Downhill	Slalom	Giant Slalom	Super Giant Slalom
1979	Ken Read	Raymond Pratte	Peter Monod	—
1980	Ken Read	Peter Monod	Peter Monod	—
1981	Robin McLeish	Peter Monod	Peter Monod	—
1982	Urs Raeber (SUI)	Peter Monod	Jim Read	—
1983	Steve Podborski	Francois Jodoin	Mike Tommy	—
1984	Steve Podborski	Mike Tommy	Jim Read	Jim Read
1985	Steven Lee (AUS)	Gordon Perry	Jim Read	Mike Brown (USA)
1986	Don Stevens	Jim Read	Jim Read	Derek Trussler
1987	Brian Stemmle	Alain Villiard	Alain Villiard	Jim Read
1988	Steven Lee (AUS)	Jack Miller (USA)	Tiger Shaw (USA)	Leonard Stock (AUT)

Women

	Downhill	Slalom	Giant Slalom	Super Giant Slalom
1979	Loni Klettl	Kathy Kreiner	Judy Richardson	—
1980	Laurie Graham	Lynn Lacasse	Ann Blackburn	—
1981	Gerry Sorensen	Lynn Lacasse	Diana Haight	—
1982	Dianne Lehodey	Lynn Lacasse	Lynn Lacasse	—
1983	Gerry Sorensen	Lynn Lacasse	Liisa Savijarvi	—
1984	Diana Haight	Andréa Bedard	Liisa Savijarvi	Laurie Graham
1985	Laurie Graham	Andréa Bedard	Liisa Savijarvi	Karen Percy
1986	Karen Percy	Josée Lacasse	Josée Lacasse	Karen Percy
1987	Liisa Savijarvi	Julie Klotz	Josée Lacasse	Karen Percy
1988	Laurie Graham	Karen Percy	Josée Lacasse	Karen Percy

World Cup Alpine Champions

Men

1967	Jean Claude Killy, France	1975	Gustavo Thoeni, Italy	1983	Phil Mahre, U.S.
1968	Jean Claude Killy, France	1976	Ingemar Stenmark, Sweden	1984	Pirmin Zurbriggen, Switzerland
1969	Karl Schranz, Austria	1977	Ingemar Stenmark, Sweden	1985	Marc Girardelli, Luxembourg
1970	Karl Schranz, Austria	1978	Ingemar Stenmark, Sweden	1986	Marc Girardelli, Luxembourg
1971	Gustavo Thoeni, Italy	1979	Peter Luescher, Switzerland	1987	Pirmin Zurbriggen, Switzerland
1972	Gustavo Thoeni, Italy	1980	Andreas Wenzel, Liechtenstein	1988	Pirmin Zurbriggen, Switzerland
1973	Gustavo Thoeni, Italy	1981	Phil Mahre, U.S.		
1974	Piero Gros, Italy	1982	Phil Mahre, U.S.		

Women

1967	Nancy Greene, Canada	1975	Annemarie Proell, Austria	1983	Tamara McKinney, U.S.
1968	Nancy Greene, Canada	1976	Rose Mittermaier, W. Germany	1984	Erika Hess, Switzerland
1969	Gertrud Gabl, Austria	1977	Lise-Marie Morerod, Switzerland	1985	Michela Figini, Switzerland
1970	Michele Jacot, France	1978	Hanni Wenzel, Liechtenstein	1986	Maria Walliser, Switzerland
1971	Annemarie Proell, Austria	1979	Annemarie Proell Moser, Austria	1987	Maria Walliser, Switzerland
1972	Annemarie Proell, Austria	1980	Hanni Wenzel, Liechtenstein	1988	Michela Figini, Switzerland
1973	Annemarie Proell, Austria	1981	Marie-Theres Nadig, Switzerland		
1974	Annemarie Proell, Austria	1982	Erika Hess, Switzerland		

Figure Skating Champions

Source: Canadian Figure Skating Association

	Canadian Champions		World Champions	
	Men	Women	Men	Women
1952	Peter Firstbrook	Marlene Smith	Richard Button, U.S.	Jacqueline du Bief, France
1953	Peter Firstbrook	Barbara Gratton	Hayes Jenkins, U.S.	Tenley Albright, U.S.
1954	Charles Snelling	Barbara Gratton	Hayes Jenkins, U.S.	Gundi Busch, W. Germany
1955	Charles Snelling	Carole Jane Pachl	Hayes Jenkins, U.S.	Tenley Albright, U.S.
1956	Charles Snelling	Carole Jane Pachl	Hayes Jenkins, U.S.	Carol Heiss, U.S.
1957	Charles Snelling	Carole Jane Pachl	Dave Jenkins, U.S.	Carol Heiss, U.S.
1958	Charles Snelling	Margaret Crosland	Dave Jenkins, U.S.	Carol Heiss, U.S.
1959	Donald Jackson	Margaret Crosland	Dave Jenkins, U.S.	Carol Heiss, U.S.
1960	Donald Jackson	Wendy Griner	Alain Giletti, France	Carol Heiss, U.S.
1961	Donald Jackson	Wendy Griner	none	none
1962	Donald Jackson	Wendy Griner	Don Jackson, Canada	Sjoukje Dijkstra, Neth.
1963	Donald McPherson	Wendy Griner	Don McPherson, Canada	Sjoukje Dijkstra, Neth.
1964	Charles Snelling	Petra Burka	Manfred Schnelldorfer, W. Germany	Sjoukje Dijkstra, Neth.

Canadian Champions

World Champions

	Men	Women	Men	Women
1965	Donald Knight	Petra Burka	Alain Calmat, France	Petra Burka, Canada
1966	Donald Knight	Petra Burka	Emmerich Danzer, Austria	Peggy Fleming, U.S.
1967	Donald Knight	Valerie Jones	Emmerich Danzer, Austria	Peggy Fleming, U.S.
1968	Jay Humphry	Karen Magnussen	Emmerich Danzer, Austria	Peggy Fleming, U.S.
1969	Jay Humphry	Linda Carbonetto	Tim Wood, U.S.	Gabriele Seyfert, E. Germany
1970	David McGillivray	Karen Magnussen	Tim Wood, U.S.	Gabriele Seyfert, E. Germany
1971	Toller Cranston	Karen Magnussen	Ondrej Nepela, Czech.	Beatrix Schuba, Austria
1972	Toller Cranston	Karen Magnussen	Ondrej Nepela, Czech.	Beatrix Schuba, Austria
1973	Toller Cranston	Karen Magnussen	Ondrej Nepela, Czech.	Karen Magnussen, Canada
1974	Toller Cranston	Lynn Nightingale	Jan Hoffman, E. Germany	Christine Errath, E. Germany
1975	Toller Cranston	Lynn Nightingale	Sergei Volkov, USSR	Dianne de Leeuw, Neth.-U.S.
1976	Toller Cranston	Lynn Nightingale	John Curry, Gr. Brit.	Dorothy Hamill, U.S.
1977	Ron Shaver	Lynn Nightingale	Vladimir Kovalev, USSR	Linda Fratianne, U.S.
1978	Brian Pockar	Heather Kemkaran	Charles Tickner, U.S.	Anett Poetzsch, E. Germany
1979	Brian Pockar	Janet Morrisey	Vladimir Kovalev, USSR	Linda Fratianne, U.S.
1980	Brian Pockar	Heather Kemkaran	Jan Hoffmann, E. Germany	Anett Poetzsch, E. Germany
1981	Brian Orser	Tracey Wainman	Scott Hamilton, U.S.	Denise Biellmann, Switzerland
1982	Brian Orser	Kay Thomson	Scott Hamilton, U.S.	Elaine Zayak, U.S.
1983	Brian Orser	Kay Thomson	Scott Hamilton, U.S.	Rosalyn Sumners, U.S.
1984	Brian Orser	Kay Thomson	Scott Hamilton, U.S.	Katarina Witt, E. Germany
1985	Brian Orser	Elizabeth Manley	Alexandre Fadeev, USSR	Katarina Witt, E. Germany
1986	Brian Orser	Tracey Wainman	Brian Boitano, U.S.	Debi Thomas, U.S.
1987	Brian Orser	Elizabeth Manley	Brian Orser, Canada	Katarina Witt, E. Germany
1988	Brian Orser	Elizabeth Manley	Brian Boitano, U.S.	Katarina Witt, E. Germany

---

Curling Champions

Source: Canadian Curling Association

Canadian Champions

World Champions

Men

Year	Province, skip	Year	Country, skip
1969	Alberta, Ron Northcott	1969	Canada, Ron Northcott
1970	Manitoba, Don Duguid	1970	Canada, Don Duguid
1971	Manitoba, Don Duguid	1971	Canada, Don Duguid
1972	Manitoba, Orest Meleschuk	1972	Canada, Orest Meleschuk
1973	Sask., Harvey Mazinke	1973	Sweden, Kjell Oscarius
1974	Alberta, Hector Gervais	1974	United States, Bud Somerville
1975	Northern Ontario, Bill Tetley	1975	Switzerland, Otto Danielli
1976	Newfoundland, Jack MacDuff	1976	United States, Bruce Roberts
1977	Quebec, Jim Ursel	1977	Sweden, Ragner Kamp
1978	Alberta, Ed Lukowich	1978	United States, Bob Nichols
1979	Manitoba, Barry Fry	1979	Norway, Kristian Soerum
1980	Saskatchewan, Rich Folk	1980	Canada, Rich Folk
1981	Manitoba, Kerry Burtnyk	1981	Switzerland, Jurg Tanner
1982	Northern Ontario, Al Hackner	1982	Canada, Al Hackner
1983	Ontario, Ed Werenich	1983	Canada, Ed Werenich
1984	Manitoba, Mike Riley	1984	Norway, Eigil Ramsfjell
1985	Northern Ontario, Al Hackner	1985	Canada, Al Hackner
1986	Alberta, Ed Lukowich	1986	Canada, Ed Luckowich
1987	Ontario, Russ Howard	1987	Canada, Russ Howard
1988	Alberta, Pat Ryan	1988	Norway, Eigil Ramsfjell

Women

Year	Province, skip	Year	Country, skip
1979	Br. Columbia, Lindsay Sparkes	1979	Switzerland, Gaby Casanova
1980	Saskatchewan, Marj Mitchell	1980	Canada, Marj Mitchell
1981	Alberta, Susan Seitz	1981	Sweden, Elizabeth Hogstrom
1982	Nova Scotia, Colleen Jones	1982	Denmark, Marianne Jorgenson
1983	Nova Scotia, Penny LaRocque	1983	Switzerland, Erika Mueller
1984	Manitoba, Connie Laliberte	1984	Canada, Connie Laliberte
1985	British Columbia, Linda Moore	1985	Canada, Linda Moore
1986	Ontario, Marilyn Darte	1986	Canada, Marilyn Darte
1987	British Columbia, Pat Saunders	1987	Canada, Pat Saunders
1988	Ontario, Heather Houston	1988	Germany, Andrea Schopp

1986 Commonwealth Games: Canadian Medal Winners

Gold Medals

Track and Field

Ben Johnson	100 m
Angella Issajenko	200 m
Atlee Mahorn	200 m
Lynn Williams	3 000 m
Graeme Fell	3 000 m steeplechase
Mark McKoy	110 m hurdles
Ben Johnson	4 × 100 m relay
Atlee Mahorn	
Mark McKoy	
Desai Williams	
Charmaine Crooks	4 × 400 m relay
Molly Killingbeck	
Marita Payne	
Jillian Richardson	
Ray Lazdins	Discus
Milt Ottey	High jump

Swimming

Mark Tewksbury	100 m backstroke
Sandy Goss	200 m backstroke
Victor Davis	100 m breaststroke
Allison Higson	100 m breaststroke
Allison Higson	200 m breaststroke
Donna McGinnis	200 m butterfly
Jane Kerr	100 m freestyle
Alex Baumann	200 m individual medley
Alex Baumann	400 m individual medley
Jane Kerr	4 × 100 m freestyle relay
Trish Noall	
Andrea Nugent	
Pam Rai	
Alex Baumann	4 × 100 m medley relay
Victor Davis	
Tom Ponting	
Mark Tewksbury	

Synchronized Swimming

Michelle Cameron	Duet
Carolyn Waldo	
Sylvie Frechette	Solo

Diving

Debbie Fuller	3 m
Debbie Fuller	10 m

Boxing

Scott Olson	48 kg
Billy Downey	57 kg
Asif Dar	60 kg
Howard Grant	63.5 kg
Dan Sherry	71 kg
Lennox Lewis	+91 kg

Wrestling

Ron Moncur	48 kg
Chris Woodcroft	52 kg
Mitch Ostberg	57 kg
Paul Hughes	62 kg
Dave McKay	68 kg
Gary Holmes	74 kg
Chris Rinke	82 kg
Clark Davis	100 kg
Wayne Brightwell	+100 kg

Weightlifting

Denis Garon	100 kg
Kevin Roy	110 kg

Rowing

Kathryn Barr	Double sculls
Andrea Schreiner	
Bruce Ford	Double sculls
Pat Walter	
Tina Clarke	Four with coxswain
Tricia Smith	
Lesley Thompson	
Jane Tregunno	
Jenny Wallinga	
Grant Main	Four without coxswain
Kevin Neufeld	
Paul Steele	
Pat Turner	

Shooting

Guy Lorion	Air rifle
Sharon Bowes	Air rifle team
Guy Lorion	
Bill Baldwin	Full bore rifle team
Alain Marion	
Claude Beaulieu	Free pistol team
Tom Guinn	
Michael Ashcroft	Small bore rifle prone team
Gale Stewart	

Silver Medals

Track and Field

Jillian Richardson	400 m
Debbie Scott-Bowker	1 500 m
Debbie Scott-Bowker	3 000 m
Donalda Duprey	400 m hurdles
Guillaume Leblanc	30 km walk
Angela Bailey	4 × 100 m relay
Angella Issajenko	
Esmie Lawrence	
Angela Phipps	
Dave Steen	Decathlon
Dave Edge	Marathon
Bob Ferguson	Pole vault

Diving

John Nash	3 m
David Bédard	10 m

Swimming

Victor Davis	200 m breaststroke
Cindy Ounpuu	200 m breaststroke
Tom Ponting	200 m butterfly
Jane Kerr	200 m freestyle
Alex Baumann	4 × 100 m freestyle relay
Vlastimil Cerny	
Sandy Goss	
Blair Hicken	
Scott Flowers	4 × 200 m freestyle relay
Sandy Goss	
Tom Ponting	
Paul Szekula	
Allison Higson	4 × 100 m medley relay
Jane Kerr	
Barb McBain	
Donna McGinnis	

Wrestling

Doug Cox	90 kg

Weightlifting

Louis Payer	75 kg
David Bolduc	+110 kg

Rowing

Heather Clarke	Double sculls
Lisa Robertson	
Lisa Wright	Single scull
Peter Tatersall	Single scull (lightweight)

Shooting

Tom Guinn	Air pistol
Sharon Bowes	Air rifle
Alain Marion	Full bore rifle
Brian Gabriel	Skeet team
Don Kwasnycia	
Michel Dion	Small bore rifle
Jean-François Senecal	3 positions team

Cycling

Alex Ongaro	Sprint

Lawn Bowling

Bill Boettger	Pairs
Ron Jones	
Dave Brown	Fours
Dave Duncalf	
Dave Houtby	
Dan Mulligan	

Badminton

Johanne Falardeau	Doubles
Denyse Julien	
Claire Backhouse-Sharpe	Team
Mike Bitten	
Mike Butler	
Linda Cloutier	
Michael de Belle	
Johanne Falardeau	
John Goss	
Denyse Julien	
Ken Poole	
Sandra Skillings	

Bronze Medals

Track and Field

Angella Issajenko	100 m
Ben Johnson	200 m
Dave Campbell	1 500 m
Lynn Williams	1 500 m
John Graham	400 m hurdles
John Graham	4 × 400 m relay
Atlee Mahorn	
Anton Skerritt	
André Smith	
Alain Metellus	High jump
Kyle McDuffie	Long jump
Odette Lapierre	Marathon

Swimming

Mike West	100 m backstroke
Sean Murphy	200 m backstroke
Tom Ponting	100 m butterfly
Jill Horstead	200 m butterfly
Chris Chalmers	1 500 freestyle
Jane Kerr	200 m individual medley
Sophie Dufour	4 × 200 m freestyle relay
Jane Kerr	
Donna McGinnis	
Trish Noall	

Diving

Kathy Kelemen	3 m

Boxing

Steve Beaupré	51 kg
John Shaw	67 kg
Brent Kosolofski	81 kg
Domenic D'Amico	91 kg

Weightlifting

Langis Côté	67.5 kg
Guy Greavette	90 kg

Rowing

Anne Drost	Four without coxswain (lightweight)
Marni Hamilton	
Marlene van der Horst	
Wendy Wiebe	
Dave Henry	Four without coxswain (lightweight)
Brian Peaker	
Bob Thomas	
Ryan Tierney	
Heather Hattin	Single scull (lightweight)

Shooting

Jean-François Senecal	Small bore rifle 3 positions
Mark Howkins	Rapid fire pistol
André Chevrefils	Rapid fire pistol team
Mark Howkins	
Brian Gabriel	Skeet

1986 Commonwealth Games Medal Winners, by Country

	Gold	Silver	Bronze	Total		Gold	Silver	Bronze	Total
England	52	42	49	143	Guernsey	0	2	0	2
Australia	40	46	33	119	Hong Kong	0	0	2	2
Canada	51	34	30	115	Isle of Man	1	0	0	1
New Zealand	8	16	14	38	Swaziland	0	1	0	1
Scotland	3	12	18	33	Malawi	0	1	0	1
Wales	6	5	12	23	Singapore	0	0	1	1
Northern Ireland	2	4	9	15	Jersey	0	0	1	1

Swimming

World Swimming Records

(As of Oct. 1988)

Women

Distance	Time	Holder	Country	Where made	Date

Freestyle

Distance	Time	Holder	Country	Where made	Date
50 m	0:24.98	Yang Wenyi	China	Seoul, S. Korea	Sept. 1988
100 m	0:54.73	Kristin Otto	E. Germany	Madrid, Spain	Aug. 1986
200 m	1:57.65	Kristin Otto	E. Germany	Seoul, S. Korea	Sept. 1988
400 m	4:03.85	Janet Evans	U.S.	Seoul, S. Korea	Sept. 1988
800 m	8:17.12	Janet Evans	U.S.	Orlando, U.S.	Mar. 1988
1 500 m	15:52.10	Janet Evans	U.S.	Orlando, U.S.	Mar. 1988

Breaststroke

100 m	1:07.91	Silke Hoerner	E. Germany	Strasbourg, France	Aug. 1987
200 m	2:26.71	Silke Hoerner	E. Germany	Seoul, S. Korea	Sept. 1988

Butterfly

100 m	0:50.00	Kristin Otto	E. Germany	Seoul, S. Korea	Sept. 1988
200 m	2:05.96	Mary T. Meagher	U.S.	Brown Deer, U.S.	Aug. 1981

Backstroke

100 m	1:00.59	Ina Kleber	E. Germany	Moscow, USSR	Aug. 1984
200 m	2:08.60	Betsy Mitchell	U.S.	Orlando, U.S.	June 1986

Individual Medley

200 m	2:10.60	Petra Schneider	E. Germany	Gainesville, Fla.	Aug. 1982
400 m	4:36.10	Petra Schneider	E. Germany	Ecuador	Aug. 1982

Freestyle Relays

4 × 100 m	3:40.57	(Otto, Stellmach, Friedrich, Schulze)	E. Germany	Madrid	Aug. 1986
4 × 200 m	7:55.47	(Stellmach, Strauss, Mohring, Friedrich)	E. Germany	Strasbourg, France	Aug. 1987

Medley Relays

4 × 100 m	4:03.69	(Kleber, Gerasch, Geissler, Meineke)	E. Germany	Moscow	Aug. 1984

Men

Distance	Time	Holder	Country	Where made	Date

Freestyle

Distance	Time	Holder	Country	Where made	Date
50 m	0:22.14	Matt Biondi	U.S.	Seoul, S. Korea	Sept. 1988
100 m	0:48.42	Matt Biondi	U.S.	Austin, U.S.	Aug. 1988
200 m	1:47.25	Duncan Armstrong	Australia	Seoul, S. Korea	Sept. 1988
400 m	3:46.95	Ewe Dassler	E. Germany	Seoul, S. Korea	Sept. 1988
800 m	7:50.64	Vladimir Salnikov	USSR	Moscow, USSR	July 1986
1 500 m	14:54.76	Vladimir Salnikov	USSR	Moscow, USSR	Feb. 1983

Breaststroke

100 m	1:01.65	Steve Lundquist	U.S.	Los Angeles, U.S.	July 1984
200 m	2:13.34	Victor Davis	Canada	Los Angeles, U.S.	Aug. 1984

Butterfly

100 m	0:52.84	Pablo Morales	U.S.	Orlando, U.S.	June 1986
200 m	1:56.24	Michael Gross	W. Germany	Bonn, W. Germ.	June 1986

Backstroke

100 m	0:55.00	Igor Polianski	USSR	Caracas, Venez.	July 1988
200 m	1:58.14	Igor Polianski	USSR	Erfurt, E. Germ.	Mar. 1985

Individual Medley

200 m	2:00.17	Tamas Darnyi	Hungary	Seoul, S. Korea	Sept. 1988
400 m	4:14.75	Tamas Darnyi	Hungary	Seoul, S. Korea	Sept. 1988

Freestyle Relays

4 × 100 m	3:16.53	(Jacobs, Dalbey, Jager, Biondi)	U.S.	Seoul, S. Korea	Sept. 1988
4 × 200 m	7:12.51	(Dalbey, Cetlinski, Gjertsen, Biondi)	U.S.	Seoul, S. Korea	Sept. 1988

Medley Relays

4 × 100 m	3:36.93	(Berkoff, Schroeder, Biondi, Jacobs)	U.S.	Seoul, S. Korea	Sept. 1988

Canadian Swimming Records

Source: Swimming Canada
(as of Oct., 1988)

Women

Event	Time	Swimmer	Site	Date
Freestyle				
50 m	26.01	Andrea Nugent	Montreal	Mar., 1987
100 m	56.60	Carol Klimpel	Heidelberg	July 29, 1981
200 m	2:00.61	Patricia Neall	Toronto	Aug. 17, 1988
400 m	4:12.83	Julie Daigneault	Montreal	July 29, 1983
800 m	8:36.24	Debbie Wurzburger	Seoul, S. Korea	Sept. 23, 1988
1 500 m	16:40.60	Elissa Purvis	Los Altos, Cal.	July, 1986
Backstroke				
100 m	1:03.28	Nancy Garapick	Montreal	July 20, 1976
200 m	2:14.23	Cheryl Gibson	Berlin	Aug. 24, 1978
Breaststroke				
100 m	1:08.83	Allison Higson	Seoul, S. Korea	Sept. 23, 1988
200 m	2:27.27	Allison Higson	Montreal	May 29, 1988
Butterfly				
100 m	1:01.27	Wendy Quirk	Etobicoke	July 22, 1980
200 m	2:11.48	Jill Horstead	Montreal	July 31, 1985
I.M.				
200 m	2:16.89	Allison Higson	Montreal	May 31, 1988
400 m	4:48.10	Cheryl Gibson	Montreal	July 24, 1976
Relays				
Freestyle				
4 × 100 m	3:46.75	1988 Olympic Team Kathy Bald Patricia Neall Andrea Nugent Jane Kerr	Seoul, S. Korea	Sept. 22, 1988
4 × 200 m	8:16.82	1987 Cdn. National Team Jane Kerr Patricia Neall Nancy Lovrinich Allison Higson	Brisbane	Aug., 1987
Medley				
4 × 100 m	4:10.49	1988 Olympic Team Lori Mellen Allison Higson Jane Kerr Andrea Nugent	Seoul, S. Korea	Sept. 24, 1988

Men

Event	Time	Swimmer	Site	Date
Freestyle				
50 m	22.88	Mark Andrews	Montreal	June 1, 1988
100 m	50.50	Sandy Goss	Toronto	Aug. 18, 1988
200 m	1:49.84	Marcel Gery	Brisbane	Aug., 1987
400 m	3:50.49	Peter Szmidt	Etobicoke	July 16, 1980
800 m	8:09.41	Harry Taylor	Montreal	June 1, 1988
1 500 m	15:16.00	Harry Taylor	Montreal	June 1, 1988
Backstroke				
100 m	55.22	Sean Murphy	Montreal	June 1, 1988
200 m	2:01.20	Mike West	Etobicoke	June 18, 1984
Breaststroke				
100 m	1:01.99	Victor Davis	Los Angeles	July 29, 1984
200 m	2:13.34	Victor Davis	Los Angeles	Aug. 2, 1984
Butterfly				
100 m	53.77	Tom Ponting	Montreal	May 29, 1988
200 m	1:58.14	Tom Ponting	Montreal	May 31, 1988
I.M.				
200 m	2:01.42	Alex Baumann	Los Angeles	Aug. 4, 1984
400 m	4:17.41	Alex Baumann	Los Angeles	July 30, 1984

Event	Time	Swimmer	Site	Date
Relays				
Freestyle				
4 × 100 m	3:21.74	1987 Cdn. National Team Vlastimil Cerny Sandy Goss Blair Hicken Marcel Gery	Brisbane	Aug., 1987
4 × 200 m	7:24.91	1988 Olympic Team Turlough O'Hare Sandy Goss Don Haddow Gary Vander Meulen	Seoul, S. Korea	Sept. 21, 1988
Medley				
4 × 100 m	3:39.28	1988 Olympic Team Mark Tewksbury Victor Davis Tom Ponting Sandy Goss	Seoul, S. Korea	Sept. 25, 1988

The America's Cup

The United States yacht *Stars & Stripes* defeated the New Zealand yacht *New Zealand* in 2 consecutive races to win the best-of-three series in the waters off San Diege, Cal. *Stars & Stripes* was skippered by Dennis Connor, as it had been when the cup was recaptured from Australia in 1987.

The New Zealand syndicate, however, is going to court to have the result of the races invalidated, claiming that the Americans did not live up to the America's Cup Deed of Gift which, they claim, says that the competing boats must be similar. The Americans used a catamaran, the New Zealanders a monohulled ship. The Cup resides at the San Diego Yacht Club, which sponsors the U.S. entry.

Competition for the America's Cup grew out of the first contest to establish a world yachting championship, one of the carnival features of the London Exposition of 1851. The race, open to all classes of yachts from all over the world, covered a 60-mile course around the Isle of Wight; the prize was a cup worth about $500, donated by the Royal Yacht Squadron of England, known as the "America's Cup" because it was first won by the United States yacht *America*. Successive efforts of British and Australian yachtsmen had failed to win the famous trophy until 1983 when the Australian yacht *Australia II* defeated the U.S. entry *Liberty*.

Winners of the America's Cup

1851	America	1934	Rainbow defeated Endeavour, England, (4-2)
1870	Magic defeated Cambria, England, (1-0)	1937	Ranger defeated Endeavour II, England, (4-0)
1871	Columbia (first three races) and Sappho (last two races) defeated Livonia, England, (4-1)	1958	Columbia defeated Sceptre, England, (4-0)
		1962	Weatherly defeated Gretel, Australia, (4-1)
1876	Madeline defeated Countess of Dufferin, Canada, (2-0)	1964	Constellation defeated Sovereign, England, (4-0)
1881	Mischief defeated Atalanta, Canada, (2-0)	1967	Intrepid defeated Dame Pattie, Australia, (4-0)
1885	Puritan defeated Genesta, England, (2-0)	1970	Intrepid defeated Gretel II, Australia, (4-1)
1886	Mayflower defeated Galatea, England, (2-0)	1974	Courageous defeated Southern Cross, Australia, (4-0)
1887	Volunteer defeated Thistle, Scotland, (2-0)	1977	Courageous defeated Australia, Australia, (4-0)
1893	Vigilant defeated Valkyrie II, England, (3-0)	1980	Freedom defeated Australia, Australia, (4-1)
1895	Defender defeated Valkyrie III, England, (3-0)	1983	Australia II, Australia defeated Liberty, (4-3)
1899	Columbia defeated Shamrock, England, (3-0)	1987	Stars & Stripes defeated Kookaburra III, Australia, (4-0)
1901	Columbia defeated Shamrock II, England, (3-0)	1988	Stars & Stripes defeated New Zealand, New Zealand, (2-0)
1903	Reliance defeated Shamrock III, England, (3-0)		
1920	Resolute defeated Shamrock IV, England, (3-2)		
1930	Enterprise defeated Shamrock V, England, (4-0)		

The World Cup of Soccer

The World Cup, emblematic of International soccer supremacy, was won by Argentina on June 29, 1986, with a 3-2 victory over W. Germany. It was the 2d time Argentina has won the event. Winners and sites of previous World Cup play follow:

Year	Winner	Final opponent	Site	Year	Winner	Final opponent	Site
1930	Uruguay	Argentina	Uruguay	1966	England	W. Germany	England
1934	Italy	Czechoslovakia	Italy	1970	Brazil	Italy	Mexico City
1938	Italy	Hungary	France	1974	W. Germany	Netherlands	W. Germany
1950	Uruguay	Brazil	Brazil	1978	Argentina	Netherlands	Argentina
1954	W. Germany	Hungary	Switzerland	1982	Italy	W. Germany	Spain
1958	Brazil	Sweden	Sweden	1986	Argentina	W. Germany	Mexico City
1962	Brazil	Czechoslovakia	Chile				

1986 Final Round

Quarterfinals

France 5, Brazil 4
W. Germany 4, Mexico 1
Argentina 2, England 1
Belgium 6, Spain 5

Semifinals

W. Germany 2, France 0
Argentina 2, Belgium 0

Championship

Argentina 3, W. Germany 2

Track and Field

World Track and Field Records

As of Oct. 1988

Men's Records

Running

Event	Record	Holder	Country	Date	Where made
100 m	09.83	Ben Johnson	Canada	Aug. 30, 1987	Rome
200 m	19.72	Pietro Mennea	Italy	Sept. 17, 1979	Mexico City
400 m	43.29	Butch Reynolds	U.S.	Aug. 1988	Zurich
800 m	1:41.73	Sebastian Coe	Gr. Britain	June 10, 1981	Florence, Italy
1 000 m	2:12.18	Sebastian Coe	Gr. Britain	July 11, 1981	Oslo
1 500 m	3:29.46	Said Aouita	Morocco	Aug. 23, 1985	W. Berlin
1 mile	3:46.32	Said Aouita	Morocco	July, 1987	Paris
2 000 m	4:50.81	Steve Cram	Gr. Britain	Aug. 4, 1985	Budapest
3 000 m	7:32.1	Henry Rono	Kenya	June 27, 1978	Oslo
5 000 m	12:58.39	Said Aouita	Morocco	July 23, 1987	Rome
10 000 m	27:13.81	Fernando Mamede	Portugal	July 2, 1984	Stockholm
20 000 m	57:24.20	Jos Hermens	Netherlands	May 1, 1976	Netherlands
25 000 m	1.13:55.80	Toshihiko Seko	Japan	Mar. 22 1981	New Zealand
30 000 m	1.29:18.80	Toshihiko Seko	Japan	Mar. 22, 1981	New Zealand
3 000 m steeplechase	8:05.40	Henry Rono	Kenya	May 13, 1978	Seattle
Marathon	2.07:12.00	Carlos Lopos	Portugal	Apr. 20, 1985	Rotterdam

Hurdles

110 m	12.93	Renaldo Nehemiah	U.S.	Aug. 19, 1981	Zurich
400 m	47.02	Edwin Moses	U.S.	Aug. 31, 1983	Koblenz, W. Germany

Relay Races

400 m	37.83	(Graddy, Brown Smith, Lewis)	U.S.	Aug. 11, 1984	Los Angeles
4 × 200 m	1:20.26	USC	U.S.	May 27, 1978	Tempe, Ariz.
4 × 400 m	2:56.16	(Matthews, Freeman, James, Evans)	U.S.	Oct. 20, 1968	Mexico City
		(Everett, Lewis, Robinzine, Reynolds)	U.S.	Sept. 1988	Seoul
4 × 800 m	7:03.89	National team	Gr. Britain	Aug. 31, 1982	London

Field Events

High jump	2.42 m	Javier Sotomaya	Cuba	Sept. 8, 1988	Spain
Long jump	8.90 m	Bob Beamon	U.S.	Oct. 18, 1968	Mexico City
Triple jump	17.97 m	Willie Banks	U.S.	June 16, 1985	Indianapolis
Pole vault	6.08 m	Sergei Bubka	USSR	July, 1988	Nice, France
16 lb. shot put	23.06 m	Ulf Timmermann	E. Germany	May, 1988	Crete
Discus throw	74.08 m	Juergen Schult	E. Germany	June 7, 1986	E. Germany
Javelin throw	104.80 m	Uwe Hohn	E. Germany	July 20, 1984	E. Berlin
16 lb. hammer throw	86.74 m	Yuri Sedykh	USSR	Aug. 30, 1986	Stuttgart
Decathlon	8 646 pts.	Daley Thompson	Gr. Britain	Aug. 8-9, 1984	Los Angeles

Walking

30 km	2.07:59.8	Jose Martin	Spain	Aug. 4, 1979	Barcelona
50 km	3.41:39	Raul Gonzales	Mexico	May 25, 1978	Norway

Women's Records

Running

100 m	10.49	Florence Griffith-Joyner	U.S.	July, 1988	Indianapolis
200 m	21.34	Florence Griffith-Joyner	U.S.	Sept. 1988	Seoul
400 m	47.60	Marita Koch	E. Germany	Oct. 6, 1986	Canberra
800 m	1:53.28	Jarmila Kratochvilova	Czech.	July 26, 1983	Munich
1 500 m	3:52.47	Tatyana Kazankina	USSR	Aug. 13, 1980	Zurich
1 mile	4:16.71	Mary Decker Slaney	U.S.	Aug. 21, 1985	Zurich
2 000 m	5:28.69	Maricica Puica	Romania	July 11, 1986	London
3 000 m	8:22.62	Tatyana Kazankina	USSR	Aug. 26, 1984	Leningrad
5 000 m	14:37.33	Ingrid Kristiansen	Norway	Aug. 5, 1986	Stockholm
10 000 m	30:13.74	Ingrid Kristiansen	Norway	July 5, 1986	Oslo
Marathon	2.21:06.00	Ingrid Kristiansen	Norway	Apr. 21, 1985	London

Hurdles

100 m	12.25	Ginka Zagorcheva	Bulgaria	Aug., 1987	Greece
400 m	52.94	Marina Stepanova	USSR	Spet. 17, 1986	USSR

Relay Races

400 m (4 × 100)	41.37	National team	E. Germany	Oct. 6, 1985	Canberra
800 m (4 × 200)	1:28.15	National team	E. Germany	Aug. 9, 1980	E. Germany
1 600 m (4 × 400)	3:15.18	National team	USSR	Sept. 1988	Seoul
3 200 m (4 × 800)	7:50.17	National team	USSR	Aug. 5, 1984	Moscow

Event	Record	Holder		Date	Where Made
		Field Events			
High jump	2.08 m	Stefka Kostadinova	Bulgaria	June 6, 1987	Moscow
Shot put	22.63 m	Natalya Lisovkaya	USSR	May 26, 1984	USSR
Long jump	7.52 m	Galina Christyakova	USSR	June, 1988	Leningrad
Discus throw	74.56 m	Zdenka Silhava	Czechoslovakia	Aug. 26, 1984	Prague
Javelin	78.90 m	Petra Felke	E. Germany	Sept., 1988	E. Berlin
Heptathlon	7 215 pts.	Jackie Joyner-Kersee	U.S.	Sept., 1988	Seoul

Evolution of the World Record for the One-Mile Run

The table below shows how the world record for the one-mile has been lowered in the past 120 years.

Year	Individual, country	Time	Year	Individual, country	Time
1868	William Chinnery, Britain	4:29	1942	Gunder Haegg, Sweden	4:04.6
1868	W. C. Gibbs, Britain	4:28.8	1943	Arne Andersson, Sweden	4:02.6
1874	Walter Slade, Britain	4:26	1944	Arne Andersson, Sweden	4:01.6
1875	Walter Slade, Britain	4:24.5	1945	Gunder Haegg, Sweden	4:01.4
1880	Walter George, Britain	4:23.2	1954	Roger Bannister, Britain	3:59.4
1882	Walter George, Britain	4:21.4	1954	John Landy, Australia	3:58
1882	Walter George, Britain	4:19.4	1957	Derek Ibbotson, Britain	3:57.2
1884	Walter George, Britain	4:18.4	1958	Herb Elliott, Australia	3:54.5
1894	Fred Bacon, Scotland	4:18.2	1962	Peter Snell, New Zealand	3:54.4
1895	Fred Bacon, Scotland	4:17	1964	Peter Snell, New Zealand	3:54.1
1895	Thomas Conneff, U.S.	4:15.6	1965	Michel Jazy, France	3:53.6
1911	John Paul Jones, U.S.	4:15.4	1966	Jim Ryun, U.S.	3:51.3
1913	John Paul Jones, U.S.	4:14.6	1967	Jim Ryun, U.S.	3:51.1
1915	Norman Taber, U.S.	4:12.6	1975	Filbert Bayi, Tanzania	3:51
1923	Paavo Nurmi, Finland.	4:10.4	1975	John Walker, New Zealand	3:49.4
1931	Jules Ladoumegue, France	4:09.2	1979	Sebastian Coe, Britain	3:49
1933	Jack Lovelock, New Zealand	4:07.6	1980	Steve Ovett, Britain	3:48.8
1934	Glenn Cunningham, U.S.	4:06.8	1981	Sebastian Coe, Britain	3:48.53
1937	Sydney Wooderson, Britain	4:06.4	1981	Steve Ovett, Britain	3:48.40
1942	Gunder Haegg, Sweden	4:06.2	1981	Sebastian Coe, Britain	3:47.33
1942	Arne Andersson, Sweden	4:06.2	1985	Steve Cram, Britain	3:46.32

Canadian Track and Field Records

Source: Canadian Track and Field Association

(As of Oct. 1988)

Men's Events

Event	Record	Holder		Date	Where Made
100 Metres	9.83	Ben Johnson		Aug. 30, 1987	Rome, Italy
200 Metres	20.20	Atlee Mahorn		June 4, 1988	Eugene, Ore.
400 Metres	45.62	Atlee Mahorn		Apr. 12, 1986	Tempe, Ariz.
		Anton Skerritt		Sept. 1, 1987	Rome, Italy
800 Metres	1:45.69	Bill Crothers		Oct. 16, 1964	Tokyo, Japan
	1:45.4¹	Simon Hoogewerf		July 23, 1988	Victoria, B.C.
1 500 Metres	3:35.82	Douglas Consiglio		June 5, 1988	Vancouver, B.C.
3 000 Metres S/C	8:12.58	Graeme Fell		Aug. 28, 1985	Koblenz, W. Germ.
5 000 Metres	13:22.68	Paul Williams		July 2, 1986	Oslo, Norway
10 000 Metres	27:50.19	Paul Williams		July 6, 1986	Oslo, Norway
Marathon	2:10.09	Jerome Drayton		July 10, 1975	Fukuoka, Japan
110 Metre Hurdles	13.17	Mark McKoy		July 24, 1988	Lausanne, France
400 Metre Hurdles	49.51	John Graham		Aug. 12, 1987	Indianapolis, U.S.A.
High Jump	2.33 m	Milt Ottey		June 21, 1986	Ottawa, Ont.
Pole Vault	5.44 m	Robert Ferguson		May 23, 1987	Cape Giradeau, U.S.A
Long Jump	8.09 m	Ian James		July 13, 1986	K.M. Stadt
Triple Jump	16.92 m	Edrick Floreal		May 22, 1987	Knoxville, U.S.A.
Shot Put	20.81 m	Bishop Dolegiewicz		Apr. 3, 1983	Austin, U.S.A.
Discus	67.32 m	Rob Gray		Apr. 30, 1984	Toronto, Ont.
Hammer Throw	72.72 m	Scott Neilson		Apr. 10, 1978	Seattle, U.S.A.
Javelin	79.04 m	Mike Mahovlich		July 17, 1988	Seattle, U.S.A.
Decathlon	8 415 pts	Dave Steen		July 16-17, 1988	Talence

Women's Events

Event	Record	Holder		Date	Where Made
100 Metres	10.97	Angella Issajenko		Aug. 16, 1987	Cologne, W. Germ.
200 Metres²	22.25	Angella Issajenko		July 20, 1982	Col. Springs, Col.
400 Metres	49.91	Marita Payne		Aug. 6, 1984	Los Angeles, Cal.
		Jillian Richardson		Sept. 25, 1988	Seoul, S. Korea
800 Metres	2:00.02	Brit McRoberts		Aug. 21, 1983	Zurich, Switz.
1 500 Metres	4:00.27	Lynn Williams		Aug. 30, 1985	Brussels, Belg.

Event	Record	Holder	Date	Where Made
3 000 Metres	8:37.30	Lynn Williams	Aug. 17, 1988	Zurich, Switz.
5 000 Metres	15:07.71	Lynn Williams	July 4, 1985	Helsinki, Fin.
10 000 Metres	31:50.51	Sue Lee	Sept. 30, 1988	Seoul, S. Korea
Marathon	2:28.36	Silvia Ruegger	Jan. 6, 1985	Houston, U.S.A.
100 Metre Hurdles	12.78	Julie Rocheleau	May 21, 1988	Provo, Ut.
400 Metre Hurdles	56.10	Gwen Wall	July 11, 1983	Edmonton, Atla.
High Jump	1.98 m	Debbie Brill	Sept. 2, 1984	Rieti, Italy
Long Jump	6.61 m	Donna Smellie	Aug. 4, 1985	Ottawa, Ont
Shot Put	17.17 m	Carmen Ionesco	June 20, 1979	Laval, Que.
Discus	62.74 m	Carmen Ionesco	Aug. 23, 1979	Montreal, Que.
Javelin	59.76 m	Celine Chartrand	June 20, 1987	Montreal, Que.
Heptathlon	6 030 pts[3]	Jill Ross-Giffen	May 22-23, 1982	Götzis, Switz.

S/C = Steeplechase. (1) Hand-timed. (2) Altitude over 1 000 metres. (3) Based on 1984 points system.

Tour de France, 1988

Pedro Delgado of Spain won the 75th Tour de France, the world's most prestigious bicycle endurance race. He completed the 21-day, 3 250-km race in 84 hours, 27 minutes and 53 seconds. Steven Rooks of the Netherlands finished second.

After leading during the early stages of the race, Steve Bauer of Fenwick, Ont., finished 4th, the best-ever showing by a Canadian.

Canadian Amateur Sports Associations

Alpine Club of Canada: P.O. Box 1026, Banff, Alta. T0L 0C0

Basketball Canada: 333 River Rd., Tower A, 11th fl., Vanier, Ont. K1L 8H9

Canadian Amateur Bobsleigh and Luge Association: 333 River Rd., Tower C, 9th fl., Vanier, Ont. K1L 8H9

Canadian Amateur Boxing Association: 333 River Rd., Tower C, 6th fl., Vanier, Ont. K1L 8H9

Canadian Amateur Diving Association: 333 River Rd., Tower A, 3rd fl., Vanier, Ont. K1L 8H9

Canadian Amateur Federation of Body Building: 115 Pickwood Cr., Pointe Claire, Que. H9R 3M3

Canadian Amateur Hockey Association: 333 River Rd., Vanier, Ont. K1L 8H9

Canadian Amateur Netball Association: P.O. Box 6044, Stn. A, Toronto, ON M5W 1P4

Canadian Amateur Rowing Association: 333 River Rd., Tower C, 10th fl., Vanier, Ont. K1L 8H9

Canadian Amateur Softball Association: 333 River Rd., Tower A, 18th fl., Vanier, Ont. K1L 8H9

Canadian Amateur Speed Skating Association: 333 River Rd., Tower A, 11th fl., Vanier, Ont. K1L 8H9

Canadian Amateur Synchronized Swimming Association Inc.: 333 River Rd., Vanier, Ont. K1L 8H9

Canadian Water Polo Association Inc.: 333 River Rd., Vanier, Ont. K1L 8H9

Canadian Amateur Wrestling Association: 333 River Rd., Vanier, Ont. K1L 8H9

Canadian Amputee Sports Association: 333 River Rd., Vanier, Ont. K1L 8H9

Canadian Association for Disabled Skiing: P.O. Box 307, Kimberley, B.C. V1A 2Y9

Canadian Badminton Association: 333 River Rd., Tower B, 11th fl., Vanier, Ont. K1L 8H9

Canadian Ballooning Association: P.O. Box 14, Grande Prairie, Alta. T8V 3A1

Canadian Blind Sports Association: 333 River Rd., Vanier, Ont. K1L 8H9

Canadian Boating Federation: 4597 Kingston Rd., Ste. 203-5, Scarborough, Ont. M1E 2P3

Canadian Broomball Federation Inc.: 76 Rita Cr., Saskatoon, Sask. S7N 2L5

Canadian Camping Association: 1806 Avenue Rd., Ste. 2, Toronto, Ont. M5M 3Z1

Canadian Canoe Association: 333 River Rd., Vanier, Ont. K1L 8H9

Canadian Cricket Association: 2041 W. 63rd Ave., Vancouver, B.C. V6P 2J2

Canadian Curling Association: 333 River Rd., Tower C, 10th fl., Vanier, Ont. K1L 8H9

Canadian Cycling Association: 333 River Rd., Vanier, Ont. K1L 8H9

Canadian Deaf Sports Association: 1367 West Broadway, Vancouver, B.C. V6H 4A7

Canadian Equestrian Federation: 333 River Rd., Tower B, 12th fl., Vanier, Ont. K1L 8H9

Canadian Federation of Amateur Baseball: 333 River Rd., Vanier, Ont. K1L 8H9

Canadian Federation of Amateur Roller Skaters: 4 Bayview Dr. S.W., Calgary, Alta. T2V 3N6

Canadian Fencing Association: 333 River Rd., Tower B, 12th fl., Vanier, Ont. K1L 8H9

Canadian Field Hockey Council: 333 River Rd., Vanier, Ont. K1L 8H9

Canadian Figure Skating Association: 333 River Rd., Vanier, Ont. K1L 8H9

Canadian Five Pin Bowlers Association: 1475 Star Top Rd., Unit 3, Gloucester, Ont. K1B 3W5

Canadian Girls Rodeo Association: Site 16, P.O. Box 9, R.R. 6, Calgary, Alta. T2M 4L5

Canadian Golf Foundation: Golf House, R.R. #2, Oakville, Ont. L6J 4Z3

Canadian Gymnastics Federation: 333 River Rd., Tower C, 10th fl., Vanier, Ont. K1L 8H9

Canadian Handball Association: 48 Eastgate, Winnipeg, Man. R3C 2C1

Canadian Highland Games Council: 63 Brant Ave., Brantford, Ont. N3T 3H2

Canadian Lacrosse Association: 333 River Rd., Vanier, Ont. K1L 8H9

Canadian Ladies Curling Association: 333 River Rd., Vanier, Ont. K1L 8H9

Canadian Ladies Golf Association: 333 River Rd., Vanier, Ont. K1L 8H9

Canadian Ladies Lawn Bowling Council: 146 Heather Ave., Pointe Claire, Que. H9R 3A4

Canadian Oldtimers' Hockey Association: 333 River Rd., Tower B, 10th fl., Vanier, Ont. K1L 8H9

Canadian Orienteering Federation: 333 River Rd., Tower A, 18th fl., Vanier, Ont. K1L 8H9

Canadian Racquetball Association: 333 River Rd., Tower A, 18th fl., Vanier, Ont. K1L 8H9

Canadian Rugby Union: 333 River Rd., Tower B, 11th fl., Vanier, Ont. K1L 8H9

Canadian Ski Association: 333 River Rd., Vanier, Ont. K1L 8H9

Canadian Ski Patrol System: 4531 South Clark Pl., R.R. 5, Box 921, Ottawa, Ont. K1G 3N3

Canadian Soccer Association: 333 River Rd., Vanier, Ont. K1L 8H9

Canadian Special Olympics Inc.: 40 St. Clair Ave. W., Ste. 209, Toronto, Ont. M4V 1M6

Canadian Sport Parachuting Association: 333 River Rd., Vanier, Ont. K1L 8H9

Canadian Squash Racquets Association: 333 River Rd., Tower C, 8th fl., Vanier, Ont. K1L 8H9

Canadian Table Soccer Association, The: P.O. Box 524, Montreal, Que. H4K 2J7

Canadian Table Tennis Association: 333 River Rd., Vanier, Ont. K1L 8H9

Canadian Tennis Association: National Tennis Centre, 3111 Steeles Ave. W., Downsview, Ont. M3J 3H2

Canadian Tenpin Federation: 544 Neil Ave., Winnipeg, Man. R2K 1E2

Canadian Track and Field Association: 333 River Rd., Vanier, Ont. K1L 8H9

Canadian Volleyball Association: 333 River Rd., Ste. B-12, Vanier, Ont. K1L 8H9

Canadian Water Ski Association: 333 River Rd., Vanier, Ont. K1L 8H9

Canadian Wheelchair Sports Association: 333 River Rd., 11th fl., Vanier, Ont. K1L 8H9

Canadian White Water Association: 319 Riverside Dr., Oakville, Ont. L6K 3N3

Canadian Women's Field Hockey Association: 333 River Rd., Vanier, Ont. K1L 8H9

Canadian Yachting Association: 333 River Rd., Vanier, Ont. K1L 8H9

Coaching Association of Canada: 333 River Rd., Vanier, Ont. K1L 8H9

Commonwealth Games Association of Canada, The: P.O. Box 129 R.R. 1, Manotick, Ont. K0A 2N0

Cross Country Canada: 333 River Rd., Vanier, Ont. K1L 8H9

Football Canada: 333 River Rd., Tower A, 10th fl., Vanier, Ont. K1L 8H9

Hockey Canada: 2 Bloor St. W., Ste. 1902, Toronto, Ont. M4W 3E2

Horseshoe Canada Association: 9828-91 Ave., Grande Prairie, Alta. T8V 0G2

Swimming Canada: 333 River Rd., Vanier, Ont. K1L 8H9

Professional Sports Directory

National Hockey League

League Headquarters
960 Sun Life Building
1155 Metcalfe St.
Montreal, Quebec H3B 2W2

Boston Bruins
150 Causeway St.
Boston, MA 02114

Buffalo Sabres
Memorial Auditorium
Buffalo, NY 14202

Calgary Flames
P.O. Box 1540
Calgary, Alta. T2P 3B9

Chicago Blackhawks
1800 W. Madison St.
Chicago, IL 60612

Detroit Red Wings
600 Civic Center Drive
Detroit, MI 48226

Edmonton Oilers
Northlands Coliseum
Edmonton, Alta. T5B 4M9

Hartford Whalers
One Civic Center Plaza
Hartford, CT 06103

Los Angeles Kings
3900 West Manchester Blvd.
Box 17013
Inglewood, CA 90306

Minnesota North Stars
7901 Cedar Ave. S.
Bloomington, MN 55425

Montreal Canadiens
2313 St. Catherine St., West
Montreal, Quebec H3H 1N2

New Jersey Devils
P.O. Box 504
E. Rutherford, NJ 07073

New York Islanders
Nassau Coliseum
Uniondale, NY 11553

New York Rangers
4 Pennsylvania Plaza
New York, NY 10001

Philadelphia Flyers
Pattison Place
Philadelphia, PA 19148

Pittsburgh Penguins
Civic Arena
Pittsburgh, PA 15219

Quebec Nordiques
2205 Ave. du Colisee
Quebec, Que. G1L 4W7

St. Louis Blues
5700 Oakland Ave.
St. Louis, MO 63110

Toronto Maple Leafs
60 Carlton St.
Toronto, Ont. M5B 1L1

Vancouver Canucks
100 North Renfrew St.
Vancouver, B.C. V5K 3N7

Washington Capitals
Capital Centre
Landover, MD 20785

Winnipeg Jets
15-1430 Maroons Road
Winnipeg, Man. R3G 0L5

Canadian Football League

League Office
1200 Bay St.
12th Floor
Toronto, Ont. M5R 2A5

B.C. Lions
B.C. Place Stadium
765 Pacific Blvd. S
Vancouver, B.C. V6B 4Y9

Calgary Stampeders
McMahon Stadium
1817 Crowchild Trail N.W.
Calgary, Alta. T2M 4R6

Edmonton Eskimos
9023-11 Ave.
Edmonton, Alta. T5B 0C3

Hamilton Tiger-Cats
75 Balsam Ave. N.
P.O. Box 172
Hamilton, Ont. L8N 3A2

Ottawa Rough Riders
Coliseum Building
Landsdowne Park
Ottawa, Ont. K1S 3W7

Saskatchewan Roughriders
2940-10th Ave.
P.O. Box 1277
Regina, Sask. S4P 3B8

Toronto Argonauts
Exhibition Stadium
Exhibition Place
Toronto, Ont. M6K 3C3

Winnipeg Blue Bombers
1465 Maroons Rd.
Winnipeg, Man. R3G 0L6

National Football League

League Office
350 Park Avenue
New York, NY 10022

Atlanta Falcons
Suwanee Road
Suwanee, GA 30174

Buffalo Bills
1 Bills Drive
Orchard Park, NY 14127

Chicago Bears
250 N. Washington
Lake Forest, IL 60045

Cincinnati Bengals
200 Riverfront Stadium
Cincinnati, OH 45202

Cleveland Browns
Cleveland Stadium
Cleveland, OH 44114

Dallas Cowboys
One Cowboy Pkwy.
Irving, TX 75063

Denver Broncos
5700 Logan St.
Denver, CO 80216

Detroit Lions
1200 Featherstone Rd.
Pontiac, MI 48057

Green Bay Packers
1265 Lombardi Ave.
Green Bay, WI 54303

Houston Oilers
P.O. Box 1516
Houston, TX 77030

Indianapolis Colts
P.O. Box 24100
Indianapolis, IN 46224

Kansas City Chiefs
1 Arrowhead Drive
Kansas City, MO 64129

Los Angeles Raiders
332 Center St.
El Segundo, CA 90245

Los Angeles Rams
2327 W. Lincoln Ave.
Anaheim, CA 92801

Miami Dolphins
4770 Biscayne Blvd.
Miami, FL 33137

Minnesota Vikings
9520 Viking Dr.
Eden Prairie, MN 55344

New England Patriots
Sullivan Stadium
Foxboro, MA 02035

New Orleans Saints
6928 Saints Dr.
Metairie, LA 70003

New York Giants
Giants Stadium
E. Rutherford, NJ 07073

New York Jets
598 Madison Ave.
New York, NY 10022

Philadelphia Eagles
Veterans Stadium
Philadelphia, PA 19148

Phoenix Cardinals
P.O. Box 888
Phoenix, AZ 85100

Pittsburgh Steelers
Three Rivers Stadium
Pittsburgh, PA 15212

San Diego Chargers
P.O. Box 20666
San Diego, CA 92120

San Francisco 49ers
711 Nevada St.
Redwood City, CA 94061

Seattle Seahawks
11220 NE 53rd St.
Kirkland, WA 98033

Tampa Bay Buccaneers
1 Buccaneer Place
Tampa, FL 33607

Washington Redskins
PO Box 17247
Dulles Intl. Airport
Washington, DC 20041

Baseball

Commissioner's Office
350 Park Ave.
New York, NY 10022

National League

National League Office
350 Park Ave.
New York, NY 10022

Atlanta Braves
PO Box 4064
Atlanta, GA 30302

Chicago Cubs
Wrigley Field
Chicago, IL 60613

Cincinnati Reds
100 Riverfront Stadium
Cincinnati, OH 45202

Houston Astros
Astrodome
Houston, TX 77001

Los Angeles Dodgers
Dodger Stadium
Los Angeles, CA 90012

Montreal Expos
PO Box 500, Station M
Montreal, Que. H1V 3P2

New York Mets
Shea Stadium
Flushing, NY 11368

Philadelphia Phillies
PO Box 7575
Philadelphia, PA 19101

Pittsburgh Pirates
Three Rivers Stadium
Pittsburgh, PA 15212

St. Louis Cardinals
Busch Stadium
St. Louis, MO 63102

San Diego Padres
PO Box 2000
San Diego, CA 92120

San Francisco Giants
Candlestick Park
San Francisco, CA 94124

American League

American League Office
350 Park Ave.
New York, NY 10022

Baltimore Orioles
Memorial Stadium
Baltimore, MD 21218

Boston Red Sox
24 Yawkey Way
Boston, MA 02215

California Angels
Anaheim Stadium
Anaheim, CA 92806

Chicago White Sox
324 W. 35th St.
Chicago, IL 60616

Cleveland Indians
Cleveland Stadium
Cleveland, OH 44114

Detroit Tigers
Tiger Stadium
Detroit, MI 48216

Kansas City Royals
P.O. Box 419969
Kansas City, MO 64141

Milwaukee Brewers
Milwaukee County Stadium
Milwaukee, WI 53214

Minnesota Twins
501 Chicago Ave. South
Minneapolis, MN 55415

New York Yankees
Yankee Stadium
Bronx, NY 10451

Oakland A's
Oakland Coliseum
Oakland, CA 94621

Seattle Mariners
P.O. Box 4100
Seattle, WA 98104

Texas Rangers
1200 Copeland Rd.
Arlington, TX 76011

Toronto Blue Jays
Box 7777
Adelaide St. PO
Toronto, Ont. M5C 2K7

National Basketball Association

League Office
645 5th Ave.
New York, NY 10022

Atlanta Hawks
100 Techwood Drive NW
Atlanta, GA 30303

Boston Celtics
Boston Garden
Boston, MA 02114

Charlotte Hornets
2 First Union Plaza
P.O. Box 30666
Charlotte, NC 28282

Chicago Bulls
980 North Michigan Ave.
Chicago, IL 60611

Cleveland Cavaliers
2923 Statesboro Rd.
Richfield, OH 44286

Dallas Mavericks
777 Sports St.
Dallas, TX 75207

Denver Nuggets
1635 Clay St.
Denver, CO 80204

Detroit Pistons
1200 Featherstone
Pontiac, MI 48057

Golden State Warriors
Oakland Coliseum
Oakland, CA 94621

Houston Rockets
The Summit
Houston, TX 77046

Indiana Pacers
2 W. Washington St.
Indianapolis, IN 46204

Los Angeles Clippers
3939 Figueroa
Los Angeles, CA 90037

New Jersey Nets
Meadowlands Arena
E. Rutherford, NJ 07073

Portland Trail Blazers
700 NE Multnomah St.
Portland, OR 97232

Seattle SuperSonics
190 Queen Ann Ave. N.
Seattle, WA 98109

Los Angeles Lakers
PO Box 10
Inglewood, CA 90306

New York Knickerbockers
4 Pennsylvania Plaza
New York, NY 10001

Sacramento Kings
1515 Sports Dr.
Sacramento, CA 95834

Utah Jazz
5 Triad Center
Salt Lake City, UT 84180

Miami Heat
100 Chopin Plaza
Miami, FL 33131

Philadelphia 76ers
PO Box 25040
Philadelphia, PA 19147

San Antonio Spurs
600 E. Market St.
San Antonio, TX 78205

Washington Bullets
Capital Centre
Landover, MD 20785

Milwaukee Bucks
901 North 4th St.
Milwaukee, WI 53203

Phoenix Suns
2910 N. Central
Phoenix, AZ 85012

Sports Halls of Fame

The following is a list of the location of the halls of fame for various sports:

Baseball, professional: Cooperstown, N.Y.
Baseball, Little League: Williamsport, Pa.
Basketball: Springfield, Mass.
Bowling: St. Louis, Mo.
Boxing: Canastota, N.Y.
Football, college: King's Island, Oh.
Football, professional: Canton, Oh.
Football, Canadian: Hamilton, Ont.
Golf, PGA: Palm Beach Gardens, Fla.

Greyhound racing: Abilene, Kan.
Hockey, NHL: Toronto, Ont.
Hockey, U.S.: Eveleth, Minn.
Lacrosse: Baltimore, Md.
Rodeo Cowboy: Oklahoma City, Okla.
Skating, figure: Colorado Springs, Col.
Skating, speed: Newburgh, N.Y.
Skiing: Ishpeming, Mich.
Soccer: Oneonta, N.Y.
Softball: Oklahoma City, Okla.

Swimming: Ft. Lauderdale, Fla.
Tennis: Newport, R.I.
Track & Field, national: Charleston, W. Va.
Track & Field, U.S.: Angola, Ind.
Trotting: Goshen, N.Y.
Volleyball: Holyoke, Mass.
Wrestling: Stillwater, Okla.

Notable Canadian Sports Personalities

Sid Abel, b. Feb. 22, 1918, Melville, Sask.: centred "Production Line" with Gordie Howe and Ted Lindsay (Detroit); won Hart trophy (1949); 4-time all-star.

Syl Apps, b. Jan. 18, 1915, Paris, Ont.: hockey player, Toronto Maple Leafs (1936-48); won Calder trophy (1937); 3-time all-star.

George Athans Jr., b. July 6, 1952, Kelowna, B.C.: 3-time world overall water-skiing champion.

Al Balding, b. Apr. 29, 1924, Toronto, Ont.: golfer, won individual and World Cup team title (1968); first Canadian winner of PGA tour event (1955).

Carling Bassett, b. Oct. 9, 1967, Toronto, Ont.: internationally-ranked tennis player.

Steve Bauer, b. June 12, 1959, Grimsby, Ont.: cyclist, won 1984 Olympic silver medal in 190 km road race; finished 4th in the 1988 Tour de France.

Alex Baumann, b. Apr. 21, 1964, Prague, Czechoslovakia: swimmer, won gold medal in 200m and 400m individual medley at 1984 Olympics; Canada's male athlete of 1984.

Jean Béliveau, b. Aug. 31, 1931, Trois-Rivières, Que.: centre, Montreal Canadiens (1953-71), won NHL scoring title (1956), Hart trophy (1956), Conn Smythe trophy (1965), 10-time all-star.

Marilyn Bell, b. Oct. 19, 1937, Toronto, Ont.: first person to swim Lake Ontario (1954).

Max Bentley (1920-1984), b. Delisle, Sask.: centre, won NHL scoring titles (1946 and 1947), Hart trophy (1946).

Trevor Berbick, b. Aug. 1, 1952, Jamaica: boxer, Canadian heavyweight champion (1978-85) and WBC world heavyweight champion (1986).

Sylvie Bernier, b. Jan. 31, 1964, Quebec, Que.: gold medalist in 3m springboard diving at 1984 Olympics.

Toe Blake, b. Aug. 21, 1912, Victoria Mines, Ont.: left winger, Montreal Canadiens (1936-48), won NHL scoring title (1939), Hart trophy (1939); coached Canadiens to 8 Stanley Cups between 1955-68.

Mike Bossy, b. Jan. 22, 1957, Montreal, Que.: right winger, New York Islanders since 1977; Calder trophy (1978), Conn Smythe trophy (1982); 8-time all-star; NHL record 9 consecutive 50-goal seasons.

Gaetan Boucher, b. May 10, 1958, Charlesbourg, Que.: speedskater, won gold medal in 1 000m and 1 500m events, bronze in 500m at 1984 Winter Olympics.

Debbie Brill, b. Mar. 10, 1953, Mission, B.C.: internationally-ranked high jump competitor during 1970s; originator of the "Brill Bend" jumping style.

Lionel Conacher, (1901-1954), b. Toronto, Ont.: named Canada's Athlete of the Half Century, 1900-50; NHL defenceman (1925-34); fullback, punter Toronto Argonauts (1921-25); also played pro baseball, lacrosse, boxed and wrestled.

Jim Corrigall, b. May 7, 1946, Barrie, Ont.: lineman with Toronto Argonauts 1970-1981; CFL outstanding defensive lineman (1975); 4-time CFL all-star.

Toller Cranston, b. Apr. 20, 1949, Hamilton, Ont.: men's singles figure skating bronze medal in 1974 World Championships and 1976 Winter Olympics; innovator in bringing artistry, creativity to men's free skating.

Petra Burka, b. Nov. 17, 1946, Amsterdam, The Netherlands: world ladies' singles figure skating champion (1965); won bronze medal at 1964 Olympics.

Tommy Burns (1881-1955), b. June 17, 1881, Hanover, Ont.: only Canadian boxer to hold world heavyweight title (1906-1908), 11 successful title defences.

Larry Cain, b. Jan. 9, 1963, Toronto, Ont.: canoeist, won gold medal in 500m CI, silver medal in 1 000m CI at 1984 Olympics.

Michelle Cameron, b. Dec. 28, 1962, Calgary, Alta.: won gold medal in synchronized swimming duet (with Carolyn Waldo) in 1988 Olympics.

John Campbell, b. Aug. 4, 1955, London, Ont.: one of North America's leading harness racing drivers.

George Chuvalo, b. Sept. 12, 1937, Toronto, Ont.: 3-time Canadian heavyweight boxing champion (1958-79); fought several world champions, including Muhammad Ali, Joe Frazier and George Foreman; never knocked off his feet.

King Clancy (1903-1986), Ottawa, Ont.: all-star defenceman with Ottawa Senators (1921-1930) and Toronto Maple Leafs (1930-1937).

Bill Crothers, b. Dec. 24, 1940, Markham, Ont.: among the world's best middle distance runners during 1960s; won silver medal in 800m at 1964 Olympics.

Dave Cutler, b. Oct. 17, 1945, Biggar, Sask.: place kicker with Edmonton Eskimos (1969-1984); 7 CFL scoring titles; all-time CFL scoring leader.

Louis Cyr (1863-1912), b. St. Cyprien de Napierville, Que.: performed many astonishing feats of strength, 1880-1900; considered the world's strongest man.

Victor Davis, b. Feb. 10, 1964, Guelph, Ont.: swimmer, gold medal in 200m breaststroke, silver medal in 100m breaststroke and 400m medley relay in 1984 Olympics.

James Day, b. July 7, 1946, Thornhill, Ont.: equestrian, team gold Paix des Nations in 1968 Olympics; team title world Prix des Nations 1970.

Cy Denneny (1891-1970), b. Farran's Point, Ont.: hockey player, among all-time NHL leaders with 26 hat tricks and a 12 game scoring streak; NHL scoring title (1924).

Marcel Dionne, b. Aug. 3, 1951, Drummondville, Que.: centre, won Art Ross trophy (1980) and goal-scoring leader.

Ken Dryden, b. Aug. 8, 1947, Hamilton, Ont.: goaltender, Montreal Canadiens, Conn Smythe trophy (1971), Calder trophy (1972), Vezina trophy (1973 and 1976-1979), 6-time all-star.

Yvon Durelle, b. Oct. 14, 1929, Baie St. Anne, N.B.: Canadian middleweight boxing title (1953), light heavyweight (1953 and 1954), British Empire light heavyweight champion (1957); lost to Archie Moore in world light heavyweight title bouts in 1958 and 1959.

Bill Durnan (1915-1972), b. Jan. 22, 1915, Toronto, Ont: goaltender, Montreal Canadiens (1943-50); 6-time Vezina trophy winner; 5-time all-star.

Alan Eagleson, b. Apr. 24, 1933, St. Catherines, Ont.: executive director NHL Players' Association; organizer of many international hockey series.

Jim Elder, b. July 27, 1934, Toronto, Ont.: equestrian, gold medal, Prix des Nations in 1968 Olympics.

Vic Emery, b. June 28, 1933, Montreal, Que.: 4-man bobsled with John Emery, Doug Anakin, Peter Kirby; pilot of gold medal teams in 1964 Olympics, 1965 World Championships.

Phil Esposito, b. Feb. 20, 1942, Sault Ste Marie, Ont.: centre, won Hart trophy (1969 and 1974), Art Ross trophy (1969 and 1971-74); 3d all-time NHL goal scorer, 4th all-time point leader.

Terry Evanshen, b. June 13, 1944, Montreal, Que.: CFL receiver (1965-78), won Schenley award as outstanding Canadian (1967 and 1971).

Hervé Filion, b. Feb. 1, 1940, Angers, Que.: harness racing's all-time leader with more than 9 000 victories and over $40 million in purses.

Steve Fonyo, b. June 29, 1965, Montreal, Que.: with an artificial leg completed 425-day, cross-country, "Journey For Lives" May 29, 1985

Terry Fox (1958-1981), b. Winnipeg, Man.: in 1980, with an artificial leg, began "Marathon of Hope" run across Canada to raise funds for cancer research; run halted by recurring cancer but succeeded in raising more than $23 million; won Lou Marsh trophy as top Canadian athlete (1980).

Anna Fraser, b. July 25, 1963, Ottawa, Ont.: freestyle skier, 1986 World Cup Aerial Champion.

Lori Fung, b. Feb. 21, 1963, Vancouver, B.C.: gymnast, won gold medal in rhythmic gymnastics in 1984 Olympics.

Tony Gabriel, b. Dec. 11, 1948, Hamilton, Ont.: football tight end, named CFL outstanding player (1978), outstanding Canadian (1974, 1976-78); holds pro football record for pass receptions in 138 straight games.

Tom Gayford, b. Nov. 21, 1928, Toronto, Ont.: equestrian, won gold medal Prix des Nations in 1968 Olympics.

Bernie Geoffrion, b. Feb. 14, 1931, Montreal, Que.: right winger, Montreal Canadiens (1950-1964); Calder Memorial trophy (1952), Hart trophy (1961), Art Ross trophy (1955 and 1961).

Avelino Gomez (1928-1980), b. Havana, Cuba: among world's leading jockeys with over 4 000 wins; 4-time Queen's Plate winner; died of injuries suffered in a racing spill.

Nancy Greene, b. May 11, 1943, Ottawa, Ont.: skier, World Cup champion (1967 and 1968); gold medal in giant slalom and silver medal in slalom at 1968 Olympics.

Gail Greenough, b. Mar. 7, 1960, Edmonton, Alta.: equestrian, won 1986 world champion individual show jumping.

Wayne Gretzky, b. Jan. 26, 1961, Brantford, Ont.: centre, Edmonton, traded to Los Angeles Kings in Aug. 1988; Hart trophy (1980-1987), Art Ross trophy (1981-1987), Conn Smythe trophy (1985 and 1988); many single season records, including most goals (92), assists (163), points (215).

Al Hackner, b. July 18, 1954, Nipigon, Ont.: curler, skip of 1982 and 1985 Brier and Silver Broom world champion rinks.

George Hainsworth (1895-1950), b. Toronto, Ont.: goaltender, won first 3 Vezina trophies (1927-1929), single season record 22 shutouts in 44 games (1929).

Glenn Hall, b. Oct. 3, 1931, Humboldt, Sask.: goaltender, won Calder trophy (1956), Vezina trophy (1963, 1967, 1969), Conn Smythe trophy (1968); 11-time all-star; a record 502 consecutive games by a goaltender.

Ned Hanlan (1855-1908), b. Toronto, Ont.: rower, first "world champion" in any sport as world champion oarsman (1880-84).

Doug Harvey, b. Dec. 19, 1924, Montreal, Que.: defenceman, won Norris trophy (1955-58 and 1960-62); 11-time all-star.

Sandy Hawley, b. Apr. 16, 1949, Oshawa, Ont.: jockey, winner of more than 5 000 races.

Anne Heggtveit, b. Jan. 11, 1939, Ottawa, Ont.: won Canada's first Olympic skiing gold medal in women's slalom (1960).

Doug Hepburn, b. Sept. 16, 1926, Vancouver, B.C.: weightlifter, won "world's strongest man" title, world heavyweight weightlifting title (1953).

Foster Hewitt (1903-1985), b. Toronto, Ont.: pioneer hockey broadcaster.

Ron Hextall, b. May 3, 1964, Brandon, Man.: goalie with Philadelphia Flyers, won Vezina and Conn Smythe trophies in 1987.

John Hiller, b. Apr. 8, 1943, Scarborough, Ont.: relief pitcher with Detroit Tigers (1965-80); tied American League record for victories by a reliever (17) in 1974.

Mathew Hilton, b. Dec. 27, 1965, Cooksville, Ont.: International Boxing Federation junior middleweight champion (1987).

George Hodgson (1893-1983), b. Montreal, Que.: first Canadian to win Olympic gold medals in swimming; 400m, 1 500m freestyle in 1912 Olympics.

Abby Hoffman, b. Feb. 11, 1947, Toronto, Ont.: national and international track and field competitor (1962-76) at 800 and 1 500m; director of Sport Canada.

Elmer Hohl (1919-1987), b. Wellesley, Ont.: 6-time world horseshoe pitching champion between 1965 and 1977.

Gordie Howe, b. Mar. 31, 1928, Floral, Sask.: right winger with Detroit Red Wings (1946-71), Houston Aeros (1973-76), New England Whalers (1977-79); 6-time Hart trophy winner, 6-time Art Ross trophy winner; all-time NHL leader in goals (801), assists (1 049), points (1 850), games (1 767), seasons (26).

Bobby Hull, b. Jan. 3, 1939, Pointe Anne, Ont.: left winger with Chicago (1957-72), Winnipeg Jets (1972-79); won Hart trophy (1965 and 1966), Art Ross trophy (1960, 1962, 1966); 12-time NHL all-star.

George Hungerford, b. Jan. 2, 1944, Vancouver, B.C.: rower, won gold medal (with Roger Jackson) in coxless pairs at 1964 Olympics.

Busher Jackson (1911-1966), b. Toronto, Ont.: left winger, won Art Ross trophy (1932); 5-time all-star.

Donald Jackson, b. Apr. 2, 1940, Oshawa, Ont.: figure skater, men's singles world champion (1962); bronze medal in 1960 Olympics.

Roger Jackson, b. Jan. 14, 1942, Toronto, Ont.: with George Hungerford, won gold medal in coxless pairs rowing in 1964 Olympics.

Russ Jackson, b. July 28, 1936, Hamilton, Ont.: quarterback with Ottawa Rough Riders (1958-69); Schenley award as outstanding player (1963, 1966, 1969), outstanding Canadian (1959, 1963, 1966, 1969).

Gerry James, b. Oct. 22, 1934, Regina, Sask.: played football with Winnipeg Blue Bombers (1952-64) and hockey with Toronto Maple Leafs (1954-59); won Schenley award as outstanding Canadian in CFL (1954 and 1957).

Otto Jelinek, b. May 20, 1940, Prague, Czechoslovakia: figure skater, with sister Maria, won world pairs championship (1962).

Ferguson Jenkins, b. Dec. 13, 1943, Chatham, Ont.: pitcher, 284-226 career won-lost; 7-time 20-game winner; National League Cy Young award (1971).

Harry Jerome (1940-1982), b. Prince Albert, Sask.: sprinter, won bronze medal in 100m at 1964 Olympics.

"Jackrabbit" Smith-Johannsen (1875-1986), b. Oslo, Norway: major force in developing cross-country skiing in Canada; active skier as a centenarian.

Ben Johnson, b. Dec. 30, 1961, Falmouth, Jamaica: sprinter, stripped of gold medal in 1988 Olympics after testing positive to drug use (steroids); set world record of 9.83 seconds in 100m sprint (1987).

Aurel Joliat (1901-1986), b. Ottawa, Ont.: left winger Montreal Canadiens (1922-38); won Hart trophy (1934).

Vicki Keith, b. Feb. 26, 1961, Winnipeg, Man.: marathon swimmer, completed crossings of all 5 Great Lakes in 1988 to raise funds for charity.

Helen Kelesi, b. Nov. 15, 1969, Victoria, B.C.: Canadian women's tennis champion, 1987 and 1988.

Sharif Khan, b. Nov. 10, 1945, Peshawar, Pakistan: North American and world hardball squash champion during 1970s.

Bruce Kidd, b. July 26, 1943, Ottawa, Ont.: won many national, U.S. and Commonwealth track titles at one, 3 and 6 miles during early 1960s; named outstanding Canadian male athlete of 1961 and 1962.

George Knudson, b. June 28, 1937, Winnipeg, Man.: golfer, with 12 PGA tour victories from 1961 to 1972; 1968 World Cup with Al Balding and World Cup individual title 1966.

Kathy Kreiner, b. May 4; 1957, Timmins, Ont.: skier, gold medallist in women's giant slalom at 1976 Winter Olympics.

Joe Krol, b. Feb. 20, 1919, Hamilton, Ont.: football player with Toronto Argonauts (1945-52); named Canada's top male athlete of 1946.

Normie Kwong, b. Oct. 24, 1929, Calgary, Alta.: fullback with Calgary Stampeders and Edmonton Eskimos (1948-1960); won Schenley award as outstanding Canadian 1955 and 1956.

Elmer Lach, b. Jan. 22, 1918, Nokomis, Sask.: centre with Montreal Canadiens (1940-55); won Hart trophy (1945), Art Ross trophy (1945 and 1948).

Guy Lafleur, b. Sept. 20, 1951, Thurso, Que.: right winger with Montreal Canadiens (1971-84); won Hart trophy (1977 and 1978); Art Ross trophy (1976, 1977 and 1978); Conn Smythe trophy (1977); Canadiens all-time scoring leader with 1 246 points.

Donny Lalonde, b. 1960, Kitchener, Ont.: boxer, WBC light-heavyweight champion, 1987-88.

Newsy Lalonde (1888-1971), b. Cornwall, Ont.: hockey player with Montreal Canadiens (1913-22); NHL scoring leader 1919 and 1921.

Mario Lemieux, b. Oct. 5, 1965, Montreal, Que.: centre with Pittsburgh Penguins since 1984; won Calder trophy (1985); led Canada to victory in 1987 Canada Cup series with 11 goals; leading scorer and Hart trophy winner in 1988.

Lennox Lewis, b. Sept. 2, 1965, London, England: boxer, won gold in super heavyweight category in 1988 Olympics.

Ted Lindsay, b. July 29, 1925, Renfrew, Ont.: left winger for 17 seasons with Detroit and Chicago; won Art Ross trophy (1950).

Tom Longboat (1887-1949), b. Brantford, Ont.: premier distance and marathon runner (1905-10); won 1907 Boston Marathon in record time; in 1906 outran a horse over a 12-mile course.

Jocelyn Lovell, b. July 19, 1950, England: Canada's premier cyclist (1970-83); won 1 000m silver medal in 1978 world championships; paralyzed in a training accident, 1983.

Cliff Lumsden, b. Apr. 13, 1931, Toronto, Ont.: among world's best marathon swimmers during 1950s.

Karen Magnussen, b. Apr. 4, 1952, North Vancouver, B.C.: figure skater, won silver medal in women's singles figure skating in 1972 Olympics and 1973 world championships.

Frank Mahovlich, b. Jan. 10, 1938, Timmins, Ont.: left winger, scored 533 goals in 17 seasons with Toronto, Detroit and Montreal (1957-74); won Calder trophy (1958).

Joe Malone (1890-1969), b. Quebec, Que.: NHL scoring leader in 1918 and 1920; scored 44 goals in 20 game season (1917-18) and 7 goals in one game.

Elizabeth Manley, b. Aug. 7, 1965, Belleville, Ont.: 1988 Olympic silver medal winner in figure skating.

Egerton Marcus, b. Feb. 2, 1965, Guyana: boxer, won silver medal in middleweight category at 1988 Olympics.

Paul Martini, b. Nov. 2, 1960, Weston, Ont.: with partner Barbara Underhill, won bronze (1983) and gold (1984) medals in world pairs figure skating.

Heather McKay, b. July 31, 1941, Queanbeyan, Australia: world's leading woman squash player during 1970s.

Jimmy McLarnin, b. Dec. 19, 1907, Belfast, Ireland: boxer, world welterweight champion (1933-35); Canada's boxer of the half century in CP poll (1950).

Stan Mikita, b. May 20, 1940, Sokolce, Czechoslovakia: centre with Chicago Blackhawks (1959-80); won Hart trophy (1967 and 1968); Art Ross trophy (1964, 1965, 1967, 1968).

Ray Mitchell, b. Mar. 22, 1931, Peace River, Alta.: bowler, 1972 Canadian and world 10-pin champion.

Howie Morenz, (1902-1937), b. Mitchell, Ont.: centre with Montreal Canadiens (1923-34 and 1936); won Hart trophy 3 times and NHL scoring championships in 1928 and 1931; Canada's hockey player of the half century in 1950 CP poll; died of hockey injury.

Alwyn Morris, b. Nov. 22, 1957, Montreal, Que.: with Hugh Fisher, won gold medal in 1 000m and bronze in 500m men's kayak doubles at 1984 Olympics.

James Naismith, (1861-1939), b. Almonte, Ont.: invented game of basketball (1891).

Susan Nattrass, b. Nov. 5, 1950, Medicine Hat, Alta.: won 6 women's world trapshooting titles (1978-82).

Cindy Nicholas, b. Aug. 20, 1957, Toronto, Ont.: marathon swimmer, record holder for swimming Lake Ontario, English Channel; first woman to complete 2-way Channel swim, 19 Channel swims, including 5 two-way crossings.

Frank Nighbor, (1893-1966), b. Pembroke, Ont.: first winner of NHL's Hart (1924), and Lady Byng (1925 and 1926) trophies.

Ron Northcott, b. Dec. 31, 1935, Innisfail, Alta.: curler, skip of Brier and world championship rinks in 1966, 1968 and 1969.

Gerry Organ, b. Dec. 4, 1944, Cheltenham, England: place kicker with Ottawa Rough Riders (1971-83); won Schenley award as outstanding Canadian (1973).

Bobby Orr, b. Mar. 20, 1948, Parry Sound, Ont.: defenceman with Boston Bruins (1966-76) and Chicago Black Hawks (1976-78); won Calder trophy (1967), Hart trophy (1970-72), Art Ross trophy (1970 and 1975), record 8 consecutive James Norris trophies (1968-75), Conn Smythe trophy (1970 and 1972); acknowledged innovator as "offensive-defenceman."

Brian Orser, b. Dec. 18, 1961, Belleville, Ont.: figure skater, 1987 men's world champion, won silver medal in 1984 and 1988 Olympics.

Anne Ottenbrite, b. May 12, 1966, Whitby, Ont.: swimmer, won gold medal in 200m, silver medal in 100m breaststroke, bronze medal in 4 × 100m medley relay at 1984 Olympics.

Robert Paul, b. June 2, 1937, Toronto, Ont.: figure skater, with partner Barbara Wagner won world pairs championship (1957-60) and Olympic gold medal in 1960.

Karen Percy, b. Oct. 10, 1966, Edmonton, Alta.: skier, won bronze medals in downhill and super giant slalom events in 1988 Olympics.

Pierre Pilote, b. Dec. 11, 1931, Kenogami, Que.: defenceman, won James Norris trophy (1963-65).

Jacques Plante, (1929-1986), b. Mt. Carmel, Que.: goalie, won Hart trophy (1962), Vezina trophy (1956-60, 1962, 1969); originated face mask and roving style for goaltenders.

Steve Podborski, b. July 25, 1957, Toronto, Ont.: skier, first North American to win World Cup downhill title (1982); won bronze medal, downhill, in 1980 Olympics.

Sam Pollock, b. Dec. 15, 1925, Montreal, Que.: general manager with Montreal Canadiens (1964-78), known for shrewd trading of extra players for future draft choices to build championship teams.

Sandra Post, b. June 4, 1943, Oakville, Ont.: golfer, Canada's first woman touring professional; LPGA tour golfer (1968-83); LPGA rookie of the year (1968).

Denis Potvin, b. Oct. 29, 1953, Ottawa, Ont.: defenceman with New York Islanders since 1973; Calder trophy (1974), James Norris trophy (1976, 1978, 1979); all-time leader among defencemen in goals and assists.

Patricia Puntous, b. Dec. 28, 1960, Montreal, Que.: with twin sister, Sylviane, among world's best female triathletes since 1983.

Sylviane Puntous, b. Dec. 28, 1960, Montreal, Que.: with twin sister, Patricia, among world's best female triathletes since 1983.

Claude Raymond, b. May 7, 1937, St. Jean, Que.: relief pitcher with Chicago White Sox, Milwaukee Braves, Houston Astros, Atlanta Braves, Montreal Expos (1962-74); 1966 National League all-star.

Ken Read, b. Nov. 6, 1955, Ann Arbor, Mich.: skier, with 5 World Cup downhill victories (1975-1980).

Maurice "Rocket" Richard, b. Aug. 4, 1921, Montreal, Que.: right winger with Montreal Canadiens (1942-60); won Hart trophy (1947); first 50-goal season scorer (1944-45 season); first 500-goal career scorer (1957); 14-time all-star.

Ernie Richardson, b. Aug. 4, 1931, Stoughton, Sask.: curler, skip of a record 4 Brier and world championship rinks between 1959 and 1963.

Blondie Robinson, b. Jan. 3, 1928, Kirkland Lake, Ont.: bowler, won world 10-pin title in 1969.

Larry Robinson, b. June 2, 1951, Winchester, Ont.: defenceman with Montreal Canadiens since 1972; James Norris trophy (1977 and 1980); Conn Smythe trophy (1978); 6-time all-star.

Bobbie Rosenfield, (1905-1969), b. Russia: won silver medal in women's 100m and gold medal in 4 × 100m relay at 1928 Olympics; named Canada's female athlete of the half-century in 1950 CP poll.

Tommy Ryan, (1882-1961), b. Guelph, Ont.: invented 5-pin bowling in 1909.

Terry Sawchuk, (1929-1970), b. Winnipeg, Man.: goaltender, won Calder trophy (1951), Vezina trophy (1952, 1953, 1955, 1965); all-time leader with 103 shutouts in 971 games.

Milt Schmidt, b. Mar. 5, 1918, Kitchener, Ont.: centre with Boston Bruins (1936-55); won Art Ross trophy (1940), Hart trophy (1951); later NHL coach and general manager.

Barbara Ann Scott, b. May 9, 1928, Ottawa, Ont.: figure skater, women's singles world champion 1947 and 1948; won gold medal in 1948 Olympics.

George Selkirk, (1899-1987), b. Huntsville, Ont.: outfielder with New York Yankees (1934-42); replaced Babe Ruth in Yankees outfield (1934).

Eddie Shore, (1902-1985), b. Ft. Qu'Apelle, Sask.: defenceman, won Hart trophy 4 times between 1933 and 1938 with Boston Bruins.

Darryl Sittler, b. Sept. 18, 1950, St. Jacob's, Ont.: centre, set NHL record 10 points in one game and tied modern record 6 goals in one game (1976) with Toronto Maple Leafs.

Graham Smith, b. May 9, 1958, Edmonton, Alta.: swimmer, won 6 gold medals in 1978 Commonwealth Games.

Conn Smythe, (1895-1980), b. Toronto, Ont.: hockey executive, owner Toronto Maple Leafs (1930-61); driving force in building Maple Leaf Gardens (1931).

Nels Stewart, (1900-1957), b. Montreal, Que.: won Hart trophy (1926 and 1930), NHL leading scorer (1926); fastest 2 goals ever (4 secs. in 1931); first NHL player to score 300 goals.

Ron Stewart, b. Sept. 25, 1934, Toronto, Ont.: running back with Ottawa Rough Riders (1958-70); Schenley award as outstanding Canadian (1960).

Marlene Stewart Streit, b. Mar. 9, 1934, Cereal, Alta.: golfer, multiple winner of national, U.S. and international amateur golf titles since 1953.

Elaine Tanner, b. Feb. 22, 1951, Vancouver, B.C.: swimmer, won silver and bronze medals in the 1968 Olympics.

Cyclone Taylor, (1883-1979), b. Tara, Ont.: hockey forward (1907-1921); scored 194 goals in 186 games; considered the best of his day during transition to the modern hockey era.

Ron Taylor, b. Dec. 13, 1937, Toronto, Ont.: relief pitcher (1962-72); member of 1964 St. Louis and 1969 N.Y. Mets world series champions.

Linda Thom, b. Dec. 30, 1943, Hamilton, Ont.: won gold medal in women's sport pistol competition at 1984 Olympics.

Cliff Thorburn, b. Jan. 16, 1948, Victoria, B.C.: among world's top ranked pro snooker players; world champion 1980.

Ron Turcotte, b. July 22, 1941, Drummond, N.B.: among North America's leading jockeys during 1960s and 1970s; rode Secretariat to Triple Crown (1973); career ended by a racing injury in 1978.

Barbara Underhill, b. June 24, 1963, Pembroke, Ont.: figure skater, with partner Paul Martini won bronze (1983) and gold (1984) medals in world pairs figure skating competition.

Gilles Villeneuve, (1952-1982), b. St. Jean, Que.: auto racer, won 6 Grand Prix victories (1978-81); died from injuries suffered in qualifying run in Belgium (1982).

Carolyn Waldo, b. Dec. 11, 1964, Montreal, Que.: won 2 gold medals in synchronized swimming at 1988 Olympics, silver medal in 1984 Olympics.

Barbara Wagner, b. May 5, 1938, Toronto, Ont.: figure skater, with partner Bob Paul won world pairs champions (1957-60); Olympic gold medal (1960).

Whipper Billy Watson, b. June 25, 1917, Toronto, Ont.: 2-time world professional wrestling champion (1947 and 1956).

Lucile Wheeler, b. Jan. 14, 1935, Montreal, Que.: skier, first Canadian to win Olympic skiing medal with downhill bronze in 1956, first North American to win world championship with 2 golds in downhill and slalom events (1958).

Percy Williams, (1908-1982), b. Vancouver, B.C.: sprinter, won 21 of 22 indoor sprints in 1929; only Canadian to win sprint double with gold medals in 100m and 200m events at 1928 Olympics; Canada's track & field athlete of the half-century in 1950 CP poll.

John Wood, b. June 7, 1950, Toronto, Ont.: canoeist, won silver medal in men's 500m canoe singles at 1976 Olympics.

Jim Young, b. June 6, 1943, Hamilton, Ont.: running back and wide receiver with B.C. Lions (1967-79); won Schenley award as outstanding Canadian (1970 and 1972).

Notable Sports Personalities

(For Notable Canadian Sports Personalities, see p. 648)

Henry Aaron, b. 1934: Milwaukee-Atlanta outfielder hit record 755 home runs; led NL 4 times.

Kareem Abdul-Jabbar, b. 1947: Milwaukee, L.A. Lakers center; MVP 6 times; leading scorer twice; playoff MVP, 1971, 1985; all-time leading NBA scorer.

Grover Cleveland Alexander, (1887-1950): pitcher won 374 NL games; pitched 16 shutouts, 1916.

Muhammad Ali, b. 1942: 3-time heavyweight champion.

Ken Anderson, b. 1949: Cinn. Bengals quarterback led AFC in passing 4 times.

Mario Andretti, b. 1940; won Indy 500, 1969; Grand Prix champ, 1978.

Eddie Arcaro, b. 1916: jockey rode 4,779 winners including the Kentucky Derby 5 times; the Preakness and Belmont Stakes 6 times each.

Arthur Ashe, b. 1943: U.S. singles champ, 1968, Wimbledon champ, 1975.

Red Auerbach, b. 1917: coached Boston Celtics to 9 NBA championships.

Ernie Banks, b. 1931: Chicago Cubs slugger hit 512 NL homers; twice MVP.

Roger Bannister, b. 1929: Briton ran first sub 4-minute mile, May 6, 1954.

Sammy Baugh, b. 1914: Washington Redskins quarterback held numerous records upon retirement after 16 pro seasons.

Elgin Baylor, b. 1934: L.A. Lakers forward; 1st team all-star 10 times.

Johnny Bench, b. 1947: Cincinnati Reds catcher; MVP twice; led league in home runs twice, RBIs 3 times.

Yogi Berra, b. 1925: N.Y. Yankees catcher; MVP 3 times; played in 14 World Series.

Raymond Berry, b. 1933: Baltimore Colts receiver caught 631 passes.

Larry Bird, b. 1956: Boston Celtics forward; chosen MVP 1984-86, playoff MVP, 1984, 1986.

George Blanda, b. 1927: quarterback, kicker; 26 years as active player, scoring record 2,002 points.

Wade Boggs, b. 1958: AL Batting champ, 1983, 1985-88.

Bjorn Borg, b. 1956: led Sweden to first Davis Cup, 1975; Wimbledon champion, 5 times.

Terry Bradshaw, b. 1948: Pittsburgh Steelers quarterback led team to 4 Super Bowl titles.

George Brett, b. 1953: Kansas City Royals 3d baseman led AL in batting, 1976, 1980; MVP, 1980.

Lou Brock, b. 1939: St. Louis Cardinals outfielder stole record 118 bases, 1974; record 938 career; led NL 8 times.

Jimmy Brown, b. 1936: Cleveland Browns fullback ran for 12,312 career yards; MVP 3 times.

Paul "Bear" Bryant, (1913-1983), college football coach with 323 victories.

Maria Bueno, b. 1939: U.S. singles champ 4 times; Wimbledon champ 3 times.

Dick Butkus, b. 1942: Chicago Bears linebacker twice chosen best NFL defensive player.

Dick Button, b. 1929: figure skater won 1948, 1952 Olympic gold medals; world titlist, 1948-52.

Roy Campanella, b. 1921: Brooklyn Dodgers catcher; MVP 3 times.

Earl Campbell, b. 1955: NFL running back; NFL MVP 1978-1980.

Rod Carew, b. 1945: AL infielder won 7 batting titles; MVP, 1977.

Steve Carlton, b. 1944: NL pitcher won 20 games 5 times, Cy Young award 4 times.

Billy Casper, b. 1931: PGA Player-of-the-Year 3 times; U.S. Open champ twice.

Wilt Chamberlain, b. 1936: center was NBA leading scorer 7 times; MVP 4 times.

Roberto Clemente, (1934-1972): Pittsburgh Pirates outfielder won 4 batting titles; MVP, 1966.

Ty Cobb, (1886-1961): Detroit Tigers outfielder had record .367 lifetime batting average, 12 batting titles.

Sebastian Coe, b. 1956: Briton won Olympic 1,500-meter run, 1980, 1984.

Nadia Comaneci, b. 1961: Romanian gymnast won 3 gold medals, achieved 7 perfect scores, 1976 Olympics.

Maureen Connolly, (1934-1969): won tennis "grand slam," 1953; AP Woman-Athlete-of-the-Year 3 times.

Jimmy Connors, b. 1952: U.S. singles champ 5 times; Wimbledon champ twice.

James J. Corbett, (1866-1933): heavyweight champion, 1892-97; credited with being the first "scientific" boxer.

Angel Cordero, b. 1942: jockey; won over 6 000 races; leading money winner 1976, 1982-83.

Margaret Smith Court, b. 1942: Australian won U.S. singles championship 5 times; Wimbledon champ 3 times.

Bob Cousy, b. 1928: Boston Celtics guard led team to 6 NBA championships; MVP, 1957.

André Dawson, b. 1954: slugger, led NL in homeruns, MVP, 1987.

Dizzy Dean, (1911-1974): colorful pitcher for St. Louis Cardinals "Gashouse Gang" in the 30s; MVP, 1934.

Jack Dempsey, (1895-1983): heavyweight champion, 1919-26.

Eric Dickerson, b. 1960: L.A. Rams running back ran for NFL record 2 105 yds., 1984.

Joe DiMaggio, b. 1914: N.Y. Yankees outfielder hit safely in record 56 consecutive games, 1941; MVP 3 times.

Leo Durocher, b. 1906: colorful manager of Dodgers, Giants, and Cubs; won 3 NL pennants.

Gertrude Ederle, b. 1906: first woman to swim English Channel, broke existing men's record, 1926.

Julius Erving, b. 1950: MVP and leading scorer in ABA 3 times; NBA MVP, 1981.

Chris Evert, b. 1954: U.S. singles champ 6 times, Wimbledon champ 3 times.

Patrick Ewing, b. 1962: center led Georgetown Univ. to 1984 NCAA championship.

Ray Ewry, (1873-1937): track and field star won 8 gold medals, 1900, 1904, and 1908 Olympics.

Juan Fangio, b. 1911: Argentine World Grand Prix champion 5 times.

Bob Feller, b. 1918: Cleveland Indians pitcher won 266 games; pitched 3 no-hitters, 12 one-hitters.

Whitey Ford, b. 1928: N.Y. Yankees pitcher won record 10 World Series games.

Jimmy Foxx, (1907-1967): Red Sox, Athletics slugger; MVP 3 times; triple crown, 1933.

A.J. Foyt, b. 1935: won Indy 500 4 times; U.S. Auto Club champ 7 times.

Joe Frazier, b. 1944: heavyweight champion, 1970-73.

Lou Gehrig, (1903-1941): N.Y. Yankees 1st baseman played record 2 130 consecutive games; MVP, 1936.

George Gervin, b. 1952: leading NBA scorer, 1978-80, 1982.

Althea Gibson, b. 1927: twice U.S. and Wimbledon singles champ.

Bob Gibson, b. 1935: St. Louis Cardinals pitcher won Cy Young award twice; struck out 3,117 batters.

Frank Gifford, b. 1930: N.Y. Giants back; MVP, 1956.

Dwight Gooden, b. 1964: N.Y. Mets pitcher was NL Rookie of Year, 1984; Cy Young award, 1985.

Steffi Graf, b. 1969: W. German, won tennis "grand slam" 1988.

Otto Graham, b. 1921: Cleveland Browns quarterback; all-pro 4 times.

Red Grange, b 1903: All-America at Univ. of Illinois; played for Chicago Bears, 1925-35.

Joe Greene, b. 1946: Pittsburgh Steelers lineman; twice NFL outstanding defensive player.

Lefty Grove, (1900-1975): pitcher won 300 AL games; 20-game winner 8 times.

Tony Gwynn, b. 1960: NL batting champion 1984, 1987, 1988.

Walter Hagen, (1892-1969): won PGA championship 5 times. British Open 4 times.

George Halas, (1895-1983): founder-coach of Chicago Bears; won 5 NFL championships.

Bill Hartack, b. 1932: jockey rode 5 Kentucky Derby winners.

Bill Haughton, b. 1923: harness racing driver won Little Brown Jug 4 times, Hambletonian 4 times.

John Havlicek, b. 1940: Boston Celtics forward scored over 26,000 NBA points.

Eric Heiden, b. 1958: speed skater won 5 1980 Olympic gold medals.

Carol Heiss, b. 1940: world champion figure skater 5 consecutive years, 1956-60; won 1960 Olympic gold medal.

Rickey Henderson, b. 1958: AL outfielder stole record 130 bases, 1982.

Sonja Henie, (1912-1969): world champion figure skater, 1927-36; Olympic gold medalist, 1928, 1932, 1936.

Ben Hogan, b. 1912: won 4 U.S. Open championships, 2 PGA, 2 Masters.

Larry Holmes, b. 1949: WBC heavyweight champ 1978-84.

Rogers Hornsby, (1896-1963): NL 2d baseman batted record .424 in 1924; twice won triple crown; batting leader, 1920-25.

Paul Hornung, b. 1935: Green Bay Packers runner-placekicker scored record 176 points, 1960.

Carl Hubbell, b. 1903: N.Y. Giants pitcher; 20-game winner 5 consecutive years, 1933-37.

Catfish Hunter, b 1946: pitched perfect game, 1968; 20-game winner 5 times.

Don Hutson, b. 1913: Green Bay Packers receiver caught NFL record 99 touchdown passes.

Reggie Jackson, b. 1946: slugger led AL in home runs 4 times; MVP, 1973; hit 5 World Series home runs, 1977.

Bruce Jenner, b. 1949: decathlon gold medalist, 1976.

Jack Johnson, (1878-1946): heavyweight champion, 1910-15.

Magic Johnson, b. 1959: NBA MVP 1987; playoff MVP 1980, 1982, 1987.

Rafer Johnson, b. 1935: decathlon gold medalist, 1960.

Walter Johnson, (1887-1946): Washington Senators pitcher won 413 games.

Bobby Jones, (1902-1971): won "grand slam of golf" 1930; U.S. Amateur champ 5 times, U.S. Open champ 4 times.

Michael Jordan, b. 1963: NBA leading scorer 1987, 1988.

Sonny Jurgensen, b. 1934: quarterback named all-pro 5 times.

Duke Kahanamoku, (1890-1968): swimmer won 1912, 1920 Olympic gold medals in 100-meter freestyle.

Harmon Killebrew, b. 1936: Minnesota Twins slugger led AL in home runs 6 times.

Jean Claude Killy, b. 1943: French skier won 3 1968 Olympic gold medals.

Ralph Kiner, b. 1922: Pittsburgh Pirates slugger led NL in home runs 7 consecutive years, 1946-52.

Billie Jean King, b. 1943: U.S. singles champ 4 times; Wimbledon champ 6 times.

Bob Knight, b. 1940: Indiana U. basketball coach, led team to NCAA championships 1976, 1981, 1987.

Olga Korbut, b. 1955: Soviet gymnast won 3 1972 Olympic gold medals.

Sandy Koufax, b. 1935: Dodgers pitcher won Cy Young award 3 times; lowest ERA in NL, 1962-66; pitched 4 no-hitters, one a perfect game.

Tom Landry, b. 1924: Dallas Cowboys head coach since 1960.

Rod Laver, b. 1938: Australian won tennis "grand slam", 1962, 1969; Wimbledon champ 4 times.

Ivan Lendl, b. 1960: U.S. singles tennis champion 1985-87.

Sugar Ray Leonard, b. 1956: former world welterweight champion.

Carl Lewis, b. 1961: track and field star won 4 gold medals in 1984 Olympics and 2 more in 1988.

Vince Lombardi, (1913-1970): Green Bay Packers coach led, team to 5 NFL championships and 2 Super Bowl victories.

Joe Louis, (1914-1981): 1914: heavyweight champion, 1937-49.

Sid Luckman, b. 1916: Chicago Bears quarterback led team to 4 NFL championships; MVP, 1943.

Connie Mack, (1862-1956): Philadelphia Athletics manager, 1901-50; won 9 pennants, 3 championships.

Bill Madlock, b. 1951: NL batting leader 4 times.

Moses Malone, b. 1955: NBA center was MVP 1979, 1982, 1983.

Mickey Mantle, b. 1931: N.Y. Yankees outfielder; triple crown, 1956; 18 World Series home runs.

Rocky Marciano, (1923-1969): heavyweight champion, 1952-56; retired undefeated.

Dan Marino, b. 1961: Miami Dolphins quarterback passed for NFL record 5,084 yds, 1984.

Roger Maris, (1934-1985): N.Y. Yankees outfielder hit record 61 home runs, 1961; MVP, 1960 and 1961.

Billy Martin, b. 1928: baseball manager led N.Y. Yankees to World Series title, 1977.

Eddie Mathews, b. 1931: Milwaukee-Atlanta 3d baseman hit 512 career home runs.

Christy Mathewson, (1880-1925): N.Y. Giants pitcher won 373 games.

Bob Mathias, b. 1930: decathlon gold medalist, 1948, 1952.

Don Mattingly, b. 1961: N.Y. Yankees 1st baseman won 1984 AL batting title; MVP, 1985.

Willie Mays, b. 1931: N.Y.-S.F. Giants center fielder hit 660 home runs; twice MVP.

Willie McCovey, b. 1938: S.F. Giants slugger hit 521 home runs; led NL 3 times.

John McEnroe, b. 1959: U.S. singles champ, 1979-81, 1984; Wimbledon champ, 1981, 1983-84.

John McGraw, (1873-1934): N.Y. Giants manager led team to 10 pennants, 3 championships.

George Mikan, b. 1924: Minneapolis Lakers center selected in a 1950 AP poll as the greatest basketball player of the first half of the 20th century.

Joe Montana, b. 1956: QB led 49ers to Super Bowl championships, 1982, 1985.

Archie Moore, b. 1913: world light-heavyweight champion, 1952-62.

Joe Morgan, b. 1943: National League MVP, 1975, 1976.

Thurman Munson, (1947-1979): N.Y. Yankees catcher; MVP, 1976.

Dale Murphy, b. 1956: Atlanta Braves outfielder chosen NL MVP 1982, 1983.

Stan Musial, b. 1920: St. Louis Cardinals star won 7 NL batting titles; MVP 3 times; NL record 3,630 hits.

Bronko Nagurski, b. 1908: Chicago Bears fullback and tackle; gained over 4,000 yds. rushing.

Joe Namath, b. 1943: quarterback led N.Y. Jets to 1969 Super Bowl title.

Martina Navratilova, b. 1956: Wimbledon champ 8 times, U.S. champ 1983-1984, 1986-87.

Byron Nelson, b. 1912: won 11 consecutive golf tournaments in 1945; twice Masters and PGA titlist.

John Newcombe, b. 1943: Australian twice U.S. singles champ; Wimbledon titlist 3 times.

Jack Nicklaus, b. 1940: PGA Player-of-the-Year, 1967, 1972; leading money winner 8 times; won Masters 6 times.

Chuck Noll, b. 1931: Pittsburgh Steelers coach led team to 4 Super Bowl titles.

Paavo Nurmi, (1897-1973): Finnish distance runner won 6 Olympic gold medals, 1920, 1924, 1928.

Al Oerter, b. 1936: discus thrower won gold medal at 4 consecutive Olympics, 1956-68.

Mel Ott, (1909-1958): N.Y. Giants outfielder hit 511 home runs; led NL 6 times.

Jesse Owens, (1913-1980): track and field star won 4 1936 Olympic golds.

Satchel Paige, (1906-1982): pitcher starred in Negro leagues, 1924-48; entered major leagues at age 42.

Arnold Palmer, b. 1929: golf's first $1 million winner; won 4 Masters, 2 British Opens.

Jim Palmer, b. 1945: Baltimore Orioles pitcher; Cy Young award 3 times; 20-game winner 7 times.

Floyd Patterson, b. 1935: twice heavyweight champion.

Walter Payton, b. 1954: Chicago Bears running back has most rushing yards in NFL history; leading NFC rusher, 1976-80.

Pele, b. 1940: Brazilian soccer star scored 1 281 goals during 22-year career.

Bob Pettit, b. 1932: first NBA player to score 20 000 points; twice NBA scoring leader.

Richard Petty, b. 1937: NASCAR national champ 6 times; 7-times Daytona 500 winner.

Laffit Pincay Jr., b. 1946: leading money-winning jockey, 1970-74, 1979.

Annemarie Proell Moser, b. 1953: Austrian skier won the World Cup championship 6 times.

Jim Rice, b. 1953: Boston Red Sox outfielder led AL in home runs, 1977-78, 1983; MVP 1978.

Branch Rickey, (1881-1965): executive instrumental in breaking baseball's color barrier, 1947; initiated farm system, 1919.

Brooks Robinson, b. 1937: Baltimore Orioles 3d baseman played in 4 World Series; MVP, 1964.

Frank Robinson, b. 1935: slugger MVP in both NL and AL; triple crown winner, 1966; first black manager in majors.

Jackie Robinson, (1919-1972): broke baseball's color barrier with Brooklyn Dodgers, 1947; MVP, 1949.

Sugar Ray Robinson, b. 1920: middleweight champion 5 times, welterweight champion.

Knute Rockne, (1888-1931): Notre Dame football coach, 1918-31; revolutionized game by stressing forward pass.

Pete Rose, b. 1941: won 3 NL batting titles; hit safely in 44 consecutive games, 1978; set record for most major league hits, 1985.

Wilma Rudolph, b. 1940: sprinter won 3 1960 Olympic gold medals.

Bill Russell, b. 1934: Boston Celtics center led team to 11 NBA titles; MVP 5 times; first black coach of major pro sports team.

Babe Ruth, (1895-1948): N.Y. Yankees outfielder hit 60 home runs, 1927; 714 lifetime; led AL 11 times.

Johnny Rutherford, b. 1938: auto racer won Indy 500 3 times.

Nolan Ryan, b. 1947: pitcher struck out record 383 batters, 1973; pitched record 5 no-hitters.

Gene Sarazen, b. 1902: won PGA championship 3 times, U.S. Open twice; developer of sand wedge.

Gale Sayers, b. 1943: Chicago Bears back twice led NFC in rushing.

Mike Schmidt, b. 1949: Phillies 3d baseman led NL in home runs, 1974-76, 1980-81, 1983-84, 1986; NL MVP, 1980, 1981, 1986.

Tom Seaver, b. 1944: pitcher won NL Cy Young award 3 times, won 311 major league games.

Bill Shoemaker, b. 1931: jockey rode 3 Kentucky Derby and 5 Belmont Stakes winners; leading career money winner.

O.J. Simpson, b. 1947: running back rushed for 2,003 yds., 1973; AFC leading rusher 4 times.

George Sisler, (1893-1973): St. Louis Browns 1st baseman had record 257 hits, 1920; batted .340 lifetime.

Sam Snead, b. 1912: PGA and Masters champ 3 times each.

Warren Spahn, b. 1921: pitcher won 363 NL games; 20-game winner 13 times; Cy Young award, 1957.

Tris Speaker, (1885-1958): AL outfielder batted .344 over 22 seasons; hit record 793 career doubles.

Mark Spitz, b. 1950: swimmer won 7 1972 Olympic gold medals.

Amos Alonzo Stagg, (1862-1965): coached Univ. of Chicago football team for 41 years, including 5 undefeated seasons; introduced huddle, man-in-motion, and end-around play.

Willie Stargell, b. 1941: Pittsburgh Pirate slugger chosen NL, World Series MVP, 1979.

Bart Starr, b. 1934: Green Bay Packers quarterback led team to 5 NFL titles and 2 Super Bowl victories.

Roger Staubach, b. 1942: Dallas Cowboys quarterback; leading NFC passer 5 times.

Casey Stengel, (1890-1975): managed Yankees to 10 pennants, 7 championships, 1949-60.

Jackie Stewart, b. 1939: Scot auto racer retired with 27 Grand Prix victories.

John L. Sullivan, (1858-1918): last bareknuckle heavyweight champion, 1882-1892.

Fran Tarkenton, b. 1940: quarterback holds career passing records for touchdowns, completions, yardage.

Gustave Thoeni, b. 1951: Italian 4-time world alpine ski champ.

Jim Thorpe, (1888-1953): football All-America, 1911, 1912; won pentathlon and decathlon, 1912 Olympics.

Bill Tilden, (1893-1953): U.S. singles champ 7 times; played on 11 Davis Cup teams.

Y.A. Tittle, b. 1926: N.Y. Giants quarterback; MVP, 1961, 1963.

Lee Trevino, b. 1939: won the U.S. and British Open championships twice.

Wyomia Tyus, b. 1945: sprinter won 1964, 1968 Olympic 100-meter dash.

Johnny Unitas, b. 1933: Baltimore Colts quarterback passed for over 40 000 yds.; MVP, 1957, 1967.

Al Unser, b. 1939: Indy 500 winner, 4 times.

Bobby Unser, b. 1934: Indy 500 winner 3 times.

Fernando Valenzuela, b. 1960: L.A. Dodgers pitcher won Cy Young award, 1981.

Norm Van Brocklin, (1926-1983): quarterback passed for game record 554 yds., 1951; MVP, 1960.

Honus Wagner, (1874-1955): Pittsburgh Pirates shortstop won 8 NL batting titles.

Tom Watson, b. 1949: golfer won British Open 5 times.

Johnny Weissmuller, (1903-1984): swimmer won 52 national championships, 5 Olympic gold medals; set 67 world records.

Jerry West, b. 1938: L.A. Lakers guard had career average 27 points per game; first team all-star 10 times.

Kathy Whitworth, b. 1939: women's golf leading money winner 8 times; first woman to earn over $300 000.

Ted Williams, b. 1918: Boston Red Sox outfielder won 6 batting titles; last major leaguer to hit over .400: .406 in 1941: .344 lifetime batting average.

Helen Wills, b. 1906: winner of 7 U.S., 8 British, 4 French women's singles titles.

John Wooden, b. 1910: coached UCLA basketball team to 10 national championships.

Carl Yastrzemski, b. 1939: Boston Red Sox slugger won 3 batting titles, triple crown, 1967.

Cy Young, (1867-1955): pitcher won record 511 major league games.

Babe Didrikson Zaharias, (1914-1956): track star won 2 1932 Olympic gold medals; won numerous golf tournaments.

The Olympics

Olympic Games Records

The modern Olympic Games, first held in Athens, Greece, in 1896, were the result of efforts by Baron Pierre de Coubertin, a French educator, to promote interest in education and culture, and also to foster better international understanding through the universal medium of youth's love of athletics.

His source of inspiration for the Olympic Games was the ancient Greek Olympic Games, most notable of the four Panhellenic celebrations. The games were combined patriotic, religious, and athletic festivals held every four years. The first such recorded festival was that held in 776 B.C., the date from which the Greeks began to keep their calendar by "Olympiads," or four-year spans between the games.

The first Olympiad is said to have consisted merely of a 180 metre foot race near the small city of Olympia, but the games gained in scope and became demonstrations of national pride. Only Greek citizens — amateurs — were permitted to participate. Winners received laurel, wild olive, and palm wreaths and were accorded many special privileges. Under the Roman emperors, the games deteriorated into professional carnivals and circuses. Emperor Theodosius banned them in 394 A.D.

Baron de Coubertin enlisted 9 nations to send athletes to the first modern Olympics in 1896; now more than 100 nations compete. Winter Olympic Games were started in 1924.

Olympic Information

Symbol: Five rings or circles, linked together to represent the sporting friendship of all peoples. The rings also symbolize the 5 continents—Europe, Asia, Africa, Australia, and America. Each ring is a different color—blue, yellow, black, green, and red.

Flag: The symbol of the 5 rings on a plain white background.

Motto: "Citius, Altius, Fortius." Latin meaning "faster, higher, braver," or the modern interpretation "swifter, higher, stronger". The motto was coined by Father Didon, a French educator, in 1895.

Creed: "The most important thing in the Olympic Games is not to win but to take part, just as the most important thing in life is not the triumph but the struggle. The essential thing is not to have conquered but to have fought well."

Oath: An athlete of the host country recites the following at the opening ceremony. "In the name of all competitors I promise that we will take part in these Olympic Games, respecting and abiding by the rules which govern them, in the true spirit of sportsmanship for the glory of sport and the honor of our teams." Both the oath and the creed were composed by Pierre de Coubertin, the founder of the modern Games.

Flame: Symbolizes the continuity between the ancient and modern Games. The modern version of the flame was adopted in 1936. The torch used to kindle the flame is first lit by the sun's rays at Olympia, Greece, and then carried to the site of the Games by relays of runners. Ships and planes are used when necessary.

The Calgary Olympics

On Feb. 13, 1988, while an estimated 2.5 billion people watched on television and 60 000 looked on from McMahon Stadium, Governor General Jeanne Sauve arrived in a horse-drawn landau escorted by scarlet-clad Mounties and members of Lord Strathcona's Horse to begin the ceremonies that officially began the XV Winter Olympic Games.

The first winter Olympics to be hosted by Canada were the largest Games ever, with approximately 1 759 athletes from 57 countries participating. When the Games closed, 15 days later, they were considered to be a resounding success of which Canada could be justifiably proud.

Canadian athletes performed better at these Olympics than any recent winter Games. Canada won 5 medals and the team recorded a dramatic increase from previous Games in the number of "personal bests" and top-8 performances. The Canadian team recorded 19 top-8 finishes, 13 personal best performances, and 3 athletes who tied their personal bests. Canadian Minister for Sport, Otto Jelinek, cited these figures to justify the "BestEver" program that the federal government sponsored for the 5 years leading up to the games. Critics, pointing to the small collection of medals, were quick to challenge the program and lament the waste of $25 million. However, Jelinek pointed out that the money was not intended just for the Olympics but also for encouraging athletic participation at the local level.

The 5 medals were shared between 4 skaters and one skier. Brian Orser won a silver in figure skating, where he had been favoured to win the gold but lost in a dramatic duel with American Brian Boitano. In the women's figure skating, the situation

was reversed. Elizabeth Manley was the dark horse who beat the odds. She upstaged superstars Katarina Witt of East Germany and Debi Thomas of the United States in the high-profile free-skating competition, and after the scores were totalled from all components of the competition, Manley captured the silver, leaving the bronze medal to Thomas and the gold to Witt. The other Canadian skating medal was a bronze that was awarded to the ice-dance duo of Tracy Wilson from Port Moody, B.C. and Rob McCall of Dartmouth, N.S.

Skier Karen Percy became a hero by producing the only Canadian multiple medal performance of the Games. The 21-year-old Banff resident won bronze in the Downhill and in the Super Giant Slalom. She narrowly missed adding a third medal, finishing fourth in the Alpine Combined event, and she was the only non-European to win any of the 30 medals in the alpine skiing events. Percy's immediate future illustrates what is at stake financially for Olympic competitors: her 9 endorsement contracts going into the games will give her $100 000, and her agent predicts she can earn up to $1 million in the next 5 years.

Canada also scored 14 first-place performances in various demonstration sports (sports that are being considered as potential future Olympic events) such as curling, disabled skiing, freestyle skiing, and short-track speed skating.

Recent Olympics have had their share of politics and the Calgary Games were no exception. The Alberta Lubicon Indian band organized a boycott of "The Spirit Sings", a dazzling display of native artifacts at the Glenbow Museum that formed the centrepiece of the colorful cultural arm of the Games. The

Lubicon's boycott was not successful: no country boycotted the games as a result of the protest, though a few major European museums refused to lend artifacts to the Glenbow. This raised publicity for the Lubicon's cause relating to a land claim dispute with the Alberta government but, ironically, it also raised the profile of the Glenbow exhibit and added to its success. Officials said that, in the end, the cultural festivities at the Games probably benefitted from the Lubicon protest.

The financial success of the Calgary Winter Olympics resulted from ingenious marketing plans, smooth organization, and the sale of the U.S. television rights to the ABC TV network for an estimated $309 million (U.S.).

ABC's multimillion dollar contribution brought a significant amount of influence and the network's clout was felt in various ways during the course of the Games. Organizers rescheduled events and even extended the length of the games by 3 days to give ABC an opportunity to cash in on an extra weekend of viewer attention. ABC also insisted on such aesthetic adjustments as spreading white British Columbia sand on the ground

at Olympic Stadium to make the TV pictures more wintery-looking for the opening ceremonies and having the ice repainted at the Olympic Saddledome to improve its appearance on the tube.

As analysts and detractors feared, the weather at these Games did become an issue. Twenty-two events were postponed at Mount Allan and Canada Olympic Park because of 9 days of above-normal temperatures caused by southern Alberta's mischievous chinook winds. Organizers were concerned that the Games might have to be extended beyond the closing ceremonies and both spectators and competitors complained bitterly about the delays. Luckily, the winds did stop and excellent conditions prevailed. However, the long period of high winds raised questions about whether the Canada Olympic Park would be used for future World Cup competitions.

As the Games were closing, organizers estimated that their efforts had realized a $32 million surplus. Most of this sum will be used to fund operations at Canada Olympic Park and Olympic Oval and to assist the development of amateur sports programs.

Winter Olympic Games Champions, 1924-1988

			Competitors		Nations repre-sented	Unofficial winners
		Date of competition	Men	Women		
1924	Chamonix, France	Jan. 25-Feb. 4	281	13	16	Norway
1928	St. Moritz, Switzerland	Feb. 11-19	468	27	25	Norway
1932	Lake Placid, United States	Feb. 4-15	274	32	17	United States
1936	Garmisch-Partenkichen, Germany	Feb. 6-16	675	80	28	Norway
1940	cancelled because of World War II					
1944	cancelled because of World War II					
1948	St. Moritz, Switzerland	Jan. 30-Feb. 8	636	77	28	Sweden
1952	Oslo, Norway	Feb. 14-25	623	109	30	Norway
1956	Cortina d'Ampezzo, Italy	Jan. 26-Feb. 5	686	132	32	U.S.S.R.
1960	Squaw Valley, United States	Feb. 18-28	521	144	30	U.S.S.R.
1964	Innsbruck, Austria	Jan. 29-Feb. 9	986	200	36	U.S.S.R.
1968	Grenoble, France	Feb. 6-18	1 081	212	37	Norway
1972	Sapporo, Japan	Feb. 3-13	1 015	217	35	U.S.S.R.
1976	Innsbruck, Austria	Feb. 4-15	900	228	37	U.S.S.R.
1980	Lake Placid, United States	Feb. 14-23	833	234	37	East Germany
1984	Sarejevo, Yugoslavia	Feb. 7-19	1 180	409	49	U.S.S.R.
1988	Calgary, Canada[1]	Feb. 13-28	1 128	317	57	U.S.S.R.
1992	Albertville, France					

(1) Including demonstration sports a total of 1 759 athletes competed in Calgary.

Final Medal Standings of the 1988 Winter Olympics

Calgary, Alberta, Canada, Feb. 13-28, 1988

	Gold	Silver	Bronze	Total		Gold	Silver	Bronze	Total
Soviet Union	11	9	9	29	Italy	2	1	2	5
East Germany	9	10	6	25	Norway	0	3	2	5
Switzerland	5	5	5	15	Canada	0	2	3	5
Austria	3	5	2	10	Yugoslavia	0	2	1	3
West Germany	2	4	2	8	Czechoslovakia	0	1	2	3
Finland	4	1	2	7	France	1	0	1	2
The Netherlands	3	2	2	7	Japan	0	0	1	1
Sweden	4	0	2	6	Liechtenstein	0	0	1	1
United States	2	1	3	6					

Canada's Winter Olympic Medal Winners

Silver
Figure Skating
Men's—Brian Orser, Orillia, Ont.
Women's—Elizabeth Manley, Ottawa, Ont.

Bronze
Alpine Skiing
Women's Downhill—Karen Percy, Banff, Alta.
Women's Super Giant Slalom—Karen Percy, Banff, Alta.
Figure Skating
Ice Dancing—Tracy Wilson, Port Moody, B.C. & Rob McCall, Dartmouth, N.S.

1988 Winter Olympics: Medal Winners

(Gold, Silver, Bronze)

Alpine Skiing

Men's Downhill—Pirmin Zurbriggen, Switzerland; Peter Mueller, Switzerland; Franck Piccard, France.
Men's Combined—Hubert Strolz, Austria; Bernhard Gstrein, Austria; Paul Accola, Switzerland.
Men's Super G—Franck Piccard, France; Helmut Mayer, Austria; Lars-Boerje Eriksson, Sweden.
Men's Giant Slalom—Alberto Tomba, Italy; Hubert Strolz, Austria; Pirmin Zurbriggen, Switzerland.
Men's Slalom—Alberto Tomba, Italy; Frank Woerndl, W. Germany; Paul Frommelt, Liechtenstein.
Women's Downhill—Marina Kiehl, W. Germany; Brigitte Oertli, Switzerland; Karen Percy, Canada.
Women's Combined—Anita Wachter, Austria; Brigitte Oertli, Switzerland; Maria Walliser, Switzerland.
Women's Super G—Sigrid Wolf, Austria; Michela Figini, Switzerland; Karen Percy, Canada.
Women's Giant Slalom—Vreni Schneider, Switzerland; Christa Kinshofer Guetlein, W. Germany; Maria Walliser, Switzerland.
Women's Slalom—Vreni Schneider, Switzerland; Mateja Svet, Yugoslavia; Christa Kinshofer Guetlein, W. Germany.

Biathlon

10 kilometre—Frank-Peter Roetsch, E. Germany; Valeri Medvedtsev, USSR; Serguei Tchepikov, USSR.
20 kilometre—Frank-Peter Roetsch, E. Germany; Valeri Medvedtsev, USSR; Johann Passler, Italy.
4 × 7.5 kilometre relay—USSR, West Germany, Italy.

Bobsledding and Luge

4-man Bobsled—Switzerland, East Germany, USSR.
2-man Bobsled—USSR, East Germany I, East Germany II.
Men's Singles—Jens Mueller, E. Germany; Georg Hackl, W. Germany; Khartchenko, USSR.
Men's Double Luge—East Germany, East Germany, West Germany.
Women's Singles—Steffi Walter, E. Germany; Ute Oberhoffner, E. Germany; Cerstin Schmidt, E. Germany.

Figure Skating

Men's Singles—Brian Boitano, U.S.; Brian Orser, Canada; Victor Petrenko, USSR.
Women's Singles—Katarina Witt, E. Germany; Elizabeth Manley, Canada; Debi Thomas, U.S.
Pairs—Ekaterina Gordeeva & Serguei Grinkov, USSR; Elena Valova & Oleg Vassiliev, USSR; Jill Watson & Peter Oppegard, U.S.
Dance—Natalia Bestemianova & Andrei Boukine, USSR; Marina Klimova & Serguei Ponomarenko, USSR; Tracy Wilson & Robert McCall, Canada.

Ice Hockey

Ice hockey—USSR, Finland, Sweden.

Nordic Skiing

Men's 15-km Cross-Country—Mikhail Deviatiarov, USSR; Pal Mikkelsplass, Norway; Vladimir Smirnov, USSR.
Men's 30-km Cross-Country—Alexei Prokourorov, USSR; Vladimir Smirnov, USSR; Vegard Ulvang, Norway.
Men's 50-km Cross-Country—Gunde Svan, Sweden; Maurillo De Zolt, Italy; Andy Gruenenfelder, Switzerland.
Men's 4 × 10-km Cross-Country Relay—Sweden, USSR, Czechoslovakia.
Men's Nordic Combined—Hippolyt Kempf, Switzerland; Klaus Sulzenbacher, Austria; Allar Levandi, USSR.
Men's Team Nordic Combined—W. Germany, Switzerland, Austria.
Women's 5-km Cross-Country—Marjo Matikainen, Finland; Tamara Tikhonova, USSR; Vida Ventsene, USSR.
Women's 10-km Cross-Country—Vida Ventsene, USSR; Raisa Smetanina, USSR; Marjo Matikainen, Finland.
Women's 20-km Cross-Country—Tamara Tikhonova, USSR; Anfissa Reztsova, USSR; Raisa Smetanina, USSR.
Women's 4 × 5-km Cross-Country Relay—USSR, Norway, Finland.

Ski Jumping

70 Metre—Matti Nykaenen, Finland; Pavel Ploc, Czechoslovakia; Jiri Malec, Czechoslovakia.
90 Metre—Matti Nykaenen, Finland; Erik Johnsen, Norway; Matjaz Debelak, Yugoslavia.
90 Metre Team Jump—Finland, Yugoslavia, Norway.

Speed Skating

Men's 500 metres—Jens-Uwe May, E. Germany; Jan Ykema, Netherlands; Akira Kuroiwa, Japan.
Men's 1 000 metres—Nikolai Gouliaev, USSR; Jens-Uwe May, E. Germany; Igor Gelezovsky, USSR.
Men's 1 500 metres—Andre Hoffman, E. Germany; Eric Flaim, U.S.; Michael Hadschieff, Austria.
Men's 5 000 metres—Tomas Gustafson, Sweden; Leo Visser, Netherlands; Gerard Kemkers, Netherlands.
Men's 10 000 metres—Tomas Gustafson, Sweden; Michael Hadschieff, Austria; Leo Visser, Netherlands.
Women's 500 metres—Bonnie Blair, U.S.; Christa Rothenburger, E. Germany; Karin Kania, E. Germany.
Women's 1 000 metres—Christa Rothenburger, E. Germany; Karin Kania, E. Germany; Bonnie Blair, U.S.
Women's 1 500 metres—Yvonne van Gennip, Netherlands; Karin Kania, E. Germany; Andrea Ehrig, E. Germany.
Women's 3 000 metres—Yvonne van Gennip, Netherlands; Andrea Ehrig, E. Germany; Gabi Zange, E. Germany.
Women's 5 000 metres—Yvonne van Gennip, Netherlands; Andrea Ehrig, E. Germany; Gabi Zange, E. Germany.

Winter Olympic Games Champions, 1924-1988

Ice Hockey

1920 Canada, U.S., Czechoslovakia
1924 Canada, U.S., Great Britain
1928 Canada, Sweden, Switzerland
1932 Canada, U.S., Germany
1936 Great Britain, Canada, U.S.

1948 Canada, Czechoslovakia, Switzerland
1952 Canada, U.S., Sweden
1956 USSR, U.S., Canada
1960 U.S., Canada, USSR
1964 USSR, Sweden, Czechoslovakia

1968 USSR, Czechoslovakia, Canada
1972 USSR, U.S., Czechoslovakia,
1976 USSR, Czechoslovakia, W. Germany

1980 U.S., USSR, Sweden
1984 USSR, Czechoslovakia, Sweden
1988 USSR, Finland, Sweden

Alpine Skiing

Men's Downhill	Time
1948 Henri Oreiller, France	2:55.0
1952 Zeno Colo, Italy	2:30.8
1956 Anton Sailer, Austria	2:52.2
1960 Jean Vuarnet, France	2:06.0
1964 Egon Zimmermann, Austria	2:18.16
1968 Jean-Claude Killy, France	1:59.85
1972 Bernhard Russi, Switzerland	1:51.43
1976 Franz Klammer, Austria	1:45.73
1980 Leonhard Stock, Austria	1:45.50
1984 Bill Johnson, U.S.	1:45:59
1988 Pirmin Zurbriggen, Switzerland	1:59.63

Women's Downhill	Time
1948 Hedy Schlunegger, Switzerland	2:28.3
1952 Trude Jochum-Beiser, Austria	1:47.1
1956 Madeleine Berthod, Switzerland	1:40.7
1960 Heidi Biebl, Germany	1:37.6
1964 Christl Haas, Austria	1:55.39
1968 Olga Pall, Austria	1:40.87
1972 Marie-Thérès Nadig, Switzerland	1:36.68
1976 Rosi Mittermaier, W. Germany	1:46.16
1980 Annemarie Moser-Pröll, Austria	1:37.52
1984 Michela Figini, Switzerland	1:13.36
1988 Marina Kiehl, W. Germany	1:25.86

Men's Slalom	Time
1948 Edi Reinalter, Switzerland	2:10.3
1952 Othmar Schneider, Austria	2:00.0
1956 Anton Sailer, Austria	3:14.72
1960 Ernst Hinterseer, Austria	2:08.9
1964 Josef Stiegler, Austria	2:11.13
1968 Jean-Claude Killy, France	1:39.73
1972 Francisco Fernandez Ochoa, Spain	1:49.27
1976 Piero Gros, Italy	2:03.29
1980 Ingemar Stenmark, Sweden	1:44.26
1984 Phil Mahre, U.S.	1:39.41
1988 Alberto Tomba, Italy	1:39.47

Women's Slalom	Time
1948 Gretchen Fraser, U.S.	1:57.2
1952 Andrea Mead Lawrence, U.S.	2:10.6
1956 Renée Colliard, Switzerland	1:52.3
1960 Anne Heggtveigt, Canada	1:49.6
1964 Christine Goitschel, France	1:29.86
1968 Marielle Goitschel, France	1:25.86
1972 Barbara Cochran, U.S.	1:31.24
1976 Rosi Mittermaier, W. Germany	1:30.54
1980 Hanni Wenzel, Liechtenstein	1:25.09
1984 Paoletta Magoni, Italy	1:36.47
1988 Vreni Schneider, Switzerland	1:36.69

Men's Giant Slalom	Time
1952 Stein Eriksen, Norway	2:25.0
1956 Anton Sailer, Austria	3:00.12
1960 Roger Staub, Switzerland	1:48.3
1964 Francois Bonlieu, France	1:46.71
1968 Jean-Claude Killy, France	3:29.28
1972 Gustav Thöni, Italy	3:09.62
1976 Heini Hemmi, Switzerland	3:26.97
1980 Ingemar Stenmark, Sweden	2:40.74
1984 Max Julen, Switzerland	2:41.18
1988 Alberto Tomba, Italy	2:06.37

Women's Giant Slalom	Time
1952 Andrea Mead Lawrence, U.S.	2:06.8
1956 Ossi Reichert, Germany	1:56.5
1960 Yvonne Rüegg, Switzerland	1:39.9
1964 Marielle Goitschel, France	1:52.24
1968 Nancy Greene, Canada	1:51.97
1972 Marie-Thérès Nadig, Switzerland	1:29.90
1976 Kathy Kreiner, Canada	1:29.13
1980 Hanni Wenzel, Liechtenstein (2 runs)	2:41.66
1984 Debbie Armstrong, U.S.	2:20.98
1988 Vreni Schneider, Switzerland	2:06.49

Men's Super Giant Slalom	Time
1988 Franck Piccard, France	1:39.66

Women's Super Giant Slalom	Time
1988 Sigrid Wolf, Austria	1:19.03

Men's Combined	Time
1988 Hubert Strolz, Austria	36.55

Women's Combined	Time
1988 Anita Wachter, Austria	29.25

Nordic Skiing

Men's 15 Kilometres	Time
1924 Thorleif Haug, Norway	1:14:31.0
1928 Johan Gröttumsbråten, Norway	1:37:01.0
1932 Sven Utterström, Sweden	1:23:07.0
1936 Erik-August Larsson, Sweden	1:14:38.0
1948 Martin Lundström, Sweden	1:13:50.0
1952 Hallgeir Brenden, Norway	1:01:34.0
1956 Hallgeir Brenden, Norway	49:39.0
1960 Håkon Brusveen, Norway	51:55.5
1964 Eero Mäntyranta, Finland	50:54.1
1968 Harald Grönningen, Norway	47:54.2
1972 Sven-Ake Lundbäck, Sweden	45:28.24
1976 Nikolai Bazhukov, USSR	43:58.47
1980 Thomas Wassberg, Sweden	41:57.63
1984 Gunde Svan, Sweden	41:25.6
1988 Mikhail Deviatiarov, USSR	41:18.9
(Note: approx. 18-km. course 1924-1952)	

Men's 50 Kilometres	Time
1924 Thorleif Haug, Norway	3:44:32.0
1928 Per Erik Hedlund, Sweden	4:52:03.0
1932 Veli Saarinen, Finland	4:28:00.0
1936 Elis Wiklund, Sweden	3:30:11.0
1948 Nils Karlsson, Sweden	3:47:48.0
1952 Veikko Hakulinen, Finland	3:33:33.0
1956 Sixten Jernberg, Sweden	2:50:27.0
1960 Kalevi Hamalainen, Finland	2:59:06.3
1964 Sixten Jernberg, Sweden	2:43:52.6
1968 Ole Ellefsaeter, Norway	2:28:45.8
1972 Päl Tyldum, Norway	2:43:14.75
1976 Ivar Formo, Norway	2:37:30.05
1980 Nikolai Zimyatov, USSR	2:27:24.60
1984 Thomas Wassberg, Sweden	2:15:55.8
1988 Gunde Svan, Sweden	2:04:30.9

4 x 10-km Cross-Country Relay	Time
1936 Finland, Norway, Sweden	2:41:33.0
1948 Sweden, Finland, Norway	2:32:08.0
1952 Finland, Norway, Sweden	2:20:16.0
1956 USSR, Finland, Sweden	2:15:30.0
1960 Finland, Norway, USSR	2:18:45.6
1964 Sweden, Finland, USSR	2:18:34.6
1968 Norway, Sweden, Finland	2:08:33.5
1972 USSR, Norway, Switzerland	2:04:47.94
1976 Finland, Norway, USSR	2:07:59.72
1980 USSR, Norway, Finland	1:57:03.46
1984 Sweden, USSR, Finland	1:55:06.30
1988 Sweden, USSR, Czechoslovakia	1:43:58.60

Men's 30 Kilometres	Time
1956 Veikko Hakulinen, Finland	1:44:06.0
1960 Sixten Jernberg, Sweden	1:51:03.9
1964 Eero Mäntyranta, Finland	1:30:50.7
1968 Franco Nones, Italy	1:35:39.2
1972 Vyacheslav Vedenine, USSR	1:36:31.15
1976 Sergei Saveliev, USSR	1:30:29.38
1980 Nikolai Zimyatov, USSR	1:27:02.80
1984 Nikolai Zimyatov, USSR	1:28:56.3
1988 Alexei Prokourorov, USSR	1:24:26.3

Nordic Combined

	Points
1924 Thorleif Haug, Norway	18.906
1928 Johan Gröttumsbräten, Norway	17.833
1932 Johan Gröttumsbräten, Norway	446.000
1936 Oddbjörn Hagen, Norway	430.300
1948 Heikki Hasu, Finland	448.800
1952 Simon Slåttvik, Norway	451.621
1956 Sverre Stenersen, Norway	455.000
1960 Georg Thoma, Germany	457.952
1964 Tormod Knutsen, Norway	469.280
1968 Franz Keller, W. Germany	449.040
1972 Ulrich Wehling, E. Germany	413.340
1976 Ulrich Wehling, E. Germany	423.390
1980 Ulrich Wehling, E. Germany	432.200
1984 Tom Sandberg, Norway	422.595
1988 Hippolyt Kempf, Switzerland	235.8

90 m Ski Jumping

	Points
1924 Jacob Tullin Thams, Norway	18.960
1928 Alfred Andersen, Norway	19.208
1932 Birger Ruud, Norway	228.1
1936 Birger Ruud, Norway	232.0
1948 Petter Hugsted, Norway	228.1
1952 Arnfinn Bergmann, Norway	226.0
1956 Antti Hyvarinen, Finland	227.0
1960 Helmut Recknagel, E. Germany	227.2
1964 Toralf Engan, Norway	230.7
1968 Vladimir Beloussov, USSR	231.3
1972 Wojciech Fortuna, Poland	219.9
1976 Karl Schnabl, Austria	234.8
1980 Jouko Törmänen, Finland	271.0
1984 Matti Nykaenen, Finland	231.2
1984 Matti Nykaenen, Finland	224.0

70 m Ski Jumping

	Points
1964 Veikko Kankkonen, Finland	229.9
1968 Jiri Raska, Czechoslovakia	216.5
1972 Yukio Kasaya, Japan	244.2
1976 Hans-Georg Aschenbach, E. Germany	252.0
1980 Anton Innauer, Austria	266.3
1984 Jens Weissflog, E. Germany	215.2
1988 Matti Nykaenen, Finland	229.1

Men's Team Ski Jumping (90m)

1988 Finland, Yugoslavia, Norway

Men's Team Nordic Combined

	Time
1988 W. Germany, Switzerland, Austria	1:20:46.0

Women's 5 Kilometres

	Time
1964 Claudia Boyarskikh, USSR	17:50.5
1968 Toini Gustafsson, Sweden	16:45.2
1972 Galina Kulakova, USSR	17:00.50
1976 Helena Takalo, Finland	15:48.69
1980 Raisa Smetanina, USSR	15:06.92
1984 Marja-Liisa Haemaelainen, Finland	17:04.0
1988 Marjo Matikainen, Finland	15:04.0

Women's 10 Kilometres

	Time
1952 Lydia Wideman, Finland	41:40.0
1956 Lyubov Kosyreva, USSR	38:11.0
1960 Maria Gusakova, USSR	39:46.6
1964 Claudia Boyarskikh, USSR	40:24.3
1968 Toini Gustafsson, Sweden	36:46.5
1972 Galina Kulakova, USSR	34:17.82
1976 Raisa Smetanina, USSR	30:13.41
1980 Barbara Petzold, E. Germany	30:31.54
1984 Marja-Liisa Haemaelainen, Finland	31:44.2
1988 Vida Ventsene, USSR	30:08.3

Women's 20 Kilometres

	Time
1984 Marja-Liisa Haemaelainen, Finland	1:01:45.0
1988 Tamara Tikhonova, USSR	55:53.6

Women's 4 x 5-km Cross-Country Relay

	Time
1956 Finland, USSR, Sweden (3 x 5 km)	1:09:01.0
1960 Sweden, USSR, Finland (3 x 5 km)	1:04:21.4
1964 USSR, Sweden, Finland (3 x 5 km)	59:20.2
1968 Norway, Sweden, USSR (3 x 5 km)	57:30.0
1972 USSR, Finland, Norway (3 x 5 km)	48:46.15
1976 USSR, Finland, E. Germany	1:07:49.75
1980 E. Germany, USSR, Norway	1:02:11.10
1984 Norway, Czechoslovakia, Finland	1:06:49.70
1988 USSR, Norway, Finland	59:51.1

Speed Skating

Men's 500 metres

	Time
1924 Charles Jewtraw, U.S.	44.0
1928 Thunberg, Finland & Evensen, Norway (tie)	43.4
1932 John A. Shea, U.S.	43.4
1936 Ivar Ballangrud, Norway	43.4
1948 Finn Helgesen, Norway	43.1
1952 Kenneth Henry, U.S.	43.2
1956 Yevgeny Grishin, USSR	40.2
1960 Yevgeny Grishin, USSR	40.2
1964 Terry McDermott, U.S.	40.1
1968 Erhard Keller, W. Germany	40.3
1972 Erhard Keller, W. Germany	39.44
1976 Yevgeny Kulikov, USSR	39.17
1980 Eric Heiden, U.S.	38.03
1984 Sergei Fokichev, USSR	38.19
1988 Jens-Uwe Mey, E. Germany	36.45

Men's 1 000 metres

	Time
1976 Peter Mueller, U.S.	1:19.32
1980 Eric Heiden, U.S.	1:15.18
1984 Gaetan Boucher, Canada	1:15.80
1988 Nikolai Gouliaev, USSR	1:13.03

Men's 1 500 metres

	Time
1924 Clas Thunberg, Finland	2:20.8
1928 Clas Thunberg, Finland	2:21.1
1932 John A. Shea, U.S.	2:57.5
1936 Charles Mathisen, Norway	2:19.2
1948 Sverre Farstad, Norway	2:17.6
1952 Hjalmar Andersen, Norway	2:20.4
1956 Grishin, & Mikhailov, both USSR (tie)	2:08.6
1960 Aas, Norway & Grishin, USSR (tie)	2:10.4
1964 Ants Antson, USSR	2:10.3
1968 Cornelis Verkerk, Netherlands	2:03.4
1972 Ard Schenk, Netherlands	2:02.96
1976 Jan Egil Storholt, Norway	1:59.38
1980 Eric Heiden, U.S.	1:55.44
1984 Gaetan Boucher, Canada	1:58.36
1988 Andre Hoffman, E. Germany	1:52.06

Men's 5 000 metres

	Time
1924 Clas Thunberg, Finland	8:39.0
1928 Ivar Ballangrud, Norway	8:50.5
1932 Irving Jaffee, U.S.	9:40.8
1936 Ivar Ballangrud, Norway	8:19.6
1948 Reidar Liaklev, Norway	8:29.4
1952 Hjalmar Andersen, Norway	8:10.6
1956 Boris Shilkov, USSR	7:48.7
1960 Viktor Kosichkin, USSR	7:51.3
1964 Knut Johannesen, Norway	7:38.4
1968 Fred Anton Maier, Norway	7:22.4
1972 Ard Schenk, Netherlands	7:23.61
1976 Sten Stensen, Norway	7:24.48
1980 Eric Heiden, U.S.	7:02.29
1984 Sven Tomas Gustafson, Sweden	7:12:28
1988 Tomas Gustafson, Sweden	6:44.63

Men's 10 000 metres

	Time
1924 Julius Skutnabb, Finland	18:04.8
1928 Event not held, thawing of ice	
1932 Irving Jaffee, U.S.	19:13.6
1936 Ivar Ballangrud, Norway	17:24.3
1948 Ake Seyffarth, Sweden	17:26.3
1952 Hjalmar Andersen, Norway	16:45.8
1956 Sigvard Ericsson, Sweden	16:35.9
1960 Knut Johannesen, Norway	15:46.6
1964 Jonny Nilsson, Sweden	15:50.1
1968 Jonny Höglin, Sweden	15:23.6
1972 Ard Schenk, Netherlands	15:01.35
1976 Piet Kleine, Netherlands	14:50.59
1980 Eric Heiden, U.S.	14:28.13
1984 Igor Malkov, USSR	14:39.90
1988 Tomas Gustafson, Sweden	13:48.20

Women's 500 metres

	Time
1960 Helga Haase, E. Germany	45.9
1964 Lydia Skoblikova, USSR	45.0
1968 Lyudmila Titova, USSR	46.1

1972	Anne Henning, U.S.	43.33
1976	Sheila Young, U.S.	42.76
1980	Karin Enke, E. Germany	41.78
1984	Christa Rothenburger, E. Germany	41.02
1988	Bonnie Blair, U.S.	39.10

Women's 1 000 metres		**Time**
1960	Klara Guseva, USSR	1:34.1
1964	Lydia Skoblikova, USSR	1:33.2
1968	Carolina Geijssen, Netherlands	1:32.6
1972	Monika Pflug, W. Germany	1:31.40
1976	Tatiana Averina, USSR	1:28.43
1980	Natalya Petruseva, USSR	1:24.10
1984	Karin Enke, E. Germany	1:21.61
1988	Christa Rothenburger, E. Germany	1:17.65

Women's 1 500 metres		**Time**
1960	Lydia Skoblikova, USSR	2:52.2
1964	Lydia Skoblikova, USSR	2:22.6

1968	Kaija Mustonen, Finland	2:22.4
1972	Dianne Holum, U.S.	2:20.85
1976	Galina Stepanskaya, USSR.	2:16.58
1980	Anne Borckink, Netherlands	2:10.95
1984	Karin Enke, E. Germany	2:03.42
1988	Yvonne von Gennip, Netherlands	2:00.68

Women's 3 000 metres		**Time**
1960	Lydia Skoblikova, USSR	5:14.3
1964	Lydia Skoblikova, USSR	5:14.9
1968	Johanna Schut, Netherlands	4:56.2
1972	Christina Baas-Kaiser, Netherlands	4:52.14
1976	Tatiana Averina, USSR	4:45.19
1980	Bjorg Eva Jensen, Norway	4:32.13
1984	Andrea Schoene, E. Germany	4:24.79
1988	Yvonne von Gennip, Netherlands	4:11.94

Women's 5 000 metres		**Time**
1988	Yvonne von Gennip, Netherlands	7:14.13

Figure Skating

Men's Singles

1908	Ulrich Salchow, Sweden
1920	Gillis Grafström, Sweden
1924	Gillis Grafström, Sweden
1928	Gillis Grafström, Sweden
1932	Karl Schäfer, Austria
1936	Karl Schäfer, Austria
1948	Richard Button, U.S.
1952	Richard Button, U.S.
1956	Hayes Alan Jenkins, U.S.
1960	David W. Jenkins, U.S.
1964	Manfred Schnelldorfer, W. Germany
1968	Wolfgang Schwarz, Austria
1972	Ondrej Nepela, Czechoslovakia
1976	John Curry, Great Britain
1980	Robin Cousins, Great Britain
1984	Scott Hamilton, U.S.
1988	Brian Boitano, U.S.

Women's Singles

1908	Madge Syers, Great Britain
1920	Magda Julin, Sweden
1924	Herma Planck-Szabó, Austria
1928	Sonja Henie, Norway
1932	Sonja Henie, Norway
1936	Sonja Henie, Norway
1948	Barbara Ann Scott, Canada
1952	Jeanette Altwegg, Great Britain
1956	Tenley Albright, U.S.
1960	Carol Heiss, U.S.
1964	Sjoukje Dijkstra, Netherlands
1968	Peggy Fleming, U.S.

1972	Beatrix Schuba, Austria
1976	Dorothy Hamill, U.S.
1980	Anett Pötzsch, E. Germany
1984	Katarina Witt, E. Germany
1988	Katarina Witt, E. Germany

Pairs

1908	Anna Hübler & Heinrich Burger, Germany
1920	Ludovika & Walter Jakobsson, Finland
1924	Helene Engelman & Alfred Berger, Austria
1928	Andrée Joly & Pierre Brunet, France
1932	Andrée Brunet (Joly) & Pierre Brunet, France
1936	Maxi Herber & Ernst Baier, Germany
1948	Micheline Lannoy & Pierre Baugniet, Belgium
1952	Ria and Paul Falk, Germany
1956	Elisabeth Schwartz & Kurt Oppelt, Austria
1960	Barbara Wagner & Robert Paul, Canada
1964	Lyudmilla Belousova & Oleg Protopopov, USSR
1968	Lyudmilla Belousova & Oleg Protopopov, USSR
1972	Irina Rodnina & Alexei Ulanov, USSR
1976	Irina Rodnina & Aleksandr Zaitsev, USSR
1980	Irina Rodnina & Aleksandr Zaitsev, USSR
1984	Elena Valova & Oleg Vassiliev, USSR
1988	Ekaterina Gordeeva & Serguei Grinkov, USSR

Ice Dancing

1976	Lyudmilla Pakhomova & Aleksandr Gorshkov, USSR
1980	Natalya Linichuk & Gennady Karponosov, USSR
1984	Jayne Torvill & Christopher Dean, Great Britain
1988	Natalia Bestemianova & Andrei Boukine, USSR

Bobsledding and Luge

4-Man Bobsled

(Driver in parentheses)		**Time**
1924	Switzerland (Eduard Scherrer)	5:45.54
1928	United States (William Fiske) (5-man)	3:20.50
1932	United States (William Fiske)	7:53.68
1936	Switzerland (Pierre Musy).	5:19.85
1948	United States (Frances Tyler)	5:20.10
1952	Germany (Andreas Ostler)	5:07.84
1956	Switzerland (Franz Kapus)	5:10.44
1964	Canada (Victor Emery)	4:14.46
1968	Italy (Eugenio Monti) (2 races)	2:17.39
1972	Switzerland (Jean Wicki)	4:43.07
1976	E. Germany (Meinhard Nehmer)	3:40.43
1980	E. Germany (Meinhard Nehmer)	3:59.92
1984	E. Germany (Wolfgang Hoppe)	3:20.22
1988	Switzerland (Ekkehard Fasser)	3:47.51

2-Man Bobsled

		Time
1932	United States (Hubert Stevens)	8:14.74
1936	United States (Ivan Brown)	5:29.29

1948	Switzerland (Felix Endrich)	5:29.20
1952	Germany (Andreas Ostler)	5:24.54
1956	Italy (Lamberto Dalla Costa)	5:30.14
1964	Great Britain (Anthony Nash)	4:21.90
1968	Italy (Eugenio Monti)	4:41.54
1972	W. Germany (Wolfgang Zimmerer)	4:57.07
1976	E. Germany (Meinhard Nehmer)	3:44.42
1980	Switzerland (Erich Schärer)	4:09.36
1984	E.Germany (Wolfgang Hoppe)	3:25.56
1988	USSR (Ianis Kipours)	3:53.48

Men's Singles Luge		**Time**
1964	Thomas Köhler, Germany.	3:26.77
1968	Manfred Schmid, Austria	2:52.48
1972	Wolfgang Scheidel, E. Germany	3:27.58
1976	Dettlef Günther, E. Germany	3:27.688
1980	Bernhard Glass, E. Germany	2:54.796
1984	Paul Hildgartner, Italy	3:04.258
1988	Jens Mueller, E. Germany.	3.05:548

Men's Doubles Luge	Time
1964 Austria	1:41.62
1968 E. Germany	1:35.85
1972 Italy, E. Germany (tie)	1:28.35
1976 E. Germany	1:25.604
1980 E. Germany	1:19.331
1984 W. Germany	1:23.620
1988 E. Germany	1:31.940

Women's Singles Luge	Time
1964 Ortrun Enderlein, E. Germany	3:24.67
1968 Erica Lechner, Italy	2:28.66
1972 Anna-Maria Müller, E. Germany	2:59.18
1976 Margit Schumann, E. Germany	2:50.621
1980 Vera Zozulya, USSR	2:36.537
1984 Steffi Martin, E. Germany	2:46.570
1988 Steffi Walter, E. Germany	3:03.973

Biathlon

10 Kilometres	Time
1980 Frank Ullrich, E. Germany	32:10.69
1984 Eirik Kvalfoss, Norway	30:53.80
1988 Frank-Peter Roetsch, E. Germany	25:08.10

	Time
1980 Anatoly Aljabiev, USSR	1:08:16.31
1984 Peter Angerer, W. Germany	1:11:52.7
1988 Frank-Peter Roetsch, E. Germany	56:33.33

4 x 7.5-Kilometre Relay	Time
1968 USSR, Norway, Sweden	2:13:02.40
1972 USSR, Finland, E. Germany	1:51:44.92
1976 USSR, Finland, E. Germany	1:57:55.64
1980 USSR, E. Germany, W. Germany	1:34:03.27
1984 USSR, Norway, W. Germany	1:38:51.70
1988 USSR, W. Germany, Italy	1:22:30.00

20 Kilometres	Time
1960 Klas Lestander, Sweden	1:33:21.6
1964 Vladimir Melanin, USSR	1:20:26.8
1968 Magnar Solberg, Norway	1:13:45.9
1972 Magnar Solberg, Norway	1:15:55.50
1976 Nikolai Kruglov, USSR	1:14:12.26

Summer Olympics

			Competitors		Nations represented	Unofficial winners
		Date of competition	Men	Women		
1896	Athens, Greece	Apr. 6-15	311	0	13	United States
1900	Paris, France	May 20-Oct. 28	1319	11	22	United States
1904	St. Louis, United States	July 1-Nov. 23	681	6	12	United States
1906[1]	Athens, Greece	Apr. 22-May 2	877	7	20	United States
1908	London, England	Apr. 27-Oct. 31	1999	36	23	United States
1912	Stockholm, Sweden	May 5-July 22	2490	57	28	United States
1916	cancelled because of World War I					
1920	Antwerp, Belgium	Apr. 20-Sept. 12	2543	64	29	United States
1924	Paris, France	May 4-July 27	2956	136	44	United States
1928	Amsterdam, Netherlands	May 17-Aug. 12	2724	290	46	United States
1932	Los Angeles, United States	July 30-Aug. 14	1281	127	37	United States
1936	Berlin, Germany	Aug. 1-16	3738	328	49	Germany
1940	cancelled because of World War II					
1944	cancelled because of World War II					
1948	London, England	July 29-Aug. 14	3714	385	59	United States
1952	Helsinki, Finland	July 19-Aug. 3	4407	518	69	United States
1956	Melbourne, Australia[2]	Nov. 22-Dec. 8	2958	384	67	U.S.S.R.
1960	Rome, Italy	Aug. 25-Sept. 11	4738	610	83	U.S.S.R.
1964	Tokyo, Japan	Oct. 10-24	4457	683	93	United States
1968	Mexico City, Mexico	Oct. 12-27	4750	781	112	United States
1972	Munich, West Germany	Aug. 26-Sept. 10	5848	1299	122	U.S.S.R.
1976	Montreal, Canada	July 17-Aug. 1	4834	1251	92[3]	U.S.S.R.
1980	Moscow, U.S.S.R.	July 19-Aug. 3	4265	1088	81	U.S.S.R.
1984	Los Angeles, United States	July 28-Aug. 12	n.a.	n.a.	140	United States
1988	Seoul, South Korea	Sept. 17-Oct. 2	n.a.	n.a.	n.a.	U.S.S.R.
1992	Barcelona, Spain					

(1) 1906 Games were not recognized by the International Olympic Committee. (2) The equestrian events were held in Stockholm, Sweden, June 10-17, 1956. (3) Most sources list this figure as 88. Cameroon, Egypt, Morocco and Tunisia all boycotted the 1976 Olympics; however, their athletes had already competed before the boycott was officially announced.
n.a. not available.

Final Medal Standings of the 1988 Summer Olympics

Seoul, S. Korea, Sept. 17-24, 1988

Final Medal Standings

	Gold	Silver	Bronze	Total		Gold	Silver	Bronze	Total
USSR	55	31	46	132	Switzerland	0	2	2	4
East Germany	37	35	30	102	Morocco	1	0	2	3
United States	36	31	27	94	Turkey	1	1	0	2
West Germany	11	14	15	40	Jarnaica	0	2	0	2
Bulgaria	10	12	13	35	Argentina	0	1	1	2
South Korea	12	10	11	33	Belgium	0	0	2	2
China	5	11	12	28	Mexico	0	0	2	2
Rumania	7	11	6	24	Austria	1	0	0	1
Great Britain	5	10	9	24	Portugal	1	0	0	1
Hungary	11	6	6	23	Suriname	1	0	0	1
France	6	4	6	16	Chile	0	1	0	1
Poland	2	5	9	16	Costa Rica	0	1	0	1
Italy	6	4	4	14	Indonesia	0	1	0	1
Japan	4	3	7	14	Iran	0	1	0	1
Australia	3	6	5	14	Netherland Antilles	0	1	0	1
New Zealand	3	2	8	13	Peru	0	1	0	1
Yugoslavia	3	4	5	12	Senegal	0	1	0	1
Sweden	0	4	7	11	Virgin Islands	0	1	0	1
Canada	3	2	5	10	Columbia	0	0	1	1
Kenya	5	2	2	9	Djibouti	0	0	1	1
Netherlands	2	2	5	9	Greece	0	0	1	1
Czechoslovakia	3	3	2	8	Mongolia	0	0	1	1
Brazil	1	2	3	6	Pakistan	0	0	1	1
Norway	2	3	0	5	Philippines	0	0	1	1
Denmark	2	1	1	4	Thailand	0	0	1	1
Finland	1	1	2	4					
Spain	1	1	2	4					

Canada's Summer Olympic Medal Winners

Gold

Boxing

Super heavyweight—Lennox, Lewis, Kitchener, Ont.

Synchronized Swimming

Solo—Carolyn Waldo, Calgary, Alta.
Duet—Carolyn Waldo and Michelle Cameron, Calgary, Alta.

Silver

Boxing

Middleweight (75 kg)—Egerton Marcus, Toronto, Ont.

Swimming

Men's 4 × 100-Metre Medley Relay—Mark Tewksbury, Calgary, Alta.; Victor Davis, Pointe-Claire, Que.; Thomas Ponting, Calgary, Alta.; Sandy Goss, Toronto, Ont.

Bronze

Boxing

Light middleweight (71 kg)—Ray Downey, Halifax, N.S.

Equestrian

Team dressage—Cindy Ishoy, King City, Ont.; Ashley Nicoll, Toronto, Ont.; Eva-Maria Pracht, Cedar Valley, Ont.; Gina Smith, Clavat, Sask.

Swimming

Women's 4 × 100-Metre Medley Relay—Lori Mellen, Whitby, Ont.; Allison Higson, Brampton, Ont.; Jane Kerr, Mississauga, Ont.; Andrea Nugent, Nanton, Alta.

Track & Field

Decathlon—Dave Steen, Toronto, Ont.

Yachting

Flying Dutchman—Frank McLaughlin & John Millen, Toronto, Ont.

Summer Olympic Games Champions, 1896-1988

(*Indicates Olympic Records)

Men's Track and Field Events

100-Metre Run

1896	Thomas Burke, United States	12.0	1948	Harrison Dillard, United States	10.3
1900	Francis W. Jarvis, United States	11.0	1952	Lindy Remigino, United States	10.4
1904	Archie Hahn, United States	11.0	1956	Bobby Morrow, United States	10.5
1908	Reginald Walker, South Africa	10.8	1960	Armin Hary, Germany	10.2
1912	Ralph Craig, United States	10.8	1964	Bob Hayes, United States	10.0
1920	Charles Paddock, United States	10.8	1968	Jim Hines, United States	9.95
1924	Harold Abrahams, Great Britain	10.6	1972	Valeri Borzov, USSR	10.14
1928	Percy Williams, Canada	10.8	1976	Hasely Crawford, Trinidad	10.06
1932	Eddie Tolan, United States	10.3	1980	Allan Wells, Great Britain	10.25
1936	Jesse Owens, United States	10.3	1984	Carl Lewis, United States	9.99
			1988	Carl Lewis, United States	9.92*

200-Metre Run

1900	Walter Tewksbury, United States	22.2
1904	Archie Hahn, United States	21.6
1908	Robert Kerr, Canada	22.6
1912	Ralph Craig, United States	21.7
1920	Allen Woodring, United States	22.0
1924	Jackson Scholz, United States	21.6
1928	Percy Williams, Canada	21.8
1932	Eddie Tolan, United States	21.2
1936	Jesse Owens, United States	20.7
1948	Mel Patton, United States	21.1
1952	Andrew Stanfield, United States	20.7
1956	Bobby Morrow, United States	20.6
1960	Livio Berruti, Italy	20.5
1964	Henry Carr, United States	20.3
1968	Tommie Smith, United States	19.83
1972	Valeri Borzov, USSR	20.00
1976	Donald Quarrie, Jamaica	20.23
1980	Pietro Mennea, Italy	20.19
1984	Carl Lewis, United States	19.80
1988	Joe Deloach, United States	19.75*

400-Metre Run

1896	Thomas Burke, United States	54.2
1900	Maxey Long, United States	49.4
1904	Harry Hillman, United States	49.2
1908	Wyndham Halswelle, Great Britain, walkover.	50.0
1912	Charles Reidpath, United States	48.2
1920	Bevil Rudd, South Africa	49.6
1924	Eric Liddell, Great Britain	47.6
1928	Ray Barbuti, United States	47.8
1932	William Carr, United States	46.2
1936	Archie Williams, United States	46.5
1948	Arthur Wint, Jamaica, B.W.I.	46.2
1952	George Rhoden, Jamaica, B.W.I.	45.9
1956	Charles Jenkins, United States	46.7
1960	Otis Davis, United States	44.9
1964	Michael Larrabee, United States	45.1
1968	Lee Evans, United States	43.8*
1972	Vincent Matthews, United States	44.66
1976	Alberto Juantorena, Cuba	44.26
1980	Viktor Markin, USSR	44.60
1984	Alonzo Babers, United States	44.27
1988	Steven Lewis, United States	13.87

800-Metre Run

1896	Edwin Flack, Australia	2:11.0
1900	Alfred Tysoe, Great Britain	2:01.2
1904	James Lightbody, United States	1:56.0
1908	Mel Sheppard, United States	1:52.8
1912	James Meredith, United States	1:51.9
1920	Albert Hill, Great Britain	1:53.4
1924	Douglas Lowe, Great Britain	1:52.4
1928	Douglas Lowe, Great Britain	1:51.8
1932	Thomas Hampson, Great Britain	1:49.7
1936	John Woodruff, United States	1:52.9
1948	Mal Whitfield, United States	1:49.2
1952	Mal Whitfield, United States	1:49.2
1956	Thomas Courtney, United States	1:47.7
1960	Peter Snell, New Zealand	1:46.3
1964	Peter Snell, New Zealand	1:45.1
1968	Ralph Doubell, Australia	1:44.3
1972	Dave Wottle, United States	1:45.9
1976	Alberto Juantorena, Cuba	1:43.50
1980	Steve Ovett, Great Britain	1:45.40
1984	Joaquim Cruz, Brazil	1:43.00*
1988	Paul Ereng, Kenya	1:43.45

1 500-Metre Run

1896	Edwin Flack, Australia	4:33.2
1900	Charles Bennett, Great Britain	4:06.2
1904	James Lightbody, United States	4:05.4
1908	Mel Sheppard, United States	4:03.4
1912	Arnold Jackson, Great Britain	3:56.8
1920	Albert Hill, Great Britain	4:01.8
1924	Paavo Nurmi, Finland	3:53.6
1928	Harry Larva, Finland	3:53.2
1932	Luigi Beccali, Italy	3:51.2
1936	Jack Lovelock, New Zealand	3:47.8
1948	Henri Eriksson, Sweden	3:49.8
1952	Josef Barthel, Luxembourg	3:45.1
1956	Ron Delany, Ireland	3:41.2
1960	Herb Elliott, Australia	3:35.6
1964	Peter Snell, New Zealand	3:38.1
1968	Kipchoge Keino, Kenya	3:34.9
1972	Pekka Vasala, Finland	3:36.3

1976	John Walker, New Zealand	3:39.17
1980	Sebastian Coe, Great Britain	3:38.4
1984	Sebastian Coe, Great Britain	3:32.53*
1988	Peter Rono, Kenya	3:35.96

3 000-Metre Steeplechase

1920	Percy Hodge, Great Britain	10:00.4
1924	Ville Ritola, Finland	9:33.6
1928	Toivo Loukola, Finland	9:21.8
1932	Volmari Iso-Hollo, Finland	10:33.4
	(About 3 460 m extra lap by error)	
1936	Volmari Iso-Hollo, Finland	9:03.8
1948	Thore Sjöstrand, Sweden	9:04.6
1952	Horace Ashenfelter, United States.	8:45.4
1956	Chris Brasher, Great Britain	8:41.2
1960	Zdzislaw Krzyszkowiak, Poland	8:34.2
1964	Gaston Roelants, Belgium	8:30.8
1968	Amos Biwott, Kenya	8:51
1972	Kipchoge Keino, Kenya	8:23.6
1976	Anders Garderud, Sweden	8:08.2
1980	Bronislaw Malinowski, Poland	8:09.7
1984	Julius Korir, Kenya	8:11.8
1988	Julius Kariuki, Kenya	8:05.51*

5 000-Metre Run

1912	Johannes Kolehmainen, Finland	14:36.6
1920	Joseph Guillemot, France	14:55.6
1924	Paavo Nurmi, Finland	14:31.2
1928	Ville Ritola, Finland	14:38
1932	Lauri Lehtinen, Finland	14:30
1936	Gunnar Hockert, Finland	14:22.2
1948	Gaston Reiff, Belgium	14:17.6
1952	Emil Zátopek, Czechoslovakia	14:06.6
1956	Vladimir Kuts, USSR	13:39.6
1960	Murray Halberg, New Zealand	13:43.4
1964	Bob Schul, United States	13:48.8
1968	Mohamed Gammoudi, Tunisia	14:05.0
1972	Lasse Viren, Finland	13:26.4
1976	Lasse Viren, Finland	13:24.76
1980	Miruts Yifter, Ethiopia	13:21.0
1984	Said Aouita, Morocco	13:05.59*
1988	John Ngugi, Kenya	13:11.70

10 000-Metre Run

1912	Johannes Kolehmainen, Finland	31:20.8
1920	Paavo Nurmi, Finland	31:45.8
1924	Ville Ritola, Finland	30:23.2
1928	Paavo Nurmi, Finland	30:18.8
1932	Janusz Kusocinski, Poland	30:11.4
1936	Ilmari Salminen, Finland	30:15.4
1948	Emil Zátopek, Czechoslovakia	29:59.6
1952	Emil Zátopek, Czechoslovakia	29:17.0
1956	Vladimir Kuts, USSR	28:45.6
1960	Ptyor Bolotnikov, USSR	28:32.2
1964	Billy Mills, United States	28:24.4
1968	Naftali Temu, Kenya	29:27.4
1972	Lasse Viren, Finland	27:38.4
1976	Lasse Viren, Finland	27:40.38
1980	Miruts Yifter, Ethiopia	27:42.7
1984	Alberto Cova, Italy	27:47.54
1988	Ibrahim Boutaidd, Morocco	27:21.46*

Marathon

1896	Spiridon Louis, Greece	2:58:50
1900	Michel Théato, France	2:59:45
1904	Thomas Hicks, United States	3:28:53
1908	John J. Hayes, United States	2:55:18.4
1912	Kenneth McArthur, South Africa	2:36:54.8
1920	Johannes Kolehmainen, Finland	2:32:35.8
1924	Albin Stenroos, Finland	2:41:22.6
1928	Boughèra El Ouafi, France	2:32:57
1932	Juan Zabala, Argentina	2:31:36
1936	Kijung Son, Japan/Korea	2:29:19.2
1948	Delfo Cabrera, Argentina	2:34:51.6
1952	Emil Zátopek, Czechoslovakia	2:23:03.2
1956	Alain Mimoun, France	2:25:00
1960	Abebe Bikila, Ethiopia	2:15:16.2
1964	Abebe Bikila, Ethiopia	2:12:11.2
1968	Mamo Wolde, Ethiopia	2:20:26.4
1972	Frank Shorter, United States	2:12:19.8
1976	Waldemar Cierpinski, E. Germany	2:09:55
1980	Waldemar Cierpinski, E. Germany	2:11:03
1984	Carlos Lopes, Portugal	2:09:21*
1988	Gelindo Bordin, Italy	2:10.32

10 000-Metre Cross-Country

1920	Paavo Nurmi, Finland	27:15*
1924	Paavo Nurmi, Finland	32:54.8

20-Kilometre Walk

1956	Leonid Spirin, USSR	1:31:27.4
1960	Vladimir Golubnichi, USSR	1:34:07.2
1964	Kenneth Mathews, Great Britain	1:29:34.0
1968	Vladimir Golubnichi, USSR	1:33:58.4
1972	Peter Frenkel, E. Germany	1:26:42.4
1976	Daniel Bautista, Mexico	1:24:40.6
1980	Maurizio Damilano, Italy	1:23:35.5
1984	Ernesto Canto, Mexico	1:23:13.0
1988	Jozef Pribilenec, Czechoslovakia	1:19.57.0*

50-Kilometre Walk

1932	Thomas Green, Great Britain	4:50:10
1936	Harold Whitlock, Great Britain	4:30:41.4
1948	John Ljunggren, Sweden	4:41:52
1952	Giuseppe Dordoni, Italy	4:28:07.8
1956	Norman Read, New Zealand	4:30:42.8
1960	Donald Thompson, Great Britain	4:25:30
1964	Abdon Pamich, Italy	4:11:12.4
1968	Christoph Hohne, E. Germany	4:20:13.6
1972	Bernd Kannenberg, W. Germany	3:56:11.6
1980	Hartwig Gauder, E. Germany	3:49:24.0
1984	Raul Gonzalez, Mexico	3:47:26.05
1988	Vyacheslav Ivanenko, USSR	3:38:29.0*

110-Metre Hurdles

1896	Thomas Curtis, United States	17.6
1900	Alvin Kraenzlein, United States	15.4
1904	Frederick Schule, United States	16.0
1908	Forrest Smithson, United States	15.0
1912	Frederick Kelly, United States	15.1
1920	Earl Thomson, Canada	14.8
1924	Daniel Kinsey, United States	15.0
1928	Sydney Atkinson, South Africa	14.8
1932	George Saling, United States	14.6
1936	Forrest Towns, United States	14.2
1948	William Porter, United States	13.9
1952	Harrison Dillard, United States	13.7
1956	Lee Calhoun, United States	13.5
1960	Lee Calhoun, United States	13.8
1964	Hayes Jones, United States	13.6
1968	Willie Davenport, United States	13.3
1972	Rod Milburn, United States	13.24
1976	Guy Drut, France	13.30
1980	Thomas Munkelt, E. Germany	13. 39
1984	Roger Kingdom, United States	13.20
1988	Roger Kingdom, United States	12.98*

400-Metre Hurdles

1900	J.W.B. Tewksbury, United States	57.6
1904	Harry Hillman, United States	53.0
1908	Charles Bacon, United States	55.0
1920	Frank Loomis, United States	54.0
1924	F. Morgan Taylor, United States	52.6
1928	Lord David Burghley, Great Britain	53.4
1932	Robert Tisdall, Ireland	51.7
1936	Glenn Hardin, United States	52.4
1948	Roy Cochran, United States	51.1
1952	Charles Moore, United States	50.8
1956	Glenn Davis, United States	50.1
1960	Glenn Davis, United States	49.3
1964	Rex Cawley, United States	49.6
1968	Dave Hemery, Great Britain	48.12
1972	John Akii-Bua, Uganda	47.82
1976	Edwin Moses, United States	47.64
1980	Volker Beck, E. Germany	48.70
1984	Edwin Moses, United States	47.75
1988	Andre Phillips, United States	47.19*

High Jump

1896	Ellery Clark, United States	1.81 m
1900	Irving Baxter, United States	1.90 m
1904	Samuel Jones, United States	1.80 m
1908	Harry Porter, United States	1.90 m
1912	Alma Richards, United States	1.93 m
1920	Richmond Landon, United States	1.93 m
1924	Harold Osborn, United States	1.98 m
1928	Robert W. King, United States	1.94 m
1932	Duncan McNaughton, Canada	1.97 m
1936	Cornelius Johnson, United States	2.03 m
1948	John L. Winter, Australia	1.98 m
1952	Walter Davis, United States	2.04 m
1956	Charles Dumas, United States	2.12 m
1960	Robert Shavlakadze, USSR	2.16 m
1964	Valery Brumel, USSR	2.18 m
1968	Dick Fosbury, United States	2.24 m
1972	Yuri Tarmak, USSR	2.23 m
1976	Jacek Wszola, Poland	2.25 m
1980	Gerd Wessig, E. Germany	2.36 m
1984	Dietmar Mogenburg, W. Germany	2.34 m
1988	Guennadi Avdeenko, USSR	2.38 m*

Long Jump

1896	Ellery Clark, United States	6.35 m
1900	Alvin Kraenzlein, United States	7.18 m
1904	Myer Prinstein, United States	7.34 m
1908	Frank Irons, United States	7.48 m
1912	Albert Gutterson, United States	7.60 m
1920	William Pettersson, Sweden	7.15 m
1924	William De Hart Hubbard, United States	7.44 m
1928	Edward B. Hamm, United States	7.73 m
1932	Edward Gordon, United States	7.64 m
1936	Jesse Owens, United States	8.06 m
1948	William Steele, United States	7.82 m
1952	Jerome Biffle, United States	7.57 m
1956	Gregory Bell, United States	7.83 m
1960	Ralph Boston, United States	8.12 m
1964	Lynn Davies, Great Britain	8.07 m
1968	Bob Beamon, United States	8.90 m*
1972	Randy Williams, United States	8.24 m
1976	Arnie Robinson, United States	8.35 m
1980	Lutz Dombrowski, E. Germany	8.54 m
1984	Carl Lewis, United States	8.54 m
1988	Carl Lewis, United States	8.73 m

4 x 100-Metre Relay

1912	Great Britain	42.4
1920	United States	42.2
1924	United States	41.0
1928	United States	41.0
1932	United States	40.0
1936	United States	39.8
1948	United States	40.6
1952	United States	40.1
1956	United States	39.5
1960	Germany (U.S. disqualified)	39.5
1964	United States	39.0
1968	United States	38.2
1972	United States	38.19
1976	United States	38.33
1980	USSR	38.26
1984	United States	37.83*
1988	USSR	38.19

4 x 400-Metre Relay

1908	United States	3:29.4
1912	United States	3:16.6
1920	Great Britain	3:22.2
1924	United States	3:16.0
1928	United States	3:14.2
1932	United States	3:08.2
1936	Great Britain	3:09.0
1948	United States	3:10.4
1952	Jamaica, B.W.I.	3:03.9
1956	United States	3:04.8
1960	United States	3:02.2
1964	United States	3:00.7
1968	United States	2:56.1*
1972	Kenya	2:59.8
1976	United States	2:58.65
1980	USSR	3:01.1
1984	United States	2:57.91
1988	United States	2:56.16

Pole Vault

1896	William Hoyt, United States	3.30 m
1900	Irving Baxter, United States	3.30 m
1904	Charles Dvorak, United States	3.50 m
1908	Alfred Gilbert, United States Edward Cook Jr., United States	3.71 m
1912	Harry Babcock, United States	3.95 m
1920	Frank Foss, United States	4.09 m
1924	Lee Barnes, United States	3.95 m
1928	Sabin W. Carr, United States	4.20 m
1932	William Miller, United States	4.31 m
1936	Earle Meadows, United States	4.35 m

1948	Guinn Smith, United States	4.30 m
1952	Robert Richards, United States	4.55 m
1956	Robert Richards, United States	4.56 m
1960	Don Bragg, United States	4.70 m
1964	Fred Hansen, United States	5.10 m
1968	Bob Seagren, United States	5.40 m
1972	Wolfgang Nordwig, E. Germany	5.50 m
1976	Tadeusz Slusarski, Poland	5.50 m
1980	Wladyslaw Kozakiewicz, Poland	5.78 m
1984	Pierre Quinon, France	5.74 m
1988	Sergei Bubka, USSR	5.90 m*

Hammer Throw

1900	John Flanagan, United States	49.73 m
1904	John Flanagan, United States	51.23 m
1908	John Flanagan, United States	51.92 m
1912	Matt McGrath, United States	54.74 m
1920	Pat Ryan, United States	52.87 m
1924	Fred Tootell, United States	53.29 m
1928	Patrick O'Callaghan, Ireland	51.39 m
1932	Patrick O'Callaghan, Ireland	53.92 m
1936	Karl Hein, Germany	56.49 m
1948	Imre Németh, Hungary	56.07 m
1952	József Csérmák, Hungary	60.34 m
1956	Harold Connolly, United States	63.19 m
1960	Vasily Rudenkov, USSR	67.10 m
1964	Romuald Klim, USSR	69.74 m
1968	Gyula Zsivotsky, Hungary	73.36 m
1972	Anatoli Bondarchuk, USSR	75.50 m
1976	Yuri Sedykh, USSR	77.52 m
1980	Yuri Sedykh, USSR	81.80 m
1984	Juha Tiainen, Finland	78.08 m
1988	Sergei Litvinov, USSR	84.80 m*

Discus Throw

1896	Robert Garrett, United States	29.15 m
1900	Rudolf Bauer, Hungary	36.04 m
1904	Martin Sheridan, United States	39.28 m
1908	Martin Sheridan, United States	40.89 m
1912	Armas Taipale, Finland	45.11 m
1920	Elmer Niklander, Finland	44.68 m
1924	Clarence Houser, United States	46.15 m
1928	Clarence Houser, United States	47.32 m
1932	John Anderson, United States	49.49 m
1936	Ken Carpenter, United States	50.48 m
1948	Adolfo Consolini, Italy	52.78 m
1952	Sim Iness, United States	55.03 m
1956	Al Oerter, United States	56.36 m
1960	Al Oerter, United States	59.18 m
1964	Al Oerter, United States	61.00 m
1968	Al Oerter, United States	64.78 m
1972	Ludvik Danek, Czechoslovakia	64.40 m
1976	Mac Wilkins, United States	67.50 m
1980	Viktor Rashchupkin, USSR	66.64 m
1984	Rolf Dannenberg, W. Germany	66.60 m
1988	Jurgen Schult	68.80 m*

Triple Jump

1896	James Connolly, United States	13.71 m
1900	Myer Prinstein, United States	14.47 m
1904	Myer Prinstein, United States	14.35 m
1908	Timothy Ahearne, Great Britain	14.92 m
1912	Gustaf Lindblom, Sweden	14.76 m
1920	Vilho Tuulos, Finland	14.50 m
1924	Anthony Winter, Australia	15.52 m
1928	Mikio Oda, Japan	15.21 m
1932	Chuhei Nambu, Japan	15.72 m
1936	Naoto Tajima, Japan	16.00 m
1948	Arne Åhman, Sweden	15.40 m
1952	Adhemar Ferriera de Silva, Brazil	16.22 m
1956	Adhemar Ferriera de Silva, Brazil	16.35 m
1960	Józef Schmidt, Poland	16.81 m
1964	Józef Schmidt, Poland	16.85 m
1968	Viktor Saneyev, USSR	17.39 m
1972	Viktor Saneyev, USSR	17.35 m

1976	Viktor Saneyev, USSR	17.29 m
1980	Jaak Uudmae, USSR	17.35 m
1984	Al Joyner, United States	17.26 m
1988	Hristo Markov, Bulgaria	17.61 m*

16 lb Shot Put

1896	Robert Garrett, United States	11.22 m
1900	Richard Sheldon, United States	14.10 m
1904	Ralph Rose, United States	14.80 m
1908	Ralph Rose, United States	14.21 m
1912	Pat McDonald, United States	15.34 m
1920	Ville Pörhölä, Finland	14.81 m
1924	Clarence Houser, United States	14.99 m
1928	John Kuck, United States	15.87 m
1932	Leo Sexton, United States	16.00 m
1936	Hans Woellke, Germany	16.20 m
1948	Wilbur Thompson, United States	17.12 m
1952	Parry O'Brien, United States	17.41 m
1956	Parry O'Brien, United States	18.57 m
1960	William Nieder, United States	19.68 m
1964	Dallas Long, United States	20.33 m
1968	Randy Matson, United States	20.54 m
1972	Wladyslaw Komar, Poland	21.18 m
1976	Udo Beyer, E. Germany	21.05 m
1980	Vladimir Kiselyov, USSR	21.35 m
1984	Alessandro Andrei, Italy	21.26 m
1988	Ulf Timmermann, E. Germany	22.47 m*

Javelin

1908	Erik Lemming, Sweden	54.82 m
1912	Erik Lemming, Sweden	60.64 m
1920	Jonni Myyra, Finland	65.78 m
1924	Jonni Myyra, Finland	62.96 m
1928	Eric Lundkvist, Sweden	66.60 m
1932	Matti Järvinen, Finland	72.71 m
1936	Gerhard Stöck, Germany	71.84 m
1948	Kai Rautavaara, Finland	69.77 m
1952	Cy Young, United States	73.78 m
1956	Egil Danielson, Norway	85.71 m
1960	Viktor Tsibulenko, USSR	84.64 m
1964	Pauli Nevala, Finland	82.66 m
1968	Janis Lusis, USSR	90.10 m
1972	Klaus Wolfermann, W. Germany	90.48 m
1976	Miklos Németh, Hungary	94.58 m*
1980	Dainis Kula, USSR	91.20 m
1984	Arto Haerkoenen, Finland	86.76 m
1988	Tapio Korjus, Finland	84.28 m

Decathlon

1912	Hugo Wieslander, Sweden	7 724 pts.[1]
1920	Helge Lövland, Norway	6 803 pts.
1924	Harold Osborn, United States	7 711 pts.
1928	Paavo Yrjölä, Finland	8 053 pts.
1932	James Bausch, United States	8 462 pts.
1936	Glenn Morris, United States	7 900 pts.
1948	Robert Mathias, United States	7 139 pts.
1952	Robert Mathias, United States	7 887 pts.
1956	Milton Campbell, United States	7 937 pts.
1960	Rafer Johnson, United States	8 392 pts.
1964	Willi Holdorf, Germany	7 887 pts.
1968	Bill Toomey, United States	8 193 pts.
1972	Nikolai Avilov, USSR	8 454 pts.
1976	Bruce Jenner, United States	8 617 pts.
1980	Daley Thompson, Great Britain	8 495 pts.
1984	Daley Thompson, Great Britain	8 798 pts.*[2]
1988	Christian Schenk, E. Germany	8 488 pts.

Former point systems used prior to 1964.

(1) Jim Thorpe of the U.S. won the 1912 Decathlon with 8 413 pts. but was disqualified and had to return his medals because he had played professional baseball prior to the Olympic games. The medals were restored posthumously in 1982. (2) Scoring change effective Apr., 1985.

Women's Track and Field Events

100-Metre Run

1928	Elizabeth Robinson, United States	12.2
1932	Stella Walsh (Stanislawa Walasiewicz), Poland	11.9
1936	Helen Stephens, United States	11.5
1948	Francina Blankers-Koen, Netherlands	11.9

1952	Marjorie Jackson, Australia	11.5
1956	Betty Cuthbert, Australia	11.5
1960	Wilma Rudolph, United States	11.0
1964	Wyomia Tyus, United States	11.4
1968	Wyomia Tyus, United States	11.0

1972	Renate Stecher, E. Germany	11.07
1976	Annegret Richter, W. Germany	11.08
1980	Lyudmila Kondratyeva, USSR	11.06
1984	Evelyn Ashford, United States	10.97
1988	Florence Griffith-Joyner, United States	10.54*

200-Metre Run

1948	Francina Blankers-Koen, Netherlands	24.4
1952	Marjorie Jackson, Australia	23.7
1956	Betty Cuthbert, Australia	23.4
1960	Wilma Rudolph, United States	24.0
1964	Edith McGuire, United States	23.0
1968	Irena Szewińska, Poland	22.5
1972	Renate Stecher, E. Germany	22.40
1976	Bärbel Eckert, E. Germany	22.37
1980	Bärbel Wockel (Eckert), E. Germany	22.03
1984	Valerie Brisco-Hooks, United States	21.81
1988	Florence Griffith-Joyner, United States	21.34*

400-Metre Run

1964	Betty Cuthbert, Australia	52.0
1968	Colette Besson, France	52.0
1972	Monika Zehrt, E. Germany	51.08
1976	Irena Szewińska, Poland	49.29
1980	Marita Koch, E. Germany	48.88
1984	Valerie Brisco-Hooks, United States	48.83
1988	Olga Bryzgina, USSR	48.65*

800-Metre Run

1928	Lina Radke, Germany	2:16.8
1960	Lyudmila Shevtsova, USSR	2:04.3
1964	Ann Packer, Great Britain	2:01.1
1968	Madeline Manning, United States	2:00.9
1972	Hildegard Falck, W. Germany	1:58.55
1976	Tatyana Kazankina, USSR	1:54.94
1980	Nadezhda Olizarenko, USSR	1:53.42*
1984	Doina Melinte, Romania	1:57.6
1988	Sigrun Wodars, E. Germany	1:56.1

1 500-Metre Run

1972	Lyudmila Bragina, USSR	4:01.4
1976	Tatyana Kazankina, USSR	4:05.48
1980	Tatyana Kazankina, USSR	3:56.6
1984	Gabriella Dorio, Italy	4:03.26
1988	Paula Ivan, Romania	3:53.96*

3 000-Metre Run

1984	Maricica Puica, Romania	8:35.96
1988	Tatiana Samolenko, USSR	8:26.53*

10 000-Metre Run

1988	Olga Bondarenko, USSR	31:44.69*

Marathon

1984	Joan Benoit, United States	2:24:52*
1988	Rosa Mota, Portugal	2:25.40

80-Metre Hurdles

1932	Mildred Didriksen, United States	11.7
1936	Trebisonda Valla, Italy	11.7
1948	Francina Blankers-Koen, Netherlands	11.2
1952	Shirley Strickland, Australia	10.9
1956	Shirley Strickland, Australia	10.7
1960	Irina Press, USSR	10.8
1964	Karin Balzer, E. Germany	10.5
1968	Maureen Caird, Australia	10.3*

100-Metre Hurdles

1972	Annelie Ehrhardt, E. Germany	12.59
1976	Johanna Schaller, E. Germany	12.77
1980	Vera Komisova, USSR	12.56
1984	Benita Brown-Fitzgerald, United States	12.84
1988	Jordanka Donkova, Bulgaria	12.38*

400-Metre Hurdles

1984	Nawal el Moutawakil, Morocco	54.61
1988	Debra Flintoff-King, Australia	53.17*

4 x 100-Metre Relay

1928	Canada	48.4
1932	United States	46.9
1936	United States	46.9
1948	Netherlands	47.5
1952	United States	45.9
1956	Australia	44.5
1960	United States	44.5
1964	Poland	43.6
1968	United States	42.8
1972	West Germany	42.81
1976	East Germany	42.55
1980	East Germany	41.60*
1984	United States	41.65
1988	United States	41.98

4 x 400-Metre Relay

1972	East Germany	3:23.0
1976	East Germany	3:19.23
1980	USSR	3:20.2
1984	United States	3:18.29
1988	USSR	3:15.18*

High Jump

1928	Ethel Catherwood, Canada	1.59 m
1932	Jean Shiley, United States	1.65 m
1936	Ibolya Csák, Hungary	1.60 m
1948	Alice Coachman, United States	1.68 m
1952	Esther Brand, South Africa	1.67 m
1956	Mildred L. McDaniel, United States	1.76 m
1960	Iolanda Balas, Romania	1.86 m
1964	Iolanda Balas, Romania	1.90 m
1968	Miloslava Resková, Czechoslovakia	1.82 m
1972	Ulrike Meyfarth, W. Germany	1.92 m
1976	Rosemarie Ackermann, E. Germany	1.93 m
1980	Sara Simeoni, Italy	1.97 m
1984	Ulrike Meyfarth, W. Germany	2.01 m
1988	Louise Ritter, United States	2.03 m*

Discus Throw

1928	Halina Konopacka, Poland	39.62 m
1932	Lillian Copeland, United States	40.58 m
1936	Gisela Mauermayer, Germany	47.63 m
1948	Micheline Ostermeyer, France	41.92 m
1952	Nina Romaschkova, USSR	51.42 m
1956	Olga Fikotová, Czechoslovakia	53.69 m
1960	Nina Ponomaryeva, USSR	55.10 m
1964	Tamara Press, USSR	57.27 m
1968	Lia Manoliu, Romania	58.28 m
1972	Faina Melnik, USSR	66.62 m
1976	Evelin Schlaak, E. Germany	69.00 m
1980	Evelin Jahl (Schlaake), E. Germany	69.96 m
1984	Ria Stalman, Netherlands	65.35 m
1988	Martina Hellman, E. Germany	72.30 m*

Javelin Throw

1932	Mildred Didriksen, United States	43.68 m
1936	Tilly Fleischer, Germany	45.18 m
1948	Herma Bauma, Austria	45.57 m
1952	Dana Zátopková, Czechoslovakia	50.47 m
1956	Inese Jaunzeme, USSR	53.86 m
1960	Elvira Ozolina, USSR	55.98 m
1964	Mihaela Penes, Romania	60.54 m
1968	Angéla Németh, Hungary	60.36 m
1972	Ruth Fuchs, E. Germany	63.88 m
1976	Ruth Fuchs, E. Germany	65.94 m
1980	Maria Colon Rueñes, Cuba	68.40 m
1984	Tessa Sanderson, Great Britain	69.54 m
1988	Petra Felke, E. Germany	74.68 m*

Shot Put (8 lbs, 13 oz.)

1948	Micheline Ostermeyer, France	13.75 m
1952	Galina Zybina, USSR	15.28 m
1956	Tamara Tishkevich, USSR	16.59 m
1960	Tamara Press, USSR	17.32 m
1964	Tamara Press, USSR	18.14 m
1968	Margitta Gummel, E. Germany	19.61 m
1972	Nadezhda Chizhova, USSR	21.03 m
1976	Ivanka Hristova, Bulgaria	21.16 m
1980	Ilona Slupianek, E. Germany	22.41 m*
1984	Claudia Losch, W. Germany	20.47 m
1988	Natalya Lisovskaya, USSR	22.24 m

Long Jump

1948	Olga Gyarmati, Hungary	5.69 m
1952	Yvette Williams, New Zealand	6.24 m
1956	Elzbieta Krzeskinska, Poland	6.35 m
1960	Vyera Krepkina, USSR	6.37 m
1964	Mary Rand (Bignal), Great Britain	6.76 m
1968	Viorica Viscopoleanu, Romania	6.82 m
1972	Heidemarie Rosendahl, W. Germany	6.78 m
1976	Angela Voigt, E. Germany	6.72 m
1980	Tatiana Kolpakova, USSR	7.06 m
1984	Anisoara Stanciu, Romania	6.96 m
1988	Jackie Joyner-Kersee, United States	7.40 m*

Pentathlon

1964	Irina Press, USSR	5 246 pts
1968	Ingrid Becker, W. Germany	5 098 pts
1972	Mary Peters, England	4 801 pts
1976	Sigrun Siegl, E. Germany	4 745 pts
1980	Nadezhda Tkachenko, USSR	5 083 pts.
	Former point system, 1964–1968	

Heptathlon

1984	Glynis Nunn, Australia	6 390 pts
1988	Jackie Joyner-Kersee, United States	7 215 pts.*

Men's Swimming

50-Metre Freestyle

1988	Matt Biondi, United States	22.14*

100-Metre Freestyle

1896	Alfréd Hajós, Hungary	1:22.2
1904	Zoltán Halmay, Hungary (100 yards)	1:02.8
1908	Charles Daniels, U.S.	1:05.6
1912	Duke Paoa Kahanamoku, U.S.	1:03.4
1920	Duke Paoa Kahanamoku, U.S.	1:01.4
1924	John Weissmuller, U.S.	59.0
1928	John Weissmuller, U.S.	58.6
1932	Yasuji Miyazaki, Japan	58.2
1936	Ferenc Csik, Hungary	57.6
1948	Wally Ris, U.S.	57.3
1952	Clark Scholes, U.S.	57.4
1956	Jon Henricks, Australia	55.4
1960	John Devitt, Australia	55.2
1964	Don Schollander, U.S.	53.4
1968	Mike Wenden, Australia	52.2
1972	Mark Spitz, U.S.	51.22
1976	Jim Montgomery, U.S.	49.99
1980	Jörg Woithe, E. Germany	50.40
1984	Rowdy Gaines, U.S.	49.80
1988	Matt Biondi, United States	48.63*

200-Metre Freestyle

1968	Mike Wenden, Australia	1:55.2
1972	Mark Spitz, U.S.	1:52.78
1976	Bruce Furniss, U.S.	1:50.29
1980	Sergei Kopliakov, USSR	1:49.81
1984	Michael Gross, W. Germany	1:47.44
1988	Duncan Armstrong, Australia	1:47.25*

400-Metre Freestyle

1904	Charles Daniels, U.S. (440 yards)	6:16.2
1908	Henry Taylor, Great Britain	5:36.8
1912	George Hodgson, Canada	5:24.4
1920	Norman Ross, U.S.	5:26.8
1924	John Weissmuller, U.S.	5:04.2
1928	Albert Zorilla, Argentina	5:01.6
1932	Clarence Crabbe, U.S.	4:48.4
1936	Jack Medica, U.S.	4:44.5
1948	William Smith, U.S.	4:41.0
1952	Jean Boiteux, France	4:30.7
1956	Murray Rose, Australia	4:27.3
1960	Murray Rose, Australia	4:18.3
1964	Don Schollander, U.S.	4:12.2
1968	Mike Burton, U.S.	4:09.0
1972	Brad Cooper, Australia	4:00.27
1976	Brian Goodell, U.S.	3:51.93
1980	Vladimir Salnikov, USSR	3:51.31
1984	George DiCarlo, U.S.	3:51.23
1988	Uwe Dassler, E. Germany	3:46.95*

1 500-Metre Freestyle

1908	Henry Taylor, Great Britain	22:48.4
1912	George Hodgson, Canada	22:00.0
1920	Norman Ross, U.S.	22:23.2
1924	Andrew Charlton, Australia	20:06.6
1928	Arne Borg, Sweden	19:51.8
1932	Kusuo Kitamura, Japan	19:12.4
1936	Noboru Terada, Japan	19:13.7
1948	James McLane, U.S.	19:18.5
1952	Ford Konno, U.S.	18:30.3
1956	Murray Rose, Australia	17:58.9
1960	Jon Konrads, Australia	17:19.6
1964	Robert Windle, Australia	17:01.7
1968	Mike Burton, U.S.	16:38.9
1972	Mike Burton, U.S.	15:52.58
1976	Brian Goodell, U.S.	15:02.40
1980	Vladimir Salnikov, USSR	14:58.27*
1984	Michael O'Brien, U.S.	15:05.20
1988	Vladimir Salnikov, USSR	15:00.40

4 x 100-Metre Medley Relay

1960	United States	4:05.4
1964	United States	3:58.4
1968	United States	3:54.9
1972	United States	3:48.16
1976	United States	3:42.22
1980	Australia	3:45.70
1984	United States	3:39.30
1988	United States	3:36.93*

4 x 100-Metre Freestyle Relay

1964	United States	3:33.2
1968	United States	3:31.7
1972	United States	3:26.42
1976	not held	
1980	not held	
1984	United States	3:19.03
1988	United States	3:16.53*

4 x 200-Metre Freestyle Relay

1908	Great Britain	10:55.6
1912	Australia/New Zealand	10:11.6
1920	United States	10:04.4
1924	United States	9:53.4
1928	United States	9:36.2
1932	Japan	8:58.4
1936	Japan	8:51.5
1948	United States	8:46.0
1952	United States	8:31.1
1956	Australia	8:23.6
1960	United States	8:10.2
1964	United States	7:52.1
1968	United States	7:52.33
1972	United States	7:35.78
1976	United States	7:23.22
1980	USSR	7:23.50
1984	United States	7:15.69
1988	United States	7:12.51*

100-Metre Backstroke

1904	Walter Brack, Germany (100 yds.)	1:16.8
1908	Arno Bieberstein, Germany	1:24.6
1912	Harry Hebner, U.S.	1:21.2
1920	Warren Paoa Kealoha, U.S.	1:15.2
1924	Warren Paoa Kealoha, U.S.	1:13.2
1928	George Kojac, U.S.	1:08.2
1932	Masaji Kiyokawa, Japan	1:08.6
1936	Adolf Kiefer, U.S.	1:05.9
1948	Allen Stack, U.S.	1:06.4
1952	Yoshi Oyakawa, U.S.	1:05.4
1956	David Thiele, Australia	1:02.2
1960	David Thiele, Australia	1:01.9
1964	not held	
1968	Roland Matthes, E. Germany	58.7
1972	Roland Matthes, E. Germany	56.58
1976	John Naber, U.S.	55.49
1980	Bengt Baron, Sweden	56.33
1984	Rick Carey, U.S.	55.79
1988	Daichi Suzuki, Japan	55.05*

200-Metre Backstroke

1964	Jed Graef, U.S.	2:10.3
1968	Roland Matthes, E. Germany	2:09.6
1972	Roland Matthes, E. Germany	2:02.82
1976	John Naber, U.S.	1:59.19*
1980	Sándor Wladár, Hungary	2:01.93
1984	Rick Carey, U.S.	2:00.23
1988	Igor Polianski, USSR	1:59.37

100-Metre Breaststroke

1968	Don McKenzie, U.S.	1:07.7
1972	Nobutaka Taguchi, Japan	1:04.94
1976	John Hencken, U.S.	1:03.11
1980	Duncan Goodhew, Great Britain	1:03.44
1984	Steve Lundquist, U.S.	1:01.65*
1988	Adrian Moorhouse, Great Britain	1:02.04

200-Metre Breaststroke

1908	Frederick Holman, Great Britain	3:09.2
1912	Walter Bathe, Germany	3:01.8
1920	Haken Malmroth, Sweden	3:04.4
1924	Robert Skelton, U.S.	2:56.6
1928	Yoshiyuki Tsuruta, Japan	2:48.8
1932	Yoshiyuki Tsuruta, Japan	2:45.4
1936	Tetsuo Hamuro, Japan	2:41.5
1948	Joseph Verdeur, U.S.	2:39.3
1952	John Davies, Australia	2:34.4
1956	Masaru Furukawa, Japan	2:34.7
1960	William Mulliken, U.S.	2:37.4
1964	Ian O'Brien, Australia	2:27.8
1968	Felipe Munoz, Mexico	2:28.7
1972	John Hencken, U.S.	2:21.55
1976	David Wilkie, Great Britain	2:15.11
1980	Robertas Zhulpa, USSR	2:15.85
1984	Victor Davis, Canada	2:13.34*
1988	Jozef Szabo, Hungary	2:13.52

Springboard Diving

		Points
1908	Albert Zürner, Germany	85.5
1912	Paul Gunther, Germany	79.23
1920	Louis Kuehn, U.S.	675.4
1924	Albert White, U.S.	696.40
1928	Pete Desjardins, U.S.	185.04
1932	Michael Galitzen, U.S.	161.38
1936	Richard Degener, U.S.	163.57
1948	Bruce Harlan, U.S.	163.57
1952	David Browning, U.S.	205.29
1956	Robert Clotworthy, U.S.	159.56
1960	Gary Tobian, U.S.	170.00
1964	Kenneth Sitzberger, U.S.	159.90
1968	Bernie Wrightson, U.S.	170.15
1972	Vladimir Vasin, USSR	594.09
1976	Phil Boggs, U.S.	619.05
1980	Aleksandr Portnov, USSR	905.02
1984	Greg Louganis, U.S.	754.41
1988	Greg Louganis, U.S.	730.80

100-Metre Butterfly

1968	Doug Russell, U.S.	55.9
1972	Mark Spitz, U.S.	54.27
1976	Matt Vogel, U.S.	54.35
1980	Pär Arvidsson, Sweden	54.92
1984	Michael Gross, W. Germany	53.08
1988	Anthony Nesty, Suriname	53.00*

200-Metre Butterfly

1956	William Yorzyk, U.S.	2:19.3
1960	Michael Troy, U.S.	2:12.8
1964	Kevin J. Berry, Australia	2:06.6
1968	Carl Robie, U.S.	2:08.7
1972	Mark Spitz, U.S.	2:00.70
1976	Mike Bruner, U.S.	1:59.23
1980	Sergei Fesenko, USSR	1:59.76
1984	Jon Sieben, Australia	1:57.04
1988	Michael Gross, W. Germany	1:56.94*

200-Metre Individual Medley

1968	Charles Hickcox, U.S.	2:12.0
1972	Gunnar Larsson, Sweden	2:07.17
1976	not held	
1980	not held	
1984	Alex Baumann, Canada	2:01.42
1988	Tamas Darnyi, Hungary	2:00.17*

400-Metre Individual Medley

1964	Dick Roth, U.S.	4:45.4
1968	Charles Hickcox, U.S.	4:48.4
1972	Gunnar Larsson, Sweden	4:31.98
1976	Rod Strachan, U.S.	4:23.68
1980	Aleksandr Sidorenko, USSR	4:22.89
1984	Alex Baumann, Canada	4:17.41
1988	Tamas Darnyi, Hungary	4:14.75*

Platform Diving

		Points
1904	George Sheldon, U.S.	12.66
1908	Hjalmar Johansson, Sweden	83.75
1912	Erik Adlerz, Sweden	73.94
1920	Clarence Pinkston, U.S.	100.67
1924	Albert White, U.S.	97.46
1928	Pete Desjardins, U.S.	98.74
1932	Harold Smith, U.S.	124.80
1936	Marshall Wayne, U.S.	113.58
1948	Sammy Lee, U.S.	130.05
1952	Sammy Lee, U.S.	156.28
1956	Joaquin Capilla, Mexico	152.44
1960	Robert Webster, U.S.	165.56
1964	Robert Webster, U.S.	148.58
1968	Klaus Dibiasi, Italy	164.18
1972	Klaus Dibiasi, Italy	504.12
1976	Klaus Dibiasi, Italy	600.51
1980	Falk Hoffmann, E. Germany	835.65
1984	Greg Louganis, U.S.	710.91
1988	Greg Louganis, U.S.	638.61

Women's Swimming

50-Metre Freestyle

1988	Kristin Otto, E. Germany	25.49*

100-Metre Freestyle

1912	Fanny Durack, Australia	1:22.2
1920	Ethelda Bleibtrey, U.S.	1:13.6
1924	Ethel Lackie, U.S.	1:12.4
1928	Albina Osipowich, U.S.	1:11.0
1932	Helene Madison, U.S.	1:06.8
1936	Hendrika Mastenbroek, Netherlands	1:05.9
1948	Greta Andersen, Denmark	1:06.3
1952	Katalin Szöke, Hungary	1:06.3
1956	Dawn Fraser, Australia	1:02.0
1960	Dawn Fraser, Australia	1:01.2
1964	Dawn Fraser, Australia	59.5
1968	Jan Henne, U.S.	1:00.0
1972	Sandra Neilson, U.S.	58.59
1976	Kornelia Ender, E. Germany	55.65
1980	Barbara Krause, E. Germany	54.79*
1984	(tie) Carrie Steinseifer, U.S.	55.92
	Nancy Hogshead, U.S.	55.92
1988	Kristin Otto, E. Germany	54.93

200-Metre Freestyle

1968	Debbie Meyer, U.S.	2:10.5
1972	Shane Gould, Australia	2:03.56
1976	Kornelia Ender, E. Germany	1:59.26
1980	Barbara Krause, E. Germany	1:58.33
1984	Mary Wayte, U.S.	1:59.23
1988	Heike Friedrich, E. Germany	1:57.65*

400-Metre Freestyle

1924	Martha Norelius, U.S.	6:02.2
1928	Martha Norelius, U.S.	5:42.8
1932	Helene Madison, U.S.	5:28.5
1936	Hendrika Mastenbroek, Netherlands	5:26.4
1948	Ann Curtis, U.S.	5:17.8
1952	Valéria Gyenge, Hungary	5:12.1
1956	Lorraine Crapp, Australia	4:54.6
1960	Susan Chris von Saltza, U.S.	4:50.6
1964	Virginia Duenkel, U.S.	4:43.3
1968	Debbie Meyer, U.S.	4:31.8
1972	Shane Gould, Australia	4:19.04
1976	Petra Thümer, E. Germany	4:09.89
1980	Ines Diers, E. Germany	4:08.76
1984	Tiffany Cohen, U.S.	4:07.10
1988	Janet Evans, U.S.	4:03.85*

800-Metre Freestyle

1968	Debbie Meyer, U.S.	9:24.0
1972	Keena Rothhammer, U.S.	8:53.68
1976	Petra Thümer, E. Germany	8:37.14
1980	Michelle Ford, Australia	8:28.90
1984	Tiffany Cohen, U.S.	8:24.95
1988	Janet Evans, U.S.	8:20.20*

100-Metre Backstroke

1924	Sybil Bauer, U.S.	1:23.3
1928	Maria Braun, Netherlands	1:22.0
1932	Eleanor Holm, U.S.	1:19.4
1936	Dina Senff, Netherlands	1:18.9
1948	Karen Margrete Harup, Denmark	1:14.4
1952	Joan Harrison, South Africa	1:14.3
1956	Judy Grinham, Great Britain	1:12.9
1960	Lynn Burke, U.S.	1:09.3
1964	Cathy Ferguson, U.S.	1:07.7
1968	Kaye Hall, U.S.	1:06.2
1972	Melissa Belote, U.S.	1:05.78
1976	Ulrike Richter, E. Germany	1:01.83
1980	Rica Reinisch, E. Germany	1:00.86*
1984	Theresa Andrews, U.S.	1:02.55
1988	Kristin Otto, E. Germany	1:00.89

200-Metre Backstroke

1968	Lillian (Pokey) Watson, U.S.	2:24.8
1972	Melissa Belote, U.S.	2:19.19
1976	Ulrike Richter, E. Germany	2:13.43
1980	Rica Reinisch, E. Germany	2:11.77
1984	Jolanda De Rover, Netherlands	2:13.38
1988	Krisztina Egerszegi, Hungary	2:09.29*

100-Metre Breaststroke

1968	Djurdjica Bjedov, Yugoslavia	1:15.8
1972	Cathy Carr, U.S.	1:13.58
1976	Hannelore Anke, E. Germany	1:11:16
1980	Ute Geweniger, E. Germany	1:10.22
1984	Petra Van Staveren, Netherlands	1:09.88
1988	Tania Dangalakova, Bulgaria	1:07.95*

200-Metre Breaststroke

1924	Lucy Morton, Great Britain	3:33.2
1928	Hilde Schrader, Germany	3:12.6
1932	Clare Dennis, Australia	3:06.3
1936	Hideko Maehata, Japan	3:03.6
1948	Petronella Van Vliet, Netherlands	2:57.2
1952	Eva Szekely, Hungary	2:51.7
1956	Ursula Happe, Germany	2:53.1
1960	Anita Lonsbrough, Great Britain	2:49.5
1964	Galina Prozumenshikova, USSR	2:46.4
1968	Sharon Wichman, U.S.	2:44.4
1972	Beverly Whitfield, Australia	2:41.71
1976	Marina Koshevaia, USSR	2:33.35
1980	Lina Kaciusytė, USSR	2:29.54
1984	Anne Ottenbrite, Canada	2:30.38
1988	Silke Hoerner, E. Germany	2:26.71*

200-Metre Individual Medley

1968	Claudia Kolb, U.S.	2:24.7
1972	Shane Gould, Australia	2:23.07
1976	not held	

1980	not held	
1984	Tracy Caulkins, U.S.	2:12.64
1988	Daniela Hunger, E. Germany	2:12.59*

400-Metre Individual Medley

1964	Donna de Varona, U.S.	5:18.7
1968	Claudia Kolb, U.S.	5:08.5
1972	Gail Neall, Australia	5:02.97
1976	Ulrike Tauber, E. Germany	4:42.77
1980	Petra Schneider, E. Germany	4:36.29*
1984	Tracy Caulkins, U.S.	4:39.24
1988	Janet Evans, U.S.	4:37.76

100-Metre Butterfly

1956	Shelley Mann, U.S.	1:11.0
1960	Carolyn Schuler, U.S.	1:09.5
1964	Sharon Stouder, U.S.	1:04.7
1968	Lynn McClements, Australia	1:05.5
1972	Mayumi Aoki, Japan	1:03.34
1976	Kornelia Ender, E. Germany	1:00.13
1980	Caren Metschuck, E. Germany	1:00.42
1984	Mary T. Meagher, U.S.	59.26
1988	Kristin Otto, E. Germany	59.00*

200-Metre Butterfly

1968	Ada Kok, Netherlands	2:24.7
1972	Karen Moe, U.S.	2:15.57
1976	Andrea Pollack, E. Germany	2:11.41
1980	Ines Geissler, E. Germany	2:10.44
1984	Mary T. Meagher, U.S.	2:06.90
1988	Kathleen Nord, E. Germany	2:09.51*

4 x 100-Metre Medley Relay

1960	United States	4:41.1
1960	United States	4:33.9
1968	United States	4:28.3
1972	United States	4:20.75
1976	East Germany	4:07.95
1980	East Germany	4:06.67
1984	United States	4:08.34
1988	East Germany	4:03.74*

4 x 100-Metre Freestyle Relay

1912	Great Britain	5:52.8
1920	United States	5:11.6
1924	United States	4:58.8
1928	United States	4:47.6
1932	United States	4:38.0
1936	Netherlands	4:36.0
1948	United States	4:29.2
1952	Hungary	4:24.4
1956	Australia	4:17.1
1960	United States	4:08.9
1964	United States	4:03.8
1968	United States	4:02.5
1972	United States	3:55.19
1976	United States	3:44.82
1980	East Germany	3:42.71*
1984	United States	3:43.43
1988	East Germany	3:40.63

	Springboard Diving	Points
1920	Aileen Riggin, U.S.	539.90
1924	Elizabeth Becker, U.S.	474.50
1928	Helen Meany, U.S.	78.62
1932	Georgia Coleman U.S.	87.52
1936	Marjorie Gestring, U.S.	89.27
1948	Victoria M. Draves, U.S.	108.74
1952	Patricia McCormick, U.S.	147.30
1956	Patricia McCormick, U.S.	142.36
1960	Ingrid Krämer, E. Germany	155.81
1964	Ingrid Engel-Krämer, E. Germany	145.00
1968	Sue Gossick, U.S.	150.77
1972	Micki King, U.S.	450.03
1976	Jenni Chandler, U.S.	506.19
1980	Irina Kalinina, USSR	725.91
1984	Sylvie Bernier, Canada	530.70
1988	Gao Min, China	580.23

	Platform Diving	Points
1912	Greta Johansson, Sweden	39.90
1920	Stefani Fryland-Clausen, Denmark	34.60
1924	Caroline Smith, U.S.	33.20
1928	Elizabeth B. Pinkston, U.S.	31.60
1932	Dorothy Poynton, U.S.	40.26
1936	Dorothy Poynton Hill, U.S.	33.93
1948	Victoria M. Draves, U.S.	68.87
1952	Patricia McCormick, U.S.	79.37
1956	Patricia McCormick, U.S.	84.85
1960	Ingrid Krämer, Germany	91.28
1964	Lesley Bush, U.S.	99.80
1968	Milena Duchkova, Czech.	109.59
1972	Ulrika Knape, Sweden	390.00
1976	Elena Vaytsekhovskaya, USSR	406.59
1980	Martina Jäschke, E. Germany	596.25
1984	Zhou Jihong, China	435.51
1988	Xu Yanmei, China	445.20

Other Summer Olympics Gold Medalists in 1988

Archery

Men—Jay Barrs, U.S.
Men's Team—South Korea.
Women—Kim Soo-nyung, S. Korea.
Women's Team—South Korea.

Basketball

Men—1. USSR; 2. Yugoslavia; 3. U.S.
Women—1. U.S.; 2. Yugoslavia 3. USSR.

Boxing

48 kg—Ivalio Hristov, Bulgaria.
51 kg—Kim Kwang-sun, S. Korea.
54 kg—Kennedy McKinney, U.S.
57 kg—Giovanni Parisi, Italy.
60 kg—Andreas Zuelow, E. Germany.
63.5 kg—Viatcheslav Janovski, USSR.
67 kg—Robert Wangila, Kenya.
71 kg—Park Si-Hun, S. Korea.
75 kg—Henry Maske, E. Germany.
81 kg—Andrew Maynard, U.S.
91 kg—Ray Mercer, U.S.
Over 91 kg—Lennox Lewis, Canada.

Men's Canoeing

500m One-Man Canoe—Olaf Huekrodt, E. Germany.
500m Two-Man Canoe—USSR.
500m One-Man Kayak—Zsolt Gyulay, Hungary.
500m Two-Man Kayak—New Zealand.
1 000m One-Man Kayak—Greg Barton, U.S.
1 000m Two-Man Kayak—U.S.
1 000m Four-Man Kayak—Hungary.
1 000m One-Man Canoe—Ivan Klementiev, USSR.
1 000m Two-Man Canoe—USSR.

Women's Canoeing

500m One-Woman Kayak—Vania Guecheva, Bulgaria.
500m Two-Woman Kayak—E. Germany.
500m Four-Woman Kayak—E. Germany.

Cycling

4 000 Individual Pursuit—Gintaoutas Umaras, USSR.
Individual Road Race—Olaf Ludwig, E. Germany.
1 000m Time Trials—Alexandre Kiritchenko, USSR.
4 000m Team Pursuit—USSR.
Sprint—Lutz Hesslich, E. Germany.
Points Race—Dan Frost, Denmark.
100 km Road Team Trials—E. Germany.
Women's Sprint—Erika Saloumiae, USSR.
Women's Individual Road Race—Monique Knol, Netherlands.

Equestrian

Individual 3-Day Event—Mark Todd, New Zealand.
Team 3-Day Event—W. Germany.
Team Jumping—W. Germany.
Team Dressage—W. Germany.
Individual Dressage—Nicole Uphoff, W. Germany.
Individual Jumping—Pierre Durand, France.

Men's Fencing

Individual Epee—Arnd Schmitt, W. Germany.
Individual Foil—Stefano Cerioni, Italy.
Individual Sabre—Jeanfrancois Lamour, France.
Team Foil—Soviet Union.
Team Epee—France.
Team Sabre—Hungary.

Women's Fencing

Individual Foil—Anja Fichtel, W. Germany.
Team Foil—W. Germany.

Field Hockey

Men—1. Great Britain; 2. W. Germany; 3. Netherlands.
Women—1. Australia; 2. S. Korea; 3. Netherlands.

Men's Gymnastics

All Around—Vladimir Artemov, USSR.
Team—USSR.
Floor Exercise—Serguei Kharikov, USSR.
Horizontal Bar—Vladimir Artemov, USSR and Valeri Lioukine, USSR (tie).
Parallel Bars—Vladimir Artemov, USSR.
Pommel Horse—Lyubomir Gueraskov, Bulgaria; Zsolt Borkai, Hungary and Dmitri Bilozertchev, USSR (tie).
Rings—Holger Behrendt, E. Germany and Dmitri Bilozertchev, USSR (tie).
Vault—Lou Yun, China.

Women's Gymnastics

Floor Exercise—Daniela Silivas, Romania.
Balance Beam—Daniela Silivas, Romania.
Vault—Svetlana Boguinskaia, USSR.
Uneven Parallel Bars—Daniela Silivas, Romania.
All-Around—Elena Shushunova, USSR.
Team—USSR.
Rhythmic—Marina Lobatch, USSR.

Team Handball

Men—1. USSR; 2. S. Korea; 3. Yugoslavia.
Women—1. S. Korea; 2. Norway; 2. USSR.

Judo

Lightweight—Mark Alexandre, France.
Extra Lightweight—Kim Jae-Yup, S. Korea.
Half Lightweight—Lee Kyung-Keun, S. Korea.
Half Middleweight—Waldemar Legien, Poland.
Middleweight—Peter Seisenbacher, Austria.
Half Heavyweight—Aurelio Miguel, Brazil.
Heavyweight—Hitoshi Saito, Japan.

Modern Pentathlon

Individual—Janos Martinek, Hungary.
Team—1. Hungary; 2. Italy.; 3. Great Britain.

Men's Rowing

Single Sculls—Thomas Lange, E. Germany.
Double Sculls—Netherlands.
Quadruple Sculls—Italy.
Pair Oars With Coxswain—Italy.
Pair Oars Without Coxswain—Great Britain.
Four Oars With Coxswain—E. Germany.
Four Oars Without Coxswain—E. Germany.
Eight Oars With Coxswain—W. Germany.

Women's Rowing

Single Sculls—Jutta Behrendt, E. Germany.
Double Sculls—E. Germany.
Quadruple Sculls with Coxswain—E. Germany.
Pair Oars Without Coxswain—Romania.
Four Oars With Coxswain—E. Germany.
Eight Oars—E. Germany.

Men's Shooting

Air Pistol—Taniou Kiriakov, Bulgaria.
Air Rifle—Goran Maksimovic, Yugoslavia.
English Small Bore Rifle—Miroslav Varga, Czechoslovakia.
Free Pistol—Sorin Babii, Romania.
Rapid-Fire Pistol—Afanasi Kouzmine, USSR.
Running Game Targets—Tor Heiestad, Norway.
Small Bore Rifle, 3 Positions—Malcolm Cooper, Great Britain.

Women's Shooting

Air Pistol—Jasna Sekaric, Yugoslavia.
Air Rifle—Irina Chilova, USSR.
Small Bore Rifle, 3 Positions—Silvia Sperber, W. Germany.
Sport Pistol—Nino Saloukvadze, USSR.

Shooting—Open

Clay Target Skeet—Axel Wegner, E. Germany
Clay Target Trap—Dmitri Monakov, USSR.

Soccer

Championship—1. USSR; 2. Brazil; 3. W. Germany.

Synchronized Swimming

Solo—Carolyn Waldo, Canada.
Duet—1. Canada; 2. U.S.; 3. Japan.

Table Tennis

Men's Singles—Yoo Nam-kyu, S. Korea.
Men's Doubles—1. China; 2. Yugoslavia; 3. S. Korea.
Women's Singles—Chen Jing, China.
Women's Doubles—1. S. Korea; 2. China; 3. Yugoslavia.

Tennis

Men's Singles—Miloslav Mecir, Czechoslovakia.
Men's Doubles—1. U.S.; 2. Spain; 3. Czechoslovakia and Sweden.
Women's Singles—Steffi Graf, W. Germany.
Women's Doubles—1. U.S.; 2. Czechoslovakia; 3. Australia and W. Germany.

Volleyball

Men—1. U.S.; 2. USSR; 3. Argentina.
Women—1. USSR; 2. Peru; 3. China.

Water Polo

Championship—1. Yugoslavia; 2. U.S.; 3. USSR.

Weight Lifting

Bantamweight—Sevdalin Marinov, Bulgaria.
Flyweight—Oxen Mirzoian, USSR.
Featherweight—Naim Suleymanoglu, Turkey.
Lightweight—Joachim Kunz, E. Germany.
Middleweight—Borislav Guidikov, Bulgaria.
Light Heavyweight—Israil Arsamakov, USSR.
Middle Heavyweight—Anatoli Khrapatyi, USSR.
100 Kilograms—Pavel Kouznetsov, USSR.
110 Kilograms—Alexander Kurlovich, USSR.
Super Heavyweight—Alexander Kurlovich, USSR.

Freestyle Wrestling

48 kg—Takashi Kobayashi, Japan.
52 kg—Mitsuru Sato, Japan.
57 kg—Serguei Beloglazov, USSR.
62 kg—John Smith, U.S.
68 kg—Arsen Fadzaev, USSR.
74 kg—Kenneth Monday, U.S.
82 kg—Han Myang-Woo, S. Korea.
90 kg—Makharbek Khadartsev, USSR.
100 kg—Vasile Puscasu, Romania.
Over 100 kg—David Gobedjichvili, USSR.

Greco-Roman Wrestling

48 kg—Vicenzo Maenza, Italy.
52 kg—Jon Ronningen, Norway.
57 kg—Andras Sike, Hungary.
62 kg—Kamandar Madjidov, USSR.
68 kg—Levon Djoulfalakian, USSR.
74 kg—Kim Young-Nam, S. Korea.
82 kg—Mikhail Mamiachvili, USSR.
90 kg—Atanas Komchev, Bulgaria.
100 kg—Andrzei Wronski, Poland.
Over 100 kg—Alexandre Kareline, USSR.

Yachting

Board Sailing—1. New Zealand; 2. Sweden; 3. U.S.
Soling Class—1. E. Germany; 2. U.S.; 3. Denmark.
Flying Dutchman Class—1. Denmark; 2. Norway; 3. Canada.
Star Class—1. Great Britain; 2. U.S. 3. Brazil.
Finn Class—Jose Luis Doreste, Spain.
Tornado Class—1. France; 2. New Zealand; 3. Brazil.
470 Class (Men)—1. France; 2. USSR; 3. U.S.
470 Class (Women)—1. Sweden; 2. Sweden; 3. USSR.

1988 Summer Olympics Medal Winners

Archery

Men—1. Jay Barrs, U.S.; 2. Park Sung Soo, S. Korea; 3. Vladimir Echeev, USSR.
Men's Team—1. S. Korea; 2. U.S.; 3. Great Britain.
Women—1. Kim Soo-Nyung, S. Korea; 2. Wang He Kyung, S. Korea; 3. Yun Young Sook, S. Korea.
Women's Team—1. S. Korea; 2. Indonesia; 3. U.S.

Basketball

Men—1. USSR; 2. Yugoslavia; 3. U.S.
Women—1. U.S.; 2. Yugoslavia; 3. USSR.

Boxing

106 lbs.—1. Ivailo Hristov, Bulgaria; 2. Michael Carbajal, U.S.; 3. Robert Isaszegi, Hungary & Leopoldo Serantes, Philippines.
112 lbs.—1. Kim Kwang Sun, S. Korea; 2. Andreas Tews, E. Germany; 3. T. Skriabin, USSR & Mario Gonzalez, Mexico.
119 lbs.—1. Kennedy McKinney, U.S.; 2. Aleksandr Hristov, Bulgaria; 3. Jorge Rocha, Colombia & Phajol Moolsan, Thailand.
126 lbs.—1. Giovanni Parisi, Italy; 2. Daniel Dumitrescu, Romania; 3.A. Achik, Morocco & Lee Jae Hyunk, S. Korea.
132 lbs.—1. Andreas Zuelow, E. Germany; 2. George Cramne, Sweden; Romallis Ellis, U.S. & Nerguy Enkhbat, Mongolia.
139 lbs.—1. Viatcheslav Janovski, USSR; 2. Grahame Cheney, Australia; 3. Lars Myrberg, Sweden & Reiner Gies, W. Germany.
147 lbs.—1. Robert Wangila, Kenya; 2. Laurent Boudouani, France; 3. Jan Dydak, Poland & Ken Gould, U.S.
157 lbs.—1. Park Si Hun, S. Korea; 2. Roy Jones, U.S.; 3. R. Woodhall, Great Britain & Ray Downey, Canada.
165 lbs.—1. Henry Maske, E. Germany; 2. Egerton Marcus, Canada; 3. Chris Sande, Kenya & Hussain Shah Syed, Pakistan.
179 lbs.—1. Andrew Maynard, U.S.; 2. N. Chanavazov, USSR; 3. Damir Skaro, Yugoslavia & Henryk Petrich, Poland.
201 lbs.—1. Ray Mercer, U.S; 2. Baik Hyun Han, S. Korea; 3. Andrzej Golota, Poland, & A. Vanderlidge, Netherlands.
Over 201 lbs.—1. Lennox Lewis, Canada; 2. Riddick Bowe, U.S.; 3. A. Mirochnitchenko, USSR & J. Zarenkiewicz, Poland.

Canoeing—Men

K1-500M—1. Zsolt Gyulay, Hungary; 2. Andreas Staehle, E. Germany; 3. Paul MacDonald, New Zealand.
K2-500M—1. Ian Ferguson, Paul MacDonald, New Zealand; 2. Igor Nagaev, Victory Denissov, USSR; 3. Attila Abraham, Ferenc Csipes, Hungary.
K1-1,000M—1. Greg Barton, U.S.; 2. Grant Davies, Australia; 3. Andre Wohliebe, E. Germany.
K2-1,000M—1. Greg Barton, N. Bellingham, U.S.; 2. Ian Ferguson, Paul MacDonald, New Zealand; 3. Peter Foster, Kevin Graham, Australia.
K4-1,000m—1. Hungary.; 2. USSR; 3. E. Germany.
C1-500M—1. Olaf Huekrodt, E. Germany; 2. Mikhail Silvinski, USSR; 3. Martin Marinov, Bulgaria.

C2-500M—1. Victor Reneiski, Nikolai Jouravski, USSR; 2. Marek Dopierala, Marek Lbik, Poland; 3. Philippe Renaud, Joel Bettin, France.
C1-1,000M—1. Ivan Klementiev, USSR; 2. Joerg Schmidt, E. Germany; 3. Andre Wohliebe, E. Germany.
C2-1,000M—1. Victor Reneiski, Nikolai Jouravski, USSR; 2. Olaf Heukrodt, Ingo Spelly, E. Germany; 3. Marek Dopierala, Marek Lbik, Poland.

Canoeing—Women

K1-500M—1. Vania Guecheva, Bulgaria; 2. Birgit Schmidt, E. Germany; 3. Izabela Dylewska, Poland.
K2-500M—1. Birgit Schmidt, Anke Nothnagel, E. Germany; 2. Vania Guecheva, Diana Paliska, Bulgaria; 3. Annemiek Derckx, Annemarie Cox, Netherlands.
K4-500M—1. E. Germany; 2. Hungary; 3. Bulgaria.

Cycling

4,000 Individual Pursuit—1. Gintaoutas Umaras, USSR; 2. Dean Woods, Australia; 3. Bernd Dittert, E. Germany.
Sprint—1. Lutz Hesslich, E. Germany; 2. Nikolai Kovche, USSR; 3. Gary Neiwand, Australia.
4,000 Team Pursuit—1. USSR; 2. E. Germany; 3. Australia.
50Km Points Race—1. Dan Frost, Denmark; 2. Leo Peelen, Netherlands; 3. Marat Ganeev, USSR.
1K Time Trial—1. Alexandr Kiritchenko, USSR; 2. Martin Vinnicombe, Australia; 3. Robert Lechner, E. Germany.
100K Team Time Trial—1. E. Germany; 2. Poland; 3. Sweden.
Road Race—1. Olaf Ludwig, E. Germany; 2. Bernd Gröne, W. Germany; 3. Christian Henn, W. Germany.
Women's Sprint—1. Erika Saloumiae, USSR; 2. Christa Rothenburg, E. Germany; 3. Connie Paraskevin Young, U.S.
Women's Road Race—1. Monique Knol, Netherlands; 2. Jutta Niehaus, W. Germany; 3. Laima Zilporitee, USSR.

Diving

Women's Platform—1. Xu Yanmei, China; 2. Michele Mitchell, U.S.; 3. Wendy Williams, U.S.
Women's Springboard—1. Gao Min, China; 2. Li Qing, China; 3. Kelly McCormick, U.S.
Men's Springboard—1. Greg Louganis, U.S.; 2. Tan Liangde, China; 3. Li Deliang, China.
Men's Platform—1. Greg Louganis, U.S.; 2. Xiong, Ni, China; 3. Jesus Mena, Mexico.

Equestrian

Individual 3-Day Event—1. Mark Todd, New Zealand; 2. Ian Stark, Great Britain; 3. Virginia Leng, Great Britain.
Team 3-Day Event—1. W. Germany; 2. Great Britain; 3. New Zealand.
Individual Dressage—1. Nicole Uphoff, W. Germany; 2. Margitt Otto-Crepin, France; Christine Stueckelberger, Switzerland.
Team Dressage—1. W. Germany; 2. Switzerland; 3. Canada.
Individual Jumping—1. Pierre Durand, France; 2. Greg Best, U.S.; 3. Karsten Huck, W. Germany.
Team Jumping—1. W. Germany; 2. U.S.; 3. France.

Fencing—Men

Foil Individual—1. Stefano Cerioni, Italy; 2. Udo Wagner, E. Germany; 3. Aleksandr Romankov, USSR.
Team Foil—1. USSR; 2. W. Germany; 3. Hungary.
Sabre Individual—1. Jean-Francois Lamour, France; 2. Janusz Olech, Poland; 3. Giovanni Scalzo, Italy.
Team Sabre—1. Hungary; 2. USSR; 3. Italy.
Epée Individual—1. Arnd Schmitt, W. Germany; 3. Phillippe Riboud, France; 3. Andrei Chouvalov, USSR.
Epée Team—1. France; 2. W. Germany; 3. USSR.

Fencing—Women

Foil Individual—1. Anja Fichtel, W. Germany; 2. Sabine Bau, W. Germany; 3. Zita Funkenhouser, W. Germany.
Team Foil—1. W. Germany; 2. Italy; 3. Hungary.

Field Hockey

Men—1. Great Britain; 2. W. Germany; 3. Netherlands.
Women—1. Australia; 2. S. Korea; 3. Netherlands.

Gymnastics—Men

Team—1. USSR; 2. E. Germany; 3. Japan.
All Around—1. Vladimir Artemov, USSR; 2. Valery Lyukin, USSR; 3. Dmitri Bilozerchev, USSR.
Floor Exercise—1. Serguei Kharikov, USSR; 2. Vladimir Artemov, USSR; 3. (tie) Yukio Iketani, Japan & Lou Yun, China.
Pommel Horse—1. Lyubomir Gueraskov, Bulgaria; Zsolt Borkai, Hungary; and Dmitri Biolozertchev, USSR.
Rings—1. Dmitri Bilozerchev, USSR; 2. Holger Behrendt, E. Germany; 3. Sven Tippelt, E. Germany.
Vault—1. Lou Yun, China; 2. Silvio Kroll, E. Germany; 3. Park Jung Hoon, S. Korea.
Parallel Bars—1. Vladimir Artemov, USSR; 2. Valeri Lyukin, E. Germany; 3. Sven Tippelt, E. Germany.
Horizontal Bar—1. Vladimir Artemov, USSR; 2. Valery Lyukin, E. Germany; 3. (tie) Holger Behrendt, E. Germany & Marius Gherman, Romania.

Gymnastics—Women

Team—1. USSR; 2. Romania; 3. E. Germany.
All-Around—1. Yelena Shoushunova, USSR; 2. Daniela Silivas, Romania; 3. Svetlana Boguinskaya, USSR.
Vault—1. Svetlana Boguinskaia, USSR; 2. Gabriela Potorac, Romania; 3. Daniela Silivas, Romania.
Uneven Parallel Bars—1. Daniela Silivas, Romania; 2. Dagmar Kersten, E. Germany; 3. Elena Shoushunova, USSR.
Balance Beam—1. Daniela Silivas, Romania; 2. Elena Shoushunova, USSR; 3. (tie) Phoebe Mills, U.S. & Gabriela Potorac, Romania.
Floor Exercise—1. Daniela Silivas, Romania; 2. Svetlana Boguinskaya, USSR; 3. Diana Doudeva, Bulgaria.

Rhythmic Gymnastics

1. Marina Lobatch, USSR; 2. Adriana Dounavska, Bulgaria; 3. Aleksandra Timochenko, USSR.

Judo

133 Pounds—1. Kim Jae Yup, S. Korea; 2. Kevin Asaon, U.S.; 3. Amiran Totikachvili, USSR & Shinji Hosokawa, Japan.
143 Pounds—1. Lee Kyung-Keun, S. Korea; 2. Janusz Pawlowski, Poland; 3. Yosuke Yamamoto, Japan & Bruno Carabetta, France.
156 Pounds—1. Marc Alexandre, France; 2. Sven Loll, E. Germany; 3. Kerrith Brown, Great Britain & Gueorgui Tenadze, USSR.
172 Pounds—1. Waldemar Legien, Poland; 2. Frank Wieneke, W. Germany; 3. Torsten Brechot, E. Germany & Bachir Varaev, USSR.
189 Pounds—1. Peter Seisenbacher, Austria; 2. Vladimir Chestakov, USSR; 3. Ben Spijkers, Netherlands & Akinobu Osako, Japan.
209 Pounds—1. Aurelio Miguel, Brazil; 2. Marc Meiling, W. Germany; 3. Dennis Stewart, Great Britain & Robert Van da Walle, Belgium.
Over 209 Pounds—1. Hitoshi Saito, Japan; 2. Henry Stoehr, E. Germany; 3. Cho Yong Chul, S. Korea & Grigori Veritchev, USSR.

Modern Pentathlon

Individual—1. Janos Martinek, Hungary; 2. Carlo Massullo, Italy; 3. Vakhtang Iagorachvili, USSR.
Team—1. Hungary; 2. Italy. 3. Great Britain.

Rowing—Men

Single Sculls—1. Tomas Lange, E. Germany; 2. Petermichael Kolbe, W. Germany; 3. Eric Verdonk, New Zealand.
Double Sculls—1. Netherlands; 2. Switzerland; 3. USSR.
Coxless Pairs—1. Great Britain; 2. Romania; 3. Yugoslavia.
Coxed Pairs—1. Italy; 2. E. Germany; 3. Great Britain.
Coxed Fours—1. E. Germany; 2. Romania; 3. New Zealand.
Coxless Fours—1. E. Germany; 2. U.S.; 3. W. Germany.
Quadruple Sculls—1. Italy; 2. Norway; 3. E. Germany.
Eights—1. W. Germany; 2. USSR; 3. U.S.

Rowing—Women

Single Sculls—1. Jutta Behrendt, E. Germany; 2. Anne Marden, U.S.; 3. Magdelena Gueorguieva, Bulgaria.
Double Sculls—1. E. Germany; 2. Romania; 3. Bulgaria.
Coxless Pairs—1. Romania; 2. Bulgaria; 3. New Zealand.
Coxless Fours—1. E. Germany; 2. China; 3. Romania.
Quadruple Sculls—1. E. Germany; 2. USSR; 3. Romania.
Eights—1. E. Germany; 2. Romania; 3. China.

Shooting—Men

Smallbore Standard Rifle—1. Miroslav Varga, Czechoslovakia; 2. Cha Young Chul, S. Korea; 3. Attila Zahonyi, Hungary.
Smallbore Free Rifle—1. Malcolm Cooper, Great Britain; 2. Alister Allan, Great Britain; Kirill Ivanov, USSR.
Free Pistol—1. Sorin Babii, Romania; 2. Ranger Skanaker, Sweden; 3. Igor Bassinski, USSR.
Air Rifle—1. Goran Maksimovic Yugoslavia; 2. Nicolas Berthelof, France; Johann Reiderer, W. Germany.
Rapid-Fire Pistol—1. Afanasi Kouzmine, USSR; 2. Ralf Schumann, E. Germany; 3. Zoltan Kovacs, Hungary.
Running Game Targets—1. Tor Heiestad, Norway; 2. Huang Shiping, China; 3. Gennadi Avramenko, USSR.
Air Pistol—1. Taniou Kiruakov, Bulgaria; 3. Erich Buljung, U.S.; Xu Haifeng, China.

Shooting—Women

Air Rifle—1. Irina Cilova, USSR; 2. Silvia Sperber, W. Germany; 3. Anna Malioukhina, USSR.
Sport Pistol—1. Nino Saloukvadze, USSR; 2. Tomoko Hasegawa, Japan; 3. Jasna Sekaric, Yugoslavia.
Air Pistol—1. Jasna Sekaric, Yugoslavia; 2. Nino Saloukvadze, USSR; 3. Marina Dobrantcheva, USSR.
Smallbore Standard Rifle—1. Silvia Sperber, W. Germany; 2. Vessela Letcheva, Bulgaria; 3. Valentina Tcherka Ssova, USSR.

Shooting—Mixed

Skeet—1. Axel Wegner, E. Germany; 2. Alfanso De iruarrizaga, Chile; 3. Jorge Guardiola, Spain.
Trap—1. Dmitri Monakov, USSR; 2. Miloslav Bednarik, Czechoslovakia; 3. Frans Peeters, Belgium.

Soccer

Championship—1. USSR; 2. Brazil; 3. W. Germany.

Swimming—Men

50M Freestyle—1. Matt Biondi, U.S.; 2. Tom Jager, U.S.; 3. Gennadi Prigoda, USSR.
100M Freestyle—1. Matt Biondi, U.S.; 2. Chris Jacobs, U.S.; 3. Stephan Caron, France.
200M Freestyle—1. Duncan Armstrong, Australia; 2. Anders Holmertz, Sweden; 3. Matt Biondi, U.S.
400M Freestyle—1. Uwe Dassler, E. Germany; 2. Duncan Armstrong, Australia; 3. Artur Wojdat, Poland.
1,500M Freestyle—1. Vladimir Salnikov, USSR; 2. Stefan Pfeiffer, W. Germany; 3. Uwe Dassler, E. Germany.
100M Breaststroke—1. Adrian Moorhouse, Great Britain; 2. Karoli Guttler, Hungary; 3. Dmitri Volkov, USSR.
200M Breaststroke—1. Jozef Szabo, Hungary; 2. Nick Gillingham, Great Britain; 3. Sergio Lopez, Spain.
100M Butterfly—1. Anthony Nesty, Suriname; 2. Matt Biondi, U.S.; 3. Andy Jameson, Great Britain.
200M Butterfly—1. Michael Gross, W. Germany; 2. Benny Nielsen, Denmark; 3. Anthony Mosse, New Zealand.
100M Backstroke—1. Daichi Suzuki, Japan; 2. David Berkoff, U.S.; 3. Igor Polyanski, USSR.
200M Backstroke—1. Igor Polyanski, USSR; 2. Frank Baltrusch, USSR; 3. Paul Kingsman, New Zealand.
200 M Individual Medley—1. Tamas Darnyi, Hungary; 2. Patrick Kuehl, E. Germany; 3. Vadim Iarochtchouk, USSR.
400M Individual Medley—1. Tamas Darnyi, Hungary; 2. Dave Wharton, U.S.; 3. Stefano Battistelli, Italy.
400M Freestyle Relay—1. U.S.; 2. USSR; 3. E. Germany.
800M Freestyle Relay—1. U.S.; 2. E. Germany; 3. W. Germany.
400M Medley Relay—1. U.S.; 2. Canada; 3. USSR.

Swimming—Women

50M Freestyle—1. Kristin Otto, E. Germany; 2. Yang Wenyi, China; 3. Jill Sterkel, U.S.
100M Freestyle—1. Kristin Otto, E. Germany; 2. Zhuang Yong, China; 3. Catherine Plewinski, France.
200M Freestyle—1. Heike Friedrich, E. Germany; 2. Silvia Poll, Costa Rica; 3. Manuela Stellmach, E. Germany.
400M Freestyle—1. Janet Evans, U.S.; 2. Heike Friedrich, E. Germany; 3. Anke Moehring, E. Germany.
800M Freestyle—1. Janet Evans, U.S.; 2. Astrid Strauss, E. Germany; 3. Julie MacDonald, Australia.
100M Breaststroke—1. Tania Dangalakova, Bulgaria; 2. Antoaneta Frenkeva, Bulgaria; 3. Silke Hörner, E. Germany.
200M Breaststroke—1. Silke Hörner, E. Germany; 2. Xiao Min Huang, China; 3. Antoaneta Fenkeva, Bulgaria.
100M Backstroke—1. Kristin Otto, E. Germany; 2. Krisztina Egerszegi, Hungary; 3. Cornelia Sirch, E. Germany.
200M Backstroke—1. Krisztina Egerszegi, Hungary; 2. Kathrin Zimmerman, E. Germany; 3. Cornelia Sirch, E. Germany.
100M Butterfly—1. Kristin Otto, E. Germany; 2. Birte Weigang, E. Germany; 3. Qian Hong, China
200M Butterfly—1. Kathleen Nord, E. Germany; 2. Birte Wiegang, E. Germany; 3. Mary T. Meagher, U.S.
200M Individual Medley—1. Daniela Hunger, E. Germany; 2. Elena Dendeberova, USSR; 3. Noemi Lung, Romania.
400M Individual Medley—1. Janet Evans, U.S.; 2. Noemi Lung, Romania; 3. Daniela Hunger, E. Germany.
400M Freestyle Relay—1. E. Germany; 2. Netherlands; 3. U.S.
400M Medley Relay—1. E. Germany; 2. U.S.; 3. Canada.

Synchronized Swimming

Solo—1. Carolyn Waldo, Canada; 2. Tracy Ruiz-Conforto, U.S.; 3. Mikako Kotani, Japan.
Duet—1. Michelle Cameron, Carolyn Waldo, Canada; 2. Sarah Josephson, Karen Josephson, U.S.; 3. Miyako Tanaka, Mikako Kotani, Japan.

Table Tennis—Men

Singles—1. Yoo Nam Kyu, S. Korea; 2. Kim Ki Taik, S. Korea; 3. Erik Lindh, Sweden.
Doubles—1. Chen Longcan, Wei Qingquang, China; 2. Ilija Lupulesku, Zoran, Primorac, Yugoslavia; 3. Ahn Jea Hyung, Yoo Nam Kyu, S. Korea.

Table Tennis—Women

Singles—1. Chen Jing, China; 2. Li Huifen, China; 3. Jiao Zhimin, China.
Doubles—1. Hyun Jung Hwa, Yang Young Ja, S. Korea; 2. Chen Jiing, Jiao Zhimin, China; 3. Jasna Fazlic, Gordana Perkucin, Yugoslavia.

Team Handball

Men—1. USSR; 2. S. Korea; 3. Yugoslavia.
Women—1. S. Korea; 2. Norway; 3. USSR.

Track and Field—Men

100M—1. Carl Lewis, U.S; ; 2. Linford Christie, Great Britain; 3. Calvin Smith, U.S.
200M—1. Joe DeLoach, U.S.; 2. Carl Lewis, U.S.; 3. Robson da Silva, Brazil.
400M—1. Steve Lewis, U.S.; 2. Butch Reynolds, U.S.; 3. Danny Everett, U.S.
800M—1. Paul Ereng, Kenya; 2. Joaquim Cruz, Brazil; 3. Said Aouita, Morocco.
1,500M—1. Peter Rono, Kenya; 2. Peter Elliott, Great Britain; 3. Jens-Peter Herold, E. Germany.
5,000M—1. John Ngugi, Kenya; 2. Dieter Baumann, W. Germany; 3. Hansjoerg Kunze, E. Germany.
10,000M—1. Brahim Boutaib, Morocco; 2. Salvatore Antibo, Italy; 3. Kipkemboi Kemeli, Kenya
110M Hurdles—1. Roger Kingdom, U.S.; 2. Colin Jackson, Great Britain; 3. Tonie Campbell, U.S.

400M Hurdles—1. Andre Phillips, U.S.; 2. Amadou Dia Ba, Senegal; 3. Edwin Moses, U.S.
4 x 100M Relay—1. USSR; 2. Great Britain; 3. France.
4 x 400M Relay—1. U.S.; 2. Jamaica; 3. W. Germany.
Shot-Put—1. Ulf Timmermann, E. Germany; 2. Randy Barnes, U.S.; 3. Werner Gunther, Switzerland.
Triple Jump—1. Hristo Markov, Bulgaria; 2. Igor Capchine, USSR ; 3. Aleksandr Kovalenko, USSR.
Javelin Throw—1. Tapio Korjus, Finland; 2. Jan Celezny, Czech.; 3. Seppo, Raty, Finland.
High Jump—1. Guennadi Avdeenko, USSR; 2. Hollis Conway, U.S.; 3. Roudolf Povarnit, USSR.
Hammer Throw—1. Sergei Litinov, USSR; 2. Yuri Sedikyh, USSR; 3. Yuri Tamm, USSR.
Long Jump—1. Carl Lewis, U.S.; 2. Mike Powell, U.S.; 3. Larry Myricks, U.S.
Pole Vault—1. Sergei Bubka, USSR; 2. Radion Gataouline, USSR; 3. Grigory Egorov, USSR.
Decathlon—1. Christian Schenk, E. Germany; 2. Torsten Voss, E. Germany; 3. Dave Steen, Canada.
Discus Throw—1. Jürgen Schult, E. Germany; 2. Romas Oubartas, USSR; 3. Rolf Danneberg, W. Germany.
20KM Walk—1. Jozef Pribilnec, Czech.; 2. Ronald Weigel, E. Germany; 3. Maurizio Damilano, Italy.
50KM Walk—1. Vayachslav Ivanenko, USSR; 2. Ronald Weigel, E. Germany; 3. Hartwig Gauder, W. Germany.
3,000M Steeplechase—1. Julius Kariuki, Kenya; 2. Peter Koech, Kenya; 3. Mark Rowland, Great Britain.
Marathon—1. Gelindo Borin, Italy; 2. Douglas Wakihuru, Kenya; 3. Ahmed Saleh, Djibouti.

Track and Field—Women

100M—1. Florence Griffith-Joyner, U.S.; 2. Evelyn Ashford, U.S.; 3. Heike Drechsler, E. Germany.
200M—1. Florence Griffith-Joyner, U.S.; 2. Grace Jackson, Jamaica; 3. Heike Drechsler, E. Germany.
400M—1. Olga Bryzgina, USSR; 2. Petra Mueller, E. Germany; 3. Olga Nazarova, USSR
800 M—1. Sigrun Wodars, E. Germany; 2. Christine Wachtel, E. Germany; 3. Kim Gallagher, U.S.
1,500M—1. Paula Ivan, Romania; 2. Tatyana Samolenko, USSR; 3. L. Baikanskaite, USSR.
3,000M—1. Tatyana Samolenko, USSR; 2. Paula Ivan, Romania; 3. Yvonne Murray, Great Britain.
10,000M—1. Olga Bondarenko, USSR; 2. Elizabeth McColgan, Great Britain; 3. Elena Joupieva, USSR.
100M Hurdles—1. Jordanka Donkova, Bulgaria; 2. Gloria Siebert, E. Germany; 3. Claudia Zackiewicz, W. Germany
400M Hurdles—1. Debra Flintoff-King, Australia; 2. Tatiana Ledovskaia, USSR; 3. Ellen Fiedler, E. Germany.
4 x 100M Relay—1. U.S.; 2. E. Germany; 3. USSR.
4 x 400M Relay—1. USSR; 2. U.S.; 3. E. Germany
Javelin Throw—1. Petra Felke, E. Germany; 2. Fatima Whitbread, Great Britain; 3. Beate Koch, E. Germany.
Long Jump—1. Jackie Joyner-Kersee, U.S.; 2. Heike Drechsler, E. Germany; 3. Galina Christakova, USSR.
High Jump—1. Louise Ritter, U.S.; 2. Stefka Kostadinova, Bulgaria; 3. Tamara Bykova, USSR.
Shot-Put—1. Natalya Lisouskava, USSR; 2. Kathrin Neimke, E. Germany; 3. Li Meisu, China.
Heptathlon—1. Jackie Joyner-Kersee, U.S.; 2. Sabine John, E. Germany; 3. Anke Behmer, E. Germany.
Marathon—1. Rosa Mota, Portugal; 2. Lisa Martin, Australia; 3. Kathrin Dorre, E. Germany.

Tennis—Men

Singles—1. Miloslav Mecir, Czech.; 2. Tim Mayotte, U.S.; Stefan Edberg, Sweden & Brad Gilbert, U.S.
Doubles—1. Ken Flach, Robert Seguso, U.S.; 2. Emilio Sánchez, Sergio Casal, Spain; 3. Stefan Edberg, Anders Jarryd, Sweden & Miloslav Mecir, Milan Srejber, Czechoslovakia.

Tennis—Women

Singles—1. Steffi Graf, W. Germany; 2. Gabriela Sabatini, Argentina; 3. Zina Garrison, U.S. & Manuela Maleeva, Bulgaria.
Doubles—1. Pam Shriver, Zina Garrison, U.S.; 2. Jana Novatnas, Helena Sukova, USSR; 3. Liz Smylie, Wendy Turnbull, Australia & Steffi Graf, Claudia Kohde Kilsch, W. Germany.

Volleyball

Men—1. U.S.; 2. USSR; 3. Argentina.
Women—1. USSR; 2. Peru; 3. China.

Water Polo

Championship—1. Yugoslavia; 2. U.S.; 3. USSR.

Weight Lifting

115 Pounds—1. Sevdalin Marinov, Bulgaria; 2. Byung Kwan Chun, S. Korea; 3. He Zhuogiang, China.
123 Pounds—1. Oxen Mirzoian, USSR; 2. He Yingqiang, China; 3. Liu Shoubin, China.
132 Pounds—1. Naim Suleymanoglu, Turkey; 2. Stefan Topourov, Bulgaria; 3. Ye Huanming, China.
149 Pounds—1. Joachim Kunz, E. Germany; 2. Israel Militossian, USSR; 3. Li Jinhe, China.
165 Pounds—1. Borislav Guidikov, Bulgaria; 2. Ingo Steinhoefel, E. Germany; 3. Aleksandr Verbanov, Bulgaria.
182 Pounds—1. Israil Arsamakov, USSR; 2. Istvan Messzi, Hungary; 3. Lee Hyung, Kun, S. Korea.
198 Pounds—1. Anatoli Khrapatyi, USSR; 2. Nail Moukhamediaro, USSR; 3. Slawomir Zawada, Poland.
220 Pounds—1. Pavel Kouzntsov, USSR; 2. Nicu Vlad, Romania; 3. Immesberger, W. Germany.
242 Pounds—1. Yuri Zakharevitch, USSR; 2. Jozsef Jacso, Hungary; 3. Ronny Weller, E. Germany.
Over 242 Pounds—1. Aleksandr Kurlovich, USSR; 2. Manfred Nerlinger, W. Germany; 3. Martin Zawieja, W. Germany.

Wrestling—Greco-Roman

106 Pounds—1. Vicenzo Maenza, Italy; 2. Andrzej Glab, Poland; 3. Bratan Tzenov, Bulgaria.
115 Pounds—1. Jon Ronningen, Norway; 2. Atsuji Miyahara, Japan; 3. Lee Jae Suk, S. Korea.
126 Pounds—1. András Sike, Hungary; 2. Stoyan Balov, Bulgaria; 3. Charalambos Holidis, Greece.
137 Pounds—1. Kamandar Madjidov, USSR; 2. Jivko Vanguelov, Bulgaria; 3. An Dae Hyun, S. Korea.
150 Pounds—1. Levon Djoulfalakian, USSR; 2. Kim Sung Moon, S. Korea; 3. Tapio Siplia, Finland.
163 Pounds—1. Kim Young Nam, S. Korea; 2. Daoulet Tourlykhanov, USSR; 3. Jozef Tracz, Poland.
181 Pounds—1. Mikhail Mamiachvili, USSR; 2. Tibor Komaromi, Hungary; 3. Kim Sang Kyu, S. Korea.
198 Pounds—1. Atanas Komchev, Bulgaria; 2. Harri Koskela, Finland; 3. Vladimir Popov, USSR.
220 Pounds—1. Andrzej Wronksi, Poland; 2. Gerhard Himmel, W. Germany; 3. Dennis Koslowski, U.S.
286 Pounds—1. Alexandre Kareline, USSR; 2. Ranguiel Guerovski, Bulgaria; 3. Tomas Johannson, Sweden.

Wrestling—Freestyle

106 Pounds—1. Takashi Kobayashi, Japan; 2. Ivan Tzonov, Bulgaria; 3. Segei Karamtchakov, USSR.
115 Pounds—1. Mitsuru Sato, Japan; 2. Saban Trestena, Yugoslavia; 3. Vladimir Togouzov, USSR.
126 Pounds—1. Serguei Beloglazov, USSR; 2. Askari Mohammadian, Iran; 3. Noh Kyung Sun, S. Korea.
137 Pounds—1. John Smith, U.S; 2. Stephan Sarkissian, USSR; 3. Simeon Chterev, Bulgaria.
150 Pounds—1. Arsen Fadzaev, USSR; 2. Park Jang Soon, S. Korea; 3. Nate Carr, U.S.
163 Pounds—1. Ken Monday, U.S.; 2. Adian Varaev, USSR; Rakhmad Sofiadi, Bulgaria.
181 Pounds—1. Han Myang-Woo, S. Korea; 2. Necmi Gencaip, Turkey; 3. Josef Lohyna, Czech.
198 Pounds—1. Makharbek Khadartsev, USSR; 2. Akira Ota, Japan; 3. Kim Tae Woo, S. Korea.
220 Pounds—1. Vasile Puscasu, Romania; 2. Leri Khabelov, USSR; 3. Bill Scherr, U.S.
286 Pounds—1. David Gobedjichvili, USSR; 2. Bruce Baumgartner, U.S.; 3. Andreas Schroeder, E. Germany.

Yachting

Board Sailing—1. Bruce Kendall, New Zealand; 2. Jan D. Boersma, Netherlands; 3. Michael Gebhardt, U.S.
Finn—1. José Luis Doreste, Spain; 2. Peter Holmberg, Virgin Islands; 3. John Cutler, New Zealand.
Flying Dutchman—1. Denmark; 2. Norway; 3. Canada.
Soling—1. E. Germany; 2. U.S.; 3. Denmark.
Star—1. Great Britain; 2. U.S.; 3. Brazil.
Tornado—1. France; 2. USSR; 3. U.S.
Men's 470—1. France; 2. New Zealand; 3. Brazil.
Women's 470—1. U.S.; 2. Sweden; 3. USSR.

Obituaries

Deaths, Nov. 1, 1987—Oct. 10, 1988

Addams, Charles, 76; cartoonist whose macabre humor appeared in the New Yorker for 5 decades; New York, Sept. 29.

Alvaraz, Luis W., 77; scientist who won the 1968 Nobel Prize in Physics; Berkeley, Cal., Sept. 1

Ameche, Alan, 55; Baltimore Colts star running back in the 1950s; Houston, Aug. 8.

Arias Madrid, Arnulfo, 86; 3-time president of Panama; Miami, Fla., Aug. 10.

Ashton, Frederick, 83; British choreographer and ballet company director; Sussex, England, Aug. 18.

Baker, Chet, 58; jazz trumpet player; Amsterdam, May 14.

Baldwin, James, 63; author, essayist, and leading voice of the civil rights movement of the 1960s; St. Paul de Vence, France, Nov. 30.

Benoit, Jehane, 83; Canada's first lady of cuisine; Sutton, Que., Nov. 24.

Benton, Brook, 56; singer who was popular in the 1950s and 1960s; New York, Apr. 9.

Berlin, Ellin, 85; novelist; wife of Irving Berlin; New York, July 29.

Besser, Joe, 80; comedian who worked with the Three Stooges and Abbott and Costello; Los Angeles, Mar. 1.

Bissell, Patrick, 30; ballet star who was a principal dancer with the American Ballet Co.; Hoboken, N.J., Dec. 29.

Bowles, Richard, 75; lawyer and lieutenant governor of Manitoba from 1965 to 1970; Winnipeg, Man., July 9.

Boyington, Gregory "Pappy", 75; Marine flying ace who led the famous Black Sheep Squadron during World War II; Fresno, Cal., Jan. 11.

Brewer, Jim, 50; relief pitcher who spent 17 years in the major leagues, mostly with the L.A. Dodgers; Carthage, Tex., Nov. 16.

Buchanan, Roy, 48; guitarist, Fairfax, Va., Aug. 14.

Butterfield, Billy, 71; trumpeter of the Big Band era; North Palm Beach, Fla., Mar. 20.

Caliguiri, Richard, 56; mayor of Pittsburgh since 1977; Pittsburgh, May 6.

Caniff, Milton, 81; cartoonist who created Steve Canyon and Terry and the Pirates strips; New York, Apr. 3.

Carignan, Jean, 71; internationally acclaimed Quebec country fiddler; Montreal, Feb. 16.

Carter, Billy, 51; colorful brother of President Jimmy Carter; Plains, Ga., Sept. 25.

Carver, Raymond, 50; poet and short-story writer; Port Angeles, Wash., Aug. 2.

Chanin, Irwin, 96; architect who built skyscrapers and theatres in New York City; New York, Feb. 24.

Chiang Ching-kuo, 77; president of Taiwan since 1978; Taiwan, Jan. 13.

Cohn, Al, 62; jazz saxophonist and arranger; East Stroudsburg, Pa., Feb. 15.

Cook, Frederick "Bun", 84; hockey star with the 1920s New York Rangers and Boston Bruins, is said to have pioneered the slapshot; Kingston, Ont., Mar. 19.

Cunningham, Glenn, 78; world record-setting miler of the 1930s; Menifee, Ark., Mar. 10.

Day, Dennis, 71; tenor who was associated with Jack Benny on radio and TV for 25 years; Bel Air, Cal., June 22.

Derringer, Paul, 81; pitcher who won 161 games with the Cincinnati Reds; 20-game winner 4 times; Sarasota, Fla., Nov. 17.

Dell, Gabriel, 68; actor known for Dead End Kids, Bowery Boys films; N. Hollywood, Cal., July 3.

Diamond, I.A.L., 67; screenwriter who was a longtime collaborator of Billy Wilder; Beverly Hills, Cal., Apr. 21.

Divine, 42; transvestite film actor; Los Angeles, Mar. 7.

Douglas, Allie, 93; distinguished astrophysicist who achieved an international reputation at a time when few astronomers were women; Kingston, Ont., July 2.

Drees, Jack, 71; radio and TV sports broadcaster; Dallas, July 27.

Drees, Willem, 101; premier of the Netherlands, 1948-58; The Hague, May 14.

Ducharme, Noel, 66; native artist known for his painting, silkscreens and carvings; Thunder Bay, Ont., Feb. 24.

Duggan, Andrew, 64; actor on TV and in films; Los Angeles, May 15.

Ebsary, Roy, 75; convicted killer of a Nova Scotian teen for whose murder Donald Marshall served 11 years; Sydney, N.S., Feb. 22.

Eldridge, Florence, 86; actress who starred in the theatre, often with husband, Frederic March; Santa Barbara, Cal., Aug. 1.

Ferrari, Enzo, 90; founder and chairman of the Italian car company; Modena, Aug. 14.

Evans, Gil, 75; jazz composer, pianist and band leader, noted for his innovative arrangements; Cuernavaca, Mexico, Mar. 20.

Eyskens, Gaston, 82; Belgium political leader who served as prime minister 6 times; Louvain, Belgium, Jan. 3.

Feeney, Thomas, 63; noted legal authority on property and wills, a founding dean of the University of Ottawa law school; Ottawa, July 16.

Fennelly, Parker, 96; actor who was best known as Titus Moody on the Fred Allen radio programs in the 1940s and 1950s; Peerskill, N.Y., Jan. 22.

Feynman, Richard, 69; a leading theoretical physicist of the postwar generation; Los Angeles, Feb. 15.

Fidler, Jimmy, 89; Hollywood gossip columnist and radio reporter; Los Angeles, Aug. 9.

Foote, Lt.-Col. John W., 83; the only Canadian chaplain to receive the Victoria Cross; Cobourg, Ont., May 2.

Foreman, Percy, 86; Texas defence lawyer, best known for persuading James Earl Ray to plead guilty to 1968 slaying of Martin Luther King; Houston, Aug. 25.

Frey, Leonard, 49; actor starred in the theater and on TV; New York, Aug. 24.

Frobe, Gert, 75; actor best known as "Goldfinger" in the James Bond film; Munich, Sept. 5.

Fuchs, Klaus, 76; physicist who passed atom secrets to the USSR; E. Germany, Jan. 28.

Galbreath, John W., 90; real estate developer, race horse breeder, and former owner of the Pittsburgh Pirates; Columbus, Oh., July 20.

Gibb, Andy, 30; teen-idol pop singer of the late 1970s; Oxfordshire, England, Mar. 10.

Gillars, Mildred, 87; U.S.-born radio propagandist for Nazi Germany who was known as "Axis Sally"; Columbus, Oh., June 25.

Greene, Vincent, 95; philatelist, regarded as Canada's "Mr. Stamps"; Toronto, July 21.

Gwathmey, Robert, 85; a leading artist of social realism; Southampton, N.Y., Sept. 21.

Heifetz, Jascha, 86; one of the most renowned violinists of the 20th century; Los Angeles, Dec. 10.

Hale, Nancy, 80 novelist and short-story writer; Charlottesville, Va., Sept. 24.

Harrison, William A., 76; respected but long-overlooked Montreal painter; Montreal, Mar. 8.

Herman, Babe, 84; Brooklyn Dodgers star in the 1920s and 1930s; Glendale, Cal., Nov. 28.

Heinlein, Robert A., 80; science fiction writer; Carmel, Cal., May 8.

Howard, Trevor, 71; British actor who appeared in over 70 films; Bushey, England, Jan. 7.

Hurkos, Peter, 77; psychic, author, and TV personality who aided many police investigations; Los Angeles, June 1.

Imlach, Punch, 69; NHL coach who led the Toronto Maple Leafs to 4 Stanley Cup championships; Toronto, Dec. 1.

Joffrey, Robert, 57; founder and artistic director of the Joffrey Ballet; New York, Mar. 25.

Johnston, Henry "Percy", 85; speed skater, former holder of 3 world records in the late 1920s, Oshawa, Ont., July 24.

Jordan, Jim, 91; actor who portrayed Fibber McGee in the classic radio show; Beverly Hills, Cal., Apr. 1.

Koster, Henry, 83; film director, *Harvey, The Bishop's Wife,* Camarillo, Cal., Sept. 21.

Kuenn, Harvey, 57; baseball player who led the AL in batting, 1959; managed Milwaukee to a pennant, 1982; Peoria, Ariz., Feb. 28.

L'Amour, Louis, 80; writer whose 101 books, many best sellers, chronicled the American West; Los Angeles, June 10.

Laurence, George C., 82; pioneer of Canada's early work in nuclear research; Deep River, Ont., Nov. 6.

Lévesque, René, 65; premier of Quebec, 1976-85, and leader of the separatist Parti Québécois, 1968-85; unsuccessful in getting Quebec voters to endorse his plan for "sovereignty-association"—a form of separation—in a 1980 referendum; Montreal, Nov. 1.

Loewe, Frederick, 86; composer of Broadway musicals, *My Fair Lady, Brigadoon;* Palm Springs, Cal., Feb. 14.

Lower, Arthur, 98; noted Canadian historian, Kingston, Ont., Jan. 7.

Logan, Joshua, 79; stage and screen director; New York, July 12.

MacDonald, Dr. John Donald Nelson, 90; Canadian credit union movement pioneer; Dartmouth, N.S. Sept.

Malavasi, Ray, 57; head football coach of the L.A. Rams, 1978-82; Santa Ana, Cal., Dec. 15.

Malenkov, Georgi, 86; prime minister of the Soviet Union, 1953-55; USSR, announced Feb. 1.

Mansfield, Irving, 80; producer, publicity agent; husband of Jacqueline Susann; New York, Aug. 24.

Maravich, Pete, 40; basketball player who set collegiate scoring marks; led NBA in scoring, 1977; Pasadena, Cal., Jan. 5.

Marchand, Jean, 69; labor union leader, prominent cabinet minister in the Pearson and Trudeau governments; St-Augustin, Que., Aug. 28.

McBride, Sean, 83; Irish revolutionary and statesman who won the 1974 Nobel Peace Prize; Dublin, Jan. 15.

McCracken, James, 61; dramatic tenor; New York, Apr. 30.

Meeker, Ralph, 67; actor who starred in the theatre and in films; Woodland Hills, Cal., Aug. 5.

Memphis Slim, 72; blues pianist and singer; Paris, Feb. 24.

Moore, Colleen, 87; silent screen star who personified the flapper of the 1920s; Templeton, Cal., Jan. 25.

Morgan, James B., 77; a member of the dynasty which founded Canada's first department store; the Morgan firm merged with the Hudson's Bay Co., in 1960; Montreal, July 2.

Murray, Henry A., 95; psychologist and educator who pioneered development of personality theory; Cambridge, Mass., June 23.

Napier, Alan, 85; British-born stage, film, and TV actor; Santa Monica, Cal., Aug. 8.

Nelson, Ralph, 71; TV and film director, *Lilies of the Field, Charly;* Santa Monica, Cal., Dec. 21.

Nevelson, Louise, 88; pioneer creator of environmental sculpture; New York, Apr. 17.

Nichol, bp, 43; award-winning Vancouver-born poet and novelist, *The Martyrology;* Toronto, Sept. 25

Norstad, Lauris, 81; NATO commander during the 1961 Berlin crisis; Tucson, Ariz., Sept. 12.

Oliver, Sy, 77; jazz composer and band leader; New York, May 27.

Olson, James E., 62; chairman and CEO of AT&T; Short Hills, N.J., Apr. 18.

O'Rourke, Heather, 12; actress who starred in the two *Poltergeist* films; San Diego, Feb. 1.

Osborn, Paul, 86; playwright and screenwriter; New York, May 12.

Paton, Alan, 85; South African apartheid foe and author, *Cry, the Beloved Country;* South Africa, Apr. 12.

Patterson, Tom, 70; decorated WWII bomber pilot, pioneer of Canadian aviation; Toronto, Oct. 5.

Pham Hung, 75; prime minister of Vietnam; Ho Chi Minh City, Mar. 10.

Philby, Kim, 76; British double agent for the Soviets; Moscow, May 11.

Plager, Barclay, 46; defenceman who played 10 seasons in the NHL, mostly with the St. Louis Blues; St. Louis, Feb. 6.

Plow, Maj.-Gen. Edward C., 83; lieutenant governor of Nova Scotia from 1958 to 1963; Toronto, Apr. 25.

Pope, Generoso 61; millionaire owner of the supermarket tabloid the National Enquirer; Lantana, Fla., Oct. 2.

Pratte, Yves, 63; controversial former chairman of Air Canada, former Supreme Court of Canada judge; Bromont, Que., June 26.

Presser, Jackie, 61; president of the International Brotherhood of Teamsters; Lakewood, Oh., July 9.

Price, Melvin, 83; U.S. representative from Illinois since 1945; Andrews AFB, Md., Apr. 22.

Rabi, Isidor Isaac, 89; scientist who pioneered exploration of the atom; won 1944 Nobel Prize in Physics; New York, Jan. 11.

Raines, Ella, 67; actress who starred in films in the 1940s; Los Angeles, May 30.

Rich, Irene, 96; silent screen star and radio personality; Hope Ranch, Cal., Apr. 22.

Righter,Carroll, 88; astrologer and syndicated columnist; Santa Monica, Cal., Apr. 30.

Ritchie, Roland, 78; former Supreme Court Judge, one of its longest serving judges; Ottawa, June 5.

Roberts, Bill, 63; pioneering political consultant; Santa Monica, Cal., June 30.

Roman, Stephan B., 66; businessman who built an international mining and energy empire, Denison Mines; Toronto, Mar. 23.

Rooney, Art, 87; owner of the Pittsburgh Steelers who helped found the NFL; Pittsburgh, Aug. 25.

Roosevelt Jr., Franklin D., 74; former U.S. representative from New York; son of FDR; Poughkeepsie, N.Y., Aug. 17.

Ross, Lanny, 82; tenor who was a popular radio star in the 1930s and 1940s; New York, Apr. 25.

Rose, George, 68; actor who won 2 Tony Awards; Dominican Republic, May 5.

Roush, Edd, 94; baseball hall of famer who had a .323 career batting average; Bradenton, Fla., Mar. 21.

Rousseau, Yvette, 71; Quebec senator, active in the labor and women's movement, founded the Quebec Council on the Status of Women; Montreal, Mar. 17.

Ruska, Ernst, 81; engineer who shared the 1986 Nobel Prize in physics; W. Berlin, May 30.

St. Johns, Adela Rogers, 94; journalist and author; Arroyo Grande, Cal., Aug. 10.

Seguin, Fernand, 66; well-known for his popular programs on radio and television about science; Montreal, June 19.

Shaara, Michael J., 58; author who won the 1975 Pulitzer Prize for fiction, *The Killer Angels;* Tallahassee, Fla.

Shulman, Max, 69; novelist, playwright and humorist who created the Dobie Gillis TV character, Los Angeles, Aug. 28.

Silva, Trinidad, 38; actor who portrayed gang leader in the Hill Street Blues TV series; Whittier, Cal., July 31.

Strickland, Brig.-Gen. Phillip W.; led Canadian soldiers into Normandy on D-Day; Orillia, Ont., Apr. 16

Strauss, Franz Josef, 73; right-wing premier of Bavaria, influential West German politician; Regensburg, West Germany, Oct. 3.

Szeryng, Henryk, 69; Polish-born violinist; Kassel, W. Germany, Mar. 3.

Vernon, Jackie, 62; night club and TV comedian; Los Angeles, Nov. 10.

Weyer, Lee, 51; National League umpire since 1961; San Mateo, Cal., July 4.

Wilentz, David, 93; prosecutor in the 1935 Lindbergh kidnapping trial; Long Branch, N.J., July 6.

Wright, J. Skelly, 77; U.S. federal judge who played a major role in promoting racial desegregation; Westmoreland Hills, Md., Aug. 6.

Wright, Sewall, 98; geneticist who was a leading evolutionary theorist of the 20th century; Madison, Wis., Mar. 3.

Zamboni, Frank, 87; inventor of the ice resurfacer; Paramount, Cal., July 28.

Zia ul-Haq, Mohammad, 64; president of Pakistan; Pakistan, Aug. 17.

Index